INTERNATIONAL LAW IN CONTEMPORARY PERSPECTIVE

W. MICHAEL REISMAN
Myres S. McDougal Professor of International Law
Yale Law School

MAHNOUSH H. ARSANJANI
Deputy Director, Codification Division, Office of Legal Affairs
United Nations Secretariat

SIEGFRIED WIESSNER
Professor of Law
Director, Graduate Program in Intercultural Human Rights
St. Thomas University School of Law

GAYL S. WESTERMAN
Professor of Law
Director, International Programs
Pace University School of Law

FOUNDATION PRESS

NEW YORK, NEW YORK

2004

THOMSON
WEST

395 Hudson Street
New York, NY 10014
Phone Toll Free 1–877–888–1330
Fax (212) 367–6799
fdpress.com

Printed in the United States of America

ISBN 1–58778–653–2

TEXT IS PRINTED ON 10% POST CONSUMER RECYCLED PAPER

In memory of Myres Smith McDougal
Master of International Law, Servant of Human Dignity

*

INTRODUCTION

International law, once a marginal and largely abstract part of the work of the lawyer and diplomat, has become one of the central facets of modern legal and political life. Domestic lawyers, no less than diplomats, appreciate that there are fewer and fewer areas of their respective practices that do not engage some aspects of the international legal process. At the same time, the media, who influence, if not shape the ideas of the public, routinely present international law as a significant factor in international - and domestic - political life. Law students, seasoned lawyers and engaged citizens alike, now confront in their daily lives the achievements - and failures - of modern international law.

For all of its current familiarity, international law continues to be one of the most intellectually difficult and often frustrating parts of the law school curriculum. International politics is more volatile and violent than the domestic political system that provides the environment for American law and the international community is far more diversified in terms of culture, language and class than its domestic counterpart. While national law in developed legal systems, like that of the United States, benefits from key common narratives of the past, many shared myths and congruent demands for the future, international law operates in an environment in which far fewer of these features obtain. And while national law is made and applied in familiar and stable institutions, international laws structures and processes are more fluid.

Contemporary international law is also undergoing rapid change in almost all of its key areas: where and how it is made and applied, who participates in these processes and the law that these processes develop. Unfortunately, much of inherited legal theory is unable to comprehend the ongoing transformations of the subject it purports to explain and has allowed itself to become a lonely, scholastic enterprise.

Our book seeks to provide the student with an intellectual framework for comprehending this extraordinarily difficult but exciting subject by focusing, first, on the processes of contemporary international law and, then, through the selection of materials covering every major area of contemporary public international law, to equip the student with the tools for performing the essential intellectual tasks of the lawyer: understanding how and why past decisions were made, assessing how future decisions are likely to be made and how they can be influenced and, no less important, how, as a matter of policy, the future direction of law should be influenced in order to advance world order and human dignity.

Because the scope and depth of international law has expanded, the designers of a contemporary casebook face several dilemmas. A short book for an introductory course, composed, perforce, of a limited number of severely pruned selections, has an appeal, but it would give a superficial and misleading picture and ill-serve the student using it. A short book focusing only on one or two topics in contemporary international law would sacrifice the breadth and surprising degree of integration of the subject.

We have decided not to sacrifice comprehensiveness and integration and, accordingly, have opted for a longer book which can be used for a general course as well as for a number of different courses and seminars in the international law field. Ideally, the entire text can be used for a two-semester course. If our text is used as a one-semester general course, we would recommend selections from Parts One, Two, Three and Four. For courses or seminars in specific areas, we would recommend that selections from Part One, which provides the student with a theoretical overview of how international law is made and applied, should be used along with the relevant Parts. For example, a seminar on Human Rights would use selections from Part One and all of Part Three. A seminar on the Law of the Sea would use selections from Part One and all of Part Four. A seminar on State Responsibility would use selections from Part One and all of Part Five. Seminars on the Law of War would use selections from Parts One and Six, as would seminars on Treaty Law. A seminar on the Establishment and Transformation of States would use all of Parts One and Part Two, with selections from Part Three (Human Rights) and Part Six. A seminar on International Jurisdiction, a subject which we believe has become an important part of contemporary international law, would use selections from Parts One and Seven.

* * *

These materials, in evolving formulations, have been used as teaching texts at our schools for many years. Each generation of students has made a significant contribution to them, through keen questions and discussions of the major issues. In assembling the materials for publication, we would like to acknowledge, in particular, the special contributions at the Yale Law School of Chris Antoniou, Jamie Baker, Anupam Chander, Alison Chase, Jacob Katz Cogan, Cheryl DeFilippo, Monica Hakimi, Kathryn Ann Hutchins, Adam Muchmore, Daniel Reich, Anna Skotko, Robert Sloane, Matthew Waxman and Andrew Willard. Gene Coakley of the Yale Law Library was an enormous help to us. Throughout the preparation of the book, Cina T. Santos was unfailingly helpful, patient, and encouraging.

At the St. Thomas University School of Law, we acknowledge the significant contributions of former and present research assistants and students Sandy Batchelor, Dana Brown, Wendy Cooper, Kimberly Kostun, Cheryl Moralez, Gabriel Pinilla, Frances Schreiber, and Ana Vallejo. Special thanks must go as well to Keith Nunes and Roza Pati who offered thoughtful advice, comments and suggestions.

At the Pace Law School, we acknowledge the invaluable contributions made by research assistants Diane Cardoso, Daniela Fuda, and Joseph Mattera. Erin Kanterman, Brian Nugent, and Mat Varughese also provided assistance. Pace Law Librarians Marie Newman, David Williams, and Gail Whittemore along with staff members Gisella Tirado and Kathleen Lambert, offered dedication, support and essential technical knowledge to the project.

Finally, for lending their particular expertise, special thanks are due to Dr. Robert Smith, Bureau of Oceans and International and Scientific Affairs, U.S. State Department; to Lawrence C. Olin; to Hiroshi Murakami, United Nations Cartographic Section; and to Matthew Smith, our graphic designer, who in the final phase of this work produced the book we had long hoped to see.

Any views expressed in this book are personal to the authors and do not necessarily reflect the views of the institutions or organizations with which the authors are affiliated.

WMR, MHA, SW, GSW

August 2004

ACKNOWLEDGEMENTS

We are indebted to the following authors and publishers for permission to reprint excerpts from copyrighted material:

Arsanjani and Reisman, The Quest for an International Liability Regime for the Protection of the Global Commons, in International Law: Theory and Practice (Karel Wellens ed. 1998). Reprinted with permission of Martinus Nijhoff Publishers.

Bodansky, International Law and the Protection of Biological Diversity, 28 Vand. J. Transnat'l L. 623 (1995). Reprinted with permission of Vanderbilt Journal of Transnational Law.

Carey and Wiessner, A New United Nations Subsidiary Organ: The Permanent Forum on Indigenous Issues, ASIL Insight No. 67, April 2001. Reprinted with permission of the American Journal of International Law.

Charney, Self-Determination: Chechnya, Kosovo, and East Timor, 34 Vand. J. Transnat'l L. 455 (2001). Reprinted with permission of Vanderbilt Journal of Transnational Law.

Charney and Reisman, Agora: Breard: The Facts, 92 Am. J. Int'l L. 666 (1998). Reprinted with permission of the American Journal of International Law.

Charnovitz, Opening the WTO to Nongovernmental Interests, 24 Fordham Int'l L.J. 173 (2000). Reprinted with permission of Fordham International Law Journal.

Cosgrove, The Sanctions Dilemma and the Case of Iraq: Human Rights and Humanitarian Challenges to the Use of Multilateral Economic Sanctions, 9 Windsor Rev. of Legal and Soc. Issues 65 (1999). Reprinted with permission of Windsor Review of Legal and Social Issues.

Edmiston, Showdown in South China: An International Incidents Analysis of the So-Called Spy Plane Crisis, 16 Emory Int'l L. Rev. 639 (2002). Reprinted with permission of the Emory International Law Review.

Forsythe, International Humanitarian Assistance: The Role of the Red Cross, 3 Buff. J. Int'l L. 235 (1996-1997). Reprinted with permission of The Buffalo Journal of International Law.

Hale, Radio Power: Propaganda and International Broadcasting (1975). Reprinted with permission of Temple University Press.

Higgins, The Abuse of Diplomatic Privileges and Immunities: Recent United Kingdom Experience, 79 Am. J. Int'l L. 641 (1985). Reprinted with permission of the American Journal of International Law.

Jennings and Watts, 1 Oppenheim's International Law, 9th ed. 1992. Reprinted with permission of Addison Wesley Publishing Company.

Kingsbury, Claims by Non-State Groups, 25 Cornell Int'l L.J. 481 (1992). Reprinted with permission of Cornell International Law Journal.

Maps: Greece, No. 3798 Rev. 2, January 2004; and East Timor, No. 4111 Rev. 8, January 2004; Reprinted with permission of the United Nations Cartographic Section.

McDougal, et al., The World Community: A Planetary Social Process, 21 U.C. Davis L. Rev. 807 (1988), copyright 1988 by the Regents of the University of California. Reprinted with permission of U.C. Davis Law Review.

McDougal and Schlei, The Hydrogen Bomb Tests in Perspective: Lawful Measures for Security, 64 Yale L.J. 648 (1955). Reprinted with permission of The Yale Law Journal.

McDougal, The Enjoyment of and Acquisition of Resources in Outer Space, 111 U. Pa. L. Rev. 521 (1963). Reprinted with permission of the University of Pennsylvania Law Review.

McDougal, The Soviet-Cuban Quarantine and Self-Defense, 57 Am. J. Int'l L. 597 (1963). Reprinted with permission of the American Journal of International Law.

McDougal and Wiessner, Law and Minimum World Public Order, in McDougal and Feliciano, The International Law of War (1994). Reprinted with permission of New Haven Press, Inc.

McDougal, Treaties and Congressional-Executive or Presidential Agreements: Interchangeable Instruments of National Policy, Studies in World Public Order (1960). Reprinted with permission of Martinus Nijhoff Publishers.

Morgan, The Shooting of Korean Air Lines Flight 007: Responses to Unauthorized Aerial Incursions, in International Incidents: The Law That Counts in World Politics (1988). Reprinted with permission of Princeton University Press.

Murphy, Contemporary Practice of the United States Relating to International Law, 93 Am. J. Int'l L. 470 (1999). Reprinted with permission of the American Journal of International Law.

Murphy, Waiver of Georgian Diplomat's Immunity from Criminal Prosecution, 93 Am. J. Int'l L. 485 (1999). Reprinted with permission of the American Journal of International Law.

Murphy, Legal Regulation of the Use of Force, 93 Am. J. Int'l L. 628 (1999). Reprinted with permission of the American Journal of International Law.

Olson, International Organized Crime: The Silent Threat to Sovereignty, 21-Fall Fletcher F. World Aff. 65 (1997). Reprinted with permission of the Fletcher Forum of World Affairs.

Pace and Thieroff, The International Criminal Court, in The Making of the Rome Statute: Issues, Negotiations, Results ch. 13 (Roy S. Lee, ed. 1999). Reprinted with permission of Kluwer Law International.

Ratner, Corporations and Human Rights: A Theory of Legal Responsibility, 111 Yale L.J. 443 (2001). Reprinted with permission of The Yale Law Journal.

Ratner, Drawing A Better Line: Unti Possidetis and the Borders of New States, 90 Am. J. Int'l L. 590 (1996). Reprinted with permission of the American Journal of International Law.

Reisman and Wiessner, 1993 Annual Meeting of the American Society of International Law, 87 Am. Soc'y Int'l L. Proc. 258 (1993). Reprinted with permission of the American Journal of International Law.

Reisman, Governments-in-Exile: Notes Toward a Theory of Formation and Operation, in Governments-in-Exile in Contemporary World Politics (1991) (Y. Shain, ed.). Reprinted with Permission of Routledge.

Reisman, Aftershocks: Reflections on the Implications of September 11, 6 Yale H.R. & Dev. L.J. 81 (2003). Reprinted with permission of Yale Human Rights and Development Law Journal.

Reisman, Appraising the Unilateral Actions of States in Terms of the Constitutive Process: The Special Problem of Humanitarian Intervention, 11 Eur. J. Int'l L. 3 (2000). Reprinted with permission of the European Journal of International Law.

Reisman, International Lawmaking: A Process of Communication, 75 Am. Soc'y Int'l L. Proc. 101 (1981). Reprinted with permission of the American Journal of International Law.

Reisman, The View from the New Haven School of International Law, 86 Am. Soc'y Int'l L. Proc. 118 (1992). Reprinted with permission of the American Society of International Law.

Reisman, International Legal Responses to International Terrorism, 22 Hous.J. Int'l L. 3 (1999). Reprinted with permission of The Houston Journal of International Law.

Reisman, Private Armies in a Global War System: Prologue to Decision, 14 Va. J. Int'l L. 1 (1973). Reprinted with permission of Virginia Journal of International Law.

Reisman, Practical Matters for Consideration in the Establishment of a Regional Human Rights Mechanism: Lessons From the Inter-American Experience, 1995 St. Louis-Warsaw Transatlantic L.J. 89. Reprinted with permission of the author.

Reisman, Jurisdiction in International Law (1999). Reprinted with permission of Ashgate Publishing Ltd.

Reisman, The Lessons of Qana, 22 Yale J. Int'l L. 381 (1997). Reprinted with permission of Yale Journal of International Law.

Reisman, A Hard Look at Soft Law, 82 Am. Soc'y Int'l L. Proc. 371 (1988). Reprinted with permission of the American Journal of International Law.

Reisman, Assessing Claims to Revise the Laws of War, 97 Am.J. Int'l L. 82 (2003). Reprinted with permission of the American Journal of International Law.

Reisman, The Constitutional Crisis in the United Nations, 87 Am. J. Int'l L. 83 (1993). Reprinted with permission of the American Journal of International Law.

Reisman, Necessary and Proper: Executive Competence to Interpret Treaties, 15 Yale J. Int'l L. 316 (1990). Reprinted with permission of the Yale Journal of International Law.

Reisman, Folded Lies (1979). Reprinted with permission of Free Press.

Reisman, The Political Consequences of the General Assembly Advisory Opinion, in International Law, The International Court of Justice and Nuclear Weapons (1999). Reprinted with permission of Cambridge University Press.

Reisman and Stevick, The Applicability of International Law Standards to United Nations Economic Sanctions Programmes, 9 Eur. J. Int'l L. 86 (1998). Reprinted with permission of the European Journal of International Law.

Reisman and Westerman, Straight Baselines in International Maritime Boundary Delimitation (1992). Reprinted with permission of St. Martin Press.

Sahurie, The International Law of Antarctica (1992). Reprinted with permission of Brill Academic Publisher.

Spiro, New Players on the International Stage, 2 Hofstra L. & Pol'y Symp. 19 (1997). Reprinted with permission of Hofstra Law and Policy Symposium.

Weiss, Invoking State Responsibility in the Twenty-first Century, 96 Am. J. Int'l L. 798 (2002). Reprinted with permission of American Journal of International Law.

Weiss, Introductory Note, United Nations Conference on Environment and Development, 31 I.L.M. 814 (1992). Reprinted with permission of the American Journal of International Law.

Westerman, The Juridical Bay (1987). Reprinted with permission of Oxford University Press.

Wiessner, Legitimacy and Accountability of NGOs: A Policy-Oriented Perspective, in Government to Governance - 2003 Hague Joint Conference on Contemporary Issues of International Law (2003). Reprinted with permission of T.M.C. Asser Press.

Wiessner, Rights and Status of Indigenous Peoples: A Global Comparative and International Legal Perspective, 12 Harv. Hum. Rts. J. 57 © (1999) by the President and Fellows of Harvard College and the Harvard Human Rights Law Journal. Reprinted with permission of the Harvard Publications Center.

Wiessner and Willard, Policy-Oriented Jurisprudence, 44 German Y.B. Int'l L. 96 (2001). Reprinted with permission of Duncker & Humblot.

Wiessner, Blessed Be the Ties that Bind: The Nexus Between Nationality and Territory, 56 Miss. L.J. 447 (1988). Reprinted with permission of The Mississippi Law Journal.

Wiessner, Human Activities in Outer Space: A Framework for Decisionmaking in Space Law: Views of the Future 7-20 (1988). Reprinted with the permission of Kluwer Law International.

Wiessner, American Indian Treaties and Modern International Law, 7 St. Thomas L. Rev. 567-602 (1995). Reprinted with permission of the St. Thomas Law Review.

Wright, The Cuban Quarantine, 57 Am. J. Int'l Law 546 (1963). Reprinted with permission of the American Journal of International Law.

TABLE OF CONTENTS

PART FOUR: ALLOCATION, PROTECTION AND REGULATION OF USE OF THE RESOURCES OF THE PLANET ---------- 645

TABLE OF CASES

Principal cases are in **bold** type. Non-principal cases are in *italics*. References are to Pages.

PART ONE: THE CONSTITUTIVE PROCESS IN THE GLOBAL COMMUNITY CONTEXT

I. How Shall We Conceive International Law?

A. Introduction

1. W. Michael Reisman, *The View from the New Haven School of International Law*
86 Am. Soc'y Int'l L. Proc. 118 (1992)

Consider, for a moment, the sorts of professional problems encountered by the contemporary international lawyer:

As a member of the International Law Commission, you are charged with adapting the inherited principles of state responsibility to the political and technological environment of the twenty-first century and, as part of this task, with establishing rules for liability without fault.

As a lawyer in the United Nations legal division, you have been asked to prepare the Secretary-General's Report on "strengthening and making more efficient within the framework and provisions of the Charter the capacity of the United Nations for preventive diplomacy, for peace-making and for peace-keeping."

As General Counsel of the National Security Council or Legal Adviser of the Department of State, you have been asked to advise the President of the United States as to whether to intercept and board, on the high seas, vessels believed to be carrying nuclear components to a Middle Eastern state.

As a professor of international law, you want to appraise the quality of work of those who perform the tasks in the preceding examples.

The way you characterize these problems, the intellectual tools you use to research them and the information you think relevant for answering them will all be determined by your conception of law. Your conception will influence the role you assume, the method you use, the ethics you adopt and the outcome.

Like the proverbial elephant, the complex of social processes and organization that are generally referred to as "the law" may be viewed from many different perspectives. People trained and sometimes locked into one perspective can scarcely believe there may be others, even less that they are equally authentic and that, for some or all tasks, they may be even more useful than the one with which they were indoctrinated and, as a result, with which they are comfortable. Each perspective is the basis for a legal jurisprudence.

Positivism views law from the perspective of the receiver of commands, the "political inferior." From this perspective, law is a body of commands. This perspective assumes the independent moral value of obedience. The essential technical problem is properly identifying the content and meaning of the command and the circumstances and procedures for obedience to it.

An entirely different perspective, deriving from the natural law tradition, is that of the person charged with making decisions. From the perspective of the decision maker, the technical and moral problems that are confronted are not framed in terms of obedience but rather in terms of making choices that are appropriate for the relevant community.

The body of rules that serves to provide the positivist with strict commands requiring obedience does not disappear, but from the perspective of the decision maker those rules are more complex communications, conveying authoritative information about community policies of varying weights that must be assessed, in each case, and then shaped into a decision. The technical and moral problems associated with obedience recede.

Selecting the right jurisprudence for a task is critical. The New Haven School of jurisprudence is an entirely secular theory of law but it takes the perspective long associated with natural law, that of the decision maker. For New Haven, the notion of decision extends across the range of social organization and through the hierarchy of power; it includes the making of law or legislation as well as its application through courts or other institutions, and it conceives of both the activities as operating at the constitutive or structural level and in all of the various value processes of a community, including the production of wealth, of enlightenment, of skill, of health and well-being, of affection, of respect and rectitude.

For the positivist, a primary jurisprudential and intellectual task is the identification of what must be obeyed. Hence the recurring concern with finding "sources" of law. From the standpoint of the New Haven School, jurisprudence is a theory about making social choices. The primary jurisprudential and intellectual tasks are the prescription and application of policy in ways that maintain community order and, simultaneously, achieve the best possible approximation of the community's social goals. The jurisprudential tools necessary for performing these tasks must address a wide range of issues, including: (1) the way one looks at oneself; (2) the way one looks at the social process one is trying to understand and influence; and (3) the way one tries to influence it.

Clarification of Standpoint

Let's return for a moment to the proverbial elephant — the question of perspective. For any phenomenon, there are many possible standpoints, each of which affects it and how it is viewed. Clarity with regard to observational standpoint is an indispensable intellectual tool. Both the reference and content of the term "law" will vary depending on whether the standpoint is that of a member of elite or the rank-and-file, whether the observer is a member of the system observed, is an outsider or is on the margin. Perception of the same phenomenon may vary depending on the culture, class, gender, age, or crisis-experience of the observer. Even within the legal establishment, reference and content will vary depending on whether the observer is a legislator, a judge, a prosecutor, a juror, a defense attorney, an accused or a victim. No standpoint is more authentic than another, but the scholar must be sensitive to the variations in perception that attend each perspective and must try to disengage himself or herself, select one that is appropriate to the task and carefully determine and consistently maintain it.

In all observation, the individual self-system is the ultimate instrument of perception, appraisal and choice. Because it is necessary to calibrate all instruments, a second preliminary intellectual task the New Haven School poses is one "self-calibration" by various techniques of self-scrutiny: the person performing a decision function is urged to examine the self for latent emotional problems or neurotic tendencies, subgroup parochialism and the distortions that may arise from professional conditioning.

Focal Lenses

The New Haven School is also concerned with the way the observer looks at things, whether State Responsibility, the ability of the United Nations to perform its security functions, or the way freedom of the oceans is accommodated with security needs.

We all look at our environment and specific issues within it "through" a variety of conceptual categories. In the physical sciences, different lenses and dyes permit the observer to bring different features or properties of the same viewed object into sharper focus for greater prominence. A comparable function may be performed in the social sciences by carefully crafted conceptual categories that serve as "focal lenses."

(1) New Haven believes that a useful theory about law must avoid the temptation, so common in conventional legal method, to drastically reduce the universe of variables to a text or a few purportedly key social factors. You cannot get far with any of the problems we started with if you limit yourself to a few texts. New Haven's theory seeks to be as comprehensive as possible regarding the various factors that influence decision.

(2) In advanced, industrial and science-based civilizations, some major decisions are ongoing and incorporate, in the collection of information and the exploration of alternative possible arrangements, the efforts of many people. New Haven recognizes the demands of economy and tries to develop various techniques of selectivity, especially for rapid decision-making.

(3) The notion of law as a body of rules, existing independently of decision makers and unchanged by their actions, is a necessary part of the intellectual and ideological equipment of the political inferior. It makes no sense in a jurisprudence which conceives of law as a proccss in which human beings try to influence the way social choices are made about the production and distribution of the

things that they want, including considerations about the ways in which those decisions should be made. New Haven reserves the word "law" for processes of decision that are both consistent with the expectations of rightness held by members of a community (authoritative decisions) and effective (controlling decisions). While the particular mix of authority and control may vary widely, a conception of law as authoritative and controlling decision avoids exercises in irrelevance, whether because of absence of authority or absence of control.

(4) A commonly observed pathology of conventional legal research is its tendency to examine only words in documents. A jurisprudence concerned with understanding and influencing the way people behave must be able to study and account for what people do as well as what they say, think and feel. Deeds, as well as words, are indicators of subjectivity, so New Haven recommends a focus on both.

(5) In any group process, some decisions will be concerned with the way decisions henceforth will be taken in what setting. We reserve the term "constitutive process" to focus attention on that portion of a group's activity concerned with establishing, maintaining or changing the fundamental institutions and procedures of decision making.

A Map of Community Processes

Focal lenses address the question of *how* observers look at pertinent data. We have yet to consider *what* observers look at. Conventional legal analyses and jurisprudences that conceive of law as a body of rules look only at a limited number of texts, characterized as legal, and those social events, "facts," to which the rules direct attention. Because New Haven's goal is understanding and influencing decision in ways that will precipitate desired social outcomes, the *what* of inquiry is necessarily broader than the *what* of conventional analysis.

The New Haven School has adapted, with a number of adjustments, a scheme of cultural anthropology in which any social process is described systematically in terms of those who engage in it (the participants), the subjective dimensions that animate them (their perspectives), the situations in which they interact, the resources upon which they draw, the ways they manipulate those resources and the aggregate outcomes of the process of interaction, which are conceived in terms of a comprehensive set of values.

The participants in any decision process include those formally endowed with decision competence, for example judges, and all those other actors who, though not endowed with formal competence, may nonetheless play important roles in influencing decisions. In international decision, the observer must examine, in addition to formal international organizations, state officials, nongovernmental organizations, pressure groups, interest groups, gangs, and individuals, who act on behalf of all other participants and on their own. I don't see how an assessment of the dangers to and assets of the international community could be realistic and useful to the Secretary-General in the second example, without this expansion of focus.

By the same token, the inventory will not be of much use if it does not take account of the ways these various actors see things. The perspectives of these actors include their specific patterns of identification and disidentification, their matter-of-fact expectations and the value demands they project. It is clear that in a complex arena such as international politics, the perspectives of the various participants actually playing a role in decision often diverge greatly in critical ways.

"Situations," as New Haven uses the term, refers generally to where decisions are made and to special properties of that "where." Conventional legal analysis generally looks to courts, secondarily examining the work of executive branches and legislatures. New Haven focuses on the range of centralized and decentralized settings in which decisions are made, their varying degree of organization and formality, the extent to which whey are specialized and the extent to which they are continuous or episodic. We also examine the extent to which participants in a particular situation perceive themselves in a state of crisis — that is, a state in which critical values are deemed to be at stake.

The resources on which participants draw their "bases of power" incorporates both effective power and symbols of authority. The New Haven School considers it appropriate for the jurist to correlate the extent, if any, to which control of power is available to support particular formulations.

In contrast to conventional legal analysis, which usually characterizes the outcome of a legal decision as a more specific statement of rule, New Haven seeks to conceive of outcomes as do those affected by them in terms of the confirmation and/or redistribution of the values at stake: of power, enlightenment, wealth, skill, well-being, affection, respect and rectitude.

Decision Functions

In most contemporary theories of jurisprudence, the term "decision" generally refers to a judge applying rules to a particular dispute in an organized setting. From the standpoint of a jurisprudence concerned with understanding and making choices, however, it is clear that the operation of making choices involves many more component functions. If one systematically separates out the elements of a decision, one can identify:

(1) intelligence-gathering or the collection, processing and dissemination of information relevant to social choices;

(2) promotion or the processes by which consciousness of a discrepancy between a desirable state and one that is or is about to take place gradually leads to a demand for some type of community intervention and regulation;

(3) prescription or lawmaking, which occurs when actors, with varying degrees of authority, select and install certain preferences about policy as community law. This may be accomplished by a legislature or some other organized lawmaker; but it is usually, and, especially in international law, largely accomplished in informal and sometimes even chaotic processes whose outcomes are generally referred to as "custom";

(4) invocation or the provisional characterization of a certain action as inconsistent with a prescription or law that has been established. Invocation is often accompanied by the demand that an appropriate community institution act;

(5) application or the conventional conception of law: the organization of the facts of a dispute, the specification of a norm or norms that apply and the fashioning of a mandatory formulation. When this takes place in a court, it is called a judgment, but it also occurs in informal, unorganized situations;

(6) termination or the abrogation of existing norms and the social arrangements based upon them, the development of transitional regimes and, where appropriate or necessary, the design of compensation programs for those who have made good-faith value investments expecting the old regime to continue;

(7) appraisal, which is concerned with evaluating the aggregate performance of all decision functions in terms of community requirements.

A jurisprudential theory concerned only with obeying rules may content itself with a few of these decision functions. But a theory that wishes to understand fully the operation of law and to equip jurists to identify and influence decisions in all settings must use a more detailed concept of decision functions.

Intellectual Tasks of the Jurist

Until now, we have examined the way in which the New Haven School recommends that jurists prepare themselves for decision by clarification of observational standpoint and scrutiny of self, conscious selection of the focal lenses recommended for examining data pertinent to decision, deployment of the map of the manifold of social reality for the organization and interrelation of those data with reference to the specific decision operations through which community policy is clarified and implemented in order to influence the production and distribution of values or desired events. That production/distribution is the major concern of both politics and law in every community.

Many of these conceptual tools are used, in varying fashion, by scholars in other disciplines. Jurists are distinctive among them in that they alone undertake, explicitly, to intervene in the social process that has been examined in order to secure changes in its pattern of authoritative decision so that it will henceforth discriminate in favor of a particular party or, one hopes, in favor of the common interest. We have found it useful to develop procedures for this juridical task. The procedures relate to each of five intellectual tasks performed by all who participate in the operations or functions of decision.

(1) *Goal Clarification.* A conception of purposive behavior requires an idea of what end that behavior seeks to secure. New Haven recommends that all who perform decision functions examine the demands of particular actors in terms of their congruence with the common interest, expressed as preferred patterns of production and distribution of every value within a system of stable minimum order.

(2) *Trend Analysis.* Once a goal has been specified, it is necessary to examine the degree to which it has been achieved in past decision. This essentially historical function identifies and organizes trends in pertinent past decision in terms of the goal expressed.

(3) *Factor Analysis.* It is important to correlate past decisions with conditions that influenced them and to note whether that context of conditions has changed in a material and pertinent way.

(4) *Predictions.* What are commonly called predictions may be made by a variety of techniques, but there is no determined future. What will be is a function, in varying measure, of what actors elect to do now. Projecting different decision options and then examining the prospective aggregate value consequences of each in terms of the goals that have been clarified permits the jurist to select and, through time, to adjust particular recommendations so that they increase the probability of the eventuation of a preferred future and minimize the eventuation of a dystopian one.

(5) *Invention of Alternatives.* Each of the problems with which we commenced demands much more than a summary of the rules of the past. When, as is often the case, predictions suggest a likely discrepancy between a goal preference and a probable future, the New Haven School recommends that the jurist explicitly explore alternative arrangements to increase the probability of the eventuation of a desired future. This intellectual task is active and interventionist and engages the fundamental responsibility of the jurist and the citizen.

Notes and Questions

1. An international decision-maker is anyone whose choice about an event can have some international significance. In addition to politicians and diplomats, businessmen, journalists, religious leaders, labor leaders, intellectuals and many others may sometimes, and perhaps frequently, find that they are making international decisions. One of the functions of international decision-makers is that of assessing the lawfulness of those claims and activities which have significant transnational characteristics. What is sometimes called "international law" is supposedly an instrument toward that end. The major emphasis in traditional conceptions of international law, an emphasis with roots extending far back into antiquity and building upon both religious and secular conceptions, as well as the *ius naturale* and *ius gentium* of the Romans, is upon certain perspectives of authority summarized in rules, which are regarded as governing relations between states. Behavior is "legal" if it can be supported by statements logically derived from these rules.

The question we raise is how helpful is this traditional conception of international law, with its emphasis upon inherited rules, in determining the "lawfulness" of the specific claims that states make against each other or that others make in relation to activities transcending state boundaries. Does this conception account for the many different types of decisions which are embraced in determinations of "lawfulness" and other community responses or for the many different factors which may in fact affect the different types of decision? Lawyers, as specialists in decision, are always performing in one form or another five intellectual tasks: they are clarifying goals, testing past trends in decision for conformity to those goals, understanding past decisions by reference to the context of conditions in which the decisions were made, trying to predict alternative trends in future decision and devising alternative courses of action. Does the traditional conception facilitate performance of these many different intellectual tasks required in the making and appraising of decisions? Consider the practical difficulties of the traditional conception. This conception appears to assume that authoritative rules are "given" or easily ascertainable. How does an observer in fact identify authoritative and controlling rules, especially when there is no widely acknowledged formal legislator? Who prescribes rules and for whom, with respect to what events or values, and by what procedures? Who takes initiative and makes effective recommendations to authoritative prescribers, by what methods, for the promotion of what policies, and with what effects? Upon what intelligence, gathered by what procedures, do authoritative prescribers and effective recommenders act?

Assuming that authoritative rules have been prescribed, who, authorized how, applies such rules to what particular controversies, by what principles of interpretation, in response to what claims, by what procedures, and with what effects? By what criteria and procedures are contradictions, ambiguities, and gaps in the prescribed rules remedied? Who is authorized to invoke the application of what rules, in what arenas, with respect to whom, and by what procedures? By what sanctioning practices are applications made effective in securing what degrees of authority? When community policies change and authoritative rules become obsolete, who, authorized how, terminates their authority? Who appraises past prescriptions and applications, for whom, and for the promotion of what policies?

2. Alternative definitions of international law include the following:

> John Austin: "[t]he law obtaining between nations is not positive law: for every positive law set by a given sovereign to a person or persons in a state of subjection to its author. . . . The law obtaining between nations is law (improperly so-called) set by general opinion. The duties which it imposes are enforced by moral sanctions: by fear on the part of nations; or by fear on the part of sovereigns, of provoking general hostility, and incurring its probable evils, in case they shall violate maxims generally received and respected." JOHN AUSTIN, THE PROVINCE OF JURISPRUDENCE DETERMINED (Wilfrid E. Rumble ed., Cambridge U. Press 1995).
>
> Professor Hyde: "The term international law may be fairly employed to designate the principles and rules of conduct declaratory thereof which states feel themselves bound to observe and, therefore, do commonly observe in their relation with each other." CHARLES C. HYDE, INTERNATIONAL LAW 1 (Little, Brown & Co. 1945) (1922);
>
> Professor Brierly: "The Law of Nations, or International Law, may be defined as the body of rules and principles of action which are binding upon civilized states in their relations with one another." JAMES L. BRIERLY, *LAW OF NATIONS: AN INTRODUCTION TO THE INTERNATIONAL LAW OF PEACE* 1 (Humphrey Waldock ed., Oxford U. Press 1949);
>
> Judge Moore: "By international law we mean the body of rules which regulate the intercourse of nations in war and peace." John Bassett Moore, *Fifty Years of International Law*, 50 HARV. L. REV. 395, 397 (1937);
>
> RESTATEMENT (THIRD) OF FOREIGN RELATIONS LAW § 101: "International Law, as used in this Restatement, consists of rules and principles of general application dealing with the conduct of states and of international organizations and with their relations *inter se*, as well as with some of their relations with persons, whether natural or juridical."

3. Definitions are not abstract statements. They are research methods prescribing what sectors of reality are to be canvassed, what material selected and how. To what extent do these definitions and the material that would be assembled in accord with them facilitate the tasks mentioned above?

4. Some definitions emphasize only power. Consider, for example, Professor Stowell:

> International law is the law of the strong States, made to preserve for strong States their possessions and also very carefully made so that it will not interfere with keen competition with their rivals. Made in this way you would expect that State system not to interfere with the very wide power of competition, and that is found to be the case when the facts are examined.

ROBERT D. SCHULZINGER, THE MAKING OF THE DIPLOMATIC MIND: THE TRAINING, OUTLOOK AND STYLE OF UNITED STATES FOREIGN SERVICE OFFICES 1908-1931, at 94 (Wesleyan U. Press 1975) (quoting Ellery C. Stowell, Lecture at the Foreign Service School, 1926).

5. Dean Acheson, a former US Secretary of State, an international lawyer, and a publicist, cast doubt on the notion that international law is law as it is conceptualized at the municipal level. Referring to the role that international law played in the Cuban Missile Crisis, Acheson said:

> [i]n my estimation, ... the quarantine is not a legal issue or an issue of international law as these terms should be understood. Much of what is called international law is a body of ethical distillation, and one must take care not to confuse this distillation with law. We should not rationalize general legal policy restricting sovereignty from international documents composed for specific purposes.

Quincy Wright, *The Cuban Quarantine,* 57 AM. SOC'Y INT'L L. PROC. 9, 14 (1963).

6. While not quite equating international law with morality, Hans Morgenthau, another prominent "realist" foreign policy expert, has argued that:

> [the] legalistic approach [to international relations] follows logically from the assumption that international politics is not a continuous struggle for power in which all great nations are of necessity involved. International politics is rather assumed to be an undertaking by peace-loving nations, if not indifferent to, certainly not greedy for power, for the purpose of making the world safe from the power-lust of aggressor nations. There is obviously but a short step from the juxtaposition of peace-loving and aggressor nations to that of law-abiding and criminal ones.

HANS J. MORGENTHAU, IN DEFENSE OF THE NATIONAL INTEREST: A CRITICAL EXAMINATION OF AMERICAN FOREIGN POLICY 101-02 (Knopf 1951).

7. Contrast the above attempts to offer an empirical account of the role that international law plays in the operation of the international system with the attack by George F. Kennan on the "legalistic-moralistic approach to international problems." GEORGE F. KENNAN, AMERICAN DIPLOMACY 95 (U. of Chicago Press 1951). According to Kennan, international law is ill-suited "to suppress the chaotic and dangerous aspirations of government in the international field." *Id.* Moreover, it tends to disrupt the natural processes of evolution that take place in the international system, "imposing a legal strait jacket on it." *Id.* at 98. Diplomacy, not the application of formal legal rules or the injection of an international tribunal into the fray, emerges as the mechanism most appropriate to achieve this end. For Kennan, international law played a subsidiary or marginal role in the settlement of disputes. Several years later, he recanted that viewpoint, saying:

> No one who has spent many years of his life in practical contact with the workings of international affairs can fail to appreciate the immense and vital value of international law in assuring the smooth functioning of that part of international life that is not concerned with such things as vital interest and military security.

GEORGE F. KENNAN, REALITIES OF AMERICAN FOREIGN POLICY 38-39 (Princeton U. Press 1954). This view, not inconsistent with the first, assigns a supportive, facilitating role to international law, "lubricating," as it were, the quest for security and vital interests.

8. Former U.S. Secretary of State Henry Kissinger has argued that the current configuration of the international system does not lend itself to the empowerment of international law as a force on the world stage. According to him:

> [i]n the emerging international order, nationalism has gained a new lease on life. Nations have pursued self-interest more frequently than high-minded principle, and have competed more than they have cooperated. There is little evidence to suggest that this age-old mode of behavior has changed, or that it is likely to change in the decades ahead.

HENRY KISSINGER, DIPLOMACY 19 (Simon & Schuster 1994).

It would appear that Kissinger's overall skepticism toward the role that international law can play in shaping international society transcends time and the recent transformations that have taken place in the organization of the international system. Almost twenty years before the publication of DIPLOMACY, during the height of the Cold War, Kissinger remarked that "in international affairs, the age-old struggle between order and anarchy has a political as well as a legal dimension. When competing national political aims are pressed to the point of unrestrained competition, the precept of law proves fragile." HENRY KISSINGER, AMERICAN FOREIGN POLICY 218 (W. W. Norton & Co. 1977).

9. While Ellery Stowell and Hans Morgenthau highlight the role that state power plays in the formation of international law, other scholars, members of the Grotian school, believe that international institutions themselves bring about limitations on the exercise of state power. Lassa Oppenheim has distinguished between these two approaches by noting that:

> [t]he legal school desires International Law to develop more or less on the lines of Municipal [domestic] Law, aiming at the codification of firm, decisive and unequivocal rules of International Law, and working for the establishment of international courts for the purpose of the administration of international justice. The diplomatic school, on the other hand, considers International Law to be, and prefers it to remain, rather a body of elastic principles than of firm precise rules. The diplomatic school opposes the establishment of international courts, because it considers diplomatic settlement of international disputes, and, failing this, arbitration, preferable to international administration of justice by international courts composed of permanently appointed judges.

LASSA OPPENHEIM, INTERNATIONAL LAW: A TREATISE 87-88 (H. Lauterpacht ed., 8th ed. Longmans, Green 1955).

10. But Oppenheim clearly aligned himself with a positivist approach for reasons that Professor Kingsbury believes were inherent in his conception of the interface of international law and international politics.

> Oppenheim saw the contested terrain in this way. He acknowledged that a positivist conception (or method, in his terminology) of international law was not generally accepted. He emphasized that much was at stake in the struggle to define the concept of international law. Thus one of his objections to natural law approaches was that their practitioners could not agree among themselves on the most basic questions about international law, let alone convince others, and that they offer a "breach through which the deniers of the law of nations can easily come in and attack the very existence of an international law." He saw perhaps a more serious threat in efforts to make international law a body of elastic principles rather than firm rules, and to exclude binding adjudication in favour of diplomatic negotiation of arbitration. Hence his view that "the progress of International Law depends to a great extent upon whether the legal school of International Jurists prevails over the diplomatic school." He asserted that judges should not assume a wide power to depart from rules without the express consent of the state

> involved, not only for the pragmatic reason that such a power would place an unsustainable responsibility on a weak system of international adjudication, but also because Oppenheim held the political view that a concept of law allowing for expansive judicial law-making was less desirable than a concept of law in which law-making was a separate institutional activity from adjudicatory law-applying.

Benedict Kingsbury, *Legal Positivism as Normative Politics: International Society, Balance of Power, and Lassa Oppenheim's Positive International Law*, 13 Eur. J. Int'l L. 401, 432-433 (2002).

11. Thomas Franck contends that international legal instruments and organizations, the products of multilateral agreements, have taken on lives of their own and are growing increasingly complex and sophisticated, relative to other actors and regimes on the world political stage. This development stems from the trends toward greater globalization that are currently unfolding, the emergence of problems that can be best dealt with through cooperation at the international level, and the breakdown of the concept of state sovereignty. Thomas M. Franck, Fairness in International Law and Institutions 3-6 (Clarendon Press 1995). Unlike Dr. Kissinger, then, Franck believes international law is likely to thrive in today's geopolitical environment.

12. Running through the abundant work of Professor Louis Henkin is the Grotian idea that the character of the relationships between the dominant category of actor in the international system, namely nation-states, as well as the political forces in play in the system will determine the making of international law and the extent to which it is adhered to. According to him:

> [i]f diplomacy can maintain a climate of order and provide lawful means for achieving change, these will induce the acceptance of law and the development of institutions for its observance. Habits of accepting and observing law, will, in turn, contribute to international order and stability. On the other hand, if international order and stability are weakened — universally, regionally, or locally — laws of a more political character will not fare well, and the observance of even the basic, 'routine' laws and agreements may be weakened.

Louis Henkin, How Nations Behave: Law and Foreign Policy 317 (Columbia U. Press 1979).

Over a decade later, Henkin concluded that "[i]n the end, State compliance with international law depends heavily on the international culture of compliance." Louis Henkin, International Law: Politics, Values, and Functions: General Course on Public International Law 86 (Dordrecht 1990).

13. Richard Falk appears to agree with Louis Henkin that "the choice to adhere or not to international law is sharply constrained by the logic and character of the evolving state system as the prevailing form of world order." Richard Falk, Revitalizing International Law (Iowa State U. Press 1989). Like Franck, Falk highlights the idea that "a major reorganization of international life is taking place at the present time that will produce drastic modifications in the world-order system that has prevailed since the Peace of Westphalia in 1648." *Id.* at 3. According to Falk, a particularly productive function for international law and lawyers to fulfill during such periods of change is to manage them by lending "self-conscious support to a set of explicit world-order goals that structure both the means and end of transition." *Id.* at 3.

14. According to Martti Koskenniemi, however, the continued relevance and vitality of international law will depend on its ability to be characterized as "simultaneously normative and concrete — that it binds a State regardless of that State's behaviour, will or interest but that its content can nevertheless be verified by reference to actual State behaviour, will or interest." Martti Koskenniemi, From Apology to Utopia: The Structure of International Legal Argument 2 (Coronet Books 1989). On one hand, if it is too closely identified with international politics and diplomacy, international law runs the risk of being labeled as unprincipled and the creation of "subjective, politically motivated State wills or interests. Law-creation is a matter of subjective, political choice." *Id.* Lying at the other extreme is the possibility that international law, as a body of rules,

will become utterly divorced from the realities of the international system. Were this to take place, international law would function as little more than a "form of natural morality, a closed narrative code which would pre-exist the opinions or interests of individual States." *Id.* at 3. *See also*, MARTTI KOSKENNIEMI, THE GENTLE CIVILIZER OF NATIONS: THE RISE AND FALL OF INTERNATIONAL LAW 1870-1960 (Cambridge U. Press 2001).

15. As a foremost participant in the critical legal studies movement, Professor David Kennedy looks to develop new or alternative approaches to international law. More specifically, he explores the effects of certain biases and polarities on the discipline. He explains:

> [T]he disciplinary sensibilities of specialists in international law, international economic law, comparative law, and international relations together overemphasize the disconnection of public and private, the apolitical nature of private law, the disconnection between governing and comprehending, the distinction between local culture and global governance. Historical progress mythologies support each of these discipline's own claims to authority and reinforce geographical divisions between the center and the periphery, while offering a narrowed definition of possible and desirable directions for reform. One result is that the interpretations ... reinforc[e] the invisibility of background norms and private arrangements and tak[e] important areas of political contestation out of the internationalist's vision at precisely the moment a turn to the market and a disaggregation of the state makes these norms and institutions potentially the most significant sites for international contestation and struggle. They reinforce the naturalness of current distributions of global wealth and poverty, focusing our attention on participation in public structures at precisely the moment questions of economic justice provide the most salient changes for the international regime as a whole. The result is a strangely passive policy-maker.

David Kennedy, *The Disciplines of International Law and Policy*, 12 LEIDEN J. INT'L L. 9, 132 (1999).

16. In the 1980s, U.S. legal scholars began focusing on the normative deficiencies of legal process, which they claimed to over-rely on precedent and on deference to elected legislatures. New legal process (NLP) expanded upon legal process' normative element while maintaining faith in the need for institutions and for institutional decision-making.

> Professor Koh, writing about this [NLP] movement, finds that these scholars "saw the law's legitimacy as resting not just on process but also on its normative content. They viewed lawmaking as not merely the rubber-stamping of a pluralistic political process, but as a process of value-creation in which courts, agencies, and the people engage in a process of democratic dialogue." Inspired by the work of new legal process, Koh has called on scholars to add the insights of the NLP and other new legal movements to international legal theory. He points to the importance of thinking beyond the functioning of a process to the normativity of that process. Koh's own work has both described the "dynamic," "non-traditional," and "non-statist" process of international law and mentioned the normativity of these processes.

Mary Ellen O'Connell, *New International Legal Process*, 93 AM. J. INT'L L. 334, 338 (1999).

17. Traditional legal process also has been criticized by feminists. Professor Charlesworth explains her view of the feminist legal method:

> Feminist methods question the possibility of objectivity in a system that effectively excludes women's voices. They are skeptical about the construction of the neutral and impartial standards, seeing them as synonyms for male perspectives. Skepticism about the hunt for the objective is, of course, shared by many critical thinkers, but they have remained curiously aloof from examining the implications for gender politics, or indeed for the situation of other marginalized groups. . . . [F]eminists pay attention to the binary

> structures of international law, but they argue that these structures also have a gendered dimension, reflecting and solidifying systems of subordination based on sex.

Hilary Charlesworth, *Feminist Methods in International Law*, 93 Am. J. Int'l L. 379, 392 (Apr. 1999). *See also*, Aaron Xavier Fellmeth, *Feminism and International Law: Theory, Methodology, and Substantive Reform*, 22.3 Hum. Rts. Q. 658 (2000); Barbara Stark, *Women and Globalization: The Failure and Postmodern Possibilities of International Law*, 33 Vand. J. Transnat'l L. 503 (2000).

18. Professors Slaughter and Ratner conclude as to the usefulness of having available a variety of legal methods from which to choose:

> conceptions of role and hence choice of method are less likely to be informed by geography than by differing understandings and beliefs about how each individual lawyer can best advance her or his normative commitments. . . . [T]he practice of a particular method is a matter of choice . . . and that is a choice that should be as self-conscious as possible.

Anne-Marie Slaughter & Steven R. Ratner, *The Method is the Message*, 93 Am. J. Int'l L. 410, 422-23 (Apr. 1999).

19. Professor Philip Allott suggests in Eunomia: New Order for a New World (Oxford U. Press 2001), that with the end of the Cold War, international order has become international disorder. Natural forces of economic and cultural integration are opposed by equal and opposite forces of national and cultural particularism. New threats to international public order have been added to centuries-old forms of international conflict. Professor Allott concludes that what is needed is a universal philosophy of society and law. *See also*, Philip Allott, The Health of Nations: Society and Law Beyond the State (Cambridge U. Press 2002).

II. How is International Law Made and Applied?

A. Introduction

Many discussions of the prescribing of international law begin and end with Article 38 of the Statute of the International Court of Justice.

1. Statute of the International Court of Justice

June 26, 1945, 59 Stat. 1055, U.N.T.S. No. 993

Article 38

1. The Court, whose function is to decide in accordance with international law such disputes as are submitted to it, shall apply:

a. international conventions, whether general or particular, establishing rules expressly recognized by the contesting states;

b. international custom, as evidence of a general practice accepted as law;

c. the general principles of law recognized by civilized nations;

d. subject to the provisions of Article 59, judicial decisions and the teachings of the most highly qualified publicists of the various nations as subsidiary means for the determination of rules of law.

2. This provision shall not prejudice the power of the Court to decide a case *ex aequo et bono,* if the parties agree thereto.

NOTES AND QUESTIONS

1. When States or non-State entities submit disputes to some form of third-party decision, they usually specify the law that is to be applied by the decision-maker. This is prudent, as there are many disputes about the content of public international law as well as the methods for determining it. Article 38 of the Statute of the International Court of Justice (ICJ) is a choice of law clause for the ICJ. Understood as such, it is a sensible formulation. The legal adviser of a government, starting from scratch, would surely propose that a tribunal apply, first, treaties to which the governments in dispute are party; second, customary law; and third, more general principles of law. Since international law does not have a systematic citator, some reference might also be made to the "subsidiary means" for determining what the law is.

2. Is a formulation such as that found in Article 38 of the Statute of the Court useful for examining how international law is made and, in particular, for increasing the effectiveness of actors in influencing what the content of future law will be? For example, does Article 38 provide instruction as to the lawmaking competences of summit meetings of Heads of State? Or of statements made by heads of government of major powers in press conferences? Should comments such as these simply be ignored because they do not fit into Article 38 or should the international lawyer develop a method that permits inquiry into the normative or norm-generating force of activities that do not fit into Article 38?

3. What is the status of formal declarations that are made at diplomatic conferences? In 2001, the United States won great praise for its statement at a meeting of the WTO Ministerial Conference in Doha, Qatar assuring that WTO rules on trade-related aspects of intellectual property would not be used to block developing countries access to pharmaceuticals. Where does this fit in Article 38 of the Statute? If it cannot be fitted there, is it part of international law? *See* Steve Charnowitz, *The Legal Status of the Doha Declarations*, 5 J. INT'L ECON. L. 207 (2002).

4. Does Article 38 provide any guidance with respect to the transformation of a treaty of limited subscription into a customary rule binding all states? In *North Sea Continental Shelf*, the International Court addressed this question with respect to the equidistance principle for lateral continental shelf boundary delimitations as laid down in Article 6 of the 1958 Geneva Convention on the Continental Shelf:

> 70.[T]he argument put forward on behalf of Denmark and the Netherlands... is to the effect that even if there was at the date of the Geneva Convention no rule of customary international law in favour of the equidistance principle, and no such rule was crystallized in Article 6 of the Convention, nevertheless such a rule has come into being since the Convention....
>
> 71. In so far as this contention is based on the view that Article 6 of the Convention has had the influence, and has produced the effect, described, it clearly involves treating that Article as a norm-creating provision which has constituted the foundation of, or has generated a rule which, while only conventional or contractual in its origin, has since passed into the general *corpus* of international law, and is now accepted as such by the *opinio juris*, so as to have become binding even for countries which have never, and do not, become parties to the Convention. There is no doubt that this process is a perfectly possible one and does from time to time occur: it constitutes indeed one of the recognized methods by which new rules of customary international law may be formed. At the same time this result is not lightly to be regarded as having been attained.

> 72. It would in the first place be necessary that the provision concerned should, at all events potentially, be of a fundamentally norm creating character such as could be regarded as forming the basis of a general rule of law. …
>
> 73. With respect to the other elements usually regarded as necessary before a conventional rule can be considered to have become a general rule of international law, it might be that, even without the passage of any considerable period of time, a very widespread and representative participation in the convention might suffice of itself, provided it included that of States whose interests were specifically affected. …
>
> 74. … Although the passage of only a short period of time is not necessarily, or of itself, a bar to the formation of a new rule of customary international law on the basis of what was originally a purely conventional rule, an indispensable requirement would be that within the period in question, short though it might be, State practice, including that of States whose interests are specially affected, should have been both extensive and virtually uniform in the sense of the provision invoked; -and should moreover have occurred in such a way as to show a general recognition that a rule of law or legal obligation is involved. …
>
> 76. To begin with, over half the States concerned, whether acting unilaterally or conjointly, were or shortly became parties to the Geneva Convention, and were therefore presumably, so far as they were concerned, acting actually or potentially in the application of the Convention. From their action no inference could legitimately be drawn as to the existence of a rule of customary international law in favour of the equidistance principle. As regards those States, on the other hand, which were not, and have not become parties to the Convention, the basis of their action can only be problematical and must remain entirely speculative. …
>
> 77. … [E]ven if these instances of action by non-parties to the Convention were much more numerous than they in fact are, they would not, even in the aggregate, suffice in themselves to constitute the *opinio juris*; -for, in order to achieve this result, two conditions must be fulfilled. Not only must the acts concerned amount to a settled practice, but they must also be such, or be carried out in such a way, as to be evidence of a belief that this practice is rendered obligatory by the existence of a rule of law requiring it. The need for such a belief, i.e., the existence of a subjective element, is implicit in the very notion of the *opinio juris sive necessitatis*. The States concerned must therefore feel that they are conforming to what amounts to a legal obligation. The frequency, or even habitual character of the acts is not in itself enough. There are many international acts, e.g., in the field of ceremonial and protocol, which are performed almost invariably, but which are motivated only by considerations of courtesy, convenience or tradition, and not by any sense of legal duty.

North Sea Continental Shelf (F.R.G. v. Den. /F.R.G. v. Neth.) 1969 I.C.J. 4, 41.

The Court has, however, often been criticized for not doing the kind of systematic analysis of practice and *opinio juris* that the judges in *North Sea Continental Shelf* recommended. *See* John Crook, *The 2002 Judicial Activity of the International Court of Justice*, 97 Am. J. Int'l L. 352, 354 (2003).

5. In line with the traditional conception of the consensual nature of international law, states that persistently object to a new limitation on their freedom to act by emerging customary law may successfully avoid being bound by it: "Although customary law may be built by the acquiescence as well as by the actions of states ... and become generally binding on all states, in principle a state that indicates its dissent from a practice while the law is still in the process of development is not bound by that rule even after it matures." Restatement (Third) Foreign Relations Law of the United States 24, 25-26 (1987). For a review of pertinent state practice, particularly that of the United States, see David A. Colson, *How Persistent Must the Persistent Objector Be?*, 61 Wash. L.

REV. 957, 969 (1986). *See also* Prosper Weil, *Towards Relative Normativity in International Law?*, 77 AM. J. INT'L L. 413, 433-34 (1983) (calling the persistent objector doctrine the "acid test of custom's voluntarist nature"). This traditional concept has been attacked, not only from the angle of peremptory norms of international law (*jus cogens*). *See* Jonathan I. Charney, *The Persistent Objector Rule and the Development of Customary International Law*, 56 BRIT. Y.B. INT'L L. 1-24 (1986); *See also* Jonathan I. Charney, *Universal International Law*, 87 AM. J. INT'L L. 529, 538-542 (1993). In light of the pressures inherited international law and its essential concepts face, can they still serve as a useful heuristic?

B. THE POLICY-ORIENTED APPROACH TO INTERNATIONAL LAW

1. W. Michael Reisman, *International Lawmaking: A Process of Communication*

75 AM. SOC'Y INT'L L. PROC. 101-13 (1981)

The problem of lawmaking has always been more urgent and, apparently, more complicated in international law. For one thing, the familiar tripartite division of formal governmental institutions — executive, legislative and judicial — does not so obviously exist in the international arena. Hence international lawyers cannot, like their domestic counterparts, simply assume that law is made by the legislature and then get on with their work. Nor do international lawyers have a reporting service. Early in the century, international lawyers developed a myth, as it was described by Harold Lasswell, functionally equivalent to Aristotle's tripartite division. Article 38 of the Statute of the International Court of Justice and of the Permanent Court before it, proclaimed that international law was made by treaties and by custom that evidenced general practice accepted as law and, in addition, international norms could be inferred from the general principles of law common to civilized states. Scholarly teachings and judgments were given a subsidiary role, facilitating the determination of the primary sources.

But if the formulae of Article 38 had any cogency in the past, how can they account for contemporary problems? Consider several examples. In 1979, pleadings in an important American case averred that the resolutions taken in formal conferences of OPEC, the Organization of Petroleum Exporting Countries, constituted international law. In 1975, the International Court held that a provision in a draft convention that failed to win the majority necessary under the parliamentary rules of the conference arena in which it took place, might nonetheless be international law. In 1980, former President Carter and the European Conference of Foreign Ministers seemed anxious to assume the same prescriptive consequence for a Security Council resolution that had been vetoed.

The League of Nations Covenant recognized the Monroe Doctrine as international law. Is it still international law? Is the Brezhnev Doctrine international law? Is the Carter Doctrine international law?

As a formal matter, the U.N. General Assembly was not endowed with lawmaking competence. Nonetheless, a number of scholars have ventured that the General Assembly "sometimes" makes law, whether by a mysterious "consensus," as mystical as transubstantiation, by "instant" custom, or, as one learned professor apparently with interests in culinary matters put it, by "pressure-cooked custom." In 1980, in the *Filartiga* case, the Court of Appeals of the 2nd Circuit seemed willing to accept the proposition that the General Assembly could and, in fact, had made international law.

Even within the confines of Article 38 of the Statute of the International Court, the problem for the scholar and the international practitioner is not a dearth of things that look like law. The international system produces documents in the legislatistic genre with promiscuous abandon. Much of it, as we all know, is not law. The phenomenon of pretended lawmaking is unusual but not unfamiliar to the domestic lawyer. Formal lawmaking bodies sometimes (and, some, often) emit communications that have the form of law but that close observers know are not law. A patent contradiction which makes the purported law unenforceable, the absence of necessary implementing legislation, insufficient enforcement machinery, an inadequate budget if a budget at all, or the delegation of implementation to a manifestly inadequate agency generally indicate that there was an intention to create not law but what I have called elsewhere *lex simulata* or *lex imperfecta*. There may be various reasons for these exercises. Thurman Arnold thought the creation of intentionally unenforceable law was an efficient and economic way of mediating between distinct classes and groups which had irreconcilably incompatible demands. Others think of it as a way of salving the conscience of a public that intends to continue to do things it still believes improper. These explanations are applicable to many international situations. But whatever the function and public value of *lex simulata*, the scholar and practitioner must be able to distinguish effective law from the enormous legislatistic babble of international politics. Assuming that an institution like the General Assembly which does not have a formal lawmaking competence may sometimes make law, or, conversely, that the treaty modality which is endowed with formal prescriptive competence may sometimes produce a document but fail to make law, the operational question for the lawyer advising private clients, the international politician bent on making law, and the scholar intent on understanding the process is *when* is law made and *how*. In response to this problem, diplomats and practitioners have begun to talk of "hard" and "soft" law. But the references of these terms are as ambiguous as the basic distinction they seek to draw. Some *soidisant* "hard law" is, and may well have been intended to be ineffective. Some "soft law," or bargains with the curious epithet of "gentlemen's agreements" may, to the consternation of elites, prove to be quite effective.

Intimately related to the question of lawmaking, and of an equal importance to practitioner and scholar, is the question of when and how a law terminates. Because we have only a rudimentary international legislature, only rarely are there formal, express abrogations of prescriptions. Some conventions allow the parties to denounce at will, with only procedural requirements. But since, according to the Vienna Convention, norms originally expressed in conventional form may ripen into custom and then apply both to parties and nonparties, independent of their original instrument, how can the lawyer or scholar determine whether unilateral denunciation is still possible?

All of these practical and professional problems require for their solution a theory about how law is made that is cogent in formal institutional settings as well as in settings in which there is little specialized, institutionalized effective law-making. This is not an academic matter. The urgency of appropriate theory is underlined by the fact that we know that international law is being prescribed continuously and that it is sometimes made in virtually all of the institutions and through all of the modalities we have mentioned. We also know that some of the law prescribed is not compatible with common interests as we understand them; some may not be compatible with the security of states, including our own. If we fail to learn *how* to prescribe, the individual and collective consequences may be grave.

Unfortunately, the theories currently available do not address these practical and theoretical concerns. The institutional theory — that law is made principally by a legislature — is ludicrous in the international arena. Yet it would be a mistake to exclude institutions that purport to be legislatures from the purview of our inquiry. Equally inapplicable is the court theory, expressed jurisprudentially by John Chipman Gray and more grandiloquently by Justice Cardozo in *New Jersey v. Delaware*:

> International law ... has at times, like the common law within states, a twilight existence during which it is hardly distinguishable from morality or justice, till at length the *imprimatur* of a court attests its jural quality.

291 U.S. 361, 383. So few international cases reach courts, that if Cardozo's judicial imprimatur were necessary, most of international law would be consigned to the twilight zone and beyond, indeed to Holland's very "vanishing point of jurisprudence." Yet one can hardly study the prescription of international law without examining international tribunals and their production.

One traditional international approach has called for an inquiry into something called *opinio juris*, what states believe law to be. Though we often say "The United States believes this" or "The Soviet Union believes that," states don't have minds. Elites who manipulate the symbols of states do, but they are rarely accessible and even more rarely cooperative. Hence the *opinio juris* test is extremely difficult to meet. But the core notion of expectations is extremely important.

Certain recent approaches seem more supple. Professor Dupuy, for example, in the Caltex Award, directly addressed the question of the prescriptive competence of the U.N. General Assembly. Noting the absence of a Charter authority, he nonetheless concluded that "it is impossible to deny that the United Nations' activities have had a significant influence on the content of contemporary international law." "In appraising the legal validity of the above-mentioned Resolutions," he continued, "this Tribunal will take account of the criteria usually taken into consideration, *i.e.*, the examination of voting conditions and the analysis of the provisions concerned." While this seems to be a better tooled instrument of inquiry, you will notice that it still focuses only on a single moment dubbed "legislation," tests its law status by reference to only two factors, and overlooks subsequent changes in thinking, talking and behaving which may be decisive in the formation or the dissolution of an erstwhile prescription. *See* Caltex (Texaco v. Libya) 53 I.L.R. 87 (1982).

The natural law theory, which holds that law is eternally there, only waiting to be expressed in explicit jural form, is inappropriate in a secular age; what is the natural law of the deep-sea mining of manganese nodules, of passage through straits or of diplomatic protection of multinational corporations? Yet natural law's emphasis on the policing role of overriding principles should not be excluded. Whether these overriding principles are transempirical in origin or are based on empirically verifiable expectations, they may provide important stabilizations in the international system. The historical approach, that law is not and cannot be a purposive human creation, but emerges organically from group processes and structures, is daily controverted by manifest and effective lawmaking activities. Yet the inquirer would be remiss if he did not pay close attention to the impact of environmental factors on lawmaking. The Marxist conception that law is never an instrument for clarifying the common interests of a community but is simply, to use the memorable phrase of the Manifesto, the directives of the executive committee of the "ruling class" masquerading as the state, has no application in the heterogeneous international arena. Yet the emphasis in that view, as well as in classical positivism, on the abiding importance of the variable of control or effective power that is often concealed behind legalism, should not be overlooked.

Thus far we have spoken of lawmaking in the rather narrow terms of our profession. In a broader sense, of moment to lawyers and politicians as well as scholars, we are concerned not only with the processes in which certain policies that self-describe as law are made, but with the aggregate of processes in a community by which political perspectives at varying levels of consciousness are shaped and changed. Whether we are speaking of new foci of attention, new patterns of identification or disidentification, new selections of what "happened" in the past and what possibilities the future holds, or new transformations of aspiration and fantasy into concrete and exigent political demands, we are obviously addressing something of extraordinary importance to the lawmaking process. These subjectivities are often the substratum and the vanguard of lobbying and lawmaking; in some cases, they may substantially determine the law that finally emerges. Institutions like the U.N. General Assembly may, as Professor Dupuy observed, perform these prelawmaking functions. But let us not focus on a single institution. In the contemporary world communications system, which supplants the obsolete concept of geographic proximity with one of global electronic simultaneity, a complex network of public and private media arrangements addressed to an extraordinarily heterogeneous and modular world audience is engaged in this comprehensive pre- or sub-lawmaking function. Events that shape the attention focus of world audiences may include, for better or worse, the terrorists' propaganda of the deed on through to the solitary artistic creation of an Uncle Tom's Cabin, a Guernica, or a Heldenleben. …

Put in simplest terms, lawmaking or the prescribing of policy as authoritative for a community is a process of communication. All groups are, perforce, communications networks. An indispensable part of the political processes of groups is communication. An ineluctable effect of all communication is political. Like any other communication process, prescription involves the mediation of subjectivities from a communicator to an audience and, in successful cases, a reception and incorporation by the intended audience, resulting in a set of appropriate expectations that are supposed to influence behavior and, contingently, to alert community enforcement responses when deviations are deemed to threaten public order. All this, of course, is obvious. The problem is how to think about it in a way that facilitates understanding and management.

In 1948, in a classic formulation, Lasswell characteristically captured it in a series of questions:

Who?

Says What?

In Which Channel?

To Whom?

With What Effect?

"Control Analysis" focuses on the Who, the communicators. "Content Analysis" focuses on the What. Those who look primarily at the institutions specialized to print, or audio or visual communication, the channels of communication, are engaged in "Media Analysis." "Audience Analysis" focuses on the Whom and "Effects Analysis" focuses on the personal and social consequences of a flow of communications. Ideally, all these types of analysis should be studied in ensemble, but any one provides a useful window on the process.

The problems of applying this to the international political arena are as great as the rewards to be reaped. One operational difficulty is the very richness of the communications process. In periods in which elites concentrated power effectively and communications media were rudimentary, the Prince communicated with his counterpart primarily by means of his own diplomatic agents. Control, content, media and audience analysis appeared comparatively simple and manageable. But from the innovation of Gutenberg in Europe to the refinement of the cathode ray tube and the perfection of the simultaneous coordinated mediation of images and sound over great distances, the quantum of communication through time and across boundaries has been growing at a dizzying pace. With satellite communication now a commonplace, it is obvious that the planet's potentialities as a comprehensively integrated, though complex, communications unit are increasingly realized.

In this unit ... each of the components of communication becomes enormously more complex. While an elite monopoly of communication is still jealously sought in many parts of the world by control of media, censorship, jamming and so on, the proliferation of media and the potentiality of rapid transborder mediation of signs and symbols provides many enhanced opportunities for wider nonofficial and counter-official participation. An aged cleric's speeches taped on cassettes, a carefully staged military action such as the *Tet* offensive, a terrorist raid virtually conceived as guerrilla theater, or a self-immolation in Vietnam or Czechoslovakia may now have enormous direct and indirect impacts on politically relevant groups throughout the globe, despite the efforts of elites to suppress them. A mass protest of Soviet human rights violations in New York, London or Paris, communicated around the globe in word and picture can reinforce demands for human rights and even punish the violator. In more indirect fashion, the exchange of goods and services itself has a substantial effect on the expectations and demands of those who enjoy and those who know they will never have access to them.

Parallel to the burst of interstitial channels of communication, there has been an explosion of official channels with specific political and lawmaking relevance. The traditional diplomatic conduits, by which territorial-based elites have communicated and clarified their common interests, continue to be important, but many other international conference and parliamentary arenas have come into operation. In some of these, nonofficial actors may participate in direct or indirect fashion. In all of them, the ever-present private media of the noncommunist, industrial world monitor and diffuse what they believe is occurring as rapidly as possible.

With extraordinary increases in the variety, number, and range of channels in international political communication, there has been a comparable increase in the size, complexity, and nature of the audience. Except for those who voluntarily and successfully privatize, virtually everyone in the world is a member of the prescription audience, though the significance and importance of different members will vary as a function of their interests and political relevance. At the same time, as a number of scholars have suggested, there may have been an increase in the complexity of the personality structure of audience members.

Not everyone has viewed this democratization of prescription favorably. A number of scholars have noted that from the 19th century on, initially as a way of discrediting popular politics after the French Revolution, then as a convenient conception of Leninism and, ironically, consumer-oriented capitalism, large audiences were referred to as a "mass," implying the passivity and characterlessness of a *tabula rasa*, to be shaped, inscribed, and jolted into action by an inundation of vast communications from some elite vanguard. Unquestionably, human beings can be manipulated, in varying degree, by signs and symbols, but the audience also communicates, ascribing expectations about authority and control, as we will see, even to the communicators themselves.

Expectations about appropriate behavior, some explicit, some at levels of consciousness so deep that people are not aware of them, are shaped in all of these processes of communication. If one is to understand and influence international lawmaking, plainly one must address the process in its rich totality.

For all of its formidable operational challenges, the communications model liberates the inquirer from the limiting and, in the international context, the distorting model of positivism, which holds that law is made by the legislature. From the standpoint of communications theory, some law may indeed be made by specialized lawmaking institutions, but any communication between elites and politically relevant groups which shapes wide expectations about appropriate future behavior must be considered as functional lawmaking. Understanding how and where this is done is vital for determining when and what law has been prescribed and often for intervening and influencing future prescriptive trends.

The only way to grasp, indeed even to speak of this, is as an ongoing process in which the inquirer can systematically identify:

(1) the full range of communicators and communicatees — including international and national officials, and nonofficial elites in every value process;

(2) the subjectivities that animate all these actors — including their identifications, the matter-of-fact expectations of past and future that comprise their phenomenological world, and their demands for values. (Manifest demands may be described as objectives; more latent demands, sometimes held at levels so deep that communicator and communicatee are unaware of them, must also be explored for they are often decisive.);

(3) the many different situations, varying from value process to value process, in which subjectivities are mediated, in word and deed, and expectations about authority and control are shaped;

(4) the resources and other bases of effective power and authority which all communicators and especially would-be prescribers employ to give weight to their words and deeds;

(5) the different modalities and strategies of communication in different constellations of target-audience and elite rank-and-file;

(6) the outcomes in shared expectation, of varying content, held with varying intensities, about appropriate future behavior.

In the international context, each of these phases of the communications process must be fleshed out if the inquirer is to track lawmaking. The first phase, communicators and communicatees, would include international and national officials, the elites of multinational enterprises, the media, many interest and pressure group leaders, and most human beings. For some norms, the relevant audience may include large numbers of people. For other norms, effectiveness may be achieved if a comparatively small group of elites comes to expect them. The second phase, the subjectivities of these participants in the communications process, would vary from those identifying with a global system to those identifying only with a most exclusive unit; demands would vary from those for world order and justice to those of exclusive self-interest; expectations would vary from the most realistic to the most wildly fantastic.

The situations in which communications take place would include formal arenas like the U.N. General Assembly, the Security Council and international conferences, as well as informal private and even secret meetings. A situation, for our purposes, is any place in which pertinent subjectivities are mediated. It is urgent that the investigator avoid preconceptions about where prescription takes place. It is commonplace that international law is sometimes prescribed in a wide range of settings, varying from the most formal and specialized, for example a lawmaking conference, to the most informal, unorganized and apparently unauthorized, for example the behavior of two naval commanders in a maritime fishing dispute. It is equally commonplace that the events in these settings sometimes do not produce prescriptions, but only legislatistic communications. Modalities of communication would exhibit a similarly wide variety, in terms of instrument and degree of persuasion or coercion. The outcomes of the process must be expectations entertained by politically relevant groups that certain policies are authoritative and controlling.

All communications involve the mediation of subjectivities or messages. While much of general communications may, as I have suggested, be relevant to law formation, what is distinctive about prescriptive or lawmaking communications is that rather than transmitting a single message, they carry simultaneously three coordinate communication flows in a fashion akin to the coaxial cables of modern telephonic communications. The three flows may be briefly referred to as the policy content, the authority signal and the control intention. Unless each of these flows is present and effectively mediated to the relevant audience, a prescription does not result. Equally important, even if the three components are initially communicated, *they must continue to be communicated* for the prescription, as such, to endure; if one or more of the components should cease to be communicated, the prescription undergoes a type of desuetude and is terminated.

Let us consider each of these communication flows in more detail. The content of a prescription, the norm — the injunction that one ought to do or refrain from doing something, or, writ large, the policy about the production and distribution of some value — is obviously an indispensable component. In statutes and the various forms of written agreements, the policy content is express, though not necessarily complete or unambiguous. But beware the fallacy of elevating form over substance. Explicit content does not automatically equal prescription. Bear in mind that not all communications in prescriptive form are intended to be prescriptions. Only some carry lawmaking intention. Some are pageantry, expressions of aspiration or *voeux,* affirmations of values with no expectation of their realization.

There may be subtle but nonetheless unmistakable indications of an absence of prescriptive intent. Consider, for a moment, the General Assembly's adoption of the New Economic Order's "Charter of Economic Rights and Duties of States"; we will return to it in more detail later. At one phase, the Assembly was invited to adopt the Charter "as a measure of codification and progressive development" of international law. Because of opposition, this self-description was abandoned when the Charter was submitted to the General Assembly for vote. But the legislatistic form of the Charter was not. It is at least arguable, as Professor Virally contends, that the deletion meant that significant parts of the group comprising the majority did not intend to make and did not believe that they were making law.

Where prescribing takes place less formally or in less organized settings, policy content may not be directly expressed, but be embedded in the situation. Where prescribing takes place behaviorally, content must often be inferred and is subject to different, inconsistent but reasonable interpretations. Consider a mundane example. In what appears to the actors within it to be a novel situation, a mother asks her child to refrain from doing something. When the child persists, the mother says, "Stop that or I'm going to tell your father." In Lasswell's terms, there are, of course, two or three decision functions being performed here: prescription, invocation and probably application. Other than the evocative or in Kelsen's terms "dynamic" norm "obey your parent," what is the policy content of the norm the erring child has violated? Though, in that particular case, both mother and child know exactly what offending behavior must stop if the child is to evade application by the father, mother and child may not know or may differ in understanding the policy content of the general norm applicable in future situations, where context and contingency may be quite different.

Similarly, consider a situation in which the Coast Guard of country A insists on escorting the fishing vessels of country B from waters that B's fishermen have plied for generations. While the specification of A's Coast Guard in that case is utterly clear, its prescriptive policy content is not. A's acts may signal a permanent closing of areas theretofore open to international maritime users, or a short-term conservation, or a pollution-control effort, or the policy of a new security zone. Key elites in A may themselves be unsure of the policy content of that communication.

Can the General Assembly or smaller aggregations of would-be lawmakers do anything they want? In the period in which natural law doctrines waned and the secular dualism, championed by Emmerich Vattel, prevailed, state elites could apparently make lawful agreements no matter how morally odious their content might have been. But in the latter part of [the twentieth] century, elites have revived the notion of *jus cogens* or peremptory norm, from which derogation is not permitted. The importance of these planks of an international bill of rights cannot be overstated. *Jus cogens* has a very special reference to the determination of policy content. Even where the message of the policy content of a purported prescription is (or was) clearly expressed, the actual prescriptive policy content may be different. A superordinate norm, for example, Article 103 of the U.N. Charter or an existing or subsequently emerged *jus cogens*, may force revisions of the content of the prescription. Many other actors besides those manifestly prescribing play a role in the prescriptive function. In this latter respect, content has certain affinities to the second component of a prescription: its authority signal.

Let us turn our attention to this second communication flow in prescription. Other than as fitting objects of criminal justice, thugs are rarely brought into polite legal discussion. It is a pity, because they are instructive as a power phenomenon. For this very reason, they were a major interest for Harold Lasswell who, like Pareto, insisted on including gangs in his itemization of political actors. Imagine four thugs sitting in a bar and deciding, meticulously following Roberts' Rules of Order, that all shopkeepers in the neighborhood will henceforth pay them 10 percent of gross receipts for "protection." Have they prescribed or made law? There is certainly a clear policy content and, alas, they may have the capacity to "enforce." But whatever the expectation of effectiveness, few would say, at least initially, that they had made law. Interestingly, if a parliament had said the same thing, few would gainsay that a prescription had been created.

Augustine remarked that a bandit is a little king and a king a big bandit. There is an important difference, in addition to size. What is missing in the thugs' enactment is what we may call the authority signal, a communication which attends the communication of policy content and control intention and which indicates to the relevant audience that the communicators are the appropriate lawmakers or, in more functional terms, have the authority to prescribe.

The base of authority may vary, from the divine or monarchical to the constitutional and democratic. It may be formal and derivative or charismatic and patently contrary to formal law: "This is the law but *I* say to ye." There may be a single base of authority or, as in heterogeneous and pluralistic systems, multiple bases requiring very complex authority signals, going through several steps or phases, each component of which is directed at a different constituent group. There may be explicit authority, as when agents plenipotentiary carefully examine each other's authorizations, and very diffuse and implicit authority. And authority changes: witness changes in the role of the House of Commons, Congress' commerce clause powers, the foreign affairs power of the President, the U.N. General Assembly's assertions of prescriptive competence. The point of emphasis is that an indispensable component of the complex communication that is a prescription is some authority signal which distinguishes demands backed up only by credible threats - the demands of the thugs in our example - from law.

The authority signal is much more complex than the communication of policy content. While the command of *what* to do is essentially unilinear, the communication of authority is more of a closed loop. It is the audience, whether or not its members realize it, that endows the prescriber with the authority that renders his communications prescription. Hence the search for authority must be empirical in the broadest sense, rather than merely documentary. In many circumstances, authority may be subtle and diffuse. But its indispensability in prescriptions is clear.

We now address the third communications flow. One of the sillier notions that surfaces in jurisprudence with an almost schizothymic regularity is that lawmaking is essentially a polite ethical conversation, a dialogue requiring only content and authority, the latter often derived implicitly from the inherent cogency of the former. If that were the case, we would maintain cadres of philosophers and rhetoricians instead of police, armies and other specialists in violence. Plainly, lawmaking involves another component: power, the capacity and willingness to make a preferential expression effective. This third component, which we prefer to call the communication of control intention, is broader than the concept of sanction. All prescriptions, by definition, contain a sanction, either a threat of deprivation for noncompliance or a promise of reward for compliance. But the fact that the drafter added a sanction does not mean that potential decision-makers whose jurisdiction will be invoked when there is a violation of the norm either have the capacity or the will to enforce the norm. Whatever the sanction that may be explicitly or implicitly designated, it is delusory to call a statement in the subjunctive mood a prescription or law if it is not accompanied by a credible communication that those who are prescribing intend to and can make it controlling. Moreover, the communication of control intention must be continuous throughout the life of the prescription. Episodic violations of a norm, among other things, have a testing function for members of the community who wish to terminate it, pushing to see whether control intention has waned and whether the prescription may henceforth be violated with diminished likelihood of sanction or with impunity.

Control intention is not synonymous with potential power. In many cases, a state elite that has, in an arithmetic sense, adequate power bases to enforce an unpopular norm, will find it inexpedient to do so if it alienates allies or undermines processes for decision-making in which the elite recognizes a continuing interest. On the other hand, where brutal use of power is the cachet of an elite group, it may seek opportunities to convey control intention in a superfluously brutal fashion and enhance the terror on which it bases itself.

Determining control intention requires, perforce, as comprehensive as possible a survey of the power process and the interests of those who are most effective in it. For each purported prescription, the inquirer must first determine which groups, official or nonofficial, constitute the effective power elite in the context in which the norm is to be implemented. This is no easy matter, for the power process is always potentially fluid. Sometimes only a few states may be critical. The inquirer must then identify the objectives of members of the elite constellation, the importance they attach to maintenance of the norm in present and projected contexts, and the actual value investment elites are willing to make to sustain the prescription. In pluralistic communities, inquiry must extend from the elite level to all relevant components of the domestic political process. Where power is widely shared, the process of control has many steps and links. …

Control intention does not require unanimity or even wide consensus. It is well to remember that norms are prescribed because they are policies which part of the community does not voluntarily or spontaneously support. Norms become effective because some elites have enough interest to make them effective. They continue to be norms only so long as some are able and willing to make them effective. Norms are not the issue of an always benign process.

Recall the familiar language in mutual defense treaties that an attack on any member will be viewed as an attack on each and all. Reflect on the brief history of the Carter Doctrine. The inquirer will frequently discover, as we will see, that elite objectives change, that support for a prescription may wane or that language or language equivalents proclaiming unqualified support for a prescription actually conceal a limit.

It is the coordination of these three message flows — policy content, authority signal and control intention — that indicates prescription or, in popular parlance, makes law. Demands on others that are backed up only by threats, only by control intention communications, may well shape the aggregate behavior of the target audience, if and so long as the demanders have and are willing to deploy the power they indicate. But it would be improper to designate their commands as prescriptive or law, though they may ultimately become such. "Power," Lasswell taught in one of his famous apothegms, "authoritizes itself."

Conversely, demands rich in authority signals but without adequate control intention communications may yield, at least for some, expressions of morality. But again it would be improper to call them law unless, in the hypothetically possible but extremely rare case, the target audience is so enchanted or enthralled by the particular authority mystique that control intention is either unnecessary, or may be deemed to have ultimately been created.

The exact mix of authority signal and control intention required to prescribe varies from context to context. In groups in which there is a high sense of collective purpose, and common interests have been internalized in the personalities of politically relevant members, authority signals alone may be sufficient to create prescriptive expectations. In aggregates in which inclusive identifications and perceptions of common interest are low or merely rhetorical, the communication of control intention may be most important. Above all, this is an approach which focuses primarily on the communications themselves, in their diverse forms, rather than on the empirically more inaccessible and hence more difficult question of the subjectivities of elites.

Human consciousness is not distinct and isolated from social process but in constant interstimulation with it. Hence, as Lasswell observed, nonauthoritative practices that endure may become prescriptive. Since the function of prescription is that the target audience come to expect that certain practices and procedures should be followed, demands that were initially not prescriptive may become prescriptive.

2. Siegfried Wiessner & Andrew R. Willard, *Policy-Oriented Jurisprudence*
44 GERMAN Y.B. INT'L L. 96, 97, 101, 107-112 (2001)

The jurisprudence Lasswell and McDougal developed starts with the delimitation of a problem as characterized by a discrepancy between predicted and desired future decisions regarding conflicting claims on any issue in society. It suggests that the problem at issue needs to be defined precisely and comprehensively in its relevant context, using all available reservoirs of knowledge. Authoritative and controlling responses to conflicting claims are analyzed as the relevant legal decisions of the past in light of their conditioning factors, including the predispositions of decision-makers and environmental elements. Only in light of these ever-changing conditioning factors can predictions about future decisions be made that are reliable. Moreover, what will be decided is not necessarily what should be decided. Accordingly, the most novel element that policy-oriented jurisprudence adds to all theories of legal realism and interdisciplinary work is that it appraises the alternative predicted futures, and recommends solution(s) to the problem(s) of concern that reflect the common interest of the community. Such solutions, policy-oriented jurisprudence posits, need to maximize access by all to all the values humans desire. This is the distinctive social interventionist feature of the approach. ...

Law as Process of Authoritative and Controlling Decision

Law, seen empirically, is a distinct social process, a process of communication of a particular nature: the relevant messages sent are statements of policy content that are transmitted by persons with authority in the relevant community, and include the express or implied threat of severe deprivations of values in the case of non-compliance and the promises of high indulgences or benefits in the case of compliance (signifying control intent). In short, law is conceived of as an *ongoing process* of *authoritative and controlling decision.* It is a human artifact, established, maintained and changed by the decisions of the politically relevant actors. In particular, law is not equated with a "body of rules" that enforce themselves. Rules always require for their implementation the "conveyor belt of human action," which is powered in large measure by human decision within particular communities. It is critical to understand that decision and law are not synonyms. For policy-oriented jurisprudence, only those decisions, i.e., communications with policy, or prescriptive, content, that are taken from community-wide perspectives of authority and backed up by control intent, are characterized as law. These are decisions that are made by the persons who are expected to make them, in accordance with criteria expected by community members, in established structures of authority, with sufficient bases in effective power to secure consequential control, and by authorized procedures. Compliance with the policy content of authoritative decision promises and/or generates significant benefits or indulgences in terms of any or all values; noncompliance is sanctioned by the threat and/or imposition of severe deprivations, again, in terms of any or all values.

The jurisprudence of positivism provides the counter-image to this empirical, dynamic conception of law. Its common focus on "existing" rules, emanating solely from entities deemed equally "sovereign," does not properly reflect the reality of how law is made, applied and changed. Positivism remains fixated on the past, trying to reap from words laid down, irrespective of the context in which they were written, the solution to a problem that arises today or tomorrow in very different circumstances. Without identifying the conditioning factors of the past decisions they rely on—such as the personality, political inclinations, gender and cultural background of the decision makers, as well as the mood of the times, and other societal factors—positivists try hard, in an ultimately futile quest for "certainty" of law, to predict future decisions. But, as they do not take into account changing and changed contexts (e.g., different legislators, judges, shifts in public opinion), their predictions are unlikely to be precise or accurate. Moreover, positivists gain no help from their theory when asked what the law "should" be. Indeed, their theory eschews any creative or prescriptive function. ...

The Decision Process, Including the Legal Process, and Its Mapping Categories

Policy-oriented jurisprudence also provides a refined way of thinking about processes of decision making. It conceives of decision processes in terms of the functions they perform. These functions include the gathering of intelligence, the promotion of preferences, the prescribing of authoritative policy or lawmaking, the invocation of prescriptions, the application of prescriptions, their termination, and the appraisal of the aggregate performance of a community's decision processes in terms of community goals.

Each decision function, in turn, can be mapped in terms of participants, perspectives, arenas, base values, strategies, and outcomes.

The Value Categories

The term "values" is used to designate the broad categories of events that gratify desire. In empirical terms, it signifies the things humans "value." They may be used in all relevant intellectual tasks. Analytically, they characterize the assets humans draw on in their efforts to achieve their goals (base values); preferentially, they relate to "preferred events" (scope values). Simply put, the concept of "base values" refers to the aggregate of assets people already have or have access to, whereas "scope values" refer to what people desire. In detail, policy-oriented jurisprudence characterizes values as follows:

Power is the making of decisions important to the social context as a whole and enforceable against challengers when necessary by the use of severe sanctions. In domestic legal systems, institutions of power include government at all levels together with parties and pressure groups specialized to influence community decisions.

Enlightenment is the gathering and spreading of information, institutionalized in agencies of research and the information media.

Wealth is the production and distribution of goods and services, institutionalized in business corporations and partnerships, trade unions and consumers' associations.

Well-being is opportunity for safety, health and comfort; relevant institutions include facilities for medical care and disease prevention.

Skill is opportunity to acquire and exercise excellence in a particular operation, including schools, artistic, vocational and professional organizations concerned with maintaining and improving standards of performance and taste.

Affection is giving and receiving intimacy, friendship and loyalty, including the institutions of family and intimate friends plus associations established to express loyalty.

Respect is the recognition and reciprocal honoring of freedom of choice. Distinctive institutions provide recognition of common merit as a human being and particular merit as a member of a group.

Rectitude refers to responsibility for conduct. Its institutions formulate and apply standards of responsibility, and justify and celebrate these norms in religious, metaphysical or ethical terms.

The social process specialized to the shaping and sharing of each value can be mapped in terms of participants, perspectives, situations, base values, strategies, and outcomes.

Five Indispensable Intellectual Tasks

In addition to what policy-oriented jurisprudence designates as principles of content, which refer to what scholars, advisers and decision makers are to focus their attention on, it provides principles of procedure, which refer to how the content is to be treated. Five intellectual or problem-solving tasks are recommended. The order in which they are carried out is not fixed. Moreover, the results of working on each task can be expected to influence how the others are performed and the outcomes they produce. The five tasks are the clarification of goals, the description of conflicting claims and past trends in decision, the analysis of factors that shape the trends in decision, the projection of future trends, and the invention, evaluation and selection of alternatives.

1. Delimitation of Problem and Clarification of Goals

The detailed clarification and specification of goals is sensitive to particular contexts. The overriding commitment of policy-oriented jurisprudence to a public order of human dignity, in which access by all to all the values humans desire is maximized, is not. This means that the commitment to preventing discrete public order violations, suspending violations that are occurring, deterring potential public order violations, restoring public order after it has been violated, correcting the behavior that generates violations, rehabilitating victims, and reconstructing the social process to remove conditions that appear likely to generate future public order violations is unyielding. Furthermore, our approach always considers progress toward achieving these goals in terms of the ways that different strategies are likely to influence the shaping and sharing of values. However, because the specification and relative priority of each value are likely to vary from context to context, the task of goal clarification and specification must take account of prevailing international and local conditions and, in particular, the perspectives of participants.

2. Identification of Conflicting Claims

Conflicting claims are important social parameters of any problem. They must be identified, together with the universe of claimants, their perspectives and their bases of power. They are context-specific.

3. Past Trends in Decision and Conditioning Factors

How has the world community responded, with authority and control intent, to these conflicting claims? We need to assess past trends in decision, i.e., determine how well the sanctioning process of the world community has performed in reaching its goals. We should investigate not only how the international system performed, but also why it succeeded or failed. This involves a close analysis of predispositional and environmental conditioning factors. Our approach would test each of the various prescriptive devices, institutional arrangements and mechanisms relevant to the problem under review for their contribution to achieving the goals for sanctioning and moving public order more in a direction compatible with human dignity. The task involves both tracking trends and appraising them against the goals established for a preferred public order.

Identification and analysis of those factors and combinations of factors that have shaped trends in decision are especially important when ascribing responsibility for successes and failures and in bringing clarity and precision to efforts at strategic intervention. This task confronts the question of why trends have been what they are. Policy-oriented jurisprudence conceptualizes the universe of potential conditioning factors most broadly in terms of predispositional and environmental factors. In differing contexts, how have these factors influenced the operation of the institutional arrangements for dealing, for example, with ruptures and potential ruptures of public order? When this question is addressed in specific contexts predispositional and environmental factors are examined in the context of particular problems, it becomes plausible to craft and put into effect alternative strategic interventions that are more likely to succeed because they are tailored to the context of conditions of concern. Factors and factor combinations that have helped in the achievement of goals can be strengthened and those that have frustrated achievement can be mitigated, neutralized or removed.

4. Projection of Future Trends

Projecting future trends requires an understanding of conditioning factors and how they might express themselves in the future. As with its assessment of past trends, policy-oriented jurisprudence is interested not only in what the future might bring, as opposed to what the past has brought, but also in how well the future is likely to approximate a public order of human dignity. To address this issue, our approach uses the projection of what are called "developmental constructs," which are both pathways and pictures of possible futures and can be quite specific to particular contexts. For example, a construct could be developed of a setting in which human rights abuses take place relatively infrequently at present, but in which they become increasingly common and virulent over time. Different institutional arrangements or mechanisms of accountability would be included in the construct or projection to show how each could operate, more or less successfully. The purpose of this construct and of developmental constructs, in general, is to provide guidance to scholars, advisers and decision makers through the provision of empirically grounded anticipations of the future. Such guidance is designed to help navigate contemporary societal rapids and enhance the likelihood of decisions that move public order toward human dignity and away from the eventuation of dystopias.

5. Alternatives and Recommendations in the Global Common Interest

The invention, evaluation and selection of alternatives is, in some measure, the culminating task in the procedure for solving problems. This can be an especially creative endeavor and builds on the results of the other tasks. Strategic intervention, whether in response to or in anticipation of human rights abuses in internal conflicts, is more likely to be accepted and successful when goals have been clarified, trends described, the conditions accounting for the trends identified and analyzed, and alternative futures projected. It is extremely context-sensitive, and it orients itself at the goal of maximizing access for all to all the values humans desire. ...

Conclusion

Policy-oriented jurisprudence does not promise or guarantee one correct, single answer to any problem posed. It does offer a comprehensive, detailed and self-aware approach to any problem. One of its distinctive features is its highly integrated stock of concepts and propositions about human behavior that can be used to focus one's attention on any problem for purposes of inquiry and action. This foundation is critical because the approach's basic framework for inquiry does not need to be invented anew whenever one is confronted by a novel problem context. Policy-oriented jurisprudence provides a stable frame of reference, including a series of heuristics for "mapping" any social, legal or decision context and an all-inclusive set of intellectual tasks that can be used by scholars, advisers or decision makers for purposes of self-orientation and strategic intervention in the flow of pertinent events. The approach is comprehensive and supple so that once one understands how to use it, one can apply it to an infinite variety of problems. Maximizing intelligence on any given issue, it enhances the making of better, more informed choices. With respect to all problems, from the heartrending to the mundane, the overriding goal of policy-oriented jurisprudence is to arrive at solutions that reflect the global common interest in approximating a world public order of human dignity.

Notes and Questions

1. The method suggested lacks the apparent certainty of Article 38. Does it, however, deal with problems with which Article 38 cannot grapple? For a further explication of the approach in a symposium on method, see Siegfried Wiessner & Andrew R. Willard, *Policy-Oriented Jurisprudence and Human Rights Abuses in Internal Conflict: Toward a World Public Order of Human Dignity*, 93 Am. J. Int'l L. 316-334 (1999). For an analysis of the differential needs of institutionalized and non-institutionalized settings, see Siegfried Wiessner, *International Law in the 21st Century: Decisionmaking in Institutionalized and Non-Institutionalized Settings*, 26 Thesaurus Acroasium 129, 146 (1997).

2. The Ninth Edition of Oppenheim's International Law also conceives the formation of customary international law as a "process." According to this work:

> In certain circumstances customary rules can develop fairly rapidly, as for example, in relation to the continental shelf, and perhaps the exclusive economic zone, this may occur particularly where the new rule has its origin in, or is soon reflected in, a multilateral treaty of appropriately general action. However, usually a customary international law is too slow a means of adapting the law to fast-changing circumstances.

Lassa Oppenheim, Oppenheim's International Law 30 (Sir Robert Jennings & Sir Arthur Watts eds., Harlow: Longman 1992).

Usage is transformed into custom "wherever and as soon as a line of international conduct frequently adopted by states is considered by states generally legally obligatory or legally right." *Id.* Indications that a given custom has become operative can be culled from bilateral treaties, the output of multilateral mechanisms, and declarations by policy-makers at the state level. *Id.* at 28. As noted, *supra*, at 15, n. 4, the ICJ has not done this systematically.

3. Sir Hersch Lauterpacht has called the so-called psychological conception of international custom "a somewhat pretentious notion which is no more than a description of the requirement of *opinio necessitatis juris*, i.e., of the consciousness that the conduct, frequently or constantly pursued, is due to the existence of a sense of legal obligation or at least of the will to undertake a legal obligation." Sir Hersch Lauterpacht, The Development of International Law by the International Court 379 (Cambridge U. Press 1958).

For Lauterpacht, it is proper to regard "all uniform conduct of Governments (or, in appropriate cases, abstention therefrom) as evidencing the *opinio necessitatis juris* except when it is shown that the conduct in question was not accompanied by such intention." *Id.* at 380.

4. Judge Rosalyn Higgins insists on the key role that the International Court of Justice plays in the development of customary international law. She contends that "at the end of the day international law is what the International Court of Justice would declare it to be." ROSALYN HIGGINS, INTERNATIONAL LAW AND HOW WE USE IT 37 (Oxford U. Press 1994). Yet, this method has not been the Court's strong suit. The problematic aspects of this approach propel Higgins to conclude that:

> [w]here the status of a treaty or a resolution at the heart of the very issue under consideration by the Court is invoked, a rather rigorous analysis of its status will ensue. But where resolutions or treaties are invoked somewhat incidentally as evidence of law, a much looser approach will suffice.

Id. at 37-38.

In fact, Higgins proceeds to set a threshold that is not very different from the classic test for confirming customary international law. While she contends that resolutions can play a role in the formation of international legal norms, accurate determinations regarding their weight should emerge from judicial inquiries aimed "at the subject-matter of the resolution in question, at whether they are binding or recommendatory, at the majorities supporting their adoption, at repeated practice in relation to them, at evidence of *opinio juris.*" *Id.* at 28.

5. Professor Anthony D'Amato suggests that for customary law to develop, there must be a pattern of states declaring specific practices they engage in as legal; "social habit, courtesy, comity, moral requirements, political expediency, plain 'usage' or any other norm" that are not explicitly characterized by states as legal, in D'Amato's view, do not qualify. ANTHONY A. D'AMATO, THE CONCEPT OF CUSTOM IN INTERNATIONAL LAW 76 (Cornell U. Press 1971). There is also a quantitative dimension to the erosion of prescriptions and the emergence of new customary international law:

> [C]ustomary law has changed over the years, and thus any theory must incorporate the possibility of change into its concept of custom. In particular, an "illegal" act by a state contains the seeds of a new legality. When a state violates an existing rule of customary international law, it undoubtedly is "guilty" of an illegal act, but the illegal act itself becomes a disconfirmatory instance of the underlying rule. The next state will find it somewhat easier to disobey the rule, until eventually a new line of conduct will replace the original rule this is a function partly of the number of acts that establishes the original rule in the first place, the remoteness in times of the previous acts, the legal authoritativeness of the participating states, and other possible factors, including the argumentative skill of the proponent or opponent of a claim of custom.

Id. at 97.

While it has been argued that the failure of a state to protest against a given customary norm functions as proof of its intent to be bound by it, D'Amato argues that:

> *if* opportunities exist to change customary law, then states need not concern themselves too much with protests. *Since* states do not often issue notes of protest, and hardly ever do so when they are not directly concerned, if follows that a relatively easy way exists for states to change customary law. One way . . . is simply to act contrary to the norm and hope that the directly affected foreign state acquiesces or at least does not complain too loudly. Another far more secure and simple way . . . is to sign a treaty.

Id. at 101.

6. In *Prosecutor v. Tadic a/k/a/ "Dule,"* Antonio Cassese, president of the UN's International Criminal Tribunal for the Former Yugoslavia, commented on how custom regarding the interpretation of Article 2 of the Statute of the International Tribunal might emerge. According to him:

> [i]n this connection the Chamber notes with satisfaction the statement in the *amicus curiae* brief submitted by the Government of the United States, where it is contended that:
>
> > the 'grave breaches' provision of Article 2 of the International Tribunal Statute apply to armed conflicts of a non-international character as well as those of an international character...
>
> This statement, unsupported by any authority, does not seem to be warranted as to the interpretation of Article 2 of the Statute. Nevertheless, seen from another viewpoint, there is no gainsaying its significance: that statement articulates the legal views of one of the permanent members of the Security Council on a delicate legal issue, on this score it provides the first indication of a possible change in *opinio juris* of States.

Prosecutor v. Tadic a/k/a"Dule," Decision on the Defense Motion for Interlocutory Appeal on Jurisdiction, at 47 (U.N. Int'l Tribunal for the Former Yugoslavia, Case No. IT-94—1-AR72, 1995).

Custom is presented in classical theory as essentially state-controlled. In light of the increasingly prominent role that actors such as corporations, non-governmental organizations, and individuals play in the international legal process, is it time for the existing theories regarding custom to be revised? Would such a shift only complicate efforts to ascertain the content of customary law?

7. Professor Reisman has questioned the capability of customary law to deal with the increasingly complicated problems that the international community faces, arguing that

> [i]t should be clear to anyone with the faintest understanding of international life that customary processes of lawmaking cannot deal with the enormous problems facing the world such as the debt crisis, the complex arrangements involved in a space station, the staggering detailed problems involved in meshing economically interdependent but functionally different national economies, the arranging of transnational defense against and suppression of terrorism and so on.

W. Michael Reisman, *The Cult of Custom in the Late 20th Century,* 17 Cal. W. Int'l L.J. 133, 143 (1987).

However, for Reisman, this reality did not necessarily mean that the UN General Assembly would loom larger in the international law-making process. Rather, he suggested that legal responses to international problems would be coordinated in regional and sectoral forums in relative secrecy. Such an approach would allow the more powerful members of the family of nations to blunt the power exercised by a majority of states in the General Assembly.

8. The fact that "the international community of the late twentieth century faces an expanding need to develop universal norms to address global concerns" causes Jonathan Charney to call for the establishment of "new rules that are binding on all subjects." Jonathan I. Charney, *Universal International Law,* 87 Am. J. Int'l L. 529 (1993). "For unless all states are bound, an exempted recalcitrant state could act as a spoiler for the entire international community." *Id.* For Charney, the most viable vehicle for establishing universal norms is multilateral mechanisms, not treaties, which require time to formulate, may not be signed by all states, and demand formal acts to be incorporated. Moreover, "the increased clarity and the more transparent process encourage widespread participation and endow the resulting law with greater legitimacy than is generally possible through the traditional customary lawmaking process." *Id.* at 551.

9. Judge Richard Baxter examined the role that treaties play in the formation of customary norms. As long as a legal instrument "purports to be declaratory of customary international law or if it can be established that such was the intent of its draftsmen, the treaty may be accepted as valid evidence of the state of customary international law." R.R. Baxter, *Multilateral Treaties as Evidence of Customary International Law,* Brit. Y.B. Int'l L. 1965-66 at 298 (1968). "As such, it

provides a sort of snapshot of or 'photographs,' the state of the law as at the time of the entry into force as to individual States . . . so long as States remain parties to it." *Id.* at 299. Given this, time is likely to diminish the validity of assertions regarding the capacity of a treaty to continue embodying the substance of customary law. The integration of a treaty into the larger body of customary international law affects states that are a party to the agreement as well as those that are not. According to Baxter, "denunciation of the treaty by a party cannot absolve that State from its obligation to observe the rules of customary international law, proof of the existence of which is to be found in the treaty." *Id.* at 300. Those arguing that a legal norm has entered the realm of international custom need not demonstrate that the signatories have actually complied with their treaty-based duties. Rather, "[t]he process of establishing the state of customary international law is one of demonstrating what States consider to be the measure of their obligations." *Id.*

10. In *Traditional and Modern Approaches to Customary International Law: A Reconciliation*, 95 AM. J. INT'L. L. 757 (2001), Anthea Elizabeth Roberts suggests that what she calls a "reflective interpretive approach" provides the best methodology for assessing asserted customs. Positing that traditional and modern approaches to custom appear to be opposed, with the traditional approach emphasizing state practice and the modern approach emphasizing *opinio juris*, Roberts has sought to create a theoretical account of custom that analyzes the competing justifications and tries to accommodate both approaches.

C. THE INTERNATIONAL LAWMAKING PROCESS IN OPERATION

A number of issues can serve to demonstrate the way the international lawmaking process works and the need for a more complex method for identification of what the law is at any moment. Indeed, most of the material that follows in this casebook will be examining trends and identifying changes, over time, in normative formulations. For purposes of discussion at this stage, however, it may be useful to look at a single issue in order to determine how law has been changed with regard to it over a period of decades and the agents and factors that have influenced those changes.

1. The Effort to Control Nuclear Weapons

a. 1945 - 1960

The Second World War was terminated by the nuclear bombing of cities in Japan by the United States. Shortly thereafter, the Cold War commenced and the United States and the then Soviet Union engaged in a fiercely competitive nuclear arms race. The programs of each of these superpowers required regular testing of nuclear weapons.

From the earliest days of the nuclear age, the scientific and political elite appreciated that nuclear explosions in the atmosphere had definite though imperfectly understood and assessed costs in terms of effects on human beings within a certain proximity, and short- and long-term effects on the natural environment of the test. Hence the more democratic states with nuclear testing programs, either anticipating or deflecting a public reaction which might have jeopardized the tests, began to move them further and further from population centers. But the earth, like a spaceship, is a closed system. The further one goes from one's own population centers, the closer perforce one gets to another's. Hence the search for distant sites was really, like the euphemistic "externalization of costs" in economic theory, a way of dumping an undesirable by-product, in this case nuclear filth, on someone else.

For the United States, in the late 1940s and early 1950s, the path of externalization went from the deserts of our own Southwest to Bikini Atoll in the Marshall Islands in 1946 and, in 1947, to what came to be the more permanent "Pacific Proving Grounds" at Eniwetok Atoll near Bikini. From time to time, areas of the high seas, initially 30,000 square miles, were closed. In 1954, an area finally including nearly 400,000 square miles of high seas was closed for almost six months.

Pacific basin states, whose elites unquestionably knew what was afoot, were in no position to lodge effective protests, even if they had wished to. We are speaking of a period before the burst of Third World membership in the U.N. General Assembly. Many of the basin states still had formal or de facto colonial status. Others, such as Japan and Australia, were part of the Western defense alliance. Australia was cooperating with some Western testing, Japan was a beneficiary of the nuclear umbrella and in any case was in no position to protest effectively. Among the Western elite there was a substantial consensus that, in Winston Churchill's words: "There is only one sane policy for the free world . . . defense through deterrents." In competition with the Soviet Union, this necessitated an ongoing nuclear development and testing program.

In 1954, the Marshall Islanders, supported by the Soviet Union and India, protested the tests to the U.N. Trusteeship Council, alleging a violation of the Trusteeship Agreement and the Charter. A majority of the Trusteeship Council rejected their move. At the time, the issue of lawfulness was primarily joined over the compatibility of the tests with the traditional freedoms of the law of the sea. Plainly, the tests closed substantial parts of the high seas, preventing the basic freedoms of transit, overflight and fishing. Some scholars, such as Dr. Margolis, argued that the U.S. tests were clear violations of the law of the sea. Other scholars, preeminently Professors McDougal and Schlei, contended that the tests were lawful. They reasoned that the law of the sea, properly understood, allowed for innovative uses, initiated by unilateral claim, if the use could be shown to be nonaggressive, inclusively advantageous, consistent with basic Charter principles, reasonable and, in the context, as considerate as possible of lawful uses engaged in by others.

(1) Myres S. McDougal & Norbert A. Schlei, *The Hydrogen Bomb Tests in Perspective: Lawful Measures for Security*
64 Yale L.J. 648, 648-63, 682-88 (1955)

Those who attack the legality of the Pacific tests ordinarily begin by implying that any use of atomic and thermonuclear weapons would be unlawful and that this conclusion has some relevance to the legality of the tests. Their principal attack is, however, cast in terms of so-called "traditional and universally accepted rules" said to be found in the international law of the sea, and an attempted "inescapable" interpretation of the U.N. Charter and the Trusteeship Agreement for the Former Japanese Mandated Islands. The most comprehensive and detailed elaboration of this attack appears in the immediately preceding article by Dr. Emanuel Margolis.

"Freedom of navigation," "freedom of fisheries," "freedom to lay submarine cables," and "freedom of aerial movement," Dr. Margolis argues, are "corollaries" of the "absolute rule" of "freedom of the seas." Although there are some "general police powers" which may be exercised on the high seas "in time of peace," and some "special police powers" which may be acquired by treaty, the bomb tests and the warning areas they make necessary fall within neither class. They are, therefore, forbidden by the "clear rule of law" that "no state can exercise sovereignty over the high seas in time of peace." It is further argued that the tests' injurious effects upon fishing, outside the zone of immediate danger, violate some ill-defined international prescription against pollution, or at least do not measure up to "justice and equity," and that the tests must therefore be stopped.

Finally, it is asserted as an "inescapable" conclusion that testing of nuclear weapons by the United States in the Pacific Proving Grounds is "at variance" with the "unqualified imperatives" of Article 73 of the U.N. Charter and Article 6 of the Trusteeship Agreement. By selective reading from that article of the Charter, it is noted that member states there recognize the principle that the interests of the inhabitants of non-self-governing territories "are paramount," and accept as a "sacred trust" the obligation to promote the "well-being" of the inhabitants and to this end to ensure their protection against "abuses." By similar exegesis upon the Trusteeship Agreement, it is added that the Administering Authority undertook to promote the economic development of the inhabitants by "the development of fisheries," to protect the inhabitants against "the loss of their lands and resources," and "to protect the health of the inhabitants." It is argued, further, that these provisions are not, at least not within the same section, "diluted" by the phrase: "subject to the requirements of security." It is then stated as a fact that injury to persons and property in connection with tests is "bound to occur," and that the tests therefore violate the Agreement. But even if danger of injury could be eliminated the tests would still be illegal, it is said, because the necessary safety measures would violate the agreement in that they would involve "removing [the inhabitants] from their land," and "depriving them of fishing grounds for months at a time." It makes no difference to this conclusion that the Agreement gives the administering authority "full powers of administration, legislation, and jurisdiction" over the territory, and the power to "establish naval, military and air bases and to erect fortifications" in the territory, as well as other broad powers with respect to security. By some curious criterion of construction, none of the powers of the administering authority are relevant in ascertaining the extent of its duties: the latter are "unqualified imperatives."

The United States' only alternatives, these critics conclude, are to cease further testing altogether, or to conduct tests in a manner which is "compatible with the basic general tenets of international law, and the specific provisions of the United Nations Charter and the Trusteeship Agreement." This can be done "only … by conducting them . . . within the … United States, or Alaska, or somewhere within the Arctic Region in the 'sector' north of Alaska."

It is our belief that all of these arguments are unsound in law and in policy, and we propose to refute them seriatim. …

Throughout the centuries of its development, one may observe the regime of the high seas as, not a static body of absolute rules, but rather a living, growing, customary law, grounded in the claims, practices, and sanctioning expectations of nation-states, and changing as the demands and expectations of decision-makers are changed by the exigencies of new social and economic interests, by the imperatives of an ever developing technology and by other continually evolving condition, in the world arena. From the perspective of realistic description, the public order of the high seas is not a mere body of rules, but a whole decision-making process, including both a structure of authorized decision-makers and a body of highly flexible, inherited prescriptions: it is a continuous process of interaction in which the decision-makers of individual nation-states unilaterally put forward claims of the most diverse and conflicting character to the use of the world's seas, and in which other decision-makers, external to the demanding nation-state and including both national and international officials, weigh and appraise these competing claims in terms of the interests of the world community and of the rival claimants, and ultimately accept or reject them.

The competing claims asserted by nation-state decision-makers to the use of the high seas, the events to which the "regime of the high seas" is a response, vary enormously in the comprehensiveness and particularity of the interests sought to be secured, in the location and size of area affected, and in the duration of the claim. They range from the comprehensive and continuous claim to all competence in the "territorial sea," through the continuous but limited claims to navigation, fishing, and cable-laying upon the "high seas," to the relatively temporary and limited claims to exercise authority and control beyond territorial boundaries for a vast array of national purposes: security and self-defense, enforcement of health, neutrality, and customs regulations, conservation or monopolization of fisheries, exploitation of the sedentary fisheries and mineral resources of the seabed and continental shelf, the conducting of naval maneuvers, military exercises, and other peacetime defensive activities, and so on.

It need cause no confusion that the authoritative decision-makers put forward by the public order of the high seas to resolve all these competing claims include, in addition to judges of international courts and other international officials, those same nation-state officials who on other occasions are themselves claimants — that, in other words, the same nation-state officials are alternatively, in a process of reciprocal interaction, both claimants and external decision-makers passing upon the claims of others. This duality in function ("*dédoublement fonctionnel*") merely reflects the present lack of specialization and centralization of policy functions in international law generally. Similarly, it may be observed, without cause for deprecation or shocked averting of the eyes, that these authoritative decision-makers projected by nation-states for creating and applying a common public order, honor each other's unilateral claims to the use of the high seas not merely by explicit agreements but also by mutual tolerances expressed in countless decisions in foreign offices, national courts, and national legislatures — which create expectations that power will be restrained and exercised in certain uniformities of pattern. This, too, is but the process by which in the present state of world organization most decisions about jurisdiction in public and private international law are, and must be, taken.

The over-riding policy which infuses this whole decision-making process, perhaps it requires explicit statement, is not the negation of use, but the encouragement of use. The major policy purpose which inspires the regime of the high seas is not merely the negation of restrictions upon navigation and fishing but also the promotion of the most advantageous — that is, the most conserving and fully utilizing — peaceful use and development by all peoples of a great common resource, covering two-thirds of the world's surface, for all contemporary values. The concept of a common and reciprocal interest in fullest utilization underlies the whole flow of decision.

For pursuing this major policy purpose in regulating the maze of conflicting claims which confront them, the authoritative decision-makers of the world community have elaborated that comprehensive body of complementary prescriptions which makes up "the regime of the high seas." One set of these prescriptions, that [are] generally referred to under the label of "freedom of the seas," was formulated, and is invoked, to honor unilateral claims to navigation, fishing, cable-laying, and other similar uses. The other set, that which includes the prescriptions summed up in a wide variety of technical terms such as "territorial sea," "contiguous zones," "jurisdiction," "continental shelf," was formulated, and is invoked, to honor all the great variety of claims, both comprehensive and particular, which may interfere, in greater or less degree, with navigation and fishing. To the initiated it is not surprising that the technical terms in which both sets of these prescriptions are formulated are at the highest level of abstraction and, hence, ambiguous in highest degree. A decision-maker confronted with the task of deciding upon the lawfulness of a challenged claim to the use of the seas must create meaning for these terms and must turn to other sources for detailed policy guidance. The sources to which such a decision-maker, like the judges of the International Court of Justice, is authorized, and may be required by the necessities of policy clarification, to turn include not only "international conventions, whether general or particular, establishing rules expressly recognized by the contesting states," but also "international custom, as evidence of a general practice accepted as law," "the general principles of law recognized by civilized nations," "judicial decisions and the teachings of the most highly qualified publicists of the various nations," and considerations "*ex aequo et bono.*"

The great ambiguity of the constituent technical terms in the principal prescriptions and the wide variety of authoritative policy sources accorded to the authorized decision-makers have given, and continue to give, to such decision-makers, a very large discretion to adjust particular controversies in terms of the multiple variables peculiar to each controversy and thus to promote the overriding policy of full-utilization. The degree to which decisions for the last century and a half, because of common interest in the sea as an efficient medium of communication and as an abundant source of food, have given a high priority to claims for freedom of navigation and fishing, is sufficiently emphasized in conventional literature. It is equally common knowledge, however, though on occasion reluctantly admitted, that a parallel flow of decisions has protected a great variety of claims to authority and control on the high seas for the protection of security, health, revenue laws, economic welfare, and so on, even against protests that they interfere with navigation and fishing, and that a still higher priority is accorded to claims of "sovereign" competence in "territorial seas" despite such interference. It has been recognized in decision, if not in the justifications summarized in the textbooks, that all of these claims, those to navigation and fishing and those that may interfere, are of a common character: they are all unilateral assertions by particular claimants to individual use of a great common resource and all such assertions are affected in equal degree — navigation and fishing no more or no less than the others — with community interest in fullest utilization and conservation, and with national interest, which, though possibly varying with geographical propinquity in particular instances, is in the sum of all instances common to all claimants. The technical prescriptions of the "freedom of the seas," on the one hand, and of "territorial sea," "contiguous zone," "jurisdiction," and so on, on the other, are not arbitrary, inelastic dogma, but rather are highly flexible policy preferences invoked by decision-makers to record or justify whatever compromise or adjustment of competing claims they may reach in any particular controversy. And for all types of controversies the one test that is invariably applied by decision-makers is that simple and ubiquitous, but indispensable, standard of what, considering all relevant policies and all variables in context, is *reasonable* as between the parties. The all-pervading importance of this test of "reasonableness" for resolving competing claims to authority and control on the high seas has been well indicated by Professor H. A. Smith, who, though as spokesman for official British policy is most opposed to extension of national power beyond territorial seas, writes:

> The law of nations which is neither enacted nor interpreted by any visible authority universally recognized, professes to be the application of reason to international conduct. From this it follows that any claim [to assert power outside the 3-mile limit] which is admittedly reasonable may fairly be presumed to be in accordance with law, and the burden of

proving that it is contrary to law should lie on the state which opposes the claim.

Without accepting Professor Smith's explanation for the use of reasonableness as a criterion, one may yet applaud the accuracy of his summary of decision-makers' perspectives.

The sections of this article which immediately follow are intended to suggest the broad outlines of relevant world prescriptions regulating the use of the high seas and to indicate in greater detail the process of decision. It will be observed that the emphasis of decision-makers upon "reasonableness" as a criterion has required them to accord a very high deference to claims to security, as against claims to unhampered navigation and fishing, in contexts of high expectations of violence. It will be made clear that the hydrogen bomb tests contravene none of the fundamental policies which underlie the "freedom of the seas" and come easily within the policies which have in the past sanctioned the greatest variety of claims more seriously interfering with navigation and fishing. It will, therefore, be concluded that the relevant world prescriptions and the process of decision-making, taken as a whole, clearly enable, and perhaps even require, decision-makers external to the United States, whether national or international, to recognize and affirm that the hydrogen bomb tests are reasonable, and hence lawful, within the regime of the high seas. ...

Plainly no existing prescriptions in the regime of the high seas are literally applicable to the unique problem presented by the tests. The United States claim bears no similarity whatever to those which, historically, "freedom of the seas" was intended to combat. Others are not excluded from the area affected in order to enable the United States to grant fishing monopolies to its nationals or to pursue the commercial aggrandizement of the United States in any way. It is apparent, also, that the claim of the United States offers no serious interference with the policies of promoting commercial navigation and fishing which underlie "freedom of the seas." Moreover, the claim does not offend against the subordinate policies against international friction which are involved in claims to exercise police powers on the high seas. No ships are seized or condemned, nor is civil or criminal jurisdiction of any kind asserted.

What is relevant, and can be applied without irrational extrapolation, to this new problem from prior prescriptions in the regime of the high seas is the test of reasonableness which underlies them all - the test by which the decision-makers of the world community have consistently during modern times decided between claims to navigation and fishing and all that great variety of claims, recounted above, which may interfere with navigation and fishing, and ranging, as we have seen, through all the labels of "territorial sea," "contiguous zones," "piracy," "self-defense," "continental shelf," and so on, even to "freedom of the seas" itself. Because of their support of this test, all the decisions sustaining claims which interfere with navigation and fishing, whether for contiguous or non-contiguous uses, may be regarded as relevant authority for appraising the claim of the United States. The claim of the United States must enjoy, of course, whatever contribution to reasonableness the factor of contiguity may make, since the United States has jurisdiction not only over the land areas within the warning zones, but also over all land areas whatsoever for nearly a thousand miles. Beyond propinquity to controlled shores, the United States may, however, point to many other factors as indices of the reasonableness of its claim, factors comparable to those which prior decision-makers have invoked to sustain so great a variety of claims to non-contiguous uses. The factors most relevant for appraising the United States claim are that it is for a purpose much honored in world prescription, that it asserts the least possible degree of authority necessary to the achievement of its purpose, that it is limited both in area and in duration to the minimum consistent with its purpose, that the area which it affects is of relatively slight importance to international trade and fishing, and that it is asserted in a context of crisis which makes its purpose of paramount importance to all who value a free world society.

The claim of the United States is in substance a claim to prepare for self-defense. It is not, as commonly in self-defense, a claim to respond with force to an attack; it is no claim to invade territory or to sink fleets in anticipation of attack or to take any of the other measures of drastic interference with others commonly subsumed under self-defense. It is, however, a claim to take certain preparatory measures under conditions comparable to those traditionally held to justify measures in self-defense. It is a claim to take certain actions in contiguous zones and upon the high seas, with the minimum possible interference with others, under conditions of high necessity. The conditions of this grave necessity and the absence of reasonable alternatives are familiar knowledge. The contemporary development of instruments of destruction makes it possible for a war-bent nation-state utterly to destroy an opponent and perhaps much of the world. It has not been possible to establish, under the United Nations, commitments and procedures of global scope which offer reasonable assurance against aggression. As expectations of imminent violence in the world arena have become ever more realistic and intense, many of the nations of the free world have organized themselves, under appropriate provisions of the U.N. Charter, into regional groupings for their more effective self-defense. The United States has undertaken its program of atomic and thermonuclear weapons development to ensure that these coalitions of free nations, are not lacking in the retaliatory power which may deter aggression, or in the weapons of self-defense if deterrence fails.

Even prior to the bipolarization of the world and the development of nuclear weapons, it was generally agreed that a nation-state could, under the necessities of self-defense, take the most drastic measures in interference with what would otherwise have been the rights of others. Some of the historic examples of the exercise of this right of self-defense have been recounted above and others may be found in all the texts. So fundamental is the underlying policy, in a world without adequate centralized authority for the maintenance of public order, that an express exception for self-defense is an integral part of the prohibition of violence which appears in the United Nations Charter. Exercised in the first instance by the nation-state whose existence is threatened, but subjected also to review for reasonableness by external decision-makers, this right is no nullification of world order but one of the few remaining instruments by which world order may be sought. If, therefore, the present legal organization of the world and posture of world affairs put so high a premium upon self-defense, with authorization of potentially the most drastic interferences with others, it cannot, we believe, be reasonably concluded that it is unreasonable for the United States to engage in temporary and limited interferences with navigation and fishing upon the high seas in preparation for defense of itself, its allies, and all the values which they cherish.

NOTES AND QUESTIONS

1. Dr. Emanuel Margolis argued against the position espoused by McDougal & Schlei in his article, *The Hydrogen Bomb Experiments in International Law,* 64 YALE L.J. 629 (1955). For Margolis, "[f]reedom of the seas is an absolute freedom to use the high seas except to the extent international custom and treaties have modified it in order to meet the needs of a continually 'smaller' and more dynamic international community." *Id.* at 634. Margolis acknowledged that the vast warning zone the United States set up which closed off so much of the Pacific, was prompted by humanitarian ends. But, he continued, "Humanitarian ends have led the United States deeper and deeper into this legal dilemma: the greater the degree of precaution, the greater the interference with freedom of navigation on the high seas." *Id.* at 636. For Margolis, the alternative was to test within the United States, which he acknowledged, "With necessary evacuation of the population from exceedingly large areas — conceivably an entire state or group of states." *Id.* at 647.

2. Note that Margolis' theory allows for no adjustment of norms to take account of other, possibly fundamental international policies. The theory propounded by McDougal and Schlei does allow for such adjustments, but they are unilaterally claimed with no effective process of review. Suppose, however, that a system of international review were available. Would this address the problem?

3. A critical factor for McDougal and Schlei was the existence of the Cold War and their contention that the United States was the bulwark of freedom against aggressive and expansive Soviet totalitarianism. Insofar as this is a justification, would it survive the Cold War?

4. Besides spreading radiation throughout a large expanse of the South Pacific, the U.S. tests sent shockwaves through diplomatic circles and were denounced by Eurocommunist political forces. According to Jonathan W. Weisgall:

> [t]he Soviet Union viewed Operation Crossroads as evidence that America was not interested in controlling atomic weapons, and it saw a direct link between the tests and the UN negotiations. . . . The Soviet line was simple: America was plotting an atomic war, and Operation Crossroads was the rehearsal. Other European Socialist and Communist parties took the same approach, denouncing the tests as a diabolical instrument of U.S. foreign policy. 'The atomic bomb is on a level with the evil deeds of the Nazis, and places conquerors and vanquished on the same plane,' proclaimed the Italian Socialist newspaper *Avanti. L'Unitá,* the Italian Communist organ, described Crossroads as a 'most startling, monstrous and at the same time tragically grotesque experiment.' Sweden's Socialist newspapers contrasted the blast to lectures in Moscow's parks on the peaceful uses of atomic energy. 'The Statute of Liberty, which reminds one of the days the United States was a model democracy,' wrote one paper, 'ought to be supplanted by a statute of the Bikini goat, symbol of American imperialism's greatest propaganda fiasco.'

JONATHAN W. WEISGALL, OPERATION CROSSROADS: THE ATOMIC TESTS AND BIKINI ATOLL 252-55 (United States Naval Institute 1994).

5. The former Soviet Union soon conducted its own hydrogen bomb tests over the Pacific. Several commentators noted the effect of U.S. and Soviet actions on developing customary law. Richard Falk wrote:

> [a] characteristic of a decentralized social system is that the political claims of the powerful nation-states serve as legal precedents for other, less powerful, members of the international community. Nuclear testing by the United States and the Soviet Union created permissive precedents that are very difficult to repudiate. Relative power plays a much greater role in creating precedents than in repudiating them. There is a kind of reciprocity and symmetry operative in international society, as in all social systems, that makes the assertion by one state of a legal claim to act in a specified way available to other states similarly situated. Such symmetry owes much to the external aspects of the ideology associated with national sovereignty, an ideology that has contributed so centrally to the constitutive structure of traditional international law through ideas of the equality of states, the absoluteness of territorial jurisdiction, and the doctrine of nonintervention.

Richard A. Falk, The Status of Law in International Society 452 (Princeton U. Press 1970).

According to another commentator, Martti Koskenniemi:

> [w]e have seen that one understanding regards custom as a 'process of reciprocal interaction' in which States constantly present claims vis-à-vis each other and acquiescence in them. The emergence of custom is, from such perspective, 'a process by which the better of two conflicting claims prevails.' The merit of this view seems to lie in its correctness. The law need not be ascertained in an abstract, *erga omnes* manner. Obligation is based on a particular legal relationship which is interpreted so as to reflect an individual norm . . . Even a rapid glance at the jurisprudence of the ICJ shows that it has tended to base obligations rather on the specific relations between the disputing States than general rules. ...
>
> Similarly, in the *Nuclear Test Cases* (1974), the Application of Australia and New Zealand seemed originally to concern the application of general law to the French nuclear weapon tests. But the Court interpreted the submission so as to aim simply at the cessation of the particular French tests, conducted in the vicinity of the Applicants' territories in the Pacific. In its effort to 'isolate the real issue in the case,' the Court construed the applicable law on the basis of the Parties' bilateral relations. Specific attention was paid to the exchange of diplomatic correspondence between them. The final solution — that France had taken a unilateral obligation to terminate testing — was not based on a general rule but on a certain interpretation of the bilateral relationship between France and the two Applicants.
>
> The Court's strategy of bilateralization — its apparent neglect for the formulations of the submissions — has been the object of severe criticism.

Martti Koskenniemi, From Apology to Utopia: The Structure of International Legal Argument 410-13 (Coronet Books 1989). Is the criticism to which Koskenniemi refers justified or is the ICJ, its name notwithstanding, ineluctably an instrument of diplomatic settlement? Discuss.

6. Besides unfolding in law journals, the debate over the legality of the American nuclear tests was also carried into US federal court. In *Pauling v. McElroy,* American citizens, residents of the Marshall Islands, and other non-resident aliens sought to:

> [e]njoin the Commissioners of the Atomic Energy Commission and the Secretary of Defense from detonating any nuclear weapons that produce radiation or radioactive atomic nuclei, on the grounds that such radiation will inflict serious genetic and somatic injury upon plaintiffs and the population of the world in general, including unborn generations. The Marshallese alien plaintiffs allege in addition that they are threatened

> with imminent danger, including destruction and contamination of their food supply, by the detonating of nuclear weapons in the Marshall Islands.

164 F. Supp. 390, 392 (D.C. Cir. 1959). In its ruling, the court held that:

> [t]he evidence presented by plaintiffs in support of their motions for preliminary injunctions does not clearly establish that the current test series will produce the serious deleterious consequences to plaintiffs and the world at large which plaintiffs assert. The plaintiffs have not shown that the considerations of possible deleterious effects to human beings claimed by plaintiffs to result from such tests outweigh the public interest involved in the development of nuclear weapons through these tests in furtherance of the national defense and safety. *Id.*

See also, Exclusion of Ships from Nonterritorial Weapons Testing Zones, 99 HARV. L. REV. 1040, 1044-45 (1986); Arnold, *The Effects of the Recent Bomb Test on Human Beings*, 10 BULL. ATOM. SCIENTISTS 347 (1954). For the statement of Lewis L. Strauss, Chairman of the Atomic Energy Commission, regarding the miscalculations of the test's effects, see N.Y. TIMES, Apr. 1, 1954, at 20. For details pertaining to the compensation paid out to the Japanese victims of the nuclear tests, see 32 Dept. St. Bull. 90 (1955) (reprinting note of Jan 4, 1955, from United States Ambassador John M. Allison to Japanese Deputy Prime Minister and Foreign Minister Mamoru Shigemitsu).

7. The fact that the requests of WHO and the General Assembly came almost fifty years after the beginning of the nuclear age raises the question of why it took so long for the legality of nuclear weapons to be challenged. Richard Falk has attempted to account for this delay:

> [o]ver the years since 1945 there have been, to be sure, a few scholarly discussions pro and con about the legality of nuclear weaponry, but somehow until the 1980's, the debate never was treated in international law circles as very important.

RICHARD FALK, REVITALIZING INTERNATIONAL LAW 107 (Iowa State U. Press 1989). For Falk, this neglect arose from:

> [t]he original popular and, in this sense, legally noncontroversial use of atomic bombs to save lives and bring peace in the closing days of World War II. ... It also seemed futile to mount a legal case against weapons so obviously useful and powerful, because of the prevailing realities and track record of geopolitics. Specifically, the inability of the West to develop sufficient nonnuclear means to defend Europe and other vital interests on the Asian mainland, in light of the perceived threat resting upon an overall Soviet superiority in conventional forces and reinforced by the logistical advantages of Soviet dominance of the Asian landmass, made it seem self-denying for Western powers to question the legal status of nuclear weapons. ... Defending the legality of nuclear weapons is such a thankless task that it undoubtedly seemed to most international lawyers, who meant to be upholding official policies, to be more desirable to maintain a discreet silence on the subject as long as this was politically possible. All of these elements contributed to the repression of 'the legal question.' *Id.*

b. 1960 - 1974

By the early 1960s, the international strategic and political landscape had changed in many pertinent ways. The process of decolonization had accelerated. As a result, many former colonies were independent and gradually coalescing into a majority in the U.N. General Assembly. The elites of these new states had not been present at the creation of the norm we are examining; many felt it served neither their interests nor the goals of the minimum world order which they pursued. Second, the environmental movement, dormant in the previous decade, was becoming a more important factor in the industrial democracies of the world; its membership was becoming increasingly alarmed at what were feared to be the irreversible effects of atmospheric testing on the biosphere. Finally, the Superpowers themselves had reached the point where atmospheric testing was deemed less vital to the progress of their own weapons' programs. A cessation of such tests could be contemplated if it were reciprocal. If a prohibition could be made universal, prevent Johnny-come-latelies to the nuclear club from engaging in this indispensable phase of development and thereby secure a Superpower nuclear monopoly — so much the better.

The conjunction of all of these forces was the "Treaty Banning Nuclear Weapon Tests in the Atmosphere, in Outer Space and Under Water" of 1963, in which each signatory undertook to prevent nuclear weapon tests in the atmosphere or anywhere else if the test deposited radioactive debris outside of the state where the test took place. Each of the Superpowers undertook to proselytize in its own sphere of influence and, in short order, well over 100 states had become party to the treaty. In 1970, the Nuclear Non-Proliferation Treaty, with a similarly wide subscription, underlined certain policies implicit in the 1963 agreement. In the meanwhile, emboldened by what was apparently a new international policy, the General Assembly began to pass resolutions conveying a majority consensus that all atmospheric testing should stop.

(1) Treaty Banning Nuclear Weapon Tests in the Atmosphere, in Outer Space and Under Water

Oct. 10, 1963, 14 U.S.T. 1313, T.I.A.S. No. 5433, 480 U.N.T.S. 43

The Governments of the United States of America, the United Kingdom of Great Britain and Northern Ireland, and the Union of Soviet Socialist Republics, hereinafter referred to as the "Original Parties",

Proclaiming as their principal aim the speediest possible achievement of an agreement on general and complete disarmament under strict international control in accordance with the objectives of the United Nations which would put an end to the armaments race and eliminate the incentive to the production and testing of all kinds of weapons, including nuclear weapons,

Seeking to achieve the discontinuance of all test explosions of nuclear weapons for all time, determined to continue negotiations to this end, and desiring to put an end to the contamination of man's environment by radioactive substances,

Have agreed as follows:

Article I

1. Each of the Parties to this Treaty undertakes to prohibit, to prevent, and not to carry out any nuclear weapon test explosion, or any other nuclear explosion, at any place under its jurisdiction or control:

(a) in the atmosphere; beyond its limits, including outer space; or under water, including territorial waters or high seas; or

(b) in any other environment if such explosion causes radioactive debris to be present outside the territorial limits of the State under whose jurisdiction or control such explosion is conducted. It is understood in this connection that the provisions of this subparagraph are without prejudice to the conclusion of a treaty resulting in the permanent banning of all nuclear test explosions, including all such explosions underground, the conclusion of which, as the Parties have stated in the Preamble to this Treaty, they seek to achieve.

2. Each of the Parties to this Treaty undertakes furthermore to refrain from causing, encouraging, or in any way participating in, the carrying out of any nuclear weapon test explosion, or any other nuclear explosion, anywhere which would take place in any of the environments described, or have the effect referred to, in paragraph 1 of this Article. …

Article IV

This Treaty shall be of unlimited duration.

Each Party shall in exercising its national sovereignty have the right to withdraw from the Treaty if it decides that extraordinary events, related to the subject matter of this Treaty, have jeopardized the supreme interests of its country. It shall give notice of such withdrawal to all other Parties to the Treaty three months in advance.

* * *

The 1963 Treaty banning atmospheric tests was followed in 1965 by a U.N. General Assembly Resolution which, if not binding on states parties, represented a growing understanding of the dangers of such weapons and a consensus that all such tests "should" be banned.

(2) U.N. General Assembly Res. 2032 (XX) Urgent Need for Suspension of Nuclear and Thermonuclear Tests

Dec. 3, 1965

The General Assembly,

Having considered the question of the cessation of nuclear and thermonuclear weapon tests and the relevant sections of the reports of the Conference of the Eighteen-Nation Committee on Disarmament,

Recalling its resolution[s] … on the cessation of all test explosions of nuclear weapons,

Noting with regret that notwithstanding these resolutions nuclear weapon tests have taken place,

Recalling the undertaking given by the original signatories to the Treaty banning nuclear weapon tests in the atmosphere, in outer space and under water, signed at Moscow on 5 August 1963, to continue negotiations for the discontinuance of all test explosions of nuclear weapons for all time,

Recognizing the mounting concern of world opinion for the fulfillment of this undertaking,

Mindful of the crucial importance of a comprehensive test ban to the issue of non-proliferation of nuclear weapons,

Noting with satisfaction the joint memorandum on a comprehensive test ban treaty submitted by Brazil, Burma, Ethiopia, India, Mexico, Nigeria, Sweden and the United Arab Republic . . .

Convinced that agreement in regard to taking this further step towards nuclear disarmament would be facilitated, *inter alia*, by the important improvements made in detection and identification techniques,

1. *Urges* that all nuclear weapon tests be suspended;

2. *Calls upon* all countries to respect the spirit and provisions of the Treaty on banning nuclear weapon tests in the atmosphere, in outer space and under water …

* * *

This important Resolution in the General Assembly was followed in 1970 by the Treaty on the Non-Proliferation of Nuclear Weapons (NPT), arguably the most important statement by the international community concerning the urgent need to control the spread of nuclear weapons technology.

(3) Treaty on the Non-Proliferation of Nuclear Weapons

March 5, 1970, 21 U.S.T. 483; T.I.A.S. No. 6839, 729 U.N.T.S. 161

The States concluding this Treaty, hereinafter referred to as the "Parties to the Treaty",

Considering the devastation that would be visited upon all mankind by a nuclear war and the consequent need to make every effort to avert the danger of such a war and to take measures to safeguard the security of peoples,

Believing that the proliferation of nuclear weapons would seriously enhance the danger of nuclear war,

In conformity with resolutions of the United Nations General Assembly calling for the conclusion of an agreement on the prevention of wider dissemination of nuclear weapons,

Undertaking to cooperate in facilitating the application of International Atomic Energy Agency safeguards on peaceful nuclear activities,

Expressing their support for research, development and other efforts to further the application, within the framework of the International Atomic Energy Agency safeguards system, of the principle of safeguarding effectively the flow of source and special fissionable materials by use of instruments and other techniques at certain strategic points, ...

Declaring their intention to achieve at the earliest possible date the cessation of the nuclear arms race and to undertake effective measures in the direction of nuclear disarmament,

Urging the cooperation of all States in the attainment of this objective,

Recalling the determination expressed by the Parties to the 1963 Treaty banning nuclear weapon tests in the atmosphere in outer space and under water in its Preamble to seek to achieve the discontinuance of all test explosions of nuclear weapons for all time and to continue negotiations to this end,

Desiring to further the easing of international tension and the strengthening of trust between States in order to facilitate the cessation of the manufacture of nuclear weapons, the liquidation of all their existing stockpiles, and the elimination from national arsenals of nuclear weapons and the means of their delivery pursuant to a treaty on general and complete disarmament under strict and effective international control,

Recalling that, in accordance with the Charter of the United Nations, States must refrain in their international relations from the threat or use of force against the territorial integrity or political independence of any State, or in any other manner inconsistent with the Purposes of the United Nations, and that the establishment and maintenance of international peace and security are to be promoted with the least diversion for armaments of the world's human and economic resources,

Have agreed as follows:

ARTICLE I

Each nuclear-weapon State Party to the Treaty undertakes not to transfer to any recipient whatsoever nuclear weapons or other nuclear explosive devices or control over such weapons or explosive devices directly, or indirectly; and not in any way to assist, encourage, or induce any non-nuclear-weapon State to manufacture or otherwise acquire nuclear weapons or other nuclear explosive devices, or control over such weapons or explosive devices.

ARTICLE II

Each non-nuclear-weapon State Party to the Treaty undertakes not to receive the transfer from any transferor whatsoever of nuclear weapons or other nuclear explosive devices or of control over such weapons or explosive devices directly, or indirectly; not to manufacture or otherwise acquire nuclear weapons or other nuclear explosive devices; and not to seek or receive any assistance in the manufacture of nuclear weapons or other nuclear explosive devices.

*   *   *

The first case concerning the legality of nuclear weapons testing came to the I.C.J. a scant three years after the adoption of the NPT.

(4) Nuclear Tests (Austl. v. Fr.)

1973 I.C.J. 98, 99 (Provisional Measures)

[Prior to the filing of the Application instituting proceedings in this case, the French Government had carried out atmospheric tests of nuclear devices at its Centre d'expérimentations du Pacifique, in the territory of French Polynesia, some 6,000 kilometers east of Australia, in the years 1966, 1967, 1968, 1970, 1971 and 1972. The French Government created "Prohibited Zones" for aircraft and "Dangerous Zones" for aircraft and shipping, and put these restrictions into effect during the testing period each year.

The United Nations Scientific Committee on the Effects of Atomic Radiation recorded in successive reports to the General Assembly that the testing of nuclear devices in the atmosphere has entailed the release into the atmosphere, and the consequent dissipation in varying degrees throughout the world, of measurable quantities of radioactive matter. It was asserted by Australia that the French atmospheric tests had caused some fall-out of this kind to be deposited on Australian territory. France maintained in particular that the radioactive matter produced by its tests was so infinitesimal that it could be regarded as negligible, and that such fall-out on Australian territory did not constitute a danger to the health of the Australian population.]

Having regard to the Application by Australia filed in the Registry of the Court on 9 May 1973, instituting proceedings against France in respect of a dispute concerning the holding of atmospheric tests of nuclear weapons by the French Government in the Pacific Ocean and asking the Court to adjudge and declare that the carrying out of further atmospheric nuclear weapon tests in the South Pacific Ocean is not consistent with applicable rules of international law, and to order that the French Republic shall not carry out any further such tests,

Makes the following Order:

1. … [T]he Government of Australia, relying on Article 33 of the General Act of 1928 for the Pacific Settlement of International Disputes and on Article 41 of the Statute and Article 66 of the Rules of Court, asks the Court to indicate, pending the final decision in the case brought before it by the Application of the same date, the following interim measures of protection:

The provisional measures should be that the French Government should desist from any further atmospheric nuclear tests pending the judgment of the Court in this case;

2. [T]he French Government was notified by telegram the same day of the filing of the Application and request for indication of interim measures of protec-

tion, and of the precise measures requested, and copies of the Application and the request were at the same time transmitted to it by express mail; ...

6. [B]y a letter dated 16 May 1973 from the Ambassador of France to the Netherlands, handed by him to the Registrar the same day, the French Government stated that it considered that the Court was manifestly not competent in the case and that it could not accept the Court's jurisdiction, and that accordingly the French Government did not intend to appoint an agent, and requested the Court to remove the case from its list; ...

11. [T]hat the French Government was not represented at the hearings ... cannot by itself constitute an obstacle to the indication of provisional measures; ...

13. ... [O]n a request for provisional measures the Court need not, before indicating them, finally satisfy itself that it has jurisdiction on the merits of the case, and yet ought not to indicate such measures unless the provisions invoked by the Applicant appear, prima facie, to afford a basis on which the jurisdiction of the Court might be founded;

14. ... [T]he Government of Australia claims to found the jurisdiction of the Court on the following provisions:

(i) Article 17 of the above-mentioned General Act of 1928, read together with Articles 36, paragraph 1, and 37 of the Statute of the Court;

(ii) Alternatively, Article 36, paragraph 2, of the Statute of the Court and the respective declarations of Australia and France made thereunder;

15. [A]ccording to the letter of 16 May 1973 handed to the Registrar by the French Ambassador to the Netherlands, the French Government considers, *inter alia*, that the General Act of 1928 was an integral part of the League of Nations system and, since the demise of the League of Nations, has lost its effectivity and fallen into desuetude; that this view of the matter is confirmed by the conduct of States in regard to the General Act of 1928 since the collapse of the League of Nations; that, in consequence, the General Act cannot serve as a basis for the competence of the Court to deliberate on the Application of Australia with respect to French nuclear tests; that in any event the General Act of 1928 is not now applicable in the relations between France and Australia and cannot prevail over the will clearly and more recently expressed in the declaration of 20 May 1966 made by the French Government under Article 36, paragraph 2, of the Statute of the Court; that paragraph 3 of that declaration excepts from the French Government's acceptance of compulsory jurisdiction "disputes concerning activities connected with national defence"; and that the present dispute concerning French nuclear tests in the Pacific incontestably falls within the exception contained in that paragraph;

16. Whereas in its oral observations the Government of Australia maintains, *inter alia,* that various matters, including certain statements of the French Government, provide indications which should lead the Court to conclude that the

General Act of 1928 is still in force between the parties to that Act; that the General Act furnishes a basis for the Court's jurisdiction in the present dispute which is altogether independent of the acceptances of compulsory jurisdiction by Australia and by France under Article 36, paragraph 2, of the Statute; that France's obligations under the General Act with respect to the acceptance of the Court's jurisdiction cannot be considered as having been modified by any subsequent declaration made by her unilaterally under Article 36, paragraph 2, of the Statute; that if the reservation in paragraph 3 of the French declaration of 20 May 1966 relating to "disputes concerning activities connected with national defence" is to be regarded as one having an objective content, it is questionable whether nuclear weapon development falls within the concept of national defence; that if this reservation is to be regarded as a self-judging reservation; it is invalid, and in consequence France is bound by the terms of that declaration unqualified by the reservation in question;

17. Whereas the material submitted to the Court leads it to the conclusion, at the present stage of the proceedings, that the provisions invoked by the Applicant appear, prima facie, to afford a basis on which the jurisdiction of the Court might be founded; and whereas the Court will accordingly proceed to examine the Applicant's request for the indication of interim measures of protection; ...

18. Whereas the Government of Australia, in replying to a question put during the oral observations, stated that it bases its request for the indication of provisional measures "first and foremost on Article 41 of the Statute of the Court", and that it bases its request on Article 33 of the above-mentioned General Act of 1928 only subsidiarily in the eventuality that the Court should find itself able, on the material now before it, to reach the conclusion that the General Act is still in force;

19. Whereas the Court is not in a position to reach a final conclusion on this point at the present stage of the proceedings, and will therefore examine the request for the indication of interim measures only in the context of Article 41 of the Statute;

20. Whereas the power of the Court to indicate interim measures under Article 41 of the Statute has as its object to preserve the respective rights of the Parties pending the decision of the Court, and presupposes that irreparable prejudice should not be caused to rights which are the subject of dispute in judicial proceedings and that the Court's judgment should not be anticipated by reason of any initiative regarding the matters in issue before the Court;

21. Whereas it follows that the Court in the present case cannot exercise its power to indicate interim measures of protection unless the rights claimed in the Application, prima facie, appear to fall within the purview of the Court's jurisdiction;

22. Whereas the claims formulated by the Government of Australia in its Application are as follows:

(i) The right of Australia and its people, in common with other States and their peoples, to be free from atmospheric nuclear weapon tests by any country is and will be violated;

(ii) The deposit of radio-active fall-out on the territory of Australia and its dispersion in Australia's airspace without Australia's consent:

(*a*) violates Australian sovereignty over its territory;

(*b*) impairs Australia's independent right to determine what acts shall take place within its territory and in particular whether Australia and its people shall be exposed to radiation from artificial sources;

(iii) the interference with ships and aircraft on the high seas and in the superjacent airspace, and the pollution of the high seas by radio-active fall-out, constitute infringements of the freedom of the high seas;

23. Whereas it cannot be assumed *a priori* that such claims fall completely outside the purview of the Court's jurisdiction, or that the Government of Australia may not be able to establish a legal interest in respect of these claims entitling the Court to admit the Application;

24. Whereas by the terms of Article 41 of the Statute the Court may indicate interim measures of protection only when it considers that circumstances so require in order to preserve the rights of either party;

25. Whereas the Government of Australia alleges, *inter alia*, that a series of atmospheric nuclear tests have been carried out by the French Government in the Pacific during the period from 1966 to 1972, including the explosion of several hydrogen bombs and a number of devices of high and medium power; that during recent months there has been a growing body of reports, not denied by the French Government, to the effect that the French Government is planning to carry out a further series of atmospheric nuclear tests in the Pacific in 1973; that this series of tests may extend to 1975 and even beyond that date; that in diplomatic correspondence and in discussions earlier in the present year the French Government would not agree to cease nuclear testing in the atmosphere in the Pacific and would not supply Australia with any information as to the dates of its proposed tests or the expected size and yield of its explosions; and that in a statement made in the French Parliament on 2 May 1973 the French Government indicated that, regardless of the protests made by Australia and other countries, it did not envisage any cancellation or modification of the programme of nuclear testing as originally planned;

26. Whereas these allegations give substance to the Australian Government's contention that there is an immediate possibility of a further atmospheric nuclear test being carried out by France in the Pacific;

27. Whereas the Government of Australia also alleges that the atmospheric nuclear explosions carried out by France in the Pacific have caused wide-spread

radio-active fall-out on Australian territory and elsewhere in the southern hemisphere, have given rise to measurable concentrations of radio-nuclides in foodstuffs and in man, and have resulted in additional radiation doses to persons living in that hemisphere and in Australia in particular; that any radio-active material deposited on Australian territory will be potentially dangerous to Australia and its people and any injury caused thereby would be irreparable; that the conduct of French nuclear tests in the atmosphere creates anxiety and concern among the Australian people; that any effects of the French nuclear tests upon the resources of the sea or the conditions of the environment can never be undone and would be irremediable by any payment of damages; and any infringement by France of the rights of Australia and her people to freedom of movement over the high seas and superjacent airspace cannot be undone;

28. Whereas the French Government, in a diplomatic Note dated 7 February 1973 and addressed to the Government of Australia, the text of which was annexed to the Application in the present case, called attention to Reports of the Australian National Radiation Advisory Committee from 1967 to 1972, which all concluded that the fall-out from the French tests did not constitute a danger to the health of the Australian population; whereas in the said Note the French Government further expressed its conviction that in the absence of ascertained damage attributable to its nuclear experiments, they did not violate any rule of international law, and that, if the infraction of the law was alleged to consist in a violation of a legal norm concerning the threshold of atomic pollution which should not be crossed, it was hard to see what was the precise rule on which Australia relied;

29. Whereas for the purpose of the present proceedings it suffices to observe that the information submitted to the Court, including Reports of the United Nations Scientific Committee on the Effects of Atomic Radiation between 1958 and 1972, does not exclude the possibility that damage to Australia might be shown to be caused by the deposit on Australian territory of radio-active fall-out resulting from such tests and to be irreparable;

30. Whereas in the light of the foregoing considerations the Court is satisfied that it should indicate interim measures of protection in order to preserve the right claimed by Australia in the present litigation in respect of the deposit of radio-active fall-out on her territory;

31. Whereas the circumstances of the case do not appear to require the indication of interim measures of protection in respect of other rights claimed by Australia in the Application; ...

Accordingly, THE COURT

Indicates, by 8 votes to 6, pending its final decision in the proceedings instituted on 9 May 1973 by Australia against France, the following provisional measures:

> The Governments of Australia and France should each of them ensure that no action of any kind is taken which might aggravate or extend

> the dispute submitted to the Court or prejudice the rights of the other Party in respect of the carrying out of whatever decision the Court may render in the case; and, in particular, the French Government should avoid nuclear tests causing the deposit of radio-active fall-out on Australian territory; …

NOTES AND QUESTIONS

1. Note that the *dispositif* of the Court does not prohibit the government of France from conducting the nuclear tests, but rather orders the French government to "avoid nuclear tests causing the deposit of radio-active fallout on Australian territory." 1973 I.C.J. 98, at para 35. Was the Court in indirect fashion indicating to France how it might comply while still pursuing its tests?

2. The Australian Government claimed a general "right to be free from atmospheric nuclear weapon tests." What is the origin of this right?

3. In granting an injunction or temporary restraining order, did the Court give at least provisional recognition to this alleged right?

(5) Nuclear Tests (Austl. v. Fr.)
1974 I.C.J. 252, 257 (Judgment)

[On June 22, 1973, the International Court of Justice ("ICJ") issued a provisional measures order under Article 41, saying that the French Government should avoid nuclear tests causing the deposit of radioactive fall-out in Australian territory. However, in July and August 1973, the French Government conducted two further series of atmospheric tests within the *Centre d'experimentations du Pacifique* region. By letters dated August 29, 1973, September 19, 1973, and November 11, 1974, the Government of Australia informed the Court that France was ignoring their provisional measures order. The letters also stated that fall-out had been recorded on Australian territory which, according to the Australian Government, was clearly attributable to these tests, and that "in the opinion of the Government of Australia, the conduct of the French Government constitutes a clear and deliberate breach of the Order of the Court of June 22, 1973."] …

16. The present case relates to a dispute between the Government of Australia and the French Government concerning the holding of atmospheric tests of nuclear weapons by the latter Government in the South Pacific Ocean. Since in the present phase of the proceedings the Court has to deal only with preliminary matters, it is appropriate to recall that its approach to a phase of this kind must be, as it was expressed in the *Fisheries Jurisdiction* cases, as follows:

> The issue being thus limited, the Court will avoid not only all expressions of opinion on matters of substance, but also any pronouncement which might prejudge or appear to prejudge any eventual decision on the merits. (*I.C.J. Reports 1973*, pp. 7 and 54.) …

19. By letters of 19 September 1973, 29 August and 11 November 1974, the Government of Australia informed the Court that subsequent to the Court's Or-

der of 22 June 1973 indicating, as interim measures under Article 41 of the Statute (*inter alia*) that the French Government should avoid nuclear tests causing the deposit of radio-active fall-out in Australian territory, two further series of atmospheric tests, in the months of July and August 1973 and June to September 1974, had been carried out at the *Centre d'expérimentations du Pacifique*. The letters also stated that fall-out had been recorded on Australian territory which, according to the Australian Government, was clearly attributable to these tests, and that "in the opinion of the Government of Australia the conduct of the French Government constitutes a clear and deliberate breach of the Order of the Court of 22 June 1973".

20. Recently a number of authoritative statements have been made on behalf of the French Government concerning its intentions as to future nuclear testing in the South Pacific Ocean. The significance of these statements, and their effect for the purposes of the present proceedings, will be examined in detail later in the present Judgment. …

21. The Application founds the jurisdiction of the Court on the following basis:

(i) Article 17 of the General Act for the Pacific Settlement of International Disputes, 1928, read together with Articles 36(1) and 37 of the Statute of the Court. Australia and the French Republic both acceded to the General Act on 21 May 1931. …

(ii) Alternatively, Article 36(2) of the Statute of the Court. Australia and the French Republic have both made declarations thereunder.

22. The scope of the present phase of the proceedings was defined by the Court's Order of 22 June 1973, by which the Parties were called upon to argue, in the first instance, questions of the jurisdiction of the Court and the admissibility of the Application. For this reason, as already indicated, not only the Parties but also the Court itself must refrain from entering into the merits of the claim. However, while examining these questions of a preliminary character, the Court is entitled, and in some circumstances may be required, to go into other questions which may not be strictly capable of classification as matters of jurisdiction or admissibility but are of such a nature as to require examination in priority to those matters.

23. In this connection, it should be emphasized that the Court possesses an inherent jurisdiction enabling it to take such action as may be required, on the one hand to ensure that the exercise of its jurisdiction over the merits, if and when established, shall not be frustrated, and on the other, to provide for the orderly settlement of all matters in dispute to ensure the observance of the "inherent limitations on the exercise of the judicial function" of the Court, and to "maintain its judicial character" (*Northern Cameroons, Judgment, I.C.J. Reports* 1963, at p. 29). Such inherent jurisdiction, on the basis of which the Court is fully empowered to make whatever findings may be necessary for the purposes just indicated, derives from the mere existence of the Court as a judicial organ estab-

lished by the consent of States, and is conferred upon it in order that its basic judicial functions may be safeguarded.

24. With these considerations in mind, the Court has first to examine a question which it finds to be essentially preliminary, namely the existence of a dispute, for, whether or not the Court has jurisdiction in the present case, the resolution of that question could exert a decisive influence on the continuation of the proceedings. It will therefore be necessary to make a detailed analysis of the claim submitted to the Court by the Application of Australia. The present phase of the proceedings having been devoted solely to preliminary questions, the Applicant has not had the opportunity of fully expounding its contentions on the merits. However the Application, which is required by Article 40 of the Statute of the Court to indicate "the subject of the dispute", must be the point of reference for the consideration by the Court of the nature and existence of the dispute brought before it.

25. The Court would recall that the submission made in the Application (paragraph 11 above) is that the Court should adjudge and declare that "the carrying out of further atmospheric nuclear weapon tests in the South Pacific Ocean is not consistent with applicable rules of international law" — the Application having specified in what respect further tests were alleged to be in violation of international law — and should order "that the French Republic shall not carry out any further such tests".

26. The diplomatic correspondence of recent years between Australia ant France reveals Australia's preoccupation with French nuclear atmospheric tests in the South Pacific region, and indicates that its objective has been to bring about their termination. Thus in a Note dated 3 January 1973 the Australian Government made it clear that it was inviting the French Government "to refrain from any further atmospheric nuclear tests in the Pacific area and formally to assure the Australian Government that no more such tests will be held in the Pacific area". In the Application, the Government of Australia observed in connection with this Note (and the French reply of 7 February 1973) that:

> It is at these Notes, of 3 January and 7 February 1973, that the Court is respectfully invited to look most closely; for it is in them that the shape and dimensions of the dispute which now so sadly divides the parties appear so clearly. The Government of Australia claimed that the continuance of testing by France is illegal and called for the cessation of tests. The Government of France asserted the legality of its conduct and gave no indication that the tests would stop. (Para. 15 of the Application.)

That this was the object of the claim also clearly emerges from the request for the indication of interim measures of protection, submitted to the Court by the Applicant on 9 May 1973, in which it was observed:

> As is stated in the Application, Australia has sought to obtain from the French Republic a permanent undertaking to refrain from further atmospheric nuclear tests in the Pacific. However, the French Republic has expressly refused to give any such undertaking. It was made clear in a statement in the French Parliament on 2 May 1973 by the French Secretary of State for the Armies that the French Government, regardless of the protests made by Australia and other countries, does not envisage any cancellation or modification of the programme of nuclear testing as originally planned. (Para. 69.)

27. Further light is thrown on the nature of the Australian claim by the reaction of Australia, through its Attorney-General, to statements, referred to in paragraph 20 above, made on behalf of France and relating to nuclear tests in the South Pacific Ocean. … [The Attorney-General] reminded the Court that "Australia has consistently stated that it would welcome a French statement to the effect that no further atmospheric nuclear tests would be conducted … but no such assurance was given". …

It is clear from these statements that if the French Government had given what could have been construed by Australia as "a firm, explicit and binding undertaking to refrain from further atmospheric tests", the applicant Government would have regarded its objective as having been achieved.

28. Subsequently, on 26 September 1974, the Attorney-General of Australia, replying to a question put in the Australian Senate with regard to reports that France had announced that it had finished atmospheric nuclear testing, said:

> From the reports I have received it appears that what the French Foreign Minister actually said was 'We have now reached a stage in our nuclear technology that makes it possible for us to continue our program by underground testing, and we have taken steps to do so as early as next year' ... this statement falls far short of a commitment or undertaking that there will be no more atmospheric tests conducted by the French Government at its Pacific Tests Centre ... There is a basic distinction between an assertion that steps are being taken to continue the testing program by underground testing as early as next year and an assurance that no further atmospheric tests will take place. It seems that the Government of France, while apparently taking a step in the right direction, is still reserving to itself the right to carry out atmospheric nuclear tests. In legal terms, Australia has nothing from the French Government which protects it against any further atmospheric tests should the French Government subsequently decide to hold them.

Without commenting for the moment on the Attorney-General's interpretation of the French statements brought to his notice, the Court would observe that it is clear that the Australian Government contemplated the possibility of "an assurance that no further atmospheric tests will take place" being sufficient to protect Australia.

29. In the light of these statements, it is essential to consider whether the Government of Australia requests a judgment by the Court which would only state the legal relationship between the Applicant and the Respondent with regard to the matters in issue, or a judgment of a type which in terms requires one or both of the Parties to take, or refrain from taking, some action. Thus it is the Court's duty to isolate the real issue in the case and to identify the object of the claim. ...

30. In the circumstances of the present case, although the Applicant has in its Application used the traditional formula of asking the Court "to adjudge and declare", the Court must ascertain the true object and purpose of the claim and in doing so it cannot confine itself to the ordinary meaning of the words used: it must take into account the Application as a whole, the arguments of the Applicant before the Court, the diplomatic exchanges brought to the Court's attention, and public statements made on behalf of the applicant Government. If these clearly circumscribe the object of the claim, the interpretation of the submissions must necessarily be affected. In the present case, it is evident that the *fons et origo* of the case was the atmospheric nuclear tests conducted by France in the South Pacific region, and that the original and ultimate objective of the Applicant was and has remained to obtain a termination of those tests; ...

32. At the hearing of 4 July 1974, in the course of a review of developments in relation to the proceedings since counsel for Australia had previously addressed the Court in May 1973, the Attorney-General of Australia made the following statement:

> You will recall that Australia has consistently stated it would welcome a French statement to the effect that no further atmospheric nuclear tests would be conducted. Indeed as the Court will remember such an assurance was sought of the French Government by the Australian Government by note dated 3 January 1973, but no such assurance was given. ...

He devoted considerable attention to a communiqué dated 8 June 1974 from the Office of the President of the French Republic, and submitted to the Court the Australian Government's interpretation of that document. Since that time, certain French authorities have made a number of consistent public statements concerning future tests, which provide material facilitating the Court's task of assessing the Applicant's interpretation of the earlier documents, and which indeed require to be examined in order to discern whether they embody any modification of intention as to France's future conduct. It is true that these statements have not been made before the Court, but they are in the public domain, and are known to the Australian Government, and one of them was commented on by the Attorney-General in the Australian Senate on 26 September 1974. It will clearly be necessary to consider all these statements, both that drawn to the Court's attention in July 1974 and those subsequently made.

33. It would no doubt have been possible for the Court, had it considered that the interests of justice so required, to have afforded the Parties the opportunity, e.g., by reopening the oral proceedings, of addressing to the Court comments on the statements made since the close of those proceedings. Such a course however would have been fully justified only if the matter dealt with in those statements had been completely new, had not been raised during the proceedings, or was unknown to the Parties. This is manifestly not the case. The essential material which the Court must examine was introduced into the proceedings by the Applicant itself, by no means incidentally, during the course of the hearings, when it drew the Court's attention to a statement by the French authorities made prior to that date, submitted the documents containing it and presented an interpretation of its character, touching particularly upon the question whether it contained a firm assurance. Thus both the statement and the Australian interpretation of it are before the Court pursuant to action by the Applicant. Moreover, the Applicant subsequently publicly expressed its comments (see paragraph 28 above) on statements made by the French authorities since the closure of the oral proceedings. The Court is therefore in possession not only of the statements made by French authorities concerning the cessation of atmospheric nuclear testing, but also of the views of the Applicant on them. Although as a judicial body the Court is conscious of the importance of the principle expressed in the maxim *audi alteram partem*, it does not consider that this principle precludes the Court from taking account of statements made subsequently to the oral proceedings, and which merely supplement and reinforce matters already discussed in the course of the proceedings, statements with which the Applicant must be familiar. Thus the Applicant, having commented on the statements of the French authorities, both that made prior to the oral proceedings and those made subsequently, could reasonably expect that the Court would deal with the matter and come to its own conclusion on the meaning and effect of those statements. The Court, having taken note of the Applicants comments, and feeling no obligation to consult the Parties on the basis for its decision finds that the reopening of the oral proceedings would serve no useful purpose.

34. It will be convenient to take the statements referred to above in chronological order. The first statement is contained in the communiqué issued by the Office of the President of the French Republic on 8 June 1974, shortly before the commencement of the 1974 series of French nuclear tests:

The Decree reintroducing the security measures in the South Pacific nuclear test zone has been published in the Official Journal of 8 June 1974:

> The Office of the President of the Republic takes this opportunity of stating that in view of the stage reached in carrying out the French nuclear defence programme France will be in a position to pass on to the stage of underground explosions as soon as the series of tests planned for this summer is completed.

A copy of the communiqué was transmitted with a Note dated 11 June 1974 from the French Embassy in Canberra to the Australian Department of Foreign Affairs, and as already mentioned, the text of the communiqué was brought to the attention of the Court in the course of the oral proceedings.

35. In addition to this, the Court cannot fail to take note of a reference to a document made by counsel at a public hearing in the proceedings, parallel to this case, instituted by New Zealand against France on 9 May 1973. At the hearing of 10 July 1974 in that case, the Attorney-General of New Zealand, after referring to the communiqué of 8 June 1974, mentioned above, stated that on 10 June 1974 the French Embassy in Wellington sent a Note to the New Zealand Ministry of Foreign Affairs, containing a passage which the Attorney General read out, and which, in the translation used by New Zealand, runs as follows:

> France, at the point which has been reached in the execution of its programme of defence by nuclear means, will be in a position to move to the stage of underground tests, as soon as the test series planned for this summer is completed.
>
> Thus the atmospheric tests which are soon to be carried out will, in the normal course of events, be the last of this type.

36. The Court will also have to consider the relevant statements made by the French authorities subsequently to the oral proceedings: on 25 July 1974 by the President of the Republic; on 16 August 1974 by the Minister of Defence; on 25 September 1974 by the Minister for Foreign Affairs in the United Nations General Assembly; and on 11 October 1974 by the Minister of Defence.

37. The next statement to be considered, therefore, will be that made on 25 July at a press conference given by the President of the Republic, when he said:

> . . . on this question of nuclear tests, you know that the Prime Minister had publicly expressed himself in the National Assembly in his speech introducing the Government's programme. He had indicated that French nuclear testing would continue. I had myself made it clear that this round of atmospheric tests would be the last, and so the members of the Government were completely informed of our intentions in this respect . . .

38. On 16 August 1974, in the course of an interview on French television, the Minister of Defence said that the French Government had done its best to ensure that the 1974 nuclear tests would be the last atmospheric tests.

39. On 25 September 1974, the French Minister for Foreign Affairs, addressing the United Nations General Assembly, said:

> We have now reached a stage in our nuclear technology that makes it possible for us to continue our programme by underground testing, and we have taken steps to do so as early as next year.

40. On 11 October 1974, the Minister of Defence held a press conference during which he stated twice, in almost identical terms, that there would not be any atmospheric tests in 1975 and that France was ready to proceed to underground tests. When the comment was made that he had not added "in the normal course of events," he agreed that he had not. This latter point is relevant in view of the passage from the Note of 10 June 1974 from the French Embassy in Wellington to the Ministry of Foreign Affairs of New Zealand, quoted in paragraph 35 above, to the effect that the atmospheric tests contemplated "will, in the normal course of events, be the last of this type". The Minister also mentioned that, whether or not other governments had been officially advised of the decision, they could become aware of it through the press and by reading the communiqués issued by the Office of the President of the Republic.

41. In view of the foregoing, the Court finds that France made public its intention to cease the conduct of atmospheric nuclear tests following the conclusion of the 1974 series of tests. The Court must in particular take into consideration the President's statement of 25 July 1974 (paragraph 37 above) followed by the Defence Minister's statement on 11 October 1974 (paragraph 40). These reveal that the official statements made on behalf of France concerning future nuclear testing are not subject to whatever proviso, if any, was implied by the expression "in the normal course of events [*normalement*]". ...

42. Before considering whether the declarations made by the French authorities meet the object of the claim by the Applicant that no further atmospheric nuclear tests should be carried out in the South Pacific, it is first necessary to determine the status and scope on the international plane of these declarations.

43. It is well recognized that declarations made by way of unilateral acts, concerning legal or factual situations, may have the effect of creating legal obligations. Declarations of this kind may be, and often are, very specific. When it is the intention of the State making the declaration that it should become bound according to its terms, that intention confers on the declaration the character of a legal undertaking, the State being thenceforth legally required to follow a course of conduct consistent with the declaration. An undertaking of this kind, if given publicly, and with an intent to be bound, even though not made within the context of international negotiations, is binding. In these circumstances, nothing in the nature of a *quid pro quo* nor any subsequent acceptance of the declaration, nor even any reply or reaction from other States, is required for the declaration to take effect, since such a requirement would be inconsistent with the strictly unilateral nature of the juridical act by which the pronouncement by the State was made.

44. Of course, not all unilateral acts imply obligation; but a State may choose to take up a certain position in relation to a particular matter with the intention of being bound—the intention is to be ascertained by interpretation of the act. When

States make statements by which their freedom of action is to be limited, a restrictive interpretation is called for.

45. With regard to the question of form, it should be observed that this is not a domain in which international law imposes any special or strict requirements. Whether a statement is made orally or in writing makes no essential difference, for such statements made in particular circumstances may create commitments in international law, which does not require that they should be couched in written form. Thus the question of form is not decisive. As the Court said in its Judgment on the preliminary objections in the case concerning the *Temple of Preah Vihear*:

> Where ... as is generally the case in international law, which places the principal emphasis on the intentions of the parties, the law prescribes no particular form, parties are free to choose what form they please provided their intention clearly results from it. (*I.C.J. Reports 1961*, p. 31.)

The Court further stated in the same case: "... the sole relevant question is whether the language employed in any given declaration does reveal a clear intention ..." (*Ibid.*, p. 32).

46. One of the basic principles governing the creation and performance of legal obligations, whatever their source, is the principle of good faith. Trust and confidence are inherent in international co-operation, in particular in an age when this co-operation in many fields is becoming increasingly essential. Just as the very rule of *pacta sunt servanda* in the law of treaties is based on good faith, so also is the binding character of an international obligation assumed by unilateral declaration. Thus interested States may take cognizance of unilateral declarations and place confidence in them, and are entitled to require that the obligation thus created be respected. ...

47. Having examined the legal principles involved, the Court will now turn to the particular statements made by the French Government. The Government of Australia has made known to the Court at the oral proceedings its own interpretation of the first such statement (paragraph 27 above). As to subsequent statements, reference may be made to what was said in the Australian Senate by the Attorney-General on 26 September 1974 (paragraph 28 above). In reply to a question concerning reports that France had announced that it had finished atmospheric nuclear testing, he said that the statement of the French Foreign Minister on 25 September (paragraph 39 above) "falls far short of an undertaking that there will be no more atmospheric tests conducted by the French Government at its Pacific Tests Centre" and that France was "still reserving to itself the right to carry out atmospheric nuclear tests" so that "In legal terms, Australia has nothing from the French Government which protects it against any further atmospheric tests".

48. It will be observed that Australia has recognized the possibility of the dispute being resolved by a unilateral declaration, of the kind specified above, on

the part of France, and its conclusion that in fact no "commitment" or "firm, explicit and binding undertaking" had been given is based on the view that the assurance is not absolute in its terms, that there is a "distinction between an assertion that tests will go underground and an assurance that no further atmospheric tests will take place", that "the possibility of further atmospheric testing taking place after the commencement of underground tests cannot be excluded" and that thus "the Government of France is still reserving to itself the right to carry out atmospheric nuclear tests". The Court must however form its own view of the meaning and scope intended by the author of a unilateral declaration which may create a legal obligation, and cannot in this respect be bound by the view expressed by another State which is in no way a party to the text.

49. Of the statements by the French Government now before the Court, the most essential are clearly those made by the President of the Republic. There can be no doubt, in view of his functions, that his public communications or statements, oral or written, as Head of State, are in international relations acts of the French State. His statements, and those of members of the French Government acting under his authority, up to the last statement made by the Minister of Defence (of 11 October 1974), constitute a whole. Thus, in whatever form these statements were expressed, they must be held to constitute an engagement of the State, having regard to their intention and to the circumstances in which they were made.

50. The unilateral statements of the French authorities were made outside the Court, publicly and *erga omnes*, even though the first of them was communicated to the Government of Australia. As was observed above, to have legal effect, there was no need for these statements to be addressed to a particular State, nor was acceptance by any other State required. The general nature and characteristics of these statements are decisive for the evaluation of the legal implications, and it is to the interpretation of the statements that the Court must now proceed. The Court is entitled to presume, at the outset, that these statements were not made *in vacuo*, but in relation to the tests which constitute the very object of the present proceedings, although France has not appeared in the case.

51. In announcing that the 1974 series of atmospheric tests would be the last, the French Government conveyed to the world at large, including the Applicant, its intention effectively to terminate these tests. It was bound to assume that other States might take note of these statements and rely on their being effective. The validity of these statements and their legal consequences must be considered within the general framework of the security of international intercourse, and the confidence and trust which are so essential in the relations among States. It is from the actual substance of these statements, and from the circumstances attending their making, that the legal implications of the unilateral act must be deduced. The objects of these statements are clear and they were addressed to the international community as a whole, and the Court holds that they constitute an undertaking possessing legal effect. …

52. Thus the Court faces a situation in which the objective of the Applicant has in effect been accomplished, inasmuch as the Court finds that France has undertaken the obligation to hold no further nuclear tests in the atmosphere in the South Pacific.

53. The Court finds that no question of damages arises in the present case, since no such claim has been raised by the Applicant either prior to or during the proceedings, and the original and ultimate objective of Applicant has been to seek protection "against any further atmospheric test" (see paragraph 28 above).

54. It would of course have been open to Australia, if it had considered that the case had in effect been concluded, to discontinue the proceedings in accordance with the Rules of Court. If it has not done so, this does not prevent the Court from making its own independent finding on the subject. It is true that "the Court cannot take into account declarations, admissions or proposals which the Parties may have made during direct negotiations between themselves, when such negotiations have not led to a complete agreement" (*Factory at Chorzów (Merits), P.C.I.J., Series A, No. 17*, p. 51). However, in the present case, that is not the situation before the Court. The Applicant has clearly indicated what would satisfy its claim, and the Respondent has independently taken action; the question for the Court is thus one of interpretation of the conduct of each of the Parties. The conclusion at which the Court has arrived as a result of such interpretation does not mean that it is itself effecting a compromise of the claim; the Court is merely ascertaining the object of the claim and the effect of the Respondent's action, and this it is obliged to do. Any suggestion that the dispute would not be capable of being terminated by statements made on behalf of France would run counter to the unequivocally expressed views of the Applicant both before the Court and elsewhere.

55. The Court, as a court of law, is called upon to resolve existing disputes between States. Thus the existence of a dispute is the primary condition for the Court to exercise its judicial function; it is not sufficient for one party to assert that there is a dispute, since "whether there exists an international dispute is a matter for objective determination" by the Court (*Interpretation of Peace Treaties with Bulgaria, Hungary and Romania (First Phase), Advisory Opinion, I.C.J. Reports 1950*, p. 74). The dispute brought before it must therefore continue to exist at the time when the Court makes its decision. It must not fail to take cognizance of a situation in which the dispute has disappeared because the object of the claim has been achieved by other means. If the declarations of France concerning the effective cessation of the nuclear tests have the significance described by the Court, that is to say if they have caused the dispute to disappear, all the necessary consequences must be drawn from this finding.

56. It may be argued that although France may have undertaken such an obligation, by a unilateral declaration, not to carry out atmospheric nuclear tests in the South Pacific Ocean, a judgment of the Court on this subject might still be of value because, if the judgment upheld the Applicant's contentions, it would

reinforce the position of the Applicant by affirming the obligation of the Respondent. However, the Court having found that the Respondent has assumed an obligation as to conduct, concerning the effective cessation of nuclear tests, no further judicial action is required. The Applicant has repeatedly sought from the Respondent an assurance that the tests would cease, and the Respondent has, on its own initiative, made a series of statements to the effect that they will cease. Thus the Court concludes that, the dispute having disappeared, the claim advanced by Australia no longer has any object. It follows that any further finding would have no *raison d'être*. …

58. The Court has in the past indicated considerations which would lead it to decline to give judgment. The present case is one in which "circumstances that have … arisen render any adjudication devoid of purpose" (*Northern Cameroons, Judgment, I.C.J. Reports* 1963, p. 38). The Court therefore sees no reason to allow the continuance of proceedings which it knows are bound to be fruitless. While judicial settlement may provide a path to international harmony in circumstances of conflict, it is none the less true that the needless continuance of litigation is an obstacle to such harmony.

59. Thus the Court finds that no further pronouncement is required in the present case. It does not enter into the adjudicatory functions of the Court to deal with issues *in abstracto*, once it has reached the conclusion that merits of the case no longer fall to be determined. The object of the claim having clearly disappeared, there is nothing on which to give judgment. …

60. Once the Court has found that a State has entered into a commitment concerning its future conduct it is not the Court's function to contemplate that it will not comply with it. However, the Court observes that if the basis of this judgment were to be affected, the Applicant could request an examination of the situation in accordance with the provisions of the Statute; the denunciation by France, by letter dated 2 January 1974, of the General Act for the Pacific Settlement of International Disputes, which is relied on as a basis of jurisdiction in the present case, cannot by itself constitute an obstacle to the presentation of such a request. …

[By nine votes to six, the Court found that the Australian claim no longer had any object, but observed that Australia might reopen the case on the same jurisdictional basis if the French commitment were violated. But three members of the majority appended separate opinions indicating support only for the narrow proposition that the suit had no object. Of this group, JUDGE PETRÉN said in part:]

As is clear from the foregoing, the admissibility of the Application depends, in my view, on the existence of a rule of customary international law which prohibits States from carrying out atmospheric tests of nuclear weapons giving rise to radio-active fall-out on the territory of other States. Now it is common knowledge, and is admitted by the Australian Government itself, that any nuclear explosion in the atmosphere gives rise to radio-active fall-out over the whole of the hemisphere where it takes place. Australia, therefore, is only one of many States on whose territory France's atmospheric nuclear tests, and likewise those of other States, have given rise to the deposit of radio-active fall-out. Since the Second World War, certain States have conducted atmospheric nuclear tests for the purpose of enabling them to pass from the atomic to the thermo-nuclear stage in the field of armaments. The conduct of these States proves that their Governments have not been of the opinion that customary international law forbade atmospheric nuclear tests. What is more, the Treaty of 1963 whereby the first three States to have acquired nuclear weapons mutually banned themselves from carrying out further atmospheric tests can be denounced. By the provision in that sense the signatories of the Treaty showed that they were still of the opinion that customary international law did not prohibit atmospheric nuclear tests.

To ascertain whether a customary rule to that effect might have come into being, it would appear more important to learn what attitude is taken up by States which have not yet carried out the tests necessary for reaching the nuclear stage. For such States the prohibition of atmospheric nuclear tests could signify the division of the international community into two groups: States possessing nuclear weapons and States not possessing them. If a State which does not possess nuclear arms refrains from carrying out the atmospheric tests which would enable it to acquire them and if that abstention is motivated not by political or economic considerations but by a conviction that such tests are prohibited by customary international law, the attitude of that State would constitute an element in the formation of such a custom. But where can one find proof that a sufficient number of States, economically and technically capable of manufacturing nuclear weapons, refrain from carrying out atmospheric nuclear tests because they consider that customary international law forbids them to do so? The example recently given by China when it exploded a very powerful bomb in the atmosphere is sufficient to demolish the contention that there exists at present a rule of customary international law prohibiting atmospheric nuclear tests. It would be unrealistic to close one's eyes to the attitude, in that respect, of the State with the largest population in the world.

To complete this brief outline, one may ask what has been the attitude of the numerous States on whose territory radio-active fall-out from the atmospheric tests of the nuclear Powers has been deposited and continues to be deposited. Have they, generally speaking, protested to these Powers, pointing out that their tests were in breach of customary international law? I do not observe that such has been the case. The resolutions passed in the General Assembly of the United Nations cannot be regarded as equivalent to legal protests made by one State to another and concerning concrete instances. They indicate the existence of a strong current of opinion in favour of proscribing atmospheric nuclear tests. That is a political task of the highest urgency, but it is one which remains to be accomplished. Thus the claim submitted to the Court by Australia belongs to the political domain and is situated outside the framework of international law as it exists today.

I consider, consequently, that the Application of Australia was, from the very institution of proceedings, devoid of any object on which the Court could give a decision, whereas the Judgment finds only that such an object is lacking now. I concur with the Judgment so far as the outcome to be given the proceedings is concerned, i.e., that the Court is not called upon to give a decision, but that does not enable me to associate myself with the grounds on which the Judgment is based. …

[Australian *ad hoc* JUDGE BARWICK, dissenting:]

Further, the Judgment, it seems to me, overlooks the fact that in all the references to assurances in the correspondence and in the oral hearings the Applicant referred to an assurance with the nature and terms of which it was satisfied. These references cannot be read in my opinion as indicating such an assurance as might be regarded as sufficient for Australia's purposes by any other judgment than its own.

The Judgment proceeds to hold that France by the communiqué of 8 June 1974, as confirmed by the subsequent Presidential and Ministerial statements to the press, did give to the international community and thus to Australia an undertaking, binding internationally, not on any occasion subsequent to the conclusion of the 1974 series of tests to test nuclear weapons in the atmosphere of the South Pacific.

My first observation is that this is a conclusion of fact. It is not in my opinion a conclusion of law. The inferences to be drawn from the issuing and the terms of the communiqué of 8 June 1974 are, in my opinion, inferences of fact, including the critical fact of the intention of France in the matter. So also, in my opinion, is the meaning to be given to the various statements which are set out in the Judgment. A decision as to those inferences and those meanings is not in my opinion an exercise in legal interpretation; it is an exercise in fact-finding.

But whether the conclusion be one of fact or one of law, my comments as to the judicial impropriety of deciding the matter without notice to the Parties of the questions to be considered, and without affording them an opportunity to make their submissions, are equally applicable.

This is a very important conclusion purporting to impose on France an internationally binding obligation of a far-reaching kind. Nothing is found as to the duration of the obligation although nothing said in the Judgment would suggest that it is of a temporary nature. There are apparently no qualifications of it related to changes in circumstances or to the varying needs of French security. Apparently it is restricted to the South Pacific area, a limitation implied from the fact that the source of the obligation is the communiqué of 8 June 1974 issued in the context of the imminence of the 1974 series of tests.

The purpose and intention of issuing the communiqué and subsequently making the various statements is to my mind far from clear. The Judgment finds an intention to enter into a binding legal obligation after giving the warning that statements limiting a State's freedom of action should receive a restrictive interpretation. The Judgment apparently finds the clear intention in the language used. I regret to say that I am unable to do so. There seems to be nothing, either in the language used or in the circumstances of its employment, which in my opinion would warrant, and certainly nothing to compel, the conclusion that those making the statements were intending to enter into a solemn and far-reaching international obligation rather than to announce the current intention of the French Government. I would have thought myself that the more natural conclusion to draw from the various statements was that they were statements of policy and not intended as undertaking to the international community such a far-reaching obligation. The Judgment does not seem to my mind to offer any reason why these statements should be regarded as expressing an intention to accept an internationally binding undertaking rather than an intention to make statements of current government policy and intention.

Further, it seems to me strange to say the least that the French Government at a time when it had not completed its 1974 series of tests and did not know that the weather conditions of the winter in the southern hemisphere would permit them to be carried out, should pre-empt itself from testing again in the atmosphere, even if the 1974 series should, apart from the effects of weather, prove inadequate for the purposes which prompted France to undertake them. A conclusion that France has made such an undertaking without any reservation of any kind, such, for example, as is found in the Moscow Treaty Banning Nuclear Weapon Tests in the Atmosphere, in Outer Space and Under Water, to which France is not a party, is quite remarkable and difficult to accept.

It is noticeable that the communiqué itself as sent to Australia makes no express reference to atmospheric testing. The message sent by the French Embassy in Wellington to the Government of New Zealand with respect to the communiqué, drew a conclusion not expressed in the communiqué itself. Somewhat guardedly the Embassy added the words "in the normal course of events" which tended to weaken the inference which apparently the Embassy had drawn from the terms of the communiqué.

In this connection it may be observed that both the Government of Australia and the Government of New Zealand in responding to the communiqué of 8 June 1974, virtually challenged France to give to them an express undertaking that no further tests would be carried out in the South Pacific. There has been ample opportunity for France to have unequivocally made such a statement: but no such express statement has been communicated to either Applicant. Without entering further into detailed criticism of the finding of fact of which personally I am not convinced, it is enough to say that there is, in my opinion, much room for grave doubt as to the correctness of the conclusion which the Court has drawn.

That circumstance underlines the essential need to have heard argument before decision.

NOTES AND QUESTIONS

1. Did Australia really want no more than cessation of the tests by France? Why would the Court choose to interpret so narrowly? What accounted for the Court's sudden reversal of position?

2. Suppose the majority of the Court had concluded that French resistance was not legally relevant and proceeded, then, to issue a judgment prohibiting nuclear testing. France would not have complied. What would the consequences have been for the Court and for international law?

3. If you were a member of the National Security Council charged with monitoring the U.S. nuclear position, would you have recommended supporting the Australia position? Explain.

4. Could (should) the Court have been influenced by an assumed U.S. position in the matter?

5. Is it reasonable to conclude that governments will be deemed to have entered "binding" agreements when they do not resort to the traditional ceremonies by which negotiators communicate serious intentions of commitment?

6. Could the Court have contributed to this part of international law by ruling that the French tests were unlawful?

7. What would have been necessary for the Court's ruling to have been effective?

8. John Dugard has identified the dangers that arise when states drag the ICJ into volatile international controversies. According to him:

> [t]he Court has handled matters of 'graver political implications' than its predecessor, but at the same time it has had quantitatively less work. If the Court is to win the confidences of those States skeptical of or hostile to international adjudication, it may have to devote less attention to controversial litigation such as the . . . Nuclear Test Cases. Since the Court itself has no power to choose the cases it will hear, the burden is upon States to be more cautious in presenting to the Court highly 'political' disputes which affect 'vital' state interests. The hasty and overzealous submission of such disputes can only result in: (a) 'avoidance decisions' along the lines of the South West Africa Cases and the Nuclear Test Cases; (b) a further decline in the number of acceptances of the compulsory opinion of the Court; and (c) the refusal of States to appear before the Court even for the purpose of contesting jurisdiction.

John Dugard, *The Nuclear Test Cases and South West Africa Cases: Some Realism About the International Judicial Decision,* 16 VA. J. INT'L L. 463, 501 (1976).

9. William K. Ris, Jr. has written on the interplay between the ICJ's ruling in *Nuclear Tests* and public opinion. He notes that:

> [i]t is, then, upon French attitudes and politics that the ICJ action, and the international response to it, may have had the most influence. Global reactions have put the French on the defensive. Following the Court order, the French Ambassador to the United States felt compelled to reply in [sic] length to a New York Times editorial on the subject. Setting the stage for a justification of the violation of the Court order which was obviously to follow in a few days, Ambassador Kosciusko-Morizet wrote that the other parties were 'the first to set themselves in contradiction with the court's request' through measures such as boycotts of French products and transportation, and the cutting off of mail and telephone communication between the two countries.

William K. Ris, *French Nuclear Testing: A Crisis for International Law,* 4 DENV. J. INT'L L & POL'Y, 111, 131 (1974).

10. Professor Reisman attempted to shed some light on the Court's behavior in *Nuclear Tests*.

> The implication that the Court was trying to duck the case was particularly puzzling because the Court had moved so boldly in the other direction a scant six months before. Equally puzzling was the sudden change in the normative status of the prohibition of atmospheric testing. Six months earlier, even the more prudent observer might have said that, with the statement of the Court at the interim phase, an inchoate norm with a "twilight existence," to borrow from Cardozo, had at last received a court's imprimatur and had emerged as real law. Now the norm had either retreated to the twilight zone or, in a more drastic move, completely vanished.
>
> It should occasion no surprise that the reasons for this sharp change are not persuasively found in the judgment. It is the style of judicial redaction and, in part, an inherent feature of the formal language of law often to conceal the most compelling policy reasons for a decision. The International Court can be presumed, here, as in many previous cases, to have been concerned about its own effectiveness. In a number of cases after the *Corfu Channel* judgment, there are reasons to suspect that jurisdiction may have been rejected precisely because of a fear of the probable ineffectiveness of a subsequent judgment, either by repudiation of the judgment itself or by a general rejection of a decisive norm on which it might have been based. But in the *Nuclear Tests* case, the communication of control intention that had appeared to accompany the prescription prohibiting atmospheric tests would have appeared ample enough to dispel the anxiety of the most timid of international judges. After all, both Superpowers appeared firmly committed to the prescription and a majority of U.N. members had expressed their support both by accession to the treaty and by voting for resolutions in the General Assembly. In those circumstances, the Court could safely conclude that the norm was law and that, should the addition of an ICJ judgment to the expectations of the world not deflect France from its intention to test, the Security Council, or the General Assembly under the Uniting for Peace Resolution, might initiate some enforcement. Once persuaded of its political base, the Court could easily have used the theory it devised in the *Reparations* case that a majority of the governments of the world could make law for the rest or, alternatively, have used the theory expressed in Article 43 of the Vienna Convention on the Law of Treaties. Either theory would have made the prohibition of the 1963 treaty operate *erga omnes*, against party and non-party alike.
>
> Curiously, in the brief period between the indication of interim measures and the judgment, the anticipated chorus of condemnation of France hardly materialized. In particular, the Superpowers, whose role in supporting the prescription in question was indispensable, took no meaningful steps indicating an ongoing commitment of control intention.
>
> The reason for this relative silence is not hard to discern. Article 4 of the 1963 Convention, while affirming that the instrument was of unlimited duration, permitted, in its second paragraph, a party to withdraw after three months advance notice "if it decides that extraordinary events, relating to the subject matter of this treaty, have jeopardized the supreme interests of its country." The parties initiating the treaty had not contemplated an absolute prohibition, but one subject to reconsideration and denunciation. If the Court had acceded to the Australian claim, it would have had to transform the contingent prohibition on atmospheric testing into a permanent ban, no longer subject to denunciation. In short, it would have been obliged to change the norm involved, not only vis-à-vis France but also vis-à-vis the Superpowers.

> From the perspective of Australia, New Zealand and other Pacific basin states that did not plan to acquire nuclear weapons, these changes may have been quite desirable. A prohibition that, for them, was already a de facto absolute became absolute de jure for all others. Since apparent nuclear parity already created the sterile balance of terror needed for world order, the non-nuclear states stood to gain nothing by further testing. To the contrary. Radio-nuclides have no nationality. Given their environmental and demographic health concerns, Pacific basin states were in a net better position if everyone, friend and foe alike, was henceforth prohibited from atmospheric testing.
>
> This perspective could not have been shared by the Superpowers. For each of them, the prospect of the excision of Article 4's denunciation privileges from the treaty imported major and potentially negative security implications. Part of the complex of motives that had produced the 1963 treaty was that a stage in weapons development had been reached by both Superpowers at which further atmospheric testing was no longer exigent if the other Superpower refrained from testing. But the situation could change and security considerations might then mandate a resumption of tests. A neutron bomb, for example, cannot be tested in the atmosphere by a party to the 1963 treaty, substantially reducing its utility, if a decision is taken to add it to the national arsenal. In some scenarios or, as Lasswell put it, constructs of possible futures, that weapon might be critical for the balance of forces in the extremely important European theater. Moreover, in a new power constellation, nuclear proliferation might not be as undesirable as it had been. The United States may have come to see certain advantages to a nuclear China, as the USSR assessed the advantages it might gain from a nuclear India. In short, there were compelling reasons why the United States and, in symmetrical fashion, the USSR would be anxious to maintain the denunciation privilege and would, hence, oppose the prescriptive transformation that the ICJ would have been obliged to craft in order to sustain the Australian claim. Hence the rather deafening silence after the interim measures phase and the absence of agitation in organized arenas such as the United Nations.
>
> France has stopped testing in the atmosphere. Perhaps the International Court can take some credit for that. It is possible that the prospect of an adverse judgment may have been an additional factor pressing France to terminate the offending tests. But the norm Australia and New Zealand sought to have confirmed was implicitly rejected. Paradoxically, the norm continued on the books as vigorously in December 1974 as it had in July 1974. Yet appraised in terms of a communications model, the modulation of control intention had been substantially changed. Henceforth, whatever the text and the authority, the norm in question could not properly be called a prescription.

W. Michael Reisman, *International Lawmaking: A Process of Communication*, 75 Am. Soc'y Int'l L. Proc. 117-19 (1981).

c. 1974 - 1996

After the I.C.J. decisions in *Nuclear Tests* in the early 1970s, the Cold War understandings of mutually-assured destruction among nuclear states and non-proliferation among non-nuclear states, was punctuated infrequently by attempts on the part of states other than the five permanent members of the Security Counsel to obtain nuclear weapons, either as an insignia of power (Iraq, North Korea, and possibly others) or as a perceived necessity for self defense (India/Pakistan; Israel). For two decades however, the common goals of the international community – the prevention of proliferation, the suspension of testing and other environmentally hazardous activities, and overall reduction in the number of weapons over time - were also a part of the Cold War landscape.

On May 11, 1995, the Review and Extension Conference of the Parties to the Treaty on the Non-Proliferation of Nuclear Weapons concluded a final document (34 I.L.M. 961 (1995)) under Article X(2) of the Treaty. That provision provided that:

> Twenty-five years after the entry into force of the Treaty, a conference shall be convened to decide whether the Treaty shall continue in force indefinitely, or shall be extended for an additional sixth period or periods. This decision shall be taken by a majority of the Parties to the Treaty.

A complex political package was concluded at the Conference. Under Decision 3, the Conference decided "The Treaty shall continue in force indefinitely." In order to accommodate the demands of the non-nuclear states, Decision 2 secured from the nuclear weapon States a reaffirmation of Article VI of the Treaty "to pursue in good faith negotiations on effective measures relating to nuclear disarmament." Section 4 of Decision 2 stated:

> The achievement of the following measures is important in the full realization and effective implementation of Article VI [of the Non-proliferation Treaty], including the programme of action as reflected below:
>
> (a) The completion by the Conference on Disarmament of the negotiations on a universal and internationally and effectively verifiable Comprehensive Nuclear-Test Ban Treaty no later than 1996. *Pending the entry into force of a Comprehensive Test-Ban Treaty, the nuclear weapon States should exercise utmost restraint.*

United Nations Decisions and Resolution of the 1995 Review and Extension Conference of the Parties to the Treaty on the Non-Proliferation of Nuclear Weapons, Decision 2, Sec. 4 (1995) *available at* http://www.mint.gov.my/policy/treaty_nuclear/npt95_rec.htm (emphasis added). Despite this commitment, President Chirac of France issued a media statement on June 13, 1995 to the effect that France would conduct a final series of eight nuclear weapons tests in the South Pacific starting in September 1995.

The 1974 Judgment in *Nuclear Tests* excerpted above provided, in paragraph 63, that:

> If the basis of this Judgment were to be affected [by French non-compliance], the Applicant could request an examination of the situation in accordance with provisions of the Statute.

Nuclear Tests (Austl. v. Fr.*)* 1974 I.C.J. 252 (Judgment).

> On August 21, 1995 New Zealand submitted to the Court a request for an examination of the situation "arising out of a proposed action announced by France which will, if carried out, affect the basis of the Judgment rendered by the Court on 20 December 1974 in *Nuclear Tests (N.Z. v. Fr.)*." In its application, New Zealand seeks recognition only of those rights that would be adversely affected by entry into the marine

> environment of radioactive material in consequence of the further tests to be carried out at Mururoa or Fangataufa Atolls, and of its entitlement to the protection and benefit of a properly conducted environmental impact assessment.

Request for an Examination of the Situation in Accordance with Paragraph 63 of the Court's 1974 Judgment in the Case Concerning Nuclear Tests (N.Z. v. Fr.), *available at* http://www.icj-cij.org/icjwww/icases/inzfr/inzfrframe.htm (1995) New Zealand asked the Court specifically:

> (i) that the conduct of the proposed nuclear tests will constitute a violation of the rights under international law of New Zealand, as well as of other States; further or in the alternative;
>
> (ii) that it is unlawful for France to conduct such nuclear tests before it has undertaken an environmental impact assessment according to accepted international standards. Unless such an assessment establishes that the tests will not give rise, directly or indirectly to radioactive contamination of the marine environment the rights under international law of New Zealand, as well as the rights of other states will be violated. *Id.*

New Zealand also asked for interim measures of protection. Two days later, Australia petitioned the Court for permission to intervene in the case under the auspices of Article 62 of the Court.

New Zealand argued that paragraph 63 of the Court's judgment in 1974 permitted New Zealand to reactivate jurisdiction if France were to act in ways incompatible with the commitments that it made and that were the basis upon which the Court found the case moot in 1974. By twelve votes to three, the International Court found that New Zealand's claims did not fall within the provisions of paragraph 63 of the 1974 Judgment and dismissed them along with New Zealand's request for provisional measures, reserving jurisdiction over nuclear testing in the atmosphere. ... *See Id.*

* * *

After the New Zealand case, both the WHO and the General Assembly asked the I.C.J. for an advisory opinion on the legality of nuclear weapons.

(1) The WHO and ICJ Advisory Opinion Requests

On May 14, 1993 the World Health Assembly of the World Health Organization (WHO) asked the International Court for an Advisory Opinion on the following question:

> In view of the health and environmental effects, would the use of nuclear weapons by a State in war or other armed conflict be a breach of its obligations under international law including the WHO Constitution?

On December 23, 1994, the U.N. General Assembly sought an Advisory Opinion as follows:

Is the threat or use of nuclear weapons in any circumstance permitted under international law?

On July 8, 1996, the International Court issued its Advisory Opinion.

(2) Legality of the Threat or Use of Nuclear Weapons

1996 I.C.J. 226 (Judgment)

23. In seeking to answer the question put to it by the General Assembly, the Court must decide, after consideration of the great corpus of international law norms available to it, what might be the relevant applicable law. …

24. Some of the proponents of the illegality of the use of nuclear weapons have argued that such use would violate the right to life as guaranteed in Article 6 of the International Covenant on Civil and Political Rights, as well as in certain regional instruments for the protection of human rights. Article 6, paragraph 1, of the International Covenant provides as follows:

Every human being has the inherent right to life. This right shall be protected by law. No one shall be arbitrarily deprived of his life.

In reply, others contended that the International Covenant on Civil and Political Rights made no mention of war or weapons, and it had never been envisaged that the legality of nuclear weapons was regulated by that instrument. It was suggested that the Covenant was directed to the protection of human rights in peacetime, but that questions relating to unlawful loss of life in hostilities were governed by the law applicable in armed conflict.

25. The Court observes that the protection of the International Covenant of Civil and Political Rights does not cease in times of war, except by operation of Article 4 of the Covenant whereby certain provisions may be derogated from in a time of national emergency. Respect for the right to life is not, however, such a provision. In principle, the right not arbitrarily to be deprived of one's life applies also in hostilities. The test of what is an arbitrary deprivation of life, however, then fails to be determined by the applicable *lex specialis*, namely, the law applicable in armed conflict which is designed to regulate the conduct of hostilities. Thus whether a particular loss of life, through the use of a certain weapon in warfare, is to be considered an arbitrary deprivation of life contrary to Article 6 of the Covenant can only be decided by reference to the law applicable in armed conflict and not deduced from the terms of the Covenant itself.

26. Some States also contended that the prohibition against genocide, contained in the Convention of 9 December 1948 on the Prevention and Punishment of the Crime of Genocide, is a relevant rule of customary international law which the Court must apply. The Court recalls that, in Article II of the Convention genocide is defined as

> any of the following acts committed with intent to destroy, in whole or in part, a national, ethnical, racial or religious group, as such:
>
> *(a)* Killing members of the group;
>
> *(b)* Causing serious bodily or mental harm to members of the group;
>
> *(c)* Deliberately inflicting on the group conditions of life calculated to being about its physical destruction in whole or in part;
>
> *(d)* Imposing measures intended to prevent births within the group;
>
> *(e)* Forcibly transferring children of the group to another group.

It was maintained before the Court that the number of deaths occasioned by the use of nuclear weapons would be enormous; that the victims could, in certain cases, include persons of a particular national, ethnic, racial or religious group; and that the intention to destroy such groups could be inferred from the fact that the use of the nuclear weapon would have omitted to take account of the well-known effects of the use of such weapons.

The Court would point out in that regard that the prohibition of genocide would be pertinent in this case if the recourse to nuclear weapons did indeed entail the element of intent, towards a group as such, required by the provisions quoted above. In the view of the Court, it would only be possible to arrive at such a conclusion after having taken due account of the circumstances specific to each case. …

27. In both their written and oral statements, some States furthermore argued that any use of nuclear weapons would be unlawful by reference to existing norms relating to the safeguarding and protection of the environment, in view of their essential importance.

Specific references were made to various existing international treaties and instruments. … These instruments and other provisions relating to the protection and safeguarding of the environment were said to apply at all times, in war as well as in peace, and it was contended that they would be violated by the use of nuclear weapons whose consequences would be widespread and would have transboundary effects.

28. Other States questioned the binding legal quality of these precepts of environmental law; or, in the context of the Convention on the Prohibition of Military or Any Other Hostile Use of weapons in hostilities; or, in the case of Additional Protocol I, denied that they were generally bound by its terms, or recalled that they had reserved their position in respect of Article 35, paragraph 3, thereof.

It was also argued by some States that the principal purpose of environmental treaties and norms was the protection of the environment in times of peace. It was said that those treaties made no mention of nuclear weapons. It was also pointed out that warfare in general, and nuclear warfare in particular, were not mentioned in their texts and that it would be destabilizing to the rule of law and to confidence in international negotiations if those treaties were now interpreted in such a way as to prohibit the use of nuclear weapons.

29. The Court recognizes that the environment is under daily threat and that the use of nuclear weapons could constitute a catastrophe for the environment. The Court also recognizes that the environment is not an abstraction but represents the living space, the quality of life and the very health of human beings, including generations unborn. The existence of the general obligation of States to ensure that activities within their jurisdiction and control respect the environment of other States or of areas beyond national control is now part of the corpus of international law relating to the environment.

30. However, the Court is of the view that the issue is not whether the treaties relating to the protection of the environment are or not applicable during an armed conflict, but rather whether the obligations stemming from these treaties were intended to be obligations of total restraint during military conflict.

The Court does not consider that the treaties in question could have intended to deprive a State of the exercise of its right of self-defence under international law because of its obligations to protect the environment. Nonetheless, States must take environmental considerations into account when assessing what is necessary and proportionate in the pursuit of legitimate military objectives. Respect for the environment is one of the elements that go to assessing whether an action is in conformity with the principles of necessity and proportionality. …

31. The Court notes furthermore that Articles 35, paragraph 3, and 55 of Additional Protocol I provide additional protection for the environment. Taken together, these provisions embody a general obligation to protect the natural environment against widespread, long-term and severe environmental damage; the prohibition of methods and means of warfare which are intended, or may be expected, to cause such damage; and the prohibition of attacks against the natural environment by way of reprisals.

These are powerful constraints for all States having subscribed to these provisions.

32. General Assembly resolution 47/37 of 25 November 1992 on the Protection of the Environment in Times of Armed Conflict, is also of interest in this context. It affirms the general view according to which environmental considerations constitute one of the elements to be taken into account in the implementation of the principles of law applicable in armed conflict …

33. The Court thus finds that while the existing international law relating to the protection and safeguarding of the environment does not specifically prohibit the use of nuclear weapons, it indicates important environmental factors that are properly to be taken into account in the context of the implementation of the principles and rules of the law applicable in armed conflict. …

34. In the light of the foregoing the Court concludes that the most directly relevant applicable law governing the question of which, it was seised, is that relating to the use of force enshrined in the United Nations Charter and the law applicable in armed conflict which regulates the conduct of hostilities, together with any specific treaties on nuclear weapons that the Court might determine to be relevant. ...

35. In applying this law to the present case, the Court cannot however fail to take into account certain unique characteristics of nuclear weapons.

The Court has noted the definitions of nuclear weapons contained in various treaties and accords. It also notes that nuclear weapons are explosive devices whose energy results from the fusion or fission of the atom. By its very nature, that process, in nuclear weapons as they exist today, releases not only immense quantities of heat and energy, but also powerful and prolonged radiation. According to the material before the Court, the first two causes of damage are vastly more powerful than the damage caused by other weapons, while the phenomenon of radiation is said to be peculiar to nuclear weapons. These characteristics render the nuclear weapon potentially catastrophic. The destructive power of nuclear weapons cannot be contained in either space or time. They have the potential to destroy all civilization and the entire ecosystem of the planet.

The radiation released by a nuclear explosion would affect health, agriculture, natural resources and demography over a very wide area. Further, the use of nuclear weapons would be a serious danger to future generations. Ionizing radiation has the potential to damage the future environment, food and marine ecosystem, and to cause genetic defects and illness in future generations.

36. In consequence, in order correctly to apply to the present case the Charter law on the use of force and the law applicable in armed conflict, in particular humanitarian law, it is imperative for the Court to take account of the unique characteristics of nuclear weapons, and in particular their destructive capacity, their capacity to cause untold human suffering, and their ability to cause damage to generations to come. ...

37. The Court will now address the question of the legality of recourse to nuclear weapons in the light of the provision of the Charter relating to the threat or use of force.

38. The Charter contains several provisions relating to the threat and use of force. In Article 2, paragraph 4, the threat or use of force against the territorial integrity or political independence of another State or in any other manner inconsistent with the purposes of the United Nations is prohibited. That paragraph provides:

> All Members shall refrain in their international relations from the threat or use of force against the territorial integrity or political independence of any State, or in any other manner inconsistent with the Purposes of the United Nations.

This prohibition of the use of force is to be considered in the light of other relevant provisions of the Charter. In Article 51, the Charter recognizes the inherent right of individual or collective self-defence if an armed attack occurs. A further lawful use of force is envisaged in Article 42, whereby the Security Council may take military enforcement measures in conformity with Chapter VII of the Charter.

39. These provisions do not refer to specific weapons. They apply to any use of force regardless of the weapons employed. The Charter neither expressly prohibits, nor permits, the use of any specific weapon, including nuclear weapons. A weapon that is already unlawful *per se,* whether by treaty or custom, does not become lawful by reason of its being used for a legitimate purpose under the Charter.

40. The entitlement to resort to self-defence under Article 51 is subject to certain constraints. Some of these constraints are inherent in the very concept of self-defence. Other requirements are specified in Article 51.

41. The submission of the exercise of the right of self-defence to the conditions of necessity and proportionality is a rule of customary international law. ...

42. The proportionality principle may thus not in itself exclude the use of nuclear weapons in self-defence in all circumstances. But at the same time, a use of force that is proportionate under the law of self-defence, must, in order to be lawful, also meet the requirements of the law applicable in armed conflict which comprise in particular the principles and rules of humanitarian law.

43. Certain States have in their written and oral pleadings suggested that in the case of nuclear weapons, the condition of proportionality must be evaluated in the light of still further factors. They contend that the very nature of nuclear weapons, and the high probability of an escalation of nuclear exchanges, mean that there is an extremely strong risk of devastation. The risk factor is said to negate the possibility of the condition of proportionality being complied with. The Court does not find it necessary to embark upon the quantification of such risks; nor does it need to inquire into the question whether tactical nuclear weapons exist which are sufficiently precise to limit those risks: it suffices for the Court to note that the very nature of all nuclear weapons and the profound risks associated therewith are further considerations to be borne in mind by States believing they can exercise a nuclear response in self-defence in accordance with the requirements of proportionality.

44. Beyond the conditions of necessity and proportionality, Article 51 specifically requires that measures taken by States in the exercise of the right of self-defence shall be immediately reported to the Security Council; this article further provides that these measures shall not in any way affect the authority and responsibility of the Security Council under the Charter to take at any time such action as it deems necessary in order to maintain or restore international peace

and security. These requirements of Article 51 apply whatever the means of force used in self-defence.

45. The Court notes that the Security Council adopted on 11 April 1995, in the context of the extension of the Treaty on the Non-Proliferation of Nuclear Weapons, resolution 984 (1995) by the terms of which, on the one hand, it "*[t]akes notes* with appreciation of the statements made by each of the nuclear-weapon States (S/1995/261, S/1995/263, S/1995/264, S/1995/265), in which they give security assurances against the use of nuclear weapons to non-nuclear weapon States that are Parties to the Treaty on the Non-Proliferation of Nuclear Weapons," and, on the other hand, it "*[w]elcomes* the intention expressed by certain States that they will provide or support immediate assistance, in accordance with the Charter, to any non-nuclear-weapon State Party to the Treaty on the Non-Proliferation of Nuclear Weapons that is a victim of an act of, or an object of a threat of, aggression in which nuclear weapons are used".

46. Certain States asserted that the use of nuclear weapons in the conduct of reprisals would be lawful. The Court does not have to examine, in this context, the question of armed reprisals in time of peace, which are considered to be unlawful. Nor does it have to pronounce on the question of belligerent reprisals save to observe that in any case any right of recourse to such reprisals would, like self-defence, be governed *inter alia* by the principle of proportionality.

47. In order to lessen or eliminate the risk of unlawful attack, States sometimes signal that they possess certain weapons to use in self-defence against any State violating their territorial integrity or political independence. Whether a signaled intention to use force if certain events occur is or is not a "threat" within Article 2, paragraph 4, of the Charter depends upon various factors. If the envisaged use of force is itself unlawful, the stated readiness to use it would be a threat prohibited under Article 2, paragraph 4. ...

48. Some States put forward the argument that possession of nuclear weapons is itself an unlawful threat to use force. Possession of nuclear weapons may indeed justify an inference of preparedness to use them. In order to be effective, the policy of deterrence, by which those States possessing or under the umbrella of nuclear weapons seek to discourage military aggression by demonstrating that it will serve no purpose, necessitates that the intention to use nuclear weapons be credible. ...

49. Moreover, the Security Council may take enforcement measures under Chapter VII of the Charter. From the statements presented to it the Court does not consider it necessary to address questions which might, in a given case, arise from the application of Chapter VII. ...

51. Having dealt with the Charter provisions relating to the threat or use of force, the Court will now turn to the law applicable in situations of armed conflict. It will first address the question whether there are specific rules in international law regulating the legality or illegality of recourse to nuclear weapons *per*

se; it will then examine the question put to it in the light of the law applicable in armed conflict proper, i.e. the principles and rules of humanitarian law applicable in armed conflict, and the law of neutrality.

52. The Court notes by way of introduction that international customary and treaty law does not contain any specific prescription authorizing the threat or use of nuclear weapons or any other weapon in general or in certain circumstances, in particular those of the exercise of legitimate self-defence. Nor, however, is there any principle or rule of international law which would make the legality of the threat or use of nuclear weapons or of any other weapons dependent on a specific authorization. State practice shows that the illegality of the use of certain weapons as such does not result from an absence of authorization but, on the contrary, is formulated in terms of prohibition.

53. The Court must therefore now examine whether there is any prohibition of recourse to nuclear weapons as such; it will first ascertain whether there is a conventional prescription to this effect.

54. In this regard, the argument has been advanced that nuclear weapons should be treated in the same way as poisoned weapons. In that case, they would be prohibited under:

(*a*) the Second Hague Declaration of 29 July 1899, which prohibits "the use of projectiles the object of which is the diffusion of asphyxiating or deleterious gases";

(*b*) Article 23 *(a)* of the Regulations respecting the laws and customs of war on land annexed to the Hague Convention IV of 18 October 1907, whereby "it is especially forbidden ... to employ poison or poisoned weapons"; and

(*c*) the Geneva Protocol of 17 June 1925 which prohibits "the use in war of asphyxiating, poisonous or other gases, and of all analogous liquids, materials or devices".

55. The Court will observe that the Regulations annexed to the Hague Convention IV do not define what is to be understood by "poison or poisoned weapons" and that different interpretations exist on the issue. Nor does the 1925 Protocol specify the meaning to be given to the term "analogous materials or devices". The terms have been understood, in the practice of States, in their ordinary sense as covering weapons whose prime, or even exclusive, effect is to poison or asphyxiate. This practice is clear, and the parties to those instruments have not treated them as referring to nuclear weapons.

56. In view of this, it does not seem to the Court that the use of nuclear weapons can be regarded as specifically prohibited on the basis of the above-mentioned provisions of the Second Hague Declaration of 1899, the Regulations annexed to the Hague Convention IV of the 1907 or the 1925 Protocol (see paragraph 54 above).

57. The pattern until now has been for weapons of mass destruction to be declared illegal by specific instruments. The most recent such instruments are the Convention of 10 April 1972 on the Prohibition of the Development, Production and Stockpiling of Bacteriological (Biological) and Toxic Weapons and on their destruction — which prohibits the possession of bacteriological and toxic weapons and reinforces the prohibition of their use — and the Convention of 13 January 1993 on the Prohibition of the Development, Production, Stockpiling and Use of Chemical Weapons and on Their Destruction — which prohibits all use of chemical weapons and requires the destruction of existing stocks. Each of these instruments has been negotiated and adopted in its own context and for its own reasons. The Court does not find any specific prohibition of recourse to nuclear weapons in treaties expressly prohibiting the use of certain weapons of mass destruction.

58. In the last two decades, a great many negotiations have been conducted regarding nuclear weapons; they have not resulted in a treaty of general prohibition of the same kind as for bacteriological and chemical weapons. However, a number of specific treaties have been concluded in order to limit:

(*a*) the acquisition, manufacture and possession of nuclear weapons ...;

(*b*) the deployment of nuclear weapons ...; and

(*c*) the testing of nuclear weapons ...

59. Recourse to nuclear weapons is directly addressed by two of these Conventions and also in connection with the indefinite extension of the Treaty on the Non-Proliferation of Nuclear Weapons of 1968:

(*a*) the Treaty of Tlatelolco of 14 February 1967 for the Prohibition of Nuclear Weapons in Latin America prohibits, in Article 1, the use of nuclear weapons by the Contracting Parties. It further includes an Additional Protocol II open to nuclear-weapon States outside the region, Article 3 of which provides:

The Governments represented by the undersigned Plenipotentiaries also undertake not to use or threaten to use nuclear weapons against the Contracting Parties of the Treaty for the Prohibition of Nuclear Weapons in Latin America.

The Protocol was signed and ratified by the five nuclear-weapon States. Its ratification was accompanied by a variety of declarations ... [allowing for the use of nuclear weapons in certain circumstances].

(*b*) the Treaty of Rarotonga of 6 August 1985 establishes a South Pacific Nuclear Free Zone in which the Parties undertake not to manufacture, acquire or possess any nuclear explosive device (Art. 3). Unlike the Treaty of Tlatelolco, the Treaty of Rarotonga does not expressly prohibit the use of such weapons. But such a prohibition is for the States parties the necessary consequence of the prohibitions stipulated by the

Treaty. The Treaty has a number of protocols. Protocol 2, open to the five nuclear-weapon States, specifies in its Article 1 that:

Each Party undertakes not to use or threaten to use any nuclear explosive device against:

(a) Parties to the Treaty; or

(b) any territory within the South Pacific Nuclear Free Zone for which a State that has become a Party to Protocol I is internationally responsible."

China and Russia are parties to that Protocol. In signing it, China and the Soviet Union each made a declaration by which they reserved the "right to reconsider" their obligations under the said Protocol; … For its part, the United Kingdom made a declaration setting out the precise circumstances in which it "will not be bound by [its] undertaking under Article 1" of the Protocol.

(*c*) as to the Treaty on the Non-Proliferation of Nuclear Weapons, at the time of its signing in 1968 the United States, the United Kingdom and the USSR gave various security assurances to the non-nuclear-weapon States that were parties to the Treaty. …

On the occasion of the extension of the Treaty of 1995, the five nuclear-weapon States gave their non-nuclear-weapon partners, by means of separate unilateral statements on 5 and 6 April 1995, positive and negative security assurances against the use of such weapons. All the five nuclear weapon States first undertook not to use nuclear weapons against non-nuclear-weapon States that were parties to the Treaty on the Non-Proliferation of Nuclear Weapons. However, these States, apart from China, made an exception in the case of an invasion or any other attack against them, their territories, armed forces or allies, or on a State towards which they had a security commitment, carried out or sustained by a non-nuclear-weapon State Party to the Non-Proliferation Treaty in association or alliance with a nuclear-weapon State. … The Security Council, in unanimously adopting resolution 984 (1995) of 11 April 1995, cited above, took note of those statements with appreciation. …

60. Those States that believe that recourse to nuclear weapons is illegal stress that the conventions that include various rules providing for the limitation or elimination of nuclear weapons in certain areas (such as the Antarctic Treaty of 1959 which prohibits the deployment of nuclear weapons in the Antarctic, or the Treaty of Tlatelolco of 1967 which creates a nuclear-weapon-free zone in Latin America), or the conventions that apply certain measures of control and limitation to the existence of nuclear weapons (such as the 1963 Partial Test-Ban Treaty or the Treaty on the Non-Proliferation of Nuclear Weapons) all set limits to the use of nuclear weapons. In their view, these treaties bear witness, in their own way, to the emergence of a rule of complete legal prohibition of all uses of nuclear weapons.

61. Those States who defend the position that recourse to nuclear weapons is legal in certain circumstances see a logical contradiction in reaching such a conclusion. According to them, those Treaties, such as the Treaty on the Non-Proliferation of Nuclear Weapons, as well as Security Council resolutions 255 (1968) and 984 (1995) which take note of the security assurances given by the nuclear-weapon States to the non-nuclear-weapon States in relation to any nuclear aggression against the latter, cannot be understood as prohibiting the use of nuclear weapons, and such a claim is contrary to the very text of those instruments. For those who support the legality in certain circumstances of recourse to nuclear weapons, there is no absolute prohibition against the use of such weapons. The very logic and construction of the Treaty on the Non-Proliferation of Nuclear Weapons, they assert, confirm this. This Treaty, whereby, they contend, the possession of nuclear weapons by the five nuclear-weapon States has been accepted, cannot be seen as a treaty banning their use by those States; to accept the fact that those States possess nuclear weapons is tantamount to recognizing that such weapons may be used in certain circumstances. Nor, they contend, could the security assurances given by the nuclear-weapon States in 1968, and more recently in connection with the Review and Extension Conference of the Parties to the Treaty on the Non-Proliferation of Nuclear Weapons in 1995, have been conceived without its being supposed that there were circumstances in which nuclear weapons could be used in a lawful manner. For those who defend the legality of the use, in certain circumstances, of nuclear weapons, the acceptance of those instruments by the different non-nuclear-weapon States confirms and reinforces the evident logic upon which those instruments are based.

62. The Court notes that the treaties dealing exclusively with acquisition, manufacture, possession, deployment and testing of nuclear weapons, without specifically addressing their threat or use, certainly point to an increasing concern in the international community with these weapons; the Court concludes from this that these treaties could therefore be seen as foreshadowing a future general prohibition of the use of such weapons, but they do not constitute such a prohibition by themselves. As to the treaties of Tlatelolco and Rarotonga and their Protocols, and also the declarations made in connection with the indefinite extension of the Treaty on the Non-Proliferation of Nuclear Weapons, it emerges from these instruments that:

(*a*) a number of States have undertaken not to use nuclear weapons in specific zones (Latin America, the South Pacific) or against certain other States (non-nuclear-weapon States which are parties to the Treaty on the Non-Proliferation of Nuclear Weapons);

(*b*) nevertheless, even within this framework, the nuclear-weapon States have reserved the right to use nuclear weapons in certain circumstances; and

(*c*) these reservations met with no objection from the parties to the Tlatelolco or Rarotonga Treaties or from the Security Council.

63. These two treaties, the security assurances given in 1995 by the nuclear-weapon States and the fact that the Security Council took note of them with satisfaction, testify to a growing awareness of the need to liberate the community of States and the international public from the dangers resulting from the existence of nuclear weapons. The Court moreover notes the signing, even more recently, on 15 December 1995, at Bangkok, of a Treaty on the Southeast Asia Nuclear-Weapon-Free Zone, and on 11 April 1996, at Cairo, of a treaty on the creation of a nuclear-weapons-free zone in Africa. It does not, however, view these elements as amounting to a comprehensive and universal conventional prohibition on the use, or the threat of use, of those weapons as such.

64. The Court will now turn to an examination of customary international law to determine whether a prohibition of the threat or use of nuclear weapons as such flows from that source of law. As the Court has stated, the substance of that law must be "looked for primarily in the actual practice and *opinio juris* of States" (*Continental Shelf (Libyan Arab Jamahiriya/Malta), Judgment. I.C.J. Reports 1985,* p. 29, para. 27).

65. States which hold the view that the use of nuclear weapons is illegal have endeavoured to demonstrate the existence of a customary rule prohibiting this use. They refer to a consistent practice of non-utilization of nuclear weapons by States since 1945 and they would see in that practice the expression of an *opinio juris* on the part of those who possess such weapons.

66. Some other States, which assert the legality of the threat and use of nuclear weapons in certain circumstances, invoked the doctrine and practice of deterrence in support of their argument. They recall that they have always, in concert with certain other States, reserved the right to use those weapons in the exercise of the right to self-defence against an armed attack threatening their vital security interests. In their view, if nuclear weapons have not been used since 1945, it is not on account of an existing or nascent custom but merely because circumstances that might justify their use have fortunately not arisen.

67. The Court does not intend to pronounce here upon the practice known as the "policy of deterrence". It notes that it is a fact that a number of States adhered to that practice during the greater part of the Cold War and continue to adhere to it. Furthermore, the Members of the international community are profoundly divided on the matter of whether non-recourse to nuclear weapons over the past fifty years constitutes the expression of an *opinio juris.* Under these circumstances the Court does not consider itself able to find that there is such an *opinio juris.*

68. According to certain States, the important series of General Assembly resolutions, beginning with resolution 1653 (XVI) of 24 November 1961, that deal with nuclear weapons and that affirm, with consistent regularity, the illegality of nuclear weapons, signify the existence of a rule of international customary law which prohibits recourse to those weapons. According to other States, however, the resolutions in question have no binding character on their own account

and are not declaratory of any customary rule of prohibition of nuclear weapons; some of these States have also pointed out that this series of resolutions not only did not meet with the approval of all of the nuclear-weapon States but of many other States as well. ...

70. The Court notes that General Assembly resolutions, even if they are not binding, may sometimes have normative value. They can, in certain circumstances, provide evidence important for establishing the existence of a rule or the emergence of an *opinio juris.* To establish whether this is true of a given General Assembly resolution, it is necessary to look at its content and the conditions of its adoption; it is also necessary to see whether an *opinio juris* exists as to its normative character. Or a series of resolutions may show the gradual evolution of the *opinio juris* required for the establishment of a new rule.

71. Examined in their totality, the General Assembly resolutions put before the Court ... fall short of establishing the existence of an *opinio juris* on the illegality of the use of such weapons. ...

74. The Court not having found a conventional rule of general scope, nor a customary rule specifically proscribing the threat or use of nuclear weapons *per se,* it will now deal with the question whether recourse to nuclear weapons must be considered as illegal in the light of the principles and rules of international humanitarian law applicable in armed conflict and of the law of neutrality.

75. A large number of customary rules have been developed by the practice of States and are an integral part of the international law relevant to the question posed. The "laws and customs of war" — as they were traditionally called -- were the subject of efforts at codification undertaken in The Hague (including the Conventions of 1899 and 1907), and were based partly upon the St. Petersburg Declaration of 1868 as well as the results of the Brussels Conference of 1874. This "Hague Law" and, more particularly, the Regulations Respecting the Laws and Customs of War on Land, fixed the rights and duties of belligerents in their conduct of operations and limited the choice of methods and means of injuring the enemy in an international armed conflict. One should add to this the "Geneva Law" (the Conventions of 1864, 1906, 1929 and 1949), which protects the victims of war and aims to provide safeguards for disabled armed forces personnel and persons not taking part in the hostilities. These two branches of law applicable in armed conflict have become so closely interrelated that they are considered to have gradually formed one single complex system, known today as international humanitarian law. The provisions of the Additional Protocols of 1977 give expression and attest to the unity and complexity of that law.

76. Since the turn of the century, the appearance of new means of combat has — without calling into question the longstanding principles and rules of international law — rendered necessary some specific prohibitions of the use of certain weapons ...

77. All this shows that the conduct of military operations is governed by a body of legal prescriptions. This is so because "the right of belligerents to adopt means of injuring the enemy is not unlimited" as stated in Article 22 of the 1907 Hague Regulations relating to the laws and "which uselessly aggravate the suffering of disabled men or make their death inevitable". ...

78. The cardinal principles contained in the texts constituting the fabric of humanitarian law are the following. The first is aimed at the protection of the civilian population and civilian objects and establishes the distinction between combatants and non-combatants. States must never make civilians the object of attack and must consequently never use weapons that are incapable of distinguishing between civilian and military targets. According to the second principle, it is prohibited to cause unnecessary suffering to combatants: it is accordingly prohibited to use weapons causing them such harm or uselessly aggravating their suffering. In application of that second principle, States do not have unlimited freedom of choice of means in the weapons they use.

The Court would likewise refer, in relation to these principles, to the Martens Clause, which was first included in the Hague Convention II with Respect to the Law and Customs of War on Land of 1899 and which has proved to be an effective means of addressing the rapid evolution of military technology. A modern version of that clause is to be found in Article 1, paragraph 2, of Additional Protocol I of 1977, which reads as follows:

> In cases not covered by this Protocol or by other international agreements, civilians and combatants remain under the protection and authority of the principles of international law derived from established custom, from the principles of humanity and from the dictates of public conscience.

In conformity with the aforementioned principles, humanitarian law, at a very early stage, prohibited certain types of weapons either because of their indiscriminate effect on combatants and civilians or because of the unnecessary suffering caused to combatants, that is to say, a harm greater than that unavoidable to achieve legitimate military objectives. If an envisaged use of weapons would not meet the requirements of humanitarian law, a threat to engage in such use would also be contrary to that law.

79. It is undoubtedly because a great many rules of humanitarian law applicable in armed conflict are so fundamental to the respect of the human person and "elementary considerations of humanity" as the Court put it in its Judgment of 9 April 1949 in the *Corfu Channel* case (*I.C.J. Reports 1949,* p. 22), that the Hague and Geneva Conventions have enjoyed a broad accession. Further, these fundamental rules are to be observed by all States whether or not they have ratified the conventions that contain them, because they constitute intransgressible principles of international customary law. ...

85. Turning now to the applicability of the principles and rules of humanitarian law to possible threat or use of nuclear weapons, the Court notes that doubts

in this respect have sometimes been voiced on the ground that these principles and rules had evolved prior to the invention of nuclear weapons and that the Conferences of Geneva of 1949 and 1974-1977 which respectively adopted the four Geneva Conventions of 1949 and the two Additional Protocols thereto did not deal with nuclear weapons specifically. Such views, however, are only held by a small minority. In the view of the vast majority of States as well as writers there can be no doubt as to the applicability of humanitarian law to nuclear weapons.

86. The Court shares that view. Indeed, nuclear weapons were invented after most of the principles and rules of humanitarian law applicable in armed conflict had already come into existence; the Conferences of 1949 and 1974-1977 left these weapons aside, and there is a qualitative as well as quantitative difference between nuclear weapons and all conventional arms. However, it cannot be concluded from this that the established principles and rules of humanitarian law applicable in armed conflict did not apply to nuclear weapons. Such a conclusion would be incompatible with the intrinsically humanitarian character of the legal principles in question which permeates the entire law of armed conflict and applies to all forms of warfare and to all kinds of weapons, those of the past, those of the present and those of the future. ...

87. Finally, the Court points to the Martens Clause, whose continuing existence and applicability is not to be doubted, as an affirmation that the principles and rules of humanitarian law apply to nuclear weapons. ...

89. The Court finds that as in the case of the principles of humanitarian law applicable in armed conflict, international law leaves no doubt that the principle of neutrality, whatever its content, which is of a fundamental character similar to that of the humanitarian principles and rules, is applicable (subject to the relevant provisions of the United Nations Charter), to all international armed conflict, whatever type of weapons might be used.

90. Although the applicability of the principles and rules of humanitarian law and of the principle of neutrality to nuclear weapons is hardly disputed, the conclusions to be drawn from this applicability are, on the other hand, controversial.

91. According to one point of view, the fact that recourse to nuclear weapons is subject to and regulated by the law of armed conflict does not necessarily mean that such recourse is as such prohibited. ...

92. Another view holds that recourse to nuclear weapons could never be compatible with the principles and rules of humanitarian law and is therefore prohibited. In the event of their use, nuclear weapons would in all circumstances be unable to draw any distinction between the civilian population and combatants, or between civilian objects and military objectives, and their effects, largely uncontrollable, could not be restricted, either in time or in space, to lawful military targets. ...

93. A similar view has been expressed with respect to the effects of the principle of neutrality. Like the principles and rules of humanitarian law, that principle has therefore been considered by some to rule out the use of a weapon the effects of which simply cannot be contained within the territories of the contending States.

94. The Court would observe that none of the States advocating the legality of the use of nuclear weapons under certain circumstances, including the "clean" use of smaller, low yield, tactical nuclear weapons, has indicated what, supposing such limited use would not tend to escalate into the all-out use of high yield nuclear weapons. This being so, the Court does not consider that it has a sufficient basis for a determination on the validity of this view.

95. Nor can the Court make a determination on the validity of the view that the recourse to nuclear weapons would be illegal in any circumstance owing to their inherent and total incompatibility with the law applicable in armed conflict. Certainly, as the Court has already indicated, the principles and rules of law applicable in armed conflict — at the heart of which is the overriding consideration of humanity — make the conduct of armed hostilities subject to a number of strict requirements. Thus, methods and means of warfare, which would preclude any distinction between civilian and military targets, or which would result in unnecessary suffering to combatants, are prohibited. In view of the unique characteristics of nuclear weapons, to which the Court has referred above, the use of such weapons in fact seems scarcely reconcilable with respect for such requirements. Nevertheless, the Court considers that it does not have sufficient elements to enable it to conclude with certainty that the use of nuclear weapons would necessarily be at variance with the principles and rules of law applicable to armed conflict in any circumstance.

96. Furthermore, the Court cannot lose sight of the fundamental right of every State to survival, and thus its right to resort to self-defence, in accordance with Article 51 of the Charter, when its survival is at stake. Nor can it ignore the practice referred to as "policy of deterrence", to which an appreciable section of the international community adhered for many years. The Court also notes the reservations which certain nuclear-weapon States have appended to the undertakings they have given, notably under the Protocols to the Treaties of Tlatelolco and Rarotonga, and also under the declarations made by them in connection with the extension of the Treaty on the Non-Proliferation of Nuclear Weapons, not to resort to such weapons.

97. Accordingly, in view of the present state of international law viewed as a whole, as examined above by the Court, and of the elements of fact at its disposal, the Court is led to observe that it cannot reach a definitive conclusion as to the legality or illegality of the use of nuclear weapons by a State in an extreme circumstance of self-defence, in which its very survival would be at stake.

Notes and Questions

1. What world order interests are at stake in the Court's Opinion?

2. In assessing the value of the Opinion in terms of world order, consider the following comment:

> The Advisory Opinion of July 8, 1996 is a striking example of a misapplication of interpretative mode that is reminiscent of ... Colonel Nicholson, in Boulle's *The Bridge on the River Kwai*, a decent and dutiful man who has, alas, lost his coordinates and, as a result, does something, otherwise splendid, at the wrong moment and in the wrong place. Analyzed in terms of ordinary canons of interpretation, parts of the Court's opinion appear to be "good" law or, as some would say, positive normative evolution. Experts will then triumphantly carry off a sentence here, a paragraph there as an indication of a major advance in their various areas of specialization. But assessed in terms of its aggregate consequences on world order, the opinion, its good intentions notwithstanding, actually undermines one of the most urgent programs in the maintenance of minimum order in contemporary international politics: non-proliferation.
>
> Kubrick's eponymous "Dr. Strangelove" was infatuated with the bomb. Virtually every other human being, whether or not he or she believes that nuclear weapons have deterred global war or that the threat or use of nuclear weapons may be lawful in certain circumstances, knows that the weapon is a scourge whose wider dissemination bodes ill for all. Everyone knows that the most urgent and fundamental common interest of humanitarian law, if not law in general, is to prevent nuclear proliferation and then to secure a general orderly and effective nuclear disarmament. The real issue, which the Court treated only glancingly and which counsel appear often to have obscured, is not over *who* is for or against nuclear weapons, but over *which* is the optimal realistic strategy for containing and finally eliminating those weapons. ...
>
> Since the early 1960s, then, the inclusive threat posed by the wider possession of nuclear weapons has been increasingly recognized as a primary threat to world order. Common goals of the international system have become the prevention of the proliferation of nuclear weapons, the suspension of testing and other uses that could contaminate the environment, the reduction of the number of nuclear weapons to ever-lower levels of parity and, ultimately, a complete nuclear disarmament. Many of the longer-term of these goals have proved difficult of achievement, all the more because some of the strongest supporters of non-proliferation have refused to consider yielding their own nuclear arsenals. Nevertheless, some very significant achievements in this regard have been registered through a complex and subtle normative metamorphosis of the status and responsibilities of the five permanent (and nuclear) members of the Security Council. That modulation must be explicated if we are to assess the critical effect of the 1996 opinion.
>
> In the early years of the nuclear era, the control of nuclear weapons was viewed as the prerogative and insignia of a great power, for each of whom untrammeled decision about their deployment and use was its single perquisite....
>
> [T]he pressure for and against nuclear weapons mounted. One of the consequences of these contrary pressures was more intense demands for containment. A by-product of containment policies was that the legitimacy of the retention by the nuclear powers themselves of nuclear weapons was put into issue. For, if non-nuclear states were not entitled to acquire the weapons, how could nuclear states justify their retention and, indeed, expansion of nuclear arsenals.
>
> By the time of the renewal of the non-proliferation treaty in 1995, a new regime had begun to take shape which may prove no less momentous for international law than the evolution of "self-defense," in the *Caroline* incident and its diplomatic aftermath, from

a political excuse to a legal doctrine. The network of agreements concluded at the time of the indefinite renewal of the NPT, which included declarations by each of the permanent members of the Security Council, established, in effect (i) that nuclear weapons were henceforth held by individual states only by virtue of the authority of the international community; (ii) that the international community henceforth prescribed the conditions under which the weapons were held; (iii) that only the permanent members of the Security Council were such lawful holders; and (iv) that all other members of the international community could not lawfully acquire such weapons.

The great novelty in this new regime was that the legitimate holders, as the price for general support for the policy of non-proliferation they actively sought and the price for the toleration of their continued retention of nuclear weapons, were being transformed into licensees rather than, as theretofore, holders of an estate in fee simple: the permanent members of the Security Council committed themselves not to use the weapons against any non-nuclear weapons state and to come to the assistance of any non-nuclear weapons state that was party to the NPT, should it be threatened or attacked by nuclear weapons. The emerging regime also included commitments to work toward reduction of nuclear weapons and total nuclear disarmament.

On May 11, 1995, in Decision 3, the Conference of the Parties to the Treaty on the Non-Proliferation of Nuclear Weapons decided that the NPT should continue in force indefinitely. 34 I.L.M. 961, 972-73 (1995). The Conference also affirmed, as an integral part of the regime, the importance of making continued advances toward nuclear disarmament, which would be achieved through a universal ban on nuclear testing, the end of production of fissile material, and reductions in the number of stockpiled weapons. *Id.* at 969-70. Other goals included the expansion of nuclear-weapon-free zones, especially in conflict-prone regions like the Middle East and the issuance of security guarantees, like that contained in Security Council Resolution 984.

Of critical importance in this package of rights, privileges, obligations and duties were the "declarations of the nuclear-weapon States concerning both negative and positive security assurances." *Id.* at 970. The systemic implications of these commitments, as soft as they were, were acknowledged by several of the permanent members of the Security Council. According to the British representative:

> [r]esolution [984] is of historic importance and it marks a very significant step forward beyond the terms of the Council's resolution 255 (1968), which was adopted in 1968. For the first time, a Council resolution relates to both positive and negative assurances. For the first time, all five nuclear-weapons States have given negative assurances in such a clear-cut and comprehensive way. For the first time, the five nuclear Powers have acted together to provide a common positive security assurance, as reflected in the resolution.

U.N. SCOR, 50th Sess., 3514th mtg. at 27, U.N. Doc. S/PV. 3514 (1995).

At the same meeting, the Russian representative repeated his country's guarantee that the:

> Russian Federation will not use nuclear weapons against non-nuclear weapon State parties to the Treaty on the Non-Proliferation of Nuclear Weapons, except in the case of an invasion or any other attack on the Russian Federation, its territory, its armed forces or other troops, its allies or on a State towards which it has a security commitment, carried out or sustained by such a non-nuclear weapon State in association or alliance with a nuclear-weapon State. *Id.* at 30.

The U.S. representative noted:

> [this] is why my Government hopes that this resolution will be seen by others as a further argument in favour of the indefinite extension of the NPT, even though these security assurances are not linked to the extensions question. As I said before, because there is a Treaty, we can offer these assurances. If the NPT is permanent; if it is fully complied with and if it is universal, not only do these assurances become more meaningful: they suggest a day when they may also prove to be unnecessary. *Id.* at 27.

Additional measures supported by the Conference included enhanced safeguards, to be implemented by the IAEA, and the development of peaceful uses of nuclear energy. 34 I.L.M. 961, 972 (1995).

The regime that had evolved and been codified in 1995 was neither final nor perfect. In theory, it still allowed the nuclear powers to conduct nuclear actions against each other. But given the effective parity and consequent balance of terror that obtained between them, the "right" to initiate nuclear action against another nuclear power was, prospectively, so costly to the initiator and so unlikely to be realized that it was all but empty. The regime was also unsatisfactory because of its gross asymmetry. But that is hardly unique to the nuclear weapons regime. The international legal system has had no choice but to come to terms with the factual realities of gross disparities in size and power; it has tried to co-opt them into the system of international security in a number of sectors. *See* W. Michael Reisman, *Toward a Normative Theory of Differential Responsibility for International Security Functions: Responsibilities of Major Powers*, Centenary Symposium, Kyoto University, Faculty of Law, Kyoto, Japan. On balance, what was achieved in 1995 was significantly better than what had preceded it. Perhaps more to the point, for all of its imperfections, what had been achieved was about all that could be expected in the context. …

The advisory opinion of July 8, 1996 of the International Court of Justice with respect to the legality of the threat or use of nuclear weapons must be appraised in terms of this evolving political and legal context. The essential question is whether the Court's holdings contribute to minimum world order by reinforcing the nuclear weapons regime that we have reviewed and pressing it further toward the desired end-goal of nuclear disarmament.

That, as Judge Higgins said with her characteristic moderation, is not clear. Rather than conceive of the issue of nuclear weapons as *sui generis* and consequently standing apart from conventional weapons and insusceptible to analysis in their terms and rather than confirm the regime that had slowly emerged and been codified in 1995, the Court elected to consider nuclear weapons in terms of the law of armed conflict. Having taken that tack, it should have been no surprise that it would ultimately conclude [as it did]. …

> In view of the present state of international law viewed as a whole, as examined above by the Court, and of the elements of fact at its disposal, the Court is led to observe that it cannot reach a definitive conclusion as to the legality or illegality of the use of nuclear weapons by a state in an extreme circumstance of self-defence in which its very survival would be at stake.

Legality of the Threat or Use of Nuclear Weapons, July 8, 1996, I.C.J., General List No. 95.

This is an interesting and debatable scholastic question, but it is no longer pertinent to the emerging regime in which non-proliferation is the *grundnorm* and the legitimate nuclear licensees operate under contingencies that are *de jure* and *de facto* more stringent. It would have been better if the Court had stated that simply and directly or, as Judge

> Oda suggested in dissent, declined to issue an opinion. Far worse, the Court's formulation raises doubts about the cogency of the new regime and revives the legitimacy of claims to use nuclear weapons for exclusive national purposes. For if international law does not hold definitively that the use of nuclear weapons by a state in an extreme circumstance of self-defense is illegal, what is the Court saying to security specialists in states that feel they are under significant threat? The conclusions of the Court, in particular, conclusion 2E of the *dispositif*, tend to legitimize the use of nuclear weapons for discrete national purposes in what the Court described as "an extreme circumstance of self-defense in which the state's very survival might be at stake." And it is, of course, the self-perceived threatened state that makes the initial, operational and irrevocable decision that it is in "an extreme circumstance of self-defense."
>
> This holding is not a theoretical abstraction. There are a number of states in the world whose elites and significant parts of whose populations have cause to believe that the price of a war that they might lose will not be in a boundary adjustment or the payment of some form of tribute or other concession. Rather, defeat will result in the extinction of their political identity and possibly the extermination of large parts of their populations. These are often people who, as the saying goes, have come by their paranoia honestly. Their impulse to acquire nuclear weapons is strong. Now the systemic restraints of the 1995 regime notwithstanding, the principal judicial organ of the United Nations has said to factions within those states that have long agitated in their internal political processes for the acquisition of the ultimate weapon and until now have received no authoritative international support, that the use of nuclear weapons for self-defense cannot be said to be prohibited by international law. That, of course, is exactly what the pro-nuclear activists in those states have been saying all along. In strengthening the hands of nuclear proponents in states with justifiable security fears, the Court has also strengthened "nuclearists" in other states, who may now point to the enhanced probability of nuclear weapons acquisition by others as justification and compulsion for their states, too, to acquire nuclear weapons. This is the essential scenario of proliferation. ...

W. Michael Reisman, *The Political Consequences of the General Assembly Advisory Opinion, in* INTERNATIONAL LAW, THE INTERNATIONAL COURT OF JUSTICE, AND NUCLEAR WEAPONS (Laurence Boisson de Chazournes & Philippe Sands eds., Cambridge U. Press 1999).

d. 1996 - 2004

Since the Court's 1996 decision in the Legality case, several nuclear flashpoints have arisen in key areas of the world, including the India/Pakistan Line of Control in Jammu Kashmir, in North Korea, and in Iraq.

(1) India/Pakistan

The Line of Control separating Indian and Pakistani troops in Jammu Kashmir has been the center of low intensity conflict and three major wars since 1947. Both nations claim Kashmir in its entirety, but agreed on a cease-fire at the Line of Control in September 1965, pending final settlement of the dispute. A settlement has proved elusive due to the seemingly irresolvable claims of Pakistan, which holds that Pakistan was created to offer a homeland to the subcontinent's Muslim population including Kashmir's Muslim majority, and India, which sees the largely Muslim territory as necessary to its mantle as a secular, multi-ethnic democracy. In more recent years, India has accused Pakistan of waging a proxy war in Kashmir by arming and training Islamic militants. Because both India and Pakistan are now nuclear powers, their conflict in Jammu Kashmir has become an even greater threat to world order.

(a) Sean D. Murphy, *Contemporary Practice of the United States Relating to International Law*

93 Am. J. Int'l L. 470, 498-501 (1999)

India-Pakistan Nuclear Weapons Tests

The Treaty on the Non-Proliferation of Nuclear Weapons (NPT) calls upon states to work toward nuclear disarmament, while at the same time preserving the right of five (and only five) member states to possess nuclear weapons (China, France, Russia, the United Kingdom, and the United States). In 1995, the NPT was extended indefinitely and unconditionally. In 1996, a Comprehensive Nuclear Test Ban Treaty (CTBT) was opened for signature. India and Pakistan joined neither the NPT nor the CTBT.

On May 11 and 13, 1998, India conducted five underground nuclear weapons tests (its first nuclear weapons test occurred in 1974). On May 28 and 30, Pakistan carried out underground nuclear tests as well. Those actions immediately triggered sanctions against both nations under U.S. foreign relations laws. Intense bilateral and multilateral diplomacy ensued. Both countries eventually announced that they would voluntarily refrain from further tests and that they intended to adhere to the CTBT by September 1999.

To assist in such diplomacy, legislation was enacted in November 1998 to provide the President with the authority to lift certain of these sanctions. Thereafter, the President waived sanctions against India and Pakistan with respect to activities of the Export-Import Bank, the Overseas Private Investment Corporation, and the Trade and Development Agency. The President also restored military education and training programs for both countries and allowed U.S. banks to make loans and provide credit to their governments. Finally, he authorized U.S. officials to vote at international financial institutions in favor of extending loans or financial or technical assistance to Pakistan. Prohibitions on sales of military and military/civilian ("dual use") items to the two countries remained in place.

On November 12, 1998, Deputy Secretary of State Strobe Talbott addressed the U.S. position on India and Pakistan's status as nuclear weapons States:

> The UN Security Council, the Group of Eight major industrialized nations, and the P-5 [five permanent members of the Security Council] have each endorsed a set of benchmarks that provide for the Indians and Pakistanis a map of the path away from the nuclear brink and back into the mainstream of those countries that are part of the solution to the problem of proliferation rather than being part of the problem itself. An unprecedented ad-hoc task force of over a dozen nuclear and non-nuclear weapons states, including several that abandoned nuclear-weapons as-

> pirations or status — countries such as Brazil, Argentina and Ukraine — joined in forging a common response. So have regional groupings such as the European Union, the Organization of American States, the ASEAN Regional Forum, the Gulf Cooperation Council, the Organization of the Islamic Conference, and several others.
>
> Two principles have guided the American side of this effort:
>
> First, we remain committed to the common position of the P-5, G-8, and South Asia Task Force, notably including on [sic] the long-range goal of universal adherence to the Nuclear Non-Proliferation Treaty. We do not and will not concede, even by implication, that India and Pakistan have established themselves as nuclear-weapons states under the NPT. Unless and until they disavow nuclear weapons and accept safeguards on all their nuclear activities, they will continue to forfeit the full recognition and benefits that accrue to members in good standing of the NPT.
>
> Our second principle applies to the near and medium term, and to the practice of diplomacy as the art of the possible. We recognize that any progress toward a lasting solution must be based on India's and Pakistan's conceptions of their own national interests. We're under no illusions that either country will alter or constrain its defense programs under duress or simply because we've asked it to. That's why we've developed proposals for near-term steps that are, we believe, fully consistent with the security requirements that my Indian and Pakistani counterparts articulated at the outset of our discussions. The Prime Ministers of both nations have said publicly that they seek to define those requirements at the lowest possible levels.
>
> In other words, while universal NPT adherence remains our long-term goal, we are not simply going to give India and Pakistan the cold shoulder until they take that step. We are working intently with both countries. ...

Strobe Talbott, *U.S. Diplomacy in South Asia: A Progress Report*, DEP'T ST. DISPATCH, Dec. 1998, at 16.

The Prime Ministers of India and Pakistan agreed on February 21, 1999, to take steps to reduce the risk of nuclear war, including bilateral discussions in areas of friction, measures to prevent the accidental launching of nuclear weapons, notification of any accidental incident that might create the risk of nuclear fallout, and notification of the testing of ballistic missiles. The two countries, however, did not jointly agree to sign the CTBT.

In 1990, when the President could no longer certify to Congress that Pakistan did not possess a nuclear explosive device, restrictions were triggered under U.S. law prohibiting the transfer to Pakistan of military equipment and technology. Among other things, these restrictions prevented delivery of F-16 aircraft that Pakistan had contracted to purchase in the late 1980s. In December 1998, the United States announced that it had agreed to pay Pakistan several hundred million dollars to settle the matter....

* * *

With the bombing of the Indian Parliament in December 2001 and the devastating attack on an army camp in the Indian-administered part of Kashmir in May 2002, both India and Pakistan initiated massive mobilizations. The use of nuclear weapons was not ruled out. India has a no first-use nuclear policy, but enjoys conventional military superiority as well as strategic space for retreat in the event Pakistan were to make territorial gains. Pakistan has none of these luxuries, and it was feared that Pakistan would activate its first-use nuclear policy.

These fears intensified on January 25, 2002, when India successfully test fired their intermediate-range Agni missile capable of carrying a nuclear warhead 700 kilometers. In response, Pakistan test fired a missile capable of carrying a nuclear warhead, and on May 30, 2002, renewed their call for Security Council action on Kashmir. With almost a million troops massed on both sides of the border, India refused a pullback until October to determine whether Pakistan had carried out its pledge to crack down on Muslim militants. On October 5, Pakistan staged a test firing of their Shaheen I missile (also called the Hatf IV) capable of carrying a nuclear warhead from 380 to 475 miles, as well as a longer-range missile, the Ghauri II, reported to be able to reach targets at a distance of 1,320 miles. Several more tests were conducted by both sides, raising the spectre of full-scale nuclear war if a diplomatic solution could not be reached.

Indian Prime Minister Atal Behari Vajpayee said in an interview that India was prepared to launch nuclear missiles at Pakistan over the dispute in Kashmir but U.S. intervention averted the war when Pakistan promised to stop supporting militants in Kashmir:

> If Pakistan had not accepted the demand to stop cross-border infiltration and the United States had not conveyed to us Pakistan's guarantee to do so, then nothing would have stopped the war.... India was prepared for an atomic war but we were confident that our neighbor would not commit such an act of madness. Stewart Bell, *U.S. Averted Kashmir War, India Says: American Intervention Persuaded Pakistan to End Support for Militants Attacking Indian Territory: Vajpayee Interview*, Nat'l Post, June 18, 2002.

In April 2003, a positive period of India/Pakistan relations began, with both sides stating through spokespersons that the rapid coalition victory in Iraq was at least in part responsible for the thaw. Peace talks between the two nuclear rivals have continued as of this writing, despite a Congress Party victory in the 2004 elections and, more importantly, the revelations in February 2004 that Dr. A.Q. Khan, the so-called "Father of the Muslim Bomb", had sold Pakistan's nuclear weapons technology over many years to countries such as Libya, Iran, and North Korea.

For further discussion, *see* V.N. KHANNA, INDIA'S NUCLEAR DOCTRINE (Samskriti 2000); PRAKASH NANDA, NUCLEARIZATION OF DIVIDED NATIONS (Manas 2001); KAMAL MATINUDDIN, THE NUCLEARIZATION OF SOUTH ASIA (Oxford U. Press 2002); GEORGE PERKOVICH, INDIA'S NUCLEAR BOMB: THE IMPACT ON GLOBAL PROLIFERATION (Oxford U. Press 2002); SUMIT GANGULY, CONFLICT UNENDING (Columbia U. Press 2002); ROBERT WIRSING, KASHMIR IN THE SHADOW OF WAR (M.E. Sharpe 2003).

(2) North Korea

The confrontation that began in 2002 between North Korea and the United States stemmed from the disintegration of a negotiated settlement that resolved the last outbreak of nuclear brinkmanship on the Korean Peninsula in 1994. In that case, North Korea promised to abandon its nuclear program and to submit to U.N./International Atomic Energy Agency (IAEA) inspections in exchange for shipments of fuel oil and the building of nuclear power plants by the United States and its allies. After disclosures in October 2002 that North Korea had been secretly pursuing the development of uranium-based nuclear weapons, the Bush administration cut the fuel shipments. Subsequently, North Korea alleged that it had begun to revive the Yongbyon nuclear reactor complex capable of producing weapons-grade plutonium. Experts stated that the complex could produce three to six nuclear weapons within the next five to nine months.

On December 31, 2002, North Korea threatened to withdraw from the 1970 Non-Proliferation Treaty ("NPT") and formally expelled the last two remaining U.N. nuclear inspectors. North Korea contended that it had been forced to reactivate its nuclear weapons program as a deterrent to the hostile policies of the United States, which had not only cut off supplies of fuel oil but was threatening North Korea with a pre-emptive military strike against its nuclear facilities. North Korea asserted that the conflict could be resolved only through bilateral negotiations with the United States. This demand was rejected by the Bush administration, which asserted that it would not reward North Korea for engaging in nuclear blackmail.

On January 10, 2003, North Korea confirmed that it was pulling out of the NPT effective immediately. Responding, the IAEA held an emergency meeting and gave North Korea a final chance to readmit its inspectors. The IAEA's board demanded that North Korea allow "the re-establishment of the required containment and surveillance measures at its nuclear facilities and the full implementation of all the required safeguard measures at all times, including the return of IAEA inspectors" or face sanctions. Res. GOV/2003/3, *International Atomic Energy Agency Board of Governors: Report by the Director General on the Implementation of the NPT Safeguards Agreement Between the Agency and the Democratic People's Republic of Korea* (2003). North Korea replied that any sanctions imposed would mean war. The Security Council, to which the matter was eventually referred, did not act.

On February 24, 2003, North Korea fired a short-range missile into the Sea of Japan. In mid-April 2003, United States, Chinese, and North Korean officials met in Beijing for talks in an effort to end the stalemate, to no effect. Various attempts at behind the scenes negotiations also proved unsuccessful. Multilateral discussions with China, South Korea, Japan, Russia and the U.S. continue sporadically. The revelation in February 2004 that Pakistani nuclear scientist Dr. A.Q. Khan sold nuclear weapons technology to North Korea has increased tensions both in and beyond the region. In June 2004, the U.S. made the first concrete proposal to North Korea offering various incentives in exchange for pulling back its nuclear program.

For further discussion, *see* Victor D. Cha & David C. Kang, Nuclear North Korea: A Debate on Strategies of Engagement (Columbia U. Press 2003); Michael O'Hanlon & Mike M. Mochizuki, Crisis on the Korean Peninsula: How to Prevent North Korea from Becoming the Next Iraq (McGraw-Hill 2003); Peggy J. Parks, North Korea (Blackbirch Press 2003).

(3) Iraq

After Iraq's defeat in the Persian Gulf War in 1991, the United Nations required Iraq to end all research on biological, chemical and nuclear weapons and stop developing missiles capable of delivering them. The Security Council imposed sweeping sanctions against the country that would remain in effect until Iraq had fully disarmed, as verified by U.N. inspectors. But the Council withdrew its last inspection team in 1998, after its leaders complained that Iraq was hampering their work. Then-U.S. President Bill Clinton ordered four days of bombing in Baghdad, arguing that Saddam Hussein posed one of the most serious threats to world order due to his known capacity to produce weapons of mass destruction and, sooner or later, must be stopped.

One year after the terrorist attacks of September 11, 2001, President George W. Bush addressed the United Nations in September 2002, describing the need for eliminating Iraq's unconventional weapons and insisting that Baghdad comply with the Security Council's longstanding disarmament orders or risk "regime change." The U.S. Congress had already given authorization for the use of force against Iraq. (*See* "Report on the Authorization for Use of Military Force Against Iraq Resolution of 2002", Washington, D.C.: U.S. G.P.O. 2003.)

In early November 2002, the United Nations Security Council unanimously adopted Resolution 1441 which gave Iraq a "final opportunity" to comply with disarmament resolutions and established a rigorous regime of inspections. The text warned of "serious consequences" if Iraq committed any violations. It was arguably understood at the time that "serious consequences" included the use of military force against Iraq. Before force could be authorized, however, the resolution required that a report be made by the newly-appointed weapons inspectors to the Council, which would then meet to decide how to proceed. The chief U.N. inspector for chemical and biological weapons, Hans Blix, announced that he would travel to Baghdad and would be accompanied by Mohamed El Baradei, the chief atomic weapons inspector for the IAEA. Saddam Hussein, the Iraqi President, had seven days to accept the resolution and pledge his compliance. Within 30 days, his government was required to produce a full and accurate list of Iraq's nuclear, chemical and biological weapons programs and secret ballistic missile developments. Shortly thereafter, at a meeting of Arab League foreign ministers, Arab governments voiced collective support for the new weapons inspections regime. However, the same Arab governments opposed the use of force and considered a strike against Iraq a threat to the national security of all Arab nations. Neil MacFarquhar, *Iraq Inspections Receive Approval from Arab League*, N.Y. TIMES, Nov. 11, 2002, at A1.

After initial reluctance on November 13, 2002, Iraq agreed to allow United Nations inspectors to enter the country, while maintaining its position that it had no weapons of mass destruction on its territory. Later, it submitted a list of pertinent programs, a list which was subsequently found to be incomplete by the U.N. weapons inspectors.

On January 27, 2003, Hans Blix reported to the Security Council that Iraq had failed to actively cooperate with the United Nations disarmament demands in that it had not facilitated interviews with scientists or resolved major discrepancies about its biological, chemical and missile programs. However, a report by the IAEA inspectors found no evidence, as of that date, that Iraq had revived its nuclear weapons program since the supposed dismantling of the program in the early 1990s.

U.S. Secretary of State Colin L. Powell informed the U.N. Security Council that in 1999 and 2000, Iraq had tried to buy from Slovenia, Romania, India and Russia gas centrifuge equipment that could be used to produce fuel for nuclear weapons. In February 2003, Romania and Slovenia confirmed United States allegations that Iraq had tried to buy equipment from them that could be used to build nuclear weapons, but reports of Iraqi efforts to purchase uranium from Africa, which the United States and Britain cited as one reason for military action, were, at least in part, based on forged documents.

Late in February 2003, the United States and Great Britain, growing increasingly impatient with the progress of U.N. inspection teams in Iraq and doubtful of Iraqi compliance, attempted to persuade nine of the fifteen members of the Security Council to back a new resolution authorizing the use of force against Iraq.

On February 25, 2003, the United States and Britain, co-sponsored by Spain, presented a "second" resolution to the Security Council. The resolution noted that Iraq had failed to take the final opportunity afforded it in Resolution 1441, thus implicitly authorizing the use of force. On the same day, France, Germany and Russia issued an informal "memorandum" calling for at least four more months of weapons inspections in Iraq. The memorandum also stated that nothing, so far, justified a war to force President Saddam Hussein to rid his country of the remnants of his nuclear, biological and chemical weapons. During these heated negotiations, a serious rift developed between the coalition partners (i.e. the U.S., the U.K., and Spain) and other countries.

In early March 2003, France and Russia made clear that they were ready to use their veto power to block passage of the U.S. and U.K.-backed "second" resolution authorizing force against Iraq. U.S. Secretary of State Colin Powell stated that the U.S. would go to war without U.N. backing if necessary. In an apparent last-ditch effort to prove compliance and avoid war, Iraq began destruction of its Al-Samoud II missiles under U.N. Monitoring, Verification and Inspection Commission ("UNMOVIC") supervision. Iraq later stated that under U.N. supervision, it had destroyed 40 Al-Samoud II missiles, about a third of its acknowledged total of 120, including 20 in various stages of construction. Inspectors cited substantial disarmament progress and no signs of a renewed nuclear arms program, but also noted that Baghdad had not answered many questions about pre-existing chemical and biological weapons that were known to exist in 1998 when inspections were halted.

On March 17, 2003, the United States, Britain and Spain pulled the proposed "second" U.N. resolution before any vote could take place due to the threatened veto by France, Russia, and China. Later that same day, President George W. Bush ordered Saddam Hussein and his sons to leave Iraq within 48 hours in order to avoid military action.

On March 19, 2003, amid widespread anti-war protest in their own countries and, in fact, throughout the world, the foreign ministers of France, Germany and Russia offered a joint declaration on the diplomatic debacle and argued that the planned American-led invasion to disarm Iraq and oust Saddam Hussein, based on the newly announced pre-emptive strike doctrine, had no basis in international law. Felicity Barringer, *Critics Say U.S. Lacks Legal Basis for Attack*, N.Y. Times, March 20, 2003, at A19. Shortly thereafter, on March 19th at 10:15 p.m., President Bush announced that the start of military action against Iraq had begun. An attack on three "leadership targets" opened the war and precision-guided military assaults on specific Iraqi targets ensued as coalition forces began their rapid march to Basra and Baghdad and completed their dislodging of the Hussein regime within four weeks.

On May 2, 2003, President Bush announced the end of major combat in Iraq. Over the course of the next year no weapons of mass destruction were found, although documentary evidence of weapons programs was uncovered. Legislative leaders in both the U.S. and the U.K. questioned whether intelligence reports used to justify the war were in fact inflated to exaggerate the threat posed by Iraqi weapons of mass destruction, and thus justify regime change. (*See*, *infra*, Part II).

In 2003, Paul Bremer, the U.S. Administrator in Iraq, appointed an Iraqi Governing Council, membership of which reflected the ethnic make-up of Iraq. In 2004 this Council approved a Constitution guaranteeing democratic freedoms to all Iraqis. As of this writing, despite substantially increased levels of violence led by insurgents in a few parts of the country, an Iraqi Interim Government has been established. The Coalition Provisional Authority handed over sovereignty to Iraq on June 28, 2004, two days ahead of schedule. The Interim Government will organize and oversee elections of a National Council and a national election for a permanent government, all by the end of 2005. Coalition forces will remain at the request of the Interim Government until no longer needed for security and training purposes.

NOTES AND QUESTIONS

1. In each of the three cases above, the world community has taken differing approaches to controlling nuclear weapons proliferation, including unilateral diplomacy between the U.S. and India, multilateral diplomacy in the case of North Korea, and full-scale war against Iraq. Why are there differences and are they legally justified?

2. The International Atomic Energy Agency (IAEA) was created shortly after the U.N. came into being at the end of World War II. Then-President Truman was anxious to turn over nuclear technology for peaceful purposes to an international body, believing that it was too powerful a tool to be left in the hands of the United States exclusively. The IAEA was created to promote the peaceful uses of the technology by nations around the world who were willing to agree to a framework of safeguards, including yearly inspections, in exchange for free access to the technology. Scores of countries took advantage of this offer throughout the 50's and 60's, receiving technical assistance from the IAEA in establishing their programs for peaceful uses, i.e., for energy, agriculture, and health services. The IAEA was not completely effective, however, in preventing nuclear proliferation. In 1968, the U.S., USSR, and the UK organized the adoption of the Non-Proliferation Treaty (NPT) by nuclear and non-nuclear states. 170 non-nuclear countries agreed to a safeguards regime, under which they promised not to develop nuclear weapons or devices, and the nuclear powers promised not to provide weapons technology to non-holders, to protect non-nuclear countries from nuclear attack by third states, and to continue to work toward an eventual nuclear disarmament. The IAEA fit well into the NPT regime, because it had already developed a cadre of nuclear inspectors who could regulate compliance with the treaty as well as continue its efforts to spread the peaceful uses of nuclear energy.

With the existence of the NPT and the IAEA returning to public consciousness during the run-up to war with Iraq, commentators have begun to evaluate the success of these dual regimes in preventing the spread of weapons technology. Some argue that for 50 years or more, only a handful of states beyond the P-5 (5 permanent members of the Security Council) have moved to nuclear status. Others say that with North Korea, India, Pakistan, Iraq, Israel, Iran and possibly others, in that club, the threat to world order has increased exponentially.

In 2004, U.S. and U.K. officials announced that Libya had agreed to hand over all its previously unacknowledged nuclear weapons technology in exchange for the removal of U.N. and unilateral sanctions. Iran also indicated a desire to cooperate with E.U. officials and the I.A.E.A. to divulge the details of its nuclear program which heretofore they had denied having.

How would you evaluate the success of these two multilateral regimes? Do they obviate unilateral coercive action? In your opinion, have inspection regimes proved effective? *See* Thomas M. Franck, *Inspections and Their Enforcement: A Modest Proposal*, 96 AM. J. INT'L L. 899 (2002).

3. For discussion of the various means by which States can prevent the further spread of unlawful nuclear technology, *see* Ellen Tauscher, *Time to Act: A Review of Legislation to Prevent the Proliferation of Nuclear Weapons*, 26 SETON HALL LEGIS. J. 325 (2002).

For current discussion of nuclear proliferation issues in general, *see* Adam Packer, *Nuclear Proliferation in South Asia*, 38 COLUM. J. TRANSNAT'L. L. 631 (2000); SAIRA KHAN, NUCLEAR PROLIFERATION DYNAMICS IN PROTRACTED CONFLICT REGIONS (Ashgate 2002); THE DYNAMICS OF MIDDLE EAST NUCLEAR PROLIFERATION (SYMPOSIUM SERIES V. 66.) (Steven L. Spiegel, Jennifer Kibbe, Elizabeth G. Matthews eds., Edwin Mellen Press 2002).

4. Iran presents particularly challenging nuclear issues at the present time. *See* KORI N. SCHAKE, THE STRATEGIC IMPLICATIONS OF A NUCLEAR-ARMED IRAN (Institute for National Strategic Studies 2001); CHEN ZAK, IRAN'S NUCLEAR POLICY AND IAEA (Washington Institute for Near East Policy 2002); C. RICHARD NELSON, MANAGING PROLIFERATION ISSUES WITH IRAN (Atlantic Council of the United States 2002); SHAHRAM CHUBIN, WHITHER IRAN? (Oxford U. Press for the International Institute of Strategic Studies 2002).

5. As of this writing, coalition forces and various agencies are carrying out an ambitious nation-building process in Iraq. For thoughtful commentary on this process, *see* EDWARD P. DJEREJIAN, FRANK G. WISNER, COUNCIL ON FOREIGN RELATIONS & LESLIE H. GELB, GUIDING PRINCIPLES FOR U.S. POST-CONFLICT POLICY IN IRAQ G GROUP REPORT: REPORT OF AN INDEPENDENT WORKING GROUP (Council on Foreign Relations Press 2003); GEOFFREY LESLIE SIMONS, FUTURE IRAQ, (Saqi 2003); CONRAD C. CRANE, RECONSTRUCTING IRAQ (Strategic Studies Institute, U.S. Army War College 2003). How would you evaluate the success of the efforts to assist the Iraqis in building a free, democratic, and prosperous state from your *current* perspective?

6. How would you characterize the law regarding nuclear weapons proliferation, at the present time? Continue the trend analysis above and consider alternative futures.

III. THE INTERACTION BETWEEN INTERNATIONAL AND NATIONAL ACTORS IN APPLYING INTERNATIONAL LAW

A. INTRODUCTION

As we have seen in the opinions we have read so far, the International Court of Justice (ICJ) takes a limited and contingent role in the application of international law due to its consensual jurisdiction. A great deal of international law therefore is applied through national courts. National courts have several advantages over an international forum, i.e., mandatory territorial jurisdiction, subpoena power and police power for enforcement. But cases that involve acute international political issues pose special problems for judges in democratic and constitutional systems, especially in countries whose constitutional structures include separation of powers, as in the United States, or parliamentary supremacy, as in the United Kingdom. On the one hand, domestic judges are committed to providing justice for parties who seek it. On the other, the judges usually appreciate that they are only one branch of a larger government and, especially in the United States, incline to defer to competences that have been constitutionally assigned to a different branch. It is not easy to find the balance between these different duties.

The traditional approach of the domestic courts of the United States has been to treat international treaties as a part of the Supreme Law of the Land. The Supremacy Clause of the U.S. Constitution provides:

> This Constitution, and the Laws of the United States which shall be made in Pursuance thereof; and all Treaties made, or which shall be made, under the Authority of the United States, shall be the supreme Law of the Land; and the Judges in every State shall be bound thereby, any Thing in the Constitution or Law of any State to the contrary notwithstanding.

U.S. CONST. art. VI, cl. 2. *See also*, *The Paquete Habana*, 175 U.S. 677, *infra*, Part Three, at 567.

B. THE JURISDICTION DILEMMA

Especially problematic for national courts are those cases which involve differing interpretations of international law by domestic and international actors. The following commentary offers a useful overview of the facts and procedural history of a landmark case.

1. Jonathan I. Charney & W. Michael Reisman, *AGORA: BREARD: The Facts*
92 AM. J. INT'L L. 666 (1998)

On February 17, 1992, police found the body of Ruth Dickie in her apartment in Arlington County, Virginia. She had been stabbed to death and her assailant had attempted to rape her. Six months later, Angel Francisco Breard was apprehended in the course of an attempted rape in Washington, D.C., and also became a suspect in Dickie's murder, for which he was subsequently indicted. As summarized in the appellate review of Breard's conviction by the Supreme Court of Virginia,[at] trial, Breard testified in his own defense. He stated that, on the night of February 17, 1992, he left his apartment armed with a knife because he thought he would "try to do someone," meaning that he "wanted to use the knife to force a woman to have sex with [him]." Breard admitted that he engaged Dickie in conversation on the street, followed her to her apartment, argued with her, and forced himself into her apartment. Breard also admitted that he stabbed Dickie, removed her pants, and got "on top of her." While he was on Dickie, he heard someone knocking on the door. He "got scared," opened a kitchen window, jumped to the ground, and fled. Breard also testified that, at the time, he believed that he was under a curse placed upon him by his ex-wife's father.

Hair, blood and other bodily fluid samples found at the scene of the crime were subjected to enzyme testing and DNA analysis. All the samples matched Breard's typing. After a jury trial, Breard was found guilty on June 24, 1993. He was sentenced to ten years' imprisonment and a fine for the attempted rape and condemned to death for the murder. The execution was set for February 17,

1994, but was stayed pending appeals. The Supreme Court of Virginia affirmed the judgment on June 10, 1994, rejecting Breard's challenges to the death sentence, the constitutionality of the trial court's review of the death sentence, jury matters, the guilt phase, the penalty phase and the sentence review. Breard petitioned the United States Supreme Court for a writ of certiorari, which was denied. On June 29, 1995, the Circuit Court of Arlington County denied Breard's state petition for habeas corpus. The Supreme Court of Virginia refused his petition for appeal on January 17, 1996, and denied his petition for rehearing on March 1, 1996.

On April 25, 1996, Breard filed a motion in the United States District Court for the Eastern District of Virginia in which he raised, along with various other new issues, an international legal claim based on violation of the Vienna Convention on Consular Relations of 1963. Article 36(1) (b) of the Convention provides that,

> if [the accused] so requests, the competent authorities of the receiving State shall, without delay, inform the consular post of the sending State if, within its consular district, a national of that State is arrested or committed to prison or to custody pending trial or is detained in any other manner. Any communication addressed to the consular post by the person arrested, in prison, custody or detention shall also be forwarded by the said authorities without delay. The said authorities shall inform the person concerned without delay of his rights under this sub-paragraph.

Breard had not made such a request; nor had the authorities of Virginia informed him of the option, as required by the Convention.

The Paraguayan consular authorities in the United States did not learn about Breard's arrest and trial until sometime in 1996. At that point, a series of discussions with the United States Department of State took place. The Department undertook an investigation and came to the following conclusions:

> Breard had almost immediate and thereafter continuing contact with his family, who were involved in his defense;
>
> Breard could not have been ignorant of American culture, as he had lived in this country since 1986 and had been married briefly to a United States citizen;
>
> Breard had a good command of English and therefore would not have needed consular assistance in interpretation;
>
> Breard was ably represented by criminal defense attorneys experienced in death penalty litigation, who worked closely with his family, some of whom traveled from Paraguay to assist in the defense;
>
> Breard decided to plead not guilty and to testify at his trial contrary to the competent advice of his attorneys, who were far better able to ex-

plain the U.S. legal system to him than any consular officer would have been;

Breard's mother, who was also Paraguayan, understood that Breard's decision to plead not guilty and to testify was a strategic error and advised him not to do what he did, and so it was implausible that cultural misunderstandings accounted for his decision;

The evidence at trial demonstrated that Breard unquestionably committed the crime, and that the jury and judge could easily have imposed the death penalty even if Breard had not testified, given ample evidence that the murder was "aggravated" within the meaning of Virginia law; and

Breard had the full protection of the criminal justice system.

On July 7, 1997, the State Department acknowledged that the non-notification of the consular authorities was a breach of the Convention and apologized for it. This communication did not satisfy the Paraguayan authorities, and the possibility of referring the matter to the International Court of Justice was broached. In February 1998, Paraguay informed the United States of its intention to approach the Court, without being specific.

In the meantime, Breard argued the international legal issue in the federal district court. On this point, the district court held:

> Virginia's persistent refusal to abide by the Vienna Convention troubles the Court. However, a violation of rights under the Convention is insufficient to permit § 2254 relief. . . . In any event, Petitioner never raised this issue in state court. Therefore, the claim is defaulted and federal review is barred. . . .
>
> Petitioner argues that the Commonwealth's failure to comply with the Vienna Convention provides just cause for the default. However, the Commonwealth's failure to comply with the Vienna Convention did not prevent Breard's counsel from raising the issue during state proceedings. The only predicate fact required to raise the claim was the knowledge of Breard's foreign nationality. The legal knowledge required to raise the claim is imputed to Breard through the various attorneys who represented him during the trial, direct appeal, and state habeas proceedings. "Attorney ignorance or inadvertence is not 'cause' because the attorney is the petitioner's agent acting, or failing to act, in furtherance of the litigation, and the petitioner must bear the risk of any attorney error."

In September 1996, the Republic of Paraguay, its Ambassador to the United States and its Consul General to the United States initiated a separate action in the United States District Court for the Eastern District of Virginia seeking a declaration of treaty violation, a vacatur of Breard's conviction and sentence, and an injunction against further violations of the treaty. The district court found that Paraguay and its officials had standing to bring their claims under the Convention (and the Paraguay-U.S. Treaty of Friendship, Commerce, and Navigation), emphasizing that Paraguay was asserting its own rights and not those of Breard, and that the Ambassador had standing to maintain a claim against the Virginia officials under the Civil Rights Act of 1871, 42 U.S.C. § 1983, because he was a "person" within the meaning of the Act. But the court decided that it did not have subject matter jurisdiction because the claimants were not alleging a "continuing violation of federal law" and therefore could not bring their claims within the exception to the immunity of states under the Eleventh Amendment permitting prospective remedies.

The U.S. Court of Appeals for the Fourth Circuit affirmed on the ground that the Eleventh Amendment precluded its jurisdiction, concluding that the various exceptions the courts had carved in it did not apply to this case. It stated:

> We share the district court's expressed "disenchantment" with the Commonwealth's conceded past violation of Paraguay's treaty rights. ... There are disturbing implications in that conduct for larger interests of the United States and its citizens. But, we conclude that because the violation of federal treaty law was not ongoing when this action was filed, nor the relief sought prospective, the Eleventh Amendment does not permit the federal courts to provide a remedy against the Commonwealth officials sued in this action for their conceded past violations.

134 F.3d at 629.

Breard pursued his own appeal to the Fourth Circuit. To Virginia's contention that he had procedurally defaulted whatever rights he had under the Vienna Convention, Breard responded "that he had no reasonable basis for raising his Vienna Convention claim until April 1996 when the Fifth Circuit decided Faulder v. Johnson," which held that an arrestee's rights under the Vienna Convention had been violated when Texas officials failed to inform him of his right to contact the Canadian Consulate. Breard also argued that he could not have raised his Vienna Convention claim because Virginia had failed to advise him of his rights in that regard. The Fourth Circuit, however, had earlier rejected the claim that a state's failure to advise a petitioner of his rights under the Vienna Convention could constitute cause for failure to raise the claim in state court, because "a reasonably diligent attorney would have discovered the applicability of the Vienna Convention to a foreign national defendant."...

Although the Court of Appeals issued a unanimous decision, Judge Butzner added a concurring opinion, "to emphasize the importance of the Vienna Convention." He wrote:

> The Vienna Convention is a self executing treaty — it provides rights to individuals rather than merely setting out the obligations of signatories. ... The text emphasizes that the right of consular notice and assistance is the citizen's. The language is mandatory and unequivocal, evidencing

> the signatories' recognition of the importance of consular access for persons detained by a foreign government.
>
> The provisions of the Vienna Convention have the dignity of an act of Congress and are binding upon the states. ... The Supremacy Clause mandates that rights conferred by a treaty be honored by the states. ... The provisions of the Convention should be implemented before trial when they can be appropriately addressed. Collateral review is too limited to afford an adequate remedy. ...
>
> The protections afforded by the Vienna Convention go far beyond Breard's case. United States citizens are scattered about the world — as missionaries, Peace Corps volunteers, doctors, teachers and students, as travelers for business and for pleasure. Their freedom and safety are seriously endangered if state officials fail to honor the Vienna Convention and other nations follow their example. Public officials should bear in mind that "international law is founded upon mutuality and reciprocity."...

Appeal was sought to the U.S. Supreme Court. Meanwhile, on April 3, 1998, Paraguay filed an Application in the International Court of Justice instituting proceedings against the United States. In that Application, Paraguay alleged the breach of certain provisions of the Vienna Convention on Consular Relations, notably Article 36, paragraph 1(b). In the Application, Paraguay asked the Court to adjudge and declare a violation of the Convention, especially its Articles 5 (relating to the consular functions) and 36, and to declare "that Paraguay is therefore entitled to "*restitutio in integrum* [meaning a retrial of Breard], and ... that the United States is under an international legal obligation not to apply the [domestic] doctrine of 'procedural default' or any other doctrine of its internal law, so as to preclude the exercise of the rights accorded under Article 36."

The Court was also asked to declare that any criminal liability imposed on Breard in violation of international legal obligations was void and should be recognized as void by the legal authorities of the United States; that the United States should restore the status quo ante, that is, reestablish the situation that had existed before the detention of, proceedings against and sentencing of Breard in violation of the legal obligations of the United States; and that the United States should guarantee to Paraguay that the illegal acts would not be repeated.

Simultaneously, Paraguay filed a request for the indication of provisional measures of protection under Article 41 of the Statute of the Court. It requested that the United States Government take the necessary measures to ensure that Breard would not be executed pending the disposition of the case; that the United States Government inform the Court of the actions it took in pursuance of that request and the results of those actions; and that the United States Government ensure that no action would be taken that might prejudice the rights of Paraguay with respect to any decision the Court might render on the merits of the case.

Paraguay also asked the Court to treat the request for provisional measures of protection as a matter of the greatest urgency.

On receipt of those documents, the Acting President notified the parties of the need to act in such a way as to enable any order the Court might make on the request for provisional measures to have its appropriate effects. Public hearings were held on April 7. The United States argued that Breard had admitted his guilt, a point Paraguay did not dispute, and while acknowledging that he had not been informed of his rights under the Vienna Convention at the time of the trial, the United States insisted that the omission was not deliberate. Nevertheless, the Government continued, Breard had all necessary legal assistance, he understood English well, and the additional assistance of consular officers would not have changed the outcome of the proceedings. Moreover, Article 36 notification is "unevenly made" and when a claim for failure to notify is lodged, the only remedy is apology. Neither the language of the Vienna Convention, nor its *travaux préparatoires* nor state practice supported a penalty of invalidation of the proceedings and return to the status quo ante. Furthermore, such a remedy would be quite unworkable. As for the actions of the United States, it alleged that "the State Department had done everything in its power to help the government of Paraguay as soon as it was informed of the situation," but that "a stay of execution depended exclusively on the United States Supreme Court and the Governor of Virginia." In any case, because Breard had not been prejudiced by the omission and his case was not likely to succeed on the merits, provisional measures should not be indicated.

At the close of oral argument, the Acting President announced that the Order containing the Court's decision would be read at a public sitting on Thursday, April 9. In that Order, the Court rejected the U.S. claim that there was no prima facie jurisdiction. . . .

Because the planned execution of Breard within that very week "would render it impossible for the Court to order the relief that Paraguay seeks and thus cause irreparable harm to the rights it claims," the Court found "that the circumstances require it to indicate, as a matter of urgency, provisional measures." Accordingly, it unanimously indicated, as provisional measures, that "the United States should take all measures at its disposal to ensure that Angel Francisco Breard is not executed pending the final decision in these proceedings, and should inform the Court of all the measures which it has taken in implementation of this Order." ...

On April 13, the Secretary of State sent a letter to the Governor of Virginia, requesting that the Governor suspend the execution [*See* full text of letter, *infra.*]

The Departments of State and Justice submitted an amicus brief to the Supreme Court urging the Court to deny a writ of certiorari and a stay. With respect to the interim measures of the International Court, the Departments contended [that an ICJ order indicating provisional measures is not binding on the parties]. … [*See* partial text of brief, *infra.*]

On April 14, 1998, the United States Supreme Court, by a vote of 6 to 3, denied the petition for habeas corpus and the petitions for certiorari. The Court found that Breard had "procedurally defaulted his claim, if any, under the Vienna Convention by failing to raise that claim in the state courts" and rejected, on two grounds, the contention by both Breard and Paraguay that the Vienna Convention claim should still be heard in a federal court because the Convention is the supreme law of the land and, as such, trumps the procedural default doctrine. First, the Court reasoned that the procedural rules of the forum state govern the implementation of a treaty in that state, unless the treaty prescribes otherwise. In the Court's reading of the Vienna Convention, no such contrary intention could be discerned. Second, the Court reasoned that the Antiterrorism and Effective Death Penalty Act of 1996 precludes a habeas petitioner from raising alleged violations of treaties of the United States if those allegations had not been developed in state court proceedings. Thus, the Court reasoned, even if Breard had a right under the Vienna Convention, the subsequent act of legislation would have precluded his raising it at this phase. Nor was the Court persuaded that a hearing would have yielded a different outcome.

The Court also concluded that the Vienna Convention did not provide a private right of action to a foreign state to set aside a criminal conviction against one of its nationals for violations of consular notification. In addition, the Court found that the Eleventh Amendment provided a separate reason why Paraguay's suit should not succeed, and it rejected the standing of the Consul General of Paraguay, as of Paraguay, to bring a section 1983 suit.

Although the Court was apprised of the indication of interim measures by the International Court of Justice and an amicus brief submitted by law professors had elaborated the implications of noncompliance with this Order in some detail, the Court did not address the international legal dimension at any length. The majority stated:

> If the Governor wishes to wait for the decision of the ICJ, that is his prerogative. But nothing in our existing case law allows us to make that choice for him.

Justice Breyer, dissenting, remarked that "more time would likely mean additional briefing and argument, perhaps, for example, on the potential relevance of proceedings in an international forum."

The Governor of Virginia refused to issue a stay. [*See* full text of statement, *infra.*]

[Mr. Breard was executed on April 14, 1998.]

2. Case Concerning The Vienna Convention on Consular Relations (Para. v. U.S.)

1998 I.C.J. 99 (Provisional Measures)

The International Court of Justice, ...

Makes the following Order:

1. Whereas, in its aforementioned Application, Paraguay bases the jurisdiction of the Court on Article 36, paragraph 1, of the Statute of the Court and on Article I of the Optional Protocol concerning the Compulsory Settlement of Disputes, which accompanies the Vienna Convention on Consular Relations ("the Optional Protocol"); ... [The Court examines the factual and procedural history.]

5. Whereas Paraguay requests the Court to adjudge and declare as follows:

> *(a)* that the United States, in arresting, detaining, trying, convicting, and sentencing Angel Francisco Breard, as described in the preceding statement of facts, violated its international legal obligations to Paraguay, in its own right and in the exercise of its right of diplomatic protection of its national, as provided by Articles 5 and 36 of the Vienna Convention;
>
> *(b)* that Paraguay is therefore entitled to *restitutio in integrum;*
>
> *(c)* that the United States is under an international legal obligation not to apply to the doctrine of 'procedural default', or any other doctrine of its internal law, so as to preclude the exercise of the rights accorded under Article 36 of the Vienna Convention; and
>
> *(d)* that the United States is under an international legal obligation to carry out in conformity with the foregoing international legal obligations any future detention of or criminal proceedings against Angel Francisco Breard or any other Paraguayan national in its territory, whether by a constituent, legislative, executive, judicial or other power, whether that power holds a superior or a subordinate position in the organization of the United States, and whether that power's functions are of an international or internal character; and that, pursuant to the foregoing international legal obligations,
>
>> (1) any criminal liability imposed on Angel Francisco Breard in violation of international legal obligations is void, and should be recognized as void by the legal authorities of the United States;
>>
>> (2) the United States should restore the *status quo ante*, that is, re-establish the situation that existed before the detention of, proceedings against, and conviction and sentencing of Paraguay's national in violation of the United States' international legal obligations took place; and

(3) the United States should provide Paraguay a guarantee of the non-repetition of the illegal acts; …

8. Whereas, in its request for the indication of provisional measures of protection, Paraguay states that, on 25 February 1998, the Circuit Court of Arlington County, Virginia, ordered that Mr. Breard be executed on 14 April 1998; whereas it emphasizes that "[t]he importance and sanctity of an individual human life are well established in international law" and "[a]s recognized by Article 6 of the International Covenant on Civil and Political Rights, every human being has the inherent right to life and this right shall be protected by law"; and whereas Paraguay states in the following terms the grounds for its request and the possible consequences of its dismissal:

> Under the grave and exceptional circumstances of this case, and given the paramount interest of Paraguay in the life and liberty of its nationals, provisional measures are urgently needed to protect the life of Paraguay's national and the ability of this Court to order the relief to which Paraguay is entitled: restitution in kind. Without the provisional measures requested, the United States will execute Mr. Breard before this Court can consider the merits of Paraguay's claims, and Paraguay will be forever deprived of the opportunity to have the *status quo ante* restored in the event of a judgment in its favour;

9. Whereas Paraguay asks that, pending final judgment in this case, the Court indicate:

> *(a)* That the Government of the United States take the measures necessary to ensure that Mr. Breard not be executed pending the disposition of this case;
>
> *(b)* That the Government of the United States report to the Court the actions it has taken in pursuance of subparagraph *(a)* immediately above and the results of those actions; and
>
> *(c)* That the Government of the United States ensure that no action is taken that might prejudice the rights of the Republic of Paraguay with respect to any decision this Court may render on the merits of the case;

and whereas it asks the Court moreover to consider its request as a matter of the greatest urgency "in view of the extreme gravity and immediacy of the threat that the authorities ... will execute a Paraguayan citizen"; …

18. Whereas at the hearing, the United States argued that Mr. Breard's guilt was well established, and pointed out that the accused had admitted his guilt, which Paraguay did not dispute; whereas it recognized that Mr. Breard had not been informed, at the time of his arrest and trial, of his rights under Article 36, subparagraph 1 *(b)*, of the Vienna Convention, and indicated to the Court that this omission was not deliberate; whereas it nonetheless maintained that the person concerned had had all necessary legal assistance, that he understood English

well and that the assistance of consular officers would not have changed the outcome of the proceedings brought against him in any way; whereas, referring to State practice in these matters, it stated that the notification provided for by Article 36, subparagraph 1 *(b)*, of the Vienna Convention is unevenly made, and that when a claim is made for failure to notify, the only consequence is that apologies are presented by the government responsible; and whereas it submitted that the automatic invalidation of the proceedings initiated and the return to the *status quo ante* as penalties for the failure to notify not only find no support in State practice, but would be unworkable;

19. Whereas the United States also indicated that the State Department had done everything in its power to help the Government of Paraguay as soon as it was informed of the situation in 1996; and whereas it stated that when, on 30 March 1998, Paraguay advised the Government of the United States of its intention to bring proceedings before the Court if the United States Government did not take steps to initiate consultation and to obtain a stay of execution for Mr. Breard, the Government of the United States had emphasized *inter alia* that a stay of execution depended exclusively on the United States Supreme Court and the Governor of Virginia;

20. Whereas the United States furthermore maintained that Paraguay's contention that the invalidation of the sentence of a person who had not been notified pursuant to Article 36, subparagraph 1 *(b)*, of the Vienna Convention could be required under that instrument, has no foundation in the relevant provisions, their *travaux préparatoires* or the practice of States, and that, in the event, Mr. Breard has not been prejudiced by the absence of notification; and whereas it pointed out that provisional measures should not be indicated where it appears that the Applicant's argument will not enable it to be successful on the merits;

21. Whereas the United States also stated that, when the Court indicates provisional measures under Article 41 of its Statute, it must take the rights of each of the Parties into consideration and ensure that it maintains a fair balance in protecting those rights; whereas that would not be the case if it acceded to Paraguay's request in these proceedings; and whereas the measures requested by Paraguay would prejudice the merits of the case;

22. Whereas the United States finally alleged that the indication of the provisional measures requested by Paraguay would be contrary to the interests of the States parties to the Vienna Convention and to those of the international community as a whole as well as to those of the Court, and would in particular be such as seriously to disrupt the criminal justice systems of the States parties to the Convention, given the risk of proliferation of cases; and whereas it stated in that connection that States have an overriding interest in avoiding external judicial intervention which would interfere with the execution of a sentence passed at the end of an orderly process meeting the relevant human rights standards; . . .

[The Court discusses the issue of jurisdiction]

34. Whereas the Court finds that, prima facie, it has jurisdiction under Article I of the aforesaid Optional Protocol to decide the dispute between Paraguay and the United States;

35. Whereas the power of the Court to indicate provisional measures under Article 41 of its Statute is intended to preserve the respective rights of the parties pending its decision, and presupposes that irreparable prejudice shall not be caused to rights which are the subject of a dispute in judicial proceedings; whereas it follows that the Court must be concerned to preserve by such measures the rights which may subsequently be adjudged by the Court to belong either to the Applicant, or to the Respondent; and whereas such measures are only justified if there is urgency; ...

37. Whereas the execution of Mr. Breard is ordered for 14 April 1998; and whereas such an execution would render it impossible for the Court to order the relief that Paraguay seeks and thus cause irreparable harm to the rights it claims;

38. Whereas the issues before the Court in this case do not concern the entitlement of the federal states within the United States to resort to the death penalty for the most heinous crimes; and whereas, further, the function of this Court is to resolve international legal disputes between States, *inter alia* when they arise out of the interpretation or application of international conventions, and not to act as a court of criminal appeal;

39. Whereas, in the light of the aforementioned considerations, the Court finds that the circumstances require it to indicate, as a matter of urgency, provisional measures in accordance with Article 41 of its Statute;

40. Whereas measures indicated by the Court for a stay of execution would necessarily be provisional in nature and would not in any way prejudge findings the Court might make on the merits; and whereas the measures indicated would preserve the respective rights of Paraguay and of the United States; and whereas it is appropriate that the Court, with the co-operation of the Parties, ensure that any decision on the merits be reached with all possible expedition;

41. For these reasons,

THE COURT, Unanimously,

I. *Indicates* the following provisional measures:

The United States should take all measures at its disposal to ensure that Angel Francisco Breard is not executed pending the final decision in these proceedings, and should inform the Court of all the measures which it has taken in implementation of this Order;

II. *Decides*, that, until the Court has given its final decision, it shall remain seised of the matters which form the subject-matter of this Order.

* * *

While the ICJ decision above was pending, the United States Supreme Court decided Breard v. Greene:

3. Breard v. Greene

523 U.S. 371(1998)

OPINION: PER CURIAM. [The Court reviewed the facts and the procedural history in U.S. state and federal courts.]

It is clear that Breard procedurally defaulted his claim, if any, under the Vienna Convention by failing to raise that claim in the state courts. Nevertheless, in their petitions for certiorari, both Breard and Paraguay contend that Breard's Vienna Convention claim may be heard in federal court because the Convention is the "supreme law of the land" and thus trumps the procedural default doctrine. This argument is plainly incorrect for two reasons.

First, while we should give respectful consideration to the interpretation of an international treaty rendered by an international court with jurisdiction to interpret such, it has been recognized in international law that absent a clear and express statement to the contrary, the procedural rules of the forum State govern the implementation of the treaty in that State. This proposition is embodied in the Vienna Convention itself, which provides that the rights expressed in the Convention "shall be exercised in conformity with the laws and regulations of the receiving State," provided that "said laws and regulations must enable full effect to be given to the purposes for which the rights accorded under this Article are intended." Article 36(2), [1970] 21 U.S.T., at 101. It is the rule in this country that assertions of error in criminal proceedings must first be raised in state court in order to form the basis for relief in habeas. Wainwright v. Sykes, 433 U.S. 72 (1977). Claims not so raised are considered defaulted. Ibid. By not asserting his Vienna Convention claim in state court, Breard failed to exercise his rights under the Vienna Convention in conformity with the laws of the United States and the Commonwealth of Virginia. Having failed to do so, he cannot raise a claim of violation of those rights now on federal habeas review.

Second, although treaties are recognized by our Constitution as the supreme law of the land, that status is no less true of provisions of the Constitution itself, to which rules of procedural default apply. We have held "that an Act of Congress . . . is on a full parity with a treaty, and that when a statute which is subsequent in time is inconsistent with a treaty, the statute to the extent of conflict renders the treaty null." Reid v. Covert, 354 U.S. 1, 18 (1957) (plurality opinion); see also Whitney v. Robertson, 124 U.S. 190, 194 (1888) (holding that if a treaty and a federal statute conflict, "the one last in date will control the other"). The Vienna Convention—which arguably confers on an individual the right to consular assistance following arrest—has continuously been in effect since 1969. But in 1996, before Breard filed his habeas petition raising claims under the Vienna Convention, Congress enacted the Antiterrorism and Effective

Death Penalty Act (AEDPA), which provides that a habeas petitioner alleging that he is held in violation of "treaties of the United States" will, as a general rule, not be afforded an evidentiary hearing if he "has failed to develop the factual basis of [the] claim in State court proceedings." 28 U.S.C. A §§ 2254(a), (e)(2) (Supp. 1998). Breard's ability to obtain relief based on violations of the Vienna Convention is subject to this subsequently-enacted rule, just as any claim arising under the United States Constitution would be. This rule prevents Breard from establishing that the violation of his Vienna Convention rights prejudiced him. Without a hearing, Breard cannot establish how the Consul would have advised him, how the advice of his attorneys differed from the advice the Consul could have provided, and what factors he considered in electing to reject the plea bargain that the State offered him. That limitation, Breard also argues, is not justified because his Vienna Convention claims were so novel that he could not have discovered them any earlier. Assuming that were true, such novel claims would be barred on habeas review under Teague v. Lane, 489 U.S. 288 (1989).

Even were Breard's Vienna Convention claim properly raised and proven, it is extremely doubtful that the violation should result in the overturning of a final judgment of conviction without some showing that the violation had an effect on the trial. Arizona *v.* Fulminante, 499 U.S. 279 (1991). In this case no such showing could even arguably be made. Breard decided not to plead guilty and to testify at his own trial contrary to the advice of his attorneys, who were likely far better able to explain the United States legal system to him than any consular official would have been. Breard's asserted prejudice—that had the Vienna Convention been followed, he would have accepted the State's offer to forgo the death penalty in return for a plea of guilty—is far more speculative than the claims of prejudice courts routinely reject in those cases were an inmate alleges that his plea of guilty was infected by attorney error.

As for Paraguay's suits … neither the text nor the history of the Vienna Convention clearly provides a foreign nation a private right of action in United States' courts to set aside a criminal conviction and sentence for violation of consular notification provisions. The Eleventh Amendment provides a separate reason why Paraguay's suit might not succeed. That Amendment's "fundamental principle" that "the States, in the absence of consent, are immune from suits brought against them … by a foreign State" was enunciated in Principality of Monaco v. Mississippi, 292 U.S. 313, 329-330 (1934). Though Paraguay claims that its suit is within an exemption dealing with continuing consequences of past violations of federal rights … we do not agree. The failure to notify the Paraguayan Consul occurred long ago and has no continuing effect. …

[The Court rejects Paraguay's civil rights claim under 42 U.S.C. §1983]

It is unfortunate that this matter comes before us while proceedings are pending before the ICJ that might have been brought to that court earlier. Nonetheless, this Court must decide questions presented to it on the basis of law. The Executive Branch, on the other hand, in exercising its authority over foreign relations may, and in this case did, utilize diplomatic discussion with Paraguay. Last night the Secretary of State sent a letter to the Governor of Virginia requesting that he stay Breard's execution. If the Governor wishes to wait for the decision of the ICJ, that is his prerogative. But nothing in our existing case law allows us to make that choice for him.

For the foregoing reasons, we deny the petition for an original writ of habeas corpus, the motion for leave to file a bill of complaint, the petitions for certiorari, and the accompanying stay applications filed by Breard and Paraguay.

JUSTICE STEVENS, dissenting.

The Court of Appeals' decision denying petitioner's first application for a federal writ of habeas corpus became final on February 18, 1998. Under this Court's Rules, a timely petition for a writ of certiorari to review that decision could have been filed as late as May 19, 1998. See Rule 13.1 ("[A] petition for a writ of certiorari to review a judgment in any case, civil or criminal, entered by … a United States court of appeals … is timely when it is filed with the Clerk of this Court within 90 days after entry of the judgment"). Ordinary review of that petition pursuant to our Rules would have given us additional time thereafter to consider its merits in the light of the response filed by the Commonwealth of Virginia. We have, however, been deprived of the normal time for considered deliberation by the Commonwealth's decision to set the date of petitioner's execution for today. There is no compelling reason for refusing to follow the procedures that we have adopted for the orderly disposition of noncapital cases. Indeed, the international aspects of this case provide an additional reason for adhering to our established Rules and procedures. I would therefore grant the applications for a stay, and I respectfully dissent from the decision to act hastily rather than with the deliberation that is appropriate in a case of this character.

JUSTICE BREYER, dissenting.

In my view, several of the issues raised here are of sufficient difficulty to warrant less speedy consideration. Breard argues, for example, that the novelty of his Vienna Convention claim is sufficient to create "cause" for his having failed to present that claim to the Virginia state courts. He might add that the nature of his claim, were we to accept it, is such as to create a "watershed rule of criminal procedure," which might overcome the bar to consideration … He additionally says that what the Solicitor General describes as Virginia's violation of the Convention "prejudiced" him by isolating him at a critical moment from Consular Officials who might have advised him to try to avoid the death penalty by pleading guilty. I cannot say, without examining the record more fully, that these arguments are obviously without merit. Nor am I willing to accept without fuller briefing and consideration the positions taken by the majority on all of the sometimes difficult issues that the majority addresses.

At the same time, the international aspects of the case have provided us with the advantage of additional briefing even in the short time available. More time would likely mean additional briefing and argument, perhaps, for example, on the potential relevance of proceedings in an international forum. ...

For these reasons, taken together I would grant the requested stay of execution and consider the petitions for certiorari in the ordinary course.

JUSTICE GINSBURG, dissenting.

I would grant the application for a stay of execution in order to consider in the ordinary course the instant petition, Breard's first federal petition for writ of habeas corpus.

* * *

Statements by a number of U.S. federal and state officials provide further insight into the complicated interplay between the various branches of government and national and international courts, with respect to the application of international law.

4. Letter from Mark Richard, Deputy Assistant Attorney General, to Charles D. Siegal, March 24, 1998

Dear Mr. Siegal:

This is in response to your letter to Attorney General Reno dated January 9, 1998, regarding the Vienna Convention on Consular Relations and other consular agreements. We fully concur that our multilateral and 'bilateral obligations are important and that all agencies are bound to comply with them. For that reason, the Department of Justice and the Department of State have undertaken and will continue to pursue vigorous and coordinated efforts to educate local, state, and federal law enforcement offices.

You suggest that some state and local law enforcement agencies do not acknowledge their obligations to comply with the treaties' notification requirements. We are not aware of any state or local government that currently takes this position. If any specific agency or agencies are brought to our attention, we will immediately and directly contact them in order to correct the situation.

With respect to the government's *amicus curiae* brief in *Republic of Paraquay v. Allen,* No.96-2770 (4th Cir., Jan. 22, 1998) , the arguments set forth therein represent the official views of the Department of Justice. Because the Government of Paraguay recently filed a petition for a writ of certiorari, we cannot comment further at this time. However, it is incorrect to assume that we view our obligations to provide consular notification as anything other than "of the highest order." To the contrary, the government understands fully that they are both binding and very important.

Finally, we appreciate your sharing with us the Draft Report of the Human Rights Committee of the American Branch of the International Law Association. Along with the Department of State, we will give careful consideration to your findings and recommendations.

5. Letter from the Legal Advisor to the U.S. Department of State, David R. Andrews, to Charles D. Siegal

Dear Mr. Siegal:

Thank you for your letter of January 9, 1998, concerning the ILA American Branch's work on consular notification, and the draft report that was enclosed with it. The Department places great importance on ensuring that the United States complies with its consular notification and access obligations. We therefore particularly appreciate receiving the Branch's ideas and suggestions for furthering this goal; while we inevitably disagree on a number of factual and legal points, many of your suggestions are consistent with actions the Department has already undertaken. In this connection, I am pleased to advise you that the Department recently published a new brochure, *Consular Notification and Access,* which we are distributing to federal, state, and local officials throughout the United States...

Given the efforts of the ILA/American Branch in this area, you may be interested to know that our information indicates that U.S. compliance with consular notification requirements compares favorably with that of other countries. We receive relatively few complaints about consular notification and access from foreign governments, particularly when considered in light of the large number of foreign nationals in the United States at any given time. We would not agree that there is pervasive noncompliance in the United States, or that "the causes of such noncompliance" are any rejection by states of the requirements or any inability to comply. Notwithstanding various statements occasionally attributed to state officials, we are not aware of any state government that in fact maintains that it is not required to comply with consular notification and access requirements, or of any agency that is "unable to comply." In our experience, failures to provide consular notification in the United States generally result from a lack of information, or a failure to recognize that a detainee is an alien, and not from any intent to ignore the obligations. We invariably have been able to address consular notification and access issues when they have been brought to our attention. In addition, we expect that our new brochure and current outreach efforts will further a deep and broad understanding of consular notification and access requirements.

Please convey to your ILA colleagues our appreciation for their work, and for sharing their views on these issues with us.

6. Letter to the Honorable James S. Gilmore III, Governor of Virginia, from Madeleine K. Albright, Secretary of State, April 13, 1998

Dear Governor Gilmore:

I am writing to request a stay of the execution of Angel Francisco Breard, who is sentenced to be executed by the Commonwealth of Virginia tomorrow, April 14.

The United States has throughout vigorously defended Virginia's right to go forward with the sentence imposed on Mr. Breard by *Virginia's* courts. Counsel for the U.S. Government argued strongly before the International Court that the Court should not *issue* the relief sought by Paraguay. We maintain, for the reasons we presented to the Court at *its* hearing last week, that consular notification would not have changed the outcome and that the Vienna Convention on Consular Relations does not require that Mr. Breard's conviction and sentence be vacated.

The International Court, however, was not prepared to decide the issues we raised in its urgent proceedings last week. Using non-binding language, the Court said that the United States should "take all measures at its disposal to ensure that Angel Francisco Breard is not executed pending the final decision in these proceedings." The Court concurrently set an expedited briefing schedule in the case, apparently intending to hold its final hearing this fall.

In light of the Court's request, the unique and difficult foreign policy issues, and other problems created by the Court's provisional measures, I therefore request that you exercise your powers as Governor and stay Mr. Breard's execution. It is only with great reluctance that I make this request, especially given the aggravated character of the crime for which Mr. Breard has been convicted and sentenced and our view of the merits of Paraguay's legal claims. As Secretary of State, however, I have a responsibility to bear in mind the safety of Americans overseas.

I am particularly concerned about: the possible negative consequences for the many U.S. citizens who live and travel abroad. The execution of Mr. Breard in the present circumstances could lead some countries to contend incorrectly that the U.S. does not take seriously its obligations under the Convention. The immediate execution of Mr. Breard in the face of the Court's April 9 action could be seen as a denial by the United States of the significance of international law and the Court's processes in its international relations and thereby limit our ability to ensure that Americans are protected when living or traveling abroad.

I appreciate the difficulty of this matter. The Legal Adviser of the Department, David Andrews, will call your Counselor, Mr. David Anderson, regarding it. ...

7. Statement by Virginia Governor Jim Gilmore Concerning the Execution of Angel Breard, April 14, 1998

Angel Breard, through his attorneys, has petitioned me to grant clemency for his crimes or, alternatively a reprieve pending the outcome or proceedings commenced by the Republic of Paraguay in the International Court of Justice. The U.S. Secretary of State has also requested that I stay Mr. Breard's execution for an indefinite period. For the following reasons, I must decline to intervene in this matter.

Breard was convicted and sentenced to death for the attempted rape and brutal murder of Ruth Dickie, a 39 year old unmarried woman. Microscopic examination of Breard's hair, together with enzyme and DNA testing of his blood, established Breard's guilt. Additionally, Breard testified in open court admitting his own guilt. Breard was represented by counsel and received a fair trial. His arguments to overturn his conviction and sentence have been heard and rejected by the Supreme Court of the Commonwealth of Virginia, the U.S. District Court for the Eastern District of Virginia, the U.S. Court of Appeals for the Fourth Circuit, and the U.S. Supreme Court. …

The Secretary specifically raises concern "about the possible negative consequences for the many U.S. citizens who live and travel abroad."

The concerns expressed by the Secretary of State are due great respect and I have given them serious consideration. However, it is but one of the various concerns that I must take into consideration in reaching my decision.

As Governor of Virginia my first duty is to ensure that those who reside within our borders — both American citizens and foreign nationals - may conduct their lives free from the fear of crime. Our criminal justice system is designed to provide the greatest degree of safety for law-abiding citizens and foreign visitors alike while ensuring substantial procedural safeguards to those accused of crime. Indeed, in this case Mr. Breard received all of the procedural safeguards that any American citizen would receive.

I am concerned that to delay Mr. Breard's execution so that the International Court of Justice may review this matter would have the practical effect of transferring responsibility from the courts of the Commonwealth and the United States to the International Court. Should the International Court resolve this matter in Paraguay's favor, it would be difficult, having delayed the execution so that the International Court could consider the case, to then carry-out the jury's sentence despite the rulings of the International Court.

The U.S. Department of Justice, together with Virginia's Attorney General, make a compelling case that the International Court of Justice has no authority to interfere with our criminal justice system. Indeed, the safety of those residing in the Commonwealth of Virginia is not the responsibility of the International Court of Justice. It is my responsibility and the responsibility of law enforcement and judicial officials throughout the Commonwealth. I cannot cede such responsibility to the International Court of Justice.

Mr. Breard having committed a heinous and depraved murder, his guilt being unquestioned, and the legal issues being resolved against him, and the U.S. Supreme Court having denied the petitions of Breard and Paraguay, I find no reason to interfere with his sentence. Accordingly, I decline to do so.

NOTES AND QUESTIONS

1. A country confronts a range of choices as it determines what status both customary and treaty-based international legal norms will have relative to its domestic laws, including its constitutional order and statutory regimes.

Some States have opted for a dualist approach. Dualists see international law as "a law between sovereign states, [while] municipal [or domestic] law applies within a state and regulates the relations of its citizens with each other and with the executive." IAN BROWNLIE, PRINCIPLES OF PUBLIC INTERNATIONAL LAW 30 (Clarendon Press 1990). Dualism also conceptualizes international law and national law as "separate, mutually independent legal orders that regulate quite different matters and have quite different sources." HANS KELSEN, PRINCIPLES OF INTERNATIONAL LAW 553 (Rynehart & Co. 1966). Indeed, some adherents to the dualist tradition see "(a) The Subjects of international law as States solely and (b) Their judicial origins are different; the source of State law is the will of the State itself, the source of international law is the common will … of States." J.G. STARKE, INTRODUCTION TO INTERNATIONAL LAW 82 (Butterworths 1977).

It is, of course, possible for an international legal norm to become part of the municipal legal system of a dualist state. However, the international law would first need to be "adopted" through a legislative "act of transformation." MALCOLM N. SHAW, INTERNATIONAL LAW 107 (Grotius Publications 1991). The leading monist, Hans Kelsen, would reduce the application of this dualist feature to legal systems expressly choosing the transformation technique in their constitutive document: "International law needs transformation into national law only when the necessity thereof is stated by the constitution of the state. If the constitution is silent on this point — as it sometimes is — the State courts are competent to apply international law directly." HANS KELSEN, GENERAL THEORY OF LAW AND STATE 378 (Harvard U. Press 1945).

Brownlie elaborates on dualism by asserting that "in case of conflict between international law and municipal law the dualist would assume that a municipal court would apply municipal law." BROWNLIE, *supra* at 30. For some dualists, the logic of imposing a barrier between international and municipal law is to preserve the power of the state. This view shares close ties to positivism. According to Brownlie, positivism "tends to deny the validity of sources of international law apart from the practice of states." *Id.*

2. Monism represents the leading alternative to dualism. Its adherents

> regard all law as a single unity composed of binding legal rules, whether those rules are obligatory on States, on individuals, or on entities other than States. In their view, the science of law is a unified field of knowledge, and the decisive point is therefore whether or not international law is true law.

J.G. STARKE, *supra* note 1, at 84. Professor Henkin has noted that according to the monist conception:

> [t]he state's constitutional system must recognize the supremacy of international law. The national legislature is bound — constitutionally bound — to respect international law in enacting legislation. The national executive is constitutionally required to take care that international law be faithfully executed, even in the face of inconsistent domes-

tic law. The national judiciary must give effect to international law, notwithstanding inconsistent domestic law, even domestic law of constitutional character.

Louis Henkin, International Law: Politics and Values 64 (Dordrecht 1995).

The principal proponent of the monist school, Professor Hans Kelsen, conceives of a unitary legal system in the form of a pyramid, in which "higher" norms invalidate "lower" prescriptions that are in substantive conflict with them. Not only would, *e.g.*, in a federal system, state law be invalidated by conflicting federal law and federal law would retain its validity only if it did not collide with constitutional law, but constitutional law itself would have to be measured against the prescriptive demands of the higher-ranked international law. At the pinnacle of this highly abstract "pyramid of norms" rests the principle of *pacta sunt servanda* ("agreements must be kept"), the "basic norm" of any legal system. Hans Kelsen, Pure Theory of Law 323-43 (Max Knight trans., U. of California Press 1967).

3. The debate between monists and dualists continues to unfold. There are several justifications for monism. In accordance with Kelsen, it is argued, for example, that international law is the most basic norm in the entire legal order. All other rules, including municipal laws, derive their validity from it. Shaw, *supra* at 103. Thus, municipal enactments must be in accordance with international law. Others defend monism on the ground that the state is an abstraction, that the primary objective of law is the protection of individuals, and that making international law supreme represents the best way to promote this goal. According to Shaw, this defense of monism is "characterized by deep suspicion of an international system based upon the sovereignty and absolute independence of states." *Id.* At the same time, because it holds that "international law is superior to or more basic than municipal law," monism has attracted a good deal of criticism. *Id.* Brownlie, for example, asserts that radical monism conflicts with "basic corollaries of the existence of sovereign states, and reduces municipal law to the status of pensioner of international law." Brownlie, *supra* note 1, at 83.

4. The U.S. legal system can be described as mitigated dualist. According to John Jackson, it "stands somewhere in between" a monist or dualist approach. John J. Jackson, *United States of America, in* The Effect of Treaties in Domestic Law 141-169, 141 (Francis G. Jacobs & Shelley Roberts eds., Sweet & Maxwell 1987). First, the U.S. has adopted a somewhat more monist approach with regard to customary international law. According to Shaw, "the current accepted position is that customary international law in the U.S. is federal law and that its determination by the federal courts is binding on the state courts." Shaw, *supra* at 118. As Professor Jordan Paust has documented in an exhaustive review of relevant case law, customary international law:

> as 'law of the United States' within the meaning of several constitutional provisions, ... is relevant both to the restraint and the enhancement of executive, congressional and judicial powers. Indeed, under Article III, section 2, clause 1 and Article VI, clause 2 of the Constitution, the judiciary is recognizably bound to identify, clarify and apply customary international law in cases otherwise properly before the courts, assuming that no unavoidable clash with some other constitutional requirement otherwise exists.

Jordan J. Paust, International Law as Law of the United States 9 (Carolina Academic Press, 1st ed. 1996). *See also* Restatement (Third) of the Foreign Relations Law of the United States § 111, Reporter's Note 4 (1987) ("Matters arising under customary international law also arise under 'the laws of the United States,' since international law is 'part of our law' ... and is federal law"). *See also Id.*, Comment e; *Id.*, § 702, Comment c.

Even a critical appraisal of this stance agrees:

> The proposition that customary international law ... is part of this country's post-*Erie* federal common law has become a well-entrenched component of U.S. foreign relations law. During the last twenty years, almost every federal court that has considered the ...

> position has endorsed it. Indeed, several courts have referred to it as "settled." The ... position also has the overwhelming approval of the academy.

Curtis A. Bradley & Jack L. Goldsmith, *Customary International Law as Federal Common Law: A Critique of the Modern Position,* 110 HARV. L. REV. 815, 816-817 (1997).

The U.S. retains a more dualist stance with regard to international agreements. Treaties are part of the United States' domestic law, as indicated in Article VI of its Constitution. Shaw notes that:

> American doctrines as to the understanding of treaty law are founded upon the distinction between 'self-executing' and 'non-self-executing' treaties. The former are able to operate automatically within the domestic sphere, without the need for any municipal legislation, while the latter require enabling acts before they can function inside the country and bind the American courts.

SHAW, *supra* note 1, at 121. For details on this distinction, and its critique, *see, infra*, Part Six, 1310-18. *See also* Julian Ku, *The State of New York Does Exist: How the States Control Compliance with International Law*, 82 N.C. L. REV. 457 (2004).

In a case of conflict between treaties and Congressional statutes, the *lex posterior* (last in time) rule applies, but with a slight preference, in effect, for the upholding of international treaty commitments. This rule is stated simply in the RESTATEMENT (THIRD) OF THE FOREIGN RELATIONS OF THE UNITED STATES:

> An act of Congress supercedes an earlier rule of international law or a provision of an international agreement as law of the United States if the purpose of the act to supercede the earlier rule or provision is clear or if the act and earlier rule or provision cannot be fairly reconciled.

RESTATEMENT (THIRD) OF FOREIGN RELATIONS LAW OF THE UNITED STATES §115 (1)(a) (1988). *See also Head Money Cases*, 112 U.S. 580 (1884). The requirement that Congressional intention to override prior treaties be manifest has always been a part of the "last in time" cases; but more recently the rule has been criticized. For a flavor of the controversy, *see e.g.,* W. Michael Reisman, *An International Farce: The Sad Case of the PLO Mission*, 14 YALE J. INT'L L. 534, 545 (1988); and Paul Szasz, *The Palestine Liberation Organization Mission Controversy*, 82 AM. SOC'Y INT'L L. PROC. 534, 538-539 (1988). Does the U.S. Supreme Court's decision in *Breard* track traditional formulation of the *lex posterior* rule?

In any event, as Paul Szasz has noted, "Articles 27 of the 1969 and 1986 Vienna Conventions on the Law of Treaties provide that a state party to a treaty may not invoke the provisions of its internal law as a justification for its failure to perform the treaty. Whatever U.S. domestic law may allow or require, the international obligation therefore remains in full force." *Id.* at 539.

5. The legal systems of many states contain both dualist and monist features. Monism is more accentuated in the domestic legal order of the Netherlands. John H. Jackson, *Status of Treaties in Domestic Legal Systems: A Policy Analysis.* 86 AM. J. INT'L L. 310, 320 (1992). According to Article 94 of the Dutch Constitution, for example, "statutory regulations in force within the Kingdom shall not be applicable if such application is in conflict with provisions of treaties that are binding on all persons or of resolutions by international institutions." ALBERT BLAUSTEIN & GISBERT FLANZ, CONSTITUTIONS OF THE COUNTRIES OF THE WORLD 105 (Oceana 1992).

Few states are dualist "in the sense that international law has no effect within the national legal system." HENRY G. SCHERMERS & DENIS WAELBROECK, JUDICIAL PROTECTION IN THE EUROPEAN COMMUNITIES 105 (Kluwer 1987). Like the United States, Italy and Germany have opted to follow a "mitigated dualist" path. *Id.* at 107. Article 59 of the Federal German Constitution, for example, establishes that the:

> [t]reaties which regulate the political relations of the Federation or relate to matters of federal legislation shall require the consent of participation, in the form of a federal law,

of the bodies competent in any specific case for such federal legislation.

Blaustein & Flanz, *supra* at 24. Article 80 of the Italian Constitution proclaims that "the Chambers authorize, by law, ratification of international treaties of a political nature, or which provide for arbitration or judicial regulation, or imply modifications to the nation's territory or financial burdens or to laws." Blaustein & Flanz, *supra* at 66. According to Schermers and Waelbroeck, however, the dualism of those provisions "is mitigated . . . by the rule [in the legal systems of each country] that the law approving the treaty simultaneously incorporates it into the national legal order." Schermers & Waelbroeck, *supra* at 107.

While treaties need legislative approval in Germany and Italy, customary international law is binding and takes immediate priority over municipal statutes in both of these countries. Article 10 of the Italian Constitution, for example, provides that "Italy's legal system conforms with the generally recognized principle of international law." Blaustein & Flanz, *supra* at 49. Similarly, Article 25 of the German Constitution states that "the general rules of public international law shall be an integral part of federal law. They shall take precedence over the laws and shall directly create rights and duties for the inhabitants of the federal territory." Blaustein & Flanz, *supra* at 91. This is a monist feature of both the Italian and German domestic legal orders.

6. Judge Rosalyn Higgins has attempted to link the "comfort level" of a state's legal culture with international law and the willingness of its domestic courts to enforce it. According to her:

> [r]elated to this great jurisprudential debate [between monism and dualism] is a further reality not to be found in the textbooks, but which must be mentioned. This is the reality of legal culture. In some jurisdictions international law will be treated as a familiar topic, one that both the judge and the counsel before him will expect to deal with on a routine basis, the introduction of which occasions no special comment or interest. Of course, this attitude is more to be expected in systems accepting the monist view. But I speak of very practical matters: the judge and lawyers in his court will have studied international law and will be familiar with it, just as they are familiar with other everyday branches of the law. But there is another culture that exists, in which it is possible to become a practicing lawyer without having studied international law, and indeed to become a judge knowing no international law. Psychologically that disposes both counsel and judge to treat international law as some exotic branch of the law, to be avoided if at all possible, and to be looked upon as if it is unreal, of no practical application in the real world. Of course, this attitude is mostly to be found in those countries that embrace (in so far as they think about it) the dualist system.

Rosalyn Higgins, Problems and Process: International Law and How We Use It 206 (Oxford U. Press 1994).

* * *

Another death penalty case followed soon after *Breard* and involved a similar variety of national and international actors. Walter LaGrand and Karl LaGrand were born in Germany in 1962 and 1963 respectively and were German nationals. While young children, they moved with their mother to live permanently in the United States. Although they never became U.S. nationals, they only returned to Germany for a period of six months in 1974. However, as noted by United States officials they both had the demeanor and speech of Americans, neither was known to speak German, and they appeared to be native citizens of the U.S. In 1982, the brothers were arrested in Arizona on suspicion of having committed an attempted armed bank robbery, in the course of which the bank manager was murdered. In 1984, they were both convicted of murder in the first degree. On December 14, 1984, in the state court of Arizona, both were sentenced to death.

At all times, both Germany and the United States were parties to the Vienna Convention on Consular Relations and the Optional Protocol. State of Arizona authorities failed to provide the LaGrands with information required by the Convention and did not inform the German Consulate of the LaGrands' arrest, thus violating the obligations of the United States under the Convention.

In 1999, the Federal Republic of Germany made a motion for a preliminary injunction against the United States of America and Jane Dee Hull, Governor of the State of Arizona, based on an order by the International Court of Justice directing the United States to prevent Arizona's scheduled execution of Walter LeGrand, a German national. The following responses ensued:

8. Statement of Governor Jane Dee Hull on the Case of Walter LaGrand, March 2, 1999

I have carefully weighed the recommendation from the Board of Executive Clemency for a reprieve in the case of Walter LaGrand.

After the board's action, I met with Dawn Lopez, one of the victims of Mr. LaGrand's crime, and also with German Ambassador Jurgen Chrobog. I appreciate the sincerity of their concerns; I also consulted with Attorney General Janet Napolitano.

However, in the interest of justice and with the victims in mind, I have decided to allow this execution to go forward as scheduled.

9. Letter from Seth P. Waxman, Solicitor General, to William Suter, Clerk of the Supreme Court of the United States, March 3, 1999

Dear Mr. Suter:

We have just received from the Clerk's Office (although we were not served), at 4:25 p.m., the Motion for Leave to File a Bill of Complaint and the Memorandum in support thereof filed by the Federal Republic of Germany. (A Motion to temporarily restrain the execution of Walter LaGrand was received 20 minutes later.) We have not had time to read the materials thoroughly or to digest the contents. Based on our understanding of the proceedings and the basis for the claim by the Federal Republic of Germany, it is our position that the Vienna Convention does not furnish a basis for this Court to grant a stay of execution.

Insofar as the United States is a named defendant, we are not aware of any applicable waiver of sovereign immunity of the United States to this original action filed by a foreign nation or its ambassador or consul. The execution is in any event to be carried out by the State of Arizona, not the United States.

Insofar as the suit is brought against the Governor of Arizona, as we explained in our response to the similar filing last year in *Paraguay v. Gilmore* and

Breard v. Greene, 118 S. Ct. 1352, neither a foreign state nor its consular officer has a judicial cause of action or remedy *in* domestic courts to obtain the vacatur of a criminal conviction on the basis of the failure by the receiving state to notify a defendant of his right to consular officials (pp. 15-28); this case is not, in any event within the core of the Court's original jurisdiction (if within the Court's jurisdiction at all) as a case "affecting" a consul (pp. 33-36); and an order of the International Court of Justice indicating provisional measures is not binding and does not furnish a basis for judicial relief (pp. 419-51). In addition, the Court held in the comparable *Breard* case that the suit against the Governor based on an alleged past violation of the Convention was barred by the Eleventh Amendment. 118 S. Ct. at 1356.

For the foregoing reasons, we respectfully submit that the alleged violation of the Vienna Convention, does not furnish a basis for this Court to grant a stay of execution.

10. The Federal Republic of Germany, *et al.* v. United States, *et al.*

526 U.S. 111 (1999)

OPINION: PER CURIAM.

The motion of the Federal Republic of Germany, et al. (plaintiffs) for leave to file a bill of complaint and the motion for preliminary injunction against the United States of America and Jane Dee Hull, Governor of the State of Arizona, both raised under this Court's original jurisdiction, are denied. Plaintiffs' motion to dispense with printing requirements is granted. Plaintiffs seek, among other relief, enforcement of an order issued this afternoon by the International Court of Justice, on its own motion and with no opportunity for the United States to respond, directing the United States to prevent Arizona's scheduled execution of Walter LaGrand. Plaintiffs assert that LaGrand holds German citizenship. With regard to the action against the United States, which relies on the ex parte order of the International Court of Justice, there are imposing threshold barriers. First, it appears that the United States has not waived its sovereign immunity. Second, it is doubtful that [U.S. Const.] Art. III, § 2. cl. 2 provides an anchor for an action to prevent execution of a German citizen who is not an ambassador or consul. With respect to the action against the State of Arizona, as in Breard v. Greene, 523 U.S. 371, (1998), a foreign government's ability here to assert a claim against a State is without evident support in the Vienna Convention and in probable contravention of Eleventh Amendment principles. This action was filed within only two hours of a scheduled execution that was ordered on January 15, 1999, based upon a sentence imposed by Arizona in 1984, about which the Federal Republic of Germany learned in 1992. Given the tardiness of the pleas and the jurisdictional barriers they implicate, we decline to exercise our original jurisdiction.

JUSTICE SOUTER with whom JUSTICE GINSBURG joins, concurring.

I join in the foregoing order, subject to the qualification that I do not rest my decision to deny leave to file the bill of complaint on any Eleventh Amendment principle. In exercising my discretion, I have taken into consideration the position of the Solicitor General on behalf of the United States.

JUSTICE BREYER and JUSTICE STEVENS dissented.

11. LaGrand Case (Ger. v. U.S.)

2001 I.C.J. 104 (Judgment of June 27)

[The Court reviews the facts and procedural history in U.S. state and federal courts]

24. On 21 December 1998, the LaGrands were formally notified by the United States authorities of their right to consular access.

25. On 15 January 1999, the Supreme Court of Arizona decided that Karl LaGrand was to be executed on 24 February 1999, and that Walter LaGrand was to be executed on 3 March 1999. Germany claims that the German Consulate learned of these dates on 19 January 1999.

26. In January and early February 1999, various interventions were made by Germany seeking to prevent the execution of the LaGrands. In particular, the German Foreign Minister and German Minister of Justice wrote to their respective United States counterparts on 27 January 1999; the German Foreign Minister wrote to the Governor of Arizona on the same day; the German Chancellor wrote to the President of the United States and to the Governor of Arizona on 2 February 1999; and the President of the Federal Republic of Germany wrote to the President of the United States on 5 February 1999. These letters referred to German opposition to capital punishment generally, but did not raise the issue of the absence of consular notification in the case of the LaGrands. The latter issue was, however, raised in a further letter, dated 22 February 1999, two days before the scheduled date of execution of Karl LaGrand, from the German Foreign Minister to the United States Secretary of State.

27. On 23 February 1999, the Arizona Board of Executive Clemency rejected an appeal for clemency by Karl LaGrand. Under the law of Arizona, this meant that the Governor of Arizona was prevented from granting clemency.

28. On the same day, the Arizona Superior Court in Pima County rejected a further petition by Walter LaGrand, based *inter alia* on the absence of consular notification, on the ground that these claims were "procedurally precluded".

29. On 24 February 1999, certain last-minute federal court proceedings brought by Karl LaGrand ultimately proved to be unsuccessful. In the course of these proceedings the United States Court of Appeals, Ninth Circuit, again held the issue of failure of consular notification to be procedurally defaulted. Karl LaGrand was executed later that same day.

30. On 2 March 1999, the day before the scheduled date of execution of Walter LaGrand, at 7.30 p.m. (The Hague time), Germany filed in the Registry of this Court the Application instituting the present proceedings against the United States (see paragraph 1 above), accompanied by a request for the following provisional measures:

> The United States should take all measures at its disposal to ensure that Walter LaGrand is not executed pending the final decision in these proceedings, and should inform the Court of all the measures which it has taken in implementation of that Order.

By a letter of the same date, the German Foreign Minister requested the Secretary of State of the United States "to urge [the] Governor [of Arizona] for a suspension of Walter LaGrand's execution pending a ruling by the International Court of Justice".

31. On the same day, the Arizona Board of Executive Clemency met to consider the case of Walter LaGrand. It recommended against a commutation of his death sentence, but recommended that the Governor of Arizona grant a 60-day reprieve having regard to the Application filed by Germany in the International Court of Justice. Nevertheless, the Governor of Arizona decided, "in the interest of justice and with the victims in mind", to allow the execution of Walter LaGrand to go forward as scheduled.

32. In an Order of 3 March 1999, this Court found that the circumstances required it to indicate, as a matter of the greatest urgency and without any other proceedings, provisional measures … in the following terms:

(a) The United States of America should take all measures at its disposal to ensure that Walter LaGrand is not executed pending the final decision in these proceedings, and should inform the Court of all the measures which it has taken in implementation of this Order;

(b) The Government of the United States of America should transmit this Order to the Governor of the State of Arizona.

33. On the same day, proceedings were brought by Germany in the United States Supreme Court against the United States and the Governor of Arizona, seeking *inter alia* to enforce compliance with this Court's Order indicating provisional measures. In the course of these proceedings, the United States Solicitor-General as counsel of record took the position, *inter alia,* that "an order of the International Court of Justice indicating provisional measures is not binding and does not furnish a basis for judicial relief". On the same date, the United States Supreme Court dismissed the motion by Germany, on the ground of the tardiness of Germany's application and of jurisdictional barriers under United States domestic law.

34. On that same day, proceedings were also instituted in the United States Supreme Court by Walter LaGrand. These proceedings were decided against him. Later that day, Walter LaGrand was executed. …

94. Germany claims that the United States committed a threefold violation of the Court's Order of 3 March 1999:

> (1) Immediately after the International Court of Justice had rendered its Order on Provisional Measures, Germany appealed to the U.S. Supreme Court in order to reach a stay of the execution of Walter LaGrand, in accordance with the International Court's Order to the same effect. In the course of these proceedings - and in full knowledge of the Order of the International Court - the Office of the Solicitor General, a section of the U.S. Department of Justice - in a letter to the Supreme Court argued once again that: 'an order of the International Court of Justice indicating provisional measures is not binding and does not furnish a basis for judicial relief'. This statement of a high-ranking official of the Federal Government ... had a direct influence on the decision of the Supreme Court.
>
> (2) In the following, the U.S. Supreme Court - an agency of the United States - refused by a majority vote to order that the execution be stayed. In doing so, it rejected the German arguments based essentially on the Order of the International Court of Justice on Provisional Measures ...
>
> (3) Finally, the Governor of Arizona did not order a stay of the execution of Walter LaGrand although she was vested with the right to do so by the laws of the State of Arizona. Moreover, in the present case, the Arizona Executive Board of Clemency - for the first time in the history of this institution - had issued a recommendation for a temporary stay, not least in light of the international legal issues involved in the case ...

95. The United States argues that it "did what was called for by the Court's 3 March Order, given the extraordinary and unprecedented circumstances in which it was forced to act". It points out in this connection that the United States Government "immediately transmitt[ed] the Order to the Governor of Arizona", that "the United States placed the Order in the hands of the one official who, at that stage, might have had legal authority to stop the execution" and that by a letter from the Legal Counsellor of the United States Embassy in The Hague dated 8 March 1999, it informed the International Court of Justice of all the measures which had been taken in implementation of the Order. The United States further states that: "[t]wo central factors constrained the United States ability to act. The first was the extraordinarily short time between issuance of the Court's Order and the time set for the execution of Walter LaGrand ... The second constraining factor was the character of the United States of America as a federal republic of divided powers."

96. The United States also alleges that the "terms of the Court's 3 March Order did not create legal obligations binding on [it]". It argues in this respect that "[t]he language used by the Court in the key portions of its Order is not the

language used to create binding legal obligations" and that "the Court does not need here to decide the difficult and controversial legal question of whether its orders indicating provisional measures would be capable of creating international legal obligations if worded in mandatory ... terms". It nevertheless maintains that those orders cannot have such effects and, in support of that view, develops arguments concerning "the language and history of Article 41 (1) of the Court's Statute and Article 94 of the Charter of the United Nations", the "Court's and State practice under these provisions", and the "weight of publicists' commentary". Concerning Germany's argument based on the "principle of effectiveness", the United States contends that "[i]n an arena where the concerns and sensitivities of States, and not abstract logic, have informed the drafting of the Court's constitutive documents, it is perfectly understandable that the Court might have the power to issue binding final judgments, but a more circumscribed authority with respect to provisional measures". ...

98. Neither the Permanent Court of International Justice, nor the present Court to date, has been called upon to determine the legal effects of orders made under Article 41 of the Statute. As Germany's third submission refers expressly to an international legal obligation "to comply with the Order on Provisional Measures issued by the Court on 3 March 1999", and as the United States disputes the existence of such an obligation, the Court is now called upon to rule expressly on this question.

99. The dispute which exists between the Parties with regard to this point essentially concerns the interpretation of Article 41, which is worded in identical terms in the Statute of each Court (apart from the respective references to the Council of the League of Nations and the Security Council). This interpretation has been the subject of extensive controversy in the literature. The Court will therefore now proceed to the interpretation of Article 41 of the Statute. It will do so in accordance with customary international law, reflected in Article 31 of the 1969 Vienna Convention on the Law of Treaties. According to paragraph 1 of Article 31, a treaty must be interpreted in good faith in accordance with the ordinary meaning to be given to its terms in their context and in the light of the treaty's object and purpose.

100. The French text of Article 41 reads as follows:

> 1. La Cour a le pouvoir *d'indiquer*, si elle estime que les circonstances l'exigent, quelles mesures conservatoires due droit de chacun *doivent* être prises à titre provisoire.
>
> 2. En attendant l'arrêt définitif, *l'indication* de ces mesures est immédiatement notifiée aux parties et au Conseil de sécurité. (Emphasis added.)

In this text, the terms "indiquer" and "l'indication" may be deemed to be neutral as to the mandatory character of the measure concerned; by contrast the words "doivent être prises" have an imperative character.

For its part, the English version of Article 41 reads as follows:

> 1. The Court shall have the power to *indicate*, if it considers that circumstances so require, any provisional measures which *ought* to be taken to preserve the respective rights of either party.
>
> 2. Pending the final decision, notice of the measures *suggested* shall forthwith be given to the parties and to the Security Council. (Emphasis added.)

According to the United States, the use in the English version of "indicate" instead of "order", of "ought" instead of "must" or "shall", and of "suggested" instead of "ordered", is to be understood as implying that decisions under Article 41 lack mandatory effect. It might however be argued, having regard to the fact that in 1920 the French text was the original version, that such terms as "indicate" and "ought" have a meaning equivalent to "order" and "must" or "shall".

101. Finding itself faced with two texts which are not in total harmony, the Court will first of all note that according to Article 92 of the Charter, the Statute "forms an integral part of the present Charter". Under Article 111 of the Charter, the French and English texts of the latter are "equally authentic". The same is equally true of the Statute. In cases of divergence between the equally authentic versions of the Statute, neither it nor the Charter indicates how to proceed. In the absence of agreement between the parties in this respect, it is appropriate to refer to paragraph 4 of Article 33 of the Vienna Convention on the Law of Treaties, which in the view of the Court again reflects customary international law. This provision reads "when a comparison of the authentic texts discloses a difference of meaning which the application of Articles 31 and 32 does not remove the meaning which best reconciles the texts, having regard to the object and purpose of the treaty, shall be adopted". The Court will therefore now consider the object and purpose of the Statute together with the context of Article 41.

102. The object and purpose of the Statute is to enable the Court to fulfill the functions provided for therein, and in particular, the basic function of judicial settlement of international disputes by binding decisions in accordance with Article 59 of the Statute. The context in which Article 41 has to be seen within the Statute is to prevent the Court from being hampered in the exercise of its functions because the respective rights of the parties to a dispute before the Court are not preserved. It follows from the object and purpose of the Statute, as well as from the terms of Article 41 when read in their context, that the power to indicate provisional measures entails that such measures should be binding, inasmuch as the power in question is based on the necessity, when the circumstances call for it, to safeguard, and to avoid prejudice to, the rights of the parties as determined by the final judgment of the Court. The contention that provisional measures indicated under Article 41 might not be binding would be contrary to the object and purpose of that Article.

103. A related reason which points to the binding character of orders made under Article 41 and to which the Court attaches importance, is the existence of a principle which has already been recognized by the Permanent Court of International Justice when it spoke of

> The principle universally accepted by international tribunals and likewise laid down in many conventions … to the effect that the parties to a case must abstain from any measure capable of exercising a prejudicial effect in regard to the execution of the decision to be given, and, in general, not allow any step of any kind to be taken which might aggravate or extend the dispute. (*Electricity Company of Sofia and Bulgaria, Order of 5 December 1939*)

104. Given the conclusions reached by the Court above in interpreting the text of Article 41 of the Statute in the light of its object and purpose, it does not consider it necessary to resort to the preparatory work in order to determine the meaning of that Article. The Court would nevertheless point out that the preparatory work of the Statute does not preclude the conclusion that orders under Article 41 have binding force. …

[The Court reviews the *travaux préparatoires* on provisional measures]

108. The Court finally needs to consider whether Article 94 of the United Nations Charter precludes attributing binding effect to orders indicating provisional measures…[and concludes that] Article 94 of the Charter does not prevent orders made under Article 41 from having a binding character.

109. In short, it is clear that none of the sources of interpretation referred to in the relevant Articles of the Vienna Convention on the Law of Treaties, including the preparatory work, contradict the conclusions drawn from the terms of Article 41 read in their context and in the light of the object and purpose of the Statute. Thus, the Court has reached the conclusion that orders on provisional measures under Article 41 have binding effect.

110. The Court will now consider the Order of 3 March 1999. This Order was not a mere exhortation. It had been adopted pursuant to Article 41 of the Statute. This Order was consequently binding in character and created a legal obligation for the United States.

111. As regards the question whether the United States has complied with the obligation incumbent upon it as a result of the Order of 3 March 1999, the Court observes that the Order indicated two provisional measures, the first of which states that "[t]he United States of America should take all measures at its disposal to ensure that Walter LaGrand is not executed pending the final decision in these proceedings, and should inform the Court of all the measures which it has taken in implementation of this Order". The second measure required the Government of the United States to "transmit this Order to the Governor of the State of Arizona". The information required on the measures taken in implementation of this Order was given to the Court by a letter of 8 March 1999 from the

Legal Counsellor of the United States Embassy at The Hague. According to this letter, on 3 March 1999 the State Department had transmitted to the Governor of Arizona a copy of the Court's Order. "In view of the extremely late hour of the receipt of the Court's Order", the letter of 8 March went on to say, "no further steps were feasible". The United States authorities have thus limited themselves to the mere transmission of the text of the Order to the Governor of Arizona. This certainly met the requirement of the second of the two measures indicated. As to the first measure, the Court notes that it did not create an obligation of result, but that the United States was asked to "take all measures at its disposal to ensure that Walter LaGrand is not executed pending the final decision in these proceedings". The Court agrees that due to the extremely late presentation of the request for provisional measures, there was certainly very little time for the United States authorities to act.

112. The Court observes, nevertheless, that the mere transmission of its Order to the Governor of Arizona without any comment, particularly without even so much as a plea for a temporary stay and an explanation that there is no general agreement on the position of the United States that orders of the International Court of Justice on provisional measures are non-binding, was certainly less than could have been done even in the short time available. The same is true of the United States Solicitor General's categorical statement in his brief letter to the United States Supreme Court that "an order of the International Court of Justice indicating provisional measures is not binding and does not furnish a basis for judicial relief"...This statement went substantially further than the amicus brief referred to in a mere footnote in his letter, which was filed on behalf of the United States in earlier proceedings before the United States Supreme Court in the case of Angel Francisco Breard. In that amicus brief, the same Solicitor General had declared less than a year earlier that "there is substantial disagreement among jurists as to whether an ICJ order indicating provisional measures is binding ... The better reasoned position is that such an order is not binding."

113. It is also noteworthy that the Governor of Arizona, to whom the Court's Order had been transmitted, decided not to give effect to it, even though the Arizona Clemency Board had recommended a stay of execution for Walter LaGrand.

114. Finally, the United States Supreme Court rejected a separate application by Germany for a stay of execution, "[g]iven the tardiness of the pleas and the jurisdictional barriers they implicate". Yet it would have been open to the Supreme Court, as one of its members urged, to grant a preliminary stay, which would have given it "time to consider, after briefing from all interested parties, the jurisdictional and international legal issues involved ...".

115. The review of the above steps taken by the authorities of the United States with regard to the Order of the International Court of Justice of 3 March 1999 indicates that the various competent United States authorities failed to take all the steps they could have taken to give effect to the Court's Order.

The Order did not require the United States to exercise powers it did not have; but it did impose the obligation to "take all measures at its disposal to ensure that Walter LaGrand is not executed pending the final decision in these proceedings ...". The Court finds that the United States did not discharge this obligation. Under these circumstances the Court concludes that the United States has not complied with the Order of 3 March 1999. ...

120. The Court observes that in its fourth submission Germany seeks several assurances. First it seeks a straightforward assurance that the United States will not repeat its unlawful acts. This request does not specify the means by which non-repetition is to be assured. Additionally, Germany seeks from the United States that "in any future cases of detention of or criminal proceedings against German nationals, the United States will ensure in law and practice the effective exercise of the rights under Article 36 of the Vienna Convention on Consular Relations". This request goes further, for, by referring to the law of the United States, it appears to require specific measures as a means of preventing recurrence.

Germany finally requests that "[i]n particular in cases involving the death penalty, this requires the United States to provide effective review of and remedies for criminal convictions impaired by a violation of the rights under Article 36". This request goes even further, since it is directed entirely towards securing specific measures in cases involving the death penalty.

121. Turning first to the general demand for an assurance of non-repetition, the Court observes that it has been informed by the United States of the "substantial measures [which it is taking] aimed at preventing any recurrence" of the breach of Article 36, paragraph 1 *(b)*. Throughout these proceedings, oral as well as written, the United States has insisted that it "keenly appreciates the importance of the Vienna Convention's consular notification obligation for foreign citizens in the United States as well as for United States citizens travelling and living abroad"; that "effective compliance with the consular notification requirements of Article 36 of the Vienna Convention requires constant effort and attention"; and that "the Department of State is working intensively to improve understanding of and compliance with consular notification and access requirements throughout the United States, so as to guard against future violations of these requirements". The United States points out that "[t]his effort has included the January 1998 publication of a booklet entitled 'Consular Notification and Access: Instructions for Federal, State and Local Law Enforcement and Other Officials Regarding Foreign Nationals in the United States and the Rights of Consular Officials to Assist Them', and development of a small reference card designed to be carried by individual arresting officers." According to the United States, it is estimated that until now over 60,000 copies of the brochure as well as over 400,000 copies of the pocket card have been distributed to federal, state and local law enforcement and judicial officials throughout the United States. The United States is also conducting training programmes reaching out to all levels of government. In the Department of State a permanent office to focus on United States and foreign

compliance with consular notification and access requirements has been created. …

124. The United States has provided the Court with information, which it considers important, on its programme. If a State, in proceedings before this Court, repeatedly refers to substantial activities which it is carrying out in order to achieve compliance with certain obligations under a treaty, then this expresses a commitment to follow through with the efforts in this regard. The programme in question certainly cannot provide an assurance that there will never again be a failure by the United States to observe the obligation of notification under Article 36 of the Vienna Convention. But no State could give such a guarantee and Germany does not seek it. The Court considers that the commitment expressed by the United States to ensure implementation of the specific measures adopted in performance of its obligations under Article 36, paragraph 1 *(b),* must be regarded as meeting Germany's request for a general assurance of non-repetition.

125. The Court will now examine the other assurances sought by Germany in its fourth submission. The Court observes in this regard that it can determine the existence of a violation of an international obligation. If necessary, it can also hold that a domestic law has been the cause of this violation. In the present case the Court has made its findings of violations of the obligations under Article 36 of the Vienna Convention when it dealt with the first and the second submission of Germany. But it has not found that a United States law, whether substantive or procedural in character, is inherently inconsistent with the obligations undertaken by the United States in the Vienna Convention. In the present case the violation of Article 36, paragraph 2, was caused by the circumstances in which the procedural default rule was applied, and not by the rule as such.

In the present proceedings the United States has apologized to Germany for the breach of Article 36, paragraph 1. …

The Court considers in this respect that if the United States, notwithstanding its commitment referred to in paragraph 124 above, should fail in its obligation of consular notification to the detriment of German nationals, an apology would not suffice in cases where the individuals concerned have been subjected to prolonged detention or convicted and sentenced to severe penalties. In the case of such a conviction and sentence, it would be incumbent upon the United States to allow the review and reconsideration of the conviction and sentence by taking account of the violation of the rights set forth in the Convention. This obligation can be carried out in various ways. The choice of means must be left to the United States. …

12. Avena and Other Mexican Nationals (Mex. v. U.S.)

2003 I.C.J. 128 (2003)

[Fifty-four Mexican nationals, currently on death row in the United States, were arrested, detained, tried, convicted, and sentenced to death following proceedings that failed to comply with the Vienna Convention. Mexico petitioned the I.C.J. to issue provisional measures to prevent the U.S. from proceeding with any executions, pending an I.C.J. decision on the matter.]

The International Court of Justice,

Makes the following Order: ...

54. Whereas "the sound administration of justice requires that a request for the indication of provisional measures founded on Article 73 of the Rules of Court be submitted in good time" *(LaGrand (Germany* v. *United States of America), Provisional Measures, Order of 3 March 1999*); whereas, moreover, the Supreme Court of the United States observed, when considering a petition seeking the enforcement of an Order of this Court, that: "It is unfortunate that this matter came before us while proceedings are pending before the ICJ that might have been brought to that court earlier" (*Breard* v. *Greene*, 523 US 371, 378 (1998)); whereas, in view of the rules and time-limits governing the granting of clemency and the fixing of execution dates in a number of the states of the United States, the fact that no such dates have been fixed in any of the cases before the Court is not *per se* a circumstance that should preclude the Court from indicating provisional measures; ...

57. Whereas it is clearly in the interest of both Parties that their respective rights and obligations be determined definitively as early as possible; whereas it is therefore appropriate that the Court, with the co-operation of the Parties, ensure that a final judgment be reached with all possible expedition;

58. Whereas the decision given in the present proceedings in no way prejudges the question of the jurisdiction of the Court to deal with the merits of the case or any questions relating to the admissibility of the Application, or relating to the merits themselves; and whereas it leaves unaffected the right of the Governments of Mexico and the United States to submit arguments in respect of those questions;

THE COURT, Unanimously

I. *Indicates* the following provisional measures:

(a) The United States of America shall take all measures necessary to ensure that Mr. César Roberto Fierro Reyna, Mr. Roberto Moreno Ramos and Mr. Osvaldo Torres Aguilera are not executed pending final judgment in these proceedings;

(b) The Government of the United States of America shall inform the Court of all measures taken in implementation of this Order.

II. *Decides* that, until the Court has rendered its final judgment, it shall remain seised of the matters which form the subject of this Order.

[For the Court's Judgment in *Avena*, *see* Part Five, *infra,* at 1018.]

NOTES AND QUESTIONS

1. In *LaGrand*, the ICJ sets forth the French version of Article 41 (permitting orders for provisional measures) and contrasts it with the English text. One argument made by U.S. Government officials and by the U.S. Supreme Court in both *Breard* and *LaGrand* was that:

> [T]he use of "indicate" instead of "order", of "ought" instead of "must" or "shall," and of "suggested" instead of "ordered", is to be understood as implying that decisions under Article 41 lack mandatory effect.

LaGrand, *supra*, at para. 100. The ICJ nevertheless concludes in paragraph 110 that an Article 41 order for provisional measures was intended to have binding effect and, thus, created a legal obligation for the United States. Judge Oda strongly dissented from the Court's position in this regard.

What in your view is the correct interpretation of Article 41? *See* Joan Fitzpatrick, *The Unreality of International Law in the United States and the LaGrand Case*, 27 YALE J. INT'L L. 427 (2002); John Quigley, *LaGrand: A Challenge to the U.S. Judiciary*, 27 YALE J. INT'L LAW 435 (2002); Jennifer Lynn Weisman, *The Clash Between U.S. Criminal Procedure and the Vienna Convention on Consular Relations: An Analysis of the International Court of Justice Decision in the LaGrand Case*, 17 AM. U. INT'L L. REV. 857 (2002); Christian J. Tams, *Recognizing Guarantees and Assurances of Non-Repetition: LaGrand and the Law of State Responsibility*, 27 YALE J. INT'L L. 441 (2002).

2. In both *Breard* and *LaGrand,* the ICJ issued orders for provisional measures that, arguably, contain non-mandatory language. For example, in paragraph 32 of *LaGrand*:

> In an order of 3 March 1999, this Court found that the circumstances required it to indicate … provisional measures in accordance with Article 41 of its Statute … in the following terms:
>
> (a) The United States of America *should* take all measures at its disposal to ensure that Walter LaGrand is not executed pending the final decision in these proceedings, and *should* inform the Court of all measures which it has taken …
>
> (b) The Government of the United States of America *should* transmit this order to the Governor of the State of Arizona.

The *Breard* order was stated in virtually identical terms. Does this presumably self-conscious use of "*should*" in orders issued under Article 41 support or detract from the Court's conclusion in *LaGrand* that such orders have binding effect on Parties? Does it really matter, now that the ICJ has decided in *LaGrand* that all provisional measures orders have binding effect?

3. In *Avena*, the ICJ changed all the "*shoulds*" to "*shalls*" in its order for provisional measures. Was the Court correcting what they saw as an error in their prior cases or simply bolstering their "binding character" holding in *LaGrand*? With this mandatory language now in the order, will United States courts be any more inclined to "obey" than they were after receiving the orders in *Breard* and *LaGrand*? Consider the following excerpt from William J. Aceves, *Case Report on the LaGrand Decision*, 96 AM. J. INT'L L. 210, 218 (2002):

> For both academics and practioners, a principal concern will be the impact of the ICJ's ruling on municipal law and practice. In this regard, the decision has numerous implications. It affirms the importance of the Convention and the right of consular assistance. It acknowledges that the Convention creates individual rights and state rights. It recognizes the binding nature of ICJ provisional measures orders. And it compels the criminal justice systems to take account of ... violations where defendants are sentenced to severe penalties. Each of these issues has been the subject of extensive debate and litigation, and the Court's decision provides some guidance on these matters.

> In the United States, past practice suggests that U.S. courts may not accord significant weight to the ICJ's ruling despite statements from the U.S. Supreme Court that courts "should give respectful consideration to the interpretation of an international treaty rendered by an international court with jurisdiction to interpret [it]." (*Breard v. Greene*, at 375.) For example, U.S. courts have disregarded the interpretation and analysis of the Convention provided by the Inter-American Court of Human Rights in its 1999 advisory opinion [*see infra* n. 5]. The U.S. Supreme Court discounted the ICJ's provisional measures orders in 1998 (*Breard v. Greene*) and in 1999 (Federal Republic of Germany v. United States). ... In the relatively brief period since the ICJ issued its judgment in LaGrand ..., most U.S. courts have accorded the decision little, if any, value. But at least one court has done more, and its approach may signal something new. In September 2001, the Oklahoma Court of Criminal Appeals stayed the execution of a Mexican national, in part because of the purported Convention violation and the broader implications of the ICJ's ruling. ... [T]he court announced the stay of execution, indicating that "this court has before it a unique and serious matter involving novel legal issues and international law." (*See* Okla. Court Postpones Execution of Mexican; International Law Cited in Ruling, WASH. POST, Sept. 22, 2001, at A 16.)
>
> It remains to be seen whether the U.S. courts will continue to disregard the rulings of international tribunals.

See also John R. Crook, *The 2001 Judicial Activity of the International Court of Justice*, 96 Am. J. Int'l L. 397 (2002); Note, *Too Sovereign But Not Sovereign Enough: Are U.S. States Beyond the Reach of the Law of Nations?*, 116 Harv. L. Rev. 2654 (2003).

4. Is this transformation of the legal effect of provisional measures a positive development for international law? In this regard, *see* Aceves, *supra* at 215-217.

5. The 1999 Advisory Opinion delivered by the Inter-American Court of Human Rights, cited *supra* in note 3, was the first decision rendered by an international tribunal regarding both the obligation of states to notify foreign nationals of their right to seek consular assistance and the municipal law implications of failing to comply with this obligation. This decision went much further than the ICJ in declaring that consular notification under the Convention had become a part of the body of international human rights law and in determining that the phrase "without delay" in Article 36 (1)(b) means that foreign nationals should be notified of their [rights] at the moment they are deprived of liberty and, in any case, before they make their first statements to the authorities. The Court pointedly reminds the parties of its earlier holding that "a state cannot use its federal structure as a basis for noncompliance with its international obligations." (1999 Advisory Opinion, para. 139).

After the Inter-American Court issued its Opinion, several foreign nationals attempted to rely upon it to bring their cases before U.S. courts, but to no avail. The First Circuit noted that the U.S. is not a party to the treaty that formed the Inter-American Court of Human Rights and therefore isn't bound by that Court's conclusions (United States v. Li, 206 F. 3d 56 (1st Cir. 2000).). The 9th Circuit *en banc* found a violation of the Convention but held that these violations could not be remedied by the judiciary (United States v. Lombera-Camorlinga, 206 F.3d 882 (9th Cir. 2000)).

How do you explain the reaction of the United States to the decisions in this section, in light of their stated policy that the interpretation of international agreements by international tribunals should be given respectful consideration by the federal courts?

6. The *Breard, LaGrand* and *Avena* decisions, although nominally about consular relations, play against a backdrop of capital punishment, a topic of great controversy in United States foreign relations. In this regard *see* William Schabas, The Abolition of the Death Penalty in International Law (3rd ed., Cambridge U. Press 2002); and Thomas Michael McDonnell, *The Death Penalty – An Obstacle to the "War Against Terrorism"?*, 39 Vand. J. Transnat'l L. 353 (2004). *See also,* The

Question of the Death Penalty, Draft Report of the UN Commission on Human Rights, 59th Sess. (2003).

IV. THE RELATION BETWEEN THE LAWFULNESS OF ACTIONS AND THE CONSTITUTIVE PROCESS

W. Michael Reisman, *Appraising the Unilateral Actions of States in Terms of the Constitutive Process: The Special Problem of Humanitarian Intervention*

11 EUR. J. INT'L L. 3, 3-8 (2000)

When a unilateral action occurs, its legal appraisal varies as a function of the constitutive configuration in which it occurs. Four constitutive configurations are relevant: first, constitutive processes without hierarchical institutions of decision; second, constitutive processes in which there are hierarchical institutions which are manifestly ineffective; third, constitutive processes in which the hierarchical institutions are generally effective, but prove to be ineffective for the application of particular norms; and fourth, constitutive processes in which hierarchical institutions are highly effective and in which unilateral actions will simply be characterized as 'taking the law into one's own hands', and hence delictual, no matter what the explanations and how passionate the justifications preferred. Let us consider each of these types.

A. *Unorganized and Non-Hierarchical Constitutive Structures*

In legal systems whose constitutive processes do not have or do not operate through hierarchical institutions for making and applying law, unilateral action is perforce the method for making decisions; the unilaterality of the action, of itself, is not a relevant consideration in the assessment of its lawfulness. Participants within the legal system may decry the absence of organized decision-making arrangements that would obviate the need for justification of unilateral action and some may even struggle to create them, but until effective institutions are brought into operation, unilateral action is perforce the lawful mode of decision. In micro-legal arrangements in the private sphere of liberal systems, coarchical decision by unilateral action is the normal mode of decision, but the stakes are usually much lower and the consequences apparently evanescent.

Wholly aside from the question of efficiency, the first type of constitutive structure raises serious political philosophical problems. Where there are clear norms, unorganized modes for appraisal of the lawfulness of the unilateral action may be quite efficient, but, by their nature, unorganized and non-hierarchical systems tend to mirror the power process, in which the quintessential grundnorm is Thucydides' 'The strong do what they will and the weak suffer what they must.'

B. *Ineffective Constitutive Structures*

In the panorama of domestic political and legal systems, many are essentially semantic: they are furnished with sometimes grandiloquent paper constitutions, along with corresponding paper institutions with elaborate legal procedures, which together purport to be their legal and political systems. Yet they have no power. Actual decisions are made by a shadow process, which may converge with the formal 'legal' system, but which operates on an entirely different value calculus. In some circumstances, the formal system will issue the actual decisions and outsiders may attribute them to the legal process. But insiders - operators who understand the 'operational code' - know that it is fruitless to seek decisions from the formal process if they have not first been certified by the actual power process.

Unfortunately, ineffective political and legal systems abound. The earliest known example is the Code of Hammurabi, an elaborate codex that was not applied. Numerous similarly ineffective systems have existed since. Rogelio Perez Perdomo has produced an indispensable study of this type of system in nineteenth century Latin America *caudillajes.* Ernst Fraenkel analyzed it in his classic study of the *Doppelstaat.* In my experience as a member of a regional human rights oversight body, I found this to be a situation so common that, for all of its frustrating ineffectiveness, one hesitates to call it 'abnormal'. I believe that, at some level of consciousness, all of us entertain the possibility that the legal system in a particular situation may be only semantic, for example, when we visit a new town and ask, 'who's the mayor?', and then, 'who's the boss?'

Yet for those who have been acculturated to and work in effective legal systems, each confrontation with semantic systems, even when recognized as such, still generates a type of what Festinger called 'cognitive dissonance'. We have been conditioned to respond affirmatively to the symbols of the law so that even if they are only symbols, with no effective legal system behind them, their presence still makes any action -whether taken by others or ourselves -that has not been pre-authorized by its paper institutions seem somehow unlawful and further corrosive of the law itself.

C. *Effective but Limited Constitutive Structures*

There are legal systems that are only partially effective. In some circumstances, this occurs over extended periods because of a lack of coordination of political power and political authority. In other circumstances, it occurs because, as McDougal put it, 'authoritative reach exceeds controlling grasp'. The phenomenon of legal over- reaching is more common than may be generally appreciated, for ineffective law is often not a failure of legal drafting or a lapse of legislative continence, but rather a conscious technique for mediating between the incompatible aspirations of different classes and interest groups by means of the device of recognizing legislatively the validity of claims while ensuring that the legal promise will neither be enforced nor otherwise fulfilled. In other circumstances, it occurs, not because of an intentionally designed incapacity, but because of a particular, unanticipated stress on the system.

Many legal systems have contingent *exceptios* for unilateral action to fill the gap for important matters for which there are clear substantive standards and prescribed procedures, but, whether generally or sporadically, insufficient power to make them effective. In modern international law, the prime example of the *exceptio* is the so-called right of self-defence. This power, which the UN Charter authorizes to its state-parties, is not, it should be emphasized, a survival from an earlier period of law as the rather archaic naturalist language that was used to frame it in the Charter would suggest. It is an intentional *exceptio,* for there was no 'right' of self-defence prior to the Charter's installation of a prohibition on the use of force. Until that time, states, as a manifestation of their sovereignty, were entitled to wage war, whether to defend existing rights or to change them, so a 'right' of self-defence was redundant, despite the word 'inherent' in the English version or 'droit naturel' in the corresponding French version of Charter Article 51, the provision was designed to function as an *exceptio* to the general assignment of the right to use force that had been made to the Security Council.

D. *Effective Constitutive Structures*

When a constitutive process has hierarchical institutions that are effective and can meet the authorized demands of those who participate in it, there is no justification for unilateral action. Hence, virtually all unilateral action in this constitutive setting is presumptively delictual. The sanctioning agents may sometimes appreciate that a particular unilateral action is different from ordinary delicts that are occasioned by negligence or presumably animated by an intention to self-enrich. Moreover, those applying the sanctions may be conscious of the moral arguments that can be marshaled to justify the particular unilateral action, nevertheless, the action will still be condemned and sanctioned, lest the constitutive process cease to be effective and degrade to the third type. In the constitutive process that has established and maintained effective structures, we encounter unique oxymorons such as 'civil disobedience' and complex multi-referential terms such as 'vigilantism'. A term such as civil disobedience is invoked by the unilateral actor, who acknowledges the authority and effectiveness of the decision process he or she is disobeying and in some theories the propriety of punishment for the 'civil disobedience'. Vigilantism is a complex term of decision-makers which at once condemns the unilateral and, as a result, more arbitrary action taken and insists that sanctions be applied, yet, in not using the term 'criminal', implies some understanding of the reasons for the action, usually the inability or refusal of the political and legal system to address through timely law-making or effective application, the issue which has excited the action of the vigilante.

Each of these four types of constitutive configurations views the category of events that we call unilateral action differently. Only in the last three systemic arrangements is unilateral action a legal problem; in the second and third, the uncertainty with regard to the lawfulness of unilateral action or its normative ambiguity arises from the cognitive dissonance caused by the realization that the constitutive process to which the prerogative of action has been assigned is either generally or momentarily unable to implement rights it has guaranteed, while in the fourth, the primary problem is one of control, as the constitutive process is effective, so unilateral actions are unnecessary to vindicate rights and hence are presumptively unlawful. Yet even in the latter type of constitutive structure, particular unilateral acts and unilateral action in general may be viewed as unlawful only by some participants.

The end of the Cold War and the disintegration of the Soviet Union signaled the apparent restoration of the consensus among the five permanent members of the Security Council. As this had been the precondition for the operation of the Charter system, for a short time, it appeared that the world community had returned to the fourth type of constitutive structure. This impression was reinforced by the response of the Security Council to Iraq's invasion of Kuwait. But the impression of effectiveness was only partially accurate, for the consensus had never gone beyond a manifest violation of an international boundary and seizure of the territory of another member of the United Nations. It had never extended to human rights, i.e. the authoritative international scrutiny of the essential techniques by which state elites control their populations. One of the five permanent and veto-franchised members was an unrepentant dictatorship that could not comply meaningfully with the international human rights standard without weakening or transforming itself, while another was in a process of transition whose ultimate outcome could not be predicted with any confidence.

The introduction of human rights into international law and the opening of an international decision process to broad and effective non-governmental participation has had a significant -and surprising -effect on the legal status of unilateral action. Recall that the absence of consensus on human rights was of little consequence for the operation of the Security Council as long as those rights were considered to be matters of domestic jurisdiction that were neither deemed to be the active responsibility of the United Nations nor within the assignment of the Security Council. Now, however, the new and expanded international decision process has taken a hitherto normatively uncertain human rights 'standard of achievement', refashioned it into the 'inter- national protection of human rights', and elevated it to an imperative level of international law. Indeed, it is increasingly characterized as a *jus cogens,* a term currently used in ways quite different from its denotation in the Vienna Convention on the Law of Treaties. But real law, which requires coercive enforcement is assigned to the Security Council. Yet the task of human rights enforcement cannot be discharged, for the members of the Council do not share a consensus on human rights norms. In a decision process in which law-makers and law-appliers are identical, non-enforcement of norms would, over time, render them caducous, but as the norms in question - international human rights norms -derive from a broader decision process than the body assigned to enforce the norms, the broader decision process sustains the norms and seeks alternative modes of enforcement.

In the fourth type of constitutive structure, the use of force - the *ultima ratio* of law - is taken from the individual state and henceforth to be effected by the Security Council. As remedies for grave human rights violations may involve the use of major coercion against a government, they, too, fall within the competence of the Security Council. But the absence of consensus on human rights means that their remedial action, requiring, as it does, agreement of all the permanent members of the Council, is unlikely. Yet the international legal process's demand for a remedy for grave violations of human rights has become so powerful and urgent that democratic governments that are susceptible to non-governmental influence and that have the wherewithal to effect a remedy are under great pressure to act unilaterally. Hence, for purposes of the enforcement of human rights, a constitutive process of the fourth type now reverts to the third type: enforcement through the Security Council, if it can be achieved, but enforcement unilaterally if it cannot.

Thus, we encounter an anomalous constitutive regime, which begins to reserve different legal treatment for different types of unilateral actions, based principally on the purpose or objective of the actions concerned. Since many participants assume that an ineluctable feature of law is generality of application, this constitutive regime engenders more normative ambiguity and cognitive dissonance.

NOTES AND QUESTIONS

1. In light of the material in this Part, how would you assess the lawfulness and effectiveness of unilateral action in the world constitutive process?

PART TWO: ESTABLISHMENT, TRANSFORMATION AND TERMINATION OF STATES AND OTHER ACTORS

I. INTRODUCTION

A wide variety of actors participate in the international legal system, in both its constitutive process and its public order: nation-states, whether independent or associated (e.g. former protectorates, colonies, "commonwealths" such as Puerto Rico), non-self-governing territories under some international régime of supervision (e.g. trusteeship territories, mandate territories), largely autonomous sub-units of composite nation-states (e.g. components of a federation, such as the U.S., Canada, Brazil, Mexico, India, the former USSR, the former Yugoslavia), regions, both within an established nation-state (Spain) and beyond (Upper Rhine Region; Carpathian Region), other largely self-governing administrative units of a special nature (Palestinian Authority in West Bank and Gaza Strip), indigenous peoples within reservations/reserves (territories allowed limited autonomous rule by, e.g., the U.S. and Canada), and without. Private entities such as multinational corporations, the media, NGO pressure groups, criminal organizations/gangs and individuals, with their effectiveness enhanced by technological innovations relatively insusceptible to control by established territorial elites exert an ever-increasing influence on the global process of authoritative and controlling decision. They are not "territorial actors," but they are actors nonetheless.

Nation-states remain the principal actors in many of the formal arenas of decision-making:

> States will continue as primary organizations and value providers. The international bureaucracy lacks the resources and the incentives necessary to fulfill the essential value demands that the individuals make on their political communities; security, productive economic arrangements, health services and the various 'safety nets' in the event of recession or calamity. Indeed, while some will decry the state as an atavism or the primary violator of human rights, the provision of internationally guaranteed human rights depends essentially on the apparatus of the state.

W. Michael Reisman, *Designing and Managing the Future of the State,* 8 EUR. J. INT'L L. 409, 416 (1997).

Other forms of territorial communities are, for the most part, pre- or post-state phenomena. Some continue to press claims for varying degrees of access to formal arenas. It is the transformations and permutations of nation-states that are the principal subject of this Part, with a focus on prescriptions, trends in practice and policy appraisal of the techniques through which internal and external elites both facilitate and restrict the "freedom" of establishment and transformation of states.

The reconfiguration of territorial communities presents the international community with difficult choices. Breakups may be exceedingly costly for the international system. In many cases, they tear up existing social structures with serious value losses for many members of the former community. They may threaten security and impede economic progress by cutting links and establishing smaller, less viable units of commercial interaction. Acting on these negative concerns, the international community has sometimes declined to recognize aspirations for self-determination.

II. THE POLICIES AT STAKE IN ESTABLISHMENT, TRANSFORMATION AND TERMINATION OF TERRITORIAL ACTORS

A. THE CONCEPT OF STATE

For convenience and economy, we will often use the term state but the student must bear in mind that the reference is to many different kinds of territorial communities, with different kinds of constitutive processes.

1. A. R. RADCLIFFE-BROWN, AFRICAN POLITICAL SYSTEMS XIII (Fortes & Evans-Pritchard eds., 1940)

In writings on political institutions there is a good deal of discussion about the nature and the origin of the State, which is usually represented as being an entity over and above the human individuals who make up a society, having as one of its attributes something called "sovereignty," and sometimes spoken of as having a will (law being often defined as the will of the State) or as issuing commands. The State, in this sense, does not exist in the phenomenal world; it is a fiction of the philosophers. What does exist is an organization, i.e., a collection of individual human beings connected by a complex system of relations. Within that organization different individuals have different roles, and some are in possession of special power or authority, as chiefs or elders capable of giving commands which will be obeyed, as legislators or judges, and so on. There is no such thing as the power of the State; there are only, in reality, powers of individuals– kings, prime ministers, magistrates, policemen, party bosses, and voters. The political organization of a society is that aspect of the total organization which is concerned with the control and regulation of the use of physical force. This, it is suggested, provides for an objective study of human societies by the methods of natural science, the most satisfactory definition of the special class of social phenomena to the investigation of which this book is a contribution.

2. Myres S. McDougal, *International Law, Power and Policy: A Contemporary Perspective*

82 Académie de Droit International, Recueil des Cours 133 (1953)

The label "nation-State," which we adopt because of its common usage, is not the happiest term for describing the participants with which we are here concerned. From a factual perspective the participants we now seek to identify may perhaps be better described as "territorially organized bodies politic" (or as "politically organized communities with a territorial base") in which active elites demand with respect to other elites in other similar bodies politic freedom of decision on both internal and external affairs and seek to preserve, or even to enhance, their territorial base for maximising all values. The term "nation-state" is commonly reserved for the bodies politic which achieve the greater degrees of freedom in decision and these are described in terms of "independence" and "sovereignty"; other bodies politic are dichotomized as "non-nation-states," given various appellations such as "protectorates," "mandates," "trusteeships," and so on, and are described as dependent and non-sovereign.

It should require no great elaboration that the criteria put forward in world prescriptions for distinguishing "nation-states" from "non-nation-states" are normatively ambiguous in high degree, referring both to the facts to which decision-makers are responding and to responses they make to such facts and embodying both descriptive and preferential judgments. Thus, in the Montevideo Convention of 1933, Article 1 prescribes: "The State as a person of international law should possess the following qualifications: (a) a permanent population; (b) a defined territory; (c) government; and (d) capacity to enter into relations with other States." When the question is whether some new elite which has emerged in apparent control of some area of the world has capacity to enter into relations with the other states, it does not clarify the grounds of decision greatly to be told that if it has such capacity it is a nation-state. The vagaries that attend decision by such traditional criteria are amply illustrated in any collection of cases.

In terms of fact it is easily observable both that the world arena today presents a great profusion of territorially organized bodies politic, of many varying degrees of formal authority and effective control, in terms both of internal control over individuals and of external relations to other bodies politic, and, further, that these numerous bodies politic are in a process of continual change in relation to each other. Inquiry that would be comprehensive and realistic must concern itself, not merely with "nation-states," but with all these bodies politic and achieve a mode of description, for clarifying policy issues in concrete controversies about access to arenas, competency to make agreements, succession to benefits and burdens of prior bodies, and so on, that is more adequate than the traditional, simple dichotomy of "nation-state" and "non-nation-state" and its attendant normatively-ambiguous criteria.

B. International Policies

In particular cases, the policies of self-determination, stability, minimum order and human rights are often difficult to accommodate. A number of scholars have struggled to find principles to balance the preferred policies. Professor Chen considers it "essential that the people directly concerned have a reasonable prospect of becoming a viable entity – politically, economically, and so on – in this increasingly interdependent world" and would consider the "effect of granting or refusing the exercise of self-determination, in terms of regional and international peace, the effectuation of authoritative governmental processes and human rights, and impacts on all value processes both regional and global." LUNG-CHU CHEN, AN INTRODUCTION TO CONTEMPORARY INTERNATIONAL LAW 34 (Yale U. Press 1989).

Professor Wiessner cautions that the "exclusive focus on ethnic ties often results in net losses for the values of human dignity." Conversely, "romantic dreams of a universal loyalty manifested by world citizenship are similarly problematic," *inter alia* because of their "potential for totalitarian abuse." Thus he would recommend the development of "loyalty to friends, ... family, ... loved ones, irrespective of immutable traits," creating a "vibrant network of social interaction" by "participating in the dynamic process of shaping and sharing values in ever-changing patterns of social configurations and identities" – "provided that the groups we join or take part in are affirmative of, not opposed to, the fundamental values of a world public order of human dignity." Siegfried Wiessner, *Faces of Vulnerability: Protecting Individuals in Organic and Non-Organic Groups, in* THE LIVING LAW OF NATIONS 217-226 (Gudmundur Alfredsson & Peter Macalister-Smith eds., 1996).

Professor Reisman concludes:

> All change, obviously, is disruptive. It benefits some and is extremely disruptive of the values of others; this is what makes it so controversial and so conflict-ridden. The question ... is, What are the strategies available to communities in transition, for their process of redefinition, and what role should the international community - an increasingly effective participant in all of these subcommunities - take in this process? Should it encourage autonomy, self-governance and independence, or, if I may draw on some of the language of Resolutions 1514 and 1541 of the UN General Assembly in 1960, should it encourage integration into the metropolitan? I will conclude with this observation: in looking at an appropriate international role for communities in transition, I think the crucial questions are these: What are the goals of the international community with regard to these lesser communities? What strategies are effective? and, What procedural values are important? I think we would all agree that any changes that now occur...should be consistent with the basic code of international human rights. Secondly, the procedures by which these changes are accomplished should meet the emerging procedural requirements - what Professor Franck has called the emerging right to

> democratic consultation - or some approximation thereof. The selection of autonomy, self-governance, integration or independence should be based on a general conviction that the particular solution selected is the one that will yield the greatest advance in terms of human rights and minimum order for all those concerned.

W. Michael Reisman, 87 AM. SOC'Y INT'L L. PROC. 249 (1993).

III. THE ROLE OF INTERNAL ELITES

A. INTERNATIONAL PRESCRIPTIONS THAT MAY ACT TO FACILITATE ESTABLISHMENT BY INTERNAL ELITES

As the major international governmental organization of the contemporary global arena, the United Nations plays an important role in prescribing policy with respect to the establishment of territorial entities. The Charter expresses a number of key policies. We consider first inclusive policies favoring, and then those restricting, establishment and change.

1. United Nations Policies That Favor Self-Determination

a. United Nations Charter

Article 1. The Purposes of the United Nations are:

(2) To develop friendly relations among nations based on respect for the principle of equal rights and self-determination of peoples, and to take other appropriate measures to strengthen universal peace; . . .

Article 55. With a view to the creation of conditions of stability and well-being which are necessary for peaceful and friendly relations among nations based on respect for the principle of equal rights and self-determination of peoples, the United Nations shall promote:

(a) higher standards of living, full employment, and conditions of economic and social progress and development;

(b) solutions of international economic, social, health, and related problems; and international cultural and educational cooperation; and

(c) universal respect for, and observation of, human rights and fundamental freedoms for all without distinction as to race, sex, language, or religion.

Article 56. All Members pledge themselves to take joint and separate action in cooperation with the Organization for the achievement of the purposes set forth in Article 55. ...

Article 73. Members of the United Nations which have or assume responsibilities for the administration of territories whose peoples have not yet attained a full measure of self-government recognize the principle that the interests of the inhabitants of these territories are paramount, and accept as a sacred trust the obligation to promote to the utmost, within the system of international peace and security established by the present Charter, the wellbeing of the inhabitants of these territories, and, to this end:

(a) to ensure, with due respect for the culture of the peoples concerned, their political, economic, social, and educational advancement, their just treatment, and their protection against abuses;

(b) to develop self-government, to take due account of the political aspirations of the peoples, and to assist them in the progressive development of their free political institutions, according to the particular circumstances of each territory and its peoples and their varying stages of advancement;

(c) to further international peace and security;

(d) to promote constructive measures of development, to encourage research, and to cooperate with one another and, when and where appropriate, with specialized international bodies with a view to the practical achievement of the social, economic, and scientific purposes set forth in this Article; and

(e) to transmit regularly to the Secretary-General for information purposes, subject to such limitation as security and constitutional considerations may require, statistical and other information of a technical nature relating to economic, social, and educational conditions in the territories for which they are respectively responsible other than those territories to which Chapters XII and XIII apply. …

Article 75. The United Nations shall establish under its authority an international trusteeship system for the administration and supervision of such territories as may be placed thereunder by subsequent individual agreements. These territories are hereinafter referred to as trust territories.

Article 76. The basic objectives of the trusteeship system, in accordance with the Purposes of the United Nations laid down in Article 1 of the present Charter, shall be:

(a) to further international peace and security;

(b) to promote the political, economic, social, and educational advancement of the inhabitants of the trust territories, and their progressive development towards self-government or independence as may be appropriate to the particular circumstances of each territory and its peoples and the freely expressed wishes of the peoples concerned, and as may be provided by the terms of each trusteeship agreement;

(c) to encourage respect for human rights and for fundamental freedoms for all without distinction as to race, sex, language, or religion, and to encourage recognition of the interdependence of the peoples of the world; and

(d) to ensure equal treatment in social, economic, and commercial matters for all Members of the United Nations and their nationals, and also equal treatment for the latter in the administration of justice, without prejudice to the attainment of the foregoing objectives and subject to the provisions of Article 80. ...

b. Declaration on the Granting of Independence to Colonial Countries and Peoples

Dec. 14, 1960, G.A.Res. 1514 (XV), 15 U.N.GAOR, Supp. (No. 16) 66, U.N. Doc. A/4684 (1961)

The General Assembly ...

Solemnly proclaims the necessity of bringing to a speedy and unconditional end colonialism in all its forms and manifestations;

And to this end

Declares that:

1. The subjection of peoples to alien subjugation, domination and exploitation constitutes a denial of fundamental human rights, is contrary to the Charter of the United Nations and is an impediment to the promotion of World peace and co-operation.

2. All peoples have the right to self-determination; by virtue of that right they freely determine their political status and freely pursue their economic, social and cultural development.

3. Inadequacy of political, economic, social or educational preparedness should never serve as a pretext for delaying independence.

4. All armed action or repressive measures of all kinds directed against dependent peoples shall cease in order to enable them to exercise peacefully and freely their right to complete independence, and the integrity of their national territory shall be respected.

5. Immediate steps shall be taken, in Trust and Non-Self-Governing Territories or all other territories which have not yet attained independence, to transfer all powers to the peoples of those territories, without any conditions or reservations, in accordance with their freely expressed will and desire, without any distinction as to race, creed or colour, in order to enable them to enjoy complete independence and freedom.

6. Any attempt aimed at the partial or total disruption of the national unity and the territorial integrity of a country is incompatible with the purposes and principles of the Charter of the United Nations.

7. All States shall observe faithfully and strictly the provisions of the Charter of the United Nations, the Universal Declaration of Human Rights and the present Declaration on the basis of equality, non-interference in the internal affairs of all States, and respect for the sovereign rights of all peoples and their territorial integrity. ...

c. Principles Which Should Guide Members in Determining Whether or Not an Obligation Exists to Transmit the Information Called for Under Article 73 E of the Charter

G.A. Res. 1541 (XV), Annex, Dec. 15, 1960

Principle I

The authors of the Charter of the United Nations had in mind that Chapter XI should be applicable to territories which were then known to be of the colonial type. An obligation exists to transmit information under Article 73(e) of the Charter in respect of such territories whose peoples have not yet attained a full measure of self-government. ...

Principle IV

Prima facie there is an obligation to transmit information in respect of a territory which is geographically separate and is distinct ethnically and/or culturally from the country administering it.

Principle V

Once it has been established that such a *prima facie* case of geographical and ethnical or cultural distinctness of a territory exists, other elements may then be brought into consideration. These additional elements may be, *inter alia,* of an administrative, political, juridical, economic or historical nature. If they affect the relationship between the metropolitan State and the territory concerned in a manner which arbitrarily places the latter in a position or status of subordination, they support the presumption that there is an obligation to transmit information under Article 73(e) of the Charter.

Principle VI

A Non-Self-Governing Territory can be said to have reached a full measure of self-government by:

(a) Emergence as a sovereign independent State;

(b) Free association with an independent State; or

(c) Integration with an independent State.

Principle VII

(a) Free association should be the result of a free and voluntary choice by the peoples of the territory concerned expressed through informed and democratic processes. It should be one which respects the individuality and the cultural

characteristics of the territory and its peoples, and retains for the peoples of the territory which is associated with an independent State the freedom to modify the status of that territory through the expression of their will by democratic means and through constitutional processes.

(b) The associated territory should have the right to determine its internal constitution without outside interference, in accordance with due constitutional processes and the freely expressed wishes of the people. This does not preclude consultations as appropriate or necessary under the terms of the free association agreed upon.

Principle VIII

Integration with an independent State should be on the basis of complete equality between the peoples of the erstwhile Non-Self-Governing Territory and those of the independent country with which it is integrated. The peoples of both territories should have equal status and rights of citizenship and equal guarantees of fundamental rights and freedoms without any distinction or discrimination; both should have equal rights and opportunities for representation and effective participation at all levels in the executive, legislative and judicial organs of government.

Principle IX

Integration should have come about in the following circumstances:

(a) The integrating territory should have attained an advanced stage of self-government with free political institutions, so that its peoples would have the capacity to make a responsible choice through informed and democratic processes;

(b) The integration should be the result of the freely expressed wishes of the territory's peoples acting with full knowledge of the change in their status, their wishes having been expressed through informed and democratic processes, impartially conducted and based on universal adult suffrage. The United Nations could, when it deems it necessary, supervise these processes.

* * *

The range of options available to peoples entitled to self-determination may have been expanded by the Declaration on Principles of International Law Concerning Friendly Relations and Co-operation Among States in Accordance with the Charter of the United Nations of October 24, 1970, G.A. Res. 2625 (XXV), 25 U.N.G.A.O.R. Supp. (No. 28), 121, U.N. Doc. A/8028 (1971), which states in part:

> The establishment of a sovereign and independent State, the free association or integration with an independent State or the emergence into any other political status freely determined by a people constitute modes of implementing the right of self-determination by that people.

NOTES AND QUESTIONS

1. The League of Nations mandate system was, in great measure, the product of President Woodrow Wilson's policy. Under Article 22 of the Covenant, certain territories inhabited by "peoples not yet able to stand by themselves under the strenuous conditions of the modern world" [sic] were entrusted to certain States, the "Mandatory Powers," for administration on behalf of the League. As the International Court of Justice put it: "[T]he Mandate was created, in the interest of the inhabitants of the territory, and of humanity in general, as an international institution with an international object - a sacred trust of civilization." *Case Concerning the Status of South West Africa,* 1950 I.C.J. 128, 132 (July 11). Three categories of mandates were established, in descending order from types "A" to "B" and "C" according to the level of political development of the territory involved. The Council of the League was to supervise the Mandatory Powers. The inhabitants of each mandated territory were entitled to petition the League. Flagrant abuses of that "sacred trust" have occurred, highlighted in the protracted ICJ litigation on the administration of South West Africa/Namibia by South Africa.

Was this system an appropriate transition mechanism toward political independence of the mandated territories? Did it properly address the aspirations of the indigenous inhabitants of these non-self-governing territories? What were the alternatives then? Should some form of trusteeship be re-established?

2. Western Sahara

a. Western Sahara
1975 I.C.J. 3, 4 (Oct. 16)

In December, 1974, the General Assembly in Resolution 3292 (XXIX) asked the International Court of Justice to render an opinion on the following questions:

I. Was Western Sahara (Rio de Oro and Sakiet El Hamra) at the time of colonization by Spain a territory belonging to no one *(terra nullius)*?

If the answer to the first question is in the negative,

II. What were the legal ties between this territory and the Kingdom of Morocco and the Mauritanian entity?

The background of the case is described succinctly in a separate opinion by Judge De Castro (1975 I.C.J. 12, 127 (Oct. 16)):

The ultimate origins of resolution 3292 (XXIX) of the United Nations General Assembly can be traced back to the determined activity of a most extraordinary personality, Si Allal El Fassi, to whom must be attributed Morocco's interest in the expansion of its frontiers. It would seem that, around 1956, Moroccans firmly believed that the Sherifian Kingdom did not extend beyond the Wad Dra'a. Government ministers were unaware even of the existence of the southern region of the Spanish Protectorate. El Fassi, on the other hand, even before Morocco's independence, was advocating the reconstitution of Greater Morocco, by claiming, on the basis of Morocco's historic rights, Mauritania, Rio de Oro, the Sakiet El Hamra, part of Algeria-Tindouf and Colomb-Béchar-and part of Mali. Speaking of what he had done, he boasted: "Originally, I was the only person to call for the liberation of the Sahara and I was greeted with laughter." He consid-

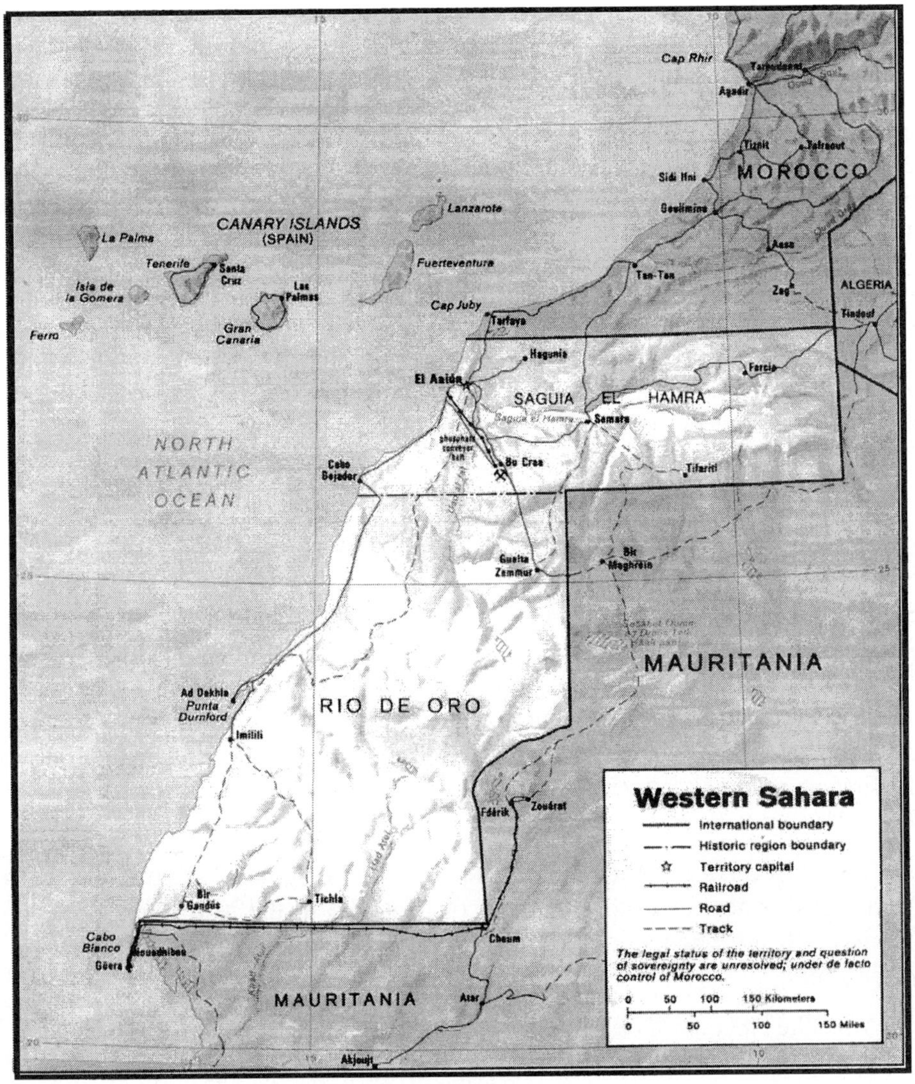

Available at: http://www.lib.utexas.edu/maps/africa/western_sahara_rel_1989.jpg
Courtesy of The General Libraries, The University of Texas at Austin.

ered those rights of Morocco over those territories as stronger than the will of the indigenous people. ...

It was on the basis of such alleged historic rights, - and similar arguments were to be used subsequently with respect to Western Sahara - that Morocco opposed in the United Nations the declaration of the independence of Mauritania. In the General Assembly, some States were in favour of Morocco's claims; others thought that the principle of self-determination of peoples was paramount. ...

The growing strength of the principle of self-determination duly had its effect upon the status of Western Sahara. Spain and the United Nations agreed to consider the territory as "non-self-governing" and thus subject to decolonization, which in pursuance of General Assembly resolution 2229 (XXI) of 20 December 1966 was to be by means of a referendum carried out on the basis of consultations between the administering Power, the Governments of Morocco and Mauritania and any other interested party.

From 1966, Morocco, too, expressed the wish that the Saharan regions should accede to independence. From then on, the policy of Morocco was to insist that the administering Power should grant independence to Western Sahara, and it voted for the General Assembly resolutions to that effect (those cited in General Assembly resolution 3292 (XXIX)). ...

But there was a further change. In his message to the Head of the Spanish State, His Majesty King Hassan II complained about Spain's "new policy in the Sahara" (A/9654). The policy announced by the Spanish Minister for Foreign Affairs-which was subsequently embodied in a communication to the Secretary-General of the United Nations-was that a decision had been taken to hold a referendum for the decolonization of the Sahara; the referendum was to be under the auspices of and supervised by the United Nations, and would be held during the first six months of 1975 on a date to be fixed sufficiently long in advance (A/9714, 21 August 1974).

The reaction of the King took the form of a letter, dated 23 September 1974, from the Minister for Foreign Affairs of Morocco to the Minister for Foreign Affairs of Spain. The letter reproduced the text of a statement made by the King to the Press:

> You, the Spanish Government, claim that the Sahara was *res nullius*; you claim that it was a territory or property left uninherited; you claim that no Power and no administration had been established over the Sahara; Morocco claims the contrary. Let us then request the arbitration of the International Court of justice. ... it will state the law of title and will then be able to enlighten the United Nations, enabling it to recommend to Morocco and Spain the course that they should follow.

The Moroccan Government accordingly presented to the Spanish Government a formal proposal:

> to submit this question jointly to the arbitration of the International Court of justice, in accordance with the spirit and the letter of Chapter VI of the United Nations Charter relating to the peaceful settlement of differences" (A/9771, 24 September 1974).

The Spanish Government did not reply; I do not know for what reason.

On 30 September 1974, Mr. Laraki, the representative of Morocco, in a statement to the General Assembly, said that the principle of self-determination was not always applicable in matters of decolonization; "for Morocco, the decolonization of the two Saharan provinces implied their reintegration into the Moroccan State" (A/PV.2249).

In Mr. Laraki's view, a dispute had existed between Morocco and Spain since 1956. To resolve it, he again proposed to submit to the Court the following questions:

> [W]ere the two Territories of the Sahara in question originally, as the Spanish Government claims, *'res nullius'* or Territories without a master, and open to occupation? Or were they at the moment of occupation under the sovereignty and administration of the Moroccan State?" (Ibid.)

If that direct method were not adopted, he added, there would remain the method of a request to the Court by the General Assembly for an advisory opinion. He commented: "The opinion given by the supreme international judicial body on a point of law could have just as considerable an effect as its arbitration." (Ibid.)

Mr. Laraki, following the lines laid down by the King, as formulated in the letter of 23 September 1974 and relying on the arguments put forward in the General Assembly, claimed the territory of Western Sahara on the grounds of Morocco's historic titles or ties. Thus no more was heard of the 11 other interested parties", and the right to self-determination of the indigenous population, which had appeared to be guaranteed by the Assembly's resolutions, was ignored.

The political understanding within the African group moderated the reaction against the Moroccan demands, but there was nevertheless a reaction -and a strong one-in favour of the principle of self-determination. ...

[The Court rendered the following opinion:]

54. The Charter of the United Nations, in Article 1, paragraph 2, indicates, as one of the purposes of the United Nations: "To develop friendly relations among nations based on respect for the principle of equal rights and self-determination of peoples . . " This purpose is further developed in Articles 55 and 56 of the Charter. Those provisions have direct and particular relevance for non-self-governing territories, which are dealt with in Chapter XI of the Charter. As the Court

stated in its Advisory Opinion of 21 June 1971 on The Legal Consequences for States of the Continued Presence of South Africa in Namibia (South West Africa) notwithstanding Security Council Resolution 276 (1970):

> [t]he subsequent development of international law in regard to non-self-governing territories, as enshrined in the Charter of the United Nations, made the principle of self-determination applicable to all of them" (I.C.J. Reports 1971, p. 31).

55. The principle of self-determination as a right of peoples, and its application for the purpose of bringing all colonial situations to a speedy end, were enunciated in the Declaration on the Granting of Independence to Colonial Countries and Peoples, General Assembly resolution 1514 (XV) [quoting Nos. 2, 5 and 6 of this resolution, and further citing, with approval, United Nations General Assembly resolutions 1541 and 2625]. …

59. The validity of the principle of self-determination, defined as the need to pay regard to the freely expressed will of peoples, is not affected by the fact that in certain cases the General Assembly has dispensed with the requirement of consulting the inhabitants of a given territory. Those instances were based either on the consideration that a certain population did not constitute a "people" entitled to self-determination or on the conviction that a consultation was totally unnecessary, in view of special circumstances. …

[The Court proceeded to review, in detail, the evolution of the General Assembly's view on the application of these principles to the territories in dispute; the Assembly consistently overrode "reminders by Morocco and Mauritania of their respective claims that Western Sahara constituted an integral part of their territory."]

70. In short, the decolonization process to be accelerated which is envisaged by the General Assembly in this provision is one which will respect the right of the population of Western Sahara to determine their future political status by their own freely expressed will. This right is not affected by the present request for an advisory opinion, nor by resolution 3292 (XXIX); on the contrary, it is expressly reaffirmed in that resolution. The right of that population to self-determination constitutes therefore a basic assumption of the questions put to the Court.

71. It remains to be ascertained whether the application of the right of self-determination to the decolonization of Western Sahara renders without object the two specific questions put to the Court. The Court has already concluded that the two questions must be considered in the whole context of the decolonization process. The right of self-determination leaves the General Assembly a measure of discretion with respect to the forms and procedures by which that right is to be realized. …

73. In any event, to what extent or degree its opinion will have an impact on the action of the General Assembly is not for the Court to decide. The function of the Court is to give an opinion based on law, once it has come to the conclusion

that the questions put to it are relevant and have a practical and contemporary effect and, consequently, are not devoid of object or purpose. ... [The Court proceeded to examine the question of whether the territory had been acquired by Spain before the critical date. Excerpts of the Court's discussion are set out in detail in Part Four, where we consider modes of acquisition of territory.]

76. [B]efore embarking on its examination of the questions, the Court has to determine what, for the purposes of the present Opinion, should be considered "the time of colonization by Spain". In this connection, it emphasizes that it is not here concerned to establish a. "critical date" in the sense given to this term in territorial disputes; for the questions do not ask the Court to adjudicate between conflicting legal titles to Western Sahara. It is here concerned only to identify the period of the historical context in which the request places the questions referred to the Court and the answers to be given to those questions.

77. In the view of the Court, for the purposes of the present Opinion, "the time of colonization by Spain" may be considered as the period beginning in 1884, when Spain proclaimed a protectorate over the Rio de Oro. It is true that Spain has mentioned certain earlier acts of alleged display of Spanish sovereignty in the fifteenth and sixteenth centuries. But it has explained that it did so only to enlighten the Court as to the remote antecedents of the Spanish presence on the west-African coast, and not to prove any continuity between those acts and "the time of colonization by Spain", which it conceded should be regarded as beginning in 1884. In any event, the information before the Court convinces it that the period beginning in 1884 represents "the time of colonization by Spain" of Western Sahara within the meaning of the request and constitutes the temporal context within which the two questions are placed by the terms of the request. ...

79. Turning to Question 1, the Court observes that the request specifically locates the question in the context of "the time of colonization by Spain", and it therefore seems clear that the words "Was Western Sahara a territory belonging to no one *(terra nullius)?"* have to be inter preted by reference to the law in force at that period. The expression *"terra nullius"* was a legal term of art employed in connection with "occupation" as one of the accepted legal methods of acquiring sovereignty over territory. "Occupation" being legally an original means of peaceably acquiring sovereignty over territory otherwise than by cession or succession, it was a cardinal condition of a valid "occupation" that the territory should be *terra nullius*-a territory belonging to no-one-at the time of the act alleged to constitute the "occupation" (cf. Legal Status of Eastern Greenland, P.C.I.J., Series A/B, No. 53, pp. 44f. and 63f.). In the view of the Court, therefore, a determination that Western Sahara was a *"terra nullius"* at the time of colonization by Spain would be possible only if it were established that at that time the territory belonged to no-one in the sense that it was then open to acquisition through the legal process of "occupation".

80. Whatever differences of opinion there may have been among jurists, the State practice of the relevant period indicates that territories inhabited by tribes

or peoples having a social and political organization were not regarded as *terrae nullius.* It shows that in the case of such territories the acquisition of sovereignty was not generally considered as effected unilaterally through "occupation" of *terra nullius* by original title but through agreements concluded with local rulers. On occasion, it is true, the word "occupation" was used in a non-technical sense denoting simply acquisition of sovereignty; but that did not signify that the acquisition of sovereignty through such agreements with authorities of the country was regarded as an "occupation" of a *"terra nullius"* in the proper sense of these terms. On the contrary, such agreements with local rulers, whether or not considered as an actual "cession" of the territory, were regarded as derivative roots of title, and not original titles obtained by occupation of *terrae nullius.*

81. In the present instance, the information furnished to the Court shows that at the time of colonization Western Sahara was inhabited by peoples which, if nomadic, were socially and politically organized in tribes and under chiefs competent to represent them. It also shows that, in colonizing Western Sahara, Spain did not proceed on the basis that it was establishing its sovereignty over *terrae nullius.* In its Royal Order of 26 December 1884, far from treating the case as one of occupation of *terra nullius,* Spain proclaimed that the King was taking the Rio de Oro under his protection on the basis of agreements which had been entered into with the chiefs of the local tribes: the Order referred expressly to "the documents which the independent tribes of this part of the coast" had "signed with the representative of the Sociedad Espaniola de Africanistas", and announced that the King had confirmed "the deeds of adherence" to Spain. Likewise, in negotiating with France concerning the limits of Spanish territory to the north of the Rio de Oro, that is, in the Sakiet El Hamra area, Spain did not rely upon any claim to the acquisition of sovereignty over a *terra nullius.*

82. Before the Court, differing views were expressed concerning the nature and legal value of agreements between a State and local chiefs. But the Court is not asked by Question I to pronounce upon the legal character or the legality of the titles which led to Spain becoming the administering Power of Western Sahara. It is asked only to state whether Western Sahara (Rio de Oro and Sakiet El Hamra) at the time of colonization by Spain was "a territory belonging to no one *(terra nullius)"*. As to this question, the Court is satisfied that, for the reasons which it has given, its answer must be in the negative. Accordingly, the Court does not find it necessary first to pronounce upon the correctness or otherwise of Morocco's view that the territory was not *terra nullius* at that time because the local tribes, so it maintains, were then subject to the sovereignty of the Sultan of Morocco; nor upon Mauritania's corresponding proposition that the territory was not *terra nullius* because the local tribes, in its view, then formed part of the "Bilad Shinguitti" or Mauritanian entity. Any conclusions that the Court may reach with respect to either of these points of view cannot change the negative character of the answer which, for other reasons already set out, it has found that it must give to Question 1.

83. The Court's answer to Question I is, therefore, in the negative and, in accordance with the terms of the request, it will now turn to Question II.

84. Question II asks the Court to state "what were the legal ties between this territory" - that is, Western Sahara - "and the kingdom of Morocco and the Mauritanian entity". The scope of this question depends upon the meaning to be attached to the expression "legal ties" in the context of the time of the colonization of the territory by Spain. That expression, however, unlike *"terra nullius"* in Question I, was not a term having in itself a very precise meaning. Accordingly, in the view of the Court, the meaning of the expression "legal ties" in Question II has to be found rather in the object and purpose of General Assembly resolution 3292 (XXIX), by which it was decided to request the present advisory opinion of the Court.

85. ... Accordingly, it appears to the Court that in Question II the words "legal ties between this territory and the Kingdom of Morocco and the Mauritanian entity" must be understood as referring to such "legal ties" as may affect the policy to be followed in the decolonization of Western Sahara. In this connection, the Court cannot accept the view that the legal ties the General Assembly had in mind in framing Question II were limited to ties established directly with the territory and without reference to the people who may be found in it. Such an interpretation would unduly restrict the scope of the question, since legal ties are normally established in relation to people. …

87. Western Sahara (Rio de Oro and Sakiet El Hamra) is a territory having very special characteristics which, at the time of colonization by Spain, largely determined the way of life and social and political organization of the peoples inhabiting it. In consequence, the legal regime of Western Sahara, including its legal relations with neighbouring territories, cannot properly be appreciated without reference to these special characteristics. The territory forms part of the great Sahara desert which extends from the Atlantic coast of Africa to Egypt and the Sudan. At the time of its colonization by Spain, the area of this desert with which the Court is concerned was being exploited, because of its low and spasmodic rainfall, almost exclusively by nomads, pasturing their animals or growing crops as and where conditions were favourable. It may be said that the territory, at the time of its colonization, had a sparse population that, for the most part, consisted of nomadic tribes the members of which traversed the desert on more or less regular routes dictated by the seasons and the wells or water-holes available to them. In general, the Court was informed, the right of pasture was enjoyed in common by these tribes; some areas suitable for cultivation, on the other hand, were subject to a greater degree to separate rights. Perennial water-holes were in principle considered the property of the tribe which put them into commission, though their use also was open to all, subject to certain customs as to priorities and the amount of water taken. Similarly, many tribes were said to have their recognized burial grounds, which constituted a rallying point for themselves and for allied tribes. Another feature of life in the region, according to the information before the Court, was that inter-tribal conflict was not infrequent.

88. These various points of attraction of a tribe to particular localities were reflected in its nomadic routes. But what is important for present purposes is the fact that the sparsity of the resources and the spasmodic character of the rainfall compelled all those nomadic tribes to traverse very wide areas of the desert. In consequence, the nomadic routes of none of them were confined to Western Sahara; some passed also through areas of southern Morocco, or of present-day Mauritania or Algeria, and some even through further countries. All the tribes were of the Islamic faith and the whole territory lay within the Dar al-Islam. In general, authority in the tribe was vested in a sheikh, subject to the assent of the "Juma'a", that is, of an assembly of its leading members, and the tribe had its own customary law applicable in conjunction with the Koranic law. Not infrequently one tribe had ties with another, either of dependence or of alliance, which were essentially tribal rather than territorial, ties of allegiance or vassalage.

89. It is in the context of such a territory and such a social and political organization of the population that the Court has to examine the question of the "legal ties" between Western Sahara and the Kingdom of Morocco and the Mauritanian entity at the time of colonization by Spain. At the conclusion of the oral proceedings, as will be seen, Morocco and Mauritania took up what was almost a common position on the answer to be given by the Court on Question II. The contentions on which they respectively base the legal ties which they claim to have had with Western Sahara at the time of its colonization by Spain are, however, different and in some degree opposed. The Court will, therefore, examine them separately.

90. Morocco's claim to "legal ties" with Western Sahara at the time of colonization by Spain has been put to the Court as a claim to ties of sovereignty on the ground of an alleged immemorial possession of the territory. This immemorial possession, it maintains, was based not on an isolated act of occupation but on the public display of sovereignty, uninterrupted and uncontested, for centuries.

91. In support of this claim Morocco refers to a series of events stretching back to the Arab conquest of North Africa in the seventh century A.D., the evidence of which is, understandably, for the most part taken from historical works. The far-flung, spasmodic and often transitory character of many of these events renders the historical material somewhat equivocal, as evidence of possession of the territory now in question. Morocco, however, invokes *inter alia* the decision of the Permanent Court of International justice in the Legal Status of Eastern Greenland case (P.C.I.J., Series A/B, No. 53). Stressing that during a long period Morocco was the only independent State which existed in the northwest of Africa, it points to the geographical contiguity of Western Sahara to Morocco and the desert character of the territory. In the light of these considerations, it maintains that the historical material suffices to establish Morocco's claim to a title based "upon continued display of authority" (op. cit., p. 45) on the same principles as those applied by the Permanent Court in upholding Denmark's claim to possession of the whole of Greenland.

92. This method of formulating Morocco's claims to ties of sovereignty with Western Sahara encounters certain difficulties. As the Permanent Court stated in the case concerning the Legal Status of Eastern Greenland, a claim to sovereignty based upon continued display of authority involves "two elements each of which must be shown to exist: the intention and will to act as sovereign, and some actual exercise or display of such authority" *(ibid.,* pp. 45f). True, the Permanent Court recognized that in the case of claims to sovereignty over areas in thinly populated or unsettled countries, "very little in the way of actual exercise of sovereign rights" (ibid., p. 46) might be sufficient in the absence of a competing claim. But, in the present instance, Western Sahara, if somewhat sparsely populated, was a territory across which socially and politically organized tribes were in constant movement and where armed incidents between these tribes were frequent. In the particular circumstances outlined in paragraphs 87 and 88 above, the paucity of evidence of actual display of authority unambiguously relating to Western Sahara renders it difficult to consider the Moroccan claim as on all fours with that of Denmark in the *Eastern Greenland* case. Nor is the difficulty cured by introducing the argument of geographical unity or contiguity. In fact, the information before the Court shows that the geographical unity of Western Sahara with Morocco is somewhat debatable, which also militates against giving effect to the concept of contiguity. Even if the geographical contiguity of Western Sahara with Morocco could be taken into account in the present connection, it would only make the paucity of evidence of unambiguous display of authority with respect to Western Sahara more difficult to reconcile with Morocco's claim to immemorial possession.

93. In the view of the Court, however, what must be of decisive importance in determining its answer to Question 11 is not indirect inferences drawn from events in past history but evidence directly relating to effective display of authority in Western Sahara at the time of its colonization by Spain and in the period immediately preceding that time (cf. Minquiers and Ecrehos, judgment, I.C.J. Reports 1953, p. 57). As Morocco has also adduced specific evidence relating to the time of colonization and the period preceding it, the Court will now consider that evidence.

94. Morocco requests that, in appreciating the evidence, the Court should take account of the special structure of the Sherifian State. No rule of international law, in the view of the Court, requires the structure of a State to follow any particular pattern, as is evident from the diversity of the forms of State found in the world today. Morocco's request is therefore justified. At the same time, where sovereignty over territory is claimed, the particular structure of a State may be a relevant element in appreciating the reality or otherwise of a display of State activity adduced as evidence of that sovereignty.

95. That the Sherifian State at the time of the Spanish colonization of Western Sahara was a State of a special character is certain. Its special character consisted in the fact that it was founded on the common religious bond of Islam existing among the peoples and on the allegiance of various tribes to the Sultan,

through their caids or sheikhs, rather than on the notion of territory. Common religious links have, of course, existed in many parts of the world without signifying a legal tie of sovereignty or subordination to a ruler. Even the Dar al-Islam, as Morocco itself pointed out in its oral statement, knows and then knew separate States within the common religious bond of Islam. Political ties of allegiance to a ruler, on the other hand, have frequently formed a major element in the composition of a State. Such an allegiance, however, if it is to afford indications of the ruler's sovereignty, must clearly be real and manifested in acts evidencing acceptance of his political authority. Otherwise, there will be no genuine display or exercise of State authority. It follows that the special character of the Moroccan State and the special forms in which its exercise of sovereignty may, in consequence, have expressed itself, do not dispense the Court from appreciating whether at the relevant time Moroccan sovereignty was effectively exercised or displayed in Western Sahara.

96. It has been stated before the Court, and not disputed in the course of the proceedings, that at the relevant period the Moroccan State consisted partly of what was called the Bled Makhzen, areas actually subject to the Sultan, and partly of what was called the Bled Siba, areas in which *de facto the* tribes were not submissive to the Sultan. Morocco states that the two expressions, Bled Makhzen and Bled Siba, merely described two types of relationship between the Moroccan local authorities and the central power, not a territorial separation; and that the existence of these different types did not affect the unity of Morocco. Because of a common cultural heritage, the spiritual authority of the Sultan was always accepted. Thus the difference between the Bled Makhzen and the Bled Siba, Morocco maintains, did not reflect a wish to challenge the existence of the central power so much as the conditions for the exercise of that power; and the Bled Siba was, in practice, a way of affecting an administrative decentralization of authority. Against this view it is stated that what characterized the Bled Siba was that it was not administered by the Makhzen; it did not contribute contingents to the Sherifian army; no taxes were collected there by the Makhzen- the government of the people was in the hands of caids appointed by the tribes, and their powers were derived more from the acquiescence of the tribes than from any delegation of authority by the Sultan; even if these local powers did not totally reject any connection with the Sherifian State, in reality they became *de facto* independent powers. It is also said that the historical evidence shows the territory between the Souss and the Dra'a to have been in a state of permanent insubordination and part of the Bled Siba; and that this implies that there was no effective and continuous display of State functions even in those areas to the north of Western Sahara. In the present proceedings, it has been common ground between Mauritania, Morocco and Spain that the Bled Siba was considered as forming part of the Moroccan State at that time, as also appears from the information before the Court.

97. That the areas immediately to the north of Western Sahara lay within the Bled Siba at the relevant period is a point which does not appear to be in dispute.

This is accordingly an element to be taken into consideration in appreciating the material which has been submitted regarding the alleged display of Moroccan authority in Western Sahara itself.

98. As evidence of its display of sovereignty in Western Sahara, Morocco has invoked alleged acts of internal display of Moroccan authority and also certain international acts said to constitute recognition by other States of its sovereignty over the whole or part of the territory.

99. The principal indications of "internal" display of authority invoked by Morocco consist of evidence alleged to show the allegiance of Saharan caids to the Sultan, including dahirs and other documents concerning the appointment of caids, the alleged imposition of Koranic and other taxes, and what were referred to as "military decisions" said to constitute acts of resistance to foreign penetration of the territory. In particular, the allegiance is claimed of the confederation of Tekna tribes, together with its allies, one part of which was stated to be established in the Noun and another part to lead a nomadic life the route of which traversed areas of Western Sahara: through Tekna caids, Morocco claims, the Sultan's authority and influence were exercised on the nomad tribes pasturing in Western Sahara. Moreover, Morocco alleges that, after the marabout Ma ul-'Aineen established himself at Smara in the Sakiet El Hamra in the late 1890s, much of the territory came under the direct authority of this sheikh, and that he himself was the personal representative of the Sultan. Emphasis is also placed by Morocco on two visits of Sultan Hassan I in person to the southern area of the Souss in 1882 and 1886 to maintain and strengthen his authority in the southern part of his realm, and on the despatch of arms by the Sultan to Ma ul-'Aineen and others in the south to reinforce their resistance to foreign penetration. In general, it is urged that Western Sahara has always been linked to the interior of Morocco by common ethnological, cultural and religious ties, and that the Sakiet El Hamra was artificially separated from the Moroccan territory of the Noun by colonization.

100. Spain, on the other hand, maintains that there is a striking absence of any documentary evidence or other traces of a display of political authority by Morocco with respect to Western Sahara. The acts of appointment of caids produced by Morocco, whether dahirs or official correspondence, do not in Spain's view relate to Western Sahara but to areas within southern Morocco such as the Noun and the Dra'a; nor has any document of acceptance by the recipients been adduced. Furthermore, according to Spain, these alleged appointments as caid were conferred on sheikhs already elected by their own tribes and were, in truth, only titles of honour bestowed on existing and *de facto* independent local rulers. As to the Tekna confederation, its two parts are said to have been in quite different relations to the Sultan: only the settled Tekna, established in southern Morocco, acknowledged their political allegiance to the Sultan, while the nomadic septs of the tribe who traversed the Western Sahara were "free" Tekna, autonomous and independent of the Sultan. Nor was Ma ul-'Aineen, according to Spain, at any time the personal representative of the Sultan's authority in Western Sa-

hara; on the contrary, he exercised his authority to the south of the Dra'a in complete independence of the Sultan; his relations with the Sultan were based on mutual respect and a common interest in resisting French expansion from the south; they were relations of equality, not political ties of allegiance or of sovereignty.

101. Further, Spain invokes the absence of any evidence of the payment of taxes by tribes of Western Sahara and denies all possibility of such evidence being adduced; according to Spain, it was a characteristic even of the Bled Siba that the tribes refused to be taxed, and in Western Sahara there was no question of taxes having been paid to the Makhzen. As to the Sultan's expeditions of 1882 and 1886, these, according to Spain, are shown by the historical evidence never to have reached Western Sahara or even the Dra'a, but only the Souss and the Noun; nor did they succeed in completely subjecting even those areas; and they cannot therefore constitute evidence of display of authority with respect to Western Sahara. Their purpose, Spain maintains, was to prevent commerce between Europeans and the tribes of the Souss and Noun, and this purpose was unrelated to Western Sahara. Again, the alleged acts of resistance in Western Sahara to foreign penetration are said by Spain to have been nothing more than occasional raids to obtain booty or hostages for ransom and to have nothing to do with display of Moroccan authority. In general, both on geographical and on other grounds, Spain questions the unity of the Saharan region with the regions of southern Morocco.

102. Mauritania's views, in so far as they relate to Morocco's pretensions to have exercised sovereignty over Western Sahara at the time of its colonization, may be summarized as follows: Mauritania does not oppose Morocco's claim to have displayed its authority in some, more northerly, areas of the territory. Thus it does not dispute the allegiance at that time of the Tekna confederation to the Sultan, nor Morocco's claim that, through the intermediary of Tekna caids in southern Morocco, it exercised a measure of authority over Tekna nomads who traversed those areas of Western Sahara. Mauritania does not, however, admit the allegiance of other tribes in Western Sahara to the Sultan, as it considers them to belong to the Bilad Shinguitti, or Mauritanian entity. In particular, like Spain, it maintains that the Regheibat were a tribe of marabout warriors wholly independent of both the Tekna caids and the Sultan, and that their links were rather with the tribes of the Bilad Shinguitti. Again, Mauritania does not admit that the marabout sheikh, Ma ul-'Aineen, represented the authority of the Sultan in Western Sahara. Instead, it insists that he was a Shinguitti personality, who acquired influence and renown as head of a religious brotherhood in the Bilad Shinguitti and also became a political figure in the Sakiet El Hamra in the later stages of his life. Like Spain also, Mauritania maintains that, as a political figure organizing and leading resistance to French penetration, Ma ul-'Aineen dealt with the Sultan on a basis of co-operation between equals; and that the relation between them was not one of allegiance but of an alliance, lasting only until the time came when the sheikh proclaimed himself Sultan.

103. The Court does not overlook the position of the Sultan of Morocco as a religious leader. In the view of the Court, however, the information and arguments invoked by Morocco cannot, for the most part, be considered as disposing of the difficulties in the way of its claim to have exercised effectively internal sovereignty over Western Sahara. The material before the Court appears to support the view that almost all the dahirs and other acts concerning caids relate to areas situated within present-day Morocco itself and do not in themselves provide evidence of effective display of Moroccan authority in Western Sahara. Nor can the information furnished by Morocco be said to provide convincing evidence of the imposition or levying of Moroccan taxes with respect to the territory. As to Sheikh Ma ul-'Aineen, the complexities of his career may leave doubts as to the precise nature of his relations with the Sultan, and different interpretations have been put upon them. The material before the Court, taken as a whole does not suffice to convince it that the activities of this sheikh should be considered as having constituted a display of the Sultan's authority in Western Sahara at the time of its colonization.

104. Furthermore, the information before the Court appears to confirm that the expeditions of Sultan Hassan I to the south in 1882 and 1886 both had objects specifically directed to the Souss and the Noun and, in fact, did not go beyond the Noun; so that they did not reach even as far as the Dra'a, still less Western Sahara. Nor does the material furnished lead the Court to conclude that the alleged acts of resistance in Western Sahara to foreign penetration could be considered as acts of the Moroccan State. Similarly, the despatch of arms by the Sultan to Ma ul-'Aineen and others to encourage their resistance to French penetration to the east of Western Sahara is, in any case, open to other interpretations than the display of the Sultan's authority. Again, although Morocco asserts that the Regheibat tribe always recognized the suzerainty of the Tekna confederation, and through them that of the Sultan himself, this assertion has not been supported by any convincing evidence. Moreover, both Spain and Mauritania insist that this tribe of marabout warriors was wholly independent.

105. Consequently, the information before the Court does not support Morocco's claim to have exercised territorial sovereignty over Western Sahara. On the other hand, it does not appear to exclude the possibility that the Sultan displayed authority over some of the tribes in Western Sahara. That this was so with regard to the Regheibat or other independent tribes living in the territory could clearly not be sustained. The position is different, however, with regard to the septs of the Tekna whose routes of migration are established as having included the territory of the Tekna caids within Morocco as well as parts of Western Sahara. True, the territory of the Tekna caids in the Noun and the Dra'a were Bled Siba at the relevant period and the subordination of the Tekna caids to the Sultan was sometimes uncertain. But the fact remains that the Noun and the Dra'a were recognized to be part of the Sherifian State and the Tekna caids to represent the authority of the Sultan. No doubt, as appears from previous paragraphs, the allegiance of the nomadic septs of the Tekna to the Tekna confedera-

tion has been in dispute in the present proceedings. The mere fact that those Tekna septs in their nomadic journeys spent periods of time within the territory of the caids of the Tekna confederation appears, however, to the Court to lend support to the view that they were subject, at least in some measure, to the authority of Tekna caids.

The Court at the same time notes that Mauritania considers these Tekna septs to have been in "Moroccan fealty".

106. Furthermore, the material before the Court contains various indications of some projection of the Sultan's authority to certain Tekna tribes or septs nomadizing in Western Sahara. Such indications are, for example, to be found in certain documents relating to the recovery of shipwrecked seamen and other foreigners held captive by Teknas in Western Sahara; in documents showing that on some occasions, notably the Sultan's visits to the south in 1882 and 1886, he received the allegiance of certain nomadic tribes which came from Western Sahara for the purpose; and in letters from the Sultan to Tekna caids requesting the performance of certain acts to the South of the Noun and the Dra'a. Accordingly, and after taking due account of any contradictory indications, the Court considers that, taken as a whole, the information before it shows the display of some authority by the Sultan, through Tekna caids, over the Tekna septs nomadizing in Western Sahara. . . .

129. The inferences to be drawn from the information before the Court concerning internal acts of Moroccan sovereignty and from that concerning international acts are, therefore, in accord in not providing indications of the existence, at the relevant period of any legal tie of territorial sovereignty between Western Sahara and the Moroccan State. At the same time, they are in accord in providing indications of a legal tie of allegiance between the Sultan and some, though only some, of the tribes of the territory, and in providing indications of some display of the Sultan's authority or influence with respect to those tribes. ...

[The review of Mauritanian claims is omitted.]

162. The materials and information presented to the Court show the existence, at the time of Spanish colonization, of legal ties of allegiance between the Sultan of Morocco and some of the tribes living in the territory of Western Sahara. They equally show the existence of rights, including some rights relating to the land, which constituted legal ties between the Mauritanian entity, as understood by the Court, and the territory of Western Sahara. On the other hand, the Court's conclusion is that the materials and information presented to it do not establish any tie of territorial sovereignty between the territory of Western Sahara and the Kingdom of Morocco or the Mauritanian entity. Thus the Court has not found legal ties of such a nature as might affect the application of resolution 1514 (XV) in the decolonization of Western Sahara and, in particular, of the principle of self-determination through the free and genuine expression of the will of the peoples of the Territory.

Notes and Questions

1. Spain had been the Western Sahara's colonial power since 1884. The United Nations first demanded a referendum on self-determination in 1965; the Organization of African Unity (OAU) echoed this request in 1972. Spain's attempt to hold the referendum in 1974 was interrupted when the U.N. General Assembly asked the International Court of Justice for the advisory opinion excerpted *supra*. Even though the World Court rejected both Morocco's and Mauritania's claims to pre-colonial territorial sovereignty over the area and upheld the Saharauis' right to self-determination, King Hassan of Morocco interpreted the ruling as an affirmation of Morocco's own claims and launched the so-called "Green March" of 350,000 Moroccans into the disputed territory.

On February 26, 1976, Spain ceded administrative control over the area to Morocco and Mauritania, in accordance with the terms of the Madrid Accords of November, 1975. The Frente Popular para la Liberación de Saguia el-Hamra y de Río de Oro (Polisario), founded in 1973 by Saharaui nationalists to liberate the territory from the Spanish, now shifted, mostly from Algerian territory, to a diplomatic and guerrilla war offensive against the Moroccan and Mauritanian troops. On February 27, 1976, Polisario proclaimed Western Sahara an independent state, named the Saharaui Arab Democratic Republic (SADR). In the first years after the occupation, Morocco and Mauritania suffered some severe military defeats. After a military coup in Mauritania, this country, on August 10, 1979, signed a peace agreement with the Polisario in Algiers. In this agreement, Mauritania renounced all "territorial or any other claims over Western Sahara" and "decide[d] to withdraw from the unjust war in the Western Sahara." Following that withdrawal, Morocco took over the sectors previously held by Mauritania.

In 1979, the U.N. General Assembly recognized the Polisario as the representative of the Saharaui people, and, in 1980, urged Morocco to begin negotiations with Polisario. In 1983, the OAU exhorted Morocco and the Polisario to undertake direct negotiations with a view to bringing about a cease-fire to create the necessary conditions for a peaceful and fair referendum of self-determination of the people of Western Sahara. Failing Morocco's compliance, the SADR was admitted to membership of the OAU in 1984. In reaction, Morocco withdrew from the OAU, and the conflict moved to the arena of the United Nations. The U.N. General Assembly lent its support to the OAU's plan for direct negotiations, a cease-fire, an interim administration in the occupied territory, and a referendum in the Western Sahara without any administrative or military constraints under the auspices of the OAU and the U.N. G.A. Res. 50, U.N. GAOR, 40th Sess., Supp. No. 53, at 268-69, U.N. Doc. A/40/53 (1985).

Pressure on Morocco mounted, and in August 1988, King Hassan agreed to a peace plan offered by then-United Nations Secretary-General Javier Perez de Cuellar. In accordance with his "settlement proposals", as accepted on 30 August 1988 by Morocco and the Polisario , the United Nations established the United Nations Mission for the Referendum in Western Sahara (MINURSO) in order to monitor a ceasefire, verify the reduction of Moroccan troops in Western Sahara, monitor the confinement of Moroccan and Polisario troops to designated locations, ensure the release of all Western Saharan political prisoners or detainees, oversee the exchange of prisoners of war, implement the repatriation program, identify and register qualified voters, organize and ensure a free and fair referendum and proclaim the results. At the time of this writing, however, the referendum has not been held – allegedly due to Morocco's dilatory tactics and crucial controversies over voter eligibility. Several U.N. officials and international legal commentators have said privately that the referendum is unlikely to be held in the foreseeable future. For further details, *see* Yahia H. Zoubir, *The Western Sahara Conflict: A Case Study in Failure of Pre-Negotiation and Prolongation of Conflict,* 26 Cal. W. Int'l L.J. 173 (1996); Tony Hodges, Western Sahara: The Roots of a Desert War (Lawrence Hill & Co. 1983); and I. William Zartman, Ripe for Resolution: Conflict and Intervention in Africa (Oxford U. Press 1985); Yahia H. Zoubir & Daniel Volman, International Dimensions of the Western Sahara Conflict (Praeger Publishers 1993);Akbarali Thobhani, Western Sahara Since 1975 Under Moroccan Administration: Social, Economic and Political Transformation (North African Studies, 1) (Edwin Mellen Press 2002).

2. Are there relevant distinguishing factors between the Saharauis' claim to self-determination and Morocco's claim to independence from its "protective" power, France? *See* Thomas M. Franck, *The Stealing of the Sahara,* 70 AM. J. INT'L L. 694 (1976); B.O. Okere, *The Western Sahara Case,* 28 INT'L & COMP. L. Q. 296 (1979); J.F. Prévost, *Observations sur l'avis consultatif de la Cour internationale de Justice relatif au Sahara occidental ("terra nullius" et autodétermination),* 103 CLUNET 813 (1976).

3. In July 2000, the Assembly of the OAU adopted the Constitutive Act of the African Union (AV), thereby terminating the prior organization. *See* NSONGURUA J. UDOMBANA, *The Unfinished Business: Conflicts, The African Union and the New Partnership for Africa's Development*, 35 GEO. WASH. INT'L L. REV. 55 (2003).

3. East Timor

a. Case Concerning East Timor (Port. v. Austl.)

1995 I.C.J. 90 (June 30)

11. The Territory of East Timor corresponds to the eastern part of the island of Timor; it includes the island of Atauro, 25 kilometres to the north, the islet of Jaco to the east, and the enclave of Oe-Cusse in the western part of the island of Timor. Its capital is Dili, situated on its north coast. The south coast of East Timor lies opposite the north coast of Australia, the distance between them being approximately 430 kilometres.

In the sixteenth century, East Timor became a colony of Portugal; Portugal remained there until 1975. The western part of the island came under Dutch rule and later became part of independent Indonesia.

12. In resolution 1542(XV) of 15 December 1960 the United Nations General Assembly recalled "differences of views ... concerning the status of certain territories under the administrations of Portugal and Spain and described by these two States as 'overseas provinces' of the metropolitan State concerned"; and it also stated that it considered that the territories under the administration of Portugal, which were listed therein (including "Timor and dependencies") were non-self-governing territories within the meaning of Chapter XI of the Charter. Portugal, in the wake of its "Carnation Revolution", accepted this position in 1974.

13. Following internal disturbances in East Timor, on 27 August 1975 the Portuguese civil and military authorities withdrew from the mainland of East Timor to the island of Atauro. On 7 December 1975 the armed forces of Indonesia intervened in East Timor. On 8 December 1975 the Portuguese authorities departed from the island of Atauro, and thus left East Timor altogether. Since their departure, Indonesia has occupied the Territory, and the Parties acknowledge that the Territory has remained under the effective control of that State. Asserting that on 31 May 1976 the people of East Timor had requested Indonesia "to accept East Timor as an integral part of the Republic of Indonesia", on 17 July 1976 Indonesia enacted a law incorporating the Territory as part of its national territory.

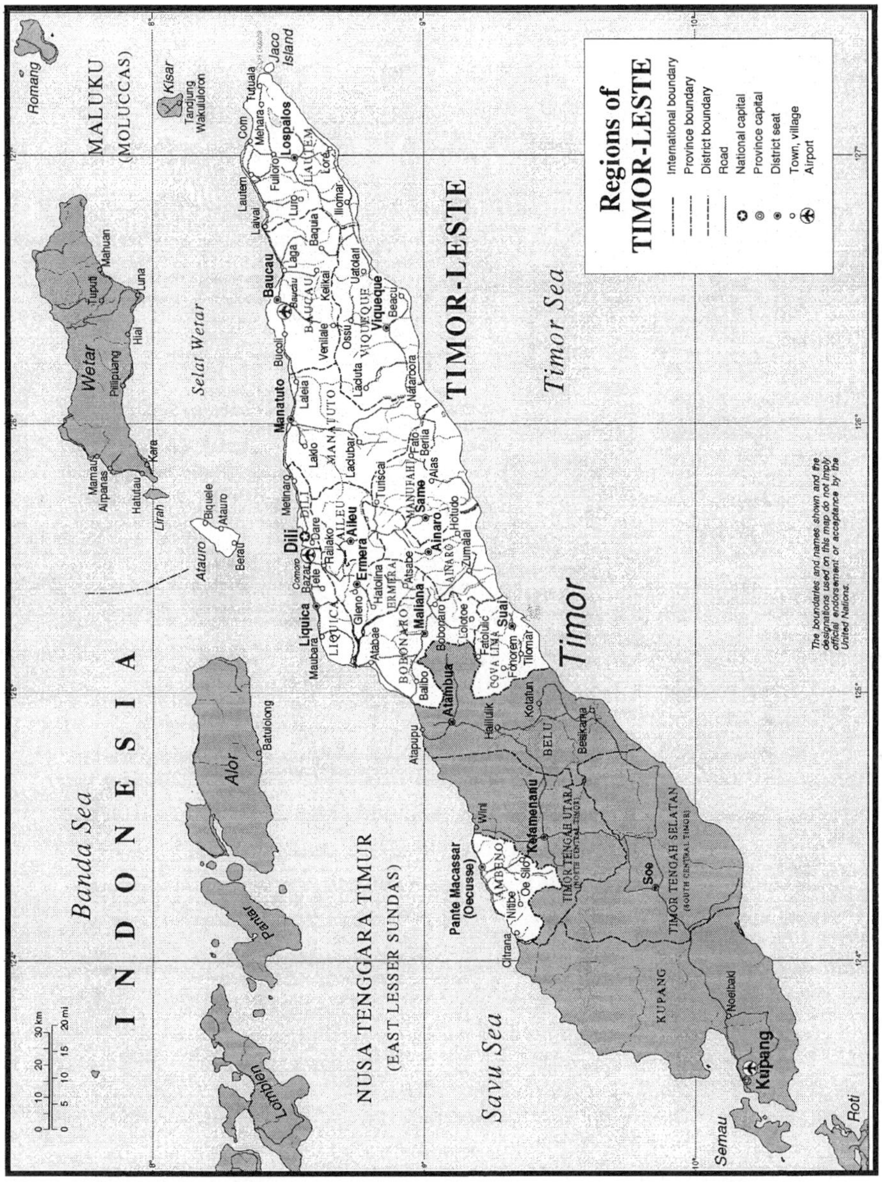

United Nations Map, DEPARTMENT OF PUBLIC INFORMATION, CARTOGRAPHIC SECTION
Map No. 4111 Rev.1 June 1999: East Timor Province

14. Following the intervention of the armed forces of Indonesia in the Territory and the withdrawal of the Portuguese authorities, the question of East Timor became the subject of two resolutions of the Security Council and of eight resolutions of the General Assembly, namely, Security Council resolutions 384 (1975) of 22 December 1975 and 389 (1976) of 22 April 1976, and General Assembly resolutions 3485(XXX) of 12 December 1975, 31/53 of 1 December 1976, 32/34 of 28 November 1977, 33/39 of 13 December 1978, 34/40 of 21 November 1979, 35/27 of 11 November 1980, 36/50 of 24 November 1981 and 37/30 of 23 November 1982.

15. Security Council resolution 384 (1975) of 22 December 1975 called upon "all States to respect the territorial integrity of East Timor as well as the inalienable right of its people to self-determination"; called upon "the Government of Indonesia to withdraw without delay all its forces from the Territory"; and further called upon

> the Government of Portugal as administering Power to co-operate fully with the United Nations so as to enable the people of East Timor to exercise freely their right to self-determination.

Security Council resolution 389 (1976) of 22 April 1976 adopted the same terms with regard to the right of the people of East Timor to self-determination; called upon "the Government of Indonesia to withdraw without further delay all its forces from the Territory"; and further called upon "all States and other parties concerned to co-operate fully with the United Nations to achieve a peaceful solution to the existing situation ...".

General Assembly resolution 3485(XXX) of 12 December 1975 referred to Portugal "as the administering Power"; called upon it "to continue to make every effort to find a solution by peaceful means"; and "strongly deplore[d] the military intervention of the armed forces of Indonesia in Portuguese Timor". In resolution 31/53 of 1 December 1976, and again in resolution 32/34 of 28 November 1977, the General Assembly rejected

> the claim that East Timor has been incorporated into Indonesia, inasmuch as the people of the Territory have not been able to exercise freely their right to self-determination and independence.

Security Council resolution 389 (1976) of 22 April 1976 and General Assembly resolutions 31/53 of 1 December 1976, 32/34 of 28 November 1977 and 33/39 of 13 December 1978 made no reference to Portugal as the administering Power. Portugal is so described, however, in Security Council resolution 384 (1975) of 22 December 1975 and in the other resolutions of the General Assembly. Also, those resolutions which did not specifically refer to Portugal as the administering Power recalled another resolution or other resolutions which so referred to it.

16. No further resolutions on the question of East Timor have been passed by the Security Council since 1976 or by the General Assembly since 1982. However, the Assembly has maintained the item on its agenda since 1982, while de-

ciding at each session, on the recommendation of its General Committee, to defer consideration of it until the following session. East Timor also continues to be included in the list of non-self-governing territories within the meaning of Chapter XI of the Charter; and the Special Committee on the Situation with Regard to the Implementation of the Declaration on the Granting of Independence to Colonial Countries and Peoples remains seised of the question of East Timor. The Secretary-General of the United Nations is also engaged in a continuing effort, in consultation with all parties directly concerned, to achieve a comprehensive settlement of the problem.

17. The incorporation of East Timor as part of Indonesia was recognized by Australia de facto on 20 January 1978. On that date the Australian Minister for Foreign Affairs stated: "The Government has made clear publicly its opposition to the Indonesian intervention and has made this known to the Indonesian Government." He added: "[Indonesia's] control is effective and covers all major administrative centres of the territory." And further:

> This is a reality with which we must come to terms. Accordingly, the Government has decided that although it remains critical of the means by which integration was brought about it would be unrealistic to continue to refuse to recognize de facto that East Timor is part of Indonesia.

On 23 February 1978 the Minister said: "we recognize the fact that East Timor is part of Indonesia, but not the means by which this was brought about".

On 15 December 1978 the Australian Minister for Foreign Affairs declared that negotiations which were about to begin between Australia and Indonesia for the delimitation of the continental shelf between Australia and East Timor, "when they start, will signify *de jure* recognition by Australia of the Indonesian incorporation of East Timor"; he added: "The acceptance of this situation does not alter the opposition which the Government has consistently expressed regarding the manner of incorporation." The negotiations in question began in February 1979.

18. Prior to this, Australia and Indonesia had, in 1971-1972, established a delimitation of the continental shelf between their respective coasts; the delimitation so effected stopped short on either side of the continental shelf between the south coast of East Timor and the north coast of Australia. This undelimited part of the continental shelf was called the "Timor Gap".

The delimitation negotiations which began in February 1979 between Australia and Indonesia related to the Timor Gap; they did not come to fruition. Australia and Indonesia then turned to the possibility of establishing a provisional arrangement for the joint exploration and exploitation of the resources of an area of the continental shelf. A Treaty to this effect was eventually concluded between them on 11 December 1989, whereby a "Zone of Cooperation" was created "in an area between the Indonesian Province of East Timor and Northern Australia". Australia enacted legislation in 1990 with a view to implementing the Treaty; this law came into force in 1991.

19. In these proceedings Portugal maintains that Australia, in negotiating and concluding the 1989 Treaty, in initiating performance of the Treaty, in taking internal legislative measures for its application, and in continuing to negotiate with Indonesia, has acted unlawfully, in that it has infringed the rights of the people of East Timor to self-determination and to permanent sovereignty over its natural resources, infringed the rights of Portugal as the administering Power, and contravened Security Council resolutions 384 and 389. Australia raised objections to the jurisdiction of the Court and to the admissibility of the Application. It took the position, however, that these objections were inextricably linked to the merits and should therefore be determined within the framework of the merits. The Court heard the Parties both on the objections and on the merits. While Australia concentrated its main arguments and submissions on the objections, it also submitted that Portugal's case on the merits should be dismissed, maintaining, in particular, that its actions did not in any way disregard the rights of Portugal.

20. According to one of the objections put forward by Australia, there exists in reality no dispute between itself and Portugal. In another objection, it argued that Portugal's Application would require the Court to rule on the rights and obligations of a State which is not a party to the proceedings, namely Indonesia. According to further objections of Australia, Portugal lacks standing to bring the case, the argument being that it does not have a sufficient interest of its own to institute the proceedings, notwithstanding the references to it in some of the resolutions of the Security Council and the General Assembly as the administering Power of East Timor, and that it cannot, furthermore, claim any right to represent the people of East Timor; its claims are remote from reality, and the judgment the Court is asked to give would be without useful effect; and finally, its claims concern matters which are essentially not legal in nature which should be resolved by negotiation within the framework of ongoing procedures before the political organs of the United Nations. Portugal requested the Court to dismiss all these objections.

21. The Court will now consider Australia's objection that there is in reality no dispute between itself and Portugal. Australia contends that the case as presented by Portugal is artificially limited to the question of the lawfulness of Australia's conduct, and that the true respondent is Indonesia, not Australia. Australia maintains that it is being sued in place of Indonesia. In this connection, it points out that Portugal and Australia have accepted the compulsory jurisdiction of the Court under Article 36, paragraph 2, of its Statute, but that Indonesia has not.

In support of the objection, Australia contends that it recognizes, and has always recognized, the right of the people of East Timor to self-determination, the status of East Timor as a non-self-governing territory, and the fact that Portugal has been named by the United Nations as the administering Power of East Timor; that the arguments of Portugal, as well as its submissions, demonstrate that Portugal does not challenge the capacity of Australia to conclude the 1989 Treaty and that it does not contest the validity of the Treaty; and that consequently there is in reality no dispute between itself and Portugal.

Portugal, for its part, maintains that its Application defines the real and only dispute submitted to the Court.

22. The Court recalls that, in the sense accepted in its jurisprudence and that of its predecessor, a dispute is a disagreement on a point of law or fact, a conflict of legal views or interests between parties (see Mavrommatis Palestine Concessions, Judgment No. 2, 1924, P.C.I.J., Series A, No. 2, p. 11; Northern Cameroons, Judgment, I.C.J. Reports 1963, p. 27; and Applicability of the Obligation to Arbitrate under Section 21 of the United Nations Headquarters Agreement of 26 June 1947, Advisory Opinion, I.C.J. Reports 1988, p. 27, para. 35). In order to establish the existence of a dispute, "It must be shown that the claim of one party is positively opposed by the other" (South West Africa, Preliminary Objections, Judgment, I.C.J. Reports 1962, p. 328); and further, "Whether there exists an international dispute is a matter for objective determination" (Interpretation of Peace Treaties with Bulgaria, Hungary and Romania, First Phase, Advisory Opinion, I.C.J. Reports 1950, p. 74).

For the purpose of verifying the existence of a legal dispute in the present case, it is not relevant whether the "real dispute" is between Portugal and Indonesia rather than Portugal and Australia. Portugal has, rightly or wrongly, formulated complaints of fact and law against Australia which the latter has denied. By virtue of this denial, there is a legal dispute.

On the record before the Court, it is clear that the Parties are in disagreement, both on the law and on the facts, on the question whether the conduct of Australia in negotiating, concluding and initiating performance of the 1989 Treaty was in breach of an obligation due by Australia to Portugal under international law.

Indeed, Portugal's Application limits the proceedings to these questions. There nonetheless exists a legal dispute between Portugal and Australia. This objection of Australia must therefore be dismissed.

23. The Court will now consider Australia's principal objection, to the effect that Portugal's Application would require the Court to determine the rights and obligations of Indonesia. The declarations made by the Parties under Article 36, paragraph 2, of the Statute do not include any limitation which would exclude Portugal's claims from the jurisdiction thereby conferred upon the Court. Australia, however, contends that the jurisdiction so conferred would not enable the Court to act if, in order to do so, the Court were required to rule on the lawfulness of Indonesia's entry into and continuing presence in East Timor, on the validity of the 1989 Treaty between Australia and Indonesia, or on the rights and obligations of Indonesia under that Treaty, even if the Court did not have to determine its validity. Portugal agrees that if its Application required the Court to decide any of these questions, the Court could not entertain it. The Parties disagree, however,

as to whether the Court is required to decide any of these questions in order to resolve the dispute referred to it.

24. Australia argues that the decision sought from the Court by Portugal would inevitably require the Court to rule on the lawfulness of the conduct of a third State, namely Indonesia, in the absence of that State's consent. In support of its argument, it cites the Judgment in the case concerning Monetary Gold Removed from Rome in 1943, in which the Court ruled that, in the absence of Albania's consent, it could not take any decision on the international responsibility of that State since "Albania's legal interests would not only be affected by a decision, but would form the very subject- matter of the decision" (I.C.J. Reports 1954, p. 32).

25. In reply, Portugal contends, first, that its Application is concerned exclusively with the objective conduct of Australia, which consists in having negotiated, concluded and initiated performance of the 1989 Treaty with Indonesia, and that this question is perfectly separable from any question relating to the lawfulness of the conduct of Indonesia. According to Portugal, such conduct of Australia in itself constitutes a breach of its obligation to treat East Timor as a non-self-governing territory and Portugal as its administering Power; and that breach could be passed upon by the Court by itself and without passing upon the rights of Indonesia. The objective conduct of Australia, considered as such, constitutes the only violation of international law of which Portugal complains.

26. The Court recalls in this respect that one of the fundamental principles of its Statute is that it cannot decide a dispute between States without the consent of those States to its jurisdiction. This principle was reaffirmed in the Judgment given by the Court in the case concerning Monetary Gold Removed from Rome in 1943 and confirmed in several of its subsequent decisions (see Continental Shelf (Libyan Arab Jamahiriya/Malta), Application for Permission to Intervene, Judgment, I.C.J. Reports 1984, p. 25, para. 40; Military and Paramilitary Activities in and against Nicaragua (Nicaragua v. United States of America), Jurisdiction and Admissibility, Judgment, I.C.J. Reports 1984, p. 431, para. 88; Frontier Dispute (Burkina Faso/Republic of Mali), Judgment, I.C.J. Reports 1986, p. 579, para. 49; Land, Island and Maritime Frontier Dispute (El Salvador/Honduras), Application to Intervene, Judgment, I.C.J. Reports 1990, pp. 114-116, paras. 54-56, and p. 112, para. 73; and Certain Phosphate Lands in Nauru (Nauru v. Australia), Preliminary Objections, Judgment, I.C.J. Reports 1992, pp. 259-262, paras. 50-55).

27. The Court notes that Portugal's claim that, in entering into the 1989 Treaty with Indonesia, Australia violated the obligation to respect Portugal's status as administering Power and that of East Timor as a non-self-governing territory, is based on the assertion that Portugal alone, in its capacity as administering Power, had the power to enter into the Treaty on behalf of East Timor; that Australia disregarded this exclusive power, and, in so doing, violated its obligations to respect the status of Portugal and that of East Timor.

The Court also observes that Australia, for its part, rejects Portugal's claim to the exclusive power to conclude treaties on behalf of East Timor, and the very fact that it entered into the 1989 Treaty with Indonesia shows that it considered that Indonesia had that power. Australia in substance argues that even if Portugal had retained that power, on whatever basis, after withdrawing from East Timor, the possibility existed that the power could later pass to another State under general international law, and that it did so pass to Indonesia; Australia affirms moreover that, if the power in question did pass to Indonesia, it was acting in conformity with international law in entering into the 1989 Treaty with that State, and could not have violated any of the obligations Portugal attributes to it. Thus, for Australia, the fundamental question in the present case is ultimately whether, in 1989, the power to conclude a treaty on behalf of East Timor in relation to its continental shelf lay with Portugal or with Indonesia.

28. The Court has carefully considered the argument advanced by Portugal which seeks to separate Australia's behaviour from that of Indonesia. However, in the view of the Court, Australia's behaviour cannot be assessed without first entering into the question why it is that Indonesia could not lawfully have concluded the 1989 Treaty, while Portugal allegedly could have done so; the very subject-matter of the Court's decision would necessarily be a determination whether, having regard to the circumstances in which Indonesia entered and remained in East Timor, it could or could not have acquired the power to enter into treaties on behalf of East Timor relating to the resources of its continental shelf. The Court could not make such a determination in the absence of the consent of Indonesia.

29. However, Portugal puts forward an additional argument aiming to show that the principle formulated by the Court in the case concerning Monetary Gold Removed from Rome in 1943 is not applicable in the present case. It maintains, in effect, that the rights which Australia allegedly breached were rights erga omnes and that accordingly Portugal could require it, individually, to respect them regardless of whether or not another State had conducted itself in a similarly unlawful manner.

In the Court's view, Portugal's assertion that the right of peoples to self-determination, as it evolved from the Charter and from United Nations practice, has an *erga omnes* character, is irreproachable. The principle of self- determination of peoples has been recognized by the United Nations Charter and in the jurisprudence of the Court (see Legal Consequences for States of the Continued Presence of South Africa in Namibia (South West Africa) notwithstanding Security Council Resolution 276 (1970), Advisory Opinion, I.C.J. Reports 1971, pp. 31-32, paras. 52-53; Western Sahara, Advisory Opinion, I.C.J. Reports 1975, pp. 31-33, paras. 54-59); it is one of the essential principles of contemporary international law. However, the Court considers that the *erga omnes* character of a norm and the rule of consent to jurisdiction are two different things. Whatever the nature of the obligations invoked, the Court could not rule on the lawfulness of the conduct of a State when its judgment would imply an evaluation of the lawfulness of the conduct of another State which is not a party to the case. Where this is so, the Court cannot act, even if the right in question is a right *erga omnes*.

30. Portugal presents a final argument to challenge the applicability to the present case of the Court's jurisprudence in the case concerning Monetary Gold Removed from Rome in 1943. It argues that the principal matters on which its claims are based, namely the status of East Timor as a non-self- governing territory and its own capacity as the administering Power of the Territory, have already been decided by the General Assembly and the Security Council, acting within their proper spheres of competence; that in order to decide on Portugal's claims, the Court might well need to interpret those decisions but would not have to decide *de novo* on their content and must accordingly take them as "givens"; and that consequently the Court is not required in this case to pronounce on the question of the use of force by Indonesia in East Timor or upon the lawfulness of its presence in the Territory.

Australia objects that the United Nations resolutions regarding East Timor do not say what Portugal claims they say; that the last resolution of the Security Council on East Timor goes back to 1976 and the last resolution of the General Assembly to 1982, and that Portugal takes no account of the passage of time and the developments that have taken place since then; and that the Security Council resolutions are not resolutions which are binding under Chapter VII of the Charter or otherwise and, moreover, that they are not framed in mandatory terms.

31. The Court notes that the argument of Portugal under consideration rests on the premise that the United Nations resolutions, and in particular those of the Security Council, can be read as imposing an obligation on States not to recognize any authority on the part of Indonesia over the Territory and, where the latter is concerned, to deal only with Portugal. The Court is not persuaded, however, that the relevant resolutions went so far.

For the two Parties, the Territory of East Timor remains a non-self-governing territory and its people has the right to self-determination. Moreover, the General Assembly, which reserves to itself the right to determine the territories which have to be regarded as non-self-governing for the purposes of the application of Chapter XI of the Charter, has treated East Timor as such a territory. The competent subsidiary organs of the General Assembly have continued to treat East Timor as such to this day. Furthermore, the Security Council, in its resolutions 384 (1975) and 389 (1976) has expressly called for respect for "the territorial integrity of East Timor as well as the inalienable right of its people to self-determination in accordance with General Assembly resolution 1514(XV)".

Nor is it at issue between the Parties that the General Assembly has expressly referred to Portugal as the "administering Power" of East Timor in a number of the resolutions it adopted on the subject of East Timor between 1975 and 1982, and that the Security Council has done so in its resolution 384 (1975). The Parties do not agree, however, on the legal implications that flow from the reference to Portugal as the administering Power in those texts.

32. The Court finds that it cannot be inferred from the sole fact that the above-mentioned resolutions of the General Assembly and the Security Council refer to Portugal as the administering Power of East Timor that they intended to establish an obligation on third States to treat exclusively with Portugal as regards the continental shelf of East Timor. The Court notes, furthermore, that several States have concluded with Indonesia treaties capable of application to East Timor but which do not include any reservation in regard to that Territory. Finally, the Court observes that, by a letter of 15 December 1989, the Permanent Representative of Portugal to the United Nations transmitted to the Secretary-General the text of a note of protest addressed by the Portuguese Embassy in Canberra to the Australian Department of Foreign Affairs and Trade on the occasion of the conclusion of the Treaty on 11 December 1989; that the letter of the Permanent Representative was circulated, at his request, as an official document of the forty-fifth session of the General Assembly, under the item entitled "Question of East Timor", and of the Security Council; and that no responsive action was taken either by the General Assembly or the Security Council.

Without prejudice to the question whether the resolutions under discussion could be binding in nature, the Court considers as a result that they cannot be regarded as "givens" which constitute a sufficient basis for determining the dispute between the Parties.

33. It follows from this that the Court would necessarily have to rule upon the lawfulness of Indonesia's conduct as a prerequisite for deciding on Portugal's contention that Australia violated its obligation to respect Portugal's status as administering Power, East Timor's status as a non-self- governing territory and the right of the people of the Territory to self-determination and to permanent sovereignty over its wealth and natural resources.

34. The Court emphasizes that it is not necessarily prevented from adjudicating when the judgment it is asked to give might affect the legal interests of a State which is not a party to the case. Thus, in the case concerning Certain Phosphate Lands in Nauru (Nauru v. Australia), it stated, inter alia, as follows:

> In the present case, the interests of New Zealand and the United Kingdom do not constitute the very subject-matter of the judgment to be rendered on the merits of Nauru's Application ... In the present case, the determination of the responsibility of New Zealand or the United Kingdom is not a prerequisite for the determination of the responsibility of Australia, the only object of Nauru's claim ... In the present case, a finding by the Court regarding the existence or the content of the responsibility attributed to Australia by Nauru might well have implications for the legal situation of the two other States concerned, but no finding in respect of that legal situation will be needed as a basis for the Court's decision on Nauru's claims against Australia. Accordingly, the Court cannot decline to exercise its jurisdiction.

I.C.J. Reports 1992, pp. 261-262, para. 55.

However, in this case, the effects of the judgment requested by Portugal would amount to a determination that Indonesia's entry into and continued presence in East Timor are unlawful and that, as a consequence, it does not have the treaty-making power in matters relating to the continental shelf resources of East Timor. Indonesia's rights and obligations would thus constitute the very subject-matter of such a judgment made in the absence of that State's consent. Such a judgment would run directly counter to the "well-established principle of international law embodied in the Court's Statute, namely, that the Court can only exercise jurisdiction over a State with its consent" (Monetary Gold Removed from Rome in 1943, Judgment, I.C.J. Reports 1954, p. 32).

35. The Court concludes that it cannot, in this case, exercise the jurisdiction it has by virtue of the declarations made by the Parties under Article 36, paragraph 2, of its Statute because, in order to decide the claims of Portugal, it would have to rule, as a prerequisite, on the lawfulness of Indonesia's conduct in the absence of that State's consent. This conclusion applies to all the claims of Portugal, for all of them raise a common question: whether the power to make treaties concerning the continental shelf resources of East Timor belongs to Portugal or Indonesia, and, therefore, whether Indonesia's entry into and continued presence in the Territory are lawful. In these circumstances, the Court does not deem it necessary to examine the other arguments derived by Australia from the non-participation of Indonesia in the case, namely the Court's lack of jurisdiction to decide on the validity of the 1989 Treaty and the effects on Indonesia's rights under that treaty which would result from a judgment in favour of Portugal.

36. Having dismissed the first of the two objections of Australia which it has examined, but upheld its second, the Court finds that it is not required to consider Australia's other objections and that it cannot rule on Portugal's claims on the merits, whatever the importance of the questions raised by those claims and of the rules of international law which they bring into play.

37. The Court recalls in any event that it has taken note in the present Judgment (paragraph 31) that, for the two Parties, the Territory of East Timor remains a non-self-governing territory and its people has the right to self-determination.

[In a long dissent, JUDGE WEERAMANTRY insisted that, "the importance of the right of the people of East Timor to self-determination and to permanent sovereignty over natural resources, [is] so important to contemporary international law [that] the duty of respect for them extends beyond mere recognition, to a duty to abstain from any State action which is incompatible with those rights or which would impair or nullify them." Case Concerning East Timor (Port. v. Austl.) 1995 I.C.J. 90 (Separate Opinion of Judge Weeramantry).]

NOTES AND QUESTIONS

1. The International Court of Justice qualifies the right to self-determination as a right *erga omnes*. What is the legal significance of this designation? Is it wise policy? On rights *erga omnes*, *see also*, *infra*, Parts Three and Five.

2. Appraise the claims of Indonesia. Was its invasion of East Timor justifiable under modern theories of international law? Contiguity? Effective occupation of a *res nullius*? Annexation? Decolonization? What is the relevance of Article 2(4) of the U.N. Charter? For further analysis, *see* Roger S. Clark, *The "Decolonization" of East Timor and the United Nations Norms on Self-Determination and Aggression,* 7 YALE J. WORLD PUB. ORD. 2 (1980). *See also* Gerry J. Simpson, *Judging the East Timor Dispute: Self-Determination at the International Court of Justice,* 17 HASTINGS INT'L & COMP. L. REV. 323 (1994). For the perspective of a leader of the independence movement (and later winner of the Nobel Peace Prize), *see* JOSÉ RAMOS HORTA, FUNU: THE UNFINISHED SAGA OF EAST TIMOR (Red Sea Press 1987).

* * *

President Suharto's July 17, 1976 designation of East Timor as Indonesia's twenty-seventh province, never recognized by the United Nations, did little to quell the resistence movement aspiring toward independence. Repression ensued. The number of East Timorese casualties during the 24 years of occupation is estimated at 200,000.

On May 1, 1998, President Suharto resigned in the midst of a crippling economic crisis and riots in Jakarta. His successor, President B. J. Habibie offered East Timor the choice of remaining a part of Indonesia with the understanding that a "no" vote was a vote for independence. An agreement with the U.N.-recognized Administering Power of East Timor, Portugal, witnessed by Kofi Annan, Secretary-General of the United Nations, paved the way for a formal consultation of the East Timorese people.

b. Agreement Between Indonesia and Portugal on East Timor

MAY 5, 1999

The Governments of Indonesia and Portugal,

Recalling General Assembly resolutions 1514 (XV), 1541(XV), 2625(XXV) and the relevant resolutions and decisions adopted by the Security Council and the General Assembly on the question of East Timor;

Bearing in mind the sustained efforts of the Governments of Indonesia and Portugal since July 1983, through the good offices of the Secretary-General, to find a just, comprehensive and internationally acceptable solution to the question of East Timor; ...

Agree as follows:

Article 1

Request the Secretary-General to put the attached proposed constitutional framework providing for a special autonomy for East Timor within the unitary Republic of Indonesia to the East Timorese people, both inside and outside East Timor, for their consideration and acceptance or rejection through a popular consultation on the basis of a direct, secret and universal ballot.

Article 2

Request the Secretary-General to establish, immediately after the signing of this Agreement, an appropriate United Nations mission in East Timor to enable him to effectively carry out the popular consultation.

Article 3

The Government of Indonesia will be responsible for maintaining peace and security in East Timor in order to ensure that the popular consultation is carried out in a fair and peaceful way in an atmosphere free of intimidation, violence or interference from any side.

Article 4

Request the Secretary-General to report the result of the popular consultation to the Security Council and the General Assembly, as well as to inform the Governments of Indonesia and Portugal and the East Timorese people.

Article 5

If the Secretary-General determines, on the basis of the result of the popular consultation and in accordance with this Agreement, that, the proposed constitutional framework for special autonomy is acceptable to the East Timorese people, the Government of Indonesia shall initiate the constitutional measures necessary for the implementation of the constitutional framework, and the Government of Portugal shall initiate within the United Nations the procedures necessary for the removal of East Timor from the list of Non-Self-Governing Territories of the General Assembly and the deletion of the question of East Timor from the agendas of the Security Council and the General Assembly.

Article 6

If the Secretary-General determines, on the basis of the result of the popular consultation and in accordance with this Agreement, that the proposed constitutional framework for special autonomy is not acceptable to the East Timorese people, the Government of Indonesia shall take the constitutional steps necessary to terminate its links with East Timor thus restoring under Indonesian law the status East Timor held prior to 17 July 1976, and the Governments of Indonesia and Portugal and the Secretary-General shall agree on arrangements for a peaceful and orderly transfer of authority in East Timor to the United Nations. The Secretary-General shall, subject to the appropriate legislative mandate, initiate the procedure enabling East Timor to begin a process of transition towards independence.

Article 7

During the interim period between the conclusion of the popular consultation and the start of the implementation of either option, the parties request the Secretary-General to maintain an adequate United Nations presence in East Timor.

c. Secretary-General Informs Security Council People of East Timor Rejected Special Autonomy Proposed by Indonesia

United Nations Press Release, U.N. Doc. SC/6721 (Sept. 3, 1999)

The people of East Timor had voted by 78.5 per cent to 21.5 per cent against the special autonomy proposed by Indonesia, Secretary-General Kofi Annan told the Security Council tonight as it met to consider the situation in East Timor.

He told Council members that the East Timorese, turning out in massive numbers for the vote, had expressed their will as to the Territory's future. The vote had resulted in 94,388 (21.5 per cent) in favour and 344,580 (78.5 per cent) against the proposed special autonomy. The East Timorese had thus rejected it and expressed their wish to begin a process of transition towards independence.

The Secretary-General said that after 24 years of conflict, East Timor stood on the threshold of an orderly and peaceful transition. The coming days, however, would require patience and calm. Now was the time for all concerned to seize the opportunity to lay a firm and lasting foundation for cooperation and peace, and to usher in an era of stability and prosperity for all.

Urging those who had voted for the proposed special autonomy not to consider the outcome a loss, and the majority not to consider it a victory, he said there had been no winners or losers. It was time to begin forging an independent East Timor.

* * *

The days following the vote were marked by thousands of civilian deaths, the displacement of almost one-half of the population, and the near-destruction of the East Timor infrastructure at the hands of Indonesian troops and para-military forces operating under their command. In two and a half weeks, almost every semblance of personal wealth in East Timor was stolen or destroyed. Unlike Kosovo, bombs were not the main weapon used. The main weapon in East Timor was gasoline. This violence necessitated action by the U.N. Security Council.

d. U.N. Security Council Resolution 1264 (1999)

Adopted by the Security Council at its 4045th meeting on 15 September 1999

The Security Council,

Recalling its previous resolutions and the statements of its President on the situation in East Timor,

Recalling also the Agreement between Indonesia and Portugal on the question of East Timor of 5 May 1999 and the Agreements between the United Nations and the Governments of Indonesia and Portugal of the same date regarding the modalities for the popular consultation of the East Timorese through a direct ballot and security arrangements (S/1999/513, Annexes I to III),

Reiterating its welcome for the successful conduct of the popular consultation of the East Timorese people of 30 August 1999 and taking note of its outcome, which it regards as an accurate reflection of the views of the East Timorese people,

Deeply concerned by the deterioration in the security situation in East Timor, and in particular by the continuing violence against and large-scale displacement and relocation of East Timorese civilians,

Deeply concerned also at the attacks on the staff and premises of the United Nations Mission in East Timor (UNAMET), on other officials and on international and national humanitarian personnel,

Recalling the relevant principles contained in the Convention on the Safety of United Nations and Associated Personnel adopted on 9 December 1994,

Appalled by the worsening humanitarian situation in East Timor, particularly as it affects women, children and other vulnerable groups,

Reaffirming the right of refugees and displaced persons to return in safety and security to their homes,

Endorsing the report of the Security Council Mission to Jakarta and Dili (S/1999/976),

Welcoming the statement by the President of Indonesia on 12 September 1999 in which he expressed the readiness of Indonesia to accept an international peacekeeping force through the United Nations in East Timor,

Welcoming the letter from the Minister for Foreign Affairs of Australia to the Secretary-General of 14 September 1999 (S/1999/975),

Reaffirming respect for the sovereignty and territorial integrity of Indonesia,

Expressing its concern at reports indicating that systematic, widespread and flagrant violations of international humanitarian and human rights law have been committed in East Timor, and stressing that persons committing such violations bear individual responsibility,

Determining that the present situation in East Timor constitutes a threat to peace and security,

Acting under Chapter VII of the Charter of the United Nations,

1. *Condemns* all acts of violence in East Timor, calls for their immediate end and demands that those responsible for such acts be brought to justice;

2. *Emphasizes* the urgent need for coordinated humanitarian assistance and the importance of allowing full, safe and unimpeded access by humanitarian organizations and calls upon all parties to cooperate with such organizations so as to ensure the protection of civilians at risk, the safe return of refugees and displaced persons and the effective delivery of humanitarian aid;

3. *Authorizes* the establishment of a multinational force under a unified command structure, pursuant to the request of the Government of Indonesia conveyed to the Secretary-General on 12 September 1999, with the following tasks: to restore peace and security in East Timor, to protect and support UNAMET in carrying out its tasks and, within force capabilities, to facilitate humanitarian assistance operations, and authorizes the States participating in the multinational force to take all necessary measures to fulfil this mandate;

4. *Welcomes* the expressed commitment of the Government of Indonesia to cooperate with the multinational force in all aspects of the implementation of its mandate and looks forward to close coordination between the multinational force and the Government of Indonesia;

5. *Underlines* the Government of Indonesia's continuing responsibility under the Agreements of 5 May 1999, taking into account the mandate of the multinational force set out in paragraph 3 above, to maintain peace and security in East Timor in the interim phase between the conclusion of the popular consultation and the start of the implementation of its result and to guarantee the security of the personnel and premises of UNAMET;

6. *Welcomes* the offers by Member States to organize, lead and contribute to the multinational force in East Timor, calls on Member States to make further contributions of personnel, equipment and other resources and invites Member States in a position to contribute to inform the leadership of the multinational force and the Secretary-General;

7. *Stresses* that it is the responsibility of the Indonesian authorities to take immediate and effective measures to ensure the safe return of refugees to East Timor;

8. *Notes* that Article 6 of the Agreement of 5 May 1999 states that the Governments of Indonesia and Portugal and the Secretary-General shall agree on arrangements for a peaceful and orderly transfer of authority in East Timor to the United Nations, and requests the leadership of the multinational force to cooperate closely with the United Nations to assist and support those arrangements;

9. *Stresses* that the expenses for the force will be borne by the participating Member States concerned and requests the Secretary-General to establish a trust fund through which contributions could be channelled to the States or operations concerned;

10. *Agrees* that the multinational force should collectively be deployed in East Timor until replaced as soon as possible by a United Nations peacekeeping operation, and invites the Secretary-General to make prompt recommendations on a peacekeeping operation to the Security Council;

11. *Invites* the Secretary-General to plan and prepare for a United Nations transitional administration in East Timor, incorporating a United Nations peacekeeping operation, to be deployed in the implementation phase of the popular

consultation (phase III) and to make recommendations as soon as possible to the Security Council;

12. *Requests* the leadership of the multinational force to provide periodic reports on progress towards the implementation of its mandate through the Secretary-General to the Council, the first such report to be made within 14 days of the adoption of this resolution;

13. *Decides* to remain actively seized of the matter.

e. The U.N. Transitional Administration in East Timor

The United Nations Transitional Administration in East Timor (UNTAET) was established in October 1999 to oversee the administration of East Timor during its transition to independence. Aid workers arrived to assist the population not only with the physical rebuilding, but also with the re-creation of the civil service, police, judiciary, education and health systems.

Until East Timor, the U.N. had never taken over the administration of a country with no preexisting institutions. The Security Council Resolution that established UNTAET effectively granted it absolute power to give birth to a free standing and democratic Timorese state. For the first time, United Nations task forces found themselves building bridges, homes, and school buildings. UNTAET was responsible for devising a currency, a banking system and a legal system. The United Nations asked German legal scholar, Hansjörg Strohmeyer, to help devise a body of laws for the embryonic country.

At this writing, the United Nations still has a presence in East Timor, albeit a steadily diminishing one. The first presidential elections were held in April 2002. Popular independence leader Xanana Gusmao became the first President of East Timor which formally gained status as an independent state in May 2002.

NOTES AND QUESTIONS

1. In line with the U.N. Security Counsel Resolution 1264 above, an Australian-led multinational force subsequently secured East Timor and disarmed rampaging pro-Indonesian militias who had engaged in a campaign of terror and destruction after the result of the popular consultation was announced. Should the widespread killing, the ransacking of East Timor's capital Dili, and the displacement of 300,000 of the nearly 800,000 East Timorese people have been foreseen and prevented by the presence of an international armed force before, during, and after the consultation? What would the effects of such a request have been on the prospects of the consultation taking place? What should the lessons be for the prospective consultation of the people of Western Sahara?

2. Note that the use of force in the case of East Timor was authorized by the Security Council, upon invitation by the Indonesian government. NATO's use of force in the case of Kosovo (*see infra*) was not similarly approved, nor consented to, by the Yugoslav government. What accounts for this differential development?

3. What progress has been made on the U.N. nation-building plan for East Timor since it became independent in May 2002? (*See Report of the Secretary-General on the United Nations Mission of Support in East Timor,* U.N. SCOR 6 Oct. 2003, U.N. Doc. S/2003/944; *Report of the Commission*

on Human Rights on its Fourth Special Session, U.N. ESCOR,4th Special Sess., U.N. Doc. E/CN.4/1999/167/Add.1,E/1999/23/Add.1 (1999); and *Report of the High Commissioner for Human Rights on the human rights situation in East Timor*, U.N. ESCOR, 4th Special Sess., U.N. Doc. E/CN.4/S-4/CRP.1 (1999)). *See also* Thomas D. Grant, *East Timor, the U.N. System, and Enforcing Non-Recognition in International Law*, 33 Vand. J. Transnat'l L. 273 (2000); Carsten Stahn, *Accommodating Individual Criminal Responsibility and National Reconciliation: The UN Truth Commission for East Timor*, 95 Am. J. Int'l L. 952 (2001); Hilary Charlesworth, *Mainstreaming Gender in International Peace and Security: The Case of East Timor*, 26 Yale J. Int'l L. 313 (2001); Mark Rothert, *U.N. Intervention in East Timor*, 39 Colum. J. Transnat'l L. 257 (2000).

4. Decolonization appears now to be virtually completed, with the major colonial powers having released most of the territories forming their transcontinental empires. Is the "right to self-determination" still an operational principle of international law?

The United Nations Secretary General Boutros-Boutros Ghali in his 1992 report entitled "An Agenda for Peace," stated:

> [F]ierce new assertions of nationalism and sovereignty spring up, and the cohesion of States is threatened by brutal ethnic, religious, social, cultural or linguistic strife. Social peace is challenged on the one hand by new assertions of discrimination and exclusion and, on the other, by acts of terrorism seeking to undermine evolution and change through democratic means. ... if every ethnic, religious or linguistic group claimed statehood, there would be no limit to fragmentation, and peace, security and economic well-being for all would become ever more difficult to achieve.
>
> 18. One requirement for solutions to theses problems lies in commitment to human rights with a special sensitivity to those of minorities, whether ethnic, religious, social or linguistic.

Report of the Secretary-General On An Agenda for Peace-Preventive Diplomacy, Peacemaking and Peace-Keeping, U.N. Doc. S/24111, *available at* 31 I.L.M. 953, 957-960 (1992).

5. Does the United Nations Charter or the International Covenant on Civil and Political Rights recognize, imply or suggest a lawful claim to secession? Who would be the holder of such a "right?" Are ethnic bonds determinative? What about other objective factors, such as common history, language, cultural traditions? What about the role of subjective factors? Should the *will* to be a nation (Ernest Renan's "plébiscite de tous les jours") be the sole determinative factor? Should the entity claiming the right to self-determination be independently economically viable? Should indigenous peoples, mostly "nations within" a recognized nation-state, still termed "sovereign" by the United States as well as other governments, have a right to secede? What about other distinct "peoples" considering themselves "trapped" within a newly-independent former colony, such as the Ibos in Nigeria? Consider these factors and their implications in the cases of a) Québec; b) the James Bay Cree Indians in Québec; c) the Basques in Spain; d) the Catholic Irish in Northern Ireland; e) the Kurds in Turkey, Iraq and Iran.

6. Consider the reconfiguration of territorial entities in the wake of the disappearance of the Soviet Union: Does the recognition of the component entities of the Soviet Union, Yugoslavia, and Czechoslovakia give rise to a customary law right of secession beyond the colonial context? Does it make a difference that the dissolutions of the Soviet Union and Czechoslovakia, on the one hand, were achieved by consensus, whereas, on the other hand, Yugoslavia's breakup was caused by unilateral actions of constituent entities of the former Socialist Federal Republic? Is the distinction consensual (treaty) vs. unilateral action (secession) empirically useful? *See* Lawrence S. Eastwood, Jr., *Secession: State Practice and International Law after the Dissolution of the Soviet Union and Yugoslavia,* 3 Duke J. Comp. & Int'l L. 299 (1993); and Lea Brilmayer, *Secession and Self-Determination: A Territorial Interpretation,* 16 Yale J. Int'l L. 177 (1991).

7. The break-up of Yugoslavia presented the world community with particular challenges. Some background on this conflict may be useful:

After a brief but bloody occupation by Nazi Germany in World War II and the interlude of a Croat fascist state, Josip Broz Tito, a Communist and leader of the Yugoslav partisan resistance, reunited the country under the name of Socialist Federal Republic of Yugoslavia (SFRY). The SFRY consisted of the member republics of Serbia, Montenegro, Croatia, Slovenia, Bosnia-Herzegovina, Macedonia, and the two autonomous provinces of Voyvodina and Kosovo. After the death of Marshall Tito in 1980, the country began to founder. The new Federal Republic of Yugoslavia (FRY), formed after Tito's death, also proved unstable after the fall of the Berlin Wall in 1989. In the early 1990's, Slovenia, Croatia, Bosnia-Herzegovina, and Macedonia declared their independence from the FRY after the first rotating President of the post-Tito Republic, Slobodan Milosevic, refused to relinquish power at the end of his term and removed or severely curtailed the autonomy of Voyvodina and Kosovo. Slovenia, with the strong support of Germany and Austria, gained recognition almost immediately, and thus avoided the tragic events that followed in Croatia, Bosnia-Herzegovina, and, to a lesser extent, Macedonia. Fuelled by a virulent form of Serbian nationalism preached by Milosevic and his followers, Serbs in Croatia and Bosnia engaged in a policy of "ethnic cleansing" of non-Serbs from putative Serbian territories and attempted to establish separate independent states. Croats conducted their own programs of ethnic cleansing against Serbian inhabitants of Croatia.

These events within the European continent shocked the international community; but strategies for effectively suppressing the violence were delayed while states and international and regional organizations debated issues such as these:

Could the former boundaries of these entities be turned again into international boundaries, thus allowing third states to offer assistance without violating their U.N. Charter obligation not to intervene in the internal affairs of another sovereign?

If so, what form could/should such intervention take?

Was it wise to recognize secessionist aspirations outside of the decolonization context, especially in light of the fall of Communism?

Or would the result be ever-increasing fragmentation along ethnic/religious/cultural lines as predicted in the Agenda for Peace (*see supra*, note 4, and *infra*, 3B(1)(c))? Couldn't., e.g., the Serbs caught within the new entities pursue their own aspirations for self-determination?

Between 1990 and 1992, while European states and others attempted to find a settlement, the violent civil war continued, resulting in thousands of deaths and deportations of Croats and Bosnian Muslims to concentration camps. In 1992, Bosnia-Herzegovina and Croatia were recognized as independent states by a majority of third states. Slovenia, Bosnia-Herzegovina, and Croatia were granted U.N. membership and were recognized by the European Union after agreeing to meet new higher conditions for recognition established by both organizations. (*See infra*, at 238-9). (Macedonia's participation was delayed over a naming dispute with Greece, which also has a province named Macedonia. In due course, Macedonia also was granted recognition and membership in international and regional organizations under the name of Former Yugoslav Republic of Macedonia (FYROM).)

Neither these activities, nor the U.N. Peacekeeping forces subsequently sent to the Balkans, served to contain or prevent continued and increased violence, such as the massacre of 7,500 Bosnian Muslims by Bosnian Serb forces in Srebrenica in July 1995. Eventually, after failing to win Security Council approval for the use of force, NATO airstrikes ended the siege of Sarajevo, and a peace agreement - the Dayton Accords - was brokered by the United States in November 1995. Since that time, an ambitious nation-building exercise has been underway in Bosnia under the auspices of the U.N., with the military support of many nations. (For further information, *see* United Nations Development Programme *available at* www.undp.org). *See also* Christine Chinkin,

Vision and Reality: Democracy and Citizenship of Women in the Dayton Peace Accords, 26 YALE J. INT'L L. 103 (2001).

In May 1993, the International Criminal Tribunal for the Former Yugoslavia was established under U.N. auspices. To date, over 100 persons have been indicted for war crimes, crimes against humanity and genocide. Ninety-one have been brought to trial in The Hague, including former President Milosevic, resulting in 37 convictions. (For updates, *see* Fact Sheet on ICTY Proceedings, *available at* http://www.un.org/icty/glance/procfact-e.htm). *See also* Guénaël Mettraux, *Crimes Against Humanity in the Jurisprudence of the International Criminal Tribunals for the Former Yugoslavia and for Rwanda*, 43 HARV. INT'L. L. REV. 237 (2002); James R. McHenry III, *The Prosecution of Rape Under International Law: Justice That is Long Overdue*, 35 VAND. J. TRANSNAT'L L. 1269 (2002); and *The Horizontal Growth of International Courts and Tribunals: Challenges or Opportunities?* 96 AM. SOC'Y INTL L. PROC. 369 (2002).

8. Does the Yugoslav incident confirm the relevant principles of international law? Consider the comment by Professor (now ICJ Judge) Rosalyn Higgins:

> In the Balkans the appreciation of loss of statehood by the former Yugoslavia has been irresistible. But the ambivalence of the international community about the new realities has been evident. On the one hand, Slovenia, Croatia, and Bosnia-Herzegovina were admitted as new member states to the United Nations in 1992. It would seem inexorably to follow that federal Yugoslavia no longer existed. And General Assembly Resolution 47/1 (1992) suspended "Socialist Federal Yugoslavia" (Serbia-Montenegro) from participation in the General Assembly. But Serbia-Montenegro was also *not* recognized as being the legal successor to federal Yugoslavia [due to the excessive use of force in their former republics]; and it was invited under the same resolution to apply *de novo* for UN membership. And for the time being 'Yugoslavia' (which surely no longer exists) remains a member of the United Nations, able to participate in everything save the Security Council. The situation can only be described as legally confused.

ROSALYN HIGGINS, PROBLEMS AND PROCESS: INTERNATIONAL LAW AND HOW WE USE IT 40-41 (Oxford U. Press 1994). Yugoslavia was called "the former Yugoslavia" by media sources and much of the world community until Milosevic was deposed. "Yugoslavia" then briefly reappeared and took its seat in the U.N. which had remained vacant since 1992. In February 2003, however, the new Federation of Serbia-Montenegro was approved and the name "Yugoslavia" was expunged from the list of U.N. member states.

9. What act completed the emergence of the various new entities as state actors in the international arena? Their unilateral declaration of independence, their admission to membership in regional organizations, admission to membership in the United Nations, recognition by other states? If the latter, by how many and which? Is context relevant, and, if yes, in what way?

10. Consider Professor Thomas Franck's assessment:

> The issue is not whether any right of self-determination has survived the era of decolonization. The clear textual evidence of the Covenants and of the Helsinki Accord places that beyond serious dispute. Less clear, however, is whether self-determination in the new post-colonial context continues to validate a right of secession, as it did in specific instances during the periods following World Wars I and II. If so, who are its beneficiaries: which 'peoples' or 'minorities'? In both of its earlier socio-political contexts, self-determination was identified as entailing a secessionist right, but only ˜*vis-à-vis* a very specific place and time: the defeat and dismemberment of the Central Powers at Versailles and the largely consensual dissolution of overseas empires under UN auspices. In the latter context, the UN's role was not to enforce a general right of 'peoples' to secede – although it had that appearance in General Assembly debates – but to oversee the interpretation and implementation of a specific right of colonized people to achieve self-government under the terms of Article 73 of the Charter and various trustee-

ship agreements to which the colonial powers had already freely and specifically assented by their adherence to the Charter and trust agreements. . .

The reaction of the system - EU, CSCE, and UN - is summarized as follows.

1. The international system does not recognize a general right of secession but may assist the government of a member state in good standing to find constructive alternatives to mitigate the conditions propelling a secessionist claim.

2. The international system regards egregious and protracted violence by and against secessionist forces as likely to give rise to a threat to international peace: by engendering flows of refugees, tempting potential external interventions, and disrupting international trade in essential goods and services. This justifies transforming a civil war from a domestic to an international dispute, validating systemic intervention in the form of debate, recommendations for settlement, demands for a cease-fire, and the imposition equally on all sides of an embargo on arms and military supplies. The international system will in this situation no longer presumptively side with governments against secessionists, nor permit individual states to do so, except perhaps where the secession is being fomented or supported by an external intervening party. Instead, the system may require neutrality.

3. With the prior consent of the government and the secessionists, the international system may provide peacekeepers charged to secure the combatants' disengagement in an agreed neutralized and demilitarized zone, and to protect and provide humanitarian aid to civilians.

4. The international system does not prohibit secession. It will recognize a secessionist territory and government *if* (a) secession is achieved by mutual agreement with the parent state, or (b) a secessionist regime has demonstrated effective continuous control over its territory *and* (c) the secessionist government has indicated its acceptance of relevant international obligations by, *inter alia,* making provision in its constitution and ratifying relevant international legal instruments for the protection of the nationality, cultural, linguistic, and religious rights of its minorities, *and* (d) it can demonstrate its democratic legitimacy, *and* (e) it has taken constitutional steps to ensure political autonomy for such of its own minorities as desire it.

5. A new state created by secession is normally entitled to those boundaries and territories which were previously administratively applicable to it, if it was then a defined unit of a parent state. Accepting those boundaries is a condition of the new state's recognition. However, this does not necessarily preclude newly created minorities within the new state from attempting to secede, providing they do so without external assistance and do not thereby create a further threat to or breach of the peace.

THOMAS M. FRANCK, FAIRNESS IN INTERNATIONAL LAW AND INSTITUTIONS 154-169 (Clarendon Press 1995).

4. Quebec

a. Supreme Court of Canada, Reference re: Secession of Quebec

File No. 25506, Aug. 20, 1998, [1998] S.C.R. 217

Pursuant to s. 53 of the *Supreme Court Act*, the Governor in Council referred the following questions to this Court:

Question 1:

Under the Constitution of Canada, can the National Assembly, legislature or government of Quebec effect the secession of Quebec from Canada unilaterally?

Question 2:

Does international law give the National Assembly, legislature or government of Quebec the right to effect the secession of Quebec from Canada unilaterally? In this regard, is there a right to self-determination under international law that would give the National Assembly, legislature or government of Quebec the right to effect the secession of Quebec from Canada unilaterally?

Question 3:

In the event of a conflict between domestic and international law on the right of the National Assembly, legislature or government of Quebec to effect the secession of Quebec from Canada unilaterally, which would take precedence in Canada? ...

Question 1

The Constitution is more than a written text. It embraces the entire global system of rules and principles which govern the exercise of constitutional authority. A superficial reading of selected provisions of the written constitutional enactment, without more, may be misleading. It is necessary to make a more profound investigation of the underlying principles animating the whole of the Constitution, including the principles of federalism, democracy, constitutionalism and the rule of law, and respect for minorities. Those principles must inform our overall appreciation of the constitutional rights and obligations that would come into play in the event that a clear majority of Quebecers votes on a clear question in favour of secession.

The Court in this Reference is required to consider whether Quebec has a right to unilateral secession. Arguments in support of the existence of such a right were primarily based on the principle of democracy. Democracy, however, means more than simple majority rule. Constitutional jurisprudence shows that democracy exists in the larger context of other constitutional values. Since Confederation, the people of the provinces and territories have created close ties of interdependence (economic, social, political and cultural) based on shared values that include federalism, democracy, constitutionalism and the rule of law, and respect for minorities. A democratic decision of Quebecers in favour of secession would put those relationships at risk. The Constitution vouchsafes order and stability, and accordingly secession of a province "under the Constitution" could not be achieved unilaterally, that is, without principled negotiation with other participants in Confederation within the existing constitutional framework.

Our democratic institutions necessarily accommodate a continuous process of discussion and evolution, which is reflected in the constitutional right of each participant in the federation to initiate constitutional change. This right implies a reciprocal duty on the other participants to engage in discussions to address any legitimate initiative to change the constitutional order. A clear majority vote in Quebec on a clear question in favour of secession would confer democratic legitimacy on the secession initiative which all of the other participants in Confederation would have to recognize.

Quebec could not, despite a clear referendum result, purport to invoke a right of self-determination to dictate the terms of a proposed secession to the other parties to the federation. The democratic vote, by however strong a majority, would have no legal effect on its own and could not push aside the principles of federalism and the rule of law, the rights of individuals and minorities, or the operation of democracy in the other provinces or in Canada as a whole. Democratic rights under the Constitution cannot be divorced from constitutional obligations. Nor, however, can the reverse proposition be accepted: the continued existence and operation of the Canadian constitutional order could not be indifferent to a clear expression of a clear majority of Quebecers that they no longer wish to remain in Canada. The other provinces and the federal government would have no basis to deny the right of the government of Quebec to pursue secession should a clear majority of the people of Quebec choose that goal, so long as in doing so, Quebec respects the rights of others. The negotiations that followed such a vote would address the potential act of secession as well as its possible terms should in fact secession proceed. There would be no conclusions predetermined by law on any issue. Negotiations would need to address the interests of the other provinces, the federal government and Quebec and indeed the rights of all Canadians both within and outside Quebec, and specifically the rights of minorities.

The negotiation process would require the reconciliation of various rights and obligations by negotiation between two legitimate majorities, namely, the majority of the population of Quebec, and that of Canada as a whole. A political majority at either level that does not act in accordance with the underlying constitutional principles puts at risk the legitimacy of its exercise of its rights, and the ultimate acceptance of the result by the international community.

The task of the Court has been to clarify the legal framework within which political decisions are to be taken "under the Constitution" and not to usurp the prerogatives of the political forces that operate within that framework. The obligations identified by the Court are binding obligations under the Constitution.

However, it will be for the political actors to determine what constitutes "a clear majority on a clear question" in the circumstances under which a future referendum vote may be taken. Equally, in the event of demonstrated majority support for Quebec secession, the content and process of the negotiations will be for the political actors to settle. The reconciliation of the various legitimate constitutional interests is necessarily committed to the political rather than the judicial realm precisely because that reconciliation can only be achieved through the give and take of political negotiations. To the extent issues addressed in the course of negotiation are political, the courts, appreciating their proper role in the constitutional scheme, would have no supervisory role. . . .

Question 2

(1) Secession at International Law

It is clear that international law does not specifically grant component parts of sovereign states the legal right to secede unilaterally from their "parent" state. This is acknowledged by the experts who provided their opinions on behalf of both the *amicus curiae* and the Attorney General of Canada. Given the lack of specific authorization for unilateral secession, proponents of the existence of such a right at international law are therefore left to attempt to found their argument (i) on the proposition that unilateral secession is not specifically prohibited and that what is not specifically prohibited is inferentially permitted; or (ii) on the implied duty of states to recognize the legitimacy of secession brought about by the exercise of the well-established international law right of "a people" to self-determination. The *amicus curiae* addressed the right of self-determination, but submitted that it was not applicable to the circumstances of Quebec within the Canadian federation, irrespective of the existence or non-existence of a referendum result in favour of secession. We agree on this point with the *amicus curiae*, for reasons that we will briefly develop.

(a) Absence of a Specific Prohibition

International law contains neither a right of unilateral secession nor the explicit denial of such a right, although such a denial is, to some extent, implicit in the exceptional circumstances required for secession to be permitted under the right of a people to self-determination, e.g., the right of secession that arises in the exceptional situation of an oppressed or colonial people, discussed below. As will be seen, international law places great importance on the territorial integrity of nation states and, by and large, leaves the creation of a new state to be determined by the domestic law of the existing state of which the seceding entity presently forms a part (R. Y. Jennings, *The Acquisition of Territory in International Law* (1963) at pp. 8-9). Where, as here, unilateral secession would be incompatible with the domestic Constitution, international law is likely to accept that conclusion subject to the right of peoples to self-determination, a topic to which we now turn.

(b) *The Right of a People to Self-determination*

While international law generally regulates the conduct of nation states, it does, in some specific circumstances, also recognize the "rights" of entities other than nation states — such as the right of a people to self-determination.

The existence of the right of a people to self-determination is now so widely recognized in international conventions that the principle has acquired a status beyond "convention" and is considered a general principle of international law (A. Cassese, *Self-determination of Peoples: A Legal Reappraisal* (1995), at pp. 171-72; K. Doehring, "Self-Determination", in B. Simma, ed., *The Charter of the United Nations: A Commentary* (1994), at p. 70).

Article 1 of the *Charter of the United Nations*, Can. T.S. 1945 No. 7, states in part that one of the purposes of the United Nations (U.N.) is:

Article 1

> ... 2. To develop friendly relations among nations based on respect for the principle of equal rights and self-determination of peoples, and to take other appropriate measures to strengthen universal peace;

Article 55 of the U.N. *Charter* further states that the U.N. shall promote goals such as higher standards of living, full employment and human rights "[w]ith a view to the creation of conditions of stability and well-being which are necessary for peaceful and friendly relations among nations based on respect for the principle of equal rights and self-determination of peoples".

This basic principle of self-determination has been carried forward and addressed in so many U.N. conventions and resolutions that, as noted by Doehring, *supra*, at p. 60:

The sheer number of resolutions concerning the right of self-determination makes their enumeration impossible.

For our purposes, reference to the following conventions and resolutions is sufficient. Article 1 of both the U.N.'s *International Covenant on Civil and Political Rights*, 999 U.N.T.S. 171, and its *International Covenant on Economic, Social and Cultural Rights*, 993 U.N.T.S. 3, states:

> 1. All peoples have the right of self-determination. By virtue of that right they freely determine their political status and freely pursue their economic, social and cultural development.

Similarly, the U.N. General Assembly's *Declaration on Principles of International Law Concerning Friendly Relations and Co-operation Among States in Accordance with the Charter of the United Nations*, GA Res. 2625 (XXV), 24 October 1970, states:

> By virtue of the principle of equal rights and self-determination of peoples enshrined in the Charter of the United Nations, all peoples have the right freely to determine, without external interference, their political status

> and to pursue their economic, social and cultural development, and every State has the duty to respect this right in accordance with the provisions of the Charter.

In 1993, the U.N. World Conference on Human Rights adopted the *Vienna Declaration and Programme of Action*, A/Conf. 157/24, 25 June 1993, that reaffirmed Article 1 of the two above-mentioned covenants. The U.N. General Assembly's *Declaration on the Occasion of the Fiftieth Anniversary of the United Nations*, GA Res. 50/6, 9 November 1995, also emphasizes the right to self-determination by providing that the U.N.'s member states will:

> 1. Continue to reaffirm the right of self-determination of all peoples, taking into account the particular situation of peoples under colonial or other forms of alien domination or foreign occupation, and recognize the right of peoples to take legitimate action in accordance with the Charter of the United Nations to realize their inalienable right of self-determination. This shall not be construed as authorizing or encouraging any action that would dismember or impair, totally or in part, the territorial integrity or political unity of sovereign and independent States conducting themselves in compliance with the principle of equal rights and self-determination of peoples and thus possessed of a Government representing the whole people belonging to the territory without distinction of any kind .
>
> . . .

The right to self-determination is also recognized in other international legal documents. For example, the *Final Act of the Conference on Security and Co-operation in Europe*, 14 I.L.M. 1292 (1975) (*Helsinki Final Act*), states (in Part VIII):

> The participating States will respect the equal rights of peoples and their right to self-determination, acting at all times in conformity with the purposes and principles of the Charter of the United Nations and with the relevant norms of international law, including those relating to territorial integrity of States.

By virtue of the principle of equal rights and self-determination of peoples, all peoples always have the right, in full freedom, to determine, when and as they wish, their internal and external political status, without external interference, and to pursue as they wish their political, economic, social and cultural development.

As will be seen, international law expects that the right to self-determination will be exercised by peoples within the framework of existing sovereign states and consistently with the maintenance of the territorial integrity of those states. Where this is not possible, in the exceptional circumstances discussed below, a right of secession may arise.

(i) Defining "Peoples"

International law grants the right to self-determination to "peoples". Accordingly, access to the right requires the threshold step of characterizing as a people the group seeking self-determination. However, as the right to self-determination has developed by virtue of a combination of international agreements and conventions, coupled with state practice, with little formal elaboration of the definition of "peoples", the result has been that the precise meaning of the term "people" remains somewhat uncertain.

It is clear that "a people" may include only a portion of the population of an existing state. The right to self-determination has developed largely as a human right, and is generally used in documents that simultaneously contain references to "nation" and "state". The juxtaposition of these terms is indicative that the reference to "people" does not necessarily mean the entirety of a state's population. To restrict the definition of the term to the population of existing states would render the granting of a right to self-determination largely duplicative, given the parallel emphasis within the majority of the source documents on the need to protect the territorial integrity of existing states, and would frustrate its remedial purpose.

While much of the Quebec population certainly shares many of the characteristics (such as a common language and culture) that would be considered in determining whether a specific group is a "people", as do other groups within Quebec and/or Canada, it is not necessary to explore this legal characterization to resolve Question 2 appropriately. Similarly, it is not necessary for the Court to determine whether, should a Quebec people exist within the definition of public international law, such a people encompasses the entirety of the provincial population or just a portion thereof. Nor is it necessary to examine the position of the aboriginal population within Quebec. As the following discussion of the scope of the right to self-determination will make clear, whatever be the correct application of the definition of people(s) in this context, their right of self-determination cannot in the present circumstances be said to ground a right to unilateral secession.

(ii) Scope of the Right to Self-determination

The recognized sources of international law establish that the right to self-determination of a people is normally fulfilled through internal self-determination — a people's pursuit of its political, economic, social and cultural development within the framework of an existing state. A right to external self-determination (which in this case potentially takes the form of the assertion of a right to unilateral secession) arises in only the most extreme of cases and, even then, under carefully defined circumstances. . . .

The establishment of a sovereign and independent State, the free association or integration with an independent State or the emergence into any other political status freely determined by a people constitute modes of implementing the right of self-determination by that people.

The international law principle of self-determination has evolved within a framework of respect for the territorial integrity of existing states. The various international documents that support the existence of a people's right to self-determination also contain parallel statements supportive of the conclusion that the exercise of such a right must be sufficiently limited to prevent threats to an existing state's territorial integrity or the stability of relations between sovereign states.

The *Declaration on Friendly Relations, supra, Vienna Declaration, supra*, and *Declaration on the Occasion of the Fiftieth Anniversary of the United Nations, supra*, are specific. They state, immediately after affirming a people's right to determine political, economic, social and cultural issues, that such rights are not to be construed as authorizing or encouraging any action which would dismember or impair, totally or in part, the territorial integrity or political unity of sovereign and independent States conducting themselves in compliance with the principle of equal rights and self-determination of peoples as described above and thus possessed of a government representing the whole people belonging to the territory without distinction...

Similarly, while the concluding document of the Vienna Meeting in 1989 of the Conference on Security and Co-operation in Europe on the follow-up to the *Helsinki Final Act* again refers to peoples having the right to determine "their internal and external political status", that statement is immediately followed by express recognition that the participating states will at all times act, as stated in the *Helsinki Final Act,* "in conformity with the purposes and principles of the Charter of the United Nations and with the relevant norms of international law, including those relating to territorial integrity of states". Principle 5 of the concluding document states that the participating states (including Canada):

> [c]onfirm their commitment strictly and effectively to observe the principle of the territorial integrity of States. They will refrain from any violation of this principle and thus from any action aimed by direct or indirect means, in contravention of the purposes and principles of the Charter of the United Nations, other obligations under international law or the provisions of the [Helsinki] Final Act, at violating the territorial integrity, political independence or the unity of a State. No actions or situations in contravention of this principle will be recognized as legal by the participating States.

Accordingly, the reference in the *Helsinki Final Act* to a people determining its external political status is interpreted to mean the expression of a people's external political status through the government of the existing state, save in the exceptional circumstances discussed below. As noted by Cassese, *supra*, at p. 287, given the history and textual structure of this document, its reference to external self-determination simply means that "no territorial or other change can be brought about by the central authorities of a State that is contrary to the will of the whole people of that State".

While the *International Covenant on Economic, Social and Cultural Rights, supra*, and the *International Covenant on Civil and Political Rights, supra*, do not specifically refer to the protection of territorial integrity, they both define the ambit of the right to self-determination in terms that are normally attainable within the framework of an existing state. There is no necessary incompatibility between the maintenance of the territorial integrity of existing states, including Canada, and the right of a "people" to achieve a full measure of self-determination. A state whose government represents the whole of the people or peoples resident within its territory, on a basis of equality and without discrimination, and respects the principles of self-determination in its own internal arrangements, is entitled to the protection under international law of its territorial integrity.

(iii) Colonial and Oppressed Peoples

Accordingly, the general state of international law with respect to the right to self-determination is that the right operates within the overriding protection granted to the territorial integrity of "parent" states. However, as noted by Cassese, *supra*, there are certain defined contexts within which the right to the self-determination of peoples does allow that right to be exercised "externally", which, in the context of this Reference, would potentially mean secession:

> [t]he right to external self-determination, which entails the possibility of choosing (or restoring) independence, has only been bestowed upon two classes of peoples (those under colonial rule or foreign occupation), based upon the assumption that both classes make up entities that are inherently distinct from the colonialist Power and the occupant Power and that their 'territorial integrity', all but destroyed by the colonialist or occupying Power, should be fully restored ...

The right of colonial peoples to exercise their right to self-determination by breaking away from the "imperial" power is now undisputed, but is irrelevant to this Reference.

The other clear case where a right to external self-determination accrues is where a people is subject to alien subjugation, domination or exploitation outside a colonial context. This recognition finds its roots in the *Declaration on Friendly Relations*, *supra*: ...

> Every State has the duty to promote, through joint and separate action, the realization of the principle of equal rights and self-determination of peoples, in accordance with the provisions of the Charter, and to render assistance to the United Nations in carrying out the responsibilities entrusted to it by the Charter regarding the implementation of the principle, in order:
>
> (a) To promote friendly relations and co-operation among States; and
>
> (b) To bring a speedy end to colonialism, having due regard to the freely expressed will of the peoples concerned; and bearing in mind that subjection of peoples to alien subjugation, domination and exploitation

> constitutes a violation of the principle, as well as a denial of fundamental human rights, and is contrary to the Charter of the United Nations. ...

A number of commentators have further asserted that the right to self-determination may ground a right to unilateral secession in a third circumstance. Although this third circumstance has been described in several ways, the underlying proposition is that, when a people is blocked from the meaningful exercise of its right to self-determination internally, it is entitled, as a last resort, to exercise it by secession. The *Vienna Declaration*, *supra*, requirement that governments represent "the whole people belonging to the territory without distinction of any kind" adds credence to the assertion that such a complete blockage may potentially give rise to a right of secession.

Clearly, such a circumstance parallels the other two recognized situations in that the ability of a people to exercise its right to self-determination internally is somehow being totally frustrated. While it remains unclear whether this third proposition actually reflects an established international law standard, it is unnecessary for present purposes to make that determination. Even assuming that the third circumstance is sufficient to create a right to unilateral secession under international law, the current Quebec context cannot be said to approach such a threshold. As stated by the *amicus curiae*, Addendum to the factum of the *amicus curiae*, at paras. 15-16:

> 15. The Quebec people is not the victim of attacks on its physical existence or integrity, or of a massive violation of its fundamental rights. The Quebec people is manifestly not, in the opinion of the *amicus curiae*, an oppressed people.
>
> 16. For close to 40 of the last 50 years, the Prime Minister of Canada has been a Quebecer. During this period, Quebecers have held from time to time all the most important positions in the federal Cabinet. During the 8 years prior to June 1997, the Prime Minister and the Leader of the Official Opposition in the House of Commons were both Quebecers. At present, the Prime Minister of Canada, the Right Honourable Chief Justice and two other members of the Court, the Chief of Staff of the Canadian Armed Forces and the Canadian ambassador to the United States, not to mention the Deputy Secretary-General of the United Nations, are all Quebecers. The international achievements of Quebecers in most fields of human endeavour are too numerous to list. Since the dynamism of the Quebec people has been directed toward the business sector, it has been clearly successful in Quebec, the rest of Canada and abroad.

The population of Quebec cannot plausibly be said to be denied access to government. Quebecers occupy prominent positions within the government of Canada. Residents of the province freely make political choices and pursue economic, social and cultural development within Quebec, across Canada, and throughout the world. The population of Quebec is equitably represented in legislative, executive and judicial institutions. In short, to reflect the phraseology of the international documents that address the right to self-determination of peoples, Canada is a "sovereign and independent state conducting itself in compliance with the principle of equal rights and self-determination of peoples and thus possessed of a government representing the whole people belonging to the territory without distinction".

The continuing failure to reach agreement on amendments to the Constitution, while a matter of concern, does not amount to a denial of self-determination. In the absence of amendments to the Canadian Constitution, we must look at the constitutional arrangements presently in effect, and we cannot conclude under current circumstances that those arrangements place Quebecers in a disadvantaged position within the scope of the international law rule.

In summary, the international law right to self-determination only generates, at best, a right to external self-determination in situations of former colonies; where a people is oppressed, as for example under foreign military occupation; or where a definable group is denied meaningful access to government to pursue their political, economic, social and cultural development. In all three situations, the people in question are entitled to a right to external self-determination because they have been denied the ability to exert internally their right to self-determination. Such exceptional circumstances are manifestly inapplicable to Quebec under existing conditions. Accordingly, neither the population of the province of Quebec, even if characterized in terms of "people" or "peoples", nor its representative institutions, the National Assembly, the legislature or government of Quebec, possess a right, under international law, to secede unilaterally from Canada.

We would not wish to leave this aspect of our answer to Question 2 without acknowledging the importance of the submissions made to us respecting the rights and concerns of aboriginal peoples in the event of a unilateral secession, as well as the appropriate means of defining the boundaries of a seceding Quebec with particular regard to the northern lands occupied largely by aboriginal peoples. However, the concern of aboriginal peoples is precipitated by the asserted right of Quebec to unilateral secession. In light of our finding that there is no such right applicable to the population of Quebec, either under the Constitution of Canada or at international law, but that on the contrary a clear democratic expression of support for secession would lead under the Constitution to negotiations in which aboriginal interests would be taken into account, it becomes unnecessary to explore further the concerns of the aboriginal peoples in this Reference.

(2) Recognition of a Factual/Political Reality: the "Effectivity" Principle

As stated, an argument advanced by the *amicus curiae* on this branch of the Reference was that, while international law may not ground a positive right to unilateral secession in the context of Quebec, international law equally does not prohibit secession and, in fact, international recognition would be conferred on such a political reality if it emerged, for example, via effective control of the territory of what is now the province of Quebec.

It is true that international law may well, depending on the circumstances, adapt to recognize a political and/or factual reality, regardless of the legality of the steps leading to its creation. However, as mentioned at the outset, effectivity, as such, does not have any real applicability to Question 2, which asks whether a right to unilateral secession exists.

No one doubts that legal consequences may flow from political facts, and that "sovereignty is a political fact for which no purely legal authority can be constituted...", H. W. R. Wade, "The Basis of Legal Sovereignty", [1955] *Camb. L.J.* 172, at p. 196. Secession of a province from Canada, if successful in the streets, might well lead to the creation of a new state. Although recognition by other states is not, at least as a matter of theory, necessary to achieve statehood, the viability of a would-be state in the international community depends, as a practical matter, upon recognition by other states. That process of recognition is guided by legal norms. However, international recognition is not alone constitutive of statehood and, critically, does not relate back to the date of secession to serve retroactively as a source of a "legal" right to secede in the first place. Recognition occurs only after a territorial unit has been successful, as a political fact, in achieving secession.

As indicated in responding to Question 1, one of the legal norms which may be recognized by states in granting or withholding recognition of emergent states is the legitimacy of the process by which the *de facto* secession is, or was, being pursued. The process of recognition, once considered to be an exercise of pure sovereign discretion, has come to be associated with legal norms. See, e.g., *European Community Declaration on the Guidelines on the Recognition of New States in Eastern Europe and in the Soviet Union*, 31 I.L.M. 1485 (1992), at p. 1487. While national interest and perceived political advantage to the recognizing state obviously play an important role, foreign states may also take into account their view as to the existence of a right to self-determination on the part of the population of the putative state, and a counterpart domestic evaluation, namely, an examination of the legality of the secession according to the law of the state from which the territorial unit purports to have seceded. As we indicated in our answer to Question 1, an emergent state that has disregarded legitimate obligations arising out of its previous situation can potentially expect to be hindered by that disregard in achieving international recognition, at least with respect to the timing of that recognition. On the other hand, compliance by the seceding province with such legitimate obligations would weigh in favour of international recognition. The notion that what is not explicitly prohibited is implicitly permitted has little relevance where (as here) international law refers the legality of secession to the domestic law of the seceding state and the law of that state holds unilateral secession to be unconstitutional.

As a court of law, we are ultimately concerned only with legal claims. If the principle of "effectivity" is no more than that "successful revolution begets its own legality" (S. A. de Smith, "Constitutional Lawyers in Revolutionary Situations" (1968), 7 *West. Ont. L. Rev.* 93, at p. 96, it necessarily means that legality follows and does not precede the successful revolution. *Ex hypothesi*, the successful revolution took place outside the constitutional framework of the predecessor state, otherwise it would not be characterized as "a revolution". It may be that a unilateral secession by Quebec would eventually be accorded legal status by Canada and other states, and thus give rise to legal consequences; but this does not support the more radical contention that subsequent recognition of a state of affairs brought about by a unilateral declaration of independence could be taken to mean that secession was achieved under colour of a legal right.

An argument was made to analogize the principle of effectivity with the second aspect of the rule of law identified by this Court in the *Manitoba Language Rights Reference*, *supra*, at p. 753, namely, avoidance of a legal vacuum. In that Reference, it will be recalled, this Court declined to strike down all of Manitoba's legislation for its failure to comply with constitutional dictates, out of concern that this would leave the province in a state of chaos. In so doing, we recognized that the rule of law is a constitutional principle which permits the courts to address the practical consequences of their actions, particularly in constitutional cases. The similarity between that principle and the principle of effectivity, it was argued, is that both attempt to refashion the law to meet social reality. However, nothing of our concern in the *Manitoba Language Rights Reference* about the severe practical consequences of unconstitutionality affected our conclusion that, as a matter of law, all Manitoba legislation at issue in that case was unconstitutional. The Court's declaration of unconstitutionality was clear and unambiguous. The Court's concern with maintenance of the rule of law was directed in its relevant aspect to the appropriate remedy, which in that case was to suspend the declaration of invalidity to permit appropriate rectification to take place.

It proclaims that an illegal act may eventually acquire legal status if, as a matter of empirical fact, it is recognized on the international plane. Our law has long recognized that through a combination of acquiescence and prescription, an illegal act may at some later point be accorded some form of legal status. In the law of property, for example, it is well-known that a squatter on land may ultimately become the owner if the true owner sleeps on his or her right to repossess the land. In this way, a change in the factual circumstances may subsequently be reflected in a change in legal status. It is, however, quite another matter to suggest that a subsequent condonation of an initially illegal act retroactively creates a legal right to engage in the act in the first place. The broader contention is not supported by the international principle of effectivity or otherwise and must be rejected.

Question 3

In the event of a conflict between domestic and international law on the right of the National Assembly, legislature or government of Quebec to effect the secession of Quebec from Canada unilaterally, which would take precedence in Canada?

In view of our answers to Questions 1 and 2, there is no conflict between domestic and international law to be addressed in the context of this Reference.

NOTES AND QUESTIONS

1. What is the legal effect of the Court's statements regarding the eventuality of a clear majority of Quebecers voting in favor of secession? Does it consider the issue a political question?

2. Is the reasoning in the international law section of the opinion convincing? Should the answer to Question 1 (re: the democratic legitimacy of a clear majority of Quebecers in favor of secession and the need for subsequent negotiations) have any impact on the answer to Question 2?

3. Should the Canadian government take account of the wishes of the majority of the population who do not live in the territory seeking independence when an independence issue comes up? To what extent should a central government weigh the disruptions likely to be caused to the rest of the people if part of the territory seeks to withdraw and declare its independence?

B. INTERNATIONAL PRESCRIPTIONS THAT MAY ACT TO LIMIT ESTABLISHMENT AND CHANGE BY INTERNAL ELITES

1. United Nations Policies That Favor Territorial Integrity

a. United Nations Charter

Article 2(4): All Members shall refrain in their international relations from the threat or use of force against the territorial integrity or political independence of any state, or in any other manner inconsistent with the Purposes of the United Nations.

b. U Thant, United Nations Secretary-General, Statement

7 U.N. MONTHLY CHRONICLE 36 (Feb. 1970)

So far as the question of secession of a particular member state is concerned, the United Nations' attitude is unequivocable. As an international organization, the United Nations has never accepted and does not accept and I do not believe that it will ever accept the principle of secession of a part of its member State.

c. Report of the United Nations Secretary-General, An Agenda for Peace - Preventive Diplomacy, Peacemaking and Peace-Keeping

U.N. Doc. S/24111, 31 I.L.M. 953, 959-960 (1992)

17. The foundation-stone of this work [by the United Nations] is and must remain the State. Respect for its fundamental sovereignty and integrity are crucial to any common international progress. The time of absolute and exclusive sovereignty, however, has passed; its theory was never matched by reality. It is the task of leaders of States today to understand this and to find a balance between the needs of good internal governance and the requirements of an ever more interdependent world. Commerce, communications and environmental matters transcend administrative borders; but inside those borders is where individuals carry out the first order of their economic, political and social lives. The United Nations has not closed its door. Yet if every ethnic, religious or linguistic group claimed statehood, there would be no limit to fragmentation, and peace, security and economic well-being for all would become ever more difficult to achieve.

18. One requirement for solutions to theses problems lies in commitment to human rights with a special sensitivity to those of minorities, whether ethnic, religious, social or linguistic. The League of Nations provided a machinery for the international protection of minorities. The General Assembly soon will have before it a declaration on the rights of minorities. That instrument, together with the increasingly effective machinery of the United Nations dealing with human rights, should enhance the situation of minorities as well as the stability of States.

19. Globalism and nationalism need not be viewed as opposing trends, doomed to spur each other on to extremes of reaction. The healthy globalization of contemporary life requires in the first instance solid identities and fundamental freedoms. The sovereignty, territorial integrity and independence of States within the established international system, and the principle of self-determination of peoples, both of great value and importance, must not be permitted to work against each other in the period ahead. Respect for democratic principles at all levels of social existence is crucial: in communities, within States and within the community of States. Our constant duty should be to maintain the integrity of each while finding a balanced design for all.

d. Rosalyn Higgins, Problems and Process: International Law and How We Use It

127-128 (Oxford U. Press 1994)

One further issue on self-determination remains to be mentioned. It follows from the principle of territorial integrity. It is often the case that self-determination is part of the armoury of rhetoric in what is essentially a dispute about territorial title. Both the case of Gibraltar and that of the Falklands illustrate the point. Title to Gibraltar is disputed between the United Kingdom and Spain. Title to the Falklands-Malvinas is disputed between the United Kingdom and Argentina. From the perspective of the United Kingdom, self-determination has a pertinent role to play. These are dependent territories, whose peoples have been given the opportunity to decide if they would like to remain in the status quo or not. From the British point of view, it is important that the wishes of the peoples of the territories be heard and heeded. But from the point of view of the Argentineans and the Spanish, that is an irrelevance. If the territory concerned belongs to Argentina, or to Spain, then the inhabitants have no right of self-determination-any more than would Spanish or Argentinean nationals happening to live in the United Kingdom. Judge Hardy Dillard's famous dictum in the *Western Sahara Case* has been much quoted: 'It is for the people to determine the destiny of the territory and not the territory the destiny of the people.'

Attractive an aphorism though it is, it still has to be said that the territorial issue *does* come first. Until it is determined where territorial sovereignty lies, it is impossible to see if the inhabitants have a right of self-determination. Thus in the *Western Sahara Case* it was necessary first to see if the territory did indeed belong to Mauritania or Morocco. If so, the peoples of Western Sahara would have had no right of self-determination (other than the ongoing right that all citizens of those countries have to determine their own political status and economic development). As neither country had sovereignty over Western Sahara, that territory was indeed a colonial dependency of Spain, whose peoples were entitled to exercise self-determination and choose their own destiny. It necessarily follows from all that I have said that I do not share the view of those who see the current problems of Hong Kong as problems of self-determination. At least so far as the leased territories are concerned, it is clear that title lies with China and must revert there in 1997. The issue in my view is to secure the generality of human rights of all in Hong Kong after that time rather than to insist that they have been denied the right of self-determination.

Notes and Questions

1. The policy underlying respect for territorial integrity is the concept of state sovereignty, a symbol justifying consolidation of power originally defined by Jean Bodin in his *Six livres de la République*, culminating in the establishment of nation-states in the wake of the Treaty of Westphalia. The Congress of Vienna was successful in preventing changes to existing borders in Europe via the 1815 Holy Alliance for more than half a century. President Lincoln won the United States Civil War against an attempt to secede with the famous argument: "[A] house divided against itself cannot stand." Abraham Lincoln, Address Accepting the Republican Nomination for U.S. Senate at Republican State Convention in Springfield, Illinois (June 16, 1858). The United Nations Charter reaffirms, though not without qualifications, this prescription of respect for territorial integrity of supposedly equal sovereigns.

2. How can the policy maker assess the advantages of preserving existing territorial configurations? An argument has been made that a right to secession is superfluous if peoples are granted the full complement of human rights, including minority rights up to far-reaching autonomy status, and if the transaction costs of secession are likely to be high in terms of human rights. *See* Hurst Hannum, Autonomy, Sovereignty, and Self-Determination: The Accommodation of Conflicting Rights (U. of Penn. Press 1990). Do you agree with that assumption? Would autonomy short of independence in combination with effective human rights and minority rights guarantees have been sufficient to satisfy the demands of, say, the Slovenes and Croats in the early 1990s? Is this satisfaction the only relevant issue?

3. In *Secession and Self-Determination: A Territorial Interpretation*, 16 YALE J. INT'L L. 177 (1991), Professor Lea Brilmayer suggests that "without a normatively sound claim to territory, self-determination arguments do not form a plausible basis for secession." *Id.* at 192. Professor David Wippman takes issue with that approach, arguing that in many secessionist disputes, e.g. the Balkans:

> [h]istorical territorial grievances are so ancient and so plentiful on all sides that they cannot be disentangled in any meaningful way ... [and]... any attempt to resolve such problems by redrawing borders to fit a particular critical date reflecting a particular historical grievance is unlikely to succeed. The predominant contemporary response to this problem has been to expand the rights available to minorities, in the hope that by doing so their legitimate concerns can be met within the confines of existing states...Unfortunately, the minority rights approach has its own difficulties. The extent of the rights at issue, and the groups entitled to claim them, remain matters of continuing uncertainty and debate, rendering self-determination a highly indeterminate and variable principle. ...

David Wippman, *Secession, Territorial Claims, and the Indeterminancy of Self-Determination*, 25 YALE J. INT'L L. 287, 289 (2000).

4. Does the context of the U.N. Charter Arts. 73 and 74 limit the scope of lawful claims to self-determination to those of "non-self-governing territories?" Wouldn't, in all other cases, the principle of territorial integrity be an essential component of the world constitutive process?

2. The Customary Principle of *uti possidetis*

Consider the limitations brought to bear on the claim to self-determination by the principle of *uti possidetis* and its application in the boundary dispute between Burkina Faso and the Republic of Mali:

a. Case Concerning the Frontier Dispute (Burk. Faso v. Mali)
1986 I.C.J. 554 (Dec. 22)

... 19. The characteristic feature of the legal context of the frontier determination to be undertaken by the Chamber is that both States involved derive their existence from the process of decolonization which has been unfolding in Africa during the past 30 years. Their territories, and that of Niger, were formerly part of the French colonies which were grouped together under the name of French West Africa (AOF). Considering only the situation which prevailed immediately before the accession to independence of the two States, and disregarding previous administrative changes, it can be said that Burkina Faso corresponds to the colony of Upper Volta, and the Republic of Mali to the colony of Sudan (formerly French Sudan). It is to be supposed that the Parties drew inspiration from the principle expressly stated in the well-known resolution (AGH/Res. 16 (I)), adopted at the first session of the Conference of African Heads of State and Government, meeting in Cairo in 1964, whereby the Conference solemnly declared that all member States of the Organization of African Unity 'solemnly ... pledge themselves to respect the frontiers existing on their achievement of national independence', inasmuch as, in the preamble to their Special Agreement, they stated that the settlement of the dispute by the Chamber must be 'based in particular on respect for the principle of the intangibility of frontiers inherited from colonization'. It is clear from this text, and from the pleadings and oral arguments of the Parties, that they are in agreement as regards both the applicable law and the starting-point for the legal reasoning which is to lead to the determination of the frontier between their territories in the disputed area.

20. Since the two Parties have, as noted above, expressly requested the Chamber to resolve their dispute on the basis, in particular, of the 'principle of the intangibility of frontiers inherited from colonization', the Chamber cannot disregard the principle of *uti possidetis juris*, the application of which gives rise to this respect for intangibility of frontiers. Although there is no need, for the purposes of the present case, to show that this is a firmly established principle of international law where decolonization is concerned, the Chamber nonetheless wishes to emphasize its general scope, in view of its exceptional importance for the African continent and for the two Parties. In this connection it should be noted that the principle of *uti possidetis* seems to have been first invoked and applied in Spanish America, inasmuch as this was the continent which first witnessed the phenomenon of decolonization involving the formation of a number of sovereign States on territory formerly belonging to a single metropolitan State. Nevertheless the principle is not a special rule which pertains solely to one specific system of international law. It is a general principle, which is logically connected with the phenomenon of the obtaining of independence, wherever it occurs. Its obvious purpose is to prevent the independence and stability of new States being endangered by fratricidal struggles provoked by the challenging of frontiers following the withdrawal of the administering power.

21. It was for this reason that, as soon as the phenomenon of decolonization characteristic of the situation in Spanish America in the 19th century subsequently appeared in Africa in the 20th century, the principle of *uti possidetis*, in the sense described above, fell to be applied. The fact that the new African States have respected the administrative boundaries and frontiers established by the colonial powers must be seen not as a mere practice contributing to the gradual emergence of a principle of customary international law, limited in its impact to the African continent as it had previously been to Spanish America, but as the application in Africa of a rule of general scope.

22. The elements of *uti possidetis* were latent in the many declarations made by African leaders in the dawn of independence. These declarations confirmed the maintenance of the territorial status quo at the time of independence, and stated the principle of respect both for the frontiers deriving from international agreements, and for those resulting from mere internal administrative divisions. The Charter of the Organization of African Unity did not ignore the principle of *uti possidetis*, but made only indirect reference to it in Article 3, according to which member States solemnly affirm the principle of respect for the sovereignty and territorial integrity of every State. However, at their first summit

conference after the creation of the Organization of African Unity, the African Heads of State, in their Resolution mentioned above (AGH/Res. 16 (I)), adopted in Cairo in July 1964, deliberately defined and stressed the principle of *uti possidetis juris* contained only in an implicit sense in the Charter of their organization.

23. There are several different aspects to this principle, in its well-known application in Spanish America. The first aspect, emphasized by the Latin genitive *juris*, is found in the pre-eminence accorded to legal title over effective possession as a basis of sovereignty. Its purpose, at the time of the achievement of independence by the former Spanish colonies of America, was to scotch any designs which non-American colonizing powers might have on regions which had been assigned by the former metropolitan State to one division or another, but which were still uninhabited or unexplored. However, there is more to the principle of *uti possidetis* than this particular aspect. The essence of the principle lies in its primary aim of securing respect for the territorial boundaries at the moment when independence is achieved. Such territorial boundaries might be no more than delimitations between different administrative divisions or colonies all subject to the same sovereign. In that case, the application of the principle of *uti possidetis* resulted in administrative boundaries being transformed into international frontiers in the full sense of the term. This is true both of the States which took shape in the regions of South America which were dependent on the Spanish Crown, and of the States Parties to the present case, which took shape within the vast territories of French West Africa. *Uti possidetis*, as a principle which upgraded former administrative delimitations, established during the colonial period, to international frontiers, is therefore a principle of a general kind which is logically connected with this form of decolonization wherever it occurs.

24. The territorial boundaries which have to be respected may also derive from international frontiers which previously divided a colony of one State from a colony of another, or indeed a colonial territory from the territory of an independent State, or one which was under protectorate, but had retained its international personality. There is no doubt that the obligation to respect pre-existing international frontiers in the event of a State succession derives from a general rule of international law, whether or not the rule is expressed in the formula *uti possidetis*. Hence the numerous solemn affirmations of the intangibility of the frontiers existing at the time of the independence of African States, whether made by senior African statesmen or by organs of the Organization of African Unity itself, are evidently declaratory rather than constitutive: they recognize and confirm an existing principle, and do not seek to consecrate a new principle or the extension to Africa of a rule previously applied only in another continent.

25. However, it may be wondered how the time-hallowed principle has been able to withstand the new approaches to international law as expressed in Africa, where the successive attainment of independence and the emergence of new States have been accompanied by a certain questioning of traditional international law. At first sight this principle conflicts outright with another one, the right

of peoples to self-determination. In fact, however, the maintenance of the territorial status quo in Africa is often seen as the wisest course, to preserve what has been achieved by peoples who have struggled for their independence, and to avoid a disruption which would deprive the continent of the gains achieved by much sacrifice. The essential requirement of stability in order to survive, to develop and gradually to consolidate their independence in all fields, has induced African States judiciously to consent to the respecting of colonial frontiers, and to take account of it in the interpretation of the principle of self-determination of peoples.

26. Thus the principle of *uti possidetis* has kept its place among the most important legal principles, despite the apparent contradiction which explained its coexistence alongside the new norms. Indeed it was by deliberate choice that African States selected, among all the classic principles, that of *uti possidetis*. This remains an undeniable fact. In the light of the foregoing remarks, it is clear that the applicability of *uti possidetis* in the present case cannot be challenged merely because in 1960, the year when Mali and Burkina Faso achieved independence, the Organization of African Unity which was to proclaim this principle did not yet exist, and the above-mentioned resolution calling for respect for the pre-existing frontiers dates only from 1964.

Separate Opinion of JUDGE ABI-SAAB:

...12. Now although I completely endorse the Judgment's general analysis of the status of maps in frontier questions ... and especially its conclusion that they have value only 'as evidence of an auxiliary or confirmatory kind' 'endorsing a conclusion at which a court has arrived by other means unconnected with the maps', I consider that here too the Judgment has failed to apply in practice what it has stated as a general principle. For, as the Judgment very clearly explains - reflecting the settled international case-law - maps in themselves never constitute a legal title of any kind, either principal or subsidiary. Yet via letter 191 CM2, which has no intrinsic legal value and is merely a verbal transcription of the 1925 Blondel la Rougery map, the Judgment manages to promote that map into a subsidiary title (what is more, it comes close in paragraph 62 to a similar result in respect of the 1960 IGN map).

13. The purpose of this frantic search for a 'written legal title', turning anything and everything into account, is to satisfy a particular conception of the *uti possidetis* principle.

However, this principle, like any other, is not to be conceived in the absolute; it has always to be interpreted in the light of its function within the international legal order.

At first sight, it may indeed seem paradoxical that peoples that have struggled for their independence should set so much store by their 'colonial heritage'. At the beginning, however, at the time when the Latin American countries were achieving independence, the principle of *uti possidetis* was formulated to serve a dual purpose: first, a defensive purpose towards the rest of the world, in the form of an outright denial that there was any land without a sovereign (or *terra nullius*) in the decolonized territories, even in unexplored areas or those beyond the control of the colonizers; secondly, a preventive purpose: to avoid or at least to minimize conflict occurring in the relationships among the successors, by freezing the carved-up territory in the format it exhibited at the moment of independence.

14. These two objectives therefore postulate the existence of a boundary, an impermeable territorial division, at the moment of independence. This hypothesis can only be factually verified in each case if a boundary is taken to mean a 'line' in the geometric sense of the word. Otherwise it will be the inevitable fate of the principle of *uti possidetis* to operate as a mere fiction that jars with reality.

This is because a minimum of two points will always suffice for the definition of a line if one starts from the geometric concept of a 'line' as 'generated by the motion of a point' (Encyclopedia Britannica, 11th ed.). In this sense there would always be a line to satisfy the logical requirements for the functioning of the *uti possidetis* principle. But if one starts from the common idea of a line as a concrete trace every point on which is specifically identifiable, it is far from likely that the postulate could be shown as realized in every instance.

15. By proceeding from the geometric concept of a line, which is alone capable of reconciling the principle of *uti possidetis* with the facts, we can state that there is always a line which defines the outer limit of lawful possession. But the scope of a court's role in identifying that line will vary inversely to the extent of its having taken concrete shape. The fewer the points (or points of reference) involved in its definition, the greater the court's 'degrees of freedom' (in the statistical sense). And it is here that considerations of equity *infra legem* (mentioned in paragraph 28 of the Judgment) come into play, to guide the court in the exercise of this freedom when interpreting and applying the law and the legal titles involved.

16. As regards the frontier line which concerns us, between the region of Toussougou/Feto Maraboule in the west and the eastern terminus (mounts N'Gouma/Kabia ford), we have only two points of reference, the pools of Soum and In Abao.

In this region, largely traversed by the Beli, no visible outline of the 'photograph of the territory' on the critical date can in my view be discerned, as I have said above, either from regulative texts, or from any sufficiently conspicuous body of administrative practice. It was up to the Chamber to give concrete shape to the line - which, defined as it is by the above-mentioned reference-points, does as such exist - on the basis of considerations of equity *infra legem.*

17. The Judgment has chosen a line coinciding with that of the maps, which do not in themselves constitute a legal title or rest upon any such genuine title, where letter 191 CM2 is concerned. This is admittedly one possible legal solution within the degrees of freedom obtaining in the circumstances of the case; and

that is why I consider it legally acceptable. But it is not the only solution which would have been legally possible, nor in my opinion the best. I would have preferred another: one which, while respecting the points of reference (and it is not by chance that both are watering-places), would have been more deeply impregnated with considerations of equity *infra legem* in the interpretation and application of law, given that the region concerned is a nomadic one, subject to drought, so that access to water is vital.

b. Steven R. Ratner, *Drawing A Better Line:* Uti Possidetis *and the Borders of New States*

90 AM. J. INT'L L. 590, 591, 598-599, 612-613, 617-624 (1996)

Should the map be drawn according to lines sketched out through processes now regarded as illegitimate and that may contribute to a worsening of human rights conditions in the new countries? Or must we resign ourselves to General Ratko Mladic's solution, where "borders are drawn with blood" and remain extralegally ordained?

At the core of the legal debate over the territory of new states is the principle of *uti possidetis*. Stated simply, *uti possidetis* provides that states emerging from decolonization shall presumptively inherit the colonial administrative borders that they held at the time of independence. It largely governed the determination of the size and shape of the states of former Spanish Latin America beginning in the early 1800s, as well as former European Africa and Southeast Asia beginning in the 1950s. The relevance of *uti possidetis* today is evidenced by the practice of states during the dissolution of the former Soviet Union, Yugoslavia and Czechoslovakia, apparently sanctifying the former internal administrative lines as interstate frontiers.

Reliance on *uti possidetis* during the post-Cold War breakups has stemmed from three arguments or assumptions. First, *uti possidetis* reduces the prospects of armed conflict by providing the only clear outcome in such situations. Absent such a policy, all borders would be open to dispute, and new states would fall prey to irredentist neighbors or internal secessionist claimants. Second, because a cosmopolitan democratic state can function within any borders, the conversion of administrative borders to international borders is as sensible as any other approach and far simpler. Third, and buttressing the other two, *uti possidetis* is asserted as a default rule of international law mandating the conversion of all administrative boundaries into international borders. This rule emerged during the decolonization of Latin America and Africa but would apply by logical extension to the breakup of states today. The most significant elaboration of this extension came from the commission chaired by Judge Robert Badinter advising the European Community on legal questions associated with the breakup of Yugoslavia.

These views seem compelling; yet the easy embrace by governments of *uti possidetis* and the suggestion that it is now a general rule of international law to govern the breakup of states lead to two distinct, yet opposite, spillover effects that endanger global order at this time of ethnic conflict. First, a policy or rule that transforms all administrative borders of modern states into international boundaries creates a significant hazard in the name of simplicity—namely, the temptation of ethnic separatists to divide the world further along administrative lines. If the Republic of Georgia's new borders must coincide with those of the former Georgian Soviet Socialist Republic, are not the future Republic of Abhazia's just as clearly those of the former Abhaz Autonomous Soviet Socialist Republic? Would the Quebecois consider secession so readily if the new state had different borders from those established by Canada and the United Kingdom for the purpose of integrating Quebec into the Dominion?

Second, the extension of *uti possidetis* to modern breakups leads to genuine injustices and instability by leaving significant populations both unsatisfied with their status in new states and uncertain of political participation there. By hiding behind inflated notions of *uti possidetis*, state leaders avoid engaging the issue of territorial adjustments—even minor ones—which is central to the process of self-determination. In the case of Yugoslavia, for instance, although *uti possidetis* hardly caused the eruption of armed conflict, the assumption by states of its applicability from the outset prevented any debate over the adjustment of boundaries and limited the universe of possible borders to one—leaving those people on the "wrong" side of the border ripe for "ethnic cleansing." Elsewhere, whether with regard to left bank Dniestrians in the Republic of Moldova or Armenians in Nagorno-Karabakh, *uti possidetis* may prove a recipe for continued denial of human dignity to minorities.

It is thus time to reexamine this oft-invoked principle of international law and relations. For application of uti possidetis to the breakup of states today both ignores critical distinctions between internal lines and international boundaries and, more important, is profoundly at odds with current trends in international law and politics. Many internal borders do merit transformation into international boundaries based on historical and other characteristics; but theassumption that all such borders must be so transformed is unwarranted. . . .

The International Court of Justice has, of course, stated in dictum in *Frontier Dispute (Burkina Faso/Mali)* that *uti possidetis* is a "general principle" and a "rule of general scope" in the case of decolonization. It has never adjudicated whether *uti possidetis* is a norm of customary law, because, in these types of border disputes, both parties have stipulated by *compromis* or otherwise that their boundary would be determined according to the borders in effect at the time of independence. Nevertheless, the repeated assumption by the Court that *uti possidetis* is a norm of international law is probative. Without definitively opining on the issue, one may thus assume some support for regarding *uti possidetis* as a norm of regional customary law in Latin America and Africa, if not a general norm as well, in the context of decolonization. . . .

The trends in state practice toward equating the right of internal self-determination with democracy do not categorically negative *uti possidetis* as the lawful response in the event of breakups. Presumably, new states based on prior internal borders could allow periodic and genuine elections, satisfying the basic element of the democratic entitlement. Just as *uti possidetis* proved a prerequisite to nation building after decolonization by promoting stability and reducing the possibility of conflict, so could it also prove a condition for true internal self-determination.

Yet the recognition in international law of the primacy of political participation does exert some pull on the sanctity of *uti possidetis.* If the overriding purpose of a state is to permit its people to advance their values through a democratic process, then the formation of a new state ought to take that goal into account. One method of promoting this policy is to ensure that the inhabitants of the new state truly seek membership in it and adjust the frontiers so as to produce an acceptable degree of participation. Of course, if the administrative borders already serve to define a polity dedicated to democracy and supported by the populace, modification will be unnecessary. ...

Uti possidetis ... represents the classic example of what Thomas Franck has called an "idiot rule"—a simple, clear norm that offers an acceptable outcome in most situations but whose very clarity undermines its legitimacy in others. The rule may assume that no border is more rational than another, or that the issue of borders is simply so complex and emotional that states will always prove unable to reallocate territory peacefully. Either way, any solution other than acceptance of past injustices would be too complicated to be applied, would lead to chaos, and would therefore prove illegitimate. This argument also won the day during the African decolonizations, usually with good reason; and it seems to underlie certain creative proposals concerning intrastate conflict today. . . .

I set out four guidelines for decision makers that suggest that the options are not so stark and lay the basis for a principled alternative to *uti possidetis*. ...

First, the functional and legal arguments against the automatic transformation of frontiers suggest a compelling need to respect the original Roman-law meaning of *uti possidetis*: to preserve the status quo only until states can resolve their competing claims, rather than apply the gloss from decolonization whereby states effectively presumed independence-day lines to be permanent. . . .

If, during the creation of states, the new entities cannot agree on an appropriate division of territory, they should respect existing lines of control—likely to be designated by administrative lines—until an authoritative determination is reached on new boundaries.

As a result, the provisional status will remain until the parties accept the costs and benefits of those borders or new ones. ...

The most immediate consequence of this starting point is an admittedly heavy burden on decision makers, whether national diplomats or international commissions or courts: to deal directly with the location of international borders, rather than retreat behind the simple, but anachronistic, decolonization form of *uti possidetis*. ...

Supplementing any proposal that states consider border changes is a requirement that the process take place through peaceful means alone. For states that have already split up, this requirement means nothing more or less than adherence to Article 2(4) of the Charter. ...

With these basic policies in mind, diplomats, conciliators and arbitrators should scrutinize administrative boundaries for their suitability as international frontiers. This process is the critical prerequisite to determining whether a substantially better alternative is available and drawing a final line. Several factors merit consideration.

First, weight must be given to the age of the line. Borders centuries old count for more than those decades old, not only because of an aversion to opening closed issues, but also because of the likelihood that the populations will have adjusted to long-standing borders. . . .

Second, the process by which the line was drawn will merit consideration. A constitutionally authorized line, for instance, ought to have a greater presumption of permanence than one determined solely at the command of a dictator. . . .

Last, because neither age nor origin directly addresses functional suitability as an international frontier, negotiators and arbitrators will have to take account of the viability of the entities that would emerge from secessions or breakups along existing lines. On the one hand, states have been unwilling to consider the size or shape of a claimant to statehood in the decision to accord recognition, especially territories emerging from colonial rule. But political geographers routinely study the effect of geography on national development; and theorists of self-determination have evaluated these issues in considering the propriety of secession. Even the ICJ has acknowledged the importance of economic issues by considering the efficient exploitation of resources in addressing disputed sea borders.

Thus, decision makers would be well-advised to consider whether the administrative lines would allow the new states—including the remnant of the prior state—to govern themselves adequately and develop economically. If the borders contain irrational elements for the governance and economy of separate states, as may well be the case given the distinct functions of internal and interstate borders, the decision makers will have to consider alternatives. ...

A provisional interpretation of *uti possidetis*, coupled with a prohibition on the use of force and scrutiny of existing administrative borders, still does not directly confront the core issue of human rights arguing against extension of the decolonization form of *uti possidetis*; namely, its failure to account for the harm to individual well-being that may result either from a lack of commitment by the new state (defined by the old borders) to protect certain groups or from their desire to locate elsewhere. That shortcoming necessitates a direct role for the affected populations in arriving at lines to replace the administrative borders. Thus, some form of consultation with the populace of a disputed territory on its future, though perhaps not a binding vote, is needed, if not already legally required. …

Principles of equity used by international courts and states in border disputes could also have an important role in drawing a final line. In the *Frontier Dispute* case, for example, Judge Abi-Saab pointed out that, when judges need to determine a border, their degrees of freedom to draw a line using equitable principles increase as the number of known border points decreases. While leaving much to the biases of arbitrators, equity offers some framework within which courts can take account of a variety of relevant factors. …

If the hallmark of an effective legal system is some degree of predictability of outcome, an assault on extending the decolonization form of *uti possidetis* to the breakup of states would appear at first to undermine the cause. For that formulation is clearly the easiest short-run method for determining the borders of a new state. But law, of course, is about justice and legitimacy as well. And self-determination, by its nature, is an enormously complex and rich process in international law. If its goal is to enable individuals and groups to realize their human rights, then the complexity of the territorial element cannot be wished away through invocation of a hallowed formula.

This article has sought to demonstrate that the default rule requiring inheritance of prior boundaries suffers from functional and normative flaws when applied to administrative lines within states. In particular, the extension of *uti possidetis* to these situations is highly suspect because of (1) the difference between internal and international borders, as well as between internal state borders and the internal colonial lines to which the principle was formerly applied; (2) the supplanting of the policy imperative underlying *uti possidetis* (decolonization) with the uncertainty surrounding state breakups; and, most important, (3) the constitutive changes in international law, principally the emphasis on internal self-determination and participatory government and the demise of *terra nullius.* These factors all require recognition in the law and policies governing modern breakups or attempts at them. The results may be unsatisfying to some, and the questions raised (including the lack of centralized enforcement mechanisms) may lead many to conclude that *uti possidetis* should develop into a rule for these situations. Even under the approach suggested here, the scrutiny of existing borders may yield a determination that many should become the boundaries of new states, and perhaps the burden of proof should lie on those who seek to challenge them.

To adopt that course of action uniformly and automatically, however, perpetuates a subterfuge: a formalized self-determination that enables a new state to form along the administrative lines of the old territorial unit but neglects the underlying territorial issues that prompted the dissatisfaction in the first place, and perhaps lays the groundwork for a new round of interstate conflicts and attempted secessions. It rewards the leaders of secessionist movements by more readily granting them a new territory, but offers uncertain prospects for the human rights and political participation of the inhabitants or the public order of the region. Only by directly engaging the territorial question, with all its dimensions, is the international community likely to control the breakup of states in an orderly manner consistent with human dignity.

NOTES AND QUESTIONS

1. Consider the following dialogue at the 1993 Annual Meeting of the American Society of International Law:

> *Professor W. Michael Reisman:* Ignoring the deep ambiguities in *uti possidetis* as to whether it refers to the *de facto* lines that exist at a certain moment or the *de jure* lines, which should exist but may not exist, *uti possidetis* says that the common interest of a particular region, or of the world if we extend the principle, now requires that there be no more adjustments in borders and that political change must take place within those borders... I think this is something we ought to think about, given the current transitions and the extraordinary costs they present... Do we need an *uti possidetis juris gentium* rather than an *uti possidetis* with only a regional application? In practice, this would mean that when group elites come forward, whether in former Czechoslovakia, former Yugoslavia, or some other state that is about to become a former state, beating the tom-toms of ethnicism, tribalism or subnationalism, the international community's response may be: "Sorry, the boundaries here are not subject to change. The fundamental entity that exists cannot be broken up. You may, however, seek all sorts of accommodations inside the national community [...]." The international community would provide some supervision in terms of a bill of human rights. I think that is one rule that may emerge as part of the guidelines for decision makers in this country and elsewhere, when they are faced with certain claims for transition. ...
>
> *Professor Siegfried Wiessner:* ... As to the *uti possidetis* rule and the desirability of such a bright-line solution for the current problems in, among others, former Yugoslavia and the former Soviet Union, I think that a return to that rule would signify a return to the futile recipe of the Holy Alliance. We cannot keep the lid on peoples who want to reorganize themselves. We cannot freeze history. It would be a betrayal of our own democratic ideals to deny groups the right to celebrate their culture and to have the ultimate choice in how to define themselves and to determine their political fate. The solution should not be to limit them to their borders as they exist now. I think that President Woodrow Wilson and the founding fathers of this country who asserted the right to revolution would be turning in their graves.
>
> *Professor Reisman:* I think that Woodrow Wilson, watching what is happening in former Yugoslavia, is turning in his grave.
>
> *Professor Wiessner:* He certainly would be very perturbed, and I share your concern. You meet this concern, however, not by denying self-determination, but by holding each new territorial entity to the fundamental tenets of international human rights.
>
> Lastly, I would like to add a suggestion amplifying Professor Franck's idea of a triad of relevant actors. Present-day international community might best be described as an architecture informed by the principle of subsidiarity, in which some functions are performed by the world community on the planetary level, some by regional communities, others by nation-states, and finally some on the local level, through formalized structures and town meetings in the Jeffersonian tradition. As a matter of preference, the communities in which we individuals organize ourselves should be communities that we

> freely enter into and continuously reaffirm. That means taking seriously Ernest Renan's plebiscite of every day. If people are organized in forced compounds such as the former Soviet Union and Yugoslavia, those communities will not survive. International law should allow for flexibility in the formation of new communities. There should, however, be an ultimate substantive restriction on what any authority may do, based on fundamental tenets of respect for the dignity of the individual, and these tenets should be forced by the international community against any new entity that arises and violates them.

87 AM. SOC'Y INT'L L. PROC. 258-259, 264-265 (1993).

2. The principle of *uti possidetis* was originally used, in international law, in the decolonization process of South America and Africa to limit the claim of now decolonized entities to the geographical extent of the former possessions of the colonial power. Later, it was also used to justify restriction of claims to self-determination of non-colonial entities to those of administrative subunits of composite states, such as member-states of a federation.

3. The Badinter Commission, adapting policies followed in the decolonization context of Africa and Latin America, and following broader statements to that effect in the Burkina Faso decision of the ICJ, determined that the new entities in Yugoslavia, to be recognizable by the EC, *inter alia,* had to be co-extensive with the territorial boundaries that had separated the component parts of the SFRY, *i.e.*, its former republics. *Conference of Yugoslavia Arbitration Commission, Opinions on Questions Arising from the Dissolution of Yugoslavia*, Jan. 11, 1992, and July 4, 1992, 31 I.L.M. 1488 (1992). For thorough analysis, *see* Matthew C. R. Craven, *The European Community Arbitration Commission on Yugoslavia*, 66 BRIT. Y.B. INT'L L. 333 (1995). Is Professor Ratner's criticism of the Commission's opinion warranted? Consider also Professor Shaw's assessment and conclusion:

> The primary justification of the principle of *uti possidetis*, first in Latin America and then in Africa, has been to seek to minimize threats to peace and security, whether they be internal, regional or international. This is achieved by entrenching territorial stability at the critical moment of the transition to independence. Precisely the same impulse lies behind the recognition of the principle outside the purely colonial context where the same dangers resulting from the break-up of existing states are evident. ...
>
> There would appear to be little lying in the way of an acceptance in international law of *uti possidetis* as applying to all situations of transition to independence.
>
> But what does the principle actually prescribe? It is clearly not an absolute rule that applies automatically. It is a presumption. That is, unless there is evidence to the contrary, defined units within one sovereignty will come to independence within that territorially defined unit. It matters not what the provenance of such units may have been. They may have arisen on the basis of ethnic or historical ties, arbitrarily, or indeed as a result of the use of force subsequently accepted. ...
>
> The applicable law with regard to the establishment of the relevant administrative borders is the domestic law of the original state in question, coupled with administrative factors and other official actions. ...
>
> [S]elf-determination and human rights questions are not irrelevant to the creation of a new state in international law. However, such issues are distinct from the question of the territorial framework of the transitional process to independence. To treat the two questions as interwoven would cause more problems than it could resolve.

Malcolm N. Shaw, *Peoples, Territorialism and Boundaries,* 8 EUR. J. INT'L L. 478, 507 (1997).

Severely critical of the Badinter Commission's assumptions, a recent monograph on the subject concludes:

> If the 'colonial *uti possidetis* principle' is to be a guiding principle in resolving current and future territorial disputes, then the basis for its application in such situations must be clarified. *Uti possidetis* represents a valid option, not a binding solution imposed under the mantle of custom.

SUZANNE LALONDE, DETERMINING BOUNDARIES IN A CONFLICTED WORLD: THE ROLE OF *UTI POSSIDETIS* 240 (McGill-Queen's U. Press 2003).

4. Does the principle of *uti possidetis* lawfully freeze the territorial aspirations of an entity intent on political independence? What if the entity did not have any federal status or any autonomy within the governmental structure from which it desires to secede? Would it not be entitled to self-determination? Would, then, the claim to self-determination be dependent on that group's partial recognition via the granting of autonomy or other distinct political status accorded by the former colonial or otherwise oppressive power? In light of the Burkina Faso opinion as well as the scholarly opinions quoted above, what are the policy arguments in its favor? What considerations militate against application of this doctrine? Could you conceive of a principle that could supplant *uti possidetis*? *Compare* Enver Hasani, Uti Possidetis Juris*: From Rome to Kosovo,* 27 FLETCHER F. WORLD AFF. 85 (2003).

c. Kosovo

The problems associated with a formal application of *uti possidetis* are highlighted by the situation of Kosovo. First, unlike the former Yugoslav Republics of Slovenia, Croatia, Bosnia-Herzegovina and Macedonia, Kosovo had never existed as an "independent" state and therefore had no former political boundaries other than those of an autonomous region, a mere administrative subunit of the Republic of Serbia. Serbia alone, not its former sub-unit, would have been legally able to secede from the SFRY under the interpretation of *uti possidetis* offered by the Badinter Commission. On the other hand, ethnic Albanians constitute 90% of the inhabitants of this formerly autonomous province of Serbia, constituting a far more ethnically homogeneous entity than the former SFRY Republic of Bosnia-Herzegovina. While the international community recognized Bosnia-Herzegovina's claim to independence despite its ethnically splintered internal make-up, similar claims for independence by the Kosovar Albanians were rejected - even though continued Serbian rule over the province, marked by atrocities, was considered unacceptable.

(1) Sean D. Murphy, *Legal Regulation of the Use of Force*
93 AM. J. INT'L L. 628, 628-635 (1999)

"Kosovo: Air Strikes Against Serbia"...

On January 27, 1999, the Clinton administration announced a plan for talks between FRY Government officials and Kosovar guerilla representatives on a political solution to the situation in Kosovo. ... From February 6 to 23, 1999, representatives of the FRY and of Kosovar Albanians engaged in talks at Rambouillet castle... outside Paris. The foreign ministers of France and the United Kingdom co-chaired the talks, which included the other "Contact Group" members: Germany, Italy, Russia, and the United States. In the course of the talks, President Clinton announced that the United States would deploy four thousand

U.S. ground forces as part of a twenty-eight thousand NATO peacekeeping force, provided a peace agreement were reached. ...

[President Clinton justified these efforts in his weekly radio address (*See* 35 WEEKLY COMP. PRES. DOC. 229 (Feb. 22, 1999)) in the following terms:]

> Last fall, using diplomacy backed [by] the threat of NATO force, we averted a humanitarian crisis and slowed the fighting. But now it's clear that only a strong peace agreement can end it. America has a national interest in achieving this peace. If the conflict persists, there likely will be a tremendous loss of life and a massive refugee crisis in the middle of Europe. There is a serious risk the hostilities would spread to the neighboring new democracies of Albania and Macedonia, and re-ignite the conflict in Bosnia we worked so hard to stop. . . .
>
> If we wait until casualties mount and war spreads, any effort to stop it will come at a higher price, under more dangerous conditions. The time to stop the war is right now.
>
> With our NATO allies and Russia, we have offered a comprehensive plan to restore peace and return self-government to Kosovo. NATO has authorized airstrikes if Serbia fails to comply with its previous commitment to withdraw forces and fails to support a peace accord. At the same time, we've made it clear to the Kosovo Albanians that if they reject our plan or continue to wage war, they will not have our support. . . .

The FRY for its part, rejected the plan to deploy any NATO troops and ordered its forces to escalate the war, later deploying thirty to forty thousand troops to Kosovo in apparent preparation for a full scale offensive. On March 23, NATO authorized airstrikes. President Clinton spoke to the nation on the eve of the NATO action, March 24, 1999, laying out the arguments for a resort to force:

> We act to protect thousands of innocent people in Kosovo from a mounting military offensive. We act to prevent a wider war, to defuse a powder keg at the heart of Europe that has exploded twice before in this century with catastrophic results. ...
>
> We've seen innocent people taken from their homes, forced to kneel in the dirt and sprayed with bullets; Kosovar men dragged from their families, fathers and sons together, lined up and shot in cold blood. This is not a war in the traditional sense. It is an attack by tanks and artillery on a largely defenseless people whose leaders have already agreed to peace. ... Ending this tragedy is a moral imperative. ...
>
> Today, we and our 18 NATO allies agreed to do what we said we would do, what we must do to restore the peace. Our mission is clear: to demonstrate the seriousness of NATO's purpose so that the Serbian leaders understand the imperative of reversing course; to deter an even bloodier offensive against innocent civilians in Kosovo; and, if necessary,

> to seriously damage the Serbian military's capacity to harm the people of Kosovo. In short, if President Milosevic will not make peace, we will limit his ability to make war.

35 WEEKLY COMP. PRES. DOC. 516, 515-517 (Mar. 29, 1999).

For the first time in its 50-year history, NATO attacked a sovereign country on March 24, 1999. Using cruise missiles launched from B-52 bombers, surface warships, submarines, and bombs dropped by manned aircraft - including for the first time in combat the U.S. B-2 "stealth" bomber - NATO targeted FRY air defenses, command and control facilities, and military infrastructure ... used for operations in Kosovo. Thirteen of NATO's nineteen members participated in the airstrike, including German aircraft flown in combat for the first time since the Second World War.

Within days, the air strikes expanded to cover other military and industrial installations, as well as attacks directly on FRY military troops, on government buildings in Belgrade, and bridges throughout Yugoslavia including over the Danube River. Eventually, the missile attacks would hit less traditional targets, such as state-run television facilities, properties of ... Milosevic's supporters, President Milosevic's own residences, and ... electrical power grids and petroleum refineries used by FRY civilians. During the course of the eleven-week air campaign, NATO planes would fly some thirty-two thousand missions, causing extensive damage in the FRY, including dozens of collateral civilian deaths and injuries when bombs went astray, mistakes were made in targeting, or when the FRY used human shields. ...

NOTES AND QUESTIONS

1. Professor Murphy notes that despite the controversial nature of the NATO/U.S. action in Kosovo, reactions to the airstrikes were largely positive, notable exceptions being Russia, Austria, Belarus, China, Cuba, India, and Ukraine. Significantly, the Security Council voted down a Russian proposal condemning the attack as a "flagrant violation" of the U.N. Charter. Secretary-General Kofi Annan implicitly endorsed the attacks, saying: "it is indeed tragic that diplomacy has failed, but there are times when the use of force may be legitimate in the pursuit of peace." Eventually, a peace agreement was reached calling for the removal of all FRY forces from Kosovo and the restoration of Kosovo's autonomous status. *Id.*

2. Even after the NATO bombings, the international community as a whole insisted upon the principle of preserving the sovereignty and territorial integrity of the Federal Republic of Yugoslavia, while installing a U.N. Interim Administration Mission (UNMIK) backed up by an international security presence under United States/NATO leadership. Is this evidence of the continuing power of the *uti possidetis* principle? Or did the external elites involved decide that Kosovo was not yet a good candidate for independence? Consider the statements of multilateral and unilateral actors which follow.

(2) U.N. Security Council Res. 1244 (1999)

U.N. SCOR, 4011th mtg., U.N. Doc. S/RES/1244 (June 10, 1999)

The Security Council,

Bearing in mind the purposes and principles of the Charter of the United Nations, and the primary responsibility of the Security Council for the maintenance of international peace and security, ...

Determined to resolve the grave humanitarian situation in Kosovo, Federal Republic of Yugoslavia, and to provide for the safe and free return of all refugees and displaced persons to their homes,

Condemning all acts of violence against the Kosovo population as well as all terrorist acts by any party, ...

Welcoming the general principles on a political solution to the Kosovo crisis adopted on 6 May 1999 (S/1999/516, annex 1 to this resolution) and welcoming also the acceptance by the Federal Republic of Yugoslavia of the principles set forth in points 1 to 9 of the paper presented in Belgrade on 2 June 1999 (S/1999/649, annex 2 to this resolution), and the Federal Republic of Yugoslavia's agreement to that paper,

Reaffirming the commitment of all Member States to the sovereignty and territorial integrity of the Federal Republic of Yugoslavia and the other States of the region, as set out in the Helsinki Final Act and annex 2,

Reaffirming the call in previous resolutions for substantial autonomy and meaningful self-administration for Kosovo,

Determining that the situation in the region continues to constitute a threat to international peace and security,

Determined to ensure the safety and security of international personnel and the implementation by all concerned of their responsibilities under the present resolution, and acting for these purposes under Chapter VII of the Charter of the United Nations,

1. *Decides* that a political solution to the Kosovo crisis shall be based on the general principles in annex 1 and as further elaborated in the principles and other required elements in annex 2;

2. *Welcomes* the acceptance by the Federal Republic of Yugoslavia of the principles and other required elements referred to in paragraph 1 above, and demands the full cooperation of the Federal Republic of Yugoslavia in their rapid implementation;

3. *Demands* in particular that the Federal Republic of Yugoslavia put an immediate and verifiable end to violence and repression in Kosovo, and begin and complete verifiable phased withdrawal from Kosovo of all military, police and

paramilitary forces according to a rapid timetable, with which the deployment of the international security presence in Kosovo will be synchronized;

4. *Confirms* that after the withdrawal an agreed number of Yugoslav and Serb military and police personnel will be permitted to return to Kosovo to perform the functions in accordance with annex 2;

5. *Decides* on the deployment in Kosovo, under United Nations auspices, of international civil and security presences, with appropriate equipment and personnel as required, and welcomes the agreement of the Federal Republic of Yugoslavia to such presences;

6. *Requests* the Secretary-General to appoint, in consultation with the Security Council, a Special Representative to control the implementation of the international civil presence, and further requests the Secretary-General to instruct his Special Representative to coordinate closely with the international security presence to ensure that both presences operate towards the same goals and in a mutually supportive manner;

7. *Authorizes* Member States and relevant international organizations to establish the international security presence in Kosovo as set out in point 4 of annex 2 with all necessary means to fulfil its responsibilities under paragraph 9 below;

8. *Affirms* the need for the rapid early deployment of effective international civil and security presences to Kosovo, and demands that the parties cooperate fully in their deployment; ...

10. *Authorizes* the Secretary-General, with the assistance of relevant international organizations, to establish an international civil presence in Kosovo in order to provide an interim administration for Kosovo under which the people of Kosovo can enjoy substantial autonomy within the Federal Republic of Yugoslavia, and which will provide transitional administration while establishing and overseeing the development of provisional democratic self-governing institutions to ensure conditions for a peaceful and normal life for all inhabitants of Kosovo;

11. *Decides* that the main responsibilities of the international civil presence will include:

(a) Promoting the establishment, pending a final settlement, of substantial autonomy and self-government in Kosovo, taking full account of annex 2 and of the Rambouillet accords (S/1999/648);

(b) Performing basic civilian administrative functions where and as long as required;

(c) Organizing and overseeing the development of provisional institutions for democratic and autonomous self-government pending a political settlement, including the holding of elections;

(d) Transferring, as these institutions are established, its administrative responsibilities while overseeing and supporting the consolidation of Kosovo's local provisional institutions and other peace-building activities;

(e) Facilitating a political process designed to determine Kosovo's future status, taking into account the Rambouillet accords (S/1999/648);

(f) In a final stage, overseeing the transfer of authority from Kosovo's provisional institutions to institutions established under a political settlement;

(g) Supporting the reconstruction of key infrastructure and other economic reconstruction;

(h) Supporting, in coordination with international humanitarian organizations, humanitarian and disaster relief aid;

(i) Maintaining civil law and order, including establishing local police forces and meanwhile through the deployment of international police personnel to serve in Kosovo;

(j) Protecting and promoting human rights;

(k) Assuring the safe and unimpeded return of all refugees and displaced persons to their homes in Kosovo; . . .

21. *Decides* to remain actively seized of the matter. ...

Annex 1: Statement by the Chairman on the conclusion of the meeting of the G-8 Foreign Ministers held at the Petersberg Centre on 6 May 1999.

The G-8 Foreign Ministers adopted the following general principles on the political solution to the Kosovo crisis:

- Immediate and verifiable end of violence and repression in Kosovo;

- Withdrawal from Kosovo of military, police and paramilitary forces;

- Deployment in Kosovo of effective international civil and security presences, endorsed and adopted by the United Nations, capable of guaran teeing the achievement of the common objectives;

- Establishment of an interim administration for Kosovo to be decided by the Security Council of the United Nations to ensure conditions for a peaceful and normal life for all inhabitants in Kosovo;

- The safe and free return of all refugees and displaced persons and unimpeded access to Kosovo by humanitarian aid organizations;

- A political process towards the establishment of an interim political framework agreement providing for a substantial self-government for Kosovo, taking full account of the Rambouillet accords and the principles of sovereignty and territorial integrity of the Federal Republic of Yugoslavia and the other countries of the region, and the demilitarization of the KLA;

- Comprehensive approach to the economic development and stabilization of the crisis region.

(3) Secretary of State Madeleine Albright, Remarks and Q&A Session at the U.S. Institute of Peace

(Feb. 4, 1999)

[We] aim to put in place a durable and fair interim agreement that will create a peaceful political framework for Kosovo while deferring the question of Kosovo's status for several years.

The people of Kosovo must be able to govern themselves democratically without interference from Belgrade while the Federal Republic of Yugoslavia's territorial integrity and sovereignty are maintained. And they must possess all the institutions a democratic government requires, from a legislature and an independent judiciary to a locally-controlled police force.

All the ethnic groups of Kosovo, of which there are several in addition to Albanians and Serbs, must be treated fairly. They must be able to control, without government interference, their identities and cultural life. And the rights of individuals of all ethnicities must be fully protected. The right to nourish and promote culture and identity is at the heart of many of the problems in the Balkans.

Finally, to ensure that these principles take effect, authority should devolve as much as possible to local communities so that they have the authority to resolve problems themselves. . . .

QUESTION: Madame Secretary, are you willing to consider independence for Kosovo at the end of this durable interim agreement, provided that could be accomplished?

SECRETARY ALBRIGHT: I think that the important point here now is that we're not asking people to give up their dreams, as Ambassador Hill has said. But it is very important for them to focus on this interim period and to build what I think as a – I guess once you're a political scientist, you're always a political scientist – what I would consider a very high degree of self-autonomy.

I think that as people begin to see the various details of this agreement, the fact that there would be a president and an assembly and an independent judiciary and power devolved to the community local level, to the creation of local police and a whole host of local units, that this is a lot more self-government than I think most people are aware of.

I think that there is a question about what independence ultimately would lead to, as I stated in my remarks, and whether, in fact, it creates different pressures in the Balkan region that would have a destabilizing effect. But I think the most important point here — and what we are focusing the parties on — is to concentrate on this three-year interim period and let democratic institutions sink their roots into the soil of Kosovo.

3. Distinguishing Between Valid and Invalid Claims for Self-Determination

a. Jonathan I. Charney, *Self-Determination: Chechnya, Kosovo, and East Timor*

34 Vand. J. Transnat'l L. 455, 455 - 467 (2001)

Hindsight always appears better than foresight. Hopefully, the reexamination of past events will provide lessons for the future. ... For me, the question is whether changes in international law might modify the behavior of major international actors such as states, intergovernmental organizations, and nongovernmental organizations. In the future they might be better prepared if situations like Chechnya, Kosovo, or East Timor were to arise...Chechnya and Kosovo have many parallels. Not only did the events take place in the same general time frame but both involved ethnic minorities seeking a degree of autonomy or independence from relatively non-democratic and dictatorial regimes. East Timor, albeit slightly different, provides interesting similarities.

At the legal heart of these matters is the law of self-determination. In its classical incarnation after the establishment of the United Nations, self- determination seemed to be only the vehicle for decolonization, resulting in a multitude of independent states. More difficult is the arguable application of this doctrine to the post colonial period. Some argue that it has no application outside of decolonization. Others argue that it may, but does not permit secession from an established state outside of the colonial context. These authorities and others might recognize so-called internal self-determination that would allow a minority group the protection of group rights and certain autonomy within the established state but no right of secession. At the far other extreme, it might be argued that a territorially-centered coherent group has the inherent right to decide for itself whether to remain part of the state in which it is located or to choose independent statehood. Debates have raged among international lawyers and diplomats over the right of self-determination in the non- colonialist context. One might even argue that this uncertainty has itself contributed to many human tragedies the world has witnessed in the post- World War II period by giving false hope to minority groups that they have rights to autonomy or independence against the states in which they are found, even absent a colonial history. That assertion may fail to take into account the many other factors that contribute to minority unrest and hopes for autonomy or independence. It is likely, however, that this legal uncertainty has encouraged minority group claims and other difficulties that have been left to fester by the international community. The rise of the general international law of human rights and the consequential erosion of the UN Charter Article 2.7 limitations on matters of domestic concern have provided further expectations of international support for minority group claims.

Thus, one task of the international community should be to clarify the right of self-determination in non-colonial situations. The clearer the law on the subject, the less likely groups will assert unfounded claims or engage in risky provocations. Reciprocally, legally supported claims of self- determination may deter egregious actions by the mother state and will encourage other states to lend appropriate support to such lawful claims of self-determination.

Although it is for the international community to develop the international law in this area, one may find the seeds of a solution in recent developments. It is interesting to compare the international community's reactions to the events in Chechnya and Kosovo. While in Kosovo the international community essentially endorsed the Albanian Kosovar's claims to self-determination, in Chechnya the reactions were more muted, essentially focusing on opposition to the violence used by the Russians against the Chechens without reference to their possible right to self-determination, within or without Russia.

This distinction may be easily dismissed by experts in international relations due to the fact that the Federal Republic of Yugoslavia (FRY) is a relatively poor country that was run by a person already indicted by the ICTY for international crimes -Slobodan Milosevic - and his supporters. On the other hand, Russia despite its troubles was a significant military power with substantial economic resources. Its government was ostensibly democratic, albeit at the margins. Furthermore, it is a permanent member of the UN Security Council, holding the veto right. These distinctions are powerful and may suffice. In the past the admitted power of the Soviet Union, however, did not immunize it from severe pressure by the international community to open its society. This pressure substantially contributed to its disintegration and the formation of several independent states out of its empire. Thus, despite differences founded in power politics, the distinction between the situations in Kosovo and Chechnya may be worth examination.

One can make historical arguments to justify conclusions about the legality or illegality under international law of the larger states' sovereignty over these two territories. Both populations have long histories of serious violent conflicts with the states within which they were situated. Both involve minority populations with major distinctions that would classify them as a separate people. There are other distinctions, however, and they may be significant in the law of self-determination, if it is applicable.

In the case of Kosovo, the Albanian Kosovars had obtained a degree of autonomy in their province within the Socialist Federal Republic of Yugoslavia (SFRY). After the demise of the SFRY, the FRY took unilateral steps to eliminate that autonomy and took draconian steps against the Albanian Kosovars. For several years, nevertheless, the Albanian Kosovars tried all peaceful means at their disposal to seek an accommodation. These efforts were rewarded only with greater suppression by the Serbs in control of the FRY. The nonviolent Kosovar actions during this period also demonstrated that there existed deep and widespread support among the Albanian Kosovars for efforts to preserve their self-determination. This led ultimately to the foundation of the Kosovo Liberation Army (KLA) that only then sought independence from the FRY and used violence to seek that goal. Those efforts were met with violence and greater suppression by the FRY. After efforts by the United Nations and NATO appeared to fail to resolve the crisis, NATO unilaterally took action to protect the Albanian Kosovars. This ultimately resulted in a UN Security Council sanctioned occupation and administration of Kosovo that operated as if Kosovo was de facto independent of the FRY.

In contrast, Chechnya's path to the declaration of independence was a unilateral process, devoid of any efforts aimed at some negotiated accommodation. It might be plausible to conclude that Chechnya managed to secede, de facto, without a major use of force between the time that the Soviet Union collapsed and a relatively stable Russian government emerged two years later. During this period of de facto independence, the Chechen government failed to build any viable institutions of an independent state, and instead turned to criminal sources of support. During that period, Chechnya became a center of criminal activities of extraordinary proportions. In the end, it is even hard to conclude that the positions of the regime represented the popular will of the Chechen people. The Russian response was indeed violent and violations of international humanitarian law can easily be attributed to both sides. While there was international condemnation of the armed force used, especially by the Russian military, no serious international support for Chechen self-determination is evident to date. One has the sense that the international community accepted the view that Chechnya should remain a part of Russia. Even the issue of Chechen minority rights has not surfaced as an international issue.

Perhaps there are distinctions between these two situations of legal significance that, in part, guided the behavior of the international community. On the one hand, the Albanian Kosovar's actions assured the international community that all efforts at peaceful settlement of the disputes had been exhausted and that, to the extent possible, the claims of self- determination represented the will of the majority of Albanian Kosovars. Furthermore, independence was sought after all other solutions proved unavailable and armed force was used only as a last resort. In contrast, the situation in Chechnya quickly escalated to the use of force and a claim to independence without significant evidence that the Chechen forces represented the will of the Chechen people.

While it is indeed possible that the facts recounted above are distorted due to limited access to information, they represent the facts generally understood by the international community. These facts thus provide the operative information that may have contributed to different reactions by this community to these superficially parallel situations. If this is true, information may be derived from these two events that reflect developments in international law that enable a people to attain the support of the international community for actions based on a claim of self- determination in the non-colonial context:

1. a bona fide exhaustion of peaceful methods of resolving the dispute between the government and the minority group claiming an unjust denial of internal self-determination, including efforts to use the good offices of other states and intergovernmental organizations;

2. a demonstration that the persons making the group's self-determination claim represent the will of the majority of that group; and

3. a resort to the use of force and a claim to independence is taken only as a means of last resort.

This is not to say that the Chechens do not deserve the benefits of the law of self-determination, but absent the above evidence it appears unlikely that the international community generally will recognize such efforts and support the claim. This may be one of the lessons to be learned from the concurrent events in Chechnya and Kosovo. If these lessons become better known, others seeking self-determination may be guided by them. Since the bona fide exhaustion of all means to find a resolution of the dispute and democratic values is critical, it may help to avoid the escalation of the dispute to violence and undesirable injuries to persons and property.

With these conclusions in mind, we might examine the somewhat different situation in East Timor. While Indonesia was not a distant colonial state in the classical sense, the situation has close parallels to the colonial past. In that situation, Indonesia recently had obtained control over East Timor by conquest. International disapprobation was severe and continuing. On these grounds alone perhaps, the doctrine of self-determination based on decolonization might apply directly. Nevertheless, if we view East Timor through the lens used for Kosovo and Chechnya, we find that a territorially-based identifiable population sought self-determination. While violence was used by some to obtain their goals shortly after the Indonesian conquest, the most salient efforts were through domestic and international means in an effort to reach the goal of self- determination, not necessarily full independence.

The appeals were denied by Indonesia but they finally bore fruit through UN efforts during the period after President Suharto was overthrown for unrelated reasons. As a consequence, a plebiscite was held resulting in an overwhelming vote for independence from Indonesia. The massive violence committed by Indonesian backed militia forces on East Timor hardened the international community's support for East Timor's independence and resulted in UN administration of the territory and substantial support from other countries. The claim of self-determination was indeed successful in a situation paralleling that of Kosovo and consistent with the three factors present there: exhaustion of peaceful methods of resolution, demonstrated support of the population for independence, and force used as a last resort—in this case by outside forces to prevent the Indonesian- backed militia from thwarting the peacefully asserted will of the East Timorese population.

This approach is very much in line with the views of the Canadian Supreme Court when it was called upon to examine the doctrine of self-determination in regard to the potential claim to secede from the Canadian Confederation by Quebec Province. Since the opinion was written in the context of the Canadian constitutional structure and the Supreme Court is an organ of the central government it may not be considered completely neutral on the subject. Nevertheless, the Court resorted to international law authorities and produced an opinion that closely tracks the behavior of third states in the Chechnya, Kosovo, and East Timor situations discussed above. This opinion provides further support for the view that the doctrine of self-determination has a role in the post colonial period and that exhaustion of peaceful settlement efforts, demonstrated representation of the minority group's will, and the use of armed force as a last resort are prerequisites to such claims outside of the decolonization context.

NOTES AND QUESTIONS

1. Do you agree with Professor Charney's assessment? If we accept his approach, are we establishing a test for recognition and/or intervention that requires that massive human rights abuses occur *before* the world community can step in? And even then, only if the abuses have been perpetrated on sympathetic victims (Kosovo) but not on the "bad guys" in Chechnya? How can we develop an early warning system that allows international assistance to flow into areas almost certain to descend into violence? *See* Report of the Independent Inquiry into the Actions of the United Nations During the 1994 Genocide in Rwanda (Dec. 15, 1999) *available at* http://www.un.org/News/ossg/rwanda_report.htm. For a historical overview of the situation in Chechnya, *see* Trent N. Tappe, *Chechnya and the State of Self-Determination in a Breakaway Region of the Former Soviet Union: Evaluating the Legitimacy of Secessionist Claims*, 34 COLUM. J. TRANSNAT'L L. 255 (1996).

2. How does Professor Charney account, if at all, for the difference between Kosovo and East Timor with respect to *uti possidetis*? *See* Valerie Epps, *Self-Determination After Kosovo and East Timor,* 6 ILSA J. INT'L & COMP. L. 445 (2000); Paul C. Szasz, *The Irresistible Force of Self-Determination Meets the Impregnable Fortress of Territorial Integrity: A Cautionary Fairy Tale About Clashes in Kosovo and Elsewhere,* 28 GA. J. INT'L & COMP. L. 1 (1999); Henry J. Richardson, *A Critical Thought on Self-Determination for East Timor and Kosovo,* 14 TEMP. INT'L & COMP. L.J. 101 (2000).

3. What progress has been made in the nation-building process in Kosovo? From your *current* perspective, how would you compare this effort with nation-building programs in East Timor, Bosnia, Afghanistan and Iraq? Is there a difference in effectiveness between programs operated by the U.N. directly (East Timor, Bosnia) and those operated by the U.S./NATO (Kosovo) or coalition forces (Iraq), with the role of the U.N. limited to humanitarian assistance? If so, how can such differences be explained at present? Laura R. Palmer, *A Very Clear and Present Danger: Hate Speech, Media Reform, and Post-Conflict Democratization in Kosovo*, 26 YALE J. INT'L L. 179 (2001).

4. For further discussion of post-conflict reconstruction in general, *see* Hansjörg Strohmeyer, *Symposium: State Reconstruction after Civil Conflict: Collapse and Reconstruction of a Judicial System: The United Nations Missions in Kosovo and East Timor*, 95 AM. J. INT'L L. 46 (2001); Michael J. Matheson, *Symposium: State Reconstruction after Civil Conflict: United Nations Governance of Postconflict Societies*, 95 AM. J. INT'L L. 76 (2001); Samuel H. Barnes, *Symposium: State Reconstruction after Civil Conflict: The Contribution of Democracy to Rebuilding Postconflict Societies*, 95 AM. J. INT'L L. 86 (2001); Frederick L. Kirgis, *Security Council Governance of Postconflict*

Societies: A Plea for Good Faith and Informed Decision Making (Editorial Comment), 96 AM. J. INT'L L. 579 (2001).

IV. THE ROLE OF EXTERNAL ELITES

There are two ways in which the other members of the international community may lawfully participate in the establishment, transformation and termination of constituent actors: (1) multilaterally, through admission to intergovernmental organizations both regional and universal, as well as through mandatory non-recognition; and (2) unilaterally, through the process of recognition.

A. THE ROLE OF COLLECTIVE ACTION IN ESTABLISHING AND TRANSFORMING STATES

1. Admission to Intergovernmental Organizations

a. United Nations Charter

Article 4

(1) Membership in the United Nations is open to all other peace-loving states which accept the obligations contained in the present Charter and, in the judgment of the Organization, are able and willing to carry out these obligations.

(2) The admission of any such state to membership in the United Nations will be effected by a decision of the General Assembly upon the recommendation of the Security Council.

b. United Nations Permanent Observer Status

For entities that do not as yet meet the requirements for admission to the United Nations as a state, but nevertheless are very much a part of the international dialogue, the U.N. created Permanent Observer Status.

(1) W. Michael Reisman, *An International Farce: The Sad Case of the PLO Mission*

14 YALE J. INT'L L. 412, 412-413 (1989)

In 1947, the United States and the United Nations, newly established in New York City, concluded what has come to be known as the Headquarters Agreement. The Agreement sets out the basic rights and obligations of each of the parties and constitutes an indispensable part of the environment necessary for an organization which, although international, must maintain and operate its headquarters within the territory of a single state…

Section 11 of the Headquarters Agreement obliged the various levels of authority within the United States not to impose impediments to transit from or to the Headquarters District upon representatives of members, officials of the United

Nations, experts performing missions, representatives of the press, representatives of non-governmental organizations recognized by the Organization and "other persons invited to the Headquarters District by the United Nations..." (*See* Agreement Between the United Nations and the United States of America Regarding the Headquarters of the United Nations, June 26, 1947, 61 Stat. 756, T.I.A.S. No. 1676, 11 U.N.T.S. 11 (1947)).

Early in its history, the General Assembly began to invite observers to its meetings – some for brief terms, some for longer terms. These observers have become important and sometimes indispensable participants in the work of the United Nations. In a relatively short period of time, the status of "Permanent Observer" was established and recognized. The U.S. government has routinely provided the benefits of the Headquarters Agreement to these Permanent Observers, on the common understanding that they fell within Section 11's category of "other persons invited to the Headquarters District." ...

Notes and Questions

1. The General Assembly has used the technique of observer status as a means of assisting groups that are trying to establish a new state. Do you think that this form of inclusive action is consistent with the United Nations Charter? Is it an appropriate role for the General Assembly?

2. When membership is denied to a territorial entity, what are the consequences? Incidents worthy of review are the U.N. treatment of Taiwan and the Federal Republic of Yugoslavia. *See* S.C. Res. 777, U.N. SCOR, 47th Sess., 3116th mtg., U.N. Doc. S/RES/777 (1992) and G.A. Res. 47/1, U.N. GAOR, 47th Sess., U.N. Doc. A/RES/47/1 (1992); *see also* Michael P. Scharf, *Musical Chairs: The Dissolution of States and Membership in the United Nations*, 28 Cornell Int'l L.J. 29 (1995); and Thomas D. Grant, *States Newly Admited to the United Nations: Some Implications,* 39 Colum. J. of Trans. L. 177 (2000-2001). Another example may be found in the Dayton Accords, *see* Dayton Peace Agreement, Dec. 14, 1995, Bosnia and Herzegovina, Croatia and the Federal Republic of Yugoslavia, *available at* http://www.state.gov/www/regions/eur/bosnia/bosagree.html.

2. Mandatory Non-Recognition

a. Legal Consequences for States of the Continued Presence of South Africa in Namibia (South West Africa) Notwithstanding Security Council Resolution 276 (1970)

1971 I.C.J. 16 (June 21)

1. ... [T]he Security Council of the United Nations had decided to submit to the Court, with the request for an advisory opinion to be transmitted to the Security Council at an early date, the question set out in the resolution, which was in the following terms: ...

> What are the legal consequences for States of the continued presence of South Africa in Namibia, notwithstanding Security Council resolution 276(1970)? ...

117. ... [T]he Court will now address itself to the legal consequences arising for States from the continued presence of South Africa in Namibia, notwithstand-

ing Security Council resolution 276 (1970). A binding determination made by a competent organ of the United Nations to the effect that a situation is illegal cannot remain without consequence. Once the Court is faced with such a situation, it would be failing in the discharge of its judicial functions if it did not declare that there is an obligation, especially upon Members of the United Nations, to bring that situation to an end. As this Court has held, referring to one of its decisions declaring a situation as contrary to a rule of international law: 'This decision entails a legal consequence, namely that of putting an end to an illegal situation' (I.C.J. Reports 1951, p. 82).

118. South Africa, being responsible for having created and maintained a situation which the Court has found to have been validly declared illegal, has the obligation to put an end to it. It is therefore under obligation to withdraw its administration from the Territory of Namibia. By maintaining the present illegal situation, and occupying the Territory without title, South Africa incurs international responsibilities arising from a continuing violation of an international obligation. It also remains accountable for any violations of its international obligations, or of the rights of the people of Namibia. The fact that South Africa no longer has any title to administer the Territory does not release it from its obligations and responsibilities under international law towards other States in respect of the exercise of its powers in relation to this Territory. Physical control of a territory, and not sovereignty or legitimacy of title, is the basis of State liability for acts affecting other States.

119. The member States of the United Nations are, for the reasons given in paragraph 115 above, under obligation to recognize the illegality and invalidity of South Africa's continued presence in Namibia. They are also under obligation to refrain from lending any support or any form of assistance to South Africa with reference to its occupation of Namibia, subject to paragraph 125 below.

120. The precise determination of the acts permitted or allowed - what measures are available and practicable, which of them should be selected, what scope they should be given and by whom they should be applied - is a matter which lies within the competence of the appropriate political organs of the United Nations acting within their authority under the Charter. Thus it is for the Security Council to determine any further measures consequent upon the decisions already taken by it on the question of Namibia. In this context the Court notes that at the same meeting of the Security Council in which the request for advisory opinion was made, the Security Council also adopted resolution 283 (1970) which defined some of the steps to be taken. The Court has not been called upon to advise on the legal effects of that resolution.

121. The Court will in consequence confine itself to giving advice on those dealings with the Government of South Africa which, under the Charter of the United Nations and general international law, should be considered as inconsistent with the declaration of illegality and invalidity made in paragraph 2 of resolu-

tion 276 (1970), because they may imply a recognition that South Africa's presence in Namibia is legal.

122. For the reasons given above, and subject to the observations contained in paragraph 125 below, member States are under obligation to abstain from entering into treaty relations with South Africa in all cases in which the Government of South Africa purports to act on behalf of or concerning Namibia. With respect to existing bilateral treaties, member States must abstain from invoking or applying those treaties or provisions of treaties concluded by South Africa on behalf of or concerning Namibia which involve active intergovernmental co-operation. With respect to multilateral treaties, however, the same rule cannot be applied to certain general conventions such as those of a humanitarian character, the non-performance of which may adversely affect the people of Namibia. It will be for the competent international organs to take specific measures in this respect.

123. Member States, in compliance with the duty of non-recognition imposed by paragraphs 2 and 5 of resolution 276 (1970), are under obligation to abstain from sending diplomatic or special missions to South Africa including in their jurisdiction the Territory of Namibia, to abstain from sending consular agents to Namibia, and to withdraw any such agents already there. They should also make it clear to the South African authorities that the maintenance of diplomatic or consular relations with South Africa does not imply any recognition of its authority with regard to Namibia.

124. The restraints which are implicit in the non-recognition of South Africa's presence in Namibia and the explicit provisions of paragraph 5 of resolution 276 (1970) impose upon member States the obligation to abstain from entering into economic and other forms of relationship or dealings with South Africa on behalf of or concerning Namibia which may entrench its authority over the Territory.

125. In general, the non-recognition of South Africa's administration of the Territory should not result in depriving the people of Namibia of any advantages derived from international co-operation. In particular, while official acts performed by the Government of South Africa on behalf of or concerning Namibia after the termination of the Mandate are illegal and invalid, this invalidity cannot be extended to those acts, such as, for instance, the registration of births, deaths and marriages, the effects of which can be ignored only to the detriment of the inhabitants of the Territory.

126. As to non-member States, although not bound by Articles 24 and 25 of the Charter, they have been called upon in paragraphs 2 and 5 of resolution 276 (1970) to give assistance in the action which has been taken by the United Nations with regard to Namibia. In the view of the Court, the termination of the Mandate and the declaration of the illegality of South Africa's presence in Namibia are opposable to all States in the sense of barring *erga omnes* the legality of a situation which is maintained in violation of international law: in particular, no State which enters into relations with South Africa concerning Namibia may

expect the United Nations or its Members to recognize the validity or effects of such relationship, or of the consequences thereof. The Mandate having been terminated by decision of the international organization in which the supervisory authority over its administration was vested, and South Africa's continued presence in Namibia having been declared illegal, it is for non-member States to act in accordance with those decisions.

127. As to the general consequences resulting from the illegal presence of South Africa in Namibia, all States should bear in mind that the injured entity is a people which must look to the international community for assistance in its progress towards the goals for which the sacred trust was instituted. ...

128. In its oral statement and in written communications to the Court, the Government of South Africa expressed the desire to supply the Court with further factual information concerning the purposes and objectives of South Africa's policy of separate development or apartheid, contending that to establish a breach of South Africa's substantive international obligations under the Mandate it would be necessary to prove that a particular exercise of South Africa's legislative or administrative powers was not directed in good faith towards the purpose of promoting to the utmost the well-being and progress of the inhabitants. It is claimed by the Government of South Africa that no act or omission on its part would constitute a violation of its international obligations unless it is shown that such act or omission was actuated by a motive, or directed towards a purpose other than one to promote the interests of the inhabitants of the Territory.

129. The Government of South Africa having made this request, the Court finds that no factual evidence is needed for the purpose of determining whether the policy of apartheid as applied by South Africa in Namibia is in conformity with the international obligations assumed by South Africa under the Charter of the United Nations. In order to determine whether the laws and decrees applied by South Africa in Namibia, which are a matter of public record, constitute a violation of the purposes and principles of the Charter of the United Nations, the question of intent or governmental discretion is not relevant; nor is it necessary to investigate or determine the effects of those measures upon the welfare of the inhabitants.

130. It is undisputed, and is amply supported by documents annexed to South Africa's written statement in these proceedings, that the official governmental policy pursued by South Africa in Namibia is to achieve a complete physical separation of races and ethnic groups in separate areas within the Territory. The application of this policy has required, as has been conceded by South Africa, restrictive measures of control officially adopted and enforced in the Territory by the coercive power of the former Mandatory. These measures establish limitations, exclusions or restrictions for the members of the indigenous population groups in respect of their participation in certain types of activities, fields of study or of training, labour or employment and also submit them to restrictions or exclusions of residence and movement in large parts of the Territory.

131. Under the Charter of the United Nations, the former Mandatory had pledged itself to observe and respect, in a territory having an international status, human rights and fundamental freedoms for all without distinction as to race. To establish instead, and to enforce, distinctions, exclusions, restrictions and limitations exclusively based on grounds of race, colour, descent or national or ethnic origin which constitute a denial of fundamental human rights is a flagrant violation of the purposes and principles of the Charter. ...

132. The Government of South Africa also submitted a request that a plebiscite should be held in the Territory of Namibia under the joint supervision of the Court and the Government of South Africa (para. 16 above). This proposal was presented in connection with the request to submit additional factual evidence and as a means of bringing evidence before the Court. The Court having concluded that no further evidence was required, that the Mandate was validly terminated and that in consequence South Africa's presence in Namibia is illegal and its acts on behalf of or concerning Namibia are illegal and invalid, it follows that it cannot entertain this proposal.

133. For these reasons, THE COURT IS OF THE OPINION,

(1) that, the continued presence of South Africa in Namibia being illegal, South Africa is under obligation to withdraw its administration from Namibia immediately and thus put an end to its occupation of the Territory;

(2) that States Members of the United Nations are under obligation to recognize the illegality of South Africa's presence in Namibia and the invalidity of its acts on behalf of or concerning Namibia, and to refrain from any acts and in particular any dealings with the Government of South Africa implying recognition of the legality of, or lending support or assistance to, such presence and administration;

(3) that it is incumbent upon States which are not Members of the United Nations to give assistance, within the scope of subparagraph (2) above, in the action which has been taken by the United Nations with regard to Namibia.

Notes and Questions

1. The 1970 Namibia Opinion by the ICJ may have gone a long way toward establishing a duty to refuse, withhold, or withdraw recognition of states or other international actors that violate fundamental human rights, at least of those states who breach the principle forbidding discrimination on the basis of race. Consider the following:

> The modern law of non-recognition may be formulated in the following terms. An act in violation of a norm having the character of *jus cogens* is illegal and is therefore null and void. This applies to the creation of States, the acquisition of territory and other situations, such as the case of Namibia. States are under a duty not to recognize such acts. Resolutions of the Security Council and General Assembly are, from a jurisprudential perspective, declaratory in the sense that they confirm an already existing duty on States not to recognize such situations.

John Dugard, Recognition and the United Nations 135 (Cambridge U. Press 1987)

The Restatement posits: A state has an obligation not to recognize or treat as a state an entity that has attained the qualification for statehood as a result of a threat or use of armed force in violation of the United Nations Charter.

RESTATEMENT OF FOREIGN RELATIONS LAW OF THE UNITED STATES (THIRD) § 202(2) (1987). How is this "obligation" enforced? Consider the East Timor decision, *supra*, in this regard.

2. During the Apartheid regime, South Africa proclaimed supposedly independent "homelands"/ bantustans. What was the legal effect of this policy? *See* JOHN DUGARD, *supra* note 1, at 98-108).

3. Are there certain acts of the effective power agent that the world community is forced to recognize? *See* the ICJ's comments in the Namibia opinion on acts of civil authority: birth, marriage, death certificates, etc. *See also* Judge Stephen M. Schwebel, *What Weight to Conquest*, 64 AM. J. INT'L L. 344 (1970).

4. The prohibition of a violation of *jus cogens*, as commonly understood, transcends the prohibition of the use of force. Dugard himself refers, additionally, to the prohibition of systematic racial discrimination, the suppression of human rights and apartheid (*supra*, at 156-158), with the problematic issue being the denial of self-determination (*Id.* at 158-162). *Ex factis jus oritur* is, in his view, no longer a mandatory principle in this field (*Id.* at 135). Do you agree with his view? Why does the RESTATEMENT appear to take a narrower stand?

5. Can a state "come into existence" without formal recognition, as such, by other states, i.e., without some acknowledgment by the external elites representing other nation-states? Does the Montevideo Convention (*see supra* at 147) express a coherent policy on this issue? What is the meaning of element (d) of this definition? Would/could a state without such "recognition" be an effective player in the world constitutive process?

B. THE ROLE OF UNILATERAL ACTION IN ESTABLISHING AND TRANSFORMING STATES

1. Recognition

a. MORTON A. KAPLAN & NICHOLAS DE BELLEVILLE KATZENBACH, THE POLITICAL FOUNDATIONS OF INTERNATIONAL LAW
121 (John Wiley & Sons 1961)

Recognition of a new government normally results in increased prestige and stability at home; access to state funds on deposit in other states; access to private and governmental loans because of legal ability to pledge the state's credit; diplomatic and consular status for its agents in the recognizing entity; access to foreign courts and immunity from foreign process; establishment of normal trade relations; a capacity to request assistance from the recognizing government in the form of financial assistance, supplies, and even military aid; respect in other states for its laws and decrees; and benefits of existing treaty arrangements. The absence of formal recognition has the effect of suspending most or all of these rights insofar as the non-recognizing state controls them. They may be accorded to another claimant, or they may simply be suspended.

Thus refusal to recognize may be a convenient way for a state to bring to bear a number of pressures by the expedient of inaction until appropriate assurances are forthcoming.

b. GREEN HACKWORTH, DIGEST OF INTERNATIONAL LAW 166-67
(Garland Pub. 1940)

Recognition is essentially a matter of intention. It may be express or implied. The mode by which it is accomplished is of no special significance. It is essential, however, that the act constituting recognition shall give a clear indication of an intention (1) to treat with the new state as such, or (2) to accept the new government as having authority to represent the state it purports to govern and to maintain diplomatic relations with it, or (3) to recognize in the case of insurgents that they are entitled to exercise belligerent rights. "Recognition cannot be accomplished by inference merely but by the full and formal entrance into international relations through the public action of the respective executives of the two countries." Secretary Colby to the Chargé d'Affaires in Mexico (Summerlin), May 25, 1920, MS. Department of State, file 812.00.24071; 1920 For.Rel. vol. III, p. 167. An act which would normally have the effect of recognition-short of one involving formal diplomatic relations with a foreign state or government - may be deprived of that quality by an express declaration of the government performing it that it is not intended to constitute recognition.

c. Memorandum on the Legal Aspects of the Problem of Representation in the United Nations
5 U.N. SCOR, Supp. No. 18, U.N. Doc. S/1466 (1950)

The recognition of a new State, or of a new government of an existing State, is a unilateral act which the recognizing government can grant or withhold. It is true that some legal writers have argued forcibly that when a new government, which comes into power through revolutionary means, enjoys, with a reasonable prospect of permanency, the habitual obedience of the bulk of the population, other States are under a legal duty to recognize it. However, while States may regard it as desirable to follow certain legal principles in according or withholding recognition, the practice of States shows that the act of recognition is still regarded as essentially a political decision, which each State decides in accordance with its own free appreciation of the situation.

An expression of this doctrine occurred during the consideration of the Palestine question in the Security Council, when the representative of Syria questioned the United States' recognition of the Provisional Government of Israel. The representative of the United States (Mr. Austin) replied:

> I should regard it as highly improper for me to admit that any country on earth can question the sovereignty of the United States of America in the exercise of that high political act of recognition of the de facto status of a State.

Moreover, I would not admit here, by implication or by direct answer, that there exists a tribunal of justice or of any other kind, anywhere, that can pass judgment upon the legality or the validity of that act of my country.

There were certain powers and certain rights of a sovereign State which were not yielded by any of the Members who signed the United Nations Charter and in particular this power to recognize the de facto authority of a provisional Government was not yielded. When it was exercised by my Government, it was done as a practical step, in recognition of realities: the existence of things, and the recognition of a change that had actually taken place. I am certain that no nation on earth has any right to question that, or to lay down a proposition that a certain length of time of the exercise of de facto authority must elapse before that authority can be recognized.

d. European Union Declaration on "Guidelines on the Recognition of New States in Eastern Europe and in the Soviet Union" of December 16, 1991

31 I.L.M. 1485 (1992)

The Community and its Member States confirm their attachment to the principles of the Helsinki Final Act and the Charter of Paris, in particular the principle of self-determination. They affirm their readiness to recognise, subject to the normal standards of international practice and the political realities in each case, those new states which, following the historic changes in the region, have constituted themselves on a democratic basis, have accepted the appropriate international obligations and have committed themselves in good faith to a peaceful process and to negotiations.

Therefore, they adopt a common position on the process of recognition of these new states, which requires:

- respect for the provisions of the Charter of the United Nations and commitments subscribed to in the Final Act of Helsinki and in the Charter of Paris, especially with regard to the rule of law, democracy and human rights;

- guarantees for the rights of ethnic and national groups and minorities in accordance with the commitments subscribed to in the framework of the CSCE;

- respect for the inviolability of all frontiers which can only be changed by peaceful means and by common agreement;

- acceptance of all relevant commitments with regard to disarmament and nuclear non-proliferation as well as to security and regional stability;

- commitment to settle by agreement, including where appropriate by recourse to arbitration, all questions concerning state succession and regional disputes.

The Community and its Member States will not recognise entities which are the result of aggression. They would take account of the effects of recognition on neighbouring states.

The commitment to these principles opens the way to recognition by the Community and its Member States and to the establishment of diplomatic relations. It could be laid down in agreements.

e. Ralph Johnson, Deputy Assistant Secretary of State for European and Canadian Affairs, Statement on U.S. Policy Toward Disintegrating Yugoslavia, Hearing before the Committee on Foreign Relations

U.S. Senate, 102nd Cong. 1st Sess., Oct. 16, 1991

Our position on the future of Slovenia is identical to that toward Yugoslavia as a whole. We will accept any future political arrangements that are decided on peacefully and democratically by the peoples of Yugoslavia, through dialog and negotiation, but we do not believe that partial solutions, unilateral actions or outcomes achieved by force and intimidation are conducive to achieving a comprehensive settlement. Let me add that the five principles that Secretary Baker enunciated in his address to the CSCE meeting in Moscow last month are also central to our policy toward Yugoslavia as a whole and its individual republics. We have made this position very clear in response to requests from Croatia and Slovenia for U.S. recognition of their independence. To reiterate, the five points are:

- Determining the future of the country peacefully and democratically, consistent with CSCE principles;
- Respect for all existing borders, both internal and external, and change to those borders only through peaceful and consensual means;
- Support for democracy and the rule of law, emphasizing the key role of elections in the democratic process;
- Safeguarding of human rights, based on full respect for the individual and including equal treatment of minorities; and
- Respect for international law and obligations, especially adherence to the Helsinki Final Act and the Charter of Paris.

Notes and Questions

1. Is recognition a discretionary or mandatory act if certain criteria of effectiveness are fulfilled? What are the pros and cons of mandatory recognition? What is the better policy? The disparity in observations of state practice is illustrated in the contrast between the U.N. Memorandum and the following view of the late Judge Lauterpacht:

> To recognize a political community as a State is to declare that it fulfills the conditions of statehood as required by international law. If these conditions are present, the existing States are under the duty to grant recognition. In the absence of an international organ competent to ascertain and authoritatively to declare the presence of requirements of full

> international personality, States already established fulfill that function in their capacity as organs of international law. In thus acting they administer the law of nations. This legal rule signifies that in granting or withholding recognition States do not claim and are not entitled to serve exclusively the interests of their national policy and convenience regardless of the principles of international law in the matter. Although recognition is thus declaratory of an existing fact, such declaration, made in the impartial fulfillment of a legal duty, is constitutive, as between the recognizing State and the community so recognized, of international rights and duties associated with full statehood. Prior to recognition such rights and obligations exist only to the extent to which they have been expressly conceded or legitimately asserted, by reference to compelling rules of humanity and justice, either by the existing members of international society or by the people claiming recognition.

H. LAUTERPACHT, RECOGNITION IN INTERNATIONAL LAW 6 (AMS Press 1947).

2. Criteria commonly projected for determining the appropriateness of recognition include such items as (1) reasonable assurance of stability and permanence in a given territory; (2) a government with the general support of (3) the population; and (4) ability and willingness to fulfill international obligations. Are they sufficient? Or have the new EU guidelines for recognition and the U.N. conditions for membership, established for the secessionist Yugoslav republics, set out above, now set a higher standard?

3. Do we witness the emergence of new criteria of legitimacy limiting the discretionary character of recognition? What are those criteria? Discuss the goals of observance of fundamental human rights, rights to democratic governance, prohibition of racial discrimination, genocide, torture in the context of the EU Declaration on Guidelines for Recognition of New States in Eastern Europe and the former Soviet Union. Are there any substantive differences between the U.S. position and that of the EU? What should be the preferred policies?

2. The Purported Duty to Recognize

a. Tinoco (Gr. Brit. v. Costa Rica)

18 AM. J. INT'L L. 147 (1924); 1 R.I. A.A. 369, 376-384 (1923)

[TAFT, Arbitrator.] In January, 1917, the Government of Costa Rica, under President Alfredo Gonzalez, was overthrown by Frederico Tinoco, the Secretary of War. Gonzalez fled. Tinoco assumed power, called an election, and established a new constitution in June, 1917. His government continued until August, 1919, when Tinoco retired, and left the country. His government fell in September following. After a provisional government under one Barquero, the old constitution was restored and elections held under it. The restored government is a signatory to this treaty of arbitration.

On the 22nd of August, 1922, the Constitutional Congress of the restored Costa Rican Government passed a law known as Law of Nullities No. 41. It invalidated all contracts between the executive power and private persons, made with or without approval of the legislative power between January 27, 1917, and September 2, 1919, covering the period of the Tinoco government. It also nullified the legislative decree No. 12 of the Tinoco government, dated June 28, 1919, authorizing the issue of the fifteen million colones currency notes. The colon is a Costa Rican gold coin or standard nominally equal to forty-six and one-half cents of an American dollar, but it is uncoined and the exchange value of the paper colon actually in circulation is much less. The Nullities Law also invalidated the legislative decree of the Tinoco government of July 8, 1919, authorizing the circulation of notes of the nomination of 1,000 colones, and annulled all transactions with such colones bills between holders and the state, directly or indirectly, by means of negotiation or contract, if thereby the holders received value as if they were ordinary bills of current issue.

The claim of Great Britain is that the Royal Bank of Canada and the Central Costa Rica Petroleum Company are British corporations whose shares are owned by British subjects; that the Banco Internacional of Costa Rica and the Government of Costa Rica are both indebted to the Royal Bank in the sum of 998,000 colones, evidenced by 998 one thousand colones bills held by the Bank; that the Central Costa Rica Petroleum Company owns, by due assignment, a grant by the Tinoco government in 1918 of the right to explore for and exploit oil deposits in Costa Rica, and that both the indebtedness and the concession have been annulled without right by the Law of Nullities and should be excepted from its operation. She asks an award that she is entitled on behalf of her subjects to have the claim of the bank paid, and the concession recognized and given effect by the Costa Rican Government.

The Government of Costa Rica denies its liability for the acts or obligations of the Tinoco government and maintains that the Law of Nullities was a legitimate exercise of its legislative governing power. It further denies the validity of such claims on the merits, unaffected by the Law of Nullities.

It is convenient to consider first the general objections to both claims of Great Britain, urged by Costa Rica, and then if such general objections cannot prevail, to consider the merits of each claim and Costa Rica's special defenses to it.

...Great Britain contends, first, that the Tinoco government was the only government of Costa Rica de facto and de jure for two years and nine months; that during that time there is no other government disputing its sovereignty, that it was in peaceful administration of the whole country, with the acquiescence of its people.

Second, that the succeeding government could not by legislative decree avoid responsibility for acts of that government affecting British subjects, or appropriate or confiscate rights and property by that government except in violation of international law; that the act of Nullities is as to British interests, therefore itself a nullity, and is to be disregarded, with the consequence that the contracts validly made with the Tinoco government must be performed by the present Costa Rican Government, and that the property which has been invaded or the rights nullified must be restored.

To these contentions the Costa Rican Government answers: First, that the Tinoco government was not a *de facto* or *de jure* government according to the rules of international law. This raises an issue of fact.

Second, that the contracts and obligations of the Tinoco government, set up by Great Britain on behalf of its subjects, are void, and do not create a legal obligation, because the government of Tinoco and its acts were in violation of the constitution of Costa Rica of 1871.

Third, that Great Britain is stopped by the fact that it did not recognize the Tinoco government during its incumbency, to claim on behalf of its subjects that Tinoco's was a government which could confer rights binding on its successor.

Fourth, that the subjects of Great Britain, whose claims are here in controversy, were either by contract or the law of Costa Rica bound to pursue their remedies before the courts of Costa Rica and not to seek diplomatic interference on the part of their home government.

Dr. John Bassett Moore, in his Digest of International Law, Volume 1, p. 249, announces the general principle which has had such universal acquiescence as to become well settled international law:

> Changes in the government or the internal policy of a state do not as a rule affect its position in international law. A monarchy may be transformed into a republic or a republic into a monarchy; absolute principles may be substituted for constitutional, or the reverse; but, though the government changes, the nation remains, with rights and obligations unimpaired.

The principle of the continuity of states has important results. The state is bound by engagements entered into by governments that have ceased to exist; the restored government is generally liable for the acts of the usurper. The governments of Louis XVIII and Louis Philippe so far as practicable indemnified the citizens of foreign states for losses caused by the government of Napoleon; and the King of the Two Cicilies made compensation to citizens of the United States for the wrongful acts of Murat.

Again Dr. Moore says:

> The origin and organization of government are questions generally of internal discussion and decision. Foreign powers deal with the existing de facto government, when sufficiently established to give reasonable assurance of its permanence, and of the acquiescence of those who constitute the state in its ability to maintain itself, and discharge its internal duties and its external obligations. ...

First, what are the facts to be gathered from the documents and evidence submitted by the two parties as to the *de facto* character of the Tinoco government?

In January, 1917, Frederico A. Tinoco was Secretary of War under Alfredo Gonzalez, the then President of Costa Rica. On the ground that Gonzalez was seeking reelection as President in violation of a constitutional limitation, Tinoco used the army and navy to seize the government, assume the provisional headship of the Republic and become Commander-in-Chief of the army. Gonzalez took refuge in the American Legation, thence escaping to the United States. Tinoco constituted a provisional government at once and summoned the people to an election for deputies to a constituent assembly on the first of May, 1917. At the same time he directed an election to take place for the Presidency and himself became a candidate. An election was held. Some 61,000 votes were cast for Tinoco and 259 for another candidate. Tinoco then was inaugurated as the President to administer his powers under the former constitution until the creation of a new one. A new constitution was adopted June 8, 1917, supplanting the constitution of 1871. For a full two years Tinoco and the legislative assembly under him peaceably administered the affairs of the Government of Costa Rica, and there was no disorder of a revolutionary character during that interval. No other government of any kind asserted power in the country. The courts sat, Congress legislated, and the government was duly administered. Its power was fully established and peaceably exercised. The people seemed to have accepted Tinoco's government with great good will when it came in, and to have welcomed the change. Even the committee of the existing government, which formulated and published a report on May 29, 1920, directing the indictment of President Tinoco for the crime of military revolution and declaring the acts of his regime as null and void and without legal value, used this language:

> Without having a constitution to establish the office of President and determine his functions, and even to indicate the period for which he was to be elected, the election was held by the sole will of the person who was violently exercising the executive power. And as was natural, the election fell to the same Mr. Tinoco, and, sad to relate, the country applauded! The act, therefore, of decreeing that said election should be held under such conditions is contrary to the most rudimentary principles of political law.

The quotation is only important to show the fact of the then acquiescence of the people in the result. Though Tinoco came in with popular approval, the result of his two years administration of the law was to rouse opposition to him. Conspiracies outside of the country were projected to organize a force to attack him. But this did not result in any substantial conflict or even a nominal provisional government on the soil until considerably more than two years after the inauguration of his government, and did not result in the establishment of any other real government until September of that year, he having renounced his Presidency in August preceding, on the score of his ill health, and withdrawn to Europe. The truth is that throughout the record as made by the case and counter case, there is no substantial evidence that Tinoco was not in actual and peaceable administration without resistance or conflict or contest by anyone until a few months before the time when he retired and resigned.

Speaking of the resumption of the present government, this passage occurs in the argument on behalf of Costa Rica:

> Powerful forces in Costa Rica were opposed to Tinoco from the outset, but his overthrow by ballot or unarmed opposition was impossible and it was equally impossible to organize armed opposition against him in Costa Rican territory.

It is true that action of the supporters of those seeking to restore the former government was somewhat delayed by the influence of the United States with Gonzalez and his friends against armed action, on the ground that military disturbances in Central America during the World War would be prejudicial to the interests of the Allied Powers. It is not important, however, what were the causes that enabled Tinoco to carry on his government effectively and peaceably. The question is, must his government be considered a link in the continuity of the Government of Costa Rica? I must hold that from the evidence that the Tinoco government was an actual sovereign government.

But it is urged that many leading Powers refused to recognize the Tinoco government, and that recognition by other nations is the chief and best evidence of the birth, existence and continuity of succession of a government. Undoubtedly recognition by other Powers is an important evidential factor in establishing proof of the existence of a government in the society of nations. …

The United States, on February 9, 1917, two weeks after Tinoco had assumed power, took this action:

> The Government of the United States has viewed the recent overthrow of the established government in Costa Rica with the gravest concern and considers that illegal acts of this character tend to disturb the peace of Central America and to disrupt the unity of the American continent. In view of its policy in regard to the assumption of power through illegal methods, clearly enunciated by it on several occasions during the past four years, the Government of the United States desires to set forth in an emphatic and distinct manner its present position in regard to the actual situation in Costa Rica which is that it will not give recognition or support to any government which may be established unless it is clearly proven that it is elected by legal and constitutional means.

And again on February 24, 1917:

> In order that citizens of the United States may have definite information as to the position of this Government in regard to any financial aid which they may give to, or any business transaction which they may have with those persons who overthrew the constitutional Government of Costa Rica by an act of armed rebellion, the Government of the United States desires to advise them that it will not consider any claims which may in the future arise from such dealings, worthy of its diplomatic support.

The Department of State issued the following in April, 1918:

> The Department of State has received reports to the effect that those citizens of Costa Rica now exercising the functions of government in the

> Republic of Costa Rica have been led to believe by those persons who are acting as their agents, that the Government of the United States was considering granting recognition to them as constituting the Government of Costa Rica.
>
> In order to correct any such impression which is absolutely erroneous, the Government of the United States desires to state clearly and emphatically that it has not altered the attitude which it has assumed in regard to the granting of recognition to the above mentioned citizens of Costa Rica and which was conveyed to them in February, 1917, and further that this attitude will not be altered in the future.

Probably because of the leadership of the United States in respect to a matter of this kind, her then Allies in the war, Great Britain, France and Italy, declined to recognize the Tinoco government. Costa Rica was, therefore, not permitted to sign the Treaty of Peace at Versailles, although the Tinoco government had declared war against Germany.

The merits of the policy of the United States in this non-recognition it is not for the arbitrator to discuss, for the reason that in his consideration of this case, he is necessarily controlled by principles of international law, and however justified as a national policy non-recognition on such a ground may be, it certainly has not been acquiesced in by all the nations of the world, which is a condition precedent to considering it as a postulate of international law.

The non-recognition by other nations of a government claiming to be a national personality, is usually appropriate evidence that it has not attained the independence and control entitling it by international law to be classed as such. But when recognition vel non of a government is by such nations determined by inquiry, not into its de facto sovereignty and complete governmental control, but into its illegitimacy or irregularity of origin, their non-recognition loses something of evidential weight on the issue with which those applying the rules of international law are alone concerned. What is true of the non-recognition of the United States in its bearing upon the existence of a de facto government under Tinoco for thirty months is probably in a measure true of the non-recognition by her Allies in the European War. Such nonrecognition for any reason, however, cannot outweigh the evidence disclosed by this record before me as to the de facto character of Tinoco's government, according to the standard set by international law.

Second. It is ably and earnestly argued on behalf of Costa Rica that the Tinoco government cannot be considered a de facto government, because it was not established and maintained in accord with the constitution of Costa Rica of 1871. To hold that a government which establishes itself and maintains a peaceful administration, with the acquiescence of the people for a substantial period of time, does not become a de facto government unless it conforms to a previous constitution would be to hold that within the rules of international law a revolution contrary to the fundamental law of the existing government cannot establish a new government. This cannot be, and is not, true. The change by revolution upsets the rule of the authorities in power under the then existing fundamental law, and sets aside the fundamental law in so far as the change of rule makes it necessary. To speak of a revolution creating a de facto government, which conforms to the limitations of the old constitution is to use a contradiction in terms. The same government continues internationally, but not the internal law of its being. The issue is not whether the new government assumes power or conducts its administration under constitutional limitations established by the people during the incumbency of the government it has overthrown. The question is, has it really established itself in such a way that all within its influence recognize its control, and that there is no opposing force assuming to be a government in its place? Is it discharging its functions as a government usually does, respected within its own jurisdiction?

Reference is further made, on behalf of Costa Rica, to the Treaty of Washington, December 20, 1907, entered into by the Republics of Central America, in which it was agreed that the governments of the contracting parties will not recognize any one who rises to power in any of the five republics in consequence of a coup d'état or by a revolution against a recognized government until the representatives of the people by free elections have reorganized the country in constitutional form.

Such a treaty could not affect the rights of subjects of a government not a signatory thereto, or amend or change the rules of international law in the matter of *de facto* governments. Their action under the treaty could not be of more weight in determining the existence of a *de facto* government under Tinoco than the policy of the United States, already considered. Moreover, it should be noted that all the signatories to the treaty but Nicaragua manifested their conviction that the treaty requirement had been met in the case of the Tinoco government, by recognizing it after the adoption of the constitution of 1917 and the election of Tinoco.

Third. It is further objected by Costa Rica that Great Britain by her failure to recognize the Tinoco government is estopped now to urge claims of her subjects dependent upon the acts and contracts of the Tinoco government. The evidential weight of such non-recognition against the claim of its de facto character I have already considered and admitted. The contention here goes further and precludes a government which did not recognize a de facto government from appearing in an international tribunal in behalf of its nationals to claim any rights based on the acts of such government.

I do not understand the arguments on which an equitable estoppel in such case can rest. The failure to recognize the de facto government did not lead the succeeding government to change its position in any way upon the faith of it. Non-recognition may have aided the succeeding government to come into power; but subsequent presentation of claims based on the de facto existence of the previous government and its dealings does not work an injury to the succeeding government in the nature of a fraud or breach of faith. An equitable estoppel to prove the truth must rest on previous conduct of the person to be estopped, which has led the person claiming the estoppel into a position in which the truth will injure him. There is no such case here.

There are other estoppels recognized in municipal law than those which rest on equitable considerations. They are based on public policy. It may be urged that it would be in the interest of the stability of governments and the orderly adjustment of international relations, and so a proper rule of international law, that a government in recognizing or refusing to recognize a government claiming admission to the society of nations should thereafter be held to an attitude consistent with its deliberate conclusion on this issue. Arguments for and against such a rule occur to me; but it suffices to say that I have not been cited to text writers of authority or to decisions of significance indicating a general acquiescence of nations in such a rule. Without this, it cannot be applied here as a principle of international law.

It is urged that the subjects of Great Britain knew of the policy of their home government in refusing to recognize the Tinoco regime and cannot now rely on protection by Great Britain. This is a question solely between the home government and its subjects. That government may take the course which the United States has done and refuse to use any diplomatic offices to promote such claims and thus to leave its nationals to depend upon the sense of justice of the existing Costa Rican Government, as they were warned in advance would be its policy, or it may change its conclusion as to the de facto existence of the Tinoco government and offer its subjects the protection of its diplomatic intervention. It is entirely a question between the claimants and their own government. It should be noted that Great Britain issued no such warning to its subjects as did the United States to its citizens in this matter.

Notes and Questions

1. Does Justice Taft rely on principles of legitimacy or of control? Consider how his reasoning would be used by a government official concerned with implementing a human rights policy in a country egregiously violating those rights.

3. The Purported Duty to Avoid Premature Recognition

a. H. Lauterpacht, Recognition in International Law
7, 8 (AMS Press 1947)

There is no doubt that at least one aspect of the matter is by general agreement governed by international law, namely, what may be called the tortious or delictual aspect of recognition. It is contrary to international law to grant premature recognition. Communities claiming recognition do so, as a rule, following upon secession from the parent State. It is generally agreed that, in relation to the latter, recognition is governed by a duty of restraint the disregard of which entails responsibility on the part of the recognizing State. ... It is generally agreed that premature recognition is more than an unfriendly act; it is an act of intervention and an international delinquency. The community claiming recognition must fulfill certain conditions of permanency and political cohesion. In particular, the parent State must in fact have ceased to make efforts, promising success, to reassert its authority. Recognition is unlawful if granted durante bello, when the outcome of the struggle is altogether uncertain. Such recognition is a denial of the sovereignty of the parent State. It has not the excuse of being dictated by the necessities of intercourse, for international law, notwithstanding the vagaries of the doctrine of implied recognition, permits various forms of intercourse short of recognition of a government or a new State. International law does not condemn rebellion or secession aiming at acquisition of independence. At the same time, save for collective measures of permissible intervention for the sake of humanity or of a general international settlement, as in the case of the recognition of Greek independence in 1830 or of Belgian independence in 1831, it forbids third States to favour insurrection by recognizing the insurgents as a State before they have succeeded in establishing themselves beyond all reasonable doubt.

NOTES AND QUESTIONS

1. How does this problem arise? Who decides whether recognition is premature? If the premature act is "tortuous," as Lauterpacht states, how is the injury gauged and how are damages assessed? What sanctions are applied?

2. Were the actions taken by Germany and Austria regarding the recognition of Croatia and Slovenia during the break-up of Yugoslavia examples of such premature action?

4. The Purported Duty to Withdraw Recognition

a. H. LAUTERPACHT, RECOGNITION IN INTERNATIONAL LAW 349 (AMS Press 1947)

De facto recognition, it has been shown, is provisional in its nature and is, therefore, liable to be withdrawn as soon as it becomes clear that there is no prospect of the requisite conditions of recognition being fulfilled. Does this mean that *de jure* recognition cannot be withdrawn? This is the view held by many. Even those who regard recognition as being in the nature of a contractual bargain or voluntary grant are emphatic that once recognition has been given it is binding on the recognizing State by virtue of the rule *pacta sunt servanda* or otherwise. The very idea that the legal personality of a State or the representative capacity of its government should be dependent on the continued good will of other States is deemed to be derogatory to the independence and the dignity of the State and inimical to the stability of international relations. Yet withdrawal of recognition is a frequent-and inevitable-feature of the practice of States. In principle there would seem to be no reason why recognition should not be liable to withdrawal so long as that act, like that of granting recognition, is conceived not as an arbitrary act of policy but as one of application of international law, namely, as a declaration that the objective requirements of recognition have ceased to exist.

5. The Recognition of "Governments-in-Exile"

Traditional international law distinguishes carefully between the recognition of states and the recognition of governments. Herbert W. Briggs, in THE LAW OF NATIONS (1952), devotes two separate chapters to this distinction. As to a classical formulation, consider:

a. 1 OPPENHEIM'S INTERNATIONAL LAW

§ 42, at 146-47 (Sir Robert Jennings & Sir Arthur Watts eds., Longman 9th ed.1992)

The position of governments in exile may be considered in this context. A government will usually establish itself in a friendly state either because its state is temporarily occupied by invaders or by usurpers and the government has had to flee to a friendly state pending its return to its own state, or because it represents a rebel community which has not yet succeeded in establishing itself in the territory of which it aspires to be the government. ... During the Second World War many governments of countries occupied by Germany fled to other countries where they were able to operate as governments in exile until it was possible for them to return to their own states. The belligerent occupation of those states did not destroy their existence, and their governments, even while in exile, could still be recognised as the government of the state in question.

A revolutionary government established outside the territory over which it claims authority and before it has acquired sufficient control in the territory to enable it to be established there will never have demonstrated that effective control of territory which is one of the requirements for recognition; and where the government in exile represents a rebel community which is trying to break away from an existing state in order to form a new state, there will not yet be a state of which it can be the government.

* * *

Professor Reisman offers a different, functional perspective on the issue of so-called "governments-in-exile:"

b. W. Michael Reisman, *Governments-in-Exile: Notes Toward a Theory of Formation and Operation*

in GOVERNMENTS-IN-EXILE IN CONTEMPORARY WORLD POLITICS 238 (Y. Shain ed., Routledge 1991)

Throughout history, some losers in domestic political struggles, whether by choice or necessity, have fled their own countries and sought haven in others. Abroad, some have assimilated while some have only dreamed of return. But some have tried to turn their exile to advantage and to continue their struggle in various ways: by trying to influence foreign governments or key foreign political forces, by organizing fellow exiles, by providing information or material to cohorts still struggling at home, by planning or executing invasions, and so on. Some of these activities must try to be clandestine. Others are necessarily public, for they require the tolerance and sometimes more active support of the state in which haven has been sought. One of the more public modes by which losers abroad have tried to continue their struggle to regain control of their governments has been by establishing what they call "governments-in-exile."

In international politics, "government" is used to denote a political organization controlling people and territory and disposing of sufficient power to fulfill those international obligations which each territorially organized community owes to every other. The term "government-in-exile" is an oxymoron, for the *soi-distant* government-in-exile does not control territory and, without that, does not control the people who inhabit it. Without those bases of power, it cannot discharge those international obligations expected of governments. The territory and the people inhabiting it are controlled by the actual government or what might be called, for purposes of clarity in this discussion, the government *in situ*. ...

The government-in-exile is, in fact and properly speaking, not a government at all, but a political and legal technique. The purpose of the technique is to influence, undermine, or replace a particular government *in situ* by trying to challenge and deprive it of its authority and through that medians strategy to undermine its control. The technique is available to exiled nationals or those abroad who identify with a real or mythic community associated with the territory controlled by the government *in situ*. The technique is also available to other governments. In any discussion of the government-in-exile technique, it is necessary to remember those indispensable other governments. From the perspective of the "others," the host or haven-granting state and of all other states who must react in some fashion to government-in-exile claims, decisions about whether to allow a government-in-exile to operate or to allow it to enjoy any of the perquisites of statehood are part of the complex practice called "recognition." ...

Like the international legal practice of recognition, the government-in-exile technique is used, presumably for different reasons, by both external political aspirants (the personnel and national or ethnic supporters of the government-in-exile) and the effective elites of other established states (all those who provide haven or some of the perquisites of statehood to the government-in-exile) to influence, indeed, intervene in the politics of another territorial community with the aim of changing its personnel, internal politics, or external alignments.

The government-in-exile technique presupposes some transnational criteria of governmental legitimacy, whether the divine right of kings, transcendental theocracy, popular government, or proletarian dictatorship. The technique cannot operate if the basic international norm is the primacy of "domestic jurisdiction," i.e., a norm requiring absolute external deference to whatever is and however it is decided domestically. In addition to this basic norm, the technique is limited in periods in which fundamental international norms emphasize stability and attenuate the operation of norms appraising, against some international standard, the legitimacy and operation of particular governments.

Thus, the technique is enhanced in periods in which the international system prescribes aspirational norms that purport to appraise governmental legitimacy by reference to a government's goals and procedures for accomplishing them. When any such transnational criteria operate, they permit insiders and outsiders to make independent evaluations of the authority or legitimacy of those who are in control of domestic processes. Where such criteria call for representative government, multi-ethnic states, for example, provide a rich setting for both irredentist politics and the government-in-exile technique. Not surprisingly, the periods immediately after the French Revolution, the Russian Revolution, and the international movement for decolonization and anti-imperialism in the United Nations context all encouraged the formation of governments-in-exile. For the most part, however, tendencies for and against the technique always coexist, with some states finding the government-in-exile technique a useful instrument, while others find it less so. ...

In terms of the classical state system, governments-in-exile may be viewed as unlawful interventions and certainly as systemically disruptive. They will always have that potential; it would be naive to assume that, if the practice is tolerated, it will not be abused in a certain number of cases. But in terms of contemporary human rights norms, governments-in-exile may acquire a consequential lawfulness precisely because they may contribute to the enhancement of human rights in particular situations. The technique of government-in-exile may permit the application of international standards of governmental comportment to both *de facto* and aspirant elite groups in particular states. The norms of popular support, popular legitimacy, and conformity to fundamental human rights standards may sometimes be focused upon and demanded with greater intensity because of the technique of governments-in-exile.

NOTES AND QUESTIONS

1. Consider the case of the Baltic Republics after the annexation by the Soviet Union in 1940. Even though they had lost effective control over territory and people, the Baltic countries' governments continued to function in exile. The United States government, for one, recognized these governments as the legitimate representatives of Lithuania, Latvia and Estonia until the Baltic states became fully independent, again, by 1991. Similarly, the Free French Government under de Gaulle, and the Polish Government during German occupation of Poland and parts of France in World War II operated from their London exile, but remained fully recognized by many nation-states. The international community of states seems to have a hard time bidding farewell to one of its members. If the idea of a "premature" recognition is based on the policy of deferring to effective power (is it?), wouldn't this policy militate in favor of a doctrine of tardy derecognition? In what way is the situation of a government that has lost control over its territory and people different from the situation of a government that has not yet established this requisite form of control?

2. With respect to recognition, is the state-government distinction still useful? What specific benefits or burdens does it entail?

3. What are the prescriptive differences between Reisman and the traditional opinion as formulated by Jennings/Watt? Should governments-in-exile set up by rebel groups fighting repressive regimes be recognized? If yes, under what conditions? The effectiveness of the Jose Ramos-Horta government based in Portugal, recognized by many States as legitimate and supported by periodic

U.N. resolutions disapproving Indonesian occupation, was important to the eventual independence of East Timor. Mr. Horta won the Nobel Peace Prize for these efforts in 1996.

6. The Claim of Regime Change

a. Introduction

The technique of recognition, as described above, is manifestly and lawfully used by states to influence transformations within other states. But it is available only at periods of state or government transition. On occasion, some states have sought a more direct intervention in the affairs of another state in order to effect a transformation of its regime and have insisted that this "regime change" is lawful. For example, in 1979, France intervened in the Central African Empire, as it was then called, in order to remove from power Emperor Bokassa and to replace him with a candidate conveniently located in Paris at that time. In the same year, Vietnam intervened in Cambodia and replaced the regime of the Khmer Rouge with a new government selected by Hanoi. And in that same year, the then-Soviet Union effected a regime change in Afghanistan. Most recently, President George W. Bush, in a series of speeches and national security statements, has claimed, for the United States, the right to engage in "regime change" in circumstances in which a particular government represents a direct threat to the United States or a threat to world order, as viewed by the United States.

George W. Bush is not the only U.S. President who has claimed the right to make a regime change in a given country although his claim may be one of the more controversial ones. President Clinton sent troops to Haiti to restore to office the newly-elected president, Aristide, who had been deposed by a military coup. President Reagan sent troops to Grenada, and the first President Bush sent troops to Panama, to depose the leaders of those states. Other historical examples abound. Although these actions were undertaken with various types of justification, e.g. humanitarian intervention (*see infra*, Part Six), they all purported to accomplish their respective objectives by forcefully changing the regime of another state.

Professor Reisman has written:

> Regime change is a euphemism for externally provoked and managed "*Coups d'Etat.*" A broad and unilateral right of regime change, by itself, can hardly be accommodated within the ensemble of policies of international law. If it became generally lawful, it would lead to more frequent internationally unsupervised meddling in the processes of choice within other states. But regime change may be internationally lawful when it is the contextually appropriate "*instrument*" of an action that is itself lawful and is, moreover, necessary and proper in its context. Recall that regime change has always been one of the strategic objectives of humanitarian intervention, a doctrine, hitherto controversial, that appears to have acquired more legitimacy after NATO bombed Serbia and Kosovo in 1999 and the various commissions established to review the lawful-

> ness of the action (*See* Independent International Commission on Kosovo, The Kosovo Report (Oct. 2000), *available at* http://www.kosovocommission.org; House of Commons, Foreign Affairs - Fourth Report (Kosovo), May 23, 2000, *available at* http://www.parliament.the-stationary-office.co.uk), essentially concluded that it was illegal but, in the circumstances, the right thing to do. If a preemptive self-defense is potentially lawful and the conditions that obtain in a particular case warrant resort to it, the lawfulness of an instrumental regime change will turn on its necessity, proportionality and discrimination.

W. Michael Reisman, *Assessing Claims to Revise the Laws of War*, 97 Am. J. Int'l L. 82, 89-90 (2003).

b. Statements by International Actors Regarding Claims to Regime Change

(1) President George W. Bush, Remarks in Address to the United Nations General Assembly in New York, NY (Sept. 12, 2002)

available at http://www.whitehouse.gov/news/releases/2002/09/20020912-1.html.

… The conduct of the Iraqi regime is a threat to the authority of the United Nations, and a threat to peace. Iraq has answered a decade of U.N. demands with a decade of defiance. All the world now faces a test, and the United Nations a difficult and defining moment. Are Security Council resolutions to be honored and enforced, or cast aside without consequence? Will the United Nations serve the purpose of its founding, or will it be irrelevant? …

My nation will work with the U.N. Security Council to meet our common challenge. If Iraq's regime defies us again, the world must move deliberately, decisively to hold Iraq to account. We will work with the U.N. Security Council for the necessary resolutions. But the purposes of the United States should not be doubted. The Security Council resolutions will be enforced – the just demands of peace and security will be met – or action will be unavoidable. And a regime that has lost its legitimacy will also lose its power.…

(2) Dr. Condoleezza Rice, National Security Advisor, Interview with BBC

available at http://news.bbc.co.uk/1/hi/world/americas /2193426.stm, Aug. 15, 2002. [Brackets in original]

This is an evil man [Saddam Hussein] who, left to his own devices, will wreak havoc again on his own population, his neighbors and, if he gets weapons of mass destruction and the means to deliver them, on all of us. It is a very powerful moral case for regime change ...We certainly do not have the luxury of doing nothing ...if Saddam Hussein is left in power, doing the things that he's doing now, this is a threat that will emerge, and emerge in a very big way.

(3) Jack Straw, Secretary of State for Foreign and Commonwealth Affairs of the United Kingdom, United Nations Weapons Inspectors Report to Security Council on Progress in Disarmament of Iraq

4714th SC Mtg., Press Release SC/7682 (Mar. 7, 2003),
available at http://www.un.org/News/Press/docs/2003/sc7682.doc.htm
(Statement summarized by the U.N. Press Office)

[T]he evidence for all to see was that Iraq had been and remained in material breach of resolution 1441 (2002). All had voted to give the Iraqi regime a final opportunity to comply with its obligations. Nobody had said Iraq was now actively and immediately in compliance with resolution 1441 (2002). The so-called clusters report was a chilling read of the failure of Iraq to comply with Council resolutions over 12 years. The UNMOVIC had not been able to resolve any outstanding issues. Iraq had refused to admit inspectors for three years and only agreed to them after forceful pressure.

(4) Colin L. Powell, United States State Department Report: "Powell says U.S. is Examining Full Range of Options on Iraq," Feb. 6, 2002

issued by U.S. Department of State International Information Programs,
available at http://usinfo.state.gov/topical/pol/arms/02020605.htm.

Regime change is something the United States might have to do alone.

(5) Donald Rumsfeld, United States Defense Department Report: Afghanistan; Iraq, June 17, 2002

issued by U.S. Department of State International Information Programs,
available at http://usinfo.state.gov/regional/nea/sasia/afghan/text/0617dodrpt.htm.

... [T]he world would be a safer place if there were a regime change in Iraq.

(6) Joschka Fischer, Vice-Chancellor and Minister for Foreign Affairs of Germany, United Nations Weapons Inspectors Report to Security Council on Progress in Disarmament of Iraq

4714th SC Mtg., Press Release SC/7682 (Mar. 7, 2003),
available at http://www.un.org/News/Press/docs/2003/sc7682.doc.htm
(Statement summarized by the U.N. Press Office)

[T]he aim of the international community remained the complete disarmament of Iraq and the elimination of the international threat posed by Iraqi weapons of mass destruction. What was at stake now was the unity of the international community, which had taken a forceful stance in its common fight against international terrorism. It fought together against the proliferation of mass destruction weapons, and it stood united in its condemnation of the Iraqi regime.

Where the views differed was in strategy on how to achieve the effective and total disarmament of Iraq. The Council must not spare any effort to find a joint approach to attain its common goal.

[T]he briefings today had made clear, once more, that Iraq's cooperation with UNMOVIC and the IAEA had not yet fully met United Nations demands. Baghdad could have taken many of the recent steps earlier and more willingly. Nevertheless, cooperation had notably improved in recent days. That was a positive development, which made it all the less comprehensible that that development should now be abandoned. There had been real progress on implementation of the relevant resolutions. In the sphere of missile technology, Iraq had begun to destroy the banned missiles within the prescribed time frame. That had shown that peaceful disarmament was possible and that there was a "real alternative" to war. That positive development also showed that Hans Blix's approach of giving the Iraqi regime concrete time frames was successful and should be used for other unresolved problems.

There had also been progress regarding the elimination of Iraq's nuclear potential and, in certain spheres, concerning biological weapons, he said. Interviews with Iraqi scientists were now taking place without monitoring or recording, and plans were being made to conduct them abroad. The inspections should be "stepped up and accelerated", and each remaining problem should be given a time frame. Drs. Blix and ElBaradei, therefore, should present the Council with a detailed, comprehensive working programme that clarified how they and their teams intended to tackle Iraq's complete disarmament. At the same time, the inspections could not go on forever. But, given the current situation, there was no need for a second resolution. "Why should we leave the path we have embarked on now that the inspections on the basis of resolution 1441 (2002) are showing viable results?" he asked. Peaceful means were far from exhausted.

(7) Dominique de Villepin, Minister for Foreign Affairs of France, United Nations Weapons Inspectors Report to Security Council on Progress in Disarmament of Iraq

4714th SC Mtg., Press Release SC/7682 (Mar. 7, 2003),
available at http://www.un.org/News/Press/docs/2003/sc7682.doc.htm
(Statement summarized by the U.N. Press Office)

... [The French] Government did not subscribe to what might be the other objectives of a war, he said. As to a regime change in Baghdad, while no one underestimated the cruelty of that dictatorship, that was not the objective of resolution 1441. And force was certainly not the best way to bring about democracy. It would encourage dangerous instability, there and elsewhere. As for fighting terrorism, war would only increase it, and the world would then be faced with a new wave of violence. As for remolding the political landscape of the Middle East, doing so ran the risk of exacerbating tensions in a region already marked by great instability.

(8) Joschka Fischer, Vice-Chancellor and Minister for Foreign Affairs of Germany, Importance of Humanitarian Aid for Iraq Stressed, as Security Council Members Voice Different Views on Disarmament Process

4721th SC Mtg., Press Release SC/7696 (Mar. 19, 2003),
available at http://www.un.org/News/Press/docs/2003/sc7696.doc.htm
(Statement summarized by the U.N. Press Office)

The Council was not responsible for what was happening outside the United Nations. Secondly, under the current circumstances, the policy of military intervention had no credibility. "It does not have the support of our people." It would not have taken much to safeguard the unity of the Council. There was no basis in the Charter for a regime change with military means. Thirdly, it was necessary to preserve the inspection regime and to endorse the work programme because both would be needed after the end of military action. Resolutions 1284 and 1441 were still in force, even if some adjustments were needed.

(9) Dominique de Villepin, Minister for Foreign Affairs of France, Importance of Humanitarian Aid for Iraq Stressed, as Security Council Members Voice Different Views on Disarmament Process

4721th SC Mtg., Press Release SC/7696 (Mar. 19, 2003),
available at http://www.un.org/News/Press/docs/2003/sc7696.doc.htm
(Statement summarized by the U.N. Press Office)

"Make no mistake about it ...The choice is indeed between two visions of the world." To those who chose to use force and thought they could resolve the world's complexity through swift preventive action, France offered in contrast resolute action over time. In international relations, nothing lasting could be built without dialogue and respect for others, without exigency and abiding by principles, especially for the democracies that must set the example. To ignore that was to run the risk of creating misunderstanding, radicalization and spiralling violence. That was even more true of the Middle East, an area of fractures and ancient conflicts, where stability must be a major objective.

c. The "Right to Liberty"?

President Bush's most far-reaching statement on regime change came on November 6, 2003, in his "Age of Liberty" address before the National Endowment for Democracy. After citing the role of prior U.S. presidents in advancing democracy and freedom around the world, the President called for an equal commitment in our own times and announced a new U.S. policy promoting freedom in the Middle East:

> Because we and our allies were steadfast, Germany and Japan are democratic nations that no longer threaten the world. A global nuclear standoff with the Soviet Union ended peacefully, as did the Soviet Union. The

nations of Europe are moving toward unity, not dividing into armed camps and descending into genocide.

Every nation has learned, or should have learned, an important lesson: Freedom is worth fighting for, dying for and standing for, and the advance of freedom leads to peace.

And now we must apply that lesson in our own time. We've reached another great turning point and the resolve we show will shape the next stage of the world democratic movement.

Our commitment to democracy is tested in countries like Cuba and Burma and North Korea and Zimbabwe, outposts of oppression in our world. The people in these nations live in captivity and fear and silence. Yet these regimes cannot hold back freedom forever. And one day, from prison camps and prison cells and from exile, the leaders of new democracies will arrive.

Communism and militarism and rule by the capricious and corrupt are the relics of a passing era. And we will stand with these oppressed peoples until the day of liberation and freedom finally arrives. …

Our commitment to democracy is also tested in the Middle East, which is my focus today and must be a focus of American policy for decades to come. In many nations in the Middle East, countries of great strategic importance, democracy has not yet taken root.

And the questions arise: Are the peoples of the Middle East somehow beyond the reach of liberty? Are millions of men and women and children condemned by history or culture to live in despotism? Are they alone never to know freedom and never even have a choice in the matter?

I, for one, do not believe it. I believe every person has the ability and the right to be free. …

The good and capable people of the Middle East all deserve responsible leadership. For too long many people in that region have been victims and subjects; they deserve to be active citizens. …

As we watch and encourage reforms in the region, we are mindful that modernization is not the same as Westernization. Representative governments in the Middle East will reflect their own cultures. They will not, and should not, look like us. …

And working democracies always need time to develop, as did our own. …

Securing democracy in Iraq is the work of many hands. …

This is a massive and difficult undertaking. It is worth our effort. It is worth our sacrifice, because we know the stakes: The failure of Iraqi

> democracy would embolden terrorists around the world and increase dangers to the American people and extinguish the hopes of millions in the region.
>
> Sixty years of Western nations excusing and accommodating the lack of freedom in the Middle East did nothing to make us safe, because in the long run stability cannot be purchased at the expense of liberty.
>
> As long as the Middle East remains a place where freedom does not flourish, it will remain a place of stagnation, resentment and violence ready for export.
>
> And with the spread of weapons that can bring catastrophic harm to our country and to our friends, it would be reckless to accept the status quo.
>
> Therefore the United States has adopted a new policy: a forward strategy of freedom in the Middle East. This strategy requires the same persistence and energy and idealism we have shown before and it will yield the same results. …
>
> With all the tests and all the challenges of our age, this is, above all, the age of liberty.

Available at http://www.nytimes.com/2003/11/06/politics/06TEXT-BUSH.html

NOTES AND QUESTIONS

1. In 2002-2003, the U.S. claimed the unilateral right to impose regime change by force in Afghanistan and Iraq. Arguments used to justify actions in Iraq have been discussed *supra*. In Afghanistan, the U. S. used the War on Terrorism to justify its military and humanitarian relief actions, basing its claim on the need to depose the government of the Taliban which had provided a base of operations for Osama Bin Laden and his Al Qaeda followers within Afghan territory. Unlike international reaction to the war in Iraq, there was virtually no negative response to the unilateral action of the U.S. in Afghanistan. What accounts for the difference?

2. In June 2003, the U.S. called for regime change in Liberia and Zimbabwe, asking their leaders to step down voluntarily. Secretary-General Kofi Annan requested the U.S. to provide military assistance to Liberia in ending their civil war within a multilateral context, a request to which the U.S. acceded. Has this more moderate form of regime change now become lawful under international law? Certainly, the new terminology "regime change" has at this writing become a standard term widely used by scholars and editorialists alike. Consider the following:

> This approach [to assist North Korea in rebuilding its economy] would not mean giving into blackmail. The United States, South Korea, Japan, China and Russia would force North Korea and modify its oppressive form of government as a condition for assistance. It would amount to a regime change – but regime change without war.

Michael O'Hanlon & Mike Mochizuki, *Rescue Its Economy*, N. Y. TIMES, August 6, 2003 *at* A17. The writers are also authors of CRISIS ON THE KOREAN PENINSULA : HOW TO PREVENT NORTH KOREA FROM BECOMING THE NEXT IRAQ, (McGraw-Hill 2003).

In a book review entitled *Regime Change, Circa 1953*, appearing in the New York Times Book Review on August 10, 2003, Warren Bass reviewed ALL THE SHAH'S MEN: AN AMERICAN COUP AND THE ROOTS OF MIDDLE EAST TERROR by Stephen Kinzer. The book details the overthrow of Mohammed

Mossadegh, Iran's nationalist prime minister, by the CIA and others in 1953, and the subsequent installation of Mohammed Reza Shah. Bass says, in part:

> Kinzer shrewdly points out that 1953 helps explain (if not excuse) the Islamist revolutionaries' baffling decision to take American hostages in 1979; the hostage-takers feared that the C.I.A. might save the shah yet again and, in part, seized prisoners as insurance. One mullah – Ayatollah Ali Khamenei, now Iran's supreme leader – warned at the time, "We are not liberals like Allende and Mossadegh, whom the C.I.A. can snuff out." Krinzer also notes that the 1953 conspiracy plunged the C.I.A. into the regime-change business, leading to coups in Guatemala, Chile and South Vietnam, as well as to the Bay of Pigs.

The term "regime change" has also become part of the general public's vocabulary:

> To the Editor:
>
> Thomas L. Friedman has, for several months, advocated regime change as a legitimate reason to go to war with Iraq, and he says the Bush administration is being sidetracked by trying to justify the war with claims of weapons of mass destruction or Iraqi ties to Al Qaeda (''Winning the Real War,'' column, July 16).
>
> But if toppling a brutal dictator because we want someone more palatable in a strategic region is reason in itself to go to war, why should we stop at Iraq? There are plenty of dictators and murderous regimes to keep us busy for years to come. If this really is the course he is advocating, then pre-emptive strikes should become a staple of our foreign policy.

Martha Wright, *Why Stop at Iraq?*, N.Y. TIMES, July 20, 2003 *at* A10.

3. Consider the abuses to which the claim of regime change is susceptible. Assuming that international law in the area of human rights now requires regime change in extreme situations, are there institutional arrangements that can control its inherent potential for abuse? *See infra*, Part Six for a discussion of the use of the military instrument in humanitarian intervention.

4. Consider the following analysis:

> When the moral case is strong and regime change appears lawful and feasible, is a military action to accomplish it wise? Is it the right thing to do? In most cases, I would suggest, it is not, for diverse moral and political reasons. Let me review them briefly.
>
> 1. It is easy to conclude that a regime is wicked and violent. It is difficult and indeed culturally arrogant to determine what sort of contextually workable regime should replace it. But once a regime has been ejected and the territory controlled, the regime changers cannot say "mission accomplished" and fly off. They must supervise a transformation. Their own model may not fit the local political culture or cultures. Leon Trotsky, the first commissar for foreign affairs after the Bolshevik Revolution, believed that, inspired by a few proclamations, all peoples would overthrow their rulers and establish communist governments. We now hear a type of democratic Trotskyism that, *mutatis mutandis*, assumes the same. Both of these theories ignore the persistent force of nationalism, culture, religion, language, and other powerful—and manipulable—focuses of identity.
>
> The great human rights instruments, of course, establish an international standard of governance. In practice, however, the standard is expressed in very general principles and norms and the "margin of appreciation" can be quite elastic. In theory, a plebiscite is the most reliable method of testing what a given group wants, but elections presuppose a minimum of internal and external agreement about what the elections are to decide. As for "governments of national unity," they are a euphemism for dividing the spoils among the

strong and not among the deserving or virtuous and may change nothing in the regime but its personnel and vocabulary.

2. The United States has continuous global interests and responsibilities. For all its overwhelming power relative to that of other states, the United States has never had enough military and political resources for all its interests and responsibilities if all or most suddenly required external action. In this respect, the United States is like a bank with vast but, relative to claims, always limited reserves. Reserves are always in danger of being overdrawn if called at once. A bank, no matter how great its reserves, avoids a run by projecting an image of solvency because it knows that the moment that image is undermined, everyone will hurry to draw down his account. Regime changes are calls on military assets, calls whose limits are difficult to gauge.

3. The process of regime change may put great strain on the economic resources of the changer and its national economy. And the longer and more widespread the economic strain, the more tenuous the domestic support for regime change becomes.

4. In liberal societies, all mobilizations for coercive action result ineluctably in a constriction of civil liberties at home. The constriction increases in direct proportion to the length of the action and, independently, the extent to which the adversary is able, credibly, to bring the threat of violence home.

5. Regime changes are likely to take a great deal of time, but tolerance for the changer is limited. An outsider is always an outsider. An army of liberation becomes an army of occupation the moment it wins. As an army of occupation, it encounters more and more resistance the longer it stays.

6. A coordinate principle operates with respect to the regime changer. Because of the predominant power it enjoys, the United States seems to be the ultimate regime changer. But, for all of its power, it does not have an aptitude for extended direct control over reluctant states. In no instance has public support for an occupation that started out with good intentions, whether in the Philippines, Haiti (on more than one occasion), or Nicaragua, been sustained. Yet regime changes are not likely to be short-lived, for the regime that is targeted for change has usually spoliated the political and economic system of the state it controlled, leaving it in shambles.

7. The new MO of resistance is likely to drain the regime changer and frustrate its intentions, leading to greater and greater violence, more and more alienation of the local population, and ever stronger resistance to the putative regime changer.

The conditions for successful regime change are difficult to meet, all the more so because the governments of democratic political systems, whose militaries will be required for regime changes, will have to present their participation in the action to their constituents as in the national interest or in self-defense. "[I]t is an arduous undertaking," Tocqueville wrote, "to excite the enthusiasm of a democratic nation for any theory which does not have a visible, direct, and immediate bearing on the occupations of their daily lives." But arguing national interest as the justification for sacrifice will run against demonstrating to outsiders that national interest plays no part in the action. Moreover, the prospect of long-term occupations over increasingly restive populations in which the methods of adversaries will be characterized as terrorist, but will be seen by them and their supporters as simply intelligent, asymmetric warfare, and will prompt military and paramilitary efforts by the regime changers that will be subjected to intense scrutiny by international criminal courts and nongovernmental custodians of human rights—this prospect will lead many democratic governments to think twice before getting involved.

W. Michael Reisman, *The Manley O. Hudson Lecture: Why Regime Change Is (Almost Always) a Bad Idea*, 98 AM. J. INT'L L. 516 (2004).

7. The Law and Policy of State Succession

One of the consequences of establishment, transformation or termination of a territorial actor is the disruption of normative arrangements which had been established on the expectation that the prior regimes would continue. Concern with the implications of disruption may account for the resistance, discussed earlier, to a broad right of self-determination and some of the doctrines, such as *uti possidetis* that restrict the right of peoples to divide existing territorial communities.

When, these policies notwithstanding, a transformation or termination is effected, the effort to regulate the consequences of change is referred to in international law as "state succession." This body of law seeks to provide guidance for the reconfiguration of territorial communities and for the adjustment of the network of economic exchanges and the status, rights and duties of the old and new entities. Ordinarily, one of the new entities will become the "successor state" to the old, inheriting the U.N. seat and other international obligations of the parent state. That does not necessarily mean, however, that the other entities are no longer bound by certain treaty and debt obligations of the parent.

The options are manifold. They range from a clean slate to an automatic devolution of status from the old to the new entity, and various arrangements in between. The failure of the FRY to become recognized as the successor state to Yugoslavia was discussed, *supra*. In the case of the Soviet Union, both the break-up and Russia's successor state status were decided by mutual agreement among the former republics of the USSR.

NOTES AND QUESTIONS

1. The international law of state succession has been described authoritatively as "uncertain and confused" (Restatement (Third) Foreign Relations Law, § 208, Reporter's Note 1). The legal effects of succession have thus often been regulated by treaty. The International Law Commission tried to remedy that situation by codifying and progressively developing the pertinent law. Based on its drafts, on August 23, 1978, the Vienna Convention on Succession of States in Respect of Treaties, U.N. Doc. A/CONF.80/31,17 I.L.M. 1488 was adopted; the Vienna Convention on Succession of States in Respect of State Property, Archives and Debts, U.N. Doc. A/Conf. 117/ 14, 22. I.L.M. 306 followed on April 7, 1983. The United Nations General Assembly adopted the ILC's Declaration of Articles on Nationality of Natural Persons in Relation to the Succession of States on December 12, 2000 (U.N. G.A. res. 55/153), *see infra* Part III.

2. While quite a number of the provisions of the 1978 Convention are uncontroversial, including the lack of effect of succession on treaties of a territorial character as expressed in Article 12, the Convention's distinction between newly-independent states, essentially former colonies, for which a modified "clean slate" approach was adopted, and other succeeding entities subjected to a continuity regime, may have prevented the emergence of a universal consensus on this codification. By 2000, the 1978 Treaty Succession Convention, although in force since 1996, had only garnered 17 ratifications, while the 1983 Convention had not even entered into force. The United States has not ratified either treaty. Thus, these treaties' provisions cannot be automatically considered expressive of customary international law.

3. Former colonies clamored for a clean slate, free from prior obligations. Is it an appropriate policy in the decolonization context? Is it an appropriate policy in a *post*-decolonization context?

4. In the Yugoslav context, practice reveals "automatic" admission to International Monetary Fund (IMF)/World Bank of all former republics and "automatic" allocation of portions of debt. *See* IMF Press Release No. 92/92 (Dec. 15, 1992), referring to the following division arrived at by the IMF: Bosnia -13.20%; Croatia -28.49%; Macedonia-5.40%; Slovenia -16.39%; and FRY -36.52%, as cited in Michael P. Scharf, *Musical Chairs: The Dissolution of States and Membership in the United Nations*, 28 CORNELL INT'L L.J. 29, 64 (1995). *See also* Paul R. Williams, *State Succession and the International Financial Institutions: Political Criteria v. Protection of Outstanding Financial Obligations*, 43 I.C.L.Q. 776 (1994); Paul Williams, *States Succession to Debts and Assets: The Modern Law and Policy*, 42 HARV. INT'L L. J. 355 (2001).

5. One of the more urgent state succession issues is determining ownership of nuclear weapons among the former republics of the U.S.S.R. *See* Lee S. Wolosky, Johnathan M. Malis & David A. Schwimmer, *Recent Development: START, START II, and Ownership of Nuclear Weapons: The Case for a "Primary Successor State"*, 34 HARV. INT'L L. J. 581 (1993).

V. ESTABLISHMENT OF INTERNATIONAL ACTORS OTHER THAN STATES

A. INTRODUCTION

1. Benedict Kingsbury, *Claims by Non-State Groups*

25 CORNELL INT'L L.J. 481, 486-488 (1992)

Five Domains of Discourse for Claims by Non-State Groups

Each of the five international domains of discourse in which claims by non-state groups are expressed is of considerable contemporary importance. Three are very general in their range of potential application. The other two domains of discourse themselves incorporate conditions of eligibility which, however open-ended, limit the range of situations in which they may effectively be invoked, and they will be mentioned only briefly.

A. Self-Determination Claims

The charismatic principle of self-determination, and the nationalism to which it gives operational expression, has had a powerful normative appeal for more than a century. The political principle of nationalities had a significant pedigree before giving way to the more sweeping doctrines of self-determination espoused by Lenin and Wilson. In the United Nations period the principal normative formulations have been the principle of "equal rights and self-determination of peoples," contained in the U.N. Charter and elaborated in various subsequent nontreaty instruments, and the right of all peoples to self-determination, which is expressed in Article 1 of the 1966 Covenants: "All peoples have the right of self-determination. By virtue of that right they freely determine their political status and freely pursue their economic, social and cultural development."

Self-determination and its socio-political analog, nationalism, are often associated, particularly in United States thinking, with liberalism. This tradition links self-determination with democratic choice, and especially with "free elections." Historically, however, nationalism has been variously associated with liberty and with the suppression of freedom, with democratization and with inequality for non-members of the nation. As Acton (who thought the theory of nationality retrogressive) wrote in 1862, nationalism "was appealed to in the name of the most contradictory principles of government, and served all parties in succession because it was one in which all could unite." Self-determination is not simply an end result or a legal process of choice: as Minogue points out, nationalism is "a spirit or style of politics."

The rhetoric of self-determination is universal, and the range of possible claimants (peoples) supported by the rhetoric is very wide. The reality of international practice has been that self-determination has been available only to a limited range of units, each of which is, in principle, eligible for separate statehood if that is the choice of the unit. Having been interpreted as a right to form separate states, the international community has endeavored to limit the right to self-determination to a very narrow range of rightholders.

Not surprisingly, the practical response of existing states to claims to separate statehood by new entities has been favorable only in a limited range of cases, which may be broken down into five principal categories:

(i) Mandated territories, trust territories, and territories treated as non-self-governing under Chapter XI of the UN Charter;

(ii) Distinct political-geographical entities subject to *carence de souveraineté* (the only entity to have achieved statehood in accordance with this criterion thus far is Bangladesh, and even this case is not easy to interpret);

(iii) Other territories in respect of which self-determination is applied by the parties, as where a plebiscite it held to determine the fate of a territory;

(iv) Highest level constituent units of a federal state which has been (or is in the process of being) dissolved by agreement among all (or, in the case of Yugoslavia, most) of the constituent units; and possibly

(v) Formerly independent entities reasserting their independence with at least the tacit consent of the established state where incorporation into the other state was illegal or of dubious legality.

Thus most secessionist entities, such as the Turkish Republic of Northern Cyprus [which is recognized only by Turkey], have received minimal international recognition. Irredentist claims on the basis of nationality, such as that espoused by Somalia before the civil war which began in 1991, have also received very little support. The general argument against accepting these claims has been that of territorial integrity and stability of frontiers. ...

B. Minority Rights Claims

There is a sharp contrast between the sweeping entitlements associated in standard international practice with the right to self-determination and the very limited provisions applicable expressly to minorities since 1945. Minority protection provisions have long been included in bilateral treaties or in multilateral treaties involving particular territories or areas, and there were several 19th century examples of diplomatic representations or military intervention in response to oppression of minorities. A more general (although far from universal) institutional system of minority protection, involving the League of Nations and the Permanent Court of International Justice, was a particular feature of the public order of Europe, 1919-39. This model fell into disfavor during and after the Second World War. The focus shifted away from minority rights to universalization of individual human rights, although several local minority protection arrangements were adopted on a case-by-case basis, and the UN was required to face a number of contentious minority questions. Minority concerns are partially addressed through equality and non-discrimination provisions, and other human rights norms. However, the cautiously-worded Article 27 of the International Covenant on Civil and Political Rights (I.C.C.P.R.) remains for the time being the only express and legally binding minority rights provision of general application. Article 27 provides:

> In those States in which ethnic, religious or linguistic minorities exist, persons belonging to such minorities shall not be denied the right, in community with the other members of their group, to enjoy their own culture, to profess and practice their own religion, or to use their own language.

This provision is narrow in scope, and does not adequately address the range of minorities issues with which the international community is again being confronted. ...

Article 27 is a limited provision. Several of the leading cases on it have in fact been brought by individual members of minority communities seeking what was in effect protection from policies of the minority community itself. As to the scope for protection of the interests of minority communities under Article 27, questions remain regarding the extent to which it places states under a duty to take positive measures, whether the right to enjoy "culture" extends to land and resource rights, and whether it effectively establishes rights for human groups as such. The case of Ominayak v. Canada was one of the most expansive decisions of the Human Rights Committee on the two latter questions. The case involved a claim brought by a group of Canadian indigenous people who had never received an adequate area of land and had suffered disastrous problems as a probable result. The Committee found that:

> Historical inequities, to which the State party refers, and certain more recent developments threaten the way of life and culture of the Lubicon Lake Band, and constitute a violation of Article 27 so long as they continue. The State party proposes to rectify the situation by a remedy that

the Committee deems appropriate within the meaning of Article 2 of the Covenant.

This implies that the right of members of a group to enjoy their culture may be violated where they are not allocated the land and control of resource development necessary to pursue economic activities of central importance to their culture, such as hunting or trapping. The right to enjoyment of culture also seems to extend to maintenance of the group's cohesiveness through, for instance, possession of a land base and pursuit of important cultural activities of an economic nature.

[The author discusses the Ominayak case in detail.]

It is clear that if some very serious conflicts are to be adequately addressed, more comprehensive and more detailed provisions for minority protection are needed, and that such provisions will only function effectively with adequate and dependable international supervision, monitoring, and national and international enforcement mechanisms. Two approaches to normative development are presently being pursued: particularized country-specific obligations, and general normative instruments.

1. Particularized Obligations

The first possible approach is to endeavor to secure the acceptance by specific states of particularized obligations with respect to minorities. Particularized obligations are naturally favored by representatives of non-target states, who are reluctant to assume potentially intrusive international obligations in this sensitive area. Policymakers from countries where potential ethnic fissures have not developed likewise do not wish to encourage latent tendencies to ethnic division within their own countries through promulgation of sweeping minority rights norms of general application, although there is debate about the risks and benefits of general normative commitments in such situations…

2. Development of General Norms on Rights of Minorities

Urgent efforts are now being directed to implementing the second approach: developing additional and more detailed normative standards, together with more effective and systematic procedures for implementation and enforcement. A Working Group of the United Nations Commission on Human Rights has, after many years of slow progress, been able to elaborate a draft Declaration on the Rights of Persons Belonging to National or Ethnic, Religious and Linguistic Minorities for consideration by the UN General Assembly. The Council of Europe is considering a European Charter for Regional or Minority Languages, and the European Commission for Democracy Through Law (the Venice Commission) in 1991 proposed that the Council of Europe adopt a European Convention for the Protection of Minorities, implementation of which would be supervised by a European Committee for the Protection of Minorities. The CSCE included a cautious provision on minorities in the Helsinki Final Act of 1975, to the effect that:

The Participating States on whose territory national minorities exist will respect the right of persons belonging to such minorities to equality before the law, will afford them the full opportunity for the actual enjoyment of human rights and fundamental freedoms and will, in this manner, protect their legitimate interests in this sphere.

C. Human Rights Claims

The principles of human rights are a major source of legitimation for claims by non-state groups. Such human rights claims have the greatest purchase when articulated as claims by aggregates of individuals who are seeking vindication only of the same rights as those enjoyed or espoused by other members of the ambient society. More difficult problems arise with this domain of discourse where the claim of the group is couched as something more than simply an aggregate of individual rights claims, or where the rights sought are not demonstrably identical with those enjoyed by the ambient population. In these and other situations the discourse of human rights and equality may lose its purchase for non-state groups, and they may find that their claims are opposed by others on human rights grounds. Equality rights, like other human rights, inure for the benefit of everyone, and may thus provide grounds for upholding or for rejecting a particular group claim. …

While the scope of existing norms is sometimes underestimated, there is a need for further normative development to deal with difficult problems in relating claims by non-state groups to human rights and equality norms. Non-state groups typically emphasize the need for greater sensitivity in accommodating their concerns within a human rights framework. It is also important that effective means be devised to hold non-state groups accountable, in appropriate circumstances, for their own violations of human rights...

D. Claims by Indigenous Peoples

Claims based on prior occupation or "indigeneity" ... have the politically important characteristic of distinguishing and narrowing the range of potential claimants. Claims based on the special status of indigenous peoples are made by non-state groups in most parts of the world, and are aired internationally in the UN's Working Group on Indigenous Populations and many other fora. The term "indigenous people" is not yet well defined and the label "Indigenous" has without doubt been arrogated on occasion to legitimize chauvinist assertions contrary to the human rights of others. Nevertheless, the category of "indigenous peoples" is a circumscribed one; it may well come to influence discourse in the other three categories, but this process is only just beginning. At present indigenous peoples also utilize other domains of discourse in pursuing their claims. Cree in Quebec, for example, have argued that if the province proceeded to exercise the right to self-determination, the Cree would have a separate international legal right to self-determination; that historically Cree sovereignty was not surrendered to Quebec and could properly be (re)asserted; and that, international norms specifically applicable to indigenous peoples would also apply.

E. Historical Sovereignty Claims

Historically-based claims to sovereignty typically involve an assertion of territorial exclusivity. Although historical assertions are an important element in many claims to sovereignty (including some by "indigenous peoples"), claims of major international political significance...in which historical revendication was the chief domain of discourse, had until recently largely been limited to: claims to retrocession of small colonial territories, such as Hong Kong, the Falklands/Malvinas, or Gibraltar; irredentist claims pursued without much immediate success, such as that of Venezuela in respect of part of Guyana and that of Guatemala in respect of Belize; certain boundary disputes; and possibly a small range of special situations where such historical assertions either accompanied or contradicted claims couched in terms of self-determination or rights of indigenous peoples. More recently, however, such assertions of historical sovereignty have been important in the dissolution or disintegration of federal states, and were crucial in legitimizing the claims to independence of Lithuania, Latvia and Estonia at a time when it seemed highly possible that decision-makers in the Soviet Union would consider trying to use military force to prevent these claims from succeeding.

F. Impact of Legal Structure on Formulation of Claims

... Not every claim by a non-state group has equal (nor necessarily any) moral merit. Blanket moral relativism about such claims attracts a strong charge of moral irresponsibility... The further question of whether it is possible or desirable to prescribe general substantive norms in these areas is highly problematic...On the other hand, it is clear that the claims of non-state groups, and the related problems of structuring relationships between states and non-state groups, are of central and enduring concern in contemporary international society. While they ought not to obscure other important questions from view, the dangers associated with abusive claims and demagoguery must be kept firmly in mind. The strategy of ignoring questions concerning the relations between states and non-state groups is neither viable nor internationally supported.

Notes and Questions

1. Decolonization brought into the fray of the world constitutive process the internal elites of embryonic, emerging and new state entities. Internal elites set up "national liberation movements" that were, or were not, recognized by colonial rulers, and/or the international community. Many gained observer status in the U.N. and its sub-agencies, and/or in regional organizations such as the OAU. Access to international arenas was an important issue, as was the recognition of representatives prior to their gaining control over territory. Controversial actors included the FLN in Algeria, SWAPO in Namibia, the various contenders in Angola, Polisario in Western Sahara, and the PLO. What kind of formal access, if any, should these representatives be granted to interstate bodies? What policies should guide decisions on their legitimacy?

B. INDIGENOUS PEOPLES

1. Siegfried Wiessner, *Rights and Status of Indigenous Peoples: A Global Comparative and International Legal Analysis*

12 HARV. HUM. RTS. J. 57, 93-128 (1999)

[International processes of decision-making are of critical importance to indigenous peoples around the globe, both with respect to content and arenas of enforcement. The author examines the two principal "sources" of international law, as traditionally understood, i.e. treaties and customary law. He details the recent and widespread domestic practice of states such as the U.S., Canada, Australia, New Zealand, Brazil and various other countries in Latin America and other parts of the world in recognizing rights and elevating the status of indigenous peoples residing within their territories, and then proceeds to a discussion of pertinent international legal efforts.]

A. Treaty Law

The "Trail of Broken Treaties," to borrow the pained formulation by Vine DeLoria, Jr., is a historical fact matched in its brutality and disrespect only by the Trail of Tears and other genocidal acts perpetrated on the Sons and Daughters of the Sun. The fact that treaties were signed, approved, and ratified, is relevant and provides much of the legal armament of indigenous peoples today. The pattern of acquiring lands and securing peace and friendship as well as regulating trade by way of formal treaty was followed in North America by, among others, the Dutch, the French, the British, the early American colonists, and even the Spanish. Trendsetters were the British, who established an extended treaty system on the North American Continent. In a Royal Proclamation of 1763, the British Empire prohibited the grant of land claimed by Indians until the Indian title lapsed by sale or a treaty of cession. Interestingly, in the ensuing battles over colonial land between the British, the French, the Spanish, and the Dutch, treaties were made with particular Indian nations to make them useful allies in fights among the colonizing peoples dividing up the pie of North America. This harnessing of Native Americans in battles of strangers over their land continued long after the Declaration of Independence of 1776. On July 13, 1787, the United States passed the North-West Ordinance, which stated, *inter alia*:

> The utmost good faith shall always be observed towards the Indians; their lands and property shall never be taken from them without their consent; and in their property, rights and liberty, they never shall be invaded or disturbed, unless in just and lawful wars authorized by Congress; but laws founded in justice and humanity shall from time to time be made, for preventing wrongs being done to them, and for preserving peace and friendship with them.

This doctrine was embodied in an act of Congress of August 7, 1789. Its actual impact faded away with the consolidation of the United States of America as a result of the second war by the Americans against the British and their allies, the northwestern tribes under Tecumseh, [i.e.] the War of 1812. Subsequently, treaties between the United States and Indian tribes were largely used to confine Indian tribes to even smaller patches of land — in exchange for solemn guarantees that this would be a final determination as to what land the white man would desire and receive.

Indigenous nations had to fight an uphill battle for their agreements with the new rulers of European origin to be recognized as prescriptions of international law. This is evident in Professor Max Huber's 1928 arbitral award in the *Island of Palmas Case*. He concluded that treaties entered into by the island's indigenous authorities and the Dutch East India Company were not, "in the international law sense, treaties or conventions capable of creating rights and obligations such as may, in international law, arise out of treaties." The 1926 *Cayuga Indians* award went so far as to say that an Indian tribe "is not a legal unit of international law."

In international law, these conclusions are no longer, if they ever were, tenable. Importantly, treaties of the United States of America with Indian Nations were entered into the same way, observing the same formalities and undergoing the same procedural treatment as agreements with any foreign nation-state. At the time of their conclusion, all of the American Indian treaties prior to 1871 appeared to have had the nature, as well as force and effect of international legal obligations. Not only the Indian Nations, but the Executive and the Legislative Branches of the United States Government conducted themselves in full accordance with the formalities and contents of international and domestic law when entering into and approving those compacts. The Judicial Branch of the United States Government worked its way up to final recognition of the international law character of these commitments in Chief Justice Marshall's famed trilogy of Indian law cases: *Johnson v. M'Intosh*, *Cherokee Nation v. Georgia*, and *Worcester v. Georgia.* Later case law and administrative practice confirmed this understanding. Treaties between Indian Nations and the United States Government are thus subject to the prescriptive regime of international law, as far as validity, interpretation and other legal ramifications are concerned. The treaty-making practices of other nations might yield similar or different outcomes.

B. Customary International Law

1. The Need for Specific Prescription

Traditional international law, in its positivist frame, permitted only nation-states to act and hold legal rights and duties. The horrors of the Nazi Holocaust prompted a rethinking of the virtually unlimited discretion states had regarding the treatment of their own citizens. The United Nations Charter put human rights and self-determination of peoples first, making them a *raison d'être* of the new worldwide organization of governments. The 1948 United Nations Declaration articulated these rights, and the 1966 United Nations Covenants as well as regional instruments codified them in legally binding agreements. There are also more specialized conventions prohibiting all forms of racial discrimination, genocide and torture, and those ensuring the human rights of women and children. These treaties ensure religious freedom, guarantee self-determination of peoples, and even protect the right of minorities to the preservation and enjoyment of their cultural heritage. The issue is whether these protections are sufficient to meet the needs of indigenous peoples, or whether separately formulated, tailor-made responses by the international community to their plight are necessary or appropriate.

It is clear that virtually all indigenous peoples share a common set of problems resulting from the tortured relationship between the conqueror and the conquered. First, Indian freely shared, not exclusively controlled land was taken away. Second, the conqueror's way of life was imposed. Third, political autonomy was drastically curtailed. Fourth, indigenous peoples have often been relegated to a status of extreme poverty, disease, and despair. Five basic claims of indigenous peoples arise from this condition: (1) traditional lands should be respected or restored, as a means to their physical, cultural, and spiritual survival; (2) indigenous peoples should have the right to practice their traditions and celebrate their culture and spirituality with all its implications; (3) they should have access to welfare, health, educational and social services; (4) conquering nations should respect and honor their treaty promises; and (5) indigenous nations should have the right to self-determination.

A number of these issues have been addressed, albeit incompletely for some, in present statements of international prescription. This goes for the right to physical survival, social and economic rights, to the extent they are accepted, and the general freedom of religion. What is missing in the broad-based international human rights instruments, however, is a specific protection of the distinctive cultural and group identity of indigenous peoples as well as the spatial and political dimension of that identity, their way of life. The clearest example of the "general human rights gap" is the indigenous peoples' need for their lands based on deep, often spiritual ties. Other such distinctive claims are those for the return of sacred remains, artifacts and sites, and their demand of governments to keep their word and honor their treaty obligations. It is hard to find these Indian-specific protections in the existing human rights covenants. The 1966 Covenants do not mention property rights at all, neither do they refer to contractual rights. The protection of sacred objects could only be seen covered, with quite a stretch, by the general right to the free exercise of religion. The Genocide Convention is not worded broadly enough to encompass acts of cultural extinction, the withdrawal of the land, material and immaterial space and other spoliation of the environment leading to the "spirit death" of an Indian nation. The Coordinator of the Indian Nations Union has stated the problem most eloquently:

> When the government took our land, ... they wanted to give us another place. ... But the State, the government, will never understand that we do not have another place to go. The only possible place for [indigenous] people to live and to re-establish our existence, to speak to our

> Gods, to speak to our nature, to weave our lives, is where our God created us. ... We are not idiots to believe that there is possibility of life for us outside of where the origin of our life is. Respect our place of living, do not degrade our living conditions, respect this life. ...The only thing we have is the right to cry for our dignity and the need to live in our land.

Because many of these cries were not heard, the concerns were not addressed domestically, the problem grew into such dimensions that international governmental action, spurred by collective action of indigenous peoples and non-governmental groups acting in their support, was finally coming to pass.

2. The Role of the International Labor Organization (ILO)

Interestingly, it was a specialized agency of the United Nations, the International Labor Organization (ILO), that first addressed indigenous concerns. Its first attempt, however, launched in 1957, proved to be guided by highly questionable policy goals. ILO Convention No. 107 Concerning the Protection and Integration of Indigenous and Other Tribal and Semi-Tribal Populations in Independent Countries placed little value on indigenous cultures as such, focusing instead on the goal of integration and assimilation rather than on the protection of the unique characteristics and lifestyles of indigenous populations. In 1986, the ILO changed direction, and started to draft a new agreement which was adopted in 1989, as ILO Convention No. 169 Concerning Indigenous and Tribal Peoples in Independent Countries. As of the fall of 1997, the Convention has been ratified by ten countries, including Norway, Mexico, Bolivia, Colombia, Costa Rica, Denmark, Guatemala, Honduras, Panama, and Peru. The convention has as its basic theme the right of indigenous people to live and develop by their own designs as distinct communities. It ensures indigenous peoples' control over their legal status, lands, internal structures, and development in environmental security. It guarantees indigenous peoples' rights to ownership and possession of the total environment they occupy or use, but it does not recognize their right to secede. On the other hand, it does not exclude it either.

3. The Role of the United Nations

In 1982, responding partly to increasing international cooperation between indigenous peoples, through non-governmental organizations such as the World Council of Indigenous Peoples and the International Indian Treaty Council, the United Nations Economic and Social Council (ECOSOC) established a "working group" charged with the task of drafting a universal declaration on the rights of indigenous "populations." Progressing with the typical "lightning speed" of United Nations bodies, the Working Group on Indigenous Populations finally agreed on a draft Declaration on the Rights of Indigenous Peoples in 1993. Similar to the Founders of the United States Constitution, the members of the Working Group went beyond their designated mandate by drafting a Declaration on the Rights of Indigenous "Peoples." Established nation-states did not appear to support that terminology, fearing that their territorial integrity might be endangered by claims to external self-determination whose rightful claimants were designated as "peoples" under the U.N. Charter's Articles 1, 2, 55, 56, and 73. Limiting their support for self-determination to colonized entities overseas ("salt-water doctrine"), nation-states wanted to define away any potential identification of legally protected claims of indigenous peoples with those of colonized communities. Thus, the "International Decade of the World's Indigenous People" deliberately kept the word "people" in the singular.

[T]he text of the 1993 Draft Declaration on the Rights of Indigenous Peoples by the U.N. Working Group on Indigenous Populations embodies the most affirmative intergovernmental response yet to the claims of indigenous peoples. Beyond recognition of the right to self-determination, it formulated an array of tailor-made collective rights, such as the right to maintain and develop their distinct political, economic, social and cultural identities and characteristics as well as their legal systems and to participate fully, "if they so choose," in the political, economic, social and cultural life of the State. They were guaranteed the right not to be subjected to genocide or ethnocide, i.e., action aimed at or affecting their integrity as distinct peoples, their cultural values and identities, including the dispossession of land, forced relocation, assimilation or integration, the imposition of foreign lifestyles and propaganda. The stated rights guaranteed to Indians as groups, not only as individual persons, include the right to observe, teach and practice tribal spiritual and religious traditions; the right to maintain and protect manifestations of their cultures, archeological-historical sites and artifacts; the right to restitution of spiritual property taken without their free and informed consent, including the right to repatriate Indian human remains; and the right to protection of sacred places and burial sites. Further listed are the rights to maintain and use tribal languages, to transmit their oral histories and traditions, to education in their language and to control over their own educational systems. They are afforded the right to maintain and develop their political, economic and social systems, and to determine and develop priorities and strategies for exercising their right to development. Their treaties with States should be recognized, observed and enforced. Last, but not least, the Draft Declaration supports the right of indigenous people to own, develop, control, and use the lands and territories which they have traditionally owned or otherwise occupied and used, including the right to restitution of lands confiscated, occupied or otherwise taken without their free and informed consent, with the option of providing just and fair compensation wherever such return is not possible. The document, in particular, goes beyond ILO Convention No. 169 in its statements on self-determination, land and resource rights, as well as political autonomy.

As important as the substantive provisions of this draft are, the procedure through which it was produced was at least as significant. It was developed, "to a large extent, ... out of a partnership between experts and indigenous people." The Working Group continues its work, and increasing numbers of indigenous people from different parts of the world attend its meetings. The Working Group has grown into "one of the largest regular human rights meetings organized by the United Nations," and has made indigenous peoples a permanent presence within that worldwide governmental organization.

In 1994, the Sub-Commission adopted the Draft Declaration without amendment and sent it to the U.N. Commission on Human Rights. The first intergovernmental meeting at the level of the Commission, held in November 1995, also did not result in any changes, although some governments voiced concern about the language on self-determination for indigenous peoples, as well as on indigenous rights over lands and resources. A second session of this group in October 1996, proved to be more difficult as opposition to collective rights and self-determination increased. Over 100 indigenous organizations, however, have been admitted to participate in the sessions of the Commission's working group, and their influence will be felt. In any event, the General Assembly has requested that the Declaration be adopted before the end of the International Decade of the World's Indigenous People in 2004.

4. The Role of the Organization of American States (OAS)

... In 1989, the OAS General Assembly recommended that the Inter-American Commission on Human Rights prepare an instrument to protect the rights of indigenous peoples. In 1991, the actual development of that instrument began, and in September 1995, under the presidency of Professor W. Michael Reisman, the first draft was sent to governments, hundreds of indigenous organizations, individual experts, and other entities for comments. Taking that feedback into account, at its ninety-fifth regular session, the Inter-American Commission for Human Rights approved the Proposed American Declaration on the Rights of Indigenous Peoples. ...

The draft offers some interesting counterpoints to the United Nations proposal. First, it defines the personal scope of the document, without, however, spelling out the meaning of the term "indigenous people" itself. The Preamble states that indigenous peoples constitute an "organized, distinctive and integral segment of their population and are entitled to be part of the national identities of the countries of the Americas." Separatism and secession, options of "external" self-determination, are expressly rejected.

On the other hand, indigenous peoples are designated a "subject of international law." "Internal" self-government, the formulation and application of indigenous law, and self-identification are broadly allowed and promoted, and forced assimilation is forbidden. The draft also states that the living conditions of Indians are "generally deplorable" and offers as one of several remedies the "right to development." The centrality, in fact the sacredness of the environment to indigenous peoples is recognized, and respect for it is to be promoted by way of indigenous culture and ecology. Indians, in turn, are to be given the right to a safe and healthy environment, including a prohibition on the introduction and deposit of radioactive and other toxic waste on their lands. Education is to take place, if so desired by the peoples themselves, in indigenous language, and it should incorporate indigenous content. Traditional collective systems for the control and use of land are to be recognized, and indigenously used property should, in principle, be returned. Maximum priority is to be accorded the demarcation of properties and areas of indigenous use.

Intrusion of illegal miners and farmers are mandated to be stopped by state authorities. Also, racism and abuses of indigenous peoples by security forces should come to an end. Rights that can only be enjoyed when exercised collectively are also recognized, including the profession and practice of spiritual beliefs and the use of indigenous language. Intellectual property rights are another important focus. Finally, indigenous persons are given the right to recognition, observance, and enforcement of treaties concluded with states or their successors — a right long contested and denied. Conflicts and disputes over such treaties, which cannot otherwise be settled, should be submitted to "competent bodies."...

In sum, the Proposed American Declaration on the Rights of Indigenous Peoples is a major step toward a more effective system of protection of indigenous rights not only in the Western hemisphere, but beyond. It reflects a growing consensus on the minimum threshold of legally enforceable claims of indigenous communities. It relies more on the remedy of empowerment and self-help than on governmental action to remove the plight of the First Nations. It places a high value on individual choice. It is conservative and, in a way, anti-Wilsonian, in that it excludes the option of secession. On the other hand, internal autonomy of indigenous nations is promoted, over a wide array of societal issues. The Declaration goes against traditional Western thought in its affirmation of the rights of groups. Its respect for indigenous spiritual beliefs and practices as constitutive of identity is reflected in a dramatic legal recognition of the traditional indigenous, inclusive ways of dealing with nature, in the use of land, air, water and other living and non-living resources of the planet.

5. The Role of the World Bank

The World Bank has become increasingly concerned about the effects of Bank-financed development projects on indigenous and tribal communities....

Its first concern with protecting small isolated tribes such as Indians in the Amazon from the adverse effects of development later changed to a more extensive promotion of conditions to Bank investments that take into account the interests of indigenous peoples broadly defined, including, wherever possible, the active participation of indigenous peoples in the development process itself. This new policy is formulated in Operational Directive 4.20 of September 17, 1991.

The Bank's objective is to ensure that the development process "fosters full respect for [indigenous people's] dignity, human rights, and cultural uniqueness, [and] ... that indigenous peoples do not suffer adverse effects during the development process, ... and that they receive culturally compatible social and economic benefits." Between the policy of insulation of indigenous communities from the modern world and the approach of acculturation or assimilation, the Bank purports to steer a middle course, proclaiming that:

> [T]he strategy for addressing the issues pertaining to indigenous peoples must be based on the informed participation of the indigenous peoples themselves. Thus, identifying local preferences through direct consultation, incorporation of indigenous knowledge into project approaches, and appropriate use of experienced specialists are core activities for any project that affects indigenous peoples and their rights to natural and economic resources. ...

III. APPRAISAL

Today, many of these proposed or actual prescriptions, coinciding, as they do, with domestic state practice as documented above, have created a new set of shared expectations about the legal status and rights of indigenous people that has matured and crystallized into customary international law. While the specific ramifications of these prescriptions are still evolving and remain somewhat ambiguous, there is widespread agreement and concordant practice, both in international and domestic law, that (a) indigenous peoples are vulnerable groups worthy of the law's heightened concern; (b) that indigenous peoples are entitled to practice their traditions, to celebrate their culture and spirituality, to protect their language, and to maintain their sacred places and artifacts; (c) that they are, in principle, entitled to demarcation, ownership, development, control, and use of the lands which they have traditionally owned or otherwise occupied and used; (d) that they have, or should be given, powers of self-government, including the administration of their own system of justice; and (e) that governments are to honor and faithfully observe their treaty commitments to indigenous nations. The draft declarations, in their tortuous way through the channels of the United Nations and the Organization of American States, have encountered virtually no government opposition regarding these issues. With respect to these claims, a consensus has emerged, and has been translated, with whatever imperfections, into widespread, virtually uniform state practice.

The controversial issues are the following: (a) how should we conceive of "indigenous peoples"?; (b) what is, and what should be, the international community's response to the claim of self-determination?; (c) what is the proper perspective regarding the issue of group or collective rights in the context of indigenous culture?; and (d) what are the prospects and best proposals for enforcement of any catalogue of indigenous rights?

A. The Issue of Definition

The concept of "indigenous people" has, perhaps surprisingly, eluded easy delimitation. The United Nations Working Group, in its 1993 Draft Declaration, consciously decided to forego any attempt at a definition; the Inter-American Human Rights Commission, in presenting its 1997 Proposed American Declaration on the Rights of Indigenous Peoples, abandoned an effort in an earlier draft at delimiting the term. The lack of success in this endeavor is not due to a lack of effort. J. Martinez Cobo, first United Nations Special Rapporteur on the issue of discrimination against indigenous peoples, offered what is perhaps the most widely acclaimed definition:

Indigenous communities, peoples and nations are those which, having a historical continuity with pre-invasion and pre-colonial societies that developed on their territories, consider themselves distinct from other sectors of the societies now prevailing in those territories, or parts of them. They form at present non-dominant sectors of society and are determined to preserve, develop and transmit to future generations their ancestral territories, and their ethnic identity, as the basis of their continued existence as peoples, in accordance with their own cultural patterns, social institutions and legal systems.

This understanding presupposes the historical event of a community suffering invasion or colonization; the group's self-identification as distinct from other parts of the national society; a present non-dominant status of the community; and the group's determination to preserve its ancestral lands. ...

[The author proceeds to critique this widely accepted definition as both under- and over-inclusive. He rejects the thesis that it is preferable to have no definitions at all, arguing primarily, that in many instances, indigenous peoples need protection from the outside against governments' attempts to deny their existence. He offers the following definition:]

Indigenous communities are ... best conceived of as peoples traditionally regarded, and self-defined, as descendants of the original inhabitants of lands with which they share a strong, often spiritual bond. These peoples are, and desire to be, culturally, socially and/or economically distinct from the dominant groups in society, at the hands of which they have suffered, in past or present, a pervasive pattern of subjugation, marginalization, dispossession, exclusion and discrimination.

B. Self-Determination

Nation-states are reluctant, to say the least, to respond affirmatively to the claims of Indian populations that they qualify as "peoples" entitled to the right of self-determination solemnly prescribed in the United Nations Charter, the 1966 International Covenant on Civil and Political Rights, and recently proclaimed as *erga omnes* obligation of all states under customary international law. Established states in the "New World," born largely from conquest, be it on paper or on the battlefield, fear the specter of secession. The indigenous peoples' claim of self-determination may mean a variety of things:

(1) "external" self-determination, i.e., the right of peoples to freely determine their international status, including the option of political independence;

(2) "internal" self-determination, the right to determine freely their form of government and their individual participation in the processes of power;

(3) their rights as "minorities" within a given nation-state structure to special rights in the cultural, economic, social and political sphere (limited autonomy).

The response to these claims by established nation-states has been mixed. While some important members of the international establishment appear to move toward even greater rights of limited autonomy, the world community of States seems to be united in the rejection of the option of full sovereignty and political independence.

The battle of the "s" (as in "peoples") is far from over. The U.N. Working Group on Indigenous Populations, taking advantage of the particular drive and influence of indigenous peoples' movements in its midst, has passed the baton in the race toward the adoption by the U.N. General Assembly of a Declaration on the Rights of Indigenous "Peoples" to the Commission on Human Rights. There, the influence of nation-states will be far more pronounced, and formulations foreclosing any option of political independence might be discussed, similar to the language of the Proposed American Declaration. In a decision of July 20, 1990, the *Mikmaq* ruling, the U.N. Human Rights Committee also refused to extend its jurisdiction to the claims of indigenous peoples to self-determination since it was not considered an "actionable" right.

To transcend this battle and the prevailing dichotomy between internal and external self-determination in the context of indigenous peoples, Professor James Anaya has suggested a reconceptualization of self-determination. He proposes a substantive concept of "constitutive" self-determination, which requires "minimum levels of participation" in processes of "creation, alteration or territorial expansion of governmental authority," coupled with "ongoing" self-determination, mandating a "governing order under which individuals and groups are able to make meaningful choices touching upon all spheres of life on a continuous basis." Since colonialism violated both of these principles, a "remedial" aspect of the principle of self-determination would come into play, which he sees implemented by the U.N. process of decolonization, allowing, *inter alia*, for the option of political independence. In the extra-colonial context, the remedies, in Professor Anaya's view, "need not entail the formation of new states," although secession "may be an appropriate remedial option in limited contexts where substantive self-determination for a particular group cannot otherwise be assured or where there is a net gain in the overall welfare of all concerned."

The controversy over self-determination and group rights of indigenous peoples is clouded by semantics. The battle over the political independence option of self-determination, the right to secede, is one that has to take into account recent successful divorces of countries in Eastern Europe, the breakup of the Soviet Union, the velvet dissolution of the unhappy marriage between the Czechs and the Slovaks, and the fragmentation of Yugoslavia. The salt-water doctrine of self-determination has been at least weakened, if not eliminated, by these powerful incidents of intra-mainland secession. In particular, the recent world community recognition of the unilateral secessions from the Socialist Federal Republic of Yugoslavia as well as the establishment of Eritrea as an independent state would appear to bolster a claim of peoples to break away from established nation-states outside and beyond the colonial context. Even the companion doctrine of *uti possidetis* has been called in question.

History cannot be frozen. If any traditional criteria of "people" exist, indigenous groupings may very well meet them. They have their own language, culture, traditions, identity – they answer, in the affirmative, to "le plebiscite de tous les jours." They might not want to choose political independence, but should they not at least be afforded the option? In addition, the monadic nature of the nation-state has waned, and formalistic concepts of sovereignty have lost much of their heuristic value in an increasingly interdependent world. Considered in comprehensive context, taking into account the interests and concerns of both the indigenous peoples and the states in which they reside, the option should be granted if, in the aggregate, it promotes the values of a public order of human dignity. In most cases, both the preferences of indigenous communities and the aggregate interest as just defined will coincide, and indigenous needs and claims will be satisfied by the granting of various forms of autonomy. In cases of serious injustice, however, where there is no other remedy available, there should be at least a moral, if not a legal right, to secede. The last-resort rationale has also been stressed by the Canadian Supreme Court in its recent opinion on the secession of Quebec.

The indigenous peoples' struggles may run up against a variety of Western legal and social concepts and institutions. One is the concept of self-determination and possible secession, as detailed above. The other is the concept of group rights that back up "dangerous" intermediate forces between the government and atomized individuals.

C. The Issue of Collective Rights

While individual rights are ascribed to an individual human being as such, who can invoke them in her own name, collective rights are ascribed to groups of people and can only be claimed by the collective entity and its authorized agents. Rights of groups go against the grain of traditional Western rights thought, which is based on the paradigm of pitting the individual against the state on the basis of a mythical, entirely fictional social contract theory. Indian thinking, at least in their traditional stateless society, is somewhat different: human beings, in their view, are born into a closely integrated network of family, kinship, social and political relations. One's clan, kinship and family identities are integral parts of one's personal identity; rights and responsibilities exist only within these networks. Indian society, thus, is horizontal, not vertical; it consists of a network of personal relationships. In the mind of indigenous people, their "nations" are not, like a Western nation-state, entities with distinct Hegelian existence separate and apart from their individual members. Members of tribal communities are existentially tied to each other in a network of deeply committed horizontal relationships. Still, there are structures of authority within tribal groups, and there is a process of formation of a common will. This process of decision-making and its cultural, geographic, social and economic environment is what the ensemble of collective rights of indigenous peoples is designed to protect. Thus, in contrast to the entirely individualistic view, both the United Nations and the IACHR draft declaration on indigenous rights acknowledge certain collective entitlements. The relevant group rights protect culture, internal decision-making, and, in particular, control and use of land.

This recognition is indispensable in order to effectuate a workable system of protection of indigenous traditions and ways of life. To "individualize" these rights would frustrate the purpose they are supposed to achieve. Culture is a group phenomenon. It includes the tribal ways of life and the natural and spiritual environment in which these traditions are maintained and developed. Prescriptions aiming at preserving such phenomena assume, of necessity, a collective character. In defining and living its culture, the community will act as such, and may override individual members' predilections. Such "overrides" are, to be sure, just as state governments' political powers, limited by legitimate individual interests within the bounds of international human rights law. Still, whether one calls the right one of "the group" or one of "the aggregate" of the "persons belonging to the group," as modern minority conventions do, the fact remains that the collective will in defining the group's identity and policy wins out over the individual aspiration.

Furthermore, to grant and specify rights to collectivities is not totally alien to Western constitutional practice. New Zealand, for example, like Fiji, grants its indigenous people a certain bloc of seats in Parliament. Canada expressly mentions "aboriginal rights" in its 1982 Charter of Rights and Freedoms, and many other countries do offer constitutional protection to ethnic minorities, in line with article 27 of the International Covenant on Civil and Political Rights. The 1835 United States Treaty with the Cherokee Nation, even though ultimately breached, guaranteed the Cherokee sanctuary and the right to exclusively govern themselves, after relocation from Georgia, in the supposed "Indian Country" of Oklahoma. Article VI of the U.S. treaty with the Delaware, the first treaty of the United States with any Indian nation, even envisioned that the Delaware and other tribes would ally with the United States, form a state, and send a delegate to Congress.

Group rights in the context of indigenous peoples are thus necessary complements to the individual rights of their members. They are properly not conceived of as exclusive of, or displacing, individual rights, but as supplementing individuals' rights in pursuit of the common goal of a public order of human dignity.

D. Enforcement

Treaties and provisions of these emerging prescriptive documents, to the extent they constitute norms of international law, partake in the general enforcement scheme of this area of jurisprudence. Like any other international law prescriptions, they are potentially invocable before international bodies, such as the United Nations Human Rights Committee. Indigenous peoples may also resort to the diplomatic, the economic, the ideological, and the military instrument, within the bounds of the modern law of war. Since they lack the formal quality of states, indigenous peoples have no access, as parties in a contested proceeding, to the International Court of Justice. Still, their legitimate concerns should be taken into account by the World Court to ensure that their legal interests are protected in any litigation that might affect them. The better solution for addressing claims of Indian treaty or other indigenous rights violations would be to create a Permanent Forum for Indigenous People as envisioned by the United Nations Working Group.

Consideration of establishment of this innovative institution is part of the objectives of the Decade of Indigenous People. Its mandate, powers, structure, and location within the United Nations system are, however, far from being defined. Various governments as well as representatives of indigenous peoples have expressed the view, in recent discussions of the U.N. Working Group, that the Forum should have a broad mandate. It should cover human rights as well as cultural, political, economic, civil, social, environmental, developmental, and educational issues. Indigenous representatives from Australia, in particular, stated that the Permanent Forum should be capable of receiving complaints about the abuse of human rights, in particular, those included in the future U.N. Declaration of the Rights of Indigenous Peoples. According to the Asian Indigenous Caucus, it should be entrusted with the power to "take appropriate action to protect the human rights of indigenous peoples." Institutionally, several governments supported the idea of placing the Forum at a high level within the United Nations structure, within the Economic and Social Council. Many indigenous representatives would like to see it established at the highest possible level, at a minimum as a subsidiary body of the Economic and Social Council. One suggestion was made to name the institution the "United Nations Commission on the Status of Indigenous Peoples. Many indigenous representatives emphasized that the Forum should consist of an equal number of members from governments and indigenous peoples on the basis of equal geographical distribution. Some indigenous persons found it useful to include independent experts as members. Also, indigenous leaders have asserted that the forum should "have teeth" and be empowered to "take action" on serious violations of human rights of their people.

The idea of a Permanent Forum of Indigenous People should be applauded for providing an important meeting ground between governments and indigenous peoples, as well as between indigenous peoples themselves. To leave its jurisdiction at this level, would, however, not transcend the power and authority of existing institutions. The Working Group on Indigenous Populations is, to a degree, already serving that function. The jurisdiction of the Permanent Forum would most usefully go beyond the concept of a place to meet and exchange ideas and information. It should be conceived as a body that responds to the aspirations of the indigenous peoples as recognized by nation-states. In particular, it could reinforce the domestic move toward negotiated solutions of festering problems by providing a neutral, international ground for the drafting of agreements on controversial bilateral disputes over land, claims of breach of treaty, and assertions of violations of indigenous rights. Such a "good offices" or mediating function with respect to particular disputes between individual nation-states and indigenous peoples could, down the line, develop into an arbitral or adjudicative role if the world community gains trust in the good judgment of the body, and both potential parties to this possible conflict-settlement mechanism subject themselves to its jurisdiction. Thus, the Permanent Forum of Indigenous People could aspire to replicate the success that international panels of arbitration and mediation have enjoyed in the context of international business transactions. Even if governments viewed the vesting of the Forum with the power of making binding decisions as too great an intrusion into their realm of sovereignty, they might still be amenable to conferring upon the Forum the measure of authority that regional human rights commissions and the United Nations Human Rights Committee enjoy, i.e., the power to receive complaints, to investigate them, to make findings of fact, and to attempt to bring about a friendly solution to the issues raised. Such complaints could go specifically to the violations of international indigenous law, be it constituted by treaties or customary law or, ultimately, the United Nations Declaration on the Rights of Indigenous Peoples.

Beyond international law's own structures of enforcement, domestic legal systems should be looked at as the main engines of enforcing international law. In most domestic legal systems, the authoritative and controlling prescriptions of international law have been incorporated as standards of domestic legal systems, invited into the categorically different normative system of internal law through, usually, prescriptions of the highest rank, such as a constitutive document. In the United States, treaties, at least those of the "self-executing" kind, form part of the "supreme Law of the Land" as defined by the United States Constitution. Customary international law is seen as a standard of federal common law to be used by the courts either on the same level of normative strength as acts of Congress, or on a level just below. Courts in the United States, as well as in other domestic systems, therefore, remain important battlegrounds for the enforcement of international indigenous rights.

IV. CONCLUSION

Indigenous peoples around the world have come a long way. They have defeated expectations that they would simply vanish, assimilate, blend in, disappear in the mainstream, or maelstrom, of "modern" society. The First Nations have found their step again, and they have risen to become important actors in this "post-modern" social process.

This rise is not limited to a few places in the most affluent parts of the globe. As this analysis demonstrates, countries around the planet have given up on the age-old goal of "integrating" the original inhabitants of their territories into their modern way of life. In that vein, whether from genuine insight, or under more or less pressure, ruling elites have modified their laws throughout the Americas and beyond. They decided that indigenous peoples have a right to their distinct identity and dignity and to the governing of their own affairs – be they the "tribal sovereigns" in the United States, the Sami in Lappland, the resguardos in Colombia, or Canada's new province of Nunavut. This move toward recognition of indigenous self-government is accompanied by an affirmation of Native communities' title to the territories they traditionally used or occupied. Unthinkable only a few years ago, be it by virtue of a peace treaty in Guatemala, via a change of the constitution, as in Brazil, or by modification of the common law, as in Australia, domestic law now mandates in many countries the demarcation and registration of First Nations' title to the lands of their ancestors. Indigenous culture, language and tradition, to the extent it survived, is increasingly inculcated and celebrated. Treaties of the distant past are being honored, and agreements are fast becoming the preferred mode of interaction between indigenous communities and the descendants of the former conquering elites.

International law expectations build on this consolidated state practice. ILO Convention No. 169 and its emancipatory policy already covers a great number of indigenous peoples around the globe. Both on the regional and universal level, declarations on the rights and status of indigenous peoples are being finalized. They can, and should, be structured in such a way as to maximize for the intended beneficiaries the access to shaping and sharing of all the values humans desire. Coupled with the widespread practice of states specially affected by the issue, these efforts at international standard-setting do provide the requisite opinio juris for the identification of specific rules of a customary international law of indigenous peoples. They relate to the following areas:

First, indigenous peoples are entitled to maintain and develop their distinct cultural identity, their spirituality, their language, and their traditional ways of life. Second, they hold the right to political, economic and social self-determination, including a wide range of autonomy and the maintenance and strengthening of their own system of justice. Third, indigenous peoples have a right to demarcation, ownership, development, control and use of the lands they have traditionally owned or otherwise occupied and used. Fourth, governments are to honor and faithfully observe their treaty commitments to indigenous nations.

What is left are issues of balancing of rights, interests, and claims. They are by no means easy to resolve. What should be the exact scope of the aforementioned guarantees? What, precisely, ought to be protected? Is it just the traditional lifestyle, the ancient pattern of culture? Such an interpretation would run the risk of caging the members of these communities into a living museum, arguably an affront against the groups' and their individual members' dignity and freedom to choose a different way of life. Also, some historical manifestations of indigenous culture, such as the Aztec practice of human sacrifice to placate the Gods, may not appear worthy of protection. Should not the preservation of culture and the exercise of the right to self-determination be tempered and legally limited by fundamental individual human rights? Then again, who decides what values should prevail? ...

All of these issues and their resolution are extremely context-sensitive. Our common goal of constructing a public order of human dignity requires a responsible response to the value aspirations and claims of indigenous peoples as well as to conflicting claims. Social Darwinism cannot be the answer.

2. Treaty-Making Power

a. Western Sahara

1975 I.C.J. 4 [Review *supra*, at 154.]

80. Whatever differences of opinion there may have been among jurists, the State practice of the relevant period indicates that territories inhabited by tribes or peoples having a social and political organization were not regarded as *terrae nullius*. It shows that in the case of such territories the acquisition of sovereignty was not generally considered as effected unilaterally through "occupation" of *terra nullius* by original title but through agreements concluded with local rulers. On occasion, it is true, the word "occupation" was used in a non-technical sense denoting simply acquisition of sovereignty; but that did not signify that the acquisition of sovereignty through such agreements with authorities of the country was regarded as an "occupation" of a "*terra nullius*" in the proper sense of these terms. On the contrary, such agreements with local rulers, whether or not considered as an actual "cession" of the territory, were regarded as derivative roots of title, and not original titles obtained by occupation of *terrae nullius*.

3. Intergovernmental Institutional Agency

a. John Carey & Siegfried Wiessner, *A New United Nations Subsidiary Organ: The Permanent Forum on Indigenous Issues*

ASIL Insight No. 67, April 2001,

available at http://www.asil.org/insights/insigh67.htm.

1) Introduction

On July 28, 2000, the United Nations Economic and Social Council decided to establish, by consensus resolution, a "Permanent Forum on Indigenous Issues" as a subsidiary organ of the Council. ECOSOC Res. 2000/22 (*available at* http://www.un.org/documents/ecosoc/dec/2000/edec2000-inf2-add2.pdf, pp. 50-52).

2) Significance

The Permanent Forum on Indigenous Issues formally integrates indigenous peoples and their representatives into the structure of the United Nations. It marks the first time that representatives of states and non-state actors have been accorded parity in a permanent representative body within the United Nations Organization proper. …

4) Structure

The Permanent Forum on Indigenous Issues will be a subsidiary organ of the Economic and Social Council. It will consist of eight members nominated by governments and elected by the Council, and eight members to be appointed by the President of the Council following broad consultations with indigenous organizations and groups. The selection process is to take into account the diversity and geographical distribution of the world's indigenous peoples as well as principles of transparency, representativeness and equal opportunity. All members of the Forum are to serve in their personal capacity as independent experts on indigenous issues for a period of three years with the possibility of re-election or reappointment for one further period. Governments, intergovernmental organizations, NGOs in consultative status with the Council, as well as organizations of indigenous people complying with procedures previously applied by the Working Group on Indigenous Populations, may participate in the Forum as observers.

5) Functions and Procedure

According to ECOSOC Resolution 2000/22, the Permanent Forum on Indigenous Issues "shall serve as an advisory body to the Council with a mandate to discuss indigenous issues within the mandate of the Council relating to economic and social development, culture, the environment, education, health and human rights."

In so doing, the Permanent Forum shall

(a) Provide expert advice and recommendations on indigenous issues to the Council, as well as to programmes, funds and agencies of the United Nations, through the Council;

(b) Raise awareness and promote the integration and coordination of activities relating to indigenous issues within the United Nations system;

(c) Prepare and disseminate information on indigenous issues." (para. 2)

Furthermore, except as modified by the Council, the rules of procedure for subsidiary organs of the Council shall apply, and "the principle of consensus shall govern the work of the Permanent Forum" (para. 3). ...

7) Evaluation

The Permanent Forum on Indigenous Issues as established does not meet the entirety of aspirations of indigenous peoples, either with respect to its name (it sidesteps continuing debate over the use of the terms "indigenous people" or "peoples"), its structure (the equal match-up between states and indigenous representatives has been criticized as ignoring the power differential between the two groups), or with respect to its mandate (the advisory, educational and recommendatory functions outlined in Resolution 2000/22 will have to be interpreted broadly to respond to indigenous peoples' concerns). Still, it constitutes a bridgehead of international agency for indigenous peoples within the formal framework of the organized global community. ... As in every organization, the personalities chosen as its members will be critical to its success.

4. Land Rights

a. The Case of the Mayagna (Sumo) Awas Tingni Community v. Nicaragua

Inter-Am. Ct. H.R., Judgment of August 31, 2001

[Facts: The Government of Nicaragua granted a thirty-year concession to a Korean-owned company to log a large area of tropical rain forest in the Atlantic Coast region inhabited by indigenous communities. This grant was attacked in domestic court as well as before the Inter-American Commission on Human Rights. In June 1998, the Inter-American Commission decided to file a complaint with the Inter-American Court of Human Rights against the Government of Nicaragua, charging it, inter alia, with a violation of the indigenous community's traditional rights to their land. The petitioning Sumo Indian community of Awas Tingni asked the Court to declare that its land and resource rights were violated, and to order the government of Nicaragua to take measures to demarcate and legally guarantee its communal rights to land as a model for all the other indigenous communities in the Atlantic Coast region.

The Court found that the State of Nicaragua had violated the Awas Tingni Community's right to judicial protection under Article 25 of the Inter-American Convention on Human Rights as well as its right to property under Article 21 of the Convention. It decided that the State had to adopt, in its domestic law, the legislative, administrative and other measures necessary to create an effective mechanism for delimitation, demarcation and titling of the property of indigenous communities in accordance with their customary law, values, customs and mores, as well as carry out the respective, delimitation, demarcation and titling with respect to the Awas Tingni community. As to the right to property, the Court conducted the following analysis:]

Violation of Article 21 — Right to Private Property

142. Article 21 of the Convention declares that:

1. Everyone has the right to the use and enjoyment of his property. The law may subordinate such use and enjoyment to the interest of society.

2. No one shall be deprived of his property except upon payment of just compensation, for reasons of public utility or social interest, and in the cases and according to the forms established by law.

3. Usury and any other form of exploitation of man by man shall by prohibited by law.

143. Article 21 of the American Convention recognizes the right to private property. In this regard, it establishes: a) that "[e]veryone has the right to the use and enjoyment of his property"; b) that such use and enjoyment can be subordinate, according to a legal mandate, to "social interest"; c) that a person may be deprived of his or her property for reasons of "public utility or social interest, and

in the cases and according to the forms established by law"; and d) that when so deprived, a just compensation must be paid.

144. "Property" can be defined as those material things which can be possessed, as well as any right which may be part of a person's patrimony; that concept includes all movables and immovables, corporeal and incorporeal elements and any other intangible object capable of having value.

145. During the study and consideration of the preparatory work for the American Convention on Human Rights, the phrase "[e]veryone has the right to the use and enjoyment of *private property*, but the law may subordinate its use and enjoyment to public interest" was replaced by "[e]veryone has the right to the n:*use and enjoyment* of his property. The law may subordinate such use and enjoyment to the social interest." In other words, it was decided to refer to the "use and enjoyment of his *property*" instead of "private property".

146. The terms of an international human rights treaty have an autonomous meaning, for which reason they cannot be made equivalent to the meaning given to them in domestic law. Furthermore, such human rights treaties are live instruments whose interpretation must adapt to the evolution of the times and, specifically, to current living conditions.

147. Article 29(b) of the Convention, in turn, establishes that no provision may be interpreted as "restricting the enjoyment or exercise of any right or freedom recognized by virtue of the laws of any State Party or by virtue of another convention to which one of the said states is a party".

148. Through an evolutionary interpretation of international instruments for the protection of human rights, taking into account applicable norms of interpretation and pursuant to article 29(b) of the Convention -which precludes a restrictive interpretation of rights-, it is the opinion of this Court that article 21 of the Convention protects the right to property in a sense which includes, among others, the rights of members of the indigenous communities within the framework of communal property, which is also recognized by the Constitution of Nicaragua.

149. Given the characteristics of the instant case, some specifications are required on the concept of property in indigenous communities. Among indigenous peoples there is a communitarian tradition regarding a communal form of collective property of the land, in the sense that ownership of the land is not centered on an individual but rather on the group and its community. Indigenous groups, by the fact of their very existence, have the right to live freely in their own territory; the close ties of indigenous people with the land must be recognized and understood as the fundamental basis of their cultures, their spiritual life, their integrity, and their economic survival. For indigenous communities, relations to the land are not merely a matter of possession and production but a material and spiritual element which they must fully enjoy, even to preserve their cultural legacy and transmit it to future generations.

150. In this regard, Law No. 28, published on October 30, 1987 in La Gaceta No. 238, the Official Gazette of the Republic of Nicaragua, which regulates the Autonomy Statute of the Regions of the Atlantic Coast of Nicaragua, states in article 36 that:

> Communal property are the lands, waters, and forests that have traditionally belonged to the Communities of the Atlantic Coast, and they are subject to the following provisions:
>
> 1. Communal lands are inalienable; they cannot be donated, sold, encumbered nor mortgaged, and they are inextinguishable.
>
> 2. The inhabitants of the Communities have the right to cultivate plots on communal property and to the usufruct of goods obtained from the work carried out.

151. Indigenous peoples' customary law must be especially taken into account for the purpose of this analysis. As a result of customary practices, possession of the land should suffice for indigenous communities lacking real title to property of the land to obtain official recognition of that property, and for consequent registration.

152. As has been pointed out, Nicaragua recognizes communal property of indigenous peoples, but has not regulated the specific procedure to materialize that recognition, and therefore no such title deeds have been granted since 1990. Furthermore, in the instant case the State has not objected to the claim of the Awas Tingni Community to be declared owner, even though the extent of the area claimed is disputed.

153. It is the opinion of the Court that, pursuant to article 5 of the Constitution of Nicaragua, the members of the Awas Tingni Community have a communal property right to the lands they currently inhabit, without detriment to the rights of other indigenous communities. Nevertheless, the Court notes that the limits of the territory on which that property right exists have not been effectively delimited and demarcated by the State. This situation has created a climate of constant uncertainty among the members of the Awas Tingni Community, insofar as they do not know for certain how far their communal property extends geographically and, therefore, they do not know until where they can freely use and enjoy their respective property. Based on this understanding, the Court considers that the members of the Awas Tingni Community have the right that the State

a) carry out the delimitation, demarcation, and titling of the territory belonging to the Community; and

b) abstain from carrying out, until that delimitation, demarcation, and titling have been done, actions that might lead the agents of the State itself, or third parties acting with its acquiescence or its tolerance, to affect the existence, value, use or enjoyment of the property located in the geographical area where the members of the Community live and carry out their activities.

Based on the above, and taking into account the criterion of the Court with respect to applying article 29(b) of the Convention (*supra* para. 148), the Court believes that, in light of article 21 of the Convention, the State has violated the right of the members of the Mayagna Awas Tingni Community to the use and enjoyment of their property, and that it has granted concessions to third parties to utilize the property and resources located in an area which could correspond, fully or in part, to the lands which must be delimited, demarcated, and titled.

154. Together with the above, we must recall what has already been established by this court, based on article 1(1) of the American Convention, regarding the obligation of the State to respect the rights and freedoms recognized by the Convention and to organize public power so as to ensure the full enjoyment of human rights by the persons under its jurisdiction. According to the rules of law pertaining to the international responsibility of the State and applicable under International Human Rights Law, actions or omissions by any public authority, whatever its hierarchic position, are chargeable to the State which is responsible under the terms set forth in the American Convention.

155. For all the above, the Court concludes that the State violated article 21 of the American Convention, to the detriment of the members of the Mayagna (Sumo) Awas Tingni Community, in connection with articles 1(1) and 2 of the Convention.

NOTES AND QUESTIONS

1. For further details on status and rights of indigenous peoples, *see* S. JAMES ANAYA, INDIGENOUS PEOPLES IN INTERNATIONAL LAW (Oxford U. Press 1996); Gudmundur Alfredsson, *The Right of Self-Determination and Indigenous Peoples, in* MODERN LAW OF SELF-DETERMINATION 41-54 (Christian Tomuschat ed. Martinus Nijhoff 1993); Russel L. Barsh, *Indigenous Peoples in the 1990s: From Object to Subject of International Law?,* 7 HARV. HUM. RTS. J. 33 (1994); Catherine J. Iorns, *Indigenous Peoples and Self-Determination: Challenging State Sovereignty,* 24 CASE W. RES. J. INT'L L. 199 (1992); ROBERT A. WILLIAMS, JR., THE AMERICAN INDIAN IN WESTERN LEGAL THOUGHT: THE DISCOURSES OF CONQUEST (Oxford U. Press 1990); Benedict Kingsbury, *"Indigenous Peoples" in International Law: A Constructivist Approach to the Asian Controversy,* 92 AM. J. INT'L L. 414 (1998); Siegfried Wiessner, *American Indian Treaties and Modern International Law,* 7 ST. THOMAS L. REV. 567 (1995); PATRICK THORNBERRY, INDIGENOUS PEOPLES AND HUMAN RIGHTS (Manchester U. Press 2002); and the collection of essays entitled INTERNATIONAL LAW AND INDIGENOUS PEOPLE (S. James Anaya ed., Ashgate 2003).

2. Is the definition of "indigenous peoples" suggested *supra* appropriate? What function does the concept have under international law? Precisely in what way are indigenous peoples different from other "peoples" entitled to self-determination? Why, if at all, do they need special protection? Aren't human rights prescriptions fashioned for individual actors sufficient?

3. Does the *Awas Tingni* decision proclaim an indigenous people's right under customary international law to the lands they traditionally occupied and held up to the present time? What about restitution of lands they lost through conquest? *See* Judith Resnick & Julie Chi-hye Suk, *Adding Insult To Injury: Questioning The Role of Dignity in Conceptions of Sovereignty*, 55 STAN. L. REV.1921 (2003).

C. International Non-Governmental Organizations (NGOs)

1. Myres S. McDougal, W. Michael Reisman & Andrew R. Willard, *The World Community: A Planetary Social Process*

21 U.C. Davis L. Rev. 807, 822-826 (1988)

Intergovernmental and Transnational Organizations

Under the pressures generated by interdependence, nation state elites have found it expedient to establish and maintain a network of official transnational organizations to accomplish a range of specific objectives. These organizations have often been handicapped by the acute concern of the most influential elements, in particular nation states, to avoid either a formal or effective surrender of control. At least in the beginning, the objectives of these structures often were strictly circumscribed. The most inclusive structures were launched at the end of World War I (the League of Nations) and World War II (the United, Nations and associated institutions).

The number of specialized agencies, giving expression on a planetary scale to every value process, has increased throughout the twentieth century. Despite their primary locus of activity being functionally limited to particular value processes, geographical sectors, or regionally bound by local elites, these organizations reflect and contribute to the fact and awareness of global community by focusing attention and energy on the inextricably transnational nature of the problems which they confront.

Transnational Political Parties and Orders

Whatever the degree of their formal authority in traditional international law, it is undeniable that transnational political parties and orders play important roles in shaping programs and politics with respect to power and other values. Communist, socialist, republican, monarchist, anarchist, and many other organizations act together across nationstate boundaries to influence elections and decisions on particular issues. They also promote comprehensive images of the past and future which orient their members and help them interpret the continuous flow of information and events. Regardless of the degree of realism of their images, these organizations provide significant opportunities for shaping and sharing power, wealth, respect, affection, and rectitude. The distinction drawn between a political party and a political order is not a conventional difference embedded in the everyday terminology of power. Rather, it is a functional distinction drawn to serve the needs of scientific observers who recognize the importance of avoiding confusion. A political party commits itself to a variety of public issues and relies principally on strategies of persuasion to obtain acceptance for the candidates and programs that it presents in its own name. On the contrary, a political order enjoys a monopoly of legality in some states, and therefore is in a position to use state coercion to exclude competitors (save, perhaps "mini-parties") from an arena. If the political order forms a political party in a country beyond its primary base, it does so as a matter of expediency that does not necessarily affect its belief in and grasp of its coercive monopoly at home.

Transnational Pressure Groups and Gangs

Many transnational organizations lack a comprehensive program or refrain from naming their own candidates. Nevertheless, these organizations often play a decisive role in the policies of parties, governments, and intergovernmental organizations. The variety of pressure groups and the intensity of their commitments is a function of context and, in particular, of the perspectives that provide the motivation for their establishment. The popularity of this mode of participation can be expected to increase as long as the demand for access to those arenas where decisions that influence the distribution of all values are made is perceived to be effective. Pressure organizations have left their mark in the struggle against slavery, prostitution, illegal drugs, ecological degradation, and scores of other targets in every process of value shaping and sharing.

A gang is parallel to a "political order" in the sense that it relies chiefly on coercion rather than persuasion." Gangs are the "enforcers" in many transnational branches of organized crime, and may coopt or be coopted by governmental and other nongovernmental actors.

Transnational Private (or Official) Associations Oriented Toward Values Other Than Power

Many transnational associations, primarily designed for the cultivation of values other than power, are actively implicated in the global community process. The point applies to mass enlightenment, for example, and includes the huge world net of scientific societies and of associations for obtaining and disseminating newsworthy information. Included in this category are transnational corporations and associations that operate in information, finance, transportation, communication, mining, fishing, agriculture, manufacturing, wholesaling and retailing, and in every other branch of economic life.

NOTES AND QUESTIONS

1. NGOs generally refer to themselves as representatives of "civil society." In democratic systems, there is a certain anomaly in their self-designation, as elected officials are the representatives of civil society, while the constituencies of the NGOs are something of a phantom. Are NGOs more than pressure and interest groups? Should they be entitled to claim a right to participate on behalf of undefined constituencies?

2. The literature on NGOs and of their role in international governance is extensive. *See*, in particular, Steve Charnovitz, *Two Centuries of Participation: NGOs and International Governance*, 18 MICH. J. INT'L L. 183 (1997; also *see* Erskine Childers and Brian Urquhart, *We, The Peoples in* RENEWING THE UNITED NATIONS SYSTEM 171 (Dag Hammarskjold Foundation 1994); Janelle M. Diller, *On the Possibilities and Limitations of NGO Participation in International Law and Its Processes: Corporate Applications*, 95 PROC. AM. SOCIETY INT'L L. 304 (2001).

3. The role of NGOs has been a continuing subject of examination and appraisal by the United Nations. *See*, in this regard, Report of the Open-Ended Working Group excerpted below:

> REPORT OF THE OPEN-ENDED WORKING GROUP ON THE REVIEW OF ARRANGEMENTS FOR CONSULTATION WITH NON-GOVERNMENTAL ORGANIZATIONS, U.N. DOC. A/49/215 (1994), at 12:
>
> 56. One delegation stressed that non-governmental organizations considered for consultative status should strictly adhere to the principles and purposes of the Charter of the United Nations, and that organizations indulging in terrorism to destabilize legitimate Governments should have no place whatsoever in the United Nations system. It suggested that a set of rights and responsibilities and a code of conduct for non-governmental organizations should be considered. …
>
> 63. Concern was expressed at the recent practice of asking non-governmental organizations to form 'coalitions' and 'constituencies' and to speak through a spokesperson. Such forced consensus would result in destroying the diversity of opinions. It was suggested that those participatory rights, warranted by Council resolution 1296 (XLIV), be fully reinstated. …
>
> 69. Some delegations suggested that in order to increase the representation of non-governmental organizations from developing countries so as to reflect the principle of equitable geographical distribution, the Committee on Non-Governmental Organizations, when considering applications for consultative status, should give priority to those emanating from non-governmental organizations in developing countries. …
>
> 89. Another delegation stated that the participation of non-governmental organizations in conferences should be decided on a case-by-case basis, and that it was essential to get a 'no objection' clearance for this from the States concerned. …

4. In what way, if any, does the status and function of indigenous peoples within the Permanent Forum on Indigenous Issues differ from the status of NGOs? What should their status be? What should be the role of the Forum?

* * *

Non-governmental organizations have not had an easy time gaining acceptance before intergovernmental bodies, although they are referred to in Article 71 of the United Nations Charter. Establishment of consultative status with the U.N. is the preferred route.

2. Arrangements for Consultation with Non-Governmental Organizations

U.N. ECOSOC Res. 1296 (XLIV) (1968)

The following principles shall be applied in establishing consultative relations with non-governmental organizations:

1. The organization shall be concerned with matters falling within the competence of the Economic and Social Council with respect to ... human rights.

2. The aims and purposes of the organization shall be in conformity with the spirit, purposes and principles of the Charter of the United Nations.

3. The organization shall undertake to support the work of the United Nations and to promote knowledge of its principles and activities. ...

4. The organization shall be of representative character and of recognized international standing; it shall represent a substantial proportion, and express the views of major sections, of the population or of the organized persons within the particular field of its competence, covering, where possible, a substantial number of countries in different regions of the world. Where there exist a number of organizations with similar objectives, interests and basic views in a given field, they shall, for the purposes of consultation with the Council, form a joint committee or other body authorized to carry on such consultation for the group as a whole. It is understood that when a minority opinion develops on a particular point within such a committee, it shall be presented along with the opinion of the majority.

5. The organization shall have an established headquarters, [and] a democratically adopted constitution. ...

3. NGO Initiatives Before the Court

Despite the fact that the statute of the Court restricts access to states and, for advisory jurisdiction, international organizations, NGOs have been able to initiate advisory jurisdiction.

a. Legality of the Threat or Use of Nuclear Weapons, Advisory Opinion, July 8, 1996, Dissenting Opinion of Judge Oda

1996 I.C.J. 226, 330, 335-36, 368
[Review, *supra,* Part One, at 76]

8. ...The idea behind the resolution whereby the General Assembly (and also the WHO [World Health Organization]) requested an advisory opinion, had previously been advanced by a handful of non-governmental organizations (NGOs) which initiated a campaign for the *total prohibition* of nuclear weapons but failed to persuade the States' delegations in the forum of the General Assembly, which has done no more during a period of more than ten years than to pass repeated resolutions suggesting a convention on the prohibition of the use or threat of use of nuclear weapons. Some NGOs seem to have tried to compensate for the vainness of their efforts by attempting to get the principal judicial organ of the United Nations to determine the *absolute illegality* of nuclear weapons, in a bid to persuade the member States of the United Nations to press for their immediate and complete prohibition in the political forum.

A statement made by an observer from the International Physicians for the Prevention of Nuclear War at the World Health Assembly in 1993 appears to shed light on what was behind the movement towards the attempt to get the International Court of Justice to render an advisory opinion on the matter in response to a request from the World Health Organization if not from the United Nations General Assembly. The observer stated that "WHO would be right to seek an opinion on the matter from the International Court of Justice".

An observer from the World Federation of Public Health Associations informed the World Health Assembly that

> it [itself] had unanimously adopted a resolution on nuclear weapons and public health which, inter alia, urged the World Health Assembly to request an advisory opinion from the International Court of Justice on the legal status of the use of nuclear weapons, so as to remove the cloud of legal doubt under which the nuclear powers continued their involvement with such weapons, as well as to provide the legal basis for the gradual creation of a nuclear-free world."

This matter is referred to in my Separate Opinion appended to the Court's Opinion in response to the request of the WHO.

Another document of interest is an essay in a newsletter of the World Government of World Citizens, a part of which reads as follows:

> The threat to humanity's existence posed by nuclear weapons has encouraged humans the world over to consider new strategies for influencing their governments. One of these initiatives — the movement to *'illegalize' nuclear weapons* — may increase participation in new governing structures being created to address global problems. The World Court Project is thus taking its place in the forefront of the antinuclear movement.. . .
>
> To crystallize a united front against nuclear weaponry, several nongovernmental organizations (NGOs) ... have established a World Court Project. These NGOs have *successfully lobbied the 'non-aligned' members of the United Nations General Assembly* and the U.N.'s World Health Organization (WHO) to establish, according to customary international law, *the illegality of nuclear weapons*. (*World Citizens News*, Vol. IX, No. 6, Dec./Jan. 1996.) (Emphasis added.) ...

This gives the impression that the request for an advisory opinion which was made by the General Assembly in 1994 originated in ideas developed by some NGOs. ...

44. ... [A] group of States stimulated by a few NGOs attempted to achieve a breakthrough by obtaining the Court's endorsement of an alleged legal axiom in order to move towards a worldwide anti-nuclear weapons convention. I have no doubt that the Request was prepared and drafted — not in order to ascertain the status of existing international law on the subject but to try to promote the total elimination of nuclear weapons — that is to say, with highly *political* motives. This reason, among others, explains why, in 1944, resolution 49/75K, although passed at the General Assembly with the support of 78 States, did meet with 43 objections while 38 States abstained from the voting.

NOTES AND QUESTIONS

1. In what respects does consultative status differ from permanent mission status discussed *supra*? Should it? Are there any functional necessities for differential treatment? *See* Erik Suy, *The Status of Observers in International Organizations,* 160 RECUEIL DES COURS 79 et seq. (1978-II); and W. Michael Reisman, *The Supervisory Jurisdiction of the International Court of Justice: International Arbitration and International Adjudication,* 258 RECUEIL DES COURS 11 et seq. (1996).

2. In situations in which governments are freely elected and parts of them are assigned the competence to represent the collectivity externally, the governmental representatives are the authorized representatives of the civil society. In these circumstances, the NGOs, rhetoric notwithstanding, are often essentially oligarchical entities, purporting to represent all of their civil societies, while, in fact, representing a narrower group defined by its financial support. In authoritarian systems, in contrast, the role of the NGO is much more likely to approximate the aspirations of a civil society that has no effective mode of expression. Ironically, the most influential NGOs in contemporary international law-making derive from Western Europe, North America and Japan.

4. Case Studies

Differential policies and impacts on the world constitutive process are exhibited by the following actors:

a. "Traditional" Actors: The ICRC

The International Committee of the Red Cross (ICRC) a private Swiss association, focuses on providing humanitarian assistance in armed conflicts of inclusive concern. Its modus operandi is determined by Red Cross principles, including low visibility, strict neutrality, and respect for the sovereignty of warring parties. For details, *see* HANDBOOK OF THE INTERNATIONAL RED CROSS AND RED CRESCENT MOVEMENT (ICRC 1971).

(1) David P. Forsythe, *International Humanitarian Assistance: The Role of the Red Cross,*
3 BUFF. J. INT'L L. 235 (1996-97)

The ICRC claims a special role in international humanitarian assistance because of history, international humanitarian law, and Red Cross principles. The organization has played a major role in assisting war victims from 1859 on, at a time when the French army had more veterinarians to care for horses than doctors to care for soldiers. It successfully lobbied for the first Geneva Convention for war victims in 1864, and thereafter played a role in the subsequent development of international humanitarian law. In the current codification of that law, the ICRC is specifically mentioned and is given certain rights and duties—to visit prisoners of war and civilian detainees in international armed conflict. Red Cross principles require it to act for humanity, on a universal basis, with impartiality and neutrality—and independence—inter alia. ...

In Geneva, the ICRC has a staff of about 600 that tracks the plight of civilians in war and complex emergencies, along with its other concerns. In the 1990s, the ICRC sent out an additional 600 persons organized into regional and subregional delegations to work in the field. In addition to its existing involvements, it planned over 20 sizable assistance programs costing about $500 million in 1995.

Since the ICRC has observer status at the United Nations, it comes in direct contact with governments. The head of the ICRC's New York office meets monthly with the president of the U.N. Security Council. The ICRC participates in two consultative groupings in New York and Geneva with NGOs involved in relief. In 1995, the ICRC opened an office in Washington D.C. The ICRC seems reasonably informed about where it should seek access to civilians in need. ...

The ICRC is not the relief actor for international humanitarian assistance in armed conflict and civil strife. The global challenge is too great and the ICRC is too small. Some crises are so massive that only states and their military establishments can provide the necessary resources and logistics—and at times security. There is growing demand for sound public policy and management of humanitarian assistance. The ICRC remains a private Swiss agency, although recognized in public international law, which answers to no one but itself—at least formally speaking. Western governments provide most of the ICRC budgets, and thus the agency must be sensitive to their concerns. Just as the ICRC failed to dominate the evolution of the Red Cross/Red Crescent Movement, with symbols and actors coming into existence that weakened the unity of the Movement, so the ICRC failed to dominate relief in armed conflict and complex emergencies.

To the extent that the current system of international humanitarian assistance continues, the ICRC is likely to remain one of the more important actors. It has performed the various tasks inherent in assistance reasonably well. It endorses horizontal or voluntary coordination among relief actors, and the current system performs better than one might expect from an initial look at its complexity.

The ICRC has not been marginalized in the provision of humanitarian assistance by the proliferation of other actors. The agency has found various important roles for itself, with donor support, that varies from case to case. In 1992 it delivered more assistance than in any year since World War II, with 70% of it going to Somalia and former Yugoslavia. The ICRC, like other relief actors, has been marginalized in some conflicts at some times by the fighting parties themselves. That the ICRC was kept from providing the assistance it wanted in places like Liberia or the Sudan was not the fault of the agency, but of the inhumane values of the combatants. That ICRC safe areas for civilian protection and assistance in Liberia worked no better than UN protected areas in Bosnia, and that the ICRC had to withdraw from Liberia for a time, reflected badly on the fighting parties but not on Geneva. ...

b. Unconventional Actors: Greenpeace

Greenpeace focuses on global environmental threats. Its means of drawing attention to its objectives are often confrontational. It does not stay away from verbal attacks on nation-state elites and multinational corporations or from intrusions on their assets. For details and appraisal, *see* Paul Kevin Wapner, Envi-

RONMENTAL ACTIVISM AND WORLD CIVIC POLITICS (State U. of New York Press 1996).

(1) Peter J. Spiro, *New Players on The International Stage*

2 HOFSTRA L. & POL'Y SYMP. 19 (1997)

NGOs are hardly new to the international scene. The Catholic Church is perhaps the original NGO, and the labor movement provides the other significant example of transnational non-governmental organizing from earlier eras. While both remain quintessential models today, they are now joined by a throng. An almost infinite variety of groupings has spawned institutional vehicles in the form of NGOs (defined as organizations of non-national definition and not- for-profit orientation). Among the more prominent NGO grouping are environmentalists, human rights advocates, women, children, gays, the elderly, consumers, and indigenous peoples, each of which has mobilized at the international level.

Many NGOs at least purport to represent memberships, and many act as advocates in and out of international institutional settings. Greenpeace and Amnesty International are perhaps the most prominent examples of the modern advocacy NGO. These advocacy NGOs are noteworthy in at least two important respects. First, they now act directly to influence international decisionmaking institutions and not only through the channel of "home states". Thus, a Greenpeace or Amnesty International will not stop at having members or national sections lobby their own governments (although they will do that, too). Rather, they will move into the international stream as transnational entities seeking leverage wherever available. For example, a Greenpeace (with a largely North Atlantic membership) has had its positions voiced and advanced by delegations from small island states and lesser developed countries. In that fashion, advocacy NGOs become players outside the control of the states from which they nominally hale.

These NGOs have also been afforded a limited formal status in some international decisionmaking contexts. Pursuant to article 71 of the U.N. Charter, the Economic and Social Council (ECOSOC) has extended "consultative status" to international NGOs satisfying certain basic criteria. Recognition entitles an NGO access to ECOSOC proceedings and, for the more prominent organizations, rights to lodge oral and written interventions as well as to propose agenda items. NGOs have also been afforded limited rights of participation at UN-sponsored world conferences in recent years, including at Rio (on the environment), Cairo (population), and Beijing (women). Conferences on multilateral pacts on climate change and endangered species have afforded NGOs a place as observers to treaty monitoring proceedings. But in no institution save the International Labour Organisation have NGOs been formally extended a status even approaching parity with that of states. Nor have NGOs been afforded standing in international judicial forums, with prominent exceptions at the level of regional organizations.

In practice, NGO influence has far exceeded that indicated by their tentative formal standing in international institutions. NGOs have prompted states to undertake significant international legal initiatives, especially with respect to human rights and environmental protection. They have also been able to pursue global political agendas outside of institutions, either by shaming states (or other relevant actors, most notably corporations) through exposure and/or by mobilizing sympathetic consumer constituencies within the integrated global economy. The former is by now a well-honed tactic of the human rights movement through which objectives are secured by public relations mechanisms. The recent controversy surrounding Royal Dutch Shell's proposed scuttling of an oil rig in the North Sea presents one recent example of the latter. Shell had received all appropriate domestic and international approvals to leave the Brent Spar rig on the ocean floor. Greenpeace objected and launched a campaign to boycott Shell gasoline. Within weeks, Shell's sales in Germany were down 30%, at which point the oil giant relented. Shell has since sought out Greenpeace for consultations in planning the decommission of other rigs. Similar tactics were deployed against France to protest its recent nuclear testing program in the South Pacific. Although the tests were completed as planned, the success of Greenpeace's consumer action campaign may have contributed to France's decision not to undertake more tests in the future.

Brent Spar-type tactics are effective in proportion to a corporation's or state's dependence on consumer trade. The potential for such activity will be enhanced by further integration of the global marketplace, which increases the exposure of target states and corporations. Granted, the mechanism may remain exceptional. Groups such as Greenpeace obviously cannot effectively attack every objective through outright confrontation. But the threat of membership mobilization will make repetitive deployment unnecessary in some cases. Potential targets may accede to NGO demands, or at least come to an informal negotiating table, out of an awareness that consumer campaigns have worked in the past. There will also be episodes in which the possible costs of boycott efforts will not outweigh the benefits of the activity that the NGO seeks to halt. This may help to explain Shell's continued presence in Nigeria notwithstanding objections to the human rights practices of the current regime there. While NGO power is not absolute, it is significant and growing.

Notes and Questions

1. For court decisions, *see Greenpeace, Inc. (U.S.A.) v. The State of France*, 946 F. Supp. 773 (1996). *See also*, *Rainbow Warrior (N.Z. v. Fr.)*, 82 I.L.R. 500 (France-New Zealand Arbitration Tribunal 1990).

2. We earlier considered the role of NGOs before the ICJ as well as the harsh criticism lodged against NGO initiatives by Judge Oda. In the area of human rights, however, a primary role of NGO's has focused on the initiation of new instruments and their invocation. In particular, the Landmine Convention was the handiwork of a coalition of NGOs led by a group in Washington. Their efforts were crowned by the adoption of the Convention in 1997, (*see* http://www.icbl.org/treaty/text.php3), and also with a Nobel Peace Prize. For further details of this process, *see* Raymond Bonner, *How a Group of Outsiders Moved Nations to Ban Land Mines,* N. Y. Times, Sept. 20, 1997, at A5.

3. The area of indigenous rights protection has figured prominently in recent human rights initiatives by NGOs. The indigenous groups themselves, such as the World Council of Indigenous Peoples and others, have played a major role in the prescription of the draft Declaration on the Rights of Indigenous Peoples which was agreed to by the Working Group on Indigenous Populations in 1993. For further details, *see* JULIAN BURGER, REPORT FROM THE FRONTIER: THE STATE OF THE WORLD'S INDIGENOUS PEOPLES (Zed Books 1988) and JULIAN BURGER & MAURICE F. STRONG, GAIA ATLAS OF FIRST PEOPLES: A FUTURE FOR THE INDIGENOUS WORLD (Doubleday 1990). *See also, infra,* Part Three.

c. Coalition-Building: NGOs and the Formation of the International Criminal Court

(1) William R. Pace & Mark Thieroff, *Participation of Non-Governmental Organizations*

in THE INTERNATIONAL CRIMINAL COURT. THE MAKING OF THE ROME STATUTE: ISSUES, NEGOTIATIONS, RESULTS, Ch. 13 (Roy S. Lee ed., 1999)

I. Formation of the NGO Coalition

For the member organizations of the NGO Coalition for an International Criminal Court, the adoption of the Rome Statute was the culmination of three and a half years of intense advocacy efforts and an unprecedented level of cooperation and coordination among non-governmental organizations (NGOs) themselves as well as between NGOs and governments and the United Nations Secretariat. The fruit of NGO involvement in the process of the establishment of the Court is the Rome Statute which, while not without its imperfections, reflects the most fundamental concerns of civil society, and exceeds the expectations of even the most optimistic observers going into the Rome Conference....

On February 25,1995, a small group of NGOs monitoring the United Nations General Assembly debate on the International Law Commission's Draft Statute for an international criminal court met in New York and formed the NGO Coalition for an International Criminal Court (CICC, or the Coalition7). The main purpose of the Coalition was to advocate the establishment of an effective and just international criminal court. The Coalition established an informal steering committee comprised largely of groups involved in these earliest stages of cooperation, including Amnesty International, *Fédération Internationale des Ligues des Droits de l'Homme,* Human Rights Watch, the International Commission of jurists, the Lawyers Committee for Human Rights, No Peace Without Justice, Parliamentarians for Global Action and the World Federalist Movement.

From its inception, the Coalition sought to bring together a broad-based network of NGOs and international law experts to develop strategies on substantive legal and political issues relating to the proposed Statute. A key goal of the Coalition was and is to foster awareness and support for the Court among a wide range of civil society organizations, including those focusing on human rights, international law, humanitarian issues, peace, the rights of women and children, religion and many other sectors. The Coalition has served as both a facilitator for civil society involvement in the negotiation process as well as, in the words of one government official, "the world's principal source of information on the ICC". Throughout the entire period of the Preparatory Committee, the Coalition secretariat arranged countless meetings for NGOs with representatives of governments, United Nations officials and others involved in the Court's negotiations; produced and maintained extensive, electronic resources and print publications on the Court; and promoted education and awareness of proposals and negotiations at relevant events and conferences around the world.

By the opening gavel of the Rome Conference, this informal grouping had grown into a movement involving more than 800 organizations. This growth in numbers was accompanied by an intensification and particularization of advocacy efforts in the run-up to Rome. Coalition members formed sectoral caucuses and working groups focusing on aspects of the Court relating to gender issues, the rights of victims, peace and disarmament questions, the protection of children and matters of faith. Vibrant national and regional networks were established in many parts of Latin America, Europe, West Africa and other areas of the world.

II. The Work of the Coalition at the Rome Conference

Of the 236 NGOs accredited to participate in the Rome Conference, all but a few were members of the Coalition. These organizations were represented by an estimated 450 individuals. Although most NGOs were able to send only one or two representatives, and most had to stagger their attendance over the five week period, a few of the larger NGO delegations, such as those of Amnesty International and Human Rights Watch, surpassed many government delegations in size.

However, the impact of NGOs at the Rome Conference was not a simple function of the size of their presence. Many governments, the Secretary General, other United Nations officials and media experts have commented on the decisive role of NGOs at the Rome Conference, and many of these comments focused on the highly organized nature of the Coalition's presence. From the much-publicized demonstrations orchestrated by No Peace Without Justice and Amnesty International, to the press conferences and briefings, to the detailed reports prepared by the Coalition's 12 monitoring teams, time and again the NGO Coalition demonstrated that it was not only the largest delegation at the Conference, but also one of the most important. …

III. The Result

While the Rome Statute does not meet all of the individual demands voiced by NGOs throughout the years of negotiations, the Rome Conference produced a Statute which is stronger than NGOs and progressive governments had realistically hoped for, and also a powerful and quiet reflection of the growth of international democracy and the rule of law in international affairs. The Court which emerged from the marathon negotiations in Rome incorporates most of the specific fundamental principles enunciated by the Coalition before the Rome Conference. Against all predictions, the Court will have jurisdiction over crimes against humanity, genocide, and war crimes, including jurisdiction over crimes occurring in internal conflicts and crimes against humanity committed in times of peace; the Court has an independent prosecutor; the Court provides new guarantees for justice for women and children, and historic advances in the, protection and rights of victims. The new Court will have, it is hoped, a strong relationship to the United Nations and Security Council, and the Statute contains protections and safeguards to ensure the proper judicial functioning of the Court. …

[The ICC received the required 60 ratifications and entered into force on July 1, 2002. On March 11, 2003, the first panel of ICC Justices was sworn in at The Hague.]

d. NGOs and International Trade

(1) Steve Charnovitz, *Opening the WTO to Nongovernmental Interests*

24 FORDHAM INT'L L.J. 173 (2000)

What is the World Trade Organization ("WTO")? A reader of the Marrakesh Agreement Establishing the World Trade Organization would see that it is an international organization set up to supervise national trade policy. As of December 2000, the WTO had 141 member governments. The WTO is located in Geneva and led by a Director-General. Unlike some other international agencies (such as the International Monetary Fund), the WTO is a consensus-based institution driven by the member governments themselves, rather than by the Director-General or the staff of the Secretariat. Thus, in some ways, the WTO is directed not only in Geneva, but also in each of the national capitals...

International trade has been a controversial issue many times in the past, as it is today in a wave of globalization. In the early 1990s, a new school of criticism developed about the impact of world trade on development, the community, the environment, and public health. This led to questions about how world trade rules are made and who makes them. Some commentators began to claim that the trade regime has a "democratic deficit" and that it is not accountable to the public. The street protestors at the WTO Ministerial Conference in Seattle in late 1999 voiced all of these concerns.

In contrast to the United Nations, the WTO operates in a closed manner. Although nongovernmental organizations ("NGOs") have always had opportunities to participate in many U.N. activities, NGOs lack equivalent opportunities at the WTO. Thus, NGOs that want to influence the WTO have to localize their campaigns. Many NGOs contend that the WTO needs to change by becoming more open to nongovernmental interests. … It is termed the "Individualist" perspective because it presents the view that, as an agency of global governance, the WTO should maintain a vital connection to the individuals who inhabit the planet. The Individualist perspective recognizes the distinction between the national and international levels of decision-making, but contends that both are appropriate for participation by individuals and their voluntary associations.

Consider, briefly, the proposition that governments are not free to establish international organizations totally shut off from the public. Such closed organizations could contradict both national and international law. At the national level, one might ask whether a democratic government - which respects the core rights of association, assembly, and petition - can bind itself to recognize the authority of a treaty and international agency in which these core rights are denied to individuals. At the international level, one might ask whether consultation with NGOs has become customary for international organizations and part of their international personality.

This line of argument is superfluous, however, because the WTO treaty already states that "the General Council may make appropriate arrangements for consultation and cooperation with non-governmental organizations concerned with matters related to those of the WTO. "This provision is based on a similar one from the Charter of the International Trade Organization of 1948. The 1948 provision expanded upon the U.N. Charter of 1945, which provides that the Economic and Social Council "may make suitable arrangements for consultation with non-governmental organizations which are concerned with matters within its competence." Thus, the founders of the trading system went beyond the formal U.N. model to explicitly seek cooperation with NGOs.

Therefore, the real issue is not whether NGOs should receive recognition from the WTO, but rather what forms of consultation and cooperation are appropriate....

In deciding what modes of cooperation are appropriate, governments are being hindered by verbal barriers. Phrases like "NGOs should be able to particiipate" or "NGOs deserve a seat at the table" are ambiguous in English and probably equally confusing in other languages. Thus, at least some of the conflict about NGOs may result from verbal misunderstanding rather than real disagreement.

With sufficient discourse, it might be possible to gain a consensus among WTO governments on the following three propositions. First, although WTO rules and decisions are applied only to members, they do in fact affect people. Second, the WTO needs to attain broader public support and improving the dialogue between governments and NGOs may be one way of achieving this. Third, no government or mainstream civil society organization is suggesting that NGOs be given a vote in the WTO, and therefore, opposition to that hypothetical NGO role should not be used as an excuse to oppose appropriate consultation and cooperation. Of course, even with these three propositions as a foundation, WTO members will still disagree on whether consultation should occur solely with governments or also with the WTO.

The case for allowing the WTO to hear nongovernmental interests is strong. When individuals are affected by an official decision, they ought to be able to have input into the decision-making at the level where the decision is being made. The claim that governments set their WTO policies at home ignores the fact that key decisions in the WTO emerge as a result of face-to-face negotiations between governments. Obviously, the best way to influence such negotiations is to be in the room (if not at the table). It may be true in some countries that amendments to the WTO treaty have to be approved by a parliament or congress. Such parliamentary votes, however, will happen too late for an NGO that wants to shape the results. An NGO can fight against ratification, but that will usually be ineffective to achieve the NGO's constructive policy goals. Moreover, in view of the growing economic importance of WTO membership, no country is likely to reject ratification of new WTO agreements.

What NGOs typically want is to increase intergovernmental cooperation. Support merely from one's own government will rarely be sufficient for achieving an NGO's international goals. This is especially true in the WTO, which needs a consensus of governments, to make a decision. …

At the national level, a citizen does not exhaust his democratic participation by what he does alone in the voting booth. He lobbies, serves on advisory groups, circulates petitions, testifies at public hearings, and participates in "town meetings." These are a manifestation of democracy, not a distortion of democracy. …

The idea that an NGO should speak only through its government has an even deeper problem. Many NGOs concerned about the WTO's activities engage in transnational relationships. This is not surprising. Throughout the 19th and 20th centuries, individuals responded to international problems by setting up transnational NGOs. This extranational activism reaches across political borders to find like-minded individuals in other countries who will work together to influence governments and international organizations. (One current example of this phenomenon is the group *Médicins Sans Frontières.*) For the WTO to send transnational environmental groups or business groups down (or back) to their "own" governments is tantamount to denigrating the causes they espouse. Daniel Esty put it well when he said that "telling these groups that they must exert influence only at the national level is to deprive them of their transnational essence."

Because key WTO policies are being determined both in national capitals and in Geneva, it is logical for a transnational NGO, like WWF, to operate simultaneously at both levels. This is not taking two bites of the apple. Rather, it is biting into two different apples, national and global.

Although the Statists claim that NGOs who want to influence the WTO should go out and win national elections, that argument is sterile. Elections are much more about picking politicians than about deciding issues. Even when the WTO is discussed in an election campaign, this issue is likely to be on a third or lower tier. So the fact that an individual is frustrated with WTO policies does not imply that the individual's preferred candidate lost the most recent election. One can vote for the winning candidate and still be disappointed in the decisions he makes regarding the WTO (or the decisions made by his agents, the trade bureaucrats).

Furthermore, even if an idea is voted down in one country, that should not necessarily put the idea to rest. An NGO in Country A could develop an idea that A's public opposes yet the rest of the world would favor. If the NGO were able to offer this idea to the WTO, then the other governments might bargain with Government A to accept it. To be sure, speaking at the WTO is not the only way for an NGO to present its idea. The NGO's chairman can write an op-ed. But the unpopularity of an idea in its country of origin should not bar it from intergovernmental discourse.

A nation of individuals does not need to speak with one voice to other nations. Each nation has a government, however, and those governments should speak with one voice to each other. Of course, governments often fail in this regard due to well-known agency problems. Even when governments do speak to each other in perfect modulation, there will be numerous sidebar conversations between individuals of different nations that will express disagreement with one or more governments. Very frequently, individuals of one nation will converse with government officials of another nation. So long as an individual does not falsely purport to speak for his national government, these everyday conversations are unproblematic.

In an important contribution to the debate, Daniel Esty explains the value of promoting more intellectual "competition" at the WTO:

In an ideal world, governments might be expected to re-evaluate their policies regularly and then be positioned to bring fresh thinking to the fore, making a prominent NGO unnecessary. But in the real world, governmental inertia is overwhelming. ... An NGO-enriched WTO decision process would offer better competition for national governments in the search for optimal policies.

Optimal policies will not necessarily emerge from a vibrant marketplace of ideas at the WTO. The initial effect may be information overload or political gridlock. But the solution can hardly be to keep a narrow bandwidth on the communications channel. ...

Furthermore, the WTO can gain more than information from NGOs. Nonstate actors can also promote compliance with WTO rules and help educate the public about the WTO and trade. In addition, NGOs are less likely to object to WTO actions when the decision-making process allows them to have their say, even when they do not get their way.

Given all these reasons for NGO involvement, why do many countries oppose it? Actually, countries do not. It is the governments in power that are opposing greater consultation and cooperation between the WTO and NGOs. At the risk of over generalizing, it seems that many of these governments, particularly from developing countries, are worried that NGO participation will diminish their sovereignty. In assessing these claims, one should consider sovereignty in its external and internal dimensions. External sovereignty today, as Abram and Antonia Handler Chayes have explained, is really about "status" or "the vindication of the state's existence as a member of the international system." Internal sovereignty refers to the authority structure within a State and to the effectiveness of its control. …

The NGO challenge to internal sovereignty can be particularly acute in non-democratic countries. Although a bare majority of WTO member governments are free and democratic, thirty-two percent are rated "Partially Free" by Freedom House and seventeen percent are rated "Not Free." These latter two groups of WTO member governments may be horrified at the idea of giving a domestic NGO greater opportunities for participation at the WTO than it has at home because the NGO may use this experience to show the backwardness of its government.

In summary, Individualists say that the world trading system is too important to leave to trade technocrats. The WTO Agreement has a provision allowing NGO involvement, but so far governments have opted for shallow participation. If they move forward to provide more opportunities, governments may improve public understanding of and support for the WTO. Opening the WTO to NGOs will not change the character of the WTO. Director-General Moore's statement that 18 million people "joined" the WTO in 2000, while intriguing, is not correct. The WTO does not have citizens. NGOs will enjoy only a consultative status.

Although I side with the Individualists in this debate, I agree that the narrow Statist perspective has coherence. Yet the current posture of Statists is ironic. To keep NGOs out of the WTO, the political conservatives glorify Leviathan over the individual.

All governments - whether national or international - require statism. So the choice we face is not statism versus individualism as absolutes, but rather how to alloy these two principles in each organization. Should the WTO move away from its state-centrism and toward greater respect for the individual? In the author's view, the answer is yes. Economic nationalism and protectionism are deeply rooted, and so providing opportunities for civil society groups to challenge these practices can help the World Trade Organization use trade to achieve a better World. …

The debate about the appropriate role of NGOs at the WTO will continue in the years ahead. Before he joined the WTO in 1999, Director-General Moore wrote about the "virtue" of civil society in exposing "the corruption and inherent dishonesty of closed minds and closed systems." Inside the WTO, Moore has butted against some closed minds. Certainly, NGOs are not more virtuous than governments. Yet as voluntary groups, NGOs consist of individuals who care enough about an issue to work for or against it. The WTO will stand a better chance of reaching enlightened decisions and implementing them if governments welcome competing views and try to get NGOs to work for a better trading system. Moreover, inviting NGOs into the WTO will keep them off the streets.

Notes and Questions

1. Charnovitz argues that NGOs should have a much larger role in the WTO. Do you agree? *See* Steve Charnovitz, *WTO Cosmopolitics*, 34 N.Y.U. J. Int'l L & Pol. 299 (2002); Daniel C. Esty, *Linkages and Governance: NGOs at the World Trade Organization*, 19 U. Pa. J. Int'l Econ. L. 709 (1998). For an historical review, *see* Steve Charnovitz, *Two Centuries of Participation: NGOs and International Governance*, 18 Mich. J. Int'l L. 183 (1997); Joost Pauwelyn, *The Role of Public International Law in the WTO: How Far Can We Go?*, 95 Am J. Int'l L. 535 (2001).

2. The WTO has become a major international organization and has increasingly been the subject of scholarly interest beyond the NGO linkage. Justice cannot be done here to this extensive literature, but interested students will want to consult the work of several key symposium participants in *Symposium: The Boundaries of the WTO*, 96 Am. J. Int'l L. 1 – 146 (2002). *See also* Steve Charnovitz, *Rethinking WTO Trade Sanctions*, 95 Am. J. Int'l L. 792 (2001) and Jan Bohanes, *Risk Regulation in WTO Law: A Procedure-Based Approach to the Precautionary Principle*, 40 Colum. J. Transnat'l L. 323 (2001-2002).

5. Siegfried Wiessner, *Legitimacy and Accountability of NGOs: A Policy-Oriented Perspective*

in From Government to Governance? 2003 Hague Joint Conference on Contemporary Issues of International Law (W.P. Heere ed., T.M.C. Asser Press, The Hague, 2004)

Gone are the days when NGOs were exemplified by the idealistic students channeled by Peter Benenson into writing polite letters to dictators around the world imploring them to let their victims go. Today's NGOs have grown to a $1 trillion industry, riding the global wave of privatization of services, and have become major channels, if not the most important conduit, of governmental aid to developing countries and other flashpoints of need. Even more threatening to established holders of power is their surprising success in the political field: for one, without them, the International Criminal Court would not be set up in [The Hague] as we speak. The idealists of yesterday have not only mushroomed, according to some estimates of reliable institutions there are now 40,000 of them, operating, and thus creating moving targets, in changing coalitions and Internet-based networks around the planet. They are no longer mere irritants to the major decision-makers in the global social process, they no longer only meddle in the corridors of power. They have arrived.

Power is a jealously guarded thing. Macchiavelli's Prince could tell you a story or two on how to achieve and maintain it. So are the other seven things humans want out of life: wealth, affection, well-being, enlightenment, respect, rectitude, and skills. NGO's should not be surprised that they have come under increasing scrutiny as they scale the fortress of entrenched international (and domestic) decision-making structures. The Empire will strike back, and try to shake the cardinal stock in trade of the self-styled vanguards of "global civic-mindedness": their credibility. Just as experienced trial lawyers will spare no effort to discredit, on personal grounds, a witness who saw their client-killer in the act. But this is only part of the story. Some NGOs have brought it on themselves: through horror stories of fiscal mismanagement, nepotism, and internecine warfare. Severe irregularities in contracting, including allegations of kickbacks, have tarnished their image. Another issue of concern raised is the absence, in many of them, of internal democratic structures of authority. And, finally, the age-old question: *quis custodiet custodes*? If you hold others to account, shouldn't you be held accountable as well? Should NGOs be entitled to hide behind the veil of private action, while public actors have to perform in the sunshine of everybody's scrutiny?

To the credit of NGOs, many have asked these questions themselves. In fact, they have entered an era of "unprecedented self-questioning." A careful response to these complex questions needs to start from the proper location of NGOs in the global social process, in particular, the process of authoritative and controlling decision commonly designated as law.

There is no question that NGOs are actors in the social process. Many studies expertly define them, and describe their role. There is an issue, however, as to whether NGOs are relevant actors in the law, in particular, international law. As discussed elsewhere, law is not properly defined as a bundle of rules, independent from their creators and the circumstances of their creation. Not only in the view of policy-oriented jurisprudence, but today predominantly so, law is a dynamic concept, a process with a past and a future, a process of decision. A decision is a policy statement, and the decisions of law emanate from persons with authority and control intent. Often, this concept of decision is reduced to its crystallization in a statute or a convention, i.e. a prescription (e.g. "if you commit genocide, you are subject to the jurisdiction of the International Criminal Court"), or the application thereof (e.g. the conviction and sentencing of a person alleged to have committed this crime). It is much more helpful, as Reisman and others have done, to unpack the concept of decision, and to discern the seven phases of a decision of law, in order to properly locate the function of any actor involved in this process. Policy-oriented jurisprudence provides a refined way of thinking about processes of decision making. It conceives of decision processes in terms of the functions they perform. These functions include the gathering of intelligence, the promotion of preferences, the prescribing of authoritative policy or lawmaking, the invocation of prescriptions, the application of prescriptions, their termination, and the appraisal of the aggregate performance of a community's decision processes in terms of community goals.

The function of NGOs in the research aspect of finding a solution to social problems, and moreover, their promotion of a preferred solution based on that analysis, is too large to be overlooked. The coalition to ban landmines provides just one example for the essential role NGOs play in this crucial field of preparing prescription. Often the final signature under a prescriptive document (here: the Ottawa Convention to Ban Landmines) is but a formality which would never have come to pass without the diligent analysis and dedicated lobbying, conventional and unconventional, of pertinent NGOs. Still, according to voices of traditional international law, this signature, a move of the hand, is the only act that matters ("legally speaking"). Prescription itself is largely reserved to entrenched actors, the traditional nation-states, even though a more realistic assessment of the creation of expectations of lawful behavior will have to take into account more supple avenues such as the passing of best practices codes by private actors, voluntary restraint undertakings, and so on – the phenomenon often described as "soft law", one concession of traditionalists to reality. Even there, NGOs have entered the field, as other authors have documented. The invocation of prescriptions in cases of perceived violations is another stronghold of NGO action. Without such invocation (especially of human rights norms), there would be little application and enforcement, taking the lifeblood out of the prescriptions enunciated by governments. The act of application, by courts or other bodies, is ever more subject to NGO participation (from the admission of NGO complaints in various intergovernmental human rights systems to the acceptance of NGO amicus briefs in WTO dispute settlement process, to mention but a few such avenues). Obviously, NGOs are also involved in constant appraisal of existing norms and try to compare them to a preferred outcome, which sometimes results in the termination of a suboptimal norm.

Having thus located NGOs, *grosso modo*, in the process of international law, we can proceed to take a closer look at the demands made of them, i.e. the claims that they establish their legitimacy to justify their recognition, set up processes of internal democratic control, and respond to the clamor for accountability and transparency. I will address these issues in the order they were presented.

Legitimacy

In our secular age, it is taken as an article of faith that power, especially political power, can only be "legitimized" by reference to the will of the people. And, since every human being is essentially valued the same, the majority of the expressions of the will of the people counts. That is why, it is argued, in any political community, the will of the majority of the people need to prevail.

Some of these assumptions are questionable. The will of the majority does not necessarily lead to good results, or wise decisions. But, so in essence Winston Churchill's argument goes, democracy is the "second-best of all forms of government," acceptable only because of our failure to know a better one. As Max Weber has demonstrated, ... there were, and are, other models of legitimacy such as tradition, religion, and charisma.

To ask "democratic legitimacy" of NGOs in the sense of them reflecting "the will of the people," however, runs against their raison d'être. In most cases, they have been founded precisely in order to counter the will of the majority. The consequence, however, is this: the majority may accept NGOs as voices in the cacophony of (international and domestic) society, but, since they are not elected by the community at large, they may be legitimately excluded from decision-making for the community at large.

Defenders of NGOs have attacked this line of reasoning by pointing out the lack, or dearth, of popular input, or representation of the true will of the people in modern mass democracies (referring, *inter alia*, to the inordinate amounts of money needed to launch a successful political campaign — the McCain critique — or the shrewd manipulation of consciousnesses of the masses of politically undereducated people – the "false consciousness" or *panem et circenses* point). The argument goes: since you (the government) are not truly representative of the will of the people, we (the NGOs) don't need to be either.

This argument does not properly address the concern about legitimacy of any organization. For one, one imperfection does not excuse another. Second, and more importantly, the argument does not take into account the function of NGOs which should drive the assessment of their legitimacy.

NGOs are best understood as associations of people who organize themselves to achieve a particular political end. More profoundly, they articulate, and combine to a pointed political force, the needs and aspirations of individual human beings with respect to a discrete policy issue. Those needs and aspirations, or things humans value, ergo "values," have conveniently been described as power, wealth, well-being, affection, enlightenment, skill, respect, and rectitude (with no particular order between them). Law, or governmental decision, effectuates distributions of these values in society. An ideal legal order maximizes access by all to all these things humans desire.

The legitimacy of an NGO in such a dynamic process of social life is tied to the authenticity of its mission, not the strength of its numbers. If the goal is not, as Bentham would have it, "the greatest happiness of the greatest number," but access to all values by all, the essential contribution of NGOs is the authentic expression of sincerely held beliefs that represent to the decision-maker in any relevant community a value preference that he/she should take into account when trying to arrive at a solution to the societal problem at issue that approximates the public order of human dignity. The most successful NGOs would be those that make the argument of their preferred solution as representing the common interest of the community most effectively and persuasively.

If authenticity of aspiration in a pluralistic society is thus the touchstone of legitimacy, a good argument can be made for the proposition that NGOs that are founded in order to disguise the real motives of their founders, or are only established to generate wealth or other hidden benefits for their leaders and administrators, would be considered illegitimate. Others, tiny as they might be, are proper amplifications of otherwise isolated and ignored "voices in the wilderness."

Ultimately, the effectiveness of any social organization committed to policy changes in an open society, especially one that has only limited resources and/or access to the media, depends on its sincerity and credibility: it needs to be authentic. Legitimacy is achieved, not conferred; and it is promoted by openness on essential facts such as mission, source of funding, activities and impact of the organization. ...

Internal Democratic Control

The issue here is the internal structuring of the organization. With the exception of Amnesty International and few others, democracy within an NGO is limited to voting with the pocketbook: if members disagree with a decision from the top, they will not try to dislodge the leaders, but simply stop paying their dues. Dissent is remedied by exiting from the organization. Some organizations aren't even membership-based such as a foundation or a trust. A corporation would not be controlled by the democratic principle of "one shareholder, one vote;" obviously, weighted voting governs decision-making in this structure.

In light of the cardinal function of NGOs as representatives of interests in society, large or small, internal democratic control would seem to carry less weight than other concerns. Ralph Nader, for example, would appear to have exactly the same impact upon decision-making processes whether he is the elected representative of an organization or not. The same, however, might not be true for leaders of other organizations. Whether membership-based organizations have their members elect their leaders, or allow dissenting members only the exit option, appears therefore to be more a matter of expediency than a matter of legitimacy.

Transparency and Accountability

The strongest point of the NGO critique is the often-encountered absence, or dearth, of transparency and accountability. There are many arguments in favor of organizational openness and responsibility. The obvious ones are the prevention of fraud and financial mismanagement, as mentioned above. This is a major goal for public order. If an NGO receives public monies, e.g. from USAID, the misuse of it through excessive administrative expenses, cost overruns by subcontractors, etc. diverts funds urgently needed for other programs essential to the community at large. If the abuse is of a criminal nature, the security of a community is at stake, and criminal accountability of the offenders is a needed response.

Beyond the misuse of money, the openness about sources of funding, in particular, and the NGO's mission, activities and expenses would check the de facto power of NGOs as much as reporting requirements on lobbyists in the legislative process do. In addition to these advantages to the general public, the benefits of transparency and accountability should be clear to the NGOs themselves. As stated above, the stock in trade of NGOs is their credibility. The sources and use of their entrusted funds should be known to the public, to actual and prospective donors. Such openness ultimately results in more effective championing of causes and endorsements of candidates for public office.

Done right, it also has a chance of significantly improving the organization. Internal evaluations, in particular, spotlight what the organization is doing, how it is doing it, with what impact, etc. Of particular use in this context appears to be Fowler's distinction between output, outcomes and impact. Also, a SWOT analysis could be a helpful method of assessment. These processes could and should be used to highlight problems, streamline internal procedures and ensure compliance with the stated mission.

The downside of strict requirements regarding transparency and accountability is the over-bureaucratization of the effort, the racing from one planning retreat to the other, the development of a cottage industry of evaluators. Also, it is not always easy to measure the impact , as exemplified in, say, an evaluation of NGOs set up to enhance the rule of law in certain countries or regions. ... [In] monitoring the American Bar Association's Central and Eastern European Law Initiative, for example, we had to use qualitative rather than quantitative data to gauge the true impact of CEELI's expert assessments of pending legislation in the target countries. Also, the over-formalization of procedures in response to evaluations may leave the organization less flexible when responding to new situations and demands. In addition, there are certain areas that should not be discussed in the sunshine, such as privacy issues of employees, issues of national security, if applicable, etc.

An argument might be made that NGOs should not be subject to the same transparency and accountability regime as government officials, since, after all, they don't make laws, and don't hold similar power over individuals. This argument of asymmetry of power is blunted, however, by reference to, say, the corporate sector, where best practices codes and regimes of voluntary self-restraint have been instituted successfully at both domestic and international levels.

The issue, then, is not whether transparency and accountability of NGOs are needed or desirable. They clearly are. The true issue concerns the ways these goals are achieved. Who does the evaluation: is it internal, external, or conducted both from the inside and the outside? Who is it that the NGOs are reporting to? Beyond the government, the internal revenue services of various countries, and the donors, openness on major data regarding the organization should exist toward the public at large. The modern means of communication, in particular the Internet, should be used effectively for that purpose. Ideally, an annual report on the institution's mission, its activities, sources of funding, its expenses, impacts and plans for the future should be published on the worldwide web.

As to power and inclusion of NGOs in formal processes of domestic and international decision-making, the prevailing debate on the "international legal subjecthood" of NGOs, limited or not, appears to be singularly unhelpful. Its sterility should be replaced by a functional analysis of areas in which such claims of participation are particularly apposite. In the context of indigenous peoples, I could well imagine, say, the newly-established Permanent Forum on Indigenous Issues, composed, in equal number, by government representatives and representatives of indigenous communities, to provide major benefits for world public order by acquiring the power to address, and decide, conflicts resulting from treaties between states and indigenous peoples.

A final point: the obligation of transparency and accountability upon an actor should be directly proportional to the degree of inclusive influence that it has. This is a principle that should not only apply to NGOs, but also to states and all other categories of actors. Power, public or private, needs to be checked as intensely as it imposes itself.

Conclusion

NGOs perform their function best by not only aggressively and authentically promoting the causes for which they have been established, but by opening themselves up to constant self- and outside scrutiny. Credibility is their major stock in trade. Public trust is gained and maintained by self-critical reporting, not only about successes, but also about failures and the paths chosen to overcome them. Best practices codes or framework conventions could be used to specify these critical requirements of transparency and accountability. Democratic legitimacy appears to be less of a concern, since the amount of support, financial or numerical, for the particular cause championed by the NGO does not necessarily indicate its fitness as a solution maximizing access by all to all the things humans desire, the touchstone of a just public order.

NOTES AND QUESTIONS

1. What is the role of NGOs in the world constitutive process? How do they contribute to the approximation of a world public order of human dignity? In what substantive areas have they had the greatest impact? What strategies promise the greatest success?

2. If NGOs have great influence or impact upon decision-making on the international plane, should they be held to standards of accountability similar to those of governments or governmental organizations? Should they have some degree of democratic legitimacy? Sustainability? How would you evaluate Professor Wiessner's recommendations in this regard?

3. A less confrontational approach than that taken by Greenpeace is pursued by Amnesty International. This organization's primary focus is assistance to political prisoners. Its main means are letter-writing campaigns, human rights reports, and the polite engagement of nation-state elites. For details, *see* THE AMNESTY INTERNATIONAL HANDBOOK (Marie Staunton, Sally Fenn & Amnesty International U.S.A. eds. Hunter House 1991).

D. MULTINATIONAL CORPORATIONS

Multinational corporations exert an informal, though at times highly significant influence on global constitutive process and nation-state elites. Those manifestations of power engender claims for prescriptive restrictions.

1. Steven R. Ratner, *Corporations and Human Rights: A Theory of Legal Responsibility*
111 YALE L.J. 443 (2001)

1. Corporations as Global Actors

The inadequacy of state responsibility stems fundamentally from trends in modern international affairs confirming that corporations may have as much or more power over individuals as governments. In analyzing the power of TNEs ["transnational enterprises"] today, Susan Strange emphasizes the need to conceptualize power beyond political power to include economic power and accordingly concludes that markets matter more than states. Whether or not the "retreat of the state" is as great as she states, corporations clearly exercise significant power over individuals in the most direct sense of controlling their well-being. Of course, corporations have always wielded significant power over their employees; and governments have to enforce their own laws as well as to protect the human rights of their citizens. So why does such power require moving beyond state responsibility?

First, the desire of many less developed states to welcome foreign investment means that some governments have neither the interest nor the resources to monitor corporate behavior, either with respect to the TNEs' employees or with respect to the broader community. Their views on investment might lead them to assist companies in violations, for instance, through deployments of security forces. In extreme cases, governments actually grant corporations de facto control over certain territories. For instance, whatever one may believe of the merits of claims against Freeport-McMoRan of human rights abuses in Irian Jaya or against Texaco in the Colombian rainforest, there seems little doubt that those entities exercise significant power in certain regions, often with little interference by the government.

Second, regardless of its position on foreign investment, the government might also use various corporate resources in its own abuses of human rights. The South African experience represents the epitome in recent times of such nefarious cooperation between public and private sectors. Because repressive governments (or opposition movements) may need to rely on businesses to supply them with material for various unacceptable activities, corporations may work in tandem with governments in abusing human rights.

Third, as firms have become more international, they have also become ever more independent of government control. Many of the largest TNEs have headquarters in one state, shareholders in others, and operations worldwide. If the host state fails to regulate the acts of the company, other states, including the state of the corporation's nationality, may well choose to abstain from regulation based on the extraterritorial nature of the acts at issue. Corporations can also shift activities to states with fewer regulatory burdens, including human rights regulations. Recognition of duties on corporations under international law could encourage home states to regulate this conduct or permit others to do so; at the very least, it would suggest a baseline standard of conduct for corporations themselves that could be monitored by interested constituencies.

If private entities might be contributing to a deleterious human rights situation, then those concerned with the behavior of such enterprises are left with three options—to continue to focus exclusively on the state, encouraging it eventually to control such enterprises; to enforce obligations against individuals (the limits of which I discuss below); or to identify and prescribe new obligations upon those private entities in international law and develop a regime of responsibility for violations they might commit.

Indeed, multinational enterprises are themselves recognizing the limits of duties on states. Unocal, for instance, has stated publicly that "human rights are not just a matter for governments." In 2000, the United Kingdom's Prince of Wales Business Leaders Forum and Amnesty International teamed up to issue Human Rights: Is It Any of Your Business?, a glossy 144-page human rights guide for senior corporate policymakers. The publication notes: "While a company is not legally obliged under international law to comply with [human rights] standards, those companies who have violated them have found, to their cost, that society at large will condemn them." And, as discussed in Section VII.A below, corporate-initiated codes of conduct represent clear evidence that normative expectations of all relevant actors— not just NGOs or governments—are now shifting.

In this sense, the need for corporate responsibility parallels the evolution of the existing corpus of law beyond state liability to cover individual responsibility, under which individuals are criminally responsible for exceptionally serious human rights abuses. Individual responsibility emerged primarily from the sense of governments and nonstate actors that holding states accountable proved inadequate to address those acts. Unlike state responsibility, accountability for individual violators might provide victims of atrocities with a sense of justice and a possibility to put the past behind them (the amorphous notion of closure). It might also help deter future abuses more effectively, send a powerful message of moral condemnation of heinous offenses, and help a society traumatized by massive human rights violations to identify perpetrators and thereby promote national reconciliation. In its ability to advance these goals, individual responsibility has become a promising alternative along a continuum of enforcement mechanisms for international human rights or international humanitarian law.

Some of the reasons for the inadequacy of state responsibility for individual human rights abuses - for example, the impact on victims of identifying and punishing their individual perpetrators (as opposed to merely blaming the state) - differ from the reasons for its inadequacy for corporate actions. But the deterrence rationale remains common to both contexts and points to the need to place obligations on entities that have the resources to violate human rights and whose conduct cannot properly be policed by the state where they operate. If international law provided for a regime whereby the corporations had duties themselves and incurred some penalty for violations of them, it would place the incentives on the party with the greatest ability and interest in addressing corporate conduct.

In one historically significant instance, the justifications for individual accountability and business accountability, and the corresponding limits of state responsibility, all came together—international efforts to outlaw the slave trade. The slave trade represented, in a sense, the worst form of private enterprise abuse of human rights. To end it, abolitionists eschewed sole reliance upon state responsibility, both because traders operated on the high seas and because many states tolerated the practice. Instead, they convinced governments to conclude a series of treaties that allowed states to seize vessels and required them to punish slave traders. Thus the first true example of international human rights law was a response to commercially oriented violations of rights. ...

NOTES AND QUESTIONS

1. Is Professor Ratner's theory of international corporate agency and responsibility convincing? As to civil liability in the context of human rights abuses, *see infra,* Part Three. *See also Presbyterian Church of Sudan v. Talisman Energy, Inc.*, 244 F. Supp. 2d 289 (S.D.N.Y. 2003).

2. To curb abuses of power by multinational corporations, "hard" and "soft" law has been developed by, *inter alia*, the United Nations Center on Transnational Corporations (UNCTC) and the "First World"-dominated Organization for Economic Cooperation and Development (OECD). Hortatory "codes" on restrictive business practices constitute an attempt to "rein in" conduct deemed unacceptable. Domestic legislation of major state actors, in particular the United States Congress, ensued as well. To combat the phenomenon of bribery highlighted in the Lockheed scandal, Congress, in 1977, passed the Foreign Corrupt Practices Act. The statute has put significant restrictions on American business. As to the role of "incentives" in doing business in various foreign countries, *see* W. MICHAEL REISMAN, FOLDED LIES: BRIBERY, CRUSADES, AND REFORMS (Free Press 1979). What is the proper policy regarding extraterritorial conduct of multinational companies?

3. The years 2001 and 2002 were marked by corporate scandals, e.g. Enron, Worldcom, Global Crossing and Vivendi, that undermined the public's confidence in corporations and their accounting firms *per se* as well as in the equity markets. New legislation in the United States has begun to address the lack of oversight on publicly traded companies and the accounting and law firms worldwide who conspired with them to mislead the public. *See, e.g.* Sarbanes-Oxley Act of 2002, H.R. 3763, 107th Cong. (2002), *available at* http://news.findlaw.com/hdocs/docs/gwbush/sarbanesoxley072302.pdf. The legislation requires corporate CEOs to certify the accuracy of their companies' financial statements, prohibits retaliation against whistle-blowers, and raises the maximum penalty for securities fraud to twenty-five years in jail. Federal legislation has also established the Interagency Corporate Fraud Task Force which has helped to bring charges against various CEOs. In addition, the White House has doubled the budget of the Securities and Exchange Commission, and it supported the establishment of a Public Company Accounting Oversight Board to make sure that auditing firms do their job properly. These efforts at reform were not enough to prevent further scandals in late 2003, this time involving allegedly illegal operations by managers of prominent mutual funds.

These events have led to increased scholarly interest in corporate governance as an international legal concern. *See* Timothy L. Fort, *Corporate Governance in a Global Environment: The Search for the Best of All Worlds*, 33 VAND. J. TRANSNAT'L L. 829 (2000); Timothy L. Fort & Cindy A. Schipani, *Corporate Governance and Sustainable Peace: Intra-Organizational Dimensions of Business Behavior and Reduced Levels of Violence*, 36 VAND. J. TRANSNAT'L L. 367 (2003); Tara J. Radin, *700 Families to Feed: The Challenge of Corporate Citizenship*, 36 VAND. J. TRANSNAT'L L. 619 (2003).

In light of the international effect of major corporate scandals, should international transparency rules be prescribed? Should the power wielded by multinational corporations be a determining factor ? Would these rules be practicable? *See also* Lee A. Tavis, *Corporate Governance and the Global Social Void*, 35 VAND. J. TRANSNAT'L L. 487 (2002).

4. Increasingly, multinational corporations have been subjected to liability for international human rights violations in domestic courts. *See infra*, Part Three. *See also* Jordan J. Paust, *Human Rights Responsibilities of Private Corporations*, 35 VAND. J. TRANSNAT'L L. 801 (2002); Scott

Greathead, *The Multinational and the "New Stakeholder": Examining the Business Case for Human Rights*, 35 VAND. J. TRANSNAT'L L. 719 (2002).

E. PRIVATE ARMIES

As effective power is an integral part of the world constitutive process, organizations seeking influence and wielding instruments of coercion and violence outside the formal structure of the nation-state become relevant to a comprehensive assessment of the arena in which law is made and changed. The French Revolution's suppression of intermediate groups between the state and the individual – the opposite of America's idea of minimal government and encouragement of broad consociation of peoples in "civil society" – reflects a larger struggle for preeminence between the elites of the nation-state, vested with authority and control intent, and the elites of subgroups in society who may not have attained the mantle of authority, but dispose of a wide variety of means that afford them access to effective power. Those "private armies" are united primarily by the desire to challenge the authority of established nation-states, and focus on maximizing, for their own members, the scope value of power.

Max Weber, in his classic ON LAW IN ECONOMY AND SOCIETY (Max Rheinstein ed. Simon & Schuster 1967), referred to the struggle this way:

> The law of the state often tries to obstruct the coercive means of other consociations. ... But the state is not always successful. There are groups stronger than the state in this respect. ... This conflict between the means of coercion of the various corporate groups is as old as the law itself. In the past it has not always ended with the triumph of the coercive means of the political body, and even today this has not always been the outcome.

Professor Reisman has highlighted the relevancy of such private armies in contemporary context, and clarified pertinent policy:

1. W. Michael Reisman, *Private Armies in a Global War System: Prologue to Decision*

14 VA. J. INT'L L. 1-7 (1973)

An army is a corps of people, sharing loyalty to a common symbol, skilled in the manual of arms and operating within a command structure one of whose manifest functions is to direct corps members or "soldiers" in the purposive exercise of violence. Given the pivotal position of effective power in almost all societies of which there is record, it is no surprise that elites who have asserted a monopoly of authority have sought as well the exclusive prerogative of maintaining armies. Characteristic of the myth of the contemporary nation-state is its claim for monopoly over the exercise of violence. Were there a rough conformity between states theory and practice, one could expect to count about as many armies in the world as there are nation-states. In fact, the equation seems perpetually imbalanced. In certain circumstances, the number of effective fighting units not affiliated with the governmental apparatus of recognized states can grow even larger. I will refer to such units as "private armies." The private army is a fact of international life. ...

The basic policy here is not only, as has often been assumed, self-defense, but also international collaboration in the prohibition of the use of force by entities not associated with or operating under delegation from a nation-state. For convenience this interlocking obligation and right will be referred to here as the "private-army rule." ...

When the logical rigor of the nation-state theory cracks under the stress of political reality, one of the first casualties is the private-army rule. A significant number of the nominal states of the world do not exercise anything approaching plenary power within their borders; they are treated as nation-states because of the tacit or express agreement or the coincidental disinterest of the effective global elites. At times private armies operate from within the borders of these states. If the private-army rule of international law were strictly applied and reprisals were undertaken, these nominal states might crumble. Hence, there are strong and effective claims for the suspension of the rule in certain circumstances. When this occurs, the private army's activities cannot even be appraised, much less regulated. A regional license for disorder is issued.

In the future, the private-army rule will probably provide an even less useful focus, with ever slacker guidelines for decision. As the contemporary nation-state system cedes to an international system with a richer diversity of effective participants often bound by much tighter links of interdependence, the use of military force by non-state entities will probably multiply. Because of this greater interdependence, violence enacted within a single state will increasingly have impacts – psychologically and material — on people in other territorial communities. More and more private armies will become international problems.

These problems will confront both official and private actors. For the official, the appropriate response would seem patent: private armies are processors of violence which have not secured the overt approval of the political institutions of states or of those territorial elites who have arrogated control of the symbols of political legitimacy. But for individuals committed to a world order of human dignity, private armies present a particularly cruel dilemma. Private armies are disruptive, whereas order seems necessarily instrumental to the realization of many other values. And there is, particularly among lawyers, an almost instinctive deference to the authority of political institutions in other communities, which is stimulated by transference, professional ideology, and the hope of reciprocity. Moreover violence itself seems inimical to the very notion of human dignity. ...

NOTES AND QUESTIONS

1. Some of the private armies referred to by Professor Reisman, have been, or are, in their self-perception, implementing a "right" under international law, *i.e.* the "right to self-determination."

They include later glorified actors in the process of decolonization ranging from Simon Bolivar to Algeria's FLN, Ché Guevara, and the SWAPO in Namibia, to name but a few. Other groups fighting for freedom from oppression outside the decolonization context narrowly defined have also used violence strategically to achieve a political end. Some of the more prominent examples would include the fighting arms of proto-state movements such as the IRA in pre-1917 Ireland, the Irgun and the "Stern Gang" in the territories of the British Mandate over Palestine prior to the independence of Israel, and the ANC in pre-Mandela South Africa. The 1970 United Nations General Assembly Declaration on Principles of International Law Concerning Friendly Relations and Co-Operation Among States in Accordance with the Charter of the United Nations addressed the conundrum posed by conflicting demands of the existing nation-states and rebelling elites by stating, in pertinent part:

> Every State has the duty to promote, through joint and separate action, realization of the principle of equal rights and self-determination of peoples, in accordance with the provisions of the Charter, and to render assistance to the United Nations in carrying out the responsibilities entrusted to it by the Charter regarding the implementation of the principle, in order:
>
> (a) To promote friendly relations and so-operation among States; and
>
> (b) To bring a speedy end to colonialism, having due regard to the freely expressed will of the peoples concerned; and bearing in mind that subjection of peoples to alien subjugation, domination and exploitation constitutes a violation of the principle as well as a denial of fundamental human rights, and is contrary to the Charter...
>
> Every State has the duty to refrain from any forcible action which deprives peoples referred to above in the elaboration of the present principle of their right to self-determination and freedom and independence. In their actions against, and resistance to, such forcible action in pursuit of the exercise of their right to self-determination, such peoples are entitled to seek and to receive support in accordance with the purposes and principles of the Charter.

G.A. Res. 2625, 25 U.N. GAOR, Supp. No. 28 (A/8028), at 121 (1970). Does this formulation constitute an exception to the traditional "private army rule" as stated by Professor Reisman? Does it go beyond the mere reflection of effective power, *i.e.* international law accepting the legitimacy of a new actor, be it a recognized nation-state or government — once, and only once, its struggle has met with success? Does it constitute good policy to consider successful such private armies as only *ex nunc*, not *ex tunc* legitimate? What are the advantages of Professor Reisman's recommendation to ground the appraisal of such entities in their overall contribution to a world public order of human dignity? Any disadvantages?

2. In the context of armed resistance to brutal dictatorships and/or genocidal regimes, who should make the determination whether that armed struggle is legitimate? Individual states or the organized world community? In cases of states with contending power centers, the United Nations credentialing process provides one method for sorting out conflicting claims of representation. If the goal of the private armies is to overthrow an entrenched government considered "dictatorial," should other countries be deemed authorized to allow private armies to operate from their soil? What about operations of Cuban exile groups opposed to the regime of Fidel Castro? For context, *see* Maria Cristina Garcia, Havana USA: Cuban Exiles and Cuban Americans in South Florida 1959-1994 (U. of Cal. Press 1996); Carlos E. Cortes, Cuban Exiles in the United States (Ayer Co. Pub. 1981).

F. TERRORISTS

1. W. Michael Reisman, *International Legal Responses to International Terrorism*

22 HOUS. J. INT'L L. 3, 4-9 (1999)

On average, from 1993 to 1998, eleven Americans died as victims of international terrorists each year, but the effect of terrorism—the quintessential "propaganda of the deed"—goes far beyond those numbers. Indeed, it may paralyze even powerful governments, as occurred to the United States when its diplomats were taken hostage in 1979. Now, the technology of transportation about the planet has advanced to the point where it has become increasingly easy to plan and implement highly destructive terrorist actions in the territory of another state, whether the technique of destruction is by electronic or kinetic intervention, or by conventional explosive, nuclear, chemical, or biological weapons. The diffusion of modern technology, the astonishing proliferation of information about the ways and means of conducting terrorist actions, and the amplification of the damage that terrorists now seem capable of wreaking, seem likely to make terrorism more attractive to would-be users and, as a result, of vastly heightened concern to an increasingly large class of potential targets. When the source of terrorism is foreign, or parts of the planning and implementation occur outside the target state, the responses of the targeted government are necessarily international political events. International law becomes engaged and, as such, it may have significant effects on the range of options available to the target state and its nationals. Yet, as we will see, the international prescriptive or law- making responses to international terrorism have manifested a remarkable resistance to comprehensive analysis and development of an appropriately diverse set of authorized responses. My remarks today are concerned, first, with inventorying the ways that international law affects the shaping of government responses to international terrorism by prescribing generally or particularly the contingencies, procedures, and scope of response—be it unilateral or multilateral—lawfully available to a target; and second, with exploring the reasons for the rather spotty record of achievement.

To make this big task more manageable, I propose to identify the key categories of potential authors of international terrorism and then to examine trends of legal decision with respect to the parameters of lawful responses that have been created for each of them. Plausible responses by targets will be appraised, not simply in terms of certain rules that are supposed to form part of a black-letter code of international law, but in terms of the acceptability of those responses, in different contexts, to the contemporary international decision process. By that decision process, I do not mean only the responses of officials of states, but the aggregate actual international decision process, comprised, as it is, of governments, intergovernmental organizations, non- governmental organizations, and, in no small measure, the media; in short, all the actors who participate in assessing, retrospectively or prospectively, the lawfulness of international actions and whose consequent reactions constitute, in sum, the international decision. The legal scholar, too, plays a distinctive role in this decision process, for the object of inquiry in all legal research is a complex variable that is influenced by its mere observation and may be adjusted, sometimes significantly, to accord more closely to the preferences of the scholar. The New Haven School explicitly acknowledges this ineluctable feature of scholarship, insisting that it is not sufficient for the scholar simply to identify and assemble trends in decision. Trends must then be tested against the requirements of world public order as a means of assessing their adequacy. Insofar as they are found wanting, scholars should take the responsibility of proposing alternative arrangements so that a better approximation of political and legal goals can be achieved in the future.

Terrorism, like any other act of unauthorized violence, has three expanding circles of effects including: an immediate effect of killing or injuring people, who are deemed, either for all purposes or in that context, to constitute an internationally prohibited target; an intermediate effect of intimidating a larger number of people and thereby influencing their political behavior and that of their government; and an aggregate effect of undermining inclusive public order. Responses to terrorism, as to any recurring threat to public order, must address a complex network of sanctioning goals that include the following: arresting the immediate threat; preventing its recurrence; deterring others who may conclude that it is a productive and economical political strategy; correcting the behavior of those who are causing the threat; repairing the social damage that the illicit actions have caused; and, insofar as there is a social etiology to the pattern of behavior that is deemed threatening; reconstructing that part of the social process that is assumed to be generating or contributing to the socially destructive behavior.

As we will see, many of the international efforts to prescribe appropriate international responses to terrorism have been stalemated by conflicting priorities as to which sanctioning goals should be pursued. The United States, Europe, and Japan have generally, though not always consistently, focused on arresting, deterring, and preventing international terrorism. Key members of the Non-Aligned Movement (NAM) in the United Nations have focused instead on what its members have deemed to be the causes of international terrorism, necessarily implying that in light of those causes, some of the terrorist tactics were justifiable, if not licit. Others in the NAM have contended that, morally and legally, the weapons of the terrorists are no different from those in the arsenal of the Great Powers. In a recent interview, Mu-amar Al-Qadhafi assailed what he characterized as "the American logic." "Those who use missiles or fighter planes and rockets are legitimate. Those who use explosives or small bombs are considered terrorists."

Qadhafi's remarks, more striking for their candor than their originality, place a major part of the problem we are addressing in direct issue. In my view, international terrorism is usually a consciously adopted rather than spontaneous or impulsive strategy. Especially with respect to the possibility of terrorists employing weapons of mass destruction, the most urgent international sanctioning goals are arresting, deterring, and preventing. Even if one sympathized with the political claims and goals of the groups that have sought to justify terrorism in their terms, the explicit selection of unlawful targets by terrorists transforms their actions from armed conflict into international legal pathologies that require arrest and deterrence as urgent international goals. Because terrorism is, in this view, an elected political strategy rather than an individual psychopathology, some of the sanctioning goals may, in some cases, promise to be economically accomplished by political indulgence rather than military deprivation, as the recent transitions in South Africa and, perhaps in more incipient and still uncertain form, in Palestine and Northern Ireland suggest. A response of indulgent accommodation often seems attractive precisely because it is non-violent. Alas, in a system of global electronic simultaneity, one of the consequences of indulgent accommodation in one sub-arena may be that putative terrorists elsewhere will conclude that the tactics they are contemplating or using, rather than leading to general revulsion and condemnation, are likely to lead to success. Accommodative responses will not only not deter terrorism, but may actually encourage it. ...

IV. Responses After the Fact

B. Responses When the State Provides Refuge to Terrorists

The 1994 Declaration on Measures to Eliminate Terrorism ... also enjoined states to "refrain ... from acquiescing in or encouraging activities within their territories directed towards the commission of" terrorist acts. Certain governments act as hosts for terrorists, whether for material gain, the contingent performance of services, or ideological affinity. Sometimes, the terrorists in a particular state will remain inactive for extended periods, but that should not make their presence there any less cognizable under international law. The terrorists are being kept, like any other weapon in an arsenal, from side-arms to nuclear missiles in a silo, for future contingencies. As such, they should be viewed as active weapons whose per se unlawfulness, in contrast to the other weapons mentioned, makes their mere retention by a government a continuing violation of international law.

When a state provides refuge to terrorists, it may appear that there is a clear distinction between the terrorists and their hosts, though in many circumstances the host government's secret service may closely follow the activities of the terrorists and prohibit certain types of actions that are deemed dangerous for the host state. In other circumstances, the terrorists are, appearances notwithstanding, instruments of the host state and function like the so-called government-in-exile, an ostensibly independent entity actually subject to whatever degree of control the host state government wishes to exercise. In this latter instance, the host state may be, in effect, the author of the terrorist acts of these groups and the analysis conducted above would apply.

The Declaration on Friendly Relations imposes a general duty on states "to refrain from ... acquiescing in organized activities within its territory directed toward the commission of such acts ..." We are concerned here with the policies that have been prescribed in contemporary international law with respect to a state in whose territory terrorist acts are planned when the state has the capacity to prohibit such action. The problem of the feckless state whose territory is used as a base for terrorist acts against other states and their nationals will be taken up below.

The trend of decisions with respect to circumstances in which a government is the author of terrorism has some implications for the problem of a state providing refuge to terrorists. The U.S. defense of the bombardment of Khartoum and Afghanistan did not make reference to particular cases or incidents that might have served as precedents, but confined itself to a statement of general principles. The most instructive incident with respect to this particular factual problem continues to be the *Caroline*. [An 1837 rebellion against the Crown in Canada excited the sympathy of, and acts in support of the rebels by private groups in the U.S. The Caroline regularly transported ammunition across the New York border to the rebels. The British Governor of Canada attempted to discuss the matter with the Governor of New York and, receiving no reply, the British Commander sent an expedition of 80 men over the U.S. border to board the ship and disperse the crew and passengers. They then set the shop afire, and towed it to a point in the river at which it was carried by the current over the falls and was destroyed. The U.S. Secretary of State protested. The defenses of the British Ambassador included self-defense and self-preservation.]

It was common ground between the parties in the *Caroline* incident that the United States government had tried to restrain the private, or to use a more modern term, "non-governmental," initiatives to provide material support to the insurrection in Canada, but it had been unsuccessful. If the United States had been unaware of the expedition that was being mounted by some of its nationals and the United Kingdom calculated (1) that the United States, if notified, would act to prevent the action; and (2) that there was time to notify the United States and await its expected action, then according to the position common to Webster and Ashburton, the United Kingdom would have been obliged to refrain from unilateral action and, instead, to refer the matter to the United States If the non-governmental support for the insurrection had already been accomplished and it was reasonable to expect that the United States, if supplied with the information, would act judicially and effectively against the private interventionists, unilateral British punitive action would not have been lawful. Transposed to the problem we are addressing here and formulated affirmatively rather than negatively, the Caroline doctrine, as agreed by Webster and Ashburton, would allow a target state to act unilaterally against a planned terrorist act emanating from the territory of another state, if it were clear that either of two conditions obtained: (1) the state from whose territory the action was emanating could not, even with the information supplied to it by the target, respond in timely fashion to prevent the terrorist act because of a shortage of time; or (2) the state from whose territory the action was emanating could not, even with adequate notice, act effectively to arrest the terrorist action. A military action against terrorists in another state would be justified only if it could be related to deterrence of further terrorist actions. In any event, as Lord Ashburton allowed, any unilateral action that was otherwise lawful would still have to be conducted in ways that minimized the damage suffered by the state in whose territory it was conducted.

Of late, the United States appears to be relying on the British claim in the *Caroline*.

On August 7, 1998, bombs exploded at the U.S. Embassies in Nairobi, Kenya, and Dar es Salaam, Tanzania, killing nearly three hundred people, including twelve Americans. Investigation into the coordinated attacks led U.S. officials to suspect the involvement of Osama bin Laden, a wealthy Saudi expatriate living in Afghanistan, who reportedly had developed an extensive network of terrorists committed to acts of violence against the United States and its nationals.

On August 20, 1998, the United States launched seventy-nine Tomahawk cruise missiles against paramilitary training camps in Afghanistan, which were associated with three militant Islamic terrorist groups, including that of bin Laden, and against a Sudanese pharmaceutical plant that the United States identified as a chemical weapons facility, which had had ties with bin Laden.[181] President Clinton explained that he had ordered the strikes at targets in Afghanistan and Sudan "because of the threat they present to our national security:"

> I ordered this action for four reasons: First, because we have convincing evidence these groups played the key role in the Embassy bombings in Kenya and Tanzania; second, because these groups have executed terrorist attacks against Americans in the past; third, because we have compelling information that they were planning additional terrorist attacks against our citizens and others with the inevitable collateral casualties we saw so tragically in Africa; and fourth, because they are seeking to acquire chemical weapons and other dangerous weapons.

At a White House press conference on August 20, 1998, National Security Adviser Samuel Berger referred to the Anti-Terrorism and Effective Death Penalty Act of 1966, in which Congress finds that "the President should use all necessary means, including covert action and military force, to disrupt, dismantle, and destroy international infrastructure used by international terrorists, including overseas terrorist training facilities and safe havens...."

The United States also notified the U.N. Security Council of the missile attacks, stating arguments redolent of the *Caroline*:

> These attacks were carried out only after repeated efforts to convince the Government of the Sudan and the Taliban regime in Afghanistan to shut these terrorist activities down and to cease their cooperation with the bin laden organization. That organization has issued a series of bla-

---

[181] Professor Sean Murphy has prepared a detailed account of the United States' reaction and I have relied on it for my account. Sean D. Murphy, *Contemporary Practice of the United States Relative to International Law*, 93 AM. J. INT'L L. 161 (1999).

> tant warnings that "strikes will continue from everywhere" against American targets, and we have convincing evidence that further such attacks were in preparation from these same terrorist facilities. The United States, therefore, had no choice but to use armed force to prevent these attacks from continuing. In doing so, the United States has acted pursuant to the right of self-defence confirmed by Article 51 of the Charter of the United Nations. The targets struck, and the timing and method of attack used, were carefully designed to minimize risks of collateral damage to civilians and to comply with international law, including the rules of necessity and proportionality.

The Government of the Sudan protested the missile strike on Sudan as did the Taliban Islamic movement, along with Iran, Iraq, Libya, Pakistan, Russia, and Yemen, Palestinian officials, and certain Islamic militant groups. The Secretariat of the League of Arab States condemned the attack on Sudan as a violation of international law, but was silent as to the attack on Afghanistan. Australia, France, Germany, Japan, Spain, and the United Kingdom expressed varying degrees of support for the United States' action.

Apparently, the United States has assumed that bin Laden is an independent terrorist, finding refuge in a third country, rather than an independent contractor who has been retained by a particular state. ...

A. Responses When the State From Whose Territory the Attack Emanates Is Unable to Exclude or Control Terrorists

International law does not ordinarily distinguish between states that are capable of controlling their territory and those that are not. In fact, a significant number of governments have control of only parts of their territories; some governments control no more than two or three districts in the capitol. Other states may exercise nominal control in their territory, but their public officials may be corrupted. In states plagued by what are now referred to as narco-terrorists, the corruption of officials may reach the very highest levels of government. States such as these prove particularly attractive to private armies, which require, in order to flourish and to pursue their special interests, space in which they are beyond the reach of governments. So the ineffective or failed state is an ideal incubator; it is itself unable to restrain the private army that uses terrorism, yet its state status insulates the private army from other states upon whom the private army may prey.

For many policy reasons, international decision makers have been reluctant to limit the status or sovereign prerogatives of ineffective states or to deprive them of the ordinary perquisites of statehood. But when the territory of such states becomes the power base of international terrorist organizations and the launchpad for their activities against other states, the target state's insistence that the host state fulfill its international legal obligations is simply beyond its capacities; this is in contrast to the state which can, but will not, fulfill those obligations. To what extent, in these circumstances, may the target state, either in anticipation of or in reaction to terrorist action emanating from the ineffective state, intervene militarily in the territory of that state to destroy the terrorist infrastructure?

Legal inquiries into this area frequently commence with an analysis of the rights of the state from which the terrorists operate and thus assume that the question is essentially one of the violation by the target state of the sovereignty of the state that is hosting the terrorists. But that is only one-half of the normative picture. It is important to recall that the host state also has important obligations to other states which are the very basis of its claim to territorial sovereignty. From this latter perspective, the sovereignty deferences that are accorded to actions within the territory of a state by other states are conditional and synallagmatic. In Island of Palmas, Max Huber, the sole arbitrator, stated that:

> Territorial sovereignty ... involves the exclusive right to display the activities of a State. This right has as corollary a duty: the obligation to protect within the territory the rights of other States, in particular their right to integrity and inviolability in peace and in war, together with the rights which each State may claim for its nationals in foreign territory.

In his dissent to the Lotus judgment, Judge John Bassett Moore stated that "it is well settled that a State is bound to use due diligence to prevent the commission within its dominions of criminal acts against another nation or its people . . . ." Thus, the issue is not simply what is owed to a state that acts as a haven for terrorists, but what are the international legal consequences and permissible responses when that state violates the obligations that it owes to other states who have theretofore respected and deferred to its sovereignty and are now suffering a consequential injury.

Some states have had to deal with terrorism emanating from ineffective states on a long-term basis and have experimented with a number of strategic devices. Israel, for example, had to contend with terrorist attacks emanating from Lebanon through long periods in which the government of Lebanon controlled little more than several districts in Beirut. When Israeli punitive raids proved ineffective and occupation of Beirut secured a withdrawal of the PLO from Lebanon, yet provoked a major international condemnation, Israel withdrew to its own territory but established a permanent nine-mile wide defense zone in the area of southern Lebanon adjoining its own northern border. This self-styled defense zone, now concerned with fending off attacks by Hezbollah forces, created an anomalous international legal situation that has spawned profound international legal problems. Within this zone, Israeli forces, and the Israeli-supported Lebanese paramilitary—the so-called Southern Lebanese Army (SLA)—have waged an ongoing battle with certain Lebanese terrorist organizations, principally the Hezbollah, or "Party of God," a militant Shi'ite faction with ties to Iran and Syria. Though punctuated by periodic cease-fires, this irregular war has persisted since 1978, incidentally claiming the lives of civilians as well as of members of the U.N. Interim Force in Lebanon (UNIFIL), a peace-keeping mission established in 1978 to "restore international peace and security and assist the Government of Lebanon in ensuring the return of its effective authority in the area . ..."

While Israel has disavowed territorial designs, it has insisted, until recently, upon the necessity of maintaining a military presence in this region as a critical "buffer zone" to protect civilians in northern Israel from Hezbollah terrorist attacks. Until Lebanon can effectively control its national territory and preclude its use as a base for terrorist operations, Israel contended that it had "no alternative but to make its own security arrangements by means of the security zone and its alliance with the SLA." The U.N. Secretary General has insisted that Israel's continuing presence "escalates the level of violence," and both Lebanon and Syria have claimed that Israeli withdrawal would end the conflict.

Short of the extended anti-terrorist intervention such as one encounters in Israel's self-styled defense zone in Lebanon, there are many examples of short-term pursuits into the territory of ineffective states in order to evict or interdict terrorists. During the Vietnam war, the North Vietnamese used Cambodian territory for a variety of military purposes. The U.S. aerial and ground interventions into Cambodia were widely criticized at the time, though, in retrospect, much of the criticism seems to have been part of a larger objection to U.S. pursuit of the war as a whole. Similarly, South African pursuit of African National Congress (ANC) personnel in Angola was condemned, though again, the international legal condemnation seemed to arise more from revulsion at South Africa and the fact that the international community had virtually unanimously condemned its apartheid system than a considered legal judgment of the lawfulness of pursuing terrorists into the territory of the state in which they have found haven. In contrast, in early 1999, after the massacre of tourists, including Americans, in Uganda by Hutu guerrillas, who operated from the Democratic Republic of the Congo, there appears to have been no protest over Ugandan President Musaveni's decision to pursue the guerrillas into Congolese territory and to kill them.

The design of a remedy, especially a unilateral action of self-help, invariably raises many acute policy issues. To say that the haven state has failed to fulfill obligations it owes to the government and nationals of the injured state does not automatically transfer into a right of unilateral action. The normal reluctance of a legal system to assign to individual members of the community competences unilaterally to use high coercion becomes even greater when there are deep divisions about whether the behavior in question constitutes a violation of law. As we saw, there has been a deep division in the international community about what terrorism is to mean, to the point that the term is used quite differently by different participants. In addition to lack of agreement about the content of the term, violent unilateral remedies can sometimes aggravate a situation and may create other acute international political and legal problems.

One can perhaps express the normative code for unilateral action here by looking to cognate areas of international law. A prerequisite to the exercise of the right of diplomatic protection of nationals is the exhaustion of local or domestic remedies. The exception to this sound policy is that "a claimant in a foreign State is not required to exhaust justice in such a State when there is no justice to exhaust." It would appear reasonable to insist on notification, protests, and demand for cooperative action when the haven state is functional and there is a plausible prospect of an effective response. In circumstances in which those conditions do not obtain, unilateral action would appear justified, but would, as anywhere else, have to meet the conditions of any lawful use of force. In particular, any action would be required to be conducted in a way that demonstrated efforts to protect the international rights of the injured state.

D. Responses When the Author Is Not a State

It is important to distinguish between private "contractors" and autonomous private operators. Carlos and the leadership of the Abu Nidal group have ideologies and psychologies that predispose them to terror and, apparently, give them satisfaction when they conduct terrorist operations. But they are, for most of their operations, contractors, who undertake assignments from governments in return for handsome fees with the understanding that they then conduct those operations as if they were entirely private initiatives. While world order is likely to be perceptibly improved when people like Carlos are not at liberty, the state which has ordered and financed the terrorist operation is served when the target state and the international community insist on focusing on the marionette and not the puppeteer. When principals try to evade responsibility, the law has long told that *qui facit per alium, facit per se*, those who do things through the medium of another are deemed to have done them themselves.

Here, however, I wish to focus on the authentic private operator, the individual or group that may share the ideology of a state or other groups but is not affiliated with any state and designs and conducts its operations on its own behalf. While it may be passively monitored by an intelligence agency of a state that is aware of its activities and possible plans, it is not actively assisted by that agency. (I exclude from this category multi-celled organisms that are intentionally segregated from each other, but follow the general lead of a territorial community; from a legal standpoint, I assume that they are agents of the territorial community and should be assimilated to cases in which a state is the author of the terrorist act.) We know that there are such groups, though we are not always certain as to who they are. Osama bin Laden, whose activities were discussed earlier and who is currently under indictment in the Southern District of New York, is ostensibly an autonomous private operator.

Sheikh Omar Abdul Rahman of Egypt, currently imprisoned in New York for his intellectual authorship of the World Trade Center bombing, is ostensibly an autonomous private operator. Timothy McVeigh and Terry Nichols were ostensibly private operators. Om Shin Rikyo is ostensibly a private and autonomous operator. I retain the adverb "ostensibly," even in cases of convictions, because it is in the very nature of international and domestic terrorism that links between the agent and principal are shadowy such that the principal retains a capacity for plausible deniability.

The international decision process has been remarkably ambivalent about the appropriate responses to be taken with respect to private terrorists. Universal jurisdiction is activated for a category of hostes humani generis, an international rogues' gallery in which terrorists are worthy of inclusion. Indeed, the Restatement of Foreign Relations Law (Third) Section 404 states that "universal jurisdiction is increasingly accepted for certain acts of terrorism, such as assaults on the life or physical integrity of diplomatic personnel, kidnapping, and indiscriminate violent assaults on people at large." Yet there has been great reluctance to extradite terrorists so that they can be tried in states that are pursuing them. Until now, the international conventions that have been concluded are all extradition treaties based on the principle of *aut judicare aut dedere.*

When a state in whose territory a terrorist is found does not extradite, does the injured state have the right to resort to self-help? United States courts apply the *Ker-Frisbie* doctrine, but there appears to be increasing international resistance to jurisdiction based on abduction. Consider the case of "*Alvarez-Machain*, an incident that is almost paradigmatic of the problems faced by the United States. The case arose out of the torture and murder of Enrique Camarena-Salazar, a DEA agent operating in Mexico. Twenty-two Mexican nationals were indicted in the United States for the murder, including Dr. Humberto Alvarez-Machain, a Mexican physician who, it was alleged, had assisted Camarena's torturers. When an agreement with a Mexican police official to deliver Alvarez for $ 50,000 fell through, Alvarez was seized in Mexico, put on a twin-engine plane and flown to El Paso, where he was arrested. A reward was paid to Alvarez's abductors. The Supreme Court ultimately confirmed U.S. jurisdiction, yet the diplomatic cost to the executive branch was heavy.

The national debate since the Reagan administration, over whether the appropriate response to terrorists should be political and military or judicial, may oversimplify the matter. Given the range and variety of terrorist activities in this fourth category, it would be a mistake to decide a priori that a political-military or legal-judicial approach should always be taken. Some cases will lend themselves to a legal-judicial approach; indeed, in some cases, a political-military approach may be too costly or be unlikely to yield any benefits. Conversely, some cases will not lend themselves to a legal-judicial approach and may only be dealt with politically or militarily. A policy of using both approaches has the additional benefit of increasing the deterrent force of United States commitments. …

VI. Responses to International Terrorism as a Nomogenic Problem of World Order

International terrorism is likely to continue to be an attractive strategic option for elites as a cheap way of heightening diplomatic pressure on adversaries without having to bear responsibility. Recruiting the foot soldiers for terrorism, even for suicidal forms, has not proved to be a problem. At the same time, continued emphasis on state sovereignty, no less than sympathy for some of the terrorists' programs are likely, alas, to limit the capacity of the international legal system to respond effectively to terrorism. Because, as we have seen, the prescriptive regime that the international decision process has created tends to shield the state principals who order or finance terrorism, this part of international law, the intentions animating it notwithstanding, may actually encourage rather than deter terrorist adventures. In this respect, this regime in international law may be called "nomogenic," for much as iatrogenic disease is disease caused by presumably well-intentioned physicians, nomogenic pathologies are caused by intentional legal arrangements themselves.

Nor is the prognosis more reassuring with respect to putative non-state affiliated terrorists. Changes in psychopersonal organization in many advanced societies are likely to lead to greater willingness on the part of disaffected individuals to resort to the techniques of terrorism. Religious extremists, as well, have already indicated a willingness to use high levels of destruction to achieve their ends. Om Shin Rikyo, in Japan, still operates. If, as many scholars insist, the objective of terrorists is publicity, the global media may encourage terrorists by the wide dissemination of their acts. And the more those acts are publicized and only sporadically punished, the more the "copy-cat" phenomenon is likely to occur.

This final projection should be more alarming because of the availability of more destructive weapons to putative terrorists and the dissemination of the basic information about how to assemble them. And, ironically, the more alarming the prognosis, the graver the danger that efforts to respond to international terrorism may be used to restrict the ambit of personal liberty that is the very heart of liberal societies and often the real target of the international terrorist.

2. Peter Bergen & Frank Smyth, *Holy Warrior*

The New Republic, Vol. 219, No. 9, August 31, 1998, at 20

Osama Bin Ladin is not an easy man to find, and he plans on keeping it that way. A multimillionaire from Saudi Arabia, he is considered by the U.S. government to be "one of the most significant financial sponsors of Islamic extremist activities in the world." Law enforcement officials from a half-dozen nations would like to question him about his possible role in at least nine terrorist conspiracies. More recently, Bin Ladin's name has surfaced in connection with last week's bombing of the American embassies in Kenya and Tanzania. He is "high on the list" of suspects, says one White House official. So maybe it's not surprising that, since 1996, Bin Ladin has taken refuge in one of the most inaccessible regions in the world: southern Afghanistan. ...

At first glance, Bin Ladin does not look like a master terrorist with a core of several thousand committed followers at his command and up to $250 million in his bank account. He is dressed simply-wearing a white turban and robe under a camouflage jacket and carrying a Kalashnikov rifle across his shoulder. But he is a tall man with an aquiline nose and an aristocratic demeanor. His followers treat him with the utmost deference, which he seems to take as his due. And, though he speaks in a near whisper, his talk is of bitter injustice and merciless revenge. The United States, he said in that CNN interview, "has committed acts that are extremely unjust, hideous, and criminal" by supporting Israel and imposing sanctions on Iraq. But it is the presence of U.S. troops in Saudi Arabia, the land of Mecca and Medina, "the holiest place of the Muslims," that most outrages Bin Ladin-this, he says, is why he has declared a jihad on the United States....

Last February [1998], as the United States seemed primed to launch strikes against Iraq, Bin Ladin joined with several other leading Islamist radicals, speaking on behalf of the World Islamic Front, in calling on Muslims "to kill the Americans and their allies-civilian and military." Significantly, the CIA Counterterrorist Center issued a statement saying: "These fatwas are the first from these groups that explicitly justify attacks on American civilians anywhere in the world . . . this is the first religious ruling sanctifying such attacks." ...

On May 26, [1998], Bin Ladin held a press conference that, in the words of a State Department advisory, implied "that some type of terrorist action could be mounted within the next several weeks."

Notes and Questions

1. The phenomenon of terrorism has been condemned worldwide. Arguably originating in trouble spots outside the United States, it has become part of the strategies of certain movements of the political or religious margin, such as the Weathermen, the Minutemen etc. The domestic wake-up call was the bombing of the Alfred R. Murrah Federal Building in Oklahoma City. The homegrown militia movement and its comfort within a certain interpretation of the Second Amendment and the right to revolution is the subject of a study by David C. Williams, *The Militia Movement and Second Amendment Revolution: Conjuring with the People,* 81 Cornell L. Rev. 879 (1996). For details on the phenomenon of terror as strategy, *see* the Terrorism Research Center's website and its various links to governmental and nongovernmental databases at www.terrorism.com.

Terrorism has met with a variety of institutional and prescriptive responses, both on the domestic and the international level. At issue are both the definition of the term and the authority, in the international context, to mete out unilateral responses. In particular, the definition of terrorism is highly controversial. Consider the Nicaraguan *contra* rebellion against the Sandinista government in the 1980s. Is one country's terrorist, the other's freedom fighter? The FBI defines terrorism as "the unlawful use of force or violence against persons or property to intimidate or coerce a government, the civilian population, or any segment thereof, in furtherance of political or social objectives." Does this definition permit distinctions? What about a contextual assessment provided by the preferred structural and substantive goal of a world public order of human dignity?

2. In a speech before the United Nations General Assembly on September 21, 1998, President Clinton said:

> If terrorism is at the top of the American agenda and should be at the top of the world agenda, what then are the concrete steps we can take together to protect our common destiny? What are our common obligations? At least, I believe, they are these:
>
> To give terrorists no support, no sanctuary, no financial assistance. To bring pressure on states that do. To act together to step up extradition and prosecution. To sign the global anti-terror convention. To strengthen the biological weapons and chemical conventions.

> To enforce the chemical weapons convention. To promote stronger domestic laws and control the manufacture and export of explosives. To raise international standards for airport security. To combat the conditions that spread violence and despair.

Barbara Crossette, *Clinton Urges World Action on Terror,* N.Y. TIMES, Sept. 22, 1998, at A12.The President did not raise the issue of unilateral reaction, as exemplified by United States strikes against targets in Afghanistan and Sudan in retaliation for terrorist attacks on the U.S. embassies in Kenya and Tanzania. Kofi Annan, Secretary General of the United Nations, stressed the preferred policy of globally concerted action:

> Terrorism is a global menace, which clearly calls for global action. Individual actions by member states, whether aimed at state or non-state actors, cannot in themselves provide a solution. *Id.*

3. September 11, 2001

"September 11, 2001" like "Dec. 7, 1941," is instantly recognizable as a code phrase for events that changed the world dramatically, both for the United States and the world community.

a. President George W. Bush: Address to a Joint Session of Congress and the American People

37 Weekly Comp. Pres. Docs. 1347 (Sept. 20, 2001)
Available at http://www.whitehouse.gov/news/releases/2001/09/text/20010920-8.html.

> ... Americans are asking: Who attacked our country? The evidence we have gathered all points to a collection of loosely affiliated terrorist organizations known as al Qaeda. They are the same murderers indicted for bombing American embassies in Tanzania and Kenya, and responsible for bombing the USS Cole.
>
> Al Qaeda is to terror what the mafia is to crime. But its goal is not making money; its goal is remaking the world - and imposing its radical beliefs on people everywhere.
>
> The terrorists practice a fringe form of Islamic extremism that has been rejected by Muslim scholars and the vast majority of Muslim clerics - a fringe movement that perverts the peaceful teachings of Islam. The terrorists' directive commands them to kill Christians and Jews, to kill all Americans, and make no distinction among military and civilians, including women and children.
>
> This group and its leader - a person named Osama bin Laden - are linked to many other organizations in different countries, including the Egyptian Islamic Jihad and the Islamic Movement of Uzbekistan. There are thousands of these terrorists in more than 60 countries. They are recruited from their own nations and neighborhoods and brought to camps in places like Afghanistan, where they are trained in the tactics of terror. They are

sent back to their homes or sent to hide in countries around the world to plot evil and destruction.

The leadership of al Qaeda has great influence in Afghanistan and supports the Taliban regime in controlling most of that country. In Afghanistan, we see al Qaeda's vision for the world. ...

Our war on terror begins with al Qaeda, but it does not end there. It will not end until every terrorist group of global reach has been found, stopped and defeated.

Americans are asking, why do they hate us? They hate what we see right here in this chamber - a democratically elected government. Their leaders are self-appointed. They hate our freedoms - our freedom of religion, our freedom of speech, our freedom to vote and assemble and disagree with each other.

They want to overthrow existing governments in many Muslim countries, such as Egypt, Saudi Arabia, and Jordan. They want to drive Israel out of the Middle East. They want to drive Christians and Jews out of vast regions of Asia and Africa. ...

We are not deceived by their pretenses to piety. We have seen their kind before. They are the heirs of all the murderous ideologies of the 20th century. By sacrificing human life to serve their radical visions - by abandoning every value except the will to power - they follow in the path of fascism, and Nazism, and totalitarianism. And they will follow that path all the way, to where it ends: in history's unmarked grave of discarded lies.

Americans are asking: How will we fight and win this war? We will direct every resource at our command — every means of diplomacy, every tool of intelligence, every instrument of law enforcement, every financial influence, and every necessary weapon of war — to the disruption and to the defeat of the global terror network.

This war will not be like the war against Iraq a decade ago, with a decisive liberation of territory and a swift conclusion. It will not look like the air war above Kosovo two years ago, where no ground troops were used and not a single American was lost in combat.

Our response involves far more than instant retaliation and isolated strikes. Americans should not expect one battle, but a lengthy campaign, unlike any other we have ever seen. It may include dramatic strikes, visible on TV, and covert operations, secret even in success. We will starve terrorists of funding, turn them one against another, drive them from place to place, until there is no refuge or no rest. And we will pursue nations that provide aid or safe haven to terrorism. Every nation, in every region, now has a decision to make. Either you are with us, or you are with the terrorists. From this day forward, any nation that continues to harbor or support terrorism will be regarded by the United States as a hostile regime. …

These measures are essential. But the only way to defeat terrorism as a threat to our way of life is to stop it, eliminate it, and destroy it where it grows. …

This is not, however, just America's fight. And what is at stake is not just America's freedom. This is the world's fight. This is civilization's fight. This is the fight of all who believe in progress and pluralism, tolerance and freedom.

We ask every nation to join us. We will ask, and we will need, the help of police forces, intelligence services, and banking systems around the world. The United States is grateful that many nations and many international organizations have already responded — with sympathy and with support. Nations from Latin America, to Asia, to Africa, to Europe, to the Islamic world. Perhaps the NATO Charter reflects best the attitude of the world: An attack on one is an attack on all. …

Americans are asking: What is expected of us? …

I ask you to uphold the values of America, and remember why so many have come here. We are in a fight for our principles, and our first responsibility is to live by them. No one should be singled out for unfair treatment or unkind words because of their ethnic background or religious faith. …

NOTES AND QUESTIONS

1. Shortly after the 9/11 disaster, NATO invoked Article 5 of its Charter for the first time in its history:

> The Parties agree that an armed attack against one or more of them in Europe or North America shall be considered an attack against them all and consequently they agree that, if such an armed attack occurs, each of them, in exercise of the right of individual or collective self-defence recognised by Article 51 of the Charter of the United Nations, will assist the Party or Parties so attacked by taking forthwith, individually and in concert with the other Parties, such action as it deems necessary, including the use of armed force, to restore and maintain the security of the North Atlantic area.
>
> Any such armed attack and all measures taken as a result thereof shall immediately be reported to the Security Council. Such measures shall be terminated when the Security Council has taken the measures necessary to restore and maintain international peace and security.

North Atlantic Treaty, Apr. 4, 1949, art. 5, 63 Stat. 2241, 2244, 34 U.N.T.S. 243, 246.

2. Is the President correct in treating all terrorists as the same and a common enemy? Does the U.S. have the power to stop terrorism everywhere? If not, what triage principles should be applied?

3. World leaders pledged their support for President Bush in his war on terrorism. Bush asked all countries to join the United States in implementing various strategies necessary to winning the

war, i.e. disrupting the financial network of terrorism, integrating police and intelligence operations among states, and so forth. Many countries followed suit. At this writing, integrated security and intelligence networks have located and disrupted terrorist cells in many cities in North America, Europe, Asia, Africa, the Middle East and Central Asia. The U.S.-led action in Afghanistan that removed the Taliban and destroyed al Qaeda training camps received widespread international support.

b. W. Michael Reisman, *Aftershocks: Reflections on the Implications of September 11*

6 Yale H.R. & Dev. L.J. 81 (2003)

During the Cold War, fictional accounts of invasion and occupation by the respective enemy became forms of entertainment as well as means of sustaining mass mobilization and willingness to sacrifice. To mention only one example of this genre, this audience will recall the motion picture "Red Dawn" which depicted a brutal Soviet occupation of large parts of North America - replete with commissars in each small town - and heroic guerrilla actions conducted by young Americans from retreats in the Rocky Mountains.

The attack on the United States on September 11 has yet to produce a new wave of such films and novels. It's not merely that the entertainment industry has not had the chance to catch up. When it does, the plots will revolve about more sabotage and terrorism, but not about invasion. Even scare fiction requires enough *vraisemblance* to make itself credible - and vendible. We are angry and indignant at the massive violation of our homeland and the murder of fellow citizens and we have no choice but to view ourselves in a war with a formidable adversary who is able to conduct the war in our territory. We require a new infrastructure of defense. But no one, whether in the Defense Department, in Governor Ridge's Office of Homeland Security, in a Department of Homeland Security when it is finally operational or, indeed, in the entertainment industry, which is ever alert for new commercial opportunities, is developing worst-case contingency plans for an invasion by Islamic militants and a long-term occupation, replete with hooded and bearded mullahs conducting forced conversions throughout the population in deconsecrated churches and synagogues that have been converted into mosques. We have been attacked and wounded and anyone who has not retreated into private fantasies accepts - as a real possibility - that we may be attacked and wounded again. But we know we are not going to be invaded. That expectation alone tells us something about the distinctive meaning of this war. This is not a classic type of war whose objective is invasion, occupation and incorporation. Nor are our enemies "mad," a soft psychologistic term we frequently call up when we cannot understand why others are doing the things they do. Nor are they driven by nihilism.

This war departs from the classic model in yet another way. Though we have been attacked, we are not the prime object of this war. This is, in large part, a war *between* Moslems in the Islamic world about the future control and social structure of the Islamic world, stretching from the Maghreb of North Africa and the largely Islamicized areas of sub-Saharan Africa, through the Middle East and the

Anatolian landmass, through Central Asia and the Islamic states of the sub-continent, through the Islamic areas of China, and through the archipelagos of South Asia. It is a war about who, among contending Islamic groups, will gain power and control the *dar al Islam*, the values that will govern it and how it will be organized.

On one side of that Islamic world stand modernizing elites and those strata of the Islamic world who wish to make their space part of the expanding global civilization based upon science and technology. These modernizing elites believe that without such engagement and incorporation, they will be unable to assure to themselves and their populations the material benefits and life-opportunities that are the products of a robust economy within a liberal system of public order. In many of their countries, some modernization has taken place. If its benefits are not widely distributed, images of life in the modern world are. Though many of these images, which are fabricated for advertising and promotional purposes, are extravagantly inaccurate, they are, nonetheless, the pictures others gain and operate with.

On the other side stand Fundamentalist conservatizing counter-elites - variously called "Islamists" or "Jihadists" - whose members' views cover a spectrum but at the core share the common belief that the civilization of science and technology is antithetical to the true values of their faith; that it will deprive them, individually and collectively, of power: that it will hollow out their religion; and that it will contaminate and corrupt their lives and the lives of their children.

Some of this reaction is familiar from many other situations of social change. Every innovation in social arrangements necessarily terminates existing ones, causing distress and deprivation to those who were secure in the older arrangements but who prove insufficiently adroit to adapt rapidly to new ones. Part of the support for the Fundamentalist conservatizers comes from these victims of rapid social change in the Islamic world. Part comes from people disenchanted with social change. The early phases of modernization are also attended by rampant and ostentatious corruption, which abounds before effective control mechanisms come into operation. Reactions to this unattractive feature of modernization account for some of the support for the Fundamentalist conservatizers, coming from those who are disgusted by the corruption and see it as an inherent - and permanent - part of the modern package. As with every social movement, some support the Fundamentalist conservatizers because they see them as a path to individual or group power. But, let us not delude ourselves: some support the conservatizers because they believe in an orthodox form of their religion and are convinced that it will be eroded and denatured by modernization.

In the long Spanish civil war, which was also a war about modernization, the lines were clearly drawn: you were either for the Roman Catholic Church or against it, for social revolution or against it, for modern values or against them. One of the things that is confusing about the struggle within the Islamic world, in contrast to the comparative clarity of the long and violent war in Spain, is that everyone, modernizers and Fundamentalist conservatizers, radicals and reactionaries, uses the language of Koranic piety. Everyone sounds like a Fundamentalist conservatizer. There are historical reasons for this anomaly. Almost all of the Islamic states were formed relatively recently, most often through the decisions of external imperial powers rather than as a result of authentic and widely supported nationalist uprisings. The peoples of these new states still lack strong national identification; loyalty systems continue to revolve around the extended family. The only vocabulary of loyalty capable of mobilizing masses of people is the language and symbols of the common religion. Hence every aspiring counter-elite in an Islamic country - whether modernizing or conservatizing - must present itself as more pious than the elite it is seeking to replace, while stigmatizing its competitors as apostates and adulterators of the faith. As for the incumbent elite - whether modernizing or conservatizing - it too has no choice but to present itself as ever more orthodox. Hence an idiosyncrasy of the modern Islamic world is a rather androgynous modernizing elite. It moves comfortably in the West, still seeks to adopt many modern programs, and often depends upon the West for its internal or external security. Yet it often cultivates a religious image in language and costume and, in particular, it indulges (and tries to control) religious institutions. For these elites, truly, the voice is the voice of Jacob, the hands are the hands of Esau.

If this is a war within the Islamic world for control of the Islamic world, why was the United States attacked - our embassies in Nairobi and Dar es Salaam, the USS Cole in the harbor of Aden, the World Trade Center in New York and the Pentagon in Washington? Why are we seen as the enemy? The answer to that question is complex but one distinct part is that we are seen as the indispensable supporter for the erstwhile modernizing elites. Many in the Islamic world believe that without our support, most of the modernizers would quickly flee, fall or molt into conservatizers. The United States was the Great Satan to the supporters of the Islamic Republic because it had reinstated the little Satan, the Shah, in 1954. U.S. support kept him in power until President Carter decided not to come to his assistance in 1979, whereupon he was, as the Iranians say, *bar bahd rafdeh*, gone with the wind. In fact, in the Islamic world, there are no explicitly modernizing leaders who have a solid democratic base of domestic support and, as a result, can survive without internal military suppression or, often, without external Western support. The modernizers know it - just ask Mr. Hamid Karzai who enjoys power, at least to the outskirts of Kabul, thanks to an international force there. The Fundamentalist conservatizers, whether in power or seeking to get it, know it too.

Our policy of support for the modernizers has not always been consistent - in the real world, few polices can be - but it is public and certainly not episodic. Consider the Carter Doctrine which President Carter declared in January, 1980: "An attempt by any outside force to gain control of the Persian Gulf region will be regarded as an assault on the vital interests of the United States of America, and such an assault will be repelled by any means necessary, including military force."

On October 1, 1981, President Reagan issued statements that the White House promptly characterized as "The Reagan Codicil to the Carter Doctrine." In response to a question, the President said, "...Saudi Arabia we will not permit to be an Iran." In clarification, the President added that "in Iran I think the United States has to take some responsibility for what happened." Immediately afterwards, a White House aide explained to the New York Times that "the President was now pledging to support the Saudi monarchy against internal as well as external threats." That codicil is still an essential plank in our foreign policy.

American engagement in the Islamic world once earned it no enmity and condemnation. As long as the Soviet Union existed and pursued an aggressive policy in the Islamic world, the United States was viewed by Fundamentalist Islamic conservatizers as a bulwark against Godless communism. That was then the major enemy and, as it is famously said in the region, "the enemy of my enemy is my friend." Now that the Soviet Union has been tossed onto the rubbish heap of history, there is no longer a fearsome enemy to the north, hence no need for a bulwark. The saying can be abbreviated: the enemy is...the enemy.

What is the war objective of the Fundamentalist conservatizers…? What, for them, would constitute victory? It is not, as I said, the conquest or destruction of the United States. There are two broad war objectives. First, the withdrawal of American support for the modernizing elites, including Israel, whereupon the conservatizers believe the modernizers will flee westward. With Fundamentalist conservatizers at the helm, true Islamic states can then be established in a type of second Caliphate, reviving the old glory of Islam. Second, and this should not be underestimated, recognition of the independent and autonomous legitimacy of Islam and, as a result, an end to the characterization of parts of Islamic dogma and many Islamic mores as violations of universal human rights standards.

NOTES AND QUESTIONS

1. Is the war on terrorism a real war, thus justifying unilateral action by the United States under a doctrine of self-defense? *See* Sean D. Murphy, *Terrorism and the Concept of "Armed Attack" in Article 51 of the U.N. Charter*, 43 HARV. INT'L L. J. 41 (2002); Steven R. Ratner, *Jus Ad Bellum and Jus in Bello after September 11*, 96 AM. J. INT'L L. 905 (2002); David Abramowitz, *The President, the Congress, and Use of Force: Legal and Political Considerations in Authorizing Use of Force Against International Terrorism*, 43 HARV. INT'L L. J. 71 (2002); Jonathan I. Charney, *The Use of Force Against Terrorism and International Law*, 95 AM. J. INT'L L. 835 (2001); Thomas M. Franck, *Terrorism and the Right of Self-Defense*, 95 AM. J. INT'L L. 839 (2001).

2. For further discussion on terrorism since 9/11, *see* M. Cherif Bassiouni, *Legal Control of International Terrorism: A Policy-Oriented Assessment*, 43 HARV. INT'L L. J. 83 (2002); George H. Aldrich, *The Taliban, al Qaeda, and the Determination of Illegal Combatants*, 96 AM. J. INT'L. L. 891 (2002); Anne-Marie Slaughter, *An International Constitutional Moment*, 43 HARV. INT'L L. J. 1 (2002); John Alan Cohan, *Formulation of State Response to Terrorism and State-Sponsored Terrorism*, 14 PACE INT'L L. REV. 77 (2002); NOAM CHOMSKY, 9-11 (Seven Stories Press 2001); DANIEL BENJAMIN & STEVEN SIMON, THE AGE OF SACRED TERROR (Random House 2002); BERNARD LEWIS, THE CRISIS OF ISLAM: HOLY WAR AND UNHOLY TERROR (Modern Library 2003).

3. For U.S. legislation enacted in response to the terrorist threat, *see* USA Patriot Act of 2001, H.R. 3162, 107th Cong. (2001), *available at* http://news.findlaw.com/hdocs/docs/terrorism/

hr3162.pdf; Homeland Security Act of 2002, H.R. 5005, 107th Cong. (2002), *available at* http://www.pfir.org/2002-hr5005.

G. Gangs

Gangs share with private armies and terrorists the characteristics of an organization with distinct command structure trained in the manual of, and purposively using, the means of violence in the achievement of their goals. Their primary objective is, however, not to maximize power, although that may be an important means to their end. The *raison d'être* of gangs appears to be, besides personal bonding, the maximization of individual and collective wealth of their members. Their impact on international affairs seems to have increased markedly in the post-Cold War environment. Gangs tend to influence political processes through intimidation, exemplary use of force, and, even more pervasively and corrosively, corruption.

1. William J. Olson, *International Organized Crime: The Silent Threat to Sovereignty*
21-FALL Fletcher F. World Aff. 65 (1997)

In a number of countries, criminal gangs now operate with a power and ruthlessness that were unthinkable just a few years ago. They openly threaten the political process, and, in some cases, undermine the efficacy of the government itself. Italy, Nigeria, Russia and the former states of the Soviet Union, South China and Mexico are only a few of the countries or regions in which major criminal organizations now operate in defiance of political authority or, as a result of corruption, with its complicity.

In addition, international financial networks are increasingly in the service, wittingly or not, of these same criminal organizations. Criminals are using the borderless world of electronic cash transactions and liberal or lax banking regulations to launder billions of illegal dollars and to defraud businesses, banks, individuals and governments. These resources are also used to corrupt and intimidate individuals and governments that try to fight back. Countries individually, and the international community collectively, are poorly positioned and woefully unprepared to cope with the extent and nature of the challenge to political order and competent government being raised by these organizations. Moreover, many political leaders and scholars of international relations do not yet recognize the nature or extent of the problem or the threat.

Accustomed to thinking in terms of national actors and of criminals as bit players on a local stage, international relations theory has not caught up with reality. Paradigms of international relations have yet to adjust to the reality that such nonstate actors as criminal organizations can, in fact, be major determinants of political patterns and outcomes within states and in international affairs. Some question whether there is even such a phenomenon as organized crime, much less whether it should be taken into consideration.

Similarly, many political leaders share this attitude or see the problem as a low-level law enforcement issue that does not require sustained policy attention. Yet, Mexico, Russia and most of the countries of the Caribbean and Latin America have described criminal organizations as a major, if not the major, threat to their national security. Italy is struggling to maintain the integrity of its political institutions in the face of direct criminal challenge. Some Chinese officials acknowledge privately that South China is virtually beyond their control because of the operations of criminal gangs. Many other countries, such as Nigeria, Taiwan or the Seychelles, have simply reached accommodations with criminal groups, either turning a blind eye to their activities or providing them the cover of national sovereignty. The United States, many members of the European Community and international donors such as the World Bank and the IMF are increasingly faced with the political, economic and social consequences of worldwide criminal activity, particularly corruption and subversion. In order to understand just how such a threat can, in fact, exist, and that it must be dealt with both conceptually and practically, it is necessary to understand the context in which this threat now operates.

Challenges to Governability

This is a bad time for government. In many parts of the world, government has failed, is failing, or has overreached its limits and capabilities. In significant stretches of the globe, governments are either waging war on their citizens, are fighting to survive assaults from their citizens, or have become a mere faction among competing forces claiming the right to govern all or part of disputed national territory.

This trend is not only evidenced in the case of organized crime—signs of it are everywhere. Few countries in the developing world are free of significant internal upheavals from religious, ethnic or political rivals who often use force to effect change, either of government or in national territory. Many countries have dissolved into vicious civil war or employ programs of ethnic cleansing. Many more face festering internal problems and poor economic performance that government seems unable to address. Corruption, malfeasance, incompetence or simple bloody-mindedness weakens governments already overwhelmed or fumbling in the face of economic, political and social problems. In many countries, the major qualification for public office appears to be a Swiss bank account for looted public funds, while infrastructure is declining, education is poor, economies are stagnating, and health is deteriorating, often in the wake of returning diseases once thought virtually eliminated.

The list of troubles is extensive, as is the number of countries affected, and it is not confined solely to the Third World: Lebanon, Liberia, Angola, Afghanistan, Yugoslavia and Somalia have effectively ceased being countries. Zaire appears to be on the same track. Whether Haiti joins this list remains a question. Much of Sub-Saharan Africa - including South Africa - India, Sri Lanka, Russia, Cambodia, Iraq, Sudan, Colombia, Mexico, Algeria and Israel, for different reasons, face major opposition or insurgent movements or dangerous political transitions that threaten peace and order. Canada, normally thought of as stable, is roiled by a powerful separatist movement that threatens to dismember the country and call into question its rationale.

In Burundi, Rwanda, and the Sudan, governments are waging near genocidal war against unwelcome ethnic or religious groups. Slavery is making a comeback in some of these areas. In Iraq and too many other countries, government is maintained by brutish force and a level of candid violence against the citizenry that clouds the very meaning of government. Many of these situations have gone on for years and show few signs of amelioration. As a result, the death lists have grown exponentially and refugee populations, whether within countries or in exile, have mushroomed to include tens of millions. By some estimates, as much as 2 percent of the population of Sub-Saharan Africa alone lives in refugee camps or in exile communities at the mercy of foreign hosts or the charity of international donors. In addition, poor economic conditions in many parts of the world, often the result of government bungling, have set many more people on the road to exile.

War and carnage are not new on the international stage. Civil war, exiles escaping tyranny, and refugee problems have an ancient lineage. Chaos is hardly an infrequent visitor in history. What, then, about the litany of the world's woes limned above is unique or an occasion for anything more than the usual anguish over folly and mayhem? The main difference lies in the fact that the present violence runs counter to expectation and to the prospect for political order and economic integration.

Three major themes have dominated history in the last few centuries: First, despite the violence and upheaval, the general trend of the last 300 years has been towards the steady grouping of peoples into large political unions of sovereign states governed by reasonably recognizable institutions and forms. Indeed, much of that history is marked by the rise of so-called nation-states and of an international order based on the interactions of those states. Second, the trend also has been toward greater international economic integration based on free trade. Third, there has been a growing formalization of rules of conduct governing state and interstate behavior. The result has been the near universal triumph of the nation-state as a form of organization for people. The nation-state has become the defining characteristic of this century. Its triumph is also a triumph of government over those peoples.

This was not a peaceful evolution, but it created a semblance of international order painfully worked out on the principle of sovereign nation- states as the embodiment of political organization. That order underwrites a wide range of activities, not the least of which are rules governing interstate conflict and an increasingly globally integrated economic system that depends to no small degree upon the local and regional order that nation-states once implied and enforced. The expectation created by this trend is for greater integration and order. To a considerable degree, economic development and prosperity are dependent upon political order and stability.

For many areas of the world today, the trend, in fact, is for the steady unraveling of many putative sovereign nation-states and the erosion of the idea that such states are the proper organizing principle for the world's people. Unfortunately, many of these new countries were not adept at self-government and incorporated ethnic or religious groups that have resisted integration or have actively sought separation. Many more lacked the resources to maintain true self-governing institutions, while others were so driven by disputes over who should govern and on what terms, that no functioning government ever emerged. The result was not so much the creation of a host of new countries but an explosion of weak or incompetent governments over much of the globe. In addition, in recent years, the trend to create nation-states, that dominated much of the recent past, now operates to dissolve those states. This process is a direct challenge not only to the survival of those states but to government as well.

As Walker Connor has noted, while the notion of a state representative of a homogeneous "nation" of racially and culturally identical people has been the ideal, most countries today are not nations in this sense. They are, rather, heterogeneous collections of people crowded together uncomfortably in shared geographic space under terminological niceties. Thus, many nation-states are not nations. Further, many groups - and the number is growing - incorporated into these nations are distinct minorities with their own developing self- awareness. One of the central elements of that self-awareness is the fact that they lack a nation of their own. Many "nations" do not have their own state, but they want one. Hence the difficulty.

In many cases, the only way to acquire one's own nation is to destroy someone else's. This commonly involves violence. Governments tend to resist their own destruction, while opponents are often unwilling to settle for less. A resort to arms is the common answer for resolving the difference. In the modern context, governments and their challengers can now call upon a variety of sources for arms, advice and support to sustain them. They are thus better able, or at least believe that they are, to achieve their goals through armed conflict. Since this results in violence, and often an assortment of human rights violations, some form of intervention by the international community soon follows. Often this does not end the violence, but it can prolong it by preventing governments or their challengers from achieving ultimate success. In such a process, a nation is neither created nor destroyed but all are involved in a protracted limbo of conflict without result and conflict resolution without peace.

The cumulative result of these various elements discussed above is the story of failed and failing governments covering much of the globe. Even in cases where failure is not manifest, many countries have only the appurtenances of government and little of the reality. In all these cases, countries lack the resources to enforce their own laws, provide security to their citizens, sustain healthy economies or maintain their own sovereignty. In many cases, they are sustained, often poorly, on international handouts or by the presence of international peacekeeping forces whose real role is to provide the needed local elements the government lacks - a sort of internationalized imperialism. In this environment, some governments and many of their rivals have resorted to criminal activities to finance their efforts, to underwrite their economies or to sustain armed forces. It is in this environment that the threat from criminal organizations must be understood in order to get a true sense of what the threat from these organizations is, why it pervades and what it means.

Enter International Organized Crime

As with many of the problems besetting nations and the international community, the threat from crime is hardly new. Nor is organized crime, even with global connections, a recent phenomenon. What is new is the profitability of criminal activities in a world in which governments are weak and opportunities for crime have grown exponentially. In this environment, the ability of criminal organizations to challenge the sovereignty of individual states has become a reality.

Organized crime differs from other types of crime in that it is organized. While this is a tautology, this fact, nevertheless, is a critical aspect in understanding the phenomenon. To phrase it another way, it is criminal activity that benefits from organization. What are the benefits? There are seven major ones. First, organization permits continuous operations over time, which means a sustained cash flow. Second, it permits diversification of activities, not only in the sense of different types of operations but also a multiplicity of similar operations, thus building in redundancy so that no single blow is fatal to the life of the business. Third, it permits diffusion of risk. Fourth, it gives flexibility and allows the organization to survive, learn from, and correct mistakes. Fifth, it provides a planning facility to adjust to market changes and to seek better ways to maximize profits. Sixth, it provides a coherent mechanism for enforcing discipline and safeguarding operations. Seventh, it provides a structure that can grow with time, enlarging on operations and increasing profits.

The organizational structure can and does vary widely. It can be vertically integrated, like the Colombian cartels, or very diffuse, like the Asian Triads. Such organizations can be largely locally based, as are many Russian groups or the Bloods and Crips in the United States; or they can have an international reach, such as the Italian Mafia, Asian Triads, Nigerian groups, Colombian Cartels and increasingly the Mexican Mafia.

While these organizations can vary widely in structure and area of expertise, they share a number of features. They are generally ethnically based, a fact that they exploit to help maximize the security of their operations and as a mechanism to spread their activities by working through expatriate communities. They are business operations whose principal purpose is to maximize profits. They tend to specialize in illegal activities - although they mix them with legitimate ones -

because they tend to be more profitable than legal efforts. They are ruthless and violence-prone, although the more sophisticated operations tend to use violence as a last resort, preferring bribery and intimidation. They exist in a hostile environment in that, operating outside the law, their operations are targets for law enforcement and competitors. They tend to grow in size and evolve in sophistication over time as they learn from mistakes and profit from their operations. And, finally, they exploit legitimate business and banking environments to disguise their activities and launder their profits.

This brief snapshot does not demonstrate, however, why such organizations are or can be a threat to governments on a scale warranting anything more than passing attention. To understand this, it is necessary to look briefly at the operations - and profitability - of these groups which make them such powerful actors, and then to set them in the context of failed or failing states as discussed above.

There are two critical features of criminal enterprise groups that makes them powerful and dangerous. The first is profitability—the money they control. The second is their ruthlessness. Being without conscience or constraint, they are formidable opponents once they pass beyond a certain size in relation to the controlling environment. To get a handle on the money at the disposal of criminal organizations, consider the profitability of the cocaine enterprise of the major Colombian cartels. Since the cartels do not file financial statements or declare their incomes, what follows are necessarily "ball park" figures, but they give a reasonable indication of orders of magnitude. ...

[T]he potential wholesale value of cocaine is roughly $10 billion annually. The net return, after overhead costs are deducted, is around $8 billion. The retail value may be five or six times this, or around $50 billion annually in the United States alone. No one knows how much of the profits from retail sales go to the Colombian cartels, but if only 3 percent is returned, that is an additional $1.5 billion dollars to the major criminal enterprises engaged in producing and marketing cocaine. This does not include annual returns on investments, stock holdings, real estate and holdings in legitimate business. Interest returns on investments over the past 10 years may yield as much as another $2 billion. The potential earnings of the cartels, then, is in the neighborhood of $11 billion to $12 billion annually.

In perspective, this represents more than 50 percent of the total revenues of Colombia ($16 billion), Bolivia ($3.7 billion), and Peru ($2 billion) combined. Excluding Puerto Rico and Cuba, cartel revenues are roughly twice that of all the countries and dependencies in the Caribbean combined. Cartel earnings are two-thirds of the GDP of Bolivia, with none of the overhead. The earnings are greater than Colombia's national debt. It is not surprising that the cartels were bold enough in the late 1980s to offer to pay off Colombia's debt if the government would leave them alone. The sum is about three-quarters of the total U.S. federal counter-drug budget for both domestic and international programs.

What these financial resources mean, when linked to utter ruthlessness in purpose and no moral or legal constraints, is that the cartels are regional superpowers with immense resources. They can outspend any individual jurisdiction. They can afford the best talent - whether accountants, computer specialists, extortionists or murderers - and the newest in equipment and technologies. They do not have to worry about legal niceties, national frontiers, human rights watch groups, environmental regulations, popular opinion or the thousand encumbrances that impede governments. Their resources are employed to bribe government officials, hire thugs to intimidate those that cannot be bought, and kill those than cannot be intimidated. The bottomless pockets mean that the cartels can move and shift their operations at will to evade local enforcement and to seek venues that are more amicable, where enforcement is lax, inadequate or pliable. As in Colombia, they can use their resources to influence the highest levels of government and to sway public opinion, as they did in 1992 in buying enough public support to influence the rewriting of the Colombian constitution to outlaw extradition—the one great fear that the cartels had. The cartels could buy Colombian justice, but they were afraid of U.S. jurisdiction.

This resource base has also enabled the Colombian cartels to internationalize their business. They now operate globally. They have struck working relationships with other major criminal organizations—such as the Italian Mafia, Mexican criminal groups, the Chinese Triads, and various Russian and Eastern European groups. They operate highly sophisticated international money-management networks that enable them to move large quantities of cash and launder billions in illegal receipts. Recently, they have begun to diversify their operations, moving into the production of heroin that they plan to market to their cocaine clientele. And, the Colombians are only one of several such international criminal organizations.

Other major groups have similar resource bases. Some, like the Chinese Triads, engage in a wide range of illegal activities from drug production and alien smuggling to extortion and international prostitution. While the figures are approximate, international organized crime generates some $500 billion to $1 trillion annually, money that goes to fund more criminal activity. In many areas of the world, where economic growth is stagnant or negative, the scale of resources can be a powerful incentive to find accommodation with illegal activity and the groups that engage in it. Corruption, intimidation and outright violence are employed when "good" business sense fails. The result, especially in an environment of failed and failing states, is to give major criminal organizations the scope to grow and escape local controls and limitations. It is the ability of criminal groups to internationalize their operations; to dispose of immense financial resources; and to use whatever means of violence, bribery or intimidation necessary to promote their activities in a world increasingly without frontiers.

Integrity at Risk

Whether the problem is drug trafficking or illegal aliens, the world's most powerful nation - with an economy around $7 trillion dollars and immense resources in manpower, technical ability, institutional sophistication, legal maturity and commitment - cannot prevent the daily violation of its sovereignty and the integrity of its frontiers from criminal organizations. In some parts of the United States, as recent congressional hearings have shown, government cannot adequately protect its own citizens from the depredations of foreign-based drug lords who menace isolated ranchers and farmers. More dangerously, the government is now itself suspect because of its seeming impotence. In some quarters of public opinion, a large percentage of the population seriously believes that the only explanation for the failure to take effective action against drug traffickers is a deliberate plan by the government to sell drugs as a way of debilitating a segment of society.

In some cities, no-go zones exist where the law seldom, if ever, reaches. Beyond local neighborhoods, criminal organizations routinely exploit trade networks and financial systems to move illegal drugs or launder money and authorities are unable to prevent it. At best, they disrupt a small fraction of the overall activity. The United States, which could forge an international coalition to expel Saddam Hussein from Kuwait, cannot put together an effective international effort to seriously disrupt the operations of major criminal gangs.

The reasons for the United States' inability to eliminate drug trafficking and dismantle the organizations that engage in it are complex and varied. However, the difficulties encountered by the United States in policing its own borders, protecting the integrity of its institutions from criminal exploitation and providing for the domestic security of its citizens despite all the resources it can bring to bear are testimony to the power and abilities of major international criminal organizations to defy or evade the best efforts of government. These difficulties are also a cautionary tale about the threat from these same organizations to countries far poorer equipped and committed to the cause than the United States.

The threat from these organizations is a threat to the sovereignty of individual countries, and in some cases to their survival. This is true not because these organizations have deliberate designs to destroy sovereignty or target individual states for extinction, but because of the consequences that their operations have for sovereignty. In this sense, the threat is a by-product of their activities. For sovereignty to be meaningful, the ability of a particular national entity claiming sovereign rights to be the only source of authority empowered to enforce laws and independently exercise the powers of government within a specified territory. Sovereignty means self-government. It means the ability to exercise legitimate authority, protect national territory from foreign encroachment, enforce and administer law and ensure domestic harmony. The activities of international criminal organizations abridge these powers, in some cases to the point of threatening the survival of states.

The threat comes in many forms, both direct and indirect. The direct threat comes from the ability of major criminal gangs overtly to challenge governments, either through violence, intimidation or corruption. The most visible form of this challenge comes as public violence directed at leading officials or others who challenge the activities of the gangs. As Colombia and Italy demonstrate, criminal gangs have been willing to wage near-open civil warfare against the main institutions of government to block efforts to enforce law and end illegal activities. Assassination, kidnapping and terror bombings have been widely used. In addition, the cartels in Colombia and Peru have forged strategic alliances with insurgent organizations to protect their activities with military cover. A similar pattern may be emerging in Mexico where corruption and violence are spreading. Criminal organizations prefer, however, to be more subtle in their measures for incapacitating government or other opponents. The favored tactic is bribery.

With immense financial resources at their disposal, the major criminal organizations have considerable ability to suborn public officials charged with enforcing the law against them. The criminal purpose is not to subvert government per se but to protect illegal enterprise from unwanted interference. Since the main threat to this enterprise is government, it is the target for efforts to incapacitate its normal functions. This results in efforts to corrupt the legitimate institutions of government and to bias their functions on the behalf of illegitimate ends.

In some countries, corruption is so pervasive in some arms of government that police and military officials actively protect criminal enterprises against other elements of the government. In less picturesque situations, key officials charged with enforcing the law simply look the other way or deliberately bungle or compromise investigations and trials. In some cases, national political leaders, legislators and heads of state are in the pay of criminal gangs—when they are not business partners or criminal leaders themselves—and use their offices to pass laws or suppress law enforcement to facilitate criminal enterprise. Criminal enterprise, however, threatens integrity and sovereignty in more indirect ways.

One of the most common means criminal organizations use to evade law and defy governments is simply exploitation of the very systems that they rely upon to sustain legitimate enterprise. In other words, they aggressively exploit legal financial networks and trading systems to hide their activities. They rely on the natural inefficiencies of governments in investigating and detecting illegal activities masquerading as, or concealed within, legal above- the-board trade or financial transactions.

Criminal gangs actively seek out environments in which local law enforcement is simply incompetent or under-staffed. Law enforcement does not have to be corrupt to be compromised. They also seek out situations where there is no law enforcement. Given the length of U.S. borders, for example, vast areas are simply uncontrolled. If they are controlled, for instance, at points of entry, the volume of traffic crossing the border is so great that effectively monitoring the flow is impossible. Of the millions of containers entering the United States every year, U.S. customs has the ability to investigate only about 2 percent of the total. Virtually none of outgoing containers are examined. Of the more than 400 million visitors crossing the borders annually by plane, train, boat and automobile, only a tiny fraction are or can be stopped. A similar situation prevails in Europe and virtually every other country involved in international trade or financial transactions.

In addition, the size and complexity of international financial networks largely put them beyond supervision. As a result, governments are perpetually at a disadvantage in trying to control money laundering or financial crime. Free trade and banking without borders are essential to modern economics, but they are also havens for the unscrupulous, and resources do not exist to cover all the possibilities. Thus, in many cases, governments simply lack the means or the institutional flexibility to deal with supple criminal organizations.

The cumulative effect of these realities on the proper function of government is another, more subtle way that criminal activities undermine the integrity of governments and thus national sovereignty. This effect is the result of the progressive discrediting of public institutions and of the basic public trust that must underlie the proper functioning of government. Corruption distorts the legitimate function of legal authority and puts its legitimacy in question. By biasing public affairs on behalf of one individual or group based on the ability to buy favors, corruption subverts the purposes of government and it makes fools out of anyone who follows the rules.

Organized crime involves the systematic use of corruption and thus subverts government's very purpose, and by doing so encourages a climate of lawlessness. It can also distort the economic process, undermining legitimate business and non-criminal enterprise. As Italy depressingly illustrates, organized criminal corruption encourages cynicism about government itself. It discredits in the public mind the institutions of self-government. For Russia, struggling with the ideas of democracy and free markets, it calls into question public commitment to the very effort to democratize. Indications suggest a considerable proportion of the public, aware of the extensive activities of criminal gangs in Russia, believe that these activities are simply the true nature of capitalism. The public increasingly resents the exploitation of public resources by uncontrollable criminal gangs. This climate of opinion may ultimately lead to hostility toward democratic institutions that seem incapable of providing adequate protection from criminal activities.

Criminal activities can also lead, as in Colombia, to major international problems. As the issue of decertification illustrates, the activities of criminal gangs can undermine relations between states. Today, U.S. relations with Columbia, Bolivia and Peru, and increasingly with Mexico, are framed by concerns about and the activities of criminal organizations. In extreme circumstances, it can mean that confidence in the integrity of key institutions is so compromised that the country is branded a pariah.

Thus, criminal organizations can weaken states through direct assault or undermine the rationale upon which government depends. In either case, government is incapacitated or is forced to surrender elements of its sovereignty to nonstate actors.

While the United States is in no danger of succumbing to this threat, the same cannot be said for other less-capable polities. Already, the activities of criminal organizations have seriously affected the political stability and the integrity of government in such major countries as Russia, Mexico, Italy, Colombia and Nigeria. Many other countries simply lack the will or the resources to take any meaningful actions against major criminal gangs. Corruption, intimidation or sheer incapacity have immobilized countless more. Greed is also a factor. Offshore banking havens in developing countries have become a boom business for many countries with depressed or emerging economies. Government and business leaders have simply winked at—when they have not actually encouraged—the proliferation of shell corporations and "brass-plate" banking to facilitate money laundering. Even in vibrant economies in Asia, the Middle East, Africa, Latin America and Europe, there is often a willingness to look the other way, not to ask inconvenient questions about the sources of money flowing into the country or not to examine too closely the activities that generate the money.

As a consequence, criminal organizations in many parts of the world have grown in size and power. They have been able to internationalize their operations and in doing so have succeeded in putting themselves beyond the capacity of any individual country to destroy them, or even seriously affect their operations. Effective responses are only possible through bilateral or multinational efforts, and, for many of the reasons noted above, many of these are stillborn. Differences in perception of the problem, conflicts in legal systems and the effects of corruption or incapacity are the rule and compromise the efficacy of combined or individual operations. What this means is that major international criminal organizations are now able to operate on a scale unimagined just a few years ago. They have the capacity to evade law enforcement in many areas and to subvert it in others. Criminal organizations are now significant international actors with the ability to compromise the integrity and sovereignty of individual states, a fact that neither public policy nor conceptual theory has caught up with. The prospects for the future are bleak.

Rising to the Challenge

While the situation is disheartening, it is too serious to ignore. Neither the United States nor other members of the international community can afford to ignore the situation or to wash their hands of it. The international community must develop timely and effective responses to protect the integrity of government itself and to prevent the criminalization of much of the world's financial processes and the subversion of many of its members. There are a number of things that can and should be done.

Many of the ideas and approaches needed to respond are already in place. International efforts to criminalize money laundering, improve detection and monitoring capabilities, strengthen legal systems, improve law enforcement capabilities of individual countries, share intelligence and coordinate international enforcement operations are important components of an effective response that is already underway. It is not a question of what as much as of how much. Current efforts are simply too fragmented and episodic to be effective. There is no adequate international framework for developing coherent, sustained, and comprehensive responses to the range of activities of major criminal organizations. There is no uniform agreement on how to respond, and awareness of the problem or willingness to deal with it is similarly fragmented.

One of the necessary elements in devising a more comprehensive approach is U.S. leadership to promote an international convention on international organized crime. While the United States has taken a number of unilateral efforts to deal with the problem, the scale and diversity of international criminal enterprise is beyond the capacity of any one country. Similarly, U.S. efforts to devise tailored bilateral arrangements are simply inadequate to the threat. Multilateral efforts are essential, but they require a common frame of reference and general agreement on principles. Efforts by the G-7 countries to develop common guidelines for financial controls are an important step in this direction, but they still lack general acceptance. Disparities in legal frameworks and poor institutional capabilities in many countries effectively abrogate meaningful counter-measures. Without a framework agreement that makes standards uniform and binding, criminal organizations will be able to evade piecemeal efforts and localized responses.

Several key elements must be incorporated into such a framework to give it the best chances of success. First, an agreement must incorporate existing efforts under G-7 Financial Action Task Force guidelines to criminalize money laundering internationally, strengthen bank supervision of and reporting on financial transactions and end bank secrecy regimes that protect illegal activities. Second, it must make stopping corruption a central component of international efforts to combat crime. This can be accomplished in many areas of the world by conditioning international assistance, from countries and international lending institutions, on effective anti-corruption programs. Third, it must include extradition agreements that will close safe havens. Fourth, it should include transparency laws that make corporate bribery illegal and that restrict the ability of countries to facilitate the creation of shell companies and brass-plate banks without adequate documentation. Fifth, it should include measures to penalize countries that fail to comply. Sixth, it should incorporate model legislation on asset forfeiture and asset sharing that will help confiscate illegal assets. Finally, it must, as with the 1988 U.N. Convention of Psychotropic Drugs, encourage efforts to share law enforcement and intelligence information, bring local laws into conformity with international practice, strengthen law enforcement capabilities, provide for adequate judicial systems and encourage an environment of cooperation.

While these measures in a comprehensive international agreement will not, in themselves, eliminate international organized crime, without such measures responses will continue to be piecemeal and inadequate. Given the growing power and influence of criminal organizations, failure to enact such measures is to invite further assaults on the sovereignty of individual countries and their ability to protect the integrity of their frontiers and institutions.

Notes and Questions

1. Does Mr. Olson, staff director for the U.S. Senate Caucus on International Narcotics Control, which is charged with monitoring U.S. international counter-narcotics policies and efforts, accurately portray the role of international criminal organizations in the world constitutive process of authoritative decision? Is his focus on the threat to sovereignty well-placed? What about the threat to substantive guiding ideas such as the rule of law, democratic governance, human rights, and the world public order of human dignity?

2. For details on drug cartels in Latin America, *see* Patrick Clawson & Rens Lee, The Andean Cocaine Industry (St. Martin's Press 1996). On policy, *see* Gregory Wilson, *The Changing Game: The United States Evolving Supply-Side Approach to Narcotics Trafficking*, 26 Vand. J. Transnat'l L. 1163 (1994). For an analysis of the phenomenon and effect of bribery in Latin American government and society, *see* W. Michael Reisman, Folded Lies: Bribery, Crusades, and Reforms (Free Press 1979). As to the increasing threat of the Russian Mafia, *see* Peter J. Vassalo, *The New Ivan the Terrible: Problems in International Criminal Enforcement and the Specter of the Russian Mafia*, 28 Case W. Res. J. Int'l L. 173-176 (1996), excerpted below:

> Unlike the Mafia of "The Godfather," which was organized in New York as five distinct families, "Russian Mafia" does not refer to a single group. Instead, it is a blanket term describing the nearly 6,000 Russian organized criminal groups operating world-wide. The groups are divided according to three main classifications: ethnicity, region, and trade. The Moscow area exemplifies this breakdown. The Dolgoprudnaya and Solntsevo derive their names from their Moscow neighborhoods. Their operational specialties include protection rackets and slot machines. Ethnic groups also specialize, such as the Azerbaijanis, who control the drug trade. Other ethnic groups, such as the Chechen, are more diversified. Chechens are particularly notorious in their breadth of activity with involvement in several areas of criminal conduct from contract killings to drug trafficking.
>
> The Moscow example is only a small slice of Russian organized crime's worldwide activities. Russian Mafia groups have established themselves throughout Europe and the United States in activities including drug trafficking, money laundering, prostitution, and, most importantly, trafficking in nuclear weapons materials. One commentator has stated:
>
> The Russian Mafia is a union of racketeers without equal. Unlike the Mafia in Sicily, which it admires and copies as a standard of excellence, it has no home seat or central command. There are no ancestral enemies or common bloodlines. Nevertheless, its proliferating clans are invading every sphere of life, usurping political power, taking over state enterprises and fleecing natural resources. They are engaged in extortion, theft, forgery, armed assault, contract killing, swindling, drug running, arms smuggling, prostitution, gambling, loan sharking, embezzling, money laundering and black marketing—all on a monumental and increasingly international scale.
>
> James Woolsey, former Director of the CIA, recently testified before Congress on the Russian Mafia's threat to U.S. security. Woolsey gave three reasons why the Russian Mafia is such a critical concern. First, Russia is a country of enormous strategic interest due to its stockpile of nuclear weapons materials. Second, the United States has an extreme interest in the outcome of Russia's transition to a market economy and democ-

racy. Finally, Russian organized crime has become a menace threatening the United States not only from abroad, but internally as well.

Due to the international nature of the Russian Mafia's activities and its lack of a central organization, it follows that international cooperation in combating it is essential. However, due to procedural barriers in international criminal law, a uniform system of transnational criminal enforcement does not exist. Traditionally, criminal law has been the responsibility of domestic legal systems. Although there have been instances of international cooperation, most enforcement efforts have been through bilateral treaties. National sovereignty and the reluctance of national courts to adjudicate foreign law have created barriers to effective transnational criminal enforcement. As a result, the system fails to recognize the international nature of modern organized crime, creating difficulties in implicating international groups such as the Russian Mafia.

This failure is exemplified by a demonstration of how "domestic" crime has developed on an international scale. Normally a local crime, Russian organized crime has taken prostitution and the sex trade to an international level. The consequences can be deadly and disruptive. Russian groups lure young women into prostitution inside Russia, and then export them to countries where the earning potential for hard currency is greater. When Russian organized crime is denied a cut of profits, situations such as the recent Frankfurt brothel murders arise. Although the prostitution and murders occurred in Germany, only German authorities were able to prosecute. The extent of Russian involvement will not be eliminated by single arrests. In cases like the Frankfurt murders, successful prosecution will not stop the problem, making related violence probable.

On a more sophisticated scale, Russian organized crime is also causing serious disruption of world financial institutions. Because Russian organized crime controls at least half of Russia's banks, it is easily able to tap into a major money supply, enabling it to take control of legitimate businesses both foreign and domestic. It is through these legitimate businesses that organized crime expands its operations, using them as cover for new operations. These tens of millions of dollars stolen from Russian banks contribute to the nearly fifteen billion dollars in cash already removed from Russia by organized crime. Since the money to finance criminal activities originates from currency shuttled out of Russia, effective international cooperation could keep some of this currency within the country. If not, Russia's economic situation will not improve, further destabilizing the country.

Nuclear smuggling poses the greatest threat to world security. The recent arrests of smugglers carrying nuclear material to Germany under scores the problem. While Germany or another third country can arrest smugglers caught with the actual material, better coordination of enforcement could stop smuggling at the source while simultaneously destroying foreign distribution networks.

Considering the grave threat the Russian Mafia poses to world security, international criminal law must begin to develop the procedural mechanisms to combat the problem on a global scale. The development of international criminal procedural mechanisms will enable effective prosecution of internally committed crimes while assisting other countries in fighting related activity.

For further discussion, *see* Sara Jankiewicz, *Glasnost and the Growth of Global Organized Crime,* 18 HOUS. J. INT'L L. 215 (1995), and Abraham Abramovsky, *Prosecuting the "Russian Mafia": Recent Russian Legislation and Increased Bilateral Cooperation May Provide the Means*, 37 VA. J. INT'L L. 191 (1996). *See also,* FEDERICO VARESE, THE RUSSIAN MAFIA: PRIVATE PROTECTION IN A NEW MARKET ECONOMY (Oxford U. Press 2001); JAMES O. FINCKENAUER & ELIN J. WARING, RUSSIAN MAFIA IN AMERICA: IMMIGRATION, CULTURE, AND CRIME (Northeastern U. Press 2001); GLENN E. SCHWEITZER

& CAROLE C. DORSCH, SUPERTERRORISM: ASSASSINS, MOBSTERS AND WEAPONS OF MASS DESTRUCTION (Perseus Publishing 1998).

3. How should the world community react to the threat posed by these international criminal groups? Should they be equated to pirates and be treated as *hostes humani generis* — enemies of all humankind? Should their offenses, like piracy, be treated as universal crimes, allowing for local authority to prosecute in any jurisdiction, even ones without territorial or nationality link to the prohibited conduct? Are effective extradition and prosecution mechanisms more realistic? Would the idea of "compound criminal liability" help? For an assessment of pertinent U.S. efforts, *see* Susan W. Brenner, *RICO, CCE, and Other Complex Crimes: The Transformation of American Criminal Law?*, 2 WM. & MARY BILL RTS. J. 239 (1993).

4. How should the world community react to the phenomenon of a government so corrupted and infiltrated by criminal organizations that it may be considered a "criminal state"? Should multilateral or unilateral sanctions be employed? What does the track record of sanctions on states sponsoring or supporting terrorist activities teach? *See infra*, Part Six at 1183-1221.

PART THREE: PROTECTION AND CONTROL OF PERSONS

I. NATIONALITY

The historical approach of international law in terms of regulating the competition among States to control human beings has evolved recently into a focus on the protection of the human being. The conceptual means to effectuate that protection are the traditional bond of "nationality" and the modern idea of "universal human rights."

A. THE NATURE AND FUNCTION OF NATIONALITY

1. Siegfried Wiessner, *Blessed Be the Ties that Bind: The Nexus between Nationality and Territory*
56 MISS. L. J. 447, 447-455 (1988)

People are, and remain, a cardinal base of power of national elites. In former times, they have been kept together by invocation and enforcement of group myths such as common ancestry, birth on common soil, or perpetual allegiance. The modern myth is the concept of nationality.

The rise of this concept is closely related to the ascent of the nation-state. Nevertheless, it was but in the aftermath of the French Revolution that it found its way into the statute books and other authoritative pronouncements of decision-makers of territorial communities. Since then, it has been a favorite object of interest for both scholars and wielders of power, not surprisingly, because it goes to the essence of the relationship between the individual and the state.

Battles over the meaning of nationality have raged since the birth of the concept. It has often been stated that nationality is a 'purely formal concept,' with no essential legal consequences flowing from it. If that were true, no distinction under customary international law between the treatment of foreigners and that of citizens would exist—be it in the area of international migration or in any other field of legally regulated behavior. The purpose of this article is to test this assumption with respect to the movement of persons across borders on a broad international and comparative legal basis—to find out whether the outcomes of the world's authoritative and controlling decision-making processes establish a definite link between nationality and home territory, and how that legal nexus is to be defined. ...

I. FOCUS OF INQUIRY: NATIONALITY

Nationality, as a term of art, is barely two-hundred years old. It has largely replaced the feudal concepts of allegiance and subjecthood. In English and in the Romance languages, it soon took on two different meaning: a politico-legal one, denoting membership of a state, and a historico-biological one, referring to membership in a nation. This inquiry focuses on the former meaning.

The 'nature' of nationality has been the subject of enduring controversy throughout the last two centuries. Basically, two theories vie for recognition: (1) the status theory, and (2) the relationship theory. The status theory maintains that nationality is an original juridical situation independent of rights and duties arising from it. The relationship theory views nationality as a legal bond between an individual and his home state that encompasses, by necessity, specific rights and duties. The latter one is prevalent in the United States.

While some states refer to their membership status as 'citizenship', others use the term 'nationality' or the *analogon* in the foreign language. In international law, the use of the term 'nationality' is overwhelming. Even those countries which call their members 'citizens' prefer the term 'nationals' when describing the members of other countries in their international treaties and domestic law. This predominant, generic use of the term 'nationality' justifies its utilization for the purposes of this inquiry.

Nationality, like any other legal concept, is a tool lawyers, judges and other decision-makers use in order to determine what ought to be done in a given situation. It is only a means to a social end, not an end in itself. Thus, inquiry focuses on the question: Why do decision-makers use a particular legal concept? In reference to nationality: Why do territorial communities confer or withdraw this particular status of membership?, and Why do individuals strive to maintain or to lose it? This functional approach may not overlook the functional consequences attached to possession of nationality. In must take into account the full array of decisions, both under domestic and international law, that are bound together in the one act of conferment or withdrawal of nationality. These implied consequences are essential features of membership in a particular community. For this reason, nationality is to be defined as an aggregate status, composed of the respective consequences attached to it by international and domestic law.

These consequences may change on both the domestic and the international plane. In fact, it has been contended that the legal content of nationality is not nearly constant since it changes with almost every new enactment. Most statutes, however, do not apply nationality as a differentiating criterion. If nationality makes a difference in the treatment of certain fact patterns, these differentiations usually have grown and matured over a long time, have been solidified by constant practice, and have become part of the engrained legal culture of a given community. Change of such features is, thus, difficult to effect. Even across borders and across legal traditions, such differentiating features may be common. As an experienced student of the area tells us, 'the concepts of nationality under municipal law have a great many common features and they show a large measure of conformity.' If there are such common functions, they form the basis for a transnational concept of nationality that establishes a crucial starting point for communication among lawyers from different legal systems. Further, in addition to providing common conceptual ground that may form the basis for scholarly insights in the comparative study of law, a transnational, functional concept of nationality may also prove useful for the drafting and interpretation of international treaties and domestic laws that utilize this term. It can be used to identify the persons who are to be considered 'nationals' of a particular state if that state has failed to enact legislation to that effect. Such identification may be necessary for the purposes of customary international law (e.g., with respect to which persons is a state entitled to exercise its right of diplomatic protection?), international conventions (which may accord certain special treatment to nationals), or the conflicts laws of other states (which may determine the applicable law according to the personal jurisdiction of the individual involved), to name but a few of the legal prescriptions involved.

The attribute of nationality is a critical factor in a variety of factual constellations, ranging, inter alia, from voting rights and diplomatic protection to access to certain professions and the common law crime of treason. The purpose of this study is to focus on one particular potential function of nationality, probably the most crucial one: the specific legal ties of a national to his or her home territory. For in the twentieth century, it is only within the home state that man may enjoy the full array of rights connected with that status; only there does man also bear all the burdens of citizenship.

This approach presupposes a broad comparative analysis of past legal trends in decision that condition the expectations of humankind as to what is right or wrong in a particular set of facts and claims.

II. METHOD OF INQUIRY

A successful comparative analysis must observe three principles: (1) it must be empirical and functional; (2) it must be sufficiently general; and (3) it must be representative.

[Because domestic legal systems are so diverse, a] transnational framework of inquiry, has to deliberately avoid the terminological codes, procedures and institutions germane to particular legal systems. It has to start from the social function of the legal terms utilized to designate the concrete societal problems addressed by the respective decision-making processes. Thus the approach has to be empirical and functional, not normative. ...

The guiding principle of functionality is joined by the principle of generality. That means that only the full membership category in any given community is analyzed; i.e., in the United Kingdom, the 'British citizen', and in the Federal Republic of Germany, the 'status as a German.' ...

It is crucial to limit the number of legal systems analyzed in detail. This is not only necessary in order not to overburden the individual researcher, but also to eliminate protracted, fruitless searches at an early stage. In our case it is possible, via careful selection of the legal systems analyzed, to determine common functions of nationality on a preliminary representative basis. If there are such common consequences, they may be tested, in a broader sample, against a wider set of state practice. The validity of this analysis depends upon a considered selection of these representative systems. In the context of people's movement across borders the major legal traditions of the world should be represented [e.g., the civil law tradition, the common law tradition, and socialist legal systems] as well as the diversity of community attitudes towards migration.

The analysis of past trends in decision and conditioning factors starts out with a historical overview, leading into the process of international legal decision-making. In reference to the latter topic, the principle of generality applied in this analysis requires the disregard of treaty law to the extent that it does not codify or evidence general international law, in particular, customary international law. Specifically, the international human rights conventions have to be matched carefully with existing state practice in order to determine whether their provisions have matured into the status of customary law. A detailed analysis of the representative domestic legal systems follows the inquiry into applicable international law. If both the analysis of international law and of representative domestic systems yield common features of differential treatment, the scope of inquiry is broadened, and the results are tested against the practice of all relevant states.

* * *

The author undertook the comprehensive comparative and cross-cultural review suggested above in a later treatise, in which he analyzed the process of ascription of nationality in the United States, Germany, and the then-U.S.S.R.

2. SIEGFRIED WIESSNER, DIE FUNKTION DER STAATSANGEHÖRIGKEIT [THE FUNCTION OF NATIONALITY] 396-397 (Tübingen U. Press 1989) [author's translation]

The hypothesis according to which certain legal consequences attached to the possession of nationality within the three representative legal systems and outside of their confines are very similar if not identical, has been confirmed. ... The various legal decisionmaking processes have established transnationally concordant consequences flowing from the possession of nationality. These legal consequences have remained constant for a long time and have stabilized during the course of this century. Taken together, they form the content of a functional transnational concept of nationality ... [which] consists of the following elements:

(1) A state if obligated to admit its members onto its territory if no other state is willing to do so.

(2) A national enjoys the right to enter, or to return to, his or her home country.

(3) Nationals must not be banished from the territory of their home state.

(4) In times of a public emergency which threatens the life of the nation, the rights listed under (2) and (3) may be limited, but only for the purpose and to the extent strictly required by the exigencies of the situation.

(5) The right to vote as well as the right to stand as a candidate for office at the national level is held exclusively by nationals.

(6) In principle, only nationals may be employed in a role that includes the exercise of strictly governmental functions.

(7) A state is entitled to diplomatic protection of its nationals validly claimed under international law vis-à-vis other states.

Notes and Questions

1. In what contexts, if any, may Professor Wiessner's transnational concept of nationality be practically relevant? Do its individual features reflect customary international law?

2. Compare Professor Peter Schuck's reference to a "positive concept" citizenship which he defines as "a relationship between individuals and the polity in which citizens owe allegiance to their polity – they must not betray it and may have to serve it – while the polity owes its citizens the fullest measure of protection that its law affords, including (except for minors and some convicted felons) the right to vote." Peter H. Schuck, *The Re-Evaluation of American Citizenship*, 12 Geo. Immigr. L.J. 1 (1997). Professor Schuck does not, however, engage in a comparative analysis and this concept may not be relevant to countries other than the U.S. *See also* Ruth Donner, The Regulation of Nationality in International Law (Transnational Publishers, 2nd ed. 1994); Kim Rubenstein & Daniel Adler, *International Citizenship: The Future of Nationality in a Globalized World*, 7 Ind. J. Global Leg. Stud. 519 (2000).

3. Professor Helen Silving has presented the idea of nationality as a *nudum jus*, an open connecting factor for unlimited discretionary use by the elites of nation-states. Helen Silving, *Nationality in Comparative Law*, 50 Am. J. Comp. L. 410 (1956). What are the pros and cons of such an idea?

B. Claims to Ascribe Nationality to People Upon Exclusively Chosen Criteria

Because people are a scarce and valuable resource, the criteria and practices by which a state may claim the right to protect as well as exercise control over them to the exclusion of other elites are extremely important. The flow of international decision has established procedures and a number of criteria for ascribing nationality. A major trend in this regard has been an increasing inclusive control over national competence to ascribe.

1. International Policies

a. Convention on Certain Questions Relating to the Conflict of Nationality Laws

Apr. 12, 1930, Ger.-Aus.-Belg.-Gr.Brit.–N.Ir.–Can. etc. 179 L.N.T.S. 89

Considering that it is of importance to settle by international agreement questions relating to the conflict of nationality laws;

Being convinced that it is in the general interest of the international community to secure that all its members should recognise that every person should have a nationality and should have one nationality only;

Recognising accordingly that the ideal towards which the efforts of humanity should be directed in this domain is the abolition of all cases both of statelessness and of double nationality;

Being of opinion that, under the economic and social conditions which at present exist in the various countries, it is not possible to reach immediately a uniform solution of all the above mentioned problems;

Being desirous, nevertheless, as a first step toward this great achievement, of settling in a first attempt at progressive codification, those questions relating to the conflict of nationality laws on which it is possible at the present time to reach international agreement; ...

[H]ave agreed as follows:

Article 1. It is for each State to determine under its own law who are its nationals. This law, shall be recognised by other States in so far as it is consistent with international conventions, international custom, and the principles of law generally recognised with regard to nationality.

Article 2. Any question as to whether a person possesses the nationality of a particular State shall be determined in accordance with the law of that State. ...

Article 18. The High Contracting Parties agree to apply the principles and rules contained in the preceding articles in their relations with each other, as from the date of the entry into force of the present Convention.

The inclusion of the above-mentioned principles and rules in the Convention shall in no way be deemed to prejudice the question whether they do or do not already form part of international law.

It is understood, that in so far as any point is not covered by any of the provisions of the preceding articles, the existing principles and rules of international law shall remain in force.

b. European Convention on Nationality

Nov. 6, 1997, 37 I.L.M. 44 (1998)

Article 3: *Competence of the State*

1. Each State shall determine under its own law who are its nationals.

2. This law shall be accepted by other States in so far as it is consistent with applicable international conventions, customary international law and the principles of law generally recognised with regard to nationality.

c. Harvard Research in International Law: *The Law of Nationality*

23 AM. J. INT'L L. SPEC. SUP. 26 (1929)

It may be difficult to precise [sic] the limitations which exist in international law upon the power of a state to confer its nationality. Yet it is obvious that some limitations do exist. They are based upon the historical development of international law and upon the fact that different states may be interested in the allegiance of the same natural person. If State A should attempt, for instance, to naturalize persons who have never had any connection with State A, who have never been within its territory, who have never acted in its territory, who have no relation whatever to any persons who have been its nationals, and who are nationals of other states, it would seem that State A would clearly have gone beyond the limits set by international law. Thus, if State A should attempt to naturalize all persons living outside its territory but within 500 miles of its frontier, it would clearly have passed those limits; or similarly if State A should attempt to naturalize all persons in the world holding a particular political or religious faith or belonging to a particular race.

2. Inclusive Competence

a. The Covenant of the League of Nations, Art. 15, para. 8

June 28, 1919, 2 Bevans 48

If the dispute between the parties is claimed by one of them, and is found by the Council, to arise out of a matter which by international law is solely within the domestic jurisdiction of that party, the Council shall so report, and shall make no recommendation as to its settlement.

* * *

The degree and method by which competence to ascribe nationality is allocated to particular states or subjected to international regulation was considered in the Nationality Decrees case.

b. Advisory Opinion on the Tunis-Morocco Nationality Decrees

1923 P.C.I.J. (Ser. B) No. 4, 7, at 21

[In 1921, France, Tunis and Morocco, both of the latter in varying forms under French control, enacted legislation, one of the effects of which would have been to ascribe Tunisian or Moroccan nationality to individuals Britain claimed as her subjects. After fruitless negotiation, Britain and France agreed that the Council of the League of Nations ask the Permanent Court of International Justice the following question:]

> Whether the dispute between France and Great Britain as to the Nationality Decrees issued in Tunis and Morocco (French zone) on November

> 8th, 1921, and their application to British subjects, is or is not, by international law, solely a matter of domestic jurisdiction. ...

Special attention must be called to the word *"exclusive"* in the French text, to which the word "solely" (within the domestic jurisdiction) corresponds in the English text. The question to be considered is not whether one of the parties to the dispute is or is not competent in law to take or to refrain from taking a particular action, but whether the jurisdiction claimed belongs *solely* to that party.

From one point of view, it might well be said that the jurisdiction of State is *exclusive* within the limits fixed by international law-using the expression in its wider sense, that is to say, embracing both customary law and general as well as particular treaty law. But a careful scrutiny of paragraph 8 of Article 15 shows that it is not in this sense that exclusive jurisdiction is referred to in that paragraph.

The words "solely within the domestic jurisdiction" seem rather to contemplate certain matters which, though they may very closely concern the interests of more than one State, are not, in principle, regulated by international law. As regards such matters, each State is sole judge.

The question whether a certain matter is or is not solely within the jurisdiction of a State is an essentially relative question; it depends upon the development of international relations. Thus, in the present state of international law, questions of nationality are, in the opinion of the Court, in principle within this reserved domain.

For the purpose of the present opinion, it is enough to observe that it may well happen that, in a matter which, like that of nationality, is not, in principle, regulated by international law, the right of a State to use its discretion is nevertheless restricted by obligations which it may have undertaken towards other States. In such a case, jurisdiction which, in principle, belongs solely to the State, is limited by rules of international law. Article 15, paragraph 8, then ceases to apply as regards those States which are entitled to invoke such rules, and the dispute as to the question whether a State has or has not the right to take certain measures becomes in these circumstances a dispute of an international character and falls outside the scope of the exception contained in this paragraph. To hold that a State has not exclusive jurisdiction does not in any way prejudice the final decision as to whether that State has a right to adopt such measures. ...

Article 15, in effect, establishes the fundamental principle that any dispute likely to lead to a rupture which is not submitted to arbitration in accordance with Article 13 shall be laid before the Council. The reservations generally made in arbitration treaties are not to be found in this Article.

Having regard to this very wide competence possessed by the League of Nations, the Covenant contains an express reservation protecting the independence of States; this reservation is to be found in paragraph 8 of Article 15. Without this reservation, the internal affairs of a country might, directly they appeared to affect the interests of another country, be brought before the Council and form the subject of recommendations by the League of Nations. Under the terms of paragraph 8, the League's interest in being able to make such recommendations as are deemed just and proper in the circumstances with a view to the maintenance of peace must, at a given point, give way to the equally essential interest of the individual State to maintain intact its independence in matters which international law recognises to be solely within its jurisdiction. ...

This consideration assumes especial importance in the case of a matter which, by international law, is, in principle, solely within the domestic jurisdiction of one Party, but in regard to which the other Party invokes international engagements which, in the opinion of that Party, are of a nature to preclude in the particular case such exclusive jurisdiction. A difference of opinion exists between France and Great Britain as to how far it is necessary to proceed with an examination of these international engagements in order to reply to the question put to the Court. ...

The main arguments developed by the Parties in support of their respective contentions are as follows:

1.

A. The French Decrees relate to persons born, not upon the territory of France itself, but upon the territory of the French Protectorates of Tunis and of the French zone of Morocco. Granted that it is competent for a State to enact such legislation within its national territory, the question remains to be considered whether the same competence exists as regards protected territory.

The extent of the powers of a protecting State in the territory of a protected State depends, first, upon the Treaties between the protecting State and the protected State establishing the Protectorate, and, secondly, upon the conditions under which the Protectorate has been recognised by third Powers as against whom there is an intention to rely on the provisions of these Treaties. In spite of common features possessed by Protectorates under international law, they have individual legal characteristics resulting from the special conditions under which they were created, and the stage of their development.

The position in the present case is determined by the international documents enumerated below: [The listing of treaties is deleted.]

The question whether the exclusive jurisdiction possessed by a protecting State in regard to nationality questions in its own territory extends to the territory of the protected State depends upon an examination of the whole situation as it appears from the standpoint of international law. The question therefore is no longer solely one of domestic jurisdiction as defined above. ...

B. The French Government contends that the public powers (*puissance publique*) exercised by the protecting State, taken in conjunction with the local sovereignty of the protected State, constitute full sovereignty equivalent to that upon which international relations are based, and that therefore the protecting State and the protected State may, by virtue of an agreement between them, exercise and divide between them within the protected territory the whole extent of the powers which international law recognises as enjoyed by sovereign States within the limits of their national territory. This contention is disputed by the British Government.

The Court observes that, in any event, it will be necessary to have recourse to international law in order to decide what the value of an agreement of this kind may be as regards third States, and that the question consequently ceases to be one which, by international law, is solely within the domestic jurisdiction of a State, as that jurisdiction is defined above.

2.

A. Great Britain denies that the Decrees of November 8th, 1921, are applicable to British subjects, and relies in support of her contention upon the Treaties concluded by her with the two States which were subsequently placed under protectorate. .. . By virtue of these Treaties, persons claimed as British subjects would enjoy a measure of extraterritoriality incompatible with the imposition of another nationality.

According to the French contention, as developed in the course of the oral statements, these Treaties, which were concluded for an indefinite period that is to say, in perpetuity, have lapsed by virtue of the principle known as the *clausula rebus sic stantibus* because the establishment of a legal and judicial regime in conformity with French legislation has created a new situation which deprives the capitulatory regime of its *raison d'être*.

It is clearly not possible to make any pronouncement upon this point without recourse to the principles of international law concerning the duration of the validity of treaties. It follows, therefore, that in this respect also the question does not, by international law, fall solely within the domestic jurisdiction of a State, as that jurisdiction is defined above.

B. As regards Tunis more especially, France contends that, following upon negotiations between the French and British Governments, Great Britain formally renounced her rights of jurisdiction in the Regency (Note from Lord Granville to M. Tissot dated June 20th, 1883, . . .) and that by the Franco-British Arrangement of September 18th, 1897, she accepted a new basis for the relations between France and herself in Tunis. It appears from the Cases and Counter-Cases that the two Governments take different views with regard to the scope of the declarations made by Great Britain in this respect and also with regard to the construction to be placed upon the Arrangement of 1897.

The appreciation of these divergent points of view involves, owing to the very nature of the divergence, the interpretation of international engagements. The question therefore does not, according to international law, fall solely within the domestic jurisdiction of a single State, as that jurisdiction is defined above.

C. As far as Morocco is concerned, it is certain that Great Britain still exercises there her consular jurisdiction. France argues that Great Britain, by consenting to the Franco-German Convention of November 4th, 1911, with regard to Morocco, agree to renounce her capitulatory rights as soon as the new judicial system contemplated by the Convention had been introduced.

The British Government, on the contrary, contends that the Franco-German Convention of 1911-its adhesion to which was conditional upon the internationalization of the town and district of Tangiers, a condition which has not yet been fulfilled-was not an agreement for the suppression of the capitulatory regime: in this respect, the relations between France and Great Britain are, it is said, still governed by the second of the Secret Articles of the Anglo-French Declaration of April 8th, 1904. …

In the case of Morocco also, therefore, as in the case of Tunis, there is a difference with regard to the interpretation of international engagements. The international character of the legal situation follows not only from the fact that the two Governments concerned place a different construction upon the obligations undertaken, but also from the fact that Great Britain exercises capitulatory rights in the territory of the French Protectorate in Morocco. Again, from this standpoint, the question does not, according to international law, fall solely within the domestic jurisdiction of a State, as that jurisdiction is defined above.

Apart from all considerations which relate to the protectorate and to the capitulations in Tunis, Great Britain relies, as regards that country, upon the most-favored-nation clause (Anglo-French Arrangement of September 18th, 1897, and the notes of March 8th and May 23rd, 1919, [thereto] exchanged …) in order to assert a claim to benefit by Article 13 of the Franco-Italian Consular Convention of September 28th, 1896. This Article expressly contemplates the preservation of their nationality by Italian subjects in Tunis. France, however, denies that the most-favored-nation clause relied upon by Great Britain is applicable in the present case, because of the exclusively economic bearing of that clause and because of the synallagmatic character of the Franco-Italian Convention.

It follows that the question is one which, by international law, does not fall solely within the domestic jurisdiction of a single State as defined above.

3.

Apart from all considerations which relate to the protectorate and to the capitulations in Tunis, Great Britain relies, as regards that country upon the most-favoured-nation clause (Anglo-French Arrangement of September 18th, 1897, and the Notes of March 8th and May 23rd, 1919, exchanged between the French and British Governments on the subject of that Arrangement; see British Case, Appendix 9, and French Counter-Case, page 64), in order to assert a claim to benefit by Article 13 of the Franco-Italian Consular convention of September 28th, 1896. This article expressly contemplates the preservation of their nationality by Italian subjects in Tunis. France, however, denies that the most-favoured-nation clause relied upon by Great Britain is applicable in the present case, because of the exclusively economic bearing of that clause and because of the synallagmatic character of the Franco-Italian Convention.

It follows that the question is one which, by international law, does not fall solely within the domestic jurisdiction of a single State as defined above.

4.

According to the French Government, paragraph 2 of Article I of the Arrangement of September 18th, 1897, should be interpreted as a formal recognition by Great Britain of the competence of France to legislate with regard to the situation of persons in Tunis, and more particularly with regard to their nationality, under the same conditions as in France. This construction is disputed by the British Government.

Since, even assuming the French contention to be correct, the question whether France possesses such competence in this respect would still depend, as regards Great Britain, on the construction to be placed upon the most-favored-nation clause mentioned under No. 3, this question is not according to international law, solely a matter of domestic jurisdiction as defined above.

The Court, not having to enter into the merits of the dispute, confines itself to consideration of the facts set down under Nos. 1, 2, 3 and 4.

In the opinion of the Court, these facts suffice, even when considered separately, to prove that the dispute arises out of a matter which, by international law, is not solely within the domestic jurisdiction of France as such jurisdiction is defined in this opinion.

NOTES AND QUESTIONS

1. How would you describe the Court's theory of national competence to ascribe nationality? Is it a matter of inclusive (international) or exclusive (national) competence? How is the competence determined over time?

2. After you have read *Nottebohm* and *Flegenheimer*, below, consider whether it is still accurate to say that "nationality is not, in principle, regulated by international law."

2. The "Genuine Link" Theory

a. Nottebohm Case (Liechtenstein v. Guatemala)

1955 I.C.J. 4, 16 (Apr. 6) (Second Phase)

[Facts: A German national from his birth in Germany in 1881, Nottebohm moved to Guatemala in 1905, residing and doing business there, without ever applying for Guatemalan citizenship. He sometimes made trips to Germany to conduct business and to Liechtenstein to visit his brother, who lived there after 1931.

On October 9, 1939, shortly after the German invasion of Poland, Nottebohm applied for naturalization in Liechtenstein while still a German national. Relieved of the three-year residence requirements, Nottebohm paid his fees and taxes to Liechtenstein and became a naturalized citizen of Liechtenstein by taking an oath of allegiance on October 20, 1939, thereby forfeiting his German nationality under the nationality law of Liechtenstein. He returned to Guatemala early in 1940 on a Liechtenstein passport to resume his business activities. At his request, the Guatemalan Ministry of External Affairs changed the Nottebohm entry in its Registrar of Aliens from "German" to "Liechtenstein" national.

In July 1941, Nottebohm was blacklisted for trade purposes by the United States and his assets in the United States were frozen. Shortly afterward, on December 11, 1941, a state of war came into existence between the United States and Germany and between Guatemala and Germany. Nottebohm was arrested in Guatemala in October 1943 and was deported to the United States, where he was interned as an enemy alien until 1946. Upon his release, Nottebohm applied for readmission to Guatemala but was refused and took up residence in Liechtenstein. Meanwhile, the Guatemalan government, after classifying him as an enemy alien, expropriated his extensive properties without compensation.

Liechtenstein instituted proceedings against Guatemala in the International Court of Justice, asking the court to declare that Guatemala had violated international law "in arresting, detaining, expelling, and refusing to readmit Mr. Nottebohm and in seizing and retaining his property." Guatemala's main contention was that Liechtenstein's claim was inadmissible because of Nottebohm's nationality. In other words, Liechtenstein's competence to protect Nottebohm was challenged.]
...

Thus, the real issue before the Court is the admissibility of the claim of Liechtenstein in respect of Nottebohm.

In order to decide upon the admissibility of the Application, the Court must ascertain whether the nationality conferred on Nottebohm by Liechtenstein by means of a naturalization which took place in the circumstances which have been described, can be validly invoked as against Guatemala, whether it bestows upon Liechtenstein a sufficient title to the exercise of protection in respect of Nottebohm as against Guatemala and therefore entitles it to seise the Court of a claim relating to him. In this connection, Counsel for Liechtenstein said: "the essential question is whether Mr. Nottebohm, having acquired the nationality of Liechtenstein, that acquisition of nationality is one which must be recognized by other States". This formulation is accurate, subject to the twofold reservation that, in the first place, what is involved is not recognition for all purposes but merely for the purposes of the admissibility of the Application, and, secondly, that what is involved is not recognition by all States but only by Guatemala.

The Court does not propose to go beyond the limited scope of the question which it has to decide, namely whether the nationality conferred on Nottebohm can be relied upon as against Guatemala in justification of the proceedings instituted before the Court. It must decide this question on the basis of international law; to do so is consistent with the nature of the question and with the nature of the Court's own function. ...

Since no proof has been adduced that Guatemala has recognized the title to the exercise of protection relied upon by Liechtenstein as being derived from the naturalization which it granted to Nottebohm, the Court must consider whether such an act of granting nationality by Liechtenstein directly entails an obligation on the part of Guatemala to recognize its effect, namely, Liechtenstein's right to exercise its protection. In other words, it must be determined whether that unilateral act by Liechtenstein is one which can be relied upon against Guatemala in regard to the exercise of protection. The Court will deal with this question without considering ... the validity of Nottebohm's naturalization according to the law of Liechtenstein.

It is for Liechtenstein, as it is for every sovereign State, to settle by its own legislation the rules relating to the acquisition of its nationality, and to confer that nationality by naturalization granted by its own organs in accordance with that legislation. It is not necessary to determine whether international law imposes any limitations on its freedom of decision in this domain. Furthermore, nationality has its most immediate, its most far-reaching and, for most people, its only effects within the legal system of the State conferring it. Nationality serves above all to determine that the person upon whom it is conferred enjoys the rights and is bound by the obligations which the law of the State in question grants to or imposes on its nationals. This is implied in the wider concept that nationality is within the domestic jurisdiction of the State.

But the issue which the Court must decide is not one which pertains to the legal system of Liechtenstein. It does not depend on the law or on the decision of Liechtenstein whether that State is entitled to exercise its protection, in the case under consideration. To exercise protection, to apply to the Court, is to place oneself on the plane of international law. It is international law which determines whether a State is entitled to exercise protection and to seise the Court.

The naturalization of Nottebohm was an act performed by Liechtenstein in the exercise of its domestic jurisdiction. The question to be decided is whether that act has the international effect here under consideration. ...

In most cases arbitrators have not strictly speaking had to decide a conflict of nationality as between States, but rather to determine whether the nationality invoked by the applicant State was one which could be relied upon as against the respondent State, that is to say, whether it entitled the applicant State to exercise protection. International arbitrators, having before them allegations of nationality by the applicant State which were contested by the respondent State, have sought to ascertain whether nationality had been conferred by the applicant State in circumstances such as to give rise to an obligation on the part of the respondent State to recognize the effect of that nationality. In order to decide this question arbitrators have evolved certain principles for determining whether full international effect was to be attributed to the nationality invoked. The same issue is now before the Court: it must be resolved by applying the same principles. ...

International arbitrators have decided...numerous cases of dual nationality, where the question arose with regard to the exercise of protection. They have given their preference to the real and effective nationality, that which accorded with the facts, that based on stronger factual ties between the person concerned and one of the States whose nationality is involved. Different factors are taken into consideration, and their importance will vary from one case to the next: the habitual residence of the individual concerned is an important factor, but there are other factors such as the center of his interests, his family ties, his participation in public life, attachment shown by him for a given country and inculcated in his children, etc. …

The same tendency prevails in the writings of publicists and in practice. This notion is inherent in the provisions of Article 3, paragraph 2, of the Statute of the Court. National laws reflect this tendency when, *inter alia,* they make naturalization dependent on conditions indicating the existence of a link, which may vary in their purpose or in their nature but which are essentially concerned with this idea. The Liechtenstein Law of January 4th, 1934, is a good example.

The practice of certain States which refrain from exercising protection in favour of a naturalized person when the latter has in fact, by his prolonged absence, severed his links with what is no longer for him anything but his nominal country, manifests the view of these States that, in order to be capable of being invoked against another State, nationality must correspond with the factual situation. A similar view is manifested in the relevant provisions of the bilateral nationality treaties concluded between the United States of America and other States since 1868, such as those sometimes referred to as the Bancroft Treaties, and in the Pan-American Convention, signed at Rio de Janeiro on August 13th, 1906, on the status of naturalized citizens who resume residence in their country of origin.

The character thus recognized on the international level as pertaining to nationality is in no way inconsistent with the fact that international law leaves it to each State to lay down the rules governing the grant of its own nationality. The reason for this is that the diversity of demographic conditions has thus far made it impossible for any general agreement to be reached on the rules relating to nationality, although the latter by its very nature affects international relations. It has been considered that the best way of making such rules accord with the varying demographic conditions in different countries is to leave the fixing of such rules to the competence of each State. On the other hand, a State cannot claim that the rules it has thus laid down are entitled to recognition by another State unless it has acted in conformity with this general aim of making the legal bond of nationality accord with the individual's genuine connection with the State which assumes the defence of its citizens by means of protection as against other States.

The requirement that such a concordance must exist is to be found in the studies carried on in the course of the last thirty years upon the initiative and under the auspices of the League of Nations and the United Nations. It explains the provision which the Conference for the Codification of International Law, held at The Hague in 1930, inserted in Article I of the Convention relating to the Conflict of Nationality Laws, laying down that the law enacted by a State for the purpose of determining who are its nationals "shall be recognized by other States in so far as it is consistent with … international custom, and the principles of law generally recognized with regard to nationality". In the same spirit, Article 5 of the Convention refers to criteria of the individual's genuine connections for the purpose of resolving questions of dual nationality which arise in third States.

According to the practice of States, to arbitral and judicial decisions and to the opinions of writers, nationality is a legal bond having as its basis a social fact of attachment, a genuine connection of existence, interests and sentiments, together with the existence of reciprocal rights and duties. It may be said to constitute the juridical expression of the fact that the individual upon whom it is conferred, either directly by the law or as the result of an act of the authorities, is in fact more closely connected with the population of the State conferring nationality than with that of any other State. Conferred by a State, it only entitles that State to exercise protection vis-à-vis another State, if it constitutes a translation into juridical terms of the individual's connection with the State which has made him its national.

Diplomatic protection and protection by means of international judicial proceedings constitute measures for the defence of the rights of the State. As the Permanent Court of International Justice has said and has repeated, "by taking up the case of one of its subjects and by resorting to diplomatic action or international judicial proceedings on his behalf, a State is in reality asserting its own rights-its right to ensure, in the person of its subjects, respect for the rules of international law" (P.C.I.J., Series A, No. 2, p. 12, and Series A/B, Nos. 20-21, p. 17).

Since this is the character which nationality must present when it is invoked to furnish the State which has granted it with a title to the exercise of protection and to the institution of international judicial proceedings, the Court must ascertain whether the nationality granted to Nottebohm by means of naturalization is of this character or, in other words, whether the factual connection between Nottebohm and Liechtenstein in the period preceding, contemporaneous with and following his naturalization appears to be sufficiently close, so preponderant in relation to any connection which may have existed between him and any other State, that it is possible to regard the nationality conferred upon him as real and effective, as the exact juridical expression of a social fact of a connection which existed previously or came into existence thereafter.

Naturalization is not a matter to be taken lightly. To seek and to obtain it is not something that happens frequently in the life of a human being. It involves his breaking of a bond of allegiance and his establishment of a new bond of allegiance. It may have far-reaching consequences and involve profound changes in the destiny of the individual who obtains it. It concerns him personally, and to consider it only from the point of view of its repercussions with regard to his property would be to misunderstand its profound significance. In order to appraise its international effect, it is impossible to disregard the circumstances in which it was conferred, the serious character which attaches to it, the real and effective, and not merely the verbal preference of the individual seeking it for the country which grants it to him.

At the time of his naturalization does Nottebohm appear to have been more closely attached by his tradition, his establishment, his interests, his activities, his family ties, his intentions for the near future to Liechtenstein than to any other State? …

At the date when he applied for naturalization Nottebohm had been a German national from the time of his birth. He had always retained his connections with members of his family who had remained in Germany and he had always had business connections with that country. His country had been at war for more than a month, and there is nothing to indicate that the application for naturalization then made by Nottebohm was motivated by any desire to dissociate himself from the Government of his country.

He had been settled in Guatemala for 34 years. He had carried on his activities there. It was the main seat of his interests. He returned there shortly after his naturalization, and it remained the center of his interests and of his business activities. He stayed there until his removal as a result of war measures in 1943. He subsequently attempted to return there, and he now complains of Guatemala's refusal to admit him. There, too, were several members of his family who sought to safeguard his interests.

In contrast, his actual connections with Liechtenstein were extremely tenuous. No settled abode, no prolonged residence in that country at the time of his application for naturalization: the application indicates that he was paying a visit there and confirms the transient character of this visit by its request that the naturalization proceedings should be initiated and concluded without delay. No intention of settling there was shown at that time or realized in the ensuing weeks, months or years-on the contrary, he returned to Guatemala very shortly after his naturalization and showed every intention of remaining there. If Nottebohm went to Liechtenstein in 1946, this was because of the refusal of Guatemala to admit him. No indication is given of the grounds warranting the waiver of the condition of residence, required by the 1934 Nationality Law, which waiver was implicitly granted to him. There is no allegation of any economic interests or of any activities exercised of to be exercised in Liechtenstein, and no manifestation of any intention whatsoever to transfer all or some of his interests and his business activities to Liechtenstein. It is unnecessary in this connection to attribute much importance to the promise to pay the taxes levied at the time of his naturalization. The only links to be discovered between the Principality and Nottebohm are the short sojourns already referred to and the presence in Vaduz of one of his brothers: but his brother's presence is referred to in his application for naturalization only as a reference to his good conduct. Furthermore, other members of his family have asserted Nottebohm's desire to spend his old age in Guatemala.

These facts clearly establish, on the one hand, the absence of any bond of attachment between Nottebohm and Liechtenstein and, on the other hand the existence of a long-standing and close connection between him and Guatemala, a link which his naturalization in no way weakened. That naturalization was not based on any real prior connection with Liechtenstein, nor did in any way alter the manner of life of the person upon whom it was conferred in exceptional circumstances of speed and accommodation. In both respects, it was lacking in the genuineness requisite to an act of such importance, if it is to be entitled to be respected by a State in the position of Guatemala. It was granted without regard to the concept of nationality adopted in international relations.

Naturalization was asked for not so much for the purpose of obtaining legal recognition of Nottebohm's membership in fact in the population of Liechtenstein, as it was to enable him to substitute for his status as a national of a belligerent State that of a national of a neutral State, with the sole aim of thus coming within the protection of Liechtenstein but not of becoming wedded to its traditions, its interests, its way of life or of assuming the obligations-other than fiscal obligations-and exercising the rights pertaining the status thus acquired.

Guatemala is under no obligation to recognize a nationality granted in such circumstances. Liechtenstein consequently is not entitled to extend its protection to Nottebohm vis-à-vis Guatemala and its claim must, for this reason, be held to be inadmissible. ...

JUDGE REED, dissenting:

. . . There have been many instances of double nationality in which international tribunals have been compelled to decide between conflicting claims. In such cases, it has been necessary to choose; and the choice has been determined by the relative strength of the association between the individual concerned and his national State. There have been many instances in which a State has refused to recognize that the naturalization of one of its own citizens has given rise to a right of diplomatic protection, or in which it has refused to treat naturalization as exempting him from the obligations incident to his original citizenship, such as military service.

But the problems presented by conflicting claims to nationality and by double nationality do not arise in this case. There can be no doubt that Mr. Nottebohm lost his German nationality of origin upon his naturalization in Liechtenstein in October 1939. I do not think that it is permissible to transfer criteria designed for cases of double nationality to an essentially different type of relationship.

It is noteworthy that, apart from the cases of double nationality, no instance has been cited to the Court in which a State has successfully refused to recognize that nationality, lawfully conferred and maintained, did not give rise to a right of diplomatic protection. ...

Nationality, and the relation between a citizen and the State to which he owes allegiance, are of such a character that they demand certainty. When one considers the occasions for invoking the relationship—emigration and immigration; travel; treason; exercise of political rights and functions; military service and the like—it becomes evident that certainty is essential. There must be objective tests, readily established, for the existence and recognition of the status. That is why the practice of States has steadfastly rejected vague and subjective tests for the right to confer nationality-sincerity, fidelity, durability, lack of substantial connection-and has clung to the rule of the almost unfettered discretionary power of the State, as embodied in Article I of The Hague Draft Convention of 1931.

NOTES AND QUESTIONS

1. Note that the ICJ, in contrast to the PCIJ, makes the mere exercise of protection over a putative national an "internationalizing act". That result requires the application of international law to the question of the ascription of nationality.

2. Nottebohm was effectively deprived of any hearing on the merits of his claim. What would have been lost if the International Court of Justice had permitted the case to be heard on the merits?

3. Would it be possible to establish a nationality only for purposes of adjudication, a sort of fictitious nationality, akin to a Doe-Roe writ of the common law or a "nationality of convenience?"

4. Who in fact was deciding whether Nottebohm was a Liechtenstein national: Liechtenstein, Guatemala, or the International Court of Justice?

5. The Court seems to presume that this is a competition between Guatemala and Liechtenstein for Nottebohm. Did Guatemala, in fact, purport to ascribe its nationality to Nottebohm?

6. Is The Hague Convention really pertinent to the Nottebohm case?

7. What was the real consequence of this decision? Consider Judge Guggenheim's dissent in *Nottebohm*:

> If the right of protection is abolished, it becomes impossible to consider the merits of certain claims alleging a violation of the rules of international law. If no other State is in a position to exercice [*sic*] diplomatic protection, as in the present case, claims put forward on behalf of an individual, whose nationality is disputed or held to be inoperative on the international level and who enjoys no other nationality, would have to be abandoned. The protection of the individual which is so precarious under existing international law would be weakened even further and I consider that this would be contrary to the basic principle embodied in Article 15 (1) of the Universal Declaration of Human Rights adopted by the General Assembly of the United Nations on December 8th, 1948, according to which everyone has the right to a nationality. Furthermore, refusal to exercise protection is not in accordance with the frequent attempts made at the present time to prevent the increase in the number of cases of stateless persons and to provide protection against acts violating the fundamental human rights recognized by international law as a minimum standard, without distinction as to nationality, religion or race. *Id.* at 63-64.

8. Articles 27 and 28 of the 1954 United Nations Convention Relating to the Status of Stateless Persons provides for the issuance of identity papers and a special travel document for stateless persons:

> Article 27. The Contracting States shall issue identity papers to any stateless person in their territory who does not possess a valid travel document.
>
> Article 28. The Contracting States shall issue to stateless persons lawfully staying in their territory travel documents for the purpose of travel outside their territory, unless compelling reasons of national security or public order otherwise require, and the provisions of the Schedule to this Convention shall apply with respect to such documents. The Contracting States may issue such a travel document to any other stateless persons

> in their territory who are unable to obtain a travel document from the country of their lawful residence.

Does the availability of this document mitigate or eliminate the concern raised by Judge Guggenheim?

b. Flegenheimer Case (United States v. Italy)

Decision of the Italian-U.S. Conciliation Commission, Sep. 20, 2958

14 R.I.A.A. 327, 337, 25 I.L.R. 91 (1958)

[Facts: Albert Flegenheimer sought invalidation of the 1941 sale of his stock in an Italian company, at a nominal sum, to which he assented because of his alleged fear of prevailing Italian anti-Semitic legislation and persecution. The Commission declared the petition filed on his behalf inadmissible on the ground that he was not a "United Nations national" within the scope of Article 78 of the Peace Treaty with Italy.

Albert's father, Samuel Flegenheimer, born in Baden, Germany, had moved to the United States in the 1860's and become a naturalized American citizen in 1873. In 1874, he returned to Germany to live in the then Kingdom of Wurttemberg, where Albert was born in 1890. On August 23, 1894, Samuel Flegenheimer was naturalized in Wurttemberg; and Albert, age 4, together with his brothers was naturalized with his father. Not until 1933, when the Nazis attained power in Germany, was Albert Flegenheimer aware of his father's former American citizenship-and hence of the possibility of his own claim to such citizenship. Thereupon he approached American consulates and embassies in Europe to obtain a determination of his citizenship status, but his inquiries were answered either ambiguously or negatively.

In 1937, because of his fear of Nazi persecution, Albert Flegenheimer left Germany for Italy, Switzerland, and eventually Canada. On November 3, 1939, he formally submitted his claim to American citizenship at the United States Consulate in Winnipeg, Canada. In response later that month, the Board of Special Inquiry of the Immigration and Naturalization Service of the United States decided (erroneously, as later appeared) that he was not an American citizen. In April 1940, he was divested of German nationality by German decree. Subsequently, he took up residence in the United States in 1941-42 on a temporary visa. In February 1942, the Immigration and Naturalization Service acknowledged that Flegenheimer was an American citizen by birth. In October 1946, the Department of State, after an earlier refusal, granted him a United States passport. Subsequent to the commencement of proceedings before the Conciliation Commission, Flegenheimer was issued, on July 10, 1952, a certificate of United States nationality by the Acting Assistant Commissioner, Inspection and Examinations Division, Immigration and Naturalization Service of the United States.]

The competence of the Commission in the instant case is not in doubt. It is based on Article 78, paragraph 3 of the Treaty of Peace which reads as follows:

> The Italian Government shall invalidate transfers involving property, rights and interests of any description belonging to United Nations nationals,

> where such transfers resulted from force or duress exerted by Axis Governments or their agencies during the war". Treaty of Peace with Italy, September 15, 1947, U.S.-Italy, art. 78, 61 Stat. 1245, 49 U.N.T.S. 3. …

On the other hand, the admissibility of the Petition of the Government of the United States is uncertain, because there exists a dispute between the High Parties on an element of fact required by Article 78, paragraph 9, letter (a) of the Treaty of Peace with Italy which provides:

> 'United Nations nationals' means individuals who are nationals of any of the United Nations, or corporations or associations organized under the laws of any of the United Nations, at the coming into force of the present Treaty, provided that the said individuals, corporations or associations also had this status on September 3, 1943, the date of the Armistice with Italy.
>
> The term 'United Nations nationals' also includes all individuals, corporations, or associations which, under the laws in force in Italy during the war, have been treated as enemy. *Id.* …

It is clear that the afore-mentioned provision of the Treaty of Peace, in explaining the meaning of "United Nations nationals" refers to an unquestionable principle of international law according to which every State is sovereign in establishing the legal conditions which must be fulfilled by an individual in order that he may be considered to be vested with its nationality.

The lengthy arguments developed both in the written proceedings and in the oral hearings by the Agents and Counsel for both Parties, on the title to nationality of the United States, suffice to establish that they [the Parties] consider this right to be determinant in deciding Albert Flegenheimer's nationality and that the Commission will have to submit to the jurisprudential or conventional legal content thereof when it has established the rules that must be applied; in other words, the Commission will have to admit or reject, at the international level, a nationality, the existence or inexistence of which shall be established, in its opinion in full compliance with the law, at the national level.

Nevertheless, the Commission recalls that, according to a well established international jurisprudence, where international law and the international bodies who must apply that law are concerned "national laws are simple facts, an indication of the will and the activity of States, just like judicial decisions or administrative measures" (P.C.I.J. Decision of May 25, 1926, case relating to certain German interests in Upper Silesia, series A, No. 7, P. 19).

The result is that, in an international dispute, official declarations, testimonials or certificates do not have the same effect as in municipal law. They are statements made by one of the Parties to the dispute which, when denied, must be proved like every other allegation. It is the duty of this Commission to establish Albert Flegenheimer's true nationality at the relevant dates specified in Article 78, paragraph 9 of the Treaty of Peace, and it has a right to go into all the elements of fact or of law which would establish whether the claimant actually was, on the aforementioned dates, vested with the nationality of the United States; these investigations are necessary in order to decide whether the international action, instituted in his behalf, fulfills the conditions required by the Treaty of Peace from which the Commission cannot deviate. It must therefore freely examine whether an administrative decision, such as that taken in favor of Albert Flegenheimer in the United States, was of such a nature as to be convincing.

The profound reason for these broad powers of appreciation which are guaranteed to an international court for resolving questions of nationality, even though coming within the reserved domain of States, is based on the principle, undenied in matters of arbitration, that complete equality must be enjoyed by both Parties to an international dispute. If it were to be ignored, one of the Parties would be placed in a state of inferiority vis-a-vis the other, because it would then suffice for the Plaintiff State to affirm that any given person is vested with its nationality for the Defendant State to be powerless to prevent an abusive practice of diplomatic protection by its Opponent.

The right of challenge of the international court authorizing it to determine whether, behind the nationality certificate or the acts of naturalization produced, the right to citizenship was regularly acquired, is in conformity with the very broad rule of effectivity which dominates the Law of Nations entirely and allows the court to fulfill its legal function and remove the inconveniences specified.

During these proceedings, the Agent of the United States and his Counsel have nevertheless persistently contended that the certificate of nationality issued to Albert Flegenheimer on July 10, 1952, under American law, constitutes legally valid proof of his nationality, and that the nature of this proof is such as to be binding on this Commission, unless it were proved that the aforesaid certificate was obtained by fraud or favoritism such as to allow the claimant to avail himself of the diplomatic protection of the United States and, as a consequence, benefit by the reparation provisions of the Treaty of Peace with Italy, and of the Commission's jurisdiction. In the latter part of their allegations, they contended that it would be sufficient for Albert Flegenheimer's American nationality to be plausibly established in order to avoid any challenge and investigation by the Commission. ...

The Commission, in conformity with the case law of international tribunals, holds that it is not bound by the provisions of the national law in question, either as regards the manner or as regards the form in which proof of nationality must be submitted. .

The Commission, on the basis of the research made in jurisprudence and authoritative doctrine, holds that its powers of investigation as to whether Albert Flegenheimer validly acquired United States nationality are all the less disputable in that no American judgment of naturalization has been introduced during these proceedings but a mere administrative statement which, according to the international practice commonly followed, is subjected to the valuation of every court, whether national or international, to which the question of the validity of a nationality is submitted.

The Commission nevertheless considers that the observations made by the commentators of the *Medina* case cannot be ignored, and that international jurisdictions must act with the greatest caution and exercise their powers of investigation only if the criticism directed by one Party against the allegations of the other, not only are not manifestly groundless, but are of such gravity as to cause serious doubts in the minds of their Members with regard to the reality and truth of the nationality invoked.

In the instant case, the grounds for doubt in connection with Albert Flegenheimer's nationality are so numerous and so patent, that the Commission could allow him to benefit by Article 78 of the Treaty of Peace with Italy only if all the doubts, raised in its mind over the facts on the basis of which the certificate of United States nationality was issued, were dispelled.

These facts are first of all connected with the validity of Samuel Flegenheimer's naturalization in the United States from which flows the acquisition *jure sanguinis*, of his son Albert's American nationality; subsequently with the loss by the latter of his American nationality as a result of his naturalization together with his father in Wurttemberg in 1894, when he was still a minor; with the long sojourn of the interested party, as a German national, in Germany from 1904 to 1937, with his entry into Canada on February 10, 1939 before the outbreak of World War II, on a German passport which was renewed to him a few days later by the German Consulate at Winnipeg, and then in 1941 by the Swiss Consul in that city, who had taken over the protection of German interests.

The Commission's grounds for doubt are further increased when acquiring knowledge, from the documents in the record, of the fact that all inquiries for information made by Albert Flegenheimer at consular offices and even at an Embassy of the United States in Europe in connection with his American nationality only resulted in negative or dubious answers; that, if he succeeded in obtaining an authorization of making, at the outset, only temporary sojourns in the United States, his case gave rise to conflicting decisions by the State Department and by the Immigration Service of the Department of justice of the United States; that at the time of the inquests to which he was subjected by American officials, he made statements which are not entirely consistent; that the authorization which was accorded to him to enter the United States as a German national was only modified by a decision of the Immigration and Naturalization Service of February 24, 1942, in the sense that he was thereafter qualified as a citizen of the United States, but that the subsequent inquests which resulted in this amendment of the record of his entry, are defined as irregular by the American counsel for the Italian Government in these proceedings.

This Commission cannot fail to take notice of the fact that the State Department on May 14, 1946 refused at first to issue an American passport to Albert Flegenheimer, and that if later on October 24, 1946, it did decide to issue a passport, it specified that this document would not be renewed; that even after the institution of legal action before this Commission on behalf of Albert Flegenheimer on June 26, 1951, the application for a certificate of citizenship made by him gave rise to a dispute between the State Department and the Department of Justice of the United States; that on May 8, 1952 Albert Flegenheimer then swore to an *ex parte* affidavit in which he explained his case; that the "Examining Officer" nevertheless concluded that his application should be refused, but the "Acting Assistant Commissioner" held that the petitioner was to be considered as a United States citizen on the basis of his own statements, on the scarcely convincing grounds that there could be no other alternative than that of considering them as completely incorrect or entirely correct; that he concluded by following this latter course which resulted in the issuance of the certificate of nationality of July 10, 1952, more than one year after the Petition was submitted to this Commission. Lastly, this Commission cannot but be impressed by the fact that the precedent of the Supreme Court of the United States in the Perkins vs. Elg case, 307 U.S. 325 (1939),, which instigated the decision of the American administrative authorities in Albert Flegenheimer's favor, was already known at the time the preceding negative decisions were rendered, and that the effects which the Bancroft Treaties might have had on the nationality of Albert Flegenheimer were not examined by the American authorities. Hence, Albert Flegenheimer's nationality is far from presenting such a character of certitude and of clarity as to entail conviction.

This Commission owes it to itself, as it owes it to the two States who have placed their confidence in it so as to assure a correct application of Article 78 of the Treaty of Peace with Italy, 49 U.N.T.S. 3 (1950), to make an objective search for the truth and to clarify the legal position which, as far as the Commission, in its capacity as an international organ, is concerned is Albert Flegenheimer's factual position. . . .

On the basis of the foregoing considerations of fact and of law, this Commission concludes:

1. that Albert Flegenheimer acquired by filiation the nationality of the United States, at birth, in Wurttemberg on July 4, 1890;

2. that he acquired German and Wurttemberg nationality as the result of his naturalization in Wurttemberg on August 23, 1894, and thereby lost, after five years' residence in his new home country, his American nationality, under the Bancroft Treaty concluded on July 2, 1868, between the United States of America and Wurttemberg;

3. that he never re-acquired his American nationality after reaching majority;

4. that he was therefore vested solely with German and Wurttemberg nationality, after five years' residence in Germany, that is, beginning from 1895 until the German decree of April 29, 1940, published on May 4, 1940, declaring he had forfeited that nationality;

5. that he became stateless beginning from this latter date, but that he did not prove that he was treated as enemy by the Italian authorities during his stay in the countries at war with Italy, Canada first and later the United States;

6. that he was never naturalized in the United States since he took up residence in that country in 1941-1942;

7. that the certificate issued to him by the United States authorities on July 10, 1952, subsequent to the filing of the Petition in the instant case with this Commission, on June 25, 1951, and after the new administrative investigations by the American authorities in 1952, which were also held subsequent to the date of the pending legal action, is not of a nature to prove, to the full satisfaction of law, that Albert Flegenheimer fulfills the conditions required by Article 78, para. g (a), sub-para. 1 of the Treaty of Peace with Italy, for the purpose of being considered as a United Nations national; nor does he fulfill the conditions required by Article V of the Lovett-Lombardo Agreement;

8. that it is not established that he fulfills the conditions of Article 78, para. 9 (a), sub-para. 2 of the aforesaid Treaty of Peace.

NOTES AND QUESTIONS

1. Is *Flegenheimer* consistent with *Nottebohm?* State the Tribunal's theory of allocation of competence with respect to ascription of nationality.

2. Do either of the above cases distinguish the competence to ascribe nationality according to the purpose for which the nationality is sought? Would this be a pertinent distinction?

3. Should ascriptions of nationality for purposes of procedural access be treated more liberally?

4. For a detailed analysis of state practice regarding genuine link, fraud, and abuse of rights claims as limiting the authority of states to confer nationality, *see* SIEGFRIED WIESSNER, DIE FUNKTION DER STAATSANGEHÖRIGKEIT, *supra,* at 66-84. The author reaches the following result:

> (1) The requirement of a genuine link does not generally limit states' power to naturalize; to view it as such would over-interpret *Nottebohm.*
>
> (2) Fraud in the process of naturalization may, however, well lead to the invalidity of the naturalization thus tainted.
>
> (3) The claim of abuse of discretion as an international legal bar to states' naturalization power is controversial; in restrictive definition it is, however, part and parcel of present-day international law.
>
> (4) There are no other factors limiting the freedom of states to naturalize.
>
> *Id.* at 79.

5. On claims that the authoritative determination of the state is conclusive in the absence of fraud, error, favoritism, and other general limits of international law, see *Flegenheimer, supra.* Hans Goldschmidt, *Recent Applications of Domestic Nationality Laws by International Tribunals,* 28 FORDHAM L. REV. 689 (1959-60); Santvinder S. Juss, *Nationality Law, Sovereignty, and the Doctrine of Exclusive Domestic Jurisdiction,* 9 FLA. J. INT'L L. 219 (1994). *See also* Mergé Claim, *infra,* at 429.

* * *

There are a number of traditional and more recent conventional prescriptions about a state's competence to ascribe nationality at birth or on certain contingencies.

3. *Jus Soli* and *Jus Sanguinis* as Bases for Ascription of Nationality

a. Harvard Research in International Law: *The Law of Nationality*

23 AM. J. INT'L L. SPEC. SUP. 13, 27-31 (1929)

It is believed that no basis other than *jus soli* or *jus sanguinis* can be found upon which nationality at birth can properly be conferred, although laws based upon either principle differ in various ways.

As to the term "place assimilated thereto," it may be noted that this draft does not attempt to define such places. For various purposes, ships, protectorates, mandated territory and leased territory have been assimilated to national territory. .

The fact that both *jus soli* and *jus sanguinis* are recognized in the convention makes it necessary to admit the existence of dual nationality at birth under some circumstances. . . [T]he complete elimination of dual nationality at birth would require the adoption of a uniform rule and the consequent elimination of either *jus soli* or *jus sanguinis*. In view of the historical antecedents of the two bases and the fact that each is now embedded in the laws and constitutions of many states, the elimination of either seems impracticable at the present time.

While *jus sanguinis* is no doubt the older of the two principles, national character having originated with membership in the family or tribe, and while this principle is now the basis of the nationality laws of most countries of the continent of Europe as well as of Asia, for many centuries *jus soli* was the basis of nationality in all countries in which the feudal system obtained. This system was in effect in France until the adoption of the Code Napoleon in 1803. ... The change in the French laws was followed by changes in the laws of other European countries. . .

Jus soli ... is still the basis of the nationality laws of Great Britain and the United States and of most of the Latin American states. ...

The nationality laws of most states which are based solely or principally on *jus sanguinis* contain no limitation upon the acquisition of their nationality by descendants of their nationals born abroad. Thus the nationality of such states may be transmitted indefinitely to successive generations of persons born and continuing to reside abroad. ...

* * *

The 1997 European Convention on Nationality found the following solution:

b. European Convention on Nationality

Nov. 6, 1997, 37 I.L.M. 44 (1998)

Article 6: *Acquisition of nationality*

1. Each State Party shall provide in its internal law for its nationality to be acquired *ex lege* by the following persons:

a. children one of whose parents possesses, at the time of the birth of these children, the nationality of that State Party, subject to any exceptions which may be provided for by its internal law as regards children born abroad. With respect to children whose parenthood is established by recognition, court order or similar procedures, each State Party may provide that the child acquires its nationality following the procedure determined by its internal law;

b. foundlings found in its territory who would otherwise be stateless.

2. Each State Party shall provide in its internal law for its nationality to be acquired by children born on its territory who do not acquire at birth another nationality. Such nationality shall be granted:

a. at birth *ex lege*; or

b. subsequently, to children who remained stateless, upon an application being lodged with the appropriate authority, by or on behalf of the child concerned, in the manner prescribed by the internal law of the State Party. Such an application may be made subject to the lawful and habitual residence on its territory for a period not exceeding five years immediately preceding the lodging of the application.

3. Each State Party shall provide in its internal law for the possibility of naturalisation of persons lawfully and habitually resident on its territory. In establishing the conditions for naturalisation, it shall not provide for a period of residence exceeding ten years before the lodging of an application.

4. Each State Party shall facilitate in its internal law the acquisition of its nationality for the following persons:

a. spouses of its nationals;

b. children of one of its nationals, falling under the exception of Article 6, paragraph 1, sub-paragraph a;

c. children one of whose parents acquires or has acquired its nationality;

d. children adopted by one of its nationals;

e. persons who were born on its territory and reside there lawfully and habitually;

f. persons who are lawfully and habitually resident on its territory for a period of time beginning before the age of 18, that period to be determined by the internal law of the State Party concerned;

g. stateless persons and recognised refugees lawfully and habitually resident on its territory.

4. An Internationally Guaranteed Right to a Nationality?

Given the fact that not only the right of a state to diplomatically protect a person is predicated upon nationality, but that there are certain legal consequences commonly attached to possession of this status, which are, for the most part, supported by international human rights instruments, it does not come as a surprise that individual claims have been made to possession of at least that root status. The plight of a stateless person has been vividly described:

a. Myres S. McDougal, Harold D. Lasswell & Lung-chu Chen, *Nationality and Human Rights*
83 YALE L.J. 900, 960 (1974)

The status of statelessness entails a most severe and dramatic deprivation of the power of an individual. Just as within the state nationality is the "right to have rights," so also on the transnational level nationality is the right to have protection in rights. The stateless person has no state to "protect" him and lacks even the freedom of movement to find a state that is willing to protect him. His participation in the value processes of any territorial community is highly restricted. As aptly stated in the preamble of one Draft Convention, statelessness

> often results in suffering and hardship shocking to conscience and offensive to the dignity of man, ...
>
> is frequently productive of friction between States, ...
>
> is inconsistent with the existing principle which postulates nationality as a condition of the enjoyment by the individual of certain rights recognized by international law. ...

Most importantly, nationality is commonly regarded as essential for a state to protect an individual vis-à-vis other entities in the transnational arena. In the words of Oppenheim-Lauterpacht,

> Since stateless individuals do not own a nationality, the principal link by which they could derive benefits from International Law is missing, and thus they lack protection as far as this Law is concerned.

Thus, a stateless person has been compared to "a *res nullius*," a "flotsam," a vessel "on the open sea not sailing under the flag of a State," "a *caput lupinum*," "a bird that flies alone," and "an international vagabond." The hardship visited upon a stateless person is dramatically evident in the *Dickson Car Wheel Company Case,* 4 R.I.A.A. 669 (1931), in which the Special Claims Commission between the United States and Mexico declared in 1931:

> A State . . . does not commit an international delinquency in inflicting an injury upon an individual lacking nationality, and consequently no State is empowered to intervene or complain on his behalf either before or after injury.

In short, statelessness means "the loss of a community willing and able to guarantee any rights whatsoever."

The powerlessness of the stateless person is most apparent in the limitation upon his freedom of movement, both of egress and of return. Because of widespread, rigorous requirements for travel documents (e. g., a valid passport, an entry visa), a stateless person, lacking necessary documents, usually experiences great difficulty in locating a state willing to receive him. Unable to enter the territory of a state lawfully, he is often compelled to do so clandestinely. His illegal entry continues to haunt him. "He will then," as has been observed, "lead an illegal existence, avoiding all contact with the authorities and living under the constant threat of discovery and expulsion."

* * *

The Universal Declaration of Human Rights of 1948 did provide a response to the claims to a nationality, albeit an inchoate one:

b. Universal Declaration of Human Rights

G.A. Res. 217, 3rd Sess., at 71, U.N. Doc. A/RES/ 217(III) (1948)

Article 15

1. Every one has the right to a nationality.

2. No one shall be arbitrarily deprived of his nationality nor denied the right to change his nationality.

* * *

The formulation of the "right to a nationality" is inchoate since it does not provide for the determination of a government that is the proper addressee of the alleged entitlement: is it, or should it be, the state on whose territory the stateless person is born? Is it the parents' home state? Is, or should any other link be relevant? In a case of statelessness after birth: Is it, or should the target country be the one who caused the instance of statelessness? The latter solution would seem to imply an absolute prohibition of deprivation of nationality in the regular case of a person with only one nationality — how would this be compatible with section 2 which prohibits only "arbitrary" deprivations of nationality?

A "right to a nationality" has not been granted in the 1966 International Covenant on Civil and Political Rights, nor has it been included in the regional human rights instruments. A general right to a nationality, although similarly unspecified as to the target state, has been formulated in the 1989 Convention on the Rights of the Child:

c. 1989 Convention on the Rights of the Child

U.N. GAOR, 44th Sess., Agenda Item 108, U.N. Doc. A/44/736 (1989)

Article 7

1. The child shall be registered immediately after birth and shall have the right from birth to a name, the right to acquire a nationality and, as far as possible, the right to know and be cared for by his or her parents.

2. States Parties shall ensure the implementation of these rights in accordance with their national law and their obligations under the relevant international instruments in this field, in particular where the child would otherwise be stateless.

* * *

The 1997 European Convention on Nationality has made the "right to a nationality" and the avoidance of statelessness basic policies of domestic nationality laws:

d. European Convention on Nationality

Nov. 6, 1997, 37 I.L.M. 44 (1998)

Article 4: *Principles*

The rules on nationality of each State Party shall be based on the following principles:

a. everyone has the right to a nationality;

b. statelessness shall be avoided;

c. no one shall be arbitrarily deprived of his or her nationality;

d. neither marriage nor the dissolution of a marriage between a national of a State Party and an alien, nor the change of nationality by one of the spouses during marriage, shall automatically affect the nationality of the other spouse.

* * *

The United Nations has adopted a specific treaty to deal with the problem of statelessness, i.e. the Convention on the Reduction of Statelessness of August 30, 1961. It addresses the aforementioned concerns:

e. United Nations Convention on the Reduction of Statelessness

Aug. 30, 1961, 989 U.N.T.S. 175

Article 1

1. A Contracting State shall grant its nationality to a person born in its territory who would otherwise be stateless. Such nationality shall be granted:

(a) At birth, by operation of law, or

(b) Upon an application being lodged with the appropriate authority, by or on behalf of the person concerned, in the manner prescribed by the national law. …

Article 2

A foundling found in the territory of a Contracting State shall, in the absence of proof to the contrary, be considered to have been born within that territory of parents possessing the nationality of that State. …

Article 4

1. A Contracting State shall grant its nationality to a person, not born in the territory of a Contracting State, who would otherwise be stateless, if the nationality of one of his parents at the time of the person's birth was that of that State. …

NOTES AND QUESTIONS

1. For details on international efforts to alleviate the situation of stateless persons, *see* A. PETER MUTHARIKA, THE REGULATION OF STATELESSNESS UNDER INTERNATIONAL AND NATIONAL LAW (Oceana Publications 1977). *See also* Paul Weis, *The United Nations Convention on the Reduction of Statelessness, 1961,* 11 INT'L & COMP. L.Q. 1073 (1962); S. Torres Bernardez, *La Conférence des Nations Unies pour l'élimination ou la réduction des cas d'apatridie dans l'avenir — La Convention sur la réduction des cas d'apatridie,* 1962 ANNUAIRE FRANÇAIS DE DROIT INTERNATIONAL 528; Milton C. Lorenz, Jr., *Aliens – Renunciation of Nationality Leaves Individual Stateless and Excludable as Any Alien,* 46 TUL. L. REV. 984 (1972); PAUL WEIS, NATIONALITY AND STATELESSNESS IN INTERNATIONAL LAW (2d ed., Hyperion Press 1979).

2. Does the 1961 Convention grant a "right to a nationality?" Should this right have been included in the 1966 Human Rights Covenant? Does a state obligation under the 1961 Convention satisfy the interests of the individual concerned?

3. How would the postulated "right to change" one's nationality under Article 15(2) of the Universal Declaration be effectuated? Is it good policy? What are the likely consequences of such an unbounded freedom to change state affiliation? What states would be the main targets of people interested in such change?

5. Inclusive Policies Against Discrimination in Ascription of Nationality

The international community, while reluctant to grant positive rights to a nationality, was more willing to concede prohibitions, in various human rights instruments, of discriminatory practices with respect to the granting of withdrawal of nationality. Compare the following multilateral treaties:

a. International Convention on the Elimination of All Forms of Racial Discrimination

Dec. 21, 1965, U.N. GAOR, U.N. Doc A/RES/2106A (1965)

Article 1

3. Nothing in this Convention may be interpreted as affecting in any way the legal provisions of States Parties concerning nationality, citizenship or naturalization, provided that such provisions do not discriminate against any particular nationality.

b. Convention on the Nationality of Married Women

Feb. 20, 1957, U.N. GAOR, U.N. Doc. A/RES/1040 (XI) (1957)

Article 3

1. Each Contracting State agrees that the alien wife of one of its nationals may, at her request, acquire the nationality of her husband through specially privileged naturalization procedures; the grant of such nationality may be subject to such limitations as may be imposed in the interests of national security or public policy.

2. Each Contracting State agrees that the present Convention shall not be construed as affecting any legislation or judicial practice by which the alien wife of one of its nationals may, at her request, acquire her husband's nationality as a matter of right.

c. Convention on the Elimination of All Forms of Discrimination Against Women

Dec. 18, 1979, U.N. GAOR, 107th Sess., U.N. Doc. A/RES/34/180(1979)

Article 9

1. States Parties shall grant women equal rights with men to acquire, change or retain their nationality. They shall ensure in particular that neither marriage to an alien nor change of nationality by the husband during marriage shall automatically change the nationality of the wife, render her stateless or force upon her the nationality of the husband.

d. European Convention on Nationality

Nov. 6, 1997, 37 I.L.M. 44 (1998)

Article 5: *Non-discrimination*

1. The rules of a State Party on nationality shall not contain distinctions or include any practice which amount to discrimination on the grounds of sex, religion, race, colour or national or ethnic origin.

2. Each State Party shall be guided by the principle of non-discrimination between its nationals, whether they are nationals by birth or have acquired its nationality subsequently.

6. Ascription of Nationality on Transfer of Territory

What policies should govern ascriptions of nationality of inhabitants when territory is transferred from one state to another? Consider the *Uhl* case.

a. United States ex rel. Schwarzkopf v. Uhl

137 F.2d 898 (2d Cir. 1943)

Acting under the presidential proclamation of December 8, 1941, No. 2526, 6 Fed,Reg. 6323 (1941), promulgated pursuant to the Act of July 6, 1798 as amended, 50 U.S.C.A. § 21, agents of the Department of Justice arrested the relator as an alien enemy. An Alien Enemy Hearing Board recommended that he be interned, and the acting attorney general so ordered. To test the legality of his detention, the relator sued out a writ of habeas corpus. . . . [T]he writ was forthwith dismissed and the relator remanded to custody; ... This appeal followed. ...

The relator is a Jew born in 1886 in the city of Prague, Bohemia, which was then within the Austro-Hungarian Empire. In 1919 Prague became part of Czechoslovakia and the relator became a citizen of that country. In 1925 he became a citizen of the German Republic by naturalization, being then in business in Berlin. In 1927 he removed from Germany to the Austrian Tyrol and in 1933 became a naturalized citizen of Austria, his former German citizenship being thereby automatically terminated. In October 1936 he arrived in the United States for permanent residence as a quota immigrant under the Czechoslovakian quota. When Hitier's forces invaded Austria in March 1938, the relator was resident in the United States and on June 17, 1938, he declared his intention to become a United States citizen. He applied for naturalization on September 26, 1941. This application was pending when he was taken into custody as an alien enemy on December 9, 1941.

The legal question for decision is whether the conceded facts bring the appellant within the class of aliens whose restraint is authorized under the statute, 50 U.S.C.A. § 21, and the presidential proclamation pursuant to which he is held. That statute provides that: "Whenever . . . any invasion or predatory incursion is . . . threatened against the territory of the United States by any foreign nation or government, and the President makes public proclamation of the event, all natives, citizens, denizens, or subjects of the hostile nation or government, being of the age of fourteen years and upward, who shall be within the United States and not actually naturalized, shall be liable to be apprehended, restrained, secured, and removed as alien enemies." The President is authorized to direct "the manner and degree" of their restraint "and in what cases," and "to establish any other regulations which are found necessary in the premises and for the public safety." On December 8, 1941, the President issued Proclamation No. 2526, published in

6 Fed.Reg. 6323 (1941), by which he proclaimed that "an invasion or predatory incursion is threatened upon the territory of the United States by Germany," and directed the attorney general to cause the apprehension of such alien enemies as in his judgment are subject to apprehension under regulations incorporated in the presidential proclamation.

With the attorney general's finding that restraint of the appellant is required as a measure of public safety the courts have no concern. . [T]he relator's writ of habeas corpus can raise only the question whether he is an alien enemy within the statutory definition, that is, whether he is a "native, citizen, denizen or subject" of Germany.

The United States attorney relies solely on the word "citizen." He argues that the relator was an Austrian citizen on March 13, 1938, the date of the annexation of Austria by Germany, and became a German citizen by virtue of the German decree of July 3, 1938, which granted German citizenship to all Austrian citizens; that the United States has recognized the de facto sovereignty of Germany over the territory formerly Austria, and our courts must recognize and give effect to the German decree of July 3rd. It is further contended that our courts must disregard the German "Executive Order" of November 25, 1941 which purports to deprive Jews residing abroad of German citizenship and to subject their property to confiscation.

It is not claimed that the United States has accorded de jure recognition to Germany's annexation of Austrian territory. Clearly no such claim could be successfully asserted in view of the public declaration by the Secretary of State that "This Government has never taken the position that Austria was legally absorbed into the German Reich." ... Even if de facto recognition be assumed it does not follow that it affects the nationality of those under the domination of the de facto power ... or that the relator thereby becomes a citizen of Germany within the meaning of a statute of the United States. Indeed, in our view, the dispute as to recognition or non-recognition by the United States of the conquest of Austria raises a wholly irrelevant issue.

The issue for decision is whether the relator is a "citizen" of Germany within the meaning of the Alien Enemy Act. The obvious purpose of that Act was to include within its ambit all aliens who by reason of ties of nativity or allegiance might be likely to favor "the hostile nation or government" and might therefore commit acts dangerous to our public safety if allowed to remain at large. Congress selected the words "natives, citizens, denizens, or subjects" as an all inclusive description. In determining who are "citizens" of a foreign nation our courts must consider not only the municipal law of the foreign nation but also the accepted rules and practices under international law. If the relator's citizenship be tested by the municipal law of Germany-disregarding for the moment the cancellation of his German citizenship by the November 1941 "Executive Order"-the claim that he is a citizen of Germany must be based upon the conquest and annexation of Austria and the decree of July 3, 1938 granting German citizenship to all citizens of Austria. But under generally accepted principles of international law Germany could impose citizenship by annexation (collective naturalization) only on those who were inhabitants of Austria in 1938. This question is discussed in Oppenheim, International Law, 5th Ed., 1, sec. 240. He states that it is the American view that only the "inhabitants" who "remain" in the territory, or by treaty are permitted to elect the new nationality, are to be deemed nationals of the annexing state. He then calls attention to a contrary opinion expressed by a Prussian court in 1868. There a cabinet minister of King George of Hanover left Hanover for Vienna, in company with the king, before the annexation of Hanover by Prussia in 1866. In 1868, while in Vienna, he was tried for high treason by a Prussian court in Berlin. This court held that he became a Prussian subject by reason of the annexation, but this view has been severely criticized as erroneous by several learned writers on the subject, and by none, so far as we know, has it been approved. … These commentators maintain that when territory is transferred to a new sovereign by conquest or cession the inhabitants of the territory become nationals of the new government only by their own consent, express or implicit. This generally accepted principle of international law has been recognized in the decisions of the Supreme Court. If the inhabitants remain within the territory their allegiance is transferred to the new sovereign. *American Insurance Co. v. 356 Bales of Cotton*, 26 U.S. 511 (1828). If they have voluntarily departed before the annexation and have never elected to accept the sovereignty of the new government, their allegiance is not so transferred. …

The respondent concedes the principle that an inhabitant of conquered or ceded territory can elect whether to retain his old nationality or accept the nationality of the new sovereign, but denies its applicability because there is no Austrian government in exile, as there is in the case of certain countries invaded by Germany, for example, Norway and Holland. Aside from the discredited Prussian case already mentioned, the only authority cited for such distinction is *Brown v. United States*, 5 Ct.Cl. 571 (1869), which does not, in our opinion, support it. On general principles of justice we think that civilized nations should not recognize the asserted distinction. If the invaded country has ceased to exist as an independent state there would seem to be all the more reason for allowing its former nationals, who have fled from the invader and established a residence abroad, the right of voluntarily electing a new nationality and remaining "stateless" until they can acquire it. In our view an invader cannot under international law impose its nationality upon non-residents of the subjugated country without their consent, express or tacit.

The statute under consideration was passed shortly after the American Revolution and the members of the Congress which enacted it were certainly not unfamiliar with the fact that British subjects resident in the Colonies did not automatically become citizens of the United States but were accorded the right to elect to retain their former nationality if they removed themselves from this country. We cannot doubt therefore that the word "citizen" as used in the statute must be construed in the light of this accepted right of election. So construed the appellant is not a citizen of Germany within the meaning of the Act. More than a year before the German conquest he fled from Austria and came to this country for permanent residence, and nothing is shown to indicate that he has ever consented to accept the sovereignty of the invader.

Moreover, if we were to deny the relator the right of election and were to look solely to German law to determine his status, he would not be a German citizen. If it be assumed that he acquired German citizenship by the annexation of Austria and the decree of July 3rd, such citizenship was lost under German law in November 1941. There is no public policy of this country to preclude an American court from recognizing the power of Germany to disclaim Schwarzkopf as a German citizen. The cases relied upon by the respondent relate to giving effect to foreign confiscation of property having an American situs-an entirely different matter from conceding that a foreign state may determine for itself who shall have the rights and privileges of citizenship. The statute does not authorize the apprehension and detention of all persons whose presence here may be found by the President to be dangerous to public safety. Unfortunately, even citizens of the United States or aliens owing allegiance to some friendly nation, may disregard their duty and commit acts favoring the enemy. But they cannot for that reason be held in custody under the statute in question. No more can the appellant. Upon the conceded facts be is not a German citizen and that is the only ground upon which the respondent justifies detention of him. The writ must be sustained and the appellant discharged from custody. It is so ordered.

b. United Nations Convention on the Reduction of Statelessness

Aug. 30, 1961, 989 U.N.T.S. 175 (1961)

Article 10

1. Every treaty between Contracting States providing for the transfer of territory shall include provisions designed to secure that no person shall become stateless as a result of the transfer. A Contracting State shall use its best endeavors to secure that any such treaty made by it with a State which is not a party to this Convention includes such provisions.

2. In the absence of such provisions a Contracting State to which territory is transferred or which otherwise acquires territory shall confer its nationality on such persons as would otherwise become stateless as a result of the transfer or acquisition.

NOTES AND QUESTIONS

1. Is the United Nations treaty perspective the best one for a global order of human dignity? What if, as in the Uhl case, the automatic conferment of nationality would result in severe deprivations of values, such as treatment as an enemy alien even if residing abroad at the time of annexation?

2. Should any resident of the transferred territory have the option to choose the nationality of the successor country? What should be the consequences of inaction? What about citizens of the transferring country now living abroad? Should they be treated differently?

3. The International Law Commission has considered the related issue of state succession and its impact on the nationality of natural and legal persons. *See* FIRST REPORT ON STATE SUCCESSION AND ITS IMPACT ON THE NATIONALITY OF NATURAL AND LEGAL PERSONS by Mr. Václav Mikulka, Special Rapporteur, U.N. Doc. A/CN.4/467, 17 April 1995; and SECOND REPORT ON STATE SUCCESSION AND ITS IMPACT ON THE NATIONALITY OF NATURAL AND LEGAL PERSONS by Mr. Václav Mikulka, Special Rapporteur, U.N. Doc. A/CN.4/474, 17 April 1996. The work resulted in Draft Articles on Nationality of Natural Persons in Relation to the Succession of States, summarized in INTERNATIONAL LAW COMMISSION: DRAFT ARTICLES ON NATIONALITY OF NATURAL PERSONS IN RELATION TO THE SUCCESSION OF STATES, U.N. Doc. A/CN.4/L.573 (May 27, 1999), ASIL INT'L LAW IN BRIEF, Sept. 13-24, 1999, and, ultimately, in the United Nations General Assembly's Articles on Nationality of Natural Persons in relation to the Succession of States of December 12, 2000:

Articles on Nationality of Natural Persons in Relation to the Succession of States
U.N. GAOR, 55th Sess., U.N. Doc. A/Res/55/153 (Dec. 12, 2000)

Article 1: *Right to a nationality*

Every individual who, on the date of the succession of States, had the nationality of the predecessor State, irrespective of the mode of acquisition of that nationality, has the right to the nationality of at least one of the States concerned, in accordance with the present articles. …

Article 4: *Prevention of statelessness*

States concerned shall take all appropriate measures to prevent persons who, on the date of the succession of States, had the nationality of the predecessor State from becoming stateless as a result of such succession.

Article 5: *Presumption of nationality*

Subject to the provisions of the present articles, persons concerned having their habitual residence in the territory affected by the succession of States are presumed to acquire the nationality of the successor State on the date of such succession. …

Article 8: *Persons concerned having their habitual residence in another State*

1. A successor State does not have the obligation to attribute its nationality to persons concerned who have their habitual residence in another State and also have the nationality of that or any other State.

2. A successor State shall not attribute its nationality to persons concerned who have their habitual residence in another State against the will of the persons concerned unless they would otherwise become stateless. ...

Article 11: *Respect for the will of persons concerned*

1. States concerned shall give consideration to the will of persons concerned whenever those persons are qualified to acquire the nationality of two or more States concerned.

2. Each State concerned shall grant a right to opt for its nationality to persons concerned who have appropriate connection with that State if those persons would otherwise become stateless as a result of the succession of States.

3. When persons entitled to the right of option have exercised such right, the State whose nationality they have opted for shall attribute its nationality to such persons.

4. When persons entitled to the right of option have exercised such right, the State whose nationality they have renounced shall withdraw its nationality from such persons, unless they would thereby become stateless.

5. States concerned should provide a reasonable time limit for the exercise of the right of option.

Article 12: *Unity of a family*

Where the acquisition or loss of nationality in relation to the succession of States would impair the unity of a family, States concerned shall take all appropriate measures to allow that family to remain together or to be reunited. ...

Article 19: *Other States*

1. Nothing in the present articles requires States to treat persons concerned having no effective link with a State concerned as nationals of that State, unless this would result in treating those persons as if they were stateless.

2. Nothing in the present articles precludes States from treating persons concerned, who have become stateless as a result of the succession of States, as nationals of the State concerned whose nationality they would be entitled to acquire or retain, if such treatment is beneficial to those persons. ...

4. In what respect, if any, does this Declaration differ from the Uhl case? What are its other innovations? Are they desirable as a matter of policy?

5. For further discussion, see Jeffrey L. Blackman, *State Successions and Statelessness: The Emerging Right to an Effective Nationality Under International Law*, 19 MICH. J. INT'L L. 1141 (1998).

7. Ascriptions of Nationality to Corporations and Other Entities

The "nationality" of a corporation may be important for purposes of regulation, responsibility, taxation, and so on. As in the preceding cases, nationality may also be important for purposes of access to an international tribunal. Many of the issues of limits to conferment of nationality on corporations, ships, aircraft, spacecraft, etc. will be dealt with, in the context of the Barcelona Traction Case (*infra,* at 443). The Restatement extrapolates from this case, with scant policy discussion, the following "rule":

a. Restatement of the Law (Third), Foreign Relations Law of the United States (1987)

§ 213. Nationality of Corporations

For purposes of international law, a corporation has the nationality of the state under the laws of which the corporation is organized. ...

Reporters' Notes 5. *Corporate nationality in United States law.* States assign nationality to corporations for various purposes and sometimes define such nationality differently for different purposes in domestic law. The United States usually refers to the place of incorporation, while European states generally look to the *siège social*, i.e., the place from which the corporation is managed or directed. In both legal systems, however, when matters of national security are involved, the law refers to the nationality of the owners of stock or of those who control and manage the corporation.

NOTES AND QUESTIONS

1. Why should corporations be treated differently than individuals regarding their nationality under international law? Should it matter that they are created, operated, and terminated differently?

2. How relevant is the nature of corporations as legal entities distinct from their shareholders? How can the *Nottebohm* requirement of a "genuine link" with the incorporating state be applied, as the Restatement suggests, given its definition as an essentially personal relationship of allegiance? Isn't a corporate entity a purely formal construct? *See* OPPENHEIM'S INTERNATIONAL LAW (Sir Robert Jennings & Sir Arthur Watts eds., 9th ed. 1992), at 861:

> The concept of nationality in relation to companies does not have the legislative basis in national laws which exists in the case of individuals, and is thus much more open to a pragmatic assessment on the basis of a company's attachment to a state. While the traditional rule is still to regard the state of incorporation as the state whose nationality the company has, there is now little hesitation in looking behind the fact of incorporation in order to determine the substantive national connection of a company. In matters of international protection and international claims, the right of an international tribunal to investigate the realities of national control and ownership of a company is now well established. However, such inquiries usually have as their purpose the need to support a claim to nationality based on incorporation, rather than to elevate some alternative criterion to the position where it could be relied on in the absence of incorporation in the claimant states.

C. CLAIMS TO WITHDRAW OR TERMINATE NATIONALITY UPON EXCLUSIVELY CHOSEN CRITERIA

1. Forms of Termination

Termination of the link of nationality may take place in two ways, each raising different policy issues. The first is termination by the state against the wishes of the individual. What is distinctive about this form of termination is that whether effected by specific executive action or by a more indirect "operation of law", it is accomplished without the express agreement of the individual. This form of termination is an attractive power base for elites, for it can be used as an effective sanction against dissidents.

The second form of termination is that initiated by the individual. State elites have generally resisted this individual competence especially during periods of national crisis. Justifications for blocking individually initiated terminations may invoke national security (e. g. the individual had access to state secrets), "brain drain" (the individual by leaving deprives the community of indispensable skills), family responsibilities and so on.

What are the appropriate policies for each of these forms of termination? Can you formulate policies that would appear to accommodate the interests of the individual and the community?

2. International Policies

Trends in international policy have varied. At the Hague Conference of 1930, the U.S. Delegate stated:

> For a century past, it has been the policy of my country that the right of expatriation is an inherent and natural right of all persons. It is true that allegiance is a duty, but it is not a chain that holds a person in bondage and that he carries with him to a new life in a new land. It is a duty and an obligation that a free man casts off when he voluntarily assumes allegiance to the country of his new home, and takes over the duties and the rights of a national there. When he accepts the new tie, the old one is loosed and gone. This principle is not a small matter. It is not a question of language, or of formulae, or of phrases. It is a principle of the rights of man and of the liberty of the human race.

* * *

Declaration and Covenant provisions dealing with withdrawal or termination of nationality include the following:

a. Universal Declaration of Human Rights

G.A. Res. 217, U.N. GAOR, 3rd Sess., U.N. Doc. A/RES/217 A (III) (1948)

Article 15

2. No one shall be arbitrarily deprived of his nationality nor denied the right to change his nationality.

b. Convention on the Elimination of All Forms of Discrimination Against Women

Dec. 18, 1979, 1249 U.N.T.S. 13

Article 9

1. States Parties shall grant women equal rights with men to acquire, change or retain their nationality. They shall ensure in particular that neither marriage to an alien nor change of nationality by the husband during marriage shall automatically change the nationality of the wife, render her stateless or force upon her the nationality of the husband.

c. Convention on the Rights of the Child

Nov. 20, 1989, 1577 U.N.T.S. 3

Article 8

1. States Parties undertake to respect the right of the child, to preserve his or her identity, including nationality, name and family relations as recognized by law without unlawful interference.

2. Where a child is illegally deprived of some or all of the elements of his or her identity, States Parties shall provide appropriate assistance and protection, with a view to speedily re-establishing his or her identity.

d. European Convention on Nationality

Nov. 6, 1997, 37 I.L.M. 44 (1998)

Article 7: *Loss of nationality* ex lege *or at the initiative of a State Party*

1. A State Party may not provide in its internal law for the loss of its nationality *ex lege* or at the initiative of the State Party except in the following cases:

a. voluntary acquisition of another nationality;

b. acquisition of the nationality of the State Party by means of fraudulent conduct, false information or concealment of any relevant fact attributable to the applicant;

c. voluntary service in a foreign military force;

d. conduct seriously prejudicial to the vital interests of the State Party;

e. lack of a genuine link between the State Party and a national habitually residing abroad;

f. where it is established during the minority of a child that the preconditions laid down by internal law which led to the *ex lege* acquisition of the nationality of the State Party are no longer fulfilled;

g. adoption of a child if the child acquires or possesses the foreign nationality of one or both of the adopting parents.

2. A State Party may provide for the loss of its nationality by children whose parents lose that nationality except in cases covered by sub-paragraphs c and d of paragraph 1. However, children shall not lose that nationality if one of their parents retains it.

3. A State Party may not provide in its internal law for the loss of its nationality under paragraphs 1 and 2 of this article if the person concerned would thereby become stateless, with the exception of the cases mentioned in paragraph 1, sub-paragraph b, of this article.

Article 8: *Loss of nationality at the initiative of the individual*

1. Each State Party shall permit the renunciation of its nationality provided the persons concerned do not thereby become stateless.

2. However, a State Party may provide in its internal law that renunciation may be effected only by nationals who are habitually resident abroad.

e. Convention on the Reduction of Statelessness

Aug. 30, 1961, 989 U.N.T.S. 175

Article 5

1. If the law of a Contracting State entails loss of nationality as a consequence of any change in the personal status of a person such as marriage, termination of marriage, legitimation, recognition or adoption, such loss shall be conditional upon possession or acquisition of another nationality. …

Article 6

If the law of a Contracting State provides for loss of its nationality by a person's spouse or children as a consequence of that person losing or being deprived of that nationality, such loss shall be conditional upon their possession or acquisition of another nationality.

Article 7

1. (a) If the law of a Contracting State entails loss or renunciation of nationality, such renunciation shall not result in loss of nationality unless the person concerned possesses or acquires another nationality. …

2. A national of a Contracting State who seeks naturalization in a foreign country shall not lose his nationality unless he acquires or has been accorded assurance of acquiring the nationality of that foreign country.

3. Subject to the provisions of paragraphs 4 and 5 of this article, a national of a Contracting State shall not lose his nationality, so as to become stateless, on the ground of departure, residence abroad, failure to register or on any similar ground.

4. A naturalized person may lose his nationality on account of residence abroad for a period, not less than seven consecutive years, specified by the law of the Contracting State concerned if he fails to declare to the appropriate authority his intention to retain his nationality.

5. In the case of a national of a Contracting State, born outside its territory, the law of that State may make the retention of its nationality after the expiry of one year from his attaining his majority conditional upon residence at that time in the territory of the State or registration with the appropriate authority.

6. Except in the circumstances mentioned in this article, a person shall not lose the nationality of a Contracting State, if such loss would render him stateless, notwithstanding that such loss is not expressly prohibited by any other provision of this Convention.

Article 8

1. A Contracting State shall not deprive a person of his nationality if such deprivation would render him stateless.

2. Notwithstanding the provisions of paragraph 1 of this article, a person may be deprived of the nationality of a Contracting State:

(a) In the circumstances in which, under paragraphs 4 and 5 of article 7, it is permissible that a person should lose his nationality;

(b) Where the nationality has been obtained by misrepresentation or fraud.

3. Notwithstanding the provisions of paragraph 1 of this article, a Contracting State may retain the right to deprive a person of his nationality, if at the time of signature, ratification or accession it specifies its retention of such right on one or more of the following grounds, being grounds existing in its national law at that time:

(a) That, inconsistently with his duty of loyalty to the Contracting State, the person:

(i) Has, in disregard of an express prohibition by the Contracting State rendered or continued to render services to, or received or continued to receive emoluments from, another State, or

(ii) Has conducted himself in a manner seriously prejudicial to the vital interests of the State;

(b) That the person has taken an oath, or made a formal declaration, of allegiance to another State, or given definite evidence of his determination to repudiate his allegiance to the Contracting State.

4. A Contracting State shall not exercise a power of deprivation permitted by paragraphs 2 or 3 of this article except in accordance with law, which shall provide for the person concerned the right to a fair hearing by a court or other independent body.

Article 9

A Contracting State may not deprive any person or group of persons of their nationality on racial, ethnic, religious or political grounds.

* * *

f. Ivcher Bronstein Case (Baruch Ivcher Bronstein v. Peru)

(Inter-American Court of Human Rights Judgment, Feb. 6, 2001)

(English translation *at* http://www.cejil.org/sentencias.cfm?id=214)

85. Article 20 of the American Convention [on Human Rights] establishes that:

1. Every person has the right to a nationality.

2. Every person has the right to the nationality of the State in whose territory he was born, if he does not have the right to any other nationality.

> 3. No one shall be arbitrarily deprived of his nationality or of the right to change it....

86. The right to nationality is recognized by international law. This Court considers that it is a right of the individual and has stated that

> [n]ationality is an inherent right of all human beings. Not only is nationality the basic requirement for the exercise of political rights, it also has an important bearing on the individual's legal capacity.

87. With regard to Article 20 of the Convention, the Court has established that this includes two aspects:

> [t]he right to a nationality provides the individual with a minimum measure of legal protection in international relations, through the link his nationality establishes between him and the State in question; and second, the protection therein accorded the individual against the arbitrary deprivation of his nationality, without which he would be deprived for all practical purposes of all his political rights as well as of those civil rights that are tied to the nationality of the individual.

88. Although it has traditionally been accepted that the determination and regulation of nationality are the competence of each State, as this Court has stated, the evolution in this matter shows that international law imposes certain limits on a State's discretionality and that, in the regulation of nationality, it is not only the competence of States, but also the requirements of the integral protection of human rights that intervene.

89. Peru's domestic legislation recognizes the right to nationality. Thus, according to Article 2(21) of the Peruvian Constitution, "[e]very person has the right ... to his nationality. No one may be deprived of it". In the same way, Article 53 of the Constitution provides that "Peruvian nationality is not lost, unless it is expressly renounced before the Peruvian authorities."

90. The Court observes that it has been proved that Mr. Ivcher was an Israeli citizen until 1984, and that, subsequently, he acquired Peruvian citizenship by naturalization. ... It should be recalled that both the American Convention and Peru's domestic legislation recognize the right to nationality without making a distinction about the way in which it was acquired, either by birth, naturalization or some other means established in the law of the respective State.

91. In this regard, the Court has declared that:

> [n]ationality can be deemed to be the political and legal bond that links a person to a given state and binds him to it with ties of loyalty and fidelity, entitling him to diplomatic protection from that State. In different ways, most States have offered individuals who did not originally possess their nationality the opportunity to acquire it at a later date, usually, through a declaration of intention made after complying with certain conditions. In these cases, nationality no longer depends on the fortuity of birth in a

> given territory or on parents having that nationality; it is based on a voluntary act aimed at establishing a relationship with a given political society, its culture, its way of life and its values.

92. The International Court of Justice has also referred to this issue:

> Requesting and obtaining [naturalization] is not a common act in the life of an individual. It entails the rupture of a relation of fidelity and the establishment of another relation of fidelity. It entails far-reaching consequences and a profound change in the destiny of the persons who obtains it.

93. In this case, it is proved that Mr. Ivcher Bronstein acquired the title of Peruvian nationality on December 7, 1984, after he had renounced his Israeli nationality. This act linked both Mr. Ivcher and his family to the political society, the culture, the way of life and the values of Peru.

94. It has also been proved that on July 11, 1997, "Directorial Resolution" No. 117-97-IN-050100000000, signed by the Director General of Migration and Naturalization, annulled this nationality title, stating that there had been "substantial omissions that invalidate[d] it [ipso jure], because the required, prior renunciation of his nationality before the competent Peruvian authorities had not been confirmed, and it had not been confirmed in writing that he had done so before his country of origin".

95. From the foregoing, it is evident that Mr. Ivcher did not expressly renounce his nationality, which is the only way of losing it, according to the Peruvian Constitution, but was deprived of it when his nationality title, without which he was unable to exercise his rights as a Peruvian national, was annulled. Moreover, the procedure used to annul the nationality title did not comply with the provisions of domestic legislation, because, according to Article 110 of Peru's Law on General Norms of Administrative Procedures, a nationality title may only be annulled within the six months following the date on which it was acquired. ... Since this certificate was annulled in July 1997, 13 years after it had been granted, the State failed to comply with the provisions of its domestic legislation and arbitrarily deprived Mr. Ivcher of his nationality, violating Article 20(3) of the Convention.

96. Furthermore, the authorities who annulled Mr. Ivcher's nationality title did not have competence. As it has been established ..., Mr. Ivcher Bronstein acquired Peruvian nationality through a "supreme resolution" of the President, and his nationality title was signed by the Minister for Foreign Affairs; however, he lost his nationality as the result of a "'directorial resolution' of the Migration and Naturalization Directorate", which is undoubtedly of a lower rank than the authority that granted the corresponding right ..., and, consequently, could not deprive the act of a superior of its effects. Once again, this demonstrates the arbitrary character of the revocation of Mr. Ivcher's nationality, in violation of Article 20(3) of the American Convention.

97. In view of the foregoing, the Court concludes that the State violated the right to nationality embodied in Article 20(1) and 20(3) of the American Convention, with regard to Baruch Ivcher Bronstein.

3. Trends in National Decision

Trends in U.S. decisions reveal the interplay of elite control and human rights considerations.

a. Kennedy v. Mendoza-Martinez

372 U.S. 144 (1963)
and

Rusk v. Cort

369 U.S. 367 (1962)

JUSTICE GOLDBERG: We are called upon in these two cases to decide the grave and fundamental problem, common to both, of the constitutionality of Acts of Congress which divest an American of his citizenship for "[d]eparting from or remaining outside of the jurisdiction of the United States in time of war or ... national emergency for the purpose of evading or avoiding training and service" in the Nation's armed forces.

The facts of both cases are not in dispute. Mendoza-Martinez, the appellee in No. 2, was born in this country in 1922 and therefore acquired American citizenship by birth. By reason of his parentage, he also, under Mexican law, gained Mexican citizenship, thereby possessing dual nationality. In 1942 he departed from this country and went to Mexico solely, as he admits, for the purpose of evading military service in our armed forces. He concedes that he remained there for that sole purpose until November 1946, when he voluntarily returned to this country. In 1947, in the United States District Court for the Southern District of California, he pleaded guilty to and was convicted of evasion of his service obligations in violation of § 11 of the Selective Training and Service Act of 1940. He served the imposed sentence of a year and a day. ... [In 1953,] after a lapse of five years, he was served with a warrant of arrest in deportation proceedings. This was premised on the assertion that, by remaining outside the United States to avoid military service after September 27, 1944, when § 401(j) took effect, he had lost his American citizenship. ...

... Mendoza-Martinez brought a declaratory judgment action in the Federal District Court for the Southern District of California, seeking a declaration of his status as a citizen, of the unconstitutionality of § 401(j) and of the voidness of all orders of deportation directed against him. .... [The District Court entered judgment against Mendoza-Martinez and the Court of Appeals for the Ninth Circuit affirmed. This Court vacated the judgment and remanded the case to the District Court.]

On September 24, 1958, the District Court announced its new decision, also unreported, that in light of Trop § 401(j) is unconstitutional because not based on any "rational nexus..... between the content of a specific power in Congress and the action of Congress in carrying that power into execution." On direct appeal under 28 U.S.C. § 1252, this Court noted probable jurisdiction, 359 U.S. 933, and then of its own motion remanded the cause, this time with permission to the parties to amend the pleadings to put in issue the question of whether the facts as determined on the draft-evasion conviction in 1947 collaterally estopped the Attorney General from now claiming that Mendoza-Martinez had lost his American citizenship while in Mexico. Mackey v. Mendoza-Martinez, 362 U.S. 384.

The District Court on remand held that the Government was not collaterally estopped because the 1947 criminal proceedings entailed no determination of Mendoza-Martinez' citizenship. The court, however, reaffirmed its previous holding that § 401 (j) is unconstitutional, adding as a further basis of invalidity that § 401(j) is "essentially penal in character and deprives the plaintiff of procedural due process. ... [T]he requirements of procedural due process are not satisfied by the administrative hearing of the Immigration Service nor in this present proceedings." The Attorney General's current appeal is from this decision. …

Cort, the appellee in No. 3, is also a native-born American, born in Boston in 1927. Unlike Mendoza-Martinez, he has no dual nationality. His wife and two young children are likewise American citizens by birth. Following receipt of his M.D. degree from the Yale University School of Medicine in 1951, he went to England for the purpose of undertaking a position as a Research Fellow at Cambridge University. He had earlier registered in timely and proper fashion for the draft and shortly before his departure supplemented his regular Selective Service registration by registering under the newly enacted Doctors Draft Act. In late 1951 he received a series of letters from the American Embassy in London instructing him to deliver his passport to it to be made "valid only for return to the United States." He did not respond to these demands because, he now says in an affidavit filed in the trial court in this proceeding, "I believed that they were unlawful and I did not wish to subject myself to this and similar forms of political persecution then prevalent in the United States. … I was engaged in important research and teaching work in physiology and I desired to continue earning a livelihood for my family." Cort had been a member of the Communist Party while he was a medical student at Yale from 1946 to 1951, except for the academic year 1948-49 when he was in England. In late 1952, while still in England at Cambridge, he accepted a teaching position for the following academic year at Harvard University Medical School. When, however, the school discovered through further correspondence that he had not yet fulfilled his military obligations, it advised him that it did not regard his teaching position as essential enough to support his deferment from military service in order to enter upon it. Thereafter, his local draft board in Brookline, Massachusetts, notified him in February 1953 that his request for deferment was denied and that he should report within 30 days for a physical examination either in Brookline or in Frankfurt, Germany. On June 4 and on July 3 the draft board again sent Cort notices to report for a physical examination, the first notice for examination on July 1 in Brookline, and the second for examination within 30 days in Frankfurt. He did not appear at either place, and the board on August 13 ordered him to report for induction on September 14, 1953. He did not report, and consequently he was indicted in December 1954 for violation of §12 (a) of the Selective Service Act of 1948 by reason of his failure to report for induction. This indictment is still outstanding. His complaint in this action states that he did not report for induction because he believed "that the induction order was not issued in good faith to secure his military services, that his past political associations and present physical disabilities made him ineligible for such service, and that he was being ordered to report back to the United States to be served with a Congressional committee subpoena or indicted under the Smith Act...." Meanwhile, the British Home Office had refused to renew his residence permit, and in mid-1954 he and his family moved to Prague, Czechoslovakia, where he took a position as Senior Scientific Worker at the Cardiovascular Institute. He has lived there since.

In April 1959, his previous United States passport having long since expired, Cort applied at the American Embassy in Prague for a new one. His complaint in this action states that he wanted the passport "in order to return to the United States with his wife and children so that he might fulfill his obligations under the Selective Service laws and his wife might secure medical treatment for multiple sclerosis." Mrs. Cort received a passport and came to this country temporarily in late 1959, both for purposes of medical treatment and to facilitate arrangements for her husband's return. Cort's application, however, was denied on the ground that he had, by his failure to report for induction on September 14, 1953, as ordered, remained outside the country to avoid military service and thereby automatically forfeited his American citizenship by virtue of § 349(a) (10) of the Immigration and Nationality Act of 1952, which had superseded § 401(j). The State Department's Passport Board of Review affirmed the finding of expatriation, and the Department's legal adviser affirmed the decision. Cort, through counsel, thereupon brought this suit in the District Court for the District of Columbia for a declaratory judgment that he is a citizen of the United States, for an injunction against enforcement of § 349(a) (10) because of its unconstitutionality, and for an order directing revocation of the certificate of loss of nationality and issuance of a United States passport to him. Pursuant to Cort's demand, a three-judge court was convened. The court held that he had remained outside the United States to evade military service, but that § 349 (a) (10) is unconstitutional because "We perceive no substantial difference between the constitutional issue in the Trop case and the one facing us." It therefore concluded that Cort is a citizen of this country and enjoined the Secretary of State from withholding a passport from Cort on the ground that he is not a citizen and from otherwise interfering with his rights of citizenship. Cort v. Herter, 187 F.Supp. 683.

The Secretary of State appealed directly to this Court, 28 U.S.C. §§ 1252, 1253, which postponed the question of jurisdiction to the hearing of the case on the merits. 365 U.S. 808. The preliminary question of jurisdiction was affirmatively resolved last Term, Rusk v. Cort, 369 U.S. 367, leaving the issue of the validity of § 349 (a) (10) for decision now, after reargument. 369 U.S., at 380. . .

Since the validity of an Act of Congress is involved, we begin our analysis mindful that the function we are now discharging is "the gravest and most delicate duty that this Court is called upon to perform." *Blodgett v. Holden*, 275 U.S. 142, 148 (1926)(separate opinion of Holmes, J.). This responsibility we here fulfill with all respect for the powers of Congress, but with recognition of the transcendent status of our Constitution.

We deal with the contending constitutional arguments in the context of certain basic and sometimes conflicting principles. Citizenship is a most precious right. It is expressly guaranteed by the Fourteenth Amendment to the Constitution, which speaks in the most positive terms. The Constitution is silent about the permissibility of involuntary forfeiture of citizenship rights. While it confirms citizenship rights, plainly there are imperative obligations of citizenship, performance of which Congress in the exercise of its powers may constitutionally exact. One of the most important of these is to serve the country in time of war and national emergency. The powers of Congress to require military service for the common defense are broad and far-reaching, for while the Constitution protects against invasions of individual rights, it is not a suicide pact. Similarly, Congress has broad power under the Necessary and Proper Clause to enact legislation for the regulation of foreign affairs. Latitude in this area is necessary to ensure effectuation of this indispensable function of government.

These principles, stemming on the one hand from the precious nature of the constitutionally guaranteed rights of citizenship, and on the other from the powers of Congress and the related obligations of individual citizens, are urged upon us by the parties here. The Government argues that §§ 401(j) and 349 (a) (10) are valid as an exercise of Congress' power over foreign affairs, of its war power, and of the inherent sovereignty of the Government. Appellees urge the provisions' invalidity as not within any of the powers asserted, and as imposing a cruel and unusual punishment.

We recognize at the outset that we are confronted here with an issue of the utmost import. "Deprivation of citizenship-particularly American citizenship, which is 'one of the most valuable rights in the world today,'... has grave practical consequences." 372 U.S. *at* 160 *quoting* Report of the President's Commission on Immigration and Naturalization 235 (1953). An expatriate who, like Cort, had no other nationality becomes a stateless person-a person who not only has no rights as an American citizen, but no membership in any national entity whatsoever. "Such individuals as do not possess any nationality enjoy, in general, no protection whatever, and if they are aggrieved by a State they have no means of redress, since there is no State which is competent to take up their case. As far as the Law of Nations is concerned, there is, apart from restraints of morality or obligations expressly laid down by treaty. . . no restriction whatever to cause a State to abstain from maltreating to any extent such stateless individuals." 1 Oppenheim, International Law (8th ed., Lauterpacht, 1955), § 291, at 640. The calamity is "[n]ot the loss of specific rights, then, but the loss of a community willing and able to guarantee any rights whatsoever ..... " Arendt, The Origins of

Totalitarianism (1951), 294. The stateless person may end up shunted from nation to nation, there being no one obligated or willing to receive him or, as in Cort's case, may receive the dubious sanctuary of a Communist regime lacking the essential liberties precious to American citizenship.

The Perez and Trop Cases

The basic principles here involved, the gravity of the issue, and the arguments bearing upon Congress' power to forfeit citizenship were considered by the Court in relation to different provisions of the Nationality Act of 1940 in two cases decided on the same day less than five years ago: *Perez v. Brownell*, 356 U.S. 44 (1958) and *Trop v. Dulles*, 356 U.S. 86 (1958).

In Perez, § 401 (e), which imposes loss of nationality for "[v]oting in a political election in a foreign state or participating in an election or plebiscite to determine the sovereignty over foreign territory," was upheld by a closely divided Court as a constitutional exercise of Congress' power to regulate foreign affairs. The Court reasoned that since withdrawal of citizenship of Americans who vote in foreign elections is reasonably calculated to effect the avoidance of embarrassment in the conduct of foreign relations, such withdrawal is within the power of Congress, acting under the Necessary and Proper Clause. Since the Court sustained the application of § 401 (e) to denationalize Perez, it did not have to deal with § 401 upon which the Government had also relied, and it expressly declined to rule on the constitutionality of that section, 356 U.S. at 62. There were three opinions written in dissent. The principal one, that of The Chief Justice, recognized "that citizenship may not only be voluntarily renounced through exercise of the right of expatriation but also by other actions in derogation of undivided allegiance to this country," id., at 68, but concluded that "[t]he mere act of voting in a foreign election, however, without regard to the circumstances attending the participation, is not sufficient to show a voluntary abandonment of citizenship." *Id.* at 78.

In Trop, § 401 (g), forfeiting the citizenship of any American who is guilty of "[d]eserting the military or naval forces of the United States in time of war, provided he is convicted thereof by court martial and as the result of such conviction is dismissed or dishonorably discharged ...," was declared unconstitutional. There was no opinion of the Court. The Chief Justice wrote an opinion for four members of the Court, concluding that § 401 (g) was invalid for the same reason that he had urged as to § 401 (e) in his dissent in Perez, and that it was also invalid as a cruel and unusual punishment imposed in violation of the Eighth Amendment. Justice Brennan conceded that it is "paradoxical to justify as constitutional the expatriation of the citizen who has committed no crime by voting in a Mexican political election, yet find unconstitutional a statute which provides for the expatriation of a soldier guilty of the very serious crime of desertion in time of war," 356 U.S. at 105. Notwithstanding, he concurred because "the requisite rational relation between this statute and the war power does not appear id., at 114. Justice Frankfurter, joined by three other justices, dissented on the ground that §

401 (g) did not impose punishment at all, let alone cruel and unusual punishment, and was within the war powers of Congress.

Sections 401 (j) and 349(a)(10) as Punishment

The present cases present for decision the constitutionality of a section not passed upon in either Perez or Trop-§ 401 (j), added in 1944, and its successor and present counterpart, § 349 (a)(10) of the Immigration and Nationality Act of 1952. We have come to the conclusion that there is a basic question in the present cases, the answer to which obviates a choice here between the powers of Congress and the constitutional guarantee of citizenship. That issue is whether the statutes here, which automatically-without prior court or administrative proceedings-impose forfeiture of citizenship, are essentially penal in character, and consequently have deprived the appellees of their citizenship without due process of law and without according them the rights, guaranteed by the Fifth and Sixth Amendments, including notice, confrontation, compulsory process for obtaining witnesses, trial by jury and assistance of counsel. . .

It is fundamental that the great powers of Congress to conduct war and to regulate the Nation's foreign relations are subject to the constitutional requirements of due process. The imperative necessity for safeguarding these rights to procedural due process under the gravest of emergencies has existed throughout our constitutional history, for it is then, under the pressing exigencies of crisis, that there is the greatest temptation to dispense with fundamental constitutional guarantees which, it is feared, will inhibit governmental action.

We hold §§ 401 (j) and 349 (a)(10) invalid because in them Congress has plainly employed the sanction of deprivation of nationality as a punishment-for the offense of leaving or remaining outside the country to evade military service-without affording the procedural safeguards guaranteed by the Fifth and Sixth Amendments. Our forefathers "intended to safeguard the people of this country from punishment without trial by duly constituted courts. . . And even the courts to which this important function was entrusted were commanded to stay their hands until and unless certain tested safeguards were observed. An accused in court must be tried by an impartial jury, has a right to be represented by counsel, [and] must be clearly informed of the charge against him . . . ." *United States v. Lovett*, 328 U.S. 303, 317 (1946). *See also Chambers v. Florida*, 309 U.S. 227, 235-238 (1940).

As the Government concedes, §§ 401 (j) and 349(a)(10) automatically strip an American of his citizenship, with concomitant deprivation "of all that makes life worth living," *Ng Fung Ho v. White*, 259 U.S. 276, 284-285 (1922), whenever a citizen departs from or remains outside the jurisdiction of this country for the purpose of evading his military obligations. Conviction for draft evasion, as Cort's case illustrates, is not prerequisite to the operation of this sanction. Independently of prosecution, forfeiture of citizenship attaches when the statutory set of facts develops. It is argued that the availability after the fact of administrative and judicial proceedings, including the machinery the Court approved last Term in

Rusk, 369 U.S. 367, to contest the validity of the sanction meets the measure of due process. But the legislative history and judicial expression with respect to every congressional enactment relating to the provisions in question dated back to 1865 establish that forfeiture of citizenship is a penalty for the act of leaving or staying outside the country to avoid the draft. This being so, the Fifth and Sixth Amendments mandate that this punishment cannot be imposed without a prior criminal trial and all its incidents, including indictment, notice, confrontation, jury trial, assistance of counsel, and compulsory process for obtaining witnesses. If the sanction these sections impose is punishment, and it plainly, is, the procedural safeguards required as incidents of a criminal prosecution are lacking.

Conclusion

It is argued that our holding today will have the unfortunate result of immunizing the draft evader who has left the United States from having to suffer any sanction against his conduct, since he must return to this country before he can be apprehended and tried for his crime. The compelling answer to this is that the Bill of Rights which we guard so jealously and the procedures it guarantees are not to be abrogated merely because a guilty man may escape prosecution or for any other expedient reason. Moreover, the truth is that even without being expatriated, the evader living abroad is not in a position to assert the vast majority of his component rights as an American citizen. If he wishes to assert those rights in any real sense he must return to this country, and by doing that he will subject himself to prosecution. In fact, while he is outside the country evading prosecution, the United States may, by proper refusal to exercise its largely discretionary power to afford him diplomatic protection, decline to invoke its sovereign power on his behalf. Since the substantial benefits of American citizenship only come into play upon return to face prosecution, the draft evader who wishes to exercise his citizenship rights will inevitably come home and pay his debt, which within constitutional limits Congress has the power to define. This is what Mendoza-Martinez did, what Cort says he is willing to do, and what others have done. Thus our holding today does not frustrate the effective handling of the problem of draft evaders who leave the United States.

We conclude, for the reasons stated, that §§ 401 (j) and 349 (a)(10) are punitive and as such cannot constitutionally stand, lacking as they do the procedural safeguards which the Constitution commands. We recognize that draft evasion, particularly in time of war, is a heinous offense, and should and can be properly punished. Dating back to Magna Carta, however, it has been an abiding principle governing the lives of civilized men that "no freeman shall be taken or imprisoned or disseised or outlawed or exiled ... without the judgment of his peers or by the law of the land. ... What we hold is only that, in keeping with this cherished tradition, punishment cannot be imposed "without due process of law." Any lesser holding would ignore the constitutional mandate upon which our essential liberties depend. Therefore the judgments of the District Courts in these cases are Affirmed.

[Justices DOUGLAS and BLACK joined in the Court's opinion but also reiterated the view that Congress has no power to deprive a person of the citizenship granted the native-born by § 1, cl. 1, of the Fourteenth Amendment.]

b. Afroyim v. Rusk

387 U.S. 253 (1967)

JUSTICE BLACK: Petitioner, born in Poland in 1893, immigrated to this country in 1912 and became a naturalized American citizen in 1926. He went to Israel in 1950, and in 1951 he voluntarily voted in an election for the Israeli Knesset, the legislative body of Israel. In 1960, when he applied for renewal of his United States passport, the Department of State refused to grant it on the sole ground that he had lost his American citizenship by virtue of § 401 (e) of the Nationality Act of 1940 which provides that a United States citizen shall "lose" his citizenship if he votes "in a political election in a foreign state." Petitioner then brought this declaratory judgment action in federal district court alleging that § 401 (e) violates both the Due Process Clause of the Fifth Amendment and § 1, cl. 1, of the Fourteenth Amendment which grants American citizenship to persons like petitioner. Because neither the Fourteenth Amendment nor any other provision of the Constitution expressly grants Congress the power to take away that citizenship once it has been acquired, petitioner contended that the only way he could lose his citizenship was by his own voluntary renunciation of it. Since the Government took the position that § 401 (e) empowers it to terminate citizenship without the citizen's voluntary renunciation, petitioner argued that this section is prohibited by the Constitution. The District Court and the Court of Appeals, rejecting this argument, held that Congress has constitutional authority forcibly to take away citizenship for voting in a foreign country based on its implied power to regulate foreign affairs. Consequently, petitioner was held to have lost his American citizenship regardless of his intention not to give it up. This is precisely what this Court held in :*Perez v. Brownell*, 356 U.S. 44.

The fundamental issue before this Court here, as it was in Perez, is whether Congress can consistently with the Fourteenth Amendment enact a law stripping an American of his citizenship which he has never voluntarily renounced or given up. The majority in Perez held that Congress could do this because withdrawal of citizenship is "reasonably calculated to effect the end that is within the power of Congress to achieve." 356 U.S. at 60. That conclusion was reached by this chain of reasoning: Congress has an implied power to deal with foreign affairs as an indispensable attribute of sovereignty; this implied power, plus the Necessary and Proper Clause, empowers Congress to regulate voting by American citizens in foreign elections; involuntary expatriation is within the "ample scope" of "appropriate modes" Congress can adopt to effectuate its general regulatory power. *Id.* at 57-60. Then, upon summarily concluding that "there is nothing in the ... Fourteenth Amendment to warrant drawing from it a restriction upon the power otherwise possessed by Congress to withdraw citizenship," *id.* at 58, n. 3, the majority specifically rejected the "notion that the power of Congress to terminate citizenship depends upon the citizen's assent." *Id.* at 61.

First we reject the idea expressed in Perez that, aside from the Fourteenth Amendment, Congress has any general power, expressed or implied to take away an American citizen's citizenship without his assent. This power cannot, as Perez indicated, be sustained as an implied attribute of sovereignty possessed by all nations. Other nations are governed by their own constitutions, if any, and we can draw no support from theirs. In our country the people are sovereign and the Government cannot sever its relationship to the people by taking away their citizenship. Our Constitution governs us and we must never forget that our Constitution limits the Government to those powers specifically granted or those that are necessary and proper to carry out the specifically granted ones. The Constitution, of course, grants Congress no express power to strip people of their citizenship, whether in the exercise of the implied power to regulate foreign affairs or in the exercise of any specifically granted power. And even before the adoption of the Fourteenth Amendment, views were expressed in Congress and by this Court that under the Constitution the Government was granted no power, even under its express power to pass a uniform rule of naturalization, to determine what conduct should and should not result in the loss of citizenship. On three occasions, in 1794, 1797, and 1818, Congress considered and rejected proposals to enact laws which would describe certain conduct as resulting in expatriation. On each occasion Congress was considering bills that were concerned with recognizing the right of voluntary expatriation and with providing some means of exercising that right. In 1794 and 1797, many members of Congress still adhered to the English doctrine of perpetual allegiance and doubted whether a citizen could even voluntarily renounce his citizenship. By 1818, however, almost no one doubted the existence of the right of voluntary expatriation, but several judicial decisions had indicated that the right could not be exercised by the citizen without the consent of the Federal Government in the form of enabling legislation. Therefore, a bill was introduced to provide that a person could voluntarily relinquish his citizenship by declaring such relinquishment in writing before a district court and then departing from the country. The opponents of the bill argued that Congress had no constitutional authority, either express or implied, under either the Naturalization Clause or the Necessary and Proper Clause, to provide that a certain act would constitute expatriation. They pointed to a proposed Thirteenth Amendment, subsequently not ratified, which would have provided that a person would lose his citizenship by accepting an office or emolument from a foreign government. ... The bill was finally defeated. It is in this setting that six years later, in Osborn v. Bank of the United States, 22 U.S. 738 (1824), this Court, speaking through Chief Justice Marshall, declared in what appears to be a mature and well-considered dictum that Congress, once a person becomes a citizen, cannot deprive him of that status:

> [The naturalized citizen] becomes a member of the society, possessing all the rights of a native citizen, and standing, in the view of the constitu-

> tion, on the footing of a native. The constitution does not authorize Congress to enlarge or abridge those rights. The simple power of the national Legislature, is to prescribe a uniform rule of naturalization, and the exercise of this power exhausts it, so far as respects the individual. *Id.*

Although these legislative and judicial statements may be regarded as inconclusive and must be considered in the historical context in which they were made, any doubt as to whether prior to the passage of the Fourteenth Amendment Congress had the power to deprive a person against his will of citizenship once obtained should have been removed by the unequivocal terms of the Amendment itself. It provides its own constitutional rule in language calculated completely to control the status of citizenship: "All persons born or naturalized in the United States ... are citizens of the United States." There is no indication in these words of a fleeting citizenship, good at the moment it is acquired but subject to destruction by the Government at any time. Rather the Amendment can most reasonably be read as defining a citizenship which a citizen keeps unless he voluntarily relinquishes it. Once acquired, this Fourteenth Amendment citizenship was not to be shifted, canceled, or diluted at the will of the Federal Government, the States, or any other governmental unit.

It is true that the chief interest of the people in giving permanence and security to citizenship in the Fourteenth Amendment was the desire to protect Negroes. The Dred Scott decision, 19 How. 393, had shortly before greatly disturbed many people about the status of Negro citizenship. But the Civil Rights Act of 1866, 14 Stat. 27, had already attempted to confer citizenship on all persons born or naturalized in the United States. Nevertheless, when the Fourteenth Amendment passed the House without containing any definition of citizenship, the sponsors of the Amendment in the Senate insisted on inserting a constitutional definition and grant of citizenship. They expressed fears that the citizenship so recently conferred on Negroes by the Civil Rights Act could be just as easily taken away from them by subsequent Congresses, and it was to provide an insuperable obstacle against every governmental effort to strip Negroes of their newly acquired citizenship that the first clause was added to the Fourteenth Amendment. ...

This undeniable purpose of the Fourteenth Amendment to make citizenship of Negroes permanent and secure would be frustrated by holding that the Government can rob a citizen of his citizenship without his consent by simply proceeding to act under an implied general power to regulate foreign affairs or some other power generally granted. Though the framers of the Amendment were not particularly concerned with the problem of expatriation, it seems undeniable from the language they used that they wanted to put citizenship beyond the power of any governmental unit to destroy. In 1868, two years after the Fourteenth Amendment had been proposed, Congress specifically considered the subject of expatriation. Several bills were introduced to impose involuntary expatriation on citizens who committed certain acts. With little discussion, these proposals were defeated. ...

The entire legislative history of the 1868 Act makes it abundantly clear that there was a strong feeling in the Congress that the only way the citizenship it conferred could be lost was by the voluntary renunciation or abandonment by the citizen himself. And this was the unequivocal statement of the Court in the case of *United States v. Wong Kim Ark*, 169 U.S. 649 (1898). The issues in that case were whether a person born in the United States to Chinese aliens was a citizen of the United States and whether, nevertheless, he could be excluded under the Chinese Exclusion Act, 22 Stat. 58. The Court first held that within the terms of the Fourteenth Amendment, Wong Kim Ark was a citizen of the United States, and then pointed out that though he might "renounce this citizenship, and become a citizen of ... any other country" he had never done so. *Won Kim Ark*, 169 U.S. at 704-705. The Court then held that Congress could not do anything to abridge or affect his citizenship conferred by the Fourteenth Amendment. Quoting Chief Justice Marshall's well-considered and oft-repeated dictum in Osborn to the effect that Congress under the power of naturalization has "a power to confer citizenship, not a power to take it away," the Court said:

> Congress having no power to abridge the rights conferred by the Constitution upon those who have become naturalized citizens by virtue of acts of Congress, a fortiori no act of Congress can affect citizenship acquired as a birthright, by virtue of the Constitution itself The Fourteenth Amendment, while it leaves the power, where it was before, in Congress, to regulate naturalization, has conferred no authority upon Congress to restrict the effect of birth, declared by the Constitution to constitute a sufficient and complete right to citizenship. *Id.*, at 703.

To uphold Congress' power to take away a man's citizenship because he voted in a foreign election in violation of § 401 (e) would be equivalent to holding that Congress has the power to "abridge," "affect," "restrict the effect of," and "take ... away" citizenship. Because the Fourteenth Amendment prevents Congress from doing any of these things, we agree with THE CHIEF JUSTICE's dissent in the Perez case that the Government is without power to rob a citizen of his citizenship under § 401 (e).

Because the legislative history of the Fourteenth Amendment and of the expatriation proposals which preceded and followed it, like most other legislative history, contains many statements from which conflicting inferences can be drawn, our holding might be unwarranted if it rested entirely or principally upon that legislative history. But it does not. Our holding we think is the only one that can stand in view of the language and the purpose of the Fourteenth Amendment, and our construction of that Amendment, we believe, comports more nearly than Perez with the principles of liberty and equal justice to all that the entire Fourteenth Amendment was adopted to guarantee. Citizenship is no light trifle to be jeopardized any moment Congress decides to do so under the name of one of its general or implied grants of power. In some instances, loss of citizenship can mean that a man is left without the protection of citizenship in any country in the world-as a man without a country. Citizenship in this Nation is a part of a cooperative affair. Its citizenry is the country and the country is its citizenry. The very nature of our free government makes it completely incongruous to have a rule of law under which a group of citizens temporarily in office can deprive another group of citizens of their citizenship. We hold that the Fourteenth Amendment was designed to, and does, protect every citizen of this Nation against a congressional forcible destruction of his citizenship, whatever his creed, color, or race. Our holding does no more than to give to this citizen that which is his own, a constitutional right to remain a citizen in a free country unless he voluntarily relinquishes that citizenship.

Perez v. Brownell is overruled. The judgment is Reversed.

c. Rogers v. Bellei

401 U.S. 815 (1971)

JUSTICE BLACKMUN: Under constitutional challenge here, primarily on Fifth Amendment due process grounds, but also on Fourteenth Amendment grounds is § 301 (b) of the Immigration and Nationality Act of June 27, 1952, 66 Stat. 236, 8 U.S.C. § 1401 (b).

Section 301 (a) of the Act, 8 U.S.C. § 1401 (a), defines those persons who "shall be nationals and citizens of the United States at birth." Paragraph (7) of § 301 (a) includes in that definition a person born abroad "of parents one of whom is an alien, and the other a citizen of the United States" who has met specified conditions of residence in this country. Section 301 (b), however, provides that one who is a citizen at birth under § 301 (a)(7) shall lose his citizenship unless, after age 14 and before age 28, he shall come to the United States and be physically present here continuously for at least five years. …

The plan thus adopted by Congress with respect to a person of this classification was to bestow citizenship at birth but to take it away upon the person's failure to comply with a post-age-14 and pre-age-28 residential requirement. It is this deprival of citizenship, once bestowed, that is under attack here.

I.

[The appellee, Aldo Mario Bellei, was born in Italy on December 22, 1939. The plaintiff's father has always been a citizen of Italy and never has acquired United States citizenship. The plaintiff's mother, however, was a native-born United States citizen. She has fulfilled the requirement of § 301 (a)(7) for physical presence in the United States for 10 years, more than five of which were after she attained the age of 14 years. The mother and father were married in Philadelphia on the mother's 24th birthday, March 14, 1939. Nine days later, the newlyweds departed for Italy and have resided there ever since. By Italian law Bellei acquired Italian citizenship upon his birth in Italy and retains that citizenship. He also acquired United States citizenship at his birth under Rev.Stat. § 1993, as amended by the Act of May 24, 1934, § 1, 48 Stat.797, then in effect. That version of the statute, as does the present one, contained a residence condition applicable to a child born abroad with one alien parent. Bellei resided in Italy from the time of his birth. He has come to the United States five different times using both his mother's passport and his own. On his fifth visit to the United States, in 1965, Bellei entered with an Italian passport as an alien visitor.

Bellei was warned in writing by United States authorities of the impact of § 301 (b) when he was in this country in January 1963 and again in November of that year when he was in Italy. Sometime after February 11, 1964, he was orally advised by the American Embassy at Rome that he had lost his United States citizenship pursuant to § 301 (b). In November 1966 he was so notified in writing by the American Consul in Rome when the plaintiff requested another American passport. On March 28, 1960, Bellei registered under the United States Selective Service laws with the American Consul in Rome. At that time he already was 20 years of age. On December 11, 1963, he was asked to report for induction in the District of Columbia. This induction, however, was then deferred because of his NATO defense program employment. At the time of deferment he was warned of the danger of losing his United States citizenship if he did not comply with the residence requirement. After February 14, 1964, Selective Service advised him by letter that, due to the loss of his citizenship, he had no further obligation for United States military service.]

Plaintiff thus concededly failed to comply with the conditions imposed by § 301 (b) of the Act.

II.

The plaintiff . . . asked that the Secretary be enjoined from carrying out and enforcing § 301 (b), and also requested a declaratory judgment that § 301 (b) is unconstitutional as violative of the Fifth Amendment's Due Process Clause, the Eighth Amendment's Punishment Clause, and the Ninth Amendment, and that he is and always has been a native-born United States citizen. ...

A three-judge District Court was convened [and]...ruled that § 301 (b) was unconstitutional. . . .

III.

[Reviewing Schneider v. Rusk, 377 U.S. 163 (1964) and Afroyim v. Rusk, 387 U.S. 253, the Court concluded] that both Mrs. Schneider and Mr. Afroyim had resided in this country for years. Each had acquired United States citizenship here by the naturalization process (in one case derivative and in the other direct) prescribed by the National Legislature. Each, in short, was covered explicitly by the Fourteenth Amendment's very first sentence: "All persons born or naturalized in the United States and subject to the jurisdiction thereof, are citizens of the United States and of the State wherein they reside." This, of course, accounts for the Court's emphasis in Afroyim upon "Fourteenth Amendment citizenship." *Id.* at 262.

IV.

[After reviewing the history of Congressional statutory efforts with regard to citizenship deprivation, the Court continued:]

The statutory pattern, therefore, developed and expanded from (a) one, established in 1790 and enduring through the Revised Statutes and until 1934, where citizenship was specifically denied to the child born abroad of a father who never resided in the United States; to (b), in 1907, a governmental protection condition for the child born of an American citizen father and residing abroad, dependent upon a declaration of intent and the oath of allegiance at majority; to (c), in 1934, a condition, for the child born abroad of one United States citizen parent and one alien parent, of five years' continuous residence in the United States before age 18 and the oath of allegiance within six months after majority; to (d), in 1940, a condition, for that child, of five years' residence here, not necessarily continuous, between ages 13 and 21; to (e), in 1952, a condition, for that child, of five years' continuous residence here, with allowance, between ages 14 and 28.

The application of these respective statutes to a person in plaintiff Bellei's position produces the following results:

1. Not until 1934 would that person have had any conceivable claim to United States citizenship. For more than a century and a half no statute was of assistance. Maternal citizenship afforded no benefit. One may observe, too, that if Mr. Bellei had been born in 1933, instead of in 1939, he would have no claim even today. …

2. Despite the recognition of the maternal root by the 1934 amendment, in effect at the time of plaintiff's birth, and despite the continuing liberalization of the succeeding statutes, the plaintiff still would not be entitled to full citizenship because, although his mother met the condition for her residence in the United States, the plaintiff never did fulfill the residential condition imposed for him by any of the statutes.

3. This is so even though the liberalizing 1940 and 1952 statutes, enacted after the plaintiff's birth, were applicable by their terms to one born abroad subsequent to May 24, 1934, the date of the 1934 Act, and were available to the plaintiff. …

Thus, in summary, it may be said fairly that, for the most part, each successive statute, as applied to a foreign-born child of one United States citizen parent, moved in a direction of leniency for the child. For plaintiff Bellei the statute changed from complete disqualification to citizenship upon a condition subsequent, with that condition being expanded and made less onerous, and, after his birth, with the succeeding liberalizing provisions made applicable to him in replacement of the stricter statute in effect when he was born. The plaintiff nevertheless failed to satisfy any form of the condition.

V.

It is evident that Congress felt itself possessed of the power to grant citizenship to the foreign born and at the same time to impose qualifications and conditions for that citizenship. …

… [I]t is conceded here both that Congress may withhold citizenship from persons like plaintiff Bellei and may prescribe a period of residence in the United States as a condition precedent without constitutional question.

Thus we have the presence of congressional power in this area, its exercise, and the Court's specific recognition of that power and of its having been properly withheld or properly used in particular situations.

VI.

This takes us, then, to the issue of the constitutionality of the exercise of that congressional power when it is used to impose the condition subsequent that confronted plaintiff Bellei. We conclude that its imposition is not unreasonable, arbitrary, or unlawful, and that it withstands the present constitutional challenge.

1. The Congress has an appropriate concern with problems attendant on dual nationality, . . . These problems are particularly acute when it is the father who is the child's alien parent and the father chooses to have his family reside in the country of his own nationality. The child is reared, at best, in an atmosphere of divided loyalty. We cannot say that a concern that the child's own primary allegiance is to the country of his birth and of his father's allegiance is either misplaced or arbitrary. …

The duality also creates problems for the governments involved. Mr. Justice Brennan recognized this when, concurring in Kennedy v. Mendoza-Martinez, 372 U.S. 144, 187 (1963), a case concerning native-born citizens, he observed: "We have recognized the entanglements which may stem from dual allegiance. … " In a famous case Mr. Justice Douglas wrote of the problem of dual citizenship. Kawakita v. United States, 343 U.S. 717, 723-736 (1952). He noted that "[o]ne who has a dual nationality will be subject to claims from both nations, claims which at times may be competing or conflicting," id., at 733; that one with dual nationality cannot turn that status "into a fair-weather citizenship," id., at 736; and that "[c]ircumstances may compel one who has a dual nationality to do acts which otherwise would not be compatible with the obligations of American citizenship," ibid. The District Court in this very case conceded:

> It is a legitimate concern of Congress that those who bear American citizenship and receive its benefits have some nexus to the United States. 296 F.Supp., at 1252.

2. There are at least intimations in the decided cases that a dual national constitutionally may be required to make an election. In *Perkins v. Elg*, 307 U.S. 325, 329 (1939), the Court observed that a native-born citizen who had acquired dual nationality during minority through his parents' foreign naturalization abroad

did not lose his United States citizenship "provided that on attaining majority he elects to retain that citizenship and to return to the United States to assume its duties." In *Kawakita v. United States*, 343 U.S. 717, 734 (1952), the Court noted that a dual national "under certain circumstances" can be deprived of his American citizenship through an Act of Congress. In *Mandoli v. Acheson*, 344 U.S. 133, 138 (1952), the Court took pains to observe that there was no statute in existence imposing an election upon that dual nationality litigant.

These cases do not flatly say that a duty to elect may be constitutionally imposed. They surely indicate, however, that this is possible, and in Mandoli the holding was based on the very absence of a statute and not on any theory of unconstitutionality. And all three of these cases concerned persons who were born here, that is, persons who possessed Fourteenth Amendment citizenship; they did not concern a person, such as plaintiff Bellei, whose claim to citizenship is wholly, and only, statutory.

3. The statutory development outlined in Part IV above, by itself and without reference to the underlying legislative history, committee reports, and other studies, reveals a careful consideration by the Congress of the problems attendant upon dual nationality of a person born abroad. This was purposeful and not accidental. It was legislation structured with care and in the light of then apparent problems.

4. The solution to the dual nationality dilemma provided by the Congress by way of required residence surely is not unreasonable. It may not be the best that could be devised, but here, too, we cannot say that it is irrational or arbitrary or unfair. Congress first has imposed a condition precedent in that the citizen parent must have been in the United States or its possessions not less than 10 years, at least five of which are after attaining age 14. It then has imposed, as to the foreign-born child himself, the condition subsequent as to residence here. The Court already had emphasized the importance of residence in this country as the talisman of dedicated attachment, *Weedin v. Chin Bow*, 274 U.S. 657, 666-667 (1927). ... The same policy is reflected in the required period of residence here for aliens seeking naturalization. 8 U.S.C. § 1427(a).

5. We feel that it does not make good constitutional sense, or comport with logic, to say, on the one hand, that Congress may impose a condition precedent, with no constitutional complication, and yet be powerless to impose precisely the same condition subsequent. Any such distinction, of course, must rest, if it has any basis at all, on the asserted "premise that the rights of citizenship of the native born and of the naturalized person are of the same dignity and are coextensive," Schneider v. Rusk, 377 U.S., at 165, and on the announcement that Congress has no "power, express or implied, to take away an American citizen's citizenship without his assent," Afroyim v. Rusk, 387 U.S., at 257. But, as pointed out above, these were utterances bottomed upon Fourteenth Amendment citizenship and that Amendment's direct reference to "persons born or naturalized in the United States. We do not accept the notion that those utterances are now to bc judically

extended to citizenship not based upon the Fourteenth Amendment and to make citizenship an absolute. That it is not an absolute is demonstrated by the fact that even Fourteenth Amendment citizenship by naturalization, when unlawfully procured, may be set aside. Afroyim v. Rusk, 387 U.S., at 267 n. 23.

6. A contrary holding would convert what is congressional generosity into something unanticipated and obviously undesired by the Congress. Our National Legislature indulged the foreign-born child with presumptive citizenship, subject to subsequent satisfaction of a reasonable residence requirement, rather than to deny him citizenship outright, as concededly it had the power to do, and relegate the child, if he desired American citizenship, to the more arduous requirements of the usual naturalization process. The plaintiff here would force the Congress to choose between unconditional conferment of United States citizenship at birth and deferment of citizenship until a condition precedent is fulfilled. We are not convinced that the Constitution requires so rigid a choice. If it does, the congressional response seems obvious.

7. Neither are we persuaded that a condition subsequent in this area impresses one with "second-class citizenship." That cliche is too handy and too easy, and, like most cliches, can be misleading. That the condition subsequent may be beneficial is apparent in the light of the conceded fact that citizenship to this plaintiff was fully deniable. The proper emphasis is on what the statute permits him to gain from the possible starting point of noncitizenship, not on what he claims to lose from the possible starting point of full citizenship to which he has no constitutional right in the first place. His citizenship, while it lasts, although conditional, is not "second-class."

8. The plaintiff is not stateless. His Italian citizenship remains. He has lived practically all his life in Italy. He has never lived in this country; although he has visited here five times, the stipulated facts contain no indication that he ever will live here. He asserts no claim of ignorance or of mistake or even of hardship. He was warned several times of the provision of the statute and of his need to take up residence in the United States prior to his 23rd birthday.

We hold that § 301 (b) has no constitutional infirmity in its application to plaintiff Bellei. The judgment of the District Court is reversed.

NOTES AND QUESTIONS

1. What accounts for the erosion of the view stated by the Court in *Afroyim*?

2. In *Bellei,* is the Court's distinction between 14th Amendment first sentence and second sentence citizenships plausible? What is its policy consequence?

3. How relevant is the notion of "loyalty" or "divided loyalty" if the issue is natural citizenship?

4. If the effect of the ruling had been to render Bellei stateless, would the Court have held to its position?

D. PROBLEMS ASSOCIATED WITH MULTIPLE NATIONALITY

1. The Issue

Techniques for ascription of nationality may overlap, and an individual may be the national of two or more states simultaneously. "The most frequent case of double nationality at birth, "observed Manley Hudson," is caused by the application of *jus soli* and *jus sanguinis* to the same individual: a person born in a country which has the jus soli, of parents who have the nationality of a country which employs *jus sanguinis*, becomes a double national or *sujet mixte*." Manley O. Hudson, *Report on Nationality, Including Statelessness,* [1952] 2 Y.B. INT'L L. COMM'N 3, 11, U.N. Doc. A/CN.4/50 (1952). As was observed by the majority in *Rogers v. Bellei (supra)*, while such an individual may enjoy multiple benefit direct access to several states and plenary civil rights within each, potential diplomatic protection by more than one state and so on, he or she can be subject to claims by the government of each nationality, with severe penalties for failure to comply.

The problems of multiple nationality become most severe during periods of intense national crisis, as exemplified in the Kawakita and Joyce cases.

2. Trends in National Decision

a. Kawakita v. United States

343 U.S. 717 (1952)

JUSTICE DOUGLAS: Petitioner, a national both of the United States and of Japan, was indicted for treason, the overt acts relating to his treatment of American prisoners of war. He was convicted of treason after a jury trial (*See* 96 F.Supp. 824) and the judgment of conviction was affirmed. 190 F.2d 506. The case is here on certiorari. 342 U.S. 932.

The important question that lies at the threshold of the case relates to expatriation. Petitioner was born in this country in 1921 of Japanese parents who were citizens of Japan. He was thus a citizen of the United States by birth (Amendment XIV, § 1) and, by reason of Japanese law, a national of Japan. See *Hirabayashi v. United States*, 320 U.S. 81, 97.

In 1939 shortly before petitioner turned 18 years of age he went to Japan with his father to visit his grandfather. He traveled on a United States passport; and to obtain it he took the customary oath of allegiance. In 1940 he registered with an American consul in Japan as an American citizen. Petitioner remained in Japan, his father returning to this country. In March, 1941, he entered Meiji University and took a commercial course and military training. In April, 1941, he renewed his United States passport, once more taking the oath of allegiance to the United States. During this period he was registered as an alien with the Japanese police. When war was declared, petitioner was still a student at Meiji University. He became of age in 1942 and completed his schooling in 1943, at which time it was impossible for him to return to the United States. In 1943 he registered in the Koseki, a family census register. Petitioner did not join the Japanese Army nor serve as a soldier. Rather, he obtained employment as an interpreter with the Oeyama Nickel Industry Co., Ltd., where he worked until Japan's surrender. He was hired to interpret communications between the Japanese and the prisoners of war who were assigned to work at the mine and in the factory of this company. The treasonable acts for which he was convicted involved his conduct toward American prisoners of war.

In December, 1945, petitioner went to the United States consul at Yokohama and applied for registration as an American citizen. He stated under oath that he was a United States citizen and had not done various acts amounting to expatriation. He was issued a passport and returned to the United States in 1946. Shortly thereafter he was recognized by a former American prisoner of war, whereupon he was arrested, and indicted, and tried for treason.

Petitioner defended at his trial on the ground that he had renounced or abandoned his United States citizenship and was expatriated. Congress has provided by § 401 of the Nationality Act of 1940, 54 Stat.1137, 1168, as amended, 8 U.S.C. § 801, that a national of the United States may lose his nationality in certain prescribed ways. It provides in relevant part,

> A person who is a national of the United States, whether by birth or naturalization, shall lose his nationality by:
>
> (a) Obtaining naturalization in a foreign state. …; or
>
> (b) Taking an oath or making an affirmation or other formal declaration of allegiance to a foreign state; or
>
> (c) Entering, or serving in, the armed forces of a foreign state unless expressly authorized by the laws of the United States, if he has or acquires the nationality of such foreign state; or
>
> (d) Accepting, or performing the duties of, any office, post, or employment under the government of a foreign state or political subdivision thereof for which only nationals of such state are eligible. …;

Petitioner asks us to hold as a matter of law that he had expatriated himself by his acts and conduct beginning in 1943. He places special emphasis on the entry of his name in the Koseki. Prior to that time he had been registered by the police as an alien. There is evidence that after that time he was considered by Japanese authorities as a Japanese and that he took action which might give rise to the inference that he had elected the Japanese nationality: he took a copy of the Koseki to the police station and had his name removed as an alien; he changed his registration at the University from American to Japanese and his address from California to Japan; he used the Koseki entry to get a job at the Oeyama camp; he went to China on a Japanese passport (see United States ex rel. Scimeca v. Husband, 2 Cir., 6 F.2d 957, 958); he accepted labor draft papers from the

Japanese government; he faced the east each morning and paid his respects to the Emperor.

The difficulty with petitioner's position is that the implications from the acts, which he admittedly performed, are ambiguous. He had a dual nationality, a status long recognized in the law. Perkins v. Elg, 307 U.S. 325, 344-349. The concept of dual citizenship recognizes that a person may have and exercise rights of nationality in two countries and be subject to the responsibilities of both. The mere fact that he asserts the rights of one citizenship does not without more mean that he renounces the other. In this setting petitioner's registration in the Koseki might reasonably be taken to mean no more than an assertion of some of the rights which his dual citizenship bestowed on him. The deposition of the Attorney General of Japan states that the entry of a person's name in the Koseki is taken to mean that one has Japanese nationality. But since petitioner already had Japanese nationality, he obviously did not acquire it by the act of registration. The Attorney General of Japan further deposed that all Japanese nationals, whether or not born abroad, are duty bound to Japanese allegiance and that registering in the Koseki is 11 not necessarily a formal declaration of allegiance but merely a reaffirmation of an allegiance to Japan which already exists." From this it would appear that the registration may have been nothing more than the disclosure of a fact theretofore not made public.

Conceivably it might have greater consequences. In other settings it might be the equivalent of "naturalization" within the meaning of § 401 (a) of the Act or the making of "an affirmation or other formal declaration of allegiance" to Japan within the meaning of § 401 (b). Certainly it was relevant to the issue of expatriation. But we cannot say as a matter of law that it was a renunciation of petitioner's American citizenship. What followed might reasonably be construed to mean no more than recognition of the Japanese citizenship which petitioner had acquired on birth-nationality that was publicly disclosed for the first time in Japan by his registration in the Koseki. Cf. 3 Hackworth, Digest of International Law (1942), p. 373. The changing of his registration at the police station and at the University, so as to conform those records to the public record of his Japanese nationality, might reasonably mean no more than announcing the fact of his Japanese nationality to the interested authorities.

As we have said, dual citizenship presupposes rights of citizenship in each country. It could not exist if the assertion of rights or the assumption of liabilities of one were deemed inconsistent with the maintenance of the other. For example, when one has a dual citizenship, it is not necessarily inconsistent with his citizenship in one nation to use a passport proclaiming his citizenship in the other. [*Id.*]Hence the use by petitioner of a Japanese passport on his trip to China, his use of the Koseki entry to obtain work at the Oeyama camp, the bowing to the Emperor, and his acceptance of labor draft papers from the Japanese government might reasonably mean no more than acceptance of some of the incidents of Japanese citizenship made possible by his dual citizenship.

Those acts, to be sure, were colored by various other acts and statements of petitioner. He testified for example that he felt no loyalty to the United States from about March, 1943, to late 1945. There was evidence that he boasted that Japan was winning and would win the war, that he taunted American prisoners of war with General MacArthur's departure from the Philippines, that he expressed his hatred towards things American and toward the prisoners as Americans. That was in 1943 and 1944. This attitude continued into 1945, although in May or June, 1945, shortly before Japan's surrender, he was saying he did not care "which way the war goes because I am going back to the States anyway."

On December 31, 1945, he applied for registration as an American citizen, and in that connection he made an affidavit in which he stated that he had been "temporarily residing" in Japan since August 10, 1939; that he came to Japan to study Japanese; that he possessed dual nationality from birth but that his name was not entered in the census register until March 8, 1943; and that he had "never been naturalized, taken an oath of allegiance, or voted as a foreign citizen or subject, or in any way held myself out as such."

The United States foreign service officer concluded that petitioner had overcome the presumption of expatriation. He reported, "In 1943 his possession of Japanese nationality was made a matter of record by the entry of his name into his uncle's Family Census Register. He states that this action was taken under severe pressure by the Japanese police and by his uncle, on whom he was financially dependent after his supply of funds from the U. S. was cut off; this office has reason to believe this statement." These representations led to the issuance of an American passport on which he returned to the United States in 1946.

If petitioner were to be believed in December, 1945, he never once renounced his American citizenship. If what petitioner now says were his thoughts, attitudes, and motives in 1943 and 1944 and in part of 1945, he did intend to renounce his American citizenship. If the latter version were believed by the jury, the signing of the family register, and the changing of his registration at the police station and at the University would assume different significance; those acts might then readily suggest the making of a declaration of allegiance to Japan within the meaning of § 401 (b). If, on the other hand, petitioner were to be believed when in 1945 he stated he had not done acts by which he renounced his American citizenship, then the Koseki incident and the changes in his police and University registration could reasonably be taken as amounting to no more than a public declaration of an established and preexisting fact, viz. his Japanese nationality. We think, in other words, that the question whether petitioner had renounced his American citizenship was on this record peculiarly for the jury to determine. The charge was that the jury must be satisfied beyond a reasonable doubt that during the period specified in the indictment, petitioner was an American citizen. We cannot say there was insufficient evidence for that finding.

Petitioner concedes he did not enter the armed services of Japan within the meaning of § 401 (c) of the Act but claims that during his tour of duty at the Oeyama camp he was "serving in" the Japanese armed services within the statutory meaning of those words. In this connection he also argues that his work in the Oeyama camp was the performance of the duties of an "office, post, or employment under the government" of Japan "for which only nationals of such state are eligible" within the meaning of § 401 (d) of the Act.

The Oeyama Nickel Industry Co., Ltd., was a private company, organized for profit. It was engaged in producing metals used for war under contracts with the Japanese government. In 1944 it was designated by the Japanese government as a munitions corporation and under Japanese law civilian employees were not allowed to change or quit their employment without the consent of the government. The company's mine and factory were manned in part by prisoners of war. They lived in a camp controlled by the Japanese army. Though petitioner took orders from the military, he was not a soldier in the armed services; he wore insignia on his uniform distinguishing him as nonmilitary personnel; he had no duties to perform in relation to the prisoners, except those of an interpreter. His employment was as an interpreter for the Oeyama Nickel Industry Co., Ltd., a private company. The regulation of the company by the Japanese government, the freezing of its labor force, the assignment to it of prisoners of war under military command were incidents of a war economy. But we find no indication that the Oeyama Company was nationalized or its properties seized and operated by the government. The evidence indicates that it was a part of a regimented industry; but it was an organization operating for private profit under private management. We cannot say that petitioner's status as an employee of a private company was changed by that regimentation of the industry.

It would require a broad and loose construction of "office, post, or employment under the government of a foreign state" as those words are used in § 401 (d) to hold that petitioner had sacrificed his American citizenship by accepting or performing the duties of interpreter. We are thinking not only of this case but of other cases to which § 401 (d) is applicable. We are reluctant to resolve the ambiguity contained in § 401 (d) so as to provide treacherous ground for the loss of the rights of citizenship by the Nisei. As the Court said in Perkins v. Elg, "Rights of citizenship are not to be destroyed by an ambiguity." It would be harsh indeed to hold that a Nisei, marooned in Japan when World War II broke out, would be expatriated merely by working for a private company whose business was supervised and whose labor supply was controlled by the Japanese government in time of war. That would give § 401 (d) a broad, pervasive sweep. Section 401 (d) not only makes acceptance of "any office, post, or employment under the government of a foreign state" the basis of expatriation; it also makes "performing the duties" of any such office, post, or employment a ground for expatriation. One who was drafted for such service would be included, as well as one who volunteered. In time of war that would bring most employees of private companies within the danger zone in view of the hold which a war economy places on industry and the supervision and control which it asserts. We therefore incline to a construction of the words "under the government of a foreign state" to mean the relationship that public employees have with their government or with the bureaus or corporations which are government owned and controlled. Support for that narrower meaning is found in the legislative history.

Section 402 creates a presumption that a national in Kawakita's category who remains six months or longer within a foreign state of which he or either of his parents shall have been a national shall be presumed to have expatriated himself under § 401 (c) or (d). Section 402 does not enlarge § 401 (c) or (d); it creates a rebuttable presumption of expatriation; and when it is shown that the citizen did no act which brought him under § 401 (c) or (d), the presumption is overcome. On that showing the person never loses his American nationality. *See* Dos Reis ex rel. Camara v. Nicolls, I Cir., 161 F.2d 860, 868. In other words, once it was shown that petitioner was not expatriated under § 401 (c) or (d), the force of § 402 was spent.

Section 408 provides, "The loss of nationality under this Act shall result solely from the performance by a national of the acts or fulfillment of the conditions specified in this Act." The District Court therefore charged the jury that the only methods of expatriation are those contained in § 401. Petitioner claims that charge was error. He argues that § 408 is applicable only to the loss of nationality "under this Act" and that there are other methods of losing it. He refers to R.S. § 1999, 8 U.S.C. § 800, which survived the Nationality Act of 1940 and is not part of it, and which proclaims the right of expatriation as "a natural and inherent right of all people." We do not undertake to resolve the question of the reason that it is not squarely presented. On this issue of expatriation, petitioner tenders no question of fact which was inadmissible under § 401. Petitioner merely says that "by his conduct" he had "expatriated himself from United States citizenship." But he has failed to show that that issue is narrower than or different from the issue presented on this record under § 401 (b) -the declaration of allegiance to Japan. As we have indicated, the major factual problem on the issue of expatriation revolved around the entry of petitioner's name in the Koseki. All of the other conduct referred to, including the paying of respects to the Emperor and the expressions of hostility to the United States, were relevant and admissible on that issue. If it could not in the eyes of the jury make the signing of the Koseki and the changes in the registration that followed that event tantamount to renunciation under § 401 (b), it hardly could do so standing alone. Hence, if there was error in the charge, it was harmless.

That conclusion is reinforced by another aspect of the case. Petitioner testified that he believed when he signed the Koseki that he lost his American citizenship. He testified that during the period charged in the indictment he believed that he was no longer an American citizen. The District Court charged that if the jury found (i) defendant had committed any overt act charged in the indictment and (2) he was an American citizen, yet they should not convict if they further found that at the time "the defendant honestly believed that he was no longer a citizen of the United States" since in that event he could not have committed the act with treasonable intent. Under this charge the belief of petitioner that he had renounced his American citizenship was sufficient to acquit if the jury believed him. His belief could not have been made more relevant to the issue of guilt if it had been admitted as proof of expatriation separate and apart from the other grounds specified in § 401 of the Act. Hence even if we assume, arguendo, that the court was wrong in charging that § 408 made the grounds specified in § 401 exclusive, the error was harmless.

Petitioner contends that a person who has a dual nationality can be guilty of treason only to the country where he resides, not to the other country which claims him as a national. More specifically, he maintains that while petitioner resided in Japan he owed his paramount allegiance to that country and was indeed, in the eyes of our law, an alien enemy.

The argument in its broadest reach is that treason against the United States cannot be committed abroad or in enemy territory, at least by an American with a dual nationality residing in the other country which claims him as a national. The definition of treason, however, contained in the Constitution contains no territorial limitation. "Treason against the United States, shall consist only in levying War against them, or in adhering to their Enemies, giving them Aid and Comfort. ..." Art. III, § 3. A substitute proposal containing some territorial limitations was rejected by the Constitutional Convention. ... The Records of the Federal Convention, pp. 347-348. The Act of April 30, 1790, 1 Stat.112, which was passed by the first Congress defining the crime of treason likewise contained no territorial limitation; and that legislation is contained in substantially the same form in the present statute. 18 U.S.C. (Supp. IV) § 2381. We must therefore reject the suggestion that an American citizen living beyond the territorial limits of the United States may not commit treason against them. See Chandler v. United States, 1 Cir., 171 F.2d 921, 929-930; Burgman v. United States, 88 U.S.App.D.C. 184,185; 188 F.2d 637, 640.

One who has a dual nationality will be subject to claims from both nations, claims which at times may be competing or conflicting. The nature of these claims has recently been stated as follows:

> A person with dual nationality may be subjected to taxes by both states of which he is a national. He is not entitled to protection by one of the two states of which he is a national while in the territorial jurisdiction of the other. Either state not at war with the other may insist on military service when the person is present within its territory. In time of war if he supports neither belligerent, both may be aggrieved. If he supports one belligerent, the other may be aggrieved. One state may be suspicious of his loyalty to it and subject him to the disabilities of an enemy alien, including sequestration of his property, while the other holds his conduct treasonable. Orfield, *The Legal Effects of Dual Nationality*, 17 GEO.WASH.L.REV. 427, 429.

Dual nationality, however, is the unavoidable consequence of the conflicting laws of different countries. One who becomes a citizen of this country by reason of birth retains it, even though by the law of another country he is also a citizen of it. He can under certain circumstances be deprived of his American citizenship through the operation of a treaty or an act of Congress; he can also lose it by voluntary action. *See* Perkins v. Elg. But American citizenship, until lost, carries obligations of allegiance as well as privileges and benefits. For one who has a dual status the obligations of American citizenship may at times be difficult to discharge. An American who has a dual nationality may find himself in a foreign country when it wages war on us. The very fact that he must make a livelihood there may indirectly help the enemy nation. In these days of total war manpower becomes critical and everyone who can be placed in a productive position increases the strength of the enemy to wage war. Of course, a person caught in that predicament can resolve the conflict of duty by openly electing one nationality or the other and becoming either an alien enemy of the country where he resides or a national of it alone. Yet, so far as the existing law of this country is concerned, he need not make that choice but can continue his dual citizenship. It has been stated in an administrative ruling of the State Department that a person with a dual citizenship who lives abroad in the other country claiming him as a national owes an allegiance to it which is paramount to the allegiance he owes the United States. That is a far cry from a ruling that a citizen in that position owes no allegiance to the United States. Of course, an American citizen who is also a Japanese national living in Japan has obligations to Japan necessitated by his residence there. There might conceivably be cases where the mere nonperformance of the acts complained of would be a breach of Japanese law. He may have employment which requires him to perform certain acts. The compulsion may come from the fact that he is drafted for the job or that his conduct is demanded by the laws of Japan. He may be coerced by his employer or supervisor or by the force of circumstances to do things which he has no desire or heart to do. That was one of petitioner's defenses in this case. Such acts-if done voluntarily and willfully-might be treasonable. But if done under the compulsion of the job or the law or some other influence, those acts would not rise to the gravity of that offense. The trial judge recognized the distinction in his charge when he instructed the jury to acquit petitioner if he did not do the acts willingly or voluntarily "but so acted only because performance of the duties of his employment required him to do so or because of other coercion or compulsion." In short, petitioner was held accountable by the jury only for performing acts of hostility toward this country which he was not required by Japan to perform.

If he can retain that freedom and still remain an American citizen, there is not even a minimum of allegiance which he owes to the United States while he resides in the enemy country. That conclusion is hostile to the concept of citizenship as we know it, and it must be rejected. One who wants that freedom can get it by renouncing his American citizenship. He cannot turn it into a fair-weather citizenship, retaining it for possible contingent benefits but meanwhile playing the part of the traitor. An American citizen owes allegiance to the United States wherever he may reside.

Circumstances may compel one who has a dual nationality to do acts which otherwise would not be compatible with the obligations of American citizenship. An American with a dual nationality who is charged with playing the role of the traitor may defend by showing that force or coercion compelled such conduct. The jury rejected that version of the facts which petitioner tendered. He is therefore forced to maintain that, being a national and a resident of Japan, he owed no allegiance to the United States even though he was an American citizen. That proposition we reject.

[The conviction was affirmed. However, President Dwight D. Eisenhower eventually commuted his death sentence. He was released from prison, stripped of his U.S. citizenship, and deported to Japan.]

b. Joyce v. Director of Public Prosecutions

[1946] A.C. 347, 364 (H.L.)

[In 1933 the appellant, an American citizen, who had resided in British territory for about twenty-four years, applied for and obtained a British passport, describing himself as a British subject by birth and stating that he required it for the purpose of holiday touring in Belgium, France, Germany, Switzerland, Italy and Austria. On its expiration, he obtained renewals on September 24, 1938 and on August 24, 1939, each for a period of one year, again describing himself as a British subject. After the outbreak of war between Great Britain and Germany and before the expiration of the validity of the renewed passport, he was proved to have been employed by the German radio company and to have delivered from enemy territory broadcast talks in English hostile to Great Britain. The passport was not found in his possession when he was arrested. Having been convicted of high treason he appealed:]

[LORD JOWITT L. C. stated his reasons for concluding that the appeal should be dismissed.]

My Lords, on November 7, 1945, the Court of Criminal Appeal dismissed the appeal of the appellant, William Joyce, who had on September 19, 1945, been convicted of high treason at the Central Criminal Court and duly sentenced to death. The Attorney-General certified under s. 1, subs. 6, of the Criminal Appeal Act 1907, that the decision of the Court of Criminal Appeal involved a point of law of exceptional public importance and that in his opinion it was desirable in the public interest that a further appeal should be brought. Hence this appeal is brought to your Lordships' House. And though, in accordance with the usual practice, the certificate of the Attorney-General does not specify the point of law raised in the appeal, it is clear that the question for your Lordships' determination is whether an alien who has been resident within the realm can be held guilty and convicted in this country of high treason in respect of acts committed by him outside the realm.

The House is called upon in the year 1945 to consider the scope and effect of a statute of the year 1351, the twenty-fifth year of the rein of Edward III. … It is proper to set out the material parts. Thus it runs: "Whereas divers opinions have been before this time in what case treason shall be said and in what not; the King, at the request of the Lords and of the Commons hath made a declaration in the manner as hereafter followeth, that is to say;" [amongst other things] "if a man do levy war against our Lord the King in his realm, or be adherent to the King's enemies in his realm, giving them aid and comfort in the realm, or elsewhere" then (I depart from the text and use modern terms) he shall be guilty of treason. It is not denied that the appellant has adhered to the King's enemies giving them aid and comfort elsewhere than in the realm. Upon this part of the case the single question is whether, having done so, he can be and in the circumstances of the case is guilty of treason. Your Lordships will observe that the statute is wide enough in Its terms to cover any man anywhere, "if a man do levy war," etc. Yet it is clear that some limitation must be placed upon the generality of the language, for the context in the preamble poses the question "in what case treason shall be said and in what not." It is necessary then to prove not only that an act was done but that, being done, it was a treasonable act. This must depend upon one thing only, namely the relation in which the actor stands to the King to whose enemies he adheres. An act that is in one man treasonable, may not be so in another. In the long discussion which your Lordships have heard upon this part of the case attention has necessarily been concentrated on the question of allegiance. The question whether a man can be guilty of treason to the King has been treated as identical with the question whether he owes allegiance to the King. An act, it is said, which is treasonable if the actor owes allegiance, is not treasonable if he does not. …

I have said, my Lords, that the question for consideration is bound up with the question of allegiance. Allegiance is owed to their sovereign Lord the King by his natural born subjects; so it is by those who, being aliens, become his subjects by denization or naturalization (I will call them all "naturalized subjects"); so it is by those who, being aliens, reside within the King's realm. … The natural-born subject owes allegiance from his birth, the naturalized subject from his naturalization, the alien from the day when he comes within the realm. By what means and when can they cast off allegiance? The natural-born subject cannot at common law at any time cast it off. "*Nemo potest exuere patriam*" is a fundamental maxim of the law from which relief was given only by recent statutes. Nor can the naturalized subjects at common law. It is in regard to the alien resident within the realm that the controversy in this case arises. Admittedly he owes allegiance while he is so resident, but it is argued that his allegiance extends no further. Numerous authorities were cited by the learned counsel for the appellant in which it is stated without any qualification or extension that an alien owes allegiance so long as he is within the realm and it has been argued with great force that the physical presence of the alien actor within the realm is necessary to make his act treasonable. It is implicit in this argument that during absence from the realm, however brief, an alien ordinarily resident within the realm cannot commit treason; he cannot in any circumstances by giving aid and comfort to the King's enemies outside the realm be guilty of a treasonable act. My Lords in my opinion this which is the necessary and logical statement of the appellant's case is not only at variance with the principle of the law, but is inconsistent with authority which your Lordships cannot disregard. I refer first to authority. It is said in

Foster's Crown Cases (3rd ed.), p. 183, "Local allegiance is founded in the protection a foreigner enjoyeth for his person, his family or effects, during his residence here; and it ceaseth, whenever he withdraweth with his family and effects." And then on p. 185 comes the statement of law upon which the passage I have cited is clearly founded "Section 4. And if such alien, seeking the protection of the Crown, and having a family and effects here, should during a war with his native country, go thither, and there adhere to the King's enemies for purposes of hostility, he might be dealt with as a traitor. For he came and settled here under the protection of the Crown; and, though his person was removed for a time, his effects and family continued still under the same protection. This rule was laid down by all the judges assembled at the Queen's command January 12, 1707." ... supposed in the resolution of 1707 an alien may be guilty of treason for an act committed outside the realm. The reason which appears in the resolution is illuminating. The principle governing the rule is established by the exception: "though his person was removed for a time, his family and effects continued under the same protection," that is, the protection of the Crown. The vicarious protection still afforded to the family, which he had left behind in this country, required of him a continuance of his fidelity. It is thus not true to say that an alien can never in law be guilty of treason to the sovereign of this realm in respect of an act committed outside the realm. My Lords, here no question arises of a vicarious protection. There is no evidence that the appellant left a family or effects behind him when he left this realm. I do not for this purpose regard parents or brother or sisters as a family. But though there was no continuing protection for his family or effects, of him too it must be asked, whether there was not such protection still afforded by the sovereign as to require of him the continuance of his allegiance. ... The material facts are these, that being for long resident here and owing allegiance he applied for and obtained a passport and, leaving the realm, adhered to the King's enemies. It does not matter that he made false representations as to his status, asserting that he was a British subject by birth, a statement that he was afterwards at pains to disprove. It may be that when he first made the statement, he thought it was true. Of this there is no evidence. The essential fact is that he got the passport and I now examine its effect. The actual passport issued to the appellant has not been produced, but its contents have been duly proved. The terms of a passport are familiar. It is thus described by Lord Alverstone C. J., in R. v. Brailsford, [1905] 2 K.B. 730, 745: "It is a document issued in the name of the sovereign on the responsibility of a minister of the Crown to a named individual, intended to be presented to the governments of foreign nations and to be used for that individual's protection as a British subject in foreign countries." By its terms it requests and requires in the name of His Majesty all those whom it may concern to allow the bearer to pass freely without let or hindrance and to afford him every assistance and protection of which he may stand in need. It is, I think, true that the possession of a passport by a British subject does not increase the sovereign's duty of protection, though it will make his path easier. For him it serves as a voucher and means of identification. But the possession of a passport by one who is not a British subject gives him rights and imposes upon the sovereign obligations which would otherwise not be given or imposed. It is immaterial that he has obtained it by misrepresentation and that he is not in law a British subject. By the possession of that document he is enabled to obtain in a foreign country the protection extended to British subjects. By his own act he has maintained the bond which while he was within the realm bound him to his sovereign. The question is not whether he obtained British citizenship by obtaining the passport, but whether by its receipt he extended his duty of allegiance beyond the moment when he left the shores of this country. As one owing allegiance to the King he sought and obtained the protection of the King for himself while abroad.

... A well known writer on international law has said (see Oppenheim, International Law, 5th ed., vol. I., p. 546) that by a universally recognized customary rule of the law of nations every state holds the right of protection over its citizens abroad. This rule thus recognized may be asserted by the holder of a passport which is for him the outward title of his rights. It is true that the measure in which the state will exercise its right lies in its discretion. But with the issue of the passport the first step is taken. Armed with that document the holder may demand from the State's representatives abroad and from the officials of foreign governments that he be treated as a British subject, and even in the territory of a hostile state may claim the intervention of the protecting power. I should make it clear that it is no part of the case for the Crown that the appellant is debarred from alleging that he is not a British subject. The contention is a different one: it is that by the holding of a passport he asserts and maintains the relation in which he formerly stood, claiming the continued protection of the Crown and thereby pledging the continuance of his fidelity. In these circumstances I am clearly of opinion that so long as he holds the passport he is within the meaning of the statute a man who, if he is adherent to the King's enemies in the realm or elsewhere commits an act of treason. There is one other aspect of this part of the case with which I must deal. It is said that there is nothing to prevent an alien from withdrawing from his allegiance when he leaves the realm. I do not dissent from this as a general proposition. It is possible that he may do so even though he has obtained a passport. But that is a hypothetical case. Here there was no suggestion that the appellant had surrendered his passport or taken any other overt step to withdraw from his allegiance, unless indeed reliance is placed on the act of treason itself as a withdrawal. That in my opinion he cannot do. For such an act is not inconsistent with his still availing himself of the passport in other countries than Germany and possibly even in Germany itself. It is not to be assumed that the British authorities could immediately advise their representatives abroad or other foreign governments that the appellant, though the holder of a British passport, was not entitled to the protection that it appeared to afford. Moreover the special value to the enemy of the appellant's services as a broadcaster was that he could be represented as speaking as a British subject and his German work book showed that it was in this character that he was employed, for which his passport was doubtless accepted as the voucher.

NOTES AND QUESTIONS

1. With respect to certain problems, international decision has established procedures and criteria for determining the consequences of multiple nationality and, in particular, which of the competing national elites is entitled to control some or all of the national's activities.

2. The multiple national is sometimes more than someone with two passports. He or she may have two identity and loyalty systems in uneasy coexistence or in shifting patterns of superordination. In the circumstances, is it fair to apply norms of absolute loyalty to the multiple national? Consider the problem in the context of the Joyce and Kawakita cases.

3. In several countries, a special duty of allegiance is expected of a national; when it is breached, the crime of treason may have been committed. *See* U.S. Const. art. III, § 3, cl. 1 ("Treason against the United States, shall consist only in levying War against them, or in adhering to their Enemies, giving them Aid and Comfort. No Person shall be convicted of Treason unless on the Testimony of two Witnesses to the same overt Act, or on Confession in open Court."), 18 U.S.C. § 2381 (2000). For recent case law regarding this crime, the only one defined in the Constitution, see Henry Mark Holzer, *Why Not Call it Treason?: From Korea to Afghanistan*, 29 S.U. L. REV. 181 (2002). Presumably because of these enhanced constitutional protections, American citizens apprehended in the War against Terrorism have not been charged with treason. *See* John Walker Lindh Formally Charged with Conspiracy to Kill United States Nationals, Supporting Terrorists and Engaging in Prohibited Action with the Taliban; Attorney General Discusses Why Government Didn't Go for Treason and Death Penalty (ABC television broadcast, Jan. 16, 2002), *available at* 2002 WL 2968446; Note, *John Walker Lindh and Yaser Esam Hamdi: Closing the Loophole in International Humanitarian Law for American Nationals Captured Abroad While Fighting with Enemy Forces*, 40 AM. CRIM. L. REV. 159 (2003); and Ryan Norwood, *None Dare Call it Treason: The Constitutionality of the Death Penalty for Peacetime Espionage*, 87 CORNELL L. REV. 820 (2002).

4. Note the policy dilemma in the cases of the multiple national who is accused of treason. On the one hand, a liberal view of self-denationalization would provide effective defense, though it would clearly reduce elite control. On the other hand, the same liberal view could lead to denationalization by operation of law without the actual consent of the individual. This would offer an extraordinarily effective instrument for elites.

c. Myres S. McDougal, Harold D. Lasswell & Lung-Chu Chen, *Nationality and Human Rights: The Protection of the Individual in External Arenas* 83 YALE L.J. 900 (1974)

The most dramatic deprivation for a person of multiple nationality relates to the burdens of military service. Intense demands for military service have appeared to be the principal source of frictions between states in their competing claims to control individuals having multiple nationality. Hence, a paramount concern at the 1930 Hague Conference was to alleviate the burdens of "multiple" military service for people of multiple nationality and thus to help lessen frictions among states. This profound concern found concrete expression in the Protocol Relating to Military Obligations in Certain Cases of Double Nationality adopted at the Conference. According to the Protocol, a person having multiple nationality "who habitually resides in one of the countries whose nationality he possesses, and who is in fact most closely connected with that country, shall be exempt from all military obligations in the other country or countries." If such a person has the right, under the law of any of these states, "on attaining his majority, to renounce or decline the nationality of that State, he shall be exempt from military service in such State during his minority." If he has lost one nationality and acquired another, he "shall be exempt from military obligations in the State of which he has lost the nationality."

Elaborate provisions regarding military obligations are found in the European Convention on Reduction of Cases of Multiple Nationality and Military Obligations in Cases of Multiple Nationality. "Persons possessing the nationality of two or more Contracting Parties shall be required to fulfill their military obligations in relation to one of those Parties only," under special arrangements to be made between any of the contracting states.

With the exception of military obligations, there is little, in terms of amelioration of value deprivations for people of multiple nationality, comparable in scope to the treatment accorded to stateless persons. Treaties are sometimes concluded to eliminate or reduce double taxation. Mention may also be made of article 3 of the European Convention on Reduction of Cases of Multiple Nationality which states:

> The Contracting Party whose nationality a person desires to renounce shall not require the payment of any special tax or charge in the event of such renunciation.

From this brief survey it can be seen that the efforts of states both to minimize the occurrence of multiple nationality and to provide ameliorations for the burdens it imposes are far from adequate. The individual is still not given full opportunity to choose between retention of multiple nationality or renunciation of nationalities which may impose burdens upon him incompatible with human rights. Multilateral conventions might be devised which would afford individuals more freedom of choice in the retention of benefits and in the renunciation of burdens, when such renunciation is not inimical to an appropriate community responsibility. Certainly the traditional doctrine that one state cannot protect an individual against another state of his nationality should be abandoned. It can only serve to deny human rights and to exaggerate state interests at the expense of the individual. The appropriate amelioration of burdens with respect to other values must of course depend upon many variables in the context in which such values are pursued.

NOTES AND QUESTIONS

1. Discuss the policy recommendations made in 1974 by Professors McDougal, Lasswell, and Chen above.

2. Service in the military as a civic duty has been abolished or suspended in many countries. Is it relevant that military service and duty of allegiance are not transnationally common features of nationality? *See* SIEGFRIED WIESSNER, DIE FUNKTION DER STAATSANGEHÖRIGKEIT, *supra*, at 263.

3. In 1998-99, the newly elected German government of Social Democrats and Greens tried to permit, by law, the maintenance of their original citizenship by foreigners, mostly Turkish citizens, who had resided and worked in Germany for decades and now tried to get naturalized in their host

country. A groundswell of popular resistance, fanned by the opposition Christian Democrats, doomed the project. *See* Jordan Bonfante, *Whose Fatherland? A Proposal to Grant Citizenship to Members of Germany's Vast Immigrant Community Stirs Passionate Debate,* 15 TIME INT'L, Jan. 25, 1999, at 153; Roger Cohen, *Schroeder's New Politics Tripped Up by Hesse Voters*, N.Y. TIMES, Feb. 8, 1999, at A3.

The special international legal problems of married women of dual nationality are exemplified in the Mergé case.

d. Mergé Claim (United States v. Italy)

Decision of the Italian-United States Conciliation Commission June 10, 1955, 14 R.I.A.A. 236 (1955)

I. THE FACTS

Mrs. F. S. Mergé, a national of the United States of America, submitted a claim under Article 78 of the Peace Treaty with Italy of 1947 for compensation for the loss, as a result of the war, of certain property in Italy owned by her. The Italian Government having contended that the claim ought to be rejected because Mrs. Mergé was, under Italian law, an Italian national by marriage, the Commission was called upon to decide the preliminary question of whether a person having dual nationality was entitled to claim compensation under the Treaty.

The following are the relevant facts: The claimant was born in the United States and so acquired United States nationality under the law of the United States. In 1933 she married an Italian national in Rome and thus acquired Italian nationality by the operation of Italian law. The claimant lived with her husband in Italy until 1937 and accompanied him when he was sent to take up a post at the Italian Embassy at Tokyo. She travelled on an Italian passport. In 1940, the claimant registered as a national of the United States at the American Consulate-General at Tokyo. She remained in Japan throughout the war and was not interned as an enemy alien. When hostilities ceased, she refused to be returned by the United States military authorities to the United States, preferring to remain in Japan with her husband. In 1946, the American Consulate at Yokohama issued to the claimant an American passport valid only for travel to the United States, on which she travelled to the United States where she remained from December 1946 until September 1947. The passport was then validated for travel to Italy; the Italian Consulate at New York granted the claimant a visa to enter Italy as a visitor; and she went to Italy, where she had resided with her husband ever since. On arrival in Italy, the claimant registered as a United States national with the consular section of the American Embassy in Rome but a few days later she there swore an affidavit explaining her protracted residence outside the United States. It appeared that her only ties with the United States were her father and mother, and that she did not pay income tax to the United States Government.

In 1950, the claimant obtained from the consular section of the Embassy in Rome a new American passport to replace that issued in 1946, which had expired. In her application she stated that her "legal residence" was in New York and that she intended to return to the United States to reside there permanently at some indefinite time in the future. …

II. THE ISSUE

(1). Position of the Government of the United States of America:

(a) The Treaty of Peace between the United Nations and Italy provides the rules necessary to a solution of the case. The first sub-paragraph of paragraph 9(a) of Article 78 states:

> "United Nations nationals" means individuals who are nationals of any of the United Nations, or corporations or associations organized under the laws of any of the United Nations, at the coming into force of the present Treaty, provided that the said individuals, corporations or associations also had this status on September 3, 1943, the date of the Armistice with Italy.

All United Nations nationals are therefore entitled to claim, and it is irrelevant for such purpose that they possess or have possessed Italian nationality as well.

(b) The intention of the drafters of the Peace Treaty was to protect both the direct and indirect interests of United Nations nationals in their property in Italy.

(c) The principle, according to which one State cannot afford diplomatic protection to one of its nationals against a State whose nationality such person also possesses, cannot be applied to the Treaty of Peace with Italy because such principle is based on the equal sovereignty of States, whereas this Treaty of Peace was not negotiated between equal Powers but between the United Nations and Italy, a State defeated and obliged to accept the clauses imposed by the victors who at that time did not consider Italy a sovereign State.

(2). Position of the Italian Government:

(a) The text governing cases of dual nationality is not the first sub-paragraph of paragraph 9(a) of Article 78 but the second sub-paragraph of the same paragraph: only in cases of treatment as enemy can the Italian national who is also a United Nations national request application of Article 78.

(b) A defeated State, even when it is obliged to undergo the imposition of the conqueror, continues to be a sovereign State. From the juridical point of view, the Treaty of Peace is an international convention, not a unilateral act. In cases of doubt, its interpretation must be that more favourable to the debtor.

(c) There exists a principle of international law, universally recognized and constantly applied, by virtue of which diplomatic protection cannot be exercised in cases of dual nationality when the claimant possesses also the nationality of the State against which the claim is being made.

The first problem to be confronted by the Commission is that concerning whether this provision does or does not govern the problem of dual nationality. …

[The Court considers the letter of the Treaty of Peace (Paragraph (a) of Article 78) and concludes that neither the first nor the second sub-paragraph of paragraph 9 (a) of Article 78 contains a definition specifically referring to dual nationality and therefore capable of being a governing rule for those cases.]

(3). Principle of equality:

As the Treaty contains no provisions governing the case of dual nationality, the Commission must turn to the general principles of international law.

In this connexion two solutions are possible: (a) the principle according to which a State may not afford diplomatic protection to one of its nationals against the State whose nationality such person also possesses; (b) the principle of effective or dominant nationality.

(1). The rules of the Hague Convention of 1930 and the customary law manifested in international precedents and in the legal writings of the authors attest the existence and the practice of two principles in the problem of diplomatic protection in dual nationality cases.

The first of these, specifically referring to the scope of diplomatic protection, as a question of public international law, is based on the sovereign equality of the States in the matter of nationality and bars protection in behalf of those who are simultaneously also nationals of the defendant State.

The second of the principles had its origin in private international law, in those cases, that is, in which the courts of a third State had to resolve a conflict of nationality Laws. Thus, the principle of effective nationality was created with relation to the individual. But decisions and legal writings, because of its evident justice, quickly transported it to the sphere of public international law.

(2). It is not a question of adopting one nationality to the exclusion of the other. Even less when it is recognized by both Parties that the claimant possesses the two nationalities. The problem to be explained is, simply, that of determining whether diplomatic protection can be exercised in such cases.

(3). A prior question requires a solution: are the two principles which have just been set forth incompatible with each other, so that the acceptance of one of them necessarily implies the exclusion of the other? If the reply is in the affirmative, the problem presented is that of a choice; if it is in the negative, one must determine the sphere of application of each one of the two principles.

The Commission is of the opinion that no irreconcilable opposition between the two principles exist; in fact, to the contrary, it believes that they complement each other reciprocally. The principle according to which a State cannot protect one of its nationals against a State which also considers him its national and the principle of effective, in the sense of dominant, nationality, have both been accepted by the Hague Convention (Articles 4 and 5) and by the International Court of Justice (Advisory Opinion of April 11, 1949 and the Nottebohm Decision of April 6, 1955). If these two principles were irreconcilable, the acceptance of both by the Hague Convention and by the International Court of Justice would be incomprehensible.

(4). The International Court of Justice, in its recent decision in the Nottebohm Case, after having said that ". . . international law leaves to each State to lay down the rules governing the grant of its own nationality", adds: "On the other hand, a State cannot claim that the rules it has thus laid down are entitled to recognition by another State unless it has acted in conformity with this general aim of making the legal bond of nationality accord with the individual's genuine connexion with the State which assumes the defence of its citizens by means of protection as against other States." ... "Conferred by a State, it only entitles that State to exercise protection vis-à-vis another State, if it constitutes a translation into juridical terms of the individual's connexion with the State which has made him its national." (Judgment of April 6, 1955, p. 23.)

For even greater reason, this theory must be understood to be applicable to the problem of dual nationality which concerns the two contesting States, in view of the fact that in such case effective nationality does not mean only the existence of a real bond, but means also the prevalence of that nationality over the other, by virtue of facts which exist in the case.

(5). The principle, based on the sovereign equality of States, which excludes diplomatic protection in the case of dual nationality, must yield before the principle of effective nationality whenever such nationality is that of the claiming State. But it must not yield when such predominance is not proved because the first of these two principles is generally recognised and may constitute a criterion of practical application for the elimination of any possible uncertainty.

(6). The question of dual nationality obviously arises only in cases where the claimant was in possession of both nationalities at the time the damage occurred and during the whole of the period comprised between the date of the Armistice (September 3, 1943) and the date of the coming into force of the Treaty of Peace (September 15, 1947). In view of the principles accepted, it is considered that the Government of the United States of America shall be entitled to protect its nationals before this Commission in cases of dual nationality, United States and Italian, whenever the United States nationality is the effective nationality.

In order to establish the prevalence of the United States nationality in individual cases, habitual residence can be one of the criteria of evaluation, but not the only one. The conduct of the individual in his economic, social, political, civic and family life, as well as the closer and more effective bond with one of the two States must also be considered.

(7). It is considered that in this connexion the following principles may serve as guides:

(a) The United States nationality shall be prevalent in cases of children born in the United States of an Italian father and who have habitually lived there.

(b) The United States nationality shall also be prevalent in cases involving Italians who, after having acquired United States nationality by naturalization and having thus lost Italian nationality, have reacquired their nationality of origin as a matter of law as a result of having sojourned in Italy for more than two years, without the intention of retransferring their residence permanently to Italy.

(c) With respect to cases of dual nationality involving American women married to Italian nationals, the United States nationality shall be prevalent in cases in which the family has had habitual residence in the United States and the interests and the permanent professional life of the head of the family were established in the United States.

(d) In case of dissolution of marriage, if the family was established in Italy and the widow transfers her residence to the United States of America, whether or not the new residence is of an habitual nature must be evaluated, case by case, bearing in mind also the widow's conduct, especially with regard to the raising of her children, for the purpose of deciding which is the prevalent nationality.

(8). United States nationals who did not possess Italian nationality but the nationality of a third State can be considered "United Nations nationals" under the Treaty, even if their prevalent nationality was the nationality of the third State.

(9). In all other cases of dual nationality, Italian and United States, when, that is, the United States nationality is not prevalent in accordance with the above, the principle of international law, according to which a claim is not admissible against a State, Italy in our case, when this State also considers the claimant as its national and such bestowal of nationality is, as in the case of Italian law, in harmony (Article I of the Hague Convention of 1930) with international custom and generally recognized principles of law in the matter of nationality, will reacquire its force.

VI. DECISION

Examining the facts of the case in bar, in the light of the aforementioned criteria, especially paragraph 6, in relation to paragraph 7(c), the Commission holds that Mrs. Mergé can in no way be considered to be dominantly a United States national within the meaning of Article 78 of the Treaty of Peace, because the family did not have its habitual residence in the United States and the interests and the permanent professional life of the head of the family were not established there. In fact, Mrs. Mergé has not lived in the United States since her marriage, she used an Italian passport in travelling to Japan from Italy in 1937, she stayed in Japan from 1937 until 1946 with her husband, an official of the Italian Embassy in Tokyo, and it does not appear that she was ever interned as a national of a country enemy to Japan.

Inasmuch as Mrs. Mergé, for the foregoing reasons, cannot be considered to be dominantly a United States national within the meaning of Article 78 of the

Treaty of Peace, the Commission is of the opinion that the Government of the United States of America is not entitled to present a claim against the Italian Government in her behalf.

The Italian-United States Conciliation Commission, having noted the statement made during the deliberations by the Italian Representative in the name of his Government, according to which Mrs. Mergé, as an Italian national, will be able to submit a suitable claim to the competent Italian authorities, under domestic law, for the damages in question, even though the time-limit for such claims has expired, unanimously, Decides:

1. The Petition of the Agent of the United States of America is rejected. …

* * *

Some countries virtually disallow the renunciation of their citizenship.

e. Case No. A/18

Decision No. DEC 32-A18-FT, Iran - United States Claims Tribunal
Apr. 6, 1984, 5 Iran-U.S. Cl. Trib. Rep. 251

A large number of claims have been filed against Iran by claimants who, under United States law, are United States citizens and, under Iranian law, are Iranian citizens.

The question … before the Tribunal is whether the Claims Settlement Declaration grants the Tribunal jurisdiction over claims against Iran filed by persons who, during the relevant period which is from the date the claim arose until 19 January 1981, were Iranian citizens under the law of Iran and United States citizens under the law of the United States.

The relevant provisions of the Claims Settlement Declaration which the Tribunal must interpret are Article II, paragraph 1, and Article VII, paragraph 1 (a).

Article II, paragraph 1, states:

> An international arbitral tribunal (the Iran-United States Claims Tribunal) is hereby established for the purpose of deciding claims of nationals of the United States against Iran and claims of nationals of Iran against the United States ...

Article VII, paragraph 1 (a), states:

> A "national" of Iran or of the United States, as the case may be, means (a) a natural person who is a citizen of Iran or the United States; …

The United States argues that the text is clear and unambiguous and that, by defining "nationals" as "citizens", a term of municipal law, it makes clear that all nationals of the United States and of Iran, including dual nationals, are entitled to bring claims in this Tribunal.

Iran also asserts that the text is clear and unambiguous in that the ordinary meaning of the word "national" excludes dual nationals, as does the use of the disjunctive article "or". …

Neither of these arguments can be accepted. The Tribunal cannot agree that the text is so clear and unambiguous as to make further analysis unnecessary. ...

Paragraph 3(c) of Article 31 of the Vienna Convention directs the Tribunal to take into account "any relevant rules of international law applicable in the relations between the parties." There is a considerable body of law and legal literature, analyzed herein, which leads the Tribunal to the conclusion that the applicable rule of international law is that of dominant and effective nationality.

1. THE 1930 HAGUE CONVENTION

On 12 April 1930, a convention was concluded at The Hague "Concerning Certain Questions relating to the Conflict of Nationality Laws" (the "Hague Convention"). As Article 1 of that Convention makes plain, a determination by one State as to who are its nationals will be respected by another State "in so far as it is consistent" with international law governing nationality. International law, then, does not determine who is a national, but rather sets forth the conditions under which that determination must be recognized by other States.

Article 4 of the Convention provides: "A State may not afford diplomatic protection to one of its nationals against a State whose nationality such person also possesses." But this provision must be interpreted very cautiously. Not only is it more than 50 years old and found in a treaty to which only 20 States are parties, but great changes have occurred since then in the concept of diplomatic protection, which concept has been expanded. … This concept continues to be in a process of transformation, and it is necessary to distinguish between different types of protection, whether consular or claims-related.

Moreover, the negotiating history of Article 4 of the Hague Convention suggests that its application is doubtful in a case, such as the present one, where a dual national, by himself, brings before an international tribunal his own claim against one of the States whose nationality he possesses. Such a proposal was made during the Conference, but it was rejected …

Another reason why the applicability of Article 4 to the claims of dual nationals before this Tribunal is debatable is that it applies by its own terms solely to "diplomatic protection" by a State. While this Tribunal is clearly an international tribunal established by treaty and while some of its cases involve disputes between the two Governments and involve the interpretation and application of public international law, most disputes (including all of those brought by dual nationals) involve a private party on one side and a Government or Government-controlled entity on the other, and many involve primarily issues of municipal law and general principles of law. In such cases it is the rights of the claimant, not of his nation, that are to be determined by the Tribunal. This should be contrasted with the situation of espousal of claims in international law which the Permanent Court of International Justice described as follows: "...in taking up the case of one of its nationals, by resorting to diplomatic action or international judicial proceedings on his behalf, a State is in reality asserting its own right, the right to ensure in the person of its nationals respect for the rules of international law." Moreover, the object and purpose of the Algiers Declaration was to resolve a crisis in relations between Iran and the United States, not to extend diplomatic protection in the normal sense. It seems clear that a major obstacle to the resolution of that crisis was the existence of much litigation in the courts of the United States brought against Iran by citizens of the United States, often involving judicial attachments of Iranian assets. In order to overcome that obstacle and permit the return of these assets and the termination of that litigation, a new substitute forum — this Tribunal — was established. ...

It is also noteworthy that Article 5 of the Hague Convention recognized the principle of the stronger link for purposes of decisions by third States in cases of dual nationality. Although this Tribunal is not an organ of a third State, it is also not, as noted above, a tribunal where claims are espoused by a State at its discretion and decided solely by reference to public international law. ...

2. PRECEDENTS

In this field, there is a considerable number of relevant judicial and arbitral decisions, most of them prior to the Second World War, supplemented and interpreted by the writings of scholars. The writing of at least one scholar, Professor E.B. Borchard, apparently had a considerable effect, not only because of the later writers who have echoed his views which favored the rule of nonresponsibility, but also because of his influence on the Hague Conference that adopted the 1930 Convention discussed above. In fact, the precedents on which Borchard relied did not generally support his conclusion, and the Parties in the present case have acknowledged that the law prior to 1930 was uncertain. Iran, however, considers the conclusion of the 1930 Convention a decisive turning point that crystallized the rule of non- responsibility. The United States, on the other hand, points to the limited number of parties to that Convention and the practice of States, particularly in the conclusion and interpretation of claims settlement agreements since the Second World War. The Tribunal, having had the benefit of extensive written and oral argument of these issues by eminent counsel, does not believe it would be worthwhile for it to recite and comment upon the many precedents cited by the Parties, for the Tribunal is satisfied that, whatever the state of the law prior to 1945, the better rule at the time the Algiers Declarations were concluded and today is the rule of dominant and effective nationality. ...

The two most important decisions on the subject in the years following the Second World War have had a decisive effect. First, the International Court of Justice, in the Nottebohm Case, on 6 April 1955, stated the following:

> International arbitrators have ... given their preference to the real and effective nationality, that which accorded with the facts, that based on stronger factual ties between the person concerned and one of the States whose nationality is involved. Different factors are taken into

> consideration, and their importance will vary from one case to the next: the habitual residence of the individual concerned is an important factor, but there are other factors such as the centre of his interests, his family ties, his participation in public life, attachment shown by him for a given country and inculcated in his children, etc.

Similarly, the courts of third States, when they have before them an individual whom two other States hold to be their national, seek to resolve the conflict by having recourse to international criteria and their prevailing tendency is to prefer the real and effective nationality. …

While *Nottebohm* itself did not involve a claim against a State of which Nottebohm was a national, it demonstrated the acceptance and approval by the International Court of Justice of the search for the real and effective nationality based on the facts of a case, instead of an approach relying on more formalistic criteria. The effects of the Nottebohm decision have radiated throughout the international law of nationality.

A few months later, on 10 June 1955, the Italian-United States Conciliation Commission set up by application of the Peace Treaty of 1947, decided in the Merge Case that the principle "... based on the sovereign equality of States, which excludes diplomatic protection in the case of dual nationality, must yield before the principle of effective nationality whenever such nationality is that of the claiming State." *Mergé Case* (U.S. v. Italy) 14 R.I.A.A. 236, 247 (1955). The Commission then applied this same analysis in numerous other similar cases involving dual nationals. The Franco-Italian Conciliation Commission also decided several claims of dual nationals according to the "link theory". *See* Rambaldi Claim (Fr. v. Italy) 13 R.I.A.A. 786 (1957); Menghi Claim (Fr. v. Italy) 13 R.I.A.A. 801 (1958); Lombroso Claim (Fr. v. Italy) 13 R.I.A.A. 804 (1958).

3. LEGAL LITERATURE

Support for the principles applied in these cases is shared by some of the most competent international lawyers. Basdevant wrote that effective nationality must prevail, because nationality is the juridical translation of a social fact. Basdevant, "Conflits de Nationalités dans les Arbitrages Venezuéliens de 1903-1905", Rev. de Droit Intern. Privé 41, 60-61 (1909). Maury in "L'Arrêt Nottebohm et la Condition de Nationalité Effective," 23 Rabels Zeitschrift 515 (1958), expressed his doubts about the alleged rule forbidding a State to act against another State in cases of dual nationality, and concluded that the Nottebohm decision has a general scope.

Recent legal literature has suggested that the "actually dominant theory", Rousseau, Droit International Public, Précis Dalloz, 112 (1976), is, at least before international tribunals, the effective nationality theory. …

This trend toward modification of the Hague Convention rule of non- responsibility by search for the dominant and effective nationality is scarcely surprising as it is consistent with the contemporaneous development of international law to accord legal protections to individuals, even against the State of which they are nationals. Moreover ... many of the relevant decisions, even in the 19th century, reflected similar concerns by giving weight to domicile.

Thus, the relevant rule of international law which the Tribunal may take into account for purposes of interpretation, as directed by Article 31, paragraph 3(c), of the Vienna Convention, is the rule that flows from the dictum of *Nottebohm*, the rule of real and effective nationality, and the search for "stronger factual ties between the person concerned and one of the States whose nationality is involved." In view of the pervasive effect of this rule since the Nottebohm decision, the Tribunal concludes that the references to "national" and "nationals" in the Algiers Declarations must be understood as consistent with that rule unless an exception is clearly stated. As stated above, the Tribunal does not find that the text of the Algiers Declarations provides such a clear exception.

For the reasons stated above, the Tribunal holds that it has jurisdiction over claims against Iran by dual Iran-United States nationals when the dominant and effective nationality of the claimant during the relevant period from the date the claim arose until 19 January 1981 was that of the United States. In determining the dominant and effective nationality, the Tribunal will consider all relevant factors, including habitual residence, center of interests, family ties, participation in public life and other evidence of attachment. ...

To this conclusion the Tribunal adds an important caveat. In cases where the Tribunal finds jurisdiction based upon a dominant and effective nationality of the claimant, the other nationality may remain relevant to the merits of the claim.

NOTES AND QUESTIONS

1. Where the dual national belongs to both the derivative claimant and respondent states, the long-standing rule of international procedure has been that the claimant state may not bring a claim on the national's behalf. Are there cogent policy justifications for such a rule?

2. Mergé acquired multiple nationality, insofar as she did, because of her status as wife of an Italian national. Are such operations of law discriminatory? Should an international tribunal police them? How?

3. In his concurring opinion in Case No. A/18, 5 Iran-U.S. Claims Tribunal, Richard M. Mosk observes that:

> Iranian law imposes Iranian nationality on a broad spectrum of people, makes it very difficult to renounce that nationality and drastically penalizes persons who succeed in doing so.
>
> Iranian citizens cannot abandon their nationality until, *inter alia*, they reach the "full age" of 25, they have the approval of the Council of Ministers and they make arrangements to transfer to Iranian nationals all rights in real property in Iran (including that which they "may acquire by inheritance"). Those who renounce their Iranian nationality must leave Iran or be expelled, and such persons can only thereafter visit Iran once, and then, only with "special permission" from the Council of Ministers. ... The following are examples of those who are deemed Iranian nationals: a woman who marries an Iranian national; children of an Iranian father; and those who have a father of foreign nationality, and who

> are born in Iran and who continue to reside in Iran for one year immediately after reaching the full age of 18. . . .
>
> Thus some United States citizens have not been able to renounce their Iranian nationality or have not been willing to do so because of their reluctance to give up their properties and foresake their right to visit family in Iran.

Case No. A/18, 5 Iran-U.S. Cl. Trib. Rep. 251 (conc. op. Mosk).

Should these factors be taken into account when deciding upon the issues presented? Is renunciation of nationality a human right? Should it be?

f. Draft Articles on Diplomatic Protection

U.N. GAOR, 59th Sess., Supp. No.10, U.N. Doc. A/59/10, chap. IV (2004)

Article 6: *Multiple nationality and claim against a third State*

1. Any State of which a dual or multiple national is a national may exercise diplomatic protection in respect of that national against a State of which that individual is not a national.

2. Two or more States of nationality may jointly exercise diplomatic protection in respect of a dual or multiple national.

Article 7: *Multiple nationality and claim against a State of nationality*

A State of nationality may not exercise diplomatic protection in respect of a person against a State of which that person is also a national unless the nationality of the former State is predominant, both at the time of the injury and at the date of the official presentation of the claim.

NOTES AND QUESTIONS

1. Do the articles adopted by the ILC in 2004 summarize the prevailing trend regarding claims on behalf of multiple nationals? Do they represent good policy?

E. CLAIMS TO PROTECT PERSONS

International decision has made only limited efforts to prescribe effective limits to an elite's control of people within its own state. But it has prescribed more forthrightly for a state's exercise of protection of its nationals when they are abroad. Such prescriptions have been necessary, for elites have frequently been bold in projecting their power abroad to protect their nationals. Moreover, the temptation to exploit such opportunities for political purposes has been great. Hitler's adroit use of alleged rights of protection of *irredenta* will be recalled. An international regime has been established with regard to the contingencies and procedures for the protection of nationals, largely on the basis of customary law.

1. Inclusive Policies

In the absence of an effective centralized transnational agency, protection of nationals is perforce a national function. The possibility of abuse may be countered in part by developing clear criteria for appraising the lawfulness of the exercise of protection. The International Law Commission at its 2477th meeting on May 15, 1997 established a Working Group to examine the topic of diplomatic protection and to study, inter alia, the "required linkage between the beneficiary and the States exercising diplomatic protection," including not only nationals, but also "aliens in the service of the State, stateless persons, non-nationals forming a minority in a group of national claimants, non-nationals with long residence in the State espousing diplomatic protection, and non-nationals in the framework of international organizations of integration." U.N. Doc. A/CN.4/L.548, para. 189. In 2004, drawing heavily on the work of Mr. John Dugard, the Special Rapporteur for the topic, the International Law Commission, on first reading, adopted the following draft articles.

a. Draft Articles on Diplomatic Protection

U.N. GAOR, 59th Sess., Supp. No.10, U.N. Doc. A/59/10, chap. IV (2004)

Part One: *General Provisions*

Article 1: *Definition and scope*

Diplomatic protection consists of resort to diplomatic action or other means of peaceful settlement by a State adopting in its own right the cause of its national in respect of an injury to that national arising from an internationally wrongful act of another State.

Article 2: *Right to exercise diplomatic protection*

A State has the right to exercise diplomatic protection in accordance with the present draft articles.

Part Two: *Nationality*

Chapter I: *General Principles*

Article 3: *Protection by the State of nationality*

1. The State entitled to exercise diplomatic protection is the State of nationality.

2. Notwithstanding paragraph 1, diplomatic protection may be exercised in respect of a non-national in accordance with draft article 8.

Chapter II: *Natural Persons*

Article 4: *State of nationality of a natural person*

For the purposes of diplomatic protection of natural persons, a State of nationality means a State whose nationality the individual sought to be protected has acquired by birth, descent, succession of States, naturalization or in any other manner, not inconsistent with international law.

Article 5: *Continuous nationality*

1. A State is entitled to exercise diplomatic protection in respect of a person who was its national at the time of the injury and is a national at the date of the official presentation of the claim.

2. Notwithstanding paragraph 1, a State may exercise diplomatic protection in respect of a person who is its national at the date of the official presentation of the claim but was not a national at the time of the injury, provided that the person has lost his or her former nationality and has acquired, for a reason unrelated to the bringing of the claim, the nationality of that State in a manner not inconsistent with international law.

3. Diplomatic protection shall not be exercised by the present State of nationality in respect of a person against a former State of nationality of that person for an injury incurred when that person was a national of the former State of nationality and not of the present State of nationality. …

[For Article 6 re *multiple nationality and claims against a third State*, and Article 7 re *multiple nationality and claims against a State of nationality*, see *supra*, at 439.]

Article 8: *Stateless persons and refugees*

1. A State may exercise diplomatic protection in respect of a stateless person who, at the time of the injury and at the date of the official presentation of the claim, is lawfully and habitually resident in that State.

2. A State may exercise diplomatic protection in respect of a person who is recognized as a refugee by that State when that person, at the time of the injury and at the date of the official presentation of the claim, is lawfully and habitually resident in that State.

3. Paragraph 2 does not apply in respect of an injury caused by an internationally wrongful act of the State of nationality of the refugee.

Chapter III: *Legal Persons*

Article 9: *State of nationality of a corporation*

For the purposes of diplomatic protection of corporations, the State of nationality means the State under whose law the corporation was formed and in whose territory it has its registered office or the seat of its management or some similar connection.

Article 10: *Continuous nationality of a corporation*

1. A State is entitled to exercise diplomatic protection in respect of a corporation which was its national at the time of the injury and is its national at the date of the official presentation of the claim.

2. Notwithstanding paragraph 1, a State continues to be entitled to exercise diplomatic protection in respect of a corporation which was its national at the

time of the injury and which, as the result of the injury, has ceased to exist according to the law of that State.

Article 11: *Protection of shareholders*

The State of nationality of the shareholders in a corporation shall not be entitled to exercise diplomatic protection on behalf of such shareholders in the case of an injury to the corporation unless:

(a) The corporation has ceased to exist according to the law of the State of incorporation for a reason unrelated to the injury; or

(b) The corporation had, at the time of the injury, the nationality of the State alleged to be responsible for causing injury, and incorporation under the law of the latter State was required by it as a precondition for doing business there.

Article 12: *Direct injury to shareholders*

To the extent that an internationally wrongful act of a State causes direct injury to the rights of shareholders as such, as distinct from those of the corporation itself, the State of nationality of any such shareholders is entitled to exercise diplomatic protection in respect of its nationals.

Article 13: *Other legal persons*

The principles contained in draft articles 9 and 10 in respect of corporations shall be applicable, as appropriate, to the diplomatic protection of other legal persons.

Part Three: *Local Remedies* [Articles 14-16, see *infra*, at 475.]

Part Four: *Miscellaneous Provisions*

Article 17: *Actions or procedures other than diplomatic protection*

The present draft articles are without prejudice to the rights of States, natural persons or other entities to resort under international law to actions or procedures other than diplomatic protection to secure redress for injury suffered as a result of an internationally wrongful act.

Article 18: *Special treaty provisions*

The present draft articles do not apply where, and to the extent that, they are inconsistent with special treaty provisions, including those concerning the settlement of disputes between corporations or shareholders of a corporation and States.

Article 19: *Ships' crews*

The right of the State of nationality of the members of the crew of a ship to exercise diplomatic protection on their behalf is not affected by the right of the State of nationality of a ship to seek redress on behalf of such crew members, irrespective of their nationality, when they have been injured in the course of an injury to the vessel resulting from an internationally wrongful act.

2. The Requirement of a "National Link"

To avoid possible abuses, practice as well as doctrine have maintained that it is the link of nationality between a State and an individual which alone gives the State the right to exercise its diplomatic protection on his or her behalf.

a. The Barcelona Traction, Light, and Power Company (Belg. v. Spain)

1970 I.C.J. 3, 31

[The Barcelona Traction, Light, and Power Company was incorporated in Toronto, Canada, in 1911, as a holding company for various wholly or substantially owned Spanish and Canadian subsidiaries, to develop and operate an electric power system in Spain. In 1948, a Spanish court declared it bankrupt and its assets were seized. As part of the company's unsuccessful efforts to resist the bankruptcy proceedings, the Belgian, British, Canadian, and United States governments made representations to Spain on behalf of the company. For reasons not of record, the Canadian government ceased its diplomatic efforts on behalf of Barcelona Traction after 1955. Since Belgian nationals owned a large majority of the stock in the company, the Belgian government, after an earlier application to the court in 1958 and its subsequent withdrawal in 1961, brought this case before the International Court of Justice in 1962. The Spanish government raised four preliminary objections, two of which were reacted by the court in 1964; the other two were joined by the court on the merits. The court's final judgment, rendered in February 1970, upheld Spain's third preliminary objection, declaring that Belgium lacked standing (*jus standi*) to espouse a claim for its nationals, shareholders in a Canadian company, for damages allegedly resulting from illegal acts of various organs of the Spanish government against the company. Belgium's application was thus dismissed and the merits of the case were not considered by the court.

The central issue was the competence of Belgium to extend protection to Belgian shareholders in a company which is a juridical entity incorporated in Canada.] …

28. …The claim is presented on behalf of natural and juristic persons, alleged to be Belgian nationals and shareholders in the Barcelona Traction, Light and Power Company, Limited. The submissions of the Belgian Government make it clear that the object of its Application is reparation for damage allegedly caused to these persons by the conduct, said to be contrary to international law, of various organs of the Spanish State towards that company and various other companies in the same group. …

30. The States which the present case principally concerns are Belgium, the national State of the alleged shareholders, Spain, the State whose organs are alleged to have committed the unlawful acts complained of, and Canada, the State under whose laws Barcelona Traction was incorporated and in whose ter-

ritory it has its registered office ("head office" in the terms of the by-laws of Barcelona Traction).

31. Thus the Court has to deal with a series of problems arising out of a triangular relationship involving the State whose nationals are shareholders in a company incorporated under the laws of another State, in whose territory it has its registered office; the State whose organs are alleged to have committed against the company unlawful acts prejudicial to both it and its shareholders; and the State under whose laws the company is incorporated, and in whose territory it has its registered office.

32. In these circumstances it is logical that the Court should first address itself to what was originally presented as the subject-matter of the third preliminary objection: namely the question of the right of Belgium to exercise diplomatic protection of Belgian shareholders in a company which is a juristic entity incorporated in Canada, the measures complained of having been taken in relation not to any Belgian national but to the company itself.

33. When a State admits into its territory foreign investments or foreign nationals, whether natural or juristic persons, it is bound to extend to them the protection of the law and assumes obligations concerning the treatment to be afforded them. These obligations, however, are neither absolute nor unqualified. In particular, an essential distinction should be drawn between the obligations of a State towards the international community as a whole, and those arising vis-à-vis another State in the field of diplomatic protection. By their very nature the former are the concern of all States. In view of the importance of the rights involved, all States can be held to have a legal interest in their protection; they are obligations *erga omnes*.

34. Such obligations derive, for example, in contemporary international law, from the outlawing of acts of aggression, and of genocide, as also from the principles and rules concerning the basic rights of the human person, including protection from slavery and racial discrimination. Some of the corresponding rights of protection have entered into the body of general international law (Reservations to the Convention on the Prevention and Punishment of the Crime of Genocide, Advisory Opinion, I.C.J. Reports 1951, P. 23); others are conferred by international instruments of a universal or quasi-universal character.

35. Obligations the performance of which is the subject of diplomatic protection are not of the same category. It cannot be held, when one such obligation in particular is in question, in a specific case, that all States have a legal interest in its observance. In order to bring a claim in respect of the breach of such an obligation, a State must first establish its right to do so, for the rules on the subject rest on two suppositions:

The first is that the defendant State has broken an obligation towards the national State in respect of its nationals. The second is that only the party to whom an international obligation is due can bring a claim in respect of its breach.

(Reparation for Injuries Suffered in the Service of the United Nations, Advisory Opinion, I.C.J. Reports 1949, pp. 181-82.)

In the present case it is therefore essential to establish whether the losses allegedly suffered by Belgian shareholders in Barcelona Traction were the consequence of the violation of obligations of which they were the beneficiaries. In other words: has a right of Belgium been violated on account of its nationals' having suffered infringement of their rights as shareholders in a company not of Belgian nationality?

36. Thus it is the existence or absence of a right, belonging to Belgium and recognized as such by international law, which is decisive for the problem of Belgium's capacity.

> This right is necessarily limited to intervention [by a State] on behalf of its own nationals because, in the absence of a special agreement, it is the bond of nationality between the State and the individual which alone confers upon the State the right of diplomatic protection, and it is as a part of the function of diplomatic protection that the right to take up a claim and to ensure respect for the rules of international law must be envisaged. (Panevezys-Saldutiskis Railway, judgment, 1939, P.C. I.J., Series A/B, No. 76, p. 16.)

It follows that the same question is determinant in respect of Spain's responsibility towards Belgium. Responsibility is the necessary corollary of a right. In the absence of any treaty on the subject between the Parties, this essential issue has to be decided in the light of the general rules of diplomatic protection.

37. In seeking to determine the law applicable to this case, the Court has to bear in mind the continuous evolution of international law. Diplomatic protection deals with a very sensitive area of international relations, since the interest of a foreign State in the protection of its nationals confronts the rights of the territorial sovereign, a fact of which the general law on the subject has had to take cognizance in order to prevent abuses and friction. From its origins closely linked with international commerce, diplomatic protection has sustained a particular impact from the growth of international economic relations, and at the same time from the profound transformations which have taken place in the economic life of nations. These latter changes have given birth to municipal institutions, which have transcended frontiers and have begun to exercise considerable influence on international relations. One of these phenomena which has a particular bearing on the present case is the corporate entity.

38. In this field international law is called upon to recognize institutions of municipal law that have an important and extensive role in the international field. This does not necessarily imply drawing any analogy between its own institutions and those of municipal law, nor does it amount to making rules of international law dependent upon categories of municipal law. All it means is that international law has had to recognize the corporate entity as an institution created by States in

a domain essentially within their domestic jurisdiction. This in turn requires that, whenever legal issues arise concerning the rights of States with regard to the treatment of companies and shareholders, as to which rights international law has not established its own rules, it has to refer to the relevant rules of municipal law. Consequently, in view of the relevance to the present case of the rights of the corporate entity and its shareholders under municipal law, the Court must devote attention to the nature and interrelation of those rights.

39. Seen in historical perspective, the corporate personality represents a development brought about by new and expanding requirements in the economic field, an entity which in particular allows of operation in circumstances which exceed the normal capacity of individuals. As such it has become a powerful factor in the economic life of nations. Of this, municipal law has had to take due account, whence the increasing volume of rules governing the creation and operation of corporate entities, endowed with a specific status. These entities have rights and obligations peculiar to themselves.

40. There, is however, no need to investigate the many different forms of legal entity provided for by the municipal laws of States, because the Court is concerned only with that exemplified by the company involved in the present case: Barcelona Traction-a limited liability company whose capital is represented by shares. There are, indeed, other associations, whatever the name attached to them by municipal legal systems, that do not enjoy independent corporate personality. The legal difference between the two kinds of entity is that for the limited liability company it is the overriding tie of legal personality which is determinant; for the other associations, the continuing autonomy of the several members.

41. Municipal law determines the legal situation not only of such limited liability companies but also of those persons who hold shares in them. Separated from the company by numerous barriers, the shareholder cannot be identified with it. The concept and structure of the company are founded on and determined by a firm distinction between the separate entity of the company and that of the shareholder, each with a distinct set of rights. The separation of property rights as between company and shareholder is an important manifestation of this distinction. So long as the company is in existence the shareholder has no right to the corporate assets.

42. It is a basic characteristic of the corporate structure that the company alone, through its directors or management acting in its name, can take action in respect of matters that are of a corporate character. The underlying justification for this is that, in seeking to serve its own best interests, the company will serve those of the shareholder too. Ordinarily, no individual shareholder can take legal steps, either in the name of the company or in his own name. If the shareholders disagree with the decisions taken on behalf of the company they may, in accordance with its articles or the relevant provisions of the law, change them or replace its officers, or take such action as is provided by law. Thus to protect the company against abuse by its management or the majority of shareholders, several municipal legal systems have vested in shareholders (sometimes a particular

number is specified) the right to bring an action for the defence of the company, and conferred upon the minority of shareholders certain rights to guard against decisions affecting the rights of the company vis-à-vis its management or controlling shareholders. Nonetheless the shareholders' rights in relation to the company and its assets remain limited, this being, moreover, a corollary of the limited nature of their liability.

43. At this point the Court would recall that in forming a company, its promoters are guided by all the various factors involved, the advantages and disadvantages of which they take into account. So equally does a shareholder, whether he is an original subscriber of capital or a subsequent purchaser of the company's shares from another shareholder. He may be seeking safety of investment, high dividends or capital appreciation-or a combination of two or more of these. Whichever it is, it does not alter the legal status of the corporate entity or affect the rights of the shareholder. In any event he is bound to take account of the risk of reduced dividends, capital depreciation or even loss, resulting from ordinary commercial hazards or from prejudice.caused to the company by illegal treatment of some kind.

44. Notwithstanding the separate corporate personality, a wrong done to the company frequently causes prejudice to its shareholders. But the mere fact that damage is sustained by both company and shareholder does not imply that both are entitled to claim compensation. Thus no legal conclusion can be drawn from the fact that the same event caused damage simultaneously affecting several natural or juristic persons. Creditors do not have any right to claim compensation from a person who, by wronging their debtor, causes them loss. In such cases, no doubt, the interests of the aggrieved are affected, but not their rights. Thus whenever a shareholder's interests are harmed by an act done to the company, it is to the latter that he must look to institute appropriate action; for although two separate entities may have suffered from the same wrong, it is only one entity whose rights have been infringed.

45. However, it has been argued in the present case that a company represents purely a means of achieving the economic purpose of its members, namely the shareholders, while they themselves constitute in fact the reality behind it. It has furthermore been repeatedly emphasized that there exists between a company and its shareholders a relationship describable as a community of destiny. The alleged acts may have been directed at the company and not the shareholders, but only in a formal sense: in reality, company and shareholders are so closely interconnected that prejudicial acts committed against the former necessarily wrong the latter; hence any acts directed against a company can be conceived as directed against its shareholders, because both can be considered in substance, i. e., from the economic viewpoint, identical. Yet even if a company is no more than a means for its shareholders to achieve their economic purpose, so long as it is *in esse* it enjoys an independent existence. Therefore the interests of the shareholders are both separable and indeed separated from those of the company, so that the possibility of their diverging cannot be denied.

46. It has also been contended that the measures complained of, although taken with respect to Barcelona Traction and causing it direct damage, constituted an unlawful act vis-à-vis Belgium, because they also, though indirectly, caused damage to the Belgian shareholders in Barcelona Traction. This again is merely a different way of presenting the distinction between injury in respect of a right and injury to a simple interest. But, as the Court has indicated, evidence that damage was suffered does not ipso facto justify a diplomatic claim. Persons suffer damage or harm in most varied circumstances. This in itself does not involve the obligation to make reparation. Not a mere interest affected, but solely a right infringed involves responsibility, so that an act directed against and infringing only the company's rights does not involve responsibility towards the shareholders, even if their interests are affected.

47. The situation is different if the act complained of is aimed at the direct rights of the shareholder as such. It is well known that there are rights which municipal law confers upon the latter distinct from those of the company, including the right to any declared dividend, the right to attend and vote at general meetings, the right to share in the residual assets of the company on liquidation. Whenever one of his direct rights is infringed, the shareholder has an independent right of action. On this there is no disagreement between the Parties. But a distinction must be drawn between a direct infringement of the shareholder's rights, and difficulties or financial losses to which he may be exposed as the result of the situation of the company.

48. The Belgian Government claims that shareholders of Belgian nationality suffered damage in consequence of unlawful acts of the Spanish authorities and, in particular, that the Barcelona Traction shares, though they did not cease to exist, were emptied of all real economic content. It accordingly contends that the shareholders had an independent right to redress, notwithstanding the fact that the acts complained of were directed against the company as such. Thus the legal issue is reducible to the question of whether it is legitimate to identify an attack on company rights, resulting in damage to shareholders, with the violation of their direct rights. ...

50. In turning now to the international legal aspects of the case, the Court must, as already indicated, start from the fact that the present case essentially involves factors derived from municipal law-the distinction and the community between the company and the shareholder-which the Parties, however widely their interpretations may differ, each take as the point of departure of their reasoning. If the Court were to decide the case in disregard of the relevant institutions of municipal law it would, without justification, invite serious legal difficulties. It would lose touch with reality, for there are no corresponding institutions of international law to which the Court could resort. Thus the Court has, as indicated, not only to take cognizance of municipal law but also to refer to it. It is to rules generally accepted by municipal legal systems which recognize the limited company whose capital is represented by shares, and not to the municipal law of a particular State, that international law refers. In referring to such rules, the Court cannot modify, still less deform them.

51. On the international plane, the Belgian Government has advanced the proposition that it is inadmissible to deny the shareholders' national State a right of diplomatic protection merely on the ground that another State possesses a corresponding right in respect of the company itself. In strict logic and law this formulation of the Belgian claim to *jus standi* assumes the existence of the very right that requires demonstration. In fact the Belgian Government has repeatedly stressed that there exists no rule of international law which would deny the national State of the shareholders the right of diplomatic protection for the purpose of seeking redress pursuant to unlawful acts committed by another State against the company in which they hold shares. This, by emphasizing the absence of any express denial of the right, conversely implies the admission that there is no rule of international law which expressly confers such a right on the shareholders' national State.

52. International law may not, in some fields, provide specific rules in particular cases. In the concrete situation, the company against which allegedly unlawful acts were directed is expressly vested with a right, whereas no such right is specifically provided for the shareholder in respect of those acts. Thus the position of the company rests on a positive rule of both municipal and international law. As to the shareholder, while he has certain rights expressly provided for him by municipal law as referred to in paragraph 42 above, appeal can, in the circumstances of the present case, only be made to the silence of international law. Such silence scarcely admits of interpretation in favour of the shareholder.

53. It is quite true, as was recalled in the course of oral argument in the present case, that concurrent claims are not excluded in the case of a person who, having entered the service of an international organization and retained his nationality, enjoys simultaneously the right to be protected by his national State and the right to be protected by the organization to which he belongs. This however is a case of one person in possession of two separate bases of protection, each of which is valid (Reparation for Injuries Suffered in the Service of the United Nations, Advisory Opinion, I.C.J. Reports 1949, p. 185). There is no analogy between such a situation and that of foreign shareholders in a company which has been the victim of a violation of international law which has caused them damage.

54. Part of the Belgian argument is founded on an attempt to assimilate interests to rights, relying on the use in many treaties and other instruments of such expressions as property, rights and interests. This is not, however, conclusive. Property is normally protected by law. Rights are *ex hypothesi* protected by law, otherwise they would not be rights. According to the Belgian Government, interests, although distinct from rights, are also protected by the aforementioned conventional rules. The Court is of the opinion that, for the purpose of interpreting the general rule of international law concerning diplomatic protection, which is its task, it has no need to determine the meaning of the term interests in the conventional rules, in other words to determine whether by this term the conventional rules refer to rights rather than simple interests.

55. The Court will now examine other grounds on which it is conceivable that the submission by the Belgian Government of a claim on behalf of shareholders in Barcelona Traction may be justified.

56. For the same reasons as before, the Court must here refer to municipal law. Forms of incorporation and their legal personality have sometimes not been employed for the sole purposes they were originally intended to serve; sometimes the corporate entity has been unable to protect the rights of those who entrusted their financial resources to it; thus inevitably there have arisen dangers of abuse, as in the case of many other institutions of law. Here, then, as elsewhere, the law, confronted with economic realties, has had to provide protective measures and remedies in the interests of those within the corporate entity as well as of those outside who have dealings with it: the law has recognized that the independent existence of the legal entity cannot be treated as an absolute. It is in this context that the process of "lifting the corporate veil" or "disregarding the legal entity" has been found justified and equitable in certain circumstances or for certain purposes. The wealth of practice already accumulated on the subject in municipal law indicates that the veil is lifted, for instance, to prevent the misuse of the privileges of legal personality, as in certain cases of fraud or malfeasance, to protect third persons such as a creditor or purchaser, or to prevent the evasion of legal requirements or of obligations.

57. Hence the lifting of the veil is more frequently employed from without, in the interest of those dealing with the corporate entity. However, it has also been operated from within, in the interest of-among others-the shareholders, but only in exceptional circumstances.

58. In accordance with the principle expounded above, the process of lifting the veil, being an exceptional one admitted by municipal law in respect of an institution of its own making, is equally admissible to play a similar role in international law. It follows that on the international plane also there may in principle be special circumstances which justify the lifting of the veil in the interest of shareholders.

59. Before proceeding, however, to consider whether such circumstances exist in the present case, it will be advisable to refer to two specific cases involving encroachment upon the legal entity, instances of which have been cited by the Parties. These are: first, the treatment of enemy and allied property, during and after the First and Second World Wars, in peace treaties and other international instruments; secondly, the treatment of foreign property consequent upon the nationalizations carried out in recent years by many States. ...

64. The Court will now consider whether there might not be, in the present case, other special circumstances for which the general rule might not take effect. In this connection two particular situations must be studied: the case of the company having ceased to exist and the case of the company's national State lacking capacity to take action on its behalf.

65. As regards the first of these possibilities the Court observes that the Parties have put forward conflicting interpretations of the present situation of Barcelona Traction. There can, however, be no question but that Barcelona Traction has lost all its assets in Spain, and was placed in receivership in Canada, a receiver and manager having been appointed. It is common ground that from the economic viewpoint the company has been entirely paralyzed. It has been deprived of all its Spanish sources of income, and the Belgian Government has asserted that the company could no longer find the funds for its legal defence, so that these had to be supplied by the shareholders.

66. It cannot however, be contended that the corporate entity of the company has ceased to exist, or that it has lost its capacity to take corporate action. It was free to exercise such capacity in the Spanish courts and did in fact do so. It has not become incapable in law of defending its own rights and the interests of the shareholders. In particular, a precarious financial situation cannot be equated with the demise of the corporate entity, which is the hypothesis under consideration: the company's status in law is alone relevant, and not its economic condition, nor even the possibility of its being "practically defunct"-a description on which argument has been based but which lacks all legal precision. Only in the event of the legal demise of the company are the shareholders deprived of the possibility of a remedy available through the company; it is only if they became deprived of all such possibility that an independent right of action for them and their government could arise.

67. In the present case, Barcelona Traction is in receivership in the country of incorporation. Far from implying the demise of the entity or of its rights, this much rather denotes that those rights are preserved for so long as no liquidation has ensued. Though in receivership, the company continues to exist. …

69. The Court will now turn to the second possibility, that of the lack of capacity of the company's national State to act on its behalf. The first question which must be asked here is whether Canada-the third apex of the triangular relationship-is, in law, the national State of Barcelona Traction.

70. In allocating corporate entities to States for purposes of diplomatic protection, international law is based, but only to a limited extent, on an analogy with the rules governing the nationality of individuals. The traditional rule attributes the right of diplomatic protection of a corporate entity to the State under the laws of which it is incorporated and in whose territory it has its registered office. These two criteria have been confirmed by long practice and by numerous international instruments. This notwithstanding, further or different links are at times said to be required in order that a right of diplomatic protection should exist. Indeed, it has been the practice of some States to give a company incorporated under their law diplomatic protection solely when it has its seat (*siège social*) or management or centre of control in their territory, or when a majority or a substantial proportion of the shares has been owned by nationals of the State concerned. Only then, it has been held, does there exist between the corporation and

the State in question a genuine connection of the kind familiar from other branches of international law. However, in the particular field of the diplomatic protection of corporate entities, no absolute test of the "genuine connection" has found general acceptance. Such tests as have been applied are of a relative nature, and sometimes links with one State have had to be weighed against those with another. In this connection reference has been made to the Nottebohm case. In fact the Parties made frequent reference to it in the course of the proceedings. However, given both the legal and factual aspects of protection in the present case the Court is of the opinion that there can be no analogy with the issues raised or the decision given in that case.

71. In the present case, it is not disputed that the company was incorporated in Canada and has its registered office in that country. The incorporation of the company under the law of Canada was an act of free choice. Not only did the founders of the company seek its incorporation under Canadian law but it has remained under that law for a period of over 50 years. It has maintained in Canada its registered office, its accounts and its share registers. Board meetings were held there for many years; it has been listed in the records of the Canadian tax authorities. Thus a close and permanent connection has been established, fortified by the passage of over half a century. This connection is in no way weakened by the fact that the company engaged from the very outset in commercial activities outside Canada, for that was its declared object. Barcelona Traction's links with Canada are thus manifold.

72. Furthermore, the Canadian nationality of the company has received general recognition. ...

76. In sum, the record shows that from 1948 onwards the Canadian Government made to the Spanish Government numerous representations which cannot be viewed otherwise than as the exercise of diplomatic protection in respect of the Barcelona Traction company. Therefore this was not a case where diplomatic protection was refused or remained in the sphere of fiction. It is also clear that over the whole period of its diplomatic activity the Canadian Government proceeded in full knowledge of the Belgian attitude and activity.

77. It is true that at a certain point the Canadian Government ceased to act on behalf of Barcelona Traction, for reasons which have not been fully revealed, though a statement made in a letter of 19 July 1955 by the Canadian Secretary of State for External Affairs suggests that it felt the matter should be settled by means of private negotiations. The Canadian Government has nonetheless retained its capacity to exercise diplomatic protection; no legal impediment has prevented it from doing so: no fact has arisen to render this protection impossible. It has discontinued its action of its own free will.

78. The Court would here observe that, within the limits ... prescribed by international law, a State may exercise diplomatic protection by whatever means and to whatever extent it thinks fit, for it is its own right that the State is asserting. Should the natural or legal persons on whose behalf it is acting consider that their

rights are not adequately protected, they have no remedy in international law. All they can do is to resort to municipal law, if means are available, with a view to furthering their cause or obtaining redress. …

81. The cessation by the Canadian Government of the diplomatic protection of Barcelona Traction cannot, then, be interpreted to mean that there is no remedy against the Spanish Government for the damage done by the allegedly unlawful acts of the Spanish authorities. It is not a hypothetical right which was vested in Canada, for there is no legal impediment preventing the Canadian Government from protecting Barcelona Traction. Therefore there is no substance in the argument that for the Belgian Government to bring a claim before the Court represented the only possibility of obtaining redress for the damage suffered by Barcelona Traction and, through it, by its shareholders. …

85. The Court will now examine the Belgian claim from a different point of view, disregarding municipal law and relying on the rule that in inter-State relations, whether claims are made on behalf of a State's national or on behalf of the State itself, they are always the claims of the State. As the Permanent Court said,

> The question, therefore, whether the … dispute originates in an injury to a private interest, which in point of fact is the case in many international disputes, is irrelevant from this standpoint. (Mavrommatis Palestine Concessions, judgment No. 2, 1924, P.C.I.J., Series A, No. 2, p. 12. See also *Nottebohm,* Second Phase, Judgment, I.C.J. Reports 1955, p. 24.)

86. Hence the Belgian Government would be entitled to bring a claim if it could show that one of its rights had been infringed and that the acts complained of involved the breach of an international obligation arising out of a treaty or a general rule of law. The opinion has been expressed that a claim can accordingly be made when investments by a State's nationals abroad are thus prejudicially affected, and that since such investments are part of a State's national economic resources, any prejudice to them directly involves the economic interest of the State.

87. Governments have been known to intervene in such circumstances not only when their interests were affected, but also when they were threatened. However, it must be stressed that this type of action is quite different from and outside the field of diplomatic protection. When a State admits into its territory foreign investments or foreign nationals it is, as indicated in paragraph 33, bound to extend to them the protection of the law. However, it does not thereby become an insurer of that part of another State's wealth which these investments represent. Every investment of this kind carries certain risks. The real question is whether a right has been violated, which right could only be the right of the State to have its nationals enjoy a certain treatment guaranteed by general international law, in the absence of a treaty applicable to the particular case. On the other hand it has been stressed that it must be proved that the investment effectively

belongs to a particular economy. This is, as it is admitted, sometimes very difficult, in particular where complex undertakings are involved. Thus the existing concrete test would be replaced by one which might lead to a situation in which no diplomatic protection could be exercised, with the consequence that an unlawful act by another State would remain without remedy.

88. It follows from what has already been stated above that, where it is a question of an unlawful act committed against a company representing foreign capital, the general rule of international law authorizes the national State of the company alone to make a claim. ...

91. With regard more particularly to human rights, to which reference has already been made in paragraph 34 of this judgment, it should be noted that these also include protection against denial of justice. However, on the universal level, the instruments which embody human rights do not confer on States the capacity to protect the victims of infringements of such rights irrespective of their nationality. It is therefore still on the regional level that a solution to this problem has had to be sought; thus, within the Council of Europe, of which Spain is not a member, the problem of admissibility encountered by the claim in the present case has been resolved by the European Convention on Human Rights, which entitles each State which is a party to the Convention to lodge a complaint against any other contracting State for violation of the Convention, irrespective of the nationality of the victim.

92. Since the general rule on the subject does not entitle the Belgian Government to put forward a claim in this case, the question remains to be considered whether nonetheless, as the Belgian Government has contended during the proceedings, considerations of equity do not require that it be held to possess a right of protection. It is quite true that it has been maintained that, for reasons of equity, a State should be able, in certain cases, to take up the protection of its nationals, shareholders in a company which has been the victim of a violation of international law. Thus a theory has been developed to the effect that the State of the shareholders has a right of diplomatic protection when the State whose responsibility is invoked is the national State of the company. Whatever the validity of this theory may be, it is certainly not applicable to the present case, since Spain is not the national State of Barcelona Traction.

93. On the other hand, the Court considers that, in the field of diplomatic protection as in all other fields of international law, it is necessary that the law be applied reasonably. It has been suggested that if in a given case it is not possible to apply the general rule that the right of diplomatic protection of a company belongs to its national State, considerations of equity might call for the possibility of protection of the shareholders in question by their own national State. This hypothesis does not correspond to the circumstances of the present case.

94. In view, however, of the discretionary nature of diplomatic protection, considerations of equity cannot require more than the possibility for some protector State to intervene, whether it be the national State of the company, by virtue

of the general rule mentioned above, or, in a secondary capacity, the national State of the shareholders who claim protection. …

95. The Belgian Government, it is true, has also contended that as high a proportion as 88 per cent. of the shares in Barcelona Traction belonged to natural or juristic persons of Belgian nationality, and it has used this as an argument for the purpose not only of determining the amount of the damages which it claims, but also of establishing its right of action on behalf of the Belgian shareholders. Nevertheless, this does not alter the Belgian Government's position, as expounded in the course of the proceedings, which implies, in the last analysis, that it might be sufficient for one single share to belong to a national of a given State for the latter to be entitled to exercise its diplomatic protection.

96. The Court considers that the adoption of the theory of diplomatic protection of shareholders as such, by opening the door to competing diplomatic claims, could create an atmosphere of confusion and insecurity in international economic relations. …

100. In the present case, it is clear from what has been said above that Barcelona Traction was never reduced to a position of impotence such that it could not have approached its national State, Canada, to ask for its diplomatic protection, and that, as far as appeared to the Court, there was nothing to prevent Canada from continuing to grant its diplomatic protection to Barcelona Traction if it had considered that it should do so.

101. For the above reasons, the Court is not of the opinion that, in the particular circumstances of the present case, *jus standi* is conferred on the Belgian Government by considerations of equity. ….

103. Accordingly, the Court rejects the Belgian Government's claim by fifteen votes to one, twelve votes of the majority being based on the reasons set out in the present judgment.

JESSUP, J., separate opinion:

50. There are three situations in which there is wide agreement that a State may extend its diplomatic protection to shareholders who are its nationals, although the company whose shares they hold has the nationality of another State. These three situations are sometimes considered "exceptions" to a general rule allowing protection of the corporation itself.

51. The first of these situations is where the corporation has been incorporated in the State which inflicts the injury on it without legal justification, and where the shareholders are of another nationality.

It is in such situations that one finds the widest agreement that a State may extend diplomatic protection to shareholders who are its nationals. The rationale seems to be based largely on equitable considerations and the result is so reasonable it has been accepted in State practice. . . By hypothesis, the respondent State has committed an unlawful act from which injury results. The corporation itself cannot seek redress and therefore the State whose nationals own the shares may protect them *ut singuli*. The equities are particularly striking when the respondent State admits foreign investment only on condition that the investors form a corporation under its law. . .

Judge Wellington Koo, in his separate opinion in this Barcelona case in 1964 asserted emphatically:

> [t]he original simple rule of protection of a company by its national State has been found inadequate and State practice, treaty regulation and international arbitral decisions have come to recognize the right of a State to intervene on behalf of its nationals, shareholders of a company which has been injured by the State of its own nationality, that is to say, a State where it has been incorporated according to its laws and therefore is regarded as having assumed its nationality (I.C.J. Reports 1964, p. 58).

Judge Wellington Koo considered it immaterial whether this rule should or should not be considered as an "exception".

52. It is curious that this "exception" should have been so widely accepted since it ignores the traditional rule that a State is not guilty of a breach of international law for injuring one of its own nationals. It rebuts also the notion that an injury to a corporation is not a direct injury to the shareholders. Moreover, if the foreign shareholders may be protected in such a situation, it is also necessary to choose one horn of a dilemma: either one admits that the right of the shareholders existed at the moment when the injury was done to the corporation, which means that the rights of shareholders may be damaged by an injury to the corporation, or, if that right came into existence subsequently, then one ignores the rule of international law that a claim must be national in origin. Moreover, the admission of this "exception" negates the argument, sometimes advanced against the diplomatic protection of shareholders, to the effect that such claims expose an accused State to a vast variety of claims on behalf of persons of whose existence it was ignorant. Since customary practice has, however, accepted this "exception", other arguments against protection of shareholders are correspondingly weakened, especially since the doctrine in question generally does not insist that the life of the corporation must have been extinguished so that it could be said the shareholders had acquired a direct right to the assets.

53. The second situation in which it is widely agreed that a State may claim on behalf of its shareholders in a foreign corporation, is where the State of incorporation has liquidated or wound up the corporation after the injury was inflicted by some third State.

This situation differs from that just considered in that the respondent State has committed its unlawful act (let us say total confiscation) against a foreign corporation. Here some doctrine would say that ordinarily State A, the State of incorporation, should be the one to extend diplomatic protection. But by hypothesis the corporate life has been extinguished by State A, so that -just as in the first situations claim can not be pressed for the corporation. Brownlie states the situation as follows:

> Where the State under the law of which the company is incorporated terminates the existence of the company in law, or other circumstances make the company practically defunct, the shareholders remain as the interests affected by government act: intervention on their behalf would seem to be justified in such a case. (Brownlie, Principles of Public International Law, 1966, p. 401.)

Here it may be said that after liquidation and payment of creditors, the shareholders-under an applicable system of municipal law-have a property interest in the assets and for that reason may be protected. But at the time of the unlawful act ("confiscation") they did not have such a property interest and therefore under the rule of continuity the claim did not have in origin the appropriate nationality on that basis. …

[Jessup did not consider … the third "exception" where shareholders may admittedly be protected, namely where the injury is inflicted directly on the shareholders and not indirectly through damage to the company.]

NOTES AND QUESTIONS

1. For the underlying details of this case, *see* John Brooks, *Annals of Finance: Privateer I and II*, THE NEW YORKER, May 21 and 28, 1979.

2. Is *Barcelona Traction* compatible with policies encouraging protection of investment and the maintenance of a productive world economy? Does *Barcelona Traction* provide adequate protection for shareholders?

3. Under the North American Free Trade Agreement, anyone who holds a share of a company is considered an "investor" with standing to make a claim to a dispute settlement panel. See Art. 1139 NAFTA.

4. Does the opinion draw any limits to the "naturalization" power of states regarding corporations? Is there a "genuine link" requirement, as in *Nottebohm* and *Flegenheimer*, to address the problem of abusive ascriptions of nationality? What about the arguable public policy drawbacks of "nationalities of convenience," such as the choosing of places of incorporation for the purpose of evading securities regulations, tax liabilities, labor law, environmental laws, etc., governing the home country of the shareholders/controlling entities? Would that be overkill? Should ascriptions for purposes of suit in international courts be deemed ineffective?

5. Should the requirement of "continuous nationality" be maintained? Traditionally, it was required that the injured entity or person possess the nationality of the claimant state at the time of the injury and maintain it throughout the process of diplomatic protection. The 2004 ILC Draft Articles on Diplomatic Protection would require continuous nationality of the claimant state at the time of injury and the date of the official presentation of the claim (Art. 5(1)). A state may exercise diplomatic protection, however, also "in respect of a person who is a national at the date of the official presentation of the claim but was not a national at the time of injury" if the acquisition of the claimant state's nationality was "unrelated to the bringing of the claim" (Art. 5(2)) – except as against the person's former state of nationality (Art. 5(3)). In the Helms-Burton Act, the United States appears to have espoused the claims of naturalized American citizens who were exclusively Cuban nationals at the time of the Cuban Government's expropriation of their assets. *See infra* Part Six, at 1216. What would be your assessment of the lawfulness of such action? Is it good policy?

Loewen v. U.S, an ICSID arbitration under NAFTA, brought the issue of continuity of nationality into sharp relief. The Loewen Group, Inc. (TLGI), a foreign (Canadian) investor brought a claim against the United States under Chapter Eleven of NAFTA, based on an alleged violation of NAFTA Article 1105(1) which mandates that "[e]ach party shall accord to investors of another party treatment in accordance with international law, including fair and equitable treatment and full protection and security." The arbitral tribunal recognized that a Mississippi trial against TLGI, resulting in a verdict of $500 million, the largest in Mississippi history, and ultimately TLGI's bankruptcy following its inability to post a bond for appeal set at 125% of the verdict, was "clearly improper and discreditable and cannot be squared with minimum standards of international law and fair and equitable treatment" (para. 137), since the trial court "permitted the jury to be influenced by persistent appeals to local favouritism as against a foreign litigant" (para. 136). In fact, "[b]y any standard of measurement, the trial involving ... Loewen was a disgrace" (para. 119). Still, the tribunal concluded that there was no violation of Article 1105 since TLGI did not file a petition for *certiorari* and seek a stay of execution in the Supreme Court of the United States (paras. 207, 217), thus violating the rule requiring exhaustion of local remedies (*see infra*, at 473-475). In addition, the tribunal concluded that it lacked jurisdiction since TLGI failed to fulfill the requirement of "continuous national identity:"

> 220. Subsequent to the October 2001 hearings on the merits, events occurred which raised questions about TLGI's capacity to pursue its NAFTA claims... TLGI had filed a voluntary petition for relief under Chapter 11 of the United States Bankruptcy Code, and a reorganization plan was approved by the bankruptcy courts... Under that plan, TLGI ceased to exist as a business entity. All of its business operations were reorganized as a United States corporation. In apparent recognition of the obvious problem that would be caused by a United States entity pursuing a claim against the United States under NAFTA, TLGI, immediately prior to its going out of business, assigned all of its right, title and interest to the NAFTA claim to a newly created corporation (discreetly called Nafcanco – a play on the words NAFTA and Canada). It would appear that the NAFTA claim is the only asset of Nafcanco, and the pursuit of the claim its only business. ...
>
> 225. Claimant TLGI urges that since it had the requisite nationality at the time the claim arose, and, antedate the time that the claim was submitted, it is of no consequence that the present real party in interest – the beneficiary of the claim – is an American citizen. Both as a matter of historical and current international precedent, this argument must fail. In international law parlance, there must be continuous national identity from the date of the events giving rise to the claim, which date is known as the *dies a quo*, through the date of the resolution of the claim, which date is known as the *dies ad quem*.
>
> 226. Claimants' first argument strand is that NAFTA itself, in Articles 1116 and 1117, require nationality only to the date of submission. However, those articles deal only with nationality requirements at the *dies a quo*, the beginning date of the claim. There is no language in those articles, or anywhere else in the treaty, which deals with the question of whether nationality must continue to the time of resolution of the claim. It is that silence in the treaty that requires the application of customary international law to resolve the question of the need for continuous national identity.
>
> 227. Nor does the recent arbitral decision in the *Mondev* case help Claimants in any way. In that case, the Tribunal dealt with the issue of whether the investment itself had to remain of the claimant's identity. Significantly, the reasoning of the Tribunal implicated other sections of NAFTA, namely Articles 1105 and 1110. The investment in *Mondev*, some Boston real estate, had been foreclosed on by an American mortgage holder. ... [T]he Tribunal appropriately found that the loss of the investment through foreclosure of the mortgage could not be the basis for denying Mondev's right to pursue its remedies under NAFTA [citing the *Mondev* Tribunals conclusion that "NAFTA should be inter-

> preted broadly to cover any legal claims arising out of the treatment of an investment ... whether or not the investment subsists as such at the time of the treatment which is complained of"]. ...
>
> 229. There is only limited dispute as to the history of the requirement of continuous nationality to the end of any international proceeding. When investment claims were negotiated and resolved only at a governmental level, any change in nationality of the claimant defeated the only reason for the nationality to continue. The claiming government no longer had a citizen to protect. This history has changed as the nature of the claim process has changed. As claimants have been allowed to prosecute claims in their own right more often, provision has been made for amelioration of the strict requirement of continuous nationality. ... Many of the bilateral investment treaties ... contain specific modifications of the requirement. But such specific provisions in other treaties and agreements only hinder TLGI's contentions, since NAFTA has no such specific provision. ...
>
> 234. TLGI urges some equitable consideration be given because it was the underlying Mississippi litigation which brought about the need for it to file bankruptcy in the first place. We have already rehearsed our view of the inequities that befell TLGI in that litigation, and a chancery court would certainly take such claims into account in assessing damages. But this is an international tribunal whose jurisdiction stems from and is limited to the words of the NAFTA treaty. Whatever the reasons for TLGI's decision to follow the bankruptcy route it chose, the consequences broke the chain of nationality that that the Treaty requires. ...
>
> 236. TLGI further contends that the International Law Commission issued a report which proposed eliminating the continuous nationality rule even in cases of diplomatic [protection, a field that would seem more nationality oriented than the protection of investors. The report itself met with criticism in many quarters and from many points of view. In any event, the ILC is far from approving any recodification based on the report. ...
>
> For the foregoing reasons the Tribunal unanimously decides ... that it lacks jurisdiction to determine TLGI's claims under NAFTA concerning the decisions of United States courts in consequences of TLGI's assignment of those claims to a Canadian corporation owned and controlled by a United States corporation.

The Loewen Group, Inc. et al. v. U.S., 42 I.L.M. 811, 846-850 (2003).

Do you agree with the Tribunal's reasoning? Should there have been more flexibility since the act complained of ultimately led to the discontinuity of nationality? Compare *NAFTA Decision on Continuous Nationality and Local Remedies*, 97 Am. J. Int'l L. 700 (2003). Would the *Mondev* policy have led to a different result? *See* NAFTA Arbitration: Final Award, *Mondev Int'l Ltd. v. United States*, ICSID Case No. ARB(AF)/99/2, (Oct. 11, 2002), available at http://www.state.gov/documents/organization/14442.pdf.

6. In its 2004 session, the ILC discussed a proposal to change the end point of the requirement of continuous nationality from the point of the "official presentation" of the claim to the date of "resolution" of the claim, referring to the Loewen decision. It ultimately retained the original language in Draft Articles 5, 7, 8, and 10, but left the door open for reconsideration on second reading in response to Governments' views on the matter. As drafted, the articles could not subject the right of a State to exercise diplomatic protection to some future date of resolution of the dispute. Also, how should situations of change in nationality be treated that occur as a result of marriage? What about changes of nationality of a corporation occasioned by succession or partition of a state? What does "date of resolution" mean? Is it necessarily identical with the date of an award or a judgment?

7. Should claims of protection be transferable? In particular, should the home state of an insurer be able to espouse a foreign claim received by subrogation?

8. In feudal times, people were viewed as the subjects or "property" of the sovereign, to be transferred at his will and, with few exceptions, to be governed as he pleased. An injury by another state to a person was deemed, in international decision, as an injury to the sovereign and not an injury to the person. Though states may continue to protect their nationals, this traditional position has been questioned for many purposes in recent international statements. Human rights law has made inroads into that traditional argument. In 2001, the ILC adopted, and the UN General Assembly referred to the attention of Governments, its Articles on State on Responsibility [ASR] (UN G.A. Res. 56/83 (Dec. 12, 2001). They include Article 48, which contemplates the invocation by a state other than the injured state of an obligation breached that is "owed to the international community as a whole" (for details, *see infra*, at Part Five). Article 17 of the Draft Articles on Diplomatic Protection now clarifies that international law "actions or procedures other than diplomatic protection" that states, natural persons or other entities can resort to "to secure redress for injury suffered as a result of an internationally wrongful act" are not excluded or in any way affected by the Draft Articles themselves ("without prejudice"). This may include, *e.g.*, states' invocations of human rights obligations *erga omnes*, as foreseen in Article 48 ASR, but also individual complaints, complaints of states, or complaints of NGOs, if available, under human rights treaty regimes.

9. States have increasingly concluded bilateral agreements dealing with investment and commercial matters including modes of dispute settlement between their investors engaged in commercial transactions in the host state. In the past, these treaties were referred to as treaties of friendship, commerce and navigation and now they are called bilateral investment treaties. Article 18 of the ILC Draft Articles on Diplomatic Protection attempts to establish a relationship between the entitlement of a state to exercise diplomatic protection and these bilateral treaties. Analyze how Article 18 applies. Assume that states A and B conclude a bilateral investment treaty. The treaty includes a provision indicating that the treaty is without prejudice to the right of any of the contracting state to diplomatic protection. Does Article 18 still apply between A and B? In your view, is it appropriate for a multilateral agreement to impose a certain interpretation on a bilateral treaty in the absence of any indication that the parties had such an intention?

3. The Requirement of Exhaustion of Local Remedies

On the nonexhaustion of local remedies, or "processes anterior" to international arbitration, one of the authors has written: "It is a general principle that an obligation to arbitrate or adjudicate becomes operative only after a number of other processes have been sought and exhausted." Elsewhere the author lists these processes as "negotiation, inquiry, mediation, and conciliation." W. MICHAEL REISMAN, NULLITY AND REVISION, *supra* at 360 (1971). "This principle is an expression of a number of policies. Economy, for example, suggests that it is preferable to resolve a dispute at its earliest manifestation and under relatively private circumstances." *Id.* at 359-60.

a. Nsongurua J. Udombana, *So Far, So Fair: The Local Remedies Rule in the Jurisprudence of the African Commission on Human and Peoples' Rights*

97 AM. J. INT'L L. 1, 36 (2003)

The principle of exhaustion of local remedies restricts the applicability of diplomatic protection by precluding resort to dispute settlement on the international level until the injured person has exhausted the legal remedies—judicial or administrative proceedings—available in the state allegedly responsible for the injury. An international tribunal can best adjudicate when the national legal system has been used not partially, but completely and exhaustively. The rule was intended to secure the equality of foreign nationals before the law and courts of a state whose national or itself was accused of committing a wrong. Brownlie has listed the "more persuasive practical considerations" that have been advanced to support application of the local remedies rule in diplomatic protection, but these considerations will equally apply to other branches of international law, including human rights law. These are:

> the greater suitability and convenience of national courts as forums for the claims of individuals and corporations, the need to avoid the multiplication of small claims on the level of diplomatic protection, the manner in which aliens by residence and business activity have associated themselves with the local jurisdiction, and the utility of a procedure which may lead to classification of the facts and liquidation of the damages.

A condition for the application of the local remedies rule is that it must first be determined whether those remedies exist, which implies the corresponding duty of the state to provide them. This is really a self-evident inference. Thus, the *process of exhaustion* is not the essence or raison d'être of the rule; it is the *actual redress* for the wrong suffered that constitutes its fundamental element and ultimate purpose. Furthermore, the remedies to be exhausted include all those that are afforded under the municipal law of the accused state and are capable of redressing the alleged wrongs and preventing diplomatic intervention. The local procedures must be such as to protect interests that "correspond *as closely as may be and in practical terms* with the interests involved in a subsequent international claim." The violation of international law will be said to persist and to generate international responsibility—which can be subjected to an international claim or to the pursuit of diplomatic protection—if it can be shown that after the exhaustion of local remedies, the initial wrong remains unrequited or inadequately redressed.

Another inherent limitation on the applicability of the rule, which, in turn, widens the possibility of diplomatic protection, is that the rule applies only to cases where national and international law are violated to the detriment of a particular individual. It does not apply to cases where only a breach of international law has occurred outside the territory or jurisdiction of the accused state or where the wrong committed rests solely on a violation of the national law of the respondent state. When the complained-of act has breached local law alone, responsibility can be generated only by the subsequent conduct of the forum state.

There has been a growing tendency, where possible, to exclude, by express agreement or by implication, the application of the domestic remedies rule in cases of diplomatic protection, as in international arbitration. However, as C. F. Amerasinghe observed:

> The fact that a State or States may agree to exclude the application of the rule in the settlement of a dispute does not detract from the quality of the rule as a customary rule of law. The incidence of this practice in recent years merely attests to the willingness of respondent States to submit for a variety of reasons disputes directly to international settlement in the interests of peace. ... It does not in fact reduce the importance of the rule or affect its relevance in the area of the diplomatic protection of aliens. Thus, it is in the interests of the international community that the rule be well-defined and reasonably developed even for the purpose of the law relating to diplomatic protection.

CHITTHARANJAN F. AMERASINGHE, STATE RESPONSIBILITY FOR INJURY TO ALIENS, at 173 (Clarendon Press 1967).

The application of the rule that local remedies must be exhausted, while appropriate in principle, may in certain instances work injustice where the respondent State is acting in less than good faith. Thus:

> In deciding on admissibility in a claim of nonexhaustion, a number of other factors should be given consideration. The temporal aspect is particularly important. The fact that a period of time will elapse before the case is resubmitted and that this period can be extended with malice by dilatory negotiation can have major impacts on the individuals and values involved in the dispute. An indication of interim measures-possible but unlikely if a finding of inadmissibility is returned -may not be an adequate remedy. The time element may, then, be a motive for seising the case despite nonexhaustion. W. MICHAEL REISMAN, NULLITY AND REVISION *supra*, at 363 (1971).

What constitutes exhaustion? In the Finnish Shipowners' Case, the Tribunal said:

> The meaning of this term "effective" has however been discussed almost exclusively in connection with the question whether there is or is not a failure of law or courts to fulfil the requirements of international law, e. g. in cases where it is suggested that, as Borchard observes . . . it is unnecessary to exhaust local remedies because, as Secretary of State Fish once said, "[there was] no justice to exhaust". This is quite natural as amongst the cases of international claims for compensation the cases of alleged failure of law or courts have been beyond comparison the most frequent. But there may arise, and have arisen, cases where, without it being suggested that there is such a failure of law or courts, it is contended that the remedies open to the individual claimant were not effective. Such cases were e. g. the prize cases, cited by Borchard ..., where it was held that in the face of a uniform course of decisions in the

> highest courts, a reversal of the condemnation being hopeless, an appeal was excused. Here, it appears, it was not a question of a failure of the courts nor of the law to fulfil the requirements of international law but the claim failed on its merits and it was hopeless to appeal.
>
> If what the parties in these respects contend is right-and the Arbitrator is of the opinion that it is so-then it appears that the raison d'être of the local remedies rule, in a case of an alleged initial breach of international law, can be solely that all the contentions of fact and propositions of law which are brought forward by the claimant Government in the international procedure as relevant to their contention that the respondent Government have committed a breach of international law by the act complained of, must have been investigated and adjudicated upon by the municipal Courts up to the last competent instance, thereby also giving the respondent Government a possibility of doing justice in their own, ordinary way.

Finland v. United Kingdom, 3 R.I.A.A. 1479 (1934).

* * *

A recent statement of this prescription is to be found in the work of the International Law Commission:

b. International Law Commission, Draft Articles on Responsibility of States for Internationally Wrongful Acts

Report of the International Law Commission on the Work of Its Fifty-third Session, U.N. GAOR, 56th Sess., Supp. No. 10, at 43, UN Doc. A/56/10 (2001)

Article 44

The responsibility of a State may not be invoked if ...

(b) The claim is one to which the rule of exhaustion of local remedies applies and any available and effective local remedy has not been exhausted.

* * *

There are certain contexts in which application of the exhaustion rule may not be appropriate on principle.

c. W. Michael Reisman, *Nullity and Revision: The Review and Enforcement of International Judgments and Awards*

359, 364 (Yale U. Press 1971)

The utility of an exhaustion rule, however, is a general and not an absolute verity. There are circumstances in which recourse to international arbitration or adjudication should be direct regardless of the availability of untried anterior processes. If, for examplc, a dispute precipitates or occurs within a context of intense crisis, the inclusive interest may call for resolution by modalities subject in high degree to community supervision. Similarly, if the effects of the dispute or of projected alternative resolutions are extremely inclusive, community supervision of the resolution and simultaneous prescription for future cases of material similarity are called for. In circumstances such as these, there are compelling reasons for ignoring the nonexhaustion of anterior processes and proceeding directly to organized international decision. The nonexhaustion rule, like all other rules, seeks to bring a number of community policies into operation. The extent to which the rule can implement these policies depends on the specific context of the dispute. The decision to insist upon or ignore exhaustion should, then, turn on examination of the context of the dispute and the probable effects of different possible decisions. …

Exhaustion of local remedies is an instrument of policy, not an inflexible rule. It will not be applied if the policies underlying it are unlikely to be realized or if other community policies at stake in the dispute will suffer. Borchard cites 31 nineteenth century arbitrations in which claims were held inadmissible on grounds of failure to exhaust local remedies. There appear to have been as many cases in which exceptions to the rule were made. The policy of economy is deemed inapplicable if the matter is submitted to arbitration by special agreement. Localization should be abandoned if the cause of action has apparently polymorphous effects. Where there have been compelling indications that no remedy satisfying international standards would be available from national arenas, the principle of good faith has been passed over. Where available local remedies are predictably incapable of changing a prior domestic decision, domestic remedies are deemed exhausted with delivery of the lower judgment.

d. The Interhandel (Switz. v. U.S.)

1959 I.C.J. 6

[Interhandel, a Swiss corporation, held a large block of shares of General Aniline and Film Corporation (GAF) of Delaware. During World War II, the shares were vested under the Trading with the Enemy Act, 1917, on the premise that Interhandel was controlled by I. G. Farben of Frankfurt or held the shares in trust for Germans. In 1945, Interhandel began proceedings to recover the assets and after more than 15 years of proceedings within the United States, the Swiss Government brought the matter to the International Court, on behalf of Interhandel, claiming that the United States was violating international agreements and general rules of international law. One of the United States defenses, presented as a preliminary objection to jurisdiction, was that diplomatic remedies had not been exhausted.]

The Third Preliminary Objection seeks a finding that "there is no jurisdiction in this Court to hear or determine the matters raised by the Swiss Application and Memorial, for the reason that Interhandel, whose case Switzerland is espousing, has not exhausted the local remedies available to it in the United States courts.

Although framed as an objection to the jurisdiction of the Court, this Objection must be regarded as directed against the admissibility of the Application of the Swiss Government. Indeed, by its nature it is to be regarded as a plea which would become devoid of object if the requirement of the prior exhaustion of local remedies were fulfilled.

The Court has indicated in what conditions the Swiss Government, basing itself on the idea that Interhandel's suit had been finally rejected in the United States courts, considered itself entitled to institute proceedings by its Application of October 2nd, 1957. However, the decision given by the Supreme Court of the United States on October 14th, 1957, on the application of Interhandel made on August 6th, 1957, granted a writ of certiorari and readmitted Interhandel into the suit. The judgment of that Court on June 16th, 1958, reversed the judgment of the Court of Appeals dismissing Interhandel's suit and remanded the case to the District Court. It was thenceforth open to Interhandel to avail itself again of the remedies available to it under the Trading with the Enemy Act, and to seek the restitution of its shares by proceedings in the United States courts. Its suit is still pending in the United States courts. The Court must have regard to the situation thus created.

The rule that local remedies must be exhausted before international proceedings may be instituted is a well-established rule of customary international law; the rule has been generally observed in cases in which a State has adopted the cause of its national whose rights are claimed to have been disregarded in another State in violation of international law. Before resort may be had to an international court in such a situation, it has been considered necessary that the State where the violation occurred should have an opportunity to redress it by its own means, within the framework of its own domestic legal system. A fortiori the rule must be observed when domestic proceedings are pending, as in the case of Interhandel, and when the two actions, that of the Swiss company in the United States courts and that of the Swiss Government in this Court, in its principal Submission, are designed to obtain the same result: the restitution of the assets of Interhandel vested in the United States.

The Swiss Government does not challenge the rule which requires that international judicial proceedings may only be instituted following the exhaustion of local remedies, but contends that the present case is one in which an exception to this rule is authorized by the rule itself.

The Court does not consider it necessary to dwell upon the assertion of the Swiss Government that "the United States itself has admitted that Interhandel had exhausted the remedies available in the United States courts". It is true that the representatives of the Government of the United States expressed this opinion on several occasions, in particular in the memorandum annexed to the Note of the Secretary of State of January 11th, 1957. This opinion was based upon a view which has proved unfounded. In fact, the proceedings which Interhandel had instituted before the courts of the United States were then in progress.

However, the Swiss Government has raised against the Third Objection other considerations which require examination.

In the first place, it is contended that the rule is not applicable for the reason that the measure taken against Interhandel and regarded as contrary to international law is a measure which was taken, not by a subordinate authority but by the Government of the United States. However, the Court must attach decisive importance to the fact that the laws of the United States make available to interested persons who consider that they have been deprived of their rights by measures taken in pursuance of the Trading with the Enemy Act, adequate remedies for the defense of their rights against the Executive.

It has also been contended on behalf of the Swiss Government that in the proceedings based upon the Trading with the Enemy Act, the United States courts are not in a position to adjudicate in accordance with the rules of international law and that the Supreme Court, in its decision of June 16th, 1958, made no reference to the many questions of international law which, in the opinion of the Swiss Government, constitute the subject of the present dispute. But the decisions of the United States courts bear witness to the fact that United States courts are competent to apply international law in their decisions when necessary. In the present case, when the dispute was brought to this Court, the proceedings in the United States courts had not reached the merits, in which considerations of international law could have been profitably relied upon.

The Parties have argued the question of the binding force before the courts of the United States of international instruments which, according to the practice of the United States, fall within the category of Executive Agreements; the Washington Accord is said to belong to that category. At the present stage of the proceedings it is not necessary for the Court to express an opinion on the matter. Neither is it practicable, before the final decision of the domestic courts, to anticipate what basis they may adopt for their judgment.

Finally, the Swiss Government laid special stress on the argument that the character of the principal Submission of Switzerland is that of a claim for the implementation of the decision given on January 5th, 1948, by the Swiss Authority of Review and based on the Washington Accord, a decision which the Swiss Government regards as an international judicial decision. "When an international decision has not been executed, there are no local remedies to exhaust, for the injury has been caused directly to the injured State." It has therefore contended that the failure by the United States to implement the decision constitutes a direct breach of international law, causing immediate injury to the rights of Switzerland as the Applicant State. The Court notes in the first place that to implement a decision is to apply its operative part. In the operative part of its decision, however, the Swiss Authority of Review "Decrees: (I) that the Appeal is sustained and the decision subjecting the appellant to the blocking of German property in Switzerland is annulled. ..." The decision of the Swiss Authority of Review relates to the unblocking of the assets of Interhandel in Switzerland; the Swiss claim is designed to secure the restitution of the assets of Interhandel in the United States. Without prejudging the validity of any arguments which the Swiss Government seeks or may seek to base upon that decision, the Court would confine itself to observing that such arguments do not deprive the dispute which has been referred to it of the character of a dispute in which the Swiss Government appears as having adopted the cause of its national, Interhandel, for the purpose of securing the restitution to that company of assets vested by the Government of the United States. This is one of the very cases which give rise to the application of the rule of the exhaustion of local remedies.

For all these reasons, the Court upholds the Third Preliminary Objection so far as the principal Submission of Switzerland is concerned.

In its alternative claim, the Swiss Government asks the Court to declare its competence to decide whether the United States is under an obligation to submit the dispute to arbitration or conciliation. The Government of the United States contends that this claim, while not identical with the principal claim, is designed to secure the same object, namely, the restitution of the assets of Interhandel in the United States, and that for this reason the Third Objection applies equally to it. It maintains that the rule of the exhaustion of local remedies applies to each of the principal and alternative Submissions which seek "a ruling by this Court to the effect that some other international tribunal now has jurisdiction to determine that very same issue, even though that issue is at the same time being actively litigated in the United States courts".

The Court considers that one interest, and one alone, that of Interhandel, which has led the latter to institute and to resume proceedings before the United States courts, has induced the Swiss Government to institute international proceedings. This interest is the basis for the present claim and should determine the scope of the action brought before the Court by the Swiss Government in its alternative form as well as in its principal form. On the other hand, the grounds on which the rule of the exhaustion of local remedies is based are the same, whether in the case of an international court, arbitral tribunal, or conciliation commission. In these circumstances, the Court considers that any distinction so far as the rule of the exhaustion of local remedies is concerned between the various claims or between the various tribunals is unfounded.

It accordingly upholds the Third Preliminary Objection also as regards the alternative Submission of Switzerland.

NOTES AND QUESTIONS

1. In the Finnish Shipowners Case, the Tribunal determined the effectiveness of the domestic remedy in terms of the integrity of the national court. If the function of the exhaustion rule is to permit a putative defendant state to resolve an issue at the domestic level before it is raised to the international level and becomes an aggravated political issue, is the question of the independence of the local courts relevant? *See* in this regard, *Mondev v. U.S.* (2002) *available at* http://www.state.gov/documents/organization/14442.pdf.

2. High transaction costs in processing a claim may ultimately preclude its prosecution. In this respect, does the exhaustion rule as interpreted in many of the precedents above tilt too much in favor of the defendant state by raising the costs and extending the time of claim prosecution such that a claimant might ultimately despair and drop the claim? In *Interhandel*, the Swiss company was obliged to pursue remedies in United States courts for almost two decades. Should there be an international policy of "justice delayed"?

3. In the *PLO Advisory Opinion*, 1988 I.C.J. 12, the International Court of Justice decided that arbitration was indicated despite the fact that the dispute was pending in United States courts, whose record of resolution of cognate issues was quite encouraging. Was this an appropriate application of the exhaustion rule?

4. Given the core policy of the exhaustion rule, should it be construed to preclude *any* contacts at the international level prior to exhaustion of diplomatic remedies? Could, for example, the government of an injured national approach the putative defendant government while matters are still *sub judice*, asking that government to submit an amicus brief to its own court indicating the international dimension of the case and urging that the matter be certified for judicial review? *See* CHITTHARANJAN FELIX AMERASINGHE, LOCAL REMEDIES IN INTERNATIONAL LAW (Cambridge U. Press, 2nd ed. 2003) (publication planned for Dec. 2004). *See also, Loewen v. U.S.* (2003) *available at* http://www.state.gov/documents/organization/22094.pdf.

5. The exhaustion rule applies to interstate disputes, even if they are precipitated by an injury caused by a state to the national of the other state. The exhaustion rule does not apply in circumstances in which an arbitration agreement exists between the putative defendant state and an injured national. Why? On the one hand, the exhaustion rule is a way of preventing disputes from aggravating at the international level. On the other, there is an independent policy in arbitration to respect arbitral commitments and to permit parties to waive an otherwise operating domestic jurisdiction.

6. In his treatise on the rule, Professor Cançado Trindade adds an interesting policy dimension, i.e. the role of the principle in human rights protection. He concludes:

> The local remedies rule, commonly regarded as a 'pre-condition of international proceedings', has ... enjoyed, in classical diplomatic protection and State responsibility for injuries to aliens, a 'negative' or preventive character, with emphasis on the process of exhaustion prior to international interposition on a discretionary State-to-State basis. This approach to the rule is hardly adequate for human rights protection, where the role of local courts and remedies is regarded as a component part of the international system of protection, and where the insertion of the rule in international instruments as a mandatory condition makes it possible to accord it detailed treatment. In a system of protection fundamentally victim-oriented, concerned with the rights of individual human beings rather than of States, an outlook of the issue which is more positive than the one by and large followed so far seems appropriate; and is likely to lead to more reassuring results than the ones ensuing from an essentially negative or formalistic approach leading to systematic, if not mechanical, rejection of applications for non-exhaustion of local remedies.

A.A. CANÇADO TRINDADE, THE APPLICATION OF THE RULE OF EXHAUSTION OF LOCAL REMEDIES IN INTERNATIONAL LAW 286-87 (Cambridge U. Press 1983).

Nsongurua Udombana comes to a similar conclusion in his analysis of the interpretation of the local remedies rule in the African system of human rights protection:

> [I]t is not adequate to view the local remedies rule in the human rights field through the same prism as it was viewed in, say, classic diplomatic protection. The Inter-American Court of Human Rights has correctly stated that, "[i]n concluding these human rights treaties, the States can be deemed to submit themselves to a legal order within which they,

> for the common good, assume various obligations, not in relation to other States, but towards all individuals within their jurisdiction." It has even been asserted that the Vienna Convention does not and cannot apply in quite the same manner to the interpretation of human rights treaties as it does to ordinary treaties and that autonomous rules may have to be developed for the interpretation of human rights instruments. Since African leaders themselves designed the African Charter to "meet the needs of Africa," the Commission should apply the Charter to meeting those needs.

Nsongurua J. Udombana, *supra*, at 36. Do you agree? How does this approach and policy differ, if at all, from the one set out by Professor Reisman above?

e. Case Concerning Elettronica Sicula S.p.A. (ELSI) (U.S. v. Italy)

1989 I.C.J. 15

50. The United States questioned whether the rule of the exhaustion of local remedies could apply at all to a case brought under Article XXVI of the FCN Treaty. That Article, it was pointed out, is categorical in its terms, and unqualified by any reference to the local remedies rule; and it seemed right, therefore, to conclude that the parties to the FCN Treaty, had they intended the jurisdiction conferred upon the Court to be qualified by the local remedies rule in cases of diplomatic protection, would have used express words to that effect; as was done in an Economic Co-operation Agreement between Italy and the United States of America also concluded in 1948. The Chamber has no doubt that the parties to a treaty can therein either agree that the local remedies rule shall not apply to claims based on alleged breaches of that treaty; or confirm that it shall apply. Yet the Chamber finds itself unable to accept that an important principle of customary international law should be held to have been tacitly dispensed with, in the absence of any words making clear an intention to do so. This part of the United States response to the Italian objection must therefore be rejected. ...

55. On the basis that the local remedies rule does apply in this case, this Judgment may now turn to the question whether local remedies were, or were not, exhausted by Raytheon and Machlett.

56. The damage claimed in this case to have been caused to Raytheon and Machlett is said to have resulted from the "losses incurred by ELSI's owners as a result of the involuntary change in the manner of disposing of ELSI's assets": and it is the requisition order that is said to have caused this change, and which is therefore at the core of the United States complaint. It was, therefore, right that any local remedy against the Italian authorities, calling in question the validity of the requisition of ELSI's plant and related assets, and raising the matter of the losses said to result from it, should be pursued by ELSI itself. In any event, both in order to attempt to recover control of ELSI's plant and assets, and to mitigate any damage flowing from the alleged frustration of the liquidation plan, the first step was for ELSI—and only ELSI could do this—to appeal to the Prefect against the requisition order. After the bankruptcy, however, the pursuit of local remedies was no longer a matter for ELSI's management but for the trustee in bankruptcy (Raytheon could, even after the bankruptcy, have influenced decisions of the committee of creditors, had it not decided against claiming in bankruptcy in

respect of sums due to it as creditor; it did exercise some influence however through its subsidiary company, Raytheon Europe, which did claim as a creditor).

57. After the trustee in bankruptcy was appointed, he, acting for ELSI, by no means left the Italian authorities and courts unoccupied with ELSI's affairs. It was he who, under an Italian law of 1934, formally requested the Prefect to make his decision within 60 days of that request; which decision was itself the subject of an unsuccessful appeal by the Mayor to the President of Italy. On 16 June 1970, the trustee, acting for the bankrupt ELSI, brought a suit against the Acting Minister of the Interior and the Acting Mayor of Palermo, asking the court to adjudge that the defendants should "pay to the bankrupt estate of Raytheon-ELSI ... damages for the illegal requisition of the plant machinery and equipment ... for the period from April 1 to September 30, 1968, in the aggregate amount of Lire 2,395,561,600 plus interests ..."

On 2 February 1973, the Court of Palermo, as indicated above (paragraph 43), rejected the claim. The trustee in bankruptcy then appealed to the Court of Appeal of Palermo; which Court gave a judgment on 24 January 1974 which "partly revising the judgment of the Court of Palermo" ordered payment by the Ministry of the Interior of damages of 114,014,711 lire with interest. Appeal was taken finally to the Court of Cassation which upheld the decision of the Court of Appeal, by a decision of 26 April 1975.

58. It is pertinent to note that this claim for damages (paragraph 42 above), as it came before the Court of Palermo in the action brought by the trustee, was described by that Court as being based (inter alia) upon the argument of the trustee in bankruptcy "that the requisition order caused an economic situation of such gravity that it immediately and directly triggered the bankruptcy of the company."...

Similarly, the Court of Appeal of Palermo had to consider whether there was a "causal link between the requisition order and the company's bankruptcy". It is thus apparent that the substance of the claim brought to the adjudication of the Italian courts is essentially the claim which the United States now brings before this Chamber. The arguments were different, because the municipal court was applying Italian law, whereas this Chamber applies international law; and, of course, the parties were different. Yet it would seem that the municipal courts had been fully seized of the matter which is the substance of the Applicant's claim before the Chamber. For both claims turn on the allegation that the requisition, by frustrating the orderly liquidation, triggered the bankruptcy, and so caused the alleged losses.

59. With such a deal of litigation in the municipal courts about what is in substance the claim now before the Chamber, it was for Italy to demonstrate that there was nevertheless some local remedy that had not been tried; or at least, not exhausted. This burden Italy never sought to deny. It contended that it was possible for the matter to have been brought before the municipal courts, citing the provisions of the treaties themselves, and alleging their violation. This was

never done. In the actions brought before the Court of Palermo, and subsequently the Court of Appeal of Palermo, and the Court of Cassation, the FCN Treaty and its Supplementary Agreement were never mentioned. This is not surprising, for, as Italy recognizes, the way in which the matter was pleaded before the courts of Palermo was not for Raytheon and Machlett to decide but for the trustee. Furthermore, the local remedies rule does not, indeed cannot, require that a claim be presented to the municipal courts in a form, and with arguments, suited to an international tribunal, applying different law to different parties: for an international claim to be admissible, it is sufficient if the essence of the claim has been brought before the competent tribunals and pursued as far as permitted by local law and procedures, and without success.

60. The question, therefore, reduces itself to this: ought Raytheon and Machlett, suing in their own right, as United States corporations allegedly injured by the requisition of property of an Italian company whose shares they held, have brought an action in the Italian courts, within the general limitation-period (five years), alleging violation of certain provisions of the FCN Treaty between Italy and the United States; this mindful of the fact that the very question of the consequences of the requisition was already in issue in the action brought by its trustee in bankruptcy, and that any damages that might there be awarded would pass into the pool of realized assets, for an appropriate part of which Raytheon and Machlett had the right to claim as creditors?

61. Italy contends that Raytheon and Machlett could have based such an action before the Italian courts on Article 2043 of the Italian Civil Code, which provides that "Any act committed either wilfully or through fault which causes wrongful damages to another person implies that the wrongdoer is under an obligation to pay compensation for those damages." According to Italy, this provision is frequently invoked by individuals against the Italian State, and substantial sums have been awarded to claimants where appropriate. If Raytheon and Machlett suffered damage caused by violations by Italian public authorities of the FCN Treaty and the Supplementary Agreement, an Italian court would, it was contended, have been bound to conclude that the relevant acts of the public authorities were wrongful acts for the purposes of Article 2043. It is common ground between the Parties that implementing legislation ("ordini di esecuzione") was enacted (Law No. 385 of 15 June 1949 and Law No. 910 of 1 August 1960), to give effect in Italy to the FCN Treaty and Supplementary Agreement, but that their provisions cannot be invoked in protection of individual rights before the Italian courts unless those provisions are regarded by the courts as self-executing. In order to show that the relevant provisions would be so regarded, decisions of the Court of Cassation have been cited by Italy in which provisions of the FCN Treaty (not the provisions relied on in the present case) have been applied for the benefit of United States nationals who have invoked them before Italian courts, and a provision of a treaty between Italy and the Federal Republic of Germany, said to be comparable with Article V of the FCN Treaty, was given effect.

62. However, those decisions were not based on Article 2043 of the Italian Civil Code; and the treaty provisions applied were given effect in conjunction with municipal legislation or the provisions of other treaties, through the mechanism of a most-favoured-nation provision. In none of the cases cited was the FCN Treaty provision relied on to establish the wrongfulness of conduct of Italian public officials. When in 1971 Raytheon consulted two Italian jurists on the question of local remedies for the purposes of a diplomatic claim, it apparently did not occur to either of them to refer even as a possibility to action under Article 2043 in conjunction with the FCN Treaty. It thus appears to the Chamber to be impossible to deduce, from the recent jurisprudence cited, what the attitude of the Italian courts would have been had Raytheon and Machlett brought an action, some 20 years ago, in reliance on Article 2043 of the Civil Code in conjunction with the provisions of the FCN Treaty and the Supplementary Agreement. Where the determination of a question of municipal law is essential to the Court's decision in a case, the Court will have to weigh the jurisprudence of the municipal courts, and "If this is uncertain or divided, it will rest with the Court to select the interpretation which it considers most in conformity with the law" (Brazilian Loans, P.C.I.J., Series A, Nos. 20/21, p. 124). In the present case, however, it was for Italy to show, as a matter of fact, the existence of a remedy which was open to the United States stockholders and which they failed to employ. The Chamber does not consider that Italy has discharged that burden.

63. It is never easy to decide, in a case where there has in fact been much resort to the municipal courts, whether local remedies have truly been "exhausted". But in this case Italy has not been able to satisfy the Chamber that there clearly remained some remedy which Raytheon and Machlett, independently of ELSI, and of ELSI's trustee in bankruptcy, ought to have pursued and exhausted. ...

NOTES AND QUESTIONS

1. The Ambatielos Arbitral Award had clarified that the local remedies to be exhausted

> [i]nclude not only reference to the courts and tribunals, but also the use of the procedural facilities which municipal law makes available to litigants before such courts and tribunals. It is the whole system of legal protection, as provided by municipal law, which must have been put to the test before a State, as the protector of its nationals, can prosecute the claim on the international plane. ... It is clear, however, that [this statement] cannot be strained too far. Taken literally, it would imply that the fact of having neglected to make use of some means of procedure, even one which is not important to the defense of the action, would suffice to allow a defendant State to claim that local remedies have not been exhausted and that therefore, an international action cannot be brought. This would confer on the rule of the prior exhaustion of local remedies a scope which is unacceptable. In the view of the Commission the non-utilization of certain means of procedure can be accepted as constituting a gap in the exhaustion of local remedies only if the use of these means of procedure were essential to establish the claimant's case before the municipal courts.

The Ambatielos Claim (Greece v. U.K.), Arbitral Award, March 6, 1956, 12 R.I.A.A. 82 (1963). Do *Interhandel* and *ELSI* follow this line of reasoning?

2. Under Article 26 of the Convention on the Settlement of Investment Disputes Between States and Nationals of Other States,

> [c]onsent of the parties to arbitration under this Convention shall, unless otherwise stated, be deemed consent to such arbitration to the exclusion of any other remedy. A Contracting State may require the exhaustion of local administrative or judicial remedies as a condition of its consent to arbitration under this Convention.

17 U.S.T. 1270, T.I.A.S. No. 6090, 575 U.N.T.S. 159 (1965).

Thus the general rule requiring exhaustion will be deemed waived unless the state party expressly demands it. The decision in *ELSI* reaches the opposite result. Which policy is preferable? For what reasons?

3. In *Loewen v. U.S.*, 42 I.L.M. 811 (2003) (facts, *supra*, at 458), the ICSID Arbitral Tribunal constituted under NAFTA arrived at a controversial interpretation of the exhaustion requirement:

> 207. ... Respondent argues that confronted with the adverse bonding decision by the Mississippi Supreme Court [upholding the requirement to post bond in the amount of $625 million], Loewen should have (i) pursued its appeal despite the risk of execution on its assets; or (ii) sought protection under Chapter Eleven of the Bankruptcy Code which would have resulted in a stay of execution against Loewen's assets; or (iii) filed a petition for *certiorari* and sought a stay of execution in the Supreme Court of the United States.
>
> 208. The first alternative suggested by Respondent raises the question whether the appeal is "a reasonably available remedy", having regard to the risk of execution against Loewen's assets if the bond was not posted. Here, the bonding requirement is attached, not to the right of appeal, but to the stay of execution. Granted the distinction, the practical impact of the requirement had severe consequences for Loewen's right of appeal. Without posting the bond, Loewen's right of appeal could be exercised only at the risk of sustaining immediate execution on Loewen's assets in Mississippi, to be followed by execution against Loewen's assets in other States, with the inevitable consequence that Loewen's share price would collapse. .... In these circumstances, if exercising the right of appeal, at the risk of immediate execution on Loewen's Mississippi assets, was the only alternative available to Loewen, it would not have been, "a reasonably available remedy" to Loewen.
>
> 209. Filing under Chapter Eleven of the Bankruptcy Code would have resulted in a stay of execution. In this respect, Chapter Eleven would have enabled Loewen's appeal to proceed without generating all the consequences that would have flowed from execution. Chapter Eleven results in re-organization not in liquidation, so that a company can continue to conduct its business under Court supervision. Although Court supervision would not necessarily bring to an end Loewen's acquisitions program, Court supervision could be expected to restrict and moderate the program. Quite apart from that consequence, a Chapter Eleven filing may have had an effect on the public market perception of Loewen with a detrimental impact on its share price. The question then is whether, in these circumstances, the need to pursue local remedies extends to requiring a claimant to file under Chapter Eleven in order to ensure that a right of appeal remains effective and reasonably available. No doubt there are some situations in which it would be reasonable to expect an impecunious claimant to file under Chapter Eleven in order to exercise an available right of appeal. Whether it was reasonable to expect Loewen to file under Chapter Eleven depends at least in part on the reasons why Loewen elected to enter into the settlement agreement in preference to exercising other options, a matter examined in paras. 214-216 (inclusive).
>
> 210. The third alternative is the petition for *certiorari* coupled with the application for a stay. There is a conflict of opinion about the prospects of success of such an application

between Professor Drew S. Days III (former United States Solicitor-General) and Professor Tribe. Professor Days is of the opinion that Loewen would have had "a reasonable opportunity" of obtaining review by the Supreme Court of the United States of the application of the Mississippi bonding requirement on the ground that it prevented, inconsistently with due process, appellate review of the Mississippi trial court judgment. Professor Tribe is of a contrary opinion. ...

211. This Tribunal is not in a position to decide whether the opinion of Professor Days or that of Professor Tribe is to be preferred. Nor is the Tribunal in a position to decide which of their conflicting opinions is to be preferred on a related question, namely whether collateral review was available in the Federal District Court. But the Tribunal notes that Professor Days does not assert that either the Supreme Court or the Federal Court would grant the relief suggested. It is fair to say that, on his view, there was a prospect, at most a reasonable prospect or possibility, of such relief being granted.

212. The decision not to relax the bonding requirement, an act for which Respondent is responsible in international law, generated the risk of immediate execution with its attendant detrimental consequences for Loewen. In this situation, was either the *certiorari* petition or the collateral review option a reasonably available and adequate remedy? The pursuit of either remedy, more particularly the Supreme Court remedy, if it resulted in a failure to obtain a stay, would worsen Loewen's position and reinforce adverse market perceptions about Loewen. So, the absence of any certainty about the outcome of either option is a significant consideration in deciding whether either option involved an adequate remedy which was reasonably available to Loewen.

213. Entry into the settlement agreement no doubt reflected a business judgment by Loewen that, of the various options then open, settlement was the most attractive, in all probability because it provided certainty. Other alternatives involved financial consequences which would not have been easy to predict.

214. Respondent argues that, because entry into the settlement agreement was a matter of business judgment, Loewen voluntarily decided not to pursue its local remedies. That submission does not dispose of the point. The question is whether the remedies in question were reasonably available and adequate. If they were not, it is not to the point that Loewen entered into the settlement, even as a matter of business judgment. It may be that the business judgment was inevitable or the natural outcome of adverse consequences generated by the impugned court decision.

215. Here we encounter the central difficulty in Loewen's case. Loewen failed to present evidence disclosing its reasons for entering into the settlement agreement in preference to pursuing other options, in particular the Supreme Court option which it had under active consideration and preparation until the settlement agreement was reached. It is a matter on which the onus of proof rested with Loewen. It is, however, not just a matter of onus of proof. If, in all the circumstances, entry into the settlement agreement was the only course which Loewen could reasonably be expected to take, that would be enough to justify an inference or conclusion that Loewen had no reasonably available and adequate remedy.

216. Although entry into the settlement agreement may well have been a reasonable course for Loewen to take, we are simply left to speculate on the reasons which led to the decision to adopt that course rather than to pursue other options. It is not a case in which it can be said that it was the only course which Loewen could reasonably be expected to take.

217. Accordingly, our conclusion is that Loewen failed to pursue its domestic remedies, notably the Supreme Court option and that, in consequence, Loewen has not shown a

> violation of customary international law and a violation of NAFTA for which Respondent is responsible.

The Loewen Group, Inc. et al. v. U.S., 42 I.L.M. 811, 844-846 (2003). Is the Tribunal's reasoning convincing? Could TLGI have avoided this result by simply disclosing its process of decision-making? See also *NAFTA Decision on Continuous Nationality and Local Remedies*, 97 AM. J. INT'L L. 700 (2003).

f. Draft Articles on Diplomatic Protection

U.N. GAOR, 59th Sess., Supp. No.10, U.N. Doc. A/59/10, chap. IV (2004)

Article 14: *Exhaustion of local remedies*

1. A State may not bring an international claim in respect of an injury to a national or other person referred to in draft article 8 before the injured person has, subject to draft article 16, exhausted all local remedies.

2. "Local remedies" means legal remedies which are open to an injured person before the judicial or administrative courts or bodies, whether ordinary or special, of the State alleged to be responsible for the injury.

Article 15: *Category of claims*

Local remedies shall be exhausted where an international claim, or request for a declaratory judgement related to the claim, is brought preponderantly on the basis of an injury to a national or other person referred to in draft article 8.

Article 16: *Exceptions to the local remedies rule*

Local remedies do not need to be exhausted where:

(a) The local remedies provide no reasonable possibility of effective redress;

(b) There is undue delay in the remedial process which is attributable to the State alleged to be responsible;

(c) There is no relevant connection between the injured person and the State alleged to be responsible or the circumstances of the case otherwise make the exhaustion of local remedies unreasonable;

(d) The State alleged to be responsible has waived the requirement that local remedies be exhausted.

NOTES AND QUESTIONS

1. How does this most recent statement of the International Law Commission relate to the policies and decisions discussed *supra*? Does it follow the policies informing *Interhandel, Ambatielos, ELSI* and/or *Loewen*? Is it authoritative? Does it represent good policy?

2. Is the exhaustion rule an anachronism or does it continue to have policy relevance?

4. Waiver of Protection? Calvo Clauses

A state may require as a condition of entry and enterprise in its territory that a foreigner waive his right to diplomatic protection. Should international law recognize such waivers? What would be the consequences for international investment? Consider the discussion in the North American Dredging Company case.

a. United States of America (North American Dredging Co. of Texas) v. United Mexican States

United States-Mexican Claims Commission, 1926 4 R.I.A.A. 26

[This was a claim on behalf of an American corporation for breach of contract between it and Mexico for dredging a port. Article 18 of the contract provided:

> The contractor and all persons, who, as employees or in any other capacity, may be engaged in the execution of the work under this contract either directly or indirectly, shall be considered as Mexicans in all matters, within the Republic of Mexico, concerning the execution of such work and the fulfillment of this contract. They shall not claim, nor shall they have, with regard to the interests and the business connected with this contract, any other rights or means to enforce the same than those granted by the laws of the Republic to Mexicans, nor shall they enjoy any other rights than those established in favor of Mexicans. They are consequently deprived of any rights as aliens, and under no conditions shall the intervention of foreign diplomatic agents be permitted, in any matter related to this contract.]

VAN VOLLENHOVEN: ... 3. The Commission is fully sensible of the importance of any judicial decision either sustaining in whole or in part, or rejecting in whole or in part, or construing the so-called "Calvo clause" in contracts between nations and aliens. It appreciates the legitimate desire on the part of nations to deal with persons and property within their respective jurisdictions according to their own laws and to apply remedies provided by their own authorities and tribunals, which laws and remedies in no wise restrict or limit their international obligations, or restrict or limit or in any wise impinge upon the correlative rights of other nations protected under rules of international law.

4. The Commission does not feel impressed by arguments either in favor of or in opposition to the Calvo clause, in so far as these arguments go to extremes. The Calvo clause is neither upheld by all outstanding international authorities and by the soundest among international awards nor is it universally rejected. The Calvo clause in a specific contract is neither a clause which must be sustained to its full length because of its contractual nature nor can it be discretionarily separated from the rest of the contract as if it were just an accidental postscript. The problem is not solved by saying yes or no; the affirmative answer exposing the rights of foreigners to undeniable dangers, the negative answer leaving to the nations involved no alternative except that of exclusion of foreigners from business. The present stage of international law imposes upon every international tribunal the solemn duty of seeking for a proper and adequate balance between the sovereign right of national jurisdiction, on the one hand, and the sovereign

right of national protection of citizens on the other. No international tribunal should or may evade the task of finding such limitations of both rights as will render them compatible within the general rules and principles of international law. …

5. At the very outset the Commission rejects as unsound a presentation of the problem according to which if article 18 of the present contract were upheld Mexico or any other nation might lawfully bind all foreigners by contract to relinquish all rights of protection by their governments. It is quite possible to recognize as valid some forms of waiving the right of foreign protection without thereby recognizing as valid and lawful every form of doing so. …

7. As civilization has progressed individualism has increased; and so has the right of the individual citizen to decide upon the ties between himself and his native country. There was a time when governments and not individuals decided if a man was allowed to change his nationality or his residence. … To acknowledge that under the existing laws of progressive, enlightened civilization a person may voluntarily expatriate himself but that short of expatriation he may not by contract, in what he conceives to be his own interest, to any extent loosen the ties which bind him to his country is neither consistent with the facts of modern international intercourse nor with corresponding developments in the field of international law and does not tend to promote good will among nations.

8. The contested provision, in this case, is part of a contract and must be upheld unless it be repugnant to a recognized rule of international law. What must be established is not that the Calvo clause is universally accepted or universally recognized, but that there exists a generally accepted rule of international law condemning the Calvo clause and denying to an individual the right to relinquish to any extent, large or small, and under any circumstances or conditions, the protection of the government to which he owes allegiance. Only in case a provision of this or any similar tendency were established could a parallel be drawn between the illegality of the Calvo clause in the present contract and the illegality of a similar clause in the Arkansas contract declared void in 1922 by the Supreme Court of the United States (257 U.S. 529) because of its repugnance to American statute provisions. …

9. The commission does not hesitate to declare that there exists no international rule prohibiting the sovereign right of a nation to protect its citizens abroad from being subject to any limitation whatsoever under any circumstances. The right of protection has been limited by treaties between nations in provisions related to the Calvo clause. While it is true that Latin-American countries-which are important members of the family of nations and which have played for many years an important and honorable part in the development of international law-are parties to most of these treaties, still such countries as France, Germany, Great Britain, Sweden, Norway, and Belgium, and in one case at least even the United States of America … have been parties to treaties containing such provisions.

10. What Mexico has asked of the North American Dredging Company of Texas as a condition for awarding it the contract which it sought is, "If all of the means of enforcing your rights under this contract afforded by Mexican law, even against the Mexican Government itself, are wide open to you, as they are wide open to our own citizens, will you promise not to ignore them and not to call directly upon your own Government to intervene in your behalf in connection with any controversy, small or large, but seek redress under the laws of Mexico through the authorities and tribunals furnished by Mexico for your protection?" and the claimant, by subscribing to this contract and seeking the benefits which were to accrue to him thereunder, has answered, "I promise."

11. Under the rules of international law may an alien lawfully make such a promise? The Commission holds that he may, but at the same time holds that he can not deprive the government of his nation of its undoubted right of applying international remedies to violations of international law committed to his damage. Such government frequently has a larger interest in maintaining the principles of international law than in recovering damage for one of its citizens in a particular case, and manifestly such citizen can not by contract tie in this respect the hands of his government. But while any attempt to so bind his government is void the Commission has not found any generally recognized rule of positive international law which would give to his government the right to intervene to strike down a lawful contract, in the terms set forth in the preceding paragraph 10, entered into by its citizen. The obvious purpose of such a contract is to prevent abuses of the right to protection, not to destroy the right itself-abuses which are intolerable to any self-respecting nation and are prolific breeders of international friction. The purpose of such a contract is to draw a reasonable and practical line between Mexico's sovereign right of jurisdiction within its own territory, on the one hand, and the sovereign right of protection of the government of an alien whose person or property is within such territory, on the other hand.

12. It being impossible to prove the illegality of the said provision, under the limitations indicated, by adducing generally recognized rules of positive international law, it apparently can only be contested by invoking its incongruity to the law of nature (natural rights) and its inconsistency with inalienable, indestructible, unprescriptible, uncurtailable rights of nations. The law of nature may have been helpful, some three centuries ago, to build up a new law of nations, and the conception of inalienable rights of men and nations may have exercised a salutary influence, some one hundred and fifty years ago, on the development of modern democracy on both sides of the ocean; but they have failed as a durable foundation of either municipal or international law. …

14. Reading [Article 18] as a whole, it is evident that its purpose was to bind the claimant to be governed by the laws of Mexico and to use the remedies existing under such laws. . . It did not take from him his undoubted right to apply to his own Government for protection if his resort to the Mexican tribunals or other authorities available to him resulted in a denial or delay of justice as that

term is used in international law. In such a case the claimant's complaint would be not that his contract was violated but that he had been denied justice. ...

16. It is quite true that this construction of article 18 of the contract does not effect complete equality between the foreigner subscribing the contract on the one hand and Mexicans on the other hand. Apart from the fact that equality of legal status between citizens and foreigners is by no means a requisite of international law-in some respects the citizen has greater rights and larger duties, in other respects the foreigner has-article 18 only purposes equality between the foreigner and Mexicans with respect to the execution, fulfillment, and interpretation of this contract and such limited equality is properly obtained. ...

20. Under article 18 of the contract declared upon the present claimant is precluded from presenting to its Government any claim relative to the interpretation or fulfillment of this contract. If it had a claim for denial of justice, for delay of justice or gross injustice, or for any other violation of international law committed by Mexico to its damage, it might have presented such a claim to its Government, which in turn could have espoused it and presented it here. Although the claim as presented falls within the first clause of Article I of the Treaty, describing claims coming within this Commission's jurisdiction, it is not a claim that may be rightfully presented by the claimant to its Government for espousal and hence is not cognizable here, pursuant to the latter part of paragraph 1 of the same Article I.

21. It is urged that the claim may be presented by claimant to its Government for espousal in view of the provision of Article V of the Treaty, to the effect "that no claim shall be disallowed or rejected by the Commission by the application of the general principle of international law that the legal remedies must be exhausted as a condition precedent to the validity or allowance of any claim." This provision is limited to the application of a general principle of international law to claims that may be presented to the Commission falling within the terms of Article I of the Treaty, and if under the terms of Article I the private claimant can not rightfully present its claim to its Government and the claim therefore can not become cognizable here, Article V does not apply to it, nor can it render the claim cognizable, nor does it entitle either Government to set aside an express valid contract between one of its citizens and the other Government.

b. ICSID: Wena Hotels Ltd. v. Arab Republic of Egypt

(Proceeding on the Jurisdiction), May 25, 1999, 41 I.L.M. 881 (2002)

This dispute arose out of agreements to develop and manage two hotels in Luxor and Cairo, Egypt.

OBJECTION 1: "THE RESPONDENT HAS NOT AGREED TO ARBITRATE WITH THE CLAIMANT AS IT IS, BY VIRTUE OF OWNERSHIP, TO BE TREATED AS AN EGYPTIAN COMPANY."

The Arab Republic of Egypt's principal object is that, "although the claimant is an English company, it is, by virtue of Mr. El-Farargy's ownership and his Egyptian nationality, to be treated as an Egyptian company pursuant to Article 8(1)." Accordingly, "as the respondent has not consented under the [Agreement between the Arab Republic of Egypt and the United Kingdom of Great Britain and Northern Ireland for the Promotion and Protection of Investments, hereinafter IPPA] to arbitrate with companies, such as the claimant, that are to be treated as Egyptian thereunder, it therefore follows from the IPPA's express terms that the respondent has not consented to the present arbitration."

In its deliberations, the Tribunal gave considerable attention to the instrument in which Egypt expressed its consent to [International Centre for the Settlement of Investment Disputes, hereinafter ICSID] arbitration—Article 8(1) of the IPPA between Egypt and the United Kingdom. The first sentence of this article contains a general consent to arbitration between a contracting State to the IPPA and a juridical person of the other contracting State to the IPPA, the situation in this case:

> Each Contracting Party hereby consents to submit to the International Centre for the Settlement of Investment Disputes … any legal dispute arising between that Contracting Party and a national or party of the other Contracting Party concerning an investment of the latter in the territory of the former.

Of considerable importance to this arbitration, however, is the second sentence of Article 8(1), which states that:

> Such a company of one Contracting Party in which before such a dispute arises a majority of shares are owned by nationals or companies of the other Contracting Party shall in accordance with Article 25(2)(b) of the Convention be treated for the purposes of the Convention as a company of the other Contracting Party.

Article 25(2)(b) of the ICSID Convention, which the second sentence expressly references, provides that, for purposes of jurisdiction under Article 25(1) of the Convention, "National of another Contracting State" means:...

> (b) any juridical person which had the nationality of the Contracting State other than the State party to the dispute on the date on which the parties consented to submit such dispute to conciliation or arbitration and any juridical person that had the nationality of the Contracting State party to the dispute on that date and which, because of foreign control, the parties have agreed should be treated as a national of another Contracting State for the purposes of this Convention. …

Egypt contends that the second sentence of Article 8(1) of the IPPA "reverses the nationality of a company incorporated in the United Kingdom but majority owned by Egyptian nationals." Thus, "a company such as the Claimant, in which the majority of shares are held by an Egyptian national, is to be treated as an Egyptian company, not a United Kingdom company." Because the first sentence of Article 8(1), quoted above, requires diversity of nationality between the "Contracting Party" and the "national or party of the other Contracting Party," Egypt argues that the second sentence of Article 8(1) has the effect of "excluding jurisdiction in cases, such as this one, where a company is majority-owned by shareholders having the nationality of the State with which the company has a dispute." …

In contrast, Wena argues that "Egypt has completely misconstrued the meaning of Article 8(1): it is a provision allowing companies incorporated in a state to sue that state where local companies are under foreign control; it does not prevent companies incorporated in that state from suing the other state." In other words, "Wena's construction of this provision is that it applies not in every case, but only to a company which has the 'nationality of the Contracting State party to the dispute,' in accordance with Article 25(2)(b) of the ICSID Convention ... to which the second sentence of Article 8(1) cross-refers." Thus, according to Wena, the "second sentence of Article 8(1) … does not apply to Wena, a company which does not have the nationality of Egypt, the Contracting State party to this dispute." …

Faced with two plausible constructions of Article 8(1) of the IPPA and no direct evidence of the intent of the United Kingdom and Egypt in drafting this provision the Tribunal gave considerable weight to this indirect evidence of the provision's purpose. Accordingly, the Tribunal agrees with Wena's interpretation (and that of most commentators) that the second sentence of Article 8(1) of the IPPA relates only to the situation in which an investment in Egypt or the United Kingdom is made through a local company, owned by companies or nationals of the other country. The provision does not reverse the consent given in the first sentence of Article 8(1) when a Contracting State is a party to a dispute with a juridical person of the other Contracting State.

NOTES AND QUESTIONS

1. What is the policy implicit in the Dredging case? Does the Wena decision express a different policy? Which one is more persuasive?

5. The Modalities of Protection

The actual modalities by which protection is extended may range from verbal, symbolic representations on through to substantial military intervention, and the protectors may be private groups, nation-states or international organizations.

a. Protection Through Diplomacy

Diplomatic protection commonly refers to any unilateral initiative short of war against a state by another state on behalf of its nationals. Diplomatic protection may be no more than an inquiry or a protest but may extend to implicit or express threats and the imposition of certain deprivations. On occasion, states have used military or naval forces against another state under the rubric of diplomatic protection. Hence the term has contrasting connotations to elites who view themselves in a particular situation as relatively weaker or stronger. To the stronger, diplomatic protection imports a benign modality; to the weaker, it imports coercion in varying degrees of subtlety. Historically, those state elites who have generally viewed themselves as weaker have sought to limit the contingencies and even the lawfulness as a whole of diplomatic protection. Elites of more powerful states have sought to extend the protection.

Amerasinghe mentions three influences on the law of diplomatic protection: (1) the right of the injured state; (2) the interests of the injured alien; and (3) the interests of the defendant state, competing national states and other entities. The confusion which characterizes this area makes it difficult to determine which one of these interests will prevail in the long-term development of the law. "Nevertheless [writes Amerasinghe], it would seem to be reasonable to assume that the interests of the national State and the interests of the alien are generally at the centre of diplomatic protection." As to the choice between these two, he concludes that while the formal structure of the law of diplomatic protection would tend to favor the interests of the national State, "[o]n a substantive plane . . . the criticism that the law should really be based on the interests of the alien, because the law of alien treatment is really a part of the law of human rights . . ., would seem to be particularly cogent and of relevance in any proposed reform." *See* C.F. AMERASINGHE, STATE RESPONSIBILITY FOR INJURIES TO ALIENS, *supra,* at 56-65.

* * *

The Court in *Barcelona Traction* discussed diplomatic protection at length.

(1) Barcelona Traction

1970 I.C.J. 3, 32 et seq. [Review paras. 33-37, 51, 53, *supra*, at 444-449]

NOTES AND QUESTIONS

1. Although the rights of the individual apart from the State have been recognized in certain areas (e. g., in claims brought before the International Center for the Settlement of Investment Disputes), the idea that a State may be legally obliged to protect the interests of its nationals has not taken hold. The question of whether or not to protect still falls within the realm of the state as an executive discretion.

2. In the United States, attempts to force executive protection through the courts have failed. *See U.S. ex rel. Boynton v. Blaine*, 139 U.S. 306 (1891). Following World War II, the United States State Department refused to extend protection to individuals with double nationality (U.S. and Soviet) who were being detained by Soviet authorities.

United States statutory law on diplomatic protection appears in 22 U.S.C. §§ 1731, 1732. Section 1731 provides that all naturalized citizens of the United States while in foreign countries are entitled to and shall receive from this Government the same protection of persons and property which is accorded to native-born citizens. R.S. § 2000. Section 1732, Release of Citizens Imprisoned by Foreign Governments, is discussed in the next case.

(2) Redpath v. Kissinger

415 F.Supp. 566 (W.D.Tex.1976) *aff'd* 545 F.2d 167 (5th Cir. 1976).

SPEARS, Chief Judge: The substance of Petitioner's allegations are that he was incarcerated by Mexican officials, subjected to torture, and that the Defendants have negligently failed and refused to accord him the assistance which he as an American citizen was entitled to receive.

... Redpath was arrested in Morelia, Michoacan, Mexico on January 22, 1975 and charged with passing bad checks. The United States Consulate General was notified, a consular officer talked to Redpath the next day, and although Redpath at that time had no attorney, the affidavit shows he was in fact afforded a court appointed attorney, ... who represented him during his trial which resulted in a sentence of five years in prison. [The Department of State] states that the sentence has been reduced, and that in due course upon good behavior the defendant will be released from imprisonment. The Gise report shows that he was a member of a panel of United States government officials which conducted an inquiry into allegations by American prisoners in Mexico about their treatment; that Redpath's allegations of torture were included in that inquiry; and that they were found to be unsubstantiated. ...

There is no doubt that a District Court has no authority to grant the requested relief by Writ of Mandamus or otherwise. The applicable statute, 22 U.S.C. § 1732, provides:

> Whenever it is made known to the President that any citizen of the United States has been unjustly deprived of his liberty by or under the authority of any foreign government, it shall be the duty of the President forthwith to demand of that government the reasons of such imprisonment; and if it appears to be wrongful and in violation of the rights of American citizenship, the President shall forthwith demand the release of such citizen, and if the release so demanded is unreasonably delayed or refused, the President shall use such means, not amounting to acts of war, as he may think necessary and proper to obtain or effectuate the release; and all the facts and proceedings relative thereto shall as soon as practicable be communicated by the President to Congress. R.S. Sec. 2001.

United States v. Dulles, 222 F.2d 390 (D.C. Cir. 1954), is dispositive of the instant petition for a Writ of Mandamus. In that case an American soldier had been tried for robbery by a French court and assessed a term of imprisonment. His wife filed a Petition for Habeas Corpus in the U.S. District Court for the District of Columbia, naming as Respondents the Secretary of State, the Secretary of Defense and the Secretary of the Army, alleging in substance that they had failed to perform their respective duties in protecting her husband from prosecution. The Respondents' Motion to Dismiss was granted on the ground that the Petitioner was not in the custody of Respondents and that the court was without jurisdiction to grant the requested writ. Upon appeal, the appellate tribunal agreed with the trial court's disposition, but reviewed and considered the case as one seeking a mandatory order requiring the Secretary of State to obtain Keith's release through diplomatic negotiations with France. Under provisions of a governing treaty, the United States was required to do certain things, among which was to have a representative of the Staff Judge Advocate present at the trial. This was done and no unconstitutional irregularities were reported. The Court of Appeals held:

> [The Secretary] was not under a legal duty to attempt through diplomatic processes to obtain Keith's release. Quite to the contrary, the commencement of diplomatic negotiations with a foreign power is completely in the discretion of the President and the head of the Department of State, who is his political agent. The Executive is not subject to judicial control or direction in such matters. *Marbury v. Madison*, 5 U.S. 137, 164 (1803). . . . Accordingly, we hold the petition was properly dismissed, even though it be regarded as seeking affirmative injunctive relief against the Secretary of State.

The Supreme Court has defined the powers of the courts of the United States with respect to the disposition of matters such as the one under consideration. In Oetjen v. Central Leather Company, 246 U.S. 297, which involved a dispute over the seizure of certain property by Mexico and the interpretation of certain treaty rights claimed by the parties, it was held that the conduct of the foreign relations of the United States is committed by the Constitution to the Executive and Legislative Departments of the government, and the propriety of what may be done in the exercise of these powers is not subject to judicial inquiry or decision.

Now, as the government points out, the Petitioner received the services of American consular officers as set forth in the Consular Affairs memorandum attached to its Motion. Nothing is found from the Petitioner himself which reflects that his arrest and conviction were improper. The Director of Special Consular Services, who is the official apparently charged with the duty of investigating the imprisonment of American nationals abroad, made special inquiry into the torture allegations of Redpath and found no substantiation for that claim. The rights of Petitioner accruing under the statute concerning citizens in prison by foreign governments, 22 U.S.C. § 1732, to have his case examined into and a report made thereof have been accorded to him. The government's response shows that the claim of Petitioner has been followed up with appropriate inquiries by the officials charged with the protection of arrested American nationals, and any further action with respect to Redpath's situation will have to be taken by the Executive through his agent, the Secretary of State. The general rule with respect to the use of mandamus which is an extraordinary writ is stated by the Court of Appeals for the Fifth Circuit as follows:

Before the writ of mandamus may properly issue three elements must coexist: (1) A clear right in the plaintiff to the relief sought; (2) a clear duty on the part of defendant to do the act in question; and (3) no other adequate remedy available." Carter v. Seamans, 411 F.2d 767 (5th Cir. 1969) *cert. den.* 397 U.S. 941 (1970). Plaintiff's petition does not satisfy this requirement. The official actions sought are not ministerial, but are clearly of a diplomatic nature involving the exercise of discretion by the Executive, or under his direction. ...

Dismissed.

NOTES AND QUESTIONS

1. The link of nationality is not the only basis on which claims to protect have been lodged. It has been argued that there is a

> [c]ustomary international legal right of quasi-diplomatic protection on behalf of ethnic, kin, speech and dialect and skill groups, for this is a phenomenon which is a necessary corollary of the very notion of the international protection of human rights. Thus, the People's Republic of China might lawfully protest and even intervene in situations in which overseas Chinese were subjected to gross deprivations of human rights. . . .

Lung-chu Chen & W. Michael Reisman, *Who Owns Taiwan: A Search for International Title*, 81 YALE L.J. 599, 652 n. 199 (1972).

2. A case of limited diplomatic protection on behalf of co-ethnics can be seen in China's reaction to the Indonesian Government's raids on Chinese property in August 1951. The raids and mass arrests, seemingly anti-Chinese as much as anti-Communist, elicited expressions of "extreme displeasure" from the Chinese Embassy and set off a Chinese press campaign against the Indonesian leadership. HERBERT FEITH, THE DECLINE OF CONSTITUTIONAL DEMOCRACY IN INDONESIA 187 (Cornell U. Press 1962).

3. Instances in which a state publicly revokes its claim to speak for its co-nationals or co-ethnics are also not unknown. In April 1954, the Chinese People's Republic announced that it would negotiate with Southeast Asian countries as to the citizenship of their resident Chinese. Under the terms of the 1955 Bandung Dual Nationality Agreement with Indonesia, China waived her traditional claim that all ethnic Chinese were her nationals. FEITH, *supra,* at 390.

4. In March of 1978, the Government of Vietnam "cracked down on private trading in the southern part of the country, largely controlled by ethnic Chinese merchants, in an attempt to nationalize commerce." (N. Y. TIMES, July 6, 1978.) Between March and July, some 140,000 ethnic Chinese left Vietnam, some of them going to Taiwan, most travelling north to the People's Republic of China. China reacted officially to the exodus in two ways: Peking launched a press campaign against Hanoi, speaking of the "persecution, ostracism and expulsion" of ethnic Chinese; and, in addition, tried to negotiate for the orderly evacuation of remaining co-ethnics. Negotiations were conducted while Chinese vessels waited off the Vietnamese coast. Interestingly, China no longer based its argument of protection on nationality, but on human rights. Hungdah Chiu, *China's Legal Position on Protecting Chinese Residents in Vietnam*, 74 AM. J. INT'L L. 685, 688-89 (1980) (referring to the fact that "by claiming that there were more than a million Chinese in Vietnam, the PRC ran the risk of being asked to accept their repatriation into China").

5. Consider, in this regard, Israeli efforts to repatriate "Falashas" from Ethiopia (Operation Moses, 1984). *See* Chaim Rosen & Steven Kaplan, *Ethiopian Jews in Israel*, 1994 AM. JEWISH Y.B., *available at* http://www.cais.com/nacoej/8.html.

6. For further discussion of the protection of co-ethnic minorities by their kin states, *see* Michael R. Geroe & Thomas K. Gump, *Hungary and a New Paradigm for the Protection of Ethnic Minorities in Central and Eastern Europe*, 32 COLUM. J. TRANSNAT'L L. 673 (1995); WILL KYMLICKA, MULTICULTURAL CITIZENSHIP: A LIBERAL THEORY OF MINORITY RIGHTS (Oxford U. Press 1995); Patrick Thornberry, *The UN Declaration on the Rights of Persons Belonging to National or Ethnic, Religious and Linguistic Minorities: Background Analysis, Observations, and an Update*, *in* UNIVERSAL MINORITY RIGHTS (Alan Phillips & Allan Rosas eds., Abo Akademi University Institute for Human Rights; Minority Rights Group (International) 1995); Steven R. Ratner, *Does International Law Matter in Preventing Ethnic Conflict?*, 32 N.Y.U. J. INT'L L. & POL'Y 591 (2000); Konrad Huber & Robert W. Mickey, *Defining the Kin-State: An Analysis of its Role and Prescriptions for Moderating its Impact*, *in* PROTECTION OF MINORITY RIGHTS THROUGH BILATERAL TREATIES: THE CASE OF CENTRAL AND EASTERN EUROPE (Kluwer Academic Publishers 1999).

7. The ILC in its Draft Articles on Diplomatic Protection adopted in 2004, *supra*, at 440, only extends the right to diplomatic protection, under great restrictions, to stateless persons and refugees. Draft Article 8 provides:

> 1. A State may exercise diplomatic protection in respect of a stateless person who, at the time of the injury and at the date of the official presentation of the claim, is lawfully and habitually resident in that State.
>
> 2. A State may exercise diplomatic protection in respect of a person who is recognized as a refugee by that State when that person, at the time of the injury and at the date of the official presentation of the claim, is lawfully and habitually resident in that State.
>
> 3. Paragraph 2 does not apply in respect of an injury caused by an internationally wrongful act of the State of nationality of the refugee.

b. Arbitration and Adjudication

The modalities of arbitration and adjudication are used comparatively infrequently for protection of nationals. One structural reason for this is the institution of "consensual jurisdiction," which requires both parties to agree to submit their dispute to a third party.

(1) Norwegian Loans Case (Fr. v. Nor.)
1957 I.C.J. 9

[In this case, a claim brought by France on behalf of its nationals against Norway failed because the French declaration on jurisdiction included a self-judging clause stating "[t]his declaration does not apply to differences relating to matters which are essentially within the national jurisdiction as understood by the Government of the French Republic." The ICJ concluded :]

[T]he Norwegian Government is entitled, by virtue of the condition of reciprocity, to invoke the reservation contained in the French Declaration...; that this reservation excludes from the jurisdiction of the Court the dispute which has been referred to it by the Application of the French Government; that consequently the Court is without jurisdiction to entertain the Application.

c. Use of Force on Behalf of Nationals and "Humanitarian Intervention"

Use of force for the purpose of rescuing endangered nationals as a measure *sine qua non* has been widely accepted by the world community. *See* N. RONZITTI, RESCUING NATIONALS ABROAD THROUGH MILITARY COERCION AND INTERVENTION ON GROUNDS OF HUMANITY (Martinus Nijhoff 1985). The Israeli rescue effort of its citizens trapped in a hijacked airplane at Entebbe, Uganda in July 1976 presents the case of a nation engaging in a limited military action for the protection of its nationals. *See* Eleanor C. McDowell, *The Entebbe Incident*, 15 I.L.M. 1224-25 (1976). U.S. Ambassador Scranton approved, for the United States, this action in the U.N. Security Council (U.N.Doc. S/PV.1941 (1976) at 31-32; 15 I.L.M. 1232 (1976)). One of the reasons offered for President Ronald Reagan's October, 1983 invasion of Grenada was the need to evacuate approximately 100 U.S. medical students. *See* Louise Doswald-Beck, *The Legality of the U.S. Intervention in Grenada*, 31 NETH. INT'L L. REV. 355 (1984); JOHN NORTON MOORE, LAW AND THE GRENADA MISSION (Georgetown U. Press 1984). For a more detailed treatment of these and other military rescue missions, *see* Part Six: Military Instrument, *infra* at, 1078-1091.

NOTES AND QUESTIONS

1. Are there any policy reasons which would counsel against unilateral rescue missions as measures of diplomatic protection by the home state? Should the Security Council be seized with matters of this type? Are the interests of the less powerful countries, either as "victims" of intervention or possible intervenors themselves, helped by a purely unilateral theory of diplomatic protection by force?

2. Since the early 1990's, humanitarian interventions involving the use of force, undertaken multilaterally or unilaterally, with or without Security Council involvement, have become more frequent and thus more controversial. This topic is extensively treated in Part Two: Regime Change, *supra,* at 252-260, and in Part Six: Military Instrument, *infra,* at 1078-91.) For a flavor of the debate, *see* SEAN D. MURPHY, HUMANITARIAN INTERVENTION (U. of Pa. Press 1996); W. Michael Reisman, *Sovereignty and Human Rights in Contemporary International Law*, 84 AM. J. INT'L L. 866 (1990); INT'L COMM'N ON INTERVENTION & STATE SOVEREIGNTY, THE RESPONSIBILITY TO PROTECT: REPORT OF THE INTERNATIONAL COMMISSION ON INTERVENTION AND STATE SOVEREIGNTY (Int'l Development Research Center 2001); SAMANTHA POWER, "A PROBLEM FROM HELL": AMERICA AND THE AGE OF GENOCIDE (Basic Books 2002); HUMANITARIAN INTERVENTION: ETHICAL, LEGAL, AND POLITICAL DILEMMAS (J.L. Holzgrefe & Robert O. Keohane eds., Cambridge U. Press 2003).

d. Protection by International Organizations

Is protection of employees of international organizations to be guided by the same principles and policies as protection of nationals by their home governments? Consider the following case:

(1) Reparations for Injuries Suffered in the Service of the United Nations

1949 I.C.J. 174, 181-184

Question I (b) is as follows:

'[H]as the United Nations, as an Organization, the capacity to bring an international claim ... in respect of the damage caused ... (b) to the victim or to persons entitled through him?'

In dealing with the question of law which arises out of Question I (b), it is unnecessary to repeat the considerations which led to an affirmative answer being given to Question I (a). It can now be assumed that the Organization has the capacity to bring a claim on the international plane, to negotiate, to conclude a special agreement and to prosecute a claim before an international tribunal. The only legal question which remains to be considered is whether, in the course of bringing an international claim of this kind, the Organization can recover 'the reparation due in respect of the damage caused ... to the victim. ...'

The traditional rule that diplomatic protection is exercised by the national State does not involve the giving of a negative answer to Question I (b).

In the first place, this rule applies to claims brought by a State. But here we have the different and new case of a claim that would be brought by the Organization.

In the second place, even in inter-State relations, there are important exceptions to the rule, for there are cases in which protection may be exercised by a State on behalf of persons not having its nationality.

In the third place, the rule rests on two bases. The first is that the defendant State has broken an obligation towards the national State in respect of its nationals. The second is that only the party to whom an international obligation is due can bring a claim in respect of its breach. This is precisely what happens when the Organization, in bringing a claim for damage suffered by its agent, does so by invoking the breach of an obligation towards itself. Thus, the rule of the nationality of claims affords no reason against recognizing that the Organization has the right to bring a claim for the damage referred to in Question I (b). On the contrary, the principle underlying this rule leads to the recognition of this capacity as belonging to the Organization, when the Organization invokes, as the ground of its claim, a breach of an obligation towards itself.

Nor does the analogy of the traditional rule of diplomatic protection of nationals abroad justify in itself an affirmative reply. It is not possible, by a strained use of the concept of allegiance, to assimilate the legal bond which exists, under Article 100 of the Charter, between the Organization on the one hand, and the Secretary-General and the staff on the other, to the bond of nationality existing between a State and its nationals.

The Court is here faced with a new situation. The questions to which it gives rise can only be solved by realizing that the situation is dominated by the provisions of the Charter considered in the light of the principles of international law.

The question lies within the limits already established; that is to say it presupposes that the injury for which the reparation is demanded arises from a breach of an obligation designed to help an agent of the Organization in the performance of his duties. It is not a case in which the wrongful act or omission would merely constitute a breach of the general obligations of a State concerning the position of aliens; claims made under this head would be within the competence of the national State and not, as a general rule, within that of the Organization.

The Charter does not expressly confer upon the Organization the capacity to include, in its claim for reparation, damage caused to the victim or to persons entitled through him. The Court must therefore begin by enquiring whether the provisions of the Charter concerning the functions of the Organization, and the part played by its agents in the performance of those functions, imply for the Organization power to afford its agents the limited protection that would consist in the bringing of a claim on their behalf for reparation for damage suffered in such circumstances. Under international law, the Organization must be deemed to have those powers which, though not expressly provided in the Charter, are conferred upon it by necessary implication as being essential to the performance of its duties. This principle of law was applied by the Permanent Court of International Justice to the International Labour Organization in its Advisory Opinion No. 13 of July 23rd, 1926 (Series B., No. 13, p. 18), and must be applied to the United Nations.

Having regard to its purposes and functions already referred to, the Organization may find it necessary, and has in fact found it necessary, to entrust its agents with important missions to be performed in disturbed parts of the world. Many missions, from their very nature, involve the agents in unusual dangers to which ordinary persons are not exposed. For the same reason, the injuries suffered by its agents in these circumstances will sometimes have occurred in such a manner that their national State would not be justified in bringing a claim for reparation on the ground of diplomatic protection, or, at any rate, would not feel disposed to do so. Both to ensure the efficient and independent performance of these missions and to afford effective support to its agents, the Organization must provide them with adequate protection.

This need of protection for the agents of the Organization, as a condition of the performance of its functions, has already been realized, and the Preamble to the Resolution of December 3rd, 1948 (supra, p. 175), shows that this was the unanimous view of the General Assembly.

For this purpose, the Members of the Organization have entered into certain undertakings, some of which are in the Charter and others in complementary agreements. The content of these undertakings need not be described here; but the Court must stress the importance of the duty to render to the Organization 'every assistance' which is accepted by the Members in Article 2, paragraph 5, of the Charter. It must be noted that the effective working of the Organization-the accomplishment of its task, and the independence and effectiveness of the work of its agents-require that these undertakings should be strictly observed. For that purpose, it is necessary that, when an infringement occurs, the Organization should be able to call upon the responsible State to remedy its default, and, in particular, to obtain from the State reparation for the damage that the default may have caused to its agent.

In order that the agent may perform his duties satisfactorily, he must feel that this protection is assured to him by the Organization, and that he may count on it. To ensure the independence of the agent, and, consequently, the independent action of the Organization itself, it is essential that in performing his duties he need not have to rely on any other protection than that of the Organization (save of course for the more direct and immediate protection due from the State in whose territory he may be). In particular, he should not have to rely on the protection of his own State. If he had to rely on that State, his independence might well be compromised, contrary to the principle applied by Article 100 of the Charter. And lastly, it is essential that- whether the agent belongs to a powerful or to a weak State; to one more affected or less affected by the complications of international life; to one in sympathy or not in sympathy with the mission of the agent-he should know that in the performance of his duties he is under the protection of the Organization. This assurance is even more necessary when the agent is stateless.

Upon examination of the character of the functions entrusted to the Organization and of the nature of the missions of its agents, it becomes clear that the capacity of the Organization to exercise a measure of functional protection of its agents arises by necessary intendment out of the Charter.

The obligations entered into by States to enable the agents of the Organization to perform their duties are undertaken not in the interest of the agents, but in that of the Organization. When it claims redress for a breach of these obligations, the Organization is invoking its own right, the right that the obligations due to it should be respected. On this ground, it asks for reparation of the injury suffered, for 'it is a principle of international law that the breach of an engagement involves an obligation to make reparation in an adequate form'; as was stated by the Permanent Court in its Judgment No. 8 of July 26th, 1927 (Series A., No. 9, p. 21). In claiming reparation based on the injury suffered by its agent, the Organization does not represent the agent, but is asserting its own right, the right to secure respect for undertakings entered into towards the Organization.

Having regard to the foregoing considerations, and to the undeniable right of the Organization to demand that its Members shall fulfil the obligations entered into by them in the interest of the good working of the Organization, the Court is of the opinion that, in the case of a breach of these obligations, the Organization has the capacity to claim adequate reparation, and that in assessing this reparation it is authorized to include the damage suffered by the victim or by persons entitled through him.

* * *

This area of protection is less developed than that involving protection by individual states. Part of the problem is the relative newness of international organizations. But much of it, at least in the case of the United Nations, has to do with the above-mentioned ambiguity as to how that body should enforce its decisions.

In some cases, an explicit mandate is imposed.

(2) Convention on the Prevention and Punishment of the Crime of Genocide

Dec. 9, 1948, 78 U.N.T.S. 277 (1951)

Article VIII

Any contracting party may call upon the competent organs of the United Nations to take such action under the Charter of the United Nations as they consider appropriate for the prevention and suppression of acts of genocide. ...

NOTES AND QUESTIONS

1. Do the policies justifying diplomatic protection of nationals apply equally to the case of agents of intergovernmental organizations?

2. Should individuals be able to enlist the assistance of their home state against injurious acts of intergovernmental organizations? What are the relevant considerations? *See* Ludwig Gramlich, *Diplomatic Protection Against Acts of Intergovernmental Organs*, 27 GERMAN Y.B. INT'L L. 386 (1984).

F. REGULATION OF INTERNAL CONSEQUENCES OF NATIONALITY

1. Claims to Control Access to Territory

Access is obviously the fundamental prerequisite to active and rewarding participation in the social process of a state. National elites claim that security interests of their communities, which encompass all values, require that they control and limit who may gain access. An optimum system of human dignity might prefer unlimited access to all communities. Are there guidelines which can be used to direct and appraise specific national decisions about permitting or excluding people?

Once access has been gained elites have traditionally demanded, and the flow of authoritative decisions has yielded, a broad competence to control the activities of people-nationals and aliens-within the national territory. Control may extend to every aspect of personal and group activity. While totalitarian systems in effect claim the authority to exercise such control, the basic prescriptions expressing international human rights would appear to establish substantial limits on legitimate elite control over people within their territory.

a. Fong Yue Ting v. United States
149 U.S. 698 (1893)

[A Chinese laborer, permanent resident of the U.S. since 1879, was subject to arrest and deportation for failing to comply with a requirement to secure a certificate of residence established by a 1892 Act of Congress. The Court concluded:]

"Chinese laborers, ... like all other aliens residing in the United States for a shorter or longer time, are entitled, so long as they are permitted by the government of the United States to remain in the country, to the safeguards of the constitution, and to the protection of the laws, in regard to their rights of person and of property, and to their civil and criminal responsibility. But they continue to be aliens, having taken no steps towards becoming citizens, and incapable of becoming such under the naturalization laws; and therefore remain subject to the power of congress to expel them, or to order them to be removed and deported from the country, whenever, in its judgment, their removal is necessary or expedient for the public interest. ...

The proceeding before a United States judge, as provided for in section 6 of the act of 1892, is in no proper sense a trial and sentence for a crime or offense. It is simply the ascertainment, by appropriate and lawful means, of the fact whether the conditions exist upon which congress has enacted that an alien of this class may remain within the country. The order of deportation is not a punishment for crime. It is not a banishment, in the sense in which that word is often applied to the expulsion of a citizen from his country by way of punishment. It is but a method of enforcing the return to his own country of an alien who has not complied with the conditions upon the performance of which the government of the nation, acting within its constitutional authority, and through the proper departments, has determined that his continuing to reside here shall depend. He has not, therefore, been deprived of life, liberty, or property without due process of law; and the provisions of the constitution, securing the right of trial by jury, and prohibiting unreasonable searches and seizures and cruel and unusual punishments, have no application.

The question whether, and upon what conditions, these aliens shall be permitted to remain within the United States being one to be determined by the political departments of the government, the judicial department cannot properly express an opinion upon the wisdom, the policy, or the justice of the measures enacted by congress in the exercise of the powers confided to it by the constitution over this subject."

Upon careful consideration of the subject, the only conclusion which appears to us to be consistent with the principles of international law, with the constitution and laws of the United States, and with the previous decisions of this court, is that in each of these cases the judgment of the circuit court dismissing the writ of habeas corpus is right, and must be affirmed.

NOTES AND QUESTIONS

1. From these and similar statements, the doctrine of Congress's "plenary power" over immigration emerged. *See, e.g., Harisiades v. Shaughnessy*, 342 U.S. 580 (1952); *The Chinese Exclusion Case (Chae Chan Ping v. United States)*, 130 U.S. 581, 599, 609 (1889); *INS v. Aguirre-Aguirre*, 526 U.S. 415, 425 (1999) (recognizing "that judicial deference to the Executive Branch is especially appropriate in the immigration context where officials 'exercise especially sensitive political functions that implicate questions of foreign relations'") (*quoting INS v. Abudu*, 485 U.S. 94, 110 (1988)); *Mathews v. Diaz*, 426 U.S. 67, 81 n.17 (1976) ("[A]ny policy toward aliens is vitally and intricately interwoven with contemporaneous policies in regard to the conduct of foreign relations, the war power, and the maintenance of a republican form of government. Such matters are so exclusively entrusted to the political branches of government as to be largely immune from judicial inquiry or interference."). *See also Nguyen v. INS*, 533 U.S. 53 (2001).

More recently, however, the Supreme Court has limited the sweep of the doctrine, declaring Congress's "plenary power" to be "subject to important constitutional limitations. *See INS v. Chadha,* 462 U.S. 919, 941-942 (1983) (Congress must choose "a constitutionally permissible means of implementing" that power); *The Chinese Exclusion Case,* 130 U.S. 581, 604 (1889) (congressional authority limited "by the Constitution itself and considerations of public policy and justice which control, more or less, the conduct of all civilized nations"); *Zadvydas v. Davis*, 121 S.Ct. 2491, 2501 (2001) (limiting indefinite detention of removable aliens who cannot be deported). Compare GERALD L. NEUMAN, STRANGERS TO THE CONSTITUTION: IMMIGRANTS, BORDERS, AND FUNDAMENTAL LAW 14 (Princeton U. Press 1996); STEPHEN H. LEGOMSKY, *Immigration Law and the Principle of Plenary Congressional Power*, 1984 SUP. CT. REV. 255 (1984).

2. United States citizens, however, are generally not subject to deportation to another country, barring banishment as "punishment of the severest kind" (*U.S. v. Ju Toy*, 198 U.S. 253, 269 (1905) (Brewer, J., dissenting), even though they may face extradition (Siegfried Wiessner, *Blessed Be the Ties That Bind: The Nexus between Nationality and Territory, supra,* at 517-528), The Supreme Court explained this differential treatment of foreigners and citizens as follows:

> The exclusion of aliens and the reservation of the power to deport have no permissible counterpart in the Federal Government's power to regulate its own citizenry. The fact that an Act of Congress treats aliens differently from citizens does not in itself imply that such disparate treatment is 'invidious'.

Mathews v. Diaz, 426 U.S. 67, 80 (1976).

b. Patel *et al.* v. United Kingdom

[1970] Y.B. Eur. Conv. on Human Rights 928, 990
(Eur. Comm'n of Human Rights)

[East African Asians, who were British nationals and holders of British passports, were denied entry to the United Kingdom or subjected to special conditions of entry and residence under the Commonwealth Immigrants Act of 1968, which was enacted when there was an influx of Asians from Africa and some strong racist reactions in the UK. The Asians complained to the European Commission. Though the issue at bar was admissibility, the substantive implications of the holding with regard to limitations imposed on governments' competence to discriminate and exclude certain groups are significant.]

I. As to the applicants' complaints that they were refused admission to the United Kingdom, or permission to remain there permanently:

[T]he applicants complained that the United Kingdom authorities refused to admit them to the United Kingdom, or to allow them to remain there permanently, when they were citizens of the United Kingdom and Colonies or of equivalent status, and holders of United Kingdom passports, and at a time when they had no other country to go to; whereas, as the respondent Government have submitted and the applicants have not disputed, no right to enter and reside in a particular country is as such guaranteed by the Convention; ... Art. 3 (2) of the Fourth Protocol, which has not been ratified by the United Kingdom Government, provides that "No-one shall be deprived of the right to enter the territory of the State of which he is a national"; and ... the aim of the Fourth Protocol, as stated in its preamble, is to ensure the collective enforcement of certain rights and freedoms other than those already included in Section I of the Convention and in Arts. 1 to 3 of the First Protocol; whereas it follows that no right for a person to enter, in particular, the territory of the State of which he is a national is as such guaranteed by the Convention or by the First Protocol;

[H]owever, the applicants have alleged that their treatment by the United Kingdom authorities amounted, in all the circumstances to "degrading treatment" within the meaning of Art. 3 of the Convention; in particular that, in refusing to admit them to the United Kingdom or to allow them to remain there permanently, the actions of the United Kingdom authorities amounted to treating them as "second-class citizens"; and ... the applicants also alleged, in relation to Art. 14 of the Convention, that the law of the United Kingdom, and the practice of the United Kingdom authorities in the application of the law, discriminated against them, in respect of this treatment, inter alia on grounds of race;

[T]he respondent Government have denied that the actions of the United Kingdom authorities could amount, in the circumstances, to degrading treatment within the meaning of Art. 3 of the Convention; ..., however, the respondent Government have admitted that the intention, and the effect, of the Commonwealth Immigrants Act 1968 were discriminatory; ... they have not disputed that the object of the Act was to exclude more than a limited number of East African Asians from entering the United Kingdom, and, further, that the Act was directed against citizens of the United Kingdom and Colonies resident in East Africa and being of Asian origin;

[T]he respondent Government have submitted in this connection, first, that the 1968 Act did not amount to discrimination within the meaning of Art. 14 of the Convention, since it did not discriminate against the applicants in their enjoyment of the rights and freedoms guaranteed by the Convention, the right to enter and reside in a particular country not being such a right; and ... the respondent Government have further submitted that, even if the law did constitute discrimination within the meaning of Art. 14, such discrimination could be justified;

[H]owever, the Commission is of the opinion that, quite apart from any consideration of Article 14, discrimination based on race could, in certain circumstances, of itself amount to degrading treatment within the meaning of Art. 3 of the Convention ... the Commission considers that it is generally recognised that a special importance should be attached to discrimination based on race, and that publicly to single out a group of persons for differential treatment on the basis of race might, in certain circumstances, constitute a special form of affront to human dignity ..., therefore, differential treatment of a group of persons on the basis of race might be capable of constituting degrading treatment in circumstances where differential treatment on some other ground, such as language, would raise no such question; ...

[T]he Commission is of the opinion that it is not its function, at the stage of admissibility, finally to determine the issues which may arise on an examination of the merits; ...

[H]owever, the Commission has just found that the complaints of the applicants raise issues of law and fact, in relation to the rights and freedoms set forth in Arts. 3 and 5 of the Convention, whose determination should depend on the examination of the merits of the cases; and ... in arriving at this finding the Commission has had special regard to the allegations of discrimination on grounds expressly included in Art. 14; ... it follows that these issues may be found to include questions arising under Article 14 of the Convention;

[C]onsequently, the applicants' complaints insofar as they raise issues under Arts. 3, 5 and 14 of the Convention cannot be declared manifestly ill-founded within the meaning of Art. 27 (2) of the Convention; ... [and thus were declared admissible.].

NOTES AND QUESTIONS

1. In August 1972, Parliament's creation of the Uganda Resettlement Board and the decision to admit large numbers of British Asians into the U.K. marked a major shift in policy. The restrictions on Asian immigration embodied in the Immigration Acts of 1968 and 1971 were largely set aside for the duration of the East African crisis.

In its final report, published in 1974, the Uganda Resettlement Board, which was set up to plan the reception and resettlement of over 28,000 Ugandan Asians holding United Kingdom passports expelled from Uganda in the autumn of 1972, said that there was evidence that the vast majority had settled down and begun with determination to make a new life in Britain. Measures undertaken to encourage Ugandan Asians to make use of the health, social security and education systems and to seek the help of the employment services are described.

In March 1974 the Home Secretary announced that the husbands of Ugandan Asian women holding British passports would be admitted for settlement even though they did not hold such passports themselves. Young people over 21 who were or had recently been studying overseas were also allowed to enter to join a parent holding a United Kingdom passport. These measures allowed a number of separated families to be reunited. [1973-74] Y.B. ON HUMAN RIGHTS 232 (United Nations). For a detailed analysis of Britain's response to and control of Asian immigration, see WILLIAM G. KUEPPER, ET AL., UGANDAN ASIANS IN GREAT BRITAIN: FORCED MIGRATION AND SOCIAL ABSORPTION 43-85 (C. Helm 1975).

2. There are two competing interests in these cases: the interest of a community to protect itself and its processes and values and the interest in avoiding discrimination by suspect classification and the protection of human rights. Under what circumstances would the United Kingdom's exclusions be found lawful, in terms of the Commission's theory? Under what circumstances, if any, should the exclusions be found lawful? Do you think the United Kingdom's restrictions were unreasonable in this context?

3. Was the Commission making law or were its conclusions plausibly derived from the Conventions discussed?

4. After the end of the Cold War, asylum/refugee law entered a period of flux as countries and regional organizations attempted to cope with mass migrations of persons. For British and European efforts, comprehensive treatments can be found in Randall Hansen, *Asylum Policy in the European Union*, 14 GEO. IMMIGR. L. J. 779 (2000); KAY HAILBRONNER, IMMIGRATION AND ASYLUM LAW AND POLICY IN THE EUROPEAN UNION (Kluwer Academic Publishers 1999). *See also* Colin Harvey, *The United Kingdom's New Asylum and Immigration Bill*, 8 INT'L J. REFUGEE L. 184 (1996); Dallal Stevens, *The Asylum and Immigration Act of 1996: Erosion of the Right to Seek Asylum*, 61 MOD. L. REV. 207 (1998); COLIN HARVEY, SEEKING ASYLUM IN THE UK: PROBLEMS AND PROSPECTS (Northwestern U. Press 2000); Catherine Phuong, *Persecution by Third Parties and European Harmonization of Asylum Policies*, 16 GEO. IMMIGR. L. J. 81 (2001); Luke T. Lee, *The London Declaration of International Law Principles on Internally Displaced Persons*, 95 AM. J. INT'L L. 454 (2001); Stephen H. Legomsky, *An Asylum Seeker's Bill of Rights in a Non-Utopian World*, 14 GEO. IMMIGR. L.J. 619 (2000); Sabine Weidlich, *First Instance Asylum Proceedings in Europe: Do Bona Fide Refugees Find Protection?*, 145 GEO. IMMIGR. L. J. 643 (2000); Gretchen Borchelt, *The Safe Third Country Practice in the European Union: A Misguided Approach to Asylum Law and a Violation of International Human Rights Standards*, 33 COLUM. HUM. RTS. L. REV. 473 (2002).

c. Boffolo Case (Italy v. Venez.)

Decision of the Venezuelan Mixed Claims Commission
10 R.I.A.A. 527, 531 (1903)

RALSTON, Umpire: The above case has been referred to the umpire on disagreement between the honorable Commissioners for Italy and Venezuela.

It appears that Gennaro Boffolo, an Italian subject, reached Venezuela in June, 1898, and in the spring of 1900 was a householder in Caracas and the publisher of an Italian weekly newspaper entitled "Il Commercio Italo-Venezuolano." In the issue of April 1, 1900, appeared an article somewhat critical of the local minor judiciary, and also referring, but in an unimportant manner, to the President. Another article recommended the reading of El Obrero, a socialistic paper. Three days later (April 4) the Gaceta Oficial contained a decree directing Boffolo's expulsion, in the following terms:

Immediately thereafter, or perhaps simultaneously, Boffolo was, as it is said, "summarily" arrested, transported by third-class ticket to Curaçao, but, through the intervention of the royal Italian legation, allowed to return about a month later.

It is further said, but no proof is offered, that during his absence his house was invaded and plundered, and articles taken belonging to others, the value of which he was compelled to reimburse, and that the claimant was subjected to police persecution, threatened with another arrest, and finally left Venezuela.

That a general power to expel foreigners, at least for cause, exists in governments can not be doubted. (See Hollander case in U. S. Foreign Relations for 1895, p. 775, and also see p. 801, same volume, citations to be found in sec. 206, vol. 2, Wharton's International Law Digest, and other citations hereinafter given.)

But it will be borne in mind that there may be a broad difference between the right to exercise a power and the rightful exercise of that power. Let us illustrate. In the Hollander case (cited above) the Government of Guatemala contended:

> The Government was not under obligation to allow him more or less time to get out of the country, nor to accommodate him in any way. All the practices of jurisprudence, supposing them to be certain and indisputable, fall down before a law clear that comes immediately from the sovereignty of a nation.

To this Secretary Olney very forcibly replied:

> The logical result of that proposition is, that whatever a state by legal formula wills to do, it may do; and that international obligations are annulled, not infringed, by legalized administrative action in contravention of those obligations. ... I construe the language used to mean that, as a rule of international law, the right of expulsion is absolute and inherent in the sovereignty of a State, and that no other State can question the exercise of this right nor the manner of exercising it. ... The modern theory and the practice of Christian nations is believed to be founded on the principle that the expulsion of a foreigner is justifiable only when his presence is detrimental to the welfare of the State, and that when expulsion is resorted to as an extreme police measure, it is to be accomplished with due regard to the convenience and the personal and property interests of the person expelled.

In the recent Ben Tillet affair between England and Belgium, the arbitrator, M. Arthur Desjardins, of France, in his sentence examined thoroughly the reasons for the expulsion of Tillet (as we shall do hereafter in this case), and also as to the treatment accorded him in connection therewith, and maintained the right of Belgium to expel under the circumstances, and, as well, justified the manner in which Tillet was treated by Belgium. (Journal du Droit International Prive, Vol. 26 (1899), p. 203.)

Hall says (International Law, p. 224):

> In such cases (expulsion of individual foreigners residing in a state) the propriety of the conduct of the expelling government must be judged with reference to the circumstances of the moment.

It appears, therefore, that the Commission may inquire into the reasons and circumstances of the expulsion.

Let us apply the principles above laid down to the case before us.

Boffolo was expelled, as the claimant Government contends (and nothing else is before the Commission), because he published a certain article supposed to reflect upon the local judiciary and referring in some purely incidental way to the President, and, as stated, recommended a socialistic paper. It is not the province of the umpire to pass upon Boffolo's taste or justice in so doing. He is, however, obliged to examine somewhat, first, as to whether in so doing he offended the laws of Venezuela, and second, whether under the laws the expulsion was permissible. ...

One is pleased to note from the foregoing that even in time of storm and stress Venezuela recognized that those subject to her jurisdiction were entitled to enjoy freedom of speech and of the press (subject only to trial for abuse thereof before competent tribunals, pursuant to the common laws, with personal freedom until after the sentence), freedom of transit and change of domicile, freedom from arrest (unless pursuant to written warrant, save when taken *in flagranti*, and except in such case not to be imprisoned unless by judicial authority), not to be deprived of liberty for political reasons, save for disturbing acts, etc.

As appears from a citation already made, the powers of the officers of Government were not autocratic, but Venezuela was a country of laws, governed even in April, 1900, by officials of limited powers; for if their powers were not limited the personal guarantees of the constitution would have been inefficacious-an impossible conclusion, as they were expressly recognized by the proclamation of General Castro.

Let us therefore see what law governed the matter of expulsion, for if none existed the power to expel was wanting. Another conclusion would make Venezuela's Government despotic-not republican or democratic. . . .

According, therefore, to the constitution of Venezuela, only as the non-domiciled foreigner might be shown to be prejudicial to public order would he be expelled. Let us pass over the fact that the Boffolo decree of expulsion declared that his presence was prejudicial to "national interests" and not to the "public order," as limited by the constitution, and see if such cause has been presented to this Commission as would justify the expulsion.

It is suggested that the expulsion may have taken place because of any one of three reasons:

1. That he spoke disrespectfully of the President.

2. That he criticized a subordinate member of the judiciary.

3. That he recommended the reading of "*El Obrero*," a socialistic paper.

The effective answer to all of these propositions is that freedom of speech and of the press are guaranteed by the constitution of Venezuela, and an expulsion for either one would have been an infringement of the constitution of Venezuela, and this is not to be presumed the President would have done. The umpire is more disposed to believe that for public reasons satisfactory to itself the

Government has chosen not to offer the basis of its action, rather preferring to submit to such judgment as to this Commission might seem meet in the case.

The further suggestion is made that Boffolo, being a foreigner, did not possess the right to criticize the Government to the same extent as Venezuelans, while the Government possessed a larger power over him. To this may be replied that the constitution of Venezuela conferred upon foreigners the same rights as were assured to natives, and for the supposed offenses not the slightest punishment could have been inflicted upon Venezuelans.

Summing up the foregoing, we may (in part repeating) say:

1. A State possesses the general right of expulsion; but,

2. Expulsion should only be resorted to in extreme instances, and must be accomplished in the manner least injurious to the person affected.

3. The country exercising the power must, when occasion demands, state the reason of such expulsion before an international tribunal, and an inefficient reason or none being advanced, accepts the consequences.

4. In the present case the only reasons suggested to the Commission would be contrary to the Venezuelan constitution, and as this is a country not of despotic power, but of fixed laws, restraining, among other things, the acts of its officials, these reasons (whatever good ones may in point of fact have existed) can not be accepted by the umpire as sufficient.

In view of the foregoing it only remains to consider the amount of damages to be awarded. The honorable representative of Italy has indicated that he would be content to accept 5,000 bolivars, and considering the harshness of expulsion as a remedy, the fact that only great provocation will, in the eyes of international law, justify its exercise, and the further fact that expulsion of foreigners so readily leads the way to the gravest international difficulties, as it may be regarded as a national affront, the amount asked seems not intrinsically unreasonable. But bearing in mind the low character of the man in question (as developed before the Commission), and that his speedy return was permitted, the umpire believes his full duty will be discharged in allowing him 2,000 bolivars, and an award of this amount will be entered.

d. Universal Declaration of Human Rights

G.A. Res. 217 (AIII), U.N. GAOR, 3rd Sess., U.N. Doc. A/810 (1948)

Article 13

1. Everyone has the right to freedom of movement and residence within the borders of each State.

2. Everyone has the right to leave any country, including his own, and to return to his country.

e. International Covenant on Civil and Political Rights

Dec. 16, 1966, 999 U.N.T.S. 171 (1966)

Article 12

1. Everyone lawfully within the territory of a State shall, within that territory, have the right to liberty of movement and freedom to choose his residence.

2. Everyone shall be free to leave any country, including his own.

3. The above-mentioned rights shall not be subject to any restrictions except those which are provided by law, are necessary to protect national security, public order (*ordre public*), public health or morals or the rights and freedoms of others, and are consistent with the other rights recognized in the present Covenant.

4. No one shall be arbitrarily deprived of the right to enter his own country.

NOTES AND QUESTIONS

1. For an overview of state practice regarding the interplay of nationality and territory, *see* Siegfried Wiessner, *Blessed Be the Ties that Bind: The Nexus Between Nationality and Territory*, *supra* at 353. He concludes that, in very rare instances of crisis, states still employ means of denying entry to nationals. However, in conformity with widely accepted human rights agreements, "one discerns an overwhelming trend toward recognition of a right of nationals to enter their home territory except in cases of public emergencies which threaten the life of the nation.... Such denials of entry must also be strictly justified by the exigencies of the situation." *Id.* at 496-97. A state also has to admit its nationals if no other state is willing to accept them.

2. While the regime of voluntary departure from a certain state does not distinguish between citizens and aliens, *id.* at 512, and the same is true for the burden of extradition, *id.* at 532, nationals, unlike aliens, may not be banished from their home state's territory unless there is a public emergency that threatens the life of the nation. Even then, this measure must be strictly required by the exigencies of the situation. *Id.* at 522. In contrast, the power to deny entry to, or to expel foreigners, appears, despite *Boffolo*, to be still jealously guarded by nation-states, see *Fong Yue Ting, supra*. Only the regional human rights systems provide for limits on the state's freedom to expel, subjecting it to the rule of law and forbidding collective expulsions of aliens. Also, a special regime of protection has been developed for refugees. For a comparison of Canadian and American asylum/refugee laws, see MARK R. VON STERNBERG, THE GROUNDS OF REFUGEE PROTECTION IN THE CONTEXT OF INTERNATIONAL RIGHTS AND HUMANITARIAN LAW (Martinus Nijhoff 2002).

3. Is this tableau of present state practice in conformity with the overall policy of a public order of human dignity? *See* OWEN FISS, A COMMUNITY OF EQUALS (Joshua Cohen & Joel Rogers eds., Beacon Press 1999). For a discussion of the legal rights of enemy aliens detained since September 11, 2001, see DAVID COLE, ENEMY ALIENS (New Press 2003,) and 2004 decisions by the U.S. Supreme Court clarifying those rights, *infra,* at 511-519.

2. Other Internal Consequences of Nationality

Besides access to territory, nationality may provide the key to participation in other value processes of the community. The most prominent exclusion of aliens is their inherent ban from sharing in the formation of the political will of the community. Beyond the right to vote and the right to stand as a candidate in national elections, countries have, to varying degrees, privileged their citizens regarding access to governmental benefits and employment, natural resources, courts and agencies, while, at times, also burdening them exclusively with the duty of allegiance, to pay taxes on their worldwide income, or to render military service. Such special privileges or burdens are not necessarily universal or "inherent." They may be subject to searching domestic judicial review.

a. Application of Griffiths
413 U.S. 717 (1973)

[Fre Le Poole Griffiths is a citizen of the Netherlands who came to the United States in 1965, originally as a visitor. In 1967 she married a citizen of the United States and became a resident of Connecticut. After her graduation from law school, she applied in 1970 for permission to take the Connecticut bar examination. The County Bar Association found her qualified in all respects save that she was not a citizen of the United States as required by Rule 8(1) of the Connecticut Practice Book (1963) and on that account refused to allow her to take the examination. She then sought judicial relief.]

POWELL, J. From its inception, our Nation welcomed and drew strength from the immigration of aliens. Their contributions to the social and economic life of the country were self-evident, especially during the periods when the demand for human resources greatly exceeded the native supply. This demand was by no means limited to the unskilled or the uneducated. In 1873, this Court noted that admission to the practice of law in the courts of a State 'in no sense depends on citizenship of the United States. It has not, as far as we know, ever been made in any State, or in any case, to depend on citizenship at all. Certainly many prominent and distinguished lawyers have been admitted to practice, both in the State and Federal courts, who were not citizens of the United States or of any State.' Bradwell v. State, 16 Wall. 130, 139. ...

But shortly thereafter, in 1879, Connecticut established the predecessor to its present rule totally excluding aliens from the practice of law. ... In subsequent decades, wide-ranging restrictions for the first time began to impair significantly the efforts of aliens to earn a livelihood in their chosen occupations. ...

In Graham v. Richardson, 403 U.S. 365 (1971), the Court concluded:

> [C]lassifications based on alienage, like those based on nationality or race, are inherently suspect and subject to close judicial scrutiny. Aliens as a class are a prime example of a 'discrete and insular' minority ... for whom such heightened judicial solicitude is appropriate.' Id., at 372.

The Court has consistently emphasized that a State which adopts a suspect classification 'bears a heavy burden of justification,' McLaughlin v. Florida, 379 U.S. 184, 196 (1964), a burden which, though variously formulated, requires the State to meet certain standards of proof. In order to justify the use of a suspect classification, a State must show that its purpose or interest is both constitutionally permissible and substantial, and that its use of the classification is 'necessary … to the accomplishment' of its purpose or the safeguarding of its interest.

Resident aliens, like citizens, pay taxes, support the economy, serve in the Armed Forces, and contribute in myriad other ways to our society. It is appropriate that a State bear a heavy burden when it deprives them of employment opportunities.

We hold that the Committee, acting on behalf of the State, has not carried its burden. The State's ultimate interest here implicated is to assure the requisite qualifications of persons licensed to practice law. It is undisputed that a State has a constitutionally permissible and substantial interest in determining whether an applicant posesses[sic] "the character and general fitness requisite for an attorney and counselor-at- law." … But no question is raised in this case as to appellant's character or general fitness. Rather, the sole basis for disqualification is her status as a resident alien.

The Committee defends Rule 8(1)'s requirement that applicants for admission to the bar be citizens of the United States on the ground that the special role of the lawyer justifies excluding aliens from the practice of law. In Connecticut, the Committee points out, the maxim that a lawyer is an 'officer of the court' is given concrete meaning by a statute which makes every lawyer a 'commissioner of the Superior Court.' As such, a lawyer has authority to 'sign writs and subpoenas, take recognizances, administer oaths and take depositions and acknowledgements of deeds.' Conn.Gen.Stat.Rev. s 51—85. In the exercise of this authority, a Connecticut lawyer may command the assistance of a county sheriff or a town constable. Conn.Gen.Stat.Rev. s 52—90. Because of these and other powers, the Connecticut Supreme Court commented that

> [t]he courts not only demand (lawyers') loyalty, confidence and respect but also require tham to function in a manner which will foster public confidence in the profession and, consequently, the judicial system. 162 Conn., at 262-263, 194 A.2d, at 287.

In order to establish a link between citizenship and the powers and responsibilities of the lawyer in Connecticut, the Committee contrasts a citizen's undivided allegiance to this country with a resident alien's possible conflict of loyalties. From this, the Committee concludes that a resident alien lawyer might in the exercise of his functions ignore his responsibilities to the courts or even his clients in favor of the interest of a foreign power.

We find these arguments unconvincing. It is no way denigrates a lawyer's high responsibilities to observe that the powers 'to sign writs and subpoenas, take recognizances, (and) administer oaths' hardly involve matters of state policy or acts of such unique responsibility as to entrust them only to citizens. Nor do we think that the practice of law offers meaningful opportunities adversely to affect the interest of the United States. Certainly the Committee has failed to show the relevance of citizenship to any likelihood that a lawyer will fail to protect faithfully the interest of his clients.

Nor would the possibility that some resident aliens are unsuited to the practice of law be a justification for a wholesale ban. …

Connecticut has wide freedom to gauge on a case- by-case basis the fitness of an applicant to practice law. Connecticut can, and does, require appropriate training and familiarity with Connecticut law. Apart from such tests of competence, it requires a new lawyer to take both an 'attorney's oath' to perform his functions faithfully and honestly and a 'commissioner's oath' to 'support the constitution of the United States, and the constitution of the state of Connecticut.' Appellant has indicated her willingness and ability to subscribe to the substance of both oaths, and Connecticut may quite properly conduct a character investigation to insure in any given case 'that an applicant is not one who 'swears to an oath pro forma while declaring or manifesting his disagreement with or indifference to the oath.' Moreover, once admitted to the bar, lawyers are subject to continuing scrutiny by the organized bar and the courts. In addition to discipline for unprofessional conduct, the range of postadmission sanctions extends from judgments for contempt to criminal prosecutions and disbarment. In sum, the Committee simply has not established that it must exclude all aliens from the practice of law in order to vindicate its undoubted interest in high professional standards. …

In its brief, the Examining Committee makes another, somewhat different argument in support of Rule 8(1). Its thrust is not that resident aliens lack the attributes necessary to maintain high standards in the legal profession, but rather that lawyers must be citizens almost as a matter of definition. The implication of this analysis is that exclusion of aliens from the legal profession is not subject to any scrutiny under the Equal Protection Clause.

The argument builds upon the exclusion of aliens from the franchise in all 50 States and their disqualification under the Constitution from holding office as President, Art. 2, s 1, cl. 5, or as a member of the House of Representatives, Art. 1, s 2, cl. 2, or of the Senate, Art. 1, s 3, cl. 3. These and numerous other federal and statutory and constitutional provisions reflect, the Committee contends, a pervasive recognition that 'participation in the government structure as voters and office holders' is inescapably an aspect of citizenship. Brief for Appellee 11. Offered in support of the claim that the lawyer is an 'office holder' in this sense is an enhanced version of the proposition, discussed above, that he is an 'officer of the court.' Specifically, the Committee states that the lawyer 'is an officer of the Court who acts by and with the authority of the State' and is entrusted with the 'exercise of actual government power.' Id., at 5.

We note at the outset that this argument goes beyond the opinion of the Connecticut Supreme Court, which recognized that a lawyer is not an officer in the ordinary sense. 162 Conn., at 254, 294 A.2d, at 283. This comports with the view of the Court expressed by Mr. Justice Black in Cammer v. United States, 350 U.S. 399 (1956):

> It has been stated many times that lawyers are 'officers of the court.' One of the most frequently repeated statements to this effect appears in Ex parte Garland, 4 Wall. 333, 378. The Court pointed out there, however, that an attorney was not an 'officer' within the ordinary meaning of that term. Certainly nothing that was said in Ex parte Garland or in any other case decided by this Court places attorneys in the same category as marshals, bailiffs, court clerks or judges. Unlike these officials a lawyer is engaged in a private profession, important though it be to our system of justice. In general he makes his own decisions, follows his own best judgment, collects his own fees and runs his own business. The word 'officer' as it has always been applied to lawyers conveys quite a different meaning from the word 'officer' as applied to people serving as officers within the conventional meaning of that term. Id., at 405.

Lawyers do indeed occupy professional positions of responsibility and influence that impose on them duties correlative with their vital right of access to the courts. Moreover, by virtue of their professional aptitudes and natural interests, lawyers have been leaders in government throughout the history of our country. Yet, they are not officials of government by virtue of being lawyers. Nor does the status of holding a license to practice law place one so close to the core of the political process as to make him a formulator of government policy.

We hold that 8(1) violates the Equal Protection Clause. The judgment of the Connecticut Supreme Court is reversed, and the case is remanded for further proceedings not inconsistent with this opinion.

b. Ambach v. Norwick

441 U.S. 68 (1979)

POWELL, J. This case presents the question whether a State, consistently with the Equal Protection Clause of the Fourteenth Amendment, may refuse to employ as elementary and secondary school teachers aliens who are eligible for United States citizenship but who refuse to seek naturalization. New York Education Law § 3001(3) (McKinney 1970) forbids certification as a public school teacher of any person who is not a citizen of the United States, unless that person has manifested an intention to apply for citizenship.

Appellee Norwick was born in Scotland and is a subject of Great Britain. She has resided in this country since 1965 and is married to a United States citizen. Appellee Dachinger is a Finnish subject who came to this country in 1966 and also is married to a United States citizen. Both Norwick and Dachinger currently meet all of the educational requirements New York has set for certification as a public school teacher, but they consistently have refused to seek citizenship in spite of their eligibility to do so. ... Both their applications [for teaching certificates] were denied because of appellees' failure to meet the requirements of § 3001(3). …

Graham v. Richardson … for the first time treated classifications based on alienage as "inherently suspect and subject to close judicial scrutiny." 403 U.S., at 372, 91 S.Ct., at 1852. Applying *Graham*, this Court has held invalid statutes that prevented aliens from entering a State's classified civil service, *Sugarman v. Dougall, 413 U.S. 634 (1973)*, practicing law, *In re Griffiths, 413 U.S. 717 (1973)*, working as an engineer, Examining Board v. Flores de Otero, 426 U.S. 572 (1976), and receiving state educational benefits, *Nyquist v. Mauclet, 432 U.S. 1 (1977)*.

…[O]ur more recent decisions … have not abandoned the general principle that some state functions are so bound up with the operation of the State as a governmental entity as to permit the exclusion from those functions of all persons who have not become part of the process of self- government. In *Sugarman*, we recognized that a State could, "in an appropriately defined class of positions, require citizenship as a qualification for office." We went on to observe:

> Such power inheres in the State by virtue of its obligation, already noted above, 'to preserve the basic conception of a political community.' ... And this power and responsibility of the State applies, not only to the qualifications of voters, but also to persons holding state elective or important nonelective executive, legislative, and judicial positions, for officers who participate directly in the formulation, execution, or review of broad public policy perform functions that go to the heart of representative government. 413 U.S., at 647. The exclusion of aliens from such governmental positions would not invite as demanding scrutiny from this Court. *Id., at 648.* …

Applying the rational-basis standard, we held last Term that New York could exclude aliens from the ranks of its police force. *Foley v. Connelie, 435 U.S. 291 (1978)*. Because the police function fulfilled "a most fundamental obligation of government to its constituency" and by necessity cloaked policemen with substantial discretionary powers, we view the police force as being one of those appropriately defined classes of positions for which a citizenship requirement could be imposed. *Id., at 297.* Accordingly, the State was required to justify its classification only "by a showing of some rational relationship between the interest sought to be protected and the limiting classification." *Id.*, at 296.

The rule for governmental functions, which is an exception to the general standard applicable to classifications based on alienage, rests on important principles inherent in the Constitution. The distinction between citizens and aliens, though ordinarily irrelevant to private activity, is fundamental to the definition and government of a State. The Constitution itself refers to the distinction no less than 11 times, see *Sugarman v. Dougall, supra, 413 U.S. at 651-652* (REHNQUIST, J., dissenting), indicating that the status of citizenship was meant to have significance in the structure of our government. The assumption of that status, whether by birth or naturalization, denotes an association with the polity which, in a democratic republic, exercises the powers of governance. See *Foley v. Connelie, supra, 435 U.S., at 295, 98 S.Ct., at 1070.* The form of this association is important: an oath of allegiance or similar ceremony cannot substitute for the unequivocal legal bond citizenship represents. It is because of this special significance of citizenship that governmental entities, when exercising the functions of government, have wider latitude in limiting the participation of noncitizens....

In determining whether, for purposes of equal protection analysis, teaching in public schools constitutes a governmental function, we look to the role of public education and to the degree of responsibility and discretion teachers possess in fulfilling that role. See *Foley v. Connelie, supra, at 297.* Each of these considerations supports the conclusion that public school teachers may be regarded as performing a task "that go[es] to the heart of representative government." *Sugarman v. Dougall, supra, 413 U.S., at 647.*

Public education, like the police function, "fulfills a most fundamental obligation of government to its constituency." *Foley, supra, 435 U.S., at 297.* The importance of public schools in the preparation of individuals for participation as citizens, and in the preservation of the values on which our society rests, long has been recognized by our decisions:

> Today, education is perhaps the most important function of state and local governments. Compulsory school attendance laws and the great expenditures for education both demonstrate our recognition of the importance of education to our democratic society. It is required in the performance of our most basic public responsibilities, even service in the armed forces. It is the very foundation of good citizenship. Today it is a principal instrument in awakening the child to cultural values, in preparing him for later professional training, and in helping him to adjust normally to his environment. *Brown v. Board of Education, 347 U.S. 483, 493, 74 S.Ct. 686, 691, 98 L.Ed. 873 (1954).* ...

Other authorities have perceived public schools as an "assimilative force" by which diverse and conflicting elements in our society are brought together on a broad but common ground. ... These perceptions of the public schools as inculcating fundamental values necessary to the maintenance of a democratic political system have been confirmed by the observations of social scientists. ...

Within the public school system, teachers play a critical part in developing students' attitude toward government and understanding of the role of citizens in our society. Alone among employees of the system, teachers are in direct, day-to-day contact with students both in the classrooms and in the other varied activities of a modern school. In shaping the students' experience to achieve educational goals, teachers by necessity have wide discretion over the way the course material is communicated to students. They are responsible for presenting and explaining the subject matter in a way that is both comprehensible and inspiring. No amount of standardization of teaching materials or lesson plans can eliminate the personal qualities a teacher brings to bear in achieving these goals. Further, a teacher serves as a role model for his students, exerting a subtle but important influence over their perceptions and values. Thus, through both the presentation of course materials and the example he sets, a teacher has an opportunity to influence the attitudes of students toward government, the political process, and a citizen's social responsibilities. This influence is crucial to the continued good health of a democracy.

Furthermore, it is clear that all public school teachers, and not just those responsible for teaching the courses most directly related to government, history, and civic duties, should help fulfill the broader function of the public school system. Teachers, regardless of their specialty, may be called upon to teach other subjects, including those expressly dedicated to political and social subjects. More importantly, a State properly may regard all teachers as having an obligation to promote civic virtues and understanding in their classes, regardless of the subject taught. Certainly a State also may take account of a teacher's function as an example for students, which exists independently of particular classroom subjects. In light of the foregoing considerations, we think it clear that public school teachers come well within the "governmental function" principle recognized in *Sugarman* and *Foley*. Accordingly, the Constitution requires only that a citizenship requirement applicable to teaching in the public schools bear a rational relationship to a legitimate state interest. …

As the legitimacy of the State's interest in furthering the educational goals outlined above is undoubted, it remains only to consider whether § 3001(3) bears a rational relationship to this interest. The restriction is carefully framed to serve its purpose, as it bars from teaching only those aliens who have demonstrated their unwillingness to obtain United States citizenship. Appellees, and aliens similarly situated, in effect have chosen to classify themselves. They prefer to retain citizenship in a foreign country with the obligations it entails of primary duty and loyalty. They have rejected the open invitation extended to qualify for eligibility to teach by applying for citizenship in this country. The people of New York, acting through their elected representatives, have made a judgment that citizenship should be a qualification for teaching the young of the State in the public schools, and § 3001(3) furthers that judgment.

NOTES AND QUESTIONS

1. A comparative study found no commonality among countries distinguishing between nationals and aliens regarding government benefits; access to education, courts, government agencies, natural resources; taxation; or service in the military. SIEGFRIED WIESSNER, DIE FUNKTION DER STAATSANGEHÖRIGKEIT, *supra*, at 396. However, only citizens have been uniformly accorded the right to vote and to stand as a candidate in national elections. Also, only nationals may, in principle, be employed in a role that includes the exercise of strictly governmental functions. *Id.*

2. Do you agree with the result and reasoning of *Griffiths* and *Ambach?* What, if any, are reasonable criteria for depriving aliens of rights and privileges available to citizens? If an alien is an exile, refugee or permanent resident, should he or she be deprived of job and educational opportunities in the same manner as a tourist or a voluntary temporary resident? What about illegal aliens? Should legal resident aliens be entitled to welfare benefits? Should the answer to this question

depend on whether they pay taxes and carry other burdens of citizenship? *See* Christopher R. Yukins, *The Measure of a Nation: Granting Excludable Aliens Fundamental Protections of Due Process*, 73 VA. L. REV. 1501 (1987); Elizabeth Larson Beyer, *A Right or a Privilege: Constitutional Protection for Detained Deportable Aliens Refused Access or Return to their Native Countries*, 35 WAKE FOREST L. REV. 1029 (2000); Howard F. Chang, *Migration Regulation Goes Local: The Role of States in U.S. Immigration Policy: Public Benefits and Federal Authorization for Alienage Discrimination by the States*, 58 N.Y.U. ANN. SURV. AM. L. 357 (2002).

c. Inter-American Commission on Human Rights Decision on Request for Precautionary Measures (Detainees at Guantanamo Bay, Cuba)

41 I.L.M. 532 (2002)

After careful deliberation on this request, the Commission decided during its 114th regular period of sessions to adopt precautionary measures, according to which we ask Your Excellency's government to take the urgent measures necessary to have the legal status of the detainees at Guantanamo Bay determined by a competent tribunal. Given the significance and implications of this request to and for the United States and the detainees concerned, the Commission wishes to articulate the basis upon which it reached this decision.

The Commission notes preliminarily that its authority to receive and grant requests for precautionary measures under Article 25(1) of its Rules of Procedure is, as with the practice of other international decisional bodies, a well-established and necessary component of the Commission's processes. Indeed, where such measures are considered essential to preserving the Commission's very mandate under the OAS Charter, the Commission has ruled that OAS member states are subject to an international legal obligation to comply with a request for such measures.

The mandate given to the Commission by OAS member states, including the United States, under Article 106 of the Charter of the Organization of American States and Articles 18, 19 and 20 of the Commission's Statute is in turn central to the Commission's consideration of the matter presently before it. Through the foregoing provisions, OAS member states have charged the Commission with supervising member states' observance of human rights in the Hemisphere. These rights include those prescribed under the American Declaration of the Rights and Duties of Man, which constitutes a source of legal obligation for all OAS member states in respect of persons subject to their authority and control. The Commission has been directed to pay particular attention to the observance of Articles I (right to life), II (right to equality before law), III (right to religious freedom and worship), IV (right to freedom of investigation, opinion, expression and dissemination), XVIII (right to a fair trial), XXV (right to protection from arbitrary arrest), and XXVI (right to due process of law) of the American Declaration.

In addition, while its specific mandate is to secure the observance of international human rights protections in the Hemisphere, this Commission has in the past looked to and applied definitional standards and relevant rules of international humanitarian law in interpreting the American Declaration and other Inter-American human rights instruments in situations of armed conflict.

In taking this approach, the Commission has drawn upon certain basic principles that inform the interrelationship between international human rights and humanitarian law. It is well-recognized that international human rights law applies at all times, in peacetime and in situations of armed conflict. In contrast, international humanitarian law generally does not apply in peacetime and its principal purpose is to place restraints on the conduct of warfare in order to limit or contain the damaging effects of hostilities and to protect the victims of armed conflict, including civilians and combatants who have laid down their arms or have been placed *hors de combat*. Further, in situations of armed conflict, the protections under international human rights and humanitarian law may complement and reinforce one another, sharing as they do a common nucleus of non-derogable rights and a common purpose of promoting human life and dignity. In certain circumstances, however, the test for evaluating the observance of a particular right, such as the right to liberty, in a situation of armed conflict may be distinct from that applicable in time of peace. In such situations, international law, including the jurisprudence of this Commission, dictates that it may be necessary to deduce the applicable standard by reference to international humanitarian law as the applicable *lex specialis.*

Accordingly, where persons find themselves within the authority and control of a state and where a circumstance of armed conflict may be involved, their fundamental rights may be determined in part by reference to international humanitarian law as well as international human rights law. Where it may be considered that the protections of international humanitarian law do not apply, however, such persons remain the beneficiaries at least of the non-derogable protections under international human rights law. In short, no person under the authority and control of a state, regardless of his or her circumstances, is devoid of legal protection for his or her fundamental and non-derogable human rights.

This basic precept is reflected in the Martens clause common to numerous long-standing humanitarian law treaties, including the Hague Conventions of 1899 and 1907 respecting the laws and customs of war on land, according to which human persons who do not fall within the protection of those treaties or other international agreements remain under the protection of the principles of the law of nations, as they result from the usages established among civilized peoples, from the laws of humanity, and the dictates of the public conscience. And according to international norms applicable in peacetime and wartime, such as those reflected in Article 5 of the Third Geneva Convention and Article XVIII of the American Declaration of the Rights and Duties of Man, a competent court or tribunal, as opposed to a political authority, must be charged with ensuring respect for the legal status and rights of persons falling under the authority and control of a state.

Specifically with regard to the request for precautionary measures presently before it, the Commission observes that certain pertinent facts concerning the detainees at Guantanamo Bay are well-known and do not appear to be the subject of controversy. These include the fact that the government of the United States considers itself to be at war with an international network of terrorists, that the United States undertook a military operation in Afghanistan beginning in October 2001 in defending this war, and that most of the detainees in Guantanamo Bay were apprehended in connection with this military operation and remain wholly within the authority and control of the United States government.

It is also well-known that doubts exists as to the legal status of the detainees. This includes the question of whether and to what extent the Third Geneva Convention and/or other provisions of international humanitarian law apply to some or all of the detainees and what implications this may have for their international human rights protections. According to official statements from the United States government, its Executive Branch has most recently declined to extend prisoner of war status under the Third Geneva Convention to the detainees, without submitting the issue for determination by a competent tribunal or otherwise ascertaining the rights and protections to which the detainees are entitled under US domestic or international law. To the contrary, the information available suggests that the detainees remain entirely at the unfettered discretion of the United States government. Absent clarification of the legal status of the detainees, the Commission considers that the rights and protections to which they may be entitled under international or domestic law cannot be said to be the subject of effective legal protection by the State.

In light of the foregoing considerations, and without prejudging the possible application of international humanitarian law to the detainees at Guantanamo Bay, the Commission considers that precautionary measures are both appropriate and necessary in the present circumstances, in order to ensure that the legal status of each of the detainees is clarified and that they are afforded the legal protections commensurate with the status that they are found to possess, which may in no case fall below the minimum standards of non-derogable rights. On this basis, the Commission hereby requests that the United States take the urgent measures necessary to have the legal status of the detainees at Guantanamo Bay determined by a competent tribunal.

d. Response of the United States to Request for Precautionary Measures – Detainees in Guantanamo Bay, Cuba

41 I.L.M. 1015 (2002)

The United States respectfully submits that the Commission has no basis in fact or law upon which it may request precautionary measures of the United States in this case.

This is because (1) the Commission lacks the requisite jurisdictional competence to apply international humanitarian law, particularly the Geneva Convention, as well as customary international humanitarian law; (2) even if the Commission had the jurisdictional competence, precautionary measures in this case are neither necessary nor appropriate; and (3) the Commission lacks the authority to request precautionary measures with respect to States such as the United States, which are not party to the American Convention on Human Rights.

* * *

In the context of the war on terrorism, Congress and the Executive undertook to redefine the scope of citizens' rights against the government, even when outside the country. The U.S. Supreme Court has set limits to such redefinitions, especially when using the rubric of "enemy combatant" with respect to a citizen.

e. Hamdi v. Rumsfeld

124 S.Ct. 2633 (2004)

JUSTICE O'CONNOR announced the judgment of the Court and delivered an opinion, in which THE CHIEF JUSTICE, JUSTICE KENNEDY, and JUSTICE BREYER join.

At this difficult time in our Nation's history, we are called upon to consider the legality of the Government's detention of a United States citizen on United States soil as an 'enemy combatant' and to address the process that is constitutionally owed to one who seeks to challenge his classification as such. The United States Court of Appeals for the Fourth Circuit held that petitioner's detention was legally authorized and that he was entitled to no further opportunity to challenge his enemy-combatant label. We now vacate and remand. We hold that although Congress authorized the detention of combatants in the narrow circumstances alleged here, due process demands that a citizen held in the United States as an enemy combatant be given a meaningful opportunity to contest the factual basis for that detention before a neutral decisionmaker. …

On September 11, 2001, the al Qaeda terrorist network used hijacked commercial airliners to attack prominent targets in the United States. Approximately 3,000 people were killed in those attacks. One week later, in response to these 'acts of treacherous violence,' Congress passed a resolution authorizing the President to 'use all necessary and appropriate force against those nations, organizations, or persons he determines planned, authorized, committed, or aided the terrorist attacks' or 'harbored such organizations or persons, in order to prevent any future acts of international terrorism against the United States by such nations, organizations or persons.' Authorization for Use of Military Force ('the AUMF'), 115 Stat. 224. Soon thereafter, the President ordered United States Armed Forces to Afghanistan, with a mission to subdue al Qaeda and quell the Taliban regime that was known to support it.

This case arises out of the detention of a man whom the Government alleges took up arms with the Taliban during this conflict. His name is Yaser Esam Hamdi. Born an American citizen in Louisiana in 1980, Hamdi moved with his family to Saudi Arabia as a child. By 2001, the parties agree, he resided in Afghanistan. At some point that year, he was seized by members of the Northern Alliance, a coalition of military groups opposed to the Taliban government, and eventually was turned over to the United States military. The Government asserts that it initially detained and interrogated Hamdi in Afghanistan before transferring him to the United States Naval Base in Guantanamo Bay in January 2002. In April 2002, upon learning that Hamdi is an American citizen, authorities transferred him to a naval brig in Norfolk, Virginia, where he remained until a recent transfer to a brig in Charleston, South Carolina. The Government contends that Hamdi is an 'enemy combatant,' and that this status justifies holding him in the United States indefinitely—without formal charges or proceedings—unless and until it makes the determination that access to counsel or further process is warranted. ...

[Hamdi's father filed this habeas petition on his behalf under 28 U. S. C. § 2241, alleging, among other things, that the Government holds his son in violation of the Fifth and Fourteenth Amendments. Although the petition did not elaborate on the factual circumstances of Hamdi's capture and detention, his father has asserted in other documents in the record that Hamdi went to Afghanistan to do 'relief work' less than two months before September 11 and could not have received military training. The Government attached to its response to the petition a declaration from Michael Mobbs (Mobbs Declaration), a Defense Department official. The Mobbs Declaration alleges various details regarding Hamdi's trip to Afghanistan, his affiliation there with a Taliban unit during a time when the Taliban was battling U. S allies, and his subsequent surrender of an assault rifle. The District Court found that the Mobbs Declaration, standing alone, did not support Hamdi's detention and ordered the Government to turn over numerous materials for *in camera* review. The Fourth Circuit reversed, stressing that, because it was undisputed that Hamdi was captured in an active combat zone, no factual inquiry or evidentiary hearing allowing Hamdi to be heard or to rebut the Government's assertions was necessary or proper. Concluding that the factual averments in the Mobbs Declaration, if accurate, provided a sufficient basis upon which to conclude that the President had constitutionally detained Hamdi, the court ordered the habeas petition dismissed. The appeals court held that, assuming that express congressional authorization of the detention was required by 18 U. S. C. § 4001(a) – which provides that '[n]o citizen shall be imprisoned or otherwise detained by the United States except pursuant to an Act of Congress'– the AUMF's 'necessary and appropriate force' language provided the authorization for Hamdi's detention. It also concluded that Hamdi is entitled only to a limited judicial inquiry into his detention's legality under the war powers of the political branches, and not to a searching review of the factual determinations underlying his seizure.] ...

Even in cases in which the detention of enemy combatants is legally authorized, there remains the question of what process is constitutionally due to a citizen who disputes his enemy-combatant status. Hamdi argues that he is owed a meaningful and timely hearing and that 'extra-judicial detention [that] begins and ends with the submission of an affidavit based on third-hand hearsay' does not comport with the Fifth and Fourteenth Amendments. ... The Government counters that any more process than was provided below would be both unworkable and 'constitutionally intolerable.' ... Our resolution of this dispute requires a careful examination both of the writ of habeas corpus, which Hamdi now seeks to employ as a mechanism of judicial review, and of the Due Process Clause, which informs the procedural contours of that mechanism in this instance. ...

Both of these positions highlight legitimate concerns. And both emphasize the tension that often exists between the autonomy that the Government asserts is necessary in order to pursue effectively a particular goal and the process that a citizen contends he is due before he is deprived of a constitutional right. The ordinary mechanism that we use for balancing such serious competing interests, and for determining the procedures that are necessary to ensure that a citizen is not 'deprived of life, liberty, or property, without due process of law,' U. S. Const., Amdt. 5, is the test that we articulated in *Mathews v. Eldridge,* 424 U. S. 319 (1976). ... *Mathews* dictates that the process due in any given instance is determined by weighing 'the private interest that will be affected by the official action' against the Government's asserted interest, 'including the function involved' and the burdens the Government would face in providing greater process. 424 U. S., at 335. The *Mathews* calculus then contemplates a judicious balancing of these concerns, through an analysis of 'the risk of an erroneous deprivation' of the private interest if the process were reduced and the 'probable value, if any, of additional or substitute safeguards.' *Ibid.* We take each of these steps in turn. ...

It is beyond question that substantial interests lie on both sides of the scale in this case. Hamdi's 'private interest ... affected by the official action,' *ibid.*, is the most elemental of liberty interests—the interest in being free from physical detention by one's own government. *Foucha v. Louisiana,* 504 U. S. 71, 80 (1992) ('Freedom from bodily restraint has always been at the core of the liberty protected by the Due Process Clause from arbitrary governmental action'); see also *Parham v. J. R.,* 442 U. S. 584, 600 (1979) (noting the 'substantial liberty interest in not being confined unnecessarily'). 'In our society liberty is the norm,' and detention without trial 'is the carefully limited exception.' *Salerno, supra*, at 755. 'We have always been careful not to 'minimize the importance and fundamental nature' of the individual's right to liberty,' *Foucha, supra*, at 80 (quoting *Salerno, supra*, at 750), and we will not do so today.

Nor is the weight on this side of the *Mathews* scale offset by the circumstances of war or the accusation of treasonous behavior, for '[i]t is clear that commitment for *any* purpose constitutes a significant deprivation of liberty that requires due process protection,' *Jones v. United States,* 463 U. S. 354, 361 (1983) (emphasis added; internal quotation marks omitted), and at this stage in the *Mathews* calculus, we consider the interest of the *erroneously* detained individual. *Carey v. Piphus,* 435 U. S. 247, 259 (1978) ('Procedural due process rules are meant to protect persons not from the deprivation, but from the mistaken or unjustified deprivation of life, liberty, or property '); see also *id.*, at 266 (noting 'the importance to organized society that procedural due process be observed,' and emphasizing that 'the right to procedural due process is 'absolute' in the sense that it does not depend upon the merits of a claimant's substantive assertions'). Indeed, as *amicus* briefs from media and relief organizations emphasize, the risk of erroneous deprivation of a citizen's liberty in the absence of sufficient process here is very real. See Brief for AmeriCares et al. as *Amici Curiae* 13-22 (noting ways in which '[t]he nature of humanitarian relief work and journalism present a significant risk of mistaken military detentions'). Moreover, as critical as the Government's interest may be in detaining those who actually pose an immediate threat to the national security of the United States during ongoing international conflict, history and common sense teach us that an unchecked system of detention carries the potential to become a means for oppression and abuse of others who do not present that sort of threat. See *Ex parte Milligan,* 4 Wall., at 125 ('[The Founders] knew—the history of the world told them—the nation they were founding, be its existence short or long, would be involved in war; how often or how long continued, human foresight could not tell; and that unlimited power, wherever lodged at such a time, was especially hazardous to freemen'). Because we live in a society in which '[m]ere public intolerance or animosity cannot constitutionally justify the deprivation of a person's physical liberty,' *O'Connor v. Donaldson,* 422 U. S. 563, 575 (1975), our starting point for the *Mathews v. Eldridge* analysis is unaltered by the allegations surrounding the particular detainee or the organizations with which he is alleged to have associated. We reaffirm today the fundamental nature of a citizen's right to be free from involuntary confinement by his own government without due process of law, and we weigh the opposing governmental interests against the curtailment of liberty that such confinement entails. ...

On the other side of the scale are the weighty and sensitive governmental interests in ensuring that those who have in fact fought with the enemy during a war do not return to battle against the United States. As discussed above, *supra*, at 10, the law of war and the realities of combat may render such detentions both necessary and appropriate, and our due process analysis need not blink at those realities. Without doubt, our Constitution recognizes that core strategic matters of warmaking belong in the hands of those who are best positioned and most politically accountable for making them. *Department of Navy v. Egan,* 484 U. S. 518, 530 (1988) (noting the reluctance of the courts 'to intrude upon the authority of the Executive in military and national security affairs'); *Youngstown Sheet & Tube Co. v. Sawyer,* 343 U. S. 579, 587 (1952) (acknowledging 'broad powers in military commanders engaged in day-to-day fighting in a theater of war').

The Government also argues at some length that its interests in reducing the process available to alleged enemy combatants are heightened by the practical difficulties that would accompany a system of trial-like process. In its view, military officers who are engaged in the serious work of waging battle would be unnecessarily and dangerously distracted by litigation half a world away, and discovery into military operations would both intrude on the sensitive secrets of national defense and result in a futile search for evidence buried under the rubble of war. ... To the extent that these burdens are triggered by heightened procedures, they are properly taken into account in our due process analysis. ...

Striking the proper constitutional balance here is of great importance to the Nation during this period of ongoing combat. But it is equally vital that our calculus not give short shrift to the values that this country holds dear or to the privilege that is American citizenship. It is during our most challenging and uncertain moments that our Nation's commitment to due process is most severely tested; and it is in those times that we must preserve our commitment at home to the principles for which we fight abroad. See *Kennedy v. Mendoza-Martinez,* 372 U. S. 144, 164-165 (1963) ('The imperative necessity for safeguarding these rights to procedural due process under the gravest of emergencies has existed throughout our constitutional history, for it is then, under the pressing exigencies of crisis, that there is the greatest temptation to dispense with guarantees which, it is feared, will inhibit government action '); see also *United States v. Robel,* 389 U. S. 258, 264 (1967) ('It would indeed be ironic if, in the name of national defense, we would sanction the subversion of one of those liberties ... which makes the defense of the Nation worthwhile').

With due recognition of these competing concerns, we believe that neither the process proposed by the Government nor the process apparently envisioned by the District Court below strikes the proper constitutional balance when a United States citizen is detained in the United States as an enemy combatant. That is, 'the risk of erroneous deprivation' of a detainee's liberty interest is unacceptably high under the Government's proposed rule, while some of the 'additional or substitute procedural safeguards' suggested by the District Court are unwarranted in light of their limited 'probable value' and the burdens they may impose on the military in such cases. *Mathews*, 424 U. S., at 335.

We therefore hold that a citizen-detainee seeking to challenge his classification as an enemy combatant must receive notice of the factual basis for his classification, and a fair opportunity to rebut the Government's factual assertions before a neutral decisionmaker. See *Cleveland Bd. of Ed. v. Loudermill,* 470 U. S. 532, 542 (1985) ('An essential principle of due process is that a deprivation of life, liberty, or property 'be preceded by notice and opportunity for hearing appropriate to the nature of the case' ...'); *Concrete Pipe & Products of Cal., Inc. v. Construction Laborers Pension Trust for Southern Cal.,* 508 U. S. 602, 617 (1993) ('due process requires a 'neutral and detached judge in the first instance' ...'). 'For more than a century the central meaning of procedural due process has been clear: 'Parties whose rights are to be affected are entitled to be heard; and in order that they may enjoy that right they must first be notified.' It is equally fundamental that the right to notice and an opportunity to be heard 'must be granted at a meaningful time and in a meaningful manner.' ' *Fuentes v. Shevin,* 407 U. S. 67, 80 (1972). ... These essential constitutional promises may not be eroded.

At the same time, the exigencies of the circumstances may demand that, aside from these core elements, enemy combatant proceedings may be tailored to alleviate their uncommon potential to burden the Executive at a time of ongoing military conflict. Hearsay, for example, may need to be accepted as the most reliable available evidence from the Government in such a proceeding. Likewise, the Constitution would not be offended by a presumption in favor of the Government's evidence, so long as that presumption remained a rebuttable one and fair opportunity for rebuttal were provided. Thus, once the Government puts forth credible evidence that the habeas petitioner meets the enemy-combatant criteria, the onus could shift to the petitioner to rebut that evidence with more persuasive evidence that he falls outside the criteria. A burden-shifting scheme of this sort would meet the goal of ensuring that the errant tourist, embedded journalist, or local aid worker has a chance to prove military error while giving due regard to the Executive once it has put forth meaningful support for its conclusion that the detainee is in fact an enemy combatant. In the words of *Mathews*, process of this sort would sufficiently address the 'risk of erroneous deprivation' of a detainee's liberty interest while eliminating certain procedures that have questionable additional value in light of the burden on the Government. 424 U. S., at 335.

We think it unlikely that this basic process will have the dire impact on the central functions of warmaking that the Government forecasts. The parties agree that initial captures on the battlefield need not receive the process we have discussed here; that process is due only when the determination is made to *continue* to hold those who have been seized. The Government has made clear in its briefing that documentation regarding battlefield detainees already is kept in the ordinary course of military affairs. Any factfinding imposition created by requiring a knowledgeable affiant to summarize these records to an independent tribunal is a minimal one. Likewise, arguments that military officers ought not have to wage war under the threat of litigation lose much of their steam when factual disputes at enemy-combatant hearings are limited to the alleged combatant's acts. This focus meddles little, if at all, in the strategy or conduct of war, inquiring only into the appropriateness of continuing to detain an individual claimed to have taken up arms against the United States. While we accord the greatest respect and consideration to the judgments of military authorities in matters relating to the actual prosecution of a war, and recognize that the scope of that discretion necessarily is wide, it does not infringe on the core role of the military for the courts to exercise their own time-honored and constitutionally mandated roles of reviewing and resolving claims like those presented here. Cf. *Korematsu v. United States*, 323 U. S. 214, 233-234 (1944) (Murphy, J., dissenting) ('[L]ike other claims conflicting with the asserted constitutional rights of the individual, the military claim must subject itself to the judicial process of having its reasonableness determined and its conflicts with other interests reconciled'); *Sterling v. Constantin*, 287 U. S. 378, 401 (1932) ('What are the allowable limits of military discretion, and whether or not they have been overstepped in a particular case, are judicial questions').

In sum, while the full protections that accompany challenges to detentions in other settings may prove unworkable and inappropriate in the enemy-combatant setting, the threats to military operations posed by a basic system of independent review are not so weighty as to trump a citizen's core rights to challenge meaningfully the Government's case and to be heard by an impartial adjudicator. ...

In so holding, we necessarily reject the Government's assertion that separation of powers principles mandate a heavily circumscribed role for the courts in such circumstances. Indeed, the position that the courts must forgo any examination of the individual case and focus exclusively on the legality of the broader detention scheme cannot be mandated by any reasonable view of separation of powers, as this approach serves only to *condense* power into a single branch of government. We have long since made clear that a state of war is not a blank check for the President when it comes to the rights of the Nation's citizens. *Youngstown Sheet & Tube*, 343 U. S., at 587. Whatever power the United States Constitution envisions for the Executive in its exchanges with other nations or with enemy organizations in times of conflict, it most assuredly envisions a role for all three branches when individual liberties are at stake. ... Likewise, we have made clear that, unless Congress acts to suspend it, the Great Writ of habeas corpus allows the Judicial Branch to play a necessary role in maintaining this delicate balance of governance, serving as an important judicial check on the Executive's discretion in the realm of detentions. See *St. Cyr*, 533 U. S., at 301 ('At its historical core, the writ of habeas corpus has served as a means of reviewing the legality of Executive detention, and it is in that context that its protections have been strongest '). Thus, while we do not question that our due process assessment must pay keen attention to the particular burdens faced by the Executive in the context of military action, it would turn our system of checks and balances on its head to suggest that a citizen could not make his way to court with a challenge to the factual basis for his detention by his government, simply because the Executive opposes making available such a challenge. Absent suspension of the writ by Congress, a citizen detained as an enemy combatant is entitled to this process.

Because we conclude that due process demands some system for a citizen detainee to refute his classification, the proposed 'some evidence' standard is inadequate. Any process in which the Executive's factual assertions go wholly unchallenged or are simply presumed correct without any opportunity for the alleged combatant to demonstrate otherwise falls constitutionally short. As the Government itself has recognized, we have utilized the 'some evidence' standard in the past as a standard of review, not as a standard of proof. Brief for Respondents 35. That is, it primarily has been employed by courts in examining an administrative record developed after an adversarial proceeding— one with process at least of the sort that we today hold is constitutionally mandated in the citizen enemy-combatant setting. See, *e.g.*, *St. Cyr, supra; Hill*, 472 U. S., at 455-457. This standard therefore is ill suited to the situation in which a habeas petitioner has received no prior proceedings before any tribunal and had no prior opportunity to rebut the Executive's factual assertions before a neutral decisionmaker.

Today we are faced only with such a case. Aside from unspecified 'screening' processes, Brief for Respondents 3-4, and military interrogations in which the Government suggests Hamdi could have contested his classification, Tr. of Oral Arg. 40, 42, Hamdi has received no process. An interrogation by one's captor, however effective an intelligence-gathering tool, hardly constitutes a constitutionally adequate factfinding before a neutral decisionmaker. Compare Brief for Respondents 42-43 (discussing the 'secure interrogation environment,' and noting that military interrogations require a controlled 'interrogation dynamic' and 'a relationship of trust and dependency' and are 'a critical source' of 'timely and effective intelligence') with *Concrete Pipe*, 508 U. S., at 617-618 ('one is entitled as a matter of due process of law to an adjudicator who is not in a situation which would offer a possible temptation to the average man as a judge . . . which might lead him not to hold the balance nice, clear and true' (internal quotation marks omitted). That even purportedly fair adjudicators 'are disqualified by their interest in the controversy to be decided is, of course, the general rule.' *Tumey v. Ohio,* 273 U. S. 510, 522 (1927). Plainly, the 'process' Hamdi has received is not that to which he is entitled under the Due Process Clause.

There remains the possibility that the standards we have articulated could be met by an appropriately authorized and properly constituted military tribunal. Indeed, it is notable that military regulations already provide for such process in related instances, dictating that tribunals be made available to determine the status of enemy detainees who assert prisoner-of-war status under the Geneva Convention. See Enemy Prisoners of War, Retained Personnel, Civilian Internees and Other Detainees, Army Regulation 190-8, § 1-6 (1997). In the absence of such process, however, a court that receives a petition for a writ of habeas corpus from an alleged enemy combatant must itself ensure that the minimum requirements of due process are achieved. Both courts below recognized as much, focusing their energies on the question of whether Hamdi was due an opportunity to rebut the Government's case against him. The Government, too, proceeded on this assumption, presenting its affidavit and then seeking that it be evaluated under a deferential standard of review based on burdens that it alleged would accompany any greater process. As we have discussed, a habeas court in a case such as this may accept affidavit evidence like that contained in the Mobbs Declaration, so long as it also permits the alleged combatant to present his own factual case to rebut the Government's return. We anticipate that a District Court would proceed with the caution that we have indicated is necessary in this setting, engaging in a factfinding process that is both prudent and incremental. We have no reason to doubt that courts faced with these sensitive matters will pay proper heed both to the matters of national security that might arise in an individual case and to the constitutional limitations safeguarding essential liberties that remain vibrant even in times of security concerns.

NOTES AND QUESTIONS

1. John Walker Lindh, the so-called "American Taliban," was accorded due process rights and a trial under the U.S. Constitution. What is the key difference, if any, to Mr. Hamdi's situation? *See Contemporary Practice of the United States Relating to International Law: U.S. Nationals Detained as Unlawful Combatants* (Sean D. Murphy ed.), 97 AM. J. INT'L L. 196 (2003); Alejandra Rodriguez, *Is the War on Terrorism Compromising Civil Liberties? A Discussion of Hamdi and Padilla*, 39 CAL. W. L. REV. 379 (2003).

2. Would you agree with Justice O'Connor's opinion in the *Hamdi* case? Does it strike a proper balance between the individual's liberty interest and the security concerns of the community? For further background on this case, see Charles I. Lugosi, *Rule of Law or Rule by Law: The Detention of Yaser Hamdi*, 30 AM. J. CRIM. L. 225 (2003).

3. What should be the proper treatment of captured terrorists? *See* Michael Ratner, *Conference: Moving Away from the Rule of Law; Military Tribunals, Executive Detentions and Torture,* 24 CARDOZO L. REV. 1513 (2003); Richard J. Wilson, *United States Detainees at Guantanamo Bay: The Inter-American Commission on Human Rights Responds to a "Legal Black Hole"*, 10 HUM. RTS. BR. 2 (2003); K. Elizabeth Dahlstrom, *Between Empire and Community: The United States and Multilateralism 2001-2003: A Mid-Term Assessment: Humanitarian Law: The Executive Policy toward Detention and Trial of Foreign Citizens at Guantanamo Bay*, 21 BERKELEY J. INT'L L. 662 (2003); Thomas J. Lepri, *Safeguarding the Enemy Within: The Need for Procedural Protections for U.S. Citizens Detained as Enemy Combatants Under* Ex Parte Quirin, 71 FORDHAM L. REV. 2565 (2003). In *Rasul v. Bush*, 124 S.Ct. 2686, decided on June 28, 2004, the U.S. Supreme Court held that the federal habeas statute conferred on district courts jurisdiction to hear challenges of aliens held at Guantanamo Bay, and that the district court was not barred from exercising jurisdiction over claims asserted under the federal question statute and the Alien Tort Statute.

II. HUMAN RIGHTS

A. INTRODUCTION

The concept of "human rights," properly delimited, refers broadly to the authoritative and controlling responses of international decision-making processes to claims by individuals to secure and maximize certain values. Those claims may vary, and they may enter into conflict with each other, depending on the identity of the claimants and their respective value preferences. It is suggested (1) that the proper focus of human rights discussion is on the individual human being; (2) that the individual human being is formed and transformed, by choice, destiny and, sometimes, the will of others, in a complex process of social interaction; (3) that the policy driving the human rights movement and its legal manifestations is the protection and full development of the individual being in his or her entire social context; and (4) that this policy can be broken down, at least initially, into the goals of protecting the physical integrity, the moral integrity, and the civic integrity of each human being.

An individual is, however, improperly conceived of as an entirely self-defining and self-regulating actor. No man or woman is an "island," a "monad" or a morally neutral or vacuous "vagabond." Total individual "autonomy" is a mirage. At least in the beginning stages of life, a human being is existentially — for sustenance and affection — dependent on one or more other individuals. The experience of community is constitutive of humanity.

An individual's identity is shaped by a complex process of social interaction. The more permanent features of his or her concept of self are determined by birth into a certain ethnic or religious group, a certain nationality, gender, race and family structure — "groups of destiny." These, at times, immutable social contexts contribute to form a person, as do subsequent institutions such as schools and religious institutions. While the early identifications do not come about by choice, individuals later develop their own web of social interaction outside of family and clan, and create often deep-seated loyalties to groups of choice, be they professional associations, religious groups, sports and entertainment clubs, political parties, etc. In turn, these chosen associations, just like the "groups of destiny," exercise a possibly transformative influence on the perception of self, the identity of their member. Social relationships sustain and enrich individuals. These relationships may solidify into group memberships, be they voluntary or not. The individual may influence decisionmaking in these bodies, and he or she is, in turn, influenced by them.

Until 1945, individuals were largely mediated by international law with States acting on their behalf. Individuals figured only as members of protected ethnic minorities, as under the Versailles Treaty, or in the arcane role of *hostis humanis generis* if they engaged in the universal crime of piracy. Any state could treat individuals on its territory as it saw fit; only foreigners could hope for some measure of protection from their home governments. The Holocaust perpetrated by Nazi Germany highlighted the moral indefensibility of the absence of international legal rules protecting individuals against their governments, and the post-World War II world order aspired to corrective action. Human rights and self-determination of peoples were the distinctive hallmarks of the United Nations Charter, the Universal Declaration of Human Rights, and the Covenant on Civil and Political Rights.

The General Assembly's 1948 Universal Declaration of Human Rights has had profound impact around the world, and has entered the spirit, if not the letter, of many constitutional documents created after World War II. The United Nations continued its leading role in developing inclusive prescriptions for the protection of human rights by drafting, and submitting for ratification by States, the 1948 Convention on the Prevention and Punishment of the Crime of Genocide, the 1951 Refugee Convention, the 1966 twin general human rights treaties — the International Covenant on Civil and Political Rights and the International Covenant on Social, Economic and Cultural Rights — as well as the trilogy of treaties of special protection — the 1966 Convention on the Elimination of All Forms of Racial Discrimination, the 1980 Convention on the Elimination of All Forms of Discrimination Against Women, and the 1989 Convention on the Rights of the Child, to name but a few of the United Nations' successful standard-setting initiatives. In terms of inclusive implementation, both the United Nations Human Rights Commission, set up in the framework of the Economic and Social Council as a Charter organ, and the United Nations Human Rights Committee, established under the Civil and Political Rights Covenant as a treaty organ, have helped greatly in refining the authoritative and controlling content of human rights law.

Regional organizations have followed this lead, and prescribed and implemented authoritative policies of human rights law, first in Europe, then in the Americas, and later, from a slightly different perspective, in Africa. The widespread acceptance and implementation, both on the international and domestic level, of internationally defined standards of protection of individual human beings, couched in the language of entitlements, has crystallized a core group of human rights prescriptions into what is traditionally called customary international law, with binding force *erga omnes.*

What are the goals pursued by these international trends? In one impressive formulation, international law under the Charter was seen as moving toward establishing a "world public order of human dignity." Within that order, all individuals were ideally to be able to maximize their access to all the processes of shaping and sharing of all values desired: power, wealth, well-being, affection, enlightenment, skills, respect and rectitude. Put more succinctly, the overriding goal of human rights law and policy was to protect and fully develop the individual human being in the complexity of his or her entire social context.

1. International Human Rights Law-Making

The prescription of human rights is a radical innovation in the structure and theory of classical international law, as it involves prescriptions that limit rather than enhance state power. Many of the major human rights prescriptions emerged from traumatic international experiences which excited a great popular demand for adjustments in international law that could prevent a recurrence of the horrors that had just been experienced. With respect to the emergence of customary international law, the usual test is a wide practice by relevant actors accompanied by certain subjective expectations of authority: the so-called *opinio juris sive necessitas*.

Many of the major human rights programs have emerged from a much more complex international law-making program that can best be understood in terms of the conceptions developed in Part One of this book, a process of communication in which authority and control signals attend certain normative formulations and render them law for the community concerned. With respect to human rights, a genealogy of many of the major human rights instruments will indicate that they often began through the exertions of one or a small group of individuals who clarified their own objective, then used the resources of modern communication to mobilize other non-governmental groups, which in turn influenced key national governments to espouse a particular program. Once the program was initially drafted, the same process increased the pressure on more reluctant members of the international community, such that an instrument might ultimately emerge. As will be seen, the initial human rights instruments were issued as Declarations rather than treaties, precisely because the states concerned were unwilling to lock themselves into a network of binding obligations. That interest notwithstanding, the same complex process of law-making has been able to transform many of these Declarations into customary international law or even, as some scholars characterize it, *jus cogens*. Hence a proper understanding of why certain human rights norms emerged and, as important for the practice in international law, how to mobilize the international political system to produce new international human rights law requires an understanding of this complex process.

Non-traditional actors have contributed greatly to the development and formulation of human rights law. One example is the role of private actors such as H.G. Wells, Quincy Wright and Hersch Lauterpacht in the genesis of the Universal Declaration of Human Rights, as chronicled by W. Michael Reisman, *Private International Declaration Initiatives*, *in* LA DÉCLARATION UNIVERSELLE DES DROITS DE L'HOMME 1948-98, 79 (Editions l'Harmattan: UNESCO 1999). Raphael Lemkin coined the term "genocide" and fought tirelessly for the formulation and adoption of the convention outlawing it. *See* Brian Urquhart, *Shameful Neglect*, N.Y. REV. BOOKS, April 25, 2002, at 12. A coalition of more than 1,000 NGOs campaigned successfully for the establishment of the International Criminal Court (see William R. Pace & Mark Thieroff, *Participation of Non-Governmental Organizations, in* THE INTERNATIONAL CRIMINAL COURT, *supra*, Part Two, at 298). Jody Williams led the campaign to ban landmines, with the support of the International

Red Cross and Diana, Princess of Wales. Ms. Williams won the Nobel Peace Prize in 1997. A similar moving force of actors other than nation-states has been discerned by Julian Burger with respect to the creation of the 1993 United Nations Draft Declaration on the Rights of Indigenous Peoples in his article, *The United Nations Draft Declaration on the Rights of Indigenous Peoples*, 9 ST. THOMAS L. REV. 209-211 (1996).

NOTES AND QUESTIONS

1. For a detailed treatment of the role of non-governmental organizations in general world constitutive process, see Part Two, *supra*, at 289-311. As to their essential role in the human rights field, see Siegfried Wiessner, *Non-State Actors and Their Impact on International Human Rights Law*, Oct. 26-28, 2000, available at www.aals.org/profdev/humanrights/weissner.html. Are there any drawbacks to the increasing role of non-governmental entities?

2. The World Council of Indigenous Peoples and the International Indian Treaty Council, among many other indigenous groups, contributed to the formulation of the 1993 U.N. Draft Declaration of the Rights of Indigenous Peoples. Is this a model for other vulnerable groups? Should ethnic groups, women, refugees or other vulnerable minorities become more actively involved in formulating standards and devising procedures for their protection? What are the costs of this involvement?

2. The Application of International Human Rights Law

In much the same way that the making of human rights law cannot be grasped without using a process framework, the application of international human rights law requires a similar approach. International courts and arbitral tribunals ordinarily do not provide standing to individuals. The UN Human Rights Commission as well as the various monitoring bodies established under human rights treaties do not have the power to render binding decisions, regional institutions such as the European and the Inter-American Courts of Human Rights notwithstanding. As a result, national courts have become the main engines for the enforcement of human rights, thanks to a convergence of demands for human rights application, a reduction of sovereign immunity for independent commercial reasons, and the accessibility of courts to ordinary citizens in many of the major democracies. In Europe, the incorporation in many jurisdictions of the European Convention on Human Rights transformed domestic courts into first-instance international human rights tribunals. In the United States, where the government ratified a number of human rights conventions, the courts responded to the pressures of the community by developing a rather elastic conception of a customary international law of human rights. This concept was first acknowledged, at the level of the International Court of Justice, in a dissenting opinion by Judge Tanaka, and was finally embraced by the Court in *Barcelona Traction*.

a. South West Africa (Second Phase) (Eth. v. S. Afr.; Liber. v. S. Afr.)

1966 I.C.J. 6, 250, 297-298 (July 18)

Dissenting Opinion, JUDGE TANAKA:

Human rights have always existed with the human being. They existed independently of, and before, the State. Alien and even stateless persons must not be deprived of them. Belonging to diverse kinds of communities and societies-ranging from family, club, corporation, to State and international community, the human rights of man must be protected everywhere in this social hierarchy, just as copyright is protected domestically and internationally. There must be no legal vacuum in the protection of human rights. Who can believe, as a reasonable man, that the existence of human rights depends upon the internal or international legislative measures, etc., of the State and that accordingly they can be validly abolished or modified by the will of the State?

If a law exists independently of the will of the State and, accordingly, cannot be abolished or modified even by its constitution, because it is deeply rooted in the conscience of mankind and of any reasonable man, it may be called 'natural law' in contrast to 'positive law'.

Provisions of the constitutions of some countries characterize fundamental human rights and freedoms as 'inalienable', 'sacred', 'eternal', 'inviolate', etc. Therefore, the guarantee of fundamental human rights and freedoms possesses a super-constitutional significance.

If we can introduce in the international field a category of law, namely *jus cogens*, recently examined by the International Law Commission, a kind of imperative law which constitutes the contrast to the *jus dispositivum*, capable of being changed by way of agreement between States, surely the law concerning the protection of human rights may be considered to belong to the *jus cogens*.

b. Case Concerning the Barcelona Traction, Light and Power Co. (Second Phase)(Belg. v. Spain)

1970 I.C.J. 3, 31 (Feb. 5)

33. … [A]n essential distinction should be drawn between the obligations of a State towards the international community as a whole, and those arising vis-à-vis another State in the field of diplomatic protection. By their very nature the former are the concern of all States. In view of the importance of the rights involved, all States can be held to have a legal interest in their protection; they are obligations *erga omnes*.

34. Such obligations derive, for example, in contemporary international law, from the outlawing of acts of aggression, and of genocide, as also from the principles and rules concerning the basic rights of the human person, including protection from slavery and racial discrimination. Some of the corresponding rights of protection have entered into the body of general international law (Reservations to the Convention on the Prevention and Punishment of the Crime of Geno-

cide, Advisory Opinion, I.C.J. Reports 1951, p. 23); others are conferred by international instruments of a universal or quasi-universal character.

NOTES AND QUESTIONS

1. Many commentators have discussed the role of national courts in the enforcement of human rights norms. *See* Jonathan I. Charney, *International Criminal Law and the Role of Domestic Courts*, 95 AM. J. INT'L L. 120 (2001); Daryl A. Mundis, *New Mechanisms for the Enforcement of International Humanitarian Law*, 95 AM. J. INT'L L. 934 (2001); Beth van Schaack, *In Defense of Civil Redress: The Domestic Enforcement of Human Rights Norms in the Context of the Proposed Hague Judgments Convention*, 42 HARV. INT'L L. J. 141 (2001); Harold Hongju Koh, *How is International Human Rights Law Enforced?*, 74 IND. L. J. 1397 (1999); Douglas Cassel, *International Human Rights Law In Practice: Does International Human Rights Law Make a Difference?*, 2 CHI. J. INT'L L. 121 (2001); FRANCISCO FORREST MARTIN, CHALLENGING HUMAN RIGHTS VIOLATIONS: USING INTERNATIONAL LAW IN U.S. COURTS (Transnational Publishers 2001); and Frederic L. Kirgis, *Restitution as a Remedy in U.S. Courts for Violations of International Law*, 95 AM. J. INT'L L. 341 (2001).

B. THE CREATION OF THE CONCEPT OF JUS COGENS

1. Reservations to the Convention on the Prevention and Punishment of the Crime of Genocide

1951 I.C.J. 15, 22-24 (May 28)

The Court recognizes that an understanding was reached within the General Assembly on the faculty to make reservations to the Genocide Convention and that it is permitted to conclude therefrom that States becoming parties to the Convention gave their assent thereto. It must now determine what kind of reservations may be made and what kind of objections may be taken to them.

The solution of these problems must be found in the special characteristics of the Genocide Convention. The origins and character of that Convention, the objects pursued by the General Assembly and the contracting parties, the relations which exist between the provisions of the Convention, inter se, and between those provisions and these objects, furnish elements of interpretation of the will of the General Assembly and the parties. The origins of the Convention show that it was the intention of the United Nations to condemn and punish genocide as 'a crime under international law' involving a denial of the right of existence of entire human groups, a denial which shocks the conscience of mankind and results in great losses to humanity, and which is contrary to moral law and to the spirit and aims of the United Nations (Resolution 96 (I) of the General Assembly, December 11th 1946). The first consequence arising from this conception is that the principles underlying the Convention are principles which are recognized by civilized nations as binding on States, even without any conventional obligation. A second consequence is the universal character both of the condemnation of genocide and of the co-operation required 'in order to liberate mankind from such an odious scourge' (Preamble to the Convention). The Genocide Convention was therefore intended by the General Assembly and by the contracting parties to be definitely universal in scope. It was in fact approved on December 9th, 1948, by a resolution which was unanimously adopted by fifty-six States.

The objects of such a convention must also be considered. The Convention was manifestly adopted for a purely humanitarian and civilizing purpose. It is indeed difficult to imagine a convention that might have this dual character to a greater degree, since its object on the one hand is to safeguard the very existence of certain human groups and on the other to confirm and endorse the most elementary principles of morality. In such a convention the contracting States do not have any interests of their own; they merely have, one and all, a common interest, namely, the accomplishment of those high purposes which are the raison d'être of the convention. Consequently, in a convention of this type one cannot speak of individual advantages or disadvantages to States, or of the maintenance of a perfect contractual balance between rights and duties. The high ideals which inspired the Convention provide, by virtue of the common will of the parties, the foundation and measure of all its provisions.The foregoing considerations, when applied to the question of reservations, and more particularly to the effects of objections to reservations, lead to the following conclusions.

The object and purpose of the Genocide Convention imply that it was the intention of the General Assembly and of the States which adopted it that as many States as possible should participate. The complete exclusion from the Convention of one or more States would not only restrict the scope of its application, but would detract from the authority of the moral and humanitarian principles which are its basis. It is inconceivable that the contracting parties readily contemplated that an objection to a minor reservation should produce such a result. But even less could the contracting parties have intended to sacrifice the very object of the Convention in favour of a vain desire to secure as many participants as possible. The object and purpose of the Convention thus limit both the freedom of making reservations and that of objecting to them. It follows that it is the compatibility of a reservation with the object and purpose of the Convention that must furnish the criterion for the attitude of a State in making the reservation on accession as well as for the appraisal by a State in objecting to the reservation. Such is the rule of conduct which must guide every State in the appraisal which it must make, individually and from its own standpoint, of the admissibility of any reservation.

NOTES AND QUESTIONS

1. Genocide is the primary crime at issue in ICJ litigation between Bosnia Herzegovina and the Federal Republic of Yugoslavia [now renamed Serbia-Montenegro]. *See* Peter H.F. Bekker & Paul C. Szasz, *Preliminary Objections of Yugoslavia to Jurisdiction of ICJ and Admissibility of Application of Bosnia-Herzegovina,* 91 AM. J. INT'L L. 80 (1997).

2. Genocide is also encompassed within the jurisdiction of the International Criminal Tribunal for the Former Yugoslavia. As to aspects of this institution's structure, operations and relevance, *see* VIRGINIA MORRIS & MICHAEL P. SCHARF, AN INSIDER'S GUIDE TO THE INTERNATIONAL TRIBUNAL FOR THE FORMER YUGOSLAVIA: A DOCUMENTARY HISTORY AND ANALYSIS, 2 vols. (Transnational Publishers 1995); George H. Aldrich, *Jurisdiction of the International Criminal Tribunal for the Former*

Yugoslavia, 90 AM. J. INT'L L. 64 (1996); M. Cherif Bassiouni, *Former Yugoslavia: Investigating Violations of International Humanitarian Law and Establishing an International Criminal Tribunal,* 18 FORDHAM INT'L L.J. 1191 (1995); Richard J. Goldstone, *The International Tribunal for the Former Yugoslavia: A Case Study in Security Council Action,* 6 DUKE J. COMP. & INT'L L. 5 (1995); Christopher C. Joyner, *Strengthening Enforcement of Humanitarian Law: Reflections on the International Criminal Tribunal for the Former Yugoslavia,* 6 DUKE J. COMP. & INT'L L. 79 (1995); Howard S. Levie, *The Statute of the International Tribunal for the Former Yugoslavia; A Comparison with the Past and a Look at the Future,* 21 SYR. J. INT'L L. & COM. 1 (1995); Michael P. Scharf, *Have We Really Learned the Lessons of Nuremberg?,* 149 MIL. L. REV. 65 (1995); Benjamin B. Ferencz, *International Trials for Internal Armed Conflicts*, 95 AM. SOC'Y INT'L L. PROC. 35 (2001); and Patricia M. Wald, *To Establish Incredible Events by Credible Evidence: The Use of Affidavit Testimony in Yugoslavia War Crimes Tribunal Proceedings*, 42 HARV. INT'L L.J. 535 (2001).

3. Implications of this tribunal's jurisdiction for international criminal law are explored in Winston P. Nagan, *International Criminal Law and the Ad Hoc Tribunal for Former Yugoslavia,* 6 DUKE J. COMP. & INT'L L. 127 (1995); Michael P. Roch, *Forced Displacement in the Former Yugoslavia: A Crime Under International Law?,* 14 DICK. J. INT'L L. 1 (1995); Alfred de Zayas, *The Right to One's Homeland, Ethnic Cleansing, and the International Criminal Tribunal for the Former Yugoslavia,* 6 CRIM. L.F. 25 (1995); and Guenael Mettraux, *Crimes Against Humanity in the Jurisprudence of the International Criminal Tribunals for the Former Yugoslavia and for Rwanda*, 43 HARV. INT'L L. J. 237 (2002).

4. The 1998 Rome Statute establishing the International Criminal Court incorporated the 1948 convention's definition of genocide in its Article 6, while defining broadly, in Article 7, the concept of crimes against humanity:

> 1. For the purpose of this Statute, "crime against humanity" means any of the following acts when committed as part of a widespread or systematic attack directed against any civilian population, with knowledge of the attack:
>
> (a) Murder;
>
> (b) Extermination;
>
> (c) Enslavement;
>
> (d) Deportation or forcible transfer of population;
>
> (e) Imprisonment or other severe deprivation of physical liberty in violation of fundamental rules of international law;
>
> (f) Torture;
>
> (g) Rape, sexual slavery, enforced prostitution, forced pregnancy, enforced sterilization, or any other form of sexual violence of comparable gravity;
>
> (h) Persecution against any identifiable group or collectivity on political, racial, national, ethnic, cultural, religious, gender as defined in paragraph 3, or other grounds that are universally recognized as impermissible under international law, in connection with any act referred to in this paragraph or any crime within the jurisdiction of the Court;
>
> (i) Enforced disappearance of persons;
>
> (j) The crime of apartheid;
>
> (k) Other inhumane acts of a similar character intentionally causing great suffering, or serious injury to body or to mental or physical health.
>
> 2. For the purpose of paragraph 1:

(a) "Attack directed against any civilian population" means a course of conduct involving the multiple commission of acts referred to in paragraph 1 against any civilian population, pursuant to or in furtherance of a State or organizational policy to commit such attack;

(b) "Extermination" includes the intentional infliction of conditions of life, inter alia, the deprivation of access to food and medicine, calculated to bring about the destruction of part of a population;

(c) "Enslavement" means the exercise of any or all of the powers attaching to the right of ownership over a person and includes the exercise of such power in the course of trafficking in persons, in particular women and children;

(d) "Deportation or forcible transfer of population" means forced displacement of the persons concerned by expulsion or other coercive acts from the area in which they are lawfully present, without grounds permitted under international law;

(e) "Torture" means the intentional infliction of severe pain or suffering, whether physical or mental, upon a person in the custody or under the control of the accused; except that torture shall not include pain or suffering arising only from, inherent in or incidental to, lawful sanctions;

(f) "Forced pregnancy" means the unlawful confinement of a woman forcibly made pregnant, with the intent of affecting the ethnic composition of any population or carrying out other grave violations of international law. This definition shall not in any way be interpreted as affecting national laws relating to pregnancy;

(g) "Persecution" means the intentional and severe deprivation of fundamental rights contrary to international law by reason of the identity of the group or collectivity;

(h) "The crime of apartheid" means inhumane acts of a character similar to those referred to in paragraph 1, committed in the context of an institutionalized regime of systematic oppression and domination by one racial group over any other racial group or groups and committed with the intention of maintaining that regime;

(i) "Enforced disappearance of persons" means the arrest, detention or abduction of persons by, or with the authorization, support or acquiescence of, a State or a political organization, followed by a refusal to acknowledge that deprivation of freedom or to give information on the fate or whereabouts of those persons, with the intention of removing them from the protection of the law for a prolonged period of time.

3. For the purpose of this Statute, it is understood that the term "gender" refers to the two sexes, male and female, within the context of society. The term "gender" does not indicate any meaning different from the above.

5. Crimes against women have received the attention of war crimes tribunals. In 2001, the Yugoslav tribunal held for the first time that rape can constitute a war crime. *See* Press Release on the 'Judgment of Trial Chamber II in the Kunarac, Kovac and Vukovic case', The Hague, 22 February 2001 JL/P.I.S./566-e. The Rwandan Tribunal, *see infra* at 538, declared that rape in its statutory context constitutes genocide. *See* MASS RAPE: THE WAR AGAINST WOMEN IN BOSNIA-HERZEGOVINA (Alexandra Stiglmayer ed., U. Nebraska Press 1994); Sharon A. Healey, *Prosecuting Rape Under the Statute of the War Crimes Tribunal for the Former Yugoslavia,* 21 BROOKLYN J. INT'L L. 327 (1995); Fionnuala Ni Aolain, *Mass Rape: The War Against Women in Former Yugoslavia* [book reviews], 8 HARV. HUM. RTS. J. 285 (1995); Catherine N. Niarchos, *Women, War, and Rape: Challenges Facing the International Tribunal for the Former Yugoslavia,* 17 HUM. RTS. Q. 649 (1995); Michele Brandt, *Redressing Non-State Acts of Gender-Specific Abuse Under the Alien Tort Statute,* 79 MINN. L. REV. 1413 (1995); James R. McHenry III, *The Prosecution of Rape under International Law: Justice that is Long Overdue*, 35 VAND. J. TRANSNAT'L L. 1269 (2002); and

Gabrielle Kirk McDonald, *Friedmann Award Address: Crimes of Sexual Violence: The Experience of the International Criminal Tribunal*, 39 COLUM. J. TRANSNAT'L L. 1 (2000-2001).

6. The Genocide Convention was a direct reaction to the Nazi Holocaust. Potential violators might be disinclined to ratify this treaty or ratify it only with debilitating reservations. How does the ICJ's opinion further the "common interest" of "safeguard[ing] the very existence of certain human groups" and of "confirm[ing] and endors[ing] the most elementary principles of morality"?

7. To what extent, if any, does the concept of *jus cogens* contribute to the achievement of this goal? *See* Art. 53 and 60 of the Vienna Convention on the Law of Treaties. Does it turn international law from a subjective, consent-based regime to an objective legal one? Is this distinction helpful?

8. Consider the Human Rights Committee's General Comment 24, set out in detail in Part Six, *infra*, at 1330. There, the body charged with monitoring the implementation of the Covenant on Civil and Political Rights concluded that the norms incorporated in that instrument were non-derogable. Is that an expansion of the notion of *jus cogens*? Does the concept serve the interests of the world community in that context? Discuss.

2. Hugo Princz v. Federal Republic of Germany

26 F.3d 1166 (D.C. Cir. 1994)

GINSBURG, Circuit Judge: Hugo Princz, a Holocaust survivor, brought suit in the district court against the Federal Republic of Germany to recover money damages for the injuries he suffered and the slave labor he performed while a prisoner in Nazi concentration camps. The district court asserted subject matter jurisdiction over Mr. Princz's claim, and Germany appealed pursuant to 28 U.S.C. § 1292. ...

We now hold, for the reasons set out below, that the district court does not have subject matter jurisdiction of Mr. Princz's claims. Assuming that the Foreign Sovereign Immunities Act of 1976, 28 U.S.C. §§ 1330, 1602-1611, applies retroactively to events occurring in 1942-1945, no exception to the general grant of sovereign immunity in that statute applies in this case. If the FSIA does not apply retroactively, then there is no federal subject matter jurisdiction over Mr. Princz's claims, which sound in tort and quasi contract.

I. BACKGROUND

When the United States declared war against Nazi Germany in 1942, Hugo Princz, an American and a Jew, was living with his parents, his sister, and his two brothers in what is now Slovakia. The Slovak police arrested the entire Princz family as enemy aliens and turned them over to the Nazi SS. Rather than allow the Princz family to return to the United States as part of the civilian prisoner exchange then being conducted by the Red Cross, because they were Jews the SS sent them to concentration camps. Mr. Princz's parents and his sister were murdered at Treblinka, while Mr. Princz and his two younger brothers were sent to Auschwitz and then to Birkenau, where they were forced to work at an I.G. Farben chemical plant. After being injured at work, Mr. Princz's brothers were starved to death in the "hospital" at Birkenau. Mr. Princz was later marched to Dachau, where he was forced to work in a Messerschmidt factory. When United

States soldiers liberated Mr. Princz at the end of the war, he was in a freight car full of concentration camp prisoners en route to another camp for extermination. The other liberated prisoners were sent to displaced persons camps, but because Mr. Princz is an American he was sent to an American military hospital for treatment.

After the war the government of the new Federal Republic of Germany established a program of reparations for Holocaust survivors. The German government denied Mr. Princz's 1955 request for reparations, however, because Mr. Princz was neither a German citizen at the time of his imprisonment nor a "refugee," within the meaning of the Geneva Convention, after the war. It appears that Mr. Princz would have qualified for reparations when the German government changed the criteria for eligibility in 1965, but he did not apply again before the statute of limitations ran in 1969.

Beginning in 1984 Mr. Princz, joined by the United States Department of State and members of the New Jersey congressional delegation, initiated a series of requests to the German government and the U.S. subsidiaries of I.G. Farben (BASF, Hoechst, and Bayer) for reparations in the form of ex gratia payments or the establishment of a pension fund; all such requests were denied. As the 1991 Treaty on the Final Settlement with Respect to Germany was awaiting ratification by the Senate, the Bush Administration attempted anew to resolve Mr. Princz's claim through diplomatic channels. That effort failed, as have the overtures that the Clinton Administration later made to the government of Germany.

In 1992, Mr. Princz finally resorted to federal district court, filing this action against Germany for false imprisonment, assault and battery, and negligent and intentional infliction of emotional distress, as well as recovery quantum meruit for the value of his labor in the I.G. Farben and Messerschmidt plants. After acceding to service of process, Germany moved to dismiss... The district court held that it had jurisdiction of the case on the ground that the FSIA "has no role to play where the claims alleged involve undisputed acts of barbarism committed by a one-time outlaw nation which demonstrated callous disrespect for the humanity of an American citizen, simply because he was Jewish." 813 F. Supp. 22, 26 (D.D.C. 1992). As we shall see below, that is not the law.

II. ANALYSIS

Germany argues that the district court lacks subject matter jurisdiction over Mr. Princz's complaint for damages sounding in tort and quasi contract because the FSIA is the only basis for obtaining jurisdiction over a foreign sovereign in the courts of the United States and this case comes within no exception to the rule of sovereign immunity codified in that Act. In the alternative, Germany argues that the FSIA does not apply retroactively to this case, and that Germany is therefore entitled to absolute sovereign immunity under the law of this circuit as it stood at the time the Nazis enslaved Mr. Princz. All of these questions concerning Germany's entitlement to sovereign immunity are matters of law for this court to consider de novo. ...

A. What Law Applies?

[The Court reviewed the development of the sovereign immunity doctrine in the U.S. from an "absolute immunity" theory in the first half of the 20th century through the gradual adoption of a restrictive theory, codified in 1976 in the Sovereign Immunities Act (Foreign Sovereign Immunities Act of 1976, 28 U.S.C. §§ 1330, 1602-1611 (1997)) and its commercial activity and other statutory exceptions. The Court concludes that even if the Nazi's leasing of Mr. Princz's labor was a "commercial activity" within the meaning of the FSIA, that activity did not have a direct effect in the United States.] …

2. The waiver exception of § 1605(a)(1).

Not surprisingly, there is no sovereign immunity in a case "in which the foreign state has waived its immunity either explicitly or by implication," 28 U.S.C. § 1605(a)(1) (with an exception not here relevant). Here the amici argue that the Third Reich impliedly waived Germany's sovereign immunity under the FSIA by violating *jus cogens* norms of the law of nations. In their own words: "A foreign state that violates these fundamental requirements of a civilized world thereby waives its right to be treated as a sovereign." With respect, we do not think that the waiver exception to the FSIA can be read so broadly.

A *jus cogens* norm is a principle of international law that is "accepted by the international community of States as a whole as a norm from which no derogation is permitted...." *Committee of U.S. Citizens in Nicaragua v. Reagan*, 859 F.2d 929, 940 (D.C. Cir. 1988) *quoting* Vienna Convention on the Law of Treaties, May 23, 1969, art. 53, 1155 U.N.T.S. 331 (1969).… Such peremptory norms are "nonderogable and enjoy the highest status within international law," *Committee of U.S. Citizens in Nicaragua*, 859 F.2d at 940; they "prevail over and invalidate international agreements and other rules of international law in conflict with them," and they are "subject to modification only by a subsequent norm of international law having the same character." Restatement, supra, § 102 comment k.

According to one authority, a state violates *jus cogens*, as currently defined, if it:

> [p]ractices, encourages, or condones (a) genocide, (b) slavery or slave trade, (c) the murder or causing the disappearance of individuals, (d) torture or other cruel, inhuman, or degrading treatment or punishment, (e) prolonged arbitrary detention, (f) systematic racial discrimination, or (g) a consistent pattern of gross violations of internationally recognized human rights.

Restatement, supra, § 702 and comment n. Before the Nuremburg trials, such outrages had not been expressly declared violations of the law of nations. … The Nuremberg Tribunal nonetheless punished Nazi officials for committing crimes against humanity:

> [The trials] for the first time made explicit and unambiguous what was theretofore, as the Tribunal has declared, implicit in International Law, namely, that to prepare, incite, or wage a war of aggression ... and that to persecute, oppress, or do violence to individuals or minorities on political, racial, or religious grounds in connection with such a war, or to exterminate, enslave, or deport civilian populations, is an international crime.

R. Jackson, Final Report to the President on the Nuremberg Trials (Oct. 7, 1946) ...

As the Ninth Circuit has explained:

> The universal and fundamental rights of human beings identified by Nuremberg–rights against genocide, enslavement, and other inhumane acts ...– are the direct ancestors of the universal and fundamental norms recognized as *jus cogens.*

Siderman de Blake v. Republic of Argentina, 965 F.2d 699, 715 (9th Cir. 1992). Indeed, it is doubtful that any state has ever violated *jus cogens* norms on a scale rivaling that of the Third Reich. ...

The amici argue that interpreting the FSIA to imply a waiver where a violation of *jus cogens* norms has occurred "would reconcile the FSIA with accepted principles of international law." Citing Adam Belsky, *Implied Waiver Under the FSIA: A Proposed Exception to Immunity for Violations of Peremptory Norms of International Law*, 77 CAL. L. REV. 365 (1989). Although no reported decision considers the amici 's specific argument that a violation of *jus cogens* norms forfeits immunity under the implied waiver provision of the FSIA, the Ninth Circuit has stated broadly that "the fact that there has been a violation of *jus cogens* does not confer jurisdiction under the FSIA." *Siderman de Blake*, 965 F.2d at 719.

Moreover, the amici's jus cogens theory of implied waiver is incompatible with the intentionality requirement implicit in § 1605(a)(1). ... That requirement is also reflected in the examples of implied waiver set forth in the legislative history of § 1605(a)(1), all of which arise either from the foreign state's agreement (to arbitration or to a particular choice of law) or from its filing a responsive pleading without raising the defense of sovereign immunity. ...

In sum, an implied waiver depends upon the foreign government's having at some point indicated its amenability to suit. Mr. Princz does not maintain, however, that either the present government of Germany or the predecessor government of the Third Reich actually indicated, even implicitly, a willingness to waive immunity for actions arising out of the Nazi atrocities. We have no warrant, therefore, for holding that the violation of *jus cogens* norms by the Third Reich constitutes an implied waiver of sovereign immunity under the FSIA.

3. The treaty provision.

Section 1604 of the FSIA provides that a foreign sovereign's immunity from suit is "subject to existing international agreements to which the United States [was] a party at the time of the enactment of [the FSIA]." One such agreement, the Hague Convention, in turn provides that the inhabitants of an occupied country may not be required to "take part in military operations against their own country," (Article 52) and that "[a] belligerent party which violates [this prohibition] shall, if the case demands, be liable to pay compensation." (Article 3).

In the Nuremberg Trial decision the Tribunal makes official what is in any event clear, that the Nazi regime acted "in flagrant violation of the terms" of the Hague Convention, including Article 52. The Nuremberg Trial, 6 F.R.D. 69, 123 (1946). Therefore, Mr. Princz argues, "the compensation provisions of the Hague Convention are in conflict with the FSIA's immunity provision, thus invoking its exception for prior existing treaty obligations." Binding precedent is clearly to the contrary, and clearly correct. ...

For the foregoing reasons, we conclude that none of the exceptions to sovereign immunity provided in the FSIA applies to the facts alleged by Mr. Princz. Therefore, we need not decide whether the FSIA applies retroactively to this case; for Mr. Princz' suit is barred by the FSIA even if we do give retroactive effect to that Act—and more to the point, to the exceptions to sovereign immunity that it recognizes.

C. Foreign Sovereign Immunity under the Circuit Law of 1942-45

What, then, if the FSIA does not apply retroactively to bar this case? In that event, Germany argues (albeit for the first time on appeal) that it is entitled to absolute sovereign immunity under the case law of this circuit as it stood during the period 1942-45, i.e. prior to the Tate Letter and to adoption of the restrictive theory of sovereign immunity. . . .

[T]his belated argument . . . is immaterial, however, because there is no present basis for subject matter jurisdiction over Mr. Princz's claims in the district court regardless of the state of the circuit law concerning immunity in the period 1942-1945.

III. CONCLUSION

The district court lacks jurisdiction of Mr. Princz's claims. If the FSIA applies retroactively to the terrible events giving rise to this case, then it bars the suit, which comes within no exception in the Act. If instead the case is governed by the pre-FSIA law of sovereign immunity, then it is not within post-FISA diversity jurisdiction of the district court. The judgment of the district court is therefore reversed and the case is Dismissed.

WALD, Circuit Judge, dissenting:

... The FSIA sets forth a general rule of foreign sovereign immunity followed by several exceptions. Jurisdiction lies whenever a litigant's claims fall within one of the statutory exceptions. One of these exceptions to immunity, the implied waiver exception, provides that a foreign state shall not be immune in any case in which the state "has waived its immunity either explicitly or by implication." 28 U.S.C. § 1605(a)(1) (1988). Because I believe that Germany implicitly waived its immunity by engaging in the barbaric conduct alleged in this case, I disagree with my colleagues' conclusion that none of the FSIA exceptions to foreign sovereign immunity apply.

Germany waived its sovereign immunity by violating the *jus cogens* norms of international law condemning enslavement and genocide. A *jus cogens* norm, also known as a "peremptory norm" of international law, "is a norm accepted and recognized by the international community of States as a whole as a norm from which no derogation is permitted and which can be modified only by a subsequent norm of general international law having the same character." Vienna Convention on the Law of Treaties, May 23, 1969, art. 53. ... *Jus cogens* norms are a select and narrow subset of the norms recognized as customary international law. ... Sitting atop the hierarchy of international law, *jus cogens* norms enjoy the greatest clout, preempting both conflicting treaties and customary international law. ...

One need not pause long before concluding that the international community's denunciation of both genocide and slavery are accepted norms of customary international law and, in particular, are *jus cogens* norms. The Restatement (Third) of Foreign Relations Law defines customary international law as the "general and consistent practice of states followed by them from a sense of legal obligation." 1 RESTATEMENT (THIRD) § 102(2). To ascertain customary international law, judges resort to "the customs and usages of civilized nations, and, as evidence of these, to the works of jurists and commentators." *The Paquete Habana*, 175 U.S. 677, 700 (1900). These same tools are used to determine whether a norm of customary international law has attained the special status of a *jus cogens* norm. *See Siderman de Blake v. Republic of Argentina*, 965 F.2d 699, 715 (9th Cir. 1992), *cert. denied* 113 S. Ct. 1812 (1993). A *jus cogens* norm exists if the international community recognizes the norm as so fundamental that it is "nonderogable." ...While commentators may disagree on the exact scope of all *jus cogens* norms, there is universal consensus on the existence of norms against genocide and enslavement. ... What could be more fundamental than an individual's right to be free from the infliction of cruel and sadistic terrors designed with the sole purpose of destroying the individual's psyche and person because of the national, ethnic, racial, or religious community to which he belongs? What could be more elementary than a prohibition against eviscerating a person's human dignity by thrusting him into the shackles of slavery? Germany clearly violated *jus cogens* norms by forcibly extracting labor from Princz at the I.G. Farben and Messerschmidt factories and by subjecting him to unconscionable physical and mental abuse at the Auschwitz and Dachau concentration camps.

The international consensus endorsing the existence and force of *jus cogens* norms solidified in the aftermath of World War II. "The universal and fundamental rights of human beings identified by Nuremberg—rights against genocide, enslavement, and other inhumane acts—are the direct ancestors of the universal and fundamental norms recognized as *jus cogens*." *Siderman*, 965 F.2d at 715After the Nuremberg war crimes trials, the General Assembly of the United Nations unanimously approved a resolution affirming "the principles of international law recognized by the Charter of the Nurnberg [sic] Tribunal and the judgment of the Tribunal." ... The Nuremberg Principles crystallized the pre-existing international condemnation of persecution and enslavement of civilians on the basis of race or religious belief, with the widescale atrocities committed by Hitler's Germany driving home the concept that certain fundamental rights may never be transgressed under international law. ...

The principle of nonderogable peremptory norms evolved due to the perception that conformance to certain fundamental principles by all states is absolutely essential to the survival of the international community. *See* Adam Belsky, *Implied Waiver*, 77 CAL. L. REV. 365, 387 (1989). Were the conscience of the international community to permit derogation from these norms, ordered society as we know it would cease. Thus, to preserve the international order, states must abdicate any "right" to ignore or violate such norms. As the German Supreme Constitutional Court has explained, *jus cogens* norms are those that "are indispensable to the existence of the law of nations as an international legal order, and the observance of which can be required by all members of the international community." ... Unlike general rules of customary international law (*jus dispositivum*), *jus cogens* norms are binding upon all nations; whereas states are not constricted by customary international law norms to which they continuously object, *jus cogens* norms do not depend on the consent of any individual state for their validity... Therefore, *jus cogens* norms have significant implications for the law of sovereign immunity, which hinges on the notion that a state's consent to suit is a necessary prerequisite to another state's exercise of jurisdiction.

To illuminate the intersection between *jus cogens* norms and the theory of foreign sovereign immunity, it is useful to begin by examining the evolution of the immunity doctrine. Granting a foreign sovereign immunity from jurisdiction has always been a matter of grace and comity, and is not required by the United States Constitution. *See Verlinden B. V. v. Central Bank of Nigeria*, 461 U.S. 480, 486 (1983). The Supreme Court first broached the question of foreign sovereign immunity in 1812, when it stated that states enjoy "exclusive and absolute" jurisdiction over their own territory. *The Schooner Exchange v. M'Faddon*, 11 U.S. 116 (1812). While Justice Marshall's seminal opinion is most often cited for the proposition that foreign sovereigns enjoy virtually absolute immunity from suit in United States courts, *see, e.g., Verlinden*, 461 U.S. at 486, the decision in fact focused on the exceptions to exclusive territorial jurisdiction, which stem from a state's explicit or implicit consent to be intruded upon. *See The Schooner Exchange*, 11 U.S. at 136-42. Such consent derives from the interest in interstate relations, "which humanity dictates and its wants require." Id. at 136. Even in the early nineteenth century, therefore, states recognized that, to facilitate international relations, they must on occasion allow infringements on their exclusive territorial jurisdiction.

Prior to the Nuremberg trials, the positivist theory of international law governed state sovereignty, and a state's treatment of its own citizens was considered immune from the dictates of international law. ... At Nuremberg, however, the four victorious powers of World War II tried German officials for "crimes against humanity," which included "murder, extermination, enslavement, deportation, and other inhuman acts committed against any civilian population, before or during the war," even if the victims were German nationals. Agreement for the Prosecution and Punishment of the Major War Criminals of the European Axis, Charter of the International Military Tribunal, Aug. 8, 1945, pt. II, art. 6, 59 Stat. 1544, 1547 ("Nuremberg Charter"). The Nuremberg trials thus permanently eroded any notion that the mantle of sovereign immunity could serve to cloak an act that constitutes a "crime against humanity," even if that act is confined within the borders of a single sovereign state.

Because the Nuremberg Charter's definition of "crimes against humanity" includes what are now termed *jus cogens* norms, a state is never entitled to immunity for any act that contravenes a *jus cogens* norm, regardless of where or against whom that act was perpetrated. The rise of *jus cogens* norms limits state sovereignty "in the sense that the "general will' of the international community of states, and other actors, will take precedence over the individual wills of states to order their relations." Mary Ellen Turpel & Phillipe Sands, *Peremptory International Law and Sovereignty: Some Questions*, 3 CONN. J. INT'L L. 364, 365 (1988). *Jus cogens* norms are by definition nonderogable, and thus when a state thumbs its nose at such a norm, in effect overriding the collective will of the entire international community, the state cannot be performing a sovereign act entitled to immunity. When the Nazis tore off Princz's clothes, exchanged them for a prison uniform and a tattoo, shoved him behind the spiked barbed wire fences of Auschwitz and Dachau, and sold him to the German armament industry as fodder for their wartime labor operation, Germany rescinded any claim under international law to immunity from this court's jurisdiction. *See* Belsky, *Implied Waiver*, 77 CAL. L. REV. at 396.

The exercise of jurisdiction over the Nazi officials at Nuremberg was by no means a single aberration in international law. Under the principle of universal jurisdiction, for certain offenses (including, but not limited to, *jus cogens* violations) a state can exercise jurisdiction over an offender in custody even if that state has neither a territorial link to the offense nor any connection to the nationality of the victim or offender. See 1 RESTATEMENT (THIRD) § 404, cmt. a & Reporter's Note 1. While it is rare for a nation to exercise universal jurisdiction, Israel asserted jurisdiction under such a theory, among others, when it abducted Adolf Eichmann, the chief executioner of Hitler's "final solution," from Argentina and prosecuted him in Israel. *See Attorney General of Israel v. Eichmann*, 36 INT'L L. REP. 277 (Sup. Ct. Israel 1962). The most recent example of a prescription of jurisdiction by the international community over *jus cogens* violations carried out within the confines of a state's own territory is the United Nations' Statute of the International War Crimes Tribunal for the former Yugoslavia ("Statute"). Enacted as a response to the appalling atrocities committed against civilians caught in the brutal conflict in the former Yugoslavia, the Statute vests the War Crimes Tribunal with jurisdiction over, inter alia, crimes against humanity and genocide committed in the territory of the former Yugoslavia since January 1, 1993. … The Statute contains absolutely no indication that foreign sovereign immunity could provide a valid defense to the exercise of the tribunal's jurisdiction. Thus the clear import of international law is to disavow a foreign sovereign's claims to immunity where that sovereign is accused of violating universally accepted norms of conduct essential to the preservation of the international order. In other words, under international law, a state waives its right to sovereign immunity when it transgresses a *jus cogens* norm.

It is a well-established canon of statutory construction that, because "international law is part of our law," *Paquete Habana*, 175 U.S. at 700, we must, wherever possible, interpret United States law consistently with international law. … Indeed, the legislative history of the FSIA indicates that Congress intended the Act to create "a statutory regime which incorporates standards recognized under international law." H.R. Rep. No. 1487, 94th Cong., 2d Sess. at 14 (1976). The only way to reconcile the FSIA's presumption of foreign sovereign immunity with international law is to interpret § 1605(a)(1) of the Act as encompassing the principle that a foreign state implicitly waives its right to sovereign immunity in United States courts by violating *jus cogens* norms. … [Construing breach of *jus cogens* norm as an implied waiver is not at odds with language and legislative history of FSIA].

Moreover, I disagree with my colleagues that the "*jus cogens* theory of implied waiver is incompatible with the intentionality requirement implicit in § 1605(a)(1)." Maj. Op. at 15. The implicit intentionality requirement stems from several decisions that have limited the implied waiver exception to cases in which the foreign sovereign "contemplated" the involvement of United States courts. In inflicting theretofore unimaginable atrocities on innocent civilians during the Holocaust, Germany could not have helped but realize that it might one day be held accountable for its heinous actions by any other state, including the United States. The magnitude of the acts put the perpetrators on notice that they were violating "principles common to the major legal systems of the world." Report to the President from Robert H. Jackson, Chief Counsel for the United States in the Prosecution of Axis War Criminals, *reprinted* in 39 Am. J. Int'l L. 178, 186 (Supp. 1945). …

In the absence of any indication that Congress intended to exclude from the scope of § 1605(a)(1) the concept that a foreign state waives its immunity by breaching a peremptory norm of international law, I believe that the only way to interpret the FSIA in accordance with international law is to construe the Act to encompass an implied waiver exception for *jus cogens* violations. Congress did not intend to thwart the opportunity of an American victim of the Holocaust to have his claims heard by the United States judicial system. Because I cannot agree that the FSIA requires us to slam the door in the face of Hugo Princz, I dissent.

NOTES AND QUESTIONS

1. Is Judge Ginsburg's construction of the FSIA convincing? In the absence of inclusive fora, doesn't denial of access to domestic courts deprive victims of the Holocaust and other genocidal action of any effective avenue to vindicate their claims?

2. Should *jus cogens* prescriptions carry with them an enforcement mechanism independent of the state's consent? Compare the examples of the Nuremberg/Tokyo and the former Yugoslavia/ Rwanda tribunals. Would the global common interest be better served if domestic courts had the authority to adjudicate cases based on causes of action sounding in international law? Or should authoritative decisions on their jurisdiction be made by domestic legislators? *See* Jack Alan Levy, *As Between* Princz *and King: Reassessing the Law of Foreign Sovereign Immunity as Applied to* Jus Cogens *Violators*, 86 GEO. L. J. 2703 (1998).

3. The notion of an "implied waiver" appears to refer to some volitional element indicative of consent by the defendant. Is the dissenting opinion based on such a notion? Are the genocidal actions by Nazi Germany indicative of its consent to the U.S. court's jurisdiction? Should Germany's implied or actual intent matter?

4. For further analysis of the Princz case, see Mathias Reimann, *A Human Rights Exception to Sovereign Immunity: Some Thoughts on* Princz v. Federal Republic of Germany, 16 MICH. J. INT'L L. 403 (1995); Marcus W. Eyth, *Princz v. Federal Republic of Germany: A Holocaust Survivor's Struggle to Bring Germany to Justice in American Courts Continues*, 9 MSU-DCL J. INT'L L. 339 (2000).

3. The Prosecutor v. Jean-Paul Akayesu

Judgment, Int'l Crim. Trib. for Rwanda, Sept. 2, 1998
Case No. ICTR-96-4-T, 37 I.L.M. 1399

[Jean-Paul Akayesu, a Rwandan national, was born in 1953. He is married, with five children. Prior to becoming bourgmestre of Taba commune in Rwanda, he was a teacher, then an inspector of schools. Akayesu entered politics in 1991 as a founding member of the Mouvement Démocratique Républicain (MDR). He was Chairman of the local wing of the MDR in Taba until April 1993 when he was elected bourgmestre of Taba. He held that position until June 1994, when he fled Rwanda. [I]n Rwanda, the bourgmestre was traditionally treated with deference by the people and had extensive powers. Akayesu appears to have discharged his various responsibilities relatively well until the period of the events described in the Indictment and to have been a respected bourgmestre.] ...

13. The Chamber then considered whether the events that took place in Rwanda in 1994 occurred solely within the context of the conflict between the RAF and the RPF, as some maintain, or whether the massacres that occurred between April and July 1994 constituted genocide. To that end...it should be noted that genocide...is defined in the Convention for the Prevention and Punishment of the Crime of Genocide, as the act of committing certain crimes, including

the killing of members of the group or causing serious physical or mental harm to members of the group with the intent to destroy, in whole or in part, a national, ethnical, racial or religious group, as such.

14. Even though the number of victims is yet to be known with accuracy, no one can reasonably refute the fact that widespread killings took place during this period throughout the country. Dr. Zachariah, who appeared as an expert witness before this Tribunal, described the piles of bodies he saw everywhere, on the roads, on the footpaths and in rivers and, particularly, the manner in which all these people had been killed. He saw many wounded people who, according to him, were mostly Tutsi and who, apparently, had sustained wounds inflicted with machetes to the face, the neck, the ankle and also to the Achilles tendon to prevent them from fleeing. Similarly, the testimony of Major-General Dallaire, former Commander of UNAMIR, before the Chamber indicated that, from 6 April 1994, the date of the crash that claimed the life of President Habyarimana, members of FAR and the Presidential Guard were going into houses in Kigali that had been previously identified in order to kill. Another witness, the British cameraman, Simon Cox, took photographs of bodies in various localities in Rwanda, and mentioned identity cards strewn on the ground, all of which were marked "Tutsi."

15. Consequently, in view of these widespread killings the victims of which were mainly Tutsi, the Trial Chamber is of the opinion that the first requirement for there to be genocide has been met, to wit, killing and causing serious bodily harm to members of a group. The second requirement is that these killings and serious bodily harm be committed with the intent to destroy, in whole or in part, a particular group targeted as such.

16. In the opinion of the Chamber, many facts show that the intention of the perpetrators of these killings was to cause the complete disappearance of the Tutsi people. In this connection, Alison DesForges, a specialist historian on Rwanda, who appeared as an expert witness, stated as follows: "on the basis of the statements made by certain political leaders, on the basis of songs and slogans popular among the interahamwe, I believe that these people had the intention of completely wiping out the Tutsi from Rwanda so that - as they said on certain occasions - their children, later on, should not know what a Tutsi looked like, unless they referred to history books." This testimony given by Dr. DesForges was confirmed by two prosecution witnesses, who testified separately before the Tribunal that one Silas Kubwimana said during a public meeting chaired by the Accused himself that all the Tutsi had to be killed so that someday Hutu children would not know what a Tutsi looked like. Dr. Zachariah also testified that the Achilles tendons of many wounded persons were cut to prevent them from fleeing. In the opinion of the Chamber, this demonstrates the resolve of the perpetrators of these massacres not to spare any Tutsi. Their plan called for doing whatever was possible to prevent any Tutsi from escaping and, thus, to destroy the whole group. Dr. Alison DesForges stated that numerous Tutsi corpses were systematically thrown into the River Nyabarongo, a tributary of the Nile, as seen,

incidentally, in several photographs shown in court throughout the trial. She explained that the intent in that gesture was "to send the Tutsi back to their origin," to make them "return to Abyssinia," in accordance with the notion that the Tutsi are a "foreign" group in Rwanda, believed to have come from the Nilotic regions. ...

19. Based on the evidence submitted to the Chamber, it is clear that the massacres which occurred in Rwanda in 1994 had a specific objective, namely the extermination of the Tutsi, who were targeted especially because of their Tutsi origin and not because they were RPF fighters. In any case, the Tutsi children and pregnant women would, naturally, not have been among the fighters. The Chamber concludes that, alongside the conflict between the RAF and the RPF, genocide was committed in Rwanda in 1994 against the Tutsi as a group. The execution of this genocide was probably facilitated by the conflict, in the sense that the conflict with the RPF forces served as a pretext for the propaganda inciting genocide against the Tutsi, by branding RPF fighters and Tutsi civilians together through the notion widely disseminated, particularly by Radio Television Libre des Mille Collines (RTLM), to the effect that every Tutsi was allegedly an accomplice of the RPF soldiers or "Inkotanyi." However, the fact that the genocide occurred while the RAF were in conflict with the RPF, obviously, cannot serve as a mitigating circumstance for the genocide.

20. Consequently, the Chamber concludes from all the foregoing that it was, indeed, genocide that was committed in Rwanda in 1994, against the Tutsi as a group. The Chamber is of the opinion that the genocide appears to have been meticulously organized. In fact, Dr. Alison Desforges testifying before the Chamber on 24 May 1997, talked of "centrally organized and supervised massacres."

Some evidence supports this view that the genocide had been planned. First, the existence of lists of Tutsi to be eliminated is corroborated by many testimonies. In this respect, Dr. Zachariah mentioned the case of patients and nurses killed in a hospital because a soldier had a list including their names.

21. The Chamber holds that the genocide was organized and planned not only by members of the RAF, but also by the political forces who were behind the "Hutu-power," that it was executed essentially by ... armed militia and ... ordinary citizens, and above all, that the majority of the Tutsi victims were non-combatants, including thousands of women and children.

22. Having said that, the Chamber then recalled that the fact that genocide was, indeed, committed in Rwanda in 1994, and more particularly in Taba, cannot influence it in its findings in the present matter. It is the Chamber's responsibility alone to assess the individual criminal responsibility of the Accused, Jean-Paul Akayesu, for the crimes alleged against him, including genocide, for which the Prosecution has to show proof. Despite the indisputable atrociousness of the crimes and the emotions evoked in the international community, the judges have examined the facts adduced in a most dispassionate manner, bearing in mind that the accused is presumed innocent. ...

26. The Chamber finds that … it has been established that, throughout the period covered in the Indictment, Akayesu, in his capacity as bourgmestre, was responsible for maintaining law and public order in the commune of Taba and that he had effective authority over the communal police. Moreover, as "leader" of Taba commune, of which he was one of the most prominent figures, the inhabitants respected him and followed his orders. Akayesu himself admitted before the Chamber that he had the power to assemble the population and that they obeyed his instructions. It has also been proven that a very large number of Tutsi were killed in Taba between 7 April and the end of June 1994, while Akayesu was bourgmestre of the Commune. Knowing of such killings, he opposed them and attempted to prevent them only until 18 April 1994, date after which he not only stopped trying to maintain law and order in his commune, but was also present during the acts of violence and killings, and sometimes even gave orders himself for bodily or mental harm to be caused to certain Tutsi, and endorsed and even ordered the killing of several Tutsi.

27. With regard to the acts alleged in paragraphs 12(A) and 12 (B) of the Indictment, the Prosecutor has shown beyond a reasonable doubt that between 7 April and the end of June 1994, numerous Tutsi who sought refuge at the Taba Bureau…were frequently beaten by members of the Interahamwe on or near the premises of the Bureau communal. Some of them were killed. Numerous Tutsi women were forced to endure acts of sexual violence, mutilations and rape, often repeatedly, often publicly and often by more than one assailant. Tutsi women were systematically raped, as one female victim testified to by saying that "each time that you met assailants, they raped you." Numerous incidents of such rape and sexual violence against Tutsi women occurred inside or near the Bureau communal. It has been proven that some communal policemen armed with guns and the accused himself were present while some of these rapes and sexual violence were being committed. Furthermore, it is proven that on several occasions, by his presence, his attitude and his utterances, Akayesu encouraged such acts, one particular witness testifying that Akayesu, addressed the Interahamwe who were committing the rapes and said that "never ask me again what a Tutsi woman tastes like." In the opinion of the Chamber, this constitutes tacit encouragement to the rapes that were being committed. …

29. As regards the facts alleged in paragraphs 14 and 15 of the Indictment, it is established that in the early hours of 19 April 1994, Akayesu joined a gathering in Gishyeshye and took this opportunity to address the public; he led the meeting and conducted the proceedings. He then called on the population to unite in order to eliminate what he referred to as the sole enemy: the accomplices of the Inkotanyi; and the population understood that he was thus urging them to kill the Tutsi. Indeed, Akayesu himself knew of the impact of his statements on the crowd and of the fact that his call to fight against the accomplices of the Inkotanyi would be understood as exhortations to kill the Tutsi in general. Akayesu who had received from the Interahamwe documents containing lists of names did, in the course of the said gathering, summarize the contents of the same to the crowd by

pointing out in particular that the names were those of RPF accomplices. He specifically indicated to the participants that Ephrem Karangwa's name was on one of the lists. Akayesu admitted before the Chamber that during the period in question, to publicly label someone as an accomplice of the RPF would put such a person in danger. The statements thus made by Akayesu at that gathering immediately led to widespread killings of Tutsi in Taba.

30. With respect to the allegations in paragraph 16 of the Indictment, it is also established that on 19 April 1994, Akayesu on two occasions threatened to kill victim U, a Tutsi woman, while she was being interrogated. He detained her for several hours at the Bureau communal, before allowing her to leave. In the evening of 20 April 1994, during a search conducted in the home of victim V, a Hutu man, Akayesu directly threatened to kill the latter. Victim V was thereafter beaten with a stick and the butt of a rifle by a communal policeman called Mugenzi and one Francois, a member of the Interahamwe militia, in the presence of the Accused. One of victim's ribs was broken as a result of the beating. ...

32. As for the allegations made in paragraph 18 of the Indictment, it is established that on or about 19 April 1994, Akayesu and a group of men under his control were looking for Ephrem Karangwa and destroyed his house and that of his mother. They then went to search the house of Ephrem Karangwa's brother-in-law, in Musambira commune and found his three brothers there. When the three brothers, namely Simon Mutijima, Thaddee Uwanyiligira and Jean-Chrysostome Gakuba, tried to escape, Akayesu ordered that they be captured, and ordered that they be killed, and participated in their killing.

33. Regarding the allegations in paragraph 19, the Chamber is satisfied that it has been established that on or about 19 April 1994, Akayesu took from Taba communal prison eight refugees from Runda commune, handed them over to Interahamwe militiamen and ordered that they be killed. They were killed by the Interahamwe using various traditional weapons, including machetes and small axes, in front of the Bureau communal and in the presence of Akayesu who told the killers "do it quickly." The refugees were killed because they were Tutsi.

34. The Prosecutor has proved that, as alleged in paragraph 20 of the Indictment, on that same day, Akayesu ordered the local people to kill intellectuals and to look for one Samuel, a professor who was then brought to the Bureau communal and killed with a machete blow to the neck. Teachers in Taba commune were killed later, on Akayesu's instructions. The victims included the following: Tharcisse Twizeyumuremye, Theogene, Phoebe Uwineze and her fiancé whose name is unknown. They were killed on the road in front of the Bureau communal by the local people and the Interahamwe with machetes and agricultural tools. Akayesu personally witnessed the killing of Tharcisse.

35. The Chamber finds that the acts alleged in paragraph 21 have been proven. It has been established that on the evening of 20 April 1994, Akayesu, and two Interahamwe militiamen and a communal policeman, one Mugenzi, who was armed at the time of the events in question, went to the house of Victim Y, a 69

year old Hutu woman, to interrogate her on the whereabouts of Alexia, the wife of Ntereye, the teacher. During the questioning which took place in the presence of Akayesu, the victim was hit and beaten several times. In particular, she was hit with the barrel of a rifle on the head by the communal policeman. She was forcibly taken away and ordered by Akayesu to lie on the ground. Akayesu himself beat her on her back with a stick. Later on, he had her lie down in front of a vehicle and threatened to drive over her if she failed to give the information he sought.

36. Furthermore, as regards the allegations in paragraphs 22 and 23 of the Indictment, it has been established that on the evening of 20 April 1994, in the course of an interrogation, Akayesu forced victim W to lay down in front of a vehicle and threatened to drive over her. That same evening, Akayesu, accompanied by Mugenzi, a communal policeman, and one Francois, an Interahamwe militiaman, interrogated victims Z and Y. The Accused put his foot on the face of victim Z, causing the said victim to bleed, while the police officer and the militiaman beat the victim with the butt of their rifles. The militiaman forced victim Z to beat victim Y with a stick. The two victims were tied together. Victim Z was also beaten on the back with the blade of a machete. …

41. On the crime of **genocide**, the Chamber recalls that the definition given by Article 2 of the Statute is echoed exactly by the Convention for the Prevention and Repression of the Crime of Genocide. The Chamber notes that Rwanda acceded, by legislative decree, to the Convention on Genocide on 12 February 1975. Thus, punishment of the crime of genocide did exist in Rwanda in 1994, at the time of the acts alleged in the Indictment, and the perpetrator was liable to be brought before the competent courts of Rwanda to answer for this crime.

42. Contrary to popular belief, the crime of genocide does not imply the actual extermination of a group in its entirety, but is understood as such once any one of the acts mentioned in Article 2 of the Statute is committed with the specific intent to destroy "in whole or in part" a national, ethnical, racial or religious group. Genocide is distinct from other crimes inasmuch as it embodies a special intent or *dolus specialis*. Special intent of a crime is the specific intention, required as a constitutive element of the crime, which requires that the perpetrator clearly seek to produce the act charged. The special intent in the crime of genocide lies in "the intent to destroy, in whole or in part, a national, ethnical, racial or religious group, as such."

43. Specifically, for any of the acts charged under Article 2(2) of the Statute to be a constitutive element of genocide, the act must have been committed against one or several individuals, because such individual or individuals were members of a specific group, and specifically because they belonged to this group. Thus, the victim is chosen not because of his individual identity, but rather on account of his being a member of a national, ethnical, racial or religious group. The victim of the act is therefore a member of a group, targeted as such; hence, the victim of the crime of genocide is the group itself and not the individual alone.

44. On the issue of determining the offender's specific intent, the Chamber considers that intent is a mental factor which is difficult, even impossible, to determine. This is the reason why, in the absence of a confession from the Accused, his intent can be inferred from a certain number of presumptions of fact. The Chamber considers that it is possible to deduce the genocidal intent inherent in a particular act charged from the general context of the perpetration of other culpable acts systematically directed against that same group, whether these acts were committed by the same offender or by others. Other factors, such as the scale of atrocities committed, their general nature, in a region or a country, or furthermore, the fact of deliberately and systematically targeting victims on account of their membership of a particular group, while excluding the members of other groups, can enable the Chamber to infer the genocidal intent of a particular act.

45. Apart from the crime of genocide, Jean-Paul Akayesu is charged with complicity in genocide and direct and public incitement to commit genocide.

46. In the opinion of the Chamber, an Accused is **an accomplice in genocide** if he knowingly aided and abetted or provoked a person or persons to commit genocide, knowing that this person or persons were committing genocide, even if the Accused himself lacked the specific intent of destroying in whole or in part, the national, ethnical, racial or religious group, as such.

47. Regarding the crime of **direct and public incitement to commit genocide**, the Chamber defines it mainly on the basis of Article 91 of the Rwandan Penal Code, as directly provoking another to commit genocide, either through speeches, shouting or threats uttered in public places or at public gatherings, or through the sale or dissemination, offer for sale or display of written material or printed matter in public places or at public gatherings or through the public display of placards or posters, or by any other means of audiovisual communication.

The moral element of this crime lies in the intent to directly encourage or provoke another to commit genocide. It presupposes the desire of the guilty to create, by his actions, within the person or persons whom he is addressing, the state of mind which is appropriate to the commission of a crime. In other words, the person who is inciting to commit genocide must have the specific intent of genocide: that of destroying in whole or in part, a national, ethnical, racial or religious group, as such. The Chamber believes that incitement is a formal offence, for which the mere method used is culpable. In other words, the offence is considered to have been completed once the incitement has taken place and that it is direct and public, whether or not it was successful. …

51. With regard to **count one on genocide**, the Chamber having regard, particularly, to the acts [of] rape and sexual violence, the Chamber wishes to underscore the fact that in its opinion, they constitute genocide in the same way as any other act as long as they were committed with the specific intent to destroy, in whole or in part, a particular group, targeted as such. Indeed, rape and sexual violence certainly constitute infliction of serious bodily and mental harm on

the victims and are even, according to the Chamber, one of the worst ways of inflicting harm on the victim as he or she suffers both bodily and mental harm. In light of all the evidence before it, the Chamber is satisfied that the acts of rape and sexual violence described above, were committed solely against Tutsi women, many of whom were subjected to the worst public humiliation, mutilated, and raped several times, often in public, in the Bureau Communal premises or in other public places, and often by more than one assailant. These rapes resulted in physical and psychological destruction of Tutsi women, their families and their communities. Sexual violence was an integral part of the process of destruction, specifically targeting Tutsi women and specifically contributing to their destruction and to the destruction of the Tutsi group as a whole.

52. The rape of Tutsi women was systematic and was perpetrated against all Tutsi women and solely against them. A Tutsi woman, married to a Hutu, testified before the Chamber that she was not raped because her ethnic background was unknown. As part of the propaganda campaign geared to mobilizing the Hutu against the Tutsi, the Tutsi women were presented as sexual objects. Indeed, the Chamber was told, for an example, that before being raped and killed, Alexia, who was the wife of the Professor, Ntereye, and her two nieces, were forced by the Interahamwe to undress and ordered to run and do exercises "in order to display the thighs of Tutsi women."

The Interahamwe who raped Alexia said, as he threw her on the ground and got on top of her, "let us now see what the vagina of a Tutsi woman tastes like." As stated above, Akayesu himself, speaking to the Interahamwe who were committing the rapes, said to them: "don't ever ask again what a Tutsi woman tastes like."

53. On the basis of the substantial testimonies brought before it, the Chamber finds that in most cases, the rapes of Tutsi women in Taba, were accompanied with the intent to kill those women. Many rapes were perpetrated near mass graves where the women were taken to be killed. A victim testified that Tutsi women caught could be taken away by peasants and men with the promise that they would be collected later to be executed.

Following an act of gang rape, a witness heard Akayesu say "tomorrow they will be killed" and they were actually killed. In this respect, it appears clearly to the Chamber that the acts of rape and sexual violence, as other acts of serious bodily and mental harm committed against the Tutsi, reflected the determination to make Tutsi women suffer and to mutilate them even before killing them, the intent being to destroy the Tutsi group while inflicting acute suffering on its members in the process.

54. The Chamber has already established that genocide was committed against the Tutsi group in Rwanda in 1994, throughout the period covering the events alleged in the Indictment. Owing to the very high number of atrocities committed against the Tutsi, their widespread nature not only in the commune of Taba, but also throughout Rwanda, and to the fact that the victims were systematically and

deliberately selected because they belonged to the Tutsi group, with persons belonging to other groups being excluded, the Chamber is also able to infer, beyond reasonable doubt, the genocidal intent of the accused in the commission of the above-mentioned crimes; to the extent that the actions and words of Akayesu during the period of the facts alleged in the Indictment, the Chamber is convinced beyond reasonable doubt, on the basis of evidence adduced before it during the hearing, that he repeatedly made statements more or less explicitly calling for the commission of genocide. Yet, according to the Chamber, he who incites another to commit genocide must have the specific intent to commit genocide: that of destroying in whole or in part, a national, ethnical, racial, or religious group, as such.

55. In conclusion, regarding **Count One on genocide**, the Chamber is satisfied beyond reasonable doubt that these various acts were committed by Akayesu with the specific intent to destroy the Tutsi group, as such. Consequently, the Chamber is of the opinion that the acts alleged in paragraphs 12, 12A, 12B, 16, 18, 19, 20, 22 and 23 of the Indictment, constitute the crimes of killing members of the Tutsi group and causing serious bodily and mental harm to members of the Tutsi group. Furthermore, the Chamber is satisfied beyond reasonable doubt that in committing the various acts alleged, Akayesu had the specific intent of destroying the Tutsi group as such.

56. Regarding **Count Two, on the crime of complicity in genocide**, the Chamber indicated *supra* that, in its opinion, the crime of genocide and that of complicity in genocide were two distinct crimes, and that the same person could certainly not be both the principal perpetrator of, and accomplice to, the same offence. Given that genocide and complicity in genocide are mutually exclusive by definition, the accused cannot obviously be found guilty of both these crimes for the same act. However, since the Prosecutor has charged the accused with both genocide and complicity in genocide for each of the alleged acts, the Chamber deems it necessary, in the instant case, to rule on Counts 1 and 2 simultaneously, so as to determine, as far as each proven fact is concerned, whether it constituted genocide or complicity in genocide.

* * *

In a later proceeding, *The Prosecutor of the Tribunal v. Jean-Paul Akayesu*, ICTR 96-4-T (Oct. 2, 1998) *available at* www.ictr.org/ENGLISH/cases/Akayesu/judgement/ak81002e.html.), the Tribunal sentenced Akayesu as follows:

The degree of magnitude of the crimes is still an essential criterion … for evaluation of sentence. A sentence must reflect the predominant standard of proportionality between the gravity of the offence and the degree of responsibility of the offender. Just sentences contribute to respect for the law and the maintenance of a just, peaceful and safe society. …

Trial Chamber I, for the foregoing reasons, delivering its decision in public *inter partes* and in the first instance, ... sentences Jean Paul Akayesu, born in 1953 in Moreshe (phonetic) sector, Taba commune, Gitarama prefecture, Rwanda;

For Count 1, life imprisonment for the crime of genocide.

For Count 3, ... life ... imprisonment for ... crimes against humanity, extermination.

For Count 4, life imprisonment for direct and public incitement to commit genocide.

For Count 5, 15 years of imprisonment for crimes against humanity, murder.

For Count 7, 15 years of imprisonment for ...crimes against humanity, murder.

For Count 9, 15 years of imprisonment for crimes against humanity, murder.

For Count 11, 10 years of imprisonment for crimes against humanity, torture.

For Count 13, 15 years imprisonment for crimes against humanity, rape.

For Count 14, 10 years of imprisonment for crimes against humanity, other inhumane acts.

The Chamber decides that the above sentences shall be served concurrently and therefore sentences Akayesu to a single sentence of life imprisonment.

NOTES AND QUESTIONS

1. The Statute of the International Criminal Tribunal for Rwanda broke new ground in establishing international criminal court jurisdiction over individuals accused of having committed genocide, crimes against humanity, which are exhaustively defined, and violations of common Article 3 of the 1949 Geneva Convention and the 1977 Additional Protocol II thereto in the context of the Hutu tribes' large-scale atrocities committed against the Tutsis in Rwanda in the summer of 1994.

2. In interpreting the crime of genocide, defined in the Rwanda Tribunal Statute in accordance with Article 2 of the 1948 Genocide Convention, the Chamber, *inter alia,* proceeds to define the target "national, ethnical, racial or religious group." In the full text of its opinion, at paras. 297-307, it states:

> On reading through the *travaux préparatoires* of the Genocide Convention, it appears that the crime of genocide was allegedly perceived as targeting only "stable" groups, constituted in a permanent fashion and membership of which is determined by birth, with the exclusion of the more "mobile" groups which one joins through individual voluntary commitment, such as political and economic groups. Therefore, a common criterion in the four types of groups protected by the Genocide Convention is that membership in such groups would seem to be normally not challengeable by its members, who belong to it automatically, by birth, in a continuous and often irremediable manner.

> Based on the *Nottebohm* decision rendered by the International Court of Justice, the Chamber holds that a national group is defined as a collection of people who are perceived to share a legal bond based on common citizenship, coupled with reciprocity of rights and duties. An ethnic group is generally defined as a group whose members share a common language or culture. The conventional definition of racial group is based on the hereditary physical traits often identified with a geographical region, irrespective of linguistic, cultural, national or religious factors. The religious group is one whose members share the same religion, denomination or mode of worship.
>
> Moreover, the Chamber considered whether the groups protected by the Genocide Convention, echoed in Article 2 of the Statute, should be limited to only the four groups expressly mentioned and whether they should not also include any group which is stable and permanent like the said four groups. In other words, the question that arises is whether it would be impossible to punish the physical destruction of a group as such under the Genocide Convention, if the said group, although stable and membership is by birth, does not meet the definition of any one of the four groups expressly protected by the Genocide Convention. In the opinion of the Chamber, it is particularly important to respect the intention of the drafters of the Genocide Convention, which according to the *travaux préparatoires,* was patently to ensure the protection of any stable and permanent group.

Does this expansive delimitation of the target group contribute to the global community interest? For an overview, *see* WILLIAM SCHABAS, GENOCIDE IN INTERNATIONAL LAW: THE CRIME OF CRIMES (Cambridge U. Press 2000).

3. Is the Chamber's linking of the term "national group" to the political-legal concept of nationality, i.e. citizenship, appropriate? *Nottebohm, supra,* required a so-called "genuine link." Is this linkage desirable? What about a linkage to the concept of "national origin," which would include, *inter alia,* former citizens of a particular country? Should the political-legal concept of national group be abandoned in favor of a broader, more empirically based idea? *See* Siegfried Wiessner, *Blessed be the Ties that Bind: The Nexus between Nationality and Territory, supra,* at 448.

4. The Rwanda and Yugoslav Tribunals were not consensually established. They were imposed by the Security Council under Chapter VII. The expansive formulations of international crimes in the statutes of both tribunals were in effect Security Council legislation which paved the way for the broad jurisdiction granted in Articles 5 through 8 of the Rome Statute. *See* Theodor Meron, *War Crimes Law Comes Of Age*, 92 AM. J. INT'L L. 462 (1998). *See also Symposium: State Reconstruction after Civil Conflict: Beyond Impunity: Can International Criminal Justice Prevent Future Atrocities*, 95 AM J. INT'L L. 7 (2001).

4. Prosecutor v. Radislav Krstic
International Tribunal for the Prosecution of Persons Responsible for Serious Violations of International Humanitarian Law Committed in the Territory of Former Yugoslavia since 1991

Aug. 2, 2001, Judgment, Trial Chamber I, Case No. IT-98-33-T

FACTS [as summarized by Presiding Judge Almiro Rodrigues at Judgment Hearing, cf. Press Release OF/P.I.S./609e, Aug. 2, 2001 *available at* http://www.un.org/icty/pressreal/p609-e.htm]:

The attack of the Serbian forces on the Srebrenica enclave followed several months, actually several years, of confrontation. Srebrenica is located in a part of eastern Bosnia, central Podrinje, which was of particular interest to both parties involved. To the Bosnian Muslims because the town was predominantly Muslim before the conflict; because it is located between Tuzla to the north and Zepa to the south both of which were under Muslim control; because the fall of Srebrenica could have extremely negative consequences for Sarajevo under siege at the time. To the Bosnian Serbs because the region known as central Podrinje was in that part of Bosnia bordering Serbia and because it was important to establish the continuity, in Bosnia like in neighbouring Serbia, of the territories under Serbian control; and, of course, for the opposite reasons of those of the Bosnian Muslims. . . .

On 16 April 1993, the United Nations Security Council declared Srebrenica a "safe area" and an agreement signed by the parties turned it into a demilitarised zone to which an UNPROFOR contingent was dispatched. …

On 8 March 1995, the President of the Bosnian Serbs, Radovan Karadzic, issued the order under the name of "Directive 7" to separate the enclaves of Srebrenica and Zepa. In respect of what concerned the Drina Corps in particular, President Karadzic wrote "By well thought out combat operations, create an unbearable situation of total insecurity with no hope of further survival or life for the inhabitants of Srebrenica and Zepa."

On the basis of this directive, on 31 March 1995, General Ratko Mladic also issued a directive which he sent *inter alia* to the Drina Corps. The Directive organised a large-scale attack known as "Sadejstvo-95" whose objective was to defend the territory of Republika Srpska on all fronts and, in particular, to avoid, and I quote, "at any cost" the lifting of the siege of Sarajevo. General Mladic foresaw that whatever the result of the events and the escalation of the conflict, UNPROFOR land forces and NATO forces would probably not be engaged, except in those cases when they come under direct physical threat. During the operation, he stated that the forces of the Republika Srpska army would collaborate in strategic camouflage and improvement of the tactical position by carrying out, among others, active combat operations.

On 2 July 1995, the Drina Corps commander, General Zivanovic signed the orders for a planned attack on Srebrenica. On 6 July the attack was launched from south of the enclave. Thousands of Bosnian Muslims fled to the town. The Bosnian Serb forces encountered no resistance. On 9 July, President Karadzic decided that, under the prevailing conditions, the town was to be taken. On 10 July, the panicked Bosnian Muslim population began to flee toward the United Nations facilities in the town (Bravo company) or out of the town towards the north, on the Bratunac road, to Potocari. The commander of the Dutch Battalion [of U.N. Peacekeepers], often called Dutchbat, asked for air support but did not receive it.

On 11 July, General Mladic, Chief-of-Staff of the Bosnian Serb army, along with General Zivanovic, General Krstic and many other VRS officers, made a triumphant entry into a Srebrenica deserted by its inhabitants. …

In the evening of 13 July, [t]here was...a forced transfer of the women, children and old people of Srebrenica. The men were systematically separated and were forced to leave behind their meager possessions, leave behind even their identify papers. They were taken to a white house several meters from the United Nations base. They were beaten. Some were taken behind the house and killed. The survivors were taken away to various detention locations, including Bratunac. ...

In all, 7,000 to 8,000 men were captured by the Serbian forces. Almost all of them were killed. Only very few survived and some of them testified before the Trial Chamber and described the horror of the mass executions which they miraculously escaped.

The mass executions began on 13 July.

Some of the executions involved only a few individuals, like the one in Jadar on the morning of 13 July. In the afternoon of 13 July, there was another execution at a relatively isolated place, the Cerska Valley. 150 bodies would be exhumed there on which 50 metal ties would be found, some of them still wrapped around the victims' wrists. Late in the afternoon, the Serbian forces indulged in a real killing spree. A large number of Bosnian Muslims, about 1,000 - 1,500, were assembled in a warehouse in Kravica. The soldiers opened fire and lobbed in grenades. Those who tried to escape were killed immediately. The next day, the Serbian forces called out to any survivors. Some of those who responded were forced to sing Serbian songs and then executed. A large machine came to carry away the bodies and, in so doing, ripped off part of the warehouse doorframe. The experts would find traces of hair, blood and human tissue on the floor and walls.

On 13 and 14 July, there were executions in Tisca also, that is, the place where the buses were to stop so that the Serbian forces could verify whether there were still men on board, and if so, to force them to get off. They were then taken to a school and, after their hands were tied, to a field where they were executed.

On 14 July, a thousand Bosnian Muslims were assembled in the Grbavci school (Orahovac) gymnasium. Their eyes were blindfolded and they were taken by truck to a field where they were executed. Machines were already digging up the ground before the executions had been completed.

There were other executions from 14 to 16 July. A group of 1,500 - 2,000 Bosnian Muslims was being detained at the Petkovci school. They were taken to an execution site next to an artificial lake, the Petkovci dam. Their hands were tied and they were barefoot. They were executed with automatic weapons.

This would also be the fate of 1,000 to 1,200 men at the Branjevo military farm. ...

In all, the experts estimate that between seven and eight thousand Bosnian Muslim men were executed between 13 and 19 July 1995.

II - Which are the crimes that were committed?

[The following discussion is taken from the official judgment, the full text of which is *available at*: http://www.un.org/icty/krstic/TrialC1/judgement/index.htm]

G. Genocide

539. General Krstic is principally charged with genocide and, in the alternative, with complicity in genocide in relation to the mass executions of the Bosnian Muslim men in Srebrenica between 11 July and 1 November 1995.

540. Article 4(2) of the Statute defines genocide as:

> any of the following acts committed with intent to destroy, in whole or in part, a national, ethnical, racial or religious group, as such:
>
> a. killing members of the group;
>
> b. causing serious bodily or mental harm to members of the group;
>
> c. deliberately inflicting on the group conditions of life calculated to bring about its physical destruction in whole or in part;
>
> d. imposing measures intended to prevent births within the group;
>
> e. forcibly transferring children of the group to another group.

541. The Trial Chamber must interpret Article 4 of the Statute taking into account the state of customary international law at the time the events in Srebrenica took place. Several sources have been considered in this respect. The Trial Chamber first referred to the codification work undertaken by international bodies. The Convention on the Prevention and Punishment of the Crime of Genocide (hereinafter "the Convention"), adopted on 9 December 1948, whose provisions Article 4 adopts d:*verbatim*, constitutes the main reference source in this respect. Although the Convention was adopted during the same period that the term "genocide" itself was coined, the Convention has been viewed as codifying a norm of international law long recognized and which case-law would soon elevate to the level of a peremptory norm of general international law (*jus cogens*).· The Trial Chamber has interpreted the Convention pursuant to the general rules of interpretation of treaties laid down in Articles 31 and 32 of the Vienna Convention on the Law of Treaties. As a result, the Chamber took into account the object and purpose of the Convention in addition to the ordinary meaning of the terms in its provisions. As a supplementary means of interpretation, the Trial Chamber also consulted the preparatory work and the circumstances which gave rise to the Convention. Furthermore, the Trial Chamber considered the international case-law on the crime of genocide, in particular, that developed by the ICTR. The Report of the International Law Commission (ILC) on the Draft Code of Crimes

against Peace and Security of Mankind received particular attention. Although the report was completed in 1996, it is the product of several years of reflection by the Commission whose purpose was to codify international law, notably on genocide: it therefore constitutes a particularly relevant source for interpretation of Article 4. The work of other international committees, especially the reports of the Sub-Commission on Prevention of Discrimination and Protection of Minorities of the UN Commission on Human Rights, was also reviewed. Furthermore, the Chamber gave consideration to the work done in producing the Rome Statute on the establishment of an international criminal court, specifically, the finalized draft text of the elements of crimes completed by the Preparatory Commission for the International Criminal Court in July 2000. Although that document post-dates the acts involved here, it has proved helpful in assessing the state of customary international law which the Chamber itself derived from other sources. In this regard, it should be noted that all the States attending the conference, whether signatories of the Rome Statute or not, were eligible to be represented on the Preparatory Commission. From this perspective, the document is a useful key to the *opinio juris* of the States. Finally, the Trial Chamber also looked for guidance in the legislation and practice of States, especially their judicial interpretations and decisions.

542. Article 4 of the Statute characterizes genocide by two constitutive elements:

- the *actus reus* of the offence, which consists of one or several of the acts enumerated under Article 4(2);

- the *mens rea* of the offence, which is described as the intent to destroy, in whole or in part, a national, ethnical, racial or religious group, as such.

1. Actus reus

543. The Trial Chamber has discussed above the murders and serious bodily and mental harm alleged by the Prosecution and has concluded they have been proved. It has been established beyond all reasonable doubt that Bosnian Muslim men residing in the enclave were murdered, in mass executions or individually. It has also been established that serious bodily or mental harm was done to the few individuals who survived the mass executions.

2. Mens rea

544. The critical determination still to be made is whether the offences were committed with the intent to destroy, in whole or in part, a national, ethnical, racial or religious group, as such. ...

546. The Trial Chamber is ultimately satisfied that murders and infliction of serious bodily or mental harm were committed with the intent to kill all the Bosnian Muslim men of military age at Srebrenica. ...

550. Genocide refers to any criminal enterprise seeking to destroy, in whole or in part, a particular kind of human group, as such, by certain means. Those are two elements of the special intent requirement of genocide:

- the act or acts must target a national, ethnical, racial or religious group;

- the act or acts must seek to destroy all or part of that group.

(a). A group, as such

551. The parties agreed that genocide must target not only one or several individuals but a group as such.

552. United Nations General Assembly resolution 96 (I) defined genocide as "a denial of the right of existence of entire human groups." On the same issue, the Secretariat explained:

> The victim of the crime of genocide is a human group. It is not a greater or smaller number of individuals who are affected for a particular reason but a group as such.

In 1951, following the adoption of the Genocide Convention, the International Court of Justice observed that the Convention looked "to safeguard the very existence of certain human groups and [...] to confirm and endorse the most elementary principles of morality." The ILC also insisted on this point in 1996:

> The group itself is the ultimate target or intended victim of this type of massive criminal conduct. [...] the intention must be to destroy the group 'as such', meaning as a separate and distinct entity.

The *Akayesu* Judgement and the *Kayishema and Ruzindana* Judgement upheld this interpretation.

553. The Convention thus seeks to protect the right to life of human groups, as such. This characteristic makes genocide an exceptionally grave crime and distinguishes it from other serious crimes, in particular persecution, where the perpetrator selects his victims because of their membership in a specific community but does not necessarily seek to destroy the community as such.

554. However, the Genocide Convention does not protect all types of human groups. Its application is confined to national, ethnical, racial or religious groups.

...

557. A group's cultural, religious, ethnical or national characteristics must be identified within the socio-historic context which it inhabits. As in the *Nikolic* and *Jelisic* cases, the Chamber identifies the relevant group by using as a criterion the stigmatization of the group, notably by the perpetrators of the crime, on the basis of its perceived national, ethnical, racial or religious characteristics.

558. Whereas the indictment in this case defined the targeted group as the Bosnian Muslims, the Prosecution appeared to use an alternative definition in its pre-trial brief by pleading the intention to eliminate the "Bosnian Muslim popula-

tion of Srebrenica " through mass killing and deportation. In its final trial brief, the Prosecution chose to define the group as the Bosnian Muslims of Srebrenica, while it referred to the Bosnian Muslims of Eastern Bosnia in its final arguments. The Defence argued in its final brief that the Bosnian Muslims of Srebrenica did not form a specific national, ethnical, racial or religious group. In particular, it contended that "one cannot create an artificial 'group' by limiting its scope to a geographical area." According to the Defence, the Bosnian Muslims constitute the only group that fits the definition of a group protected by the Convention.

559. Originally viewed as a religious group, the Bosnian Muslims were recognized as a "nation" by the Yugoslav Constitution of 1963. The evidence tendered at trial also shows very clearly that the highest Bosnian Serb political authorities and the Bosnian Serb forces operating in Srebrenica in July 1995 viewed the Bosnian Muslims as a specific national group. Conversely, no national, ethnical, racial or religious characteristic makes it possible to differentiate the Bosnian Muslims residing in Srebrenica, at the time of the 1995 offensive, from the other Bosnian Muslims. The only distinctive criterion would be their geographical location, not a criterion contemplated by the Convention. In addition, it is doubtful that the Bosnian Muslims residing in the enclave at the time of the offensive considered themselves a distinct national, ethnical, racial or religious group among the Bosnian Muslims. Indeed, most of the Bosnian Muslims residing in Srebrenica at the time of the attack were not originally from Srebrenica but from all around the central Podrinje region. Evidence shows that they rather viewed themselves as members of the Bosnian Muslim group.

560. The Chamber concludes that the protected group, within the meaning of Article 4 of the Statute, must be defined, in the present case, as the Bosnian Muslims. The Bosnian Muslims of Srebrenica or the Bosnian Muslims of Eastern Bosnia constitute a part of the protected group under Article 4. The question of whether an intent to destroy a part of the protected group falls under the definition of genocide is a separate issue that will be discussed below.

561. The Prosecution and the Defence, in this case, concur in their belief that the victims of genocide must be targeted *by reason of* their membership in a group. This is the only interpretation coinciding with the intent which characterizes the crime of genocide. The intent to destroy a group as such, in whole or in part, presupposes that the victims were chosen by reason of their membership in the group whose destruction was sought. Mere knowledge of the victims' membership in a distinct group on the part of the perpetrators is not sufficient to establish an intention to destroy the group as such. As the ILC noted:

> [...] the intention must be to destroy a group and not merely one or more individuals who are coincidentally members of a particular group. The [...] act must be committed against an individual because of his membership in a particular group and as an incremental step in the overall objective of destroying the group.

562. As a result, there are obvious similarities between a genocidal policy and the policy commonly known as ''ethnic cleansing''. In this case, acts of discrimination are not confined to the events in Srebrenica alone, but characterize the whole of the 1992-95 conflict between the Bosnian Serbs, Muslims and Croats. The Report of the Secretary-General comments that "a central objective of the conflict was the use of military means to terrorize civilian populations, often with the goal of forcing their flight in a process that came to be known as 'ethnic cleansing'." The Bosnian Serbs' war objective was clearly spelt out, notably in a decision issued on 12 May 1992 by Momcilo Krajisnik, then President of the National Assembly of the Bosnian Serb People. The decision indicates that one of the strategic objectives of the Serbian people of Bosnia-Herzegovina was to reunite all Serbian people in a single State, in particular by erasing the border along the Drina which separated Serbia from Eastern Bosnia, whose population was mostly Serbian.

563. The accused himself defined the objective of the campaign in Bosnia during an interview in November 1995, when he explained that the Podrinje region should remain "Serbian forever, while the Eastern part of Republika Srpska and the Drina river would be an important meeting point for the entire Serbian people from both sides of the Drina." ...

(b). Intent to destroy the group in whole or in part

(i). Intent to destroy

569. The Prosecution urges a broad interpretation of Article 4's requirement of an intent to destroy all or part of the group. It contends that the acts have been committed with the requisite intent if "the accused consciously desired his acts to result in the destruction, in whole or in part, of the group, as such; or he knew his acts were destroying, in whole or in part, the group, as such; or he knew that the likely consequence of his acts would be to destroy, in whole or in part, the group, as such." The Prosecution is of the opinion that, in this case, General Krstic and others "consciously desired their acts to lead to the destruction of part of the Bosnian Muslim people as a [...] group."

570. Conversely, the Defence claims that the perpetrator of genocide must "have the specific intent to destroy the [...] group" and concludes that "the *dolus specialis* constitutes a higher form of premeditation."

571. The preparatory work of the Genocide Convention clearly shows that the drafters envisaged genocide as an enterprise whose goal, or objective, was to destroy a human group, in whole or in part. United Nations General Assembly resolution 96 (I) defined genocide as "the *denial* of the right of existence of entire human groups." The draft Convention prepared by the Secretary-General presented genocide as a criminal act which aims to destroy a group, in whole or in part, and specified that this definition excluded certain acts, which may result in the total or partial destruction of a group, but are committed in the absence of an intent to destroy the group. The International Law Commission upheld this inter-

pretation and indicated that "a general intent to commit one of the enumerated acts combined with a general awareness of the probable consequences of such an act with respect to the immediate victim or victims is not sufficient for the crime of genocide. The definition of this crime requires a "*particular state of mind* or a *specific intent* with respect to the overall consequence of the prohibited act." The International Court of Justice insisted, in its Opinion on the *Legality of the Threat or Use of Nuclear Weapons,* that specific intent to destroy was required and indicated that "the prohibition of genocide would be pertinent in this case if the recourse to nuclear weapons did indeed entail the element of intent, towards a group as such, required by the provision quoted above." The ICTR adopted the same interpretation. In *The Prosecutor v. Jean Kambanda,* the Trial Chamber stated: "the crime of genocide is unique because of its element of *dolus specialis* (special intent) which requires that the crime be committed with the intent 'to destroy in whole or in part, a national, ethnic, racial or religious group as such'." In *Kayishema, Ruzindana*, the Trial Chamber also emphasized that "genocide requires the aforementioned specific intent to exterminate a protected group (in whole or in part)." Moreover, the Chamber notes that the domestic law of some States distinguishes genocide by the existence of a plan to destroy a group. Some legal commentators further contend that genocide embraces those acts whose foreseeable or probable consequence is the total or partial destruction of the group without any necessity of showing that destruction was the goal of the act. Whether this interpretation can be viewed as reflecting the status of customary international law at the time of the acts involved here is not clear. For the purpose of this case, the Chamber will therefore adhere to the characterization of genocide which encompass only acts committed with the *goal* of destroying all or part of a group.

572. Article 4 of the Statute does not require that the genocidal acts be premeditated over a long period. It is conceivable that, although the intention at the outset of an operation was not the destruction of a group, it may become the goal at some later point during the implementation of the operation. For instance, an armed force could decide to destroy a protected group during a military operation whose primary objective was totally unrelated to the fate of the group. The Appeals Chamber, in a recent decision, indicated that the existence of a plan was not a legal ingredient of the crime of genocide but could be of evidential assistance to prove the intent of the authors of the criminal act(s). Evidence presented in this case has shown that the killings were planned: the number and nature of the forces involved, the standardized coded language used by the units in communicating information about the killings, the scale of the executions, the invariability of the killing methods applied, indicate that a decision was made to kill all the Bosnian Muslim military aged men.

573. The Trial Chamber is unable to determine the precise date on which the decision to kill all the military aged men was taken. Hence, it cannot find that the killings committed in Potocari on 12 and 13 July 1995 formed part of the plan to kill all the military aged men. Nevertheless, the Trial Chamber is confident that

the mass executions and other killings committed from 13 July onwards were part of this plan.

574. The manner in which the destruction of a group may be implemented so as to qualify as a genocide under Article 4 must also be discussed. The physical destruction of a group is the most obvious method, but one may also conceive of destroying a group through purposeful eradication of its culture and identity resulting in the eventual extinction of the group as an entity distinct from the remainder of the community.

575. The notion of genocide, as fashioned by Raphael Lemkin in 1944, originally covered all forms of destruction of a group as a distinct social entity. As such, genocide closely resembled the crime of persecution. In this regard, the ILC stated, in its 1996 report, that genocide as currently defined corresponds to the second category of crime against humanity established under Article 6(c) of the Nuremberg Tribunal's Statute, namely the crime of persecution. There is consensus that the crime of persecution provided for by the Statute of the Nuremberg Tribunal was not limited to the physical destruction of the group but covered all acts designed to destroy the social and/or cultural bases of a group. Such a broad interpretation of persecution was upheld *inter alia* in the indictment against *Ulrich Greifelt et al.,* before the United States Military Tribunal in Nuremberg. The accused were charged with implementing a systematic program of genocide which sought to destroy foreign nations and ethnic groups. The indictment interpreted destruction to mean not only the extermination of the members of those groups but also the eradication of their national characteristics. It should be noted that this interpretation was supported by the working group established to report on the human rights violations in South Africa in 1985. While recognizing that the Convention literally covered only the physical or material destruction of the group, the report explained that it was adopting a broader interpretation that viewed as genocidal any act which prevented an individual "from participating fully in national life," the latter being understood "in its more general sense."

576. Although the Convention does not specifically speak to the point, the preparatory work points out that the "cultural" destruction of a group was expressly rejected after having been seriously contemplated. The notion of cultural genocide was considered too vague and too removed from the physical or biological destruction that motivated the Convention. The ILC noted in 1996:

> As clearly shown by the preparatory work for the Convention, the destruction in question is the material destruction of a group either by physical or by biological means, not the destruction of the national, linguistic, religious, cultural or other identity of a particular group. The national or religious element and the racial or ethnic element are not taken into consideration in the definition of the word "destruction," which must be taken only in its material sense, its physical or biological sense.

577. Several recent declarations and decisions, however, have interpreted the intent to destroy clause in Article 4 so as to encompass evidence relating to acts that involved cultural and other non physical forms of group destruction.

578. In 1992, the United Nations General Assembly labeled ethnic cleansing as a form of genocide.

579. The Federal Constitutional Court of Germany said in December 2000 that:

> [t]he statutory definition of genocide defends a supra-individual object of legal protection, i.e. the *social* existence of the group [...] the intent to destroy the group [...] extends beyond physical and biological extermination [...] The text of the law does not therefore compel the interpretation that the culprit's intent must be to exterminate physically at least a substantial number of the members of the group.

580. The Trial Chamber is aware that it must interpret the Convention with due regard for the principle of *nullum crimen sine lege*. It therefore recognizes that, despite recent developments, customary international law limits the definition of genocide to those acts seeking the physical or biological destruction of all or part of the group. Hence, an enterprise attacking only the cultural or sociological characteristics of a human group in order to annihilate these elements which give to that group its own identity distinct from the rest of the community would not fall under the definition of genocide. The Trial Chamber however points out that where there is physical or biological destruction there are often simultaneous attacks on the cultural and religious property and symbols of the targeted group as well, attacks which may legitimately be considered as evidence of an intent to physically destroy the group. In this case, the Trial Chamber will thus take into account as evidence of intent to destroy the group the deliberate destruction of mosques and houses belonging to members of the group.

(ii). "In part"

581. Since in this case primarily the Bosnian Muslim men of military age were killed, a second issue is whether this group of victims represented a sufficient part of the Bosnian Muslim group so that the intent to destroy them qualifies as an " intent to destroy the group in whole or in part" under Article 4 of the Statute.

582. Invoking the work of the ILC and the *Jelisic* Judgement, the Prosecution interprets the expression "in whole or in part" to mean a "substantial" part in quantitative or qualitative terms. However, the Prosecution states that "it is not necessary to consider the global population of the group. The intent to destroy a multitude of persons because of their membership in a particular group constitutes genocide even if these persons constitute only part of a group either within a country or within a region or within a single community." The Prosecution relies on, *inter alia*, the *Akayesu* Judgement which found the accused guilty of genocide for acts he committed within a single commune and the *Nikolic* Deci-

sion taken pursuant to Rule 61, which upheld the characterization of genocide for acts committed within a single region of Bosnia-Herzegovina, in that case, the region of Vlasenica. The Prosecution further cites the *Jelisic* Judgement which declared that "international custom admitted the characterization of genocide even when the exterminatory intent only extended to a limited geographic zone."

583. The Defence contends that the term "in part" refers to the scale of the crimes actually committed, as opposed to the intent, which would have to extend to destroying the group as such, *i.e.* in its entirety. The Defence relies for this interpretation on the intention of the drafters of the Convention, which it contends was confirmed by the subsequent commentary of Raphael Lemkin in 1950 before the American Congress during the debates on the Convention's ratification and by the implementing legislation proposed by the United States during the Nixon and Carter administrations. That is, any destruction, even if only partial, must have been carried out with the intent to destroy the entire group, as such.

584. The Trial Chamber does not agree. Admittedly, by adding the term "in part," some of the Convention's drafters may have intended that actual destruction of a mere part of a human group could be characterized as genocide, only as long as it was carried out with the intent to destroy the group as such. The debates on this point during the preparatory work are unclear, however, and a plain reading of the Convention contradicts this interpretation. Under the Convention , the term ''in whole or in part'' refers to the intent, as opposed to the actual destruction, and it would run contrary to the rules of interpretation to alter the ordinary meaning of the terms used in the Convention by recourse to the preparatory work which lacks clarity on the issue. The Trial Chamber concludes that any act committed with the intent to destroy a part of a group, as such, constitutes an act of genocide within the meaning of the Convention.

585. The Genocide Convention itself provides no indication of what constitutes intent to destroy "in part." The preparatory work offers few indications either. The draft Convention submitted by the Secretary-General observes that "the systematic destruction even of a fraction of a group of human beings constitutes an exceptionally heinous crime." Early commentaries on the Genocide Convention opined that the matter of what was substantial fell within the ambit of the Judges' discretionary evaluation. Nehemia Robinson was of the view that the intent to destroy could pertain to only a region or even a local community if the number of persons targeted was substantial. Pieter Drost remarked that any systematic destruction of a fraction of a protected group constituted genocide.

586. A somewhat stricter interpretation has prevailed in more recent times. According to the ILC, the perpetrators of the crime must seek to destroy a quantitatively substantial part of the protected group:

> It is not necessary to intend to achieve the complete annihilation of a group from every corner of the globe. None the less the crime of genocide by its very nature requires the intention to destroy at least a substantial part of a particular group.

The *Kayishema and Ruzindana* Judgement stated that the intent to destroy a part of a group must affect a "considerable" number of individuals. The Judgement handed down on Ignace Bagilishema, on 7 June 2001, also recognized that the destruction sought must target at least a substantial part of the group.

587. Benjamin Whitaker's 1985 study on the prevention and punishment of the crime of genocide holds that the partial destruction of a group merits the characterization of genocide when it concerns a large portion of the entire group or a significant section of that group.

'In part' would seem to imply a reasonably significant number, relative to the total of the group as a whole, or else a significant section of a group, such as its leadership.

The "Final Report of the Commission of Experts established pursuant to Security Council resolution 780 (1992)" (hereinafter "Report of the Commission of Experts") confirmed this interpretation, and considered that an intent to destroy a specific part of a group, such as its political, administrative, intellectual or business leaders, "may be a strong indication of genocide regardless of the actual numbers killed." The report states that extermination specifically directed against law enforcement and military personnel may affect "a significant section of a group in that it renders the group at large defenseless against other abuses of a similar or other nature." However, the Report goes on to say that "the attack on the leadership must be viewed *in the context of the fate of what happened to the rest of the group*. If a group suffers extermination of its leadership and in the wake of that loss, a large number of its members are killed or subjected to other heinous acts, for example deportation, the cluster of violations ought to be considered in its entirety in order to interpret the provisions of the Convention in a spirit consistent with its purpose."

588. Judge Elihu Lauterpacht, the *ad hoc* Judge nominated by Bosnia-Herzegovina in the case before the International Court of Justice regarding the application of the Convention on the Prevention and Punishment of the Crime of Genocide, spoke similarly in his separate opinion. Judge Lauterpacht observed that the Bosnian Serb forces had murdered and caused serious mental and bodily injury to the Bosnian Muslims and had subjected the group to living conditions meant to bring about its total or partial physical destruction. He went on to take into account "the forced migration of civilians, more commonly known as 'ethnic cleansing'" in order to establish the intent to destroy all or part of the group. In his view, this demonstrated the Serbs' intent "to eliminate Muslim control of, and presence in, substantial parts of Bosnia-Herzegovina." Judge Lauterpacht concluded that the acts which led to the group's physical destruction had to be characterized as "acts of genocide" since they were "directed against an ethnical or religious group as such, and they were intended to destroy that group, if not in whole, certainly in part, to the extent necessary to ensure that that group would no longer occupy the parts of Bosnia-Herzegovina coveted by the Serbs."

589. Several other sources confirm that the intent to eradicate a group within a limited geographical area such as the region of a country or even a municipality may be characterized as genocide. The United Nations General Assembly characterized as an act of genocide the murder of approximately 800 Palestinians detained at Sabra and Shatila, most of whom were women, children and elderly. The *Jelisic* Judgement held that genocide could target a limited geographic zone. Two Judgements recently rendered by German courts took the view that genocide could be perpetrated within a limited geographical area. The Federal Constitutional Court of Germany, in the *Nikola Jorgic* case, upheld the Judgement of the Düsseldorf Supreme Court, interpreting the intent to destroy the group "in part" as including the intention to destroy a group within a limited geographical area. In a Judgement against Novislav Djajic on 23 May 1997, the Bavarian Appeals Chamber similarly found that acts of genocide were committed in June 1992 though confined within the administrative district of Foca.

590. The Trial Chamber is thus left with a margin of discretion in assessing what is destruction "in part" of the group. But it must exercise its discretionary power in a spirit consonant with the object and purpose of the Convention which is to criminalize specified conduct directed against the existence of protected *groups* , as such. The Trial Chamber is therefore of the opinion that the intent to destroy a group, even if only in part, means seeking to destroy a distinct part of the group as opposed to an accumulation of isolated individuals within it. Although the perpetrators of genocide need not seek to destroy the entire group protected by the Convention, they must view the part of the group they wish to destroy as a distinct entity which must be eliminated as such. A campaign resulting in the killings, in different places spread over a broad geographical area, of a finite number of members of a protected group might not thus qualify as genocide, despite the high total number of casualties, because it would not show an intent by the perpetrators to target the very existence of the group as such. Conversely, the killing of all members of the part of a group located within a small geographical area, although resulting in a lesser number of victims, would qualify as genocide if carried out with the intent to destroy the part of the group as such located in this small geographical area. Indeed, the physical destruction may target only a part of the geographically limited part of the larger group because the perpetrators of the genocide regard the intended destruction as sufficient to annihilate the group as a distinct entity in the geographic area at issue. In this regard, it is important to bear in mind the total context in which the physical destruction is carried out.

591. The parties have presented opposing views as to whether the killings of Bosnian Muslim men in Srebrenica were carried out with intent to destroy a substantial part of the Bosnian Muslim group. …

594. The Trial Chamber concludes from the evidence that the VRS forces sought to eliminate all of the Bosnian Muslims in Srebrenica as a community. Within a period of no more than seven days, as many as 7,000 - 8,000 men of military age were systematically massacred while the remainder of the Bosnian

Muslim population present at Srebrenica , some 25,000 people, were forcibly transferred to Kladanj. The Trial Chamber previously described how the VRS attempted to kill all the Bosnian Muslim men of military age, regardless of their civilian or military status; wounded men were spared only because of the presence of UNPROFOR and the portion of the column that managed to get through to government-held territory owed its survival to the fact that the VRS lacked the military resources to capture them.

595. Granted, only the men of military age were systematically massacred, but it is significant that these massacres occurred at a time when the forcible transfer of the rest of the Bosnian Muslim population was well under way. The Bosnian Serb forces could not have failed to know, by the time they decided to kill all the men, that this selective destruction of the group would have a lasting impact upon the entire group. Their death precluded any effective attempt by the Bosnian Muslims to recapture the territory. Furthermore, the Bosnian Serb forces had to be aware of the catastrophic impact that the disappearance of two or three generations of men would have on the survival of a traditionally patriarchal society, an impact the Chamber has previously described in detail. The Bosnian Serb forces knew, by the time they decided to kill all of the military aged men, that the combination of those killings with the forcible transfer of the women, children and elderly would inevitably result in the physical disappearance of the Bosnian Muslim population at Srebrenica. Intent by the Bosnian Serb forces to target the Bosnian Muslims of Srebrenica as a group is further evidenced by their destroying homes of Bosnian Muslims in Srebrenica and Potocari and the principal mosque in Srebrenica soon after the attack.

596. Finally, there is a strong indication of the intent to destroy the group as such in the concealment of the bodies in mass graves, which were later dug up, the bodies mutilated and reburied in other mass graves located in even more remote areas , thereby preventing any decent burial in accord with religious and ethnic customs and causing terrible distress to the mourning survivors, many of whom have been unable to come to a closure until the death of their men is finally verified.

597. The strategic location of the enclave, situated between two Serb territories , may explain why the Bosnian Serb forces did not limit themselves to expelling the Bosnian Muslim population. By killing all the military aged men, the Bosnian Serb forces effectively destroyed the community of the Bosnian Muslims in Srebrenica as such and eliminated all likelihood that it could ever re-establish itself on that territory.

598. The Chamber concludes that the intent to kill all the Bosnian Muslim men of military age in Srebrenica constitutes an intent to destroy in part the Bosnian Muslim group within the meaning of Article 4 and therefore must be qualified as a genocide.

599. The Trial Chamber has thus concluded that the Prosecution has proven beyond all reasonable doubt that genocide, crimes against humanity and violations of the laws or customs of war were perpetrated against the Bosnian Muslims, at Srebrenica, in July 1995. …

[The Court found Radislav Krstic guilty of Genocide; Persecution for murders, cruel and inhumane treatment, terrorizing the civilian population; Forcible transfer and destruction of personal property of Bosnian Muslim civilians; Murder as a violation of the Laws and Customs of War. He was sentenced to 40 years imprisonment.]

NOTES AND QUESTIONS

1. The ICTY Trial Chamber considered several sources in its interpretation of Article 4 of the Statute, including the prepatory work and circumstances surrounding the creation of the Genocide Convention, case law developed by the ICTR, the Draft ILC Report and other reports, and the preparatory work on the Rome Statute establishing the International Criminal Court. Some, if not many, of the sources given significant weight by the Trial Chamber post-date the events in Srebrenica. Could the Trial Chamber have reached the same final judgment without looking to these documents? Does the use of post-dated sources, specifically in the tribunal's interpretation of customary international law at the time of the events in Srebenica, strengthen or weaken the precedential value of this decision? What impact, if any, will it have on the continued development of customary international law?

2. Judge Richard Goldstone, in an International Bar Association Task Force Report on legal responses to terrorism, suggests that terrorism can be considered a potential mode of genocide but only if utilized with the requisite intent:

> The terrorist acts of September 11 do not qualify as acts of genocide [under Article 6 of the ICC Statute]. While the act of murder may be an element of both genocide and terrorism, the underlying motive for the two will generally be distinct. Terrorist acts are commonly committed with the intent of destabilising states or other groups by instilling terror, without an intent to wipe out a particular group. If there is such an intent then the act becomes one of genocide.

INTERNATIONAL TERRORISM: LEGAL CHALLENGES AND RESPONSES, A REPORT FROM THE INTERNATIONAL BAR ASSOCIATION'S TASK FORCE ON INTERNATIONAL TERRORISM 157-158 (Transnat'l Publishers, Inc. 2003). Do you agree? *See* Alfred P. Rubin, *Focus: September 11, 2001 – Legal Response to Terror: An International Criminal Court*, 43 HARV. INT'L L. J. 65 (2002).

3. The International Criminal Court is tasked with the international prosecution and sanctioning of genocide, crimes against humanity, war crimes, and, in the future, the crime of aggression; its jurisdiction is established by treaty, i.e. state consent. What are the advantages of a permanent tribunal as opposed to the ad hoc tribunals? What are its disadvantages? *See* Louise Arbour, *Friedmann Award Address: Litigation Before the ICC: Not If and When, but How*, 40 COLUM. J. TRANSNAT'L L. 1 (2001-2002). Some commentators have drawn attention to potential defects in the procedures of these tribunals. *See* Maryam Kamali, *Accountability for Human Rights Violations: A Comparison of Transitional Justice in East Germany and South Africa*, 40 COLUM. J. TRANSNAT'L L. 89 (2001-2002); Jacob Katz Cogan, *International Criminal Courts and Fair Trials: Difficulties and Prospects*, 27 YALE J. INT'L L. 111 (2002); James Blount Griffin, *A Predictive Framework for the Effectiveness of International Criminal Tribunals*, 34 VAND. J. TRANSNAT'L L. 405 (2001).

4. War crimes tribunals represent some of, but by no means the only, authoritative and controlling world community responses to serious violations of public order. Seen in broader context, the pertinent goals of a world community faced with the phenomena described are to restore minimum

order, reduce the expectation of violence, reestablish practices of a productive civil society, eliminate or mitigate the factors that could, in varying combination, reignite particular conflicts, and deter in the society at issue and in others that are watching the occurrence of comparable offending behavior. What other mechanisms to achieve these goals are available? How important is the context of the violations? For details, *see* W. Michael Reisman, *Institutions and Practices for Restoring and Maintaining Public Order,* 6 DUKE J. COMP. & INT'L L. 175 (1995); M. Cherif Bassiouni, *Searching for Peace and Achieving Justice: The Need for Accountability, in* ASSOCIATION INTERNATIONAL DE DROIT PÉNAL, REINING IN IMPUNITY FOR INTERNATIONAL CRIMES AND SERIOUS VIOLATIONS OF FUNDAMENTAL HUMAN RIGHTS: PROCEEDINGS OF THE SIRACUSA CONFERENCE 17-21 SEPTEMBER 1998 45, 57-64 (Christopher C. Joyner, special ed., 1998). Siegfried Wiessner and Andrew R. Willard, in *Policy Oriented Jurisprudence and Human Rights Abuses in Internal Conflict: Toward a World Public Order of Human Dignity,* 93 AM. J. INT'L L. 316, 333 (1999) present a synopsis of the responses available to the international community:

> With respect to any instance of large-scale human rights atrocities, a variety of community responses are available, judging from the experience of the past and the imagination of the future. These responses may involve authoritative action by local and/or international or foreign decision makers. Pertinent arrangements include, but are not limited to:
>
> – prescription of human rights law, humanitarian law, the law of state responsibility, and the law relating to civil and criminal individual responsibility for international crimes;
>
> – prosecution before national courts of so-called universal crimes based on established theories of "jurisdiction," such as passive personality and the concept of "universal jurisdiction";
>
> – prosecution before international criminal tribunals, ad hoc or permanent;
>
> – judicial assistance and extradition to foreign or international criminal courts;
>
> – denial of sovereign or diplomatic immunity for international crimes;
>
> – national lustration mechanisms;
>
> – national civil remedies;
>
> – international compensation mechanisms;
>
> – gathering of facts through commissions of inquiry and truth commissions, both national and international;
>
> – national and international reconciliation commissions;
>
> – refusal to allow violators the beneficial consequences of actions deemed unlawful; and
>
> – individual pardons and general amnesties.
>
> Each of these arrangements, ... and others that have yet to be considered, can be utilized alone or in combination as the facts suggests. Id.

C. CUSTOMARY AND TREATY-BASED INTERNATIONAL LAW OF HUMAN RIGHTS

Earlier, we considered the emergence of the concept of a customary international law of human rights. The application of this body of human rights law falls to domestic courts and a number of formal international bodies, in particular, those established under the Charter of the United Nations. Domestic courts in states that have ratified the major instruments will apply those treaties as domestic law, if their Constitutions so provide and the pertinent treaty obligations are considered self-executing. But for those states that have not become party to all or many of the human rights instruments, domestic courts must, if they are so empowered and disposed, apply the standards of the customary international law of human rights. One important such vehicle of empowerment in the United States is 28 U.S.C. § 1350, the Alien Tort Claims Act of 1789.

1. Domestic Courts

a. Filartiga v. Pena-Irala

630 F.2d 876 (2d Cir. 1980)

The appellants, plaintiffs below, are citizens of the Republic of Paraguay. Dr. Joel Filartiga, a physician, describes himself as a longstanding opponent of the government of President Alfredo Stroessner, which has held power in Paraguay since 1954. His daughter, Dolly Filartiga, arrived in the United States in 1978 under a visitor's visa, and has since applied for permanent political asylum. The Filartigas brought this action in the Eastern District of New York against Americo Norberto Pena-Irala (Pena), also a citizen of Paraguay, for wrongfully causing the death of Dr. Filartiga's seventeen-year old son, Joelito. Because the district court dismissed the action for want of subject matter jurisdiction, we must accept as true the allegations contained in the Filartigas' complaint and affidavits for purposes of this appeal.

The appellants contend that on March 29, 1976, Joelito Filartiga was kidnapped and tortured to death by Pena, who was then Inspector General of Police in Asuncion, Paraguay. Later that day, the police brought Dolly Filartiga to Pena's home where she was confronted with the body of her brother, which evidenced marks of severe torture. As she fled, horrified, from the house, Pena followed after her shouting, "Here you have what you have been looking for for so long and what you deserve. Now shut up." The Filartigas claim that Joelito was tortured and killed in retaliation for his father's political activities and beliefs.

Shortly thereafter, Dr. Filartiga commenced a criminal action in the Paraguayan courts against Pena and the police for the murder of his son. As a result, Dr. Filartiga's attorney was arrested and brought to police headquarters where, shackled to a wall, Pena threatened him with death. This attorney, it is alleged, has since been disbarred without just cause.

During the course of the Paraguayan criminal proceeding, which is apparently still pending after four years, another man, Hugo Duarte, confessed to the murder. Duarte, who was a member of the Pena household, claimed that he had discovered his wife and Joelito in flagrante delicto, and that the crime was one of passion. The Filartigas have submitted a photograph of Joelito's corpse showing injuries they believe refute this claim. Dolly Filartiga, moreover, has stated that she will offer evidence of three independent autopsies demonstrating that her brother's death "was the result of professional methods of torture." Despite his confession, Duarte, we are told, has never been convicted or sentenced in connection with the crime.

In July of 1978, Pena sold his house in Paraguay and entered the United States under a visitor's visa. He was accompanied by Juana Bautista Fernandez Villalba, who had lived with him in Paraguay. The couple remained in the United States beyond the term of their visas, and were living in Brooklyn, New York, when Dolly Filartiga, who was then living in Washington, D. C., learned of their presence. Acting on information provided by Dolly the Immigration and Naturalization Service arrested Pena and his companion, both of whom were subsequently ordered deported on April 5, 1979 following a hearing. They had then resided in the United States for more than nine months.

Almost immediately, Dolly caused Pena to be served with a summons and civil complaint at the Brooklyn Navy Yard, where he was being held pending deportation. The complaint alleged that Pena had wrongfully caused Joelito's death by torture and sought compensatory and punitive damages of $10,000,000. The Filartigas also sought to enjoin Pena's deportation to ensure his availability for testimony at trial. The cause of action is stated as arising under "wrongful death statutes; the U.N. Charter; the Universal Declaration on Human Rights; the U.N. Declaration Against Torture; the American Declaration of the Rights and Duties of Man; and other pertinent declarations, documents and practices constituting the customary international law of human rights and the law of nations," as well as 28 U.S.C. § 1350, Article II, sec. 2 and the Supremacy Clause of the U.S. Constitution. Jurisdiction is claimed under the general federal question provision, 28 U.S.C. § 1331 and, principally on this appeal, under the Alien Tort Statute, 28 U.S.C. § 1350.

Judge Nickerson stayed the order of deportation, and Pena immediately moved to dismiss the complaint on the grounds that subject matter jurisdiction was absent and for forum non conveniens. On the jurisdictional issue, there has been no suggestion that Pena claims diplomatic immunity from suit. The Filartigas submitted the affidavits of a number of distinguished international legal scholars, who stated unanimously that the law of nations prohibits absolutely the use of torture as alleged in the complaint. Pena, in support of his motion to dismiss on the ground of forum non conveniens, submitted the affidavit of his Paraguayan counsel, Jose Emilio Gorostiaga, who averred that Paraguayan law provides a full and adequate civil remedy for the wrong alleged. Dr. Filartiga has not commenced such an action, however, believing that further resort to the courts of his own country would be futile.

Judge Nickerson heard argument on the motion to dismiss on May 14, 1979, and on May 15 dismissed the complaint on jurisdictional grounds. The district judge recognized the strength of appellants' argument that official torture violates an emerging norm of customary international law. Nonetheless, he felt constrained by dicta contained in two recent opinions of this Court, Dreyfus v. Von Finck, 534 F.2d 24 (2d Cir.), cert. denied, 429 U.S. 835 (1976); IIT v. Vencap,

Ltd., 519 F.2d 1001 (2d Cir. 1975), to construe narrowly "the law of nations," as employed in § 1350, as excluding that law which governs a state's treatment of its own citizens.

The district court continued the stay of deportation for forty-eight hours while appellants applied for further stays. These applications were denied by a panel of this Court on May 22, 1979, and by the Supreme Court two days later. Shortly thereafter, Pena and his companion returned to Paraguay.

II.

Appellants rest their principal argument in support of federal jurisdiction upon the Alien Tort Statute, 28 U.S.C. § 1350, which provides: "The district courts shall have original jurisdiction of any civil action by an alien for a tort only, committed in violation of the law of nations or a treaty of the United States." Since appellants do not contend that their action arises directly under a treaty of the United States, a threshold question on the jurisdictional issue is whether the conduct alleged violates the law of nations. In light of the universal condemnation of torture in numerous international agreements, and the renunciation of torture as an instrument of official policy by virtually all of the nations of the world (in principle if not in practice), we find that an act of torture committed by a state official against one held in detention violates established norms of the international law of human rights, and hence the law of nations.

The Supreme Court has enumerated the appropriate sources of international law. The law of nations "may be ascertained by consulting the works of jurists, writing professedly on public law; or by the general usage and practice of nations; or by judicial decisions recognizing and enforcing that law." United States v. Smith, 18 U.S. (5 Wheat.) 153, 160-61 (1820). In Smith, a statute proscribing "the crime of piracy (on the high seas) as defined by the law of nations," 3 Stat. 510(a) (1819), was held sufficiently determinate in meaning to afford the basis for a death sentence. The Smith Court discovered among the works of Lord Bacon, Grotius, Borchard and other commentators a genuine consensus that rendered the crime "sufficiently and constitutionally defined." Smith, supra, 18 U.S. (5 Wheat.) at 162.

The Paquete Habana, 175 U.S. 677 (1900), reaffirmed that

> where there is no treaty, and no controlling executive or legislative act or judicial decision, resort must be had to the customs and usages of civilized nations; and, as evidence of these, to the works of jurists and commentators, who by years of labor, research and experience, have made themselves peculiarly well acquainted with the subjects of which they treat. Such works are resorted to by judicial tribunals, not for the speculations of their authors concerning what the law ought to be, but for trustworthy evidence of what the law really is.

Id. at 700. Modern international sources confirm the propriety of this approach.

Habana is particularly instructive for present purposes, for it held that the traditional prohibition against seizure of an enemy's coastal fishing vessels during wartime, a standard that began as one of comity only, had ripened over the preceding century into "a settled rule of international law" by "the general assent of civilized nations." Id. at 694. Thus it is clear that courts must interpret international law not as it was in 1789, but as it has evolved and exists among the nations of the world today. See Ware v. Hylton, 3 U.S. (3 Dall.) 198.

The requirement that a rule command the "general assent of civilized nations" to become binding upon them all is a stringent one. Were this not so, the courts of one nation might feel free to impose idiosyncratic legal rules upon others, in the name of applying international law. Thus, in Banco Nacional de Cuba v. Sabbatino, 376 U.S. 398 (1964), the Court declined to pass on the validity of the Cuban government's expropriation of a foreign-owned corporation's assets, noting the sharply conflicting views on the issue propounded by the capital-exporting, capital-importing, socialist and capitalist nations. Id. at 428-30.

The case at bar presents us with a situation diametrically opposed to the conflicted state of law that confronted the Sabbatino Court. Indeed, to paraphrase that Court's statement, id. at 428, there are few, if any, issues in international law today on which opinion seems to be so united as the limitations on a state's power to torture persons held in its custody.

The United Nations Charter (a treaty of the United States, see 59 Stat. 1033 (1945)) makes it clear that in this modern age a state's treatment of its own citizens is a matter of international concern. It provides:

> With a view to the creation of conditions of stability and well-being which are necessary for peaceful and friendly relations among nations . . . the United Nations shall promote . . . universal respect for, and observance of, human rights and fundamental freedoms for all without distinctions as to race, sex, language or religion. Id. Art. 55.

And further:

> All members pledge themselves to take joint and separate action in cooperation with the Organization for the achievement of the purposes set forth in Article 55. Id. Art. 56.

While this broad mandate has been held not to be wholly self-executing, Hitai v. Immigration and Naturalization Service, 343 F.2d 466, 468 (2d Cir. 1965), this observation alone does not end our inquiry. For although there is no universal agreement as to the precise extent of the "human rights and fundamental freedoms" guaranteed to all by the Charter, there is at present no dissent from the view that the guaranties include, at a bare minimum, the right to be free from torture. This prohibition has become part of customary international law, as evidenced and defined by the Universal Declaration of Human Rights, General Assembly Resolution 217 (III)(A) (Dec. 10, 1948) which states, in the plainest of terms, "no one shall be subjected to torture." The General Assembly has declared that the Charter precepts embodied in this Universal Declaration "constitute basic principles of international law." G.A.Res. 2625 (XXV) (Oct. 24, 1970).

Particularly relevant is the Declaration on the Protection of All Persons from Being Subjected to Torture, General Assembly Resolution 3452, 30 U.N. GAOR Supp. (No. 34) 91, U.N. Doc. A/1034 (1975). ... The Declaration expressly prohibits any state from permitting the dastardly and totally inhuman act of torture. Torture, in turn, is defined as "any act by which severe pain and suffering, whether physical or mental, is intentionally inflicted by or at the instigation of a public official on a person for such purposes as ... intimidating him or other persons." The Declaration goes on to provide that "(w)here it is proved that an act of torture or other cruel, inhuman or degrading treatment or punishment has been committed by or at the instigation of a public official, the victim shall be afforded redress and compensation, in accordance with national law." This Declaration, like the Declaration of Human Rights before it, was adopted without dissent by the General Assembly. ...

Article 1

1. For the purpose of this Declaration, torture means any act by which severe pain or suffering, whether physical or mental, is intentionally inflicted by or at the instigation of a public official on a person for such purposes as obtaining from him or a third person information or confession, punishing him for an act he has committed or is suspected of having committed, or intimidating him or other persons. It does not include pain or suffering arising only from, inherent or incidental to lawful sanctions to the extent consistent with the Standard Minimum Rules for the Treatment of Prisoners.

2. Torture constitutes an aggravated and deliberate form of cruel, inhuman or degrading treatment or punishment.

Article 2

Any act of torture or other cruel, inhuman or degrading treatment or punishment is an offense to human dignity and shall be condemned as a denial of the purposes of the Charter of the United Nations and as a violation of human rights and fundamental freedoms proclaimed in the Universal Declaration of Human Rights. ... [quoting the remaining provisions, arts. 3-12].

These U.N. declarations are significant because they specify with great precision the obligations of member nations under the Charter. Since their adoption, "[m]embers can no longer contend that they do not know what human rights they promised in the Charter to promote." ... Moreover, a U.N. Declaration is, according to one authoritative definition, "a formal and solemn instrument, suitable for rare occasions when principles of great and lasting importance are being enunciated." 34 U.N. ESCOR, Supp. (No. 8) 15, U.N. Doc. E/CN.4/1/610 (1962) (memorandum of Office of Legal Affairs, U.N. Secretariat). Accordingly, it has been observed that the Universal Declaration of Human Rights "no longer fits into the dichotomy of 'binding treaty' against 'non-binding pronouncement,' but is rather an authoritative statement of the international community." ... Thus, a Declaration creates an expectation of adherence, and "insofar as the expectation is gradually justified by State practice, a declaration may by custom become recognized as laying down rules binding upon the States." 34 U.N. ESCOR, supra. Indeed, several commentators have concluded that the Universal Declaration has become, in toto, a part of binding, customary international law. ...

Turning to the act of torture, we have little difficulty discerning its universal renunciation in the modern usage and practice of nations. Smith, supra, 18 U.S. (5 Wheat.) at 160-61. The international consensus surrounding torture has found expression in numerous international treaties and accords. The substance of these international agreements is reflected in modern municipal, i.e. national law as well. Although torture was once a routine concomitant of criminal interrogations in many nations, during the modern and hopefully more enlightened era it has been universally renounced. According to one survey, torture is prohibited, expressly or implicitly, by the constitutions of over fifty-five nations, including both the United States and Paraguay. Our State Department reports a general recognition of this principle:

> There now exists an international consensus that recognizes basic human rights and obligations owed by all governments to their citizens. ... There is no doubt that these rights are often violated; but virtually all governments acknowledge their validity.

We have been directed to no assertion by any contemporary state of a right to torture its own or another nation's citizens. Indeed, United States diplomatic contacts confirm the universal abhorrence with which torture is viewed:

> In exchanges between United States embassies and all foreign states with which the United States maintains relations, it has been the Department of State's general experience that no government has asserted a right to torture its own nationals. Where reports of torture elicit some credence, a state usually responds by denial or, less frequently, by asserting that the conduct was unauthorized or constituted rough treatment short of torture.

Memorandum of the United States as Amicus Curiae at 16 n.34.

Having examined the sources from which customary international law is derived the usage of nations, judicial opinions and the works of jurists we conclude that official torture is now prohibited by the law of nations. The prohibition is clear and unambiguous, and admits of no distinction between treatment of aliens and citizens. Accordingly, we must conclude that the dictum in Dreyfus v. Von Finck, supra, 534 F.2d at 31, to the effect that "violations of international law do not occur when the aggrieved parties are nationals of the acting state," is clearly out of tune with the current usage and practice of international law. The treaties and accords cited above, as well as the express foreign policy of our own government, all make it clear that international law confers fundamental rights upon all people vis-à-vis their own governments. While the ultimate scope of those rights will be a subject for continuing refinement and elaboration, we hold that the right to be free from torture is now among them. We therefore turn to the question whether the other requirements for jurisdiction are met.

III.

Appellee submits that even if the tort alleged is a violation of modern international law, federal jurisdiction may not be exercised consistent with the dictates of Article III of the Constitution. The claim is without merit. Common law courts of general jurisdiction regularly adjudicate transitory tort claims between individuals over whom they exercise personal jurisdiction, wherever the tort occurred. Moreover, as part of an articulated scheme of federal control over external affairs, Congress provided, in the first Judiciary Act, § 9(b), 1 Stat. 73, 77 (1789), for federal jurisdiction over suits by aliens where principles of international law are in issue. The constitutional basis for the Alien Tort Statute is the law of nations, which has always been part of the federal common law. …

The law of nations forms an integral part of the common law, and a review of the history surrounding the adoption of the Constitution demonstrates that it became a part of the common law of the United States upon the adoption of the Constitution. Therefore, the enactment of the Alien Tort Statute was authorized by Article III.

During the eighteenth century, it was taken for granted on both sides of the Atlantic that the law of nations forms a part of the common law. 1 Blackstone, Commentaries 263-64 (1st Ed. 1765-69); 4 id. at 67. …

As ratified, the judiciary article contained no express reference to cases arising under the law of nations. Indeed, the only express reference to that body of law is contained in Article I, sec. 8, cl. 10, which grants to the Congress the power to "define and punish … offenses against the law of nations." Appellees seize upon this circumstance and advance the proposition that the law of nations forms a part of the laws of the United States only to the extent that Congress has acted to define it. This extravagant claim is amply refuted by the numerous decisions applying rules of international law uncodified in any act of Congress. E. g., Ware v. Hylton, 3 U.S. (3 Dall.) 198 (1796); The Paquete Habana, supra, 175 U.S. 677; Sabbatino, supra, 376 U.S. 398 (1964). A similar argument was offered to and rejected by the Supreme Court in United States v. Smith, supra, 18 U.S. (5 Wheat.) 153, 158-60 and we reject it today. As John Jay wrote in The Federalist No. 3, at 22 (1 Bourne ed. 1901), "Under the national government, treaties and articles of treaties, as well as the laws of nations, will always be expounded in one sense and executed in the same manner, whereas adjudications on the same points and questions in the thirteen states will not always accord or be consistent." Federal jurisdiction over cases involving international law is clear.

Thus, it was hardly a radical initiative for Chief Justice Marshall to state in The Nereide, 13 U.S. (9 Cranch) 388 (1815), that in the absence of a congressional enactment, United States courts are "bound by the law of nations, which is a part of the law of the land." These words were echoed in The Paquete Habana, supra, 175 U.S. at 700: "(i)nternational law is part of our law, and must be ascertained and administered by the courts of justice of appropriate jurisdiction, as often as questions of right depending upon it are duly presented for their determination."

The Filartigas urge that 28 U.S.C. § 1350 be treated as an exercise of Congress's power to define offenses against the law of nations. While such a reading is possible, ... we believe it is sufficient here to construe the Alien Tort Statute, not as granting new rights to aliens, but simply as opening the federal courts for adjudication of the rights already recognized by international law. The statute nonetheless does inform our analysis of Article III, for we recognize that questions of jurisdiction "must be considered part of an organic growth part of an evolutionary process," and that the history of the judiciary article gives meaning to its pithy phrases. ... The Framers' overarching concern that control over international affairs be vested in the new national government to safeguard the standing of the United States among the nations of the world therefore reinforces the result we reach today. ...

Pena argues that the customary law of nations, as reflected in treaties and declarations that are not self-executing, should not be applied as rules of decision in this case. In doing so, he confuses the question of federal jurisdiction under the Alien Tort Statute, which requires consideration of the law of nations, with the issue of the choice of law to be applied, which will be addressed at a later stage in the proceedings. The two issues are distinct. Our holding on subject matter jurisdiction decides only whether Congress intended to confer judicial power, and whether it is authorized to do so by Article III. The choice of law inquiry is a much broader one, primarily concerned with fairness, see Home Insurance Co. v. Dick, 281 U.S. 397 (1930); consequently, it looks to wholly different considerations. See Lauritzen v. Larsen, 345 U.S. 571 (1954). Should the district court decide that the Lauritzen analysis requires it to apply Paraguayan law, our courts will not have occasion to consider what law would govern a suit under the Alien Tort Statute where the challenged conduct is actionable under the law of the forum and the law of nations, but not the law of the jurisdiction in which the tort occurred.

Pena also argues that "(i)f the conduct complained of is alleged to be the act of the Paraguayan government, the suit is barred by the Act of State doctrine." This argument was not advanced below, and is therefore not before us on this appeal. We note in passing, however, that we doubt whether action by a state official in violation of the Constitution and laws of the Republic of Paraguay, and wholly unratified by that nation's government, could properly be characterized as an act of state. See Banco Nacional de Cuba v. Sabbatino, supra, 376 U.S. 398; Underhill v. Hernandez, 168 U.S. 250 (1897). Paraguay's renunciation of torture as a legitimate instrument of state policy, however, does not strip the tort of its character as an international law violation, if it in fact occurred under color of government authority. See Declaration on the Protection of All Persons from Being Subjected to Torture, supra note 11; cf. Ex parte Young, 209 U.S. 123 (1908) (state official subject to suit for constitutional violations despite immunity of state). …

In the twentieth century the international community has come to recognize the common danger posed by the flagrant disregard of basic human rights and particularly the right to be free of torture. Spurred first by the Great War, and then the Second, civilized nations have banded together to prescribe acceptable norms of international behavior. From the ashes of the Second World War arose the United Nations Organization, amid hopes that an era of peace and cooperation had at last begun. Though many of these aspirations have remained elusive goals, that circumstance cannot diminish the true progress that has been made. In the modern age, humanitarian and practical considerations have combined to lead the nations of the world to recognize that respect for fundamental human rights is in their individual and collective interest. Among the rights universally proclaimed by all nations, as we have noted, is the right to be free of physical torture. Indeed, for purposes of civil liability, the torturer has become like the pirate and slave trader before him hostis humani generis, an enemy of all mankind. Our holding today, giving effect to a jurisdictional provision enacted by our First Congress, is a small but important step in the fulfillment of the ageless dream to free all people from brutal violence.

* * *

Contrast the following opinion:

b. Tel-Oren v. Libyan Arab Republic

726 F.2d 774 (D.C. Cir. 1984)

PER CURIAM: [Plaintiffs in this action, mostly Israeli citizens, are survivors and representatives of persons murdered in an armed attack on a civilian bus in Israel in March 1978. They filed suit for compensatory and punitive damages in the District Court, naming as defendants the Libyan Arab Republic, the Palestine Liberation Organization, the Palestine Information Office, the National Association of Arab Americans, and the Palestine Congress of North America. In their complaint, plaintiffs alleged that defendants were responsible for multiple tortious acts in violation of the law of nations, treaties of the United States, and criminal laws of the United States, as well as the common law.

The District Court dismissed the action for lack of subject matter jurisdiction and the action was barred by the applicable statute of limitations. In affirming the District Court's dismissal, the Court of Appeals was sharply divided with three judges writing three separate concurring opinions, including that of Judge Bork.]

BORK, CIRCUIT JUDGE. ... The question in this case is whether appellants have a cause of action in courts of the United States for injuries they suffered in Israel. Judge Edwards contends, and the Second Circuit in Filartiga assumed, that Congress' grant of jurisdiction also created a cause of action. That seems to me fundamentally wrong and certain to produce pernicious results. For reasons I will develop, it is essential that there be an explicit grant of a cause of action before a private plaintiff be allowed to enforce principles of international law in a federal tribunal. It will be seen below, however, that no body of law expressly grants appellants a cause of action; the relevant inquiry, therefore, is whether a cause of action is to be inferred. That inquiry is guided by general principles that apply whenever a court of the United States is asked to act in a field in which its judgment would necessarily affect the foreign policy interests of the nation. ...

An analysis of the appropriateness of providing appellants with a cause of action must take into account the concerns that are inherent in and peculiar to the field of international relations. ... The factors counselling hesitation are constitutional; they derive from principles of separation of powers.

The crucial element of the doctrine of separation of powers in this case is the principle that "the conduct of the foreign relations of our Government is committed by the Constitution to the Executive and Legislative - the 'political' - Departments." Oetjen v. Central Leather Co., 246 U.S. 297, 302 (1918). That principle has been translated into a limitation on judicial power in the international law area principally through the act of state and political question doctrines. Whether or not this case falls within one of these categories, the concerns that underlie them are present and demand recognition here. ...

Questions touching on the foreign relations of the United States make up what is likely the largest class of questions to which the political question doctrine has been applied. See id. at 211-14. If it were necessary, I might well hold that the political question doctrine bars this lawsuit, since it is arguable, as much of the remainder of this opinion will show, that this case fits several of the categories listed in Baker v. Carr. Such a determination is not necessary, however, because many of the same considerations that govern application of the political question doctrine also govern the question of the appropriateness of providing appellants with a cause of action.

Neither is there a need to consider whether the act of state doctrine applies to bar this case from going forward. Although the act of state doctrine might well apply to Libya's alleged role in the 1978 bus attack, it would seem not to apply, in its current formulation, to the alleged acts of the PLO, the PIO, and the NAAA, none of which would seem to be a state under international law. ... Nevertheless, to the extent the act of state doctrine is based predominantly, if not exclusively, on separation of powers concerns (as it has increasingly come to be), its own rationale might justify extending it to cover the acts of such entities as the PLO where adjudication of the validity of those acts would present problems of judicial competence and of judicial interference with foreign relations. Such an extension would bring the act of state doctrine closer, especially in its flexibility, to the political question doctrine. ...

Those [separation of powers] principles counsel against recognition of a cause of action for appellants if adjudication of their claims would raise substantial problems of judicial interference with nonjudicial functions, such as the conduct of foreign relations. Appellants' complaint requires a determination, either at the jurisdictional stage or at the stage of defining and applying a rule of decision, whether international law has been violated. I am therefore guided in large measure by the Supreme Court's observation in Sabbatino that the greater the degree of codification or consensus concerning a particular area of international law, the more appropriate it is for the judiciary to render decisions regarding it, since the courts can then focus on the application of an agreed principle to circumstances of fact rather than on the sensitive task of establishing a principle not inconsistent with the national interest or with international justice. It is also evident that some aspects of international law touch more sharply on national nerves than do others; the less important the implications of an issue are for our foreign relations, the weaker the justification for exclusivity in the political branches. 376 U.S. at 428. There is no need to decide here under what circumstances considerations such as these might deprive an individual of a cause of action clearly given by a state, by Congress, by a treaty, or by international law. In the absence of such a cause of action, they lead to the conclusion that adjudication of appellants' claims would present grave separation of powers problems. It is therefore inappropriate to recognize a cause of action allowing appellants to bring this suit.

Most important, perhaps, even appellants concede that the incidents described in appellants' complaint are properly understood only when viewed in the context of the continuing conflicts in the Middle East. Indeed, appellants point out that "one of the primary purposes of the March 11 attack was to sabotage the foreign relations of the United States and its negotiations by destroying the positive efforts made in the Camp David accords." Brief for Appellants at 15. The Camp David accords, of course, were but one of the major efforts made by the United States to resolve the myriad problems behind the series of military and political conflicts that have kept the Middle East at or near the center of American foreign relations for at least the last fifteen years. A judicial pronouncement on the PLO's responsibility for the 1978 bus attack would likely interfere with American diplomacy, which is actively concerned with the Middle East today as it has ever been. ...

Customary international law may well forbid states from aiding terrorist attacks on neighboring states. ... Although that principle might apply in a case like this to a state such as Libya (which is not a proper party here, see supra note 13), it does not, at least on its face, apply to a nonstate like the PLO. More important, there is less than universal consensus about whether PLO-sponsored attacks on Israel are lawful. One important sign of the lack of consensus about terrorism generally, and about PLO activities in particular, is that accusations of terrorism are often met not by denial of the fact of responsibility but by a justification for the challenged actions. …

There is, of course, no occasion here to state what international law should be. Nor is there a need to consider whether an extended and discriminating analysis might plausibly maintain that customary international law prohibits the actions alleged in the complaint. It is enough to observe that there is sufficient controversy of a politically sensitive nature about the content of any relevant international legal principles that litigation of appellants' claims would present, in acute form, many of the problems that the separation of powers principles inherent in the act of state and political question doctrines caution courts to avoid. The lack of clarity in, and absence of consensus about, the legal principles invoked by appellants, together with the political context of the challenged actions and the PLO's impingement upon American foreign relations, lead to the conclusion that appellants' case is not the sort that is appropriate for federal-court adjudication, at least not without an express grant of a cause of action.

I turn next to examine treaties, common law, congressional enactments, and customary international law to determine whether any of these sources of law provides a cause of action for appellants. In light of what has been said, it would require a very clear showing that these other bodies of law grant appellants a cause of action before my concerns about the principles of separation of powers could be overcome. But, as will be seen, there is no clear grant of a cause of action to be found. In truth, the law concerning treaties and customary international law of its own force appears actually to deny appellants any cause of action.

III.

Treaties of the United States, though the law of the land, do not generally create rights that are privately enforceable in courts. … Absent authorizing legislation, an individual has access to courts for enforcement of a treaty's provisions only when the treaty is self-executing, that is, when it expressly or impliedly provides a private right of action. … When no right is explicitly stated, courts look to the treaty as a whole to determine whether it evidences an intent to provide a private right of action. …

In Count III of the complaint, appellants alleged that defendants violated the following "treaties of the United States": [provides list of treaties]. …

Only the first five of these alleged treaties are treaties currently binding on the United States. See Treaties Affairs Staff, Office of the Legal Adviser, Department of State, Treaties in Force (1983). Even if the remaining eight are relevant to Count II of the complaint as evidence of principles of international law, they are not treaties of the United States. Since Count III (tortious actions in violation of the treaties of the United States) purports to state a cause of action distinct from that stated in Count II (tortious actions in violation of the law of nations), the last eight of the thirteen alleged treaties of the United States can provide no basis for jurisdiction over the claims in Count III under the treaty components of sections 1331 and 1350.

Of the five treaties in force, none provides a private right of action. Three of them — the Geneva Convention for the Protection of Civilian Persons in Time of War, the Geneva Convention Relative to the Treatment of Prisoners of War, and the OAS Convention to Prevent and Punish Acts of Terrorism — expressly call for implementing legislation. A treaty that provides that party states will take measures through their own laws to enforce its proscriptions evidences its intent not to be self-executing. ... These three treaties are therefore not self-executing. Indeed, with respect to the first Geneva Convention, one court has already so held. Huynh Thi Anh v. Levi, 586 F.2d 625, 629 (6th Cir. 1978).

Articles 1 and 2 of the United Nations Charter are likewise not self-executing. They do not speak in terms of individual rights but impose obligations on nations and on the United Nations itself. They address states, calling on them to fulfill in good faith their obligations as members of the United Nations. Sanctions under article 41, the penultimate bulwark of the Charter, are to be taken by states against other states. Articles 1 and 2, moreover, contain general "purposes and principles," some of which state mere aspirations and none of which can sensibly be thought to have been intended to be judicially enforceable at the behest of individuals. These considerations compel the conclusion that articles 1 and 2 of the U.N. Charter were not intended to give individuals the right to enforce them in municipal courts, particularly since appellants have provided no evidence of a contrary intent. ...

The Hague Conventions similarly cannot be construed to afford individuals the right to judicial enforcement. ... The Second Circuit has drawn the same conclusion, Dreyfus v. Von Finck, 534 F.2d at 30, and appellants have pointed to no case holding otherwise in the more than three-quarters of a century since the Conventions were adopted.

None of the five treaties relied on by appellants thus even impliedly grants individuals the right to seek damages for violation of their provisions. Appellants have, therefore, failed to state a cause of action for violation of any treaties of the United States.

IV.

Appellants' argument that they may recover damages for violations of international law is simple. International law, they point out, is part of the common law of the United States. This proposition is unexceptionable. See e.g., The Paquete Habana, 175 U.S. 677 (1900); United States v. Smith, 18 U.S. (5 Wheat.) (1820). But appellants then contend that federal common law automatically provides a cause of action for international law violations, as it would for violations of other federal common law rights. I cannot accept this conclusion.

Appellants' argument reflects a confusion of two distinct meanings of "common law". That term has long referred to the body of court-made law whose origins can be traced to the medieval English legal system. It has also come to refer generally to law (mostly court-made) not based on a statute or constitution. "Federal common law", in particular, has been used "to refer generally to federal rules of decision where the authority for a federal rule is not explicitly or clearly found in federal statutory or constitutional command." P. Bator, P. Mishkin, D. Shapiro & H. Wechsler, Hart and Wechsler's The Federal Courts and the Federal System 770 (2d ed. 1973) ("Hart & Wechsler"). To say that international law is part of federal common law is to say only that it is nonstatutory and nonconstitutional law to be applied, in appropriate cases, in municipal courts. It is not to say that, like the common law of contract and tort, for example, by itself it affords individuals the right to ask for judicial relief.

Thus, the step appellants would have us take — from the phrase "common law" to the implication of a cause of action — is not a simple and automatic one. Neither is it advisable. The considerations of separation of powers rehearsed above provide ample reason for refusing to take a step that would plunge federal courts into the foreign affairs of the United States.

Appellants, seeking to recover for a violation of international law, might look to federal statutes either for a grant of a cause of action or for evidence that a cause of action exists. These notions may be quickly dismissed. The only plausible candidates are the two jurisdictional statutes relied on by appellants, section 1331 and 1350 of Title 28 of the United States Code. Neither of those statutes either expressly or impliedly grants a cause of action. Both statutes merely define a class of cases federal courts can hear; they do not themselves even by implication authorize individuals to bring such cases. As the Supreme Court has stated, "the Judicial Code, in vesting jurisdiction in the District Courts, does not create causes of action, but only confers jurisdiction to adjudicate those arising from other sources which satisfy its limiting provisions." Montana-Dakota Utilities Co. v. Northwestern Public Service Co., 341 U.S. 246, 249 (1951). ...

Although the jurisdictional statutes relied on by appellants cannot be read to provide a cause of action, those statutes might conceivably provide evidence of Congress' recognition (as opposed to creation) of one. ...

The broadest reading of section 1350 as evidence of congressional recognition of such a cause of action is that it merely requires that a plaintiff prove that the actions complained of violated international law. If that jurisdictional prerequisite is met, according to appellants, the plaintiff has a cause of action for tort damages, as he would for any tort. This approach is adopted by the Second Circuit in Filartiga, as well as by Judge Edwards. I believe, nonetheless, that this construction of section 1350 must be rejected for several reasons.

First, appellants' broad reading would have to apply equally to actions brought to recover damages for torts committed in violation of treaties, since treaties stand in exactly the same position in section 1350 as principles of customary international law (the law of nations). Such an application would render meaningless, for alien plaintiffs, the well-established rule that treaties that provide no cause of action cannot be sued on without (express or implied) federal law authorization.

Judge Edwards' approach, as well as the analysis of the Second Circuit in Filartiga, would also make all United States treaties effectively self-executing. As appellants here seek evidence of a cause of action to vindicate an asserted international law right that they do not assert itself affords them a private right of action, their claim is indistinguishable, under the language of section 1350, from a claim brought to vindicate rights set forth in a non-self-executing treaty.

In addition, appellants' construction of section 1350 is too sweeping. It would authorize tort suits for the vindication of any international legal right. As demonstrated below, that result would be inconsistent with the severe limitations on individually initiated enforcement inherent in international law itself, and would run counter to constitutional limits on the role of federal courts. Those reasons demand rejection of appellants' construction of section 1350 unless a narrow reading of the provision is incompatible with congressional intent. There is no evidence, however, that Congress intended the result appellants suggest.

What is known of the origins of section 1350 was perhaps best described by Judge Friendly in IIT v. Vencap, Ltd., 519 F.2d 1001, 1015 (2d Cir. 1975): "This old but little used section is a kind of legal Lohengrin; ... no one seems to know whence it came." Section 1350 was enacted, in almost its current form, as part of the Judiciary Act of 1789, ch. 20, 1 Stat. 73, 77. I have discovered no direct evidence of what Congress had in mind when enacting the provision. The debates over the Judiciary Act in the House — the Senate debates were not recorded — nowhere mention the provision, not even, so far as we are aware, indirectly. See 1 Annals of Cong. 782-833 (J. Gales ed. 1789).

Historical research has not yet disclosed what section 1350 was intended to accomplish. The fact poses a special problem for courts. A statute whose original meaning is hidden from us and yet which, if its words are read incautiously with modern assumptions in mind, is capable of plunging our nation into foreign conflicts, ought to be approached by the judiciary with great circumspection. It will not do simply to assert that the statutory phrase, the "law of nations," whatever it may have meant in 1789, must be read today as incorporating all the modern rules of international law and giving aliens private causes of action for violations of those rules. It will not do because the result is contrary not only to what we know of the framers' general purposes in this area but contrary as well to the appropriate, indeed the constitutional, role of courts with respect to foreign affairs.

What little relevant historical background is now available to us indicates that those who drafted the Constitution and the Judiciary Act of 1789 wanted to open federal courts to aliens for the purpose of avoiding, not provoking, conflicts with other nations. The Federalist No. 80 (A. Hamilton). A broad reading of section 1350 runs directly contrary to that desire. It is also relevant to a construction of this provision that until quite recently nobody understood it to empower courts to entertain cases like this one or like Filartiga. …

Clearly, cases like this and Filartiga were beyond the framers' contemplation. Id. at 24-26. That problem is not avoided by observing that the law of nations evolves. It is one thing for a case like The Paquete Habana to find that a rule has evolved so that the United States may not seize coastal fishing boats of a nation with which we are at war. It is another thing entirely, a difference in degree so enormous as to be a difference in kind, to find that a rule has evolved against torture by government so that our courts must sit in judgment of the conduct of foreign officials in their own countries with respect to their own citizens. The latter assertion raises prospects of judicial interference with foreign affairs that the former does not. A different question might be presented if section 1350 had been adopted by a modern Congress that made clear its desire that federal courts police the behavior of foreign individuals and governments. But section 1350 does not embody a legislative judgment that is either current or clear and the statute must be read with that in mind.

What kinds of alien tort actions, then, might the Congress of 1789 have meant to bring into federal courts? According to Blackstone, a writer certainly familiar to colonial lawyers, "the principal offences against the law of nations, animadverted on as such by the municipal laws of England, [were] of three kinds; 1. Violation of safe-conducts; 2. Infringement of the rights of ambassadors; and 3. Piracy." 4 W. BLACKSTONE, COMMENTARIES 68, 72, quoted in 1 W. W. CROSSKEY, POLITICS AND CONSTITUTION IN THE HISTORY OF THE UNITED STATES 459 (U. Chicago Press 1953). One might suppose that these were the kinds of offenses for which Congress wished to provide tort jurisdiction for suits by aliens in order to avoid conflicts with other nations.

The Constitution, of course, gave particular attention to piracy and to the rights of ambassadors [refers, inter alia, to Article I, section 8 and Article III, section 2]. …

These thoughts as to the possible original intention underlying section 1350 are admittedly speculative, and those who enacted the law may well have had additional torts in mind. I offer these possibilities merely to show that the statute could have served a useful purpose even if the larger tasks assigned it by Filartiga and Judge Edwards are rejected. …

Congress' understanding of the "law of nations" in 1789 is relevant to a consideration of whether Congress, by enacting section 1350, intended to open the federal courts to the vindication of the violation of any right recognized by international law. Examining the meaning of the "law of nations" at the time does not, contrary to my colleague's charges, "avoid the dictates of The Paquete Habana" and "limit the 'law of nations' to its 18th Century definition." Edwards' op. at 29. The substantive rules of international law may evolve and perhaps courts may apply those new rules, but that does not solve the problem of the existence of a cause of action. …

V.

Whether current international law itself gives appellants a cause of action requires more extended discussion. Appellants' claim, in Count II of their complaint, is that appellees have committed the "torts of terror, torture, hostage-taking and genocide," Brief for Appellants at 29, in violation of various customary principles of international law. Such principles become law by virtue of the "general assent of civilized nations." The Paquete Habana, 175 U.S. at 694. Unlike treaties and statutes, such law is not authoritatively pronounced by promulgation in a written document but must be found in the "customs and usages of civilized nations" as evidenced by the works of "jurists and commentators." Id. at 700; see Statute of the International Court of Justice, art. 38, 59 Stat. 1055 (1945), T.S. No. 993; Restatement of the Foreign Relations Law of the United States (Revised) §§ 102-103, at 24-38 (Tent. Draft No. 1, 1980). Consequently, any cause of action that might exist, like the precise meaning of the customary principles themselves, must be inferred from the sources that are evidence of and attempt to formulate the legal rules. The district court found, and appellants have not argued to the contrary, that none of the documents appellants have put forth as stating the international legal principles on which they rely expressly state that individuals can bring suit in municipal courts to enforce the specified rights. See 517 F. Supp. at 548-49. Moreover, we have been pointed to nothing in their language, structure, or circumstances of promulgation that suggests that any of those documents should be read as implicitly declaring that an individual should be able to sue in municipal courts to enforce the specified rights. In any event, there is no need to review those documents and their origins in further detail, for, as a general rule, international law does not provide a private right of action, and an exception to that rule would have to be demonstrated by clear evidence that civilized nations had generally given their assent to the exception. …

International law typically does not authorize individuals to vindicate rights by bringing actions in either international or municipal tribunals. " 'Like a general treaty, the law of nations has been held not to be self-executing so as to vest a plaintiff with individual legal rights. '" Dreyfus v. Von Finck, 534 F.2d 24, 31 (2nd Cir. 1974) quoting Pauling v. McElroy, 164 F. Supp. 390, 393(D.D.C. 1958). "The usual method for an individual to seek relief is to exhaust local remedies and then repair to the executive authorities of his own state to persuade them to champion his claim in diplomacy or before an international tribunal." Banco Nacional de Cuba v. Sabbatino, 376 U.S. at 422-23.

This general relegation of individuals to a derivative role in the vindication of their legal rights stems from "the traditional view of international law … that it establishes substantive principles for determining whether one country has wronged another." 376 U.S. at 422. …

International law, unlike municipal law (at least in the United States), is not widely regarded as a tool of first or frequent resort and as the last word in the legitimate resolution of conflicts. Nations rely chiefly on diplomacy and other political tools in their dealings with each other, and these means are frequently incompatible with declarations of legal rights. Diplomacy demands great flexibility and focuses primarily on the future rather than on the past, often requiring states to refrain, for the sake of their future relations, from pronouncing judgment on past conduct. ...

This remains true even as international law has become increasingly concerned with individual rights. Some of the rights specified in the documents relied upon by appellants as stating principles of international law recognizing individual rights are clearly not expected to be judicially enforced throughout the world. E.g., Universal Declaration of Human Rights ... (1948) (right to life, liberty, and security of person; right to freedom from arbitrary detention; right to leave country; right to practice religion; right to speak and assemble; right to freely elected government); International Covenant on Civil and Political Rights ... (1966) (similar list of rights); American Convention on Human Rights, Nov. 22, 1969 ... (similar list of rights). Some of the key documents are meant to be statements of ideals and aspirations only; they are, in short, merely precatory. ... Some expressly oblige states to enact implementing legislation, thus impliedly denying a private cause of action. E.g., International Covenant on Civil and Political Rights, art. 2, supra; American Convention on Human Rights, art. 2, supra.

It may be doubted that courts should understand documents of this sort as having been assented to as law by all civilized nations since enforcement of the principles enunciated would revolutionize most societies. For that reason, among others, courts should hesitate long before finding violations of a "law of nations" evidenced primarily by the resolutions and declarations of multinational bodies. ... Current international human rights law, in whatever sense it may be called "law," is doubtless growing. But it remains true that even that branch of international law does not today generally provide a private right of action.

Appellants, therefore, are not granted a private right of action to bring this lawsuit either by a specific international legal right or impliedly by the whole or parts of international law.

VI.

In Filartiga v. Pena-Irala, 630 F.2d 876 (2d Cir. 1980), the Second Circuit, which did not address the issue of the existence of a cause of action, held that section 1350 afforded jurisdiction over a claim brought by Paraguayan citizens against a former Paraguayan official. The plaintiffs, a father and daughter, alleged that the defendant had tortured his son, her brother, in violation of international law's proscription of official torture. To highlight what I believe should be the basis for our holding, it is worth pointing out several significant differences between this case and Filartiga.

First, unlike the defendants in this case, the defendant in Filartiga was a state official acting in his official capacity. Second, the actions of the defendant in Filartiga were in violation of the constitution and laws of his state and were "wholly unratified by that nation's government." 630 F.2d at 889. Third, the international law rule invoked in Filartiga was the proscription of official torture, a principle that is embodied in numerous international conventions and declarations, that is "clear and unambiguous" in its application to the facts in Filartiga, id. at 884, and about which there is universal agreement "in the modern usage and practice of nations." Id. at 883.

Thus, in Filartiga the defendant was clearly the subject of international-law duties, the challenged actions were not attributed to a participant in American foreign relations, and the relevant international law principle was one whose definition was neither disputed nor politically sensitive. None of that can be said about this case. For these reasons, not all of the analysis employed here would apply to deny a cause of action to the plaintiffs in Filartiga.

I differ with the Filartiga decision, however, because the court there did not address the question whether international law created a cause of action that the private parties before it could enforce in municipal courts. For the reasons given, that inquiry is essential.

* * *

The meandering course of U.S. case law dealing with international human rights law and its enforcement is continued in a case arising from the violent context of Bosnia-Herzegovina.

c. Kadic v. Karadzic

70 F.3d 232 (2d Cir. 1995)

NEWMAN, C.J.: The plaintiffs-appellants are Croat and Muslim citizens of the internationally recognized nation of Bosnia-Herzegovina, formerly a republic of Yugoslavia. Their complaints, which we accept as true for purposes of this appeal, allege that they are victims, and representatives of victims, of various atrocities, including brutal acts of rape, forced prostitution, forced impregnation, torture, and summary execution, carried out by Bosnian-Serb military forces as part of a genocidal campaign conducted in the course of the Bosnian civil war. Karadzic, formerly a citizen of Yugoslavia and now a citizen of Bosnia-Herzegovina, is the President of a three-man presidency of the self-proclaimed Bosnian-Serb republic within Bosnia-Herzegovina, sometimes referred to as "Srpska," which claims to exercise lawful authority, and does in fact exercise actual control, over large parts of the territory of Bosnia-Herzegovina. In his capacity as President, Karadzic possesses ultimate command authority over the Bosnian-Serb military forces, and the injuries perpetrated upon plaintiffs were committed as part of a pattern of systematic human rights violations that was directed by Karadzic and carried out by the military forces under his command. The complaints allege that Karadzic acted in an official capacity either as the titular head of Srpska or in collaboration with the government of the recognized nation of the former Yugoslavia and its dominant constituent republic, Serbia.

The two groups of plaintiffs asserted causes of action for genocide, rape, forced prostitution and impregnation, torture and other cruel, inhuman, and degrading treatment, assault and battery, sex and ethnic inequality, summary execution, and wrongful death. They sought compensatory and punitive damages, attorney's fees, and, in one of the cases, injunctive relief. Plaintiffs grounded subject-matter jurisdiction in the Alien Tort Act, the Torture Victim Protection Act of 1991 ("Torture Victim Act"), Pub.L. No. 102- 256, 106 Stat. 73 (1992), codified at 28 U.S.C. § 1350 note (Supp. V 1993), the general federal-question jurisdictional statute, 28 U.S.C. § 1331 (1988), and principles of supplemental jurisdiction, 28 U.S.C. § 1367 (Supp. V 1993).

In early 1993, Karadzic was admitted to the United States on three separate occasions as an invitee of the United Nations. According to affidavits submitted by the plaintiffs, Karadzic was personally served with the summons and complaint in each action during two of these visits while he was physically present in Manhattan. Karadzic admits that he received the summons and complaint in the Kadic action, but disputes whether the attempt to serve him personally in the Doe action was effective. ...

Karadzic contends that appellants have not alleged violations of the norms of international law because such norms bind only states and persons acting under color of a state's law, not private individuals. In making this contention, Karadzic advances the contradictory positions that he is not a state actor, ... even as he asserts that he is the President of the self-proclaimed Republic of Srpska. ...

We do not agree that the law of nations, as understood in the modern era, confines its reach to state action. Instead, we hold that certain forms of conduct violate the law of nations whether undertaken by those acting under the auspices of a state or only as private individuals. An early example of the application of the law of nations to the acts of private individuals is the prohibition against piracy. Later examples are prohibitions against the slave trade and certain war crimes.

The liability of private persons for certain violations of customary international law and the availability of the Alien Tort Act to remedy such violations was early recognized by the Executive Branch in an opinion of Attorney General Bradford in reference to acts of American citizens aiding the French fleet to plunder British property off the coast of Sierra Leone in 1795. See Breach of Neutrality, 1 Op. Att'y Gen. 57, 59 (1795). The Executive Branch has emphatically restated in this litigation its position that private persons may be found liable under the Alien Tort Act for acts of genocide, war crimes, and other violations of international humanitarian law. See Statement of Interest of the United States at 5-13.

The Restatement (Third) of the Foreign Relations Law of the United States (1986) proclaims: "Individuals may be held liable for offenses against international law, such as piracy, war crimes, and genocide." Restatement (Third) pt. II, introductory note. The Restatement is careful to identify those violations that are actionable when committed by a state, Restatement (Third) § 702, and a more limited category of violations of "universal concern," id. § 404, partially overlapping with those listed in section 702. Though the immediate focus of section 404 is to identify those offenses for which a state has jurisdiction to punish without regard to territoriality or the nationality of the offenders, cf. id. § 402(1)(a), (2), the inclusion of piracy and slave trade from an earlier era and aircraft hijacking from the modern era demonstrates that the offenses of "universal concern" include those capable of being committed by non-state actors. Although the jurisdiction authorized by section 404 is usually exercised by application of criminal law, international law also permits states to establish appropriate civil remedies, id. § 404 cmt. b, such as the tort actions authorized by the Alien Tort Act. Indeed, the two cases invoking the Alien Tort Act prior to Filartiga both applied the civil remedy to private action.

Karadzic disputes the application of the law of nations to any violations committed by private individuals. …

(a) Genocide. … The Convention on the Prevention and Punishment of the Crime of Genocide, 78 U.N.T.S. 277, entered into force Jan. 12, 1951, for the United States Feb. 23, 1989 (hereinafter "Convention on Genocide"), provides a more specific articulation of the prohibition of genocide in international law [provides language of Article II] … Especially pertinent to the pending appeal, the Convention makes clear that "[p]ersons committing genocide ... shall be punished, whether they are constitutionally responsible rulers, public officials or private individuals." Id. art. IV (emphasis added). These authorities unambiguously reflect that, from its incorporation into international law, the proscription of genocide has applied equally to state and non-state actors. …

(b) War crimes. … The offenses alleged by the appellants, if proved, would violate the most fundamental norms of the law of war embodied in common article 3, which binds parties to internal conflicts regardless of whether they are recognized nations or roving hordes of insurgents. The liability of private individuals for committing war crimes has been recognized since World War I and was confirmed at Nuremberg after World War II, see Telford Taylor, Nuremberg Trials: War Crimes and International Law, 450 Int'l Conciliation 304 (April 1949) (collecting cases), and remains today an important aspect of international law, see Jordan Paust, After My Lai: The Case for War Crimes Jurisdiction Over Civilians in Federal District Courts, in 4 The Vietnam War and International Law 447 (R. Falk ed., 1976). The District Court has jurisdiction pursuant to the Alien Tort Act over appellants' claims of war crimes and other violations of international humanitarian law.

(c) Torture and summary execution. In Filartiga, we held that official torture is prohibited by universally accepted norms of international law, see 630 F.2d at 885, and the Torture Victim Act confirms this holding and extends it to cover summary execution. Torture Victim Act §§ 2(a), 3(a). However, torture and summary execution—when not perpetrated in the course of genocide or war crimes—are proscribed by international law only when committed by state officials or under color of law. See Declaration on Torture art. 1 (defining torture as being "inflicted by or at the instigation of a public official"); Convention Against Torture and Other Cruel, Inhuman, or Degrading Treatment or Punishment pt. I, art. 1, 23 I.L.M. 1027 (1984), as modified, 24 I.L.M. 535 (1985), entered into force June 26, 1987, ratified by United States Oct. 21, 1994, 34 I.L.M. 590, 591 (1995) (defining torture as "inflicted by or at the instigation of or with the consent or acquiescence of a public official or other person acting in an official capacity"); Torture Victim Act § 2(a) (imposing liability on individuals acting "under actual or apparent authority, or color of law, of any foreign nation"). ...

It suffices to hold at this stage that the alleged atrocities are actionable under the Alien Tort Act, without regard to state action, to the extent that they were committed in pursuit of genocide or war crimes, and otherwise may be pursued against Karadzic to the extent that he is shown to be a state actor. ...

Appellants contend that they are entitled to prove that Srpska satisfies the definition of a state for purposes of international law violations and, alternatively, that Karadzic acted in concert with the recognized state of the former Yugoslavia and its constituent republic, Serbia. ...

Although the Restatement's definition of statehood requires the capacity to engage in formal relations with other states, it does not require recognition by other states. Recognized states enjoy certain privileges and immunities relevant to judicial proceedings. Our courts have regularly given effect to the "state" action of unrecognized states.

The customary international law of human rights, such as the proscription of official torture, applies to states without distinction between recognized and unrecognized states. See Restatement (Third) §§ 207, 702. It would be anomalous indeed if non-recognition by the United States, which typically reflects disfavor with a foreign regime — sometimes due to human rights abuses — had the perverse effect of shielding officials of the unrecognized regime from liability for those violations of international law norms that apply only to state actors.

Appellants' allegations entitle them to prove that Karadzic's regime satisfies the criteria for a state, for purposes of those international law violations requiring state action. Srpska is alleged to control defined territory, control populations within its power, and to have entered into agreements with other governments. It has a president, a legislature, and its own currency. These circumstances readily appear to satisfy the criteria for a state in all aspects of international law. Moreover, it is likely that the state action concept, where applicable for some violations like "official" torture, requires merely the semblance of official authority. The inquiry, after all, is whether a person purporting to wield official power has exceeded internationally recognized standards of civilized conduct, not whether statehood in all its formal aspects exists. ...

Appellants also sufficiently alleged that Karadzic acted under color of law insofar as they claimed that he acted in concert with the former Yugoslavia, the statehood of which is not disputed. The "color of law" jurisprudence of 42 U.S.C. § 1983 is a relevant guide to whether a defendant has engaged in official action for purposes of jurisdiction under the Alien Tort Act. A private individual acts under color of law within the meaning of section 1983 when he acts together with state officials or with significant state aid. The appellants are entitled to prove their allegations that Karadzic acted under color of law of Yugoslavia by acting in concert with Yugoslav officials or with significant Yugoslavian aid.

B. The Torture Victim Protection Act

The Torture Victim Act, enacted in 1992, provides a cause of action for official torture and extrajudicial killing:

> An individual who, under actual or apparent authority, or color of law, of any foreign nation—
>
> (1) subjects an individual to torture shall, in a civil action, be liable for damages to that individual; or
>
> (2) subjects an individual to extrajudicial killing shall, in a civil action, be liable for damages to the individual's legal representative, or to any person who may be a claimant in an action for wrongful death.

Torture Victim Act § 2(a). The statute also requires that a plaintiff exhaust adequate and available local remedies, id. § 2(b), imposes a ten-year statute of limitations, id. § 2(c), and defines the terms "extrajudicial killing" and "torture," id. § 3.

By its plain language, the Torture Victim Act renders liable only those individuals who have committed torture or extrajudicial killing "under actual or apparent authority, or color of law, of any foreign nation." Legislative history confirms that this language was intended to "make[ ] clear that the plaintiff must establish some governmental involvement in the torture or killing to prove a claim," and that the statute "does not attempt to deal with torture or killing by purely private groups." H.R.Rep. No. 367, 102d Cong., 2d Sess., at 5 (1991), reprinted in 1992 U.S.C.C.A.N. 84, 87. In construing the terms "actual or apparent authority" and "color of law," courts are instructed to look to principles of agency law and to jurisprudence under 42 U.S.C. § 1983, respectively. Id.

Though the Torture Victim Act creates a cause of action for official torture, this statute, unlike the Alien Tort Act, is not itself a jurisdictional statute. The Torture Victim Act permits the appellants to pursue their claims of official torture under the jurisdiction conferred by the Alien Tort Act and also under the general federal question jurisdiction of section 1331. ...

II. Service of Process and Personal Jurisdiction

Appellants aver that Karadzic was personally served with process while he was physically present in the Southern District of New York. In the Doe action, the affidavits detail that on February 11, 1993, process servers approached Karadzic in the lobby of the Hotel Intercontinental at 111 East 48th St. in Manhattan, called his name and identified their purpose, and attempted to hand him the complaint from a distance of two feet, that security guards seized the complaint papers, and that the papers fell to the floor. Karadzic submitted an affidavit of a State Department security officer, who generally confirmed the episode, but stated that the process server did not come closer than six feet of the defendant. In the Kadic action, the plaintiffs obtained from Judge Owen an order for alternate means of service, directing service by delivering the complaint to a member of defendant's State Department security detail, who was ordered to hand the complaint to the defendant. The security officer's affidavit states that he received the complaint and handed it to Karadzic outside the Russian Embassy in Manhattan. Karadzic's statement confirms that this occurred during his second visit to the United States, sometime between February 27 and March 8, 1993. Appellants also allege that during his visits to New York City, Karadzic stayed at hotels outside the "headquarters district" of the United Nations and engaged in non-United Nations-related activities such as fund-raising.

Fed.R.Civ.P. 4(e)(2) specifically authorizes personal service of a summons and complaint upon an individual physically present within a judicial district of the United States, and such personal service comports with the requirements of due process for the assertion of personal jurisdiction.

Nevertheless, Karadzic maintains that his status as an invitee of the United Nations during his visits to the United States rendered him immune from service of process. He relies on both the Agreement Between the United Nations and the United States of America Regarding the Headquarters of the United Nations, reprinted at 22 U.S.C. § 287 note (1988) ("Headquarters Agreement"), and a claimed federal common law immunity. We reject both bases for immunity from service. …

In sum, if appellants personally served Karadzic with the summons and complaint while he was in New York but outside of the U.N. headquarters district, as they are prepared to prove, he is subject to the personal jurisdiction of the District Court.

NOTES AND QUESTIONS

1. Access to federal court is provided by the Alien Tort Claims Act, 28 U.S.C. §1350, originally included in the Judiciary Act of 1789. How does the difficulty in discerning legislative history of this enactment affect the various opinions rendered? Why did it remain in relative obscurity until *Filartiga*?

2. Is *Filartiga* sound policy? Should U.S. courts act as an international ombudsman? What effect will *Filartiga*-type decisions have on anti-humanitarian practices in foreign states? Do they support a trend toward universal jurisdiction regarding the enforcement of human rights prescriptions? *See* Beth Stephens, *Translating Filartiga: A Comparative and International Law Analysis of Domestic Remedies for International Human Rights Violations*, 27 YALE J. INT'L L. 1 (2002); Beth van Schaack, *In Defense of Civil Redress: The Domestic Enforcement of Human Rights Norms in the Context of the Proposed Hague Judgments Convention*, 42 HARV. INT'L L. J. 141 (2001).

3. What, exactly, separates the opinions of Judges Kaufman and Newman from the one rendered by Judge Bork? Does international law include the right to an effective remedy? In domestic courts?

4. Does Judge Bork imply that international law applies only between states? Or does it only bind states, as opposed to individuals? Note the development on this issue in Chief Judge Newman's opinion.

5. What is the effect of opening up U.S. courts to a volatile situation on the ground? Consider the situation in war-torn Bosnia and *Kadic v. Karadzic*. Theodore Posner analyzed the Kadic opinion in 90 AM. J. INT'L L. 658 (1996).

6. The Second Circuit carefully distinguished *Tel-Oren* and *Amerada Hess*, first, by classifying Mr. Karadzic as a non-state actor not shielded by immunity of states or state agencies under the Foreign Sovereign Immunities Act (FSIA); second, by holding that individual non-state actors are capable of violating international law prohibiting genocide and war crimes; and third, by holding that a U.S. district court may exercise jurisdiction under the Alien Tort Claims Act (ATCA) over a non-state actor accused of these offenses. Is this opinion convincing? Why wouldn't Mr. Karadzic qualify as President of the Bosnian-Serb Republic (Republika Srpska) and thus enjoy immunities accorded a head of state? Does the FSIA only apply to state agencies and instrumentalities? After *Amerada Hess*, other lower courts have held that FSIA immunity also applies to individuals acting as agents of the state. *Chuidian v. Philippine Nat'l Bank*, 912 F.2d 1095, 1102 (9th Cir. 1990); *Herbage v. Meese*, 747 F.Supp. 60, 66-67 (D.D.C. 1990), *aff'd*, 947 F.2d 1564 (D.C. Cir. 1991).

7. Why should torture, for purposes of establishing U.S. courts' jurisdiction, be treated as a crime that can be committed only by state actors, while genocide and war crimes can be committed by non-state actors as well?

8. What is the effect of allowing service of process on officials of foreign states visiting the United Nations under the Headquarters Agreement? *See* Mary Margaret Penrose, *It's Good to Be the King: Prosecuting Heads of State and Former Heads of State under International Law*, 39 COLUM. J. TRANSNAT'L L. 193 (2000-2001).

d. Hawa Abdi Jama v. United States I.N.S.

22 F. SUPP.2D 353 (D.N.J. 1998)

DEBEVOISE, J.: Plaintiffs, aliens who sought asylum and who were detained at a facility in Elizabeth, New Jersey, brought this action against defendants Correctional Services Corporation, a number of its officers and employees, the United States Immigration and Naturalization Service ("INS"), and various INS officials, alleging mistreatment while detained in that facility and asserting claims under federal, state and international law. The INS moves to dismiss the complaint under Fed.R.Civ.P. 12(b)(1) and 12(b)(6) or, in the alternative, for summary judgment. ...

The allegations of the amended complaint can be summarized as follows:

Every moment of plaintiffs' detention was filled with abuse. They could not escape from these abuses even in their dreams, as they were not permitted to sleep—bright lights shone on them 24 hours a day, and guards woke them up just to taunt them.

Esmor's layout contributed to and exacerbated the unrelenting abuses defendants inflicted on plaintiffs. Esmor was separated into several dormitories which were filthy and constantly smelled of human waste and other noxious odors. … Between twenty and forty asylees were packed into each room, which lacked natural light, telephones, and recreational materials ... The rooms were separated from each other and the communal hallways by thick dark glass so that persons in the halls could peer into the dormitories. ... The dorms were not cleaned by defendants and were filthy. ... In response to plaintiffs' repeated requests for cleaning materials, the guards beat plaintiffs. …

The shower and toilet in each dormitory were in the same room as the eating and sleeping areas, forcing the plaintiffs to eat meals only inches away from the bathroom areas. ... Thus, as they ate, plaintiffs could observe and smell other detainees using the toilets. ... Additionally, the bathroom facilities had no curtain or divider—allowing the other asylees, guards and anyone passing in the hallway to observe the naked bodies of the plaintiffs who were using the toilets and taking showers. ... This was traumatic, humiliating and degrading to many detainees particularly the women, many of whom had never exposed their bodies to anyone before. … When women detainees showered, guards made crude sexual comments about their bodies. This exacerbated the women plaintiffs' feelings of shame and humiliation. ...

In a variety of ways defendants physically, mentally and sexually abused plaintiffs. In addition to beating them they yelled racial and ethnic epithets at them such as "African Monkeys" from the "jungle". ... The guards woke plaintiffs before sunrise and forced them to stand facing a wall, with their legs spread, for up to an hour at a time. ... Upon searching male plaintiffs' genital areas the guards forcefully yanked their genitals causing severe pain. There was inappropriate touching of both male and female plaintiffs. ... Sexual favors were sought of female plaintiffs. ...

Defendants deprived plaintiffs of clothing and personal hygiene necessities. ... Changes of clothing were infrequent and the clothing provided was often filthy and could not be worn. ...

Defendants served spoiled food and insufficient amounts. The kitchen served rotten meat and sour milk. … Esmor officials and guards ordered detainees not to report food problems to INS inspectors who visited the facility. ...

Guards regularly locked plaintiffs in solitary confinement cells without warning or explanation, without a hearing, ranging from several days to several months. The defendants often shackled plaintiffs to their beds. ...

Guards performed strip searches and body cavity searches in a manner designed to degrade and humiliate plaintiffs. ...

Defendants prevented plaintiffs from practicing their religious rituals. ... Defendants forced plaintiffs to work without compensation. ... They took plaintiffs' property and never returned it. Guards stole money from plaintiffs. ...

Plaintiffs were denied adequate medical treatment. ... They were denied access to legal representation. For example, guards, without any justification, often would refuse to allow plaintiffs to use the telephone to discuss their asylum cases with their counsel. ... Additionally, defendants continuously failed to transport plaintiffs promptly to their asylum hearings. ... As a result, plaintiffs often missed important asylum meetings (which resulted in a postponement of their asylum hearings) and prolonged their detention at Esmor. ... Moreover, female detainees were forced to choose between being sexually assaulted and contacting their lawyers, as guards premised using the telephones on submitting to their unwanted sexual advances. ...

Plaintiffs allege that at all times during the events that gave rise to the complaint the individual Esmor defendants were employees and agents of both Esmor and the INS. They also assert that Esmor officers and INS officials either were or should have been aware of the pattern of abuses taking place at the Esmor facility.

The Esmor facility was closed after a revolt by the detainees on June 18, 1995. Some of the plaintiffs are still subject to detention at other facilities; some have been granted political asylum, and some have been deported.

On the basis of their factual allegations, plaintiffs assert numerous claims against each category of defendants. Counts 68-84 accuse the Esmor guards of violations of the First, Fifth, and Thirteenth Amendments to the United States Constitution, numerous provisions of the New Jersey Constitution, the ICCPR, customary international law, the ATCA, the RFRA, the Fair Labor Standards Act, and New Jersey law. ....

In counts 50-67 plaintiffs make corresponding allegations against Esmor officers - predicating the officers' liability for the actions of the guards on "failing to curb" the pattern of abuse, on "deliberate indifference," and, in the case of the New Jersey tort law claims, on theories of respondeat superior and of negligent hiring, training, and supervision.

The claims against Esmor as a corporation (counts 31-49) are equivalent to those against the Esmor officers, with the addition of a breach of contract claim (count 33) alleging that the plaintiffs' were third-party beneficiaries of Esmor's contract with the INS and that they were harmed by Esmor's breach of that contract. ....

In counts 13-30 plaintiffs invoke the same rights against the INS officials as they do against the Esmor officers - advancing theories of liability based on omissions - "failing to curb" and "deliberate indifference." ....

Finally, in counts 1-12 plaintiffs assert claims against the INS - invoking New Jersey tort and contract law, the ICCPR, customary international law, the RFRA, and the ATCA. In all counts other than those invoking New Jersey law, INS liability is predicated upon its failure to curb abuses at the Esmor facility. ....

ANALYSIS

I. Claims Under International Law

Plaintiffs rely heavily upon international law to establish claims against all of the defendants, including the INS and its officers. This might seem like an unnecessary journey in view of the state and federal law remedies which at least at the outset were available to plaintiffs. Since some of those remedies may have slipped from their grasp, however, it is necessary to examine the international law claims. This involves a two step process. The first step is to determine if plaintiffs have a claim under international law. If they do have such a claim the second step is to determine whether it may be asserted against the various categories of defendants in this case.

28 U.S.C. § 1350 ("ATCA") provides that "The district courts shall have original jurisdiction of any civil action by an alien for a tort only, committed in violation of the law of nations or a treaty of the United States." Plaintiffs have included among their papers in opposition to the motion to dismiss nineteen treaties, charters on human rights, conventions and other international instruments articulating the rights of refugees and seekers of asylum and condemning or prohibiting in general or specific terms many of the kinds of abuses which are alleged in the complaint.

In order for a treaty to confer rights enforceable by private parties it must be self-executing, that is, a treaty which requires no legislation to make it operative. *Frolova v. Union of Soviet Socialist Republics*, 761 F.2d 370 (7th Cir.1985). Unless a treaty is self-executing, it must be implemented by legislation before it can give rise to a private right of action enforceable in a court of the United States. *Dreyfus v. Van Fink*, 534 F.2d 24 (2d Cir.1976), cert. denied, 429 U.S. 835 (1976).

None of the treaties or other international instruments which plaintiffs have submitted are self-executing. Plaintiffs recognize that these treaties do not per se provide a basis for suit under the ATCA. Rather, they are submitted for another purpose — to support a claim under the "law of nations" or international law, which is also a basis for an ATCA action: "The complaint alleges violations of customary international law and not specific treaties... ...."

In *Filartiga v. Pena-Irala*, 630 F.2d 876 (2nd Cir.1980) the court breathed new life into the ATCA. Originally enacted in 1789, it held that "[t]he constitutional basis for the Alien Tort Statute is the law of nations, which has always been part of the federal common law" Id. at 885, and that "courts must interpret international law not as it was in 1789, but as it has evolved and exists among the nations of the world today." Id at 881. "[E]volving standards of international law govern who is within the [Alien Tort Act's] jurisdictional grant." *Amerada Hess Shipping Corp. v. Argentine Republic,* 830 F.2d 421, 425 (2nd Cir.1987), rev'd on other grounds, 488 U.S. 428 (1989). Depending upon the nature of the offense, an ATCA claim may be brought against private individuals as well as state actors. *Kadic v. Karadzic*, 70 F.3d 232 (2nd Cir.1995), cert. denied, 518 U.S. 1005 (1996).

Many courts have concluded that the ATCA provides both jurisdiction and a cause of action for claims under customary international law. ...

Not all jurists interpret the ATCA as broadly as these courts and the Court of Appeals for the Second Circuit ... However, Congress has left untouched the *Filartiga* approach even as it legislated in this field. The Torture Victim Act, enacted in 1992, for example, creates a cause of action for official torture and extrajudicial killing. "Congress enacted the Torture Victim Act to codify the cause of action recognized by this Circuit in *Filartiga,* and to further extend that cause of action to plaintiffs who are U.S. citizens." *Kadic*, 70 F.3d at 241. The reasoning of *Filartiga* and cases which have followed it is sound, and it will be followed in this case.

For the purposes of the present motions, the allegations of the complaint must be accepted as true and all reasonable inferences favorable to plaintiffs must be drawn from them. When this is done, it is evident that the totality of the treatment to which plaintiffs were subjected violated customary international law as it is now established. A multitude of sources establishes this rule of international law, and the references below are by way of example only. ...

A number of international instruments prescribe cruel, unhuman or degrading treatment. For example, the European Convention on the Protection of Human Rights and Fundamental Freedom, Nov. 4, 1950, Europ. T.S. 5, 213 U.N.T.S. 221, 224 (1956) provides that "[n]o one shall be subjected to torture or to inhuman or degrading treatment or punishment." The United States has recognized this customary international human rights norm. In *United States v. Iran*, 1980 I.C.J. 3, the United States argued that even though at that time neither the United States nor Iran had ratified treaties proscribing such conduct, they were nevertheless bound by the norm.

American Courts have recognized that the right to be free from cruel, unhuman or degrading treatment is a universally accepted customary human rights norm. ... Each of these cases involved extreme forms of abuse, but the entirety of the conduct in which the Esmor guards were alleged to have engaged over a considerable period of time approaches the abuses in certain of these cases and would clearly violate the Eighth Amendment's prohibition against cruel and unusual punishment. ...

The mental and physical abuses which are alleged to have been inflicted upon plaintiffs violate the international human rights norm of the right to be free from cruel, unhuman and degrading treatment. The ATCA confers federal subject matter jurisdiction when i) an alien sues, ii) for a tort iii) committed in violation of the law of nations (i.e., international law), *Kadic*, 70 F.3d at 238. The complaint sufficiently alleges all three jurisdictional requirements. ...

Defendants contend that because United States laws provide constitutional and legislative protection which afford plaintiffs adequate relief, plaintiffs are precluded from bringing international law claims under the ATCA.

Contrary to defendants' argument, there is no absolute preclusion of international law claims by the availability of domestic remedies for the same alleged harm. ...

Perhaps if there were domestic law in conflict with the norms of international law, domestic law should prevail. That is not the case here where domestic law is consistent with international norms. There is nothing in the ATCA which limits its application to situations where there is no relief available under domestic law. There is no reason why plaintiffs cannot seek relief on alternative grounds. ...

The second step in the ATCA analysis is to determine whether the various defendants are subject to suit under the statute. The defendant categories are: i) the INS, ii) officials of the INS, iii) Esmor, iv) supervisory employees of Esmor and v) the guards who are alleged to have committed the abuses.

1. INS: The INS moves to dismiss the ATCA claims against it because the United States has not waived its sovereign immunity with respect to that statute. Absent a specific waiver of such immunity the United States and its agencies are immune from suit and courts lack jurisdiction over them. FDIC v. Meyer, 510 U.S. 471, 474-75 (1994). ...

The intent to waive sovereign immunity must be expressed in clear, unambiguous language. It is difficult to discern an unambiguous waiver (or even an ambiguous waiver) when the Senate ratified the ICCPR, stated that it was not self-executing and made no mention of the 200 year old ATCA.

The United States has not waived its sovereign immunity under the ATCA. *See Sanchez-Espinoza v. Reagan*, 770 F.2d 202, 206-07 (D.C.Cir.1985) *citing Canadian Transp. Co. v. United States*, 663 F.2d 1081, 1092, (D.C.Cir.1980)(holding that even if customary international law may be applied to foreign sovereigns under the ATCA as interpreted in *Filartiga v. Pena-Irala,* 630 F.2d 876 (2d Cir.1980), it cannot be applied to the United States, as there is no waiver of immunity). The ATCA, in providing jurisdiction and a right of action under the law of nations, does nothing to displace sovereign immunity, and plaintiffs' claims against the INS based on the ATCA must be dismissed.

2. INS Officials: Plaintiffs sue the INS officials in their individual capacities, alleging that they failed to ensure that the plaintiffs were not treated in the manner previously described and that they acted with deliberate indifference to the wrongs committed against plaintiffs.

The INS officials contend that none of the acts with which they are charged constitute violations of customary international law. They allege that Esmor operated the facility under a contract and that there is no allegation in the First Amended Complaint that the INS officials either in their individual or official capacities had the authority or ability to manage the facility. At this stage in the proceedings it would be premature to hold as a matter of law that plaintiffs cannot prove that the INS officials violated customary international law. The viability of plaintiffs' ATCA claim against the INS officials had best be decided in the context of a motion for summary judgment.

The INS officials also claim the protection of sovereign immunity citing *Sanchez-Espinoza v. Reagan*, 770 F.2d 202 (D.C.Cir.1985). The facts of the present case are substantially different from those in *Sanchez*. The INS officials are being sued in their individual capacities and are not entitled to sovereign immunity. Melo v. Hafer, 912 F.2d 628, 634-35 (3d Cir.1990).

The motions of the INS officials to dismiss the ATCA claims will be denied.

3. Esmor, Its Officials, Directors and Employees: These categories of defendants move for dismissal of the claims based on international law. …

It should be noted that Esmor, its officers, directors and employees (including the guards) were acting under contract with the INS and were performing governmental services. Thus they were state actors and it is unnecessary to address the question raised in *Kadic*, namely the extent to which non-state actors can be sued under the ATCA.

All of the other contentions of the Esmor defendants were addressed above and decided adversely to them. Consequently, their motion to dismiss the ATCA claims will be denied. ...

Notes and Questions

1. What is the exact novelty in the Court's holding? Is it in line with *Filartiga, Tel-Oren* and *Kadic v. Karadzic*? How would Judge Bork address this case?

e. Presbyterian Church of Sudan v. Talisman Energy, Inc.
244 F.Supp.2d 289 (S.D.N.Y. 2003)

Plaintiffs, current and former residents of the Republic of the Sudan … bring this purported class action against Talisman Energy, Inc. ("Talisman") and Sudan, alleging violations of international law stemming from oil exploration activities conducted in that country. Specifically, plaintiffs allege that defendants collaborated to commit gross human rights violations, including extrajudicial killing, forcible displacement, war crimes, confiscation and destruction of property, kidnapping, rape, and enslavement. Collectively, plaintiffs claim that these activities amount to genocide. … Talisman's motion to dismiss is denied.

Talisman Energy, Inc. is the largest independent Canadian oil producer and is headquartered in Calgary, Alberta. … It conducts activities throughout the world, with operations in Canada, the United States, the North Sea, Indonesia, Algeria, Trinidad, Colombia, and Sudan. ...

Talisman commenced its operations in Sudan in October 1998. … Plaintiffs contend that Talisman worked with the Government to devise a plan of security for the oil fields and related facilities. ... Talisman hired its own military advisors to coordinate military strategy with the Government. ... Specifically, Talisman would have regular meetings with Sudan's army intelligence unit and the Ministry of Energy and Mining during which the parties would discuss "how to dispose of civilians" in areas in which Talisman intended to operate. ... Based on the joint Talisman-Government strategy, "Government troops and allied militia engaged in an ethnic cleansing operation to execute, enslave or displace the non-Muslim, African Sudanese civilian population from areas that are near the pipeline or where Talisman wanted to drill." ... Talisman was and is aware that Government's "protection" of oil operations entailed "ethnic cleansing" or genocide, including the murder of substantial numbers of civilians (including women and children); the destruction of civilian residences and villages; and the capture and enslavement of civilians who survived the military attacks. ... Defendants' concerted actions are purportedly demonstrated by, *inter alia,* a May 7, 1999 communication from the Government's Petroleum Security Office in Khartoum to a satellite office in Heglig. ... This directive, denominated as "very urgent," reads as follows:

> In accordance with directives of His Excellency the Minister of Energy and Mining and fulfilling the request of the Canadian Company...the armed forces will conduct cleaning up operations in all villages from Heglig to Pariang.

Plaintiffs claim that thousands of villages and at least seventeen churches were destroyed in the areas surrounding Talisman's oil fields, and that one, el-Toor, was located within walking distance of a Talisman site. ...

Plaintiffs claim the Presbyterian Church's churches have been bombed and destroyed and that its church leaders and parishioners have been displaced by Government forces because of their religion and proximity to the oil fields. ...

Talisman contends that the Court lacks subject matter jurisdiction because corporations are legally incapable of violating the laws of nations. It argues that international law applies to states and in some cases to individuals, but that "the law of nations simply does not encompass principles of corporate liability." ... Talisman relies primarily on affidavits submitted by two renowned international law scholars, James Crawford and Christopher Greenwood. Both scholars, consulting a variety of international sources, conclude that there is no basis in existing international law for the liability of corporations. Nonetheless, a considerable body of United States and international precedent indicates that corporations may be liable for violations of international law, particularly when their actions constitute *jus cogens* violations.

a. United States Precedent

As noted *supra,* interpretations of international law of the Supreme Court and Second Circuit are binding upon this Court. Talisman fails to cite a single Supreme Court, Second Circuit, or even Southern District of New York case holding that a corporation is "legally incapable of violating the law of nations." … Similarly, Messrs. Crawford and Greenwood, while citing a variety of international law sources, fail to cite a single United States case upholding their position. In fact, numerous Second Circuit cases, as well as cases from courts outside the Second Circuit, make it clear that corporations can be held liable for *jus cogens* violations.

i. Second Circuit Precedent

Neither party cites any Supreme Court decision for the proposition that corporations are or are not potentially liable under the ATCA for violations of international law, nor is the Court aware of any such decision. Therefore, the Court is obligated to follow the Second Circuit's interpretation of international law. While the Supreme Court has not yet addressed the question of whether corporations may be liable for international law violations under the ATCA, the Second Circuit has. …

Kadic established that individuals, even those not acting under color of law, can be held liable for certain violations of the law of nations (i.e., *jus cogens* violations) whether or not they acted under color of state authority. In *Jota v. Texaco Inc.,* 157 F.3d 153 (2d Cir.1998), Ecuadorian residents brought a class action under the ATCA against a corporation, Texaco, for alleged environmental and personal injuries resulting from the corporation's exploitation of certain oil fields. The district court dismissed the suit on the basis of *forum non conveniens,* international comity, and failure to join an indispensable party. In *Jota,* the Second Circuit addressed these issues, and ultimately vacated the district court's decision and remanded the case. It did not explicitly address the question of subject matter jurisdiction, and the parties had apparently not raised the issue on appeal. However, "even when no party has questioned the court's subject matter jurisdiction, the court has the duty to dismiss *sua sponte* when such jurisdiction is lacking." … The fact that the Second Circuit did not address an obvious jurisdictional question *sua sponte* indicates that it had no reservations about the ATCA reaching the acts of corporations. The Second Circuit's holdings in later cases confirm this impression. Talisman's claim that in *Jota* and other cases the Second Circuit merely "assumed the possibility of liability" is not compelling, because subject matter jurisdiction, unlike other issues, represents the most fundamental question of whether a court has the legal power to hear a case, and a court has a duty to determine the issue of subject matter jurisdiction, whether or not the parties raise the issue. By reaching the merits in *Jota,* the Second Circuit tacitly acknowledged that subject matter jurisdiction lay in that case.

In *Wiwa v. Royal Dutch Petroleum Co.,* 226 F.3d 88 (2d Cir.2000), the Second Circuit again confronted a situation in which a corporation was sued under the ATCA. As in the instant case, the defendant was alleged to have committed violations of international human rights law. The court did not directly address the question of subject matter jurisdiction. As noted above, this fact indicates that the court believed that subject matter jurisdiction lay in that action.

Moreover, the Second Circuit reiterated its recent holding in *Kadic* that "the ATCA reaches the conduct of private parties provided that their conduct is undertaken under the color of state authority or violates a norm of international law that is recognized as extending to the conduct of private parties." *Wiwa, 226 F.3d at 104.* Both of the two defendants in *Wiwa* were private corporations. In light of that fact, *Wiwa* clearly extended the decision in *Kadic* to apply the ATCA to the acts of corporations that constitute *jus cogens* violations.

Only months after the *Wiwa* decision, the Second Circuit decided *Bigio v. Coca-Cola Co.,* 239 F.3d 440 (2d Cir.2000). In that case, Canadian citizens and an Egyptian corporation sued the Coca-Cola Company and the Coca-Cola Export Company (collectively, "Coca-Cola"), both Delaware corporations. The plaintiffs in *Bigio* stated that the Egyptian government had unlawfully seized their property in Egypt because they were Jewish. Coca-Cola then allegedly purchased or leased the plaintiffs' property with full knowledge of the unlawful manner in which it was seized. Unlike in *Jota* or *Wiwa,* in *Bigio* subject matter jurisdiction was squarely before the court: "if the complaint did not plead a violation of the law of nations by Coca-Cola, the district court was without subject matter jurisdiction under the Alien Tort Claims Act, and neither it nor we may consider the matter further under the Act." *Bigio, at 447.* The Second Circuit emphasized the centrality of the question of subject matter jurisdiction, stating that the "first issue we must address is whether Coca-Cola can have violated 'the law of nations' if it acted solely as a non-governmental entity." *Bigio, at 447.* The Second Circuit noted that the plaintiffs only alleged that Coca-Cola had acquired property that it knew had been discriminatorily expropriated. The Second Circuit rightly pointed out that although such discriminatory expropriation was "reprehensible," it was not an act of "universal concern" or a *jus cogens* violation. *Bigio, at 448.* Additionally, the Second Circuit found that the *Bigio* plaintiffs had not alleged that Coca-Cola conspired with the Egyptian government in conducting the unlawful expropriation.

The Second Circuit's reasoning in *Bigio* is instructive. Although it ultimately held that the district court lacked subject matter jurisdiction under the ATCA, it did so because it was unclear that the acts allegedly committed by Coca-Cola actually violated international law. At the very least, the court held, the acts alleged to have been committed by Coca-Cola only violated international law when committed by state actors. *See Bigio,* at 448. The *Bigio* court contrasted these acts with slave trading, genocide, and war crimes, citing *Kadic* and Restatement (Third) of Foreign Relations § 404 (1987). The clear implication is that subject matter jurisdiction would have existed if the *Bigio* plaintiffs had alleged *jus cogens* violations such as enslavement, genocide, or war crimes—exactly the acts alleged in the instant case—rather than procurement of unlawfully expropriated property.

The Second Circuit recently delivered an opinion in *Aguinda v. Texaco, Inc.,* 303 F.3d 470 (2d Cir.2002) which also involved a suit against a private corporation under the ATCA for alleged violations of international law. The court ultimately affirmed the district court's dismissal of the case on the basis of *forum non conveniens.* In so doing, however, the court merely held that Ecuador was the most convenient forum for the action; it did not hold that the action could not be brought in the Southern District of New York. Indeed, in deciding the *forum non conveniens* motion, the Second Circuit painstakingly weighed the various factors militating for and against trying the action in the United States. Such analysis would have been wholly superfluous if there was no subject matter jurisdiction to try the case in federal court in the first place. Thus, the recent *Aguinda* decision adds credence to the notion that corporations may be held liable for international law violations under the ATCA.

As noted, Talisman contends that the Second Circuit has never squarely addressed the question of whether corporations are potentially liable for international law violations under the ATCA. While the Second Circuit has not explicitly held that corporations are potentially liable for violations of the law of nations, it has considered numerous cases, as noted above, where a plaintiff sued a corporation under the ATCA for alleged breaches of international law: *Jota, Wiwa, Bigio,* and *Aguinda.* In each of these cases, the Second Circuit acknowledged that corporations are potentially liable for violations of the law of nations that ordinarily entail individual responsibility, including *jus cogens* violations.

ii. Other Circuit Precedent

In addition to Second Circuit precedent, other circuit courts have held that corporations may be held liable under the ATCA for certain international law violations. Earlier this year, the Ninth Circuit decided *Deutsch v. Turner Corp.,* 317 F.3d 1005 (9th Cir.2003). In that case, plaintiffs, who alleged that they had been forced to work as slave laborers during World War II, sued a myriad of German and Japanese corporations under various statutes, including the ATCA. The Ninth Circuit, while dismissing the ATCA claims on statute of limitations grounds, tacitly acknowledged subject matter jurisdiction by not addressing that issue *sua sponte. See Deutsch,* 317 F.3d at 1028-29.

The Ninth Circuit more explicitly recognized that a corporation could be sued under the ATCA in *Doe v. Unocal Corp.,* — F.3d ——, 2002 WL 31063976 (9th Cir. 2002).... The court, citing *Kadic,* held that because the complaint alleged *jus cogens* violations (including rape, torture, and summary execution), no state action was necessary and Unocal could be held liable. ... [In 2003, the Ninth Circuit ordered this case to be "reheard by the *en banc* court", ___F.3d___ 2003 WL 359787 (9th Cir.)]

The Fifth Circuit also confronted the issue of corporate liability under the ATCA in *Beanal v. Freeport-McMoran, Inc.,* 197 F.3d 161 (5th Cir.1999). The Fifth Circuit dismissed the ATCA claims, but did so based on the fact that the alleged acts, including surveillance, mental torture, death threats, house arrest, and environmental abuse did not clearly violate the law of nations. *See id.* at 165-66. The court did not question the fact that it had jurisdiction over the subject matter of the action. More than a decade earlier, the Fifth Circuit explicitly assumed without deciding that it had subject matter jurisdiction in an ATCA action against a corporation for violations of international law. *See Carmichael v. United Technologies Corp.,* 835 F.2d 109, 113-14 (5th Cir.1988).

iii. [Court discusses other U.S. district court precedent holding that corporations are subject to suit under ATCA] …

b. International Precedent

As noted *supra,* this Court is obliged to follow international law as interpreted by the Supreme Court and Second Circuit. In light of the precedent cited above, the Court must reject Talisman's claim that it is legally incapable of violating the law of nations. A further examination of international legal precedent similarly reveals that Talisman's position is "anachronistic." Declaration of Professor Ralph G. Steinhardt, at ¶ 8, appended to Declaration of Stephen A. Whinston dated June 26, 2002 as Exhibit 1. A review of international precedent and practice reveals that corporate liability, at least for *jus cogens* violations, is contemplated under international law.

i. International Tribunal Precedent

The concept of corporate liability for *jus cogens* violations has its roots in the trials of German war criminals after World War II. The Nuremberg Charter permitted the prosecution of "a group or organization" and allowed the tribunal to declare that entity a "criminal organization." Agreement for the Prosecution and Punishment of Major War Criminals of the European Axis, and Establishing the Charter of the International Military Tribunal, 1951, arts. 9, 10, 82 U.N.T.S. 279. In *United States v. Flick, United States v. Krauch,* and *United States v. Krupp,* the heads of major German corporations were prosecuted for, *inter alia,* war crimes and crimes against humanity. *See* Steven R. Ratner, *Corporations and Human Rights: A Theory of Legal Responsibility,* 111 YALE L.J. 443, 477-78 (2001). Talisman points out, correctly, that in each of these cases, individuals, and not corporate entities, were put on trial. However, it ignores the fact that the court consistently spoke in terms of corporate liability. …

The Nuremberg precedent cited above is particularly significant not merely because it constitutes a basis for finding corporate liability for violations of international law, but because the language ascribes to the corporations involved the necessary *mens rea* for the commission of war crimes and crimes against humanity; the types of criminal behavior at issue in the instant case. …

ii. International Treaty Precedent

As a preliminary note, several of the major conventions protecting basic human rights, such as the Genocide Convention and common article 3 of the Geneva Convention, do not explicitly reach corporations. Nonetheless, such instruments may reach conduct by corporations:

These regimes do not distinguish between natural and juridical individuals, and it is implausible that international law would protect a corporation that engaged in the slave trade or produced the contemporary equivalent of Zyklon B for the destruction of Jews in concentration camps.

Declaration of Professor Ralph G. Steinhardt, at ¶ 14. ... Thus, corporations may be liable under codified international law. As noted below, a variety of international treaties hold corporations directly responsible for tort violations.

Treaties, by definition, are concluded between states. ... Nonetheless, international treaties occasionally hold corporate defendants, as opposed to states, liable for certain acts. ...

For example, the 1960 Paris Convention on Third Party Liability in the Field of Nuclear Energy states that "[t]he operator of a nuclear installation shall be liable" for, *inter alia,* "damage to or loss of life of any person" and damage to property. Convention on Third Party Liability in the Field of Nuclear Energy of 29th July 1960, as amended by the Additional Protocol of 28th January 1964 and by the Protocol of 16th November 1982, July 29, 1960, art. 3(a), 956 U.N.T.S. 251. Similarly, the International Convention on Civil Liability for Oil Pollution Damage holds that "the owner of a ship at the time of an incident [...] shall be liable for any pollution damage caused by oil which has escaped or been discharged from the ship as a result of the incident." International Convention on Civil Liability for Oil Pollution Damage, Nov. 29, 1969, art. 3(1), 26 U.S.T. 765, 973 U.N.T.S. 3. ...

Significantly, all of these treaties impose corporate liability for actions or omissions by companies that have major deleterious effects such as nuclear accidents and oil spills. While most treaties do not bind corporations, the line of instruments cited above indicates that precedent does exist for holding corporations liable for large-scale torts. If corporations can be held liable for unintentional torts such as oil spills or nuclear accidents, logic would suggest that they can be held liable for intentional torts such as complicity in genocide, slave trading, or torture.

iii. International Organization Precedent

The practice of several international organizations indicates that corporations are potentially subjects of international law. The United Nations Universal Declaration of Human Rights enumerates a series of rights, the most basic of which have become part of customary international law (such as the prohibition on slavery and torture). By its terms, it is binding on states as well as corporations:

> The General Assembly proclaims this Universal Declaration of Human Rights as a common standard of achievement for all peoples and all nations, to the end that every individual and every organ of society, keeping this Declaration constantly in mind, shall strive by teaching and education to promote respect for these rights and freedoms and by progressive measures, national and international, to secure their universal and effective recognition and observance. ...

G.A. Res. 217 A(III), Dec. 10, 1948 ("Universal Declaration of Human Rights"). Noted legal scholar and Chief Reporter for the RESTATEMENT (THIRD) OF FOREIGN RELATIONS has stated that "[e]very individual includes juridical persons. Every individual and every organ of society excludes no one, no company, no market, no cyberspace. The Universal Declaration applies to them all." Louis Henkin, *The Universal Declaration at 50 and the Challenge of Global Markets,* 25 BROOK. J. INT'L L. 17, 25 (1999). Consequently, corporations are obligated to respect basic human rights of individuals, such as the right to life, the right to freedom from slavery, and the right to be free from torture and cruel and inhuman treatment.

Other United Nations precedent indicates that corporations have duties under international law. For example, the United Nations Security Council has frequently utilized economic sanctions to punish the unlawful acts of states. While such sanctions are formally directed at states, they also entail certain duties for corporations. For example, corporations wishing to purchase oil from Iraq following the implementation of sanctions were required by the Security Council to follow certain procedures. ...

The practice of the European Union indicates that corporations may be subject to international law. Indeed, the Treaty Establishing the European Community and the binding decisions of the European Council and Commission have "created a vast body of legal obligations which apply directly to corporate entities" including, for example, a prohibition on anticompetitive behavior. ... Beyond commercial regulations, precedent from the European Court of Justice has held that corporations may be held liable for human rights violations such as discrimination. ...

c. Conclusion

Historically, states, and to a lesser extent individuals, have been held liable under international law. However, ... substantial international and United States precedent indicates that corporations may also be held liable under international law, at least for gross human rights violations. Extensive Second Circuit precedent further indicates that actions under the ATCA against corporate defendants for such substantial violations of international law, including *jus cogens* violations, are the norm rather than the exception.

Such a result should hardly be surprising. A private corporation is a juridical person and has no *per se* immunity under U.S. domestic or international law. *See* Jordan J. Paust, *Human Rights Responsibilities of Private Corporations,* 35 VAND. J. TRANSNAT'L L. 801, 803 (2002). As noted above, a corporation may be imputed with having the requisite specific intent to commit a criminal action. *See supra* note 28. Given that private individuals are liable for violations of international law in certain circumstances, there is no logical reason why corporations should not be held liable, at least in cases of *jus cogens* violations. Indeed, while Talisman disputes the fact that corporations are capable of violating the law of nations, it provides no logical argument supporting its claim. As noted at length *supra,* substantial U.S. and international precedent indicates that corporations may be responsible, in certain cases, for violations of international law. In this case, where plaintiffs allege *jus cogens* violations, corporate liability may follow. Consequently, the Court denies Talisman's motion to dismiss for lack of subject matter jurisdiction on this basis.

NOTES AND QUESTIONS

1. Does *Presbyterian Church of Sudan* eliminate the distinction between the state and private actors as addressees of human rights prescriptions? Would this be a positive development?

2. For further discussion of corporate liability for violations of fundamental human rights, see Craig Forcese, *ATCA's Achilles Heel: Corporate Complicity, International Law and the Alien Tort Claims Act*, 26 YALE J. INT'L L. 487 (2001); *Alien Tort Claims and Business Liability*, 95 AM SOC'Y INT'L L. PROC. 42 (2001); Ronald J. Bettauer, *Holocaust Claims: The Role of the United States Government in Recent Holocaust Claims Resolution*, 95 AM SOC'Y INT'L L. PROC. 37 (2001). For a critical assessment of the ATCA, see GARY C. HUFBAUER, AWAKENING MONSTER: THE ALIEN TORT STATUTE OF 1789 (Institute for International Economics 2003).

f. Sosa v. Alvarez-Machain; U.S. v. Alvarez-Machain
124 S.Ct. 2739 (2004)

In 1985, an agent of the Drug Enforcement Administration (DEA), Enrique Camarena-Salazar, was captured on assignment in Mexico and taken to a house in Guadalajara, where he was tortured over the course of a 2-day interrogation, then murdered. Based in part on eyewitness testimony, DEA officials in the United States came to believe that respondent Humberto Alvarez-Machain (Alvarez), a Mexican physician, was present at the house and acted to prolong the agent's life in order to extend the interrogation and torture. *Id.*, at 657.

In 1990, a federal grand jury indicted Alvarez for the torture and murder of Camarena-Salazar, and the United States District Court for the Central District of California issued a warrant for his arrest. 331 F. 3d 604, 609 (CA9 2003) (en banc). The DEA asked the Mexican Government for help in getting Alvarez into the United States, but when the requests and negotiations proved fruitless, the DEA approved a plan to hire Mexican nationals to seize Alvarez and bring him to the United States for trial. As so planned, a group of Mexicans, including petitioner Jose Francisco Sosa, abducted Alvarez from his house, held him overnight in a motel, and brought him by private plane to El Paso, Texas, where he was arrested by federal officers. *Ibid.*

Once in American custody, Alvarez moved to dismiss the indictment on the ground that his seizure was "outrageous governmental conduct," *Alvarez-Machain,* 504 U. S., at 658, and violated the extradition treaty between the United States and Mexico. The District Court agreed, the Ninth Circuit affirmed, and we reversed, *id.*, at 670, holding that the fact of Alvarez's forcible seizure did not affect the jurisdiction of a federal court. The case was tried in 1992, and ended at the close of the Government's case, when the District Court granted Alvarez's motion for a judgment of acquittal.

In 1993, after returning to Mexico, Alvarez began the civil action before us here. He sued Sosa, Mexican citizen and DEA operative Antonio Garate-Bustamante, five unnamed Mexican civilians, the United States, and four DEA agents. 331 F. 3d, at 610. So far as it matters here, Alvarez sought damages from the United States under the FTCA, alleging false arrest, and from Sosa under the ATS, for a violation of the law of nations. The former statute authorizes suit "for ... personal injury ... caused by the negligent or wrongful act or omission of any employee of the Government while acting within the scope of his office or employment." 28 U. S. C. §1346(b)(1). The latter provides in its entirety that "[t]he district courts shall have original jurisdiction of any civil action by an alien for a tort only, committed in violation of the law of nations or a treaty of the United States." §1350.

The District Court granted the Government's motion to dismiss the FTCA claim, but awarded summary judgment and $25,000 in damages to Alvarez on the ATS claim. A three-judge panel of the Ninth Circuit then affirmed the ATS judgment, but reversed the dismissal of the FTCA claim. 266 F. 3d 1045 (2001).

A divided *en banc* court came to the same conclusion. 331 F. 3d, at 641. As for the ATS claim, the court called on its own precedent, "that [the ATS] not only provides federal courts with subject matter jurisdiction, but also creates a cause of action for an alleged violation of the law of nations." *Id.*, at 612. The Circuit then relied upon what it called the "clear and universally recognized norm prohibiting arbitrary arrest and detention," *id.*, at 620, to support the conclusion that Alvarez's arrest amounted to a tort in violation of international law. On the FTCA claim, the Ninth Circuit held that, because "the DEA had no authority to effect Alvarez's arrest and detention in Mexico," *id.*, at 608, the United States was liable to him under California law for the tort of false arrest, *id.*, at 640-641.

We granted certiorari in these companion cases to clarify the scope of both the FTCA and the ATS. 540 U. S.1045 (2003). We now reverse in each.

[The Court reversed the lower Court's holding allowing suit to proceed against the United States under the FTCA.] ...

Alvarez has also brought an action under the ATS against petitioner, Sosa, who argues (as does the United States supporting him) that there is no relief under the ATS because the statute does no more than vest federal courts with jurisdiction, neither creating nor authorizing the courts to recognize any particular right of action without further congressional action. Although we agree the statute is in terms only jurisdictional, we think that at the time of enactment the jurisdiction enabled federal courts to hear claims in a very limited category defined by the law of nations and recognized at common law.

We do not believe, however, that the limited, implicit sanction to entertain the handful of international law *cum* common law claims understood in 1789 should be taken as authority to recognize the right of action asserted by Alvarez here. …

"When the *United States* declared their independence, they were bound to receive the law of nations, in its modern state of purity and refinement." *Ware* v. *Hylton,* 3 Dall. 199, 281 (1796) (Wilson, J.). In the years of the early Republic, this law of nations comprised two principal elements, the first covering the general norms governing the behavior of national states with each other: "*the science which teaches the rights subsisting between nations or states, and the obligations correspondent to those rights,*" E. de Vattel, The Law of Nations, Preliminaries §3 (J. Chitty et al. transl. and ed. 1883). . . , or "that code of public instruction which defines the rights and prescribes the duties of nations, in their intercourse with each other," 1 James Kent Commentaries. This aspect of the law of nations thus occupied the executive and legislative domains, not the judicial. See 4 W. Blackstone, Commentaries on the Laws of England 68 (1769) ("[O]ffenses against" the law of nations are "principally incident to whole states or nations").

The law of nations included a second, more pedestrian element, however, that did fall within the judicial sphere, as a body of judge-made law regulating the conduct of individuals situated outside domestic boundaries and consequently carrying an international savor. To Blackstone, the law of nations in this sense was implicated "in mercantile questions, such as bills of exchange and the like; in all marine causes, relating to freight, average, demurrage, insurances, bottomry …; [and] in all disputes relating to prizes, to shipwrecks, to hostages, and ransom bills." *Id.*, at 67. The law merchant emerged from the customary practices of international traders and admiralty required its own transnational regulation. And it was the law of nations in this sense that our precursors spoke about when the Court explained the status of coast fishing vessels in wartime grew from "ancient usage among civilized nations, beginning centuries ago, and gradually ripening into a rule of international law … ." *The Paquete Habana,* 175 U. S. 677, 686 (1900).

There was, finally, a sphere in which these rules binding individuals for the benefit of other individuals overlapped with the norms of state relationships. Blackstone referred to it when he mentioned three specific offenses against the law of nations addressed by the criminal law of England: violation of safe conducts, infringement of the rights of ambassadors, and piracy. 4 Commentaries 68. An assault against an ambassador, for example, impinged upon the sovereignty of the foreign nation and if not adequately redressed could rise to an issue of war. See Vattel 463-464. It was this narrow set of violations of the law of nations, admitting of a judicial remedy and at the same time threatening serious consequences in international affairs, that was probably on minds of the men who drafted the ATS with its reference to tort. …

... [T]here is every reason to suppose that the First Congress did not pass the ATS as a jurisdictional convenience to be placed on the shelf for use by a future Congress or state legislature that might, some day, authorize the creation of causes of action or itself decide to make some element of the law of nations actionable for the benefit of foreigners. ...

The second inference to be drawn from the history is that Congress intended the ATS to furnish jurisdiction for a relatively modest set of actions alleging violations of the law of nations. Uppermost in the legislative mind appears to have been offenses against ambassadors, see *id.*, at 118; violations of safe conduct were probably understood to be actionable, *ibid.*, and individual actions arising out of prize captures and piracy may well have also been contemplated. *Id.*, at 113-114. But the common law appears to have understood only those three of the hybrid variety as definite and actionable, or at any rate, to have assumed only a very limited set of claims. As Blackstone had put it, "offences against this law [of nations] are principally incident to whole states or nations," and not individuals seeking relief in court. 4 Commentaries 68. ...

We think it is correct, then, to assume that the First Congress understood that the district courts would recognize private causes of action for certain torts in violation of the law of nations, though we have found no basis to suspect Congress had any examples in mind beyond those torts corresponding to Blackstone's three primary offenses: violation of safe conducts, infringement of the rights of ambassadors, and piracy. We assume, too, that no development in the two centuries from the enactment of §1350 to the birth of the modern line of cases beginning with *Filartiga* v. *Pena-Irala*, 630 F. 2d 876 (CA2 1980), has categorically precluded federal courts from recognizing a claim under the law of nations as an element of common law; Congress has not in any relevant way amended §1350 or limited civil common law power by another statute. Still, there are good reasons for a restrained conception of the discretion a federal court should exercise in considering a new cause of action of this kind. Accordingly, we think courts should require any claim based on the present-day law of nations to rest on a norm of international character accepted by the civilized world and defined with a specificity comparable to the features of the 18th-century paradigms we have recognized. This requirement is fatal to Alvarez's claim.

A series of reasons argue for judicial caution when considering the kinds of individual claims that might implement the jurisdiction conferred by the early statute.

First, the prevailing conception of the common law has changed since 1789 in a way that counsels restraint in judicially applying internationally generated norms. When §1350 was enacted, the accepted conception was of the common law as "a transcendental body of law outside of any particular State but obligatory within it unless and until changed by statute." *Black and White Taxicab & Transfer Co.* v. *Brown and Yellow Taxicab & Transfer Co.*, 276

U. S. 518, 533 (1928) (Holmes, J., dissenting). Now, however, in most cases where a court is asked to state or formulate a common law principle in a new context, there is a general understanding that the law is not so much found or discovered as it is either made or created. Holmes explained famously in 1881 that

> [i]n substance the growth of the law is legislative … [because t]he very considerations which judges most rarely mention, and always with an apology, are the secret root from which the law draws all the juices of life. I mean, of course, considerations of what is expedient for the community concerned. The Common Law 31-32 (Howe ed. 1963).

One need not accept the Holmesian view as far as its ultimate implications to acknowledge that a judge deciding in reliance on an international norm will find a substantial element of discretionary judgment in the decision.

Second, along with, and in part driven by, that conceptual development in understanding common law has come an equally significant rethinking of the role of the federal courts in making it. *Erie R. Co.* v. *Tompkins,* 304 U. S. 64 (1938), was the watershed in which we denied the existence of any federal "general" common law, *id.*, at 78, which largely withdrew to havens of specialty, some of them defined by express congressional authorization to devise a body of law directly, *e.g.*, *Textile Workers* v. *Lincoln Mills of Ala.*, 353 U. S. 448 (1957) (interpretation of collective-bargaining agreements); Fed. Rule Evid. 501 (evidentiary privileges in federal-question cases). Elsewhere, this Court has thought it was in order to create federal common law rules in interstitial areas of particular federal interest. *E.g., United States* v. *Kimbell Foods, Inc.,* 440 U. S. 715, 726-727 (1979). And although we have even assumed competence to make judicial rules of decision of particular importance to foreign relations, such as the act of state doctrine, see *Banco Nacional de Cuba* v. *Sabbatino*, 376 U. S. 398, 427 (1964), the general practice has been to look for legislative guidance before exercising innovative authority over substantive law. It would be remarkable to take a more aggressive role in exercising a jurisdiction that remained largely in shadow for much of the prior two centuries.

Third, this Court has recently and repeatedly said that a decision to create a private right of action is one better left to legislative judgment in the great majority of cases. *Correctional Services Corp.* v. *Malesko,* 534 U. S. 61, 68 (2001); *Alexander* v. *Sandoval,* 532 U. S. 275, 286-287 (2001). The creation of a private right of action raises issues beyond the mere consideration whether underlying primary conduct should be allowed or not, entailing, for example, a decision to permit enforcement without the check imposed by prosecutorial discretion. Accordingly, even when Congress has made it clear by statute that a rule applies to purely domestic conduct, we are reluctant to infer intent to provide a private cause of action where the statute does not supply one expressly. While the absence of congressional action addressing private rights of action under an international norm is more equivocal than its failure to provide such a right when it creates a statute, the possible collateral consequences of making international rules privately actionable argue for judicial caution.

Fourth, the subject of those collateral consequences is itself a reason for a high bar to new private causes of action for violating international law, for the potential implications for the foreign relations of the United States of recognizing such causes should make courts particularly wary of impinging on the discretion of the Legislative and Executive Branches in managing foreign affairs. It is one thing for American courts to enforce constitutional limits on our own State and Federal Governments' power, but quite another to consider suits under rules that would go so far as to claim a limit on the power of foreign governments over their own citizens, and to hold that a foreign government or its agent has transgressed those limits. Cf. *Sabbatino*, *supra*, at 431-432. Yet modern international law is very much concerned with just such questions, and apt to stimulate calls for vindicating private interests in §1350 cases. Since many attempts by federal courts to craft remedies for the violation of new norms of international law would raise risks of adverse foreign policy consequences, they should be undertaken, if at all, with great caution. Cf. *Tel-Oren* v. *Libyan Arab Republic*, 726 F. 2d 774, 813 (CADC 1984) (Bork, J., concurring) (expressing doubt that §1350 should be read to require "our courts [to] sit in judgment of the conduct of foreign officials in their own countries with respect to their own citizens").

The fifth reason is particularly important in light of the first four. We have no congressional mandate to seek out and define new and debatable violations of the law of nations, and modern indications of congressional understanding of the judicial role in the field have not affirmatively encouraged greater judicial creativity. …

Whereas Justice SCALIA sees these developments as sufficient to close the door to further independent judicial recognition of actionable international norms, other considerations persuade us that the judicial power should be exercised on the understanding that the door is still ajar subject to vigilant doorkeeping, and thus open to a narrow class of international norms today. *Erie* did not in terms bar any judicial recognition of new substantive rules, no matter what the circumstances, and post-*Erie* understanding has identified limited enclaves in which federal courts may derive some substantive law in a common law way. For two centuries we have affirmed that the domestic law of the United States recognizes the law of nations. See, *e.g.*, *Sabbatino,* 376 U.S., at 423 ("[I]t is, of course, true that United States courts apply international law as a part of our own in appropriate circumstances"): *The Paquete Habana,* 175 U.S., at 700 ("International law is part of our law, and must be ascertained and administered by the courts of justice of appropriate jurisdiction, as often as questions of right depending upon it are duly presented for their determination"); *The Nereide,* 9 Cranch 388, 423 (1815) (Marshall, C.J.) ("[T]he Court is bound by the law of nations which is a part of the law of the land"); see also *Texas Industries, Inc. v. Radcliff*

Materials, Inc., 451 U.S. 630, 641 (1981) (recognizing that "international disputes implicating ... our relations with foreign nations" are one of the "narrow areas" in which "federal common law" continues to exist). It would take some explaining to say now that federal courts must avert their gaze entirely from any international norm intended to protect individuals. ...

We think an attempt to justify such a position would be particularly unconvincing in light of what we know about congressional understanding bearing on this issue lying at the intersection of the judicial and legislative powers. The First Congress, which reflected the understanding of the framing generation and included some of the Framers, assumed that federal courts could properly identify some international norms as enforceable in the exercise of § 1350 jurisdiction. We think it would be unreasonable to assume that the First Congress would have expected federal courts to lose all capacity to recognize enforceable international norms simply because the common law might lose some metaphysical cachet on the road to modern realism. Later Congresses seem to have shared our view. The position we take today has been assumed by some federal courts for 24 years, ever since the Second Circuit decided *Filartiga v. Pena-Irala,* 630 F.2d 876 (C.A.2 1980), and for practical purposes the point of today's disagreement has been focused since the exchange between Judge Edwards and Judge Bork in *Tel-Oren v. Libyan Arab Republic,* 726 F.2d 774 (C.A.D.C.1984), Congress, however, has not only expressed no disagreement with our view of the proper exercise of the judicial power, but has responded to its most notable instance by enacting legislation supplementing the judicial determination in some detail. See *supra,* ... (discussing the Torture Victim Protection Act).

While we agree with Justice SCALIA to the point that we would welcome any congressional guidance in exercising jurisdiction with such obvious potential to affect foreign relations, nothing Congress has done is a reason for us to shut the door to the law of nations entirely. It is enough to say that Congress may do that at any time (explicitly, or implicitly by treaties or statutes that occupy the field) just as it may modify or cancel any judicial decision so far as it rests on recognizing an international norm as such. ...

We must still, however, derive a standard or set of standards for assessing the particular claim Alvarez raises, and for this case it suffices to look to the historical antecedents. Whatever the ultimate criteria for accepting a cause of action subject to jurisdiction under § 1350, we are persuaded that federal courts should not recognize private claims under federal common law for violations of any international law norm with less definite content and acceptance among civilized nations than the historical paradigms familiar when § 1350 was enacted. See, *e.g., United States v. Smith,* 5 Wheat. 153, 163-180, n. a (1820) (illustrating the specificity with which the law of nations defined piracy). This limit upon judicial recognition is generally consistent with the reasoning of many of the courts and judges who faced the issue before it reached this Court. See *Filartiga, supra,* at 890 ("[F]or purposes of civil liability, the torturer has become—like the pirate and slave trader before him—*hostis humani generis,* an enemy of all mankind"); *Tel-Oren, supra,* at 781 (Edwards, J., concurring) (suggesting that the "limits of section 1350's reach" be defined by "a handful of heinous actions—each of which violates definable, universal and obligatory norms"); see also *In re Estate of Marcos Human Rights Litigation,* 25 F.3d 1467, 1475 (C.A.9 1994) ("Actionable violations of international law must be of a norm that is specific, universal, and obligatory"). And the determination whether a norm is sufficiently definite to support a cause of action [20] should (and, indeed, inevitably must) involve an element of judgment about the practical consequences of making that cause available to litigants in the federal courts. [21]

Another possible limitation that we need not apply here is a policy of case-specific deference to the political branches. For example, there are now pending in federal district court several class actions seeking damages from various corporations alleged to have participated in, or abetted, the regime of apartheid that formerly controlled South Africa. See *In re South African Apartheid Litigation,* 238 F.Supp.2d 1379 (JPML 2002) (granting a motion to transfer the cases to the Southern District of New York). The Government of South Africa has said that these cases interfere with the policy embodied by its Truth and Reconciliation Commission, which "deliberately avoided a 'victors' justice' approach to the crimes of apartheid and chose instead one based on confession and absolution, informed by the principles of reconciliation, reconstruction, reparation and goodwill." Declaration of Penuell Mpapa Maduna, Minister of Justice and Constitutional Development, Republic of South Africa, reprinted in App. to Brief for Government of Commonwealth of Australia et al. as *Amici Curiae* 7a, ¶ 3.2.1 (emphasis deleted). The United States has agreed. See Letter of William H. Taft IV, Legal Adviser, Dept. of State, to Shannen W. Coffin, Deputy Asst. Atty. Gen., Oct. 27, 2003, reprinted in *id.,* at 2a. In such cases, there is a strong argument that federal courts should give serious weight to the Executive Branch's view of the case's impact on foreign policy. Cf. *Republic of Austria v. Altmann,* 541 U.S. 2240 (2004) (discussing the State Department's use of statements of inter-

---

[20] A related consideration is whether international law extends the scope of liability for a violation of a given norm to the perpetrator being sued, if the defendant is a private actor such as a corporation or individual. Compare *Tel-Oren v. Libyan Arab Republic,* 726 F.2d 774, 791- 795 (C.A.D.C.1984) (Edwards, J., concurring) (insufficient consensus in 1984 that torture by private actors violates international law), with *Kadic v. Karadzic,* 70 F.3d 232, 239-241 (C.A.2 1995) (sufficient consensus in 1995 that genocide by private actors violates international law)

[21] This requirement of clear definition is not meant to be the only principle limiting the availability of relief in the federal courts for violations of customary international law, though it disposes of this case. For example, the European Commission argues as *amicus curiae* that basic principles of international law require that before asserting a claim in a foreign forum, the claimant must have exhausted any remedies available in the domestic legal system, and perhaps in other fora such as international claims tribunals. See Brief for European Commission as *Amicus Curiae* 24, n. 54 (citing I. Brownlie, Principles of Public International Law 472-481 (6th ed.2003)); cf. Torture Victim Protection Act of 1991, § 2(b), 106 Stat. 73 (exhaustion requirement). We would certainly consider this requirement in an appropriate case.

est in cases involving the Foreign Sovereign Immunities Act of 1976, 28 U.S.C. § 1602 *et seq.*).

Thus, Alvarez's detention claim must be gauged against the current state of international law, looking to those sources we have long, albeit cautiously, recognized.

To begin with, Alvarez cites two well-known international agreements that, despite their moral authority, have little utility under the standard set out in this opinion. He says that his abduction by Sosa was an "arbitrary arrest" within the meaning of the Universal Declaration of Human Rights (Declaration). ... And he traces the rule against arbitrary arrest not only to the Declaration, but also to article nine of the International Covenant on Civil and Political Rights (Covenant) ..., to which the United States is a party, and to various other conventions to which it is not. But the Declaration does not of its own force impose obligations as a matter of international law. ... And, although the Covenant does bind the United States as a matter of international law, the United States ratified the Covenant on the express understanding that it was not self-executing and so did not itself create obligations enforceable in the federal courts. ... Accordingly, Alvarez cannot say that the Declaration and Covenant themselves establish the relevant and applicable rule of international law. He instead attempts to show that prohibition of arbitrary arrest has attained the status of binding customary international law. ...

Alvarez's failure to marshal support for his proposed rule is underscored by the Restatement (Third) of Foreign Relations Law of the United States (1987), which says in its discussion of customary international human rights law that a "state violates international law if, as a matter of state policy, it practices, encourages, or condones ... prolonged arbitrary detention." *Id.*, § 702. Although the Restatement does not explain its requirements of a "state policy" and of "prolonged" detention, the implication is clear. Any credible invocation of a principle against arbitrary detention that the civilized world accepts as binding customary international law requires a factual basis beyond relatively brief detention in excess of positive authority. Even the Restatement's limits are only the beginning of the enquiry, because although it is easy to say that some policies of prolonged arbitrary detentions are so bad that those who enforce them become enemies of the human race, it may be harder to say which policies cross that line with the certainty afforded by Blackstone's three common law offenses. In any event, the label would never fit the reckless policeman who botches his warrant, even though that same officer might pay damages under municipal law. ...

Whatever may be said for the broad principle Alvarez advances, in the present, imperfect world, it expresses an aspiration that exceeds any binding customary rule having the specificity we require. Creating a private cause of action to further that aspiration would go beyond any residual common law discretion we think it appropriate to exercise. It is enough to hold that a single illegal detention of less than a day, followed by the transfer of custody to lawful authorities and a prompt arraignment, violates no norm of customary international law so well defined as to support the creation of a federal remedy.

NOTES AND QUESTIONS

1. Note the Court's sensitivity to assuming a law-making role when the impacts are felt on other states. Compare this holding with the Court's decision in the *Hoffman LaRoche* opinion (see Part Seven, *infra,* at 1428), which was issued in the same term.

2. What is the policy underlying the Supreme Court's opinion in *Sosa*? Is it in line with an overall order of human dignity?

3. After *Sosa*, what violations of customary international law may still give rise to a claim under the Alien Tort Claims Act? Could corporations still be sued under it?

2. INTERNATIONAL BODIES

Present-day review mechanisms at the universal and regional level are limited. If a country has not ratified any of the human rights treaties, but is a member of the United Nations, the only inclusive forum to review its conduct is the United Nations Human Rights Commission. Its review, instituted on the basis of Articles 55 and 56 of the Charter by ECOSOC Res. 1503, is predicated on a "consistent pattern of gross and reliably attested violations of human rights." It is limited to the finding of facts; fact-finding missions to the country under investigation require the cooperation of its government; and the effect of the Commission's findings as well as of any hortatory statements it makes depend heavily, if not exclusively, on the good will of the country concerned and the support of third governments and world opinion

Other human rights implementation bodies, both regional and universal, are set up by treaties and require special consent by the states to be reviewed. Some are limited to fact-finding and the suggestion of "friendly settlements." Others again, such as the European and the Inter-American Court of Human Rights, make binding legal decisions. Consider the following account of the Inter-American experience:

a. W. Michael Reisman, *Practical Matters for Consideration in the Establishment of a Regional Human Rights Mechanism: Lessons from the Inter-American Experience*

1995 ST. LOUIS-WARSAW TRANSATLANTIC L.J. 89, 90-94

I. THE INTER-AMERICAN SYSTEM OF HUMAN RIGHTS

The Organization of American States (OAS) is a pioneer of modern human rights law. The OAS Charter of 1948 incorporates the "fundamental rights of the individual" as one of the Organization's founding principles. The American Declaration of the Rights and Duties of Man (American Declaration), prepared by the Inter-American Juridical Committee in 1947, was adopted by the OAS in Bogotá, Colombia, in 1948 to elaborate upon the Charter's general commitment to human rights.

The Inter-American Commission of Human Rights (Commission) was created in 1959 to serve as a mechanism for overseeing national implementation of such human rights commitments. Composed of seven members elected in their individual capacity, the Commission started operating in 1960 with a vague mandate. In 1965, its competence was expanded to accept communications, request information from governments, and make recommendations "with the objective of bringing about more effective observance of human rights." In 1967, the OAS Charter was amended, and the Commission became a principal organ of the OAS. The American Convention of Human Rights (American Convention), signed in 1969, incorporated the Commission and assigned it specified conventional competences. It also created the Inter-American Court of Human Rights (Inter-American Court). The American Convention entered into force in 1978. Currently there are twenty-five parties to the Convention.

The Commission has three forms of jurisdiction. Its conventional jurisdiction applies to the twenty-five states that have, to date, become parties to the American Convention. Its judicial invocative jurisdiction provides the competence to invoke the Inter-American Court; it applies to the state-parties to the American Convention that have accepted the Inter-American Court's jurisdiction. While these two forms of jurisdiction depend upon adherence to the American Convention, the Commission's declaration jurisdiction applies to all parties to the OAS Charter, indeed, to all states in the Americas. Hence, every independent state in the Western Hemisphere, even those which have not yet become party to the American Convention, is subject, in some form, to the Commission's jurisdiction.

The Commission's jurisdiction may be invoked by citizens and organizations within the hemisphere. On its own initiative, the Commission may also prepare country reports. To facilitate both of these activities, the Commission conducts on-site visits to individual countries. The Commission also plays a role in regional codification and progressive development. It has drafted a number of important human rights instruments for the OAS, provided technical assistance to state-parties in matters concerning the American Convention, and litigated cases before the Inter-American Court.

Human rights are about individuals; therefore, it is no surprise that a substantial part of the daily work of the Commission comes from individual petitions. Article 44 of the American Convention states:

> Any person or group of persons, or any nongovernmental entity legally recognized in one or more member states of the Organization, may lodge petitions with the Commission containing denunciations or complaints of violation of this Convention by a State Party.

A case begins on receipt of a petition alleging a violation of human rights. Petitions about the same event often come from a number of different sources. The Commission examines each petition in terms of the basic requirements of Articles 46 and 47: whether the petition contains names and signatures, whether it states facts that tend to establish a violation of the American Convention or whether it is manifestly groundless, whether domestic remedies have been exhausted, whether the petition has been lodged within specified time limits, and whether the petition is pending in another international proceeding or has already been before the Commission.

If the petition satisfies these threshold requirements, it is relayed to the named government for the latter's information and views. The information supplied by the government may lay the matter to rest, in which case the Commission is required by Article 48(b) to order that the record be closed. It is also possible that the information provided may establish that the petition is inadmissible, which also terminates the procedure. If neither occurs, the Commission, with the knowledge of the parties, must proceed to investigate the matter, asking for information it deems necessary, hearing oral arguments, and receiving written statements. It also puts itself at the disposal of the parties with the objective of reaching an amicable settlement.

If an amicable settlement can be arranged, the Commission issues a short report to that effect to the Secretary-General of the OAS. If there is no settlement, the Commission draws up a report stating the facts, its conclusions, and its recommendations. The report is then sent only to the state concerned, which may not publicize it. If, within three months, the matter has not been settled, the Commission has two options: the provisions of Article 50 state that it may issue a final report, which becomes part of the Annual Report to the General Assembly of the OAS; or according to Article 51, the Commission may refer the matter to the Inter-American Court, if the state concerned has accepted the Inter-American Court's jurisdiction.

Aside from petitions, the Commission must stay abreast of general trends in order to perform the various functions prescribed by Article 41 of the American Convention. It accomplishes this by using a wide-ranging methodology. In addition to its scrutiny of all relevant documents, the Commission devotes a great deal of its efforts to meeting with numerous government officials, spokespersons for non-governmental human rights organizations, and citizens. This methodology is important, for Article 41 also specifies that the Commission is to prepare "reports" or "studies" as it considers advisable.

One form of report is a country report. Country reports have been prepared on the Commission's own initiative, upon instruction from an organ of the OAS, or even at the spontaneous request of the country concerned. A country report examines the aggregate human rights situation in the particular country on which it focuses and, where appropriate, makes recommendations to the government. Every application of a legal instrument requires interpretation and judgment; thus, governments do not always agree with all of the conclusions the Commission may reach in its country reports. Nevertheless, many governments accept the reports in a positive way and have entered into a dialogue with the Commission about ways of dealing with the problems indicated in the reports, of which the government may have already been aware. A number of governments have been critical of the Commission, feeling that they were singled out unfairly or arbitrarily. In no case, however, is a country report about a member-state of the OAS prepared without consultation with government officials or without giving the government ample opportunity to express its views on the issues in the report.

Sometimes, as a result of the methodology described above and other information received, the Commission finds that essentially the same discrepancies from the standards prescribed by the Convention are occurring in many countries. Some human rights violations are widespread, if not virtually universal. In some cases, these violations are the result of major political, moral, or technological changes to which national laws or institutional practices have not yet adapted. If the Commission were only to confront such pathologies through the petition procedure, case-by-case and country-by- country, remedies might only be secured in the individual cases that are lodged. The underlying factors that precipitated the problem and the broader pattern of abuses, however, would continue. Some of these problems call for fundamental institutional change, as contemplated in Articles 2 and 41(b) of the American Convention. Moreover, it does not seem fair to single out in a country report only one of the many countries engaged in a practice inconsistent with the American Convention.

To deal with these types of problems, the Commission may prepare "studies" as provided for by Article 41(c) of the Convention. These studies enable the Commission to see things in a hemispheric perspective and to develop recommendations on a hemispheric scale. Currently, the Commission is studying the status of women in national legislation in the hemisphere and practices in national prisons throughout the hemisphere. A study of the consequences of large-scale migration on the rights in the American Convention, both interstate and intrastate, is also being considered. This would follow a recommendation made by the General Assembly of the OAS to the Commission on a cognate subject.

The Commission faces a daunting mandate. It is, as stated, responsible for thirty-four countries and more than 600 million human beings, yet the Commission has only seven members, a staff of ten lawyers, a secretarial staff of seven, and an annual budget of less than $1.6 million. The Commission's tasks are rendered even more difficult by the social and economic heterogeneity of the Americas, the intermittent civil strife that still afflicts many countries, the terrorism and narcotics traffic that compound existing human rights problems and present special human rights problems of their own, and the sporadic coups. Incidentally, the suspension of constitutional order has never meant a "time-out" or a suspension of the Commission's jurisdiction. Indeed, constitutional order itself is a requirement of the American Convention as well as a precondition for the fulfillment of many other rights set out therein. In fact, the Commission has played an important role in reestablishing constitutional order on a few occasions.

The Commission has not always been successful; however, it regularly examines its performance, carefully heeds the OAS's annual review of its activities, and studies responsible non-governmental appraisals, some of which have been quite critical. Moreover, the Commission closely follows jurisprudence and developments in international and other regional human rights systems. To facilitate cross-fertilization, some of the Commission's staff have been lent to other human rights institutions, and the Commission offers short-term internships to lawyers from other systems.

NOTES AND QUESTIONS

1. In light of the experiences of the Inter-American and other international review bodies, should the powers of these agencies be expanded? Should every person complaining of a violation of his or her human rights be provided an inclusive judicial forum? Should an inclusive *actio popularis* be instituted, allowing for every person aware of human rights violations to bring the case before an international judicial body?

2. In many respects, the international system is not yet equipped to handle a potential flood of complaints on possibly minor matters, a process which could end up trivializing human dignity. On the other hand, a significant number of states do not yet have the infrastructure at their disposal to implement international human rights. Others have failed, or acted *mala fide.* In these situations, exemplified by the genocidal contexts of Rwanda, Bosnia and Somalia, inclusive review and action appear particularly appropriate. Would an *actio popularis* of the kind mentioned produce mischief and abuse?

3. A policy of subsidiarity could be structured the following way: Nation-states are encouraged to efficiently prescribe and enforce a public order of human rights. Local remedies are to be exhausted before the international arena could be entered. Even with respect to rogue governments, the policies inherent in the "last clear chance" doctrine would apply. Would this policy be appropriate? Are there any drawbacks?

The Inter-American experience has not suffered from a lack of dramatic decisions. Consider the following case:

b. Inter-American Court of Human Rights: Judgment, Velasquez Rodriguez Case

(Forced Disappearance and Death of Individual in Honduras)
July 29, 1988, 28 I.L.M. 291 (1989)

1. The Inter-American Commission on Human Rights (hereinafter "the Commission") submitted the instant case to the Inter-American Court of Human Rights (hereinafter the "Court") on April 24, 1986. It originated in a petition (No. 7920) against the State of Honduras (hereinafter "Honduras" or "the Government"), which the Secretariat of the Commission received on October 7, 1981.

2. In submitting the case, the Commission invoked Articles 50 and 51 of the American Convention on Human Rights (hereinafter "the Convention" or "the American Convention") and requested that the Court determine whether the State in question had violated Articles 4 (Right to Life), 5 (Right to Humane Treatment) and 7 (Right to Personal Liberty) of the Convention in the case of Angel Manfredo Velasquez Rodriguez (also known as Manfredo Velasquez). In addition, the Commission asked the Court to rule that "the consequences of the

situation that constituted the breach of such right or freedom be remedied and that fair compensation be paid to the injured party or parties." …

148. Based upon the above, the Court finds that the following facts have been proven in this proceeding: (1) a practice of disappearances carried out or tolerated by Honduran officials existed between 1981 and 1984; (2) Manfredo Velasquez disappeared at the hands of or with the acquiescence of those officials within the framework of that practice; and (3) the Government of Honduras failed to guarantee the human rights affected by that practice. …

154. Without question, the State has the right and duty to guarantee its security. It is also indisputable that all societies suffer some deficiencies in their legal orders. However, regardless of the seriousness of certain actions and the culpability of the perpetrators of certain crimes, the power of the State is not unlimited, nor may the State resort to any means to attain its ends. The State is subject to law and morality. Disrespect for human dignity cannot serve as the basis for any State action.

155. The forced disappearance of human beings is a multiple and continuous violation of many rights under the Convention that the States Parties are obligated to respect and guarantee. The kidnapping of a person is an arbitrary deprivation of liberty, an infringement of a detainee's right to be taken without delay before a judge and to invoke the appropriate procedures to review the legality of the arrest, all in violation of Article 7 of the Convention which recognizes the right to personal liberty. …

156. Moreover, prolonged isolation and deprivation of communication are in themselves cruel and inhuman treatment, harmful to the psychological and moral integrity of the person and a violation of the right of any detainee to respect for his inherent dignity as a human being. Such treatment, therefore, violates Article 5 of the Convention, which recognizes the right to the integrity of the person. …

In addition, investigations into the practice of disappearances and the testimony of victims who have regained their liberty show that those who are disappeared are often subjected to merciless treatment, including all types of indignities, torture and other cruel, inhuman and degrading treatment, in violation of the right to physical integrity recognized in Article 5 of the Convention.

157. The practice of disappearances often involves secret execution without trial, followed by concealment of the body to eliminate any material evidence of the crime and to ensure the impunity of those responsible. This is a flagrant violation of the right to life, recognized in Article 4 of the Convention. …

158. The practice of disappearances, in addition to directly violating many provisions of the Convention, such as those noted above, constitutes a radical breach of the treaty in that it shows a crass abandonment of the values which emanate from the concept of human dignity and of the most basic principles of the inter-American system and the Convention. The existence of this practice,

moreover, evinces a disregard of the duty to organize the State in such a manner as to guarantee the rights recognized in the Convention, as set out below. ...

159. The Commission has asked the Court to find that Honduras has violated the rights guaranteed to Manfredo Velasquez by Articles 4, 5 and 7 of the Convention. The Government has denied the charges and seeks to be absolved.

160. This requires the Court to examine the conditions under which a particular act, which violates one of the rights recognized by the Convention, can be imputed to a State Party thereby establishing its international responsibility.

161. Article 1(1) of the Convention provides:

> Article 1. Obligation to Respect Rights
>
> 1. The States Parties to this Convention undertake to respect the rights and freedoms recognized herein and to ensure to all persons subject to their jurisdiction the free and full exercise of those rights and freedoms, without any discrimination for reasons of race, color, sex, language, religion, political or other opinion, national or social origin, economic status, birth, or any other social condition.

162. This article specifies the obligation assumed by the States Parties in relation to each of the rights protected. Each claim alleging that one of those rights has been infringed necessarily implies that Article 1(1) of the Convention has also been violated.

163. The Commission did not specifically allege the violation of Article 1(1) of the Convention, but that does not preclude the Court from applying it. The precept contained therein constitutes the generic basis of the protection of the rights recognized by the Convention and would be applicable, in any case, by virtue of a general principle of law, *iura novit curia*, on which international jurisprudence has repeatedly relied and under which a court has the power and the duty to apply the juridical provisions relevant to a proceeding, even when the parties do not expressly invoke them ("Lotus", Judgment No. 9, 1927, P.C.I.J., Series A No. 10, p. 31 and Eur. Court H.R., Handyside Case, Judgment of 7 December 1976, Series A No. 24, para. 41).

164. Article 1(1) is essential in determining whether a violation of the human rights recognized by the Convention can be imputed to a State Party. In effect, that article charges the States Parties with the fundamental duty to respect and guarantee the rights recognized in the Convention. Any impairment of those rights which can be attributed under the rules of international law to the action or omission of any public authority constitutes an act imputable to the State, which assumes responsibility in the terms provided by the Convention.

165. The first obligation assumed by the States Parties under Article 1(1) is "to respect the rights and freedoms" recognized by the Convention. The exercise of public authority has certain limits which derive from the fact that human rights

are inherent attributes of human dignity and are, therefore, superior to the power of the State. ....

166. The second obligation of the States Parties is to "ensure" the free and full exercise of the rights recognized by the Convention to every person subject to its jurisdiction. This obligation implies the duty of the States Parties to organize the governmental apparatus and, in general, all the structures through which public power is exercised, so that they are capable of juridically ensuring the free and full enjoyment of human rights. As a consequence of this obligation, the States must prevent, investigate and punish any violation of the rights recognized by the Convention and, moreover, if possible attempt to restore the right violated and provide compensation as warranted for damages resulting from the violation.

167. The obligation to ensure the free and full exercise of human rights is not fulfilled by the existence of a legal system designed to make it possible to comply with this obligation — it also requires the government to conduct itself so as to effectively ensure the free and full exercise of human rights. ...

169. According to Article 1(1), any exercise of public power that violates the rights recognized by the Convention is illegal. Whenever a State organ, official or public entity violates one of those rights, this constitutes a failure of the duty to respect the rights and freedoms set forth in the Convention.

170. This conclusion is independent of whether the organ or official has contravened provisions of internal law or overstepped the limits of his authority: under international law a State is responsible for the acts of its agents undertaken in their official capacity and for their omissions, even when those agents act outside the sphere of their authority or violate internal law.

171. This principle suits perfectly the nature of the Convention, which is violated whenever public power is used to infringe the rights recognized therein. If acts of public power that exceed the State's authority or are illegal under its own laws were not considered to compromise that State's obligations under the treaty, the system of protection provided for in the Convention would be illusory.

172. Thus, in principle, any violation of rights recognized by the Convention carried out by an act of public authority or by persons who use their position of authority is imputable to the State. However, this does not define all the circumstances in which a State is obligated to prevent, investigate and punish human rights violations, nor all the cases in which the State might be found responsible for an infringement of those rights. An illegal act which violates human rights and which is initially not directly imputable to a State (for example, because it is the act of a private person or because the person responsible has not been identified) can lead to international responsibility of the State, not because of the act itself, but because of the lack of due diligence to prevent the violation or to respond to it as required by the Convention.

173. Violations of the Convention cannot be founded upon rules that take psychological factors into account in establishing individual culpability. For the

purposes of analysis, the intent or motivation of the agent who has violated the rights recognized by the Convention is irrelevant — the violation can be established even if the identity of the individual perpetrator is unknown. What is decisive is whether a violation of the rights recognized by the Convention has occurred with the support or the acquiescence of the government, or whether the State has allowed the act to take place without taking measures to prevent it or to punish those responsible. Thus, the Court's task is to determine whether the violation is the result of a State's failure to fulfill its duty to respect and guarantee those rights, as required by Article 1(1) of the Convention.

174. The State has a legal duty to take reasonable steps to prevent human rights violations and to use the means at its disposal to carry out a serious investigation of violations committed within its jurisdiction, to identify those responsible, to impose the appropriate punishment and to ensure the victim adequate compensation.

175. This duty to prevent includes all those means of a legal, political, administrative and cultural nature that promote the protection of human rights and ensure that any violations are considered and treated as illegal acts, which, as such, may lead to the punishment of those responsible and the obligation to indemnify the victims for damages. It is not possible to make a detailed list of all such measures, since they vary with the law and the conditions of each State Party. Of course, while the State is obligated to prevent human rights abuses, the existence of a particular violation does not, in itself, prove the failure to take preventive measures. On the other hand, subjecting a person to official, repressive bodies that practice torture and assassination with impunity is itself a breach of the duty to prevent violations of the rights to life and physical integrity of the person, even if that particular person is not tortured or assassinated, or if those facts cannot be proven in a concrete case.

176. The State is obligated to investigate every situation involving a violation of the rights protected by the Convention. If the State apparatus acts in such a way that the violation goes unpunished and the victim's full enjoyment of such rights is not restored as soon as possible, the State has failed to comply with its duty to ensure the free and full exercise of those rights to the persons within its jurisdiction. The same is true when the State allows private persons or groups to act freely and with impunity to the detriment of the rights recognized by the Convention.

177. In certain circumstances, it may be difficult to investigate acts that violate an individual's rights. The duty to investigate, like the duty to prevent, is not breached merely because the investigation does not produce a satisfactory result. Nevertheless, it must be undertaken in a serious manner and not as a mere formality preordained to be ineffective. An investigation must have an objective and be assumed by the State as its own legal duty, not as a step taken by private interests that depends upon the initiative of the victim or his family or upon their offer of proof, without an effective search for the truth by the government. This

is true regardless of what agent is eventually found responsible for the violation. Where the acts of private parties that violate the Convention are not seriously investigated, those parties are aided in a sense by the government, thereby making the State responsible on the international plane.

178. In the instant case, the evidence shows a complete inability of the procedures of the State of Honduras, which were theoretically adequate, to carry out an investigation into the disappearance of Manfredo Velasquez, and of the fulfillment of its duties to pay compensation and punish those responsible, as set out in Article 1(1) of the Convention.

179. As the Court has verified above, the failure of the judicial system to act upon the writs brought before various tribunals in the instant case has been proven. Not one writ of habeas corpus was processed. No judge had access to the places where Manfredo Velasquez might have been detained. The criminal complaint was dismissed.

180. Nor did the organs of the Executive Branch carry out a serious investigation to establish the fate of Manfredo Velasquez. There was no investigation of public allegations of a practice of disappearances nor a determination of whether Manfredo Velasquez had been a victim of that practice. ... The offer of an investigation in accord with Resolution 30/83 of the Commission resulted in an investigation by the Armed Forces, the same body accused of direct responsibility for the disappearances. This raises grave questions regarding the seriousness of the investigation. The Government often resorted to asking relatives of the victims to present conclusive proof of their allegations even though those allegations, because they involved crimes against the person, should have been investigated on the Government's own initiative in fulfillment of the State's duty to ensure public order. This is especially true when the allegations refer to a practice carried out within the Armed Forces, which, because of its nature, is not subject to private investigations. ... All of the above leads to the conclusion that the Honduran authorities did not take effective action to ensure respect for human rights within the jurisdiction of that State as required by Article 1(1) of the Convention.

181. The duty to investigate facts of this type continues as long as there is uncertainty about the fate of the person who has disappeared. Even in the hypothetical case that those individually responsible for crimes of this type cannot be legally punished under certain circumstances, the State is obligated to use the means at its disposal to inform the relatives of the fate of the victims and, if they have been killed, the location of their remains.

182. The Court is convinced, and has so found, that the disappearance of Manfredo Velasquez was carried out by agents who acted under cover of public authority. However, even had that fact not been proven, the failure of the State apparatus to act, which is clearly proven, is a failure on the part of Honduras to

fulfill the duties it assumed under Article 1(1) of the Convention, which obligated it to ensure Manfredo Velasquez the free and full exercise of his human rights.

183. The Court notes that the legal order of Honduras does not authorize such acts and that internal law defines them as crimes. The Court also recognizes that not all levels of the Government of Honduras were necessarily aware of those acts, nor is there any evidence that such acts were the result of official orders. Nevertheless, those circumstances are irrelevant for the purposes of establishing whether Honduras is responsible under international law for the violations of human rights perpetrated within the practice of disappearances. …

185. The Court, therefore, concludes that the facts found in this proceeding show that the State of Honduras is responsible for the involuntary disappearance of Angel Manfredo Velasquez Rodriguez. Thus, Honduras has violated Articles 7, 5 and 4 of the Convention.

186. As a result of the disappearance, Manfredo Velasquez was the victim of an arbitrary detention, which deprived him of his physical liberty without legal cause and without a determination of the lawfulness of his detention by a judge or competent tribunal. Those acts directly violate the right to personal liberty recognized by Article 7 of the Convention (supra 155) and are a violation imputable to Honduras of the duties to respect and ensure that right under Article 1(1).

187. The disappearance of Manfredo Velasquez violates the right to personal integrity recognized by Article 5 of the Convention (supra 156). First, the mere subjection of an individual to prolonged isolation and deprivation of communication is in itself cruel and inhuman treatment which harms the psychological and moral integrity of the person, and violates the right of every detainee under Article 5(1) and 5(2) to treatment respectful of his dignity. Second, although it has not been directly shown that Manfredo Velasquez was physically tortured, his kidnapping and imprisonment by governmental authorities, who have been shown to subject detainees to indignities, cruelty and torture, constitute a failure of Honduras to fulfill the duty imposed by Article 1(1) to ensure the rights under Article 5(1) and 5(2) of the Convention. The guarantee of physical integrity and the right of detainees to treatment respectful of their human dignity require States Parties to take reasonable steps to prevent situations which are truly harmful to the rights protected.

188. The above reasoning is applicable to the right to life recognized by Article 4 of the Convention (*supra* 157). The context in which the disappearance of Manfredo Velasquez occurred and the lack of knowledge seven years later about his fate create a reasonable presumption that he was killed. Even if there is a minimal margin of doubt in this respect, it must be presumed that his fate was decided by authorities who systematically executed detainees without trial and concealed their bodies in order to avoid punishment. This, together with the failure to investigate, is a violation by Honduras of a legal duty under Article 1(1) of the Convention to ensure the rights recognized by Article 4(1). That duty is to ensure to every person subject to its jurisdiction the inviolability of the right to life

and the right not to have one's life taken arbitrarily. These rights imply an obligation on the part of States Parties to take reasonable steps to prevent situations that could result in the violation of that right.

NOTES AND QUESTIONS

1. For practitioner perspectives, see Juan Méndez and José Miguel Vivanco, *Disappearances and the Inter-American Court: Reflections on a Litigation Experience,* 13 HAMLINE L. REV. 507 (1990); and Richard J. Wilson, *Researching the Jurisprudence of the Inter-American Commission on Human Rights: A Litigator's Perspective*, 10 AM. U. J. INT'L L. & POL'Y 1 (1994). *See also* Christina M. Cerna, *The Structure and Functioning of the Inter-American Court of Human Rights (1979-1992)*, BRIT. Y.B. INT'L L. 135 (1992); THE INTER-AMERICAN SYSTEM OF HUMAN RIGHTS (David J. Harris & Stephen Livingstone eds., Oxford U. Press 1998).

2. Is "causing disappearance" now internationally proscribed? *See Forti v. Suarez-Mason*, 694 F. Supp. 707 (N.D. Cal. 1988 (Forti II)).

3. The human rights abuses by the military dictatorship in Argentina were originally resolved by trying and convicting some of the individual abusers and then granting them amnesty. *See* David Weissbrodt & Maria Luisa Bartolomei, *The Effectiveness of International Human Rights Pressures: The Case of Argentina, 1976-1983*, 75 MINN. L. REV. 1009 (1991); IAIN GUEST, BEHIND THE DISAPPEARANCES: ARGENTINA'S DIRTY WAR AGAINST HUMAN RIGHTS AND THE UNITED NATIONS (U. Pa. Press 1990). This constitutional solution was challenged by President Nestor Kirchner in 2003. *See* Larry Rohter, *Argentine Congress Likely to Void 'Dirty War' Amnesties*, N.Y. TIMES, Aug. 21, 2003 at A3.

For further discussion of amnesty legislation in other countries, see William W. Burke-White, *Reframing Impunity: Applying Liberal International Law Theory to an Analysis of Amnesty Legislation*, 42 HARV. INT'L L. J. 467 (2001).

4. For compensation issues under *Velasquez Rodriguez*, see Jo M. Pasqualucci, *Victim Reparations in the Inter-American Human Rights System: A Critical Assessment of Current Practice and Procedure,* 18 MICH. J. INT'L L. 1 (1996).

D. UNIVERSAL HUMAN RIGHTS AND CLAIMS OF CULTURAL RELATIVITY: SELECTED SUBSTANTIVE ISSUES

1. The Treatment of Women

Women are a non-organic group in the sense that the members of this group, formed by accident of birth, are not united in the will to form a self-contained unit, an entity of common purpose. Their claims are, therefore, not oriented toward the goals of group autonomy or self-determination. Siegfried Wiessner, *Faces of Vulnerability: Protecting Individuals in Organic and Non-Organic Groups, supra*, at 224. Rather, what they are concerned about are violations of their integrity - physical, moral and civic - that occur because they are women. Those violations may be classified into simple unequal treatment where there is no justifiable gender-based reason; unequal treatment justified by gender difference; and situations of equal treatment where unequal treatment would be appropriate. Examples of violations of women's physical integrity include the *sati*, the ancient Hindu custom of burning widows; other homicides of females; the modern slavery of prostitution; systematic rape and forced impregnation of women; forced abortions and sterilizations; physical beatings and other forms of violence against women in societies around the globe; as well as female circumcision/genital mutilation practiced in some countries of Africa and Asia. While some of these actions are committed by government officials, most of them are not, and the government stands accused of letting them happen. It may actively encourage them, turn a blind eye, or fail to outlaw or effectively prosecute them.

Some of these practices (e.g., homicide, forced prostitution, rape, and forced impregnation) are viewed as bad, unacceptable and repugnant to any credible moral or legal system. Other practices are justified by the moral authority of the community in which they take place. *See* Courtney W. Howland, *The Challenge of Religious Fundamentalism to the Liberty and Equality Rights of Women: An Analysis Under the United Nations Charter,* 35 COLUM. J. TRANSNAT'L L. 271 (1997). However, other practices, such as female circumcision, the *sati*, the *hijab,* and other depredations of the physical and social integrity of women, are often justified as being a valid part of the individual's cultural environment. In the case of circumcision, it is argued that a woman can only fulfill her role as a woman in her culture by undergoing such "rites of initiation". Further, by forestalling this act she will be impaired in her personality development, will not be able to marry, and will most likely have to resort to prostitution for her economic survival. Perhaps ironically, these arguments are often made most forcefully by the other women of her community.

a. Abankwah v. INS

185 F.3d 18, 25-26 (2d Cir. 1999)

[Adelaide Abankwah, a 29-year old native of Ghana sought asylum in the United States and withholding of deportation on the grounds that should she return to Ghana, she would be forced to undergo FGM [Female Genital Mutilation] as a consequence of having engaged in premarital sex.

The Immigration Judge ("IJ") denied Abankwah's request for asylum and withholding of deportation. He determined that Abankwah was a credible witness, that she was clearly very fearful of returning to Ghana, and that she could not escape her tribe within Ghana because tribal members could eventually find her as they did in Accra. However, the IJ concluded that Abankwah had failed to establish that her fear of FGM as punishment for her lack of virginity was objectively reasonable…

Abankwah appealed this decision to the Board of Immigration Appeals ("BIA"), which dismissed it on a somewhat different basis. Unlike the IJ, the BIA did not dispute that Abankwah's fear of genital mutilation was on account of her membership in a cognizable social group. Rather, the BIA held that Abankwah had failed to meet her burden of proof in establishing past persecution, and that the "evidence is insufficient to support her claims of persecution based upon her membership in a social group, specifically "women of the Nkumssa tribe who did not remain virgins until marriage." On appeal, the Second Circuit determined that Abankwah did present sufficient evidence to support her claims:]

A reading of Abankwah's testimony in its entirety, combined with her affidavit, reveals that Abankwah's fear that she will be mutilated is based on her knowledge of and experience with the customs of her tribe. Having established that Abankwah is credible, we accept as fact her assertion that Nkumssa custom includes FGM as a punishment for premarital sex. Abankwah's position is particularly compelling in light of the general conditions present in Ghana. In 1997, the United States Department of State estimated that between 15 and 30 percent of all women and girls in Ghana had been subjected to FGM. See United States Department of State Report on Female Genital Mutilation (FGM) in Ghana (Feb. 5, 1997) at 1. Although the government of Ghana clearly recognizes that the practice of FGM exists and criminalized it in 1994, the number of prosecutions has been insignificant. The record indicates that there have been only seven arrests for this crime since 1994. …

Abankwah's fear of FGM is thus sufficiently "grounded in reality" to satisfy the objective element of the test for well-founded fear of persecution. Given the customs of the Nkumssa tribe, a reasonable person who knew that she had disobeyed a tribal taboo and knew that discovery by the tribe of her disobedience was imminent would share Abankwah's fears. For the reasons stated above, the decision of the BIA that Abankwah is not eligible for asylum is reversed and remanded for further proceedings not inconsistent with this opinion.

* * *

Professor Reisman has commented on the problem of imposing international human rights standards on culturally distinct societies, in particular those in which key women's rights are seen as a threat to the very survival of the culture.

b. W. Michael Reisman, *Aftershocks: Reflections on the Implications of September 11*

6 YALE H.R. & DEV. L.J. 81 (2003)

Since 1945, the international legal system, at the initiative of leading Western modernizing states, has established a set of ground rules of political and other social organization based upon what it considers to be universally valid and self-evident principles. It is the Universal Declaration of Human Rights, concluded by the United Nations General Assembly in 1948, which we now present as the universal "standard of achievement." With minor variations, regional human rights treaties in Europe and the Americas have adopted the principles and even the language of the Universal Declaration. Since 1948, a network of institutions of varying degrees of compulsoriness and effectiveness have worked to implement them. Let me briefly remind you of some of those rights by quoting from the Universal Declaration:

> Article 2(1): Everyone is entitled to all the rights and freedom set forth in this Declaration, without distinction of any kind, such as race, color, sex, language, religion, political or other opinion, national or social origin, property, birth or other status Article 5: No one shall be subjected to torture or to cruel, inhuman or degrading treatment or punishment.
>
> Article 5: No one shall be subjected to torture or to cruel, inhuman or degrading treatment or punishment.
>
> Article 16(1): Men and women of full age, without any limitation due to race, nationality or religion, have the right to marry and to found a family. They are entitled to equal rights as to marriage, during marriage and at its dissolution.
>
> Article 16(2): Marriage shall be entered into only with the free and full consent of the intending spouses. …
>
> Article 19: Everyone has the right to freedom of opinion and expression; this right includes freedom to hold opinions without interference and to seek, receive and impart information and ideas through any media and regardless of frontiers. …

Although the United Nations Charter purported to reserve the domestic jurisdiction of states from international concern, Western governments and the human rights lobby have vigorously diminished the scope of domestic jurisdiction so that it no longer buffers the internal legal arrangements of states from the application of international human rights law. We press them as a precondition for regional and world peace because we believe that democracies do not wage war against each other. We press them as a precondition for economic development, because we assume that it requires a free and open society in order to flourish. These instrumental calculations aside, we also advance our values for their own sake. In the part of the planet which we inhabit, we accept these human rights as basic, necessary and self-evident principles of political and social organization. So quite naturally, we characterize as pathological and pathogenic many of the cultural practices in other parts of the world that deviate from them.

The values we designate as "universal" are, indeed, "universalizable," in contrast with tribal or other ethnically or religiously restrictive values which limit their reach and confine their benefits to members of a particular group. But "universalizable" values are not necessarily universally held. Nor are they "natural." Many of our values are the result of momentous conflicts in our own civilization. It was the Reformation, an event attended by great violence, that laid the basis for the idea, not self-evident to true believers then or, I daresay, now, that different religions are equally legitimate, can flourish side by side and require the concept of freedom of expression. Civilizations that have not gone through something comparable to the Reformation - one thinks of the systems of public order in Latin America and Asia and not simply in Islam - have great difficulty even understanding the notion of freedom of religion and freedom of expression. Indeed, in certain parts of the world, freedom of religions, in the plural, is viewed as a contradiction in terms: allowing other faiths to proselytize your co-religionists is complicity in apostasy. As for sexual equality and sexual freedom, now so central to individual self-expression in our civilization, these values are viewed in other civilizations as the official installation of a policy of promiscuity and constitute a particularly pernicious form of evil, both corrupt and corrupting. …

…[What our universal standards] mean to many of those who are being targeted for "development" is a coercive dismantling of their own cultural system, "self-amputations of [their] own being," to use Marshall McLuhan's vivid expression. McLuhan wrote, "All social changes are the effect of new technologies...on the order of our sensory lives. It is the shift in this order, altering the images that we make of ourselves and our world, that guarantees that every major technical innovation will so disturb our inner lives that wars necessarily result as misbegotten efforts to recover the old images." (MARSHALL MCLUHAN & QUINTIN FIORE, WAR AND PEACE IN THE GLOBAL VILLAGE 4 (1968)). …

While we may support modernizing elites in the Islamic world for programmatic political reasons, we press our values for ideological ones. And it is hard to see how we can stop without changing who we are and how we are organized, for while Islam historically allowed for zones of believers and zones of non-believers, our conception of human dignity is inherently universal and presses its exponents to project and demand values worldwide.

* * *

Women have been prey to fundamentalist religious dogma regardless of the society or religious culture in which they live. In 1996, the Taliban government in Afghanistan ordered the public stoning of a man and a woman charged with adultery. The incident was widely and graphically reported in the press.

The reaction of much of the world community was reflected in Security Council Resolution 1076:

c. Security Council Resolution 1076 (1996)

Adopted by the Security Council at its 3706th meeting, on 22 October 1996

The Security Council,

Having considered the situation in Afghanistan…

Deeply concerned about the discrimination against women and other abuses of human rights in Afghanistan, …

11. *Denounces* the discrimination against girls and women and other violations of human rights and international humanitarian law in Afghanistan, and notes with deep concern possible repercussions on international relief and reconstruction programmes in Afghanistan;…

NOTES AND QUESTIONS

1. What should be the proper solution to conflicts between an individual woman's interest in physical integrity and claims to moral integrity raised by the dominant forces of the community in which she lives? Protection of life and limb would seem to be a fundamental tenet of the human rights regimes. Should physical intrusion be the baseline of individual human dignity against which claims of culture and community cannot prevail? If so, should the state and others be prohibited from the use of such intrusions? Female circumcision would, under this theory of limitation, be outlawed, along with *sati* and forced sterilization. What about criminal sanctions that involve mere physical punishment? Public flogging? The stoning of adulterers? *See* Tracy E. Higgins, *Anti-Essentialism, Relativism, and Human Rights,* 19 HARV. WOMEN'S L.J. 89 (1996); Elene G. Mountis, *Cultural Relativity and Universalism: Reevaluating Gender Rights in a Multicultural Context,* 15 DICK. J. INT'L L. 113 (1996).

2. Despite the focus on individuals in the major international human rights conventions, a number of instruments have elaborated special protection regimes and policies for particular groups, *e.g.*, women and children, refugees and targets of racial or religious discrimination. The justification for these special treatments is to be found in the indignities and deprivations that members of these groups have suffered because the patterns of discrimination appear to be interwoven, as noted above, into the cultures in which they operate. Instruments specifically designed to protect women include the Convention on the Elimination of All Forms of Discrimination Against Women, (18 Dec. 1979, 34 U.N. GAOR, Supp. No. 21 (A/34/46), at 193, U.N. Doc. A/RES/34/180, 1249 U.N.T.S. 14 (entered into force 3 Sept. 1981)), and the Inter-American Convention on the Prevention, Punishment and Eradication of Violence Against Women, Inter-American Commission on Women, June 9, 1994, 33 I.L.M. 1534 (1994). *See also,* Rebecca J. Cook & Valerie L. Oosterveld, *A Select Bibliography of Women's Human Rights,* 44 AM. U. L. REV. 1429 (1995); HUMAN RIGHTS OF WOMEN: NATIONAL AND INTERNATIONAL PERSPECTIVES (Rebecca J. Cook ed., U. Pa. Press 1994); FROM BASIC NEEDS TO BASIC RIGHTS: WOMEN'S CLAIM TO HUMAN RIGHTS (Margaret Schuler ed. Women Law & Development Intl 1995); Winston Langley, *The Rights of Women, the African Charter, and the Economic Development of Africa,* 7 B.C. THIRD WORLD L.J. 215 (1987); Kristin J. Miller, *Human Rights of Women in Iran: The Universalist Approach and the Relativist Response,* 10 EMORY INT'L L. REV. 779 (1996); M.H.A. Reisman, *Some Reflections on Human Rights and Clerical Claims to Political Power,* 19 YALE J. INT'L L. 509 (1994).

3. Many women, particularly in economically under-developed countries, view as their most critical problem the absence of economic opportunity and social status. Their economic situation often forces them into prostitution and other statuses of subjugation. If they are mobile enough, they may cross borders, but, then again, they may end up in first-world situations of subordination and exploitation, thanks to the globalizing sex industry and the burgeoning mail-order bride business. It has been proposed that these exploitative schemes be regulated internationally. Christine S.Y. Chun, *The Mail-Order Bride Industry: The Perpetuation of Transnational Economic Inequalities and Stereotypes,* 17 U. PA. J. INT'L ECON. L. 1155 (1996). *See also* Nora V. Demleitner, *Forced Prostitution: Naming an International* Offense, 18 FORDHAM INT'L L.J. 163 (1994); Mary De Ming Fan, *The Fallacy of the Sovereign Prerogative to Set De Minimis Liability Rules for Sexual Slavery,* 27 YALE J. INT'L L. 395 (2002); Barbara Stark, *After/word(s): 'Violations of Human Dignity' and Postmodern International Law*, 27 YALE J. INT'L L. 315 (2002). As to violence against women, see Margareth Etienne, *Addressing Gender-Based Violence in an International Context,* 18 HARV. WOMEN'S L.J. 139 (1995); Elizabeth Dietz, *Violence Against Women in the United States: An International Solution,* 13 ARIZ. J. INT'L & COMP. L. 551 (1996).

4. The deprivations of women are often justified by reference to the dominant religious beliefs of their communities. Those beliefs have often been given full effect in the positive law of the state. Discussion of the relationship between state and religion, in the recent past, largely oscillated between the poles of negative and positive toleration. What was untouched, on a global basis, was the post-Westphalian principle: the individual freedom to choose and practice one's religion

subject to minimal governmental constraints. This principle was enshrined in the various human rights instruments at the global and the regional levels. In particular, Article 20(2) of the International Covenant on Civil and Political Rights prohibits "any advocacy of ... religious hatred that constitutes incitement to discrimination, hostility or violence." The 1981 General Assembly Declaration on the Elimination of All Forms of Intolerance, and of Discrimination Based on Religion and Belief, goes even further than that and states, in Article 3, that "[d]iscrimination between human beings on the grounds of religion or belief constitutes an affront to human dignity and a disavowal of the principles of the Charter of the United Nations." U.N.G.A. Res. 36/55 (1981).

5. The rise of modern fundamentalism in the Islamic World and beyond attacks this pillar of the post-Westphalian order. Divided amongst themselves as the communities of, say post-Shah Iran or Taliban-governed Afghanistan may appear, they agree on one principle: the preeminence of religious over secular law, and the need for uniform enforcement of the social order rules of the dominant state religion. In instituting repression of other faiths, they throw the gauntlet to the prevailing theory of religious toleration, leaving the international decision-making process with the vexing problem. For proposed methods of dealing with this *compare* MICHAEL WALZER, ON TOLERATION (Yale U. Press, 1997); W. Michael Reisman, *Autonomy, Interdependence, and Responsibility,* 103 YALE L.J. 401 (1993). *See also* Leslie C. Griffin, *Fundamentalism from the Perspective of Liberal Tolerance*, 24 CARDOZO L. REV. 1631 (2003); Steven Mailloux, *Contingent Universals: Religious Fundamentalism, Academic Post-modernism, and Public Intellectuals in the Aftermath of September 11*, 24 CARDOZO L. REV. 1583 (2003).

6. One argument for exempting these regimes from the post-Westphalian consensus is based on "cultural relativism": it claims that there are no legitimate cross-cultural standards, no "universal truths" in terms of rules of conduct; all cultures are, in this respect, "equally valid." The moral integrity of the individual as defined by his or her social context is deemed a value superior to the individual's freedom of choice. The dominant group's system of rectitude could thus legitimately run counter, and ultimately trump, an individual right universally defined. *See* Douglas Lee Donoho, *Relativism Versus Universalism in Human Rights: The Search for Meaningful Standards,* 27 STAN. J. INT'L L. 345 (1991); Christina M. Cerna, *Universality of Human Rights and Cultural Diversity: Implementation of Human Rights in Different Socio-Cultural Cont*exts, 16 HUM. RTS. Q. 740, 741-42 (1994); Robert D. Sloane, *Outrelativizing Relativism: A Liberal Defense of the Universality of International Human Rights*, 34 VAND. J. TRANSNAT'L L. 527 (2001).

7. Several issues arise: Can claims to cultural relativity and to universal human rights be reconciled? More fundamentally: Is a religious state at all compatible with the idea of human rights? Why shouldn't a religious majority, in accordance with the principle of democratic rule, be able to enact laws based on its moral judgments? If yes, are there any limits, such as the physical integrity of individuals? Should there be rights of exit from such a community? As to some of these problems, *see* MICHAEL WALZER, *supra* note 2; Adeno Addis, *On Human Diversity and the Limits of Toleration,* 39 NOMOS 112 (1997); Donald E. Smith, *Religion and the Good Polity,* 4 CARDOZO J. INT'L & COMP. L. 277 (1996); Steven D. Smith, *The Restoration of Tolerance,* 78 CALIF. L. REV. 305 (1990); *Has Religion Served as a Catalyst or Impediment to International Law?,* 87 AM. SOC'Y INT'L L. PROC. 321 (1993); Jay Schiffman, *Tolerance as Understanding*, 3 MARGINS 1 (2003).

3. Sexual Conduct and the Right to Privacy

Conflicts between universal human rights as interpreted by inclusive review bodies and community values may not only occur in "fundamentalist" societies. Consider the issue of criminalization of homosexual conduct.

a. Bowers v. Hardwick
478 U.S. 186 (1986)

WHITE, J.: In August 1982, respondent Hardwick (hereafter respondent) was charged with violating the Georgia statute criminalizing sodomy by committing that act with another adult male in the bedroom of respondent's home. After a preliminary hearing, the District Attorney decided not to present the matter to the grand jury unless further evidence developed.

Respondent then brought suit in the Federal District Court, challenging the constitutionality of the statute insofar as it criminalized consensual sodomy. He asserted that he was a practicing homosexual, that the Georgia sodomy statute, as administered by the defendants, placed him in imminent danger of arrest, and that the statute for several reasons violates the Federal Constitution. The District Court granted the defendants' motion to dismiss for failure to state a claim. ... A divided panel of the Court of Appeals for the Eleventh Circuit reversed. ... We agree with petitioner that the Court of Appeals erred, and hence reverse its judgment.

This case does not require a judgment on whether laws against sodomy between consenting adults in general, or between homosexuals in particular, are wise or desirable. It raises no question about the right or propriety of state legislative decisions to repeal their laws that criminalize homosexual sodomy, or of state-court decisions invalidating those laws on state constitutional grounds. The issue presented is whether the Federal Constitution confers a fundamental right upon homosexuals to engage in sodomy and hence invalidates the laws of the many States that still make such conduct illegal and have done so for a very long time. The case also calls for some judgment about the limits of the Court's role in carrying out its constitutional mandate.

We first register our disagreement with the Court of Appeals and with respondent that the Court's prior cases have construed the Constitution to confer a right of privacy that extends to homosexual sodomy and for all intents and purposes have decided this case. ...

[N]one of the rights announced in those cases bears any resemblance to the claimed constitutional right of homosexuals to engage in acts of sodomy that is asserted in this case. No connection between family, marriage, or procreation on the one hand and homosexual activity on the other has been demonstrated. ... Moreover, any claim that these cases nevertheless stand for the proposition that any kind of private sexual conduct between consenting adults is constitutionally insulated from state proscription is unsupportable. ...

Precedent aside, however, respondent would have us announce, as the Court of Appeals did, a fundamental right to engage in homosexual sodomy. This we are quite unwilling to do. It is true that despite the language of the Due Process Clauses of the Fifth and Fourteenth Amendments, which appears to focus only on the processes by which life, liberty, or property is taken, the cases are legion in which those Clauses have been interpreted to have substantive content, subsuming rights that to a great extent are immune from federal or state regulation or proscription. Among such cases are those recognizing rights that have little or no textual support in the constitutional language. *Meyer*, *Prince*, and *Pierce* fall in this category, as do the privacy cases from *Griswold* to *Carey*.

Striving to assure itself and the public that announcing rights not readily identifiable in the Constitution's text involves much more than the imposition of the Justices' own choice of values on the States and the Federal Government, the Court has sought to identify the nature of the rights qualifying for heightened judicial protection. In *Palko v. Connecticut*, 302 U.S. 319, 325, 326 (1937), it was said that this category includes those fundamental liberties that are "implicit in the concept of ordered liberty," such that "neither liberty nor justice would exist if [they] were sacrificed." A different description of fundamental liberties appeared in *Moore v. East Cleveland*, 431 U.S. 494, 503 (1977)(opinion of POWELL, J.), where they are characterized as those liberties that are "deeply rooted in this Nation's history and tradition." Id., at 503 (POWELL, J.). ...

It is obvious to us that neither of these formulations would extend a fundamental right to homosexuals to engage in acts of consensual sodomy. Proscriptions against that conduct have ancient roots. ... Sodomy was a criminal offense at common law and was forbidden by the laws of the original thirteen States when they ratified the Bill of Rights. In 1868, when the Fourteenth Amendment was ratified, all but 5 of the 37 States in the Union had criminal sodomy laws. In fact, until 1961, all 50 States outlawed sodomy, and today, 24 States and the District of Columbia continue to provide criminal penalties for sodomy performed in private and between consenting adults. ... Against this background, to claim that a right to engage in such conduct is "deeply rooted in this Nation's history and tradition" or "implicit in the concept of ordered liberty" is, at best, facetious. ...

Respondent, however, asserts that the result should be different where the homosexual conduct occurs in the privacy of the home. He relies on *Stanley v. Georgia*, 394 U.S. 557 (1969), where the Court held that the First Amendment prevents conviction for possessing and reading obscene material in the privacy of one's home: "If the First Amendment means anything, it means that a State has no business telling a man, sitting alone in his house, what books he may read or what films he may watch." Id., at 565.

Stanley did protect conduct that would not have been protected outside the home, and it partially prevented the enforcement of state obscenity laws; but the decision was firmly grounded in the First Amendment. The right pressed upon us here has no similar support in the text of the Constitution, and it does not qualify for recognition under the prevailing principles for construing the Fourteenth Amendment. Its limits are also difficult to discern. Plainly enough, otherwise illegal conduct is not always immunized whenever it occurs in the home. Victimless crimes, such as the possession and use of illegal drugs, do not escape the law where they are committed at home. *Stanley* itself recognized that its holding offered no protection for the possession in the home of drugs, firearms, or stolen goods. *Id.*, at 568, n. 11. And if respondent's submission is limited to the voluntary sexual conduct between consenting adults, it would be difficult, except by fiat, to limit the claimed right to homosexual conduct while leaving exposed to prosecution adultery, incest, and other sexual crimes even though they are committed in the home. We are unwilling to start down that road.

Even if the conduct at issue here is not a fundamental right, respondent asserts that there must be a rational basis for the law and that there is none in this case other than the presumed belief of a majority of the electorate in Georgia that homosexual sodomy is immoral and unacceptable. This is said to be an inadequate rationale to support the law. The law, however, is constantly based on notions of morality, and if all laws representing essentially moral choices are to be invalidated under the Due Process Clause, the courts will be very busy indeed. Even respondent makes no such claim, but insists that majority sentiments about the morality of homosexuality should be declared inadequate. We do not agree, and are unpersuaded that the sodomy laws of some 25 States should be invalidated on this basis.

Accordingly, the judgment of the Court of Appeals is Reversed.

b. Toonen v. Australia

Case No. 488/1992, Apr. 4, 1994
U.N. GAOR Human Rights Committee, 15th Sess.,
U.N. Doc. CCPR/C/50/D/488/1992 (1994)

1. The author of the communication is Nicholas Toonen, an Australian citizen born in 1964, currently residing in Hobart in the state of Tasmania, Australia. He is a leading member of the Tasmanian Gay Law Reform Group (TGLRG) and claims to be a victim of violations by Australia of articles 2, paragraphs 1, 17 and 26 of the International Covenant on Civil and Political Rights.

The facts as submitted by the author:

2.1 The author is an activist for the promotion of the rights of homosexuals in Tasmania, one of Australia's six constitutive states. He challenges two provisions of the Tasmanian Criminal Code, namely Sections 122(a) and (c) and 123, which criminalize various forms of sexual contacts between men, including all forms of sexual contacts between consenting adult homosexual men in private.

2.2 The author observes that the above sections of the Tasmanian Criminal Code empower Tasmanian police officers to investigate intimate aspects of his private life and to detain him, if they have reason to believe that he is involved in sexual activities which contravene the above sections. He adds that the Director of Public Prosecutions announced, in August 1988, that proceedings pursuant to

Sections 122(a), (c) and 123 would be initiated if there was sufficient evidence of the commission of a crime.

2.3 Although in practice the Tasmanian police has not charged anyone either with "unnatural sexual intercourse" or "intercourse against nature" (Section 122) nor with "indecent practice between male persons" (Section 123) for several years, the author argues that because of his long-term relationship with another man, his active lobbying of Tasmanian politicians and the reports about his activities in the local media, and because of his activities as a gay rights activist and gay HIV/AIDS worker, his private life and his liberty are threatened by the continued existence of Sections 122(a), (c) and 123 of the Criminal Code.

2.4 Mr. Toonen further argues that the criminalization of homosexuality in private has not permitted him to expose openly his sexuality and to publicize his views on reform of the relevant laws on sexual matters, as he felt that this would have been extremely prejudicial to his employment. In this context, he contends that Sections 122(a), (c) and 123 have created the conditions for discrimination in employment, constant stigmatization, vilification, threats of physical violence and the violation of basic democratic rights. …

Examination of the merits:

8.1 The Committee is called upon to determine whether Mr. Toonen has been the victim of an unlawful or arbitrary interference with his privacy, contrary to article 17, paragraph 1, and whether he has been discriminated against in his right to equal protection of the law, contrary to article 26.

8.2 Inasmuch as article 17 is concerned, it is undisputed that adult consensual sexual activity in private is covered by the concept of "privacy", and that Mr. Toonen is actually and currently affected by the continued existence of the Tasmanian laws. The Committee considers that Sections 122(a), (c) and 123 of the Tasmanian Criminal Code "interfere" with the author's privacy, even if these provisions have not been enforced for a decade. In this context, it notes that the policy of the Department of Public Prosecutions not to initiate criminal proceedings in respect of private homosexual conduct does not amount to a guarantee that no actions will be brought against homosexuals in the future, particularly in the light of undisputed statements of the Director of Public Prosecutions of Tasmania in 1988 and those of members of the Tasmanian Parliament. The continued existence of the challenged provisions therefore continuously and directly "interferes" with the author's privacy.

8.3 The prohibition against private homosexual behaviour is provided for by law, namely, Sections 122 and 123 of the Tasmanian Criminal Code. As to whether it may be deemed arbitrary, the Committee recalls that pursuant to its General Comment 16 on article 17, the "introduction of the concept of arbitrariness is intended to guarantee that even interference provided for by the law should be in accordance with the provisions, aims and objectives of the Covenant and should be, in any event, reasonable in the circumstances". The Committee interprets the requirement of reasonableness to imply that any interference with privacy must be proportional to the end sought and be necessary in the circumstances of any given case.

8.4 While the State party acknowledges that the impugned provisions constitute an arbitrary interference with Mr. Toonen's privacy, the Tasmanian authorities submit that the challenged laws are justified on public health and moral grounds, as they are intended in part to prevent the spread of HIV/AIDS in Tasmania, and because, in the absence of specific limitation clauses in article 17, moral issues must be deemed a matter for domestic decision.

8.5 As far as the public health argument of the Tasmanian authorities is concerned, the Committee notes that the criminalization of homosexual practices cannot be considered a reasonable means or proportionate measure to achieve the aim of preventing the spread of AIDS/HIV. The Australian Government observes that statutes criminalizing homosexual activity tend to impede public health programmes "by driving underground many of the people at the risk of infection". Criminalization of homosexual activity thus would appear to run counter to the implementation of effective education programmes in respect of the HIV/AIDS prevention. Secondly, the Committee notes that no link has been shown between the continued criminalization of homosexual activity and the effective control of the spread of the HIV/AIDS virus.

8.6 The Committee cannot accept either that for the purposes of article 17 of the Covenant, moral issues are exclusively a matter of domestic concern, as this would open the door to withdrawing from the Committee's scrutiny a potentially large number of statutes interfering with privacy. It further notes that with the exception of Tasmania, all laws criminalizing homosexuality have been repealed throughout Australia and that, even in Tasmania, it is apparent that there is no consensus as to whether Sections 122 and 123 should not also be repealed. Considering further that these provisions are not currently enforced, which implies that they are not deemed essential to the protection of morals in Tasmania, the Committee concludes that the provisions do not meet the "reasonableness" test in the circumstances of the case, and that they arbitrarily interfere with Mr. Toonen's right under article 17, paragraph 1.

8.7 The State party has sought the Committee's guidance as to whether sexual orientation may be considered an "other status" for the purposes of article 26. The same issue could arise under article 2, paragraph 1, of the Covenant. The Committee confines itself to noting, however, that in its view the reference to "sex" in articles 2, paragraph 1, and 26 is to be taken as including sexual orientation.

9. The Human Rights Committee, acting under article 5, paragraph 4, of the Optional Protocol to the International Covenant on Civil and Political Rights, is of the view that the facts before it reveal a violation of articles 17, paragraph 1, juncto 2, paragraph 1, of the Covenant.

10. Under article 2(3)(a) of the Covenant, the author, victim of a violation of articles 17, paragraph 1, juncto 2, paragraph 1, of the Covenant, is entitled to a remedy. In the opinion of the Committee, an effective remedy would be the repeal of Sections 122(a), (c) and 123 of the Tasmanian Criminal Code.

11. Since the Committee has found a violation of Mr. Toonen's rights under articles 17(1) and 2(1) of the Covenant requiring the repeal of the offending law, the Committee does not consider it necessary to consider whether there has also been a violation of article 26 of the Covenant.

12. The Committee would wish to receive, within 90 days of the date of the transmittal of its Views, information from the State party on the measures taken to give effect to the Views.

* * *

By 1981, the European Court of Human Rights had already held laws proscribing homosexual conduct violative of the privacy right of Article 8 of the European Convention on Human Rights. *Dudgeon v. United Kingdom,* 45 Eur. Ct. H.R. (1981). See also *Norris v. Ireland,* 142 Eur. Ct. H.R. (1988); *Modinos v. Cyprus,* 259 Eur. Ct. H.R. (1993); and *P.G. & J.H. v. United Kingdom,* App. No. 00044787/98 (Eur.Ct.H. R., Sept. 25, 2001). In 2003, the U.S. Supreme Court revisited the issue.

c. Lawrence v. Texas

539 U.S. 558 (2003)

KENNEDY, J.: The question before the Court is the validity of a Texas statute making it a crime for two persons of the same sex to engage in certain intimate sexual conduct.

In Houston, Texas, officers of the Harris County Police Department were dispatched to a private residence in response to a reported weapons disturbance. They entered an apartment where one of the petitioners, John Geddes Lawrence, resided. The right of the police to enter does not seem to have been questioned. The officers observed Lawrence and another man, Tyron Garner, engaging in a sexual act. The two petitioners were arrested, held in custody over night, and charged and convicted before a Justice of the Peace.

The complaints described their crime as "deviate sexual intercourse, namely anal sex, with a member of the same sex (man)." ... The applicable state law is Tex. Penal Code Ann. § 21.06(a) (2003). It provides: "A person commits an offense if he engages in deviate sexual intercourse with another individual of the same sex." The statute defines "[d]eviate sexual intercourse" as follows:

> (A) any contact between any part of the genitals of one person and the mouth or anus of another person; or (B) the penetration of the genitals or the anus of another person with an object. § 21.01(1).

The petitioners exercised their right to a trial *de novo* in Harris County Criminal Court. They challenged the statute as a violation of the Equal Protection Clause of the Fourteenth Amendment and of a like provision of the Texas Constitution. Tex. Const., Art. 1, § 3a. Those contentions were rejected. The petitioners, having entered a plea of *nolo contendere,* were each fined $200 and assessed court costs of $141.25. …

We conclude the case should be resolved by determining whether the petitioners were free as adults to engage in the private conduct in the exercise of their liberty under the Due Process Clause of the Fourteenth Amendment to the Constitution. For this inquiry we deem it necessary to reconsider the Court's holding in *Bowers.* …

The Court began its substantive discussion in *Bowers* as follows: "The issue presented is whether the Federal Constitution confers a fundamental right upon homosexuals to engage in sodomy and hence invalidates the laws of the many States that still make such conduct illegal and have done so for a very long time." *Id., at 190, 106 S.Ct. 2841.* That statement, we now conclude, discloses the Court's own failure to appreciate the extent of the liberty at stake. To say that the issue in *Bowers* was simply the right to engage in certain sexual conduct demeans the claim the individual put forward, just as it would demean a married couple were it to be said marriage is simply about the right to have sexual intercourse. The laws involved in *Bowers* and here are, to be sure, statutes that purport to do no more than prohibit a particular sexual act. Their penalties and purposes, though, have more far-reaching consequences, touching upon the most private human conduct, sexual behavior, and in the most private of places, the home. The statutes do seek to control a personal relationship that, whether or not entitled to formal recognition in the law, is within the liberty of persons to choose without being punished as criminals.

This, as a general rule, should counsel against attempts by the State, or a court, to define the meaning of the relationship or to set its boundaries absent injury to a person or abuse of an institution the law protects. It suffices for us to acknowledge that adults may choose to enter upon this relationship in the confines of their homes and their own private lives and still retain their dignity as free persons. When sexuality finds overt expression in intimate conduct with another person, the conduct can be but one element in a personal bond that is more enduring. The liberty protected by the Constitution allows homosexual persons the right to make this choice.

Having misapprehended the claim of liberty there presented to it, and thus stating the claim to be whether there is a fundamental right to engage in consensual sodomy, the *Bowers* Court said: "Proscriptions against that conduct have ancient roots." *Id., at 192.* In academic writings, and in many of the scholarly *amicus* briefs filed to assist the Court in this case, there are fundamental criticisms of the historical premises relied upon by the majority and concurring opinions in *Bowers.* … We need not enter this debate in the attempt to reach a definitive historical judgment, but the following considerations counsel against adopting the definitive conclusions upon which *Bowers* placed such reliance.

At the outset it should be noted that there is no longstanding history in this country of laws directed at homosexual conduct as a distinct matter. Beginning in colonial times there were prohibitions of sodomy derived from the English criminal laws passed in the first instance by the Reformation Parliament of 1533. The English prohibition was understood to include relations between men and women as well as relations between men and men. ... Nineteenth-century commentators similarly read American sodomy, buggery, and crime-against-nature statutes as criminalizing certain relations between men and women and between men and men. ... The absence of legal prohibitions focusing on homosexual conduct may be explained in part by noting that according to some scholars the concept of the homosexual as a distinct category of person did not emerge until the late 19th century. ... Thus early American sodomy laws were not directed at homosexuals as such but instead sought to prohibit nonprocreative sexual activity more generally. This does not suggest approval of homosexual conduct. It does tend to show that this particular form of conduct was not thought of as a separate category from like conduct between heterosexual persons.

Laws prohibiting sodomy do not seem to have been enforced against consenting adults acting in private. A substantial number of sodomy prosecutions and convictions for which there are surviving records were for predatory acts against those who could not or did not consent, as in the case of a minor or the victim of an assault. ...

It was not until the 1970's that any State singled out same-sex relations for criminal prosecution, and only nine States have done so. ... Post-*Bowers* even some of these States did not adhere to the policy of suppressing homosexual conduct. Over the course of the last decades, States with same-sex prohibitions have moved toward abolishing them. ...

In summary, the historical grounds relied upon in *Bowers* are more complex than the majority opinion and the concurring opinion by Chief Justice Burger indicate. Their historical premises are not without doubt and, at the very least, are overstated.

It must be acknowledged, of course, that the Court in *Bowers* was making the broader point that for centuries there have been powerful voices to condemn homosexual conduct as immoral. The condemnation has been shaped by religious beliefs, conceptions of right and acceptable behavior, and respect for the traditional family. For many persons these are not trivial concerns but profound and deep convictions accepted as ethical and moral principles to which they aspire and which thus determine the course of their lives. These considerations do not answer the question before us, however. The issue is whether the majority may use the power of the State to enforce these views on the whole society through operation of the criminal law. ...

Chief Justice Burger joined the opinion for the Court in *Bowers* and further explained his views as follows: "Decisions of individuals relating to homosexual conduct have been subject to state intervention throughout the history of Western civilization. Condemnation of those practices is firmly rooted in Judeao-Christian moral and ethical standards." 478 U.S., at 196, 106 S.Ct. 2841. As with Justice White's assumptions about history, scholarship casts some doubt on the sweeping nature of the statement by Chief Justice Burger as it pertains to private homosexual conduct between consenting adults. See, *e.g.,* Eskridge, Hardwick and Historiography, 1999 U. Ill. L.Rev. 631, 656. In all events we think that our laws and traditions in the past half century are of most relevance here. These references show an emerging awareness that liberty gives substantial protection to adult persons in deciding how to conduct their private lives in matters pertaining to sex. "[H]istory and tradition are the starting point but not in all cases the ending point of the substantive due process inquiry." *County of Sacramento v. Lewis, 523 U.S. 833, 857 (1998)* (KENNEDY, J., concurring).

This emerging recognition should have been apparent when *Bowers* was decided. In 1955 the American Law Institute promulgated the Model Penal Code and made clear that it did not recommend or provide for "criminal penalties for consensual sexual relations conducted in private." ALI, Model Penal Code § 213.2, Comment 2, p. 372 (1980). It justified its decision on three grounds: (1) The prohibitions undermined respect for the law by penalizing conduct many people engaged in; (2) the statutes regulated private conduct not harmful to others; and (3) the laws were arbitrarily enforced and thus invited the danger of blackmail. ALI, Model Penal Code, Commentary 277-280 (Tent. Draft No. 4, 1955). In 1961 Illinois changed its laws to conform to the Model Penal Code. Other States soon followed. ...

In *Bowers* the Court referred to the fact that before 1961 all 50 States had outlawed sodomy, and that at the time of the Court's decision 24 States and the District of Columbia had sodomy laws. 478 U.S., at 192-193. Justice Powell pointed out that these prohibitions often were being ignored, however. Georgia, for instance, had not sought to enforce its law for decades. *Id.,* at 197-198, n. 2 ("The history of nonenforcement suggests the moribund character today of laws criminalizing this type of private, consensual conduct").

The sweeping references by Chief Justice Burger to the history of Western civilization and to Judeo-Christian moral and ethical standards did not take account of other authorities pointing in an opposite direction. A committee advising the British Parliament recommended in 1957 repeal of laws punishing homosexual conduct. The Wolfenden Report: Report of the Committee on Homosexual Offenses and Prostitution (1963). Parliament enacted the substance of those recommendations 10 years later. Sexual Offences Act 1967, § 1.

Of even more importance, almost five years before *Bowers* was decided the European Court of Human Rights considered a case with parallels to *Bowers* and to today's case. An adult male resident in Northern Ireland alleged he was a practicing homosexual who desired to engage in consensual homosexual conduct. The laws of Northern Ireland forbade him that right. He alleged that he had been questioned, his home had been searched, and he feared criminal prosecution. The court held that the laws proscribing the conduct were invalid under the European Convention on Human Rights. *Dudgeon v. United Kingdom,* 45 Eur. Ct. H.R. (1981) & ¶ 52. Authoritative in all countries that are members of the Council of Europe (21 nations then, 45 nations now), the decision is at odds with the premise in *Bowers* that the claim put forward was insubstantial in our Western civilization.

In our own constitutional system the deficiencies in *Bowers* became even more apparent in the years following its announcement. The 25 States with laws prohibiting the relevant conduct referenced in the *Bowers* decision are reduced now to 13, of which 4 enforce their laws only against homosexual conduct. In those States where sodomy is still proscribed, whether for same- sex or heterosexual conduct, there is a pattern of nonenforcement with respect to consenting adults acting in private. The State of Texas admitted in 1994 that as of that date it had not prosecuted anyone under those circumstances. *State v. Morales, 869 S.W.2d 941, 943.*

Two principal cases decided after *Bowers* cast its holding into even more doubt. In *Planned Parenthood of Southeastern Pa. v. Casey, 505 U.S. 833 (1992)*, the Court reaffirmed the substantive force of the liberty protected by the Due Process Clause. The *Casey* decision again confirmed that our laws and tradition afford constitutional protection to personal decisions relating to marriage, procreation, contraception, family relationships, child rearing, and education. *Id.,* at 851. ...

Persons in a homosexual relationship may seek autonomy for these purposes, just as heterosexual persons do. The decision in *Bowers* would deny them this right.

The second post-*Bowers* case of principal relevance is *Romer v. Evans, 517 U.S. 620 (1996)*. There the Court struck down class-based legislation directed at homosexuals as a violation of the Equal Protection Clause. *Romer* invalidated an amendment to Colorado's constitution which named as a solitary class persons who were homosexuals, lesbians, or bisexual either by "orientation, conduct, practices or relationships," *id.,* at 624, and deprived them of protection under state antidiscrimination laws. We concluded that the provision was "born of animosity toward the class of persons affected" and further that it had no rational relation to a legitimate governmental purpose. *Id., at 634.*

As an alternative argument in this case, counsel for the petitioners and some *amici* contend that *Romer* provides the basis for declaring the Texas statute invalid under the Equal Protection Clause. That is a tenable argument, but we conclude the instant case requires us to address whether *Bowers* itself has continuing validity. ... The central holding of *Bowers* has been brought in question by this case, and it should be addressed. Its continuance as precedent demeans the lives of homosexual persons.

The stigma this criminal statute imposes, moreover, is not trivial. The offense, to be sure, is but a class C misdemeanor, a minor offense in the Texas legal system. Still, it remains a criminal offense with all that imports for the dignity of the persons charged. The petitioners will bear on their record the history of their criminal convictions. Just this Term we rejected various challenges to state laws requiring the registration of sex offenders. ... We are advised that if Texas convicted an adult for private, consensual homosexual conduct under the statute here in question the convicted person would come within the registration laws of a least four States were he or she to be subject to their jurisdiction. ... This underscores the consequential nature of the punishment and the state-sponsored condemnation attendant to the criminal prohibition. Furthermore, the Texas criminal conviction carries with it the other collateral consequences always following a conviction, such as notations on job application forms, to mention but one example.

The foundations of *Bowers* have sustained serious erosion from our recent decisions in *Casey* and *Romer.* When our precedent has been thus weakened, criticism from other sources is of greater significance. In the United States criticism of *Bowers* has been substantial and continuing, disapproving of its reasoning in all respects, not just as to its historical assumptions. See, *e.g.,* C. Fried, Order and Law: Arguing the Reagan Revolution—A Firsthand Account 81-84 (1991); R. Posner, Sex and Reason 341- 350 (1992). ...

To the extent *Bowers* relied on values we share with a wider civilization, it should be noted that the reasoning and holding in *Bowers* have been rejected elsewhere. The European Court of Human Rights has followed not *Bowers* but its own decision in *Dudgeon v. United Kingdom.* See *P.G. & J.H. v. United Kingdom,* App. No. 00044787/98, & ¶ 56 (Eur.Ct.H. R., Sept. 25, 2001); *Modinos v. Cyprus,* 259 Eur. Ct. H.R. (1993); *Norris v. Ireland,* 142 Eur. Ct. H.R. (1988). Other nations, too, have taken action consistent with an affirmation of the protected right of homosexual adults to engage in intimate, consensual conduct. See Brief for Mary Robinson et al. as *Amici Curiae* 11-12. The right the petitioners seek in this case has been accepted as an integral part of human freedom in many other countries. There has been no showing that in this country the governmental interest in circumscribing personal choice is somehow more legitimate or urgent.

The doctrine of *stare decisis* is essential to the respect accorded to the judgments of the Court and to the stability of the law. It is not, however, an inexorable command. ... In *Casey* we noted that when a Court is asked to overrule a precedent recognizing a constitutional liberty interest, individual or societal reliance on the existence of that liberty cautions with particular strength against reversing course. 505 U.S., at 855-856; see also *id.,* at 844 ("Liberty finds no refuge in a jurisprudence of doubt"). The holding in *Bowers,* however, has not induced detrimental reliance comparable to some instances where recognized individual rights are involved. Indeed, there has been no individual or societal reliance on *Bowers* of the sort that could counsel against overturning its holding once there are compelling reasons to do so. *Bowers* itself causes uncertainty, for the precedents before and after its issuance contradict its central holding.

The rationale of *Bowers* does not withstand careful analysis. In his dissenting opinion in *Bowers* Justice STEVENS came to these conclusions:

> Our prior cases make two propositions abundantly clear. First, the fact that the governing majority in a State has traditionally viewed a particular practice as immoral is not a sufficient reason for upholding a law prohibiting the practice; neither history nor tradition could save a law prohibiting miscegenation from constitutional attack. Second, individual decisions by married persons, concerning the intimacies of their physical relationship, even when not intended to produce offspring, are a form of 'liberty' protected by the Due Process Clause of the Fourteenth Amendment. Moreover, this protection extends to intimate choices by unmarried as well as married persons. 478 U.S., at 216.

Justice STEVENS' analysis, in our view, should have been controlling in *Bowers* and should control here. *Bowers* was not correct when it was decided, and it is not correct today. It ought not to remain binding precedent. *Bowers v. Hardwick* should be and now is overruled. ...

JUSTICE SCALIA, with whom THE CHIEF JUSTICE and JUSTICE THOMAS join, dissenting:

... *Bowers*' conclusion that homosexual sodomy is not a fundamental right "deeply rooted in this Nation's history and tradition" is utterly unassailable.

Realizing that fact, the Court instead says: "[W]e think that our laws and traditions in the past half century are of most relevance here. These references show *an emerging awareness* that liberty gives substantial protection to adult persons in deciding how to conduct their private lives *in matters pertaining to sex.*" ... Apart from the fact that such an "emerging awareness" does not establish a "fundamental right," the statement is factually false. States continue to prosecute all sorts of crimes by adults "in matters pertaining to sex": prostitution, adult incest, adultery, obscenity, and child pornography. Sodomy laws, too, have been enforced "in the past half century," in which there have been 134 reported cases involving prosecutions for consensual, adult, homosexual sodomy. ...

In any event, an "emerging awareness" is by definition not "deeply rooted in this Nation's history and tradition[s]," as we have said "fundamental right" status requires. Constitutional entitlements do not spring into existence because some States choose to lessen or eliminate criminal sanctions on certain behavior. Much less do they spring into existence, as the Court seems to believe, because *foreign nations* decriminalize conduct. The *Bowers* majority opinion *never* relied on "values we share with a wider civilization," but rather rejected the claimed right to sodomy on the ground that such a right was not " 'deeply rooted in *this Nation's* history and tradition.' " ... *Bowers*' rational-basis holding is likewise devoid of any reliance on the views of a "wider civilization," see *id., at 196, 106 S.Ct. 2841.* The Court's discussion of these foreign views (ignoring, of course, the many countries that have retained criminal prohibitions on sodomy) is therefore meaningless dicta. Dangerous dicta, however, since "this Court ... should not impose foreign moods, fads, or fashions on Americans." *Foster v. Florida,* 537 U.S. 990 (THOMAS, J., concurring in denial of certiorari). ...

I turn now to the ground on which the Court squarely rests its holding: the contention that there is no rational basis for the law here under attack. This proposition is so out of accord with our jurisprudence—indeed, with the jurisprudence of *any* society we know—that it requires little discussion.

The Texas statute undeniably seeks to further the belief of its citizens that certain forms of sexual behavior are "immoral and unacceptable," *Bowers, supra,* at 196—the same interest furthered by criminal laws against fornication, bigamy, adultery, adult incest, bestiality, and obscenity. *Bowers* held that this *was* a legitimate state interest. The Court today reaches the opposite conclusion. The Texas statute, it says, "furthers *no legitimate state interest* which can justify its intrusion into the personal and private life of the individual." ... The Court embraces instead Justice STEVENS' declaration in his *Bowers* dissent, that "the fact that the governing majority in a State has traditionally viewed a particular practice as immoral is not a sufficient reason for upholding a law prohibiting the practice" ... This effectively decrees the end of all morals legislation. If, as the Court asserts, the promotion of majoritarian sexual morality is not even a *legitimate* state interest, none of the above-mentioned laws can survive rational-basis review.

Today's opinion is the product of a Court, which is the product of a law-profession culture, that has largely signed on to the so-called homosexual agenda, by which I mean the agenda promoted by some homosexual activists directed at eliminating the moral opprobrium that has traditionally attached to homosexual conduct. I noted in an earlier opinion the fact that the American Association of Law Schools (to which any reputable law school *must* seek to belong) excludes from membership any school that refuses to ban from its job-interview facilities a law firm (no matter how small) that does not wish to hire as a prospective partner a person who openly engages in homosexual conduct. See *Romer, supra, at 653.*

One of the most revealing statements in today's opinion is the Court's grim warning that the criminalization of homosexual conduct is "an invitation to subject homosexual persons to discrimination both in the public and in the private spheres." ... It is clear from this that the Court has taken sides in the culture war, departing from its role of assuring, as neutral observer, that the democratic rules of engagement are observed. Many Americans do not want persons who openly engage in homosexual conduct as partners in their business, as scoutmasters for their children, as teachers in their children's schools, or as boarders in their home. They view this as protecting themselves and their families from a lifestyle that they believe to be immoral and destructive. The Court views it as "discrimination" which it is the function of our judgments to deter. So imbued is the Court with the law profession's anti-anti-homosexual culture, that it is seemingly unaware that the attitudes of that culture are not obviously "mainstream"; that in most States what the Court calls "discrimination" against those who engage in homosexual acts is perfectly legal; that proposals to ban such "discrimination" under Title VII have repeatedly been rejected by Congress ...; and that in some cases such "discrimination" is a constitutional right, see *Boy Scouts of America v. Dale, 530 U.S. 640* (2000).

Notes and Questions

1. Note that the U.S. Supreme Court in its majority opinion in *Lawrence* invokes decisions by the European Court of Human Rights as expressions of "values we share with a wider civilization." Does this reference begin a trend toward an interpretation of U.S. Constitutional rights in light of international human rights standards? Would this be a desirable development?

2. Consider the U.S. armed forces' "don't ask, don't tell" policy in light of the following summarized decision of the European Court of Human Rights:

Lustig-Prean and Beckett v. United Kingdom; Smith and Grady v. United Kingdom
Nos. 31417/96, 32377/96; 33985/96, 33986/96 (Sept. 27, 1999)
ASIL Int'l Law in Brief, Sept. 27 - Oct. 1, 1999

> The four applicants, all British nationals, were homosexual members of the United Kingdom armed forces. The U.K. Ministry of Defense applies a policy which excludes homosexuals from the armed forces. During an investigation by the service police concerning their homosexuality, the applicants admitted their sexual orientation and were administratively discharged on that sole ground. The Court of Appeal subsequently rejected their applications.
>
> Mr. Lustig-Prean and Mr. Beckett brought this action before the European Court of Human Rights ("Court") alleging both a violation of Article 8 (right to respect for private and family life) of the European Convention of Human Rights ("Convention") and discrimination under Article 14.
>
> Ms. Smith and Mr. Grady made the same complaints under Articles 8 and 14. They additionally argued that the Ministry of Defense policy against homosexuals, and the consequent investigation and discharge, were degrading in violation of Article 3 (prohibition of inhuman or degrading treatment or punishment). Mr. Smith and Mr. Grady also argued that the policy violated Article 10 (freedom of expression), and that an effective domestic remedy was not available as required by Article 13.
>
> In deciding the case of Lustig-Prean and Beckett, the Court focused first on the alleged violation of Article 8. Article 8, Sect. 1 establishes that "Everyone has the right to respect for his private and family life. ..." Section 2 provides that no interference by a public authority is permitted "except such as is in accordance with the law and is necessary in a democratic society in the interests of national security. ..." After finding: 1) that the investigation had been "exceptionally intrusive"; 2) that the administrative discharges had a "profound effect" on the applicant's careers and prospects; and 3) the policy adopted by the Ministry of Defense was "striking", the Court had to determine whether

the Government had demonstrated "particularly convincing and weighing reasons" to justify those interferences.

The Court concluded that the Government did not meet its burden of proof. The Court particularly rejected a Government argument, based on a 1996 Report, that the presence of homosexuals in the armed forces would have a substantial and negative effect on morale and, consequently, on the fighting power and operational effectiveness of the armed forces. The Court noted that the views expressed in the Report were founded solely upon the negative attitude of heterosexual personnel towards homosexual personnel. According to the Court, "[t]o the extent that they represent a predisposed bias on the part of a heterosexual majority against a homosexual minority, these negative attitudes cannot, of themselves, be considered by the Court to amount to sufficient justification for the interferences with the applicant's rights . . . any more than similar negative attitudes toward those of a different race, origin or colour." The Court acknowledged that certain conduct-based difficulties could arise with a change of policy, but it also said that as in the cases of racial minorities and women in the military these difficulties could be addressed by a strict code of conduct and disciplinary rules. The Court held that, given its decision under Article 8, there was no need to separately consider an Article 14 claim of discrimination.

In deciding the case of Smith and Grady the Court adopted the same reasoning and reached the same conclusion as in Lustig-Prean and Beckett regarding Articles 8 and 14. However, the Court concluded that there had been no violation of Article 3, either alone or in conjunction with Article 14. The Court held that the applicant's treatment did not rise to the level of severity necessary to establish a violation of Article 3. The Court declined to consider the Article 10 complaint, holding that the freedom of expression element was subsidiary to the applicant's principal claim, the right to respect in their private lives. The Court further held that the applicants did not have an effective domestic remedy, in that UK courts were bound to conclude that the Ministry of Defense policy was not "irrational."

In both cases, Judge Loucaides partially dissented from the majority holding that there had been an Article 8 violation by reason of the applicant's discharge. Loucaides stated that "the sexual orientation of homosexuals does create the problems highlighted by the Government as a result of the communal accommodation with heterosexuals." For details, see http://www.dhcour.coe.fr/eng/Judgments.htm.

PART FOUR: ALLOCATION, PROTECTION AND REGULATION OF USE OF THE RESOURCES OF THE PLANET

An historic function of international law has been to prescribe policy for the allocation of planetary resources among states and, more recently, policy for the regulation of use and conservation of these resources.

I. General Principles Governing Resource Use

A. Resources: A Contextual Definition

There is a tendency among scholars to view resources as a fixed inventory with the permanence of the Table of Elements. In fact, resources are a legal and cultural artifact, determined at each moment in time by the convergence of human imagination and aspiration and technological capacity. Modern "resources" were not characterized as such in previous centuries. Consider aluminum, one of the struts of modern civilization. It is refined from clay having a certain percentage of neolin. Until its nature was understood and until the high amounts of energy necessary for transforming neolin into alumina and then aluminum were available, it was not a resource. Or consider petroleum. It was only in the last century that hydrocarbons were recognized as a major source of energy. Likewise, the once-flourishing market in quills reached its nadir more than a century ago.

The point of emphasis is that the material of our planet, understood as an earth and space continuum, is protean and may undergo many transformations, in which different components will be characterized as resources for a period and then discarded. This conception of resource is important both for understanding past decision and for planning and appraising future options.

B. Policies For Resource Use

A number of basic policies may be postulated with respect to the exploitation of resources. Some of these policies are generally accepted in contemporary international law. Others are not, as we will see later in Part Four.

1. Efficiency:

Resources should be explored, exploited and their benefits should be distributed in an optimally efficient fashion.

2. Conservation:

Patterns of exploitation, exploration and utilization of resources should allow for conservation of renewable and non-renewable resources so as to preserve resources and to maintain diversity of resources and species.

3. Biodiversity:

As an aspect of conservation, all uses of resources should be consistent with preserving and maintaining the diversity among living species and of ecosystems.

4. Scientific Development:

All patterns of uses of resources should encourage scientific development and creation of new and substitute resources.

5. Economic Development:

The uses of resources should be structured in such a way that it encourages the development of those sectors of the global economy that lag behind the international standard.

6. Sustainable Development:

All uses of resources, whether for purposes of exploration, exploitation or distribution, should be accomplished in ways that do not deplete the resources themselves.

7. Structuring Patterns of Use In Ways That Benefit The Commonweal:

The traditional vocabulary for appraising claims distinguished only between "international" or "national" (or "domestic") competence, preferring one or the other on some general principle. But if one takes into account such factors as the *nature* of different resources, the conditions necessary for their optimum use (including their conservation) and the prevailing socio-economic context, the inadequacy of the traditional dichotomy becomes apparent. Some resources will actually be used in ways that benefit the entire community if they are under the control of a single state, while other resources will yield optimum benefits to the community if they are "owned" by no state but are available for use by all. Such benefits are the only reason that resources are important; unfortunately, the traditional terms permit no appraisal in this meaningful sense. We suggest that the competences to make and apply law about resources be appraised in terms of those in the "common interest." Common interests may be achieved by allocating competence with regard to specific resources "inclusively," *i.e.*, in ways that preserve uses for the entire community, or "exclusively," *i.e.*, in ways that reserve uses for a single state. Whether a particular inclusive or exclusive arrangement of competence is in the common interest will depend upon the nature of the resource, the state of technology, the socio-economic context and other factors deemed relevant at a given time.

8. Precautionary Principle:

As a procedural and evidentiary principle, uncertainty should not be a "green light," but rather a "yellow light" for exploitation of resources. In other sectors, the burden of proof with respect to the initiation of development is on the putative regulator. Absence of certain knowledge means that regulation cannot be justified. With respect to the protection of the environment, however, uncertainty should not be a general license to exploit resources.

C. The Inclusive Concern for the Environment

In the past 30 years, there has been a growing common realization that the environment is a critical resource of humankind that requires international protection. The first timid expression of this was found in the Stockholm Declaration of the United Nations Conference on the Human Environment in 1972, where it was said, in relevant part:

> The protection and improvement of the human environment is a major issue which affects the well-being of peoples and economic development throughout the world; it is the urgent desire of the peoples of the whole world and the duty of all Governments.

Report of the United Nations Conference on the Human Environment, Stockholm June 5-16, U.N. GAOR, 27th Sess., U.N. Doc. A/CONF.48/14 (1972), 11 I.L.M. 1416, 1420 (1972).

This very carefully bounded expression of policy may be contrasted with a statement by the International Court of Justice in its Advisory Opinion of July 8, 1996:

> The existence of the general obligation of States to ensure that activities within their jurisdiction and control respect the environment of other States or of areas beyond national control is now part of the corpus of international law relating to the environment. …

Legality of the Threat or Use of Nuclear Weapons, 1996 I.C.J. 226 ¶ 29 (July 8).

II. Water

A. Ocean Maritime Zones

1. Gayl S. Westerman, The Juridical Bay
14-19, 181-184 (Oxford U. Press 1987)

The principal features of the international law of the sea have been formed through the effort over several centuries to accommodate the exclusive interests of individual states in maximizing areas of maritime sovereignty and the inclusive interests of all states in maximizing freedom of the seas. The legal presumption favoring freedom of the seas remains in place today, but since World War II there has been a radical change in the international context within which that principle gained temporary ascendancy. Many new nation-states, largely poor and conscious of their solidarity, have used their newfound political power to press for a review of traditional international doctrines which do not favor their interests. In addition, the rapid advance of marine and undersea technology has precipitated demands by both developed and developing states for increased authority and use of their contiguous waters.

The *mare liberum* or free seas principle entered the law of nations as a reaction against broad claims to territorial sovereignty over vast sea areas put forward by major sea powers in the sixteenth and seventeenth centuries. It is familiar history that common interests eventually triumphed over monopoly; and that until the present, most states have, to a greater or lesser degree, shared the conviction that the greatest production of community values can be achieved by permitting and protecting the widest possible sharing of ocean space. ...

When the modern concept of a marginal belt of territorial waters around the shore of a coastal state developed in the eighteenth and nineteenth centuries, the distances claimed were usually modest, the baseline for measuring the marginal waters was generally accepted to be the shoreline, and those affected by such delimitation were for the most part fishermen, smugglers, and the warships of belligerent nations. The boundary of the territorial sea was close enough to the shore for a mariner to determine his position easily, and no great precision nor expertise was or could be required of either the delimitation method or the delimitator.

In the twentieth century, however, as increasing requirements for protein, oil, and other ocean resources led to expansive national claims to areas of the sea and seabed previously held to be *res communes*, a need emerged, where none had previously existed, to determine boundaries with precision and to develop a body of rules capable of making sophisticated differentiations between various zones of national and international jurisdiction.

The 1958 Geneva Conventions were adopted in response to the general recognition among states that the time had come to address the problems presented by the radical political and economic changes which had transformed society in the postwar era. By codifying existing law which remained relevant and creating new law to respond to newly perceived needs, the world community sought to place acceptable, if in some cases compromisory, limits on the expansive claims and demands of coastal states. ...

The dynamic forces set in motion by rapid change could not be wholly addressed nor checked by international agreement in 1958, however. Since that time, the demand for ever wider sovereignty over ocean space has only intensified and has been joined in its assault on freedom of the seas by a new adversary, the demand by developing states to restrict the use of the seabed of the high seas under a new species of *res communes*, the common heritage of mankind. The adoption of the U.N. Convention on the Law of the Sea, [hereinafter UNCLOS] in 1982, a mere fifteen years after Geneva, reflects wide community acquiescence in these demands. ...

Both the 1958 Geneva Conventions and ... [UNCLOS] codify community recognition of a series of sea zones which extend landward and seaward of a state's "baseline." The delimitation of this baseline is fundamental to the determination of all other sea boundaries, for it is this line which marks the seaward limit of a state's internal waters as well as the landward limit of the territorial sea. It is from this baseline that every sea zone extending from the coast of a given state is measured.

Within each zone, different coastal competences are honored. All waters landward of the baseline are *internal* or *inland waters*, over which a coastal state may exercise exclusive control, identical to that exercised over its land territory. This sovereign authority includes the right to exploit the resources of the surface waters, the seabed, and the subsoil, as well as the right to arbitrarily deny access to foreign vessels. Directly seaward from the baseline lies the *territorial sea*, over which the coastal state may exercise some of the attributes of sovereignty, such as the preservation of fishery resources for its own nationals, but through which must be allowed the innocent passage of foreign vessels. Overlapping with the territorial sea and extending twelve miles [further] seaward from the baseline lies the *contiguous zone*, wherein the coastal state enjoys extraterritorial jurisdiction to enforce its own customs, tax, sanitary, and pollution laws, but no sovereign power to deny access to foreign vessels outside the territorial limit. As one proceeds further seaward through the *continental shelf*, and ... the newly conceived *exclusive economic zone*, the state may lay claim to various ocean resources but must increasingly compromise its interests with those of other states. The last zone, the *high seas* [a zone that technically begins at the seaward limit of the *territorial sea*], lies beyond the reach of any exclusive regime and is open to all. Of critical importance to this system of competences is the location of the baseline, for whatever the width of the territorial sea claimed by the littoral state, any movement of the baseline landward or seaward affects the limits of the state's exclusive authority.

The most significant effect of a *seaward* extension of this crucial boundary line is to increase the area of ocean space over which the littoral state may exercise the most comprehensive control and thereby to decrease the total sea area over which all states share inclusive authority and use. Because what is ultimately at stake is the distribution of authority over the use of the oceans, the issue of baseline delimitation poses a classic conflict between the legitimate interests of an individual state in obtaining as large a share of ocean space as is deemed necessary to pursue wealth, power, and national security, and the wider interests of the community of states in preserving the maximum sea area possible for navigation, communication, fishing, and other inclusive pursuits. ...

[Since the 1950's, this balance has been increasingly struck in favor of the coastal state.] Commentators now estimate that as a result of state claims permitted by international agreement, between 30 and 40% of ocean space has been placed under some form of state control, primarily via claims to expanded territorial seas, claims to legal continental shelves, and claims to exclusive economic or fishing zones. When one further reflects on the fact that all exploitable offshore hydrocarbons, all commercially exploitable minerals in unconsolidated sediments (from sand and gravel to tin), most phosphorite nodules, a significant portion of recently discovered polymetallic sulphide deposits, cobalt crusts, and manganese nodule deposits, over 90% of the commercially exploitable living resources of the sea, nearly all marine plants, and all known sites suitable to the production of energy are to be found in the contiguous offshore areas currently under state control, the magnitude of the policy shift in favor of the exclusive interests of coastal states becomes apparent.

Despite intense international competition for resources and increasing demand for national ownership of ever larger areas of the oceans, the freedom of the seas principle has not disappeared from international prescription. Both the 1958 Geneva Convention on the High Seas and UNCLOS preserve the freedom of all states in the use of the high seas for navigation, fishing, overflight, the laying of submarine cables and pipelines, and specifically in UNCLOS, for scientific research and the construction of artificial islands. Yet, these freedoms can in no sense be termed absolute. … [O]ther compelling inclusive interests in pollution control and fishery conservation must occasionally take precedence if ocean resources are to be truly preserved to the common good of all. Nor can it be inferred that the widespread acceptance of the free seas principle absolutely precludes all claims to exclusive authority and use. Individual states are routinely granted permission for special uses of ocean space which only temporarily affect community access. More controversy is a certainty when a state lays claim to permanent and exclusive use of expanded water areas under the principle of territorial sovereignty.

2. High Seas

a. Le Louis

2 Dods. 210 (1817), 165 Eng. Rep. 1464

A French vessel, sailing from Martinique on January 30, 1816, on a voyage to the coast of Africa and back, was captured on March 11 ten or twelve leagues to the southward of Cape Mesurada, by the "Queen Charlotte" cutter, and carried to Sierra Leone, where it was condemned to His Majesty in the Vice-Admiralty Court. On Appeal.

[Sir W. SCOTT looked first at the authority of the seizer to effect this "capture." He found that a commission existed professing to be issued by the governor of Sierra Leone and founded on the Slave Trade Act, 51 G.3, authorizing seizure and detention of all ships and vessels offending against that act or any other act abolishing the slave trade. But the Court stated that no British Act of Parliament could affect the rights of foreigners unless it was consistent with the law of nations. A commission authorizing seizures in time of peace must also conform to the law of nations regarding the rights of foreigners.] …

Upon the first question, whether the right of search exists in time of peace, I have to observe, that two principles of public law are generally recognized as fundamental. One is the perfect equality and entire independence of all distinct states. Relative magnitude creates no distinction of right; relative imbecility, whether permanent or casual, gives no additional right to the powerful neighbour; and any advantage seized upon that ground is mere usurpation. This is the great foundation of public law, which ... mainly concerns the peace of mankind, both in their politic and private capacities, to preserve inviolate. The second is that, all nations being equal, all have an equal right to the uninterrupted use of the unappropriated parts of the ocean for their navigation. In places where no local authority exists, where the subjects of all states meet upon a footing of entire equality and independence, no one state, or any of its subjects, has a right to assume or exercise authority over the subjects of another. I can find no authority that gives the right of interruption to the navigation of states in amity upon the high seas, excepting that which the rights of war give to both belligerents against neutrals. This right, incommodious as its exercise may occasionally be to those who are subjected to it, has been fully established in the legal practice of nations, having for its foundation the necessities of self-defence, in preventing the enemy from being supplied with the instruments of war, and from having his means of annoyance augmented by the advantages of maritime commerce. Against the property of his enemy each belligerent has the extreme rights of war. Against that of neutrals, the friends of both, each has the right of visitation and search, and of pursuing an enquiry whether they are employed in the service of his enemy, the right being subject, in almost all cases of an enquiry wrongfully pursued, to a compensation in costs and damages.

With professed pirates there is no state of peace. They are the enemies of every country, and at all times; and therefore are universally subject to the extreme rights of war. An ancient authority, the laws of Oleron (Section 45), composed at the time of the Crusades, and, as supposed by an eminent leader in those expeditions, our own Rich. I, [King Richard I of England] represents *infidels* as equally subject to those rights; but this rests partly upon the ground of notions long ago exploded, that such persons could have no fellowship, no peaceful communion with the faithful; and still more upon the ground of fact that they were for many centuries engaged in real hostilities with the Christian states. Another exploded practice was that of princes granting private letters of marque against the subjects of powers in amity, by whom they had been injured, without being able to obtain redress from the sovereign or tribunals of that country. But at present, under the law, as now generally understood and practiced, no nation can exercise a right of visitation and search upon the common and unappropriated parts of the sea, save only on the belligerent claim. If it be asked why the right of search does not exist in time of peace as well as in war, the answer is prompt; that it has not the same foundation on which alone it is tolerated in war, - the necessities of self-defence. They introduced it in war; and practice has established it. No such necessities have introduced it in time of peace, and no such practice has established it. It is true, that wild claims (alluded to in the argument) have been occasionally set up by nations, particularly those of Spain and Portugal, in the East and West Indian seas: but these are claims of a nature quite foreign to the present question, being claims not of a general right of visitation and search upon the high seas unappropriated, but extravagant claims to the appropriation of particular seas, founded upon some grants of a pretended authority, or upon some ancient exclusive usurpation. Upon a principle much more just in itself and more temperately applied, maritime states have claimed a right of visitation and enquiry within those parts of the ocean adjoining to their shores, which the common courtesy of nations has for their common convenience allowed to be considered as parts of their dominions for various domestic purposes, and particularly for fiscal or defensive regulations more immediately affecting their safety and welfare. Such are our hovering laws, which within certain limited distances more or less moderately assigned, subject foreign vessels to such examination. This has nothing in common with a right of visitation and search upon the unappropriated parts of the ocean. ...

It is next said that every country has a right to enforce its own navigation laws; and so it certainly has, so far as it does not interfere with the rights of others. It has a right to see that its own vessels are duly navigated, but it has no right in consequence to visit and search all the apparent vessels of other countries on the high seas, in order to institute an enquiry whether they are not in truth British vessels violating British laws. No such right has ever been claimed, nor can it be exercised without the oppression of interrupting and harassing the real and lawful navigation of other countries; for the right of search when it exists at all, is universal, and will extend to vessels of all countries, whether they tolerate the slave trade or not; and whether the vessels are employed in slave trading or in any other traffic. It is no objection to say that British ships may thus by disguise elude the obligations of British law. The answer of the foreigner is ready that you have no right to provide against the inconvenience by imposing a burden upon his navigation. If the question were even reduced to this, that either all British ships might fraudulently escape, or all foreign ships be injuriously harassed, Great Britain could not claim the option to embrace the latter branch of the alternative. When you complain that the regulation cannot be enforced without the exercise of such a right, the answer again is, that you ought not to make regulations which you cannot enforce without trespassing on the rights of others. If it were a matter by which your own safety was affected the necessities of self-defence would fully justify; but in a matter in which your own safety is in no degree concerned, you have no right to prevent a suspected injustice towards another by committing an actual injustice of your own.

[The judgment below was reversed.]

NOTES AND QUESTIONS

1. *Le Louis* expresses a clear policy preference for a public order of the oceans in which, in time of peace, no state may exercise any jurisdiction over the vessels of any other state. To a great extent, that policy continues to be authoritative. Does the effective enforcement of international criminal

laws require exceptions to this long-standing norm? What about the pursuit of the war on terrorism since September 11, 2001?

2. Consider in this regard, the Proliferation Security Initiative (PSI) established in Paris on September 3, 2003. The Statement of Interdiction Principles provides, in part:

PSI participants are committed to the following interdiction principles to establish a more coordinated and effective basis through which to impede and stop shipments of WMD, delivery systems, and related materials flowing to and from states and non-state actors of proliferation concern, consistent wit national legal authorities and relevant international law and frameworks, including the UN Security Council. They call on all states concerned with this threat to international peace and security to join in similarly committing to:

Take specific actions in support of interdiction efforts regarding cargoes of WMD, their delivery systems, or related materials, to the extent their national legal authorities permit and consistent with their obligations under international law and frameworks, to include:

... take appropriate actions to (1) stop and/or search in their internal waters, territorial seas, or contiguous zones (when declared) vessels that are reasonably suspected of carrying such cargoes to or from states or non-state actors of proliferation concern and to seize such cargoes that are identified; and (2) to enforce conditions on vessels entering or leaving their ports, internal waters or territorial seas that are reasonable suspected of carrying such cagoes, such as requiring that such vessels be subject to boarding, search, and seizure of such cargoes prior to entry.

Proliferation Security Initiative:Statement of Interdiction Principles, The White House, Office of the Press Secretary, Washington, DC. (Sept 4, 2003), *available at* http://www.state.gov/t/np/rls/fs/23764.htmal□.

3. In contemporary practice, wireless communications now minimize many of the potential conflicts that *Le Louis* situations might present. If, for example, a vessel flying the flag of State X is hovering beyond the territorial sea of State Y, the Coast Guard of State Y may be patched through to the Ministry of Shipping of State X and determine in several seconds whether the vessel in question is indeed part of the fleet of State X and whether it may be boarded to in order to determine whether or not it is violating some international law.

The essential policy in *Le Louis* was confirmed in the 1958 Convention on the High Seas.

b. Convention on the High Seas

Apr. 29, 1958, 13 U.S.T. 2312; T.I.A.S. No. 5200, 450 U.N.T.S. 82

Article 2

The high seas being open to all nations, no State may validly purport to subject any part of them to its sovereignty. Freedom of the high seas is exercised under the conditions laid down by these articles and by the other rules of international law. It comprises, *inter alia*, both for coastal and non-coastal States:

(1) Freedom of navigation;

(2) Freedom of fishing;

(3) Freedom to lay submarine cables and pipelines;

(4) Freedom to fly over the high seas.

These freedoms, and others which are recognized by the general principles of international law, shall be exercised by all States with reasonable regard to the interests of other States in their exercise of the freedom of the high seas.

* * *

The 1982 United Nations Convention on the Law of the Sea may have moved away from the sharp dualism of the earlier formulations.

c. 1982 United Nations Convention on the Law of the Sea

Dec. 10, 1982, 1833 U.N.T.S. 3

Article 87: *Freedom of the high seas*

1. The high seas are open to all States, whether coastal or land-locked. Freedom of the high seas is exercised under the conditions laid down by this Convention and by other rules of international law. It comprises, *inter alia,* both for coastal and land-locked States:

(a) freedom of navigation;

(b) freedom of overflight;

(c) freedom to lay submarine cables and pipelines, subject to Part VI;

(d) freedom to construct artificial islands and other installations permitted under international law, subject to Part VI;

(e) freedom of fishing, subject to the conditions laid down in section 2;

(f) freedom of scientific research, subject to Parts VI and XIII.

2. These freedoms shall be exercised by all States with due regard for the interests of other States in their exercise of the freedom of the high seas, and also with due regard for the rights under this Convention with respect to activities in the Area. …

Article 89: *Invalidity of claims of sovereignty over the high seas*

No State may validly purport to subject any part of the high seas to its sovereignty.

Article 90: *Right of navigation*

Every State, whether coastal or land-locked, has the right to sail ships flying its flag on the high seas.

Article 91: *Nationality of ships*

1. Every State shall fix the conditions for the grant of its nationality to ships, for the registration of ships in its territory, and for the right to fly its flag. Ships have the nationality of the State whose flag they are entitled to fly. There must exist a genuine link between the State and the ship.

2. Every State shall issue to ships to which it has granted the right to fly its flag documents to that effect.

Article 92: *Status of ships*

1. Ships shall sail under the flag of one State only and, save in exceptional cases expressly provided for in international treaties or in this Convention, shall be subject to its exclusive jurisdiction on the high seas. A ship may not change its flag during a voyage or while in a port of call, save in the case of a real transfer of ownership or change of registry.

2. A ship which sails under the flags of two or more States, using them according to convenience, may not claim any of the nationalities in question with respect to any other State, and may be assimilated to a ship without nationality.

Article 94: *Duties of the flag State*

6. A State which has clear grounds to believe that proper jurisdiction and control with respect to a ship have not been exercised may report the facts to the flag State. Upon receiving such a report, the flag State shall investigate the matter and, if appropriate, take any action necessary to remedy the situation.

7. Each State shall cause an inquiry to be held by or before a suitably qualified person or persons into every marine casualty or incident of navigation on the high seas involving a ship flying its flag and causing loss of life or serious injury to nationals of another State or serious damage to ships or installations of another State or to the marine environment. The flag State and the other State shall co-operate in the conduct of any inquiry held by that other State into any such marine casualty or incident of navigation.

Article 95: *Immunity of warships on the high seas*

Warships on the high seas have complete immunity from the jurisdiction of any State other than the flag State.

Article 96: *Immunity of ships used only on government non-commercial service*

Ships owned or operated by a State and used only on government non-commercial service shall, on the high seas, have complete immunity from the jurisdiction of any State other than the flag State.

Article 99: *Prohibition of the transport of slaves*

Every State shall take effective measures to prevent and punish the transport of slaves in ships authorized to fly its flag and to prevent the unlawful use of its flag for that purpose. Any slave taking refuge on board any ship, whatever its flag, shall *ipso facto* be free.

Notes and Questions

1. Because of its dissatisfaction with Part XI of UNCLOS which established the "Area," (see *infra*, at 721), the United States refused to sign UNCLOS. Yet it accepted virtually all other parts

of UNCLOS as representative of customary international law. On March 10, 1983, President Reagan issued a statement on United States Oceans Policy, which said, in relevant part:

> Last July, I announced that the United States will not sign the United Nations Law of the Sea Convention that was opened for signature on December 10. We have taken this step because several major problems in the Convention's deep seabed mining provisions are contrary to the interests and principles of industrialized nations and would not help attain the aspirations of developing countries.
>
> The United States does not stand alone in those concerns. Some important allies and friends have not signed the convention. Even some signatory states have raised concerns about these problems.
>
> However, the convention also contains provisions with respect to traditional uses of the oceans which generally confirm existing maritime law and practice and fairly balance the interests of all states.
>
> Today I am announcing three decisions to promote and protect the oceans interests of the United States in a manner consistent with those fair and balanced results in the Convention and international law.
>
> First, the United States is prepared to accept and act in accordance with the balance of interests relating to traditional uses of the oceans—such as navigation and overflight. In this respect, the United States will recognize the rights of other states in the waters off their coasts, as reflected in the Convention, so long as the rights and freedoms of the United States and others under international law are recognized by such coastal states.
>
> Second, the United States will exercise and assert its navigation and overflight rights and freedoms on a worldwide basis in a manner that is consistent with the balance of interests reflected in the convention. The United States will not, however, acquiesce to unilateral acts of other states designed to restrict the rights and freedoms of the international community in navigation and overflight and other related high seas uses. ...

President's Statement on United States Oceans Policy, PUBLIC PAPERS OF THE PRESIDENTS OF THE UNITED STATES, Book 1 at 378-379 (March 10, 1983).

2. If UNCLOS, apart from Part XI, *has* become a part of customary international law since 1982, is it now binding on all non-states parties including the United States?

3. UNCLOS, which is now widely accepted as general international law, incorporates a number of reductions in the high seas freedoms that existed theretofore. First, as Professor Westerman has noted above, the Convention assigns to coastal states exclusive economic zones of 200 miles from the baselines within which the coastal state has sovereign rights. Comparable rights are assigned to coastal states in the continental shelf or seabed extending 200 miles and, in some geological formations, further. Thus the area in which the high seas freedoms of the earlier regime are now enjoyed is considerably smaller than in the past. *See* W. MICHAEL REISMAN & GAYL S. WESTERMAN, STRAIGHT BASELINES IN MARITIME BOUNDARY DELIMITATION (St. Martin's Press 1992). Second, the immunity assigned to ships of one state from the jurisdiction of any other state is less certain. Article 95, quoted above, ensures "complete immunity" from jurisdiction to warships and Article 96 ensures "complete immunity" to ships owned or operated by a state and used only on government non-commercial service on the high seas. By implication, all other ships flying the flag of another state do not have complete immunity. They would have had such immunity under the older regime. For a current discussion of the rights of coastal states in regard to the ships of third states on the high seas, *see* Anne Bardin, *Coastal State's Jurisdiction Over Foreign Vessels*, 14 PACE INT'L L. REV. 27 (2002).

4. UNCLOS rules on rights of states to board the ships of other states at sea can be modified by agreement. For example, the Caribbean has established itself as a major drug producing region and

some nations are said to be on the border of de-certification from the United States. The region has also served as a transhipment point for drug cartels in South America. Recently, the discussions have intensified because of Washington's drafting of the Shiprider Agreements which allow U.S. officials to pursue suspected drug trafficking vessels into an agreed nation's territory without requesting permission from the local authorities nor even notifying those authorities. The fourteen member states, in addition to the U.S., are Guyana, Antigua and Barbuda, The Bahamas, Barbados, Belize, Grenada, Jamaica, Montserrat, St. Kitts and Nevis, Saint Lucia, St. Vincent and the Grenadines, Trinidad and Tobago, Dominica, and Suriname. Do you foresee any problems with such agreements? Do they modify or supplant the UNCLOS rules above?

3. Internal Waters

Internal waters are assimilated to the territory of the state concerned, with no rights reserved for international users.

a. Delimitation

1982 United Nations Convention on the Law of the Sea

Article 5: *Normal baseline*

Except where otherwise provided in this Convention, the normal baseline for measure the breadth of the territorial sea is the low-water line along the coast as marked on large-scale charts officially recognized by the coastal State.

Article 7: *Straight baselines*

1. In localities where the coastline is deeply indented and cut into, or if there is a fringe of islands along the coast in its immediate vicinity, the method of straight baselines joining appropriate points may be employed in drawing the baseline from which the breadth of the territorial sea is measured.

2. Where because of the presence of a delta and other natural conditions the coastline is highly unstable, the appropriate points may be selected along the furthest seaward extent of the low-water line and, notwithstanding subsequent regression of the low-water line, the straight baselines shall remain effective until changed by the coastal State in accordance with this Convention.

3. The drawing of straight baselines must not depart to any appreciable extent from the general direction of the coast, and the sea areas lying within the lines must be sufficiently closely linked to the land domain to be subject to the regime of internal waters.

4. Straight baselines shall not be drawn to and from low-tide elevations, unless lighthouses or similar installations which are permanently above sea level have been built on them or except in instances where the drawing of baselines to and from such elevations has received general international recognition.

5. Where the method of straight baselines is applicable under paragraph 1, account may be taken, in determining particular baselines, of economic interests peculiar to the region concerned, the reality and the importance of which are clearly evidenced by long usage.

6. The system of straight baselines may not be applied by a State in such a manner as to cut off the territorial sea of another State from the high seas or an exclusive economic zone.

Article 8: *Internal waters*

1. Except as provided in Part IV, waters on the landward side of the of the territorial sea form part of the internal waters of the State.

2. Where the establishment of a straight baseline in accordance with the method set forth in article 7 has the effect of enclosing as internal waters areas which had not previously been considered as such, a right of innocent passage as provided in this Convention shall exist in those waters.

Article 9: *Mouths of rivers*

If a river flows directly into the sea, the baseline shall be a straight line across the mouth of the river between points on the low-water line of its banks.

Article 10: *Bays*

1. This article relates only to bays the coasts of which belong to a single State.

2. For the purposes of this Convention, a bay is a well-marked indentation whose penetration is in such proportion to the width of its mouth as to contain land-locked waters and constitute more than a mere curvature of the coast. An indentation shall not, however, be regarded as a bay unless its area is as large as, or larger than, that of the semi-circle whose diameter is a line drawn across the mouth of that indentati

3. For the purpose of measurement, the area of an indentation is that lying between the low-water mark around the shore of the indentation and a line joining the low-water mark of its natural entrance points. Where, because of the presence of islands, an indentation has more than one mouth, the semicircle shall be drawn on a line as long as the sum total of the lengths of the lines across the different mouths. Islands within an indentation shall be included as if they were part of the water area of the indentation.

4. If the distance between the low-water marks of the natural entrance points of a bay does not exceed 24 nautical miles, a closing line may be drawn between these two low-water marks, and the waters enclosed thereby shall be considered as internal waters.

5. Where the distance between the low-water marks of the natural entrance points of a bay exceeds 24 nautical miles, a straight baseline of 24 nautical miles shall be drawn within the bay in such a manner as to enclose the maximum area of water that is possible with a line of that length.

6. The foregoing provisions do not apply to so-called "historic" bays, or in any case where the system of straight baselines provided for in article 7 is applied.

Article 11: *Ports*

For the purpose of delimiting the territorial sea, the outermost permanent harbour works which form an integral part of the harbour system are regarded as forming part of the coast. Off-shore installations and artificial islands shall not be considered as permanent harbour works.

* * *

The UNCLOS Article 5 rule above that locates the normal baseline at the"low water mark along the coast" of a given state would appear to be easily understood and applied. All coasts, however, are not created equal. Two species of internal waters involve indentations into the coastal landmass and require special rules. The Article 10 rules for enclosing juridical bays and the Article 7 rules for establishing straight baseline systems along complex coastlines legitimize the drawing of water-crossing baselines across the mouths of various indentations. These "closing lines" then become the "coast" for maritime boundary delimitation purposes.

Article 10 codified customary international law that had developed over many centuries, as the discussion below indicates. Article 7 was derived in its entirety from the ICJ case which follows.

b. GAYL S. WESTERMAN, THE JURIDICAL BAY, *supra*, at 3-4

History reveals that from the earliest times, the inhabitants of coastal lands settled near small, protected indentations in the coastal littoral. The land surrounding the indentation sheltered it from the full force of nature while man labored to extract benefit from a thus protected arm of the sea. In its provision of an easily obtained and abundant food supply, of an efficient transportation system for persons and goods, and of easily protected coastal boundaries, this sheltered sea area contributed even more than the surrounding land mass or the open sea to man's basic requirement for food, security, services and goods.

Throughout centuries of fluctuating international norms in regard to the sea as a whole, these indentations lying within the land mass of a single state and variously termed bays, gulfs, locks, firths, estuaries and the like, were perceived by coastal states as so vitally entwined with life on the shore as to be valid components of their own territory. For the most part, this perception was shared by the world community as part of a broader effort to accommodate the exclusive interests of individual states in preserving their respective shares of natural resources and the security of their borders with the inclusive interests of the community as a whole in resource exploitation and navigation. Within this equation the exclusive interests of a given state were seen to attach most particularly to waters lying *inter fauces terrae,* literally within the jaws of the land.

c. Fisheries Case (U.K. v. Nor.)

1951 I.C.J. 116 (Judgment of Dec.18)

[British fishermen refrained from fishing in Norwegian coastal waters from 1616-1618 until 1906, as a result of complaints from the King of Denmark and Norway at the beginning of the 17th century.

British vessels reappeared in 1906, and increased in number from 1908 onward. Trawlers with improved gear perturbed the local population and the Norwegian government took steps to specify areas prohibited to foreign fishing.

In 1911 a British trawler was seized and condemned for violating the limits. Negotiations between the two governments were interrupted in 1914 by the war, but were resumed (after incidents in 1922 and 1923) in 1924. In 1932, arrests increased when the British extended activities off the Norwegian coast west of the North Cape. On July 27th, 1933, the United Kingdom government complained in a memorandum to the Norwegian government that unjustifiable baselines delimited the Norwegian territorial sea. On July 12th, 1935, a Norwegian Royal Decree was enacted delimiting the Norwegian fisheries zone north of 66°28.8' North latitude.

The United Kingdom protested to Oslo, and the Norwegian government announced a policy of leniency regarding enforcement of the Decree, pending the result of negotiations. Negotiations failed to resolve the issues, and in 1948 the leniency policy ended. Arrests and incidents became more frequent and the U. K. government instituted proceedings before the International Court of Justice.]

On September 28th, 1949, the Government of the United Kingdom of Great Britain and Northern Ireland filed in the Registry an Application instituting proceedings before the Court against the Kingdom of Norway, the subject of the proceedings being the validity or otherwise, under international law, of the lines of delimitation of the Norwegian fisheries zone laid down by the Royal Decree of July 12th, 1935, as amended by a Decree of December 10th, 1937, for that part of Norway which is situated northward of 66°28.8' (or 66°28' 48") N. latitude. The Application refers to the Declarations by which the United Kingdom and Norway have accepted the compulsory jurisdiction of the Court in accordance with Article 36, paragraph 2, of the Statute.

This Application asked the Court

(*a*) to declare the principles of international law to be applied in defining the base-lines, by reference to which the Norwegian Government is entitled to delimit a fisheries zone, extending to seaward 4 sea miles from those lines and exclusively reserved for its own nationals, and to define the said base-lines in so far as it appears necessary, in the light of the arguments of the Parties, in order to avoid further legal differences between them;

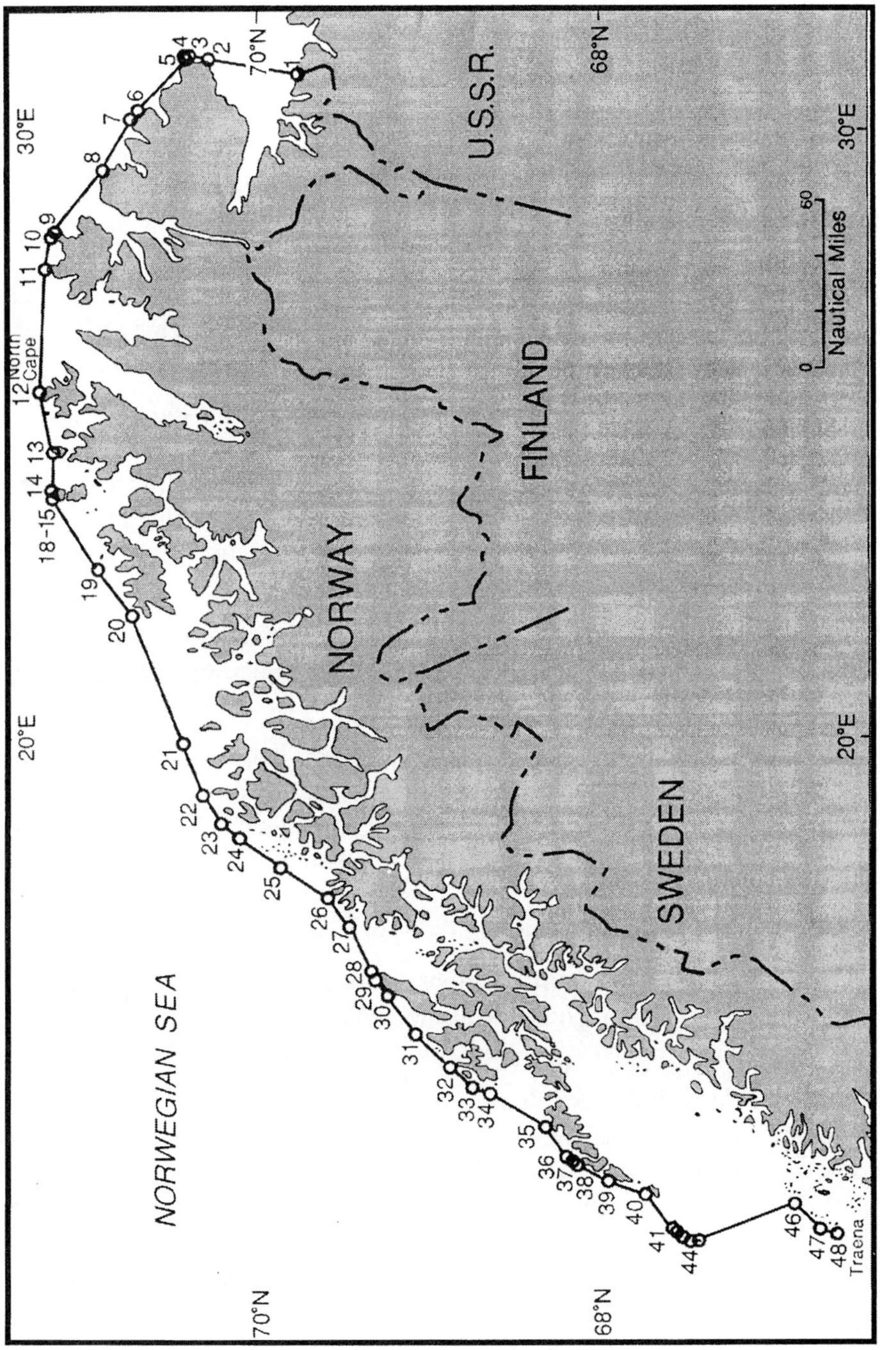

"Figure 2.1 Norwegian Straight Baselines. 1935", *reprinted from* W. MICHAEL REISMAN & GAYL S. WESTERMAN, *supra* at 25.

> (*b*) to award damages to the Government of the United Kingdom in respect of all interferences by the Norwegian authorities with British fishing vessels outside the zone which, in accordance with the Court's decision under (*a*), the Norwegian Government is entitled to reserve for its nationals. …

The Norwegian Royal Decree of July 12th, 1935, concerning the delimitation of the Norwegian fisheries zone sets out in the preamble the considerations on which its provisions are based. In this connection it refers to "well established national titles of right", "the geographical conditions prevailing on the Norwegian coasts", "the safeguard of the vital interests of the inhabitants of the northernmost parts of the country"; it further relies on the Royal Decrees of February 22nd, 1812, October 17th, 1869, January 5th, 1881, and September 9th, 1889.

The Decree provides that "lines of delimitation towards the high sea of the Norwegian fisheries zone as regards that part of Norway which is situated northward of 66°28'8 N[orth] latitude … shall run parallel with straight baselines drawn between fixed points on the mainland, on islands or rocks, starting from the final point of the boundary line of the Realm in the easternmost part of the Varangerfjord and going as far as Træna in the County of Nordland". …

The claim of the United Kingdom Government is founded on what it regards as the general international law applicable to the delimitation of the Norwegian fisheries zone.

The Norwegian Government does not deny that there exist rules of international law to which this delimitation must conform. It contends that the propositions formulated by the United Kingdom Government in its "Conclusions" do not possess the character attributed to them by that Government. It further relies on its own system of delimitation which it asserts to be in every respect in conformity with the requirements of international law.

The Court will examine in turn these various aspects of the claim of the United Kingdom and of the defence of the Norwegian Government. …

The coastal zone concerned in the dispute is of considerable length. It lies north of latitude 66°28.8' N., that is to say, north of the Arctic Circle, and it includes the coast of the mainland of Norway and all the islands, islets, rocks and reefs, known by the name of the "skjærgaard" (literally, rock rampart), together with all Norwegian internal and territorial waters. The coast of the mainland, which, without taking any account of fjords, bays and minor indentations, is over 1,500 kilometres in length, is of a very distinctive configuration. Very broken along its whole length, it constantly opens out into indentations often penetrating for great distances inland : the Porsangerfjord, for instance, penetrates 75 sea miles inland. To the west, the land configuration stretches out into the sea : the large and small islands, mountainous in character, the islets, rocks and reefs, some always above water, others emerging only at low tide, are in truth but an extension of the Norwegian mainland. The number of insular formations, large and small, which make up the "skjærgaard", is estimated by the Norwegian Government to be one hundred and twenty thousand. From the southern extremity of the disputed area to the North Cape, the "skjærgaard" lies along the whole of the coast of the mainland; east of the North Cape, the "skjærgaard" ends, but the coast line continues to be broken by large and deeply indented fjords.

With the "skjærgaard", almost every island has its large and its small bays; countless arms of the sea, straits, channels and mere waterways serve as a means of communication for the local population which inhabits the islands as it does the mainland. The coast of the mainland does not constitute, as it does in practically all other countries, a clear dividing line between land and sea. What matters, what really constitutes the Norwegian coast line, is the outer line of the "skjærgaard".

The whole of this region is mountainous. The North Cape, a sheer rock little more than 300 metres high, can be seen from a considerable distance; there are other summits rising to over a thousand metres, so that the Norwegian coast, mainland and "skjaergaard", is visible from far off.

Along the coast are situated comparatively shallow banks, veritable underwater terraces which constitute fishing grounds where fish are particularly abundant; these grounds were known to Norwegian fishermen and exploited by them from time immemorial. Since these banks lay within the range of vision, the most desirable fishing grounds were always located and identified by means of the method of alignments ("*meds*"'), at points where two lines drawn between points selected on the coast or on islands intersected.

In these barren regions the inhabitants of the coastal zone derive their livelihood essentially from fishing.

Such are the realities which must be borne in mind in appraising the validity of the United Kingdom contention that the limits of the Norwegian fisheries zone laid down in the 1935 Decree are contrary to international law.

The Parties being in agreement on the figure of 4 miles for the breadth of the territorial sea, the problem which arises is from what base-line this breadth is to be reckoned. The Conclusions of the United Kingdom are explicit on this point : the base-line must be low-water mark on permanently dry land which is a part of Norwegian territory, or the proper closing line of Norwegian internal waters.

The Court has no difficulty in finding that, for the purpose of measuring the breadth of the territorial sea, it is the low-water mark as opposed to the high-water mark, or the mean between the two tides, which has generally been adopted in the practice of States. This criterion is the most favourable to the coastal State and clearly shows the character of territorial waters as appurtenant to the land territory. The Court notes that the Parties agree as to this criterion, but that they differ as to its application. ...

The Court finds itself obliged to decide whether the relevant low-water mark is that of the mainland or of the "skjærgaard". Since the mainland is bordered in its western sector by the "skjærgaard", which constitutes a whole with the mainland, it is the outer line of the "skjærgaard" which must be taken into account in delimiting the belt of Norwegian territorial waters. This solution is dictated by geographic realities. ...

The arcs of circles method, which is constantly used for determining the position of a point or object at sea, is a new technique in so far as it is a method for delimiting the territorial sea. This technique was proposed by the United States delegation at the 1930 Conference for the codification of international law. Its purpose is to secure the application of the principle that the belt of territorial waters must follow the line of the coast. It is not obligatory by law, as was admitted by Counsel for the United Kingdom Government in his oral reply. In these circumstances, and although certain of the Conclusions of the United Kingdom are founded on the application of the arcs of circles method, the Court considers that it need not deal with these Conclusions in so far as they are based upon this method.

The principle that the belt of territorial waters must follow the general direction of the coast makes it possible to fix certain criteria valid for any delimitation of the territorial sea; these criteria will be elucidated later. The Court will confine itself at this stage to noting that, in order to apply this principle, several States have deemed it necessary to follow the straight base-lines method and that they have not encountered objections of principle by other States. This method consists of selecting appropriate points on the low-water mark and drawing straight lines between them. This has been done, not only in the case of well-defined bays, but also in cases of minor curvatures of the coast line where it was solely a question of giving a simpler form to the belt of territorial waters.

It has been contended, on behalf of the United Kingdom, that Norway may draw straight lines only across bays. The Court is unable to share this view. If the belt of territorial waters must follow the outer line of the "skjærgaard", and if the method of straight base-lines must be admitted in certain cases, there is no valid reason to draw them only across bays, as in Eastern Finnmark, and not also to draw them between islands, islets and rocks, across the sea areas separating them, even when such areas do not fall within the conception of a bay. It is sufficient that they should be situated between the island formations of the "skjærgaard", *inter fauces terrarum*.

The United Kingdom Government concedes that straight lines, regardless of their length, may be used only subject to the conditions set out in point 5 of its Conclusions, as follows:

> Norway is entitled to claim as Norwegian internal waters, on historic grounds, all fjords and sunds which fall within the conception of a bay as defined in international law (see No. (6) below), whether the proper closing line of the indentation is more or less than 10 sea miles long.

A preliminary remark must be made in respect of this point.

In the opinion of the United Kingdom Government, Norway is entitled, on historic grounds, to claim as internal waters all fjords and sunds which have the character of a bay. She is also entitled on historic grounds to claim as Norwegian territorial waters all the waters of the fjords and sunds which have the character of legal straits ... and, either as internal or as territorial waters, the areas of water lying between the island fringe and the mainland. …

By "historic waters" are usually meant waters which are treated as internal waters but which would not have that character were it not for the existence of an historic title. The United Kingdom Government refers to the notion of historic titles both in respect of territorial waters and internal waters, considering such titles, in both cases, as derogations from general international law. In its opinion Norway can justify the claim that these waters are territorial or internal on the ground that she has exercised the necessary jurisdiction over them for a long period without opposition from other States, a kind of *possessio longi temporis,* with the result that her jurisdiction over these waters must now be recognized although it constitutes a derogation from the rules in force. Norwegian sovereignty over these waters would constitute an exception, historic titles justifying situations which would otherwise be in conflict with international law.

As has been said, the United Kingdom Government concedes that Norway is entitled to claim as internal waters all the waters of fjords and sunds which fall within the conception of a bay as defined in international law whether the closing line of the indentation is more or less than ten sea miles long. But the United Kingdom Government concedes this only on the basis of historic title; it must therefore be taken that that Government has not abandoned its contention that the ten-mile rule is to be regarded as a rule of international law.

In these circumstances the Court deems it necessary to point out that although the ten-mile rule has been adopted by certain States both in their national law and in their treaties and conventions, and although certain arbitral decisions have applied it as between these States, other States have adopted a different limit. Consequently, the ten-mile rule has not acquired the authority of a general rule of international law.

In any event the ten-mile rule would appear to be inapplicable as against Norway inasmuch as she has always opposed any attempt to apply it to the Norwegian coast.

The Court now comes to the question of the length of the base-lines drawn across the waters lying between the various formations of the "skjærgaard" Basing itself on the analogy with the alleged general rule of ten miles relating to bays, the United Kingdom Government still maintains on this point that the length of straight lines must not exceed ten miles.

In this connection, the practice of States does not justify the formulation of any general rule of law. The attempts that have been made to subject groups of islands or coastal archipelagoes to conditions analogous to the limitations concerning bays (distance between the islands not exceeding twice the breadth of the territorial waters, or ten or twelve sea miles), have not got beyond the stage of proposals.

Furthermore, apart from any question of limiting the lines to ten miles, it may be that several lines can be envisaged. In such cases the coastal State would seem to be in the best position to appraise the local conditions dictating the selection.

Consequently, the Court is unable to share the view of the United Kingdom Government, that "Norway, in the matter of base-lines, now claims recognition of an exceptional system". As will be shown later, all that the Court can see therein is the application of general international law to a specific case. …

It does not at all follow that, in the absence of rules having the technically precise character alleged by the United Kingdom Government, the delimitation undertaken by the Norwegian Government in 1935 is not subject to certain principles which make it possible to judge as to its validity under international law. The delimitation of sea areas has always an international aspect; it cannot be dependent merely upon the will of the coastal State as expressed in its municipal law. Although it is true that the act of delimitation is necessarily a unilateral act, because only the coastal State is competent to undertake it, the validity of the delimitation with regard to other States depends upon international law.

In this connection, certain basic considerations inherent in the nature of the territorial sea bring to light certain criteria which, though not entirely precise, can provide courts with an adequate basis for their decisions, which can be adapted to the diverse facts in question.

Among these considerations, some reference must be made to the close dependence of the territorial sea upon the land domain. It is the land which confers upon the coastal State a right to the waters off its coasts. It follows that while such a State must be allowed the latitude necessary in order to be able to adapt its delimitation to practical needs and local requirements, the drawing of base-lines must not depart to any appreciable extent from the general direction of the coast.

Another fundamental consideration, of particular importance in this case, is the more or less close relationship existing between certain sea areas and the land formations which divide or surround them. The real question raised in the choice of base-lines is in effect whether certain sea areas lying within these lines are sufficiently closely linked to the land domain to be subject to the regime of internal waters. This idea, which is at the basis of the determination of the rules relating to bays, should be liberally applied in the case of a coast, the geographical configuration of which is as unusual as that of Norway.

Finally there is one consideration not to be overlooked, the scope of which extends beyond purely geographical factors: that of certain economic interests peculiar to a region, the reality and importance of which are clearly evidenced by a long usage.

[The Court, by a vote of ten to two, upheld the Norwegian method of straight base-lines as not contrary to international law and, by a vote of eight to four, upheld the specific lines employed in application of this method as not contrary to international law.]

NOTES AND QUESTIONS

1. The Court's judgment set off a great "sea-rush."

> Few judgments of the International Court have been so clearly and directly responsible for a major change in international law. The 1951 Judgment precipitated two lines of development. One was a veritable explosion of unilateral straight baseline delimitations ... Coincident with this widespread usage was a codification and progressive development exercise, under the direction of the International Law Commission, which refashioned the *ratio* of the Judgment. The preparatory work of the ILC was then adopted in treaty form in 1958 and reaffirmed in 1982. ...

W. MICHAEL REISMAN & GAYL S. WESTERMAN, *supra* at 37.

2. Many states seek to enlarge their maritime jurisdiction by extending their internal waters. As the provisions of UNCLOS above indicate, these extensions may be accomplished by enclosing a juridical bay under Art. 10 or an historic bay under historical title. Both of these options have sometimes been abused by states. GAYL S. WESTERMAN, THE JURIDICAL BAY, *supra* at 28, n. 46. An even more exorbitant extension of internal waters jurisdiction can be accomplished by coastal states which utilize UNCLOS, Art. 7, to enclose areas of previously territorial and high seas behind illegitimate straight baselines. If these baselines are very long, substantial areas of continental shelf can also be gained. This unilateral action, often not opposed by third states, has two deleterious effects: to expand the exclusive use of these waters by coastal states and to subsume all prior legitimate claims to bays rivers, ports, and so forth along their mainland coasts, often rendering those delimitation regimes anachronistic. W. MICHAEL REISMAN & GAYL S. WESTERMAN, STRAIGHT BASELINES IN INTERNATIONAL MARITIME BOUNDARY DELIMITATION, *supra* at 105-107.

3. Exemplifying the more problematic straight baseline claims are those off the southern coast of Vietnam, *see* map, *infra,* at 668. Fringed with islands along portions of the northeastern coast, the remainder of the Vietnamese coastline except for the Mekong River delta is relatively smooth without a fringe of islands in the immediate vicinity. Nonetheless, baseline segments A1 to A6 enclose the entire coast with infrequent basepoints located on the islands of Dao Tho Chu, Hon Khoai, Con Dao and the Phu Qui group (Chatwick Islands). As can be readily seen, the configuration of these islands and their distance from the coast deny them any status as a group of fringing islands under [UNCLOS Article 7].

Even if the Mekong delta qualifies the coastline in this locality as deeply indented, the islands selected are not appropriate as basepoints. Typical of this type of pathology, the baseline veers from the general direction of the coast and encloses waters which cannot be characterized as internal. ... In addition, the length of segment Al to A2 is 99.94 n.m., segment A2 to A3 is 103.9 n.m., and segment A5 to A6 is 162.3 n.m. The enormous increase in maritime area gained by Vietnam from these claims has been illustrated ... in Fig. 5.1 [below]. When combined with the Cambodian straight baseline claims, these baselines represent a likely infringement upon Thailand's rights in this ocean region. *Id.* at 133-136.

4. As will be seen throughout Part Four, the I.C.J. has assigned itself a major role in the development of maritime boundary delimitation jurisprudence. *See* BARBARA KWIATKOWSKA, THE CONTRIBUTION OF THE WORLD COURT TO THE DEVELOPMENT OF THE LAW OF THE SEA (Bookworld 2002).

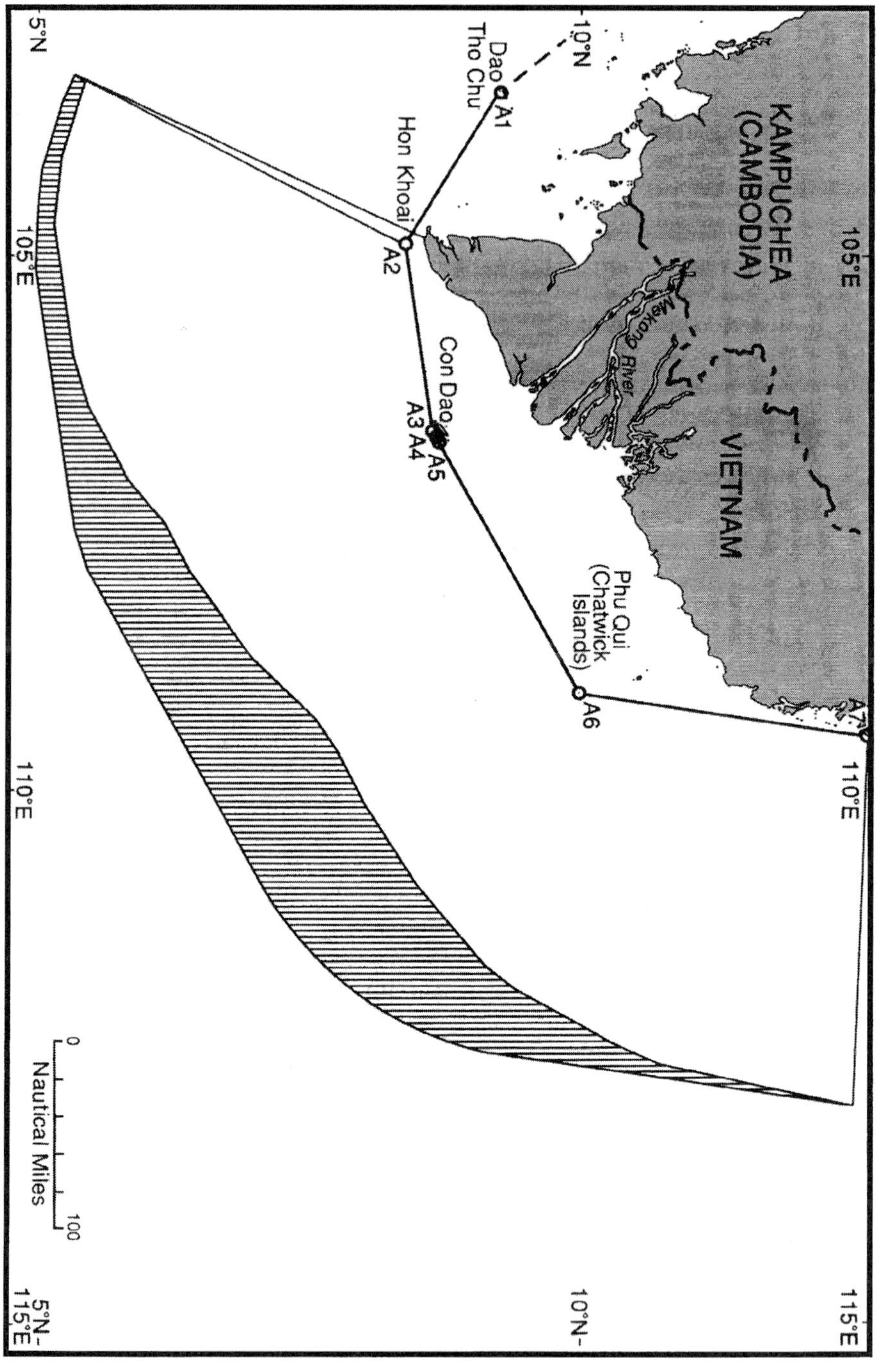

"Figure 5. 1 Vietnam" *reprinted from* W. MICHAEL REISMAN & GAYL S. WESTERMAN, *supra* at 109.

5. United States courts have turned to international law for construction of cognate terms. In *United States v. California*, 381 U.S. 139 (1965), *reh. den.* 382 U.S. 889, the Supreme Court adopted the Geneva Convention on the Territorial Sea and the Contiguous Zone for purposes of evaluating California's inland waters claims, which are illustrated, *infra*, at 670.

The Court characterized the "focal point of this case" as "the interpretation to be placed on 'inland waters' as used in the Act" and adopted the definition provided by the 1958 Convention on the Territorial Sea and the Contiguous Zone for purposes of the Submerged Lands Act, 43 U.S.C. §§ 1301 *et seq.*)

HARLAN, J. Once it is decided that the definitions of the Convention on the Territorial Sea and the Contiguous Zone apply, many of the subsidiary issues before us fall into place.

> 1. *Straight Base Lines.*—California argues that because the Convention permits a nation to use the straight-base-line method for determining its seaward boundaries if its "coast line is deeply indented and cut into, or if there is a fringe of islands along the coast in its immediate vicinity," California is therefore free to use such boundary lines across the openings of its bays and around its islands. We agree with the United States that the Convention recognizes the validity of straight base lines used by other countries, Norway for instance, and would *permit* the United States to use such base lines if it chose, but that California may not use such base lines to extend our international boundaries beyond their traditional international limits against the expressed opposition of the United States. ... We conclude that the choice under the Convention to use the straight-base-line method for determining inland waters claimed against other nations is one that rests with the Federal Government, and not with the individual States. ...
>
> 2. *Twenty-four-mile Closing Rule.*—The Convention recognizes, and it is the present United States position, that a 24-mile closing rule together with the semicircle test should be used for classifying bays in the.United States. Applying these tests to the segments of California's coast here in dispute, it appears that Monterey Bay is inland water and that none of the other coastal segments in dispute fulfill these aspects of the Convention test. We so hold.
>
> California asserts that the Santa Barbara Channel may be considered a "fictitious bay" because the openings at both ends of the channel and between the islands are each less than 24 miles. The United States argues that the channel is no bay at all; that it is a strait which serves as a useful route of communication between two areas of open sea and as such may not be classified as inland waters. ...
>
> Evidence submitted to the Special Master on the extent of international use made of the Santa Barbara Channel was sparse. What evidence there was indicated the usefulness of the route, but did not specify whether the ships so using it were domestic or international. California now regards the point as important, for under international law as expressed in the *Corfu Channel Case*, [1949] I.C.J. Rep. 4, the International Court of Justice held that a country could not claim a strait as inland water if, in its natural state, it served as a useful route for *international* passage. We do not consider the point of controlling importance. The United States has not in the past claimed the Santa Barbara Channel as inland water and opposes any such claim now. The channel has not been regarded as a bay either historically or geographically. In these circumstances, as with the drawing of straight base lines, we hold that if the United States does not choose to employ the concept of a "fictitious bay" in order to extend our international boundaries around the islands framing Santa Barbara Channel, it cannot be forced to do so by California. ...
>
> 3. *Historic Inland Waters.*— By the terms of the Convention the 24-mile closing rule does not apply to so-called "historic" bays. Essentially these are bays over which a

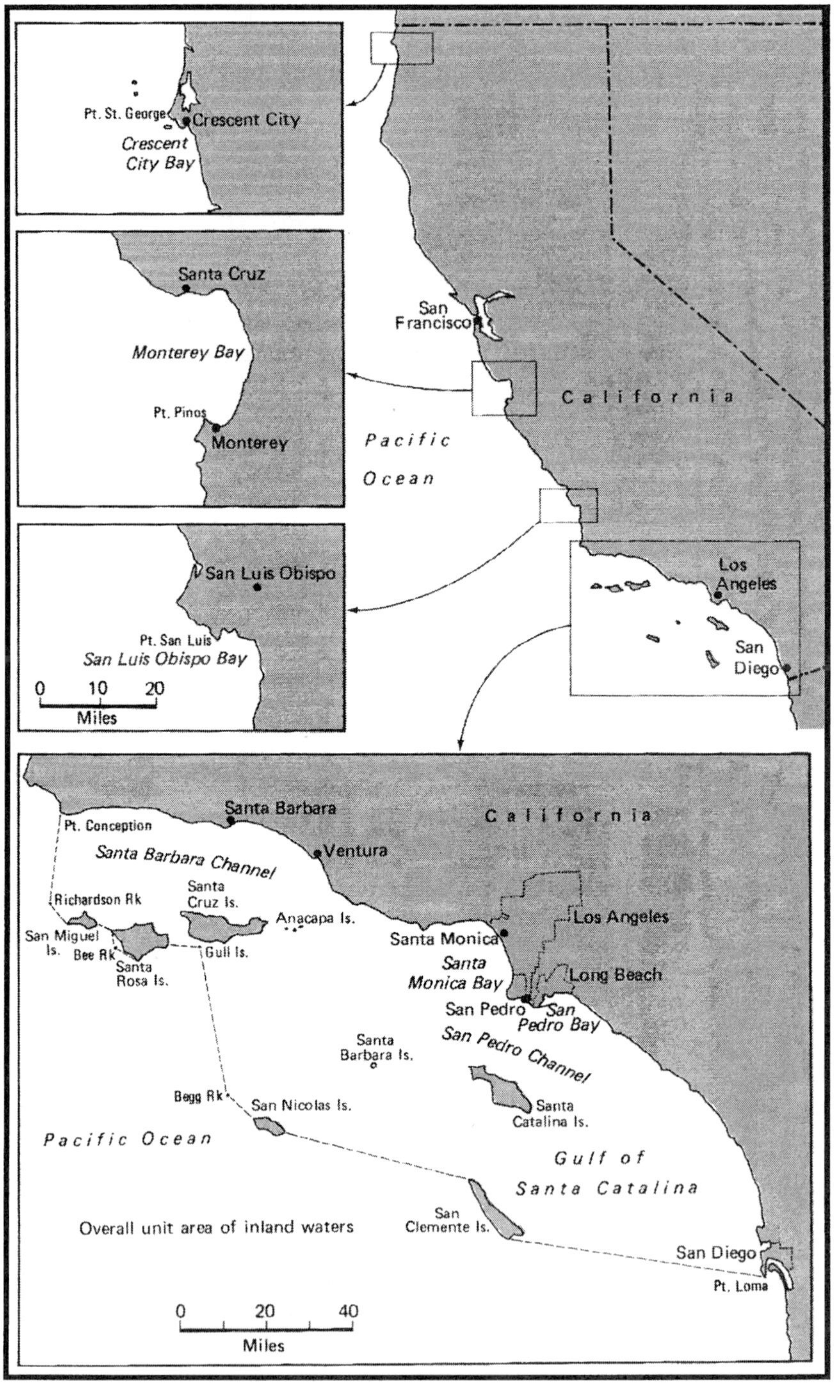

"Figure 12. Inland waters claimed by California," *reprinted from* GAYL S. WESTERMAN, THE JURIDICAL BAY, *supra* at 206.

coastal nation has traditionally asserted and maintained dominion with the acquiescence of foreign nations. California claims that virtually all the waters here in dispute are historic inland waters as the term is internationally understood. It relies primarily on an interpretation of its State Constitution to the effect that the state boundaries run three miles outside the islands and bays, plus several court decisions which so interpret it as applied to Monterey, Santa Monica, and San Pedro Bays. The United States counters that, as with straight base lines, California can maintain no claim to historic inland waters unless the claim is endorsed by the United States. ... Since the 24-mile rule includes Monterey Bay, we do not consider it here. As to Santa Monica Bay, San Pedro Bay, and the other water areas in dispute, we agree with the Special Master that they are not historic inland waters of the United States. ... Id.

6. Why would the Federal Government *not* want to claim straight baselines on behalf of the U.S.?

4. Territorial Sea

The territorial sea pertains to the coastal state but, in contrast to internal waters, is subject to certain servitudes for the benefit of international users.

a. Delimitation

1982 United Nations Convention on the Law of the Sea

Article 3: *Breadth of the territorial sea*

Every State has the right to establish the breadth of its territorial sea up to a limit not exceeding 12 nautical miles, measured from baselines determined in accordance with this Convention.

Article 4: *Outer limit of the territorial sea*

The outer limit of the territorial sea is the line every point of which is at a distance from the nearest point of the baseline equal to the breadth of the territorial sea. ...

Article 17: *Right of innocent passage*

Subject to this Convention, ships of all States, whether coastal or land-locked enjoy the right of innocent passage through the territorial sea.

Article 18: *Meaning of passage*

1. Passage means navigation through the territorial sea for the purpose of:

(a) traversing that sea without entering internal waters or calling at a roadstead or port facility outside internal waters; or

(b) proceeding to or from internal waters or a call at such roadstead or port facility.

2. Passage shall be continuous and expeditious. However, passage includes stopping and anchoring, but only in so far as the same are incidental to ordinary navigation or are rendered necessary by force majeure or distress or for the purpose of rendering assistance to persons, ships or aircraft in danger or distress.

Article 19: *Meaning of innocent passage*

1. Passage is innocent so long as it is not prejudicial to the peace, good order or security of the coastal State. Such passage shall take place in conformity with this Convention and with other rules of international law.

2. Passage of a foreign ship shall be considered to be prejudicial to the peace, good order or security of the coastal State if in the territorial sea it engages in any of the following activities:

(a) any threat or use of force against the sovereignty, territorial integrity or political independence of the coastal State, or in any other manner in violation of the principles of international law embodied in the Charter of the United Nations;

(b) any exercise or practice with weapons of any kind;

(c) any act aimed at collecting information to the prejudice of the defence or security of the coastal State;

(d) any act of propaganda aimed at affecting the defence or security of the coastal State;

(e) the launching, landing or taking on board of any aircraft;

(f) the launching, landing or taking on board of any military device;

(g) the loading or unloading of any commodity, currency or person contrary to the customs, fiscal, immigration or sanitary laws and regulations of the coastal State;

(h) any act of willful and serious pollution contrary to this Convention;

(i) any fishing activities;

(j) the carrying out of research or survey activities;

(k) any act aimed at interfering with any systems of communication or any other facilities or installations of the coastal State;

(1) any other activity not having a direct bearing on passage. …

Article 24: *Duties of the coastal State*

1. The coastal State shall not hamper the innocent passage of foreign ships through the territorial sea except in accordance with this Convention. In particular, in the application of this Convention or of any laws or regulations adopted in conformity with this Convention, the coastal State shall not:

(a) impose requirements on foreign ships which have the practical effect of denying or impairing the right of innocent passage; or

(b) discriminate in form or in fact against the ships of any State or against ships carrying cargoes to, from or on behalf of any State.

2. The coastal State shall give appropriate publicity to any danger to navigation, of which it has knowledge, within its territorial sea.

Article 25: *Rights of protection of the coastal State*

1. The coastal State may take the necessary steps in its territorial sea to prevent passage which is not innocent.

2. In the case of ships proceeding to internal waters or a call at a port facility outside internal waters, the coastal State also has the right to take the necessary steps to prevent any breach of the conditions to which admission of those ships to internal waters or such a call is subject.

3. The coastal State may, without discrimination in form or in fact among foreign ships, suspend temporarily in specified areas of its territorial sea the innocent passage of foreign ships if such suspension is essential for the protection of its security, including weapons exercises. Such suspension shall take effect only after having been duly published.

Notes and Questions

1. With respect to the exercise of jurisdiction over ships transiting Territorial Seas, UNCLOS establishes a specific regime that admonishes the coastal state not to exercise criminal jurisdiction on board save if the consequences of the crime extend to the coastal state; if the assistance of local authorities has been requested by the master or a diplomatic agent of the flag state; or if it is necessary for the suppression of drugs. With respect to civil jurisdiction over foreign ships transiting the Territorial Seas the coastal state is admonished not to stop or divert the ship for the purpose of exercising civil jurisdiction, subject to very limited exceptions. For a more thorough discussion of these issues, see Ann Bardin, *Coastal States Jurisdiction Over Foreign Vessels,* 14 Pace Int'l L. Rev. 27, 32-39 (2002).

2. Warships are subject to a special regime in the Territorial Sea. Article 29 provides a definition of warships and Article 30 limits the coastal state, when it is confronted with a warship that is not complying with its laws and regulations, to require it to leave the Territorial Sea promptly. Article 31 establishes the international responsibility of the flag state of a warship for any resulting loss or damage to the coastal state. *Id.* at 39.

5. Contiguous Zone

Historically, coastal states have insisted on projecting jurisdiction, for specific purposes, beyond the territorial sea.

a. Delimitation

1982 United Nations Convention on The Law of the Sea

Article 33: *Contiguous zone*

1. In a zone contiguous to its territorial sea, described as the contiguous zone, the coastal State may exercise the control necessary to:

(a) prevent infringement of its customs, fiscal, immigration or sanitary laws and regulations within its territory or territorial sea;

(b) punish infringement of the above laws and regulations committed within its territory or territorial sea.

2. The contiguous zone may not extend beyond 24 nautical miles from the baselines from which the breadth of the territorial sea is measured.

b. Church v. Hubbart
6 U.S. 187(1804)

[Suit by owner of the brigantine *Aurora.* The Aurora was seized by the Portuguese off Pará, Brazil, beyond the territorial sea limit. The insurers defended by citing a contract clause stating "the insurers are not liable for seizure by the Portuguese for illicit trade." The plaintiff contended, *inter alia,* that the seizure was not for illicit trade, and that the seizure was not justified by Portuguese law because the ship lay outside Portuguese territorial jurisdiction at the time of seizure. The lower courts found for the insurers.]

MARSHALL, Ch. J.: That the law of nations prohibits the exercise of any act of authority over a vessel in the situation of the *Aurora*, and that this seizure is, on that account, a mere marine trespass, not within the exception, cannot be admitted. To reason from the extent of protection a nation will afford to foreigners, to the extent of the means it may use for its own security, does not seem to be perfectly correct. It is opposed by principles which are universally acknowledged. The authority of a nation, within its own territory, is absolute and exclusive. The seizure of a vessel within the range of its cannon by a foreign force is an invasion of that territory, and is a hostile act which it is its duty to repel. But its power to secure itself from injury may certainly be exercised beyond the limits of its territory. Upon this principle the right of a belligerent to search a neutral vessel on the high seas for contraband of war, is universally admitted, because the belligerent has a right to prevent the injury done to himself by the assistance intended for his enemy : so too a nation has a right to prohibit any commerce with its colonies. Any attempt to violate the laws made to protect this right, is an injury to itself which it may prevent, and it has a right to use the means necessary for its prevention. These means do not appear to be limited within any certain marked boundaries, which remain the same at all times and in all situations. If they are such as unnecessarily to vex and harass foreign lawful commerce, foreign nations will resist their exercise. If they are such as are reasonable and necessary to secure their laws from violation, they will be submitted to.

In different seas and on different coasts, a wider or more contracted range, in which to exercise the vigilance of the government, will be assented to. Thus in the channel, where a very great part of the commerce to and from all the north of Europe, passes through a very narrow sea, the seizure of vessels on suspicion of attempting an illicit trade, must necessarily be restricted to very narrow limits, but on the coast of *South America*, seldom frequented by vessels but for the purpose of illicit trade, the vigilance of the government may be extended somewhat further ; and foreign nations submit to such regulations as are reasonable in themselves, and are really necessary to secure that monopoly of colonial commerce, which is claimed by all nations holding distant possessions.

If this right be extended too far, the exercise of it will be resisted. It has occasioned long and frequent contests, which have sometimes ended in open war. The *English*, it will be well recollected, complained of the right claimed by *Spain* to search their vessels on the high seas, which was carried so far, that the *guarda costas* of that nation, seized vessels not in the neighbourhood of their coasts. This practice was the subject of long and fruitless negotiations, and at length, of open war. The right of the *Spaniards* was supposed to be exercised unreasonably and vexatiously, but it never was contended that it could only be exercised within the range of the cannon from their batteries. Indeed the right given to our own revenue cutters, to visit vessels four leagues from our coast, is a declaration that in the opinion of the American government, no such principle as that contended for, has a real existence. …

Notes and Questions

1. In the President's transmittal of the 1982 Convention to the Senate Committee on Foreign Relations, the President said, "[i]n the contiguous zone, vessels and aircraft enjoy the same high seas freedoms of navigation and overflight as in the EEZ." Message from the President of the United States Transmitting the United Nations Convention on the Law of the Sea, *supra*, Treaty Doc. 103-39 at 23. Is the President's interpretation consistent with the powers assigned to the coastal state in Article 33?

2. Consider the following hypothetical: Travel Galore, an American cruise vessel, is making its way through the Persian Gulf with a large number of American tourists on board. When it is in the Contiguous Zone of Iran, Iranian naval personnel board the ship to determine whether alcohol is on board and is being served. Is this lawful under UNCLOS?

6. Straits

Straits are maritime passages connecting two parts of the high seas. These choke points are critical for the movement on, below and above the oceans and have been sources of acute conflict in international politics and law, particularly after the extension of the breadth of the territorial sea.

a. Delimitation

1982 United Nations Convention on the Law of the Sea

Article 37: *Scope of this section*

This section applies to straits which are used for international navigation between one part of the high seas or an exclusive economic zone and another part of the high seas or an exclusive economic zone.

Article 38: *Right of transit passage*

1. In straits referred to in article 37, all ships and aircraft enjoy the right of transit passage, which shall not be impeded; except that, if the strait is formed by an island of a State bordering the strait and its mainland, transit passage shall not

apply if there exists seaward of the island a route through the high seas or through an exclusive economic zone of similar convenience with respect to navigational and hydrographical characteristics.

2. Transit passage means the exercise in accordance with this Part of the freedom of navigation and overflight solely for the purpose of continuous and expeditious transit of the strait between one part of the high seas or an exclusive economic zone and another part of the high seas or an exclusive economic zone. However, the requirement of continuous and expeditious transit does not preclude passage through the strait for the purpose of entering, leaving or returning from a State bordering the strait, subject to the conditions of entry to that State.

3. Any activity which is not an exercise of the right of transit passage through a strait remains subject to the other applicable provisions of this Convention.

Article 39: *Duties of ships and aircraft during transit passage*

1. Ships and aircraft, while exercising the right of transit passage, shall:

(a) proceed without delay through or over the strait;

(b) refrain from any threat or use of force against the sovereignty, territorial integrity or political independence of States bordering the strait, or in any other manner in violation of the principles of international law embodied in the Charter of the United Nations;

(c) refrain from any activities other than those incident to their normal modes of continuous and expeditious transit unless rendered necessary *by force majeure* or by distress;

(d) comply with other relevant provisions of this Part.

2. Ships in transit passage shall:

(a) comply with generally accepted international regulations, procedures and practices for safety at sea, including the International Regulations for Preventing Collisions at Sea;

(b) comply with generally accepted international regulations, procedures and practices for the prevention, reduction and control of pollution from ships.

3. Aircraft in transit passage shall:

(a) observe the Rules of the Air established by the International Civil Aviation Organization as they apply to civil aircraft; state aircraft will normally comply with such safety measures and will at all times operate with due regard for the safety of navigation;

(b) at all times monitor the radio frequency assigned by the competent internationally designated air traffic control authority or the appropriate international distress radio frequency. …

Article 44: *Duties of States bordering straits*

States bordering straits shall not hamper transit passage and shall give appropriate publicity to any danger to navigation or overflight within or over the strait of which they have knowledge. There shall be no suspension of transit passage

Article 45: *Innocent Passage*

1. The régime of innocent passage, in accordance with Part 11, section 3, shall apply in straits used for international navigation:

(a) excluded from the application of the regime of transit passage under article 38, paragraph 1; or

(b) between a part of the high seas or an exclusive economic zone and the territorial sea of a foreign State.

2. There shall be no suspension of innocent passage through such straits.

b. The Corfu Channel Case (U.K. v. Alb.)
1949 I.C.J. 4 (Judgment of Dec. 15)

By the first part of the Special Agreement, the following question is submitted to the Court:

> (I) Is Albania responsible under international law for the explosions which occurred on the 22nd October 1946 in Albanian waters and for the damage and loss of human life which resulted from them and is there any duty to pay compensation?

On October 22nd, 1946, a squadron of British warships, the cruisers *Mauritius* and *Leander* and the destroyers *Saumarez* and *Volage,* left the port of Corfu and proceeded northward through a channel previously swept for mines in the North Corfu Strait. The cruiser *Mauritius* was leading, followed by the destroyer *Saumarez*; at a certain distance thereafter came the cruiser *Leander* followed by the destroyer *Volage.* Outside the Bay of Saranda, *Saumarez* struck a mine and was heavily damaged. *Volage* was ordered to give her assistance and to take her in tow. Whilst towing the damaged ship, *Volage* struck a mine and was much damaged. Nevertheless, she succeeded in towing the other ship back to Corfu.

Three weeks later, on November 13th the North Corfu Channel was swept by British minesweepers and twenty-two moored mines were cut. Two mines were taken to Malta for expert examination. During the minesweeping operation it was thought that the mines were of the German GR type, but it was subsequently established that they were of the German GY type. ...

It is clear that knowledge of the minelaying cannot be imputed to the Albanian Government by reason merely of the fact that a minefield discovered in Albanian territorial waters caused the explosions of which the British warships were the victims. It is true, as international practice shows, that a State on whose territory or in whose waters an act contrary to international law has occurred,

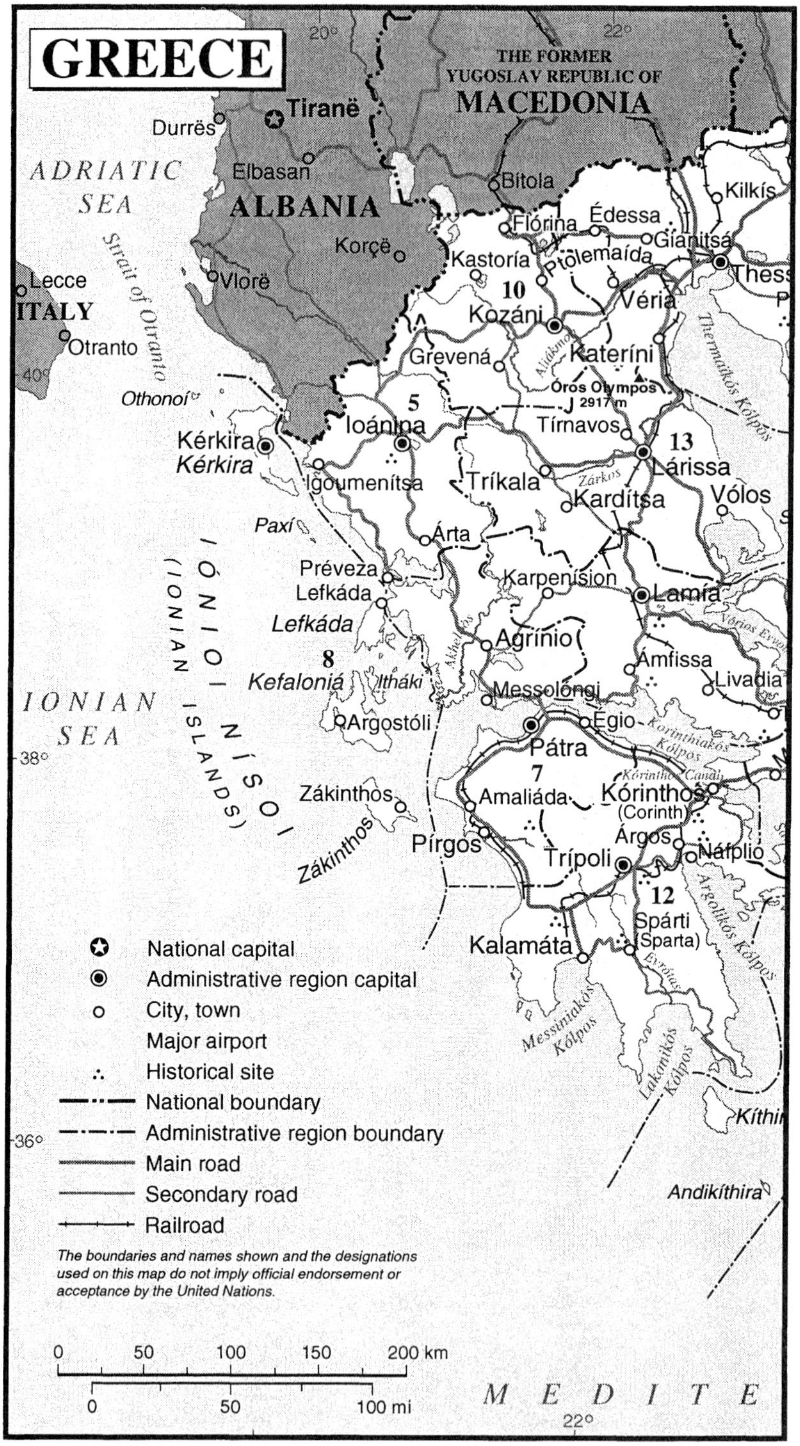

Partial United Nations Map of Greece, DEPARTMENT OF PEACEKEEPING OPERATIONS, CARTOGRAPHIC SECTION, Map No. 3798 Rev. 1 (October 2002), showing Corfu (as Kérkira) and the Corfu Channel between Corfu and the Albanian mainland

may be called upon to give an explanation. It is also true that that State cannot evade such a request by limiting itself to a reply that it is ignorant of the circumstances of the act and of its authors. The State may, up to a certain point, be bound to supply particulars of the use made by it of the means of information and inquiry at its disposal. But it cannot be concluded from the mere fact of the control exercised by a State over its territory and waters that that State necessarily knew, or ought to have known, of any unlawful act perpetrated therein, nor yet that it necessarily knew, or should have known, the authors. This fact, by itself and apart from other circumstances, neither involves *prima facie* responsibility nor shifts the burden of proof.

On the other hand, the fact of this exclusive territorial control exercised by a State within its frontiers has a bearing upon the methods of proof available to establish the knowledge of that State as to such events. By reason of this exclusive control, the other State, the victim of a breach of international law, is often unable to furnish direct proof of facts giving rise to responsibility. Such a State should be allowed a more liberal recourse to inferences of fact and circumstantial evidence. This indirect evidence is admitted in all systems of law, and its use is recognized by international decisions. It must be regarded as of special weight when it is based on a series of facts linked together and leading logically to a single conclusion.

The Court must examine therefore whether it has been established by means of indirect evidence that Albania has knowledge of minelaying in her territorial waters independently of any connivance on her part in this operation. The proof may be drawn from inferences of fact, provided that they leave *no room* for reasonable doubt. The elements of fact on which these inferences can be based may differ from those which are relevant to the question of connivance. …

From all the facts and observations mentioned above, the Court draws the conclusion that the laying of the minefield which caused the explosions on October 22nd, 1946, could not have been accomplished without the knowledge of the Albanian Government.

The obligations resulting for Albania from this knowledge are not disputed between the Parties. Counsel for the Albanian Government expressly recognized that [*translation*] "if Albania had been informed of the operation before the incidents of October 22nd, and in time to warn the British vessels and shipping in general of the existence of mines in the Corfu Channel, her responsibility would be involved …".

The obligations incumbent upon the Albanian authorities consisted in notifying, for the benefit of shipping in general, the existence of a minefield in Albanian territorial waters and in warning the approaching British warships of the imminent danger to which the minefield exposed them. Such obligations are based, not on the Hague Convention of 1907, No. VIII, which is applicable in time of war, but on certain general and well-recognized principles, namely: elementary considerations of humanity, even more exacting in peace than in war ; the principle of the freedom of maritime communication ; and every State's obligation not to allow knowingly its territory to be used for acts contrary to the rights of other States.

In fact, Albania neither notified the existence of the minefield, nor warned the British warships of the danger they were approaching.

But Albania's obligation to notify shipping of the existence of mines in her waters depends on her having obtained knowledge of that fact in sufficient time before October 22nd; and the duty of the Albanian coastal authorities to warn the British ships depends on the time that elapsed between the moment that these ships were reported and the moment of the first explosion. ...

In fact, nothing was attempted by the Albanian authorities to prevent the disaster. These grave omissions involve the international responsibility of Albania.

The Court therefore reaches the conclusion that Albania is responsible under international law for the explosions which occurred on October 22nd, 1946, in Albanian waters, and for the damage and loss of human life which resulted from them, and that there is a duty upon Albania to pay compensation to the United Kingdom. ...

In the second part of the Special Agreement, the following question is submitted to the Court:

> (2) Has the United Kingdom under international law violated the sovereignty of the Albanian People's Republic by reason of the acts of the Royal Navy in Albanian waters on the 22nd October and on the 12th and 13th November 1946 and is there any duty to give satisfaction?

The Court will first consider whether the sovereignty of Albania was violated by reason of the acts of the British Navy in Albanian waters on October 22nd, 1946.

On May 15th, 1946, the British cruisers *Orion* and *Superb,* while passing southward through the North Corfu Channel, were fired at by an Albanian battery in the vicinity of Saranda. It appears from the report of the commanding naval officer dated May 29th, 1946, that the firing started when the ships had already passed the battery and were moving away from it; that from 12 to 20 rounds were fired; that the firing lasted 12 minutes and ceased only when the ships were out of range; but that the ships were not hit although there were a number of "shorts" and of "overs". An Albanian note of May 21st states that the Coastal Commander ordered a few shots to be fired in the direction of the ships "in accordance with a General Order founded on international law."

The United Kingdom Government at once protested to the Albanian Government, stating that innocent passage through straits is a right recognized by international law. There ensued a diplomatic correspondence in which the Albanian Government asserted that foreign warships and merchant vessels had no right to pass through Albanian territorial waters without prior notification to, and the permission of, the Albanian authorities. This view was put into effect by a communication of the Albanian Chief of Staff, dated May 17th, 1946, which purported to subject the passage of foreign warships and merchant vessels in Albanian territorial waters to previous notification to and authorization by the Albanian Government. The diplomatic correspondence continued, and culminated in a United Kingdom note of August 2nd, 1946, in which the United Kingdom Government maintained its view with regard to the right of innocent passage through straits forming routes for international maritime traffic between two parts of the high seas. The note ended with the warning that if Albanian coastal batteries in the future opened fire on any British warship passing through the Corfu Channel, the fire would be returned.

The contents of this note were, on August 1st, communicated by the British Admiralty to the Commander-in-Chief, Mediterranean, with the instruction that he should refrain from using the Channel until the note had been presented to the Albanian Government. On August 10th, he received from the Admiralty the following telegram: "The Albanians have now received the note. North Corfu Strait may now be used by ships of your fleet, but only when essential and with armament in fore and aft position. If coastal guns fire at ships passing through the Strait, ships should fire back." On September 21st, the following telegram was sent by the Admiralty to the Commander-in-Chief, Mediterranean: "Establishment of diplomatic relations with Albania is again under consideration by His Majesty's Government who wish to know whether the Albanian Government have learnt to behave themselves. Information is requested whether any ships under your command have passed through the North Corfu Strait since August and, if not, whether you intend them to do so shortly." The Commander-in-Chief answered the next day that his ships had not done so yet, but that it was his intention that *Mauritius* and *Leander* and two destroyers should do so when they departed from Corfu on October 22nd.

It was in such circumstances that these two cruisers together with the destroyers *Saumarez* and *Volage* were sent through the North Corfu Strait on that date.

The Court will now consider the Albanian contention that the United Kingdom Government violated Albanian sovereignty by sending the warships through this Strait without the previous authorization of the Albanian Government.

It is, in the opinion of the Court, generally recognized and in accordance with international custom that States in time of peace have a right to send their warships through straits used for international navigation between two parts of the high seas without the previous authorization of a coastal State, provided that the passage is *innocent.* Unless otherwise prescribed in an international convention, there is no right for a coastal State to prohibit such passage through straits in time of peace.

The Albanian Government does not dispute that the North Corfu Channel is a strait in the geographical sense; but it denies that this Channel belongs to the class of international highways through which a right of passage exists, on the grounds that it is only of secondary importance and not even a necessary route between two parts of the high seas, and that it is used almost exclusively for local traffic to and from the ports of Corfu and Saranda.

It may be asked whether the test is to be found in the volume of traffic passing through the Strait or in its greater or lesser importance for international navigation. But in the opinion of the Court the decisive criterion is rather its geographical situation as connecting two parts of the high seas and the fact of its being used for international navigation. Nor can it be decisive that this Strait is not a necessary route between the Ægean and the Adriatic Seas. It has nevertheless been a useful route for international maritime traffic. In this respect, the Agent of the United Kingdom Government gave the Court the following information relating to the period from April 1st, 1936, to December 31st, 1937: "The following is the total number of ships putting in at the Port of Corfu after passing through or just before passing through the Channel. During the period of one year nine months, the total number of ships was 2,884. The flags of the ships are Greek, Italian, Roumanian, Yugoslav, French, Albanian and British. Clearly, very small vessels are included, as the entries for Albanian vessels are high, and of course one vessel may make several journeys, but 2,884 ships for a period of one year nine months is quite a large figure. These figures relate to vessels visited by the Customs at Corfu and so do not include the large number of vessels which went through the Strait without calling at Corfu at all." There were also regular sailings through the Strait by Greek vessels three times weekly, by a British ship fortnightly, and by two Yugoslav vessels weekly and by two others fortnightly. The Court is further informed that the British Navy has regularly used this Channel for eighty years or more, and that it has also been used by the navies of other States.

One fact of particular importance is that the North Corfu Channel constitutes a frontier between Albania and Greece, that a part of it is wholly within the territorial waters of these States, and that the Strait is of special importance to Greece by reason of the traffic to and from the port of Corfu.

Having regard to these various considerations, the Court has arrived at the conclusion that the North Corfu Channel should be considered as belonging to the class of international highways through which passage cannot be prohibited by a coastal State in time of peace.

On the other hand, it is a fact that the two coastal States did not maintain normal relations, that Greece had made territorial claims precisely with regard to a part of Albanian territory bordering on the Channel, that Greece had declared that she considered herself technically in a state of war with Albania, and that Albania, invoking the danger of Greek incursions, had considered it necessary to take certain measures of vigilance in this region. The Court is of opinion that

Albania, in view of these exceptional circumstances, would have been justified in issuing regulations in respect of the passage of warships through the Strait, but not in prohibiting such passage or in subjecting it to the requirement of special authorization.

For these reasons, the Court is unable to accept the Albanian contention that the Government of the United Kingdom has violated Albanian sovereignty by sending the warships through the Strait without having obtained the previous authorization of the Albanian Government.

In these circumstances, it is unnecessary to consider the more general question, much debated by the Parties, whether States under international law have a right to send warships in time of peace through territorial waters not included in a strait.

The Albanian Government has further contended that the sovereignty of Albania was violated because the passage of the British warships on October 22nd, 1946, was not an *innocent passage.* The reasons advanced in support of this contention may be summed up as follows: The passage was not an ordinary passage, but a political mission; the ships were maneuvering and sailing in diamond combat formation with soldiers on board; the position of the guns was not consistent with innocent passage; the vessels passed with crews at action stations; the number of the ships and their armament surpassed what was necessary in order to attain their object and showed an intention to intimidate and not merely to pass; the ships had received orders to observe and report upon the coastal defences and this order was carried out.

It is shown by the Admiralty telegram of September 21st, cited above, and admitted by the United Kingdom Agent, that the object of sending the warships through the Strait was not only to carry out a passage for purposes of navigation, but also to test Albania's attitude. As mentioned above, the Albanian Government, on May 15th, 1946, tried to impose by means of gunfire its view with regard to the passage. As the exchange of diplomatic notes did not lead to any clarification, the Government of the United Kingdom wanted to ascertain by other means whether the Albanian Government would maintain its illegal attitude and again impose its view by firing at passing ships. The legality of this measure taken by the Government of the United Kingdom cannot be disputed, provided that it was carried out in a manner consistent with the requirements of international law. The "mission" was designed to affirm a right which had been unjustly denied. The Government of the United Kingdom was not bound to abstain from exercising its right of passage, which the Albanian Government had illegally denied.

It remains, therefore, to consider whether the *manner* in which the passage was carried out was consistent with the principle of innocent passage and to examine the various contentions of the Albanian Government in so far as they appear to be relevant.

When the Albanian coastguards at St. George's Monastery reported that the British warships were sailing in combat formation and were maneuvering, they must have been under a misapprehension. It is shown by the evidence that the ships were not proceeding in combat formation, but in line, one after the other, and that they were not maneuvering until after the first explosion. Their movements thereafter were due to the explosions and were made necessary in order to save human life and the mined ships. It is shown by the evidence of witnesses that the contention that soldiers were on board must be due to a misunderstanding probably arising from the fact that the two cruisers carried their usual detachment of marines.

It is known from the above-mentioned order issued by the British Admiralty on August 10th, 1946, that ships, when using the North Corfu Strait, must pass with armament in fore and aft position. That this order was carried out during the passage on October 22nd is stated by the Commander-in-Chief, Mediterranean, in a telegram of October 26th to the Admiralty. The guns were, he reported, "trained fore and aft, which is their normal position at sea in peace time, and were not loaded". It is confirmed by the commanders of *Saumarez* and *Volage* that the guns were in this position before the explosions. The navigating officer on board *Mauritius* explained that all guns on that cruiser were in their normal stowage position. The main guns were in the line of the ship, and the anti-aircraft guns were pointing outwards and up into the air, which is the normal position of these guns on a cruiser both in harbour and at sea. In the light of this evidence, the Court cannot accept the Albanian contention that the position of the guns was inconsistent with the rules of innocent passage.

In the above-mentioned telegram of October 26th, the Commander-in-Chief reported that the passage "was made with ships at action stations in order that they might be able to retaliate quickly if fired upon again". In view of the firing from the Albanian battery on May 15th, this measure of precaution cannot, in itself, be regarded as unreasonable. But four warships—two cruisers and two destroyers—passed in this manner, with crews at action stations, ready to retaliate quickly if fired upon. They passed one after another through this narrow channel, close to the Albanian coast, at a time of political tension in this region. The intention must have been, not only to test Albania's attitude, but at the same time to demonstrate such force that she would abstain from firing again on passing ships. Having regard, however, to all the circumstances of the case, as described above, the Court is unable to characterize these measures taken by the United Kingdom authorities as a violation of Albania's sovereignty.

The Admiralty Chart, Annex 21 to the Memorial, shows that coastal defences in the Saranda region had been observed and reported. In a report of the commander of *Volage,* dated October 23rd, 1946—a report relating to the passage on the 22nd—it is stated: "The most was made of the opportunities to study Albanian defences at close range. These included, with reference to XCU...."—and he then gives a description of some coastal defences.

In accordance with Article 49 of the Statute of the Court and Article 54 of its Rules, the Court requested the United Kingdom Agent to produce the documents referred to as XCU for the use of the Court. Those documents were not produced, the Agent pleading naval secrecy; and the United Kingdom witnesses declined to answer questions relating to them. It is not therefore possible to know the real content of these naval orders. The Court cannot, however, draw from this refusal to produce the orders any conclusions differing from those to which the actual events gave rise. The United Kingdom Agent stated that the instructions in these orders related solely to the contingency of shots being fired from the coast—which did not happen. If it is true, as the commander of *Volage* said in evidence, that the orders contained information concerning certain positions from which the British warships might have been fired at, it cannot be deduced therefrom that the vessels had received orders to reconnoiter Albanian coastal defences. Lastly, as the Court has to judge of the innocent nature of the passage, it cannot remain indifferent to the fact that, though two warships struck mines, there was no reaction, either on their part or on that of the cruisers that accompanied them.

With regard to the observations of coastal defences made after the explosions, these were justified by the fact that two ships had just been blown up and that, in this critical situation, their commanders might fear that they would be fired on from the coast, as on May 15th.

Having thus examined the various contentions of the Albanian Government in so far as they appear to be relevant, the Court has arrived at the conclusion that the United Kingdom did not violate the sovereignty of Albania by reason of the acts of the British Navy in Albanian waters on October 22nd, 1946. …

In addition to the passage of the United Kingdom warships on October 22nd, 1946, the second question in the Special Agreement relates to the acts of the Royal Navy in Albanian waters on November 12th and 13th, 1946. This is the minesweeping operation called "Operation Retail" by the Parties during the proceedings. This name will be used in the present Judgment. …

The United Kingdom Government does not dispute that "Operation Retail" was carried out against the clearly expressed wish of the Albanian Government. It recognizes that the operation had not the consent of the international mine clearance organizations, that it could not be justified as the exercise of a right of innocent passage, and lastly that, in principle, international law does not allow a State to assemble a large number of warships in the territorial waters of another State and to carry out minesweeping in those waters. The United Kingdom Government states that the operation was one of extreme urgency, and that it considered itself entitled to carry it out without anybody's consent. …

But, in fact, the explosions of October 22nd, 1946, in a channel declared safe for navigation, and one which the United Kingdom Government, more than any other government, had reason to consider safe, raised quite a different problem from that of a routine sweep carried out under the orders of the mine clearance organizations. These explosions were suspicious; they raised a question of responsibility.

Accordingly, this was the ground on which the United Kingdom Government chose to establish its main line of defence. According to that Government, the *corpora delicti* must be secured as quickly as possible, for fear they should be taken away, without leaving traces, by the authors of the minelaying or by the Albanian authorities. This justification took two distinct forms in the United Kingdom Government's arguments. It was presented first as a new and special application of the theory of intervention, by means of which the State intervening would secure possession of evidence in the territory of another State, in order to submit it to an international tribunal and thus facilitate its task.

The Court cannot accept such a line of defence. The Court can only regard the alleged right of intervention as the manifestation of a policy of force, such as has, in the past, given rise to most serious abuses and such as cannot, whatever be the present defects in international organization, find a place in international law. Intervention is perhaps still less admissible in the particular form it would take here; for, from the nature of things, it would be reserved for the most powerful States, and might easily lead to perverting the administration of international justice itself.

The United Kingdom Agent, in his speech in reply, has further classified "Operation Retail" among methods of self-protection or self-help. The Court cannot accept this defence either. Between independent States, respect for territorial sovereignty is an essential foundation of international relations. The Court recognizes that the Albanian Government's complete failure to carry out its duties after the explosions, and the dilatory nature of its diplomatic notes, are extenuating circumstances for the action of the United Kingdom Government. But to ensure respect for international law, of which it is the organ, the Court must declare that the action of the British Navy constituted a violation of Albanian sovereignty.

This declaration is in accordance with the request made by Albania through her Counsel, and is in itself appropriate satisfaction. …

NOTES AND QUESTIONS

1. The Corfu Channel decision was made in the context of the Cold War. The United Kingdom and the United States were supporting the Royalist Government in Greece against a Soviet-supported Communist insurrection which was using Albania, a contiguous state, as a safe-haven for mounting operations in Greece. The passage by British cruisers through the Straits of Corfu and along the Albanian coast was intended to convey to the Albanian government British capacity to respond militarily. A critical part of the case turned on the question of whether states may use the oceans for purposes of conveying such threats. The Judgment vindicated the U.K. and the interests of other large maritime powers, but it was revised in the 1982 Convention. Contrast the regime created by UNCLOS with the holding of the International Court in *Corfu Channel*: "[T]he North Corfu Channel should be considered as belonging to the class of international highways through which passage cannot be prohibited by a coastal State in time of peace."

2. The straits regime of UNCLOS has been a subject of conflict among scholars. Consider one comment:

> The straits regime ... poses two problems: the absence of an express right of submerged passage in a context of other provisions, many of which could be inconsistent with an allegedly implied right, and, second, the more general problem, common to the innocent passage regime, of the enhanced primary competence of the coastal state to characterize any passage below, on, or above the surface as violating "transit" requisites and hence not "transit passage."
>
> The language of the Camp David agreement of 1978 dealing with straits passage may be contrasted with that of the UNCLOS text. It is particularly instructive for, though bilateral, it purports to enunciate many general norms and is the first major diplomatic statement on the subject since the ICNT draft. Moreover, the United States played a significant role in its formulation. Rather than adopting or even intimating any relation with the UNCLOS formula, the Camp David formula states in part: "[T]he Strait of Tiran and the Gulf of Aqaba are international waterways to be open to all nations for unimpeded and nonsuspendable freedom of navigation and overflight." With this sort of formula, tortured, casuistic interpretations are not necessary. Indeed, Camp David is redundant in emphasizing precisely what the ICNT overlooks. The waterways are characterized as "international," and any hint of a territorial competence with regard to passage is repeatedly excluded; there is no "right of transit" characterizable by the coastal state, but instead and only the traditional freedom of navigation, and that right may not be impeded or suspended. Interpreted logically or teleologically, Camp David produces freedom of navigation and, were it necessary, even a right of submerged transit. The ICNT achieves nothing approaching that clarity.

W. M. Reisman, *The Regime of Straits and National Security: An Appraisal of International Lawmaking*, 74 AM. J. INT'L L. 48, 75-76 (1980). *See also* John Norton Moore, *The Regime of Straits and the Third United Nations Conference on the Law of the Sea*, 74 AM. J. INT'L L. 77 (1980).

3. The following summary of the UNCLOS regime for straits may prove helpful:

International Straits

Legal Regime

Part III of ... [UNCLOS] addressed five different kinds of straits used for international navigation, each with a distinct legal regime:

> 1. Straits connecting one part of the high seas/EEZ and another part of the high seas/ EEZ (Article 37- governed by transit passage).
>
> 2. Straits connecting a part of the high seas/EEZ and the territorial sea of a foreign state (Article 45(1)(a) – regulated by nonsuspendable innocent passage).
>
> 3. Straits connecting one part of the high seas/EEZ and another part of the high seas/ EEZ where the strait is formed by an island of a state bordering the strait and its mainland, if there exists seaward of the island a route through the high seas/EEZ of similar convenience with regard to navigation and hydrographic characteristics (Article 38(1) – regulated by nonsuspendable innocent passage).
>
> 4. Straits regulated in whole or in part by international conventions (Article 35(c)). The LOS Convention does not alter the legal regime in straits regulated by long-standing international conventions in force specifically relating to such straits.
>
> 5. Straits through archipelagic waters governed by archipelagic sea lanes passage (Article 53(4)).

Bureau of Oceans and International and Scientific Affairs, U.S. Dept. of State, Limits in the Seas No. 112, United States Response to Excessive National Maritime Claims 64 (Robert W. Smith ed., 1992), *available at* http://www.law.fsu.edu/library/collection/LimitsinSeas/ls112.pdf.

Which of these passage regimes would now apply to a geographic situation like Corfu Channel? Is the Corfu Channel decision still good law?

7. Archipelagic Waters

UNCLOS represents a fundamental historic compromise between long-distance maritime users and archipelagic states. Archipelagic states have won a special recognition of their unique situation, and a degree of national control over archipelagic waters has been assigned to them that would have been unthinkable under the Grotian *mare liberum* regime. In brief, states composed wholly of archipelagos and islands may enclose their outermost islands with baselines, transforming the waters within those lines into "archipelagic" waters.

a. Delimitation

1982 United Nations Convention on the Law of the Sea

Article 46: *Use of terms*

For the purposes of this Convention:

(a) "archipelagic State" means a State constituted wholly by one or more archipelagos and may include other islands;

(b) "archipelago" means a group of islands, including parts of islands, interconnecting waters and other natural features which are so closely interrelated that such islands, waters and other natural features form an intrinsic geographical, economic and political entity, or which historically have been regarded as such.

Article 47: *Archipelagic baselines*

1. An archipelagic State may draw straight archipelagic baselines joining the outermost points of the outermost islands and drying reefs of the archipelago provided that within such baselines are included the main islands and an area in which the ratio of the area of the water to the area of the land, including atolls, is between 1 to 1 and 9 to 1.

2. The length of such baselines shall not exceed 100 nautical miles, except that up to 3 per cent of the total number of baselines enclosing any archipelago may exceed that length, up to a maximum length of 125 nautical miles.

3. The drawing of such baselines shall not depart to any appreciable extent from the general configuration of the archipelago.

4. Such baselines shall not be drawn to and from low-tide elevations, unless lighthouses or similar installations which are permanently above sea level have

been built on them or where a low-tide elevation is situated wholly or partly at a distance not exceeding the breadth of the territorial sea from the nearest island.

5. The system of such baselines shall not be applied by an archipelagic State in such a manner as to cut off from the high seas or the exclusive economic zone the territorial sea of another State.

6. If a part of the archipelagic waters of an archipelagic State lies between two parts of an immediately adjacent neighbouring State, existing rights and all other legitimate interests which the latter State has traditionally exercised in such waters and all rights stipulated by agreement between those States shall continue and be respected.

7. For the purpose of computing the ratio of water to land under paragraph 1, land areas may include waters lying within the fringing reefs of islands and atolls, including that part of a steep-sided oceanic plateau which is enclosed or nearly enclosed by a chain of limestone islands and drying reefs lying on the perimeter of the plateau.

8. The baselines drawn in accordance with this article shall be shown on charts of a scale or scales adequate for ascertaining their position. Alternatively, lists of geographical co-ordinates of points, specifying the geodetic datum, may be substituted.

9. The archipelagic State shall give due publicity to such charts or lists of geographical co-ordinates and shall deposit a copy of each such chart or list with the Secretary-General of the United Nations.

Article 48: *Measurement of the breadth of the territorial sea, the contiguous zone, the exclusive economic zone and the continental shelf*

The breadth of the territorial sea, the contiguous zone, the exclusive economic zone and the continental shelf shall be measured from archipelagic baselines drawn in accordance with article 47.

Article 49: *Legal status of archipelagic waters, of the air space over archipelagic waters and of their bed and subsoil*

1. The sovereignty of an archipelagic State extends to the waters enclosed by the archipelagic baselines drawn in accordance with article 47, described as archipelagic waters, regardless of their depth or distance from the coast.

2. This sovereignty extends to the air space over the archipelagic waters, as well as to their bed and subsoil, and the resources contained therein.

3. This sovereignty is exercised subject to this Part.

4. The régime of archipelagic sea lanes passage established in this Part shall not in other respects affect the status of the archipelagic waters, including the

sea lanes, or the exercise by the archipelagic State of its sovereignty over such waters and their air space, bed and subsoil, and the resources contained therein. . . .

Article 52: *Right of innocent passage*

1. Subject to article 53 and without prejudice to article 50, ships of all States enjoy the right of innocent passage through archipelagic waters, in accordance with Part II, section 3.

2. The archipelagic State may, without discrimination in form or in fact among foreign ships, suspend temporarily in specified areas of its archipelagic waters the innocent passage of foreign ships if such suspension is essential for the protection of its security. Such suspension shall take effect only after having been duly published.

Article 53: *Right of archipelagic sea lanes passage*

1. An archipelagic State may designate sea lanes and air routes thereabove, suitable for the continuous and expeditious passage of foreign ships and aircraft through or over its archipelagic waters and the adjacent territorial sea.

2. All ships and aircraft enjoy the right of archipelagic sea lanes passage in such sea lanes and air routes.

3. Archipelagic sea lanes passage means the exercise in accordance with this Convention of the rights of navigation and overflight in the normal mode solely for the purpose of continuous, expeditious and unobstructed transit between one part of the high seas or an exclusive economic zone and another part of the high seas or an exclusive economic zone. ...

12. If an archipelagic State does not designate sea lanes or air routes, the right of archipelagic sea lanes passage may be exercised through the routes normally used for international navigation.

b. Trends in State Practice

(1) W. Michael Reisman & Gayl S. Westerman, Straight Baselines in International Maritime Boundary Delimitation
153-158; 160-63 (St. Martin's Press 1992)

The rules for drawing archipelagic baselines [can be summarized briefly]: an archipelagic state may draw baselines joining the outermost islands and drying reefs of the archipelago as long as the following basic rules are followed:

1. the baselines must include the main islands and an area of water in which the ratio of water to land, including atolls is between 1 to 1 and 9 to 1;

2. the length of the baseline segments must not exceed 100 n.m. except for 3 per cent of the total, which may be between 100 n.m. and 125 n.m. in length;

3. baselines shall not depart to any appreciable extent from the general configuration of the archipelago.

The remaining...guidelines are similar to those of [UNCLOS Article 7], in that baselines cannot be drawn to low-tide elevations except in certain specified cases, nor in such a way as to cut off the territorial sea of another state from the high seas; the rights of competing states in the waters enclosed must be respected and all baselines must be given due publicity. The remaining sections of [UNCLOS] Part IV: Archipelagic States, specify the rights and duties of archipelagic and third states in the waters internalized. ...

Under the [UNCLOS] Article 46(a) definition set forth above, there are currently thirty-five states which could be considered archipelagic in that they are composed entirely of islands. Of these, perhaps only twelve can legitimately enclose their entire island territory... under the guidelines in [UNCLOS] Article 47. Fifteen archipelagic states are prevented from drawing archipelagic baselines because they fail to meet the [UNCLOS] Article 47(1) [water to land ratio]. ... Several of these states have nonetheless entered straight baseline claims along all or part of their coasts.

* * *

(a) Indonesia

Indonesia was one of the states that advocated most strongly for the adoption of an archipelagic baseline regime. It is in fact a paradigmatic archipelagic state under UNCLOS, Article 46, in that it is entirely composed of islands or archipelagos (*see* map, *infra,* at 692). With over 17,000 islands, Indonesia is the largest archipelagic state in the world. Prior to the adoption of the new regime in 1982, Indonesia established a system of straight baselines in 1960 based upon the then unrecognized "archipelago theory" which, they claimed, allowed them to enclose their entire territory within a system of baselines connecting the outermost points of the islands of the archipelago. *See* Act No. 4 Prp. Of 1960 (State Gazette of 1960 No. 22. Supplementary State Gazette Number 1942.) *See also* Limits in the Seas, No. 35: Straight Baselines: Indonesia, at 1-8. By Act No. 6 of 8 August 1966 Regarding Indonesian Waters, the Indonesian government formally established an archipelagic baseline system under UNCLOS. (For full text and baseline coordinates, *see* Act of the Republic relating to the Indonesian Waters, Act No.6 (1966), *available at* http://www.un.org/Depts/los/LEGISLATIONANDTREATIES/PDFFILES/IDN_1996_Act .pdf.

(b) Maldives

Certainly one of the more exceptional baseline systems is that devised by the Republic of Maldives, which has enclosed its entire archipelago within a so-called "constitutional rectangle" defined by geographical coordinates (*see* map, *infra,* at 693). Because none of these coordinates touches land, the baseline system is inconsistent with [UNCLOS] Article 47(1) which states that "[an ar-

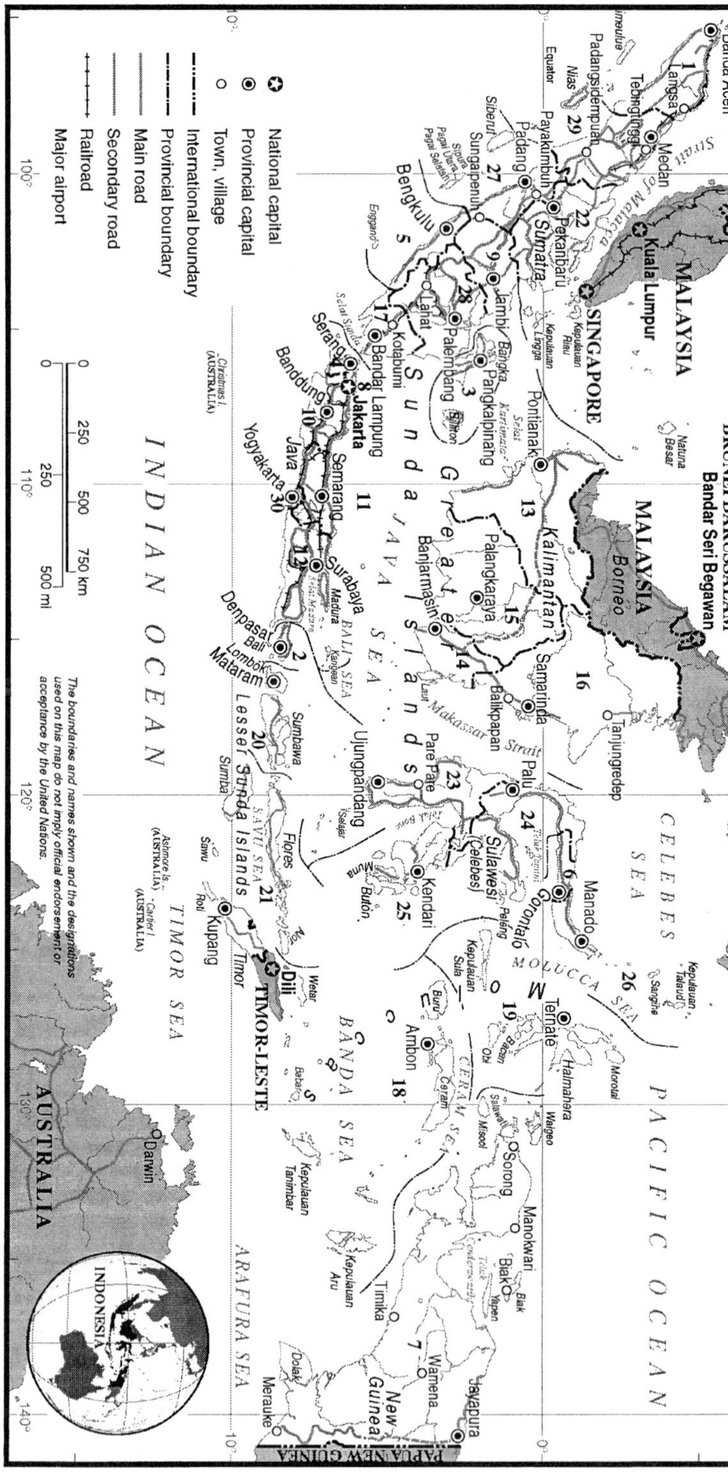

Partial United Nations Map of Indonesia, DEPARTMENT OF PEACEKEEPING OPERATIONS, CARTOGRAPHIC SECTION, Map No. 4110 Rev. 4 (Jan. 2004).

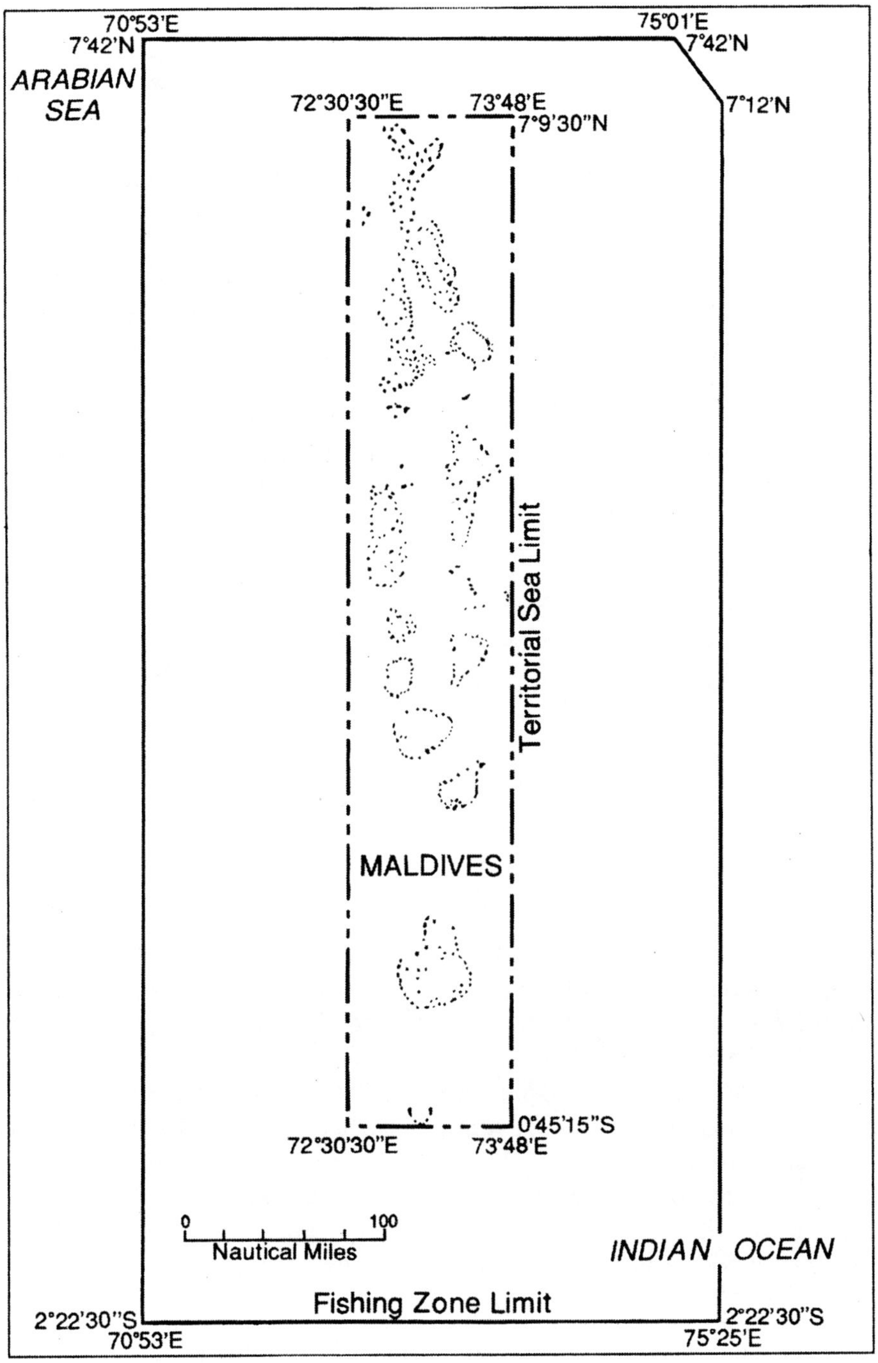

"Figure 5.28 Maldives Islands" *reprinted from id.* at 162.

chipelagic State may draw straight archipelagic baselines joining the outermost points of the outermost islands and drying reefs of the archipelago. ...] This violation would seem to render the baseline invalid *per se.*

As to the other requirements set forth under [UNCLOS] Article 47, the configuration of the Maldives Islands is rather linear and, therefore, the "constitutional rectangle" does appear to comport with the [UNCLOS] Article 47(3) requirement that baselines "shall not depart to any appreciable extent from the general configuration of the archipelago." However, if each side of the rectangle is considered as one baseline, the length of these segments will certainly violate the [UNCLOS] Article 47(2) rule limiting archipelagic baselines to 100 n.m., except for "3 per cent which may extend to a maximum of 125 n.m. The north and south segments of the rectangle each measure 472.4 n.m., and the east and west segments each measure 77.085 n.m. An exact hydrographic measurement will be needed in order to determine whether the area of the waters enclosed within the baselines equals or exceeds that of the land territory, as required under [UNCLOS] Article 47(1). *See* REISMAN & WESTERMAN, *supra,* at 160-163.

Having failed to pass muster under [UNCLOS] Article 47 guidelines, this baseline system would be even more inappropriate under those of [UNCLOS Article 7] for reasons discussed above. *See* REISMAN & WESTERMAN, *supra* at 161-162. [At this writing, a new baseline map for Maldives is in production at the U.S. State Department for their "Limits in the Seas" series.]

(c) Ecuador

[Some mainland states, such as Ecuador, fail the UNCLOS Article 46 definition but have nonetheless established archipelagic baselines as indicated on the maps, *infra,* at 696 and 697.]

Segment 1-2 encloses a mere curvature of the coast. Basepoint 3 is located on the non-fringing Isla la Plata, which causes the baseline to depart appreciably from the general direction of the coast. Basepoint 5 is located at sea at an arbitrary point on the Ecuador-Peru maritime boundary, producing an even more appreciable departure. Baseline segments 2-3 and 3-4 together total 192 nautical miles. ... Ecuador has also sought to enclose the so-called Archipiélago de Colon (Galapagos Islands) with another straight baseline system. This enclosure is invalid under [UNCLOS] Article 46(a), for Ecuador is by definition not an archipelagic state. Although some scholars are now suggesting that the [UNCLOS] definition [should] be expanded to include continental states with archipelagic territories, such baselines are currently invalid *per se.* ...

If, alternatively, the basis of Ecuador's claim is [UNCLOS Article 7: *Straight Baselines*], the baseline system is also invalid. First, the mainland coast of Ecuador, as we have said, is not deeply indented and cut-into such that it would justify a system of straight baselines; and second, the Galapagos Islands cannot be characterized as a fringe of islands in the immediate vicinity of that coast. As to the validity of an [UNCLOS Article 7] baseline around the islands themselves, it is possible that the waters surrounding the Galapagos have been historically considered as internal between the main islands, but the enormous water area between Isla Darwin and Isla Isabella could never have been so considered. Thus, the enclosure of the Archipelago de Colon by Ecuador is impermissible under [UNCLOS] Article 46 as well as [UNCLOS] Article 7. *See* REISMAN & WESTERMAN, *supra* at 154-157.

NOTES AND QUESTIONS

1. The transmittal of the 1982 Convention by the President of the United States to the Committee on Foreign Relations of the Senate, stated, with regard to the archipelagic States section:

> Part IV represents a successful resolution, following years of controversy, of the effort, led by Indonesia and The Philippines, to achieve a special regime for archipelagic States. The United States and other maritime States were willing to recognize the concept of archipelagic States only if its application were limited... and did not impede rights of navigation and overflight. In effect, the concept of archipelagic States creates a geographic situation requiring the same kind of solution as transit passage of straits, i.e., the right of navigation and overflight on, over, and under the waters enclosed. Acceptance of this principle guarantees critical U.S. military and commercial navigation rights.

Message from the President of the United States transmitting United Nations Convention on the Law of the Sea, with annexes ... October 7, 1994, 103d Cong., 2nd Sess., Sen. Treaty Doc. 103-39.

2. Based on the examples of state practice noted above, has the historic compromise designed to benefit archipelagic states proven to be a wise one for major ocean users? In fact, many issues raised by the archipelagic regime have yet to be resolved. For example, no archipelagic State, other than Indonesia, has yet established archipelagic sea lanes, a determination which will have major effects on United States interests as well as those of international users in common.

3. Should archipelagic regimes be extended to include states, such as Ecuador above, that are comprised of both archipelagos and mainland components? Is there any policy for ocean use that would be put more at risk if the regime were expanded to archipelagos wherever located, even those under the control of a mainland state?

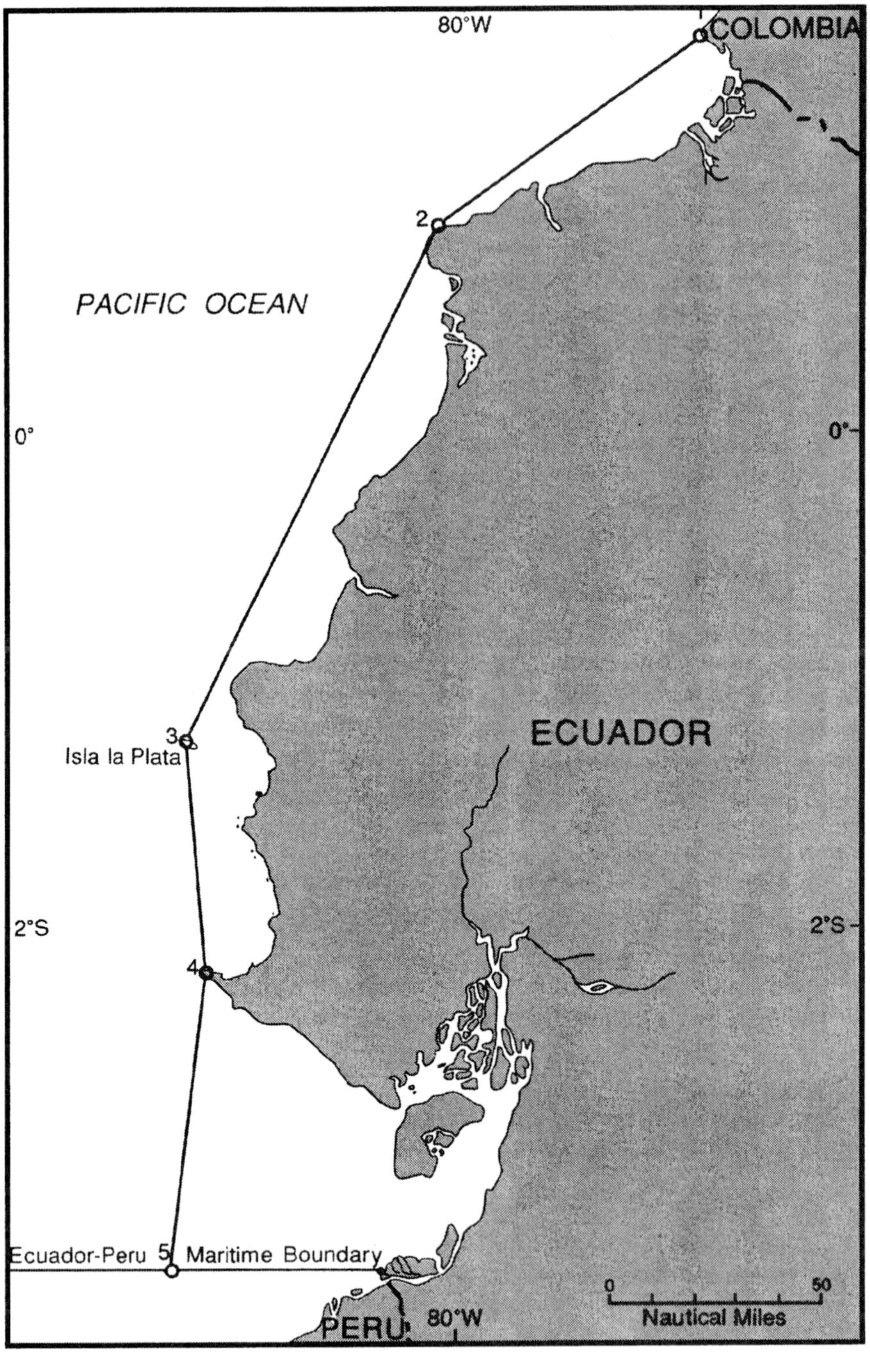

"Figure 5.24 Ecuador" *reprinted from id.* at 155

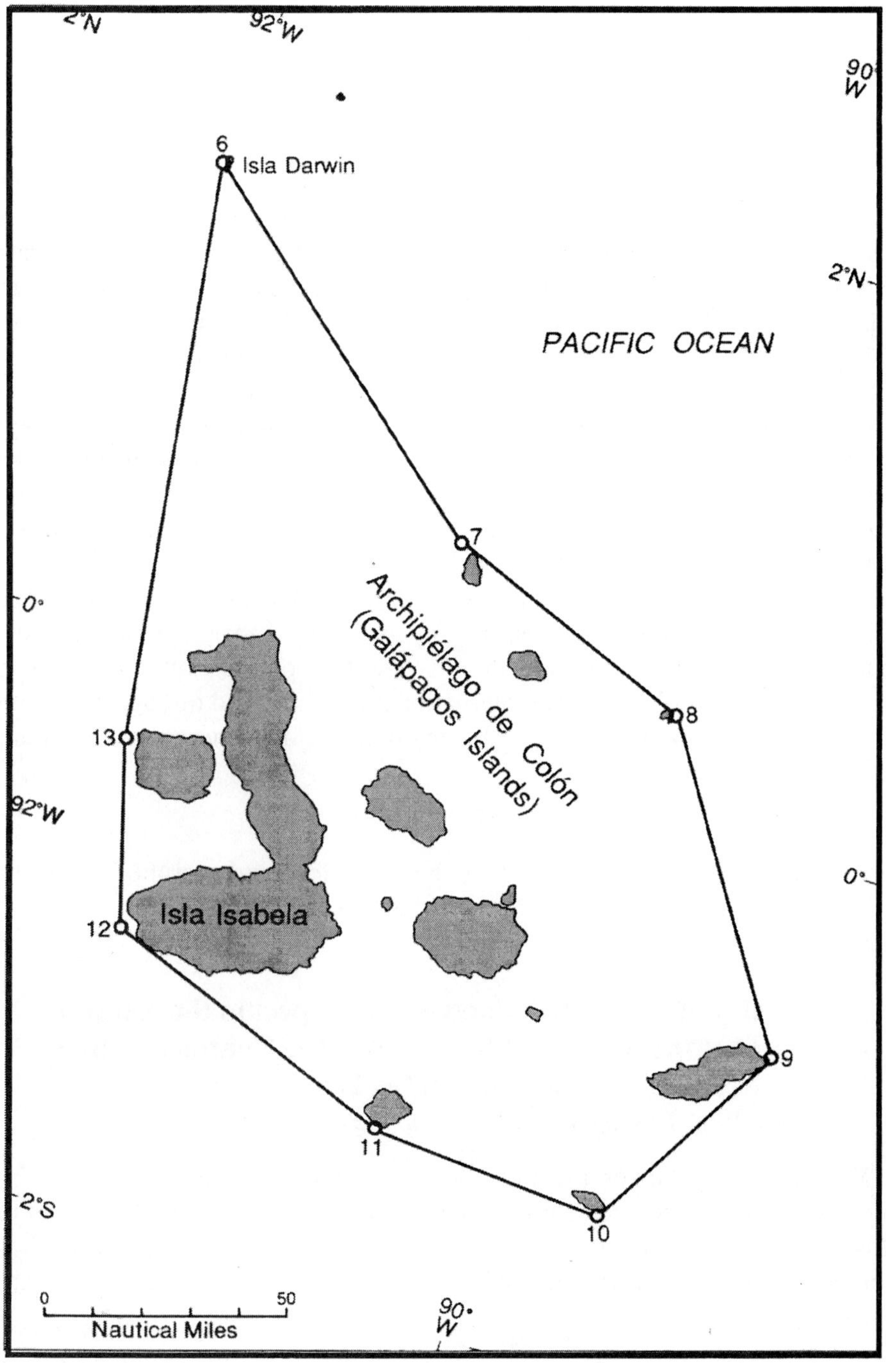

Figure 5.25 Ecuador- Galapagos Islands", *reprinted from id.* at 157.

8. Continental Shelf

a. The Development of a New Regime

(1) W. MICHAEL REISMAN & GAYL S. WESTERMAN
STRAIGHT BASELINES IN MARITIME BOUNDARY DELIMITATION
19-20 (St. Martin's Press 1992)

In retrospect, it is clear that from the third decade of this century on, many political forces were coalescing in a common effort to expand coastal control over increasingly broad areas of the contiguous high seas. Pride of place for the initiative is usually claimed by the Latin American states, but many states and publicists had begun to act and write in support of such seaward expansion prior to the Second World War. The reasons for these new demands for coastal state jurisdiction were hardly recondite. The world had entered the hydrocarbon age, and the technical possibilities of offshore production had put deposits in the continental shelf within reach. But other interests groups, including long distance fishermen and naval and air force elements, continued to resist such expansions in favor of the traditional three-mile limit. Where these groups proved to be the dominant domestic force, they mobilized their respective governments into opposition to domestic and foreign pressures for seaward expansion of national jurisdiction. Those nations and groups that favored the continuation of a regime of narrow coastal control and broad international use prevailed through the 1950s. But by 1958, and certainly by 1960, the broad lines of the emerging expansionist regime were becoming clear.

* * *

One of the first unilateral claims with respect to rights over the Continental Shelf was issued by the United States in the Truman Proclamation, which provides:

(2) Policy of the United States With Respect to the Natural Resources of the Subsoil and Sea Bed of the Continental Shelf, Proclamation No. 2667
10 Fed. Reg. 12303 (Sept 28, 1945) (President Harry S. Truman)

WHEREAS the Government of the United States of America, aware of the long range world-wide need for new sources of petroleum and other minerals, holds the view that efforts to discover and make available new supplies of these resources should be encouraged; and

WHEREAS its competent experts are of the opinion that such resources underlie many parts of the continental shelf off the coasts of the United States of America, and that with modern technological progress their utilization is already practicable or will become so at an early date; and

WHEREAS it is the view of the Government of the United States that the exercise of jurisdiction over the natural resources of the subsoil and sea bed of the continental shelf by the contiguous nation is reasonable and just, since the effectiveness of measures to utilize or conserve these resources would be contingent upon cooperation and protection from the shore, since the continental shelf may be regarded as an extension of the land-mass of the coastal nation and thus naturally appurtenant to it, since these resources frequently form a seaward extension of a pool or deposit lying within the territory, and since self-protection compels the coastal nation to keep close watch over activities off its shores which are of the nature necessary for utilization of these resources;

> NOW THEREFORE, I, HARRY S. TRUMAN, President of the United States of America, do hereby proclaim the following policy of the United States of America with respect to the natural resources of the subsoil and sea bed of the continental shelf.

Having concern for the urgency of conserving and prudently utilizing its natural resources, the Government of the United States regards the natural resources of the subsoil and sea bed of the continental shelf beneath the high seas but contiguous to the coasts of the United States as appertaining to the United States, subject to its jurisdiction and control. In cases where the continental shelf extends to the shores of another State, or is shared with an adjacent State, the boundary shall be determined by the United States and the State concerned in accordance with equitable principles. The character as high seas of the waters above the continental shelf and the right to their free and unimpeded navigation are in no way thus affected.

* * *

By 1958, as a consequence of an increasing number of unilateral claims to exploit the resources in the ocean floor and its subsoil contiguous to the territorial sea, the international community realized that a regime was necessary and its first effort was found in the Convention on the Continental Shelf.

(3) 1958 Convention on the Continental Shelf

Apr. 29, 1958, 15 U.S.T. 471, T.I.A.S. No. 5578, 499 U.N.T.S. 311.

Article 1

For the purpose of these articles, the term "continental shelf" is used as referring (*a*) to the seabed and subsoil of the submarine areas adjacent to the coast but outside the area of the territorial sea, to a depth of 200 metres or, beyond that limit, to where the depth of the superjacent waters admits of the exploitation of the natural resources of the said areas; (*b*) to the seabed and subsoil of similar submarine areas adjacent to the coasts of islands.

Article 2

1. The coastal State exercises over the continental shelf, sovereign rights for the purpose of exploring it and exploiting its natural resources.

2. The rights referred to in paragraph 1 of this article are exclusive in the sense that if the coastal State does not explore the continental shelf or exploit its natural resources, no one may undertake these activities, or make a claim to the continental shelf, without the express consent of the coastal State.

3. The rights of the coastal State over the continental shelf do not depend on occupation, effective or notional, or on any express proclamation.

4. The natural resources referred to in these articles consist of the mineral and other non-living resources of the seabed and subsoil together with living organisms belonging to sedentary species, that is to say, organisms which, at the harvestable stage, either are immobile on or under the seabed or are unable to move except in constant physical contact with the seabed or the subsoil.

Article 3

The rights of the coastal State over the continental shelf do not affect the legal status of the superjacent waters as high seas, or that of the air space above those waters. ...

Article 6

1. Where the same continental shelf is adjacent to the territories of two or more States whose coasts are opposite each other, the boundary of the continental shelf appertaining to such States shall be determined by agreement between them. In the absence of agreement, and unless another boundary line is justified by special circumstances, the boundary is the median line, every point of which is equidistant from the nearest points of the baselines from which the breadth of the territorial sea of each State is measured.

2. Where the same continental shelf is adjacent to the territories of two adjacent States, the boundary of the continental shelf shall be determined by agreement between them. In the absence of agreement, and unless another boundary line is justified by special circumstances, the boundary shall be determined by application of the principle of equidistance from the nearest points of the baselines from which the breadth of the territorial sea of each State is measured.

3. In delimiting the boundaries of the continental shelf, any lines which are drawn in accordance with the principles set out in paragraphs 1 and 2 of this article should be defined with reference to charts and geographical features as exist at a particular date, and reference should be made to fixed permanent identifiable points on the land.

Notes and Questions

1. The 1958 Convention was a major technical achievement. Doubts about the breadth of the Shelf were finessed by a formula that provided a specific bathymetric test as well as an infinitely expandable exploitable test.

2. Because the creation of a new national area inevitably raised questions as to the boundaries between different claimants, Article 6 of the Convention, (*supra*) provided an equidistance formula for resolution of disputes that could not be resolved by negotiation.

3. There were two conceptual flaws in the paradigm of the Article 6 approach. First, Article 6 assumed a universe in which maritime boundary conflicts were bilateral. Second, and related to the first, Article 6 assumed a universe in which the spatial conflicts between the two states arose from either their coastal adjacency or their coastal opposition. By 1969, when three states with coasts on the North Sea turned to the International Court for instruction on the principles of law relevant to the delimitation of their maritime boundary, the paradigmatic limitations of the regime forged in 1958 had become clear. The decision of the ICJ in 1969 initiated a search for a more complex and nuanced code that came to be known as the rule of equitable principles and whose major postulates included far more general standards, such as norms holding that each state was entitled to its "natural prolongation," no state could be cut off from the sea and, as between states competing for ocean space, the distribution should be roughly proportional to their relative lengths of coastlines. Equidistance and special circumstances were reduced to optional techniques, among others, for reaching an equitable result. The problems became apparent within a decade in a dispute over the delimitation of the Continental Shelf in the North Sea.

(4) North Sea Continental Shelf Cases (F.R.G. v. Den.; F.R.G. v. Neth.)

1969 I.C.J. 12 (Judgment of Feb. 20)

[As the map *infra,* at 702 indicates, the application of Article 6 of the 1958 Convention to the Continental Shelf boundary dispute between The Netherlands, Germany, and Denmark would have produced a relatively small shelf for Germany, if the Netherlands and Denmark applied the regime for coastal opposition. Article 6 ... did not take account of the distortion that arose from concave coastlines.

Germany had not ratified the Convention and would not have been bound by it unless it was deemed to have become customary international law. The Court held that Articles I and II were customary but that Article 6 was not. The Court stated:]

46. The conclusion drawn by the Court from the foregoing analysis is that the notion of equidistance as being logically necessary, in the sense of being an inescapable *a priori* accompaniment of basic continental shelf doctrine, is incorrect. It is said not to be possible to maintain that there is a rule of law ascribing certain areas to a State as a matter of inherent and original right (see paragraphs 19 and 20), without also admitting the existence of some rule by which those areas can be obligatorily delimited. The Court cannot accept the logic of this view. The problem arises only where there is a dispute and only in respect of the marginal areas involved. The appurtenance of a given area, considered as an entity, in no way governs the precise delimitation of its boundaries, any more than uncertainty as to boundaries can affect territorial rights. There is for instance no rule that the land frontiers of a State must be fully delimited and defined, and often in various places and for long periods they are not, as is shown by the case of the entry of Albania into the League of Nations (*Monastery of Saint Naoum, Advisory Opinion, 1924, P.C.I.J., Series B, No. 9,* at p. 10).

47. A review of the genesis and development of the equidistance method of delimitation can only serve to confirm the foregoing conclusion. Such a review may appropriately start with the instrument, generally known as the "Truman

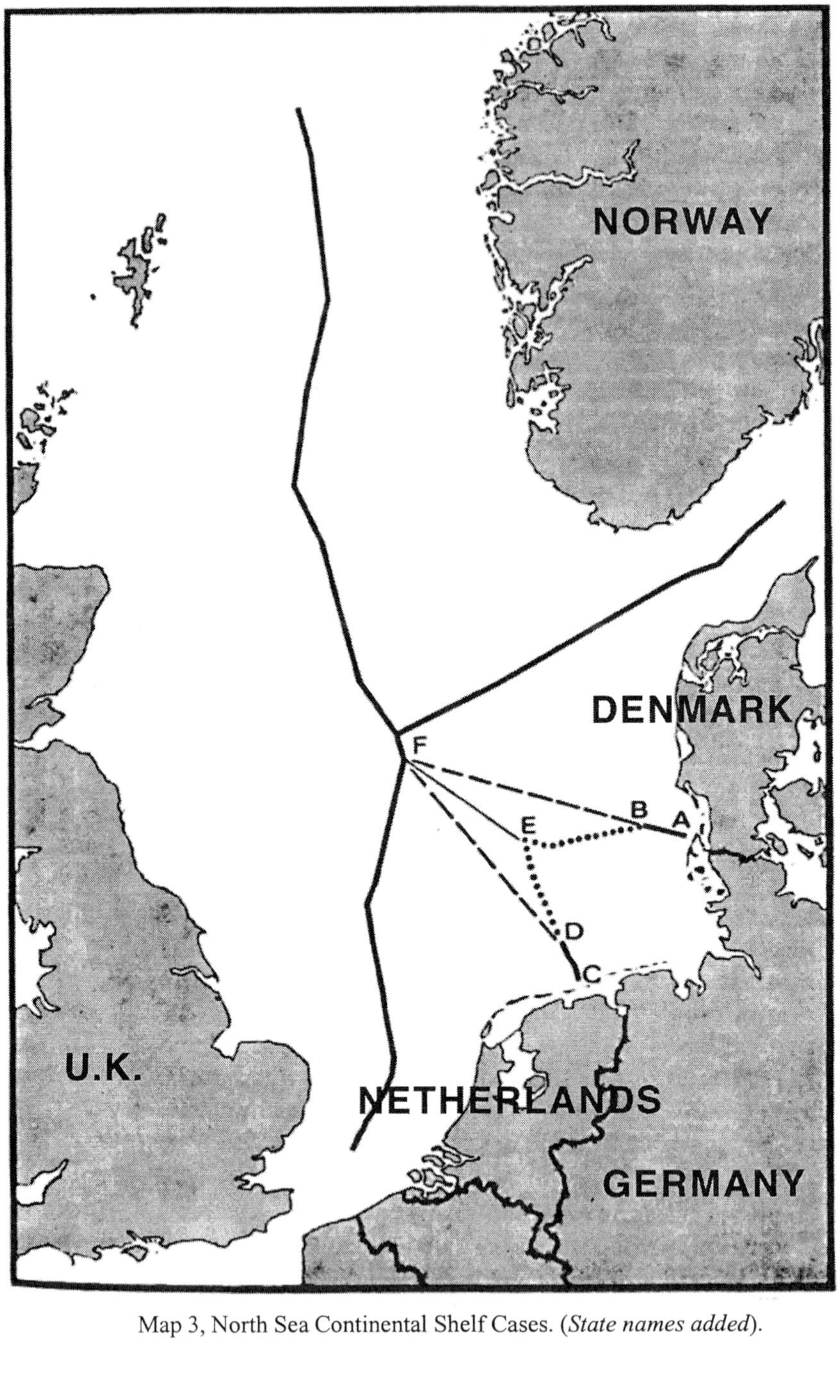

Map 3, North Sea Continental Shelf Cases. (*State names added*).

Proclamation", issued by the Government of the United States on 28 September 1945. Although this instrument was not the first or only one to have appeared, it has in the opinion of the Court a special status. Previously, various theories as to the nature and extent of the rights relative to or exercisable over the continental shelf had been advanced by jurists, publicists and technicians. The Truman Proclamation however, soon came to be regarded as the starting point of the positive law on the subject, and the chief doctrine it enunciated, namely that of the coastal State as having an original, natural, and exclusive (in short a vested) right to the continental shelf off its shores, came to prevail over all others, being now reflected in Article 2 of the 1958 Geneva Convention on the Continental Shelf. With regard to the delimitation of lateral boundaries between the continental shelves of adjacent States, a matter which had given rise to some consideration on the technical, but very little on the juristic level, the Truman Proclamation stated that such boundaries "shall be determined by the United States and the State concerned in accordance with equitable principles". These two concepts, of delimitation by mutual agreement and delimitation in accordance with equitable principles, have underlain all the subsequent history of the subject. They were reflected in various other State proclamations of the period, and after, and in the later work on the subject. ...

80. There are of course plenty of cases (and a considerable number were cited) of delimitations of waters, as opposed to seabed, being carried out on the basis of equidistance—mostly of internal waters (lakes, rivers, etc.), and mostly median-line cases. The nearest analogy is that of adjacent territorial waters... the Court does not consider this case to be analogous to that of the continental shelf.

81. The Court accordingly concludes that if the Geneva Convention was not in its origins or inception declaratory of a mandatory rule of customary international law enjoining the use of the equidistance principle for the delimitation of continental shelf areas between adjacent States, neither has its subsequent effect been constitutive of such a rule; and that State practice up-to-date has equally been insufficient for the purpose. ...

85. It emerges from the history of the development of the legal régime of the continental shelf, which has been reviewed earlier, that the essential reason why the equidistance method is not to be regarded as a rule of law is that, if it were to be compulsorily applied in all situations, this would not be consonant with certain basic legal notions which ... have from the beginning reflected the *opinio juris* in the matter of delimitation; those principles being that delimitation must be the object of agreement between the States concerned, and that such agreement must be arrived at in accordance with equitable principles. On a foundation of very general precepts of justice and good faith, actual rules of law are here involved which govern the delimitation of adjacent continental shelves—that is to say, rules binding upon States for all delimitations;—in short, it is not a question of applying equity simply as a matter of abstract justice, but of applying a rule of law which itself requires the application of equitable principles, in accordance with

the ideas which have always underlain the development of the legal regime of the continental shelf in this field, namely:

(*a*) the parties are under an obligation to enter into negotiations with a view to arriving at an agreement, and not merely to go through a formal process of negotiation as a sort of prior condition for the automatic application of a certain method of delimitation in the absence of agreement; they are under an obligation so to conduct themselves that the negotiations are meaningful, which will not be the case when either of them insists upon its own position without contemplating any modification of it;

(*b*) the parties are under an obligation to act in such a way that, in the particular case, and taking all the circumstances into account, equitable principles are applied,—for this purpose the equidistance method can be used, but other methods exist and may be employed, alone or in combination, according to the areas involved;

(*c*) for the reasons given in paragraphs 43 and 44, the continental shelf of any State must be the natural prolongation of its land territory and must not encroach upon what is the natural prolongation of the territory of another State.

93. In fact, there is no legal limit to the considerations which States may take account of for the purpose of making sure that they apply equitable procedures, and more often than not it is the balancing-up of all such considerations that will produce this result rather than reliance on one to the exclusion of all others. The problem of the relative weight to be accorded to different considerations naturally varies with the circumstances of the case.

94. In balancing the factors in question it would appear that various aspects must be taken into account. Some are related to the geological, others to the geographical aspect of the situation, others again to the idea of the unity of any deposits. These criteria, though not entirely precise, can provide adequate bases for decision adapted to the factual situation. …

97. Another factor to be taken into consideration in the delimitation of areas of continental shelf as between adjacent States is the unity of any deposits. The natural resources of the subsoil of the sea in those parts which consist of continental shelf are the very object of the legal régime established subsequent to the Truman Proclamation. Yet it frequently occurs that the same deposit lies on both sides of the line dividing a continental shelf between two States, and since it is possible to exploit such a deposit from either side, a problem immediately arises on account of the risk of prejudicial or wasteful exploitation by one or other of the States concerned. To look no farther than the North Sea, the practice of States shows how this problem has been dealt with, and all that is needed is to refer to the undertakings entered into by the coastal States of that sea with a view to ensuring the most efficient exploitation or the apportionment of the products extracted—(see in particular the agreement of 10 March 1965 between the United Kingdom and Norway, Article 4; the agreement of 6 October 1965 between the

Netherlands and the United Kingdom relating to "the exploitation of single geological structures extending across the dividing line on the continental shelf under the North Sea"; and the agreement of 14 May 1962 between the Federal Republic and the Netherlands concerning a joint plan for exploiting the natural resources underlying the area of the Ems Estuary where the frontier between the two States has not been finally delimited.) The Court does not consider that unity of deposit constitutes anything more than a factual element which it is reasonable to take into consideration in the course of the negotiations for a delimitation. The Parties are fully aware of the existence of the problem as also of the possible ways of solving it.

98. A final factor to be taken account of is the element of a reasonable degree of proportionality which a delimitation effected according to equitable principles ought to bring about between the extent of the continental shelf appertaining to the States concerned and the lengths of their respective coastlines,— these being measured according to their general direction in order to establish the necessary balance between States with straight, and those with markedly concave or convex coasts, or to reduce very irregular coastlines to their truer proportions. The choice and application of the appropriate technical methods would be a matter for the parties. One method discussed in the course of the proceedings, under the name of the principle of the coastal front, consists in drawing a straight baseline between the extreme points at either end of the coast concerned, or in some cases a series of such lines. Where the parties wish to employ in particular the equidistance method of delimitation, the establishment of one or more baselines of this kind can play a useful part in eliminating or diminishing the distortions that might result from the use of that method.

* * *

One of the first cases to interpret the language of the ICJ in the North Sea Cases was the Channel Arbitration in 1979.

(5) Arbitration between the United Kingdom of Great Britain and Northern Ireland and the French Republic on the Delimitation of the Continental Shelf: The Channel Arbitration

18 I.L.M. 397 (1979)

[T]he Parties have requested the Court to decide, in accordance with the rules of international law applicable in the matter as between them, the following question:

> What is the course of the boundary (or boundaries) between the portions of the continental shelf appertaining to the United Kingdom and the Channel Islands and to the French Republic, respectively, westward of 30 minutes west of the Greenwich Meridian as far as the 1,000 metre isobath?

3. The English Channel stretches westwards from the Straits of Dover (Pas de Calais) in a south-westerly and then in a west-south-westerly direction, sepa-

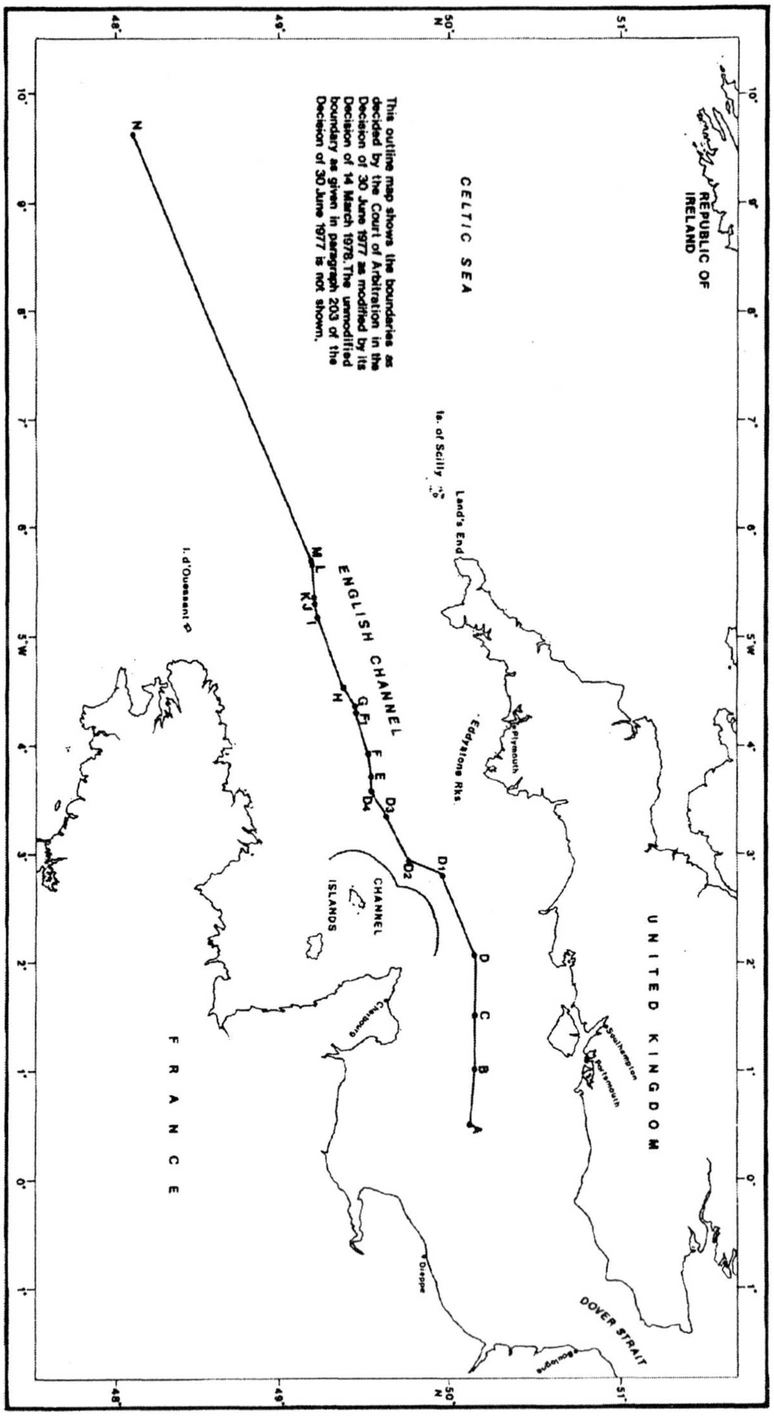

Map from Channel Islands Arbitration (1979).

rating the south coast of Great Britain from the north coast of France over a distance of some 300 nautical miles. …

146. In this region the Parties remain agreed that the geographical and legal framework for determining the boundary is one of States the coasts of which are opposite each other; and that, in consequence, the boundary should, in principle, be the median line. They are, however, in sharp disagreement as to the role which should be allowed to the coasts of the Channel Islands as coasts of the United Kingdom "opposite" to those of France. …

182. [W]here the coastlines of two opposite States are themselves approximately equal in their relation to the continental shelf not only should the boundary in normal circumstances [should] be the median line. … Clearly, if the Channel Islands did not exist, this is precisely how the delimitation of the boundary of the continental shelf in the English Channel would present itself.

183. The Channel Islands, however, do exist and are situated not only on the French side of a median line drawn between the two mainlands but practically within the arms of a gulf on the French coast. …

187. [T]he Court has to take account of the fact that, apart from their three-mile zone of territorial sea the Channel Islands have an existing fishery zone of 12 miles, expressly recognized by the French Republic, and the potentiality of an extension of their territorial sea from three to 12 miles. …

195. The legal rules to be applied in the Channel Islands region … are those of customary international law, rather than of Article 6 of the Convention. Under customary law, the method adopted for delimiting the boundary must, while applying the principle of natural prolongation of territory, also ensure that the resulting delimitation of the boundary accords with equitable principles. …

201. In the actual circumstances of the Channel Islands region, where the extent of the continental shelf is comparatively modest and the scope for adjusting the equities correspondingly small, the Court considers that the situation demands a twofold solution. First, in order to maintain the appropriate balance between the two States in relation to the continental shelf as riparian States of the Channel with approximately equal coastlines, the Court decides that the primary boundary between them shall be a median line, linking Point D of the agreed eastern segment to Point E of the western agreed segment. In the light of the Court's previous decisions regarding the course of the boundary in the English Channel, this means that throughout the whole length of the Channel comprised within the arbitration area the primary boundary of the continental shelf will be a mid-Channel median line. In delimiting its course in the Channel Islands region, that is between Points D and E, the Channel Islands themselves are to be disregarded, since their continental shelf must be the subject of a second and separate delimitation.

202. The second part of the solution is to delimit a second boundary … *vis-à-vis* the Channel Islands. … This second boundary must not … be so drawn

as to allow the continental shelf of the French Republic to encroach upon the established 12-mile fishery zone of the Channel Islands. [T]his boundary shall be drawn at a distance of 12 nautical miles from the established baselines of the territorial sea of the Channel Islands. The effect will be to accord to the French Republic a substantial band of continental shelf in mid-Channel which is continuous with its continental shelf to the east and west of the Channel Islands region; and at the same time to leave to the Channel Islands, to their north and to their west, a zone of seabed and subsoil extending 12 nautical miles from the baselines. ... The result, so far as the Channel Islands are concerned, is to enclose them in an enclave formed, to their north and west, by the boundary of the 12-mile zone … and, to their east, south and south-west by the boundary between them and the coasts of Normandy and Brittany, the exact course of which it is outside the competence of the Court to specify. …

NOTES AND QUESTIONS

1. In *North Sea Continental Shelf Cases,* the Court's rejection of the relatively automatic geometric method for Continental Shelf Delimitation in favor of the application of "equitable principles" required the Court and other tribunals to articulate precisely what those equitable principles were for a variety of different circumstances.

2. In *Channel Islands Arbitration* discussed above, the arbitral tribunal established that where islands pertaining to one state were on the "wrong" side of the median line between the coasts of the two states, the median line would not deviate, but an enclave would be described around each of the Channel Islands.

3. In 1982, the ICJ, in *Continental Shelf (Tunisia/Libyan Arab Jamahiriya),* determined that islands on the "right" side of the median line projected provisionally from the mainland of each state would be given "partial effect" rather than full effect in determining the boundary of the shelf. *Case Concerning the Continental Shelf (Tunisia/Libyan Arab Jamahirya),* 1982 I.C.J.18 (1982).

4. Islands, defined in UNCLOS Art. 121 as "a naturally formed area of land, surrounded by water, which is above water at high tide", create special problems in maritime boundary delimitation due to the fact that, like all land territory, they are entitled under UNCLOS to claim a 12 mile territorial sea, a further 12 mile contiguous zone, a 200 mile, or further, continental shelf, and a 200 mile exclusive economic zone. This gives even the smallest island an exorbitant share of resources, often exceeding its importance as a landmass. The current system fosters conflict among States claiming the same islands (e.g., all states surrounding the Spratley Islands and other island groups in the South China Sea), often escalating into military conflict. A separate problem is caused when States extend their baselines through island claims (as in *Channel Islands Arbitration*) and therefore infringe upon the maritime boundary claims of their neighbors.

The importance of the issues raised by islands and low-tide elevations in maritime boundary delimitation is witnessed in the disputes reaching the ICJ and the amount of legal scholarship devoted to the problem since 1982. *See* JONATHAN CHARNEY, INTERNATIONAL MARITIME BOUNDARIES (Kluwer Law International 1998); Jonathan Charney, *Central East Asian Maritime Boundaries and the Law of the Sea,* 89 AM. J. INT'L L. 724 (1995). *See also,* Hugo Inacio Llanos, *Low-Tide Elevations: Reassessing their Impact on Maritime Delimitation,* 14 PACE INT'L L. REV. 255 (2002).

b. Delimitation

The ICJ in *North Sea Continental Shelf Cases* made Article 6 of the 1958 Geneva Convention on the Continental Shelf obsolete. The decision of the Court to rely on equitable principles for Continental Shelf boundary delimitation was reflected in 1982 in UNCLOS.

1982 United Nations Convention on the Law of the Sea

Article 76: *Definition of the continental shelf*

1. The continental shelf of a coastal State comprises the sea-bed and subsoil of the submarine areas that extend beyond its territorial sea throughout the natural prolongation of its land territory to the outer edge of the continental margin, or to a distance of 200 nautical miles from the baselines from which the breadth of the territorial sea is measured where the outer edge of the continental margin does not extend up to that distance.

2. The continental shelf of a coastal State shall not extend beyond the limits provided for in paragraphs 4 to 6.

3. The continental margin comprises the submerged prolongation of the land mass of the coastal State, and consists of the sea-bed and subsoil of the shelf, the slope and the rise. It does not include the deep ocean floor with its oceanic ridges or the subsoil thereof.

4. (a) For the purposes of this Convention, the coastal State shall establish the outer edge of the continental margin wherever the margin extends beyond 200 nautical miles from the baselines from which the breadth of the territorial sea is measured, by either:

(i) a line delineated in accordance with paragraph 7 by reference to the outermost fixed points at each of which the thickness of sedimentary rocks is at least 1 per cent of the shortest distance from such point to the foot of the continental slope; or

(ii) a line delineated in accordance with paragraph 7 by reference to fixed points not more than 60 nautical miles from the foot of the continental slope.

(b) In the absence of evidence to the contrary, the foot of the continental slope shall be determined as the point of maximum change in the gradient at its base.

5. The fixed points comprising the line of the outer limits of the continental shelf on the sea-bed, drawn in accordance with paragraph 4 (a)(i) and (ii), either shall not exceed 350 nautical miles from the baselines from which the breadth of the territorial sea is measured or shall not exceed 100 nautical miles from the 2,500 metre isobath, which is a line connecting the depth of 2,500 metres.

6. Notwithstanding the provisions of paragraph 5, on submarine ridges, the outer limit of the continental shelf shall not exceed 350 nautical miles from the

baselines from which the breadth of the territorial sea is measured. This paragraph does not apply to submarine elevations that are natural components of the continental margin, such as its plateaux, rises, caps, banks and spurs.

7. The coastal State shall delineate the outer limits of its continental shelf, where that shelf extends beyond 200 nautical miles from the baselines from which the breadth of the territorial sea is measured, by straight lines not exceeding 60 nautical miles in length, connecting fixed points, defined by coordinates of latitude and longitude.

8. Information on the limits of the continental shelf beyond 200 nautical miles from the baselines from which the breadth of the territorial sea is measured shall be submitted by the coastal State to the Commission on the Limits of the Continental Shelf set up under Annex II on the basis of equitable geographical representation. The Commission shall make recommendations to coastal States on matters related to the establishment of the outer limits of their continental shelf. The limits of the shelf established by a coastal State on the basis of these recommendations shall be final and binding.

9. The coastal State shall deposit with the Secretary-General of the United Nations charts and relevant information, including geodetic data, permanently describing the outer limits of its continental shelf. The Secretary-General shall give due publicity thereto.

10. The provisions of this article are without prejudice to the question of delimitation of the continental shelf between States with opposite or adjacent coasts.

Article 77: *Rights of the coastal State over the continental shelf*

1. The coastal State exercises over the continental shelf sovereign rights for the purpose of exploring it and exploiting its natural resources.

2. The rights referred to in paragraph 1 are exclusive in the sense that if the coastal State does not explore the continental shelf or exploit its natural resources, no one may undertake these activities without the express consent of the coastal State.

3. The rights of the coastal State over the continental shelf do not depend on occupation, effective or notional, or on any express proclamation.

4. The natural resources referred to in this Part consist of the mineral and other non-living resources of the sea-bed and subsoil together with living organisms belonging to sedentary species, that is to say, organisms which, at the harvestable stage, either are immobile on or under the sea-bed or are unable to move except in constant physical contact with the sea-bed or the subsoil.

Article 78: *Legal status of the superjacent waters and air space and the rights and freedoms of other States*

1. The rights of the coastal State over the continental shelf do not affect the legal status of the superjacent waters or of the air space above those waters.

2. The exercise of the rights of the coastal State over the continental shelf must not infringe or result in any unjustifiable interference with navigation and other rights and freedoms of other States as provided for in this Convention. …

Article 83: *Delimitation of the continental shelf between States with opposite or adjacent coasts*

1. The delimitation of the continental shelf between States with opposite or adjacent coasts shall be effected by agreement on the basis of international law, as referred to in Article 38 of the Statute of the International Court of Justice, in order to achieve an equitable solution.

2. If no agreement can be reached within a reasonable period of time, the States concerned shall resort to the procedures provided for in Part XV.

3. Pending agreement as provided for in paragraph 1, the States concerned, in a spirit of understanding and co-operation, shall make every effort to enter into provisional arrangements of a practical nature and, during this transitional period, not to jeopardize or hamper the reaching of the final agreement. Such arrangements shall be without prejudice to the final delimitation.

4. Where there is an agreement in force between the States concerned, questions relating to the delimitation of the continental shelf shall be determined in accordance with the provisions of that agreement.

c. Trends in State Practice Since 1982

Since 1982, there has been a steady erosion in the "equitable principles" approach established by the ICJ in the North Sea Continental Shelf cases and later codified in the UNCLOS provisions set forth above. In a series of cases (*see Continental Shelf (Libyan Arab Jamahirya/Malta)*, Judgment, 1985 I.C.J.13; *Delimitation of Maritime Areas Between Canada and the French Republic (St. Pierre and Miquelon) (Can./Fr.)* 95 ILR 645; *Case Concerning Maritime Delimitation in the Area Between Greenland and Jan Mayen (Denmark v. Norway)*, 1993 I.C.J. 38; *Award of the Arbitral Tribunal in the Second Stage of the Proceedings (Maritime Delimitation), Eritrea/Yemen* (Dec. 17, 1999) (obtainable at Permanent Court of Arbitration, http://www.pca-cpa.org; and *Maritime Delimitation and Territorial Questions between Qatar and Bahrain (Qatar v. Bahrain)*, below), both the ICJ and tribunals of the Permanent Court of Arbitration have returned to the "equidistance line, corrected for special circumstances" approach of Article 6 of the 1958 Geneva Convention on the Continental Shelf, as exemplified in the *Qatar/Bahrain* case below.

(1) Maritime Delimitation and Territorial Questions between Qatar and Bahrain (Qatar v. Bahrain)

2001 I.C.J. 87 (Judgment of Mar.16)

[The State of Qatar and the State of Bahrain are both located in the southern part of the Arabian/Persian Gulf (hereinafter, "the Gulf"), almost halfway between the mouth of the Shatt al Arab and the Strait of Hormuz. Both states' land territory is partially composed of islands and low-tide elevations. After reviewing the history of the region and determining the territorial sovereignty as between Qatar and Bahrain over a number of these maritime features, the Court concluded that low-tide elevations cannot establish a part of the coast of Bahrain for delimitation purposes, nor is Bahrain entitled to apply the method of straight baselines for determining the coastal baseline for measuring the other sea zones. In the end, the Court appears to go back to the "most logical and widely practiced" approach, which is first to:]

... draw provisionally an equidistance line and then to consider whether that line must be adjusted in the light of the existence of special circumstances. ...

166. The Court will now turn to the question of the maritime delimitation.

167. The Parties are in agreement that the Court should render its decision on the maritime delimitation in accordance with international law. Neither Bahrain nor Qatar is party to the Geneva Conventions on the Law of the Sea of 29 April 1958; Bahrain has ratified the United Nations Convention on the Law of the Sea of 10 December 1982 but Qatar is only a signatory to it. Customary international law, therefore, is the applicable law. Both Parties, however, agree that most of the provisions of the 1982 Convention which are relevant for the present case reflect customary law. ...

169. It should be kept in mind that the concept of "single maritime boundary" may encompass a number of functions. In the present case the single maritime boundary will be the result of the delimitation of various jurisdictions. In the southern part of the delimitation area, which is situated where the coasts of the Parties are opposite to each other, the distance between these coasts is nowhere more than 24 nautical miles. The boundary the Court is expected to draw will, therefore, delimit exclusively their territorial seas and, consequently, an area over which they enjoy territorial sovereignty.

170. More to the north, however, where the coasts of the two States are no longer opposite to each other but are rather comparable to adjacent coasts, the delimitation to be carried out will be one between the continental shelf and exclusive economic zone belonging to each of the Parties, areas in which States have only sovereign rights and functional jurisdiction. Thus both Parties have differentiated between a southern and a northern sector. ...

173. The Court observes that the concept of a single maritime boundary does not stem from multilateral treaty law but from State practice, and that it finds its explanation in the wish of States to establish one uninterrupted boundary line

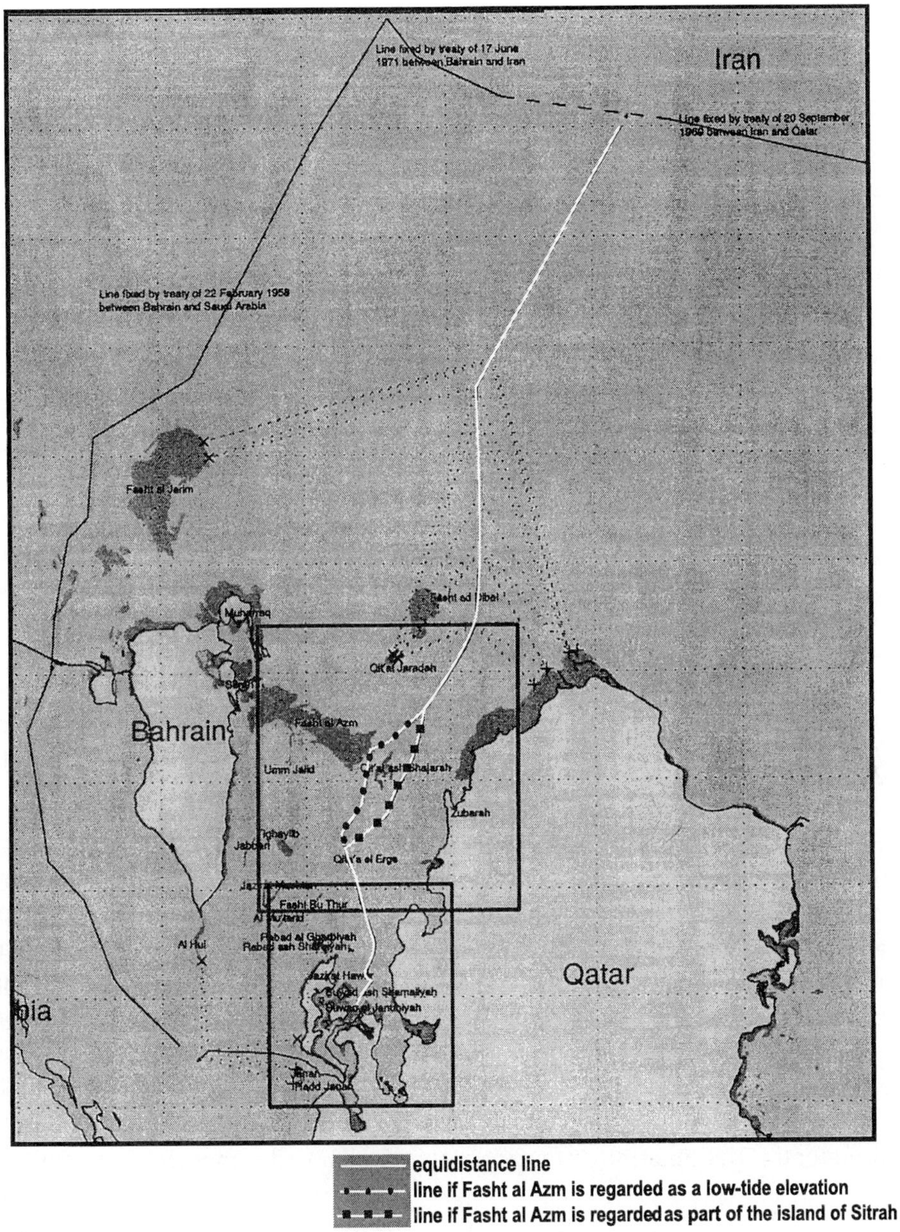

Partial Map: Bahrain & Qatar: Various Maritime Boundary Lines, 2001 I.C.J. 87 (Judgment Mar. 16) *(Original color lines retouched for grayscale reproduction)*

delimiting the various - partially coincident - zones of maritime jurisdiction appertaining to them. In the case of coincident jurisdictional zones, the determination of a single boundary for the different objects of delimitation

> can only be carried out by the application of a criterion, or combination of criteria, which does not give preferential treatment to one of these . . . objects to the detriment of the other, and at the same time is such as to be equally suitable to the division of either of them,

as was stated by the Chamber of the Court in the *Gulf of Maine* case (*I.C.J. Reports 1984*, p. 327, para. 194). In that case, the Chamber was asked to draw a single line which would delimit both the continental shelf and the superjacent water column. ...

175. The Parties agree that the provisions of Article 15 of the 1982 Convention on the Law of the Sea, headed "Delimitation of the territorial sea between States with opposite or adjacent coasts", are part of customary law. This Article provides:

> Where the coasts of two States are opposite or adjacent to each other, neither of the two States is entitled, failing agreement between them to the contrary, to extend its territorial sea beyond the median line every point of which is equidistant from the nearest point on the baselines from which the breadth of the territorial seas of each of the two States is measured. The above provision does not apply, however, where it is necessary by reason of historic title or other special circumstances to delimit the territorial seas of the two States in a way which is at variance therewith.

176. Article 15 of the 1982 Convention is virtually identical to Article 12, paragraph 1, of the 1958 Convention on the Territorial Sea and the Contiguous Zone, and is to be regarded as having a customary character. It is often referred to as the "equidistance/special circumstances" rule. The most logical and widely practised approach is first to draw provisionally an equidistance line and then to consider whether that line must be adjusted in the light of the existence of special circumstances. Once it has delimited the territorial seas belonging to the Parties, the Court will determine the rules and principles of customary law to be applied to the delimitation of the Parties' continental shelves and their exclusive economic zones or fishery zones. The Court will further decide whether the method to be chosen for this delimitation differs from or is similar to the approach just outlined.

...

224. The Court will now deal with the drawing of the single maritime boundary in that part of the delimitation area which covers both the continental shelf and the exclusive economic zone (see paragraph 170 above). ...

226. The Court itself referred to the close relationship between continental shelf and exclusive economic zone for delimitation purposes in its Judgment in the case concerning the *Continental Shelf (Libya/Malta)*. It observed that

> even though the present case relates only to the delimitation of the continental shelf and not to that of the exclusive economic zone, the principles and rules underlying the latter concept cannot be left out of consideration. As the 1982 Convention demonstrates the two institutions - continental shelf and exclusive economic zone - are linked together in modern law. (*I.C.J. Reports 1985*, p. 33, para. 33.)

And the Court went on to say that, in case of delimitation, "greater importance must be attributed to elements, such as distance from the coast, which are common to both concepts" *(ibid.)*.

227. A similar approach was taken by the Court in the *Jan Mayen* case, where it was also asked to draw a single maritime boundary. With regard to the delimitation of the continental shelf the Court stated that

> even if it were appropriate to apply . . . customary law concerning the continental shelf as developed in the decided cases [the Court had referred to the *Gulf of Maine* and the *Libya/Malta* cases], it is in accord with precedents to begin with the median line as a provisional line and then to ask whether 'special circumstances' [the term used in Art. 6 of the 1958 Convention on the Continental Shelf, which was the applicable law in the case] require any adjustment or shifting of that line. (*I.C.J. Reports 1993*, p. 61, para. 51)

228. After having come to a similar conclusion with regard to the fishery zones, the Court stated:

> It thus appears that, both for the continental shelf and for the fishery zones in this case, it is proper to begin the process of delimitation by a median line provisionally drawn. (*Ibid.*, p. 62, para. 53.) …

230. The Court will follow the same approach in the present case. For the delimitation of the maritime zones beyond the 12-mile zone it will first provisionally draw an equidistance line and then consider whether there are circumstances which must lead to an adjustment of that line.

231. The Court further notes that the equidistance/special circumstances rule, which is applicable in particular to the delimitation of the territorial sea, and the equitable principles/relevant circumstances rule, as it has been developed since 1958 in case-law and State practice with regard to the delimitation of the continental shelf and the exclusive economic zone, are closely interrelated. …

244. The Court will now consider whether there are other reasons which might require an adjustment of the course of the equidistance line in order to achieve an equitable solution.

245. In drawing the line which delimits the continental shelves and exclusive economic zones of the Parties the Court cannot ignore the location of Fasht al

Jarim, a sizeable maritime feature partly situated in the territorial sea of Bahrain. The Parties have expressed differing views on the legal nature of this maritime feature but, in any event, given the feature's location, its low-water line may be used as the baseline from which the breadth not only of the territorial sea, but also of the continental shelf and the exclusive economic zone, is measured.

246. The Court recalls that in the *Libya/Malta* case, referred to above, it stated:

> the equitableness of an equidistance line depends on whether the precaution is taken of eliminating the disproportionate effect of certain 'islets, rocks and minor coastal projections', to use the language of the Court in its 1969 Judgment. (*I.C.J. Reports 1985*, p. 48, para. 64).

247. The Court further recalls that in the northern sector the coasts of the Parties are comparable to adjacent coasts abutting on the same maritime areas extending seawards into the Gulf. The northern coasts of the territories belonging to the Parties are not markedly different in character or extent; both are flat and have a very gentle slope. The only noticeable element is Fasht al Jarim as a remote projection of Bahrain's coastline in the Gulf area, which, if given full effect, would "distort the boundary and have disproportionate effects" (*Continental Shelf* case (*France/United Kingdom*), United Nations, *Reports of International Arbitral Awards*, Vol. XVIII, p. 114, para. 244).

248. In the view of the Court, such a distortion, due to a maritime feature located well out to sea and of which at most a minute part is above water at high tide, would not lead to an equitable solution which would be in accord with all other relevant factors referred to above. In the circumstances of the case considerations of equity require that Fasht al Jarim should have no effect in determining the boundary line in the northern sector.

* * *

A number of separate and dissenting opinions were submitted. For further discussion, see W. Michael Reisman, *International Decision: Maritime Delimitation Between Opposite States ...*, 94 AM. J. INT'L L. 721 (2000); and Glen Plant, *International Decision: Delimitation of Single Maritime Boundary, Including Territorial Seas ...*, 96 AM J. INT'L L. 198 (2002).

9. Exclusive Economic Zone (EEZ)

Church v. Hubbart, considered above, was a manifestation of claims by the coastal state to exercise limited jurisdiction beyond the territorial sea. In the twentieth century, a significant group of states pressed for a much broader competence over areas of ocean space beyond their territorial waters. The ICJ's 1974 decision in favor of Iceland gave weight to the concept of an exclusive fisheries or economic zone.

a. Fisheries Jurisdiction Case (U.K. v. Ice.)
1974 I.C.J. 3 (Judgment of July 26)

[In violation of their commitments to Germany and the U.K., Iceland in 1948 passed a law that established strict conservation zones within the limits of the Continental Shelf of Iceland and placed all fisheries under exclusive Icelandic control. Iceland justified the new regulations based on the concept of "preferential rights" due to coastal states whose economies, like that of Iceland, depended almost entirely on fishing in the vicinity of their coasts. The U.K. protested, claiming historic rights in the same waters, and this led to several violent incidents at sea and protracted negotiations.]

62. The concept of preferential rights is not compatible with the exclusion of all fishing activities of other States. A coastal State entitled to preferential rights is not free, unilaterally and according to its own uncontrolled discretion, to determine the extent of those rights. The characterization of the coastal State's rights as preferential implies a certain priority, but cannot imply the extinction of the concurrent rights of other States, and particularly of a State which, like the Applicant, has for many years been engaged in fishing in the waters in question, such fishing activity being important to the economy of the country concerned. The coastal State has to take into account and pay regard to the position of such other States, particularly when they have established an economic dependence on the same fishing grounds. Accordingly, the fact that Iceland is entitled to claim preferential rights does not suffice to justify its claim unilaterally to exclude the Applicant's fishing vessels from all fishing activity in the waters beyond the limits agreed to in the 1961 Exchange of Notes. …

65. Iceland has for its part admitted the existence of the Applicant's historic and special interests in the fishing in the disputed waters. The Exchange of Notes as a whole and in particular its final provision requiring Iceland to give advance notice to the United Kingdom of any extension of its fishery limits impliedly acknowledged the existence of United Kingdom fishery interests in the waters adjacent to the 12-mile limit. The discussions which have taken place between the two countries also imply an acknowledgement by Iceland of the existence of such interests. Furthermore, the Prime Minister of Iceland stated on 9 November 1971:

> … the British have some interests to protect in this connection. For a long time they have been fishing in Icelandic waters … The well-being of specific British fishing towns may nevertheless to some extent be connected with the fisheries in Icelandic waters. …

66. Considerations similar to those which have prompted the recognition of the preferential rights of the coastal State in a special situation apply when coastal populations in other fishing States are also dependent on certain fishing grounds. In both instances the economic dependence and the livelihood of whole communities are affected. Not only do the same considerations apply, but the same interest in conservation exists. In this respect the Applicant has recognized that

the conservation and efficient exploitation of the fish stocks in the Iceland area are of importance not only to Iceland but also to the United Kingdom.

68. The findings stated by the Court in the preceding paragraphs suffice to provide a basis for the decision of the present case, namely: that Iceland's extension of its exclusive fishery jurisdiction beyond 12 miles is not opposable to the United Kingdom; that Iceland may on the other hand claim preferential rights in the distribution of fishery resources in the adjacent waters; that the United Kingdom also has established rights with respect to the fishery resources in question; and that the principle of reasonable regard for the interests of other States enshrined in Article 2 of the Geneva Convention on the High Seas of 1958 requires Iceland and the United Kingdom to have due regard to each other's interests, and to the interests of other States, in those resources.

69. It follows from the reasoning of the Court in this case that in order to reach an equitable solution of the present dispute it is necessary that the preferential fishing rights of Iceland, as a State specially dependent on coastal fisheries, be reconciled with the traditional fishing rights of the Applicant. Such a reconciliation cannot be based, however, on a phasing-out of the Applicant's fishing, as was the case in the 1961 Exchange of Notes in respect of the 12-mile fishery zone. In that zone, Iceland was to exercise exclusive fishery rights while not objecting to continued fishing by the Applicant's vessels during a phasing-out period. In adjacent waters outside that zone, however, a similar extinction of rights of other fishing States, particularly when such rights result from a situation of economic dependence and long-term reliance on certain fishing grounds, would not be compatible with the notion of preferential rights as it was recognized at the Geneva Conferences of 1958 and 1960, nor would it be equitable. At the 1960 Conference, the concept of preferential rights of coastal States in a special situation was recognized in the joint amendment referred to in paragraph 57 above, under such limitations and to such extent as is found "necessary by reason of the dependence of the coastal State on the stock or stocks of fish, while having regard to the interests of any other State or States in the exploitation of such stock or stocks of fish". The reference to the interests of other States in the exploitation of the same stocks clearly indicates that the preferential rights of the coastal State and the established rights of other States were considered as, in principle, continuing to co-exist.

70. This is not to say that the preferential rights of a coastal State in a special situation are a static concept, in the sense that the degree of the coastal State's preference is to be considered as fixed for ever at some given moment. On the contrary, the preferential rights are a function of the exceptional dependence of such a coastal State on the fisheries in adjacent waters and may, therefore, vary as the extent of that dependence changes. Furthermore, as was expressly recognized in the 1961 Exchange of Notes, a coastal State's exceptional dependence on fisheries may relate not only to the livelihood of its people but to its economic development. In each case, it is essentially a matter of appraising the dependence

of the coastal State on the fisheries in question in relation to that of the other State concerned and of reconciling them in as equitable a manner as is possible. …

72. It follows that even if the Court holds that Iceland's extension of its fishery limits is not opposable to the Applicant, this does not mean that the Applicant is under no obligation to Iceland with respect to fishing in the disputed waters in the 12-mile to 50-mile zone. On the contrary, both States have an obligation to take full account of each other's rights and of any fishery conservation measures the necessity of which is shown to exist in those waters. It is one of the advances in maritime international law, resulting from the intensification of fishing, that the former *laissez-faire* treatment of the living resources of the sea in the high seas has been replaced by a recognition of a duty to have due regard to the rights of other States and the needs of conservation for the benefit of all. Consequently, both Parties have the obligation to keep under review the fishery resources in the disputed waters and to examine together, in the light of scientific and other available information, the measures required for the conservation and development, and equitable exploitation, of those resources, taking into account any international agreement in force between them, such as the North-East Atlantic Fisheries Convention of 24 January 1959, as well as such other agreements as may be reached in the matter in the course of further negotiation.

73. The most appropriate method for the solution of the dispute is clearly that of negotiation. Its objective should be the delimitation of the rights and interests of the Parties, the preferential rights of the coastal State on the one hand and the rights of the Applicant on the other, to balance and regulate equitably questions such as those of catch-limitation, share allocations and "related restrictions concerning areas closed to fishing, number and type of vessels allowed and forms of control of the agreed provisions" …

78. In the fresh negotiations which are to take place on the basis of the present Judgment, the Parties will have the benefit of the above appraisal of their respective rights, and of certain guidelines defining their scope. The task before them will be to conduct their negotiations on the basis that each must in good faith pay reasonable regard to the legal rights of the other in the waters around Iceland outside the 12-mile limit, thus bringing about an equitable apportionment of the fishing resources based on the facts of the particular situation, and having regard to the interests of other States which have established fishing rights in the area. It is not a matter of finding simply an equitable solution, but an equitable solution derived from the applicable law. As the Court stated in the North Sea Continental Shelf cases:

> . . . it is not a question of applying equity simply as a matter of abstract justice, but of applying a rule of law which itself requires the application of equitable principles. 1969 I.C.J. at 47.

b. Delimitation

The position of states that identified their interests with Iceland was largely vindicated in UNCLOS:

1982 United Nations Convention on the Law of the Sea

Article 55: *Specific legal régime of the exclusive economic zone*

The exclusive economic zone is an area beyond and adjacent to the territorial sea, subject to the specific legal regime established in this Part, under which the rights and jurisdiction of the coastal State and the rights and freedoms of other States are governed by the relevant provisions of this Convention.

Article 56: *Rights, jurisdiction and duties of the coastal State in the exclusive economic zone*

1. In the exclusive economic zone, the coastal State has:

(a) sovereign rights for the purpose of exploring and exploiting, conserving and managing the natural resources, whether living or non-living, of the waters superjacent to the sea-bed and of the sea-bed and its subsoil, and with regard to other activities for the economic exploitation and exploration of the zone, such as the production of energy from the water, currents and winds;

(b) jurisdiction as provided for in the relevant provisions of this Convention with regard to:

(i) the establishment and use of artificial islands, installations and structures;

(ii) marine scientific research;

(iii) the protection and preservation of the marine environment;

(c) other rights and duties provided for in this Convention.

2. In exercising its rights and performing its duties under this Convention in the exclusive economic zone, the coastal State shall have due regard to the rights and duties of other States and shall act in a manner compatible with the provisions of this Convention.

3. The rights set out in this article with respect to the sea-bed and subsoil shall be exercised in accordance with Part VI.

Article 57: *Breadth of the exclusive economic zone*

The exclusive economic zone shall not extend beyond 200 nautical miles from the baselines from which the breadth of the territorial sea is measured.

Notes and Questions

1. UNCLOS Article 61 addresses the conservation of living resources of the EEZ and imposes obligations with respect to catch limits. Article 62 addresses the utilization of the living resources of the EEZ and requires the coastal state to promote optimum utilization of those resources.

2. What is the equitable basis by which Iceland can claim a larger competence to determine load limits and conservation programs in waters that are in the high seas than can historic users of those waters such as the United Kingdom and Germany?

3. It is ironic that the Third Law of the Sea Convention that produced UNCLOS was animated by the notion of the oceans as a "common heritage of mankind." In fact, institutions like the Exclusive Economic Zone (EEZ) effectively transferred control of a theretofore common resource to a relatively small number of states. The United States, which has one of the longest aggregate coastlines in the world, was one of the major beneficiaries of the EEZ. On the other hand, almost one-third of the participants in the Conference who were either landlocked or "geographically disadvantaged" in the sense that they have very small coastlines, received very little, while being locked out of areas in which most of the fish consumed by our species are to be found.

10. The Area

"The Area" refers to the sea-bed and ocean floor and the sub-soil thereof, as well as all resources therein, beyond the limits of national jurisdiction.

In 1982, the UNCLOS drafters concretized in Part XI a regime to regulate the use of the Area and established the International Sea-Bed Authority to carry out such regulation. But the actual advocacy for the creation of the regime began much earlier, culminating in a series of U.N. General Assembly Resolutions which declared the Area and its resources to be "the common heritage of mankind."

a. The Deepsea Ventures Incident

In 1970, the United Nations General Assembly resolved:

> The sea-bed and ocean floor, and the subsoil thereof, beyond the limits of national jurisdiction (hereinafter referred to as the area, as well as the resources of the area, are the common heritage of mankind

and imposed a moratorium on exploitation pending the establishment of an international regime.

Declaration of Principles Governing the Sea-Bed and the Ocean Floor, and Subsoil Thereof, Beyond the Limits of National Jurisdiction, G.A. Res. 2749 (XXV), U.N. GAOR, 25th Sess., 1933rd Plenary Meeting, , 25 G.A.O.R. Supp. 28 (A/8028) at 24 (Dec. 17, 1970).

* * *

The General Assembly had already resolved that

... pending the establishment of the aforementioned international régime:

(a) States and persons, physical or juridical, are bound to refrain from all activities of exploitation of the resources of the area of the sea-bed and ocean floor, and the subsoil thereof, beyond the limits of national jurisdiction;

(b) No claim to any part of that area or its resources shall be recognized.

The U.N. Moratorium Resolution, G.A.Res. 2547D, 24 G.A.O.R. Supp. 30 (A/7630) at 11 (1969).

* * *

Multinational consortia of mineral extracting companies that wished to mine manganese nodules ... thus found themselves precluded by the General Assembly from staking claims. Without a claim guaranteed by international law, a consortium that sank funds into locating manganese nodules and then developing the technology for scooping them off the ocean floor would likely find another company moving into part of the Area that had been identified and beginning to scoop as well. Without some way of ensuring tenure over the areas, exploration and exploitation of this particular resource of the ocean could not commence.

In 1974, one such consortium, Deepsea Ventures, Inc., wrote to then-Secretary of State Kissinger:

My dear Mr. Secretary:

Deepsea Ventures, Inc., a Delaware corporation having its principal place of business in the County of Gloucester, The Commonwealth of Virginia, U.S.A., respectfully makes of record, by filing with your office this *Notice of Discovery and Claim of Exclusive Mining Rights and Request for Diplomatic Protection and Protection of Investment, by Deepsea Ventures, Inc.* (hereinafter "Claim"), as authorized by its Board of Directors by resolution dated 30 October 1974, a certified copy of which is annexed hereto as Exhibit A. [not reproduced].

Deepsea Ventures, Inc., (hereinafter "Deepsea"), hereby gives public notice that it has discovered and taken possession of, and is not engaged in developing and evaluating, as the first stages of mining, a deposit of seabed manganese nodules (hereinafter "Deposit"). The Deposit, illustrated by the sketch annexed as Exhibit B, is encompassed by, and extends to, lines drawn between the coordinates numbered in series below. [deleted]

These lines include approximately 60,000 square kilometers for purposes of development and evaluation of the Deposit encompassed therein, which area will be reduced by Deepsea to 30,000 square kilometers upon expiration of a term of 15 years (absent force majeure) from the date of this notice or upon commencement (absent force majeure) of commercial production from the Deposit, whichever event occurs first. The Deposit lies on the abyssal ocean floor, in water depths ranging between 2300 to 5000 meters and is more than 1000 kilometers from the nearest island, and more than 1300 kilometers seaward of the outer edge of the nearest continental margin. It is beyond the limits of seabed jurisdiction presently claimed by any State. The overlying waters are, of course, high seas.

The general area of the Deposit was identified in August of 1964 by the predecessor in interest of Deepsea, and the Deposit was discovered by Deepsea on August 31, 1969.

Further exploration, evaluation, engineering development and processing research have been carried out to enable the recovery of the specific manganese nodules of the Deposit and the production of products and byproducts therefrom. ...

Deepsea respectfully requests the diplomatic protection of the United States Government with respect to the exclusive mining rights described and asserted in the foregoing Claim, and any other rights which may hereafter accrue to Deepsea as a result of its activities at the site of the Deposit, and similar protection of the integrity of its investments heretofore made and now being undertaken, and to be undertaken in the future.

Notice of Discovery and Claim of Exclusive Mining Rights, and Request for Diplomatic Protection and Protection of Investment, by Deepsea Ventures, Inc., 14 I.L.M. 51 (1975).

* * *

The United States Department of State responded:

> The Department of States does not grant or recognize exclusive mining rights to the mineral resources of an area of the seabed beyond the limits of national jurisdiction.
>
> The appropriate means for the development of the law of the sea is the Third United Nations Conference on the Law of the Sea and not unilateral claims. The United States supports the achievement of a widely acceptable and comprehensive law of the sea treaty in 1975 that would include a regime and machinery for the exploration for and exploitation of the mineral resources of the deep seabed beyond the limits of national jurisdiction.

Responses of Governments to Deepsea Ventures Claim, 14 I.L.M. 66, 69, 795, 796 (1975).

* * *

A number of other governments responded to the circular letter sent by Deepsea Ventures indicating their opposition, as a matter of law and policy, to the multinational's claim of exclusive mining rights in an area of the deepsea. Deepsea Ventures thereupon turned to the U.S. Congress, from which it secured the Deep Seabed Hard Mineral Resources Act of 1980.

Deep Seabed Hard Mineral Resources Act

June 28, 1980, Pub.L. No. 96-283, §§ 2, 3, 101, 111, 201, 202, 94 Stat. 553 (1980) (codified in 30 U.S.C. §§ 1401, 1402, 1411, 1421, 1441, 1442.)

(12) it is the legal opinion of the United States that exploration for and commercial recovery of hard mineral resources of the deep seabed are freedom of the high seas subject to a duty of reasonable regard to the interests of other states in their exercise of those and other freedoms recognized by general principles of international law;

(13) pending a Law of the Sea Treaty, and in the absence of agreement among states on applicable principles of international law, the uncertainty among potential investors as to the future legal regime is likely to discourage or prevent the investments necessary to develop deep seabed mining technology;

(14) pending a Law of the Sea Treaty, the protection of the marine environment from damage caused by exploration or recovery of hard mineral resources of the deep seabed depends upon the enactment of suitable interim national legislation;

(15) a Law of the Sea Treaty is likely to establish financial arrangements which obligate the United States or United States citizens to make payments to an international organization with respect to exploration or recovery of the hard mineral resources of the deep seabed; and

(16) legislation is required to establish an interim legal regime under which technology can be developed and the exploration and recovery of the hard mineral resources of the deep seabed can take place until such time as a Law of the Sea Treaty enters into force with respect to the United States.

(b) Purposes. The Congress declares that the purposes of this Act are:

(1) to encourage the successful conclusion of a comprehensive Law of the Sea Treaty, which will give legal definition to the principle that the hard mineral resources of the deep seabed are the common heritage of mankind and which will assure, among other things, nondiscriminatory access to such resources for all nations;

(2) pending the ratification by, and entering into force with respect to, the United States of such a Treaty, to provide for the establishment of an international revenue-sharing fund the proceeds of which shall be used for sharing with the international community pursuant to such Treaty;

(3) to establish, pending the ratification by, and entering into force with respect to, the United States of such a Treaty, an interim program to regulate the exploration for and commercial recovery of hard mineral resources of the deep seabed by United States citizens;

(4) to accelerate the program of environmental assessment of exploration for and commercial recovery of hard mineral resources of the deep seabed and

assure that such exploration and recovery activities are conducted in a manner which will encourage the conservation of such resources, protect the quality of the environment, and promote the safety of life and property at sea; and

(5) to encourage the continued development of technology necessary to recover the hard mineral resources of the deep seabed.

NOTES AND QUESTIONS

1. The Deepsea Ventures story is instructive in at least two ways. First, as we saw in Part one, it is representative of the complex interactions between national and international actors involved in the process of making international law, this time, the law which would govern the allocation of control over and the use of a special area of the deep-sea bed beyond national jurisdiction. Second, it is gratifying to note that such allocations of control are not always made on the basis of power alone. The United States, then one of two superpowers, was unable to effectuate the claim of an influential, multinational American corporation because the international system was unprepared to recognize claims that were unsupported by the new legal regime that had been designed to operate in the common interest of all States.

2. The Law of the Sea Conference, underway while the events discussed above were unfolding, established an international regime for the development of deep ocean resources under Part XI of UNCLOS. The U.S. government opposed the regime. Indeed, as noted, President Ronald Reagan refused to sign the 1982 Treaty, largely because of the inclusion of Part XI. Even without the support of the United States, however, the Preparatory Commission for the Deep Seabed Authority, established by UNCLOS, went into operation. U.S. multinational corporations watched as multinationals in other countries began to stake claims in The Area.

In 1993, the United States secured a substantial revision of Part XI with respect to the exploitation of deepsea minerals and indicated that it would now become a party to UNCLOS. The United States signed the Part XI Agreement on July 29, 1994. On October 7, 1994, President Clinton submitted UNCLOS including the Part XI Agreement to the Senate for its advice and consent.

Even without U.S. ratification, the Part XI Agreement, which is to be interpreted and applied together with the revised Part XI as a single instrument, entered into force on July 28, 1996. States ratifying UNCLOS after this date also consent to be bound by Part XI, and no state may consent to be bound by the Agreement without also accepting UNCLOS. The more interesting question was "What about States parties who ratified UNCLOS *before* July 28, 1996, when the original version of Part XI was still operative?" According to John Noyes, these states "could choose among a variety of mechanisms to express their consent...[including] definitive signature of the Part XI Agreement, ratification after signature, accession, or a simplified procedure consisting of signature of the Agreement followed by lack of notice within 12 months of an intent not to use the simplified procedure." John E. Noyes, *International Legal Developments in Review: 1996, International Law of the Sea*, 31 INT'L LAW 703, 703-704.

The various institutions created under Part XI, such as the International Tribunal for the Law of the Sea (headquartered in Hamburg, Germany), and the International Seabed Authority ("the Authority", headquartered in Kingston, Jamaica), along with its main organs (the Assembly, the Council, and a Secretariat) and various subsidiary organs, have been established at this writing. In addition, the Commission on the Limits of the Continental Shelf was established in 1997. The Commission makes recommendations to coastal states concerning the establishment of their continental shelves, where those limits extend beyond 200 n.m. from their coasts. (Noyes, *supra*, at 705-706). *See* UNCLOS, Annex II, at Arts. 1-9. According to Dr. Robert Smith, who edits the Limits in the Seas Series for the U.S. State Department, the number of continental shelf claims brought before the Commission by states is increasing each year. *See* David Colson, *Some Perspectives on Adjudicating Before the World Court: The Gulf of Maine Case,* 79 AM. J. INT'L L. 578; PETER

J. COOK & CHRIS M. CARLETON, CONTINENTAL SHELF LIMITS: THE SCIENTIFIC AND LEGAL INTERFACE (Oxford U. Press 2000). *See also*, Donald L. Morgan, *Implications of the Proliferation of International Legal Fora: The Example of the Southern Bluefin Tuna Cases*, 43 HARV. INT'L L. J. 541 (2002); John Shamsey, *ITLOS vs. Goliath: The International Tribunal for the Law of the Sea Stands Tall with the Appellate Body in the Chilean-EU Swordfish Dispute*, 12 TRANSNAT'L L. & CONTEMP. PROBS. 513 (2002).

B. OTHER INTERNATIONAL WATERS

1. International Rivers

a. Convention and Statute on the Regime of Navigable Waterways of International Concern

Barcelona, April 20, 1921, 7 U.N.T.S. 37 (1921)
[hereinafter: "The Barcelona Convention"]

Article 1

In the application of the Statute, the following are declared to be navigable waterways of international concern:

1. All parts which are naturally navigable to and from the sea of a waterway which in its course, naturally navigable to and from the sea, separates or traverses different States, and also any part of any other waterway naturally navigable to and from the sea, which connects with the sea a waterway naturally navigable which separates or traverses different States.

It is understood that:

(*a*) Transshipment from one vessel to another is not excluded by the words "navigable to and from the sea";

(*b*) Any natural waterway or part of a natural waterway is termed "naturally navigable" if now used for ordinary commercial navigation, or capable by reason of its natural conditions of being so used; by "ordinary commercial navigation" is to be understood navigation which, in view of the economic condition of the riparian countries, is commercial and normally practicable;

(*c*) Tributaries are to be considered as separate waterways;

(*d*) Lateral canals constructed in order to remedy the defects of a waterway included in the above definition are assimilated thereto.

(*e*) The different States separated or traversed by a navigable waterway of international concern, including its tributaries of international concern, are deemed to be "riparian States".

2. Waterways, or parts of waterways, whether natural or artificial, expressly declared to be placed under the regime of the General Convention regarding navigable waterways of international concern either in unilateral Acts of the States under whose sovereignty or authority these waterways or parts of waterways are situated, or in agreements made with the consent, in particular, of such States.

Article 2

For the purpose of Articles 5, 10, 12 and 14 of this Statute, the following shall form a special category of navigable waterways of international concern:

(*a*) Navigable waterways for which there are international Commissions upon which non-riparian States are represented;

(*b*) Navigable waterways which may hereafter be placed in this category, either in pursuance of unilateral Acts of the States under whose sovereignty or authority they are situated, or in pursuance of agreements made with the consent, in particular, of such States. …

Article 3

Subject to the provisions contained in Articles 5 and 17, each of the Contracting States shall accord free exercise of navigation to the vessels flying the flag of any one of the other Contracting States on those parts of navigable waterways specified above which may be situated under its sovereignty or authority.

Article 4

In the exercise of navigation referred to above, the nationals, property and flags of all Contracting States shall be treated in all respects on a footing of perfect equality. No distinction shall be made between the nationals, the property and the flags of the different riparian States, including the riparian State exercising sovereignty or authority over the portion of the navigable waterway in question: similarly, no distinction shall be made between the nationals, the property and the flags of riparian and non-riparian States. It is understood, in consequence, that no exclusive right of navigation shall be accorded on such navigable waterways to companies or to private persons.

No distinction shall be made in the said exercise, by reason of the point of departure or of destination, or of the direction of the traffic.

Article 5

As an exception to the two preceding Articles, and in the absence of any Convention or obligation to the contrary:

1. A riparian State has the right of reserving for its own flag the transport of passengers and goods loaded at one port situated under its sovereignty or authority and unloaded at another port also situated under its sovereignty or authority. A State which does not reserve the above-mentioned transport to its own flag may, nevertheless, refuse the benefit of equality of treatment with regard to such transport to a co-riparian which does reserve it.

On the navigable waterways referred to in Article 2, the Act of Navigation shall only allow to riparian States the right of reserving the local transport of passengers or of goods which are of national origin or are nationalised. In every case, however, in which greater freedom, of navigation may have been already established, in a previous Act of Navigation, this freedom shall not be reduced.

2. When a natural system of navigable waterways of international concern which does not include waterways of the kind referred to in Article 2 separates or traverses two States only, the latter have the right to reserve to their flags by mutual agreement the transport of passengers and goods loaded at one port of this system and unloaded at another port of the same system, unless this transport takes place between two ports which are not situated under the sovereignty or authority of the same State in the course of a voyage, effected without transshipment on the territory of either of the said States, involving a sea-passage or passage over a navigable waterway of international concern which does not belong to the said system.

b. The River Oder Case

1929 P.C.I.J. (Ser. A), No. 23 (Sept. 10)

102. In the case concerning *Territorial Jurisdiction of the International Commission of the River Oder,* the PCIJ was asked to determine whether, under the Treaty of Versailles of 1919, the jurisdiction of the International Commission of the Oder extended to certain tributaries of that river. The Oder rises in Czechoslovakia, flows into Poland, forms the border between Poland and eastern Germany, and empties into the Baltic. Article 331 of the Treaty of Versailles provided that all navigable parts of these river systems [including the Oder] which naturally provided more than one State with access to the sea possessed international status. Article 341 of the Treaty placed the Oder under the administration of an International Commission, whose task it was to define the sections of the river or its tributaries to which the international regime would be applied.

103. The question before the PCIJ was whether the jurisdiction of the Commission should extend to two tributaries of the Oder situated in Poland, the Netze (Notéc) and the Warthe (Warta): Poland maintained that the Commission's jurisdiction should end where the Oder crossed the Polish border, whereas the six other members of the Commission contended that it should extend to the point at which each of the tributaries ceased to be navigable, even if that point were situated within Polish territory. The navigability of the Warthe and the Netze was not disputed, but Poland claimed that the sections of those rivers situated in Polish territory provided only Poland with "access to the sea" under article 331.

104. The issue in the case thus concerned the competence of the Oder Commission in particular and navigation rights in general. However, because the PCIJ found that it was unable to answer the question before it solely on the basis of the provisions of the Treaty of Versailles, it resorted to "the principles underlying the matter to which the text refers," namely those "governing international fluvial law in general". 1929 P.C.I.J. at 26. The Court acknowledged that providing upstream States with access to the sea played an important role "in the formation of the principle of freedom of navigation on so-called international rivers." But, it continued:

> [W]hen consideration is given to the manner in which States have regarded the concrete situations arising out of the fact that a single waterway traverses or separates the territory of more than one State, and the possibility of fulfilling the requirements of justice and the considerations of utility which this fact places in relief, it is at once seen that a solution of the problem has been sought not in the idea of a right of passage in favor of upstream States, but in that of a community of interest of riparian States. This community of interest in a navigable river becomes the basis of a common legal right, the essential features of which are the perfect equality of all riparian States in the use of the whole course of the river and the exclusion of any preferential privilege of any one riparian State in relation to the others.

Id. at 26-27. The Court went on to hold that, under the Treaty of Versailles, the jurisdiction of the Commission extended to the sections of the Oder tributaries that were situated in Polish territory.

c. The Faber Case

Commission under the Agreement of February 13, 1903 Senate Doc. 316, 58th Cong. 2nd Sess. 1904; JACKSON H. RALSTON, VENEZUELAN ARBITRATIONS OF 1903 600 (GPO 1904)

DUFFIELD, *Umpire*: This is one of several claims which grow out of the suspension of river traffic on the river Zulia by Executive decrees of Venezuela in 1900, 1901, and 1902. The claimant Faber is a German subject who resides and has his place of business in Cúcuta, in Colombia. …

As to the main objection of the Commissioner for Venezuela that her acts in closing the ports in question were fully within the attributes of her sovereignty, the Commissioner for Germany insists to the contrary. In the course of a very able discussion of the question, to which he has brought great research, he maintains:

> To begin, it can not be denied that a sovereign state possesses absolute authority over its rivers and water courses as far as the boundary lines of other states. This principle is nevertheless limited in two ways in international law. When a river is the only route of communication and indispensable to the existence of another state or part of it, its use can not be entirely prohibited.

He also cites Heffter, Puffendorf, Groot, and Vattel, that a state can not deny to another nation without committing an act of hostility, and no state can prevent another from getting its commerce to the market of a third without giving offence and inflicting injury, and he claims "these international maxims whose object is to draw nations together have been at different times embraced in treaties," a number of which he cites, and concludes:

> It must be considered as an international doctrine that the navigation of rivers passing through the territory of several states, together with all their affluent, must be free from the point where they begin to be navigable to the point where they empty into the sea. …

We are met on the threshold of the discussion with the fact that no direct oceanic navigation was interrupted. Physical limitations deprive Colombia of the enjoyment of direct oceanic traffic through Venezuelan territory. No seagoing vessels can thus pass into Colombian territory. All must stop at Maracaibo, where all ocean freight must be reshipped. The case, therefore, is not one in which a foreigner is deprived by the act of Venezuela of the use of waters to which nature has given him direct access. That right Venezuela has not attempted to restrict. She permits him to carry his goods in the vessel in which they entered her territory as far as nature permits him. But the claimant insists that because of the nature of his business he suffers damage because goods are not permitted to be twice reshipped in the territory of Venezuela and thus transported into Colombia. Obviously this is a very different matter. First, it of necessity involves the use of land of Venezuela not incidental to navigation merely, but for the transshipment, carriage, and handling of freight on her shores. Second, it extends the claim of free navigation of rivers to a new case, for which I have found no precedent.

It is one thing for a foreigner to claim, "I have a right to navigation for my vessels wherever natural conditions permit, and Venezuela can not restrict it." But it is quite another thing to claim, "I have a right to send my goods over the inland waters of Venezuela, reshipping them into smaller and smaller vessels as often as the lessening depth of water may require." The question seems to be one of regulating commerce, rather than restricting internal navigation. It also appears that the laws of Venezuela with reference to internal navigation over its rivers and lakes require a nationalization of the vessels engaged therein. They also define interior maritime commerce of coast or river trade to be that which is established between ports and points on the banks of the rivers or shores of Venezuela in national boats with foreign merchandise which has paid duty, or fruits or other productions of the country. Another provision of law requires captains of vessels engaged in this trade to be Venezuelan citizens.

That these provisions were within the proper exercise of Venezuela's sovereignty can not be doubted. It results, therefore, that in the lawful exercise of such sovereignty she has excluded from her internal commerce boats of other nationalities and required even the boats of Venezuelan nationality to be commanded by Venezuelans.

For a considerable period before the decree of September 11, 1900, was issued there were internal political disturbances in the territory tributary to the Catatumbo and Zulia rivers. The relations between Venezuela and Colombia were at the same time seriously strained, and the former complained that revolutionist plans and movements found moral and material support on Colombian territory, which afforded a secure base of operations for them.

In this state of affairs the various decrees complained of were promulgated. It is evident that their purpose was to control the passage of vessels, especially steamers, to and fro between Colombia and Venezuela. The language of some of the decrees intimate fears of hostile forces entering Venezuela in that way. In July, 1901, Gen. Rángel Garbiras had begun his insurrection, which at one time seemed threatening, from Colombia. A part of his forces came into Venezuela by way of the Zulia and Catatumbo rivers. It may be reasonably presumed that this was the cause of the decree of July 29, 1901, revoking the permission given in that of March 4, 1901.

The concrete question, therefore, in the case is whether, under these physical and political conditions, Venezuela had the right to suspend the traffic on these rivers by the closing of these ports. She was in full possession of them and they were actually under her sovereignty. This distinguishes the case from that of the Orinoco Asphalt Company. [Ralston's Report, p. 586.]

As has been shown above, there is no substantial contradiction of authorities as to the rights of a state to regulate, and, if necessary to the peace, safety, and convenience of her own citizens, to prohibit temporarily navigation on rivers which flow to the sea. What is necessary to peace, safety, and convenience of her own citizens she must judge, and it seems to the umpire quite clear that in any case calling for an exercise of that judgment her decision is final. That a case for the exercise of this discretion did exist at the dates of the various decrees complained of is obvious, and in the opinion of the umpire the decision of Venezuela in the premises can not be reviewed by this Commission or any other tribunal. Being of the opinion that the closing of the ports of the Catatumbo and Zulia rivers under the circumstances which existed at the time was a lawful exercise of sovereignty by the Republic of Venezuela, the claim is disallowed. …

The theory of Grotius was that on the establishment of separate property, which he conceived grew by agreement out of an original community of goods, there were reserved for the public benefit certain of the preexisting natural rights, and that one of these was the passage over territory, whether by land or by water, and whether in the form of navigation of rivers for commercial purposes, or of an army over neutral ground, which he held to be an innocent use, the concession of which it was not competent to a nation to refuse.

It is on this doctrine that some writers on international law uphold the principle of the freedom of river navigation. …

It is to be observed that distinctions are drawn by some of the above text writers, some declaring that the right of innocent use is confined to time of peace; others that only the inhabitants of those countries through which the river passes have the right of innocent use, while still others sustain the right without any limitation, save the right of the state to make necessary and proper regulations in respect to the use of the stream within its boundaries.

The theory of Grotius, mentioned above, has been said to be the "root of such legal authority as is now possessed by the principle of the freedom of river navigation." ... It does not appear to have been adopted by the best annotators on international law. Hall says: "It can no longer be accepted as an argumentative starting point." (Hall's Treatise on International Law, p. 139.)

The other theory, also of Grotius, was because the use of rivers belonged to the class of things "*utilitatis innoxiae*," the value of streams being in no way whatever diminished to the proprietors by this innocent use of them by others, inasmuch as the use of them is inexhaustible. …

Most of the advocates of the innocent use of rivers base their claim upon the grounds that the inhabitants of lands traversed by another portion of the stream have a special right of use of the other portions because such use is highly advantageous to them. If the proprietary right of the state to the portion of the river within its boundaries be conceded, as it must be generally, there can be no logical defense of this position. It certainly is a novel proposition that because one may be so situated that the use of the property of another will be of special advantage to him he may on that ground demand such use *as a right*. The rights of an individual are not created or determined by his wants or even his necessities. The starving man who takes the bread of another without right is none the less, a thief, legally, although the immorality of the act is so slight as to justify it. Wants or necessities of individuals can not create legal rights for them, or infringe the existing rights of others.

However, it is no longer to be doubted that the reason of the thing and the opinion of other jurists, spoken generally, seem to agree in holding that the right can only be what is called (however improperly) by Vattel and other writers imperfect, and that the state through whose domain the charge is to be made "*must be the sole judge* as to whether it is innocent or injurious in its character." …

From this review of the authorities it seems that even in respect of rivers capable of navigation by sea-going vessels carrying oceanic commerce the weight of authority sustains the right of Venezuela to make the decrees complained of. But in the opinion of the umpire there are other considerations which control the decision in this case.

If the case before the umpire turned upon this general question of international law, the umpire is inclined to the opinion that he would be compelled to sustain the right of Venezuela to the complete control of navigation of the Catatumbo and Zulia rivers. In his opinion it is not necessary to decide the case on this ground. As has been shown above, there is no contradiction of authority as to the right of Venezuela to regulate, and, if necessary to the peace, safety, or convenience of her own citizens, to prohibit altogether navigation on these rivers. It is also equally without doubt that her judgment in the premises cannot be reviewed by this Commission or any other tribunal. That a case for the exercise of discretion did exist is obvious. …

Notes and Questions

1. Given the inclusive interest in exchange of goods and services with every part of the planet, should there be an inclusive policy in favor of unrestricted innocent passage over international rivers such as those of concern in *Faber*?

2. In most situations, questions of navigation on international rivers have been settled via bilateral or multilateral treaties. In *Faber*, Venezuela's authority to inhibit navigation was affirmed. Would the result have been the same if there had been no threat to Venezuela's security?

2. International Canals

A fundamental international policy with respect to international canals was expressed by the Permanent Court of International Justice in *The S.S. "Wimbledon"* (*see* facts and holding, *infra* at 901): "when an artificial waterway connecting two open seas has been permanently dedicated to the use of the whole world, such waterway is assimilated to natural straits ..." Actual practice with respect to the different canals has not approximated this high standard.

a. The Suez Canal

(1) Convention between Great Britain, Austria-Hungary, France, Germany, Italy, the Netherlands, Russia, Spain, and Turkey, Respecting the Free Navigation of the Suez Maritime Canal

3 Am. J. Int'l L. (Supp.) 123 (1909)

Article 1. The Suez Maritime Canal shall always be free and open, in time of war as in time of peace, to every vessel of commerce or of war, without distinction of flag.

Consequently, the high contracting parties agree not in any way to interfere with the free use of the canal, in time of war as in time of peace.

The canal shall never be subject to the exercise of the right of blockade.

Article 2. The high contracting parties, recognizing that the Fresh-Water Canal is indispensable to the Maritime Canal, take note of the engagements of His Highness the Khedive towards the Universal Suez Canal company as regards the Fresh-Water Canal; which engagements are stipulated in a convention dated 18th March, 1863, containing an exposé and four articles.

They undertake not to interfere in any way with the security of that canal and its branches, the working of which shall not be exposed to any attempt at obstruction.

Article 3. The high contracting parties likewise undertake to respect the plant, establishments, buildings and work of the Maritime Canal and of the Fresh-Water Canal.

Article 4. The Maritime Canal remaining open in time of war as a free passage, even to ships of war of the belligerents, according to the terms of article

I of the present treaty, the high contracting parties agree that no right of war, no act of hostility, nor any act having for its object to obstruct the free navigation of the canal, shall be committed in the canal and its ports of access, as well as within a radius of three marine miles from those ports, even though the Ottoman Empire should be one of the belligerent powers.

Vessels of war of belligerents shall not revictual or take in stores in the canal and its ports of access, except in so far as may be strictly necessary. The transit of the aforesaid vessels through the canal shall be effected with the least possible delay, in accordance with the regulations in force, and without any other intermission than that resulting from the necessities of the service.

Their stay at Port Said and the roadstead of Suez shall not exceed 24 hours, except in case of distress. In such case, they shall be bound to leave as soon as possible. An interval of 24 hours shall always elapse between the sailing of a belligerent ship from one of the ports of access and the departure of a ship belonging to the hostile power.

ARTICLE 5. In time of war belligerent powers shall not disembark nor embark within the canal and its ports of access either troops, munitions, or materials of war. But in case of an accidental hindrance in the canal, men may be embarked or disembarked at the ports of access by detachments not exceeding 1,000 men, with a corresponding amount of war material. …

ARTICLE 14. The high contracting parties agree that the engagements resulting from the present treaty shall not be limited by the duration of the acts of concession of the Universal Suez Canal Company.

NOTES AND QUESTIONS

1. On July 26, 1956, President Nasser of Egypt issued a decree stating that "The Universal Company of the Suez Maritime Canal … is hereby nationalized. All its assets, rights and obligations are transferred to the Nation and all the organizations and committees that now operate its management are hereby dissolved." On August 2, 1956, the U.S., U. K. and France issued a Tripartite Statement stating, *inter alia*, "The present action involves far more than the simple act of nationalization. It involves the arbitrary and unilateral seizure by one nation of an international agency which has the responsibility to maintain and operate the Suez Canal. …" France, the U.K. and Israel invaded Egypt, but were obliged to withdraw by the United Nations, strongly supported by the United States.

Thereafter, Egypt refused passage to vessels coming from Israeli ports. *See* generally JOSÉ OBIETA CHALBAUD, THE INTERNATIONAL STATUS OF THE SUEZ CANAL 110 (The Hague, Nijhoff 1970). At the end of the Six-Day War, Security Council Resolution 242 (1967) affirmed, *inter alia*, "The necessity (a) for guaranteeing freedom of navigation through international waterways in the area." On a number of occasions thereafter, however, the Egyptian government denied passage to states with which it viewed itself at war or some of whose policies it opposed. *Id.* at 130-39.

2. What procedures or adjustments could be taken to insure that the Suez Canal operates in accord with the Convention of Constantinople?

b. Panama Canal

(1) Isthmian Canal Convention

U.S.- Pan., 33 Stat. 2234 (1904)

Article XVIII

The Canal, when constructed, and the entrances thereto shall be neutral in perpetuity, and shall be opened upon the terms provided for by Section I of Article three of, and in conformity with all the stipulations of, the treaty entered into by the Governments of the United States and Great Britain on November 18, 1901.

(2) Treaty Between the United States and Great Britain to Facilitate the Construction of a Ship Canal

Nov.18, 1901 [Hay-Pauncefote Treaty]
U.S.-U.K., 32 Stat. 1903 (1902) Doc. No. 474, 292, at 293-94 (1914)

Article III

The United States adopts, as the basis of the neutralization of such ship canal, the following Rules, substantially as embodied in the Convention of Constantinople, signed the 28th October, 1888, for the free navigation of the Suez Canal, that is to say:

1. The canal shall be free and open to the vessels of commerce and of war of all nations observing these Rules, on terms of entire equality, so that there shall be no discrimination against any such nation, or its citizens or subjects, in respect of the conditions or charges of traffic, or otherwise. Such conditions and charges of traffic shall be just and equitable.

2. The canal shall never be blockaded, nor shall any right of war be exercised nor any act of hostility be committed within it. The United States, however, shall be at liberty to maintain such military police along the canal as may be necessary to protect it against lawlessness and disorder.

3. Vessels of war of a belligerent shall not revictual nor take any stores in the canal except so far as may be strictly necessary; and the transit of such vessels through the canal shall be effected with the least possible delay in accordance with the Regulations in force, and with only such intermission as may result from the necessities of the service.

Prizes shall be in all respects subject to the same Rules as vessels of war of the belligerents.

4. No belligerent shall embark or disembark troops, munitions of war, or warlike materials in the canal, except in case of accidental hindrance of the transit, and in such case the transit shall be resumed with all possible dispatch.

5. The provisions of this Article shall apply to waters adjacent to the canal, within 3 marine miles of either end. Vessels of war of a belligerent shall not remain in such waters longer than twenty-four hours at any one time, except in

case of distress, and in such case shall depart as soon as possible; but a vessel of war of one belligerent shall not depart within twenty-four hours from the departure of a vessel of war of the other belligerent.

6. The plant, establishments, buildings, and all works necessary to the construction, maintenance, and operation of the canal shall be deemed to be part thereof, for the purposes of this Treaty, and in time of war, as in time of peace, shall enjoy complete immunity from attack or injury by belligerents, and from acts calculated to impair their usefulness as part of the canal.

Notes and Questions

1. The Isthmian Canal Convention, *supra*, was revised for the first time in 1936. The United States withdrew its guarantee of Panama's independence which had been embodied in Article 1, raised the annual payments to $430,000 per year, and agreed to bar all commercial enterprise within the Canal Zone except that directly concerned with shipping. (U.S.T.S. No. 945.) In 1955 a second revision increased the annual payment to $1,930,000, transferred millions of dollars of real estate to Panama, guaranteed equal pay and opportunity to non-citizen employees, and made other concessions to Panama. [Treaty in 32 Dept. of State Bull. 238 (1955)] In 1960 the United States informed Panama that in recognition of the titular sovereignty residing in the Republic of Panama with respect to the Canal Zone, the Panamanian flag "will hereafter be flown together with the United States flag on a daily basis. ..." (See Text of Note, 43 State Dept. Bull. 558 (1960).) The Note added that this action in no way modified previous treaties and agreements in force between the United States and Panama.

2. In 1977, the United States and Panama concluded a new "Panama Canal Treaty" providing for the phased return of the Canal to Panama with certain reserved rights during the transition for the United States. 1280 U.N.T.S. 4.

3. With respect to the issue of neutrality of the Panama Canal, consider the following commentary by Dr. Mohamed Y. Olwan:

> By Article I of the Treaty concerning the Permanent Neutrality and Operation of the Panama Canal, Panama declared that the canal would be permanently neutral. It would remain open in peace time and in war time to the peaceful passage of vessels of all nations without discrimination. Nevertheless, Article VI (1) provided for an exception to the equality of treatment rule. By that article, U.S. and Panamanian warships and auxiliary vessels had the right to pass through the Canal at the greatest speed. The interpretative declaration of the two Heads of State of 14 October 1977 makes it clear that this stipulation grants preferential treatment to the ships of the Contracting Parties, which may, in case of need or urgency, traverse the Canal ahead of all other shipping. However, warships and auxiliary ships of all nations are entitled to use the Canal at all times without having to submit to inspection, investigation or surveillance and without having to declare their births, origin, armaments, cargo or destination.

Mohamed Olwan, *International Canals, in* INTERNATIONAL LAW, ACHIEVEMENTS AND PROSPECTS 1011 (Bedjaoui, ed., U.N. Educational 1991).

c. The Kiel Canal

The Treaty of Peace with Germany after World War I established an international regime for the Kiel Canal.

(1) The Treaty of Versailles

June 28, 1919, 13 Am. J. Int'l L. Supp. 359-361 (1919)

Article 380

The Kiel Canal and its approaches shall be maintained free and open to the vessels of commerce and of war of all nations at peace with Germany on terms of entire equality.

Article 381

The nationals, property and vessels of all Powers shall, in respect of charges, facilities, and in all other respects, be treated on a footing of perfect equality in the use of the Canal, no distinction being made to the detriment of nationals, property and vessels of any Power between them and the nationals, property and vessels of Germany or of the most favoured nation.

No impediment shall be placed on the movement of persons or vessels other than those arising out of police, customs, sanitary, emigration or immigration regulations and those relating to the import or export of prohibited goods. Such regulations must be reasonable and uniform and must not unnecessarily impede traffic.

Article 382

Only such charges may be levied on vessels using the Canal or its approaches as are intended to cover in an equitable manner the cost of maintaining in a navigable condition, or of improving, the Canal or its approaches, or to meet expenses incurred in the interests of navigation. The schedule of such charges shall be calculated on the basis of such expenses, and shall be posted up in the ports.

These charges shall be levied in such a manner as to render any detailed examination of cargoes unnecessary, except in the case of suspected fraud or contravention.

Article 383

Goods in transit may be placed under seal or in the custody of customs agents; the loading and unloading of goods, and the embarkation and disembarkation of passengers, shall only take place in the ports specified by Germany.

Article 384

No charges of any kind other than those provided for in the present Treaty shall be levied along the course or at the approaches of the Kiel Canal.

Article 385

Germany shall be bound to take suitable measures to remove any obstacle or danger to navigation, and to ensure the maintenance of good conditions of navigation. She shall not undertake any works of a nature to impede navigation on the canal or its approaches.

Article 386

In the event of violation of any of the conditions of Articles 380 to 386, or of disputes as to the interpretation of these Articles, any interested Power can appeal to the jurisdiction instituted for the purpose by the League of Nations. ...

NOTES AND QUESTIONS

1. In *The S.S. "Wimbledon"*, *infra*, at 785,901, the Permanent Court of International Justice declared that the Kiel Canal was assimilated to the status of natural straits.

2. In 1936, Germany denounced the clause of the Treaty of Versailles and established a new regime under which the passage of foreign warships needed prior German authorization. 1 OPPENHEIM'S INTERNATIONAL LAW 595 (Robert Jennings & Arthur Watts eds., 9th ed. Longman 1992).

3. International Lakes

a. The Lake Lanoux Arbitration *(Fr. v. Spain)*

12 R.I.A.A. 281 (1957), 24 I.L.R. 101 (1957)

[Lake Lanoux is situated on the southern slope of the Pyrenees and on the territory of the French Republic, in the Department of the Eastern-Pyrenees. It is fed by streams, all of which arise in and cross only French territory. Its waters flow out only through the stream called Font-Vive, which is one of the sources of the Carol River. This river, after flowing about 25 kilometers in French territory, counting from Lake Lanoux, crosses the Spanish border at Puigcerda and continues to flow in Spain for about six kilometers before joining the River Sègre, which empties into the Ebro. Before entering Spain, the waters of the Carol feed the canal of Puigcerda which is privately owned by that Spanish town. An Additional Act to the Boundary Treaties concluded December 1, 1856, April 14, 1862 and May 26, 1866, signed at Bayonne, May 26, 1866, provided:]

> *Article* 9: For watercourses which flow from one Country to the other, or which constitute a boundary, each Government recognizes, subject to the exercise of a right of verification when appropriate, the legality of irrigations, of works and of enjoyment for domestic uses currently existing in the other State, by virtue of concession, title or prescription, with the reservation that only that volume of water necessary to satisfy actual needs will be used, that abuses must be eliminated, and that this recognition will in no way injure the respective rights of the Governments to authorize works of public utility, on condition that proper compensation is paid.
>
> *Article* 10: If, after having satisfied the actual needs of users recognized on each side as regular, there remains at low tide water available where the frontier is crossed, such water will be shared in advance between the two countries, in proportion to the areas of the irrigable lands belonging to the immediate respective riparian owners, *minus* land already irrigated.

Article 11: When in one of the two States it is proposed to construct works or to grant new concessions which might change the regime or the volume of a watercourse of which the lower or opposite part is being used by the riparian owners of the other country, prior notice will be given to the highest administrative authority of the Department or of the Province to which such riparian owners are subject by the corresponding authority in the jurisdiction where such projects are proposed, so that, if they might threaten the rights of the riparian owners of the adjoining Sovereignty, a claim may be lodged in due time with the competent authorities, and thus the interests that may be involved on both sides will be safeguarded. If the work and concessions are to take place in a *Commune* contiguous to the border, the engineers of the other Country will have the option, upon proper notice given to them reasonably in advance, of inspecting the site with those in charge of it.

[The French project for the development of Lake Lanoux includes the following features:

Without changing the sources and streams which presently feed the lake, it would be transformed, notably, by the construction of a barrage in such a manner as to accumulate a quantity of water which will increase its capacity from 17 to 70 million cubic meters. The waters of the lake flowing out naturally by a stream which is a tributary of the Carol and from there toward Spain would normally cease to follow this course. They would be used for the production of electric energy by a diversion which would conduct them to the Ariège, a tributary of the Garonne. These waters would therefore flow into the Atlantic Ocean and no longer into the Mediterranean. To compensate for this withdrawal of the waters feeding the Carol, an underground tunnel for their restitution would conduct a part of the waters of the Ariege to the Carol, to which river they would be returned on French territory upstream from the intake of the Puigcerda Canal.

This project therefore proposes the construction of a large reservoir on the very favorable site of Lake Lanoux, and proposes to utilize the waters of this basin under a great vertical drop and to return to the Carol, by borrowing from the Ariège, a volume of water equal to that which is contributed to Lake Lanoux by the natural sources and streams.] …

3. The present dispute can be reduced to two fundamental questions:

(A). Do the works for utilizing the waters of Lake Lanoux in the conditions laid down in the French scheme and proposals mentioned in the Preamble of the *Compromis*, constitute an infringement of the rights of Spain recognized by the principal provisions of the Treaty of Bayonne of May 26, 1866 and the Additional Act of the same date?

(B). If the reply to the preceding question be negative, does the execution of said works constitute an infringement of the provisions of the Treaty of Bayonne of May 26, 1866, and of the Additional Act of the same date, because those provisions would in any event make such execution subject to a prior agreement between the two Governments or because other rules of Article 11 of the Additional Act concerning dealings between the two Governments have not been observed?

[The first question was answered in the negative.]

As to question (B):

10. In the *Compromis,* the Spanish Government had already declared that, in its opinion, the French scheme required for its execution 'the previous agreement of both Governments, in the absence of which the country making the proposal is not at liberty to undertake the works'.

In the written as well as oral proceedings, that Government developed this point of view, completing it by the recital of the principles which ought to govern dealings leading to such prior agreement. Two obligations, therefore, would seem to rest upon the State which desires to undertake the works envisaged, the most important being to reach a prior agreement with the other interested State; …

The argument put forward by the Spanish Government is stated on two planes—the Spanish Government takes its stand, on the one hand, on the Treaty and the Additional Act, on the other hand on the system of *faceries* or *compascuites* which exists on the Pyrenean frontier, as well as on the rules of international common law. The two latter sources would permit, first of all, the interpretation of the Treaty and the Additional Act of 1866, and then, in a larger perspective, the demonstration of the existence of an unwritten general rule of international law. The latter (it is contended) has precedents which would permit its establishment in the traditions of the system of *faceries,* in the provisions of the Pyrenean Treaties and in the international practice of States in the matter of the industrial use of international watercourses.

11. Before proceeding to an examination of the Spanish argument, the Tribunal believes it will be useful to make some very general observations on the very nature of the obligations invoked against the French Government. To admit that jurisdiction in a certain field can no longer be exercised except on the condition of, or by way of, an agreement between two States, is to place an essential restriction on the sovereignty of a State, and such restriction could only be admitted if there were clear and convincing evidence. Without doubt, international practice does reveal some special cases in which this hypothesis has become reality; thus, sometimes two States exercise conjointly jurisdiction over certain territories (joint ownership, *co-imperium*, or *condominium*); likewise, in certain international arrangements, the representatives of States exercise conjointly a certain jurisdiction in the name of the States or in the name of the organizations. But these cases are exceptional, and international judicial decisions are slow to recognize their existence, especially when they impair the territorial sovereignty of a State, as would be the case in the present matter.

In effect, in order to appreciate in its essence the necessity for prior agreement, one must envisage the hypothesis in which the interested States cannot reach agreement. In such a case, it must be admitted that the State which is normally competent has lost its right to act alone as a result of the unconditional and arbitrary opposition of another State. This amounts to admitting a 'right of assent', a 'right of veto', which at the discretion of one State paralyzes the exercise of the territorial jurisdiction of another.

That is why international practice prefers to resort to less extreme solutions by confining itself to obliging the States to seek, by preliminary negotiations, terms for an agreement, without subordinating the exercise of their competences to the conclusion of such an agreement. Thus, one speaks, although often inaccurately, of the 'obligation of negotiating an agreement'. In reality, the engagements thus undertaken by States take very diverse forms and have a scope which varies according to the manner in which they are defined and according to the procedures intended for their execution; but the reality of the obligations thus undertaken is incontestable and sanctions can be applied in the event, for example, of an unjustified breaking off of the discussions, abnormal delays, disregard of the agreed procedures, systematic refusals to take into consideration adverse proposals or interests, and, more generally, in cases of violation of the rules of good faith (*Tacna-Arica Arbitration: Reports of International Arbitral Awards*, vol. 11, pp. 921, *et seq.; Case of Railway Traffic between Lithuania and Poland*: P.C.I.J., Series A/B No. 42, pp. 108, *et seq.*).

In the light of these general observations, and in relation to the present case, we will now examine in turn whether a prior agreement is necessary and whether the other rules laid down by Article 11 of the Additional Act have been observed.

...

A. The necessity for a prior agreement ...

13. The Spanish Government endeavoured to establish similarly the content of current positive international law. Certain principles which it demonstrates are, assuming the demonstration to be accepted, of no interest for the problem now under examination. Thus, if it is admitted that there is a principle which prohibits the upstream State from altering the waters of a river in such a fashion as seriously to prejudice the downstream State, such a principle would have no application to the present case, because it has been admitted by the Tribunal, in connection with the first question examined above, that the French scheme will not alter the waters of the Carol. In fact, States are today perfectly conscious of the importance of conflicting interests brought into play by the industrial use of international rivers, and of the necessity to reconcile them by mutual concessions. The only way to arrive at such compromises of interests is to conclude agreements on an increasingly comprehensive basis. International practice reflects the conviction that States ought to strive to conclude such agreements: there would thus appear to be an obligation to accept in good faith all communications and contacts which could, by a broad comparison of interests and by reciprocal good

will, provide States with the best conditions for concluding agreements. This point will be referenced to again later on, when enquiring what obligations rest on France and Spain in connection with the contracts and the communications preceding the putting in hand of a scheme such as that relating to Lake Lanoux.

But international practice does not so far permit more than the following conclusion: the rule that States may utilize the hydraulic power of international watercourses only on condition of a *prior* agreement between the interested States cannot be established as a custom, even less as a general principle of law. The history of the formulation of the multilateral Convention signed at Geneva of December 9, 1923, relative to the Development of Hydraulic Power Affecting More than One State, is very characteristic in this connection. The initial project was based on the obligatory and paramount character of agreements whose purpose was to harness the hydraulic forces of international watercourses. But this formulation was rejected, and the Convention, in its final form, provides (Article 1) that

> [The present Convention] in no way alters the freedom of each State, within the framework of international law, to carry out on its territory all operations for the development of hydraulic power which it desires;

there is provided only an obligation upon the interested signatory States to join in a common study of a development programme; the execution of this programme is obligatory only for those States which have formally subscribed to it.

Customary international law, like the traditional Law of the Pyrenees, does not supply evidence of a kind to orient the interpretation of the Treaty and of the Additional Act of 1866 in the direction of favouring the necessity for prior agreement; even less does it permit us to conclude that there exists a general principle of law or a custom to this effect.

14. As between Spain and France, the existence of a rule requiring prior agreement for the development of the water resources of an international watercourse can therefore result only from a Treaty. ...

24. In the case of Lake Lanoux, France has maintained to the end the solution which consists in diverting the waters of the Carol to the Ariège with full restitution. By making this choice France is only making use of a right; the development works of Lake Lanoux are on French territory, the financing of and responsibility for the enterprise fall upon France, and France alone is the judge of works of public utility which are to be executed on her own territory, save for the provisions of Articles 9 and 10 of the Additional Act, which, however, the French scheme does not infringe.

On her side, Spain may not invoke a right to insist on a development of Lake Lanoux based on the needs of Spanish agriculture. In effect, if France were to renounce all of the works envisaged on her territory, Spain could not demand that other works in conformity to her wishes be carried out. Therefore, she can only urge her interests to obtain, within the framework of the scheme decided upon by France, terms which reasonably safeguard them.

It remains to be established whether this requirement has been fulfilled.

In whatever fashion one regards the course of dealings covering the period 1917-1954, it is beyond doubt that the French position became very flexible and even transformed. From a promise of compensation but without restoration of diverted water, it passed to a partial restoration; then, in 1954, to complete restoration. In 1955, in the proposals which are an integral part of the scheme itself, France added to complete restoration the guarantee of a minimum restoration of 20 million cubic metres; that offer was possible only within the framework of the diversion of water from the Atlantic into the Mediterranean, since, moreover, France was going to ensure the complete restoration of the waters of the Carol. In 1956, at the time of the second meeting of experts, in March, France made two new proposals to Spain. The restoring of the water by the French, instead of following the rhythm of the natural feeding of Lake Lanoux, would be modified according to the needs of Spanish agriculture; during the irrigation period, all the water would be diverted into the Carol while during the winter period, on the other hand, France would reduce the flow so as to ensure over the year an equality of water diverted and restored (a system known as 'running account of water'). On the other hand, an inter-annual reserve would permit Spain to draw from a supplementary source in an exceptionally dry year (Annex 11 of the French Memorial, p. 147). On March 5, 1956, the president of the Spanish delegation replied, according to the *procès-verbal*, as follows:

> The new proposals formulated by the French delegation cannot be taken into consideration because any solution which pre-supposes the diversion of the waters of Lake Lanoux out of their natural course is unacceptable to Spain. He adds that the attitude of the Spanish delegation does not result from a desire to obtain compensation either by an increase in volume of water guaranteeing Spanish irrigation or by more electric energy, so that it is quite useless to discuss the volume of water proposed by way of compensation, seeing that there is no agreement on the basic question. (French Memorial, p. 156).

When one examines the question of whether France, either in the course of the dealings or in her proposals, has taken Spanish interests into sufficient consideration, it must be stressed how closely linked together are the obligation to take into consideration, in the course of negotiations, adverse interests and the obligation to give a reasonable place to these interests in the solution finally adopted. A State which has conducted negotiations with understanding and good faith in accordance with Article 11 of the Additional Act is not relieved from giving a reasonable place to adverse interests in the solution it adopts simply because the conversations have been interrupted, even though owing to the intransigence of its partner. Conversely, in determining the manner in which a scheme has taken into consideration the interests involved, the way in which negotiations have developed, the total number of the interests which have been presented, the price which each Party was ready to pay to have those interests safeguarded, are all essential factors in establishing, with regard to the obligations set out in Article 11 of the Additional Act, the merits of this scheme.

Having regard to all the circumstances of the case, set out above, the Tribunal is of the opinion that the French scheme complies with the obligations of Article 11 of the Additional Act.

For these reasons:

The Tribunal decides to reply affirmatively to the question set out in the first Article of the *Compromis*. In carrying out, without prior agreement between the two Governments, works for the utilization of the waters of Lake Lanoux in the conditions mentioned in the Scheme for the Utilization of the Waters of Lake Lanoux notified to the Governor of the Province of Gerona on January 21, 1954, and brought to the notice of the representatives of Spain on the Commission for the Pyrenees at its session held from November 3 to 14, 1955, and according to the proposals submitted by the French delegation to the Special Mixed Commission on December 13, 1955, the French Government was not committing a breach of the provisions of the Treaty of Bayonne of May 26, 1866, and the Additional Act of the same date.

b. Convention on the Law of the Non-navigational Uses of International Watercourses

U.N. GAOR, 51st Sess., Supp. No. 49, U.N. Doc. A/Res/51/229 Annex (1997)

Article 1: *Scope of the present Convention*

1. The present Convention applies to uses of international watercourses and of their waters for purposes other than navigation and to measures of protection, preservation and management related to the uses of those watercourses and their waters.

2. The uses of international watercourses for navigation is not within the scope of the present Convention except insofar as other uses affect navigation or are affected by navigation.

Article 2: *Use of terms*

For the purposes of the present Convention:

(a) "Watercourse" means a system of surface waters and groundwaters constituting by virtue of their physical relationship a unitary whole and normally flowing into a common terminus;

(b) "International watercourse" means a watercourse, parts of which are situated in different States; ...

Article 5: *Equitable and reasonable utilization and participation*

1. Watercourse States shall in their respective territories utilize an international watercourse in an equitable and reasonable manner. In particular, an international watercourse shall be used and developed by watercourse States with a view to attaining optimal and sustainable utilization thereof and benefits therefrom, taking into account the interests of the watercourse States concerned, consistent with adequate protection of the watercourse.

2. Watercourse States shall participate in the use, development and protection of an international watercourse in an equitable and reasonable manner. Such participation includes both the right to utilize the watercourse and the duty to cooperate in the protection and development thereof, as provided in the present Convention.

Article 6: *Factors relevant to equitable and reasonable utilization*

1. Utilization of an international watercourse in an equitable and reasonable manner within the meaning of article 5 requires taking into account all relevant factors and circumstances, including:

(a) Geographic, hydrographic, hydrological, climatic, ecological and other factors of a natural character;

(b) The social and economic needs of the watercourse States concerned;

(c) The population dependent on the watercourse in each watercourse State;

(d) The effects of the use or uses of the watercourses in one watercourse State on other watercourse States;

(e) Existing and potential uses of the watercourse;

(f) Conservation, protection, development and economy of use of the water resources of the watercourse and the costs of measures taken to that effect;

(g) The availability of alternatives, of comparable value, to a particular planned or existing use.

2. In the application of article 5 or paragraph 1 of this article, watercourse States concerned shall, when the need arises, enter into consultations in a spirit of cooperation.

3. The weight to be given to each factor is to be determined by its importance in comparison with that of other relevant factors. In determining what is a reasonable and equitable use, all relevant factors are to be considered together and a conclusion reached on the basis of the whole.

Article 7: *Obligation not to cause significant harm*

1. Watercourse States shall, in utilizing an international watercourse in their territories, take all appropriate measures to prevent the causing of significant harm to other watercourse States.

2. Where significant harm nevertheless is caused to another watercourse State, the States whose use causes such harm shall, in the absence of agreement to such use, take all appropriate measures, having due regard for the provisions of articles 5 and 6, in consultation with the affected State, to eliminate or mitigate such harm and, where appropriate, to discuss the question of compensation.

NOTES AND QUESTIONS

1. For further information, *see* the International Law Commission Commentaries to the Draft Articles on the Law of the Non-navigational Uses of International Watercourses, [1994] Y.B.INT'L L. COMM'N, pt. 2 at 88-135.

2. What is the relationship between Articles 5 and 7 of the Convention on the Non-navigational Uses of International Watercourses? In case of conflict, which article prevails?

3. What kind of an obligation is created under Articles 5 and 7? Obligation of conduct or obligation of result?

4. What does equitable utilization mean? Is it compatible with optimal utilization as required by Article 5(1) of the Convention?

III. Land

A. CHARACTERISTICS AND POLICIES

1. Myres S. McDougal, Harold D. Lasswell, Ivan A.Vlasic & Joseph C. Smith, *The Enjoyment of and Acquisition of Resources in Outer Space*

111 U. PA. L. REV. 521, 573-4 (1963)

The factors which have influenced decisions favoring exclusive enjoyment with respect to the territorial sea, the airspace over land masses, internal rivers, and the land mass of the Arctic are inseparably connected with the factors which have influenced comparable decision with respect to the land masses of the Earth. Hence we first examine the latter and then briefly note the former.

1. Physical Characteristics

The most significant difference between the land masses and other spatial-extension resources is that the land masses are relatively solid, while the other resources, except for parts of the polar regions, lack this quality. This relative solidity of the land masses has of course facilitated the establishment of permanent sedentary communities with exclusive claim. Another significant difference is the fact that the land masses are filled with natural barriers such as mountain ranges, streams, bodies of water, deserts, and forests. These barriers have had the effect of reinforcing the parochial nature of organizations arising from blood, family, and racial ties, and thus intensifying man's tendency to organize into territorial communities. Such natural barriers do not, in contrast, exist in the other spatial-extension resources, and with technological development these resources have become avenues of, rather than roadblocks to, communication and movement. Although transportation modalities of the modern era have now in some areas of the world overcome these barriers, the social organization of mankind into territorial communities has been much too firmly established to be suddenly changed.

2. Participants

The participants in the process of acquisition of the land masses of the Earth have been from prehistoric times organized together upon the basis of first family, then tribal and racial, and finally cultural ties, and inherent in this structure has been the exclusion of the stranger and groups not sharing these common characteristics. Thus, the land masses slowly became organized along territorial rather than functional lines.

3. Objectives

The objectives of the participants with respect to the land masses have been largely parochial and exclusive. Minimum order has been sought through the exclusion of the stranger and the strengthening of identifications along territorial lines, thus favoring exclusive decision. The achievement of optimum order has been sought in terms of the individual community rather than on a regional or global scale, consequently objectives in this regard have often been exclusive rather than inclusive.

4. Situations

Probably the most important factor influencing developments favorable to exclusivity has been that much of the land masses of the Earth are in a geographical relationship with other resources which facilitates a sedentary type of social structure. Where land is rich in stock and flow resources, the relevant uses of the land are commonly of a more permanent nature than in the cases of other areas of land masses, such as deserts, or of other spatial-extension resources, such as the oceans or airspace. A vessel or aircraft may quickly pass over the oceans or through the airspace; but, in the case of land, the houses, communities, and cities are so constructed as to make it impossible for the same space to be used by other participants. Where most territorial communities have developed, there have been a plentiful supply of water, moderate temperature, a variety of plant and animal life, rich supplies of stock resources, such as minerals and soil nutrients, and naturally a breathable atmosphere. Under such circumstances the spatial-extension quality of the land mass has been subordinated to the enjoyment and development of the various resources which it contains.

B. ACQUISITION

1. Effective Occupation and Effectivités

a. Island of Palmas Case (U.S. v. Neth.)

2 R.I.A.A. 829 (1928)

Max HUBER, Arbitrator: ... The *subject of the dispute* is the sovereignty over the Island of Palmas (or Miangas). The Island in question is indicated with precision in the preamble to the Special Agreement, its latitude and longitude being specified. The fact that in the diplomatic correspondence prior to the conclusion of the Special Agreement, and in the documents of the arbitration proceedings, the United States refer to the "Island of Palmas" and the Netherlands to the "Island of Miangas", does not therefore concern the identity of the subject of the dispute. Such difference concerns only the question whether certain assertions made by the Netherlands Government really relate to the island described in the Special Agreement or another island or group of islands which might be designated by the name of Miangas or a similar name.

It results from the evidence produced by either side that Palmas (or Miangas) is a single, isolated island, not one of several islands clustered together. It lies about half way between Cape San Augustin (Mindanao, Philippine Islands) and the most northerly island of the Nanusa (Nanoesa) group (Netherlands East Indies).

[The dispute originated with a visit to the Island by General Leonard Wood of the U.S., on January 21, 1906. That visit was regarded as the first contact with the Island by American authorities.

As a result of that visit, the U.S. considered the Island to be included in the Philippine Island archipelago, as delimited by Article III of the 1898 Peace Treaty between the U.S. and Spain. The Netherlands considered the Island to be part of their East Indies possessions.] ...

The claim of the United States to sovereignty over the Island of Palmas (or Miangas) is derived from Spain by way of cession under the Treaty of Paris. The latter Treaty, though it comprises the island in dispute within the limits of cession, and in spite of the absence of any reserves or protest by the Netherlands as to these limits, has not created in favour of the United States any title of sovereignty such as was not already vested in Spain. The essential point is therefore to decide whether Spain had sovereignty over Palmas (or Miangas) at the time of the coming into force of the Treaty of Paris.

The United States base their claim on the titles of discovery, of recognition by treaty and of contiguity, i.e. titles relating to acts or circumstances leading to the acquisition of sovereignty; they have however not established the fact that sovereignty so acquired was effectively displayed at any time.

The Netherlands on the contrary found their claim to sovereignty essentially on the title of peaceful and continuous display of State authority over the island.

Since this title would in international law prevail over a title of acquisition of sovereignty not followed by actual display of State authority, it is necessary to ascertain in the first place, whether the contention of the Netherlands is sufficiently established by evidence, and, if so, for what period of time.

In the opinion of the Arbitrator the Netherlands have succeeded in establishing the following facts:

a. The Island of Palmas (or Miangas) is identical with an island designated by this or a similar name, which has formed, at least since 1700, successively a part of two of the native States of the Island of Sangi (Talautse Isles).

b. These native States were from 1677 onwards connected with the East India Company, and thereby with the Netherlands, by contracts of suzerainty, which conferred upon the suzerain such powers as would justify his considering the vassal State as a part of his territory.

c. Acts characteristic of State authority exercised either by the vassal State or by the suzerain Power in regard precisely to the Island of Palmas (or Miangas) have been established as occurring at different epochs between 1700 and 1898, as well as in the period between 1898 and 1906.

The acts of indirect or direct display of Netherlands sovereignty at Palmas (or Miangas), especially in the 18th and early 19th centuries are not numerous, and there are considerable gaps in the evidence of continuous display. But apart from the consideration that the manifestations of sovereignty over a small and distant island, inhabited only by natives, cannot be expected to be frequent, it is not necessary that the display of sovereignty should go back to a very far distant period. It may suffice that such display existed in 1898, and had already existed as continuous and peaceful before that date long enough to enable any Power who might have considered herself as possessing sovereignty over the island, or having a claim to sovereignty, to have, according to local conditions, a reasonable possibility for ascertaining the existence of a state of things contrary to her real or alleged rights.

It is not necessary that the display of sovereignty should be established as having begun at a precise epoch; it suffices that it had existed at the critical period preceding the year 1898. It is quite natural that the establishment of sovereignty may be the outcome of a slow evolution, of a progressive intensification of State control. This is particularly the case, if sovereignty is acquired by the establishment of the suzerainty of a colonial Power over a native State, and in regard to outlying possessions of such a vassal State.

Now the evidence relating to the period after the middle of the 19th century makes it clear that the Netherlands Indian Government considered the island distinctly as a part of its possessions and that, in the years immediately preceding 1898, an intensification of display of sovereignty took place.

Since the moment when the Spaniards, in withdrawing from the Moluccas in 1666, made express reservations as to the maintenance of their sovereign rights, up to the contestation made by the United States in 1906, no contestation or other action whatever or protest against the exercise of territorial rights by the Netherlands over the Talautse (Sangi) Isles and their dependencies (Miangas included) has been recorded. The peaceful character of the display of Netherlands sovereignty for the entire period to which the evidence concerning acts of display relates (1700-1906) must be admitted.

There is moreover no evidence which would establish any act of display of sovereignty over the island by Spain or another Power, such as might counterbalance or annihilate the manifestations of Netherlands sovereignty. As to third Powers, the evidence submitted to the Tribunal does not disclose any trace of such action, at least from the middle of the 17th century onwards. These circumstances, together with the absence of any evidence of a conflict between Spanish and Netherlands authorities during more than two centuries as regards Palmas (or Miangas), are an indirect proof of the exclusive display of Netherlands sovereignty.

This being so, it remains to be considered first whether the display of State authority might not be legally defective and therefore unable to create a valid title of sovereignty, and secondly whether the United States may not put forward a better title to that of the Netherlands.

As to the conditions of acquisition of sovereignty by way of continuous and peaceful display of State authority (so-called prescription), some of which have been discussed in the United States Counter-Memorandum, the following must be said:

The display has been open and public, that is to say that it was in conformity with usages as to exercise of sovereignty over colonial States. A clandestine exercise of State authority over an inhabited territory during a considerable length of time would seem to be impossible. An obligation for the Netherlands to notify to other Powers the establishment of suzerainty over the Sangi States or of the display of sovereignty in these territories did not exist.

Such notification, like any other formal act, can only be the condition of legality as a consequence of an explicit rule of law. A rule of this kind adopted by the Powers in 1885 for the African continent does not apply *de plano* to other regions, and thus the contract with Taruna of 1885, or with Kandahar-Taruna of 1889, even if they were to be considered as the first assertions of sovereignty over Palmas (or Miangas) would not be subject to the rule of notification.

There can further be no doubt that the Netherlands exercised the State authority over the Sangi States as sovereign in their own right, not under a derived or precarious title.

Finally it is to be observed that the question whether the establishment of the Dutch on the Talautse Isles (Sangi) in 1677 was a violation of the Treaty of

Münster and whether this circumstance might have prevented the acquisition of sovereignty even by means of prolonged exercise of State authority, need not be examined, since the Treaty of Utrecht recognized the state of things existing in 1714 and therefore the suzerain right of the Netherlands over Tabukan and Miangas.

The conditions of acquisition of sovereignty by the Netherlands are therefore to be considered as fulfilled. It remains now to be seen whether the United States as successors of Spain are in a position to bring forward an equivalent or stronger title. This is to be answered in the negative.

The title of discovery, if it had not been already disposed of by the Treaties of Münster and Utrecht would, under the most favourable and most extensive interpretation, exist only as an inchoate title, as a claim to establish sovereignty by effective occupation. An inchoate title however cannot prevail over a definite title founded on continuous and peaceful display of sovereignty.

The title of contiguity, understood as a basis of territorial sovereignty, has no foundation in international law.

The title of recognition by treaty does not apply, because even if the Sangi States, with the dependency of Miangas, are to be considered as "held and possessed" by Spain in 1648, the rights of Spain to be derived from the Treaty of Münster would have been superseded by those which were acquired by the Treaty of Utrecht. Now if there is evidence of a state of possession in 1714 concerning the island of Palmas (or Miangas), such evidence is exclusively in favour of the Netherlands. But even if the Treaty of Utrecht could not be taken into consideration, the acquiescence of Spain in the situation created after 1677 would deprive her and her successors of the possibility of still invoking conventional rights at the present time.

The Netherlands title of sovereignty, acquired by continuous and peaceful display of State authority during a long period of time going probably back beyond the year 1700, therefore holds good.

The same conclusion would be reached, if for argument's sake, it were admitted that the evidence laid before the Tribunal in conformity with the rules governing the present procedure did not—as it is submitted by the United States—suffice to establish continuous and peaceful display of sovereignty over the Island of Palmas (or Miangas). In this case no Party would have established its claims to sovereignty over the Island and the decision of the Arbitrator would have to be founded on the relative strength of the titles invoked by each Party.

A solution on this ground would be necessary under the Special Agreement. The terms adopted by the Parties in order to determine the point to be decided by the Arbitrator (Article I) presuppose for the present case that the Island of Palmas (or Miangas) can belong only either to the United States or to the Netherlands, and must form in its entirety a part of the territory either of the one or of the other of these two Powers, Parties to the dispute. For since, according to the terms of its Preamble, the Agreement of January 23rd, 1925, has for object to "terminate" the dispute, it is the evident will of the Parties that the arbitral award shall not conclude by a "non liquet", but shall in any event decide that the island forms a part of the territory of one or the other of two litigant Powers.

The possibility for the Arbitrator to found his decision on the relative strength of the titles invoked on either side must have been envisaged by the Parties to the Special Agreement, because it was to be foreseen that the evidence produced as regards sovereignty over a territory in the circumstances of the island in dispute might prove not to be sufficient to lead to a clear conclusion as to the existence of sovereignty.

For the reasons given above, no presumption in favour of Spanish sovereignty can be based on international law on the titles invoked by the United States as successors of Spain. Therefore, there would not be sufficient grounds for deciding the case in favour of the United States, even if it were admitted, in accordance with their submission, that the evidence produced by the Netherlands in support of their claim either does not relate to the Island in dispute or does not suffice to establish a continuous display of State authority over the island. For, in any case, the exercise of some acts of State authority and the existence of external signs of sovereignty, e.g. flags and coat of arms, has been proved by the Netherlands, even if the Arbitrator were to retain only such evidence as can, in view of the trustworthy and sufficiently accurate nautical observations given to support it, concern solely the island of Palmas (or Miangas), namely that relating to the visits of the steamer *Raaf* in 1895, of H.M.S. *Edi* in 1898 and of General Wood in 1906.

These facts at least constitute a beginning of establishment of sovereignty by continuous and peaceful display of State authority, or a commencement of occupation of an island not yet forming a part of the territory of a State; and such a state of things would create in favour of the Netherlands an inchoate title for completing the conditions of sovereignty. Such inchoate title, based on display of State authority, would, in the opinion of the Arbitrator, prevail over an inchoate title derived from discovery, especially if this latter title has been left for a very long time without completion by occupation; and it would equally prevail over any claim which, in equity, might be deduced from the notion of contiguity. International law, like law in general, has the object of assuring the coexistence of different interests which are worthy of legal protection. If, as in the present instance, only one of two conflicting interests is to prevail, because sovereignty can be attributed to but one of the Parties, the interest which involves the maintenance of a state of things having offered at the critical time to the inhabitants of the disputed territory and to other States a certain guarantee for the respect of their rights ought, in doubt, to prevail over an interest which—supposing it to be recognized in international law—has not yet received any concrete form of development.

Supposing that, at the time of the coming into force of the Treaty of Paris, the Island of Palmas (or Miangas) did not form part of the territory of any State, Spain would have been able to cede only the rights which she might possibly derive from discovery or contiguity. On the other hand, the inchoate title of the Netherlands could not have been modified by a treaty concluded between third Powers; and such a treaty could not have impressed the character of illegality on any act undertaken by the Netherlands with a view to completing their inchoate title—at least as long as no dispute on the matter had arisen, i.e. until 1906.

Now it appears from the report on the visit of General Wood to Palmas (or Miangas), on January 21st, 1906, that the establishment of Netherlands authority, attested also by external signs of sovereignty, had already reached such a degree of development, that the importance of maintaining this state of things ought to be considered as prevailing over a claim possibly based either on discovery in very distant times and unsupported by occupation, or on mere geographical position.

This is the conclusion reached on the ground of the relative strength of the titles invoked by each Party, and founded exclusively on a limited part of the evidence concerning the epoch immediately preceding the rise of the dispute.

This same conclusion must impose itself with still greater force if there be taken into consideration—as the Arbitrator considers should be done—all the evidence which tends to show that there were unchallenged acts of peaceful display of Netherlands sovereignty in the period from 1700 to 1906, and which—as has been stated above—may be regarded as sufficiently proving the existence of Netherlands sovereignty.

For these reasons the Arbitrator, in conformity with Article I of the Special Agreement of January 23rd, 1925, decides that: The Island of Palmas (or Miangas) forms in its entirety a part of Netherlands territory.

NOTES AND QUESTIONS

1. It is clear from Judge Huber's analysis that the international legal process has been quite contextually sensitive to the varieties of resources in assessing what constitutes occupation. Consider one commentary:

> [T]he effective occupation required in community consensus is not some single isolated act but rather a complex process which may include a wide variety of activities and extend over a considerable period of time. The merest pretense to synoptic observation of the flow of claims and authoritative responses in recent centuries must reveal, further, that the kind of effective occupation which has been asserted and honored has not been uniform but has differed widely in degrees of completeness and other details, depending upon many variables in the process of interaction and, most especially, upon the characteristics of the resources claimed. Thus, the participants who have sought to engage in effective occupation have ranged from nation-states, through differing officials, to private individuals, such as traders, trappers, explorers, and missionaries, having varying degrees of authorization from their states; other group claimants have included religious orders, private groups seeking to escape religious persecution, and corporations, such as the Hudson's Bay Company, the Virginia Company, and the French East Indies company. The objectives exhibited by claimants have embraced the extremes, both of the

> most formal statement of *animus occupandi*, intent to appropriate, through ceremonies and symbolic acts, such as discussed above, and of the most informal demands for transient trading rights, such as made for the temporary enjoyment of local resources. The areas sought to be occupied have sometimes been in close proximity to other areas of unquestioned sovereignty, and on occasion at remote distances, even separated by vast oceans; sometimes the activities alleged to constitute occupation have endured through long periods of time, sometimes they have been most fleeting; often activities in occupation have been attended by intense expectations of violence or other crisis, while at other times by expectations only of continuing peaceful cooperation. The capabilities which claimants have had at their disposal for insuring the effectiveness of alleged occupation have varied historically as have the bases of power of the states which have come and gone in the world arena. The strategies employed by claimants have ranged over the whole panoply of diplomatic, ideological, economic, and military—exhibiting many varying degrees of persuasion and coercion, and of triviality and consequentiality. The outcomes in corpus of occupation achieved have, finally, included many differing degrees (from none to maximum) in effective control, the establishment of authority or display of the activities of a state in varying comprehensiveness and modality, and success or failure in the exploitation and development of resources in all possible degree.

Myres S. McDougal, Harold D. Lasswell, Ivan A.Vlasic & Joseph C. Smith, *The Enjoyment of and Acquisition of Resources in Outer Space*, 111 U. PA. L. REV. 521, 611-13 (1963).

2. Note that no effect is given to the continuous occupation of the territory in question by indigenous peoples. Consider, in this regard, the following commentary:

> In the past, if the indigenous peoples survived disease, economic exploitation and sometimes genocide (and many did not), they were consigned to a kind of international legal shadow land. The international law of the newcomers allowed them the weakest of rights of title to the lands they inhabited and even weaker rights to equal treatment under the law. . . .
>
> Despite the moral relevance of decolonization to the situation of indigenous peoples, decolonization rarely encompassed indigenous peoples. In the New World, decolonization benefited mostly so-called Creole or local elites of European extraction. Legal doctrines such as *uti possidetis juris*, which the elites of the new states appropriated in the nineteenth century, effectively precluded any recognition of rights to the lands that indigenous peoples had historically inhabited. *Uti possidetis juris* was a Latin neologism (and, at that, an inversion of the Praetorian edict whose terms it purloined so as to give itself the illusion of the authority of antiquity); it bestowed an aura of historical legality to the expropriation of the lands of indigenous peoples. The new elites divided territory among themselves exactly as had the former imperial powers—in other words, without regard to the claims or interests of the aboriginal inhabitants.

W. Michael Reisman, *Protecting Indigenous Rights in International Adjudication* 89 AM.. J. INT'L L. 350, 352 (1995). For further discussion of indigenous rights, *see supra* Part Three. *See also* M.F.LINDLEY, THE ACQUISITION AND GOVERNMENT OF BACKWARD TERRITORY IN INTERNATIONAL LAW (1926).

3. The ICJ's *Western Sahara* opinion (see *supra* Part Two) as well as subsequent efforts by the international community to raise the legal status of, and recognize rights held by, indigenous peoples have rejected this doctrine of *terra nullius*. (*See* Siegfried Wiessner, *Rights and Status of Peoples: A Global Comparative and International Legal Analysis*, 12 HARV. HUM. RTS. J. 57 (1999)). So did the Australian High Court in *Mabo v. Queensland*, 107 A.L.R. 1 (1992). Justice Brennan's opinion, with ample references to international and comparative law, called the denial of tribal title to the Murray Islands in the Torres Strait a "discriminatory denigration of indigenous inhabitants, their social organization and habits." *Id.* at para. 39. Speaking for the Court, he continued:

> [T]he fiction by which the rights and interests of indigenous inhabitants in land were treated as nonexistent was justified by a policy which has no place in the contemporary law of this country. ... Whatever the justification advanced in earlier days for refusing to recognise the rights and interests in land of the indigenous inhabitants of settled colonies, an unjust and discriminatory doctrine of that kind can no longer be accepted.

Id. at para. 42. In the case of *Awas Tingni* (*see supra* Part Two), the Inter-American Court of Human Rights also recognized a communal right to ownership, title and demarcation of the lands an indigenous community had traditionally possessed.

4. As to nation-states' sovereign rights to land, however, the question remains as to what kind and what quality and quantity of activity was, and is, considered sufficient to establish effective occupation.

5. The regimes established to apportion water resources and those established for land are quite different. Can you detect a reason for such differences? *See* Natalie Klein & Lea Brilmayer, *Land and Sea: Two Sovereignty Regimes in Search of a Common Denominator*, 33 N.Y.U. J. Int'l L. & Pol. 703 (2001).

b. Sovereignty Over Clipperton Island (Fr. v. Mex.)

26 Am. J. Int'l L. 390 (1932)

[On November 17, 1858, Lieutenant Le Coat de Kerwéguen of the French Navy, while one-half mile from Clipperton Island, drew up an act claiming the Island for France. One landing on the Island was made, but no sign of sovereignty was left. The declaration of sovereignty was published in Hawaii, and that government notified.

Prior to the above expedition, on April 8, 1858, the French government issued a commission for exploitation of guano beds on the Island, but this exploitation was never begun.

On November 24, 1897, three Americans were found on the Island collecting guano. The U.S. stated that it had issued no commission and intended no claim.

One month later a Mexican ship approached the Island, and on December 13, 1897, a detachment landed on the Island. Two of the Americans left the Island. Their U.S. flag was lowered and the Mexican flag raised.] ...

On January 8, France, having learned of the Mexican expedition, reminded that Power of its rights over Clipperton. From then a very long diplomatic discussion took place which lasted until the date when, by the agreement of March 2, 1909, the two governments decided to refer to our arbitration the solution of the difference relative to sovereignty over the island.

In Law, it is opportune to examine, in the first instance, the principal thesis maintained by Mexico that Clipperton Island already belonged to her before France had proclaimed her sovereignty over the said island. If this claim should be recognized as founded, it would be necessary to conclude that the occupation of the said Island by France was unlawful.

According to Mexico, Clipperton Island, which had been given the name of the famous English adventurer who, at thc bcginning of the 18th century, used it as a place of refuge, was none other than Passion Island, called also Medano or Medanos Island, that this island had been discovered by the Spanish Navy and, by virtue of the law then in force, fixed by the Bull of Alexander VII, had belonged to Spain, and afterwards, from 1836, to Mexico as the successor state of the Spanish state.

But according to the actual state of our knowledge, it has not been proven that this island, by whatever name one may call it, had been actually discovered by the Spanish navigators. That they might have known it before the log-books on board the French vessels *La Princesse* and *La Découverte* dated in 1711, had identified and described it, is a conjecture more or less probable, but from which one cannot draw any decisive argument. However, even admitting that the discovery had been made by Spanish subjects, it would be necessary, to establish the contention of Mexico, to prove that Spain not only had the right, as a state, to incorporate the island in her possessions, but also had effectively exercised the right. But that has not been demonstrated at all. Mexico produces to support her thesis a geographical map printed from the Archives of the Mexican Society of Geography and Statistics, where the island figures as comprised within the "Political and Military Governments of Spain in North America." But the official character of this map cannot be affirmed, because it is not certain that it was drawn by order and under the care of the state, or because the manuscript memorandum which one reads there, namely, that it was used at the Royal Tribunal of the Consulate of Mexico, does not confer official character upon it.

Moreover, the proof of an historic right of Mexico's is not supported by any manifestation of her sovereignty over the island, a sovereignty never exercised until the expedition of 1897; and the mere conviction that this was territory belonging to Mexico, although general and of long standing, cannot be retained.

Consequently, there is ground to admit that, when in November, 1858, France proclaimed her sovereignty over Clipperton, that island was in the legal situation of *territorium nullius*, and, therefore, susceptible of occupation.

The question remains whether France proceeded to an effective occupation, satisfying the conditions required by international law for the validity of this kind of territorial acquisition. In effect, Mexico maintains, secondarily to her principal contention which has just been examined, that the French occupation was not valid, and consequently her own right to occupy the island which must still be considered as *nullius* in 1897.

In whatever concerns this question, there is, first of all, ground to hold as incontestable, the regularity of the act by which France in 1858 made known in a clear and precise manner, her intention to consider the island as her territory.

On the other hand, it is disputed that France took effective possession of the island, and it is maintained that without such a taking of possession of an effective character, the occupation must be considered as null and void.

It is beyond doubt that by immemorial usage having the force of law, besides the *animus occupandi,* the actual, and not the nominal, taking of possession is a necessary condition of occupation. This taking of possession consists in the act, or series of acts, by which the occupying state reduces to its possession the territory in question and takes steps to exercise exclusive authority there. Strictly speaking, and in ordinary cases, that only takes place when the state establishes in the territory itself an organization capable of making its laws respected. But this step is, properly speaking, but a means of procedure to the taking of possession, and, therefore, is not identical with the latter. There may also be cases where it is unnecessary to have recourse to this method. Thus, if a territory, by virtue of the fact that it was completely uninhabited, is, from the first moment when the occupying state makes its appearance there, at the absolute and undisputed disposition of that state, from that moment the taking of possession must be considered as accomplished, and the occupation is thereby completed. There is no reason to invoke the obligation contained in Art. 35 of the Act of Berlin of 1885 assuring to occupied territories the existence of an authority sufficient to cause acquired rights to be respected and, the case occurring, the liberty of commerce and of transit in the conditions upon which it may be stipulated. Since this Act of Berlin was subsequent to the French occupation here under consideration, concerns only territories on the coasts of Africa, and binds only the signatory states, of which Mexico is not one, in their mutual relations, it can have no weight in the present case. Besides, Art. 35, strictly speaking, has nothing to do with the taking of possession, but imposes an obligation which presupposes an occupation which has already taken place and is already valid.

The regularity of the French occupation has also been questioned because the other Powers were not notified of it. But it must be observed that the precise obligation to make such notification is contained in Art. 34 of the Act of Berlin cited above, which, as before mentioned, is not applicable to the present case. There is good reason to think that the notoriety given to the act, by whatever means, sufficed at the time, and that France provoked that notoriety by publishing the said act in the manner above indicated.

It follows from these premises that Clipperton Island was legitimately acquired by France on November 17, 1858. There is no reason to suppose that France has subsequently lost her right by *derelictio,* since she never had the *animus* of abandoning the island, and the fact that she has not exercised her authority there in a positive manner does not imply the forfeiture of an acquisition already definitively perfected.

NOTES AND QUESTIONS

1. The contextual relativity of *Palmas* and *Clipperton* operates on two axes. The first axis is determined by reference to the degree of habitability of the territory in question and the second axis

is established by reference to the comparative occupational activities of other contenders. In this regard, see *Minquiers & Ecrehos, (Fr. v. U.K.)* 1953 I.C.J. 47 (Nov. 17).

2. The 1966 Arbitral Award between Argentina and Chile, 16 R.I. A. A. 109 (1966) is noteworthy for its detailing of materials often used to document effective occupation:

> Chile has introduced a great deal of evidence designed to show effective Chilean administration over the disputed area. ... The evidence consists of material frequently employed for substantiating claims to territorial sovereignty, e.g., registration of land titles; imposition of land tax: registration of settlers with the police; registration of births, marriages and deaths; animal brand registers - imposition of military service; electoral rolls; legal transactions; administrative, police and judicial activity of various kinds; taking of censuses; provision of health and educational facilities and so on. Even unofficial acts are relied upon, such as ministrations by priests coming under the Apostolic Vicarage of Aysen in Chile, and strenuous efforts have also been made to show that the settlers of the disputed area have Chilean loyalties and have "by their conduct attorned to the Chilean authorities." *Id.*

c. Legal Status of Eastern Greenland
1933 P.C.I.J. (Ser. A/B) No. 53 (Apr. 5).

[On July 10, 1931, Norway promulgated a Royal Resolution confirming the occupation of a portion of Eastern Greenland and announcing that "police powers" in the area were vested in two named individuals. The Norwegian action came after a lengthy controversy with Denmark regarding Danish claims to sovereignty over the whole of Greenland. On July 12, 1931, Denmark instituted proceedings before the Permanent Court of International Justice.]

The Danish submission in the written pleading, that the Norwegian occupation of July 10th, 1931, is invalid, is founded upon the contention that the area occupied was at the time of the occupation subject to Danish sovereignty; that the area is part of Greenland, and at the time of the occupation Danish sovereignty existed over all Greenland ; consequently it could not be occupied by another Power.

In support of this contention, the Danish Government advances two propositions. The first is that the sovereignty which Denmark now enjoys over Greenland has existed for a long time, has been continuously and peacefully exercised and, until the present dispute, has not been contested by any Power. This proposition Denmark sets out to establish as a fact. The second proposition is that Norway has by treaty or otherwise herself recognized Danish sovereignty over Greenland as a whole and therefore cannot now dispute it.

The Norwegian submissions are that Denmark possessed no sovereignty over the area which Norway occupied on July 10th, 1931, and that at the time of the occupation the area was *terra nullius*. Her contention is that the area lay outside the limits of the Danish colonies in Greenland and that Danish sovereignty extended no further than the limits of these colonies. ...

The first Danish argument is that the Norwegian occupation of part of the East coast of Greenland is invalid because Denmark has claimed and exercised sovereign rights over Greenland as a whole for a long time and has obtained thereby a valid title to sovereignty. The date at which such Danish sovereignty must have existed in order to render the Norwegian occupation invalid is the date at which the occupation took place, viz., July 10th 1931.

The Danish claim is not founded upon any particular act of occupation but alleges—to use the phrase employed in the Palmas Island decision of the Permanent Court of Arbitration, April 4th, 1928—a title "founded on the peaceful and continuous display of State authority over the island". It is based upon the view that Denmark now enjoys all the rights which the King of Denmark and Norway enjoyed over Greenland up till 1814. Both the existence and the extent of these rights must therefore be considered, as well as the Danish claim to sovereignty since that date.

It must be borne in mind, however, that as the critical date is July 10th, 1931, it is not necessary that sovereignty over Greenland should have existed throughout the period during which the Danish Government maintains that it was in being. Even if the material submitted to the Court might be thought insufficient to establish the existence of that sovereignty during the earlier periods, this would not exclude a finding that it is sufficient to establish a valid title in the period immediately preceding the occupation.

Before proceeding to consider in detail the evidence submitted to the court, it may be well to state that a claim to sovereignty based not upon some particular act or title such as a treaty of cession but merely upon continued display of authority, involves two elements each of which must be shown to exist: the intention and will to act as sovereign, and some actual exercise or display of such authority.

Another circumstance which must be taken into account by any tribunal which has to adjudicate upon a claim to sovereignty over a particular territory, is the extent to which the sovereignty is also claimed by some other Power. In most of the cases involving claims to territorial sovereignty which have come before an international tribunal, there have been two competing claims to the sovereignty, and the tribunal has had to decide which of the two is the stronger. One of the peculiar features of the present case is that up to 1931 there was no claim by any Power other than Denmark to the sovereignty over Greenland. Indeed, up till 1921, no Power disputed the Danish claim to sovereignty.

It is impossible to read the records of the decisions in cases as to territorial sovereignty without observing that in many cases the tribunal has been satisfied with very little in the way of the actual exercise of sovereign rights, provided that the other State could not make out a superior claim. This is particularly true in the case of claims to sovereignty over areas in thinly populated or unsettled countries. ...

[The Court then examined some of the history of Greenland, beginning with the establishment of Nordic settlements in the 13th century. The Court concluded that the disappearance of these colonies did not end the period of sovereignty, either on the basis of conquest (by Eskimos) or abandonment (since hope of finding survivors continued). In the 18th century, interest in Greenland reawakened, and a new colony was established in 1721. The Court held this was sufficient to establish the two elements of sovereignty (intention and exercise) and the claim over Greenland was not a mere pretense. The Court then examined Norway's claim that the term "Greenland" only applied to the colonized western portions, and not the eastern coast. The court rejected this argument after examining trading ordinances which applied to all of Greenland. It held that Norway had not met its burden of showing the term had only some limited meaning.] ...

The conclusion to which the Court is led is that, bearing in mind the absence of any claim to sovereignty by another Power and the Arctic and inaccessible character of the uncolonized parts of the country, the King of Denmark and Norway displayed during the period from the founding of the colonies by Hans Egede in 1721 up to 1814 his authority to an extent sufficient to give his country a valid claim to sovereignty, and that his rights over Greenland were not limited to the colonized area.

Up to the date of the Treaty of Kiel of 1814, the rights which the King possessed over Greenland were enjoyed by him as King of Norway. It was a Norwegian possession that Greenland was dealt with in Article 4 of that Treaty, whereby the King ceded to the King of Sweden the Kingdom of Norway, "*la Groënland ... non comprise ....*" The result of the Treaty was that what had been a Norwegian possession remained with King of Denmark and became for the future a Danish possession. Except in this respect, the Treaty of Kiel did not affect or extend the King's rights over Greenland.

In order to establish the Danish contention that Denmark has exercised in fact sovereignty over all Greenland for a long time, Counsel for Denmark have laid stress on the long series of conventions—mostly commercial in character—which have been concluded by Denmark and in which, with the concurrence of the other contracting Party, a stipulation has been inserted to the effect that the convention shall not apply to Greenland. In the case of multilateral treaties, the stipulation usually takes the form of a Danish reserve at the time of signature. In date, these conventions cover the period from 1782 onwards. As pointed out in the earlier part of the judgment, the exclusion of Greenland is, with one exception, made without qualification. In that case alone it is "the Danish colonies in Greenland" to which the treaty is not to apply. In many of these cases, the wording is quite specific; for instance, Article 6 of the Treaty of 1826 with the United States of America : "The present Convention shall not apply to the Northern possessions of His Majesty the King of Denmark, that is to say Iceland, the Færö Islands and Greenland. ..."

The importance of these treaties is that they show a willingness on the part of the States with which Denmark has contracted to admit her right exclude Greenland. To some of these treaties, Norway has herself been a Party, and these must be dealt with later because they are relied on by Denmark as constituting binding admissions by Norway that Greenland is subject to Danish sovereignty. For the purpose of the present argument, the importance of these conventions, with whatever States they have been concluded, is due to the support which they lend to the Danish argument that Denmark possesses sovereignty over Greenland as a whole.

It has been contended on behalf of Norway that no importance should be attached to these conventions because, when they were concluded, the Parties had no such question in mind as whether Danish sovereignty was limited or not to the colonies, and whether in consequence "Greenland" meant more than the colonized area. Both as to these conventions, and also as to the Treaty of Kiel, Counsel for Norway adhere to the contention that the word "Greenland" is used in the sense of the area comprised within the colonies.

It is true that when they conclude a commercial convention, States are not dealing with such questions as the extent of their respective territories, but the usual object of a commercial convention is to give to each of the Parties facilities for trade and navigation in the territories of the other ; consequently, the area within which such facilities are, or are not, accorded is a point of some importance. It is a question on which disputes may arise if there is any uncertainty. If the Parties were agreed that the treaty was not to apply in a particular area and the area is only designated by name, the natural conclusion is that no difference existed between them as to the extent of the area which that name covered. The Court is therefore once more led back to the question as to what the contracting Parties meant when they excluded "Greenland". The natural meaning of the term is its geographical meaning as shown in the maps. If it is argued on behalf of Norway that these treaties use the term "Greenland" in some special sense, it is for her to establish it, and it is not decisive in this respect that the northern part of Greenland was still unknown. She has not succeeded in showing that in these treaties the word "Greenland" means only the colonized area.

To the extent that these treaties constitute evidence of recognition of her sovereignty over Greenland in general, Denmark is entitled to rely upon them.

These treaties may also be regarded as demonstrating sufficiently Denmark's will and intention to exercise sovereignty over Greenland. There remains the question whether during this period, i.e. 1814 to 1915, she exercised authority to the uncolonized area sufficiently to give her a valid claim to sovereignty therein. In their arguments, Counsel for Denmark have relied chiefly on the concession granted in 1863 to Tayler of exclusive rights on the East coast for trading, hunting, mining etc. The result of all the documents connected with the grant of the concession is to show that, on the one side, it was granted upon the footing that the King of Denmark was in a position to grant a valid monopoly on the East coast and that his sovereign rights entitled him to do so, and, on the other, that the concessionaries in England regarded the grant of a monopoly as essential to the success of their projects and had no doubt as to the validity of the rights conferred. ...

The concessions granted for the erection of telegraph lines and the legislation fixing the limits of territorial waters in 1905 are also manifestations of the exercise of sovereign authority.

In view of the above facts, when taken in conjunction with the legislation she had enacted applicable to Greenland generally, the numerous treaties in which Denmark, with the concurrence of the other contracting Party, provided for the non-application of the treaty to Greenland in general, and absence of all claim to sovereignty over Greenland by any other Power, Denmark must be regarded as having displayed during this period of 1814 to 1915 her authority over the uncolonized part of the country to a degree sufficient to confer a valid title to the sovereignty.

[The Court then summarized the activities of Denmark between 1921 and 1930, noting an increase in activity, and holding that Norwegian protests did not alter their sovereign character.] ...

These acts, coupled with the activities of the Danish hunting expeditions which were supported by the Danish Government, the increase in the number of scientific expeditions engaged in mapping and exploring the country with the authorization and encouragement of the Government, even though the expeditions may have been organized by non-official institutions, the occasions on which the *Godthaab,* a vessel belonging to the State and placed at one time under the command of a naval officer, was sent to the East coast on inspection duty, the issue of permits by the Danish authorities, under regulations issued in 1930, to persons visiting the eastern coast of Greenland, show to a sufficient extent—even when separated from the history of the preceding periods—the two elements necessary to establish a valid title to sovereignty namely : the intention and will to exercise such sovereignty and the manifestation of State activity.

The conclusion of the 1924 Convention with Norway, to which reference must again be made later, though signed by that State on the footing that she maintained her point of view as to the territorial status of Eastern Greenland (*terra nullius*) and that the conclusion of the Convention did not prejudice her point of view, does not exclude the right of Denmark to maintain her point of view that she was entitled to and was in fact enjoying sovereignty over all Greenland, nor does it exclude her right to show that the elements which go to establish a valid claim to sovereignty were both present.

Except for the verbal change that the phrase "*territoire de Groënland*" is more often employed than "*Groënland*", the commercial arrangements concluded by Denmark during the period continue to provide that, on the Danish side, the agreement is not to apply to Greenland, showing thereby that the States with which Denmark was concluding these agreements were not disposed to dispute her claim to be sovereign over the area which the agreement denominates as Greenland. As also is the case with regard to the previous periods, it lies on Norway to show that the word "Greenland" in these agreements is used in some special sense which does not include the uncolonized part of the East coast, and in the opinion of the Court Norway has not shown that this is so.

Even if the period from 1921 to July 10th, 1931, is taken by itself and without reference to the preceding periods, the conclusion reached by the Court is that during this time Denmark regarded herself as possessing sovereignty over all Greenland and displayed and exercised her sovereign rights to an extent sufficient to constitute a valid title to sovereignty. When considered in conjunction with the facts of the preceding periods, the case in favour of Denmark is confirmed and strengthened.

It follows from the above that the Court is satisfied that Denmark has succeeded in establishing her contention that at the critical date, namely, July 10th, 1931, she possessed a valid title to the sovereignty over all Greenland.

This finding constitutes by itself sufficient reason for holding that the occupation of July 10th, 1931, and any steps taken in this connection by the Norwegian Government, were illegal and invalid. …

[The Court also found that a written statement by the Norwegian Minister for Foreign Affairs to his Danish counterpart to the effect that the Norwegian Government "*ne fera pas de difficultés*" bound Norway.]

NOTES AND QUESTIONS

1. Note that the Permanent Court seemed willing to accept as indication of occupation the passage of legislation. But the legislative activity is one which is accomplished in Copenhagen. As such, it may be indicative of intention, but unless there are corresponding acts in Greenland, to what extent does the legislation indicate occupation?

2. What, if anything, does the Greenland decision add to the concept of "effective occupation"?

3. The Greenland case is often cited in articles discussing claims to sovereignty in Antarctica. The decision is said to establish the proposition that in polar areas with inaccessible or uninhabitable regions, a lesser standard of "occupation" is applied to determine sovereignty. The term "effective control" is sometimes used. *See* J.P.A. Bernhardt, *Sovereignty in Antarctica*, 5 CAL. W. INT'L L. J. 297 (1975). Why should the difficulty of meeting the test of sovereignty (intention and exercise) allow a claimant to establish sovereignty even though there has been very little "exercise"? Is "intent" more important?

d. Frontier Dispute (Burk. Faso v. Mali)

1986 I.C.J. 554, 586-587 (Judgment of Dec. 22)
[Review facts, *supra,* Part Two, at 206]

63. Apart from the texts and maps listed above, the Parties have invoked in support of their respective contentions the "colonial *effectivités*", in other words, the conduct of the administrative authorities as proof of the effective exercise of territorial jurisdiction in the region during the colonial period. For Burkina Faso,

the *effectivités* can support an existing title, whether written or cartographical, but when their probative value has to be assessed they must be systematically compared with the title in question; in no circumstances can they be substituted for the title. For its part, Mali admits that in principle the *effectivités* cannot be brought into operation where they are contrary to the text of a treaty, but argues that in a situation where there is no boundary described in conventional or legislative form, it is necessary to ascertain the boundary by other methods, and an investigation of the *effectivités* then becomes essential. The role played in this case by such *effectivités* is complex, and the Chamber will have to weigh carefully the legal force of these in each particular instance. It must however state forthwith, in general terms, what legal relationship exists between such acts and the titles on which the implementation of the principle of *uti possidetis* is grounded. For this purpose, a distinction must be drawn among several eventualities. Where the act corresponds exactly to law, where effective administration is additional to the *uti possidetis juris*, the only role of *effectivité* is to confirm the exercise of the right derived from a legal title. Where the act does not correspond to the law, where the territory which is the subject of the dispute is effectively administered by a State other than the one possessing the legal title, preference should be given to the holder of the title. In the event that the *effectivité* does not co-exist with any legal title, it must invariably be taken into consideration. Finally, there are cases where the legal title is not capable of showing exactly the territorial expanse to which it relates. The *effectivités* can then play an essential role in showing how the title is interpreted in practice.

e. Gulf of Fonseca Case (El Sal. v. Hond.)

1992 I.C.J. 351 (Judgment of Sept. 11)

67. There has also been some argument between the Parties about the "critical date" in relation to this dispute. The principle of *uti possidetis juris* is sometimes stated in almost absolute terms, suggesting that the position at the date of independence is always determinative; in short, that no other critical date can arise. As appears from the discussion above, this cannot be so. A later critical date clearly may arise, for example, either from adjudication or from a boundary treaty. Thus, in the previous Latin American boundary arbitrations it is the award that is now determinative, even though it be based upon a view of the *uti possidetis juris* position. The award's view of the *uti possidetis juris* position prevails and cannot now be questioned juridically, even if it could be questioned historically. So for such a boundary the date of the award has become a new and later critical date. Likewise there can be no question that the parts of the El Salvador/Honduras boundary fixed by the General Treaty of Peace of 1980 now constitute the boundary and 1980 is now the critical date. If the *uti possidetis juris* position can be qualified by adjudication and by treaty, the question then arises whether it can be qualified in other ways, for example, by acquiescence or recognition. There seems to be no reason in principle why these factors should not operate, where there is sufficient evidence to show that the parties have in

effect clearly accepted a variation, or at least an interpretation, of the *uti possidetis juris* position. ...

80. As already explained (paragraph 67 above), the Chamber does not consider that the effect of the application of the principle of the *uti possidetis juris* in Spanish America was to freeze for all time the provincial boundaries which, with the advent of independence, became the frontiers between the new States. It was obviously open to those States to vary the boundaries between them by agreement; and some forms of activity, or inactivity, might amount to acquiescence in a boundary other than that of 1821. Even on the hypothesis that Honduras's analysis of the legal effect, under Spanish colonial law, of the grant of the Citalá *título ejidal* is correct, so that from 1776 onward the provincial boundary remained to the south-west of the land comprised in that title (and followed the line E-F-G-H-J-A), the conclusion does not follow that that is the course of the international frontier today. The situation was susceptible of modification by acquiescence in the lengthy intervening period; and the Chamber finds that the conduct of Honduras from 1881 until 1972 may be regarded as amounting to such acquiescence in a boundary corresponding to the boundary between the Tepangüisir lands granted to Citalá and those of Ocotepeque.

f. Case Concerning the Land and Maritime Boundary between Cameroon and Nigeria (Cameroon v. Nig.)

2002 I.C.J. 303 (Judgment of Oct. 10)

65. The Court will now examine Nigeria's argument based on historical consolidation of title.

The Court observes in this respect that in the *Fisheries* case (*United Kingdom v. Norway*) (*I.C.J. Reports 1951*, p. 130) it had referred to certain maritime delimitation decrees promulgated by Norway a century earlier which had been adopted for decades without any opposition. These decrees were said by the Court to represent "a well-defined and uniform system ... which would reap the benefit of general toleration, the basis of an historical consolidation which would make it enforceable as against all states" (*ibid.*, p. 137). The Court notes, however, that the notion of historical consolidation has never been used as a basis of title in other territorial disputes, whether in its own or other case law.

Nigeria contends that the notion of historical consolidation has been developed by academic writers, and relies on that theory, associating it with the maxim *quieta non movere*.

The Court notes that the theory of historical consolidation is highly controversial and cannot replace the established modes of acquisition of title under international law, which take into account many other important variables of fact and law. It further observes that nothing in the Fisheries Judgment suggests that the "historical consolidation" referred to, in connection with the external boundaries of the territorial sea, allows land occupation to prevail over an established treaty title. ... Nigeria's arguments on this point cannot therefore be upheld.

66. Nigeria further states that the peaceful possession on which it relies, coupled with acts of administration, represents a manifestation of sovereignty and is thus a specific element of its other two heads of title, namely: on the one hand, effective administration by Nigeria, acting as sovereign, and the absence of protests; and, on the other, manifestations of sovereignty by Nigeria over Darak and the neighboring villages, together with acquiescence by Cameroon in such sovereignty.

67. In this regard, it may be observed that the gradual settling of Nigerians in the villages was followed in turn by support provided by the Ngala Local Government in Nigeria, along with a degree of administration and supervision. ...

Some of these activities – the organization of public health and education facilities, policing, the administration of justice – could normally be considered to be acts *à titre de souverain*. The Court notes, however, that, as there was a pre-existing title held by Cameroon in this area of the lake, the pertinent legal test is whether there was thus evidenced acquiescence by Cameroon in the passing of title from itself to Nigeria.

68. In this context the Court also observes that Cameroon's own activities in the Lake Chad area have only a limited bearing on the issue of title. ... [Court refers to *Burkina Faso v. Republic of Mali.*]

... Cameroon held the legal title to territory lying to the east of the boundary as fixed by the applicable instruments. ... Hence the conduct of Cameroon in that territory has pertinence only for the question of whether it acquiesced in the establishment of a change in treaty title, which cannot be wholly precluded as a possibility in law [Court refers to *El Salvador v. Honduras*, 1992 I.C.J. at para. 80.].

69. It appears from the case file that the control of certain local Cameroonian officials over the area was limited. As Nigerian settlements, and the organization within them of village life, became supplemented from 1987 onwards by Nigerian administration and the presence of Nigerian troops, Cameroon restricted its protests to a few "incidents" (notably the taking over of the fisheries training station at Katti Kime), rather than to the evolving situation as such. There is some evidence however that Cameroon continued sporadically to seek to exercise some administrative control in these areas, albeit with little success in this later period.

Cameroon has put to the Court that it did not regard the activities of Nigeria in Lake Chad in the years 1984 to 1994 as *à titre de souverain*, because Nigeria was in those years fully participating in the work entrusted to the LCBC [Lake Chad Basin Commission] and its contractors, and agreed that they should work on the basis of the various treaty instruments which governed title. ...

On 14 April 1994, Nigeria, in a diplomatic Note, for the first time claimed sovereignty over Darak. Cameroon firmly protested in a Note Verbale of 21 April 1994, expressing "its profound shock at the presumption that Darak is part of Nigerian territory", and reiterating its own sovereignty. Shortly after, it also enlarged the scope of its Application to the Court.

70. The Court finds that the above events, taken together, show that there was no acquiescence by Cameroon in the abandonment of its title in the area in favour of Nigeria. Accordingly, the Court concludes that the situation was essentially one where the *effectivités* adduced by Nigeria did not correspond to the law, and that accordingly "preference should be given to the holder of the title." *Burkina Faso*, 1986 I.C.J. at 587.

g. Eritrea-Ethiopia Boundary Commission Decision Regarding Delimitation of the Border

Apr. 13, 2002, *available at* http://www.un.org/NewLinks/eebcarbitration/EEBC-Decision-TOC.pdf

Effectivités

3.29 As to activity on the ground, the actions of a State pursued *à titre de souverain* can play a role either as assertive of that State's position or, expressly or impliedly, contradictory of the conduct of the opposing State. Such actions may comprise legislative, administrative or judicial assertions of authority over the disputed area. There is no set standard of duration and intensity of such activity. Its effect depends on the nature of the terrain and the extent of its population, the period during which it has been carried on and the extent of any contradictory conduct (including protests) of the opposing State. It is also important to bear in mind that conduct does not by itself produce an absolute and indefeasible title, but only a title relative to that of the competing State. The conduct of one Party must be measured against that of the other. Eventually, but not necessarily so, the legal result may be to vary a boundary established by a treaty.

Notes and Questions

1. For the ICJ, *effectivités*, i.e. exercises of effective governmental control over a certain area, appear to play only a secondary role with respect to a state whose boundaries were set by *uti possidetis* (*see supra* Part Two) or by treaty. They may help in clarifying an unclear "legal" title; and they are critical when such title does not exist. *Effectivités contra legem*, i.e. those which run against a title clearly established under *uti possidetis* or a treaty will, in the opinion of the *Burkina Faso* and the *Cameroon* courts, lose out against the legal title. What are the advantages and disadvantages of this position?

2. The *Gulf of Fonseca* decision, as reaffirmed in *Cameroon v. Nigeria*, allows for correction of established legal title by later agreement or acquiescence. What is the difference between acquiescence and *effectivités*?

2. Allegiance

Morocco's claims in the *Western Sahara* case were based in part on the voluntary submission of largely nomadic inhabitants of the region to the Sultan of

Morocco, and on the religious ties between the Kingdom and the Islamic tribes. As we saw, these claims were not recognized as valid.

a. Western Sahara

1975 I.C.J. 4 (May 22) [Review *supra* Part Two, at 154]

NOTES AND QUESTIONS

1. What are the policies underlying Morocco's claim? Are they backed by a traditional, albeit dated, "principle" of international law, such as effective occupation of a "terra nullius"? How does effective occupation accommodate with a people's right to self-determination?

2. Is Morocco's title a derivative one, founded on the voluntary submission of the largely nomadic inhabitants of the region and the religious ties between the (Islamic) tribes and the Sultan of Morocco? Are these factors legally relevant? To what extent, if any, does the *East Timor* decision, *supra* Part Two, at 170, expand the right to self-determination as defined in *Western Sahara*?

3. Is allegiance by local tribes a valid root of title? How does it differ, if at all, from voluntary submission? From effective occupation? Compare the following two cases.

b. Dubai-Sharjah Border Dispute

91 I.L.R. 543 (1993)

[Dubai and Sharjah had been under the protection of Great Britain from 1892, and their common boundary depended on the allegiance of the nomadic tribes to one or the other of them. The tribes occasionally changed allegiances, but even when they did not, their nomadic lifestyles made their "dirahs" or homelands extremely imprecise. In 1937, however, when the discovery of oil led oil companies to seek concessions from the rulers, Great Britain attempted to define the Dubai/Sharjah boundary more clearly.

A British political agent, Mr. Tripp, used the surveys of another British official, Mr. Walker, to issue a series of "awards" regarding the Dubai/Sharjah boundary. Because Dubai never accepted these awards, the Dubai/Sharjah boundary had remained uncertain, especially as regards the Al Mamzer Peninsula (part of the coast adjacent to Dubai and separated from Sharjah by Khan Creek) and the Hadhib Azana (an area further inland). In order to resolve this controversy, the two Emirates signed an agreement to arbitrate on November 30, 1976.] ...

The applicable rules of international law relating to boundary disputes are those which are concerned with the resolution of claims to sovereignty over territory. Yet to apply these rules, in their contemporary form, to peoples which have had, until very recently, a totally different conception of sovereignty would be highly artificial. As the International Court of Justice said in its Advisory Opinion in the *Western Sahara* case:

> It is in the context of such a territory and such a social and political organisation of the population that the Court has to examine the question

of the "legal ties" between Western Sahara and the Kingdom of Morocco and the Mauritanian entity ... *(I.C.J. Reports, 1975, p. 42.)*

It is not appropriate for this Court to examine the social and political organisation of the Emirates as it evolved during the course of their history. It is sufficient to note here that until the mid-twentieth century this region was largely desert and sparsely populated. Except for the coastal fringe, the population was nomadic or semi nomadic and for such people the modern concept of "boundary" or "frontier" had no meaning. They were concerned only with areas or localities within which they moved from place to place.

An expert, Mr. Morsy Abdullah, has written that, before the 1930s:

> [t]he concept of a state with clearly defined boundaries was totally alien to the political notions of the rulers and the tribes of the area. (Muhammed Morsy Abdullah, *The United Arab Emirates: A Modern History* (London, 1978), p. 291.)

The tribes owed allegiance to a Ruler. The form of allegiance varied, but might, for instance, involve the payment of the religious tax known as "zakat". The link between a tribe and a Ruler might be close or tenuous, dependent on the degree of independence manifested by the people concerned. It was, however, by way of this allegiance that a Ruler was able to exercise a form of sovereignty over a region where nomadic tribesmen were regularly moving from place to place. There was no direct control by a Ruler over a given territory but a control exercised through the tribal system, which might indeed, if a particular tribe displayed a high degree of' independence, become more or less theoretical. Mr. Morsy Abdullah has very well summarised the position in these words:

> Political boundaries were dependent on tribal loyalties to particular shaikhs and consequently were subject to frequent change. Therefore, the frontier between the Trucial States and the Sultanate of Muscat and the inter-state boundaries changed frequently during the nineteenth and twentieth centuries as it was based on the *dirah* of the tribes. *Dirah* in Arabia at this time was a flexibly defined area, changing in size according to the strength of the tribe which wandered within it. In addition, a tribe's loyalty was determined by its own interests and could, and at this time often did, alter. *(loc. cit.)*

The term "dirah" indicates a region within which a nomadic people moves. The term "haram" means, however, an area in the vicinity of a town or settlement upon which such town or settlement has a claim of exclusive rights for the purpose of obtaining the necessities of its existence.

Such was the situation confronting the British authorities when the prospect of the exploration of the oil resources of the region made it necessary for them to consider the delimitation of boundaries. In a letter of 10 July 1937, from the Political Agent to the Political Resident in the Persian Gulf, it was said:

> The present boundaries between the States are not demarcated with any accuracy and I am doubtful if any of the Trucial Shaikhs themselves can accurately describe where their territorial boundaries run ... Some of the Shaikhs have been gradually losing control and what was considered an integral part of the Shaikhdom ten years or more ago has now become separated and under the Ruler of the Shaikh of one of the nomadic tribes. (D. R. vol. 2, pp. 25-6.)

Mr Walker very well understood that the modern idea of sovereignty could not apply to the region at the time when he undertook his task of investigating the boundaries. He indicated, in his 1955 report, the criteria he adopted in assessing and evaluating the various territorial claims: ...

> They are listed in approximate order of importance.
>
> 1. *De facto* control of several years' standing in an area, and the recognition of that control by local and neighbouring tribesmen and authorities.
>
> 2. The collection of zakat (on crops).
>
> 3. The allegiance of tribesmen settled in the area.
>
> 4. Historical evidence:
> (a) agreements
> (b) zakat
> (c) settlement of disputes
> (d) past occupation
> (e) development and use of territory
>
> 5. Ownership of property. (Sh. M. vol. 11, pp. 7-8.)

In the view of the Court these criteria may be reduced essentially to the following two—(i) control, and (ii) allegiance. It is by reference to these two criteria that this Court will be able to determine what was the legal situation in the disputed boundary areas. It is necessary to emphasis, however, that the relative weight and importance to be placed on each of these criteria must vary with the period and the region under consideration.

As far as the period is concerned, it is clear that the weight to be placed upon the criterion of allegiance cannot be the same in the 1960s and 1970s as it would have been in the nineteenth century. Allegiance becomes of less significance as the Emirates' economic and political development leads to fundamental changes in their internal organisation and structure. Difficulties over the identification of boundaries sprang originally, as has been seen, from the nomadic life of the population; the predominant influence of that style of life was itself progressively diminished in the course of time. A similar variation is true in assessing the criterion of control. At a time when allegiance is important, actual control plays a role of secondary significance. As the Court has indicated, the Ruler controlled a given territory only through the operation of the tribal system; the quotations given above indicate how variable, even nominal, may have been such control at one time or another.

The two criteria of allegiance and control must also, in their application, have regard to the region under consideration. In the interior of the disputed boundary area the criterion of control may be of very limited significance in the distant past, but perhaps of slightly greater significance in the more recent past. This is still a desert region with a nomadic population. However, in the coastal area, and more especially in the immediate neighbourhood of the towns of Dubai and Sharjah, the criterion of control becomes of greater significance, since the population is more settled and the disputed area, extremely limited in size, is too closely linked with the townships for the criterion of allegiance to be of much significance.

Of course, the nature and extent of control is itself extremely variable. As long as the towns of Dubai and of Sharjah had few inhabitants and only a limited economic life, acts of' authority demonstrating such control could only have been infrequent and the opportunities for their exercise very restricted. This situation, of course, changed as the economic life of the two towns began to develop. …

Doubtless during the last century, through the allegiance of the population of Abu Hail, Sharjah had a legal title over the Al Mamzer peninsula and well beyond, but, with the disappearance of the town, the development of Dubai and its increasing economic and political weight caused Sharjah gradually to lose this title. Lorimer noted this already in 1908, since he gives the boundary as passing half a mile from Khan. In any event from the beginning of the present century neither reference to allegiance nor to the ownership of property was appropriate for the determination of legal title, because, as far as the former is concerned, the Court has already indicated that the population of the area was both mixed and occasional, and, as far as the latter is concerned, the British authorities in 1920 admitted the existence of control by Dubai irrespective of the property rights of individuals in the area. The only other possibility was to refer to effective control and this control was no longer exercised by Sharjah. In consequence, by this time, the former legal title of Sharjah was lost.

[The Court therefore grants Dubai the Al Mamzer Peninsula.]

c. Case Concerning Maritime Delimitation and Territorial Questions between Qatar and Bahrain

2001 I.C.J. 87 (Judgment of Mar. 16)

85. Bahrain maintains … that the Al-Khalifah continued to exercise control over Zubarah through a Naim-led tribal confederation loyal to them, notwithstanding that at the end of the eighteenth century they had moved the seat of their government to the islands of Bahrain.

86. The Court cannot accept this contention. While there may have been, at different times, ties of personal allegiance between some members of the Naim and the Ruler of Bahrain, there is also evidence that some members of the Naim

served both the Al-Khalifah and the Al-Thani. In any event, there is no evidence that members of the Naim exercised sovereign authority on behalf of the Sheikh of Bahrain within Zubarah. Indeed, they came under the jurisdiction of the local territorial sovereign, which was not Bahrain and had not been Bahrain at least since the events of 1868.

3. Cession

a. Egypt-Israel Arbitration: Taba

27 I.L.M. 1421 (1988)

[In 1979, Egypt and Israel concluded a Treaty of Peace which provided for a joint commission to demarcate the international boundary. The commission was unable to identify the precise location of several of the nearly 100 pillars. An arbitration tribunal, under the Treaty of Peace, was charged with identifying the location of the pillars in controversy. The historical facts of the case were complex.

During the nineteenth century, the areas of present-day Egypt and Israel both were within the territorial domain of the Ottoman Empire. In 1841, the Empire created in Egypt a privileged vassal state. Starting in 1881, Great Britain occupied Egypt as a means to secure its route to India via the Suez Canal. Great Britain did not, however, make any attempt to change Egypt's status as a vassal state within the Ottoman Empire. Egypt's boundaries with Palestine remained undefined until 1906, at which point the countries involved in the area formally agreed on the issue. After the Agreement of 1906, the border was demarked with "pillars." Great Britain then undertook to map out the new boundary.] ...

The Mandate Period (1923-1948)

71. By the time the Council of the League of Nations had approved the text of the Mandate for Palestine on 24 July 1922, and later when the Mandate finally entered into force on 29 September 1923, no boundaries had been established for the mandated territory. The Preamble to the Mandate Resolution recites that the Principal Allied Powers had decided to entrust to Great Britain the mandate for Palestine, "within such boundaries as may be fixed by them". Article 5 of the Mandate stipulated, however, that:

> The Mandatory shall be responsible for seeing that no Palestine territory is ceded or leased to, or in any way placed under the control of, the Government of any foreign Power.

72. A few years later, in answer to a question raised on 16 July 1925 in the British House of Commons with regard to the status of Aqaba, Mr. McNeill answered for the Government of Great Britain that "[t]he line dividing the territories under Egyptian and Turkish administration respectively was defined in 1906 by a boundary commission and has not since been modified." He informed the questioner that "Akaba lies a few miles to the east of this line."

73. On 6 October 1925, Great Britain invited Egypt to recognize the special situation of Great Britain in the territory of Palestine. The Egyptian Prime Minister and Minister for Foreign Affairs, Ahmed Ziwer Pasha, did so in a letter to the British High Commissioner in Cairo of 4 February 1926, but reserved Egypt's position regarding the Egyptian frontier with Palestine since the Mandate provided that the frontiers of Palestine would be decided at a later date "by the Principal Allied Powers". The letter concluded that the Egyptian frontier with Palestine could not in any way be affected by the delimitation of the frontiers of Palestine.

74. Following consultations with the relevant British authorities, the British High Commissioner informed the Egyptian Foreign Minister by letter of 25 June 1926 in response to the letter of 4 February that "the Palestine and Egyptian frontier as defined in the year 1906 will be in no way affected by the delimitation of the frontiers of the mandated territory of Palestine."

75. In 1926 the Survey of Egypt published the 1915 British Map of the Sinai at the scale of 1:250,000. The Tribunal was not informed when the 1915 British Map was made public by Great Britain. It remained the only map for some time which plotted the position of individual boundary pillars along the line. In subsequent years, the authorities of mandated Palestine repeatedly sought survey information from the Survey of Egypt concerning the locations of the boundary pillars in order to describe accurately the south-western boundary of Palestine, but the Survey of Egypt replied that the boundary pillars had never been surveyed.

76. On 4 April 1932, the Eastern Department of the British Foreign Office issued a lengthy memorandum on the question of the frontiers of mandated territories in the Middle East due to a question raised in the League of Nations concerning the necessity of submitting the frontiers of mandated territories to the Principal Allied Powers or to the Council of the League for approval. Attached to this memorandum was an annex describing the frontiers of each of the mandated territories. The description of the Egypt-Palestine frontier affirmed that the then-present frontier was the same as the "Separative Administrative Line" established by the 1 October 1906 Agreement, but remarked, that the line "does not appear at any stage to have been formally constituted an international frontier." After noting the letter of 4 February 1926 from the Egyptian Government to the British High Commissioner, the annex stated that the assurance given in response to Egypt's reservation "seems to imply recognition by His Majesty's Government and the Egyptian Government of the 1906 line as the definitive frontier between Palestine and Egypt." ...

111. Egypt contends that the task of the Tribunal under Article II of the Compromis is to identify the locations of the disputed pillars of the boundary defined in Article II of the Treaty of Peace. In Egypt's contention, the formulation of the boundary between Egypt and Israel as "the recognized international boundary between Egypt and the former mandated territory of Palestine" implies

that 24 July 1922 is the critical date at which time the Tribunal must establish the factual location of boundary pillars as representing the legal boundary between Egypt and Palestine. This date, being the date when the Council of the League of Nations adopted the Mandate for Palestine, was selected since it constituted the first date on which the two distinct entities of Egypt and mandated Palestine could be said both to have attained status on the international plane. Egypt contends that this early date is the appropriate one in terms of application of the concept of the critical date. In the course of the proceedings, however, Egypt conceded that 14 May 1948, the date on which the Mandate expired, or any date within the period of the Mandate, could just as well serve as the critical date since the Parties were in agreement that no changes had occurred in the boundary during that period. ...

142. With respect to the task of the Tribunal, Israel contends that the Tribunal must decide, in conformity with Article II of the Compromis, the course of the legal boundary adopted by the Parties in Article II of the Treaty of Peace and express the line in terms of the location of boundary pillars where these are in dispute. The legal boundary, according to Israel, is "the recognized international boundary" which separated Egypt from the mandated territory of Palestine.

143. Israel alleges that Great Britain, as mandatory power in Palestine, and Egypt had both explicitly recognized in 1926 the line defined in 1906 as that boundary, and that Great Britain had assured Egypt that its boundary would not be affected by the delimitation of the boundaries of Palestine. By virtue of a renvoi, or referral, to the 1906 Agreement made by Egypt and Great Britain in 1926, and in the absence of any explicit agreement between Egypt and Great Britain defining the frontier of Egypt and Palestine, Israel contends that the Tribunal is, pursuant to the Treaty of Peace and the Compromis, referred to the terms of the 1906 Agreement to determine the course of the legal boundary. For Israel, any pillars or pillar remains which are at variance with the terms of the 1906 Agreement are of no significance since no pillars of whatever nature, type, or designation were ever recognized as boundary pillars during the period of the Mandate, which Israel agrees is the legally relevant period according to the Treaty of Peace for the definition of the boundary between Egypt and Israel. Israel further contends that the several conventions between the Parties related to the boundary, with their implicit reference to the 1906 Agreement, are sufficient for the Tribunal's task and that the Egyptian reliance on general principles of law is unnecessary. ...

170. As has been stated above in paragraph 143, Israel submits that both Great Britain, as mandatory power, and Egypt in 1926 explicitly recognized the line defined in 1906 as the boundary between Egypt and Palestine. By virtue of this renvoi to the 1906 Agreement, Israel contends, the Tribunal is referred to the line defined in the 1906 Agreement, not to the boundary pillars established pursuant thereto. The Tribunal cannot share this view. First of all, the expressions "defined in 1906" and 'defined by the 1906 Agreement", which were used in British and Egyptian declarations in 1926, do not have a particular technical mean-

ing in the sense that they refer only to the description of the boundary line in the Agreement to the exclusion of the demarcation of the boundary also expressly provided for by the 1906 Agreement. It can hardly have been the meaning of the declarations of Great Britain and Egypt in 1926 that the demarcation of the boundary, as it took place in 1906-07, could be disregarded. It is important in this respect that both Great Britain and Egypt were well acquainted with the demarcated boundary. Egypt had taken part in the demarcation of the boundary. Both States had made surveys and produced maps of the region, both before and during the time of the British mandate over Palestine. The 1915 British map and the 1926 and 1935-38 Egyptian maps even indicate the location of boundary pillars. Neither State ever questioned the demarcated line.

171. It would also hardly be understandable why the Treaty of Peace and the Compromis should refer to "the recognized international boundary between Egypt and the former mandated territory of Palestine" if reference could just as well have been made directly to the 1906 Agreement. Moreover, Israel's contention that the boundary line proposed by it corresponds to "the legal line" as defined by the 1906 Agreement, while the Egyptian line, which in its southern part is based on boundary pillars, deviates from the Agreement, has not been confirmed by the evidence submitted to the Tribunal, as will be shown later in the Award.

172. The Tribunal will therefore have to decide the locations of the fourteen boundary pillars on the basis of the boundary between Egypt and the former mandated territory of Palestine as it was demarcated, consolidated, and commonly understood during the period of the Mandate (29 September 1923 - 14 May 1948, also referred to as "the critical period"). Although both Parties referred to 24 July 1922 as the starting date of the Mandate, the Tribunal considers that 29 September 1923, the date of the formal entry into force of the Mandate, is the appropriate date in the circumstances.

173. In so far as there are doubts as to where the boundary pillars stood during the period of the Mandate or for confirmation of its findings, the Tribunal, for its part, will also consider the 1906 Agreement, but merely as an indice among others, as to what was the situation on the ground during the critical period. In the same way, the Tribunal will consider any relevant evolution with regard to the delimited and demarcated boundary prior to the critical period.

174. In this context it is worth mentioning that even when the Annex to the Compromis refers to "the final boundary pillar No. 91" it adopts literally and without qualifications the following words from the translation of the 1906 Agreement included in Owen's General Report: "at the point of Ras Taba on the western shore of the Gulf of Akaba".

175. Events subsequent to the critical period can in principle also be relevant, not in terms of a change of the situation, but only to the extent that they may reveal or illustrate the understanding of the situation as it was during the critical period. However, in the present case the Tribunal has felt it to be of only limited use to consider events belonging to the troublesome period after the termination

of the Mandate and during which period also the nations involved were not the same as before.

[The Tribunal decided, with one member dissenting, in favor of Egypt.]

NOTES AND QUESTIONS

1. In *Libya v. Chad*, 1994 I.C.J. 6 (Feb. 3), the Court said "a boundary established by treaty thus achieves a permanence which the treaty itself does not necessarily enjoy. The treaty can cease to be enforced without in anyway affecting the continuance of the boundary." This and similar statements by the Court indicate deference to boundary treaties because they serve the policy of stability and finality of title and boundaries thereto.

2. In its 2001 *Qatar v. Bahrain* decision, the ICJ even accorded an unratified treaty conclusive effect:

> 89. The Court observes that signed but unratified treaties may constitute an accurate expression of the understanding of the parties at the time of signature. In the circumstances of this case the Court has come to the conclusion that the Anglo-Ottoman Convention does represent evidence of the views of Great Britain and the Ottoman Empire as to the factual extent of the authority of the Al-Thani Ruler in Qatar up to 1913.
>
> 90. The text of Article 11 of the Anglo-Ottoman Convention is clear: "it is agreed between the two Governments that the said peninsula will, as in the past, be governed by the Sheikh Jasim-bin-Sani and his successors". Thus Great Britain and the Ottoman Empire did not recognize Bahrain's sovereignty over the peninsula, including Zubarah. In their opinion the whole Qatar peninsula would continue to be governed by Sheikh Jassim Al-Thani, who had formerly been nominated *kaimakam* by the Ottomans, and by his successors.

Case Concerning Maritime Delimitation and Territorial Questions between Qatar and Bahrain, 2001 I.C.J. 87 (Judgment, Mar. 16).

C. REGULATING THE USE OF LAND

1. Permanent Sovereignty over Natural Resources

a. Declaration on Permanent Sovereignty over Natural Resources

G.A. Res. 1803, U.N. GAOR, 17th Sess., Supp. No. 17, at 15, U.N. Doc. A/5217 (1962)

1. The right of peoples and nations to permanent sovereignty over their natural wealth and resources must be exercised in the interest of their national development and of the well-being of the people of the State concerned.

2. The exploration, development and disposition of such resources, as well as the import of the foreign capital required for these purposes, should be in conformity with the rules and conditions which the peoples and nations freely consider to be necessary or desirable with regard to the authorization, restriction or prohibition of such activities.

3. In cases where authorization is granted, the capital imported and the earnings on that capital shall be governed by the terms thereof, by the national legis-

lation in force, and by international law. The profits derived must be shared in the proportions freely agreed upon, in each case, between the investors and the recipient State, due care being taken to ensure that there is no impairment, for any reason, of that State's sovereignty over its natural wealth and resources.

4. Nationalization, expropriation or requisitioning shall be based on grounds or reasons of public utility, security or the national interest which are recognized as overriding purely individual or private interests, both domestic and foreign. In such cases the owner shall be paid appropriate compensation, in accordance with the rules in force in the State taking such measures in the exercise of its sovereignty and in accordance with international law. In any case where the question of compensation gives rise to a controversy, the national jurisdiction of the State taking such measures shall be exhausted. However, upon agreement by sovereign States and other parties concerned, settlement of the dispute should be made through arbitration or international adjudication. ...

8. Foreign investment agreements freely entered into by or between sovereign States shall be observed in good faith: States and international organizations shall strictly and conscientiously respect the sovereignty of peoples and nations over their natural wealth and resources in accordance with the Charter and the principles set forth in the present resolution.

b. Caltex (Texaco v. Libya)

53 I.L.R. 87 (1982)

[The case submitted to arbitration originates from fourteen Deeds of Concession concluded between 1955 and 1968 between the State of Libya and two American companies, Texaco Overseas Petroleum Company and California Asiatic Oil Company. Nine of the Deeds were amended in 1963 in order to make them compatible with new Libyan regulatory and legislative provisions relating to petroleum. The question that the Tribunal considers is whether, by adopting nationalization measures in 1973 and 1974, the Libyan Government breached its obligations under the contracts with Texaco and California Asiatic.] ...

80. This Tribunal has stated that it intends to rule on the basis of positive law, but now it is necessary to determine precisely the content of positive law and to ascertain the place which resolutions by the General Assembly of the United Nations could occupy therein.

In its Preliminary Award of 27 November 1975, this Tribunal postponed the examination of the objection raised by the Libyan Government in its Memorandum of 26 July 1974 according to which:

> Nationalization is an act related to the sovereignty of the State. This fact has been recognized by the consecutive Resolutions of the United Na-

> tions on the sovereignty of States over their natural resources, the last being Resolution No. 3171 of the United Nations General Assembly adopted on December 13, 1973, G.A. Res. 3171, U.N. GAOR, 28th Sess., U.N. Doc. A/RES/3171 [1974], as well as paragraph (4/E) of Resolution No. 3201 (S. VI) adopted on 1 May, 1974. The said Resolutions confirm that every State maintains complete right to exercise full sovereignty over its natural resources... Nationalization, being related to the sovereignty of the State, is not subject to foreign jurisdiction. Provisions of the International Law do not permit a dispute with a State to be referred to any Jurisdiction other than its national Jurisdiction. In affirmance of this principle, Resolutions of the General Assembly provide that any dispute related to Nationalization or its consequences should be settled in accordance with provisions of domestic law of the State. ...

The practice of the United Nations, referred to in the Libyan Government's Memorandum, does not contradict in any way the status of international law as indicated above. This Tribunal wishes first to recall the relevant passages for this case of Resolution 1803 (XVII) entitled "Permanent Sovereignty over Natural Resources", as adopted by the General Assembly on 14 December 1962 [recites paras. 3 and 4, supra]. ...

82. The Memorandum of the Libyan Government which has just been quoted relies, however, on more recent Resolutions of the General Assembly (3171 and 3201 (S-VI), in particular) which, according to this Government would as a practical matter rule out any recourse to international law and would confer an exclusive and unlimited competence upon the legislation and courts of the host country.

Although not quoted in the Libyan Memorandum, since subsequent to the date of 26 July 1974, Resolution 3281 (XXIX), proclaimed under the title "Charter of Economic Rights and Duties of the States" and adopted by the General Assembly on 12 December 1974, should also be mentioned with the two Resolutions in support of the contention made by the Libyan Government. Two portions of such Resolutions are of particular interest in the present case:

—Resolution 3201 (S-VI) adopted by the General Assembly on 1 May 1974 under the title "Declaration on the Establishment of a New International Economic Order", Article 4, paragraph (e):

> Full permanent sovereignty of every State over its natural resources and all economic activities. In order to safeguard these resources, each State is entitled to exercise effective control over them and their exploitation with means suitable to its own situation, including the right to nationalization or transfer of ownership to its nationals, this right being in expression of the full permanent sovereignty of the State. No State may be subjected to economic political or any other type of coercion to prevent the free and full exercise of this inalienable right.

—Article 2 of Resolution 3281 (XXIX):

1. Every State has and shall freely exercise full permanent sovereignty, including possession, use and disposal, over all its wealth, natural resources and economic activities.

2. Each State has the right …

c) To nationalize, expropriate or transfer ownership of foreign property, in which case appropriate compensation should be paid by the State adopting such measures, taking into account its relevant laws and regulations and all circumstances that the State considers pertinent. In any case where the question of compensation gives rise to a controversy, it shall be settled under the domestic law of the nationalizing State and by its tribunals, unless it is freely and mutually agreed by all States concerned that other peaceful means be sought on the basis of the sovereign equality of States and in accordance with the principal of free choice of means.

Substantial differences thus exist between Resolution 1803 (XVII) and the subsequent Resolutions as regards the role of international law in the exercise of permanent sovereignty over natural resources. This aspect of the matter is directly related to the instant case under consideration; this Tribunal is obligated to consider the legal validity of the above-mentioned Resolutions and the possible existence of a custom resulting therefrom.

83. The general question of the legal validity of the Resolutions of the United Nations has been widely discussed by the writers. This Tribunal will recall first that, under Article 10 of the U.N. Charter, the General Assembly only issues "recommendations", which have long appeared to be texts having no binding force and carrying no obligations for the Member States. …

Refusal to recognize any legal validity of United Nations Resolutions must, however, be qualified according to the various texts enacted by the United Nations. These are very different and have varying legal value, but it is impossible to deny that the United Nations' activities have had a significant influence on the content of contemporary international law. In appraising the legal validity of the above-mentioned Resolutions, this Tribunal will take account of the criteria usually taken into consideration, *i.e.,* the examination of voting conditions and the analysis of the provisions concerned.

84. (1) With respect to the first point, Resolution 1803 (XV-II) of 14 December 1962 was passed by the General Assembly by 87 votes to 2, with 12 abstentions. It is particularly important to note that the majority voted for this text, including many States of the Third World, but also several Western developed countries with market economies including the most important one, the United States. The principles stated in this Resolution were therefore assented to by a great many States representing not only all geographical areas but also all economic systems.

From this point of view, this Tribunal notes that the affirmative vote of several developed countries with a market economy was made possible in particular by the inclusion in the Resolution of two references to international law, and one passage relating to the importance of international cooperation for economic development. According to the representative of Tunisia:

> [t]he result of the debate on this question was that the balance of the original draft resolution was improvedbalance between, on the one hand, the unequivocal affirmation of the inalienable right of States to exercise sovereignty over their natural resources and, on the other hand, the reconciliation or adaptation of this sovereignty to international law, equity and the principles of international cooperation. (17 U.N. GAOR 1122, U.N. Doc. A/PV. 1193 (1962).)

The reference to international law, in particular in the field of nationalization, was therefore an essential factor in the support given by several Western countries to Resolution 1803 (XVII).

85. On the contrary, it appears to this Tribunal that the conditions under which Resolutions 3171 (XXVII), 3201 (S-VI) and 3281 (XXIX) (Charter of the Economic Rights and Duties of States) were notably different:

— Resolution 3171 (XXVII) was adopted by a recorded vote of 108 votes to 1, with 16 abstentions, but this Tribunal notes that a separate vote was requested with respect to the paragraph in the operative part mentioned in the Libyan Government's Memorandum whereby the General Assembly stated that the application of the principle according to which nationalizations effected by States as the expression of their sovereignty implied that it is within the right of each State to determine the amount of possible compensation and the means of their payment, and that any dispute which might arise should be settled in conformity with the national law of each State instituting measures of this kind. As a consequence of a roll-call, this paragraph was adopted by 86 votes to 11 … with 28 abstentions. …

This specific paragraph concerning nationalizations, disregarding the role of international law, not only was not consented to by the most important Western countries, but caused a number of the developing countries to abstain.

— Resolution 3201 (S-VI) was adopted without a vote by the General Assembly, but the statements made by 38 delegates showed clearly and explicitly what was the position of each main group of countries. The Tribunal should therefore note that the most important Western countries were opposed to abandoning the compromise solution contained in Resolution 1803 (XVII).

— The conditions under which Resolution 3281 (XXIX), proclaiming the Charter of Economic Rights and Duties of States, was adopted also show unambiguously that there was no general consensus of the States with respect to the most important provisions and in particular those concerning nationalization. Having been the subject matter of a roll-call vote, the Charter was adopted by 118 votes to 6, with 10 abstentions. … From this point of view, paragraph 2 (c) of Article 2 of the Charter, which limits consideration of the characteristics of compensation to the State and does not refer to international law, was voted by 104 to 16, with 6 abstentions, all of the industrialized countries with market economies having abstained or having voted against it. …

86. … As this Tribunal has already indicated, the legal value of the resolutions which are relevant to the present case can be determined on the basis of circumstances under which they were adopted and by analysis of the principles which they state:

— With respect to the first point, the absence of any binding force of the resolutions of the General Assembly of the United Nations implies that such resolutions must be accepted by the members of the United Nations in order to be legally binding. In this respect, the Tribunal notes that only Resolution 1803 (XVII) of 14 December 1962 was supported by a majority of Member States representing all of the various groups. By contrast, the other Resolutions mentioned above, and in particular those referred to in the Libyan Memorandum, were supported by a majority of States but not by any of the developed countries with market economies which carry on the largest part of international trade.

87. (2) With respect to the second point, to wit the appraisal of the legal value on the basis of the principles stated, it appears essential to this Tribunal to distinguish between those provisions stating the existence of a right on which the generality of the States has expressed agreement and those provisions introducing new principles which were rejected by certain representative groups of States and having nothing more than a *de lege ferenda* value only in the eyes of the States which have adopted them; as far as the others are concerned, the rejection of these same principles implies that they consider them as being *contra legem.* With respect to the former, which proclaim rules recognized by the community of nations, they do not create a custom but confirm one by formulating it and specifying its scope, thereby making it possible to determine whether or not one is confronted with a legal rule. As has been noted by Ambassador Castañeda, "[such resolutions] do not create the law; they have a declaratory nature of noting what does exist" (129 R.C.A.D.T. 204 (1970), at 315).

On the basis of the circumstances of adoption mentioned above and by expressing an *opinio juris communis*, Resolution 1803 (XVII) seems to this Tribunal to reflect the state of customary law existing in this field. Indeed, on the occasion of the vote on a resolution finding the existence of a customary rule, the States concerned clearly express their views. The consensus by a majority of States belonging to the various representative groups indicates without the slightest doubt universal recognition of the rules therein incorporated, *i.e.,* with respect to nationalization and compensation the use of the rules in force in the nationalizing State, but all this in conformity with international law.

88. … [T]his is not at all the case with respect to the other Resolutions mentioned above… In particular, as regards the Charter of Economic Rights and

Duties of States, several factors contribute to denying legal value to those provisions....

— In the first place, Article 2 of this Charter must be analyzed as a political rather than as a legal declaration concerned with the ideological strategy of development and, as such, supported only by non-industrialized States.

— In the second place, this Tribunal notes that ... the General Assembly was invited to adopt the Charter "as a first measure of codification and progressive development" within the field of the international law of development. However, because of the opposition of several States, this description was deleted from the text submitted to the vote of the Assembly. This important modification led Professor Virally to declare:

> It is therefore clear that the Charter is not a first step to codification and progressive development of international law, within the meaning of Article 13, para. 1 (a) of the Charter of the United Nations, that is to say an instrument purporting to formulate in writing the rules of customary law and intended to better adjust its content to the requirements of international relations. The persisting difference of opinions in respect to some of its articles prevented reaching this goal and it is healthy that people have become aware of this. *La Charte des Droits et Devoirs Economiques des Etats. Notes de Lecture*, 20 ANN. FRANÇAIS DE DROIT INT'L 57, 59 (1974).

... [S]everal developing countries, although having voted favorably on the Charter of Economic Rights and Duties of States as a whole, in explaining their votes regretted the absence of any reference to international law.

89. Such an attitude is further reinforced by an examination of the general practice of relations between States with respect to investments. ... [A] great many investment agreements entered into between industrial States or their nationals ... and developing countries ... state... the standards of compensation and further provide, in case of dispute regarding the level of such compensation, the possibility of resorting to an international tribunal. ...

90. The argument of the Libyan Government... that any dispute relating to nationalization or its consequences should be decided in conformity with the provisions of the municipal law of the nationalizing State and only in its courts, is also negated by a complete analysis of the whole text of the Charter of Economic Rights and Duties of States.

[T]his Tribunal concludes that the provisions referred to in this Article do not escape all norms of international law. Article 33, paragraph 2, of this Resolution states as follows: "2. In their interpretation and application, the provisions of the present Charter are interrelated and each provision should be construed in the context of the other provisions". Now, among the fundamental elements of international economic relations quoted in the Charter, principle (j) is headed as follows: "Fulfillment in good faith of international obligations". ...

91. Therefore, one should note that the principle of good faith... has an important place even in ... The Charter of Economic Rights and Duties of States. One should conclude that a sovereign State which nationalizes cannot disregard the commitments undertaken by the contracting State: to decide otherwise would in fact recognize that all contractual commitments undertaken by a State have been undertaken under a purely permissive condition on its part and are therefore lacking of any legal force and any binding effect. From the point of view of its advisability, such a solution would gravely harm the credibility of States since it would mean that contracts signed by them did not bind them; it would introduce in such contracts a fundamental imbalance because in these contracts only one party—the party contracting with the State—would be bound. In law, such an outcome would go directly against the most elementary principle of good faith and for this reason it cannot be accepted.

2. Servitudes

The exclusive control assigned to the nation-state over its territorial domain rests on the policy of optimalization of resource exploitation and conservation. Yet, in domestic law, it is appreciated that the corresponding right of "ownership," in its various forms, can sometimes impede uses that maximize common interests. Hence the doctrine of servitude, which can be traced back to Roman law, subordinates territory otherwise owned by one person to certain community uses in favor of others. Without such servitudes, some parts of the territorial domain of a community might suffer a reduction in value because of lack of access. International decision has struggled with the question of servitudes in a number of critical cases.

a. The North Atlantic Coast Fisheries Case (U.K. v. U.S.)

11 R.I.A.A. 167 (1910)

[In a dispute concerning the rights of U.S. nationals to take fish in certain parts of the British North Atlantic coastal waters and to enter bays and harbors for purposes of repairs and certain other activities associated with fishing, which was based on an earlier treaty, the United States contended, among other things, that the rights assigned to it were in the nature of a servitude and, hence, could not be regulated or subjected to conditions by the United Kingdom.] ...

The Tribunal is unable to agree with this contention:

(*a*) Because there is no evidence that the doctrine of international servitudes was one with which either American or British Statesmen were conversant in 1818, no English publicists employing the term before 1818, and the mention of it in Mr. GALLITIN's report being insufficient;

(*b*) Because a servitude in the French law, referred to by Mr. GALLATIN, can, since the Code, be only real and can not be personal (Code Civil, art. 686);

(*c*) Because a servitude in International law predicates an express grant of a sovereign right and involves an analogy to the relation of a *praedium dominans* and a *praedium serviens*; whereas by the Treaty of 1818 one State grants a liberty to fish, which is not a sovereign right, but a purely economic right, to the inhabitants of another State;

(*d*) Because the doctrine of international servitude in the sense which is now sought to be attributed to it originated in the peculiar and now obsolete conditions prevailing in the Holy Roman Empire of which the *domini terrae* were not fully sovereigns; they holding territory under the Roman Empire, subject at least theoretically, and in some respects also practically, to the courts of that Empire; their right being, moreover, rather of a civil than of a public nature, partaking more of the character of *dominium* than of *imperium,* and therefore certainly not a complete sovereignty. And because in contradistinction to this quasi-sovereignty with its incoherent attributes acquired at various times, by various means, and not impaired in its character by being incomplete in any one respect or by being limited in favor of another territory and its possessor, the modern State, and particularly Great Britain, has never admitted partition of sovereignty, owing to the constitution of a modern State requiring essential sovereignty and independence;

(*e*) Because this doctrine being but little suited to the principle of sovereignty which prevails in States under a system of constitutional government such as Great Britain and the United States, and to the present International relations of Sovereign States, has found little, if any, support from modern publicists. It could therefore in the general interest of the Community of Nations, and of the parties to this treaty, be affirmed by this tribunal only on the express evidence of an international contract;

(*f*) Because even if these liberties of fishery constituted an International servitude, the servitude would derogate from the sovereignty of the servient State only in so far as the exercise of the rights of sovereignty by the servient State would be contrary to the exercise of the servitude right by the dominant State. Whereas it is evident that, though every regulation of the fishery is to some extent a limitation, as it puts limits to the exercise of the fishery at will, yet such regulations as are reasonable and made for the purpose of securing and preserving the fishery and its exercise for the common benefit, are clearly to be distinguished from those restrictions and "molestations", the annulment of which was the purpose of the American demands formulated by MR. ADAMS in 1782, and such regulations consequently can not be held to be inconsistent with a servitude;

(*g*) Because the fishery to which the inhabitants of the United States were admitted in 1783, and again in 1818, was a regulated fishery…

(*h*) Because the fact that Great Britain rarely exercised the right of regulation in the period immediately succeeding 1818 is to be explained by various circumstances and is not evidence of the non-existence of the right;

(*i*) Because the words "in common with British subjects" tend to confirm the opinion that the inhabitants of the United States were admitted to a regulated fishery;

(*j*) Because the statute of Great Britain, 1819, which gives legislative sanction to the Treaty of 1818, provides for the making of "regulations with relation to the taking, drying and curing of fish by inhabitants of the United States in 'common.'"

b. The S.S. "Wimbledon" (U.K. v. Ger.)

1923 P.C.I.J. (Ser.A) No.1 (Jun. 28)

[During the Russo-Polish War in 1921, an English steamship, the *Wimbledon*, that had been chartered by a French company, sought to carry munitions and artillery stores to the Polish naval base at Danzig, by way of the Kiel Canal in Northern Germany. The German Government refused to allow the vessel to pass through the Canal, because, it alleged, it violated German neutrality law which prohibited such cargoes for Poland or Russia.] ...

The question upon which the whole case depends is whether the German authorities were entitled to refuse access to and passage through the Kiel Canal to the S.S. "Wimbledon" on March 21st, 1921, under the conditions and circumstances in which they did so.

The reply to this question must be sought in the provisions devoted by the Peace Treaty of Versailles to the Kiel Canal, in Part XII, entitled "Ports, Waterways and Railways", Section VI. This Section commences with a provision of a general and peremptory character, contained in Article 380, which is as follows:

> The Kiel Canal and its approaches shall be maintained free and open to the vessels of commerce and of war of all nations at peace with Germany on terms of entire equality..
>
> Then follow various provisions intended to facilitate and regulate the exercise of this right of free passage. ...

The Court considers that the terms of Article 380 are categorical and give rise to no doubt. It follows that the canal has ceased to be an internal and national navigable waterway, the use of which by the vessels of states other than the riparian state is left entirely to the discretion of that state, and that it has become an international waterway intended to provide under treaty guarantee easier access to the Baltic for the benefit of all nations of the world. Under its new regime, the Kiel Canal must be open on a footing of equality, to all vessels, without making any distinction between war vessels and vessels of commerce, but on one express condition, namely, that these vessels must belong to nations at peace with Germany.

The right of the Empire to defend herself against her enemies by refusing to allow their vessels to pass through the canal is therefore proclaimed and recognized. In making this reservation in the event of Germany not being at peace with the nation whose vessels of war or of commerce claim access to the canal, the Peace Treaty clearly contemplated the possibility of a future war in which Germany was involved. If the conditions of access to the canal were also to be modified in the event of a conflict between two Powers remaining at peace with the German Empire, the Treaty would not have failed to say so. It has not said so and this omission was no doubt intentional. ...

In order to dispute, in this case, the right of the S.S. "Wimbledon" to free passage through the Kiel Canal under the terms of Article 380, the argument has been urged upon the Court that this right really amounts to a servitude by international law resting upon Germany and that, like all restrictions or limitations upon the exercise of sovereignty, this servitude must be construed as restrictively as possible and confined within its narrowest limits, more especially in the sense that it should not be allowed to affect the rights consequent upon neutrality in an armed conflict. The Court is not called upon to take a definite attitude with regard to the question, which is moreover of a very controversial nature, whether in the domain of international law, there really exist servitudes analogous to the servitudes of private law. Whether the German Government is bound by virtue of a servitude or by virtue of a contractual obligation undertaken towards the Powers entitled to benefit by the terms of the Treaty of Versailles, to allow free access to the Kiel Canal in time of war as in time of peace to the vessels of all nations, the fact remains that Germany has to submit to an important limitation of the exercise of the sovereign rights which no one disputes that she possesses over the Kiel Canal. This fact constitutes a sufficient reason for the restrictive interpretation, in case of doubt, of the clause which produces such a limitation. But the Court feels obliged to stop at the point where the so-called restrictive interpretation would be contrary to the plain terms of the article and would destroy what has been clearly granted.

The argument has also been advanced that the general grant of a right of passage to vessels of all nationalities through the Kiel Canal cannot deprive Germany of the exercise of her rights as a neutral power in time of war, and place her under an obligation to allow the passage through the canal of contraband destined for one of the belligerents; for, in this wide sense, this grant would imply the abandonment by Germany of a personal and imprescriptible right, which forms an essential part of her sovereignty and which she neither could nor intended to renounce by anticipation. This contention has not convinced the Court; it conflicts with general considerations of the highest order. It is also gainsaid by consistent international practice and is at the same time contrary to the wording of Article 380 which clearly contemplated time of war as well as time of peace. The Court declines to see in the conclusion of any Treaty by which a State undertakes to perform or refrain from performing a particular act an abandonment of its sovereignty. No doubt any convention creating an obligation of this kind places a restriction upon the exercise of the sovereign rights of the State, in the sense that it requires them to be exercised in a certain way. But the right of entering into international engagements is [also] an attribute of State sovereignty.

As examples of international agreements placing upon the exercise of the sovereignty of certain states restrictions which though partial are intended to be perpetual, thc rules established with regard to the Suez and Panama Canals were cited before the Court. These rules are not the same in both cases; but they are of equal importance in that they demonstrate that the use of the great international waterways, whether by belligerent men-of-war, or by belligerent or neutral merchant ships carrying contraband, is not regarded as incompatible with the neutrality of the riparian sovereign.

[The Court discussed the treaties governing the use of both the Suez and Panama Canals, and held that although the treaties differed (the Suez could be used by nations belligerent to the sovereign), in neither case was the neutrality of the sovereign compromised.]

The precedents therefore afforded by the Suez and Panama Canals invalidate in advance the argument that Germany's neutrality would have necessarily been imperiled if her authorities had allowed the passage of the "Wimbledon" through the Kiel Canal, because that vessel was carrying contraband of war consigned to a state then engaged in an armed conflict. Moreover they are merely illustrations of the general opinion according to which when an artificial waterway connecting two open seas has been permanently dedicated to the use of the whole world, such waterway is assimilated to natural straits in the sense that even the passage of a belligerent man-of-war does not compromise the neutrality of the sovereign State under whose jurisdiction the waters in question lie. ...

[The Court held that Germany had improperly barred passage through the Kiel Canal to the *"Wimbledon"*, for which damages, which the Court liquidated, were to be paid.]

c. Right of Passage Over Indian Territory (Port. v. India)

1960 I.C.J. 6 (Judgment of Apr. 12)

[Portugal sued India for, among other things, refusing to allow passage over Indian territory into Portuguese enclaves.]

[T]he British found the Portuguese in occupation of the villages and exercising full and exclusive administrative authority over them. They accepted the situation as they found it and left the Portuguese in occupation of, and in exercise of exclusive authority over, the villages. The Portuguese held themselves out as sovereign over the villages. The British did not, as successors of the Marathas, themselves claim sovereignty, nor did they accord express recognition of Portuguese sovereignty, over them. The exclusive authority of the Portuguese over the villages was never brought in question. Thus Portuguese sovereignty over the villages was recognized by the British in fact and by implication and was subsequently tacitly recognized by India. As a consequence the villages comprised in the Maratha grant acquired the character of Portuguese enclaves within Indian territory. ...

With regard to Portugal's claim of a right of passage as formulated by it on the basis of local custom, it is objected on behalf of India that no local custom could be established between only two States. It is difficult to see why the number of States between which a local custom may be established on the basis of long practice must necessarily be larger than two. The Court sees no reason why long continued practice between two States accepted by them as regulating their relations should not form the basis of mutual rights and obligations between the two States.

As already stated, Portugal claims a right of passage to the extent necessary for the exercise of its sovereignty over the enclaves, without any immunity and subject to the regulation and control of India. In the course of the written and oral proceedings, the existence of the right was discussed with reference to the different categories making up the right, namely private persons, civil officials, goods in general, armed forces, armed police, and arms and ammunition. ...

It is common ground between the Parties that the passage of private persons and civil officials was not subject to any restrictions, beyond routine control, during these periods. There is nothing on the record to indicate the contrary.

Goods in general, that is to say, all merchandise other than arms and ammunition, also passed freely between Daman and the enclaves during the periods in question, subject only, at certain times, to customs regulations and such regulation and control as were necessitated by considerations of security or revenue....[and]... therefore, concludes that, with regard to private persons, civil officials and goods in general there existed during the British and post-British periods a constant and uniform practice allowing free passage between Daman and the enclaves. This practice having continued over a period extending beyond a century and a quarter unaffected by the change of regime in respect of the intervening territory which occurred when India became independent, the Court is, in view of all the circumstances of the case, satisfied that that practice was accepted as law by the Parties and has given rise to a right and a correlative obligation.

The Court therefore holds that Portugal had in 1954 a right of passage over intervening Indian territory between coastal Daman and the enclaves and between the enclaves, in respect of private persons, civil officials and goods in general, to the extent necessary, as claimed by Portugal, for the exercise of its sovereignty over the enclaves, and subject to the regulation and control of India.

As regards armed forces, armed police and arms and ammunition, the position is different.

It appears that during the British period up to 1878 passage of armed forces and armed police between British and Portuguese possessions was regulated on a basis of reciprocity. …

[A]fter 1878, such passage could only take place with previous authorization by the British and later by India, accorded either under a reciprocal arrangement already agreed to, or in individual cases. Having regard to the special circumstances of the case, this necessity for authorization before passage could take place constitutes, in the view of the Court, a negation of passage as of right. The practice predicates that the territorial sovereign had the discretionary power to withdraw or to refuse permission. It is argued that permission was always granted, but this does not, in the opinion of the Court, affect the legal position. There is nothing in the record to show that grant of permission was incumbent on the British or on India as an obligation.

As regards arms and ammunition, paragraph 4 of Article XVIII of the Treaty of 1878 provided that the exportation of arms, ammunition or military stores from the territories of one party to those of the other "shall not be permitted, except with the consent of, and under rules approved of by, the latter".

Rule 7A, added in 1880 … provided that "nothing in rules 5, 6, or 7 shall be deemed to authorize the grant of licenses … to import any arms, ammunition or military stores from Portuguese India, [or] to export to Portuguese India … [such objects] … except … by a special license". Subsequent practice shows that this provision applied to transit between Daman and the enclaves.

There was thus established a clear distinction between the practice permitting free passage of private persons, civil officials and goods in general, and the practice requiring previous authorization, as in the case of armed forces, armed police, and arms and ammunition.

The Court is, therefore, of the view that no right of passage in favour of Portugal involving a correlative obligation on India has been established in respect of armed forces, armed police, and arms and ammunition. …

Portugal also invokes general international custom, as well as the general principles of law recognized by civilized nations, in support of its claim of a right of passage as formulated by it. Having arrived at the conclusion that the course of dealings between the British and Indian authorities on the one hand and the Portuguese on the other established a practice, well understood between the Parties, by virtue of which Portugal had acquired a right of passage in respect of private persons, civil officials and goods in general, the Court does not consider it necessary to examine whether general international custom or the general principles of law recognized by civilized nations may lead to the same result.

As regards armed forces, armed police and arms and ammunition, the finding of the Court that the practice established between the Parties required for passage in respect of these categories the permission of the British or Indian authorities, renders it unnecessary for the Court to determine whether or not, in the absence of the practice that actually prevailed, general international custom or the general principles of law recognized by civilized nations could have been relied upon by Portugal in support of its claim to a right of passage in respect of these categories.

NOTES AND QUESTIONS

1. In negotiations between Israel and the Palestinian Authority over the establishment of a Palestinian state, the Palestinians have demanded guarantees that they will be able to pass from the West Bank to Gaza without being subjected to Israeli discretion about passage. The claims which states make for rights in the territory of other states are commonly discussed under the heading of "servitudes." Their utility in international law, especially for landlocked states which wish access to the sea, for military bases, or to situations like the Middle East example, is obvious. But none of the three cases above recognized the concept of "servitudes" in international law, relying instead on prior treaties or prior practice for their decisions. On what legal basis can Palestinians rely to establish the right to contiguous territory or a future state?

2. On the situation of the U.S. base at Guantánamo, Cuba, see Agreement for the Lease to the United States of Lands in Cuba for Naval and Coaling Stations 1 Malloy, Treaties 358-59 (1903). *See also* Article 3, Treaty between the United States and Cuba defining their relations, June 9, 1934, 48 Stat. 1682 (1934).

3. For further discussion, *see* F.A. VALI, SERVITUDES OF INTERNATIONAL LAW: A STUDY OF RIGHTS IN FOREIGN TERRITORY (Fred B. Rothman & Company 1986); *See also*, James R. Gordley, *Servitudes*, 3 GLOBAL JURIST FRONTIERS 1 (2003).

IV. AIRSPACE

A. CHARACTERISTICS AND POLICY

The airspace over the land masses, the territorial seas, and internal rivers have been regarded as generally non-sharable because of their physical proximity to, or intimate interdependence with, the land masses of the nation-state. This proximity and interdependence have made all use, and potential use, of such resources an integral part of the social process of the land masses they attend. Neither the security, nor the protection and appropriate development, of the various value processes upon the land masses could have been achieved without a high degree of exclusive control over these auxiliary resources. Even though modern developments in weapons make contiguity of considerably less relevance to military security than in the past, some degree of exclusive control over such resources remains necessary for the protection of many common exclusive interests.

Myres S. McDougal, Harold D. Lasswell, Ivan A. Vlasic & Joseph C. Smith, *The Enjoyment and Acquisition of Resources in Outer Space*, 111 U. PA. L.REV. 521, 575 (1963).

B. Allocation and Regulation of Use

1. Chicago Convention on International Civil Aviation

61 Stat. 1180 (1944)

Article 1: *Sovereignty*

The contracting States recognize that every State has complete and exclusive sovereignty over the airspace above its territory.

Article 2: *Territory*

For the purposes of this Convention the territory of a State shall be deemed to be the land areas and territorial waters adjacent thereto under the sovereignty, suzerainty, protection or mandate of such State.

Article 3: *Civil and state aircraft*

(*a*) This Convention shall be applicable only to civil aircraft, and shall not be applicable to state aircraft.

(*b*) Aircraft used in military, customs and police services shall be deemed to be state aircraft.

(*c*) No state aircraft of a contracting State shall fly over the territory of another State or land thereon without authorization by special agreement or otherwise, and in accordance with the terms thereof.

(*d*) The contracting States undertake, when issuing regulations for their state aircraft, that they will have due regard for the safety of navigation of civil aircraft. ...

Article 5: *Right of non-scheduled flight*

Each contracting State agrees that all aircraft of the other contracting States, being aircraft not engaged in scheduled international air services shall have the right, subject to the observance of the terms of this Convention, to make flights into or in transit non-stop across its territory and to make stops for non-traffic purposes without the necessity of obtaining prior permission, and subject to the right of the State flown over to require landing. Each contracting State nevertheless reserves the right, for reasons of safety of flight, to require aircraft desiring to proceed over regions which are inaccessible or without adequate air navigation facilities to follow prescribed routes, or to obtain special permission for such flights.

Such aircraft, if engaged in the carriage of passengers, cargo, or mail for remuneration or hire on other than scheduled international air services, shall also, subject to the provisions of Article 7, have the privilege of taking on or discharging passengers, cargo, or mail, subject to the right of any State where such embarkation or discharge takes place to impose such regulations, conditions or limitations as it may consider desirable.

Article 6: *Scheduled air services*

No scheduled international air service may be operated over or into the territory of a contracting State, except with the special permission or other authorization of that State, and in accordance with the terms of such permission or authorization.

2. Customary Law

While the air space above land territory is assimilated, as a legal matter, to the territory below, many special problems arise which are not completely clarified by the Chicago Convention or other international instruments.

a. Military Surveillance Flights

(1) Statement by President Eisenhower Proposing Reciprocal Aerial Inspection

July 21, 1955, The Geneva Conference of Heads of Governments, July 18-23, 1955 (Dept. of State Pub. 6044) at 54-55, *reprinted in* Documents on American Foreign Relations 1955, at 215-16

Gentlemen, since I have been working on this memorandum to present to this Conference, I have been searching my heart and mind for something that I could say here that could convince everyone of the great sincerity of the United States in approaching this problem of disarmament.

I should address myself for a moment principally to the Delegates from the Soviet Union, because our two great countries admittedly possess new and terrible weapons in quantities which do give rise in other parts of the world, or reciprocally, to the fears and dangers of surprise attack.

I propose, therefore, that we take a practical step, that we begin an arrangement, very quickly, as between ourselves—immediately. These steps would include:

To give to each other a complete blueprint of our military establishments, from beginning to end, from one end of our countries to the other; lay out the establishments and provide the blueprints to each other.

Next, to provide within our countries facilities for aerial photography to the other country—we to provide you the facilities within our country, ample facilities for aerial reconnaissance, where you can make all the pictures you choose and take them to your own country to study, you to provide exactly the same facilities for us and we to make these examinations, and by this step to convince the world that we are providing as between ourselves against the possibility of great surprise attack, thus lessening danger and relaxing tension. Likewise we will make more easily attainable a comprehensive and effective system of inspection and disarmament, because what I propose, I assure you, would be but a beginning.

Notes and Questions

1. President Eisenhower had occasion to reaffirm the principle he had enunciated in 1955, when a U.S. pilot in a U2 reconnaissance plane was brought down over the Soviet Union in 1960. In a news conference, President Eisenhower emphasized that his proposal was designed "to permit aerial observation over the United States and the Soviet Union which would assure that no surprise attack was being prepared against anyone." (News conference statement, May 11, 1960, 42 Dept. of State Bulletin. 851, 851-52 (1960)).

2. Within a decade, the Eisenhower proposal of mutual toleration on the part of the two Superpowers of surveillance of the air space of each had been incorporated into fundamental arms control instruments such as SALT I, SALT II and Article XII of the Anti-Ballistic Missile Agreement, which reads, in part:.

> Article XII
>
> 1. For the purpose of providing assurance or compliance with the provisions of this Treaty, each Party shall use national technical means of verification at its disposal in a manner consistent with generally recognized principles of international law.
>
> 2. Each Party undertakes not to interfere with the national technical means of verification of the other Party operating in accordance with paragraph 1 of this Article.
>
> 3. Each Party undertakes not to use deliberate concealment measures which impede verification by national technical means of compliance with the provisions of this Treaty. This obligation shall not require changes in current construction, assembly, conversion, or overhaul practices.

The threat of violent encounters between military aircraft of the subjacent state and the military surveillance aircraft of third states did not end with the Cold War, as the 2001 incident between the People's Republic of China and the United States confirms.

(2) W. Allan Edmiston, III, *Showdown in the South China Sea: An International Incidents Analysis of the So-Called Spy Plane Crisis*
16 Emory Int'l L. Rev. 639 (2002)

Early on April 1, 2001, a United States Navy EP-3 turboprop aircraft left the United States air base at Kadena on Okinawa, Japan, en route for the South China Sea. The EP-3 is an electronic surveillance plane. Although it is outfitted with highly sensitive equipment capable of collecting radio and radar emissions originating deep within the subject country's territory, and well beyond the reach of spy satellites, it carries no weapons. Its crews affectionately call the EP-3, with a maximum speed of 403 miles per hour, the "flying pig," for its lumbering pace and sluggish maneuverability.

After the EP-3 was detected by Chinese radar about seventy miles off the coast of Hainan Island, two Chinese F-8 fighter jets were scrambled from their airfield at Lingshui, on Hainan, to intercept it. Although China and the United States dispute the cause, the EP-3 and one of these F-8 fighters calamitously collided. Predictably, United States officials claimed that the Chinese pilot caused the collision, while Chinese officials claimed that the United States pilot caused it. Whatever the cause, the impact destroyed one of the EP-3's propellers, damaged a second, and detached part of its nose cone. And it so badly damaged the F-8 that its pilot was forced to eject. The Chinese pilot's body was never recovered.

The EP-3 plunged 8,000 feet before its pilot regained control. It made an emergency landing on Hainan, apparently the closest airstrip to the point of collision. Although the plane's crew insisted that repeated Mayday calls were transmitted on an internationally recognized frequency, the Chinese denied receiving these. Nevertheless, both sides later stipulated that the EP-3 did not receive permission, oral or otherwise, by Chinese authorities to land. After landing, the EP-3's crew was instructed to disembark. [The EP-3] was then conveyed to a nearby Chinese barracks, where it was detained for ten days. Despite the protests of United States officials, the Chinese boarded the plane, apparently to perform an investigation of it and its contents.

China and the United States presented conflicting versions of the circumstances leading up to the event, and discrepant understandings of the relevant legal norms. Both countries' legal arguments centered around three main issues of international law: (1) whether military overflight by an unarmed surveillance aircraft in a country's Exclusive Economic Zone (EEZ) is permissible; (2) whether violation of a country's territorial integrity by a military aircraft in distress is permitted without advance authorization; and (3) whether a military aircraft which lands in distress on another country's territory constitutes the sovereign territory of the aircraft's flag state. …

III. Outcome

... [T]he plane's crew was ultimately released on April 11, 2001, following receipt by the Chinese Minister of Foreign Affairs of a letter sent by the United States Ambassador to China, Joseph W. Prueher. In this letter Ambassador Prueher officially conveyed his, the Secretary of State's, and the President's "sincere regret" about the missing pilot and aircraft, and requested that the Minister of Foreign Affairs assure the Chinese people and the family of the missing pilot that the United States is "very sorry for their loss." Although this carefully worded letter prompted the Chinese to release the detained crewmembers, the dispute nevertheless continued.

With regard to future surveillance activity, both sides' positions were clear. China demanded that the United States cease surveillance activity off its coast. But the United States … [announced] its intention to continue to fly reconnaissance and surveillance flights in "international airspace" around the world.…

[T]he EP-3 remained stranded on the Hainan Island airfield until July 3, 2001, when it was finally disassembled and removed by a Russian cargo plane. This method of removal was the result of a carefully crafted compromise. Chinese officials feared a public outcry if further flights by United States military aircraft were permitted through Chinese airspace. Therefore, they adamantly opposed the United States' suggestion that its personnel should repair the plane in China, before flying it to its home airbase in Japan. However, both sides seemed satisfied with the agreement: Chinese Foreign Minister Sun Yuxi expressed his hope that "bilateral relations [c]ould come back to th[eir] normal track," while Department of Defense spokesman Rear Admiral Quigley allowed, "[w]e're glad to get the airplane back in a condition that it can be repaired and used again."

The international community's official reactions to the spy plane crisis were cautiously restrained and carefully measured. Its reactions were, for the most part, limited to routine expressions of hope that the standoff would be resolved peacefully and expeditiously, and in accordance with international law. ... There were no attempts to characterize the dispute as an intractable one requiring third party intervention. Nor were there any real efforts to condemn or criticize either of the participant parties. This would seem to suggest that even if the outcome of this incident was not completely consistent with the international community's perceptions of the relevant and applicable norms, neither was it sufficiently inconsistent with those perceptions to provoke an unequivocal response. So viewed, the international community's reaction appears to implicitly, if not explicitly, affirm that: (1) overflight by state-aircraft, for the purpose of military surveillance, is permissible in a coastal State's EEZ; (2) an emergency landing on the sovereign territory of another state is permissible, if advance authorization is sought, though not received; and (3) when a military aircraft makes a distress landing on another State's territory, that State may, without violation of international law, inspect the plane and its contents. ...

Still, clarification of a norm of international law in this manner does not ensure that the participants will abide by that norm in all future instances. Indeed, "[e]xpectations of lawfulness tend to guide rather than predetermine the behavior of participants." Therefore, to prevent occurrence of another similar dispute, these norms should be fortified, or else redefined, either through a multilateral agreement between the global military powers, or through a bilateral agreement between China and the United States. This agreement should accomplish two things. First, it should constitute a "standing consultative mechanism" to prevent future military incidents. Second, it should provide a clear statement of rights and procedures, binding on all signatories, in the event future military incidents occur. The latter might resemble the Agreement on the Prevention of Dangerous Military Activities concluded by the United States and the former Soviet Union on June 12, 1989. Under that agreement both countries committed to, *inter alia*, certain procedures for the resolution of incidents related to *force majeure* entry by one signatory into the national territory of the other. Specifically, the agreement provided that, in such circumstances, military personnel should be: (1) accorded an opportunity to contact their Defense Attaché or consular authorities as soon as possible; (2) cared for properly and their equipment protected; and (3) assisted in repairing their equipment in order to facilitate their departure. Clearly, both China and the United States would benefit from the certainty, consistency, and constancy that such an agreement would provide.

NOTES AND QUESTIONS

1. The author is engaging in an "international incidents analysis". For more on the technique, see INTERNATIONAL INCIDENTS: THE LAW THAT COUNTS IN WORLD POLITICS (W. Michael Reisman & Andrew R. Willard eds., Princeton U. Press 1988).

2. What factors, in your view, explain the ability of the United States and China to resolve the crisis peacefully?

3. The author's own recommendations for averting such conflicts in the future are included in the final paragraph above. Do they appear reasonable?

b. The Shooting Down of Civilian Aircraft

(1) Korean Airlines Flight 007 and Other Incidents

(a) Craig A. Morgan, *The Shooting of Korean Air Lines Flight 007: Responses to Unauthorized Aerial Incursions* in INTERNATIONAL INCIDENTS: THE LAW THAT COUNTS IN WORLD POLITICS (W. Michael Reisman & Andrew R. Willard eds., Princeton U. Press 1988)

In the early morning of September 1, 1983, a Korean Air Lines (KAL) Boeing 747 was shot down by a Soviet fighter while on a regularly scheduled flight from Anchorage, Alaska, to Seoul, South Korea. The Korean airliner had penetrated restricted airspace over a sensitive military base located on Sakhalin Island, on the northern Pacific coast of the Soviet Union. All 269 people aboard were killed. The downing resulted in the greatest loss of life and produced the strongest international reaction of any use of military force against civilian aircraft to date....

The incident is instructive for three reasons. First, the issues raised by the use of such force have never been formally adjudicated. Second, the only relevant international agreement in effect at the time of the incident did not settle the issue. Third, the most recent preceding incident had resulted in international behavior seemingly inconsistent with that of the four prior incidents.

The KAL 007 incident seems to indicate that the use of lethal force against intruding aircraft is subject to a set of widely shared normative expectations among participants in the international community. These expectations require that, at least in peacetime, lethal force not be used against civilian aircraft intruding into territorial airspace unless such aircraft display hostile intent. Civil aircraft are to be presumed nonhostile even when flying at night through restricted airspace over sensitive military installations. The subjacent state has an affirmative duty to identify properly such an aircraft as civilian. Whether an intruder's failure to respond to obvious warnings would constitute sufficient hostile intent to warrant the use of lethal force is still unclear. A number of states, however, apparently subscribe to what could be the emerging norm: the only appropriate response in such a situation is diplomatic, at least when the intruding aircraft does not appear to be armed.

The Previous Incidents

Prior to the downing of KAL Flight 007, there had been five peacetime incidents in which civilian airliners were fired on by the military forces of a subjacent state and casualties resulted. The international community, however, reacted to these incidents inconsistently, indicating no clearly shared normative expectation. Furthermore, there were factual considerations in the KAL downing that were not present in the earlier incidents. As a result, any community judgment of those earlier incidents may not provide a complete basis for assessing the expectations of participants in the KAL 007 incident.

The first of these prior incidents occurred on April 29, 1952, when an Air France plane en route from Frankfurt to Berlin was attacked by Soviet fighters over the Soviet-occupied zone of Germany. Three people aboard were injured, but the plane, although badly damaged, was able to land safely in Berlin. The Soviet Union claimed that its fighter had fired warning shots because the plane was not flying in the approved corridor and had thus violated Soviet airspace. The British, French, and American Allied High Commissioners issued a joint statement vehemently protesting the shooting, denying that the airliner was outside the corridor, and arguing that it should not matter if it were: "Quite apart from these questions of fact, to fire in any circumstances, even by way of warning, on an unarmed aircraft in time of peace, wherever that aircraft may be, is entirely inadmissible and contrary to all standards of civilized behavior." They requested that the Soviets conduct an investigation, punish those responsible, and pay compensation for the injuries and property damage. It seems that these requests were never officially answered.

A second incident occurred on July 23, 1954, when a Cathay Pacific airliner flying from Singapore to Hong Kong was shot down by fighters from the People's Republic of China, killing ten of the eighteen people on board. Following protests from the British and American governments, the Chinese, in a diplomatic note to the British, took responsibility for the incident, claiming that they had mistakenly identified the airliner as a Nationalist Chinese military aircraft on a mission of aggression. They expressed their willingness to consider compensation and subsequently paid in full the British demands submitted on behalf of all claimants.

One year later, on July 27, 1955, Bulgarian fighters shot down an El Al Israel plane near the Graeco-Bulgarian border, killing all fifty-eight on board. Protests and demands for compensation were lodged by the Israeli, British, American, French, and Swedish governments on behalf of their nationals killed in the incident. In an official statement, the Bulgarian government claimed that the airliner had violated its airspace and ignored signals to land, but nonetheless admitted that its air defenses had "shown hastiness" by firing on the airliner before exhausting other means of forcing it to land. The Bulgarian government promised to punish those responsible, take measures to prevent a recurrence, and pay compensation to the victims' families. However, it later denied any fault in the incident, insisting that its offer of compensation was strictly *ex gratia*, and suggested an amount that Israel, the United States, and the United Kingdom all rejected as unacceptably small. These three states then brought suit in the International Court of Justice, but Bulgaria refused to submit to the jurisdiction of the court and the case was never decided.

The most serious incident prior to Flight 007 occurred on February 21, 1973, when a Libyan Airlines plane, en route from Benghazi, Libya, apparently overshot its destination, Cairo, and intruded over the Israeli-occupied Sinai. It was shot down by Israeli fighters and 106 of the 118 people on board were killed instantly or died shortly thereafter. Israel maintained that the aircraft had penetrated airspace "over a most highly sensitive Israeli-controlled military area," had behaved in a suspicious manner, and had acknowledged but ignored signals to land from the intercepting fighters. Israeli officials claimed that the fighters had shot at the wings of the plane to force it to land, not to destroy it, and had done so only as a last resort. As further justification, they cited intelligence reports, received a month before, warning that Arab terrorists were planning to crash an aircraft loaded with explosives, or a hijacked airliner, into an Israeli city. Nonetheless, Israel admitted that the shooting had been a mistake, although one that could only be known after the fact, and offered to pay compensation on an *ex gratia* basis. The international community condemned Israel for this incident. The Libyan foreign minister declared the shooting a "criminal act," and Syria, Lebanon, Algeria, and Egypt joined in denouncing Israel. The United Nations Commission on Human Rights called the shooting "cruel and unjustified." The International Federation of Airline Pilots' Associations concluded that it could find "no justification for the excessive use of force," but decided against calling for sanctions. The International Civil Aviation Organization (ICAO) Secretariat conducted an investigation of the incident. The ICAO Council, after examining the Secretariat's report, adopted a resolution on June 4, 1973, strongly condemning Israel.

The fifth incident occurred on the night of April 20-21, 1978, and involved a Korean Air Lines flight from Paris to Seoul, South Korea, that flew into Soviet airspace over a restricted military area south of Murmansk. A Soviet fighter shot at the airliner, killing two passengers and injuring sixteen others. The airliner was able to crash-land on a frozen lake with no additional injuries. The Soviet Union released all of the passengers and most of the crew two days later, but detained the pilot and navigator for a week of questioning. This incident is noteworthy for its lack of strong adverse international reaction. The Soviet Union did not publicly charge that the airliner was spying, and South Korea did not condemn the shooting as unjustified. The president of South Korea, in fact, thanked the Soviet Union for the speedy return of the airliner's passengers and crew. Neither South Korea nor the Soviet Union offered a public explanation of why the airliner was several hundred miles off course. …

These five incidents suggest that, prior to 1983, international normative expectations prohibited shooting an intruding aircraft simply because it was in one's airspace. "Exclusive sovereignty" over airspace above a state was not enough to justify employing force. In each of these incidents the territorial state felt it had to allege aggravating circumstances-such as failure to heed warnings or presence over sensitive areas-to justify using such force. Beyond this rejection of a rather absolute position, the governing norms were unclear. …

The principle of proportionality, as a limit upon a state's lawful use of sovereign force, has emerged [after the KAL 007 incident] as an appropriate standard for judging the lawfulness of response to aerial intrusions. …

The subjacent state must justify shooting an intruding aircraft and cannot rely on a presumption that the action is lawful merely because the aircraft violated territorial airspace. Such a shooting must be justified even when the foreign aircraft has penetrated a sensitive and clearly restricted area at night. Some overt demonstration of hostile intent is required to support the use of violence, and the burden rests upon the intercepting state to take reasonable measures to determine that intent and to take measures short of lethal force to divert the plane. Specifically, the ICAO requirement to warn an intruding civilian aircraft has become a widely accepted norm. …

Moreover, a minority of states feel that during peacetime the threat of an intruding airliner's potential for reconnaissance can never be sufficiently hostile to justify endangering innocent lives. This view may represent the emerging norm. …

NOTES AND QUESTIONS

1. Shooting down civilian aircraft can invite retaliatory strikes of a devastating character, such as the blowing up by terrorists of Pan Am Flight 103 over Lockerbie, Scotland, in 1988, an act that was widely seen as a response to the following incident:

> On July 3, 1988, the U.S.S. Vincennes, already involved in an exchange of fire with a group of Iranian naval craft (Boghammar boats) in the international waters of the Persian Gulf, shot down an unidentified aircraft that had just departed from the joint military-civilian airfield at Bandar-e Abbas. After repeated, unsuccessful efforts by the Vincennes to establish contact with the unidentified aircraft, the captain, believing that his vessel might be attacked within minutes by an Iranian military aircraft sent to assist the gunboats engaged in the surface exchange, ordered the still unidentified aircraft to be fired upon. The aircraft was shot down, and was only afterwards identified as a civil airliner, Iran Air Flight 655. The incident resulted in the deaths of 290 individuals from six nations. President Reagan, learning the true identity of the aircraft later the same day, defended the defensive action by the Vincennes as "proper" and issued a statement of sympathy and condolences for the passengers, crew and families concerned.… On July 11, 1988, the White House announced that the President, personally saddened at the tragic deaths of the innocent victims of the "accident" and prompted by the humanitarian traditions of the United States, had decided that the United States would offer compensation on an *ex gratia* basis to their families.
>
> Then-Vice President Bush representing the U.S. before the Security Council on July 14, 1988, justified the attack as an act of self-defense during hostilities and urged Iran to accept S.C. Resolution 598 which called for a cease fire between Iran and the U.S. Subsequently, the President of the Islamic Republic of Iran, Seyed Ali Khamenei, in-

formed UN Secretary-General Javier Pérez de Cuéllar by a letter dated July 17, 1988, that Iran accepted Resolution 598.

Marian N. Leich, *AGORA: The Downing of Iran Air Flight 655, Denial Of Liability: Ex Gratia Compensation on a Humanitarian Basis*, 83 AM. J. INT'L L. 319 (1989). *See also* Andreas F. Lowenfeld, *AGORA: The Downing of Iran Air Flight 655, Looking Back and Looking Ahead,* 83 AM. J. INT'L L. 336 (1989).

2. *Alejandre v. Republic of Cuba*, 42 F.Supp. 2d 1317 (1999), was a suit against the Republic of Cuba and the Cuban Air Force by three of the four victims of a shoot-down of two "Brothers to the Rescue" (BTTR) aircraft in 1996. On December 17, 1997, this Court entered Final Judgment on behalf of Plaintiffs and against Defendants Cuba and CAF for total compensatory damages of $49,927,911. In addition, the Court entered Final Judgment on behalf of Plaintiffs and against only Defendant CAF for punitive damages in the sum of $137,000,000. This Court concluded its Order with the following unambiguous statement: "The total compensatory and punitive damages here-with awarded to Plaintiffs are $187,627,911, for which execution may issue forthwith against the Defendants Cuba and the Cuban Air Force and against any of their assets wherever situated."

3. Related to the same matter, Florida criminal indictments were issued on August 21, 2003, against General Ruben Martinez Puente and the Cuban Air Force crew members who shot down the BTTR planes. Charges include murder, destruction of aircraft, and conspiracy, carrying a possible death sentence. Extradition is impossible, however, because no diplomatic relations exist between Cuba and the U.S.

4. On the basis of the above incidents, how would you analyze customary international law in regard to the shooting down of civilian aircraft prior to September 2001? What effect might the War on Terrorism have on those developing norms? *See* also, Maj. Stephen M. Shrewsbury, *September 11th and the Single European Sky: Developing Concepts of Airspace Sovereignty*, 68 J. AIR L. & COM. 115 (2003).

V. ANTARCTICA

A. CHARACTERISTICS AND POLICIES

1. EMILIO J. SAHURIE, THE INTERNATIONAL LAW OF ANTARCTICA xxi-xxvi (New Haven Press 1992)

Antarctica ... covers some 13.5 million square kilometers, a landmass larger than the size of the United States and Mexico combined. ...

Only when larger ships were built and transoceanic voyages took place could Antarctic seas be reached. In the eighteenth century Captain Cook, while circumnavigating the globe, twice crossed the Antarctic Circle, and found his way hampered by ice fields. His reports of fur seal colonies and whales gave rise to the period of early exploitation of Antarctic marine living resources.

By the end of the eighteenth and the beginning of the nineteenth century, commercial expeditions of American, Argentine, Australian, British, Chilean, and French nationals had hunted seals and had visited several Antarctic and sub-Antarctic islands. During these voyages the Antarctic continent was sighted, and man landed there for the first time early in the nineteenth century. When seals were exterminated, commercial activities centered on whales; and Germans and New Zealanders joined in the trade.

Antarctic exploration began at the turn of the twentieth century. Several major expeditions were organized from Belgium, Germany, Sweden, Britain, Scotland, France, Japan, Australia, and other nations. Their heroism is highlighted by the dramatic race for the South Pole in 1911 between Amundsen's Norwegian expedition and Scott's British expedition. Assertions of territorial claims by several states traced early exploration of the continent. Between 1908 and 1942 national claims to Antarctic territory were put forward by Britain, France, Australia, New Zealand, Chile, Norway, and Argentina. These pie-shaped claims converge at the South Pole and cover some 85% of the continent and its adjacent islands. The remaining 15% of the continental territory is still unclaimed. The Argentine, British and Chilean claims overlap and conflict with each other — indeed, Antarctica has not escaped conflict.

Discord in Antarctica began early in the twentieth century, but it reached serious proportions only in the midst of World War II, when British warships seeking German submarines and stations in Antarctica found that Argentines had taken possession of some Antarctic islands located within the disputed region. Chile and Argentina made a common cause against the British claim over the "American" Antarctic, and after the World War, the dispute worsened in both tone and action, and included the use of force. A situation soon developed that posed a serious threat to the peace of the region.

In part, that conflict had a geopolitical aspect, which awakened the interest of the superpowers. The strategic importance of Antarctica for the control of the oceans became evident in World War II as it was used as a pass through the Atlantic, the Pacific, and the Indian Oceans. Thus, although the United States and the Soviet Union had neither recognized nor made any claim to Antarctica, by the end of the 1940s both had asserted their interest in the area. Whereas in the 1920s and 1930s U.S. expeditions organized to Antarctica had been privately sponsored, in 1946-47 the U.S. government launched the largest expedition ever sent to the region. For its part, in 1949 the Soviet Union, after more than a hundred years of passivity, suddenly claimed that the Russian Admiral von Bellingshausen was the first discoverer of the Antarctic continent. A year later the Soviet government sent a note to the interested governments stating that it could not recognize any settlement of Antarctica reached without its participation.

By the 1950s it was obvious that the problems, relating to Antarctica were more numerous and more complex than in the preceding decade. Clearly Antarctica was part of the larger international process, but it was as yet unclear whether its order was to be fully absorbed into such a process (characterized by the bipolarism of the superpowers' antagonism and systems of resource allocation of territorial sovereignty, freedom of access, and common spaces) or whether a more differentiated pattern of practices better suited to the sharing and shaping of values attainable from the area was to develop.

Unexpectedly, events took a course which shifted the concerns of the participants from security to enlightenment and greatly affected future political and legal developments. These events originated with the International Geophysical Year (IGY) held in 1957-58, which was to be undertaken in different parts of the globe, including Antarctica. All the states with territorial claims or other interests in Antarctica participated. The success of the IGY as a scientific achievement and example of international cooperation helped to create a propitious atmosphere to negotiate an institutional arrangement for the management of Antarctica. The IGY also produced another important political effect: by establishing scientific stations for both superpowers, the IGY created a situation in which both the United States and the Soviet Union were present in Antarctica and willing to remain there. The presence of the United States and the Soviet Union was viewed by claimant states as precluding any attempt to enforce their territorial claims and made it necessary to formalize the modus vivendi in the area which had evolved from situations of violence and expectations of conflict to peaceful activities and international cooperation.

The patterns of interaction that had developed were formalized in the Antarctic Treaty of 1959, which took effect in 1961. The twelve original signatories include the territorial claimants, Argentina, Australia, Britain, Chile, France, New Zealand, and Norway, together with the other interested states, Belgium, Japan, South Africa, the United States, and the Soviet Union. All had actively participated in the IGY. The Treaty prohibits the establishment of military bases, the testing of weapons, nuclear explosions, and the disposal of radioactive waste. Territorial claims were put in abeyance, and new claims were barred during the life of the Treaty. The Treaty also framed a system of decision-making under which more than one hundred resolutions and regulations have been reached so far.

During the 1960s and the 1970s the resulting order of Antarctica was perceived to have functioned satisfactorily. The institutional practices developed achieved a remarkable degree of stability and congruence not only with basic community expectations but even with formal documents - the wording of the Antarctic Treaty has been upheld and respected in actual practice. Indeed, Antarctica became a unique place on earth, where confrontation between East and West and North and South, as well as traditional national rivalries, were avoided and did not strain cooperation and scientific exchange.

But a new period is now characterized by the organization of exploitation of resources, and by broader international awareness of Antarctica; in fact, one has led to the other. Because it was considered unfeasible to exploit resources in Antarctica, and because it was a matter in which the position of claimants and non-claimants seemed irreconcilable, the Antarctic Treaty is silent on resource exploitation; therefore the Antarctic order contemplates no authoritative policies on the issue. This is despite the apparent fact that the area is rich in most minerals and in living resources. Krill, a small crustacean abundant in Antarctic seas, holds great commercial and nutritional potentialities. With respect to minerals, important deposits of iron, coal, uranium, gold, silver, copper, nickel, chromium, tin, and others have been traced. However, hydrocarbons have attracted the most attention. It is believed that oil and gas abound both on land and offshore. Certainly, offshore exploitation of hydrocarbons presents the most immediate possibility of exploitation in Antarctica.

The Antarctic powers realized that the balance created through the Antarctic Treaty System could be seriously threatened unless its umbrella were extended to cover the issue of resources; nevertheless, there was confidence that the problems of creating a resources regime could be dealt with, since the Treaty System had worked well for so many years. Thus the Antarctic powers negotiated, and in 1980 concluded, a comprehensive Convention on Antarctic Marine Living Resources. Since 1982 they had been negotiating a minerals regime, which was adopted in 1988. However, in September, 1989, the French and Australian governments withdrew from the agreement reached in 1988. The agreement was finally rejected in 1991, when the present book was in production, and a protocol to the Antarctic Treaty on environmental protection was adopted.

The international community perceived these actions as a prelude to intense resource exploitation in Antarctica. In a world hungry for proteins and energy, this apparent preparation was enough to lead other nations to demand participation in the riches of an area whose status seemed so undefined. In 1983, for the first time, Antarctica was included in the agenda of the U.N. General Assembly at the request of Malaysia, Antigua, and Barbuda, which received the support of other LDCs [Least Developed Countries]. Since then, Antarctica has become part of the U.N. debate. Those countries pressing the issue claim that the area is, or should be, part of the common heritage of mankind. They want to replace the Antarctic Treaty System and to establish a new institutional arrangement for the management of Antarctica within the U.N. system.

While the Antarctic Treaty System is being challenged, it is also growing larger and gathering substantial support. More than twenty states have joined the original twelve parties to the Treaty, and eight of them, Poland, West Germany, Brazil, India, China, Uruguay, East Germany, and Sweden, now enjoy a status within the Treaty System comparable to that of the original parties.

The unsolved conflicts about Antarctica are many and profound. Disputes exist among the territorial claimants, between them and other Antarctic powers, and between the latter and the rest of the international community. Individuals, environmentalists, scientists, and business groups also have distinctive interests. Underlying these divergent claims is the current and potential importance of Antarctica for global processes relating to power and security, to wealth and the exploitation of resources, to enlightenment and scientific research, to well-being and the protection of the environment, as well as to international prestige and respect.

B. ALLOCATION, PROTECTION AND REGULATION OF USE

Consider the various prescriptive regimes accepted or proposed:

1. Antarctic Treaty

402 U.N.T.S. 71 (1959).

The Government of Argentina, Australia, Belgium, Chile, the French Republic, Japan, New Zealand, Norway, the Union of South Africa, the Union of Soviet Socialist Republics, the United Kingdom of Great Britain and Northern Ireland, and the United States of America,

Recognizing that it is in the interest of all mankind that Antarctica shall continue forever to be used exclusively for peaceful purposes and shall not become the scene or object of international discord;

Acknowledging the substantial contributions to scientific knowledge resulting from international cooperation in scientific investigation in Antarctica;

Convinced that the establishment of a firm foundation for the continuation and development of such cooperation on the basis of freedom of scientific investigation in Antarctica as applied during the International Geophysical Year accords with the interests, of science and the progress of all mankind;

Convinced also that a treaty ensuring the use of Antarctica for peaceful purposes only and the continuance of international harmony in Antarctica will further the purposes and principles embodied in the Charter of the United Nations;

Have agreed as follows:

Article I

(1) Antarctica shall be used for peaceful purposes only. There shall be prohibited, inter alia, any measures of a military nature, such as the establishment of military bases and fortifications, the carrying out of military maneuvers, as well as the testing of any type of weapons.

(2) The present Treaty shall not prevent the use of military personnel or equipment for scientific research or for any other peaceful purpose.

Article II

Freedom of scientific investigation in Antarctica and cooperation toward that end, as applied during the International Geophysical Year, shall continue, subject to the provisions of the present Treaty. …

Article IV

(1) Nothing contained in the present Treaty shall be interpreted as:

(a) a renunciation by any Contracting Party of previously asserted rights of or claims to territorial sovereignty in Antarctica;

(b) a renunciation or diminution by any Contracting Party of any basis of claim to territorial sovereignty in Antarctica which it may have whether as a result of its activities or those of its nationals in Antarctica, or otherwise;

(c) prejudicing the position of any Contracting Party as regards its recognition or non-recognition of any other State's right of or claim or basis of claim to territorial sovereignty in Antarctica.

(2) No acts or activities taking place while the present Treaty is in force shall constitute a basis for asserting, supporting or denying a claim to territorial sovereignty in Antarctica or create any rights of sovereignty in Antarctica. No new claim, or enlargement of an existing claim, to territorial sovereignty in Antarctica shall be asserted while the present Treaty is in force.

Article V

(1) Any nuclear explosions in Antarctica and the disposal there of radioactive waste material shall be prohibited. …

Article VI

The provisions of the present Treaty shall apply to the area south of 60' South Latitude, including all ice shelves, but nothing in the present Treaty shall prejudice or in any way affect the rights, or the exercise of the rights, of any State under international law with regard to the high seas within that area.

2. Convention on the Regulation of Antarctic Mineral Resource Activities

27 I.L.M. 859 (1988)

The States Parties to this Convention, ...

Reaffirming that it is in the interest of all mankind that the Antarctic Treaty area shall continue forever to be used exclusively for peaceful purposes and shall not become the scene or object of international discord;

Noting the possibility that exploitable mineral resources may exist in Antarctica; …

Believing that a regime governing Antarctic mineral resource activities will further strengthen the Antarctic Treaty system;

Convinced that participation in Antarctic mineral resource activities should be open to all States which have an interest in such activities and subscribe to a regime governing them and that the special situation of developing country Parties to the regime should be taken into account;

Believing that the effective regulation of Antarctic mineral resource activities is in the interest of the international community as a whole;

HAVE AGREED as follows:

Article 2: *Objectives and General Principles*

1. This Convention is an integral part of the Antarctic Treaty system, comprising the Antarctic Treaty, the measures in effect under that Treaty, and its associated separate legal instruments, the prime purpose of which is to ensure that Antarctica shall continue forever to be used exclusively for peaceful purposes and shall not become the scene or object of international discord. The Parties provide through this Convention, the principles it establishes, the rules it prescribes, the institutions it creates and the decisions adopted pursuant to it, a means for:

(a) assessing the possible impact on the environment of Antarctic mineral resource activities;

(b) determining whether Antarctic mineral resource activities are acceptable;

(c) governing the conduct of such Antarctic mineral resource activities as may be found acceptable; and

(d) ensuring that any Antarctic mineral resource activities are undertaken in strict conformity with this Convention.

2. In implementing this Convention, the Parties shall ensure that Antarctic mineral resource activities, should they occur, take place in a manner consistent with all the components of the Antarctic Treaty system and the obligations flowing therefrom.

3. In relation to Antarctic mineral resource activities, should they occur, the Parties acknowledge the special responsibility of the Antarctic Treaty Consultative Parties for the protection of the environment and the need to:

(a) protect the Antarctic environment and dependent and associated ecosystems;

(b) respect Antarctica's significance for, and influence on, the global environment;

(c) respect other legitimate uses of Antarctica;

(d) respect Antarctica's scientific value and aesthetic and wilderness qualities;

(e) ensure the safety of operations in Antarctica;

(f) promote opportunities for fair and effective participation of all Parties; and

(g) take into account the interests of the international community as a whole.

Article 3: *Prohibition of Antarctic Mineral Resource Activities Outside this Convention*

No Antarctic mineral resource activities shall be conducted except in accordance with this Convention and measures in effect pursuant to it and, in the case of exploration or development, with a Management Scheme approved pursuant to Article 48 or 54.

3. Protocol on Environmental Protection to the Antarctic Treaty

30 I.L.M. 1461 (1991)

Article 2: *Objective and Designation*

The Parties commit themselves to the comprehensive protection of the Antarctic environment and dependent and associated ecosystems and hereby designate Antarctica as a natural reserve, devoted to peace and science.

Article 3: *Environmental Principles*

1. The protection of the Antarctic environment and dependent and associated ecosystems and the intrinsic value of Antarctica, including its wilderness an aesthetic values and its value as an area for the conduct of scientific research, in particular research essential to understanding the global environment, shall be fundamental considerations in the planning and conduct all activities in the Antarctic Treaty area.

2. To this end:

(a) activities in the Antarctic Treaty area shall be planned and conducted so as to limit adverse impacts on the Antarctic environment and dependent a associated ecosystems;

(b) activities in the Antarctic Treaty area shall be planned and conducted so as to avoid:

(i) adverse effects on climate or weather patterns;

(ii) significant adverse effects on air or water quality;

(iii) significant changes in the atmospheric, terrestrial (including aquatic), glacial or marine environments;

(iv) detrimental changes in the distribution, abundance or productivity species or populations of species of fauna and flora;

(v) further jeopardy to endangered or threatened species or populations such species; or

(vi) degradation of, or substantial risk to, areas of biological, scientific, historic, aesthetic or wilderness significance;

(c) activities in the Antarctic Treaty area shall be planned and conducted on the basis of information sufficient to allow prior assessments of, and informed judgments about, their possible impacts on the Antarctic environment and dependent and associated ecosystems and on the value of Antarctica for the conduct of scientific research …

3. Activities shall be planned and conducted in the Antarctic Treaty area s as to accord priority to scientific research and to preserve the value of Antarctica as an area for the conduct of such research, including research essential to understanding the global environment. …

Article 7: *Prohibition of Mineral Resource Activities*

Any activity relating to mineral resources, other than scientific research, shall be prohibited.

Article 8: *Environmental Impact Assessment*

1. Proposed activities referred to in paragraph 2 below shall be subject to the procedures set out in Annex I for prior assessment of the impacts of those activities on the Antarctic environment or on dependent or associated ecosystems …

2. Each Party shall ensure that the assessment procedures set out in Annex I are applied in the planning processes leading to decisions about any activities undertaken in the Antarctic Treaty area pursuant to scientific research programmes, tourism and all other governmental and non-governmental activities in the Antarctic Treaty area … including associated logistic support activities.

3. The assessment procedures set out in Annex I shall apply to any change in any activity whether the change arises from an increase or decrease in the intensity of an existing activity, from the addition of an activity, the decommissioning of a facility, or otherwise. …

Article 25: *Modification or Amendment*

1. Without prejudice to the provisions of Article 9, this Protocol may be modified or amended at any time in accordance with the procedures set forth in Article XII (1) (a) and (b) of the Antarctic Treaty.

2. If, after the expiration of 50 years from the date of entry into force of this Protocol, any of the Antarctic Treaty Consultative Parties so requests by a communication addressed to the Depositary, a conference shall be held as so as practicable to review the operation of this Protocol.

3. A modification or amendment proposed at any Review Conference called pursuant to paragraph 2 above shall be adopted by a majority of the Parties, including 3/4 of the States which are Antarctic Treaty Consultative Parties at the time of adoption of this Protocol.

4. A modification or amendment adopted pursuant to paragraph 3 above shall enter into force upon ratification, acceptance, approval or accession by 3/4 the Antarctic Treaty Consultative Parties, including ratification, acceptance approval or accession by all States which are Antarctic Treaty Consultative Parties at the time of adoption of this Protocol.

5. (a) With respect to Article 7, the prohibition on Antarctic mineral resource activities contained therein shall continue unless there is in force a binding legal regime on Antarctic mineral resource activities that includes an agreed means for determining whether, and, if so, under which conditions, any such activities would be acceptable. This regime shall fully safeguard the interests of all States referred to in Article IV of the Antarctic Treaty and apply the principles thereof. Therefore, if a modification or amendment to Article 7 is proposed at a Review Conference referred to in paragraph 2 above, it shall include such a binding legal regime.

(b) If any such modification or amendment has not entered into force within 3 years of the date of its adoption, any Party may at any time thereafter notify to the Depositary of its withdrawal from this Protocol, and such withdrawal shall take effect 2 years after receipt of the notification by the Depositary.

NOTES AND QUESTIONS

1. Management and control of Antarctica is presently exercised in the joint decision-making processes of the twenty-two Consultative Parties to the Antarctic Treaty. This model of resource use has exclusionary features. What, if anything, differentiates the Antarctic treaty regime from a condominium arrangement, i.e. shared territorial sovereignty, viz. the joint control of co-riparians over a common lake such as the The Gulf of Fonseca or the Lake of Constance? Is there a difference regarding the degree to which states parties pursue exclusively their own interests? Is the Antarctic Treaty regime committed exclusively to the global common, i.e. the inclusive interest? *See, generally,* EMILIO J. SAHURIE, THE INTERNATIONAL LAW OF ANTARCTICA, *supra*, at 373-378; THE ANTARCTIC LEGAL REGIME (Christopher C. Joyner & Sudhir K. Chopra eds., 1988); Donald R. Rothwell, *Governing the Antarctic: The Effectiveness and Legitimacy of the Antarctic Treaty System*, 92 AM. J. INT'L L. 170 (1998); David J. Bederman, *Theory on Ice: Antarctica in International Law and Relations*, 39 VA. J. INT'L L. 467 (1999).

2. Territorial sectoral claims remain "frozen." Are those claims to sovereignty possibly in the best interest of the world community, given a general tendency of neglect of shared or common resources? *See* Garrett Hardin, *The Tragedy of the Commons*, 162 SCIENCE 1243 (1968). Wouldn't exclusive owners be more concerned about protecting and conserving the resource? Have the sectoral claims been established in conformity with universal policies regarding effective occupation? Is recognition of "constructive possession," by virtue of the Hinterland theory (see *Eastern Greenland*, *supra*, at 758), still an appropriate policy choice? The U.S. now maintains a year-round research facility (McMurdo station) directly on the South Pole. To establish territorial sovereignty, shouldn't there be a requirement of a more extensive and intensive presence? Would that be ecologically wise? In case the territorial claims were "unfrozen," could the United States, by virtue of McMurdo, claim the center of Antarctica and truncate the sectoral claims of the other claimants? Compare D. Michael Hinkley, *Protecting American Interests in Antarctica: The Territorial Claims Dilemma*, 39 NAVAL L. REV. 43 (1990), and Bernard N. Oxman, *Antarctica and the New Law of the Sea*, 19 CORNELL INT'L L.J. 211 (1986).

3. The relatively exclusionary Antarctic Treaty regime justifies itself by the States Parties' professed real interest and stake in the area as evidenced by the establishment of research stations and the carrying-out of research functions. Are the reasons for this virtual "closed shop" persuasive? With the exception of South Africa, no African country is a member of the "Antarctic Club." Is it fair, or in the global common interest, to exclude them? Is it fair to impose a requirement such as the carrying-out of significant research on the continent as the test of sincerity of a country's interest in the resource? Isn't such a "demonstrated interest" just a reflection of the relative economic power of the claimant state? Isn't the present regime reflecting the existing global economic and technological imbalance by requiring massive investment prior to gaining any benefits from the regime? See a similar arrangement with respect to the Deep Sea-Bed Authority: under Article 161 of the 1982 Law of the Sea Convention, affected states are conferred rights of special representation on this administrative body. For an analysis of the regulation of this "comparable" resource, *see* SAHURIE, *supra,* at 379-390. The other, equally imperfect analogy is to the legal regulation of the Arctic region, ID. at 390-419, or ice in general, *see* Christopher C. Joyner, *The International Law of the Hydrologic Cycle: Ice-Covered Regions in International Law,* 31 NAT. RESOURCES J. 213 (1991). Or is a *sui generis* regime based on the functional necessities and explicit policy choices the better way? *See* SAHURIE, at 420-423; 574-586. For a wide-ranging discussion, *see The Future of the Antarctic Regime: New Directions,* 85 PROC. AM. SOC'Y INT'L L. 461 (1991).

4. As stated *supra*, the special status of Antarctica was created as an outgrowth of the International Geophysical Year, 1957. Should its only use remain as object of scientific research? *See* Colin C. Deihl, *Antarctica: An International Laboratory,* 18 B.C. ENVTL. AFF. L. REV. 423 (1991). Is research for military purposes excluded? Should it be?

5. Prevailing geological theory holds that Antarctica formed part of the original landmass of Gondvanaland. Following this theory, and studying the morphology of the former composite parts of this broken-up continent, scientists conclude that it is very likely that the Antarctic landmass harbors precious minerals and elements such as gold, uranium and diamonds. The 1988 Wellington Convention (CRAMRA) was designed to pave the way to ultimate exploration and exploitation of these mineral resources. *See* its analysis in the ASIL panel discussion, *The Antarctic Minerals Agreement,* 83 PROC. AM. SOC'Y INT'L L. 204 (1989); Douglas M. Zang, *Frozen in Time: The Antarctic Mineral Resource Convention,* 76 CORNELL L. REV. 722 (1991). The 50-year moratorium of the 1991 Madrid Protocol stopped these activities in their tracks. Deborah Cook Waller, *Death of a Treaty: The Decline and Fall of the Antarctic Minerals Convention,* 22 VAND. J. TRANSNAT'L L. 631 (1989).

But shouldn't there be some harnessing of the riches of the Seventh Continent, at least if essential resources dwindle and become scarce in the remainder of the planet? Who should make the decision on whether to proceed — the home states of the potential investors, the Antarctic Treaty Consultative Parties, or the entire world community? Is the constellation of interests and balance of equities the same as with respect to the deep sea-bed? *See* Barbara Heim, *Exploring the Last Frontiers for Mineral Resources: A Comparison of International Law Regarding the Deep Seabed, Outer Space, and Antarctica,* 23 VAND. J. TRANSNAT'L L. 819 (1990); Douglas Miller, *Who has the Right to Exploitation, and the Right to Prevent Exploitation, of the Minerals in Antarctica,* 79 PROC. AM. SOC'Y INT'L L. 58 (1985); and Jonathan D. Weiss, *The Balance of Nature and Human Needs in Antarctica: The Legality of Mining,* 9 TEMP. INT'L & COMP. L.J. 387 (1995).

6. The 1991 Madrid Protocol was signed by all the 26 nations of the "Antarctic Club." To enter into force, it needs to be ratified by all 26 member states (art. 23). Ratification, however, has stalled in many countries. *See* Comment, *A Call for U.S. Ratification of the Protocol on Antarctic Environmental Protection,* 21 ECOLOGY L.Q. 163 (1994). Can you think of a reason why?

The Protocol and its annexes provide for a 50-year moratorium on mineral and oil exploitation, new systems of protected areas, and some guidelines for conduct of human activity in the region. They establish limits to tourism, including a maximum number of visitors per boat and year, severe restrictions on their movement, as well as the exclusion of dogs, foreign microorganisms and other life forms that might endanger the pristine environment. For details, *see* S.K.N. Blay, *New Trends in the Protection of the Antarctic Environment: The 1991 Madrid Protocol,* 86 AM. J. INT'L L. 377 (1992); Andrew Neuman, *Closing the Frozen Treasure Chest: Antarctica's New Environmental Protocol,* 3 FORDHAM ENVTL. L. REP. 57 (1991). Critical comments include Francisco Orrego Vicuña, *The Protocol on Environmental Protection to the Antarctic Treaty: Questions of Effectiveness,* 7 GEO. INT'L ENVTL. L. REV. 1 (1994); Comment, *A Certain False Security: The Madrid Protocol to the Antarctic Treaty,* 4 COLO. J. INT'L ENVTL. L. & POL'Y 458 (1993); and Elaine F. Forman, *Protecting the Antarctic Environment: Will a Protocol Be Enough?,* 7 AM. U. J. INT'L L. & POL'Y 843 (1992).

For pertinent U.S. domestic law and policy, see the Antarctic Protection Act as discussed by Joan M. Bondareff, *The Congress Acts to Protect Antarctica,* 1 TERR. SEA J. 223 (1991); West's Legal News, *Senate Clears Legislation Amending Antarctic Protection Act,* Environmental Law: The News 9-11-96, WLN 9499); Smith v. United States, 32 ILM 516 (1993)(declines application of the Federal Tort Claims Act to Antarctica in suit of widow of person killed at the McMurdo Station while working under contract to federal agency); and Environmental Defense Fund, Inc. v. Massey, 32 ILM 505 (1993)(application to Antarctica of the National Environmental Policy Act). *See also* Bosire Maragia, *Defining the Jurisdictional Reach of NEPA: An Analysis of the Extraterritorial Application of NEPA in* Environmental Defense Fund, Inc. v. Massey, 4 WIDENER J. PUB. L. 129 (1994); Retenya Shepard, *The United States in Antarctica: The Legality, Practicality, and Morality of Applying the National Environmental Policy Act,* 14 GEO. MASON U. L. REV. 373 (1991). *See also* Robert M. Andersen, *Leading International Efforts to Improve Environmental Controls in Antarctica While Navigating National Politics,* 6 GEO. INT'L ENVTL. L. REV. 303 (1994).

7. The waters around the Antarctic landmass and their living resources have been the object of an earlier, pathbreaking treaty regarding environmental protection. The 1980 Convention on the Conservation of Antarctic Marine Living Resources (CCAMLR) heralded the advent of a comprehensive, ecosystem approach to international environmental law. Its role has been analyzed by Anne Batchelor in her seminal article *The Preservation of Wildlife Habitat in Ecosystems: Towards a Direction Under International Law to Prevent Species' Extinction,* 3 FLA. INT'L L.J. 307 (1988):

> Although limited in its participation by the members of the international community, the Convention on the Conservation of Antarctic Marine Living Resources (CCAMLR) bridges the essential evolutionary gap in wildlife conservation by incorporating into the agreement consideration of the whole ecosystem where the animal is found. CCAMLR's ecosystem approach can serve as a laudable model for the future drafting of an essential global wildlife treaty aimed at the protection of endangered species by preserving their critical habitat. Finally, other conservation measures which would support a world-wide wildlife habitat agreement are the more aggressive enforcement of existing wildlife treaties, the creation of international parks, the encouraged participation by nongovernmental organizations (NGOs), and the pursuit of scientific knowledge on ecosystem dynamics.

See also Christopher C. Joyner, *Fragile Ecosystems: Preclusive Restoration in the Antarctic,* 34 NAT. RESOURCES J. 879 (1994).

8. What is the most appropriate policy regarding control over and use of Antarctica? Shouldn't the yardstick be the best arrangement to harness the resource to the benefit of all? Should the interest of people be in the forefront, or the "interest of nature"? *See,* Comment, *Conflicting Interests in Antarctica: People or Nature? Who Decides?,* 5 TEMP. INT'L & COMP. L.J. 109 (1991).

The idea of turning Antarctica into a "world park" has been vigorously pursued by NGOs such as Greenpeace — a non-state actor who briefly established a research base in Antarctica, reviewed the conduct, regarding pollution, etc. of other actors in that field, and laudably removed the station without leaving a trace after accomplishing its purpose. *See* Ellen Tenenbaum, *A World Park in Antarctica: The Common Heritage of Mankind,* 10 VA. ENVTL. L.J. 109 (1990). In what aspects does the idea of a world park differ from the regime established by the Madrid Protocol? Could the idea of a World Park be reconciled with limited exploitation of resources? *See* Bernard P. Herber, *Mining or World Park? A Politico-Economic Analysis of Alternative Land Use Regimes in Antarctica,* 31 NAT. RESOURCES J. 839 (1991); and J.M. Spectar, *Saving the Ice Princess: NGOs, Antarctica & International Law in the New Millennium,* 23 SUFFOLK TRANSNAT'L L. REV. 57 (1999).

VI. OUTER SPACE AND CELESTIAL BODIES

A. CHARACTERISTICS AND POLICIES

The allocation of rights of access best designed to promote the common interests of all peoples would appear ... that which accords the utmost priority to inclusive access and uses, with only an occasional honoring for limited and temporary purposes of any exclusive control of areas in space. It is only by the maintenance of inclusive access and enjoyment that the general community can have assurance both that the great potential gains from the vast resources of space will in fact be achieved and that these gains will be appropriately shared among all peoples.

MYRES S. MCDOUGAL, HAROLD D. LASSWELL & IVAN A. VLASIC, LAW AND PUBLIC ORDER IN SPACE 198-199 (Yale U. Press 1963).

B. ALLOCATION, PROTECTION AND REGULATION OF USE

1. Treaty on Principles Governing the Activities of States in the Exploration and Use of Outer Space, including the Moon and Other Celestial Bodies

610 U.N.T.S. 205 (1966)

The States Parties to this Treaty,

Inspired by the great prospects opening up before mankind as a result of man's entry into outer space,

Recognizing the common interest of all mankind in the progress of the exploration and use of outer space for peaceful purposes,

Believing that the exploration and use of outer space should be carried on for the benefit of all peoples irrespective of the degree of their economic or scientific development,

Desiring to contribute to broad international co-operation in the scientific as well as the legal aspects of the exploration and use of outer space for peaceful purposes,

Believing that such co-operation will contribute to the development of mutual understanding and to the strengthening of friendly relations between States and peoples,

Recalling resolution 1962 (XVIII), entitled "Declaration of Legal Principles Governing the Activities of States in the Exploration and Use of Outer Space", which was adopted unanimously by the United Nations General Assembly on 13 December 1963,

Recalling resolution 1884 (XVIII), calling upon States to refrain from placing in orbit around the earth any objects carrying nuclear weapons or any other kinds of weapons of mass destruction or from installing such weapons on celestial bodies, which was adopted unanimously by the United Nations General Assembly on 17 October 1963,

Taking account of United Nations General Assembly resolution 110 (II) of 3 November 1947, which condemned propaganda designed or likely to provoke or encourage any threat to the peace, breach of the peace or act of aggression, and considering that the aforementioned resolution is applicable to outer space,

Convinced that a Treaty on Principles Governing the Activities of States in the Exploration and Use of Outer Space, including the Moon and Other Celestial Bodies, will further the purposes and principles of the Charter of the United Nations,

Have agreed on the following:

Article I

The exploration and use of outer space, including the moon and other celestial bodies, shall be carried out for the benefit and in the interests of all countries, irrespective of their degree of economic or scientific development, and shall be the province of all mankind.

Outer space, including the moon and other celestial bodies, shall be free for exploration and use by all States without discrimination of any kind, on a basis of equality and in accordance with international law, and there shall be free access to all areas of celestial bodies.

There shall be freedom of scientific investigation in outer space, including the moon and other celestial bodies, and States shall facilitate and encourage international co-operation in such investigation.

Article II

Outer space, including the moon and other celestial bodies, is not subject to national appropriation by claim of sovereignty, by means of use or occupation, or by any other means.

2. Agreement Governing the Activities of States on the Moon and Other Celestial Bodies

1363 U.N.T.S. 3 (1979)

Article 11

1. The moon and its natural resources are the common heritage of mankind, which finds its expression in the provisions of this Agreement, in particular in paragraph 5 of this article.

2. The moon is not subject to national appropriation by any claim of sovereignty, by means of use or occupation, or by any other means.

3. Neither the surface nor the subsurface of the moon, nor any part thereof or natural resources in place, shall become property of any State, international intergovernmental or non- governmental organization, national organization or non-governmental entity or of any natural person. The placement of personnel, space vehicles, equipment, facilities, stations and installations on or below the surface of the moon, including structures connected with its surface or subsurface, shall not create a right of ownership over the surface or the subsurface of the moon or any areas thereof. The foregoing provisions are without prejudice to the international régime referred to in paragraph 5 of this article.

4. States Parties have the right to exploration and use of the moon without discrimination of any kind, on the basis of equality and in accordance with international law and the terms of this Agreement.

5. States Parties to this Agreement hereby undertake to establish an international régime, including appropriate procedures, to govern the exploitation of the natural resources of the moon as such exploitation is about to become feasible. This provision shall be implemented in accordance with article 18 of this Agreement.

6. In order to facilitate the establishment of the international régime referred to in paragraph 5 of this article, States Parties shall inform the Secretary-General of the United Nations as well as the public and the international scientific community, to the greatest extent feasible and practicable, of any natural resources they may discover on the moon.

7. The main purposes of the international régime to be established shall include:

(a) The orderly and safe development of the natural resources of the moon;

(b) The rational management of those resources;

(c) The expansion of opportunities in the use of those resources;

(d) An equitable sharing by all States Parties in the benefits derived from those resources, whereby the interests and needs of the developing countries, as well as the efforts of those countries which have contributed either directly or indirectly to the exploration of the moon, shall be given special consideration.

8. All the activities with respect to the natural resources of the moon shall be carried out in a manner compatible with the purposes specified in paragraph 7 of this article and the provisions of article 6, paragraph 2, of this Agreement.

3. Siegfried Wiessner, *Human Activities in Outer Space: A Framework for Decisionmaking*

in SPACE LAW: VIEWS OF THE FUTURE 7, 8-16 (Tanja L. Zwaan et al. eds., Kluwer Law & Taxation Pub.1988), *reprinted in* THE SPIRIT OF AMERICAN LAW 514-521 (George S. Grossman ed., Westview Press 2000)

The dawn of the Space Age has produced quite an assortment of multilateral treaties dealing with human activities in this newly-conquered arena. The most inclusive such document is the Treaty on Principles Governing the Activities of States in the Exploration and Use of Outer Space, Including the Moon and Other Celestial Bodies of 27 January, 1967. Its broad and general nature and content made that agreement, for a long time, the "constitution" of outer space, boasting membership of 93 states including all the spacefaring nations. Essentially non-controversial, it met the criteria for a document evidencing the content of customary international law, in fact, constituting the *fons et origo* of it.

This consensus about the Outer Space Treaty may be waning. It was the product of highflying dreams of its time, but it was also limited to the then-present technology and the then-held expectations about future technology and human aspirations. Among other issues, the Treaty failed to foresee, and thus take into account, the scramble for scarce resources in the geostationary orbit, the problems of privacy and national security to be created by rampant remote sensing, and the filling of the near-Earth environment with "exotic" battle stations. Scholars had substantial input. The Treaty reflected a world in which globalism and the common interest of humankind were not yet unmasked by the ruling elites of dominant powers as ringing oratory, designed to disguise selfish claims by the have-nots to most generous transfers of wealth and technology. ...

Problems with the 1967 Treaty

1. The first, unresolved problem revolves around the scope of application of this agreement: What do we mean when we refer to *outer space?* Wisely, the international community did not delve into the various demarcation lines suggested by the so-called "spatialist" school for the clearcut separation of airspace and outer space, the realm of state sovereignty, and the domain of international law, respectively. With the impending development of the aerospace plane, the "functionalists" advocating a flexible approach depending on the type of activity conducted seem to have gained a decisive upper hand.

2. At the beginning of the Space Age, expectations flew high that outer space was *to be used exclusively for peaceful purposes.* In the late fifties, the General Assembly of the United Nations, as well as the top leaders of the

spacefaring nations, expressed this as a common aspiration that would have outlawed any kind of military activities in outer space. The United States and the Soviet Union, however, soon toned down the rhetoric. In the early sixties, they pressed for U.N. General Assembly resolutions adopting a more limited view of "peaceful purposes" and split up the legal regime of outer space into differently treated arenas.

The 1967 Treaty follows this line. The aspirations of humankind were relegated to the oratory of the preamble:

> The States Parties to this Treaty, ... Recognising the common interest of all mankind in the progress of die exploration and use of outer space for peaceful purposes, ... Have agreed on the following ...
>
> And these States, the major space powers, agreed, in Article III, that they,
>
> shall carry on activities in the exploration and use of outer space ... in the interest of maintaining international peace and security and promoting international co-operation and understanding.

The only teeth that were put into this Treaty with respect to military uses of outer space were mild and enumerated in Article IV:

> (1) States Parties to the Treaty undertake not to place in orbit around the Earth any objects carrying nuclear weapons or any other kinds of weapons of mass destruction, install such weapons on celestial bodies, or station such weapons in outer space in any other manner.
>
> (2) The moon and other celestial bodies shall be used by all States Parties to die Treaty exclusively for peaceful purposes. The establishment of military bases, installations and fortifications, the testing of any type of weapons and the conduct of military maneuvers on celestial bodies shall be forbidden...

Thus, the only parts of outer space which were to be "demilitarised" were the moon and other celestial bodies. Nuclear weapons and other weapons of mass destruction were banned from being *stationed* in outer space. Thus, Articles III and IV did not prevent the buildup of ICBM's, SLBM's, and intermediate-range nuclear missiles that employ the medium of outer space merely to reach their targets.

Beyond that, the U.S. and the USSR have put into Earth orbit a barrage of "national technical means of verification" which are crucial for gathering intelligence about the military strengths and movements of the other side, for verification of arms control agreements, and for early warning of nuclear attacks. In fact, such missiles and reconnaissance satellites have been considered essential for the maintaining of international peace and security, under the superpowers' "open skies" policy.

The next step, beyond the passive reconnaissance function, was the stationing of antisatellite systems (ASATs) in outer space. Their presence was justified as defensive, perfectly legitimate "non-aggressive military use" of outer space. Scientists soon pointed out that such devices could easily be used for offensive purposes. Ultimately, however, any weapon may be perceived as contributing to the overall balance of deterrence designed to uphold the peace.

New military strategies go far beyond mere ASAT capability. The U.S. Strategic Defense Initiative, using several layers of defence against ICBM's, would employ weapons systems in outer space that can be used offensively as well as defensively. They include nuclear driven devices such as particle beams, microwaves, hypervelocity pellets, X-ray lasers, and optical lasers. In particular, the proposed X-ray laser would not only be powered by nuclear energy, but would set free a nuclear explosion if operated. It has thus been called a "third generation nuclear weapon". As such, the X-ray laser would seem to violate the proscription against nuclear weapons in Earth orbit, laid down in Article IV (1) of the 1967 Treaty.

Soviet proposals, in the United Nations, to completely "deweaponise" outer space have proven unsuccessful.

We have to realise that the competition of contending value systems on Earth cannot be prevented from entering the arena of outer space. Security is a nation's vital need, the *conditio sine qua non of* a territorial community. Without a world government and a consensus on the basic social values, this competition between contending value systems, by its own dynamics, will not spare the critical arena of outer space. How can outer space be preserved as the fairy place of peace if, on Earth, the consensus on the most basic restriction on the use of force, Article 2(4) of the United Nations Charter, is breaking down? We might end up settling for agreed-upon astronautical rules of the road that govern, as a sort of a regulation on the lowest common denominator, the use of the ever-shrinking voids of outer space.

3. The universalistic spirit of the 1967 Treaty also found its expression in Article I (1):

> The exploration and use *of* outer space ... shall be carried out for the benefit and in the interests of all countries, irrespective of their degree of economic or scientific development, and shall be the *province of all mankind.*

What does this clause mean? In the U.S. Senate hearings on advice and consent to the Treaty, it was made clear that this prescription would not translate into obligations by the haves of space technology to the have-nots. At best, the term "province of all mankind" was "embryonic". It did not carry with it the distinctive connotations of equitable sharing and common inclusive management which are packed in the standard of a "common heritage of mankind". The latter term, used in the 1979 Moon Agreement, was decisively rejected by the space superpowers, together with the Moon Agreement itself. Outer space thus remains a free-for-all; the benefits clause of Article I (1) vanishes into legal nirvana before the freedoms of use, exploration and exploitation of outer space as enumerated in Article 1 (2) and (3).[25] This is another example of the inadequacies of the 1967 text.

4. A fundamental presumption of the 190 Treaty is that outer space and the celestial bodies cannot be appropriated. In the context of SDI, it has been contended that the array of objects to be placed in Earth orbit and the necessity to create "keep-out" zones around them would constitute an appropriation of outer space, contrary to Article II of the Treaty. I confess to having some problems with this proposition: Would the declaration and enforcement of any keep-out zone constitute an appropriation? If so, what about the semi-permanent satellite positions on the geostationary orbit and their assigned latitudes? Is that not also an appropriation of outer space? If not, how large must the zones be to be considered "appropriations"? Should the difference between these security zones be one of quality rather than quantity, depending on the intent of the parties?

Another issue concerning appropriation arises in the context of possible future space mining. It may lead not only to the exploitation of valuable parts of the moon, but to the virtual consumption of entire asteroids. By what twist of the language can this still be called mere "use", and not "appropriation", of the celestial body?

5. The 1967 Treaty fails to take into account, to the extent needed, the numerous activities of *private enterprise* which enter into the use of outer space. Soviet Scholars have asserted that the emergence of international private space law under the 1967 Treaty is not likely.

The 1967 Treaty is largely State-oriented: Article VI provides that a State has to "authorise and supervise" the activities of its non-governmental entities in outer space. Article VII establishes liability by the launching state, and Article VIII requires retention of jurisdiction and control over space objects by the States "on whose registry" such objects are launched.

One does notice private parties operating in the first commercial arena: communications satellites. Important business needs are satisfied by these space stations. They provide for telephone, telex, and record traffic, but also TV, radio, data transmissions, videoconferencing, weather forecasting, and navigation. Remote sensing is being privatized: the Land Remote-Sensing Commercialisation Act of 1984 moved control over civilian remote sensing to private EOSAT, which

---

[25] This does not mean that the *res communis* standard of unrestricted use governs each and every area and resource situated in outer space. A case in point is the geostationary satellite orbit. Its heavy, and growing, inclusive regulation makes it a prime example of a *res publica internationalis*. *See* Siegfried Wiessner, *Access to a* Res Publica Internationalis*: The Case of the Geostationary Orbit*, PROCEEDINGS OF THE 29TH COLLOQUIUM ON THE LAW OF OUTER SPACE 147 (1987); and Siegfried Wiessner, *The Public Order of the Geostationary Orbit: Blueprints for the Future,* 9 YALE J. WORLD PUB. ORD. 217, 263-266 (1983).

now has to compete with SPOT-Image, a private French company with some Dutch and Swedish participation. The media are considering operating their own satellite, raising grave concerns of national security and foreign policy (will the media be able to independently verify the Government's accounts of interventions?) and individual privacy. The future aerospace plane will be a most appreciated means of intercontinental transportation, beyond its initial, predominantly military, use. Even launching may be taken over by private parties. Materials processing will take place on the space station envisaged by President Reagan.

All these activities presuppose some kind of supervision and control of the participant private parties' activities by nation-states. Whereas the attribution of space objects to individual states was dealt with by the 1975 Registration Convention, the issue of the minimum degree of control of a nation-state over its private "national" space object remains as it was - barely touched on by the 1967 Treaty.

6. The problem of liability is addressed only most generally in the 1967 Treaty. Article VII provides that the launching state is internationally liable for the damage caused by its space object. The 1971 Liability Convention provides more detail. New issues, however, will arise with the advent of the aerospace plane. Should liability for its operation and its registration be determined by the established rules of air law or space law, or should we strive to tailor a special regime for that particular object?

7. Space debris has become a major threat to human activities in outer space. Current regimes of liability, based as they are on negligence theories of negative obligations, duties not to commit certain acts, even the 1967 Treaty's strict liability for the harmful effects emanating from one's own space object, might no longer be enough - in view of both the increasing "contamination" of the area, and the increasing difficulties in identifying whose country's space object has caused the damage. It seems to be advisable to contemplate positive dudes to remove dangerous debris, similar to the duty to perform necessary repairs in domestic property law. This duty might be incumbent upon a country that is predominantly active in one particular area of outer space, or on the international community as a whole who might commission such mine-sweeping missions from the leading space powers.

8. This, by necessity, incomplete list of problems may be concluded for now by reference to the novel legal issues created by the establishment of an international space station. Looming large are the jurisdictional and substantive law conflicts on such a complex, "international" space structure. Who owns the station? Who decides which disputes where? On board the station? According to which law?

9. One may conclude that the 1967 Treaty fails to address major novel issues of space law, and that some of its fundamental policies are honoured today only in their breach. This state of things will worsen in the future with increasing military and commercial use. Thus, beyond the 1967 Treaty, it is up to scholars to ascer-

tain what are the expectations about lawfulness or unlawfulness of specific human activities in outer space. Where evidence on the outcome of the world's constitutive process of decision-making in relation to a particular problem is lacking or inconclusive, it is the critical task of scholars to advance solutions in the global common interest. Such recommendations should ideally promote the abundant and economic use of great sharable resources for the benefit of the whole of humankind.

* * *

Compare the more recent formulation of space policy by the United States:

4. National Space Policy

The White House National Science and Technology Council, Sept. 19, 1996

(1) For over three decades, the United States has led the world in the exploration and use of outer space. Our achievements in space have inspired a generation of Americans and people throughout the world. We will maintain this leadership role by supporting a strong, stable and balanced national space program that serves our goals in national security, foreign policy, economic growth, environmental stewardship and scientific and technical excellence. Access to and use of space is central for preserving peace and protecting U.S. national security as well as civil and commercial interests. The United States will pursue greater levels of partnership and cooperation in national and international space activities and work with other nations to ensure the continued exploration and use of outer space for peaceful purposes.

(2) The goals of the U.S. space program are to:

(a) Enhance knowledge of the Earth, the solar system and the universe through human and robotic exploration;

(b) Strengthen and maintain the national security of the United States;

(c) Enhance the economic competitiveness, and scientific and technical capabilities of the United States;

(d) Encourage State, local and private sector investment in, and use of, space technologies;

(e) Promote international cooperation to further U.S. domestic, national security, and foreign policies.

(3) The United States is committed to the exploration and use of outer space by all nations for peaceful purposes and for the benefit of all humanity. "Peaceful purposes" allow defense and intelligence-related activities in pursuit of national security and other goals. The United States rejects any claims to sovereignty by any nation over outer space or celestial bodies, or any portion thereof, and rejects any limitations on the fundamental right of sovereign nations to acquire data from space. The United States considers the space systems of any nation to be na-

tional property with the right of passage through and operations in space without interference. Purposeful interference with space systems shall be viewed as an infringement on sovereign rights. …

Civil Space Guidelines

(1) The National Aeronautics and Space Administration is the lead agency for research and development in civil space activities.

(2) NASA, in coordination with other departments and agencies as appropriate, will focus its research and development efforts in: space science to enhance knowledge of the solar system, the universe, and fundamental natural and physical sciences; Earth observation to better understand global change and the effect of natural and human influences on the environment; human space flight to conduct scientific, commercial, and exploration activities; and space technologies and applications to develop new technologies in support of U.S. Government needs and our economic competitiveness.

(3) To enable these activities, NASA will:

(a) Develop and operate the International Space Station to support activities requiring the unique attributes of humans in space and establish a permanent human presence in Earth orbit. The International Space Station will support future decisions on the feasibility and desirability of conducting further human exploration activities.

(b) Work with the private sector to develop flight demonstrators that will support a decision by the end of the decade on development of a next-generation reusable launch system.

(c) Continue a strong commitment to space science and Earth science programs. …

National Security Space Guidelines

(1) The United States will conduct those space activities necessary for national security. These activities will be overseen by the Secretary of Defense and the Director of Central Intelligence (DCI). ...

(2) Improving our ability to support military operations worldwide, monitor and respond to strategic military threats, and monitor arms control and non-proliferation agreements and activities are key priorities for national security space activities. The Secretary of Defense and DCI shall ensure that defense and intelligence space activities are closely coordinated; that space architectures are integrated to the maximum extent feasible; and will continue to modernize and improve their respective activities to collect against, and respond to, changing threats, environments and adversaries.

(3) National security space activities shall contribute to U.S. national security by:

(a) providing support for the United States' inherent right of self-defense and our defense commitments to allies and friends;

(b) deterring, warning, and if necessary, defending against enemy attack;

(c) assuring that hostile forces cannot prevent our own use of space;

(d) countering, if necessary, space systems and services used for hostile purposes;

(e) enhancing operations of U.S. and allied forces;

(f) ensuring our ability to conduct military and intelligence space-related activities;

(g) satisfying military and intelligence requirements during peace and crisis as well as through all levels of conflict;

(h) supporting the activities of national policy makers, the intelligence community, the National Command Authorities, combatant commanders and the military services, other federal officials, and continuity of government operations. …

Commercial Space Guidelines

(1) The fundamental goal of U.S. commercial space policy is to support and enhance U.S. economic competitiveness in space activities while protecting U.S. national security and foreign policy interests. Expanding U.S. commercial space activities will generate economic benefits for the Nation and provide the U.S. Government with an increasing range of space goods and services.

(2) U.S. Government agencies shall purchase commercially available space goods and services to the fullest extent feasible and shall not conduct activities with commercial applications that preclude or deter commercial space activities except for reasons of national security or public safety. A space good or service is "commercially available" if it is currently offered commercially, or if it could be supplied commercially in response to a government service procurement request. "Feasible" means that such goods or services meet mission requirements in a cost-effective manner.

(3) The United States will pursue its commercial space objectives without the use of direct Federal subsidies. Commercial Sector space activities shall be supervised or regulated only to the extent required by law, national security, international obligations and public safety.

(4) To stimulate private sector investment, ownership, and operation of space assets, the U.S. Government will facilitate stable and predictable U.S. commercial sector access to appropriate U.S. Government space-related hardware, facilities and data. The U.S. Government reserves the right to use such hardware, facilities and data on a priority basis to meet national security and critical civil sector requirements.

Government Space Sectors shall:

(a) Enter into appropriate cooperative agreements to encourage and advance private sector basic research, development, and operations while protecting the commercial value of the intellectual property developed.

(b) Identify, and propose appropriate amendments to or the elimination of, applicable portions of United States laws and regulations that unnecessarily impede commercial space sector activities.

(c) Consistent with national security, provide for the timely transfer of government-developed space technology to the private sector in such a manner as to protect its commercial value, including retention of technical data rights by the private sector.

(d) To the extent feasible, pursue innovative methods for procurement of space products and services.

(5) Free and fair trade in commercial space launch services is a goal of the United States. In support of this goal, the United States will implement, at the expiration of current space launch agreements, a strategy for transitioning from negotiated trade in launch services towards a trade environment characterized by the free and open interaction of market economies. …

Intersector Guidelines

The following paragraphs identify priority intersector guidance to support major United States space policy objectives.

(1) International Cooperation

The United States will pursue and conduct international cooperative space-related activities that achieve scientific, foreign policy, economic, or national security benefits for the nation. …

(3) Space-based Earth Observation

(a)The United States requires a continuing capability for space-based Earth observation to provide information useful for protecting public health, safety, and national security. Such a capability contributes to economic growth and stimulates educational, scientific and technological advancement. …

(4) Nonproliferation, Export Controls, and Technology Transfer

(a) The MTCR Guidelines are not designed to impede national space programs or international cooperation in such programs as long as such programs could not contribute to delivery systems for weapons of mass destruction. Consistent with U.S. nonproliferation policy, the United States will continue to oppose missile programs of proliferation concern, and will exercise particular restraint in missile-related cooperation. The United States will continue to retain a strong presumption of denial against exports of complete space launch vehicles or other MTCR Category I components. ...

(5) Arms Control

The United States will consider and, as appropriate, formulate policy positions on arms control and related measures governing activities in space, and will conclude agreements on such measures only if they are equitable, effectively verifiable, and enhance the security of the United States and our allies. ...

(6) Space Nuclear Power

The Department of Energy will maintain the necessary capability to support space missions which may require the use of space nuclear power systems. U.S. Government agency proposals for international cooperation involving space nuclear power systems are subject to normal interagency review procedures. Space nuclear reactors will not be used in Earth orbit without specific approval by the President or his designee. Such requests for approval will take into account public safety, economic considerations, international treaty obligations, and U.S. national security and foreign policy interests. ...

(7) Space Debris

(a) The United States will seek to minimize the creation of space debris. NASA, the Intelligence Community, and the DoD, in cooperation with the private sector, will develop design guidelines for future government procurements of spacecraft, launch vehicles, and services. The design and operation of space tests, experiments and systems, will minimize or reduce accumulation of space debris consistent with mission requirements and cost effectiveness.

(b) It is in the interest of the U.S. Government to ensure that space debris minimization practices are applied by other spacefaring nations and international organizations. The U.S. Government will take a leadership role in international fora to adopt policies and practices aimed at debris minimization and will cooperate internationally in the exchange of information on debris research and the identification of debris mitigation options.

* * *

The Bush Administration ordered a complete overhaul of U.S. space policy on June 28, 2002, with a final report due to the National Security Council by February 28, 2003 (see National Security Presidential Directive/NSPD-15, available at http://www.ostp.gov/html/02_7_15_2.html). As of this writing, the report has not been received.

NOTES AND QUESTIONS

1. In what way, exactly, do these treaty regimes of outer space and the Moon differ? Do references to space as "the province of all mankind" in the Outer Space Treaty of 1966 and the

Moon being the "common heritage of mankind" as described in the 1979 Moon Treaty denote categorically different resource régimes? Note that in the 1970s and '80s, the Third World's push for inclusive use and administration of global common resources led to the creation of the concept of "common heritage of mankind," codified in the controversial legal regime of the deep sea-bed ("The Area") , Part IX of UNCLOS 1982. For analysis and discussion, *see supra* at 721-726.

2. By 1998, the 1967 Outer Space Treaty had been ratified by well over 100 countries, including all major space powers, while the Moon Treaty could only claim nine states parties, with France being the only major space power among them. UNITED NATIONS, MULTILATERAL TREATIES DEPOSITED WITH THE SECRETARY-GENERAL, Status as at 31 December 1997, at 869 (1998). What, in your opinion, contributed to that outcome? Do you agree with Professor Wiessner's comments on the 1967 Treaty? Are they dated? Does the 1996 United States National Space Policy address all regulatory and inclusive policy concerns? What are the prospects of its review by the Bush Administration? What is the appropriate "public order of outer space?" *See, supra,* MYRES S. MCDOUGAL, HAROLD D. LASSWELL & IVAN A. VLASIC, LAW AND PUBLIC ORDER OF SPACE (1963).

3. Nation-states, despite many attempts, particularly by the then-Soviet Union and its allies, have not achieved agreement on a fixed boundary between exclusively controlled airspace and inclusively regulated outer space. The key argument by the United States against such delimitation has been the need to vary prescriptive regimes according to the activities envisioned in the respective area. That functional approach has carried the day. Are there any downsides to such relative indeterminacy?

4. Private activities in outer space are increasing in number and have become important factors of the global economy. Revenues from communication satellites alone were projected at over $35 billion in 2002. In addition to the uses mentioned *supra* — i.e. communication, navigation, reconnaissance, remote sensing and mining of the earth's resources, etc. – "exotic" uses of outer space include space-based advertisements, tourism to a low-earth orbit space resort or a lunar base, even space burials and disposal of hazardous wastes on the far side of the Moon or in deep space. Sean P. Curley, *Near Term Prospects for Mass Commercialization of Space*, at http://members.tripod.com/SeanCurley/Space Commercialization.html (visited Oct. 19, 1999). The first sub-orbital space flight in June 2004 by a private company with an eye toward developing the lucrative market of space tourism makes such ventures appear ever less extraordinary. These novel entrepreneurial actions illustrate the need to develop proper inclusive (and exclusive) policies.

VII. THE ENVIRONMENT

A. INTRODUCTION

The increasing perception that intense industrial and scientific uses of the environment may cause serious degradation to it has necessitated the accommodation of environmental concerns within other important parts of contemporary international law. In the Gabcíkovo-Nagymaros case, below, Hungary and Czechoslovakia had begun joint construction between their countries of a dam for hydroelectric purposes. When the project was well advanced, Hungary concluded, on the basis of new evidence, that the dam would cause major environmental harm and sought to terminate the project. The matter was submitted to the International Court of Justice which acknowledged the significance of emerging international rules on the protection of the environment but was unwilling to bend a treaty arrangement to take account of new environmental information, insisting, instead, on the primacy of prior treaty commitments.

1. Case Concerning Gabcíkovo-Nagymaros Project (Hung. v. Slovk.)

1997 I.C.J. 1 (Sept. 25)

[In 1977, Hungary and Czechoslovakia signed a treaty which provided for the construction and operation of the Gabcíkovo-Nagymaros system of locks on the Danube. The project was designed to attain broad utilization of the natural resources of the Bratislava-Budapest section of the Danube River for the development of water resources, energy, transport, agriculture and other sectors of the national economies of the parties. As a result of the intense public criticism which the new environmental information generated in Hungary, the Hungarian government decided on 13 May 1989 to suspend the works at Nagymaros pending the completion of various studies which the competent authorities were to finish before 31 July 1989. The Hungarian government extended the suspension of the works until 31 October 1989. On 27 October 1989, Hungary decided to abandon the works at Nagymaros and to maintain the status quo elsewhere. During this period, Czechoslovakia began to explore alternative solutions. One of the projects, subsequently known as "Variant C", began in November 1991. Discussion between the two governments failed to resolve the dispute. On 19 May 1992, the Hungarian government terminated the 1977 Treaty with effect from 25 May 1992. On 15 October 1992, Czechoslovakia began work to enable the Danube to be closed and proceeded to dam the river. In 1993 Slovakia became an independent State.]

[One issue presented to the Court and not discussed below was whether a treaty concluded with one state remained enforceable when that state, Czechoslovakia, had been transformed into two successor states, the Czech Republic and Slovakia. The Court concluded that the treaty remained in force, despite the changed identity of one of the parties.] ...

53. The Court has no difficulty in acknowledging that the concerns expressed by Hungary for its natural environment in the region affected by the Gabcíkovo-Nagymaros Project related to an "essential interest" of that State, within the meaning given to that expression in Article 33 of the Draft [Articles on State Responsibility] of the International Law Commission.

The Commission, in its Commentary, indicated that one should not, in that context, reduce an "essential interest" to a matter only of the "existence" of the State, and that the whole question was, ultimately, to be judged in the light of the particular case (*see* Yearbook of the International Law Commission, 1980, Vol. II, Part 2, p. 49, para. 32); at the same time, it included among the situations that could occasion a state of necessity, "a grave danger to ... the ecological preservation of all or some of [the] territory [of a State]" *(Ibid.*, p. 35, para. 3); and specified, with reference to State practice, that "It is primarily in the last two decades that safeguarding the ecological balance has come to be considered an 'essential interest' of all States." (*Ibid.*, p. 39, para. 14.)

The Court recalls that it has recently had occasion to stress, in the following terms, the great significance that it attaches to respect for the environment, not only for States but also for the whole of mankind:

> [t]he environment is not an abstraction but represents the living space, the quality of life and the very health of human beings, including generations unborn. The existence of the general obligation of States to ensure that activities within their jurisdiction and control respect the environment of other States or of areas beyond national control is now part of the corpus of international law relating to the environment. (Legality of the Threat or Use of Nuclear Weapons, Advisory Opinion, I.C.J. Reports 1996, pp. 241-242, para. 29.) …

111. Finally, the Court will address Hungary's claim that it was entitled to terminate the 1977 Treaty because new requirements of international law for the protection of the environment precluded performance of the Treaty.

112. Neither of the Parties contended that new peremptory norms of environmental law had emerged since the conclusion of the 1977 Treaty, and the Court will consequently not be required to examine the scope of Article 64 of the Vienna Convention on the Law of Treaties. On the other hand, the Court wishes to point out that newly developed norms of environmental law are relevant for the implementation of the [1977] Treaty and that the parties could, by agreement, incorporate them through the application of Articles 15, 19 and 20. … These articles do not contain specific obligations of performance but require the parties, in carrying out their obligations to ensure that the quality of water in the Danube is not impaired and that nature is protected, to take new environmental norms into consideration when agreeing upon the means to be specified in the Joint Contractual Plan.

By inserting these evolving provisions in the [1977] Treaty, the parties recognized the potential necessity to adapt the Project. Consequently, the Treaty is not static, and is open to adapt to emerging norms of international law. By means of Articles 15 and 19, new environmental norms can be incorporated in the Joint Contractual Plan.

The responsibility to do this was a joint responsibility. The obligations … are, by definition, general and have to be transformed into specific obligations of performance through a process of consultation and negotiation. Their implementation thus requires a mutual willingness to discuss in good faith actual and potential environmental risks. …

The awareness of the vulnerability of the environment and the recognition that environmental risks have to be assessed on a continuous basis have become much stronger in the years since the Treaty's conclusion. These new concerns have enhanced the relevance of Articles 15, 19 and 20.

113. The Court recognizes that both Parties agree on the need to take environmental concerns seriously and to take the required precautionary measures, but they fundamentally disagree on the consequences this has for the joint Project. In such a case, third-party involvement may be helpful and instrumental in finding a solution, provided each of the Parties is flexible in its position.

* * *

The Court's response to this dispute is symptomatic of much of the international environmental initiative in the current international legal setting. One might well ask, "What exactly has the Court required the parties to do?" Environmental provisions are generally referred to as "soft law", in the sense of stating a clear policy, with an appropriately clear signal of authority, but omitting incorporation of a control or sanction mechanism. The technique of "standard-setting" may enhance sensitivity to the environmental needs of the international community; but by refusing to establish policy in the form of hard law, it often raises expectations without providing the legal means for their satisfaction.

2. W. Michael Reisman, *A Hard Look at Soft Law*

82 AM. SOC'Y INT'L L. PROC. 371, 371-377 (1988)

Whenever we talk about law, … in whatever jurisprudential mode, we are speaking about a communication of these three related elements: content, asking you to do or forbear from doing something; certain signals of authority that distinguish this as law from other statements in the subjunctive mood; and finally, communications of intention to make that effective, and to distinguish it from all the "you ought's" and "you should's" that bombard us every day. …

In contemporary international legal scholarship, soft law has come to refer to a diverse range of phenomena related to lawmaking and frequently presented as law. For some scholars, the phenomenon is supposedly so lacking in the third component, control intention, as to be mislabelled law. These same scholars are apparently unaware that scholars in many weak and small states view some very "hard" law, that is, communications backed by compelling control intention but of questionable authority, as naked power. In fact, law can be soft in all its dimensions: in terms of its content, in terms of its authority, and in terms of control intention.

Let me give you one example of a formula that is very soft in terms of its content. In 1951 the International Court of Justice in the *Anglo-Norwegian Fisheries Case*, (U.K. v. Nor.), 1951 I.C.J. 116 (Dec. 15), purporting to establish limits on what a state could do in establishing straight baselines, said as follows: "[W]hile such a state must be allowed the latitude necessary in order to be able to adapt its delimitation to practical needs and local requirements, the drawing of baselines must not depart to any appreciable extent from the general direction of the coast." "General direction of the coast" is not defined, "appreciable extent" is not defined, "departure" is not defined; this becomes in many ways a very permissive formula. It is very soft in terms of content.

Authority signals can be soft as well. We know, for example, that when the Security Council is discharging its function to maintain the peace it is operating on a very firm authority base. We know that when the General Assembly purports to make new law, or to resolve matters that have not been assigned to it, its authority, though it may be present in some fashion, is much more ambiguous; it is softer.

And of course, we all know of many cases of law that is legislated, ... without capacity to put it into effect. In this respect, we encounter softness in terms of sanction or control intention.

Soft law in all these senses is presented as a new, unusual, and pathological phenomenon. The term is new, but what it refers to is not, nor is it a quintessentially international phenomenon. Although like anything else it can be abused, it is not *per se* a legal pathology. In some circumstances, it may perform very important legal functions.

* * *

See also W. Michael Reisman, *The Concept and Functions of Soft Law in International Politics*, *in* ESSAYS IN HONOUR OF JUDGE TASLIM OLAWALE ELIAS: 1 CONTEMPORARY INTERNATIONAL LAW AND AFRICAN LAW: AFRICAN LAW AND COMPARATIVE PUBLIC LAW 135-144 (Emmanuel G. et al. eds., Martinus Nijhoff 1992).

Another factor also makes the enforcement of environmental norms problematic. As we saw in the area of human rights, the more inclusive the concerns which international law seeks to regulate, the wider the demand for participation in fashioning policy and implementation. This phenomenon is particularly evident in the area of international environmental law, where NGOs have been recognized as "stake-holders" and increasingly have been incorporated in much of the promotion, prescription and invocation function of this area of law. While such wider participation increases the likelihood of an expression of common interest, it also makes the achievement of agreements and their implementation more difficult.

B. CHARACTERISTICS AND GENERAL POLICIES

An increasingly urgent challenge to contemporary international law is that of devising effective and workable policies and regulations for the protection of the environment. It has not been easy to accomplish this in ways that accommodate other important and traditional international policies. International environmental law depends on the accuracy of the available scientific knowledge. Moreover, the rapid development of technology introduces an element of impermanence in this area. International environmental law is still developing its own language, logic and style of debate and persuasion. As noted above, many of its principles are cast in the form of soft law. The fact remains, however, that the protection of the environment will be an increasingly important concern in the conduct of many activities and, consequently, it will have a significant bearing on other well-established principles of international law.

To date, most if not all international agreements for the protection of the environment have primarily set out rules for consultations and negotiations by those concerned, with inconclusive or weak compliance and liability mechanisms. Because of their voluntary character, it has been difficult to interpret new environmental regulations together with those aspects of international law which provide definite rights and obligations for states.

A review of international environmental instruments and decisions indicates inconsistency in approach to a variety of issues, in particular the question of definition of such terms as "environment", "environmental damage", and others.

1. The Stockholm Declaration

U.N. Doc. A/Conf.48/14 and Corr. 1; 11 I.L.M. 1416 (1972)

Principle 1

Man has the fundamental right to freedom, equality and adequate conditions of life, in an environment of a quality that permits a life of dignity and well-being, and he bears a solemn responsibility to protect and improve the environment for present and future generations. ...

Principle 2

The natural resources of the earth including the air, water, land, flora and fauna and especially representative samples of natural ecosystems must be safeguarded for the benefit of present and future generations through careful planning or management, as appropriate.

Principle 3

The capacity of the earth to produce vital renewable resources must be maintained and, wherever practicable, restored or improved.

Principle 4

Man has a special responsibility to safeguard and wisely manage the heritage of wildlife and its habitat which are now gravely imperilled by the combination of adverse factors. Nature conservation including wildlife must therefore receive importance in planning for economic development.

Principle 5

The non-renewable resources of the earth must be employed in such a way as to guard against the danger of their future exhaustion and to ensure the benefits from such employment are shared by all mankind.

Principle 6

The discharge of toxic substances or of other substances and the release of heat, in such quantities or concentrations as to exceed the capacity of the environment to render them harmless, must be halted in order to ensure that serious or irreversible damage is not inflicted upon ecosystems. ...

Principle 7

States shall take all possible steps to prevent pollution to the seas by substances that are liable to create hazards to human health, to harm living resources and marine life, to damage amenities or to interfere with other legitimate uses of the sea. ...

Principle 9

Environmental deficiencies generated by the conditions of underdevelopment and natural disasters pose grave problems and can best be remedied by accelerated development through the transfer of substantial quantities of financial and technological assistance as a supplement to the domestic effort of the developing countries and such timely assistance as may be required. ...

Principle 21

States have, in accordance with the Charter of the United Nations and the principles of Environmental law, the sovereign right to exploit their own resources pursuant to their own environmental policies, and the responsibility to ensure that activities within their jurisdiction or control do not cause damage to the environment of other states or of areas beyond the limits of national jurisdiction.

Principle 22

States shall cooperate to develop further the international law regarding liability and compensation for the victims of pollution and other environmental damage caused by activities within the jurisdiction or control of such states to areas beyond their jurisdiction. …

Principle 24

International matters concerning the protection and improvement of the environment should be handled in a co-operative spirit by all countries, big or small, on an equal footing. ...

2. The Rio Declaration

U.N. GAOR, 46th Sess., princ. 2, U.N. Doc. A/CONF.151/5/Rev.1 (1992)

Principle 2

States have, in accordance with the Charter of the United Nations and the principles of international law, the sovereign right to exploit their own resources pursuant to their own environmental and developmental policies, and the responsibility to ensure that activities within their jurisdiction or control do not cause damage to the environment of other States or of areas beyond the limits of national jurisdiction.

Principle 3

The right to development must be fulfilled so as to equitably meet developmental and environmental needs of present and future generations.

Principle 4

In order to achieve sustainable development, environmental protection shall constitute an integral part of the development process and cannot be considered in isolation from it. …

Principle 6

The special situation and needs of developing countries, particularly the least developed and those most environmentally vulnerable, shall be given special priority. International actions in the field of environment and development should also address the interests and needs of all countries.

Principle 7

States shall cooperate in a spirit of global partnership to conserve, protect and restore the health and integrity of the Earth's ecosystem. In view of the different contributions to global environmental degradation, States have common but differentiated responsibilities. The developed countries acknowledge the responsibility that they bear in the international pursuit of sustainable development in view of the pressures their societies place on the global environment and of the technologies and financial resources they command. …

Principle 11

States shall enact effective environmental legislation. Environmental standards, management objectives and priorities should reflect the environmental and developmental context to which they apply. Standards applied by some countries may be inappropriate and of unwarranted economic and social cost to other countries, in particular developing countries.

Principle 12

... Trade policy measures for environmental purposes should not constitute a means of arbitrary or unjustifiable discrimination or a disguised restriction on international trade. Unilateral actions to deal with environmental challenges outside the jurisdiction of the importing country should be avoided. Environmental measures addressing transboundary or global environmental problems should, as far as possible, be based on an international consensus.

Principle 13

States shall develop national law regarding liability and compensation for the victims of pollution and other environmental damage. States shall also cooperate in an expeditious and more determined manner to develop further international law regarding liability and compensation for adverse effects of environmental damage caused by activities within their jurisdiction or control to areas beyond their jurisdiction.

Principle 14

States should effectively cooperate to discourage or prevent the relocation and transfer to other States of any activities and substances that cause severe environmental degradation or are found to be harmful to human health.

Principle 15

In order to protect the environment, the precautionary approach shall be widely applied by States according to their capabilities. Where there are threats of serious or irreversible damage, lack of full scientific certainty shall not be used as a reason for postponing cost-effective measures to prevent environmental degradation.

Principle 16

National authorities should endeavour to promote the internalization of environmental costs and the use of economic instruments, taking into account the approach that the polluter should, in principle, bear the cost of pollution, with due regard to the public interest and without distorting international trade and investment.

Principle 17

Environmental impact assessment, as a national instrument, shall be undertaken for proposed activities that are likely to have a significant adverse impact on the environment and are subject to a decision of a competent national authority.

Principle 18

States shall immediately notify other States of any natural disasters or other emergencies that are likely to produce sudden harmful effects on the environment of those States. Every effort shall be made by the international community to help States so afflicted.

Principle 19

States shall provide prior and timely notification and relevant information to potentially affected States on activities that may have a significant adverse transboundary environmental effect and shall consult with those States at an early stage and in good faith. …

Principle 24

Warfare is inherently destructive of sustainable development. States shall therefore respect international law providing protection for the environment in times of armed conflict and cooperate in its further development, as necessary.

3. Agenda 21

U.N. Conference on Environment and Development,
U.N. Doc. A/CONF.151.6 (1992)

a. E. B. Weiss, *Introductory Note, United Nations Conference on Environment and Development*

31 I.L.M. 814 (1992)

The Rio Conference resulted in a suite of documents which will set the agenda for the next several decades. These include an approximately 800-page Agenda 21, which is a complex document setting forth actions that need to be taken in relevant sectors, a Rio Declaration, Conventions on Climate Change and on Biological Diversity, and a Statement of Principles on Forests. ...

Agenda 21.

Countries began negotiations for the Rio Conference in Nairobi, Kenya in August 1990. Since then, they held preparatory committee meetings every few months, during which they negotiated the contents of the Agenda 21. The Agenda includes a set of priority actions and a basket of means for accomplishing these priority actions. Priorities are grouped into the following categories:

- achieving sustainable growth, as through integrating environment and development in decision-making;

- fostering an equitable world, as by combating poverty and protecting human health;

- making the world habitable by addressing issues of urban water supply, solid waste management, and urban pollution;

- encouraging efficient resource use, a category which includes management of energy resources, care and use of fresh water, forest development, management of fragile eco systems, conservation of biological diversity, and management of land resources;

- protecting global and regional resources, including the atmosphere, oceans and seas, and living marine resources; and

- managing chemicals and hazardous and nuclear wastes.

Many of the action items in this agenda are very specific and advance significantly beyond the actions now in place in many countries.

The most controversial section of this part of Agenda 21 during the Rio Conference was the section on protecting the atmosphere. Saudi Arabia did not want this section to address renewable energy resources as environmentally sound energy resources. This is the only section in this part of Agenda 21 which was completely rewritten during the UNCED Conference.

The other part of Agenda 21 addresses the instruments for achieving environmentally sustainable development, which include legal instruments, international institutional arrangements, and finances, among others.

In the section on international legal instruments, countries identify four priorities; review and assessment of relevant international law; further development of implementation mechanisms and compliance measures; effective participation by all countries in the international law-making process; and attention to the range and effectiveness of dispute resolution techniques. ...

On the crucial issue of financing environmentally sustainable development, countries agreed that new and additional resources were needed, and that all available mechanisms of financing should be used. This includes the Global Environmental Facility of the World Bank ... but does not limit financing to it. The industrialized countries did not agree to commit 0.7% of their GNP to assist developing countries, as the Group of 77 had demanded.

C. KEY ENVIRONMENTAL REGIMES

1. Maritime

a. Introduction

In the last few decades of the twentieth century, the uses of the oceans intensified significantly. Marine ecosystems became destabilized due to increased levels of marine pollution caused by vessels, either through discharge of oil as a by-product of normal operations; or as a result of accidents, such as the Torrey Canyon or Exxon Valdez incidents; or by land based sources and the dumping of wastes. Several treaties were enacted from 1954 on, but they were limited in scope and enforcement mechanisms.

There are many treaties dealing with regional seas and the protection of the marine environment. Some of these treaties existed prior to the 1982 Convention (UNCLOS) but have been developed by subsequent instruments adjusting and expanding their regimes. For a summary of characteristic regional seas treaties see PATRICIA W. BIRNIE & ALAN E. BOYLE, INTERNATIONAL LAW AND THE ENVIRONMENT (2d ed., Oxford U. Press 2002), at 358-359.

The 1954 International Convention for the Prevention of Pollution of the Sea by Oil (London) [327 U.N.T.S. 3] was the first attempt to regulate oil pollution by vessels. The Convention regulated discharge of oil by ships, requiring from the coastal state adequate port facilities and indicating prohibited areas for discharge of oil. The Convention applied to ships registered in any of the territories of a contracting government and to unregistered ships having the nationality of a contracting party. The limitation of the Convention both in terms of enforcement and its scope of protection were reasons for the adoption of the 1973 International Convention for the Prevention of Pollution from Ships. The new Convention extended the scope of maritime pollution protection from oil to other harmful substances by minimizing the accidental discharges of such substances. The new Convention also provided for a more rigorous enforcement mechanism. This Convention was amended in 1978.

Ultimately, the prevention of marine pollution was seen to require a global approach which could not be achieved by the various bilateral, regional, and international treaties that preceded UNCLOS, the Rio Declaration and Agenda 21.

Part XII of UNCLOS provides a comprehensive approach to the protection of the marine environment dealing with all sources of pollution. One of the most important contributions of UNCLOS has been that "pollution no longer [can] be regarded as an implicit freedom of the seas". BIRNIE & BOYLE, *supra,* at 348. UNCLOS, the Rio Declaration and Agenda 21 have substantially influenced the framework for dealing with the protection of the environment in general and the marine environment in particular, and have modified certain existing regional seas treaties.

Protection of the marine environment is established as a general "obligation" of states in UNCLOS, Article 192. To counter-balance this general obligation, Article 193 reaffirms the sovereign right of States to exploit their natural resources. In practice, achieving the balance between the obligation and the right has proved to be very difficult.

b. 1982 United Nations Convention on the Law of the Sea

1833 U.N.T.S. 3

Article 192: *General obligation*

States have the obligation to protect and preserve the marine environment.

Article 193: *Sovereign right of States to exploit their natural resources*

States have the sovereign right to exploit their natural resources pursuant to their environmental policies and in accordance with their duty to protect and preserve the marine environment.

Article 194: *Measures to prevent, reduce and control Pollution of the marine environment*

1. States shall take, individually or jointly as appropriate, all measures consistent with this Convention that are necessary to prevent, reduce and control pollution of the marine environment from any source, using for this purpose the best practicable means at their disposal and in accordance with their capabilities, and they shall endeavour to harmonize their policies in this connection.

2. States shall take all measures necessary to ensure that activities under their jurisdiction or control are so conducted as not to cause damage by pollution to other States and their environment, and that pollution arising from incidents or activities under their jurisdiction or control does not spread beyond the areas where they exercise sovereign rights in accordance with this Convention

3. The measures taken pursuant to this Part shall deal with all sources of pollution of the marine environment. These measures shall include, *inter alia*, those designed to minimize to the fullest possible extent:

(a) the release of toxic, harmful or noxious substances, especially those which are persistent, from land-based sources, from or through the atmosphere or by dumping;

(b) pollution from vessels, in particular measures for preventing accidents and dealing with emergencies, ensuring the safety of operations at sea, preventing intentional and unintentional discharges, and regulating the design, construction, equipment, operation and manning of vessels;

(c) pollution from installations and devices used in exploration or exploitation of the natural resources of the seabed and subsoil, in particular measures for preventing accidents and dealing with emergencies, ensuring the safety of operations at sea, and regulating the design, construction, equipment, operation and manning of such installations or devices;

(d) pollution from other installations and devices operating in the marine environment, in particular measures for preventing accidents and dealing with emergencies, ensuring the safety of operations at sea, and regulating the design, construction, equipment, operation and manning of such installations or devices.

4. In taking measures to prevent, reduce or control pollution of the marine environment, States shall refrain from unjustifiable interference with activities carried out by other States in the exercise of their rights and in pursuance of their duties in conformity with this Convention.

5. The measures taken in accordance with this Part shall include those necessary to protect and preserve rare or fragile ecosystems as well as the habitat of depleted, threatened or endangered species and other forms of marine life. ...

Article 197: *Cooperation on a global or regional basis*

States shall cooperate on a global basis and, as appropriate, on a regional basis, directly or through competent international organizations, in formulating and elaborating international rules, standards and recommended practices and procedures consistent with this Convention, for the protection and preservation of the marine environment, taking into account characteristic regional features.

* * *

Following the 1972 Stockholm Conference, the Convention on the Prevention of Marine Pollution by Dumping of Wastes and Other Matter was adopted. Under Article 3 of the Convention, "dumping" is defined as "any deliberate disposal at sea of wastes or other matter from vessels, aircraft, platforms or other man-made structures at sea" as well as "any deliberate disposal at sea of vessels, aircraft, platforms or other man-made structures at sea". Wastes or other matters incidental to the normal operations of vessels, aircraft, platforms or other man-made structures at sea are not included in the definition. Under the same Article, "waste or other matter" is defined as "material and substance of any kind, form or description." Annex I to the Convention lists prohibited substances and includes mercury, crude oil, materials produced for biological and chemical warfare and "high-level radio-active wastes or other high-level radio-active matter". Annex II lists substances requiring a prior special permit and includes arsenic, lead, copper, zinc, pesticides, radio-active wastes or other radio-active matter not included in Annex I. The dumping of all other wastes requires a prior general permit. The Convention has been updated several times. The 1996 Protocol to the Convention includes a number of substantive changes to the 1972 Convention taking into account the 1982 United Nations Convention on the Law of Sea and the Rio Declaration on the Environment and Development.

c. Convention on Prevention of Marine Pollution by Dumping of Wastes and other Matter, 1972: 1996 Protocol and Resolutions

Nov. 8, 1996, 36 I.L.M. 1, IMO Doc. LC/SM 1/6 (1996).

Article 2: *Objectives*

Contracting Parties shall individually and collectively protect and preserve the marine environment from all sources of pollution and take effective measures, according to their scientific, technical and economic capabilities, to prevent, reduce and where practicable eliminate pollution caused by dumping or incineration at sea of wastes or other matter....

Article 3: *General Obligations*

1. In implementing this Protocol, Contracting Parties shall apply a precautionary approach to environmental protection from dumping of waters or other matter whereby appropriate preventative measures are taken when there is reason to believe that wastes or other matter introduced into the marine environment

are likely to cause harm even when there is no conclusive evidence to prove a causal relation between inputs and their effects.

2. Taking into account the approach that the polluter should, in principle, bear the cost of pollution, each Contracting Party shall endeavour to promote practices whereby those it has authorized to engage in dumping or incineration at sea bear the cost of meeting the pollution prevention and control requirements for the authorized activities, having due regard to the public interest. …

Article 5: *Incineration at Sea*

Contracting Parties shall prohibit incineration at sea of wastes or other matter.

Article 6: *Export of Wastes or Other Matter*

Contracting Party shall not allow the export of wastes or other matter to other countries for dumping or incineration at sea. …

d. Southern Bluefin Tuna (Austl. & N. Z. v. Japan)
39 I.L.M. 1359 (2000)

[In 1993, Australia, Japan and New Zealand concluded the Convention for the Conservation of Southern Bluefin Tuna [hereinafter SBT Convention] which established the Commission for the Conservation of Southern Bluefin Tuna. By May 1994, the Commission set a Total Allowable Catch Level (hereinafter TAC) at 11,750 tons, with national allocation among Japan, Australia and New Zealand. Japan from 1994 sought an increase in the TAC level and in its allotment. But any increase was opposed by Australia and New Zealand. While the Commission initially maintained the TAC at existing levels due to the impasse, since 1998 it has been unable to agree upon any TAC. In the absence of a Commission decision, the Parties in practice have maintained their TAC as set in 1994. At a Commission meeting in 1998 Japan stated that, while it would voluntarily adhere to its previous quota for commercial SBT fishing, it would commence a unilateral, three-year Experimental Fishing Programme [hereinafter EFP] as of the summer of 1998. Despite vigorous protests by Australia and New Zealand over pursuance of any unilateral EFP, Japan conducted a pilot program with an estimated catch of 1,464 mt. in the summer of 1998. Parties were unable to resolve their dispute under the 1993 Convention. Australia and New Zealand invoked the compulsory arbitration provisions of the UN Convention on the Law of the Sea and requested provisional measures from the International Tribunal for the Law of the Sea (hereinafter ITLOS) pending an arbitration tribunal under Annex VII ITLOS, by an order of August 27, 1999, found that *prima facia* the arbitration tribunal would have jurisdiction and prescribed provisional measures. In its award of August 4, 2000, the Arbitration Tribunal decided that it lacked jurisdiction and revoked the provisional measures prescribed by ITLOS.] …

63. The second consideration of a general character that the Tribunal has taken into account is the fact that a significant number of international agreements with maritime elements, entered into after the adoption of UNCLOS, ex-

63. The second consideration of a general character that the Tribunal has taken into account is the fact that a significant number of international agreements with maritime elements, entered into after the adoption of UNCLOS, exclude with varying degrees of explicitness unilateral reference of a dispute to compulsory adjudicative or arbitral procedures. Many of these agreements effect such exclusion by expressly requiring disputes to be resolved by mutually agreed procedures, whether by negotiation and consultation or other method acceptable to the parties to the dispute or by arbitration or recourse to the International Court of Justice by common agreement of the parties to the dispute. Other agreements preclude unilateral submission of a dispute to compulsory binding adjudication or arbitration, not only by explicitly requiring disputes to be settled by mutually agreed procedures, but also, as in Article 16 of the 1993 [SBT] Convention, by requiring the parties to continue to seek to resolve the dispute by any of the various peaceful means of their own choice. The Tribunal is of the view that the existence of such a body of treaty practice – postdating as well as antedating the conclusion of UNCLOS – tends to confirm the conclusion that States Parties to UNCLOS may, by agreement, preclude subjection of their disputes to section 2 procedures in accordance with Article 281(1). To hold that disputes implicating obligations under both UNCLOS and an implementing treaty such as the 1993 Convention – as such disputes typically may – must be brought within the reach of section 2 of Part XV of UNCLOS would be effectively to deprive of substantial effect the dispute settlement provisions of those implementing agreements which prescribe dispute resolution by means of the parties' choice.

64. The Tribunal does not exclude the possibility that there might be instances in which the conduct of a State Party to UNCLOS and to a fisheries treaty implementing it would be so egregious, and risk consequences of such gravity, that a Tribunal might find that the obligations of UNCLOS provide a basis for jurisdiction, having particular regard to the provisions of Article 300 of UNCLOS. While Australia and New Zealand in the proceedings before ITLOS invoked Article 300, in the proceedings before this Tribunal they made clear that they do not hold Japan to any independent breach of an obligation to act in good faith.

65. It follows from the foregoing analysis that this Tribunal lacks jurisdiction to entertain the merits of the dispute brought by Australia and New Zealand against Japan. …

NOTES AND QUESTIONS

1. Compare Article 194 of UNCLOS with Principle 21 of the Stockholm Declaration and Principle 2 of the Rio Declaration. What are the differences between them? For further discussion of the problem of vessel-source pollution, *see* Christopher P. Mooradian, *Protecting "Sovereign Rights": The Case for Increased Coastal State Jurisdiction over Vessel-Source Pollution in the Exclusive Economic Zone*, 82 B.U.L. REV. 767 (2002); Andrew Schulkin, *Safe Harbors: Crafting an International Solution to Cruise Ship Pollution*, 15 GEO. INT'L ENVTL. L. REV. 105 (2002); Meredith Dahl, *The Federal Regulation of Waste From Cruise Ships in U.S. Waters*, 9 ENVTL. LAW. 609 (2003).

2. Interpret the obligations contained in paragraph 2 of UNCLOS Article 194 in the light of the language of paragraph 1, in particular the words "best practicable means at their disposal and in accordance with their capabilities". What does the phrase "States shall take all measures necessary to ensure…" in paragraph 2 mean? What are the consequences of a state's failure to take such measures?

3. How do you interpret the precautionary principle in Article 3(2) of the Protocol to the Convention on Prevention of Marine Pollution by dumping of Wastes and Other Matter, in view of Article 2 language limiting the obligation of states parties "to their scientific, technical and economic capabilities"?

4. What is the relationship between UNCLOS and many other fisheries treaties and treaties dealing with marine environment which were drafted prior to or after UNCLOS? What conclusions in this regard can you draw from the Southern Bluefin Tuna award? *See* in particular paragraph 64 of the award. *See also*, Christian C. Polychron, *Towards a Solution to the Problem of the Common Anadromous Stocks of the North Pacific*, 4 SAN DIEGO INT'L L. J. 543 (2003).

5. For further discussion of Agenda 21, see AGENDA 21: EARTH'S ACTION PLAN, (N.A. Robinson, ed., Oceana 1993); AGENDA 21 & THE UNCED PROCEEDINGS (N.A. Robinson, ed., Oceana 1993).

6. Increasingly, environmental claims are being adjudicated in international tribunals. *See* Donald L. Morgan, *Implications of the Proliferation of International Legal Fora: The Example of the Southern Bluefin Tuna Cases*, 43 Harv. Int'l L. J. 531 (2002). For further commentary, *see also* Barbara Kwiatkowska's summary of *Southern Blue Fin Tuna* at 95 Am.J. Int'l L. 162 (2001).

2. Transboundary Pollution

a. Trail Smelter Arbitration (U.S. v. Can.)

3 R.I.A.A. 1911 (1938), 35 AM. J. INT'L. L. 684 (1941)

[The Consolidated Mining and Smelting Company Limited of Canada operated a zinc and lead smelter along the Columbia river at Trail, British Columbia, about 10 miles north of the international boundary with the State of Washington. In the period between 1928 and 1935, the United States filed complaints with the Canadian government asserting that sulfur dioxide emissions from the Trail smelter had damaged the Columbia River Valley. The main concern of the United States was that the smelter's sulfur dioxide emissions were harming the land and the trees that were used for logging, farming, and cattle grazing; the three industries crucial to the area. The main species affected were yellow pines, Douglas firs, larch, and cedar. Affected harvests included alfalfa, wheat, and oats. On August 7, 1928, the issue was referred to the International Joint Commission by the United States and Canada (IJC-UC) for settlement. The IJC-UC decided on February 28, 1931 that the Trail smelter should limit its sulfur dioxide emissions and that Canada should pay the United States US$350,000 as compensation for damages.

Despite the IJC-UC decision, the conditions at the Trail smelter did not improve. Consequently in February 1933 the United States renewed its complaints. This set of complaints led to an emissions convention between the United States of America and Canada (hereinafter termed "the Convention") which was signed by the two parties on April 15, 1935. The Convention called for the creation of a Tribunal to determine the answers to four questions:

2. If the smelter was found to have done damage, should it be made to refrain from doing so in the future?

3. Should the smelter operate under any restrictions?

4. Should any compensation be paid in light of the answers to questions 2 and 3?]

The controversy is between two Governments, involving damage occurring, or having occurred, in the territory of one of them (the United States of America) and alleged to be due to an agency situated in the territory of the other (the Dominion of Canada) …

As between the two countries involved, each has an equal interest that if a nuisance is proved, the indemnity to damaged parties for proven damage shall be just and adequate and each has also an equal interest that unproven or unwarranted claims shall not be allowed. For, while the United States interests may now be claimed to be injured by the operations of a Canadian corporation, it is equally possible that at some time in the future Canadian interests might be claimed to be injured by an American corporation. As has well been said: "It would not be to the advantage of the two countries concerned that industrial effort should be prevented by exaggerating the interests of the agricultural community. Equally it would not be to the advantage of the two countries that the agricultural community should be oppressed to advance the interest of industry."

Considerations like the above are reflected in the provisions of the Convention in article IV, that "the desire of the High Contracting Parties" is "to reach a solution just to all parties concerned". And the phraseology of the questions submitted to the Tribunal clearly evinces a desire and an intention that, to some extent, in making its answers to the questions, the Tribunal should endeavour to adjust the conflicting interests by some "just solution" which would allow the continuance of the operation of the Trail Smelter but under such restrictions and limitations as would, as far as foreseeable, prevent damage in the United States, and as would enable indemnity to be obtained, if, in spite of such restrictions and limitations, damage should occur in the future in the United States.

In arriving at this decision, the Tribunal has had always to bear in mind the further fact that in the preamble to the Convention, it is stated that it is concluded with the recognition of "the desirability and necessity of affecting a permanent settlement." …

Part Three

The second question under article III of the Convention is as follows:

In the event of this answer to the first part of the preceding question being in the affirmative, whether the Trail Smelter should be required to refrain from causing damage in the State of Washington in the future and, if so, to what extent.

Damage has occurred since January 1, 1932, as fully set forth in the previous decision. To that extent, the first part of the preceding question has thus been answered in the affirmative.

The first problem which arises is whether the question should be answered on the basis of the law followed in the United States or on the basis of international law. The Tribunal, however, finds that this problem need not be solved here, as the law followed in the United States in dealing with the quasi-sovereign rights of the States of the Union, in the matter of air pollution, whilst more definite, is in conformity with the general rules of international law.

Particularly, in reaching its conclusions as regards this question as well as the next, the Tribunal has given consideration to the desire of the High Contracting Parties "to reach a solution just to all parties concerned". ...

As Professor Eagleton puts it (see *Responsibility of States in International Law,* 1928, p. 80): "A State owes at all times a duty to protect other States against injurious acts by individuals from within its jurisdiction". A great number of such general pronouncements by leading authorities concerning the duty of a State to respect other States and their territory have been presented to the Tribunal. These and many others have been carefully examined. International decisions, in various matters, ... are based on the same general principle, and indeed, this principle, as such, has not been questioned by Canada. But the real difficulty often arises rather when it comes to determine what ... is deemed to constitute an injurious act. ...

No case of air pollution dealt with by an international tribunal has been brought to the attention of the Tribunal nor does the Tribunal know of any such case. The nearest analogy is that of water pollution. But, here also, no decision of an international tribunal has been cited or has been found.

There are, however, as regards both air pollution and water pollution, certain decisions of the Supreme Court of the United States which may legitimately be taken as a guide in this field of international law, for it is reasonable to follow by analogy, in international cases, precedents established by that Court in dealing with controversies between States of the Union or with other controversies concerning the quasi-sovereign rights of such States, where no contrary rule prevails in international law and no reason for rejecting such precedents can be adduced from the limitations of sovereignty inherent in the Constitution of the United States. ...

[After having considered some of the cases decided by the United States Supreme Court, the Tribunal concluded:]

The Tribunal therefore, finds that the above decisions, taken as a whole, constitute an adequate basis for its conclusions, namely that, under the principles of international law, as well as of the law of the United States, no State has the right to use or permit the use of its territory in such a manner as to cause injury by fumes in or to the territory of another of the properties or persons therein, when the case is of serious consequence and the injury is established by clear and convincing evidence.

The decisions of the Supreme Court of the United States which are the basis of these conclusions are decisions in equity and a solution inspired by them, together, with the regime hereinafter prescribed, will, in the opinion of the Tribunal, be "just to all parties concerned", as long, at least, as the present conditions in the Columbia River Valley continue to prevail.

Considering the circumstances of the case, the Tribunal holds that the Dominion of Canada is responsible in international law for the conduct of the Trail Smelter. Apart from the undertakings in the Convention, it is therefore, the duty of the Government of the Dominion of Canada to see to it that this conduct should be in conformity with the obligation of the Dominion under international law as herein determined.

NOTES AND QUESTIONS

1. What is the holding in *Trail Smelter*? Does it create customary law binding on states other than the United States and Canada? Does the prior acceptance by Canada of its responsibility for injuries by the Smelter prior to 1932 as well as any damage determined by the Tribunal subsequent to that date; affect the holding of the arbitration tribunal that "under the principles of international law, ... no State has the right to use or permit the use of its territory in such a manner as to cause injury by fumes in or to the territory of another or the properties or persons therein, when the case is of serious consequence and the injury is established by clear and convincing evidence?" Is this "good law" for the international community? In this context, *see* L. Goldie, *A General View of International Environmental Law – A Survey of Capabilities, Trends and Limits*, *in* HAGUE ACADEMY OF INTERNATIONAL LAW, Colloquium (1973); *see also* S. Bleicher, *An Overview of International Environmental Regulation*, 2 ECOLOGY L.Q.1, 22 (1972).

2. If Canada had not accepted responsibility for damage, would, in your view, the Tribunal have held Canada responsible for extraterritorial damage caused by an act of a private person?

3. Did the Tribunal order cessation of the work of the Trail Smelter? Did the United States ask for complete cessation of any transboundary damage? What were the factors deemed relevant by the United States? *See* J. Read, *The Trail Smelter Dispute*, 1963 CAN. Y.B. INT'L. L. 213, 224-225 (1963).

4. If the injury in the United States was only potential, but had not yet occurred, what do you think the decision of the Tribunal would have been?

b. Lake Lanoux Arbitration (Fr. v. Spain)

12 R.I.A.A. 281 (1957)

Translated in 1974 Y.B. INT'L L. COMM'N, VOL. II, PT. II, 194-9

[The court discusses the geographic features of the Lake Lanoux area, the facts of this case, and the features of the French project for Lake Lanoux, *supra*, this Part at 738.]

3. This dispute may be reduced to two fundamental questions:

(a) Would the works for the use of the waters of Lake Lanoux, on the terms laid down in the project and in the French proposals mentioned in the preamble to the *compromis*, constitute in themselves a violation of the rights granted to Spain by the substantive provisions of the Treaty of Bayonne of 26 May 1866 and the Additional Act of the same date?

(b) If the answer to the preceding questions [sic] is in the negative, would the execution of these works constitute a violation of the provisions of the Treaty of Bayonne of 26 March 1866 and of the Additional Act of the same date, because these provisions made the said execution subject in any circumstances to preliminary agreement between the two Governments or because other rules of [A]rticle 11 of the Additional Act concerning the negotiations between the two Governments had not been observed?

[With respect to the first question stated in paragraph 3(a), the Tribunal observed:]

In reality, it seems that the Spanish thesis is twofold and covers, on the one hand, the prohibition, without the consent of the other Party, of compensation between two basins, in spite of the equivalence of withdrawal and return and, on the other hand, the prohibition, without the consent of the other Party, of all actions that may create along with a *de facto* inequality, the physical possibility of a violation of law. The two points should be examined in order.

8. The prohibition of compensation between two basins, without the consent of the other Party, despite the equivalence of withdrawal and return, would result in a general bar to the taking of water from a waterway belonging to the river basin A for the benefit of river basin B, even if this withdrawal was offset by a strictly equivalent return from a waterway of river basin B for the benefit of river basin A. The Tribunal, from the viewpoint of physical geography, cannot disregard the reality of each river basin, which constitutes, as the Spanish case contends, "a whole". But this fact does not justify the absolute consequences which the Spanish thesis seeks to draw from it. The unity of a basin is supported at the legal level only to the extent that it conforms to the realities of life. Water, which is by nature a fungible thing, may be restored without alteration of its qualities from the viewpoint of human needs. A withdrawal with return, as contemplated in the French project, does not alter a state of affairs established in response to the demands of life in society.

The state of modern technology leads more and more frequently to the acknowledgement that water used in the generation of electric power need not be returned to its natural course.

The Tribunal considers, therefore, that withdrawal with return, as provided in the French project and proposals, is not in conflict with the Treaty and the Additional Act of 1866.

9. In another connexion, the Spanish Government challenged the legality of works carried out on the territory of one of the signatories of the Treaty and of the Additional Act, if they were calculated to enable it, even in violation of its international commitments, to bring pressure to bear on the other signatory. This

rule was said to follow from the fact that the treaties in question established the principle of equality among States. Specifically, Spain feels that France does not have the right to procure for itself, by public works, the physical possibility of stopping the flow of the Lanoux water or the return of an equivalent quantity of water. It is not for the Tribunal to judge the reasons or experiences which might lead the Spanish Government to give expression to a certain anxiety. But it is not alleged that the purpose of the works in question, aside from the satisfaction of French interests, is to create a means of at least potential injury to Spanish interests; that would be all the more unlikely as France could only partially exhaust the resources represented by the discharge of the Carol, it would also affect all the French land irrigated by the Carol, and it would be open along the whole boundary to formidable reprisals.

Moreover, the French Government's proposals, which are an integral part of its project, include "the assurance that it will not, in any case, interfere with the regime thus established", ... The Tribunal must, therefore, answer the question submitted by the *compromis* on the basis of this assurance. It could not be alleged that despite this commitment Spain would not have a sufficient guarantee, for it is a well-established general principle of law that bad faith is not presumed. Moreover, it has not been contended that either of the two States at any time intentionally infringed a rule relating to the water economy to the detriment of the other. Moreover, although based on a just spirit of reciprocity, the Treaties of Bayonne established only equality in law and not equality in fact. If it were otherwise, they would have had to forbid on both sides of the boundary any installations and works of a military order which could give to one of the States a *de facto* predominance which it might use to violate its international commitments. But it is necessary to go farther still; man's growing mastery of the forces and secrets of nature has placed in his hands instruments which he may use to violate his obligations or for the common good; the danger of misuse has not resulted, up to the present, in making the possession of these means dependent on the authorization of the States which may be threatened. Even if viewed solely from the standpoint of the relations of neighbours, the political danger alleged by the Spanish Government would be no more exceptional than the technical risk mentioned above. In any case, there is not, in the Treaty and Additional Act of 26 May 1866 or in the generally accepted principles of international law, a rule which forbids a State, acting to protect its legitimate interests, from placing itself in a situation which enables it in fact, in violation of its international obligations, to do even serious injury to a neighbouring State.

It remains still to be determined whether the French project conflicts with the substantive rules laid down by article 11. This question will be examined farther on, in connexion with the general terms of this article. ...

Subject to this last reservation, the Tribunal replies in the negative to the first question, set forth in paragraph 3 a. ...

11. Before considering the Spanish arguments, the Tribunal believes it would be useful to make some very general observations on the nature of the obligations alleged to be incumbent on the French Government. To admit that in a given matter competence may no longer be exercised except on the condition of or by means of an agreement between two States is to place an essential restriction on the sovereignty of a State, and it may be allowed only if there is conclusive proof. Undoubtedly international practice discloses some specific cases in which this assumption is proved; thus, sometimes two States exercise jurisdiction jointly over certain territories (indivisum, coimperium or condominium); similarly, in certain international institutions, the representatives of States exercise jointly a certain competence on behalf of States or on behalf of organizations. But these cases are exceptional and international case law does not readily recognize their existence, especially when they infringe upon the territorial sovereignty of a State, which would be true in the present case.

In fact, to evaluate in its essence the need for a preliminary agreement, it is necessary to adopt the hypothesis that the States concerned cannot arrive at an agreement. In that case, it would have to be admitted that a State which ordinarily is competent has lost the right to act alone as a consequence of the unconditional and discretionary opposition of another State. This is to admit a "right of consent", a "right of veto", which at the discretion of one State paralyses another State's exercise of its territorial competence.

For this reason, international practice prefers to resort to less extreme solutions, limiting itself to requiring States to seek the terms of an agreement by preliminary negotiations without making the exercise of their competence conditional on the conclusion of this agreement. Thus reference is made, although often incorrectly, to "an obligation to negotiate an agreement". In reality, the commitments thus assumed by States take very diverse forms, and their scope varies according to the way in which they are defined and according to the procedures for their execution; but the reality of the obligations thus assumed cannot be questioned, and they may be enforced, for example, in the case of an unjustified breaking off of conversations, unusual delays, disregard of established procedures, systematic refusal to give consideration to proposals or adverse interests, and more generally in the case of infringement of the rules of good faith. ...

[On the requirement of prior agreement the Tribunal said:]

12. We shall consider first, therefore, whether the proposition that the execution of the French project is conditional on the preliminary consent of the Spanish Government is justified by reference to the system of joint community pasturage rights or to the generally accepted principles of international law. ...

The Spanish Government desired in particular to show that "the demarcation line of the Pyrénées boundary constituted, not a limit to the sovereign rights of the bordering States, but a zone organized in accordance with a special customary law, incorporated into international law by the boundary Treaties which recognized that zone" ... The most characteristic expression of this customary law was said to be the existence of joint community pasturage rights; … these were themselves said to be the residue of a wider community system, which in the Pyrénées valleys was based on the rule that matters of common interest should be settled by freely negotiated agreements.

In fact, the French project does not affect the rights of pasturage on French territory guaranteed by the treaties to certain Spanish towns. In particular, it appears, according to the replies of the Parties to a question put by the Tribunal, that the rights of pasturage on French territory held by the Spanish town of Llivia in no way affect the waters of Lanoux or of the Carol. …

13. … Thus, while admittedly there is a rule prohibiting the upper riparian State from altering the waters of a river in circumstances calculated to do serious injury to the lower riparian State, such a principle has no application to the present case, since it was agreed by the Tribunal, with respect to the first question considered above, that the French project did not alter the waters of the Carol. In fact, States today are well aware of the importance of the conflicting interests involved in the industrial use of international rivers and of the necessity of reconciling some of these interests with others through mutual concessions. The only way to achieve these adjustments of interest is the conclusion of agreements on a more and more comprehensive basis. International practice reflects the conviction that States should seek to conclude such agreements; there would thus be an obligation for States to agree in good faith to all negotiations and contacts which should, through a wide confrontation of interests and reciprocal goodwill, place them in the best circumstances to conclude agreements. This point will be considered later on in establishing the obligations of France and Spain concerning contacts and negotiations prior to the execution of a project such as the one for Lake Lanoux.

But international practice does not permit us, so far, to go beyond this conclusion; the rule that States may use the hydraulic power of international waterways only if a *preliminary* agreement between the States concerned has been concluded cannot be established as a customary rule or, still less, as a general principle of law. …

[As to other obligations arising from Article 11 of the Additional Act, the Tribunal said:]

21. Article 11 of the Additional Act imposes a twofold obligation on States in which works or new concessions calculated to change the administration or the volume of a waterway traversing the two States are proposed. One is to give prior notice to the competent authorities of the neighbouring country; the other is to develop a system of complaints and of safeguards for all the interests involved on one side and the other. …

The fact that France satisfied the obligation of notice as far as the development of Lake Lanoux was concerned has not been contested.

22. The content of the second obligation is more difficult to determine. The "complaints" mentioned in article 11 relate to the various rights protected by the Additional Act, but the main question is to establish how "all the interests involved on one side and the other" should be safeguarded.

First, it is necessary to determine which "interests" should be safeguarded. A strict interpretation of [A]rticle 11 would support the conclusion that only interests corresponding to a right of the riparian population were involved. Various considerations already pointed out by the Tribunal lead however to a broader interpretation. Consideration must be given to all interests, whatever their nature, which may be affected by the works undertaken, even if they do not amount to a right. Only this solution is in accord with the terms of article 16, the spirit of the Pyrénées Treaties, and the trends apparent in current international practice as regards hydro-electric development.

The second question is to determine the procedure whereby these interests can be safeguarded. Although this procedure necessarily involves negotiations, it cannot be reduced to purely formal requirements, such as taking note of complaints, protests or expressions of regret submitted by the lower riparian State. The Tribunal considers that the upper riparian State, under the rules of good faith, has an obligation to take into consideration the various interests concerned, to seek to give them every satisfaction compatible with the pursuit of its own interests and to show that it has, in this matter, a real desire to reconcile the interests of the other riparian with its own.

It is difficult to determine if such an obligation has been met. Nevertheless, without substituting himself for the Parties, the judge is able to undertake this determination on the basis of the evidence furnished by the negotiations.

23. In the present case, the Spanish Government charges that the French Government did not draw up the development project for the waters of Lake Lanoux on a basis of absolute equality. This charge is twofold: it relates to both form and substance. In the matter of form, it is suggested that the French Government imposed its project unilaterally without associating the Spanish Government in a joint search for an acceptable solution. As to substance, it is contended that the French project does not maintain an equitable balance between French interests and Spanish interests. The French project, it is argued, perfectly serves French interests, but does not take sufficient account of Spanish interests in the matter of irrigation. …

From the standpoint of principle, the Spanish thesis cannot be accepted by the Tribunal, for it is inclined to put rights and mere interests on the same level. Article 11 of the Additional Act makes a distinction between them, which both Parties have reproduced in the fundamental statement of their theses at the beginning of the *compromis:*

> Considering that, in the opinion of the French Government, the carrying out of its project … would not prejudice any of the rights or interests

referred to in the Treaty of Bayonne of 26 May 1866 and in the Additional Act of the same date;

Considering that, in the opinion of the Spanish Government, the carrying out of this project would prejudice Spanish interests and rights.

France may use its rights; it may not disregard Spanish interests.

Spain may demand respect for its rights and consideration of its interests. …

24. In the case of Lake Lanoux, France adhered throughout to the solution which involved a diversion of the water of the Carol to the Ariège, with complete return. In making this choice, France is merely exercising a right: the Lake Lanoux development works are being carried out on French territory, the burden and the responsibility of the undertaking rests on France, and France is the sole judge of the public works to be carried out on its territory, subject to articles 9 and 10 of the Additional Act, which the French project does not infringe.

For its part, Spain may not invoke a right to have the development of Lake Lanoux based on the needs of Spanish agriculture. In fact, if France renounced all the works planned on its territory, Spain could not require other works which conformed to its wishes to be carried out. It, therefore, may assert its interests simply to obtain terms providing reasonable safeguards for them within the limits of the project adopted by France.

It remains to be decided whether this requirement has been met. …

In determining whether France, both in its negotiations and in its proposals, took Spanish interests sufficiently into consideration, note must be taken of the intimate connexion between the obligation to take adverse interests into account in the course of negotiations and the obligation to give a reasonable place to such interests in the solution adopted. A State which has conducted negotiations with understanding and good faith, according to article 11 of the Additional Act, is not released from the obligation to give a reasonable place to adverse interests in the solution adopted because the conversations have been interrupted, even by the intransigence of its partner. Inversely, when it is a question of appraising the way in which a project takes account of the interests concerned, the manner in which the negotiations have been conducted, the list of the interests which might have been presented in them and the price which each of the Parties was prepared to pay in order to obtain their safeguard, are the main factors in establishing the merit of this project in relation to the obligations of article 11 of the Additional Act.

In view of all the above-mentioned circumstances of the case, the Tribunal is of the opinion that the French project satisfies the obligations of article 11 of the Additional Act.

For these reasons, the Tribunal decided to reply in the affirmative to the question set forth in article 1 of the *compromis*. In carrying out, without a preliminary agreement between the two Governments, works for the use of the waters of Lake Lanoux on the terms laid down in the project for the use of the waters of Lake Lanoux, due notice of which was given to the Governor of Gerona Province on 21 January 1954 and of which the representatives of Spain on the Pyrénées Commission were informed during the Commission's session from 3 to 14 November 1955, and in accordance with the proposals submitted by the French delegation to the Special Joint Commission on 13 December 1955, the French Government would not commit a violation of the provisions of the Treaty of Bayonne of 26 May 1866 and of the Additional Act of that date.

c. Corfu Channel (U.K. v. Alb.)

1949 I.C.J. 4 (Apr. 9)

[Review, *supra,* at 677. *See also* Part Five, *infra*, at 910.]

NOTES AND QUESTIONS

1. How does the *Lake Lanoux* Tribunal interpret the obligation of negotiation?

2. In 1928, Max Huber, the sole arbitrator, in *Island of Palmas* (U.S. v. Neth.), 2 R.I.A.A. 829, 839 held that the exclusive right to territorial sovereignty "has as corollary a duty: the obligation to protect within the territory the rights of other states, in particular their right to integrity and inviolability in peace and in war, together with the rights which each state may claim for its nationals in foreign territory". The ICJ in Order No. 3 of 26 January 1971 in *Legal Consequences for States of the Continued Presence of South Africa in Namibia (South West Africa) Notwithstanding Security Council Resolution 276 (1970)* stated that "physical control of a territory, and not sovereignty or legitimacy of title, is the basis of State liability for acts affecting other States" 1971 I.C.J. Rep. 42, para. 118. What is the significance of these statements, and those in *Corfu Channel*, that it is "every State's obligation not to allow knowingly its territory to be used for acts contrary to the rights of other States" for transboundary pollution problems? Compare the above with *Trail Smelter*. In your view, what would have been the decision of the Court in *Corfu Channel* if it were confronted with a failed government in Albania that had no physical control outside the capital?

d. Nuclear Tests (Austl. v. Fr.)

1973 I.C.J. 99 (Order of June 22)

[Review facts, *supra*, Part One, at 51 .]

25. Whereas the Government of Australia alleges, *inter alia*, that a series of atmospheric nuclear tests have been carried out by the French Government in the Pacific during the period from 1966 to 1972, including the explosion of several hydrogen bombs and a number of devices of high and medium power; that during recent months there has been a growing body of reports, not denied by the French Government, to the effect that the French Government is planning to carry out a further series of atmospheric nuclear tests in the Pacific in 1973; that this series of tests may extend to 1975 and even beyond that date; that in diplomatic correspondence and in discussions earlier in the present year the French Government would not agree to cease nuclear testing in the atmosphere in the Pacific and would not supply Australia with any information as to the dates of its proposed tests or the expected size and yield of its explosions; and that in a statement made in the French Parliament on 2 May 1973 the French Government indicated that, regardless of the protests made by Australia and other countries, it did not envis-

age any cancellation or modification of the programme of nuclear testing as originally planned;

26. Whereas these allegations give substance to the Australian Government's contention that there is an immediate possibility of a further atmospheric nuclear test being carried out by France in the Pacific;

27. Whereas the Government of Australia ... alleges that the atmospheric nuclear explosions carried out by France in the Pacific have caused wide-spread radio-active fall-out on Australian territory and elsewhere in the southern hemisphere, have given rise to measurable concentrations of radio-nuclides in foodstuffs and in man, and have resulted in additional radiation doses to persons living in that hemisphere and in Australia in particular; that any radio-active material deposited in Australian territory will be potentially dangerous to Australia and its people and any injury caused thereby would be irreparable; that the conduct of French nuclear tests in the atmosphere creates anxiety and concern among the Australian people; that any effects of the French nuclear tests upon the resources of the sea or the conditions of the environment can never be undone and would be irremediable by any payment of damages; and any infringement by France of the rights of Australia and her people to freedom of movement over the high seas and superjacent airspace cannot be undone;

28. Whereas the French Government, in a diplomatic Note dated 7 February 1973 and addressed to the Government of Australia, the text of which was annexed to the Application in the present case, called attention to Reports of the Australian National Radiation Advisory Committee from 1967 to 1972, which all concluded that the fall-out from the French tests did not constitute a danger to the health of the Australian population; whereas in the said Note the French Government further expressed its conviction that in the absence of ascertained damage attributable to its nuclear experiments, they did not violate any rule of international law, and that, if the infraction of the law was alleged to consist in a violation of a legal norm concerning the threshold of atomic pollution which should not be crossed, it was hard to see what was the precise rule on which Australia relied;

29. Whereas for the purpose of the present proceedings it suffices to observe that the information submitted to the Court, including Reports of the United Nations Scientific Committee on the Effects of Atomic Radiation between 1958 and 1972, does not exclude the possibility that damage to Australia might be shown to be caused by the deposit on Australian territory of radio-active fall-out resulting from such tests and to be irreparable;

30. Whereas in the light of the foregoing considerations the Court is satisfied that it should indicate interim measures of protection in order to preserve the right claimed by Australia in the present litigation in respect of the deposit of radio-active fall-out on her territory; ...

Accordingly, THE COURT

Indicates, by 8 votes to 6, pending its final decision in the proceeding instituted on 9 May 1973 by Australia against France, the following provisional measures:

The Governments of Australia and France should each of them ensure that no action of any kind is taken which might aggravate or extend the dispute submitted to the Court or prejudice the rights of the other Party in respect of the carrying out of whatever decision the Court may render in the case; and, in particular, the French Government should avoid nuclear tests causing the deposit of radio-active fall-out on Australian territory;

e. Nuclear Tests (Austl. v. Fr.)

1974 I.C.J. 253 (Judgment of Dec. 20)

[As discussed *supra,* in Part One, where a more complete text appears (*see* ¶¶ 52-62), France ignored the Court order by continuing atmospheric nuclear testing in the South Pacific. In 1974, the Court held hearings on jurisdiction and admissibility in the absence of French participation. A few weeks prior to the hearings, France publicly stated that it would no longer conduct nuclear atmospheric tests. The public announcement was made by the French President and later confirmed and repeated by the French Ministers of Defense and of Foreign Affairs. Following this statement, the Court held by 9 votes to 6, that the claim of Australia no longer had any object and that the Court was therefore not called upon to give a decision on the claim. The Court did not discuss the environmental damage issue raised by Australia even though the irreparable nature of that harm had led it to issue provisional measures against France.]

Separate Opinion of JUDGE PETRÉN: [Judge Petrén notes that international tribunals have failed to modify their jurisdictional rules so that issues of human rights can be brought to international adjudication.] …

We can see a similar evolution taking place today in an allied field, that of the protection of the environment. Atmospheric nuclear tests, envisaged as the bearers of a particularly serious risk of environmental pollution, are a source of acute anxiety for present-day mankind, and it is only natural that efforts should be made on the international plane to erect legal barriers against that kind of test. In the present case, the question is whether such barriers existed at the time of the filing of the Australian Application. That Application cannot be considered admissible if, at the moment when it was filed, international law had not reached the stage of applicability to the atmospheric testing of nuclear weapons. It has been argued that it is sufficient for two parties to be in dispute over a right for an application from one of them on that subject to be admissible. Such would be the situation in the present case, but to my mind the question of the admissibility of an application cannot be reduced to the observance of so simple a formula. It is still necessary that the right claimed by the applicant party should belong to a domain governed by international law. In the present case, the Application is based upon an allegation that France's nuclear tests in the Pacific have given rise to radio-active fall-out on the territory of Australia. The Australian Government considers that its sovereignty has thereby been infringed in a manner contrary to international law. As there is no treaty link between Australia and France in the matter of nuclear tests, the Application presupposes the existence of a rule of customary international law whereby States are prohibited from causing, through atmospheric nuclear tests, the deposit of radio-active fall-out on the territory of other States. It is therefore the existence or non-existence of such a customary rule which has to be determined. ...

It is common knowledge, and is admitted by the Australian Government itself, that any nuclear explosion in the atmosphere gives rise to radio-active fall-out over the whole of the hemisphere where it takes place. Australia, therefore, is only one of many States on whose territory France's atmospheric nuclear tests, and likewise those of other States, have given rise to the deposit of radio-active fall-out. Since the Second World War, certain States have conducted atmospheric tests for the purpose of enabling them to pass from the atomic to the thermo-nuclear stage in the field of armaments. The conduct of these States proves that their Governments have not been of the opinion that customary international law forbade atmospheric nuclear tests. What is more, the Treaty of 1963 whereby the first three States to have acquired nuclear weapons mutually banned themselves from carrying out further atmospheric tests can be denounced. By the provision in that sense the signatories of the Treaty showed that they were still of the opinion that customary international law did not prohibit atmospheric nuclear tests.

To ascertain whether a customary rule to that effect might have come into being, it would appear more important to learn what attitude is taken up by States which have not yet carried out the tests necessary for reaching the nuclear stage. For such States the prohibition of atmospheric nuclear tests could signify the division of the international community into two groups: States possessing nuclear weapons and States not possessing them. If a State which does not possess nuclear arms refrains from carrying out the atmospheric tests which would enable it to acquire them and if that abstention is motivated not by political or economic considerations but by a conviction that such tests are prohibited by customary international law, the attitude of that State would constitute an element in the formation of such a custom. But where can one find proof that a sufficient number of States, economically and technically capable of manufacturing nuclear weapons, refrain from carrying out atmospheric nuclear tests because they consider that customary international law forbids them to do so? The example recently given by China when it exploded a very powerful bomb in the atmosphere is sufficient to demolish the contention that there exists at present a rule of customary international law prohibiting atmospheric nuclear tests. It would be unrealistic to close one's eyes to the attitude, in that respect, of the State with the largest population in the world.]

f. Request for an Examination of the Situation in Accordance with Paragraph 63 of the Court's Judgment of 20 December 1974 in Nuclear Tests (N.Z. v. Fr.)

1995 I.C.J. 288 (Order of Sept. 22)

[Following the decision by France to resume a final series of eight nuclear weapons tests in the South Pacific starting in September 1995, New Zealand requested the ICJ to resume the case on the basis of paragraph 63 of judgment of the Court. Paragraph 63 of judgment is identical to paragraph 60 of the Court's judgment in the same case involving Australia against France. The Court rejected the request on the ground that paragraph 63 of its judgment dealt only with atmospheric nuclear tests.]

NOTES AND QUESTIONS

1. What is the contribution of the ICJ decision in *Nuclear Tests* to the development of the law on transboundary pollution?

2. The International Law Commission (ILC) began consideration of a topic entitled "International Liability for Injurious Consequences Arising out of Acts Not Prohibited by International Law" in 1978. In essence this topic dealt with transboundary environmental harm. The difficulty for the ILC in adopting a coherent approach to this topic has been evident since the beginning of its work, both in terms of conceptualising it as a separate and coherent topic from its sister topic of State Responsibility as well as incorporating the concepts of liability for risk or without fault in a meaningful way.

The earlier work of the ILC viewed prevention of transboundary harm and some form of liability for such harm as requiring an integrated approach. Opposition in the ILC as well as among governments on accepting any form of "liability" led the Commission to divide the topic into two subtopics, one dealing with prevention of transboundary harm and the other with the question of liability. The ILC has completed drafting a set of 19 articles on "Prevention of Transboundary Harm from Hazardous Activities" (GA Off. Records, Fifty-Sixth Sess. Supp. No. 10 A/ 56/10, pp. 370-436). The articles require impact assessment for activities with significant risk of transboundary effect, prior consultations and negotiations and exchange of information. Article 5 (Implementation) provides that "[s]tates concerned shall take necessary legislative, administrative or other action including the establishment of suitable monitoring mechanisms to implement the provisions of the present articles." Accordingly, the obligation of states is limited to putting in place certain domestic procedural mechanisms for implementation. The obligation of states, in case of a private person within their territory engaged in an activity that causes transboundary harm, would be limited to sanctions against such a person. This approach imposes a relatively minor obligation on states which might be insufficient to lead to their liability for transboundary harm. The draft articles proposed by the ILC, contrary to most conventions dealing with transboundary pollution, have a broad scope and do not identify any particular activity.

In considering the draft articles, the Sixth Committee of the General Assembly, at its fifty-seventh session (2001), expressed disappointment with the ILC approach, which did not address the liability question. The General Assembly refused to take any action on the draft pending receipt of further work on liability. The ILC began work on liability for transboundary harm in 2002. The adoption of the Convention on Civil Liability for Damage resulting from Activities Dangerous to the Environment (1993 Lugano Convention), June 21, 1993, Eur. T.S. No. 150 and the Protocol on Civil Liability and Compensation for Damage Caused by the Transboundary Effects of Industrial Accidents on Transboundary Waters (Kiev Protocol, 2003) [MP.WAT/2003/1] *available at* http://untreaty.un.org/English/notpub/27_16E.pdf (last visited Sept. 30, 2003), all of which were drafted by the European states, seem to provide possible models for a global approach to the liability question.

3. For a discussion of the particular harm caused to both air and water environments by persistent organic pollutants ("POP's"), *see* Peter L. Lallas, *The Stockholm Convention on Persistent Organic Pollutants*, 95 AM. J. INT'L L. 692 (2001).

g. Convention on Long-Range Transboundary Air Pollution

Nov.13, 1979, 1302 U.N.T.S. 217 (1979)

Article 1

For the purposes of the present Convention:

(a) 'air pollution' means the introduction by man, directly or indirectly, of substances or energy into the air resulting in deleterious effects of such a nature as to endanger human health, harm living resources and ecosystems and material property and impair or interfere with amenities and other legitimate uses of the environment, and 'air pollutants' shall be construed accordingly.

(b) 'Long-range transboundary air pollution' means air pollution whose physical origin is situated wholly or in part within the area under the national jurisdiction of one State and which has adverse effects in the area under the jurisdiction of another State at such a distance that it is not generally possible to distinguish the contribution of individual emission sources or groups of sources.

Article 2

The Contracting Parties, taking due account of the facts and problems involved, are determined to protect man and his environment against air pollution and shall endeavour to limit and, as far as possible, gradually reduce and prevent air pollution including long-range transboundary air pollution.

Article 3

The Contracting Parties, within the framework of the present Convention, shall by means of exchanges of information, consultation, research and monitoring, develop without undue delay policies and strategies which shall serve as a means of combating the discharge of air pollutants, taking into account efforts already made at national and international levels.

Article 4

The Contracting Parties shall exchange information on and review their policies, scientific activities and technical measures aimed at combating, as far as possible, the discharge of air pollutants which may have adverse effects, thereby contributing to the reduction of air pollution including long-range transboundary air pollution.

Article 5

Consultations shall be held, upon request, at any early stage between, on the one hand, Contracting Parties which are actually affected by or exposed to a significant risk of long-range transboundary air pollution and, on the other hand, Contracting Parties within which and subject to whose jurisdiction a significant contribution to long-range transboundary air pollution originates, or could originate, in connexion with activities carried on or contemplated therein. …

Article 13: *Settlement of Disputes*

If a dispute arises between two or more Contracting Parties to the present Convention as to the interpretation or application of the Convention, they shall seek a solution by negotiation or by any other method of dispute settlement acceptable to the parties to the dispute.

h. Protocol on Further Reduction of Sulphur Emissions

U.N. Doc. ECE/EB.AIR/40 (1994), 33 I.L.M. 1540 (1994)

Article 2: *Basic Obligations*

1. The Parties shall control and reduce their sulphur emissions in order to protect human health and the environment from adverse effects, in particular acidifying effects, and to ensure, as far as possible, without entailing excessive costs, that depositions of oxidized sulphur compounds in the long term do not exceed critical loads for sulphur given, in annex I, as critical sulphur depositions, in accordance with present scientific knowledge.

2. As a first step, the Parties shall, as a minimum, reduce and maintain their annual sulphur emissions in accordance with the timing and levels specified in annex II. …

4. Furthermore, the Parties shall make use of the most effective measures for the reduction of sulphur emissions, appropriate in their particular circumstances, for new and existing sources, which include, *inter alia,*

— Measures to increase energy efficiency,

— Measures to increase the use of renewable energy,

— Measures to reduce the sulphur content of particular fuels and to encourage the use of fuel with a low sulphur content, including the combined use of high-sulphur with low-sulphur or sulphur-free fuel,

— Measures to apply best available control technologies not entailing excessive cost, using the guidance in annex IV. …

6. The Parties may, in addition, apply economic instruments to encourage the adoption of cost-effective approaches to the reduction of sulphur emissions.

7. The Parties to this Protocol may, at a session of the Executive Body, in accordance with rules and conditions which the Executive Body shall elaborate and adopt, decide whether two or more Parties may jointly implement the obligations set out in annex II. These rules and conditions shall ensure the fulfilment of the obligations set out in paragraph 2 above and also promote the achievement of the environmental objectives set out in paragraph 1 above.

Article 7: *Compliance*

1. An Implementation Committee is hereby established to review the implementation of the present Protocol and compliance by the Parties with their obligations. It shall report to the Parties at sessions of the Executive Body and may make such recommendations to them as it considers appropriate.

2. Upon consideration of a report, and any recommendations, of the Implementation Committee, the Parties, taking into account the circumstances of a matter and in accordance with Convention practice, may decide upon and call for action to bring about full compliance with the present Protocol, including measures to assist a Party's compliance with the Protocol, and to further the objectives of the Protocol.

3. The Parties shall, at the first session of the Executive Body after the entry into force of the present Protocol, adopt a decision that sets out the structure and functions of the Implementation Committee as well as procedures for its review of compliance.

4. The application of the compliance procedure shall be without prejudice to the provisions of article 9 of the present Protocol.

NOTES AND QUESTIONS

1. The Convention on Long Range Transboundary Air Pollution, as is the case of a number of other environmental agreements, does not deal with the issue of liability. Is there any relief under the treaty? What methods of implementation are available?

2. During the Gulf War in 1991, Iraq, before withdrawing from Kuwait, set oil wells on fire in Kuwait causing not only economic loss but also environmental damage to Kuwait and neighbouring states. The Security Council in Resolution 687 of 3 April 1991 condemned Iraq for its actions and stated that Iraq was "liable under international law for any direct loss, damage – including environmental damage and the depletion of natural resources ... to foreign Governments, nationals and corporations as a result of its unlawful invasion and occupation of Kuwait". The United Nations established a Compensation Commission to deal with the claims. The Governing Council of the United Nations Compensation Commission agreed on a set of criteria for processing claims, U.N. Doc. S/AC.26/1991/7/Rev.1. Paragraph 35 of this decision provides:

> These payments are available with respect to direct environmental damage and the depletion of natural resources as a result of Iraq's unlawful invasion and occupation of Kuwait. This will include losses or expenses resulting from:
>
> (a) Abatement and prevention of environmental damage, including expenses directly relating to fighting oil fires and stemming the flow of oil in coastal and international waters;
>
> (b) Reasonable measures already taken to clean and restore the environment or future measures which can be documented as reasonably necessary to clean and restore the environment;
>
> (c) Reasonable monitoring and assessment of the environmental damage for the purposes of evaluating and abating the harm and restoring the environment;

(d) Reasonable monitoring of public health and performing medical screenings for the purposes of investigation and combating increased health risks as a result of the environmental damage; and

(e) Depletion of or damage to natural resources.

What is the significance of Resolution 687 for confirming the liability of a state for transboundary pollution? To compare the liability mechanism under U.S. law., *see* Jeffrey Miller, *Liability for War-Caused Environmental Damage: Models from the United States*, in the ENVIRONMENTAL CONSEQUENCES OF WAR (Cambridge U. Press 2000). *See also*, John H. Knox, *The Myth and Reality of Transboundary Environmental Impact Assessment*, 96 AM. J. INT'L L. 291 (2002).

3. The UN Compensation Commission has not made any decision with respect to environmental claims. In your view what is the scope of "environmental damage" under the guidelines?

4. The International Court of Justice, in their Advisory Opinion on the *Legality of the Threat or Use of Nuclear Weapons* in 1996 held that the threat or use of nuclear weapons would generally be contrary to the rules of international law applicable in armed conflict, and in particular the principles of and rules of humanitarian law. Both the majority opinions and the dissenting opinion by Judge Weeramantry noted the devastating environmental effects of nuclear weapons.

3. Climate Change

a. 1 PHILIPPE SANDS, PRINCIPLES OF INTERNATIONAL ENVIRONMENTAL LAW 271 (Manchester U. Press 1995)

The earth's climate is determined in large part by the presence in the atmosphere of naturally occurring greenhouse gases, including in particular water vapour, carbon dioxide (CO_2), methane (CH_4), CFCs, nitrous oxide (N_2O) and tropospheric ozone (O_3). These are transparent to incoming shortwave solar radiation but absorb and trap longwave radiation emitted by the earth's surface. Their presence exerts a warming influence on the earth. Scientific evidence suggests that continued increases in atmospheric concentrations of selected greenhouse gases due to human activities will lead to an enhanced 'greenhouse effect' and global climatic change. Carbon dioxide from emissions from the combustion of fossil fuels, production of cement, and agricultural and other land use (including deforestation) is widely considered to be the most significant contribution to the threat of climate change, but global emissions of CFC-11 and 12, methane and nitrous oxide also pose a significant threat.

b. United Nations Framework Convention on Climate Change 1771 U.N.T.S. 107 (1992)

Article 2: *Objective*

The ultimate objective of this Convention and any related legal instruments that the Conference of the Parties may adopt is to achieve, in accordance with the relevant provisions of the Convention, stabilization of greenhouse gas concentrations in the atmosphere at a level that would prevent dangerous anthropogenic interference with the climate system. Such a level should be achieved within a time-frame sufficient to allow ecosystems to adapt naturally to climate change, to ensure that food production is not threatened and to enable economic development to proceed in a sustainable manner.

Article 3: *Principles*

In their actions to achieve the objective of the Convention and to implement its provisions, the Parties shall be guided, *inter alia*, by the following:

1. The Parties should protect the climate system for the benefit of present and future generations of humankind, on the basis of equity and in accordance with their common but differentiated responsibilities and respective capabilities. Accordingly, the developed country Parties should take the lead in combating climate change and the adverse effects thereof.

2. The specific needs and special circumstances of developing country Parties, especially those that are particularly vulnerable to the adverse effects of climate change, and of those Parties, especially developing country Parties, that would have to bear a disproportionate or abnormal burden under the Convention, should be given full consideration.

3. The Parties should take precautionary measures to anticipate, prevent or minimize the causes of climate change and mitigate its adverse effects. Where there are threats of serious or irreversible damage, lack of full scientific certainty should not be used as a reason for postponing such measures, taking into account that policies and measures to deal with climate change should be cost-effective so as to ensure global benefits at the lowest possible cost. To achieve this, such policies and measures should take into account different socio-economic contexts, be comprehensive, cover all relevant sources, sinks and reservoirs of greenhouse gases and adaptation, and comprise all economic sectors. Efforts to address climate change may be carried out cooperatively by interested Parties.

4. The Parties have a right to, and should, promote sustainable development. Policies and measures to protect the climate system against human-induced change should be appropriate for the specific conditions of each Party and should be integrated with national development programmes, taking into account that economic development is essential for adopting measures to address climate change.

5. The Parties should cooperate to promote a supportive and open international economic system that would lead to sustainable economic growth and development in all Parties, particularly developing country Parties, thus enabling them better to address the problems of climate change. Measures taken to combat climate change, including unilateral ones, should not constitute a means of arbitrary or unjustifiable discrimination or a disguised restriction on international trade.

Notes and Questions

1. As is clear from Article 2, the negotiators of the 1992 Convention assumed some degree of climate change as part of the normal process of industrialization and aimed only at "stabilization of greenhouse gas concentrations in the atmosphere at a level that would prevent dangerous anthropogenic interference with the climate system." The influence of the Rio Declaration is evident in

Article 3 paragraph 3 declaring the duty of states to protect the climate system for the benefit of present and future generations on the basis of differentiated responsibilities and requesting developed countries to take the lead to this end. Following two years of negotiation, the Kyoto Protocol to the Convention was concluded in 1997. (37 I.L.M. 22 (1998)). The Protocol establishes emission targets for certain greenhouse gases. States have flexibility in meeting these targets unilaterally or jointly in cooperation with other states. Article 1 of the Protocol instructs states parties to elaborate and approve measures dealing with non-compliance, indicating the consequences for non-compliance. Such measures have not yet been agreed on. In 2001, the George W. Bush administration announced that it would not ratify the Kyoto Protocol. For a review of the climate change regime, *see* Clare Breidenich, Daniel Magraw, Anne Rowley and James W. Rubin, *Current Development: The Kyoto Protocol to the United Nations Framework Convention on Climate Change*, 92 AM. J. INT'L. L. 317 (1998) ; Patricia W. Birnie and Alan E. Boyle *supra* at 523-535. *See also*, Daniel Bodansky, *United Nations Framework Convention on Climate Change*, 18 YALE J. INT'L L. 451 (1993).

2. What is a "framework convention"? *See* Richard L. Ottinger, *Global Climate Change Kyoto Protocol Implementation: Legal Frameworks for Implementing Clean Energy Solutions*, 18 PACE ENVTL. L. REV. 19 (2000); David A. Wirth, *The Sixth Session (Part Two) and the Seventh Session of the Conference of the Parties to the Framework Convention on Climate Change*, 96 AM. J. INT'L L. 647 (2002).

3. What are the consequences for a State Party of non-compliance with the Climate Change Convention or the Kyoto Protocol? Does this make the Climate Change Convention soft law? *See* Prue Taylor, *Heads in the Sand as the Tide Rises: Environmental Ethics and the Law on Climate Change*, 19 UCLA J. ENVTL. & POL'Y 247 (2001).

4. For a discussion of sustainability from an energy perspective, *see* Richard L. Ottinger, *Renewable Energy Sources for Development*, 32 ENVTL. L. 331 (2002); SOCIAL COSTS AND SUSTAINABLE MOBILITY (Klaus Remmings et al. eds., Springer Verlag 2000); ENERGY LAW AND SUSTAINABLE DEVELOPMENT (Adrian Bradbrook & Richard L. Ottinger eds., International Union for the Conservation of Nature 2003).

4. Conservation, Endangered Species and Biological Diversity

Over-exploitation of natural resources was the primary concern for earlier conventions dealing with fisheries and other wildlife. The goal of these conventions was to reach a level for sustainable exploitation. These conventions dealt with the protection and preservation of specific types of species such as migratory species of wild animals, dolphins, elephants, fur seals, polar bears, tigers, whales, etc. There are also a number of conventions dealing with fishing. The precautionary principle has influenced the development of a more modern approach to resource management which takes a broader view of ways by which resources should be preserved. The most prominent implementation of this approach is the 1995 United Nations Agreement Relating to the Conservation and Management of Straddling Fish Stocks and Migratory Fish Stocks. 34 I.L.M. 1542 (1995).

The Convention on International Trade in Endangered Species of Wild Fauna and Flora, 993 U.N.T.S. 243 (1973), was drafted as an effort to preserve these species by regulating the international trade in them with a view to their survival. The Convention drafted in 1973 lists protected species in three appendices which have been amended several times. An export permit for trading of species listed in Appendix I is required. Such a permit may be granted under certain conditions specified in article 3(2) of the Convention, which regulates international trade and not domestic. Reservations may be made to lists in the Appendices, within 90 days before the entry into force of the lists. While the Convention has been credited with the protection of endangered species, its effectiveness in view of the large volume of illegal trade which continues, its inadequate infrastructure for enforcement, and lack of sanctions for non-compliance, has now been questioned.

a. Daniel M. Bodansky, *International Law and the Protection of Biological Diversity*

28 VAND. J. TRANSNAT'L. L. 623, 626-28 (1995)

There are two reasons why the problem of protecting even seemingly local species has an international dimension. One reason is that, in some cases, the threats to species have an international character. For instance, international trade can lead to poaching and other activities that deplete a species that the source country wishes to protect. In these types of situations, international cooperation is needed to effectively implement national conservation measures. The rationale for international cooperation is similar to the rationale for international cooperation in law enforcement. Although punishment of crimes is ordinarily a national matter, international cooperation is often required in order to gather evidence, obtain custody of the offender, and thereby make national laws more effective. This interest in international cooperation was the rationale for Appendix III of the 1973 Convention on International Trade in Endangered Species 993 U.N.T.S. 243 (1973).

The other reason for international concern about biological resources found within a particular country is that the benefits of conservation are, in part, global in character. To the extent that the benefits of conservation are global, they are a positive externality. International action helps internalize that externality, giving states where the resources are found an incentive to conserve, by sharing in the benefits of conservation.

There are several global benefits of biodiversity that the international community should seek to internalize. First, biological resources are a repository of valuable information in the form of genetic codes. Preserving that information may eventually make possible the development of new drugs or crops. Second, biodiversity provides insurance against events that might devastate a particular species (e.g., pests or disease). Just as diversifying an investment portfolio reduces risk, maintaining biological diversity, in essence, provides insurance against catastrophes that might befall a particular species. Finally, ecosystem diversity provides global benefits in terms of ecological services, such as purifying water supplies and preventing land degradation.

Over the last twenty to twenty-five years, international environmental law has developed a number of general principles that are relevant to biodiversity protection. Whether these general principles constitute customary international law is a morass into which this article will not delve. Regardless of whether these principles have the status of customary international law, however, they represent an orientation or framework for international discussions of environmental issues.

The three principles most relevant to biological diversity are: (1) the precautionary principle, (2) the principle of intergenerational equity, and (3) the principle of differentiated responsibilities. The precautionary principle says that the international community need not await scientific certainty before taking action to protect the environment, particularly when the potential environmental harms are irreversible. This principle is clearly relevant to the biodiversity question, given the substantial uncertainties about the magnitude of the problem. Some skeptics argue that there is insufficient evidence to conclude that the world is on the brink of mass extinctions. However, the precautionary principle, which is explicitly recognized in the preamble to the Biological Diversity Convention, responds that certainty is not necessary before undertaking action.

The second relevant principle is intergenerational equity, which says that people have a duty to conserve resources for the benefit not only of the present generation but of future generations as well. Intergenerational equity is relevant to the biological diversity problem because some of the values of biological diversity mentioned previously, namely as a source of information and as an insurance policy, largely benefit future generations.

Finally, the principle of differentiated responsibilities addresses the concerns of developing countries, where most biodiversity is found. According to this principle, countries should contribute differently to international environmental efforts, depending on their capabilities and their historical responsibility. In practice, this principle has meant preferential treatment of poor, developing countries, and a greater contribution by wealthy, developed countries.

These three principles provide the general framework for efforts to conserve biological resources. However, they are not a panacea. They do not answer the hard questions about exactly how much evidence is needed before undertaking conservation measures or how much protection is warranted, nor do they dictate any particular regulatory policies.

b. Convention on Biological Diversity

June 5, 1992, 31 I.L.M. 818

Article 1: *Objectives*

The objectives of this Convention, to be pursued in accordance with its relevant provisions, are the conservation of biological diversity, the sustainable use of its components and the pair and equitable sharing of the benefits arising out of the utilization of genetic resources, including by appropriate access to genetic resources and by appropriate transfer of relevant technologies, taking into account all rights over those resources and to technologies, and by appropriate funding.

Article 2: *Use of Terms*

For the purposes of this Convention:

"*Biological diversity*" means the variability among living organisms from all sources including, *inter alia*, terrestrial, marine and other aquatic ecosystems and the ecological complexes of which they are part; this includes diversity within species, between species and of ecosystems.

"*Biological resources*" Includes genetic resources, organisms or parts thereof, populations, or any other biotic component of ecosystems with actual or potential use or value for humanity.

"*Biotechnology*" means any technological application that uses biological systems, living organisms, or derivatives thereof, to make or modify products or processes for specific use.

Article 3: *Principle*

States have, in accordance with the Charter of the United Nations and the principles of international law, the sovereign right to exploit their own resources pursuant to their own environmental policies, and the responsibility to ensure that activities within their jurisdiction or control do not cause damage to the environment of other States or of areas beyond the limits of national jurisdiction.

Article 4: *Jurisdictional Scope*

Subject to the rights of other States, and except as otherwise expressly provided in this Convention, the provisions of this Convention apply, in relation to each Contracting Party:

(a) In the case of components of biological diversity, in areas within the limits of its national jurisdiction; and

(b) In the case of processes and activities, regardless of where their effects occur, carried out under its jurisdiction or control, within the area of its national jurisdiction or beyond the limits of national jurisdiction. ...

Article 6: *General Measures for Conservation and Sustainable Use*

Each Contracting Party shall, in accordance with its particular conditions and capabilities:

(a) Develop national strategies, plans or programmed for the conservation and sustainable use of biological diversity or adapt for this purpose existing strategies, plans or programmes which shall reflect, inter alia, the measures set out in this Convention relevant to the Contracting Party concerned; and

(b) Integrate, as far as possible and as appropriate, the conservation and sustainable use of biological diversity into relevant sectoral or cross-sectoral plans, programmes and policies. ...

Article 10: *Sustainable Use of Components of Biological Diversity*

Each Contracting Party shall, as far as possible and as appropriate:

(a) Integrate consideration of the conservation and sustainable use of biological resources into national decision-making;

(b) Adopt measures relating to the use of biological resources to avoid or minimize adverse impacts on biological diversity;

(c) Protect and encourage customary use of biological resources in accordance with traditional cultural practices that are compatible with Conservation or sustainable use requirements;

(d) Support local populations to develop and implement remedial action in degraded areas where biological diversity has been reduced; and

(e) Encourage cooperation between L.S. governmental authorities and tic private sector in developing methods for sustainable use of biological resources

Article 11: *Incentive Measures*

Each Contracting Party shall, as far as possible and as appropriate, adopt economically and socially sound measures that act as incentives for the conservation and sustainable use of components of biological diversity. ...

Article 22: *Relationship with Other International Conventions*

1. The provisions of this Convention shall not affect the rights and obligations of any Contracting Party deriving from any existing international agreement, except where the exercise of those rights and obligations would cause a serious damage or threat to biological diversity.

2. Contracting Parties shall implement this Convention with respect to the marine environment consistently with the rights and obligations of States under the law of the sea.

Declaration of the United States of America

1. In signing the Final Act, the United States recognizes that this negotiation has drawn to a close.

2. The United States strongly supports the conservation of biodiversity and, as is known, was an original proponent of a convention on this important subject. We continue to view international cooperation in this area as extremely desirable.

3. It is deeply regrettable to us that - whether because of the haste with which we have completed our work or the result of substantive disagreement - a number of issues of serious concern in the United States have not been ad-

equately addressed in the course of this negotiation. As a result, in our view, the text is seriously flawed in a number of important respects.

4. As a matter of substance, we find particularly unsatisfactory the text's treatment of intellectual property rights; finances, including, importantly, the role of the Global Environmental Facility (GEF); technology transfer and biotechnology.

5. In addition, we are disappointed with the development of issues related to environmental impact assessments, the legal relationship between this Convention and other international agreements, and the scope of obligations with respect to the marine environment.

NOTES AND QUESTIONS

1. In January 2000, the Cartagena Protocol on Biosafety 39 I.L.M. 1027 (2000) to the Convention on Biological Diversity was adopted dealing with transboundary movement, transit, handling and use of all living modified organisms that may have adverse effects on the conservation and sustainable use of biological diversity, taking also into account risks to human health. The Protocol is based on the concept of the precautionary principle (Principle 15 of the Rio Declaration) and relies on the requirements of risk assessment, prior consultations and negotiations and monitoring.

The Protocol does not deal with the question of liability. It provides in Article 27: "The Conference of the Parties ... shall, at its first meeting, adopt a process with respect to the appropriate elaboration of international rules and procedures in the field of liability and redress for damage resulting from transboundary movements of living modified organisms, analysing and taking due account of the ongoing processes in international law on these matters, and shall endeavour to complete this process within four years."

2. Why is the protection of biodiversity deemed to be a matter of international concern? Does the Convention provide adequate protection?

3. What are the concerns of the United States about the Convention?

4. What are the consequences to states of breach of the Convention on Biodiversity? Bearing in mind that the Cartagena Protocol to the Convention does not provide any liability mechanism and states specifically in article 27 that at some future time the parties should draft such rules, is there any legal remedy for a state party that is injured as a result of the breach of the Protocol by another state party? *See* Sean D. Murphy, *Biotechnology and International Law*, 42 HARV. INT'L L. J. 47 (2001).

D. EFFORTS TO ACCOMMODATE THE POLICIES FOR INTERNATIONAL TRADE AND ENVIRONMENTAL PROTECTION

Liberalization of and free trade are the main objectives of the present international trading system, which was put in place by the 1949 General Agreement on Tariffs and Trade (GATT) and supplemented by the Marrakesh Agreement of 1994. Free trade policy will inevitably come into conflict with some environmental agreements and with some domestic environmental standards. In addition many multilateral environmental agreements have been based on the requirement of cooperation and negotiation with weak compliance mechanisms. The "soft" character of environmental agreements is yet a further reason for sidestepping them when they are incongruent with the "hard" character of trade regulations. However, the multiplicity of international environmental agreements and their promotion at the governmental and non-governmental level have influenced some aspects of international trade. Now states and dispute settlement bodies acting under major international trade agreements have been forced to take into account environmental concerns in the application of regulatory provisions dealing with trade restrictions, ostensibly for the protection of the domestic environment as well as the environment outside the territory of a state. Dispute settlement bodies have become more responsive to environmental concerns by correcting their earlier decisions viewed as insensitive to such concerns.

1. The General Agreement on Tariffs and Trade

55 U.N.T.S. 194 (1949)

Article I: *General Most-Favoured Nation Treatment*

1. With respect to customs duties and charges of any kind imposed on or in connection with importation or exportation or imposed on the international transfer of payments for imports or exports, and with respect to the method of levying such duties and charges, and with respect to all rules and formalities in connection with importation and exportation, and with respect to all matters referred to in paragraphs 2 and 4 of Article III, any advantage, favour, privilege or immunity granted by any contracting party to any product originating in or destined for any other country shall be accorded immediately and unconditionally to the like product originating in or destined for the territories of all other contracting parties. …

Article III: *National Treatment on Internal Taxation and Regulation*

4. The products of the territory of any contracting party imported into the territory of any other contracting party shall be accorded treatment no less favourable than that accorded to like products of national origin in respect of all laws, regulations, and requirements affecting their internal sale, offering for sale, purchase, transportation, distribution or use. The provisions of this paragraph shall not prevent the application of differential internal transportation charges which are based exclusively on the economic operation of the means of transport and not on the nationality of the product. …

Article XI: *General Elimination of Quantitative Restrictions*

1. No prohibitions or restrictions other than duties, taxes or other charges, whether made effective through quotas, import or export licenses or other measures, shall be instituted or maintained by any contracting party on the importation of any product of the territory of any other contracting party or on the exportation or sale for export of any product destined for the territory of any other contracting party. …

Article XX: *General Exemptions*

Subject to the requirement that such measures are not applied in a manner which would constitute a means of arbitrary or unjustifiable discrimination between countries where the same conditions prevail, or a disguised restriction on international trade, nothing in this Agreement shall be construed to prevent the adoption or enforcement by any contracting party of measures:

(a) necessary to protect public morals;

(b) necessary to protect human, animal or plant life or health;

(c) relating to the importations or exportations of gold or silver; ...

(e) relating to the products of prison labour;

(f) imposed for the protection of national treasures of artistic, historic or archaeological value;

(g) relating to the conservation of exhaustible natural resources if such measures are made effective in conjunction with restriction on domestic production or consumption; ...

2. GATT Dispute Settlement Panel Report on United States Restrictions on Imports of Tuna (Tuna-Dolphin I)

30 I.L.M. 1594, 1598 (1991)

[Dolphins often swim beneath yellowfin tuna. The United States Mammal Protection Act, 16 U.S.C. §§ 1361-1421h (2000), to protect dolphins sets standards for the American fishing fleet and for other countries whose fishing fleet catch yellowfin tuna in eastern tropical areas of the Pacific Ocean. A country that cannot prove that it meets the dolphin protection standards of the Act ... will be prohibited from exporting tuna or tuna products to the United States. Mexico complained under the GATT dispute settlement procedure that the US cannot embargo imports of tuna products from Mexico because Mexican regulations with respect to methods for catching tuna do not comply with U.S. regulations. Mexico further complained that under GATT a state cannot use trade regulation as way to extraterritorially apply its domestic rules even to protect animal health or exhaustible natural resources. A number of other countries which fell into the category, i.e., states exporting processed tuna from countries whose fishing standard did not meet the U.S. regulations, joined Mexico. The dispute was submitted to a Panel which reported 3 September 1991. Mexico and the U.S. held bilateral consultations to reach agreement outside of GATT.]

5.27. The Panel further noted that Article XX(b) allows each contracting party to set its human, animal or plant life or health standards. The conditions set out in Article XX(b) which limit resort to this exception, namely that the measure taken must be "necessary" and not "constitute a means of arbitrary or unjustifiable discrimination or a disguised restriction on international trade", refer to the trade measure requiring justification under Article XX(b), not however to the life or health standard chosen by the contracting party. The Panel recalled the finding of a previous panel that this paragraph of Article XX was intended to allow contracting parties to impose trade restrictive measures inconsistent with the General Agreement to pursue overriding public policy goals to the extent that such inconsistencies were unavoidable. The Panel considered that if the broad interpretation of Article XX(b) suggested by the United States were accepted, each contracting party could unilaterally determine the life or health protection policies from which other contracting parties could not deviate without jeopardizing their rights under the General Agreement. The General Agreement would then no longer constitute a multilateral framework for trade among all contracting parties but would provide legal security only in respect of trade between a limited number of contracting parties with identical internal regulations.

5.28. The Panel considered that the United States' measures, even if Article XX(b) were interpreted to permit extra jurisdictional protection of life and health, would not meet the requirement of necessity set out in that provision. The United States had not demonstrated to the Panel – as required of the party invoking an Article XX exception – that it had exhausted all options reasonably available to it to pursue its dolphin protection objectives through measures consistent with the General Agreement, in particular through the negotiation of international cooperative arrangements, which would seem to be desirable in view of the fact that dolphins roam the waters of many states and the high seas. Moreover, even assuming that an import prohibition were the only resort reasonably available to the United States, the particular measure chosen by the United States could in the Panel's view not be considered to be necessary within the meaning of Article XX(b). The United States linked the maximum incidental dolphin taking rate which Mexico had to meet during a particular period in order to be able to export tuna to the United States to the taking rate actually recorded for United States fishermen during the same period. Consequently, the Mexican authorities could not know whether, at a given point of time, their policies conformed to the United States' dolphin protection standards. The Panel considered that a limitation on trade based on such unpredictable conditions could not be regarded as necessary to protect the health or life of dolphins.

5.29. On the basis of the above considerations, the Panel found that the United States' direct import prohibition imposed on certain yellowfin tuna and certain yellowfin tuna products of Mexico and the provisions of the MMPA under which it is imposed could not be justified under the exception in Article XX(b). ...

5.30. The Panel proceeded to examine whether the prohibition on imports of certain yellowfin tuna and certain yellowfin tuna products from Mexico and the MMPA provisions under which it was imposed could be justified under the exception in Article XX(g). The Panel noted that the United States, in invoking Article XX(g) with respect to its direct import prohibition under the MMPA, had argued that the measures taken under the MMPA are measures primarily aimed at the conservation of dolphin, and that the import restrictions on certain tuna and tuna products under the MMPA are "primarily aimed at rending effective restrictions on domestic production or consumption" of dolphin. The Panel also noted that Mexico had argued that the United States measures were not justified under the exception in Article XX(g) because, *inter alia*, this provision could not be applied extra jurisdictionally.

5.31. The Panel noted that Article XX(g) required that the measures relating to the conservation of exhaustible natural resources be taken "in conjunction with restrictions on domestic production or consumption". A previous panel had found that a measure could only be considered to have been taken "in conjunction with" production restrictions "if it was primarily aimed at rendering effective these restrictions". A country can effectively control the production or consumption of an exhaustible natural resource only to the extent that the production or consumption is under its jurisdiction. This suggests that Article XX(g) was intended to permit contracting parties to take trade measures primarily aimed at rendering effective restrictions on production or consumption within their jurisdiction.

5.32. The Panel further noted that Article XX(g) allows each contracting party to adopt its own conservation policies. The conditions set out in Article XX(g) which limit resort to this exception, namely that the measures taken must be related to the conservation of exhaustible natural resources, and that they not "constitute a means of arbitrary or unjustifiable discrimination ... or a disguised restriction on international trade" refer to the trade measure requiring justification under Article XX(g), not however to the conservation policies adopted by the contracting party. The Panel considered that if the extra jurisdictional interpretation of Article XX(g) suggested by the United States were accepted, each contracting party could unilaterally determine the conservation policies from which other contracting parties could not deviate without jeopardizing their rights under the General Agreement. The considerations that led the Panel to reject an extra jurisdictional application of Article XX(b) therefore apply also to Article XX(g).

5.33. The Panel did not consider that the United States measures, even if Article XX(g) could be applied extra jurisdictionally, would meet the conditions set out in that provision. A previous panel found that a measure could be considered as "relating to the conservation of exhaustible natural resources" within the meaning of Article XX(g) only if it was primarily aimed at such conservation. The Panel recalled that the United States linked the maximum incidental dolphin-taking rate which Mexico had to meet during a particular period in order to be able to export tuna to the United States to the taking rate actually recorded for United States fishermen during the same period. Consequently, the Mexican authorities could not know whether, at a given point of time, their conservation policies conformed to the United States conservation standards. The Panel considered that a limitation on trade based on such unpredictable conditions could not be regarded as being primarily aimed at the conservation of dolphins.

5.34. On the basis of the above considerations, the Panel found that the United States direct import prohibition on certain yellowfin tuna and certain yellowfin tuna products of Mexico directly imported from Mexico, and the provisions of the MMPA under which it is imposed, could not be justified under Article XX(g).

3. GATT Dispute Settlement Panel Report on United States Restrictions on Imports of Tuna (Tuna-Dolphin II)

33 I.L.M. 839 (1994)

[The facts are the same as in Tuna-Dolphin I. The complaint was brought by the European Economic Commission against the United States. The Panel's report was never adopted by GATT members.]

5.28 The Panel noted the United States argument that both the primary and intermediary nation embargoes, even if inconsistent with Articles III or XI, were justified by Article XX (b) as measures necessary to protect the life and health of dolphins. The United States argued that there was no requirement in Article XX (b) that the animals whose life or health was to be protected had to be within the jurisdiction of the country taking the measure. The United States further argued that the measures were necessary to fulfil the policy goal of protecting the life and health of dolphins. Finally, it argued that the measures met the requirement of the preamble to Article XX. The EEC and the Netherlands disagreed, stating that the animals whose life or health was to be protected had to be within the jurisdiction of the country taking the measure. The EEC and the Netherlands were further of the view that the United States measures were not necessary within the meaning of Article XX (b).

5.29 The Panel proceeded first to examine the text of Article XX(b), which, together with its preamble, states:

Subject to the requirement that such measures are not applied in a manner which would constitute a means of arbitrary or unjustifiable discrimination between countries where the same conditions prevail, or a disguised restriction on international trade, nothing in this Agreement shall be construed to prevent the adoption or enforcement by any contracting party of measures: ...

(b) necessary to protect ... animal... life or health.

The Panel observed that the text of Article XX(b) suggested a three-step analysis:

— First, it had to be determined whether the policy in respect of which these provisions were invoked fell within the range of policies referred to in these provisions, that is policies to protect human, animal or plant life or health;

— Second, it had to be determined whether the measure for which the exception was being invoked - that is the particular trade measure inconsistent with the obligations under the General Agreement - was "necessary" to protect human, animal or plant life or health;

— Third, it had to be determined whether the measure was applied in a manner consistent with the requirement set out in the preamble to Article XX, namely that the measure not be applied in a manner which would constitute a means of arbitrary or unjustifiable discrimination between countries where the same conditions prevail or in a manner which would constitute a disguised restriction on international trade.

5.30 Turning to the first of the above three questions, the Panel noted that the parties did not disagree that the protection of dolphin life or health was a policy that could come within Article XX (b). The EEC argued, however, that Article XX (b) could not justify measures taken to protect living things located outside the territorial jurisdiction of the party taking the measure. The United States disagreed. The arguments on this issue advanced by the parties were similar to those made under Article XX (g).

5.31 The Panel recalled its reasoning under Article XX (g). It observed that the text of Article XX (b) does not spell out any limitation on the location of the living things to be protected. It noted that the conditions set out in the text of Article XX (b) and the preamble qualify only the trade measure requiring justification ("necessary to") or the manner in which the trade measure is applied ("arbitrary or unjustifiable discrimination", "disguised restriction on international trade"). The nature and precise scope of the policy area named in the Article, the protection of living things, is not specified in the text of the Article, in particular with respect to the location of the living things to be protected.

5.32 The Panel further recalled its observation that elsewhere in the General Agreement measures according different treatment to products of different origins could in principle be taken with respect to things located, or actions occurring, outside the territorial jurisdiction of the party taking the measure. It could not therefore be said that the General Agreement proscribed in an absolute manner such measures. The Panel further recalled its observation that, under general international law, states are not in principle barred from regulating the conduct of their nationals with respect to persons, animals, plants and natural resources outside of their territory (see paragraph 5.17 above).

5.33 The Panel noted that the United States and the EEC, as under Article XX (g), based many of their arguments regarding the location of the living things to protected under Article XX (b) on environmental and trade treaties other than the General Agreement. However, for the reasons advanced under its discussion of Article XX (g), the Panel did not consider that the treaties were relevant for the interpretation of the text of the General Agreement (see paragraphs 5.19-5.20). The Panel also noted that the statements and drafting changes made during the negotiation of the Havana Charter and the General Agreement did not clearly support any particular contention of the parties with respect to the location of the living thing to be protected under Article XX (b). The Panel did not see the need to settle the issue argued by the parties as to whether the intent of the drafters was to restrict measures justifiable under Article XX to sanitary measures. The Panel therefore found that the policy to protect the life and health of dolphins in the eastern tropical Pacific Ocean, which the United States pursued within its jurisdiction over its nationals and vessels, fell within the range of policies covered by Article XX (b). …

5.34 The Panel then examined the second of the above three questions, namely whether the primary and intermediary nation embargoes imposed by the United States on yellowfin tuna could be considered to be "necessary" for the protection of the living things within the meaning of Article XX (b). The United States argued that its measures met this requirement, since "necessary" in this sense simply meant "needed". The EEC disagreed, stating that the normal meaning of the term "necessary" was "indispensable" or "unavoidable". The EEC further argued that adopted panel reports had stated that a measure otherwise inconsistent with the General Agreement could only be justified as necessary under Article XX (b) if no other consistent measure, or more consistent measure, were reasonably available to fulfil the policy objective.

5.35 The Panel proceeded first to examine the relationship established by Article XX (b) between the trade measure and the policy of protecting living things. It noted that, in the ordinary meaning of the term, "necessary" meant that no alternative existed. A previous panel, in discussing the use of the same term in Article XX (d), stated that

> [a] contracting party cannot justify a measure inconsistent with another GATT provision as "necessary" in terms of Article XX(d) if an alternative measure which it could reasonably be expected to employ and which is not inconsistent with other GATT provisions is available to it. By the same token, in cases where a measure consistent with other GATT provisions is not reasonably available, a contracting party is bound to use, among the measures reasonably available to it, that which entails the least degree of inconsistency with other GATT provisions.

This interpretation had also been accepted by another panel specifically examining Article XX (b). The Panel agreed with the reasoning of these previous panels. The Panel then proceeded to examine whether the trade embargoes imposed by the United States could be considered to be "necessary" in this sense to protect the life or health of dolphins.

5.36 The Panel noted that measures taken under the intermediary nation embargo prohibited imports from a country of any tuna, whether or not the particular tuna was harvested in a manner that harmed or could harm dolphins, and whether or not the country had tuna harvesting practices and policies that harmed or could harm dolphin, as long as it was from a country that imported tuna from countries maintaining tuna harvesting practices and policies not comparable to those of the United States. The Panel observed that the prohibition on imports of tuna into the United States taken under the intermediary nation embargo could not, by itself, further the United States conservation objectives. The intermediary nation embargo would achieve its intended effect only if it were followed by changes in policies or practices, not in the country exporting tuna to the United States, but in third countries from which the exporting country imported tuna.

5.37 The Panel also recalled that measures taken under the primary nation embargo prohibited imports from a country of any tuna, whether or not the particular tuna was harvested in a way that harmed or could harm dolphins, as long as the country's tuna harvesting practices and policies were not comparable to those of the United States. The Panel observed that, as in the case of the intermediary nation embargo, the prohibition on imports of tuna into the United States taken under the primary nation embargo could not possibly, by itself, further the United States objective of protecting the life and health of dolphins. The primary nation embargo could achieve its desired effect only if it were followed by changes in policies and practices in the exporting countries. In view of the foregoing, the Panel observed that both the primary and intermediary nation embargoes on tuna were taken by the United States so as to force other countries to change their policies with respect to persons and things within their own jurisdiction, since the embargoes required such changes in order to have any effect on the protection of the life or health of dolphins.

5.38 The Panel then examined whether, under Article XX (b), measures necessary to protect the life or health of animals could include measures taken so as to force other countries to change their policies within their own jurisdictions, and requiring such changes in order to be effective. The Panel noted that the text of Article XX is not explicit on this question. The Panel then recalled its reasoning under its examination of Article XX (g) that Article XX, as a provision for exceptions, should be interpreted narrowly and in a way that preserves the basic objectives and principles of the General Agreement. If Article XX (b) were interpreted to permit contracting parties to deviate from the basic obligations of the General Agreement by taking trade measures to implement policies within their own jurisdiction, including policies to protect living things, the objectives of the General Agreement would be maintained. If however Article XX (b) were interpreted to permit contracting parties to impose trade embargoes so as to force other countries to change their policies within their jurisdiction, including policies to protect living things, and which required such changes to be effective, the objectives of the General Agreement would be seriously impaired.

5.39 The Panel concluded that measures taken so as to force other countries to change their policies, and that were effective only if such changes occurred, could not be considered "necessary" for the protection of animal life or health in the sense of Article XX (b). Since an essential condition of Article XX (b) had not been met, the Panel did not consider it necessary to examine the further issue of whether the United States measures had also met the other requirements of Article XX. The Panel accordingly found that the import prohibitions on tuna and tuna products maintained by the United States inconsistently with Article XI:1 were not justified by Article XX (b).

4. United States – Import Prohibition of Certain Shrimp and Shrimp Products (Shrimp-Turtle I)

WTO Appellate Body, Oct. 8, 1998, 38 I.L.M. 118 (1999)

[The United States appealed the report of the Panel with regard to certain issues of law. The Panel was constituted at the request of India, Malaysia, Pakistan and Thailand with respect to their complaint against the United States regarding a prohibition imposed by the United States on the importation of certain shrimp and shrimp products by Section 609 of Public Law 101-162 and associated regulations and judicial rulings.]

2. … The United States issued regulations in 1987 pursuant to the Endangered Species Act of 1973 requiring all United States shrimp trawl vessels to use approved Turtle Excluder Devices ("TEDs") or tow-time restrictions in specified areas where there was a significant mortality of sea turtles in shrimp harvesting. These regulations, which became fully effective in 1990, were modified so as to require the use of approved TEDs at all times and in all areas where there is a likelihood that shrimp trawling will interact with sea turtles, with certain limited exceptions.

3. Section 609 was enacted on 21 November 1989. Section 609(a) calls upon the United States Secretary of State, in consultation with the Secretary of Commerce, inter alia, to "initiate negotiations as soon as possible for the development of bilateral or multilateral agreements with other nations for the protection and conservation of sea turtles" and to "initiate negotiations as soon as possible with all foreign governments which are engaged in, or which have persons or companies engaged in, commercial fishing operations which, as determined by the Secretary of Commerce, may affect adversely such species of sea turtles, for the purpose of entering into bilateral and multilateral treaties with such countries to protect such species of sea turtles; … " Section 609(b)(1) imposed, not later than 1 May 1991, an import ban on shrimp harvested with commercial fishing technology which may adversely affect sea turtles. Section 609(b)(2) provides that the import ban on shrimp will not apply to harvesting nations that are certified. Two kinds of annual certifications are required for harvesting nations, details of which were further elaborated in regulatory guidelines in 1991, 1993 and 1996: First, certification shall be granted to countries with a fishing environment which does not pose a threat of the incidental taking of sea turtles in the course of shrimp harvesting. According to the 1996 Guidelines, the Department of State "shall certify any harvesting nation meeting the following criteria without the need for action on the part of the government of the harvesting nation: (a) Any harvesting nation without any of the relevant species of sea turtles occurring in waters subject to its jurisdiction; (b) Any harvesting nation that harvests shrimp exclusively by means that do not pose a threat to sea turtles, e.g., any nation that harvests shrimp exclusively by artisanal means; or (c) Any nation whose commercial shrimp trawling operations take place exclusively in waters subject to its jurisdiction in which sea turtles do not occur." …

4. Second, certification shall be granted to harvesting nations that provide documentary evidence of the adoption of a regulatory program governing the incidental taking of sea turtles in the course of shrimp trawling that is comparable to the United States program and where the average rate of incidental taking of sea turtles by their vessels is comparable to that of United States vessels. According to the 1996 Guidelines, the Department of State assesses the regulatory program of the harvesting nation and certification shall be made if the program includes: (i) the required use of TEDs that are "comparable in effectiveness to those used in the United States. Any exceptions to this requirement must be comparable to those of the United States program …"; and (ii) "a credible enforcement effort that includes monitoring for compliance and appropriate sanctions." The regulatory program may be in the form of regulations, or may, in certain circumstances, take the form of a voluntary arrangement between industry and government. Other measures that the harvesting nation undertakes for the protection of sea turtles will also be taken into account in making the comparability determination. The average incidental take rate "will be deemed comparable if the harvesting nation requires the use of TEDs in a manner comparable to that of the U.S. program ...".

5. The 1996 Guidelines provide that all shrimp imported into the United States must be accompanied by a Shrimp Exporter's Declaration form attesting that the shrimp was harvested either in the waters of a nation currently certified under Section 609 or "under conditions that do not adversely affect sea turtles", that is: (a) "Shrimp harvested in an aquaculture facility in which the shrimp spend at least 30 days in ponds prior to being harvested"; (b) "Shrimp harvested by commercial shrimp trawl vessels using TEDs comparable in effectiveness to those required in the United States"; (c) "Shrimp harvested exclusively by means that do not involve the retrieval of fishing nets by mechanical devices or by vessels using gear that, in accordance with the U.S. program … , would not require TEDs"; and (d) "Species of shrimp, such as the pandalid species, harvested in areas where sea turtles do not occur." On 8 October 1996, the United States Court of International Trade ruled that the 1996 Guidelines were in violation of Section 609 in allowing the import of shrimp from non-certified countries if accompanied by a Shrimp Exporter's Declaration form attesting that they were caught with commercial fishing technology that did not adversely affect sea turtles. A 25 November 1996 ruling of the United States Court of International Trade clarified that shrimp harvested by manual methods which did not harm sea turtles could still be imported from non-certified countries. On 4 June 1998, the United States Court of Appeals for the Federal Circuit vacated the decisions of the United States Court of International Trade of 8 October and 25 November 1996. In practice, however, exemption from the import ban for TED-caught shrimp from non-certified countries remained unavailable while this dispute was before the Panel and before us.

6. The 1991 Guidelines limited the geographical scope of the import ban imposed by Section 609 to countries in the wider Caribbean/western Atlantic

region, and granted these countries a three-year phase-in period. The 1993 Guidelines maintained this geographical limitation. On 29 December 1995, the United States Court of International Trade held that the 1991 and 1993 Guidelines violated Section 609 by limiting its geographical scope to shrimp harvested in the wider Caribbean/western Atlantic region, and directed the Department of State to extend the ban worldwide not later than 1 May 1996. On 10 April 1996, the United States Court of International Trade refused a subsequent request by the Department of State to postpone the 1 May 1996 deadline. On 19 April 1996, the United States issued the 1996 Guidelines, extending Section 609 to shrimp harvested in all foreign countries effective 1 May 1996.

7. In the Panel Report, the Panel reached the following conclusions:

In the light of the findings above, we conclude that the import ban on shrimp and shrimp products as applied by the United States on the basis of Section 609 of Public Law 101-162 is not consistent with Article XI:1 of GATT 1994, and cannot be justified under Article XX of GATT 1994.and made this recommendation:

> The Panel recommends that the Dispute Settlement Body request the United States to bring this measure into conformity with its obligations under the WTO Agreement.

8. On 13 July 1998, the United States notified the DSB of its decision to appeal certain issues of law covered in the Panel Report and certain legal interpretations developed by the Panel, pursuant to paragraph 4 of Article 16 of the DSU, and filed a notice of appeal 29 with the Appellate Body pursuant to Rule 20 of the Working Procedures for Appellate Review. ...

113. Article XX of the GATT 1994 reads, in its relevant parts:

> Article XX: *General Exceptions*
>
> Subject to the requirement that such measures are not applied in a manner which would constitute a means of arbitrary or unjustifiable discrimination between countries where the same conditions prevail, or a disguised restriction on international trade, nothing in this Agreement shall be construed to prevent the adoption or enforcement by any Member of measures: ...
>
> (b) necessary to protect human, animal or plant life or health; ...
>
> (g) relating to the conservation of exhaustible natural resources if such measures are made effective in conjunction with restrictions on domestic production or consumption;...

114. The Panel did not follow all of the steps of applying the "customary rules of interpretation of public international law" as required by Article 3.2 of the DSU. As we have emphasized numerous times, these rules call for an examination of the ordinary meaning of the words of a treaty, read in their context, and in the light of the object and purpose of the treaty involved. A treaty interpreter must begin with, and focus upon, the text of the particular provision to be interpreted. It

is in the words constituting that provision, read in their context, that the object and purpose of the states parties to the treaty must first be sought. Where the meaning imparted by the text itself is equivocal or inconclusive, or where confirmation of the correctness of the reading of the text itself is desired, light from the object and purpose of the treaty as a whole may usefully be sought.

115. In the present case, the Panel did not expressly examine the ordinary meaning of the words of Article XX. The Panel disregarded the fact that the introductory clauses of Article XX speak of the "manner" in which measures sought to be justified are "applied". In United States - Gasoline, we pointed out that the chapeau of Article XX "by its express terms addresses, not so much the questioned measure or its specific contents as such, but rather the manner in which that measure is applied." The Panel did not inquire specifically into how the application of Section 609 constitutes "a means of arbitrary or unjustifiable discrimination between countries where the same conditions prevail, or a disguised restriction on international trade." What the Panel did, in purporting to examine the consistency of the measure with the chapeau of Article XX, was to focus repeatedly on the design of the measure itself. For instance, the Panel stressed that it was addressing "a particular situation where a Member has taken unilateral measures which, by their nature, could put the multilateral trading system at risk."

116. ... Moreover, the Panel did not look into the object and purpose of the chapeau of Article XX. Rather, the Panel looked into the object and purpose of the whole of the GATT 1994 and the WTO Agreement, which object and purpose it described in an overly broad manner. Thus, the Panel arrived at the very broad formulation that measures which "undermine the WTO multilateral trading system" must be regarded as "not within the scope of measures permitted under the chapeau of Article XX." Maintaining, rather than undermining, the multilateral trading system is necessarily a fundamental and pervasive premise underlying the WTO Agreement; but it is not a right or an obligation, nor is it an interpretative rule which can be employed in the appraisal of a given measure under the chapeau of Article XX. In United States - Gasoline, we stated that it is "important to underscore that the purpose and object of the introductory clauses of Article XX is generally the prevention of 'abuse of the exceptions of [Article XX]'." The Panel did not attempt to inquire into how the measure at stake was being applied in such a manner as to constitute abuse or misuse of a given kind of exception. ...

1. "Exhaustible Natural Resources"

127. We begin with the threshold question of whether Section 609 is a measure concerned with the conservation of "exhaustible natural resources" within the meaning of Article XX(g). The Panel, of course, with its "chapeau-down" approach, did not make a finding on whether the sea turtles that Section 609 is designed to conserve constitute "exhaustible natural resources" for purposes of Article XX(g). In the proceedings before the Panel, however, the parties to the dispute argued this issue vigorously and extensively. India, Pakistan and Thailand

contended that a "reasonable interpretation" of the term "exhaustible" is that the term refers to "finite resources such as minerals, rather than biological or renewable resources." ... Moreover, they argued, if "all" natural resources were considered to be exhaustible, the term "exhaustible" would become superfluous. They also referred to the drafting history of Article XX(g), and, in particular, to the mention of minerals, such as manganese, in the context of arguments made by some delegations that "export restrictions" should be permitted for the preservation of scarce natural resources. For its part, Malaysia added that sea turtles, being living creatures, could only be considered under Article XX(b), since Article XX(g) was meant for "nonliving exhaustible natural resources". It followed, according to Malaysia, that the United States cannot invoke both the Article XX(b) and the Article XX(g) exceptions simultaneously.

128. We are not convinced by these arguments. Textually, Article XX(g) is not limited to the conservation of "mineral" or "non-living" natural resources. The complainants' principal argument is rooted in the notion that "living" natural resources are "renewable" and therefore cannot be "exhaustible" natural resources. We do not believe that "exhaustible" natural resources and "renewable" natural resources are mutually exclusive. One lesson that modern biological sciences teach us is that living species, though in principle, capable of reproduction and, in that sense, "renewable", are in certain circumstances indeed susceptible of depletion, exhaustion and extinction, frequently because of human activities. Living resources are just as "finite" as petroleum, iron ore and other non-living resources.

129. The words of Article XX(g), "exhaustible natural resources", were actually crafted more than 50 years ago. They must be read by a treaty interpreter in the light of contemporary concerns of the community of nations about the protection and conservation of the environment. While Article XX was not modified in the Uruguay Round, the preamble attached to the WTO Agreement shows that the signatories to that Agreement were, in 1994, fully aware of the importance and legitimacy of environmental protection as a goal of national and international policy. The preamble of the WTO Agreement — which informs not only the GATT 1994, but also the other covered agreements — explicitly acknowledges "the objective of sustainable development":

> The Parties to this Agreement,
>
> Recognizing that their relations in the field of trade and economic endeavour should be conducted with a view to raising standards of living, ensuring full employment and a large and steadily growing volume of real income and effective demand, and expanding the production of and trade in goods and services, while allowing for the optimal use of the world's resources in accordance with the objective of sustainable development, seeking both to protect and preserve the environment and to enhance the means for doing so in a manner consistent with their respective needs and concerns at different levels of economic development...

130. From the perspective embodied in the preamble of the WTO Agreement, we note that the generic term "natural resources" in Article XX(g) is not "static" in its content or reference but is rather "by definition, evolutionary". It is, therefore, pertinent to note that modern international conventions and declarations make frequent references to natural resources as embracing both living and non-living resources. For instance, the 1982 United Nations Convention on the Law of the Sea ("UNCLOS"), [articles 56, 61 and 62]... The Convention on Biological Diversity uses the concept of "biological resources". Agenda 21 speaks most broadly of "natural resources" and goes into detailed statements about "marine living resources". In addition, the Resolution on Assistance to Developing Countries, adopted in conjunction with the Convention on the Conservation of Migratory Species of Wild Animals, recites:

> Conscious that an important element of development lies in the conservation and management of living natural resources and that migratory species constitute a significant part of these resources; ....

131. Given the recent acknowledgement by the international community of the importance of concerted bilateral or multilateral action to protect living natural resources, and recalling the explicit recognition by WTO Members of the objective of sustainable development in the preamble of the WTO Agreement, we believe it is too late in the day to suppose that Article XX(g) of the GATT 1994 may be read as referring only to the conservation of exhaustible mineral or other non-living natural resources. Moreover, two adopted GATT 1947 panel reports previously found fish to be an "exhaustible natural resource" within the meaning of Article XX(g). We hold that, in line with the principle of effectiveness in treaty interpretation, measures to conserve exhaustible natural resources, whether living or non-living, may fall within Article XX(g). ...

132. We turn next to the issue of whether the living natural resources sought to be conserved by the measure are "exhaustible" under Article XX(g). That this element is present in respect of the five species of sea turtles here involved appears to be conceded by all the participants and third participants in this case. The exhaustibility of sea turtles would in fact have been very difficult to controvert since all of the seven recognized species of sea turtles are today listed in Appendix 1 of the Convention on International Trade in Endangered Species of Wild Fauna and Flora ("CITES"). The list in Appendix 1 includes "all species threatened with extinction which are or may be affected by trade." ...

134. For all the foregoing reasons, we find that the sea turtles here involved constitute "exhaustible natural resources" for purposes of Article XX(g) of the GATT 1994.

2. "Relating to the Conservation of [Exhaustible Natural Resources]" ...

142. In our view, therefore, Section 609 is a measure "relating to" the conservation of an exhaustible natural resource within the meaning of Article XX(g) of the GATT 1994. ...

166. Another aspect of the application of Section 609 that bears heavily in any appraisal of justifiable or unjustifiable discrimination is the failure of the United States to engage the appellees, as well as other Members exporting shrimp to the United States, in serious, across-the-board negotiations with the objective of concluding bilateral or multilateral agreements for the protection and conservation of sea turtles, before enforcing the import prohibition against the shrimp exports of those other Members. ….

168. …, the protection and conservation of highly migratory species of sea turtles, that is, the very policy objective of the measure, demands concerted and cooperative efforts on the part of the many countries whose waters are traversed in the course of recurrent sea turtle migrations. …

172. Clearly, the United States negotiated seriously with some, but not with other Members (including the appellees), that export shrimp to the United States. The effect is plainly discriminatory and, in our view, unjustifiable. …

176. When the foregoing differences in the means of application of Section 609 to various shrimp exporting countries are considered in their cumulative effect, we find, and so hold, that those differences in treatment constitute "unjustifiable discrimination" between exporting countries desiring certification in order to gain access to the United States shrimp market within the meaning of the chapeau of Article XX. …

185. In reaching these conclusions, we wish to underscore what we have not decided in this appeal. We have not decided that the protection and preservation of the environment is of no significance to the Members of the WTO. Clearly, it is. We have not decided that the sovereign nations that are Members of the WTO cannot adopt effective measures to protect endangered species, such as sea turtles. Clearly, they can and should. And we have not decided that sovereign states should not act together bilaterally, plurilaterally or multilaterally, either within the WTO or in other international fora, to protect endangered species or to otherwise protect the environment. Clearly, they should and do.

186. What we have decided in this appeal is simply this: although the measure of the United States in dispute in this appeal serves an environmental objective that is recognized as legitimate under paragraph (g) of Article XX of the GATT 1994, this measure has been applied by the United States in a manner which constitutes arbitrary and unjustifiable discrimination between Members of the WTO, contrary to the requirements of the chapeau of Article XX. For all of the specific reasons outlined in this Report, this measure does not qualify for the exemption that Article XX of the GATT 1994 affords to measures which serve certain recognized, legitimate environmental purposes but which, at the same time, are not applied in a manner that constitutes a means of arbitrary or unjustifiable discrimination between countries where the same conditions prevail or a disguised restriction on international trade. As we emphasized in United States - Gasoline, WTO Members are free to adopt their own policies aimed at protecting

the environment as long as, in so doing, they fulfill their obligations and respect the rights of other Members under the WTO Agreement. …

188. The Appellate Body recommends that the DSB request the United States to bring its measure found in the Panel Report to be inconsistent with Article XI of the GATT 1994, and found in this Report to be not justified under Article XX of the GATT 1994, into conformity with the obligations of the United States under that Agreement.

5. United States – Import Prohibition of Certain Shrimp and Shrimp Products (Shrimp-Turtle II)

WTO Appellate Body, Oct. 22, 2001, 41 I.L.M. 149 (2002)

[Malaysia appealed to the Appellate Body for a ruling that the United States had not complied with the recommendations and rulings of the DSB in Shrimp-Turtle I.]

3. Malaysia's complaint relates to a measure taken by the United States in the form of an import prohibition to protect and conserve certain species of sea turtles, considered to be an endangered species. …

4. Section 609, the Revised Guidelines, and their application, are described in the Panel Report. In the following paragraphs, we set out those aspects of the Revised Guidelines that are pertinent to the consideration of the issues raised in this appeal.

5. Section 609(b)(2) provides that the import prohibition on shrimp does not apply to harvesting nations that are "certified" according to criteria set by the United States. The Revised Guidelines set forth the criteria for certification. The stated goal of the programme set out in the Revised Guidelines is the same as that set out in the programme of the original guidelines, namely, to protect endangered sea turtle populations from further decline by reducing their incidental mortality in commercial shrimp trawling. A central element of the United States programme is that commercial shrimp trawlers are required to use Turtle Excluder Devices ("TEDs") approved in accordance with standards established by the United States National Marine Fisheries Service. Where the government of a harvesting country seeks certification on the basis of having adopted a programme that is based on TEDs, certification will be granted if this government's programme includes a requirement that commercial shrimp trawlers use TEDs that are "comparable in effectiveness" to those used in the United States, and a credible enforcement effort that includes monitoring for compliance.

6. Under the original guidelines, the practice of the Department of State was to certify countries only after they had shown that they required the use of TEDs. Under the Revised Guidelines, countries may apply for certification even if they do not require the use of TEDs. In such cases, a harvesting country has to demonstrate that it has implemented, and is enforcing, a "comparably effective" regulatory programme to protect sea turtles without the use of TEDs. The Department of State is required "to take fully into account any demonstrated differences

between the shrimp fishing conditions in the United States and those in other nations, as well as information available from other sources."

7. An exporting country may also be certified if its shrimp fishing environment does not pose a threat of incidental capture of sea turtles. The Revised Guidelines provide that the Department of State shall certify a harvesting country pursuant to Section 609 if it meets any of the following criteria: the relevant species of sea turtles do not occur in waters subject to that country's jurisdiction; in that country's waters, shrimp is harvested exclusively by means that do not pose a threat to sea turtles, for example, any country that harvests shrimp exclusively by artisanal means; or, commercial shrimp trawling operations take place exclusively in waters in which sea turtles do not occur.

8. Before the Panel, Malaysia argued that the United States had failed to comply with the recommendations and rulings of the DSB, and ... the Panel found as follows:

(a) [T]he measure adopted by the United States in order to comply with the recommendations and rulings of the DSB violates Article XI.1 of the GATT 1994;

(b) in light of the recommendations and rulings of the DSB, Section 609 of Public Law 101-162, as implemented by the Revised Guidelines of 8 July 1999 and as applied so far by the [United States] authorities, is justified under Article XX of the GATT 1994 as long as the conditions stated in the findings of this Report, in particular the ongoing serious good faith efforts to reach a multilateral agreement, remain satisfied.

9. The Panel urged "Malaysia and the United States to cooperate fully in order to conclude as soon as possible an agreement which will permit the protection and conservation of sea turtles to the satisfaction of all interests involved and taking into account the principle that States have common but differentiated responsibilities to conserve and protect the environment."

10. On 23 July 2001, Malaysia notified the DSB of its intention to appeal certain issues of law covered in the Panel Report and certain legal interpretations developed by the Panel....

137. We recall that, in United States - Shrimp, we stated:

> It appears to us that conditioning access to a Member's domestic market on whether exporting Members comply with, or adopt, a policy or policies unilaterally prescribed by the importing Member may, to some degree, be a common aspect of measures falling within the scope of one or another of the exceptions (a) to (j) of Article XX. Paragraphs (a) to (j) comprise measures that are recognized as exceptions to substantive obligations established in the GATT 1994, because the domestic policies embodied in such measures have been recognized as important and legitimate in character. It is not necessary to assume that requiring from

> exporting countries compliance with, or adoption of, certain policies (although covered in principle by one or another of the exceptions) prescribed by the importing country, renders a measure a priori incapable of justification under Article XX. Such an interpretation renders most, if not all, of the specific exceptions of Article XX inutile, a result abhorrent to the principles of interpretation we are bound to apply.

138. In our view, Malaysia overlooks the significance of this statement. Contrary to what Malaysia suggests, this statement is not "dicta". As we said before, it appears to us "that conditioning access to a Member's domestic market on whether exporting Members comply with, or adopt, a policy or policies unilaterally prescribed by the importing Member may, to some degree, be a common aspect of measures falling within the scope of one or another of the exceptions (a) to (j) of Article XX." This statement expresses a principle that was central to our ruling in United States - Shrimp. ...

144. In our view, there is an important difference between conditioning market access on the adoption of essentially the same programme, and conditioning market access on the adoption of a programme comparable in effectiveness. Authorizing an importing Member to condition market access on exporting Members putting in place regulatory programmes comparable in effectiveness to that of the importing Member gives sufficient latitude to the exporting Member with respect to the programme it may adopt to achieve the level of effectiveness required. It allows the exporting Member to adopt a regulatory programme that is suitable to the specific conditions prevailing in its territory. As we see it, the Panel correctly reasoned and concluded that conditioning market access on the adoption of a programme comparable in effectiveness, allows for sufficient flexibility in the application of the measure so as to avoid "arbitrary or unjustifiable discrimination". We, therefore, agree with the conclusion of the Panel on "comparable effectiveness".

145. Malaysia also argues that the measure at issue is not flexible enough to meet the requirement of the chapeau of Article XX relating to "unjustifiable or arbitrary discrimination" because the Revised Guidelines do not provide explicitly for the specific conditions prevailing in Malaysia.

146. We note that the Revised Guidelines contain provisions that permit the United States authorities to take into account the specific conditions of Malaysian shrimp production, and of the Malaysian sea turtle conservation programme, should Malaysia decide to apply for certification. The Revised Guidelines explicitly state that "[if] the government of a harvesting nation demonstrates that it has implemented and is enforcing a comparably effective regulatory program to protect sea turtles in the course of shrimp trawl fishing without the use of TEDs, that nation will also be eligible for certification." Likewise, the Revised Guidelines provide that the "Department of State will take fully into account any demonstrated differences between the shrimp fishing conditions in the United States and those in other nations as well as information available from other sources."

147. Further, the Revised Guidelines provide that the import prohibitions that can be imposed under Section 609 do not apply to shrimp or products of shrimp "harvested in any other manner or under any other circumstances that the Department of State may determine, following consultations with the [United States National Marine Fisheries Services], does not pose a threat of the incidental taking of sea turtles." Under Section II.B(c)(iii) of the Revised Guidelines (Additional Sea Turtle Protection Measures), the "Department of State recognizes that sea turtles require protection throughout their life-cycle, not only when they are threatened during the course of commercial shrimp trawl harvesting." Additionally, Section II.B(c)(iii) states that "[i]n making certification determinations, the Department shall also take fully into account other measures the harvesting nation undertakes to protect sea turtles, including national programmes to protect nesting beaches and other habitat, prohibitions on the direct take of sea turtles, national enforcement and compliance programmes, and participation in any international agreement for the protection and conservation of sea turtles." With respect to the certification process, the Revised Guidelines specify that a country that does not appear to qualify for certification will receive a notification that "will explain the reasons for this preliminary assessment, suggest steps that the government of the harvesting nation can take in order to receive a certification, and invite the government of the harvesting nation to provide any further information." Moreover, the Department of State commits itself to "actively consider any additional information that the government of the harvesting nation believes should be considered by the Department in making its determination concerning certification."

148. These provisions of the Revised Guidelines, on their face, permit a degree of flexibility that, in our view, will enable the United States to consider the particular conditions prevailing in Malaysia if, and when, Malaysia applies for certification. As Malaysia has not applied for certification, any consideration of whether Malaysia would be certified would be speculation.

149. We need only say here that, in our view, a measure should be designed in such a manner that there is sufficient flexibility to take into account the specific conditions prevailing in any exporting Member, including, of course, Malaysia. Yet this is not the same as saying that there must be specific provisions in the measure aimed at addressing specifically the particular conditions prevailing in every individual exporting Member. Article XX of the GATT 1994 does not require a Member to anticipate and provide explicitly for the specific conditions prevailing and evolving in every individual Member.

150. We are, therefore, not persuaded by Malaysia's argument that the measure at issue is not flexible enough because the Revised Guidelines do not explicitly address the specific conditions prevailing in Malaysia.

151. Malaysia argues, finally, that the Panel should have scrutinized the decision of the CIT [U.S. Court of International Trade] in the Turtle Island case and assessed, in the light of that decision, the likelihood and consequences of the

Revised Guidelines being modified in the future. According to Malaysia, the Panel should have come to the conclusion that the Revised Guidelines are not flexible enough because the CIT ruled that the part of the Revised Guidelines allowing TED-caught shrimp from non-certified harvesting countries to be imported into the United States is contrary to Section 609. As we have already ruled, we are of the view that, when examining the United States measures, the Panel took into account the status of municipal law at the time, and reached the correct conclusion. The CIT decision in the Turtle Island case has not modified the legal effect or the application of the Revised Guidelines; hence, we are not persuaded by this argument of Malaysia.

152. For all these reasons, we uphold the finding of the Panel, in paragraph 6.1 of the Panel Report, that "Section 609 of Public Law 101-162, as implemented by the Revised Guidelines of 8 July 1999 and as applied so far by the [United States] authorities, is justified under Article XX of the GATT 1994 as long as the conditions stated in the findings of this Report, in particular the ongoing serious, good faith efforts to reach a multilateral agreement, remain satisfied".

Notes and Questions

1. Do you agree with the Panel's interpretation of the Chapeau of Article XX?

2. Compare the Report of the Panel in *Tuna-Dolphin I* and *II* with *Shrimp-Turtle I* and *II*.

3. In what way could international environmental law be used to interpret Article XX (b) and (g) of GATT?

4. What is the view of the Appellate Body in the two Shrimp-Turtle opinions with regard to unilateral actions by WTO members to protect the environment?

5. Why did the United States lose in *Shrimp-Turtle I*?

6. In both Shrimp-Turtle opinions the Appellate Body went further than in its first case, World Trade Organization Report of the Appellate Body, *United States Standards for Reformulated and Conventional Gasoline(U.S. v. Brazil)*, WT/DS2/AB/R (April 29, 1996), where it held in 1996 that:

> The "general rule of interpretation" set out ... [in Article III] has been relied upon by all of the participants ...[t]hat general rule of interpretation has attained the status of a rule of customary or general international law. As such, it forms part of the "customary rules of interpretation of public international law" which the Appellate Body has been directed, by Article 3(2) of the *DSU*, to apply in seeking to clarify the provisions of the *General Agreement* and the other "covered agreements" of the *Marrakesh Agreement Establishing the World Trade Organization* (the "*WTO Agreement*"). That direction reflects a measure of recognition that the *General Agreement* is not to be read in *clinical isolation* from public international law."(Emphasis added)

7. In the Shrimp-Turtle opinions, the Appellate Body stated that Article XX of GATT must be interpreted in accordance with the Vienna Convention on the Law of Treaties and international law including other relevant multilateral and bilateral agreements. The opinions further emphasized the importance of agreements on the protection of the environment. It has been suggested that uncertainty about the implication of these two opinions was the reason for a ministerial declaration which was adopted two weeks after the decision in *Shrimp-Turtle II* in Doha:

WTO Ministerial Conference, Fourth Session, Doha 9-14 November 2001
Ministerial Declaration

WT/MIN (01)/DEC/W/1 (Nov. 14, 2001).

31. With a view to enhancing the mutual supportiveness of trade and environment, we agree to negotiations, without prejudging their outcome, on:

(i) the relationship between existing WTO rules and specific trade obligations set out in multilateral environmental agreements (MEAs). The negotiations shall be limited in scope to the applicability of such existing WTO rules as among parties to the MEA in question. The negotiations shall not prejudice the WTO rights of any Member that is not a party to the MEA in question;

(ii) procedures for regular information exchange between MEA Secretariats and the relevant WTO committees, and the criteria for the granting of observer status;

(iii) the reduction or, as appropriate, elimination of tariff and non-tariff barriers to environmental goods and services.

We note that fisheries subsidies form part of the negotiations provided for in paragraph 28.

32. We instruct the Committee on Trade and Environment, in pursuing work on all items on its agenda within its current terms of reference, to give particular attention to:

(i) the effect of environmental measures on market access, especially in relation to developing countries, in particular the least-developed among them, and those situations in which the elimination or reduction of trade restrictions and distortions would benefit trade, the environment and development;

(ii) the relevant provisions of the Agreement on Trade-Related Aspects of Intellectual Property Rights; and

(iii) labelling requirements for environmental purposes.

Work on these issues should include the identification of any need to clarify relevant WTO rules. The Committee shall report to the Fifth Session of the Ministerial Conference, and make recommendations, where appropriate, with respect to future action, including the desirability of negotiations. The outcome of this work as well as the negotiations carried out under paragraph 31(i) and (ii) shall be compatible with the open and non-discriminatory nature of the multilateral trading system, shall not add to or diminish the rights and obligations of members under existing WTO agreements, in particular the Agreement on the Application of Sanitary and Phytosanitary Measures, nor alter the balance of these rights and obligations, and will take into account the needs of developing and least-developed countries.

33. We recognize the importance of technical assistance and capacity building in the field of trade and environment to developing countries, in particular the least-developed among them. We also encourage that expertise and experience be shared with members wishing to perform environmental reviews at the national level. A report shall be prepared on these activities for the Fifth Session.

8. For further discussion of trade/environment conflicts, *see* M. J. TREBILCOCK AND R. HOWSE, THE REGULATION OF INTERNATIONAL TRADE (Routledge 1999) at 406-420; PATRICIA W. BIRNIE AND ALAN E. BOYLE *supra* at 709-714; N.A. Robinson, *Trade and Environment Disputes: Mediating Common But Differentiated Responsibilities*, 1999 THE COURT JOURNAL 320 (Supreme Court of the Philippines); L. de La Fayette, *United States-Import Prohibition of Certain Shrimp and Shrimp Products-Recourse to Article 21.5 of the DSU by Malaysia,* 96 AM. J. INT'L L. 685, 685-693 (2002);

James Salzman, Note: *Executive Order 13,141 and the Environmental Review of Trade Agreements*, 95 AM. J. INT'L L. 366 (2001); Donald O. Mayer, *Corporate Governance in the Cause of Peace: An Environmental Perspective*, 35 VAND. J. TRANSNAT'L L. 585 (2002); Steve Charnovitz, *Law of Environmental "PPMs" in the WTO: Debunking the Myth of Illegality*, 27 YALE J. INT'L L. 59 (2002).

E. THE NEED FOR AN EFFECTIVE LIABILITY REGIME

1. Mahnoush H. Arsanjani & W. Michael Reisman *The Quest for an International Liability Regime for the Protection of the Global Commons* *in* INTERNATIONAL LAW: THEORY AND PRACTICE 469-73 (Karel Wellens ed., Martinus Nijhoff 1998)

[As we have seen above,] [e]fforts to establish a regime for the protection of the environment and the global commons have gone through a number of stages. Early conventions focused primarily on the preservation and exploitation of certain natural resources. ... The method was regulation of the use of resources in order to preserve their quantity or quality. The targets were patterns of exploitation that threatened the resources. The vehicles of regulation were agreements, e.g., fisheries agreements and those dealing with whaling.

With the increasingly intensive use of the oceans and the availability of more scientific data about the short-term and long-term effects of pollution of the marine environment, the method for protection of the global commons evolved from limiting exploitation of resources to the prevention and regulation of pollution of the oceans themselves. Part of this change of focus is attributable to new information about ecological changes. Transportation of goods and services across the globe, an essential strut in the international trade infrastructure, was incontrovertibly polluting the marine environment. Regulatory action to reduce pollution was perceived as necessary. ...

A third stage in the development of the law relating to the protection of the global commons is distinctive in its concern for the injurious impacts of certain types of marine pollution on individuals rather than on the commons itself. The approach in the second stage was exemplified by the civil liability conventions. These instruments aimed at providing remedies for injuries to private and judicial persons, caused as the result of certain types of physical use of the environment. Although these conventions address the liability of the operator or the state for harm caused by certain types of activities in the global commons, the focus of the conventions is not on harm to the commons as such, but rather on injury to states, their citizens or entities and their property. ...

State practice with respect to claims for compensation for activities affecting the global commons reflects this third stage.... In *Nuclear Tests*, the claims of both Australia and New Zealand against French atmospheric nuclear tests were based on the alleged impacts of such tests on their territories and peoples. Earlier, when the United States announced that it would conduct a series of tests in the Pacific, the Japanese Ambassador to the United States requested assurances from the United States that compensation would be forthcoming in the event of damage or economic loss to Japanese fishermen as a result of the tests. The Japanese claims for suspension of the tests and a contingent assurance of compensation were based on the possible harmful impacts that such tests might have on Japan and its fishermen. The Ambassador referred to the "Japanese diet" which relied on the fish in that area, but not to the area itself.

The Japanese protest was symptomatic of the general flow of practice with respect to harm to the commons. Harmful consequences of lawful activities... were examined primarily in relation to the legally recognised and protected rights of other states that were being exercised in the global commons. The point was made dramatically in a remarkable historic debate in the United States about the lawfulness of nuclear testing in oceans areas. Most of the theories of the illegality of such tests were based on their interference with the rights of other states with respect to free navigation, exploitation of fishing resources of the ocean, etc. A legal doctrine prohibiting an activity or imposing liability for harm to the global commons *per se* was not developed.

There were some exceptions. In an article in the Yale Law Journal in 1955, Dr. Emanuel Margolis argued the unlawfulness of the American hydrogen bomb tests in the Pacific on the basis of pollution *per se:* "[t]he injurious effects of the thermo-nuclear explosions may be viewed also within the juridical context of the responsibility of states to prevent pollution of international waters and air space." [Emanuel Margolis, *The Hydrogen Bomb Experiments and International Law*, 64 YALE L. J. 629, 641 (1955).] Margolis admitted that, up to that time, concern over the problem of pollution of international waters had been restricted almost exclusively to pollution from the discharge of oil by ships. He felt, however, that general principles of law and equity could be used in resolving disputes concerning pollution and thus imposing responsibility on States for causing pollution. Margolis also invoked the criterion of "serious consequence" of injury that had earlier been established by *Trail Smelter*; he felt it could be applied to serious injuries to persons and property on the high seas. He also invoked a dictum of the S.S. "*Lotus*": "a ship on the high seas in assimilated to the territory of the State, the flag of which it flies."[*Id.* at 642, (quoting 1 OPPENHEIM INTERNATIONAL LAW, 215 (Lauterpacht 1952))].

But Margolis admitted that it was less than clear as to whether "the Trail Smelter rule may be carried beyond injury to foreign nationals and foreign territory and applied to the contamination of high seas fisheries, except perhaps by invoking a *res communis* theory with respect to the natural resources of the seas." [*Id.*] He also admitted that without specific treaty arrangements, and in the absence of international decisions "squarely in point, the duty of states under international law to prevent pollution of international waters is as yet an inchoate one". [*Id.* at 643.]

In the same issue of the Yale Law Journal, Professor Myres McDougal and his student Norbert Schlei [Myres S. McDougal & Norbert Schlei, *The Hydrogen Bomb Test in Perspective: Lawful Measures for Security*, 64 YALE L. J. 648 (1955), *supra* Part One] challenged Margolis' legal assumptions: "no international tribunal has ever held a nation-state liable in damages for pollution of the sea or declared the existence of a duty to desist". McDougal and Schlei felt that an argument against the tests based on "pollution" merely focused attention on one modality of possible interference with the competing lawful uses of navigation and fishing. For them, the criterion of pollution had to be tested against its impact upon other key lawful uses, namely navigation and fishing of the high seas. Accordingly, they felt that the criterion of "serious magnitude" of damage cannot be a sole legal test, as Margolis had proposed.

McDougal and Schlei neatly expressed the view that then prevailed. The international regulation of pollution is at its merest inception, with prescriptions yet to be formulated. In this state of affairs, a decision-maker confronted with competing claims with respect to pollution and freedom of navigation and fishing can only resort to such sources as general principles of law recognized by civilised nations, and considerations *ex aequo et bono*.

The decision-maker thus resorting to national prescriptions with respect to "nuisance" generally, and the pollution of waters in particular, finds himself despite an elaborate facade of technical terms, instructed only to apply the familiar and indispensable test of reasonableness. The innumerable forms which such controversies may indeed take make it impracticable to adopt any standard more explicit than that of reasonableness, determined by the familiar process of balancing of "utility of the conduct" causing damage, and the "gravity of the harm" to the injured party.

McDougal and Schlei concluded that, by analogy from municipal law, even under the criteria of reasonableness for performing an act with injurious consequences, a State which is conducting such activities is only responsible in damages for inevitable injuries to innocent parties.

The Stockholm Declaration on the Human Environment and later the Rio Declaration on Environment and Development attempted to introduce a different legal perspective about harm to the global commons. Principle 21 of the Stockholm Declaration and Principle 2 of the Rio Declaration, after reaffirming the right of States to exploit their own natural resources pursuant to their own environmental and developmental policy, proclaimed that States have the responsibility "to ensure that activities within their jurisdiction or control do not cause damage to the environment of other Sates or of areas beyond the limits of national jurisdiction." This was one of the first authoritative attempts to make pollution or harm to the global commons unlawful *per se*.

But the Stockholm initiative was tentative and uncertain. The correlative Principle 22, dealing with the concepts of liability and compensation, regressed to the focus on victims of pollution. The same approach was adopted in 1992, in Principle 13 of the Rio Declaration....

The cooperation of states was to be limited to the development of international law regarding liability and compensation for the victims of pollution and the victims of other environmental damage caused by the activities. Now victims are, in juridical parlance, juridical or natural persons. An activity causing environmental damage to areas beyond national jurisdiction would come within the scope of Principle 22, only if it caused harm to a juridical or a natural person. Hence, the impact of the environmental harm is assessed in terms of the injury to a juridical or a natural person and not the global environment itself. Thus, the Stockholm Declaration, in its Principle 21, while stipulating generally that states should not cause damage to the environment beyond the limits of national jurisdiction, confined liability and compensation for such harm to the victims of pollution.

The 1982 United Nations Convention on the Law of Sea seems to move beyond Stockholm with respect to the protection of the marine environment. Article 235, entitled "Responsibility and Liability", holds states responsible for non-compliance with their international obligations for the protection of the marine environment. It provides, in terms, that states shall ensure that "recourse is available in accordance with their legal systems for prompt and adequate compensation or other relief in respect of damage caused by pollution of the marine environment to natural or juridical persons under their jurisdiction". Unlike Stockholm, ... neither paragraph 2 nor 3 of [A]rticle 235 limits prompt and adequate compensation to juridical or natural persons. Yet it does not indicate who is to be compensated.

The most explicit international agreement on liability for injury to the global commons *per se* is to be found in the 1988 Convention on the Regulation of Antarctic Mineral Resources Activities [*see supra* at ____]. [The Preamble of the Convention] recognizes "the unique ecological, scientific and wilderness value of Antarctica and the importance of Antarctica to the global environment" and provides liability for "damage to the Antarctic environment or dependent or associated ecosystem" arising from Antarctic mineral resources activities. Article 1 (15) defines "damage to the Antarctic environment or dependent or associated ecosystem" as "any impact on the living or non-living components of that environment or other systems, including harm to atmospheric, marine or terrestrial life, beyond that which is negligible or which has been assessed and judged to be acceptable pursuant to this Convention". Under Article 8 (3), if the operator of the activity which caused damage to the environment fails to fulfil its obligation under the Convention, the sponsoring state becomes liable for that portion of liability not satisfied by the operator.

This is the first time that an international convention explicitly holds an operator or a state liable for harm to the environment, independent of its consequences for juridical or natural persons. The liability of the sponsoring state is not strict, but is limited in a number of ways. It is limited only to damage caused due to its violation of the Convention, which may not cover other damage done to the commons. The liability is also limited to damage which would not have occurred or continued if the state had carried out is obligation under the Convention with respect to its operator. The Convention is, nevertheless, the first significant step toward explicitly establishing the legal regime for accountability for having caused harm to one segment of the global commons. [The Convention was adopted on June 2, 1988. It has been signed by 19 states and ratified by none. As of this writing the Convention has not come into force.]

The Council of Europe's Convention on Liability for Damage Resulting from Activities Dangerous to the Environment [June 21, 1993 Eur. T.S. No. 150 (1993)], adopted in 1993 is certainly unique.. It aims at ensuring adequate compensation for damage resulting from activities dangerous to the environment. Loss or damage by impairment of the environment has been included in the [Convention's] definition of "damage". Even within the European setting, however, this Convention has not attracted sufficient support to bring it into force.

[The search for an international liability regime that will adequately protect the global commons, therefore, continues at this writing.]

PART FIVE: STATE RESPONSIBILITY

I. INTRODUCTION

A. 1 OPPENHEIM'S INTERNATIONAL LAW

500-02 (R. Jennings & A. Watts eds., Longman 9th ed.1992)

In international law ... a state bears responsibility for its conduct in breach of its international obligations. Such responsibility attaches to a state by virtue of its position as an international person. The sovereignty of the state affords it no basis for denying that responsibility. Failure to comply with an international obligation constitutes an international wrong by the state giving rise to international responsibility of that state from which flow certain legal consequences, both for that state (such as the obligation to make reparation) and for others (such as certain rights for the injured state to seek redress or take counter-measures, or even an obligation in certain cases for all other states to respond to the wrongful act). The most usual consequence of an international wrong is to enable the injured state to avail itself of the measures and procedures available to it in accordance with international law to compel the delinquent state to fulfill its obligations, or to obtain from that state reparation for the failure. Specific forms of redress or other legal consequences may be provided in treaties dealing with particular subjects in the event of a party acting in breach of their provisions. A state may, depending on the circumstances, be jointly responsible with one or more other states, as in the case of joint occupation of enemy territory.

A distinction is sometimes made between the original and so-called vicarious responsibility of a state. 'Original' responsibility is borne by a state for acts which are directly imputable to it, such as acts of its government, or those of its officials or private individuals performed at the government's command or with its authorization. 'Vicarious' responsibility, on the other hand, arises out of certain internationally injurious acts of private individuals (whether nationals, or aliens in the state's territory), and of officials acting without authorization. It is apparent that the essential difference between original and vicarious responsibility in this sense is that whereas the former involves a state being in direct breach of legal obligations binding on it, and is accordingly a particularly serious matter, with the latter the state's responsibility is at one remove from the injurious conduct complained of: in such cases the state's responsibility calls for it to take certain preventive measures and requires it to secure that as far as possible the wrongdoer makes suitable reparation, and if necessary to punish him. But these preventive and remedial obligations of the state in cases of 'vicarious' responsibility are themselves obligations for the breach of which (as by refusing to take the remedial action which is required) the state bears direct responsibility.

NOTES AND QUESTIONS

1. Traditionally, state responsibility was viewed in terms of injuries to aliens and their property. This was the approach taken by the International Law Commission (ILC) when it began working on the codification of the topic of in 1956. In 1962, the ILC reconsidered its approach to the topic both as the result of the reaction in the General Assembly and of internal debates within the ILC itself. The Commission adopted a new approach expanding the scope to general rules of responsibility of states covering a broader field and focusing on what are called the "secondary rules" as opposed to "primary rules" of international responsibility. Roberto Ago, the second special rapporteur , substantially shaped this approach to the topic. The ILC completed the codification of state responsibility in 2001 and submitted a set of 59 articles to the General Assembly. This time the Assembly welcomed the work of the Commission, but was not yet ready to adopt it as a convention. In the view of many governments, while some articles had codified customary international law in the field, other articles reflected the so-called "progressive development" of international law or what the law ought to be. The General Assembly decided to take note of the work of the ILC, attaching the articles to a resolution (hereinafter ASR), and agreed to come back to the issue in the future. This would allow time for governments to determine if they are prepared to accept all the articles and to give them a formal legal authority.

The approach of the ILC to this topic and its work over many years has already influenced the development of the law of state responsibility. The work of the Commission has been referred to by the International Court of Justice and other international tribunals, as well as by legal scholars. For overview and discussion, *see Symposium: The ILC's State Responsibility Articles*, 96 AM. J. INT'L L. 773 (Daniel Bodansky & John R. Crook eds.) (2002). Because of this influence, this part of the casebook has followed the ILC's approach. The issue of responsibility of a state for the protection of aliens and their property is covered in Part Three under Diplomatic Protection.

2. One important characteristic of the approach to the codification of the law of state responsibility by the International Law Commission is the emphasis on "secondary" norms. In defining what "secondary norms of international law" means, the Commission's general commentary to the articles states:

> (1) These articles seek to formulate, by way of codification and progressive development, the basic rules of international law concerning the responsibility of States for their internationally wrongful acts. The emphasis is on the secondary rules of State responsibility: that is to say, the general conditions under international law for the State to be considered responsible for wrongful actions or omissions, and the legal consequences which flow therefrom. The articles do not attempt to define the content of the international obligations breach of which gives rise to responsibility. This is the function of the primary rules, whose codification would involve restating most of substantive international law, customary and conventional. …
>
> (3) Given the existence of a primary rule establishing an obligation under international law for a State, and assuming that a question has arisen as to whether that State has complied with the obligation, a number of further issues of a general character arise. These include:
>
> (*a*) The role of international law as distinct from the internal law of the State concerned in characterizing conduct as unlawful;
>
> (*b*) Determining in what circumstances conduct is to be attributed to the State as a subject of international law;
>
> (*c*) Specifying when and for what period of time there is or has been a breach of an international obligation by a State;
>
> (*d*) Determining in what circumstances a State may be responsible for the conduct of another State which is incompatible with an international obligation of the latter;

(*e*) Defining the circumstances in which the wrongfulness of conduct under international law may be precluded;

(*f*) Specifying the content of State responsibility, i.e. the new legal relations that arise from the commission by a State of an internationally wrongful act, in terms of cessation of the wrongful act, and reparation for any injury done;

(*g*) Determining any procedural or substantive preconditions for one State to invoke the responsibility of another State, and the circumstances in which the right to invoke responsibility may be lost;

(*h*) Laying down the conditions under which a State may be entitled to respond to abreach of an international obligation by taking countermeasures designed to ensure the fulfilment of the obligations of the responsible State under these articles.

This is the province of the secondary rules of State responsibility.

Report of the International Law Commission on the Work of its Fifty-third Session, U.N. GAOR, 56th Sess., Supp. No. 10, at 59-60, U.N. Doc. A/56/10 (2001).

II. Responsibility for Breach of an International Legal Obligation

A. Report of the International Law Commission on the Work of its Fifty-third Session: Articles 1-3, 12-15 ASR

U.N. GAOR 56th Sess., Supp. No. 10, at 155-168, U.N. Doc. A/56/10 (2001) [hereinafter ILC Report 2001]

Article 1: *Responsibility of a State for its internationally wrongful acts*

Every internationally wrongful act of a State entails the international responsibility of that State.

Article 2: *Elements of an internationally wrongful act of a State*

There is an internationally wrongful act of a State when conduct consisting of an action or omission:

(a) Is attributable to the State under international law; and

(b) Constitutes a breach of an international obligation of the State.

Article 3: *Characterization of an act of a State as internationally wrongful*

The characterization of an act of a State as internationally wrongful is governed by international law. Such characterization is not affected by the characterization of the same act as lawful by internal law. ...

Article 12: *Existence of a breach of an international obligation*

There is a breach of an international obligation by a State when an act of that State is not in conformity with what is required of it by that obligation, regardless of its origin or character.

Article 13: *International obligation in force for a State*

An act of a State does not constitute a breach of an international obligation unless the State is bound by the obligation in question at the time the act occurs.

Article 14: *Extension in time of the breach of an international obligation*

1. The breach of an international obligation by an act of a State not having a continuing character occurs at the moment when the act is performed, even if its effects continue.

2. The breach of an international obligation by an act of a State having a continuing character extends over the entire period during which the act continues and remains not in conformity with the international obligation.

3. The breach of an international obligation requiring a State to prevent a given event occurs when the event occurs and extends over the entire period during which the event continues and remains not in conformity with that obligation.

Article 15: *Breach consisting of a composite act*

1. The breach of an international obligation by a State through a series of actions or omissions defined in aggregate as wrongful, occurs when the action or omission occurs which, taken with the other actions or omissions, is sufficient to constitute the wrongful act.

2. In such a case, the breach extends over the entire period starting with the first of the actions or omissions of the series and lasts for as long as these actions or omissions are repeated and remain not in conformity with the international obligation.

B. ILC REPORT 2001: RELATED COMMENTARIES

[Commentary to article 2]

(4) Conduct attributable to the State can consist of actions or omissions. Cases in which the international responsibility of a State has been invoked on the basis of an omission are at least as numerous as those based on positive acts, and no difference in principle exists between the two. ...

(5) For particular conduct to be characterized as an internationally wrongful act, it must firstbe attributable to the State. The State is a real organized entity, a legal person with full authority to act under international law. But to recognize this is not to deny the elementary fact that the State cannot act of itself. An "act of the State" must involve some action or omission by a human being or group: "States can act only by and through their agents and representatives." The question is which persons should be considered as acting on behalf of the State, i.e. what constitutes an "act of the State" for the purposes of State responsibility.

[Commentary to article 3]

(1) … [T]he characterization of a given act as internationally wrongful is independent of its characterization as lawful under the internal law of the State concerned. There are two elements to this. First, an act of a State cannot be characterized as internationally wrongful unless it constitutes a breach of an international obligation, even if it violates a provision of the State's own law. Secondly and most importantly, a State cannot, by pleading that its conduct conforms to the provisions of its internal law, escape the characterization of that conduct as wrongful by international law. …

(7) The rule that the characterization of conduct as unlawful in international law cannot be affected by the characterization of the same act as lawful in internal law makes no exception for cases where rules of international law require a State to conform to the provisions of its internal law, for instance by applying to aliens the same legal treatment as to nationals. It is true that in such a case, compliance with internal law is relevant to the question of international responsibility. But this is because the rule of international law makes it relevant, e.g. by incorporating the standard of compliance with internal law as the applicable international standard or as an aspect of it. …

[Commentary to article 12]

(3) … International obligations may be established by a customary rule of international law, by a treaty or by a general principle applicable within the international legal order. States may assume international obligations by a unilateral act. An international obligation may arise from provisions stipulated in a treaty (a decision of an organ of an international organization competent in the matter, a judgment given between two States by the International Court of Justice or another tribunal, etc.) …

(5) … As far as the origin of the obligation breached is concerned, there is a single general regime of State responsibility. Nor does any distinction exist between the "civil" and "criminal" responsibility as is the case in internal legal systems.

(6) State responsibility can arise from breaches of bilateral obligations or of obligationsowed to some States or to the international community as a whole. It can involve relatively minor infringements as well as the most serious breaches of obligations under peremptory norms of general international law. Questions of the gravity of the breach and the peremptory character of the obligation breached can affect the consequences which arise for the responsible State and, in certain cases, for other States also. …

(12) … Certain obligations may be breached by the mere passage of incompatible legislation. Where this is so, the passage of the legislation without more entails the international responsibility of the enacting State, the legislature itself being an organ of the State for the purposes of the attribution of responsibility. In other circumstances, the enactment of legislation may not in and of itself amount

to a breach, especially if it is open to the State concerned to give effect to the legislation in a way which would not violate the international obligation in question. In such cases, whether there is a breach will depend on whether and how the legislation is given effect.

[Commentary to article 13]

(5) … [E]ven when a new peremptory norm of general international law comes into existence, …, this does not entail any retrospective assumption of responsibility. …

(7) … [O]nce responsibility has accrued as a result of an internationally wrongful act, it is not affected by the subsequent termination of the obligation, whether as a result of the termination of the treaty which has been breached or of a change in international law. …

(9) … The evolutionary interpretation of treaty provisions is permissible in certain cases but this has nothing to do with the principle that a State can only be held responsible for breach of an obligation which was in force for that State at the time of its conduct. Nor does the principle of the intertemporal law mean that facts occurring prior to the entry into force of a particular obligation may not be taken into account where these are otherwise relevant. …

[Commentary to article 14]

(1) The problem of identifying when a wrongful act begins and how long it continues is one which arises frequently and has consequences in the field of State responsibility, including the important question of cessation of continuing wrongful acts. …

(5) Moreover, the distinction between completed and continuing acts is a relative one. A continuing wrongful act itself can cease: thus a hostage can be released, or the body of a disappeared person returned to the next of kin. In essence a continuing wrongful act is one which has been commenced but has not been completed at the relevant time. …

(6) An act does not have a continuing character merely because its effects or consequences extend in time. It must be the wrongful act as such which continues. In many cases of internationally wrongful acts, their consequences may be prolonged. The pain and suffering caused by earlier acts of torture or the economic effects of the expropriation of property continue even though the torture has ceased or title to the property has passed. …

(13) A question common to wrongful acts whether completed or continuing is when a breach of international law occurs, as distinct from being merely apprehended or imminent. … [T]hat question can only be answered by reference to the particular primary rule. Some rules specifically prohibit threats of conduct, incitement or attempt, in which case the threat, incitement or attempt is itself a wrongful act. On the other hand where the internationally wrongful act is the

occurrence of some event - e.g. the diversion of an international river - mere preparatory conduct is not necessarily wrongful.

[Commentary to article 15]

(1) ...Composite acts give rise to continuing breaches, which extend in time from the first of the actions or omissions in the series of acts making up the wrongful conduct.

(2) Composite acts ...are limited to breaches of obligations which concern some aggregate of conduct and not individual acts as such. In other words their focus is "a series of acts or omissions defined in aggregate as wrongful". Examples include the obligations concerning genocide, apartheid or crimes against humanity, systematic acts of racial discrimination, systematic acts of discrimination prohibited by a trade agreement, etc. Some of the most serious wrongful acts in international law are defined in terms of their composite character. ...

(3) Even though it has special features, the prohibition of genocide, formulated in identical terms in the 1948 Convention and in later instruments, may be taken as an illustration of a "composite" obligation. It implies that the responsible entity (including a State) will have adopted a systematic policy or practice. .... Genocide is not committed until there has been an accumulation of acts of killing, causing harm, etc., committed with the relevant intent, so as to satisfy the definition in article II [of the 1948 Convention]. Once that threshold is crossed, the time of commission extends over the whole period during which any of the acts was committed, and any individual responsible for any of them with the relevant intent will have committed genocide.

(4) It is necessary to distinguish composite obligations from simple obligations breached by a "composite" act. Composite acts may be more likely to give rise to continuing breaches, but simple acts can cause continuing breaches as well. The position is different, however, where the obligation itself is defined in terms of the cumulative character of the conduct, i.e. where the cumulative conduct constitutes the essence of the wrongful act. Thus apartheid is different inkind from individual acts of racial discrimination, and genocide is different in kindfrom individual acts even of ethnically or racially motivated killing. ...

(7) A consequence of the character of a composite act is that the time when the act is accomplished cannot be the time when the first action or omission of the series takes place. It is only subsequently that the first action or omission will appear as having, as it were, inaugurated the series. Only after a series of actions or omissions takes place will the composite act be revealed, not merely as a succession of isolated acts, but as a composite act, i.e. an act defined in aggregate as wrongful.

Notes & Questions

1. In the language of traditional international law, what would be the "source" of the "binding nature" of the Articles on State Responsibility? If it is customary international law, would it be

sufficient for its establishment if the ILC cites the ICJ (e.g. *Gabcíkovo* and *LaGrand*), while the ICJ refers back to the ILC's draft articles for support (*see supra*, General Commentary)? Isn't that argument circular, representing a citation carousel? In *Changing the Premise of International Legal Remedies: The Unfounded Adoption of Assurances and Guarantees of Non-Repetition*, 7 UCLA J. INT'L L. & FOR. AFF. 265, 300-01 (2002-2003), Scott M. Sullivan concludes:

> The ILC in its Draft Articles on State Responsibility and the ICJ in *LaGrand* attempt to bypass customary international law by relying on the authority of each other. The ILC work on Article 30 was designed to move away from state consent and domestic responsibility in tailoring international obligations. Faced with the reality that AGNRs [Assurances and Guarantees of Non-Repetition] lack both consistent state practice and *opinio juris*, but unwilling to label them as progressive development, the ILC waited for ICJ adoption of such measures in *LaGrand*. The ICJ did so while declining to exercise the large scope of this new remedy, which kept the focus of the case on the death penalty and provisional measures.
>
> The ICJ's and ILC's surreptitious movement toward AGNRs resulted in an illegitimate and artificial production of an international rule, which is both bad public policy and which stains both the institutions and the principle. A change in international law to a future-oriented approach empowered to interfere directly with domestic law redefines international court power under the doubtful guise of custom.

2. Is it relevant, in this context, that members of the ILC, trusted members of the scholarly and/ or diplomatic establishment of their respective home countries, in a familiar career pattern, are often moved on to become judges of the ICJ (e.g., the appointment of Professor Roberto Ago first to the ILC, then to the ICJ)? For further criticism of the ILC-ICJ "feedback loop," exemplified by the narrowing interpretation of the proportionality requirement for countermeasures in *Gabcíkovo-Nagymaros Project* (Hung. v. Slovk.), 1997 I.C.J. 7 (Sept. 25)(Judgment) and Art. 51 ASR, *see* David J. Bederman, *Counterintuiting Countermeasures*, 96 AM. J. INT'L L. 817, 819 (2002):

> The ICJ and the ILC have enjoyed a cozy historical relationship. It is not only that ILC members have often been elected to the Court, but also that the Court uniquely privileges some of the drafts, reports, and other work product of the Commission through citations in its decisions. In return, the Commission is careful to incorporate the doctrinal pronouncements of the ICJ in its codification efforts. Indeed, sometimes the ILC may have no other practical course, insofar as its work products are reviewed by the Sixth Committee of the United Nations General Assembly and by member states convened at plenipotentiary conferences to consider and conclude treaty texts. ... This dynamic produces a "feedback loop" of jurisprudence, variously reinforcing certain norms previously found in state practice and judicial decisions, or, alternatively, perpetuating certain doctrines of uncertain origin or dubious validity. ...
>
> [Author discusses the proprotionality requirement of Art. 51 and concludes:] The use of countermeasures for purely punitive reasons—without any hope or expectation that the malefactor state will actually back down from its offensive conduct —appears to be now precluded by the articles. This change in emphasis on the nature and purpose of countermeasures likewise places in some doubt the Commission's use of earlier international law sources.
>
> Thus, what we appear to have in Article 51 is a provision whose key term is based exclusively on isolated language in a recent World Court decision [i.e. the *Gabcikovo-Nagymaros Project* Judgment]. Perhaps even more disconcerting is that, to the extent that "commensurability" can be traced to the 1971 report of Roberto Ago, he took a strikingly different approach to the topic. Unlike the final draft of the article, Ago's version recognized that limited forms of escalation were consistent with a proportional response, especially in light of the need to "induce" a malefactor state to abide by its

international obligations. In short, Article 51 indicates the hazards of relying on ostensibly neutral and superior legal authority (ICJ decisions) to reach codification outcomes, rather than on state practice, the weight of previous arbitral decisions, and the Commission's own *doctrine*. Absent such traditional indicia of authority in international law, which go beyond the conclusory pronouncements of the ICJ, the articles' intellectual support and coherence must come from other sources or policy preferences. These considerations are not meant to suggest that many of the articles suffer from this kind of authority deficit, but the surprising lack of support for the crucial clause on proportionality in the use of countermeasures does give one pause about what other difficulties may be lurking in the construction of the articles.

3. With respect to the criticism offered by Bederman and Sullivan, it has to be acknowledged that it is difficult to find state practice as such, absent any judicial or arbitral pronouncement, in the technical field of state responsibility. In addition, it has now become "fashionable" to refer disputes to some form of judicial forum, and to rely on the decisions emanating from such fora as newly-binding law. Many states, in particular developing and smaller ones, believe that their interests will be better served in a judicial or arbitral environment. Many representatives of developing countries, and even some from developed countries, feel that a good part of customary law was created by a limited number of states and did not reflect a universal acceptance of the norm in question, as opposed to more recent judicial and arbitral decisions, conventions, etc. which are more reflective of a much larger participation of states. This view is reflected in the membership of the ILC, hence the attention it pays to judicial decisions of the ICJ, regional courts, and arbitral awards.

4. If and to the extent they can not be classified as part and parcel of customary law, can the Articles on State Responsibility be seen as "general principles of law recognized by civilized nations" (Article 38(1)(c) ICJ Statute)? What would be the problem with that classification? Note that domestic legal systems, regarding issues such as attribution, circumstances precluding wrongfulness, countermeasures and consequences of breach of an obligation, differ substantially not only *between* themselves (civil and common law traditions primarily), but also *within* themselves (different attribution rules for tort law and criminal law; or different consequences for breaches of contracts as opposed to torts)? Can domestic legal prescriptions for private liability be proper bases for analogies to the responsibility of states?

C. THE S.S "WIMBLEDON" (U.K., FR., ITALY, JAPAN V. GER.)

1923 P.C.I.J.(Ser. A) No. 1 at 29-30 (Aug. 17)

[Under the terms of Article 380 of the Treaty of Versailles, "The Kiel Canal and its approaches shall be maintained free and open to the vessels of commerce and war of all nations at peace with Germany on terms of entire equality." On March 21, 1921, the British steamship "Wimbledon" chartered by the French armament firm "Les Affrêteurs réunis", proceeding from Salonika to Danzig with a cargo of 4,000 tons of military material was refused access to and free passage through the Kiel Canal by the German authorities on the ground that the cargo was destined for Poland which was at war with Russia and that German regulations regarding neutrality forbade the transit across German territory of war material destined for these two countries.]. . .

The precedents therefore afforded by the Suez and Panama Canals invalidate in advance the argument that Germany's neutrality would have necessarily been imperilled if her authorities had allowed the passage of the "Wimbledon" through the Kiel Canal, because that vessel was carrying contraband of war consigned to a state then engaged in an armed conflict. Moreover they are merely illustrations of the general opinion according to which when an artificial waterway connecting two open seas has been permanently dedicated to the use of the whole world, such waterway is assimilated to natural straits in the sense that even the passage of a belligerent man-of-war does not compromise the neutrality of the sovereign State under whose jurisdiction the waters in question lie.

The next question to be considered is whether Germany was entitled to invoke her rights and duties as a neutral power and the provisions of her Neutrality Orders issued in connection with the Russo-Polish war as a ground for her refusal to allow the "Wimbledon" to enter the Kiel Canal, in spite of the categorical terms of Article 380 of the Treaty of Versailles.

The first of the Orders above mentioned dated July 25th, 1920, contains the following:

> In consequence of Germany's neutrality in the war which has arisen between the Republic of Poland and the Federal Socialist Republic of the Russian Soviets ... the Government enacts as follows:
>
> Article I: The export and transit of arms, munitions, powder and explosives and other articles of war material is prohibited in so far as these articles are consigned to the territories of the Polish Republic or of the Federal Socialist Republic of the Russian Soviets.

A detailed list of the substances and articles, the export and transit of which are forbidden, was given some days later in a further Order, dated July 30th, 1920.

The export prohibition contained in the German Neutrality Orders clearly could not apply to the passage through the Canal of the articles enumerated when such articles were dispatched from one foreign country and consigned to another foreign country. Nor does the word "transit" appear to refer to the Kiel Canal; it no doubt only refers to the German territory to which the stipulations of Article 380 are not applicable. In any case a neutrality order, issued by an individual State, could not prevail over the provisions of the Treaty of Peace.

Since Article 380 of the Treaty of Versailles lays down that the Kiel Canal shall be maintained free and open to the vessels of commerce and war of all nations at peace with Germany, it is impossible to allege that the terms of this article preclude, in the interests of the protection of Germany's neutrality, the transport of contraband of war. The German Government had not at the time when the "Wimbledon" incident took place claimed any right to close the Canal to ships of war of belligerent nations at peace with Germany. On the contrary, in the note of the President of the German Delegation to the President of the Conference of Ambassadors of April 20th, 1921, it is expressly stated that the German Government claimed to apply its neutrality orders only to vessels of commerce and not to vessels of war. The Court is not called upon to give an opinion in regard to the legal effect of such statement; but if, as seems certain, it contains, in regard to the passage of belligerent war vessels through the Kiel Canal, an accurate interpretation of the Treaty of Versailles, it follows *a fortiori* that the passage of neutral vessels carrying contraband of war is authorised by Article 380, and cannot be imputed to Germany as a failure to fulfill its duties as a neutral. If, therefore, the "Wimbledon", making use of the permission granted by Article 380, had passed through the Kiel Canal, Germany's neutrality would have remained intact and irreproachable.

From the foregoing, therefore, it appears clearly established that Germany not only did not, in consequence of her neutrality, incur the obligation to prohibit the passage of the "Wimbledon" through the Kiel Canal, but, on the contrary, was entitled to permit it. Moreover, under Article 380 of the Treaty of Versailles, it was her definite duty to allow it. She could not advance her neutrality orders against the obligations which she had accepted under this Article. Germany was perfectly free to declare and regulate her neutrality in the Russo-Polish war, but subject to the condition that she respected and maintained intact the contractual obligations which she entered into at Versailles on June 28th, 1919.

In these circumstances it will readily be seen that it would be useless to consider in this case whether the state of war between Russia and Poland, and with it Germany's neutrality, had or had not terminated at the date on which the "Wimbledon" incident occurred. In war time as in peace time the Kiel Canal should have been open to the "Wimbledon" just as to every vessel of every nation at peace with Germany.

The Court having arrived at the conclusion that the respondent, Germany, wrongfully refused passage through the Canal to the vessel "Wimbledon", that country is responsible for the loss occasioned by this refusal, and must compensate the French Government, acting on behalf of the Company known as "Les Affrêteurs réunis", which sustained the loss.

Notes & Questions

1. What are the elements that lead to characterizing an act as a breach of an international obligation of a state? Examine the effect of the claim by a state that it had complied with its domestic law as a defense to its responsibility for a breach of an international obligation, as expressed in *S.S. "Wimbledon"* and the Articles on State Responsibility.

2. A Chamber of the ICJ, in *Elettronica Sicula S.p.A. (ELSI)* (U.S. v. Italy), 1989 I.C.J. 15 (July 20) (discussed in Part Three, *supra*), dealt with the relationship between domestic law and international law for the purposes of establishment of a breach of an international obligation by a state:

> Compliance with municipal law and compliance with the provisions of a treaty are different questions. What is a breach of treaty may be lawful in the municipal law and what is unlawful in the municipal law may be wholly innocent of violation of a treaty provision. Even had thePrefect held the requisition to be entirely justified in Italian law, this would not exclude the possibility that it was a violation of the FCN Treaty. ...
>
> The fact that an act of a public public authority may have been unlawful in municipal law does not necessarily mean that that act was unlawful in international law, as a breach of treaty or otherwise. A finding of the local courts that an act was unlawful may well be

> relevant to an argument that it was also arbitrary; but by itself, and without more, unlawfulness cannot be said to amount to arbitrariness ... Nor does it follow from a finding by a municipal court that an act was unjustified, or unreasonable, or arbitrary, that that act is necessarily to be classed as arbitrary in international law, though the qualification given to the impugned act by a municipal authority may be a valuable indication.

Id. paras. 73 and 124.

3. Note that the *Wimbledon* tribunal refers to the regimes of the Suez and the Panama Canals as illustrations of a presumably customary law rule ("general opinion") regarding access by vessels carrying contraband to an artificial waterway permanently dedicated to the whole world and connecting two open seas. Interestingly, the 1923 Treaty of Lausanne provided that Turkey could prohibit passage of warships through the Bosporus and the Dardanelles in time of war when Turkey was not a belligerent. 1 OPPENHEIM'S INTERNATIONAL LAW 641 (R. Jennings & A. Watts eds., Longman 9th ed. 1992).

4. On November 14, 1936 Germany declared it would "no longer recognize as binding the provisions of the Versailles Treaty which concern the German waterways..." *Id.* at 595. There was no protest against this declaration on the part of a majority of the interested signatories of the Treaty. *Id.* What was the legal consequence of this declaration?

5. Do the 1982 United Nations Convention on the Law of the Sea and its provisions on innocent or transit passage apply, to whom do they apply, and do they embody the customary law rule enunciated in *Wimbledon*? *See* Part Four, *supra*, at 672, 675-677.

III. ATTRIBUTION OF AN ACT TO A STATE

A. ILC REPORT 2001: ARTICLES 4-11 ASR

Article 4: *Conduct of organs of a State*

1. The conduct of any State organ shall be considered an act of that State under international law, whether the organ exercises legislative, executive, judicial or any other functions, whatever position it holds in the organization of the State, and whatever its character as an organ of the central government or of a territorial unit of the State.

2. An organ includes any person or entity which has that status in accordance with the internal law of the State.

Article 5: *Conduct of persons or entities exercising elements of governmental authority*

The conduct of a person or entity which is not an organ of the State under article 4 but which is empowered by the law of that State to exercise elements of the governmental authority shall be considered an act of the State under international law, provided the person or entity is acting in that capacity in the particular instance.

Article 6: *Conduct of organs placed at the disposal of a State by another State*

The conduct of an organ placed at the disposal of a State by another State shall be considered an act of the former State under international law if the organ is acting in the exercise of elements of the governmental authority of the State at whose disposal it is placed.

Article 7: *Excess of authority or contravention of instructions*

The conduct of an organ of a State or of a person or entity empowered to exercise elements of the governmental authority shall be considered an act of the State under international law if the organ, person or entity acts in that capacity, even if it exceeds its authority or contravenes instructions.

Article 8: *Conduct directed or controlled by a State*

The conduct of a person or group of persons shall be considered an act of a State under international law if the person or group of persons is in fact acting on the instructions of, or under the direction or control of, that State in carrying out the conduct.

Article 9: *Conduct carried out in the absence or default of the official authorities*

The conduct of a person or group of persons shall be considered an act of a State under international law if the person or group of persons is in fact exercising elements of the governmental authority in the absence or default of the official authorities and in circumstances such as to call for the exercise of those elements of authority.

Article 10: *Conduct of an insurrectional or other movement*

1. The conduct of an insurrectional movement which becomes the new government of a State shall be considered an act of that State under international law.

2. The conduct of a movement, insurrectional or other, which succeeds in establishing a new State in part of the territory of a pre-existing State or in a territory under its administration shall be considered an act of the new State under international law.

3. This article is without prejudice to the attribution to a State of any conduct, however related to that of the movement concerned, which is to be considered an act of that State by virtue of articles 4 to 9.

Article 11: *Conduct acknowledged and adopted by a State as its own*

Conduct which is not attributable to a State under the preceding articles shall nevertheless be considered an act of that State under international law if and to the extent that the State acknowledges and adopts the conduct in question as its own.

B. ILC REPORT 2001: RELATED COMMENTARIES

[Commentary to Chapter II of Part One]

(2) In theory, the conduct of all human beings, corporations or collectivities linked to the State by nationality, habitual residence or incorporation might be attributed to the State, whether or not they have any connection to the government. In international law, such an approach is avoided, both with a view to limiting responsibility to conduct which engages the State as an organization, and also so as to recognize the autonomy of persons acting on their own account and not at the instigation of a public authority. Thus the general rule is that the only conduct attributed to the State at the international level is that of its organs of government, or of others who have acted under the direction, instigation or control of those organs, i.e., as agents of the State. …

(4) The attribution of conduct to the State as a subject of international law is based on criteria determined by international law and not on the mere recognition of a link of factual causality. As a normative operation, attribution must be clearly distinguished from the characterization of conduct as internationally wrongful. Its concern is to establish that there is an act of the State for the purposes of responsibility. To show that conduct is attributable to the State says nothing, as such, about the legality or otherwise of that conduct, and rules of attribution should not be formulated in terms which imply otherwise. But the different rules of attribution … have a cumulative effect, such that a State may be responsible for the effects of the conduct of private parties, if it failed to take necessary measures to prevent those effects. For example a receiving State is not responsible, as such, for the acts of private individuals in seizing an embassy, but it will be responsible if it fails to take all necessary steps to protect the embassy from seizure, or to regain control over it. In this respect there is often a close link between the basis of attribution and the particular obligation said to have been breached, even though the two elements are analytically distinct.

(5) The question of attribution of conduct to the State for the purposes of responsibility is to be distinguished from other international law processes by which particular organs are authorized to enter into commitments on behalf of the State. Thus the head of State or government or the minister of foreign affairs is regarded as having authority to represent the State without any need to produce full powers. Such rules have nothing to do with attribution for the purposes of State responsibility. In principle, the State's responsibility is engaged by conduct incompatible with its international obligations, irrespective of the level of administration or government at which the conduct occurs….

(6) In determining what constitutes an organ of a State for the purposes of responsibility, the internal law and practice of each State are of prime importance. The structure of the State and the functions of its organs are not, in general, governed by international law. It is a matter for each State to decide how its administration is to be structured and which functions are to be assumed

by government. But while the State remains free to determine its internal structure and functions through its own law and practice, international law has a distinct role. For example, the conduct of certain institutions performing public functions and exercising public powers (e.g. the police) is attributed to the State even if those institutions are regarded in internal law as autonomous and independent of the executive government. Conduct engaged in by organs of the State in excess of their competence may also be attributed to the State under international law, whatever the position may be under internal law.

C. ORIGINS OF STATE RESPONSIBILITY

1. British Claims in the Spanish Zone of Morocco

2 R.I.A.A. 617 (1929), *translated in* 1978 Int'l L. Comm'n Y.B., vol. II, Pt.I,171-2

[During the years 1913 to 1921, a number of British subjects and British protected persons suffered losses and sustained injuries from acts of bandits and tribal rebels, and by military operations in the Spanish Zone of Morocco. By the Special Agreement of 29 May 1923, Spain and the United Kingdom submitted the claims to arbitration, M. Max Huber being the sole arbitrator.

In a memorial dated 16 March 1924, the British Government contended, *inter alia*, that for a long period of time the action of the Spanish authorities in Morocco had resulted in a denial of justice to British subjects and British protégés, and added the following as the expression of the attitude customarily followed by the United Kingdom:]

Where claims are made for compensation for damage done by insurgents in armed insurrection against a Government which was unable to control them, claimants should be informed that His Majesty's Government does not regard a Government as liable in such cases, unless that Government was negligent and might have prevented the damage arising or unless it pays compensation either to its own citizens or subjects or to other foreigners in similar cases, or unless the rebellion has been successful and the insurgent party has been installed in power. . . .

[With regard to the responsibility of a state in situations caused by uprisings, revolts andwars, characterizing them as cases of *force majeure* and the duty of a state to take preventive measures, Max Huber stated:]

The fact that it is an alien who is the victim of an offence under the *ordinary law*, for example, theft or looting, does not place the event on an international plane; the same is true if the criminal prosecution to which the act is liable does not take place, and if a claim for restitution or damages and interest receives no positive and satisfactory response. No police force or administration of justice is perfect, and undoubtedly a considerable margin in which tolerance is necessary must be accepted, even in the best administered countries. But the restriction thus placed on the right of States to intervene to protect their nationals presupposes that general security in the latters' countries of residence should not fall below a certain level, and that at least their protection by justice should not become purely illusory. It is for this reason that interventions by States to obtain indemnification for their injured nationals arise most often in situations where the authorities are no longer in a position to guarantee the security that may rightly be expected.

3. It is in this connexion that the principle of the non-responsibility of States for damages caused by *popular uprisings, revolts and wars* becomes important, for it is in precisely these cases that insecurity is particularly great and judicial protection becomes problematical. It would appear indisputable that the State is not responsible for the fact of an uprising, revolt, civil war or international war, or for the fact that these events provoke damages within its territory. It may be that it was more or less possible to show proof of errors committed by the Government, but failing specific clauses in a treaty or agreement the investigation necessary for this purpose is not acceptable. These events must be regarded as cases of *force majeure*. ...

But does non-responsibility for the event as such exonerate the territorial State from all responsibility? Does the simple fact that the damages sustained have a certain connexion with events of the nature of war or rebelling make it possible to rule out, by virtue of the theory of non-responsibility for those events, all consideration of the responsibility possibly incurred by the State in that respect? ...

Even admitting the argument that the responsibility of the State ceases altogether when there is a connexion between a damage sustained and a revolt, etc., it would still not be possible to reject a claim in that respect out of hand, for it would always be necessary first to examine and decide on a point of fact, namely the effective nexus between the two events. Furthermore, the principle of non-responsibility in no way precludes the duty to exercise a certain vigilance. Though the State is not responsible for the revolutionary events themselves, it may nevertheless be responsible for what the authorities do or do not do to mitigate the consequences as far as possible. Responsibility for the action or inaction of the public authorities is quite different from responsibility for acts that may be imputed to persons outside the control of the authorities or openly hostile to them. The principle of non-intervention in the relations between a State and the aliens established in its territory presupposes not only normal conditions of justice and administration but also the will of the State to carry out its primary purpose: the maintenance of domestic peace and social order. The State is bound to exercise a certain vigilance. Although it is the authorities of the country which decide what is to be done or left undone with a view to the suppression of a revolt, etc., a State cannot require another State, the interests of whosenationals are injured, to remain unmoved if possibilities of assistance are, for no good reason, openly neglected, or if the authorities, despite ample warning, take no preventive measures, or again, if equal protection is not afforded to aliens of all nationalities. ...

[As far as the responsibility for acts of plunder is concerned, Max Huber stated:]

Is the territorial State then exonerated if it has done what may reasonably be demanded of it, given its effective situation? Or is it bound to guarantee a certain degree of security, being responsible for possible inability to provide it? Such an argument has been put forward and has been applied in respect of certain States. However, it seems highly disputable that this manner of viewing the case is well-founded, and it is far from having been accepted in the decisions of international tribunals. Doctrine is clearly opposed to it. In the branch of international law in which the problem of the negligence of the State in regard to the prevention of acts possibly contrary to international law has played a particularly important role, namely in the realm of neutrality in time of war at sea, the end result has been recognition that the State is only bound to exercise that degree of vigilance that corresponds to the means at its disposal. To demand that these means should be commensurate with the circumstances would be to impose on the State a burden which it might often be unable to support. Therefore, the argument that the vigilance to be exercised must correspond to the importance of the interests at stake could not succeed. The vigilance which the State, from the point of view of international law, is bound to ensure may be characterized, by applying by analogy a term from Roman law, as *diligentia quam in suis*. This rule, in conformity with the primary principle of the independence of States in their domestic affairs, in fact offers States, as far as their nationals are concerned, the degree of security they may reasonably expect. As soon as the vigilance exercised falls obviously short of that level in respect of the nationals of a particular foreign State, that State is entitled to regard itself as injured in respect of interests that should enjoy the protection of international law.

What has just been stated on the subject of due vigilance in relation to the general insecurity resulting from the activities of brigands applies even more strongly to the two other situations envisaged above, namely criminal offences under the originary law and rebellion. In the first case, vigilance pressed further than *diligentia quam in suis* would impose on the State the obligation to organize a special security service for aliens, which would certainly go beyond the bounds of recognized international obligations (apart from cases involving persons entitled by law to special protection). In the second hypothesis, that of rebellion, etc., responsibility is limited because the authorities are faced with exceptional resistance. ...

[T]he state may incur responsibility in the situations in question, not only through a lack of vigilance in preventing injurious acts, but also through a lack of diligence in the criminal prosecution of the offenders, as well as in applying the appropriate civil penalties.

NOTES & QUESTIONS

1. Do the obligations imposed by contemporary international human rights instruments invalidate Judge Huber's theory? *See supra* Part Three, Human Rights, at 520 et seq. Note that Article 2(1) of the 1966 International Covenant on Civil and Political Rights formulates a state party's "duty to ensure these rights to all individuals within its territory and subject to its jurisdiction." It also imposes a duty to enact appropriate implementing legislation (Art. 2(2)) and provide effective remedies (Art. 2(3)). Does it contain a *force majeure* exception similar to the one enunciated by Judge Huber? Would the emergency provision, i.e. Article 4 ICCPR, apply in these circumstances? Do these primary rules leave open the application of the Articles on State Responsibility, or are they a special regime excluding the Articles under their Article 55 on *lex specialis*?

2. Note also that the 1965 Convention on the Elimination of All Forms of Racial Discrimination requires states parties to prevent abuses by private actors. Does it apply in circumstances such as those dealt with above?

3. How do the ASR allocate state responsibility for acts of insurgents? *See,* in particular, Art. 10.

2. Corfu Channel (U.K. v. Alb.)

1949 I.C.J. 4, 22-23 (Apr. 9) (Merits)

[As discussed *supra*, Part Four, at 677, the Corfu Channel Case arose from incidents that occurred on October 22nd 1946, in the Corfu Strait. Two British destroyers struck mines in Albanian waters and suffered damage, including serious loss of life. The United Kingdom first seized the Security Council of the United Nations which, by a Resolution of April 9th, 1947, recommended to the two Governments to submit the dispute to the Court. On March 25, 1948, Albania and the United Kingdom concluded a Special Agreement asking the Court to give judgment on a number of questions including: Is Albania responsible for the explosions, and is there a duty to pay compensation?]

From all the facts and observations mentioned above, the Court draws the conclusion that the laying of the minefield which caused the explosions on October 22nd, 1946, could not have been accomplished without the knowledge of the Albanian Government.

The obligations resulting for Albania from this knowledge are not disputed between the Parties. Counsel for the Albanian Government expressly recognized that *[translation]* "if Albania had been informed of the operation before the incidents of October 22nd, and in time to warn the British vessels and shipping in general of the existence of mines in the Corfu Channel her responsibility would be involved...".

The obligations incumbent upon the Albanian authorities consisted in notifying, for the benefit of shipping in general, the existence of a minefield in Albanian territorial waters and in warning the approaching British warships of the imminent danger to which the minefield exposed them. Such obligations are based, not on the Hague Convention of 1907, No. VIII, which is applicable in time of war, but on certain general and well-recognized principles, namely: elementary considerations of humanity, even more exacting in peace than in war; and every

State's obligation not to allow knowingly its territory to be used for acts contrary to the rights of other States.

In fact, Albania neither notified the existence of the minefield, nor warned the British warships of the danger they were approaching.

But Albania's obligation to notify shipping of the existence of mines in her waters depends on her having obtained knowledge of that fact in sufficient time before October 22nd; and the duty of the Albanian coastal authorities to warn the British ships depends on the time that elapsed between the moment that these ships were reported and the moment of the first explosion.

On this subject, the Court makes the following observations. As has already been stated, the Parties agree that the mines were recently laid. It must be concluded that the minelaying, whatever may have been its exact date, was done at a time when there was a close Albanian surveillance over the Strait. If it be supposed that it took place at the last possible moment, i.e., in the night of October 21st-22nd, the only conclusion to be drawn would be that a general notification to the shipping of all States before the time of the explosions would have been difficult, perhaps even impossible. But this would certainly not have prevented the Albanian authorities from taking, as they should have done, all necessary steps immediately to warn ships near the danger zone, especially those that were approaching that zone. When on October 22nd about 13:00 hours the British warships were reported by the look-out post at St. George's Monastery to the Commander of the Coastal Defences as approaching Cape Long, it was perfectly possible for the Albanian authorities to use the interval of almost two hours that elapsed before the explosion affecting *Saumarez* (14.53 hours or 14.55 hours) to warn the vessels of the danger into which they were running.

In fact, nothing was attempted by the Albanian authorities to prevent the disaster. These grave omissions involve the international responsibility of Albania.

The Court therefore reaches the conclusion that Albania is responsible under international law for the explosions which occurred on October 22nd, 1946, in Albanian waters, and for the damage and loss of human life which resulted from them, and that there is a duty upon Albania to pay compensation to the United Kingdom.

D. Acts Ultra Vires

1. Thomas H. Youmans Case (U.S. v. Mex.)

4 R.I.A.A. 110 (1926)

1. Claim for damages [is] made in this case by the United States of America against the United Mexican States on behalf of Thomas H. Youmans, the son of Henry Youmans, an American citizen, who, together with two other Americans, John A. Connelly and GeorgeArnold, was killed at the hands of a mob on March 14, 1880, at Angangueo, State of Michoacán, Mexico. …

11. The claim made by the United States is predicated on the failure of the Mexican Government to exercise due diligence to protect the father of the claimant from the fury of the mob at whose hands he was killed, and the failure to take proper steps looking to the apprehension and punishment of the persons implicated in the crime. In connection with the contention with respect to the failure of the authorities to protect Youmans from the acts of the mob, particular emphasis is laid on the participation of soldiers which is asserted to be in itself a ground of liability. In behalf of the respondent Government it is contended that the Mexican Government and the Government of the State of Michoacán acted with due diligence in arresting and bringing to justice all persons against whom a reasonable suspicion of guilt existed; that the charge that some State troops participated in the riot is not proved by the evidence; and that, even if it were assumed that the soldiers were guilty of such participation, the Mexican Government should not be held responsible for the wrongful acts of ten soldiers and one officer of the State of Michoacán, who, after having been ordered by the highest official in the locality to protect American citizens, instead of carrying out orders given them acted in violation of them in consequence of which the Americans were killed. …

13. With respect to the question of responsibility for the acts of soldiers there are citations in the Mexican Government's brief of extracts from a discussion of a subcommittee of the League of Nations Committee of Experts for the Progressive Codification of International Law. The passage quoted, which deals with the responsibility of a State for illegal acts of officials resulting in damages to foreigners, begins with a statement relative to the acts of an official accomplished "outside the scope of his competency, that is to say, if he has exceeded his powers." An illegal act of this kind, it is stated n the quotation, is one that can not be imputed to the State. Apart from the question whether the acts of officials referred to in this discussion have any relation to the rule of international law with regard to responsibility for acts of soldiers, it seems clear that the passage to which particular attention is called in the Mexican Government's brief is concerned solely with the question of the authority of an officer as defined by domestic law to act for his Government with reference to some particular subject. Clearly it is not intended by the rule asserted to say that no wrongful act of an official acting in the discharge of duties entrusted to him can impose responsibility on a Government under international law because any such wrongful act must be considered to be "outside the scope of his competency." If this were the meaning intended by the rule it would follow that no wrongful acts committed by an official could be considered as acts for which his Government could be held liable. We do not consider that any of these passages from the discussion of the subcommittee quoted in the Mexican brief are at variance with the view which we take that the action of the troops in participating in the murder at Angangueo imposed a direct responsibility on the Government of Mexico.

14. … Certain cases coming before the international tribunals may have revealed some uncertainty whether the acts of soldiers should properly be regarded as private acts for which there was no liability on the State, or acts for which the State should be held responsible. But we do not consider that the

participation of the soldiers in the murder at Angangueo can be regarded as acts of soldiers committed in their private capacity when it is clear that at the time of the commission of these acts the men were on duty under the immediate supervision and in the presence of a commanding officer. Soldiers inflicting personal injuries or committing wanton destruction or looting always act in disobedience of some rules laid down by superior authority. There could be no liability whatever for such misdeeds if the view were taken than any acts committed by soldiers in contravention of instructions must always be considered as personal acts.

2. Jean-Baptiste Caire Case

Fr. & Mex. Mixed Claims Comm'n 1929, 5 Ann. Dig. 146

THE FACTS.—This was a claim arising out of the death, in December, 1914, of a French citizen, Caire, which occurred in the following circumstances: Caire kept a boarding-house in Mexico City. He had as a boarder a certain major who was attached to the brigade of General Tomás Urbina of the Northern Division of the Conventionist forces which at that time occupied the city of Mexico. On 11 December the major, accompanied by two armed soldiers, presented himself to Caire and demanded from him the sum of 5,000 pesos in gold. This sum Caire declared himself unable to procure. The major appeared again later with a captain of the same brigade, conveyed Caire to the barracks, left him there for some hours, carried him back to his house and there repeated his demand for 5,000 pesos, under the threat to shoot him. Caire having offered them all he possessed, namely, 200 pesos in paper money, the two officers again took him to the barracks. There he was undressed, taken by car to a neighbouring village and put to death, together with a Mexican friend who had intervened on his behalf. ... [T]he Mexican Government alleged that Mexico was not liable for the murder for two reasons: (t:*a*) the two officers being no more than a couple of bandits with the worst antecedents, they should be classified under the category of "bandits," mentioned in item (*v*) of Article III of the French-Mexican Claims Convention of 25 September, 1924, or, alternatively, they should be recognised as military forces, under the category of "insurrectionary forces" mentioned in the same category (*v*), in neither case fault having been established on the part of the competent authorities; (*b*) if the Conventionist forces were to be considered as revolutionary forces under (ii) of Article III, the responsibility of Mexico would be excluded for the reason: (1) that the authors of the crime were isolated soldiers; (2) that they had acted without the knowledge, if not against orders, of the commander of the brigade; (3) that the crime bore no relation whatever to the aims and objects of the revolution.

Held (by the President): that Mexico was liable:

(*a*) The general principles of international law in the matter of State responsibility must be interpreted in the light of the doctrine of the "*responsabilité objective*" of the State. According to that doctrine international responsibility might be incurred by a State notwithstanding the absence of any fault on its side, seeing that a State was responsible for all acts committed by its officers or organs and constituting delinquencies from the point of view of the lawof nations, regardless of whether the officers or organs in question have acted within the limits of their competence or have exceeded it. "In order, however, to justify the admission of this "*responsabilité objective*" of the State for acts committed by its officers outside the limits of their competencies, it is necessary either that they should have acted, at least apparently, as authorised officers, or that, in acting, they should have exercised powers or measures connected with their official character."

(*b*) The responsibility of Mexico under the Claims Convention, considered in the light of the general principles of international law relating to State responsibility, could not be denied, on the following grounds: Article 3 of Convention No. IV of the Second Hague Peace Conference of 1907, enacting regulations concerning the laws of war on land, which established the responsibility of a belligerent State for all acts perpetrated in violation of those regulations by persons forming part of its armed forces, had no direct bearing on civil wars, nor should its operation be extended thereto by simple analogy, since the Article quoted was a rather exceptional provision of limited applicability. The questions must be decided according to the general principles of customary international law. In particular, the special characteristics which distinguished the military from civil officers necessarily affected the conditions and the extent of the responsibility of the State for their acts; they aggravate the responsibility of the State.

Moreover, State responsibility for acts of State organs was an absolute responsibility and not a responsibility based on fault. In the case under consideration the murderers had acted in their capacity of military officers and had taken advantage of the power and compulsory means at their disposal by reason of that very capacity. The fact that their criminal act was not subservient to the interests of the revolutionary movement in which they were engaged could not discharge Mexico from its responsibility since neither the text nor the origin of the Convention nor the general principles of customary international law admitted such a restriction. Indeed, "the international responsibility of a State has never been made dependent on the aims to be attained by the injurious acts; on the contrary, if there were any reason to limit the extent of State responsibility, it would rather be in the sense of excluding it in all cases where the acts were imperatively required by the state o fnecessity through which the State had to struggle, but not in cases where the aims of the State or of the revolution did not necessitate them at all." Otherwise international responsibility would be excluded in the very cases where justice and equity demand it, for instance, when the commander-in-chief of the armed forces of a legitimate Government or of victorious revolutionary troops ordered the bombardment of undefended towns or hospitals or declared that no quarter would be given, and so on.

(*c*) The classification of the authors of damage either under one of the forces enumerated in Article III or under the category of "bandits" did not depend upon the more or less criminal character of themselves of their acts, but exclusively upon their incorporation in the military forces. The Villist

(Conventionist) forces of the Northern Division were in December, 1914, doubtless revolutionary forces in the sense of sub-section (ii) of Article III, in the same way as the forces of the "*Ejército Libertador*" of Zapata.

NOTES AND QUESTIONS

1. Are the acts of revolutionaries as opposed to the faction that is ultimately successful attributable to the State?

2. Note that Pancho Villa's insurrection was ultimately not successful. *See* FRIEDRICH KATZ, THE LIFE & TIMES OF PANCHO VILLA 497 (1998). *See also* Steve Sheppard, *Passion and Nation: War, Crime and Guilt in the Individual and the Collective*, 78 NOTRE DAME L. REV. 751 (2003). Compare the opinion's reference to "victorious" rebels and Art. 10 ASR. Why did Mexico then have to assume responsibility for the acts of Villa's armed forces?

3. Is there any difference between the responsibility of a State for wrongful acts of members of its armed forces and acts of other government employees?

4. In the 1986 *Rainbow Warrior Case* (Case Concerning The Differences Between New Zealand and France Arising From the *Rainbow Warrior* Affair (N.Z. v. Fr.) 19 R.I.A.A. 199 (1986)), *infra* at 952, French security agents blew up the *Rainbow Warrior*, a Greenpeace vessel in Auckland Harbour, New Zealand. The Secretary-General of the United Nations, acting as an arbitrator, ruled that France should apologize to New Zealand for "the violation of its sovereignty and its rights under international law". *Id.* France admitted that the agents acted on orders of the French security service. Would France be responsible if the two agents had acted on their own, without the French Government's knowledge, but having used French Secret Service facilities and material for blowing up the vessel?

E. ACTS BY NON-STATE ACTORS

1. United States Diplomatic and Consular Staff in Tehran (U.S. v. Iran)

1980 I.C.J. 3 (Judgment of May 24)

[After the Iranian Revolution, on 4 November 1979, the United States Embassy compound in Tehran was overrun by an armed group of several hundred people. During the three hours or more of the assault, despite repeated calls for help from the Embassy to the Iranian Foreign Ministry, no Iranian Security Forces were sent in time to provide protection.] ...

56. [The] facts have to be looked at by the Court from two points of view. First, it must determine how far, legally, the acts in question may be regarded as imputable to the Iranian State. Secondly, it must consider their compatibility or incompatibility with the obligations of Iran under treaties in force or under any other rules of international law that may be applicable. The events which are the subject of the United States' claims fall into two phases which it will be convenient to examine separately.

57. The first of these phases covers the armed attack on the United States Embassy by militants on 4 November 1979, the overrunning of its premises, the seizure of its inmates as hostages, the appropriation of its property and archives

and the conduct of the Iranian authorities in the face of those occurrences. The attack and the subsequent overrunning, bit by bit, of the whole Embassy premises, was an operation which continued over a period of some three hours without any body of police, any military unit or any Iranian official intervening to try to stop or impede it from being carried through to its completion. The result of the attack was considerable damage to the Embassy premises and property, the forcible opening and seizure of its archives, the confiscation of the archives and other documents found in the Embassy and, most grave of all, the seizure by force of its diplomatic and consular personnel as hostages, together with two United States nationals.

58. No suggestion has been made that the militants, when they executed their attack on the Embassy, had any form of official status as recognized "agents" or organs of the Iranian State. Their conduct in mounting the attack, overrunning the Embassy and seizing its inmates as hostages cannot, therefore, be regarded as imputable to that State on that basis. Their conduct might be considered as itself directly imputable to the Iranian State only if it were established that, in fact, on the occasion in question the militants acted on behalf of the State, having been charged by some competent organ of the Iranian State to carry out a specific operation. The information before the Court does not, however, suffice to establish with the requisite certainty the existence at that time of such a link between the militants and any competent organ of the State.

59. Previously, it is true, the religious leader of the country, the Ayatollah Khomeini, had made several public declarations inveighing against the United States as responsible for all his country's problems. In so doing, it would appear, the Ayatollah Khomeini was giving utterance to the general resentment felt by supporters of the revolution at the admission of the former Shah to the United States. The information before the Court also indicates that a spokesman for the militants, in explaining their action afterwards, did expressly refer to a message issued by the Ayatollah Khomeini, on 1 November 1979. In that message the Ayatollah Khomeini had declared that it was "up to the dear pupils, students and theological students to expand with all their might their attacks against the United States and Israel, so they may force the United States to return the deposed and criminal shah, and to condemn this great plot" (that is, a plot to stir up dissension between the main streams of Islamic thought). In the view of the Court, however, it would be going too far to interpret such general declarations of the Ayatollah Khomeini to the people or students of Iran as amounting to an authorization from the State to undertake the specific operation of invading and seizing the United States Embassy. To do so would, indeed, conflict with the assertions of the militants themselves who are reported to have claimed credit for having devised and carried out the plan to occupy the Embassy. Again, congratulations after the event, such as those reportedly telephoned to the militants by the Ayatollah Khomeini on the actual evening of the attack, and other subsequent statements of official approval, though highly significant in another context shortly to

be considered, do not alter the initially independent and unofficial character of the militants' attack on the Embassy.

60. The first phase, here under examination, of the events complained of also includes the attacks on the United States Consulates at Tabriz and Shiraz. Like the attack on the Embassy, they appear to have been executed by militants not having an official character, and successful because of lack of sufficient protection.

61. The conclusion just reached by the Court, that the initiation of the attack on the United States Embassy on 4 November 1979, and of the attacks on the Consulates at Tabriz and Shiraz the following day, cannot be considered as in itself imputable to the Iranian State does not mean that Iran is, in consequence, free of any responsibility in regard to those attacks; for its own conduct was in conflict with its international obligations. By a number of provisions of the Vienna Conventions of 1961 and 1963, Iran was placed under the most categorical obligations, as a receiving State, to take appropriate steps to ensure the protection of the United States Embassy and Consulates, their staffs, their archives, their means of communication and the freedom of movement of the members of their staffs.

62. Thus, after solemnly proclaiming the inviolability of the premises of a diplomatic mission, Article 22 of the 1961 Convention continues in paragraph 2:

> *The receiving State is under a special duty to take all appropriate steps to protect the premises of the mission against any intrusion or damage and to prevent* any disturbance of the peace of the mission or impairment of its dignity. (Emphasis added.)

So, too, after proclaiming that the person of a diplomatic agent shall be inviolable, and that he shall not be liable to any form of arrest or detention, Article 29 provides:

> The receiving State shall treat him with due respect and *shall take all appropriate steps to prevent any attack on his person, freedom or dignity*. (Emphasis added.)

The obligation of a receiving State to protect the inviolability of the archives and documents of a diplomatic mission is laid down in Article 24, which specifically provides that they are to be "inviolable at any time and wherever they may be". Under Article 25 it is required to "accord full facilities for the performance of the functions of the mission", under Article 26 to "ensure to all members of the mission freedom of movement and travel in its territory", and under Article 27 to "permit and protect free communication on the part of the mission for all official purposes". Analogous provisions are to be found in the 1963 Convention regarding the privileges and immunities of consular missions and their staffs (Art. 31, para. 3, Arts. 40, 33, 28, 34 and 35). In the view of the Court, the obligations of the Iranian Government here in question are not merely contractual obligations established by the Vienna Conventions of 1961 and 1963, but also obligations under general international law.

63. The facts set out in paragraphs 14 to 27... establish to the satisfaction of the Court that on 4 November 1979 the Iranian Government failed altogether to take any "appropriate steps" to protect the premises, staff and archives of the United States' mission against attack by the militants, and to take any steps either to prevent this attack or to stop it before it reached its completion. They also show that on 5 November 1979 the Iranian Government similarly failed to take appropriate steps for the protection of the United States Consulates at Tabriz and Shiraz. In addition they show, in the opinion of the Court, that the failure of the Iranian Government to take such steps was due to more than mere negligence or lack of appropriate means.

64. The total inaction of the Iranian authorities on that date in face of urgent and repeated requests for help contrasts very sharply with its conduct on several other occasions of a similar kind. Some eight months earlier, on 14 February 1979, the United States Embassy in Tehran had itself been subjected to the armed attack mentioned above (paragraph 14), in the course of which the attackers had taken the Ambassador and his staff prisoner. On that occasion, however, a detachment of Revolutionary Guards, sent by the Government, had arrived promptly, together with a Deputy Prime Minister, and had quickly succeeded in freeing the Ambassador and his staff and restoring the Embassy to him. On 1 March 1979, moreover, the Prime Minister of Iran had sent a letter expressing deep regret at the incident, giving an assurance that appropriate arrangements had been made to prevent any repetition of such incidents, and indicating the willingness of his Government to indemnify the United States for the damage. On 1 November 1979, only three days before the events which gave rise to the present case, the Iranian police intervened quickly and effectively to protect the United States Embassy when a large crowd of demonstrators spent several hours marching up and down outside it. Furthermore, on other occasions in November 1979 and January 1980, invasions or attempted invasions of other foreign embassies in Tehran were frustrated or speedily terminated.

65. A similar pattern of facts appears in relation to consulates. In February 1979, at about the same time as the first attack on the United States Embassy, attacks were made by demonstrators on its Consulates in Tabriz and Shiraz; but the Iranian authorities then took the necessary steps to clear them of the demonstrators. On the other hand, the Iranian authorities took no action to prevent the attack of 5 November 1979, or to restore the Consulates to the possession of the United States. In contrast, when on the next day militants invaded the Iraqi Consulate in Kermanshah, prompt steps were taken by the Iranian authorities to secure their withdrawal from the Consulate. Thus in this case, the Iranian authorities and police took the necessary steps to prevent and check the attempted invasion or return the premises to their rightful owners.

66. As to the actual conduct of the Iranian authorities when faced with the events of 4 November 1979, the information before the Court establishes that, despite assurances previously given by them to the United States Government and despite repeated and urgent calls for help, they took no apparent steps either

to prevent the militants from invading the Embassy or to persuade or to compel them to withdraw. Furthermore, after the militants had forced an entry into the premises of the Embassy, the Iranian authorities made no effort to compel or even to persuade them to withdraw from the Embassy and to free the diplomatic and consular staff whom they had made prisoner.

67. This inaction of the Iranian Government by itself constituted clear and serious violation of Iran's obligations to the United States under the provisions of Article 22, paragraph 2, and Articles 24, 25, 26, 27 and 29 of the 1961 Vienna Convention on Diplomatic Relations, and Articles 5 and 36 of the 1963 Vienna Convention on Consular Relations. Similarly, with respect to the attacks on the Consulates at Tabriz and Shiraz, the inaction of the Iranian authorities entailed clear and serious breaches of its obligations under the provisions of several further articles of the 1963 Convention on Consular Relations. So far as concerns the two private United States nationals seized as hostages by the invading militants, that inaction entailed, albeit incidentally, a breach of its obligations under Article II, paragraph 4, of the 1955 Treaty of Amity, Economic Relations, and Consular Rights which, in addition to the obligations of Iran existing under general international law, requires the parties to ensure "the most constant protection and security" to each other's nationals in their respective territories.

2. Kenneth P. Yeager v. Iran

17 Iran-U.S. Cl. Trib. Rep. 92 (1987)

6. In October 1977, the Claimant was offered a job by the Bell Helicopter International Company ("BHI") to work as a Program Manager providing management, supervision and training services to the Iranian Helicopter Support and Renewal Depot at Mehrabad Airport in Tehran. The Claimant accepted the offer and departed for Iran on 6 January 1978. …

8. The Claimant alleges that, beginning in October 1978, United States citizens in Iran were subjected increasingly to harassment and violence by Iranian militants and revolutionaries. …

12. The Claimant alleges that, at about 10 a.m. on 13 February 1979, his landlord came to his apartment together with two men his landlord identified as "Revolutionary Guards". The Claimant described them as being dressed in everyday clothes, but wearing distinctive arm bands indicating association with the new Government, and armed with rifles. He asserts that these Guards announced that he and his wife had to leave on the same day, and that they had 30 minutes to pack whatever they could carry; the rest of their belongings they had to leave behind. The Claimant alleges that they were then taken by car to the Hilton Hotel in Tehran.

13. On arrival at the Hilton Hotel, the Claimant learned that the Hotel had been attacked by revolutionaries the previous day, and that it had since then been under the revolutionaries' control. The Claimant alleges that he and his wife were forced to remain inside the Hotel until 16 February 1979, as "Revolutionary

Guards" manned the exits, and that they were unable to recover property left in their apartment during that time.

14. According to the Claimant, on 17 February 1979, BHI employees were evacuated from Iran pursuant to instructions by the BHI management. They were taken to Mehrabad Airport in a convoy of buses. . . . Thereafter, Claimant left Iran on a flight to Germany. …

37. The Claimant … argues that he was expelled by "Revolutionary Guards" who forced him to leave his apartment. The Respondent asserts first that these "Revolutionary Guards" were not authentic, and second that their conduct is not attributable to Iran. In the Tribunal's view, these arguments are interrelated: in order to attribute an act to the State, it is necessary to identify with reasonable certainty the actors and their association with the State.

39. It is beyond doubt that the vast majority within the revolutionary movement supported Ayatollah Khomeini and his policies. Many of Ayatollah Khomeini's supporters were organized in local revolutionary committees, so-called Komitehs, which often emerged from the "neighborhood committees" formed before the victory of the revolution. These Komitehs served as local security forces in the immediate aftermath of the revolution. … While there were complaints about a lack of discipline among the numerous Komitehs, Ayatollah Khomeini stood behind them, and the Komitehs, in general, were loyal to him and the clergy. Soon after the victory of the Revolution, the Komitehs, contrary to other groups, obtained a firm position within the State structure and were eventually conferred a permanent place in the State budget. …

42. The question then arises whether the acts at issue are attributable to Iran under international law. While there is some doubt as to whether revolutionary "Komitehs" or "Guards" can be considered "organs" of the Government of Iran, since they were not formally recognized during the period relevant to this Case, attributability of acts to the State is not limited to acts of organs formally recognized under internal law. Otherwise a State could avoid responsibility under international law merely by invoking its internal law. It is generally accepted in international law that a State is also responsible for acts of persons, if it is established that those persons were in fact acting on behalf of the State. ... An act is attributable even if a person or group of persons was in fact merely exercising elements of governmental authority in the absence of the official authorities and in circumstances which justified the exercise of those elements of authority. …

43. The Tribunal finds sufficient evidence in the record to establish a presumption that revolutionary "Komitehs" or "Guards" after 11 February 1979 were acting in fact on behalf of the new government, or at least exercised elements of governmental authority in the absence of official authorities, in operations of which the new Government must have had knowledge and to which it did not specifically object. Under those circumstances, and for the kind of measures involved here, the Respondent has the burden of coming forward with evidence showing that members of "Komitehs" or "Guards" were in fact *not* acting on its behalf, or

were not exercising elements of government authority, or that it could not control them.

44. The Tribunal is convinced that the evacuation of BHI employees, subsequent to 12 February 1979, was controlled by revolutionary "Komitehs" or "Guards" loyal to the new government, ... and that an operation of this size and nature was known to the new government. Under those circumstances, the Respondent has failed, in the Tribunal's view, to offer satisfactory evidence that these "Komitehs" or "Guards" did not act in fact on behalf of the new government, or that they did not exercise elements of governmental authority. Rather, the evidence suggests that the new government, despite occasional complaints about a lack of discipline, stood behind them. The Tribunal is persuaded, therefore, that the revolutionary "Komitehs" or "Guards" involved in this Case, were acting "for" Iran.

45. Nor has the Respondent established that it could not control the revolutionary "Komitehs" or "Guards" in this operation. Because the new government accepted their activity in principle and their role in the maintenance of public security, calls for more discipline, phrased in general rather than specific terms, do not meet the standard of control required in order to effectively prevent those groups from committing wrongful acts against United States nationals. Under international law Iran cannot, on the one hand, tolerate the exercise of governmental authority by revolutionary "Komitehs" or "Guards" and at the same time deny responsibility for wrongful acts committed by them. On the basis of the evidence in this Case, therefore, the Tribunal finds the acts of the two men who took the Claimant to the Hilton Hotel attributable to Iran.

NOTES AND QUESTIONS

1. Did the ICJ in *U.S. Diplomatic Staff* require a formal authorization of the private actors by the state? *See* para. 59. Is *Yeager* easily subsumed under Article 9 ASR, or do other rules justify its outcome? Compare the reasoning of the ICJ in *US Diplomatic Staff* and the Tribunal in *Kenneth P. Yeager v. Iran* in attributing an act to the state. Are they compatible? Which better serves world order? *See* Alwyn V. Freeman, *Responsibility of States for Unlawful Acts of Their Armed Forces*, 88 RECUEIL DES COURS 267 (1956); IAN BROWNLIE, SYSTEM OF THE LAWS OF NATIONS: RESPONSIBILITY, Part I, 132-166 (Oxford U. Press 1983); David Caron, *The Basis of Responsibility: Attribution and Other Trans-Substantive Rules, in* THE IRAN-UNITED STATES CLAIMS TRIBUNAL: ITS CONTRIBUTION TO THE LAW OF STATE RESPONSIBILITY 109 (R. Lillich & D. Magraw eds., Transnational Publ. 1998).

2. In *Alfred Short*, Chamber Three of the Iran-U.S. Claims Tribunal, in a case concerning the forcible expulsion of the Claimant from Iran, stated that the question was whether the departure of the Claimant from Iran was "attributable to Iran, either directly or indirectly as a result of its deliberate policies, or whether they reveal a lack of due diligence in meeting Iran's international duties towards the Claimant." (para. 19) The Chamber held, by a majority vote that the act of self-appointed revolutionaries or the supporters of the revolution were insufficient to engage the responsibility of the State. Judge Brower, the American judge in the Chamber, wrote a dissenting opinion. He argued that the continuous theme of the revolution was to rid Iran completely of Americans and their influence in any form. He maintained that it would be unrealistic to view statements of the leader of the revolution as insufficient to engage state responsibility. He also argued that in considering any wrongful expulsion case such as *Alfred Short,* one must explore the:

> 23. ... relationship of the will of the Claimant to that of his American employer and the effects this relationship might have under varying hypotheses. The doctrine of wrongful expulsion is applied only in the case of natural persons. The answer as to why it never is discussed in relation to a juridical person is that such persons have access to other legal concepts which address their concrete problems in a less drastic way, or at least in a more familiar one. Thus American corporations who as a practical matter might feel that they, too, were "expelled" from Iran normally allege a breach of the contract that probably took them to Iran in the first place or an expropriation, or both. An individual who was present in Iran solely for the purpose of being employed there by such a company is not likely to have the same remedies.
>
> 24. The interposition of an individual's employer into the complex of legal relations between the host State and the individual raises particular questions. Such an employee may be dependent upon his employer for transportation out of the country and is not in a position to flee no matter how great and justified his terror at the thought of staying. That is to say, a constructive expulsion may require, for actual effectuation, an act of the employer in addition to thed: employee having drawn his justified conclusions. By the same token, an individual who himself might choose to persevere through even the worst hostility to which the succeeding revolution might subject him necessarily is prevented from doing so if his employer sees it differently and evacuates him. The question arises whether the departing employee is any less expelled in the second case than in the first. To resolve the question of expulsion in any given case ideally requires examination of the treatment to which the employer was subjected, yet the Parties here have devoted precious little time to the situation of Claimant's employer. Lockheed, even though it claims here, too, in a separate case, and the Tribunal is not thus very fully informed.

Short v. Iran, 16 Iran-U.S. Cl. Trib. Rep. 76, 97-98 (1987).

3. Military and Paramilitary Activities In and Against Nicaragua (Nicar. v. U.S.)

1986 I.C.J. 14 (June 27) (Merits)

[On 9 April 1984, Nicaragua instituted a proceeding against the United States at the International Court of Justice concerning a dispute with regard to certain military and paramilitary activities. To establish the jurisdiction of the Court, Nicaragua relied on declarations made by the Parties accepting the jurisdiction of the Court under Article 36 of the Statute. Nicaragua also relied on its 1956 Treaty of Friendship, Commerce and Navigation with the United States to establish the jurisdiction of the Court. El Salvador's request to intervene was struck down by the Court on the ground that it was unrelated to that phase of the proceedings relating to the jurisdiction of the Court. The United States challenged the jurisdiction of the Court.

By a judgment on 26 November 1984, the Court found that it had jurisdiction to entertain the application by Nicaragua on the basis of Article 36 (2) and (5) of the Court's Statute and that it had jurisdiction to entertain the application in so far as it related to a dispute concerning the interpretation or application of the Treaty of Friendship, Commerce and Navigation, on the basis of article XXIV of that treaty.

Subsequent to the fall of the Government of President Anastasio Somoza Debayle in Nicaragua in July 1979, and following his departure, a Junta of National Reconstruction and an 18-member government was installed by the Frente Sandinista de Liberacion Nacional (FSLN), the body that led the armed opposition to Somoza. That body had initially an extensive share in the new government and later became its sole component. Certain opponents of the new government primarily supporting the former Somoza government and in particular ex-members of that National Guard, formed themselves into irregular military forces, and commenced a policy of armed opposition. The United States initially had a favourable attitude to the new government and extended to it economic aid. By 1981, the U.S. had changed its attitude and suspended economic aid. The United States explained the change of attitude on the ground that the government of Nicaragua was providing logistical support including provision of arms for guerrillas in El Salvador. According to Nicaragua, as of September 1981, the United States had decided to plan and undertake activities directed against Nicaragua.

The armed opposition to the new government in Nicaragua, which originally was comprised of various movements, subsequently became organized into two main groups: Fuerza Democratica Nicaraguense (hereinafter FDN) and Alianza Revolucionaria Democratica (hereinafter ARDE). FDN grew from 1981 into a trained fighting force, operating along the boarders with Honduras; ARDE, formed in 1982, operated along the borders with Costa Rica. These opposition groups were referred to as the *contras*. Nicaragua contended that the United States effectively controlled the activities of the *contras*, and that it devised their strategy and directed their tactics to overthrow the government of Nicaragua. Nicaragua further claimed that certain military and paramilitary operations against it were carried out, not by the *contras*, who at the time claimed responsibility, but by persons in the pay of the United States Government, and under the direct command of United States personnel, who also participated to some extent in the operations, including the mining of certain Nicaraguan ports in early 1984, and attacks on ports, oil installations, a naval base, etc. Nicaragua also complained of over-flights of its territory by United States aircraft, not only for purposes of intelligence-gathering and supply to the *contras* in the field, but also in order to intimidate the population. The United States also withdrew economic aid from Nicaragua and drastically reduced the quota for imports of sugar from Nicaragua and imposed a trade embargo on it.

Nicaragua claimed that the United States acted *inter alia*, in violation of Article 2, paragraph 4 of the United Nations Charter, and of a customary international law obligation to refrain from the threat or use of force; that its actions amount to intervention in the internal affairs of Nicaragua, in breach of the Charter of the Organization of American States and of the rule of customary international law forbidding intervention.

The United States did not appear before the Court on the merits, but in its Counter-Memorial on the questions of jurisdiction and admissibility stated that "by providing, upon request, proportionate and appropriate assistance to third States not before the Court" it claims to be acting in reliance on the inherent right of self-defence "guaranteed ... by Article 51 of the Charter" of the United Nations, that is to say the right of collective self-defence.] ...

109. What the Court has to determine at this point is whether or not the relationship of the contras to the United States Government was so much one of dependence on the one side and control on the other that it would be right to equate the *contras*, for legal purposes, with an organ of the United States Government, or as acting on behalf of that Government. Here it is relevant to note that in May 1983 the assessment of the Intelligence Committee, in the Report referred to in paragraph 95 above [Report of the Permanent Select Committee on Intelligence of the House of Representatives], was that the contras "constitute[d] an independent force" and that the "only element of control that could be exercised by the United States" was "cessation of aid". Paradoxically this assessment serves to underline, *a contrario*, the potential for control inherent in the degree of the *contras*' dependence on aid. Yet despite the heavy subsides and other support provided to them by the United States, there is no clear evidence of the United States having actually exercised such a degree of control in all fields as to justify treating the *contras* as acting on its behalf. ...

113. The question of the degree of control of the *contras* by the United States Government is relevant to the claim of Nicaragua attributing responsibility to the United States for activities of the contras whereby the United States has, it is alleged, violated an obligation of international law not to kill, wound or kidnap citizens of Nicaragua. The activities in question are said to represent a tactic which includes "the spreading of terror and danger to non-combatants as an end in itself with no attempt to observe humanitarian standards and no reference to the concept of military necessity". In support of this, Nicaragua has catalogued numerous incidents, attributed to "CIA-trained mercenaries" or "mercenary forces", of kidnapping, assassination, torture, rape, killing of prisoners, and killing of civilians not dictated by military necessity. The declaration of Commander Carrion annexed to the Memorial lists the first such incident in December 1981, and continues up to the end of 1984. Two of the witnesses called by Nicaragua (Father Loison and Mr. Glennon) gave oral evidence as to events of this kind. By way of examples of evidence to provide "direct proof of the tactics adopted by the contras under United States guidance and control", the Memorial of Nicaragua offers a statement, reported in the press, by the ex-FDN leader Mr. Edgar Chamorro, repeated in the latter's affidavit, of assassinations in Nicaraguan villages; the alleged existence of a classified Defence Intelligence Agency report of July 1982, reported in the New York Times on 21 October 1984, disclosing that the contras were carrying out assassinations; and the preparation by the CIA in 1983 of a manual of psychological warfare. At the hearings, reliance was also placed on the affidavit of Mr. Chamorro.

114. In this respect, the Court notes that according to Nicaragua, the contras are no more than bands of mercenaries which have been recruited, organized, paid and commanded by the Government of the United States. This would mean that they have no real autonomy in relation to that Government. Consequently,

any offences which they have committed would be imputable to the Government of the United States, like those of any other forces placed under the latter's command. In the view of Nicaragua, "*stricto sensu*, the military and paramilitary attacks launched by the United States against Nicaragua do not constitute a case of civil strife. They are essentially the acts of the United States." If such a finding of the imputability of the acts of the contras to the United States were to be made, no question would arise of mere complicity in those acts, or of incitement of the contras to commit them.

115. The Court has taken the view ... that United States participation, even if preponderant or decisive in the financing, organizing, training, supplying and equipping of the *contras*, the selection of its military or paramilitary targets, and the planning of the whole of its operation, is still insufficient in itself, on the basis of the evidence in the possession of the Court, for the purpose of attributing to the United States the acts committed by the *contras* in the course of their military or paramilitary operations in Nicaragua. All the forms of United States participation mentioned above, and even the general control by the respondent State over a force with a high degree of dependency on it, would not in themselves mean, without further evidence, that the United States directed or enforced the perpetration of the acts contrary to human rights and humanitarian law alleged by the applicant State. Such acts could well be committed by members of the contras without the control of the United States. For this conduct to give rise to legal responsibility of the United States, it would in principle have to be proved that that State had effective control of the military or paramilitary operations in the course of which the alleged violations were committed.

116. The Court does not consider that the assistance given by the United States to the *contras* warrants the conclusion that these forces are subject to the United States to such an extent that any acts they have committed are imputable to that State. It takes the view that the *contras* remain responsible for their acts, and that the United States is not responsible for the acts of the *contras*, but for its own conduct vis-à-vis Nicaragua, including conduct related to the acts of the *contras*. What the Court has to investigate is not the complaints relating to alleged violations of humanitarian law by the *contras*, regarded by Nicaragua as imputable to the United States, but rather unlawful acts for which the United States may be responsible directly in connection with the activities of the *contras*. The lawfulness or otherwise of such acts of the United States is a question different from the violations of humanitarian law of which the contras may or may not have been guilty. It is for this reason that the Court does not have to determine whether the violations of humanitarian law attributed to the *contras* were in fact committed by them. At the same time, the question whether the United States Government was, or must have been, aware at the relevant time that allegations of breaches of humanitarian law were being made against the *contras* is relevant to an assessment of the lawfulness of the action of the United States. In this respect, the material facts are primarily those connected with the issue in 1983 of a manual of psychological operations.

117. Nicaragua has in fact produced in evidence before the Court two publications which it claims were prepared by the CIA and supplied to the contras in 1983. The first of these, in Spanish, is entitled "Operaciones sicologicas en guerra de guerrillas" (Psychological Operations in Guerrilla Warfare), by "Tayacan"; the certified copy supplied to the Court carries no publishers name or date. In its Preface, the publication is described as "a manual for the training of guerrillas in psychological operations, and its application to the concrete case of the Christian and democratic crusade being waged in Nicaragua by the Freedom Commandos". The second is entitled the Freedom Fighter's Manual, with the subtitle "Practical guide to liberating Nicaragua from oppression and misery by paralyzing the military-industrial complex of the traitorous marxist state without having to use special tools and with minimal risk for the combatant". The text is printed in English and Spanish, and illustrated with simple drawings: it consists of guidance for elementary sabotage techniques. The only indications available to the Court of its authorship are reports in the New York Times, quoting a United States Congressman and Mr. Edgar Chamorro as attributing the book to the CIA. Since the evidence linking the Freedom Fighter's Manual to the CIA is no more than newspaper reports the Court will not treat its publication as an act imputable to the United States Government for the purposes of the present case.

118. The Court will therefore concentrate its attention on the other manual, that on "Psychological Operations". That this latter manual was prepared by the CIA appears to be clearly established: a report published in January 1985 by the Intelligence Committee contains a specific statement to that effect. It appears from this report that the manual was printed in several editions; only one has been produced and it is of that text that the Court will take account. The manual is devoted to techniques for winning the minds of the population, defined as including the guerrilla troops, the enemy troops and the civilian population. In general, such parts of the manual as are devoted to military rather than political and ideological matters are not in conflict with general humanitarian law; but there are marked exceptions. A section on "Implicit and Explicit Terror", while emphasizing that "the guerrillas should be careful not to become an explicit terror, because this would result in a loss of popular support", and stressing the need for good conduct toward the population, also includes directions to destroy military or police installations, cut lines of communication, kidnap officials of the Sandinista government, etc. Reference is made to the possibility that "it should be necessary … to fire on a citizen who was trying to leave the town", to be justified by the risk of his informing the enemy. Furthermore, a section on "Selective Use of Violence for Propagandistic Effects" begins with the words:

> It is possible to neutralize carefully selected and planned targets, such as court judges, mesta judges, police and State Security officials, CDS chiefs, etc. For psychological purposes it is necessary to take extreme precautions, and it is absolutely necessary to gather together the population affected, so that they will be present, take part in the act, and formulate accusations against the oppressor.

In a later section on "Control of mass concentrations and meetings", the following guidance is given (*inter alia*):

> If possible, professional criminals will be hired to carry out special selective jobs'. ... Specific tasks will be assigned to others, in order to create a 'martyr' for the cause, taking the demonstrators to a confrontation with the authorities, in order to bring about uprisings or shootings, which will cause the death of one or more persons, who would become the martyrs, a situation that should be made use of immediately against the regime, in order to create greater conflicts. ...

186. It is not to be expected that in the practice of States the application of the rules in question should have been perfect, in the sense that States should have refrained, with complete consistency, from the use of force or from intervention in each other's internal affairs. The Court does not consider that, for a rule to be established as customary, the corresponding practice must be in absolutely rigorous conformity with the rule. In order to deduce the existence of customary rules, the Court deems it sufficient that the conduct of States should, in general, be consistent with such rules, and that instances of State conduct inconsistent with a given rule should generally have been treated as breaches of that rule, not as indications of the recognition of a new rule. If a State acts in a way prima facie incompatible with a recognized rule, but defends its conduct by appealing to exceptions or justifications contained within the rule itself, then whether or not the State's conduct is in fact justifiable on that basis, the significance of that attitude is to confirm rather than to weaken the rule. ...

226. The Court, having outlined both the facts of the case as proved by the evidence before it, and the general rules of international law, which appear to it to be in issue as a result of these facts, and the applicable treaty-law, has now to appraise the facts in relation to the legal rules applicable. In so far as acts of the Respondent may appear to constitute violations of the relevant rules of law, the Court will then have to determine whether there are present any circumstances excluding unlawfulness, or whether such acts may be justified upon any other ground. ...

283. The third submission of Nicaragua in its Memorial on the merits, set out in paragraph 15 above, requests the Court to adjudge and declare that compensation is due to Nicaragua and "to receive evidence and to determine, in a subsequent phase of the present proceedings, the quantum of damages to be assessed as the compensation due to the Republic of Nicaragua." The fourth submission requests the Court to award to Nicaragua the sum of 370,200,000 United States dollars, "which sum constitutes the minimum valuation of the direct damages" claimed by Nicaragua. In order to decide on these submissions, the Court must satisfy itself that it possesses jurisdiction to do so. In general, jurisdiction to determine the merits of a dispute entails jurisdiction to determine reparation. More specifically, the Court notes that in its declaration of acceptance of jurisdiction under the Optional Clause of 26 August 1946, the United States expressly ac-

cepted the Court's jurisdiction in respect of disputes concerning "the nature or extent of the reparation to be made for the breach of an international obligation". The corresponding declaration by which Nicaragua accepted the Court's jurisdiction contains no restriction of the powers of the Court under Article 36, paragraph 2 (d), of its Statute; Nicaragua has thus accepted the "same obligation". Under the 1956 FCN Treaty, the Court has jurisdiction to determine "any dispute between the Parties as to the interpretation or application of the present Treaty" (Art. XXIV, para. 2); and as the Permanent Court of International Justice stated in the case concerning the *Factory at Chorzów*,

> Differences relating to reparations, which may be due by reason of failure to apply a convention, are consequently differences relating to its application. (*The Factory at Chorzów* (Ger. v. Pol.), 1927 P.C.I.J. (ser. A) No. 9, at 21.) ...

Notes and Questions

1. What is the degree of control that must be exercised by a state in order for the act to be attributable to it?

2. The Nicaragua judgment is seen as applying an exacting effective control test to the issue of attribution of the acts of insurgents to a supporting state. At the end of para. 115, the Court required that it would "in principle have to be proved that that State had effective control of the military or paramilitary operations in the course of which the alleged violations were committed."

3. In the same opinion, the ICJ rejected the United States' claim of collective self-defence in support of El Salvador fending off a Nicaragua-backed rebellion by the Farabundo Marti National Liberation Front. Would the Court have had to accept the U.S. claim if it had used a lower threshold of attribution?

4. The Appeals Chamber of the International Criminal Tribunal for the Former Yugoslavia (ICTY) rejected the approach taken by the ICJ in the Nicaragua case. In *Prosecutor v. Tadic*, the Tribunal held:

> 117. The principles of international law concerning the attribution to States of acts performed by private individuals are not based on rigid and uniform criteria. ... In other words, States are not allowed on the one hand to act *de facto* through individuals and on the other to disassociate themselves from such conduct when these individuals breach international law. The requirement of international law for the attribution to States of acts performed by private individuals is that the State exercises control over the individuals. The *degree of control* may, however, vary according to the factual circumstances of each case. The Appeals Chamber fails to see why in each and every circumstance international law should require a high threshold for the test of control. Rather, various situations may be distinguished."

Prosecutor v. Tadic, 38 I.L.M. 1518 (ICTY 1999).

Do you agree with the analysis of the Appeals Chamber of the ICTY? What are the implications of the tests set out by the Appeals Chamber as opposed to the ones set out by the ICJ in the Nicaragua case? In your view which ones are more persuasive?

5. Does Article 8 ASR lean more toward the "effective control" test of *Nicaragua* or more toward the "overall control" criterion of *Tadic*?

F. Conduct Adopted by a State as its Own

1. X. & Y. v. Switzerland

App. No. 1289/75 and 7349/76,
1977 Y.B. Eur. Conv. on H.R. (Eur. Comm'n on H.R) 372, 402-406

[Applicants, a German and an Austrian, complained to the European Commission of Human Rights for alleged violation of the European Convention of Human Rights by Switzerland because of denial by the Swiss police of one of the applicant's entry into Liechtenstein. At that time, Liechtenstein was not party to the Convention while Switzerland was. By an agreement between the two countries, Switzerland exercised Swiss customs and immigration in Liechtenstein. The issue was whether Switzerland's exercise of its customs and immigration in Liechtenstein with the consent of that state should be considered as conduct of Liechtenstein and not of Switzerland. The European Commission of Human Rights held:]

... [T]he responsibility of Switzerland under the Convention can only be engaged if the measures of which the applicants complain are imputable to Switzerland rather than to Liechtenstein.

Liechtenstein is a sovereign State which has not ratified the Convention. It is clear that the Convention is not binding upon the Liechtenstein authorities themselves.

In the present case, however, it is exclusively the Swiss authorities which have acted, although with effect in the territory of Liechtenstein.

The Swiss authorities exercised their functions on the basis of the treaty relationship between the two countries.

The basic instrument is the treaty of 1923 concerning the inclusion of Liechtenstein within the Swiss customs area. Art. 33 (I) of this treaty provides that Switzerland waives the control of foreigners on the Swiss-Liechtenstein border while Liechtenstein undertakes to ensure that the Swiss regulations on aliens are not circumvented on its territory.

This treaty provision has been implemented by successive agreements on the exercise of the aliens' police in Liechtenstein. The two agreements at present in force date from 1963. One of them concerns the treatment of the citizens of each of the Contracting States in the territory of the other. It has no relevance to the present case as neither applicant possesses the nationality of the Contracting States. The second agreement, which has been applied in the present case, concerns the exercise of the aliens' police in respect of third-country nationals in Liechtenstein, and Swiss-Liechtenstein co-operation in matters of the aliens' police.

This agreement provides the following:

(a) The Swiss laws and decrees (*Erlasse*) concerning the entry, exit, residence and establishment of foreigners are in principle applicable with regard to third country nationals in Liechtenstein (Art. I (I) 1st sentence).

(b) The administration of these matters is in principle entrusted to the Swiss Federal authorities. The authorities of Liechtenstein have only the powers and functions of the corresponding authorities of a Swiss canton in this respect (Art. I (I) 2nd sentence).

(c) Expulsions and restrictions or prohibitions of entry pronounced for the whole of Switzerland have automatically effect in Liechtenstein. This effect can be excluded by a special decision of the Swiss aliens' police. The Liechtenstein authorities themselves cannot derogate from such a measure pronounced by the competent Swiss authority (Art. 3).

(d) The Liechtenstein authorities have, however, reserved certain functions of the aliens' police. They can e.g. expel a person from Liechtenstein territory alone (with no effect for Swiss territory) (Art. 2 (b) of the agreement), and they are not under an obligation to admit or tolerate a third-country national on their territory although he has been admitted to Switzerland (Art. 2 (c)).

What matters in the Commission's opinion is the circumstance that according to the system established by the above agreement a prohibition of entry pronounced by the Swiss authorities while producing its effect first of all in Swiss territory is automatically extended to Liechtenstein by virtue of Article 3 of the agreement and the Liechtenstein authorities themselves have no possibility to exclude this effect. On the contrary, the exclusion of Liechtenstein from the territorial application of a prohibition of entry is expressly reserved to the Swiss authority.

Switzerland is certainly responsible, under Art. I of the Convention, for the procedure and for the effect which the prohibition of entry produced in its own territory. But it must also held responsible insofar as the prohibition of entry produced an effect in Liechtenstein. According to the special treaty relationship existing between Switzerland and Liechtenstein Swiss authorities when acting for Liechtenstein do not act in distinction from their national competences. In fact on the basis of the treaty they act exclusively in conformity with Swiss law and it is only the effect of this act which is extended to Liechtenstein territory. That means that it was Swiss jurisdiction which was used and extended to Liechtenstein. Acts by Swiss authorities with effect in Liechtenstein bring all those to whom they apply under Swiss jurisdiction within the meaning of Art. I of the Convention.

It follows that the present applications are not *ratione personae* incompatible with the provisions of the Convention.

The Commission therefore considers that it is fully competent *ratione loci* and *ratione personae* to deal with the applications. …

2. United States Diplomatic and Consular Staff in Tehran (U.S. v. Iran)

1980 I.C.J. 3, 33-35 (Judgment of June 24)

71. … [E]xpressions of approval of the take-over of the Embassy, and indeed also of the Consulates at Tabriz and Shiraz, by militants came immediately from numerous Iranian authorities, including religious, judicial, executive, police and broadcasting authorities. Above all, the Ayatollah Khomeini himself made crystal clear the endorsement by the State both of the take-over of the Embassy and Consulates and of the detention of the Embassy staff as hostages. At a reception in Qom on 5 November, the Ayatollah Khomeini left his audience in no doubt as to his approval of the action of the militants in occupying the Embassy, to which he said they had resorted 'because they saw that the shah was allowed in America'. Saying that he had been informed that the 'centre occupied by our young men . . . has been a lair of espionage and plotting', he asked how the young people could be expected 'simply to remain idle and witness all these things'. Furthermore he expressly stigmatized as 'rotten roots' those in Iran who were 'hoping we would mediate and tell the young people to leave this place'. The Ayatollah's refusal to order 'the young people' to put an end to their occupation of the Embassy, or the militants in Tabriz and Shiraz to evacuate the United States Consulates there, must have appeared the more significant when, on 6 November, he instructed 'the young people' who had occupied the Iraqi Consulate in Kermanshah that they should leave it as soon as possible. The true significance of this was only reinforced when, next day, he expressly forbade members of the Revolutionary Council and all responsible officials to meet the special representatives sent by President Carter to try and obtain the release of the hostages and evacuation of the Embassy. …

73. The seal of official government approval was finally set on this situation by a decree issued on 17 November 1979 by the Ayatollah Khomeini. His decree began with the assertion that the American Embassy was 'a centre of espionage and conspiracy' and that 'those people who hatched plots against our Islamic movement in that place do not enjoy international diplomatic respect'. He went on expressly to declare that the premises of the Embassy and the hostages would remain as they were until the United States had handed over the former Shah for trial and returned his property to Iran. This statement of policy the Ayatollah qualified only to the extent of requesting the militants holding the hostages to 'hand over the blacks and the women, if it is proven that they did not spy, to the Ministry of Foreign Affairs so that they may be immediately expelled from Iran'. As to the rest of the hostages, he made the Iranian Government's intentions all too clear 'The noble Iranian nation will not give permission for the release of the rest of them. Therefore, the rest of them will be under arrest until the American Government acts according to the wish of the nation.'

74. The policy thus announced by the Ayatollah Khomeini, of maintaining the occupation of the Embassay and the detention of its inmates as hostages for the purpose of exerting pressure on the United States Government was complied with by other Iranian authorities and endorsed by them repeatedly in statements made in various contexts. The result of that policy was fundamentally to transform the legal nature of the situation created by the occupation of the Embassy and the detention of its diplomatic and consular staff as hostages. The approval given to these facts by the Ayatollah Khomeini and other organs of the Iranian State, and the decision to perpetuate them, translated continuing occupation of the Embassy and detention of the hostages into acts of that State. The militants, authors of the invasion and jailers of the hostages, had now become agents of the Iranian State for whose acts the State itself was internationally responsible. On 6 May 1980, the Minister for Foreign Affairs, Mr. Ghotbzadeh, is reported to have said in a television interview that the occupation of the United States Embassy had been 'done by our nation'.

NOTES AND QUESTIONS

1. Could Switzerland's responsibility now be based on Articles 4, 5, 6 or 11 ASR?

2. What distinguishes Ayatollah Khomeini's statements before and during the seizure of the embassy from those held to be adopting the students' illegal conduct? *See* Art. 11 ASR.

G. RESPONSIBILITY OF A STATE FOR THE WRONGFUL ACT OF ANOTHER STATE

1. Robert E. Brown Case (U.S. v. Gr. Brit.)

6 R.I.A.A. 120 (1923)

The United States claims £330,000, with interest, from Great Britain on account of the alleged denial of certain real property rights contended to have been acquired in 1895, by one Robert E. Brown in the territory of the South African Republic which was conquered and annexed by Great Britain on September 1, 1900.

[The British Government denied any responsibility for the denial of justice suffered by Mr. Brown in the hands of the South African government. The Tribunal held:]

[T] his liability [for denial of justice] never passed to or was assumed by the British Government. Neither in the terms of peace granted at the time of the surrender of the Boer Forces … nor in the Proclamation of Annexation … can there be found any provision referring to the assumption of liabilities of this nature. It should be borne in mind that this was simply a pending claim for damages against certain officials and had never become a liquidated debt of the former State. Nor is there, properly speaking, any question of State succession here involved. The United States plants itself squarely on two propositions: first, that the British Government, by the acts of its own officials with respect to Brown's case, has become liable to him; and, secondly, that in some way a liability was imposed upon the British Government by reason of the peculiar relation of suzerainty which is maintained with respect to the South African Republic.

The first of these contentions is set forth in the reply as follows:

> The United States reaffirms that Brown suffered a denial of justice at the hands of authorities of the South African Republic. Had it not been for this denial of justice, it may be assumed that a diplomatic claim would not have arisen. But it does not follow that, as is contended in His Majesty's Government's answer, it is incumbent on the United States to show that there is a rule of international law imposing liability on His Majesty's Government for the tortious acts of the South African Republic. Occurrences which took place during the existence of the South African Republic are obviously relevant and important in connexion with the case before the Tribunal, but the United States contends that acts of the British Government and of British officials and the general position taken by them with respect to Brown's case have fixed liability on His Majesty's Government.
>
> ... We have searched the record for any indication that the British authorities did more than leave this matter exactly where it stood when annexation took place. They did not redress the wrong which had been committed nor did they place any obstacles in Brown's path; they took no action one way or the other. No British official nor any British court undertook to deny Brown justice or to perpetuate the wrong. The Attorney General of the Colony, in his opinion, declared that the courts were still open to the claimant. The contention of the American Agent amounts to an assertion that a succeeding State acquiring a territory by conquest without any undertaking to assume such liabilities is bound to take affirmative steps to right the wrongs done by the former State. We cannot indorse this doctrine.

The point as to suzerainty is likewise not well taken. It is not necessary to trace the vicissitudes of the South African State in its relation to the British Crown, from the Sand River Convention of 1852, through the annexation of 1877, the Pretoria Convention of 1881, and the London Convention of 1884, to the definitive annexation in 1900. We may grant that a special relation between Great Britain and the South African State, varying considerably in its scope and significance from time to time, existed from the beginning. No doubt Great Britain's position in South Africa imposed upon her a peculiar status and responsibility. She repeatedly declared and asserted her authority as the so-called paramount Power in the region; but the authority which she exerted over the South African Republic certainly at the time of the occurrences here under consideration, in our judgment fell far short of what would be required to make her responsible for the wrong inflicted upon Brown. Concededly, the general relation of suzerainty created by the Pretoria Convention of 1881 ... survived after the concluding of the London Convention of 1884. ... Nevertheless, the specific authority of the suzerain power was materially changed, and under the 1884 Convention it is plain that Great Britain as suzerain, reserved only a qualified control over the relations of the South African Republic with foreign powers. The Republic agreed to conclude no "treaty or engagement" with any State or nation other than the Orange Free State, without the approval of Great Britain, but such approval was to be taken for granted if the latter did not give notice that the treaty was in conflict with British interests within six months after it was brought to the attention of Her Majesty's Government. Nowhere is there any clause indicating that Great Britain had any right to interest herself in the internal administration of the country, legislative, executive or judicial; nor is there any evidence that Great Britain ever did undertake to interfere in this way. Indeed, the only remedy which Great Britain ever had for maladministration affecting British subjects and those of other Powers residing in the South African Republic was, as the event proved, the resort to war. If there had been no South African war, we hold that the United States Government would have been obliged to take up Brown's claim with the Government of the Republic and that there would have been no ground for bringing it to the attention of Great Britain. The relation of suzerain did not operate to render Great Britain liable for the acts complained of.

2. 1 Georg Schwarzenberger, International Law
624 (3d ed., Stevens & Sons 1957)

International responsibility for dependent States which have maintained a modicum of international personality cannot possibly rest on the agency established between the protecting power and the protected State. In relation to third powers, this is *res inter alios acta.* In any case, even if such an agency were *opposable* to third States, it would be possible to establish on this basis responsibility only of the principal for the agent, that is to say, of the protected State for the protecting power.

In fact, third States are not interested in any vicarious responsibility of this kind, but in holding protecting or administering powers responsible for acts and omissions in areas to which they have international access only through such powers. Their international responsibility is one of the implications of the acts of recognition, consent or acquiescence by which third States make such an agency *opposable* to themselves. To the extent to which they accept this position, they treat protecting powers, or States in similar positions, as if they were sovereign in the area in question. Correspondingly, such States are estopped from denying their international responsibility. They must allow themselves to be treated as if international illegal acts and omissions relating to such areas were attributable to themselves: "As in relation to third States, the situation of the protecting power is the same as that of a sovereign State, its responsibility must be the same."

Conversely, to the extent to which a dependent State maintains its own international personality in relation to third States, no scope for such "derivative" responsibility exists. *Pro tanto,* the dependent State remains internationally responsible for any illegal acts and omissions as are attributable to it. Thus, in the *Brown* Claim (1923), the British-United States Claims Arbitral Tribunal established that British suzerainty over the South African Republic before the Boer War did not extend to the internal affairs of the Republic. If the Republic had survived, international claims on matters within its exclusive jurisdiction could have been addressed only to the Republic, and not to Great Britain.

Notes and Questions

1. Compare the decision in *Brown* with Max Huber's report in *British Claims in the Spanish Zone of Morocco, supra*, at 907. What distinguishes the role of the British as suzerain from the role of the Spanish as protecting power?

H. Complicity and Coercion

1. ILC Report 2001: Arts. 16-19 ASR

Article 16: *Aid or assistance in the commission of an internationally wrongful act*

A State which aids or assists another State in the commission of an internationally wrongful act by the latter is internationally responsible for doing so if:

(a) That State does so with knowledge of the circumstances of the internationally wrongful act; and

(b) The act would be internationally wrongful if committed by that State.

Article 17: *Direction and control exercised over the commission of an internationally wrongful act*

A State which directs and controls another State in the commission of an internationally wrongful act by the latter is internationally responsible for that act if:

(a) That State does so with knowledge of the circumstances of the internationally wrongful act; and

(b) The act would be internationally wrongful if committed by that State.

Article 18: *Coercion of another State*

A State which coerces another State to commit an act is internationally responsible for that act if:

(a) The act would, but for the coercion, be an internationally wrongful act of the coerced State; and

(b) The coercing State does so with knowledge of the circumstances of the act.

Article 19: *Effect of this chapter*

This chapter is without prejudice to the international responsibility, under other provisions of these articles, of the State which commits the act in question, or of any other State.

2. ILC Report 2001: Related Commentaries

[Commentary to Chapter IV of Part One]

(5) … [T[here may be cases where conduct of the organ of one State, not acting as an organ or agent of another State, is nonetheless chargeable to the latter State, and this may be so even though the wrongfulness of the conduct lies, or at any rate primarily lies, in a breach of the international obligations of the former. …

(9) …The incitement of wrongful conduct is generally not regarded as sufficient to give rise to responsibility on the part of the inciting State, if it is not accompanied by concrete support or does not involve direction and control on the part of the inciting State. However, there can be specific treaty obligations prohibiting incitement under certain circumstances. Another concerns the issue which is described in some systems of internal law as being an "accessory after the fact". It seems that there is no general obligation on the part of third States to cooperate in suppressing internationally wrongful conduct of another State which may already have occurred. Again it is a matter for specific treaty obligations to establish any such obligation of suppression after the event. There are, however, two important qualifications here. First, in some circumstances assistance given by one State to another after the latter has committed an internationally wrongful act may amount to the adoption of that act by the former State. … Secondly, special obligations of cooperation in putting an end to an unlawful situation arise in the case of serious breaches of obligations under peremptory norms of general international law. By definition, in such cases States will have agreed that no derogation from such obligations is to be permitted and, faced with a serious breach of such an obligation, certain obligations of cooperation arise…

[Commentary to article 16]

(3) Article 16 limits the scope of responsibility for aid or assistance in three ways. First, the relevant State organ or agency providing aid or assistance must be aware of the circumstances making the conduct of the assisted State internationally wrongful; secondly, the aid or assistance must be given with a view to facilitating the commission of that act, and must actually do so; and thirdly, the completed act must be such that it would have been wrongful had it been committed by the assisting State itself. …

[Commentary to article 17]

(4) … [R]elationships of dependency, such as dependent territories fall entirely outside the scope of article 17, which is concerned only with the responsibility of one State for the conduct of another State. In most relationships of dependency between one territory and another, the dependent territory, even if it may possess some international personality, is not a State. Even in cases where a component unit of a federal State enters into treaties or other international legal relations in its own right, and not by delegation from the federal State, the compo-

nent unit is not itself a State in international law. So far as State responsibility is concerned, the position of federal States is no different from that of any other States: the normal principles specified in articles 4 to 9 of the draft articles apply, and the federal State is internationally responsible for the conduct of its component units even though that conduct falls within their own local control under the federal constitution.

(5) Nonetheless, instances exist or can be envisaged where one State exercises the power to direct and control the activities of another State, whether by treaty or as a result of a military occupation or for some other reason. …

(7) In the formulation of article 17, the term "controls" refers to cases of domination over the commission of wrongful conduct and not simply the exercise of oversight, still less mere influence or concern. Similarly, the word "directs" does not encompass mere incitement or suggestion but rather connotes actual direction of an operative kind. Both direction and control must be exercised over the wrongful conduct in order for a dominant State to incur responsibility. …

(8) … [T]he dominant State is only responsible if it has knowledge of the circumstances making the conduct of the dependent State wrongful. … [It also] has to be shown that the completed act would have been wrongful had it been committed by the directing and controlling State itself. This condition is significant in the context of bilateral obligations, which are not opposable to the directing State. In cases of multilateral obligations and especially of obligations to the international community, it is of much less significance. The essential principle is that a State should not be able to do through another what it could not do itself.

(9) … The defence of "superior orders" does not exist for States in international law. … Conversely it is no excuse for the directing State to show that the directed State was a willing or even enthusiastic participant in the internationally wrongful conduct, if in truth the conditions laid down in article 17 are met.

[Commentary to article 18]

(1) … Article 18 is concerned with the specific problem of coercion deliberately exercised in order to procure the breach of one State's obligation to a third State. In such cases the responsibility of the coercing State with respect to the third State derives not from its act of coercion, but rather from the wrongful conduct resulting from the action of the coerced State. …

(6) A State which sets out to procure by coercion a breach of another State's obligations to a third State will be held responsible to the third State for the consequences, regardless of whether the coercing State is also bound by the obligation in question. …

Notes and Questions

1. The notion of the responsibility of a State for the breach of an obligation of another State to which the former State acted as an accomplice or aided or assisted or coerced the other state is relatively new. While there have been claims to that effect, they were denied by the State that was

accused. During the Iran-Iraq war, Iran accused the United Kingdom of supplying Iraq with weapons including chemical weapons. The United Kingdom rejected the accusation. N.Y. TIMES, March 5, 1984, p. A1, col. 1 and March 6, 1984, p. A3, col. 1. A similar accusation was made by Libya against the United Kingdom for having allowed its airfield to be used by American airplanes which bombed Tripoli in 1986. The United Kingdom asserted that the bombing by the United States was an act of lawful self-defense. *See* U.S. Dep't of State Bulletin, No. 2111, June 1986, p.8 and 57 BRIT. YB. INT'L L. 638 (1986).

2. Similarly with regard to coercion, while there have been a few incidents, there have been no formal claims. An early example cited as such is the termination of the employment by the Persian government in 1911 of Morgan Shuster, an American who was hired for a period of 3 years by Persia on the recommendation of the American government in order to advise the Persian government as Treasurer-General on economic matters. The Russian government, which was unhappy with the possible American influence in Persia, intervened militarily in Persia, effectively overthrowing the constitutional government and forcing Persia to terminate Morgan Shuster's contract. Clement L. Bouve, *Russia's Liability in Tort for Persia's Breach Contract*, 6 AM. J. INT'L L. 389 (1912).

3. In another incident, shortly after Romania entered World War I in 1916, the British and other allied governments, in anticipation of an invasion of Romania by Germany, agreed with Romania to destroy Romanian oil properties and its large supplies of oil and grain to prevent Germany from gaining access to them. Among the property destroyed was that of Romano-Americana, a subsidiary of the Standard Oil Corp. The United States demanded compensation from the United Kingdom on the ground that:

> The work of destruction was thus an essentially British war measure carried out pursuant to the deliberate British policy under British direction on Roumanian soil. It reveals a situation where a strong belligerent for a purpose primarily its own arising from its defensive requirements at sea, compelled a weaker Ally to acquiesce in an operation which it carried out on the territory of that Ally. Instead of placing an efficient weapons of destruction at the disposal or Roumania, Great Britain itself made use of that weapon on Roumanian soil and compelled Roumania to yield consent. From the consent no freedom from responsibility was attained by the primary actor.

While the British admitted that the destruction was encouraged by the Allies, it contended that it was carried out on Romanian soil on the order of that government by individuals acting on behalf of and in cooperation with its military authorities. Britain also admitted that the Allies agreed to compensate Romania for any loss which it might sustain as a result of the destruction. Ultimately Standard Oil settled its claim by accepting an offer of compensation by the Romanian government. (GREEN HACKWORTH, DIGEST OF INTERNATIONAL LAW, vol. V, pp. 702-705)

4. In 1952 when France held a protectorate over Morocco, it instituted proceedings against the United States before the ICJ (*Case Concerning Rights of Nationals of the United States in Morocco* (*Fr. v. U.S.*), 1952 I.C.J. 176 (Aug. 27)), with respect to certain rights granted to the United States in a treaty of 1836 between Morocco and the United States. The United States raised a preliminary objection on the grounds that the judgment could not bind Morocco, which was not a party to the dispute. France confirmed that it was acting also as the protecting power of Morocco and that the judgment would be binding on them both. The Court relied on that understanding and proceeded with the case. Compare this case with *Robert E. Brown, supra,* and the ASR. Do the latter apply?

5. Assume that after the Iraq war of 2003, the United States and the United Kingdom, as occupying powers, ask the transitional authority of Iraq to terminate a number of contracts that were concluded during the Saddam Hussein regime with French, German and Russian companies so that it can conclude contracts on better terms for Iraq with other contractors. Is there any responsibility on the part of the United States or the United Kingdom for such termination of contracts? Assume that in the same situation, the transitional authority in Iraq in the absence of any request

from either the United States of the United Kingdom terminates contracts with French, German and Russian companies, knowing that such terminations would please the occupying powers. How is responsibility allocated? Consider the relevant provisions of the ASR.

6. *See also,* IAN BROWNLIE, SYSTEM OF LAW OF NATIONS: STATE RESPONSIBILITY (PART I) 189-92 (1983), and John Quigley, *Complicity in International Law: A New Direction in the Law of State Responsibility*, 57 BRIT. YB. INT'L L. 77 (1986).

IV. CIRCUMSTANCES PRECLUDING WRONGFULNES

Circumstances precluding wrongfulness are to be distinguished from other arguments which may have the effect of allowing a State to avoid responsibility. They have nothing to do with questions of the jurisdiction of a court or tribunal over a dispute or the admissibility of a claim. They are to be distinguished from the constituent requirements of the obligation, i.e., those elements which have to exist for the issue of wrongfulness to arise in the first place and which are in principle specified by the obligation itself. In this sense the circumstances precluding wrongfulness operate like defences or excuses in internal legal systems...

ILC Report 2001: Commentary to Chapter V of Part One, para. 7, at 172.

A. CONSENT

1. ILC Report 2001: Art. 20 ASR

Article 20: *Consent*

Valid consent by a State to the commission of a given act by another State precludes the wrongfulness of that act in relation to the former State to the extent that the act remains within the limits of that consent.

2. ILC Report 2001: Related Commentary

[Commentary to article 20]

(4) In order to preclude wrongfulness, consent dispensing with the performance of an obligation in a particular case must be "valid". Whether consent has been validly given is a matter addressed by international law rules outside the framework of State responsibility. Issues include whether the agent or person who gave the consent was authorized to do so on behalf of the State (and if not, whether the lack of that authority was known or ought to have been known to the acting State), or whether the consent was vitiated by coercion or some other factor. Indeed there may be a question whether the State could validly consent at all. The reference to a "valid consent" in article 20 highlights the need to consider these issues in certain cases.

3. The Savarkar Case (Fr. v. Gr. Brit.)

Hague Ct. Rep. (Scott) 275 (Perm. Ct. Arb. 1911) (first ser.).

This case arose as the result of the escape of Savarkar, a Hindoo, who was being transported from England to India for trial on a charge of abetment of murder, and who at Marseilles on July 8, 1910, escaped to the shore from the *Morea,* a British merchant vessel, which was carrying him. While being pursued by Indian policemen from the vessel, he was captured by a French police officer, who returned him to the *Morea,* which sailed with the fugitive on board on the following day. Subsequently, France demanded the restitution of the fugitive on the ground that his delivery to the British officers on board the vessel was contrary to the rules of international law, and, upon Great Britain's refusal to comply, the questions of law and fact involved were, by a *compromis* signed October 25, 1910, submitted to the arbitration of a tribunal. ...

The tribunal found that previously to the arrival of the *Morea* at Marseilles arrangements had been made between the British and French police to prevent the escape of the fugitive, and that, although the French officer who arrested him may have been ignorant of his identity, there was no fraud or force used to obtain possession of him and the failure of the French authorities to disavow the arrest and delivery before the ship sailed might naturally have led the British police to believe that the French officer acted in accordance with instructions or that his conduct was approved. The tribunal held that while an irregularity was committed in the arrest of Savarkar and his delivery to the British police, there is no rule of international law which imposes under these circumstances any obligation on the Power which has the custody of the prisoner to restore him because of a mistake made by the foreign agent who delivered him up.

4. The Russian Indemnity Case (Russ. v. Turk.)

Hague Ct. Rep. (Scott) 297 (Perm. Ct. Arb. 1912) (first ser.)

[Under the treaty of January 27/February 8, 1879, which ended Russo-Turkish War, Turkey and Russia agreed on a settlement of claims by Russian subjects in Turkey. Payments by Turkey, however, were delayed and were made only under constant pressure by Russia. The case was brought to arbitration. Russia claimed interest on delayed payments. Turkey refused. The Tribunal held:]

When the tribunal recognized that, according to the general principles and custom of public international law, there was a similarity between the condition of a State and that of an individual, which are debtors for a clear and exigible conventional sum, it is equitable and juridical also to apply by analogy the principles of private law common to cases where the demand for payment must be considered as removed and the benefit to be derived therefrom as eliminated. In private law, the effects of demand for payment are eliminated when the creditor, after having made legal demand upon the debtor, grants one or more extensions for the payment of the principal obligation, without reserving the rights acquired by the legal demand (Toullier-Duvergier, *Droit français,* vol. iii, p. 159, No. 256), or again, when "the creditor does not follow up the summons to the debtor," and "these rules apply to interest-damages, and also to interest due for the non-fulfilment of an obligation . . . or for delay in its fulfilment" (Duranton, *Droit français*, x, p. 470; Aubry and Rau, *Droit Civil,* 1871, iv, p. 99; Berney, *De la demeure,* etc., Lausanne, 1886, p. 62; Windscheid, *Lehrbuch des Pandektenrechts,* 1879, p. 99; Demolombe, x, p. 49; Laronbière i, art. 1139, No. 22, etc.).

In the relations between the Imperial Russian Government and the Sublime Porte, Russia therefore renounced its right to interest, since its Embassy repeatedly accepted without discussion or reservation and mentioned again and again in its own diplomatic correspondence the amount of the balance of the indemnity as identical with the amount of the balance of the principal. In other words, the correspondence of the last few years proves that the two parties interpreted, in fact, the acts of 1879 as implying that the payment of the balance of the principal and the payment of the balance to which the claimants had a right were identical, and this implied the relinquishment of the right to interest or moratory interest-damages.

The Imperial Russian Government can not, when the principal of the indemnity has been paid or placed at its disposal, validly reconsider one-sidedly an interpretation accepted and practised in its name by its Embassy.

The arbitral tribunal, basing its conclusion upon the statements of law and fact which precede, is of the opinion

> [t]hat in principle the Imperial Ottoman Government was liable to moratory indemnities to the Imperial Russian Government from December 31, 1890/January 12, 1891, the date of the receipt of the explicit and regular demand for payment.

But that, in fact, the benefit to the Imperial Russian Government of this legal demand having ceased as a result of the subsequent relinquishment by its Embassy at Constantinople, the Imperial Ottoman Government is not held liable to pay interest-damages by reason of the dates on which the payment of the indemnities was made.

5. Military Intervention by Belgium in Congo

U.N. SCOR, 15th Yr., 873d mtg., U.N. Doc. S/PV.873 (1960)

[After the independence of Congo from Belgium and the civil war that followed, Belgium intervened militarily in certain parts of Congo. Belgium was accused of unlawful intervention. Belgium defended its intervention on a number of grounds, but primarily on the ground of consent by a provincial government in Congo. Below are excerpts from the statement of Belgium's representative in the Security Council:]

186. Thus we did not intervene at Elisabethville until after five Europeans had been killed and when we intervened we did so only because we learnt that rioters were advancing on the town in a threatening manner. The Belgian inter-

vention took place with the full agreement of the head of the provincial government.

187. We shall be told that authorization should have been given by the Central Government, not by the provincial government. But in the state of anarchy at present existing in the Congo, is it possible to refuse assistance to the lawful, constitutional head of a provincial government constituted in accordance with the fundamental law of the Congolese State? Should such aid be refused when it is requested to save human lives?

188. It is worthy of note that Mr. Lumumba, the head of the Congolese Government, has not objected to the action or to the agreement concluded with Mr. Tshombé. Indeed Mr. Lumumba and Mr. Kasavubu, the Head of State, even countersigned an agreement between the Congolese authorities and the Belgian authorities requesting Belgium to intervene to re-establish security at Luluabourg and in Kasaï.

189. Again, we shall be told that it is a limited agreement. That is true, and I will even say that it was more or less by chance that Mr. Lumumba and Mr. Kasavubu signed the agreement. It was because they happened to be at Luluabourg at that time. If they had not been there, we should not be able to produce this document bearing the signatures of the Head of State and of the Head of the Government.

190. This agreement stipulates: "In view of the gravity of the situation, Belgian troops will remain for at least two months in Kasaï " That is the document signed by Mr. Kasavubu as Commander-in-Chief of the national armed forces and by Mr. Lumumba, as Prime Minister and Minister of National Defence.

191. At Leopoldville the intervention took place when the situation became extremely tense. Arbitrary arrests of Europeans were taking place on a large scale. The men arrested were generally stripped and held without clothing. We have freed over a hundred of them. There were increasingly frequent cases of molestation of Europeans. Thousands of refugees at the airport were prevented by the mutineers from boarding aircraft to take them to places of safety. Representatives of foreign powers requested Belgian representatives to send reinforcements from Kamina to ensure safety in the city. Had the Belgian Government the right to refuse to respond to this appeal? Had it the right not to take the measures necessary to ensure respect for the human person?

192. The intervention of Belgian metropolitan troops is thus justified, first, by the total inability of the Congolese national authorities to ensure respect for fundamental rules which must be observed in any civilized community and by the Belgian Government's sacred duty to take the measures required by morality and by public international law.

193. Secondly, it is justified by the complete absence of interference by the Belgian Government in the internal affairs of the Republic of the Congo, I wish to

make it absolutely clear that Belgian military operations have no political objective. I am able to state that in places where intervention by Belgian metropolitan troops was possible, security prevails. In most cases, the mere presence of the troops and the show of force were sufficient to restore order. It was unnecessary to fire a shot. As I have already told you, there have been hardly any casualties on the Congolese side. At all events not a single Congolese woman has been raped, not a single Congolese house has been looted, not a single Congolese citizen has been maltreated or harassed, or been forced to flee, to leave his home to seek safety elsewhere. There has not been a single case of that kind.

194. In contrast, security is seriously in doubt in places in which there are no Belgian troops and where military intervention has not been possible. The Belgian Government still hopes that the Congolese Government will be able and willing to act vigorously in the towns where there are no Belgian troops. However, we learn with some alarm that repeated inflammatory calls to action are being broadcast in the Congo. In view of these calls there is a danger of general massacres of the white population in the towns and other places where Belgian forces are not in a position to protect human life. You will understand that in these circumstances the Belgian Government cannot accept the ultimatum addressed to it by the Congolese Government calling for the withdrawal of its metropolitan troops within a few hours. The Belgian Government cannot be satisfied with the Congolese authorities' purely verbal undertaking to ensure the safety of Belgian nationals and Europeans with their own armed forces. Unfortunately the facts have so far been at variance with this assurance. The withdrawal of Belgian troops will not be possible until security has been genuinely established and properly assured by a responsible authority.

195. It is in the light of these considerations that I was instructed this morning to inform the Secretary-General of the United Nations that Belgium requested and hoped for United Nations military aid to collaborate in the restoration of security and the protection of human life. The Belgian Government is able to support the proposal for United Nations intervention which was made today by the Secretary-General. The Secretary-General proposes that United Nations troops shall be sent to ensure security in the Republic of the Congo where security is at present ensured only by Belgian troops, as a result of the total failure of the Congolese authorities in this field.

196. The Belgian Government can only interpret the statement just made by Mr. Hammarskjold as recognition of the material necessity for Belgian military intervention in the Congo, and indeed as an implicit acknowledgement of the legality of the action my country was compelled to take in order to protect its nationals and in the interests of the Congo and of the international community at large. This intervention, which was, I believe I have shown, imperative and unavoidable, is strictly proportional. …

NOTES AND QUESTIONS

1. Nazi Germany justified the annexation of Austria on the ground of consent by Austria expressed by a law signed by its President after German troops were already in Austria. Having reviewed the sequence of events leading to the adoption of that law, the Nuremberg Tribunal stated the following:

> It was contended before the Tribunal that the annexation of Austria was justified by the strong desire expressed in many quarters for the union of Austria and Germany; that there were many matters in common between the two peoples and made this union desirable; and that in the result the object was achieved without bloodshed.
>
> These matters, even if true, are really immaterial, for the facts plainly prove that the methods employed to achieve the object were those of an aggressor. The ultimate factor was the armed might of Germany ready to be used if any resistance was encountered. Moreover, none of these considerations appear from the Hossbach account of the meetings of 5 November 1937 to have been the motives which actuated Hitler on the contrary, all the emphasis is there laid on the advantage to be gained by Germany in her military strength by the annexation of Austria.

41 AM. J. INT'L L. 172, 194 (1947). Was the Nuremberg Tribunal correct?

2. What are the ways in which a State can validly express consent? Can consent be presumed or implied? If so, how? Can consent by a "puppet" government be considered valid? Can consent be after-the-fact?

3. In 1994, approximately 800,000 persons, primarily Tutsis in Rwanda, were systematically murdered by rival Hutu government officials and civilians. Many of these acts were determined to be genocide by the Rwanda War Crimes Tribunal. In 2002-2003, a long-standing civil war in Congo once again flared into mass killings by rival groups. How would you evaluate Belgium's argument before the Security Council in 1960, if a provincial government or a tribal chief in Rwanda or Congo had asked for intervention by another state?

4. In the situation of failed states, i.e. Somalia or Congo, where there is no central government or one that is not recognized by substantial numbers of states or the United Nations, would the consent by a provincial chief, or military commander, for assistance from another state to intervene in the locality under his or her control constitute valid consent?

5. Can a State consent to violation of its rights by another State which at the same time amounts to violation of a *jus cogens*? Would consent (by popular vote) of a State to come under the administration of a larger State be valid?

6. Would the decision of the Tribunal in the Russian Indemnity case be upheld today? *See* Art. 38 ASR.

7. The United States intervened in Grenada in 1983 on the ground of the request from a regional organization, or, in the alternative, on the invitation of Sir Paul Scoon, Governor General, who could be conceived of as standing in for the overthrown government of Prime Minister Maurice Bishop. *See The United States Action in Grenada* (Agora), 78 AM. J. INT'L L. 131-175 (1984). Does the consent of a regional organization in the absence of consent by the government suffice for a lawful intervention?

8. For further discussion of humanitarian intervention, *see, supra,* Part Three at 487; *infra*, Part Six, Military Instrument, at 1078-1091.

B. Self-Defense

1. ILC Report 2001: Art. 21 ASR.

Article 21: *Self-defence*

The wrongfulness of an act of a State is precluded if the act constitutes a lawful measure of self-defence taken in conformity with the Charter of the United Nations.

2. ILC Report 2001: Related Commentaries

[Commentary to article 21]

(1) The existence of a general principle admitting self-defence as an exception to the prohibition against the use of force in international relations is undisputed. Article 51 of the Charter of the United Nations preserves a State's "inherent right" of self-defence in the face of an armed attack and forms part of the definition of the obligation to refrain from the threat or use of force laid down in Article 2, paragraph (4). Thus a State exercising its inherent right of self-defence as referred to in Article 51 of the Charter is not, even potentially, in breach of Article 2, paragraph (4).

(2) Self-defence may justify non-performance of certain obligations other than that under Article 2, paragraph (4), of the Charter, provided that such non-performance is related to the breach of that provision. Traditional international law dealt with these problems by instituting a separate legal regime of war, defining the scope of belligerent rights and suspending most treaties in force between the belligerents on the outbreak of war. …

3. Legality of the Threat or Use of Nuclear Weapons

1996 I.C.J. 226 (July 8) (Advisory Opinion)

1. The question upon which the advisory opinion of the Court has been requested is set forth in resolution 49/75 K adopted by the General Assembly of the United Nations (hereinafter called the "General Assembly") on 15 December 1994. [The relevant paragraph of the resolution read as follows:]

> *Decides*, pursuant to Article 96, paragraph 1, of the Charter of the United Nations, to request the International Court of Justice urgently to render its advisory opinion on the following question: 'Is the threat or use of nuclear weapons in any circumstance permitted under international law?'"

[In its advisory opinion, the Court reviewed whether there were certain obligations which need not be complied with on the grounds of self-defence.] …

25. The Court observes that the protection of the International Covenant of Civil and Political Rights does not cease in times of war, except by operation of Article 4 of the Covenant whereby certain provisions may be derogated from in a time of national emergency. Respect for the right to life is not, however, such a

provision. In principle, the right not arbitrarily to be deprived of one's life applies also in hostilities. The test of what is an arbitrary deprivation of life, however, then falls to be determined by the applicable *lex specialis*, namely, the law applicable in armed conflict which is designed to regulate the conduct of hostilities. Thus whether a particular loss of life, through the use of a certain weapon in warfare, is to be considered an arbitrary deprivation of life contrary to Article 6 of the Covenant, can only be decided by reference to the law applicable in armed conflict and not deduced from the terms of the Covenant itself.

26. Some States also contended that the prohibition against genocide, contained in the Convention of 9 December 1948 on the Prevention and Punishment of the Crime of Genocide, is a relevant rule of customary international law which the Court must apply. …

The Court would point out in that regard that the prohibition of genocide would be pertinent in this case if the recourse to nuclear weapons did indeed entail the element of intent, towards a group as such, required by the provision quoted above [article II of the Genocide Convention]. In the view of the Court, it would only be possible to arrive at such a conclusion after having taken due account of the circumstances specific to each case.

27. In both their written and oral statements, some States furthermore argued that any use of nuclear weapons would be unlawful by reference to existing norms relating to the safeguarding and protection of the environment, in view of their essential importance. Specific references were made to various existing international treaties and instruments. …These instruments and other provisions relating to the protection and safeguarding of the environment were said to apply at all times, in war as well as in peace, and it was contended that they would be violated by the use of nuclear weapons whose consequences would be widespread and would have transboundary effects.

28. Other States questioned the binding legal quality of these precepts of environmental law; or, in the context of the Convention on the Prohibition of Military or Any Other Hostile Use of Environmental Modification Techniques, denied that it was concerned at all with the use of nuclear weapons in hostilities; or, in the case of Additional Protocol I, denied that they were generally bound by its terms, or recalled that they had reserved their position in respect of Article 35, paragraph 3, thereof.

It was also argued by some States that the principal purpose of environmental treaties and norms was the protection of the environment in time of peace. It was said that those treaties made no mention of nuclear weapons. It was also pointed out that warfare in general, and nuclear warfare in particular, were not mentioned in their texts and that it would be destabilizing to the rule of law and to confidence in international negotiations if those treaties were now interpreted in such a way as to prohibit the use of nuclear weapons. …

30. ...[T]he Court is of the view that the issue is not whether the treaties relating to the protection of the environment are or not applicable during an armed conflict, but rather whether the obligations stemming from these treaties were intended to be obligations of total restraint during military conflict. The Court does not consider that the treaties in question could have intended to deprive a State of the exercise of its right of self-defence under international law because of its obligations to protect the environment. Nonetheless, States must take environmental considerations into account when assessing what is necessary and proportionate in the pursuit of legitimate military objectives. Respect for the environment is one of the elements that go to assessing whether an action is in conformity with the principles of necessity and proportionality. ...

34. In the light of the foregoing the Court concludes that the most directly relevant applicable law governing the question of which it was seised, is that relating to the use of force enshrined in the United Nations Charter and the law applicable in armed conflict which regulates the conduct of hostilities, together with any specific treaties on nuclear weapons that the Court might determine to be relevant. ...

37. The Court will now address the question of the legality or illegality of recourse to nuclear weapons in the light of the provisions of the Charter relating to the threat or use of force.

38. The Charter contains several provisions relating to the threat and use of force. In Article 2, paragraph 4, the threat or use of force against the territorial integrity or political independence of another State or in any other manner inconsistent with the purposes of the United Nations is prohibited. That paragraph provides:

> All Members shall refrain in their international relations from the threat or use of force against the territorial integrity or political independence of any State, or in any other manner inconsistent with the Purposes of the United Nations.

This prohibition of the use of force is to be considered in the light of other relevant provisions of the Charter. In Article 51, the Charter recognizes the inherent right of individual or collective self-defence if an armed attack occurs. A further lawful use of force is envisaged in Article 42, whereby the Security Council may take military enforcement measures in conformity with Chapter VII of the Charter. ...

46. Certain States asserted that the use of nuclear weapons in the conduct of reprisals would be lawful. The Court does not have to examine, in this context, the question of armed reprisals in time of peace, which are considered to be unlawful. Nor does it have to pronounce on the question of belligerent reprisals save to observe that in any case any right of recourse to such reprisals would, like self-defence, be governed *inter alia* by the principle of proportionality. ...

79. It is undoubtedly because a great many rules of humanitarian law applicable in armed conflict are so fundamental to the respect of the human person and "elementary considerations of humanity" as the Court put it in its Judgment of 9 April 1949 in the *Corfu Channel* case *(I.C.J. Reports 1949*, p. 22), that the Hague and Geneva Conventions have enjoyed a broad accession. Further these fundamental rules are to be observed by all States whether or not they have ratified the conventions that contain them, because they constitute intransgressible principles of international customary law …

89. The Court finds that as in the case of the principles of humanitarian law applicable in armed conflict, international law leaves no doubt that the principle of neutrality, whatever its content, which is of a fundamental character similar to that of the humanitarian principles and rules, is applicable (subject to the relevant provisions of the United Nations Charter), to all international armed conflict, whatever type of weapons might be used.

96. Furthermore, the Court cannot lose sight of the fundamental right of every State to survival, and thus its right to resort to self-defence, in accordance with Article 51 of the Charter, when its survival is at stake. Nor can it ignore the practice referred to as "policy of deterrence", to which an appreciable section of the international community adhered for many years. The Court also notes the reservations which certain nuclear-weapon States have appended to the undertakings they have given, notably under the Protocols to the Treaties of Tlatelolco and Rarotonga, and also under the declarations made by them in connection with the extension of the Treaty on the Non-Proliferation of Nuclear Weapons, not to resort to such weapons.

97. Accordingly, in view of the present state of international law viewed as a whole, as examined above by the Court, and of the elements of fact at its disposal, the Court is led to observe that it cannot reach a definitive conclusion as to the legality or illegality of the use of nuclear weapons by a State in an extreme circumstance of self-defence, in which its very survival would be at stake.

NOTES AND QUESTIONS

1. What is the difference between self-defense and reprisals? Is the purpose of the (re)action determinative? For details, *see infra* Part Six, Military Instrument, at 1049-78.

2. On March 28, 1964, the British Royal Air Force carried out attacks against the Yemen Arab Republic. The British argued that their action was in self-defense:

> At the 1109th meeting on 7 April 1964, the representative of the United Kingdom declared that the action against Yemen "was not a retaliation or a reprisal. On the contrary, the action was taken in response to an urgent request from ministers of the Federation to protect the interests and integrity of their country. It was a measure of defence". He went on to explain that in existing law there was a clear distinction between the two forms of self-help. One, which was of a retributive, or punitive nature, was termed retaliation or reprisal; the other which was to expressly contemplated or authorized by the Charter was self-defence against armed attack. The term "counter-attack" previously used by his delegation might have led to some misunderstanding and might have implied action of the nature of reprisals only. However, the use of force to repel or

> prevent an attack, "that is, legitimate action of a defensive nature", might sometimes have to take the form of a counter-attack. The territory of the Federation had been subjected to a series of acts of aggression over a considerable period of time and against which its people had asked to be defended. In that connexion the destruction of the fort at Harib "with the minimum use of force, was therefore a defensive measure proportionate and confined to the necessities of the case", and lacked the essential element of vengeance or retribution. It was the latter use of force which was condemned by the Charter "and not the use of force for defensive purposes such as warding off future attacks".

Repertoire of the Practice of the Security Council, Supplement 1964-1965 (United Nations publication, Sales No. E.68, VII.1), chap. XI, part IV, Case No. 7.

The British argued in the Yemen case that the essential element of an act of reprisal is "vengeance or retribution". Does the absence of such an element preclude an action from being characterized as reprisal? Are there legal limits to reprisals?

3. After September 11, 2001, the United States attacked Taliban and Al Qaeda positions in Afghanistan, overthrowing the Taliban government and installing an interim government. The United States' claim was based on the right to self-defense. In April 2003, the United States attacked Iraq claiming, among other things, the right to self-defense. Was the U.S. argument persuasive? *See* William H. Taft IV & Todd F. Buchwald, *Agora: Future Implications of the Iraq Conflict: Preemption, Iraq and International Law,* 97 Am. J. Int'l L. 557 (2003). *See also* W. Michael Reisman, *Assessing Claims to Revise the Laws of War*, 97 Am. J. Int'l L. 82-90 (2003), *infra* Part Six, Military Instrument, at 1175-82.

C. *Force Majeure*, Distress and Necessity

1. ILC Report 2001: Arts. 23-25 ASR

Article 23: *Force majeure*

1. The wrongfulness of an act of a State not in conformity with an international obligation of that State is precluded if the act is due to *force majeure*, that is the occurrence of an irresistible force or of an unforeseen event, beyond the control of the State, making it materially impossible in the circumstances to perform the obligation.

2. Paragraph 1 does not apply if:

(*a*) The situation of *force majeure* is due, either alone or in combination with other factors, to the conduct of the State invoking it; or

(b) The State has assumed the risk of that situation occurring.

Article 24: *Distress*

1. The wrongfulness of an act of a State not in conformity with an international obligation of that State is precluded if the author of the act in question has no other reasonable way, in a situation of distress, of saving the author's life or the lives of other persons entrusted to the author's care.

2. Paragraph 1 does not apply if:

(*a*) The situation of distress is due, either alone or in combination with other factors, to the conduct of the State invoking it; or *(b)* The act in question is likely to create a comparable or greater peril.

Article 25: *Necessity*

1. Necessity may not be invoked by a State as a ground for precluding the wrongfulness of an act not in conformity with an international obligation of that State unless the act:

(*a*) Is the only way for the State to safeguard an essential interest against a grave and imminent peril; and

(*b*) Does not seriously impair an essential interest of the State or States towards which the obligation exists, or of the international community as a whole.

2. In any case, necessity may not be invoked by a State as a ground for precluding wrongfulness if:

(*a*) The international obligation in question excludes the possibility of invoking necessity; or

(*b*) The State has contributed to the situation of necessity.

2. ILC Report 2001: Related Commentaries

[Commentary to article 23]

(2) A situation of *force majeure* precluding wrongfulness only arises where three elements are met: (a) the act in question must be brought about by an irresistible force or an unforeseen event, (b) which is beyond the control of the State concerned, and (c) which makes it materially impossible in the circumstances to perform the obligation. The adjective "irresistible" qualifying the word "force" emphasizes that there must be a constraint which the State was unable to avoid or oppose by its own means. To have been "unforeseen" the event must have been neither foreseen nor of an easily foreseeable kind. Further the "irresistible force" or "unforeseen event" must be causally linked to the situation of material impossibility, as indicated by the words "due to *force majeure* ... making it materially impossible". Subject to paragraph 2, where these elements are met the wrongfulness of the State's conduct is precluded for so long as the situation of *force majeure* subsists.

(3) Material impossibility of performance giving rise to *force majeure* may be due to a natural or physical event ... or to human intervention ... or some combination of the two. Certain situations of duress or coercion involving force imposed on the State may also amount to *force majeure* if they meet the various requirements of article 23. In particular the situation must be irresistible, so that the State concerned has no real possibility of escaping its effects. *Force majeure* does not include circumstances in which performance of an obligation has become more difficult, for example due to some political or economic crisis. Nor does it cover situations brought about by the neglect or default of the State concerned, even if the resulting injury itself was accidental and unintended.

[Commentary to article 24]

(1) Article 24 deals with the specific case where an individual whose acts are attributable to the State is in a situation of peril, either personally or in relation to persons under his or her care. The article precludes the wrongfulness of conduct adopted by the State agent in circumstances where the agent had no other reasonable way of saving life. Unlike situations of *force majeure* dealt with in article 23, a person acting under distress is not acting involuntarily, even though the choice is effectively nullified by the situation of peril. Nor is it a case of choosing between compliance with international law and other legitimate interests of the State, such as characterize situations of necessity under article 25. The interest concerned is the immediate one of saving people's lives, irrespective of their nationality.

[Commentary to article 25]

(2) The plea of necessity … arises where there is an irreconcilable conflict between an essential interest on the one hand and an obligation of the State invoking necessity on the other. These special features mean that necessity will only rarely be available to excuse non-performance of an obligation and that it is subject to strict limitations to safeguard against possible abuse.

3. Case Concerning the Payment of Various Serbian Loans Issued in France (Fr. v. Serb.)

1929 P.C.I.J. (ser. A) No. 20 (July 12)

[France brought a claim before the PCIJ on behalf of the French creditors maintaining that the kingdom of Serbs, Croats and Slovenes was under the obligation to pay the creditors on a gold franc basis and not on a paper franc basis as maintained by the defendant. The Serb-Croat-Slovene Government invoked the existence of *force majeure* consisting of material impossibility of making a payment in gold francs.]

Force majeure.— It cannot be maintained that the war itself, despite its grave economic consequences, affected the legal obligations of the contracts between the Serbian Government and the French bondholders. The economic dislocations caused by the ward did not release the debtor State, although they may present equities which doubtless will receive appropriate consideration in the negotiations and – if resorted to – the arbitral determination for which Article II of the Special Agreement provides.

It is contended that under the operation of the forced currency régime of France, pursuant to the law of August 5th, 1914, payment in gold francs, that is, in specie, became impossible. But if the loan contracts be deemed to refer to the gold franc as a standard of value, payments of the equivalent amount of francs, calculated on that basis, could still be made. Thus, when the Treaty of Versailles became effective, it might be said that "gold francs", as stipulated in Article 262, of the weight and fineness as defined by law on January 1st, 1914, were no longer obtainable, and have not since been obtainable as gold coins *in specie.* But it could hardly be said that for this reason the obligation of the Treaty was discharged in this respect on the ground of impossibility of performance. That is the case of a treaty between States, and this is a case of loan contracts between a State and private persons or lenders. But, viewing the question, not as one of the source or basis of the original obligation, but as one of impossibility of performance, it appears to be quite as impossible to obtain "gold francs" of the sort stipulated in Article 262 of the Treaty of Versailles as it is to obtain gold francs of the sort deemed to be required by the Serbian loan contracts.

4. Rainbow Warrior (N. Z. v. Fr.)

20 R.I.A.A. 217 (1990)

[On 10 July 1985, a civilian vessel, the *Rainbow Warrior*, not flying the New Zealand flag, was sunk at its moorings in Auckland Harbour, New Zealand, as a result of extensive damage caused by two high-explosive devices. One person, a Netherlands citizen was killed as a result of this action. Two agents of French Directorate General of External Security were arrested and prosecuted and found guilty. The two French agents Alain Mafart and Dominique Prieur were sentenced by the Chief Justice of New Zealand to a term of 10 years imprisonment. Following negotiation between the two States the conflict was submitted to the Secretary-General of the United Nations for a ruling. On July 6 1986, the Secretary-General issued a ruling among which the two French agents were immediately to be transferred to the French military facility on the isolated island of Hao in French Polynesia for a period of three years and they could not be removed from that island without the consent of New Zealand. In accordance with this ruling the French agents were transferred to the island of Hao on 23 July 1986. In late 1987 and early 1988 both French agents were moved back to France without the consent of New Zealand. This issue was submitted to arbitration.]

. . .

15. On 7 December 1987 the French Ministry of Defence was advised by the commander of the Hao military base that the condition of Major Mafart's health required examinations and immediate care, which could not be carried out locally. The Minister of Defence then decided to send a medical team to the site. This team was led by a principal Army doctor, Dr. Maurel, from the Val-de-Grace Hospital in Paris.

16. On 10 December 1987 (Hao date), Dr. Maurel sent the Ministry of Defence a message, received in Paris on Friday 11 December, stating that Major Mafart "poses the etiological and therapeutic problem of stabbing abdominal pains in a patient with a history of similar, and still unlabeled, problems. The results of today's examination indicate the need for explorations in a highly specialized environment. His condition justifies an emergency return to a hospital in mainland France. . . .

[France and New Zealand could not agree on arrangements for a doctor appointed by New Zealand to visit Major Mafart in Hao. He was, however, visited by a New Zealand Doctor who indicated in its report that there was no evidence produced to show that Major Mafart had an impending obstruction at the time he was evacuated from Hao.] ...

45. According to the French Counter-Memorial Alain Mafart, who was evacuated in December 1987 for health reasons, was declared "repatriated for health reasons" on 11 March 1988. After a temporary assignment at the Head Office of the Nuclear Experimentation Center, he was assigned on 1 September 1988 to the War College in Paris, after passing the entrance examination, for which he had taken the written part in Hao and the oral part in Paris. On 1 October 1988, he was promoted to the rank of Lieutenant Colonel. ...

47. The French Counter-Memorial states that on 3 May 1988, the French Ministry of Foreign Affairs received a medical report indicating that Dominique Prieur was 6 weeks pregnant. The report stated that this pregnancy should be treated with special care for several reasons: Mrs. Prieur was almost 39 years old; her gynecological history; the fact that this would be her first child. It also indicated that the medical facilities existing on Hao were unable to provide the necessary medical examinations and the care required by Mrs. Prieur's condition. ...

52. On 5 May 1988 at 11.00 a.m. (French time), the New Zealand Ambassador in Paris was told that the French Government had been informed of a "new development", namely, that Dominique Prieur's father, hospitalized for treatment of a cancer, was dying. The French Government informed the Ambassador that "for obvious humanitarian reasons" Dominique Prieur had to see her father before his death. ...

58. On 16 May 1988 the father of Captain Prieur died.

59. On 21 July 1988 Dr. Croxson examined both Major Mafart and Captain Prieur and advised as to the latter as follows:

> The investigations and examinations by the French medical attendants and my clinical examination would all be consistent with an approximately 18-week pregnancy which is proceeding uneventfully. Results of the amniocentesis to exclude important chromosome abnormalities are awaited. No special arrangements for later pregnancy or delivery are planned, and I formed the opinion that management would be conducted on usual clinical criteria for a 39-year-old, fit, healthy woman in her first pregnancy.

60. According to the French Counter-Memorial, Dominique Prieur was assigned to the Head Office of the Nuclear Experimentation Center in Villacoublay. She was on leave until 7 November 1988, corresponding to military furlough that she had not taken previously. She then received twenty-two weeks maternity

leave, pursuant to French labor law. She gave birth to her child on 15 December 1988. …

62. New Zealand contends that France has committed six separate breaches of the international obligations it assumed under Clauses 3 to 7 of the First Agreement of 9 July 1986, three in respect of each agent. New Zealand submits that, taken chronologically, these breaches of obligations were: first, France's failure to seek in good faith its consent to the removal of the two agents from Hao; second, the removal of the two agents without New Zealand's consent; and, third, the continued failure to return the two agents to Hao. …

66. For its part, the French Republic maintains that the clause prohibiting the two agents from leaving the island except with the consent of the two Governments is intended for one of the two following possibilities: either a special situation, particularly illness, or, as in the case of Captain Prieur, pregnancy, which would render their remaining on the island inconceivable, or a joint desire by the two Governments to shorten the total length of their stay. It stresses that, both in December 1987, for Major Mafart, and in May 1988, for Captain Prieur, the first possibility was involved.

France acknowledges that it did not obtain New Zealand's prior consent, but it nevertheless seems to France that, bearing in mind the reason that made the transfer to Paris necessary, and the very special circumstances under which that transfer was made, its action bore no stain of illegality under the 1986 Agreement and the rules and principles of international law. It believes, moreover, that legitimate reasons have prevented the return of the officers in question to their island, and that in any case, the obligation to return can have no existence after 22 July 1989, the expiration date of the 1986 Agreement. …

77. … [With respect to *force majeure,* the Tribunal agreed it was not] of relevance in this case because the test of its applicability of absolute and material impossibility, and because a circumstance rendering performance more difficult or burdensome does not constitute a case of *force majeure*. Consequently, this excuse is of no relevance in the present case.

78. … [As regard the claim of distress, the Tribunal stated] [t]he question therefore is to determine whether the circumstances of distress in a case of extreme urgency involving elementary humanitarian considerations affecting the acting organs of the State may exclude wrongfulness in this case.

79. In accordance with the previous legal considerations, three conditions would be required to justify the conduct followed by France in respect to major Mafart and Captain Prieur:

> 1) The existence of very exceptional circumstances of extreme urgency involving medical or other considerations of an elementary nature, provided always that a prompt recognition of the existence of those exceptional circumstances is subsequently obtained from the other interested party or is clearly demonstrated.

> 2) The reestablishment of the original situation of compliance with the assignment in Hao as soon as the reasons of emergency invoked to justify the repatriation had disappeared.
>
> 3) The existence of a good faith effort to try to obtain the consent of New Zealand in terms of the 1986 Agreement. …

As for the case of Major Mafart …

88. … Both parties recognized that the return of Major Mafart to Hao depended mainly on his state of health. Thus, the French Ministry of Foreign Affairs in its note of 30 December 1987 to the New Zealand Embassy referring to France's respect for the 1986 Agreement had said that Major Mafart will return to Hao when his state of health allowed.

Consequently, there was no valid ground for Major Mafart continuing to remain in metropolitan France and the conclusion is unavoidable that this omission constitutes a material breach by the French Government of the First Agreement.

For the foregoing reasons the Tribunal:

> -by a majority declares that the French Republic did not breach its obligations to New Zealand by removing Major Mafart from the island of Hao on 13 December 1987;
>
> -declares that the French Republic committed a material and continuing breach of its obligation to New Zealand by failing to order the return of Major Mafart to the island of Hao as from 12 February 1988. …

As for the case of Captain Prieur …

93. The facts above, which are not disputed, show that New Zealand would not oppose Captain Prieur's departure, if that became necessary because of special care which might be required by her pregnancy. They also indicate that France and New Zealand agreed that Captain Prieur would be examined by Dr. Brenner, a New Zealand physician, before returning to Paris. Only because of the strike by the U.T.A. airline, the examination that was to take place in Hao on Thursday 5 May had to be postponed until Friday 6 May, since Dr. Brenner would be arriving in Papeete at 3.25 p.m. local time, via Air New Zealand. As the French Republic acknowledges in its Counter- Memorial, "It seemed that we were moving towards a satisfactory solution; New Zealand's approval of Mrs. Prieur's departure seemed probable". Reconciliation of respect for the Agreement of 9 July 1986 and the humanitarian concerns due to the particular circumstances of Mrs. Prieur's pregnancy thus seemed to have been achieved.

94. On the other hand, it appears that during the day of 5 May the French Government suddenly decided to present the New Zealand Government with *the fait accompli* of Captain Prieur's hasty return for a new reason, the health of Mrs. Prieur's father, who was seriously ill, hospitalized for cancer. Indisputably the health of Mrs. Prieur's father, who unfortunately would die on 16 May, and the concern for allowing Mrs. Prieur to visit her dying father constitute humani-

tarian reasons worthy of consideration by both Governments under the 1986 Agreement. But the events of 5 May (French date) prove that the French Republic did not make efforts in good faith to obtain New Zealand's consent. First of all, it must be remembered that France and New Zealand agreed that Captain Prieur would be examined in Hao on 6 May, which would allow her to return to France immediately. For France, in this case, it was only a question of gaining 24 or 36 hours. Of course, the health of Mrs Prieur's father, who had been hospitalized for several months, could serve as grounds for such acute and sudden urgency; but, in this case, New Zealand would have had to be informed very precisely and completely, and not be presented with a decision that had already been made.

However, when the French Republic notified the Ambassador of New Zealand on 5 May at 11.00 a.m. (French time), the latter was merely told that Mrs. Dominique Prieur's father, hospitalized for cancer treatment, was dying. Of course, it was explained that the New Zealand Government could verify "the validity of this information" using a physician of its choice, but the telegram the French Minister of Foreign Affairs sent to the Embassy of France in Wellington on 5 May 1988 clearly stated that the decision to repatriate was final. And this singular announcement was addressed to New Zealand: "After all, New Zealand should understand that it would be incomprehensible for both French and New Zealand opinion for the New Zealand Government to stand in the way of allowing Mrs. Prieur to see her father on his death bed …" Thus, New Zealand was really not asked for its approval, as compliance with France's obligations required, even under extremely urgent circumstances; it was indeed demanded so firmly that it was bound to provoke a strong reaction from New Zealand. …

96. Pondering the reasons for the haste of France, New Zealand contended that Captain Prieur's "removal took place against the back drop of French presidential elections in which the Prime Minister was a candidate" and New Zealand pointed out that Captain Prieur's departure and arrival in Paris had been widely publicized in France. During the oral proceedings, New Zealand produced the text of an interview given on 27 September 1989 by the Prime Minister at the relevant time, explaining the following on the subject of the "Turenge couple": "I take responsibility for the decision that was made, and could not imagine how these two officers could be abandoned after having obeyed the highest authorities of the State. Because it was the last days of my Government, I decided to bring Mrs. Prieur, who was pregnant, back from the Pacific atoll where she was stationed. Had I failed to do so, she would surely still be there today". New Zealand alleges that the French Government acted in this way for reasons quite different from the motive or pretext invoked. The Tribunal need not search for the French Government's motives, nor examine the hypotheses alleged by New Zealand. It only observes that, during the day of 5 May 1988, France did not seek New Zealand's approval in good faith for Captain Prieur's sudden departure; and accordingly, that the return of Captain Prieur, who left Hao on Thursday, 5 May

at 11.30 p.m. (French time) and arrived in Paris on Friday, 6 May, thus constituted a violation of the obligations under the 1986 Agreement.

This violation seems even more regrettable because, as of 12 February 1988, France had been in a state of continuing violation of its obligations concerning Major Mafart, as stated above, which normally should have resulted in special care concerning compliance with the Agreement in Captain Prieur's case.

97. Moreover, France continued to fall short of its obligations by keeping Captain Prieur in Paris after the unfortunate death of her father on 16 May 1988. No medical report supports or demonstrates the original claim by French authorities to the effect that Captain Prieur's pregnancy required "particular care" and demonstrating that "the medical facilities on Hao are not equipped to carry out the necessary medical examinations and to give Mrs. Prieur the care required by her condition". There is no evidence either which demonstrates that the facilities in Papeete, originally suggested by the New Zealand Ambassador in Paris, were also inadequate: on the contrary, positive evidence has been presented by New Zealand as to their adequacy and sophistication. ...

So, the record provides no justification for the failure to return Captain Prieur to Hao some time after the death of her father.

98. The fact that "pregnancy in itself normally constitutes a contra-indication for overseas appointment" is not a valid explanation, because the return to Hao was not an assignment to service, or "an assignment" or military posting, for the reasons already indicated in the case of Major Mafart. Likewise, the fact that Captain Prieur benefited, under French regulations, from "military leave which she had not taken previously", as well as "the maternity and nursing leaves established by French law" may be measures provided by French military laws or regulations.

But in this case, as in that of Major Mafart, French military laws or regulations do not constitute the limit of the obligations of France or of the consequential rights deriving for New Zealand from those obligations. ...

99. In summary, the circumstances of distress, of extreme urgency and the humanitarian considerations invoked by France may have been circumstances excluding responsibility for the unilateral removal of Major Mafart without obtaining New Zealand's consent, but clearly these circumstances entirely fail to justify France's responsibility for the removal of Captain Prieur and from the breach of its obligations resulting from the failure to return the two officers to Hao (in the case of Major Mafart once the reasons for their removal had disappeared). There was here a clear breach of its obligations and a breach of a material character.

5. Gabcíkovo-Nagymaros Project (Hung. v. Slovk.)

1997 I.C.J. 7 (Sept. 25)

[Facts and further discussion, *supra,* Part Four, at 826.]

49. The Court will now consider the question of whether there was, in 1989, a state of necessity which would have permitted Hungary, without incurring international responsibility, to suspend and abandon works that it was committed to perform in accordance with the 1977 Treaty and related instruments. ...

51. The Court considers, first of all, that the state of necessity is a ground recognized by customary international law for precluding the wrongfulness of an act not in conformity with an international obligation. It observes moreover that such ground for precluding wrongfulness can only be accepted on an exceptional basis. The International Law Commission was of the same opinion when it explained that it had opted for a negative form of words in Article 33 of its Draft

> in order to show, by this formal means also, that the case of invocation of a state of necessity as a justification must be considered as really constituting an exception – and one even more rarely admissible than is the case with the other circumstances precluding wrongfulness ... (*ibid.*, p. 51, para. 40).

Thus, according to the Commission, the state of necessity can only be invoked under certain strictly defined conditions which must be cumulatively satisfied; and the State concerned is not the sole judge of whether those conditions have been met.

52. In the present case, the following basic conditions set forth in Draft Article 33 are relevant: it must have been occasioned by an "essential interest" of the State which is the author of the act conflicting with one of its international obligations; that interest must have been threatened by a "grave and imminent peril"; the act being challenged must have been the "only means" of safeguarding that interest; that act must not have "seriously impair[ed] an essential interest" of the State towards which the obligation existed; and the State which is the author of that act must not have "contributed to the occurrence of the state of necessity". Those conditions reflect customary international law. The Court will now endeavour to ascertain whether those conditions had been met at the time of the suspension and abandonment, by Hungary, of the works that it was to carry out in accordance with the 1977 Treaty.

53. The Court has no difficulty in acknowledging that the concerns expressed by Hungary for its natural environment in the region affected by the Gabcíkovo-Nagymaros Project related to an "essential interest" of that State, within the meaning given to that expression in Article 33 of the Draft of the International Law Commission. The Commission, in its Commentary, indicated that one should not, in that context, reduce an "essential interest" to a matter only of the "existence" of the State, and that the whole question was, ultimately, to be judged in the light of the particular case (see *Yearbook of the International*

Law Commission, 1980, Vol. II, Part 2, p. 49, para. 32); at the same time, it included among the situations that could occasion a state of necessity, "a grave danger to … the ecological preservation of all or some of [the] territory [of a State]" (*ibid.*, p. 35, para. 3); and specified, with reference to State practice, that "It is primarily in the last two decades that safeguarding the ecological balance has come to be considered an 'essential interest' of all States." (*Ibid.*, p. 39, para. 14.) The Court recalls that it has recently had occasion to stress, in the following terms, the great significance that it attaches to respect for the environment, not only for States but also for the whole of mankind:

> [t]he environment is not an abstraction but represents the living space, the quality of life and the very health of human beings, including generations unborn. The existence of the general obligation of States to ensure that activities within their jurisdiction and control respect the environment of other States or of areas beyond national control is now part of the corpus of international law relating to the environment. (*Legality of the Threat or Use of Nuclear Weapons, Advisory Opinion, I.C.J. Reports 1996,* pp. 241-242, para. 29.)

54. The verification of the existence, in 1989, of the "peril" invoked by Hungary, of its "grave and imminent" nature, as well as of the absence of any "means" to respond to it, other than the measures taken by Hungary to suspend and abandon the works, are all complex processes. As the Court has already indicated (see paragraphs 33 *et seq.* above), Hungary on several occasions expressed, in 1989, its "uncertainties" as to the ecological impact of putting in place the Gabcikovo-Nagymaros barrage system, which is why it asked insistently for new scientific studies to be carried out. The Court considers, however, that, serious though these uncertainties might have been they could not, alone, establish the objective existence of a "peril" in the sense of a component element of a state of necessity. The word "peril" certainly evokes the idea of "risk"; that is precisely what distinguishes "peril" from material damage. But a state of necessity could not exist without a "peril" duly established at the relevant point in time; the mere apprehension of a possible "peril" could not suffice in that respect. It could moreover hardly be otherwise, when the "peril" constituting the state of necessity has at the same time to be "grave" and "imminent". "Imminence" is synonymous with "immediacy" or "proximity" and goes far beyond the concept of "possibility". As the International Law Commission emphasized in its commentary, the "extremely grave and imminent" peril must "have been a threat to the interest at the actual time" (*Yearbook of the International Law Commission,* 1980, Vol. II, Part 2, p. 49, para. 33). That does not exclude, in the view of the Court, that a "peril" appearing in the long term might be held to be "imminent" as soon as it is established, at the relevant point in time, that the realization of that peril, however far off it might be, is not thereby any less certain and inevitable. The Hungarian argument on the state of necessity could not convince the Court unless it was at least proven that a real, "grave" and "imminent" "peril" existed in

1989 and that the measures taken by Hungary were the only possible response to it.

NOTES AND QUESTIONS

1. In the *Société Commerciale de Belgique* case between Greece and Belgium where two arbitral awards required the Greek government to make payments to a Belgian company for a debt it owed the Company, the Greek government did not comply, invoking the country's serious budgetary and monetary situation. Counsel for Greece, in an oral statement of 16 and 17 May 1939, stated the following:

> There occur from time to time external circumstances beyond all human control which make it impossible for Governments to discharge their duty to creditors and their duty to the people; the country's resources are insufficient to perform both duties at once. It is impossible to pay the debt in full and at the same time to provide the people with a fitting administration and to guarantee the conditions essential for its moral, social and economic development. The painful problem arises of making a choice between the two duties; one of them must give way to the other in some measure: which?
>
> Doctrine and the decisions of the courts have therefore had occasion to concern themselves with the question . . .
>
> Doctrine recognizes in this matter that the duty of a Government to ensure the proper functioning of its essential public services outweighs that of paying its debts. No State is required to execute, or to execute in full, its pecuniary obligation if this jeopardizes the functioning of its public services and has the effect of disorganizing the administration of the country. In the case in which payment of its debt endangers economic life or jeopardizes the administration, the Government is, in the opinion of authors, authorized to suspend or even to reduce the service of debt.

"Force Majeure" and "Fortuitous Event" as Circumstances Precluding Wrongfulness: Survey of State Practice, International Judicial Decisions and Doctrine – Survey Prepared by the Secretariat, INT'L L. COMM'N Y.B. 1978, Vol. II (Part Two), p. 61, para. 281.

International decision makers have manifested a great reluctance to find a situation of *force majeure*. Even in circumstances of major political and economic disruption, international tribunals and courts have still resisted a finding of *force majeure*. *See e.g.* Société Commerciale de Belgique, 1939 P.C.I.J. (Ser. A/B) No. 78, at 160 (June 15)(Judgment). In your view, is the international response cogent? Should it be reconsidered and should there be a more flexible approach to the application of *force majeure*? Discuss. *See* in this regard, W. Michael Reisman, *The Supervisory Jurisdiction of the International Court of Justice: International Arbitration and International Adjudication*, 258 RECUEIL DES COURS (1996), pp 233-253.

2. Could severe hardship on the population now be justified as grounds for non-payment of otherwise valid debts? Is there a connection here with certain international human rights?

3. What are the differences between *force majeure*, distress and necessity?

D. COUNTERMEASURES

1. ILC Report 2001: Arts. 22; 49-54; and 26 ASR

Article 22: *Countermeasures in respect of an internationally wrongful act*

The wrongfulness of an act of a State not in conformity with an international obligation towards another State is precluded if and to the extent that the act constitutes a countermeasure taken against the latter State in accordance with chapter II of Part Three.

Article 26: *Compliance with peremptory norms*

Nothing in this chapter precludes the wrongfulness of any act of a State which is not in conformity with an obligation arising under a peremptory norm of general international law.

Article 49: *Object and limits of countermeasures*

1. An injured State may only take countermeasures against a State which is responsible for an internationally wrongful act in order to induce that State to comply with its obligations under Part Two.

2. Countermeasures are limited to the non-performance for the time being of international obligations of the State taking the measures towards the responsible State.

3. Countermeasures shall, as far as possible, be taken in such a way as to permit the resumption of performance of the obligations in question.

Article 50: *Obligations not affected by countermeasures*

1. Countermeasures shall not affect:

(a) The obligation to refrain from the threat or use of force as embodied in the Charter of the United Nations;

(b) Obligations for the protection of fundamental human rights;

(c) Obligations of a humanitarian character prohibiting reprisals;

(d) Other obligations under peremptory norms of general international law.

2. A State taking countermeasures is not relieved from fulfilling its obligations:

(a) Under any dispute settlement procedure applicable between it and the responsible State;

(b) To respect the inviolability of diplomatic or consular agents, premises, archives and documents.

Article 51: *Proportionality*

Countermeasures must be commensurate with the injury suffered, taking into account the gravity of the internationally wrongful act and the rights in question.

Article 52: *Conditions relating to resort to countermeasures*

1. Before taking countermeasures, an injured State shall:

(a) Call on the responsible State, in accordance with article 43, to fulfil its obligations under Part Two;

(b) Notify the responsible State of any decision to take countermeasures and offer to negotiate with that State.

2. Notwithstanding paragraph 1 (b), the injured State may take such urgent countermeasures as are necessary to preserve its rights.

3. Countermeasures may not be taken, and if already taken must be suspended without undue delay if:

(a) The internationally wrongful act has ceased; and

(b) The dispute is pending before a court or tribunal which has the authority to make decisions binding on the parties.

4. Paragraph 3 does not apply if the responsible State fails to implement the dispute settlement procedures in good faith.

Article 53: *Termination of countermeasures*

Countermeasures shall be terminated as soon as the responsible State has complied with its obligations under Part Two in relation to the internationally wrongful act.

Article 54: *Measures taken by States other than an injured State*

This chapter does not prejudice the right of any State, entitled under article 48, paragraph 1 to invoke the responsibility of another State, to take lawful measures against that State to ensure cessation of the breach and reparation in the interest of the injured State or of the beneficiaries of the obligation breached.

2. ILC Report 2001: Related Commentaries.

[Commentary to article 22]

(1) In certain circumstances, the commission by one State of an internationally wrongful act may justify another State injured by that act in taking non-forcible countermeasures in order to procure its cessation and to achieve reparation for the injury. Article 22 deals with this situation from the perspective of circumstances precluding wrongfulness. ...

(4) Where countermeasures are taken in accordance with article 22, the underlying obligation is not suspended, still less terminated; the wrongfulness of the conduct in question is precluded for the time being by reason of its character as a countermeasure, but only provided that and for so long as the necessary conditions for taking countermeasures are satisfied. ... As a response to internationally wrongful conduct of another State countermeasures may be justified only in relation to that State. ... An act directed against a third State would not fit this definition and could not be justified as a countermeasure. On the other hand, indirect or consequential effects of countermeasures on third parties, which do

not involve an independent breach of any obligation to those third parties, will not take a countermeasure outside the scope of article 22.

[Commentary to article 26]

(3) Where there is an apparent conflict between primary obligations, one of which arises for a State directly under a peremptory norm of general international law, it is evident that such an obligation must prevail. The processes of interpretation and application should resolve such questions without any need to resort to the secondary rules of State responsibility. In theory one might envisage a conflict arising on a subsequent occasion between a treaty obligation, apparently lawful on its face and innocent in its purpose, and a peremptory norm. If such a case were to arise it would be too much to invalidate the treaty as a whole merely because its application in the given case was not foreseen. But in practice such situations seem not to have occurred. Even if they were to arise, peremptory norms of general international law generate strong interpretative principles which will resolve all or most apparent conflicts.

(4) It is however desirable to make it clear that the circumstances precluding wrongfulness … do not authorize or excuse any derogation from a peremptory norm of general international law. For example, a State taking countermeasures may not derogate from such a norm: for example, a genocide cannot justify a counter-genocide. The plea of necessity likewise cannot excuse the breach of a peremptory norm. …

[Commentary to article 49]

(1) … Countermeasures may only be taken by an injured State in order to induce the responsible State to comply with its obligations …, namely, to cease the internationally wrongful conduct, if it is continuing, and to provide reparation to the injured State. Countermeasures are not intended as a form of punishment for wrongful conduct….

[Commentary to article 50]

(1) Article 50 specifies certain obligations the performance of which may not be impaired by countermeasures. An injured State is required to continue to respect these obligations in its relations with the responsible State, … So far as the law of countermeasures is concerned, they are sacrosanct.

(2) The obligations dealt with in article 50 fall into two basic categories. Paragraph 1 deals with certain obligations which by reason of their character must not be the subject of countermeasures at all. Paragraph 2 deals with certain obligations relating in particular to the maintenance of channels of communication between the two States concerned, including machinery for the resolution of their disputes.

[Commentary to article 51]

(1) Article 51 establishes an essential limit on the taking of countermeasures by an injured State in any given case, based on considerations of proportionality.

It is relevant in determining what countermeasures may be applied and their degree of intensity. Proportionality provides a measure of assurance inasmuch as disproportionate countermeasures could give rise to responsibility on the part of the State taking such measures. ...

(6) Considering the need to ensure that the adoption of countermeasures does not lead to inequitable results, proportionality must be assessed taking into account not only the purely "quantitative" element of the injury suffered, but also "qualitative" factors such as the importance of the interest protected by the rule infringed and the seriousness of the breach....

(7) Proportionality is concerned with the relationship between the internationally wrongful act and the countermeasure. In some respects proportionality is linked to the requirement of purpose. ...

[Commentary to article 52]

(1) Article 52 lays down certain procedural conditions relating to the resort to countermeasures by the injured State. Before taking countermeasures an injured State is required to call on the responsible State ... to comply with its obligations.... The injured State is also required to notify the responsible State that it intends to take countermeasures and to offer to negotiate with that State. Notwithstanding this second requirement, the injured State may take certain urgent countermeasures to preserve its rights. If the responsible State has ceased the internationally wrongful act and the dispute is before a competent court or tribunal, countermeasures may not be taken; if already taken, they must be suspended. However this requirement does not apply if the responsible State fails to implement dispute settlement procedures in good faith. In such a case countermeasures do not have to be suspended and may be resumed.

[Commentary to article 54]

(1) ...[Injured] States, ... are not the only States entitled to invoke the responsibility of a State for an internationally wrongful act.... Article 48 allows such invocation by any State, in the case of the breach of an obligation to the international community as a whole, or by any member of a group of States, in the case of other obligations established for the protection of the collective interest of the group. By virtue of article 48 (2), such States may also demand cessation and performance in the interests of the beneficiaries of the obligation breached. ... The question is to what extent these States may legitimately assert a right to react against unremedied breaches.

(2) It is vital for this purpose to distinguish between individual measures, whether taken by one State or by a group of States each acting in its individual capacity and through its own organs on the one hand, and institutional reactions in the framework of international organisations on the other. The latter situation, for example where it occurs under the authority of Chapter VII of the United Nations Charter, is not covered by the Articles. More generally the Articles do not cover

the case where action is taken by an international organization, even though the member States may direct or control its conduct.

3. The Naulilaa (Port. v. Ger.)

4 Ann. Dig. 526 (Spec. Arb. Trib. 1928)

THE FACTS. On 19 October, 1914, a German official and two German officers of German South-West Africa were killed by members of a Portuguese frontier post at Naulilaa. Two other Germans were wounded and interned. As a measure of reprisals, and at the order of the Governor of German South-West Africa, German forces attacked and destroyed a number of forts and posts in the frontier region of Portuguese territory. In addition, the German Governor sent a military expedition in the direction of the fort of Naulilaa, whose garrison offered resistance but was finally forced to give up the fort and to retire. The retreat continued well into Portuguese territory, although the German troops withdrew, after the engagement, into the German colony. As the result of the Portuguese retreat the evacuated regions were subjected to looting and pillage on the part of the native population. … Portugal contended that the reprisals were unjustified, and that Germany was responsible for the damage caused by the invasion.

After examining the circumstances accompanying the death of the three Germans on 19 October, 1914, the Commission found that the incident was entirely due to a misunderstanding caused largely by the fact that the Germans did not speak Portuguese and that the Portuguese officer who gave the order to fire believed himself to be in danger.

Held: That Germany was responsible.

Justification of reprisals. A necessary condition for the legitimate exercise of the right of reprisals is the violation of a rule of international law by the State against which the reprisals are directed. There was no such violation in the present case, seeing that the death of the German officers was due to an accident caused by a misunderstanding. Neither could the internment of the two surviving Germans be regarded as an act contrary to the law of nations. A neutral State is entitled to disarm and intern members of belligerent forces which come into its territory.

Necessity of Request to Redress the Injury.—Reprisals are illegal if they are not preceded by a request to remedy the alleged wrong. There is no justification for using force except in cases of necessity. It was true that this principle was not denied by Germany, who pleaded that the German Governor informed all German posts by wireless of the assassination of German officers, and this notice, which must have reached the Portuguese authorities, should have been sufficient warning. Germany also pleaded that the Governor refrained from sending a party with a flag of truce because he feared that the members of the party might be put to death or imprisoned. However, the Tribunal was not prepared to regard these reasons as sufficient.

Question of Proportionality.—Reprisals which are altogether out of proportion with the act which prompted them, are excessive and therefore illegal. This is so even if it is not admitted that international law requires that reprisals should be approximately of the same degree as the injury to which they are meant as an answer. In addition, Germany did not, in the pleadings, deny the requirement of proportionality. There was an obvious lack of proportion between the incident of Naulilaa and the reprisals which followed the incident.

4. The Cysne (Port v. Ger.)

2 R.I.A.A. 1053 (1930)

The Facts.– This was a claim under § 4 of the Annex to Articles 297 and 298 of the Treaty of Versailles. The Tribunal was called upon to decide in regard "to acts committed by the German Government or by any German authority in the period between 31 July, 1914, and 9 March, 1916, namely, the date on which Portugal entered the war." On 28 May, 1915, The Cysne, a Portuguese cargo steamer, sailed with a cargo of pit props from Porto (Portugal) to New Port. When in the Channel she was stopped by a German submarine which, after examining the ship's papers, ordered the crew to take to the boats within five minutes and then sank the steamer. Subsequently, there took place between the Portuguese and German Governments an exchange of notes, but the correspondence was not produced before the Tribunal. On 3 September, 1915, the German Prize Court at Hamburg fixed a time limit of two months within which the owners of the Cysne and of the cargo were asked to put forward their claims, if any. They abstained from doing so. On 27 November, 1915, the Hamburg Prize Court held that the capture and destruction of the Cysne and her cargo were in accordance with the law. The sole reason of the decision was that the vessel carried absolute contraband the hostile destination of which had been duly established in accordance with German Prize Law.

At the beginning of the World War the British, German, and other Governments declared that, subject to certain conditions and modifications, they would adhere to the provisions of the Declaration of London of 1909. On 18 April, 1915, Germany published a decree in which, as a measure of reprisals, she considerably enlarged the list of articles of absolute contraband. The enlarged list included pit props.

Both Governments admitted before the Tribunal that although the Declaration of London, not having been ratified, had no binding force, it was to be regarded as codifying agreed principles of international law.

Germany contended that the Tribunal had no jurisdiction on the ground that, in view of the confirmation by the German Prize Court of the seizure and of the destruction of the vessel, the matter was res judicata. Portugal invoked Article 440 of the Treaty of Versailles in which the Allied and Associated Powers reserved the right "to examine in such manner as they may determine all decisions and orders of German Prize Courts, whether affecting the property rights of nationals of those Powers or of neutral Powers."

On the merits of the claim Portugal maintained that Germany was responsible on the ground that:

(a) the destruction of the vessel was contrary to Articles 48 and 50 of the Declaration of London which prohibited as a rule destruction of neutral prizes and which laid down that in any case sufficient provision must be made for the safety of the crew; (b) that the putting of pit props, which were not exclusively employed for war purposes (Art. 23), on the list of goods of absolute contraband was contrary to the Declaration of London, and that for this reason the vessel was immune from destruction (Art. 36); (c) that the cargo was not liable to capture seeing that it was not consigned to a government contractor or any other agency enumerated in Article 34 of the Declaration.

The German Government submitted: (a) that the submarine could not consistently with its safety conduct the Cysne to a port and that the destruction of the vessel was therefore in accordance with Article 49 of the Declaration; (b) that the placing of pit props on the list of absolute contraband was a measure adopted in pursuance of reprisals against similar measures by Great Britain and her allies; (c) that the goods were consigned both to a recognised government contractor and to a port which was to be regarded as a "fortified place and other place" within the meaning of Article 34 of the Declaration. ...

(d) Reprisals and Neutral States. As pit props, when sent to a country rich in mines, could not be regarded as employed exclusively for war purposes, it was contrary to international law to put them on the absolute contraband list except as an act of reprisals. Such a measure of reprisals was not contrary to international law so far as the enemies of Germany were concerned. But reprisals are not admissible against neutrals. There is no legal justification for reprisals except when they have been provoked by an act contrary to international law. This means that they are not admissible except against the State held guilty of the original violation of international law. It is conceivable that such legitimate reprisals may indirectly injure subjects of the innocent neutral (e.g., when the property of neutral subjects suffers in the course of a bombardment). But in the present case the reprisals were aimed directly and deliberately against neutral subjects. As Portugal had not violated, in relation to Germany, any rule of international law, acts of reprisals directed against her were contrary to international law.

5. Case Concerning the Air Services Agreement of 27 March 1946 between the United States of America and France (U.S. v. Fr.)

18 R.I.A.A. 415 (1979)

[The United States claimed that France violated a 1946 agreement on air services by disallowing Panam airlines to fly airplanes smaller than a Boeing 747 between London and Paris. The French claimed that the change of plane was a change of gauge, i.e. aircraft size, not authorized by the 1946 agreement. After unsuccessful negotiations, the United States suspended French flights to Los Angeles, which were authorized by the 1946 agreement, and also proposed arbitration. Two questions were put to the Tribunal: First, did the United States have the right to change gauge under the 1946 agreement; second, did the United States have the right to suspend French flights to Los Angeles authorized under the 1946 agreement. The Tribunal found that the United States had the right to change gauge. With regard to the second question the Tribunal held:] ...

80. Having thus recalled some of the essential circumstances of the case, the Tribunal will consider, in turn, the principle of the legitimacy of "counter-measures" and the limits on those measures in the light either of the existence of a machinery of negotiations or of a mechanism of arbitration or judicial settlement.

81. Under the rules of present-day international law, and unless the contrary results from special obligations arising under particular treaties, notably from mechanisms created within the framework of international organisations, each State establishes for itself its legal situation vis-à-vis other States. If a situation arises which, in one State's view, results in the violation of an international obligation by another State, the first State is entitled, within the limits set by the general rules of international law pertaining to the use of armed force, to affirm its rights through "counter-measures".

82. At this point, one could introduce various doctrinal distinctions and adopt a diversified terminology dependent on various criteria, in particular whether it is the obligation allegedly breached which is the subject of the counter-measures or whether the latter involve another obligation, and whether or not all the obligations under consideration pertain to the same convention. The Tribunal, however, does not think it necessary to go into these distinctions for the purposes of the present case. Indeed, in the present case, both the alleged violation and the counter-measure directly affect the operation of air services provided for in the Agreement and the Exchange of Notes of 5 April 1960.

83. It is generally agreed that all counter-measures must, in the first instance, have some degree of equivalence with the alleged breach; this is a well-known rule. In the course of the present proceedings, both Parties have recognised that the rule applies to this case, and they both have invoked it. It has been observed, generally, that judging the "proportionality" of counter-measures is not an easy task and can at best be accomplished by approximation. In the Tribunal's view, it is essential, in a dispute between States, to take into account not only the injuries suffered by the companies concerned but also the importance of the questions of principle arising from the alleged breach. The Tribunal thinks that it will not suffice, in the present case, to compare the losses suffered by Pan Am on account of the suspension of the projected services with the losses which the French companies would have suffered as a result of the counter-measures; it will also be necessary to take into account the importance of the positions of principle which were taken when the French authorities prohibited changes of gauge in third countries. If the importance of the issues is viewed within the

framework of the general air transport policy adopted by the United States Government and implemented by the conclusion of a large number of international agreements with countries other than France, the measures taken by the United States do not appear to be clearly disproportionate when compared to those taken by France. Neither Party has provided the Tribunal with evidence that would be sufficient to affirm or reject the existence of proportionality in these terms, and the Tribunal must be satisfied with a very approximative appreciation.

84. Can it be said that the resort to such counter-measures, which are contrary to international law but justified by a violation of international law allegedly committed by the State against which they are directed, is restricted if it is found that the Parties previously accepted a duty to negotiate or an obligation to have their dispute settled through a procedure of arbitration or of judicial settlement?

85. It is tempting to assert that when Parties enter into negotiations, they are under a general duty not to aggravate the dispute, this general duty being a kind of emanation of the principle of good faith.

86. Though it is far from rejecting such an assertion, the Tribunal is of the view that, when attempting to define more precisely such a principle, several essential considerations must be examined.

87. First, the duty to negotiate may, in present times, take several forms and thus have a greater or lesser significance. There is the very general obligation to negotiate which is set forth by Article 33 of the Charter of the United Nations and the content of which can be stated in some quite basic terms. But there are other, more precise obligations.

88. The Tribunal recalls the terms of Article VIII of the 1946 Agreement, which reads as follows:

> In a spirit of close collaboration, the aeronautical authorities of two Contracting Parties will consult regularly with a view to assuring the observance of the principles and the implementation of the provisions outlined in the present Agreement and its Annex.

This Article provides for an obligation of continuing consultation between the Parties. In the context of this general duty, the Agreement establishes a clear mandate to the Parties to make god faith efforts to negotiate on issues of potential controversy. Several other provisions of the Agreement and the Annex state requirements to consult in specific circumstances, when the possibility of a dispute might be particularly acute. Finally, Article X imposes on the Parties a special consultation requirement when, in spite of previous efforts, a dispute has arisen.

89. But the present problem is whether, on the basis of the above-mentioned texts, counter-measures are prohibited. The Tribunal does not consider that either general international law or the provisions of the Agreement allow it to go that far.

90. Indeed, it is necessary carefully to assess the meaning of counter-measures in the framework of proportionality. Their aim is to restore equality between the Parties and to encourage them to continue negotiations with mutual desire to reach an acceptable solution. In the present case, the United States of America holds that a change of gauge is permissible in third countries; that conviction defined its position before the French refusal came into play; the United States counter-measures restore in a negative way the symmetry of the initial positions.

91. It goes without saying that recourse to counter-measures involves the great risk of giving rise, in turn, to a further reaction, thereby causing an escalation which will lead to a worsening of the conflict. Counter-measures therefore should be a wager on the wisdom, not on the weakness of the other Party. They should be used with a spirit of great moderation and be accompanied by a genuine effort at resolving the dispute. but the Arbitral Tribunal does not believe that it is possible, in the present state of international relations, to lay down a rule prohibiting the use of counter-measures during negotiations, especially where such counter-measures are accompanied by an offer for a procedure affording the possibility of accelerating the solution of the dispute.

92. That last consideration is particularly relevant in disputes concerning air service operations: the network of air services is in fact an extremely sensitive system, disturbances of which can have wide and unforeseeable consequences.

93. With regard to the machinery of negotiations, the actions by the United States Government do not appear, therefore, to run counter to the international obligations of that Government.

94. However, the lawfulness of such counter-measures has to be considered still from another viewpoint. It may indeed be asked whether they are valid in general, in the case of a dispute concerning a point of law, where there is arbitral or judicial machinery which can settle the dispute. Many jurists have felt that while arbitral or judicial proceedings were in progress, recourse to counter-measures, even if limited by the proportionality rule, was prohibited. Such an assertion deserves sympathy but requires further elaboration. If the proceedings form part of an institutional framework ensuring some degree of enforcement of obligations, the justification of counter-measures will undoubtedly disappear, but owing to the existence of that framework rather than solely on account of the existence of arbitral or judicial proceedings as such.

95. Besides, the situation during the period in which a case is not yet before a tribunal is not the same as the situation during the period in which that case is *sub judice*. So long as a dispute has not been brought before the tribunal, in particular because an agreement between the Parties is need to set the procedure in motion, the period of negotiation is not over and the rules mentioned above remain applicable. This may be a regrettable solution, as the Parties in principle did agree to resort to arbitration or judicial settlement, but it must be conceded that under present-day international law States have not renounced their right to take counter-measures in such situations. In fact, however, this solution may be

preferable as it facilitates States' acceptance of arbitration or judicial settlement procedures.

96. The situation changes once the tribunal is in a position to act. To the extent that the tribunal has the necessary means to achieve the objectives justifying the counter-measures, it must be admitted that the right of the Parties to initiate such measures disappears. In other words, the power of a tribunal to decide on interim measures of protection, regardless of whether this power is expressly mentioned or implied in its statute (at least as the power to formulate recommendations to this effect), leads to the disappearance of the power to initiate counter-measures and may lead to an elimination of existing counter-measures to the extent that the tribunal so provides as an interim measure of protection. As the object and scope of the power of the tribunal to decide on interim measures of protection may be defined quite narrowly, however, the power of the Parties to initiate or maintain countermeasures, too, may not disappear completely.

97. In a case under the terms of a provision like Article X of the Air Services Agreement of 1946, as amended by the Exchange of Notes of 19 March 1951, the arbitration may be set in motion unilaterally. Although the arbitration need not be binding, the Parties are obliged to "use their best efforts under the powers available to them to put into effect the opinion expressed" by the Tribunal. In the present case, the Parties concluded a *Compromis* that provides for a binding decision on Question (A) and expressly authorises the Tribunal to decide on interim measures.

98. As far as the action undertaken by the United States Government in the present case is concerned, the situation is quite simple. Even if arbitration under Article X of the Agreement is set in motion unilaterally, implementation may take time, and during this period counter-measures are not excluded; a State resorting to such measures, however, must do everything in its power to expedite the arbitration. This is exactly what the Government of the United States has done.

The Tribunal's Reply to Question (B) consists of the above observations as a whole. These observations lead to the conclusion that, under the circumstances in question, the Government of the United States had the right to undertake the action that it undertook under Part 213 of the Economic Regulations of the C. A. B. [to suspend French flights to Los Angeles].

6. United States Diplomatic and Consular Staff in Tehran (U.S. v. Iran)

1980 I.C.J. 3 (May 24)

53. The point has also been raised whether, having regard to certain counter-measures taken by the United States vis-à-vis Iran, it is open to the United States to rely on the Treaty of Amity, Economic Relations, and Consular Rights in the present proceedings. However, all the measures in question were taken by the United States after the seizure of its Embassy by an armed group and subsequent

detention of its diplomatic and consular staff as hostages. They were measures taken in response to what the United States believed to be grave and manifest violations of international law by Iran, including violations of the 1955 Treaty itself. In any event, any alleged violation of the Treaty by either party could not have the effect of precluding that party from invoking the provisions of the Treaty concerning pacific settlement of disputes. …

83. In any case, even if the alleged criminal activities of the United States in Iran could be considered as having been established, the question would remain whether they could be regarded by the Court as constituting a justification by Iran's conduct and thus a defence to the United States/'claims in the present case. The Court, however, is unable to accept that they can be so regarded. This is because diplomatic law itself provides the necessary means of defence against, and sanction for, illicit activities by members of diplomatic or consular missions.

7. Gabcíkovo -Nagymaros Project (Hung. v. Slovk.)

1997 I.C.J. Rep. 7 (Sept. 25)

83. In order to be justifiable, a countermeasure must meet certain conditions (see Military and Paramilitary Activities in and against Nicaragua (Nicaragua v. United States of America) Merits, Judgment, I.C.J. Reports 1986, p. 127, para. 249. See also Arbitral Award of 9 December 1978 in the case concerning the Air Service Agreement of 27 March 1946 between the United States of America and France, United Nations, Reports of International Arbitral Awards (RIAA), Vol. XVIII, pp. 443 et seq.; also Articles 47 to 50 of the Draft Articles on State Responsibility adopted by the International Law Commission on first reading, "Report of the International Law Commission on the work of its forty-eighth session, 6 May-26 July 1996", Official Records of the General Assembly, Fifty-first Session, Supplement No. 10 (A/51/10), pp. 144-145.) In the first place it must be taken in response to a previous international wrongful act of another State and must be directed against that State. Although not primarily presented as a countermeasure, it is clear that Variant C was a response to Hungary's suspension and abandonment of works and that it was directed against that State; and it is equally clear, in the Court's view, that Hungary's actions were internationally wrongful. …

84. Secondly, the injured State must have called upon the State committing the wrongful act to discontinue its wrongful conduct or to make reparation for it. It is clear from the facts of the case, as recalled above by the Court (see paragraphs 61 et seq.), that Czechoslovakia requested Hungary to resume the performance of its treaty obligations on many occasions.

85. In the view of the Court, an important consideration is that the effects of a countermeasure must be commensurate with the injury suffered, taking account of the rights in question. In 1929, the Permanent Court of International Justice, with regard to navigation on the River Oder, stated as follows:

> "[the] community of interest in a navigable river becomes the basis of a common legal right, the essential features of which are the perfect equality of all riparian States in the user of the whole course of the river and the exclusion of any preferential privilege of any one riparian State in relation to the others" (Territorial Jurisdiction of the International Commission of the River Oder, Judgment No. 16, 1929, P.C.I.J., Series A, No. 23, p. 27).

Modern development of international law has strengthened this principle for non-navigational uses of international watercourses as well, as evidenced by the adoption of the Convention of 21 May 1997 on the Law of the Non-Navigational Uses of International Watercourses by the United Nations General Assembly. The Court considers that Czechoslovakia, by unilaterally assuming control of a shared resource, and thereby depriving Hungary of its right to an equitable and reasonable share of the natural resources of the Danube — with the continuing effects of the diversion of these waters on the ecology of the riparian area of the Szigetköz — failed to respect the proportionality which is required by international law. ...

87. The Court thus considers that the diversion of the Danube carried out by Czechoslovakia was not a lawful countermeasure because it was not proportionate. It is therefore not required to pass upon one other condition for the lawfulness of a countermeasure, namely that its purpose must be to induce the wrongdoing State to comply with its obligations under international law, and that the measure must therefore be reversible.

8. Report of the WTO Dispute Settlement Panel, *United States - Sections 301-310 of The Trade Act of 1974*

Dec. 22,1999, WT/DS152/R

[The question is whether under the WTO dispute settlement system, a member state may suspend concessions or other WTO obligations in response to a failure by another member to comply with recommendations and rulings of a WTO panel or the Appellate Body.

Under Section 301 of the United States 1974 Trade Act, the president may take action against foreign states believed to be engaged in unlawful import restrictions, export subsidies and other discriminatory actions or policies. Office of the Trade Representative may take such actions under Section 301 on its own initiative or at the request of an interested person. If the USTR is satisfied that a state is engaged in acts violating U.S. rights, it will negotiate with that state or will engage in formal dispute settlement procedures. If the dispute is not resolved, USTR may retaliate with trade restrictions against that state in an amount equal to the burden caused or restrictions imposed by that state on U.S. trade. Foreign states have criticized the unilateral action under Section 301 on the grounds that it was inconsistent with U.S. obligations under the WTO system, in particular the rules for Dispute Settlement Understanding (DSU), insofar as the eighteen-month time-limit for determining whether U.S. rights have been violated by a foreign state does not allow sufficient time for WTO panel proceedings to be completed.

The European Communities requested the establishment of a WTO panel to address this complaint.]

The European Communities claims that:

> By imposing specific, strict time limits within which unilateral determinations must be made and trade sanctions must be taken, Sections 306 and 305 of the Trade Act of 1974 do not allow the United States to comply with the rules of the DSU in situations where a prior multilateral ruling under the DSU on the conformity of implementing measures has not yet been adopted by the DSB. Where measures have been taken to implement DSB recommendations, the DSU rules require either agreement between the parties to the dispute or a multilateral finding on non-conformity under Article 21.5 DSU before any determination of non-conformity can be made, let alone any measures of retaliation can be announced or implemented. The DSU procedure resulting in a multilateral finding, even if initiated immediately at the end of the reasonable period of time for implementation, cannot be finalised, nor can the subsequent DSU procedure for seeking compensation or suspension of concessions be complied with, within the time limits of Sections 306 and 305. The European Communities considers that Title III, chapter 1 (Sections 301 - 310) of the Trade Act of 1974, as amended, and in particular Sections 306 and 305 of that Act, are inconsistent with, in particular, but not necessarily exclusively, the following WTO provisions.

[The European Communities particularly refer to article 23, paras.(1) and (2)(a) which provide:

> 1. When Members seek the redress of a violation of obligations or other nullification or impairment of benefits under the covered agreements or an impediment to the attainment of any objective of the covered agreements, they shall have recourse to, and abide by, the rules and procedures of this Understanding.
>
> 2. In such cases, Members shall:
>
> (a) not make a determination to the effect that a violation has occurred, that benefits have been nullified or impaired or that the attainment of any objective of the covered agreements has been impeded, except through recourse to dispute settlement in accordance with the rules and procedures of this Understanding, and shall make any such determination consistent with the findings contained in the panel or Appellate Body report adopted by the DSB or an arbitration award rendered under this Understanding;]

4.61 The United States argues that the question in this dispute, and the only question, is whether Sections 301-310 command the United States to violate specific WTO obligations. ...

4.62 The United States further states that if ever there were a case which emphasised the importance of the rule of law, this is that case. The law is the protector of both the weak and the strong, equally. It protects the small and the large, equally. It protects the popular and the unpopular, equally. While there are cases where the small and weak are grateful for the restraints it places on the powerful, there are others in which the law provides a shelter to the unpopular, whatever its size, when it has done no wrong. The United States knows that Sections 301-310 are not popular. But the WTO and the DSU are not a club to be used in a popularity contest against any one Member. If they are credibly to protect the weak, they must also protect the strong against attacks not on what they have done, but on who they are. And a statute does no wrong unless it commands authorities to violate their WTO obligations.

4.63 According to the United States, here at the WTO, the law, the substantive provisions of the WTO Agreement and its annexes, enforced through the provisions of the dispute settlement system, provides security and predictability to all WTO Members. That security and predictability rests firmly on a mode of legal analysis which focuses first and foremost on the text of the Agreement, because that is what the Members have agreed to. It is the text which they signed; it is the text which they submitted to their legislatures for approval by the representatives of their people. The Members brought to the negotiation of the text a number of objectives and purposes, some of which are explicitly listed in the text, and some of which are not. In either case, however, those objectives and purposes are reflected in the agreement text itself. There can be no security and predictability in the multilateral trading system if the explicit rules Members have agreed to may be ignored in favour of a mode of analysis driven by a desire to achieve a specific result. The law must apply equally to all, and in all cases.

4.64 The United States notes that by its terms of reference, this dispute is not about something the United States has done. Because of this, it is not proper to speculate about what the United States might do, any more than it would be proper for the United States to bring a case based on speculation that another Member will not act in accordance with its obligations. The only way that a panel may rule on something that a Member might do in the future is if that Member's law commands it to do it. It may not be assumed that they will not fulfill their solemn international obligations if they are in a position to do so. Only when a Member has crossed the line, by enacting a law which does not permit compliance with its international obligations, has it created a situation in which other Members have a legitimate and non-speculative basis for assuming that another Member will not abide by its international obligations. Only then will those Members find the security and predictability of their trade threatened in a manner distinguishable from the ever-present uncertainty as to whether other Members will fulfill their obligations.

4.65 The United States contends that as has been clear from the outset of this case, Sections 301-310 allow the USTR to comply fully with US obligations under the WTO Agreement and its annexes. This law does not command the USTR to violate the WTO obligations of the United States. This law by its mere existence violates none of these obligations. The EC's transparent efforts to turn this proceeding into a forum for making political attacks on US trade policy only highlight the absolute void at the center of its legal case. It has none. This Panel must find that the European Communities has failed to meet its burden of establishing that Sections 301-310 of the Trade Act of 1974 are inconsistent with DSU Article 23, WTO Agreement Article XVI:4 and GATT 1994 Articles I, II, III, VIII and XI, and that Sections 301-310 are therefore not inconsistent with these obligations. ...

4.67 The European Communities claims that these provisions [Article 23, paras (1) and (2)(a)] clearly oblige the United States to refrain from unilaterally determining whether another Member has denied rights or benefits under a WTO agreement to the United States and whether DSB rulings and recommendations have been implemented. They also leave no doubt that obligations under the GATT and the GATS may be suspended in response to a failure to comply with DSB rulings and recommendations only upon the grant of an authorization by the DSB. ...

4.71 The European Communities adds that international customary law recognises that a party to a treaty breached by another party may reciprocally suspend proportional obligations under the treaty. However, it is also recognised that this right may only be exercised in accordance with any provision in the treaty applicable in the event of a breach.

4.72 The European Communities maintains that Articles XXII and XXIII of the GATT 1947 were such provisions. Clair Wilcox, a drafter of the Havana Charter for an International Trade Organisation (ITO), from which these provisions derived, explained their rationale as follows:

> We have introduced a new principle in international economic relations. We have asked the nations of the world to confer upon an international organisation the right to limit their power to retaliate. We have sought to tame retaliation, to discipline it, to keep it within bounds. By subjecting it to the restraints of international control, we have endeavoured to check its spread and growth, to convert it from a weapon of economic warfare to an instrument of international order.

4.73 The European Communities states that this idea was forcefully expressed in Article 92 of the Havana Charter:

> Reliance on the Procedures of the Charter
>
> 1. The Members undertake that they will not have recourse, in relation to other Members and to the Organisation, to any procedure other than the

procedures envisaged in this Charter for complaints and the settlement of differences arising out of its operation.

2. The Members also undertake, without prejudice to any other international agreement, that they will not have recourse to unilateral economic measures of any kind contrary to the provisions of this Charter.

4.74 According to the European Communities, international customary law also recognises that a fundamental change of circumstances not foreseen by the parties to a treaty may, under certain conditions, bc invoked as a ground for terminating or withdrawing from the treaty. However, the right of a party to such action may in principle be exercised only with respect to the treaty as a whole. International customary law does not entitle a party to a treaty to perform its obligations selectively on the ground that the balance of interest under the treaty has shifted to its disadvantage.

4.75 The European Communities argues that in respect of the GATT 1947, the United States did not consider itself prevented from taking unilateral restrictive trade actions. In its view, unilateral measures were justified because the dispute settlement procedures of Article XXIII were based on consensus and the approval of the suspension of obligations in response to another contracting party's failure to observe obligations could therefore be blocked by the defendant party.

4.76 In the view of the European Communities, the United States also did not consider itself bound by the unconditional most-favoured-nation principle of the GATT 1947 because it enabled contracting parties to obtain the benefit of negotiated market access commitments or new rules even if they had not contributed to the liberalisation efforts or accepted the new rules.

4.77 According to the European Communities, the United States believed that these features of the GATT 1947 justified resorting to unilateral trade measures inconsistent with the GATT whenever the GATT mechanisms did not produce results meeting its expectations. …

[Decision of the Panel]

7.35 Article 23 of the DSU deals, as its title indicates, with the "Strengthening of the Multilateral System". Its overall design is to prevent WTO Members from unilaterally resolving their disputes in respect of WTO rights and obligations. It does so by obligating Members to follow the multilateral rules and procedures of the DSU.

7.36 Article 23.1 provides as follows:

Strengthening of the Multilateral System

When Members seek the redress of a violation of obligations or other nullification or impairment of benefits under the covered agreements or an impediment to the attainment of any objective of the covered agreements, they shall have recourse to, and abide by, the rules and procedures of this Understanding.

7.37 Article 23.2 specifies three elements that need to be respected as part of the multilateral DSU dispute settlement process. It provides as follows:

> In such cases [referred to in Article 23.1, i.e. when Members seek the redress of WTO inconsistencies], Members shall:
>
> (a) not make a determination to the effect that a violation has occurred, that benefits have been nullified or impaired or that the attainment of any objective of the covered agreements has been impeded, except through recourse to dispute settlement in accordance with the rules and procedures of this Understanding, and shall make any such determination consistent with the findings contained in the panel or Appellate Body report adopted by the DSB or an arbitration award rendered under this Understanding;
>
> (b) follow the procedures set forth in Article 21 to determine the reasonable period of time for the Member concerned to implement the recommendations and rulings; and
>
> (c) follow the procedures set forth in Article 22 to determine the level of suspension of concessions or other obligations and obtain DSB authorization in accordance with those procedures before suspending concessions or other obligations under the covered agreements in response to the failure of the Member concerned to implement the recommendations and rulings within that reasonable period of time.

7.38 On this basis, we conclude as follows:

(a) It is for the WTO through the DSU process - not for an individual WTO Member - to determine that a WTO inconsistency has occurred (Article 23.2(a)).

(b) It is for the WTO or both of the disputing parties, through the procedures set forth in Article 21 - not for an individual WTO Member - to determine the reasonable period of time for the Member concerned to implement DSB recommendations and rulings (Article 23.2(b)).

(c) It is for the WTO through the procedures set forth in Article 22 - not for an individual WTO Member - to determine, in the event of disagreement, the level of suspension of concessions or other obligations that can be imposed as a result of a WTO inconsistency, as well as to grant authorization for the actual implementation of these suspensions.

7.39 Article 23.2 clearly, thus, prohibits specific instances of unilateral conduct by WTO Members when they seek redress for WTO inconsistencies in any given dispute. This is, in our view, the first type of obligations covered under Article 23.

7.40 It is not, however, our task in these proceedings to assess the WTO conformity of specific determinations made under Section 304 in a given dispute but to determine, instead, whether Section 304 as such violates Article 23 of the DSU. This leads us to the second type of obligations covered under Article 23.

7.41 As a general proposition, GATT *acquis*, confirmed in Article XVI:4 of the WTO Agreement and recent WTO panel reports, make abundantly clear that legislation as such, independently from its application in specific cases, may breach GATT/WTO obligations:

(a) In GATT jurisprudence, to give one example, legislation providing for tax discrimination against imported products was found to be GATT inconsistent even before it had actually been applied to specific products and thus before any given product had actually been discriminated against.

(b) Article XVI:4 of the WTO Agreement explicitly confirms that legislation as such falls within the scope of possible WTO violations. It provides as follows:

> Each Member shall ensure the conformity of its laws, regulations and administrative procedures with its obligations as provided in the annexed Agreements.

The three types of measures explicitly made subject to the obligations imposed in the WTO agreements - "laws, regulations and administrative procedures" - are measures that are applicable generally; not measures taken necessarily in a specific case or dispute. Article XVI:4, though not expanding the material obligations under WTO agreements, expands the type of measures made subject to these obligations.

(c) Recent WTO panel reports confirm, too, that legislation as such, independently from its application in a specific case, can be inconsistent with WTO rules.

7.42 Legislation may thus breach WTO obligations. This must be true, too, in respect of Article 23 of the DSU. This is so, in our view, not only because of the above-mentioned case law and Article XVI:4, but also because of the very nature of obligations under Article 23.

7.43 Article 23.1 is not concerned only with specific instances of violation. It prescribes a general duty of a dual nature. First, it imposes on all Members to "have recourse to" the multilateral process set out in the DSU when they seek the redress of a WTO inconsistency. In these circumstances, Members have to have recourse to the DSU dispute settlement system to the exclusion of any other system, in particular a system of unilateral enforcement of WTO rights and obligations. This, what one could call "exclusive dispute resolution clause", is an important new element of Members' rights and obligations under the DSU. Second, Article 23.1 also prescribes that Members, when they have recourse to the dispute settlement system in the DSU, have to "abide by" the rules and procedures set out in the DSU. This second obligation under Article 23.1 is of a confirmatory nature: when having recourse to the DSU Members must abide by all DSU rules and procedures.

7.44 Turning to the second paragraph under Article 23, Article 23.2 - which, on its face, addresses conduct in specific disputes - starts with the words "[i]n such cases". It is, thus, explicitly linked to, and has to be read together with and subject to, Article 23.1.

7.45. Indeed, two of the three prohibitions mentioned in Article 23.2 - Article 23.2(b) and (c) - are but egregious examples of conduct that contradicts the rules and procedures of the DSU which, under the obligation in Article 23.1 to "abide by the rules and procedures" of the DSU, Members are obligated to follow. These rules and procedures clearly cover much more than the ones specifically mentioned in Article 23.2. There is a great deal more State conduct which can violate the general obligation in Article 23.1 to have recourse to, and abide by, the rules and procedures of the DSU than the instances especially singled out in Article 23.2.

7.46. Article 23 interdicts, thus, more than action in specific disputes, it also provides discipline for the general process WTO Members must follow when seeking redress of WTO inconsistencies. A violation of the explicit provisions of Article 23 can, therefore, be of two different kinds. It can be caused

(a) by an ad hoc, specific action in a given dispute, or

(b) by measures of general applicability, e.g. legislation or regulations, providing for a certain process to be followed which does not, say, include recourse to the DSU dispute settlement system or abide by the rules and procedures of the DSU.

[On January 27, 2000, the WTO Dispute Settlement Body adopted the panel's report.]

NOTES AND QUESTIONS

1. What is the purpose of a countermeasure? *See* Art. 49(1) ASR. Do the ASR (in particular, Art. 50(1)(a)) purport to outlaw the use of force in reaction to any violation of international law? What are the differences between reprisals and countermeasures?

2. What are the differences between reciprocity and countermeasures?

3. Are countermeasures impermissible once a dispute between two States is submitted to judicial determination or other forms of dispute settlement? Discuss in this regard The United States Diplomatic and Consular Staff case, as well as the Air Services Agreement case and the United States Trade Act case. Why do the outcomes in the last two cases differ?

4. What, exactly, does the requirement of "proportionality" of countermeasures mean? Does the countermeasure have to be "commensurate" with the injury suffered, as stated in Art. 51 ASR and in the Gabcíkovo case, or does it only have to be "not out of proportion" or "clearly disproportionate" to the injury, allowing for a certain escalation and, thus, deterrence of the initial violation of international law, as stated in *Naulilaa* and the Air Services Agreement case? For pertinent criticism of Art. 51 ASR, *see* David J. Bederman, *Counterintuiting Countermeasures*, 96 AM. J. INT'L L. 817, 821-822 (2002):

> [T]he Commission's adoption of the ICJ's proportionality language in *Gabcíkovo-Nagymaros* raises some troubling concerns. The first is whether the substitution of the relative neologism "commensurate" can at all be regarded as preferable to the continued elaboration of the concept of proportionality. Although state practice on proportionality is admittedly sparse, it often does lie in the interstices of states' reactions to international

incidents. Even while acknowledging the difficulty of assembling and analyzing such evidence, the Commission might well be faulted for failing to cite any source other than a published arbitral or judicial decision. Through its change in terminology, the Commission has raised questions regarding the weight of a century's worth of state practice on proportionality. Second, "commensurate" is nowhere defined in Article 51, nor in the *Gabcikovo-Nagymaros* decision itself, exposing the articles to the criticism, made by some national governments, that "commensurate" was intended to have a meaning rather narrower than "proportional." This conclusion, however, does not necessarily follow either logically or semantically from the Commission's text. Moreover, no discussion by the Commission gives any hint that the commensurability analysis should focus on the level of response required to induce a responsible state to conform its conduct to international obligations. This was an important aspect of earlier ILC considerations of countermeasures but appears to have been collapsed into the threshold requisites of Article 49(1) for the imposition of countermeasures—that they be taken only against a state responsible for an internationally wrongful act as a way to implement the remedies set forth in part 2 of the articles. The use of countermeasures for purely punitive reasons—without any hope or expectation that the malefactor state will actually back down from its offensive conduct —appears to be now precluded by the articles. This change in emphasis on the nature and purpose of countermeasures likewise places in some doubt the Commission's use of earlier international law sources.

See also, Part Six, Military Instrument, at 1092, for discussion of proportionality in the Oil Platforms case.

5. May countermeasures be directed against the nationals of the target State located in the State taking the countermeasures? Discuss *Sardino* v. *Federal Reserve,* 361 F. 2d. 106 (2d Cir, 1996) and *Narenji* v. *Civiletti,* 617 F. 2d. 745 (D.C. Cir, 1979).

6. Are there any legal limits to countermeasures in respect of violations of multilateral treaties or other international law obligations? Or when such countermeasures affect the rights of third States? In this connection, consider the relevance of General Comment 8 (adopted on December 4, 1997) of the Committee on Economic, Social and Cultural Rights on the effect of economic sanctions on civilian populations:

> 4. In considering sanctions, it is essential to distinguish between the basic objective of applying political and economic pressure upon the governing élite of the country to persuade them to conform to international law, and the collateral infliction of suffering upon the most vulnerable groups within the targeted country. For that reason, the sanctions regimes established by the Security Council now include humanitarian exemptions designed to permit the flow of essential goods and services destined for humanitarian purposes. It is commonly assumed that these exemptions ensure basic respect for economic, social and cultural rights within the targeted country. ...
>
> 7. The Committee considers that the provisions of the Covenant, virtually all of which are also reflected in a range of other human rights treaties as well as the Universal Declaration of Human Rights, cannot be considered to e inoperative, or in any way inapplicable, solely because a decision has been taken that considerations of international peace and security warrant the imposition of sanctions. Just as the international community insists that any targeted State must respect the civil and political rights of its citizens, so too must that State and the international community itself do everything possible to protect at least the core content of the economic, social and cultural rights of the affected peoples of the State. ...
>
> 16. In adopting this general comment the sole aim of the Committee is to draw attention to the fact that the inhabitants of a given country do not forfeit their basic economic, social and cultural rights by virtue of any determination that their leaders have violated

> norms relating to international peace and security. The is not to give support or encouragement to such leaders, nor is it to undermine the legitimate interests of the international community in enforcing respect for the provisions of the Charter of the United Nations and the general principle of international law. Rather, it is to insist that lawlessness of one kind should not be met by lawlessness of another kind which pays no heed to the fundamental rights that underlie and give legitimacy to any such collective action.

UN.Doc. E/C.12/1997/8 of 12 December 1997.

7. May a State respond in kind to grave human rights abuses against its nationals in another State? *See* Art. 50 ASR. Do "peremptory norms" limit countermeasures?

8. Can States limit their right to countermeasures by a bilateral or multilateral agreement? Discuss the WTO Panel Report in *United States – Sections 301-310 of the Trade Act of 1974, supra.*

9. What are the differences between countermeasures and retorsion?

10 Are there any legal limits to retorsion?

V. CONSEQUENCES OF RESPONSIBILITY

A. CONTINUED PERFORMANCE OF OBLIGATION, CESSATION AND ASSURANCES OF NON-REPETITION

1. ILC Report 2001: Arts. 28-31; 33 ASR

Article 28: *Legal consequences of an internationally wrongful act*

The international responsibility of a State which is entailed by an internationally wrongful act in accordance with the provisions of Part One involves legal consequences as set out in this Part.

Article 29: *Continued duty of performance*

The legal consequences of an internationally wrongful act under this Part do not affect the continued duty of the responsible State to perform the obligation breached.

Article 30: *Cessation and non-repetition*

The State responsible for the internationally wrongful act is under an obligation:

(a) To cease that act, if it is continuing;

(b) To offer appropriate assurances and guarantees of non-repetition, if circumstances so require. …

Article 33: *Scope of international obligations set out in this Part*

1. The obligations of the responsible State set out in this Part may be owed to another State, to several States, or to the international community as a whole, depending in particular on the character and content of the international obligation and on the circumstances of the breach.

2. This Part is without prejudice to any right, arising from the international responsibility of a State, which may accrue directly to any person or entity other than a State.

2. ILC Report 2001: Related Commentaries

[Commentary to article 29]

(2) Article 29 states the general principle that the legal consequences of an internationally wrongful act do not affect the continued duty of the State to perform the obligation it has breached. As a result of the internationally wrongful act, a new set of legal relations is established between the responsible State and the State or States to whom the international obligation is owed. But this does not mean that the pre-existing legal relation established by the primary obligation disappears. Even if the responsible State complies with its obligations... to cease the wrongful conduct and to make full reparation for the injury caused, it is not relieved thereby of the duty to perform the obligation breached. The continuing obligation to perform an international obligation, notwithstanding a breach, underlies the concept of a continuing wrongful act ... and the obligation of cessation.

[Commentary to article 30]

(1) Article 30 deals with two separate but linked issues raised by the breach of an international obligation: the cessation of the wrongful conduct and the offer of assurances and guarantees of non-repetition by the responsible State if circumstances so require. Both are aspects of the restoration and repair of the legal relationship affected by the breach. Cessation is, as it were, the negative aspect of future performance, concerned with securing an end to continuing wrongful conduct, whereas assurances and guarantees serve a preventive function and may be described as a positive reinforcement of future performance. The continuation in force of the underlying obligation is a necessary assumption of both, since if the obligation has ceased following its breach, the question of cessation does not arise and no assurances and guarantees can be relevant.

(4) Cessation of conduct in breach of an international obligation is the first requirement in eliminating the consequences of wrongful conduct. With reparation, it is one of the two general consequences of an internationally wrongful act. Cessation is often the main focus of the controversy produced by conduct in breach of an international obligation. It is frequently demanded not only by States but also by the organs of international organizations such as the General Assembly and Security Council in the face of serious breaches of international law. By contrast reparation, important though it is in many cases, may not be the central issue in a dispute between States as to questions of responsibility.

3. Fisheries Jurisdiction (F.R.G. v. Ice.)

1974 I.C.J. 175, 201-205 (July 25) (Merits)

[In 1948, Iceland passed a law concerning the Scientific Conservation of the Continental Shelf Fisheries which empowered the Government to establish conservation zones wherein all fisheries would be subject to Icelandic rules and control, to the extent compatible with agreements with other countries. In 1958 Iceland issued regulations extending the limits of its exclusive right of fishing off its coasts to 12 nautical miles., and in 1959 the Althing declared by a resolution "that recognition should be obtained of Iceland's right to the entire continental shelf area in conformity with the policy adopted by the Law of 1948". After refusing to recognize the validity of the new Regulations, the Federal Republic negotiated with Iceland and, on July 19, 1961, concluded with it an Exchange of Notes which specified *inter alia* that the Federal Republic would no longer object to a 12-mile fishery zone, that Iceland would continue to work for the implementation of the 1959 Resolution regarding the extension of fisheries jurisdiction but would give the Federal Republic six months' notice of such extension and that "in case of a dispute in relation to such an extension, the matter shall, at the request of either Party, be referred to the International Court of Justice".

In 1971 the Icelandic Government announced that the agreement on fisheries jurisdiction with the Federal Republic would be terminated and that the limit of Iceland's exclusive fisheries jurisdiction would be extended to 50 miles. By an aide-mémoire of February 24, 1972 the Federal Republic was formally notified of that intention and replied that, in its view, the measures contemplated would be "incompatible with the general rules of international law" and that the Exchange of Notes could not be denounced unilaterally. On July 14, 1972 new Regulations were introduced whereby Iceland's fishery limits would be extended to 50 miles as from September 1, 1972 and all fishing activities by foreign vessels inside those limits would be prohibited.

On May 26, 1972, Germany instituted a proceeding before the ICJ against Iceland. The negotiations between Germany and Iceland, while the proceedings before the Court were continuing did not lead to any agreement.

Germany asked to Court to adjudge and declare *inter alia* that:

> -the unilateral extension by Iceland of its zone of exclusive fisheries jurisdiction to 50 nautical miles from the baselines has, as against the Federal Republic of Germany no basis in international law and shall not be enforced against Germany or vessels registered therein; ...
>
> -while it does not, at present, submit a claim against Iceland for payment of a certain amount of money as compensation for the damage already suffered, it does, however, request the Court to declare that Iceland is, in principle, responsible for the damage inflicted upon German fishing vessels and is under an obligation to pay full compensation for the all the

> damage which Germany and its nationals have actually suffered as a result of the unlawful act of Iceland.

On August 17, 1972, the Court issued interim measures of protection which, *inter alia,* fixed a catch-limitation for German vessels.] …

65. The most appropriate method for the solution of the dispute is clearly that of negotiation. Its objective should be the delimitation of the rights and interests of the Parties, the preferential rights of the coastal State on the one hand and the rights of the Applicant on the other, to balance and regulate equitably questions such as those of catch-limitation, share allocations and "related restrictions concerning areas closed to fishing, number and type of vessels allowed and forms of control of the agreed provisions" (*Fisheries Jurisdiction* (Federal Republic of Germany v. Iceland), Interim Measures, Order of 12 July 1973, I.C.J. Reports 1973, p. 314, para. 7). This necessitates detailed scientific knowledge of the fishing grounds. It is obvious that the relevant information and expertise would be mainly in the possession of the Parties. The Court would, for this reason, meet with difficulties if it were itself to attempt to lay down a precise scheme for an equitable adjustment of the rights involved.

66. It is implicit in the concept of preferential rights that negotiations are required in order to define or delimit the extent of those rights, as was already recognized in the 1958 Geneva Resolution on Special Situations relating to Coastal Fisheries, which constituted the starting point of the law on the subject. This Resolution provides for the establishment, through collaboration between the coastal State and any other States fishing in the area, of agreed measures to secure just treatment of the special situation.

67. The obligation to negotiate thus flows from the very nature of the respective rights of the Parties; to direct them to negotiate is therefore a proper exercise of the judicial function in this case. This also corresponds to the Principles and provisions of the Charter of the United Nations concerning peaceful settlement of disputes. As the Court stated in the *North Sea Continental Shelf* cases:

> [t]his obligation merely constitutes a special application of a principle which underlies all international relations, and which is moreover recognized in Article 33 of the Charter of the United Nations as one of the methods for the peaceful settlement of international disputes (I.C.J. Reports 1969, p. 47, para. 86).

68. In this sense negotiations were initiated by the Parties from the date when Iceland gave notice of its intention to extend its fisheries jurisdiction, but these negotiations reached an early deadlock and could not come to any conclusion. In its Memorial, the Applicant has asked the Court to give the Parties some guidance as to the principles which they should take into account in their negotiations for the most equitable management of the fishery resources, and has declared its readiness to enter into meaningful discussions with the Government of Iceland for the purpose of a permanent settlement of the fisheries problem. As to

Iceland, its policy was clearly stated in paragraph 3 of the Althing Resolution of 15 February 1972, namely to continue efforts to reach a solution of the problems connected with the extension through discussions with the Applicant.

69. In the fresh negotiations which are to take place on the basis of the present Judgment, the Parties will have the benefit of the above appraisal of their respective rights and of certain guidelines defining their scope. The task before them will be to conduct their negotiations on the basis that each must in good faith pay reasonable regard to the legal rights of the other in the waters around Iceland outside the 12-mile limit, thus bringing about an equitable apportionment of the fishing resources based on the facts of the particular situation, and having regard to the interests of other States which have established fishing rights in the area. It is not a matter of finding simply an equitable solution, but an equitable solution derived from the applicable law. As the Court stated in the *North Sea Continental Shelf* cases:

> it is not a question of applying equity simply as a matter of abstract justice, but of applying a rule of law which itself requires the application of equitable principles. (1969 I.C.J. 47, at para. 85).

70. The Court must take into account the situation which will result from the delivery of its Judgment, with respect to the interim measures indicated on 17 August 1972 and which, *inter alia*, fixed a catch-limitation figure of 119,000 tons for vessels registered in the Federal Republic of Germany. These interim measures will cease to have effect as from the date of the present Judgment, since the power of the Court to indicate Interim measures under Article 41 of the Statute of the Court is only exercisable *pendente lite*. Notwithstanding the fact that the Parties have not entered into any provisional arrangement, they are not at liberty to conduct their fishing activities in the disputed waters without limitation. Negotiations in good faith, which are ordered by the Court in the present Judgment, involve in the circumstances of the case an obligation upon the Parties to pay reasonable regard to each other's rights and to conservation requirements pending the conclusion of the negotiations. While this statement is of course a reaffirmation of a self-evident principle, it refers to the rights of the Parties as indicated in the present Judgment. It is obvious that both in regard to merits and to jurisdiction, the Court only pronounces on the case which is before it and not on any hypothetical situation which might arise in the future. At the same time, the Court must add that its Judgment cannot preclude the Parties from benefiting from any subsequent developments in the pertinent rules of international law.

71. By the fourth submission in its Memorial, maintained in the oral proceedings, the Federal Republic of Germany raised the question of compensation for alleged acts of harassment of its fishing vessels by Icelandic coastal patrol boats; the submission reads as follows:

> That the acts of interference by Icelandic coastal patrol boats with fishing vessels registered in the Federal Republic of Germany or with their fishing operations by the threat or use of force are unlawful under inter-

> national law, and that Iceland is under an obligation to make compensation therefor to the Federal Republic of Germany.

72. The Court cannot accept the view that it would lack jurisdiction to deal with this submission. The matter raised therein is part of the controversy between the Parties, and constitutes a dispute relating to Iceland's extension of its fisheries jurisdiction. The submission is one based on facts subsequent to the filing of the Application, but arising directly out of the question which is the subject-matter of that Application. As such it falls within the scope of the Court's jurisdiction defined in the compromissory clause of the Exchange of Notes of 19 July 1961.

73. In its Memorial, and in the oral proceedings, when presenting its submission on compensation, the Federal Republic of Germany stated that:

> [it] reserves all its rights to claim full compensation from M Government of Iceland for all unlawful acts that have been committed, or may yet be committed ... [it] does not, at present, submit a claim against the Republic of Iceland for the payment of a certain amount of money as compensation for the damage already inflicted upon the fishing vessels of the Federal Republic. [It does] however, request the Court to adjudge and declare that the Republic of Iceland is, in principle, responsible for the damage inflicted upon German fishing vessels ... and under an obligation to pay full compensation for all the damage which the Federal Republic of Germany and its nationals have actually suffered thereby.

74. The manner of presentation of this claim raises the question whether the Court is in a position to pronounce on a submission maintained in such an abstract form. The submission does not ask for an assessment of compensation for certain specified acts but for a declaration of principle that Iceland is under an obligation to make compensation to the Federal Republic in respect of all unlawful acts of interference with fishing vessels of the Federal Republic. The Applicant is thus asking for a declaration adjudicating, with definitive effect, that Iceland is under an obligation to pay full compensation for all the damage suffered by the Applicant as a consequence of the acts of interference specified in the proceedings. In its Memorial the Federal Republic has listed a large number of incidents involving its vessels and Icelandic coastal patrol boats, and continues:

> The Government of the Federal Republic does ... request the Court to adjudge and declare that the Republic of Iceland is, in principle, responsible for the damage inflicted upon German fishing vessels by the illegal acts of the Icelandic coastal patrol boats *described in the preceding paragraphs*, and under an obligation to pay full compensation for *all the damage* which the Federal Republic of Germany and its nationals have actually suffered *thereby*. (Emphasis added.)

The final submission, which refers to "the acts of interference" and the "obligation to make compensation therefore", confirms the above interpretation.

75. Part V of the Memorial on the merits contains a general account of what the Federal Republic describes as harassment of its fishing vessels by Iceland, while Annexes G, H, I and K give some further details in diplomatic Notes and Annex L lists the incidents, with a statement of the kind of each incident. Some information concerning incidents is also to be found in the Federal Republic's reports regarding the implementing of the Court's Order for provisional measures.

76. The documents before the Court do not however contain in every case an indication in a concrete form of the damages for which compensation is required or an estimation of the amount of those damages. Nor do they furnish evidence concerning such amounts. In order to award compensation the Court can only act with reference to a concrete submission as to the existence and the amount of each head of damage. Such an award must be based on precise grounds and detailed evidence concerning those acts which have been committed, taking into account all relevant facts of each incident and their consequences in the circumstances of the case. It is only after receiving evidence on these matters that the Court can satisfy itself that each concrete claim is well founded in fact and in law. It is possible to request a general declaration establishing the principle that compensation is due, provided the claimant asks the Court to receive evidence and to determine, in a subsequent phase of the same proceedings, the amount of damage to be assessed. Moreover, while the Applicant has reserved all its rights "to claim compensation", it has not requested that these damages be proved and assessed in a subsequent phase of the present proceedings. It would not be appropriate for the Court, when acting under Article 53 of the Statute, and after the Applicant has stated that it is not submitting a claim for the payment of a certain amount of money as compensation, to take the initiative of requesting specific information and evidence concerning the indemnity which, in the view of the Applicant, would correspond to each incident and each head of damage. In these circumstances, the Court is prevented from making an all-embracing finding of liability which would cover matters as to which it has only limited information and slender evidence. Accordingly, the fourth submission of the Federal Republic of Germany as presented to the Court cannot be acceded to.

4. Gabcíkovo-Nagymaros Project (Hung. v. Slovk.)

1997 I.C.J. 7 (Sept. 25)

114. Finally, Hungary maintained that by their conduct both parties had repudiated the Treaty and that a bilateral treaty repudiated by both parties cannot survive. The Court is of the view, however, that although it has found that both Hungary and Czechoslovakia failed to comply with their obligations under the 1977 Treaty, this reciprocal wrongful conduct did not bring the Treaty to an end nor justify its termination. The Court would set a precedent with disturbing implications for treaty relations and the integrity of the rule *pacta sunt servanda* if it were to conclude that a treaty in force between States, which the parties have implemented in considerable measure and at great cost over a period of years,

might be unilaterally set aside on grounds of reciprocal non-compliance. It would be otherwise, of course, if the parties decided to terminate the Treaty by mutual consent. But in this case, while Hungary purported to terminate the Treaty, Czechoslovakia consistently resisted this act and declared it to be without legal effect. …

125. The Court now turns to the other legal consequences arising from its Judgment. As to this, Hungary argued that future relations between the Parties, as far as Variant C is concerned, are not governed by the 1977 Treaty. It claims that it is entitled, pursuant to the Convention of 1976 on the Regulation of Water Management Issues of Boundary Waters, to "50% of the natural flow of the Danube at the point at which it crosses the boundary below Cunovo" and considers that the Parties

> are obliged to enter into negotiations in order to produce the result that the water conditions along the area from below Cunovo to below the confluence at Sap become jointly defined water conditions as required by Article 3 (a) of the 1976 Convention.

Hungary moreover indicated that any mutually accepted long-term discharge régime must be "capable of avoiding damage, including especially damage to biodiversity prohibited by the [1992 Rio Convention on Biological Diversity]". It added that "a joint environmental impact assessment of the region and of the future of Variant C structures in the context of the sustainable development of the region" should be carried out.

126. Hungary also raised the question of financial accountability for the failure of the original project and stated that both Parties accept the fact that the other has "proprietary and financial interests in the residues of the original Project and that an accounting has to be carried out". Furthermore, it noted that:

> Other elements of damage associated with Variant C on Hungarian territory also have to be brought into the accounting . . ., as well as electricity production since the diversion

and that:

> The overall situation is a complex one, and it may be most easily resolved by some form of lump sum settlement.

127. Hungary stated that Slovakia had incurred international responsibility and should make reparation for the damage caused to Hungary by the operation of Variant C. In that connection, it referred, in the context of reparation of the damage to the environment, to the rule of *restitutio in integrum*, and called for the re-establishment of "joint control by the two States over the installations maintained as they are now", and the "re-establishment of the flow of [the] waters to the level at which it stood prior to the unlawful diversion of the river". It also referred to reparation of the damage to the fauna, the flora, the soil, the sub-soil, the groundwater and the aquifer, the damages suffered by the Hungarian population on account of the increase in the uncertainties weighing on its future (*pretium doloris*), and the damage arising from the unlawful use, in order to divert

the Danube, of installations over which the two Parties exercised joint ownership. Lastly, Hungary called for the "cessation of the continuous unlawful acts" and a "guarantee that the same actions will not be repeated", and asked the Court to order "the permanent suspension of the operation of Variant C". …

[The Court did not require the permanent suspension of the operation of Variant C. Instead, it stated the following:]

146. The Court also concludes that Variant C, which it considers operates in a manner incompatible with the Treaty, should be made to conform to it. By associating Hungary, on an equal footing, in its operation, management and benefits, Variant C will be transformed from a de facto status into a treaty-based régime.

It appears from various parts of the record that, given the current state of information before the Court, Variant C could be made to function in such a way as to accommodate both the economic operation of the system of electricity generation and the satisfaction of essential environmental concerns.

Regularization of Variant C by making it part of a single and indivisible operational system of works also appears necessary to ensure that Article 9 of the Treaty, which provides that the contracting parties shall participate in the use and in the benefits of the System of Locks in equal measure, will again become effective.

147. Re-establishment of the joint régime will also reflect in an optimal way the concept of common utilization of shared water resources for the achievement of the several objectives mentioned in the Treaty, in concordance with Article 5, paragraph 2, of the Convention on the Law of the Non-Navigational Uses of International Watercourses. …

5. LaGrand (Ger. v. U.S.)

2001 I.C.J. 104 (June 27) (Merits)

121. Turning first to the general demand for an assurance of non-repetition, the Court observes that it has been informed by the United States of the "substantial measures [which it is taking] aimed at preventing any recurrence" of the breach of Article 36, paragraph 1 *(b)*. Throughout these proceedings, oral as well as written, the United States has insisted that it "keenly appreciates the importance of the Vienna Convention's consular notification obligation for foreign citizens in the United States as well as for United States citizens travelling and living abroad"; that "effective compliance with the consular notification requirements of Article 36 of the Vienna Convention requires constant effort and attention"; and that

> [t]he Department of State is working intensively to improve understanding of and compliance with consular notification and access requirements throughout the United States, so as to guard against future violations of these requirements.

The United States points out that

> [t]his effort has included the January 1998 publication of a booklet entitled 'Consular Notification and Access: Instructions for Federal, State and Local Law Enforcement and Other Officials Regarding Foreign Nationals in the United States and the Rights of Consular Officials to Assist Them', and development of a small reference card designed to be carried by individual arresting officers.

According to the United States, it is estimated that until now over 60,000 copies of the brochure as well as over 400,000 copies of the pocket card have been distributed to federal, state and local law enforcement and judicial officials throughout the United States. The United States is also conducting training programmes reaching out to all levels of government. In the Department of State a permanent office to focus on United States and foreign compliance with consular notification and access requirements has been created.

122. Germany has stated that it "does not consider the so-called 'assurances' offered by the Respondent as adequate". It says

> [v]iolations of Article 36 followed by death sentences and executions cannot be remedied by apologies or the distribution of leaflets. An effective remedy requires certain changes in US law and practice.

In order to illustrate its point, Germany has presented to the Court a "[l]ist of German nationals detained after January 1, 1998, who claim not to have been informed of their consular rights". The United States has criticized this list as misleading and inaccurate.

123. The Court notes that the United States has acknowledged that, in the case of the LaGrand brothers, it did not comply with its obligations to give consular notification. The United States has presented an apology to Germany for this breach. The Court considers however that an apology is not sufficient in this case, as it would not be in other cases where foreign nationals have not been advised without delay of their rights under Article 36, paragraph 1, of the Vienna Convention and have been subjected to prolonged detention or sentenced to severe penalties.

In this respect, the Court has taken note of the fact that the United States repeated in all phases of these proceedings that it is carrying out a vast and detailed programme in order to ensure compliance by its competent authorities at the federal as well as at the state and local levels with its obligation under Article 36 of the Vienna Convention.

124. The United States has provided the Court with information, which it considers important, on its programme. If a State, in proceedings before this Court, repeatedly refers to substantial activities which it is carrying out in order to achieve compliance with certain obligations under a treaty, then this expresses a commitment to follow through with the efforts in this regard. The programmc in question certainly cannot provide an assurance that there will never again be a

failure by the United States to observe the obligation of notification under Article 36 of the Vienna Convention. But no State could give such a guarantee and Germany does not seek it. The Court considers that the commitment expressed by the United States to ensure implementation of the specific measures adopted in performance of its obligations under Article 36, paragraph 1 *(b),* must be regarded as meeting Germany's request for a general assurance of non-repetition.

125. The Court will now examine the other assurances sought by Germany in its fourth submission. The Court observes in this regard that it can determine the existence of a violation of an international obligation. If necessary, it can also hold that a domestic law has been the cause of this violation. In the present case the Court has made its findings of violations of the obligations under Article 36 of the Vienna Convention when it dealt with the first and the second submission of Germany. But it has not found that a United States law, whether substantive or procedural in character, is inherently inconsistent with the obligations undertaken by the United States in the Vienna Convention. In the present case the violation of Article 36, paragraph 2, was caused by the circumstances in which the procedural default rule was applied, and not by the rule as such.

In the present proceedings the United States has apologized to Germany for the breach of Article 36, paragraph 1, and Germany has not requested material reparation for this injury to itself and to the LaGrand brothers. It does, however, seek assurances:

> [t]hat, in any future cases of detention or of criminal proceedings against German nationals, the United States will ensure in law and practice the effective exercise of the rights under Article 36 of the Vienna Convention on Consular Relations,

and that

> [i]n particular in cases involving the death penalty, this requires the United States to provide effective review of and remedies for criminal convictions impaired by the violation of the rights under Article 36.

The Court considers in this respect that if the United States, notwithstanding its commitment referred to in paragraph 124 above, should fail in its obligation of consular notification to the detriment of German nationals, an apology would not suffice in cases where the individuals concerned have been subjected to prolonged detention or convicted and sentenced to severe penalties. In the case of such a conviction and sentence, it would be incumbent upon the United States to allow the review and reconsideration of the conviction and sentence by taking account of the violation of the rights set forth in the Convention. This obligation can be carried out in various ways. The choice of means must be left to the United States.

126. Given the foregoing ruling by the Court regarding the obligation of the United States under certain circumstances to review and reconsider convictions and sentences, the Court need not examine Germany's further argument which seeks to found a like obligation on the contention that the right of a detained

person to be informed without delay pursuant to Article 36, paragraph 1, of the Vienna Convention is not only an individual right but has today assumed the character of a human right.

127. In reply to the fourth submission of Germany, the Court will therefore limit itself to taking note of the commitment undertaken by the United States to ensure implementation of the specific measures adopted in performance of its obligations under Article 36, paragraph 1 *(b),* of the Vienna Convention, as well as the aforementioned duty of the United States to address violations of that Convention should they still occur in spite of its efforts to achieve compliance.

6. Case Concerning Avena and other Mexican Nationals (Mex. v. U.S.)

I.C.J. Provisional Measures Order of Feb. 5, 2003, *available at* http://www.icj-cij.org/icjwww/idocket/imus/imusorder/imus_iorder_20030205.PDF
[Review facts, *supra*, Part One at 136.]

[Mexico complained that competent authorities of the United States — namely, officials of the States of California, Texas, Illinois, Arizona, Arkansas, Florida, Nevada, Ohio, Oklahoma, and Oregon arrested, detained, tried, convicted, and sentenced to death no fewer than 54 Mexican nationals, following proceedings in which competent authorities failed to comply with their obligations under Article 36 (1) *(b)* of the Vienna Convention.]

5. Whereas in the Application Mexico explains that it has made numerous démarches to the competent authorities of the United States with a view to vindicating its rights and those of its nationals, but that these authorities have consistently refused to provide relief adequate to put an end to these violations and to ensure Mexico that they will not reoccur in the future;

6. Whereas Mexico further notes that the diplomatic démarches which it has made over the last six years to the executive branch of the federal Government of the United States and to the competent authorities of the constituent States have been ineffective; whereas, despite many diplomatic protests during that period, those authorities carried out the execution of several Mexican nationals whose rights under the Vienna Convention had been violated; and whereas the only response ever received by Mexico from those authorities has consisted of formal apologies made after the executions;

7. Whereas in its Application Mexico maintains that the United States, by breaching its obligations under Article 36, paragraph 1 *(b),* of the Vienna Convention, prevented Mexico from exercising its rights and performing its consular functions pursuant to Articles 5 and 36 of the Convention, which "could have prevented the convictions and death sentences"; whereas it contends that the steps taken by the United States to improve compliance with the Vienna Convention do not enable full effect to be given to the rights established by the Conven-

tion; whereas it claims that apologies by the United States in cases of breaches of the Convention are an insufficient remedy; and whereas Mexico accordingly asserts that it has suffered injury, in its own right and in the form of injury to its nationals [Application of Mexico, para. 2], and that it is entitled to *restitutio in integrum*, that is to say, to the "reestablish[ment of] the situation which would, in all probability, have existed if [the violations] had not been committed"; …

11. Whereas in the request for the indication of provisional measures Mexico states that three Mexican nationals, namely Messrs. César Roberto Fierro Reyna, Roberto Moreno Ramos and Osvaldo Torres Aguilera, risk execution within the next six months and that many other Mexican nationals could be executed before the end of 2003; and whereas Mexico further states that César Roberto Fierro Reyna's execution could take place as early as 14 February 2003;

12. Whereas in the request for the indication of provisional measures Mexico notes that the Court indicated provisional measures to prevent executions in two prior cases involving claims brought under the Vienna Convention by States whose nationals were subject to execution in the United States as a result of criminal proceedings conducted in violation of the Convention; whereas it states that "[t]here can be no question of the importance of the interests at stake", that "[i]nternational law recognizes the sanctity of human life" and that "Article 6 of the International Covenant on Civil and Political Rights, to which the United States is a State party, establishes that every human being has an inherent right to life and mandates that States protect that right by law"; and whereas Mexico states in the following terms the grounds for its request and the possible consequences if it is denied:

> Unless the Court indicates provisional measures directing the United States to halt any executions of Mexican nationals until this Court's decision on the merits of Mexico's claims, the executive officials of constituent states of the United States will execute Messrs. Fierro [Reyna], Moreno Ramos, Torres [Aguilera], or other Mexican nationals on death row before the Court has had the opportunity to consider those claims. In that event, Mexico would forever be deprived of the opportunity to vindicate its rights and those of its nationals. As the Court recognized in the *LaGrand* case, such circumstances would constitute irreparable prejudice …;

13. Whereas Mexico concludes that "[p]rovisional measures are therefore clearly justified in order both to protect Mexico's paramount interest in the life and liberty of its nationals and to ensure the Court's ability to order the relief Mexico seeks";

14. Whereas Mexico adds in its request that "[t]here can also be no question about the urgency of the need for provisional measures";

15. Whereas Mexico states that, while it recognizes that the Court may wish to leave to the United States the choice of means to ensure compliance with the provisional measures ordered, it nevertheless requests that the Court "leave no doubt as to the required result";

16. Whereas Mexico notes specifically in its request that "[a]s a matter of international law, both the United States and its constituent political subdivisions have an obligation to abide by the international legal obligations of the United States"; and whereas Mexico takes the view that,

> [h]aving undertaken international obligations on behalf of its constituent political entities, the United States should not now be heard to suggest that it cannot enforce their compliance with its obligations;

17. Whereas Mexico further states that,

> [g]iven the clarity of both international law and United States municipal law, there can be no doubt that the United States has the means to ensure compliance with an order of provisional measures issued by this Court pursuant to article 41 (1) [of its Statute]; ...

37. Whereas at the hearings a Member of the Court put the following question to the Agent of the United States:

> Under what circumstances will the Legal Adviser of the State Department notify an appellate court rather than later notify a clemency body of the obligations of the United States consequent upon an admitted violation of Article 36 of the Vienna Convention? Is the matter simply one of timing?;

whereas, in response to that question, the Agent stated *inter alia* the following:

> We ... have made a conscious choice to focus our efforts on clemency proceedings for providing the review and reconsideration this Court called for in *LaGrand*. [That Judgment] expressly left the choice of means of providing the review and reconsideration to the United States[.] ... [C]lemency proceedings provide a more flexible process that is best suited for achieving, without procedural obstacles, the review and reconsideration this Court called for;

and whereas the Agent added that his

> Government would ... inform a court upon request, at any time, of the international legal obligations of the United States, and how in the particular posture of a given case they [might] or [might] not apply and whether and how they might be carried out under the applicable domestic law in that court,

while explaining that "a court [might] determine ... that domestic law principles still preclude[d] an express judicial remedy for a failure of consular notification";

...

44. Whereas the United States acknowledges that, in certain cases, Mexican nationals have been prosecuted and sentenced without being informed of their rights pursuant to Article 36, paragraph 1 *(b)*, of the Vienna Convention; whereas it argues, however, that in such cases, in accordance with the Court's Judgment

in the *LaGrand* case, the United States has the obligation "by means of its own choosing, [to] allow the review and reconsideration of the conviction and sentence by taking account of the violation of the rights set forth in that Convention"; whereas it submits that in the specific cases identified by Mexico the evidence indicates the commitment of the United States to providing such review and reconsideration; whereas the United States contends that such review and reconsideration can occur through the process of executive clemency — an institution "deeply rooted in the Anglo-American system of justice" — which may be initiated by the individuals concerned after the judicial process has been completed; whereas it claims that such review and reconsideration has already occurred in several cases during the last two years; that none of the Mexicans "currently under sentence of death will be executed unless there has been a review and reconsideration of the conviction and sentence that takes into account any failure to carry out the obligations of Article 36 of the Vienna Convention"; that, under the terms of the Court's decision in the *LaGrand* case, this is a sufficient remedy for its breaches, and that there is accordingly no need to indicate provisional measures intended to preserve the rights to such remedies; ...

49. Whereas "the power of the Court to indicate provisional measures under Article 41 of its Statute is intended to preserve the respective rights of the parties pending its decision, and presupposes that irreparable prejudice shall not be caused to rights which are the subject of a dispute in judicial proceedings" (*LaGrand (Germany* v. *United States of America), Provisional Measures, Order of 3 March 1999, I.C.J. Reports 1999 (I)*, pp. 14-15, para. 22);

50. Whereas, moreover, "provisional measures under Article 41 of the Statute are indicated 'pending the final decision' of the Court on the merits of the case, and are therefore only justified if there is urgency in the sense that action prejudicial to the rights of either party is likely to be taken before such final decision is given" (*Passage through the Great Belt (Finland* v. *Denmark)), Provisional Measures, Order of 29 July 1991, I.C.J. Reports* 1991, p. 17, para. 23); ...

55. Whereas it is apparent from the information before the Court in this case that three Mexican nationals, Messrs. César Roberto Fierro Reyna, Roberto Moreno Ramos and Osvaldo Torres Aguilera, are at risk of execution in the coming months, or possibly even weeks;

whereas their execution would cause irreparable prejudice to any rights that may subsequently be adjudged by the Court to belong to Mexico; and whereas the Court accordingly concludes that the circumstances require that it indicate provisional measures to preserve those rights, as Article 41 of its Statute provides;

56. Whereas the other individuals listed in Mexico's Application, although currently on death row, are not in the same position as the three persons identified in the preceding paragraph of this Order; whereas the Court may, if appropriate,

indicate provisional measures under Article 41 of the Statute in respect of those individuals before it renders final judgment in this case;

57. Whereas it is clearly in the interest of both Parties that their respective rights and obligations be determined definitively as early as possible; whereas it is therefore appropriate that the Court, with the co-operation of the Parties, ensure that a final judgment be reached with all possible expedition;

58. Whereas the decision given in the present proceedings in no way prejudges the question of the jurisdiction of the Court to deal with the merits of the case or any questions relating to the admissibility of the Application, or relating to the merits themselves; and whereas it leaves unaffected the right of the Governments of Mexico and the United States to submit arguments in respect of those questions;

59. For these reasons,

THE COURT, Unanimously,

I. *Indicates* the following provisional measures:

(a) The United States of America shall take all measures necessary to ensure that Mr. César Roberto Fierro Reyna, Mr. Roberto Moreno Ramos and Mr. Osvaldo Torres Aguilera are not executed pending final judgment in these proceedings;

(b) The Government of the United States of America shall inform the Court of all measures taken in implementation of this Order.

II. *Decides* that, until the Court has rendered its final judgment, it shall remain seised of the matters which form the subject of this Order.

NOTES AND QUESTIONS

1. Reparation is not always the central issue in a dispute. In light of the *Fisheries Jurisdiction* case, analyze the main concerns of the parties in the cases set out above.

2. What is the difference between restitution and cessation of a wrongful act?

3. Compare the decision of the ICJ in *Gabcíkovo-Nagymaros* with article 60 of the Vienna Convention on the Law of Treaties which provides in paragraph (1) that: "A material breach of a bilateral treaty by one of the parties entitles the other to invoke the breach as a ground for terminating the treaty or suspending its operation in whole or in part." Is the Vienna Convention on the Law of Treaties *lex specialis*? Are there remedies available to a state party to a bilateral treaty other than those which article 60 of the Vienna Convention provides?

4. What is the significance of guarantees of non-repetition and when is it reasonable to make such a request? In considering this question, bear in mind a statement made by President Johnson with respect to demonstrations against the United States Embassy in Moscow in 1964-1965:

> The U.S. Government must insist that its diplomatic establishments and personnel be given the protection which is required by international law and custom and which is necessary for the conduct of diplomatic relations between States. Expressions of regret and compensation are no substitute for adequate protection.

4 ILM 698 (1965). Compare the statement of President Johnson with the U.S. position in the *LaGrand* case.

5. As to the newly-minted obligation to provide assurances of non-repetition, *see* Christian J. Tams, *Symposium: Reflection on the ICJ's* LaGrand *Decision, Recognizing Guarantees and Assurances of Non-Repetition:* LaGrand *and the Law of State Responsibility*, 26 YALE J. INT'L L. 441 (2002). The requirement of assurances and guarantees of non-repetition in *LaGrand* and Art. 30(b) ASR have been attacked as insufficiently authorized by state practice. *See* Scott M. Sullivan, *Changing the Premise of International Legal Remedies: The Unfounded Adoption of Assurances and Guarantees of Non-Repetition*, 7 UCLA J. INT'L L. & FOR. AFF. 265, 300-01 (2002-2003). Do you agree? If they are part of the ILC's "progressive development" agenda, should these assurances and guarantees of non-repetition be viewed as an important and desirable element of a system of state responsibility designed to enhance compliance with international law?

B. REPARATION

1. ILC Report 2001: Arts. 31, 32, 34-39 ASR

Article 31: *Reparation*

1. The responsible State is under an obligation to make full reparation for the injury caused by the internationally wrongful act.

2. Injury includes any damage, whether material or moral, caused by the internationally wrongful act of a State.

Article 32: *Irrelevance of internal law*

The responsible State may not rely on the provisions of its internal law as justification for failure to comply with its obligations under this Part [articles 28 to 41 dealing with consequences of responsibility].

Article 34: *Forms of reparation*

Full reparation for the injury caused by the internationally wrongful act shall take the form of restitution, compensation and satisfaction, either singly or in combination, in accordance with the provisions of this chapter.

Article 35: *Restitution*

A State responsible for an internationally wrongful act is under an obligation to make restitution, that is, to re-establish the situation which existed before the wrongful act was committed, provided and to the extent that restitution:

(a) Is not materially impossible;

(b) Does not involve a burden out of all proportion to the benefit deriving from restitution instead of compensation.

Article 36: *Compensation*

1. The State responsible for an internationally wrongful act is under an obligation to compensate for the damage caused thereby, insofar as such damage is not made good by restitution.

2. The compensation shall cover any financially assessable damage including loss of profits insofar as it is established.

Article 37: *Satisfaction*

1. The State responsible for an internationally wrongful act is under an obligation to give satisfaction for the injury caused by that act insofar as it cannot be made good by restitution or compensation.

2. Satisfaction may consist in an acknowledgement of the breach, an expression of regret, a formal apology or another appropriate modality.

3. Satisfaction shall not be out of proportion to the injury and may not take a form humiliating to the responsible State.

Article 38: *Interest*

1. Interest on any principal sum due under this chapter shall be payable when necessary in order to ensure full reparation. The interest rate and mode of calculation shall be set so as to achieve that result.

2. Interest runs from the date when the principal sum should have been paid until the date the obligation to pay is fulfilled.

Article 39: *Contribution to the injury*

In the determination of reparation, account shall be taken of the contribution to the injury by wilful or negligent action or omission of the injured State or any person or entity in relation to whom reparation is sought.

2. ILC Report: Related Commentaries

[Commentary to article 31]

(4) The general obligation of reparation is formulated in article 31 as the immediate corollary of a State's responsibility, i.e., as an obligation of the responsible State resulting from the breach, rather than as a right of an injured State or States. This formulation avoids the difficulties that might arise where the same obligation is owed simultaneously to several, many or all States, only a few of which are specially affected by in the breach. …

(5) The responsible State's obligation to make full reparation relates to the "injury caused by the internationally wrongful act". The notion of "injury"… is to be understood as including any damage caused by that act. … [It] includes any material or moral damage caused thereby. This formulation is intended both as inclusive, covering both material and moral damage broadly understood, and as limitative, excluding merely abstract concerns or general interests of a State which is individually unaffected by the breach. "Material" damage here refers to damage to property or other interests of the State and its nationals which is assessable in financial terms. "Moral" damage includes such items as individual pain and suffering, loss of loved ones or personal affront associated with an intrusion on one's home or private life. …

(10) The allocation of injury or loss to a wrongful act is, in principle, a legal and not only a historical or causal process. Various terms are used to describe the link which must exist between the wrongful act and the injury in order for the obligation of reparation to arise. For example, reference may be made to losses "attributable [to the wrongful act] as a proximate cause", or to damage which is "too indirect, remote, and uncertain to be appraised", or to "any direct loss, damage, including environmental damage and the depletion of natural resources, or injury to foreign Governments, nationals and corporations as a result of" the wrongful act. Thus causality in fact is a necessary but not a sufficient condition for reparation. There is a further element, associated with the exclusion of injury that is too "remote" or "consequential" to be the subject of reparation. In some cases, the criterion of "directness" may be used, in others "foreseeability" or "proximity". But other factors may also be relevant: for example, whether State organs deliberately caused the harm in question, or whether the harm caused was within the ambit of the rule which was breached, having regard to the purpose of that rule. In other words, t-he requirement of a causal link is not necessarily the same in relation to every breach of an international obligation. In international as in national law, the question of remoteness of damage "is not a part of the law which can be satisfactorily solved by search for a single verbal formula". The notion of a sufficient causal link which is not too remote is embodied in the general requirement ... that the injury should be in consequence of the wrongful act, ...

(11) A further element affecting the scope of reparation is the question of mitigation of damage. Even the wholly innocent victim of wrongful conduct is expected to act reasonably when confronted by the injury. Although often expressed in terms of a "duty to mitigate", this is not a legal obligation which itself gives rise to responsibility. It is rather that a failure to mitigate by the injured party may preclude recovery to that extent. ...

[Commentary to article 32]

(1) ... Article 32 makes clear the irrelevance of a State's internal law to compliance with the obligations of cessation and reparation. It provides that a State which has committed an internationally wrongful act may not invoke its internal law as a justification for failure to comply with its obligations ... [of cessation and reparation]

[Commentary to article 35]

(1) ... [R]estitution is the first of the forms of reparation available to a State injured by an internationally wrongful act. Restitution involves the re-establishment as far as possible of the situation which existed prior to the commission of the internationally wrongful act, to the extent that any changes that have occurred in that situation may be traced to that act. .....

(2) The concept of restitution is not uniformly defined. According to one definition, restitution consists in re-establishing the *status quo ante*, i.e. the situ-

ation that existed prior to the occurrence of the wrongful act. Under another definition, restitution is the establishment or re-establishment of the situation that would have existed if the wrongful act had not been committed. The former definition is the narrower one; … [t]he latter definition absorbs into the concept of restitution other elements of full reparation and tends to conflate restitution as a form of reparation and the underlying obligation of reparation itself. …

(3) … [B]ecause restitution most closely conforms to the general principle that the responsible State is bound to wipe out the legal and material consequences of its wrongful act by re-establishing the situation that would exist if that act had not been committed, it comes first among the forms of reparation. …

[Commentary to article 36]

(1) Article 36 deals with compensation for damage caused by an internationally wrongful act, to the extent that such damage is not made good by restitution. The notion of "damage" is defined inclusively … as any damage whether material or moral. Article 36 (2) develops this definition by specifying that compensation shall cover any financially assessable damage including loss of profits so far as this is established in the given case. The qualification "financially assessable" is intended to exclude compensation for what is sometimes referred to as "moral damage" to a State, i.e., the affront or injury caused by a violation of rights not associated with actual damage to property or persons: this is the subject matter of satisfaction, dealt with in article 37.

(2) Of the various forms of reparation, compensation is perhaps the most commonly sought in international practice. … It is … well-established that an international court or tribunal which has jurisdiction with respect to a claim of State responsibility has, as an aspect of that jurisdiction, the power to award compensation for damage suffered. …

(7) As to the appropriate heads of compensable damage and the principles of assessment to be applied in quantification, these will vary, depending upon the content of particular primary obligations, an evaluation of the respective behaviour of the parties and, more generally, a concern to reach an equitable and acceptable outcome. …

[Commentary to article 37]

(1) Satisfaction is … not a standard form of reparation, in the sense that in many cases the injury caused by an internationally wrongful act of a State may be fully repaired by restitution and/or compensation. The rather exceptional character of the remedy of satisfaction, and its relationship to the principle of full reparation, are emphasized by the phrase "insofar as [the injury] cannot be made good by restitution or compensation". It is only in those cases where those two forms have not provided full reparation that satisfaction may be required.

[Commentary to article 38]

(1) Interest is not an autonomous form of reparation, nor is it a necessary part of compensation in every case. ... Nevertheless, an award of interest may be required in some cases in order to provide full reparation for the injury caused by an internationally wrongful act, and it is normally the subject of separate treatment in claims for reparation and in the awards of tribunals.

(2) As a general principle, an injured State is entitled to interest on the principal sum representing its loss, if that sum is quantified as at an earlier date than the date of the settlement of, or judgment or award concerning, the claim and to the extent that it is necessary to ensure full reparation. ...

[Commentary to article 39]

(2) Article 39 recognizes that the conduct of the injured State, or of any person or entity in relation to whom reparation is sought, should be taken into account in assessing the form and extent of reparation. This is consonant with the principle that full reparation is due for the injury - but nothing more - arising in consequence of the internationally wrongful act. It is also consistent with fairness as between the responsible State and the victim of the breach..

3. Case Concerning the Factory at Chorzów (Ger. v. Pol.)

1928 P.C.I.J. (Ser. A) No. 17,at 46-48 (Sept. 13)

[The German Reich entered into an agreement in 1915 with a Bavarian company (*Bayerische Stickstoffwerke)* to set up a factory at Chorzów in Upper Silesia in which the Reich would have interests. The necessary lands were to be acquired on behalf of the Reich and entered in its name in the land register. The Bavarian company undertook to manage the factory until March 1941 making use of all patents, licences, experience gained, innovations and improvements, as also of all supply and delivery contracts of which it had the benefit. For this purpose a special section of the company was to be formed, which was, to a certain extent, to be subject to the supervision of the Reich which had the right to a share of the surplus resulting from the working of the Factory during each financial year. The Reich had the right, commencing in March 1926, to terminate the contract for the management of the factory by the Bavarian company subject to fifteen months' notice.

In December 1919, after the Versailles Treaty had been signed but before it went into effect, the Reich transferred all its interests to a newly formed company, the Upper Silesian Stickstoffwerke (*Oberschlesische Stickstoffwerke*). The management and working of the factory at Chorzów were to remain in the hands of the Bavarian company. These relations between the two companies were confirmed by means of letters in 1919. In 1920, the Upper Silesian Stickstoffwerke was duly entered in the Chorzów land registery, as owner of the landed property constituting the nitrate factory of Chorzów.

Under both the Treaty of Versailles and the Geneva Convention (concerning Upper Silesia concluded on May 15th 1922 between Germany and Poland), Poland was obliged to respect German private interests with her jurisdiction but was allowed certain expropriatory privileges, particularly to property held by the German Reich. While the property of German nationals could be seized, it could not be liquidated.

In 1920, the Polish government promulgated a law concerning transfer of rights of the German Treasury and of members of German reigning houses to the Polish Treasury. Article 1 of this law incorporated the expropriation privileges of Versailles and ordered Polish courts to substitute the Polish Treasury for property in the former Prussian provinces owned by the German government. But article 2 stated that alienations or transfers by the Reich after November 11, 1918 would be struck from the registry and the courts were to revert ownership to the former status. This allowed expropriation of the Chorzów factory under article 1 and the Treaty of Versailles. In 1922, the Polish court of Upper Silesia decided that the transfer and register of the Chorzów factory to Upper Silesian Stickstoffwerke were void and returned the interests to the Reich.

Germany challenged Poland's act and took the matter to the Permanent Court. The Permanent Court held that the application of Polish Law of 1922, insofar as it affected German nationals, was contrary to the Geneva Convention concerning Upper Silesia concluded on May 15, 1922 between Germany and Poland. [*German Interests in Polish Upper Silesia*, [1926] P.C.I.J, Ser. A. No. 7]. On the basis of the judgment, the two governments began negotiation to settle compensation, but the negotiations failed. Finally Germany referred the issue back to the Permanent Court requesting the Court to declare that Poland was under an obligation to make good the consequent damage sustained by two companies (the Bavarian company and the Upper Silesian Stickstoffwerke) and to fix the method of payment. The Permanent Court ruled in favour of Germany that Poland was under an obligation to pay compensation corresponding to the damage sustained by the two companies.] ...

The existence of a damage to be made good being recognized by the respondent Party as regards the Bayerische, and the objections raised by the same Party against the existence of any damage that would justify compensation to the Oberschlesische being set aside, the Court must now lay down the guiding principles according to which the amount of compensation due may be determined.

The action of Poland which the Court has judged to be contrary to the Geneva Convention is not an expropriation — to render which lawful only the payment of fair compensation would have been wanting; it is a seizure of property, rights and interests which could not be expropriated even against compensation, save under the exceptional conditions fixed by Article 7 of the said Convention. As the Court has expressly declared in Judgment No. 8, reparation is in this case the consequence not of the application of Articles 6 to 22 of the Geneva Convention, but of acts contrary to those articles.

It follows that the compensation due to the German Government is not necessarily limited to the value of the undertaking at the moment of dispossession, plus interest to the day of payment. This limitation would only be admissible if the Polish Government had had the right to expropriate, and if its wrongful act consisted merely in not having paid to the two Companies the just price of what was expropriated; in the present case, such a limitation might result in placing Germany and the interests protected by the Geneva Convention, on behalf of which interests the German Government is acting, in a situation more unfavourable than that in which Germany and these interests would have been if Poland had respected the said Convention. Such a consequence would not only be unjust, but also and above all incompatible with the aim of Article 6 and following articles of the Convention — that is to say, the prohibition, in principle, of the liquidation of the property, rights and interests of German nationals and of companies controlled by German nationals in Upper Silesia — since it would be tantamount to rendering lawful liquidation and unlawful dispossession indistinguishable in so far as their financial needs are concerned.

The essential principle contained in the actual notion of an illegal act — a principle which seems to be established by international practice and in particular by the decisions of arbitral tribunals — is that reparation must, as far as possible, wipe out all the consequences of the illegal act and re-establish the situation which would, in all probability, have existed if that act had not been committed. Restitution in kind, or if this is not possible, payment of a sum corresponding to the value which a restitution in kind would bear; the award, if need be, of damages for loss sustained which would not be covered by restitution in kind or payment in place of it — such are the principles which should serve to determine the amount of compensation due for an act contrary to international law.

This conclusion particularly applies as regards the Geneva Convention, the object of which is to provide for the maintenance of economic life in Upper Silesia on the basis of respect for the *status quo*. The dispossession of an industrial undertaking — the expropriation of which is prohibited by the Geneva Convention — then involves the obligation to restore the undertaking and, if this be not possible, to pay its value at the time of the indemnification, which value is designed to take the place of restitution which has become impossible. To this obligation, in virtue of the general principles of international law, must be added that of compensating loss sustained as the result of the seizure. The impossibility, on which the Parties are agreed, of restoring the Chorzów factory could therefore have no other effect but that of substituting payment of the value of the undertaking for restitution; it would not be in conformity either with the principles of law or with the wish of the Parties to infer from that agreement that the question of compensation must henceforth be dealt with as though an expropriation properly so called was involved.

4. BP Exploration Co. (Libya) Ltd. v. Government of the Libyan Arab Republic

53 I.L.R. 297 (1979) (Arbitral Award of Oct. 10, 1973 and Aug. 1, 1974)

On 18 December 1957 Libya granted a concession in conformity with Libyan Petroleum Law of 1955 to Mr. Hunt, an American national. In 1960 the Claimant company, BP Exploration Company (Libya) Limited, acquired from Mr. Hunt an undivided one half interest in that concession (concession 65). The concession granted a 50-year exclusive right to search for and extract petroleum in a designated area of Libya, and to sell the oil thus produced. Clause 16 of the Concession provided *inter alia* that

> the contractual rights expressly created by this concession shall not be altered except by mutual consent of the parties.

Clause 28 of the Concession provided for the settlement of disputes by arbitration and stated that the Concession

> shall be governed by and interpreted in accordance with the principles of law of Libya common to the principles of international law and in the absence of such common principles then by and in accordance with the general principles of law, including such of those principles as may have been applied by international tribunals.

On 7 December 1971 Libya nationalized the activities of the claimant with respect to the concession. The Libyan government stated that the nationalization is a retaliation for certain actions by the British Government in the Gulf. The Nationalization Law provided that the Libya should pay compensation to be determined within three months by a committee to be appointed by the Libyan Minister of Petroleum. The Committee did not report within that period.

The claimant started arbitration proceedings on 11 December 1971, contending that the nationalization amounted to a unilateral and unacceptable repudiation of the Concession. As the Libyan government did not respond, the claimants applied to the President of the International Court of Justice for the appointment of a sole arbitrator pursuant to the arbitration clause. The President nominated Judge Lagergren as Sole Arbitrator.

The claimant asked the Tribunal to declare *inter alia* that:

(i) the Libyan Nationalization Law was a breach of the concession;

(ii) the breach was ineffective to terminate the concession;

(iii) the claimant is entitled to be restored to the full enjoyment of its rights under the concession;

(iv) the claimant is the owner of its share of any oil extracted from the concession area after, as well as before, the date of nationalization;

(v) the claimant is entitled to damages.

[The Tribunal] *Held:* - (*inter alia*) that:

(i) the Nationalization Law was a breach of the concession;

(ii) the Nationalization Law "was effective to terminate the BP concession except in the sense that the BP concession forms the basis of the jurisdiction of the Tribunal and of the right of the claimant to claim damages from the Respondent before the Tribunal";

(iii) no declaration could be made that the claimant is entitled to be restored to the full enjoyment of its rights under the concession;

(iv) no declaration could be made that the claimant is the owner of any oil extracted after the date of nationalization;

(v) the claimant is entitled to damages arising from the wrongful act of the respondent, to be assessed by the Tribunal in subsequent proceedings.

With regard to the question of the availability of the remedies of specific performance and *restitutio in integrum* in customary international law, it is important at the outset to stress that the inquiry below will be restricted to the general field of economic interests and especially to long-term contracts of a commercial or industrial character and property and other assets employed in industrial undertakings. The relevant issues may be fundamentally different in other contexts, such as disputes concerning sovereignty over territory. A decision by a tribunal with respect to the alignment of a boundary between two States naturally implies that when the judgment has become effective, the State which is in possession of territory declared in the judgment to be the territory of the other State must cede it. Thus the judgment can be characterised as decreeing *restitutio in integrum* if the territory to be so ceded has been occupied by the wrongful possessor in the near or distant past. If the decision of the tribunal is based on a treaty, such restitution may be said to be of a contractual nature. Every international decision on a boundary at least impliedly presents this feature. The International Court of Justice in the *Temple of Preah Vihear (Merits)* case expressly decided not only that the temple in dispute was situated in territory under the sovereignty of Cambodia but also held that Thailand was under an obligation to withdraw any military or police forces or other guards or keepers stationed by her at the temple or in its vicinity on Cambodian territory. The Court went even further by ordering Thailand to restore to Cambodia any object which Thai authorities might have removed from the temple or the temple area since the date of the occupation of the temple by Thailand in 1954. *(Case concerning the Temple of Preah Vihear (Cambodia v. Thailand) (Merits),* Judgment of 15 June 1962: *I.C.J. Reports* 1962, pp. 36-37.) The restitution in kind ordered by the Court in this instance, it may be noted, comprised not only the temple and the territory on which it was situated but specific, unique works of art of religious significance.

If territory to a State always represents more than the economic market value of the real estate there are other situations also in which restitution in kind from one State to another of thins appropriated in violation of an international obligation may be indicated for particular reasons. This is why the limitation is made in the inquiry below to cases and other materials relating to matters which in essence are of an economic character, such as industrial enterprises and their like.

Professor Schwebel, addressing himself to the question whether specific performance is, or should be, available to parties to a contract between a State and a foreign national, concludes, *de lege lata*, that "the fact that specific performance normally is not afforded against a state in the national sphere suggests that it normally will not be accorded in the international sphere" (Schwebel, "Speculations on Specific Performance of a Contract Between a State and a Foreign National" in *The Rights and Duties of Private Investors Abroad,* 1965, p. 201, at p. 210). However, he continues:

> Good faith observance of international contracts imports performance of the terms of the contract by both parties. Where there is a breach of contract, the remedy to repair it may be specific performance — especially where it is the only remedy which can repair it effectively. If a state, as is sometimes the case, lacks the capacity to pay the damages it would be obliged to pay were monetary compensation required, it may be said that good faith requires the contract to be performed specifically.
> ...

The Tribunal concludes, ... that it is arguable that when an international contractual obligation is unlawfully abrogated by one party, the other party may regard the agreement as still existing until it elects, within a reasonable time, to terminate it, and that such innocent party further, during the intervening period, may suspend its performance thereunder. However, the stated principle of the continuing validity of the agreement rests only on a basis of extreme generality and has never been fully considered in the context of facts as those which are at issue here where one party is a sovereign State.

The important question is what remedies would be available to the party claiming the continuance of the agreement.

The survey of cases and other relevant materials ... demonstrates that there is no explicit support for the proposition that specific performance, and even less so *restitution in integrum*, are remedies of public international law available at the option of a party suffering a wrongful breach by a co-contracting party. An analysis of the cases shows instead that while declaratory awards have often been made in terms of defining the rights and obligations of parties to a concession contract, these cases have never involved the total expropriation or taking by the State of the property, rights and interests of the concessionaire; and indeed in the most important of the cases the validity and continued existence of the contract has not been questioned. The case analysis also demonstrates that the responsibility incurred by the defaulting party for breach of an obligation to perform a contractual undertaking is a duty to pay damages, and that the concept of *restitutio in integrum* has been employed merely as a vehicle for establishing the amount of damages. This becomes nowhere more apparent than in certain remarks on the concept made in 1927 by the late Sir Hersch Lauterpacht:

> A problem of a similar kind is involved in the question as to how far the general principle of private law, that in awarding damages *restitution in integrum* should, as a rule, be aimed at, applies in cases when damages are to be awarded under international law. That principle means that the injured person is placed in the position he occupied before the occurrence of the injurious act or omission; it means that, to use the Roman law terminology, not only the *damnum emergens* but also *lucrum cessans* is taken into consideration...

Hence *restitutio in integrum* is not to be understood in its literal sense of being a remedy for physical reinstatement of a concessionaire party into a position from which it has been effectively and definitively removed by the other, sovereign party. ...

Taking a broad view of State practice over the past decades, there is reason to believe that the sovereignty actually claimed and exercised by modern nations over their natural wealth and resources (with the tacit or explicit acquiescence of other States) constitutes weak support for the contentions of the Claimant in this case as to the remedies available to a concessionaire in circumstances such as the present. The trend of practice has gone another way, and may have become a custom and acquired the force of law.

5. Texaco Overseas Petroleum Co. and California Asiatic Oil Co. v. The Government of Libyan Arab Republic

17 I.L.M. 1 (1978)

On September 1, 1973 and February 11, 1974, Libya promulgated decrees purporting to nationalize all of the rights, interests and property of Texaco Overseas Petroleum Company and California Asiatic Oil Company (the "Companies") in Libya granted to them jointly under 14 Deeds of Concession. The Companies objected to the decrees and claimed that such action by the Libyan Government violated the terms and conditions of their Deeds of Concession.

Exercising their rights under their Deeds of Concession, the Companies requested arbitration and appointed an arbitrator. The Libyan Government refused to accept arbitration and did not appoint an arbitrator. Pursuant to the arbitration provision in their Deeds of Concession, the Companies requested the President of the International Court of Justice to appoint a sole arbitrator to hear and determine the disputes. The Libyan Government opposed such request and filed a memorandum with the President contending, *inter alia*. that the disputes were not subject to arbitration because the nationalizations were acts of sovereignty. This memorandum represented the only appearance by the Libyan Government in the arbitration proceedings.

After considering the Libyan Government's objections, the President of the International Court of Justice, on December 18, 1974, appointed René-Jean Dupuy, Secretary General of The Hague Academy of International Law and Professor of Law at the University of Nice, as the Sole Arbitrator.

On January 19, 1977, the Sole Arbitrator delivered an Award on the Merits in favor of the Companies. The Sole Arbitrator held that (1) the Deeds of Concession are binding on the parties (b) by adopting the measures of nationalization, the Libyan Government breached its obligations arising under the Deeds of Concession and (c) the Libyan Government is legally bound to perform the Deeds of Concession and to give them their full force and effect. The Award on the Merits was delivered in the French language and the following version is the Companies' authorized English translation. Approximately eight months after the Award on the Merits was rendered, Libya and the Companies reached a settlement of their disputes. ...

53. The Tribunal must now rule on the point whether, in adopting nationalization measures in 1973 and 1974, the defendant Government has, or has not, breached its obligations arising from the contracts it executed. For this purpose, this Tribunal should examine the various reasons which could be envisaged in order to justify the defendant Government's behavior and which, if established, would constitute reasons for freeing or exonerating it from the obligation which it had assumed and from its related responsibilities. ...

59. ... [T]he right of a State to nationalize is unquestionable today. It results from international customary law, established as the result of general practices considered by the international community as being the law. The exercise of the national sovereignty to nationalize is regarded as the expression of the State's territorial sovereignty. Territorial sovereignty confers upon the State an exclusive competence to organize as it wishes the economic structures of its territory and to introduce therein any reforms which may seem to be desirable to it. It is an essential prerogative of sovereignty for the constitutionally authorized authorities of the State to choose and build freely an economic and social system. International law recognizes that a State has this prerogative just as it has the prerogative to determine freely its political regime and its constitutional institutions. The exclusive nature of such a right is in fact confirmed by the fact that in practice a decision to nationalize very often is made by the organ which is regarded as the supreme level in the internal hierarchy of State institutions.

60. Diplomatic precedents confirm the right of a State to nationalize. ...

1. Even though, for a State, the decision of nationalizing is an expression of its sovereignty, which this Tribunal fully recognizes, does not the exercise of the right to nationalize know some limits in the international order? In particular, does the act of sovereignty which constitutes the nationalization authorize a State to disregard its international commitments assumed by it within the framework of its sovereignty?

It is clear from an international point of view that it is not possible to criticize a nationalization measure concerning nationals of the State concerned, or any measure affecting aliens in respect of whom the State concerned has made no particular commitment to guarantee and maintain their position. ...But the case is totally different where the State has concluded with a foreign contracting party an internationalized agreement, either because the contract has been subjected to the municipal law of the host country, viewed as a mere law of reference, applicable as of the effective date of the contract, and "stabilized" on that same date by specific clauses, or because it has been placed directly under the aegis of international law. Under these two assumptions, the State has placed itself within the international legal order in order to guarantee vis-à-vis its foreign contracting party a certain legal and economic status over a certain period of time. In consideration for this commitment, the partner is under an obligation to make a certain amount of investments in the country concerned and to explore and exploit at its own risks the petroleum resources which have been conceded to it.

Thus, the decision of a State to take nationalizing measures constitutes the exercise of an internal legal jurisdiction but carries international consequences when such measures affect international legal relationships in which the nationalizing State is involved.

63. In order to appreciate the scope of the nationalization measures, one must therefore investigate whether the nationalizing State has undertaken international obligations which prevent it from resorting to such nationalizing measures for a certain period of time and whether the disregard of such obligations is justified by the sovereign nature of such nationalization measures. Such an investigation, in the instant case, can only be conducted in the light of the agreements binding the two parties and in the light of the applicable law; it therefore is not purely theoretical but falls within the examination of the pertinent existing law.

64. (a) There is no doubt that in the exercise of its sovereignty, a State has the power to make international commitments. Is this rule, which is accepted in general law, confirmed by the law applicable to the agreements between the parties in the present case? In other words, is this rule confirmed both by Libyan law and by international law? And does it therefore constitute a "common principle" in the sense of Clause 28 of the Deeds of Concession?

First, as regards Libyan municipal law, it does not seem possible for this Tribunal to question the principle that the Libyan State can validly contract with subjects of foreign law. This is the case whether one considers the legal traditions deriving from Muslim law or those deriving from the Libyan Civil Code. ...

66. There is no need to dwell at any length on the existence and value of the principle under which a State may, within the framework of its sovereignty, undertake international commitments with respect to a private party. This rule results from the discretionary competence of the State in this area and also from

the principle which confers upon the parties to a contract the right to choose the law governing their relationship.

The right of a state to undertake commitments under a treaty concluded with another State is unquestionable; this has always been recognized by international case law, in particular by the Permanent Court of International Justice in its judgment in the *Wimbledon* case, a decision which emphasized that sovereignty is not negated by the conclusion of a treaty but, quite the contrary, that the conclusion of a treaty is a manifestation of such sovereignty. This observation has logically the same scope and significance in the case of an agreement entered into by a given State with a foreign private company. Of course, this agreement is not a treaty commitment because a treaty can be entered into only as between States, but it is an agreement which falls within the international legal order since the contracting State agreed to submit the agreement not to the exclusive, and unlimited in time, application of its municipal law, but to rules falling at least in part within the framework of international law or of general principles of law. ..

67. … [T]he State, by entering into an international agreement with any partner whatsoever, exercises its sovereignty whenever the State is not subject to duress and where the State has freely committed itself through an untainted consent. …

68. Lastly, and without prejudice to anything which may be said later as to the legal value of the Resolutions of the General Assembly of the United Nations, it should be noted that dismissing the objections made by certain delegations, this body has stated in Resolution 1803, dated 14 December 1962, on the permanent sovereignty over natural resources, that "[f]oreign investment agreements freely entered into by, or between, sovereign States shall be observed in good faith. ... " Thus, this text places on the same footing agreements entered into between States and agreements concluded by a State and foreign private enterprises.

The result is that a State cannot invoke its sovereignty to disregard commitments freely undertaken through the exercise of this same sovereignty and cannot, through measures belonging to its internal order, make null and void the rights of the contracting party which has performed its various obligations under the contract. …

[After having considered international case law and doctrine the tribunal stated:]

109. Thus, for the general reasons mentioned above, this Tribunal must hold that *restitutio in integrum* is, both under the principles of Libyan law and under the principles of international law, the normal sanction for non-performance of contractual obligations and that it is inapplicable only to the extent that restoration of the c:*status quo ante* is impossible. To these general grounds should be added other grounds, which are specific to the present case.

6. Amoco International Finance Corp. v. Iran
15 Iran-U.S. Cl. Trib. Rep. 189 (1987)

1. The present claim arises out of the Khemco Agreement, entered into on 12 July 1966 between Amoco and NPC, pursuant to which the parties thereto agreed to form a joint venture company, Khemco, for the purpose of building and operating a plant for the production and marketing of sulfur, natural gas liquids and liquified petroleum gas derived from natural gas.

2. The Claimant, AIFC, contends that the Government of the Islamic Republic of Iran ("Iran"), independently and through its agencies and instrumentalities, deprived AIFC of its 50% property interest in Khemco. AIFC now seeks recovery of the value of its property interest in Khemco. The factual circumstances relevant to the present Case are generally not in dispute, but the Parties disagree as to the legal characterization and effects of these factual circumstances. The Parties also disagree as to the applicable standards of valuation of AIFC's property interest and the appropriate method of quantifying any damages or compensation to which AIFC may be entitled. ...

104. As discussed further below, the Treaty [Treaty of Amity, Economic Relations and Consular Rights of 1955 between Iran and the U.S.] recognizes the right of each party to nationalize the assets of the nationals and companies of the other party, under stated conditions. This recognition does not mean that any nationalization automatically is lawful, since this will be the case only if the conditions listed in Article IV are actually met. The Tribunal will consider at a later stage in this Award whether or not the expropriation here at issue was made in conformity with the requisites of the Treaty. ...

108. Clearly the purpose of the second sentence of Article IV, paragraph 2 [of the Treaty] is to protect the property of the nationals of one party against expropriation by the other party. Expropriation, which can be defined as a compulsory transfer of property rights, may extend to any right which can be the object of a commercial transaction, *i.e.,* freely sold and bought, and thus has a monetary value. ...

110. As to the Respondents' objection that Amoco, as a Swiss corporation, is outside the protection of the Treaty, the Tribunal agrees that the legal protection afforded by the Treaty applies only to nationals of the parties to the Treaty. As a Swiss corporation, Amoco could not invoke such protection, just as it is not allowed to bring a claim before this Tribunal, which under the CSD has jurisdiction only over claims submitted by nationals of Iran or of the United States. In the present Case, however, the Claimant is not Amoco, but AIFC, the United States corporation which wholly owns and controls Amoco. AIFC relies on the terms of Article VII, paragraph 2 of the CSD, which defines "claims of nationals" as including claims that are owned indirectly by such nationals through ownership of capital stock or other proprietary interests in judicial persons, provided that the

ownership interests of such nationals, collectively, were sufficient at the time the claim arose to control the corporation or other entity, and provided, further, that the corporation or other entity is not itself entitled to bring a claim under the terms of this agreement. ...

(ii) Customary International Law

112. As a *lex specialis* in the relations between the two countries, the Treaty supersedes the *lex generalis,* namely customary international law. This does not mean, however, that the latter is irrelevant in the instant Case. On the contrary, the rules of customary law may be useful in order to fill in possible *lacunae* of the Treaty, to ascertain the meaning of undefined terms in its text or, more generally, to aid interpretation and implementation of its provisions.

113. It is worthwhile, in this context, to compare the provisions of Article IV, paragraph 2 of the Treaty with the customary rules of international law in the field of expropriation. A leading expression of these rules is the judgment of the Permanent Court of International Justice in the *Case Concerning Certain German Interests in Polish Upper Silesia* (Germany v. Poland), 1926 P.C.I.J., Ser. A, No. 7, (Judgment of 25 May 1926). As reflected in this case, the principles of international law generally accepted some sixty years ago in regard to the treatment of foreigners recognized very few exceptions to the principle of respect for vested rights. The Court listed among such exceptions only "expropriation for reasons of public utility, judicial liquidation and similar measures." *Id.* at 22. A very important evolution in the law has taken place since then, with the progressive recognition of the right of States to nationalize foreign property for a public purpose. This right is today unanimously accepted, even by States which reject the principle of permanent sovereignty over natural resources, considered by a majority of States as the legal foundation of such a right. ...

(iii) Discrimination

139. In support of its contention that the expropriation was discriminatory, the Claimant relies on the fact that, in another of NPC's joint ventures, the Japanese share of a consortium, the Iran-Japan Petrochemical Company ("IJPC"), was not expropriated. In contrast, all American interests in petrochemical joint ventures with NPC were expropriated. The Claimant thus argues that the expropriation of Amoco's interest in Khemco was based on discrimination against American interests and was unlawful for this reason.

140. Discrimination is widely held as prohibited by customary international law in the field of expropriation. Although Article IV, paragraph 2 does not expressly prohibit a discriminatory expropriation, paragraph 1 of the same article obliges each party to "refrain from applying unreasonable or discriminatory measures that would impair [the] legally acquired rights and interests" of the nationals and companies of the other party. This wording is so broad that it certainly applies to expropriations. In any event, the Respondents recognize that a discriminatory expropriation is wrongful, but deny that the expropriation was discriminatory in the instant Case.

141. The Respondents assert that the Single Article Act applied to the entire oil industry, irrespective of the nationality of the foreign companies involved in this industry. In the event, it was applied to non-United States corporations as well as United States corporations. Therefore, it can not be held to be discriminatory. That the Special Commission did not include the contract with IJPC among those which were nullified, the Respondents submit, was an exception due to specific circumstances. They mention specifically the fact that the operation of the IJPC joint venture was not closely linked with other contracts relating to the exploitation of oil fields, whereas the operation of the Khemco plant was linked to the supply of gas from the oil fields operated jointly by Amoco and NIOC pursuant to the JSA. Furthermore, the Respondents emphasize that IJPC was not yet an operational concern at the relevant time, a point that was confirmed by the Claimant.

142. The Tribunal finds it difficult, in the absence of any other evidence, to draw the conclusion that the expropriation of a concern was discriminatory only from the fact that another concern in the same economic branch was not expropriated. Reasons specific to the non-expropriated enterprise, or to the expropriated one, or to both, may justify such a difference of treatment. Furthermore, as observed by the arbitral tribunal in *Kuwait* v. *American Independent Oil Company (AMINOIL)*, ..., *reprinted in* 21 *Int'l Legal Mat'ls* 976, 1019, a coherent policy of nationalization can reasonably be operated gradually in successive stages. In the present Case, the peculiarities discussed by the Parties can explain why IJPC was not treated in the same manner as Khemco. The Tribunal declines to find that Khemco's expropriation was discriminatory. ...

(v) Lack of Public Purpose ...

145. A precise definition of the "public purpose" for which an expropriation may be lawfully decided has neither been agreed upon in international law nor even suggested. It is clear that, as a result of the modern acceptance of the right to nationalize, this term is broadly interpreted, and that States, in practice, are granted extensive discretion. An expropriation, the only purpose of which would have been to avoid contractual obligations of the State or of an entity controlled by it, could not, nevertheless, be considered as lawful under international law. ... Such an expropriation, indeed, would be contrary to the principle of good faith and to accept it as lawful would run counter to the well-settled rule that a State has the right to commit itself by contract to foreign corporations. ... It is also generally accepted that a State has no right to expropriate a foreign concern only for financial purposes. It must, however, be observed that, in recent practice and mostly in the oil industry, States have admitted expressly, in a certain number of cases, that they were nationalizing foreign properties primarily in order to obtain a greater share, or even the totality, of the revenues drawn from the exploitation of a national natural resource, which, according to them, should accrue to the development of the country. Such a purpose has not generally been denounced as unlawful and illegitimate.

146. The Tribunal need not determine the delicate legal issues raised in the preceding paragraph. It cannot be doubted that the Single Article Act was adopted for a clear public purpose, namely to complete the nationalization of the oil industry in Iran initiated by the 1951 Nationalization of the Iranian Oil Industry Act, with a view to implementing one of the main economic and political objectives of the new Islamic Government. The decision of the Special Commission relative to Khemco was taken in apparent conformity with the Single Article Act. Even in financial considerations were considered in the adoption of such a decision — which would have been only natural, but which has not been evidenced — this fact would not be sufficient, in the opinion of the Tribunal, to prove that this decision was not taken for a public purpose.

147. In conclusion the Tribunal finds that the Claimant's arguments so far considered do not sustain the contention that the expropriation of Khemco was unlawful. The Tribunal has yet to consider the allegation that the Respondents breached the Khemco Agreement. This question and its possible consequences on the lawfulness of the expropriation will be discussed in the following section.

. . .

2. *The Effects of Lawfulness or Unlawfulness of Expropriation on the Standard of Compensation*

189. Both Parties consider that this issue must be decided by reference to customary international law. The Tribunal agrees. Article IV, paragraph 2 of the Treaty determines the conditions that an expropriation should meet in order to be in conformity with its terms and therefore defines the standard of compensation only in case of a lawful expropriation. A nationalization in breach of the Treaty, on the other hand, would render applicable the rules relating to State responsibility, which are to be found not in the Treaty but in customary law.

190. The Claimant asserts that in case of unlawful expropriation compensation would be more than the "full equivalent" standard which applies to lawful expropriation. The Respondents argue that in case of lawful expropriation the measure of compensation must be substantially less than for a wrongful expropriation and assert that in such a case compensation is limited to the unjustified enrichment realized by the nationalizing State, with no compensation for lost profit.

. . .

192. Undoubtedly, the first principle established by the Court is that a clear distinction must be made between lawful and unlawful expropriations, since the rules applicable to the compensation to be paid by the expropriating State differ according to the legal characterization of the taking. ...

194. The difficulty, obviously, is in determining the practical consequences of the distinction between reparation of the damage caused by a wrongful expropriation and payment of compensation in case of lawful expropriation. The legal bases of the two concepts are totally different and, logically, the practical methods to be used in order to derive the amount due should also differ. ...

197. Obviously the value of an expropriated enterprise does not vary according to the lawfulness or the unlawfulness of the taking. This value can not depend on the legal characterization of a fact totally foreign to the economic constituents of the undertaking, namely the conduct of the expropriating State. In the traditional language of international law it equates the *damnum emergens,* which must be compensated in any case. ... The difference is that if the taking is lawful the value of the undertaking at the time of the dispossession is the measure and the limit of the compensation, while if it is unlawful, this value is, or may be, only a part of the reparation to be paid. In any event, even in case of unlawful expropriation the damage actually sustained is the measure of the reparation, and there is no indication that "punitive damages" could be considered.

[The Tribunal proceeded to examine various methods for valuating an enterprise and, in particular, distinguishing between *lucrum cessans* and *damnum emergens*.]

198. What can be added to the value of the enterprise in order to meet the requirements of *restitutio*? An answer to this question can be found in the formulation of the questions on which an expert inquiry was arranged by the Court. *See Chorzów Factory, supra,* at 51. These questions are an integral part of the judgment, with the same authority as all the other parts, and have the advantage, with the benefit of explanations which the Court added to their terms, of being much more precise and concrete than the general principles previously enunciated. ...

3. The Standard of Compensation in Case of Lawful Expropriation

207. The standard of "just compensation" for a lawful expropriation referred to in Article IV, paragraph 2, of the Treaty is more precisely defined in the last sentence of the paragraph, which provides that "such compensation shall be in an effectively realizable form and shall represent the full equivalent of the property taken."

208. As previously noted, by the phrase "just compensation" the parties to the Treaty chose one of the various ways of describing the compensation due in case of nationalization. It is therefore apparent that the wording chose in Article IV, paragraph 2, has as a first purpose and effect to exclude consideration of factors foreign to the value of the expropriated assets, such as excessive past profits or the rate of return on the initial investment, which have been invoked in a few cases of nationalization in order to reduce the compensation due to an amount less than the full value of these assets. Although counsel for the Respondents made some references to the rate of return on Amoco's initial investment, the Respondents do not appear to suggest that this factor should enter into the calculation of the compensation due, and no other factor of this kind was invoked.

209. "Just compensation" has generally been understood as a compensation equal to the full value of the expropriated assets. This is confirmed in the wording of Article IV, paragraph 2, which refers to "the full equivalent of the property

taken." The Tribunal does not see any material difference between this phrase and the usual term of "just compensation." …Such a finding, however, leaves without a precise answer the difficult question of the proper method to be used in order to determine what the "full value" or "full equivalent" of the property taken means in figures. This question of method goes beyond the issue of the standard of compensation, because several methods are available and the choice between them depends on the particular circumstances of each case. …

7. LaGrand (Ger. v. U.S.)

2001 I.C.J. 104, 116 (June 27) (Merits)

55. According to the United States, Germany's late filing compelled the Court to respond to its request for provisional measures by acting *ex parte*, without full information. The United States claims that the procedure followed was inconsistent with the principles of "equality of the Parties" and of giving each Party a sufficient opportunity to be heard, and that this would justify the Court in not addressing Germany's third submission which is predicated wholly upon the Order of 3 March 1999.

56. Germany acknowledges that delay on the part of a claimant State may render an application inadmissible, but maintains that international law does not lay down any specific time-limit in that regard. It contends that it was only seven days before it filed its Application that it became aware of all the relevant facts underlying its claim, in particular, the fact that the authorities of Arizona knew of the German nationality of the LaGrands since 1982. According to Germany, it cannot be accused of negligence in failing to obtain the 1984 pre-sentence reports earlier. It also maintains that in the period between 1992, when it learned of the LaGrands' cases, and the filing of its Application, it engaged in a variety of activities at the diplomatic and consular level. It adds that it had been confident for much of this period that the United States would ultimately rectify the violations of international law involved.

57. The Court recognizes that Germany may be criticized for the manner in which these proceedings were filed and for their timing. The Court recalls, however, that notwithstanding its awareness of the consequences of Germany's filing at such a late date, it nevertheless considered it appropriate to enter the Order of 3 March 1999, given that an irreparable prejudice appeared to be imminent. In view of these considerations, the Court considers that Germany is now entitled to challenge the alleged failure of the United States to comply with the Order. Accordingly, the Court finds that Germany's third submission is admissible. …

116. The Court observes finally that in the third submission Germany requests the Court to adjudge and declare only that the United States violated its international legal obligation to comply with the Order of 3 March 1999; it contains no other request regarding that violation. Moreover, the Court points out that the United States was under great time pressure in this case, due to the circumstances in which Germany had instituted the proceedings. The Court notes more-

over that at the time when the United States authorities took their decision the question of the binding character of orders indicating provisional measures had been extensively discussed in the literature, but had not been settled by its jurisprudence. The Court would have taken these factors into consideration had Germany's submission included a claim for indemnification.

8. Case Concerning Avena and other Mexican Nationals (Mex. v. U.S.)

Judgment of 31 March 2004

[Review facts, *supra,* Part One at 136.]

Legal consequences of the breach

115. Having concluded that in most of the cases brought before the Court by Mexico in the 52 instances, there has been a failure to observe the obligations prescribed by Article 36, paragraph 1 *(b)*, of the Vienna Convention, the Court now proceeds to the examination of the legal consequences of such a breach and of what legal remedies should be considered for the breach.

116. Mexico in its fourth, fifth and sixth submissions asks the Court to adjudge and declare:

> (4) that pursuant to the injuries suffered by Mexico in its own right and in the exercise of diplomatic protection of its nationals, Mexico is entitled to full reparation for these injuries in the form of *restitutio in integrum*;
>
> (5) that this restitution consists of the obligation to restore the *status quo ante* by annulling or otherwise depriving of full force or effect the conviction and sentences of all 52 Mexican nationals; [and]
>
> (6) that this restitution also includes the obligation to take all measures necessary to ensure that a prior violation of Article 36 shall not affect the subsequent proceedings.

117. In support of its fourth and fifth submissions, Mexico argues that "It is well-established that the primary form of reparation available to a State injured by an internationally wrongful act is *restitutio in integrum*", and that "The United States is therefore obliged to take the necessary action to restore the *status quo ante* in respect of Mexico's nationals detained, tried, convicted and sentenced in violation of their internationally recognized rights". ... Mexico therefore asks in its submissions that the convictions and sentences of the 52 Mexican nationals be annulled, and that, in any future criminal proceedings against these 52 Mexican nationals, evidence obtained in breach of Article 36 of the Vienna Convention be excluded.

118. The United States on the other hand argues:

> *LaGrand*'s holding calls for the United States to provide, in each case, 'review and reconsideration' that 'takes account of' the violation, not 'review and reversal', not across-the-board exclusions of evidence or

nullification of convictions simply because a breach of Article 36 (1) occurred and without regard to its effect upon the conviction and sentence and, not … 'a precise, concrete, stated result: to re-establish the *status quo ante*'.

119. The general principle on the legal consequences of the commission of an internationally wrongful act was stated by the Permanent Court of International Justice in the *Factory at Chorzów* case as follows: "It is a principle of international law that the breach of an engagement involves an obligation to make reparation in an adequate form." (*Factory at Chorzów, Jurisdiction, 1927, P.C.I.J., Series A, No. 9*, p. 21.) What constitutes "reparation in an adequate form" clearly varies depending upon the concrete circumstances surrounding each case and the precise nature and scope of the injury, since the question has to be examined from the viewpoint of what is the "reparation in an adequate form" that corresponds to the injury. …

120. In the *LaGrand* case the Court made a general statement on the principle involved as follows:

> The Court considers in this respect that if the United States, notwithstanding its commitment [to ensure implementation of the specific measures adopted in performance of its obligations under Article 36, paragraph 1 *(b)*], should fail in its obligation of consular notification to the detriment of German nationals, an apology would not suffice in cases where the individuals concerned have been subjected to prolonged detention or convicted and sentenced to severe penalties. In the case of such a conviction and sentence, it would be incumbent upon the United States to allow the review and reconsideration of the conviction and sentence by taking account of the violation of the rights set forth in the Convention. This obligation can be carried out in various ways. The choice of means must be left to the United States. (*I.C.J. Reports 2001*, pp. 513-514, para. 125.)

121. Similarly, in the present case the Court's task is to determine what would be adequate reparation for the violations of Article 36. It should be clear from what has been observed above that the internationally wrongful acts committed by the United States were the failure of its competent authorities to inform the Mexican nationals concerned, to notify Mexican consular posts and to enable Mexico to provide consular assistance. It follows that the remedy to make good these violations should consist in an obligation on the United States to permit review and reconsideration of these nationals' cases by the United States courts, as the Court will explain further in paragraphs 128 to 134 below, with a view to ascertaining whether in each case the violation of Article 36 committed by the competent authorities caused actual prejudice to the defendant in the process of administration of criminal justice.

122. The Court reaffirms that the case before it concerns Article 36 of the Vienna Convention and not the correctness as such of any conviction or sentencing. …

124. Mexico has further contended that the right to consular notification and consular communication under the Vienna Convention is a fundamental human right that constitutes part of due process in criminal proceedings and should be guaranteed in the territory of each of the Contracting Parties to the Vienna Convention; according to Mexico, this right, as such, is so fundamental that its infringement will *ipso facto* produce the effect of vitiating the entire process of the criminal proceedings conducted in violation of this fundamental right. Whether or not the Vienna Convention rights are human rights is not a matter that this Court need decide. The Court would, however, observe that neither the text nor the object and purpose of the Convention, nor any indication in the *travaux préparatoires*, support the conclusion that Mexico draws from its contention in that regard.

125. For these reasons, Mexico's fourth and fifth submissions cannot be upheld.

126. The reasoning of the Court on the fifth submission of Mexico is equally valid in relation to the sixth submission of Mexico. In elaboration of its sixth submission, Mexico contends that "As an aspect of *restitutio in integrum*, Mexico is also entitled to an order that in any subsequent criminal proceedings against the nationals, statements and confessions obtained prior to notification to the national of his right to consular assistance be excluded". Mexico argues that "The exclusionary rule applies in both common law and civil law jurisdictions and requires the exclusion of evidence that is obtained in a manner that violates due process obligations", and on this basis concludes that

> The status of the exclusionary rule as a general principle of law permits the Court to order that the United States is obligated to apply this principle in respect of statements and confessions given to United States law enforcement officials prior to the accused Mexican nationals being advised of their consular rights in any subsequent criminal proceedings against them.

127. The Court does not consider that it is necessary to enter into an examination of the merits of the contention advanced by Mexico that the "exclusionary rule" is "a general principle of law under Article 38(1) (c) of the ... Statute" of the Court. The issue raised by Mexico in its sixth submission relates to the question of what legal consequences flow from the breach of the obligations under Article 36, paragraph 1, a question which the Court has already sufficiently discussed above in relation to the fourth and the fifth submissions of Mexico. The Court is of the view that this question is one which has to be examined under the concrete circumstances of each case by the United States courts concerned in the process of their review and reconsideration. For this reason, the sixth submission of Mexico cannot be upheld.

128. While the Court has rejected the fourth, fifth and sixth submissions of Mexico relating to the remedies for the breaches by the United States of its international obligations under Article 36 of the Vienna Convention, the fact remains that such breaches have been committed, as the Court has found, and it is thus incumbent upon the Court to specify what remedies are required in order to redress the injury done to Mexico and to its nationals by the United States through non-compliance with those international obligations. As has already been observed in paragraph 120, the Court in the *LaGrand* Judgment stated the general principle to be applied in such cases by way of a remedy to redress an injury of this kind (*I.C.J. Reports 2001*, pp. 513-514, para. 125).

129. In this regard, Mexico's seventh submission also asks the Court to adjudge and declare:

> That to the extent that any of the 52 convictions or sentences are not annulled, the United States shall provide, by means of its own choosing, meaningful and effective review and reconsideration of the convictions and sentences of the 52 nationals, and that this obligation cannot be satisfied by means of clemency proceedings or if any municipal law rule or doctrine [that fails to attach legal significance to an Article 36 (1) violation] is applied.

130. On this question of "review and reconsideration", the United States takes the position that it has indeed conformed its conduct to the *LaGrand* Judgment. In a further elaboration of this point, the United States argues that "[t]he Court said in *LaGrand* that the choice of means for allowing the review and reconsideration it called for 'must be left' to the United States", but that "Mexico would not leave this choice to the United States but have the Court undertake the review instead and decide at once that the breach requires the conviction and sentence to be set aside in each case".

131. In stating in its Judgment in the *LaGrand* case that "the United States of America, *by means of its own choosing*, shall allow the review and reconsideration of the conviction and sentence" (*I.C.J. Reports 2001*, p. 516, para. 128; emphasis added), the Court acknowledged that the concrete modalities for such review and reconsideration should be left primarily to the United States. It should be underlined, however, that this freedom in the choice of means for such review and reconsideration is not without qualification: as the passage of the Judgment quoted above makes abundantly clear, such review and reconsideration has to be carried out "by taking account of the violation of the rights set forth in the Convention" (*I.C.J. Reports 2001*, p. 514, para. 125), including, in particular, the question of the legal consequences of the violation upon the criminal proceedings that have followed the violation.

132. The United States argues (1) "that the Court's decision in *LaGrand* in calling for review and reconsideration called for a process to re-examine a conviction and sentence in light of a breach of Article 36"; (2) that "in calling for a

process of review, the Court necessarily implied that one legitimate result of that process might be a conclusion that the conviction and sentence should stand"; and (3) "that the relief Mexico seeks in this case is flatly inconsistent with the Judgment in *LaGrand*: it seeks precisely the award of a substantive outcome that the *LaGrand* Court declined to provide".

133. However, the Court wishes to point out that the current situation in the United States criminal procedure, as explained by the Agent at the hearings, is that "If the defendant alleged at trial that *a failure of consular information resulted in harm to a particular right essential to a fair trial*, an appeals court can *review how the lower court handled that claim of prejudice*", but that "*If the foreign national did not raise his Article 36 claim at trial, he may face procedural constraints* [i.e., the application of the procedural default rule] on raising that particular claim in direct or collateral judicial appeals" (emphasis added). As a result, a claim based on the violation of Article 36, paragraph 1, of the Vienna Convention, however meritorious in itself, could be barred in the courts of the United States by the operation of the procedural default rule. ...

134. It is not sufficient for the United States to argue that "[w]hatever label [the Mexican defendant] places on his claim, his right ... must and will be vindicated if it is raised *in some form* at trial" (emphasis added), and that

> In that way, even though a failure to label the complaint as a breach of the Vienna Convention may mean that he has technically speaking forfeited his right to raise this issue as a Vienna Convention claim, on appeal that failure would not bar him from independently asserting *a claim that he was prejudiced because he lacked this critical protection needed for a fair trial.* (Emphasis added.)

The crucial point in this situation is that, by the operation of the procedural default rule as it is applied at present, the defendant is effectively barred from raising the issue of the violation of his rights under Article 36 of the Vienna Convention and is limited to seeking the vindication of his rights under the United States Constitution.

135. Mexico, in the latter part of its seventh submission, has stated that "this obligation [of providing review and reconsideration] cannot be satisfied by means of clemency proceedings". Mexico elaborates this point by arguing first of all that "the United States's reliance on clemency proceedings is wholly inconsistent with its obligation to provide a remedy, as that obligation was found by this Court in *LaGrand*". ...

Furthermore, Mexico argues that the clemency process is in itself an ineffective remedy to satisfy the international obligations of the United States. It concludes: "clemency review is standardless, secretive, and immune from judicial oversight".

Finally, in support of its contention, Mexico argues that

> [t]he failure of state clemency authorities to pay heed to the intervention of the U.S. Department of State in cases of death-sentenced Mexican nationals refutes the [United States] contention that clemency review will provide meaningful consideration of the violations of rights conferred under Article 36.

136. Against this contention of Mexico, the United States claims that it "gives 'full effect' to the 'purposes for which the rights accorded under [Article 36, paragraph 1,] are intended' through executive clemency". It argues that "[t]he clemency process … is well suited to the task of providing review and reconsideration". The United States explains that "Clemency ... is more than a matter of grace; it is part of the overall scheme for ensuring justice and fairness in the legal process" and that "Clemency procedures are an integral part of the existing 'laws and regulations' of the United States through which errors are addressed".

137. Specifically in the context of the present case, the United States contends that the following two points are particularly noteworthy:

> First, these clemency procedures allow for broad participation by advocates of clemency, including an inmate's attorney and the sending state's consular officer. … Second, these clemency officials are not bound by principles of procedural default, finality, prejudice standards, or any other limitations on judicial review. They may consider any facts and circumstances that they deem appropriate and relevant, including specifically Vienna Convention claims.

138. The Court would emphasize that the "review and reconsideration" prescribed by it in the *LaGrand* case should be effective. Thus it should "tak[e] account of the violation of the rights set forth in [the] Convention" [I.C.J. Reports 2001, p. 516, para. 128 (7)] and guarantee that the violation and the possible prejudice caused by that violation will be fully examined and taken into account in the review and reconsideration process. Lastly, review and reconsideration should be both of the sentence and of the conviction.

139. Accordingly, in a situation of the violation of rights under Article 36, paragraph 1, of the Vienna Convention, the defendant raises his claim in this respect not as a case of "harm to a particular right essential to a fair trial" - a concept relevant to the enjoyment of due process rights under the United States Constitution - but as a case involving the infringement of his rights under Article 36, paragraph 1. The rights guaranteed under the Vienna Convention are treaty rights which the United States has undertaken to comply with in relation to the individual concerned, irrespective of the due process rights under United States constitutional law. In this regard, the Court would point out that what is crucial in the review and reconsideration process is the existence of a procedure which guarantees that full weight is given to the violation of the rights set forth in the

Vienna Convention, whatever may be the actual outcome of such review and reconsideration.

140. As has been explained in paragraphs 128 to 134 above, the Court is of the view that, in cases where the breach of the individual rights of Mexican nationals under Article 36, paragraph 1 *(b)*, of the Convention has resulted, in the sequence of judicial proceedings that has followed, in the individuals concerned being subjected to prolonged detention or convicted and sentenced to severe penalties, the legal consequences of this breach have to be examined and taken into account in the course of review and reconsideration. The Court considers that it is the judicial process that is suited to this task.

141. The Court in the *LaGrand* case left to the United States the choice of means as to how review and reconsideration should be achieved, especially in the light of the procedural default rule. Nevertheless, the premise on which the Court proceeded in that case was that the process of review and reconsideration should occur within the overall judicial proceedings relating to the individual defendant concerned.

142. As regards the clemency procedure, the Court notes that this performs an important function in the administration of criminal justice in the United States and is "the historic remedy for preventing miscarriages of justice where judicial process has been exhausted" (*Herrera* v. *Collins*, 506 U.S. 390 (1993) at pp. 411-412). The Court accepts that executive clemency, while not judicial, is an integral part of the overall scheme for ensuring justice and fairness in the legal process within the United States criminal justice system. It must, however, point out that what is at issue in the present case is not whether executive clemency as an institution is or is not an integral part of the "existing laws and regulations of the United States", but whether the clemency process as practised within the criminal justice systems of different states in the United States can, in and of itself, qualify as an appropriate means for undertaking the effective "review and reconsideration of the conviction and sentence by taking account of the violation of the rights set forth in the Convention", as the Court prescribed in the ~:*LaGrand* Judgment (*I.C.J. Reports 2001*, p. 514, para. 125).

143. It may be true, as the United States argues, that in a number of cases "clemency in fact results in pardons of convictions as well as commutations of sentences". In that sense and to that extent, it might be argued that the facts demonstrated by the United States testify to a degree of effectiveness of the clemency procedures as a means of relieving defendants on death row from execution. The Court notes, however, that the clemency process, as currently practised within the United States criminal justice system, does not appear to meet the requirements described in paragraph 138 above and that it is therefore not sufficient in itself to serve as an appropriate means of "review and reconsideration" as envisaged by the Court in the *LaGrand* case. The Court considers nevertheless that appropriate clemency procedures can supplement judicial review and reconsideration, in particular where the judicial system has failed to

take due account of the violation of the rights set forth in the Vienna Convention, as has occurred in the case of the three Mexican nationals referred to in paragraph 114 above.

144. Finally, the Court will consider the eighth submission of Mexico, in which it asks the Court to adjudge and declare:

> That the [United States] shall cease its violations of Article 36 of the Vienna Convention with regard to Mexico and its 52 nationals and shall provide appropriate guarantees and assurances that it shall take measures sufficient to achieve increased compliance with Article 36 (1) and to ensure compliance with Article 36 (2). …

148. Mexico emphasizes the necessity of requiring the cessation of the wrongful acts because, it alleges, the violation of Article 36 with regard to Mexico and its 52 nationals still continues. The Court considers, however, that Mexico has not established a continuing violation of Article 36 of the Vienna Convention with respect to the 52 individuals referred to in its final submissions; it cannot therefore uphold Mexico's claim seeking cessation. The Court would moreover point out that, inasmuch as these 52 individual cases are at various stages of criminal proceedings before the United States courts, they are in the state of *pendente lite*; and the Court has already indicated in respect of them what it regards as the appropriate remedy, namely review and reconsideration by reference to the breach of the Vienna Convention.

149. The Mexican request for guarantees of non-repetition is based on its contention that beyond these 52 cases there is a "regular and continuing" pattern of breaches by the United States of Article 36. In this respect, the Court observes that there is no evidence properly before it that would establish a general pattern. …

150. …The Court believes that as far as the request of Mexico for guarantees and assurances of non-repetition is concerned, what the Court stated in this passage of the *LaGrand* Judgment remains applicable, and therefore meets that request [para. 124 of the LaGrand Judgment].

151. … [T] he fact that in this case the Court's ruling has concerned only Mexican nationals cannot be taken to imply that the conclusions reached by it in the present Judgment do not apply to other foreign nationals finding themselves in similar situations in the United States.

152. By its Order of 5 February 2003 the Court, acting on a request by Mexico, indicated by way of provisional measure that "The United States of America shall take all measures necessary to ensure that Mr. César Roberto Fierro Reyna, Mr. Roberto Moreno Ramos and Mr. Osvaldo Torres Aguilera are not executed pending final judgment in these proceedings" (*I.C.J. Reports 2003*, pp. 91-92, para. 59 (I)) (see paragraph 21 above). The Order of 5 February 2003, according to its terms and to Article 41 of the Statute, was effective pending final judgment, and the obligations of the United States in that respect are, with effect

from the date of the present Judgment, replaced by those declared in this Judgment. The Court has rejected Mexico's submission that, by way of *restitutio in integrum*, the United States is obliged to annul the convictions and sentences of all of the Mexican nationals the subject of its claims (see above, paragraphs 115-125). The Court has found that, in relation to these three persons (among others), the United States has committed breaches of its obligations under Article 36, paragraph 1 *(b)*, of the Vienna Convention and Article 36, paragraphs 1 *(a)* and *(c)*, of that Convention; moreover, in respect of those three persons alone, the United States has also committed breaches of Article 36, paragraph 2, of the said Convention. The review and reconsideration of conviction and sentence required by Article 36, paragraph 2, which is the appropriate remedy for breaches of Article 36, paragraph 1, has not been carried out. The Court considers that in these three cases it is for the United States to find an appropriate remedy having the nature of review and reconsideration according to the criteria indicated in paragraphs 138 *et seq.* of the present Judgment.

153. For these reasons, THE COURT,

(1) By thirteen votes to two,

Rejects the objection by the United Mexican States to the admissibility of the objections presented by the United States of America to the jurisdiction of the Court and the admissibility of the Mexican claims;

(2) Unanimously,

Rejects the four objections by the United States of America to the jurisdiction of the Court;

(3) Unanimously,

Rejects the five objections by the United States of America to the admissibility of the claims of the United Mexican States;

(4) By fourteen votes to one,

Finds that, by not informing, without delay upon their detention, the 51 Mexican nationals referred to in paragraph 106 (1) above of their rights under Article 36, paragraph 1 *(b)*, of the Vienna Convention on Consular Relations of 24 April 1963, the United States of America breached the obligations incumbent upon it under that subparagraph;

(5) By fourteen votes to one,

Finds that, by not notifying the appropriate Mexican consular post without delay of the detention of the 49 Mexican nationals referred to in paragraph 106 (2) above and thereby depriving the United Mexican States of the right, in a timely fashion, to render the assistance provided for by the Vienna Convention to the individuals concerned, the United States of America breached the obligations incumbent upon it under Article 36, paragraph 1 *(b)*;

(6) By fourteen votes to one,

Finds that, in relation to the 49 Mexican nationals referred to in paragraph 106 (3) above, the United States of America deprived the United Mexican States of the right, in a timely fashion, to communicate with and have access to those nationals and to visit them in detention, and thereby breached the obligations incumbent upon it under Article 36, paragraph 1 *(a)* and *(c)*, of the Convention;

(7) By fourteen votes to one,

Finds that, in relation to the 34 Mexican nationals referred to in paragraph 106 (4) above, the United States of America deprived the United Mexican States of the right, in a timely fashion, to arrange for legal representation of those nationals, and thereby breached the obligations incumbent upon it under Article 36, paragraph 1 *(c)*, of the Convention;

(8) By fourteen votes to one,

Finds that, by not permitting the review and reconsideration, in the light of the rights set forth in the Convention, of the conviction and sentences of Mr. César Roberto Fierro Reyna, Mr. Roberto Moreno Ramos and Mr. Osvaldo Torres Aguilera, after the violations referred to in subparagraph (4) above had been established in respect of those individuals, the United States of America breached the obligations incumbent upon it under Article 36, paragraph 2, of the Convention;

(9) By fourteen votes to one,

Finds that the appropriate reparation in this case consists in the obligation of the United States of America to provide, by means of its own choosing, review and reconsideration of the convictions and sentences of the Mexican nationals referred to in subparagraphs (4), (5), (6) and (7) above, by taking account both of the violation of the rights set forth in Article 36 of the Convention and of paragraphs 138 to 141 of this Judgment;

(10) Unanimously,

Takes note of the commitment undertaken by the United States of America to ensure implementation of the specific measures adopted in performance of its obligations under Article 36, paragraph 1 *(b)*, of the Vienna Convention; and *finds* that this commitment must be regarded as meeting the request by the United Mexican States for guarantees and assurances of non-repetition;

(11) Unanimously,

Finds that, should Mexican nationals nonetheless be sentenced to severe penalties, without their rights under Article 36, paragraph 1 *(b)*, of the Convention having been respected, the United States of America shall provide, by means of its own choosing, review and reconsideration of the conviction and sentence, so as to allow full weight to be given to the violation of the rights set forth in the Convention, taking account of paragraphs 138 to 141 of this Judgment.

9. "I'm Alone" (Can. v. U.S.)

3 R.I.A.A. 1609, 1617 (1935)

[A Canadian vessel owned by United States nationals was sunk by the United States Coast Guard. The Commission did not award any damages for the loss but stated :]

The vessel was a British ship of Canadian registry; after her construction she was employed for several years in rum running, the cargo being destined for illegal introduction into, and sale in, the United States. In December, 1928, and during the early months of 1929, down to the sinking of the vessel on the 22nd of March of that year, she was engaged in carrying liquor from Belize, in British Honduras, to an agreed point or points in the Gulf of Mexico, in convenient proximity to the coast of Louisiana, where the liquor was taken from her in smaller craft, smuggled into the United States, and sold there.

We find as a fact that, from September 1928 down to the date when she was sunk, the *I'm Alone,* although a British ship of Canadian registry, was *de facto* owned, controlled, and at the critical times, managed, and her movements directed and her cargo dealt with and disposed of, by a group of persons acting in concert who were entirely, or nearly so, citizens of the United States, and who employed her for the purposes mentioned. The possibility that one of the group may not have been of United States nationality we regard as of no importance in the circumstances of this case.

The Commissioners considers that, in view of the facts, no compensation ought to be paid in respect of the loss of the ship or the cargo.

The act of sinking the ship, however, by officers of the United States Coast Guard, was, as we have already indicated, an unlawful act; and the Commissioners consider that the United States ought formally to acknowledge its illegality, and to apologize to His Majesty's Canadian Government therefor; and, further, that as a material amend in respect of the wrong the United States should pay the sum of $25,000 to His Majesty's Canadian Government; and they recommend accordingly.

The Commissioners have had under consideration the compensation which ought to be paid by the United States to His Majesty's Canadian Government for the benefit of the captain and members of the crew, none of whom was a party to the illegal conspiracy to smuggle liquor into the United States and sell the same there.

10. W. Michael Reisman, *The Lessons of Qana*

22 YALE J. INT'L L. 381, 397-398 (1997)

The dynamic linking choice of weapons to domestic political considerations will challenge humanitarian law, which may have to develop other techniques and doctrines. One, I submit, should be a *general* obligation to compensate for unintended injuries to civilians. Article 3 of the 1907 Hague Convention on Land Warfare established the principle of compensation, and it is restated in article 91 of Protocol I: "A Party to the conflict which violates the provisions of the Conventions or of this Protocol shall, if the case demands, be liable to pay compensation. It shall be responsible for all acts committed by persons forming part of its armed forces." A slightly better formula, focusing on the persons actually injured, is found in article 24(5) of the Hague Rules of Aërial Warfare of 1923: "A belligerent is liable to pay compensation for injuries to person or to property caused by the violation of its officers or forces of the provisions of this article." But all of these provisions make compensation conditional of a *violation* of the laws of war. This is inertial treaty law and not proactive humanitarian law, for it confuses two entirely different sanction objectives: punishing the law violator, on the one hand, and succoring the victims who suffer, on the other, whether or not the cause of their injury was a violation of the law of war.

The euphemism "collateral damage" means death and injury of noncombatants and destruction of their property. That term of art may insulate the party that has caused this damage from international *criminal* responsibility and, perhaps, moral self-doubt. It should not absolve it from a civil obligation to compensate, directly and promptly, the victims or their survivors, regardless of whether the actions of the damage-feasor violated the laws of war or merely caused "collateral damage." An appropriate example may be found in the downing of the Iranian Airbus by the U.S.A. *Vincennes* in the Persian Gulf. President Reagan insisted that the U.S. action did not violate the law of war; nevertheless, he promptly offered compensation directly to the families of the victims. The United States has now paid. It is unimportant if offers and payments such as these are made *ex gratia*, as they usually are, because self-characterization of an action as lawful is not legally binding on others. What is important is that payments to innocent injured parties be made as soon as possible.

Compensation in humanitarian law should be conceived on two levels, with two measures of damages. First, and without regard to the question of violation of the law of war, belligerents must compensate injured noncombatants or their survivors promptly, in proportion to the degree to which each caused the injuries suffered. Measure of damages here may be determined by general principles of compensation for civil liability on which there is ample agreement and for which there are detailed models. Thus, compensation will be a humanitarian instrument for repair of an injury suffered by an innocent party. The issue is not absolute liability, for a state may substantially reduce, if not eliminate, liability by using more discriminating (and hence more operator-vulnerable) weapons, thereby "externalising" what would otherwise be collateral damage. But it is surely incompatible with the postulates of humanitarian law, indeed law in general, to allow an actor to externalise heavy costs onto innocent people—without engaging responsibility to compensate.

Second, compensation should also be conceived of as a sanction for violations of treaty terms—in short, an international expiation for criminal responsibility. Measure of damages here will be determined in sanction terms by reference to such factors as the gravity of the offense, intentionality, etc.

In particular cases, both liabilities may not be present. In some circumstances, the liability may fall heavily or even entirely on the other belligerent; for example, when it uses noncombatants as human shields. This two-level approach is needed because, without the sanction component, incentives for compliance with the laws of war will decline; without the personal compensation component, incentives to reduce collateral damage, already declining because of concern for retro-vulnerability, will sink further. A humane law of armed conflict should resist both of these tendencies.

In an incident like Qana, the party causing injury should be obliged to assume a civil liability to the victims and their survivors, proportional to its responsibility. Whether or not its actions were internationally criminal or were marked by a chain of grievous errors, innocent victims are entitled to the repair of their injuries. That repair should not come from the international community, but from the party that, arguably in ways compatible with the law of war, elected to reduce its own exposure and contain its own injuries by shifting the danger and consequent injury onto others. In imposing the costs of the engagement onto innocent parties, a belligerent should, like anyone in war or peace, be obliged to repair the injuries it has caused in a measure proportional to its contribution to them.

Notes and Questions

1. International law has not recognized punitive damages. This position has been reiterated in *Velasquez Rodriguez* by the Inter-American Court of Human Rights (Inter-Am. C.H.R., Series C, No.7 (1989) and *Re Letelier and Moffit*, 88 I.L.R. 727 (1992)). *See also* N. Jorgensen, *A Reappraisal of Punitive Damages in International Law,* 68 Brit. Yb. Int'l L. 247 (1997). This principle has been accepted by the International Law Commission in the draft articles on responsibility of states for internationally wrongful acts.

2. What is the role of "satisfaction" and "apology" as remedies and how are they different from punitive damages? In *Rainbow Warrior* (N.Z. v. Fr.), the Tribunal held that:

> There is a long established practice of States and international Courts and Tribunals of using satisfaction as remedy or form of reparation (in the wide sense) for the breach of an international obligation. This practice relates particularly to the case of moral or legal damage done directly to the State, especially as opposed to the case of damage to persons involving international responsibilities.

20 R.I.A.A. 122 (1990).

3. Restitution may take different forms: return of territory, property, persons, restoration, reestablishment of the legal situation which existed between the parties. *See* the following cases in

this regard: *U.S. Diplomatic and Consular Staff in Tehran*; *Temple of Preah Vihear*, (1962 I.C.J. 6 (June 15)); *Buzau-Nehoiasi Railway*, (3 R.I.A.A. 1839 (1939); *Free Zones of Upper Savoy and the District of Gex* (1932 P.C.I.J. (ser. A/B) No. 46, at 96).

4. How did the ICJ interpret the notion of restitution in *LaGrand* and *Avena*?

5. Why did the ICJ decide in its judgment in *Avena* that executive clemency proceedings do not meet the requirement of judicial "review and reconsideration"?

6. What are the conditions under which restitution may not be granted?

7. As to reparations, see, generally, Dinah Shelton, *Righting Wrongs: Reparations in the Articles on State Responsibility*, 96 Am. J. Int'l L. 833 (2002). For remedies in violation of human rights see Dinah Shelton, Remedies in International Human Rights Law 214-279 (Oxford U. Press1999). *See also*, Michael Reisman, *Compensation for Human Rights Violations: the Practice of the Past Decade in the Americas*, *in* State Responsibility and the Individual: Reparation in instances of Grave Violations of Human Rights 63-108 (Albrecht Randelzhofer & Christian Tomuschat eds., 1999).

8. Compare the function of compensation with satisfaction. What are common forms of satisfaction under Art. 37 ASR?

9. Why is compensation the most common form of reparation?

10. In cases of nationalization, is there any difference between the amount of compensation when the taking is lawful or unlawful?. *See* The Jurisprudence of the Iran-United States Claims Tribunal, chaps. 5, 6 & 12 (George H. Aldrich ed. 1996); The Iran-United States Claims Tribunal: Its Contribution to the Law of State Responsibility, 185-266 & 325-385 (R.B. Lillich & D.B. McGraw eds. 1999).

11. Is there any basis for requiring a state to pay compensation for damage caused as a result of an act of self-defense? Review Professor Reisman's article, *The Lessons of Qana*, *supra*.

VI. Serious Violations of Peremptory Norms

A. ILC Report 2001: Arts. 40-41 ASR

Article 40: *Application of this chapter*

1. This chapter applies to the international responsibility which is entailed by a serious breach by a State of an obligation arising under a peremptory norm of general international law.

2. A breach of such an obligation is serious if it involves a gross or systematic failure by the responsible State to fulfil the obligation.

Article 41: *Particular consequences of a serious breach of an obligation under this chapter*

1. States shall cooperate to bring to an end through lawful means any serious breach within the meaning of article 40.

2. No State shall recognize as lawful a situation created by a serious breach within the meaning of article 40, nor render aid or assistance in maintaining that situation.

3. This article is without prejudice to the other consequences referred to in this Part and to such further consequences that a breach to which this chapter applies may entail under international law.

B. ILC Report 2001: Related Commentaries

[General Commentary to articles 40 and 41]

(1) ...[Articles 40 and 41 set] out certain consequences of specific types of breaches of international law, identified by reference to two criteria: first, they involve breaches of obligations under peremptory norms of general international law; second, the breaches concerned are in themselves serious, having regard to their scale or character. ...

(2) Whether a qualitative distinction should be recognized between different breaches of international law has been the subject of a major debate....

(7) Accordingly the present Articles do not recognize the existence of any distinction between State "crimes" and "delicts" for the purposes of Part One. On the other hand, it is necessary for the Articles to reflect that there are certain *consequences* flowing from the basic concepts of peremptory norms of general international law and obligations to the international community as a whole within the field of State responsibility. Whether or not peremptory norms of general international law and obligations to the international community as a whole are aspects of a single basic idea, there is at the very least substantial overlap between them....

1. Barcelona Traction, Light and Power Company, Limited, Second Phase (Belg. v. Spain)

1970 I.C.J. 3 (Feb. 5), paras 33, 34 (Review *supra* Part Three, at 443)

2. East Timor (Port. v. Austl.)

1995 I.C.J. 90 (June 30)

[In the sixteenth century East Timor became a colony of Portugal, and Portugal remained there until 1975. The western part of East Timor came under Dutch rule and later became part of Indonesia. In 1960, the UN General Assembly recognized East Timor as a non-self-governing territory, administered by Portugal, within the meaning of Chapter XI of the UN Charter. Following internal disturbances in East Timor in 1975, the Portuguese civil and administrative authorities withdrew from the mainland of East Timor to the island of Atauro and by the end of that year they left East Timor altogether. Indonesia occupied East Timor and it remained under its effective control. Following the intervention of Indonesia and the withdrawal of the Portuguese authorities, the Security Council and the General Assembly of the United Nations adopted resolutions requesting all states to respect the territorial integrity of East Timor as well as the inalienable right of its people to self-determination. Some of the resolutions called upon

Portugal, as the administrating power to cooperate with the United Nations. No further actions, however, were taken by the United Nations.

The incorporation of East Timor as part of Indonesia was recognized by Australia *de facto* in 1978, but not the means by which this was brought about. In 1979, Australia began negotiation with Indonesia for the delimitation of the continental shelf between itself and East Timor. The negotiations did not come to fruition. The two countries then agreed to establish a provisional arrangement for the joint exploration and exploitation of the resources of an area of the continental shelf between Australia and East Timor. A treaty to that effect was concluded between Australia and Indonesia in 1989 which entered into force in 1991.

In February 1991, Portugal instituted a proceeding against Australia at the International Court of Justice, on the basis of article 36, paragraph 2 of the Statute of the Court invoking the responsibility of Australia. Portugal claimed that Australia by concluding the treaty with Indonesia, *inter alia* had infringed the rights of the people of East Timor to self-determination and to permanent sovereignty over their natural resources and the rights of Portugal as the administrating power of East Timor.

The Court declined jurisdiction on the ground that, it would have to rule as a prerequisite, on the lawfulness of Indonesia's conduct in the absence of that state's consent to the jurisdiction of the Court.

In its judgment, the Court addressed the question of rights *erga omnes*.] …

29. However, Portugal puts forward an additional argument aiming to show that the principle formulated by the Court in the case concerning *Monetary Gold Removed from Rome in 1943* is not applicable in the present case. It maintains, in effect, that the right which Australia allegedly breached were rights *erga omnes* and that accordingly Portugal could require it, individually, to respect them regardless of whether or not another State had conducted itself in a similarly unlawful manner.

In the Court's view, Portugal's assertion that the right of peoples to self-determination, as it evolved from the Charter and from United Nations practice, has an *erga omnes* character, is irreproachable. The principle of self-determination of peoples has been recognized by the United Nations Charter and in the jurisprudence of the Court …; it is one of the essential principles of contemporary international law. However, the Court considers that the *erga omnes* character of a norm and the rule of consent to jurisdiction are two different things. Whatever the nature of the obligations involved, the Court could not rule on the lawfulness of the conduct of a State when its judgment would imply an evaluation of the lawfulness of the conduct of another State which is not a party to the case. Where this is so, the Court cannot act, even if the right in question in a right *erga omnes*.

3. Application of the Convention on the Prevention and Punishment of the Crime of Genocide (Bosn. & Herz. v. Yug.)

1996 I.C.J. 595 (July 11) (Preliminary Objections)

[On 20 March 1993, Bosnia-Herzegovina filed a claim against Yugoslavia for violation of the 1948 Convention on the Prevention and Punishment of the Crime of Genocide. Bosnia-Herzegovina claimed that Yugoslavia (Serbia and Montenegro), directly, or through the use of its surrogates, had violated the Genocide Convention of the Prevention and Punishment of the Crime of Genocide, by destroying in part, and attempting to destroy in whole, national, ethnic or religious groups within, but not limited to the territory of Bosnia-Herzegovina, including in particular the Muslim population, by killing members of the group; causing deliberate bodily or mental harm to members of the group; deliberately inflicting on the group conditions of life calculated to bring about its physical destruction in whole or in part; imposing measures intended to prevent births within the group.

Bosnia-Herzegovina invoked Article IX of the Genocide Convention as the basis of the jurisdiction of the Court.

Yugoslavia challenged the Court's Jurisdiction on *inter alia* the ground that the case involved internal armed conflict; the claims based on allegations of State responsibility fell outside the scope of the Genocide Convention and of its compromissory clause; and that certain allegations were related to events which occurred prior to entry into force of the Genocide Convention for Bosnia-Herzegovina and therefore do not fall within the jurisdiction of the Court.

The Court rejected the objections to its jurisdiction by Yugoslavia and in doing so also relied on the notion of obligations *erga omnes*.]

30. To found its jurisdiction, the Court must, however, still ensure that the dispute in question does indeed fall within the provisions of Article IX of the Genocide Convention.

Yugoslavia disputes this. It contests the existence in this case of an "international dispute" within the meaning of the Convention, basing itself on two propositions: first, that the conflict occurring in certain parts of the Applicant's territory was of a domestic nature, Yugoslavia was not party to it and did not exercise jurisdiction over that territory at the time in question; and second, that State responsibility, as referred to in the requests of Bosnia-Herzegovina, was excluded from the scope of application of Article IX.

31. The Court will begin with a consideration of Yugoslavia's first proposition.

In doing so, it will start by recalling the terms of Article I of the Genocide Convention, worded as follows:

> The Contracting Parties confirm that genocide, whether committed in time of peace or in time of war, is a crime under international law which they undertake to prevent and to punish.

The Court sees nothing in this provision which would make the applicability of the Convention subject to the condition that the acts contemplated by it should have been committed within the framework of a particular type of conflict. The contracting parties expressly state therein their willingness to consider genocide as "a crime under international law", which they must prevent and punish independently of the context "of peace" or "of war" in which it takes place. In the view of the Court, this means that the Convention is applicable, without reference to the circumstances linked to the domestic or international nature of the conflict, provided the acts to which it refers in Articles II and III have been perpetrated. In other words, irrespective of the nature of the conflict forming the background to such acts, the obligations of prevention and punishment which are incumbent upon the States parties to the Convention remain identical.

As regards the question whether Yugoslavia took part — directly or indirectly in the conflict at issue, the Court would merely note that the Parties have radically differing viewpoints in this respect and that it cannot, at this stage in the proceedings, settle this question, which clearly belongs to the merits.

Lastly, as to the territorial problems linked to the application of the Convention, the Court would point out that the only provision relevant to this, Article VI, merely provides for persons accused of one of the acts prohibited by the Convention to "be tried by a competent tribunal of the State in the territory of which the act was committed ...". It would also recall its understanding of the object and purpose of the Convention, as set out in its Opinion of 28 May 1951, cited above:

> The origins of the Convention show that it was the intention of the United Nations to condemn and punish genocide as 'a crime under international law' involving a denial of the right of existence of entire human groups, a denial which shocks the conscience of mankind and results in great losses to humanity, and which is contrary to moral law and to the spirit and aims of the United Nations (Resolution 96 (I) of the General Assembly, December 11th 1946). The first consequence arising from this conception is that the principles underlying the Convention are principles which are recognized by civilized nations as binding on States, even without any conventional obligation. A second consequence is the universal character both of the condemnation of genocide and of the co-operation required 'in order to liberate mankind from such an odious scourge' (Preamble to the Convention). (*I.C.J. Reports 1951*, p. 23.)

It follows that the rights and obligations enshrined by the Convention are rights and obligations *erga omnes*. The Court notes that the obligation each State thus has to prevent and to punish the crime of genocide is not territorially limited by the Convention.

32. The Court now comes to the second proposition advanced by Yugoslavia, regarding the type of State responsibility envisaged in Article IX of the Convention. According to Yugoslavia, that Article would only cover the responsibility flowing from the failure of a State to fulfil its obligations of prevention and punish-

ment as contemplated by Articles V, VI and VII; on the other hand, the responsibility of a State for an act of genocide perpetrated by the State itself would be excluded from the scope of the Convention.

The Court would observe that the reference in Article IX to "the responsibility of a State for genocide or for any of the other acts enumerated in Article III", does not exclude any form of State responsibility.

Nor is the responsibility of a State for acts of its organs excluded by Article IV of the Convention, which contemplates the commission of an act of genocide by "rulers" or "public officials".

NOTES AND QUESTIONS

1. In its earlier work on the topic of state responsibility, the International Law Commission had introduced the notion of "international crimes" of states as separate from "international delicts." It had defined an "international crime" as "an internationally wrongful act which results from the breach by a State of an international obligation so essential for the protection of fundamental interests of the international community that its breach is recognized as a crime by that community as a whole.." (II Y.B. Int'l L. Comm'n 32 (1980) (Part Two)). This proposal became the subject of great controversy within the ILC, among governments in the General Assembly of the United Nations and among scholars. The approach was finally abandoned by the ILC in favor of new articles 40 and 41. *See* INTERNATIONAL CRIMES OF STATES (J. Weiler et al. eds. 1989) and NINA JORGENSEN, THE RESPONSIBILITY OF STATES FOR INTERNATIONAL CRIMES (2000). For strong arguments in favor of the retention of draft Article 19, the provision on state crimes, *see* Georges Abi-Saab, *The Uses of Article 19*, 10 EUR. J. INT'L L. 339 (1999), and Giorgio Gaja, *Should All References to International Crimes Disappear from the ILC Draft Articles on State Responsibility?,* 10 EUR. J. INT'L L. 365 (1999). *See also* Alain Pellet, *Can a State Commit a Crime? Definitely, Yes!,* 10 EUR. J. INT'L L. 425 (1999).

2. Although the earlier references to crimes of states in the draft articles of State Responsibility by the ILC were deleted in the final version, substantive references to the equivalent of international crimes remain, e.g. Art. 40 ASR. In your view, has this concept contributed to an improved world order? Should crimes of States have been dropped entirely or expanded?

3. *See* Articles 53 and 64 of the Vienna Convention on the Law of Treaties on *jus cogens*. *See also* Part Six, *infra* at 1300. For obligations *erga omnes* see MAURIZIO RAGAZZI, THE CONCEPT OF INTERNATIONAL OBLIGATIONS *ERGA OMNES* (1997). What are the differences between obligations *erga omnes* and *jus cogens* norms?

4. Discuss the decisions of the International Court of Justice in *Barcelona Traction, East Timor* and the *Application of the Convention on the Prevention of the Crime of Genocide* with regard to obligations *erga omnes*. Compare Part Three, Human Rights, *supra*, at 524-526.

VII. Invocation of State Responsibility

A. ILC Report 2001: Arts. 42-48 ASR

Article 42: *Invocation of responsibility by an injured State*

A State is entitled as an injured State to invoke the responsibility of another State if the obligation breached is owed to:

(a) That State individually; or

(b) A group of States including that State, or the international community as a whole, and the breach of the obligation:

(i) Specially affects that State; or

(ii) Is of such a character as radically to change the position of all the other States to which the obligation is owed with respect to the further performance of the obligation.

Article 43: *Notice of claim by an injured State*

1. An injured State which invokes the responsibility of another State shall give notice of its claim to that State.

2. The injured State may specify in particular:

(a) The conduct that the responsible State should take in order to cease the wrongful act, if it is continuing;

(b) What form reparation should take in accordance with the provisions of Part Two.

Article 44: *Admissibility of claims*

The responsibility of a State may not be invoked if:

(a) The claim is not brought in accordance with any applicable rule relating to the nationality of claims;

(b) The claim is one to which the rule of exhaustion of local remedies applies and any available and effective local remedy has not been exhausted.

Article 45: *Loss of the right to invoke responsibility*

The responsibility of a State may not be invoked if:

(a) The injured State has validly waived the claim;

(b) The injured State is to be considered as having, by reason of its conduct, validly acquiesced in the lapse of the claim.

Article 46: *Plurality of injured States*

Where several States are injured by the same internationally wrongful act, each injured State may separately invoke the responsibility of the State which has committed the internationally wrongful act.

Article 47: *Plurality of responsible States*

1. Where several States are responsible for the same internationally wrongful act, the responsibility of each State may be invoked in relation to that act.

2. Paragraph 1:

(a) Does not permit any injured State to recover, by way of compensation, more than the damage it has suffered;

(b) Is without prejudice to any right of recourse against the other responsible States.

Article 48: *Invocation of responsibility by a State other than an injured State*

1. Any State other than an injured State is entitled to invoke the responsibility of another State in accordance with paragraph 2 if:

(a) The obligation breached is owed to a group of States including that State, and is established for the protection of a collective interest of the group; or

(b) The obligation breached is owed to the international community as a whole.

2. Any State entitled to invoke responsibility under paragraph 1 may claim from the responsible State:

(a) Cessation of the internationally wrongful act, and assurances and guarantees of non-repetition in accordance with article 30; and

(b) Performance of the obligation of reparation in accordance with the preceding articles, in the interest of the injured State or of the beneficiaries of the obligation breached.

3. The requirements for the invocation of responsibility by an injured State under articles 43, 44 and 45 apply to an invocation of responsibility by a State entitled to do so under paragraph 1.

B. ILC Report 2001: Related Commentaries

[General Commentary to articles 42-48]

(2) Central to the invocation of responsibility is the concept of the injured State. This is the State whose individual right has been denied or impaired by the internationally wrongful act or which has otherwise been particularly affected by that act. This concept is introduced in article 42 and various consequences are drawn from it in other articles.... In keeping with the broad range of international

obligations covered by the Articles, it is necessary to recognize that a broader range of States may have a legal interest in invoking responsibility and ensuring compliance with the obligation in question. Indeed in certain situations, all States may have such an interest, even though none of them is individually or specially affected by the breach. This possibility is recognized in article 48. Articles 42 and 48 are couched in terms of the entitlement of States to invoke the responsibility of another State. They seek to avoid problems arising from the use of possibly misleading terms such as "direct" versus "indirect" injury or "objective" versus "subjective" rights.

[Commentary to article 42] ...

(2) Invocation [of state responsibility] should be understood as taking measures of a relatively formal character, for example, the raising or presentation of a claim against another State or the commencement of proceedings before an international court or tribunal. A State does not invoke the responsibility of another State merely because it criticizes that State for a breach and calls for observance of the obligation, or even reserves its rights or protests. ...

[Commentary to article 43]

(2) Although State responsibility arises by operation of law on the commission of an internationally wrongful act by a State, in practice it is necessary for an injured State and/or other interested State(s) to respond, if they wish to seek cessation or reparation. Responses can take a variety of forms, from an unofficial and confidential reminder of the need to fulfil the obligation through formal protest, consultations, etc. Moreover the failure of an injured State which has notice of a breach to respond may have legal consequences, including even the eventual loss of the right to invoke responsibility by waiver or acquiescence: this is dealt with in article 45.

[Commentary to article 45]

(4) A waiver is only effective if it is validly given. ... The use of the term "valid waiver" is intended to leave to the general law the question of what amounts to a valid waiver in the circumstances. Of particular significance in this respect is the question of consent given by an injured State following a breach of an obligation arising from a peremptory norm of general international law, especially one to which article 40 applies. Since such a breach engages the interest of the international community as a whole, even the consent or acquiescence of the injured State does not preclude that interest from being expressed in order to ensure a settlement in conformity with international law.

(5) Although it may be possible to infer a waiver from the conduct of the States concerned or from a unilateral statement, the conduct or statement must be unequivocal. ...

[Commentary to article 46]

(2) Several States may qualify as "injured" States. ... In a situation of a plurality of injured States each may seek cessation of the wrongful act if it is continuing, and claim reparation in respect of the injury to itself. ...

[Commentary to article 48]

(1) ... It deals with the invocation of responsibility by States other than the injured State acting in the collective interest. A State which is entitled to invoke responsibility under article 48 is acting not in its individual capacity by reason of having suffered injury but in its capacity as a member of a group of States to which the obligation is owed, or indeed as a member of the international community as a whole. ...

1. Edith Brown Weiss, *Invoking State Responsibility in the Twenty-first Century*

96 AM. J. INT'L L. 798, 799-805 (2002)

An Overview of the Articles

Chapter I (of part 3) on invocation contains seven articles, Articles 42-48. Article 42 addresses invocation of responsibility by an injured state, while Article 48 turns to invocation of responsibility by a state other than an injured state. This is an important and potentially controversial distinction, which is discussed below. The articles in between, Articles 43-47, deal with procedural aspects of the invocation of state responsibility: the obligation to provide notice of a claim, the admissibility of claims (requirements concerning nationality of claims and exhaustion of local remedies), the loss of the right to invoke responsibility, the ability of a plurality of states injured by the same "internationally wrongful act" to make claims, and the rights of invocation when there are a plurality of responsible states. The first three of these articles apply equally to states invoking responsibility as an injured state or as a noninjured state.

Articles 43-47 generally codify international law and are relatively straightforward. However, Articles 45, 46, and 47 deserve special note. Article 46 (plurality of injured states) and Article 47 (plurality of responsible states) were added in the year 2000 after the draft articles were adopted on first reading. They make clear that if there is a plurality of injured states or a plurality of responsible states, each one is entitled to make a claim against any responsible state subject to the limitation that no injured state may recover compensation exceeding its damages. Since problems such as environmental protection usually engage more than one injured state and more than one responsible state, Articles 46 and 47 may be especially useful. Article 45 addresses when a state may lose the right to invoke state responsibility, namely, by waiving its claim or by conduct indicating that it has "validly acquiesced in the lapse of the claim." The last condition gives considerable flexibility to a court in determining whether the right has been lost and, as the commentary indicates, reflects the somewhat varying judgments on this point of the International Court of Justice (ICJ) in the *Certain Phosphate Lands in Nauru* and *LaGrand* cases.

Definition of Invocation

The articles define "invocation" narrowly. The commentary to Article 42 indicates that the term "should be understood as taking measures of a relatively formal character, for example, the raising or presentation of a claim against another State or the commencement of proceedings before an international court or tribunal." Protests, criticisms, or calls for other states to abide by an obligation do not by themselves qualify as "invoking" the responsibility of a state under Article 42. However, claims before intergovernmental human rights commissions, for example, or before other intergovernmental bodies should suffice. While the ILC may have defined invocation narrowly, the articles are likely to be applied when states make less formal claims of international law violations. On the other hand, by keeping the definition narrow, the Commission may have intentionally left undisturbed the right of "noninjured" states to make less formal claims that a state has breached its international obligations, as well as any rights of individuals and nonstate entities to make less formal claims.

II. WHO MAY INVOKE STATE RESPONSIBILITY UNDER THE ARTICLES

Historically, there has been considerable jurisprudential disagreement as to whether international agreements create only bilateral obligations between pairs of individual states, whether they may also create an indivisible whole so that the treaty obligations are to be performed in relation to every other state party to the agreement, or whether they may in some cases reflect obligations of a state toward the international community as a whole. If the first approach is accepted, then correlative rights and obligations exist between individual states, and the state holding the right can invoke state responsibility as against the holder of the obligation. This theory provides an orderly approach to international law, for it makes it relatively easy to identify who has the obligation and who the right of invocation. This bilateralist approach formed the basis of the traditional law of treaties and underlies the 1969 Vienna Convention on the Law of Treaties.

The second approach is more complicated, because it posits that some agreements create rights and obligations that are indivisible for all states party to the treaty and that each state owes an obligation to every other state party to perform those treaty obligations. The 1963 Limited Test Ban Treaty and the 1991 Protocol on Environmental Protection to the Antarctic Treaty exemplify this approach. The Vienna Convention on the Law of Treaties considers this problem in Article 60 by defining when a state party to a multilateral agreement may terminate or suspend its performance in response to a material breach by another contracting party. Article 60 provides that any state party may invoke a material breach to suspend the treaty in whole or in part if the "treaty is of such a character" that a material breach "radically changes the position of every party with respect to the further performance of its obligations under the treaty."

The third approach posits that multilateral agreements or customary international law may create obligations that run to the international community as a whole, as the International Court of Justice suggested in the *Barcelona Traction* case (referring to them as obligations *erga omnes*). Determining which states have the right to invoke a breach of these obligations as grounds for taking remedial or counter-measures has proved controversial. In theory, states should be able to claim a breach of these obligations even if they have suffered no direct injury, but the Court did not go that far in *Barcelona Traction* and, indeed, in the earlier *South West Africa* cases ultimately declined to find that the applicant states had legal rights or interests sufficient for jurisdiction.

The International Law Commission, to its credit, considers all three categories of obligations and does so in an innovative, if perhaps controversial, way. The first two categories are addressed in Article 42(a) and (b), respectively. The last is handled through the mechanism of Article 48(1)(b), which provides that a state may invoke state responsibility if the obligation breached "is owed to the international community as a whole." Article 48(1)(a) concerns the breach of those obligations owed to a group of states and established for the protection of the collective interest of the group. These obligations are distinct from those covered by Article 42(b) (in which the breach must specially affect one state or radically change the position of the other states to which the obligation is owed). Arguably, Article 48(1)(a) develops a different class of obligation, which derives from the traditional second category but contains elements of the third. It is linked to the important distinction that the ILC draws between the injured and the noninjured states, which is analyzed below. Notably, in this chapter the ILC does not address or even acknowledge the important role of nonstate entities and individuals in invoking state responsibility.

Article 42 and the Injured State

The articles distinguish between injured states (Art. 42) and states that have not been injured (Art. 48). The distinction replaces distinctions raised in previous Commission deliberations, such as between states with direct and indirect injuries. Article 42 entitles a state as an injured State to invoke the responsibility of another State if the obligation breached is owed to:

(a) that State individually; or

(b) a group of States including that State, or the international community as a whole, and the breach of the obligation:

(i) specially affects that State; or

(ii) is of such a character as radically to change the position of all the other States to which the obligation is owed with respect to the further performance of the obligation.

The commentary makes clear that the definition of injury in Article 42 is "closely modelled on article 60 of the Vienna Convention on the Law of Treaties," which deals with material breaches of treaties. Under paragraph (a), a state is injured if the breached obligation was owed to it individually. This could occur under a bilateral agreement; a unilateral commitment (such as not to use a particular weapon or not to fish in a specific zone); a general rule of international law that gives rise to obligations between two states, such as those governing relations between riparian states on an international watercourse; or a multilateral agreement in which states have specific obligations toward each other, as in the Vienna Convention on Diplomatic Relations. Under paragraph (b), a state qualifies as an injured state, according to the commentary, if it is "affected by the breach in a way which distinguishes it from the generality of other States to which the obligation is owed" or the breach affects "*per se* every other State to which the obligation is owed." A breach of the Limited Test Ban Treaty or the prohibition on sovereign territorial claims in the Treaty on Antarctica exemplifies the latter. The Commission chose in Article 42 to define the injured state narrowly, and has left the issues raised by the *Barcelona Traction* case and the *South West Africa* cases to Article 48.

The Commission's distinction in Articles 42 and 48 between an injured and a noninjured state assumes that when a state violates obligations such as the prohibition on genocide or slavery and the right to self-determination, other states are not injured. But this assumption is questionable. While they may not be injured in the sense of Article 42, they nonetheless suffer injury from the fact that an obligation to which they subscribe has been breached and its status could therefore be threatened unless action is taken to enforce the obligation. States often put down "markers" in the form of statements when they observe other states breaching international obligations, such as by the use of chemical or biological agents, even though they are not directly injured by that use. They do so to secure the integrity of the rule and prevent its dissolution through unchallenged practice. In this sense, the development of a separate article to deal with a noninjured state is arguably misleading.

The old Article 40, the predecessor to Articles 42 and 48, did not distinguish between states on this point and treated all states as equally injured. This approach, too, had problems because not all states were equally injured. James Crawford, noting that this treatment was not conducive to developing public international law (rather than private international law), argued that it was important to distinguish between the primary beneficiaries (the right holders) and those states with a legal interest in compliance, "irrespective of how or whether the breach has affected [them]."

Article 48 and the Noninjured State

When the Commission thus decided to create a new article (Article 48) in which states could invoke responsibility for a breach of an obligation owed to the international community as a whole, even though the states had suffered no "injury" in the traditional use of that word, it made an important innovation. The distinction could provide a reasonable basis for later recognition of the rights of actors other than states to invoke state responsibility in these circumstances. If injury is not required, then nonstate actors (who similarly may find it difficult to show direct injury) should have an easier time in asserting competence to claim for breaches of obligations owed to the international community as a whole. As discussed later in this article, there is precedent at the national level for the right of groups and individuals to raise claims for breaches of environmental obligations even though the group or individual has not been directly injured. Article 48 reflects more recent developments in international law and represents its progressive development.

Under Article 48(1), states other than injured states can invoke the responsibility of another state in two contexts: if "(a) the obligation breached is owed to a group of States including that State, and is established for the protection of a collective interest of the group; or (b) the obligation breached is owed to the international community as a whole." The commentary indicates that the former category, Article 48(1)(a), encompasses such agreements as regional security arrangements, regional systems for protecting human rights, and regional agreements for protecting the environment. It reflects the *S.S. Wimbledon* case, in which the Permanent Court of International Justice (PCIJ) granted standing to states party to a multilateral treaty even when some of them had suffered no direct injury.

The most interesting and presumably still controversial part of Article 48 is subparagraph (1)(b), which covers breaches of obligations "owed to the international community as a whole." Here the Commission draws upon the International Court of Justice's famous dictum in *Barcelona Traction* that there is a distinction between obligations owed to particular states and those owed to "the international community as a whole" and that as regards the latter, "all States can be held to have a legal interest in their protection." Although the Court referred to these as obligations *erga omnes*, the Commission eschews this term on the grounds that it has sometimes been confused with obligations owed to all parties to a treaty. Article 48 essentially reverses the Court's position in the *South West Africa* cases, where the ICJ declined to recognize the standing of Ethiopia and Liberia to seek a declaration on the illegality of South Africa's actions in South West Africa (now Namibia). It permits states to raise claims regarding obligations owed to the community as a whole. This category of obligations is likely to grow, especially in human rights and environmental protection. In the *Barcelona Traction* case, the Court enunciated a handful of such obligations: acts of aggression, genocide, slavery, and racial discrimination. As noted in the commentary, the Court in the East Timor case added the principle of "self-determination" as an *erga omnes* obligation. Arguably, other obligations have also emerged, such as an obligation not to dispose of high-or medium-level nuclear wastes in the oceans. Thus, the ILC not only reflects the Court's assertion in the *Barcelona Traction* case, but sets the stage for states to invoke state responsibility for the breach of any obligation owed to the international community.

The text is significant for what it does not say. Article 48 refers to the "international community as a whole," not to the international community of states as a whole, which is the phrase used in the Vienna Convention on the Law of Treaties. The commentary to Article 25, where the phrase is first introduced, indicates that the Commission intentionally adopted the broader phrasing used in the *Barcelona Traction* case and subsequent international agreements, and rejected including the phrase "of States." This formulation conforms with the view that the international community now comprises important actors other than states.

Article 48(2) provides that any state that is entitled to invoke the responsibility of another state may ask not only for the cessation of the act and assurances that it will not recur, but also for reparation of the interest of the injured state or of the beneficiaries of the obligation that has been breached. It does not make clear whom the latter includes and the commentary does not elaborate on the point. The beneficiaries could extend, for example, to the individuals who benefit from human rights treaties. The provision expands the domain within which state responsibility operates and in this sense represents progressive international legal development.

The inclusion of the new Article 48(1)(b) was not accepted without controversy in the Commission. One member wanted to delete the article entirely because it was not a core issue of state responsibility. In finalizing the articles, the Commission agreed to delete any provision articulating the notion of international crimes, a controversial concept that had been included in earlier versions.

Article 48's extension to any state of the right to invoke state responsibility for breaches of obligations owed to the international community as a whole is a welcome development. If states were not allowed to do so, then many breaches could occur without the threat of a claim by any state against the wrongful act. This approach, however, poses potential dangers. Because no collective decision or third-party decision about a breach need be made, the provision leaves it to each state to determine whether a breach of an obligation owed to the international community as a whole has occurred and whether to make a claim. In writing about the potential inclusion of international crimes in the ILC articles, D. N. Hutchinson referred to this latitude as letting loose "'a sort of international vigilantism', with States being wrongly accused of crimes and subjected to damaging measures without good cause." The fear is that the rights conferred by Article 48(1) could be used to justify politically motivated acts or unilateral interventions by a state to enforce international law. To guard against the possibility that a state might be subjected to countermeasures based on a spurious legal claim that it has breached an obligation toward the international community as a whole, the chapter on countermeasures, in Article 54, limits the right of any state entitled to invoke the responsibility of another state under Article 48(1) to "lawful measures." The commentary indicates that the use of "lawful measures" rather than "countermeasures" in reference to Article 48(1) is deliberate; it permits practice to evolve in this area.

While the argument that Article 48 could be used for spurious ends to justify unilateral interventions is a serious one, it should nonetheless be given limited weight today. The Commission's language anticipates that the obligations addressed in Article 48 will, at least for now, be relatively few and of a status comparable to those outlined by the Court in *Barcelona Traction* as obligations *erga omnes*. Moreover, the costs of a potentially frivolous or politically motivated claim, which can be disposed of as such, may be the price for a system in which states will now have the right to hold other states accountable for breaching obligations owed to the international community as a whole.

2. Interhandel Case (Switz. v. U.S.)

1959 I.C.J. 6 (Mar. 21) (Preliminary Objections)
(Review paras. 24-27, *supra,* Part Three, at 464).

3. Case Concerning Elettronica Sicula S.p.A. (ELSI) (U.S. v. Italy)

1989 I.C.J. 15 (July 20)
(Review paras. 49-63, *supra,* Part Three, at 469).

Notes and Questions

1. The ICJ in its decision in *United States Diplomatic and Consular Staff,* referring to the unlawful character of Iran's detention of the diplomatic and consular staff in Tehran, stated:

> [t]he attention of the entire international community, of which Iran has been a member since time immemorial, to the irreparable harm that may be caused by events of the kind now before the Court. Such events cannot fail to undermine the edifice of law carefully constructed by mankind over a period of centuries, the maintenance of which is vital for the security and well-being of the complex international community of the present day, to which its more essential than ever that the rules developed to ensure the ordered progress of relations between its members should be constantly and scrupulously respect. (para. 92 of the judgment)

Bearing in mind the above quotation, do you think that states other than the United States could have sued Iran for the taking of American diplomatic staff as hostages? Why or why not?

2. Does the injured state have the right to elect its remedy? If so what are the limits to its choice? In this context, see Art. 43 ASR.

3. On the requirement of exhaustion of local remedies, see *Mavrommatis Palestine Concession Case* (1924 P.C.I.J. (Ser. A) No. 2, at 12); Chittharanjan F. Amerasinghe, Local Remedies in International Law (Cambridge U. Press, 2d ed. 2003) (Publication planned for Dec. 2004); A. A. Cançado Trindade, The Application of the Rule of Exhaustion of Local Remedies in International Law: Its Rationale in the International Protection of Individual Rights (Cambridge U. Press 1983). For further details, *see supra* Part Three, Diplomatic Protection, at 460-475.

4. What are the limits to the requirement of exhaustion of local remedies? *See*, in this regard, the discussion of the Loewen case in Part Three, *supra,* at 473.

PART SIX: STRATEGIES

I. Regulating The Use of the Military Instrument

The strategies available to participants are considered in terms of a persuasive-coercive continuum and their reliance on the diplomatic, ideological, economic and military instruments. In most instances, combinations or assemblages of these instruments are mobilized and deployed. The most coercive strategy involves the use of force, more precisely, the use of the military instrument.

A. Introduction

Traditional international law drew a clear line of distinction between the "laws of war" and the "laws of peace." This dichotomy relates back to Hugo Grotius' foundational treatise De iure belli ac pacis (1670), and is reflected in the two corresponding volumes of Oppenheim's International Law. Not only with the advent of global terrorism, but on a more fundamental basis, this dichotomy may have outlived its usefulness.

1. Myres S. McDougal & Siegfried Wiessner, *Law and Minimum World Public Order*

in Myres S. McDougal & Florentino P. Feliciano, The International Law of War xix, xxvi-xxviii (New Haven Press 1994)

In traditional literature international law is commonly divided into a most imprecise dichotomy of "war" and "peace." These words are characteristically employed to make simultaneous reference both to the presence or absence of the facts of transnational coercion and violence and to the legal consequences to be attached by authoritative decision to different intensities in coercion and violence. The facts to which reference is made are those of the global process of effective power in which many different participants (state and other), for many varying objectives in expansion or conservation, employ all instruments of policy (military, diplomatic, ideological, and economic), in varying stages of acceleration and deceleration in intensity of violence and coercion, in attack upon the bases of power (people, resources, institutions) of other participants, and are themselves in turn the targets of attack. The legal policies and sanctioning consequences that the authoritative decision-makers of the global community apply to the different aspects of this continuous process of violence and coercion vary with many particular problems. These problems may be categorized … in terms of the minimization of major coercions, the conduct of hostilities, the termination of hostilities, the regulation of minor coercions, and so on. In a first effort to minimize major violence and coercion, through a law of "aggression" and "self-defense," authoritative decision-makers seek … to prevent alterations in the existing distribution of values among nation-states by processes of unilateral and unauthorized coercion and to promote value changes and adjustments by processes of persuasion or by community-sanctioned coercion. A second effort, when persuasive strategies fail and violence and coercion break out, is to reduce to a minimum the unnecessary destruction of values by defining, with as much specificity as possible, the permissible maximum of violence and destruction in particular types of situations. It has been many times documented that our inherited concepts of "peace" and "war," making such ambiguous reference to this vast maze of facts and legal policies, cast but a darkening light upon the difficult problems in public order that presently confront humankind.

It is suggested that a more relevant conception of peace can be found through employment of contemporary notions of world public order. A distinction is sometimes made between "minimum order," in the sense of the minimization of unauthorized violence and coercion, and "optimum order," as the arrangements that provide the greatest access of the individual human being to the shaping and sharing of all the values of human dignity.

It would appear, however, that both these kinds of allegedly different public order goals are indispensable to any workable conception of peace. Even when conceived in the minimum sense of freedom from the fact and expectation of arbitrary violence and coercion, peace may increasingly be observed to be dependent upon maintaining people's expectations that the processes of authoritative and effective decision will be responsive to their demands for a reasonable access to all the values we today characterize as those of human dignity. When peace is more broadly conceived as security in position, expectation, and potential with regard to all basic community values, the interrelationship of peace and human rights quite obviously passes beyond that of interdependence and approaches that of identity. Hence, there is much in President John F. Kennedy's question "Is not peace, in the last analysis, basically a matter of human rights?"

It may be generalized that the basic policies that underlie contemporary conceptions of peace and human rights are the same policies that, in any democratic community, underlie all law. It is no metaphor to conclude that peace and law may appropriately be described as one side of the coin (in community process and effective power) of which arbitrary violence and coercion are the opposite side. A major goal of an international law of human dignity must be to make the persuasion component of the global process of effective power increasingly dominant over the coercive component.

* * *

Another inherited distinction is the one between the law relating to the initiation of the use of force (*jus ad bellum*) and the law relating to the conduct of hostilities (*jus in bello*). For purposes of expediency, this chapter is organized using this sequence of fact. We will first discuss the law and policy of initiation of hostilities, then analyze the law regarding the conduct of armed conflict, proceed to a discussion of individual criminal liability for violating the laws of war, and end with the paradigm-shattering phenomenon of global terrorism and the laws and policies of combating it.

B. BASES FOR INITIATING THE USE OF FORCE

1. Self-Defense

a. W. Michael Reisman, *Assessing Claims to Revise the Laws of War*

97 AM. J. INT'L L. 82, 83-90 (2003)

The law setting the conditions under which states may resort to military force, the *jus ad bellum,* was shaped in the early part of the twentieth century and largely codified in the United Nations Charter. The unilateral and discretionary use of proactive military force, until then lawful, was henceforth prohibited; reactive military force was to be limited to self-defense and then only insofar as, and until, the international community could come to the assistance of a victim of unlawful military force. All uses of force were to be necessary, proportional, and discriminating.

Among the factors that made such a novel legal regime acceptable to those charged with the maintenance of national security within states was the unprecedented undertaking by the major powers in the Security Council to cooperate to ensure the collective defense of victims of aggression. Even those who assumed that the Security Council would wield the power the Charter assigned it in each appropriate case did not imagine that it would act quickly. But time was less of the essence then than now, given the character and potential of the arsenals of adversaries. Arsenals consisted essentially of kinetic weapons of relatively limited range, often requiring significant time for pre-positioning before activation. Prior to the expanded development and refinement of air warfare, weapons were usually limited in reach to the peripheries of the territorial communities that might come under attack. A surprise attack could thus be costly to its victim but not decisive. Most important, critical weapons were likely to be available in militarily significant quanta only to other states whose elites, however different their cultures and values, generally shared a continuing interest in the maintenance of the state system, of which all were part. Each elite's own territorial base made it at once member and beneficiary of, as well as hostage to, the system, susceptible to the ongoing dynamic of reciprocity and retaliation that generates the effectiveness of international law.

All of these factors shaped a common interest in a legal regime restricting the contingencies for self-defense to an actual armed attack. Indeed, as late as 1986, the International Court of Justice, in the watershed decision in the *Nicaragua* case, purported to limit the right of self-defense even further to an armed attack *of significant scale*, thereby prohibiting unilateral acts of self-defense in response to what came to be called "low-level warfare." One may question the wisdom of the Court's decision, but it indubitably represented a considered policy. At times when the Security Council was frozen by the Cold War, self-defense would become the only real response to attack. As long as determining the contingency for resort to defensive violence was left to the discretion of a beleaguered state, the Court apparently reasoned, international violence would be minimized if the legal threshold for resort to self-defense were set higher rather than lower.

III.

The development of weapons roared on, as did their proliferation. Wholly apart from the doubts that had arisen about the effectiveness of the Security Council, the introduction of vastly more destructive and rapidly delivered weapons began to put the efficacy of the legal regime itself into question. The reason was simple: the opportunity for meaningful self-defense could be irretrievably lost if an adversary, armed with much more destructive weapons and poised to attack, had to be allowed to initiate (which could mean, in effect, to accomplish) its attack before the right of self-defense came into operation. This development prompted a claim to expand the right of reactive self-defense to "anticipatory self-defense."

Anticipatory self-defense, the claim to "do unto others *before* they do unto you," promised to vouchsafe the security of the intended victim when he who struck first could deliver an unacceptable measure of damage, if not win outright. But the move from reactive to anticipatory self-defense required replacing the objectively verifiable prerequisite of an "armed attack" with the subjective perception of a "threat" of such an attack that, in the sole judgment of the state believing itself about to become a target, was so palpable, imminent, and prospectively destructive that the only defense was its prevention.

While all these considerations were redolent of the *Caroline* incident and could thus respond to the defensive needs of the putative victim, they did not fit easily into the Charter formula and presented serious systemic challenges. Anticipatory self-defense was, and is, open to abuse by self-serving interpretations in ways that the older right of reactive self-defense was not. Hence, the authority of anticipatory self-defense remained cloudy and much of formal legal doctrine rejected its lawfulness. Nevertheless, security planners could not afford to exclude the possibility of its eventuation. …

VI.

One of the factors that had made the inherited *jus ad bellum* effective was the concentration of weapons in the hands of territorial elites who were subject to the dynamic of reciprocity and retaliation that underlies international law. That dynamic does not operate for nonstate actors, for they are neither beneficiaries of nor hostages to the territorial system. As long as nonstate actors did not amass significant arsenals, their indifference or even hostility to world public order was inconsequential.

The proliferation of atomic, biological, and chemical weapons, the so-called ABC weapons, and their diffusion into the hands of nonstate actors has changed that. Even if an ABM system could screen the few nuclear weapons likely to be fired intercontinentally from the territory of an adversary, the United States, on the morning of September 11, 2001, awoke to a new reality. There are many other ways that the cluster of nonstate groups referred to as Al Qaeda can deliver highly destructive weapons to what has since come to be called "the homeland." Biological and chemical weapons cannot be screened by an ABM system. Nor can the most effective ABM system prevent the infiltration and detonation of a "dirty bomb." Nor can deterrence operate without an address to deter. As President Bush confessed, "Deterrence—the promise of massive retaliation against nations—means nothing against shadowy terrorist networks with no nations or citizens to defend." These developments have given new impetus to a claim of preemptive, as opposed to anticipatory, self-defense.

"Preemptive self-defense" is broader than anticipatory self-defense. Although different definitions have been proffered, preemptive self-defense is essentially a "nip in the bud" strategy. It is a claim to use unilaterally, and without prior international authorization, high levels of violence to arrest an incipient development that is not yet operational, hence not yet *directly* threatening, but that, if permitted to mature, could then be neutralized only at a higher and possibly unacceptable cost. A credible claim for anticipatory self-defense must point to a palpable and imminent threat. A claim for preemptive self-defense can point only to a possibility, a contingency. As one moves from an actual armed attack as the requisite threshold of reactive self-defense, to the palpable and imminent threat of attack, which is the threshold of preventive self-defense, and from there to the conjectural and contingent threat of *possible* attack, which is the threshold of preemptive self-defense, the need for interpretive latitude of the would-be unilateralist and his burden of proof become ever greater. In an international system marked by radically different values and factual perceptions, an act of preemptive self-defense will often look like a serious or hysterical misjudgment to some actors and like naked aggression to others.

Analytically, the claim to engage, in certain circumstances, in a "regime change" is a corollary of preemptive self-defense. For if a regime that is animated by unlawful ambitions against its neighbors continues to develop the ABC weapons, and especially if it does so in violation of international commitments, the deprivation of those weapons in a single instance may only reinforce the regime's intentions to try even harder the next time to develop and deploy the weapons so that it can then paralyze subsequent efforts to control it.

VII.

The United States claim to engage in preemptive self-defense is not new. It was made implicitly by the Clinton administration with respect to aerial military action to "degrade" Iraqi military capacities, actions that continue to the present. There may have been more explicit applications. President Clinton recently stated that "[w]e actually drew up plans to attack North Korea and to destroy their reactors and we told them we would attack unless they ended their nuclear programme." That threat was apparently an effective preemption. But if threats or overt acts aimed at degradation of an adversary's arsenal fail, will further and even more intrusive preemptive acts against the adversary be deemed permissible under the rubric of self-defense?

On June 1, 2002, President Bush stated: "We must take the battle to the enemy, disrupt his plans, and confront the worst threats before they emerge." On September 17, 2002, he made explicit and expanded the claim to preemptive action that had been an active part of America's legal arsenal in the previous decade. He said:

> We will disrupt and destroy terrorist organizations by:
>
> • direct and continuous action using all the elements of national and international power. Our immediate focus will be those terrorist organizations of global reach and any terrorist or state sponsor of terrorism which attempts to gain or use weapons of mass destruction (WMD) or their precursors;
>
> • defending the United States, the American people, and our interests at home and abroad by identifying and destroying the threat before it reaches our borders. While the United States will constantly strive to enlist the support of the international community, we will not hesitate to act alone, if necessary, to exercise our right of self-defense by acting preemptively against such terrorists, to prevent them from doing harm against our people and our country; and
>
> • denying further sponsorship, support, and sanctuary to terrorists by convincing or compelling states to accept their sovereign responsibilities.

Even more explicitly, the President's *National Strategy to Combat Weapons of Mass Destruction*, issued in December 2002, stated:

> Because deterrence may not succeed, and because of the potentially devastating consequences of WMD use against our forces and civilian population, U.S. military forces and appropriate civilian agencies must have the capability to defend against WMD-armed adversaries, including in appropriate cases through preemptive measures.

The unilateralism of these claims has been decried by some critics as if it were the major innovation here. In fact, it is not very different from the approach of the previous [Clinton] administration, which had said, famously, "We act in concert with the international community whenever possible, but do not hesitate to act unilaterally when necessary." The issue is not the lawfulness of unilateral action in self-defense, which, after all, is the essential formula of Charter Article 51. The issue is, rather, an explicit claim to preemptive self-defense.

VIII.

International law has been grappling with the claim of preemptive self-defense for decades. In 1967 the initiation of the Six-Day War by an Israeli air attack on Egyptian airports was not condemned by the institutions of the international community. The relation that prevailed between Egypt and Israel at the time may have already been one of belligerency, so that the air attack could have been seen as anticipatory or even reactive, rather than preemptive, self-defense. If a state of war exists, a belligerent need not wait until its adversary strikes in order to respond militarily, but is entitled, itself, to select the moment of initiation or resumption of overt conflict. Since the relation between Al Qaeda and the United States can generally be characterized as a state of war, it would be inappropriate to characterize unilateral United States actions after September 11 as falling in the area of preemptive self-defense. In contrast, the Israeli destruction of the Osirak reactor near Baghdad in 1981 was a quintessential preemptive action. At the time, it was widely condemned as a violation of international law. Scarcely a decade later, after the lethal and aggressive character of the regime in Baghdad was exposed, opinions about the preemptive action of 1981 underwent revision in many quarters, suggesting that there may be unarticulated, but operative, criteria for assessing the lawfulness of preemptive actions.

By their nature, all acts of self-defense are initiated unilaterally and evaluated for their lawfulness only after the fact. In all claims to self-defense, the international legal review of the action will be based upon a prudential contextual assessment of factors such as the degree of the threat presented, the availability of a meaningful organized international response, the urgency of unilateral action to prevent or deflect the attack, and the proportionality of the means chosen to the necessity presented by the threat. Thus, on a case-by-case basis, the legal danger of an abuse of preemptive self-defense is no greater than for anticipatory self-defense, which also does not require an "armed attack" to justify it. Humanitarian intervention does not even require a demonstration of a real or conjectural threat against the intervening state or states. The danger presented by the installation of a doctrine of preemptive self-defense is systemic: if writ large and generally available in international law, it is even more likely than anticipatory self-defense to lead to greater resort to international violence by further lowering the threshold for unilaterally determined contingencies that warrant acts of self-defense. This potential could create an imperative for all latent adversaries to strike sooner so as to strike first, raising the general expectation of violence and the likelihood of its eventuation.

Fear of an inexorable slide down that precipitous slope appeared to have been the concern of the International Court of Justice in *Nicaragua,* where, as noted above, the Court set the legal bar for the initiation of actions in self-defense at a rather high notch and, in effect, asked targeted populations simply to endure the consequences of protracted low-level conflict. In transposing the Court's policy prescription from a context of low-level protracted conflict conducted with relatively primitive and inherently focused weapons to a situation in which nonstate actors, armed with weapons of mass destruction, animated by manifestly hostile intentions, and impervious to the controls of reciprocity and retaliation that operate on territorial elites, are preparing the wherewithal for attack or actually readying to attack, international law would now be demanding that target states tolerate a much higher toll of death and destruction without trying to prevent it by prior unilateral action. Such a transposition of the International Court's policy position in *Nicaragua* puts international law on a head-on collision course with democratic politics, for a government in a functioning democracy whose population faces such violence will not last long if, in the circumstances, it tells its electorate that international law prevents it from taking anticipatory or preemptive action.

IX.

A critical factor in the acceptance and incorporation of a new claim into the corpus of international law is whether it serves the common interests of the aggregate of actors. Thus, the responsibility of the international lawyer here is to assess innovative claims carefully for their contribution, in present and projected contexts, to the essential goals of law.

For all the fury it provoked, the claim to develop an ABM system posed no challenge to the international security system. It does not threaten the effectiveness of the deterrence mechanism operating between the major nuclear powers, while an operational ABM system would provide an entirely passive self-defense mode to states likely to be targets of surprise ABC missile attacks. It is, by its nature, only defensive. Moreover, the denunciation of the ABM Treaty did not undermine the viability of the international treaty regime, for the treaty in question was susceptible, by its terms, to termination, on notice.

"Regime change" is a euphemism for externally provoked and managed coups d'état. A broad and unilateral right of regime change, by itself, can hardly be accommodated within the ensemble of policies of international law. If it became generally lawful, it would lead to more frequent unsupervised meddling in the processes of choice within other states. But regime change may be internationally lawful when it is the contextually appropriate *instrument* of an intrinsically lawful action. Recall that regime change has always figured as one of the strategic objectives of humanitarian intervention, a claim to use force unilaterally, hitherto controversial, that appears to have acquired more legitimacy since NATO bombed Serbia and Kosovo in 1999 and the various commissions established to review the lawfulness of the action essentially concluded that it was illegal but, in the circumstances, the right thing to do. If preemptive self-defense is potentially lawful and the conditions that obtain in a particular case warrant resort to it, the legality of an instrumental regime change will turn on its necessity, proportionality, and discrimination.

But can a preemptive self-defense action be lawful? It is not hard to imagine circumstances in which such action might appear justified. Yet the claim, if universalized, could increase the expectation of and resort to violence and undermine minimum order. Its challenge to international law, at least with respect to a prospective preemptive strike against Iraq, may be finessed by construing various Security Council resolutions under Chapter VII as fully authorizing the action for the material breach of prior resolutions. Alternatively, the claim to engage in preemptive action may be partially rejected by being confined to the status of an American "doctrine," rather like the Monroe Doctrine in the days of the League of Nations.

In modern international law, a doctrine—such as the Brezhnev, Carter, and Reagan doctrines—consists of a formal and credible statement by a significant international actor of a firm policy and the resolve to implement it upon certain contingencies. Doctrines are positioned at the interface of law and power. They are not based on a general right that is theoretically available to other states. By their nature, they constitute a demand for an exception. Not all doctrines conform with existing international law, but doctrines do contribute to minimum order by stabilizing the expectations of all actors as to the consequences of certain types of action and thus aid in avoiding adventures and mistakes.

If preemptive self-defense is only an American doctrine, reserved to the global superpower for its episodic forays as international policeman, at least the danger of its rampant use by many other states is contained. The danger of its abuse by an uncontrolled superpower is not. But the potential for abuse here does not derive from the power of a single state. Rather, it inheres in a legal system that continues to maintain weak central institutions and accordingly reserves to each state, in the words of the French text of Article 51 of the Charter, a *droit naturel* to engage in unilateral action when necessary for its self-defense, while assigning the residual responsibility for global security to a small group of powerful states.

Until the installation of an effective world constitutive process, which will remove the need to rely upon unilateral action for the achievement of key international goals, it will be for the college of international lawyers to establish criteria for the lawfulness of the initiation and application of unilateral anticipatory and preemptive defensive actions. Their lodestar will be the legitimacy of self-defense insofar as it is implemented in accordance with the venerable policies of necessity, proportionality, and discrimination. But because the context has changed, the legal arrangements to implement these policies of international law must change as well. Legal creativity and factual realism in this area are called for in equally urgent measure, for if the effectiveness and soundness of a future international regime about the unilateral use of force remain clouded in uncertainty, the insufficiency of the inherited regime, which was designed for a context of weapons and adversaries that has changed forever, is certain beyond peradventure.

b. Inclusive Policies

(1) United Nations Charter

Article 2

The Organization and its Members, in pursuit of the Purposes stated in Article 1, shall act in accordance with the following Principles. ...

4. All Members shall refrain in their international relations from the threat or use of force against the territorial integrity or political independence of any state, or in any other manner inconsistent with the Purposes of the United Nations. ...

Article 24

1. In order to ensure prompt and effective action by the United Nations, its Members confer on the Security Council primary responsibility for the maintenance of international peace and security, and agree that in carrying out its duties under this responsibility the Security Council acts on their behalf. …

Article 25

The Members of the United Nations agree to accept and carry out the decisions of the Security Council in accordance with the present Charter. …

Article 39

The Security Council shall determine the existence of any threat to the peace, breach of the peace, or act of aggression and shall make recommendations, or decide what measures shall be taken in accordance with Articles 4 and 42, to maintain or restore international peace and security.

Article 40

In order to prevent an aggravation of the situation, the Security Council may, before making the recommendations or deciding upon the measures provided for in Article 39, call upon the parties concerned to comply with such provisional measures as it deems necessary or desirable. Such provisional measures shall be without prejudice to the rights, claims, or position of the parties concerned. The Security Council shall duly take account of failure to comply with such provisional measures.

Article 41

The Security Council may decide what measures not involving the use of armed force are to be employed to give effect to its decisions, and it may call upon the Members of the United Nations to apply such measures. These may include complete or partial interruption of economic relations and of rail, sea, air, postal, telegraphic, radio, and other means of communication, and the severance of diplomatic relations.

Article 42

Should the Security Council consider that measures provided for in Article 41 would be inadequate or have proved to be inadequate, it may take such action by air, sea, or land forces as may be necessary to maintain or restore international peace and security. Such action may include demonstrations, blockade, and other operations by air, sea, or land forces of Members of the United Nations.

Article 43

1. All Members of the United Nations, in order to contribute to the maintenance of international peace and security, undertake to make available to the Security Council, on its call and in accordance with a special agreement or agreements, armed forces, assistance, and facilities, including rights of passage, necessary for the purpose of maintaining international peace and security.

2. Such agreement or agreements shall govern the numbers and types of forces, their degree of readiness and general location, and the nature of the facilities and assistance to be provided.

3. The agreement or agreements shall be negotiated as soon as possible on the initiative of the Security Council. They shall be concluded between the Security Council and Members or between the Security Council and groups of Members and shall be subject to ratification by the signatory states in accordance with their respective constitutional processes. ...

Article 51

Nothing in the present Charter shall impair the inherent right of individual or collective self-defense if an armed attack occurs against a Member of the United Nations, until the Security Council has taken measures necessary to maintain international peace and security. Measures taken by Members in the exercise of this right of self-defense shall be immediately reported to the Security Council and shall not in any way affect the authority and responsibility of the Security Council under the present Charter to take at any time such action as it deems necessary in order to maintain or restore international peace and security.

Article 52

1. Nothing in the present Charter precludes the existence of regional arrangements or agencies for dealing with such matters relating to the maintenance of international peace and security as are appropriate for regional action, provided that such arrangements or agencies and their activities are consistent with the Purposes and Principles of the United Nations.

2. The Members of the United Nations entering into such arrangements or constituting such agencies shall make every effort to achieve pacific settlement of local disputes through such regional arrangements or by such regional agencies before referring them to the Security Council.

3. The Security Council shall encourage the development of pacific settlement of local disputes through such regional arrangements or by such regional agencies either on the initiative of the states concerned or by reference from the Security Council.

(2) Aggression and Self-Defense

The most fundamental policy of any community with regard to strategies must be the prohibition of unauthorized coercion. The international community expresses that policy in the United Nations Charter, Article 2 (4), above.

Article 2(4) does not flatly prohibit all coercion but only that which in the circumstances operates against the territorial integrity or political independence of a state or is inconsistent with the purposes of the United Nations. The context in which coercion has been or will be used is indispensable for the evaluation of lawfulness. The requirements of self-defense, for example, may in certain contexts permit the use of high levels of coercion.

Much of the legal effort in this area has been directed to providing guidelines for the Security Council determining, in each case, aggression and its correlative, self-defense.

Consider the following regional definition:

(a) Inter-American Treaty of Reciprocal Assistance

62 Stat. 1681 (1947)

Article IX

In addition to other acts which the Organ of Consultation may characterize as aggression, the following shall be considered as such:

a. Unprovoked armed attack by a State against the territory, the people, or the land, sea or air forces of another State;

b. Invasion, by the armed forces of a State, of the territory of an American State, through the trespassing of boundaries demarcated in accordance with a treaty, judicial decision, or arbitral award, or, in the absence of frontiers thus demarcated, invasion affecting a region which is under the effective jurisdiction of another State.

* * *

On December 14, 1974, the General Assembly adopted without vote a "Definition of Aggression":

(b) Definition of Aggression

G.A. Res. 3314, 29 U.N. GAOR, Supp. (No. 31) 142, U.N.DOC. A/9631 (1974)

Article 1. Aggression is the use of armed force by a State against the sovereignty, territorial integrity or political independence of another State, or in any other manner inconsistent with the Charter of the United Nations, as set out in this Definition.

[*Explanatory note:* In this Definition the term "State":

(a) Is used without prejudice to questions of recognition or to whether a State is a Member of the United Nations;

(b) Includes the concept of a "group of States" where appropriate.]

Article 2. The first use of armed force by a State in contravention of the Charter shall constitute *prima facie* evidence of an act of aggression although the Security Council may, in conformity with the Charter, conclude that a determination that an act of aggression has been committed would not be justified in the light of other relevant circumstances, including the fact that the acts concerned or their consequences are not of sufficient gravity.

Article 3. Any of the following acts, regardless of a declaration of war, shall, subject to and in accordance with the provisions of article 2, qualify as an act of aggression:

(a) The invasion or attack by the armed forces of a State of the territory of another State, or any military occupation, however temporary, resulting from such invasion or attack, or any annexation by the use of force of the territory of another State or part thereof;

(b) Bombardment by the armed forces of a State against the territory of another State or the use of any weapons by a State against the territory of another State;

(*c*) The blockade of the ports or coasts of a State by the armed forces of another State;

(*d*) An attack by the armed forces of a State on the land, sea or air forces, or marine and air fleets of another State;

(e) The use of armed forces of one State which are within the territory of another State with the agreement of the receiving State, in contravention of the conditions provided for in the agreement or any extension of their presence in such territory beyond the termination of the agreement;

(*f*) The action of a State in allowing its territory, which it has placed at the disposal of another State, to be used by that other State for perpetrating an act of aggression against a third State;

(*g*) The sending by or on behalf of a State of armed bands, groups, irregulars or mercenaries, which carry out acts of armed force against another State of such gravity as to amount to the acts listed above, or its substantial involvement therein,

Article 4. The acts enumerated above are not exhaustive and the Security Council may determine that other acts constitute aggression under the provisions of the Charter,

Article 5. 1. No consideration of whatever nature, whether political, economic, military or otherwise, may serve as a justification for aggression.

2. A war of aggression is a crime against international peace. Aggression gives rise to international responsibility.

3. No territorial acquisition or special advantage resulting from aggression is or shall be recognized as lawful.

Article 6. Nothing in this Definition shall be construed as in any way enlarging or diminishing the scope of the Charter, including its provisions concerning cases in which the use of force is lawful.

Article 7. Nothing in this Definition, and in particular article 3, could in any way prejudice the right to self-determination, freedom and independence, as derived from the Charter, of peoples forcibly deprived of that right and referred to in the Declaration on Principles of International Law concerning Friendly Relations and Co-operation among States in accordance with the Charter of the United Nations, particularly peoples under colonial and racist regimes or other forms of alien domination; nor the right of these peoples to struggle to that end and to seek and receive support, in accordance with the principles of the Charter and in conformity with the above-mentioned Declaration.

Article 8. In their interpretation and application the above provisions are interrelated and each provision should be construed in the context of the other provisions.

NOTES AND QUESTIONS

1. The "Definition" was not intended to be definitional. Paragraph 4 of the Resolution recommended that the Security Council "should, as appropriate, take account of that Definition, as guidance in determining, in accordance with the Charter, the existence of an act of aggression." For an overview of the development of the concept of aggression, see *Historical Review of Developments Relating to Aggression*, UNITED NATIONS PUBLICATION, U.N. Sales No. E.03.V.10.

2.. Do any of the definitions of aggression provide adequate guidelines for decision and appraisal?

c. Determining Aggression in Practice

Determining when a use of force is aggression or self-defense has proved to be extremely difficult and controversial.

(1) The Cuban Quarantine

(a) The Cuban Quarantine, 1962

4 Whiteman, Digest of Int'l Law 523-24

On the evening of October 22, 1962, President John F. Kennedy announced to his fellow U.S. citizens that "This Government, as promised, has maintained the closest surveillance of the Soviet military buildup on the island of Cuba. Within the past week unmistakable evidence has established the fact that a series of offensive missile sites is now in preparation on that imprisoned island." He added that "This urgent transformation of Cuba into an important strategic base - by the presence of these large, long-range, and clearly offensive weapons of sudden mass destruction - constitutes an explicit threat to the peace and security of all the Americas, in flagrant and deliberate defiance of the Rio Pact of 1947, the traditions of this nation and hemisphere, the joint Resolution of the 87th Congress, the Charter of the United Nations, and my own public warnings to the Soviets on September 4, and 13 [1962]." On the following day, October 23, the Council of the Organization of American States, meeting as the Provisional Organ of Consultation, called for "the immediate dismantling and withdrawal from Cuba of all missiles and other weapons with any offensive capability" and recommended that "the member states, in accordance with Articles 6 and 8 of the Inter-American Treaty of Reciprocal Assistance [1947], take all measures, individually and collectively, including the use of armed force, which they may deem necessary to ensure that the Government of Cuba cannot continue to receive supplies which may threaten the peace and security of the Continent and to prevent the missiles in Cuba with offensive capability from ever becoming an active threat to the peace and security of the Continent".

On that same day—October 23, 1962—President Kennedy by Proclamation ordered the interdiction by U.S. forces of the delivery of offensive weapons to Cuba. The substantive portions of the Proclamation provided that in accordance with the resolution of the Organ of Consultation of the American Republics of October 23, 1962, "and to defend the security of the United States", the forces under the President's command were ordered, beginning at 2 p.m. Greenwich time October 24, 1962, to interdict the delivery of offensive weapons and associated materiel to Cuba. To enforce this order, the Secretary of Defense was ordered to take appropriate measures to prevent the delivery of the prohibited materiel to Cuba, "employing the land, sea and air forces of the United States in cooperation with any forces that may be made available by other American States".

* * *

The U.S. and the U.S.S.R. convened the Security Council on October 23. The U.S. contended that Soviet missiles in Cuba were a threat to the peace. Cuba accused the U.S. of aggression. The U.S. called its action a "quarantine." The Soviets claimed the missiles were for defensive purposes only.

The lawfulness of the U.S. response was strongly attacked by Professor Quincy Wright and defended by Professor Myres McDougal.

(b) Quincy Wright, *The Cuban Quarantine*

57 AM. J. INT'L L. 546 (1963)

Under general principles of international law and several treaties, the United States was in principle bound to respect the sovereignty of Cuba in its airspace. Consequently, the evidence concerning the "offensive missiles" in Cuba, on the basis of which the "quarantine" was instituted, was illegally obtained, unless authority for such surveillance can be found in instruments to which Cuba had consented. …

It is difficult to find that the Soviet Union violated any obligation of international law in shipping missiles to, and installing them in Cuba at the request of the Castro government. Under general international law, states are free to engage in trade in any articles whatever in time of peace. Treaties have been made restricting trade in arms, but no such treaty had been ratified by the Soviet Union, and the United States has refused to ratify such treaties on the ground, among others, that they might prevent countries without arms manufacture from providing for their defense. …

There is no rule of international law that requires publicity for collective defense measures, though such a rule may be desirable and indeed necessary if the installations are to have deterrent influence. While Soviet deception, asserted by President Kennedy and Ambassador Stevenson, certainly could not improve relations and would render any agreement based on such deception voidable, it could not clearly demonstrate that the purpose of the missiles was not defensive. If disclosed prior to installation, the missiles might be intercepted at sea, and, furthermore, it is not clear that the Soviet officials did not intend to assert by the alleged deceptive statements that the weapons were intended to be used only for defense and to reject the United States contention that medium-range missiles were inherently offensive.

An effort to justify the quarantine by the historic doctrine of pacific blockade, therefore, fails because the United States did not make it clear what illegal act of Cuba it was trying to remedy and, if it had been claimed that Castro's installation of the missiles manifested allegiance to Communism in violation of obligations of Cuba under O.A.S. resolutions, non-coercive means of settlement had not been exhausted. Indeed, negotiations to remedy the situation could not be utilized because the United States had broken diplomatic relations with Castro and induced his expulsion from the O.A.S. at the Punta del Este Conference of January, 1962. …

It cannot be doubted that the United States Government acted skillfully to obtain the removal of the long-range missiles from Cuba. The form and timing of the quarantine declaration, the organization of naval forces, the procurement of consent by the O. A. S. and the NATO allies, and the utilization of the United

Nations as a forum for discussion and explanation and as an instrument of mediation and supervision, achieved the results desired without hostilities or United Nations criticism. The United States Government had gained in experience since the Bay of Pigs episode of the spring of 1961. Most Americans were happy that a conditional agreement was reached with Khrushchev, that the missiles were withdrawn, and that peace was maintained. It cannot be easily argued, however, that the United States has lived up to its legal obligations to respect the freedom of the seas, to submit threats to the peace to the United Nations before taking unilateral action, and to refrain from use or threat of force in international relations except in individual or collective self-defense against armed attack, under authority of the United Nations, or with consent of the state against which the force is used.

(c) Myres S. McDougal, *The Soviet-Cuban Quarantine and Self-Defense*

57 Am.J. Int'l L. 597 (1963)

The broad outlines of a different approach may be indicated by briefly noting, first, the more important characteristics of the traditional, customary right of self-defense, secondly, the considerations which should guide a genuine, as contrasted with a spurious, interpretation of the whole United Nations Charter, and, thirdly, the more obvious factors in the context of this particular confrontation between the United States and the Soviets which should be taken into account in any serious assessment of the necessity and proportionality of the United States' action.

Historically, states have demanded, and reciprocally honored, a right of self-defense of considerable, though not unlimited, scope. In broadest formulation, this right of self-defense, as established by traditional practice authorizes a state which, being the target of activities by another state, reasonably decides, as third-party observers may determine reasonableness, that such activities imminently require it to employ the military instrument to protect its territorial integrity and political independence, to use such force as may be necessary and proportionate for securing its defense. In a still primitively organized world in which expectations are low about the effective capability of the general community to protect its individual members, this right has been regarded as indispensable to the maintenance of even the most modest minimum order.

The more important limitations imposed by the general community upon this customary right of self-defense have been, in conformity with the overriding policy it serves of minimizing coercion and violence across state lines, those of necessity and proportionality. The conditions of necessity required to be shown by the target state have never, however, been restricted to "actual armed attack"; imminence of attack of such high degree as to preclude effective resort by the intended victim to non-violent modalities of response has always been regarded as sufficient justification, and it is now generally recognized that a determination of imminence requires an appraisal of the total impact of an initiating state's coercive activities upon the target state's expectations about the costs of preserving its territorial integrity and political independence. Even the highly restrictive language of Secretary of State Webster in the *Caroline* case specifying a "necessity of self defense, instant, overwhelming, leaving no choice of means and no moment for deliberation," did not require "actual armed attack," and the understanding is now widespread that a test formulated in the previous century for a controversy between two friendly states is hardly relevant to contemporary controversies, involving high expectations of violence, between nuclear-armed protagonists. The requirement of proportionality, in further expression of the policy of minimizing coercion, stipulates that the responding use of the military instrument by the target state be limited in intensity and magnitude to what is reasonably necessary promptly to secure the permissible objectives of self-defense under the established conditions of necessity.

The honoring in international law of a customary right of self-defense has not meant - the point may bear emphasis - the exaltation of unilateral decision by particular states over inclusive decision by the general community. It has indeed been accepted ... that a target state may make a first, provisional decision that the conditions of necessity are such as to require it immediately to employ the military instrument for preservation of its territorial integrity and political independence. Given the continuing ineffectiveness of the general community organization to act quickly and certainly for the protection of states, no other principle could be either acceptable to states or conducive to minimum order. Save for an occasional uninformed and uniformly rejected whisper, it has, however, been generally agreed that both this first provisional decision by a claimant target state and the measures it actually takes are subject to review for their necessity and proportionality by the general community of states. The principle of auto-interpretation, that each state is authorized to interpret customary principles, has never been applied, any more to claims of self-defense than to claims about other matters, to preclude other states from passing upon the degree to which the actions of a particular state conform to general community expectations. Fortunately, today the authority structures of the United Nations, despite all their other weaknesses, do provide quickly available and convenient fora for general community review of the lawfulness of particular claims to employ the military instrument.

The position taken by Professor Wright that Article 51 of the United Nations Charter must be construed to limit the customary right of self-defense by states to reactions against "actual armed attack" would not appear to be supported by any of the commonly accepted principles for the interpretation of international agreements. It may be recalled that the appropriate goal in interpreting great constitutional agreements, such as the United Nations Charter, is that of ascertaining the genuine expectations, created by the framers and by successive appliers of the agreement, in contemporary community members about what future decisions should be; the words and behavior in the past are relevant only as they affect contemporary expectations about the requirements of future decision. There is not the slightest evidence that the framers of the United Nations Charter, by inserting one provision which expressly reserves a right of self-defense, had the intent of imposing by this provision new limitations upon the traditional right of states. In fact, as Professor Bowett summarizes, the preparatory work suggests "only that the article should safeguard the right of self-defence, not restrict it." Thus, Committee 1/I stressed in its report, approved by both Commission I and the Plenary Conference, that "The use of arms in legitimate self defense remains admitted and unimpaired." The apparent purpose of the inept language of Article 51, commonly ascribed to the late Senator Vandenburg, was only that of accommodating regional organizations, as specifically envisioned for the inter-American system by the Act of Chapultepec, with the more comprehensive, centralized system of collective security projected by the Charter.

A serious review from general community perspectives of the conditions of necessity confronting the United States when it imposed the quarantine would of course require systematic and disciplined appraisal of many features of the context of the particular events to which the United States reacted. Some of the more important of these features may be briefly indicated under certain category headings useful for the description of any social process, persuasive or coercive: participants, objectives, situation, base values, strategies, and outcomes.

Participants. The threat against which the United States reacted came from the Soviet Union, not Cuba. The Castro regime contributed to the threat, but more as puppet or as potential irresponsible brandisher of borrowed nuclear weapons. The suggestion by Professor Wright that in the "Cuban quarantine" the United States was dealing with "unpalatable action or attitudes of a small state" scarcely accords with reality.

Objectives. The objectives of the Soviet Union in moving major military power into the Western Hemisphere were clearly expansionist. The missiles, had their installation been achieved, would have been directly pointed toward the "territorial integrity" of all states within range. The explicit and consistent public utterances of its official spokesmen, the totalitarian character of its internal structures of authority, and the monolithic character of its demanded system of world public order raised grave question about the genuineness of the Soviet Union's dedication to the basic principle of minimum order, that violence and coercion are not to be used as instruments of expansion across state lines.

Situation. The general geographic area into which the Soviet Union was moving was one which the United States and other states in the Hemisphere had long specified, through the Monroe Doctrine and otherwise, as of especial strategic concern to them. The specific location being sought by the Soviet Union for its missiles would, in more particular, have by-passed the Dewline warning system maintained by the United States for securing advance notice of the launching of missiles from the Soviet Union. The bypassing of the Dewline would have grievously reduced the United States' reaction time to possible attacks from the Soviet Union, thus causing a serious disruption in the whole world balance of power between the totalitarian and non-totalitarian states. Even a few days' delay by the United States in taking appropriate measures would have meant that the missiles would be in place and the situation irreversible.

Expectations of crisis in the world arena as a whole were high, and estimates of prompt and effective action from the organized community of states for ameliorating particular crises were realistically low.

Bases of Power. The Soviet Union, as one of the world's two major powers, obviously disposed of ample bases of power to put into effect the threats explicit in its behavior.

Strategies. The strategies employed by the Soviet Union included manipulation of the military instrument in its most awesome and gruesome contemporary form. Special advantage was at first sought clandestinely, but this use of the military instrument was at all times accompanied by a fanfare of other instruments - ideological, economic, and diplomatic - with an explicit promise of still more to come in all areas of the Hemisphere. The reference by Professor Wright to the shipping and installation of missiles as "trade" between the Soviet Union and Cuba in "time of peace" would appear at least mildly euphemistic.

Outcomes. The outcome almost within the grasp of the Soviet Union was that of a new, more direct military threat to the whole of the Americas, with most major cities and military bases brought within the reach of momentary nuclear destruction. The intensity of the coercion which this nearly achieved threat imposed upon the United States and the other Members of the Organization of American States was accurately reflected in the unanimity, celerity, and effectiveness with which they acted, once the character and dimensions of the threat became apparent.

Responsible appraisal from general community perspectives of the proportionality of the action taken by the United States in response to the threat from the Soviet Union must require a similarly comprehensive reference to the major features of the context of that action. We may note some of the more important features by the same headings:

Participants. Though the decision to impose the quarantine was first taken by the United States alone, quick confirmation that this decision was not an egocentric one, in the special interest of the United States only, came from the other Members of the Organization of American States in associating themselves with the United States.

Objectives. The immediate, manifest objectives of the United States were defensive: to secure the withdrawal and elimination of nuclear weapons from Cuba. The historic precedent by which Cuba was initially set free, the generally democratic internal structures of authority in the United States, and the pluralistic world order of independent states traditionally demanded and supported by the United States did not suggest covert, expansionist objectives.

Situation. The geographic area within which the United States applied its power was located largely upon the high seas, entailing the least possible interference within the internal territorial domain of any state. The duration of the interference was limited to that necessary to the effectiveness of defense.

Bases of Power. The bases of power of the United States and its associates, though great, were not sufficiently disparate from those of the Soviet Union and its associates to suggest disguised duress.

Strategies. The use by the United States of the military instrument was as limited as could have been fashioned, extending only to the selective interdiction of certain types of weapons. The United States acted openly, after advance warning that the establishment of an offensive military base in Cuba would be regarded as a threat to its security. The United States immediately reported its action to the United Nations Security Council, asking for appropriate measures from that body.

Outcomes. The quarantine was a reversible action, causing no irremediable destruction. The employment of force which it authorized was clearly limited in intensity and magnitude to that necessary to removal of the provoking threat.

Even this impressionistic recall of some of the more salient features of the larger context of threat and response should suffice to suggest that a third-party observer, genuinely concerned to clarify the common interests of all peoples, could reasonably conclude that the action taken by the United States was in accord with traditional general community expectations about the requirements of self-defense. The flow of pertinent comment and decision since the incident would indeed seem to confirm that this has been the overwhelming conclusion of world public opinion.

In a better organized world, mankind might be able to dispense with a conception of self-defense which confers upon a claimant target state as much initial discretion as does the conception so long honored in customary international law. Until that better organization is more nearly achieved, the task which confronts free peoples is, however, that of clarifying and applying a conception of self-defense which will serve their common interests in minimum order without imposing upon them paralysis in the face of attacks from community members who do not genuinely accept the principle of minimum order. The importance of the incident of the Soviet-Cuban quarantine is in its indication that such a clarification and application can effectively be made and that free peoples do not, as some have insisted, have to choose between the historic restraints of international law and their own survival.

NOTES AND QUESTIONS

1. Comparable issues were raised during the 1967 "Six Day War". For a detailed historical recitation, see Charles Yost, *The Arab-Israeli War: How It Began, in* 2 THE ARAB-ISRAELI CONFLICT 5 (John N. Moore ed., 1974). *See also* Stuart S. Malawer, *Anticipatory Self-Defense under Article 51 of the United Nations Charter*, STUDIES IN INTERNATIONAL LAW 191 (1977).

(2) The Corfu Channel Case

1949 I.C.J. 4, 32-35 (April 9) (Merits)

[*See* facts and more complete text, *supra* Part Four, at 677]

In addition to the passage of the United Kingdom warships on October 22nd, 1946, the second question in the Special Agreement relates to the acts of the Royal Navy in Albanian waters on November 12th and 13th, 1946. This is the minesweeping operation called 'Operation Retail'. ...

The United Kingdom Government does not dispute that 'Operation Retail' was carried out against the clearly expressed wish of the Albanian Government. It recognizes that the operation had not the consent of the international mine clearance organizations, that it could not be justified as the exercise of a right of innocent passage, and lastly that, in principle, international law does not allow a State to assemble a large number of warships in the territorial waters of another State and to carry out minesweeping in those waters. The United Kingdom Government states that the operation was one of extreme urgency, and that it considered itself entitled to carry it out without anybody's consent. ...

[T]he explosions of October 22nd, 1946, in a channel declared safe for navigation, and one which the United Kingdom Government, more than any other government, had reason to consider safe, raised quite a different problem from that of a routine sweep carried out under the orders of the mine clearance organizations. These explosions were suspicious; they raised a question of responsibility.

Accordingly, this was the ground on which the United Kingdom Government chose to establish its main line of defence. According to that Government, the *corpora delicti* must be secured as quickly as possible, for fear they should be taken away, without leaving traces, by the authors of the minelaying or by the Albanian authorities. This justification took two distinct forms in the United Kingdom Government's arguments. It was presented first as a new and special application of the theory of intervention, by means of which the State intervening would secure possession of evidence in the territory of another State, in order to submit it to an international tribunal and thus facilitate its task.

The Court cannot accept such a line of defence. The Court can only regard the alleged right of intervention as the manifestation of a policy of force, such as has, in the past, given rise to most serious abuses and such as cannot, whatever be the present defects in international organization, find a place in international law. Intervention is perhaps still less admissible in the particular form it would take here; for, from the nature of things, it would be reserved for the most powerful States, and might easily lead to perverting the administration of international justice itself.

The United Kingdom Agent, in his speech in reply, has further classified 'Operation Retail' among methods of self-protection or self-help. The Court cannot accept this defence either. Between independent States, respect for territorial sovereignty is an essential foundation of international relations. The Court recognizes that the Albanian Government's complete failure to carry out its duties after the explosions, and the dilatory nature of its diplomatic notes, are extenuating circumstances for the action of the United Kingdom Government. But to ensure respect for international law, of which it is the organ, the Court must declare that the action of the British Navy constituted a violation of Albanian sovereignty.

This declaration is in accordance with the request made by Albania through her Counsel, and is in itself appropriate satisfaction.

(3) Case Concerning Military and Paramilitary Activities In and Against Nicaragua (Nicar. v. U.S.)

1986 I.C.J. 13 (Jan. 10)

[*See* facts and more complete text, *supra* Part Five, at 915]

227. The Court will first appraise the facts in the light of the principle of the non-use of force. ... What is unlawful, in accordance with that principle, is recourse to either the threat or the use of force against the territorial integrity or political independence of any State. ...

228. Nicaragua has ... claimed that the United States has violated Article 2, paragraph 4, of the Charter, and has used force against Nicaragua in breach of its obligation under customary international law in as much as it has engaged in 'recruiting, training, arming, equipping, financing, supplying and otherwise encouraging, supporting, aiding, and directing military and paramilitary actions in and against Nicaragua'. ...

So far as the claim concerns breach of the Charter, it is excluded from the Court's jurisdiction by the multilateral treaty reservation. As to the claim that United States activities in relation to the contras constitute a breach of the customary international law principle of the non-use of force, the Court finds that, subject to the question whether the action of the United States might be justified as an exercise of the right of self-defence, the United States has committed a prima facie violation of that principle by its assistance to the contras in Nicaragua, by 'organizing or encouraging the organization of irregular forces or armed bands ... for incursion into the territory of another State', and 'participating in acts of civil strife ... in another State', in the terms of General Assembly resolution 2625 (XXV). According to that resolution, participation of this kind is contrary to the principle of the prohibition of the use of force when the acts of civil strife referred to 'involve a threat or use of force'. In the view of the Court, while the arming and training of the contras can certainly be said to involve the threat or use of force against Nicaragua, this is not necessarily so in respect of all the assistance given by the United States Government. In particular, the Court considers that the mere supply of funds to the contras, while undoubtedly an act of intervention in the internal affairs of Nicaragua, as will be explained below, does not in itself amount to a use of force.

229. The Court must thus consider whether… the acts in question of the United States are justified by the exercise of its right of collective self-defence against an armed attack. The Court must therefore establish whether the circumstances required for the exercise of this right of self-defence are present and, if so, whether the steps taken by the United States actually correspond to the requirements of international law. For the Court to conclude that the United States was lawfully exercising its right of collective self-defence, it must first find that Nicaragua engaged in an armed attack against El Salvador, Honduras or Costa Rica.

230. As regards El Salvador, the Court has found … that it is satisfied that between July 1979 and the early months of 1981, an intermittent flow of arms was routed via the territory of Nicaragua to the armed opposition in that country. The Court was not however satisfied that assistance has reached the Salvadorian armed opposition, on a scale of any significance, since the early months of 1981, or that the Government of Nicaragua was responsible for any flow of arms at either period. Even assuming that the supply of arms to the opposition in El Salvador could be treated as imputable to the Government of Nicaragua, to justify invocation of the right of collective self-defence in customary international law, it would have to be equated with an armed attack by Nicaragua on El Salvador. As stated above, the Court is unable to consider that, in customary international law, the provision of arms to the opposition in another State constitutes an armed attack on that State. Even at a time when the arms flow was at its peak, and again assuming the participation of the Nicaraguan Government, that would not constitute such armed attack.

231. Turning to Honduras and Costa Rica, the Court has also stated …that it should find established that certain transborder incursions into the territory of those two States, in 1982, 1983 and 1984, were imputable to the Government of Nicaragua. Very little information is however available to the Court as to the circumstances of these incursions or their possible motivations, which renders it difficult to decide whether they may be treated for legal purposes as amounting, singly or collectively, to an 'armed attack' by Nicaragua on either or both States. The Court notes that during the Security Council debate in March/April 1984, the representative of Costa Rica made no accusation of an armed attack, emphasizing merely his country's neutrality and support for the Contadora process … [t]he representative of Honduras however stated that my country is the object of aggression made manifest through a number of incidents by Nicaragua against our territorial integrity and civilian population (ibid., p. 37).

There are however other considerations which justify the Court in finding that neither these incursions, nor the alleged supply of arms to the opposition in El Salvador, may be relied on as justifying the exercise of the right of collective self-defence.

232. The exercise of the right of collective self-defence presupposes that an armed attack has occurred; and it is evident that it is the victim State, being the

most directly aware of that fact, which is likely to draw general attention to its plight. It is also evident that if the victim State wishes another State to come to its help in the exercise of the right of collective self-defence, it will normally make an express request to that effect. Thus in the present instance, the Court is entitled to take account, in judging the asserted justification of the exercise of collective self-defence by the United States, of the actual conduct of El Salvador, Honduras and Costa Rica at the relevant time, as indicative of a belief by the State in question that it was the victim of an armed attack by Nicaragua, and of the making of a request by the victim State to the United States for help in the exercise of collective self-defence.

233. The Court has seen no evidence that the conduct of those States was consistent with such a situation, either at the time when the United States first embarked on the activities which were allegedly justified by self-defence, or indeed for a long period subsequently. So far as El Salvador is concerned, it appears to the Court that while El Salvador did in fact officially declare itself the victim of an armed attack, and did ask for the United States to exercise its right of collective self-defence, this occurred only on a date much later than the commencement of the United States activities which were allegedly justified by this request. The Court notes that on 3 April 1984, the representative of El Salvador before the United Nations Security Council, while complaining of the 'open foreign intervention practised by Nicaragua in our internal affairs' … refrained from stating that El Salvador had been subjected to armed attack, and made no mention of the right of collective self-defence which it had supposedly asked the United States to exercise. Nor was this mentioned when El Salvador addressed a letter to the Court in April 1984, in connection with Nicaragua's complaint against the United States. It was only in its Declaration of Intervention filed on 15 August 1984, that El Salvador referred to requests addressed at various dates to the United States for the latter to exercise its right of collective self-defence (para. XII), asserting on this occasion that it had been the victim of aggression from Nicaragua 'since at least 1980'. In that Declaration, El Salvador affirmed that initially it had 'not wanted to present any accusation or allegation [against Nicaragua] to any of the jurisdictions to which we have a right to apply', since it sought 'a solution of understanding and mutual respect' (para. III).

234. As to Honduras and Costa Rica, they also were prompted by the institution of proceedings in this case to address communications to the Court; in neither of these is there mention of armed attack or collective self-defence. As has already been noted …, Honduras in the Security Council in 1984 asserted that Nicaragua had engaged in aggression against it, but did not mention that a request had consequently been made to the United States for assistance by way of collective self-defence. On the contrary, the representative of Honduras emphasized that the matter before the Security Council 'is a Central American problem, without exception, and it must be solved regionally', … i.e., through the Contadora process. The representative of Costa Rica also made no reference to collective self-defence. Nor, it may be noted, did the representative of the United States

assert during that debate that it had acted in response to requests for assistance in that context.

235. There is also an aspect of the conduct of the United States which the Court is entitled to take into account as indicative of the view of that State on the question of the existence of an armed attack. At no time, up to the present, has the United States Government addressed to the Security Council, in connection with the matters the subject of the present case, the report which is required by Article 51 of the United Nations Charter in respect of measures which a State believes itself bound to take when it exercises the right of individual or collective self-defence. The Court, whose decision has to be made on the basis of customary international law, has already observed that in the context of that law, the reporting obligation enshrined in Article 51 of the Charter of the United Nations does not exist. It does not therefore treat the absence of a report on the part of the United States as the breach of an undertaking forming part of the customary international law applicable to the present dispute. But the Court is justified in observing that this conduct of the United States hardly conforms with the latter's avowed conviction that it was acting in the context of collective self-defence as consecrated by Article 51 of the Charter. This fact is all the more noteworthy because, in the Security Council, the United States has itself taken the view that failure to observe the requirement to make a report contradicted a State's claim to be acting on the basis of collective self-defence. ...

236. Similarly, while no strict legal conclusion may be drawn from the date of El Salvador's announcement that it was the victim of an armed attack, and the date of its official request addressed to the United States concerning the exercise of collective self-defence, those dates have a significance as evidence of El Salvador's view of the situation. The declaration and the request of El Salvador, made publicly for the first time in August 1984, do not support the contention that in 1981 there was an armed attack capable of serving as a legal foundation for United States activities which began in the second half of that year. The states concerned did not behave as though there were an armed attack at the time when the activities attributed by the United States to Nicaragua, without actually constituting such an attack, were nevertheless the most accentuated; they did so behave only at a time when these facts fell furthest short of what would be required for the Court to take the view that an armed attack existed on the part of Nicaragua against El Salvador.

237. Since the Court has found that the condition sine qua non required for the exercise of the right of collective self-defence by the United States is not fulfilled in this case, the appraisal of the United States activities in relation to the criteria of necessity and proportionality takes on a different significance. As a result of this conclusion of the Court, even if the United States activities in question had been carried on in strict compliance with the canons of necessity and proportionality, they would not thereby become lawful. If however they were not, this may constitute an additional ground of wrongfulness. On the question of necessity, the Court observes that the United States measures taken in Decem-

ber 1981 (or, at the earliest, March of that year...cannot be said to correspond to a 'necessity' justifying the United States action against Nicaragua on the basis of assistance given by Nicaragua to the armed opposition in El Salvador. First, these measures were only taken, and began to produce their effects, several months after the major offensive of the armed opposition against the Government of El Salvador had been completely repulsed (January 1981), and the actions of the opposition considerably reduced in consequence. Thus it was possible to eliminate the main danger to the Salvadorian Government without the United States embarking on activities in and against Nicaragua. Accordingly, it cannot be held that these activities were undertaken in the light of necessity. Whether or not the assistance to the contras might meet the criterion of proportionality, the Court cannot regard the United States activities ... relating to the mining of the Nicaraguan ports and the attacks on ports, oil installations, etc., as satisfying that criterion. Whatever uncertainty may exist as to the exact scale of the aid received by the Salvadorian armed opposition from Nicaragua, it is clear that these latter United States activities in question could not have been proportionate to that aid. Finally on this point, the Court must alsoo: observe that the reaction of the United States in the context of what it regarded as self-defence was continued long after the period in which any presumed armed attack by Nicaragua could reasonably be contemplated.

238. Accordingly, the Court concludes that the plea of collective self-defence against an alleged armed attack on El Salvador, Honduras or Costa Rica, advanced by the United States to justify its conduct toward Nicaragua, cannot be upheld; and accordingly that the United States has violated the principle prohibiting recourse to the threat or use of force by the acts listed in paragraph 227 above, and by its assistance to the contras to the extent that this assistance 'involve[s] a threat or use of force' (paragraph 228 above). ...

JUDGE SCHWEBEL, dissenting.

6. Without any pretense, still less actuality, of provocation, Nicaragua since 1979 has assisted and persisted in efforts to overthrow the Government of El Salvador by providing large-scale, significant and sustained assistance to the rebellion in El Salvador - a rebellion which, before the rendering of Nicaraguan and other foreign assistance, was ill-organized, ill-equipped and ineffective. The delictual acts of the Nicaraguan Government have not been confined to provision of very large quantities of arms, munitions and supplies (an act which of itself might be viewed as not tantamount to an armed attack); Nicaragua (and Cuba) have joined with the Salvadoran rebels in the organization, planning and training for their acts of insurgency; and Nicaragua has provided the Salvadoran insurgents with command-and-control facilities, bases, communications and sanctuary, which have enabled the leadership of the Salvadoran insurgency to operate from Nicaraguan territory. Under both customary and conventional international law, that scale of Nicaraguan subversive activity not only constitutes unlawful intervention in the affairs of El Salvador; it is cumulatively tantamount to an armed attack upon El Salvador. (It is striking that both Nicaragua and the United States, in

their pleadings before the Court, agree that significant material support by a State of foreign armed irregulars who endeavour forcibly to overthrow the Government of another State is tantamount to armed attack upon the latter State by the former State.) Not only is El Salvador entitled to defend itself against this armed attack; it can, and has, called upon the United States to assist it in the exercise of collective self-defence. The United States is legally entitled to respond. It can lawfully respond to Nicaragua's covert attempt to overthrow the Government of El Salvador by overt or covert pressures, military and other, upon the Government of Nicaragua, which are exerted either directly upon the Government, territory and people of Nicaragua by the United States, or indirectly through the actions of Nicaraguan rebels - the 'contras' - supported by the United States. ...

13. As to the law, the Court holds that, even if the shipment of arms through Nicaragua to Salvadoran insurgents could be imputed to the Nicaraguan Government, such shipment would not be legally tantamount to an armed attack upon El Salvador. In the absence of armed attack, the Court holds, El Salvador is not entitled to react in self-defence - and did not - and the United States is not entitled to react in collective self-defence - and did not. I find the Court's interpretation of what is tantamount to an armed attack, and of the consequential law, inconsonant with accepted international law and with the realities of international relations. And I find its holdings as to what El Salvador and the United States actually did inconsistent with the facts.

14. The truth is that the State which first intervened with the use of force in the affairs of another State in the dispute before the Court was Nicaragua, which initiated and has maintained its efforts to subvert or overthrow the governments of its neighbours, particularly of El Salvador. In contemporary international law, the State which first undertakes specified unprovoked, unlawful uses of force against another State - such as substantial involvement in the sending of armed bands onto its territory - is, prima facie, the aggressor. On examination, Nicaragua's status as the prima facie aggressor can only be definitively confirmed. Moreover, Nicaragua has compounded its delictual behaviour by pressing false testimony on the Court in a deliberate effort to conceal it. Accordingly, on both grounds, Nicaragua does not come before the Court with clean hands. Judgment in its favour is thus unwarranted, and would be unwarranted even if it should be concluded - as it should not be - that the responsive actions of the United States were unnecessary or disproportionate.

(4) Case Concerning Oil Platforms (Iran v. U.S.)

2003 I.C.J. No. 90 (Nov. 6) (Merits)
available at http://212.153.43.18/icjwww/idocket/iop/iopframe.htm

23. ... [T]he factual background to the case, as it emerges from the pleadings of both parties [is]... not disputed, being a matter of historical record. The actions giving rise to both the claim and the counter-claim occurred in the context of the general events that took place in the Persian Gulf between 1980 and 1988, in particular the armed conflict that opposed Iran and Iraq. That conflict began

on 22 September 1980, when Iraqi forces advanced into the western areas of Iranian territory, and continued until the belligerent parties accepted a ceasefire in the summer of 1988, pursuant to United Nations Security council resolution 598 (1987) of 20 July 1987. During the war, combat occurred in the territories of both States, but the conflict also spread to the Persian Gulf – which is an international commercial route and line of communication of major importance – and affected commerce and navigation in the region. From the very beginning of the conflict, on 22 September 1980, Iran established a defence exclusion zone around its coasts; shortly after, in early October 1980, Iraq declared a "prohibited war zone" and later established a "naval total exclusive zone" in the northern area of the Persian Gulf. In 1984, Iraq commenced attacks against ships in the Persian Gulf, notably tankers carrying Iranian oil. These were the first incidents of what later became known as the "Tanker War": in the period between 1984 and 1988, a number of commercial vessels and warships of various nationalities, including neutral vessels, were attacked by aircraft, helicopters, missiles or warships, or struck mines in the waters of the Persian Gulf. Naval forces of both belligerent parties were operating in the region, but Iran has denied responsibility for any actions other than incidents involving vessels refusing a proper request for stop and search. The United States attributes responsibility for certain incidents to Iran whereas Iran suggests that Iraq was responsible for them.

24. A number of States took measures at the time aimed at ensuring the security of their vessels navigating in the Persian Gulf. In late 1986 and early 1987, the Government of Kuwait expressed its preoccupation at Iran's alleged targeting of its merchant vessels navigating the Persian Gulf. It therefore requested the United States, the Untied Kingdom and the Soviet Union to "reflag" some of these vessels to ensure their protection. Following this request, the Kuwaiti Oil Tanker company was able to charter a number of Soviet vessels, and to flag four ships under United Kingdom registry and 11 ships under United States registry. In addition, the Government of the United States agreed to provide all United States-flagged vessels with a naval escort when transiting the Persian Gulf, in order to deter further attacks; these escort missions were initiated in July 1987, under the designation "Operation Earnest Will". Other foreign Powers, including Belgium, France, Italy, the Netherlands and the United Kingdom, took parallel action, sending warships to the region to protect international shipping. Despite these efforts, a number of ships, including reflagged Kuwaiti vessels, merchant tankers carrying Kuwaiti oil and warships participating in "Operation Earnest Will", suffered attacks or struck mines in the Persian Gulf between 1987 and the end of the conflict.

25. Two specific attacks on shipping are of particular relevance in the case. On 16 October 1987, the Kuwaiti tanker *Sea Isle City*, reflagged to the United States, was hit by a missile near Kuwait harbour. The United States attributed this attack to Iran, and three days later, on 19 October 1987, it attacked Iranian offshore oil production installations, claiming to be acting in self-defence. …

51. … [I]n order to establish that it was legally justified in attacking the Iranian platforms in exercise of the right of individual self-defence, the United States has to show that attacks had been made upon it for which Iran was responsible; and that those attacks were of such a nature as to be qualified as "armed attacks" within the meaning of that expression in Article 51 of the United Nations Charter, and as understood in customary law on the use of force. As the Court observed in the case concerning *Military and Paramilitary Activities in and against Nicaragua*, it is necessary to distinguish "the most grave forms of the use of force (those constituting an armed attack) from other less grave forms" (I.C.J. Reports 1986, p.101, para. 191), since "In the case of individual self-defence, the exercise of this right is subject to the State concerned having been the victim of an armed attack" (*ibid.*, p. 103, para. 195). The United States must also show that its actions were necessary and proportional to the armed attack made on it, and that the platforms were a legitimate military target open to attack in the exercise of self-defence. …

64. On the hypothesis that all the incidents complained of are to be attributed to Iran, and thus setting aside the question, examined above, of attribution to Iran of the specific attack on the *Sea Isle City*, the question is whether that attack, either in itself or in combination with the rest of the "series of … attacks" cited by the United States can be categorized as an "armed attack" on the United States justifying self-defence. The Court notes first that the *Sea Isle City* was in Kuwaiti waters in the time of the attack on it, and that a Silkworm missile fired from (it is alleged) more than 100 km away could not have been aimed at the specific vessel, but simply programmed to hit some target in Kuwaiti waters. Secondly, the *Texaco Caribbean,* whatever its ownership, was not flying a United States flag, so that an attack on the vessel is not itself to be equated with an attack on that State. As regards the alleged firing on United States helicopters from Iranian gunboats and from the Reshadat oil platform, no persuasive evidence has been supplied to support this allegation. There is no evidence that the minelaying alleged to have been carried out by the *Iran Ajr*, at a time when Iran was at war with Iraq, was aimed specifically at the United States; and similarly it has not been established that the mine struck by the *Bridgeton* was laid with the specific intention of harming that ship, or other United States vessels. Even taken cumulatively, and reserving, as already noted, the question of Iranian responsibility, these incidents do not seem to the Court to constitute an armed attack on the United States, of the kind that the Court, in the case concerning *Military and Paramilitary Activities in and against Nicaragua*, qualified as a "most grave" form of the use of force (see paragraph 51 above).

68. The Court notes that the attacks on the Salman and Nasr platforms were not an isolated operation, aimed simply at the oil installations, as had been the case with the attacks of 19 October 1987; they formed part of a much more extensive military action, designated "Operation Praying Mantis", conducted by the United States against what it regarded as "legitimate military targets"; armed

force was used, and damage done to a number of targets, including destruction of two Iranian frigates and other Iranian naval vessels and aircraft.

Notes and Questions

1. What type and intensity of outside involvement in anti-government activity would constitute an "armed attack" in the eyes of the *Nicaragua* Court? Is its finding of customary law correct? Is it desirable? Is it in line with the *Corfu Channel* holding?

2. Has the International court in *Oil Platforms* further restricted the trigger mechanism of "armed attack"? What are the implications of this judgment for a state that finds its ships or aircraft under attack?

d. The National Security Strategy of the United States of America

The White House, September 17, 2002,
available at http://www.whitehouse.gov/nsc/nss.html

For centuries, international law recognized that nations need not suffer an attack before they can lawfully take action to defend themselves against forces that present an imminent danger of attack. Legal scholars and international jurists often conditioned the legitimacy of preemption on the existence of an imminent threat—most often a visible mobilization of armies, navies, and air forces preparing to attack.

We must adapt the concept of imminent threat to the capabilities and objectives of today's adversaries. Rogue states and terrorists do not seek to attack us using conventional means. They know such attacks would fail. Instead, they rely on acts of terror and, potentially, the use of weapons of mass destruction—weapons that can be easily concealed, delivered covertly, and used without warning.

The targets of these attacks are our military forces and our civilian population, in direct violation of one of the principal norms of the law of warfare. As was demonstrated by the losses on September 11, 2001, mass civilian casualties is the specific objective of terrorists and these losses would be exponentially more severe if terrorists acquired and used weapons of mass destruction.

The United States has long maintained the option of preemptive actions to counter a sufficient threat to our national security. The greater the threat, the greater is the risk of inaction— and the more compelling the case for taking anticipatory action to defend ourselves, even if uncertainty remains as to the time and place of the enemy's attack. To forestall or prevent such hostile acts by our adversaries, the United States will, if necessary, act preemptively.

The United States will not use force in all cases to preempt emerging threats, nor should nations use preemption as a pretext for aggression. Yet in an age where the enemies of civilization openly and actively seek the world's most destructive technologies, the United States cannot remain idle while dangers gather. We will always proceed deliberately, weighing the consequences of our actions. To support preemptive options, we will:

· build better, more integrated intelligence capabilities to provide timely, accurate information on threats, wherever they may emerge;

· coordinate closely with allies to form a common assessment of the most dangerous threats; and

· continue to transform our military forces to ensure our ability to conduct rapid and precise operations to achieve decisive results.

The purpose of our actions will always be to eliminate a specific threat to the United States or our allies and friends. The reasons for our actions will be clear, the force measured, and the cause just.

* * *

The preemptive self-defense claim put forward by the United States was sharply criticized during the Security Council debates prior to the Iraq war. For a more thorough discussion, *see supra*, Part Two, at 252-260.

NOTES AND QUESTIONS

1. Please review, *supra*, W. Michael Reisman, *Assessing Claims to Revise the Laws of War*, 97 AM. J. INT'L L. 82 (2003). Has the doctrine of preemptive self-defense risen to the level of customary law? Should it? In October 2003, following the suicide bombing of a Haifa restaurant that killed 19 Jewish and Arab Israelis, Israel bombed an alleged Islamic Jihad training facility inside Syria. Syria immediately brought the matter to the Security Council, asking for a strong denunciation of Israel's action. It was widely predicted that the act would re-ignite hostilities between Israel and Syria, seriously inflame the region, and greatly exacerbate the Israeli-Palestinian conflict. In fact, Syria received only a tepid response from the world community, suicide bombings against Israeli targets ceased for two months, and Israel and the Palestinians re-started, for a time, their long-dormant peace negotiations. What do these facts add to your assessment of the status of preemptive strike doctrine under customary international law?

2. As a matter of global order, should this defense only be available to the United States, as the world's sole superpower? Compare similar doctrines from the era of the Cold War (Brezhnev Doctrine, Carter Doctrine, etc.) *See also* Harold Hongju Koh, *On American Exceptionalism*, 55 STAN. L. REV. 1479 (2003).

3. What level of threat must be reached before the use of force against a target country is justified? Must the threat be one that would lead a "third-party observer, genuinely concerned to clarify the common interests of all people," to "reasonably conclude" that self-defense is warranted under the circumstances? MYRES S. MCDOUGAL, THE SOVIET-CUBAN QUARANTINE AND SELF-DEFENSE, *supra* at 1063. Does the 2003 invasion of Iraq meet these criteria?

2. Humanitarian Intervention

a. Introduction

State elites are using the ancient doctrine of "humanitarian intervention" not infrequently to justify initial uses of force against other states in order to protect their nationals or to stop mass slaughter, genocide, or other significant violations of fundamental human rights. Humanitarian intervention, while it might preserve international peace, and thus benefit the intervenor, is apt to be perceived more as an act of charity than as one directly in the national interest. W. Michael Reisman

& Myres S. McDougal, *Humanitarian Intervention to Protect the Ibos, in* HUMANITARIAN INTERVENTION AND THE UNITED NATIONS 167, 172 (Lillich ed. 1973) [hereinafter Reisman & McDougal].

McDougal and Bebr once lamented "[t]he failure of traditional international law to develop doctrines and procedures for protecting the fundamental rights of the individual. . . ." Myres S. McDougal & Gerhard Bebr, *Human Rights in the United Nations*, 58 AM.J. INT'L L. 603, 608 (1964). Reisman and McDougal have termed humanitarian intervention "an extraordinary remedy, an exception to the postulates of State sovereignty and territorial inviolability that are fundamental to the traditional theory if not the actual practice of international law." Reisman & McDougal, at 168. Unformalized as it is, humanitarian intervention has long been authorized by international law where essential rights are habitually violated. EDWIN BORCHARD, THE DIPLOMATIC PROTECTION OF CITIZENS ABROAD 14 (William S. Hein & Co. 1915).

Franck and Rodley have questioned the justifiability of the unilateral use of force in humanitarian intervention. In examining India's 1971 military intervention in East Bengal, they concluded:

> It is our contention that: (1) use of unilateral force remains and should remain illegal except in instances of self-defense against an actual attack, and (2) the Bangladesh case, although containing important mitigating factors in India's favor, does not constitute the basis for a definable, workable, or desirable new rule of law which, in the future, would make certain kinds of unilateral military interventions permissible.

Thomas M. Franck and Nigel S. Rodley, *After Bangladesh: The Law of Humanitarian Intervention by Military Force*, 67 AM. J. INT'L L. 275, 276 (1973).

There is a risk that any "right" to intervene unilaterally will be used for "some very peculiar purposes"— aims governed less by humanitarian than nationalistic impulses. *Id.* at 282. There was considerable debate on this point. Consider the following commentary, also from 1973:

> The Preamble of the Charter expresses the determination of the peoples of the world "to reaffirm faith in fundamental human rights, in the dignity and worth of the human person, equal rights of men and women..." It is significant that, in the following paragraph of the Preamble, there is a commitment "to ensure, by the acceptance of principles and the institution of methods, that armed force shall not be used, save in the common interest..." Hence, the preambular statements of the Charter confirm that the use of force in common interest, such as for self-defense or humanitarian purposes, continues to be lawful. The repeated emphasis upon the common interest in human rights indicates that the use of force for the urgent protection of such rights is no less authorized than other forms of self-help. ...
>
> If, then, intervention is justified, how is it to be effected?

> A number of fundamental policies are obvious. First, action within the frame of an authorized organization is most preferable; such action would include direct organizational intervention as well as delegated organizational intervention. Second, barring organizational action, a collective intervention is preferable to an intervention by a single State. There are obviously advantages and disadvantages to collective forces of a global, regional, unilingual, or multilingual composition, and so on. Where circumstances require a unilateral humanitarian intervention, the operation should be submitted to inclusive authoritative appraisal as soon as possible. It remains then to examine the specific organs and entities that are authorized coordinately under international law to perform humanitarian interventions.
>
> The organizational authority of the United Nations to perform humanitarian intervention is subsumed under a number of different jurisdictional bases. Under differing circumstances, the Security Council, the General Assembly, the Economic and Social Council, and the Secretariat may play key roles in such activities. The Charter authorization for regional organizations brings these bodies into a possible role. Since the actual composition of a humanitarian intervention and the modalities which it employs are functions of necessity, available capacity, context, and creative statesmanship, a number of specialized agencies with human rights jurisdiction as well as several nongovernmental associations of international scope can be integrated where appropriate in a humanitarian intervention.

Reisman & McDougal, *supra*, at 172 and 188.

* * *

Appraise the following cases of humanitarian intervention in light of the preceding discussion.

b. Entebbe

(1) Overview

The Israeli rescue effort at Entebbe, Uganda in July 1976 presents the case of a nation engaging in a limited military action for the protection of its nationals on board a plane hijacked by terrorists. For details, see Eleanor C. McDowell, *The Entebbe Incident*, 15 I.L.M. 1224, 1224-25 (1976).

The U.K. and the U.S. presented a draft resolution to the UN Security Council which, *inter alia*, condemned hijacking and called on states to prevent and punish all such terrorist acts, while reaffirming the need to respect the sovereignty and territorial integrity of all states. It failed for lack of the 9 affirmative votes required for adoption. The vote was 6 in favor (U.S., U.K., France, Italy, Japan, Sweden), with 2 abstentions (Panama, Romania), and 7 countries not participating in the vote (Benin, the People's Republic of China, Guyana, Libya, Pakistan, Tanzania, and the U.S.S.R.).

In the analysis of the Entebbe rescue, one line of thought was that, while the operation had infringed the sovereignty of Uganda, it was, under the circumstances, justified and could not be deemed a violation of international law. This is the approach taken by commentators such as L.C. Green, *Rescue at Entebbe-Legal Aspects*, 6 Israel Y.B. Hum. Rts., 312 at 319ff. (1976). It was also the official position of the United States Government in the Security Council on July 12, 1976, where Ambassador Scranton stated:

> Israel's action in rescuing the hostages necessarily involved a temporary breach of the territorial integrity of Uganda. Normally, such a breach would be impermissible under the Charter of the United Nations. However, there is a well established right to use limited force for the protection of one's own nationals from an imminent threat of injury or death in a situation where the State in whose territory they are located is either unwilling or unable to protect them. The right, flowing from the right of self-defence, is limited to such use of force as is necessary and appropriate to protect threatened nationals from injury.

U.N.Doc. S/PV.1941 (1976) at 31-32; 15 I.L.M. 1232 (1976). Speaking before the Sixth Committee of the United Nations General Assembly in December 1976, the United States Representative, Monroe Leigh, remarked that "[g]overnments have a paramount obligation to protect the lives of their citizens." 76 U.S. Dept. of State Bulletin 75, 76).

(2) Myres S. McDougal & W. Michael Reisman, *Entebbe*

New York Times, July 16, 1976 at A20, cols. 3-4

There is a bizarre Newspeak quality to the denunciations, in terms of asserted international law, of the Israeli rescue of hijacked passengers from the Entebbe airport in Uganda on July 4.

The initial act of air piracy at Athens was a violation of international law, as was the holding of the hostages for political purposes thereafter. At least one of these acts, piracy, is an international crime subject to universal jurisdiction.

The Israeli action would appear justified as a humanitarian intervention, a doctrine whose roots go back, at least, to Hugo Grotius. Where gross violations of human rights are taking place within a state whose government will not or cannot prevent them, the organs of the international community, or in exigent circumstances a single state, may enter the territory of the defaulting state for the sole purpose of terminating the outrage.

c. Other Interventions in Africa

In May 1978, Katangan rebel troops, operating out of Angola, invaded the Shaba province of Zaire and occupied Kolwezi and Mutshalsha, two of the principal towns. Zaire's President Mobutu Sese Seko requested military aid from a number of European and African countries. France and Belgium responded with 600 and 700 troops, respectively, and began to evacuate the area of Europeans and to hold it against further rebel incursions. Premier Tindemans of Belgium characterized his country's operations as being solely of a humanitarian nature, although, it should be noted, Belgium had over $1 billion worth of investments in the country. At the same time, Tindemans accused France of other, less honorable, purposes, i.e., trying to usurp Belgium's economic position. The French effort was certainly the more military of the two. While the Belgian troops were engaged primarily in evacuating the area, the French, who did most of the fighting, determined to remain in force at least until all French nationals had been rescued.

Whether the Belgian-French operations constituted a hostile "intervention" or, to borrow from Borchard, a "non-belligerent interposition" may depend on the matter of consent. *See* R. Lillich, *Forcible Self-Help by States to Protect Human Rights*, 53 IOWA L. REV. 325, 331 (1967). Though the difficulty of distinguishing between coerced and uncoerced consent has been emphasized (Reisman & McDougal, *supra*, at 184), the Shaba case seems a clear example of the latter. The fact that Mobutu criticized Belgium for showing hesitation in coming to his aid and the fact that he later asked for assistance from other West African states, would seem to indicate an uncoerced consent. (Belgium had also intervened in certain parts of the Congo in 1960, at the request of a provincial government. For a discussion of that intervention, Belgium's defense of it before the Security Council and the issue of consent, see *supra,* Part Five at 941-943; and notes 1-7 at 944.)

In January, 1966, Jean-Bedel Bokassa overthrew Central African Republic's President David Dacko. As opposition to his regime grew, Bokassa proclaimed himself emperor and committed increasingly ruthless atrocities. After a particularly bloody massacre in September 1979, some 1,800 French commandos were flown in to restore President Dacko to power. The French Government justified its intervention on the basis of humanitarian concerns for its own nationals. For details, see FERNANDO TESÓN, HUMANITARIAN INTERVENTION: AN INQUIRY INTO LAW AND MORALITY 177 (Transnat'l Pub. 1988)(hereinafter TESÓN).

In Sierra Leone, a brutal civil war that had lasted for decades was effectively resolved when 1,000 British troops intervened in 2000. An *ad hoc* war crimes tribunal has been established for Sierra Leone to prosecute individuals for crimes committed during the civil war. In 2003, French troops intervened in both Ivory Coast and Congo. *See* Jeremy Levitt, *Humanitarian Intervention by Regional Actors in Internal Conflicts: The Cases of ECOWAS in Liberia and Sierra Leone*, 12 TEMP. INT'L & COMP. L.J. 333 (1998); Babafemi Akinrinade, *International Humanitarian Law and the Conflict in Sierra Leone*, 15 NOTRE DAME J. L. ETHICS & PUB. POL'Y 391 (2001); Eleanor Lumsden, *An Uneasy Peace: Multilateral Military Intervention in Civil Wars*, 35 N.Y.U. J. INT'L L. & POL. 795 (2003).

Former colonies themselves, now independent states, have used the rationale of humanitarian intervention to take military action against neighboring states in Africa. One example is Tanzania's 1979 intervention in Uganda, which put an end to Idi Amin's terror regime which had claimed some 300,000 deaths. TESÓN, at 159-175. *See also* U. Umozurike, *Tanzania's Intervention in Uganda*, 20 ARCHIV DES VÖLKERRECHTS 301 (1982). Other actions include a regional intervention in Liberia, led ineffectually by Nigeria with the support of the United States in the 1990s. *See* K. Kufuor, *The Legality of the Intervention in the Liberian Civil War by the Economic Community of West African States*, 5 AFRICAN J. INT'L & COMP. L. 525 (1993). The United Nations intervened in Liberia in 2003, authorizing the use of a Nigerian peacekeeping force with the logistical support of the United States to restore order and effectuate regime change. President Charles Taylor was ousted and given sanctuary in Nigeria. Taylor was indicted for war crimes by the Sierra Leone *ad hoc* tribunal. *See* Levi Woodward, *Taylor's Liberia and the U.N.'s Involvement*, 19 N.Y.L. SCH. J. HUM. RTS. 923 (2003).

d. The Tehran Hostage Rescue Mission

United States actions to protect nationals included the attempted rescue of United States embassy personnel held hostage in Tehran.

(1) W. Michael Reisman, *Humanitarian Intervention: The Rescue Mission*

The Nation, May 24, 1980, at 612-13

Until full details of the abortive attempt to rescue U.S. hostages in Teheran become available, disturbing questions about tactical feasibility, international political wisdom and constitutional propriety will have to wait. But the question of international legality must not be deferred. ...

Plainly, humanitarian intervention and diplomatic protection are susceptible to abuse by larger states. More than a few interventions, self-characterized as humanitarian, have generally and correctly been deemed unlawful. Our own humanitarian intervention in the Dominican Republic in 1965 is, to say the least, controversial. But it is virtually impossible on the evidence now available to say that the U.S. effort in Iran was aimed at anything other than securing the release of illegally detained U.S. diplomats, after moderate means had failed.

On December 15, 1979, the International Court ordered Iran to release the hostages immediately. It also admonished both states not to "take any action and ... [to] ensure that no action is taken which may aggravate the tension between the two countries or render the dispute more difficult of solution." Americans interpreted this as prohibiting the trial of the detained diplomats. Europeans, fearful of escalation and expansion of the conflict, viewed it as also prohibiting the United States from any forceful acts against the hostages, any U.S. action would plainly have been unlawful. Since Iran ignored the directive, Washington, after waiting a reasonable interval to see if compliance would be forthcoming, was probably entitled to undertake self-help measures.

Whether the United States justifies its action as humanitarian intervention, diplomatic protection of its nationals or as forcible self-help, the case for the lawfulness, apart from the wisdom, of the attempt is quite compelling. The seizure of hostages had been universally condemned, and efforts at peacefully ending their detention appeared exhausted; the operation finally mounted was, as far as is known, limited in object and scope to hostage release.

e. Pro-Democratic Intervention

(1) Grenada

President Ronald Reagan's October, 1983 invasion of Grenada led to the replacement of a hard-line Marxist-Leninist regime on the island that was engaged in a bloody coup attempt. The United States justified the action by referring to an invitation from the Grenadan Governor General to restore order to the island, a collective security request from the Organization of Eastern Caribbean States (OECS), and the need to evacuate about 100 U.S. medical students. The legality of the invasion was heavily debated. The U.N. General Assembly condemned the intervention as a violation of international law. G.A. Res. 38/7, U.N. GAOR, 38th Sess., Supp. No. 47, at 19, U.N. Doc. A/38/47 (1983). For a flavor of the debate, compare the following:

(2) W. Michael Reisman, *Coercion and Self-Determination: Construing Charter Article 2(4)*

78 AM. J. INT'L L. 642, 643-644 (1984)

Article 2(4), like so much in the Charter and in contemporary international politics, rests on and must be interpreted in terms of this key postulate of political legitimacy in the 20th century. Each application of Article 2(4) must enhance opportunities for ongoing self-determination. Though all interventions are lamentable, the fact is that some may serve, in terms of aggregate consequences, to increase the probability of the free choice of peoples about their government and political structure. Others have the manifest objective and consequence of doing exactly the opposite. There is neither need nor justification for treating in a mechanically equal fashion Tanzania's intervention in Uganda to overthrow Amin's despotism, on the one hand, and Soviet intervention in Hungary in 1956 or Czechoslovakia in 1966 to overthrow popular governments and to impose an undesired regime on a coerced population, on the other. Here, as in all other areas of law, it is important to remember that norms are instruments devised by human beings to precipitate desired social consequences. One should not seek point-for-point conformity to a rule without constant regard for the policy or principle that animated its prescription, and with appropriate regard for the factual constellation in the minds of the drafters.

(3) Oscar Schachter, *The Legality of Pro-Democratic Invasion*
78 AM. J. INT'L L. 645, 647-648 (1984)

In my view, this [approach suggested by Reisman] is an inadequate and seriously flawed approach. I would not question his initial proposition that the will and consent of the governed is (or at least should be) a key principle of political legitimacy. Indeed, in that connection, I strongly agree with Reisman's criticism of foreign support for repressive regimes. My doubts arise regarding the propositions that follow. The first doubt concerns the assertion that "the main purpose" of international law is the "enhancement" of "ongoing self-determination." This is said to be obvious; no independent support is given for the proposition. In presenting that as an *ipse dixit* proposition, Reisman provides no reason to accept it. We are left to wonder why that purpose is now accorded primacy and treated as a "higher law" to which other aims and principles must be subordinated. One would have expected that a proposition so far-reaching in character would have been presented with an appropriate legal and empirical foundation. As it is, it is almost startling to be told that Article 2(4) is now only a means and that such aims as the maintenance of peace and the prevention of aggression are secondary to the enhancement of popular rule.

It is hardly necessary for readers of this Journal to be reminded that from the very inception of the present Charter system, there has been general agreement that the rule against unilateral recourse to force (except in self-defense) is a fundamental tenet of international law. In recent years, it has been widely characterized as *jus cogens*. To argue that it must now be "reinterpreted" so as to subordinate its prohibition to the right of states to overthrow despotic governments by force is a radical departure from that principle. Even the democratic governments in the United Nations have not claimed a right to intervene forcibly to bring about the free choice of peoples in other countries. The United States, despite occasional "rollback" oratory, has never justified its military interventions elsewhere on the ground suggested by Reisman. In Vietnam and currently in Central America, the legal justification for intervention has rested on the claim that foreign intervention had taken place and that U.S. action in response to the request of the government was justified on the basis of the collective self-defense provisions of the Charter. It is true the Grenada intervention (which Reisman may have in mind but does not mention) was considered by many in the United States as politically desirable because it would lead to democratic rule in place of a repressive regime. However, significantly, the U.S. Government did not assert that as a legal ground. Its statements clearly presented three other grounds, which, in combination, were said to provide a legal basis for the U.S. action. Whether these grounds were well founded in law and in fact are independent issues. The point here is that the United States did not present the argument that it had the right to intervene to restore popular rule in Grenada. Nor have other states taken that position.

* * *

On the legality of the Grenada action, see also Louise Doswald-Beck, *The Legality of the U.S. Intervention in Grenada*, 31 NETH. INT'L L. REV. 355 (1984); JOHN NORTON MOORE, LAW AND THE GRENADA MISSION (Center for Strategic and International Studies, Georgetown University 1984); Francis A. Boyle et al., *International Lawlessness in Grenada*, 78 AM. J. INT'L L. 172 (1984); Ved P. Nanda, *The United States Armed Intervention in Grenada: Impact on World Order*, 14 CAL. W. INT'L L.J. 395 (1984); Detlev Vagts, *International Law Under Time Pressure: Grading the Grenada Take-Home Examination*, 78 AM. J. INT'L L. 169 (1984).

(4) Haiti

Significantly less controversial was the action undertaken by the United States with respect to the Caribbean nation of Haiti in 1994. A military dictatorship had installed itself in 1991, overthrowing democratically elected President Jean-Bertrand Aristide and commencing a rule of brutal disregard of fundamental human rights by killing political opponents, raping their wives and daughters, slaying priests and orphans, and leaving the bodies or body parts of those slain as a warning to others. Unable to remove the illegitimate regime by force of diplomacy and an international embargo, the United Nations Security Council authorized the use of force on July 31, 1994.

(a) U.N. Security Council Resolution 940 (1994)

U.N.SCOR, 49th Sess., 3413th mtg., U.N. Doc. S/RES/940 (1994)

The Security Council,

... *Condemning* the continuing disregard of [Governors Island and other agreements to return to democratic rule] by the illegal de facto regime, and the regime's refusal to cooperate with efforts by the United Nations and the Organization of American States (OAS) to bring about their implementation,

Gravely concerned by the significant further deterioration of the humanitarian situation in Haiti, in particular the continuing escalation by the illegal de facto regime of systematic violations of civil liberties, the desperate plight of Haitian refugees and the recent expulsion of the staff of the International Civilian Mission (MICIVIH), which was condemned in its Presidential statement of 12 July 1994 (S/PRST/1994/32), ...

Reaffirming that the goal of the international community remains the restoration of democracy in Haiti and the prompt return of the legitimately elected President, Jean-Bertrand Aristide, within the framework of the Governors Island Agreement, ...

Determining that the situation in Haiti continues to constitute a threat to peace and security in the region,...

4. *Acting* under Chapter VII of the Charter of the United Nations, authorizes Member States to form a multinational force under unified command and

control and, in this framework, to use all necessary means to facilitate the departure from Haiti of the military leadership, consistent with the Governors Island Agreement, the prompt return of the legitimately elected President and the restoration of the legitimate authorities of the Government of Haiti, and to establish and maintain a secure and stable environment that will permit implementation of the Governors Island Agreement, on the understanding that the cost of implementing this temporary operation will be borne by the participating Member States.

* * *

With Brazil and China abstaining, the vote on this resolution was twelve to zero. In the Security Council debate, the action was justified by the massive human rights violations and the need to restore the democratically elected government. The United States led the effort and secured commitments of support for a post-invasion force by several Caribbean states. On September 15, in a nationally televised speech graphically illustrating the reign of terror in Haiti, President Clinton prepared the nation for military action, which was only averted, on September 18, 1994, by former President Carter's successful conclusion of dramatic last-minute negotiations with the Haitian rulers. On September 19, the first contingent of U.S. forces landed in Haiti; on October 10, the military rulers fled to Panama; and, on October 15, 1994, President Aristide returned to the island. For details, *see* SEAN D. MURPHY, HUMANITARIAN INTERVENTION 260-275 (1996).

In 2004, a rebellion against President Aristide once again threatened to remove him from power. Ironically, in light of the 1994 intervention which restored him to office, U.S., and later, French troops intervened to remove President Aristide from the presidential palace and restore order. At this writing, an interim government has been established, supported by a U.N. Peacekeeping Force until new elections can be held.

NOTES AND QUESTIONS

1. Intervention for the limited purposes of rescuing endangered nationals seems to find relatively broad acceptance. *See* N. RONZITTI, RESCUING NATIONALS ABROAD THROUGH MILITARY COERCION AND INTERVENTION ON GROUNDS OF HUMANITY 1 (Martinus Nijhoff 1985). Are there any policy reasons which would counsel against unilateral rescue missions as measures of diplomatic protection by the home state? Should the Security Council be seized with this matter? What about less powerful countries? Are their interests, either as "victims" of intervention or possible intervenors themselves, helped by a purely unilateral theory of diplomatic protection by force? *See* COREY GIDEON GUNDERSON, WHEN DIPLOMACY FAILS (Abdo & Daughters 2003); LAW IN HUMANITARIAN CRISES (Office for Official Publications of the European Communities 1995). *See also, supra* Part Three, at 487.

2. Could or should force be lawfully used to restore or establish a free and democratic government? The arguments for pro-democratic invasion were discussed in the above-quoted articles of Professors Reisman and Schachter. In fact, United States unilateral action in Panama installing an elected government and U.N.-approval of the effort to restore, by force, a similarly legitimized ruler in Haiti might provide some support for the backers of "pro-democratic invasion." *See* Anthony D'Amato, *The Invasion of Panama Was a Lawful Response to Tyranny*, 84 AM. J. INT'L L. 516 (1990). *See also* W. Michael Reisman, *Sovereignty and Human Rights in Contemporary International Law*, 84 AM. J. INT'L L. 866 (1990); *Thomas M. Franck, The Emerging Right to Democratic Governance,* 86 AM. J. INT'L L. 46 (1992); CHARLOTTE KU & HAROLD K. JACOBSON, ACCOUNTABILITY

AND DEMOCRACY IN THE CASE OF USING FORCE UNDER INTERNATIONAL AUSPICES (Gale Group 2000); Nsongurua J. Udombana, *Articulating the Right to Democratic Governance in Africa*, 24 MICH. J. INT'L L. 1209 (2003).

While the "right to democratic governance" has not been counted among the prescriptions accorded the rank of *jus cogens* (*see supra,* at 525-529), should its possible inclusion in the *erga omnes* right of self-determination (*see East Timor Case, supra,* Part Two at 170) and its constitutive role for the world community not justify establishment or restoration of a democratic government by force? If yes, should such an action only be undertaken with authority granted by the Security Council? Prof. Murphy suggests:

> In the end, Resolution 940 on Haiti stands as a striking precedent for a very expansive view of what can constitute a threat to international peace, and in the future may be used as support by those who favor Security Council action to promote the development (or at least the preservation) of democracies worldwide.

SEAN D. MURPHY, HUMANITARIAN INTERVENTION 281 (U. Penn. Press 1996). Have more recent events in Haiti affected this trend, or was that also a "pro-democratic" invasion?

3. Another, more controversial justification for "humanitarian intervention" is the intent to stop a genocide or other ongoing and massive violations of fundamental human rights at the level of *jus cogens*. While Tanzania's invasion of Uganda and India's action in East Pakistan/Bangladesh received widespread support from the world community, as did the recent, albeit belated intervention in Rwanda, Vietnam's invasion of Cambodia to stop the murderous Khmer Rouge failed to garner the same degree of approval. In particular, the United States withheld its approbation. What may have been the underlying rationale for the United States denunciation of Vietnam's action? Must the intervenor be "disinterested"? Should such humanitarian interventions be limited in time, and strictly confined to the restoration of minimum order and a system of human dignity? For an argument that humanitarian intervention in situations of massive violations of fundamental human rights is a time-honored exception to the rule that prohibits the use of force, *see* Myres S. McDougal & Siegfried Wiessner, *Law and Minimum World Public Order, in* MYRES S. MCDOUGAL & FLORENTINO P. FELICIANO, THE INTERNATIONAL LAW OF WAR xix, lii (New Haven Press, 1994).

4. In Kosovo, ongoing atrocities committed by Serbian government forces against ethnic Albanian citizens were considered sufficient by NATO to intervene even though Security Council authorization was arguably not secured. In 2003, one of the justifications of the U.S.-led coalition to invade Iraq and overthrow the regime of Saddam Hussein was the latter's brutal human rights record. Again, authorization by the Security Council was arguably not secured. Were the two situations substantially different? Should humanitarian intervention be allowed without Security Council authorization? If yes, under what circumstances? For an effort at establishing principles for lawful intervention, see George K. Walker, *Principles for Collective Humanitarian Intervention to Succor Other Countries' Imperiled Indigenous Nationals*, 18 AM. U. INT'L L. REV. 35, 160-162 (2002).

5. A private effort by a group of seasoned international and national political leaders proposed a possible duty of military intervention based on a "responsibility to protect". *See* the report by the members of the INT'L COMM'N ON INTERVENTION & STATE SOVEREIGNTY, THE RESPONSIBILITY TO PROTECT: REPORT OF THE INTERNATIONAL COMMISSION ON INTERVENTION AND STATE SOVEREIGNTY (2001), *available at* http://www.dfait-maeci.gc.ca/iciss-ciise/report2-en.asp, excerpted below:

THE RESPONSIBILITY TO PROTECT: CORE PRINCIPLES

(1) Basic Principles

> A. State sovereignty implies responsibility, and the primary responsibility for the protection of its people lies with the state itself.

B. Where a population is suffering serious harm, as a result of internal war, insurgency, repression or state failure, and the state in question is unwilling or unable to halt or avert it, the principle of non-intervention yields to the international responsibility to protect.

(2) Foundations

The foundations of the responsibility to protect, as a guiding principle for the international community of states, lie in:

A. obligations inherent in the concept of sovereignty;

B. the responsibility of the Security Council, under Article 24 of the UN Charter, for the maintenance of international peace and security;

C. specific legal obligations under human rights and human protection declarations, covenants and treaties, international humanitarian law and national law;

D. the developing practice of states, regional organizations and the Security Council itself.

(3) Elements

The responsibility to protect embraces three specific responsibilities:

A. The responsibility to prevent: to address both the root causes and direct causes of internal conflict and other man-made crises putting populations at risk.

B. The responsibility to react: to respond to situations of compelling human need with appropriate measures, which may include coercive measures like sanctions and international prosecution, and in extreme cases military intervention.

C. The responsibility to rebuild: to provide, particularly after a military intervention, full assistance with recovery, reconstruction and reconciliation, addressing the causes of the harm the intervention was designed to halt or avert.

(4) Priorities

A. Prevention is the single most important dimension of the responsibility to protect: prevention options should always be exhausted before intervention is contemplated, and more commitment and resources must be devoted to it.

B. The exercise of the responsibility to both prevent and react should always involve less intrusive and coercive measures being considered before more coercive and intrusive ones are applied. "

THE RESPONSIBILITY TO PROTECT:
PRINCIPLES FOR MILITARY INTERVENTION

(1) The Just Cause Threshold

Military intervention for human protection purposes is an exceptional and extraordinary measure. To be warranted, there must be serious and irreparable harm occurring to human beings, or imminently likely to occur, of the following kind:

A. large scale loss of life, actual or apprehended, with genocidal intent or not, which is the product either of deliberate state action, or state neglect or inability to act, or a failed state situation; or

B. large scale 'ethnic cleansing', actual or apprehended, whether carried out by killing, forced expulsion, acts of terror or rape.

(2) The Precautionary Principles

A. Right intention: The primary purpose of the intervention, whatever other motives intervening states may have, must be to halt or avert human suffering. Right intention is better assured with multilateral operations, clearly supported by regional opinion and the victims concerned.

B. Last resort: Military intervention can only be justified when every non-military option for the prevention or peaceful resolution of the crisis has been explored, with reasonable grounds for believing lesser measures would not have succeeded.

C. Proportional means: The scale, duration and intensity of the planned military intervention should be the minimum necessary to secure the defined human protection objective.

D. Reasonable prospects: There must be a reasonable chance of success in halting or averting the suffering which has justified the intervention, with the consequences of action not likely to be worse than the consequences of inaction.

(3) Right Authority

A. There is no better or more appropriate body than the United Nations Security Council to authorize military intervention for human protection purposes. The task is not to find alternatives to the Security Council as a source of authority, but to make the Security Council work better than it has.

B. Security Council authorization should in all cases be sought prior to any military intervention action being carried out. Those calling for an intervention should formally request such authorization, or have the Council raise the matter on its own initiative, or have the Secretary-General raise it under Article 99 of the UN Charter.

C. The Security Council should deal promptly with any request for authority to intervene where there are allegations of large scale loss of human life or ethnic cleansing. It should in this context seek adequate verification of facts or conditions on the ground that might support a military intervention.

D. The Permanent Five members of the Security Council should agree not to apply their veto power, in matters where their vital state interests are not involved, to obstruct the passage of resolutions authorizing military intervention for human protection purposes for which there is otherwise majority support.

E. If the Security Council rejects a proposal or fails to deal with it in a reasonable time, alternative options are:

I. consideration of the matter by the General Assembly in Emergency Special Session under the "Uniting for Peace" procedure; and

II. action within area of jurisdiction by regional or sub-regional organizations under Chapter VIII of the Charter, subject to their seeking subsequent authorization from the Security Council.

F. The Security Council should take into account in all its deliberations that, if it fails to discharge its responsibility to protect in conscience-shocking situations crying out for action, concerned states may not rule out other means to meet the gravity and urgency of that situation - and that the stature and credibility of the United Nations may suffer thereby.

(4) Operational Principles

A. Clear objectives; clear and unambiguous mandate at all times; and resources to match.

B. Common military approach among involved partners; unity of command; clear and unequivocal communications and chain of command.

C. Acceptance of limitations, incrementalism and gradualism in the application of force, the objective being protection of a population, not defeat of a state.

D. Rules of engagement which fit the operational concept; are precise; reflect the principle of proportionality; and involve total adherence to international humanitarian law.

E. Acceptance that force protection cannot become the principal objective.

F. Maximum possible coordination with humanitarian organizations.

* * *

Applying these principles to the Iraqi intervention, was this intervention justified? *See also* Fernando R. Tesón, *The Liberal Case for Humanitarian Intervention, in* HUMANITARIAN INTERVENTION: ETHICAL, LEGAL AND POLITICAL DILEMMAS (J.L. Holzgrefe & Robert O. Keohane eds., Cambridge U. Press 2003); Jeremy I. Levitt, *The Responsibility to Protect: A Beaver Without a Dam?*, 24 MICH. J. INT'L L. 153 (2003).

6. The counter-argument is made by Professor Jack Goldsmith:

> … Liberal democratic government is more powerful than civil society. But it can generally only act in ways that enhance national welfare. Often, it is possible for a State to enhance its welfare in ways that helps others. By treaty, nations can set terms of cooperation with other nations that can make all better off. Or by intervention, one State can serve its strategic interests in ways that help local populations in other States. The limiting principle here, however, is national interest ... This means that the best we can hope for is uneven humanitarian intervention that comports with the strategic and security interests that would be furthered by the potentially intervening nations. …
>
> The resulting uneven patterns of enforcement are often derided as hypocritical. Opportunistic interventions are also what give rise to the (not unjustified) concern that many so-called humanitarian interventions are ruses for invasions motivated in large part by strategic ends. A clear-eyed analysis of interventions would realize that such mixed-motive cases are probably the best we can hope for. The presence of mixed motives does not detract from the fact that some such interventions might help local populations, as the Kosovo intervention arguably did. Those who want to eliminate double standards aim to increase intervention to all cases of massive human rights abuses. But the much more likely possibility is that the elimination of double standards would be achieved by eliminating all humanitarian interventions.

Jack Goldsmith, *Liberal Democracy and Cosmopolitan Duty*, 55 STAN. L. REV. 1667, 1694-95 (2003).

7. Which arguments do you find compelling? What is the proper role of humanitarian intervention in world public order?

C. THE CONDUCT OF HOSTILITIES

1. Overview

a. Case Concerning Oil Platforms (Iran v. U.S.)

2003 I.C.J. __ (Nov. 6) (Merits)
available at http://212.153.43.18/icjwww/idocket/iop/iopframe.htm
[*See* facts, *supra* at 1074.]

25. Two specific attacks on shipping are of particular relevance in this case. On 16 October 1987, the Kuwaiti tanker *Sea Isle City*, reflagged to the United States, was hit by a missile near Kuwait harbour. The United States attributed this attack to Iran, and three days later, on 19 October 1987, it attacked Iranian offshore oil production installations, claiming to be acting in self-defence. United States naval forces launched an attack against the Reshadat ["Rostam"] and Resalat ["Rakhsh"] complexes; the R-7 and R-4 platforms belonging the Reshadat complex were destroyed in the attack. On 14 April 1988, the warship USS *Samuel B. Roberts* struck a mine in international waters near Bahrain while returning from an escort mission; four days later the United States, again asserting the right of self-defence, employed its naval forces to attack and destroy simultaneously the Nasr ["Sirri"] and Salman ["Sassan"] complexes.

26. These attacks by United States forces on the Iranian oil platforms are claimed by Iran to constitute breaches of the 1955 Treaty; and the attacks on the *Sea Isle City* and the USS *Samuel B. Roberts* were invoked in support of the United States' claim to act in self-defence. The counter-claim of the United States is however not limited to those attacks; according to the United States, Iran was in breach of its obligations under Article X, paragraph 1, of the 1955 Treaty, "in attacking vessels in the Gulf with mines and missiles and otherwise engaging in military actions that were dangerous and detrimental to commerce and navigation between the territories of the United States and the Islamic Republic of Iran". According to the United States, Iran conducted an aggressive policy and was responsible for more than 200 attacks against neutral shipping in international waters and the territorial seas of Persian Gulf States. Iran denies responsibility for those attacks, suggesting that they were committed by Iraq and drawing attention to Iraq's interest in internationalizing the conflict. Furthermore, Iran claims that the attitude of the Iranian authorities and the measures taken by its naval forces in the Persian Gulf were solely defensive in nature. It has emphasized that Iraq was the aggressor State in the conflict, and has claimed that Iraq received diplomatic, political, economic and military support from a number of third countries that were not formally parties to the conflict, including Kuwait, Saudi Arabia and the United States. …

73. As noted above (paragraph 43), in the present case a question of whether certain action is "necessary arises both as an element of international law relating to self-defence and on the basis of the actual terms of Article XX, paragraph 1(*d*), of the 1955 Treaty, already quoted, whereby the Treaty does "not

preclude…measures…necessary to protect [the] essential security interests" of either party. In this latter respect, the United States claims that it considered in good faith that the attacks on the platforms were necessary to protect its essential security interests, and suggests that "A measure of discretion should be afforded to a party's good faith application of measures to protect its essential security interests". Iran was prepared to recognize some of the interests referred to by the United States – the safety of United States vessels and crew, and the uninterrupted flow of maritime commerce in the Persian Gulf – as being reasonable security interests of the United States interpretation of Article XX, paragraph 1 (a:*d*), on this point is correct, since the requirement of international law that measures taken avowedly in self-defence must have been necessary for that purpose is strict and objective, leaving no room for any "measure of discretion". The Court will therefore turn to the criteria of necessity and proportionality in the context of international law on self-defence.

74. In its decision in the case concerning *Military and Paramilitary Activities in and against Nicaragua*, the Court endorsed the shared view of the parties to that case that in customary law "whether the response to the [armed] attack is lawful depends on observance of the criteria of the necessity and the proportionality of the measures taken in self-defence" (*I.C.J. Reports 1986,* p. 103, para. 194). One aspect of these criteria is the nature of the target of the force used avowedly in self-defence. In its communications to the Security Council, in particular in that of 19 October 1987 (paragraph 46 above), the United States indicated the grounds on which it regarded the Iranian platforms as legitimate targets for an armed action in self-defence. In the present proceedings, the United States has continued to maintain that they were such, and has presented evidence directed to showing that the platforms collected and reported intelligence concerning passing vessels, acted as a military communication link coordinating Iranian naval forces and served as actual staging bases to launch helicopter and small boat attacks on neutral commercial shipping. The United States has referred to documents and materials found by its forces aboard the vessel *Iran Air* (see paragraph 63 above, allegedly establishing that the Reshadat platforms served as military communication facilities. It has also affirmed that the international shipping community at the time was aware of the military use of the platforms, as confirmed by the costly steps commercial vessels took to avoid them, and by various witness reports describing Iranian attacks. The United States has also submitted expert analysis of the conditions and circumstances surrounding these attacks, examining their pattern and location in the light of the equipment at Iran's disposal. Finally, the United States has produced a number of documents found on the Reshadat complex when it was attacked, allegedly corroborating the platforms' military function. In particular, it contends that these documents prove that the Reshadat platforms had monitored the movements of the *Sea Isle City* on 8 August 1987. On the other hand, the forces that attacked the Salman and Nasr complexes were not able to board the platforms containing the control centers, and did not therefore seize any material (if indeed such existed) tending to show the use of those complexes for military purposes. …

77. As to the requirement of proportionality, the attack of 19 October 1987 might, had the Court found that it was necessary in response to the *Sea Isle City* incident as an armed attack committed by Iran, have been considered proportionate. In the case of the attacks of 18 April 1988, however, they were conceived and executed as part of a more extensive operation entitled "Operation Praying Mantis" (see paragraph 68 above). The question of the lawfulness of other aspects of that operation is not before the Court, since it is solely the action against the Salman and Nasr complexes that is presented as a breach of the 1955 Treaty; but the Court cannot assess in isolation the proportionality of that action to the attack to which it was said to be a response; it cannot close its eyes to the scale of the whole operation, which involved, *inter alia*, the destruction of two Iranian frigates and a number of other naval vessels and aircraft. As a response to the mining, by an unidentified agency, of a single United States warship, which was severely damaged but not sunk, and without loss of life, neither "Operation Praying Mantis" as a whole, nor even that part of it that destroyed the Salman and Nasr platforms, can be regarded, in the circumstances of this case, as a proportionate use of force in self-defence.

78. The Court thus concludes from the foregoing that the actions carried out by United States forces against Iranian oil installations on 19 October 1987 and 18 April 1988 cannot be justified under Article XX, paragraph 1(*d*), of the 1955 Treaty, as being measures necessary to protect the essential security interests of the United States, since those actions constituted recourse to armed force not qualifying under international law on the question, as acts of self-defence, and thus did not fall within the category of measures contemplated, upon its correct interpretation, by that provision of the Treaty.

Separate Opinion of JUDGE SIMMA:

14. In the present case, I agree with the Court that neither the broad pattern of unlawful use of force by Iran against United States vessels and their naval escorts nor the two specific attacks against the *Sea Isle City* and the *Samuel B. Roberts* amounted to an "armed attack" within the meaning of Article 51 of the United Nations Charter. These hostile activities could, as I have pointed out, have been countered immediately by "proportionate countermeasures" also of a military nature, consisting of defensive measures designed to eliminate the specific source of the threat or harm to affected ships in, and at the time of, the specific incidents. The Iranian oil platforms and their possible non-commercial activities during the Gulf War were too remote from these incidents (in every sense of this word) to provide a legitimate target for countermeasures within the meaning given to this term in the *Nicaragua* Judgment. Also, there is in the international law on the use of force no "qualitative jump" from iterative activities remaining below the threshold of Article 51 of the Charter to the type of "armed attack" envisaged there. However, as I read the facts of the present case, there was on the part of Iran no iterative or continued pattern of armed attacks against the United States ships to begin with. Attacks on ships flying foreign flags could not be relied on by the United States in order to trigger Article 51 action. Further-

more, not a single Security Council resolution adopted at the material time determined that it was Iran (alone) which had engaged in "armed attacks" against neutral shipping in the Gulf.

15. But even if we assume, for the sake of discussion, that the United States had been the victim of an armed attack by Iran within the meaning of Article 51 of the United Nations Charter the United States attacks on oil platforms would not qualify as legitimate acts of self-defence under the provision. The United States actions fulfilled neither the condition of necessity nor that of proportionality. In the light of the material before the Court relating to the political and military considerations on the part of United States authorities that led to the attacks on the oil platforms, the selection of these platforms as targets was made on the basis of decisions by military efficiency, etc., but to which the notion of "self-defence", was quite foreign. It is possible, indeed probable, that some monitoring of United States as well as any other neutral shipping had actually taken place from aboard the oil platforms. Obviously this was a nuisance to United States military decision-makers. The United States authorities might also have been right in assuming a connection between information flowing as it were, from the oil platforms and the harassing of the neutral shipping in the Gulf. Thus, as I see it, either following the incidents involving the *Sea Isle City* and the *Samuel B. Roberts*, the United States military considered that enough was enough, and thus decided to neutralize the oil platforms, or, rather, the United States used these two incidents to teach Iran a broader lesson. The material put before the Court by the United States contains several more or less convincing reasons as to why it was the oil platforms and not some other military targets that were chosen for the purpose of a "reply" to the specific incidents involving the *Sea Isle City* and the *Samuel B. Roberts*, respectively the broader pattern of unlawful force engaged in by Iran. But nowhere in these materials do we encounter any trace of the considerations that an international lawyer would regard as necessary in order to justify action taken in self-defence.

16. I arrive at the conclusion that the United States military actions against the oil platforms were not of the defensive nature required both by Article 51 of the United Nations Charter and the general international law governing "proportionate counter-measures", to refer again to the *Nicaragua* Court's tantalizing phrase. As I interpret the law on the limits of unilateral use of armed force as it has evolved since 1945, there is no way to regard such actions as lawful or justified.

NOTES AND QUESTIONS

1. Under the facts, as the Court describes them, do you think that the U.S. actions against the platforms met the necessity and proportionality tests?

2. Under the legal framework of the Court and Judge Simma's separate opinion, what actions would have been lawfully available to the U.S.?

3. Does the Court's understanding of necessity and proportionality in cases of self-defense differ from the same requirements in cases of countermeasures in the context of articles 25 and 51 of the 2001 Articles on State Responsibility? *See* Part Five, *supra,* at 960-965.

2. W. Michael Reisman, *The Lessons of Qana*

22 YALE J. INT'L L. 381 (1997)

On April 18, 1996, Israeli artillery fired on a United Nations compound in Qana, southern Lebanon. In less than ten minutes, more than 100 Lebanese civilians sheltered in the compound died. Then U.N. Secretary-General Boutros-Ghali ordered his military adviser, General van Kappen, to conduct an inquiry. Van Kappen's report itself became a subject of controversy and a source of acute tension between the Secretary-General and the United States. ...

According to the van Kappen Report, between noon and 2 p.m. on April 18, Hesbollah fighters fired two or three rockets from a location 350 meters south-east of the compound. Between 12:30 and 1 p.m., they fired four or five Katyushas from a location 600 meters south of the compound. Van Kappen also reported that a 120 mm mortar was installed between 150 and 200 meters from the compound between 11 a.m. and noon. The 120 mm mortar is considered a heavy weapon in that category of artillery, with a high range (5000 to 9000 meters) and heavy firepower.

Several reports refer to an Israeli ground unit that had crossed the red line on April 18 into the range of the 120 mm mortar near the UNIFIL compound. One source quotes a UNIFIL officer opining that the Israeli ground unit was laying sophisticated mines, but that speculation was unsupported in other reports. It seems more probable, given the coincidence in time and the absence of any other Israeli counteraction, that the ground unit was advancing on Qana either for the purpose of engaging the authors of the Katyusha attacks intervisibly and hence with more precision than artillery could bring to bear, or to provide more accurate target information ("forward observation"), given the proximity of the rocket and mortar sites to the U.N. compound.

Whatever their mission, the Israeli unit came under mortar fire from Qana. Van Kappen cites Lebanese witnesses who reported that shortly before 2 p.m.—about fifteen minutes before the Israeli shelling—between five and eight rounds were fired from the heavy mortar that had been installed less than 200 meters from the UNIFIL compound. Van Kappen quotes Israeli military sources who indicated that the 120 mm mortar fire fell within forty meters of the Israeli unit that had advanced north of the red line. Israeli press reports indicate that the commander of the ground unit under mortar attack radioed that his unit had taken casualties. That report proved to be incorrect, but its misinformation may help to explain part of what transpired thereafter.

Van Kappen reports that the Israeli target acquisition system then identified, at 1:52 and 1:58 p.m., two separate targets in the vicinity of Qana. The target locations that the Israelis gave to General van Kappen corresponded to the sites of the 120 mm mortar and of the Katyusha attacks. The information was relayed automatically to the Northern Command and to an artillery battalion on the Israeli-Lebanese border, about twelve kilometers from the sea.

The commander of the Israeli artillery battalion confirmed that one of the targets was within 300 meters of the compound. Consequently, he did not fire before securing explicit authorization. Northern Command, which presumably also had the "information" that the ground unit had come under mortar fire and taken casualties, checked the data and granted permission to fire. Apparently, the reason for overriding the rules of engagement that preclude using such weapons within 300 meters of a U.N. area was that the ground unit had suffered casualties.

The precipitating event of the Israeli action then was the mortar attack on the ground unit north of the red line. Israeli command undertook a number of responses. First, as mentioned, it authorized artillery fire. The Israeli battalion comprised three batteries, each with four M-109A2 guns. According to information that Israel supplied to General van Kappen, the first target, the 120 mm mortar, was engaged by one battery, using all four guns and firing thirty-eight shells, two-thirds of which had impact fuses and one-third proximity fuses. The firing took less than five minutes, from 2:07 p.m. to 2:12 p.m. Israel reported to van Kappen that the two types of fuses had been distributed randomly.

According to Israel, another battery engaged the second target by firing forty rounds from 2:11 p.m. to 2:17 p.m. Thus, according to Israel, seventy-eight shells would have been fired from its batteries between 2:07 p.m. and 2:17 p.m. at the two targets in Qana. As a consequence of the bombardment, more than 100 Lebanese noncombatants were killed and many more were wounded. No UNIFIL personnel were killed.

General van Kappen found thirty-six impacts in the Qana area, in two distinct concentrations, with two "stray" impacts. Seventeen shells, sixteen with impact fuses and one with a proximity fuse, landed about 100 meters south of the U.N. compound, some seventy-five meters northwest of the point from which the mortar had been firing. Thirteen detonations struck inside or directly above the compound and four very close to it. General van Kappen also found that "[d]uring the shelling, there was a perceptible shift in the weight of fire from the mortar site to the United Nations compound." Based on the evidence remaining after the clean-up, General van Kappen estimated that eight shells with proximity fuses detonated over the compound and one such shell exploded just outside it. Five high explosive shells with impact fuses struck the compound and three exploded close to it. It is not certain which shell type was responsible for the deaths of the civilians or whether a different mix of shells might have averted or minimized the tragedy.

The initial Israeli response to General van Kappen's inquiries had been that two-thirds of the shells fired were armed with impact fuses and one-third with proximity fuses. The Israeli command later confessed error; the mix was the reverse. The battalion commander had indicated that the shells were fired in random order. The precise type of shells used is usually determined according to a formula that is designed for maximum impact on the particular target. Proximity fuses, which explode while the shell in which they are incorporated is still in the air, are designed to rain shrapnel downward onto soldiers crawling on their bellies. They are an antipersonnel weapon. Impact fuses explode laterally and upward, thus doing maximum damage to standing or running soldiers. The mix-formula can be calculated by the artillery computer or by hand. Proximity and impact fuses likely will be mixed for infantry targets. That Israel used more proximity than impact fuses suggests it may have thought the guerillas were dug-in or crawling, not running or standing.

Thus, if Israel fired into the compound accidentally, the use of more proximity fuses makes sense; it could have believed that the Hesbollah irregulars were dug-in, pinning down Israeli infantry with rifle and mortar fire. Israel probably would have used more impact fuses if it believed that the irregulars were running toward the U.N. compound. If the Israeli decisionmakers were unaware of the refugees, but assumed that Hesbollah irregulars had entered the camp and that UNIFIL soldiers had entered their bunkers, proximity-fused shells would have discriminated between Hesbollah and UNIFIL. Reports that Israeli helicopters or satellites actually observed Hesbollah irregulars running into the U.N. compound and mingling with refugees, if true, would support this interpretation, but only if Israel fired the artillery after the irregulars were observed running into the compound, as opposed to while they were running.

Assuming that Israel's action was not intentional, the cause *sine qua non* of the death of the civilians and the destruction within the compound was not the initial targeting or the selection of the mix of ammunition, but a change in the direction of fire in the course of the attack. General van Kappen states: "Several witnesses reported that during the shelling there had been a perceptible shift in the weight of fire from an area south-west of the compound (the mortar site) to the compound itself." Van Kappen asked the commanding officer of the artillery battalion about this.

Asked if he had shifted fire during the shelling, [the commanding officer] said he had not; he added that the mission had taken only three to four minutes (the time given by the Israeli forces was from 1407 to 1412 hours) and there would have been no time to change target data. General Harel, who responded to the van Kappen Report on behalf of Israel, could not explain the shift in fire. Reports in the Israeli and international press speculated on possible explanations.

Israel initially stated that there had been no aircraft, helicopters, or remotely piloted vehicles (RPVs) over Qana before, during, or after the shelling. Witnesses in Lebanon, however, reported seeing an RPV over Qana. A videotape by a UNIFIL soldier shows an RPV and two helicopters. Van Kappen and the Time analysis indicate that Israeli helicopters were within two kilometers of Qana at the time. The Israeli military acknowledged that two helicopters had been sent north "to locate and attack the sources of fire." But Israel averred that the helicopters had been unable to find the target and had left the area. Subsequent to the report, Israel claimed that after receiving reports that the U.N. camp had been hit, they diverted an RPV "in order to ascertain the validity of the reports," and the RPV confirmed the report despite poor weather conditions.

According to some accounts, U.N. investigators believe that Israeli helicopters had observed Hesbollah irregulars fleeing into the U.N. compound and mingling with the refugees, and even had a satellite spy camera trained on the source of rocket fire. The Times of London reported that an amateur video of the massacre taken by a Norwegian soldier showed two Israeli helicopters observing the attack. The investigation also discovered an Israeli satellite stationed over Qana at the time, which showed hundreds of civilians milling around inside the UN base.

In response to the van Kappen Report, Israel attributed the mistargeting to two errors: the placement of a pin on a map with a scale of one to 20,000 about 100 meters north of its actual location, and targeting calculations that did not take account of the space covered by the compound, making the target seem as if it were 350 meters from the compound rather than the 180 meters it actually was. The Time investigation quotes a U.N. spokesman doubting the Israeli explanation and insisting that when the Israelis withdrew from the area of Qana in 1985, they videotaped every building and street and used aerial photography to mark every house on their maps. Whether such information was used in the maps available to the Israeli soldiers engaged in targeting and firing is not clear.

General van Kappen does not focus on whether the firing could or should have been suspended when it became clear that the shells were falling on civilians and on the UNIFIL camp, perhaps because his team did not think that this was a realistic option. Time quotes the commander of the UNIFIL compound at Qana as saying: "We made the effort to make them stop. But they kept firing." The efforts apparently involved three neighboring U.N. posts firing red warning flares. These would not have been visible to the artillery battalion but might have been visible to aircraft. The RPV that was videotaped in the vicinity was reportedly of the type that has a real-time communications link. But even if the information had been conveyed, one wonders if it could have been absorbed, interpreted, and acted on in the remaining two or three minutes of the shelling.

Israeli television had shown civilians in U.N. compounds the day before the incident at Qana. General van Kappen did not explore the question of whether Israeli officers knew that a large number of civilians had sought shelter there because he felt it was irrelevant: "[T]he United Nations compound was not a legitimate target." There were, however, 152 compounds, and none of the reports indicate whether the media information specified which were refugee centers or whether the Israeli command had issued a general advisory about the presence of refugees in all UNIFIL compounds. Van Kappen quotes Israeli officers to the effect that "it was not Israeli policy to target civilians or the United Nations." Immediately after the incident, Shimon Peres averred that Israel had not known of the presence of the civilians; had it known, according to Peres, it would have acted differently.

General van Kappen did not find any of the Israeli explanations persuasive. In his report of May 1, he concluded, "While the possibility cannot be ruled out completely, it is unlikely that the shelling of the United Nations compound was the result of gross technical and/or procedural errors." Reviewing the official Israeli responses on May 7, General van Kappen reaffirmed his earlier conclusion: "As I stated in my report, it is unlikely that gross technical and/or procedural errors led to the shelling of the United Nations compound. However, it cannot be ruled out completely." The report of May 1 stated that Israel had informed the commander of UNIFIL "of new precautions adopted by the Israeli forces with regard to firing at targets near United Nations positions," but does not indicate what they were.

International legal and political statements condemned the shelling of civilians, but were less vocal about the law concerning such operations against U.N. posts. On April 19, 1996, the International Committee of the Red Cross (ICRC) condemned the action, reiterating its earlier appeal to the belligerents "to comply with the rules of international humanitarian law, including the absolute ban on indiscriminate attacks of a nature to strike civilians or civilian property." On May 10, 1996, the U.N. General Assembly passed a resolution that, among other things, expressed grave concern at actions that seriously threaten the safety of the United Nations Interim Force in Lebanon and impede the implementation of its mandate, in particular the incident that occurred on 18 April 1996 in which shelling resulted in heavy loss of life among civilians at a site of the Interim Force. In its operative paragraphs, the Assembly condemned "the Israeli military attacks against the civilian population in Lebanon, especially against the United Nations base at Qana, which violate the rules of international humanitarian law pertaining to the protection of civilians." The Assembly also resolved that "Lebanon is entitled to appropriate redress for the destruction it has suffered and that Israel is responsible for such compensation." The resolution, however, made no further mention of the issue of UNIFIL's status. An initiative in the Security Council, which included condemnation of Israel, a call for compensation, steps by Israel to prevent recurrence, and steps by the Secretary-General to prevent such attacks in the future, was aborted. ...

What was distinctive in the Qana incident was the large number of civilian casualties. Noncombatants are a key object of concern of contemporary humanitarian law, yet the law is proving ineffective for incidents like these because of intersecting technical and political factors.

Article 51 of the First Additional Protocol to the Geneva Convention affords the civilian population and individual civilians "general protection," which includes a prohibition on "indiscriminate attacks." Subsection 5 provides examples of indiscriminate attacks: a) an attack by bombardment by any methods or means which treats as a single military objective a number of clearly separated and distinct military objectives located in a city, town ... and b) an attack which may be expected to cause incidental loss of civilian life, injury to civilians, damage to civilian objects, or a combination thereof, which would be excessive in relation to the concrete and direct military advantage anticipated. Article 57 requires a belligerent to do "everything feasible" for verification of the presence of civilians and to take all feasible precautions in the choice of means and methods of attack with a view to avoiding injury to civilians.

Moreover, article 57(2)(b) states that an attack shall be cancelled or suspended if it becomes apparent that the objective is not a military one or is subject to special protection or that the attack may be expected to cause incidental loss of civilian life . . . which would be excessive in relation to the concrete and direct military advantage anticipated. The ICRC Commentary makes clear that, though the law of war balances the necessities of war and humanitarian requirements, the principle of proportionality is secondary to the principles of protection: "[A]n attack cannot be justified only on grounds of proportionality if it contravenes the above-mentioned principles."

Many commentators and ICRC spokespersons suggest that proportionality should be a complex equation, taking into account factors such as the military importance or exigency of the target. A single sniper in the turret of a church or the top floor of a hospital will not justify destruction of the church or hospital; a highly destructive weapon placed there by an adversary may warrant it. In the first instance, the deployment of weapons that are more discriminating and less collaterally destructive is expected, even though the costs in terms of lives and casualties of the belligerent seeking to neutralize the sniper may be higher than would the use of a larger weapon, applied from a relatively safer remove.

How will that be applied to incidents like Qana? Assume the threatened destruction of part of a patrol of, let us say, twelve soldiers by mortar fire from the vicinity of a U.N. compound known to be sheltering more than 800 noncombatants. According to some commentators, knowledge of the presence of the noncombatants would severely restrict the choice of the weapons to be used to extricate the patrol because the application of a relatively undiscriminating weapon in this context, though it might be the only one that could be deployed rapidly enough to help the patrol, could cause great loss of civilian life. Even though the selection of a more discriminating weapon in this context— assuming that such weapons were available in real time—would probably increase the losses of the actor seeking to defend its unit, it is, according to this argument, legally required.

This agreement was unacceptable to Israel. The rules of engagement inferred from the record suggest that Israel was willing to defer to humanitarian considerations with respect to rockets emanating from the zone of the compound as long as there was no direct threat to its units. When such a threat eventuated, Israel responded vigorously in defense of the unit. Though it expressed regret for the deaths of noncombatants, it did not acknowledge improper action.

In circumstances like these, any democratic polity engaged in elective conflict will insist on a comparable version of the law. Its elites will encounter two potentially conflicting imperatives: on the one hand, the imperative of using force in a limited fashion in an external arena and, on the other, the imperative of retaining the support of an internal constituency to whom the relation of such an operation to national interest may not appear vividly self-evident. For such actions, it is assumed that the public's tolerance for casualties is low, in contrast to circumstances in which national security or integrity are widely believed to be at stake, and in which tolerance for casualties may, for a time, be extremely high. Because some determinate casualty figure is believed, both by the democracy and its adversary, to be the cutoff point, the democracy's political-military leadership will make every effort to keep low or "zero" casualties as its adversaries try to push them up. To an extent, democratic leadership will seek to avoid elective military action. When it cannot, it will select and deploy weapons that provide maximum safety to its own forces.

Because of the increasing legal and moral force of humanitarian law, this strategy will be justified by a touting of "smart" weapons that are supposed to increase accuracy while reducing the exposure of the soldier operating them. The promise of these weapons is true—to an extent. Silicon chips may make a weapon more accurate, but that same weapon, corrected by an operator and intervisible with the target, will be even more accurate—meaning less injury to people with the misfortune to be in the way. Yet intervisibility means "retro-vulnerability": The operator is more vulnerable to injury by the adversary. Hence one may hypothesize that in order to minimize retro-vulnerability, human correction will be reduced or avoided in elective conflicts in which a democratic polity's tolerance of losses is expected to be inelastic. Unfortunately, in armed conflict, the safety equation is zero-sum: the more safety reserved for your forces, the more unintended and, of course, regrettable injury to civilians.

* * *

The legal prescriptions designed to "tame the dogs of war" have been codified, for the main part, in the Hague Conventions of 1899 and 1907 and the four Geneva Conventions of 1949. *See* MYRES S. MCDOUGAL & FLORENTINO P. FELICIANO, THE INTERNATIONAL LAW OF WAR (New Haven Press 1994), in particular at 384-832.

Arguably the most important provision, applying to both international and certain non-international armed conflicts, is Common Article 3 of the Four Geneva Conventions of 1949, excerpted below.

3. Common Article 3, Four Geneva Conventions of 1949

Aug. 12, 1949, art. 3, 6 U.S.T. 3114, 3116-3118

In the case of armed conflict not of an international character occurring in the territory of one of the High Contracting Parties, each Party to the conflict shall be bound to apply, as a minimum, the following provisions:

(1) Persons taking no active part in the hostilities, including members of armed forces who have laid down their arms and those placed *hors de combat* by sickness, wounds, detention, or any other cause, shall in all circumstances be treated humanely, without any adverse distinction founded on race, colour, religion or faith, sex, birth or wealth, or any other similar criteria.

To this end, the following acts are and shall remain prohibited at any time and in any place whatsoever with respect to the above-mentioned persons:

(a) violence to life and person, in particular murder of all kinds, mutilation, cruel treatment and torture;

(b) taking of hostages;

(c) outrages upon personal dignity, in particular humiliating and degrading treatment;

(d) the passing of sentences and the carrying out of executions without previous judgement pronounced by a regularly constituted court, affording all the judicial guarantees which are recognized as indispensable by civilized peoples.

(2) The wounded and sick shall be collected and cared for.

An impartial humanitarian body, such as the International Committee of the Red Cross, may offer its services to the Parties to the conflict.

* * *

In reaction to changes in world social process, two protocols to the 1949 Geneva Conventions were adopted in 1977. Protocol I offers the following modifications: Part II (Articles 8-34) updates the rules of the First and Second Geneva Conventions on the wounded, sick and shipwrecked. Part III restates the basic prohibition of methods and means of warfare that inflict unnecessary suffering and superfluous injury and notably projects, in Article 35 (3), the fundamental policy to ban methods of warfare which are "intended, or may be expected, to cause widespread, long-term and severe damage to the natural environment." Articles 43 and 44 modify the conception of permissible combatancy in land warfare, and relate to the requirements compliance with which entitles members of armed forces to claim prisoner of war status upon capture by the enemy. These two provisions, reflecting experience with guerilla warfare during World War II and in subsequent decades, have deemphasized, by passing over *sub silentio,* the traditional prerequisite of exhibiting fixed, distinctive and recognizable signs. At the same time, they stress that the more realistic customary law requirement of carrying arms openly be complied with during actual military engagements and immediately preceding military deployment.

Part IV, excerpted below, reaffirms the basic policy of reducing to the minimum the unnecessary or militarily irrelevant destruction of values by requiring belligerents to distinguish between "civilian objects" and "specific military objectives" and confining permissible objects of attack to the latter. Protection of the civilian population is sought by prohibiting "indiscriminate attacks" and defining these as attacks which are not or cannot be directed at or limited to a "specific military objective" (Article 51(4)). Military objectives are characterized in terms of the extent to which they, in particular circumstances, constitute effective bases of military power (Article 52(2)).

The protection of the civilian population as designed in Protocol I has become a major factor in modern warfare.

Protocol II is designed to address the fact that approximately 80% of the casualties of armed conflicts since 1945 have been victims of non-international conflicts, often fought more cruelly than international conflicts. The aim is to extend the essential rules of humanitarian warfare to internal wars. Ironically, Protocol II's scope of application *ratione materiae is* narrower and will thus apply to a smaller range of internal wars than Common Article 3.

4. Protocol Additional to the Geneva Conventions of 12 August 1949, and relating to the Protection of Victims of International Armed Conflicts (Protocol I)

Dec. 12, 1977, 1125 U.N.T.S. 3 (1979)

Article 50. *Definition of civilians and civilian population*

1. A civilian is any person who does not belong to one of the categories of persons referred to in Article 4 (A) (1), (2), (3) and (6) of the Third Convention and in Article 43 of this Protocol. In case of doubt whether a person is a civilian, that person shall be considered to be a civilian.

2. The civilian population comprises all persons who are civilians.

3. The presence within the civilian population of individuals who do not come within the definition of civilians does not deprive the population of its civilian character.

Article 51. *Protection of the civilian population*

1. The civilian population and individual civilians shall enjoy general protection against dangers arising from military operations. To give effect to this protection, the following rules, which are additional to other applicable rules of international law, shall be observed in all circumstances.

2. The civilian population as such, as well as individual civilians, shall not be the object of attack. Acts or threats of violence the primary purpose of which is to spread terror among the civilian population are prohibited.

3. Civilians shall enjoy the protection afforded by this section, unless and for such time as they take a direct part in hostilities.

4. Indiscriminate attacks are prohibited. Indiscriminate attacks are:

(a) those which are not directed at a specific military objective;

(b) those which employ a method or means of combat which cannot be directed at a specific military objective; or

(c) those which employ a method or means of combat the effects of which cannot be limited as required by this Protocol; and consequently, in each such case, are of a nature to strike military objectives and civilians or civilian objects without distinction.

5. Among others, the following types of attacks are to be considered as indiscriminate:

(a) an attack by bombardment by any methods or means which treats as a single military objective a number of clearly separated and distinct military objectives located in a city, town, village or other area containing a similar concentration of civilians or civilian objects; and

(b) an attack which may be expected to cause incidental loss of civilian life, injury to civilians, damage to civilian objects, or a combination thereof, which would be excessive in relation to the concrete and direct military advantage anticipated.

6. Attacks against the civilian population or civilians by way of reprisals are prohibited.

7. The presence or movements of the civilian population or individual civilians shall not be used to render certain points or areas immune from military operations, in particular in attempts to shield military objectives from attacks or to shield, favour or impede military operations. The Parties to the conflict shall not direct the movement of the civilian population or individual civilians in order to attempt to shield military objectives from attacks or to shield military operations.

8. Any violation of these prohibitions shall not release the Parties to the conflict from their legal obligations with respect to the civilian population and civilians, including the obligation to take the precautionary measures provided for in Article 57.

Article 52. *General Protection of civilian objects*

1. Civilian objects shall not be the object of attack or of reprisals. Civilian objects are all objects which are not military objectives as defined in paragraph 2.

2. Attacks shall be limited strictly to military objectives. In so far as objects are concerned, military objectives are limited to those objects which by their nature, location, purpose or use make an effective contribution to military action and whose total or partial destruction, capture or neutralization, in the circumstances ruling at the time, offers a definite military advantage.

3. In case of doubt whether an object which is normally dedicated to civilian purposes, such as a place of worship, a house or other dwelling or a school, is being used to make an effective contribution to military action, it shall be presumed not to be so used.

5. HCJ 4764/04: Physicians for Human Rights *et al.* v. Commander of the IDF Forces in the Gaza Strip

Israel Supreme Court, May 30, 2004

BARAK, C.J.: [Four human rights organizations in Israel petitioned the Israel Supreme Court] ... that the IDF allow medical teams and ambulances to reach and evacuate the wounded in Rafah, that such evacuation not require coordination with the Hotline, that medical teams be neither threatened nor harmed, and that the transport of medical equipment into Rafah be allowed. The petition further asks that electricity and water provisions be restored to the neighborhood of Tel A-Sultan, that the IDF allow the provision of food and medicines to the residents of that neighborhood, and that a medical team of Petitioner 1 be allowed to enter hospitals in the Gaza Strip and assess the medical situation there. Finally, petitioners ask that a full investigation be made into an incident in which a number of residents were killed when a crowd of protesting civilians was shelled. Moreover, petitioners ask for an order prohibiting the shelling of civilians, even when among them are armed combatants, who do not pose an immediate threat to life. ...

7. "Israel is not an isolated island. She is a member of an international system." HCJ 5592/02 *Yassin v. Commander of the Kziot Military Camp*. The military operations of the IDF are not conducted in a legal vacuum. There are legal norms – of customary international law, of treaties to which Israel is party, and of the fundamental principles of Israeli law – which set out how military operations should be conducted. In HCJ 3451/02 *Almandi v. The Minister of Defense*, I noted that:

> Israel finds itself in the middle of a difficult battle against a furious wave of terrorism. Israel is exercising its right of self defense. *See* The Charter of the United Nations, art. 51. This combat is not taking place in a normative void. It is being carried out according to the rules of international law, which provide principles and rules for combat activity. The saying, "When the cannons roar, the muses are silent," is incorrect. Cicero's aphorism that laws are silent during war does not reflect modern reality...
>
> The foundation of this approach is not only the pragmatic consequence of a political and normative reality. Its roots lie much deeper. It is an expression of the difference between a democratic state fighting for its life and the aggression of terrorists rising up against it. The state fights in the name of the law and in the name of upholding the law. The terrorists fight against the law and exploit its violation. The war against terror is also the law's war against those who rise up against it. See HCJ 320/80 *Kawasma v. The Minister of Defense*, at 132. Moreover, the State of Israel is founded on Jewish and democratic values. We established a state that upholds the law—it fulfills its national goals, long the vision of its generations, while upholding human rights and ensuring human dignity. Between these—the vision and the law— there lies only harmony, not conflict.

Indeed, all of the IDF's operations are subject to international law. For example, in HCJ 3114/02 *Barake v. Minister of Defense* I noted that "[e]ven in a time of combat, the laws of war must be followed. Even in a time of combat, all must be done in order to protect the civilian population." …

9. We do not review the wisdom of the decision to take military action. We review the legality of the military operations. As such, we presume that the operations in Rafah are necessary from a military standpoint. The question before us is only whether these military operations adhere to domestic and international law. The fact that operations are necessary from a military standpoint does not automatically mean that they fulfill legal requirements. Of course, with regard to issues of military concern, we do not stand in the stead of the military commander, and we do not substitute our discretion for his own. That is his expertise. We examine the legal import of his decisions. That is our expertise. …

34. According to the humanitarian principles of international law, military activities require the following: First, that the rules of conduct be taught to, and that they be internalized by, all combat soldiers, from the Chief of General Staff down to new recruits. *See Physicians for Human Rights*, at 5. Second, that procedures be drawn up that allow implementation of these rules, and which allow them to be put into practice during combat. An examination of the conduct of the army while fighting in Rafah, as detailed in the petition before us – and we have nothing other than what has been presented to us – indicates significant progress compared to the situation two years ago. *See Barake*; *Physicians for Human Rights* and other decisions. This is the case regarding the implementation of the duty to ensure water, medical equipment, medicines, food, evacuation of the wounded, and the burial of the dead. This is also the case regarding the preparation of the army, and the design of procedures that allow humanitarian obligations to be satisfied. The establishment of the Humanitarian Hotline and the District Coordination Office, as well as the assignment of a liaison officer of the Coordination Office to every battalion, greatly aided the implementation of humanitarian principles.

35. In the framework of our discussion regarding the internalization of humanitarian laws, we emphasize that it is the duty of the military commander not only to prevent the army from harming the lives and dignity of the local residents (the "negative" duty: *see supra* para. 11). He also has a "positive" duty (*para.* 11). He must protect the lives and dignity of the local residents. For example, regarding the burial of local residents, the military commander was satisfied that the corpses were transferred to A-Najar Hospital. But this was not enough. He is obligated to do his utmost to ensure that the bodies be brought to a dignified burial according to local custom. He must make prior arrangements in order to ensure there are sufficient supplies of food and water. Damage to the water supply is something that can be anticipated from the outset, and if it cannot be avoided, a solution to this problem must be prearranged. Supplies of medicines, medical equipment and food should also be prepared in advance. Harm to local residents is expected and if, despite every effort to limit this, in the end there will be casu-

alties among residents, this must be prepared for from the outset. Respondent should not rely solely on international and Israeli aid organizations to solve these problems, though their aid is important. The recognition that the basic duty belongs to the military commander must be internalized, and it is his job to adopt different measures from the outset so that he can fulfill his duty on the battlefield.

36. Additional measures should be adopted so that the established institutional arrangements (*see supra* para. 3) will be more effective. We were informed that those who called the Humanitarian Hotline had to wait many hours. Col. Mordechai noted several times that some issues should have been referred to him, and not to the Humanitarian Hotline. The lack of information led, on several occasions, to inefficiency in aid efforts by third parties. Thus, for example, a vehicle of Petitioner 1 laden with medical equipment and medicines waited at Erez Crossing while the entrance point was Karni Crossing. However, at Karni Crossing their entrance was again denied, since Israeli doctors were among the passengers in the vehicle, and the army was only prepared to allow the entry of non-Israeli doctors. These issues and others need to be addressed. It is possible that the Humanitarian Hotline needs to be expanded, and there needs to be more effective communication between it and the District Coordination Office and the Coordination Office's liaison officers placed with the combat battalions. It is possible that there is a need, with regard to international and Israeli organizations whose humanitarian involvement is anticipated, to bypass the Humanitarian Hotline and facilitate direct contact with the DCO. It is possible that there is a need to take other measures. This matter is for the respondent to address; it must learn from the events of the day.

37. With the conclusion of the arguments in the petition, we ordered that the military staff in the area ensure that they solve not only the problems raised by petitioners, but also anticipate new problems that, in the nature of things, will arise in the future. For this reason it has been decided that Col. Mordechai will appoint a senior officer who will remain in direct contact with petitioners. This is the least that should have been done at the time the events were unfolding. The main thing is that it must be done now in order to learn lessons from the episode.

Notes and Questions

1. On the issue of prohibited weapons, consider the following comment.

I. The Cluster Bomb

> Unlike the general-purpose bomb or the penetration bomb, a cluster bomb contains smaller bombs inside. It is a highly developed fragmentation bomb. Essentially, each cluster bomb consists of a large canister, the dispenser, which holds anywhere from 10 to 500 small fragmentation bombs (submunitions), euphemistically called "bomblets." When dropped from an aircraft, the dispenser of the cluster bomb hurtles to earth, but, well before making impact, releases the small bomblets. The dispenser is designed to spin so on dispersal it spreads the bomblets over a large area.

> Cluster bombs endanger the civilian population in two principal ways. A cluster bomb consists of a great number of small, but extraordinarily powerful bombs. ... The cluster bomb is an "area weapon," so called because a single dispenser can spread its cluster bombs over a huge area, from one to five football fields. Each of the small bombs contains over a hundred tiny pieces of shrapnel, which can cause physical injury at especially long distances. If dropped on a military target in a populated area, cluster bombs, because of their enormous footprint and because of each small bomb's terrific destructive power, almost certainly will kill, maim, or otherwise wound a large number of innocent civilians.
>
> Secondly, five to thirty percent of the small cluster bombs are duds. But they can remain dangerous years after launch; a slight vibration can detonate them. At least in some models, the passage of time makes the cluster bomb more dangerous, as the fuzing mechanism deteriorates. Since the small cluster bombs often look like toys, children tend to pick them up, ... resulting in death or amputation. The question here is whether the cluster bomb violates international law.

Thomas Michael McDonnell, *Cluster Bombs over Kosovo: A Violation of International Law?*, 44 Ariz. L. Rev. 31, 31-42 (2002). Should cluster bombs be considered prohibited weapons in all circumstances? *See also* Protection of War Victims (Oceana Publications 1979); Frits Kalshoven, Constraints on the Waging of War (International Committee of the Red Cross 2001).

2. *See also* Armed Conflict and the New Law (Michael A. Meyer ed., British Institute of International and Comparative Law 1989); Lindsay Moir, The Law of Internal Armed Conflict (Cambridge U. Press 2002); Adir Waldman, *Clashing Behavior, Converging Interests: A Legal Convention Regulating a Military Conflict*, 27 Yale J. Int'l L. 249 (2002).

3. In a Memorandum of January 9, 2002 of the U.S. Department of Justice, Deputy Assistant Attorney General John Yoo developed a theory about the Application of Treaties and Laws to al Qaeda and Taliban Detainees. He concluded:

> For the foregoing reasons, we conclude that neither the federal War Crimes Act nor the Geneva Conventions would apply to the detention conditions in Guantánamo Bay, Cuba, or to trial by military commission of al Qaeda or Taliban prisoners. We also conclude that customary international law has no binding legal effect on either the President or the military because it is not federal law as recognized by the Constitution. Nonetheless, we also believe that the President, as Commander in Chief, has the constitutional authority to impose the customary laws of war on both the al Qaeda and Taliban groups and the U.S. Armed Forces.

U.S. Department of Justice, Office of Legal Counsel, Memorandum for William J. Haynes II from John Yoo, Deputy Assistant Attorney General, Robert J. Delahunty, Special Counsel, January 9, 2002. Would you agree?

6. Legal Consequences of the Construction of a Wall in the Occupied Palestinian Territory

2004 I.C.J. No. 131 (July 9) (Advisory Opinion)

available at http://www.icj-cij.org/icjwww/idocket/imwp/imwp/imwpframe.htm

[On December 8, 2003, the UN General Assembly asked the Court for an advisory opinion on the following question:

> What are the legal consequences arising from the construction of the wall being built by Israel, the occupying Power, in the Occupied Palestinian Territory, including in and around East Jerusalem, as described in the report of the Secretary-General, considering the rules and principles of

international law, including the Fourth Geneva Convention of 1949, and relevant Security Council and General Assembly resolutions? ...]

67. ... [T]he "wall" in question is a complex construction, so that that term cannot be understood in a limited physical sense. However, the other terms used, either by Israel ("fence") or by the Secretary-General ("barrier"), are no more accurate if understood in the physical sense. In this Opinion, the Court has therefore chosen to use the terminology employed by the General Assembly. ...

82. According to the description in the report and the Written Statement of the Secretary-General, the works planned or completed have resulted or will result in a complex consisting essentially of:

(1) a fence with electronic sensors;

(2) a ditch (up to 4 metres deep);

(3) a two-lane asphalt patrol road;

(4) a trace road (a strip of sand smoothed to detect footprints) running parallel to the fence;

(5) a stack of six coils of barbed wire marking the perimeter of the complex.

The complex has a width of 50 to 70 metres, increasing to as much as 100 metres in some places. "Depth barriers" may be added to these works.

The approximately 180 kilometres of the complex completed or under construction as of the time when the Secretary-General submitted his report included some 8.5 kilometres of concrete wall. These are generally found where Palestinian population centres are close to or abut Israel (such as near Qalqiliya and Tulkarm or in parts of Jerusalem).

83. According to the report of the Secretary-General, in its northernmost part, the wall as completed or under construction barely deviates from the Green Line. It nevertheless lies within occupied territories for most of its course. The works deviate more than 7.5 kilometres from the Green Line in certain places to encompass settlements, while encircling Palestinian population areas. A stretch of 1 to 2 kilometres west of Tulkarm appears to run on the Israeli side of the Green Line. Elsewhere, on the other hand, the planned route would deviate eastward by up to 22 kilometres. In the case of Jerusalem, the existing works and the planned route lie well beyond the Green Line and even in some cases beyond the eastern municipal boundary of Jerusalem as fixed by Israel.

84. On the basis of that route, approximately 975 square kilometres (or 16.6 per cent of the West Bank) would, according to the report of the Secretary-General, lie between the Green Line and the wall. This area is stated to be home to 237,000 Palestinians. If the full wall were completed as planned, another 160,000 Palestinians would live in almost completely encircled communities, described as enclaves in the report. As a result of the planned route, nearly 320,000 Israeli

settlers (of whom 178,000 in East Jerusalem) would be living in the area between the Green Line and the wall.

85. Lastly, it should be noted that the construction of the wall has been accompanied by the creation of a new administrative régime. Thus in October 2003 the Israeli Defence Forces issued Orders establishing the part of the West Bank lying between the Green Line and the wall as a "Closed Area". Residents of this area may no longer remain in it, nor may non-residents enter it, unless holding a permit or identity card issued by the Israeli authorities. According to the report of the Secretary-General, most residents have received permits for a limited period. Israeli citizens, Israeli permanent residents and those eligible to immigrate to Israel in accordance with the Law of Return may remain in, or move freely to, from and within the Closed Area without a permit. Access to and exit from the Closed Area can only be made through access gates, which are opened infrequently and for short periods.

86. The Court will now determine the rules and principles of international law which are relevant in assessing the legality of the measures taken by Israel. Such rules and principles can be found in the United Nations Charter and certain other treaties, in customary international law and in the relevant resolutions adopted pursuant to the Charter by the General Assembly and the Security Council. However, doubts have been expressed by Israel as to the applicability in the Occupied Palestinian Territory of certain rules of international humanitarian law and human rights instruments. The Court will now consider these various questions.

87. The Court first recalls that, pursuant to Article 2, paragraph 4, of the United Nations Charter:

> All Members shall refrain in their international relations from the threat or use of force against the territorial integrity or political independence of any State, or in any other manner inconsistent with the Purposes of the United Nations.

On 24 October 1970, the General Assembly adopted resolution 2625 (XXV), entitled "Declaration on Principles of International Law concerning Friendly Relations and Co-operation among States" (hereinafter "resolution 2625 (XXV)"), in which it emphasized that "No territorial acquisition resulting from the threat or use of force shall be recognized as legal." As the Court stated in its Judgment in the case concerning *Military and Paramilitary Activities in and against Nicaragua (Nicaragua* v. *United States of America)*, the principles as to the use of force incorporated in the Charter reflect customary international law (see *I.C.J. Reports 1986*, pp. 98-101, paras. 187-190); the same is true of its corollary entailing the illegality of territorial acquisition resulting from the threat or use of force.

88. The Court also notes that the principle of self-determination of peoples has been enshrined in the United Nations Charter and reaffirmed by the General Assembly in resolution 2625 (XXV) cited above, pursuant to which "Every State

has the duty to refrain from any forcible action which deprives peoples referred to [in that resolution] ... of their right to self-determination." Article 1 common to the International Covenant on Economic, Social and Cultural Rights and the International Covenant on Civil and Political Rights reaffirms the right of all peoples to self-determination, and lays upon the States parties the obligation to promote the realization of that right and to respect it, in conformity with the provisions of the United Nations Charter....

The Court has referred to this principle on a number of occasions in its jurisprudence (*ibid.*; see also *Western Sahara, Advisory Opinion, I.C.J. Reports 1975*, p. 68, para. 162). The Court indeed made it clear that the right of peoples to self-determination is today a right *erga omnes* (see *East Timor (Portugal* v. *Australia), Judgment, I.C.J. Reports 1995*, p. 102, para. 29).

89. As regards international humanitarian law, the Court would first note that Israel is not a party to the Fourth Hague Convention of 1907, to which the Hague Regulations are annexed. The Court observes that, in the words of the Convention, those Regulations were prepared "to revise the general laws and customs of war" existing at that time. Since then, however, the International Military Tribunal of Nuremberg has found that the "rules laid down in the Convention were recognised by all civilised nations, and were regarded as being declaratory of the laws and customs of war" (Judgment of the International Military Tribunal of Nuremberg, 30 September and 1 October 1946, p. 65). The Court itself reached the same conclusion when examining the rights and duties of belligerents in their conduct of military operations (*Legality of the Threat or Use of Nuclear Weapons, Advisory Opinion, I.C.J. Reports 1996 (I)*, p. 256, para. 75). The Court considers that the provisions of the Hague Regulations have become part of customary law, as is in fact recognized by all the participants in the proceedings before the Court.

The Court also observes that, pursuant to Article 154 of the Fourth Geneva Convention, that Convention is supplementary to Sections II and III of the Hague Regulations. Section III of those Regulations, which concerns "Military authority over the territory of the hostile State", is particularly pertinent in the present case.

90. Secondly, with regard to the Fourth Geneva Convention, differing views have been expressed by the participants in these proceedings. Israel, contrary to the great majority of the other participants, disputes the applicability *de jure* of the Convention to the Occupied Palestinian Territory. In particular, in paragraph 3 of Annex I to the report of the Secretary-General, entitled "Summary Legal Position of the Government of Israel", it is stated that Israel does not agree that the Fourth Geneva Convention "is applicable to the occupied Palestinian Territory", citing "the lack of recognition of the territory as sovereign prior to its annexation by Jordan and Egypt" and inferring that it is "not a territory of a High Contracting Party as required by the Convention".

91. The Court would recall that the Fourth Geneva Convention was ratified by Israel on 6 July 1951 and that Israel is a party to that Convention. Jordan has

also been a party thereto since 29 May 1951. Neither of the two States has made any reservation that would be pertinent to the present proceedings.

Furthermore, Palestine gave a unilateral undertaking, by declaration of 7 June 1982, to apply the Fourth Geneva Convention. Switzerland, as depositary State, considered that unilateral undertaking valid. It concluded, however, that it "[was] not as a depositary in a position to decide whether" "the request [dated 14 June 1989] from the Palestine Liberation Movement in the name of the 'State of Palestine' to accede" *inter alia* to the Fourth Geneva Convention "can be considered as an instrument of accession".

92. Moreover, for the purpose of determining the scope of application of the Fourth Geneva Convention, it should be recalled that under common Article 2 of the four Conventions of 12 August 1949:

> In addition to the provisions which shall be implemented in peacetime, the present Convention shall apply to all cases of declared war or of any other armed conflict which may arise between two or more of the High Contracting Parties, even if the state of war is not recognized by one of them.
>
> The Convention shall also apply to all cases of partial or total occupation of the territory of a High Contracting Party, even if the said occupation meets with no armed Resistance.
>
> Although one of the Powers in conflict may not be a party to the present Convention, the Powers who are parties thereto shall remain bound by it in their mutual relations. They shall furthermore be bound by the Convention in relation to the said Power, if the latter accepts and applies the provisions thereof.

93. After the occupation of the West Bank in 1967, the Israeli authorities issued an order No. 3 stating in its Article 35 that: "the Military Court ... must apply the provisions of the Geneva Convention dated 12 August 1949 relative to the Protection of Civilian Persons in Time of War with respect to judicial procedures. In case of conflict between this Order and the said Convention, the Convention shall prevail."

Subsequently, the Israeli authorities have indicated on a number of occasions that in fact they generally apply the humanitarian provisions of the Fourth Geneva Convention within the occupied territories. However, according to Israel's position as briefly recalled in paragraph 90 above, that Convention is not applicable *de jure* within those territories because, under Article 2, paragraph 2, it applies only in the case of occupation of territories falling under the sovereignty of a High Contracting Party involved in an armed conflict. Israel explains that Jordan was admittedly a party to the Fourth Geneva Convention in 1967, and that an armed conflict broke out at that time between Israel and Jordan, but it goes on to observe that the territories occupied by Israel subsequent to that conflict had not previously fallen under Jordanian sovereignty. It infers from this that that Convention is not applicable *de jure* in those territories. According however to the great majority of other participants in the proceedings, the Fourth Geneva Convention is applicable to those territories pursuant to Article 2, paragraph 1, whether or not Jordan had any rights in respect thereof prior to 1967.

94. The Court would recall that, according to customary international law as expressed in Article 31 of the Vienna Convention on the Law of Treaties of 23 May 1969, a treaty must be interpreted in good faith in accordance with the ordinary meaning to be given to its terms in their context and in the light of its object and purpose. Article 32 provides that: "Recourse may be had to supplementary means of interpretation, including the preparatory work of the treaty and the circumstances of its conclusion, in order to confirm the meaning resulting from the application of article 31, or to determine the meaning when the interpretation according to article 31 ... leaves the meaning ambiguous or obscure; or ... leads to a result which is manifestly obscure or unreasonable." ...

95. The Court notes that, according to the first paragraph of Article 2 of the Fourth Geneva Convention, that Convention is applicable when two conditions are fulfilled: that there exists an armed conflict (whether or not a state of war has been recognized); and that the conflict has arisen between two contracting parties. If those two conditions are satisfied, the Convention applies, in particular, in any territory occupied in the course of the conflict by one of the contracting parties.

The object of the second paragraph of Article 2 is not to restrict the scope of application of the Convention, as defined by the first paragraph, by excluding therefrom territories not falling under the sovereignty of one of the contracting parties. It is directed simply to making it clear that, even if occupation effected during the conflict met no armed resistance, the Convention is still applicable.

This interpretation reflects the intention of the drafters of the Fourth Geneva Convention to protect civilians who find themselves, in whatever way, in the hands of the occupying Power. Whilst the drafters of the Hague Regulations of 1907 were as much concerned with protecting the rights of a State whose territory is occupied, as with protecting the inhabitants of that territory, the drafters of the Fourth Geneva Convention sought to guarantee the protection of civilians in time of war, regardless of the status of the occupied territories, as is shown by Article 47 of the Convention. That interpretation is confirmed by the Convention's *travaux préparatoires*. ...

96. The Court would moreover note that the States parties to the Fourth Geneva Convention approved that interpretation at their Conference on 15 July 1999. They issued a statement in which they "reaffirmed the applicability of the Fourth Geneva Convention to the Occupied Palestinian Territory, including East Jerusalem". Subsequently, on 5 December 2001, the High Contracting Parties, referring in particular to Article 1 of the Fourth Geneva Convention of 1949, once again reaffirmed the "applicability of the Fourth Geneva Convention to the Occupied Palestinian Territory, including East Jerusalem". They further reminded the

Contracting Parties participating in the Conference, the parties to the conflict, and the State of Israel as occupying Power, of their respective obligations.

97. Moreover, the Court would observe that the ICRC, whose special position with respect to execution of the Fourth Geneva Convention must be "recognized and respected at all times" by the parties pursuant to Article 142 of the Convention, has also expressed its opinion on the interpretation to be given to the Convention. In a declaration of 5 December 2001, it recalled that "the ICRC has always affirmed the *de jure* applicability of the Fourth Geneva Convention to the territories occupied since 1967 by the State of Israel, including East Jerusalem".

98. The Court notes that the General Assembly has, in many of its resolutions, taken a position to the same effect. Thus on 10 December 2001 and 9 December 2003, in resolutions 56/60 and 58/97, it reaffirmed "that the Geneva Convention relative to the Protection of Civilian Persons in Time of War, of 12 August 1949, is applicable to the Occupied Palestinian Territory, including East Jerusalem, and other Arab territories occupied by Israel since 1967".

99. The Security Council, for its part, had already on 14 June 1967 taken the view in resolution 237 (1967) that "all the obligations of the Geneva Convention relative to the Treatment of Prisoners of War ... should be complied with by the parties involved in the conflict". Subsequently, on 15 September 1969, the Security Council, in resolution 271 (1969), called upon "Israel scrupulously to observe the provisions of the Geneva Conventions and international law governing military occupation". Ten years later, the Security Council examined "the policy and practices of Israel in establishing settlements in the Palestinian and other Arab territories occupied since 1967". In resolution 446 (1979) of 22 March 1979, the Security Council considered that those settlements had "no legal validity" and affirmed "*once more* that the Geneva Convention relative to the Protection of Civilian Persons in Time of War, of 12 August 1949, is applicable to the Arab territories occupied by Israel since 1967, including Jerusalem". It called "*once more upon* Israel, as the occupying Power, to abide scrupulously" by that Convention. On 20 December 1990, the Security Council, in resolution 681 (1990), urged "the Government of Israel to accept the *de jure* applicability of the Fourth Geneva Convention ... to all the territories occupied by Israel since 1967 and to abide scrupulously by the provisions of the Convention". It further called upon "the high contracting parties to the said Fourth Geneva Convention to ensure respect by Israel, the occupying Power, for its obligations under the Convention in accordance with article 1 thereof". Lastly, in resolutions 799 (1992) of 18 December 1992 and 904 (1994) of 18 March 1994, the Security Council reaffirmed its position concerning the applicability of the Fourth Geneva Convention in the occupied territories.

100. The Court would note finally that the Supreme Court of Israel, in a judgment dated 30 May 2004, also found that: "The military operations of the [Israeli Defence Forces] in Rafah, to the extent they affect civilians, are governed by Hague Convention IV Respecting the Laws and Customs of War on

Land 1907 ... and the Geneva Convention Relative to the Protection of Civilian Persons in Time of War 1949."

101. In view of the foregoing, the Court considers that the Fourth Geneva Convention is applicable in any occupied territory in the event of an armed conflict arising between two or more High Contracting Parties. Israel and Jordan were parties to that Convention when the 1967 armed conflict broke out. The Court accordingly finds that that Convention is applicable in the Palestinian territories which before the conflict lay to the east of the Green Line and which, during that conflict, were occupied by Israel, there being no need for any enquiry into the precise prior status of those territories.

102. The participants in the proceedings before the Court also disagree whether the international human rights conventions to which Israel is party apply within the Occupied Palestinian Territory. Annex I to the report of the Secretary-General states: "4. Israel denies that the International Covenant on Civil and Political Rights and the International Covenant on Economic, Social and Cultural Rights, both of which it has signed, are applicable to the occupied Palestinian territory. It asserts that humanitarian law is the protection granted in a conflict situation such as the one in the West Bank and Gaza Strip, whereas human rights treaties were intended for the protection of citizens from their own Government in times of peace." Of the other participants in the proceedings, those who addressed this issue contend that, on the contrary, both Covenants are applicable within the Occupied Palestinian Territory.

103. On 3 October 1991 Israel ratified both the International Covenant on Economic, Social and Cultural Rights of 19 December 1966 and the International Covenant on Civil and Political Rights of the same date, as well as the United Nations Convention on the Rights of the Child of 20 November 1989. It is a party to these three instruments.

104. In order to determine whether these texts are applicable in the Occupied Palestinian Territory, the Court will first address the issue of the relationship between international humanitarian law and human rights law and then that of the applicability of human rights instruments outside national territory.

105. In its Advisory Opinion of 8 July 1996 on the *Legality of the Threat or Use of Nuclear Weapons*, the Court had occasion to address the first of these issues in relation to the International Covenant on Civil and Political Rights. In those proceedings certain States had argued that "the Covenant was directed to the protection of human rights in peacetime, but that questions relating to unlawful loss of life in hostilities were governed by the law applicable in armed conflict" (*I.C.J. Reports 1996 (I)*, p. 239, para. 24).

The Court rejected this argument, stating that:

> [t]he protection of the International Covenant of Civil and Political Rights does not cease in times of war, except by operation of Article 4 of the Covenant whereby certain provisions may be derogated from in a time

> of national emergency. Respect for the right to life is not, however, such a provision. In principle, the right not arbitrarily to be deprived of one's life applies also in hostilities. The test of what is an arbitrary deprivation of life, however, then falls to be determined by the applicable *lex specialis*, namely, the law applicable in armed conflict which is designed to regulate the conduct of hostilities. (*Ibid.*, p. 240, para. 25.)

106. More generally, the Court considers that the protection offered by human rights conventions does not cease in case of armed conflict, save through the effect of provisions for derogation of the kind to be found in Article 4 of the International Covenant on Civil and Political Rights. As regards the relationship between international humanitarian law and human rights law, there are thus three possible situations: some rights may be exclusively matters of international humanitarian law; others may be exclusively matters of human rights law; yet others may be matters of both these branches of international law. In order to answer the question put to it, the Court will have to take into consideration both these branches of international law, namely human rights law and, as *lex specialis*, international humanitarian law.

107. It remains to be determined whether the two international Covenants and the Convention on the Rights of the Child are applicable only on the territories of the States parties thereto or whether they are also applicable outside those territories and, if so, in what circumstances.

108. The scope of application of the International Covenant on Civil and Political Rights is defined by Article 2, paragraph 1, thereof, which provides:

> Each State Party to the present Covenant undertakes to respect and to ensure to all individuals within its territory and subject to its jurisdiction the rights recognized in the present Covenant, without distinction of any kind, such as race, colour, sex, language, religion, political or other opinion, national or social origin, property, birth or other status.

This provision can be interpreted as covering only individuals who are both present within a State's territory and subject to that State's jurisdiction. It can also be construed as covering both individuals present within a State's territory and those outside that territory but subject to that State's jurisdiction. The Court will thus seek to determine the meaning to be given to this text.

109. The Court would observe that, while the jurisdiction of States is primarily territorial, it may sometimes be exercised outside the national territory. Considering the object and purpose of the International Covenant on Civil and Political Rights, it would seem natural that, even when such is the case, States parties to the Covenant should be bound to comply with its provisions.

The constant practice of the Human Rights Committee is consistent with this. Thus, the Committee has found the Covenant applicable where the State exercises its jurisdiction on foreign territory. It has ruled on the legality of acts by Uruguay in cases of arrests carried out by Uruguayan agents in Brazil or Argentina (case No. 52/79, *López Burgos* v. *Uruguay*; case No. 56/79, *Lilian Celiberti de Casariego* v. *Uruguay*). It decided to the same effect in the case of the confiscation of a passport by a Uruguayan consulate in Germany (case No. 106/ 81, *Montero* v. *Uruguay*).

The *travaux préparatoires* of the Covenant confirm the Committee's interpretation of Article 2 of that instrument. These show that, in adopting the wording chosen, the drafters of the Covenant did not intend to allow States to escape from their obligations when they exercise jurisdiction outside their national territory. They only intended to prevent persons residing abroad from asserting, vis-à-vis their State of origin, rights that do not fall within the competence of that State, but of that of the State of residence (see the discussion of the preliminary draft in the Commission on Human Rights, E/CN.4/SR.194, para. 46; and United Nations, *Official Records of the General Assembly, Tenth Session, Annexes*, A/2929, Part II, Chap. V, para. 4 (1955)).

110. The Court takes note in this connection of the position taken by Israel, in relation to the applicability of the Covenant, in its communications to the Human Rights Committee, and of the view of the Committee. In 1998, Israel stated that, when preparing its report to the Committee, it had had to face the question "whether individuals resident in the occupied territories were indeed subject to Israel's jurisdiction" for purposes of the application of the Covenant (CCPR/C/SR.1675, para. 21). Israel took the position that "the Covenant and similar instruments did not apply directly to the current situation in the occupied territories" (*ibid.*, para. 27). The Committee, in its concluding observations after examination of the report, expressed concern at Israel's attitude and pointed "to the long-standing presence of Israel in [the occupied] territories, Israel's ambiguous attitude towards their future status, as well as the exercise of effective jurisdiction by Israeli security forces therein" (CCPR/C/79/Add.93, para. 10). In 2003 in face of Israel's consistent position, to the effect that "the Covenant does not apply beyond its own territory, notably in the West Bank and Gaza ...", the Committee reached the following conclusion: "in the current circumstances, the provisions of the Covenant apply to the benefit of the population of the Occupied Territories, for all conduct by the State party's authorities or agents in those territories that affect the enjoyment of rights enshrined in the Covenant and fall within the ambit of State responsibility of Israel under the principles of public international law" (CCPR/CO/78/ISR, para. 11).

111. In conclusion, the Court considers that the International Covenant on Civil and Political Rights is applicable in respect of acts done by a State in the exercise of its jurisdiction outside its own territory.

112. The International Covenant on Economic, Social and Cultural Rights contains no provision on its scope of application. This may be explicable by the fact that this Covenant guarantees rights which are essentially territorial. However, it is not to be excluded that it applies both to territories over which a State party has sovereignty and to those over which that State exercises territorial

jurisdiction. Thus Article 14 makes provision for transitional measures in the case of any State which "at the time of becoming a Party, has not been able to secure in its metropolitan territory or other territories under its jurisdiction compulsory primary education, free of charge".

It is not without relevance to recall in this regard the position taken by Israel in its reports to the Committee on Economic, Social and Cultural Rights. In its initial report to the Committee of 4 December 1998, Israel provided "statistics indicating the enjoyment of the rights enshrined in the Covenant by Israeli settlers in the occupied Territories". The Committee noted that, according to Israel, "the Palestinian population within the same jurisdictional areas were excluded from both the report and the protection of the Covenant" (E/C.12/1/Add. 27, para. 8). The Committee expressed its concern in this regard, to which Israel replied in a further report of 19 October 2001 that it has "consistently maintained that the Covenant does not apply to areas that are not subject to its sovereign territory and jurisdiction" (a formula inspired by the language of the International Covenant on Civil and Political Rights). This position, continued Israel, is "based on the well-established distinction between human rights and humanitarian law under international law".

It added: "the Committee's mandate cannot relate to events in the West Bank and the Gaza Strip, inasmuch as they are part and parcel of the context of armed conflict as distinct from a relationship of human rights" (E/1990/6/Add. 32, para. 5). In view of these observations, the Committee reiterated its concern about Israel's position and reaffirmed "its view that the State party's obligations under the Covenant apply to all territories and populations under its effective control" (E/C.12/1/Add.90, paras. 15 and 31).

For the reasons explained in paragraph 106 above, the Court cannot accept Israel's view. It would also observe that the territories occupied by Israel have for over 37 years been subject to its territorial jurisdiction as the occupying Power. In the exercise of the powers available to it on this basis, Israel is bound by the provisions of the International Covenant on Economic, Social and Cultural Rights. Furthermore, it is under an obligation not to raise any obstacle to the exercise of such rights in those fields where competence has been transferred to Palestinian authorities.

113. As regards the Convention on the Rights of the Child of 20 November 1989, that instrument contains an Article 2 according to which "States Parties shall respect and ensure the rights set forth in the ... Convention to each child within their jurisdiction ...". That Convention is therefore applicable within the Occupied Palestinian Territory.

114. Having determined the rules and principles of international law relevant to reply to the question posed by the General Assembly, and having ruled in particular on the applicability within the Occupied Palestinian Territory of international humanitarian law and human rights law, the Court will now seek to as-

certain whether the construction of the wall has violated those rules and principles.

115. In this regard, Annex II to the report of the Secretary-General, entitled "Summary Legal Position of the Palestine Liberation Organization", states that "The construction of the Barrier is an attempt to annex the territory contrary to international law" and that "The de facto annexation of land interferes with the territorial sovereignty and consequently with the right of the Palestinians to self-determination." This view was echoed in certain of the written statements submitted to the Court and in the views expressed at the hearings. *Inter alia*, it was contended that: "The wall severs the territorial sphere over which the Palestinian people are entitled to exercise their right of self-determination and constitutes a violation of the legal principle prohibiting the acquisition of territory by the use of force." In this connection, it was in particular emphasized that "The route of the wall is designed to change the demographic composition of the Occupied Palestinian Territory, including East Jerusalem, by reinforcing the Israeli settlements" illegally established on the Occupied Palestinian Territory. It was further contended that the wall aimed at "reducing and parcelling out the territorial sphere over which the Palestinian people are entitled to exercise their right of self-determination".

116. For its part, Israel has argued that the wall's sole purpose is to enable it effectively to combat terrorist attacks launched from the West Bank. Furthermore, Israel has repeatedly stated that the Barrier is a temporary measure (see report of the Secretary-General, para. 29). It did so *inter alia* through its Permanent Representative to the United Nations at the Security Council meeting of 14 October 2003, emphasizing that "[the fence] does not annex territories to the State of Israel", and that Israel is "ready and able, at tremendous cost, to adjust or dismantle a fence if so required as part of a political settlement" (S/PV.4841, p. 10). Israel's Permanent Representative restated this view before the General Assembly on 20 October and 8 December 2003. On this latter occasion, he added: "As soon as the terror ends, the fence will no longer be necessary. The fence is not a border and has no political significance. It does not change the legal status of the territory in any way." (A/ES-10/PV.23, p. 6.)

117. The Court would recall that both the General Assembly and the Security Council have referred, with regard to Palestine, to the customary rule of "the inadmissibility of the acquisition of territory by war" (see paragraphs 74 and 87 above). Thus in resolution 242 (1967) of 22 November 1967, the Security Council, after recalling this rule, affirmed that:

> the fulfilment of Charter principles requires the establishment of a just and lasting peace in the Middle East which should include the application of both the following principles:
>
> (i) Withdrawal of Israel armed forces from territories occupied in the recent conflict;

(ii) Termination of all claims or states of belligerency and respect for and acknowledgement of the sovereignty, territorial integrity and political independence of every State in the area and their right to live in peace within secure and recognized boundaries free from threats or acts of force.

It is on this same basis that the Council has several times condemned the measures taken by Israel to change the status of Jerusalem (see paragraph 75 above).

118. As regards the principle of the right of peoples to self-determination, the Court observes that the existence of a "Palestinian people" is no longer in issue. Such existence has moreover been recognized by Israel in the exchange of letters of 9 September 1993 between Mr. Yasser Arafat, President of the Palestine Liberation Organization (PLO) and Mr. Yitzhak Rabin, Israeli Prime Minister. In that correspondence, the President of the PLO recognized "the right of the State of Israel to exist in peace and security" and made various other commitments. In reply, the Israeli Prime Minister informed him that, in the light of those commitments, "the Government of Israel has decided to recognize the PLO as the representative of the Palestinian people". The Israeli-Palestinian Interim Agreement on the West Bank and the Gaza Strip of 28 September 1995 also refers a number of times to the Palestinian people and its "legitimate rights" (Preamble, paras. 4, 7, 8; Article II, para. 2; Article III, paras. 1 and 3; Article XXII, para. 2). The Court considers that those rights include the right to self-determination, as the General Assembly has moreover recognized on a number of occasions (see, for example, resolution 58/163 of 22 December 2003).

119. The Court notes that the route of the wall as fixed by the Israeli Government includes within the "Closed Area" (see paragraph 85 above) some 80 per cent of the settlers living in the Occupied Palestinian Territory. Moreover, it is apparent from an examination of the map mentioned in paragraph 80 above that the wall's sinuous route has been traced in such a way as to include within that area the great majority of the Israeli settlements in the occupied Palestinian Territory (including East Jerusalem).

120. As regards these settlements, the Court notes that Article 49, paragraph 6, of the Fourth Geneva Convention provides: "The Occupying Power shall not deport or transfer parts of its own civilian population into the territory it occupies." That provision prohibits not only deportations or forced transfers of population such as those carried out during the Second World War, but also any measures taken by an occupying Power in order to organize or encourage transfers of parts of its own population into the occupied territory.

In this respect, the information provided to the Court shows that, since 1977, Israel has conducted a policy and developed practices involving the establishment of settlements in the Occupied Palestinian Territory, contrary to the terms of Article 49, paragraph 6, just cited.

The Security Council has thus taken the view that such policy and practices "have no legal validity". It has also called upon "Israel, as the occupying Power, to abide scrupulously" by the Fourth Geneva Convention and: "to rescind its previous measures and to desist from taking any action which would result in changing the legal status and geographical nature and materially affecting the demographic composition of the Arab territories occupied since 1967, including Jerusalem and, in particular, not to transfer parts of its own civilian population into the occupied Arab territories" (resolution 446 (1979) of 22 March 1979).

The Council reaffirmed its position in resolutions 452 (1979) of 20 July 1979 and 465 (1980) of 1 March 1980. Indeed, in the latter case it described "Israel's policy and practices of settling parts of its population and new immigrants in [the occupied] territories" as a "flagrant violation" of the Fourth Geneva Convention.

The Court concludes that the Israeli settlements in the Occupied Palestinian Territory (including East Jerusalem) have been established in breach of international law.

121. Whilst the Court notes the assurance given by Israel that the construction of the wall does not amount to annexation and that the wall is of a temporary nature (see paragraph 116 above), it nevertheless cannot remain indifferent to certain fears expressed to it that the route of the wall will prejudge the future frontier between Israel and Palestine, and the fear that Israel may integrate the settlements and their means of access. The Court considers that the construction of the wall and its associated régime create a "fait accompli" on the ground that could well become permanent, in which case, and notwithstanding the formal characterization of the wall by Israel, it would be tantamount to *de facto* annexation.

122. The Court recalls moreover that, according to the report of the Secretary-General, the planned route would incorporate in the area between the Green Line and the wall more than 16 per cent of the territory of the West Bank. Around 80 per cent of the settlers living in the Occupied Palestinian Territory, that is 320,000 individuals, would reside in that area, as well as 237,000 Palestinians. Moreover, as a result of the construction of the wall, around 160,000 other Palestinians would reside in almost completely encircled communities (see paragraphs 84, 85 and 119 above).

In other terms, the route chosen for the wall gives expression *in loco* to the illegal measures taken by Israel with regard to Jerusalem and the settlements, as deplored by the Security Council (see paragraphs 75 and 120 above). There is also a risk of further alterations to the demographic composition of the Occupied Palestinian Territory resulting from the construction of the wall inasmuch as it is contributing, as will be further explained in paragraph 133 below, to the departure of Palestinian populations from certain areas. That construction, along with measures taken previously, thus severely impedes the exercise by the Palestinian people of its right to self-determination, and is therefore a breach of Israel's obligation to respect that right.

123. The construction of the wall also raises a number of issues in relation to the relevant provisions of international humanitarian law and of human rights instruments.

124. With regard to the Hague Regulations of 1907, the Court would recall that these deal, in Section II, with hostilities and in particular with "means of injuring the enemy, sieges, and bombardments". Section III deals with military authority in occupied territories. Only Section III is currently applicable in the West Bank and Article 23 *(g)* of the Regulations, in Section II, is thus not pertinent.

Section III of the Hague Regulations includes Articles 43, 46 and 52, which are applicable in the Occupied Palestinian Territory. Article 43 imposes a duty on the occupant to "take all measures within his power to restore, and, as far as possible, to insure public order and life, respecting the laws in force in the country". Article 46 adds that private property must be "respected" and that it cannot "be confiscated". Lastly, Article 52 authorizes, within certain limits, requisitions in kind and services for the needs of the army of occupation.

125. A distinction is also made in the Fourth Geneva Convention between provisions applying during military operations leading to occupation and those that remain applicable throughout the entire period of occupation. ... Since the military operations leading to the occupation of the West Bank in 1967 ended a long time ago, only those Articles of the Fourth Geneva Convention referred to in Article 6, paragraph 3, remain applicable in that occupied territory.

126. These provisions include Articles 47, 49, 52, 53 and 59 of the Fourth Geneva Convention. [Court quotes these provisions.] ...

127. The International Covenant on Civil and Political Rights also contains several relevant provisions. Before further examining these, the Court will observe that Article 4 of the Covenant allows for derogation to be made, under various conditions, to certain provisions of that instrument.

Israel made use of its right of derogation under this Article by addressing the following communication to the Secretary-General of the United Nations on 3 October 1991:

> Since its establishment, the State of Israel has been the victim of continuous threats and attacks on its very existence as well as on the life and property of its citizens.
>
> These have taken the form of threats of war, of actual armed attacks, and campaigns of terrorism resulting in the murder of and injury to human beings.
>
> In view of the above, the State of Emergency which was proclaimed in May 1948 has remained in force ever since. This situation constitutes a public emergency within the meaning of article 4 (1) of the Covenant.

> The Government of Israel has therefore found it necessary, in accordance with the said article 4, to take measures to the extent strictly required by the exigencies of the situation, for the defence of the State and for the protection of life and property, including the exercise of powers of arrest and detention.
>
> In so far as any of these measures are inconsistent with article 9 of the Covenant, Israel thereby derogates from its obligations under that provision.

The Court notes that the derogation so notified concerns only Article 9 of the International Covenant on Civil and Political Rights, which deals with the right to liberty and security of person and lays down the rules applicable in cases of arrest or detention. The other Articles of the Covenant therefore remain applicable not only on Israeli territory, but also on the Occupied Palestinian Territory.

128. Among these mention must be made of Article 17, paragraph 1 of which reads as follows: "No one shall be subjected to arbitrary or unlawful interference with his privacy, family, home or correspondence, nor to unlawful attacks on his honour and reputation." Mention must also be made of Article 12, paragraph 1, which provides: "Everyone lawfully within the territory of a State shall, within that territory, have the right to liberty of movement and freedom to choose his residence."

129. In addition to the general guarantees of freedom of movement under Article 12 of the International Covenant on Civil and Political Rights, account must also be taken of specific guarantees of access to the Christian, Jewish and Islamic Holy Places. The status of the Christian Holy Places in the Ottoman Empire dates far back in time, the latest provisions relating thereto having been incorporated into Article 62 of the Treaty of Berlin of 13 July 1878. The Mandate for Palestine given to the British Government on 24 July 1922 included an Article 13, under which: "All responsibility in connection with the Holy Places and religious buildings or sites in Palestine, including that of preserving existing rights and of securing free access to the Holy Places, religious buildings and sites and the free exercise of worship, while ensuring the requirements of public order and decorum, is assumed by the Mandatory ..." Article 13 further stated: "nothing in this mandate shall be construed as conferring . . . authority to interfere with the fabric or the management of purely Moslem sacred shrines, the immunities of which are guaranteed".

In the aftermath of the Second World War, the General Assembly, in adopting resolution 181 (II) on the future government of Palestine, devoted an entire chapter of the Plan of Partition to the Holy Places, religious buildings and sites. Article 2 of this Chapter provided, in so far as the Holy Places were concerned: "the liberty of access, visit and transit shall be guaranteed, in conformity with existing rights, to all residents and citizens [of the Arab State, of the Jewish State] and of the City of Jerusalem, as well as to aliens, without distinction as to nationality, subject to requirements of national security, public order and decorum". Subsequently, in the aftermath of the armed conflict of 1948, the 1949 General Armistice Agreement between Jordan and Israel provided in Article VIII for the establishment of a special committee for "the formulation of agreed plans and arrangements for such matters as either Party may submit to it" for the purpose of enlarging the scope of the Agreement and of effecting improvement in its application. Such matters, on which an agreement of principle had already been concluded, included "free access to the Holy Places". This commitment concerned mainly the Holy Places located to the east of the Green Line. However, some Holy Places were located west of that Line. This was the case of the Room of the Last Supper and the Tomb of David, on Mount Zion. In signing the General Armistice Agreement, Israel thus undertook, as did Jordan, to guarantee freedom of access to the Holy Places. The Court considers that this undertaking by Israel has remained valid for the Holy Places which came under its control in 1967. This undertaking has further been confirmed by Article 9, paragraph 1, of the 1994 Peace Treaty between Israel and Jordan, by virtue of which, in more general terms, "Each party will provide freedom of access to places of religious and historical significance."

130. As regards the International Covenant on Economic, Social and Cultural Rights, that instrument includes a number of relevant provisions, namely: the right to work (Articles 6 and 7); protection and assistance accorded to the family and to children and young persons (Article 10); the right to an adequate standard of living, including adequate food, clothing and housing, and the right "to be free from hunger" (Art. 11); the right to health (Art. 12); the right to education (Arts. 13 and 14).

131. Lastly, the United Nations Convention on the Rights of the Child of 20 November 1989 includes similar provisions in Articles 16, 24, 27 and 28.

132. From the information submitted to the Court, particularly the report of the Secretary-General, it appears that the construction of the wall has led to the destruction or requisition of properties under conditions which contravene the requirements of Articles 46 and 52 of the Hague Regulations of 1907 and of Article 53 of the Fourth Geneva Convention.

133. That construction, the establishment of a closed area between the Green Line and the wall itself and the creation of enclaves have moreover imposed substantial restrictions on the freedom of movement of the inhabitants of the Occupied Palestinian Territory (with the exception of Israeli citizens and those assimilated thereto). Such restrictions are most marked in urban areas, such as the Qalqiliya enclave or the City of Jerusalem and its suburbs. They are aggravated by the fact that the access gates are few in number in certain sectors and opening hours appear to be restricted and unpredictably applied. ... There have also been serious repercussions for agricultural production, as is attested by a number of sources. ... In a recent survey conducted by the World Food Programme, it is stated that the situation has aggravated food insecurity in the region, which reportedly numbers 25,000 new beneficiaries of food aid. ... It has

further led to increasing difficulties for the population concerned regarding access to health services, educational establishments and primary sources of water. … At Qalqiliya, according to reports furnished to the United Nations, some 600 shops or businesses have shut down, and 6,000 to 8,000 people have already left the region. … In addition, … in the view of the Court, since a significant number of Palestinians have already been compelled by the construction of the wall and its associated régime to depart from certain areas, a process that will continue as more of the wall is built, that construction, coupled with the establishment of the Israeli settlements mentioned in paragraph 120 above, is tending to alter the demographic composition of the Occupied Palestinian Territory.

134. To sum up, the Court is of the opinion that the construction of the wall and its associated régime impede the liberty of movement of the inhabitants of the Occupied Palestinian Territory (with the exception of Israeli citizens and those assimilated thereto) as guaranteed under Article 12, paragraph 1, of the International Covenant on Civil and Political Rights. They also impede the exercise by the persons concerned of the right to work, to health, to education and to an adequate standard of living as proclaimed in the International Covenant on Economic, Social and Cultural Rights and in the United Nations Convention on the Rights of the Child. Lastly, the construction of the wall and its associated régime, by contributing to the demographic changes referred to in paragraphs 122 and 133 above, contravene Article 49, paragraph 6, of the Fourth Geneva Convention and the Security Council resolutions cited in paragraph 120 above.

135. The Court would observe, however, that the applicable international humanitarian law contains provisions enabling account to be taken of military exigencies in certain circumstances.

Neither Article 46 of the Hague Regulations of 1907 nor Article 47 of the Fourth Geneva Convention contain any qualifying provision of this type. With regard to forcible transfers of population and deportations, which are prohibited under Article 49, paragraph 1, of the Convention, paragraph 2 of that Article provides for an exception in those cases in which "the security of the population or imperative military reasons so demand". This exception however does not apply to paragraph 6 of that Article, which prohibits the occupying Power from deporting or transferring parts of its own civilian population into the territories it occupies. As to Article 53 concerning the destruction of personal property, it provides for an exception "where such destruction is rendered absolutely necessary by military operations".

The Court considers that the military exigencies contemplated by these texts may be invoked in occupied territories even after the general close of the military operations that led to their occupation. However, on the material before it, the Court is not convinced that the destructions carried out contrary to the prohibition in Article 53 of the Fourth Geneva Convention were rendered absolutely necessary by military operations.

136. The Court would further observe that some human rights conventions, and in particular the International Covenant on Civil and Political Rights, contain provisions which States parties may invoke in order to derogate, under various conditions, from certain of their conventional obligations. In this respect, the Court would however recall that the communication notified by Israel to the Secretary-General of the United Nations under Article 4 of the International Covenant on Civil and Political Rights concerns only Article 9 of the Covenant, relating to the right to freedom and security of person (see paragraph 127 above); Israel is accordingly bound to respect all the other provisions of that instrument.

The Court would note, moreover, that certain provisions of human rights conventions contain clauses qualifying the rights covered by those provisions. There is no clause of this kind in Article 17 of the International Covenant on Civil and Political Rights. On the other hand, Article 12, paragraph 3, of that instrument provides that restrictions on liberty of movement as guaranteed under that Article "shall not be subject to any restrictions except those which are provided by law, are necessary to protect national security, public order *(ordre public)*, public health or morals or the rights and freedoms of others, and are consistent with the other rights recognized in the present Covenant". As for the International Covenant on Economic, Social and Cultural Rights, Article 4 thereof contains a general provision as follows:

> The States Parties to the present Covenant recognize that, in the enjoyment of those rights provided by the State in conformity with the present Covenant, the State may subject such rights only to such limitations as are determined by law only in so far as this may be compatible with the nature of these rights and solely for the purpose of promoting the general welfare in a democratic society.

The Court would observe that the restrictions provided for under Article 12, paragraph 3, of the International Covenant on Civil and Political Rights are, by the very terms of that provision, exceptions to the right of freedom of movement contained in paragraph 1. In addition, it is not sufficient that such restrictions be directed to the ends authorized; they must also be necessary for the attainment of those ends. As the Human Rights Committee put it, they "must conform to the principle of proportionality" and "must be the least intrusive instrument amongst those which might achieve the desired result" (CCPR/C/21/Rev.1/Add.9, General Comment No. 27, para. 14).

On the basis of the information available to it, the Court finds that these conditions are not met in the present instance.

The Court would further observe that the restrictions on the enjoyment by the Palestinians living in the territory occupied by Israel of their economic, social and cultural rights, resulting from Israel's construction of the wall, fail to meet a condition laid down by Article 4 of the International Covenant on Economic, Social and Cultural Rights, that is to say that their implementation must be "solely for the purpose of promoting the general welfare in a democratic society".

137. To sum up, the Court, from the material available to it, is not convinced that the specific course Israel has chosen for the wall was necessary to attain its security objectives. The wall, along the route chosen, and its associated régime gravely infringe a number of rights of Palestinians residing in the territory occupied by Israel, and the infringements resulting from that route cannot be justified by military exigencies or by the requirements of national security or public order. The construction of such a wall accordingly constitutes breaches by Israel of various of its obligations under the applicable international humanitarian law and human rights instruments.

138. The Court has thus concluded that the construction of the wall constitutes action not in conformity with various international legal obligations incumbent upon Israel. However, Annex I to the report of the Secretary-General states that, according to Israel: "the construction of the Barrier is consistent with Article 51 of the Charter of the United Nations, its inherent right to self-defence and Security Council resolutions 1368 (2001) and 1373 (2001)". More specifically, Israel's Permanent Representative to the United Nations asserted in the General Assembly on 20 October 2003 that "the fence is a measure wholly consistent with the right of States to self-defence enshrined in Article 51 of the Charter"; the Security Council resolutions referred to, he continued, "have clearly recognized the right of States to use force in self-defence against terrorist attacks", and therefore surely recognize the right to use non-forcible measures to that end (A/ES-10/PV.21, p. 6).

139. Under the terms of Article 51 of the Charter of the United Nations: "Nothing in the present Charter shall impair the inherent right of individual or collective self-defence if an armed attack occurs against a Member of the United Nations, until the Security Council has taken measures necessary to maintain international peace and security." Article 51 of the Charter thus recognizes the existence of an inherent right of self-defence in the case of armed attack by one State against another State. However, Israel does not claim that the attacks against it are imputable to a foreign State.

The Court also notes that Israel exercises control in the Occupied Palestinian Territory and that, as Israel itself states, the threat which it regards as justifying the construction of the wall originates within, and not outside, that territory. The situation is thus different from that contemplated by Security Council resolutions 1368 (2001) and 1373 (2001), and therefore Israel could not in any event invoke those resolutions in support of its claim to be exercising a right of self-defence.

Consequently, the Court concludes that Article 51 of the Charter has no relevance in this case.

140. The Court has, however, considered whether Israel could rely on a state of necessity which would preclude the wrongfulness of the construction of the wall. In this regard the Court is bound to note that some of the conventions at issue in the present instance include qualifying clauses of the rights guaranteed or provisions for derogation (see paragraphs 135 and 136 above).

Since those treaties already address considerations of this kind within their own provisions, it might be asked whether a state of necessity as recognized in customary international law could be invoked with regard to those treaties as a ground for precluding the wrongfulness of the measures or decisions being challenged. However, the Court will not need to consider that question. As the Court observed in the case concerning the *Gabcíkovo-Nagymaros Project (Hungary/Slovakia)*, "the state of necessity is a ground recognized by customary international law" that "can only be accepted on an exceptional basis"; it "can only be invoked under certain strictly defined conditions which must be cumulatively satisfied; and the State concerned is not the sole judge of whether those conditions have been met" (*I.C.J. Reports 1997*, p. 40, para. 51). One of those conditions was stated by the Court in terms used by the International Law Commission, in a text which in its present form requires that the act being challenged be "the only way for the State to safeguard an essential interest against a grave and imminent peril" (Article 25 of the International Law Commission's Articles on Responsibility of States for Internationally Wrongful Acts; see also former Article 33 of the Draft Articles on the International Responsibility of States, with slightly different wording in the English text). In the light of the material before it, the Court is not convinced that the construction of the wall along the route chosen was the only means to safeguard the interests of Israel against the peril which it has invoked as justification for that construction.

141. The fact remains that Israel has to face numerous indiscriminate and deadly acts of violence against its civilian population. It has the right, and indeed the duty, to respond in order to protect the life of its citizens. The measures taken are bound nonetheless to remain in conformity with applicable international law.

142. In conclusion, the Court considers that Israel cannot rely on a right of self-defence or on a state of necessity in order to preclude the wrongfulness of the construction of the wall resulting from the considerations mentioned in paragraphs 122 and 137 above. The Court accordingly finds that the construction of the wall, and its associated régime, are contrary to international law. …

147. Since the Court has concluded that the construction of the wall in the Occupied Palestinian Territory, including in and around East Jerusalem, and its associated régime, are contrary to various of Israel's international obligations, it follows that the responsibility of that State is engaged under international law.

148. The Court will now examine the legal consequences resulting from the violations of international law by Israel by distinguishing between, on the one hand, those arising for Israel and, on the other, those arising for other States and, where appropriate, for the United Nations. The Court will begin by examining the legal consequences of those violations for Israel.

149. The Court notes that Israel is first obliged to comply with the international obligations it has breached by the construction of the wall in the Occupied Palestinian Territory (see paragraphs 114-137 above). Consequently, Israel is bound to comply with its obligation to respect the right of the Palestinian people to

self-determination and its obligations under international humanitarian law and international human rights law. Furthermore, it must ensure freedom of access to the Holy Places that came under its control following the 1967 War (see paragraph 129 above).

150. The Court observes that Israel also has an obligation to put an end to the violation of its international obligations flowing from the construction of the wall in the Occupied Palestinian Territory. The obligation of a State responsible for an internationally wrongful act to put an end to that act is well established in general international law. ...

151. Israel accordingly has the obligation to cease forthwith the works of construction of the wall being built by it in the Occupied Palestinian Territory, including in and around East Jerusalem.

Moreover, in view of the Court's finding (see paragraph 143...that Israel's violations of its international obligations stem from the construction of the wall and from its associated régime, cessation of those violations entails the dismantling forthwith of those parts of that structure situated within the Occupied Palestinian Territory, including in and around East Jerusalem. All legislative and regulatory acts adopted with a view to its construction, and to the establishment of its associated régime, must forthwith be repealed or rendered ineffective, except in so far as such acts, by providing for compensation or other forms of reparation for the Palestinian population, may continue to be relevant for compliance by Israel with the obligations referred to in paragraph 153 below.

152. Moreover, given that the construction of the wall in the Occupied Palestinian Territory has, *inter alia*, entailed the requisition and destruction of homes, businesses and agricultural holdings, the Court finds further that Israel has the obligation to make reparation for the damage caused to all the natural or legal persons concerned. The Court would recall that the essential forms of reparation in customary law were laid down by the Permanent Court of International Justice in the following terms: [Court quotes *Factory at Chorzów, Merits, Judgment No. 13, 1928, P.C.I.J., Series A, No. 17*, p. 47.] ...

153. Israel is accordingly under an obligation to return the land, orchards, olive groves and other immovable property seized from any natural or legal person for purposes of construction of the wall in the Occupied Palestinian Territory. In the event that such restitution should prove to be materially impossible, Israel has an obligation to compensate the persons in question for the damage suffered. The Court considers that Israel also has an obligation to compensate, in accordance with the applicable rules of international law, all natural or legal persons having suffered any form of material damage as a result of the wall's construction.

154. The Court will now consider the legal consequences of the internationally wrongful acts flowing from Israel's construction of the wall as regards other States.

155. The Court would observe that the obligations violated by Israel include certain obligations *erga omnes*. As the Court indicated in the *Barcelona Traction* case, such obligations are by their very nature "the concern of all States" and, "In view of the importance of the rights involved, all States can be held to have a legal interest in their protection." (*Barcelona Traction, Light and Power Company, Limited, Second Phase, Judgment, I.C.J. Reports 1970*, p. 32, para. 33.)

The obligations *erga omnes* violated by Israel are the obligation to respect the right of the Palestinian people to self-determination, and certain of its obligations under international humanitarian law.

156. As regards the first of these, the Court has already observed (paragraph 88 above) that in the *East Timor* case, it described as "irreproachable" the assertion that "the right of peoples to self-determination, as it evolved from the Charter and from United Nations practice, has an *erga omnes* character" (*I.C.J. Reports 1995*, p. 102, para. 29). The Court would also recall that under the terms of General Assembly resolution 2625 (XXV), already mentioned above (see paragraph 88),

> Every State has the duty to promote, through joint and separate action, realization of the principle of equal rights and self-determination of peoples, in accordance with the provisions of the Charter, and to render assistance to the United Nations in carrying out the responsibilities entrusted to it by the Charter regarding the implementation of the principle …

157. With regard to international humanitarian law, the Court recalls that in its Advisory Opinion on the *Legality of the Threat or Use of Nuclear Weapons*, it stated that "a great many rules of humanitarian law applicable in armed conflict are so fundamental to the respect of the human person and 'elementary considerations of humanity' ...", that they are "to be observed by all States whether or not they have ratified the conventions that contain them, because they constitute intransgressible principles of international customary law" (*I.C.J. Reports 1996 (I)*, p. 257, para. 79). In the Court's view, these rules incorporate obligations which are essentially of an *erga omnes* character.

158. The Court would also emphasize that Article 1 of the Fourth Geneva Convention, a provision common to the four Geneva Conventions, provides that "The High Contracting Parties undertake to respect and to ensure respect for the present Convention in all circumstances." It follows from that provision that every State party to that Convention, whether or not it is a party to a specific conflict, is under an obligation to ensure that the requirements of the instruments in question are complied with.

159. Given the character and the importance of the rights and obligations involved, the Court is of the view that all States are under an obligation not to recognize the illegal situation resulting from the construction of the wall in the Occupied Palestinian Territory, including in and around East Jerusalem. They are

also under an obligation not to render aid or assistance in maintaining the situation created by such construction. It is also for all States, while respecting the United Nations Charter and international law, to see to it that any impediment, resulting from the construction of the wall, to the exercise by the Palestinian people of its right to self-determination is brought to an end. In addition, all the States parties to the Geneva Convention relative to the Protection of Civilian Persons in Time of War of 12 August 1949 are under an obligation, while respecting the United Nations Charter and international law, to ensure compliance by Israel with international humanitarian law as embodied in that Convention.

160. Finally, the Court is of the view that the United Nations, and especially the General Assembly and the Security Council, should consider what further action is required to bring to an end the illegal situation resulting from the construction of the wall and the associated régime, taking due account of the present Advisory Opinion.

161. The Court, being concerned to lend its support to the purposes and principles laid down in the United Nations Charter, in particular the maintenance of international peace and security and the peaceful settlement of disputes, would emphasize the urgent necessity for the United Nations as a whole to redouble its efforts to bring the Israeli-Palestinian conflict, which continues to pose a threat to international peace and security, to a speedy conclusion, thereby establishing a just and lasting peace in the region.

162. The Court has reached the conclusion that the construction of the wall by Israel in the Occupied Palestinian Territory is contrary to international law and has stated the legal consequences that are to be drawn from that illegality. The Court considers itself bound to add that this construction must be placed in a more general context. Since 1947, the year when General Assembly resolution 181 (II) was adopted and the Mandate for Palestine was terminated, there has been a succession of armed conflicts, acts of indiscriminate violence and repressive measures on the former mandated territory. The Court would emphasize that both Israel and Palestine are under an obligation scrupulously to observe the rules of international humanitarian law, one of the paramount purposes of which is to protect civilian life. Illegal actions and unilateral decisions have been taken on all sides, whereas, in the Court's view, this tragic situation can be brought to an end only through implementation in good faith of all relevant Security Council resolutions, in particular resolutions 242 (1967) and 338 (1973). The "Roadmap" approved by Security Council resolution 1515 (2003) represents the most recent of efforts to initiate negotiations to this end. The Court considers that it has a duty to draw the attention of the General Assembly, to which the present Opinion is addressed, to the need for these efforts to be encouraged with a view to achieving as soon as possible, on the basis of international law, a negotiated solution to the outstanding problems and the establishment of a Palestinian State, existing side by side with Israel and its other neighbours, with peace and security for all in the region.

[The Court decided, by fourteen to one, that

The construction of the wall being built by Israel, the occupying Power, in the Occupied Palestinian Territory, including in and around East Jerusalem, and its associated régime, are contrary to international law; ...

Israel is under an obligation to terminate its breaches of international law; it is under an obligation to cease forthwith the works of construction of the wall being built in the Occupied Palestinian Territory, including in and around East Jerusalem, to dismantle forthwith the structure therein situated, and to repeal or render ineffective forthwith all legislative and regulatory acts relating thereto, in accordance with paragraph 151 of this Opinion; ...

Israel is under an obligation to make reparation for all damage caused by the construction of the wall in the Occupied Palestinian Territory, including in and around East Jerusalem; ...

The United Nations, and especially the General Assembly and the Security Council, should consider what further action is required to bring to an end the illegal situation resulting from the construction of the wall and the associated régime, taking due account of the present Advisory Opinion.

The Court decided by thirteen to two, that

All States are under an obligation not to recognize the illegal situation resulting from the construction of the wall and not to render aid or assistance in maintaining the situation created by such construction; all States parties to the Fourth Geneva Convention relative to the Protection of Civilian Persons in Time of War of 12 August 1949 have in addition the obligation, while respecting the United Nations Charter and international law, to ensure compliance by Israel with international humanitarian law as embodied in that Convention; ...]

7. HCJ 2056/04: Beit Sourik Village Council v. Israel

Israel Supreme Court, June 30, 2004

BARAK, C.J.: [In 2004, Israel proceeded with the construction of a security barrier (the "Fence") in the occupied West Bank, which it has controlled as a belligerent occupant since 1967. (A more detailed description of the barrier is set out in the International Court's Advisory Opinion, *Legal Consequences of the Construction of a Wall in the Occupied Palestinian Territory*, *supra* at 1109.)

Part of the Fence in the area near Jerusalem was to be built on land seized from Arab villagers. Moreover, the location of the Fence would separate the villagers from access to their land and water. The villagers petitioned the High Court of Justice to enjoin the construction of the Fence for violation, *inter alia*, of international law.]

33. The focus of this petition is the legality of the route chosen for the construction of the Separation Fence. This question stands on its own, and it requires a straightforward, real answer. It is not sufficient that the Fence be motivated by security considerations, as opposed to political considerations. The military commander is not at liberty to pursue, in the area he holds in belligerent occupation, every activity primarily motivated by security considerations. The discretion of the military commander is restricted by the normative system in which he acts, which is the source of his authority. Indeed, the military commander is not the sovereign in the occupied territory. *See* Oppenheim, *The Legal Relations Between an Occupying Power and the Inhabitants*, 33 Law Q. Rev., 363, 364 (1917); Y. Dinstein, The Law of War 210 (1983). He must act within the law that establishes his authority in a situation of belligerent occupation. What is the content of this law?

34. The law of belligerent occupation recognizes the authority of the military commander to maintain security in the area and to protect the security of his country and her citizens. However, it imposes conditions on the use of this authority. This authority must be properly balanced against the rights, needs, and interests of the local population. . .

> This Court has emphasized, in its case law since the Six Day War, that "together with the right to administer comes the obligation to provide for the well being of the population." . . .
>
> The Hague Convention authorizes the military commander to act in two central areas: one – ensuring the legitimate security interest of the holder of the territory, and the other – providing for the needs of the local population in the territory held in belligerent occupation .... The first need is military and the second is civilian-humanitarian. The first focuses upon the security of the military forces holding the area, and the second focuses upon the responsibility for ensuring the well being of the residents. In the latter area the military commander is responsible not only for the maintenance of the order and security of the inhabitants, but also for the protection of their rights, especially their constitutional human rights. The concern for human rights stands at the center of the humanitarian considerations which the military commander must take into account. *Hess*, at paragraph 8 (Procaccia, J.).

35. The approach of this Court is well anchored in the humanitarian law of public international law. This is set forth in Regulation 46 of the Hague Regulations and Article 46 of the Fourth Geneva Convention. Regulation 46 of the Hague Regulations provides:

> Family honour and rights, the lives of persons, and private property, as well as religious convictions and practice, must be respected. Private property cannot be confiscated.
>
> Article 27 of the Fourth Geneva Convention provides:

> Protected persons are entitled, in all circumstances, to respect for their persons, their honour, their family rights, their religious convictions and practices, and their manners and customs. They shall at all times be humanely treated, and shall be protected especially against all acts of violence or threats thereof .... However, the Parties to the conflict may take such measures of control and security in regard to protected persons as may be necessary as a result of the war.

These rules are founded upon a recognition of the value of man and the sanctity of his life.... Interpreting Article 27 of the Fourth Geneva Convention, Pictet writes:

> Article 27 ... occupies a key position among the articles of the Convention. It is the basis of the Convention, proclaiming as it does the principles on which the whole "Geneva Law" is founded. It proclaims the principle of respect for the human person and the inviolable character of the basic rights of individual men and women ... the right of respect for the person must be understood in its widest sense: it covers all the rights of the individual, that is, the rights and qualities which are inseparable from the human being by the very fact of his existence and his mental and physical powers, it includes, in particular, the right to physical, moral and intellectual integrity – one essential attribute of the human person.

The rules in Regulation 46 of the Hague Regulations and in Article 27 of the Fourth Geneva Convention cast a double obligation upon the military commander: he must refrain from actions that injure the local inhabitants. This is his "negative" obligation. He must take the legally required actions in order to ensure that the local inhabitants shall not be injured. This is his "positive" obligation..... In addition to these fundamental provisions, there are additional provisions that deal with specifics, such as the seizure of land. *See* Regulation 23(g) and 52 of the Hague Regulations; Article 53 of the Fourth Geneva Convention. These provisions create a single tapestry of norms that recognize both human rights and the needs of the local population as well security needs from the perspective of the military commander. Among these conflicting norms, a proper balance must be found. What is that balance?

Proportionality

36. The problem of balancing security and liberty is not specific to the discretion of a military commander of an area under belligerent occupation. It is a general problem in the law, both domestic and international. Its solution is universal. It is found deep in the general principles of law, which include reasonableness and good faith... One of these foundational principles, which balances the legitimate objective with the means for achieving it, is the principle of proportionality. According to this principle, the liberty of the individual can be limited (in this case, the liberty of the local inhabitants under belligerent occupation), on the

condition that the restriction is proportionate. This approach applies to all types of law. In the framework of the petition before us, its importance is twofold: first, it is a basic principle in international law in general and specifically in the law of belligerent occupation; second, it is a central standard in Israeli administrative law, which applies to the area under belligerent occupation. We shall now briefly discuss each of these.

37. Proportionality is recognized today as a general principle of international law. ...

The Meaning of Proportionality and its Elements

40. According to the principle of proportionality, the decision of an administrative body is legal only if the means used to realize its governmental objective is of proper proportion. The principle of proportionality focuses, therefore, on the relationship between the objective whose achievement is attempted, and the means used to achieve it. This principle is a general one. It requires application. As such, both in international law, which deals with different national systems – from both the common law family (such as Canada) and the continental family (such as Germany) – as well as in domestic Israeli law, three subtests grant specific content to the principle of proportionality. . . .

41. The first subtest is that the objective must be related to the means. The means that the administrative body uses must be constructed to achieve the precise objective that the administrative body is trying to achieve. The means used by the administrative body must rationally lead to the realization of the objective. This is the "appropriate means" or "rational means" test. According to the second subtest, the means used by the administrative body must injure the individual to the least extent possible. In the spectrum of means that can be used to achieve the objective, the least injurious means must be used. This is the "least injurious means" test. The third test requires that the damage caused to the individual by the means used by the administrative body in order to achieve its objectives must be of proper proportion to the gain brought about by that means. That is the "proportionate means" test (or proportionality "in the narrow sense.") The test of proportionality "in the narrow sense" is commonly applied with "absolute values," by directly comparing the advantage of the administrative act with the damage that results from it. However, it is also possible to apply the test of proportionality in the narrow sense in a "relative manner." According to this approach, the administrative act is tested vis-à-vis an alternate act, whose benefit will be somewhat smaller than that of the former one. The original administrative act is disproportionate in the narrow sense if a certain reduction in the advantage gained by the original act – by employing alternate means, for example – ensures a substantial reduction in the injury caused by the administrative act.

42. It is possible to say that the means used by an administrative authority are proportionate only if all three subtests are satisfied. Satisfaction of one or two of these subtests is insufficient. All three of them must be satisfied simultaneously. Not infrequently, there are a number of ways that the requirement of

proportionality can be satisfied. In these situations a "zone of proportionality" must be recognized (similar to a "zone of reasonableness.") Any means chosen by the administrative body that is within the zone of proportionality is proportionate. . . .

43. This principle of proportionality also applies to the exercise of authority by the military commander in an area under belligerent occupation. Thus, for example, in *Ajuri*, the question arose whether restricting the area in which one can live – in that case, the transfer of local inhabitants from the area of Judea and Samaria to the Gaza Strip – was proportionate. Regarding the proportionality test, as applied in that case, I wrote:

> Like the use of any other means, the means of restricting the area in which one can live must be also be used proportionately. The individual's offense must be proportionate to the means employed by the authorities ... an appropriate link is necessary between the objective of preventing danger from the person whose living area is restricted, and the danger if this means is not employed ... it is necessary that the injury caused by the means employed be minimal; it is also necessary that the means of restricting the living area be of proper proportion to the security benefit to the area. *Id.*, at 373.

44. The principle of proportionality applies to our examination of the legality of the Separation Fence. This approach is accepted by respondents. It is reflected in the government decision (of October 1, 2003) that "during the planning, every effort shall be made to minimize, to the extent possible, the disturbance to the daily lives of the Palestinians due to the construction of the obstacle." The argument that the damage caused by the Separation Fence route is proportionate was the central argument of respondents. Indeed, our point of departure is that the Separation Fence is intended to realize a security objective that the military commander is authorized to achieve. The key question regarding the route of the Fence is: is the route of the Separation Fence proportionate? The proportionality of the Separation Fence must be decided by the three following questions, which reflect the three subtests of proportionality. First, does the route pass the "appropriate means" test (or the "rational means" test)? The question is whether there is a rational connection between the route of the Fence and the goal of the construction of the Separation Fence. Second, does it pass the test of the "least injurious" means? The question is whether, among the various routes which would achieve the objective of the Separation Fence, is the chosen one the least injurious. Third, does it pass the test of proportionality in the narrow sense? The question is whether the Separation Fence route, as set out by the military commander, injures the local inhabitants to the extent that there is no proper proportion between this injury and the security benefit of the Fence. According to the "relative" examination of this test, the Separation Fence will be found disproportionate if an alternate route for the Fence is suggested that has a smaller security advantage than the route chosen by respondent, but which will cause significantly less damage than that original route.

46. The first question deals with the military character of the route. It examines whether the route chosen by the military commander for the Separation Fence achieves its stated objectives, and whether there is no route that achieves this objective better. It raises issues within the realm of military expertise. We, Justices of the Supreme Court, are not experts in military affairs. We will not examine whether the military commander's military opinion corresponds to ours – to the extent that we have an opinion regarding the military character of the route. So we act in all questions that are matters of professional expertise, and so we act in military affairs as well. All we can determine is whether a reasonable military commander would have set out the route as this military commander did.. ...

Therefore, in our examination of the contrasting military considerations in this case, we give special weight to the fact that the commander of the area is responsible for security. Having employed this approach, we are of the opinion – the details of which we shall explain below – that petitioners have not carried their burden, and have not convinced us that we should prefer the professional expert opinion of members of the Council for Peace and Security over the security stance of the commander of the area. We are dealing with two military approaches. Each of them has military advantages and disadvantages. In this state of affairs, we must place the expert opinion of the military commander at the foundation of our decision.

The Proportionality of the Route of the Separation Fence

48. The second question regards the proportionality of the route of the Separation Fence, as determined by the military commander. This question raises no problems in the field of military considerations. Rather, it relates to the severity of the injury caused to the local inhabitants by the route decided upon by the military commander. Within the context of this question, we are dealing not with military considerations, but rather with humanitarian considerations. The question is not the proportionality of different military considerations. The question is the proportionality between the military consideration and the humanitarian consideration. The question is not whether to prefer the military approach of the military commander to that of the experts of the Council for Peace and Security. The question is whether the route of the Separation Fence, according to the approach of the military commander, is proportionate. The standard for this question is not the subjective standard of the military commander. The question is not whether the military commander believed, in good faith, that the injury was proportionate. The standard is objective. The question is whether, by legal standards, the route of the Separation Fence passes the tests of proportionality. This is a legal question, the expertise for which is held by the Court. ...

The military commander is the expert on the military aspects of the Fence's route. We are the experts of the humanitarian aspects of the route. The military commander can determine the geographical placement of the Fence—across mountain or plane. This is his expertise. We review whether the military commander's route inflicts disproportionate injury upon the local inhabitants. This is our expertise.

From the General to the Specific

49. The key question before us is whether the route of the Separation Fence is proportionate. The question is: is the injury to local inhabitants by the Separation Fence proportionate, or is it is possible to satisfy the main security concerns while establishing a Fence route whose injury to the local inhabitants is lesser and, as such, proportionate? ...

58. The second subtest examines whether it is possible to attain the security objectives of the Separation Fence in a way that causes less injury to the local inhabitants. There is no doubt – and the issue is not even disputed – that the route suggested by the members of the Council for Peace and Security causes less injury to the local inhabitants than the injury caused by the route determined by the military commander. The question is whether the former route satisfies the security objective of the security Fence to the same extent as the route set out by the military commander. We cannot answer this question in the affirmative. The position of the military commander is that the route of the Separation Fence, as proposed by members of the Council for Peace and Security, grants less security than his proposed route. By our very determination that we shall not intervene in that position, we have also determined that there is no alternate route that fulfills, to a similar extent, the security needs while causing lesser injury to the local inhabitants. In this state of affairs, our conclusion is that the second subtest of proportionality, regarding the issue before us, is satisfied.

59. The third subtest examines whether the injury caused to the local inhabitants by the construction of the Separation Fence stands in proper proportion to the security benefit from the Security Fence in its chosen route. This is the proportionate means test (or proportionality "in the narrow sense"). Concerning this topic, Professor Y. Zamir wrote:

> The third element is proportionality itself. According to this element, it is insufficient that the administrative authority chose the proper and most moderate means for achieving the objective; it must also weigh the benefit reaped by the public against the damage that will be caused to the citizen by this means under the circumstances of the case at hand. It must ask itself if, under these circumstances, there is a proper proportion between the benefit to the public and the damage to the citizen. The proportion between the benefit and the damage – and it is also possible to ... say the proportion between means and objective – must be proportionate.

This subtest weighs the costs against the benefits. *See Stamka*, at 776. According to this subtest, a decision of an administrative authority must reach a reasonable balance between communal needs and the damage done to the individual. The objective of the examination is to determine whether the severity of the damage to the individual and the reasons brought to justify it stand in proper proportion to each other. This judgment is made against the background of the general normative structure of the legal system, which recognizes human rights and the necessity of ensuring the provision of the needs and welfare of the local inhabitants, and which preserves "family honour and rights" (Regulation 46 of the Hague Regulations). All these are protected in the framework of the humanitarian provisions of the Hague Regulations and the Geneva Convention. The question before us is: does the severity of the injury to local inhabitants, by the construction of the Separation Fence along the route determined by the military commander, stand in reasonable (proper) proportion to the security benefit from the construction of the Fence along that route?

60. Our answer is that there relationship between the injury to the local inhabitants and the security benefit from the construction of the Separation Fence along the route, as determined by the military commander, is not proportionate. The route disrupts the delicate balance between the obligation of the military commander to preserve security and his obligation to provide for the needs of the local inhabitants. This approach is based on the fact that the route which the military commander established for the Security Fence – which separates the local inhabitants from their agricultural lands – injures the local inhabitants in a severe and acute way, while violating their rights under humanitarian international law. Here are the facts: more than 13,000 farmers (falahin) are cut off from thousands of dunams of their land and from tens of thousands of trees which are their livelihood, and which are located on the other side of the Separation Fence. No attempt was made to seek out and provide them with substitute land, despite our oft repeated proposals on that matter. The separation is not hermetic: the military commander announced that two gates will be constructed, from each of the two villages, to its lands, with a system of licensing. This state of affairs injures the farmers severely, as access to their lands (early in the morning, in the afternoon, and in the evening), will be subject to restrictions inherent to a system of licensing. Such a system will result in long lines for the passage of the farmers themselves; it will make the passage of vehicles (which themselves require licensing and examination) difficult, and will distance the farmer from his lands (since only two daytime gates are planned for the entire length of this segment of the route). As a result, the life of the farmer will change completely in comparison to his previous life. The route of the Separation Fence severely violates their right of property and their freedom of movement. Their livelihood is severely impaired. The difficult reality of life from which they have suffered (due, for example, to high unemployment in that area) will only become more severe.

NOTES AND QUESTIONS

1. What are the essential differences between the decisions of the Israeli Supreme Court and the ICJ? In what aspects do they agree?

2. How do you assess the ICJ's evaluation of Israel's claim of self-defense against terrorism in light of recent legal developments in the war against terrorism? Should the ICJ have rendered its advisory opinion even though Israel did not submit its view of the facts and legal issues at stake?

3. The ICJ classified humanitarian law as *lex specialis* to general human rights law, which leaves human rights law applicable even in armed conflict if the law of armed conflict does not address the issue. Does this statement accord with the Court's treatment of this issue in *Legality of Nuclear Weapons* (see Part One, *supra*, at 76)?

4. Consider the ICJ's observation in paragraph 139 on the inherent right of self-defense under Article 51 of the Charter, that "Israel does not claim that the attacks against it are imputable to a foreign State." What implications does the sentence hold for United States self-defense actions against Al Qaeda?

D. INDIVIDUAL CRIMINAL LIABILITY IN WAR

Individual criminal liability has become a strong, if not the strongest, instrument of enforcement of the laws of war. Arising from the legacy of the International Military Tribunals in Nuremberg and Tokyo, the pertinent categories are crimes against peace, i.e. aggression, and war crimes *per se*, i.e. violations of the laws and customs of war (*jus in bello*).

1. The Crime Against Peace: Aggression

a. Judgment of The International Military Tribunal For the Trial of German Major War Criminals

Nuremberg, Sept. 30 & Oct. 1, 1946, Cmd. 6964;
41 AM. J. INT'L L. 172 (1947)

On the 8th August, 1945, the Government of the United Kingdom of Great Britain and Northern Ireland, the Government of the United States of America, the Provisional Government of the French Republic, and the Government of the Union of Soviet Socialist Republics entered into an Agreement establishing this Tribunal for the trial of War Criminals whose offences have no particular geographical location. ...

The Tribunal was invested with power to try and punish persons who had committed crimes against peace, war crimes and crimes against humanity as defined in the Charter.

In Berlin, on the 18th October, 1945, in accordance with Article 14 of the Charter, an Indictment was lodged against the defendants named ... who had been designated by the Committee of the Chief Prosecutors of the signatory Powers as major war criminals.

... The Trial which was conducted in four languages - English, Russian, French and German - began on the 20th November, 1945 ... The hearing of evidence and the speeches of Counsel concluded on 31st August, 1946. ...

Much of the evidence presented to the Tribunal on behalf of the Prosecution was documentary evidence, captured by the Allied armies in German army headquarters, Government buildings, and elsewhere. Some of the documents were found in salt mines, buried in the ground, hidden behind false walls and in other places thought to be secure from discovery. The case, therefore, against the defendants rests in a large measure on documents of their own making, the authenticity of which has not been challenged except in one or two cases.

THE CHARTER PROVISIONS

The individual defendants are indicted under Article 6 of the Charter, which is as follows:

Article 6. The Tribunal established by the Agreement referred to in Article 1 hereof for the trial and punishment of the major war criminals of the European Axis countries shall have the power to try and punish persons who, acting in the interests of the European Axis countries, whether as individuals or as members of organisations, committed any of the following crimes:

The following acts, or any of them, are crimes, coming within the jurisdiction of the Tribunal for which there shall be individual responsibility:

(a) Crimes against Peace: namely, planning, preparation, initiation or waging of a war of aggression, or a war in violation of international treaties, agreements or assurances, or participation in a common plan or conspiracy for the accomplishment of any of the foregoing:

(b) War Crimes: namely, violations of the laws or customs of war. Such violations shall include, but not be limited to, murder ill-treatment or deportation to slave labour or for any other purpose of civilian population of or in occupied territory, murder or ill-treatment of prisoners of war or persons on the seas, killing of hostages, plunder of public or private property, wanton destruction of cities, towns or villages, or devastation not justified by military necessity:

(c) Crimes against Humanity: namely, murder, extermination, enslavement, deportation, and other inhumane acts committed against any civilian population, before or during the war, or persecutions on political, racial or religious grounds in execution of or in connection with any crime within the jurisdiction of the Tribunal, whether or not in violation of the domestic law of the country where perpetrated.

Leaders, organisers, instigators and accomplices participating in the formulation or execution of a common plan or conspiracy to commit any of the foregoing crimes are responsible for all acts performed by any persons in execution of such plan.

These provisions are binding upon the Tribunal as the law to be applied to the case. The Tribunal will later discuss them in more detail; but before doing so, it is necessary to review the facts. For the purpose of showing the background of the aggressive war and war crimes charged in the Indictment, the Tribunal will begin by reviewing some of the events that followed the first world war, and in particular, by tracing the growth of the Nazi Party under Hitler's leadership to a position of supreme power from which it controlled the destiny of the whole German people, and paved the way for the alleged commission of all the crimes charged against the defendants. [The Tribunal discusses the Origins and Aims of the Nazi Party.]

THE COMMON PLAN OR CONSPIRACY AND AGGRESSIVE WAR

The Tribunal now turns to the consideration of the Crimes against peace charged in the Indictment. Count One of the Indictment charges the defendants with conspiring or having a common plan to commit crimes against peace.

Count Two of the Indictment charges the defendants with committing specific crimes against peace by planning, preparing, initiating, and waging wars of aggression against a number of other States. It will be convenient to consider the question of the existence of a common plan and the question of aggressive war together, and to deal later in this Judgment with the question of the individual responsibility of the defendants.

The charges in the Indictment that the defendants planned and waged aggressive wars are charges of the utmost gravity. War is essentially an evil thing. Its consequences are not confined to the belligerent states alone, but affect the whole world.

To initiate a war of aggression, therefore, is not only an international crime; it is the supreme international crime differing only from other war crimes in that it contains within itself the accumulated evil of the whole.

The first acts of aggression referred to in the Indictment are the seizure of Austria and Czechoslovakia and the first war of aggression charged in the Indictment is the war against Poland begun on the 1st September, 1939. …

The war against Poland did not come suddenly out of an otherwise clear sky; the evidence has made it plain that this war of aggression, as well as the seizure of Austria and Czechoslovakia, was pre-meditated and carefully prepared, and was not undertaken until the moment was thought opportune for it to be carried through as a definite part of the pre-ordained scheme and plan.

For the aggressive designs of the Nazi Government were not accidents arising out of the immediate political situation in Europe and the world; they were a deliberate and essential part of Nazi foreign policy.

From the beginning, the National Socialist movement claimed that its object was to unite the German people in the consciousness of their mission and destiny, based on inherent qualities of race, and under the guidance of the Fuehrer.

For its achievement, two things were deemed to be essential: the disruption of the European order as it had existed since the Treaty of Versailles, and the creation of a Greater Germany beyond the frontiers of 1914. This necessarily involved the seizure of foreign territories.

War was seen to be inevitable, or at the very least, highly probable, if these purposes were to be accomplished. The German people, therefore, with all their resources were to be organised as a great political-military army, schooled to obey without question any policy decreed by the State.

The making of the Charter was the exercise of the sovereign legislative power by the countries to which the German Reich unconditionally surrendered; and the undoubted right of these countries to legislate for the occupied territories has been recognised by the civilised world. The Charter is not an arbitrary exercise of power on the part of the victorious nations, but in the view of the Tribunal, as will be shown, it is the expression of international law existing at the time of its creation; and to that extent is itself a contribution to international law.

The Signatory Powers created this Tribunal, defined the law it was to administer, and made regulations for the proper conduct of the Trial. In doing so, they have done together what any one of them might have done singly; for it is not to be doubted that any nation has the right thus to set up special courts to administer law. With regard to the constitution of the court, all that the defendants are entitled to ask is to receive a fair trial on the facts and law.

The Charter makes the planning or waging of a war of aggression or a war in violation of international treaties a crime; and it is therefore not strictly necessary to consider whether and to what extent aggressive war was a crime before the execution of the London Agreement. But in view of the great importance of the questions of law involved, the Tribunal has heard full argument from the Prosecution and the Defense, and will express its view on the matter.

It was urged on behalf of the defendants that a fundamental principle of all law -international and domestic - is that there can be no punishment of crime without a pre -existing law. "*Nullum crimen sine lege, nulla poena sine lege.*" It was submitted that ex post facto punishment is abhorrent to the law of all civilised nations, that no sovereign power had made aggressive war a crime at the time the alleged criminal acts were committed, that no statute had defined aggressive war, that no penalty had been fixed for its commission, and no court had been created to try and punish offenders.

In the first place, it is to be observed that the maxim *nullum crimen sine lege* is not a limitation of sovereignty, but is in general a principle of justice. To assert that it is unjust to punish those who in defiance of treaties and assurances have attacked neighbouring states without warning is obviously untrue, for in such circumstances the attacker must know that he is doing wrong, and so far from it being unjust to punish him, it would be unjust if his wrong were allowed to go unpunished. Occupying the positions they did in the government of Germany, the defendants, or at least some of them must have known of the treaties signed by Germany, outlawing recourse to war for the settlement of international disputes; they must have known that they were acting in defiance of all international law when in complete deliberation they carried out their designs of invasion and aggression. On this view of the case alone, it would appear that the maxim has no application to the present facts.

This view is strongly reinforced by a consideration of the state of international law in 1939, so far as aggressive war is concerned. The General Treaty for the Renunciation of War of 27th August, 1928, more generally known as the Pact of Paris or the Kellogg-Briand Pact, was binding on sixty-three nations, including Germany, Italy and Japan at the outbreak of war in 1939. In the preamble, the signatories declared that they were:

> Deeply sensible of their solemn duty to promote the welfare of mankind; persuaded that the time has come when a frank renunciation of war as an instrument of national policy should be made to the end that the peaceful and friendly relations now existing between their peoples should be perpetuated all changes in their relations with one another should be sought only by pacific means … thus uniting civilised nations of the world in a common renunciation of war as an instrument of their national policy.

The first two Articles are as follows:

Article I: The High Contracting Parties solemnly declare in the names of their respective peoples that they condemn recourse to war for the solution of international controversies and renounce it as a instrument of national policy in their relations to one another.

Article II: The High Contracting Parties agree that the settlement or solution of all disputes or conflicts of whatever nature or of whatever origin they may be, which may arise among them, shall never be sought except by pacific means.

The question is, what was the legal effect of this Pact? The nations who signed the Pact or adhered to it unconditionally condemned recourse to war for the future as an instrument of policy, and expressly renounced it. After the signing of the Pact, any nation resorting to war as an instrument of national policy breaks the Pact. In the opinion of the Tribunal, the solemn renunciation of war as an instrument of national policy necessarily involves the proposition that such a war is illegal in international law; and that those who plan and wage such a war, with its inevitable and terrible consequences, are committing a crime in so doing. War for the solution of international controversies undertaken as an instrument of national policy certainly includes a war of aggression, and such a war is therefore outlawed by the Pact. …

But it is argued that the Pact does not expressly enact that such wars are crimes, or set up courts to try those who make such wars. To that extent the same is true with regard to the laws of war contained in the Hague Convention. The Hague Convention of 1907 prohibited resort to certain methods of waging war. These included the inhumane treatment of prisoners, the employment of poisoned weapons, the improper use of flags of truce, and similar matters. Many of these prohibitions had been enforced long before the date of the Convention;

but since 1907 they have certainly been crimes, punishable as offenses against the laws of war; yet the Hague Convention nowhere designates such practices as criminal, nor is any sentence prescribed, nor any mention made of a court to try and punish offenders. For many years past, however, military tribunals have tried and punished individuals guilty of violating the rules of land warfare laid down by this Convention. In the opinion of the Tribunal, those who wage aggressive war are doing that which is equally illegal, and of much greater moment than a breach of one of the rules of the Hague Convention. In interpreting the words of the Pact, it must be remembered that international law is not the product of an international legislature, and that such international agreements as the Pact of Paris have to deal with general principles of law, and not with administrative matters of procedure. The law of war is to be found not only in treaties, but in the customs and practices of states which gradually obtained universal recognition, and from the general principles of justice applied by jurists and practised by military courts. This law is not static, but by continual adaptation follows the needs of a changing world. Indeed, in many cases treaties do no more than express and define for more accurate reference the principles of law already existing.

The view which the Tribunal takes of the true interpretation of the Pact is supported by the international history which preceded it. In the year 1923 the draft of a Treaty of Mutual Assistance was sponsored by the League of Nations. ...

Although the Protocol was never ratified, it was signed by the leading statesmen of the world, representing the vast majority of the civilised states and peoples and may be regarded as strong evidence of the intention to brand aggressive war as an international crime. ...

All these expressions of opinion, and others that could be cited, so solemnly made, reinforce the construction which the Tribunal placed upon the Pact of Paris, that resort to a war of aggression is not merely illegal but is criminal. ...

It is also important to remember that Article 227 of the Treaty of Versailles provided for the constitution of a special Tribunal, composed of representatives of five of the Allied and Associated Powers which had been belligerents in the first World War opposed to Germany, to try the former German Emperor "for a supreme offense against international morality and the sanctity of treaties." The purpose of this trial was expressed to be "to vindicate the solemn obligations of international undertakings, and the validity of international morality." In Article 228 of the Treaty, the German Government expressly recognised the right of the Allied Powers "to bring before military tribunals persons accused of having committed acts of violation of the laws and customs of war."

It was submitted that international law is concerned with the action of sovereign States, and provides no punishment for individuals; and further, that where the act in question is an act of state, those who carry it out are not personally responsible, but are protected by the doctrine of the sovereignty of the State. In the opinion of the Tribunal, both these submissions must be rejected. That international law imposes duties and liabilities upon individuals as well as upon States has long been recognised. In the recent case of *Ex Parte Quirin*, 317 U.S. 1 (1942), before the Supreme Court of the United States persons were charged during the war with landing in the United States for purposes of spying and sabotage. The late Justice Stone, speaking for the Court, said:

> From the very beginning of its history this Court has applied the law of war as including that part of the law of nations which prescribes for the conduct of war the status, rights and duties of enemy nations as well as enemy individuals.

He went on to give a list of cases tried by the Courts, where individual offenders were charged with offences against the laws of nations, and particularly, the laws of war. Many other authorities could be quoted, but enough has been said to show that individuals can be punished for violations of international law. Crimes against international law are committed by men, not by abstract entities, and only by punishing individuals who commit such crimes can the provisions of international law be enforced.

The principle of international law, which under certain circumstances, protects the representatives of a state, cannot be applied to acts which are condemned as criminal by international law. The authors of these facts cannot shelter themselves behind their official position in order to be freed from punishment in appropriate proceedings. Article 7 of the Charter expressly declares:

> The official position of defendants, whether as Heads of State, or responsible officials in government departments, shall not be considered as freeing them from responsibility, or mitigating punishment.

On the other hand the very essence of the Charter is that individuals have international duties which transcend the national obligations of obedience imposed by the individual State. He who violates the laws of war cannot obtain immunity while acting in pursuance of the authority of the State if the State in authorising action moves outside its competence under international law.

It was also submitted on behalf of most of these defendants that in doing what they did they were acting under the orders of Hitler, and therefore cannot be held responsible for the acts committed by them in carrying out these orders. The Charter specially provides in Article 8:

> The fact that the defendant acted pursuant to order of his Government or of a superior shall not free him from responsibility, but may the considered in mitigation of punishment.

The provisions of this Article are in conformity with the law of all nations. That a soldier was ordered to kill or torture in violation of the international law of war has never been recognised as a defence to such acts of brutality, though, as the Charter here provides, the order may be urged in mitigation of the punishment. The true test, which is found in varying degrees in the criminal law of most nations, is not the existence of the order, but whether moral choice was in fact possible.

THE LAW AS TO THE COMMMON PLAN OR CONSPIRACY

Planning and preparation are essential to the making of war. In the opinion of the Tribunal aggressive war is a crime under international law. The Charter defines this offence as planning, preparation, initiation or waging of a war of aggression " or participation in a common plan or conspiracy for the accomplishment … of the foregoing." The Indictment follows this distinction. Count One charges the common plan or conspiracy. Count Two charges the planning and waging of war. The same evidence has been introduced to support both counts. We shall therefore discuss both counts together, as they are in substance the same. The defendants have been charged under both counts, and their guilt under each count must be determined.

The "common plan or conspiracy" charged in the Indictment covers twenty-five years, from the formation of the Nazi party in 1919 to the end of the war in 1945. …

In the opinion of the Tribunal, the evidence establishes the common planning to prepare and wage war by certain of the defendants. It is immaterial to consider whether a single conspiracy to the extent and over the time set out in the Indictment has been conclusively proved. Continued planning, with aggressive war as the objective, has been established beyond doubt. …

The argument that such common planning cannot exist where there is complete dictatorship is unsound. A plan in the execution of which a number of persons participate is still a plan, even though conceived by only one of them; and those who execute the plan do not avoid responsibility by showing that they acted under the direction of the man who conceived it. Hitler could not make aggressive war by himself. He had to have the co-operation of statesmen, military leaders, diplomats, and business men. When they, with knowledge of his aims, gave him their co-operation, they made themselves parties to the plan he had initiated. They are not to be deemed innocent because Hitler made use of them, if they knew what they were doing. That they were assigned to their tasks by a dictator does not absolve them from responsibility for their acts. The relation of leader and follower does not preclude responsibility here any more than it does in the comparable tyranny of organised domestic crime.

NOTES AND QUESTIONS

1. The Charter of the International Military Tribunal provided, among other things, that:

   The following acts …are crimes…

   (a) Crimes against peace: namely, planning, preparation, initiation or waging of a war of aggression, or a war in violation of international treaties, agreements or assurances, or participation in a common plan or conspiracy for the accomplishment of any of the foregoing.

This and the other principles of international law recognized by the Charter of the Nuremberg Tribunal were affirmed by the General Assembly at its first session. G.A.Res. 95(I), U.N. Doc. A/64, at 188 (1946).

2. Given the intense expectation of violence characteristic of international politics and the resultant pattern of planning logistical and military exercises, is this a realistic norm? If it is unrealistic, why was it prescribed?

3. As part of their defensive preparations, ministries and departments of defense are constantly preparing "contingency plans" for every conceivable type of operation. Do these plans deter or stimulate war? Are those who prepare contingency plans war criminals?

4. Due to heavy political controversy over the definition of aggression, the "crime against peace" has not been defined in the Rome Statute of the International Criminal Court. According to Article 5(2) of the Statute, "[t]he Court shall exercise jurisdiction over the crime of aggression once a provision is adopted in accordance with articles 121 and 123 defining the crime and setting out the conditions under which the Court shall exercise jurisdiction with respect to this crime. Such a provision shall be consistent with the relevant provisions of the Charter of the United Nations."

2. War Crimes

a. Judgment of The International Military Tribunal for the Trial of German Major War Criminals

Nuremberg, Sept. 30 & Oct. 1, 1946, Cmd. 6964;
41 AM. J. INT'L L. 172 (1947).
[Review Nuremberg Charter Provisions, *supra* at 1142]

WAR CRIMES AND CRIMES AGAINST HUMANITY

The evidence relating to war crimes has been overwhelming, in its volume and its detail. It is impossible for this Judgment adequately to review it, or to record the mass of documentary and oral evidence that has been presented. The truth remains that war crimes were committed on a vast scale, never before seen in the history of war. They were perpetrated in all the countries occupied by Germany, and on the High Seas, and were attended by every conceivable circumstance of cruelty and horror. There can be no doubt that the majority of them arose from the Nazi conception of "total war ", with which the aggressive wars were waged. For in this conception of "total war", the moral ideas underlying the conventions which seek to make war more humane are no longer regarded as having force or validity. Everything is made subordinate to the overmastering dictates of war. Rules, regulations, assurances and treaties all alike are of no moment, and so, freed from the restraining influence of international law, the aggressive war is conducted by the Nazi leaders in the most barbaric way. Accordingly, war crimes were committed when and wherever the Fuehrer and his close associates thought them to be advantageous. They were for the most part the result of cold and criminal calculation.

On some occasions, war crimes were deliberately planned long in advance. In the case of the Soviet Union, the plunder of the territories to be occupied, and the ill-treatment of the civilian population, were settled in minute detail before the attack was begun....

Similarly, when planning to exploit the inhabitants of the occupied countries for slave labour on the very greatest scale, the German Government conceived it as an integral part of the war economy, and planned and organised this particular war crime down to the last elaborate detail.

Other war crimes, such as the murder of prisoners of war who had escaped and been recaptured, or the murder of Commandos or captured airmen, or the destruction of the Soviet Commissars, were the result of direct orders circulated through the highest official channels.

Prisoners of war were ill-treated and tortured and murdered, not only in defiance of the well-established rules of international law, but in complete disregard of the elementary dictates of humanity. Civilian populations in occupied territories suffered the same fate. Whole populations were deported to Germany for the purposes of slave labour upon defence works, armament production and similar tasks connected with the war effort. Hostages were taken in very large numbers from the civilian populations in all the occupied countries, and were shot as suited the German purposes. Public and private property was systematically plundered and pillaged in order to enlarge the resources of Germany at the expense of the rest of Europe. Cities and towns and villages were wantonly destroyed without military justification or necessity. ... [The Tribunal reviews further evidence on the murder and ill-treatment of prisoners of war.]

MURDER AND ILL-TREATMENT OF CIVILIAN POPULATION

Article 6(b) of the Charter provides that "ill-treatment ... of civilian population of or in occupied territory ... killing of hostages ... wanton destruction of cities, towns or villages " shall be a war crime. In the main these provisions are merely declaratory of the existing laws of war as expressed by the Hague Convention, Article 46, which stated:

> Family honour and rights, the lives of persons and private property, as well as religious convictions and practices must be respected.

The territories occupied by Germany were administered in violation of the laws of war. The evidence is quite overwhelming of a systematic rule of violence, brutality and terror. ...

One of the most notorious means of terrorising the people in occupied territories was the use of concentration camps. They were first established in Germany at the moment of the seizure of power by the Nazi Government. Their original purpose was to imprison without trial all those persons who were opposed to the Government, or who were in any way obnoxious to German authority. With the aid of a secret police force, this practice was widely extended and in course of time concentration camps became places of organised and systematic murder, where millions of people were destroyed.

In the administration of the occupied territories the concentration camps were used to destroy all opposition groups. The persons arrested by the Gestapo were as a rule sent to concentration camps.

A certain number of the concentration camps were equipped with gas chambers for the wholesale destruction of the inmates, and with furnaces for the burning of the bodies. Some of them were in fact used for the extermination of Jews as part of the "final solution " of the Jewish problem. Most of the non-Jewish inmates were used for labour, although the conditions under which they worked made labour and death almost synonymous terms. Those inmates who became ill and were unable to work were either destroyed in the gas chambers or sent to special infirmaries, where they were given entirely inadequate medical treatment, worse food if possible than the working inmates, and left to die.

The murder and ill-treatment of civilian populations reached its height in the treatment of the citizens of the Soviet Union and Poland. … [The Tribunal reviews the evidence of crimes committed against Polish and Soviet civilians.]

SLAVE LABOUR POLICY

Article 6 (b) of the Charter provides that the "ill-treatment, or deportation to slave labour or for any other purpose, of civilian population of or in occupied territory" shall be a war crime. The laws relating to forced labour by the inhabitants of occupied territories are found in Article 52 of The Hague Convention, which provides:

> Requisition in kind and services shall not be demanded from municipalities or inhabitants except for the needs of the army of occupation. They shall be in proportion to the resources of the country, and of such a nature as not to involve the inhabitants in the obligation of taking part in military operations against their own country.

The policy of the German occupation authorities was in flagrant violation of the terms of this Convention. Some idea of this policy may be gathered from the statement made by Hitler in a speech on 9th November, 1941:

> The territory which now works for us contains more than 250,000,000 men, but the territory which works indirectly for us includes now more than 350,000,000. In the measure in which it concerns German territory, the domain which we have taken under our administration, it is not doubtful that we shall succeed in harnessing the very last man to this work.

The actual results achieved were not so complete as this, but the German occupation authorities did succeed in forcing many of the inhabitants of the occupied territories to work for the German war effort, and in deporting at least 5,000,000 persons to Germany to serve German industry and agriculture. [The Tribunal reviews evidence on slave labour.]

Reference should also be made to the policy which was in existence in Germany by the summer of 1940, under which all aged, insane, and incurable people, " useless eaters," were transferred to special institutions where they were killed, and their relatives informed that they had died from natural causes. The victims were not confined to German citizens, but included foreign labourers, who were no longer able to work, and were therefore useless to the German war machine. It has been estimated that at least some 275,000 people were killed in this manner in nursing homes, hospitals and asylums. ... How many foreign workers were included in this total it has been quite impossible to determine.

PERSECUTION OF THE JEWS

The persecution of the Jews at the hands of the Nazi Government has been proved in the greatest detail before the Tribunal. It is a record of consistent and systematic inhumanity on the greatest scale. ...

The anti-Jewish policy was formulated in Point 4 of the [Nazi] Party Programme which declared "Only a member of the race can be a citizen. A member of the race can only be one who is of German blood, without consideration of creed. Consequently, no Jew can be a member of the race." Other points of the programme declared that Jews should be treated as foreigners, that they should not be permitted to hold public office, that they should be expelled from the Reich if it were impossible to nourish the entire population of the State, that they should be denied any further immigration into Germany, and that they should be prohibited from publishing German newspapers. ... "Der Stuermer" and other publications were allowed to disseminate hatred of the Jews, and in the speeches and public declarations of the Nazi leaders, the Jews were held up to public ridicule and contempt.

With the seizure of power, the persecution of the Jews was intensified. A series of discriminatory laws were passed, which limited the offices and professions permitted to Jews; and restrictions were placed on their family life and their rights of citizenship. By the autumn of 1938, the Nazi policy towards the Jews had reached the stage where it was directed towards the complete exclusion of Jews from German life. Pogroms were organised which included the burning and demolishing of synagogues, the looting of Jewish businesses, and the arrest of prominent Jewish business men. A collective fine of one billion marks was imposed on the Jews, the seizure of Jewish assets was authorised, and the movement of Jews was restricted by regulations to certain specified districts and hours. The creation of ghettoes was carried out on an extensive scale, and by an order of the Security Police Jews were compelled to wear a yellow star to be worn on the breast and back.

It was contended for the Prosecution that certain aspects of this anti-Semitic policy were connected with the plans for aggressive war. The violent measures taken against the Jews in November, 1938, were nominally in retaliation for the killing of an official of the German Embassy in Paris. But the decision to seize Austria and Czechoslovakia had been made a year before. The imposition of a fine of one billion marks was made, and the confiscation of the financial holdings of the Jews was decreed, at a time when German armament expenditure had put the German treasury in difficulties, and when the reduction of expenditure on armaments was being considered. ...

The Nazi persecution of Jews in Germany before the war, severe and repressive as it was, cannot compare, however, with the policy pursued during the war in the occupied territories. Originally the policy was similar to that which had been in force inside Germany. Jews were required to register, were forced to live in ghettoes, to wear the yellow star, and were used as slave labourers. In the summer of 1941, however, plans were made for the "final solution" of the Jewish question in all of Europe. This " final solution " meant the extermination of the Jews, which early in 1939 Hitler had threatened would be one of the consequences of an outbreak of war, and a special section in the Gestapo under Adolf Eichmann, as head of Section B4 of the Gestapo, was formed to carry out the policy. ...

[A]nother Part of the "final solution " was the gathering of Jews from all German-occupied Europe in concentration camps. Their physical condition was the test of life or death. All who were fit to work were used as slave labourers in the concentration camps; all who were not fit to work were destroyed in gas chambers and their bodies burnt. Certain concentration camps such as Treblinka and Auschwitz were set aside for this main purpose. With regard to Auschwitz, the Tribunal heard the evidence of Hoess, the Commandant of the camp from 1st May, 1940, to 1st December, 1943. He estimated that in the camp of Auschwitz alone in that time 2,500,000 persons were exterminated, and that a further 500,000 died from disease and starvation. Hoess described ... the actual killing by stating:

> It took from three to fifteen minutes to kill the people in the death chamber, depending upon climatic conditions. We knew when the people were dead because their screaming stopped. We usually waited about one half-hour before we opened the doors and removed the bodies. After the bodies were removed our special commandos took off the rings and extracted the gold from the teeth of the corpses.

Adolf Eichmann, who had been put in charge of this programme by Hitler, has estimated that the policy pursued resulted in the killing of 6,000,000 Jews, of which 4,000,000 were killed in the extermination institutions. [*See* Eichmann case, *infra,* Part Seven at 1457.]

THE LAW RELATING TO WAR CRIMES AND CRIMES AGAINST HUMANITY

As heretofore stated, the Charter does not define as a separate crime any conspiracy except the one set out in Article 6 (a), dealing with crimes against peace.

The Tribunal is of course bound by the Charter, in the definition which it gives both of war crimes and crimes against humanity. With respect to war crimes, however, as has already been pointed out, the crimes defined by Article 6, section (b), of the Charter were already recognised as war crimes under international law. They were covered by Articles 46, 50, 52, and 56 of the Hague Convention of 1907, and Articles 2, 3, 4, 46 and 51 of the Geneva Convention of 1929. That violations of these provisions constituted crimes for which the guilty individuals were punishable is too well settled to admit of argument.

With regard to crimes against humanity, there is no doubt whatever that political opponents were murdered in Germany before the war, and that many of them were kept in concentration camps in circumstances of great horror and cruelty. The policy of terror was certainly carried out on a vast scale, and in many cases was organised and systematic. The policy of persecution, repression and murder of civilians in Germany before the war of 1939, who were likely to be hostile to the Government, was most ruthlessly carried out. The persecution of Jews during the same period is established beyond all doubt. To constitute crimes against humanity, the acts relied on before the outbreak of war must have been in execution of, or in connection with, any crime within the jurisdiction of the Tribunal. The Tribunal is of the opinion that revolting and horrible as many of these crimes were, it has not been satisfactorily proved that they were done in execution of, or in connection with, any such crime. The Tribunal therefore cannot make a general declaration that the acts before 1939 were crimes against humanity within the meaning of the Charter, but from the beginning of the war in 1939 war crimes were committed on a vast scale, which were also crimes against humanity; and insofar as the inhumane acts charged in the Indictment, and committed after the beginning of the war, did not constitute war crimes, they were all committed in execution of, or in connection with, the aggressive war, and therefore constituted crimes against humanity.

THE ACCUSED ORGANIZATIONS

... A criminal organisation is analogous to a criminal conspiracy in that the essence of both is cooperation for criminal purposes. There must be a group bound together and organised for a common purpose. The group must be formed or used in connection with the commission of crimes denounced by the Charter. Since the declaration with respect to the organisations and groups will, as has been pointed out, fix the criminality of its members, that definition should exclude persons who had no knowledge of the criminal purposes or acts of the organisation and those who were drafted by the State for membership, unless they were personally implicated in the commission of acts declared criminal by Article 6 of the Charter as members of the organisation. Membership alone is not enough to come within the scope of these declarations. ...

The Indictment asks that the Tribunal declare to be criminal the following organisations: The Leadership Corps of the Nazi Party; The Gestapo; The S.D.; The S.S.; The S.A.; The Reich Cabinet, and The General Staff and High Command of the German Armed Forces. ... [The Tribunal reviews the evidence and declares that the Nazi Party, the Gestapo, The S.D., and The S.S. are criminal organizations but that The S.A., The Reich Cabinet and The General Staff and High Command of the German Armed Forces are not. The Tribunal continues however that] although the Tribunal is of the opinion that the term "group" in Article 9 must mean something more than this collection of military officers, it has heard much evidence as to the participation of these officers in planning and waging aggressive war, and in committing war crimes and crimes against humanity. This evidence is, as to many of them, clear and convincing.

They have been responsible in large measure for the miseries and suffering that have fallen on millions of men, women and children. They have been a disgrace to the honourable profession of arms. Without their military guidance the aggressive ambitions of Hitler and his fellow Nazis would have been academic and sterile. Although they were not a group falling within the words of the Charter they were certainly a ruthless military caste. The contemporary German militarism flourished briefly with its recent ally, National Socialism, as well as or better than it had in the generations of the past.

Many of these men have made a mockery of the soldier's oath of obedience to military orders. When it suits their defence they say they had to obey; when confronted with Hitler's brutal crimes, which are shown to have been within their general knowledge, they say they disobeyed. The truth is they actively participated in all these crimes, or sat silent and acquiescent, witnessing the commission of crimes on a scale larger and more shocking than the world has ever had the misfortune to know. This must be said.

Where the facts warrant it, these men should be brought to trial so that those among them who are guilty of these crimes should not escape punishment. …

* * *

b. The International Criminal Tribunal for the Former Yugoslavia The Prosecutor of the Tribunal against Slobodan Milosevic, Indictment

Oct. 8, 2001, Case No. IT-01-50-I,
available at http://www.un.org/icty/indictment/english/mil-ii011008e.htm

24. From 1987 until late 2000, Slobodan Milosevic was the dominant political figure in Serbia. He acquired control of all facets of the Serbian government, including the police and other state security services. In addition, he gained control over the political leaders of Kosovo, Vojvodina, and Montenegro.

25. In his capacity as the President of Serbia and through his leading position in the SPS [Socialist Party of Serbia (hereinafter SPS)] party, Slobodan Milosevic exercised effective control or substantial influence over the above-listed participants in the joint criminal enterprise and either alone or acting in concert with them and additional known and unknown persons effectively controlled or substantially influenced the actions of the Federal Presidency of the SFRY [Socialist Federal Republic of Yugoslavia (hereinafter SFRY)] and later the FRY [Federal Republic of Yugoslavia (hereinafter FRY)], the Serbian Ministry of Internal Affairs ("MUP"), the JNA[Yugoslav People's Army (hereinafter JNA)], the Serb-run TO [Territorial Defense (hereinafter TO)] staff in the territories subject to this indictment as well as Serb volunteer groups.

26. Slobodan Milosevic, acting alone and in concert with other members of the joint criminal enterprise, participated in the joint criminal enterprise in the following ways:

a) provided direction and assistance to the political leadership of the SAO SBWS [Serbian Autonomous District Slavonia, Baranja and Western Srem (hereinafter SAO SBWS)], the SAO Western Slavonia, the SAO Krajina and RSK [Republic of Serbian Krajina (hereinafter RSK)] on the take-over of these areas and the subsequent forcible removal of the Croat and other non-Serb population.

b) provided financial, material and logistical support for the regular and irregular military forces necessary for the take-over of these areas and the subsequent forcible removal of the Croat and other non-Serb population.

c) directed organs of the government of the Republic of Serbia to create armed forces separate from the federal armed forces to engage in combat activities outside the Republic of Serbia, in particular in the said areas in Croatia and the subsequent forcible removal of the Croat and other non-Serb population.

d) participated in the formation, financing, supply, support and direction of special forces of the Republic of Serbia Ministry of Internal Affairs. These special forces were created and supported to assist in the execution of the purpose of the joint criminal enterprise through the commission of crimes which are in violation of Articles 2, 3 and 5 of the Statute of the Tribunal.

e) participated in providing financial, logistical and political support and direction to Serbian irregular forces and paramilitaries. Such support was given in furtherance of the joint criminal enterprise through the commission of crimes which are in violation of Articles 2, 3 and 5 of the Statute of the Tribunal.

f) participated in the planning and preparation of the take-over of the SAO SBWS, the SAO Western Slavonia, the SAO Krajina and the Dubrovnik Republic and the subsequent forcible removal of the Croat and other non-Serb population.

g) exerted effective control or substantial influence over the JNA which participated in the planning, preparation and execution of the forcible removal of the Croat and other non-Serb population from the SAO SBWS, the SAO Western Slavonia, the SAO Krajina and the Dubrovnik Republic.

h) provided financial, logistical and political support to TO units and Serb volunteer units acting in the SAO SBWS, the SAO Western Slavonia, the SAO Krajina and the Dubrovnik Republic, which assisted in the execution of the purpose of the joint criminal enterprise through the commission of crimes which are in violation of Articles 2, 3 and 5 of the Statute of the Tribunal.

i) effectively ordered the passage of laws and regulations relative to the involvement of the JNA, the TO and Serb volunteer units in Croatia.

j) directed, commanded, controlled, or otherwise provided substantial assistance or support to the JNA, the Serb-run TO staff, and volunteer forces deployed in the SAO SBWS, the SAO Western Slavonia, the SAO Krajina and the Dubrovnik Republic engaged in the execution of the purpose of the joint criminal enterprise through the commission of crimes which are in violation of Articles 2, 3 and 5 of the Statute of the Tribunal.

k) directed, commanded, controlled, or otherwise provided substantial assistance or support to the police forces within the MUP of the Republic of Serbia, including the DB [State Security (hereinafter DB)], whose members assisted in the execution of the purpose of the joint criminal enterprise in the SAO SBWS, the SAO Western Slavonia, the SAO Krajina and the Dubrovnik Republic.

l) financed Serb military, police, and irregular soldiers in Croatia who perpetrated crimes as specified in this indictment.

m) controlled, contributed to, or otherwise utilised Serbian state-run media outlets to manipulate Serbian public opinion by spreading exaggerated and false messages of ethnically based attacks by Croats against Serb people in order to create an atmosphere of fear and hatred among Serbs living in Serbia and Croatia. The propaganda generated by the Serbian media was an important tool in contributing to the perpetration of crimes in Croatia.

27. Slobodan Milosevic knowingly and wilfully participated in the joint criminal enterprise, sharing the intent of other participants in the joint criminal enterprise or aware of the foreseeable consequences of their actions. On this basis, he bears individual criminal responsibility for these crimes under Article 7 (1) of the Statute of the Tribunal in addition to his responsibility under the same Article for having planned, instigated, ordered or otherwise aided and abetted in the planning, preparation and execution of these crimes.

28. The accused and other participants in the joint criminal enterprise shared the intent and state of mind required for the commission of each of the crimes charged in counts 1 to 32.

* * *

Slobodan Milosevic was also indicted for genocide by the ICTY for his key role in "ethnic cleansing" in Bosnia and Herzegovinia

c. The International Criminal Tribunal for the Former Yugoslavia The Prosecutor of the Tribunal against Slobodan Milosevic, Indictment

Nov. 22, 2001, Case No. IT-01-50-I [Bosnia],
available at:http://www.un.org/icty/indictment/english/mil-ii011008e.htm

25. Slobodan Milosevic, acting alone and in concert with other members of the joint criminal enterprise participated in the joint criminal enterprise in the following ways:

a) He exerted effective control over elements of the JNA and VJ [Yugoslav Army (hereinafter VJ)] which participated in the planning, preparation, facilitation and execution of the forcible removal of the majority of non-Serbs, principally Bosnian Muslims and Bosnian Croats, from large areas of Bosnia and Herzegovina.

b) He provided financial, logistical and political support to the VRS [Bosnian Serb Army (hereinafter VRS)]. These forces subsequently participated in the execution of the joint criminal enterprise through the commission of crimes which are in violation of Articles 2, 3, 4 and 5 of the Statute of the Tribunal.

c) He exercised substantial influence over, and assisted, the political leadership of Republika Srpska in the planning, preparation, facilitation and execution of the take-over of municipalities in Bosnia and Herzegovina and the subsequent forcible removal of the majority of non-Serbs, principally Bosnian Muslims and Bosnian Croats, from those municipalities.) He controlled, manipulated or otherwise utilised Serbian state-run media to spread exaggerated and false messages of ethnically based attacks by Bosnian Muslims and Croats against Serb people intended to create an atmosphere of fear and hatred among Serbs living in Serbia, Croatia and Bosnia and Herzegovina which contributed to the forcible removal of the majority of non-Serbs, principally Bosnian Muslims and Bosnian Croats, from large areas of Bosnia and Herzegovina.

d) He participated in the planning and preparation of the take-over of municipalities in Bosnia and Herzegovina and the subsequent forcible removal of the majority of non-Serbs, principally Bosnian Muslims and Bosnian Croats, from those municipalities. He provided the financial, material and logistical support necessary for such take-over.

e) He participated in the formation, financing, supply, support and direction of special forces of the Republic of Serbia Ministry of Internal Affairs. These special forces participated in the execution of the joint criminal enterprise through the commission of crimes which are in violation of Articles 2, 3, 4 and 5 of the Statute of the Tribunal.

f) He participated in providing financial, logistical and political support and direction to Serbian irregular forces or paramilitaries. These forces participated in the execution of the joint criminal enterprise through the commission of crimes which are in violation of Articles 2, 3, 4 and 5 of the Statute of the Tribunal.

g) He controlled, manipulated or otherwise utilised Serbian state-run media to spread exaggerated and false messages of ethnically based attacks by Bosnian Muslims and Croats against Serb people intended to create an atmosphere of fear and hatred among Serbs living in Serbia, Croatia and Bosnia and Herzegovina which contributed to the forcible removal of the majority of non-Serbs, principally Bosnian Muslims and Bosnian Croats, from large areas of Bosnia and Herzegovina.

* * *

Building upon the work of the Nuremberg, Yugoslavia, and Rwanda war crimes tribunals, the Rome Statute defines "war crimes" in great detail.

d. Rome Statute of the International Criminal Court

U.N. Doc. A/CONF.183/9 (1998)

Article 8. *War crimes*

1. The Court shall have jurisdiction in respect of war crimes in particular when committed as a part of a plan or policy or as part of a large-scale commission of such crimes.

2. For the purpose of this Statute, "war crimes" means:

(a) Grave breaches of the Geneva Conventions of 12 August 1949, namely, any of the following acts against persons or property protected under the provisions of the relevant Geneva Convention:

(i) Wilful killing;

(ii) Torture or inhuman treatment, including biological experiments;

(iii) Wilfully causing great suffering, or serious injury to body or health;

(iv) Extensive destruction and appropriation of property, not justified by military necessity and carried out unlawfully and wantonly;

(v) Compelling a prisoner of war or other protected person to serve in the forces of a hostile Power;

(vi) Wilfully depriving a prisoner of war or other protected person of the rights of fair and regular trial;

(vii) Unlawful deportation or transfer or unlawful confinement;

(viii) Taking of hostages.

(b) Other serious violations of the laws and customs applicable in international armed conflict, within the established framework of international law, namely, any of the following acts:

(i) Intentionally directing attacks against the civilian population as such or against individual civilians not taking direct part in hostilities;

(ii) Intentionally directing attacks against civilian objects, that is, objects which are not military objectives;

(iii) Intentionally directing attacks against personnel, installations, material, units or vehicles involved in a humanitarian assistance or peacekeeping mission in accordance with the Charter of the United Nations, as long as they are entitled to the protection given to civilians or civilian objects under the international law of armed conflict;

(iv) Intentionally launching an attack in the knowledge that such attack will cause incidental loss of life or injury to civilians or damage to civilian objects or widespread, long-term and severe damage to the natural environment which would be clearly excessive in relation to the concrete and direct overall military advantage anticipated;

(v) Attacking or bombarding, by whatever means, towns, villages, dwellings or buildings which are undefended and which are not military objectives;

(vi) Killing or wounding a combatant who, having laid down his arms or having no longer means of defence, has surrendered at discretion;

(vii) Making improper use of a flag of truce, of the flag or of the military insignia and uniform of the enemy or of the United Nations, as well as of the distinctive emblems of the Geneva Conventions, resulting in death or serious personal injury;

(viii) The transfer, directly or indirectly, by the Occupying Power of parts of its own civilian population into the territory it occupies, or the deportation or transfer of all or parts of the population of the occupied territory within or outside this territory;

(ix) Intentionally directing attacks against buildings dedicated to religion, education, art, science or charitable purposes, historic monuments, hospitals and places where the sick and wounded are collected, provided they are not military objectives;

(x) Subjecting persons who are in the power of an adverse party to physical mutilation or to medical or scientific experiments of any kind which are neither justified by the medical, dental or hospital treatment of the person concerned nor carried out in his or her interest, and which cause death to or seriously endanger the health of such person or persons;

(xi) Killing or wounding treacherously individuals belonging to the hostile nation or army;

(xii) Declaring that no quarter will be given;

(xiii) Destroying or seizing the enemy's property unless such destruction or seizure be imperatively demanded by the necessities of war;

(xiv) Declaring abolished, suspended or inadmissible in a court of law the rights and actions of the nationals of the hostile party;

(xv) Compelling the nationals of the hostile party to take part in the operations of war directed against their own country, even if they were in the belligerent's service before the commencement of the war;

(xvi) Pillaging a town or place, even when taken by assault;

(xvii) Employing poison or poisoned weapons;

(xviii) Employing asphyxiating, poisonous or other gases, and all analogous liquids, materials or devices;

(xix) Employing bullets which expand or flatten easily in the human body, such as bullets with a hard envelope which does not entirely cover the core or is pierced with incisions;

(xx) Employing weapons, projectiles and material and methods of warfare which are of a nature to cause superfluous injury or unnecessary suffering or which are inherently indiscriminate in violation of the international law of armed conflict, provided that such weapons, projectiles and material and methods of warfare are the subject of a comprehensive prohibition and are included in an annex to this Statute, by an amendment in accordance with the relevant provisions set forth in articles 121 and 123;

(xxi) Committing outrages upon personal dignity, in particular humiliating and degrading treatment;

(xxii) Committing rape, sexual slavery, enforced prostitution, forced pregnancy, as defined in article 7, paragraph 2 (f), enforced sterilization, or any other form of sexual violence also constituting a grave breach of the Geneva Conventions;

(xxiii) Utilizing the presence of a civilian or other protected person to render certain points, areas or military forces immune from military operations;

(xxiv) Intentionally directing attacks against buildings, material, medical units and transport, and personnel using the distinctive emblems of the Geneva Conventions in conformity with international law;

(xxv) Intentionally using starvation of civilians as a method of warfare by depriving them of objects indispensable to their survival, including wilfully impeding relief supplies as provided for under the Geneva Conventions;

(xxvi) Conscripting or enlisting children under the age of fifteen years into the national armed forces or using them to participate actively in hostilities.

(c) In the case of an armed conflict not of an international character, serious violations of Article 3 common to the four Geneva Conventions of 12 August 1949, namely, any of the following acts committed against persons taking no active part in the hostilities, including members of armed forces who have laid down their arms and those placed hors de combat by sickness, wounds, detention or any other cause:

(i) Violence to life and person, in particular murder of all kinds, mutilation, cruel treatment and torture;

(ii) Committing outrages upon personal dignity, in particular humiliating and degrading treatment;

(iii) Taking of hostages;

(iv) The passing of sentences and the carrying out of executions without previous judgment pronounced by a regularly constituted court, affording all judicial guarantees which are generally recognized as indispensable.

(d) Paragraph 2 (c) applies to armed conflicts not of an international character and thus does not apply to situations of internal disturbances and tensions, such as riots, isolated and sporadic acts of violence or other acts of a similar nature.

(e) Other serious violations of the laws and customs applicable in armed conflicts not of an international character, within the established framework of international law, namely, any of the following acts:

(i) Intentionally directing attacks against the civilian population as such or against individual civilians not taking direct part in hostilities;

(ii) Intentionally directing attacks against buildings, material, medical units and transport, and personnel using the distinctive emblems of the Geneva Conventions in conformity with international law;

(iii) Intentionally directing attacks against personnel, installations, material, units or vehicles involved in a humanitarian assistance or peacekeeping mission in accordance with the Charter of the United Nations, as long as they are entitled to the protection given to civilians or civilian objects under the law of armed conflict;

(iv) Intentionally directing attacks against buildings dedicated to religion, education, art, science or charitable purposes, historic monuments, hospitals and places where the sick and wounded are collected, provided they are not military objectives;

(v) Pillaging a town or place, even when taken by assault;

(vi) Committing rape, sexual slavery, enforced prostitution, forced pregnancy, as defined in article 7, paragraph 2 (f), enforced sterilization, and any other form of sexual violence also constituting a serious violation of article 3 common to the four Geneva Conventions;

(vii) Conscripting or enlisting children under the age of fifteen years into armed forces or groups or using them to participate actively in hostilities;

(viii) Ordering the displacement of the civilian population for reasons related to the conflict, unless the security of the civilians involved or imperative military reasons so demand;

(ix) Killing or wounding treacherously a combatant adversary;

(x) Declaring that no quarter will be given;

(xi) Subjecting persons who are in the power of another party to the conflict to physical mutilation or to medical or scientific experiments of any kind which are neither justified by the medical, dental or hospital treatment of the person concerned nor carried out in his or her interest, and which cause death to or seriously endanger the health of such person or persons;

(xii) Destroying or seizing the property of an adversary unless such destruction or seizure be imperatively demanded by the necessities of the conflict;

(f) Paragraph 2 (e) applies to armed conflicts not of an international character and thus does not apply to situations of internal disturbances and tensions, such as riots, isolated and sporadic acts of violence or other acts of a similar nature. It applies to armed conflicts that take place in the territory of a State when there is protracted armed conflict between governmental authorities and organized armed groups or between such groups.

3. Nothing in paragraphs 2 (c) and (d) shall affect the responsibility of a Government to maintain or reestablish law and order in the State or to defend the unity and territorial integrity of the State, by all legitimate means. ...

Article 9. *Elements of Crimes*

[Pursuant to Article 9 of the Rome Statute, and one of the Statute's several innovations, the elements of crimes of Genocide, Crimes against Humanity and War Crimes were identified. The Elements of Crimes are intended to assist the Court in the interpretation and application of the crimes defined in the Statute. They also make the element of intent crucial to any ICC indictment and conviction. *See* Assembly of States Parties to the Rome Statute of the International Criminal Court, First Session, New York, 3-10 September 2002, Official Records, ICC-ASP/1/3, 112-155. For a commentary to the elements of crimes, see The International Criminal Court: Elements of Crimes and Rules of Procedure and Evidence (Roy Lee ed. 2001). *See also,* Knut Dörmann, Elements of War Crimes under the Rome Statute of the International Criminal Court: Sources and Commentary (2003).]

3. The Issue of Command Responsibility

a. Yamashita v. Styer, Commanding General, U.S. Army Forces, Western Pacific

327 U.S. 1, 8 (1946)

Mr. Chief Justice STONE: From the petitions and supporting papers it appears that prior to September 3, 1945, petitioner was the Commanding General of the Fourteenth Army Group of the Imperial Japanese Army in the Philippine Islands. On that date he surrendered to and became a prisoner of war of the United States Army Forces in Baguio, Philippine Islands. On September 25th, by order of respondent, Lieutenant General Wilhelm D. Styer, Commanding General of the United States Army Forces, Western Pacific, which command embraces the Philippine Islands, petitioner was served with a charge prepared by the Judge Advocate General's Department of the Army, purporting to charge petitioner with a violation of the law of war. On October 8, 1945, petitioner, after pleading not guilty to the charge, was held for trial before a military commission of five Army officers appointed by order of General Styer. The order appointed six Army officers, all lawyers, as defense counsel. Throughout the proceedings which followed, including those before this Court, defense counsel have demonstrated their professional skill and resourcefulness and their proper zeal for the defense with which they were charged.

On the same date a bill of particulars was filed by the prosecution, and the commission heard a motion made in petitioner's behalf to dismiss the charge on the ground that it failed to state a violation of the law of war. On October 29th the commission was reconvened, a supplemental bill of particulars was filed, and the motion to dismiss was denied. The trial then proceeded until its conclusion on December 7, 1945, the commission hearing two hundred and eighty-six witnesses, who gave over three thousand pages of testimony. On that date petitioner was found guilty of the offense as charged and sentenced to death by hanging.

The petitions for habeas corpus set up that the detention of petitioner for the purpose of the trial was unlawful for reasons which are now urged as showing that the military commission was without lawful authority or jurisdiction to place petitioner on trial, as follows: ...

(b) that the charge preferred against petitioner fails to charge him with a violation of the law of war; ....

The Charge. Neither Congressional action nor the military orders constituting the commission authorized it to place petitioner on trial unless the charge preferred against him is of a violation of the law of war. The charge, so far as now relevant, is that petitioner, between October 9, 1944 and September 2, 1945, in the Philippine Islands, 'while commander of armed forces of Japan at war with the United States of America and its allies, unlawfully disregarded and failed to discharge his duty as commander to control the operations of the members of his command, permitting them to commit brutal atrocities and other high crimes against people of the United States and of its allies and dependencies, particularly the Philippines; and he ... thereby violated the laws of war.'

Bills of particulars, filed by the prosecution by order of the commission, allege a a series of acts, one hundred and twenty-three in number, committed by members of the forces under petitioner's command, during the period mentioned. The first item specifies the execution of a 'a deliberate plan and purpose to massacre and exterminate a large part of the civilian population of Batangas Province, and to devastate and destroy public, private and religious property therein, as a result of which more than 25,000 men, women and children, all unarmed noncombatant civilians, were brutally mistreated and killed, without cause or trial, and entire settlements were devastated and destroyed wantonly and without military necessity.' Other items specify acts of violence, cruelty and homicide inflicted upon the civilian population and prisoners of war, acts of wholesale pillage and the wanton destruction of religious monuments.

It is not denied that such acts directed against the civilian population of an occupied country and against prisoners of war are recognized in international law as violations of the law of war. Articles 4, 28, 46, and 47, Annex to Fourth Hague Convention, 1907, 36 Stat. 2277, 2296, 2303, 2306, 2307. But it is urged that the charge does not allege that petitioner has either committed or directed the commission of such acts, and consequently that no violation is charged as against him. But this overlooks the fact that the gist of the charge is an unlawful breach of duty by petitioner as an army commander to control the operations of the members of his command by 'permitting them to commit' the extensive and widespread atrocities specified. The question then is whether the law of war imposes on an army commander a duty to take such appropriate measures as are within his power to control the troops under his command for the prevention of the specified acts which are violations of the law of war and which are likely to attend the occupation of hostile territory by an uncontrolled soldiery, and whether he may be charged with personal responsibility for his failure to take such measures when violations result. That this was the precise issue to be tried was made clear by the statement of the prosecution at the opening of the trial.

It is evident that the conduct of military operations by troops whose excesses are unrestrained by the orders or efforts of their commander would almost certainly result in violations which it is the purpose of the law of war to prevent. Its purpose to protect civilian populations and prisoners of war from brutality would largely be defeated if the commander of an invading army could with impunity neglect to take reasonable measures for their protection. Hence the law of war presupposes that its violation is to be avoided through the control of the operations of war by commanders who are to some extent responsible for their subordinates.

This is recognized by the Annex to Fourth Hague Convention of 1907, respecting the laws and customs of war on land. Article I lays down as a condition which an armed force must fulfill in order to be accorded the rights of lawful belligerents, that it must be 'commanded by a person responsible for his subordinates.' 36 Stat. 2295. Similarly Article 19 of the Tenth Hague Convention, relating to bombardment by naval vessels, provides that commanders in chief of the belligerent vessels 'must see that the above Articles are properly carried out.' 36 Stat. 2389. And Article 26 of the Geneva Red Cross Convention of 1929, 47 Stat. 2074, 2092, for the amelioration of the condition of the wounded and sick in armies in the field, makes it 'the duty of the commanders-in-chief of the belligerent armies to provide for the details of execution of the foregoing articles (of the convention), as well as for unforeseen cases.' And, finally, Article 43 of the Annex of the Fourth Hague Convention, 36 Stat. 2306, requires that the commander of a force occupying enemy territory, as was petitioner, 'shall take all the measures in his power to restore, and ensure, as far as possible, public order and safety, while respecting, unless absolutely prevented, the laws in force in the country.'

These provisions plainly imposed on petitioner, who at the time specified was military governor of the Philippines, as well as commander of the Japanese forces, an affirmative duty to take such measures as were within his power and appropriate in the circumstances to protect prisoners of war and the civilian population. This duty of a commanding officer has heretofore been recognized, and its breach penalized by our own military tribunals. A like principle has been applied so as to impose liability on the United States in international arbitrations. ...

Congress, in the exercise of its constitutional power to define and punish offenses against the law of nations, of which the law of war is a part, has recognized the 'military commission' appointed by military command, as it had previously existed in United States army practice, as an appropriate tribunal for the trial and punishment of offenses against the law of war. ...

We do not make the laws of war but we respect them so far as they do not conflict with the commands of Congress or the Constitution. There is no contention that the present charge, thus read, is without the support of evidence, or that the commission held petitioner responsible for failing to take measures which were beyond his control or inappropriate for a commanding officer to take in the circumstances.[4] We do not here appraise the evidence on which petitioner was convicted. We do not consider what measures, if any, petitioner took to prevent the commission, by the troops under his command, of the plain violations of the law of war detailed in the bill of particulars, or whether such measures as he may have taken were appropriate and sufficient to discharge the duty imposed upon him. These are questions within the peculiar competence of the military officers composing the commission and were for it to decide. See Smith v. Whitney, 116 U.S. 167. It is plain that the charge on which petitioner was tried charged him with a breach of his duty to control the operations of the members of his command, by permitting them to commit the specified atrocities. This was enough to require the commission to hear evidence tending to establish the culpable failure of petitioner to perform the duty imposed on him by the law of war and to pass upon its sufficiency to establish guilt.

b. International Criminal Tribunal for the Former Yugoslavia Prosecutor v. Dario Kordic and Mario Cerkez

Trial Chamber, Judgment, 26 Feb. 26, 2001, Case No. IT-95-14.
available at http://www.un.org/icty/kordic/trialc/judgement/index.htm

1. ... Both accused are Bosnian Croats who played prominent parts in the conflict in the Central Bosnian region of Bosnia and Herzegovina in the early 1990s. Dario Kordic was a politician at the time, described as the most important Bosnian Croat political figure in the area. On the other hand, Mario Cerkez was a military man and Commander of a Brigade of the Croatian Defence Council.

[4] In its findings the commission took account of the difficulties 'faced by the accused, with respect not only to the swift and overpowering advance of American forces, but also to errors of his predecessors, weakness in organization, equipment, supply ... training, communication, discipline and morale of his troops,' and 'the tactical situation, the character, training and capacity of staff officers and subordinate commanders, as well as the traits of character of his troops.' It nonetheless found that petitioner had not taken such measures to control his troops as were 'required by the circumstances.' We do not weigh the evidence. We merely hold that the charge sufficiently states a violation against the law of war, and that the commission, upon the facts found, could properly find petitioner guilty of such a violation.

The conflict between the Bosnian Muslims and the Bosnian Croats, with which this case is concerned, took place mainly in 1992 and 1993. The accused are charged with offences arising from that conflict. ….

5. The Indictment may be summarised in this way:

(a) The background is the break-up of the former Yugoslavia. The declaration of independence by the Republic of Croatia occurred in June 1991 and its recognition by the European Community in January 1992. The declaration of independence by the Republic of Bosnia and Herzegovina followed in March 1992 and its recognition by the European Community in April 1992.

(b) The principal Bosnian Croat political party was the Croatian Democratic Union of Bosnia and Herzegovina ("HDZ-BiH"), an offshoot of its Croatian parent, the HDZ , a nationalist party. As the Indictment sets out, the goal of the HDZ-BiH party was to secure the right of the Croatian people to self-determination, including the right to secession.

(c) To this end, in November 1991 the HDZ-BiH set up a new community or entity for the Bosnian Croats, called the Croatian Community of Herceg-Bosna ("HZ H-B") which was described as 'a separate and distinct cultural, economic and territorial whole'. (This community covered the area of Central Bosnia with which this case is concerned.) The HZ H-B then created another new body, the Croatian Defence Council ("HVO ") in April 1992 which was to be the supreme executive and defence authority of the HZ H-B. Local municipal HVO units were subsequently established from June 1992 as the executive and military power in the municipalities.

(d) Dario Kordic rose rapidly in the HDZ-BiH, becoming its President in the Municipality of Busovaca, President of the Travnik Regional Community and a Vice-President of the HZ H-B. In August 1993 the HZ H-B turned itself into the Croatian Republic of Herceg Bosna ("HR H-B") with Dario Kordic continuing as a Vice-President. He became President of the HDZ-BiH in July 1994.

(e) The Indictment alleges that from November 1991 to March 1994 persons and groups "directed, instigated, supported or aided or abetted by the HDZ, the HDZ-BiH, the HZ H-B/HR H-B and HVO … planned … and engaged in a campaign of persecutions and ethnic cleansing and committed serious violations of international humanitarian law against the Bosnian Muslim population residing in the HZ H-B/HR H-B …". The charges in the Indictment arise from this campaign and relate, inter alia, to the persecution, killing, inhuman treatment and unlawful imprisonment of Bosnian Muslims.

(f) The Indictment also alleges that Dario Kordic exerted "power, influence and control over the political and military aims and operations of the HDZ-BiH, the HZ H-B, the HR H-B and HVO" and, from November 1991 to March 1994, was individually responsible, under Article 7(1) of the Statute of the International Tribunal, for committing, planning, instigating or ordering the preparation or execution of the crimes charged against him in the Indictment. Further, or alternatively, it is alleged that Dario Kordic was criminally responsible, under Article 7(3) of the Statute, as a superior, for the acts of his subordinates since he knew, or had reason to know, that persons subordinate to him were about to commit these crimes and failed to take the necessary and reasonable measures to prevent the crimes or punish the perpetrators. …

363. Alongside the charges of individual criminal responsibility based on personal participation in criminal conduct, the Indictment charges Dario Kordic and Mario Cerkez with criminal responsibility on the basis of their alleged positions as superiors to the perpetrators of the crimes alleged in the Indictment. Article 7 of the Statute, entitled "Individual criminal responsibility", provides:

> 1. A person who planned, instigated, ordered, committed or otherwise aided and abetted in the planning, preparation or execution of a crime referred to in articles 2 to 5 of the present Statute, shall be individually responsible for the crime. …
>
> 3. The fact that any of the acts referred to in articles 2 to 5 of the present Statute was committed by a subordinate does not relieve his superior of criminal responsibility if he knew or had reason to know that the subordinate was about to commit such acts or had done so and the superior failed to take the necessary and reasonable measures to prevent such acts or to punish the perpetrators thereof.

364. Article 7 is clearly intended to assign individual criminal responsibility at different levels, both subordinate and superior, for the commission of crimes listed in Articles 2 to 5 of the Statute. Article 7 gives effect to a general principle of criminal law that an individual is responsible for his acts and omissions. It provides that an individual may be held criminally responsible for the direct commission of a crime, whether as an individual or jointly, or through his omissions for the crimes of his subordinates when under an obligation to act. Article 7(3) of the Statute sets forth the principle governing the responsibility of superiors commonly referred to as "command responsibility". …

II. FINDINGS AS TO RESPONSIBILITY UNDER ARTICLE 7(1) OF THE STATUTE

A. Counts 1 and 2: Persecution …

827. The Trial Chamber has already defined persecution under Article 5(h) of the Statute as the occurrence of discriminatory acts on racial, religious or political grounds committed with intent to cause an infringement of an individual's basic or fundamental rights; and in fact doing so. The Trial Chamber finds, on overwhelming evidence, that there was a campaign of persecution throughout the Indictment period in Central Bosnia (and beyond) aimed at the Bosnian Muslims. This campaign was led by the HDZ-BiH and conducted through the instruments of the HZ H-B and the HVO and orchestrated from Zagreb. It took the form of the most extreme expression of persecution, i.e., of attacking towns and villages with the concomitant destruction and plunder, killing, injuring and detain-

ing Bosnian Muslims. The Trial Chamber has already held that the allegations relating to the encouragement and promotion of hatred, etc., and the dismissal of Bosnian Muslims from employment do not amount to persecution for the purposes of this case or, in the case of the latter allegation, at all. The purpose of this campaign was the subjugation of the Bosnian Muslim population. All this, in the Trial Chamber's view, has been comprehensively proved and thus all the elements of the underlying offence made out. The defence case that these events amounted to a civil war in which the Bosnian Croats were on the defensive, and themselves subject to persecution, is rejected. …

829. The Trial Chamber has already held that planning is an autonomous form of responsibility under Article 7(1) and that no formal superior-subordinate relationship is required for a finding of "ordering". Its findings to date amount to this: Dario Kordic was the political leader of the Bosnian Croats in Central Bosnia with particular authority in the Lasva Valley and although having no formal position in the chain of command he was associated with the military leadership; as such he participated in the HVO take-over of the municipalities and the attacks on Busovaca in January and the Lasva Valley in April and Kiseljak in June 1993. Whatever positions he may have held, the evidence does not support the contention that Dario Kordic was in the very highest echelons of the Bosnian Croat leadership or that he conceived the campaign of persecution. He was a regional political leader and lent himself enthusiastically to the common design of persecution by planning, preparing and ordering those parts of the campaign which fell within his sphere of authority. (It is to be inferred that he did so intending to advance the policy and sharing the discriminatory intent from his active participation in the campaign.) The evidence on which the Trial Chamber relies in making this finding is of the accused's positions as Vice-President of the HDZ-BiH and President of the Busovaca HDZ, his role in the HVO take-over and attack on Busovaca and his role in the attacks in the Lasva Valley and Kiseljak and in the confinement of Muslims.

B. Counts 3-44: Unlawful Attacks, Wilful Killing, Inhuman Treatment , Detention and Destruction

832. The prosecution case on these counts is that Kordic was responsible for planning and ordering the crimes which were committed by HVO units implementing his commands and instructions. The coordinated fashion and number of crimes is an indication of the existence of an organised scheme. Kordic had the necessary mens rea since he intended the crimes or accepted the risk that they would be committed.On the other hand the Kordic Final Brief begins by asserting that the case deals with crimes committed by soldiers whereas Dario Kordic was a local political leader who helped his community organise itself for defence: the core issue is the "lack of linkage" of any credible evidence that the accused had any criminal responsibility for crimes by soldiers. …

834. The Trial Chamber finds that in those cases where Kordic participated in the HVO attacks he intended to commit the crimes associated with them and

did so. His role was as political leader and his responsibility under Article 7(1) was to plan, instigate and order the crimes. In making this finding the Trial Chamber relies on the evidence already referred to in relation to persecution. As a result the Trial Chamber finds the accused Dario Kordic liable under Article 7(1) on the following counts [detailed account follows]. ...

III. FINDINGS AS TO RESPONSIBILITY UNDER ARTICLE 7(3) OF THE STATUTE

A. Dario Kordic ...

838. Dario Kordic was a civilian and a politician with tremendous influence and power in Central Bosnia. He occupied an important position in the leadership of the HZ H-B, but was not in the top echelon, being answerable to Mate Boban.

839. While he played an important role in military matters, even at times issuing orders, and exercising authority over HVO forces, he was, and remained throughout the Indictment period, a civilian, who was not part of the formal command structure of the HVO.

840. Although liability under Article 7(3) may attach to civilians as well as military personnel, once it is established that the requisite power to prevent or punish exists, the Chamber holds that great care must be taken in assessing the evidence to determine command responsibility in respect of civilians, lest an injustice is done. In the first place, it is established that substantial influence (such as Kordic had), by itself, is not indicative of a sufficient degree of control for liability under Article 7(3). Secondly, while liability under Article 7(3) may attach not only to persons in formal positions of command, but also to those who are effectively in command of more informal structures, the Chamber finds that Kordic lacked effective control, which the Appeals Chamber in the Celebici case defined as "a material ability to prevent or punish criminal conduct, however that control is exercised".

841. In sum, the Chamber finds that Kordic was neither a commander nor a superior in respect of the HVO, since he possessed neither the authority to prevent the crimes that were committed, nor to punish the perpetrators of those crimes, and as such, he is not liable under Article 7(3) of the Statute.

Notes and Questions

1. Are there any differences between the *Yamashita* and the *Kordic* decisions regarding the scope of command responsibility?

2. Article 25(3)(b) of the Rome Statute ("orders...the commission of...a crime") appears to track closely Article 7(1) of the Yugoslav Tribunal's statute. As to Article 7(3) compare Articles 27 and 28 of the Rome Statute:

Article 27: *Irrelevance of official capacity*

1. This Statute shall apply equally to all persons without any distinction based on official capacity. In particular, official capacity as a Head of State or Government, a member of a Government or parliament, an elected representative or a government official shall in no case exempt a person from criminal responsibility under this Statute, nor shall it, in and of itself, constitute a ground for reduction of sentence.

2. Immunities or special procedural rules which may attach to the official capacity of a person, whether under national or international law, shall not bar the Court from exercising its jurisdiction over such a person.

Article 28: *Responsibility of commanders and other superiors*

In addition to other grounds of criminal responsibility under this Statute for crimes within the jurisdiction of the Court:

(a) A military commander or person effectively acting as a military commander shall be criminally responsible for crimes within the jurisdiction of the Court committed by forces under his or her effective command and control, or effective authority and control as the case may be, as a result of his or her failure to exercise control properly over such forces, where:

(i) That military commander or person either knew or, owing to the circumstances at the time, should have known that the forces were committing or about to commit such crimes; and

(ii) That military commander or person failed to take all necessary and reasonable measures within his or her power to prevent or repress their commission or to submit the matter to the competent authorities for investigation and prosecution.

(b) With respect to superior and subordinate relationships not described in paragraph (a), a superior shall be criminally responsible for crimes within the jurisdiction of the Court committed by subordinates under his or her effective authority and control, as a result of his or her failure to exercise control properly over such subordinates, where:

(i) The superior either knew, or consciously disregarded information which clearly indicated, that the subordinates were committing or about to commit such crimes;

(ii) The crimes concerned activities that were within the effective responsibility and control of the superior; and

(iii) The superior failed to take all necessary and reasonable measures within his or her power to prevent or repress their commission or to submit the matter to the competent authorities for investigation and prosecution.

Is this allocation of responsibility appropriate?

E. TERRORISM

1. W. Michael Reisman, *International Legal Responses to International Terrorism*

22 HOUS. J. INT'L L. 3 (1999)

Another anticipatory method for dealing with international terrorism involves multilateral initiatives to create a supportive normative environment for the prevention of terrorism or apprehension of those who have engaged in it. Thanks to political divisions over what constitutes terrorism, this approach has not been marked with great success until now. As early as 1937, the Convention for the Prevention and Punishment of Terrorism allowed a state to decline extradition for acts it determined fell within the political offense exception.

Conventional initiatives have been a major focus of international activity since the 1970s and have produced a great deal of paper, but not a great deal of useful law. The Hague Convention of 1970 against the capture of civil aircraft and the Montreal Convention of 1971 on illegal acts against civil aircraft are essentially extradition and judicial assistance treaties. As the Lockerbie case in the International Court and thereafter in the United Nations made clear, these treaties by themselves are of little use if the terrorism in question is state-sponsored and the terrorist state is expected to cooperate in its own investigation and conviction. If, as parallel indictments in the United States and the United Kingdom contend, the government of Libya was the author of the destruction of Pan Am 103, in which 188 Americans were killed, a legal regime that requires voluntary Libyan cooperation in investigation and trial of the perpetrators will fail. We may refer to this as the "Lockerbie problem."

In 1972, the U.N. Secretary General initiated legal efforts with a view toward conclusion of a comprehensive treaty banning terrorism. The United States vigorously supported the initiative, but it was effectively resisted by the NAM [i.e., non-aligned member states of the U.N.], which proposed instead a study of the underlying causes of terrorism. The NAM was concerned to exclude from international criminalization violent actions, whatever their nature, that were undertaken by groups fighting in the "struggle of national liberation movements." As a statement of the Government of Cyprus put it, there was a distinction to be drawn between "international terrorist acts, which the international community abhors, and militant forms of liberation activity by people struggling for their inalienable rights to freedom, independence and sovereignty, which are internationally accepted as legitimate liberation struggles." This terrorist parallel to *bellum justum* (just war) precluded agreement on a common understanding of terrorism, since the discussion had shifted from the lawfulness of a technique to the lawfulness of the purpose for which it was deployed, on which there was fundamental disagreement.

Viewed in this fashion, enough states in the United Nations believed that terrorism used for so-called "national liberation" was lawful, for Oscar Schachter to conclude that "no single inclusive definition of international terrorism has been accepted by the United Nations or in a generally accepted multilateral treaty." During this period, an ad hoc committee established by the United Nations produced a number of nonbinding recommendations admonishing states, in general terms, to "refrain from ... terrorist acts in another State. ..." In the meanwhile, a majority of the Security Council criticized Israeli and United States anti-terrorist retaliatory strikes, while the General Assembly, though calling on all states to "refrain from organizing, instigating, assisting or participating in terrorist acts in other States, or acquiescing in activities within their territory directed towards the commission of such acts," tended to be critical of all retaliatory actions, even, apparently, when they were the only meaningful option available to the victim.

Because of this fundamental fault-line in the political topography, a series of conventions were produced for specific crimes: the Diplomats and Internationally Protected Persons Convention of 1973, the Hostage Convention of 1979, the Protection of Nuclear Materials Convention of 1980, the Protocol to the Montreal Convention of 1988 (extending its reach to acts of violence in airports), the Navigation Security Convention of 1988, the Protocol on Platforms on the Continental Shelf, and the Terrorists Explosives Convention of 1997. Each, as its title indicates, addressed a particular type of terrorist action, but none essayed a more general definition of terrorism. As for mode of implementation, each was essentially an extradition treaty.

In 1986, Syria called for a diplomatic conference to define terrorism and distinguish it from actions in pursuit of national liberation. The proposal was enthusiastically supported by the Arab states, but staunchly opposed by the West. The prescriptive stalemate was broken in the early 1990s when Algeria, and then other North African states, now compelled to view terrorism from the victims' perspective, broke ranks with the NAM and called for a more comprehensive diplomatic approach. Even then, however, resistance to a general definition persisted and it continued to be easier to address particular acts. A qualitative change was, nonetheless, registered and its first explicit manifestation was a declaration in 1994, followed by a declaration in 1996. Both were nonbinding instruments. The 1994 Declaration declared:

> 1. The States Members of the United Nations solemnly reaffirm their unequivocal condemnation of all acts, methods and practices of terrorism, as criminal and unjustifiable, wherever and by whomever committed, including those which jeopardize the friendly relations among States and peoples and threaten the territorial integrity and security of States;
>
> 2. Acts, methods and practices of terrorism constitute a grave violation of the purposes and principles of the United Nations, which may pose a threat to international peace and security, jeopardize friendly relations among States, hinder international cooperation and aim at the destruction of human rights, fundamental freedoms and the democratic bases of society;
>
> 3. Criminal acts intended or calculated to provoke a state of terror in the general public, a group of persons or particular persons for political purposes are in any circumstance unjustifiable, whatever the considerations of a political, philosophical, ideological, racial, ethnic, religious or any other nature that may be invoked to justify them;
>
> 4. States, guided by the purposes and principles of the Charter of the United Nations and other relevant rules of international law, must refrain from organizing, instigating, assisting or participating in terrorist acts in

> territories of other States, or from acquiescing in or encouraging activities within their territories directed towards the commission of such acts.

The 1996 declaration continued the trend of reprehending, by implication, unilateral, forceful action. The 1994 declaration was accompanied by a request that the Secretariat study the way terrorism was treated in national laws and treaties. An ad hoc committee was established, but again, its mandate was focused on a particular pathology rather than the general problem. The first result of this effort, the Convention for the Suppression of Terrorist Bombings, adopted in 1997, may represent a sea-change, for it criminalizes a general technique, which it explicitly insulates from characterization "as a political offence or as an offence connected with a political offence or as an offence inspired by political motives." Article 11 continues: "A request for extradition or for mutual legal assistance based on such an offence may not be refused on the sole ground that it concerns a political offence or an offence connected with a political offence or an offence inspired by political motives."

The Convention now has forty-two signatures and one ratification; twenty-two ratifications are required for entry into force. In 1996, the Assembly adopted a resolution calling for a convention on nuclear terrorism. Article 12 of this draft convention relieves the state from an obligation to extradite if the purpose of the prosecution arises from, inter alia, the "political opinion" of the person sought.

All of these instruments are essentially extradition and judicial assistance treaties and, with the exception of the 1998 Terrorist Bombing Convention, would apparently allow extradition to be refused on the basis of the political offense exception. These instruments also purport to prohibit direct action in the territory of a state that may harbor a terrorist. In this respect, they do not address the "Lockerbie" problem. This is not a minor technical defect. Even when a terrorist is apprehended in a state that does not practice terrorism, there may still be substantial resistance to extraditing, as the rather bizarre case of the pursuit and apprehension of Abdullah Ocalan, the leader of the PKK (a Kurdish separatist organization in Turkey), demonstrates. Italy refused to extradite Ocalan to Turkey, and Germany, despite an outstanding warrant for his arrest there, declined to request extradition, presumably because of fear of the reactions of its sizable Turkish and Kurdish minorities. Ocalan was finally apprehended in Nairobi, Kenya by means of a unilateral covert action, whose details and participants remain obscure, and returned to Turkey, where he was tried and condemned to death. The Ocalan case demonstrates that some states, even those prominently involved in efforts to create international regimes against terrorism, may still grant or withhold rendition of terrorists in particular cases, depending on whether they seek some other accommodation from the state seeking the terrorist.

2. Inclusive Policies

a. U.N. Security Council Resolution 1267

Res. 1267, U.N. SCOR, U.N. Doc. S/RES/1267 (1999)

The Security Council, ...

Recalling the relevant international counter-terrorism conventions and in particular the obligations of parties to those conventions to extradite or prosecute terrorists,

Strongly condemning the continuing use of Afghan territory, especially areas controlled by the Taliban, for the sheltering and training of terrorists and planning of terrorist acts, and reaffirming its conviction that the suppression of international terrorism is essential for the maintenance of international peace and security,

Deploring the fact that the Taliban continues to provide safe haven to Usama bin Laden and to allow him and others associated with him to operate a network of terrorist training camps from Taliban-controlled territory and to use Afghanistan as a base from which to sponsor international terrorist operations,

Noting the indictment of Usama bin Laden and his associates by the United States of America for, inter alia, the 7 August 1998 bombings of the United States embassies in Nairobi, Kenya, and Dar es Salaam, Tanzania and for conspiring to kill American nationals outside the United States, and noting also the request of the United States of America to the Taliban to surrender them for trial (S/1999/1021),

Determining that the failure of the Taliban authorities to respond to the demands in paragraph 13 of resolution 1214 (1998) constitutes a threat to international peace and security,

Stressing its determination to ensure respect for its resolutions,

Acting under Chapter VII of the Charter of the United Nations,

1. *Insists* that the Afghan faction known as the Taliban, which also calls itself the Islamic Emirate of Afghanistan, comply promptly with its previous resolutions and in particular cease the provision of sanctuary and training for international terrorists and their organizations, take appropriate effective measures to ensure that the territory under its control is not used for terrorist installations and camps, or for the preparation or organization of terrorist acts against other States or their citizens, and cooperate with efforts to bring indicted terrorists to justice;

2. *Demands* that the Taliban turn over Usama bin Laden without further delay to appropriate authorities in a country where he has been indicted, or to appropriate authorities in a country where he will be returned to such a country, or to appropriate authorities in a country where he will be arrested and effectively brought to justice;

3. *Decides* that on 14 November 1999 all States shall impose the measures set out in paragraph 4 below, unless the Council has previously decided, on the basis of a report of the Secretary-General, that the Taliban has fully complied with the obligation set out in paragraph 2 above;

4. *Decides further* that, in order to enforce paragraph 2 above, all States shall:

(a) Deny permission for any aircraft to take off from or land in their territory if it is owned, leased or operated by or on behalf of the Taliban as designated by the Committee established by paragraph 6 below, unless the particular flight has been approved in advance by the Committee on the grounds of humanitarian need, including religious obligation such as the performance of the Hajj;

(b) Freeze funds and other financial resources, including funds derived or generated from property owned or controlled directly or indirectly by the Taliban, or by any undertaking owned or controlled by the Taliban, as designated by the Committee established by paragraph 6 below, and ensure that neither they nor any other funds or financial resources so designated are made available, by their nationals or by any persons within their territory, to or for the benefit of the Taliban or any undertaking owned or controlled, directly or indirectly, by the Taliban, except as may be authorized by the Committee on a case-by-case basis on the grounds of humanitarian need;

5. *Urges* all States to cooperate with efforts to fulfil the demand in paragraph 2 above, and to consider further measures against Usama bin Laden and his associates;

6. *Decides* to establish, in accordance with rule 28 of its provisional rules of procedure, a Committee of the Security Council consisting of all the members of the Council to undertake the following tasks and to report on its work to the Council with its observations and recommendations:

(a) To seek from all States further information regarding the action taken by them with a view to effectively implementing the measures imposed by paragraph 4 above;

(b) To consider information brought to its attention by States concerning violations of the measures imposed by paragraph 4 above and to recommend appropriate measures in response thereto;

(c) To make periodic reports to the Council on the impact, including the humanitarian implications, of the measures imposed by paragraph 4 above;

(d) To make periodic reports to the Council on information submitted to it regarding alleged violations of the measures imposed by paragraph 4 above, identifying where possible persons or entities reported to be engaged in such violations;

(e) To designate the aircraft and funds or other financial resources referred to in paragraph 4 above in order to facilitate the implementation of the measures imposed by that paragraph;

(f) To consider requests for exemptions from the measures imposed by paragraph 4 above as provided in that paragraph, and to decide on the granting of an exemption to these measures in respect of the payment by the International Air Transport Association (IATA) to the aeronautical authority of Afghanistan on behalf of international airlines for air traffic control services;

(g) To examine the reports submitted pursuant to paragraph 9 below;

7. *Calls upon* all States to act strictly in accordance with the provisions of this resolution, notwithstanding the existence of any rights or obligations conferred or imposed by any international agreement or any contract entered into or any licence or permit granted prior to the date of coming into force of the measures imposed by paragraph 4 above;

8. *Calls upon* States to bring proceedings against persons and entities within their jurisdiction that violate the measures imposed by paragraph 4 above and to impose appropriate penalties;

9. *Calls upon* all States to cooperate fully with the Committee established by paragraph 6 above in the fulfilment of its tasks, including supplying such information as may be required by the Committee in pursuance of this resolution;

10. *Requests* all States to report to the Committee established by paragraph 6 above within 30 days of the coming into force of the measures imposed by paragraph 4 above on the steps they have taken with a view to effectively implementing paragraph 4 above;

11. *Requests* the Secretary-General to provide all necessary assistance to the Committee established by paragraph 6 above and to make the necessary arrangements in the Secretariat for this purpose;

12. *Requests* the Committee established by paragraph 6 above to determine appropriate arrangements, on the basis of recommendations of the Secretariat, with competent international organizations, neighbouring and other States, and parties concerned with a view to improving the monitoring of the implementation of the measures imposed by paragraph 4 above;

13. *Requests* the Secretariat to submit for consideration by the Committee established by paragraph 6 above information received from Governments and public sources on possible violations of the measures imposed by paragraph 4 above;

14. *Decides* to terminate the measures imposed by paragraph 4 above once the Secretary-General reports to the Security Council that the Taliban has fulfilled the obligation set out in paragraph 2 above;

15. *Expresses its readiness to* consider the imposition of further measures, in accordance with its responsibility under the Charter of the United Nations, with the aim of achieving the full implementation of this resolution;

16. *Decides* to remain actively seized of the matter.

b. U.N. Security Council Resolution 1368

Res. 1368, U.N. SCOR, U.N. Doc. S/Res/1368 (2001)

The Security Council,

Reaffirming the principles and purposes of the Charter of the United Nations,

Determined to combat by all means threats to international peace and security caused by terrorist acts,

Recognizing the inherent right of individual or collective self-defence in accordance with the Charter,

1. *Unequivocally condemns* in the strongest terms the horrifying terrorist attacks which took place on 11 September 2001 in New York, Washington, D.C. and Pennsylvania and *regards* such acts, like any act of international terrorism, as a threat to international peace and security;

2. *Expresses* its deepest sympathy and condolences to the victims and their families and to the people and Government of the United States of America;

3. *Calls* on all States to work together urgently to bring to justice the perpetrators, organizers and sponsors of these terrorist attacks and *stresses* that those responsible for aiding, supporting or harbouring the perpetrators, organizers and sponsors of these acts will be held accountable;

4. *Calls also* on the international community to redouble their efforts to prevent and suppress terrorist acts including by increased cooperation and full implementation of the relevant international anti-terrorist conventions and Security Council resolutions, in particular resolution 1269 (1999) of 19 October 1999;

5. *Expresses* its readiness to take all necessary steps to respond to the terrorist attacks of 11 September 2001, and to combat all forms of terrorism, in accordance with its responsibilities under the Charter of the United Nations;

6. *Decides* to remain seized of the matter.

c. U.N. Security Council Resolution 1373 (2001)

Res. 1373, U.N. SCOR, U.N. Doc. S/2002/15 (2002)

The Security Council,

Reaffirming its resolutions 1269 (1999) of 19 October 1999 and 1368 (2001) of 12 September 2001,

Reaffirming also its unequivocal condemnation of the terrorist attacks which took place in New York, Washington, D.C. and Pennsylvania on 11 September 2001, and expressing its determination to prevent all such acts,

Reaffirming further that such acts, like any act of international terrorism, constitute a threat to international peace and security,

Reaffirming the inherent right of individual or collective self-defence as recognized by the Charter of the United Nations as reiterated in resolution 1368 (2001),

Reaffirming the need to combat by all means, in accordance with the Charter of the United Nations, threats to international peace and security caused by terrorist acts,

Deeply concerned by the increase, in various regions of the world, of acts of terrorism motivated by intolerance or extremism,

Calling on States to work together urgently to prevent and suppress terrorist acts, including through increased cooperation and full implementation of the relevant international conventions relating to terrorism,

Recognizing the need for States to complement international cooperation by taking additional measures to prevent and suppress, in their territories through all lawful means, the financing and preparation of any acts of terrorism,

Reaffirming the principle established by the General Assembly in its declaration of October 1970 (resolution 2625 (XXV)) and reiterated by the Security Council in its resolution 1189 (1998) of 13 August 1998, namely that every State has the duty to refrain from organizing, instigating, assisting or participating in terrorist acts in another State or acquiescing in organized activities within its territory directed towards the commission of such acts,

Acting under Chapter VII of the Charter of the United Nations,

1. *Decides* that all States shall:

(a) Prevent and suppress the financing of terrorist acts;

(b) Criminalize the wilful provision or collection, by any means, directly or indirectly, of funds by their nationals or in their territories with the intention that the funds should be used, or in the knowledge that they are to be used, in order to carry out terrorist acts;

(c) Freeze without delay funds and other financial assets or economic resources of persons who commit, or attempt to commit, terrorist acts or participate in or facilitate the commission of terrorist acts; of entities owned or controlled directly or indirectly by such persons; and of persons and entities acting on behalf of, or at the direction of such persons and entities, including funds derived or generated from property owned or controlled directly or indirectly by such persons and associated persons and entities;

(d) Prohibit their nationals or any persons and entities within their territories from making any funds, financial assets or economic resources or financial or other related services available, directly or indirectly, for the benefit of persons who commit or attempt to commit or facilitate or participate in the commission of terrorist acts, of entities owned or controlled, directly or indirectly, by such persons and of persons and entities acting on behalf of or at the direction of such persons;

2. *Decides also* that all States shall:

(a) Refrain from providing any form of support, active or passive, to entities or persons involved in terrorist acts, including by suppressing recruitment of members of terrorist groups and eliminating the supply of weapons to terrorists;

(b) Take the necessary steps to prevent the commission of terrorist acts, including by provision of early warning to other States by exchange of information;

(c) Deny safe haven to those who finance, plan, support, or commit terrorist acts, or provide safe havens;

(d) Prevent those who finance, plan, facilitate or commit terrorist acts from using their respective territories for those purposes against other States or their citizens;

(e) Ensure that any person who participates in the financing, planning, preparation or perpetration of terrorist acts or in supporting terrorist acts is brought to justice and ensure that, in addition to any other measures against them, such terrorist acts are established as serious criminal offences in domestic laws and regulations and that the punishment duly reflects the seriousness of such terrorist acts;

(f) Afford one another the greatest measure of assistance in connection with criminal investigations or criminal proceedings relating to the financing or support of terrorist acts, including assistance in obtaining evidence in their possession necessary for the proceedings;

(g) Prevent the movement of terrorists or terrorist groups by effective border controls and controls on issuance of identity papers and travel documents, and through measures for preventing counterfeiting, forgery or fraudulent use of identity papers and travel documents;

3. *Calls* upon all States to:

(a) Find ways of intensifying and accelerating the exchange of operational information, especially regarding actions or movements of terrorist persons or networks; forged or falsified travel documents; traffic in arms, explosives or sensitive materials; use of communications technologies by terrorist groups; and the threat posed by the possession of weapons of mass destruction by terrorist groups;

(b) Exchange information in accordance with international and domestic law and cooperate on administrative and judicial matters to prevent the commission of terrorist acts;

(c) Cooperate, particularly through bilateral and multilateral arrangements and agreements, to prevent and suppress terrorist attacks and take action against perpetrators of such acts;

(d) Become parties as soon as possible to the relevant international conventions and protocols relating to terrorism, including the International Convention for the Suppression of the Financing of Terrorism of 9 December 1999;

(e) Increase cooperation and fully implement the relevant international conventions and protocols relating to terrorism and Security Council resolutions 1269 (1999) and 1368 (2001);

(f) Take appropriate measures in conformity with the relevant provisions of national and international law, including international standards of human rights, before granting refugee status, for the purpose of ensuring that the asylum-seeker has not planned, facilitated or participated in the commission of terrorist acts;

(g) Ensure, in conformity with international law, that refugee status is not abused by the perpetrators, organizers or facilitators of terrorist acts, and that claims of political motivation are not recognized as grounds for refusing requests for the extradition of alleged terrorists;

4. *Notes* with concern the close connection between international terrorism and transnational organized crime, illicit drugs, money-laundering, illegal armstrafficking, and illegal movement of nuclear, chemical, biological and other potentially deadly materials, and in this regard *emphasizes* the need to enhance coordination of efforts on national, subregional, regional and international levels in order to strengthen a global response to this serious challenge and threat to international security;

5. *Declares* that acts, methods, and practices of terrorism are contrary to the purposes and principles of the United Nations and that knowingly financing, planning and inciting terrorist acts are also contrary to the purposes and principles of the United Nations;

6. *Decides* to establish, in accordance with rule 28 of its provisional rules of procedure, a Committee of the Security Council, consisting of all the members of the Council, to monitor implementation of this resolution, with the assistance of appropriate expertise, and *calls upon* all States to report to the Committee, no later than 90 days from the date of adoption of this resolution and thereafter according to a timetable to be proposed by the Committee, on the steps they have taken to implement this resolution;

7. *Directs* the Committee to delineate its tasks, submit a work programme within 30 days of the adoption of this resolution, and to consider the support it requires, in consultation with the Secretary-General;

8. *Expresses* its determination to take all necessary steps in order to ensure the full implementation of this resolution, in accordance with its responsibilities under the Charter;

9. *Decides* to remain seized of this matter.

NOTES AND QUESTIONS

1. The use of force against the Taliban government in Afghanistan in 2002 was widely seen as a legitimate act of self-defense. W. Michael Reisman, *In Defense of World Public Order*, 85 AM. J. INT'L L. 833 (2001); Thomas M. Franck, *Terrorism and the Right of Self-Defense*, 95 AM. J. INT'L L. 839 (2001); Steven R. Ratner, Jus Ad Bellum *and* Jus in Bello *after September 11*, 96 AM. J. INT'L L. 905 (2002). Both Security Council Resolutions 1368 and 1373 refer in the context of the September 11 attack to "inherent right of individual or collective self-defense." Nevertheless, Professor Charney argued that, in this context, an express authorization of the use of force by the Security Council would have been preferable. Jonathan I. Charney, *The Use of Force Against Terrorism and International Law*, 95 AM. J. INT'L L. 835 (2001). Do you agree? *See also* Ilias Bantekas, *The International Law of Terrorist Financing*, 97 AM. J. INT'L L. 315 (2003).

2. Are the traditional categories and protections of the laws of war applicable in the context of terrorism? Are they appropriate? Should the reactions and preventive actions by victim and potential victim governments be limited by the Geneva Conventions? If not, should regular human rights law apply? For an affirmative answer, see the Inter-American Commission on Human Rights' decision on the request for precautionary measures for the detainees at Guantánamo Bay, *supra*. Do you agree? Under the U.S. response, what are the international legal contours of the status of Guantánamo detainees? What are they based on? *Compare* January 9, 2002 Memorandum by Deputy Assistant Attorney General John Yoo, *supra*, at 1109. *See also* Part Three, *supra*, at 511-519 for a more detailed discussion of these as well as other detainees in Afghanistan and Iraq.

3. In *Yamashita*, the U.S. Supreme Court stated:

> Congress, in the exercise of its constitutional power to define and punish offenses against the law of nations, of which the law of war is a part, has recognized the 'military commission' appointed by military command, as it had previously existed in United States army practice, as an appropriate tribunal for the trial and punishment of offenses against the law of war. Espionage Act 1917, tit. 1, s 7, 50 U.S.C.A. s 38; Articles of War, arts. 2, 12, 15, 10 U.S.C.A. ss 1473, 1483, 1486; U.S.C.A. Const. art. 1, s 8, cl. 10.

Yamashita v. Styer, Commanding General, U.S. Army Forces, Western Pacific, 327 U.S. 1, 8 (1946).

The legitimacy of the military tribunals established after the war in Afghanistan has been hotly debated. Are such tribunals internationally lawful? *AGORA: Military Commissions*, 96 AM J. INT'L L. 320 (2002).

II. Regulating the Use of the Economic Instrument

A. Issues and Policies

In politics, the economic instrument is used not only for the accumulation of wealth, but also as a means of influencing power outcomes. From earliest times, state elites have used the promise of economic indulgence or the threat of economic deprivation as part of the ensemble of means for influencing others. In contemporary world politics, rewards such as most-favored-nation status, full or associate membership in a common market or customs union, loans, credits and foreign aid, not to speak of bribes to specific persons, are regularly employed. Deprivatory techniques classically called retorsions such as selective tariffs, embargos, boycotts, expropriation and dumping are just as commonplace.

A comprehensive exposition of the legal regulation of the economic instrument would embrace a huge flow of decisions about all aspects of the movement of goods and services across state lines. At a much more general level, our concern is the extent to which prescriptions exist that delineate the appropriate use of the different economic strategies, the effectiveness of the prescriptions in practice and their adequacy from the standpoint of world public order.

B. Regulation of Economic Deprivation

1. W. Michael Reisman & Douglas L. Stevick, *The Applicability of International Law Standards to United Nations Economic Sanctions Programmes*

9 Eur. J. Int'l L. 86 (1998)

'Economic sanctions' may take many forms and may be applied unilaterally or multilaterally. They involve the purposive threat or actual granting or withholding of economic indulgences, opportunities and benefits by one actor or group of actors in order to induce another actor or group of actors to change a policy. Targeted policies may be external, such as the withdrawal of the target state from territory it has seized or illegally occupied (e.g., South Africa's long occupation of Namibia in defiance of the United Nations' termination of the Mandate), or internal, such as ending patterns of human rights violations (as in present-day China). Economic sanctions may even seek the replacement of the elite in the target state (e.g., Peron in Argentina after the Second World War or Saddam Hussein in Iraq …).

A. Prevalence

Economic sanctions are often used as a unilateral technique in international politics, though not necessarily explicitly - indeed, sometimes demurrers or denials are declared by the sanction-feasor, who may insist that the consequences, which are, of course, regrettable, are the ineluctable result of some other lawful action. An agriculture-exporting state's perishable products aboard a ship in harbour may slowly compost, as the importing state's customs inspectors, with unprecedented care, examine each hold 'by the book', all this occurring at a moment when the two states are engaged in a critical negotiation. Denials or not, the target state always gets the message.

Uses of power by one actor against another are, by definition, based on a general or momentary power-superiority, whose fluidity can be obscured by stereotyping terms, in common parlance, such as the 'strong' and the 'weak'. Economic sanctions are not quite 'equal opportunity' instruments, but their use is certainly not limited to the greatest states against the smallest states. Any disparity in power - in general or as a result even of a transitory situation - can provide the basis for the design and application of an economic sanctions programme. For example, during the stormy election of the Secretary-General of the Organization of American States (OAS) some three years ago, some Caribbean states angrily accused Costa Rica of using banana diplomacy to persuade certain states to support the candidate it had put forward. Costa Rica is hardly a superpower.

Conversely, immunity from economic sanctions is a matter of degree. Even large and powerful states such as the United States may be targeted effectively. The People's Republic of China has mounted an extraordinarily effective economic sanctions programme against the United States, through which it has secured virtually all the adjustments it seeks in America's China policy. One of the most fascinating aspects of this particular economic sanctions programme is that the target, the United States, seems possessed of the idea that *it* is the economic sanctioner, while China is the target! The seemingly interminable national debate about the utility and wisdom of economic sanctions proceeds on this flawed assumption. The point of emphasis is that opportunities to use economic sanctions unilaterally are rather widely distributed.

B. Effectiveness of Economic Sanctions

Are economic sanctions effective? If that question means: 'When used without the military strategy, can and do economic sanctions induce desired adjustments in the external or internal policies of the target?', the answer is, under certain conditions, yes, decisively and demonstrably so. In 1919, Woodrow Wilson, one of the great enthusiasts of economic sanctions, said:

> A nation that is boycotted is a nation that is in sight of surrender. Apply this economic, peaceful, silent, deadly remedy and there will be no need for force. It is a terrible remedy. It does not cost a life outside the nation boycotted, but it brings a pressure upon the nation which, in my judgment, no modern nation could resist.

Wilson was speaking as a propagandist for the League of Nations and did not need, in that role, to specify the conditions for the success of the instrument. But his basic point still holds: economic sanctions can be highly effective.

Part of Wilson's subtext - that economic sanctions are, in his words, silent, deadly and terrible - also holds. Another part of his subtext, however - that the instruments are 'peaceful' - certainly does not apply to the targets of the sanctions. It is that comfortable astigmatism that prompts the present inquiry. Precisely because economic sanctions are now used more frequently by the international community, a re-examination of what they are, how they stake and how they miss, and how they should be normatively organized is timely.

Economic sanctions are a potentially powerful instrument in the right circumstances. They are also of great potential destructiveness. If nothing else, the case of Haiti, which we consider in detail below, where sanctions were used with tremendous and indiscriminate force, should prompt a fundamental reconsideration - in terms of social science, international law and natural law - of the mechanisms, politics, and law of the use of non-lethal sanctions in the international arsenal and of the contingencies and policies that should be applied to their role in international enforcement action.

C. Strategic Instruments of Enforcement

To understand the way economic sanctions are used, it is necessary to locate them in the context of all strategic instruments and to understand the sequences in which these instruments are deployed. Analytically, policies can be implemented by combinations of four strategic instruments: the military instrument, involving the application of varying degrees of coercion by specialists in violence against a target; the economic instrument, involving the granting or withholding of indulgences or deprivations from a target; the diplomatic instrument, involving communications ranging from persuasion to coercion, directed against the elite of a target; and the ideologic or propagandic instrument, involving the modulation of carefully selected signs and symbols to politically relevant parts of the rank and file as a means of influencing the elite that governs it.

All strategic instruments are directed toward reducing the ambit of choice of the target by constraining it to adopt policies or positions it would otherwise eschew. Indulgent techniques seek to secure this compliance by promising rewards or giving bribes. The consequence of an indulgent strategy is still to attenuate the freedom of choice of the target, which must forego advantages or opportunities it expected to gain, but neither the target nor the people nor things on its peripheries suffer manifest damage. Deprivatory techniques, in contrast, try to secure compliance by sequestering or destroying certain power bases or instruments of influence of the target elite.

D. Sanctions and Threat Theory

Threats are an actor's credible communication of interest, capacity, and contingent intention; they are designed to warn another actor that if it does not desist from or adjust certain behaviour, more destructive instruments will be applied. Although the term 'threat' suffers a generally pejorative connotation in ordinary language usage, threats are a critical, indeed indispensable, part of politics. Like anything else, they can be abused, but they can be beneficial to certain public order configurations, precisely because they facilitate adjustments without requiring overt conflict.

Sanctions are, in part, an application of the theory of threats. Like threats, all instruments of strategy are designed to change the attitudes and behaviour of the target. They do this in two stages. The first stage involves the credible communication of capacity and intention to carry out a particular programme: 'do such and such *or else*'. Let us refer to this stage as the 'communication' stage. The second stage involves the effective application of the sanctions, the actual delivery of the 'or else'. We shall call this the 'application' stage. Sanctions accomplished by the communication stage alone certainly have transaction costs, but they involve fewer costs to the sanctioner and the target than do sanctions that require the second, applicative phase.

Generally, insofar as the actors involved are rational, the communication stage should ensure the desired change in behaviour if two cumulative conditions are met: (i) the content of the programme is clearly sufficient to accomplish its manifest objectives; and (ii) the communication of capacity and intention ('political will') is credible. The target will obviously not comply when the content of the threatened programme is manifestly inadequate, for instance, where the target perceives the programme as essentially symbolic, staged for certain internal or external audiences. Nor will the target comply when the content of the programme is manifestly adequate, but the target has reason to believe that the sanctioner will not follow through. For example, the target, monitoring the sanctioner's internal political processes, may detect at the elite level a most fragile unity of purpose. Or the target may conclude from prior cases that the sanctioner's political will often collapses when sanctions are resisted by a target. Under both conditions, the target will have cause to believe that the sanctioner will be unable to initiate or to sustain the application stage of the programme. Whether the target's perceptions are correct or not, the communication phase alone will not suffice to ensure compliance, and the enforcement programme will have to proceed to application.

The relevance of threat theory varies depending on the strategic instrument being used. The communications stage of a credible military sanctions programme is more likely to be a successful application of threat theory than is the communications stage of a credible economic sanctions programme and, *a fortiori,* a credible propaganda programme. Excluding for the moment military actions such as quarantines, which are actually economic deprivations accomplished by carefully defined and limited military means, the effect of the military instrument is generally rapid and, if effective, irreversible. When the economic instrument is used, in contrast, the effects are slow and cumulative, especially if they are being 'cranked up' in measured increments. Faced with a credible threat of overt military sanctions, a 'wait-and-see' attitude is not a rational option for the target. But 'wait-and-see' could be rational if the programme about to be mounted against the target is an economic or propagandic one, for the target can still haggle over terms of compliance or, indeed, turn off the programme directed against it at any time, simply by saying 'yes'. That is not to say that 'wait-and-see' has no costs for the target. The infrastructural costs of sanctions and the sunk costs of reactive attempts to transform the economy may prove as durable and politically costly as those following limited use of the military instrument, even if the target subsequently responds affirmatively. Indeed, in some ways it may prove more politically costly, for damage from the military instrument is easily and plausibly blamed on outsiders; damage from internal preventive, anticipatory action is not.

'Wait-and-see' is not always the strategy that a target will or should follow. In at least two instances, economic sanctions have obtained the desired policy goals at the communication stage: the League of Nations' sanctions against Yugoslavia in 1921 and the American and Canadian sanctions against South Korea to stop nuclear reprocessing in 1975. Whether the target should follow such a passive strategy depends on the credibility of the threat, based on the target's observation of the sanctioner's previous behaviour and other contextual indications of authority and control intent, and on the ability of the target's elites to hedge the impact of the threatened economic shocks.

The target's elites may adopt a defensive strategy at the communication stage. But, as suggested above, such a strategy is not costless and its adoption will depend on a balancing of expected costs and rewards. These strategies may include, but are not limited to, transforming the economy's structure toward import substitution or seeking temporary alternative markets in which to purchase and sell goods and services. The expected benefit from these strategies, in turn, will depend on the costs of redirecting production, on the size of the internal market, and on the elasticity of world supply and demand for those goods in which the target trades.

In most cases, the costs of adopting these reactive strategies at the communication stage may be prohibitively high. As a result, economic sanctions would tend to be less effective at the communication stage than uses of the military instrument, unless the sanctioner has a well-known record of threatening sanctions and carrying them out if necessary. Mere assertions of power or authority are unlikely to make the target change its policies at this stage for they convey little information about the sanctioner's credibility. The differential effect of threat theory on enforcement instruments means that the quantum and nature of damage flowing from a sanctions programme will vary depending on which instrument is selected as the primary sanction tool.

E. Collateral Damage

The destruction of people and objects on the periphery of a target is called, euphemistically, 'collateral damage'. Some collateral damage is a virtually inescapable feature of destructive strategies, for no weapon regularly delivers its punch with the `surgical precision' claimed by its manufacturers and operators. Customary international law, now codified, has long tried to define lawful primary targets and to establish boundaries of tolerance for collateral damage. Weapons are not *per se* lawful or unlawful, but must be selected for particular contexts and missions, taking account of their properties and, in particular, their capacities to discriminate between the combatants and non-combatants in the actual circumstances of the case.

The critical notions of damage and collateral damage have been conceived for and applied primarily to uses of the military instrument. Some scholars and politicians believe that the other strategic instruments are essentially, or at least comparatively, non-damage-causing. But if one examines facts contextually and systematically, it is readily apparent that none of the four instruments of policy is inherently non-destructive. Each may be used in ways that produce significant destruction, often on the peripheries rather than on the target itself.

This is obviously the case with military weapons in many contexts. Consider a recent example: the destruction, by 'smart' missiles, of Iraqi intelligence headquarters in Baghdad, which President Clinton ordered in reaction to the Iraqi plot to assassinate former President Bush, produced some collateral damage in the suburb of Baghdad in which the intelligence headquarters was situated.

The inevitability of collateral damage is less obvious for some of the other instruments. The propagandic instrument - the purposive modulation of signs and symbols by one side to a conflict against the rank and file of the adversary - was used prior to, during and after Desert Storm, to encourage the Shi'a in the south of Iraq and the Kurds in the north of Iraq to rise against the Ba'ath regime. In both cases, it could be anticipated that the propaganda, if it were successful, would ignite a chain of events ultimately causing substantial collateral damage in the insurrection and the brutal suppression that would follow it, especially if the coalition that had encouraged the insurrection did not come to its assistance.

Two points must be emphasized. First, damage - in an empirically referential sense - is not caused exclusively by uses of the *military* instrument. The other instruments are often used in highly destructive ways. In fact, though often counter-intuitive, the military instrument, as we have seen, in its communicative or threat stage, can be and usually is used in non-destructive and essentially communicative ways. The sequence is quite simple. Threats and coordinate demonstrations of power are perceived by the intended target; they concentrate its mind in a way that words alone do not; and they stimulate careful assessments of relative power positions correlated with the degree of importance of the issues at stake. Where the assessments indicate probabilities of net losses, they lead to appropriate non-belligerent adjustments. The military instrument is more likely than the other instruments to be effective in this stage, precisely because 'wait-and-see' is an inappropriate response.

Second, damage is not caused exclusively by the application of *material* assets, the 'sticks and stones' of the arsenal. Words can cause direct and collateral damage as well… [authors expound on propaganda and "psychological warfare"].

In sum, then, considered in terms of threat theory, the collateral damage caused by non-military instruments - the economic and propagandic - may be greater than that of the military instrument, precisely because the elite, presented with a credible threat of the application of one of these non-military instruments, will often adopt, quite rationally, a 'wait-and-see' posture. During the time that this posture is followed, collateral damage can accumulate. Precisely because 'wait-and-see' is always irrational in the face of a credible threat to use the military instrument, its effective employment may actually cause less collateral damage than the use of non-military instruments.

F. The 'Appeal' of Economic Sanctions

Economic sanctions are unquestionably the flavour of the year nationally and internationally for enforcement action. They are preferred in advanced industrial democracies because they engage comparatively less *internal* political resistance than other candidate strategies. Comparatively speaking, economic sanctions are politically cheap. To be sure, they do have retro-costs, which may be considerable, that are borne by particular sectors of the national economy of the sanctioning state. But economic sanctions do not generate sombre processions of body bags bringing home the mortal remains of the sons and daughters of the constituents. Even when it is glaringly obvious that economic sanctions are not going to be effective, as for example with the US grain embargo mounted against the Soviet Union in response to its invasion of Afghanistan in 1979, or when it is clear in advance that economic sanctions will actually prove more costly to the party imposing them than to the target, the sanctions are not without important political consequences: they still reinforce public commitment to the norm that has been violated and generate a sense of civic virtue, without incurring unacceptable domestic political costs. Whatever their economic costs, they are often likely to be the cheapest feasible political option. When, as often happens in democratic polities, political forces cannot agree on the appropriateness of response to some perceived international delict, economic sanctions become an easy point for compromise: not necessarily the most rational of options, but certainly the lowest common denominator.

Yet international tolerance for unilaterally applied economic sanctions may be declining. Economic interdependence is a long-standing fact. The *perception* of just how integrated the international economy has become, however, and how inclusively disruptive some heretofore tolerated unilateral actions can be to that interdependence has increased. One manifestation of this perception is the growing criticism of the unilateral application of economic sanctions. But the concern about the use of these sanctions has been motivated entirely by self-interest rather than by a concern for the essential lawfulness and morality of the general or particular use of economic sanctions. Indeed, those who press for general or particular economic sanctions programmes feel that it is they who control the moral high ground.

It is the militant sense of virtue and moral superiority that attaches to the application of economic sanctions that is so fascinating. Economic sanctions have enjoyed great popularity among people of pacifistic bent because they seem to offer wholly non-violent and non-destructive ways of implementing international policy. 'At least,' one hears again and again, 'we're not killing anyone.' 'At least, we're giving non-lethal sanctions a chance.' In this line of thinking, economic sanctions are always to be preferred to the application of military strategy and, in any case, are always to be exhausted before military action is initiated. As we have seen, however, such assumptions are unfounded.

G. The Relevance of the Law of Armed Conflict

The basic postulates of the law of armed conflict are the sharp distinction between combatants and non-combatants and the imperative that any use of force be demonstrably necessary, proportional to the necessity, and capable of discriminating between combatants and non-combatants. It is a cardinal principle of the international law of armed conflict that military strategies are to be planned and appraised taking due account of these criteria. Prospectively, rules of engagement must be designed to accommodate these principles in the anticipated context. Major military campaigns are subjected to critical post-mortems to determine the extent to which those principles were met and whether the application of coercion in that case was internationally lawful.

The same type of examination is not transposed, *mutatis mutandis*, for prospective assessment of applications of the other three instruments. The apparent reason for this persistent blind spot in international legal analysis has been the incorrect assumption that only the military instrument is destructive. The assumption that non-military strategies are inherently non-destructive or non-lethal has also insulated their prospective and retrospective appraisal in terms of basic human rights instruments. The consequences of this blind spot can be very grave. State-sponsored propaganda, for example, is often used to exacerbate hatred between different groups. Surely this is a violation of the Convention on the Elimination of Racial Discrimination.

Non-military instruments should be tested rigorously against the criteria of the international law of armed conflict and other relevant norms of contemporary international law *before* a decision is made to initiate or to continue to apply them. If the non-military instruments were so tested, it is quite probable that, in some cases, they would be found to fail and to require adjustment or abandonment. The economic and propagandic instruments are problematic, mainly because of their relative incapacity to discriminate between licit targets and because of their durable resultant collateral injuries, which persist long after the conclusion of the campaign in which they were deployed.

These considerations should apply, *a fortiori*, to international organizations when they elect to use the economic instrument. Since GATT and WTO prescriptions are placing an increasing number of limitations on the unilateral uses of economic sanctions, their most common and intensive lawful use in the future is likely to be through international organizations. Our thesis is that in these applications, compliance with international law, and particularly the criteria of lawfulness of the law of armed conflict, is mandatory. A preliminary, factual question is whether and to what extent the international organizations that have mounted economic sanctions programmes have complied with this requirement. Thereafter, we will turn our attention to the question of under what circumstances and through which procedures economic sanctions programmes should be planned and applied in the future. …

3. The Application of Economic Sanctions by the United Nations

Although the UN General Assembly has periodically passed non-binding resolutions calling on all Member States to apply economic sanctions, it is the UN Security Council that has decided upon and applied the regimes of UN-enforced economic sanctions. In the first 50 years of existence of the United Nations, the Security Council, acting pursuant to Chapter VII, has on ten different occasions mandated that Member States implement economic sanctions of varying degrees of stringency against offending states. Our question here is not whether these sanctions programmes succeeded in achieving their objectives, a subject that is keenly disputed among scholars and policy-makers. We are concerned, rather, with the question whether UN bodies and decision-makers have considered the requisite legal issues of proportionality and discrimination when using any coercive instrument and, if so, the procedures and criteria by which key UN actors have reached their judgments. As the following case studies reveal, UN practice has generally been to either ignore the legal issues raised by the effects of economic sanctions on the population of target states or to address these issues only on an ad hoc basis. It is only as a result of the persistent complaints of Iraq regarding the allegedly unjust impact of post-Gulf War sanctions on its populace and the perception among many in the international community that UN economic measures against Haiti primarily harmed the impoverished people of the country rather than the Haitian military and its supporters that the legal questions raised by sanctions have become a subject of sustained international concern.

A. Southern Rhodesia, 1965 - 1979

The Security Council first acted under Chapter VII to define and enforce a mandatory programme of economic sanctions in 1968 in response to the crisis in Southern Rhodesia. The genesis of the Security Council's actions lay in the illegal unilateral declaration of Rhodesian independence (UDI) from the United Kingdom made by the white minority government of Prime Minister Ian Smith on 11 November 1965. Acting on behalf of the British Commonwealth, the United Kingdom immediately imposed a series of economic sanctions against Southern Rhodesia to pressure the Smith Government into renouncing the UDI and guaranteeing political participation by the disenfranchised black African majority. By early 1966, the UK sanctions included a complete ban on imports from and exports to Southern Rhodesia as well as a series of drastic financial measures ranging from the removal of Rhodesia from the sterling area and a prohibition on capital exports to Rhodesia to the freezing of Rhodesian assets in the United Kingdom. Other nations, including France and the United States, also implemented selective sanctions programmes, and the OAU declared a total economic boycott. In November 1965 the Security Council also acted, passing Resolution 217, which recommended that all states 'break off all economic relations' with Southern Rhodesia.

When the sanctions failed to achieve the quick reversal of the UDI that had been hoped for, the Security Council turned to a programme of mandatory sanctions under Chapter VII. In December 1966, the Security Council decided that Member States should implement selective mandatory sanctions against the Smith Government, including a prohibition on exports to Rhodesia of petroleum, armaments, vehicles and aircraft, and a ban on imports of Rhodesian agricultural products and minerals. These selective sanctions also failed to bring about an end to the Rhodesian 'rebellion' or to persuade the Smith regime to terminate its racist policies.

Accordingly, in May 1968 the Security Council passed Resolution 253, which imposed a ban on all exports to and imports from Rhodesia, prohibited the transfer of funds to Rhodesia for investment, denounced the purported Rhodesian passport, and severed air links with the country. A limited humanitarian exception existed for exports to Rhodesia of foodstuffs and medical, educational and informational materials. Because this resolution was expressly passed under Chapter VII, it was binding on all Member States. Resolution 253 also established a special Sanctions Committee of the Security Council to monitor compliance of Member States with the mandatory sanctions.

The compulsory UN sanctions regime endured for eleven years, expanding to prohibit, *inter alia*, transportation to or from Southern Rhodesia; insuring exports to and imports from the territory; licensing trade names, trademarks and franchises there; and transferring Southern Rhodesian funds to or from, or using such funds in, Member States. By the time the Security Council terminated the economic sanctions in late 1979, after the signing of the British-mediated Lancaster House agreement that provided for a constitutional transition to African-majority rule and an independent Zimbabwe, the programme of mandatory economic sanctions was, at least on paper, quite comprehensive.

In framing this sanctions regime, UN bodies did periodically discuss the effects that sanctions might have or were having on the Rhodesian economy. Prior to the passing of Resolution 253, for example, the UN Secretary-General commissioned a report on the effects on Southern Rhodesia of an embargo on petroleum products. In debates in the Security Council leading up to the enactment of comprehensive economic sanctions by Resolution 253, the representatives of many countries noted the ambiguous effects on the Rhodesian economy of the selective sanctions mandated by Resolution 232. The only formal measure that the Security Council expressly took to ascertain the impact of the sanctions on

Rhodesia, however, was extending the mandate of the Sanctions Committee to study ways to increase the sanctions' effectiveness. As a minor part of its activities, the Sanctions Committee did analyze the Rhodesian economy in recommending measures to expand the sanctions. Yet despite the comprehensive nature of the sanctions, for the thirteen years in which they were in force against Southern Rhodesia, there was virtually no formal consideration within the United Nations of the extent to which these sanctions were having a disproportionately injurious impact on the Rhodesian populace and economy.

Three features of the sanctions programme account for this omission. First, the United Nations was primarily concerned with sanctions evasion by both Member States *and* non-members, which was widespread throughout the life of the sanctions. Western multinationals continued to engage furtively in commerce with Southern Rhodesia, many African regimes closed their eyes to trade links between their nationals and Rhodesia, and the US Congress disregarded the mandatory Security Council resolutions by enacting the Byrd Amendment in 1971, which permitted the import of chrome, a strategic mineral, from Southern Rhodesia. Portugal, which still ruled Southern Rhodesia's eastern neighbour, Mozambique, and South Africa, the regional power directly to Rhodesia's south, condemned and openly flouted the UN sanctions regime: for the first decade of the sanctions' operation, the governments of both nations sympathized with Smith's white minority regime and actively sought to help Southern Rhodesia mitigate the effects of the sanctions.

Thus, it was the issue of non-compliance with the sanctions regime which virtually monopolized the Security Council's consideration of Southern Rhodesia. This was the near-exclusive concern of the thirteen reports filed by the special sanctions committee of the Security Council established by Resolution 253. Moreover, rather than considering the moral issues raised by the impact of the sanctions on the target populace, the General Assembly repeatedly called on the Security Council to widen the scope of the sanctions to include all measures permissible under Charter Article 41, condemned Member States (particularly the United States) for failing to comply with Security Council resolutions imposing sanctions, and demanded that the Security Council extend the sanctions to Portugal and South Africa. This crisis in sanctions enforcement left little space for considering whether the sanctions were disproportionate.

The second reason that neither the United Nations nor its Member States considered the effects of the sanctions programme on the Rhodesian populace was the manifestly limited impact that the sanctions were having on Southern Rhodesia's economy. In short, at least for the first decade or so of their imposition, the sanctions were ineffective. Anticipating such a response to UDI, the Smith government had taken preparatory measures, such as encouraging the formation of long-term contracts, in order to minimize the impact of the sanctions. Furthermore, after sanctions were imposed, Southern Rhodesia did a remarkable job at thwarting them by internalizing its economy, successfully promoting rapid import-substitution and economic diversification, and minimizing harm to the white settlers who constituted its political base. Indeed, morale remained high in the white community as it rallied around the common purpose of defying the UN. Although traditional export sectors, such as tobacco and mining, were initially hard hit, and other sectors, including petroleum imports, never fully adjusted to economic isolation, after the first year of sanctions the Rhodesian economy - much to the exasperation of the international community - resumed its rapid growth. Not until the mid-1970s did the economic distortions caused by the sanctions, factored, at this point, by the withdrawal of Portuguese and South African support, the external shock of the 1973 OPEC oil embargo, and intensifying guerrilla warfare, truly begin to bite. In such a situation of ambiguous effects, questions about a disproportionate or discriminatory impact of the sanctions on the population of the target state and its economic bases of support simply did not arise.

A third possible reason for the world community's obliviousness to the plight of the bulk of the African population caused by the sanctions may have been a self-serving stereotypical view of a 'Third World' dual economy. In this stereotype, all the Europeans in Rhodesia were exclusively engaged in the modern sector and were most likely to be affected by international sanctions, while Africans were exclusively engaged in the traditional sector, which was not incorporated into the global economy and, hence, not susceptible to injury by the sanctions. This, however, was not a realistic appraisal of the Rhodesian economy.

The Security Council and other UN bodies had ample opportunity to consider such questions. For example, evidence indicated that the sanctions disproportionately harmed Rhodesia's black population, which was particularly concentrated in the sanctions-sensitive sector of tobacco cultivation. Moreover, the Security Council did authorize relief measures for Zambia, Rhodesia's neighbour to the north, to alleviate the considerable economic harm and dislocation that this nation suffered as result of the sanctions. The predominant attitude towards the Africans' plight, however, was symbolized by the chairman of Zimbabwe's African National Council, who declared in a statement before the Security Council that sanctions should not be weakened solely because they were hurting Africans; pain was a price for freedom, and the white minority was suffering as well. The ease with which these self-authorized affirmations and waivers of others' human rights were accepted by a United Nations ostensibly bent on protecting human rights manifested a troubling disregard for the welfare of 'non-combatants'. The presumed consent of African Rhodesians to the hardships engendered by the sanctions was, thus, a fourth feature that contributed to the failure of the United Nations systematically to address questions of proportionality. In brief, the persistent problem of sanctions evasion and the extraordinary ability Rhodesia demonstrated to minimize the impact of the sanctions did not create the conditions for considering the legal implications of the disproportionate impact of an economic sanctions programme on the population of a target state. The Sanctions Committee set up by the Security Council to monitor the sanctions regime addressed itself exclusively to technical problems of enforcement and effectiveness.

B. Iraq: 1991 – Present [1998]

The United Nations adopted its most comprehensive programme of mandatory sanctions under Chapter VII against Iraq in response to that country's invasion of Kuwait on 1 August 1990. On 6 August, the Security Council adopted Resolution 661, which forbade all imports from and exports to Iraq, froze the assets of the Iraqi government and nationals abroad, and suspended pre-existing commercial contracts with Iraqis and Iraqi entities. The trade embargo did not apply to 'supplies intended strictly for medical purposes, and, in humanitarian circumstances, foodstuffs', or to the financial transactions necessary to effect such supplies. Resolution 661 also established a Sanctions Committee, whose membership consisted of the members of the Security Council, to monitor implementation of the sanctions. The original intent of the sanctions was to peacefully compel Iraq to withdraw from Kuwait.

The sanctions programme was quickly modified and expanded. In Resolution 666, the Security Council delegated to the Sanctions Committee the task of determining what constituted 'humanitarian circumstances' under Resolution 661. To minimize sanctions evasion, the Council also reiterated that humanitarian shipments of foodstuffs and medical supplies should be provided under the auspices of international humanitarian agencies, not the Iraqi government. The extent of the 'humanitarian circumstances' exemption became a point of concern in the Sanctions Committee, particularly among those states with nationals working as expatriates or guest workers in Iraq and Kuwait.

To enforce the trade embargo, the Security Council authorized Member States to halt Iraq's inward and outward maritime shipping in order to inspect the cargoes of ships suspected of trading with Iraq or Kuwait. The Council also banned air traffic to and from Iraq and required Member States to deny overflight rights to Iraqi aircraft. When the Council judged that the sanctions regime had failed peacefully to dislodge Iraqi forces from Kuwait, it passed Resolution 678, which authorized Member States to 'use all necessary means' to ensure Iraq's withdrawal.

Pursuant to this authorization, Member States whose forces had been deployed in the Persian Gulf region launched air and land operations against the Iraqi armed forces in January and February of 1991, and decisively expelled Iraq's army from Kuwait. As part of the ceasefire that ended the Gulf War, the Security Council decided in Resolution 687 to maintain the programme of sanctions against Iraq. Medical and health supplies were completely exempted from the trade embargo, and proposed shipments of foodstuffs were also exempted so long as they were notified to the Sanctions Committee. The Council also authorized the Sanctions Committee to approve 'materials and supplies for essential civilian needs' under an accelerated no-objection procedure. The trade and financial embargo would terminate when Iraq complied with the provisions of Resolution 687 requiring it to destroy its weapons of mass destruction and to permit international monitoring to ensure that it did not resume its nuclear, chemical and biological weapons programmes. Because Iraq refused fully to comply with Resolution 687, particularly its provisions regarding the destruction of weapons of mass destruction, the Chapter VII sanctions regime remained in effect without significant modification from August 1990 to December 1996.

The continued maintenance of mandatory UN sanctions against Baghdad has been controversial, in part due to the harm that the sanctions have inflicted on the Iraqi people. The Security Council and the Sanctions Committee have been aware of the injuries suffered by Iraqis and have sought to minimize the impact of the sanctions on innocent Iraqi civilians by creating a liberal regime of humanitarian exceptions to the sanctions programme. Indeed, in 1994 the Sanctions Committee received $6 billion in requests for humanitarian shipments to Iraq, leading the Committee's former deputy secretary to charge that 'the magnitudes eventually came to resemble normal commercial deliveries of no particular humanitarian merit'. In 1991, the Security Council approved arrangements whereby Iraq could export oil to earn funds to purchase food and other humanitarian goods. However, Iraq initially refused to participate in the oil-for-food scheme, claiming that the arrangement would violate Iraqi sovereignty.

The sanctions have caused a significant deterioration in the economic and social welfare of the Iraqi populace. The Iraqi economy virtually collapsed. Prior to the embargo, oil accounted for 95 per cent of Iraq's foreign exchange earnings, and medical and other advanced services were largely operated by (since-departed) foreign expatriates. The dinar deteriorated from $ .60 to the dollar in 1990 to 1,200 dinars to the dollar in April 1995. By mid-1994, inflation since 1990 had reached 6,000 per cent. In 1993, industry was operating at only 10 to 15 per cent of capacity, and industrial unemployment was estimated to exceed 70 per cent. The sanctions-induced economic collapse hit the poor particularly hard: the prices of staples such as bread, infant formula and flour have increased by several thousand per cent, and the World Food Programme estimated that the cost of the average basket of goods had increased 50 times by 1993. The middle and professional classes have also seen their incomes dramatically erode and have been reduced to selling durable goods and family heirlooms to survive. By 1993, living standards had been reduced by one-third, and the situation has since worsened considerably. The deterioration of the economy has led to skyrocketing levels of crime, particularly in urban areas.

Iraq's economic collapse has precipitated a crisis in health, nutrition and education. An oft-cited 1992 study published in *The New England Journal of Medicine* reported that the Gulf War, civil strife and UN economic sanctions caused a threefold increase in infant mortality in Iraq between January and August 1991. International organizations warned in 1993 that only 50 per cent of water purification and sewage treatment plants were functioning; UNICEF, for example, found in January 1993 that only twenty-five of Basra's 135 waste-water pumps worked. In November 1993, Food and Agriculture Organization (FAO) nutritionists reported 'pre-famine' conditions characterized by 'very high food prices, collapse of private incomes, depletion of personal assets and rapidly increasing numbers of the destitute'. The food ration that had previously provided most of the daily calorie intake of most Iraqis was cut by up to half by the government in October 1994. In December 1994, UNICEF issued a report estimating that 3.5 million Iraqi civilians were at a significant health risk of malnutrition and death due to the sanctions, including 1.58 million children under the age of fifteen and 230,000 pregnant or nursing women. A 1995 World Health Organization report noted shortages of medicine, medical supplies, foodstuffs, and water purification and sanitation parts and equipment. At one point, Iraq had less than one-tenth of the medicines needed, and minor surgeries were performed without anesthesia. The UN reported in May 1995 that 23 per cent of children under the age of five suffered from malnutrition and that water treatment systems had fallen apart, leading to water-borne diseases such as malaria and tuberculosis. Alarms about the crisis in the health of the Iraqi people have also been sounded by British medical groups, a German medical study group and the Red Cross. Furthermore, the UN estimates that one in five students has dropped out of school because of shortages in educational materials and financial hardship.

While many have excoriated the Security Council for maintaining economic sanctions in the face of the economic, health and educational crisis endured by innocent Iraqi civilians, others have charged that Iraqi policy has aggravated the harmful impact of the sanctions on the populace and that Iraq has overstated the effects of the sanctions to garner support for their lifting. In October 1991, Saddam Hussein's regime pulled all government workers and services out of Kurdish Iraq in the north, forcing the United Nations to provide humanitarian aid. The Iraqi government pursued the same policies towards the Shiite provinces in the south, which had rebelled after the termination of the Gulf War. Most of the nation's transportation and energy infrastructure has been rebuilt, particularly around Baghdad, and a 1993 US Congressional investigation found that Iraq had rebuilt most of its conventional weapons arsenal. The government also initiated a massive self-sufficiency campaign in agriculture that was successful for the first few years of the sanctions; even in December 1996, when the oil-for-food deal was implemented, there was food on the shelves - poor Iraqis just lack the resources to buy much of it. Poor management of the Iraqi economy over the past four years, which resulted from Saddam Hussein's decision to become personally involved in economic policy, has aggravated the deteriorating humanitarian situation provoked by the sanctions. Saddam Hussein has also insulated his family, the military command, and his supporters in the ruling Ba'ath party from the impact of the sanctions. The Iraqi regime's deliberate policy of using the sanctions for domestic political purposes has resulted in a situation in which, in the words of a Catholic Relief Services official, '[t]he rich and the strong survive, the poor and the weak starve'.

Pressure that had been building for the Security Council to modify or terminate economic sanctions against Iraq initially diminished following revelations in the fall of 1995 that Iraq had consistently deceived international monitors about the extent of its programme to develop weapons of mass destruction. Some of that pressure, at least in the Security Council, arose more from the desire of European countries to do business with Iraq than from concern over the impact of the sanctions on innocent Iraqi civilians. Nevertheless, many developing countries continued to urge the Security Council to repeal or lighten the sanctions, and the humanitarian situation for the majority of Iraqis steadily worsened. Accordingly, in 1995 the Security Council passed a resolution that would permit Iraq to export $1 billion in oil every three months to generate the funds to import food and medicine. In January 1996, the UN and Iraq began a series of negotiations to finalize the oil-for-food agreement, with areas of disagreement centering on, *inter alia*, monitoring Iraqi imports and the 'equitable distribution' of food and medicines to the Kurds in the north and the Shiites in the south. Indeed, the mere announcement of negotiations in January 1996 caused food prices in Iraq to fall from 30 to 50 per cent overnight and the Iraqi dinar to stabilize.

The oil-for-food arrangement was not finalized, however, until early December 1996, after six months of negotiations between the Iraqi government, the Security Council and the Secretary-General. The final plan permitted Iraq to sell $2 billion worth of oil over six months to raise funds to buy food, medicines and other humanitarian goods. Funds earned from the oil sales were to be placed in an escrow account in New York administered by the United Nations. About $260 million was to be reserved for the Kurdish population of northern Iraq, and $600,000 placed in a special fund established to compensate victims of the Iraqi 1990 invasion. The UN Special Commission charged with monitoring Iraq's destruction of its weapons of mass destruction was to receive $20 million to cover operating expenses, with the remainder of the money to be distributed in Iraq. The Security Council could renew the oil-for-food plan after six months if Iraq complied with conditions; finding no major violations, the Council extended the plan for a second six-month term in June 1997. Diplomats were confident that Iraq could not easily evade the restrictions: in the words of the US Deputy Representative to the United Nations, 'We designed a resolution for a cheater.... We know [Saddam Hussein] well.' Since its implementation, the oil-for-food scheme has been criticized for chronic administrative delays.

The plight of innocent Iraqi civilians raises one of the thorniest legal dilemmas of any comprehensive, effective sanctions programme: the proper response of the UN to the government of a target state that deliberately adopts policies which aggravate the sanctions' impact on the most vulnerable, who are then exploited in public relations as a way of eroding the legitimacy of the sanctions programme. As one international aid worker characterized the dilemma, 'If [Saddam Hussein's] last weapon is the sacrifice of millions of Iraqis to the horrors of starvation and disease until the Western alliance is shocked into saying, 'Enough!' and relaxing sanctions, then Mr. Hussein will not hesitate to reach for this weapon.'

C. Libya, 1992 – Present [1998]

In the spring of 1992 the UN Security Council imposed mandatory sanctions against the Qadhafi regime in Libya. The primary rationale for the sanctions was Libya's failure to extradite to the United Kingdom or the United States two Libyan nationals allegedly responsible for the bombing of Pan Am Flight 103 over Lockerbie, Scotland, in 1988.

The Security Council had previously passed a non-binding resolution urging the Libyan government, in effect, to extradite the two individuals. Libya promptly filed suit in the International Court of Justice (ICJ) against the United States and the United Kingdom, invoking its rights under the Montreal Convention not to extradite the accused Libyans. After oral argument in the provisional measures phase of the case, the Security Council, acting under Chapter VII, passed Resolution 748, which imposed sanctions on Libya. The ICJ refused to disturb the UN sanctions regime and denied the provisional measures requested by Libya, holding, by virtue of Charter Articles 25 and 103, that the Security Council's decision pursuant to Chapter VII trumped Libya's rights under the Montreal Convention.

Resolution 748 banned air travel to and from Libya; prohibited supplying, servicing and insuring Libyan aircraft; imposed an embargo on arms shipments and military training and assistance to Libya; and directed all states to prevent the operation of Libyan Arab Airlines offices. The Council established a Sanctions Committee to monitor implementation of the sanctions, report on violations, consider special economic problems that implementing the sanctions might cause for any state, and approve special flights to or from Libya on grounds of significant humanitarian need. The sanctions programme went into effect on 15 April 1992, and the Council was to review the sanctions measures every 120 days (or sooner if necessary) in light of the compliance by the Libyan government with the requests that Libya extradite the two accused Libyan nationals and that it cease supporting terrorism.

Despite regular reviews of the sanctions measures, the Security Council elected not to modify the sanctions. Indeed, mounting frustration with Libya's perceived non-cooperation led the Council in November 1993 to pass a resolution significantly tightening the sanctions regime. The new Resolution 883, also enacted under Chapter VII, directed all states to freeze the assets of the government or public authorities of Libya and of any Libyan undertaking, and to ensure that none of the frozen assets be made available to any of those Libyan entities. The resolution forbade the sale, supply or maintenance of specified equipment used in oil refining and the petrochemicals production process. Finally, the Council tightened the measures relating to servicing and supplying Libyan aircraft and to Libyan Arab Airlines. But in a significant concession to Western European states, many of which are heavily dependent on Libyan oil and have major oil-related investments in Libya, the resolution did not freeze assets derived from the sale or supply of Libyan petroleum, natural gas and agricultural products after 1 December 1993. The sanctions took effect on that date.

The Security Council insisted that it had considered the possible effects of the sanctions on the Libyan people in designing and imposing the initial sanctions regime of Resolution 748 in March 1992. Representatives from Iraq and Zimbabwe, for example, called the Council's attention to the impact that sanctions would have on innocent civilians. In response, the US Ambassador to the UN argued that '[t]he means chosen in this resolution are appropriate; these sanctions are measured, precise and limited. ... They are tailored to fit the offence - Libya's wanton and criminal destruction of civilian aviation - and are designed to penalize the Government of Libya, not its neighbors or any other State.' The UK and French representatives similarly argued that the sanctions, which were targeted to aviation and diplomatic privileges, fitted the crime, with the French Ambassador stating that the sanctions were 'not aimed at the Libyan people, who are not responsible for the acts of their leaders'.

Similar exchanges occurred when the Security Council expanded the sanctions in November 1993. The Libyan representative reported that the air embargo had had deleterious effects on the populace because of the government's inability to arrange medical evacuations. Egypt warned that intensifying the sanctions would increase the harm to the Libyan people and called on the Council to monitor the humanitarian situation. In response, US Ambassador Albright flatly asserted that the sanctions were 'balanced and precisely targeted'.

Since the tightening of the sanctions in December 1993, however, the Security Council has not investigated, or even formally considered, the possibility that the sanctions might be having a disproportionate or discriminatory impact on the Libyan populace. Indeed, there has been sentiment in the Council, particularly on the part of the United States, for widening the sanctions to prohibit the sale of Libyan oil abroad as well as foreign investment in oil-related projects in Libya. Such a move, opposed by Western European states dependent on Libyan oil, would have a devastating effect generally on the Libyan economy. The Sanctions Committee established by Resolution 748 has issued only one report on its activities; that report did not address the issue of the effects of the sanctions on the Libyan people. Of the Council's permanent members, only China has questioned the sanctions on the humanitarian grounds that they aggravate the suffering of the Libyan people, without, however, supplying confirming data. In fact, the impact of the sanctions on the Libyan people has been relatively mild, at least until recently. The prolonged internal debates in the Security Council prior to the adoption of Resolution 883, which tightened the sanctions programme, permitted Libya to anticipate and minimize the impact of the sanctions by concealing its overseas assets. Furthermore, financial maneuvering by Libya and half-hearted enforcement of the sanctions by some Middle Eastern and Western European governments have led to widespread sanctions evasion.

Despite the difficulties in gathering data on the Libyan economy, it appears that the sanctions have recently become more effective. The oil-refining, petrochemicals and tourism sectors have experienced sanctions-induced setbacks. In 1994, it was reported that Libyan factories were running at about 50 per cent of capacity due to a shortage of raw materials. Inflation in mid-1995 was estimated at around 300 per cent. The value of dinar-denominated salaries has plummeted, while the prices of imports and unsubsidized agricultural products (such as fruits) have risen dramatically. The economy experienced a 7 per cent contraction in 1993 and 1994, and unemployment, which has been growing, hovers at about 30 per cent. High and rising unemployment led Libya to seek permission from the Security Council to expel over a million African and Palestinian immigrant workers in the fall of 1995. Col. Qadhafi has also put down at least one coup attempt since the sanctions were imposed.

Libya has aggressively sought to portray the sanctions as having a devastating impact on its people, particularly in the area of health. In August 1994, the Qadhafi government submitted a report to the Security Council that detailed the allegedly 'extremely harmful' effects of the sanctions on the Libyan health care system and on the agricultural, stock-raising, transportation, communications, industrial, financial and commercial sectors of the economy.

The Libyan initiative was not without effect. Support for UN sanctions against Libya among developing and Arab states, which had initially implemented the measures, has weakened. In 1994, the League of Arab States and the Non-Aligned Movement expressed 'concern' over the negative impact that the sanctions were having on the Libyan populace. The OAU, '[g]reatly concerned about the human and material damage that the Libyan Arab people and those of the neighbouring States are suffering as a result of the unjust sanctions imposed on Libya,' has called on the Security Council to lift the sanctions. Some outside observers, however, regard the primary impact of the sanctions as 'psychological' - It is generally recognized that irritating though the current sanctions might be, they come nowhere near exerting sufficient economic pressure on the Libyan regime to make it think seriously about complying with the UN demands.'

D. Yugoslavia (now Serbia and Montenegro), 1992-1995

The Security Council imposed mandatory sanctions against the Federal Republic of Yugoslavia (Serbia and Montenegro) (FRY) in 1992 as part of an international effort to contain and end the violent strife associated with the disintegration of the former Socialist Federal Republic of Yugoslavia. War in the Balkans broke out in the summer of 1991 between the Serb-dominated federal government and army and the republics of Slovenia and Croatia after the latter declared their independence from the federal state. In an effort to contain the conflict, the Security Council on 25 September 1991, imposed a Chapter VII arms embargo on the former Yugoslavia, and in December of 1991 the Council created a special committee of the Council to monitor its implementation.

The arms embargo failed to bring an end to the Balkan conflict. Moreover, many in the international community concluded that primary responsibility for prolonging the war rested with the FRY, led by Serbia, and the Bosnian Serbs. Accordingly, on 30 May 1992, the Security Council, acting under Chapter VII, passed Resolution 757, which imposed an expansive, mandatory trade embargo against the FRY. Resolution 757 prohibited exports to and imports from the FRY; banned foreign financial assistance to enterprises in the FRY; cut off the FRY's air links to the rest of the world; and severed scientific, technical and cultural cooperation and sporting exchanges with the FRY. Foodstuffs and medical supplies were exempted from the trade embargo. The Security Council also expanded the mandate of the special committee, established by Resolution 713, to monitor the arms embargo, to overseeing the implementation of the economic sanctions. Two weeks later, another Security Council resolution permitted the sanctions committee to approve, via its accelerated, no-objection procedure, requests to export to the FRY any non-food, non-medical 'commodities and products for essential humanitarian needs'.

Over the next three-and-a-half years, the UN modulated the economic sanctions programme against the FRY in repeated attempts to compel the government of Serbian President Slobodan Milosevic to bring about an end to the war in neighbouring Bosnia and Herzegovina. When the economic sanctions and arms embargo proved porous, the Security Council sought to prevent shipments of strategic goods, such as fuel and industrial inputs, through the FRY. At the same time, NATO and Western European Union forces began to monitor the FRY's borders and ply the Adriatic Sea to minimize sanctions evasion. In April 1993, the Security Council tightened the sanctions by freezing the FRY's financial assets and overseas property and by extending the economic sanctions regime against the FRY to areas of Bosnia and Herzegovina controlled by the Bosnian Serbs. Sanctions against Bosnian Serb territory were eventually widened to include a ban on all 'commercial, financial, and industrial activities and transactions 'with Bosnian Serb persons and entities and a freeze of Bosnian Serb assets held abroad.

In deciding whether to remove sanctions against the FRY, the UN pursued a carrot-and-stick approach that focused on influencing the behaviour of President Milosevic, with scant concern for the possible disproportionate or discriminatory impact that the sanctions might have had on the FRY populace. In September 1994, the Council partially suspended the sanctions programme pending certification that the FRY had closed its border with Serb-controlled Bosnia and Herzegovina and had ceased to provide military and financial support to the Bosnian Serbs. International passenger air traffic with Serbia and Montenegro, passenger ferry service to Bari, Italy, and FRY participation in international sporting and cultural exchanges were permitted - measures which benefited primarily the people of the FRY, not their rulers. Similar partial suspensions of the sanctions programme occurred in 1995 to reward the Milosevic regime for continuing to deny support to the Bosnian Serbs. Only when FRY President Milosevic agreed to the Dayton Peace Accords on 21 November 1995, did the Security Council completely lift the economic sanctions against the FRY and provide for the gradual lifting of the arms embargo against all republics of the former Yugoslavia. Moreover, continued relief from the sanctions depends on Serbia and Montenegro's fulfillment of the Dayton Agreement; sanctions can be reimposed without a Security Council vote if there is evidence that the FRY is violating the peace accords.

The empirical evidence indicates that UN sanctions contributed to a significant decline in the Serbian economy, but socialist mismanagement of the economy and the dislocations produced by the war were also important factors in the FRY's economic collapse. When UN sanctions were first imposed, it appeared that the FRY might be able to withstand them. The Belgrade government had stockpiled goods and fuel; the Serbian economy had a relatively low dependence on foreign trade; domestic oil production was constant and geared towards industry, rather than (dramatically reduced) consumer demand; and analysts believed that the FRY could be agriculturally self-sufficient for some time.

In fact, however, the Serbian economy quickly began to deteriorate. By early 1994, industrial production was estimated to be at about 20 to 30 per cent of its pre-war capacity. Shortages of petroleum for industrial use and of heating oil for homes threatened the country's economy and health. Food self-sufficiency was jeopardized when farmers began to hoard their harvests instead of selling them to the government for nearly worthless Yugoslav dinars. Analysts estimate that the Serbian economy shrank anywhere from 35 to 65 per cent between 1989 and 1995.

With the economic collapse came massive unemployment, which reached levels of 60 to 70 per cent. Aggravating the effects of such high levels of unemployment on family income was a hyperinflation that rivalled that of Germany after World War I; the Belgrade government had taken to printing money to subsidize the economy and household consumption, and annual inflation in January 1994 reached the incredible level of 313 million per cent before being halted. At the same time, real wages were declining: a Red Cross study found that real household income had fallen to one-tenth of its 1990 level by 1994. The same study showed that 2.2 million of the FRY's 10.5 million people lived in poverty, and half a million of those individuals lived in extreme poverty. Competing for scarce domestic and international resources were 850,000 refugees from other parts of the former Yugoslavia. Such dire circumstances provoked the emigration of professionals and the middle class - those most likely to oppose the Milosevic policies that had led to UN sanctions.

The sanctions also took a toll on the health of the populace. The government in Belgrade and international health officials claimed that the FRY had exhausted its foreign currency reserves and was thus unable to buy medical supplies, medical equipment and pharmaceuticals, which had been exempted from the trade embargo. Raw materials for manufacturing drugs domestically, however, were not exempted. FRY doctors who headed three Belgrade hospitals warned that UN sanctions had caused a sharp rise in suicides and heart attacks in Serbia and Montenegro. Mental health services also deteriorated; international observers reported a tripling of mortality in mental institutions in less than one year, and mental health budgets were cut drastically.

Accordingly, preventive health care suffered; the government claimed that it declined by 50 per cent between mid-1992 and late 1993. A report issued by the Milosevic government also claimed that because the sanctions regime prohibited the import of chemicals used to purify water, the incidence of preventable contagious diseases rose substantially: in the first six months of 1993, 108 people died of contagious diseases, a figure that was 5.4 times higher than the same period in 1992. The Red Cross found that a decrease in vaccinations also contributed to the increase in disease. FRY officials noted, both during and after the sanctions programme, that malnutrition and infant mortality had increased significantly, assertions confirmed by the Red Cross. This situation was aggravated by growing food shortages, which led the FRY to begin rationing food in September 1994 for the first time since 1948.

However, throughout the life of the sanctions, despite the economic downturn and declining health situation, stores in the FRY were filled with goods, restaurants remained open, and gas was freely available on the black market. Indeed, it was estimated that 40 per cent of all economic activity occurred in the black market, a phenomenon that the Belgrade government encouraged in order to meet the large needs left unfulfilled by its relatively unsuccessful reassumption of socialist-like control of the economy. On the other hand, profits from black marketeering went primarily to the criminal gangs that controlled it.

Four factors must be taken into account in evaluating the legality of UN sanctions against the FRY. First, it is difficult to measure how much of Serbia and Montenegro's post-1991 economic crisis is attributable to the sanctions and how much to other factors, such as economic mismanagement. Second, it is not clear that the Yugoslav people suffered disproportionately from the sanctions: while some claim that the average family struggled just to meet its basic needs, others argue that the sanctions did not unduly burden the populace and that they brought about long-needed changes in the FRY's previously state-dominated and inefficient economy. Third, at least some evidence supports the conclusion that the Serbian and Montenegran people were not innocent victims of UN sanctions; in December 1992, voters in the FRY chose Slobodan Milosevic, and his vision of a Greater Serbia, over Milan Panic, who had 'promised a change of policies that could have led to a lifting of the sanctions'. The question that must be faced in such a situation of apparent consent by citizens in the target state to the governmental policies that brought on international economic sanctions is what role such consent should play in assessing the legality of the impact of sanctions on innocent parties, such as children. Finally, the sanctions did appear to have influenced policy-makers in the FRY: Western diplomats attribute Milosevic's willingness to cease supporting the Bosnian Serbs and to negotiate the Dayton Peace Agreement in part to the effects that sanctions had on his country.

E. Haiti, 1993–1994

The UN Security Council imposed economic sanctions under Chapter VII most recently against Haiti. On 30 September 1991, the Haitian military, under the command of General Raoul Cedras and supported by the country's small and wealthy elite, overthrew the left-wing populist government of President Jean-Bertrand Aristide. The Haitian electorate had voted for Aristide by a large majority in December 1990 in an election that international monitors, including the UN and the OAS, had judged to be free and fair. Following the coup, President Aristide went into exile in the United States.

While both the UN General Assembly and the OAS condemned the coup, the locus of the first phase of sanctions against Haiti was the OAS. Within ten days of the coup, the Ministers of Foreign Affairs of OAS Member States had passed two resolutions recommending diplomatic, economic and financial sanctions against the Haitian government, requesting the suspension of non-humanitarian aid, and urging OAS Member States to freeze the assets of the Haitian government and to impose a trade embargo on all but humanitarian goods. By mid-1992, the OAS was calling upon Member States to reinforce the embargo, to freeze the private assets of the Haitian military and those who supported the coup, and to deny port access to ships trading with Haiti. Consistent with the OAS resolutions, the Bush Administration froze Haitian government assets in the United States and imposed an embargo on imports from and exports to Haiti.

Implementation of the OAS sanctions programme by OAS Member States was haphazard. Sanctions evasion was particularly egregious along Haiti's porous eastern border with the Dominican Republic. The Haitian military and its supporters further minimized the impact of the sanctions by continuing to trade with countries from other regions, such as Western Europe, that were not subject to the OAS regime. In sum, the sanctions failed to dislodge the Haitian military, which had begun a savage campaign of repression to eliminate domestic supporters of President Aristide.

When the ineffectiveness of the OAS sanctions became manifest, the focus of activities shifted to the UN Security Council. In June 1993, acting under Chapter VII of the Charter, it passed Resolution 841, which imposed an embargo on the sale and supply of oil and arms to Haiti, froze the funds of the Haitian government and its officials, and established a Sanctions Committee to monitor compliance with the sanctions regime as well as to approve requests, on a no-objection basis, to ship petroleum to Haiti 'for essential humanitarian needs'. The sanctions were suspended when UN and US negotiators brokered an agreement between General Cedras and Haiti's government-in-exile at Governors Island, New York in July 1994 for the gradual return of President Aristide to power by 30 October 1993. The Security Council reimposed the sanctions when the Haitian military violated the Governors Island Agreement by refusing to allow US military personnel to land in Haiti in mid-October as part of a UN mission.

In view of the failure of renewed efforts to mediate an end to military rule, the ongoing human rights violations and the deteriorating economic situation in Haiti, the Security Council in May 1994 passed Resolution 917. This resolution required UN Member States to deny landing and overfly permission to all but regularly scheduled commercial passenger flights flying to or from Haiti; to deny entry into their territories of members of the Haitian military, its agents, and Haitian government officials; to ban imports to or exports from Haiti; and to observe a trade embargo with the nation. The resolution also strongly urged, but did not require, Member States to freeze the funds of members of the Haitian military, its agents, and Haitian government officials. The Sanctions Committee that had been established by Resolution 841 was authorized to use the no-objection procedure to grant individual exemptions to the ban on the export to Haiti of food and fuel for humanitarian purposes.

With international frustration mounting at the failure of the sanctions to dislodge the Haitian military or to persuade it to agree to a negotiated solution, the Security Council approved Resolution 940, under Chapter VII, in July 1994. This resolution authorized Member States 'to form a multinational force ... to use all necessary means to facilitate the departure from Haiti of the military leadership'. Economic sanctions were to be lifted only upon the return of President Aristide to power. Acting under the authority of this resolution, President Clinton gave the Haitian military an ultimatum: surrender power by 19 September 1994, or face invasion by a multinational force under the leadership of the United States. Following a frenzied weekend of negotiations between General Cedras and President Clinton's special emissaries, former President Jimmy Carter, former Chairman of the Joint Chiefs of Staff Colin Powell, and Senator Sam Nunn, the Haitian military agreed to relinquish power and permit President Aristide to return and resume power. On 19 September 1994, a multinational force led by the United States was deployed in Haiti pursuant to the Cedras-Carter agreement. President Aristide returned to a tumultuous welcome in Haiti on 15 October 1994, and economic sanctions against the country were lifted the next day pursuant to Security Council resolutions.

Because of their devastating effects on the Haitian economy and their impact on the health and social well-being of the mass of impoverished Haitians, the OAS and UN sanctions programmes against Haiti were particularly controversial. Within four months of the imposition of OAS sanctions, Representative Robert Torricelli of New Jersey was urging President Bush to terminate the embargo and intervene militarily to oust the Haitian military regime because the economic situation in Haiti had reached the point where military intervention was 'the most humane solution'. In October 1992, one year after the coup, an interagency committee under the direction of the UN Secretariat's Department of Humanitarian Affairs issued a report detailing the desperate economic and humanitarian situation in Haiti. As a result of the OAS sanctions, tens of thousands of jobs in the industrial and service sectors had been lost and unemployment had risen. Farm income and production had dropped off and deforestation had accelerated due to the embargo on petroleum imports.

The resulting decline in family purchasing power had led to increased levels of malnutrition, particularly among children. Other indicators of social welfare, such as the delivery of health services and education, had also reached a state of crisis. An influential study by the Harvard Center for Population and Development Studies found that the embargo and cessation of foreign aid may have caused up to 1,000 extra child deaths per month.

The impoverished majority of Haitians continued to suffer the brunt of OAS and UN sanctions. Particularly galling to many in the international community was the ease with which Haiti's economic elite and military avoided their impact; indeed, many military officers amassed huge fortunes by controlling the black market in food and fuel spawned by the sanctions.

The international community, and in particular the United Nations, was slow to consider formally the disproportionate and discriminatory impact of the sanctions on Haiti's poor and negligent in tailoring sanctions so as to maximize their impact on the Haitian military and its supporters. In addition to reports from humanitarian agencies in Haiti and accounts in the popular press, UN decision-makers were apprised through official channels of the disproportionate effects of the sanctions on Haiti's poor. In November 1992, the Secretary-General bluntly informed the General Assembly that Haiti's economy was 'in a state of free fall' and detailed the effects of the OAS sanctions regime on different sectors of the Haitian economy and on the social welfare of the impoverished masses. The Secretary-General repeated these characterizations to the Security Council after it imposed mandatory UN sanctions in 1993, noting, for example, that Haiti was 'economically paralysed' and that [t]he Haitian economy is on the verge of collapse. Since last month, the national currency has lost 40 per cent of its value. There is galloping inflation, and shortages are becoming more severe. The prices of staple food products have more than doubled. According to international economists, almost four fifths of the population are unemployed. Despite the early evidence that the sanctions were crippling Haiti's poor, the world community was generally slow to react. In February 1992, the Bush Administration lifted US implementation of the OAS embargo on a case-by-case basis for US-owned maquiladora plants in Haiti. The State Department characterized this measure as 'fine-tuning' and 'retarget[ing]' the sanctions so as not to 'hurt innocent people' - in this case, the 40,000 Haitians who had been employed in the US-owned maquiladoras prior to the coup. Critics charged that the measure was ill-conceived and that the Bush Administration had merely caved in to pressure from corporate lobbyists.

There was no mention of the possibly disproportionate or discriminatory impact of economic sanctions on the poor in the Security Council meeting in which UN sanctions were first imposed. The Council, however, did gradually refine the sanctions regime in the face of the public outcry over the ravages the sanctions inflicted on the Haitian economy. During the interregnum in the summer and fall of 1993 during which the sanctions were suspended pending implementation of the Governors Island accord, the Council repeatedly issued Presidential Statements warning the Haitian military that non-compliance with the agreement would result in the reinstatement of sanctions 'appropriate to the situation, with particular emphasis on those measures aimed at those deemed responsible for the non-compliance with the Agreement'. When the Haitian military disregarded the Governors Island Agreement and the Security Council reimposed the sanctions regime set up under Resolution 841, the Council's president stated that it was 'deeply concerned by the suffering of the Haitian people'. The Council attributed responsibility for that suffering 'directly' to 'the refusal of the military authorities to comply with the Governors Island Process'. Two weeks later in another Presidential Statement, however, the Council did express 'its determination to minimize the impact of the present situation on the most vulnerable groups and call[ed] upon Member States to continue, and to intensify, their humanitarian assistance to the people of Haiti'.

Such expressions of concern for the plight of the Haitian people surfaced with more frequency in centres of power in the United Nations over the following few months. For example, when the 'Friends of the Secretary-General on Haiti'- France, Canada, Venezuela and the United States - called for 'new comprehensive trade sanctions' against Haiti in February 1994, they were careful to note that the sanctions should be 'aimed at the military authorities in Haiti and their supporters'. Nevertheless, not until May 1994 did the Security Council specifically target its sanctions at the wrongdoers, when the Council required that Member States deny entry visas to the Haitian military and its supporters. In the same resolution, however, the Council merely 'strongly urge[d],' rather than required, Member States to freeze the financial resources of those persons. Furthermore, the sanctions imposed by Resolution 917 supplemented UN sanctions already in place; none of the previous sanctions that had placed such an onerous burden on the destitute Haitian economy were lifted or adjusted.

Statements by representatives of Member States in the Security Council in the meeting in which Resolution 917 was approved show the Council's awareness of the desperate situation of the Haitian people. The representatives of Canada, Venezuela, Argentina, Spain, the United States, France and Brazil all expressly referred to the suffering that sanctions had inflicted on Haiti's poor. US Ambassador to the UN Madeline Albright acknowledged that sanctions are 'a blunt instrument'. Many Security Council members attempted to shift blame for the economic and human crisis to the Haitian military: in the words of Canada's representative, '[i]t is the failure of the military authorities to fulfil their commitments which is solely responsible for the plight of the Haitian population'. Other Security Council members, in what can charitably be regarded as an expression of pious hope rather than a hard-headed assessment of the probable real-world effects of policy, echoed France's declaration that

> [t]he Council has seen to it that that objective [of returning Aristide to power] will not be achieved at the cost of the infliction of intolerable suffering on the Haitian people, which has suffered too much already. The Council intends to censure a minority, including through the use of measures that are exceptional in that they are aimed at individuals. In so doing, the Council has also made sure that the poorest people will not be crushed even more.

Although the Brazilian representative expressed some trepidation about the additional suffering that the expanded sanctions might engender in Haiti, only the Chinese representative addressed the Security Council's responsibility to craft proportionate and discriminatory sanctions:

> Ironically, this suffering [of the Haitian people] is at least partially attributable to the sanctions already applied to Haiti by the Security Council and by other bodies. The question is then whether the newly introduced sanctions regime, if applied, could possibly increase the suffering of the ordinary people in Haiti; and we cannot but express concern about this.

While some Council members undertook to continue to review the humanitarian situation in Haiti, the economic plight of the Haitian people caused by the sanctions subsequently received virtually no formal attention from the Security Council and played no explicit role in its decision to authorize a multinational force to remove the Haitian military and restore President Aristide to his post. Two reasons account for the world community's delay in recognizing the disproportionately harmful impact the sanctions were having on the Haitian people and the inadequate tailoring of sanctions to affect primarily the Haitian armed forces and their supporters. First, Jean-Bertrand Aristide, Haiti's elected president, strongly supported wide-ranging economic sanctions against his country from the time of the coup up to the day the multinational force was deployed in Haiti. President Aristide's unwavering support for imposing, maintaining and expanding economic sanctions would have made it politically difficult for the OAS or the Security Council to loosen the sanctions programme, even had it been inclined to do so.

A more important factor in the poorly-designed sanctions regime was Haiti's strategic insignificance to the great powers on the Security Council. On the one hand, the human rights violations committed by the Haitian military and the desperate economic plight of the Haitian people aroused international and popular outrage. The Haitian coup also bucked the post-Cold War trend toward democratization in the Western Hemisphere, a matter of particular concern to the OAS. On the other hand, no state - and, in particular, not the United States - had a strategic interest in intervening militarily in Haiti. Caught on the horns of this dilemma, the international community took the path of least resistance: It demonstrated its moral outrage by imposing 'tough' sanctions, but took the politically safe course of not intervening militarily, despite the manifest mistargeting of the impact of the sanctions. Indeed, President Clinton's September 1994 ultimatum to the Cedras regime to relinquish power or face UN-authorized military intervention was arguably motivated more by the Clinton Administration's need to shore up its sagging international credibility than concern for the suffering that the indiscriminately applied sanctions had inflicted on the Haitian people.

F. Mandatory UN Arms Embargoes and Other Measures

A less comprehensive instrument applied by the United Nations to influence the behaviour of elites in target states is the mandatory arms embargo. Since 1992, the Security Council, acting pursuant to Chapter VII of the Charter, has imposed mandatory embargoes on supplying weapons and military assistance to Somalia, Liberia, Angola and Rwanda. In these situations, the Security Council has acted in response to ongoing civil strife that has led to internal anarchy and humanitarian crises of international dimensions.

In Somalia, the Security Council imposed an arms embargo in January 1992 in an effort to limit intense factional fighting among the country's clans and to prevent the collapse of civil authority. In November 1992, the Council decreed an arms embargo with respect to Liberia, where the 1989 rebellion of forces led by Charles Taylor and the 1990 assassination of President Samuel Doe plummeted the country into an anarchy from which it has yet to fully emerge. The refusal of Jonas Savimbi's National Union for the Total Independence of Angola (UNITA) to recognize the legitimacy of the results of UN-supervised elections in 1992 and to lay down its arms led the Security Council to impose an embargo on the supply of arms and petroleum to UNITA on 15 September 1993. Finally, the Security Council imposed an arms embargo against Rwanda in May 1994, when the country descended into genocidal carnage after the Rwandan President's plane was shot down over Burundi.

A universal arms embargo is a useful tool that the international community can make use of when it is foreseeable that mandatory economic sanctions will either be ineffective or will unjustly impact the innocent. For example, imposing economic sanctions against Somalia would have served only to deepen the existing humanitarian crisis by harming the starving civilians who were caught in the crossfire of the degradations of contending warlords. Liberia, Somalia and Rwanda have effectively been without national governments for much of the periods during which these countries have been subject to UN arms embargoes. Thus, it would have been difficult in these cases to identify a target elite whose behaviour could have been influenced by the application of sanctions - and the brunt of sanctions would likely have been felt most of all by the already-pressed civilian populace rather than by the fighters responsible for the violence. Finally, an arms embargo against a particular faction in a country can be an appropriate policy tool in some situations. The arms and petroleum embargo against UNITA in Angola, for example, is easier for the Security Council to apply than a programme of economic sanctions, and it avoids the danger that the Angolan government might use an international sanctions regime in a less than humanitarian fashion to advance its domestic political agenda. Furthermore, in Angola UNITA is the primary wrongdoer, and the civilian population already suffers tremendously from the effects of war alone.

Nevertheless, there are situations in which mandatory economic sanctions are preferable to, or should be a complement of, an arms embargo. For example, an arms embargo against Libya in response to the latter's involvement in the bombing of civilian aircraft would not have been adequately tailored to the illegal acts involved. Alternatively, as was the case with Iraq, countering an aggressor's threat to international peace and security can at times require not only cutting off a state's access to armaments, but also undermining its ability to make war by using economic sanctions to weaken its economy.

There are also situations when the imprecise application of an arms embargo can unjustifiably endanger a state to which the embargo applies. Thus, many have argued that the UN's maintenance of the arms embargo against all the republics of the former Yugoslavia prolonged the Balkan wars by indirectly giving an international imprimatur to Serbia and Montenegro's military advantages over the state of Bosnia and Herzegovina. Thus, even arms embargoes must be measured against the criteria of proportionality and discrimination.

The Council has also recently enacted Chapter VII measures that fall short of an arms embargo or a comprehensive programme of economic sanctions. In 1995, the Sudanese government gave refuge to terrorists who had attempted to assassinate Egyptian President Hosni Mubarak in Addis Ababa. In response, the Council passed a series of resolutions designed to increase pressure on Sudan to extradite the terrorists to Ethiopia for trial. After unsuccessfully calling on Sudan to extradite the accused individuals, the Council acted under Chapter VII first by mandating diplomatic sanctions against Sudan and then by requiring states to deny aircraft substantially owned or controlled by the Sudanese government permission to take off from, land in or overfly their territories. Such measures represent, in appropriate circumstances, viable alternatives to arms embargoes and economic sanctions programmes.

2. Erica Cosgrove, *The Sanctions Dilemma and the Case of Iraq: Human Rights and Humanitarian Challenges to the Use of Multilateral Economic Sanctions*

9 Windsor Rev. of Legal and Soc. Issues 65 (1999)

Since the primary stated objective of the initial sanctions against Iraq — forcing it to withdraw from Kuwait — was achieved through the use of military force in 1991, the continuation of sanctions has fostered discord in the international community. The increasing number of exemptions to the Iraq sanctions has resulted in a progressive weakening of the sanctions regime in order to ease the suffering of civilians. This process has contributed to two negative perceptions: that sanctions are not effective, and that they are inherently inhumane, as it is continually necessary to soften their blow.

In light of these developments, several fundamental questions are raised:

1. Can the UN deploy economic sanctions that will bring about compliance with its decisions and enforce the norms of the international community?

2. If so, can it impose sanctions that address humanitarian concerns?

3. Will the UN have the political will to employ economic sanctions that incorporate humanitarian concerns?

First, regarding the efficacy of sanctions, their record of success is mixed. In 1995, the UN special commission (UNSCOM) overseeing Iraqi disarmament reported that most of its requirements had been fulfilled after four years of sanctions, and commended Iraq for its cooperation. Yet many problems persist. UNSCOM's pronouncements regarding Iraqi compliance were shown to have been premature after Hussein Kamel, a senior Iraqi defence official, defected and revealed the extent of Iraq's secret weapons programs. Iraq has not yet fully cooperated with UN demands and continues to withhold vital information and deny access to certain sites from weapons inspectors. The current impasse with regard to weapons inspections — Iraq having refused to cooperate with UNSCOM since August 1998, and the Security Council having ceased its regular reviews of the sanctions against Iraq — does not bode well for an end to sanctions or Iraqi intransigence in the near future. The result is that the Security Council continues to disagree as to precisely what conditions Iraq must meet in order for sanctions to be eased, while Iraq insists that it has met the conditions, and demands that the sanctions be lifted. It remains to be seen whether the ongoing application of sanctions will ultimately realize the Security Council's aims. As noted throughout this paper, however, the consensus to continue enforcing sanctions against Iraq has been weakened, and it cannot be assumed that sanctions will be maintained indefinitely.

Many arguments have been put forth suggesting that sanctions are inherently unjust and violate humanitarian norms. For sanctions to be useful, a balance must be found that addresses humanitarian concerns without so weakening sanctions as to render them useless. Although the international community has gradually tried to "redesign mechanisms for humanitarian provision to make them effective", the profound suffering which persists in Iraq is proof of failure in this regard. The following are some steps that could be taken to address these concerns:

1. From the outset, sanctions and exemptions should conform to requirements of general international law, and the law of war in particular, as well as to general expectations regarding basic needs of a population. Peter Walker, the director of disaster and refugee policy at the IFRC, suggests that sanctions should not be allowed free rein, but like warfare, should operate within prescribed limits.

2. The UN must also interpret exemptions in the most generous way possible and actively seek to fulfill the spirit of the exemptions. It is not enough to include a humanitarian exemption in UN resolutions, and then proceed to limit or negate these exemptions through other actions. Christiansen and Powers, as well as others, have criticized humanitarian exemptions for being too narrowly defined. They recommend that exemptions should be defined broadly enough that there can be no threat to human health or life. I propose a modified version of their formula, providing for exemptions to ensure that sanctions pose a *minimal* "threat to human health or life". With this modification, the formula might be acceptable to those who argue that any exemptions weaken sanctions to the point that they

are rendered useless, and might help to ensure that sanctions could be effective and just.

3. Sanctions should be crafted and applied so as to minimize their effect on civilians and maximize their effect on the rogue governments that are the true targets.

4. These changes to the way sanctions are implemented would open the way for allowing sanctions time to work. Sanctions cannot be expected to work as a swift punishment. Rather, they should be regarded as an attempt to bring about changes to the policy or ideology of their target regimes, which are neither lightly held nor likely to be abandoned quickly

There is a danger that the measures recommended above will limit the effectiveness of sanctions, but the Iraq case strongly suggests that it is also dangerous to enforce economic measures that inflict profound suffering on civilians. As Christiansen and Powers note, "broader exemptions than those permitted under existing sanctions regimes could make the enforcement of sanctions regimes more difficult, and might diminish the effectiveness of sanctions, but due care for civilian populations seems to require that these added difficulties be accepted if adequate provision is to be made for civilians." This is particularly true for countries like Iraq, where leaders show a callous disregard for the well-being of the population.

The international community achieved an unprecedented level of consensus regarding its response to Iraq's invasion of Kuwait in 1990, yet significant challenges to this consensus and to the sanctions against Iraq have emerged over time. The steps taken by the UN to address these concerns — from the initial humanitarian exemptions to the oil-for-food plan — have been inadequate. The situation in Iraq appears to have contributed to a diminished willingness in the international community to impose sanctions in other situations and has called into question the efficacy and morality of sanctions generally. Effective steps must be taken to better address humanitarian concerns and to incorporate these concerns into the structure of future sanctions regimes. Unless this occurs, it is unlikely that sanctions will receive sufficient support to allow them to achieve their goals. For all the difficulties associated with their use, sanctions are a powerful element in the international community's repertory of potential responses to violations of international law. Their loss would be serious. Without the option of imposing sanctions, the international community seems likely to revert to a pattern experienced too often throughout the Cold War: either to resort to armed force in the face of grave transgressions, or to do nothing. Neither option is attractive.

3. General Comment 8 of the Committee on Economic, Social and Cultural Rights on the Effect of Economic Sanctions on Civilian Populations

UN.Doc. E/C.12/1997/8 (Dec. 12, 1997)

4. In considering sanctions, it is essential to distinguish between the basic objective of applying political and economic pressure upon the governing élite of the country to persuade them to conform to international law, and the collateral infliction of suffering upon the most vulnerable groups within the targeted country. For that reason, the sanctions regimes established by the Security Council now include humanitarian exemptions designed to permit the flow of essential goods and services destined for humanitarian purposes. It is commonly assumed that these exemptions ensure basic respect for economic, social and cultural rights within the targeted country. …

7. The Committee considers that the provisions of the Covenant, virtually all of which are also reflected in a range of other human rights treaties as well as the Universal Declaration of Human Rights, cannot be considered to be inoperative, or in any way inapplicable, solely because a decision has been taken that considerations of international peace and security warrant the imposition of sanctions. Just as the international community insists that any targeted State must respect the civil and political rights of its citizens, so too must that State and the international community itself do everything possible to protect at least the core content of the economic, social and cultural rights of the affected peoples of the State. …

16. In adopting this general comment the sole aim of the Committee is to draw attention to the fact that the inhabitants of a given country do not forfeit their basic economic, social and cultural rights by virtue of any determination that their leaders have violated norms relating to international peace and security. The is not to give support or encouragement to such leaders, nor is it to undermine the legitimate interests of the international community in enforcing respect for the provisions of the Charter of the United Nations and the general principle of international law. Rather, it is to insist that lawlessness of one kind should not be met by lawlessness of another kind which pays no heed to the fundamental rights that underlie and give legitimacy to any such collective action.

NOTES AND QUESTIONS

1. How do you view the use of inclusive economic sanctions as a strategy for achieving a world public order of human dignity? When and under what circumstances are unilateral uses of economic sanctions more effective than a multilateral imposition of economic sanctions as a means of bringing about a desired outcome? *See*, in general, Sarah H. Cleveland, *Norm Internalization and U.S. Economic Sanctions*, 26 YALE J. INT'L L. 1 (2001).

2. Why are economic sanctions a strategy preferred over the use of the military instrument in most industrialized economies, notwithstanding the severity of the "collateral damage" experienced in the targeting nations? Former U.S. Attorney General Ramsey Clark argued that sanctions in Iraq constituted weapons of mass destruction. What arguments can be made for and against the proposition that sanctions, as an economic instrument, are inherently unjust and violate humanitar-

ian norms? For a critical perspective, see Adeno Addis, *Economic Sanctions and the Problem of Evil,* 25 Hum. Rts. Q. 573 (2003); and August Reinisch, *Developing Human Rights and Humanitarian Law Accountability of the Security Council for the Imposition of Economic Sanctions*, 95 Am. J. Int'l L. 851 (2001).

3. The materials above were written prior to the 2003 war with Iraq, the renewal of nuclear tensions with North Korea, and the U.N. intervention in Liberia. If the world community had been fully apprised of the effect of economic sanctions in these and other areas, would that knowledge have affected the multilateral and/or unilateral decisions made in these cases? If so, in what way?

4. What similarities and differences are there between the imposition of economic sanctions against Haiti and the present economic sanctions against Cuba? How can a reassessment of the decision to impose economic sanctions under principles of necessity and proportionality alter the use of economic sanctions as a diplomatic tool in these cases?

5. In 1997 the WTO Dispute Resolution Settlement Body ruled that the EU's preferential treatment towards ACP Bananas was a violation of the quantity restriction and the Most Favored Nation Clause of GATT, a decision upheld by the WTO Appellate Body. The EU was given fifteen months, until January 1, 1999, to implement this ruling; however, the EU did not comply. The United Stated retaliated by imposing sanctions on some EU goods. Is this an appropriate use of the economic instrument? *See* Bozena Ziedalski, *The World Trade Organization and the Transatlantic Banana Split,* 5 New England Int'l & Comp. L. Annual (1999), *available at* http://www.nesl.edu/intljournal/vol5/zield.htm.

6. Are Free Trade Areas inherently a form of economic sanctioning against those who are outside the area? Aren't measures such as those embraced by the LOME Convention in favor of former colonies a legitimate form of positive discrimination or affirmative action? *See* Hale Sheppard, *The LOME Convention in the Next Millennium: Modification of the Trade/Aid Package and Support for Regional Integration*, 7 Kan. J.L.& Pub. Pol'y 84 (1998).

4. Cuba: Embargo on All Trade

22 U.S.C. § 2370 (1979)

(a) (1) No assistance shall be furnished under this chapter to the present government of Cuba; nor shall any such assistance be furnished to any country which furnishes assistance to the present government of Cuba unless the President determines that such assistance is in the national interest of the United States. As an additional means of implementing and carrying into effect the policy of the preceding sentence, the President is authorized to establish and maintain a total embargo upon all trade between the United States and Cuba.

(2) Except as may be deemed necessary by the President in the interest of the United States, no assistance shall be furnished under this chapter to any government of Cuba, nor shall Cuba be entitled to receive any quota authorizing the importation of Cuban sugar into the United States or to receive any other benefit under any law of the United States, until the President determines that such government has taken appropriate steps according to international law standards to return to United States citizens, and to entities not less than 50 per centum beneficially owned by United States citizens, or to provide equitable compensation to such citizens and entities for property taken from such citizens and entities on or after January 1, 1959, by the Government of Cuba.

(3) No funds authorized to be made available under this chapter (except under section 2174 of this title) shall be used to furnish assistance to any country which has failed to take appropriate steps, not later than 60 days after December 16, 1963-

(A) to prevent ships or aircraft under its registry from transporting to Cuba (other than to United States installations in Cuba)-

(i) any items of economic assistance,

(ii) any items which are, for the purposes of title I of the Mutual Defense Assistance Control Act of 1951, as amended, arms, ammunition and implements of war, atomic energy materials, petroleum, transportation materials of strategic value, or items of primary strategic significance used in the production of arms, ammunition, and implements of war, or

(iii) any other equipment, materials, or commodities, so long as Cuba is governed by the Castro regime; and

(B) to prevent ships or aircraft under its registry from transporting any equipment, materials, or commodities from Cuba (other than from United States installations in Cuba) so long as Cuba is governed by the Castro regime.

(b) No assistance shall be furnished under this chapter to the government of any country unless the President determines that such country is not dominated or controlled by the international Communist movement.

5. Cuban Liberty and Democratic Solidarity (LIBERTAD) Act of 1996

22 U.S.C. §§ 6021-6091(1996) (hereinafter Helms-Burton Act)

§ 6022. The purposes of this Act are—

(1) to assist the Cuban people in regaining their freedom and prosperity, as well as in joining the community of democratic countries that are flourishing in the Western Hemisphere;

(2) to strengthen international sanctions against the Castro government;

(3) to provide for the continued national security of the United States in the face of continuing threats from the Castro government of terrorism, theft of property from United States nationals by the Castro government, and the political manipulation by the Castro government of the desire of Cubans to escape that results in mass migration to the United States;

(4) to encourage the holding of free and fair democratic elections in Cuba, conducted under the supervision of internationally recognized observers;

(5) to provide a policy framework for United States support to the Cuban people in response to the formation of a transition government or a democratically elected government in Cuba; and

(6) to protect United States nationals against confiscatory takings and the wrongful trafficking in property confiscated by the Castro regime. …

§ 6032. (a) Policy

(1) Restrictions by other countries

The Congress hereby reaffirms section 1704(a) of the Cuban Democracy Act of 1992, which states that the President should encourage foreign countries to restrict trade and credit relations with Cuba in a manner consistent with the purposes of that Act.

(2) Sanctions on other countries

The Congress further urges the President to take immediate steps to apply the sanctions described in section 1704(b)(1) of that Act against countries assisting Cuba. …

(b) Diplomatic efforts

The Secretary of State should ensure that United States diplomatic personnel abroad understand and, in their contacts with foreign officials, are communicating the reasons for the United States economic embargo of Cuba, and are urging foreign governments to cooperate more effectively with the embargo.

(c) Existing regulations

The President shall instruct the Secretary of the Treasury and the Attorney General to enforce fully the Cuban Assets Control Regulations set forth in part 515 of title 31, Code of Federal Regulations. …

(h) Codification of economic embargo

The economic embargo of Cuba, as in effect on March 1, 1996, including all restrictions under part 515 of title 31, Code of Federal Regulations, shall be in effect on March 12, 1996, and shall remain in effect, subject to section 6064 of this title. …

§ 6081. The Congress makes the following findings:

(1) Individuals enjoy a fundamental right to own and enjoy property which is enshrined in the United States Constitution.

(2) The wrongful confiscation or taking of property belonging to United States nationals by the Cuban Government, and the subsequent exploitation of this property at the expense of the rightful owner, undermines the comity of nations, the free flow of commerce, and economic development.

(3) Since Fidel Castro seized power in Cuba in 1959—

(A) he has trampled on the fundamental rights of the Cuban people; and

(B) through his personal despotism, he has confiscated the property of—

(i) millions of his own citizens;

(ii) thousands of United States nationals; and

(iii) thousands more Cubans who claimed asylum in the United States as refugees because of persecution and later became naturalized citizens of the United States.

(4) It is in the interest of the Cuban people that the Cuban Government respect equally the property rights of Cuban nationals and nationals of other countries.

(5) The Cuban Government is offering foreign investors the opportunity to purchase an equity interest in, manage, or enter into joint ventures using property and assets some of which were confiscated from United States nationals.

(6) This "trafficking" in confiscated property provides badly needed financial benefit, including hard currency, oil, and productive investment and expertise, to the current Cuban Government and thus undermines the foreign policy of the United States—

(A) to bring democratic institutions to Cuba through the pressure of a general economic embargo at a time when the Castro regime has proven to be vulnerable to international economic pressure; and

(B) to protect the claims of United States nationals who had property wrongfully confiscated by the Cuban Government.

(7) The United States Department of State has notified other governments that the transfer to third parties of properties confiscated by the Cuban Government "would complicate any attempt to return them to their original owners".

(8) The international judicial system, as currently structured, lacks fully effective remedies for the wrongful confiscation of property and for unjust enrichment from the use of wrongfully confiscated property by governments and private entities at the expense of the rightful owners of the property.

(9) International law recognizes that a nation has the ability to provide for rules of law with respect to conduct outside its territory that has or is intended to have substantial effect within its territory.

(10) The United States Government has an obligation to its citizens to provide protection against wrongful confiscations by foreign nations and their citizens, including the provision of private remedies.

(11) To defer trafficking in wrongfully confiscated property, United States nationals who were the victims of these confiscations should be endowed with a judicial remedy in the courts of the United States that would deny traffickers any profits from economically exploiting Castro's wrongful seizures.

§ 6082. (a) Civil remedy

(1) Liability for trafficking

(A) Except as otherwise provided in this section, any person that, after the end of the 3-month period beginning on the effective date of this subchapter, traffics in property which was confiscated by the Cuban Government on or after January 1, 1959, shall be liable to any United States national who owns the claim to such property for money damages in an amount equal to the sum of—

(i) the amount which is the greater of—

(I) the amount, if any, certified to the claimant by the Foreign Claims Settlement Commission under the International Claims Settlement Act of 1949 [22 U.S.C.A. § 1621 et seq.], plus interest;

(II) the amount determined under section 6083(a)(2) of this title, plus interest; or

(III) the fair market value of that property, calculated as being either the current value of the property, or the value of the property when confiscated plus interest, whichever is greater; and

(ii) court costs and reasonable attorneys' fees.

(B) Interest under subparagraph (A)(i) shall be at the rate set forth in section 1961 of Title 28, computed by the court from the date of confiscation of the property involved to the date on which the action is brought under this subsection. …

§ 6085. … (c) Other authorities

(1) Suspension

After this subchapter and the amendments of this subchapter have taken effect—

(A) no person shall acquire a property interest in any potential or pending action under this subchapter; and

(B) the President may suspend the right to bring an action under this subchapter with respect to confiscated property for a period of not more than 6 months if the President determines and reports in writing to the appropriate congressional committees at least 15 days before the suspension takes effect that such suspension is necessary to the national interests of the United States and will expedite a transition to democracy in Cuba.

(2) Additional suspensions

The President may suspend the right to bring an action under this subchapter for additional periods of not more than 6 months each, each of which shall begin on the day after the last day of the period during which a suspension is in effect under this subsection, if the President determines and reports in writing to the appropriate congressional committees at least 15 days before the date on which the additional suspension is to begin that the suspension is necessary to the national interests of the United States and will expedite a transition to democracy in Cuba. …

§ 6091. (a) Grounds for exclusion

The Secretary of State shall deny a visa to, and the Attorney General shall exclude from the United States, any alien who the Secretary of State determines is a person who, after March 12, 1996—

(1) has confiscated, or has directed or overseen the confiscation of, property a claim to which is owned by a United States national, or converts or has converted for personal gain confiscated property, a claim to which is owned by a United States national;

(2) traffics in confiscated property, a claim to which is owned by a United States national;

(3) is a corporate officer, principal, or shareholder with a controlling interest of an entity which has been involved in the confiscation of property or trafficking in confiscated property, a claim to which is owned by a United States national; or

(4) is a spouse, minor child, or agent of a person excludable under paragraph (1), (2), or (3).

* * *

Upon the Castro government's spring 2003 crackdown on dissidents as well as execution of hijackers trying to flee the island, the European Union also imposed a measure of economic sanctions on Cuba:

6. Declaration by the Presidency, on behalf of the European Union, on Cuba

Brussels, June 5, 2003, 9961/03 (Presse 157), P 65/03

Following the recent deplorable actions of the Cuban authorities aiming not only at violating fundamental freedoms in Cuba, but also at depriving civilians of the ultimate human right, that of life, the EU regrets that the Cuban authorities broke the de-facto moratorium on the death penalty and wishes to inform the international community that on 5 June it addressed the following demarche to the Cuban authorities:

> The EU, deeply concerned about the continuing flagrant violation of human rights and of fundamental freedoms of members of the Cuban opposition and of independent journalists, being deprived of their freedom for having expressed freely their opinion, calls once again the Cuban authorities to release immediately all political prisoners.
>
> While expecting a favourable response from the Cuban authorities, the EU, mindful of increasing reports about poor detention conditions of prisoners with serious health problems, appeals to the Cuban authorities

that, in the meantime, the prisoners do not suffer unduly and are not exposed to inhumane treatment.

Furthermore and vis-à-vis the current situation in Cuba, the EU has unanimously decided to:

- limit the bilateral high-level governmental visits

- reduce the profile of member states' participation in cultural events

- invite Cuban dissidents at national days celebrations

- proceed to the re-evaluation of the EU common position.

The Acceding Countries Cyprus, the Czech Republic, Estonia, Hungary, Latvia, Lithuania, Malta, Poland, the Slovak Republic and Slovenia, the Associated Countries Bulgaria and Romania and the EFTA countries, members of the European Economic Area align themselves with this declaration.

Notes and Questions

1. Even though the application of one of the more controversial provisions of the Act, *i.e* the right to bring an action relating to confiscated Cuban property, has been suspended by Presidents Clinton and Bush (*see infra*, Part Seven, at 1440), the Helms-Burton Act has generated a fierce debate. As to the statute's legality and desirability, see Brice M. Clagett, *The Controversy over Title III of Helms-Burton: Who Is Breaking International Law—The United States, or the States that Have Made Themselves Co-Conspirators with Cuba in Its Unlawful Confiscations*, 30 Geo. Wash. J. Int'l L. & Econ. 271 (1996-97); Brice M. Clagett, *Agora: The Cuban Liberty and Democratic Solidarity (LIBERTAD) Act, Continued, A Reply to Professor Lowenfeld,* 90 Am. J. Int'l L. 641 (1996) (hereinafter Agora); Lucien J. Dhooge, *Fiddling with Fidel: An Analysis of the Cuban Liberty and Democratic Solidarity Act of 1996*, 14 Ariz. J. Int'l & Comp. L. 575 (1997); William S. Dodge, *The Helms-Burton Act and Transnational Legal Process*, 20 Hastings Int'l & Comp. L. Rev. 713 (1997); David P. Fidler, *LIBERTAD v. Liberalism: An Analysis of the Helms-Burton Act from Within Liberal International Relations Theory*, 4 Ind. J. Global Legal Stud. 297 (1997); Andreas F. Lowenfeld, *Congress & Cuba: The Helms-Burton Act*, 90 Am. J. Int'l L. 419 (1996); Ralph G. Steinhardt, *Helms-Burton and the Virtues of a Good Course in Pathology*, 30 Geo. Wash. J. Int'l L. & Econ. 201 (1996-97); Jeannette M.E. Tramhel, *Helms-Burton Invites a Closer Look at Counter-Measures*, 30 Geo. Wash. J. Int'l L. & Econ. 317 (1996-97); John Yoo, *Federal Courts as Weapons of Foreign Policy: The Case of the Helms-Burton Act,* 20 Hastings Int'l & Comp. L. Rev. 747 (1997); W. Fletcher Fairey, Comment, *The Helms-Burton Act: The Effect of International Law on Domestic Implementation,* 46 Am. U. L. Rev. 1289 (1997); Christian Franken, Note, *The Helms-Burton Act: Force or Folly of the World's Leader?*, 7 Minn. J. Global Trade 157 (1998); Jonathan R. Ratchik, Note, *Cuban Liberty and Democratic Solidarity Act of 1995*, 11 Am. U. J. Int'l L. & Pol'y 343 (1996); Anthony M. Solis, Comment, *The Long Arm of U.S. Law: The Helms-Burton Act*, 19 Loy. L.A. Int'l & Comp. L.J. 709 (1997); Brian J. Welke, Comment, *GATT & NAFTA v. The Helms-Burton Act: Has the United States Violated Multilateral Agreements?*, 4 Tulsa J. Comp. & Int'l L. 361 (1997); Cassandra LaRae-Perez, *Economic Sanctions as a Use of Force: Re-Evaluating the Legality of Sanctions from an Effects-Based Perspective*, 20 B.U. Int'l L.J. 161 (2002). Digna B. French, *Economic Sanctions Imposed by the United States Against Cuba: The Thirty Nine Year Embargo Culminating With the Cuban Liberty and Democratic Solidarity Act (LIBERTAD) Act of 1996*, 7 U. Miami Int'l Comp. L. Rev. 1 (1999). C. Todd Piczak, *The Helms-Burton Act: U.S. Foreign Policy Toward Cuba, the National Security Exception to the GATT and the Political Question Doctrine*, 61 U. Pitt. L. Rev. 287 (1999).

2. What is your assessment of the effectiveness and continued desirability of the Cuban embargo?

C. Regulation of Economic Indulgence

One of the two basic methods of securing compliance with one's wishes is the proffering or granting of rewards. Rewards that are offered to secure the defection of someone from an authoritative duty are called bribes. Since so much of international politics takes place in a context of competing authority systems, opportunities for bribing are rife. Consider the following.

1. W. Michael Reisman, Folded Lies
63-64 (Free Press 1979)

Bribery ... is a routine strategy. Though it is apparently prohibited in customary and conventional international law, there is substantial reason to assume that it is one of the most frequent of covert operations undertaken by the intelligence agencies of nation-states. For there is nothing quite like having someone in the adversary's government secretly working for you. Miles Copeland, a candid, international Machiavellian, counsels, "Buy the man, not his information, it's the regularity and dependability of the pay that matters, not the amount."

Bribery as a means for securing national objectives is used in high theater as well as offstage. In the United Nations, bribery assumes as many guises as it does in the United States Government. In 1976, the New York Times reported that Daniel Moynihan, former United States representative to the United Nations, said "he was aware during his term last fall that votes on critical General Assembly resolutions were bought and sold by diplomats." Major powers were not party to such transactions because they could gain support through the licit bribal techniques of loans or profitable trade agreements. Moynihan "did not find it shocking that countries engaged in bargaining and saw not much difference in whether votes went for cash or wheat. 'All countries sell their votes in one way or the other,' he commented. 'I don't find it surprising or shocking what countries do to maximize their interests.' "

The vicious competitive character of the war system is not restricted to the political arena. Because all the institutional processes of the nation-state are components of its power, security may require supervision or even control over them "in the national interest." One of the results of these factors has been the use of political power abroad to secure national economic and trade advantages. One political gambit in 1976 may thus be considered a peerless macro-bribe. "Secretary Kissinger has apparently promised leaders of copper-producing nations in Africa (Zambia and Zaire) that he would try to halt the slump in metal prices generally." His plan called for the stockpiling of copper. In return, the African nations reportedly offered to assist in Kissinger's peace efforts in southern Africa. In this case either the African countries used their potential political leverage to extort the economic concessions from Kissinger or Kissinger offered copper stockpiling in exchange for the African nations' cooperation. …

Most operators would accept as appropriate, if not necessarily "nice," that officials, overt or covert, of one nation-state might tender bribes to officials of others in the line of duty. Thus Secretary of State Cyrus Vance, when pressed in a public forum to distinguish Korean bribery of United States congressmen from United States bribery of Korean politicians, claimed that he could "draw a clear distinction between a government-to-government operation and one that deals with individuals, such as the Korean situation." Theirs, he said, "was not a government-to-government kind of operation" and that rendered it unlawful. All governmental bribe operations are, of course, not automatically lawful, but most operators would be somewhat un- easy with the assertion that any other social organization operating in the international arena might just as properly use the bribe technique as a way of securing its objectives.

Official attitudes about bribery vary, according to the role or responsibility of the official concerned in the governmental system. For those charged with responsibility for the balance of payments or the balance of power, "extraordinary payments" may be viewed as a necessary evil, if an evil at all; in Intelligence activities and in foreign trade, all sorts of things that may not be done at home can be done abroad if they are property approved. But other officials view bribery as an intolerable evil.

* * *

If such a prescription should not be applied to nation-states, as then-Secretary of State Cyrus Vance implied, should it be applied to corporations in their dealings with foreign countries?

The first General Assembly position on corporate bribery was formulated in Resolution 3514:

2. Measures Against Corrupt Practices of Transnational and Other Corporations, Their Intermediaries and Others Involved

GA Res. 3514, 30 U.N.GAOR, Supp. (No. 34) 69, U.N. Doc. A/10034 (1975)

The General Assembly,

Concerned by the corrupt practices of certain transnational and other corporations, their intermediaries and others involved, …

Recalling also the provisions of section V of the Programme of Action on the Establishment of a New International Economic Order emphasizing, inter alia, the need to formulate, adopt and implement the code of conduct referred to in the report of the Commission on Transnational Corporations on its first session;

Recalling further the provisions of the Charter of Economic Rights and Duties of States, according to which such corporations should not operate in a manner that violates the laws and regulations of the host countries, …

1. *Condemns* all corrupt practices, including bribery, by transnational and other corporations, their intermediaries and others involved, in violation of the laws and regulations of the host countries;

2. *Reaffirms* the right of any State to adopt legislation and to investigate and take appropriate legal action, in accordance with its national laws and regulations, against transnational and other corporations, their intermediaries and others involved, for such corrupt practices;

3. *Calls upon* both home and host Governments to take, within their respective national jurisdictions, all necessary measures which they deem appropriate, including legislative measures, to prevent such corrupt practices, and to take consequent measures against the violators;

4. *Calls upon* Governments to collect information on such corrupt practices, as well as on measures taken against such practices, and to exchange information bilaterally and, as appropriate, multilaterally, particularly through the United Nations Centre on Transnational Corporations;

5. *Calls upon* home Governments to co-operate with Governments of the host countries to prevent such corrupt practices, including bribery, and to prosecute, within their national jurisdictions, those who engage in such acts;

6. *Requests* the Economic and Social Council to direct the Commission on Transnational Corporations to include in its programme of work the question of corrupt practices of transnational corporations and to make recommendations on ways and means whereby such corrupt practices can be effectively prevented;

7. *Requests* the Secretary-General to report to the General Assembly at its thirty-first session, through the Economic and Social Council, on the implementation of the present resolution.

* * *

See also U.N. Declaration Against Corruption and Bribery in International Commercial Transactions, U.N. GAOR, 51st Sess., Agenda Item 12, U.N. Doc. A/RES/51/191 (1997).

Given the widespread practice of bribery - of both the national and international sort - how effective will Resolution 3514 be? In setting a norm? In curtailing corruption? Consider these questions as you read the following materials.

The U.S. response has been a statutory enactment.

3. Foreign Corrupt Practices Act

15 U.S.C. § 78dd-2 (Supp. 1980)

(a) Prohibited practices

It shall be unlawful for any domestic concern, other than an issuer which is subject to section 78dd-I of this title, or any officer, director, employee, or agent of such domestic concern or any stockholder thereof acting on behalf of such quently, in the aftermath of the armed conflict of 1948, the 1949 General Armistice Agreement between Jordan and Israel provided in Article VIII for the establishment of a special committee for "the formulation of agreed plans and arrangements for such matters as either Party may submit to it" for the purpose of enlarging the scope of the Agreement and of effecting improvement in its application. Such matters, on which an agreement of principle had already been concluded, included "free access to the Holy Places". This commitment concerned mainly the Holy Places located to the east of the Green Line. However, some Holy Places were located west of that Line. This was the case of the Room of the Last Supper and the Tomb of David, on Mount Zion. In signing the General Armistice Agreement, Israel thus undertook, as did Jordan, to guarantee freedom of access to the Holy Places. The Court considers that this undertaking by Israel has remained valid for the Holy Places which came under its control in 1967. This undertaking has further been confirmed by Article 9, paragraph 1, of the 1994 Peace Treaty between Israel and Jordan, by virtue of which, in more general terms, "Each party will provide freedom of access to places of religious and historical significance."

130. As regards the International Covenant on Economic, Social and Cultural Rights, that instrument includes a number of relevant provisions, namely: the right to work (Articles 6 and 7); protection and assistance accorded to the family and to children and young persons (Article 10); the right to an adequate standard of living, including adequate food, clothing and housing, and the right "to be free from hunger" (Art. 11); the right to health (Art. 12); the right to education (Arts. 13 and 14).

131. Lastly, the United Nations Convention on the Rights of the Child of 20 November 1989 includes similar provisions in Articles 16, 24, 27 and 28.

132. From the information submitted to the Court, particularly the report of the Secretary-General, it appears that the construction of the wall has led to the destruction or requisition of properties under conditions which contravene the requirements of Articles 46 and 52 of the Hague Regulations of 1907 and of Article 53 of the Fourth Geneva Convention.

133. That construction, the establishment of a closed area between the Green Line and the wall itself and the creation of enclaves have moreover imposed substantial restrictions on the freedom of movement of the inhabitants of the Occupied Palestinian Territory (with the exception of Israeli citizens and those assimilated thereto). Such restrictions are most marked in urban areas, such as the Qalqiliya enclave or the City of Jerusalem and its suburbs. They are aggravated by the fact that the access gates are few in number in certain sectors and opening hours appear to be restricted and unpredictably applied. ... There have also been serious repercussions for agricultural production, as is attested by a number of sources. ... In a recent survey conducted by the World Food Programme, it is stated that the situation has aggravated food insecurity in the region, which reportedly numbers 25,000 new beneficiaries of food aid. ... It has

(2) Any officer or director of a domestic concern, or stockholder acting on behalf of such domestic concern, who willfully violates subsection (a) of this section shall, upon conviction, be fined not more than $10,000, or imprisoned not more than five years, or both.

(3) Whenever a domestic concern is found to have violated subsection (a) of this section, any employee or agent of such domestic concern who is a United States citizen, national, or resident or is otherwise subject to the jurisdiction of the United States (other than an officer, director, or stock- holder acting on behalf of such domestic concern), and who willfully carried out the act or practice constituting such violation shall, upon conviction, be fined not more than $10,000, or imprisoned not more than five years, or both.

(4) Whenever a fine is imposed under paragraph (2) or (3) of this subsection upon any officer, director, stockholder, employee, or agent of a domestic concern, such fine shall not be paid, directly or indirectly, by such domestic concern.

4. Kirkpatrick Co. v. Environmental Tectronics Corp.
493 U.S. 400 (1990)

Justice SCALIA: In this case we must decide whether the act of state doctrine bars a court in the United States from entertaining a cause of action that does not rest upon the asserted invalidity of an official act of a foreign sovereign, but that does require imputing to foreign officials an unlawful motivation (the obtaining of bribes) in the performance of such an official act.

I.

The facts as alleged in respondent's complaint are as follows: In 1981, Harry Carpenter, who was then chairman of the board and chief executive officer of petitioner W.S. Kirkpatrick & Co., Inc. (Kirkpatrick), learned that the Republic of Nigeria was interested in contracting for the construction and equipment of an aeromedical center at Kaduna Air Force Base in Nigeria. He made arrangements with Benson "Tunde" Akindele, a Nigerian citizen, whereby Akindele would endeavor to secure the contract for Kirkpatrick. It was agreed that, in the event the contract was awarded to Kirkpatrick, Kirkpatrick would pay to two Panamanian entities controlled by Akindele a "commission" equal to 20% of the contract price, which would in turn be given as a bribe to officials of the Nigerian Government. In accordance with this plan, the contract was awarded to petitioner W.S. Kirkpatrick & Co., International (Kirkpatrick International), a wholly owned subsidiary of Kirkpatrick; Kirkpatrick paid the promised "commission" to the appointed Panamanian entities; and those funds were disbursed as bribes. All parties agree that Nigerian law prohibits both the payment and the receipt of bribes in connection with the award of a government contract.

Respondent Environmental Tectonics Corporation, International, an unsuccessful bidder for the Kaduna contract, learned of the 20% "commission" and brought the matter to the attention of the Nigerian Air Force and the United

States Embassy in Lagos. Following an investigation by the Federal Bureau of Investigation, the United States Attorney for the District of New Jersey brought charges against both Kirkpatrick and Carpenter for violations of the Foreign Corrupt Practices Act of 1977, 91 Stat. 1495, as amended, 15 U.S.C. § 78dd-1 *et seq.,* and both pleaded guilty.

Respondent then brought this civil action in the United States District Court for the District of New Jersey against Carpenter, Akindele, petitioners, and others, seeking damages under the Racketeer Influenced and Corrupt Organizations Act, 18 U.S.C. § 1961 *et seq.,* the Robinson-Patman Act, 49 Stat. 1526, 15 U.S.C. § 13 *et seq.,* and the New Jersey Anti-Racketeering Act, N.J.Stat.Ann. § 2C:41-2 *et seq.* (West 1982). The defendants moved to dismiss the complaint under Rule 12(b)(6) of the Federal Rules of Civil Procedure on the ground that the action was barred by the act of state doctrine.

The District Court, having requested and received a letter expressing the views of the legal adviser to the United States Department of State as to the applicability of the act of state doctrine, treated the motion as one for summary judgment under Rule 56 of the Federal Rules of Civil Procedure and granted the motion. 659 F.Supp. 1381 (1987). The District Court concluded that the act of state doctrine applies "if the inquiry presented for judicial determination includes the motivation of a sovereign act which would result in embarrassment to the sovereign or constitute interference in the conduct of foreign policy of the United States." *Id.,* at 1392-1393 (citing *Clayco Petroleum Corp. v. Occidental Petroleum Corp.,* 712 F.2d 404, 407 (CA9 1983)). Applying that principle to the facts at hand, the court held that respondent's suit had to be dismissed because in order to prevail respondent would have to show that "the defendants or certain of them intended to wrongfully influence the decision to award the Nigerian Contract by payment of a bribe, that the Government of Nigeria, its officials or other representatives knew of the offered consideration for awarding the Nigerian Contract to Kirkpatrick, that the bribe was actually received or anticipated and that 'but for' the payment or anticipation of the payment of the bribe, ETC would have been awarded the Nigerian Contract." 659 F.Supp., at 1393 (footnote omitted).

The Court of Appeals for the Third Circuit reversed. 847 F.2d 1052 (1988). Although agreeing with the District Court that "the award of a military procurement contract can be, in certain circumstances, a sufficiently formal expression of a government's public interests to trigger application" of the act of state doctrine, *id.,* at 1058, it found application of the doctrine unwarranted on the facts of this case. The Court of Appeals found particularly persuasive the letter to the District Court from the legal adviser to the Department of State, which had stated that in the opinion of the Department judicial inquiry into the purpose behind the act of a foreign sovereign would not produce the "unique embarrassment, and the particular interference with the conduct of foreign affairs, that may result from the judicial determination that a foreign sovereign's acts are invalid." *Id.,* at 1061. The Court of Appeals acknowledged that "the Department's legal conclusions as to the reach of the act of state doctrine are not controlling on the courts," but concluded that "the Department's factual assessment of whether fulfillment of its responsibilities will be prejudiced by the course of civil litigation is entitled to substantial respect." *Id.,* at 1062. In light of the Department's view that the interests of the Executive Branch would not be harmed by prosecution of the action, the Court of Appeals held that Kirkpatrick had not met its burden of showing that the case should not go forward; accordingly, it reversed the judgment of the District Court and remanded the case for trial. *Id.,* at 1067. We granted certiorari, 492 U.S. 905 (1989).

II.

This Court's description of the jurisprudential foundation for the act of state doctrine has undergone some evolution over the years. We once viewed the doctrine as an expression of international law, resting upon "the highest considerations of international comity and expediency," *Oetjen v. Central Leather Co.,* 246 U.S. 297, 303-304 (1918). We have more recently described it, however, as a consequence of domestic separation of powers, reflecting "the strong sense of the Judicial Branch that its engagement in the task of passing on the validity of foreign acts of state may hinder" the conduct of foreign affairs, *Banco Nacional de Cuba v. Sabbatino,* 376 U.S. 398, 423 (1964). Some Justices have suggested possible exceptions to application of the doctrine, where one or both of the foregoing policies would seemingly not be served: an exception, for example, for acts of state that consist of commercial transactions, since neither modern international comity nor the current position of our Executive Branch accorded sovereign immunity to such acts, see *Alfred Dunhill of London, Inc. v. Republic of Cuba,* 425 U.S. 682, 695-706 (1976) (opinion of WHITE, J.); or an exception for cases in which the Executive Branch has represented that it has no objection to denying validity to the foreign sovereign act, since then the courts would be impeding no foreign policy goals, see *First National City Bank v. Banco Nacional de Cuba,* 406 U.S. 759, 768-770 (1972) (opinion of REHNQUIST, J.).

The parties have argued at length about the applicability of these possible exceptions, and, more generally, about whether the purpose of the act of state doctrine would be furthered by its application in this case. We find it unnecessary, however, to pursue those inquiries, since the factual predicate for application of the act of state doctrine does not exist. Nothing in the present suit requires the Court to declare invalid, and thus ineffective as "a rule of decision for the courts of this country," *Ricaud v. American Metal Co.,* 246 U.S. 304, 310 (1918), the official act of a foreign sovereign.

In every case in which we have held the act of state doctrine applicable, the relief sought or the defense interposed would have required a court in the United States to declare invalid the official act of a foreign sovereign performed within its own territory. In *Underhill v. Hernandez,* 168 U.S. 250, 254 (1897), holding the defendant's detention of the plaintiff to be tortious would have required denying legal effect to "acts of a military commander representing the authority of the revolutionary party as government, which afterwards succeeded and was recognized by the United States." In *Oetjen v. Central Leather Co., supra,* and in *Ricaud v. American Metal Co., supra,* denying title to the party who claimed through purchase from Mexico would have required declaring that government's prior seizure of the property, within its own territory, legally ineffective. See *Oetjen, supra,* 246 U.S., at 304; *Ricaud, supra,* 246 U.S., at 310. In *Sabbatino,* upholding the defendant's claim to the funds would have required a holding that Cuba's expropriation of goods located in Havana was null and void. In the present case, by contrast, neither the claim nor any asserted defense requires a determination that Nigeria's contract with Kirkpatrick International was, or was not, effective.

Petitioners point out, however, that the facts necessary to establish respondent's claim will also establish that the contract was unlawful. Specifically, they note that in order to prevail respondent must prove that petitioner Kirkpatrick made, and Nigerian officials received, payments that violate Nigerian law, which would, they assert, support a finding that the contract is invalid under Nigerian law. Assuming that to be true, it still does not suffice. The act of state doctrine is not some vague doctrine of abstention but a "*principle of decision* binding on federal and state courts alike." *Sabbatino, supra,* 376 U.S., at 427 (emphasis added). As we said in *Ricaud,* "the act within its own boundaries of one sovereign State ... becomes ... a rule of decision for the courts of this country." 246 U.S., at 310. Act of state issues only arise when a court *must decide*—that is, when the outcome of the case turns upon—the effect of official action by a foreign sovereign. When that question is not in the case, neither is the act of state doctrine. That is the situation here. Regardless of what the court's factual findings may suggest as to the legality of the Nigerian contract, its legality is simply not a question to be decided in the present suit, and there is thus no occasion to apply the rule of decision that the act of state doctrine requires. Cf. *Sharon v. Time, Inc.,* 599 F.Supp. 538, 546 (SDNY 1984) ("The issue in this litigation is not whether [the alleged] acts are valid, but whether they occurred").

In support of their position that the act of state doctrine bars any factual findings that may cast doubt upon the validity of foreign sovereign acts, petitioners cite Justice Holmes' opinion for the Court in *American Banana Co. v. United Fruit Co.,* 213 U.S. 347 (1909). That was a suit under the United States antitrust laws, alleging that Costa Rica's seizure of the plaintiff's property had been induced by an unlawful conspiracy. In the course of a lengthy opinion Justice Holmes observed, citing *Underhill,* that "a seizure by a state is not a thing that can be complained of elsewhere in the courts." 213 U.S., at 357-358. The statement is concededly puzzling. *Underhill* does indeed stand for the proposition that a seizure by a state cannot be complained of elsewhere—in the sense of being sought to be declared *ineffective* elsewhere. The plaintiff in *American Banana,* however, like the plaintiff here, was not trying to undo or disregard the governmental action, but only to obtain damages from private parties who had procured it. Arguably, then, the statement did imply that suit would not lie if a foreign state's actions would be, though not invalidated, impugned.

Whatever Justice Holmes may have had in mind, his statement lends inadequate support to petitioners' position here, for two reasons. First, it was a brief aside, entirely unnecessary to the decision. *American Banana* was squarely decided on the ground (later substantially overruled, see *Continental Ore Co. v. Union Carbide & Carbon Corp.*, 370 U.S. 690, 704-705 (1962)) that the antitrust laws had no extraterritorial application, so that "what the defendant did in Panama or Costa Rica is not within the scope of the statute." 213 U.S., at 357. Second, whatever support the dictum might provide for petitioners' position is more than overcome by our later holding in *United States v. Sisal Sales Corp.*, 274 U.S. 268 (1927). There we held that, *American Banana* notwithstanding, the defendant's actions in obtaining Mexico's enactment of "discriminating legislation" could form part of the basis for suit under the United States antitrust laws. 274 U.S., at 276. Simply put, *American Banana* was not an act of state case; and whatever it said by way of dictum that might be relevant to the present case has not survived *Sisal Sales.*

Petitioners insist, however, that the policies underlying our act of state cases—international comity, respect for the sovereignty of foreign nations on their own territory, and the avoidance of embarrassment to the Executive Branch in its conduct of foreign relations—are implicated in the present case because, as the District Court found, a determination that Nigerian officials demanded and accepted a bribe "would impugn or question the nobility of a foreign nation's motivations," and would "result in embarrassment to the sovereign or constitute interference in the conduct of foreign policy of the United States." 659 F.Supp., at 1392-1393. The United States, as *amicus curiae,* favors the same approach to the act of state doctrine, though disagreeing with petitioners as to the outcome it produces in the present case. We should not, the United States urges, "attach dispositive significance to the fact that this suit involves only the 'motivation' for, rather than the 'validity' of, a foreign sovereign act," Brief for United States as *Amicus Curiae* 37, and should eschew "any rigid formula for the resolution of act of state cases generally," *id.,* at 9. In some future case, perhaps, "litigation ... based on alleged corruption in the award of contracts or other commercially oriented activities of foreign governments could sufficiently touch on 'national nerves' that the act of state doctrine or related principles of abstention would appropriately be found to bar the suit," *id.,* at 40 (quoting *Sabbatino,* 376 U.S., at 428), and we should therefore resolve this case on the narrowest possible ground, viz., that the letter from the legal adviser to the District Court gives sufficient indication that, "in the setting of this case," the act of state doctrine poses no bar to adjudication, *ibid.*

Even if we agreed with the Government's fundamental approach, we would question its characterization of the legal adviser's letter as reflecting the absence of any policy objection to the adjudication. The letter, which is reprinted as an appendix to the opinion of the Court of Appeals, see 847 F.2d 1052, 1067-1069 (CA3 1988), did not purport to say whether the State Department would like the suit to proceed, but rather responded (correctly, as we hold today) to the question whether the act of state doctrine was applicable.

These urgings are deceptively similar to what we said in *Sabbatino,* where we observed that sometimes, even though the validity of the act of a foreign sovereign within its own territory is called into question, the policies underlying the act of state doctrine may not justify its application. We suggested that a sort of balancing approach could be applied—the balance shifting against application of the doctrine, for example, if the government that committed the "challenged act of state" is no longer in existence. 376 U.S., at 428. But what is appropriate in order to avoid unquestioning judicial acceptance of the acts of foreign sovereigns is not similarly appropriate for the quite opposite purpose of expanding judicial incapacities where such acts are not directly (or even indirectly) involved. It is one thing to suggest, as we have, that the policies underlying the act of state doctrine should be considered in deciding whether, despite the doctrine's technical availability, it should nonetheless not be invoked; it is something quite different to suggest that those underlying policies are a doctrine unto themselves, justifying expansion of the act of state doctrine (or, as the United States puts it, unspecified "related principles of abstention") into new and uncharted fields.

The short of the matter is this: Courts in the United States have the power, and ordinarily the obligation, to decide cases and controversies properly presented to them. The act of state doctrine does not establish an exception for cases and controversies that may embarrass foreign governments, but merely requires that, in the process of deciding, the acts of foreign sovereigns taken within their own jurisdictions shall be deemed valid. That doctrine has no application to the present case because the validity of no foreign sovereign act is at issue.

The judgment of the Court of Appeals for the Third Circuit is affirmed.

* * *

On 21 November 1997, OECD member countries and five non-member countries, Argentina, Brazil, Bulgaria, Chile and the Slovak Republic, adopted a Convention on Combating Bribery of Foreign Public Officials in International Business Transactions. Signature of the Convention took place in Paris on 17 December 1997.

5. OECD Convention on Combating Bribery of Foreign Public Officials in International Business Transactions

Dec. 17, 1997, 37 I.L.M. 1 (1998)

Article 1 - *The Offence of Bribery of Foreign Public Officials*

1. Each Party shall take such measures as may be necessary to establish that it is a criminal offence under its law for any person intentionally to offer, promise or give any undue pecuniary or other advantage, whether directly or through intermediaries, to a foreign public official, for that official or for a third party, in

order that the official act or refrain from acting in relation to the performance of official duties, in order to obtain or retain business or other improper advantage in the conduct of international business.

2. Each Party shall take any measures necessary to establish that complicity in, including incitement, aiding and abetting, or authorisation of an act of bribery of a foreign public official shall be a criminal offence. Attempt and conspiracy to bribe a foreign public official shall be criminal offences to the same extent as attempt and conspiracy to bribe a public official of that Party.

3. The offences set out in paragraphs 1 and 2 above are hereinafter referred to as "bribery of a foreign public official".

4. For the purpose of this Convention:

a. "foreign public official" means any person holding a legislative, administrative or judicial office of a foreign country, whether appointed or elected; any person exercising a public function for a foreign country, including for a public agency or public enterprise; and any official or agent of a public international organisation;

b. "foreign country" includes all levels and subdivisions of government, from national to local;

c. "act or refrain from acting in relation to the performance of official duties" includes any use of the public official's position, whether or not within the official's authorised competence.

Article 2 - *Responsibility of Legal Persons*

Each Party shall take such measures as may be necessary, in accordance with its legal principles, to establish the liability of legal persons for the bribery of a foreign public official.

Article 3 - *Sanctions*

1. The bribery of a foreign public official shall be punishable by effective, proportionate and dissuasive criminal penalties. The range of penalties shall be comparable to that applicable to the bribery of the Party's own public officials and shall, in the case of natural persons, include deprivation of liberty sufficient to enable effective mutual legal assistance and extradition.

2. In the event that, under the legal system of a Party, criminal responsibility is not applicable to legal persons, that Party shall ensure that legal persons shall be subject to effective, proportionate and dissuasive non-criminal sanctions, including monetary sanctions, for bribery of foreign public officials.

3. Each Party shall take such measures as may be necessary to provide that the bribe and the proceeds of the bribery of a foreign public official, or property the value of which corresponds to that of such proceeds, are subject to seizure and confiscation or that monetary sanctions of comparable effect are applicable.

4. Each Party shall consider the imposition of additional civil or administrative sanctions upon a person subject to sanctions for the bribery of a foreign public official. ...

Article 7 - *Money Laundering*

Each Party which has made bribery of its own public official a predicate offence for the purpose of the application of its money laundering legislation shall do so on the same terms for the bribery of a foreign public official, without regard to the place where the bribery occurred.

Article 8 - *Accounting*

1. In order to combat bribery of foreign public officials effectively, each Party shall take such measures as may be necessary, within the framework of its laws and regulations regarding the maintenance of books and records, financial statement disclosures, and accounting and auditing standards, to prohibit the establishment of off-the-books accounts, the making of off-the-books or inadequately identified transactions, the recording of non-existent expenditures, the entry of liabilities with incorrect identification of their object, as well as the use of false documents, by companies subject to those laws and regulations, for the purpose of bribing foreign public officials or of hiding such bribery.

2. Each Party shall provide effective, proportionate and dissuasive civil, administrative or criminal penalties for such omissions and falsifications in respect of the books, records, accounts and financial statements of such companies.

Article 9 - *Mutual Legal Assistance*

1. Each Party shall, to the fullest extent possible under its laws and relevant treaties and arrangements, provide prompt and effective legal assistance to another Party for the purpose of criminal investigations and proceedings brought by a Party concerning offences within the scope of this Convention and for non-criminal proceedings within the scope of this Convention brought by a Party against a legal person. The requested Party shall inform the requesting Party, without delay, of any additional information or documents needed to support the request for assistance and, where requested, of the status and outcome of the request for assistance.

2. Where a Party makes mutual legal assistance conditional upon the existence of dual criminality, dual criminality shall be deemed to exist if the offence for which the assistance is sought is within the scope of this Convention.

3. A Party shall not decline to render mutual legal assistance for criminal matters within the scope of this Convention on the ground of bank secrecy.

Article 10 - *Extradition*

1. Bribery of a foreign public official shall be deemed to be included as an extraditable offence under the laws of the Parties and the extradition treaties between them.

2. If a Party which makes extradition conditional on the existence of an extradition treaty receives a request for extradition from another Party with which it has no extradition treaty, it may consider this Convention to be the legal basis for extradition in respect of the offence of bribery of a foreign public official.

3. Each Party shall take any measures necessary to assure either that it can extradite its nationals or that it can prosecute its nationals for the offence of bribery of a foreign public official. A Party which declines a request to extradite a person for bribery of a foreign public official solely on the ground that the person is its national shall submit the case to its competent authorities for the purpose of prosecution.

4. Extradition for bribery of a foreign public official is subject to the conditions set out in the domestic law and applicable treaties and arrangements of each Party. Where a Party makes extradition conditional upon the existence of dual criminality, that condition shall be deemed to be fulfilled if the offence for which extradition is sought is within the scope of Article 1 of this Convention.

NOTES AND QUESTIONS

1 Bribery has been described as a routine strategy in many countries and an important weapon in securing national economic and trade advantage. It is a practice woven into the political and diplomatic fabric of many countries. *See* Corruption Reports, A Sampler of Corruption Cases from Around the World, Transparency International Newsletter, Sept. 1999, *available at* http://www.transparency.de/documents/newsletter/99.3/report.html. The Foreign Corrupt Practice Act makes bribery of foreign government officials unlawful. Does this impede the ability of U.S. companies to compete effectively in international business transactions, particularly with countries which have not implemented similar prohibitions? In other words, is FCPA sound national and/or international policy? For diverging assessments, see Steven R. Salbu, *The Foreign Corrupt Practices Act as a Threat to Global Harmony,* 20 MICH. J. INT'L L. 419 (1999); David A. Gantz, *The Foreign Corrupt Practices Act: Professional and Ethical Challenges for Lawyers*, 14 ARIZ. J. INT'L & COMP. L. 97 (1997); Lee C. Buchheit & Ralph Reisner, *Why Has the FCPA Prospered?,* 18 NW. J. INT'L L. & BUS. 263 (1998); Melysa Sperber, *Foreign Corrupt Practices Act*, 39 AM. CRIM. L. REV. 679 (2002); and Peter W. Schroth, *American Law in a Time of Global Interdependence: U.S. National Reports to the XVIth International Congress of Comparative Law: Section V – The United States and the International Bribery Conventions*, 50 AM. J. COMP. L. 593 (2002).

2. What is the approach taken by the OECD Convention? What are its advantages and disadvantages? For background, see Lucinda Low, *Transnational Corruption: New Rules for Old Temptations, New Players to Combat a Perennial Evil,* 92 PROC. AM. SOC'Y INT'L L. 151 (1998); Gregory J. Wallace, *Morality Triumphs: The Foreign Corrupt Practices Act Goes Global*, 1057 PLI/Corp 1241 (1998); Philip M. Nichols, *Regulating Transnational Bribery in Times of Globalization and Fragmentation*, 24 YALE J. INT'L L. 257 (1999); and Christopher K. Carlberg, *A Truly Level Playing Field for International Business: Improving the OECD Convention on Combating Bribery Using Clear Standards*, 26 B.C. INT'L & COMP. L. REV. 95 (2003).

III. Regulating the Use of the Ideological Instrument

A. Issues and Policies

From earliest times, elites have tried to influence popular perspectives in other states, initially by sending in or retaining agents who might secretly disseminate information or misinformation through the myriad networks of folk exchange and rumor, later by financing local newspapers, radios or individual opinion leaders or groups. In this century, with the extraordinary growth of communications technology, the communication of messages to mass audiences in other states has become a major means of shaping a national identity, changing values and behavior and influencing a foreign state's policy.

By the ideological strategy we refer to the beaming of messages, whatever their content, to a mass audience for the purpose of influencing the behavior of the body-politic which the audience composes. The ideological strategy is thus the analogue of the diplomatic strategy, the latter aimed, as we will see, at communicating to an elite audience. Our primary concern is the international legal regulation of the use of the ideological strategy, the agreement among effective elites about the appropriate use of this strategy, the effectiveness of the regulation, the extent to which it contributes to improved world order, and the ways in which it can be improved. Though casebooks do not ordinarily treat this strategy, its importance cannot be over- stated. Popular support for governments and/or their specific programs is an important base of power. Since media technology now permits outsiders to beam messages at foreign internal audiences, the use of the strategy, with its high potential, is greater than ever before.

The key characteristic of this strategy has been its intended audience; rather than the government or the elite, the target has been non-elite or rank- and-file. At times, the content of the messages may have been designed to support for the incumbent government or certain of its programs, but in many other cases, the purpose of the communications has been to weaken or over- throw the government or to erode support for particular programs thereby indirectly forcing the foreign government to change that program in ways it would not otherwise have done. The key factors which have accounted for the increased use of the ideological instrument have been the growth of mass-based politics, particularly after the French Revolution, and the contemporaneous growth of communications media. The first of these factors made the masses more relevant, the second facilitated communication with them.

Mediation of signs and symbols across political boundaries, though frequently criticized by national elites as a violation of sovereignty, must be viewed as an indispensable modality for the creation of a world community. Hence the problem presented to the policy maker committed to a world order of human dignity is not to "stop" the ideological instrument, but to shape its use in ways that contribute optimally to a humane world order.

Thanks to developments in communications technology, non-state actors have been able to play an increasingly effective role in the use of the ideological instrument. The Islamic Revolution in Iran was facilitated by the wide dissemination of cassettes of the Ayatollah Khomeini's speeches. Osama Bin Laden has been extremely skillful at using this instrument.

It is desirable to encourage the maximum exchange of ideas through media across boundaries and to all members of community process and, insofar as possible, to seek to protect freedom of speech from elite control. Yet, public order will require some distinctions: the modulation of signs and symbols whose effect on the intended audience is coercive rather than persuasive, modulation of messages aimed at disrupting minimum order, modulation of messages violating key values of human dignity and so on.

B. PROPAGANDA

1. W. Michael Reisman & Douglas L. Stevick, *The Applicability of International Law Standards to United Nations Economic Sanctions Programmes* 9 EUR. J. INT'L L. 86 (1998)

One of the common methods of propaganda - 'psychwar' - seeks to exacerbate latent conflicts between different ethnic groups within the adversary in order to undermine elite control or to require the elite to divert resources to suppress internal resistance. Propaganda of this sort is hardly without potentially severe collateral damage: tensions between ethnic groups may produce violent incidents or even widespread pogroms. Even if they do not, long after the particular conflict has ended, the residue of hatred that has been endorsed and made more acute will lurk in people's consciousness, like a time bomb or a quiescent virus to be transmitted from one generation to the next until it bursts forth or is detonated. Propaganda, unlike lawful land mines, cannot be set to self-destruct.

2. JULIAN ANTHONY STUART HALE, RADIO POWER: PROPAGANDA AND INTERNATIONAL BROADCASTING 1-9 (Temple U. Press 1975)

In 1933, when the Nazi Party came to power in Germany, radio 'was a novelty. Its propaganda potential was virtually untried. Yet the Nazi leaders' faith in it was unbounded. Eugene Hadamowski, chief of German Radio, wrote in his autobiography:

> We spell radio with three exclamation marks because we are possessed in it of a miraculous power-the strongest weapon ever given to the spirit-that opens hearts and does not stop at the borders of cities and does not

> turn back before closed doors; that jumps rivers, mountains, and seas; that is able to force peoples under the spell of one powerful spirit.

And Hitler wrote of radio in *Mein Kampf*:

> It is a terrible weapon in the hands of those who know how to make use of it.

Goebbels at the opening of the 1933 Berlin Radio Exhibition declared that in the twentieth century radio would take over the role that the press played in the nineteenth.

Had television been available as a national propaganda medium in the thirties, there is no doubt that Goebbels would have welcomed the combination of sound and pictures. At a time 'when British politicians ' were less aware, even unaware, of television's political implications, Goebbels was telling one of Baird TV's directors how wonderful it would be for the German people to have Hitler and himself in every home.

But the war put a stop to television's development, leaving radio to lead the propaganda assault. Nevertheless, for all its peculiar powers and its leading role, radio was only one of an arsenal of propaganda weapons. It was part of a tightly integrated network organized and coordinated by the *Propagandaministerium*. The techniques and the media used by the Nazi Party so successfully in their bid for power in Germany were, after 1933, fitted in to the entire coercive apparatus of the state. As Zeman has written:

> [Goebbels] interfered with the lives of the people to an extent unparalleled in history. The news and even the comments in their papers were centrally supplied; a dissenting opinion could never take the form of the legally printed word. The films they saw and the broadcasts they listened to all carried an indelible Nazi stamp. The Party took care of their leisure time, their travel, their social activities; it presented newly married couples with copies of *Mein Kampf*.

Under Goebbels control was everything that could be used as propaganda: not just the media, but the organization of Party speakers and rallies, of tourism, literature, the arts in general, the cinema, and entertainment for the troops. Propaganda was perhaps the Nazis' one new contribution to the science of politics. Propaganda workers, whether in the Reich Chambers of Culture, the *Reichsrundfunkgesellschaft*, or any of the other bodies which formed the pyramid of which Goebbels was the apex, were specially selected, examined and trained. All were compelled to belong to the Nazi federations. Propaganda was regarded as a science, a mixture of politics, psychology and elocution. People who wanted to broadcast but were not on the RRG staff were tested by a 'microphone examination committee' which formed part of the Reich Chamber of Broadcasting and issued certificates of proficiency.

The point here is the faith that was placed in the medium. It was a faith confirmed as early as 1934 by the evidence of a radio campaign to reincorporate the Saarland into Germany. Goebbels had set up a special office to coordinate the broadcasts, and cheap radio sets were distributed in the target area. The message was not one of political reasoning, but a frank emotional appeal to German feelings. In January 1935, ninety-one per cent of those who voted in the plebiscite opted for the return of the Saar to Germany. From this point on, the Nazi leaders felt they could achieve almost anything through the planned use of radio propaganda.

In retrospect it is clear that the effect was greatest within the confines of the Reich itself. Inside Germany, all the media spoke with one voice, obstacles were placed in the way of outside sources of information, and through intimate knowledge of the home audience the propagandists were able to adapt their psychological tools to fit the audience's fears, hopes and prejudices. The very nature of German propaganda required it to be both monopolistic and singleminded. As Hitler put it in *Mein Kampf*:

As soon as by one's own propaganda even a glimpse of right on the other side is admitted, the cause for doubting one's own right is laid.

The object was to create a captive audience which could be manipulated by the 'leader' and the army of propagandists whose job it was to interpret and to publicize his will.

Ironically, it was radio that presented the greatest danger to the Propaganda Ministry's monopoly. Although the BBC did not start its German-language service until 1938, and the Nazis succeeded in negotiating temporary non-aggression pacts with the Soviet Union and Poland which covered the use of mutual propaganda, the signals from foreign radio which penetrated German jamming, especially during the latter years of the war, were a constant worry to the Nazis. As for the German people, however, the vast majority were deflected not at all from a behaviour pattern dictated by the Nazi media and backed by the sanctions of physical power.

But the Nazi External Service, broadcasting from Zeesen, was in open Competition with local information sources and the radio output of a whole range of hostile nations. The German answer was to concentrate on the foreign audience that they knew best—Germans living abroad. During the campaign against Czechoslovakia, for example, Nazi Propaganda was directed solely towards the German minority, in the German language.

This is not to say that they ignored foreign-language broadcasting. On the contrary, Zeesen was putting out programmes in fifty-five languages by the end of the war. But the primary aim was to create a fifth column of convinced believers in the Nazi cause and to use them as a lobby to back up the work of the German embassies. … During the war, of course, the emphasis in enemy countries had to switch to undermining the morale of the citizens as a whole. But even then the logic of an internal propaganda designed to rally a committed audience around the catchphrases of total fascist power spread into the sphere of foreign propaganda. There was no consistent attempt to understand the psychology of the anti-fascist foreign audience, little attempt to modify the hate-language and emotional racist appeals that characterized the RRG's output. When the tone sometimes lapsed into friendly chattiness, or into highbrow monologues on German culture, the intention was only to make more relevant and more respectable the uncompromising political message.

[Hitler and Goebbels] believed that propaganda should be aimed at the masses. The audience was no more than a manipulable crowd. Ideally the aim was to create a hyponotic effect, a mindless reaction. People who resisted the message would preferably be eliminated physically rather than persuaded round. To the committed, Goebbels would then supply the symbols of Nazi power. The radio would match the appeal of flags and swastikas. He would identify and attack the targets of hatred: the Jews, communists, 'Windsy' Churchill, and senile plutocrats. ... From the outbreak of war the German Radio built up a large audience of French listeners who had grown suspicious of the statements of their home press and radio. As the invasion began the weapon was already in contact with its objective.

To din the Nazi message into people's minds and, above all, hearts, the propagandists used a number of specific techniques which were more or less consciously based on psychological theory. One of the most important was repetition. The audience was bombarded, saturated with the same information, the same slogan, endlessly repeated phrases. This was done partly to reinforce the stereotypes, partly to Jay the propaganda on so thick that no other voice could compete. People would start to believe things they initially, and reasonably, rejected because it would become too much of a strain to resist the concentrated bombardment.

However low their estimate of the masses' intelligence, the propagandists took no chances. Broadcasting in Germany contained 'hardly anything except, on the one hand, concentrated propaganda hammering home the daily directive of the Propaganda Ministry, and, on the other, distraction which releases the mind from thought'. The only danger was that the most resistant and discriminating elements would be encouraged to disbelieve everything they heard and, despite all attempts to prevent them, turn to outside sources for their information. There were some non-conformists who took this course, and it was mainly to these that the BBC and others directed their German-language propaganda. But the Nazis were less concerned about losing a few dissenters among the intellectuals than they were about keeping their grip on the masses.

The slogan was an important element of the repetition/ritual technique. Some of the crudest methods of early Madison Avenue were seized on by the Nazis. Hitler always referred to the *'Diktat of Versailles'*. Other slogans varied from the most punchy-*'Sieg Heil!'*-to the most arch-Austria was before *Anschluss* a mere 'hallucination'.

The concept of propaganda by bludgeoning extended also to the use of obscenity and atrocity propaganda.

In the contemporary world virtually every state maintains some foreign broadcasting services. In some places, radio is a major instrument of foreign policy and foreign broadcasts are a significant problem for foreign elites, a target for jamming and a subject for diplomatic protest.

In one way, the expanded use of the ideological strategy has led to an increase in power sharing, for by recognizing the political potential of the rank-and-file and trying to use it, ideological communication necessarily realizes some of that political potential. In other ways, however, it has sterilized wider participation, especially when its messages are manifestly false or are so intimidating as to paralyze the intended audience.

C. INCITEMENT TO GENOCIDE

1. The Prosecutor v. Jean-Paul Akayesu

Case No. ICTR-96-4-T, Judgment, Sept. 2, 1998

6.3.3. Direct and Public Incitement to Commit Genocide

THE CRIME OF DIRECT AND PUBLIC INCITEMENT TO COMMIT GENOCIDE, PUNISHABLE UNDER ARTICLE 2(3)(c) OF THE STATUTE

Under count 4, the Prosecutor charges Akayesu with direct and public incitement to commit genocide, a crime punishable under Article 2(3)(c) of the Statute. Perhaps the most famous conviction for incitement to commit crimes of international dimension was that of Julius Streicher by the Nuremberg Tribunal for the virulently anti-Semitic articles which he had published in his weekly newspaper *Der Stürmer*. The Nuremberg Tribunal found that: "Streicher's incitement to murder and extermination, at the time when Jews in the East were being killed under the most horrible conditions, clearly constitutes persecution on political and racial grounds in connection with War Crimes, as defined by the Charter, and constitutes a Crime against Humanity". Nuremberg Proceedings, Vol. 22, p. 502. At the time the Convention on Genocide was adopted, the delegates agreed to expressly spell out direct and public incitement to commit genocide as a specific crime, in particular, because of its critical role in the planning of a genocide, with the delegate from the USSR stating in this regard that, "It was impossible that hundreds of thousands of people should commit so many crimes unless they had been incited to do so and unless the crimes had been premeditated and carefully organized. He asked how in those circumstances, the inciters and organizers of the crime could be allowed to escape punishment, when they were the ones really responsible for the atrocities committed. ...

Under Common law systems, incitement tends to be viewed as a particular form of criminal participation, punishable as such. Similarly, under the legislation of some Civil law countries, including Argentina, Bolivia, Chili, Peru, Spain, Uruguay and Venezuela, provocation, which is similar to incitement, is a specific form of participation in an offence ..., but in most Civil law systems, incitement is most often treated as a form of complicity. The Rwandan Penal Code is one such legislation. Indeed, as stated above, in the discussion on complicity in genocide, it does provide that direct and public incitement or provocation is a form of complicity. In fact, Article 91 subparagraph 4 provides that an accomplice shall mean "A person or persons who, whether through speeches, shouting or threats uttered in public places or at public gatherings, or through the sale or dissemination, offer for sale or display of written material or printed matter in public places or at public gatherings or through the public display of placards or posters, directly incite(s) the perpetrator or perpetrators to commit such an action without prejudice to the penalties applicable to those who incite others to commit offences, even where such incitement fails to produce results". ... Under the Statute, direct and public incitement is expressly defined as a specific crime, punishable as such, by virtue of Article 2(3)(c). With respect to such a crime, the Chamber deems it appropriate to first define the three terms: incitement, direct and public. Incitement is defined in Common law systems as encouraging or persuading another to commit an offence "... someone who instigates or encourages another person to commit an offence should be liable to conviction for those acts of incitement, both because he is culpable for trying to cause a crime and because such liability is a step towards crime prevention." ... One line of authority in Common law would also view threats or other forms of pressure as a form of incitement. "The conduct required for incitement is some form of encouragement or persuasion to commit an offence, although there is authority which would regard threats or other forms of pressure as incitement." ... As stated above, Civil law systems punish direct and public incitement assuming the form of provocation, which is defined as an act intended to directly provoke another to commit a crime or a misdemeanour through speeches, shouting or threats, or any other means of audiovisual communication. ... Such a provocation, as defined under Civil law, is made up of the same elements as direct and public incitement to commit genocide covered by Article 2 of the Statute, that is to say it is both direct and public.

The public element of incitement to commit genocide may be better appreciated in light of two factors: the place where the incitement occurred and whether or not assistance was selective or limited. A line of authority commonly followed in Civil law systems would regard words as being public where they were spoken aloud in a place that were public by definition. ... According to the International Law Commission, public incitement is characterized by a call for criminal action to a number of individuals in a public place or to members of the general public at large by such means as the mass media, for example, radio or television. The element of public incitement requires communicating the call for criminal action to a number of individuals in a public place or to members of the general public at large. Thus, an individual may communicate the call for criminal action in person in a public place or by technical means of mass communication, such as by radio or television. Draft Code of Crimes Against the Peace and Security of Mankind, art. 2(3)(f); Report of the International Law Commission to the General Assembly, 51 U.N. ORGA Supp. (No. 10), at 26, U.N. Doc. A/51/10(1996). It should be noted in this respect that at the time the Convention on Genocide was adopted, the delegates specifically agreed to rule out the possibility of including private incitement to commit genocide as a crime, thereby underscoring their commitment to set aside for punishment only the truly public forms of incitement. ...

The "direct" element of incitement implies that the incitement assume a direct form and specifically provoke another to engage in a criminal act, and that more than mere vague or indirect suggestion goes to constitute direct incitement. "The element of direct incitement requires specifically urging another individual to take immediate criminal action rather than merely making a vague or indirect suggestion." Draft Code of Crimes Against the Peace and Security of Mankind, art. 2(3)(f); Report of the International Law Commission to the General Assembly, 51 U.N. ORGA Supp. (No. 10), at 26, U.N. Doc. A/51/10(1996). Under Civil law systems, provocation, the equivalent of incitement, is regarded as being direct where it is aimed at causing a specific offence to be committed. The prosecution must prove a definite causation between the act characterized as incitement, or provocation in this case, and a specific offence. ...

However, the Chamber is of the opinion that the direct element of incitement should be viewed in the light of its cultural and linguistic content. Indeed, a particular speech may be perceived as "direct" in one country, and not so in another, depending on the audience. On this subject, see above, in the findings of the Chamber on Evidentiary Matters, the developments pertaining to the analysis of the Kinyarwanda language presented by the expert witness Professor Mathias Ruzindana.. The Chamber further recalls that incitement may be direct, and nonetheless implicit. Thus, at the time the Convention on Genocide was being drafted, the Polish delegate observed that it was sufficient to play skillfully on mob psychology by casting suspicion on certain groups, by insinuating that they were responsible for economic or other difficulties in order to create an atmosphere favourable to the perpetration of the crime. ...

The Chamber will therefore consider on a case-by-case basis whether, in light of the culture of Rwanda and the specific circumstances of the instant case, acts of incitement can be viewed as direct or not, by focusing mainly on the issue of whether the persons for whom the message was intended immediately grasped the implication thereof. In light of the foregoing, it can be noted in the final analysis that whatever the legal system, direct and public incitement must be defined for the purposes of interpreting Article 2(3)(c), as directly provoking the perpetrator(s) to commit genocide, whether through speeches, shouting or threats uttered in public places or at public gatherings, or through the sale or dissemination, offer for sale or display of written material or printed matter in public places or at public gatherings, or through the public display of placards or posters, or through any other means of audiovisual communication.

The *mens rea* required for the crime of direct and public incitement to commit genocide lies in the intent to directly prompt or provoke another to commit genocide. It implies a desire on the part of the perpetrator to create by his actions a particular state of mind necessary to commit such a crime in the minds of the person(s) he is so engaging. That is to say that the person who is inciting to commit genocide must have himself the specific intent to commit genocide, namely, to destroy, in whole or in part, a national, ethnical, racial or religious group, as such. Therefore, the issue before the Chamber is whether the crime of direct and public incitement to commit genocide can be punished even where such incitement was unsuccessful. It appears from the *travaux préparatoires* of the Convention on Genocide that the drafters of the Convention considered stating explicitly that incitement to commit genocide could be punished, whether or not it was successful. In the end, a majority decided against such an approach. Nevertheless, the Chamber is of the opinion that it cannot thereby be inferred that the intent of the drafters was not to punish unsuccessful acts of incitement. In light of the overall *travaux,* the Chamber holds the view that the drafters of the Convention simply decided not to specifically mention that such a form of incitement could be punished.

There are under Common Law so-called inchoate offences, which are punishable by virtue of the criminal act alone, irrespective of the result thereof, which may or may not have been achieved. The Civil Law counterparts of inchoate offences are known as [*infractions formelles*] (acts constituting an offence per se irrespective of their results), as opposed to [*infractions matérielles*] (strict liability offences). Indeed, as is the case with inchoate offenses, in [*infractions formelles*], the method alone is punishable. Put another way, such offenses are "deemed to have been consummated regardless of the result achieved" … Indeed, Rwandan lawmakers appear to characterize the acts defined under Article 91(4) of the Rwandan Penal Code as so-called [*infractions formelles*], since provision is made for their punishment even where they proved unsuccessful. It should be noted, however, that such offences are the exception, the rule being that in theory, an offence can only be punished in relation to the result envisaged by the lawmakers. In the opinion of the Chamber, the fact that such acts are in themselves particularly dangerous because of the high risk they carry for society, even if they fail to produce results, warrants that they be punished as an exceptional measure. The Chamber holds that genocide clearly falls within the category of crimes so serious that direct and public incitement to commit such a crime must be punished as such, even where such incitement failed to produce the result expected by the perpetrator. …

7.5. Count 4 - Direct and Public Incitement to Commit Genocide

Count 4 deals with the allegations described in paragraphs 14 and 15 of the Indictment, relating, essentially, to the speeches that Akayesu reportedly made at a meeting held in Gishyeshye on 19 April 1994. The Prosecutor alleges that, through his speeches, Akayesu committed the crime of direct and public incitement to commit genocide, a crime punishable under Article 2(3)(c) of the Statute. The Trial Chamber made the following factual findings on the events described in paragraphs 14 and 15 of the Indictment. The Chamber is satisfied beyond a reasonable doubt that:

(i) Akayesu, in the early hours of 19 April 1994, joined a crowd of over 100 people which had gathered around the body of a young member of the Interahamwe in Gishyeshye.

(ii) He seized that opportunity to address the people and, owing, particularly, to his functions as bourgmestre and his authority over the population, he led the gathering and the proceedings.

(iii) It has been established that Akayesu then clearly urged the population to unite in order to eliminate what he termed the sole enemy: the accomplices of the Inkotanyi.

(iv) On the basis of consistent testimonies heard throughout the proceedings and the evidence of Dr. Ruzindana, appearing as expert witness on linguistic matters, the Chamber is satisfied beyond a reasonable doubt that the population understood Akayesu's call as one to kill the Tutsi. Akayesu himself was fully aware of the impact of his speech on the crowd and of the fact that his call to fight against the accomplices of the Inkotanyi would be construed as a call to kill the Tutsi in general.

(v) During the said meeting, Akayesu received from the Interahamwe documents which included lists of names, and read from the lists to the crowd by stating, in particular, that the names were those of RPF accomplices.

(vi) Akayesu testified that the lists contained, especially, the name of Ephrem Karangwa, whom he named specifically, while being fully aware of the consequences of doing so. Indeed, he admitted before the Chamber that, at the time of the events alleged in the Indictment, to label anyone in public as an accomplice of the RPF would put such a person in danger.

(vii) The Chamber is of the opinion that there is a causal relationship between Akayesu's speeches at the gathering of 19 April 1994 and the ensuing widespread massacres of Tutsi in Taba.

From the foregoing, the Chamber is satisfied beyond a reasonable doubt that, by the above-mentioned speeches made in public and in a public place, Akayesu had the intent to directly create a particular state of mind in his audience necessary to lead to the destruction of the Tutsi group, as such. Accordingly, the Chamber finds that the said acts constitute the crime of direct and public incitement to commit genocide, as defined above. In addition, the Chamber finds that the direct and public incitement to commit genocide as engaged in by Akayesu, was indeed successful and did lead to the destruction of a great number of Tutsi in the commune of Taba.

NOTES AND QUESTIONS

1. Several treaties have prohibited the use of the ideological instrument for purposes of human rights. Foremost among them is the Genocide Convention, 78 U.N.T.S. 277 (1951). Article III(c) defines as punishable direct and public incitement to genocide. In *Akayesu*, the incitement to commit genocide is interpreted as constituting an independent international crime, whether the genocide actually occurred or not. Do you agree with that conclusion? Should there be a "clear and present danger" requirement akin to U.S. First Amendment doctrine?

2. Compare Article 4 of The International Convention on the Elimination of All Forms of Racial Discrimination, Dec. 21, 1965, 660 U.N.T.S. 195:

> States Parties condemn all propaganda and all organizations which are based on ideas or theories of superiority of one race or group of persons of one colour or ethnic origin, or which attempt to justify or promote racial hatred and discrimination in any form, and undertake to adopt immediate and positive measures designed to eradicate all incitement to, or acts of, such discrimination, and to this end, with due regard to the principles embodied in the Universal Declaration of Human Rights and the rights expressly set forth in article 5 of this Convention, *inter alia:*
>
> (a) Shall declare an offence punishable by law all dissemination of ideas based on racial superiority or hatred, incitement to racial discrimination, as well as all acts of violence or incitement to such acts against any race or group of persons of another colour or ethnic origin, and also the provision of any assistance to racist activities, including the financing thereof;
>
> (b) Shall declare illegal and prohibit organizations, and also organized and all other propaganda activities, which promote and incite racial discrimination, and shall recognize participation in such organizations or activities as an offence punishable by law;
>
> (c) Shall not permit public authorities or public institutions, national of local, to promote or incite racial discrimination.

3. International Covenant on Civil and Political Rights, G.A. Res. 2200A, 21 U.N. GAOR, Supp. (No. 16) 49, 55, U.N. Doc. 6316 (1966) prescribes in Article 20, "(1) Any propaganda for war shall be prohibited by law. (2) Any advocacy of national, racial or religious hatred that constitutes incitement to discrimination, hostility or violence shall be prohibited by law."

4.. Thanks to the Internet, the channels for modulating signs and symbols that affect political behavior have been greatly expanded. There is, however, little international regulation of the use of the ideological instrument through this and other available channels. One of the reasons is the concern over limiting the freedom of expression. Another is the disagreement among élites as to what constitutes unlawful use of the ideological instrument and what is deemed to be use of the instrument in support of public order. Could you argue that Al Jazeera is facilitating terrorism by broadcasting tapes allegedly from Osama bin Laden calling for a jihad against Americans and Jews? On tapes allegedly made by Saddam Hussein calling on loyal Iraqis to kill the American occupiers? Where does balanced reporting begin and end?

5. In 1978, UNESCO issued a Declaration on Fundamental Principles Concerning the Contribution of the Mass Media to Strengthening Peace and International Understanding to the Promotion of Human Rights and to Countering War Propaganda, Racialism, Apartheid and Incitement to War (20 UNESCO GCOF Resolutions 100, UNESCO Doc.20C/Resolution 3/3.1/2 (1978). The effort was widely viewed in Europe and North America as an attempt to muzzle the free media in those countries by encouraging "a free flow and wider and better balanced dissemination of information" (Art. X). THE ECONOMIST, for example, called the text "an undisguised assault on freedom of the press, arguing, *inter alia*, that the "free ... and balanced" flow of information goals are "contradic-

tory[:] ...who does the balancing of the reporting of, say, a dissident's trial in Russia or a gun battle in Northern Ireland?" No, No, UNESCO, THE ECONOMIST, Sep. 16, 1978, at 17. Do you agree?

IV. REGULATING THE USE OF THE DIPLOMATIC INSTRUMENT

A. ISSUES AND POLICIES

The world constitutive process has long been concerned with maintaining channels of communication between elites. The reason has been the perception that the clearer communications between the managers of territorial communities, the clearer will be the understanding of the intentions and capacities of each and the less likely will be the eruption of overt conflict. All of the institutional characteristics of diplomacy, such as diplomatic immunity, inviolability of diplomatic premises, etc., have been crafted to facilitate political communication. Every one of these institutions is susceptible to abuse. Diplomatic immunity may shield a beneficiary from criminal or civil responsibility; immunity may permit widespread espionage; the inviolability of the diplomatic premises may allow contraband and smuggling opportunities. Despite these periodic abuses, the constitutive process and a flow of decisions in public order have consistently upheld the immunity policy. The reason, in the past, was often attributed to reciprocal respect by monarchs for their peers. In fact, the reason was the need for the maintenance of open channels.

These channels of communication are important in times of low expectation of violence. They are far more important in periods of crisis. Paradoxically, it is precisely in periods of crisis that demands are heard to ignore diplomatic immunity. As adversaries diabolize each other and their respective minions, the willingness to allow any immunity decreases. Until now, the international system has resisted these understandable tendencies.

In the past decade, however, new challenges to the immunities that appear to be indispensable to international political communication have been raised. The international protection of human rights movement and, in particular, the International Criminal Court, have challenged diplomatic immunity, contending that it can never be a shield against the exercise of international jurisdiction for the grave crimes over which the ICC will have jurisdiction. The question for the student of international law in the coming generation will be whether the intentional erosion of diplomatic immunity in favor of these new jurisdictions will enhance minimum world order and human dignity or undermine it.

1. Vienna Convention on Diplomatic Relations

Apr. 18, 1961, 23 U.S.T. 3227; T.I.A.S. 7502; 500 U.N.T.S. 95

Article 2. The establishment of diplomatic relations between States, and of permanent diplomatic missions, takes place by mutual consent.

Article 3. (1) The functions of a diplomatic mission consist *inter alia* in:

(a) representing the sending State in the receiving State;

(b) protecting in the receiving State the interests of the sending state and of its nationals, within the limits permitted by international law;

(c) negotiating with the Government of the receiving State;

(d) ascertaining by all lawful means conditions and developments in the receiving State, and reporting thereon to the Government of the sending State;

(e) promoting friendly relations between the sending State and the receiving State, and developing their economic, cultural and scientific relations. …

Article 4. (l) The sending State must make certain that the *agrément* of the receiving State has been given for the person it proposes to accredit as head of the mission to that State.

(2) The receiving State is not obliged to give reasons to the sending State for a refusal of *agrément.* …

Article 9. (l) The receiving State may at any time and without having to explain its decision, notify the sending State that the head of the mission or any member of the diplomatic staff of the mission is *persona non grata* or that any other member of the staff of the mission is not acceptable. In any such case, the sending State shall, as appropriate, either recall the person concerned or terminate his functions with the mission. A person may be declared *non grata* or not acceptable before arriving in the territory of the receiving State.

(2) If the sending State refuses or fails within a reasonable period to carry out its obligations under paragraph 1 of this Article, the receiving State may refuse to recognize the person concerned as a member of the mission. …

Article 22. (1) The premises of the mission shall be inviolable. The agents of the receiving State may not enter them, except with the consent of the head of the mission.

(2) The receiving State is under a special duty to take all appropriate steps to protect the premises of the mission against any intrusion or damage and to prevent any disturbance of the peace of the mission or impairment of its dignity.

(3) The premises of the mission, their furnishings and other property thereon and the means of transport of the mission shall be immune from search, requisition, attachment or execution. …

Article 24. The archives and documents of the mission shall be inviolable at any time and wherever they may be.

Article 25. The receiving State shall accord full facilities for the performance of the functions of the mission. …

Article 27. (1) The receiving State shall permit and protect free communication on the part of the mission of all official purposes. In communicating with the Government and the other missions and consulates of the sending State, wherever situated, the mission may employ an appropriate means, including diplomatic couriers and messages in code or cipher. However, the mission may install and use a wireless transmitter only with the consent of the receiving State.

(2) The official correspondence of the mission shall be inviolable. Official correspondence means all correspondence relating to the mission and its functions.

(3) The diplomatic bag shall not be opened or detained.

(4) The packages constituting the diplomatic bag must bear visible external marks of their character and may contain only diplomatic documents or articles intended for official use.

(5) The diplomatic courier, who shall be provided with an official document indicating his status and the number of packages constituting the diplomatic bag, shall be protected by the receiving State in the performance of his functions. He shall enjoy personal inviolability and shall not be liable to any form of arrest or detention.

(6) The sending State or the mission may designate diplomatic couriers *ad hoc*. In such cases the provisions of paragraph 5 of this Article shall also apply, except that the immunities therein mentioned shall cease to apply when such a courier has delivered to the consignee the diplomatic bag in his charge.

(7) A diplomatic bag may be entrusted to the captain of a commercial aircraft scheduled to land at an authorized port of entry. He shall be provided with an official document indicating the number of packages constituting the bag but he shall not be considered to be a diplomatic courier. The mission may send one of its members to take possession of the diplomatic bag directly and freely from the captain of the aircraft. ...

Article 29. The person of a diplomatic agent shall be inviolable. He shall not be liable to any form of arrest or detention. The receiving State shall treat him with due respect and shall take all appropriate steps to prevent any attack on his person, freedom or dignity.

Article 30. (1) The private residence of a diplomatic agent shall enjoy the same inviolability and protection as the premises of the mission.

(2) His papers, correspondence and, except as provided in paragraph 3 of Article 31, his property, shall likewise enjoy inviolability.

Article 31. (1) A diplomatic agent shall enjoy immunity from the criminal jurisdiction of the receiving State. He shall also enjoy immunity from its civil and administrative jurisdiction, except in the case of:

(a) a real action relating to private immovable property situated in the territory of the receiving State, unless he holds it on behalf of the sending State for the purposes of the mission;

(b) an action relating to succession in which the diplomatic agent is involved as executor, administrator, heir or legatee as a private person and not on behalf of the sending States;

(c) an action relating to any professional or commercial activity exercised by the diplomatic agent in the receiving State outside his official functions.

(2) A diplomatic agent is not obliged to give evidence as a witness.

(3) No measures of execution may be taken in respect of a diplomatic agent except in the cases coming under sub-paragraphs (a), (b) and (c) of paragraph 1 of this Article, and provided that the measures concerned can be taken without infringing the inviolability of his person or of his residence.

(4) The immunity of a diplomatic agent from the jurisdiction of the receiving State does not exempt him from the jurisdiction of the sending State.

Article 32. (1) The immunity from jurisdiction of diplomatic agents and of persons enjoying immunity under Article 37 may be waived by the sending State.

(2)Waiver must always be express.

(3) The initiation of proceedings by a diplomatic agent or by a person enjoying immunity from jurisdiction under Article 37 shall preclude him from invoking immunity from jurisdiction in respect of any counterclaim directly connected with the principal claim.

(4) Waiver of immunity from jurisdiction in respect of civil or administrative proceedings shall not be held to imply waiver of immunity in respect of the execution of the judgment, for which a separate waiver shall be necessary. ...

Article 41. (1) Without prejudice to their privileges and immunities, it is the duty of all persons enjoying such privileges and immunities to respect the laws and regulations of the receiving State. They also have a duty not to interfere in the internal affairs of that State.

(2) All official business with the receiving State entrusted to the mission by the sending State shall be conducted with or through the Ministry for Foreign Affairs of the receiving State or such other ministry as may be agreed.

(3) The premises of the mission must not be used in any manner incompatible with the functions of the mission as laid down in the present Convention or by other rules of general international law or by any special agreements in force between the sending and the receiving State.

2. Case Concerning United States Diplomatic and Consular Staff in Iran (U.S. v. Iran)

1980 I.C.J. 3 (May 24)

17. At approximately 10.30 a. m. on 4 November 1979, during the course of a demonstration of approximately 3,000 persons, the United States Embassy compound in Tehran was overrun by a strong armed group of several hundred people. The Iranian security personnel are reported to have simply disappeared from the scene; at all events it is established that they made no apparent effort to deter or prevent the demonstrators from seizing the Embassy's premises. The invading group (who subsequently described themselves as "Muslim Student Followers of the Imam's Policy", who will hereafter be as referred to as "the militants") gained access by force to the compound and to the ground floor of the Chancery building. Over two hours after the beginning of the attack, and after the militants had attempted to set fire to the Chancery building and to cut through the upstairs steel doors with a torch, they gained entry to the upper floor; one hour later they gained control of the main vault. The militants also seized the other buildings, including the various residences, on the Embassy compound. In the course of the attack all the diplomatic and consular personnel and other persons present in the premises were seized as hostages, and detained in the Embassy compound; subsequently other United States personnel and one United States private citizen seized elsewhere in Tehran were brought to the compound and added to the number of hostages.

18. During the three hours or more of the assault, repeated calls for help were made from the Embassy to the Iranian Foreign Ministry, and repeated efforts to secure help from the Iranian authorities were also made through direct discussions by the United States Chargé d'affaires, who was at the Foreign Ministry at the time, together with two other members of the mission. From there he made contact with the Prime Minister's Office and with Foreign Ministry officials. A request was also made to the Iranian Chargé d'affaires in Washington for assistance in putting an end to the seizure of the Embassy. Despite these repeated requests, no Iranian security forces were sent in time to provide relief and protection to the Embassy. In fact when Revolutionary Guards ultimately arrived on the scene, dispatched by the Government "to prevent clashes", they considered that their task was merely to "protect the safety of both the hostages and the students", according to statements subsequently made by the Iranian Government's spokesman, and by the operations commander of the Guards. No attempt was made by the Iranian Government to clear the Embassy premises, to rescue the persons held hostage, or to persuade the militants to terminate their action against the Embassy.

19. During the morning of 5 November, only hours after the seizure of the Embassy, the United States Consulates in Tabriz and Shiraz were also seized; again the Iranian Government took no protective action. The operation of these Consulates had been suspended since the attack in February 1979 (paragraph 14 above), and therefore no United States personnel were seized on these premises.

20. The United States diplomatic mission and consular posts in Iran were not the only ones whose premises were subjected to demonstrations during the revolutionary period in Iran. On 5 November 1979, a group invaded the British Embassy in Tehran but was ejected after a brief occupation. On 6 November 1979 a brief occupation of the Consulate of Iraq at Kermanshah occurred but was brought to an end on instructions of the Ayatollah Khomeini; no damage was done to the Consulate or its contents. On 1 January 1980 an attack was made on the Embassy in Tehran of the USSR by a large mob, but as a result of the protection given by the Iranian authorities to the Embassy, no serious damage was done. …

26. From the outset of the attack upon its Embassy in Tehran, the United States protested to the Government of Iran both at the attack and at the seizure and detention of the hostages. …

28. … The Security Council then adopted resolution 457 (1979) [and resolution 461 (1979)], calling on Iran to release the personnel of the Embassy immediately, to provide them with protection and to allow them to leave the country. …

35. In its letter of 9 December 1979 the Government of Iran maintained that the Court could not and should not take cognizance of the present case for another reason, namely that the case submitted to the Court by the United States, is "confined to what is called the question of the 'hostages of the American Embassy in Tehran' ". It then went on to explain why it considered this to preclude the Court from taking cognizance of the case:

> For this question only represents a marginal and secondary aspect of an overall problem, one such that it cannot be studied separately, and which involves, *inter alia*, more than 25 years of continual interference by the United States in the internal affairs of Iran, the shameless exploitation of our country, and numerous crimes perpetrated against the Iranian people, contrary to and in conflict with all international and humanitarian norms.
>
> The problem involved in the conflict between Iran and the United States is thus not one of the interpretation and the application of the treaties upon which the American Application is based, but results from an overall situation containing much more fundamental and more complex elements. Consequently, the Court cannot examine the American Application divorced from its proper context, namely the whole political dossier of the relations between Iran and the United States over the last 25 years. This dossier includes, *inter alia*, all the crimes perpetrated in Iran by the American Government, in particular the *coup d'etat* of 1953, stirred up and carried out by the CIA, the overthrow of the lawful national government of Dr. Mossadegh, the restoration of the Shah and of his regime which was under the control of American interests, and all the social, economic, cultural and political consequences of the direct interventions in our internal affairs, as well as grave, flagrant and continuous violations of all international norms, committed by the United States in Iran.

36. The Court, however, in its Order of 15 December 1979, made it clear that the seizure of the United States Embassy and Consulates and the detention of internationally protected persons as hostages cannot be considered as something "secondary" or "marginal", having regard to the importance of the legal principles involved. It also referred to a statement of the Secretary-General of the United Nations, and to Security Council Resolution 457 (1979), as evidencing the importance attached by the international community as a whole to the observance of those principles in the present case as well as its concern at the dangerous level of tension between Iran and the United States. The Court, at the same time, pointed out that no provision of the Statute or Rules contemplates that the Court should decline to take cognizance of one aspect of a dispute merely because that dispute has other aspects, how- ever important. It further underlined that, if the Iranian Government considered the alleged activities of the United States in Iran legally to have a close connection with the subject-matter of the United States' Application, it was open to that Government to present its own arguments regarding those activities to the Court either by way of defence in a Counter-Memorial or by way of a counter-claim. …

69. The second phase of the events which are the subject of the United States' claims comprises the whole series of facts which occurred following the completion of the occupation of the United States Embassy by the militants, and the seizure of the Consulates at Tabriz and Shiraz. The occupation having taken place and the diplomatic and consular personnel of the United States mission having been taken hostage, the action required of the Iranian Government by the Vienna Conventions and by general international law was manifest. Its plain duty was at once to … take every appropriate step … to re-establish the status quo and to offer reparation for the damage. …

70. No such step was, however, taken by the Iranian authorities. At a press conference on 5 November the Foreign Minister, Mr. Yazdi, conceded that "according to international regulations the Iranian Government is duty-bound to safeguard the life and property of foreign nationals". But he made no mention of Iran's obligation to safeguard the inviolability of foreign embassies and diplomats. …

75. … The Court's Order of 15 December 1979 indicating provisional measures, which called for the immediate restoration of the Embassy to the United States and the release of the hostages, was publicly rejected by the Minister for Foreign Affairs on the following day and has been ignored by all Iranian authorities. …

76. The Iranian authorities' decision to continue the subjection of the premises of the United States Embassy to occupation by militants and of the Embassy staff to detention as hostages, clearly gave rise to repeated and multiple breaches of the applicable provisions of the Vienna Conventions even more serious than those which arose from their failure to take any steps to prevent the attacks on the inviolability of these premises and staff.

77. In the first place, these facts constituted breaches additional to those already committed of paragraph 2 of Article 22 of the 1961 Vienna Convention on Diplomatic Relations which requires Iran to protect the premises of the mission against any intrusion or damage and to prevent any disturbance of its peace or impairment of its dignity. Paragraphs I and 3 of that Article have also been infringed, and continue to be infringed, since they forbid agents of a receiving State to enter the premises of a mission without consent or to undertake any search, requisition, attachment or like measure on the premises. Secondly, they constitute continuing breaches of Article 29 of the same Convention which forbids any arrest or detention of a diplomatic agent and any attack on his person, freedom or dignity. Thirdly, the Iranian authorities are without doubt in continuing breach of the provisions of Articles 25, 26 and 27 of the 1961 Vienna Convention and of pertinent, provisions of the 1963 Vienna Convention concerning facilities for the performance of functions, freedom of movement and communications for diplomatic and consular staff, as well as of Article 24 of the former Convention and Article 33 of the latter, which provide for the absolute inviolability of archives and documents of diplomatic missions and consulates. This particular violation has been made manifest to the world by repeated statements by the militants occupying the Embassy, who claim to be in possession of documents from the archives, and by various government authorities, purporting to specify the contents thereof. Finally, the continued detention as hostages of the two private individuals of United States nationality entails a renewed breach of the obligations of Iran under Article 11, paragraph 4, of the 1955 Treaty of Amity, Economic Relations, and Consular Rights.

78. Inevitably, in considering the compatibility … of the conduct of the Iranian authorities with the requirements of the Vienna Conventions, the Court has focused its attention primarily on the occupation of the Embassy and the treatment of the United States diplomatic and consular personnel within the Embassy. It is however evident that the question of the compatibility of their conduct with the Vienna Conventions also arises in connection with the treatment of the United States Chargé d'affaires and two members of his staff in the Ministry of Foreign Affairs on 4 November and since that date. The facts of this case establish to the satisfaction Court that on 4 November 1979 and thereafter the Iranian authorities withheld from the Chargé d'affaires and the two members of his necessary protection and facilities to permit them to leave the Ministry in safety. Accordingly it appears to the Court that with respect to these three members of the United States' mission the Iranian authorities have committed a continuing breach of their obligations under Articles 26 and 29 of the Vienna Convention on Diplomatic Relations. It further appears to the Court that the continuation of that situation over a long period has, in the circumstances, amounted to detention in the Ministry.

79. The Court moreover cannot conclude its observations on the series of acts which it has found to be imputable to the Iranian State and to entry inconsistent with its international obligations under the Vienna Conventions of 1961 and

1963 without mention also of another fact. This is that judicial authorities of the Islamic Republic of Iran and the Minister of Foreign Affairs have frequently voiced or associated themselves with, a threat first announced by the militants, of having some of the hostages submitted to trial before a court or some other body. These threats may at present be acts in contemplation. But the Court considers it necessary here and now to stress that, if the intention to submit the hostages to any form of criminal trial or investigation were to be put into effect, that would constitute breach by Iran of its obligations under Article 31, paragraph 1, of the Vienna Convention. This paragraph states in the most express terms: "A diplomatic agent shall enjoy immunity from the criminal jurisdiction of the receiving State." Again, if there were an attempt to compel the hostages to bear witness, a suggestion renewed at the time of the visit to Iran of the Secretary-General's Commission, Iran would without question be violating paragraph 2 of that same Article of the 1961 Vienna Convention stating that: "A diplomatic agent is not obliged to give evidence as a witness."

80. The facts of the present case, viewed in the light of the applicable rules of law, thus speak loudly and clearly of successive and still continuing breaches by Iran of its obligations to the United States under the Vienna Conventions of 1961 and 1963, as well as under the Treaty of 1955. Before drawing from this finding the conclusions which flow from it, in terms the international responsibility of the Iranian State vis-à-vis the United States of America, the Court considers that it should examine one further point. The Court cannot overlook the fact that on the Iranian side, in often imprecise terms, the idea has been put forward that the conduct of the Iranian Government, at the time of the events of 4 November 1979 and subsequently, might be justified by the existence of special circumstances.

81. In his letters of 9 December 1979 and 16 March 1980, as previously recalled, Iran's Minister for Foreign Affairs referred to the present case as only "a marginal and secondary aspect of an overall problem". This problem, he maintained, "involves, *inter alia*, more than 25 years of continual interference by the United States in the internal affairs of Iran. . . [T]he Iranian Foreign Minister took the position that the United States' Application could not be examined by the Court divorced from its proper context, which he insisted was "the whole political dossier of the relations between Iran and the United States over the last 25 years".

82. The Court must however observe, first of all, that the matters alleged in the Iranian Foreign Minister's letters of 9 December 1979 and 16 March 1980 are of a kind which, if invoked in legal proceedings, must clearly be established to the satisfaction of the tribunal with all the requisite proof. The Court, in its Order of 15 December 1979, pointed out that if the Iranian Government considered the alleged activities of the United States in Iran legally to have a close connection with the subject-matter of the Application it was open to Iran to present its own case regarding those activities to the Court by way of defence to the United States' claims. The Iranian Government, however, did not appear before the

Court. Moreover, even in his letter of 16 March 1980, transmitted to the Court some three months after the issue of that Order, the Iranian Foreign Minister did not furnish the Court with any further information regarding the alleged criminal activities of the United States in Iran, or explain on what legal basis he considered these allegations to constitute a relevant answer to the United States' claims.

83. In any case, even if the alleged criminal activities of the United States in Iran could be considered as having been established, the question would remain whether they could be regarded by the Court as constituting a justification of Iran's conduct and thus a defence to the United States' claims in the present case. The Court, however, is unable to accept that they can be so regarded. This is because diplomatic law itself provides the necessary means of defence against, and sanction for, illicit activities by members of diplomatic or consular missions.

84. The Vienna Conventions of 1961 and 1963 contain express provisions to meet the case when members of an embassy staff, under the cover of diplomatic privileges and immunities, engage in such abuses of their functions as espionage or interference in the internal affairs of the receiving State. It is precisely with the possibility of such abuses in contemplation that Article 41, paragraph 1, of the Vienna Convention on Diplomatic Relations, and Article 55, paragraph 1, of the Vienna Convention on Consular Relations, provide:

> Without prejudice to their privileges and immunities, it is the duty of all persons enjoying such privileges and immunities to respect the laws and regulations of the receiving State. They also have a duty not to interfere in the internal affairs of that State.

Paragraph 3 of Article 41 of the 1961 Convention further states: "The premises of the mission must not be used in any manner incompatible with the functions of the mission..."; an analogous provision, with respect to consular premises is to be found in Article 55, paragraph 2, of the 1963 Convention.

85. Thus, it is for the very purpose of providing a remedy for such possible abuses of diplomatic functions that Article 9 of the 1961 Convention on Diplomatic Relations stipulates:

> 1. The receiving State may at any time and without having to explain its decision, notify the sending State that the head of the mission or any member of the diplomatic staff of the mission is *persona non grata* or that any other member of the staff of the mission is not acceptable. In any such case, the sending State shall, as appropriate, either recall the person concerned or terminate his functions with the mission. A person may be declared *non grata* or not acceptable before arriving in the territory of the receiving State.
>
> 2. If the sending State refuses or fails within a reasonable period to carry out its obligations under paragraph 1 of this Article, the receiving State may refuse to recognize the person concerned as a member of the mission.

The 1963 Convention contains ... analogous provisions in respect of consular officers and consular staff. Paragraph 1 of Article 9 of the 1961 Convention, and paragraph 4 of Article 23 of the 1963 Convention, take account of the difficulty that may be experienced in practice of proving such abuses in every case or, indeed, of determining exactly when exercise of the diplomatic function, expressly recognized in Article 3 (I) (*d*) of the 1961 Convention, of "ascertaining by all lawful means conditions and developments in the receiving State" may be considered as involving such acts as "espionage" or "interference in internal affairs." The way in which Article 9, paragraph 1, takes account of any such difficulty is by providing expressly in its opening sentence that the receiving State may "at any time and without having to explain its decision" notify the sending State that any particular member of its diplomatic mission is "*persona non grata*" or "not acceptable" (and similarly Article 23, paragraph 4, of the 1963 Convention provides that "the receiving State is not obliged to give to the sending State reasons for its decision"). Beyond that remedy for dealing with abuses of the diplomatic function by individual members of a mission, a receiving State has in its hands a more radical remedy if abuses of their functions by members of a mission reach serious proportions. This is the power which every receiving State has, at its own discretion, to break off diplomatic relations with a sending State and to call for the immediate closure of the offending mission.

86. The rules of diplomatic law, in short, constitute a self-contained régime which, on the one hand, lays down the receiving State's obligations regarding the facilities, privileges and immunities to be accorded to diplomatic missions and, on the other, foresees their possible abuse by members of the mission and specifies the means at the disposal of the receiving State to counter any such abuse. These means are, by their nature, entirely efficacious, for unless the sending State recalls the member of the mission objected to forthwith, the prospect of the almost immediate loss of his privileges and immunities, because of the withdrawal by the receiving State of his recognition as a member of the mission, will in practice compel that person, in his own interest, to depart at once. But the principle of the inviolability of the persons of diplomatic missions is one of the very ... foundations of this long-established regime, to the evolution of which the traditions of Islam made a substantial contribution. The fundamental character of the principle of inviolability is, moreover, strongly underlined by the provisions of Articles 44 and 45 of the Convention of 1961 ... Even in the case of armed conflict or in the case of a breach in diplomatic relations those provisions require that both the inviolability of the members of a diplomatic mission and of the premises, property and archives of the mission must be respected by the receiving State. Naturally, the observance of this principle does not mean - and this the Applicant Government expressly acknowledges - that a diplomatic agent caught in the act of committing an assault or other offence may not, on occasion, be briefly arrested by the police of the receiving State in order to prevent the commission of the particular crime. But such eventualities bear no relation at all to what occurred in the present case.

87. In the present case, the Iranian Government did not break off diplomatic relations with the United States; and in response to a question put to him by a Member of the Court, the United States Agent informed the Court that at no time before the events of 4 November 1979 had the Iranian Government declared, or indicated any intention to declare, any member of the United States diplomatic or consular staff in Tehran persona non grata. The Iranian Government did not, therefore, employ the remedies placed at its disposal by diplomatic law specifically for dealing with activities of the kind of which it now complains. Instead, it allowed a group of militants to attack and occupy the United States Embassy by force, and to seize the diplomatic and consular staff as hostages; instead, it has endorsed that action of those militants and has deliberately maintained their occupation of the Embassy and detention of its staff as a means of coercing the sending State. It has, at the same time, refused altogether to discuss this situation with representatives of the United States. The Court, therefore, can only conclude that Iran ...resorted to coercive action against the United States Embassy and its staff.

88. In an address given on 5 November 1979, the Ayatollah Khomeini traced the origin of the operation carried out by the Islamic militants on the previous day to the news of the arrival of the former Shah of Iran in the United States. That fact may no doubt have been the ultimate catalyst of the resentment felt in certain circles in Iran and among the Iranian population against the former Shah for his alleged misdeeds, and also against the United States Government... But whatever be the truth in regard to those matters, they could hardly be considered as having provided a justification for the attack on the United States Embassy and its diplomatic mission. Whatever extenuation of the responsibility to be attached to the conduct of the Iranian authorities may be found in the offence felt by them because of the admission of the Shah to the United States, that feeling of offence could not affect the imperative character of the legal obligations incumbent upon the Iranian Government which is not altered by a state of diplomatic tension between the two countries. Still less could a mere refusal or failure on the part of the United States to extradite the Shah to Iran be considered to modify the obligations of the Iranian authorities, quite apart from any legal difficulties in internal or international law, there might be in acceding to such a request for extradition.

89. Accordingly, the Court finds that no circumstances exist in the present case which are capable of negating the fundamentally unlawful character of the conduct pursued by the Iranian State on 4 November 1979, and thereafter. This finding does not however exclude the possibility that some of the circumstances alleged, if duly established, may later be found to have some relevance in determining the consequences of the responsibility incurred by the Iranian State with respect to that conduct, although they could not be considered to alter its unlawful character.

90. On the basis of the foregoing detailed examination of the merit of the case, the Court finds that Iran, by committing successive and continuing breaches of the obligations laid upon it by the Vienna Conventions in 1961 and 1963 on

Diplomatic and Consular Relations, the Treaty of Amity, Economic Relations, and Consular Rights of 1955, and the applicable rules of general international law, has incurred responsibility towards the United States. As to the consequences of this finding, it clearly entails an obligation on the part of the Iranian State to make reparation.

NOTES AND QUESTIONS

1. Is it historically and/or legally possible to separate the Iranian grievance and the hostage issue?

2. Are there policy justifications for the "self-contained régime" of diplomatic relations? Doesn't it invite abuse? What if an embassy is used to manufacture anthrax or another weapon of mass destruction?

3. Rosalyn Higgins, *The Abuse of Diplomatic Privileges and Immunities: Recent United Kingdom Experience*

79 AM. J. INT'L L. 641 (1985)

Diplomatic law governs the conduct of relations between representative organs of a state operating within the territory of another state, and the receiving state. Its purpose is to facilitate international diplomacy, balancing the pursuit of the foreign policy interests of the sending state with respect for the territorial sovereignty of the receiving state. Diplomatic immunity is an exception to the general rule of territorial jurisdiction. It allows diplomats to be able to carry out their functions within the framework of necessary security and confidentiality. But it still contributes to the balancing of interests between the sending and receiving state, because immunity does not entitle diplomats to flout local laws.

There are many types of missions for the conduct of international diplomacy. To a certain extent, each type has become governed by its own specific body of diplomatic law. But permanent missions established by states within each other's territory have become the mainstay of international intercourse. Until the end of the 1950s, the sources of law governing the missions were largely customary. In 1961 there was concluded the Vienna Convention on Diplomatic Relations. This treaty is agreed to be largely confirmatory of existing customary law, and it has been ratified by the great majority of states, including states as diverse as the United States and Iran, the United Kingdom and Libya.

For about 15 years it was fairly generally felt that the provisions of the Vienna Convention did indeed provide a fair balance between the interests of the sending and receiving states. But in many of the major capitals of the world, it came to be felt that diplomats were abusing the privileged status given to their vehicles, and in particular parking illegally, causing obstructions and failing to pay traffic fines. This feeling was, of course, compounded in a country such as the United States, which was also host in New York to the United Nations and important specialized agencies. By contrast, there was much less public awareness of traffic violations by the diplomatic community in London. On the other hand, London has seemed an attractive venue for shoplifting and other offenses. In the period 1974 mid

1984, there were 546 occasions on which persons avoided arrest or prosecution for alleged serious offenses (i.e., offenses carrying a potential sentence of 6 months' imprisonment or greater) because of diplomatic immunity.

In the mid 1970s, more worrying problems developed. It became clear that certain diplomatic missions were holding firearms, contrary to the provisions of local law. Further, it seemed that these firearms were often being imported through the diplomatic bag. In recent years in various Western countries, there have also been terrorist incidents, in which it was believed that the weapons used were provided from diplomatic sources. It was widely thought that certain foreign governments were promoting state terrorism against dissident exiles, through the involvement of their embassies in the country concerned. Normal diplomatic communication with the Libyan Embassy in London was complicated by the fact that (as in other Western capitals) so called revolutionary committees had taken over the embassy, renamed the embassy the Libyan People's Bureau and refused to designate a person in charge of the mission. The bizarre events of this period, and the response of the United Kingdom Government to them, are beyond the scope of these editorial comments. In February 1980, further internal upheavals occurred in the Libyan People's Bureau in London, giving rise to further diplomatic problems.

On April 17, 1984, an orderly demonstration was held by Libyan opponents of Colonel Qaddafi's Government, on the pavement in St. James's Square, London, opposite the People's Bureau. Both the Foreign Office in London and the British Ambassador in Tripoli had been warned the day before that if the demonstration were to be allowed to go ahead, Libya "would not be responsible for its consequences." Shots were fired from the windows of the Bureau, killing Woman Police Constable Fletcher, who was on duty in the square. The events immediately following were these:

> 74. … The Libyan authorities in Tripoli were immediately asked to instruct those inside the Bureau to leave the building and to allow it to be searched for weapons and explosives. This request was refused. The British Embassy in Tripoli was the scene of hostile demonstrations and certain British citizens were unjustifiably arrested and detained.
>
> 75. Her Majesty's Government proposed that "as a basis for terminating relations by agreement" that:
>
> (1) Occupants of the Bureau and all other Libyan diplomatic staff in the country should have safe conduct out of the country. (It will be noted that the proposal covered, so far as those on Bureau premises were concerned, those who had no diplomatic status as well as any who might have had such status. The Government indicated that in its view evidence capable of sustaining criminal charges would in any event have been difficult to achieve in respect of such persons.)
>
> (2) Our own diplomats were to leave Libya in safety.

(3) We should be satisfied that all weapons and explosives were removed from the Bureau and that it could no longer be used for terrorist acts.

These proposals were refused.

76. On 20 April a bomb exploded in the luggage hall of Heathrow airport injuring 25 people. The Government have reserved their position as to whether it was connected with the incidents in St. James's Square, though there was wide press speculation that this was in fact the case. On 22 April the Libyans were notified that diplomatic relations would terminate at 6.00 p.m. that day and that all diplomatic staff and other persons in the Bureau were to leave by midnight 29 30 April. Two Libyans (not at the Bureau) were deported after the shooting of WPC Fletcher. Various measures were announced by the Home Secretary for tightening the exercise of his discretionary powers in respect of Libyans already in the country or wishing to enter.

77. The Bureau was evacuated on 27 April 1984. Those leaving were questioned and electronically searched. Diplomatic bags that left the Bureau were not searched or scanned. The Bureau was sealed, and on 30 April 1984 was entered by the British authorities, in the presence of a representative of the Saudi Arabian Embassy, and searched. Weapons and relevant forensic evidence were found.

There was, as might be expected, general outrage at these events. The public and many legislators were clearly deeply disturbed that the international law of diplomatic immunity apparently prevented the Bureau from being entered, and those responsible from being arrested. More specifically, it was widely felt that diplomats acting in a way incompatible with their diplomatic status should not benefit from an immunity granted to assist the orderly conduct of diplomatic relations. It was suggested that some way should be found of searching diplomatic bags that were suspected of containing either drugs or weapons. And there was a widespread sentiment that premises which were a base for unlawful acts should not be accorded inviolability. It was argued variously that a proper interpretation of the Vienna Convention would support the view that immunity and inviolability fell away when diplomats and missions abused their positions; but that if the Vienna Convention made these desirable outcomes impossible, then the Convention should be amended or denounced.

These and related issues have now been systematically reviewed in a study prepared by the Foreign Affairs Committee of the United Kingdom House of Commons.

Many detailed points of interest are found in the report. In addition, some important general points emerged. It became clear that diplomatic law is not only about the balancing of legitimate interests between the sending state and the receiving state. There is another factor often at play: the presence abroad, in the territory of the sending state, of an expatriate community of the receiving state. (There were, for example, some 8,000 Britons resident in Libya in April 1984.) The extent to which countries will avail themselves of the opportunities for lawful response to abuse of diplomatic immunities will depend in large measure upon whether that expatriate community is perceived to be at risk. That is something that the balanced text of the Vienna Convention cannot provide against and by the same token, any amendment of that text or withdrawal from its obligations would not change that reality.

As has been briefly explained above, the Libyan Bureau incident in April 1984 concerned the inviolability of the embassy, the protection of the diplomatic bag from being opened or detained, and the personal immunity of the diplomats in the Bureau.

INVIOLABILITY OF THE PREMISES OF AN EMBASSY

Article 22(1) of the Convention provides that "[t]he premises of the mission shall be inviolable. The agents of the receiving State may not enter them, except with the consent of the head of the mission." Article 22(3) further provides that "[t]he premises of the mission ... shall be immune from search, requisition, attachment or execution." It is clear, notwithstanding popular and ill informed views to the contrary, that inviolability of premises is not lost by the perpetration from them of unlawful acts. Both the International Law Commission in its preparatory work and the conference at which the Vienna Convention was drafted deliberately rejected the idea of specified exceptions in the face of manifest abuse. Inviolability had to be absolute if the door was not to be opened to possible abuse by the receiving state.

That being said, there are still two difficult related issues that require mention. They concern, respectively, the relationship of general treaty principles on the one hand, and of the concept of self defense on the other, to the notions of inviolability under the Convention. Although a fundamental breach of treaty (which the use of embassy premises for terrorism surely is) would normally allow another state party to the treaty to be relieved of its obligations vis à vis the violating state, the drafting history of the Vienna Convention seems to make the operation of this principle inappropriate. This conclusion is buttressed by the fact that the Vienna Convention provides for its own remedies in case it is violated the severing of diplomatic relations is available as a response to what one could term "a fundamental breach."

Is there a principle of self defense that continues to exist side by side with the Convention, allowing the authorities of the receiving state to take certain action against an embassy, notwithstanding Article 22 of the Convention? In a very interesting statement, the Legal Adviser to the Foreign and Commonwealth Office took the view that "self defence applies not only to action taken directly against a state but also to action directed against members of that state." Sir John Freeland thought that where the classic requirements ("A necessity of self defence, instant, overwhelming, leaving no choice of means and moment for deliberation") were met, forcible entry of embassy premises might be justified in self defense. (He did not believe that the events as they unfolded in London on April 17, 1984 met that test.) This writer remains skeptical as to the applicability at all of the international law concept of self defense to violent acts by the representatives of one state within the territory of another, directed against the latter's citizens.

SEARCHING OF DIPLOMATIC BAGS

Two main grounds have been advanced for suggesting that one does not have to treat as mandatory the provision in Article 27(3) of the Convention that "[t]he diplomatic bag shall not be opened or detained." The first is that the inviolability of the bag is to protect diplomatic materials, but not materials that do not fall in that category and indeed constitute an abuse of the diplomatic bag. The second is that abuse by members of a mission of the functions protected under the Convention entails forfeiture of the protection of the Convention. The travaux préparatoires of the Convention are not quite as categorical on these related points as they are on the lack of any exception allowing uninvited entry onto diplomatic premises. But they are still clear enough, and the policy considerations are the same. There is no way of ascertaining that a bag contains illicit materials save by examination; and that possibility gives too much opportunity to a receiving state to interfere with the proper flow of diplomatic materials. Even those states that have suffered most in recent years from the abusive use of the diplomatic bag that has undoubtedly occurred show little enthusiasm for a departure from the prohibition of search in Article 27(3).

The Legal Adviser to the Foreign and Commonwealth Office took the view, on balance, that electronic scanning is not unlawful under the Convention. Acknowledging that some regard scanning as "constructive opening," Sir John Freeland noted that Article 27 of the Convention requires only that the bag not be "opened or detained" and does not accord full inviolability. In the view of the Government, scanning or other remote examination by equipment or dogs would not be unlawful under Article 27. However, the Government was at pains to point out that it did not in fact scan, nor did it wish to do so. It expressed doubts on technical grounds about the advantage to be gained from doing so (scanning can identify the existence of a problem, but its precise nature would often require the opening of the bag); further, various techniques exist for disguising the exact identity of items that might be revealed by a scan. Obviously, there was also concern about adverse reciprocal consequences if scanning were to be introduced. It is not correct that states acting lawfully have nothing to fear from scanning: such a practice might reveal sensitive information about, e.g., types of ciphers in use by the sending state.

The United Kingdom's decision not to search the diplomatic bags of the Libyans expelled from the Bureau was generally assumed by the press and television reporters at the time to be part and parcel of the obligations laid upon the United Kingdom by the Vienna Convention. The United Kingdom Government, while not positively affirming this, did not take any of the parliamentary opportunities to explain that this was not quite the case. In fact, Libya's accession to the Vienna Convention had been qualified by a reservation that provided that were it to entertain strong doubts that the contents of a diplomatic pouch include items which may not be sent by diplomatic pouch in accordance with paragraph 4 of article 27 of said Convention, the Socialist People's Libyan Arab Jamahiriya reserves its right to request the opening of such pouch in the presence of an official representative of the diplomatic mission concerned. If such request is denied by the authorities of the sending state, the diplomatic pouch shall be returned to its place of origin.

The United Kingdom made no objection to this reservation, believing that it was not incompatible with the object and purpose of the Convention, and that it represented customary international law as it was before the Convention. Indeed, the United Kingdom had introduced an unsuccessful amendment to Article 27 to much the same effect.

In fact, the Libyans have never relied upon this reservation to ask for a search. Nonetheless, the potential effect of the reservation was there. The Libyan reservation had opened the possibility of searching the bag and it was not necessary for Libya to have made even a request for a search for that reservation to be used reciprocally by a nonobjecting party to the Convention. In response to questioning by the committee, the Legal Adviser to the Foreign and Commonwealth Office confirmed the legal position, and further agreed that, therefore, the decision not to search the bags was political and not legal. The committee in its report did not dissent from the political judgment made.

Whether remedies available under and within the Convention should be used will always be subject to political judgment. And sometimes it may be convenient for a government to let it be supposed, in exercising political judgment, that its hands are tied by the requirements of international law.

CRIMINAL OFFENSES AND PERSONAL IMMUNITIES

39. The person of a diplomatic agent is inviolable and he may not be arrested or detained (Article 29, Vienna Convention on Diplomatic Relations). A diplomatic agent is immune from the criminal jurisdiction of the receiving State, and immune from the civil and administrative jurisdiction save in certain specified cases (Article 39). He is further exempt from local taxes (Article 34). These privileges and immunities are extended to the members of his family forming part of his household, provided that they are not nationals of the receiving State (Article 37). The same privileges and immunities are extended to the members of the administrative and technical staffs of the mission, with the same provisions for their families. The only difference is that immunity from civil and administrative jurisdiction will only be in respect of acts performed within the course of their duties. …

42. All persons enjoying privileges and immunities under the Convention (or similar conventions applicable to consular staff or staff of international organisations) are under a duty to respect the laws and regulations of the receiving State, and not to interfere in its internal affairs (Article 41). That a diplomat is indeed bound by the laws of the receiving State is underlined by the provision of Article 31(1) that his immunity does not exempt him from the jurisdiction of the sending State. At the same time, it is not correct that when a diplomat violates this duty he loses his immunity. Such a reading is inconsistent with the immunities given, which operate precisely in respect of such alleged violations, and which, in the case of diplomatic agents, apply even to unofficial acts. An argument can be made that when diplomats act in fact as terrorists, they are not diplomats at all, and thus must lose the benefit of those immunities that diplomats are entitled to. But the right view seems to be that a person remains an accredited diplomat until the receiving State requires him to be withdrawn. This view would seem to accord with the general ethos of the Convention that there should be no exceptions to its terms.

The Foreign Affairs Committee felt that this was not an intolerable situation and that the Convention provided a remedy in the ability of the receiving state to declare a diplomat *persona non grata*. In cases concerning offenses against the security of the state, offending diplomats were routinely declared *persona non grata*. But there had been other occasions where interference in internal affairs was suspected, or where local law has been violated, or where threats had been issued, and no request had been made for the person or persons to be withdrawn. The committee recommended a greater readiness to use this remedy.

This study was based, as has been explained above, on the submission of detailed evidence from a wide variety of interested parties, and oral examination of witnesses. It concluded that amendment of the Vienna Convention was not only virtually impossible to achieve, but of doubtful desirability:

> [I]t is doubtful whether, from the UK's point of view, amendment is even desirable. In respect of all these matters we were constantly reminded of the importance of reciprocity namely, that the privileges and immunities operate to provide a very real protection for our diplomats and their families overseas, and that action should not be taken which would expose them to personal danger or make the carrying out of their diplomatic tasks more difficult or even impossible. The UK maintains a substantial number of diplomatic posts overseas and there is little doubt that, in many of these posts, the protections afforded by the Convention are necessary for the effective and safe performance of their functions.

More difficult was the issue whether security in the streets of London could and should be facilitated by changing the practice regarding demonstrations outside embassies. Unlike the United States and certain other states, the United Kingdom has no statutory requirement prohibiting demonstrations within a specified distance of diplomatic premises. The matter is simply dealt with by local acts following for the direction of routes of processions and demonstrations, the maintenance of order and prevention of obstructions, and the control of public order generally. There is no special power given to police commissioners in respect of offenses at or near diplomatic premises.

Article 22 of the Vienna Convention nonetheless places on the receiving state "a special duty to prevent disturbance of the peace of the mission or impairment of its dignity." Article 22 (together with other articles) is given the force of law in the United Kingdom by the Diplomatic Privileges Act 1964. The view was offered in certain quarters that the absence of legislation to keep demonstrations at a certain distance from embassies is incompatible with the obligations under Article 22.

Is the peace of the mission or the impairment of its dignity prevented by peaceful demonstrations in the immediate vicinity? Or is the better view that Article 22 is not meant to insulate the foreign mission from expressions of public opinion within the receiving state (provided always that there is free and safe access and egress for the members of the mission, and no real fear of danger to mission staff or damage to the premises)?

During the summer of 1984, a police commander moved a demonstration away from the east pavement of Trafalgar Square outside the South African High Commission, arresting those who refused to move. This incident was interesting in several respects. Demonstrations had taken place on the east pavement of Trafalgar Square every Friday for 2 years. On this occasion, though the demonstration did not differ from those held previously, the responsible police commander took the view that it violated the Diplomatic Privileges Act. He arrived at this view without consulting the Foreign and Commonwealth Office. The Magistrates Court that dealt with the case of one of the persons arrested found that impairment of dignity required abusing or insulting behavior, and that political demonstrations per se do not amount to such.

The present writer welcomes this robust approach to Article 22 of the Convention, and also the decision of the Foreign Affairs Committee not to recommend statutory distances for demonstrations. As the committee noted, a breakdown of public order outside the mission premises (for which there are appropriate statutory powers) would put in jeopardy the fulfilling of obligations under Article 22; "an orderly expression of opposition to the policies of the sending State cannot of itself do so."

At the end of the day, terroristic abuse of diplomatic status can be controlled neither by moving demonstrations away from embassies nor by trying to amend the Vienna Convention. What is needed is close coordination between the various parts of government, and international security cooperation. Governments must keep themselves more fully informed than they have sometimes appeared to be in the past, and should not, for the sake of promoting trade or other reasons, seek to accommodate those who are reluctant to conform to the requirements of the Vienna Convention. Above all, those remedies available for abuse in the Convention especially the power to limit the size of the mission, to declare a diplomat persona non grata should be used with firmness and vigor, and not just reserved for matters related to espionage.

As is so often the case, legal means are at hand; but they need to be matched by political will.

* * *

On April 23, 1985, the British Government issued its reply to the Foreign Affairs Committee's report (Cmd. 9497).

4. Rosalyn Higgins, *UK Foreign Affairs Committee Report on the Abuse of Diplomatic Immunities and Privileges: Government Response and Report*
80 AM. J. INT'L L. 135 (1986)

The Foreign Affairs Committee had made a detailed set of recommendations. In a very rare act, the Government has indicated that it accepts all the major recommendations made by the committee. Thus, the Government has accepted that it would be difficult to achieve any restrictive amendment to the Vienna Convention, that it would be of doubtful net benefit to do so, and that it should "not ... concentrate on amendment of the Convention as a major element in new policies to restrict abuse of immunities"; that a firmer policy in the application of the Convention should be preserved; that electronic scanning of diplomatic bags should take place on specific occasions if the need arises; that it should be made clear to all diplomats that they may well be required to leave the country if they violate the criminal law (other than in minor matters); that the Government should be "significantly readier than in the past" to limit the size of a mission where there is cause for significant concern about the overall nature of the mission's activities; and that the Foreign and Commonwealth Office should take all steps, as early as possible, to inform itself about those arriving to take up mission posts.

NOTES AND QUESTIONS

1. Are the historical justifications for immunity persuasive by contemporary standards? What about the necessity of "insuring free communication between states"? What about the host state's "right of self-defense"? *See* Veronica L. Maginnis, *Limiting Diplomatic Immunity: Lessons Learned from the 1946 Convention on the Privileges and Immunities of the United Nations*, 28 BROOK. J. INT'L L. 989 (2003).

2. Rational policy must be concerned not only for communications but also for efficiency in the use of peaceful procedures for the promotion of all values. With respect to remedies available for violation of doctrines concerning diplomatic immunity, it is easily observed that the sanctions of reciprocity and retaliation work effectively and effortlessly. The right of agréation and the power to demand recall afford considerable protection against abuse of diplomatic immunities.

3. Sometimes, however, these remedies don't work too smoothly. See Sean D. Murphy, *Expulsion of Cuban Diplomat for Spying*, 94 AM. J. INT'L L. 535 (2000):

On February 17, 2000, U.S. law enforcement officers arrested a U.S. Immigration and Naturalization Service (INS) official, Mariano Faget, on charges of violating the Espionage Act by leaking classified information to, and lying about a meeting with agents of, the government of Cuba. On February 19, the U.S. Department of State requested that Cuba withdraw José Imperatori, a vice consul of the Cuban interests section in Washington, D.C., from the United States within seven days; the charge was that Imperatori was an intelligence contact for Faget. Cuba refused to comply, however, stating that Imperatori should "remain in the United States to testify and prove full falseness to that accusation no matter what the consequences might be." The refusal to withdraw Imperatori resulted in the State Department's declaring Imperatori *persona non grata* and ordering him to depart the United States no later than 1:30 P.M. on February 26. The State Department further asserted that if Imperatori failed to leave, "he will no longer enjoy the privileges and immunities conferred by the Vienna Convention on Diplomatic Relations" and will "become subject to the laws of the United States."

On the morning of February 26, the day that Imperatori had been order to leave, he informed reporters that he had resigned from the Cuban interests section, had given up his diplomatic immunity, and was prepared to be arrested and tried for what he considered to be false accusations. Imperatori's subsequent failure to depart represented the first time that a foreign diplomat had defied a U.S. expulsion order. Later that day, at 8:45 P.M., agents of the FBI went to Imperatori's apartment, seized him, and took him to Reagan National Airport. An FBI airplane then flew him to Montreal, Canada. According to the State Department, Imperatori no longer enjoyed privileges and immunities under the Vienna Convention and was expelled for not departing the United States when ordered to do so. Although the expulsion to Canada was coordinated in advance by Canadian, Cuban, and U.S. officials, Imperatori also initially refused to leave Canada. He eventually returned to Cuba on March 2.

4. For a critical review of the need for protection of the diplomatic bag, see Gregory L. Stangle, *When Diplomacy Meets Illegality: Reevaluating the Need for the Diplomatic Bag*, 3 Dig. Int'l L. 51 (1995-96). The United States has protested violations of the status of the diplomatic bag vigorously.

* * *

Another intra-diplomatic regime remedy is the waiver of immunity by the sending state.

5. Sean D. Murphy, *Waiver of Georgian Diplomat's Immunity from Criminal Prosecution*

93 Am. J. Int'l L. 485 (1999)

On January 3, 1997, a diplomat posted at the Embassy of Georgia in Washington, D.C., Gueorgui Makharadze, was speeding in his car when it crashed, causing a multicar collision that killed sixteen year old Joviane Waltrick and injured four other persons. At the time of her death, Waltrick was a citizen of Brazil on a tourist visa in the United States.

The U.S. Attorney's office for the District of Columbia informed the Department of State that its initial review of the evidence indicated that Makharadze could be charged with negligent homicide, involuntary manslaughter, or second degree murder. Consequently, on January 9, the Department of State requested that the Georgian Embassy waive Makharadze's immunity from criminal prosecution. On January 10, President Eduard A. Shevardnadze of the Republic of Georgia announced that Georgia was prepared to waive the diplomat's immunity.

After further discussions between the two governments regarding the charges that would be brought against Makharadze, the Department of State, on February 11, 1997, transmitted to the Embassy of Georgia an affidavit setting forth the U.S. Attorney's evidence in the case and providing information on the maximum sentence that could be imposed if Makharadze were charged and convicted of involuntary manslaughter and aggravated assault. By diplomatic note dated February 14, the Embassy responded as follows:

> The Government of Georgia has considered the request of the United States Department of State and according to Article 32 of the Vienna Convention on Diplomatic Relations has waived the diplomatic immunity for Mr. George Makharadze, so he can be prosecuted in the United States, for the accident that took place on January 3, 1997, in Washington, DC.

After welcoming this decision, State Department spokesman Nicholas Burns noted that it was "highly unusual in modern diplomacy for a head of state to take a step like this. But given the emotions in the United States, given the feelings of the family and the local community here in Washington, D.C., we think it's the appropriate step for the Government of Georgia to take."

On February 20, 1997, Makharadze was charged with one count of involuntary manslaughter and four counts of aggravated assault for the death of Waltrick and injuries to four others. In October, Makharadze pleaded guilty. As part of a plea bargain, prosecutors agreed not to object to the diplomat's request to serve his sentence in a federal prison instead of in the District's Lorton Correctional Complex. He was sentenced to seven to twenty one years in prison on December 19.

On December 31, 1997, the estate of Joviane Waltrick filed a civil suit in federal court against various parties: Makharadze, the Republic of Georgia (for letting Makharadze drive despite a history of traffic violations), Yanni's Greek Tavern (where Makharadze drank wine immediately prior to the accident), the Ford Motor Co. and Jerry's Ford Sales (based on Makharadze's claims that the brakes had failed), and certain insurance and credit companies. In order to establish the responsibility of the Republic of Georgia, the complaint alleged that Makharadze had been acting within the scope of his employment since the accident occurred after he had consumed alcohol at an official dinner function and while he was using a vehicle leased by the Embassy.

On January 9, 1998, plaintiff's counsel in the case requested that the Department of State seek a waiver from the Republic of Georgia of Makharadze's immunity from civil suit. The Department of State responded, in part:

> Mr. Makharadze was a diplomatic agent accredited to the Embassy of Georgia. However, when he was incarcerated after having entered guilty pleas to criminal charges arising from the accident in which Miss

> Waltrick was killed, he ceased to perform diplomatic functions. Therefore, pursuant to Article 39(2) of the Vienna Convention on Diplomatic Relations, Mr. Makharadze has residual immunity from civil jurisdiction of U.S. courts only "with respect to acts performed ... in the exercise of his functions as a member of the mission."
>
> It is not the Department's practice to seek the waiver of immunity in civil cases in instances where the defendant's immunity is limited to acts done within the scope of his diplomatic functions. We note that Mr. Makharadze would be amenable to suit if the court were to determine that his actions were nondiplomatic in nature. If the court finds otherwise, your clients would continue to have recourse against the insurance company and other named defendants.

On April 22, 1998, counsel for Makharadze sought his dismissal from the civil case on grounds of diplomatic immunity. On May 29, U.S. District Judge Thomas F. Hogan granted the motion, concluding:

> Plaintiff has not established a waiver of defendant Makharadze's immunity from civil jurisdiction. Neither the Republic of Georgia's explicit waiver of criminal immunity nor the circumstances surrounding that waiver support such a conclusion. Furthermore, although defendant Makharadze no longer enjoys the blanket immunity granted to acting diplomatic officers, he enjoys residual immunity for actions taken in performance of his former duties. Because plaintiff explicitly pleads that the accident occurred in the course of defendant Makharadze' official duties, the Court must conclude that residual immunity attaches. Therefore, because defendant Makharadze enjoys immunity from the civil jurisdiction of this Court, the Court must dismiss him from the case.

On October 14, 1998, all remaining defendants except Yanni's Greek Tavern agreed to settle the lawsuit for an undisclosed amount in excess of $250,000.

NOTES AND QUESTIONS

1. Was the waiver of criminal immunity by the sending state the best possible solution to the situation at hand? What about declaring the diplomat *persona non grata* and expelling him?

2. Diplomatic immunity is granted by the host state via the *agrément*. Are other states bound to respect it, especially in the context of state succession? For an interesting factual constellation, see Bardo Fassbender, *S. v. Berlin Court of Appeal and District Court of Berlin Tiergarten. German Federal Constitutional Court, June 10, 1997,* 92 AM. J. INT'L L. 74 (1998):

> On July 21, 1994, the District Court (Amtsgericht) of Berlin Tiergarten issued a warrant for the arrest of S., the former Ambassador of Syria to the German Democratic Republic (GDR), on charges of having assisted in the commission of murder and the bringing about of a bomb explosion in West Berlin in August 1983. The court of appeal reinstated the warrant after the Higher District Court (Landgericht) of Berlin revoked it. The German Federal Constitutional Court dismissed the constitutional complaint against the decisions of the lower courts, holding that none of the fundamental rights guaranteed by the Basic Law had been violated.

> In the central part of its reasoning on the international issues involved, the Court held that S. had rightfully been denied diplomatic immunity by the Berlin courts. Only the GDR, as the receiving state, and not the Federal Republic of Germany, as a "third state," was obliged to respect the subsisting immunity of a diplomat with regard to acts performed in the exercise of his official functions according to Article 39, paragraph 2 of the Vienna Convention on Diplomatic Relations of 1961. International law, the Court said, also did not provide for the devolution of that obligation to the Federal Republic as the GDR's successor. ...
>
> The German Court presented its decision as being completely in line with the law as it stands and previous state practice. But it actually introduced a severe limitation on diplomatic immunity. Diplomatic agents are subjected to the jurisdiction of all states but the receiving state, even with respect to acts committed in the receiving state. Among the many judicial rulings cited by the Court there is, as far as I can see, not one in favor of trying a diplomat accredited, or previously accredited, to a third state for an act performed by him in his official capacity on the territory of the third state.
>
> Some may regret that states have not yet agreed on a limitation of diplomatic immunity with regard to participation in terrorist acts. Others may fear that such a limitation could expose the effective performance of diplomatic functions to arbitrary determinations of what constitutes such participation. Be that as it may, in the absence of such a limitation, the decision rendered by the German Constitutional Court appears to be questionable.

Do you agree?

3. *See Regina v. Bow Street Metro. Stipendiary Magistrate, ex parte Pinochet Ugarte,* [1998] 3 W.L.R. 1456 (H.L.), 37 I.L.M. 1302 (1998). In a remarkable opinion, set aside only because of the perceived bias of another judge, Lord Nicholls of Birkenhead stated:

> ...[I]t hardly needs saying that torture of his subjects, or of aliens, would be regarded by international law as a function of a head of state. All states disavow the use of torture as abhorrent, although from time to time still resort to it. Similarly, the taking of hostages, as much as torture, has been outlawed by the international community as an offence. International law recognizes, of course, that the function of head of state may include activities which are wrongful, even illegal, by the laws of his own state or by the laws of other states. But international law has made plain that certain types of conduct, including torture and hostage-taking, are not acceptable conduct on the part of anyone. This applies as much to heads of state, or even more so, as it does to everyone else; the contrary conclusion would make a mockery of international law. 37 I.L.M. at 1333.

See also DARREN G. HAWKINS, INTERNATIONAL HUMAN RIGHTS AND AUTHORITARIAN RULE IN CHILE (U. of Nebraska Press 2002); Kerry Creque O'Neill, *A New Customary Law of Head of State Immunity?: Hirohito and Pinochet*, 38 STAN. J. INT'L L. 289 (2002). For additional discussion of the *Pinochet* case, see Jose E. Alvarez, *Pinochet Revisited*, 95 AM. SOC. INT'L L. PROC. 139 (2001).

4. Assume there is evidence of war crimes committed by an ambassador of one of the successor countries to the former Yugoslavia. The International Criminal Tribunal for Yugoslavia demands of his host state extradition to The Hague. Should it be granted? *See* Adam Isaac Hasson, *Extraterritorial Jurisdiction and Sovereign Immunity on Trial: Noriega, Pinochet, and Milosevic – Trends in Political Accountability and Transnational Criminal Law*, 25 B.C. INT'L & COMP. L. REV. 125 (2002); and Michael A. Tunks, *Diplomats or Defendants? Defining the Future of Head-of-State Immunity*, 52 DUKE L. J. 651 (2002).

6. Rome Statute of the International Criminal Court

July 17, 1998, 37 I.L.M. 999 (1998)

Article 27: *Irrelevance of official capacity*

1. This Statute shall apply equally to all persons without any distinction based on official capacity. In particular, official capacity as a Head of State or Government, a member of a Government or parliament, an elected representative or a government official shall in no case exempt a person from criminal responsibility under this Statute, nor shall it, in and of itself, constitute a ground for reduction of sentence.

2. Immunities or special procedural rules which may attach to the official capacity of a person, whether under national or international law, shall not bar the Court from exercising its jurisdiction over such a person.

7. Case Concerning the Arrest Warrant of 11 April 2000 (Dem. Rep. of Congo v. Belg.)

2002 I.C.J. 121 (Feb. 14)

13. On 11 April 2000 an investigating judge of the Brussels *tribunal de première instance* issued "an international arrest warrant *in absentia*" against Mr. Abdulaye Yerodia Ndombasi, charging him, as perpetrator or co-perpetrator, with offences constituting grave breaches of the Geneva Conventions of 1949 and of the Additional Protocols thereto, and with crimes against humanity.

At the time when the arrest warrant was issued Mr. Yerodia was the Minister for Foreign Affairs of the Congo.

14. The arrest warrant was transmitted to the Congo on 7 June 2000, being received by the Congolese authorities on 12 July 2000. According to Belgium, the warrant was at the same time transmitted to the International Criminal Police Organization (Interpol), an organization whose function is to enhance and facilitate cross-border criminal police co-operation worldwide; through the latter, it was circulated internationally.

15. In the arrest warrant, Mr. Yerodia is accused of having made various speeches inciting racial hatred during the month of August 1998 [In particular, as detailed in para. 67, "[t]hese speeches allegedly had the effect of inciting the population to attack Tutsi residents of Kinshasa: there were dragnet searches, manhunts (the Tutsi enemy) and lynchings. The speeches inciting racial hatred thus are said to have resulted in several hundred deaths, the internment of Tutsis, summary executions, arbitrary arrests and unfair trials."]. The crimes with which Mr. Yerodia was charged were punishable in Belgium under the Law of 16 June 1993 "concerning the Punishment of Grave Breaches of the International Geneva Conventions of 12 August 1949 and of Protocols I and II of 8 June 1977 Additional Thereto", as amended by the Law of 19 February 1999 "concerning the Punishment of Serious Violations of International Humanitarian Law" (hereinafter referred to as the "Belgian Law").

Article 7 of the Belgian Law provides that "The Belgian courts shall have jurisdiction in respect of the offences provided for in the present Law, wheresoever they may have been committed". In the present case, according to Belgium, the complaints that initiated the proceedings as a result of which the arrest warrant was issued emanated from 12 individuals all resident in Belgium, five of whom were of Belgian nationality. It is not contested by Belgium, however, that the alleged acts to which the arrest warrant relates were committed outside Belgian territory, that Mr. Yerodia was not a Belgian national at the time of those acts, and that Mr. Yerodia was not in Belgian territory at the time that the arrest warrant was issued and circulated. That no Belgian nationals were victims of the violence that was said to have resulted from Mr. Yerodia's alleged offences was also uncontested.

Article 5, paragraph 3, of the Belgian Law further provides that "[i]mmunity attaching to the official capacity of a person shall not prevent the application of the present Law".

16. At the hearings, Belgium further claimed that it offered "to entrust the case to the competent authorities [of the Congo] for enquiry and possible prosecution", and referred to a certain number of steps which it claimed to have taken in this regard from September 2000, that is, before the filing of the Application instituting proceedings. The Congo for its part stated the following: "We have scant information concerning the form [of these Belgian proposals]." It added that "these proposals . . . appear to have been made very belatedly, namely *after* an arrest warrant against Mr. Yerodia had been issued."

17. On 17 October 2000, the Congo filed in the Registry an Application instituting the present proceedings ... in which the Court was requested "to declare that the Kingdom of Belgium shall annul the international arrest warrant issued on 11 April 2000". The Congo relied in its Application on two separate legal grounds. First, it claimed that "[t]he *universal jurisdiction* that the Belgian State attributes to itself under Article 7 of the Law in question"constituted a "[v]iolation of the principle that a State may not exercise its authority on the territory of another State and of the principle of sovereign equality among all Members of the United Nations, as laid down in Article 2, paragraph 1, of the Charter of the United Nations".

Secondly, it claimed that "[t]he non-recognition, on the basis of Article 5 ... of the Belgian Law, of the immunity of a Minister for Foreign Affairs in office" constituted a "[v]iolation of the diplomatic immunity of the Minister for Foreign Affairs of a sovereign State, as recognized by the jurisprudence of the Court and following from Article 41, paragraph 2, of the Vienna Convention of 18 April 1961 on Diplomatic Relations".

18. On the same day that it filed its Application instituting proceedings, the Congo submitted a request to the Court for the indication of a provisional measure under Article 41 of the Statute of the Court. During the hearings devoted to consideration of that request, the Court was informed that in November 2000 a

ministerial reshuffle had taken place in the Congo, following which Mr. Yerodia had ceased to hold office as Minister for Foreign Affairs and had been entrusted with the portfolio of Minister of Education. Belgium accordingly claimed that the Congo's Application had become moot and asked the Court, as has already been recalled, to remove the case from the List. By Order of 8 December 2000, the Court rejected both Belgium's submissions to that effect and also the Congo's request for the indication of provisional measures.

19. From mid-April 2001, with the formation of a new Government in the Congo, Mr. Yerodia ceased to hold the post of Minister of Education. He no longer holds any ministerial office today. ...

[The Court first finds that the dispute is not moot.]

45. As indicated above ..., in its Application instituting these proceedings, the Congo originally challenged the legality of the arrest warrant of 11 April 2000 on two separate grounds: on the one hand, Belgium's claim to exercise a universal jurisdiction and, on the other, the alleged violation of the immunities of the Minister for Foreign Affairs of the Congo then in office. However, in its submissions in its Memorial, and in its final submissions at the close of the oral proceedings, the Congo invokes only the latter ground.

46. As a matter of logic, the second ground should be addressed only once there has been a determination in respect of the first, since it is only where a State has jurisdiction under international law in relation to a particular matter that there can be any question of immunities in regard to the exercise of that jurisdiction. However, in the present case, and in view of the final form of the Congo's submissions, the Court will address first the question whether, assuming that it had jurisdiction under international law to issue and circulate the arrest warrant of 11 April 2000, Belgium in so doing violated the immunities of the then Minister for Foreign Affairs of the Congo. ...

51. The Court would observe at the outset that in international law it is firmly established that, as also diplomatic and consular agents, certain holders of high-ranking office in a State, such as the Head of State, Head of Government and Minister for Foreign Affairs, enjoy immunities from jurisdiction in other States, both civil and criminal. For the purposes of the present case, it is only the immunity from criminal jurisdiction and the inviolability of an incumbent Minister for Foreign Affairs that fall for the Court to consider.

52. A certain number of treaty instruments were cited by the Parties in this regard. These included, first, the Vienna Convention on Diplomatic Relations of 18 April 1961, which states in its preamble that the purpose of diplomatic privileges and immunities is "to ensure the efficient performance of the functions of diplomatic missions as representing States". It provides in Article 32 that only the sending State may waive such immunity. On these points, the Vienna Convention on Diplomatic Relations, to which both the Congo and Belgium are parties, reflects customary international law. The same applies to the corresponding provi-

sions of the Vienna Convention on Consular Relations of 24 April 1963, to which the Congo and Belgium are also parties.

The Congo and Belgium further cite the New York Convention on Special Missions of 8 December 1969, to which they are not, however, parties. They recall that under Article 21, paragraph 2, of that Convention:

> The Head of the Government, the Minister for Foreign Affairs and other persons of high rank, when they take part in a special mission of the sending State, shall enjoy in the receiving State or in a third State, in addition to what is granted by the present Convention, the facilities, privileges and immunities accorded by international law.

These conventions provide useful guidance on certain aspects of the question of immunities. They do not, however, contain any provision specifically defining the immunities enjoyed by Ministers for Foreign Affairs. It is consequently on the basis of customary international law that the Court must decide the questions relating to the immunities of such Ministers raised in the present case.

53. In customary international law, the immunities accorded to Ministers for Foreign Affairs are not granted for their personal benefit, but to ensure the effective performance of their functions on behalf of their respective States. In order to determine the extent of these immunities, the Court must therefore first consider the nature of the functions exercised by a Minister for Foreign Affairs. He or she is in charge of his or her Government's diplomatic activities and generally acts as its representative in international negotiations and intergovernmental meetings. Ambassadors and other diplomatic agents carry out their duties under his or her authority. His or her acts may bind the State represented, and there is a presumption that a Minister for Foreign Affairs, simply by virtue of that office, has full powers to act on behalf of the State (see, e.g., Art. 7, para. 2 *(a)*, of the 1969 Vienna Convention on the Law of Treaties). In the performance of these functions, he or she is frequently required to travel internationally, and thus must be in a position freely to do so whenever the need should arise. He or she must also be in constant communication with the Government, and with its diplomatic missions around the world, and be capable at any time of communicating with representatives of other States. The Court further observes that a Minister for Foreign Affairs, responsible for the conduct of his or her State's relations with all other States, occupies a position such that, like the Head of State or the Head of Government, he or she is recognized under international law as representative of the State solely by virtue of his or her office. He or she does not have to present letters of credence: to the contrary, it is generally the Minister who determines the authority to be conferred upon diplomatic agents and countersigns their letters of credence. Finally, it is to the Minister for Foreign Affairs that *chargés d'affaires* are accredited.

54. The Court accordingly concludes that the functions of a Minister for Foreign Affairs are such that, throughout the duration of his or her office, he or she when abroad enjoys full immunity from criminal jurisdiction and inviolability.

That immunity and that inviolability protect the individual concerned against any act of authority of another State which would hinder him or her in the performance of his or her duties.

55. In this respect, no distinction can be drawn between acts performed by a Minister for Foreign Affairs in an "official" capacity, and those claimed to have been performed in a "private capacity", or, for that matter, between acts performed before the person concerned assumed office as Minister for Foreign Affairs and acts committed during the period of office. Thus, if a Minister for Foreign Affairs is arrested in another State on a criminal charge, he or she is clearly thereby prevented from exercising the functions of his or her office. The consequences of such impediment to the exercise of those official functions are equally serious, regardless of whether the Minister for Foreign Affairs was, at the time of arrest, present in the territory of the arresting State on an "official" visit or a "private" visit, regardless of whether the arrest relates to acts allegedly performed before the person became the Minister for Foreign Affairs or to acts performed while in office, and regardless of whether the arrest relates to alleged acts performed in an "official" capacity or a "private" capacity. Furthermore, even the mere risk that, by travelling to or transiting another State a Minister for Foreign Affairs might be exposing himself or herself to legal proceedings could deter the Minister from travelling internationally when required to do so for the purposes of the performance of his or her official functions.

56. The Court will now address Belgium's argument that immunities accorded to incumbent Ministers for Foreign Affairs can in no case protect them where they are suspected of having committed war crimes or crimes against humanity. In support of this position, Belgium refers in its Counter-Memorial to various legal instruments creating international criminal tribunals, to examples from national legislation, and to the jurisprudence of national and international courts. Belgium begins by pointing out that certain provisions of the instruments creating international criminal tribunals state expressly that the official capacity of a person shall not be a bar to the exercise by such tribunals of their jurisdiction. Belgium also places emphasis on certain decisions of national courts, and in particular on the judgments rendered on 24 March 1999 by the House of Lords in the United Kingdom and on 13 March 2001 by the Court of Cassation in France in the *Pinochet* and *Qaddafi* cases respectively, in which it contends that an exception to the immunity rule was accepted in the case of serious crimes under international law. Thus, according to Belgium, the *Pinochet* decision recognizes an exception to the immunity rule when Lord Millett stated that "[i]nternational law cannot be supposed to have established a crime having the character of a *jus cogens* and at the same time to have provided an immunity which is co-extensive with the obligation it seeks to impose", or when Lord Phillips of Worth Matravers said that "no established rule of international law requires state immunity *rationae materiae* to be accorded in respect of prosecution for an international crime". As to the French Court of Cassation, Belgium contends that, in holding that, "under international law as it currently stands, the crime alleged [acts of terrorism],

irrespective of its gravity, does not come within the exceptions to the principle of immunity from jurisdiction for incumbent foreign Heads of State", the Court explicitly recognized the existence of such exceptions.

57. The Congo, for its part, states that, under international law as it currently stands, there is no basis for asserting that there is any exception to the principle of absolute immunity from criminal process of an incumbent Minister for Foreign Affairs where he or she is accused of having committed crimes under international law. In support of this contention, the Congo refers to State practice, giving particular consideration in this regard to the *Pinochet* and *Qaddafi* cases, and concluding that such practice does not correspond to that which Belgium claims but, on the contrary, confirms the absolute nature of the immunity from criminal process of Heads of State and Ministers for Foreign Affairs. Thus, in the *Pinochet* case, the Congo cites Lord Browne-Wilkinson's statement that "[t]his immunity enjoyed by a head of state in power and an ambassador in post is a complete immunity attached to the person of the head of state or ambassador and rendering him immune from all actions or prosecutions . . .." According to the Congo, the French Court of Cassation adopted the same position in its *Qaddafi* judgment, in affirming that "international custom bars the prosecution of incumbent Heads of State, in the absence of any contrary international provision binding on the parties concerned, before the criminal courts of a foreign State". As regards the instruments creating international criminal tribunals and the latter's jurisprudence, these, in the Congo's view, concern only those tribunals, and no inference can be drawn from them in regard to criminal proceedings before national courts against persons enjoying immunity under international law.

58. The Court has carefully examined State practice, including national legislation and those few decisions of national higher courts, such as the House of Lords or the French Court of Cassation. It has been unable to deduce from this practice that there exists under customary international law any form of exception to the rule according immunity from criminal jurisdiction and inviolability to incumbent Ministers for Foreign Affairs, where they are suspected of having committed war crimes or crimes against humanity.

The Court has also examined the rules concerning the immunity or criminal responsibility of persons having an official capacity contained in the legal instruments creating international criminal tribunals, and which are specifically applicable to the latter (see Charter of the International Military Tribunal of Nuremberg, Art. 7; Charter of the International Military Tribunal of Tokyo, Art. 6; Statute of the International Criminal Tribunal for the former Yugoslavia, Art. 7, para. 2; Statute of the International Criminal Tribunal for Rwanda, Art. 6, para. 2; Statute of the International Criminal Court, Art. 27). It finds that these rules likewise do not enable it to conclude that any such an exception exists in customary international law in regard to national courts.

Finally, none of the decisions of the Nuremberg and Tokyo international military tribunals, or of the International Criminal Tribunal for the former Yugoslavia, cited by Belgium deal with the question of the immunities of incumbent Ministers for Foreign Affairs before national courts where they are accused of having committed war crimes or crimes against humanity. The Court accordingly notes that those decisions are in no way at variance with the findings it has reached above.

In view of the foregoing, the Court accordingly cannot accept Belgium's argument in this regard.

59. It should further be noted that the rules governing the jurisdiction of national courts must be carefully distinguished from those governing jurisdictional immunities: jurisdiction does not imply absence of immunity, while absence of immunity does not imply jurisdiction. Thus, although various international conventions on the prevention and punishment of certain serious crimes impose on States obligations of prosecution or extradition, thereby requiring them to extend their criminal jurisdiction, such extension of jurisdiction in no way affects immunities under customary international law, including those of Ministers for Foreign Affairs. These remain opposable before the courts of a foreign State, even where those courts exercise such a jurisdiction under these conventions.

60. The Court emphasizes, however, that the *immunity* from jurisdiction enjoyed by incumbent Ministers for Foreign Affairs does not mean that they enjoy *impunity* in respect of any crimes they might have committed, irrespective of their gravity. Immunity from criminal jurisdiction and individual criminal responsibility are quite separate concepts. While jurisdictional immunity is procedural in nature, criminal responsibility is a question of substantive law.

Jurisdictional immunity may well bar prosecution for a certain period or for certain offences; it cannot exonerate the person to whom it applies from all criminal responsibility.

61. Accordingly, the immunities enjoyed under international law by an incumbent or former Minister for Foreign Affairs do not represent a bar to criminal prosecution in certain circumstances.

First, such persons enjoy no criminal immunity under international law in their own countries, and may thus be tried by those countries' courts in accordance with the relevant rules of domestic law.

Secondly, they will cease to enjoy immunity from foreign jurisdiction if the State which they represent or have represented decides to waive that immunity.

Thirdly, after a person ceases to hold the office of Minister for Foreign Affairs, he or she will no longer enjoy all of the immunities accorded by international law in other States. Provided that it has jurisdiction under international law, a court of one State may try a former Minister for Foreign Affairs of another State in respect of acts committed prior or subsequent to his or her period of office, as well as in respect of acts committed during that period of office in a private capacity.

Fourthly, an incumbent or former Minister for Foreign Affairs may be subject to criminal proceedings before certain international criminal courts, where they have jurisdiction. Examples include the International Criminal Tribunal for the former Yugoslavia, and the International Criminal Tribunal for Rwanda, established pursuant to Security Council resolutions under Chapter VII of the United Nations Charter, and the future International Criminal Court created by the 1998 Rome Convention. The latter's Statute expressly provides, in Article 27, paragraph 2, that "[i]mmunities or special procedural rules which may attach to the official capacity of a person, whether under national or international law, shall not bar the Court from exercising its jurisdiction over such a person".

NOTES AND QUESTIONS

1. Could Belgium now turn around and issue a new international arrest warrant against Mr. Yerodia, based on the same facts? Should it be able to?

2. On August 1, 2003, BBC News reported the following:

> **Belgium Amends War Crimes Law**
>
> The Belgian Senate has given final approval to a new version of a war crimes law which had led to cases being filed against several world leaders.
>
> The bill was passed by 39 votes in favour to four against and 20 abstentions.
>
> The revised law drops a controversial "universal competence" clause which led to complaints being filed against US President George W Bush, UK Prime Minister Tony Blair and Israeli Prime Minister Ariel Sharon.
>
> The lower house of parliament approved the bill amending the controversial law earlier this week.
>
> It now only needs the signature of King Albert II - a formality - to become law.
>
> "Unhappily, the noble cause that prompted the parliament to adopt this law was hit with abuse and manipulated for political ends," Foreign Minister Louis Michel told the Senate before the vote.
>
> Previously, Belgian courts could try anyone for war crimes, genocide or crimes against humanity, regardless of their nationality and of where the alleged crimes were committed.
>
> The new bill will limit the jurisdiction of the courts to cases only involving Belgian citizens and residents.
>
> The US had threatened to block further funding for Nato's new headquarters in Belgium until the law was withdrawn.
>
> After his re-election in May, Prime Minister Guy Verhofstadt promised the law would be scrapped.

BBC News, Belgium Amends War Crimes Law (Aug. 1, 2003), *available at* http://news.bbc.co.uk/2/hi/europe/3116975.stm. For the full text of the amended law, *see* Loi relative aux violations graves du droit humanitaire (Moniteur Belge du 7 août 2003), arts. 14-16; *see also* the report of the House Justice Committee, July 28, 2003, Parliamentary Doc. 51 0103/003, at 4-5, *available at* http://www1.dekamer.be/FLWB/pdf/51/0103/51K0103003.pdf [hereinafter Justice Committee Report].

Does the new law make any further action in the case above impossible?

V. REGULATING INTERNATIONAL AGREEMENTS

A. Issues and Policies

The special importance of agreements among the strategies of states resides in the fact that, in the absence of centralized legislative institutions in the world arena, agreements offer one of the closest approaches to the considered and deliberate prescription of future policies which is the characteristic function of constitutive and legislative institutions in municipal arenas. The most fundamental policy of any law of contracts, expressing a fundamental preference for the shaping and sharing of values by persuasion rather than coercion, that agreements must be kept is expressed in the familiar maxim *pacta sunt servanda*. Thus Article 26 of the 1969 Vienna Convention on the Law of Treaties, largely reflective of customary international law, provides that "Every treaty in force is binding upon the parties to it and must be per-formed by them in good faith."

All agreements between states project policies into the future. Even the "conveyance" of territory implies a pattern of future rights and duties with respect to the territory transferred. Hence, the traditional distinction between "law-making" and other treaties adumbrates only a very vague reference to the number of parties to an agreement and the comprehensiveness of policies projected.

Agreements between states do, however, differ in the number of parties sharing commitment, in the scope and detail of policies projected, and in the expectations of permanence or impermanence attending commitment. The very different functions performed by such agreements may be summarized as:

(1) Constitutive—the establishment of the basic features of a comprehensive process of authoritative decision as in the constitutional charters of the United Nations and the specialized agencies.

(2) Legislative—the prescription of particular policies about particular events in public order for varying numbers of states, with expectations on occasion that conformity will be required even of non-parties.

(3) Contractual—the establishment of shared expectations of commitment between two or more states for policies of varying scope and importance, but not creating expectations of general community prescription.

(4) Exchange transactions—the division or transfer of existing values, with a minimum projection of future policy as in "conveyance."

The debate over whether differences in legal prescriptions attend the various phases in the making, interpretation, performance, and termination of agreements, depending upon differences in function and values at stake, will require for its resolution a very careful study of past trends in decision. Highest level prescriptions are projected as applicable to all agreements and the detailed application of these principles varies of course as does the application of other principles, with many varying factors in particular contexts. Note should be taken of these variations during our inquiry. The designation of such agreements, whether they be called "treaties," "conventions," "covenants," "protocols," etc. is immaterial; the prevailing generic term is "treaty" as reflected in the 1969 Vienna Convention (Article 2(1)(a)).

Agreements between states also play a most important role in the development of customary international law. Because of the dual function of state officials in the world arena—acting alternately as claimants and decision makers—agreements may both express the demands or claims of certain states against the general community of states and establish the uniformities in expectation which ultimately add up to lawfulness. The fact that many uniform agreements have been made, and tolerated without protest, over a period of time is often adduced as good evidence of customary international law.

The making, performance, and termination of international agreements, as of other agreements, involves, of course, much more than mere shapes on paper or agitations in the air. Most comprehensively described, what is involved is a complex of component sub-processes: the making of a commitment, the performance or non-performance of a commitment, and the termination or other modification of a commitment. A full exposition of the law of international agreements would require the examination of each of these sub-processes in terms of the familiar institutional categories of participants, perspectives, situations, bases of power, strategies, and outcomes. Here we can offer only illustrative specification with respect to the more important, or more disputed, features of each of these sub-processes.

B. The Formation of International Agreements

The "making" of an international agreement is not a simple single act. It is rather a complex process, requiring performance of a variety of different functions or tasks by the officials of a participating state.

Among the functions which must be distinguished for even minimal clarity are the following: (1) the formulation of rational policies to guide the conduct of negotiations with other states; (2) the conduct of negotiations with the representatives of other states; (3) the approval of an agreement for internal application within the state, when such internal application is contemplated; (4) the approval of an agreement for the external commitment of the state; (5) the final utterance of the agreement as the external commitment of the state to other states.

The fulfillment of this external commitment may involve many events, subsequent to final utterance, and requires a similarly comprehensive analysis, as developed below.

Treaties are negotiated by agents of states involved. Usually, once the agents agree on a text, the authenticity of this agreed-upon mutual commitment is confirmed by the agents placing their initials on the draft agreement ("initialing"). Their principals, usually the heads of state or their representatives, then sign the treaty within a time period specified in the treaty, and submit it to internal processes, usually legislative authorities, for approval. Once this approval is secured, the heads of state express the consent of their state to be bound by depositing an instrument of ratification with the depositary power (in the case of a multilateral treaty) or with the other state party (in the case of a bilateral treaty). In the case of a multilateral treaty not signed in time, a state can still validly declare its consent to be bound by submitting an instrument of accession.

The Secretary-General of the United Nations is the main depositary of multilateral treaties. For a detailed account of the pertinent practice of the United Nations Secretariat, see the UNITED NATIONS TREATY HANDBOOK, U.N. Doc. E.02.V.2.

The competency of state agents in the treaty-making process will be discussed in the following section.

1. Regulating the Competency of Participants

The processes of authority within states, as we have seen, project certain officials into interactions in the world arena with apparent authority to commit their states to future policies.

In some contexts, the authority, both of the bodies politic which officials purport to represent and of the particular officials themselves, may be questioned for conformity to international law. In other contexts, the authority of particular officials to represent or commit their state may be questioned by the standards of their internal, constitutional law. On occasion, when the requirements of international law and national law differ, decision-makers representing the general community must choose between the two. More fundamentally, the adequacy of the internal processes of authority established by states for engaging in processes of persuasion with other states most drastically affects the whole flow of interactions between states.

Our inquiry must accordingly extend to both international and national prescriptions relating to competency.

a. International Prescriptions

(1) Vienna Convention on the Law of Treaties

May 23, 1969, Arts. 6, 7, 8, 27, 46 & 47,
1155 U.N.T.S. 331, 340 (1969)

Article 6. Every state possesses capacity to conclude treaties.

Article 7. (1) A person is considered as representing a State for the purpose of adopting or authenticating the text of a treaty or for the purpose of expressing the consent of the State to be bound by a treaty if:

(*a*) he produces appropriate full powers; or

(*b*) it appears from the practice of the States concerned or from other circumstances that their intention was to consider that person as representing the State for such purposes and to dispense with full powers.

(2) In virtue of their functions and without having to produce full powers, the following are considered as representing their State:

(*a*) Heads of State, Heads of Government and Ministers for Foreign Affairs, for the purpose of performing all acts relating to the conclusion of a treaty;

(*b*) heads of diplomatic missions, for the purpose of adopting the text of a treaty between the accrediting State and the State to which they are accredited;

(*c*) representatives accredited by States to an international conference or to an international organization or one of its organs, for the purpose of adopting the text of a treaty in that conference, organization or organ.

Article 8. An act relating to the conclusion of a treaty performed by a person who cannot be considered under article 7 as authorized to represent a State for that purpose is without legal effect unless afterwards confirmed by that State. …

Article 27. A party may not invoke the provisions of its internal law as justification for its failure to perform a treaty. This rule is without prejudice to article 46. …

Article 46. (1) A State may not invoke the fact that its consent to be bound by a treaty has been expressed in violation of a provision of its internal law regarding competence to conclude treaties as invalidating its consent unless that violation was manifest and concerned a rule of its internal law of fundamental importance.

(2) A violation is manifest if it would be objectively evident to any State conducting itself in the matter in accordance with normal practice and in good faith.

Article 47. If the authority of a representative to express the consent of a State to be bound by a particular treaty has been made subject to a specific restriction, his omission to observe that restriction may not be invoked as invalidating the consent expressed by him unless the restriction was notified to the other negotiating States prior to his expressing such consent.

b. National Prescriptions: The American Constitutional Design

The constitutional distribution of competence among the different governmental institutions (executive, legislative, judicial) for performance of these different functions might of course differ greatly from state to state, and the states of the world today obviously do exhibit many apparent differences in such distribution. It is believed, however, that most of the major states present an astonishingly similar pattern.

We will make detailed examination of the constitutional structures and practices of the United States as an illustration of this pattern.

(1) The Treaty-Making Power

(a) U. S. Const. art. II, § 2, cl. 2

He [the President] shall have power by and with the Advice and Consent of the Senate to make Treaties, provided two thirds of the Senators present concur.

(b) Missouri v. Holland

252 U.S. 416 (1920)

Justice HOLMES: This is a bill in equity brought by the State of Missouri to prevent a game warden of the United States from attempting to enforce the Migratory Bird Treaty Act of July 3, 1918, c. 128, 40 Stat. 755, and the regulations made by the Secretary of Agriculture in pursuance of the same. The ground of the bill is that the statute is an unconstitutional interference with the rights reserved to the States by the Tenth Amendment, and that the acts of the de-fendant done and threatened under that authority invade the sovereign right of the State and contravene its will manifested in statutes. The State also al-leges a pecuniary interest, as owner of the wild birds within its borders and otherwise, admitted by the Government to be sufficient, but it is enough that the bill is a reasonable and proper means to assert the alleged quasi sovereign rights of a State. ... A motion to dismiss was sustained by the District Court on the ground that the act of Congress is constitutional. … The State appeals.

On December 8, 1916, a treaty between the United States and Great Britain was proclaimed by the President. It recited that many species of birds in their annual migrations traversed certain parts of the United States and of Canada, that they were of great value as a source of food and in de-stroying insects injurious to vegetation, but were in danger of extermination through lack of adequate protection. It therefore provided for specified close seasons and protection in other forms, and agreed that the two powers would take or propose to their lawmaking bodies the necessary measures for carrying the treaty out. 39 Stat. 1702. The above mentioned Act of July 3, 1918, entitled an act to give effect to the convention, prohibited the killing, capturing or selling any of the migratory birds included in the terms of the treaty except as permitted by regulations compatible with those terms, to be made by the Secretary of Agriculture. Regulations were proclaimed on July 31, and October 25, 1918. 40 Stat. 1812, 1863. It is unnecessary to go into any details, because, as we have said, the question raised is the general one whether the treaty and statute are void as an interference with the rights reserved to the States.

To answer this question it is not enough to refer to the Tenth Amendment, reserving the powers not delegated to the United States, because by Article 11, § 2, the power to make treaties is delegated expressly, and by Article VI treaties made under the authority of the United States, along with the Constitution and laws of the United States made in pursuance thereof, are declared the supreme law of the land. If the treaty is valid there can be no dispute about the validity of the statute under Article I, § 8, as a necessary and proper means to execute the powers of the Government. The language of the Constitution as to the supremacy of treaties being general, the question before us is narrowed to an inquiry into the ground upon which the present supposed exception is placed.

It is said that a treaty cannot be valid if it infringes the Constitution, that there are limits, therefore, to the treaty-making power, and that one such limit is that what an act of Congress could not do unaided, in derogation of the powers reserved to the States, a treaty cannot do. An earlier act of Congress that attempted by itself and not in pursuance of a treaty to regulate the killing of migratory birds within the States had been held bad in the District Court. . . . Those decisions were supported by arguments that migratory birds were owned by the States in their sovereign capacity for the benefit of their people, and that under cases like *Geer v. Connecticut*, 161 U.S. 519, this control was one that Congress had no power to displace. The same argument is supposed to apply now with equal force.

Whether the two cases cited were decided rightly or not they cannot be accepted as a test of the treaty power. Acts of Congress are the supreme law of the land only when made in pursuance of the Constitution, while treaties are declared to be so when made under the authority of the United States. It is open to question whether the authority of the United States means more than the formal acts prescribed to make the convention. We do not mean to imply that there are no qualifications to the treaty-making power; but they must be ascertained in a different way. It is obvious that there may be matters of the sharpest exigency for the national well-being that an act of Congress could not deal with but that a treaty followed by such an act could, and it is not lightly to be assumed that, in matters requiring national action, "a power which must belong to and somewhere reside in every civilized government" is not to be found. *Andrews v. Andrews*, 188 U.S. 14, 33. What was said in that case with regard to the powers of the States applies with equal force to the powers of the nation in cases where the States individually are incompetent to act. We are not yet discussing the particular case before us but only are considering the validity of the test proposed. With regard to that we may add that when we are dealing with words that also are a constituent act, like the Constitution of the United States, we must realize that they have called into life a being the development of which could not have been foreseen completely by the most gifted of its begetters. It was enough for them to realize or to hope that they had created an organism; it has taken a century and has cost their successors much sweat and blood to prove that they created a nation. The case before us must be considered in the light of our whole experience and not merely in that of what was said a hundred years ago. The treaty in question does not contravene any prohibitory words to be found in the Constitution. The only question is whether it is forbidden by some invisible radiation from the general terms of the Tenth Amendment. We must consider what this country has become in deciding what that Amendment has reserved.

The State as we have intimated founds its claim of exclusive authority upon an assertion of title to migratory birds, an assertion that is embodied in statute. No doubt it is true that as between a State and its inhabitants the State may regulate the killing and sale of such birds, but it does not follow that its authority is exclusive of paramount powers. To put the claim of the State upon title is to lean upon a slender reed. Wild birds are not in the possession of anyone; and possession is the beginning of ownership. The whole foundation of the State's rights is the presence within their jurisdiction of birds that yesterday had not arrived, tomorrow may be in another State and in a week a thousand miles away. If we are to be accurate we cannot put the case of the State upon higher ground than that the treaty deals with creatures that for the moment are within the state borders, that it must be carried out by officers of the United States within the same territory, and that but for the treaty the State would be free to regulate this subject itself.

As most of the laws of the United States are carried out within the States and as many of them deal with matters which in the silence of such laws the State might regulate such general grounds are not enough to support Missouri's claim. Valid treaties of course "are as binding within the territorial limits of the States as they are elsewhere throughout the dominion of the United States." Baldwin v. Franks, 120 U.S. 678, 683. No doubt the great body of private relations usually fall within the control of the State, but a treaty may override its power. We do not have to invoke the later developments of constitutional law for this proposition; it was recognized as early as *Hopkirk v. Bell*, 3 Cranch, 454, with regard to statutes of limitation, and even earlier, as to confiscation, in *Ware v. Hylton*, 3 Dall. 199. ... Further illustration seems unnecessary, and it only remains to consider the application of established rules to the present case.

Here a national interest of very nearly the first magnitude is involved. It can be protected only by national action in concert with that of another power. The subject-matter is only transitorily within the State and has no permanent habitat therein. But for the treaty and the statute there soon might be no birds for any powers to deal with. We see nothing in the Constitution that compels the Government to sit by while a food supply is cut off and the protectors of our forests and our crops are destroyed. It is not sufficient to rely upon the States. The reliance is vain, and were it otherwise, the question is whether the United States is forbidden to act. We are of opinion that the treaty and statute must be upheld. Carey v. South Dakota, 250 U.S. 118.

NOTES AND QUESTIONS

1. Does the Court in *Missouri v. Holland* find a federal legislative power in the Constitution that is independent from other powers of Congress? If yes, are there any limits to this power?

2. For a more restrictive view of the treaty power, emphasizing state sovereignty, see Curtis A. Bradley, *The Treaty Power and American Federalism*, 97 MICH. L. REV. 390 (1998); for the counter-argument, see David Golove, *Treaty-Making and the Nation: The Historical Foundations of the Nationalist Conception of the Treaty Power*, 98 MICH. L. REV. 1075 (2000).

(2) Congressional-Executive Agreements

(a) Myres S. McDougal & Asher Lans, *Treaties and Congressional-Executive Agreements*

54 YALE L.J. 181, 186 (PT. 1) (1945)

The wise statesmen who drafted the Constitution of the United States not only gave the President a *permissive* power, "with the advice and consent of the Senate," "to make treaties, provided two-thirds of the Senators present concur," but they also gave both to the President and to the whole Congress broad powers of control over the external relations of the government which are meaningless if they do not include the instrumental powers, first, to authorize the making of intergovernmental agreements and, secondly, to make these agreements the law of the land. Throughout our national history, these broad grants to the President and the Congress have, furthermore, been in fact interpreted, by all branches of the government, in hundreds of instances, to include such instrumental powers. The result is that our constitutional law today makes available two parallel and completely interchangeable procedures, wholly applicable to the same subject matters and of identical domestic and international legal consequences, for the consummation of intergovernmental agreements. In addition to the treaty-making procedure, which may—as the nation has found from bitter experience—be subjected to minority control, there is what may be called an "agreement-making procedure," which may operate either under the combined powers of the Congress and the President or in some instances under the powers of the President alone. The practices of successive administrations, supported by the Congress and by numerous court decisions, have for all practical purposes made the congressional-executive agreement authorized or sanctioned by both houses of Congress interchangeable with the agreements ratified under the treaty clause by two-thirds of the Senate. The same decisive authorities have likewise made agreements negotiated by the President, on his own responsibility and within the scope of his own constitutional powers, appropriate instruments for handling many important aspects of our foreign relations. Initial choice of the procedure to be followed for securing validation of any particular intergovernmental agreement lies with the President since it is constitutional practice unquestioned since Washing-ton's day that the President alone has the power to propose or dispose in the actual conduct of negotiations with other governments. When a specific agreement is submitted to the Congress for approval or implementation, the Congress may of course question the procedure by which the President seeks validation of the agreement, but if the Congress is to act rationally—that is, appropriately to secure the best long-term interests of the whole nation—it should shape its action in terms of the policy issues involved in the specific agreement and not in terms of some misleading and unhistorical notion that the treaty-making procedure is the exclusive mode of making important inter-national agreements under our Constitution.

(b) State Department Procedures on Treaties and Other International Agreements

11 F.A.M. §700 (1974)

§721.2 …

(3) Agreements Pursuant to the Constitutional Authority of the President

The President may conclude an international agreement on any subject within his constitutional authority so long as the agreement is not inconsistent with legislation enacted by the Congress in the exercise of its constitutional authority. The constitutional authority for the President to conclude international agreements include:

(a) The President's authority as Chief Executive to represent the nation in foreign affairs;

(b) The President's authority to receive ambassadors and other public ministers;

(c) The President's authority as "Commander-in-Chief "; and

(d) The President's authority to "take care that the laws be faithfully executed."

§721.3 Considerations for Selecting Among Constitutionally Authorized Procedures

In determining a question as to the procedure which should be followed for any particular international agreement, due consideration is given to the following factors along with those in section 721.2:

a. The extent to which the agreement involves commitments or risks affecting the nation as a whole;

b. Whether the agreement is intended to affect State laws;

c. Whether the agreement can be given effect without the enactment of subsequent legislation by the Congress;

d. Past United States practice with respect to similar agreements;

e. The preference of the Congress with respect to a particular type of agreement;

f. The degree of formality desired for an agreement;

g. The proposed duration of the agreement, the need for prompt conclusion of an agreement, and the desirability of concluding a routine or short-term agreement; and

h. The general international practice with respect to similar agreements.

In determining whether any international agreement should be brought into force as a treaty or as an international agreement other than a treaty, the utmost care is to be exercised to avoid any invasion or compromise of the constitutional powers of the Senate, the Congress as a whole, or the President.

§721.4 Questions as to Type of Agreement to Be Used; Consultation With Congress

a. All legal memorandums accompanying Circular 175 requests (see section 722.3e) will discuss thoroughly the bases for the type of agreement recommended.

b. When there is any question whether an international agreement should be concluded as a treaty or as an international agreement other than a treaty, the matter is brought to the attention of the Legal Adviser of the Department. If the Legal Adviser considers the question to be a serious one that may warrant congressional consultation, a memorandum will be transmitted to the Assistant Secretary for Congressional Relations and other officers concerned. Upon receiving their views on the subject, the Legal Adviser shall, if the matter has not been resolved, transmit a memorandum thereon to the Secretary for his decision. Every practicable effort will be made to identify such questions at the earliest possible date so that consultations may be completed in sufficient time to avoid last-minute consideration.

c. Consultations on such questions will be held with congressional leaders and committees as may be appropriate. Arrangements for such con-sultations shall be made by the Assistant Secretary for Congressional Relations and shall be held with the assistance of the Office of the Legal Adviser and such other offices as may be determined. Nothing in this section shall be taken as derogating from the requirement of appropriate consultations with the Congress in accordance with section 723.1e in connection with the initiation of, and developments during, negotiations for international agreements, particularly where the agreements are of special interest to the Con-gress.

(c) The Case Act

1 U.S.C. § 112(b) (1988)

(a) The Secretary of State shall transmit to the Congress the text of any international agreement (including the text of any oral international agreement, which agreement shall be reduced to writing), other than a treaty, to which the United States is a party as soon as practicable after such agreement has entered into force with respect to the United States but in no event later than sixty days thereafter. However, any such agreement the immediate public disclosure of which would, in the opinion of the President, be prejudicial to the national security of the United States shall not be so transmitted to the Congress but shall be transmitted to the Committee on Foreign Relations of the Senate and the Committee on International Relations of the House of Representatives under an appropriate injunction of secrecy to be removed only upon due notice from the President. Any department or agency of the United States Government which enters into any international agreement on behalf of the United States shall transmit to the Department of State the text of such agreement not later than twenty days after such agreement has been signed.

(b) Not later than March 1, 1979, and at yearly intervals thereafter, the President shall, under his own signature, transmit to the Speaker of the House of Representatives and the chairman of the Committee on Foreign Relations of the Senate a report with respect to each international agreement which, during the preceding year, was transmitted to the Congress after the expiration of the 60-day period referred to in the first sentence of subsection (a), describing fully and completely the reasons for the late transmittal.

(c) Notwithstanding any other provision of law, an international agreement may not be signed or otherwise concluded on behalf of the United States without prior consultation with the Secretary of State. Such consultation may encompass a class of agreements rather than a particular agreement.

(d) The Secretary of State shall determine for and within the executive branch whether an arrangement constitutes an international agreement within the meaning of this section.

(e) The President shall, through the Secretary of State, promulgate such rules and regulations as may be necessary to carry out this section.

NOTES AND QUESTIONS

1. How would you generalize the competence of the President to make international agreements with respect to security, wealth, and other values? Was it wise of the founding fathers to leave this competence relatively undefined?

2. In *Consumers Union of United States v. Kissinger,* 506 F.2d 136 (D.C. Cir. 1974), *cert. denied,* 421 U.S. 1004 (1975), the legal effect of voluntary restraint undertakings by foreign producers of steel was at issue. The court treated them as non-agreements, not affecting the Congress's preemption of such commitments if they were held to be legally enforceable.

3. The Constitution, in particular the Bill of Rights, places limits on the Congress's treaty power. In *Reid v. Covert,* 354 U.S. 1 (1956), the court-martial conviction of a U.S. citizen who had murdered her husband on a U.S. airbase in England was overturned; the defendant, not part of the U.S. armed forces herself, could not be deprived by the pertinent Status of Forces Agreement of her right as a citizen to a trial by jury. In *Seery v. United States,* 27 F. Supp. 601 (Ct. Cl. 1955) the Court held that a U.S. citizen whose property was taken in the course of the U.S. occupation of Austria could avail herself of the protection of the takings clause in spite of a more restrictive executive agreement covering these issues between the U.S. and Austria.

4. For a positive answer to the question of constitutionality of congressional-executive agreements, in particular, fast-track trade agreements, see Bruce Ackerman & David Golove, *Is NAFTA Constitutional?*, 108 HARV. L. REV. 799 (1995). *Contra* Laurence H. Tribe, *Taking Text and Struc-*

ture Seriously: Reflections on Free Form Method in Constitutional Interpretation, 108 HARV. L. REV. 1221 (1995) ("[The] text and structure of Articles I and II are not nearly as amenable to the congressional executive agreement form as has been suggested. . . . Considerations of constitutional topology demand that constitutional interpretation take into account the precise ways that powers under Article I and Article II intersect."). The salvo back in this debate is fired by David M. Golove, *Against Free-Form Formalism*, 73 N.Y.U. L. REV. 1791 (1998).

(d) Dames & Moore v. Regan
453 U.S. 654 (1981)

JUSTICE REHNQUIST: On November 4, 1979, the American Embassy in Tehran was seized and our diplomatic personnel were captured and held hostage. In response to that crisis, President Carter, acting pursuant to the International Emergency Economic Powers Act, 91 Stat. 1626, 50 U.S.C. §§ 1701 1706 (1976 ed., Supp. III) (hereinafter IEEPA), declared a national emergency on November 14, 1979, and blocked the removal or transfer of "all property and interests in property of the Government of Iran, its instrumentalities and controlled entities and the Central Bank of Iran which are or become subject to the jurisdiction of the United States. ..." Exec. Order No. 12170, 3 CFR 457 (1980), note following 50 U.S.C. § 1701 (1976 ed., Supp. III). President Carter authorized the Secretary of the Treasury to promulgate regulations carrying out the blocking order. On November 15, 1979, the Treasury Department's Office of Foreign Assets Control issued a regulation providing that "[u]nless licensed or authorized ... any attachment, judgment, decree, lien, execution, garnishment, or other judicial process is null and void with respect to any property in which on or since [November 14, 1979,] there existed an interest of Iran." 31 CFR § 535.203(e) (1980). The regulations also made clear that any licenses or authorizations granted could be "amended, modified, or revoked at any time." § 535.805.

On November 26, 1979, the President granted a general license authorizing certain judicial proceedings against Iran but which did not allow the "entry of any judgment or of any decree or order of similar or analogous effect..." § 535.504(a). On December 19, 1979, a clarifying regulation was issued stating that "the general authorization for judicial proceedings contained in § 535.504(a) includes pre judgment attachment." § 535.418.

On December 19, 1979, petitioner Dames & Moore filed suit in the United States District Court for the Central District of California against the Government of Iran, the Atomic Energy Organization of Iran, and a number of Iranian banks. In its complaint, petitioner alleged that its wholly owned subsidiary, Dames & Moore International, S. R. L., was a party to a written contract with the Atomic Energy Organization, and that the subsidiary's entire interest in the contract had been assigned to petitioner. Under the contract, the subsidiary was to conduct site studies for a proposed nuclear power plant in Iran. As provided in the terms of the contract, the Atomic Energy Organization terminated the agreement for its own convenience on June 30, 1979. Petitioner contended, however, that it was owed $3,436,694.30 plus interest for services performed under the contract prior to the date of termination. The District Court issued orders of attachment directed against property of the defendants, and the property of certain Iranian banks was then attached to secure any judgment that might be entered against them.

On January 20, 1981, the Americans held hostage were released by Iran pursuant to an Agreement entered into the day before and embodied in two Declarations of the Democratic and Popular Republic of Algeria. ...The Agreement stated that "[i]t is the purpose of [the United States and Iran] ... to terminate all litigation as between the Government of each party and the nationals of the other, and to bring about the settlement and termination of all such claims through binding arbitration." In furtherance of this goal, the Agreement called for the establishment of an Iran United States Claims Tribunal which would arbitrate any claims not settled within six months. Awards of the Claims Tribunal are to be "final and binding" and "enforceable ... in the courts of any nation in accordance with its laws." Under the Agreement, the United States is obligated

> [t]o terminate all legal proceedings in United States courts involving claims of United States persons and institutions against Iran and its state enterprises, to nullify all attachments and judgments obtained therein, to prohibit all further litigation based on such claims, and to bring about the termination of such claims through binding arbitration.

In addition, the United States must "act to bring about the transfer" by July 19, 1981, of all Iranian assets held in this country by American banks. One billion dollars of these assets will be deposited in a security account in the Bank of England, to the account of the Algerian Central Bank, and used to satisfy awards rendered against Iran by the Claims Tribunal.

On January 19, 1981, President Carter issued a series of Executive Orders implementing the terms of the agreement. These Orders revoked all licenses permitting the exercise of "any right, power, or privilege" with regard to Iranian funds, securities, or deposits; "nullified" all non Iranian interests in such assets acquired subsequent to the blocking order of November 14, 1979; and required those banks holding Iranian assets to transfer them "to the Federal Reserve Bank of New York, to be held or transferred as directed by the Secretary of the Treasury."

On February 24, 1981, President Reagan issued an Executive Order in which he "ratified" the January 19th Executive Orders. Moreover, he "suspended" all "claims which may be presented to the ... Tribunal" and provided that such claims "shall have no legal effect in any action now pending in any court of the United States." The suspension of any particular claim terminates if the Claims Tribunal determines that it has no jurisdiction over that claim; claims are discharged for all purposes when the Claims Tribunal either awards some recovery and that amount is paid, or determines that no recovery is due.

II.

The parties and the lower courts, confronted with the instant questions, have all agreed that much relevant analysis is contained in *Youngstown Sheet & Tube Co. v. Sawyer*, 343 U.S. 579 (1952). Justice Black's opinion for the Court in that case, involving the validity of President Truman's effort to seize the country's steel mills in the wake of a nationwide strike, recognized that "[t]he President's power, if any, to issue the order must stem either from an act of Congress or from the Constitution itself." Id., at 585. Justice Jackson's concurring opinion elaborated in a general way the consequences of different types of interaction between the two democratic branches in assessing Presidential authority to act in any given case. When the President acts pursuant to an express or implied authorization from Congress, he exercises not only his powers but also those delegated by Congress. In such a case the executive action "would be supported by the strongest of presumptions and the widest latitude of judicial interpretation, and the burden of persuasion would rest heavily upon any who might attack it." Id., at 637. When the President acts in the absence of congressional authorization he may enter "a zone of twilight in which he and Congress may have concurrent authority, or in which its distribution is uncertain." Ibid. In such a case the analysis becomes more complicated, and the validity of the President's action, at least so far as separation of powers principles are concerned, hinges on a consideration of all the circumstances which might shed light on the views of the Legislative Branch toward such action, including "congressional inertia, indifference or quiescence." Ibid. Finally, when the President acts in contravention of the will of Congress, "his power is at its lowest ebb," and the Court can sustain his actions "only by disabling the Congress from acting upon the subject." Id., at 637 638.

Although we have in the past found and do today find Justice Jackson's classification of executive actions into three general categories analytically useful, we should be mindful of Justice Holmes' admonition, quoted by Justice Frankfurter in *Youngstown*, *supra*, at 597 (concurring opinion), that "[t]he great ordinances of the Constitution do not establish and divide fields of black and white." *Springer v. Philippine Islands*, 277 U.S. 189, 209 (1928) (dissenting opinion). Justice Jackson himself recognized that his three categories represented "a somewhat over simplified grouping," 343 U.S., at 635, and it is doubtless the case that executive action in any particular instance falls, not neatly in one of three pigeonholes, but rather at some point along a spectrum running from explicit congressional authorization to explicit congressional prohibition. This is particularly true as respects cases such as the one before us, involving responses to international crises the nature of which Congress can hardly have been expected to anticipate in any detail.

III.

In nullifying post November 14, 1979, attachments and directing those persons holding blocked Iranian funds and securities to transfer them to the Federal

Reserve Bank of New York for ultimate transfer to Iran, President Carter cited five sources of express or inherent power. The Government, however, has principally relied on § 203 of the IEEPA, 91 Stat. 1626, 50 U.S.C. § 1702(a)(1) (1976 ed., Supp. III), as authorization for these actions. Section 1702(a)(1) provides in part:

At the times and to the extent specified in section 1701 of this title, the President may, under such regulations as he may prescribe, by means of instructions, licenses, or otherwise—

> (A) investigate, regulate, or prohibit
>
> (i) any transactions in foreign exchange,
>
> (ii) transfers of credit or payments between, by, through, or to any banking institution, to the extent that such transfers or payments involve any interest of any foreign country or a national thereof,
>
> (iii) the importing or exporting of currency or securities, and
>
> (B) investigate, regulate, direct and compel, nullify, void, prevent or prohibit, any acquisition, holding, withholding, use, transfer, withdrawal, transportation, importation or exportation of, or dealing in, or exercising any right, power, or privilege with respect to, or transactions involving, any property in which any foreign country or a national thereof has any interest;

by any person, or with respect to any property, subject to the jurisdiction of the United States. ...

We ... refuse to read out of § 1702 all meaning to the words "transfer," "compel," or "nullify." Nothing in the legislative history of either § 1702 or § 5(b) of the TWEA requires such a result. To the contrary, we think both the legislative history and cases interpreting the TWEA fully sustain the broad authority of the Executive when acting under this congressional grant of power. See, e. g., Orvis v. Brownell, 345 U.S. 183 (1953). Although Congress intended to limit the President's emergency power in peacetime, we do not think the changes brought about by the enactment of the IEEPA in any way affected the authority of the President to take the specific actions taken here. We likewise note that by the time petitioner instituted this action, the President had already entered the freeze order. Petitioner proceeded against the blocked assets only after the Treasury Department had issued revocable licenses authorizing such proceedings and attachments. The Treasury Regulations provided that "unless licensed" any attachment is null and void, 31 CFR § 535.203(e) (1980), and all licenses "may be amended, modified, or revoked at any time." § 535.805. As such, the attachments obtained by petitioner were specifically made subordinate to further actions which the President might take under the IEEPA. Petitioner was on notice of the contingent nature of its interest in the frozen assets.

This Court has previously recognized that the congressional purpose in authorizing blocking orders is "to put control of foreign assets in the hands of the President. ..." *Propper v. Clark*, 337 U.S. 472, 493 (1949). Such orders permit the President to maintain the foreign assets at his disposal for use in negotiating the resolution of a declared national emergency. The frozen assets serve as a "bargaining chip" to be used by the President when dealing with a hostile country. Accordingly, it is difficult to accept petitioner's argument because the practical effect of it is to allow individual claimants throughout the country to minimize or wholly eliminate this "bargaining chip" through attachments, garnishments, or similar encumbrances on property. Neither the purpose the statute was enacted to serve nor its plain language supports such a result.

Because the President's action in nullifying the attachments and ordering the transfer of the assets was taken pursuant to specific congressional authorization, it is "supported by the strongest of presumptions and the widest latitude of judicial interpretation, and the burden of persuasion would rest heavily upon any who might attack it." *Youngstown*, 343 U.S., at 637 (Jackson, J., concurring). Under the circumstances of this case, we cannot say that petitioner has sustained that heavy burden. A contrary ruling would mean that the Federal Government as a whole lacked the power exercised by the President, see id., at 636 637, and that we are not prepared to say. ...

Although we have declined to conclude that the IEEPA or the Hostage Act directly authorizes the President's suspension of claims for the reasons noted, we cannot ignore the general tenor of Congress' legislation in this area in trying to determine whether the President is acting alone or at least with the acceptance of Congress. As we have noted, Congress cannot anticipate and legislate with regard to every possible action the President may find it necessary to take or every possible situation in which he might act. Such failure of Congress specifically to delegate authority does not, "especially ... in the areas of foreign policy and national security," imply "congressional disapproval" of action taken by the Executive. *Haig v. Agee*, 453 U.S. 280, 291. On the contrary, the enactment of legislation closely related to the question of the President's authority in a particular case which evinces legislative intent to accord the President broad discretion may be considered to "invite" "measures on independent presidential responsibility," *Youngstown*, 343 U.S., at 637 (Jackson, J., concurring). At least this is so where there is no contrary indication of legislative intent and when, as here, there is a history of congressional acquiescence in conduct of the sort engaged in by the President. It is to that history which we now turn.

Not infrequently in affairs between nations, outstanding claims by nationals of one country against the government of another country are "sources of friction" between the two sovereigns. *United States v. Pink*, 315 U.S. 203, 225 (1942). To resolve these difficulties, nations have often entered into agreements settling the claims of their respective nationals. As one treatise writer puts it, international agreements settling claims by nationals of one state against the government of another "are established international practice reflecting traditional international theory." L. Henkin, Foreign Affairs and the Constitution 262 (1972). Consistent with that principle, the United States has repeatedly exercised its sovereign authority to settle the claims of its nationals against foreign countries. Though those settlements have sometimes been made by treaty, there has also been a longstanding practice of settling such claims by executive agreement without the advice and consent of the Senate. Under such agreements, the President has agreed to renounce or extinguish claims of United States nationals against foreign governments in return for lump sum payments or the establishment of arbitration procedures. To be sure, many of these settlements were encouraged by the United States claimants themselves, since a claimant's only hope of obtaining any payment at all might lie in having his Government negotiate a diplomatic settlement on his behalf. But it is also undisputed that the "United States has sometimes disposed of the claims of its citizens without their consent, or even without consultation with them, usually without exclusive regard for their interests, as distinguished from those of the nation as a whole." Henkin, supra, at 262 263. Accord, Restatement (Second) of Foreign Relations Law of the United States § 213 (1965) (President "may waive or settle a claim against a foreign state ... [even] without the consent of the [injured] national"). It is clear that the practice of settling claims continues today. Since 1952, the President has entered into at least 10 binding settlements with foreign nations, including an $80 million settlement with the People's Republic of China.

Crucial to our decision today is the conclusion that Congress has implicitly approved the practice of claim settlement by executive agreement. This is best demonstrated by Congress' enactment of the International Claims Settlement Act of 1949, 64 Stat. 13, as amended, 22 U.S.C. § 1621 et seq. (1976 ed. and Supp. IV). The Act had two purposes: (1) to allocate to United States nationals funds received in the course of an executive claims settlement with Yugoslavia, and (2) to provide a procedure whereby funds resulting from future settlements could be distributed. To achieve these ends Congress created the International Claims Commission, now the Foreign Claims Settlement Commission, and gave it jurisdiction to make final and binding decisions with respect to claims by United States nationals against settlement funds. 22 U.S.C. § 1623(a). By creating a procedure to implement future settlement agreements, Congress placed its stamp of approval on such agreements. Indeed, the legislative history of the Act observed that the United States was seeking settlements with countries other than Yugoslavia and that the bill contemplated settlements of a similar nature in the future. H.R.Rep. No. 770, 81st Cong., 1st Sess., 4, 8 (1949).

Over the years Congress has frequently amended the International Claims Settlement Act to provide for particular problems arising out of settlement agreements, thus demonstrating Congress' continuing acceptance of the President's claim settlement authority. With respect to the Executive Agreement with the People's Republic of China, for example, Congress established an allocation formula for distribution of the funds received pursuant to the Agreement. 22 U.S.C. § 1627(f) (1976 ed. and Supp. IV). As with legislation involving other executive agreements, Congress did not question the fact of the settlement or the power of the President to have concluded it. In 1976, Congress authorized the Foreign Claims Settlement Commission to adjudicate the merits of claims by United States nationals against East Germany, prior to any settlement with East Germany, so that the Executive would "be in a better position to negotiate an adequate settlement ... of these claims." S.Rep. No. 94 1188, p. 2 (1976), U. S. Code Cong. & Admin. News, 1976, pp. 5582, 5583; 22 U.S.C. § 1644b. Similarly, Congress recently amended the International Claims Settlement Act to facilitate the settlement of claims against Vietnam. 22 U.S.C. §§ 1645, 1645a(5) (1976 ed., Supp. IV). The House Report stated that the purpose of the legislation was to establish an official inventory of losses of private United States property in Vietnam so that recovery could be achieved "through future direct Government to Government negotiation of private property claims." H.R.Rep. No. 96 915, pp. 2 3 ... Finally, the legislative history of the IEEPA further reveals that Congress has accepted the authority of the Executive to enter into settlement agreements. Though the IEEPA was enacted to provide for some limitation on the President's emergency powers, Congress stressed that "[n]othing in this act is intended ... to interfere with the authority of the President to [block assets], or to impede the settlement of claims of U. S. citizens against foreign countries." S.Rep. No. 95 466, p. 6 (1977) ...; 50 U.S.C. § 1706(a)(1) (1976 ed., Supp. III).

In addition to congressional acquiescence in the President's power to settle claims, prior cases of this Court have also recognized that the President does have some measure of power to enter into executive agreements without obtaining the advice and consent of the Senate. In *United States v. Pink*, 315 U.S. 203 (1942), for example, the Court upheld the validity of the Litvinov Assignment, which was part of an Executive Agreement whereby the Soviet Union assigned to the United States amounts owed to it by American nationals so that outstanding claims of other American nationals could be paid. The Court explained that the resolution of such claims was integrally connected with normalizing United States' relations with a foreign state:

> Power to remove such obstacles to full recognition as settlement of claims of our nationals ... certainly is a modest implied power of the President.... No such obstacle can be placed in the way of rehabilitation of relations between this country and another nation, unless the historic conception of the powers and responsibilities...is to be drastically revised. Id., at 229 230.

Similarly, Judge Learned Hand recognized:

> The constitutional power of the President extends to the settlement of mutual claims between a foreign government and the United States, at least when it is an incident to the recognition of that government; and it would be unreasonable to circumscribe it to such controversies. The continued mutual amity between the nation and other powers again and again depends upon a satisfactory compromise of mutual claims; the

> necessary power to make such compromises has existed from the earliest times and been exercised by the foreign offices of all civilized nations. *Ozanic v. United States*, 188 F.2d 228, 231 (CA2 1951).

Petitioner raises two arguments in opposition to the proposition that Congress has acquiesced in this longstanding practice of claims settlement by executive agreement. First, it suggests that all pre 1952 settlement claims, and corresponding court cases such as Pink, should be discounted because of the evolution of the doctrine of sovereign immunity. Petitioner observes that prior to 1952 the United States adhered to the doctrine of absolute sovereign immunity, so that absent action by the Executive there simply would be no remedy for a United States national against a foreign government. When the United States in 1952 adopted a more restrictive notion of sovereign immunity, by means of the so called "Tate" letter, it is petitioner's view that United States nationals no longer needed executive aid to settle claims and that, as a result, the President's authority to settle such claims in some sense "disappeared." Though petitioner's argument is not wholly without merit, it is refuted by the fact that since 1952 there have been at least 10 claims settlements by executive agreement. Thus, even if the pre 1952 cases should be disregarded, congressional acquiescence in settlement agreements since that time supports the President's power to act here.

Petitioner next asserts that Congress divested the President of the authority to settle claims when it enacted the Foreign Sovereign Immunities Act of 1976 (hereinafter FSIA), 28 U.S.C. §§ 1330, 1602 et seq. The FSIA granted personal and subject matter jurisdiction in the federal district courts over commercial suits brought by claimants against those foreign states which have waived immunity. 28 U.S.C. § 1330. Prior to the enactment of the FSIA, a foreign government's immunity to suit was determined by the Executive Branch on a case by case basis. According to petitioner, the principal purpose of the FSIA was to depoliticize these commercial lawsuits by taking them out of the arena of foreign affairs—where the Executive Branch is subject to the pressures of foreign states seeking to avoid liability through a grant of immunity—and by placing them within the exclusive jurisdiction of the courts. Petitioner thus insists that the President, by suspending its claims, has circumscribed the jurisdiction of the United States courts in violation of Art. III of the Constitution.

We disagree. In the first place, we do not believe that the President has attempted to divest the federal courts of jurisdiction. Executive Order No. 12294 purports only to "suspend" the claims, not divest the federal court of "jurisdiction." As we read the Executive Order, those claims not within the jurisdiction of the Claims Tribunal will "revive" and become judicially enforceable in United States courts. This case, in short, illustrates the difference between modifying federal court jurisdiction and directing the courts to apply a different rule of law. See *United States v. Schooner Peggy*, 1 Cranch 103 (1801). The President has exercised the power, acquiesced in by Congress, to settle claims and, as such, has simply effected a change in the substantive law governing the lawsuit. Indeed, the very example of sovereign immunity belies petitioner's argument. No one would suggest that a determination of sovereign immunity divests the federal courts of "jurisdiction." Yet, petitioner's argument, if accepted, would have required courts prior to the enactment of the FSIA to reject as an encroachment on their jurisdiction the President's determination of a foreign state's sovereign immunity.

Petitioner also reads the FSIA much too broadly. The principal purpose of the FSIA was to codify contemporary concepts concerning the scope of sovereign immunity and withdraw from the President the authority to make binding determinations of the sovereign immunity to be accorded foreign states. ... The FSIA was thus designed to remove one particular barrier to suit, namely sovereign immunity, and cannot be fairly read as prohibiting the President from settling claims of United States nationals against foreign governments. It is telling that the Congress which enacted the FSIA considered but rejected several proposals designed to limit the power of the President to enter into executive agreements, including claims settlement agreements. It is quite unlikely that the same Congress that rejected proposals to limit the President's authority to conclude executive agreements sought to accomplish that very purpose sub silentio through the FSIA. And, as noted above, just one year after enacting the FSIA, Congress enacted the IEEPA, where the legislative history stressed that nothing in the IEEPA was to impede the settlement of claims of United States citizens. It would be surprising for Congress to express this support for settlement agreements had it intended the FSIA to eliminate the President's authority to make such agreements.

In light of all of the foregoing the inferences to be drawn from the character of the legislation Congress has enacted in the area, such as the IEEPA and the Hostage Act, and from the history of acquiescence in executive claims settlement we conclude that the President was authorized to suspend pending claims pursuant to Executive Order No. 12294. As Justice Frankfurter pointed out in Youngstown, 343 U.S., at 610 611, "a systematic, unbroken, executive practice, long pursued to the knowledge of the Congress and never before questioned ... may be treated as a gloss on 'Executive Power' vested in the President by § 1 of Art. II." Past practice does not, by itself, create power, but "long continued practice, known to and acquiesced in by Congress, would raise a presumption that the [action] had been [taken] in pursuance of its consent...." *United States v. Midwest Oil Co.*, 236 U.S. 459, 474 (1915). *See Haig v. Agee*, 453 U.S., at 291, 292. Such practice is present here and such a presumption is also appropriate. In light of the fact that Congress may be considered to have consented to the President's action in suspending claims, we cannot say that action exceeded the President's powers.

Our conclusion is buttressed by the fact that the means chosen by the President to settle the claims of American nationals provided an alternative forum, the Claims Tribunal, which is capable of providing meaningful relief. The Solicitor General also suggests that the provision of the Claims Tribunal will actually enhance the opportunity for claimants to recover their claims, in that the Agreement removes a number of jurisdictional and procedural impediments faced by claimants in United States courts. Although being overly sanguine about the chances of United States claimants before the Claims Tribunal would require a degree of naïveté which should not be demanded even of judges, the Solicitor General's point cannot be discounted. Moreover, it is important to remember that we have already held that the President has the statutory authority to nullify attachments and to transfer the assets out of the country. The President's power to do so does not depend on his provision of a forum whereby claimants can recover on those claims. The fact that the President has provided such a forum here means that the claimants are receiving something in return for the suspension of their claims, namely, access to an international tribunal before which they may well recover something on their claims. Because there does appear to be a real "settlement" here, this case is more easily analogized to the more traditional claim settlement cases of the past.

Just as importantly, Congress has not disapproved of the action taken here. Though Congress has held hearings on the Iranian Agreement itself, Congress has not enacted legislation, or even passed a resolution, indicating its displeasure with the Agreement. Quite the contrary, the relevant Senate Committee has stated that the establishment of the Tribunal is "of vital importance to the United States." S.Rep.No. 97 71, p. 5 (1981). We are thus clearly not confronted with a situation in which Congress has in some way resisted the exercise of Presidential authority.

Finally, we re emphasize the narrowness of our decision. We do not decide that the President possesses plenary power to settle claims, even as against foreign governmental entities. As the Court of Appeals for the First Circuit stressed, "[t]he sheer magnitude of such a power, considered against the background of the diversity and complexity of modern international trade, cautions against any broader construction of authority than is necessary." *Chas T. Main Int'l, Inc. v. Khuzestan Water & Power Authority*, 651 F.2d, at 814. But where, as here, the settlement of claims has been determined to be a necessary incident to the resolution of a major foreign policy dispute between our country and another, and where, as here, we can conclude that Congress acquiesced in the President's action, we are not prepared to say that the President lacks the power to settle such claims.

NOTES AND QUESTIONS

1. In light of these cases, what are the constitutional limitations, if any, on the content of executive agreements? Do these limitations apply to treaties?

2. On the similarities in the constitutional structures of major nation states, see Julia Yoo, *Participation in the Making of Legislative Treaties: The United States and Other Federal Systems*, 41 COLUM. J. TRANSNAT'L L. 455 (2003). On the relationship of internal and international law in general, *see supra*, Part One, at 103-140.

3. Many of the major states have constitutional structures much like that of the United States. The generalized picture appears to be as follows:

–the formulation of policies to guide negotiation is largely reserved to the legislature, but with some executive participation;

–the negotiating function is usually entrusted to the executive;

–the final commitment as a binding international obligation may, on some agreements, be made by the executive, but legislative approval may be required on others;

–the prescription of policies as the internal law of the land may some-times be made by the executive, but more commonly legislative action is required;

–the final utterance is commonly made by the executive.

2. Regulating the Genesis and Content of Agreements

a. International Prescriptions

Articles 46-53 of the Vienna Convention on the Law of Treaties contain a negative list of illicit ways of making internationally binding commitments as well as impermissible purposes of such agreements. Sanctions range from categorical invalidity (as in the case of *jus cogens*) to voidability (as in most cases of defects in the formative stage of treaties).

(1) Peremptory Norms

(a) Vienna Convention on the Law of Treaties

Article 53. A treaty is void if, at the time of its conclusion, it conflicts with a peremptory norm of general international law. For the purposes of the present Convention, a peremptory norm of general international law is a norm accepted and recognized by the international community of States as a whole as a norm from which no derogation is permitted and which can be modified only by a subsequent norm of general international law having the game character.

(b) Myres S. McDougal, Harold D. Lasswell & Ivan A. Vlasic, Law and Public Order in Space
153 (Yale U. Press 1963)

The most important contemporary prescriptions by which the general community seeks to police international agreements are of course those relating to minimum order. Through the Pact of Paris, the United Nations Charter, the Nuremberg Charter and Verdict, and many other authoritative formulations, the peoples of the world have clarified, … a set of prescrip-tions whose design is, in general, to minimize the deliberate use of unauthorized coercion across state lines as an instrument of policy, and in particular relation to major coercions, to prohibit the employment of violence in attacks upon the territorial integrity and political independence of peoples. It would only be self-stultification for the community to honor agreements designed to subvert these prescriptions, and the common assumption is that such agreements are unlawful.

(c) The Case of Aloeboetoe

15 Inter-Am. Ct. H.R. (Ser. C) (1993)

56. The Saramakas are a tribe that lives in Surinamese territory and was formed by African slaves fleeing from their Dutch owners. The Commission's brief affirms that the Saramakas enjoy internal autonomy by virtue of a treaty dated September 19, 1762, which granted them permission to be governed by their own laws. It also states that these people "acquired their rights on the basis of a treaty entered into with the Netherlands, which recognizes, among other things, the local authority of the Saramaka (sic) over their own territory." The text of the treaty is attached to the brief in question, which adds that "the obligations of the treaty are applicable, by succession, to the state (sic) of Suriname."

57. The Court does not deem it necessary to investigate whether or not that agreement is an international treaty. Suffice it to say that even if that were the case, the treaty would today be null and void because it contradicts the norms of *jus cogens superveniens*. In point of fact, under that treaty the Saramakas undertake to, among other things, capture any slaves that have deserted, take them prisoner and return them to the Governor of Suriname, who will pay from 10 to 50 florins per slave, depending on the distance of the place where they were apprehended. Another article empowers the Saramakas to sell to the Dutch any other prisoners they might take, as slaves. No treaty of that nature may be invoked before an international human rights tribunal.

(2) Illegal Deprivations upon Third States

(a) Vienna Convention on the Law of Treaties

Article 34. A treaty does not create either obligations or rights for a third State without its consent.

(b) McDougal, Lasswell & Vlasic, *supra,* at 153-154

Still another principle, commonly asserted to be authoritative prescrip-tion, condemns agreements designed to impose illegal deprivations upon third parties. The often quoted wording of Lord McNair is: "It is believed that a treaty between two States the execution of which contemplates the infliction upon a third State of what customary international law regards as a wrong is illegal and invalid *ab initio.* ..." The broad application of this princi-ple would outlaw agreements designed to encourage piracy or to achieve the monopolization of shareable resources not subject to exclusive appropriation by a single state.

(c) Eritrea v. Yemen

Award of the Arbitral Tribunal in the First Stage of the Proceedings, 9 October 1998 Permanent Court of Arbitration, 40 I.L.M. 900 (2001)

153. … Boundary and territorial treaties made between two parties are *res inter alios acta* vis-à-vis third parties. But this special category of treaties also represents a legal reality which necessarily impinges upon third states, because they have effect *erga omnes*. If State A has title to territory and passes it to State B, then it is legally without purpose for State C to invoke the principle *res inter alios acta*, unless its title is better than that of A (rather than of B). In the absence of such better title, a claim of *res inter alios acta* is without import.

(3) Agreements Conflicting with Other Agreements

(a) McDougal, Lasswell & Vlasic, *supra*, at 936 (1963)

One final principle, quite generally accepted, is that which accords a priority to the obligations of an earlier agreement over those of a subsequent agreement. An exception is of course made for the United Nations Charter which, because of its constitutional character, is accorded priority over both earlier and subsequent agreements. Thus, Article 103 of the Charter provides:

> In the event of a conflict between the obligations of the Members of the United Nations under the present Charter and their obligations under any other international agreement, their obligations under the present Charter shall prevail.

The importance of this constitutional character of the obligations of the Charter is enhanced when it is recalled that Article 2(6) has created expectations that they may be enforced against nonmembers "so far as may be necessary for the maintenance of international peace and security."

(b) W. Michael Reisman, *The Constitutional Crisis in the United Nations*

87 Am. J. Int'l L. 83 (1993)

[Libya's] suit in the International Court against the United States and the United Kingdom for alleged violations of its rights under the 1971 Montreal Convention was widely viewed as the cynical ruse of a government implicated in state terrorism to evade condemnation and sanction by the Security Council. But claimants, no matter how ignoble, sometimes raise important issues. In dealing with Libya's request for interim measures and the jurisdictional boundary between the International Court and the Security Council, the Court collided with world constitutional issues that had been taking shape over the previous five years.

In Resolution 731 (1992), the Council had asked Libya, in effect, to surrender for trial two Libyan officials who had been indicted in the United States and

Scotland for causing the destruction of an American civilian airliner over Lockerbie, Scotland. Relying on the Montreal Convention, to which all the relevant states are party, Libya insisted on its treaty and customary right *aut dedere aut judicare* and indicated that it would try the officials itself if its investigating magistrate—who, it averred, had begun to review the evidence—found sufficient grounds. As the Libyan Government purported to see it, three permanent members of the Council—the United States, the United Kingdom and France—were exploiting their powers under the Charter to deprive Libya of its rights under conventional and customary international law. Because the Montreal Convention incorporates the International Court's jurisdiction, Libya asked the Court to stop them. Though the Court's decision responds to a request for interim measures and could be reconsidered at a hypothetical merits phase, the majority, concurring and dissenting opinions provide a remarkable window on the Court's thinking about a critical constitutional problem.

The nominal issue in Lockerbie was thus the sequencing, as between Council and Court, of the exercise of jurisdiction in part held concurrently by both of them. This is not an unusual phenomenon in advanced legal systems where different organs with different competences are created over time and often find themselves seized of all or different parts of the same dispute. The solution lies in the development of various codes for allocating and sequencing competences. Behind this nominal issue, however, lay a more difficult constitutional question that fused an apparently technical interpretation of the Charter about the boundary between the competences of Council and Court with an increasingly acute struggle over the most fundamental allocations of power in the United Nations system.

The nominal constitutional issue in Lockerbie is easily resolved. When the Security Council makes a decision under chapter VII of the Charter that concerns a state and the decision is inconsistent with some other treaty based right claimed by that state, the Council decision prevails. The interim measures decision in Lockerbie thus reached the right legal conclusion on this point. Unfortunately, the Court seems to have reached its decision on the basis of unsound constitutional policy reasoning, which may prove to be troublesome in subsequent cases.

In Lockerbie the Council action that proved determinative, Resolution 748, only came several days after cloture of the proceedings in the Court. As a result, the focus of the parties' arguments before the Court had perforce been Resolution 731, which was cast in recommendatory language. (Indeed, it was not clear from the terms of Resolution 731 whether it had been adopted pursuant to chapter VI, or as a nonbinding recommendation under Article 39 of chapter VII.) The structure of the majority opinion, as well as several of the declarations and separate opinions, suggests that more than a few of the judges believed that Resolution 731, by itself, would not have preempted the rights Libya had claimed under the Montreal Convention.

Perhaps the defendants, the United States and the United Kingdom, had sensed this judicial inclination during the proceedings. In pleadings, the Court was reminded that the Council was still seized of the matter and might be moving toward an explicit chapter VII decision. Whatever the reason, after oral argument in the Peace Palace had ended, but before judgment was rendered, the Security Council issued Resolution 748. This time, the Council used very precise language. The new resolution said *expressis verbis* that it was a decision being taken under chapter VII of the Charter and that "the Libyan Government must now comply without any further delay with paragraph 3 of Resolution 731."

The effect on the Court of this new resolution was immediate and dispositive. Every judge who joined the majority (and, indeed, some of the dissenters) relied on Resolution 748 and not on 731. The Court said: "whatever the situation previous to the adoption of that resolution [748], the rights claimed by Libya under the Montreal Convention cannot now be regarded as appropriate for protection by the indication of provisional measures." By relying exclusively on Resolution 748, the Court tended to confirm, after the fact, the fears of the defendants that the judges might well view Resolution 731 by itself as insufficient to trump the Montreal Convention.

In the most basic terms, the Court's legal reason for the supremacy of Resolution 748 over rights based on the Montreal Convention or on customary international law was that (1) Council "decisions" taken under the authority of chapter VII are accepted in advance as obligations by member states by virtue of Charter Article 25; and (2) obligations under the Charter prevail over obligations under any other international agreement by virtue of Charter Article 103. It is not, as one separate opinion was at pains to point out, so much that the Court is shouldered aside by a chapter VII decision, as that the applicant state loses whatever conventional or customary legal basis it may have had for making its application before the chapter VII decision. Superficially, this line of reasoning seems to preserve the dignity and organic equality of the Court vis à vis the Council. Implicit in this reasoning, however, is the notion that Resolution 731 would not have prevailed over treaty based Court jurisdiction.

This notion is extremely problematic in light of the constitutional policy that animates the law in this area. The Council was assigned the primary responsibility for the maintenance of international peace and security, conditions that are, by their nature, basic and prerequisite to the achievement of all the other legal goals of the Charter. When the Council is involved in discharging that primary responsibility, states may not oppose to it inconsistent treaty or customary based rights. If they could, the Council's function might be checked in some cases and the UN scheme for the maintenance of international peace and security could fail.

NOTES AND QUESTIONS

1. The August 27, 1999 order on provisional measures by the International Tribunal for the Law of the Sea in the *Southern Bluefin Tuna Case* (ITLOS Cases 3 and 4), *available at* http://www.un.org/depts/los/itlos/order-tuna34.htm, has been summarized by Professor Barbara Kwiatkowska:

The Southern Bluefin Tuna cases resulted from a disagreement between Australia and New Zealand, on the one hand, and Japan, on the other, that arose within the framework of the Convention for the Conservation of Southern Bluefin Tuna (CSBT Convention) concluded by the three states. Using an experimental fishing program (EFP), Japan had exceeded its previously agreed limit for southern bluefin tuna (SBT), a highly migratory stock that is harvested by nationals of all three states and also by others-notably Indonesia, South Korea, and Taiwan-that are not parties to the CSBT Convention. Through the adoption of the CSBT Convention, which went into effect in 1994, the cooperation of the three states was institutionalized in the Commission for the Conservation of Southern Bluefin Tuna, which establishes a total allowable catch (TAC) and its distribution by national allocations. Since 1996, the Commission has also been responsible for implementing an EFP.

This case was the first in which the Tribunal acted on a request for provisional measures under paragraph 5 of Article 290. According to this provision, pending the constitution of an arbitral tribunal under the Convention, the Tribunal may prescribe provisional measures "if it considers that prima facie the tribunal which is to be constituted would have jurisdiction and that the urgency of the situation so requires." The standard for provisional measures specified in Article 290(1)-namely, "to preserve the respective rights of the parties to the dispute or to prevent serious harm to the marine environment"-differs on its face from the comparable standard established in Article 41 of the Statute of the ICJ, which authorizes the Court to "indicate," rather than "prescribe," provisional measures which ought to be taken "to preserve the respective rights of either party."

In concluding that the arbitral tribunal would prima facie have jurisdiction over the dispute, the Tribunal rejected all of Japan's contentions to the contrary. Invoking the ICJ's definition of a legal dispute, the Tribunal rejected Japan's arguments that the dispute is scientific rather than legal and that it concerns the interpretation or application of the CSBT Convention rather than Law of the Sea Convention; the applicability of the CSBT Convention between the parties did not preclude their right to invoke the Law of the Sea Convention, specifically Articles 64 and 116-11 (these articles are the ones that, along with rules of customary international law, Japan's unilateral EFP had allegedly violated in 1998 and 1999, with regard to both the high seas and the applicants' 200-mile exclusive economic zones). A related point of disagreement between the parties was whether the applicants had exhausted (through negotiation or other agreed peaceful means) the procedures under Part XV, Section 1, specifically Articles 281 and 283; doing so was a precondition of submitting the dispute to compulsory settlement under Part XV, Section 2, of the Law of the Sea Convention. Japan, which consistently regarded the dispute as falling exclusively within the scope of the CSBT Convention, maintained that the applicants had failed to seek settlement in good faith under Article 16(1) of the CSBT Convention. By the same token, Japan argued that applicants had made no effort to reach a settlement under Part XV, Section 1, of the Law of the Sea Convention. Consequently, Japan argued, they were not entitled to resort to compulsory procedures under Section 2, and the Tribunal lacked prima facie jurisdiction. Nevertheless, in view of the applicants' contentions that their negotiations with the respondent had, in effect, terminated, the Tribunal found that the requirements for invoking the procedures under Section 2 had been fulfilled. Moreover, since none of the three states had made a declaration under Article 287(1) of the Law of the Sea Convention to select a means for the settlement of disputes under that Convention, the parties were deemed to have accepted arbitration in accordance with Annex VII.

94 AM. J. INT'L L. 150, 150-152 (2000). Does this decision reflect a "primacy" of universal (Law of the Sea) over regional (CSBT) international treaties? Should widely-subscribed multilateral treaties of global reach be analogized to federal legislation and "pre-empt" regional or bilateral treaty arrangements, or do different policies operate in international law?

(4) Coercion

The legal significance of coercion on the treaty-making process has varied through time. As long as force was considered a licit activity, coercion *per se* could not be invoked to invalidate agreements. This changed with the U.N. Charter and its invalidation of aggression in Article 2(4).

(a) Vienna Convention on the Law of Treaties

Article 51. The expression of a State's consent to be bound by a treaty which has been procured by the coercion of its representative through acts or threats directed against him shall be without any legal effect.

Article 52. A treaty is void if its conclusion has been procured by the threat or use of force in violation of the principles of international law embodied in the Charter of the United Nations.

NOTES AND QUESTIONS

1. What effect should this new policy have on older treaties still in force?

2. Theories of the "sovereign equality" of states and the demanded consensual character of agreements have given rise to a set of claims regarding lawful modalities in the making of agreements and, in particular, whether con-sent has been fully given or coerced. At an extreme, some states seek to in-validate agreements by inferring coercion from the unequal power position of the parties. The lopsidedness of agreements, as a result of unequal bargaining power between states, has traditionally not been considered an impediment to their validity under traditional international law. Werner Morvay, *Unequal Treaties*, *in* 7 ENC. PUB. INT'L L. 514, 514-16 (Rudolf Bernhardt ed., 1984) (referring to treaties signed by a weak Chinese government that were upheld under customary law).

3. For the most part, claims and decisions have skirted the ambiguities of alleged "unequal treaties" and focused on more precise claims, such as actual duress and fraudulent misrepresentation. In the interest of minimum order, international law, like national law, polices the commitment process in an effort to insure that apparent agreements are not disguised coercion.

(5) Voidability Due to Manifest Violations of Fundamental Rules of Internal Law, Error, Fraud or Corruption of State Representative

(a) Vienna Convention on the Law of Treaties

Articles 46 and 47. [*supra*, at 1282]

Article 48. (1) A State may invoke an error in a treaty as invalidating its con-sent to be bound by the treaty if the error relates to a fact or situation which was assumed by that State to exist at the time when the treaty was concluded and formed an essential basis of its consent to be bound by the treaty.

(2) Paragraph 1 shall not apply if the State in question contributed by its own conduct to the error or if the circumstances were such as to put that State on notice of a possible error.

(3) An error relating only to the wording of the text of a treaty does not affect its validity; article 79 then applies.

Article 49. If a State has been induced to conclude a treaty by the fraudulent conduct of another negotiating State, the State may invoke the fraud as invalidating its consent to be bound by the treaty.

* * *

After an exhaustive study, the Harvard Research in International Law concluded: "In practice no instances of the actual employment of fraud in the negotiation of treaties are known, and there appear to be no decisions either of national or international tribunals involving the question." *Research in International Law, The Law of Treaties*, 29 AM. J. INT'L L. SUPP. 1145 (1935).

(6) Excursus: American Indian Treaties

(a) Siegfried Wiessner, *American Indian Treaties and Modern International Law*

7 ST. THOMAS L. REV. 567, 591-599 (1995)

1. Traditional international law scholarship, applied in intellectual honesty, would have a hard time denying commitments arising from U.S.-Indian treaties the effect of international legal obligations. Even if it follows the dated axiom that treaties could only be entered into between "sovereign states," there is no credible way to interpret out of existence the fact that the budding new player in the international arena of the 18th and 19th century, the United States, for whatever reason, did enter into treaties of friendship and alliance on a perfectly level playing field with the Indian nations. It treated them with the same respect, extending to them the same courtesies as to other nations of the then overwhelmingly European international legal order. Later, the balance of power shifted, the [Indian] allies (and few enemies) in the war of independence became designated "wards," [and] the horizontal tended to shift to a more vertical relationship. Still, the United States Government never treated Indian nations as fully subjugated, leaving them with the dignity of the designation as sovereign, as well as with a range of autonomy in internal decision-making both substantively and procedurally. Thus, the Indian nations in the United States can hardly be compared with extinct subjugated entities such as the formerly independent state of Texas prior to its joining the Union in 1845, or even only fictionally continuing states without a functioning government such as the Baltic states between 1941 and 1990. Thus, no issues as to state succession arise.

2. Even if one considers United States' declarations of Indian nations as "sovereign" as disingenuous, contrary to fact, and hardly in line with reality in Indian country, the United States' continued designation of Indian nations as "sovereign" might work to estop the U.S. government from denying the treaties entered into with these entities international legal effect. The principle of estoppel is a general principle of law recognized by civilized nations, as defined by Article 38(1)(c) of the Statute of the International Court of Justice, and as such a source of the law of nations. Its policy, binding a state to its unilateral declarations at least if another subject of international law relied to its detriment on this declara-

tion, underlies the World Court's decisions in the *Eastern Greenland* and the *Nuclear Tests* cases.

3. Even if Indian nations somehow lost their character as "sovereign states" under international law between 1776 and 1871, the obligations under their treaties did not disappear with that designation. First, and foremost, the United States government still feels bound by these treaties, to the extent Congress has not abrogated them, and to the extent they have not been replaced by later treaties. Contrary to the *Cayuga Indians* and *Island of Palmas* arbitral awards of the 1920s, the International Court of Justice in its 1975 advisory opinion on the status of the *Western Sahara* has confirmed the international legal effect of agreements between indigenous tribes and clearly recognized sovereign states. The Court found that agreements between colonizing States and local rulers could be "regarded as derivative roots of title, and not original titles obtained by occupation of terrae nullius." In addition, even agreements between sovereign states and foreign private entities have been held to be subject, in very limited circumstances, to international law. The fact is that the United States dealt with Indian nations, at least until 1871, the same way as with foreign nation-states, i.e. it made treaties with them. The only difference is that it did not exchange ambassadors with them, and it reserved "plenary power" over them, a claim which was never exercised to its theoretical maximum. It never did integrate the tribal governments fully into its constitutional scheme; they are left out of the dual sovereignty concept, which implies shared original powers allocated by the Constitution between the federal government and the states.

4. Whatever controversy there may be over content and meaning of "tribal sovereignty," traditional international lawyers may thus be forced to conclude that American Indian treaties have international legal character.

What are the consequences of such a characterization?

One, the substantive international law regarding formation and interpretation of treaties would apply. The 1969 Vienna Convention on the Law of Treaties would be of help regarding the content of customary law in this area to the extent it codified pre-existing customary international law in this area. According to this convention, treaties procured by the use or threat of force, coercion of a representative, or fraud, are void or voidable. Treaties materially breached can be suspended or terminated by the other side. Also, a fundamental change in circumstances not foreseen by the parties, may lead to (optional) invalidation.

One (intertemporal) caution: the customary law of treaties can only be applied in the form and with the content it had at the time of the making of the treaty. Prior to 1945, peace treaties between the victor and the vanquished, though based on manifest coercion, were considered valid; war was considered the continuation of politics by other means. Still, customary law of the time considered treaties invalid if they were procured by physical coercion of a country's representative. The invalidity for fraud prescriptions also predated 1945. Even though such practice is sparse, its validity can be based on the notion of general principles of law recognized by civilized nations. The corruption of a state representative as a ground for invalidating a state's consent has been characterized as an example of progressive development of law in the Vienna Convention; still, a number of delegations at the codification conference considered it only another form of fraud. Also, the potential invalidity of a treaty made on behalf of a State by an organ not competent to conclude treaties or that kind of treaty, predates the Vienna Convention as customary international law. The same is true for the right to terminate or suspend a treaty, or to receive damages in case of material breach by one party.

The interpretation provisions of the Vienna Convention, to the extent it codifies customary law, are also potentially different from domestic law. United States courts have handled the interpretation of Indian treaties with a decidedly pro-Indian slant. In exchange for upholding the validity of such agreements, they have decided to fashion three special canons of construction that reflect the historic circumstances of often unilateral imposition of these obligations: Indian treaties should be construed as the Indians would have understood them; ambiguous expressions must be resolved in favor of the Indians; and treaties must be liberally construed in favor of the Indians. Traditional scholars applying the horizontal rules of interpretation of treaties under international law, would not be ready to afford such, at least verbal, preference, to one side. Then, again, they usually do not deal with such lopsided agreements. A hybrid theory of the character of American Indian treaties might apply the international law rules regarding the validity of treaties, while adding to the Vienna rules of interpretation the domestic rules of preferential treatment regarding interpretation. This "picking and choosing" attitude, however, is subject to the criticism that it is as result-oriented as the United States case law it criticizes. The better solution, at least for traditional scholars, might thus be that one has to "take the bitter with the sweet" and place the entire system of legal evaluation of such treaties, both with respect to validity and to meaning, under the regime of international law. This would make Indian treaties entirely ones of international law in character, receiving their validity domestically through the affirmative action of the Senate and the promulgation, and subsequent ratification, by the President.

Authors in this field have rejected the international law "analogy" by referring to the disproportionately better treatment of Indians in the interpretation of treaties under domestic law. Some have referred to the likeness of Indian treaties to domestic adhesion contracts. The modern doctrine of adhesion contracts is, however, one that is not limited to the ambience of American law. The unequal bargaining power of many actors in the domestic field, the prevalence of standard form contracts, etc. has led to legislative reactions in many legal systems around the globe that favor the weaker party, the one upon which the contract terms have been imposed, including strict rules of interpretation of such a contract against the party who dictated its terms (rule *contra proferentem*). Thus, a general principle of law recognized by civilized nations, derived from the "common core" of domestic legal systems, applicable international law under Article

38(1)(c) of the Statute of the International Court of Justice, may most arguably have emerged that would mandate such an unequal regime of enforcement and interpretation in the case of extremely lopsided agreements. Given the context and genesis of at least a great number of the post-1812 American Indian treaties, the conclusion may be warranted that they constitute international treaties of adhesion. Their interpretation would by necessity, then, have to depart from the horizontal, neutral rules of the Vienna Convention.

These rules of international law regarding validity and meaning would have to applied by the courts of the United States of America, both on the state and the federal level. After all, the treaties with Indian nations have domestic effect on the same level of validity as Acts of Congress under the supremacy clause of Article VI of the Constitution. As any other treaty with foreign nations, the treaty is incorporated into United States law as a "creature" of international law, still subject to international law criteria of validity and interpretation. In other words, if the treaty loses its validity internationally, it loses its effect domestically as well. The same holds true for the interpretation of such an agreement. It is subject to the customary international law of treaties.

b. National Prescriptions

The United States Constitution in Article VI(2) provides:

> This Constitution, and the laws of the United States which shall be made in pursuance thereof, and all treaties made, or which shall be made under the authority of the United States, shall be the Supreme law of the land; and the judges in every State shall be bound thereby, anything in the Constitution or laws of any State to the contrary notwithstanding.

When the President and the Senate are forewarned, there is no difficulty in explicitly making a treaty "self-executing" within the United States. When the President and the Senate do not make their intent unambiguously explicit, the problem becomes one of interpretation, requiring a careful contextual examination of all circumstances that might bear upon in-tent.

A judge-made conception, however, determines the domestic legal effect of American agreements with other countries: the key distinction between "self-executing" and "non-self-executing" treaties. Chief Justice Marshall, in *Foster v. Neilson*, 27 U.S. 253 (1829),, introduced the heretofore unknown distinction between "self-executing" and "non-self-executing" treaties. This construction of the Supremacy Clause, originally based on the nature of the treaty (i.e., treaties of the "self-executing" kind were legislative in character, while the others contained only promises by the United States to take further action) ran against the text of the Constitution ("all Treaties ... shall be the supreme Law of the Land") as well as President George Washington's interpretation of 1796 ("every Treaty [properly ratified] ... thenceforward becomes the law of the land"). JORDAN PAUST, INTERNATIONAL LAW AS LAW OF THE UNITED STATES 51 (Carolina Academic Press 1996). Still, courts have followed Marshall's distinction and have declared a variety of international commitments, including the United Nations Charter, non-self-executing, i.e., incapable of being invoked in United States courts without the presence of enabling or implementing legislation. At times, when the treaty was of a clearly legislative character - an example being the International Covenant on Civil and Political Rights, the U.S. Government has declared it non-self-executing in the process of ratification. Although this practice has attracted some domestic and international criticism, the Restatement concludes, "In general, agreements that can be readily given effect by executive or judicial bodies, federal or state, without further legislation, are deemed self- executing, unless a contrary intention is manifest. Obligations not to act, or to act only subject to limitations, are generally self-executing." Restatement (Third) of Foreign Relations Law Of the United States §111, Reporter's Note 5 (1987).

(1) Sei Fujii v. State

242 P.2d 617 (Cal. 1952)

GIBSON, Chief Justice: Plaintiff, an alien Japanese who is ineligible for citizenship under our naturalization laws, appeals from a judgment declaring that certain land purchased by him in 1948 had escheated to the state. There is no treaty between this country and Japan which confers upon plaintiff the right to own land, and the sole question presented on this appeal is the validity of the California alien land law.

It is first contended that the land law has been invalidated and superseded by the provisions of the United Nations Charter pledging the member nations to promote the observance of human rights and fundamental freedoms without distinction as to race. Plaintiff relies on statements in the preamble and in Articles 1, 55 and 56 of the Charter, 59 Stat. 1035.

It is not disputed that the charter is a treaty, and our federal Constitution provides that treaties made under the authority of the United States are part of the supreme law of the land and that the judges in every state are bound thereby. U.S. Const., art. VI. A treaty, however, does not automatically supersede local laws which are inconsistent with it *unless the treaty provisions are self-executing*. In the words of Chief Justice Marshall: A treaty is "to be regarded in courts of justice as equivalent to an act of the Legislature, whenever it operates of itself, without the aid of any legislative provision. But when the terms of the stipulation import a contract - when either of the parties engages to perform a particular act - the treaty addresses itself to the political, not the judicial department; and the Legislature must execute the contract, before it can become a rule for the court." Foster v. Neilson, 1829, 2 Pet. 253, 314.

In determining whether a treaty is self-executing courts look to the in-tent of the signatory parties as manifested by the language of the instrument, and, if the instrument is uncertain, recourse may be had to the circumstances surrounding its execution. ... In order for a treaty provision to be operative without the aid of implementing legislation and to have the force and effect of a statute, it must appear that the framers of the treaty intended to prescribe a rule that, standing alone, would be enforceable in the courts. ...

It is clear that the provisions of the preamble and of Article 1 of the Charter which are claimed to be in conflict with the alien land law are not self-executing. They state general purposes and objectives of the United Nations Organization and do not purport to impose legal obligations on the individual member nations or to create rights in private persons. It is equally clear that none of the other provisions relied on by plaintiff is self-executing. Article 55 declares that the United Nations "shall promote: ... universal respect for, and observance of, human rights and fundamental freedoms for all without distinction as to race, sex, language, or religion," and in Article 56, the member nations "pledge themselves to take joint and separate action in cooperation with the Organization for the achievement of the pur-poses set forth in Article 55." Although the member nations have obligated themselves to cooperate with the international organization in promoting respect for, and observance of, human rights, it is plain that it was contemplated that future legislative action by the several nations would be required to accomplish the declared objectives, and there is nothing to indicate that these provisions were intended to become rules of law for the courts of this country upon the ratification of the Charter.

The language used in Articles 55 and 56 is not the type customarily employed in treaties which have been held to be self-executing and to create rights and duties in individuals. For example, the treaty involved in Clark v. Allen, 331 U.S. 503, 507-508, relating to the rights of a national of one country to inherit real property located in another country, specifically provided that "such national shall be allowed a term of three years in which to sell the [property] ... and withdraw the proceeds ..." free from any discriminatory taxation. ... In other instances treaty provisions were enforced without implementing legislation where they prescribed in detail the rules governing rights and obligations of individuals or specifically provided that citizens of one nation shall have the same rights while in the other country as are enjoyed by that country's own citizens. ...

It is significant to note that when the framers of the Charter intended to make certain provisions effective without the aid of implementing legislation they employed language which is clear and definite and manifests that intention. For example, Article 104 provides: "The Organization shall enjoy in the territory of each of its Members such legal capacity as may be necessary for the exercise of its functions and the fulfillment of its purposes." Article 105 provides: "1. The Organization shall enjoy in the territory of each of its Members such privileges and immunities as are necessary for the fulfillment of its purposes. 2. Representatives of the Members of the United Nations and officials of the Organization shall similarly enjoy such privileges and immunities as are necessary for the independent exercise of their functions in connection with the Organization." In *Curran v. City of New York*, 191 Misc. 229, 77 N.Y.S.2d 206, 212, these articles were treated as being self-executory. ...

The provisions in the charter pledging cooperation in promoting observance of fundamental freedoms lack the mandatory quality and definiteness which would indicate an intent to create justiciable rights in private persons immediately upon ratification. Instead, they are framed as a promise of fu-ture action by the member nations. Secretary of State Stettinius, Chairman of the United States delegation at the San Francisco Conference where the Char-ter was drafted, stated in his report to President Truman that Article 56 pledges the various countries to cooperate with the organization by joint and separate action in the achievement of the economic and social objectives of the organization without infringing upon their right to order their national affairs according to their own best ability, in their own way, and in accord-ance with their own political and economic institutions and processes. ... The same view was repeatedly expressed by delegates of other na-tions in the debates attending the drafting of article 56. ...

The humane and enlightened objectives of the United Nations Charter are, of course, entitled to respectful consideration by the courts and Legislatures of every member nation, since that document expresses the universal de-sire of thinking men for peace and for equality of rights and opportunities. The charter represents a moral commitment of foremost importance, and we must not permit the spirit of our pledge to be compromised or disparaged in either our domestic or foreign affairs. We are satisfied, however, that the Charter provisions relied on by plaintiff were not intended to supersede existing domestic legislation, and we cannot hold that they operate to invalidate the alien land law. ... [The Court eventually held the Alien Land Law invalid under the 14th Amendment.]

(2) People of Saipan v. United States Dept. of Interior

502 F.2d 90 (9th Cir. 1974), *cert. denied*, 420 U.S. 1003 (1975)

ALFRED T. GOODWIN, Circuit Judge: Plaintiffs, citizens of the Trust Territory of the Pacific Islands (known also as Micronesia), sued in the district court to challenge the execution by the High Commissioner of the Trust Territory of a lease permitting Continental Airlines to construct and operate a hotel on public land adjacent to Micro Beach, Saipan. Plaintiffs appeal a judgment of dismissal. ...

Continental applied in 1970 to the Trust Territory government for permission to build a hotel on public land adjacent to Micro Beach, Saipan, an important historical, cultural, and recreational site for the people of the islands. Pursuant to the requirements of the Trust Territory Code, 67 T.T.C. § 53, Continental's application was submitted to the Mariana Islands District Land Advisory Board for its consideration. In spite of the Board's unanimous recommendation that the area be reserved for public park pur-poses, the District Administrator of the Marianas District recommended approval of a lease. The High Commissioner himself executed the lease on be-half of the Trust Territory government. An officer appointed by the President of the United States with the advice and consent of the Senate (48 U.S.C. § 1681a), the High Commissioner is the highest official in the executive branch of the Trust Territory government.

Following its execution in 1972, the lease was opposed by virtually every official body elected by the people of Saipan. Indeed, the record in this case shows that the High Commissioner's decision was officially supported only by the United States Department of the Interior, the Trust Territory Attorney General (a United States citizen), and the District Administrator of the Marianas District (appointed by the High Commissioner, serving directly under him, and subject to removal by him).

Later in 1972, an action against some of the parties here was commenced before the High Court of the Trust Territory to enjoin construction of the hotel. The High Court, while denying defendants' motions to dismiss on certain nonfederal causes of action, held that NEPA did not apply to actions of the Trust Territory government, as plaintiffs had contended. Soon after-ward, the plaintiffs filed this action in the United States District Court for the District of Hawaii, and the High Court thereupon stayed proceedings be-fore it pending the outcome of this action.

The district court relying upon its earlier decision in *People of Enewetak v. Laird*, 353 F. Supp. 811 (D. Haw. 1973), again held that NEPA applies to federal agencies operating in the Trust Territory. It also held that approval of the lease agreement was "major" action, within the meaning of NEPA. However, although the district court rejected the defendants' contention that the Trust Territory government is a foreign government immune to suits in United States courts, it accepted the defendants' alternate contention that the local government is a government of a United States territory or possession, within the meaning of the exclusionary clause in the Administrative Procedure Act, 5 U.S.C. § 701 (b)(1)(C). Having concluded that the Trust Territory government was exempt from review under the APA, the district court reasoned that the same standards on the scope of review should be applied to NEPA, and concluded that the action of the High Commissioner in approving and executing the lease agreement was not "federal" action cover-ed by the National Environmental Policy Act, 42 U.S.C. § 4332.

We affirm these conclusions of the district court. ...

Plaintiffs also asserted below and assert here that the action of the governmental defendants in leasing public land to an American corporation against the expressed opposition of the elected representatives of the people of Saipan and without compliance with [the National Environmental Policy Act, hereinafter NEPA] NEPA is a violation of their duties under the Trusteeship Agreement. The district court rejected this argument, holding that the Trusteeship Agreement did not vest the citizens of the Trust Territory with rights which they can assert in a district court.

We cannot accept the full implications of this holding. We do not dispute the district court's conclusion that compliance with NEPA was not required by the Trusteeship Agreement. We do, however, disagree with the holding insofar as it can be read to say that the Trusteeship Agreement does not create for the islanders substantive rights that are judicially enforceable.

The district court relied for its conclusion on language in *Pauling v. McElroy*, 164 F. Supp. 390, 393 (D.D.C.1958), aff'd on other grounds, 278 F.2d 252, cert. denied, 364 U.S. 835 (1960). Pauling concerned an attempt to enjoin United States officials from proceeding with nuclear tests in the Marshall Islands, an area within the trusteeship. The controversy there, unlike the one here, involved the Trusteeship Agreement's grant of broad discretion to use the area for military purposes. *See* Trusteeship Agreement arts. 1, 5, 13, 61 Stat. 3301, 3302, 3304. We do not find *Pauling* to support the defendants' contention here that the plaintiffs cannot invoke the provisions of the Trusteeship Agreement to challenge the High Commissioner's power to lease local public land for commercial exploitation by private developers.

The right of Rhodesian and American citizens to maintain an action in the courts of the United States seeking enforcement of the United Nations embargo against Rhodesia was recently recognized in *Diggs v. Shultz*, 470 F.2d 461 (1972), cert. denied, 411 U.S. 931 (1973). On the merits, the court denied specific relief because of Congressional action which was held to have abrogated the United Nations Security Council Resolution, but the right to seek enforcement in federal court was firmly established. That decision, if correct, suggests that the islanders here can enforce their treaty rights, if need be in federal court.

Article 73 of the United Nations Charter, 59 Stat. 1031, 1048, T.S. No. 993 (1945), which discusses non-self-governing territories generally, provides:

> Members of the United Nations which have or assume responsibilities for the administration of territories whose peoples have not yet attained a full measure of self-government recognize the principle that the interests of the inhabitants of these territories are paramount, and accept as sacred trust the obligation to promote to the utmost, within the system of international peace and security established by the present Charter, the well-being of the inhabitants of these territories, and, to this end:
>
> a. To ensure, with due respect for the culture of the peoples concerned, their political, economic, social, and educational advancement, their just treatment, and their protections against abuses …

See also United Nations Charter art. 76, describing the basic objectives of the trusteeship system. Although the plaintiffs have argued that these articles of the United Nations Charter, standing alone, create affirmative and judicially enforceable obligations, we assume without deciding that they do not.

However, pursuant to Article 79 of the Charter, the general principles governing the administration of trust territories were covered in more detail in a specific trusteeship agreement for the Trust Territory of the Pacific Islands. … Specifically, Article 6 of the Trusteeship Agreement re-quires the United States to "promote the economic advancement and self-sufficiency of the inhabitants, and to this end … regulate the use of natural resources and to protect the inhabitants against the loss of their lands and resources. …"

Defendants contend, though, that provisions of the Trusteeship Agreement, including Article 6, can be enforced only before the Security Council of the United Nations. We disagree, concluding that the Trusteeship Agreement can be a source of rights enforceable by an individual litigant in a domestic court of law.

The extent to which an international agreement establishes affirmative and judicially enforceable obligations without implementing legislation must be determined in each case by reference to many contextual factors: the purposes of the treaty and the objectives of its creators, the existence of domestic procedures and institutions appropriate for direct implementation, the avail-ability and feasibility of alternative enforcement methods, and the immediate and long-range social consequences of self- or non-self-execution. *See* generally M. McDougal, H. Lasswell, & J. Miller, The Interpretation of Agreements and World Public Order: Principles of Content and Procedure, (Yale University Press, 1967).

The preponderance of features in this Trusteeship Agreement suggests the intention to establish direct, affirmative, and judicially enforceable rights. The issue involves the local economy and environment, not security; the concern with natural resources and the concern with political development are explicit in the agreement and are general international concerns as well; the enforcement of these rights requires little legal or administrative innovation in the domestic fora; and the alternative forum, the Security Council, would present to the plaintiffs obstacles so great as to make their rights virtually unenforceable.

Moreover, the Trusteeship Agreement constitutes the plaintiffs' basic constitutional document …, and is codified into the law of the Trust Territory, I T.T.C. § 101(i). For all these reasons, we believe that the rights asserted by the plaintiffs are judicially enforceable. However, we see no reason why they could not and should not have been enforced in the High Court of the Trust Territory. The district court found that:

> The lease approval was a 'local' decision of the High Commissioner acting within the scope of his duties as chief executive of the Trust Territory Government. The officials of the Interior Department did not negotiate, counsel, advise or participate in the decision. Nor was the lease ever sent to the Department for approval or concurrence in any form. … 356 F.Supp. at 657 n. 28.

Surely, the judicial branch of the Trust Territory government has the authority to determine whether or not the action of its chief executive complies with a provision in its own constitutional document.

We recognize that the Trusteeship Agreement purports to obligate the United States, not the individual who happens to be High Commissioner. Nonetheless, because of the process of his appointment, the High Commissioner has the responsibility to act in a manner consistent with the duties assumed by the United States itself in the Trusteeship Agreement.

Thus, although we hold that the Trusteeship Agreement is a source of individual legal rights, we also hold that, in a case involving actions by the High Commissioner within the scope of his duties as chief executive, these rights are not initially enforceable in United States courts. Rather, upon principles of comity, they should be asserted before the High Court of the Trust Territory.

Admittedly, the substantive rights guaranteed through the Trusteeship Agreement are not precisely defined. However, we do not believe that the agreement is too vague for judicial enforcement. Its language is no more general than such terms as "due process of law," "seaworthiness," "equal protection of the law . . . good faith," or "restraint of trade," which courts interpret every day. Moreover, the High Court can look for guidance to its own recently enacted environmental quality and protection act, T.T.Pub.L. No. 4C-78 of Apr. 14, 1972, *codified at* 63 T.T.C. §§ 501-509, to the relevant principles of international law and resource use which have achieved a substantial degree of codification and consensus ... and to the general direction, al-though not necessarily the specific provisions, of NEPA.

These sources should provide a sufficiently definite standard against which to test the High Commissioner's approval of a 50-year lease of unique public lands to an American corporation, allegedly in disregard of the protests of the islands' elected officials and without a showing of consideration of cultural and environmental factors. ...

Notes and Questions

1. Compare and appraise the application of the "self-executing" doctrine in the *Sei Fujii* and *People of Saipan* cases. *See also* Part One, *supra,* at 124.

2. The U.S. Government, in its ratification of the 1966 International Covenant on Civil and Political Rights, formally declared the treaty non-self-executing, thereby averting a private cause of action in U.S. courts arising out of an alleged Covenant violation. U.S. Senate Committee on Foreign Relations, Report on the International Covenant on Civil and Political Rights, at 620, 102nd Cong., 2d Sess., Mar. 24, 1992, *reprinted in* 31 I.L.M. 645, 651-57 (1992). Professor Paust comments:

> It was a sad day in American legal history when President Bush reiterated previously suggested reservations, understandings, and declarations concerning the 1966 International Covenant on Civil and Political Rights, and sadder still when the U.S. Senate, so miserably compliant with the Executive, unquestionably accepted the Executive's declaration that the treaty should not be self-executing. Rarely has a formal attempt at adherence to a treaty been so blatantly meaningless and so openly defiant of its terms, the needed efficacy of its norms, and the very possibility of its direct application as supreme law of the land.

Jordan J. Paust, International Law as Law of the United States 361 (Carolina Academic Press 1996). *See* also Lori Fisler Damrosch, *The Role of the United States Senate Concerning "Self-Executing" and "Non-Self-Executing" Treaties*, 67 Chi.-Kent L. Rev. 515, 516-18 (1991); Jordan J. Paust, *Self-Executing Treaties*, 82 Am. J. Int'l L. 760 (1988); Stefan A. Riesenfeld & Frederick M. Abbott, *The Scope of U.S. Senate Control Over the Conclusion and Operation of Treaties*, 67 Chi.-Kent L. Rev. 571, 631 (1991); Carlos Manuel Vazquez, *Treaty-Based Rights and Remedies of Individuals*, 92 Colum. L. Rev. 1082, 1084 (1992); Carlos Manuel Vazquez, *The Four Doctrines of*

Self-Executing Treaties, 89 AM. J. INT'L L. 695 (1995); David Sloss, *Non-Self-Executing Treaties: Exposing a Constitutional Fallacy*, 36 U.C. DAVIS L. REV. 1 (2002).

A recent assessment of the efficacy of this declaration is not as bleak:

> While non-self-execution forestalls immediate and direct effects on U.S. domestic law comparable to those wrought in Europe by the European Convention, the Covenant, over time, probably will have some incremental effects within the United States. Litigants in state and federal courts will argue its relevance as an aid to interpretation (including in the context of state constitutions); activists will use the Covenant and the Human Rights Committee's interpretations to complain about actions by state officials or police; and lobbyists and nongovernmental organizations will deploy them to promote legislative agendas.

José E. Alvarez, *International Law: Some Recent Developments,* 46 J. LEGAL EDUCATION 557, 56-61 (1996). *See also* Ann Woolhandler, *Treaties, Self-Execution, and the Public Law Litigation Model*, 42 VA. J. INT'L L. 757 (2002); Caleb Nelson, *The Treaty Power and Self-Execution: A Comment on Professor Woolhandler's Article*, 42 VA. J. INT'L L. 801 (2002).

3. Is the distinction between self-executing and non-self-executing character of a treaty undertaking one properly made by a prospective party? What if such a determination runs against the object and purpose of a treaty? As to the U.S. declaration, see General Comment Adopted by the Human Rights Committee Under Article 40, Paragraph 4, of the International Covenant on Civil and Political Rights, CCPR/C/21/Rev.1/Add.6 (Nov. 2, 1994), see *infra*, at 1333 , para. 12:

> Of particular concern are widely formulated reservations which essentially render ineffective all Covenant rights which would require any change in national law to ensure compliance with Covenant obligations. No real international rights or obligations have thus been accepted. And when there is an absence of provisions to ensure that Covenant rights may be sued on in domestic courts, and, further, a failure to allow individual complaints to be brought to the Committee under the first Optional Protocol, all the essential elements of the Covenant guarantees have been removed.

4. How would you bring more clarity to the distinction between "self-executing" and "non-self executing"? What are the consequences for an international treaty régime that permits non-enforcement on these grounds?

C. CONSENT TO BE BOUND

1. Final Utterance of Commitment

There are elaborate provisions about the formalities of expression of consent to be bound. Do they serve an important contemporary function or are they no more than relics of a more ritualistic age?

a. Vienna Convention on the Law of Treaties

Article 11. The consent of a State to be bound by a treaty may be ex-pressed by signature, exchange of instruments constituting a treaty, ratification, acceptance, approval or accession, or by any other means if so agreed.

Article 12. (1) The consent of a State to be bound by a treaty is ex-pressed by the signature of its representative when:

(a) the treaty provides that signature shall have that effect,

(b) it is otherwise established that the negotiating States were agreed that signature should have that effect, or

(c) the intention of the State to give that effect to the signature appears from the full powers of its representative or was expressed during the negotiation.

2) For the purposes of paragraph 1:

(a) the initialling of a text constitutes a signature of the treaty when it is established that the negotiating States so agreed,

(b) the signature *ad referendum* of a treaty by a representative, if confirmed by his State, constitutes a full signature of the treaty.

Article 13. The consent of States to be bound by a treaty constituted by instruments exchanged between them is expressed by that exchange when:

(a) the instruments provide that their exchange shall have that effect; or

(b) it is otherwise established that those States were agreed that the exchange of instruments should have that effect.

Article 14. (1) The consent of a State to be bound by a treaty is expressed by ratification when:

(a) the treaty provides for such consent to be expressed by means of ratification,

(b) it is otherwise established that the negotiating States were agreed that ratification should be required;

(c) the representative of the State has signed the treaty subject to ratification; or

(d) the intention of the State to sign the treaty subject to ratification appears from the full powers of its representative or was expressed during the negotiation.

(2) The consent of a State to be bound by a treaty is expressed by acceptance or approval under conditions similar to those which apply to ratification.

Article 18. A State is obliged to refrain from acts which would defeat the object and purpose of a treaty when:

(a) it has signed the treaty or has exchanged instruments constituting the treaty subject to ratification, acceptance or approval, until it shall have made its intention clear not to become a party to the treaty; or

(b) it has expressed its consent to be bound by the treaty, pending the entry into force of the treaty and provided that such entry into force is not unduly delayed.

b. International Criminal Court

(1) Letter from Under Secretary of State for Arms Control and International Security, John R. Bolton to U.N. Secretary-General Kofi Annan

Released on May 6, 2002, available at http://www.state.gov/r/pa/prs/ps/2002/9968.htm

Dear Mr. Secretary-General:

This is to inform you, in connection with the Rome Statute of the International Criminal Court adopted on July 17, 1998, that the United States does not intend to become a party to the treaty. Accordingly, the United States has no legal obligations arising from its signature on December 31, 2000. The United States requests that its intention not to become a party, as expressed in this letter, be reflected in the depositary's status lists relating to this treaty.

Sincerely,

S/John R. Bolton

Notes and Questions

1. The legal effect of the Bolton letter has at times been erroneously characterized as "unsigning" the Rome Statute. Whether one agrees with the U.S. policy or not, the Bolton letter was consistent with Article 18 of the 1969 Vienna Convention on the Law of Treaties and was the appropriate measure once the U.S. had resolved not to become a party. Does it matter that the United States has signed, but not ratified the 1969 Vienna Convention on the Law of Treaties? *See* David C. Scott, *Management and Control of the Modern Business Corporation: Presidential Power to "Unsign" Treaties*, 69 U. Chi. L. Rev. 1447 (2002); Edward T. Swaine, *Unsigning*, 55 Stan L. Rev. 2061 (2003).

2. As to Article 18, *see* Jan Klabbers, *How to Defeat a Treaty's Object and Purpose Pending Entry into Force: Toward Manifest Intent*, 34 Vand. J. Transnat'l L. 283 (2001).

2. Reservations to Commitment

a. Vienna Convention on The Law of Treaties

1155 U.N.T.S. 331 (1969)

Article 19. A State may, when signing, ratifying, accepting, approving or acceding to a treaty, formulate a reservation unless:

(*a*) the reservation is prohibited by the treaty;

(b) the treaty provides that only specified reservations, which do not include the reservation in question, may be made; or

(*c*) in cases not falling under sub-paragraphs (a) and *(b),* the reservation is incompatible with the object and purpose of the treaty.

Article 20. (1) A reservation expressly authorized by a treaty does not require any subsequent acceptance by the other contracting States unless the treaty so provides.

(2) When it appears from the limited number of the negotiating States and the object and purpose of a treaty that the application of the treaty in its entirety between all the parties is an essential condition of the consent of each one to be bound by the treaty, a reservation requires acceptance by all the par-ties.

(3) When a treaty is a constituent instrument of an international organization and unless it otherwise provides, a reservation requires the acceptance of the competent organ of that organization.

(4) In cases not failing under the preceding paragraphs and unless the treaty otherwise provides:

(*a*) acceptance by another contracting State of a reservation constitutes the reserving State a party to the treaty in relation to that other State if or when the treaty is in force for those States;

(*b*) an objection by another contracting State to a reservation does not preclude the entry into force of the treaty as between the objecting and reserving States unless a contrary intention is definitely expressed by the objecting State;

(*c*) an act expressing a State's consent to be bound by the treaty and containing a reservation is effective as soon as at least one other contracting State has accepted the reservation.

(5) For the purposes of paragraphs 2 and 4 and unless the treaty other-wise provides, a reservation is considered to have been accepted by a State if it shall have raised no objection to the reservation by the end of a period of twelve months after it was notified of the reservation or by the date on which it expressed its consent to be bound by the treaty, whichever is later.

Article 21. (1) A reservation established with regard to another party in accordance with articles 19, 20 and 23:

(*a*) modifies for the reserving State in its relations with that other party the provisions of the treaty to which the reservation relates to the extent of the reservation; and

(*b*) modifies those provisions to the same extent for that other party in its relations with the reserving State.

(2) The reservation does not modify the provisions of the treaty for the other parties to the treaty *inter se.*

(3) When a State objecting to a reservation has not opposed the entry into force of the treaty between itself and the reserving State, the provisions to which the reservation relates do not apply as between the two States to the extent of the reservation.

Article 22. (1) Unless the treaty otherwise provides, a reservation may be withdrawn at any time and the consent of a State which has accepted the reservation is not required for its withdrawal.

(2) Unless the treaty otherwise provides, an objection to a reservation may be withdrawn at any time.

(3) Unless the treaty otherwise provides, or it is otherwise agreed:

(*a*) the withdrawal of a reservation becomes operative in relation to another contracting State only when notice of it has been received by that State;

(*b*) the withdrawal of an objection to a reservation becomes operative only when notice of it has been received by the State which formulated the reservation.

Article 23. (1) A reservation, an express acceptance of a reservation and an objection to a reservation must be formulated in writing and communicated to the contracting States and other States entitled to become parties to the treaty.

(2) If formulated when signing the treaty subject to ratification, acceptance or approval, a reservation must be formally confirmed by the reserving State when expressing its consent to be bound by the treaty. In such a case the reservation shall be considered as having been made on the date of its confirmation.

b. Reservations to the Convention on Genocide

1951 I.C.J. 15, 20-26 (May 28)

The Court observes that the three questions which have been referred to it for an Opinion have certain common characteristics. ...

The three questions are purely abstract in character. They refer neither to the reservations which have, in fact, been made to the Convention by certain States, nor to the objections which have been made to such reservations by other States. They do not even refer to the reservations which may in future be made in respect of any particular article; nor do they refer to the objections to which these reservations might give rise.

Question 1 is framed in the following terms:

> Can the reserving State be regarded as being a party to the Convention while still maintaining its reservation if the reservation is object-ed to by one or more of the parties to the Convention but not by others?

The Court observes that this question refers, not to the possibility of making reservations to the Genocide Convention, but solely to the question whether a contracting State which has made a reservation can, while still maintaining it, be regarded as being a party to the Convention, when there is a divergence of views between the contracting parties concerning this reservation, some accepting the reservation, others refusing to accept it.

It is well established that in its treaty relations a State cannot be bound without its consent, and that consequently no reservation can be effective against any State without its agreement thereto. It is also a generally recognized principle that a multilateral convention is the result of an agreement freely concluded upon its clauses and that consequently none of the contract-ing parties is entitled to frustrate or impair, by means of unilateral decisions or particular agreements, the purpose and *raison d'être* of the convention. To this principle was linked the notion of the integrity of the convention as adopted, a notion which in its traditional concept involved the proposition that no reservation was valid unless it was accepted by all the contracting par-ties without exception, as would have been the case if it had been stated during the negotiations.

This concept, which is directly inspired by the notion of contract, is of undisputed value as a principle. However, as regards the Genocide Convention, it is proper to refer to a variety of circumstances which would lead to a more flexible application of this principle. Among these circumstances may be noted the clearly universal character of the United Nations under whose auspices the Convention was concluded, and the very wide degree of participation envisaged by Article XI of the Convention. Extensive participation in conventions of this type has already given rise to greater flexibility in the international practice concerning multilateral conventions. More general re-sort to reservations, very great allowance made for tacit assent to reservations, the existence of practices which go so far as to admit that the author of reservations which have been rejected by certain contracting parties is nevertheless to be regarded as a party to the convention in relation to those contracting parties that have accepted the reservations—all these factors are manifestations of a new need for flexibility in the operation of multilateral conventions.

It must also be pointed out that although the Genocide Convention was finally approved unanimously, it is nevertheless the result of a series of majority votes. The majority principle, while facilitating the conclusion of multilateral conventions, may also make it necessary for certain States to make reservations. This observation is confirmed by the great number of reservations which have been made of recent years to multilateral conventions.

In this state of international practice, it could certainly not be inferred from the absence of an article providing for reservations in a multilateral convention that the contracting States are prohibited from making certain reservations. Account should also be taken of the fact that the absence of such an article or even the decision not to insert such an article can be explained by the desire not to invite a multiplicity of reservations. The character of a multilateral convention, its purpose, provisions, mode of preparation and adoption, are factors which must be considered in determining, in the absence of any express provision on the subject, the possibility of making reservations, as well as their validity and effect.

Although it was decided during the preparatory work not to insert a special article on reservations, it is none the less true that the faculty for States to make reservations was contemplated at successive stages of the drafting of the Convention. In this connection, the following passage may be quoted from the comments on the draft Convention prepared by the Secretary-General:

> (1) It would seem that reservations of a general scope have no place in a convention of this kind which does not deal with the private interests of a State, but with the preservation of an element of international order. ; (2) perhaps in the course of discussion in the General Assembly it will be possible to allow certain limited reservations.

Even more decisive in this connection is the debate on reservations in the Sixth Committee at the meetings (December 1st and 2nd, 1948) which immediately preceded the adoption of the Genocide Convention by the General Assembly. Certain delegates clearly announced that their governments could only sign or ratify the Convention subject to certain reservations.

Furthermore, the faculty to make reservations to the Convention appears to be implicitly admitted by the very terms of Question 1.

The Court recognizes that an understanding was reached within the General Assembly on the faculty to make reservations to the Genocide Convention and that it is permitted to conclude therefrom that States becoming parties to the Convention gave their assent thereto. It must now determine what kind of reservations may be made and what kind of objections may be taken to them.

The solution of these problems must be found in the special characteristics of the Genocide Convention. The origins and character of that Convention, the objects pursued by the General Assembly and the contracting parties, the relations which exist between the provisions of the Convention, *inter se,* and between those provisions and these objects, furnish elements of interpretation of the will of the General Assembly and the parties. The origins of the Convention show that it was the intention of the United Nations to condemn and punish genocide as "a crime under international law" involving a denial of the right of existence of entire human groups, a denial which shocks the conscience of mankind and results in great losses to humanity, and which is contrary to moral law and to the spirit and aims of the United Nations (Resolution 96(1) of the General Assembly, December 11th, 1946). The first consequence arising from this conception is that the principles underlying the Convention are principles which are recognized by civilized na-tions as binding on States, even without any conventional obligation. A sec-ond consequence is the universal character both of the condemnation of geno-cide and of the co-operation required "in order to liberate mankind from such an odious scourge" (Preamble to the Convention). The Genocide Conven-tion was therefore intended by the General Assembly and by the contracting parties to be definitely universal in scope. It was in fact approved on December 9th, 1948, by a resolution which was unanimously adopted by fifty-six States.

The objects of such a convention must also be considered. The Convention was manifestly adopted for a purely humanitarian and civilizing purpose. It is indeed difficult to imagine a convention that might have this dual character to a greater degree, since its object on the one hand is to safeguard the very existence of certain human groups and on the other to confirm and endorse the most elementary principles of morality. In such a convention the contracting States do not have any interests of their own; they merely have, one and all, a common interest, namely, the accomplishment of those high purposes which are the *raison d'être* of the convention. Consequently, in a convention of this type one cannot speak of individual advantages or disadvantages to States, or of the maintenance of a perfect contractual balance between rights and duties. The high ideals which inspired the Convention pro-vide, by virtue of the common will of the parties, the foundation and measure of all its provisions.

The foregoing considerations, when applied to the question of reservations, and more particularly to the effects of objections to reservations, lead to the following conclusions.

The object and purpose of the Genocide Convention imply that it was the intention of the General Assembly and of the States which adopted it that as many States as possible should participate. The complete exclusion from the Convention of one or more States would not only restrict the scope of its application, but would detract from the authority of the moral and humanitarian principles which are its basis. It is inconceivable that the contracting parties readily contemplated that an objection to a minor reservation should produce such a result. But even less could the contracting parties have intended to sacrifice the very object of the Convention in favour of a vain desire to secure as many participants as possible. The object and purpose of the Convention thus limit both the freedom of making reservations and that of objecting to them. It follows that it is the compatibility of a reservation with the object and purpose of the Convention that must furnish the criterion for the attitude of a State in making the reservation on accession as well as for the appraisal by a State in objecting to the reservation. Such is the rule of conduct which must guide every State in the appraisal which it must make, individually and from its own standpoint, of the admissibility of any reservation.

Any other view would lead either to the acceptance of reservations which frustrate the purposes which the General Assembly and the contracting parties had in mind, or to recognition that the parties to the Convention have the power of excluding from it the author of a reservation, even a minor one, which may be quite compatible with those purposes.

It has nevertheless been argued that any State entitled to become a party to the Genocide Convention may do so while making any reservation it chooses by virtue of its sovereignty. The Court cannot share this view. It is obvious that so extreme an application of the idea of State sovereignty could lead to a complete disregard of the object and purpose of the Convention.

On the other hand, it has been argued that there exists a rule of international law subjecting the effect of a reservation to the express or tacit assent of all the contracting parties. This theory rests essentially on a contractual conception of the absolute integrity of the convention as adopted. This view, however, cannot prevail if, having regard to the character of the convention, its purpose and its mode of adoption, it can be established that the parties intended to derogate from that rule by admitting the faculty to make reservations thereto.

It does not appear, moreover, that the conception of the absolute integrity of a convention has been transformed into a rule of international law. The considerable part which tacit assent has always played in estimating the effect which is to be given to reservations scarcely permits one to state that such a rule exists, determining with sufficient precision the effect of objections made to reservations. In fact, the examples of objections made to reservations appear to be too rare in international practice to have given rise to such a rule. It cannot be recognized that the report which was adopted on the subject by the Council of the League of Nations on June 17th, 1927, has had this effect. At best, the recommendation made on that date by the Council constitutes the point of departure of an administrative practice which, after being observed by the Secretariat of the League of Nations, imposed itself, so to speak, in the ordinary course of things on the Secretary-General of the United Nations in his capacity of depositary of conventions concluded under the auspices of the League. But it cannot be concluded that the legal problem of the effect of objections to reservations has in this way been solved. The opinion of the Secretary-General of the United Nations himself is embodied in the following passage of his report of September 21st, 1950: "While it is universally recognized that the consent of the other governments concerned must be sought before they can be bound by the terms of a reservation, there has not been unanimity either as to the procedure to be followed by a depositary in obtaining the necessary consent or as to the legal effect of a State's objecting to a reservation."

It may, however, be asked whether the General Assembly of the United Nations, in approving the Genocide Convention, had in mind the practice according to which the Secretary-General, in exercising his functions as a depositary, did not regard a reservation as definitively accepted until it had been established that none of the other contracting States objected to it. If this were the case, it might be argued that the implied intention of the contracting par-ties was to make the effectiveness of any reservation to the Genocide Convention conditional on the assent of all the parties.

The Court does not consider that this view corresponds to reality. It must be pointed out, first of all, that the existence of an administrative practice does not in itself constitute a decisive factor in ascertaining what views the contracting States to the Genocide Convention may have had concerning the rights and duties resulting therefrom. It must also be pointed out that there existed among the American States members, both of the United Nations and of the Organization of American States, a different practice which goes so far as to permit a reserving State to become a party irrespective of the nature of the reservations or of the objections raised by other contracting States. The preparatory work of the Convention contains nothing to justify the statement that the contracting States implicitly had any definite practice in mind. Nor is there any such indication in the subsequent attitude of the contracting States: neither the reservations made by certain States nor the position adopted by other States towards those reservations permit the conclusion that assent to one or the other of these practices had been given. Finally, it is not without interest to note, in view of the preference generally said to attach to an established practice, that the debate on reservations to multilateral treaties which took place in the Sixth Committee at the fifth session of the General Assembly reveals a profound divergence of views, some delegations being attached to the idea of the absolute integrity of the Convention, others favouring a more flexible practice which would bring about the participation of as many States as possible.

It results from the foregoing considerations that Question 1, on account of its abstract character, cannot be given an absolute answer. The appraisal of a reservation and the effect of objections that might be made to it depend upon the particular circumstances of each individual case.

c. United States: Genocide Convention Implementation Act

18 U.S.C. § 109 (1988)

Reservations:

(1) That with reference to article IX of the Convention, before any dispute to which the United States is a party may be submitted to the jurisdiction of the International Court of Justice under this article, the specific consent of the United States is required in each case.

(2) That nothing in the Convention requires or authorizes legislation or other action by the United States of America prohibited by the Constitution of the United States as interpreted by the United States.

Understandings:

(1) That the term "intent to destroy, in whole or in part, a national, ethnical, racial, or religious group as such" appearing in article II means the specific intent to destroy, in whole or in substantial part, a national, ethnical, racial or religious group as such by the acts specified in article II.

(2) That the term "mental harm" in article II(b) means permanent impairment of mental faculties through drugs, torture or similar techniques.

(3) That the pledge to grant extradition in accordance with a state's laws and treaties in force found in article VII extends only to acts which are criminal under the laws of both the requesting and the requested state and nothing in article VI affects the right of any state to bring to trial before its own tribunals any of its nationals for acts committed outside a state.

(4) That acts in the course of armed conflicts committed without the specific intent required by article II are not sufficient to constitute genocide as defined by this Convention.

(5) That with regard to the reference to an international penal tribunal in article VI of the Convention, the United States declares that it reserves the right to effect its participation in any such tribunal only by a treaty entered into specifically for that purpose with the advice and consent of the Senate.

d. U.S. Senate Committee on Foreign Relations, Report on the International Covenant on Civil and Political Rights

102nd Cong. 6-20 (1992), *reprinted in* 31 I.L.M. 645, 658-57 (1992).

I. The Senate's advice and consent is subject to the following reservations:

(1) That Article 20 does not authorize or require legislation or other action by the United States that would restrict the right of free speech and association protected by the Constitution and laws of the United States.

(2) That the United States reserves the right, subject to its Constitutional constraints, to impose capital punishment on any person (other than a pregnant woman) duly convicted under existing or future laws permitting the imposition of capital punishment, including such punishment for crimes committed by persons below 18 years of age.

(3) That the United States considers itself bound by Article 7 to the extent that "cruel, inhuman or degrading treatment or punishment" means the cruel and unusual treatment or punishment prohibited by the Fifth, Eighth and/or Fourteenth Amendments to the Constitution of the United States.

(4) That because U.S. law generally applies to an offender the penalty in force at the time the offense was committed, the United States does not adhere to the third clause of paragraph 1 of Article 15.

(5) That the policy and practice of the United States are generally in compliance with and supportive of the Covenant's provisions regarding treatment of juveniles in the criminal justice system. Nevertheless, the United States reserves the right, in exceptional circumstances, to treat juveniles as adults, notwithstanding paragraphs 2(b) and 3 of Article 10 and paragraph 4 of Article 14. The United States further reserves to these provisions with respect to individuals who volunteer for military service prior to age 18.

II. The Senate's advice and consent is subject to the following understandings, which shall apply to the obligations of the United States under this Covenant:

(1) That the Constitution and laws of the United States guarantee all persons equal protection of the law and provide extensive protections against discrimination. The United States understands distinctions based upon race, colour, sex, language, religion, political or other opinion, national or social origin, property, birth or any other status—as those terms are used in Article 2, paragraph 1 and Article 26—to be permitted when such distinctions are, at minimum, rationally related to a legitimate governmental objective. The United States further understands the prohibition in paragraph 1 of Article 4 upon discrimination, in time of

public emergency, based "solely" on the status of race, colour, sex, language, religion or social origin not to bar distinctions that may have a disproportionate effect upon persons of a particular status.

(2) That the United States understands the right to compensation referred to in Articles 9(5) and 14(6) to require the provision of effective and enforceable mechanisms by which a victim of an unlawful arrest or detention or a miscarriage of justice may seek and, where justified, obtain compensation from either the responsible individual or the appropriate governmental entity. Entitlement to compensation may be subject to the reasonable requirements of domestic law.

(3) That the United States understand the reference to "exceptional circumstances" in paragraph 2(a) of Article 10 to permit the imprisonment of an accused person with convicted persons where appropriate in light of an individual's overall dangerousness, and to permit accused persons to waive their right to segregation from convicted persons. The United States further understands that paragraph 3 of Article 10 does not diminish the goals of punishment, deterrence, and incapacitation as additional legitimate purposes for a penitentiary system.

(4) That the United States understands that subparagraphs 3(b) and (d) of Article 14 do not require the provision of a criminal defendant's counsel of choice when the defendant is provided with court-appointed counsel on grounds of indigence, when the defendant is financially able to retain alternative counsel, or when imprisonment is not imposed. The United States further understands that paragraph 3(e) does not prohibit a requirement that the defendant make a showing that any witness whose attendance he seeks to compel is necessary for his defense. The United States understands the prohibition upon double jeopardy in paragraph 7 to apply only when the judgment of acquittal has been rendered by a court of the same governmental unit, whether the Federal Government or a constituent unit, as is seeking a new trial for the same cause.

(5) That the United States understands that this Convention shall be implemented by the Federal Government to the extent that it exercises legislative and judicial jurisdiction over the matters covered therein, and otherwise by the state and local governments; to the extent that state and local governments exercise jurisdiction over such matters, the Federal Government shall take measures appropriate to the Federal system to the end that the competent authorities of the state or local governments may take appropriated measures for the fulfillment of the Convention.

III. The Senate's advice and consent is subject to the following declarations:

(1) That the United States declares that the provisions of Articles 1 through 27 of the Covenant are not self-executing.

(2) That it is the view of the United States that States Party to the Covenant should wherever possible refrain from imposing any restrictions or limitations on the exercise of the rights recognized and protected by the Covenant, even when such restrictions and limitations are permissible under the terms of the Covenant.

For the United States, Article 5, paragraph 2, which provides that fundamental human rights existing in any State Party may not be diminished on the pretext that the Covenant recognizes them to a lesser extent, has particular relevance to Article 19, paragraph 3, which would permit certain restrictions on the freedom of expression. The United States declares that it will continue to adhere to the requirements and constraints of its Constitution in respect to all such restrictions and limitations.

(3) That the United States declares that it accepts the competence of the Human Rights Committee to receive and consider communications under Article 41 in which a State Party claims that another State Party is not fulfilling its obligations under the Covenant.

(4) That the United States declares that the right referred to in Article 47 may be exercised only in accordance with international law.

IV. The Senate's advice and consent is subject to the following proviso, which shall not be included in the instrument of ratification to be deposited by the President:

Nothing in this Covenant requires or authorizes legislation, or other action, by the United States of America prohibited by the Constitution of the United States as interpreted by the United States.

e. General Comment No. 24: On Issues Relating to Reservations Made upon Ratification or Accession to the Covenant or the Optional Protocols Thereto, or in Relation to Declarations under Article 41 of the Covenant, United Nations Human Rights Committee

CCPR/C/21/Rev.1/Add.6 (1994) *reprinted in* 34 I.L.M. 839 (1995)

1. As of 1 November 1994, 46 of the 127 States parties to the International Covenant on Civil and Political Rights had, between them, entered 150 reservations of varying significance to their acceptance of the obligations of the Covenant. Some of these reservations exclude the duty to provide and guarantee particular rights in the Covenant. Others are couched in more general terms, often directed to ensuring the continued paramountcy of certain domestic legal provisions. Still others are directed at the competence of the Committee. The number of reservations, their content and their scope may undermine the effective implementation of the Covenant and tend to weaken respect for the obligations of States Parties. Is it important for States Parties to know exactly what obligations they, and other States Parties, have in fact undertaken. And the Committee, in the performance of its duties under either Article 40 of the Covenant or under the Optional Protocols, must know whether a State is bound by a particular obligation or to what extent. This will require a determination as to whether a unilateral statement is a reservation or an interpretative declaration and a determination of its acceptability and effects.

2. For these reasons the Committee has deemed it useful to address in a General Comment the issues of international law and human rights policy that arise. The General Comment identifies the principles of international law that apply to the making of reservations and by reference to which their acceptability is to be tested and their purport to be interpreted. It addresses the role of States Parties in relation to the reservations of others. It further addresses the role of the Committee itself in relation to reservations. And it makes certain recommendations to present States Parties for a reviewing of reservations and to those States that are not yet parties about legal and human rights policy considerations to be borne in mind should they consider ratifying or acceding with particular reservations.

3. It is not always easy to distinguish a reservation from a declaration as to a State's understanding of the interpretation of a provision, or from a statement of policy. Regard will be had to the intention of the State, rather than the form of the instrument. If a statement, irrespective of its name or title, purports to exclude or modify the legal effect of a treaty in its application to the State, it constitutes a reservation. Conversely, if a so called reservation merely offers a State's understanding of a provision but does not exclude or modify that provision in its application to that State, it is, in reality, not a reservation.

4. The possibility of entering reservations may encourage States which consider that they have difficulties in guaranteeing all the rights in the Covenant nonetheless to accept the generality of obligations in that instrument. Reservations may serve a useful function to enable States to adapt specific elements in their laws to the inherent rights of each person as articulated in the Covenant. However, it is desirable in principle that States accept the full range of obligations, because the human rights norms are the legal expression of the essential rights that every person is entitled to as a human being.

5. The Covenant neither prohibits reservations nor mentions any type of permitted reservation. The same is true of the first Optional Protocol. The Second Optional Protocol provides, in article 2, paragraph 1, that "No reservation is admissible to the present Protocol, except for a reservation made at the time of ratification or accession that provides for the application of the death penalty in time of war pursuant to a conviction for a most serious crime of a military nature committed during wartime". Paragraphs 2 and 3 provide for certain procedural obligations.

6. The absence of a prohibition on reservations does not mean that any reservation is permitted. The matter of reservations under the Covenant and the first Optional Protocol is governed by international law. Article 19(3) of the Vienna Convention on the Law of Treaties provides relevant guidance. It stipulates that where a reservation is not prohibited by the treaty or falls within the specified permitted categories, a State may make a reservation provided it is not incompatible with the object and purpose of the treaty. Even though, unlike some other human rights treaties, the Covenant does not incorporate a specific reference to

the object and purpose test, that test governs the matter of interpretation and acceptability of reservations.

7. In an instrument which articulates very many civil and political rights, each of the many articles, and indeed their interplay, secures the objectives of the Covenant. The object and purpose of the Covenant is to create legally binding standards for human rights by defining certain civil and political rights and placing them in a framework of obligations which are legally binding for those States which ratify; and to provide an efficacious supervisory machinery for the obligations undertaken.

8. Reservations that offend peremptory norms would not be compatible with the object and purpose of the Covenant. Although treaties that are mere exchanges of obligations between States allow them to reserve inter se application of rules of general international law, it is otherwise in human rights treaties, which are for the benefit of persons within their jurisdiction. Accordingly, provisions in the Covenant that represent customary international law (and a fortiori when they have the character of peremptory norms) may not be the subject of reservations. Accordingly, a State may not reserve the right to engage in slavery, to torture, to subject persons to cruel, inhuman or degrading treatment or punishment, to arbitrarily deprive persons of their lives, to arbitrarily arrest and detain persons, to deny freedom of thought, conscience and religion, to presume a person guilty unless he proves his innocence, to execute pregnant women or children, to permit the advocacy of national, racial or religious hatred, to deny to persons of marriageable age the right to marry, or to deny to minorities the right to enjoy their own culture, profess their own religion, or use their own language. And while reservations to particular clauses of Article 14 may be acceptable, a general reservation to the right to a fair trial would not be.

9. Applying more generally the object and purpose test to the Covenant, the Committee notes that, for example, reservation to article 1 denying peoples the right to determine their own political status and to pursue their economic, social and cultural development, would be incompatible with the object and purpose of the Covenant. Equally, a reservation to the obligation to respect and ensure the rights, and to do so on a non discriminatory basis (Article 2(1) would not be acceptable. Nor may a State reserve an entitlement not to take the necessary steps at the domestic level to give effect to the rights of the Covenant (Article 2(2)).

10. The Committee has further examined whether categories of reservations may offend the "object and purpose" test. In particular, it falls for consideration as to whether reservations to the non derogable provisions of the Covenant are compatible with its object and purpose. While there is no hierarchy of importance of rights under the Covenant, the operation of certain rights may not be suspended, even in times of national emergency. This underlines the great importance of non derogable rights. But not all rights of profound importance, such as articles 9 and 27 of the Covenant, have in fact been made non derogable. One

reason for certain rights being made non derogable is because their suspension is irrelevant to the legitimate control of the state of national emergency (for example, no imprisonment for debt, in article 11). Another reason in that derogation may indeed be impossible (as, for example, freedom of conscience). At the same time, some provisions are non derogable exactly because without them there would be no rule of law. A reservation to the provisions of article 4 itself, which precisely stipulates the balance to be struck between the interests of the State and the rights of the individual in times of emergency, would fall in this category. And some non derogable rights, which in any event cannot be reserved because of their status as peremptory norms, are also of this character—the prohibition of torture and arbitrary deprivation of life are examples. While there is no automatic correlation between reservations to non derogable provisions, and reservations which offend against the object and purpose of the Covenant, a State has a heavy onus to justify such a reservation.

11. The Covenant consists not just of the specified rights, but of important supportive guarantees. These guarantees provide the necessary framework for securing the rights in the Covenant and are thus essential to its object and purpose. Some operate at the national level and some at the international level. Reservations designed to remove these guarantees are thus not acceptable. Thus, a State could not make a reservation to article 2, paragraph 3, of the Covenant, indicating that it intends to provide no remedies for human rights violations. Guarantees such as these are an integral part of the structure of the Covenant and underpin its efficacy. The Covenant also envisages, for the better attainment of its stated objectives, a monitoring role for the Committee. Reservations that purport to evade that essential element in the design of the Covenant, which is also directed to securing the enjoyment of the rights, are also incompatible with its object and purpose. A State may not reserve the right not to present a report and have it considered by the Committee. The Committee's role under the Covenant, whether under article 40 or under the Optional Protocols, necessarily entails interpreting the provisions of the Covenant and the development of a jurisprudence. Accordingly, a reservation that rejects the Committee's competence to interpret the requirements of any provisions of the Covenant would also be contrary to the object and purpose of that treaty.

12. The intention of the Covenant is that the rights contained therein should be ensured to all those under a State's party's jurisdiction. To this end certain attendant requirements are likely to be necessary. Domestic laws may need to be altered properly to reflect the requirements of the Covenant; and mechanisms at the domestic level will be needed to allow the Covenant rights to be enforceable at the local level. Reservations often reveal a tendency of States not to want to change a particular law. And sometimes that tendency is elevated to a general policy. Of particular concern are widely formulated reservations which essentially render ineffective all Covenant rights which would require any change in national law to ensure compliance with Covenant obligations. No real international rights or obligations have thus been accepted. And when there is an ab-

sence of provisions to ensure that Covenant rights may be sued on in domestic courts, and, further, a failure to allow individual complaints to be brought to the Committee under the first Optional Protocol, all the essential elements of the Covenant guarantees have been removed.

13. The issue arises as to whether reservations are permissible under the first Optional Protocol and, if so, whether any such reservation might be contrary to the object and purpose of the Covenant or of the first Optional Protocol itself. It is clear that the first Optional Protocol is itself an international treaty, distinct from the Covenant but closely related to it. Its object and purpose is to recognise the competence of the Committee to receive and consider communications from individuals who claim to be victims of a violation by a State party of any of the rights in the Covenant. States accept the substantive rights of individuals by reference to the Covenant, and not the first Optional Protocol. The function of the first Optional Protocol is to allow claims in respect of those rights to be tested before the Committee. Accordingly, a reservation to an obligation of a State to respect and ensure a right contained in the Covenant, made under the first Optional Protocol when it has not previously been made in respect of the same rights under the Covenant, does not affect the State's duty to comply with its substantive obligation. A reservation cannot be made to the Covenant through the vehicle of the Optional Protocol but such a reservation would operate to ensure that the State's compliance with that obligation may not be tested by the Committee under the first Optional Protocol. And because the object and purpose of the first Optional Protocol is to allow the rights obligatory for a State under the Covenant to be tested before the Committee, a reservation that seeks to preclude this would be contrary to the object and purpose of the first Optional Protocol, even if not of the Covenant. A reservation to a substantive obligation made for the first time under the first Optional Protocol would seem to reflect an intention by the State concerned to prevent the Committee from expressing its views relating to a particular article of the Covenant in an individual case.

14. The Committee considers that reservations relating to the required procedures under the first Optional Protocol would not be compatible with its object and purpose. The Committee must control its own procedures as specified by the Optional Protocol and its rules of procedure. Reservations have, however, purported to limit the competence of the Committee to acts and events occurring after entry into force for the State concerned of the first Optional Protocol. In the view of the Committee this is not a reservation but, most usually, a statement consistent with its normal competence ratione temporis. At the same time, the Committee has insisted upon its competence, even in the face of such statements or observations, when events or acts occurring before the date of entry into force of the first Optional Protocol have continued to have an effect on the rights of a victim subsequent to that date. Reservations have been entered which effectively add an additional ground of inadmissibility under article 5, paragraph 2, by precluding examination of a communication when the same matter has already been examined by another comparable procedure. Insofar as the most basic

obligation has been to secure independent third party review of the human rights of individuals, the Committee has, where the legal right and the subject matter are identical under the Covenant and under another international instrument, viewed such a reservation as not violating the object and purpose of the first Optional Protocol.

15. The primary purpose of the Second Optional Protocol is to extend the scope of the substantive obligations undertaken under the Covenant, as they relate to the right to life, by prohibiting execution and abolishing the death penalty. It has its own provision concerning reservations, which is determinative of what is permitted. Article 2, paragraph 1, provides that only one category of reservation is permitted, namely one that reserves the right to apply the death penalty in time of war pursuant to a conviction for a most serious crime of a military nature committed during wartime. Two procedural obligations are incumbent upon State parties wishing to avail themselves of such a reservation. Article 2, paragraph 1, obliges such a State to inform the Secretary General, at the time of ratification or accession, of the relevant provisions of its national legislation during warfare. This is clearly directed towards the objectives of specificity and transparency and in the view of the Committee a purported reservation unaccompanied by such information is without legal effect. Article 2, paragraph 3, requires a State making such a reservation to notify the Secretary General of the beginning or ending of a state of war applicable to its territory. In the view of the Committee, no State may seek to avail itself of its reservation (that is, have execution in time of war regarded as lawful) unless it has complied with the procedural requirement of article 2, paragraph 3.

16. The Committee finds it important to address which body has the legal authority to make determinations as to whether specific reservations are compatible with the object and purpose of the Covenant. As for international treaties in general, the International Court of Justice has indicated in the Reservations to the Genocide Convention Case (1951) that a State which objected to a reservation on the grounds of incompatibility with the object and purpose of a treaty could, through objecting, regard the treaty as not in effect as between itself and the reserving State. Article 20, paragraph 4, of the Vienna Convention on the Law of Treaties 1969 contains provisions most relevant to the present case on acceptance of and objection to reservations. This provides for the possibility of a State to object to a reservation made by another State. Article 21 deals with the legal effects of objections by States to reservations made by other States. Essentially, a reservation precludes the operation, as between the reserving and other States, of the provision reserved; and an objection thereto leads to the reservation being in operation as between the reserving and objecting State only to the extent that it has not been objected to.

17. As indicated above, it is the Vienna Convention on the Law of Treaties that provides the definition of reservations and also the application of the object and purpose test in the absence of other specific provisions. But the Committee believes that its provisions on the role of State objections in relation to reserva-

tions are inappropriate to address the problem of reservations to human rights treaties. Such treaties, and the Covenant specifically, are not a web of inter State exchanges of mutual obligations. They concern the endowment of individuals with rights. The principle of inter State reciprocity has no place, save perhaps in the limited context of reservations to declarations on the Committee's competence under article 41. And because the operation of the classic rules on reservations is so inadequate for the Covenant, States have often not seen any legal interest in or need to object to reservations. The absence of protest by States cannot imply that a reservation is either compatible or incompatible with the object and purpose of the Covenant. Objections have been occasional, made by some States but not others, and on grounds not always specified; when an objection is made, it often does not specify a legal consequence, or sometimes even indicates that the objecting party nonetheless does not regard the Covenant as not in effect as between the parties concerned. In short, the pattern is so unclear that it is not safe to assume that a non objecting State thinks that a particular reservation is acceptable. In the view of the Committee, because of the special characteristics of the Covenant as a human rights treaty, it is open to question what effect objections have between States inter se. However, an objection to a reservation made by States may provide some guidance to the Committee in its interpretation as to its compatibility with the object and purpose of the Covenant. . . .

20. It necessarily falls to the Committee to determine whether a specific reservation is compatible with the object and purpose of the Covenant. This is in part because, as indicated above, it is an inappropriate task for States parties in relation to human rights treaties, and in part because it is a task that the Committee cannot avoid in the performance of its functions. In order to know the scope of its duty to examine a State's compliance under article 40 or a communication under the first Optional Protocol, the Committee has necessarily to take a view on the compatibility of a reservation with the object and purpose of the Covenant and with general international law. Because of the special character of a human rights treaty, the compatibility of a reservation with the object and purpose of the Covenant must be established objectively, by reference to legal principles, and the Committee is particularly well placed to perform this task. The normal consequence of an unacceptable reservation is not that the Covenant will not be in effect at all for a reserving party. Rather, such a reservation will generally be severable, in the sense that the Covenant will be operative for the reserving party without benefit of the reservation.

21. Reservations must be specific and transparent, so that the Committee, those under the jurisdiction of the reserving State and other States parties may be clear as to what obligations of human rights compliance have or have not been undertaken. Reservations may thus not be general, but must refer to a particular provision of the Covenant and indicate in precise terms its scope in relation thereto. When considering the compatibility of possible reservations with the object and purpose of the Covenant, States should also take into consideration the overall

effect of a group of reservations, as well as the effect of each reservation on the integrity of the Covenant, which remains an essential consideration. States should not enter so many reservations that they are in effect accepting a limited number of human rights obligations, and not the Covenant as such. So that reservations do not lead to a perpetual non attainment of international human rights standards, reservations should not systematically reduce the obligations undertaken only to the presently existing in less demanding standards of domestic law. Nor should interpretative declarations or reservations seek to remove an autonomous meaning to Covenant obligations, by pronouncing them to be identical, or to be accepted only insofar as they are identical, with existing provisions of domestic law. States should not seek through reservations or interpretative declarations to determine that the meaning of a provision of the Covenant is the same as that given by an organ of any other international treaty body.

22. States should institute procedures to ensure that each and every reservation is compatible with the object and purpose of the Covenant. It is desirable for a State entering a reservation to indicate in precise terms the domestic legislation or practices which it believes to be incompatible with the Covenant obligation reserved; and to explain the time period it requires to render its own laws and practices compatible with the Covenant, or why it is unable to render its own laws and practices compatible with the Covenant. States should also ensure that the necessity for maintaining reservations is periodically reviewed, taking into account any observations and recommendations made by the Committee during examination of their reports. Reservations should be withdrawn at the earliest possible moment. Reports to the Committee should contain information on what action has been taken to review, reconsider or withdrawn reservations.

f. Belilos v. Switzerland

10 E.H.R.R. 466 (1988)

[The applicant, Mrs. Belilos, who was convicted and fined for having participated in an unauthorized demonstration, complained that the procedure before the Police Board of the municipality of Lausanne and the higher courts which heard her appeal did not conform with the requirements of Article 6(1). The respondent Government, relying on an interpretative declaration made by Switzerland upon ratification of the Convention, argued that the application was incompatible with the international obligations entered into by that country under Article 6(1).] …

38. [Switzerland's] interpretative declaration … is worded as follows:

The Swiss Federal Council considers that the guarantee of fair trial in Article 6(1) of the Convention, in the determination of civil rights and obligations or any criminal charge against the person in question is intended solely to ensure ultimate control by the judiciary over the acts or decisions of the public authorities relating to such rights or obligations or the determination of such a charge.

In [the Government's] submission, the Commission should have declined to exercise jurisdiction as the application related to a right that was not recognised by the Confederation.

39. The Court will examine the nature of the declaration in issue and then, if appropriate, its validity for the purposes of Article 64 of the Convention, which reads as follows:

> 1. Any State may, when signing the Convention or when depositing its instrument of ratification, make a reservation in respect of any particular provision of the Convention to the extent that any law then in force in its territory is not in conformity with the provision. Reservations of a general character shall not be permitted under this Article.
>
> 2. Any reservation made under this Article shall contain a brief statement of the law concerned.

A. The nature of the declaration...

40. The applicant contended that the declaration could not be equated with a reservation. When ratifying the Convention, Switzerland had made two ' reservations' and two 'interpretative declarations'; in so doing, it had adopted a terminology that had been chosen quite deliberately. A reservation resulted in the Convention's being inapplicable in respect of a particular point, whereas a declaration on the other hand was only provisional in nature, pending a decision of the Strasbourg organs. ...

41. The Commission likewise reached the conclusion that the declaration was a mere interpretative declaration which did not have the effect of a reservation ...

42. In the Government's submission, on the other hand, the declaration was a 'qualified' interpretative declaration. It consequently was in the nature of a reservation within the meaning of Article 2(1)(d) of the Vienna Convention on the Law of Treaties of 23 May 1969, which provides:

> "Reservation" means a unilateral statement, however phrased or named, made by a State, when signing, ratifying, accepting, approving or acceding to a treaty, whereby it purports to exclude or to modify the legal effect of certain provisions of the treaty in their application to that State. ...

49. ... In order to establish the legal character of such a declaration, one must look behind the title given to it and seek to determine the substantive content. In the present case, it appears that Switzerland meant to remove certain categories of proceedings from the ambit of Article 6(1) and to secure itself against an interpretation of that Article which it considered to be too broad. However, the Court must see to it that the obligations arising under the Convention are not subject to restrictions which would not satisfy the requirements of Article 64 as regards reservations. Accordingly, it will examine the validity of the interpreta-

tive declaration in question, as in the case of a reservation, in the context of this provision.

B. The validity of the declaration …

55. By 'reservation of a general character' in Article 64 is meant in particular a reservation couched in terms that are too vague or broad for it to be possible to determine their exact meaning and scope. While the preparatory work and the Government's explanations clearly show what the respondent State's concern was at the time of ratification, they cannot obscure the objective reality of the actual wording of the declaration. The words 'ultimate control by the judiciary over the acts or decisions of the public authorities relating to [civil] rights or obligations or the determination of [a criminal] charge' do not make it possible for the scope of the undertaking by Switzerland to be ascertained exactly, in particular as to which categories of dispute are included and as to whether or not the 'ultimate control by the judiciary' takes in the facts of the case. They can therefore be interpreted in different ways, whereas Article 64(1) requires precision and clarity. In short, they fall foul of the rule that reservations must not be of a general character. …

58. In the Commission's view, the undeniable practical difficulties put forward by the Government could not justify the failure to comply with paragraph 2 of Article 64. The latter applied to all the States Parties without any distinction, whether they were unitary or federal and whether or not they had a unified body of procedural law. … The scope of the rule whose application the State wished to prevent by means of a reservation or interpretative declaration was a relevant factor here, because the wider the rule's scope, the greater was the need to include a statement of the law.

59. The Court concurs on the whole with the Commission's view on this point. It would add that the 'brief statement of the law concerned' both constitutes an evidential factor and contributes to legal certainty. The purpose of Article 64(2) is to provide a guarantee—in particular for the other Contracting Parties and the Convention institutions—that a reservation does not go beyond the provisions expressly excluded by the State concerned. This is not a purely formal requirement but a condition of substance. The omission in the instant case therefore cannot be justified even by important major practical difficulties.

C. Conclusion

60. In short, the declaration in question does not satisfy two of the requirements of Article 64 of the Convention, with the result that it must be held to be invalid. At the same time, it is beyond doubt that Switzerland is, and regards itself as, bound by the Convention irrespective of the validity of the declaration. Moreover, the Swiss Government recognised the Court's competence to determine the latter issue, which it argued before it. The Government's preliminary objection must therefore be rejected.

NOTES AND QUESTIONS

1. For a flavor of the debate on the legal effect, in particular the severability, of reservations to human rights treaties, *see* Ryan Goodman, *Human Rights Treaties, Invalid Reservations, and State Consent,* 96 AM. J. INT'L L. 531 (2002) and the response by Professor Elena A. Baylis, at 97 AM. J. INT'L L. 107 (2003). *See also,* Elena A. Baylis, *Commentary 24: Confronting the Problem of Reservations to Human Rights Treaties*, 17 BERKELEY J. INT'L L. 277 (1999).

2. Is it desirable to limit the range of reservations to human rights treaties? Would it discourage potential new parties from joining these treaties? As to the "special nature" of human rights treaties, in particular, the Inter-American Convention on Human Rights, with respect to withdrawal and reservations, see the Inter-American Court of Human Rights' Judgment in the *Ivcher Bronstein Case*, Competence, of September 24, 1999 (*infra*, at 1369).

3. The ILC Preliminary Conclusions on Reservations to Normative Multilateral Treaties including Human Rights Treaties was written in response to Commentary 24. (*See Report of the ILC at its Forty-Ninth Session,* [1997] Y.B. INT'L L. COMM'N para. 157 U.N. Doc. A/52/10.)

4. In response to the Commission's request for comments by human rights monitoring bodies, the Sub-Commission on Prevention of Discrimination and Protection of Minorities established a Working Group. Ms. Francoise Hampton prepared a working paper on "Reservations to Human Rights Treaties." *See* U.N. ESCOR, 51st Sess., U.N. Doc. E/CN.4/Sub.2/1999/28 (1999). *See also* the report by the Secretariat of the Committee on the Elimination of Discrimination Against Women, which *inter alia* addresses the question of "practices of human rights treaty bodies on reservations", U.N. CEDAW, 25th Sess., part III, paras. 20-56, U.N. Doc. CEDAW/C.2001/II/4 (2001).

D. THE INTERPRETATION OF INTERNATIONAL AGREEMENTS

1. Issues and Policies

a. W. Michael Reisman, *Necessary and Proper: Executive Competence to Interpret Treaties*
15 YALE J. INT'L L. 316 (1990)

The question of what was agreed, externally or internally, is only part of the problem. Whatever was agreed inevitably changes. Life is Heracleitian. Nothing stands still. Once a policy has been prescribed, in a statute or a contract or a treaty, the pertinent parties begin to modulate their behavior in accord with and in reliance on it. Things may seem fairly simple in single performance treaties, like the return of the crown of St. Stephen—one crown; one return; one receipt; end of treaty. In performing continuing treaties, however, the other party or parties (including their distinct internal decision components) must each interpret or decide what is proper, in each instance in which the treaty concerns something it is doing. And each of these performance interpretations is made in contexts in which myriad other bilateral and multilateral concerns, some evanescent, some more durable, shape and limit options.

Some of the ensuing unilateral interpretations, expressed in performance, are readily accepted by other treaty partners. Some are protested or challenged in the various ways provided by the treaty itself or available in international law. Some provoke bargaining, winning concessions in treaty related or other matters. Some may redefine the proposed action or the treaty itself, and some may secure a retraction. Depending on the outcomes of those sub processes, that particular performance adapts, changes or prevails, as the case may be.

These successive performance interpretations are not picaresque events that occur and are forgotten. They become, under international law, part of the continuing expectations of the parties as to what their obligations are. In more than a figurative sense, performance constantly becomes part of the agreement. Documents uttered in solemn fashion, let us say, by hearings and advice and consent, continue to evolve in the course of their performance. That evolution or development may go in ways that some of the parties or some components within some of the parties had not anticipated or possibly wished. Yet, at the international level, the agreement will continue to be valid until some event occurs which international treaty law characterizes as terminable or terminating.

This evolution or development of treaties and laws is not due to faithless executives or courts consciously deciding not to follow text and trying to aggrandize power. In the political hurly burly, that sort of indictment is frequently levelled against courts and the executive. That is a fundamental misunderstanding of what is necessarily involved in performance interpretation. It rests on the assumption that performance interpretation is simply a matter of identifying and following a single rule.

If that were the case, we would hardly need lawyers; the matter could be turned over to people at the clerk typist level equipped with little handbooks like those used by customs clerks making ad valorem assessments. We need lawyers precisely because many rules and authorized policies are engaged in particular performances and disputes about them, because the international context of decision is extraordinarily complex and always changing and because the aggregate consequences of different performance interpretation options will have different effects on the ensemble of national legal objectives. The art of decision making involves acquiring the sensitivity to, identifying, and then taking account of, all of these and fashioning a response that realizes or optimalizes as many of the policies and values as possible.

Performance interpretation is aggravated by the boundary uncertainties mentioned earlier, but most of the problems arise in longer term and general agreements which may not have dealt with the sort of issue that now arises, or when contexts, technologies and other policies that may have prevailed at the time of the making of the agreement have changed, or when the identify, alignment or behavior of some of the other parties changes in unanticipated ways. In these circumstances, performance interpretation always involves at least four intellectual operations:

1. identification of the text or texts and a provisional construction of their meaning;

2. identifying and supplementing other pertinent authoritative policies that are not in the invoked instrument but are parts of the encompassing and often changing legal system and are pertinent to the problem at hand;

3. policing or actualizing parts of the agreement that are no longer consistent with contemporary community policies, whose force must now be limited;

4. testing the aggregate consequences of alternative projected applications in terms of all the legal objectives that are pertinent.

These operations are not an exclusive American prerogative. All other treaty parties engage in performance interpretation when they perform or when they react to other parties' performance interpretations and then themselves decide whether to protest, insist on a modification, declare the treaty void, or acquiesce. International tribunals engage in comparable operations. Because of all of these factors, the international agreement is, by its nature, dynamic and changing, sometimes in dramatic ways.

Now you may say, why have all this interpretation? If I say something, just do what I say. Don't interpret me. In fact, appliers have no choice but to interpret and reinterpret in all treaty performance. There is simply no practical alternative to this reinterpretation. And here's why.

The jealous prince or parliament may give its ministers or courts a single command and order them to execute exactly as prescribed or return for additional instructions. In this type of regime, if things are unclear, the minister returns for further instructions or the courts, in the language of Roman and continental jurisprudence, render a decision of non liquet, in which they say they cannot decide. But because ministers would be constantly at the door and the courts would constantly be issuing non liquets, jealous princes and parliaments learn to express their jealousy in other ways. Ministers who cannot make up their minds and perform are fired and, in continental systems, judges are ordered by the Code to supplement or else suffer criminal penalties.

Our own system would grind to a halt if, in each instance in which courts were faced with instruments that required input from them, they suspended operations and referred the matter back to Congress. Thc system would grind to a halt if, in cases in which executive agents had to interpret or had to respond to another party's performance interpretation, they got in line on the Hill for additional legislation, which would, in its performance interpretation, require additional instruction ad infinitum. Wholly aside from the swelling of the power of the legislature over the Executive and the shriveling of checks and balances, it simply could not work.

... Dean [Eugene] Rostow, from a vantage of academic and practical experience that few others can claim, has written:

> The phenomenon of presidential interpretation and reinterpretation of treaties ... occurs daily in every nook and cranny of the law. When the President sends instructions to representatives of the United States at the United Nations ... and at international conferences on dozens if not hundreds of subjects ... he is interpreting and reinterpreting treaties as he "faithfully executes" the law. ... This process of change and development is inherent in the growth of the law. Sometimes the changes are incremental and interstitial. Sometimes they are considerable. They are in fact inevitable as law confronts life every day of the week.

The issue is simply the competence to perform treaties internationally. If you cannot interpret, you cannot perform. If you cannot perform, power shifts to the authorized interpreter who de facto becomes the Executive. And if that putative Executive is structurally unable to perform, we are in deep trouble.

So, wholly apart from explicit constitutional assignments, the Executive must interpret in the course of performance of bilateral treaties and multilateral instruments, as courts must interpret them in the course of their adjudication. And with an equal inevitability, these instruments are prone to an evolution that involves a drift from what the parties thought when they concluded the agreement. Treaties have a greater propensity to drift because all the parties must interpret in the course of their own respective performances, while the rest constantly examine the interpretations in terms of their own interests and decide whether to protest, acquiesce or terminate. International courts and tribunals may accelerate the drift. National legislatures themselves contribute to this drift when they enact legislation which interprets or impacts on treaties and becomes part of that flow of practice that is, through time, the agreement.

2. The Goals and Methods of Interpretation

a. International Prescriptions

(1) Vienna Convention on the Law of Treaties

Article 31. (1) A treaty shall be interpreted in good faith in accordance with the ordinary meaning to be given to the terms of the treaty in their context and in the light of its object and purpose.

(2) The context for the purpose of the interpretation of a treaty shall comprise, in addition to the text, including its preamble and annexes:

(*a*) any agreement relating to the treaty which was made between all the parties in connexion with the conclusion of the treaty;

(*b*) any instrument which was made by one or more parties in connexion with the conclusion of the treaty and accepted by the other par-ties as an instrument related to the treaty.

(3) There shall be taken into account, together with the context:

(*a*) any subsequent agreement between the parties regarding the interpretation of the treaty or the application of its provisions;

(b) any subsequent practice in the application of the treaty which establishes the agreement of the parties regarding its interpretation;

(*c*) any relevant rules of international law applicable in the relations between the parties.

(4) A special meaning shall be given to a term if it is established that the parties so intended.

Article 32. Recourse may be had to supplementary means of interpretation, including the preparatory work of the treaty and the circumstances of its conclusion, in order to confirm the meaning resulting from the application of article 31, or to determine the meaning when the interpretation according to article 31:

(*a*) leaves the meaning ambiguous or obscure; or

(b) leads to a result which is manifestly absurd or unreasonable.

Article 33. (1) When a treaty has been authenticated in two or more languages, the text is equally authoritative in each language, unless the treaty provides or the parties agree that, in case of divergence, a particular text shall prevail.

(2) A version of the treaty in a language other than one of those in which the text was authenticated shall be considered an authentic text only if the treaty so provides or the parties so agree.

(3) The terms of the treaty are presumed to have the same meaning in each authentic text.

(4) Except where a particular text prevails in accordance with para-graph 1, when a comparison of the authentic texts discloses a difference of meaning which the application of articles 31 and 32 does not remove, the meaning which best reconciles the texts, having regard to the object and pur-pose of the treaty, shall be adopted. …

* * *

Do the provisions of the Vienna Convention outline a viable method for the interpretation of international agreements? Is it possible for an interpreter in fact to comply with its terms? Consider the following appraisal.

(2) Myres S. McDougal, *The International Law Commission's Draft Articles upon Interpretation: Textuality* Redivivus

61 AM. J. INT'L L. 992, 999 (1967)

Scire leges non hoc est verba earum tenere, sed vim ac potestatem—Celsus, DIG. 1.3.17.

The great defect, and tragedy, in the International Law Commission's final recommendations about the interpretation of treaties is in their insistent emphasis upon an impossible, conformity-imposing textuality. This unhappy emphasis makes an appearance in, and dominates, the goal for interpretation which the Commission implicitly postulates but never critically examines; the deprecatory appraisal which the Commission offers of the potentialities that inhere in the rational employment of principles of interpretation; and the content and ordering of the particular principles which the Commission puts forward for canonization as "obligatory" rules of law.

In explicit rejection of a quest for the "intentions of the parties as a subjective element distinct from the text," the Commission adopts a "basic approach" which demands merely the ascription of a meaning to a text. The only justification offered, and several times repeated as if in an effort to carry conviction, is that "the text [of a treaty] must be presumed to be the authentic expression of the intentions of the parties" and hence that "the starting point of interpretation is the elucidation of the meaning of the text, not an investigation *ab initio* into the intentions of the parties." ...

A broad sampling of past decision, practice and opinion would suggest that the Commission's formulations accurately reflect neither the aggregate flow of past decision and practice nor general expectations about the requirements of future decision. Certainly, it would not appear to be in the common interest for a community, which depends upon agreement not merely as a modality for the peaceful shaping and sharing of values among members but even as a principal instrument for establishing its constitution and for the prescription of authoritative community policy, deliberately to accept and project as authoritative prescription, formulations so esoteric and potentially so destructive of the foundations of genuine agreement as those put forward by the Commission.

* * *

Some indications of the methods and problems of inquiring into intentions and interpreting teleologically are offered in the following decisions:

(3) Dispute Concerning Access to Information under Article 9 of the OSPAR Convention (Ir. v. U.K.), Final Award

(Perm. Ct. of Arb. 2003), available at http://www.pca-cpa.org/PDF/OSPAR%20Award.pdf.

103. Lest it produce anachronistic results that are inconsistent with current international law, a tribunal must certainly engage in *actualization* or

contemporization when construing an international instrument that was concluded in an earlier period (*Legal Consequences for States of the Continued Presence of South Africa in Namibia (South West Africa) Notwithstanding Security Council Resolution 276 (1970)*, Advisory Opinion, 1971 ICJ Rep., at p. 3). Oppenheim, after restating the so-called law of inter-temporality (i.e., that an instrument is to be interpreted in the light of the general rules of international law in force at the time of its conclusion), adds the qualification that "in some respects the interpretation of a treaty's provisions cannot be divorced from developments in the law subsequent to its adoption" (OPPENHEIM'S INTERNATIONAL LAW, NINTH EDITION, at 1281-1282 (Sir Robert Jennings and Sir Arthur Watts eds., Longman, 1996). But the reference in the Court's *dictum* and the doctrinal statement in Oppenheim based upon it is to developments in *law*. Wholly apart from the question of the need for actualization of a treaty made scarcely ten years earlier, the Court's reference in *Gabcíkovo-Nagymaros* is to new *law* "in a great number of *instruments*" [italics supplied] and not material that has not yet become law. As stated, a tribunal must also adjust application of a treaty insofar as one of its provisions proves inconsistent with a *jus cogens* that subsequently emerged. The present case does not raise questions of *jus cogens.*

(4) Eritrea-Ethiopia Boundary Commission, Decision Regarding Delimitation of the Border

April 13, 2002,

available at http://pca-cpa.org/PDF/EEBC/EEBC%20Decision-L.pdf

5.16 The resolution of this issue [i.e. Eritrea-Ethiopia border in the Western sector] depends initially upon a proper interpretation of the Treaty [i.e. 1902 treaty between Ethiopia, Italy and the U.K.]. That interpretation in turn depends upon the text of Article I, read in the light of its object and purpose, its context and negotiating history, and the subsequent course of conduct of the Parties in its application – all of which are tools for determining "the common will" of the parties. …

5.44 In order to complete its task of interpreting the Treaty in the light of applicable international law, the Commission now turns to an examination of the principal items evidencing subsequent conduct or practice of the Parties that the Commission considers relevant for this purpose. …

(5) Dr. Horst Reineccius v. Bank for International Settlements Partial Award on the Lawfulness of the Recall of Privately Held Shares on 8 January 2001 and the Applicable Standards for Valuation of Those Shares

(Perm. Ct. of Arb. 2002), available at http://www.pca-cpa.org/PDF/BIS%20Partial%20Award.pdf.

Conformity of the Recall to the Statutes

143. Given the importance of the text, it will be useful to set out again the language of Articles 57 and 58 of the Statutes. Article 57 provides:

> Amendments of any Articles of these Statutes other than those enumerated in Article 58 may be proposed by a two-thirds majority of the Board to the General Meeting and if adopted by a majority of the General Meeting shall come into force, provided that such amendments are not inconsistent with the provisions of the Articles enumerated in Article 58.

Articles 58 provides:

> Articles 2, 3, 8, 14, 19, 24, 27, 44, 51, 54, 57 and 58 cannot be amended except subject to the following conditions: the amendment must be adopted by a two-thirds majority of the Board, approved by a majority of the General Meeting and sanctioned by a law supplementing the Charter of the Bank.

With the exception of the requirement of Swiss legislation to supplement the Charter of the Bank for amendment of the enumerated articles in Article 58, the procedures in Article 57 and Article 58 are actually the same, except that Article 58 specifies that a change of the capital requires a two-thirds majority of the General Meeting rather than a simple majority.

144. The language of Article 57 introduces no substantive limitation on the amendment competence of the General Meeting other than the requirement that those amendments not be inconsistent with the enumerated articles in Article 58. Hence, as a simple textual matter, an amendment to the Statutes accomplished according to the procedures required by Article 57 would be *intra vires* and valid as long as it were not inconsistent with one of the enumerated reserved provisions in Article 58. There is no indication in Article 57 that the mode of formulation of an amendment, whether as an addition to an existing article or as an entirely new article designated by a new number, has any legal significance. Hence, an interpretation of the Statutes in good faith in accordance with the ordinary meaning to be given to the terms of the Treaty, must find the amendment under discussion as valid and *intra vires* the Statutes.

145. Article 31(3)(b) of the Vienna Convention on the Law of Treaties requires that account be taken of "any subsequent practice in the application of the Treaty which establishes the agreement of the Parties regarding its interpretation." This provision takes on special meaning when applied, in accordance with

Article 5 of the Vienna Convention, to the constituent instruments of international organizations. In *Reparations for Injuries Suffered in the Service of the United Nations*, the International Court of Justice held that "the rights and duties of an entity such as the Organization [the United Nations] must depend upon its purposes and functions as specified or implied in its constituent documents and *developed in practice*." The fact that the Bank has, on a number of occasions, amended its Statutes by the introduction of a new article appears to be probative of the authoritative interpretation of the Statutes in this regard.

146. Mr. Mathieu stated that a strict interpretation of the powers of the Bank had been sought by the drafters lest the Bank, once established, escape their control and take liberties with the powers that had been accorded to them. But the decision structure of the Bank, as established in Chapters IV and V of the Statutes, requires two-thirds of the Board to propose amendments and a majority of the General Meeting to approve them. Article 27 of the Statutes, which established the membership of the Board, gave the central banks of the founding States of the Bank a permanent position. Hence it would not appear that Mr. Mathieu's concern is relevant to the interpretation of this part of the Statutes.

147. Article 18A concerning the compulsory repurchase of the privately held shares cannot be plausibly construed as engaging any of the reserved articles in Article 58 or any of the concerns that animated that provision. While the Bank would have been obliged to secure the approval of Switzerland (in agreement with the other signatory governments; see Article 1 of the Convention) if an amendment of one of the articles enumerated in Article 58 were planned, such approval would only have been required for amendment of a reserved article. In fact, as was reported at the Hearing, the Bank did notify Switzerland of the proposed amendment and Switzerland did not register any demand or objection. Similarly, all the central banks that were members of the Bank were given notice, as required by the Statutes of the Bank, from which fact it is fair to assume that their Governments were also made aware of the pending change. Nor would there appear to be anything implicit in the Statutes or the Charter that would have precluded the change.

148. For the above reasons, the Tribunal finds that the Bank had the authority to add Article 18A to its Statutes and that the compulsory recall of the shares, including the procedures by which it was accomplished, was *intra vires* the Statutes and was, accordingly, a valid exercise of the Bank's powers.

NOTES AND QUESTIONS

1. How does the "common will" of the parties as defined in the Eritrea-Ethiopia Boundary Commission's decision differ from the parties' "shared expectations" emphasized by Professor McDougal?

2. Do you find the recourse to subsequent institutional practice as a tool of interpretation of the constitutive instruments of the Bank convincing? Isn't there an issue regarding the created body exceeding the powers given it by its creators?

3. For a similar argument regarding the interpretation of the United Nations Charter, see Rosalyn Higgins, The Development of International Law Through the Political Organs of the United Nations (Oxford U. Press 1963); and Thomas Franck, *Interrogating the Treaty and the Future of the Treaty*, Lauterpacht Lecture, October 10, 2003, Cambridge University (forthcoming) *see* http://www.biicl.org/events/2003Events/x10%20October/October%202003%20Events.htm.

b. National Prescriptions

(1) Air France v. Saks

105 S.Ct. 1338 (1985)

[Passenger brought an action against the airline for permanent deafness allegedly caused by negligent maintenance and operation of the aircraft's pressurization system. The issue was whether the passenger had been subjected to an "accident" for which airline could be held liable under the Warsaw Convention.]

O'Connor J.: ... The proper answer turns on interpretation of a clause in an international treaty to which the United States is a party. "[T]reaties are construed more liberally than private agreements, and to ascertain their meaning we may look beyond the written words to the history of the treaty, the negotiations, and the practical construction adopted by the parties." *Choctaw Nation of Indians v. United States,* 318 U.S. 423, 431-432 (1943). The analysis must begin, however, with the text of the treaty and the context in which the written words are used. See *Maximov v. United States,* 373 U.S. 49, 53-54 (1963).

Article 17 of the Warsaw Convention establishes the liability of international air carriers for harm to passengers. Article 18 contains parallel provisions regarding liability for damage to baggage. The governing text of the Convention is in the French language. ...

Two significant features of these provisions stand out in both the French and the English texts. First, Article 17 imposes liability for injuries to passengers caused by an "accident," whereas Article 18 imposes liability for destruction or loss of baggage caused by an "occurrence." This difference in the parallel language of Articles 17 and 18 implies that the drafters of the Convention understood the word "accident" to mean something different than the word "occurrence," for they otherwise logically would have used the same word in each article. ... The language of the Convention accordingly renders suspect the opinion of the Court of Appeals that "accident" means "occurrence." Second, the text of Article 17 refers to an accident *which caused* the passenger's injury, and not to an accident which *is* the passenger's injury. ...

In Article 17, the drafters of the Warsaw Convention apparently did make an attempt to discriminate between "the cause and the effect"; they specified that air carriers would be liable if an accident *caused* the passenger's injury. The text of the Convention thus implies that, however we define "accident," it is the *cause* of the injury that must satisfy the definition rather than the occurrence of the injury alone. ...

While the text of the Convention gives these two clues to the meaning of "accident," it does not define the term. Nor is the context in which the term is used illuminating. ...To determine the meaning of the term "accident" in Article 17 we must consider its French legal meaning. See *Reed v. Wiser,* 555 F.2d 1079 (CA2), cert. denied, 434 U.S. 922 (1977); *Block v. Compagnie Nationale Air France,* 386 F.2d 323 (CA5 1967), cert. denied, 392 U.S. 905 (1968). This is true not because "we are forever chained to French law" by the Convention, see *Rosman v. Trans World Airlines, Inc.,* 34 N.Y.2d 385, 394 (1974), but because it is our responsibility to give the specific words of the treaty a meaning consistent with the shared expectations of the contracting parties. *Reed, supra,* at 1090; *Day v. Trans World Airlines, Inc.,* 528 F.2d 31 (CA2 1975), cert. denied, 429 U.S. 890 (1976). We look to the French legal meaning for guidance as to these expectations because the Warsaw Convention was drafted in French by continental jurists. ...

[A survey of French cases and dictionaries indicates that the French legal meaning of the term "accident" differs little from the meaning of the term in Great Britain, Germany, or the United States.] ... The text of the Convention consequently suggests that the passenger's injury must be caused by an unexpected or unusual event. ...

This interpretation of Article 17 is consistent with the negotiating history of the Convention, the conduct of the parties to the Convention, and the weight of precedent in foreign and American courts. In interpreting a treaty it is proper, of course, to refer to the records of its drafting and negotiation. *Choctaw Nation of Indians v. United States,* 318 U.S., at 431, 63 S.Ct., at 677. In part because the "travaux préparatoires" of the Warsaw Convention are published and generally available to litigants, courts frequently refer to these materials to resolve ambiguities in the text. *See Trans World Airlines, Inc. v. Franklin Mint Corp.,* 466 U.S. 243, 259 (1984). ...

The treaty that became the Warsaw Convention was first drafted at an international conference in Paris in 1925. The protocol resulting from the Parish Conference contained an article specifying: "The carrier is liable for accidents, losses, breakdowns, and delays. It is not liable if it can prove that it has taken reasonable measures designed to preempt damage ...." The protocol drafted at Paris was revised several times by a committee of experts on air law, and then submitted to a second international conference that convened in Warsaw in 1929. ...

Article 22 of this draft, like the original Paris draft, permitted the carrier to avoid liability by proving it had taken reasonable measures to avoid the damage. ... None of the early drafts required that an accident *cause* the passenger's injury [proceeds to detail legislative history]. ...

The records of the negotiation of the Convention accordingly support what is evident from its text: A passenger's injury must be caused by an accident, and an accident must mean something different than an "occurrence" on the plane. Like the text of the Convention, however, the records of its negotiation offer no precise definition of "accident."

Reference to the conduct of the parties to the Convention and the subsequent interpretations of the signatories helps clarify the meaning of the term. At a Guatemala City International Conference on Air Law in 1971, representatives of many of the Warsaw signatories approved an amendment to Article 17 which would impose liability on the carrier for an "event which caused the death or injury" rather than for an "accident which caused" the passenger's injury, but would exempt the carrier from liability if the death or injury resulted "solely from the state of health of the passenger." ... The Guatemala City Protocol of 1971 and the Montreal Protocols Nos. 3 and 4 of 1975 include this amendment, see S.Exec.Rep. No. 98-1 (1983), but have yet to be ratified by the Senate, and therefore do not govern the disposition of this case. The statements of the delegates at Guatemala City indicate that they viewed the switch from "accident" to "event" as expanding the scope of carrier liability to passengers. ...

In determining precisely what causes can be considered accidents, we "find the opinions of our sister signatories to be entitled to considerable weight." *Benjamins v. British European Airways,* 572 F.2d 913, 919 (CA2 1978), cert. denied, 439 U.S. 1114, 99 S.Ct. 1016, 59 L.Ed.2d 79 (1979). While few decisions are precisely on point, we note that, in *Air France v. Haddad, Judgment of June 19, 1979,* Cour d'appel de Paris, Première Chambre Civile, 1979 Revue Francaise de Droit Aérien, at 328, a French court observed that the term "accident" in Article 17 of the Warsaw Convention embraces causes of injuries that are fortuitous or unpredictable. European legal scholars have generally construed the word "accident" in Article 17 to require that the passenger's injury be caused by a sudden or unexpected event other than the normal operation of the plane. ... These observations are in accord with American decisions which, while interpreting the term "accident" broadly, *Maugnie v. Compagnie Nationale Air France,* 549 F.2d, at 1259, nevertheless refuse to extend the term to cover routine travel procedures that produce an injury due to the peculiar internal condition of a passenger. ...

We conclude that liability under Article 17 of the Warsaw Convention arises only if a passenger's injury is caused by an unexpected or unusual event or happening that is external to the passenger. This definition should be flexibly applied after assessment of all the circumstances surrounding a passenger's injuries. For example, lower courts in this country have interpreted Article 17 broadly enough to encompass torts committed by terrorists or fellow passengers. ... In cases where there is contradictory evidence, it is for the trier of fact to decide whether an "accident" as here defined caused the passenger's injury. ... But when the injury indisputably results from the passenger's own internal reaction to the usual, normal, and expected operation of the aircraft, it has not been caused by an accident, and Article 17 of the Warsaw Convention cannot apply. ...

Until Article 17 of the Warsaw Convention is changed by the signatories, it cannot be stretched to impose carrier liability for injuries that are not caused by accidents. It remains "[o]ur duty ... to enforce the ... treaties of the United States, whatever they might be, and ... the Warsaw Convention remains the supreme law of the land." *Reed,* 555 F.2d, at 1093.

NOTES AND QUESTIONS

1. Does Justice O'Connor's opinion differ from the interpretive approach prescribed by the Vienna Convention? How do you conceive of her reference to the parties' "shared expectations"?

2. *See also Sumitomo Shoji America, Inc. v. Avagliano*, 457 U.S. 176 (1982) (stating that the clear import of treaty language controls unless application of the words of the treaty according to their obvious meaning "effects a result inconsistent with the intent or expectations of its signatories").

E. THE SUSPENSION AND/OR TERMINATION OF INTERNATIONAL AGREEMENTS

The deliberate efforts by parties, during the course of performing, or not performing an agreement, to change the original expectations created by that agreement include many varying degrees of change from modification, amendment, withdrawal, and suspension, to complete denunciation and termination. It is the claims to denunciation and termination that have been most controverted in practice, and it is to these claims that we denote major attention.

In a well-organized state there are commonly specialized institutions for terminating policy prescriptions when they cease to register community consensus. Despite the rapidity of social change and the constant obsolescing of existing agreements, the world arena offers still the most rudimentary institutions for the performance of this function. In the absence of appropriate institutions, the function is executed largely by the parties to agreements, by application of certain inherited doctrines. These doctrines authorize termination both by new agreement between the parties and by unilateral decision without the consent of some parties.

Some writers seek to confine methods of termination entirely to those based on consent. Most writers rightly deplore the too easy acceptance of practices of unilateral denunciation.

It is believed, however, that in the absence of appropriate international institutions, with compulsory jurisdiction, both realistic description and rational preference must admit methods of termination not based upon the consent of all parties.

The problem from community perspectives is that of maintaining an appropriate balance between the honoring of the reasonable expectations of the parties to agreements (maintaining a reasonable stability in the relations between the parties) and permitting or encouraging a continual, progressive reformulation of policies to keep them in accord with changing perspectives and conditions.

The enquiry which follows distinguishes, accordingly, between (1) termination based on mutual consent and (2) termination on the ground of changed conditions, with varying degrees of mutual consent.

1. International Prescriptions

a. Termination by Mutual Consent

(1) Termination in Accordance with Terms of the Original Agreement

(a) Vienna Convention on the Law of Treaties

Article 39. A treaty may be amended by agreement between the par-ties. The rules laid down in Part 11 apply to such an agreement except in so far as the treaty may otherwise provide.

Article 40. (1) Unless the treaty otherwise provides, the amendment of multilateral treaties shall be governed by the following paragraphs.

(2) Any proposal to amend a multilateral treaty as between all the par-ties must be notified to all the contracting States, each one of which shall have the right to take part in:

(a) the decision as to the action to be taken in regard to such proposal;

(b) the negotiation and conclusion of any agreement for the amendment of the treaty.

(3) Every State entitled to become a party to the treaty shall also be en-titled to become a party to the treaty as amended.

(4) The amending agreement does not bind any State already a party to the treaty which does not become a party to the amending agreement; article 30, paragraph 4 (b), applies in relation to such State.

(5) Any State which becomes a party to the treaty after the entry into force of the amending agreement shall, failing an expression of a different intention by that State:

(a) be considered as a party to the treaty as amended; and

(b) be considered as a party to the unamended treaty in relation to any party to the treaty not bound by the amending agreement.

Article 41. (1) Two or more of the parties to a multilateral treaty may conclude an agreement to modify the treaty as between themselves alone if:

(a) the possibility of such a modification is provided for by the treaty; or

(b) the modification in question is not prohibited by the treaty and:

(i) does not affect the enjoyment by the other parties of their rights under the treaty or the performance of their obligations;

(ii) does not relate to a provision, derogation from which is incompatible with the effective execution of the object and purpose of the treaty as a whole.

(2) Unless in a case falling under paragraph 1(a) the treaty otherwise provides, the parties in question shall notify the other parties of their intention to conclude the agreement and of the modification to the treaty for which it provides....

Article 54. The termination of a treaty or the withdrawal of a party may take place:

(*a*) in conformity with the provisions of the treaty; or

(*b*) at any time by consent of all the parties after consultation with the other contracting States. ...

Article 56. (1) A treaty which contains no provision regarding its termination and which does not provide for denunciation or withdrawal is not subject to denunciation or withdrawal unless:

(*a*) it is established that the parties intended to admit the possibility of denunciation or withdrawal; or

(*b*) a right of denunciation or withdrawal may be implied by the nature of the treaty.

(2) A party shall give not less than twelve months' notice of its intention to denounce or withdraw from a treaty under paragraph 1.

Article 57. The operation of a treaty in regard to all the parties or to a particular party may be suspended:

(*a*) in conformity with the provisions of the treaty; or

(*b*) at any time by consent of all the parties after consultation with the other contracting States.

(2) Termination by a New Agreement

(a) Vienna Convention on the Law of Treaties (1969)

Article 59. (1) A treaty shall be considered as terminated if all the parties to it conclude a later treaty relating to the same subject-matter and:

(*a*) it appears from the later treaty or is otherwise established that the parties intended that the matter should be governed by that treaty; or

(*b*) the provisions of the later treaty are so far incompatible with those of the earlier one that the two treaties are not capable of being applied at the same time.

(2) The earlier treaty shall be considered as only suspended in operation if it appears from the later treaty or is otherwise established that such was the intention of the parties.

(3) Renunciation of Claims by the Party Benefited

(a) *The Law of Treaties*

29 Am. J. Int'l L. Supp. 653, 1161-62 (1935)

As to termination by renunciation, it is often said by writers, and it is so declared in the Havana Convention on Treaties (Art. 14), that a bipartite treaty which creates rights or benefits only for one party without imposing obligations on it for the benefit of the other party—that is a bipartite, unilateral or non-synallagmatic treaty—may be terminated by the express renunciation by the beneficiary party of its rights thereunder. It hardly seems Justifiable, however, to regard this procedure as one by which treaties may be terminated. In any case, it would no, be correct to say that the renunciation by one party of its rights under such a treaty would have the effect of terminating the treaty. The consent of the other party would still be necessary to its termination and it is conceivable that the other party might be unwilling to give its consent. In these circumstances it would be arbitrary to lay down a rule to the effect that the renunciation by a party of its rights under a bipartite treaty has the effect of automatically terminating the treaty.

b. Termination in the Absence of Mutual Consent

(1) Vienna Convention on the Law of Treaties

1155 U.N.T.S. 331 (1969)

Article 60. (1) A material breach of a bilateral treaty by one of the parties entities the other to invoke the breach as a ground for terminating the treaty or suspending its operation in whole or in part.

(2) A material breach of a multilateral treaty by one of the parties entities:

(a) the other parties by unanimous agreement to suspend the operation of the treaty in whole or in part or to terminate it either:

(i) in the relations between themselves and the defaulting State, or

(ii) as between all the parties;

(b) a party specially affected by the breach to invoke it as a ground for suspending the operation of the treaty in whole or in part in the relations between itself and the defaulting State;

(c) any party other than the defaulting State to invoke the breach as a ground for suspending the operation of the treaty in whole or in part with respect to itself if the treaty is of such a character that a material breach of its provisions by one party radically changes the position of every party with respect to the further performance of its obligation, under the treaty.

(3) A material breach of a treaty, for the purposes of this article, consists in:

(a) a repudiation of the treaty not sanctioned by the present Convention: or

(b) the violation of a provision essential to the accomplishment of the object or purpose of the treaty.

(4) The foregoing paragraphs are without prejudice to any provision in the treaty applicable in the event of a breach.

(5) Paragraphs 1 to 3 do not apply to provisions relating to the protection of the human person contained in treaties of a humanitarian character, in particular to provisions prohibiting any form of reprisals against persons protected by such treaties.

Article 61. (1) A party may invoke the impossibility of performing a treaty as a ground for terminating or withdrawing from it if the impossibility results from the permanent disappearance or destruction of an object indispensable for the execution of the treaty. If the impossibility is temporary, it may be invoked only as a ground for suspending the operation of the treaty.

(2) Impossibility of performance may not be invoked by a party as a ground for terminating, withdrawing from or suspending the operation of a treaty if the impossibility is the result of a breach by that party either of an obligation under the treaty or of any other international obligation owed to any other party to the treaty.

Article 62. (1) A fundamental change of circumstances which has occurred with regard to those existing at the time of the conclusion of a treaty, and which was not foreseen by the parties, may not be invoked as a ground for terminating or withdrawing from the treaty unless:

(*a*) the existence of those circumstances constituted an essential basis of the consent of the parties to be bound by the treaty; and

(*b*) the effect of the change is radically to transform the extent of obligations still to be performed under the treaty.

(2) A fundamental change of circumstances may not be invoked as a ground for terminating or withdrawing from a treaty:

(*a*) if the treaty establishes a boundary; or

(*b*) if the fundamental change is the result of a breach by the party invoking it either of an obligation under the treaty or of any other international obligation owed to any other party to the treaty.

(3) If, under the foregoing paragraphs, a party may invoke a fundamental change of circumstances as a ground for terminating or withdrawing from a treaty it may also invoke the change as a ground for suspending the operation of the treaty.

(2) Case Concerning the Gabcíkovo-Nagymaros Project (Hung. v. Slovk.)
1997 I.C.J. 7 (Sept. 25)

[Review facts and procedural history, *supra,* Part Four: Environment at 826.]

27. The Court will now turn to a consideration of the questions submitted by the Parties. In terms of Article 2, paragraph 1 *(a)*, of the Special Agreement, the Court is requested to decide first

> [w]hether the Republic of Hungary was entitled to suspend and subsequently abandon, in 1989, the works on the Nagymaros Project and on the part of the Gabcíkovo Project for which the Treaty attributed responsibility to the Republic of Hungary.

28. The Court would recall that the Gabcíkovo-Nagymaros System of Locks is characterized in Article 1, paragraph 1, of the 1977 Treaty as a "single and indivisible operational system of works". ...

38. ... In spring 1990, the new Hungarian Government, in presenting its National Renewal Programme, announced that the whole of the Gabcíkovo-Nagymaros Project was a "mistake" and that it would initiate negotiations as soon as possible with the Czechoslovak Government "on remedying and sharing the damages". On 20 December 1990, the Hungarian Government adopted a resolution for the opening of negotiations with Czechoslovakia on the termination of the Treaty by mutual consent and the conclusion of an agreement addressing the consequences of the termination. On 15 February 1991, the Hungarian Plenipotentiary transmitted a draft agreement along those lines to his Czechoslovak counterpart. ...

39. The two Parties to this case concur in recognizing that the 1977 Treaty, the above-mentioned Agreement on mutual assistance of 1977 and the Protocol of 1989 were validly concluded and were duly in force when the facts recounted above took place. ... [Hungary's state of ecological necessity arguments are set out in Part Four: Environment, *supra* at 827-828.]

47. ... A determination of whether a convention is or is not in force, and whether it has or has not been properly suspended or denounced, is to be made pursuant to the law of treaties. On the other hand, an evaluation of the extent to which the suspension or denunciation of a convention, seen as incompatible with the law of treaties, involves the responsibility of the State which proceeded to it, is to be made under the law of State responsibility.

Thus the Vienna Convention of 1969 on the Law of Treaties confines itself to defining— in a limitative manner—the conditions in which a treaty may lawfully be denounced or suspended; while the effects of a denunciation or suspension seen as not meeting those conditions are, on the contrary, expressly excluded from the scope of the Convention by operation of Article 73. It is moreover well established that, when a State has committed an internationally wrongful act, its international responsibility is likely to be involved whatever the nature of the obligation it has failed to respect (cf. *Interpretation of Peace Treaties with Bulgaria, Hungary and Romania, Second Phase, Advisory Opinion, I.C.J. Reports 1950*, p. 228; and see Article 17 of the Draft Articles on State Responsibility provisionally adopted by the International Law Commission on first reading, *Yearbook of the International Law Commission*, 1980, Vol. II, Part 2, p. 32).

48. The Court cannot accept Hungary's argument to the effect that, in 1989, in suspending and subsequently abandoning the works for which it was still responsible at Nagymaros and at Dunakiliti, it did not, for all that, suspend the application of the 1977 Treaty itself or then reject that Treaty. The conduct of Hungary at that time can only be interpreted as an expression of its unwillingness to comply with at least some of the provisions of the Treaty and the Protocol of 6 February 1989, as specified in the Joint Contractual Plan. The effect of Hungary's conduct was to render impossible the accomplishment of the system of works that the Treaty expressly described as "single and indivisible".

The Court moreover observes that, when it invoked the state of necessity in an effort to justify that conduct, Hungary chose to place itself from the outset within the ambit of the law of State responsibility, thereby implying that, in the absence of such a circumstance, its conduct would have been unlawful. The state of necessity claimed by Hungary—supposing it to have been established—thus could not permit of the conclusion that, in 1989, it had acted in accordance with its obligations under the 1977 Treaty or that those obligations had ceased to be binding upon it. It would only permit the affirmation that, under the circumstances, Hungary would not incur international responsibility by acting as it did. Lastly, the Court points out that Hungary expressly acknowledged that, in any event, such a state of necessity would not exempt it from its duty to compensate its partner.

49. The Court will now consider the question of whether there was, in 1989, a state of necessity which would have permitted Hungary, without incurring international responsibility, to suspend and abandon works that it was committed to perform in accordance with the 1977 Treaty and related instruments. [For details of this analysis, see Part Five, State Responsibility, *supra* at 958-960]. ...

57. ...The Court infers from all these elements that, in the present case, even if it had been established that there was, in 1989, a state of necessity linked to the performance of the 1977 Treaty, Hungary would not have been permitted to rely upon that state of necessity in order to justify its failure to comply with its treaty obligations, as it had helped, by act or omission to bring it about. ...

59. In the light of the conclusions reached above, the Court ... finds that Hungary was not entitled to suspend and subsequently abandon, in 1989, the works on the Nagymaros Project and on the part of the Gabcíkovo Project for which the 1977 Treaty and related instruments attributed responsibility to it.

60. By the terms of Article 2, paragraph 1*(b)*, of the Special Agreement, the Court is asked in the second place to decide

> *(b)* whether the Czech and Slovak Federal Republic was entitled to proceed, in November 1991, to the 'provisional solution' and to put into operation from October 1992 this system, described in the Report of the Working Group of Independent Experts of the Commission of the European Communities, the Republic of Hungary and the Czech and Slovak Federal Republic dated 23 November 1992 (damming up of the Danube at river kilometre 1851.7 on Czechoslovak territory and resulting consequences on water and navigation course). [known and explained later as "Variant C"]

64. ... Hungary considered, as it indicated in a Note Verbale of 14 February 1992, that Variant C was in contravention

> of [the Treaty of 1977] … and the convention ratified in 1976 regarding the water management of boundary waters.

> .Letter from Under Secretary of State for Arms Control and International Security, John R. BoltoLetter from Under Secretary of State for Arms Control and International Security, John R. Bolton

> with the principles of sovereignty, territorial integrity, with the inviolability of State borders, as well as with the general customary norms on international rivers and the spirit of the 1948 Belgrade Danube Convention;

and the suspension of the implementation of Variant C was, in its view, a prerequisite. As for Czechoslovakia, it took the view that recourse to Variant C had been rendered inevitable, both for economic and ecological as well as navigational reasons, because of the unlawful suspension and abandonment by Hungary of the works for which provision was made in the 1977 Treaty. …

72. Before dealing with the arguments advanced by the Parties, the Court wishes to make clear that it is aware of the serious problems with which Czechoslovakia was confronted as a result of Hungary's decision to relinquish most of the construction of the System of Locks for which it was responsible by virtue of the 1977 Treaty. Vast investments had been made, the construction at Gabcíkovo was all but finished, the bypass canal was completed, and Hungary itself, in 1991, had duly fulfilled its obligations under the Treaty in this respect in completing work on the tailrace canal. It emerges from the report, dated 31 October 1992, of the tripartite fact-finding mission the Court has referred to in paragraph 24 of the present Judgment, that not using the system would have led to considerable financial losses, and that it could have given rise to serious problems for the environment.

73. Czechoslovakia repeatedly denounced Hungary's suspension and abandonment of works as a fundamental breach of the 1977 Treaty and consequently could have invoked this breach as a ground for terminating the Treaty; but this

would not have brought the Project any nearer to completion. It therefore chose to insist on the implementation of the Treaty by Hungary, and on many occasions called upon the latter to resume performance of its obligations under the Treaty.

When Hungary steadfastly refused to do so—although it had expressed its willingness to pay compensation for damage incurred by Czechoslovakia—and when negotiations stalled owing to the diametrically opposed positions of the parties, Czechoslovakia decided to put the Gabcíkovo system into operation unilaterally, exclusively under its own control and for its own benefit.

74. That decision went through various stages and, in the Special Agreement, the Parties asked the Court to decide whether Czechoslovakia "was entitled to proceed, in November 1991" to Variant C, and "to put [it] into operation from October 1992".

75. With a view to justifying those actions, Slovakia invoked what it described as "the principle of approximate application", expressed by Judge Sir Hersch Lauterpacht in the following terms:

> It is a sound principle of law that whenever a legal instrument of continuing validity cannot be applied literally owing to the conduct of one of the parties, it must, without allowing that party to take advantage of its own conduct, be applied in a way approximating most closely to its primary object. To do that is to interpret and to give effect to the instrument—not to change it. (*Admissibility of Hearings of Petitioners by the Committee on South West Africa*, separate opinion of Sir Hersch Lauterpacht, *I.C.J. Reports 1956*, p. 46.)

It claimed that this is a principle of international law and a general principle of law.

76. It is not necessary for the Court to determine whether there is a principle of international law or a general principle of law of "approximate application" because, even if such a principle existed, it could by definition only be employed within the limits of the treaty in question. In the view of the Court, Variant C does not meet that cardinal condition with regard to the 1977 Treaty.

77. As the Court has already observed, the basic characteristic of the 1977 Treaty is, according to Article 1, to provide for the construction of the Gabcíkovo-Nagymaros System of Locks as a joint investment constituting a single and indivisible operational system of works. This element is equally reflected in Articles 8 and 10 of the Treaty providing for joint ownership of the most important works of the Gabcíkovo-Nagymaros project and for the operation of this joint property as a co-ordinated single unit. By definition all this could not be carried out by unilateral action. In spite of having a certain external physical similarity with the original Project, Variant C thus differed sharply from it in its legal characteristics.

78. Moreover, in practice, the operation of Variant C led Czechoslovakia to appropriate, essentially for its use and benefit, between 80 and 90 per cent of the waters of the Danube before returning them to the main bed of the river, despite

the fact that the Danube is not only a shared international watercourse but also an international boundary river.

Czechoslovakia submitted that Variant C was essentially no more than what Hungary had already agreed to and that the only modifications made were those which had become necessary by virtue of Hungary's decision not to implement its treaty obligations. It is true that Hungary, in concluding the 1977 Treaty, had agreed to the damming of the Danube and the diversion of its waters into the bypass canal. But it was only in the context of a joint operation and a sharing of its benefits that Hungary had given its consent. The suspension and withdrawal of that consent constituted a violation of Hungary's legal obligations, demonstrating, as it did, the refusal by Hungary of joint operation; but that cannot mean that Hungary forfeited its basic right to an equitable and reasonable sharing of the resources of an international watercourse.

The Court accordingly concludes that Czechoslovakia, in putting Variant C into operation, was not applying the 1977 Treaty but, on the contrary, violated certain of its express provisions, and, in so doing, committed an internationally wrongful act.

79. The Court notes that between November 1991 and October 1992, Czechoslovakia confined itself to the execution, on its own territory, of the works which were necessary for the implementation of Variant C, but which could have been abandoned if an agreement had been reached between the parties and did not therefore predetermine the final decision to be taken. For as long as the Danube had not been unilaterally dammed, Variant C had not in fact been applied.

Such a situation is not unusual in international law or, for that matter, in domestic law. A wrongful act or offence is frequently preceded by preparatory actions which are not to be confused with the act or offence itself. It is as well to distinguish between the actual commission of a wrongful act (whether instantaneous or continuous) and the conduct prior to that act which is of a preparatory character and which "does not qualify as a wrongful act" (see for example the Commentary on Article 41 of the Draft Articles on State Responsibility, "Report of the International Law Commission on the work of its forty-eighth session, 6 May-26 July 1996", *Official Records of the General Assembly, Fifty-first Session, Supplement No. 10* (A/51/10), p. 141 and *Yearbook of the International Law Commission*, 1993, Vol. II, Part 2, p. 57, para. 14). … [The Court proceeds to examine the requirements of a justified countermeasure, as reproduced *supra* in Part Five, State Responsibility, at 972-973.]

89. By the terms of Article 2, paragraph 1 *(c)*, of the Special Agreement, the Court is asked, thirdly, to determine what are the legal effects of the notification, on 19 May 1992, of the termination of the Treaty by the Republic of Hungary. …

92. During the proceedings, Hungary presented five arguments in support of the lawfulness, and thus the effectiveness, of its notification of termination. These were the existence of a state of necessity; the impossibility of performance of the

Treaty; the occurrence of a fundamental change of circumstances; the material breach of the Treaty by Czechoslovakia; and, finally, the development of new norms of international environmental law. Slovakia contested each of these grounds. ...

98. The question, as formulated in Article 2, paragraph 1 *(c)*, of the Special Agreement, deals with treaty law since the Court is asked to determine what the legal effects are of the notification of termination of the Treaty. The question is whether Hungary's notification of 19 May 1992 brought the 1977 Treaty to an end, or whether it did not meet the requirements of international law, with the consequence that it did not terminate the Treaty.

99. The Court has referred earlier to the question of the applicability to the present case of the Vienna Convention of 1969 on the Law of Treaties. The Vienna Convention is not directly applicable to the 1977 Treaty inasmuch as both States ratified that Convention only after the Treaty's conclusion. ... Consequently only those rules which are declaratory of customary law are applicable to the 1977 Treaty. As the Court has already stated above, this is the case, in many respects, with Articles 60 to 62 of the Vienna Convention, relating to termination or suspension of the operation of a treaty. On this, the Parties, too, were broadly in agreement.

100. The 1977 Treaty does not contain any provision regarding its termination. Nor is there any indication that the parties intended to admit the possibility of denunciation or withdrawal. On the contrary, the Treaty establishes a long-standing and durable régime of joint investment and joint operation. Consequently, the parties not having agreed otherwise, the Treaty could be terminated only on the limited grounds enumerated in the Vienna Convention.

101. The Court will now turn to the first ground advanced by Hungary, that of the state of necessity. In this respect, the Court will merely observe that, even if a state of necessity is found to exist, it is not a ground for the termination of a treaty. It may only be invoked to exonerate from its responsibility a State which has failed to implement a treaty. Even if found justified, it does not terminate a Treaty; the Treaty may be ineffective as long as the condition of necessity continues to exist; it may in fact be dormant, but—unless the parties by mutual agreement terminate the Treaty—it continues to exist. As soon as the state of necessity ceases to exist, the duty to comply with treaty obligations revives.

102. Hungary also relied on the principle of the impossibility of performance as reflected in Article 61 of the Vienna Convention on the Law of Treaties. Hungary's interpretation of the wording of Article 61 is, however, not in conformity with the terms of that Article, nor with the intentions of the Diplomatic Conference which adopted the Convention. Article 61, paragraph 1, requires the "permanent disappearance or destruction of an object indispensable for the execution" of the treaty to justify the termination of a treaty on grounds of impossibility of performance. During the conference, a proposal was made to extend the scope of the article by including in it cases such as the impossibility to make

certain payments because of serious financial difficulties (*Official Records of the United Nations Conference on the Law of Treaties, First Session, Vienna, 26 March-24 May 1968*, Doc. A/CONF.39/11, Summary records of the plenary meetings and of the meetings of the Committee of the Whole, 62nd Meeting of the Committee of the Whole, pp. 361-365). Although it was recognized that such situations could lead to a preclusion of the wrongfulness of non-performance by a party of its treaty obligations, the participating States were not prepared to consider such situations to be a ground for terminating or suspending a treaty, and preferred to limit themselves to a narrower concept.

103. Hungary contended that the essential object of the Treaty—an economic joint investment which was consistent with environmental protection and which was operated by the two contracting parties jointly—had permanently disappeared and that the Treaty had thus become impossible to perform. It is not necessary for the Court to determine whether the term "object" in Article 61 can also be understood to embrace a legal régime as in any event, even if that were the case, it would have to conclude that in this instance that régime had not definitively ceased to exist. The 1977 Treaty—and in particular its Articles 15, 19 and 20—actually made available to the parties the necessary means to proceed at any time, by negotiation, to the required readjustments between economic imperatives and ecological imperatives. The Court would add that, if the joint exploitation of the investment was no longer possible, this was originally because Hungary did not carry out most of the works for which it was responsible under the 1977 Treaty; Article 61, paragraph 2, of the Vienna Convention expressly provides that impossibility of performance may not be invoked for the termination of a treaty by a party to that treaty when it results from that party's own breach of an obligation flowing from that treaty.

104. Hungary further argued that it was entitled to invoke a number of events which, cumulatively, would have constituted a fundamental change of circumstances. In this respect it specified profound changes of a political nature, the Project's diminishing economic viability, the progress of environmental knowledge and the development of new norms and prescriptions of international environmental law.

The Court recalls that, in the *Fisheries Jurisdiction* case (*I.C.J. Reports 1973*, p. 63, para. 36), it stated that,

Article 62 of the Vienna Convention on the Law of Treaties, ... may in many respects be considered as a codification of existing customary law on the subject of the termination of a treaty relationship on account of change of circumstances.

The prevailing political situation was certainly relevant for the conclusion of the 1977 Treaty. But the Court will recall that the Treaty provided for a joint investment programme for the production of energy, the control of floods and the improvement of navigation on the Danube. In the Court's view, the prevalent political conditions were thus not so closely linked to the object and purpose of the Treaty that they constituted an essential basis of the consent of the parties and, in changing, radically altered the extent of the obligations still to be performed. The same holds good for the economic system in force at the time of the conclusion of the 1977 Treaty. Besides, even though the estimated profitability of the Project might have appeared less in 1992 than in 1977, it does not appear from the record before the Court that it was bound to diminish to such an extent that the treaty obligations of the parties would have been radically transformed as a result.

The Court does not consider that new developments in the state of environmental knowledge and of environmental law can be said to have been completely unforeseen. What is more, the formulation of Articles 15, 19 and 20, designed to accommodate change, made it possible for the parties to take account of such developments and to apply them when implementing those treaty provisions.

The changed circumstances advanced by Hungary are, in the Court's view, not of such a nature, either individually or collectively, that their effect would radically transform the extent of the obligations still to be performed in order to accomplish the Project. A fundamental change of circumstances must have been unforeseen; the existence of the circumstances at the time of the Treaty's conclusion must have constituted an essential basis of the consent of the parties to be bound by the Treaty. The negative and conditional wording of Article 62 of the Vienna Convention on the Law of Treaties is a clear indication moreover that the stability of treaty relations requires that the plea of fundamental change of circumstances be applied only in exceptional cases.

105. The Court will now examine Hungary's argument that it was entitled to terminate the 1977 Treaty on the ground that Czechoslovakia had violated its Articles 15, 19 and 20 (as well as a number of other conventions and rules of general international law); and that the planning, construction and putting into operation of Variant C also amounted to a material breach of the 1977 Treaty.

106. As to that part of Hungary's argument which was based on other treaties and general rules of international law, the Court is of the view that it is only a material breach of the treaty itself, by a State party to that treaty, which entitles the other party to rely on it as a ground for terminating the treaty. The violation of other treaty rules or of rules of general international law may justify the taking of certain measures, including countermeasures, by the injured State, but it does not constitute a ground for termination under the law of treaties.

107. Hungary contended that Czechoslovakia had violated Articles 15, 19 and 20 of the Treaty by refusing to enter into negotiations with Hungary in order to adapt the Joint Contractual Plan to new scientific and legal developments regarding the environment. Articles 15, 19 and 20 oblige the parties jointly to take, on a continuous basis, appropriate measures necessary for the protection of water quality, of nature and of fishing interests. Articles 15 and 19 expressly provide that the obligations they contain shall be implemented by the means specified in the Joint Contractual Plan. The failure of the parties to agree on those means cannot, on the basis of the record before the Court, be attributed solely to one party. The Court has not found sufficient evidence to conclude that Czecho-

slovakia had consistently refused to consult with Hungary about the desirability or necessity of measures for the preservation of the environment. The record rather shows that, while both parties indicated, in principle, a willingness to undertake further studies, in practice Czechoslovakia refused to countenance a suspension of the works at Dunakiliti and, later, on Variant C, while Hungary required suspension as a prior condition of environmental investigation because it claimed continuation of the work would prejudice the outcome of negotiations. In this regard it cannot be left out of consideration that Hungary itself, by suspending the works at Nagymaros and Dunakiliti, contributed to the creation of a situation which was not conducive to the conduct of fruitful negotiations.

108. Hungary's main argument for invoking a material breach of the Treaty was the construction and putting into operation of Variant C. As the Court has found in paragraph 79 above, Czechoslovakia violated the Treaty only when it diverted the waters of the Danube into the bypass canal in October 1992. In constructing the works which would lead to the putting into operation of Variant C, Czechoslovakia did not act unlawfully.

In the Court's view, therefore, the notification of termination by Hungary on 19 May 1992 was premature. No breach of the Treaty by Czechoslovakia had yet taken place and consequently Hungary was not entitled to invoke any such breach of the Treaty as a ground for terminating it when it did.

109. In this regard, it should be noted that, according to Hungary's Declaration of 19 May 1992, the termination of the 1977 Treaty was to take effect as from 25 May 1992, that is only six days later. Both Parties agree that Articles 65 to 67 of the Vienna Convention on the Law of Treaties, if not codifying customary law, at least generally reflect customary international law and contain certain procedural principles which are based on an obligation to act in good faith. As the Court stated in its Advisory Opinion on the *Interpretation of the Agreement of 25 March 1951 between the WHO and Egypt* (in which case the Vienna Convention did not apply):

> Precisely what periods of time may be involved in the observance of the duties to consult and negotiate, and what period of notice of termination should be given, are matters which necessarily vary according to the requirements of the particular case. In principle, therefore, it is for the parties in each case to determine the length of those periods by consultation and negotiation in good faith." (*I.C.J. Reports 1980*, p. 96, para. 49.)

The termination of the Treaty by Hungary was to take effect six days after its notification. On neither of these dates had Hungary suffered injury resulting from acts of Czechoslovakia. The Court must therefore confirm its conclusion that Hungary's termination of the Treaty was premature.

110. Nor can the Court overlook that Czechoslovakia committed the internationally wrongful act of putting into operation Variant C as a result of Hungary's

own prior wrongful conduct. As was stated by the Permanent Court of International Justice:

> It is, moreover, a principle generally accepted in the jurisprudence of international arbitration, as well as by municipal courts, that one Party cannot avail himself of the fact that the other has not fulfilled some obligation or has not had recourse to some means of redress, if the former Party has, by some illegal act, prevented the latter from fulfilling the obligation in question, or from having recourse to the tribunal which would have been open, to him. (*Factory at Chorzów, Jurisdiction, Judgment No. 8, 1927, P.C.I.J., Series A, No. 9*, p. 31.)

Hungary, by its own conduct, had prejudiced its right to terminate the Treaty; this would still have been the case even if Czechoslovakia, by the time of the purported termination, had violated a provision essential to the accomplishment of the object or purpose of the Treaty. ...

114. Finally, Hungary maintained that by their conduct both parties had repudiated the Treaty and that a bilateral treaty repudiated by both parties cannot survive. The Court is of the view, however, that although it has found that both Hungary and Czechoslovakia failed to comply with their obligations under the 1977 Treaty, this reciprocal wrongful conduct did not bring the Treaty to an end nor justify its termination. The Court would set a precedent with disturbing implications for treaty relations and the integrity of the rule *pacta sunt servanda* if it were to conclude that a treaty in force between States, which the parties have implemented in considerable measure and at great cost over a period of years, might be unilaterally set aside on grounds of reciprocal non-compliance. It would be otherwise, of course, if the parties decided to terminate the Treaty by mutual consent. But in this case, while Hungary purported to terminate the Treaty, Czechoslovakia consistently resisted this act and declared it to be without legal effect.

115. In the light of the conclusions it has reached above, the Court, in reply to the question put to it in Article 2, paragraph 1 *(c)*, of the Special Agreement, finds that the notification of termination by Hungary of 19 May 1992 did not have the legal effect of terminating the 1977 Treaty and related instruments.

NOTES AND QUESTIONS

1. With regard to the effect of change on treaties, state practice clearly does not require a basis in the original intentions of the parties or resort to independent decision-makers. Parties to agreements cannot be expected to anticipate all future events. In the present context of world organization, state elites are unlikely to accept compulsory jurisdiction on matters that may affect survival.

Would it be better to recognize the doctrine in a more flexible formulation? The ordinary sanctions - in reciprocities and retaliations - can be relied upon to minimize its abuse. For the better operation of these sanctions, effort might be devoted to the clarification of common policies as these might vary with type of change (peaceful or violent), type of treaty (alliance or exchange of information), the duration and past observance of the treaty, the degree to which the parties anticipated or might have anticipated the change, the interest of the one party in change, the damage to the values of the other party by change, the modality by which the claim to change was asserted, and so on.

With reference to each particular type of change alleged, it is necessary to examine whether the agreement has been executed or calls for a continuous performance and whether the duration of the agreement is indefinite, or for a limited period, or permanent. Distinctions must also be made between agreements in terms of their major objectives (whether relating to security, power, wealth, human rights, and so on).

The major types of change that have been controverted in the past include:

(1) The severance of diplomatic relations.

(2) Changes in the extent of territory.

(3) Changes in governmental institutions in one of the parties.

(4) The extinction of a "state" party to the agreement.

(5) Non-performance and violation by the other party, supra.

(6) The outbreak of hostilities between the parties.

To what extent should the "Reunification of States" be added to the list above? *See* Cecilia Y. Oh, *The Effect of Reunification of North and South Korea on Treaty Status*, 16 Emory Int'l L. Rev. 311 (2002).

2. The problem created by an outbreak of hostilities offers an excellent illustration of the number of relevant variables. Consider this assessment:

> It is doubtful if any statesman today would claim that it is "a rule of international law universally accepted" that war terminates all treaties between opposing belligerents. If so, the proposition could not be successfully defended. Nearly all writers on international law today hold that ipso facto termination is the exception rather than the rule. ...
>
> The abandonment of the old theory and the recognition of the principle that at most it can only be said that certain kinds of treaties are ipso facto an-nulled by the outbreak of war between the parties, that certain others are merely suspended, while others still are not affected, was a necessary corollary of the increasing interdependence of States, the establishment of a vast net work of treaty-relationships and a clearer appreciation of the general inconvenience of a practice which would result in the complete upsetting, under modern conditions, of these relationships. It has come more and more to be realized that there is no necessary incompatibility between the existence of a state of war between two or more States and the maintenance in force of their treaties, even though it may be necessary to suspend their execution during the period of hostilities. There is no reason of public policy or national defense why any treaties should be regarded as ipso facto annulled or terminated by the outbreak of war between the parties, Likewise it is more and more realized that there may be treaties or particular stipulations of treaties of which no consideration of public policy or belligerent interest requires that they should even be suspended. In this class are such treaties as those which do not require for their execution direct relations between the enemy parties such as would be incompatible with the carrying on of hostilities.

Research in International Law, The Law of Treaties, 29 Am. J. Int'l L. Supp. 1185-86 (1935). Rational decision about the effect of war must obviously depend upon a considerable range of factors including the type of treaty in terms of the whole process of agreement (i.e., variations in terms of participants, objectives, base values, situations); the type of war (total or limited, aggressive or defensive); the type of claim (from minor modification to complete ab-rogation); the time when the claim is asserted (during war, afterwards); express provision in the treaty about termination; and the decisionmaker to whom the claim is addressed.

3. Multilateral treaties often make elaborate provision for revision or for withdrawal. Consider, for example, the 1963 Limited Test Ban Treaty (Part One, *supra*, at 47-48). In the absence of such

a provision, are the parties to a treaty, absent Vienna Convention termination grounds, forever bound to the terms of the treaty they ratified?

4. Both the League of Nations and the United Nations have offered more generalized constitutive provisions for change:

COVENANT OF THE LEAGUE OF NATIONS

> *Article 19.* The Assembly may from time to time advise the reconsideration by Members of the League of treaties which have become inapplicable and the consideration of international conditions whose continuance might endanger the peace of the world.

CHARTER OF THE UNITED NATIONS

> *Article 14.* Subject to the provisions of Article 12, the General Assembly may recommend measures for the peaceful adjustment of any situation, regardless of origin, which it deems likely to impair the general welfare or friendly relations among nations, including situations resulting from a violation of the provisions of the present Charter setting forth the Purposes and Principles of the United Nations.

5. One example of the operation of these more generalized constitutive provisions is offered in the *Namibia* case, 1971 I.C.J. 16 [Facts are set out *supra*, Part Two, at 231]:

> 91. One of the fundamental principles governing the international relationship thus established is that a party which disowns or does not fulfil its own obligations cannot be recognized as retaining the rights which it claims to derive from the relationship.
>
> 92. The terms of the preamble and operative part of resolution 2145(XXI) leave no doubt as to the character of the resolution. In the preamble the General Assembly declares itself "*Convinced* that the administration of the Mandated Territory by South Africa has been conducted in a manner contrary" to the two basic international instruments directly imposing obligations upon South Africa, the Mandate and the Charter of the United Nations, as well as to the Universal Declaration of Human Rights. In another paragraph of the preamble the conclusion is reached that, after having insisted with no avail upon performance for more than twenty years, the moment has arrived for the General Assembly to exercise the right to treat such violation as a ground for termination.
>
> 93. In paragraph 3 … the General Assembly "*Declares* that South Africa has failed to fulfil its obligations in respect of the administration of the Mandated Territory and to ensure the mor-al and material well-being and security of the indigenous inhabitants of South West Africa and has, in fact, disavowed the Mandate". In paragraph 4 the decision is reached, as a consequence of the previous declaration "that the Mandate conferred upon His Britannic Majesty to be exercised on his behalf by the Government of the Union of South Africa is *therefore* terminated ..." (Emphasis added.) It is this part of the resolution which is relevant in the present proceedings.
>
> 94. In examining this action of the General Assembly it is appropriate to have regard to the general principles of international law regulating termination of a treaty relationship on account of breach. For even if the mandate is viewed as having the character of an institution, as is maintained, it depends on those international agreements which created the system and regulated its application. As the Court indicated in 1962, "this Mandate, like practically all other similar Mandates," was "a special type of instrument composite in nature and instituting a novel international régime. It incorporates a definite agreement (I.C.J. Reports 1962, p. 331) The Court stated conclusively in that judgment that the Mandate " … in fact and in law, is an international agreement having the character of a treaty or convention" (I.C.J. Reports 1962, p. 330). The rules laid down by the Vienna Convention on the Law of Treaties concerning termination of a treaty relationship on account of breach (adopted without a dissenting vote) may in many respects be consid-

ered as a codification of existing customary law on the subject. In the light of these rules, only a material breach of a treaty justifies termination, such breach being defined as:

(a) a repudiation of the treaty not sanctioned by the present Convention; or

(b) the violation of a provision essential to the accomplishment of the object or purpose of the treaty (Art. 60, para. 3).

95. General Assembly resolution 2145 (XXI) determines that both forms of material breach had occurred in this case. By stressing that South Africa "has, in fact, disavowed the Mandate", the General Assembly declared in fact that it had repudiated it. The resolution in question is therefore to be viewed as the exercise of the right to terminate a relationship in case of a de-liberate and persistent violation of obligations which destroys the very object and purpose of that relationship.

International law may prescribe a special régime for human rights. *Compare* General Comment No. 24 by the United Nations Human Rights Committee (*supra* at 1330) and the Inter-American Court of Human Rights' *Bronstein* decision:

(3) Ivcher Bronstein Case (Baruch Ivcher Bronstein v. Peru) Competence Judgment of Sept. 24, 1999

Inter-Am. Ct. H.R. (Ser. C) No. 54 (1999)

English translation *at* http://www.law.monash.edu.au/humanrts/iachr/C/54-ing.html

A. FACTS:

25. The Commission submitted the application in the Ivcher Bronstein case on March 31, 1999. The Court forwarded note CDH-11,762/002 to the State on May 10, 1999, wherein it notified Peru of the application and sent it a copy of both the application and its attachments. The Court also advised the State that it had one month to designate an agent and alternate agent, two months to file preliminary objections and four months to answer the application.

26. By a second note of May 10, 1999, CDH-11,762/003, the Court informed the State that it had 30 days in which to designate an *ad hoc* judge.

27. On May 17, 1999, Peru advised the Secretariat that it had received notification of the case on May 12, 1999. On June 8, it designated its agent and alternate agent and gave Peru's Embassy in San José, Costa Rica, as the address to which communications should be directed.

28. By note of July 16, 1999, received at the Secretariat of the Court on July 27 of that year, the General Secretariat of the OAS reported that on July 9, 1999, Peru had presented an instrument wherein it advised that it was withdrawing its declaration consenting to the optional clause in the American Convention recognizing the contentious jurisdiction of the Court.

It also sent a copy of the original of that instrument, dated Lima, July 8, 1999. There, the Minister of Foreign Affairs of Peru stated that by Legislative Resolution No. 27,152 of July 8, 1999, the Congress of the Republic had approved the withdrawal in the following terms:

> that in accordance with the American Convention on Human Rights, the Republic of Peru is withdrawing the declaration whereby it consents to the optional clause recognizing the contentious jurisdiction of the Inter-American Court of Human Rights, a declaration given by the Peruvian government at the time.

This withdrawal of recognition of the Inter-American Court's contentious jurisdiction will take effect immediately and will apply to all cases in which Peru has not answered the application filed with the Court.

29. On August 4, 1999, the Minister and Counselor of the Embassy of Peru in Costa Rica appeared at the Secretariat of the Inter-American Court and stated that they were returning the application in the Ivcher Bronstein case and its appendices. The Secretariat made a record of these documents' return.

30. Peru has been a State Party to the American Convention since July 28, 1978. In its instrument of ratification of the Convention, the Government noted that the Convention had been approved by Decree Law No. 22,231, of July 11, 1978, and had become State law. On the honor of the Republic, it pledged to abide by the Convention. On January 21, 1981, Peru recognized the contentious jurisdiction of the Court as follows:

> [a]s prescribed in paragraph 1 of Article 62 of the American Convention, the Government of Peru hereby declares that it recognizes as binding, *ipso facto*, and not requiring special agreement, the jurisdiction of the Court on all matters relating to the interpretation or application of the Convention.

This recognition of jurisdiction is for an unspecified period and on condition of reciprocity.

31. Exercising its jurisdiction, the Court took cognizance of the Ivcher Bronstein case on March 31, 1999, the date on which it formally received the corresponding application, filed in accordance with articles 48, 50, and 51 of the Convention and Article 32 of the Court's Rules of Procedure.

B. LAW:

32. The Court must settle the question of Peru's purported withdrawal of its declaration recognizing the contentious jurisdiction of the Court and of its legal effects. The Inter-American Court, as with any court or tribunal, has the inherent authority to determine the scope of its own competence (*compétence de la compétence/Kompetenz-Kompetenz*).

33. The Court cannot abdicate this prerogative, as it is a duty that the Convention imposes upon it, requiring it to exercise its functions in accordance with Article 62(3) thereof. That provision reads as follows:

> The jurisdiction of the Court shall comprise all cases concerning the interpretation and application of the provisions of this Convention that are submitted to it, provided that the States Parties to the case recognize or

have recognized such jurisdiction, whether by special declaration pursuant to the preceding paragraphs, or by a special agreement.

34. The jurisdiction of the Court cannot be contingent upon events extraneous to its own actions. The instruments consenting to the optional clause concerning recognition of the Court's binding jurisdiction (Article 62(1) of the Convention) presuppose that the States submitting them accept the Court's right to settle any controversy relative to its jurisdiction. An objection or any other action taken by the State for the purpose of somehow affecting the Court's jurisdiction has no consequence whatever, as the Court retains the *compétence de la compétence*, as it is master of its own jurisdiction.

35. Interpreting the Convention in accordance with its object and purpose ... the Court must act in a manner that preserves the integrity of the mechanism provided for in Article 62(1) of the Convention. That mechanism cannot be subordinated to any restrictions that the respondent State might add to the terms of its recognition of the Court's binding jurisdiction, as that would adversely affect the efficacy of the mechanism and could obstruct its future development.

36. Acceptance of the Court's binding jurisdiction is an ironclad clause to which there can be no limitations except those expressly provided for in Article 62(1) of the American Convention. Because the clause is so fundamental to the operation of the Convention's system of protection, it cannot be at the mercy of limitations not already stipulated but invoked by States Parties for internal reasons.

37. The States Parties to the Convention must guarantee compliance with its provisions and its effects (*effet utile*) within their own domestic laws. This principle applies not only to the substantive provisions of human rights treaties (in other words, the clauses on the protected rights), but also to the procedural provisions, such as the one concerning recognition of the Tribunal's contentious jurisdiction. That clause, essential to the efficacy of the mechanism of international protection, must be interpreted and applied in such a way that the guarantee that it establishes is truly practical and effective, given the special nature of human rights treaties (*cf. infra* 42 to 45) and their collective enforcement.

38. Article 31(1) of the 1969 Vienna Convention on the Law of Treaties (hereinafter "the Vienna Convention") provides that:

> A treaty shall be interpreted in good faith in accordance with the ordinary meaning to be given to the terms of the treaty in their context and in the light of its object and purpose...

39. Article 62(1) of the American Convention stipulates that a State Party may, upon depositing its instrument of ratification or adherence to this Convention, or at any subsequent time, declare "that it recognizes as binding, *ipso facto*, and not requiring any special agreement, the jurisdiction of the Court on all matters relating to the interpretation or application of this Convention." There is no provision in the Convention that expressly permits the States Parties to withdraw

their declaration of recognition of the Court's binding jurisdiction. Nor does the instrument in which Peru recognizes the Court's jurisdiction, dated January 21, 1981, allow for that possibility.

40. An interpretation of the Convention done "in good faith in accordance with the ordinary meaning to be given to the terms of the treaty in their context and in light of its object and purpose" leads this Court to the view that a State Party to the American Convention can only release itself of its obligations under the Convention by following the provisions that the treaty itself stipulates. In the instant case, under the Convention, the only avenue the State has to disengage itself from the Court's binding contentious jurisdiction is to denounce the Convention as a whole...; if this happens, then the denunciation will only have effect if done in accordance with Article 78, which requires one year's advance notice.

41. Article 29(a) of the American Convention provides that no provision of the Convention shall be interpreted as permitting any State Party, group, or person to suppress the enjoyment or exercise of the rights and freedoms recognized in the Convention or to restrict them to a greater extent than is provided for therein. Any interpretation of the Convention that allows a State Party to withdraw its recognition of the Court's binding jurisdiction, as Peru would in the instant case, would imply suppression of the exercise of the rights and freedoms recognized in the Convention, would be contrary to its object and purpose as a human rights treaty, and would deprive all the Convention's beneficiaries of the additional guarantee of protection of their human rights that the Convention's jurisdictional body affords.

42. The American Convention and the other human rights treaties are inspired by a set of higher common values (centered around the protection of the human person), are endowed with specific supervisory mechanisms, are applied as a collective guarantee, embody essentially objective obligations, and have a special character that sets them apart from other treaties. The latter govern mutual interests between and among the States Parties and are applied by them, with all the juridical consequences that follow therefrom for the international and domestic legal systems.

43. In its Advisory Opinion OC-2/82, of September 24, 1982, titled *The Effect of Reservations on the Entry into Force of the American Convention on Human Rights (Arts. 74 and 75)*, the Court found that:

> [m]odern human rights treaties in general, and the American Convention in particular, are not multilateral treaties of the traditional type concluded to accomplish the reciprocal exchange of rights for the mutual benefit of the contracting States. Their object and purpose is the protection of the basic rights of individual human beings irrespective of their nationality, both against the State of their nationality and all other contracting States. In concluding these human rights treaties, the States can be deemed to submit themselves to a legal order within which they, for the common

> good, assume various obligations, not in relation to other States, but towards all individuals within their jurisdiction. (paragraph 29)

44. That finding is consistent with the case-law of other international jurisdictional bodies. For example, in its Advisory Opinion on *Reservations to the Convention for the Prevention and Punishment of the Crime of Genocide* (1951), the International Court of Justice held that with treaties of this nature, "the contracting States do not have any individual advantages or disadvantages nor interests of their own, but merely a common interest; hence the Convention's raison d'être is to accomplish its purposes."

45. For their part, the European Commission and Court of Human Rights (hereinafter "the European Commission" and "the European Court") have arrived at similar findings. In the *Austria vs. Italy* case (1961), the European Commission declared that the obligations undertaken by the States Parties to the European Convention on Human Rights (hereinafter "the European Convention") "are essentially objective in nature, and intended to protect the fundamental rights of human beings against violations on the part of the High Contracting Parties, rather than to create subjective and reciprocal rights between the High Contracting Parties." Similarly, in *Ireland vs. the United Kingdom* (1978), the European Court held the following:

> Unlike international treaties of the classic kind, the Convention comprises more than mere reciprocal engagements between contracting States. It creates, over and above a network of mutual, bilateral undertakings, objective obligations which, in the words of the Preamble, benefit from a "collective enforcement".

In the *Soering vs. United Kingdom* case (1989), the European Court declared that in interpreting the European Convention "regard must be had to its special character as a treaty for the collective enforcement of human rights and fundamental freedoms.... Thus, the object and purpose of the Convention as an instrument for the protection of individual human beings require that its provisions be interpreted and applied so as to make its safeguards practical and effective."

46. The optional clause recognizing the contentious jurisdiction of the Inter-American Court is of particular importance to the operation of the system of protection embodied in the American Convention. When a State consents to that clause, it binds itself to the whole of the Convention and is fully committed to guaranteeing the international protection of human rights that the Convention embodies. A State Party may only release itself from the Court's jurisdiction by renouncing the treaty as a whole...The instrument whereby it recognizes the Court's jurisdiction must, therefore, be weighed in light of the object and purpose of the Convention as a human rights treaty.

47. No analogy can be drawn between the State practice detailed under Article 36(2) of the Statute of the International Court of Justice and acceptance of the optional clause concerning recognition of the binding jurisdiction of this

Court, given the particular nature and the object and purpose of the American Convention. The European Court of Human Rights ruled similarly in its judgment on preliminary objections in the *Loizidou vs. Turkey* case (1995), in connection with optional recognition of the European Court's binding jurisdiction (Article 46 of the European Convention, before Protocol XI to the European Convention entered into force on January 1, 1998). The European Court held that the European Convention was a law-making treaty.

48. In effect, international settlement of human rights cases (entrusted to tribunals like the Inter-American and European Courts of Human Rights) cannot be compared to the peaceful settlement of international disputes involving purely interstate litigation (entrusted to a tribunal like the International Court of Justice); since, as is widely accepted, the contexts are fundamentally different, States cannot expect to have the same amount of discretion in the former as they have traditionally had in the latter.

49. A unilateral juridical act carried out in the context of purely interstate relations (e.g. recognition, promise, protest, renunciation) and independently self-consummated, can hardly be compared with a unilateral juridical act carried out within the framework of treaty law, such as acceptance of an optional clause recognizing the binding jurisdiction of an international court. That acceptance is determined and shaped by the treaty itself and, in particular, through fulfillment of its object and purpose.

50. A State that recognized the binding jurisdiction of the Inter-American Court under Article 62(1) of the Convention, is thenceforth bound by the Convention as a whole ... The goal of preserving the integrity of the treaty obligations is from Article 44(1) of the Vienna Convention, which is based on the principle that the denunciation (or "withdrawal" of recognition of a treaty's mechanism) can only be vis-à-vis the treaty as a whole, unless the treaty provides or the Parties thereto agree otherwise.

51. The American Convention is very clear that denunciation is of "this Convention" (Article 78) as a whole, and not denunciation of or "release" from parts or clauses thereof, since that would undermine the integrity of the whole. Applying the criteria of the Vienna Convention (Article 56(1)), it does not appear to have been the Parties' intention to allow this type of denunciation or release; nor can denunciation or release be inferred from the character of the American Convention as a human rights treaty.

52. Even supposing, for the sake of argument, that "release" was possible – a hypothetical that this Court rejects -, it could not take effect immediately. Article 56(2) of the Vienna Convention stipulates that a State Party must give "not less than 12 months' notice" of its intention to denounce or withdraw from a treaty. This is to protect the interests of the other Parties to the treaty. The international obligation in question, even when undertaken by means of a unilateral declaration, is binding for the State. The latter is thenceforth "legally re-

quired to follow a course of conduct consistent with its declaration", and the other States Parties are authorized to demand that that obligation be honored.

53. Despite the fact that it is optional, the declaration of recognition of the contentious jurisdiction of an international tribunal, once made, does not give the State the authority to change its content and scope at will at some later date: "... The right of immediate termination of declarations with indefinite duration is far from established. It appears from the requirements of good faith that they should be treated, by analogy, according to the law of treaties, which requires a reasonable time for withdrawal from or termination of treaties that contain no provision regarding the duration of their validity." Thus, in order for an optional clause to be unilaterally terminated, the pertinent rules of the law of treaties must be applied. Those rules clearly preclude any possibility of a termination or "release" with "immediate effect".

54. For the foregoing reasons, the Court considers inadmissible Peru's purported withdrawal of the declaration recognizing the contentious jurisdiction of the Court effective immediately, as well as any consequences said withdrawal was intended to have, among them the return of the application, which is irrelevant.

* * *

For a further discussion of the special character of human rights treaties in regard to termination rules, *see* Ryan Goodman, *Human Rights Treaties, Invalid Reservations, and State Consent*, 96 Am. J. Int'l L. 531 (2001).

2. National Prescriptions

International agreements may, as we have seen in inquiring about the process of performance, be prescribed as the internal policies of states, committing officials, individuals and private associations to their observance. Such internal prescription may be abrogated by appropriate constitutional authorities without in any way releasing the state from its external obligations to other states. The abrogation of the internal prescription may be a violation of the external obligations, but it does not release it. The two obligations must be kept distinct.

The methods by which the internal prescriptive effect of international agreements may be abrogated are established by the constitutional procedures of the different nation-states.

For purposes of illustration, the procedures within the United States may be outlined.

a. Myres S. McDougal & Asher Lans, *Treaties and Congressional-Executive or Presidential Agreements: Inter-changeable Instruments of National Policy*

in MYRES SMITH MCDOUGAL, STUDIES IN WORLD PUBLIC ORDER 404, 594-99 (Martinus Nijhoff 1960)

There are seven procedures by which the domestic status of treaties as the "law of the land" may be terminated. First, provisions of a treaty lose their operative effect if inconsistent terms or an express stipulation of repeal are included in a later treaty. In the second place, following a precedent established in 1784 when the Treaty of Commerce and Amity with France was modified by an exchange of notes between the French Foreign Minister and Benjamin Franklin, executive agreements have not infrequently been utilized as a method of altering treaties. Thirdly, a treaty may be terminated in whole or in part by a congressional act or joint resolution expressly providing for its denunciation. This procedure, advocated by Presidents Hayes and Grant, has been upheld in a series of court decisions, culminated by the Supreme Court's recent opinion in *Van der Weyde v. Ocean Transport Company*. With reference to the question of congressional denunciation, the Court said:

> In this instance, the Congress requested and directed the President to give notice of the termination of the treaty provisions in conflict with the act. From every point of view, it was incumbent upon the President, charged with the conduct of negotiations with foreign governments and also with the duty to take care that the laws of the United States are faithfully executed, to reach a conclusion as to the inconsistency between the provisions of the treaty and the provisions of the new law. It is not possible to say that his conclusion as to articles 13 and 14 are arbitrary or inadmissible. Having determined that their termination was necessary, the President through the Secretary of State took appropriate steps to effect it.

In the fourth place, treaties have frequently been terminated indirectly, by the enactment of conflicting or inconsistent legislation. In the fifth place, Congress may nullify a treaty by refusing to pass supplementary legislation need-ed for its enforcement or by mere failure to appropriate necessary funds. These last two methods, while not formally denominated terminations of a treaty, palpably have the same operative effect. In the sixth place, termination may be effected by executive denunciation, with or without prior congressional authorization. The administrations of Presidents Madison, Grant, McKinley, Taft, and possibly Lincoln furnish precedent for this type of executive action. President Franklin D. Roosevelt denounced at least two treaties on his own initiative: in 1933, the extradition treaty with Greece, and in 1939, the treaty of commerce and amity with Japan. There are dicta in the 1910 decision of the Supreme Court in *Charlton v. Kelly* indicating the validity of direct Presidential termination. In the seventh place, a treaty may be terminated by the President after enactment of a resolution of denunciation by two-thirds of the Senate. It is an illuminating example of the pervasive-ness of constitutional usage to note that this procedure-which appears to ac-cord with the language of the treaty-making clause of the Constitution more closely than do the methods commonly followed-has been utilized only twice: in 1854 when the Senate authorized President Pierce to denounce a treaty with Denmark "at his discretion," and in 1920.

An executive agreement authorized by act of Congress, such as a postal convention or reciprocal trade agreement, is subject to termination by the first six of the procedures indicated in the preceding paragraph, and presumably may be automatically terminated by repeal of the authorizing act. The status of an agreement negotiated by the President on his own authority is more in-definite. Clearly any President has power to terminate the internal status of such agreements as the law of the land. If the agreements deal with questions, such as the war power, where Congress has concurrent jurisdiction, it is possible that such agreements may also be terminated by legislation. But where such agreements are predicated upon the President's independent constitutional powers, such as in the field of foreign relations, under the separation of powers doctrine, congressional action might not affect either the domestic effect of the agreement or its status as an international contract. These are obviously uncharted problems to which it is impossible to give dogmatic answers.

The existence of this variety of techniques for terminating the municipal life of international agreements does not imply that Presidents or Congresses will behave irresponsibly in ignoring the expectations created by their promises to other nations. But - speaking purely of power - a treaty clearly may be terminated by as many procedures as a congressional-executive agreement and, paradoxical though it may seem, even appears to be subject to termination in more ways than in a direct presidential agreement.

* * *

The constitutional issues have been raised in sharp relief by the Presidential termination in 1978 of the 1954 Defense Treaty with Taiwan. The lawfulness of the termination was challenged in the courts in *Goldwater v. Carter*, 481 F. Supp. 949 (D.D.C. 1979), *rev'd*, 617 F.2d 697 (D.C. Cir. 1979) (en banc), *vacated and remanded with directions to dismiss*, 444 U.S. 996 (1980). In the Supreme Court, the justices seemed sharply divided as to whether and why the case should have been dismissed. Goldwater v. Carter, 444 U.S. 996 (1979). Justice Rehnquist (with whom the Chief Justice, Stewart, J. and Stevens, J. concurred) said:

> I am of the view that the basic question presented by the petitioners in this case is "political" and therefore nonjusticiable because it involves the authority of the President in the conduct of our country's foreign relations and the extent to which the Senate or the Congress is authorized to negate the action of the President. In *Coleman v. Miller,* 307 U.S. 433, 59 S.Ct. 972, 83 L.Ed. 1385 (1939), a case in which members of the

Kansas Legislature brought an action attacking a vote of the State Senate in favor of the ratification of the Child Labor Amendment, Mr. Chief Justice Hughes wrote in what is referred to as the "Opinion of the Court":

> We think that ... the question of the efficacy of ratifications by state legislatures, in the light of previous rejection or attempted withdrawal, should be regarded as a political question pertaining to the political departments, with the ultimate authority in the Congress in the exercise of its control over the promulgation of the adoption of the Amendment.
>
> The precise question as now raised is whether, when the legislature of the State, as we have found, has actually ratified the proposed amendment, the Court should restrain the state officers from certifying the ratification to the Secretary of State, because of an earlier rejection, and thus prevent the question from coming before the political departments. We find no basis in either Constitution or statute for such judicial action. Article V, speaking solely of ratification, contains no provision as to rejection. ... *Id.,* at 450, 59 S.Ct. 972.

Thus, Mr. Chief Justice Hughes' opinion concluded that "Congress in controlling the promulgation of the adoption of a constitutional amendment has the final determination of the question whether by lapse of time its proposal of the amendment had lost its vitality prior to the required ratifications." *Id.,* at 456, 59 S.Ct. 972.

I believe it follows *a fortiori* from *Coleman* that the controversy in the instant case is a nonjusticiable political dispute that should be left for resolution by the Executive and Legislative Branches of the Government. Here, while the Constitution is express as to the manner in which the Senate shall participate in the ratification of a treaty, it is silent as to that body's participation in the abrogation of a treaty. In this respect the case is directly analogous to *Coleman, supra.* As stated in *Dyer v. Blair,* 390 F.Supp. 1291, 1302 (N.D.Ill.1975) (three-judge court):

> A question that might be answered in different ways for different amendments must surely be controlled by political standards rather than standards easily characterized as judicially manageable.

In light of the absence of any constitutional provision governing the termination of a treaty, and the fact that different termination procedures may be appropriate for different treaties (see, *e. g.,* n. 1, *infra*), the instant case in my view also "must surely be controlled by political standards."

I think that the justifications for concluding that the question here is political in nature are even more compelling than in *Coleman* because it involves foreign relations—specifically a treaty commitment to use military force in the defense of a foreign government if attacked. In *United States v. Curtiss-Wright Corp.,* 299 U.S. 304, 57 S.Ct. 216, 81 L.Ed. 255 (1936), this Court said:

> Whether, if the Joint Resolution had related solely to internal affairs it would be open to the challenge that it constituted an unlawful delegation of legislative power to the Executive, we find it unnecessary to determine. The whole aim of the resolution is to affect a situation entirely external to the United States, and falling within the category of foreign affairs. ... *Id.*, at 315, 57 S.Ct. 216.

The present case differs in several important respects from *Youngstown Sheet & Tube Co. v. Sawyer,* 343 U.S. 579, 72 S.Ct. 863, 96 L.Ed. 1153 (1952), cited by petitioners as authority both for reaching the merits of this dispute and for reversing the Court of Appeals. In *Youngstown,* private litigants brought a suit contesting the President's authority under his war powers to seize the Nation's steel industry, an action of profound and demonstrable domestic impact. Here, by contrast, we are asked to settle a dispute between coequal branches of our Government, each of which has resources available to protect and assert its interests, resources not available to private litigants outside the judicial forum. Moreover, as in *Curtiss-Wright,* the effect of this action, as far as we can tell, is "entirely external to the United States, and [falls] within the category of foreign affairs." Finally, as already noted, the situation presented here is closely akin to that presented in *Coleman,* where the Constitution spoke only to the procedure for ratification of an amendment, not to its rejection.

* * *

Consider the following appraisal.

b. Michael Reisman & Myres S. McDougal, *Who Can Terminate Mutual Defense Treaties?*

National L.J., May 21, 1979, at 19, and May 28, 1979, at 17

Congress' legal position in this matter has been correct. In consenting to the peace treaty with Japan, Congress declared as part of its constitutional act that the agreement did not resolve the status of Taiwan, an issue which participants at the peace conference had said was to be decided later according to the principles of the U.N. Charter. When this declaration is read with the mutual defense treaty and with the subsequent explicit direction to the president not to terminate the treaty without consulting Congress, it is clear that one of the functions of the treaty was to hold open the possibility of an internationally proper resolution of the status issue. That possibility has been seriously undermined by the president's unilateral action. It is doubly tragic that such a deed should have been committed by an administration that avows the international protection of human rights.

While the document of 1789 makes no express reference to termination, the fundamental principles of a democratic sharing of power, and of checks and balances to protect that sharing, require that the Congress be accorded a role in the termination of all agreements, whatever the modality of their making, other than purely presidential agreements. Virtually all practice with regard to agreements other than presidential has historically involved either an express or implicit authorization by Congress to the president to terminate. Departures from this practice which have not been denounced as unlawful have only occurred in periods of national crisis. The postwar mutual defense treaties arise from legislation which did delegate to the president certain termination powers, but only for certain types of agreements and for carefully spelled-out contingencies. There was no implied authorization to terminate mutual defense treaties; indeed congressional communications indicated exactly the opposite expectation. Nor does the treaty itself authorize the president to terminate.

Even if our historic constitutional practice were ambiguous, the key problem would remain: to shape a future policy in a most critical area in the life of this republic. A rational policy must retain that balancing of power which our national experience has confirmed is necessary for the preservation of freedom while retaining a requisite efficiency in decision-making. Such a policy plainly requires a continuing congressional role in treaty termination.

Notes and Questions

1. Under the U.S. Constitution, should all branches involved in the making of a treaty also be involved in its unmaking? *See* Joshua P. O'Donnell, *The Anti-Ballistic Missile Treaty Debate: Time for Some Clarification of the President's Authority to Terminate a Treaty*, 35 Vand. J. Transnat'l L. 1601 (2002).

PART SEVEN: JURISDICTION: ALLOCATIONS OF COMPETENCE TO MAKE AND APPLY LAW

I. Introduction

A. W. Michael Reisman, Jurisdiction in International Law

xi, xi-xiii (Ashgate 1999)

Politically, our planet is divided into a grid of territorially-based communities: states, federations of states and unions of diverse sorts, to which member states have assigned various legal competences. Each unit's competence within its territory is expressed through its acts of legislation and the application of its law. The government of each territorial community or state tries to police its borders, while seeking to make and apply its policies, expressed as law, within its territorial domain with respect to the events vital to it.

Conflicting Claims to Competence

When exchanges occur between territorial communities, two or more states will often try—simultaneously or sequentially—to make or apply their own law to the same persons, things or events. Lawyers refer to these encounters as "conflicts of laws," but they are, in the most profound sense, conflicts of power, for they engage the very essence of state sovereignty: a state's exercise of its political power by making and applying its law. These conflicts arise from two inextricable yet incompatible features of international politics: territorial communities that are, at once, autonomous, to varying degrees, and interdependent, to varying degrees. The more interactive and interdependent the putatively autonomous states are, the more frequent and acute the jurisdictional conflicts.

The Function of International Jurisdiction Law

The prescriptions within the corpus of public international law that are called, in English, "jurisdiction" seek to resolve systematically these conflicts by allocating to particular states the competence to make or apply law to particular persons, things or events that are, simultaneously or sequentially, claimed by or subject to, the control of two or more states. While the term "jurisdiction" in some languages refers solely to judicial competences, the international usage of the term encompasses the exercise of official power by the full range of legislative, executive and judicial institutions by which states purport to make and apply law. This sector of law is often referred to as "private international law," because particular disputes to which it is applied frequently involve private parties. But the term "private" is a misnomer, for what is transpiring is a fundamental inter-state competition for power that falls squarely within the province of public international law.

The Sources of International Law

Until the middle of this century, the process of allocating competences as between competing states within the Western system of international law was essentially "horizontal," in the sense that relatively little law which was authentically international restricted the substantive lawmaking competences of states. In this sense, the law of international jurisdiction was essentially allocative, a switching mechanism sending a dispute to one or another system of law or to its courts. But since the Second World War, an increasing number of international norms of both customary and conventional provenance—human rights norms, *jus cogens*, state responsibility, substantive international commercial law, macroeconomic adjustments in the form of "structural readjustments" imposed by the International Monetary Fund, and so on—now restrict or displace specific law-making and applying competences of states. They, too, are competitors in "conflict" cases and must be considered in any inquiry about international jurisdiction. Since states themselves compose the hierarchical or super-ordinated institutions which make and apply these norms, the content of these new international norms may reflect the values and interests of the stronger states.

In modern international politics, non-state entities have also sought to participate in lawmaking and applying. At the law-making level, non-governmental organizations have long initiated and promoted legislative programs. Moreover, explicit and customary arrangements between multinational corporations have been accepted by international tribunals as international law. As long as the application of this non-state law depended upon the action of international or national courts, it could not be considered to be on a par with national law creation, because the institutions of the state, whether courts or legislatures acting internally or in collaboration with other states, retained the competence to review and decide whether particular formulations by non-state entities would be enforced by state power. Now, however, with the expansion of international commercial arbitration, law of non-state origin—the so-called *lex mercatoria*—may be applied by non-state tribunals, in a regime in which the possibilities of control by the judicial apparatus of the state have been considerably attenuated.

After two efforts under the auspices of the League of Nations, the United Nations Convention on the Recognition and Enforcement of International Arbitral Awards has rationalized a system under which private parties may, by agreement, "privatize" dispute resolution for transnational commercial matters, with the role of national courts restricted to supervision of arbitral compliance with essentially formal requirements. Coupled with the growth of *lex mercatoria*, modern arbitration has, in many economic sectors, removed the issue of legislative conflicts of jurisdiction from states and assigned them to a network of private tribunals. While this does not obviate jurisdictional conflicts, it substantially limits the inter-state dimension of this conflict. In this respect, theoretical as well as practical inquiries into the vital sources of the modern international law of jurisdiction must now take account of both state and non-state claims. Nonetheless, the fundamental claims of states for control over key internal processes continue to be both precipitating factors and central concerns of this part of international law.

B. POLICY

1. Myres S. McDougal, *Act of State in Policy Perspective: The International Law of an International Economy* *in* PRIVATE INVESTORS ABROAD: STRUCTURES AND SAFEGUARDS 327 (Virginia Shook Cameron ed., 1966)

The principal function of our inherited international law for the protection of an international economy and private rights has been that of facilitating international cooperation in principles of jurisdiction [that] are, again, of two kinds: first, those which honor or legitimize an initial, first-instance making or application of law by a claimant state which regards itself as substantially affected by certain events; secondly, those which suggest or require that some state which has enough effective control over people or resources to make or apply law for certain events should not assert its own competence but should rather abstain and defer to the prior prescriptions or applications of another state. The responses of states to claims under this second set of principles are sometimes described as "secondary" or "indirect" assertions of competence, in contrast with the initial or "direct" assertions under the first set of principles.

The principles which confer upon states competence to make or prescribe law are those stated, in highest level abstraction, in terms of "territoriality," "nationality," "protection of interests," "passive personality," and "universality of interest." In somewhat lower abstraction, these principles are commonly refined to take into account many different features of any particular context of "contract," "tort," "crime," and "property," such as the plea of making an agreement, the plea of performance or impact, the habitual residence of parties, the physical location of assets, and so on. Taken in sum, these principles confer upon any state the competence to make law for any events by which it is substantially affected. In an interdependent world, in which everything affects everything else and markets and resources are widely distributed, it should not be surprising that such broad grants of competence often confer jurisdiction upon more than one state over the same event. In the absence of "priorities" among principles, it may, further, be emphasized that the "territoriality" principle does not exclude the application by states of any of the other principles.

The principles which confer upon states the competence to apply law (whether their own or that of another state) derive from somewhat different polices. When a claim to apply ("judicial jurisdiction") is asserted, the context is one of immediate adjudication of the rights of immediately identifiable parties in a proceeding uniquely related to them. Considerations of fairness and convenience complement the more general community interest in requiring that account be taken of such factors as the domicile of the parties, the presence of persons and assets within the arena, and consent or submission of the parties to adjudication. The Anglo-Americans and the Europeans formulate the various technical principles by which these factors are taken into account quite differently, and both are inclined to regard the formulations of the other as barbarous.

C. The Struggle for a Constitutional Principle

1. The Case of the S.S. "Lotus"

(Fr. v. Turk.), 1927 P.C.I.J. (Ser. A) No. 10 (Sept. 7)

[In 1926, a collision occurred between a French ship, the Lotus, and a Turkish ship, the Boz-Kourt, in international waters off Turkey. The Boz-Kourt sank and Turkish nationals perished; the Lotus picked up survivors and proceeded to Constantinople, where the French officer of the watch on the Lotus was arrested on a charge of manslaughter. Subsequently, Lieutenant Demons was sentenced to 80 days imprisonment and a fine. Because of differences between France and Turkey as to the propriety of the exercise of Turkish jurisdiction against Lieutenant Demons, the case was referred, by agreement, to the Permanent Court of International Justice. Turkey defended its application of jurisdiction by reference to its Penal Code which provides for Turkish jurisdiction for "any foreigner who … commits an offense abroad to the prejudice of Turkey or the Turkish subject, for which offense Turkish law proscribes a penalty ... provided that he is arrested in Turkey."]

I.

The Court, having to consider whether there are any rules of international law which may have been violated by the prosecution in pursuance of Turkish law of Lieutenant Demons, is confronted in the first place by a question of principle which, in the written and oral arguments of the two Parties, has proved to be a fundamental one. The French Government contends that the Turkish Courts, in order to have jurisdiction, should be able to point to some title to jurisdiction recognized by international law in favour of Turkey. On the other hand, the Turkish Government takes the view that Article 15 allows Turkey jurisdiction whenever such jurisdiction does not come into conflict with a principle of international law.

The latter view seems to be in conformity with the special agreement itself, No. 1 of which asks the Court to say whether Turkey has acted contrary to the principles of international law and, if so, what principles. According to the special agreement, therefore, it is not a question of stating principles which would permit Turkey to take criminal proceedings, but of formulating the principles, if any, which might have been violated by such proceedings.

This way of stating the question is also dictated by the very nature and existing conditions of international law.

International law governs relations between independent States. The rules of law binding upon States therefore emanate from their own free will as expressed in conventions or by usages generally accepted as expressing principles of law and established in order to regulate the relations between these co-existing independent communities or with a view to the achievement of common aims. Restrictions upon the independence of States cannot therefore be presumed.

Now the first and foremost restriction imposed by international law upon a State is that—failing the existence of a permissive rule to the contrary—it may not exercise its power in any form in the territory of another State. In this sense jurisdiction is certainly territorial; it cannot be exercised by a State outside its territory except by virtue of a permissive rule derived from international custom or from a convention.

It does not, however, follow that international law prohibits a State from exercising jurisdiction in its own territory, in respect of any case which relates to acts which have taken place abroad, and in which it cannot rely on some permissive rule of international law. Such a view would only be tenable if international law contained a general prohibition to States to extend the application of their laws and the jurisdiction of their courts to persons, property and acts outside their territory, and if, as an exception to this general prohibition, it allowed States to do so in certain specific cases. But this is certainly not the case under international law as it stands at present. Far from laying down a general prohibition to the effect that States may not extend the application of their laws and the jurisdiction of their courts to persons, property and acts outside their territory, it leaves them in this respect a wide measure of discretion which is only limited in certain cases by prohibitive rules; as regards other cases, every State remains free to adopt the principles which it regards as best and most suitable.

This discretion left to States by international law explains the great variety of rules which they have been able to adopt without objections or complaints on the part of other States; it is in order to remedy the difficulties resulting from such variety that efforts have been made for many years past, both in Europe and America, to prepare conventions the effect of which would be precisely to limit the discretion at present left to States in this respect by international law, thus making good the existing lacuna in respect of jurisdiction or removing the conflicting jurisdictions arising from the diversity of the principles adopted by the various States.

In these circumstances, all that can be required of a State is that it should not overstep the limits which international law places upon its jurisdiction; within these limits, its title to exercise jurisdiction rests in its sovereignty.

It follows from the foregoing that the contention of the French Government to the effect that Turkey must in each case be able to cite a rule of international law authorizing her to exercise jurisdiction is opposed to the generally accepted international law to which Article 15 of the Convention of Lausanne refers. Having regard to the terms of Article 15 and to the construction which the Court has just placed upon it, this contention would apply in regard to civil as well as to criminal cases, and would be applicable on conditions of absolute reciprocity as between Turkey and the other contracting Parties; in practice, it would therefore in many cases result in paralyzing the action of the courts, owing to the impossibility of citing a universally accepted rule on which to support the exercise of their jurisdiction.

Nevertheless, it has to be seen whether the foregoing considerations really apply as regards criminal jurisdiction, or whether this jurisdiction is governed by a different principle: this might be the outcome of the close connection which for a long time existed between the conception of supreme criminal jurisdiction and that of a State, and also by the especial importance of criminal jurisdiction from the point of view of the individual.

Though it is true that in all systems of law the principle of the territorial character of criminal law is fundamental, it is equally true that all or nearly all these systems of law extend their action to offences committed outside the territory of the State which adopts them, and they do so in ways which vary from State to State. The territoriality of criminal law, therefore, is not an absolute principle of international law and by no means coincides with territorial sovereignty.

This situation may be considered from two different standpoints corresponding to the points of view respectively taken up by the Parties. According to one of these standpoints, the principle of freedom, in virtue of which each State may regulate its legislation at its discretion, provided that in so doing it does not come in conflict with a restriction imposed by international law, would also apply as regards law governing the scope of jurisdiction in criminal cases. According to the other standpoint, the exclusively territorial character of law relating to this domain constitutes a principle which, except as otherwise expressly provided, would, *ipso facto,* prevent States from extending the criminal jurisdiction of their courts beyond their frontiers; the exceptions in question, which include for instance extraterritorial jurisdiction over nationals and over crimes directed against public safety, would therefore rest on special permissive rules forming part of international law.

Adopting, for the purposes of the argument, the standpoint of the latter of these two systems, it must be recognized that, in the absence of a treaty provision, its correctness depends upon whether there is a custom having the force of law establishing it. The same is true as regards the applicability of this system—assuming it to have been recognized as sound—in the particular case. It follows that, even from this point of view, before ascertaining whether there may be a rule of international law expressly allowing Turkey to prosecute a foreigner for an offence committed by him outside Turkey, it is necessary to begin by establishing both that the system is well-founded and that it is applicable in the particular case. Now, in order to establish the first of these points, one must, as has just been seen, prove the existence of a principle of international law restricting the discretion of States as regards criminal legislation.

Consequently, whichever of the two systems described above be adopted, the same result will be arrived at in this particular case: the necessity of ascertaining whether or not under international law there is a principle which would have prohibited Turkey, in the circumstances of the case before the Court, from prosecuting Lieutenant Demons. And moreover, on either hypothesis, this must be ascertained by examining precedents offering a close analogy to the case under consideration; for it is only from precedents of this nature that the existence of a general principle applicable to the particular case may appear. For if it were found, for example, that, according to the practice of States, the jurisdiction of the State whose flag was flown was not established by international law as exclusive with regard to collision cases on the high seas, it would not be necessary to ascertain whether there were a more general restriction; since, as regards that restriction—supposing that it existed—the fact that it had been established that there was no prohibition in respect of collision on the high seas would be tantamount to a special permissive rule.

The Court therefore must, in any event, ascertain whether or not there exists a rule of international law limiting the freedom of States to extend the criminal jurisdiction of their courts to a situation uniting the circumstances of the present case.

II.

The Court will now proceed to ascertain whether general international law, to which Article 15 of the Convention of Lausanne refers, contains a rule prohibiting Turkey from prosecuting Lieutenant Demons.

For this purpose, it will in the first place examine the value of the arguments advanced by the French Government, without however omitting to take into account other possible aspects of the problem, which might show the existence of a restrictive rule applicable in this case.

The arguments advanced by the French Government, other than those considered above, are, in substance, the three following:

(1) International law does not allow a State to take proceedings with regard to offences committed by foreigners abroad, simply by reason of the nationality of the victim; and such is the situation in the present case because the offence must be regarded as having been committed on board the French vessel.

(2) International law recognizes the exclusive jurisdiction of the State whose flag is flown as regards everything which occurs on board a ship on the high seas.

(3) Lastly, this principle is especially applicable in a collision case.

As regards the first argument, the Court feels obliged in the first place to recall that its examination is strictly confined to the specific situation in the present case, for it is only in regard to this situation that its decision is asked for.

As has already been observed, the characteristic features of the situation of fact are as follows: there has been a collision on the high seas between two vessels flying different flags, on one of which was one of the persons alleged to be guilty of the offence, whilst the victims were on board the other.

This being so, the Court does not think it necessary to consider the contention that a State cannot punish offences committed abroad by a foreigner simply by reason of the nationality of the victim. For this contention only relates to the case where the nationality of the victim is the only criterion on which the criminal jurisdiction of the State is based. Even if that argument were correct generally speaking—and in regard to this the Court reserves its opinion—it could only be used in the present case if international low forbade Turkey to take into consideration the fact that the offence produced its effects on the Turkish vessel and consequently in a place assimilated to Turkish territory in which the application of Turkish criminal law cannot be challenged, even in regard to offences committed there by foreigners. But no such rule of international law exists. No argument has come to the knowledge of the Court from which it could be deduced that States recognize themselves to be under an obligation towards each other only to have regard to the place where the author of the offence happens to be at the time of the offence. On the contrary, it is certain that the courts of many countries, even of countries which have given their criminal legislation a strictly territorial character, interpret criminal law in the sense that offences, the authors of which at the moment of commission are in the territory of another State, are nevertheless to be regarded as having been committed in the national territory, if one of the constituent elements of the offence, and more especially its effects, have taken place there. French courts have, in regard to a variety of situations, given decisions sanctioning this way of interpreting the territorial principle. Again, the Court does not know of any cases in which governments have protested against the fact that the criminal law of some country contained a rule to this effect or that the courts of a country construed their criminal law in this sense. Consequently, once it is admitted that the effects of the offence were produced on the Turkish vessel, it becomes impossible to hold that there is a rule of international law which prohibits Turkey from prosecuting Lieutenant Demons because of the fact that the author of the offence was on board the French ship. Since, as has already been observed, the special agreement does not deal with the provision of Turkish law under which the prosecution was instituted, but only with the question whether the prosecution should be regarded as contrary to the principles of international law, there is no reason preventing the Court from confining itself to observing that, in this case, a prosecution may also be justified from the point of view of the so-called territorial principle.

Nevertheless, even if the Court had to consider whether Article 6 of the Turkish Penal Code was compatible with international law, and if it held that the nationality of the victim did not in all circumstances constitute a sufficient basis for the exercise of criminal jurisdiction by the State of which the victim was a national, the Court would arrive at the same conclusion for the reasons just set out. For even were Article 6 to be held incompatible with the principles of international law, since the prosecution might have been based on another provision of Turkish law which would not have been contrary to any principle of international law, it follows that it would be impossible to deduce from the mere fact that Article 6 was not in conformity with those principles, that the prosecution itself was contrary to them. The fact that the judicial authorities may have committed an error in their choice of the legal provision applicable to the particular case and compatible with international law only concerns municipal law and can only affect international law in so far as a treaty provision enters into account, or the possibility of a denial of justice arises.

It has been sought to argue that the offence of manslaughter cannot be localized at the spot where the mortal effect is felt; for the effect is not intentional and it cannot be said that there is, in the mind of the delinquent, any culpable intent directed towards the territory where the mortal effect is produced. In reply to this argument it might be observed that the effect is a factor of outstanding importance in offences such as manslaughter, which are punished precisely in consideration of their effects rather than of the subjective intention of the delinquent. But the Court does not feel called upon to consider this question, which is one of interpretation of Turkish criminal law. It will suffice to observe that no argument has been put forward and nothing has been found from which it would follow that international law has established a rule imposing on States this reading of the conception of the offence of manslaughter.

The second argument put forward by the French Government is the principle that the State whose flag is flown has exclusive jurisdiction over everything which occurs on board a merchant ship on the high seas.

It is certainly true that—apart from certain special cases which are defined by international law—vessels on the high seas are subject to no authority except that of the State whose flag they fly. In virtue of the principle of the freedom of the seas, that is to say, the absence of any territorial sovereignty upon the high seas, no State may exercise any kind of jurisdiction over foreign vessels upon them. Thus, if a war vessel, happening to be at the spot where a collision occurs between a vessel flying its flag and a foreign vessel, were to send on board the latter an officer to make investigations or to take evidence, such an act would undoubtedly be contrary to international law.

But it by no means follows that a State can never in its own territory exercise jurisdiction over acts which have occurred on board a foreign ship on the high seas. A corollary of the principle of the freedom of the seas is that a ship on the high seas is assimilated to the territory of the State the flag of which it flies, for, just as in its own territory, that State exercises its authority upon it, and no other State may do so. All that can be said is that by virtue of the principle of the freedom of the seas, a ship is placed in the same position as national territory; but there is nothing to support the claim according to which the rights of the State under whose flag the vessel sails may go farther than the rights which it exercises within its territory properly so called. It follows that what occurs on board a vessel on the high seas must be regarded as if it occurred on the territory of the State whose flag the ship flies. If, therefore, a guilty act committed on the high seas produces its effects on a vessel flying another flag or in foreign territory, the same principles must be applied as if the territories of two different States were concerned, and the conclusion must therefore be drawn that there is no rule of international law prohibiting the State to which the ship on which the effects of the offence have taken place belongs, from regarding the offence as having been committed in its territory and prosecuting, accordingly, the delinquent.

This conclusion could only be overcome if it were shown that there was a rule of customary international law which, going further than the principle stated above, established the exclusive jurisdiction of the State whose flag was flown. The French Government has endeavoured to prove the existence of such a rule, having recourse for this purpose to the teachings of publicists, to decisions of municipal and international tribunals, and especially to conventions which, whilst creating exceptions to the principle of the freedom of the seas by permitting the war and police vessels of a State to exercise a more or less extensive control over the merchant vessels of another State, reserve jurisdiction to the courts of the country whose flag is flown by the vessel proceeded against.

In the Court's opinion, the existence of such a rule has not been conclusively proved.

In the first place, as regards teachings of publicists, and apart from the question as to what their value may be from the point of view of establishing the existence of a rule of customary law, it is no doubt true that all or nearly all writers teach that ships on the high seas are subject exclusively to the jurisdiction of the State whose flag they fly. But the important point is the significance attached by them to this principle; now it does not appear that in general, writers bestow upon this principle a scope differing from or wider than that explained above and which is equivalent to saying that the jurisdiction of a State over vessels on the high seas is the same in extent as its jurisdiction in its own territory. On the other hand, there is no lack of writers who, upon a close study of the special question whether a State can prosecute for offences on board a foreign ship on the high seas, definitely come to the conclusion that such offences must be regarded as if they had been committed in the territory of the State whose flag the ship flies, and that consequently the general rules of each legal system in regard to offences committed abroad are applicable.

In regard to precedents, it should first be observed that, leaving aside the collision cases which will be alluded to later, none of them relates to offences affecting two ships flying the flags of two different countries, and that consequently they are not of much importance in the case before the Court. The case of the *Costa Rica Packet* is no exception, for the [prow] on which the alleged depredations took place was adrift without flag or crew, and this circumstance certainly influenced, perhaps decisively, the conclusion arrived at by the arbitrator.

On the other hand, there is no lack of cases in which a State has claimed a right to prosecute for an offence, committed on board a foreign ship, which it regarded as punishable under its legislation. Thus Great Britain refused the request of the United States for the extradition of John Anderson, a British seaman who had committed homicide on board an American vessel, stating that she did not dispute the jurisdiction of the United States but that she was entitled to exercise hers concurrently. This case, to which others might be added, is relevant in spite of Anderson's British nationality, in order to show that the principle of the exclusive jurisdiction of the country whose flag the vessel flies is not universally accepted.

The cases in which the exclusive jurisdiction of the State whose flag was flown has been recognized would seem rather to have been cases in which the foreign State was interested only by reason of the nationality of the victim, and in which, according to the legislation of that State itself or the practice of its courts, that ground was not regarded as sufficient to authorize prosecution for an offence committed abroad by a foreigner.

Finally, as regards conventions expressly reserving jurisdiction exclusively to the State whose flag is flown, it is not absolutely certain that this stipulation is to be regarded as expressing a general principle of law rather than as corresponding to the extraordinary jurisdiction which these conventions confer on the state-owned ships of a particular country in respect of ships of another country on the high seas. Apart from that, it should be observed that these conventions relate to matters of a particular kind, closely connected with the policing of the seas, such as the slave trade, damage to submarine cables, fisheries, etc., and not to common law offences. Above all it should be pointed out that the offences contemplated by the conventions in question only concern a single ship; it is impossible therefore to make any deduction from them in regard to matters which concern two ships and consequently the jurisdiction of two different States.

The Court therefore has arrived at the conclusion that the second argument put forward by the French Government does not, any more than the first, establish the existence of a rule of international law prohibiting Turkey from prosecuting Lieutenant Demons.

It only remains to examine the third argument advanced by the French Government and to ascertain whether a rule specially applying to collision cases has grown up, according to which criminal proceedings regarding such cases come exclusively within the jurisdiction of the State whose flag is flown.

In this connection, the Agent for the French Government has drawn the Court's attention to the fact that questions of jurisdiction in collision cases, which frequently arise before civil courts, are but rarely encountered in the practice of criminal courts. He deduces from this that, in practice, prosecutions only occur before the courts of the State whose flag is flown and that that circumstance is proof of a tacit consent on the part of States and, consequently, shows what positive international law is in collision cases.

In the Court's opinion, this conclusion is not warranted. Even if the rarity of the judicial decisions to be found among the reported cases were sufficient to prove in point of fact the circumstance alleged by the Agent for the French Government, it would merely show that States had often, in practice, abstained from instituting criminal proceedings, and not that they recognized themselves as being obliged to do so; for only if such abstention were based on their being conscious of having a duty to abstain would it be possible to speak of an international custom. The alleged fact does not allow one to infer that States have been conscious of having such a duty; on the other hand, as will presently be seen, there are other circumstances calculated to show that the contrary is true.

So far as the Court is aware there are no decisions of international tribunals in this matter; but some decisions of municipal courts have been cited. Without pausing to consider the value to be attributed to the judgments of municipal courts in connection with the establishment of the existence of a rule of international law, it will suffice to observe that the decisions quoted sometimes support one view and sometimes the other. …

Lengthy discussions have taken place between the Parties as to the importance of each of these decisions as regards the details of which the Court confines itself to a reference to the Cases and Counter-Cases of the Parties. The Court does not think it necessary to stop to consider them. It will suffice to observe that, as municipal jurisprudence is thus divided, it is hardly possible to see in it an indication of the existence of the restrictive rule of international law which alone could serve as a basis for the contention of the French Government.

On the other hand, the Court feels called upon to lay stress upon the fact that it does not appear that the States concerned have objected to criminal proceedings in respect of collision cases before the courts of a country other than that the flag of which was flown, or that they have made protests: their conduct does not appear to have differed appreciably from that observed by them in all cases of concurrent jurisdiction. This fact is directly opposed to the existence of a tacit consent on the part of States to the exclusive jurisdiction of the State whose flag is flown, such as the Agent for the French Government has thought it possible to deduce from the infrequency of questions of jurisdiction before criminal courts. It seems hardly probable, and it would not be in accordance with international practice, that the French Government … would have omitted to protest against the exercise of criminal jurisdiction by the Italian and Belgian Courts, if they had really thought that this was a violation of international law. …

In support of the theory in accordance with which criminal jurisdiction in collision cases would exclusively belong to the State of the flag flown by the ship, it has been contended that it is a question of the observance of the national regulations of each merchant marine and that effective punishment does not consist so much in the infliction of some months' imprisonment upon the captain as in the cancellation of his certificate as master, that is to say, in depriving him of the command of his ship.

In regard to this, the Court must observe that in the present case a prosecution was instituted for an offence at criminal law and not for a breach of discipline. Neither the necessity of taking administrative regulations into account (even ignoring the circumstance that it is a question of uniform regulations adopted by States as a result of an international conference) nor the impossibility of applying certain disciplinary penalties can prevent the application of criminal law and of penal measures of repression.

The conclusion at which the Court has therefore arrived is that there is no rule of international law in regard to collision cases to the effect that criminal proceedings are exclusively within the jurisdiction of the State whose flag is flown.

This conclusion moreover is easily explained if the manner in which the collision brings the jurisdiction of two different countries into play be considered.

The offence for which Lieutenant Demons appears to have been prosecuted was an act—of negligence or imprudence—having its origin on board the *Lotus,* whilst its effects made themselves felt on board the *Boz-Kourt.* These two elements are, legally, entirely inseparable, so much so that their separation renders the offence non-existent. Neither the exclusive jurisdiction of either State, nor the limitations of the jurisdiction of each to the occurrences which took place on the respective ships would appear calculated to satisfy the requirements of justice and effectively to protect the interests of the two States. It is only natural that each should be able to exercise jurisdiction and to do so in respect of the incident as a whole. It is therefore a case of concurrent jurisdiction.

The Court, having arrived at the conclusion that the arguments advanced by the French Government either are irrelevant to the issue or do not establish the existence of a principle of international law precluding Turkey from instituting the prosecution which was in fact brought against Lieutenant Demons, observes that in the fulfilment of its task of itself ascertaining what the international law is, it has not confined itself to a consideration of the arguments put forward, but has included in its researches all precedents, teachings and facts to which it had access and which might possibly have revealed the existence of one of the principles of international law contemplated in the special agreement. The result of these researches has not been to establish the existence of any such principle. It must therefore be held that there is no principle of international law, within the meaning of Article 15 of the Convention of Lausanne of July 24th, 1923, which precludes the institution of the criminal proceedings under consideration. Consequently, Turkey, by instituting, in virtue of the discretion which international law leaves to every sovereign State, the criminal proceedings in question, has not, in the absence of such principles, acted in a manner contrary to the principles of international law within the meaning of the special agreement.

[The Court was equally divided and decision was reached by the President's casting vote. The Court decided that Turkey had not acted in conflict with the principles of international law.]

NOTES AND QUESTIONS

1. In many ways, the Permanent Court in *Lotus* evaded a decision by developing a theory that is entirely permissive, and that frequently produces a "concurrent" jurisdictional finding. Does this serve the interest of the international community? If you think that it disserves the interest of the international community, why would the International Court have selected such an approach when the opportunity was presented to establish a clear allocation of competence in matters like these?

2. Shortly after *Lotus* was decided, the law with respect to maritime jurisdiction was changed. In 1929, the International Association of Mercantile Marine Officers questioned the judgment in a communication to the League of Nations. International Maritime Committee conferences in 1930 and 1933, as well as 1940 Montevideo Conference, debated the issue. The 1940 conference ultimately adopted a treaty on International Penal Law, article 8 of which read: "crimes committed on the high seas, whether on board airplanes, men-of-war or merchant ships, must be tried and punished according to the law of the State whose flag the vessel flies." Article 11 of the 1958 Geneva Convention on the High Seas gave jurisdiction either to the flag State or the State of nationality of the accused, while Article 1 of the 1952 Brussels Convention gives jurisdiction only to the flag State. *See* C. JOHN COLOMBOS, THE INTERNATIONAL LAW OF THE SEA 306-07 (6th ed., David McKay Co. 1967); Philip C. Jessup, *The Growth of the Law*, 29 AM. J. INT'L L. 495 (1935).

3. The 1982 Law of the Sea Convention introduces a number of changes with respect to the *Lotus* theory of jurisdiction for events on ships. *See supra* Part Four.

4. In *Legality of the Threat or Use of Nuclear Weapons*, 1996 I.C.J. 226 (July 8)), the International Court of Justice addressed the issue raised in the *Lotus* as follows:

> 20. The Court must next address certain matters arising in relation to the formulation of the question put to it by the General Assembly. The English text asks: "Is the threat or use of nuclear weapons in any circumstance permitted under international law?" ... It was suggested that the Court was being asked by the General Assembly whether it was permitted to have recourse to nuclear weapons in every circumstance, and it was contended that such a question would inevitably invite a simple negative answer...
>
> 21. The use of the word "permitted" in the question put by the General Assembly was criticized before the Court by certain States on the ground that this implied that the threat or the use of nuclear weapons would only be permissible if authorization could be found in a treaty provision or in customary international law. Such a starting point, those States submitted, was incompatible with the very basis of international law, which rests upon the principles of sovereignty and consent; accordingly, and contrary to what was implied by use of the word "permitted", States are free to threaten or use nuclear weapons unless it can be shown that they are bound not to do so by reference to a prohibition in either treaty law or customary international law. Support for this contention was found in dicta of the Permanent Court of International Justice in the "Lotus" case that "restrictions upon the independence of States cannot ... be presumed" and that international law leaves to States "a wide measure of discretion which is only limited in certain cases by prohibitive rules" (P.C.I.J., Series A, No. 10, pp. 18 and 19). Reliance was also placed

on the dictum of the present Court in the case concerning Military and Paramilitary Activities in and against Nicaragua (Nicaragua v. United States of America) that:

> [i]n international law there are no rules, other than such rules as may be accepted by the State concerned, by treaty or otherwise, whereby the level of armaments of a sovereign State can be limited (I.C.J. Reports 1986, p. 135, para. 269).

For other States, the invocation of these dicta in the "Lotus" case was inapposite; their status in contemporary international law and applicability in the very different circumstances of the present case were challenged. It was also contended that the above-mentioned dictum of the present Court was directed to the possession of armaments and was irrelevant to the threat or use of nuclear weapons.

Finally, it was suggested that, were the Court to answer the question put by the Assembly, the word "permitted" should be replaced by "prohibited".

22. The Court notes that the nuclear-weapon States appearing before it either accepted, or did not dispute, that their independence to act was indeed restricted by the principles and rules of international law, more particularly humanitarian law, as did the other States which took part in the proceedings.

Hence, the argument concerning the legal conclusions to be drawn from the use of the word "permitted", and the questions of burden of proof to which it was said to give rise, are without particular significance for the disposition of the issues before the Court.

5. The *Lotus* opinion was considered critical in the separate opinion of Judges Higgins, Kooijmans and Buergenthal in the *Arrest Warrant* case. For discussion of this case, see *infra* at 1479-1494.

II. Competence to Make Law

A. The Problem

What if any, are the legal limits to national law-making competences with respect to both internal and external people, events, and things? To what extent does the international community impose such restrictions or impose obligations with respect to the reach and content of the national law?

1. Island of Palmas Case (U.S. v. Neth.)

2 R.I.A.A. 829 (1928)

[For the facts of this case, *see supra*, Part Four at 748.]

MAX HUBER, Arbitrator:

Territorial sovereignty, as has already been said, involves the exclusive right to display the activities of a State. This right has as corollary a duty: the obligation to protect within the territory the rights of other States, in particular their right to integrity and inviolability in peace and in war, together with the rights which each State may claim for its nationals in foreign territory. Without manifesting its territorial sovereignty in a manner corresponding to circumstances, the State cannot fulfill this duty. Territorial sovereignty cannot limit itself to its negative side, i.e. to excluding the activities of other States; for it serves to divide between nations the space upon which human activities are employed, in order to assure them at all points the minimum of protection of which international law is the guardian.

B. POLICY

1. W. MICHAEL REISMAN, JURISDICTION IN INTERNATIONAL LAW
xiv, xiv-xv (Ashgate 1999)

The demands for autonomy of each territorial community, however it may be organized, continue to be the predicate and driving force of the system of international jurisdiction. The crisis in the law of jurisdiction is to be found in the increasing number of conflicts, as well as in the advent of different types of conflicts. World-wide communications and movements of persons, goods and services and the resultant economic links have created new interdependences. This has meant more jurisdictional conflicts, some of which present special problems. In more and more social sectors, activities that cross borders can no longer be regulated effectively by the parts of the state apparatus that have been responsible for them. Whether it is health, criminal activity, including terrorism and other forms of purposive political violence, economic organization, immigration or border control, protection of intellectual and material property—whatever—the state, acting alone, seems less and less able to accomplish what is expected of it without locking itself into increasingly complex and durable inter-governmental arrangements. Each of these arrangements requires some yielding of national competence.

With this growth of transnational activity, the relevance, *raison d'être* and future of the state and the consequent law of international jurisdiction have been brought into question. But hold the funerary crepe. Anticipation of the demise of the state is premature. The exclusive territorial community, to which the individual accords and insists that others accord primary loyalty, is neither an atavistic nor transient nor pathological phenomenon. It is, rather, a response to a persisting set of human demands. There are cogent, "rational" reasons why human beings stubbornly continue to organize themselves in exclusive rather than the most inclusive of groups, why group boundaries are "a functional necessity, not simply an inert artifact of primordial cultural identities." As Professor Snyder has observed:

> According to collective action theory, successful groups need to establish clear boundaries. Groups producing collective goods, such as defense and economic infrastructure, need boundaries in order to exclude non-contributors and to identify outsiders who might act opportunistically in transactions with group members. They also need boundaries to prevent crowding, which would diminish the value of membership in the club: tribes keep strangers from crowding their scarce land, and the

> United States bars access to immigrants seeking high wages. In addition, boundaries may help to limit commitments to people whose contributions to the collective good would be outweighed by the cost of defending them.

Jack Snyder, "Civic versus Ethnic Nation-Building: A Collective-Action Approach," unpublished paper read at Yale University on February 14, 1994 at p. 17.

Claims of states for law making and law applying competences sufficient to protect the various social and economic processes that render each of them viable will remain a continuing source of conflict and efforts at securing their resolution a common feature of international politics.

2. Timberlane Lumber Co. v. Bank of America, N.T. & S.A.

549 F.2d 597 (9th Cir. 1976)

[Timberlane Lumber company, an Oregon partnership owning the Honduran corporations Danli Industrial and Maya Lumber and engaged in milling operations for the production of export lumber in Honduras, sued Bank of America and others in Federal Court in California for conspiring to exclude Timberlane and its companies from Honduras.]

CHOY, CIRCUIT JUDGE:

The conspiracy sketched by Timberlane actually started before the plaintiffs entered the scene. The Lima family operated a lumber mill in Honduras, competing with Lamas and Casanova, in both of which the Bank had significant financial interests. The Lima enterprise was also indebted to the Bank. By 1971, however, the Lima business was in financial trouble. Timberlane alleges that driving Lima under was the first step in the conspiracy which eventually crippled Timberlane's efforts, but the particulars do not matter for this appeal. What does matter is that various interests in the Lima assets, including its milling plant, passed to Lima's creditors: Casanova, the Bank, and the group of Lima employees who had not been paid the wages and severance pay due them. Under Honduran law, the employees' claim had priority.

Enter Timberlane, with a long history in the lumber business, in search of alternative sources of lumber for delivery to its distribution system on the East Coast of the United States. After study, it decided to try Honduras. In 1971, Danli was formed, tracts of forest land were acquired, plans for a modern log-processing plant we prepared, and equipment was purchased and assembled for shipment from the United States to Danli in Honduras. Timberlane became aware that the Lima plant might be available and began negotiating for its acquisition. Maya was formed, purchased the Lima employees' interest in the machinery and equipment in January 1972, despite opposition from the conspirators, and reactivated and [sic] the Lima mill.

Realizing that they were faced with better-financed and more vigorous competition from Timberlane and its Honduran subsidiaries, the defendants and others extended the anti-Lima conspiracy to disrupt Timberlane's efforts. The primary weapons employed by the conspirators were the claim still held by the Bank in the remaining assets of the Lima enterprise under the all-inclusive mortgage Lima had been forced to sign and another claim held by Casanova. Maya made a substantial cash offer for the Bank's interest in an effort to clear its title, but the Bank refused to sell. Instead, the Bank surreptitiously conveyed the mortgage to Casanova for questionable consideration, Casanova paying nothing and agreeing only to pay the Bank a portion of what it collected. Casanova immediately assigned the Bank's claim and its own on similar terms to Caminals, who promptly set out to disrupt the Timberlane operation.

Caminals is characterized as the "front man" in the campaign to drive Timberlane out of Honduras, with the Bank and other defendants intending and carrying responsibility for his actions. Having acquired the claims of Casanova and the Bank, Caminals went to court to enforce them, ignoring throughout Timberlane's offers to purchase or settle them. Under the laws of Honduras, an "embargo" on property is a court-ordered attachment, registered with the Public Registry, which precludes the sale of that property without a court order. Honduran law provides, upon embargo, that the court appoint a judicial officer, called an "interventor" to ensure against any diminution in the value of the property. In order to paralyze the Timberlane operation, Caminals obtained embargoes against Maya and Danli. Acting through the interventor, since accused of being on the payroll of the Bank, guards and troops were used to cripple and, for a time, completely shut down Timberlane's milling operation. The harassment took other forms as well: the conspirators caused the manager of Timberlane's Honduras operations, Gordon Sloan Smith, to be falsely arrested and imprisoned and were responsible for the publication of several defamatory articles about Timberlane in the Honduran press.

As a result of the conspiracy, Timberlane's complaint claimed damages then estimated in excess of $5,000,000. Plaintiffs also allege that there has been a direct and substantial effect on United States foreign commerce, and that defendants intended the results of the conspiracy, including the impact on United States commerce.

Act of State

The classic enunciation of the act of state doctrine is found in *Underhill v. Hernandez*, 168 U.S. 250, 252:

> Every sovereign State is bound to respect the independence of every other sovereign State, and the courts of one county will not sit in judgment on the acts of the government of another done within its own territory.

From the beginning, this principle has been applied in foreign trade antitrust cases. In *American Banana Co. v. United Fruit Co.*, 213 U.S. 347 (1909), the first such case of significance, the American owner of a banana plantation caught in a border dispute between Panama and Costa Rica claimed that competitors violated the Sherman Act by persuading the Costa Rican government to seize his lands. The act complained of would have required an adjudication of the legality of the Costa Rican seizure, an action which the Supreme Court said our courts could not challenge. More recently, see *Occidental Petroleum Corp. v. Buttes Gas & Oil Co.*, 331 F. Supp. 92 (C.D.Cal.1971), *affirmed* 461 F.2d 1261 (9th Cir.), *cert. denied*, 409 U.S. 950 (1972), the case mentioned from the bench by the district court here in ruling in favor of the defense motion to dismiss.

The defendants argue—as the district court apparently held—that the injuries allegedly suffered by Timberlane resulted from acts of the Honduran government, principally in connection with the enforcement of the security interests in the Maya plant, which American courts cannot review. Such an application of the act of state doctrine seems to us to be erroneous. Even if the *coup de grace* to Timberlane's enterprise in Honduras was applied by official authorities, we do not agree that the doctrine necessarily shelters these defendants or requires dismissal of the Timberlane action.

The leading modern statement of the act of state doctrine appears in *Banco Nacional de Cuba v. Sabbatino*, 376 U.S. 398 (1964). Despite contrary implications in *Underhill* and *American Banana*, the Court concluded that the doctrine was not compelled by the nature of sovereignty, by international law, or by the text of the Constitution. 376 U.S. at 421-23. Rather, it derives from the judiciary's concern for its possible interference with the conduct of foreign affairs by the political branches of the government ... The Court recognized that not every case is identical in its potential impact on our relations with other nations. ... Thus the Court explicitly rejected "laying down or reaffirming an inflexible and all-encompassing rule." *Id.* Whether forbearance by an American court in a given situation is advisable or appropriate depends upon the "balance of relevant considerations." *Id.*

It is apparent that the doctrine does not bestow a blank-check immunity upon a conduct blessed with some imprimatur of a foreign government. In *Continental Ore Co. v. Union Carbide & Carbon Corp.*, 370 U.S. 690 (1962), the Canadian government had made a private corporation its exclusive agent for the purchase of vanadium, a material used in steel production. The Canadian corporation, acting in concert with an affiliated American company, used its position to exclude a competitor of the American affiliate from the Canadian market. The Court held that the Canadian corporation's activity was not entitled to immunity, carefully noting that the plaintiff did not question the validity of any action taken by the Canadian government and that there was no indication that any Canadian government official "approved or would have approved" of the monopolizing efforts. *Id.* at 706.

In *Alfred Dunhill of London, Inc. v. The Republic of Cuba*, 425 U.S. 682 (1976), … the Court … [refused] to conclude that "the conduct in question was the public act of those with authority to exercise sovereign authority and was entitled to respect in our courts." *Id.* at 694. There was no proof that the failure of the interventors to repay the money reached the level of an "act of state," a sovereign assertion of the Cuban government. …

A corollary to the act of state doctrine in the foreign trade antitrust field is the often-recognized principle that corporate conduct which is compelled by a foreign sovereign is also protected from antitrust liability, as if it were an act of the state itself. Thus, in *Interamerican Refining Corp. v. Texaco Maracaibo, Inc.*, 307 F. Supp. 1291 (D. Del.1970), a refusal by defendants to sell Venezuelan crude oil to plaintiff was held not to be an illegal restraint of trade because it was a complete defense that the Venezuelan government had imposed a boycott forbidding such sales. The court there observed that "[w]hen a nation compels a trade practice, firms there have no choice but to obey. Acts of business become effectively acts of the sovereign." *Id.* at 1298.

On the other hand, mere governmental approval or foreign governmental involvement which the defendants had arranged does not necessarily provide a defense. In *U.S. v. Sisal Sales Corp.*, 274 U.S. 268 (1927), the defendants were accused of conspiring to monopolize sales of sisal, a material used in making rope, from Mexico to the United States by inducing Mexican officials to recognize the conspirators as the exclusive traders and to impose discriminatory taxes on rival sellers. The Court rejected the defendants' claim to act of state protection, ruling that a conspiracy formed in the United States for the purpose of monopolizing sales to the United States was not protected simply because one element of the conspiracy involved securing favorable action by foreign officials. In *Continental Ore*, the Court indicated that it continued to accept the *Sisal* reasoning. *See* 370 U.S. at 705.

The distinction was recognized and relied upon in *U.S. v. The Watchmakers of Switzerland Information Center, Inc.*, 1963 Trade Cases (S.D.N.Y.1962), *order modified,* 1965 Trade Cases (S.D.N.Y.1965), the "*Swiss Watch*" case:

> If, of course, the defendants' activities had been required by Swiss law, this court could indeed do nothing. An American court would have under such circumstances no right to condemn the governmental activity of another sovereign nation. In the present case, however, the defendants' activities were not required by the laws of Switzerland. They were agreements formulated privately without compulsion on the part of the Swiss Government. It is clear that these private agreements were then recognized as facts of economic and industrial life by that nation's government. Nonetheless, the fact that the Swiss Government may, as a practical matter, approve of the effects of this private activity cannot convert what is essentially a vulnerable private conspiracy into an unassailable system resulting from foreign governmental mandate. …

The touchstone of *Sabbatino*—the potential for interference with our foreign relations—is the crucial element in determining whether deference should be accorded in any given case. We wish to avoid "passing on the validity" of foreign acts. ... Similarly, we do not wish to challenge the sovereignty of another nation, the wisdom of its policy, or the integrity and motivation of its action. On the other hand, repeating the terms of *Sabbatino, id.* at 428, "the less important the implications of an issue are for our foreign relations, the weaker the justification for exclusivity in the political branches."

While we do not wish to impugn or question the nobility of a foreign nation's motivation, we are necessarily interested in the depth and nature of its interest. The Restatement (Second) of Foreign Relations Law of the United States § 41 (1965) makes an important distinction on this basis in limiting the deference of American courts:

> [A] court in the United States ... will refrain from examining the validity of an act of a foreign state by which that state has exercised its jurisdiction *to give effect to its public interests*. [*Emphasis added.*]

The "public interest" qualification is intentional and significant in the context of Timberlane's action, as a comment to § 41 makes plain:

> *Comment d. Nature of act of state*. An "act of state" as the term is used in this Title involves the public interests of a state as a state, as distinct from its interest in providing the means of adjudicating disputes or claims that arise within its territory. ... A judgment of a court may be an act of state. Usually it is not, because it involves the interests of private litigants or because court adjudication is not the usual way in which state exercises its jurisdiction to give e feet to public interests. *Id.* at 127.

On the basis of the foregoing analysis, we conclude that the court below erred in dismissing the instant suit on the authority of *Occidental Petroleum Corp. v. Buttes Gas & Oil Co.*, 331 F. Supp. 92, 108-13 (C.D.Cal.1971), *aff'd,* 461 F.2d 1261 (9th Cir.) *cert. denied*, 409 U.S. 950 (1972). The actions of the Honduran government that are involved here—including the application by its court and their agents of the Honduran laws concerning security interests and the protection of the underlying property against diminution—are clearly distinguishable from the sovereign decrees laying claim to off-shore waters that were at issue in *Occidental Petroleum,* ... at 99-101 & n.11. Here, the allegedly "sovereign" acts of Honduras consisted of judicial proceedings which were initiated by Caminals, a private party and one of the alleged co-conspirators, not by the Honduran government itself. Unlike the *Occidental Petroleum* plaintiffs, *see id* at 110, Timberlane does not seek to name Honduras or any Honduran officer as a defendant or co-conspirator, nor does it challenge Honduran policy or sovereignty in any fashion that appears on its face to hold any threat to relations between Honduras and the United States. In fact, there is no indication that the actions of the Honduran court and authorities reflected a sovereign decision that Timberlane's efforts should be crippled or that trade with the United States should be restrained. ... Moreover, and once again unlike the situation in *Occidental Petroleum*, ... plaintiffs here apparently complain of additional agreements and actions which are totally unrelated to the Honduran government. These separate activities would clearly be unprotected even if procurement of a Honduran act of state were one part of defendants' overall scheme. ...

Under these circumstances, it is clear that the "act of state" doctrine does not require dismissal of the Timberlane action.

Extraterritorial Reach of the United States Antitrust Laws

There is no doubt that American antitrust laws extend over some conduct in other nations. There was language in the first Supreme Court case on point, *American Banana Co. v. United Fruit Co.,* 213 U.S. 347 (1909), casting doubt on the extension of the Sherman Act to acts outside United States territory. But subsequent cases have limited *American Banana* to its particular facts, and the Sherman Act—and with it other antitrust laws—has been applied to extraterritorial conduct. ...The act may encompass the foreign activities of aliens as well as American citizens. ...

That American law covers some conduct beyond this nation's borders does not mean that it embraces all, however. Extraterritorial application is understandably a matter of concern for the other countries involved. Those nations have sometimes resented and protested, as excessive intrusions into their own spheres, broad assertions of authority by American courts. ... Our courts have recognized this concern and have, at times, responded to it, even if not always enough to satisfy all the foreign critics. ... In any event, it is evident that at some point the interests of the United States are too weak and the foreign harmony incentive for restraint too strong to justify an extraterritorial assertion of jurisdiction.

What that point is or how it is determined is not defined by international law. ... Nor does the Sherman Act limit itself. In the domestic field the Sherman Act extends to the full reach of the commerce power. ... To define it somewhat more modestly in the foreign commerce area courts have generally, and logically, fallen back on a narrower construction of congressional intent, such as expressed in Judge Learned Hand's oft-cited opinion in *Alcoa,* 148 F.2d at 443:

> [T]he only question open is whether Congress intended to impose the liability and whether our own Constitution permitted it to do so: as a court of the United States we cannot look beyond our own law. Nevertheless, it is quite true that we are not to read general words, such as those in this Act, without regard to the limitations customarily observed by nations upon the exercise of their powers; limitations which generally correspond to those fixed by the "Conflict of Laws.' We should not impute to Congress an intent to punish all whom its courts can catch, for conduct which has no consequences within the United States.

It is the effect on American foreign commerce which is usually cited to support extraterritorial jurisdiction. *Alcoa* set the course, when Judge Hand declared:

> [I]t is settled law ... that any state may impose liabilities, even upon persons not within its allegiance, for conduct outside its borders that has consequences within its borders which the state reprehends; and these liabilities other states will ordinarily recognize. *Id.*

Despite its description as "settled law," *Alcoa*'s assertion has been roundly disputed by many foreign commentators as being in conflict with international law, comity, and good judgment. Nonetheless, American courts have firmly concluded that there is some extraterritorial jurisdiction under the Sherman Act.

Even among American courts and commentators, however, there is no consensus on how far the jurisdiction should extend. The district court here concluded that a "direct and substantial effect" on United States foreign commerce was a prerequisite, without stating whether other factors were relevant or considered. The same formula was employed, to some extent, by the district courts in the *Swiss Watch* case, 1963 Trade Cases, in *U.S. v. R. P. Oldham Co.*, 152 F.Supp. 818, 822 (N.D. Cal.1957), and in *General Electric,* 82 F.Supp. at 891. It has been identified and advocated by several commentators. ...

Other courts have used different expressions, however. ... ("the combination affected the foreign commerce of this country"); ... (" intended to affect imports and exports [and] ... is shown actually to have had some effect on them"); ... ("a conspiracy ... which affects American commerce"); ... ("a direct and influencing effect on trade"). ...

Different standards have been urged by other commentators. Julian von Kalinowski ... advocates a "direct *or* substantial" effect test—"any effect that is not *both* insubstantial and indirect" should support jurisdiction, a view that was adopted by the district court in *Occidental Petroleum v. Buttes Gas & Oil Co.,* 331 F. Supp. 92, 102-03 (C.D.Cal.1971), *affirmed on other grounds,* 461 F.2d 1261 (9th Cir.), *cert. denied,* 409 U.S. 950 (1972). James Rahl turns away from a flat requirement of effects by concluding that the Sherman Act should reach a restraint either "(1) if it occurs *in the course of* foreign commerce, *or* (2) if it *substantially affects* either foreign or interstate commerce." Rahl, *Foreign Commerce Jurisdiction of the American Antitrust Laws*, 43 ANTITRUST L.J. 521, 523 (1974). In essence, as Dean Rahl observes, "[t]here is no agreed black-letter rule articulating the Sherman Act's commerce coverage" in the international context. *Id.*

Few cases have discussed the nature of the effect required for jurisdiction, perhaps because most of the litigated cases have involved relatively obvious offenses and rather significant and apparent effects on competition within the United States. ... It is probably in part because the standard has not often been put to a real test that it seems so poorly defined. William Fugate, who has identified the "direct and substantial" standard as the rule, has described the meaning of that phrase as being "quite broad." ... What the threshold of significance is, however, has not been identified. Nor is it quite clear what the "direct-indirect" distinction is supposed to mean. It might well be, as was said in the context of transnational securities regulation:

> Although courts have spoken in terms of the *Restatement* and of congressional policy, findings that an American effect was direct, substantial, and foreseeable, or within the scope of congressional intent, have little independent analytic significance. Instead, cases appear to turn on a reconciliation of American and foreign interests in regulating their respective economies and business affairs. ...

Note, *American Adjudication of Transnational Securities Fraud*, 89 HARV.L.REV. 563, 563 (1976).

> Implicit in that observation, as it is in several of the cases and commentaries employing the "effects" test, is the suggestion that factors other than simply the effect on the United States are weighed, and rightly so. As former Attorney General (then Professor) Katzenbach observed, the effect on American commerce is not, by itself, sufficient information on which to base a decision that the United States is the nation primarily interested in the activity causing the effect. "[A]nything that affects the external trade and commerce of the United States also affects the trade and commerce of other nations, and may have far greater consequences for others than for the United States." Katzenbach, *Conflicts on an Unruly Horse*, 65 YALE L.J. 1087, 1150 (1956).

The effects test by itself is incomplete because it fails to consider other nations' interests. Nor does it expressly take into account the full nature of the relationship between the actors and this country. Whether the alleged offender is an American citizen, for instance, may make a big difference; applying America's laws to American citizens raises fewer problems than application to foreigners. As was observed in *Pacific Seafarers, Inc. v. Pacific Far East Line, Inc.*, 404 F.2d 804, 815 (1968), *cert. denied,* 393 U.S. 1093 (1969):

> If ... [American antitrust] policy cannot extend to the full sweep of American foreign commerce because of the international complications involved, then surely the test which determines whether United States law is applicable must focus on the nexus between the parties and their practices and the United States, not on the mechanical circumstances of effect on commodity exports or imports.

American courts have, in fact, often displayed a regard for comity and the prerogatives of other nations and considered their interests as well as other parts of the factual circumstances, even when professing to apply an effects test. To some degree, the requirement for a "substantial" effect may silently incorporate these additional considerations, with "substantial" as a flexible standard that varies with other factors. The intent requirement suggested by *Alcoa,* 148 F.2d at 443-44, is one example of an attempt to broaden the court's perspective, as is drawing a distinction between American citizens and non-citizens.

The failure to articulate these other elements in addition to the standard effects analysis is costly, however, for it is more likely that they will be overlooked or slighted in interpreting past decisions and reaching new ones. Placing emphasis on the qualification that effects be "substantial" is also risky, for the term has a meaning in the interstate antitrust context which does not encompass all the factors relevant to the foreign trade case.

Indeed, that "substantial effects" element of interstate antitrust analysis may well be responsible for the use of an effects test for foreign commerce. The Sherman Act reaches restraints directly intended to limit the flow of interstate trade or whose sole impact is on interstate commerce, but it also reaches "wholly local business restraints" if the particular restraint "substantially and adversely affects interstate commerce." ... Such a test is necessary in the interstate context to separate the restraints which fall within the federal ambit under the interstate commerce clause from those which, as purely intrastate burdens, remain the province of the states. ... Since, however, no comparable constitutional problem exists in defining the scope of congressional power to regulate *foreign* commerce, it may be unwise blindly to apply the "substantiality" test to the international setting. ... Only respect for the role of the executive and for international notions of comity and fairness limit that constitutional grant.

A tripartite analysis seems to be indicated. As acknowledged above, the antitrust laws require in the first instance that there be some effect—actual or intended—on American foreign commerce before the federal courts may legitimately exercise subject matter jurisdiction under those statutes. Second, a greater showing of burden or restraint may be necessary to demonstrate that the effect is sufficiently large to present a cognizable injury to the plaintiffs and, therefore, a civil *violation* of the antitrust laws. ... Third, there is the additional question which is unique to the international setting of whether the interests of, and links to, the United States—including the magnitude of the effect on American foreign commerce are sufficiently strong, vis-à-vis those of other nations, to justify an assertion of extraterritorial authority.

It is this final issue which is both obscured by undue reliance on the "substantiality" test and complicated to resolve. An effect on United States commerce, although necessary to the exercise of jurisdiction under the antitrust laws, is alone not a sufficient basis on which to determine whether American authority *should* be asserted in a given case as a matter of international comity and fairness. In some cases, the application of the direct and substantial test in the international context might open the door too widely by sanctioning jurisdiction over an action when these considerations would indicate dismissal. At other times, it may fail in the other direction, dismissing a case for which comity and fairness do not require forbearance, thus closing the jurisdictional door too tightly—for the Sherman Act does reach some restraints which do not have both a direct and substantial effect on the foreign commerce of the United States. A more comprehensive inquiry is necessary. We believe that the field of conflict of laws presents the proper approach, as was suggested, if not specifically employed, in 5*Alcoa* in expressing the basic limitation on application of American laws:

> [W]e are not to read general words, such as those in this Act, without regard to the limitations customarily observed by nations upon the exercise of their powers; limitations which generally correspond to those fixed by the "Conflict of Laws."

148 F.2d at 443. The same idea is reflected in Restatement (Second) of Foreign Relations Law of the United States § 40:

> Where two states have jurisdiction to prescribe and enforce rules of law and the rules they may prescribe require inconsistent conduct upon the part of a person, each state is required by international law to consider, in good faith, moderating the exercise of its enforcement jurisdiction. …

The act of state doctrine discussed earlier demonstrates that the judiciary is sometimes cognizant of the possible foreign implications of its action. Similar awareness should be extended to the general problems of extraterritoriality. Such acuity is especially required in private suits, like this one, for in these cases there is no opportunity for the executive branch to weigh the foreign relations impact, nor any statement implicit in the filing of the suit that that consideration has been outweighed.

What we prefer is an evaluation and balancing of the relevant considerations in each case—in the words of Kingman Brewster, a "jurisdictional rule of reason." Balancing of the foreign interests involved was the approach taken by the Supreme Court in *Continental Ore Co. v. Union Carbide Carbon Co.,* 370 U.S. 690 (1962), where the involvement of the Canadian government in the alleged monopolization was held not to require dismissal. The Court stressed that there was no indication that the Canadian authorities approved or would have approved of the monopolization, meaning that the Canadian interest, if any, was slight and was outweighed by the American interest in condemning the restraint. Similarly, in *Lauritzen v. Larsen,* 345 U.S. 571 (1953), the Court used a like approach in declining to apply the Jones Act to a Danish seaman, injured in Havana on a Danish ship, although he had signed on to the ship in New York.

The elements to be weighed include the degree of conflict with foreign law or policy, the nationality or allegiance of the parties and the locations or principal places of business of corporations, the extent to which enforcement by either state can be expected to achieve compliance, the relative significance of effects on the United States as compared with those elsewhere, the extent to which there is explicit purpose to harm or affect American commerce, the foreseeability of such effect, and the relative importance to the violations charged of conduct within the United States as compared with conduct abroad. A court evaluating these factors should identify the potential degree of conflict if American authority is asserted. A difference in law or policy is one likely sore spot, though one which may not always be present. Nationality is another; though foreign governments may have some concern for the treatment of American citizens and business residing there, they primarily care about their own nationals. Having assessed the conflict, the court should then determine whether in the face of it the contacts and interests of the United States are sufficient to support the exercise of extraterritorial jurisdiction.

We conclude, then, that the problem should be approached in three parts: Does the alleged restraint affect, or was it intended to affect, the foreign commerce of the United States? Is it of such a type and magnitude so as to be cognizable as a violation of the Sherman Act? As a matter of international comity and fairness, should the extraterritorial jurisdiction of the United States be asserted to cover it? The district court's judgment found only that the restraint involved in the instant suit did not produce a direct and substantial effect on American foreign commerce. That holding does not satisfy any of these inquiries.

The Sherman Act is not limited to trade restraints which have both a direct and substantial effect on our foreign commerce. Timberlane has alleged that the complained of activities were intended to, and did, affect the export of lumber from Honduras to the United States—the flow of United States foreign commerce, and as such they are within the jurisdiction of the federal courts under the Sherman Act. Moreover, the magnitude of the effect alleged would appear to be sufficient to state a claim.

The comity question is more complicated. From Timberlane's complaint it is evident that there are grounds for concern as to at least a few of the defendants, for some are identified as foreign citizens: Laureano Gutierrez Falla, Michael Casanova and the Casanova firms, of Honduras and Patrick Byrne, of Canada. Moreover, it is clear that most of the activity took place in Honduras, though the conspiracy may have been directed from San Francisco, and that the most direct economic effect was probably on Honduras. However, there has been no indication of any conflict with law or policy of the Honduran government, nor any comprehensive analysis of the relative connections and interests of Honduras and the United States. Under these circumstances, the dismissal by the district court cannot be sustained on jurisdictional grounds.

We, therefore, vacate the dismissal and remand the Timberlane action.

Notes and Questions

1. In *Mannington Mills, Inc. v. Congoleum Corp.*, 595 F.2d 1287 (3d Cir. 1979), Mannington Mills, Inc., a flooring manufacturer, sued the Congoleum Corporation for violations of Section 2 of the Sherman Antitrust Act arising from its alleged fraud in securing foreign patents to vinyl floor coverings. The Third Circuit found that: 1) "when two American litigants are contesting alleged antitrust activity abroad that results in harm to the export business of one, a federal court does have subject matter jurisdiction"; 2) the act of state doctrine did not apply since "[t]he grant of patents for floor coverings is not the type of sovereign activity that would be of substantial concern to the executive branch in its conduct of international affairs"; 3) the district court should follow the balancing process suggested by the Ninth Circuit in *Timberlane* in order to determine whether to exercise jurisdiction.

2. *See* William Sugden, *Global Antitrust and the Evolution of an International Standard*, 35 VAND. J. TRANSNAT'L L. 989 (2002); William S. Dodge, *Understanding the Presumption Against Extraterritoriality*, 16 BERKELEY J. INT'L L. 85 (1998); Jake S. Tyshow, *Informal Foreign Affairs Formalism: The Act of State Doctrine and the Reinterpretation of International Comity*, 43 VA. J. INT'L L. 275 (2002).

3. Restatement (Third) of Foreign Relations Law of the United States (1987)

§ 402. *Bases of Jurisdiction to Prescribe*

Subject to § 403, a state has jurisdiction to prescribe law with respect to

(1) (a) conduct that, wholly or in substantial part, takes place within its territory;

(b) the status of persons, or interests in things, present within its territory;

(c) conduct outside its territory that has or is intended to have substantial effect within its territory;

(2) the activities, interests, status, or relations of its nationals outside as well as within its territory; and

(3) certain conduct outside its territory by persons not its nationals that is directed against the security of the state or against a limited class of other state interests.

§ 403. *Limitations on Jurisdiction to Prescribe*

(1) Even when one of the bases for jurisdiction under § 402 is present, a state may not exercise jurisdiction to prescribe law with respect to a person or activity having connections with another state when the exercise of such jurisdiction is unreasonable.

(2) Whether exercise of jurisdiction over a person or activity is unreasonable is determined by evaluating all relevant factors, including, where appropriate:

(a) the link of the activity to the territory of the regulating state, i.e., the extent to which the activity takes place within the territory, or has substantial, direct, and foreseeable effect upon or in the territory;

(b) the connections, such as nationality, residence, or economic activity, between the regulating state and the person principally responsible for the activity to be regulated, or between that state and those whom the regulation is designed to protect;

(c) the character of the activity to be regulated, the importance of regulation to the regulating state, the extent to which other states regulate such activities, and the degree to which the desirability of such regulation is generally accepted.

(d) the existence of justified expectations that might be protected or hurt by the regulation;

(e) the importance of the regulation to the international political, legal, or economic system;

(f) the extent to which the regulation is consistent with the traditions of the international system;

(g) the extent to which another state may have an interest in regulating the activity; and

(h) the likelihood of conflict with regulation by another state.

(3) When it would not be unreasonable for each of two states to exercise jurisdiction over a person or activity, but the prescriptions by the two states are in conflict, each state has an obligation to evaluate its own as well as the other state's interest in exercising jurisdiction, in light of all the relevant factors, including those set out in Subsection (2); a state should defer to the other state if that state's interest is clearly greater.

C. Traditional Grounds on Which Prescriptive Competence Has Been Claimed

States have demanded prescriptive competence on a wide range of grounds: territoriality, i.e., that the acts in question occurred within the territory of the claimant state; impact territoriality, i.e., that the acts in question had an impact on the territory of the claimant state even though they occurred abroad; nationality, i.e. that either the perpetrator or the victim of the act is a national of the claimant state, without regard to where the actions giving rise to the claim occurred (active and passive personality); the protective principle, i.e. that a state is entitled to make and apply law to events that occurred abroad if necessary to protect its essential interests; and universal jurisdiction, i.e. that a state may exercise jurisdiction over events wherever they may occur if they are prohibited by international law.

1. Territoriality

a. American Banana Co. v. United Fruit Co.

213 U.S. 347 (1909)

HOLMES, J.: This is an action brought to recover threefold damages under the Act to Protect Trade against Monopolies. July 2, 1890, c. 647, § 7. 26 Stat. 209, 210 (15 U.S.C. § 15). …

The allegations of the complaint may be summed up as follows: The plaintiff is an Alabama corporation, organized in 1904. The defendant is a New Jersey corporation, organized in 1899. Long before the plaintiff was formed, the defendant, with intent to prevent competition and to control and monopolize the banana trade, bought the property and business of several of its previous competitors, with provision against their resuming the trade, made contracts with others, including a majority of the most important, regulating the quantity to be purchased and the price to be paid, and acquired a controlling amount of stock in still others. For the same purpose it organized a selling company, of which it held the stock, that by agreement sold at fixed prices all the bananas of the combining parties. By this and other means it did monopolize and restrain the trade and maintained unreasonable prices. The defendant being in this ominous attitude, one McConnell in 1903 started a banana plantation in Panama, then part of the United States of Colombia, and began to build a railway (which would afford his only means of export), both in accordance with the laws of the United States of Colombia. He was notified by the defendant that he must either combine or stop. Two months later, it is believed at the defendant's instigation, the governor of Panama recommended to his national government that Costa Rica be allowed to administer the territory through which the railroad was to run, and this although that territory had been awarded to Colombia under an arbitration agreed to by treaty. The defendant, and afterwards, in September, the government of Costa Rica, it is believed by the inducement of the defendant, interfered with McConnell. In November, 1903, Panama revolted and became an independent republic, declaring its boundary to be that settled by the award. In June, 1904, the plaintiff bought out McConnell and went on with the work, as it had a right to do under the laws of Panama. But in July, Costa Rican soldiers and officials, instigated by the defendant, seized a part of the plantation and a cargo of supplies and have held them ever since, and stopped the construction and operation of the plantation and railway. In August one Astua, by *ex parte* proceedings, got a judgment from a Costa Rican court, declaring the plantation to be his, although, it is alleged, the proceedings were not within the jurisdiction of Costa Rica, and were contrary to its laws and void. Agents of the defendant then bought the lands from Astua. The plaintiff has tried to induce the government of Costa Rica to withdraw its soldiers and also has tried to persuade the United States to interfere, but has been thwarted in both by the defendant and has failed. The government of Costa Rica remained in possession down to the bringing of the suit.

As a result of the defendant's acts the plaintiff has been deprived of the use of the plantation, and the railway, the plantation and supplies have been injured. The defendant also, by outbidding, has driven purchasers out of the market and has compelled producers to come to its terms, and it has prevented the plaintiff from buying for export and sale. This is the substantial damage alleged. There is thrown in a further allegation that the defendant has "sought to injure" the plaintiff's business by offering positions to its employees and by discharging and threatening to discharge persons in its own employ who were stockholders of the plaintiff. But no particular point is made of this. It is contended, however, that, even if the main argument fails and the defendant is held not to be answerable for acts depending on the cooperation of the government of Costa Rica for their effect, a wrongful conspiracy resulting in driving the plaintiff out of business is to be gathered from the complaint and that it was entitled to go to trial upon that.

It is obvious that, however stated, the plaintiff's case depends on several rather startling propositions. In the first place the acts causing the damage were done, so far as appears, outside the jurisdiction of the United States and within that of other states. It is surprising to hear it argued that they were governed by the act of Congress.

No doubt in regions subject to no sovereign, like the high seas, or to no law that civilized countries would recognize as adequate, such countries may treat some relations between their citizens as governed by their own law, and keep to some extent the old notion of personal sovereignty alive. ... They go further, at times, and declare that they will punish any one, subject or not, who shall do certain things, if they can catch him, as in the case of pirates on the high seas. In cases immediately affecting national interests they may go further still and may make, and, if they get the chance, execute similar threats as to acts done within another recognized jurisdiction. ... But the general and almost universal rule is that the character of an act as lawful or unlawful must be determined wholly by the law of the country where the act is done. *Slater v. Mexican National R.R.. Co.*, 194 U. S. 120, 126. This principle was carried to an extreme in *Milliken v. Pratt,* 125 Massachusetts, 374. For another jurisdiction, if it should happen to lay hold of the actor, to treat him according to its own notions rather than those of the place where he did the acts, not only would be unjust, but would be an interference with the authority of another sovereign, contrary to the comity of nations, which the other state concerned justly might resent. ...

Law is a statement of the circumstances in which the public force will be brought to bear upon men through the courts. But the word commonly is confined to such prophecies or threats when addressed to persons living within the power of the courts. A threat that depends upon the choice of the party affected to bring himself within that power hardly would be called law in the ordinary sense. We do not speak of blockade running by neutrals as unlawful. And the usages of speech correspond to the limit of the attempts of the lawmaker, except in extraordinary cases. It is true that domestic corporations remain always within the power of the domestic law, but in the present case, at least, there is no ground for distinguishing between corporations and men.

The foregoing considerations would lead in case of doubt to a construction of any statute as intended to be confined in its operation and effect to the territorial limits over which the lawmaker has general and legitimate power. "All legislation is *prima facie* territorial." *Ex parte Blain, In re Sawers,* 12 Ch. Div. 522, 528; ... Words having universal scope, such as "Every contract in restraint of trade," "Every person who shall monopolize," etc., will be taken as a matter of course to mean only every one subject to such legislation, not all that the legislator subsequently may be able to catch. In the case of the present statute the improbability of the United States attempting to make acts done in Panama or Costa Rica criminal is obvious, yet the law begins by making criminal the acts for which it gives a right to sue. We think it entirely plain that what the defendant did in Panama or Costa Rica is not within the scope of the statute so far as the present suit is concerned. Other objections of a serious nature are urged but need not be discussed.

For again, not only were the acts of the defendant in Panama or Costa Rica not within the Sherman Act, but they were not torts by the law of the place and therefore were not torts at all, however contrary to the ethical and economic postulates of that statute. The substance of the complaint is that, the plantation being within the *de facto* jurisdiction of Costa Rica, that state took and keeps possession of it by virtue of its sovereign power. But a seizure by a state is not a thing that can be complained of elsewhere in the courts. *Underhill v. Hernandez,* 168 U. S. 250. The fact, if it be one, that *de jure* the estate is in Panama does not matter in the least; sovereignty is pure fact. The fact has been recognized by the United States, and by the implications of the bill is assented to by Panama.

The fundamental reason why persuading a sovereign power to do this or that cannot be a tort is not that the sovereign cannot be joined as a defendant or because it must be assumed to be acting lawfully. The intervention of parties who had a right knowingly to produce the harmful result between the defendant and the harm has been thought to be a non-conductor and to bar responsibility, ... but it is not clear that this is always true, for instance, in the case of the privileged repetition of a slander ... or the malicious and unjustified persuasion to discharge from employment. . . . The fundamental reason is that it is a contradiction in terms to say that within its jurisdiction it is unlawful to persuade a sovereign power to bring about a result that it declares by its conduct to be desirable and proper. It does not, and foreign courts cannot, admit that the influences were improper or the results bad. It makes the persuasion lawful by its own act. The very meaning of sovereignty is that the decree of the sovereign makes law. ... In the case of private persons it consistently may assert the freedom of the immediate parties to an injury and yet declare that certain persuasions addressed to them are wrong. . . .

The plaintiff relied a good deal on *Rafael v. Verelst*, 2 Wm. Bl. 983; *Ib.* 1055. But in that case, although the Nabob who imprisoned the plaintiff was called a sovereign for certain purposes, he was found to be the mere tool of the defendant, an English Governor. That hardly could be listened to concerning a really independent state. But of course it is not alleged that Costa Rica stands in that relation to the United Fruit Company.

The acts of the soldiers and officials of Costa Rica are not alleged to have been without the consent of the government and must be taken to have been done by its order. It ratified them, at all events, and adopted and keeps the possession taken by them. ... The injuries to the plantation and supplies seem to have been the direct effect of the acts of the Costa Rican government, which is holding them under an adverse claim of right. The claim for them must fall with the claim for being deprived of the use and profits of the place. As to the buying at a high price, etc., it is enough to say that we have no ground for supposing that it was unlawful in the countries where the purchases were made. Giving to this complaint every reasonable latitude of interpretation we are of opinion that it alleges no case under the act of Congress and discloses nothing that we can suppose to have been a tort where it was done. A conspiracy in this country to do acts in another jurisdiction does not draw to itself those acts and make them unlawful, if they are permitted by the local law.

Further reasons might be given why this complaint should not be upheld, but we have said enough to dispose of it and to indicate our general point of view.

b. Wildenhus's Case (Mali v. Keeper of the Common Jail)

120 U.S. 1 (1887)

[Wildenhus, a Belgian national, working on a Belgian flag vessel, murdered another Belgian while the vessel was in the port of Jersey City. The Article XI of a Consular Convention between Belgium and the United States provided:

> The respective consuls-general, consuls, vice-consuls, and consular agents shall have exclusive charge of the internal order of the merchant vessels of their nation, and shall alone take cognizance of all differences which may arise, either at sea or in port, between the captains, officers, and crews, without exception, particularly with reference to the adjustment of wages and the execution of contracts. The local authorities shall not interfere, except when the disorder that has arisen is of such a nature as to disturb tranquillity and public order on shore, or in the port, or when a person of the country or not belonging to the crew, shall be concerned therein.
>
> In all other cases, the aforesaid authorities shall confine themselves to lending aid to the consuls and vice-consuls or consular agents, if they are requested by them to do so, in causing the arrest and imprisonment of any person whose name is inscribed on the crew list, whenever, for any cause, the said officers shall think proper.

Nonetheless, Wildenhus was arrested and prosecuted by the authorities in Jersey City. A *habeas corpus* was sought to secure his release.]

By §§ 751 and 753 of the Revised Statutes the courts of the United States have power to issue writs of *habeas corpus* which shall extend to prisoners in jail when they are in "custody in violation of the Constitution or a law or treaty of the United States," and the question we have to consider is, whether these prisoners are held in violation of the provisions of the existing treaty between the United States and Belgium.

It is part of the law of civilized nations that when a merchant vessel of one country enters the ports of another for the purposes of trade, it subjects itself to the law of the place to which it goes, unless by treaty or otherwise the two countries have come to some different understanding or agreement; for, as was said by Chief Justice Marshall in *The Exchange,* 7 Cranch, 116, 144, "it would be obviously inconvenient and dangerous to society, and would subject the laws to continual infraction, and the government to degradation, if such ... merchants did not owe temporary and local allegiance, and were not amenable to the jurisdiction of the country." …

From experience, however, it was found long ago that it would be beneficial to commerce if the local government would abstain from interfering with the internal discipline of the ship, and the general regulation of the rights and duties of the officers and crew towards the vessel or among themselves. And so by comity it came to be generally understood among civilized nations that all matters of discipline and all things done on board which affected only the vessel or those belonging to her, and did not involve the peace or dignity of the country, or the tranquillity of the port, should be left by the local government to be dealt with by the authorities of the nation to which the vessel belonged as the laws of that nation or the interests of its commerce should require. But if crimes are committed on board of a character to disturb the peace and tranquillity of the country to which the vessel has been brought, the offenders have never by comity or usage been entitled to any exemptions from the operation of the local laws for their punishment, if the local tribunals see fit to assert their authority. Such being the general public law on this subject, treaties and conventions have been entered into by nations having commercial intercourse, the purpose of which was to settle and define the rights and duties of the contracting parties with respect to each other in these particulars, and thus prevent the inconvenience that might arise from attempts to exercise conflicting jurisdictions. …

The form of the provision found in the present convention with Belgium first appeared in a convention with Austria concluded in 1870, Art. XI, 17 Stat. 827, and it is found now in substantially the same language in all the treaties and conventions which have since been entered into by the United States on the same subject. …

It thus appears that at first provision was made only for giving consuls police authority over the interior of the ship and jurisdiction in civil matters arising out of disputes or differences on board, that is to say, between those belonging to the vessel. Under this police authority the duties of the consuls were evidently confined to the maintenance of order and discipline on board. This gave them no power to punish for crimes against the peace of the country. In fact, they were expressly prohibited from interfering with the local police in matters of that kind. …

In the next conventions consuls were simply made judges and arbitrators to settle and adjust differences between those on board. This clearly related to such differences between those belonging to the vessel as are capable of adjustment and settlement by judicial decision or by arbitration, for it simply made the consuls judges or arbitrators in such matters. That would of itself exclude all idea of punishment for crimes against the State which affected the peace and tranquillity of the port; but, to prevent all doubt on this subject, it was expressly provided that it should not apply to differences of that character.

Next came a form of convention which in terms gave the consuls authority to cause proper order to be maintained on board and to decide disputes between the officers and crew, but allowed the local authorities to interfere if the disorders taking place on board were of such a nature as to disturb the public tranquillity, and that is substantially all there is in the convention with Belgium which we have now to consider. This treaty is the law which now governs the conduct of the United States and Belgium towards each other in this particular. Each nation has granted to the other such local jurisdiction within its own dominion as may be necessary to maintain order on board a merchant vessel, but has reserved to itself the right to interfere if the disorder on board is of a nature to disturb the public tranquillity.

The treaty is part of the supreme law of the United States, and has the same force and effect in New Jersey that it is entitled to elsewhere. If it gives the consul of Belgium exclusive jurisdiction over the offence which it is alleged has been committed within the territory of New Jersey, we see no reason why he may not enforce his rights under the treaty by writ of *habeas corpus* in any proper court of the United States. This being the case, the only important question left for our determination is whether the thing which has been done—the disorder that has arisen—on board this vessel is of a nature to disturb the public peace, or, as some writers term it, the "public repose" of the people who look to the state of New Jersey for their protection. If the thing done—"the disorder," as it is called in the treaty—is of a character to affect those on shore or in the port when it becomes known, the fact that only those on the ship saw it when it was done is a matter of no moment. Those who are not on the vessel pay no special attention to the mere disputes or quarrels of the seamen while on board, whether they occur under deck or above. Neither do they as a rule care for anything done on board which relates only to the discipline of the ship, or to the preservation of order and authority. Not so, however, with crimes which from their gravity awaken a public interest as soon as they become known, and especially those of a character which every civilized nation considers itself bound to provide a severe punishment for when committed within its own jurisdiction. In such cases inquiry is certain to be instituted at once to ascertain how or why the thing was done, and the popular excitement rises or falls as the news spreads and the facts become known. It is not alone the publicity of the act, or the noise and clamor which attends it, that fixes the nature of the crime, but the act itself. If that is of a character to awaken public interest when it becomes known, it is a "disorder" the nature of which is to affect the community at large, and consequently to invoke the power of the local government whose people have been disturbed by what was done. The very nature of such an act is to disturb the quiet of a peaceful community, and to create, in the language of the treaty, a "disorder" which will "disturb tranquillity and public order on shore or in the port." The principle which governs the whole matter is this: Disorders which disturb only the peace of the ship or those on board are to be dealt with exclusively by the sovereignty of the home of the ship, but those which disturb the public peace may be suppressed, and, if need be, the offenders punished by the proper authorities of the local jurisdiction. It may not be easy at all times to determine to which of the two jurisdictions a particular act of disorder belongs. Much will undoubtedly depend on the attending circumstances of the particular case, but all must concede that felonious homicide is a subject for the local jurisdiction, and that if the proper authorities are proceeding with the case in a regular way, the consul has no right to interfere to prevent it. That, according to the petition for the *habeas corpus*, is this case.

This is fully in accord with the practice in France, where the government has been quite as liberal towards foreign nations in this particular as any other, and where, as we have seen in the cases of *The Sally* and *The Newton*, by a decree of the Council of State, representing the political department of the government, the French courts were prevented from exercising jurisdiction. But afterwards, in 1859, in the case of *Jally*, the mate of an American merchantman, who had killed one of the crew and severely wounded another on board the ship in the port of Havre, the Court of Cassation, the highest judicial tribunal of France, upon full consideration held, while the Convention of 1853 was in force, that the French courts had rightful jurisdiction, for reasons which sufficiently appear in the following extract from its judgment:

> Considering that it is a principle of the law of nations that every state has sovereign jurisdiction throughout its territory;
>
> Considering that by the terms of Article 3 of the Code Napoleon the laws of police and safety bind all those who inhabit French territory, and that consequently foreigners, even *transeuntes*, find themselves subject to those laws;
>
> Considering that merchant vessels entering the port of a nation other than that to which they belong cannot be withdrawn from the territorial jurisdiction, in any case in which the interest of the state of which that port forms part finds itself concerned, without danger to good order and to the dignity of the government;
>
> Considering that every state is interested in the repression of crimes and offences that may be committed in the ports of its territory, not only by the men of the ship's company of a foreign merchant vessel towards men not forming part of that company, but even by men of the ship's company among themselves, whenever the act is of a nature to compromise the tranquillity of the port, or the intervention of the local authority is invoked, or the act constitutes a crime by common law," *(droit commun,* the law common to all civilized nations,) "the gravity of which does not permit any nation to leave it unpunished, without impugning its rights of jurisdictional and territorial sovereignty, because that crime is in itself

the most manifest as well as the most flagrant violation of the laws which it is the duty of every nation to cause to be respected in all parts of its territory." 1 Ortolan Diplomatie de la Mer (4th ed.), pp. 455, 456; Sirey (N. S.), 1859, p. 189.

The judgment of the Circuit Court is affirmed.

c. Strathearn Steamship Co. v. Dillon
252 U.S. 348 (1920)

MR. JUSTICE DAY. This case presents questions arising under the Seamen's Act of March 4, 1915, c. 153, 38 Stat. 1164. It appears that Dillon, the respondent, was a British subject, and shipped at Liverpool on the eighth of May, 1916, on a British vessel. The shipping articles provided for a voyage of not exceeding three years, commencing at Liverpool and ending at such port in the United Kingdom as might be required by the master, the voyage including ports of the United States. The wages which were fixed by the articles were made payable at the end of the voyage. At the time of the demand for one-half wages, and at the time of the beginning of the action, the period of the voyage had not been reached. The articles provided that no cash should be advanced abroad or liberty granted other than at the pleasure of the master. This, it is admitted, was a valid contract for the payment of wages under the laws of Great Britain. The ship arrived at the Port of Pensacola, Florida, on July 31, 1916, and while she was in that port, Dillon, still in the employ of the ship, demanded from her master one-half part of the wages theretofore earned, and payment was refused. Dillon had received nothing for about two months, and after the refusal of the master to comply with his demand for one-half wages, he filed in the District Court of the United States a libel against the ship, claiming $125.00, the amount of wages earned at the time of demand and refusal.

The District Court found against Dillon upon the ground that his demand was premature. The Circuit Court of Appeals reversed this decision, and held that Dillon was entitled to recover. 256 Fed. Rep. 631. A writ of certiorari brings before us for review the decree of the Circuit Court of Appeals.

In *Sandberg v. McDonald*, 248 U. S. 185, and *Neilson v. Rhine Shipping Co.*, 248 U. S. 205, we had occasion to deal with § 11 of the Seamen's Act, and held that it did not invalidate advancement of seamen's wages in foreign countries when legal where made. The instant case requires us to consider now § 4 of the same act. That section amends § 4530, Rev. Stats., and so far as pertinent provides: "Sec. 4530. Every seaman on a vessel of the United States shall be entitled to receive on demand from the master of the vessel to which he belongs one-half part of the wages which he shall have then earned at every port where such vessel, after the voyage has been commenced, shall load or deliver cargo before the voyage is ended and all stipulations in the contract to the contrary shall be void: *Provided,* Such a demand shall not be made before the expiration of, nor oftener than once in five days. Any failure on the part of the master to comply with this demand shall release the seaman from his contract and he shall be entitled to full payment of wages earned. … *And provided further*, That this section shall apply to seamen on foreign vessels while in harbors of the United States, and the courts of the United States shall be open to such seamen for its enforcement." …

The section, of which the statute now under consideration is an amendment, expressly excepted from the right to recover one-half of the wages those cases in which the contract otherwise provided. In the amended section all such contract provisions are expressly rendered void, and the right to recover is given the seamen notwithstanding contractual obligations to the contrary. The language applies to all seamen on vessels of the United States, and the second proviso of the section as it now reads makes it applicable to seamen on foreign vessels while in harbors of the United States. The proviso does not stop there, for it contains the express provision that the courts of the United States shall be open to seamen on foreign vessels for its enforcement. The latter provision is of the utmost importance in determining the proper construction of this section of the act. It manifests the purpose of Congress to give the benefit of the act to seamen on foreign vessels, and to open the doors of the federal courts to foreign seamen. No such provision was necessary as to American seamen, for they had the right independently of this statute to seek redress in the courts of the United States, and, if it were the intention of Congress to limit the provision of the act to American seamen, this feature would have been wholly superfluous.

It is said that it is the purpose to limit the benefit of the act to American seamen, notwithstanding this provision giving access to seamen on foreign vessels to the courts of the United States, because of the title of the act in which its purpose is expressed "to promote the welfare of American seamen in the merchant marine of the United States." But the title is more than this, and not only declares the purposes to promote the welfare of American seamen but further to abolish arrest and imprisonment as a penalty for desertion and to secure the abrogation of treaty provisions in relation thereto; and to promote safety at sea. But the title of an act cannot limit the plain meaning of its text, although it may be looked to to aid in construction in cases of doubt. *Cornell v. Coyne*, 192 U.S. 418, 530, and cases cited. Apart from the text, which we think plain, it is by no means clear that, if the act were given a construction to limit its application to American seamen only, the purposes of Congress would be subserved, for such limited construction would have a tendency to prevent the employment of American seamen, and to promote the engagement of those who were not entitled to sue for one-half wages under the provisions of the Law. But, taking the provisions of the act as the same are written, we think it plain that it manifests the purpose of Congress to place American and foreign seamen on an equality of right in so far as the privileges of this section are concerned, with equal opportunity to resort to the courts of the United States for the enforcement of the act. Before the amendment, as we have already pointed out, the right to recover one-half the wages could not be enforced in face of a contractual obligation to the contrary. Congress, for reasons which it deemed sufficient, amended the act so as to permit the recovery upon the conditions named in the statute. In the case of *Sandberg v. McDonald*, 248 U.S. supra, we found no purpose manifested by Congress in § 11 to interfere with wages advanced in foreign ports under contracts legal where made. That section dealt with advancements, and contained no provision such as we find in § 4. Under § 4 all contracts are avoided which run counter to the purposes of the statute. Whether consideration for contractual rights under engagements legally made in foreign countries would suggest a different course is not our province to inquire. It is sufficient to say that Congress has otherwise declared by the positive terms of this enactment, and if it had authority to do so, the law is enforceable in the courts.

We come then to consider the contention that this construction renders the statute unconstitutional as being destructive of contract rights. But we think this contention must be decided adversely to the petitioner upon the authority of previous cases in this court. The matter was fully considered in *Patterson v. Bark Eudora*, 190 U.S. 169, in which the previous decisions of this court were reviewed, and the conclusion reached that the jurisdiction of this Government over foreign merchant vessels in our ports was such as to give authority to Congress to make provisions of the character now under consideration; that it was for this Government to determine upon what terms and conditions vessels of other countries might be permitted to enter our harbors, and to impose conditions upon the shipment of sailors in our own ports, and make them applicable to foreign as well as domestic vessels. Upon the authority of that case, and others cited in the opinion therein, we have no doubt as to the authority of Congress to pass a statute of this sort, applicable to foreign vessels in our ports and controlling the employment and payment of seamen as a condition of the right of such foreign vessels to enter and use the ports of the United States. ...

We find no error in the decree of the Circuit Court of Appeals and the same is *Affirmed*.

Notes and Questions

1. In a series of cases from *U.S. v. Sisal Sales Corp.* , 274 U.S. 268 (1927) through *Continental Ore Co. v. Union Carbide & Carbon Corp.*, 370 U.S. 690 (1962), the Supreme Court retreated from the position taken in *American Banana, supra*.

2. In a highly interactive system, the effects of actions undertaken in one state may have significant public order consequences in another. Hence, the demand to abandon territoriality as a basis for jurisdiction and to install a doctrine that permits a state to protect its social and economic processes even from events that occur beyond its boundaries. While an "effects" theory of jurisdiction equips a state to protect itself, it also introduces chaos into allocation of jurisdiction, for the more interactive a system of states, the more different states will be insisting on exercising law-making and law-applying jurisdiction over events that are initiated in another state and are subject to their jurisdiction. It is precisely the logical consequence of an effects doctrine that has led, as in *Occidental Petroleum Corp. v. Buttes Gas & Oil Co.*, 331 F. Supp. 92 (C.D. Cal. 1971), *aff'd on other grounds*, 461 F.2d 1261 (9th Cir. 1972), *cert. denied*, 409 U.S. 950 (1972) to a revival of a judicial demand for territoriality. *See* in this regard Gary J. Simson, *The Return of* American Banana*: A Contemporary Perspective on American Antitrust Abroad*, 9 J. Int'l L. Econ. 233 (1974); Hannah

L. Buxbaum, *The Private Attorney General in a Global Age: Public Interests in Private International Antitrust Litigation*, 26 YALE J. INT'L L. 219 (2001); EXTRATERRITORIAL JURISDICTION IN THEORY AND PRACTICE (Karl M. Meessen, ed., Kluwer Law International 1996); James E. Ward, *"Is That Your Final Answer?" The Patchwork Jurisprudence Surrounding the Presumptioin Against Extraterritoriality*, 70 U. CIN. L. REV. 715 (2002).

d. U.S. v. Aluminum Co. of America

148 F.2d 416 (2d Cir. 1945)

[The government brought an antitrust action under Sections 1 and 2 of the Sherman Act against various producers (both domestic and foreign) of aluminum ingot. One of the counts alleged that various foreign producers ("shareholders") had created a cartel, Aluminum Limited ("Limited"), in order to restrict import of aluminum ingot into the United States. To implement this plan, the foreign producers entered into an agreement in 1931 limiting their output of ingots. This agreement was replaced in 1936 by a system of quotas and royalties, with the royalties (which were paid to "Limited" and then redistributed among the shareholders) rising drastically when a producer's quota was exceeded. Such agreements would be illegal if entered into in the United States. On appeal, Limited, a Swiss corporation, raised the issue whether American courts had jurisdiction over those involved, since the agreements were entered into, and carried out, wholly outside the United States.]

HAND, J. ... Did either the agreement of 1931 or that of 1936 violate § 1 of the Act? The answer does not depend upon whether we shall recognize as a source of liability a liability imposed by another state. On the contrary we are concerned only with whether Congress chose to attach liability to the conduct outside the United States of persons not in allegiance to it. That being so, the only question open is whether Congress intended to impose the liability, and whether our own Constitution permitted it to do so: as a court of the United States, we cannot look beyond our own law. Nevertheless, it is quite true that we are not to read general words, such as those in this Act, without regard to the limitations customarily observed by nations upon the exercise of their powers; limitations which generally correspond to those fixed by the "Conflict of Laws." We should not impute to Congress an intent to punish all whom its courts can catch, for conduct which has no consequences within the United States. ... On the other hand, it is settled law—as "Limited" itself agrees—that any state may impose liabilities, even upon persons not within its allegiance, for conduct outside its borders that has consequences within its borders which the state reprehends; and these liabilities other states will ordinarily recognize. ... It may be argued that this Act extends further. Two situations are possible. There may be agreements made beyond our borders not intended to affect imports, which do affect them, or which affect exports. Almost any limitation of the supply of goods in Europe, for example, or in South America, may have repercussions in the United States if there is trade between the two. Yet when one considers the international complications likely to arise from an effort in this country to treat such agreements as unlawful, it is safe to assume that Congress certainly did not intend the

Act to cover them. Such agreements may on the other hand intend to include imports into the United States, and yet it may appear that they have had no effect upon them. That situation might be thought to fall within the doctrine that intent may be a substitute for performance in the case of a contract made within the United States or it might be thought to fall within the doctrine that a statute should not be interpreted to cover acts abroad which have no consequence here. We shall not choose between these alternatives; but for argument we shall assume that the Act does not cover agreements, even though intended to affect imports or exports, unless its performance is shown actually to have had some effect upon them. Where both conditions are satisfied, the situation certainly falls within such decisions as *U.S. v. Pacific & Arctic R. & Navigation Co.*, 228 U.S. 87. ... It is true that in those cases the persons held liable had sent agents into the United States to perform part of the agreement; but an agent is merely an animate means of executing his principal's purposes, and, for the purposes of this case, he does not differ from an inanimate means; besides, only human agents can import and sell ingot.

Both agreements would clearly have been unlawful, had they been made within the United States; and it follows from what we have just said that both were unlawful, though made abroad, if they were intended to affect imports and did affect them. Since the shareholders almost at once agreed that the agreement of 1931 should not cover imports, we may ignore it and confine our discussion to that of 1936: indeed that we should have to do anyway, since it superseded the earlier agreement. The judge found that it was not the purpose of the agreement to "suppress or restrain the exportation of aluminum to the United States for sale in competition with "Alcoa." By that we understand that he meant that the agreement was not specifically directed to "Alcoa," because it only applied generally to the production of the shareholders. If he meant that it was not expected that the General restriction upon production would have an effect upon imports, we cannot agree, for the change made in 1936 was deliberate and was expressly made to accomplish just that. It would have been an idle gesture, unless the shareholders had supposed that it would, or at least might, have that effect. The first of the conditions which we mentioned was therefore satisfied; the intent was to set up a quota system for imports.

The judge also found that the 1936 agreement did not "materially affect the ... foreign trade or commerce of the United States"; apparently because the imported ingot was greater in 1936 and 1937 than in earlier years. We cannot accept this finding, based as it was upon the fact that, in 1936, 1937 and the first quarter of 1938, the gross imports of ingot increased. It by no means follows from such an increase that the agreement did not restrict imports; and incidentally it so happens that in those years such inference as is possible at all, leads to the opposite conclusion. It is true that the average imports—including "Alcoa's"—for the years 1932-1935 inclusive were about 15 million pounds, and that for 1936, 1937 and one-fourth of 1938 they were about 33 million pounds; but the average domestic ingot manufacture in the first period was about 96 million and in the second about 262 million; so that the proportion of imports to domestic ingot was about 15.6 per cent for the first period and about 12.6 per cent for the second. We do not mean to infer from this that the quota system of 1936 did in fact restrain imports, as these figures might suggest; but we do mean that nothing is to be inferred from the gross increase of imports. We shall dispose of the matter therefore upon the assumption that, although the shareholders intended to restrict imports, it does not appear whether in fact they did so. Upon our hypothesis the plaintiff would therefore fail, if it carried the burden of proof upon this issue as upon others. We think, however, that, after the intent to affect imports was proved; the burden of proof shifted to "Limited." In the first place a depressant upon production which applies generally may be assumed, ceteris paribus, to distribute its effect evenly upon all markets. Again, when the parties took the trouble specifically to make the depressant apply to a given market, there is reason to suppose that they expected that it would have some effect, which it could have only by lessening what would otherwise have been imported. If the motive they introduced was over-balanced in all instances by motives which induced the shareholders to import, if the United States market became so attractive that the royalties did not count at all and their expectations were in fact defeated, they to whom the facts were more accessible than to the plaintiff ought to prove it, for a prima facie case had been made. Moreover, there is an especial propriety in demanding this of "Limited," because it was "Limited" which procured the inclusion in the agreement of 1936 of imports in the quotas.

There remains only the question whether this assumed restriction had any influence upon prices. ... To that *Socony-Vacuum Oil Co. v. United States, supra,* 310 U.S. 150, is an entire answer. It will be remembered that, when the defendants in that case protested that the prosecution had not proved that the "distress" gasoline had affected prices, the court answered that that was not necessary, because an agreement to withdraw any substantial part of the supply from a market would, if carried out, have some effect upon prices, and was as unlawful as an agreement expressly to fix prices. The underlying doctrine was that all factors which contribute to determine prices, must be kept free to operate unhampered by agreements. For these reasons we think that the agreement of 1936 violated § 1 of the Act. [Affirmed.]

e. Hartford Fire Insurance Co. v. California

509 U.S. 764 (1993)

[A group of states "allege[d] that both domestic and foreign defendants . . . violated the Sherman Act by engaging in various conspiracies to affect the American insurance market." The defendants argued "that the principle of international comity requires the District Court to refrain from exercising jurisdiction over certain claims against it."]

JUSTICE SOUTER, writing for JUSTICES WHITE, BLACKMUN, STEVENS, and REHNQUIST: At the outset, we note that the District Court undoubtedly had jurisdiction of these Sherman Act claims, as the London reinsurers apparently concede. See Tr. of Oral Arg. 37 ("Our position is not that the Sherman Act does not apply in the sense that a minimal basis for the exercise of jurisdiction doesn't exist here. Our position is that there are certain circumstances, and that this is one of them, in which the interests of another State are sufficient that the exercise of that jurisdiction should be restrained"). Although the proposition was perhaps not always free from doubt, see *American Banana Co. v. United Fruit Co.*, 213 U.S. 347 (1909), it is well established by now that the Sherman Act applies to foreign conduct that was meant to produce and did in fact produce some substantial effect in the United States. Such is the conduct alleged here: that the London reinsurers engaged in unlawful conspiracies to affect the market for insurance in the United States and that their conduct in fact produced substantial effect.

According to the London reinsurers, the District Court should have declined to exercise such jurisdiction under the principle of international comity. The Court of Appeals agreed that courts should look to that principle in deciding whether to exercise jurisdiction under the Sherman Act. This availed the London reinsurers nothing, however. To be sure, the Court of Appeals believed that "application of [American] antitrust laws to the London reinsurance market 'would lead to significant conflict with English law and policy,'" and that "[s]uch a conflict, unless out-weighed by other factors, would by itself be reason to decline exercise of jurisdiction." But other factors, in the court's view, including the London reinsurers' express purpose to affect United States commerce and the substantial nature of the effect produced, out-weighed the supposed conflict and required the exercise of jurisdiction in this litigation.

When it enacted the Foreign Trade Antitrust Improvements Act of 1982 (FTAIA), Congress expressed no view on the question whether a court with Sherman Act jurisdiction should ever decline to exercise such jurisdiction on grounds of international comity. See H. R. Rep. No. 97-686, p. 13 (1982) ("If a court determines that the requirements for subject matter jurisdiction are met, [the FTAIA] would have no effect on the court['s] ability to employ notions of comity ... or otherwise to take account of the international character of the transaction") (citing *Timberlane*). We need not decide that question here, however, for even assuming that in a proper case a court may decline to exercise Sherman Act jurisdiction over foreign conduct (or, as JUSTICE SCALIA would put it, may conclude by the employment of comity analysis in the first instance that there is no jurisdiction), international comity would not counsel against exercising jurisdiction in the circumstances alleged here. The only substantial question in this litigation is whether "there is in fact a true conflict between domestic and foreign law." *Société Nationale Industrielle Aérospatiale v. United States Dist. Court for Southern Dist. of Iowa,* 482 U.S. 522, 555 (1987) (BLACKMUN, J., concurring in part and dissenting in part). The London reinsurers contend that applying the Act to their conduct would conflict significantly with British law, and the British Government, appearing before us as amicus curiae, concurs. They assert that Parliament has established a comprehensive regulatory regime over the London reinsurance market and that the conduct alleged here was perfectly consistent with British law and policy. But this is not to state a conflict. ... No conflict exists, for these purposes, "where a person subject to regulation by two states can comply with the laws of both." Restatement (Third) Foreign Relations Law § 403, Comment e. Since the London reinsurers do not argue that British law requires them to act in some fashion prohibited by the law of the United States or claim that their compliance with the laws of both countries is otherwise impossible, we see no conflict with British law. We have no need in this litigation to address other considerations that might inform a decision to refrain from the exercise of jurisdiction on grounds of international comity.

JUSTICE SCALIA, writing for JUSTICES O'CONNOR, KENNEDY, and THOMAS, dissenting:

[The] extraterritorial reach of the Sherman Act [has] nothing to do with the jurisdiction of the courts. It is a question of substantive law turning on whether, in enacting the Sherman Act, Congress asserted regulatory power over the challenged conduct. *See EEOC v. Arabian American Oil Co.*, 499 U.S. 244, 248 (1991) (*Aramco*) ("It is our task to determine whether Congress intended the protections of Title VII to apply to United States citizens employed by American employers outside of the United States"). If a plaintiff fails to prevail on this issue, the court does not dismiss the claim for want of subject-matter jurisdiction—want of power to adjudicate; rather, it decides the claim, ruling on the merits that the plaintiff has failed to state a cause of action under the relevant statute. *See Romero*, supra, at 384 (holding no claim available under the Jones Act); *American Banana Co. v. United Fruit Co.*, 213 U.S. 347, 359 (1909) (holding that complaint based upon foreign conduct "alleges no case under the [Sherman Act]").

There is, however, a type of "jurisdiction" relevant to determining the extraterritorial reach of a statute; it is known as "legislative jurisdiction," *Aramco*, supra, at 253; Restatement (First) Conflict of Laws § 60 (1934), or "jurisdiction to prescribe," 1 Restatement (Third) of Foreign Relations Law of the United States 235 (1987). This refers to "the authority of a state to make its law applicable to persons or activities," and is quite a separate matter from "jurisdiction to adjudicate," see id., at 231. There is no doubt, of course, that Congress possesses legislative jurisdiction over the acts alleged in this complaint: Congress has broad power under Article I, § 8, cl. 3, "to regulate Commerce with foreign Nations," and this Court has repeatedly upheld its power to make laws applicable to persons or activities beyond our territorial boundaries where United States interests are affected. But the question in this litigation is whether, and to what extent, Congress has exercised that undoubted legislative jurisdiction in enacting the Sherman Act.

Two canons of statutory construction are relevant in this inquiry. The first is the "longstanding principle of American law 'that legislation of Congress, unless a contrary intent appears, is meant to apply only within the territorial jurisdiction of the United States.'" *Aramco*, at 248 ... Applying that canon in *Aramco*, we held that the version of Title VII of the Civil Rights Act of 1964 then in force, 42 U.S.C. §§ 2000e to 2000e-17 (1988 ed.), did not extend outside the territory of the United States even though the statute contained broad provisions extending its prohibitions to, for example, "'any activity, business, or industry in commerce.'" Id., at 249 (quoting 42 U.S.C. § 2000e(h)). We held such "boilerplate language" to be an insufficient indication to override the presumption against extraterritoriality. Id., at 251. The Sherman Act contains similar "boilerplate language," and if the question were not governed by precedent, it would be worth considering whether that presumption controls the outcome here. We have, however, found the presumption to be overcome with respect to our antitrust laws; it is now well established that the Sherman Act applies extraterritorially.

But if the presumption against extraterritoriality has been overcome or is otherwise inapplicable, a second canon of statutory construction becomes relevant: "An act of congress ought never to be construed to violate the law of nations if any other possible construction remains." *Murray v. Schooner Charming Betsy*, 6 U.S. 64 (1804) (Marshall, C.J.). This canon is "wholly independent" of the presumption against extraterritoriality. *Aramco*, supra, at 264 (Marshall, J., dissenting). It is relevant to determining the substantive reach of a statute because "the law of nations," or customary international law, includes limitations on a nation's exercise of its jurisdiction to prescribe. See Restatement (Third) §§ 401-416. Though it clearly has constitutional authority to do so, Congress is generally presumed not to have exceeded those customary international-law limits on jurisdiction to prescribe.

Consistent with that presumption, this and other courts have frequently recognized that, even where the presumption against extraterritoriality does not apply, statutes should not be interpreted to regulate foreign persons or conduct if that regulation would conflict with principles of international law. For example, in *Romero v. International Terminal Operating Co.*, 358 U.S. 354 (1959), the plaintiff, a Spanish sailor who had been injured while working aboard a Spanish-flag and Spanish-owned vessel, filed a Jones Act claim against his Spanish employer. The presumption against extraterritorial application of federal statutes was inapplicable to the case, as the actionable tort had occurred in American waters. See id., at 383. The Court nonetheless stated that, "in the absence of a contrary congressional direction," it would apply "principles of choice of law that are consonant with the needs of a general federal maritime law and with due recognition of our self-regarding respect for the relevant interests of foreign nations in the regulation of maritime commerce as part of the legitimate concern of the international community." Id., at 382-383. "The controlling considerations" in this choice-of-law analysis were "the interacting interests of the United States and of foreign countries." Id., at 383.

Romero referred to, and followed, the choice-of-law analysis set forth in *Lauritzen v. Larsen*, 345 U.S. 571 (1953). As previously mentioned, *Lauritzen* also involved a Jones Act claim brought by a foreign sailor against a foreign employer. The *Lauritzen* Court recognized the basic problem: "If [the Jones Act were] read literally, Congress has conferred an American right of action which requires nothing more than that plaintiff be 'any seaman who shall suffer personal injury in the course of his employment.'" Id., at 576. The solution it adopted was to construe the statute "to apply only to areas and transactions in which American law would be considered operative under prevalent doctrines of international law." Id., at 577. To support application of international law to limit the facial breadth of the statute, the Court relied upon—of course—Chief Justice Marshall's statement in *Schooner Charming Betsy*, quoted supra, at 814-815. It then set forth "several factors which, alone or in combination, are generally conceded to influence choice of law to govern a tort claim." 345 U.S. at 583.

Lauritzen, *Romero*, and *McCulloch* were maritime cases, but we have recognized the principle that the scope of generally worded statutes must be construed in light of international law in other areas as well. ... More specifically, the principle was expressed in *U.S. v. Aluminum Co. of America*, 148 F.2d 416 (CA2 1945), the decision that established the extraterritorial reach of the Sherman Act. In his opinion for the court, Judge Learned Hand cautioned "we are not to read general words, such as those in [the Sherman] Act, without regard to the limitations customarily observed by nations upon the exercise of their powers; limitations which generally correspond to those fixed by the 'Conflict of Laws.'" Id., at 443.

More recent lower court precedent has also tempered the extraterritorial application of the Sherman Act with considerations of "international comity." The "comity" they refer to is not the comity of courts, whereby judges decline to exercise jurisdiction over matters more appropriately adjudged elsewhere, but rather what might be termed "prescriptive comity": the respect sovereign nations afford each other by limiting the reach of their laws. That comity is exercised by legislatures when they enact laws, and courts assume it has been exercised when they come to interpreting the scope of laws their legislatures have enacted. It is a traditional component of choice-of-law theory. See J. Story, Commentaries on the Conflict of Laws § 38 (1834) (distinguishing between the "comity of the courts" and the "comity of nations," and defining the latter as "the true foundation and extent of the obligation of the laws of one nation within the territories of another"). Comity in this sense includes the choice-of-law principles that, "in the absence of contrary congressional direction," are assumed to be incorporated into our substantive laws having extraterritorial reach. *Romero*, supra, at 382-383; see also *Lauritzen*, supra, at 578-579; *Hilton v. Guyot*, 159 U.S. 113, 162-166 (1895). Considering comity in this way is just part of determining whether the Sherman Act prohibits the conduct at issue.

In sum, the practice of using international law to limit the extraterritorial reach of statutes is firmly established in our jurisprudence. In proceeding to apply that practice to the present cases, I shall rely on the Restatement (Third) for the relevant principles of international law. Its standards appear fairly supported in the decisions of this Court construing international choice-of-law principles

(*Lauritzen*, *Romero*, and *McCulloch*) and in the decisions of other federal courts, especially Timberlane. Whether the Restatement precisely reflects international law in every detail matters little here, as I believe this litigation would be resolved the same way under virtually any conceivable test that takes account of foreign regulatory interests.

Under the Restatement, a nation having some "basis" for jurisdiction to prescribe law should nonetheless refrain from exercising that jurisdiction "with respect to a person or activity having connections with another state when the exercise of such jurisdiction is unreasonable." Restatement (Third) § 403(1). The "reasonableness" inquiry turns on a number of factors including, but not limited to: "the extent to which the activity takes place within the territory [of the regulating state]," id., § 403(2)(a); "the connections, such as nationality, residence, or economic activity, between the regulating state and the person principally responsible for the activity to be regulated," id., § 403(2)(b); "the character of the activity to be regulated, the importance of regulation to the regulating state, the extent to which other states regulate such activities, and the degree to which the desirability of such regulation is generally accepted," id., § 403(2)(c); "the extent to which another state may have an interest in regulating the activity," id., § 403(2)(g); and "the likelihood of conflict with regulation by another state," id., § 403(2)(h). Rarely would these factors point more clearly against application of United States law. The activity relevant to the counts at issue here took place primarily in the United Kingdom, and the defendants in these counts are British corporations and British subjects having their principal place of business or residence outside the United States. Great Britain has established a comprehensive regulatory scheme governing the London reinsurance markets, and clearly has a heavy "interest in regulating the activity." Finally, § 2(b) of the McCarran-Ferguson Act allows state regulatory statutes to override the Sherman Act in the insurance field, subject only to the narrow "boycott" exception set forth in § 3(b)—suggesting that "the importance of regulation to the [United States]," Restatement (Third) § 403(2)(c), is slight. Considering these factors, I think it unimaginable that an assertion of legislative jurisdiction by the United States would be considered reasonable, and therefore it is inappropriate to assume, in the absence of statutory indication to the contrary, that Congress has made such an assertion.

It is evident from what I have said that the Court's comity analysis, which proceeds as though the issue is whether the courts should "decline to exercise ... jurisdiction," rather than whether the Sherman Act covers this conduct, is simply misdirected. I do not at all agree, moreover, with the Court's conclusion that the issue of the substantive scope of the Sherman Act is not in the cases. To be sure, the parties did not make a clear distinction between adjudicative jurisdiction and the scope of the statute. Parties often do not, as we have observed (and have declined to punish with procedural default) before. It is not realistic, and also not helpful, to pretend that the only really relevant issue in this litigation is not before us. In any event, if one erroneously chooses, as the Court does, to make adjudicative jurisdiction (or, more precisely, abstention) the vehicle for taking account of the needs of prescriptive comity, the Court still gets it wrong. It concludes that no "true conflict" counseling nonapplication of United States law (or rather, as it thinks, United States judicial jurisdiction) exists unless compliance with United States law would constitute a violation of another country's law. That breathtakingly broad proposition, which contradicts the many cases discussed earlier, will bring the Sherman Act and other laws into sharp and unnecessary conflict with the legitimate interests of other countries—particularly our closest trading partners.

f. F. Hoffman-LaRoche Ltd. v. Empagran S.A.

124 S.Ct. 2359 (2004)

JUSTICE BREYER delivered the opinion of the Court.

The Foreign Trade Antitrust Improvements Act of 1982 (FTAIA) excludes from the Sherman Act's reach much anticompetitive conduct that causes only foreign injury. It does so by setting forth a general rule stating that the Sherman Act "shall not apply to conduct involving trade or commerce ... with foreign nations." 96 Stat. 1246, 15 U.S.C. § 6a. It then creates exceptions to the general rule, applicable where (roughly speaking) that conduct significantly harms imports, domestic commerce, or American exporters.

We here focus upon anticompetitive price-fixing activity that is in significant part foreign, that causes some domestic antitrust injury, and that independently causes separate foreign injury. We ask two questions about the price-fixing conduct and the foreign injury that it causes. First, does that conduct fall within the FTAIA's general rule excluding the Sherman Act's application? That is to say, does the price-fixing activity constitute "conduct involving trade or commerce ... with foreign nations"? We conclude that it does.

Second, we ask whether the conduct nonetheless falls within a domestic-injury exception to the general rule, an exception that applies (and makes the Sherman Act nonetheless applicable) where the conduct (1) has a "direct, substantial, and reasonably foreseeable effect" on domestic commerce, and (2) "such effect gives rise to a [Sherman Act] claim." § § 6a(1)(A), (2). We conclude that the exception does not apply where the plaintiff's claim rests solely on the independent foreign harm.

To clarify: The issue before us concerns (1) significant foreign anticompetitive conduct with (2) an adverse domestic effect and (3) an independent foreign effect giving rise to the claim. In more concrete terms, this case involves vitamin sellers around the world that agreed to fix prices, leading to higher vitamin prices in the United States and independently leading to higher vitamin prices in other countries such as Ecuador. We conclude that, in this scenario, a purchaser in the United States could bring a Sherman Act claim under the FTAIA based on domestic injury, but a purchaser in Ecuador could not bring a Sherman Act claim based on foreign harm. ...

The plaintiffs in this case originally filed a class-action suit on behalf of foreign and domestic purchasers of vitamins under, *inter alia,* § 1 of the Sherman Act, 26 Stat. 209, as amended, 15 U.S.C. § 1, and §§ 4 and 16 of the Clayton Act, 38 Stat. 731, 737, as amended, 15 U.S.C. §§ 15, 26. Their complaint alleged that petitioners, foreign and domestic vitamin manufacturers and distributors, had engaged in a price-fixing conspiracy, raising the price of vitamin products to customers in the United States and to customers in foreign countries.

As relevant here, petitioners moved to dismiss the suit as to the *foreign* purchasers (the respondents here), five foreign vitamin distributors located in Ukraine, Australia, Ecuador, and Panama, each of which bought vitamins from petitioners for delivery outside the United States. 2001 WL 761360, (D.D.C., June 7, 2001) (describing the relevant transactions as "wholly foreign"). Respondents have never asserted that they purchased any vitamins in the United States or in transactions in United States commerce, and the question presented assumes that the relevant "transactions occurr[ed] entirely outside U.S. commerce." The District Court dismissed their claims. *Ibid.* It applied the FTAIA and found none of the exceptions applicable. ... Thereafter, the *domestic* purchasers transferred their claims to another pending suit and did not take part in the subsequent appeal. 315 F.3d 338, 343 (C.A.D.C.2003). ...

The FTAIA seeks to make clear to American exporters (and to firms doing business abroad) that the Sherman Act does not prevent them from entering into business arrangements (say, joint-selling arrangements), however anticompetitive, as long as those arrangements adversely affect only foreign markets. ... It does so by removing from the Sherman Act's reach, (1) export activities and (2) other commercial activities taking place abroad, *unless* those activities adversely affect domestic commerce, imports to the United States, or exporting activities of one engaged in such activities within the United States.

The FTAIA says:

> Sections 1 to 7 of this title [the Sherman Act] shall not apply to conduct involving trade or commerce (other than import trade or import commerce) with foreign nations unless—
>
> (1) such conduct has a direct, substantial, and reasonably foreseeable effect—
>
> > (A) on trade or commerce which is not trade or commerce with foreign nations [*i.e.,* domestic trade or commerce], or on import trade or import commerce with foreign nations; or
> >
> > (B) on export trade or export commerce with foreign nations, of a person engaged in such trade or commerce in the United States [*i.e.,* on an American export competitor]; and
>
> (2) such effect gives rise to a claim under the provisions of sections 1 to 7 of this title, other than this section.

> If sections 1 to 7 of this title apply to such conduct only because of the operation of paragraph (1)(B), then sections 1 to 7 of this title shall apply to such conduct only for injury to export business in the United States. 15 U.S.C. § 6a.

This technical language initially lays down a general rule placing *all* (non-import) activity involving foreign commerce outside the Sherman Act's reach. It then brings such conduct back within the Sherman Act's reach *provided that* the conduct *both* (1) sufficiently affects American commerce, *i.e.,* it has a "direct, substantial, and reasonably foreseeable effect" on American domestic, import, or (certain) export commerce, *and* (2) has an effect of a kind that antitrust law considers harmful, *i.e.,* the "effect" must "giv[e] rise to a [Sherman Act] claim." §§ 6a(1), (2).

We ask here how this language applies to price-fixing activity that is in significant part foreign, that has the requisite domestic effect, and that also has independent foreign effects giving rise to the plaintiff's claim. ... [The Court examined the legislative history.]

We turn now to the basic question presented, that of the exception's application. Because the underlying antitrust action is complex, potentially raising questions not directly at issue here, we reemphasize that we base our decision upon the following: The price-fixing conduct significantly and adversely affects both customers outside the United States and customers within the United States, but the adverse foreign effect is independent of any adverse domestic effect. In these circumstances, we find that the FTAIA exception does not apply (and thus the Sherman Act does not apply) for two main reasons.

First, this Court ordinarily construes ambiguous statutes to avoid unreasonable interference with the sovereign authority of other nations. ...

This rule of statutory construction cautions courts to assume that legislators take account of the legitimate sovereign interests of other nations when they write American laws. It thereby helps the potentially conflicting laws of different nations work together in harmony—a harmony particularly needed in today's highly interdependent commercial world.

No one denies that America's antitrust laws, when applied to foreign conduct, can interfere with a foreign nation's ability independently to regulate its own commercial affairs. But our courts have long held that application of our antitrust laws to foreign anticompetitive conduct is nonetheless reasonable, and hence consistent with principles of prescriptive comity, insofar as they reflect a legislative effort to redress *domestic* antitrust injury that foreign anticompetitive conduct has caused. See *United States v. Aluminum Co. of America,* 148 F.2d 416, 443-444 (C.A.2 1945) (L.Hand, J.); 1 P. Areeda & D. Turner, Antitrust Law ¶ 236 (1978).

But why is it reasonable to apply those laws to foreign conduct *insofar as that conduct causes independent foreign harm and that foreign harm alone gives rise to the plaintiff's claim?* Like the former case, application of those laws creates a serious risk of interference with a foreign nation's ability independently to regulate its own commercial affairs. But, unlike the former case, the justification for that interference seems insubstantial. See Restatement § 403(2) (determining reasonableness on basis of such factors as connections with regulating nation, harm to that nation's interests, extent to which other nations regulate, and the potential for conflict). Why should American law supplant, for example, Canada's or Great Britain's or Japan's own determination about how best to protect Canadian or British or Japanese customers from anticompetitive conduct engaged in significant part by Canadian or British or Japanese or other foreign companies?

We recognize that principles of comity provide Congress greater leeway when it seeks to control through legislation the actions of *American* companies, see Restatement § 402; and some of the anticompetitive price-fixing conduct alleged here took place in *America.* But the higher foreign prices of which the foreign plaintiffs here complain are not the consequence of any domestic anticompetitive conduct *that Congress sought to forbid,* for Congress did not seek to forbid any such conduct insofar as it is here relevant, *i.e.,* insofar as it is intertwined with foreign conduct that causes independent foreign harm. Rather Congress sought to *release* domestic (and foreign) anticompetitive conduct from Sherman Act constraints when that conduct causes foreign harm. Congress, of course, did make an exception where that conduct also causes domestic harm. See House Report 13, U.S.Code Cong. & Admin.News 1982, 2487, 2498 (concerns about American firms' participation in international cartels addressed through "domestic injury" exception). But any independent domestic harm the foreign conduct causes here has, by definition, little or nothing to do with the matter.

We thus repeat the basic question: Why is it reasonable to apply this law to conduct that is significantly foreign *insofar as that conduct causes independent foreign harm and that foreign harm alone gives rise to the plaintiff's claim?* We can find no good answer to the question.

The Areeda and Hovenkamp treatise notes that under the Court of Appeals' interpretation of the statute

> [a] Malaysian customer could ... maintain an action under United States law in a United States court against its own Malaysian supplier, another cartel member, simply by noting that unnamed third parties injured [in the United States] by the American [cartel member's] conduct would also have a cause of action. Effectively, the United States courts would provide worldwide subject matter jurisdiction to any foreign suitor wishing to sue its own local supplier, but unhappy with its own sovereign's provisions for private antitrust enforcement, provided that a different plaintiff had a cause of action against a different firm for injuries that were within U.S. [other-than-import] commerce. It does not seem ex-

cessively rigid to infer that Congress would not have intended that result. P. Areeda & H. Hovenkamp, Antitrust Law ¶ 273, pp. 51-52 (Supp.2003).

We agree with the comment. We can find no convincing justification for the extension of the Sherman Act's scope that it describes.

Respondents reply that many nations have adopted antitrust laws similar to our own, to the point where the practical likelihood of interference with the relevant interests of other nations is minimal. Leaving price fixing to the side, however, this Court has found to the contrary. See, *e.g., Hartford Fire,* 509 U.S. at 797-799, 113 S.Ct. 2891 (noting that the alleged conduct in the London reinsurance market, while illegal under United States antitrust laws, was assumed to be perfectly consistent with British law and policy) …

Regardless, even where nations agree about primary conduct, say price fixing, they disagree dramatically about appropriate remedies. The application, for example, of American private treble-damages remedies to anticompetitive conduct taking place abroad has generated considerable controversy. … And several foreign nations have filed briefs here arguing that to apply our remedies would unjustifiably permit their citizens to bypass their own less generous remedial schemes, thereby upsetting a balance of competing considerations that their own domestic antitrust laws embody. *E.g.,* Brief for Federal Republic of Germany et al. as *Amici Curiae* 2 (setting forth German interest "in seeing that German companies are not subject to the extraterritorial reach of the United States' antitrust laws by private foreign plaintiffs—whose injuries were sustained in transactions entirely outside United States commerce—seeking treble damages in private lawsuits against German companies"); Brief for Government of Canada as *Amicus Curiae* 14 ("treble damages remedy would supersede" Canada's "national policy decision"); Brief for Government of Japan as *Amicus Curiae* 10 (finding "particularly troublesome" the potential "interfere[nce] with Japanese governmental regulation of the Japanese market").

These briefs add that a decision permitting independently injured foreign plaintiffs to pursue private treble-damages remedies would undermine foreign nations' own antitrust enforcement policies by diminishing foreign firms' incentive to cooperate with antitrust authorities in return for prosecutorial amnesty. …

Respondents alternatively argue that comity does not demand an interpretation of the FTAIA that would exclude independent foreign injury cases *across the board.* Rather, courts can take (and sometimes have taken) account of comity considerations case by case, abstaining where comity considerations so dictate. Cf., *e.g., Hartford Fire, supra,* at 797, n. 24, 113 S.Ct. 2891; *United States v. Nippon Paper Industries Co.,* 109 F.3d 1, 8 (C.A.1 1997); *Mannington Mills, Inc. v. Congoleum Corp.,* 595 F.2d 1287, 1294-1295 (C.A.3 1979).

In our view, however, this approach is too complex to prove workable. The Sherman Act covers many different kinds of anticompetitive agreements. Courts would have to examine how foreign law, compared with American law, treats not only price fixing but also, say, information-sharing agreements, patent- licensing price conditions, territorial product resale limitations, and various forms of joint venture, in respect to both primary conduct and remedy. The legally and economically technical nature of that enterprise means lengthier proceedings, appeals, and more proceedings—to the point where procedural costs and delays could themselves threaten interference with a foreign nation's ability to maintain the integrity of its own antitrust enforcement system. Even in this relatively simple price-fixing case, for example, competing briefs tell us (1) that potential treble-damage liability would help enforce widespread anti-price-fixing norms (through added deterrence) and (2) the opposite, namely that such liability would hinder antitrust enforcement (by reducing incentives to enter amnesty programs). ... How could a court seriously interested in resolving so empirical a matter— a matter potentially related to impact on foreign interests—do so simply and expeditiously?

We conclude that principles of prescriptive comity counsel against the Court of Appeals' interpretation of the FTAIA. Where foreign anticompetitive conduct plays a significant role and where foreign injury is independent of domestic effects, Congress might have hoped that America's antitrust laws, so fundamental a component of our own economic system, would commend themselves to other nations as well. But, if America's antitrust policies could not win their own way in the international marketplace for such ideas, Congress, we must assume, would not have tried to impose them, in an act of legal imperialism, through legislative fiat. ...

Nevertheless, respondents now have called to our attention six cases, three decided by this Court and three decided by lower courts. ...

The upshot is that no pre-1982 case provides significant authority for application of the Sherman Act in the circumstances we here assume. Indeed, a leading contemporaneous lower court case contains language suggesting the contrary. See *Timberlane Lumber Co. v. Bank of America,* 549 F.2d 597, 613 (C.A.9 1976) (insisting that the foreign conduct's domestic effect be "sufficiently large to present a cognizable injury *to the plaintiffs*" (emphasis added)).

Taken together, these two sets of considerations, the one derived from comity and the other reflecting history, convince us that Congress would not have intended the FTAIA's exception to bring independently caused foreign injury within the Sherman Act's reach. ...

We have assumed that the anticompetitive conduct here independently caused foreign injury; that is, the conduct's domestic effects did not help to bring about that foreign injury. Respondents argue, in the alternative, that the foreign injury was not independent. Rather, they say, the anticompetitive conduct's domestic effects were linked to that foreign harm. Respondents contend that, because vitamins are fungible and readily transportable, without an adverse domestic effect (*i.e.,* higher prices in the United States), the sellers could not have maintained their international price-fixing arrangement and respondents would not have suffered their foreign injury. They add that this "but for" condition is sufficient to bring the price-fixing conduct within the scope of the FTAIA's exception.

The Court of Appeals, however, did not address this argument … and, for that reason, neither shall we. Respondents remain free to ask the Court of Appeals to consider the claim. The Court of Appeals may determine whether respondents properly preserved the argument, and, if so, it may consider it and decide the related claim.

For these reasons, the judgment of the Court of Appeals is vacated, and the case is remanded for further proceedings consistent with this opinion. …

JUSTICE SCALIA, with whom JUSTICE THOMAS joins, concurring in the judgment.

I concur in the judgment of the Court because the language of the statute is readily susceptible of the interpretation the Court provides and because only that interpretation is consistent with the principle that statutes should be read in accord with the customary deference to the application of foreign countries' laws within their own territories.

NOTES AND QUESTIONS

1. *Hoffman-La Roche* stimulated the following comment by Professor George Priest:

> The Court, appropriately, did not discuss the broader public policy issues regarding globalization. It based its decision on the importance of avoiding interference with the sovereign authority of other nations and on its interpretation of congressional intent. But the implications of the values defined in the Court's opinion are clear.
>
> Democrats, including Messrs. Gephardt and Kerry, claim that it is only fair to American workers if the foreign competition that they face is subjected to identical levels of labor and environmental regulation that the workers are subjected to in the U.S. Thus, they demand that free trade agreements be conscribed by the requirement that the foreign nation adopt standards similar to those that prevail in the U.S. Practically, these demands are only relevant to trade agreements with developing nations, subjecting them to much stricter levels of regulation than the nations themselves desire.
>
> However protective of U.S. workers, these demands constitute harmful economic policy. They destroy the comparative advantage of the developing nations and cripple the extent to which workers in these nations can make use of their developing workplace abilities. Put starkly, these demands keep developing nations poor.
>
> The Supreme Court recognized this problem in the Hoffman-La Roche case and established, at least for antitrust regulation, the principle of allowing each nation to define its own regulatory policy.

George Priest, *Supreme Wisdom*, WALL ST. J., June 18, 2004, at A10.

2. Consider the following cases: *U.S. v. Nippon Paper Industries Co.,* 109 F.3d 1 (1st Cir. 1997) (holding that activities that took place entirely abroad that had a substantial and intended effect in the U.S. could serve as the basis for a criminal prosecution under Section One of the Sherman Antitrust Act); *U.S. v. Vasquez-Velasco*, 15 F.3d 833 (9th Cir. 1994) (affirming conviction under federal racketeering statute of defendant accused of committing violent crimes to further his position in drug trafficking enterprise in Mexico); *Independent Union of Flight Attendants v. Pan Am*,

923 F.2d 678 (9th Cir. 1991) (holding that the Railway Labor Act did not apply extraterritorially with respect to purely foreign flights); *Pfeiffer v. Wm. Wrigley Jr. Co.*, 755 F.2d 554 (7th Cir. 1985) (finding that the Age Discrimination in Employment Act did not apply extraterritorially to apply to a German subsidiary of an American employer). *See also* William Dubois, *New Drug Research, The Extraterritorial Application of FDA Regulations, and the Need for International Cooperation*, 36 VAND. J. TRANSNAT'L L. 161 (2003); William J. Tuttle, *The Return of Timberlane?: The Fifth Circuit Signals a Return to Restrictive Notions of Extraterritorial Antitrust*, 36 VAND. J. TRANSNAT'L L. 319 (2003).

3. European jurisprudence and scholarship had long been critical of the American judicial practice of extensive extraterritorial jurisdiction. But *Re Wood Pulp Cartel*, 1988 E.C.R. 5193, the then Court of Justice of the European Communities essentially adopted an effects approach:

> It should be observed that an infringement of Article 85, such as the conclusion of an agreement which has had the effect of restricting competition within the Common Market, consists of conduct made up of two elements, the formation of the agreement, decision or concerted practice and the implementation thereof. If the applicability of prohibitions laid down under competition law were made to depend on the place where the agreement, decision or concerted practice was formed, the result would obviously be to give undertakings an easy means of evading those prohibitions. The decisive factor is therefore the place where it is implemented.
>
> The producers in this case implemented their pricing agreement within the Common Market. It is immaterial in that respect whether or not they had recourse to subsidiaries, agents, sub-agents, or branches within the Community in order to make their contacts with purchasers within the Community.
>
> Accordingly the Community's jurisdiction to apply its competition rules to such conduct is covered by the territoriality principle as universally recognised in public international law. …

4. What are the reasons that account for the European Court, after many years of criticizing the imperial and expansive character of effects jurisdiction, adopting this jurisdiction itself? Is the increasing interdependence and integration of the economies of territorial communities a factor that necessarily pushes each of them toward an effects jurisdiction as a way of protecting their social and economic processes? *See* Salil K. Mehra, *Deterrence: The Private Remedy and International Antitrust Cases*, 40 COLUM. J. TRANSNAT'L L. 275 (2001-2002); Robert Wai, *Transnational Liftoff and Juridical Touchdown: The Regulatory Function of Private International Law in an Era of Globalization*, 40 COLUM. J. TRANSNAT'L L. 209 (2001-2002).

5. The E.C. and the United States have recently signed an agreement that commits them to cooperate in the application of their antitrust laws. *See* Agreement between the European Communities and the Government of the United States of America on the Application of Positive Comity Principles in the Enforcement of Their Competition Laws, 37 I.L.M. 1070 (1998).

g. The Helms-Burton Incident

In 1996, Congress passed the Cuban Liberty and Democratic Solidarity (Libertad) Act (104 Pub. L. 114; 110 Stat. 785) which, among other things, established liability, with civil remedies in United States courts, for trafficking in confiscated property in Cuba claimed by United States nationals. (The text of the legislation is set out in Part Six, *supra*.) The European Union reacted sharply to the United States legislation.

(1) European Union: Demarches Protesting the Cuban Liberty and Democratic Solidarity (Libertad) Act

35 I.L.M. 397 (1996)

The Presidency of the Council of the European Union and the European Commission present their compliments to the Department of State and wish to refer to the Cuban Liberty and Democratic Solidarity (LIBERTAD) Act of 1996.

The European Union (EU) has consistently expressed its opposition, as a matter of law and policy, to extraterritorial applications of US jurisdiction which would also restrict EU trade in goods and services with Cuba, as already stated in various diplomatic demarches made in Washington last year, including a letter from Sir Leon Brittan to Secretary of State Warren Christopher. Although the EU is fully supportive of a peaceful transition in Cuba, it cannot accept that the US unilaterally determine and restrict EU economic and commercial relations with third countries.

The EU is consequently extremely concerned by the latest developments in the House-Senate Conference in relation to this legislation, including the position now apparently taken by the US Administration. The legislation contains several objectionable elements. In addition, provisions relating to trafficking in confiscated property and those concerning denial of visas to executives or shareholders of companies involved in transactions concerning confiscated properties in Cuba, which had been removed during the adoption procedure by the Senate last 19 October 1995, have now been reintroduced by the House-Senate Conference. These provisions, if enacted and implemented, risk leading to legal chaos.

The EU cannot accept the prohibition for US-owned or controlled firms from financing other firms that might be involved in certain economic transactions with Cuba. The EU has stated on many occasions that such an extraterritorial extension of US jurisdiction is unacceptable as a matter of law and policy. Therefore, the EU takes the position that the United States has no basis in international law to claim the right to regulate in any way transactions taking place outside the United States with Cuba undertaken by subsidiaries of US companies incorporated outside the US.

Nor can … we accept the immediate impact of the legislation on the trade interests of the EU by prohibiting the entry of its sugars, syrups and molasses into the US, unless the former certifies that it will not import such products from Cuba. The EU considers such requests, designed to enforce a US policy which is not applied by the EU, as illegitimate. Such measures would appear unjustifiable under GATT 1994 and would appear to violate the general principles of international law and sovereignty on independent states.

In these circumstances, the EU would appreciate it if you would inform Congress that the EU is currently examining the compatibility of this legislation with WTO rules and that the EU will react to protect all its legitimate rights.

The EU is also worried by the provisions that would lead the US to unilaterally reduce payments to international institutions, such as the IMF. This measure would run counter to collectively agreed upon obligations vis-à-vis those institutions and would represent an attempt to influence improperly their internal decision-making processes.

The EU also finds most worrying the reduction of US assistance to the Russian Federation as a possible consequence of this legislation. Such a measure would not only weaken Western leverage in favour of reforms, but comes at a critical junction in time.

Finally the EU objects, as a matter of principle, to those provisions that seek to assert extraterritorial jurisdiction of US Federal courts over disputes between the US and foreign companies regarding expropriated property located overseas. This measure would risk complicating not only third country economic relations with Cuba, but also any transitional process in Cuba itself. Furthermore, these provisions offer the possibility to US firms for legal harassment against foreign competitors that choose to do business in Cuba. The threat of denial of a US visa for corporate officers and shareholders accentuates this concern.

The EU considers that the collective effects of these provisions have the potential to cause grave damage to bilateral EU-US relations. For these reasons, the EU urges the US Administration to use its influence to seek appropriate modifications to the proposed legislation, or if this should not be feasible, to prevent it from being enacted.

Should the legislation be adopted, the European Union intends to defend its legitimate interests in the appropriate international fora.

(2) Council Regulation (EC) No 2271/96, of 22 November 1996 Protecting Against the Effects of the Extra-territorial Application of Legislation Adopted by a Third Country, and Actions Based Thereon or Resulting Therefrom

36 I.L.M. 125 (1997)

Whereas the objectives of the Community include contributing to the harmonious development of world trade and to the progressive abolition of restrictions on international trade;

Whereas the Community endeavours to achieve to the greatest extent possible the objective of free movement of capital between Member States and third countries, including the removal of any restrictions on direct investment—including investment in real estate—establishment, the provision of financial services or the admission of securities to capital markets;

Whereas a third country has enacted certain laws, regulations, and other legislative instruments which purport to regulate activities of natural and legal persons under the jurisdiction of the Member State;

Whereas by their extra-territorial application such laws, regulations and other legislative instruments violate international law and impede the attainment of the aforementioned objectives;

Whereas such laws, including regulations and other legislative instruments, and actions based thereon or resulting therefrom affect or are likely to affect the established legal order and have adverse effects on the interests of the Community and the interests of natural and legal persons exercising rights under the Treaty establishing the European Community;

Whereas, under these exceptional circumstances, it is necessary to take action at the Community level to protect the established legal order, the interests of the Community and the interests of the said natural and legal persons, in particular by removing, neutralising, blocking or otherwise countering the effects of the foreign legislation concerned; ...

Whereas the actions provided for in this Regulation are necessary to attain objectives of the Treaty establishing the European Community; ...

HAS ADOPTED THIS REGULATION:

Article 1

This Regulation provides protection against and counteracts the effects of the extra-territorial application of the laws specified in the Annex of this Regulation, including regulations and other legislative instruments, and of actions based thereon or resulting therefrom, where such application affects the interests of persons, referred to in Article 11, engaging in international trade and/or the movement of capital and related commercial activities between the Community and third countries.

Acting in accordance with the relevant provisions of the Treaty and notwithstanding the provisions of Article 7 (c), the Council may add or delete laws to or from the Annex to this Regulation.

Article 2

Where the economic and/or financial interests of any person referred to in Article 11 are affected, directly or indirectly, by the laws specified in the Annex or by actions based thereon or resulting therefrom, that person shall inform the Commission accordingly within 30 days from the date on which it obtained such information; insofar as the interests of a legal person are affected, this obligation applies to the directors, managers and other persons with management responsibilities.

At the request of the Commission, such person shall provide all information relevant for the purposes of this Regulation in accordance with the request from the Commission within 30 days from the date of the request.

All information shall be submitted to the Commission either directly or through the competent authorities of the Member States. Should the information be submitted directly to the Commission, the Commission will inform immediately the competent authorities of the Member States in which the person who gave the information is resident or incorporated. …

Article 4

No judgment of a court or tribunal and no decision of an administrative authority located outside the Community giving effect, directly or indirectly, to the laws specified in the Annex or to actions based thereon or resulting therefrom, shall be recognized or be enforceable in any manner.

Article 5

No person referred to in Article 11 shall comply, whether directly or through a subsidiary or other intermediary person, actively or by deliberate omission, with any requirement or prohibition, including requests of foreign courts, based on or resulting, directly or indirectly, from the laws specified in the Annex or from actions based thereon or resulting therefrom.

Persons may be authorized, in accordance with the procedures provided in Articles 7 and 8, to comply fully or partially to the extent that non- compliance would seriously damage their interests or those of the Community. The criteria for the application of this provision shall be established in accordance with the procedure set out in Article 8. When there is sufficient evidence that non-compliance would cause serious damage to a natural or legal person, the Commission shall expeditiously submit to the committee referred to in Article 8 a draft of the appropriate measures to be taken under the terms of the Regulation.

Article 6

Any person referred to in Article 11, who is engaging in an activity referred to in Article 1 shall be entitled to recover any damages, including legal costs, caused to that person by the application of the laws specified in the Annex or by actions based thereon or resulting therefrom.

Such recovery may be obtained from the natural or legal person or any other entity causing the damages or from any person acting on its behalf or intermediary.

The Brussels Convention of 27 September 1968 on jurisdiction and the enforcement of judgments in civil and commercial matters shall apply to proceedings brought and judgments given under this Article. Recovery may be obtained on the basis of the provisions of Sections 2 to 6 of Title II of that Convention, as well as, in accordance with Article 57 (3) of that Convention, through judicial proceedings instituted in the Courts of any Member State where that person, entity, person acting on its behalf or intermediary holds assets.

Without prejudice to other means available and in accordance with applicable law, the recovery could take the form of seizure and sale of assets held by those persons, entities, persons acting on their behalf or intermediaries within the Community, including shares held in a legal person incorporated within the Community. …

Article 11

This Regulation shall apply to:

1. any natural person being a resident in the Community and a national of a Member State,

2. any legal person incorporated within the Community,

3. any natural or legal person referred to in Article 1 (2) of Regulation (EEC) No 4055/86,

4. any other natural person being a resident in the Community, unless that person is in the country of which he is a national,

5. any other natural person within the Community, including its territorial waters and air space and in any aircraft or on any vessel under the jurisdiction or control of a Member State, acting in a professional capacity.

* * *

On January 3, 1997, President Clinton suspended the operation of the right to file suit under the Cuban Liberty and Democratic Solidarity Act for an additional six months, ostensibly "to consolidate and build on the momentum we have generated for democratic change in Cuba." Statement by the President on suspending Title III of the Helms-Burton Act, January 3, 1997, 36 ILM 216 (1997).

The suspension has been continued by President George W. Bush:

(3) Statement by the President, The Cuban Liberty and Democratic Solidarity Act Title III

July 16, 2001, *available at* http://usinfo.state.gov/regional/ar/us-cuba/burton17.htm

Today, I transmitted to Congress my decision to exercise the authority granted to me under the Cuban Liberty and Democratic Solidarity(LIBERTAD) Act to suspend for six months, from August 1 through January 31, the right to bring actions under Title III of that Act. In exercising this authority, I do so taking into account that it is necessary for the national interest of the United States and will expedite the transition to democracy in Cuba.

Real differences remain between the United States and our allies concerning the best methods for pursuing change in Cuba. However, for its part, the European Union has again renewed its Common Position on Cuba and has reaffirmed its goal of promoting a peaceful transition to democracy in Cuba. Our actions will encourage support for the embargo and further strengthen, not weaken, the growing multilateral, multi-faceted movement to promote democracy and human rights in Cuba.

My Administration is firmly committed to a proactive Cuba policy that will assist the Cuban people in their struggle for freedom. On Friday, I reaffirmed my commitment to maintain existing sanctions against the Cuban regime and to strengthening pro-democracy movements in Cuba. I call upon the European Union and the international community to work together with us toward the fundamental goals that should unite us: free speech, free elections, and respect for basic human rights in Cuba.

(4) Understanding with Respect to Disciplines for the Strengthening of Investment Protection EU-U.S. Summit in London, May 18, 1998

available at http://www.eurunion.org/news/invest.htm

The United States and the European Union (hereinafter, 'the participants').

Recalling the Understanding of April 11, 1997, which stated, inter alia: 'The EU and the U.S agree to step up their efforts to develop agreed disciplines and principles for the strengthening of investment protection, bilaterally and in the context of the Multilateral Agreement on Investment (MAI) or other appropriate international fora.

Recognising that the standard of protection governing expropriation and nationalisation embodied in international law and envisioned in the MAI should be respected by all States. These disciplines should inhibit and deter the future acquisition of investments from any State which has expropriated or nationalised such investments in contravention of international law, and subsequent dealings in covered investments.'

Wish to confirm in this Understanding their intention to propose jointly in negotiation of the Multilateral Agreement on Investment (MAI) the disciplines reflected in Part I of this Understanding and to apply those disciplines as a matter of policy, in accordance with Part II prior to entry into force of the MAI. …

II. MODALITIES

4. The U.S. Administration will continue intensive consultations with the Congress with a view to obtaining an amendment to Title IV of the Libertad Act that would provide authority for a waiver that would apply, with respect to the EU, without a specific time limit, so long as this Understanding is in effect. Application of the disciplines and exercise of such waiver authority will be simultaneous.

5. The U.S. Administration is prepared, in the light of the EU's developing efforts to promote democracy and human rights in Cuba, to take soundings of Congressional opinion and consult Congress with a view to obtaining a Title III waiver provision that would have no specific time limit, so long as these efforts continue and bearing in mind the duration of the presumption of a Title III waiver in the April 1997 Understanding.

6. Taking into account paragraph 5(b) of Annex B, neither participant will prevent the making of settlements with respect to property as to which there is a claim of expropriation in contravention of international law while this Understanding is in effect.

7. The participants will consider whether there should be future work to further their objective of strengthening the international protection of property rights in the context of investment protection. …

NOTES AND QUESTIONS

1. Consider also: Inter-American Juridical Committee Opinion Examining the U.S. Helms-Burton Act, 35 I.L.M. 1322 (1996); United Nations General Assembly: Resolution on the Necessity of Ending the Economic, Commercial and Financial Embargo Imposed by the United States of America Against Cuba, U.N. Doc. A/RES/52/10, November 5, 1997, 37 I.L.M. 247 (1998); Cuba: Reaffirmation of Cuban Dignity and Sovereignty Act 36 I.L.M. 472 (1997); Canada: Foreign Extraterritorial Measures Act Incorporating the Amendments Countering the U.S. Helms-Burton Act, 36 I.L.M. 111 (1997); Mexico: Act to Protect Trade and Investment from Foreign Norms that Contravene International Law, 36 I.L.M. 133 (1997). *See also* Bernadette Atuahene, *The Effectiveness of International Legislative Responses to the Helms-Burton Act*, 69 REV. JUR. U.P.R. 809 (2000); Manuel A. Rodriguez, *III The Helms-Burton Act: U.S. vs. European Union, Helms Burton: Social Policy and Norm Definition*, 10 U. MIAMI INT'L & COMP. L. REV. 63 (2002); Runa Kinzel, *III The Helms-Burton Act: U.S. vs. European Union, Helms Burton: A View from Abroad*, 10 U. MIAMI INT'L & COMP. L. REV. 81 (2002); H. Scott Fairley, *Relating to and Doing Business With Cuba: A Canadian Perspective*, 36 INT'L LAW. 1117 (2002); and James E. Ward, *"Is That Your Final Answer?" The Patchwork Jurisprudence Surrounding the Presumption Against Extraterritoriality*, 70 U. CIN. L. REV. 715 (2002).

2. To what extent does Helms-Burton conflict with obligations assumed by the United States under the GATT and the World Trade Organization? *See*, in this regard, Hannes L. Schloemann & Stefan Ohlhoff, *"Constitutionalization" and Dispute Settlement in the WTO: National Security as an Issue of Competence*, 93 AM. J. INT'L L. 424 (1999).

3. Section 5(a) of the Iran and Libya Sanctions Act of 1996, Public. L. No. 104-172, 110 Stat. 1541 (codified at 50 U.S.C. 1701), provides that "the President shall impose 2 or more of the sanctions ... [provided for in] section 6 if the President determines that a person has, with actual knowledge, … made an investment of $40,000,000 or more ... that directly and significantly contributed to the enhancement of Iran's ability to develop petroleum resources of Iran." Section 5(b)(2) applies an identical provision to Libya. Sanctions provided for in section 6 include: the denial of Export-Import Bank financing; the denial of export licenses; the prohibition on U.S. financial institutions from making loans greater than $10,000,000 per year to sanctioned persons; the prohibition of sanctioned persons from acting as dealers of U.S. government bonds; the banning of U.S. government procurement of goods from sanctioned persons; presidential import sanctioning in accordance with the International Emergency Economic Powers Act.

4. A number of U.S laws restrict the importation of fish caught using certain techniques, ostensibly for environmental reasons. These have been subject to challenges under GATT. *See, e.g.*, GATT Dispute Settlement Panel Report on United States Restrictions on Imports of Tuna, 33 I.L.M. 839 (1994).

2. Nationality

a. Active Personality

Protection of nationals, as we saw in Parts Three and Four, has been a frequently invoked basis for a state's claiming competence to impose responsibility upon other states. In addition to protection, states frequently seek to regulate the behavior of their nationals abroad, as in The Foreign Corrupt Practices Act, Pub. L. 95-213, 91 Stat. 1496 (1977) (codified as amended at 15 U.S.C. 78dd-1 to -2 (1994)).

The claim to prescribe for the conduct of a state's nationals within shared domains or in other countries is often subsumed under the more general claim to prescribe for the conduct of nationals *wherever* the conduct takes place. *See* Restatement (Third) § 402.

In a case involving a Florida regulation of sponge fishing which reached beyond territorial waters into the Gulf of Mexico, Chief Justice Hughes stated:

> The argument based on the limits of the territorial waters of the United States, as these are described by this Court in *Cunard Steamship Co. v. Mellon*, 262 U.S. 100, 122, and in diplomatic correspondence and statements of the political department of our Government, is thus beside the point. For, aside from the question of the extent of control which the United States may exert in the interest of self-protection over waters near its borders, although beyond its territorial limits, the United States is not debarred by any rule of international law from governing the conduct of its own citizens upon the high seas or even in foreign countries when the rights of other nations or their nationals are not infringed. With respect to such an exercise of authority there is no question of international law, but solely of the purport of the municipal law which establishes the duty of the citizen in relation to his own government. ...\
>
> If the United States may control the conduct of its citizens upon the high seas, we see no reason why the State of Florida may not likewise govern the conduct of its citizens upon the high seas with respect to matters in which the State has a legitimate interest and where there is no conflict with acts of Congress. Save for the powers committed by the Constitution to the Union, the State of Florida has retained the status of a sovereign. Florida was admitted to the Union "on equal footing with the original States, in all respects whatsoever." *Skiriotes v. Florida*, 313 U.S. 69, 73, 77 (1941).

The question of how far competence to prescribe for conduct of one's nationals in shared domains extends has been neatly focused in the cases of so-called "pirate broadcasters", private commercial radio entrepreneurs who typically locate their transmitters on vessels just outside territorial seas to escape regulation.

What demands can be made with regard to which values, under what theories and for what duration, by a state on conduct outside its borders by an actor deemed by that state to be its national? Are there authoritative criteria for appraising ascriptions for these purposes? Does it matter whether or not the actor was once present in the territory of the state and then removed? How relevant are actual or imaginable claims by other states that the actor is *their* agent; are authoritative criteria available to distinguish between concurrent and contradictory multiple claims of nationality? What effect is to be given the actor's own claim as to nationality?

It will be noted that these claims may involve an assertion by one state of competence over events taking place in the territory of another.

The Mexican Supreme Court reasoned as follows in assuming penal jurisdiction over the acts of a Mexican national in the U.S.:

> It is well known that it is the federal judge who has jurisdiction notwithstanding that it is the principle of territoriality which fundamentally regulates the special application of the penal law in accordance with Article 4 of the Federal Criminal Code, even though this precept, in its first hypothesis—a crime committed abroad by a Mexican national admits the principle of personal law. This is so because of the respect due ... to the ties of allegiance which should bind the subject to his State, or because it is not possible to conceive that a State should be transformed into a safe refuge for its own nationals who have committed crimes outside its frontiers, or because the rule of prosecution is merely a just corollary to the nonextradition of nationals, which is the practice of the majority of countries.

Re Gutierrez, 24 INT'L L. REP. 265, 266 (1961).

(1) Steele v. Bulova Watch Co.
344 U.S. 280 (1952)

[The Supreme Court held that under the Lanham Trade-Mark Act of 1946, a federal district court has jurisdiction to award relief to an American corporation against acts of trade-mark infringement and unfair competition in a foreign country by a United States national who purchases parts here and some of whose products, sold abroad, enter the U.S. Justice Clark's opinion read in part:]

Bulova Watch Company, Inc., a New York corporation, sued Steele, petitioner here, in the United States District Court for the Western District of Texas. The gist of its complaint charged that "Bulova," a trade-mark properly registered under the laws of the United States, had long designated the watches produced and nationally advertised and sold by the Bulova Watch Company; and that petitioner, a United States citizen residing in San Antonio, Texas, conducted a watch business in Mexico City where, without Bulova's authorization and with the purpose of deceiving the buying public, he stamped the name "Bulova" on watches there assembled and sold. Basing its prayer on these asserted violations of the trade-mark laws of the United States, Bulova requested injunctive and monetary relief. Personally served with process in San Antonio, petitioner answered by challenging the court's jurisdiction over the subject matter of the suit and by interposing several defenses, including his due registration in Mexico of the mark "Bulova" and the pendency of Mexican legal proceedings thereon, to the merits of Bulova's claim. The trial judge, having initially reserved disposition of the jurisdictional issue until a hearing on the merits, interrupted the presentation of evidence and dismissed the complaint "with prejudice," on the ground that the court lacked jurisdiction over the cause. This decision rested on the court's findings that petitioner had committed no illegal acts within the United States. With one judge dissenting, the Court of Appeals reversed; it held that the pleadings and evidence disclosed a cause of action within the reach of the Lanham Trade-Mark Act of 1946. ... The dissenting judge thought that "since the conduct complained of substantially related solely to acts done and trade carried on under full authority of Mexican law, and were confined to and affected only that Nation's internal commerce, [the District Court] was without jurisdiction to enjoin such conduct." We granted certiorari. ...

Petitioner concedes, as he must, that Congress in prescribing standards of conduct for American citizens may project the impact of its laws beyond the territorial boundaries of the United States. ... Resolution of the jurisdictional issue in this case therefore depends on construction of exercised congressional power, not the limitations upon that power itself. And since we do not pass on the merits of Bulova's claim, we need not now explore every facet of this complex and controversial Act.

The Lanham Act, on which Bulova posited its claims to relief, confers broad jurisdictional powers upon the courts of the United States. The statute's expressed intent is "to regulate commerce within the control of Congress by making actionable the deceptive and misleading use of marks in such commerce; to protect registered marks used in such comme[r]ce from interference by State, or territorial legislation; to protect persons engaged in such commerce against unfair competition; to prevent fraud and deception in such commerce by the use of reproductions, copies, counterfeits, or colorable imitations of registered marks; and to provide rights and remedies stipulated by treaties and conventions respecting trade-marks, trade names, and unfair competition entered into between the United States and foreign nations." ... To that end, § 32 (1) holds liable in a civil action by a trade-mark registrant."[a]ny person who shall, in commerce," infringe a registered trade-mark in a manner there detailed. "Commerce" is defined as "all commerce which may lawfully be regulated by Congress." ... The district courts of the United States are granted jurisdiction over all actions "arising under" the Act, ... and can award relief which may include injunctions, "according to the principles of equity," to prevent the violation of any registrant's rights. ...

The record reveals the following significant facts which for purposes of a dismissal must be taken as true: Bulova Watch Company, one of the largest watch manufacturers in the world, advertised and distributed "Bulova" watches in the United States and foreign countries. Since 1929, its aural and visual advertising, in Spanish and English, has penetrated Mexico. Petitioner, long a resident of San Antonio, first entered the watch business there in 1922, and in 1926 learned of the trade-mark "Bulova." He subsequently transferred his business to Mexico City and, discovering that "Bulova" had not been registered in Mexico, in 1933 procured the Mexican registration of that mark. Assembling Swiss watch movements and dials and cases imported from that country and the United States, petitioner in Mexico City stamped his watches with "Bulova" and sold them as such. As a result of the distribution of spurious "Bulovas," Bulova Watch Company's Texas sales representative received numerous complaints from retail jewelers in the Mexican border area whose customers brought in for repair defective "Bulovas" which upon inspection often turned out not to be products of that company. Moreover, subsequent to our grant of certiorari in this case the prolonged litigation in the courts of Mexico has come to an end. On October 6, 1952, the Supreme Court of Mexico rendered a judgment upholding an administrative ruling which had nullified petitioner's Mexican registration of "Bulova."

On the facts in the record we agree with the Court of Appeals that petitioner's activities, when viewed as a whole, fall within the jurisdictional scope of the Lanham Act. This Court has often stated that the legislation of Congress will not extend beyond the boundaries of the United States unless a contrary legislative intent appears. ... The question thus is "whether Congress intended to make the law applicable" to the facts of this case. *Ibid.* For "the United States is not debarred by any rule of international law from governing the conduct of its own citizens upon the high seas or even in foreign countries when the rights of other nations or their nationals are not infringed. With respect to such an exercise of authority there is no question of international law, but solely of the purport of the municipal law which establishes the duty of the citizen in relation to his own government." *Skiriotes v. Florida,* 313 U.S. 69, 73 (1941). As Mr. Justice Minton, then sitting on the Court of Appeals, applied the principle in a case involving unfair methods of competition: "Congress has the power to prevent unfair trade practices in foreign commerce by citizens of the United States, although some of the acts are done outside the territorial limits of the United States." *Branch v. Federal Trade Commission,* 141 F.2d 31, 35 (1944). Nor has this Court in tracing the commerce scope of statutes differentiated between enforcement of legislative policy by the Government itself or by private litigants proceeding under a statutory right. ... The public policy subserved is the same in each case. In the light of the broad jurisdictional grant in the Lanham Act, we deem its scope to encompass petitioner's activities here. His operations and their effects were not confined within the territorial limits of a foreign nation. He bought component parts of his wares in the United States, and spurious "Bulovas" filtered through the Mexican border into this country; his competing goods could well reflect adversely on Bulova Watch Company's trade reputation in markets cultivated by advertising here as well as abroad. Under similar factual circumstances, courts of the United States have awarded relief to registered trade-mark owners, even prior to the advent of the broadened commerce provisions of the Lanham Act. ... Even when most jealously read, that Act's sweeping reach into "all commerce which may lawfully be regulated by Congress" does not constrict prior law or deprive courts of jurisdiction previously exercised. We do not deem material that petitioner affixed the mark "Bulova" in Mexico City rather than here, or that his purchases in the United States when viewed in isolation do not violate any of our laws. They were essential steps in the course of business consummated abroad; acts in themselves legal lose that character when they become part of an unlawful scheme. ... "[I]n such a case it is not material that the source of the forbidden effects upon ... commerce arises in one phase or another of that program." ... In sum, we do not think that petitioner by so simple a device can evade the thrust of the laws of the United States in a privileged sanctuary beyond our borders.

(2) Blackmer v. U.S.

284 U.S. 421 (1932)

MR. CHIEF JUSTICE HUGHES. ... The petitioner, Harry M. Blackmer, a citizen of the United States resident in Paris, France, was adjudged guilty of contempt of the Supreme Court of the District of Columbia for failure to respond to subpoenas served upon him in France and requiring him to appear as a witness on behalf of the United States at a criminal trial in that court. Two subpoenas were issued, for appearances at different times, and there was a separate proceeding with respect to each. The two cases were heard together, and a fine of $30,000 with costs was imposed in each case, to be satisfied out of the property of the petitioner which had been seized by order of the court. ...

The subpoenas were issued and served, and the proceedings to punish for contempt were taken, under the provisions of the Act of July 3, 1926, c. 762, 44 Stat. 835, U.S.C, Tit. 28, §§ 711-718. The statute provides that whenever the attendance at the trial of a criminal action of a witness abroad, who is "a citizen of the United States or domiciled therein," is desired by the Attorney General, or any assistant or district attorney acting under him, the judge of the court in which the action is pending may order a subpoena to issue, to be addressed to a consul of the United States and to be served by him personally upon the witness with a tender of travelling expenses. §§ 2, 3. Upon proof of such service and of the failure of the witness to appear, the court may make an order requiring the witness to show cause why he should not be punished for contempt, and upon the issue of such an order the court may direct that property belonging to the witness and within the United States may be seized and held to satisfy any judgment which may be rendered against him in the proceeding. §§ 4, 5. Provision is made for personal service of the order upon the witness and also for its publication in a newspaper of general circulation in the district where the court is sitting. § 6. If, upon the hearing, the charge is sustained, the court may adjudge the witness guilty of contempt and impose upon him a fine not exceeding $100,000, to be satisfied by a sale of the property seized. § 7. This statute and the proceedings against the petitioner are assailed as being repugnant to the Constitution of the United States.

First. The principal objections to the statute are that it violates the due process clause of the Fifth Amendment. These contentions are (1) that the "Congress has no power to authorize United States consuls to serve process except as permitted by treaty"; (2) that the Act does not provide "a valid method of acquiring judicial jurisdiction to render personal judgment against defendant and judgment against his property"; (3) that the Act "does not require actual or any other notice to defendant of the offense or of the Government's claim against his property"; (4) that the provisions "for hearing and judgment in the entire absence of the accused and without his consent" are invalid; and (5) that the Act is "arbitrary, capricious and unreasonable."

While it appears that the petitioner removed his residence to France in the year 1924, it is undisputed that he was, and continued to be, a citizen of the United States. He continued to owe allegiance to the United States. By virtue of the obligations of citizenship, the United States retained its authority over him, and he was bound by its laws made applicable to him in a foreign country. Thus, although resident abroad, the petitioner remained subject to the taxing power of the United States. *Cook v. Tait*, 265 U.S. 47, 54, 56. For disobedience to its laws through conduct abroad he was subject to punishment in the courts of the United States. *U.S. v. Bowman*, 260 U. S. 94, 102. With respect to such an exercise of authority, there is no question of international law, but solely of the purport of the municipal law which establishes the duties of the citizen in relation to his own government. While the legislation of the Congress, unless the contrary intent appears, is construed to apply only within the territorial jurisdiction of the United States, the question of its application, so far as citizens of the United States in foreign countries are concerned, is one of construction, not of legislative power. ... Nor can it be doubted that the United States possesses the power inherent in sovereignty to require the return to this country of a citizen, resident elsewhere, whenever the public interest requires it, and to penalize him in case of refusal. ... What in England was the prerogative of the sovereign in this respect, pertains under our constitutional system to the national authority which may be exercised by the Congress by virtue of the legislative power to prescribe the duties of the citizens of the United States. It is also beyond controversy that one of the duties which the citizen owes to his government is to support the administration of justice by attending its courts and giving his testimony whenever he is properly summoned. ... And the Congress may provide for the performance of this duty and prescribe penalties for disobedience.

Decrees affirmed.

Notes and Questions

1. The Third Circuit, in *U.S. v. Harvey*, 2 F.3d 1318 (1993), rejected the defendant's claim that federal sentencing guidelines did not apply when the underlying act (here, sexually exploiting children in the Philippines) occurred outside the United States. The Court held that "No tenet of international law prohibits Congress from punishing the wrongful conduct of its citizens, even if some of that conduct occurs abroad." The First Circuit, however, in *U.S. v. Azeem*, 946 F.2d 13 (1991), refused to include a foreign drug transaction as part of the base level calculation under the sentencing guidelines in a conspiracy case. This specific transaction, conducted in Cairo, "was not a crime against the United States."

(3) Code of Federal Regulations

31 C.F.R. § 500.329 (1998)

The term, person subject to the jurisdiction of the United States, includes:

(a) Any individual, wherever located, who is a citizen or resident of the United States;

(b) Any person within the United States as defined in § 500.330;

(c) Any corporation organized under the laws of the United States or of any state, territory, possession, or district of the United States; and

(d) Any corporation, partnership, or association, wherever organized or doing business, that is owned or controlled by persons specified in paragraph (a) or (c) of this section.

b. Passive Personality

(1) U.S. v. Yunis

924 F.2d 1086 (D.C. Cir. 1991)

MIKVA, CHIEF JUDGE: Appellant Fawaz Yunis challenges his convictions on conspiracy, aircraft piracy, and hostage-taking charges stemming from the hijacking of a Jordanian passenger aircraft in Beirut, Lebanon. He appeals from orders of the district court denying his pretrial motions relating to jurisdiction, illegal arrest, alleged violations of the Posse Comitatus Act, and the government's withholding of classified documents during discovery. Yunis also challenges the district court's jury instructions as erroneous and prejudicial.

Although this appeal raises novel issues of domestic and international law, we reject Yunis' objections and affirm the convictions.

I. Background

On June 11, 1985, appellant and four other men boarded Royal Jordanian Airlines Flight 402 ("Flight 402") shortly before its scheduled departure from Beirut, Lebanon. They wore civilian clothes and carried military assault rifles, ammunition bandoleers, and hand grenades. Appellant took control of the cockpit and forced the pilot to take off immediately. The remaining hijackers tied up Jordanian air marshals assigned to the flight and held the civilian passengers, including two American citizens, captive in their seats. The hijackers explained to the crew and passengers that they wanted the plane to fly to Tunis, where a conference of the Arab League was under way. The hijackers further explained that they wanted a meeting with delegates to the conference and that their ultimate goal was removal of all Palestinians from Lebanon.

After a refueling stop in Cyprus, the airplane headed for Tunis but turned away when authorities blocked the airport runway. Following a refueling stop at Palermo, Sicily, another attempt to land in Tunis, and a second stop in Cyprus, the plane returned to Beirut, where more hijackers came aboard. These reinforcements included an official of Lebanon's Amal Militia, the group at whose direction Yunis claims he acted. The plane then took off for Syria, but was turned away and went back to Beirut. There, the hijackers released the passengers, held a press conference reiterating their demand that Palestinians leave Lebanon, blew up the plane, and fled from the airport.

An American investigation identified Yunis as the probable leader of the hijackers and prompted U.S. civilian and military agencies, led by the Federal Bureau of Investigation (FBI), to plan Yunis' arrest. After obtaining an arrest warrant, the FBI put "Operation Goldenrod" into effect in September 1987. Undercover FBI agents lured Yunis onto a yacht in the eastern Mediterranean Sea with promises of a drug deal, and arrested him once the vessel entered international waters. The agents transferred Yunis to a United States Navy munitions ship and interrogated him for several days as the vessel steamed toward a second rendezvous, this time with a Navy aircraft carrier. Yunis was flown to Andrews Air Force Base from the aircraft carrier, and taken from there to Washington, D.C. In Washington, Yunis was arraigned on an original indictment charging him with conspiracy, hostage taking, and aircraft damage. A grand jury subsequently returned a superseding indictment adding additional aircraft damage counts and a charge of air piracy. …

Yunis admitted participation in the hijacking at trial but denied parts of the government's account and offered the affirmative defense of obedience to military orders, asserting that he acted on instructions given by his superiors in Lebanon's Amal Militia. The jury convicted Yunis of conspiracy, 18 U.S.C. § 371 (1988), hostage taking, 18 U.S.C. § 1203 (1988), and air piracy, 49 U.S.C. App. § 1472(n) (1988). However, it acquitted him of three other charged offenses that went to trial: violence against people on board an aircraft, 18 U.S.C. § 32(b)(1) (1988), aircraft damage, 18 U.S.C. § 32(b)(2) (1988), and placing a destructive device aboard an aircraft, 18 U.S.C. § 32(b)(3) (1988). The district court imposed concurrent sentences of five years for conspiracy, thirty years for hostage taking, and twenty years for air piracy. Yunis appeals his conviction and seeks dismissal of the indictment.

II. Analysis

Yunis argues that the district court lacked subject matter and personal jurisdiction to try him on the charges of which he was convicted, that the indictment should have been dismissed because the government seized him in violation of the Posse Comitatus Act and withheld classified materials useful to his defense, and that the convictions should be reversed because of errors in the jury instructions. We consider these claims in turn.

A. Jurisdictional Claims

Yunis appeals first of all from the district court's denial of his motion to dismiss for lack of subject matter and personal jurisdiction. Appellant's principal claim is that, as a matter of domestic law, the federal hostage taking and air piracy statutes do not authorize assertion of federal jurisdiction over him. Yunis also suggests that a contrary construction of these statutes would conflict with established principles of international law, and so should be avoided by this court. Finally, appellant claims that the district court lacked personal jurisdiction because he was seized in violation of American law.

1. Hostage Taking Act

The Hostage Taking Act provides, in relevant part:

> (a) Whoever, whether inside or outside the United States, seizes or detains and threatens to kill, to injure, or to continue to detain another person in order to compel a third person or a governmental organization to do or to abstain from any act . . . shall be punished by imprisonment by any term of years or for life.
>
> (b)(1) It is not an offense under this section if the conduct required for the offense occurred outside the United States unless -
>
> (A) the offender or the person seized or detained is a national of the United States;
>
> (B) the offender is found in the United States; or
>
> (C) the governmental organization sought to be compelled is the Government of the United States.

18 U.S.C. § 1203. Yunis claims that this statute cannot apply to an individual who is brought to the United States by force, since those convicted under it must be "found in the United States." But this ignores the law's plain language. Subsections (A), (B), and (C) of section 1203(b)(1) offer independent bases for jurisdiction where "the offense occurred outside the United States." Since two of the passengers on Flight 402 were U.S. citizens, section 1203(b)(1)(A), authorizing assertion of U.S. jurisdiction where "the offender or the person seized or detained is a national of the United States," is satisfied. The statute's jurisdictional requirement has been met regardless of whether or not Yunis was "found" within the United States under section 1203(b)(1)(B).

Appellant's argument that we should read the Hostage Taking Act differently to avoid tension with international law falls flat. Yunis points to no treaty obligations of the United States that give us pause. Indeed, Congress intended through the Hostage Taking Act to execute the International Convention Against the Taking of Hostages, which authorizes any signatory state to exercise jurisdiction over persons who take its nationals hostage "if that State considers it appropriate." International Convention Against the Taking of Hostages, opened for signature Dec. 18, 1979, art. 5, para. 1, 34 U.N. GAOR Supp. (No. 39), 18 I.L.M. 1456, 1458.

Nor is jurisdiction precluded by norms of customary international law. The district court concluded that two jurisdictional theories of international law, the "universal principle" and the "passive personal principle," supported assertion of U.S. jurisdiction to prosecute Yunis on hijacking and hostage-taking charges. Under the universal principle, states may prescribe and prosecute "certain offenses recognized by the community of nations as of universal concern, such as piracy, slave trade, attacks on or hijacking of aircraft, genocide, war crimes, and perhaps certain acts of terrorism," even absent any special connection between the state and the offense. See Restatement (Third) of the Foreign Relations Law of the United States §§ 404, 423 (1987). Under the passive personal principle, a state may punish non-nationals for crimes committed against its nationals outside of its territory, at least where the state has a particularly strong interest in the crime.

Relying primarily on the Restatement, Yunis argues that hostage taking has not been recognized as a universal crime and that the passive personal principle authorizes assertion of jurisdiction over alleged hostage takers only where the victims were seized because they were nationals of the prosecuting state. Whatever merit appellant's claims may have as a matter of international law, they cannot prevail before this court. Yunis seeks to portray international law as a self-executing code that trumps domestic law whenever the two conflict. That effort misconceives the role of judges as appliers of international law and as participants in the federal system. Our duty is to enforce the Constitution, laws, and treaties of the United States, not to conform the law of the land to norms of customary international law. See U.S. Const. art. VI. As we said in *Committee of U.S. Citizens Living in Nicaragua v. Reagan,* 859 F.2d 929 (D.C. Cir. 1988): "Statutes inconsistent with principles of customary international law may well lead to international law violations. But within the domestic legal realm, that inconsistent statute simply modifies or supersedes customary international law to the extent of the inconsistency." Id. at 938.

To be sure, courts should hesitate to give penal statutes extraterritorial effect absent a clear congressional directive. Similarly, courts will not blind themselves to potential violations of international law where legislative intent is ambiguous. But the statute in question reflects an unmistakable congressional intent, consistent with treaty obligations of the United States, to authorize prosecution of those who take Americans hostage abroad no matter where the offense occurs or where the offender is found. Our inquiry can go no further.

2. Antihijacking Act

The Antihijacking Act provides for criminal punishment of persons who hijack aircraft operating wholly outside the "special aircraft jurisdiction" of the United States, provided that the hijacker is later "found in the United States." 49 U.S.C. App. § 1472(n). Flight 402, a Jordanian aircraft operating outside of the United States, was not within this nation's special aircraft jurisdiction. Yunis urges this court to interpret the statutory requirement that persons prosecuted for air piracy must be "found" in the United States as precluding prosecution of alleged hijackers who are brought here to stand trial. But the issue before us is more fact-specific, since Yunis was indicted for air piracy while awaiting trial on hostage-taking and other charges; we must determine whether, once arrested and brought to this country on those other charges, Yunis was subject to prosecution under the Antihijacking Act as well.

The Antihijacking Act of 1974 was enacted to fulfill this nation's responsibilities under the Convention for the Suppression of Unlawful Seizure of Aircraft (the "Hague Convention"), which requires signatory nations to extradite or punish hijackers "present in" their territory. Convention for the Suppression of Unlawful Seizure of Aircraft, Dec. 16, 1970, art. 4, para. 2, Dec. 16, 1970, 22 U.S.T. 1643, 1645. This suggests that Congress intended the statutory term "found in the United States" to parallel the Hague Convention's "present in [a contracting state's] territory," a phrase which does not indicate the voluntariness limitation urged by Yunis. Moreover, Congress interpreted the Hague Convention as requiring the United States to extradite or prosecute "offenders in its custody," evidencing no concern as to how alleged hijackers came within U.S. territory. S. Rep. No. 13, 93d Cong., 1st Sess. at 3; see H. Rep. No. 885, 93d Cong., 2d Sess. at 10 1974 U.S. Code Cong. & Admin. News 3975, 3978 (Hague Convention designed to close "gap" in Tokyo Convention, which did not require states to prosecute or extradite hijackers "in [their] custody"). From this legislative history we conclude that Yunis was properly indicted under section 1472(n) once in the United States and under arrest on other charges.

The district court correctly found that international law does not restrict this statutory jurisdiction to try Yunis on charges of air piracy. Aircraft hijacking may well be one of the few crimes so clearly condemned under the law of nations that states may assert universal jurisdiction to bring offenders to justice, even when the state has no territorial connection to the hijacking and its citizens are not involved. But in any event we are satisfied that the Antihijacking Act authorizes assertion of federal jurisdiction to try Yunis regardless of hijacking's status vel non as a universal crime. Thus, we affirm the district court on this issue.

3. Legality of Seizure

[The Court found that the government's conduct in bringing Yunis to the United States was not "outrageous" and affirmed the conviction.]

(2) Extraterritorial Jurisdiction over Terrorist Acts Abroad Against U.S. Nationals

18 U.S.C.A. §§ 2331-2339B (West Supp. 1998)

§ 2331. Definitions

As used in this chapter—

(1) the term "international terrorism" means activities that—

(A) involve violent acts or acts dangerous to human life that are a violation of the criminal laws of the United States or of any State, or that would be a criminal violation if committed within the jurisdiction of the United States or of any State

(B) appear to be intended—

(i) to intimidate or coerce a civilian population

(ii) to influence the policy of a government by intimidation or coercion; or

(iii) to affect the conduct of a government by assassination or kidnapping; and

(C) occur primarily outside the territorial jurisdiction of the United States, or transcend national boundaries in terms of the means by which they are accomplished, the persons they appear intended to intimidate or coerce, or the locale in which their perpetrators operate or seek asylum;

(2) the term "national of the United States" has the meaning given such term in section 101(a)(22) of the Immigration and Nationality Act;

(3) the term "person" means any individual or entity capable of holding a legal or beneficial interest in property, and

(4) the term "act of war" means any act occurring in the course of—

(A) declared war;

(B) armed conflict, whether or not war has been declared, between two or more nations; or

(C) armed conflict between military forces of any origin,

§ 2332. Criminal penalties

(a) HOMICIDE.—Whoever kills a national of the United States, while such national is outside the United States, shall—

(1) if the killing is murder (as defined in section 1111(a)), be fined under this title, punished by death or imprisonment for any term of years or for life, or both;

(2) if the killing is a voluntary manslaughter as defined in section 1112(a) of this title, be fined under this title or imprisoned not more than ten years, or both; and

(3) if the killing is an involuntary manslaughter as defined in section 1112(a) of this title, be fined under this title or imprisoned not more than three years, or both.

(b) Attempt or Conspiracy With Respect to Homicide.—Whoever outside the United States attempts to kill, or engages in a conspiracy to kill, a national of the United States shall—

(1) in the case of an attempt to commit a that is a murder as defined in this chapter, be fined under this title or imprisoned not more than 20 years, or both; and

(2) in the case of a conspiracy by two or more persons to commit a killing that is a murder as defined in section 1111(a) of this title. if one or more of such persons do any Overt act to effect the object of the conspiracy, be fined under this title or imprisoned for any term of years or for life, or both so fined and so imprisoned.

(c) Other Conduct.—Whoever outside the United States engages in physical violence—

(1) with intent to cause serious bodily injury to a national of the United States; or

(2) with the result that serious bodily injury is caused to a national of the United States;

shall be fined under this title or imprisoned not more than five years, or both.

(d) Limitation on Prosecution.—No prosecution for any offense described in this section shall be undertaken by the United States except on written certification of the Attorney General or the highest ranking subordinate of the Attorney General with responsibility for criminal prosecutions that, in the judgment of the certifying official, such offense was intended to coerce, intimidate, or retaliate against a government or a civilian population.

§ 2332a. Use of weapons of mass destruction

(a) Offense.—A person who uses, or attempts or conspires to use, a weapon of mass destruction—

(1) against a national of the United States while such national is outside of the United States;

(2) against any person within the United States; or

(3) against any property that is owned, leased or used by the United States or by any department or agency of the United States, whether the property is within or outside of the United States,

shall be imprisoned for any term of years or for life, and if death results, shall be punished by death or imprisoned for any term of years or for life. …

§ 2333. Civil remedies

(a) ACTION AND JURISDICTION.—Any national of the United States injured in his or her person, property, or business by reason of an act of international terrorism, or his or her estate, survivors, or heirs, may sue therefor in any appropriate district court of the United States and shall recover threefold the damages he or she sustains and the cost of the suit, including attorney's fees. …

§ 2339A. Providing material support to terrorists

DEFINITION.—In this section, "material support or resources" means currency or other financial securities, financial services, lodging, training, safehouses, false documentation or identification, communications equipment, facilities, weapons, lethal substances, explosives, personnel, transportation, and other physical assets, but does not include humanitarian assistance to persons not directly involved in such violations.

OFFENSE.—A person who, within the United States, provides material support or resources or conceals or disguises the nature, location, source, or ownership of material support or resources, knowing or intending that they are to be used in preparation for, or in carrying out, a violation of section 32, 36, 351, 844(f) or (i), 1114, 1116, 1203, 1361, 1363, 1751, 2280, 2281, 2331, or 2339 of this title or section 46502 of title 49, or in preparation for or carrying out the concealment of 3 an escape from the commission of any such violation, shall be fined under this title, imprisoned not more than 10 years, or both. …

§ 2339B. Providing material support or resources to designated foreign terrorist organizations

(a) PROHIBITED ACTIVITIES.—

(1) Unlawful conduct.—Whoever, within the United States or subject to the jurisdiction of the United States, knowingly provides material support or resources to a foreign terrorist organization, or attempts or conspires to do so, shall be fined under this title or imprisoned not more than 10 years, or both.

(2) Financial institutions.—Except as authorized by the Secretary, any financial institution that becomes aware that it has possession of, or control over, any funds in which a foreign terrorist organization, or its agent, has an interest, shall—

(A) retain possession of, or maintain control over, such funds; and

(B) report to the Secretary the existence of such funds in accordance with regulations issued by the Secretary.

(b) Civil penalty.—Any financial institution that knowingly fails to comply with subsection (a)(2) shall be subject to a civil penalty in an amount that is the greater of—

(A) $50,000 per violation; or

(B) twice the amount of which the financial institution was required under subsection (a)(2) to retain possession or control.

(c) Injunction.—Whenever it appears to the Secretary or the Attorney General that any person is engaged in, or is about to engage in, any act that constitutes, or would constitute, a violation of this section, the Attorney General may initiate civil action in a district court of the United States to enjoin such violation.

(d) Extraterritorial jurisdiction.—There is extraterritorial Federal jurisdiction over an offense under this section. . . .

(g) Definitions.—As used in this section— …

(6) the term "terrorist organization" means an organization designated as a terrorist organization under section 219 of the Immigration and Nationality Act.

3. Protective Principle

(a) Attorney-General of the Government of Israel v. Eichmann

36 I.L.R. 5 (Dist. Ct., Jm. 1961), aff'd, 36 I.L.R. 277 (Israel 1962)

[Adolf Eichmann was abducted from Argentina and brought to trial in Israel under the Nazi Collaborators (Punishment) Law, enacted after Israel became a state and after the events charged against Eichmann during the Nazi era in Germany. Section 1 (a) of the law provides:

A person who has committed one of the following offences—

(1) did, during the period of the Nazi regime, in a hostile country, an act constituting a crime against the Jewish people;

(2) did, during the period of the Nazi regime, in a hostile country, an act constituting a crime against humanity;

(3) did, during the period of the Second World War, in a hostile country, an act constituting a war crime;

is liable to the death penalty.

Counsel for Eichmann objected to the jurisdiction of the Court, *inter alia,* on grounds based on international law.] [Excerpted opinion follows.]

Learned Counsel does not ignore the fact that the Israel law applicable to the acts attributed to the accused vests in us the jurisdiction to try this case. His contention against the jurisdiction of the Court is not based on this law, but on international law. He contends—

> (a) that the Israel law, by inflicting punishment for acts done outside the boundaries of the State and before its establishment, against persons who were not Israel citizens, and by a person who acted in the course of duty on behalf of a foreign country ("Act of State") conflicts with international law and exceeds the powers of the Israel legislator; …

We have discussed at length the international character of the crimes in question because this offers the broadest possible, though not the only, basis for Israel's jurisdiction according to the law of nations. No less important from the point of view of international law is the special connection the State of Israel has with such crimes, seeing that the people of Israel (Am Israel)—the Jewish people (Ha'am Ha'yehudi—to use the term in the Israel legislation)—constituted the target and the victim of most of the crimes in question. The State of Israel's "right to punish" the accused derives, in our view, from two cumulative sources: a universal source (pertaining to the whole of mankind) which vests the right to prosecute and punish crimes of this order in every State within the family of nations; and a specific or national source which gives the victim nation the right to try any who assault their existence.

This second foundation of penal jurisdiction conforms, according to the acknowledged terminology, to the protective principle or the *compétence réelle.* In England, which, until a short time ago, was considered a country that does not rely on such jurisdiction … it was said in *Joyce v. D.P.P.* [1946] A.C. 347 (p. 372):

> The second point of appeal … was that in any case no English Court has jurisdiction to try an alien for a crime committed abroad. ... There is, I think, a short answer to this point. The statute in question deals with the crime of treason committed within or ... without the realm. … No principle of comity demands that a state should ignore the crime of treason committed against it outside its territory. On the contrary a proper regard for its own security requires that all those who commit that crime, whether they commit it within or without the realm, should be amenable to its laws.

Oppenheim-Lauterpacht I § 147, p. 333 says that the penal jurisdiction of the State includes "crimes injuring its subjects or serious crimes against its own safety."

Most European countries go much farther than this. …

Dahm says in his "Zur Problematik des Völkerstrafrechts," 1956 p. 28, that the protective principle is not confined to foreign offences that threaten the "vital interests" of the State, and goes on to explain (pp. 38-39) in his reference to "immanent limitations" of the jurisdiction of the State that a departure therefrom would constitute an "abuse" of its sovereignty. He says:

> Penal jurisdiction is not a matter for everyone to exercise. There must be a "linking point," a legal connection that links the punisher with the punished. The State may, insofar as international law does not con-

> tain rules contradicting this, punish only persons and acts *which concern it more than they concern other States* (italics by author).

Learned Counsel has summed up his pleadings against the jurisdiction of the Israel legislator by stressing ... that under international law there must be a connection between the State and the person who committed the crime, and that in absence of an "acknowledged linking point" it was ultra vires the State to inflict punishment for foreign offences.

The doctrine of the "linking point" is not new. Dahm (ibid.) bases himself on *Mendelssohn-Bartholdy,* Vergleichende Darstellung des deutschen und ausländischen Strafrechts, Allg. Teil VI (1908) 111 ff. And Mendelssohn-Bartholdy himself (ibid.) quotes Rolin-Jaequemyns as having said in 1874:

> *Tout le monde est d'accord sur ce point qu'il faut un lien de droit entre celui qui punit et celui qui subit le châtiment.*

We have already stated above the view of Grotius on "the right to punish," a view which is also based on a "linking point" between the criminal an his victim: Grotius holds that the very commission of the crime creates a legal connection between the offender and the victim, and one that vests in the victim the right to punish the offender or demand his punishment. According to natural justice the victim may himself punish the offender, but the organisation of society has delegated that natural right to the sovereign State. One of the main objects of the punishment is—continues the author of "The Law of Peace and War" (Book 2, chapter 20)—to ensure that "the victim shall not in future suffer a similar infliction at the hands of the same person or at the hands of others (*ne post hac tale quid patiatur aut ab oedem aut ab aliis*)."

Grotius also quotes an ancient authority who said that the punishment is necessary to

> defend the honour or the authority of him who was hurt by the offence so that the failure to punish may not cause his degradation': ... and he adds that all that has been said of the jurisdiction applies to the infringement of all his rights. ...
>
> In order that the victim may not be hurt by others, there must be no mere punishment but a public and striking punishment that will serve as an example.

Not all jurists use the term "linking point" in an equal connotation. Thus Mendelssohn-Bartholdy holds the opinion that the sovereignty of a country in determining its penal jurisdiction is unlimited, and he resorts to the "linking point" doctrine solely as a scientific device for the classification of the offences specified in positive law: "The number of linking points is as large as the number of offences" (*ibid.*, p. 112). On the other hand, Hyde (*ibid.*, p. 804) demands, as already mentioned,

> a close and definite connection between that act and the prosecutor, and one which is commonly acknowledged to excuse the exercise of jurisdiction. There are few situations where the requisite connection is deemed to exist ... The connection ... is ... apparent when the act complained of is to be fairly regarded as directed against the safety of the prosecuting State.

Between these two extreme views is the view of *Dahm* (*ibid.*).

Notwithstanding the difference of opinion as to the closeness of the requisite link, the very term "connection" or "linking point" is useful for the elucidation of the problem before us. The question is: What is the special connection between the State of Israel and the offences attributed to the accused, and whether this connection is sufficiently close to form a foundation for Israel's right of punishment as against the accused. This is no merely technical question but a wide and universal one; for the principles of international law are wide and universal principles and no articles in an express code.

When the question is presented in its widest form, as stated above, it seems to us that there can be no doubt as to what the answer will be. The "linking point" between Israel and the accused (and for that matter between Israel and any person accused of a crime against the Jewish people under this Law) is striking and glaring in a "crime manifest against the Jewish people," a crime that postulates an intention to exterminate the Jewish people in whole or in part. Indeed, even without such specific definition—and it must be noted that the draft law had only defined "crimes against humanity" and "war crimes" (Bills of Law of the year 5710 No. 36, p. 119)—there was a subsisting "linking point," seeing that most of the Nazi crimes of this kind were perpetrated against the Jewish people; but viewed in the light of the definition of "crime against the Jewish people," the legal position is clearer. The "crime against the Jewish people," as defined in the Law, constitutes in effect an attempt to exterminate the Jewish people, or a partial extermination of the Jewish people. If there is an effective link (and not necessarily an identity) between the State of Israel and the Jewish people, then a crime intended to exterminate the Jewish people has a very striking connection with the State of Israel.

The connection between the State of Israel and the Jewish people needs no explanation. The State of Israel was established and recognised as the State of the Jews. The proclamation of Iyar 5, 5705 (14.5.48) (Official Gazette No. 1) opens with the words: "It was in the Land of Israel that the Jewish people was born," dwells on the history of the Jewish people from ancient times until the Second World War, refers tot he Resolution of the United Nations Assembly of 29.11.47 which demands the establishment of a Jewish State in Eretz Israel, determines the "natural right of the Jewish people to be, like every other people, self-governing, in its sovereign State." It would appear that there is hardly need for any further proof of the very obvious connection between the Jewish people and the State of Israel: this is the sovereign State of the Jewish people.

Moreover, the proclamation of the establishment of the State of Israel makes mention of the very special tragic link between the Nazi crimes, which form the theme of the law in question, and the establishment of the State:

> The recent holocaust which consumed millions of Jews in Europe, provides fresh and unmistakable proof of the necessity of solving the problem of the homelessness and lack of independence of the Jewish people by re-establishing the Jewish State which would fling open the gates of the fatherland to every Jew and would endow the Jewish people with equality of status within the family of nations.
>
> The remnants of the disastrous slaughter of the Nazis in Europe together with Jews from other lands persisted in making their way to the Land of Israel in defiance of all difficulties, obstacles and dangers. They have not ceased to claim their right to a life of dignity, freedom and honest toil in their ancestral home.
>
> In the Second World War the Jewish people in Palestine made its full contribution to the struggle of the freedom and peace-loving nations against the Nazi forces of evil. Its war effort and the blood of its soldiers entitled it to rank with the peoples that made the covenant of the United Nations.

These words are no mere rhetoric, but historical facts, which international law does not ignore.

In the light of the recognition by the United Nations of the right of the Jewish people to establish their State, and in the light of the recognition of the established Jewish State by the family of nations, the connection between the Jewish people and the State of Israel constitutes an integral part of the Law of Nations. …

Counsel contended that the protective principle cannot apply to this case because that principle is designed to protect only an existing State, its security and its interests, while the State of Israel had not existed at the time of the commission of the crime. He further submitted that the same contention was effective with respect to the principle of the "passive personality" which stemmed from the protective principle, and of which some States have made use for the protection of their citizens abroad through their penal legislation. Counsel pointed out that in view of the absence of a sovereign Jewish State at the time of the catastrophe the victims of the Nazis were not, at the time they were murdered, citizens of the State of Israel.

The retroactive application of the law to a period precedent to the establishment of the State of Israel does not in itself constitute in respect to the accused (and for that matter, to any accused under this law) a problem on which we have already dwelt above. Goodhart says in his "The Legality of the Nurnberg Trial," Juridical Review, April 1946, (p. 8), *inter alia:*

> Many of the national courts now functioning in the liberated countries have been established recently, but no one has argued that they are not

> competent to try the cases that arose before their establishment. ... No defendant can complain that he is being tried by a Court which did not exist when he committed the act.

What is here said of a court which did not exist at the time of the commission of the crime is also valid with respect to a State which was not sovereign at the time of the commission of the crime. The whole political landscape of the Continent of occupied Europe has changed after the war; there, too, boundaries have changed as has also changed the very identity of States that had existed before, but all this does not concern the accused.

All this is said in relation to the accused; but may a new State, at all, try crimes that were committed before it was established? The reply to this question was given in *Katz-Cohen v. Attorney-General*, C.A. 3/48 (Pesakim II, p. 225) wherein it was decided that the Israel courts have full jurisdiction to try offences committed before the establishment of the State, and that "in spite of the changes in sovereignty there subsisted a continuity of law." "I cannot see," said President Smoira, "why that community in the country against whom the crime was committed should not demand the punishment of the offender solely because that community is now governed by the Government of Israel instead of by the Mandatory Power." This was said with respect to a crime committed in the country, but there is no reason to assume that the law would be different with respect to foreign offences. Had the Mandatory legislator enacted at the time an extraterritorial law for the punishment of war criminals (as, to give on example, the Australian legislator had done in the War Criminals Act, 1945, see Section 12) it is clear that the Israel Court would have been competent to try under such law offences which were committed abroad prior to the establishment of the State. The principle of continuity also applies to the power to legislate; the Israel Legislator is empowered to amend or supplement the mandatory legislation retroactively, by enacting laws applicable to criminal acts which were committed prior to the establishment of the State.

Indeed, this retroactive law is designed to supplement a gap in the laws of Mandatory Palestine, and the interests protected by this law had existed also during the period of the Jewish National Home. The Balfour Declaration and the Palestine Mandate given by the League of Nations to Great Britain constituted an international recognition of the Jewish people, (see *N. Feinberg,* "The Recognition of the Jewish People in International Law," Jewish Yearbook of International Law 1948, p. 15, and authorities there were cited), the historical link of the Jewish people with Eretz Israel and their right to re-establish their National Home in that country. The Jewish people has actually made use of that right, and the National Home has grown and developed until it reached a sovereign status. During the period preceding the establishment of the sovereign State the Jewish National Home may be seen as reflecting the rule "nasciturus pro jam nato habetur" (see Feinberg *ibid*.). The Jewish "Yishuv" in Palestine constituted during that period a "State-on-the-way," as it were, which reached in due time a sovereign status. The want of sovereignty made it impossible for the Jewish "Yishuv" in the country to enact a criminal law against the Nazi crimes at the time of the commission thereof, but these crimes were also directed against that "Yishuv" who constituted an integral part of the Jewish people, and the enactment with retroactive application of the law in question by the State of Israel filled the need which had already existed previously.

The historical facts explain the background of the legislation in question; but it seems to us that from a legal point of view the power of the new State to enact retroactive legislation does not depend on that background alone, and is not conditioned by the continuity of law between Palestine and the State of Israel. Let us take an extreme example and assume that the Gypsy survivors, an ethnic group or a nation who were also, like the Jewish people, victims of the "crime of genocide," would have gathered after the War and established a sovereign State in any part of the world. It seems to us that no principle of international law could have denied the new State the natural power to put on trial all those killers of their people who fell into their hands. The right of the 'hurt' group to punish offenders derives directly, as Grotius explained (see *supra*), from the crime committed against them by the offender, and it was only want of sovereignty that denied them the power to try and punish the offender. If the hurt group or people thereafter reaches political sovereignty in any territory, it may make use of such sovereignty for the enforcement of its natural right to punish the offender who hurt them.

All this holds good in respect to the crime of genocide (including the crime against the Jewish people) which, it is true, is committed by the killing of the individuals, but is intended to exterminate the nation as a group. According to Hitler's murderous racialism the Nazis singled out Jews from all other citizens in all countries of their domination, and carried the Jews to their death solely because of their racial origin. Even as the Jewish people constituted the object against which the crime was directed, so it is now the competent subject to place on trial those who assailed their existence. The fact that that people has become after the catastrophe a subject, where it had hitherto been an object, and has turned from the victim of a racial crime to the wielder of authority to punish the criminals is a great historic right that cannot be dismissed. The State of Israel, the sovereign State of the Jewish people, performs through its legislation the task of carrying into effect the right of the Jewish people to punish the criminals who killed their sons with intent to put an end to the survival of this people. We are convinced that this power conforms to the principles of the law of nations in force. For all these reasons we have dismissed the first contention of Counsel against the jurisdiction of the Court.

We should add that the well-known judgment of the International Court of Justice at The Hague in the "Lotus Case" has ruled that the principle of territoriality does not limit the power of the State to try crimes and, moreover, any argument against such power must point to a specific rule in international law which negates the power. We have not guided ourselves by this which devolves, so to speak, the "onus of proof" upon him who contends against such power, but have preferred to base ourselves on positive reasons which establish the jurisdiction of the State of Israel.

4. Universality

(a) Demjanjuk v. Petrovsky

776 F.2d 571 (6th Cir. 1985), *cert. denied*, 475 U.S. 1016 (1986)

LIVELY, CHIEF JUDGE. This international extradition case is before the court on appeal from the denial of a petition for a writ of habeas corpus.

The petitioner, John Demjanjuk, is a native of the Ukraine, one of the republics of the Soviet Union. Demjanjuk was admitted to the United States in 1952 under the Displaced Persons Act of 1948 and became a naturalized United States citizen in 1958. He has resided in the Cleveland, Ohio area since his arrival in this country.

In 1981 the United States District Court for the Northern District of Ohio revoked Demjanjuk's certificate of naturalization and vacated the order admitting him to United States citizenship. Chief Judge Battisti of the district court entered extensive findings of fact from which he concluded that the certificate and order "were illegally procured and were procured by willful misrepresentation of material facts under 8 U.S.C. § 1451(a)."

The district court found that Demjanjuk was conscripted into the Soviet Army in 1940 and was captured by the Germans in 1942. After short stays in several German POW camps and a probable tour at the Trawniki SS training camp in Poland, Demjanjuk became a guard at the Treblinka concentration camp, also in Poland, late in 1942. In his various applications for immigration to the United States the petitioner misstated his place of residence during the period 1937-1948 and did not reveal that he had worked for the SS at Treblinka or served in a German military unit later in the war. In the denaturalization proceedings Demjanjuk admitted that his statements concerning residence were false and that he had in fact served in a German military unit. He steadfastly denied that he had been at Trawniki or Treblinka, though documentary evidence placed him at Trawniki and five Treblinka survivors and one former German guard at the camp identified Demjanjuk as a Ukrainian guard who was known as "Ivan or Iwan Grozny," that is, "Ivan the Terrible."

Following the denaturalization order the government began deportation proceedings against Demjanjuk. While these proceedings were underway the State of Israel filed with the United States Department of State a request for the extradition of Demjanjuk. The United States Attorney for the Northern District of Ohio, acting on behalf of the State of Israel, filed a complaint in the district court seeking the arrest of Demjanjuk and a hearing on the extradition request. Following a hearing the district court entered an order certifying to the Secretary of State that Demjanjuk was subject to extradition at the request of the State of Israel pursuant to a treaty on extradition between the United States and Israel signed December 10, 1962, effective December 5, 1963. Bond previously granted Demjanjuk was revoked and he was committed to the custody of the Attorney General of the United States pending the issuance of a warrant of surrender by the Secretary of State. …

A separate jurisdictional argument concerns the territorial reach of the statutory law of Israel. Demjanjuk relies on two facts to question the power of the State of Israel to proceed against him. He is not a citizen or resident of Israel and the crimes with which he is charged allegedly were committed in Poland. He also points out that the acts which are the basis of the Israeli arrest warrant allegedly took place in 1942 or 1943, before the State of Israel came into existence. Thus, Demjanjuk maintains that the district court had no jurisdiction because Israel did not charge him with extraditable offenses.

The scope of this nation's international extradition power and the function of the federal courts in the extradition process are set forth in 18 U.S.C. § 3184:

> § 3184. Fugitives from foreign country to United States
>
> Whenever there is a treaty or convention for extradition between the United States and any foreign government, any justice or judge of the United States, or any magistrate authorized so to do by a court of the United States, or any judge of a court of record of general jurisdiction of any State, may, upon complaint made under oath, charging any person found within his jurisdiction, with having committed within the jurisdiction of any such foreign government any of the crimes provided for by such treaty or convention, issue his warrant for the apprehension of the person so charged, that he may be brought before such justice, judge, or magistrate, to the end that the evidence of criminality may be heard and considered. If, on such hearing, he deems the evidence sufficient to sustain the charge under the provisions of the proper treaty or convention, he shall certify the same, together with a copy of all the testimony taken before him, to the Secretary of State, that a warrant may issue upon the requisition of the proper authorities of such foreign government, for the surrender of such person, according to the stipulations of the treaty or convention; and he shall issue his warrant for the commitment of the person so charged to the proper jail, there to remain until such surrender shall be made.

Section 3184 clearly provides that the extradition complaint must charge the person sought to be extradited with having committed crimes "within the jurisdiction of any such foreign government," that is, the requesting state. This same condition is reflected in § 486(a) of the Restatement, which requires the requested state to comply with the request to arrest and deliver a person sought "on charges of having committed a serious crime within the jurisdiction of the requesting state." The question is whether the murder of Jews in a Nazi extermination camp in Poland during the 1939-1945 war can be considered, for purposes of extradition, crimes within the jurisdiction of the State of Israel.

B.

We look first at the Treaty. Article III provides that when an offense has been committed outside the territorial jurisdiction of the requesting party, "extradition need not be granted unless the laws of the requested party provide for the punishment of such an offense committed in similar circumstances." Demjanjuk maintains that the "need not" language of Article III prohibits extradition in this case because the laws of the United States do not provide punishment for war crimes or crimes against humanity. He places principal reliance on *Valentine v. United States ex rel. Neidecker*, 299 U.S. 5 (1936). In Valentine the treaty provided in part, "Neither of the contracting parties shall be bound to deliver up its own citizens or subjects under the stipulations of this convention." The Supreme Court concluded that this language did not grant discretion to the government to extradite citizens of the United States. Demjanjuk argues that the "need not ... unless" language in the Treaty presently before us similarly precludes an exercise of discretion to extradite for any offense for which the laws of the United States provide no punishment under similar circumstances. ...

In our view the treaty language makes two things clear: (1) the parties recognize the right to request extradition for extra territorial crimes, and (2) the requested party has the discretion to deny extradition if its laws do not provide for punishment of offenses committed under similar circumstances. This provision does not affect the authority of a court to certify extraditability; it merely distinguishes between cases where the requested party is required to honor a request and those where it has discretion to deny a request. That the specific offense charged is not a crime in the United States does not necessarily rule out extradition.

The Israeli statute under which Demjanjuk was charged deals with "crimes against the Jewish people," "crimes against humanity" and "war crimes" committed during the Nazi years. It is clear from the language defining the crimes, and other references to acts directed at persecuted persons and committed in places of confinement, that Israel intended to punish under this law those involved in carrying out Hitler's "final solution." This was made explicit in the prosecution of Adolph Eichmann in 1961. Such a claim of extraterritorial jurisdiction over criminal offenses is not unique to Israel. For example, statutes of the United States provide for punishment in domestic district courts for murder or manslaughter committed within the maritime jurisdiction (18 U.S.C. § 1111) and murder or manslaughter of internationally protected persons wherever they are killed (18 U.S.C. § 1116(c)). We conclude that the reference in 18 U.S.C. § 3184 to crimes committed within the jurisdiction of the requesting government does not refer solely to territorial jurisdiction. Rather, it refers to the authority of a nation to apply its laws to particular conduct. In international law this is referred to as "jurisdiction to prescribe." Restatement § 401(1).

C.

The law of the United States includes international law. *The Paquete Habana*, 175 U.S. 667, 712 (1900). International law recognizes a "universal jurisdiction" over certain offenses. This "universality principle" is based on the assumption that some crimes are so universally condemned that the perpetrators are the enemies of all people. Therefore, any nation which has custody of the perpetrators may punish them according to its law applicable to such offenses. This principle is a departure from the general rule that "the character of an act as lawful or unlawful must be determined wholly by the law of the country where the act is done." *American Banana Co. v. United Fruit Co.,* 213 U.S. 347, 356 (1909).

The wartime allies created the International Military Tribunal which tried major Nazi officials at Nuremberg and courts within the four occupation zones of post-war Germany which tried lesser Nazis. All were tried for committing war crimes, and it is generally agreed that the establishment of these tribunals and their proceedings were based on universal jurisdiction.

Demjanjuk argues that the post-war trials were all based on the military defeat of Germany and that with the disestablishment of the special tribunals there are no courts with jurisdiction over alleged war crimes. This argument overlooks the fact that the post-war tribunals were not military courts, though their presence in Germany was made possible by the military defeat of that country. These tribunals did not operate within the limits of traditional military courts. They claimed and exercised a much broader jurisdiction which necessarily derived from the universality principle. Whatever doubts existed prior to 1945 have been erased by the general recognition since that time that there is a jurisdiction over some types of crimes which extends beyond the territorial limits of any nation.

Turning again to the Restatement, § 443 appears to apply to the present case:

> § 443. *Jurisdiction to Adjudicate in Aid of Universal and Other Non-Territorial Crimes.*
>
> A state's courts may exercise jurisdiction to enforce the state's criminal laws which punish universal crimes (§ 404) or other non-territorial offenses within the state's jurisdiction to prescribe (§§ 402-403).

Israel is seeking to enforce its criminal law for the punishment of Nazis and Nazi collaborators for crimes universally recognized and condemned by the community of nations. The fact that Demjanjuk is charged with committing these acts in Poland does not deprive Israel of authority to bring him to trial.

Further, the fact that the State of Israel was not in existence when Demjanjuk allegedly committed the offenses is no bar to Israel's exercising jurisdiction under the universality principle. When proceeding on that jurisdictional premise, neither the nationality of the accused or the victim(s), nor the location of the crime is significant. The underlying assumption is that the crimes are offenses against the law of nations or against humanity and that the prosecuting nation is acting for all nations. This being so, Israel or any other nation, regardless of its status in 1942 or 1943, may undertake to vindicate the interest of all nations by seeking to punish the perpetrators of such crimes. ...

The judgment of the district court is affirmed.

NOTES AND QUESTIONS

1. Demjanjuk was extradited to Israel, where he was tried, but ultimately acquitted at the Israeli Supreme Court level. Cr. A. 347/88, *Demjanjuk v. Israel*, P.D. 447 (July 29, 1993).

2. For a further discussion of extradition law, *see* Abraham Abramovsky & Jonathan I. Edelstein, *The Post-Sheinbein Israeli Extradition Law: Has it Solved the Extradition Problems Between Israel and the United States or Has it Merely Shifted the Battleground?*, 35 VAND. J. TRANSNAT'L L. 1 (2002); Thomas Rose, *A Delicate Balance: Extradition, Sovereignty, and Individual Rights in the United States and Canada*, 27 YALE J. INT'L L. 193 (2002).

Compare the cautionary note on universal jurisdiction sounded in the next case.

(b) U.S. v. Yousef
327 F.3d 56 (2d Cir. 2003)

[Defendant, a non-U.S. citizen or resident, was convicted, inter alia, of charges relating to a conspiracy to bomb United States commercial airliners in southeast Asia.]

Count Nineteen, the bombing of Philippine Airlines Flight 434, appears to present a less straight-forward jurisdictional issue because the airplane that was bombed was not a United States-flag aircraft, it was flying between two destinations outside of the United States, and there is no evidence that any United States citizens were aboard the flight or were targets of the bombing. The District Court nevertheless concluded that jurisdiction over Yousef for the offenses charged in Count Nineteen was proper, *inter alia,* under the principle of "universal jurisdiction." *Yousef,* 927 F. Supp. at 681-82. ...

The District Court erred in holding that the universality principle provides a basis for jurisdiction over Yousef for the acts charged in Count Nineteen because the universality principle permits jurisdiction over only a limited set of crimes that cannot be expanded judicially, as discussed in full below. The District Court's reliance on the qualified language in *Yunis* that aircraft- related crime "*may well be*" one of the few crimes supporting universal jurisdiction, *Yousef, 927 F.Supp. at 681*, ... is facially at odds with this requirement because such language reflects that these crimes are not unequivocally condemned by all States. ...

The universality principle permits a State to prosecute an offender of any nationality for an offense committed outside of that State and without contacts to that State, but only for the few, near-unique offenses uniformly recognized by the "civilized nations" as an offense against the "Law of Nations." The strictly limited set of crimes subject to universal jurisdiction cannot be expanded by drawing an analogy between some new crime such as placing a bomb on board an airplane and universal jurisdiction's traditional subjects. Nor … can universal jurisdiction be created by reliance on treatises or other scholarly works consisting of aspirational propositions that are not themselves good evidence of customary international law, much less primary sources of customary international law. …

The class of crimes subject to universal jurisdiction traditionally included only piracy. … In modern times, the class of crimes over which States can exercise universal jurisdiction has been extended to include war crimes and acts identified after the Second World War as "crimes against humanity." *See, e.g., Demjanjuk v. Petrovsky,* 776 F.2d 571, 582-83 (6th Cir.1985), *vacated on other grounds,* 10 F.3d 338 (6th Cir.1993).

The concept of universal jurisdiction has its origins in prosecutions of piracy, which States and legal scholars have acknowledged for at least 500 years as a crime against all nations both because of the threat that piracy poses to orderly transport and commerce between nations and because the crime occurs statelessly on the high seas. …

Universal jurisdiction over violations of the laws of war was not suggested until the Second World War. … Following the Second World War, the United States and other nations recognized "war crimes" and "crimes against humanity," including "genocide," as crimes for which international law permits the exercise of universal jurisdiction. *Demjanjuk, 776 F.2d at 582.*

A commentator of the time explained that war crimes are "similar to piratical acts" because "[i]n both situations there is ... a lack of any adequate judicial system operating on the spot where the crime takes place—in the case of piracy it is because the acts are on the high seas and in the case of war crimes because of a chaotic condition or irresponsible leadership in time of war." Willard B. Cowles, *Universality of Jurisdiction Over War Crimes,* 33 Cal. L. Rev. 177, 194 (1945).

The historical restriction of universal jurisdiction to piracy, war crimes, and crimes against humanity demonstrates that universal jurisdiction arises under customary international law only where crimes (1) are universally condemned by the community of nations, and (2) by their nature occur either outside of a State or where there is no State capable of punishing, or competent to punish, the crime (as in a time of war).

Unlike those offenses supporting universal jurisdiction under customary international law—that is, piracy, war crimes, and crimes against humanity—that now have fairly precise definitions and that have achieved universal condemnation, "terrorism" is a term as loosely deployed as it is powerfully charged. [Court discusses *Tel-Oren v. Libyan Arab Republic, 726 F.2d 774 (D.C.Cir.1984), supra* Part Three, at 573, and Judges Edwards, Bork and Robb's agreement on the absence of a consensus on the definition of terrorism].

We regrettably are no closer now than eighteen years ago to an international consensus on the definition of terrorism or even its proscription; [41] the mere existence of the phrase "state-sponsored terrorism" proves the absence of agreement on basic terms among a large number of States that terrorism violates public international law. Moreover, there continues to be strenuous disagreement among States about what actions do or do not constitute terrorism, nor have we shaken ourselves free of the cliché that "one man's terrorist is another man's freedom fighter." We thus conclude that the statements of Judges Edwards, Bork, and Robb remain true today, and that terrorism—unlike piracy, war crimes, and crimes against humanity—does not provide a basis for universal jurisdiction.

Terrorism is defined variously by the perpetrators' motives, methods, targets, and victims. Motive-based definitions suffer from confusion because of the attempt to carve out an exception for assertedly legitimate armed struggle in pursuit of self-determination. For example, under one of the various United Nations resolutions addressing terrorism, armed and violent acts do not constitute "terrorism" if committed by peoples seeking self-determination in opposition to a violently enforced occupation. *See, e.g.,* Declaration on Principles of International Law Concerning Friendly Relations Among Co-operating States in Accordance with the Charter of the United Nations, Oct. 24, 1970, G.A. Res. 2625. ... This attempt to distinguish "terrorists" from "freedom fighters" potentially could legitimate as non-terrorist certain groups nearly universally recognized as terrorist, including the Irish Republican Army, Hezbollah, and Hamas. ...

By contrast, the European Convention on the Suppression of Terrorism defines terrorism solely based on the methods of violence the perpetrator employs, and explicitly removes political judgment of the acts by defining most violent acts as "non-political" (regardless of the perpetrator's claimed motive). European Convention on the Suppression of Terrorism, Nov. 10, 1976, Europ. T.S. No. 90. Thus, in Article I, the Convention defines as terrorism any offenses, *inter alia,* "involving the use of a bomb, grenade, rocket, automatic firearm, or letter or

---

[41]For example, each side of the Israeli-Palestinian conflict charges the other with "terrorism," sentiments echoed by their allies. *See, e.g.,* Todd S. Purdum, *What Do You Mean, "Terrorist"?,* N.Y. Times, Apr. 7, 2002, Week in Review, at 1 ("If Israel sees its military campaign in the West Bank as a justifiable echo of Mr. Bush's assault on Al Qaeda, Palestinians claim affinity with the American colonists' revolt against an occupying power."). The Organization of the Islamic Conference met in Kuala Lumpur, Malaysia, in April 2002, to define terrorism; the host of the conference, Malaysian Prime Minister Mahathir Mohamad, proposed a definition of terrorism as "all attacks on civilians"; the conference's final declaration, however, stated that terrorism consists only of attacks on civilians perpetrated by non-Palestinians, stating that the Conference " 'rejects any attempt to link terrorism to the struggle of the Palestinian people in the exercise of their inalienable right to establish their independent state.' " *Id.* (quoting statements by Mohamad and contained in the conference's final declaration). Sentiments at the conference were far from uniform, however: The deputy foreign minister of Bosnia-Herzegovina stated that "if a person kills or harms a civilian ... he is a terrorist" irrespective of the "race or religion" of the perpetrator and the victims. *Terrorism Issue Splits Muslim Conferees,* Chi. Trib., April 2, 2002, at 10 (quoting statements of Bosnian-Herzegovinian delegate to conference).

parcel bomb if this use endangers persons," a definition that may fail to circumscribe the offense adequately.

The Arab Convention on the Suppression of Terrorism (Cairo, Apr. 22, 1998), *reprinted in* International Instruments Related to the Prevention and Suppression of International Terrorism, 152-73 (United Nations 2001), while condemning terrorism, takes a uniquely restrictive approach to defining it, stating that offenses committed against the interests of Arab states are "terrorist offenses," while offenses committed elsewhere or against other peoples or interests are not. *Id.* at Art. I.3 (defining "terrorist offence" as any of several defined violent actions that occur "in any of the Contracting States, or against their nationals, property or interests"). The Convention further defines as legitimate (non-terrorist) "[a]ll cases of struggle by whatever means, including armed struggle," unless such struggles "prejudic[e] the territorial integrity of any Arab State." *Id.* at Art. II(a).

United States legislation has adopted several approaches to defining terrorism, demonstrating that, even within nations, no single definition of "terrorism" or "terrorist act" prevails. There are numerous statutes defining "terrorism" or "acts of terrorism." *see, e.g.,* 18 U.S.C. § 2331 (defining terrorism by motive, stating that "international terrorism" is comprised of certain acts that "appear to be intended (i) to intimidate or coerce a civilian population; (ii) to influence the policy of a government by intimidation or coercion; or (iii) to affect the conduct of a government by mass destruction, assassination or kidnapping"); 50 U.S.C. § 1801(c)(2) (substantially the same); 6 U.S.C. § 444(2)(B) (defining terrorism by its effect on United States interests, stating that "acts of terrorism" are any acts that are "unlawful" and that cause damage to any "person, property, or entity" in the United States, or to any United States-flag craft or air carrier); 8 U.S.C. § 1182(a)(3)(B)(ii) (in the context of what acts cause an alien to be excludable based on participation in "terrorist activity," defining "terrorist activity" apart from any nexus to United States interests, as "any activity which is unlawful under the laws of the place where it is committed (or which, if committed in the United States, would be unlawful under the laws of the United States or any State)" and that involves, *inter alia,* attacks on third parties to influence the policy of any government, attacks on aircraft and other vessels, or the use of chemical, biological or nuclear weapons).

Still other definitions of "terrorism" may focus on the victims of the attacks or the relationship between the perpetrators and the victims. *See, e.g.,* Alex P. Schmid & Albert J. Jongman, Political Terrorism 1-2 (1988) ("Terrorism is a method of combat in which ... symbolic victims serve as an instrumental target of violence. These instrumental victims share group or class characteristics which form the basis for their selection for victimization. Through previous use of violence or the credible threat of violence other members of that group or class are put in a state of chronic fear (terror).").

b. *Jurisdiction Is Proper Under United States Laws Giving Effect to Its Obligations Under the Montreal Convention*

While it is true, as Yousef asserts, that the District Court erred in concluding that the universality principle conferred jurisdiction over the crimes charged in Count Nineteen, Yousef's claim that principles of customary international law constrain Congress's power to enact laws that proscribe extraterritorial conduct is simply wrong.

In Count Nineteen, Yousef was charged with, and convicted of, violating 18 U.S.C. § 32(b)(3). Title 18 U.S.C. § 32 was enacted as part of the Aircraft Sabotage Act of 1984, Pub. L. No. 98-473, 98 Stat. 1837, 2187-88, which, as discussed above, implements the Montreal Convention. Section 32(a) proscribes offenses, and attempts and conspiracies to commit offenses, against United States-flag aircraft; Section 32(b) proscribes the same offenses when committed against the aircraft of all other nations. Absent § 32(b)'s extension of jurisdiction over perpetrators of offenses against non-United States-flag aircraft, the statute would not effectuate the purpose of the Convention—to forbid all States parties to the Convention from affording aircraft terrorists a safe haven by requiring each party to the Convention to extradite offenders to another party State or to prosecute the offender. As noted above, treaties may diverge broadly from customary international law, yet nevertheless may be enforced, provided that they do not violate one of the strictly limited "peremptory norms" of international law.

In the absence of requests for extradition by other States vested with jurisdiction, the Montreal Convention requires, and § 32 authorizes, the United States to prosecute Yousef for the acts charged in Counts Twelve through Nineteen of the indictment. [43] Thus, in this case, far from exceeding its jurisdictional competence, as Yousef claims, the United States merely met its non-discretionary obligation under the Convention to prosecute Yousef for the acts charged in these Counts. Article 7 of the Convention, as enacted into domestic law in § 32, unequivocally requires the United States to prosecute Yousef. Article 7 states that a State party to the Convention "shall ... be obliged, without exception whatsoever" and "whether or not the offence was committed in its territory" to prosecute (or extradite) an individual found within its borders who has committed one of the offenses proscribed by the Convention. 24 U.S.T. at 565. Moreover, the Convention does not condition the requirement that a State party extradite or prosecute such an individual found within the State on the existence of any additional con-

---

[43]Other States colorably could have asserted jurisdiction over Yousef or requested his extradition from Pakistan, where he was arrested. These States include the Philippines, because the attack was on a Philippine-flag aircraft and also because the aircraft was flying between two points in the Philippines when Yousef placed the bomb under his seat; Japan, because the aircraft was en route from the Philippines to Japan when the bomb exploded and because one Japanese national was injured and another was murdered in the attack; and Pakistan, because Yousef is believed to be a Pakistani national. Each of these States had jurisdiction to prosecute under customary international law, and, as parties to the Montreal Convention, under the Convention…

tacts between that State and either the offender or the offense. In other words, no nexus requirement delimits the obligation of parties to the Convention to prosecute offenders. In the instant case, because the Philippines, Japan, and Pakistan, each of which could have asserted jurisdiction to prosecute Yousef for this particular offense, did not seek to prosecute Yousef, the United States "was obliged" by the Convention—"without exception whatsoever"—to indict Yousef once he was within the United States and irrespective of whether his acts were aimed at the United States.

Moreover, as noted above, "courts of the United States are ... obligated to give effect to an unambiguous exercise by Congress of its [power to grant jurisdiction to agencies or to courts] *even if such an exercise would exceed the limitations imposed by international law.*" *Federal Trade Comm'n v. Compagnie de Saint-Gobain-Pont-a-Mousson, 636 F.2d 1300, 1323 (D.C.Cir.1980)* (emphasis added); *see also* Brown, 12 U.S. (8 Cranch) at 127 (stating that rules of customary international law "may be disregarded" by Congress); *Comm. of United States Citizens Living in Nicaragua, 859 F.2d at 939* (holding that Congressional acts are not subject to challenge on the basis that they violate customary international law).[44]

This statement could be read to imply that United States lawmaking with respect to extraterritorial acts is constrained by an international law principle of "reasonableness"—and, by extrapolation, by sometimes elusive, and generally malleable and evolving, customary international law standards. But the statute at issue in *Javino* did *not* expressly apply to extraterritorial conduct. *Id. at 1142.* Accordingly, to the extent that *Javino* could be read to state that customary international law imposes limits on the ability of Congress, acting under its constitutional power, to extend the jurisdiction of our courts to extraterritorial conduct, such statements constituted mere dicta.

Moreover, any such reading of *Javino*'s assertion in dicta that Congress may be constrained by principles of customary international law in its ability to legislate in respect of extraterritorial conduct is flatly contradicted by a long-settled Supreme Court precedent. Chief Justice Marshall, writing for the Court, held in *The Nereide, 13 U.S. (9 Cranch) 388 (1815)*, that Congress may "manifest [its] will" to apply a rule different from that of customary international law "by passing an act for the purpose." *Id. at 423*. The Court reaffirmed this principle in *McCulloch v. Sociedad Nacional de Marineros de Honduras, 372 U.S. 10*

---

[44] In *U.S. v. Javino, 960 F.2d 1137, 1143 (2d Cir.1992)*, we noted that Congress may be constrained by a "reasonableness" standard in enacting legislation that asserts jurisdiction over extraterritorial criminal conduct, stating that "[t]he reasonableness of an attempt to exercise extraterritorial control depends on such factors as the extent to which the conduct 'has substantial, direct, and foreseeable effect' in the legislating country, and the extent to which other states 'may have an interest in regulating the activity.' " *Id.* (quoting Restatement (Third) of the Foreign Relations Law of the United States § 403(2)(a), (g) (1987)).

(1963), stating that Congress may enact laws superseding "the law of nations," *id. at 21-22,* and we summarized this principle succinctly in *U.S. v. Pinto-Mejia, 720 F.2d 248 (2d Cir.1983)*, in which we stated, "Congress is not bound by international law." *Id. at 259.*

Title 18 U.S.C. § 32 carefully tracks the text of the Montreal Convention; even if § 32 diverged from the Convention, however, jurisdiction under the statute still would be valid. The Supreme Court has held explicitly that legislative acts trump treaty-made international law, stating that "when a statute which is subsequent in time [to a treaty] is inconsistent with a treaty, the statute to the extent of conflict renders the treaty null." *Breard v. Greene, 523 U.S. 371, 376 (1998)* (quoting *Reid v. Covert, 354 U.S. 1, 18 (1957)* (plurality opinion)); *see also Whitney v. Robertson*, 124 U.S. 190, 194 (1888) (holding that if a treaty and a federal statute conflict, "the one last in date will control the other").

In sum, even though Yousef's prosecution under Count Nineteen did not comport with the universality principle, jurisdiction was properly predicated on the Montreal Convention and the United States' own statutes giving effect to the Convention.

c. *In Any Event, Jurisdiction Over Count Nineteen Is Proper under the Protective Principle of Customary International Law*

Although the government is not required to prove that its prosecution of Yousef comported with any of the customary international law bases of criminal jurisdiction, we note that, in fact, Yousef's prosecution by the United States *is* consistent with the "protective principle" of international law. The protective (or "security") principle permits a State to assume jurisdiction over non-nationals for acts done abroad that affect the security of the State. *Rocha v. United States, 288 F.2d 545, 549 (9th Cir.1961)* ... The protective principle generally is invoked to obtain jurisdiction over politically motivated acts but is not limited to acts with a political purpose. *In re Marc Rich & Co., 707 F.2d 663, 666 (2d Cir.1983)* (stating that the protective principle provides jurisdiction over acts committed outside of a State's territory that are directed at interfering with the State's "governmental functions," provided that the act also is contrary to the laws of the host State, if such State has a "reasonably developed" legal system). ...

The stated purpose of Yousef's plot to destroy United States commercial aircraft was to influence United States foreign policy, the making of which clearly constitutes a "governmental function." The bombing of the Philippine Airlines flight at issue in Count Nineteen, which killed one Japanese national and maimed another, was merely a test-run that Yousef executed to ensure that the tactics and devices the conspirators planned to use on United States aircraft operated properly.

Documentation stored on Yousef's laptop computer and adduced at trial, demonstrates that the Philippine Airlines bombing constituted part of the co-conspirators' plan to detonate numerous bombs on United States-flag aircraft. A letter, with a file date of November 19, 1994, found in Yousef's laptop states, in pertinent part:

> We, the Fifth Division of the Liberation Army ... declare our responsibility for striking at some American targets in the near future in retaliation for the financial, political, and military support extended by the American government to the Jewish State .... [T]he Jewish State continues its massacres ... with American money, weapons, and ammunition, in addition to the support and blessing given ... by the U.S. Congress. The American people are quite aware of all this. [Therefore] [we] *will consider all American nationals as part of our legitimate targets because they are responsible for the behavior of their government and its foreign policies,* for the policy of the government represents the will of the people.
>
> Letter from Fifth Division of the Liberation Army (Nov. 19, 1994) (emphasis added).

Extensive additional documentation was found on Yousef's laptop and presented at trial. These documents, which set forth, *inter alia,* the flight schedules and paths of United States-flag aircraft and detailed plans for planting bombs on these flights, confirmed that the co-conspirators intended to bomb United States-flag aircraft using a *modus operandi* identical to that which permitted them to place the bomb on Philippine Airlines flight 434. All of these flights were scheduled to depart from cities in Southeast Asia where the bomber would board the plane, make a stopover in that region where the bomber would disembark, and then continue on to a United States destination, at which point the previously-planted explosive device would detonate. *Id.* This is more than enough to permit the United States to claim jurisdiction over Yousef under the protective principle.

To summarize, we hold that the District Court erred in holding that jurisdiction over the acts charged in Count Nineteen is proper under the customary international law principle of universal jurisdiction, but conclude that the District Court properly asserted jurisdiction over Counts Twelve through Nineteen under United States law (18 U.S.C. § 32), the treaty obligations of the United States, and various principles of customary international law other than the universality principle. We reject Yousef's claim that the absence of jurisdiction under the universality principle over so-called "terrorist" acts precludes his prosecution under United States law.

Notes and Questions

1. Do you agree with the Court's assessment of jurisdictional grounds? Its discussion of the relationship between international and domestic law? Compare materials *supra* Part One, at 124, which appear to state the "last in time" rule far less categorically than the 2nd Circuit in *Yousef.*

2. Ultimately, this decision might not be known as much for its rejection of universal jurisdiction for terrorist acts as for its broadside on "some" international law scholars fired on pp. 101-102:

Some contemporary international law scholars assert that they themselves are an authentic source of customary international law, perhaps even more relevant than the practices and acts of States. The most candid and aggressive formulation of the unfounded claim to legal suzerainty by the international law professoriate has been made by the eminent Louis B. Sohn, the emeritus Bemis Professor of International Law at the Harvard Law School, who stated: I submit that states really never make international law on the subject of human rights. *It is made by the people that care,* the professors, the writers of textbooks and casebooks, and the authors of articles in the leading international law journals .... This is the way international law is made, *not by states, but by "silly" professors writing books*[.] Louis B. Sohn, *Sources of International Law, 25 Ga. J. Int'l & Comp. L. 399, 399, 401 (1996)* (emphasis added). This notion—that professors of international law enjoy a special competence to prescribe the nature of customary international law wholly unmoored from legitimating territorial or national responsibilities, the interests and practices of States, or (in countries such as ours) the processes of democratic consent—may not be unique, but it is certainly without merit.

What is the role, if any, of professors and scholars in the clarification of international law?

c. Rome Statute of the International Criminal Court

37 I.L.M. 999 (1998)

Article 5: *Crimes within the jurisdiction of the Court*

1. The jurisdiction of the Court shall be limited to the most serious crimes of concern to the international community as a whole. The Court has jurisdiction in accordance with this Statute with respect to the following crimes:

(a) The crime of genocide [Article 6 — definition *supra* Part Three, at 551];

(b) Crimes against humanity [Article 7 – definition *supra* Part Three,

at 527-528];

(c) War crimes [Article 8 — definition *supra* Part Six, at 1159-1163];

(d) The crime of aggression.

2. The Court shall exercise jurisdiction over the crime of aggression once a provision is adopted in accordance with articles 121 and 123 defining the crime and setting out the conditions under which the Court shall exercise jurisdiction with respect to this crime. Such a provision shall be consistent with the relevant provisions of the Charter of the United Nations. ...

Article 12: *Preconditions to the exercise of jurisdiction*

1. A State which becomes a Party to this Statute thereby accepts the jurisdiction of the Court with respect to the crimes referred to in article 5.

2. In the case of article 13, paragraph (a) or (c), the Court may exercise its jurisdiction if one or more of the following States are Parties to this Statute or have accepted the jurisdiction of the Court in accordance with paragraph 3:

(a) The State on the territory of which the conduct in question occurred or, if the crime was committed on board a vessel or aircraft, the State of registration of that vessel or aircraft;

(b) The State of which the person accused of the crime is a national.

3. If the acceptance of a State which is not a Party to this Statute is required under paragraph 2, that State may, by declaration lodged with the Registrar, accept the exercise of jurisdiction by the Court with respect to the crime in question. The accepting State shall cooperate with the Court without any delay or exception in accordance with Part 9.

Article 13: *Exercise of jurisdiction*

The Court may exercise its jurisdiction with respect to a crime referred to in article 5 in accordance with the provisions of this Statute if:

(a) A situation in which one or more of such crimes appears to have been committed is referred to the Prosecutor by a State Party in accordance with article 14;

(b) A situation in which one or more of such crimes appears to have been committed is referred to the Prosecutor by the Security Council acting under Chapter VII of the Charter of the United Nations; or

(c) The Prosecutor has initiated an investigation in respect of such a crime in accordance with article 15.

Article 14: *Referral of a situation by a State Party*

1. A State Party may refer to the Prosecutor a situation in which one or more crimes within the jurisdiction of the Court appear to have been committed requesting the Prosecutor to investigate the situation for the purpose of determining whether one or more specific persons should be charged with the commission of such crimes.

2. As far as possible, a referral shall specify the relevant circumstances and be accompanied by such supporting documentation as is available to the State referring the situation.

Article 15: *Prosecutor*

1. The Prosecutor may initiate investigations *proprio motu* on the basis of information on crimes within the jurisdiction of the Court.

2. The Prosecutor shall analyse the seriousness of the information received. For this purpose, he or she may seek additional information from States, organs of the United Nations, intergovernmental or non-governmental organizations, or other reliable sources that he or she deems appropriate, and may receive written or oral testimony at the seat of the Court.

3. If the Prosecutor concludes that there is a reasonable basis to proceed with an investigation, he or she shall submit to the Pre-Trial Chamber a request for authorization of an investigation, together with any supporting material collected. Victims may make representations to the Pre-Trial Chamber, in accordance with the Rules of Procedure and Evidence.

4. If the Pre-Trial Chamber, upon examination of the request and the supporting material, considers that there is a reasonable basis to proceed with an investigation, and that the case appears to fall within the jurisdiction of the Court, it shall authorize the commencement of the investigation, without prejudice to subsequent determinations by the Court with regard to the jurisdiction and admissibility of a case.

5. The refusal of the Pre-Trial Chamber to authorize the investigation shall not preclude the presentation of a subsequent request by the Prosecutor based on new facts or evidence regarding the same situation.

6. If, after the preliminary examination referred to in paragraphs 1 and 2, the Prosecutor concludes that the information provided does not constitute a reasonable basis for an investigation, he or she shall inform those who provided the information. This shall not preclude the Prosecutor from considering further information submitted to him or her regarding the same situation in the light of new facts or evidence.

Article 16: *Deferral of investigation or prosecution*

No investigation or prosecution may be commenced or proceeded with under this Statute for a period of 12 months after the Security Council, in a resolution adopted under Chapter VII of the Charter of the United Nations, has requested the Court to that effect; that request may be renewed by the Council under the same conditions.

Article 17: *Issues of admissibility*

1. Having regard to paragraph 10 of the Preamble and article 1, the Court shall determine that a case is inadmissible where:

(a) The case is being investigated or prosecuted by a State which has jurisdiction over it, unless the State is unwilling or unable genuinely to carry out the investigation or prosecution;

(b) The case has been investigated by a State which has jurisdiction over it and the State has decided not to prosecute the person concerned, unless the decision resulted from the unwillingness or inability of the State genuinely to prosecute;

(c) The person concerned has already been tried for conduct which is the subject of the complaint, and a trial by the Court is not permitted under article 20, paragraph 3;

(d) The case is not of sufficient gravity to justify further action by the Court.

2. In order to determine unwillingness in a particular case, the Court shall consider, having regard to the principles of due process recognized by international law, whether one or more of the following exist, as applicable:

(a) The proceedings were or are being undertaken or the national decision was made for the purpose of shielding the person concerned from criminal responsibility for crimes within the jurisdiction of the Court referred to in article 5;

(b) There has been an unjustified delay in the proceedings which in the circumstances is inconsistent with an intent to bring the person concerned to justice;

(c) The proceedings were not or are not being conducted independently or impartially, and they were or are being conducted in a manner which, in the circumstances, is inconsistent with an intent to bring the person concerned to justice.

3. In order to determine inability in a particular case, the Court shall consider whether, due to a total or substantial collapse or unavailability of its national judicial system, the State is unable to obtain the accused or the necessary evidence and testimony or otherwise unable to carry out its proceedings.

(d) Case Concerning the Arrest Warrant of 11 April 2000 (Congo v. Belg.)

2002 I.C.J. __ (Judgment of Feb. 14)

JUDGES HIGGINS, KOOIJMANS and BUERGENTHAL, separate opinion:

19. We ... turn to the question whether States are entitled to exercise jurisdiction over persons having no connection with the forum State when the accused is not present in the State's territory. The necessary point of departure must be the sources of international law identified in Article 38, paragraph 1 *(c)*, of the Statute of the Court, together with obligations imposed upon all United Nations Members by Security Council resolutions, or by such General Assembly resolutions as meet the criteria enunciated by the Court in the case concerning *Legality of the Threat or Use of Nuclear Weapons, Advisory Opinion (I.C.J. Reports 1996*, p. 226, para. 70).

20. Our analysis may begin with national legislation, to see if it evidences a State practice. Save for the Belgian legislation of 10 February 1999, national legislation, whether in fulfilment of international treaty obligations to make certain international crimes offences also in national law, or otherwise, does not suggest a universal jurisdiction over these offences. Various examples typify the more qualified practice. The Australian War Crimes Act of 1945, as amended in 1988, provides for the prosecution in Australia of crimes committed between 1 September 1939 and 8 May 1945 by persons who were Australian citizens or residents at the times of being charged with the offences (ss. 9 and 11). The United Kingdom War Crimes Act of 1991 enables proceedings to be brought for murder, manslaughter or culpable homicide, committed between 1 September 1935 and 5 June 1945, in a place that was part of Germany or under German occupation, and in circumstances where the accused was at the time, or has become, a British

citizen or resident of the United Kingdom. The statutory jurisdiction provided for by France, Germany and (in even broader terms) the Netherlands, refer for their jurisdictional basis to the jurisdictional provisions in those international treaties to which the legislation was intended to give effect. It should be noted, however, that the German Government on 16 January 2002 has submitted a legislative proposal to the German Parliament, section 1 of which provides:

> This Code governs all the punishable acts listed herein violating public international law, [and] in the case of felonies listed herein [this Code governs] even if the act was committed abroad and does not show any link to [Germany].

The Criminal Code of Canada 1985 allows the execution of jurisdiction when at the time of the act or omission the accused was a Canadian citizen or "employed by Canada in a civilian or military capacity"; or the "victim is a Canadian citizen or a citizen of a State that is allied with Canada in an armed conflict", or when "at the time of the act or omission Canada could, in conformity with international law, exercise jurisdiction over the person on the basis of the person's presence in Canada" (Art. 7).

21. All of these illustrate the trend to provide for the trial and punishment under international law of certain crimes that have been committed extraterritorially. But none of them, nor the many others that have been studied by the Court, represent a classical assertion of a universal jurisdiction over particular offences committed elsewhere by persons having no relationship or connection with the forum State.

22. The case law under these provisions has largely been cautious so far as reliance on universal jurisdiction is concerned. In the *Pinochet* case in the English courts, the jurisdictional basis was clearly treaty based, with the double criminality rule required for extradition being met by English legislation in September 1988, after which date torture committed abroad was a crime in the United Kingdom as it already was in Spain. In Australia the Federal Court referred to a group of crimes over which international law granted universal jurisdiction, even though national enabling legislation would also be needed (*Nulyarimma*, 1999: genocide). The High Court confirmed the authority of the legislature to confer jurisdiction on the courts to exercise a universal jurisdiction over war crimes (*Polyukhovich*, 1991). In Austria (whose Penal Code emphasizes the double-criminality requirement), the Supreme Court found that it had jurisdiction over persons charged with genocide, given that there was not a functioning legal system in the State where the crimes had been committed nor a functioning international criminal tribunal at that point in time (*Cvjetkovic*, 1994). In France it has been held by a *juge d'instruction* that the Genocide Convention does not provide for universal jurisdiction (*In re Javor*, reversed in the *Cour d'Appel* on other grounds. The *Cour de Cassation* ruling equally does not suggest universal jurisdiction). The *Munyeshyaka* finding by the *Cour d'Appel* (1998) relies for a finding — at first sight inconsistent — upon cross-reference into the Statute of the International Tribunal for Rwanda as the jurisdictional basis. In the *Qaddafi*

case the *Cour d'Appel* relied on passive personality and not on universal jurisdiction (in the *Cour de Cassation* it was immunity that assumed central importance).

23. In the *Bouterse* case the Amsterdam Court of Appeal concluded that torture was a crime against humanity, and as such an "extraterritorial jurisdiction" could be exercised over a non-national. However, in the *Hoge Raad*, the Dutch Supreme Court attached conditions to this exercise of extraterritorial jurisdiction (nationality, or presence within the Netherlands at the moment of arrest) on the basis of national legislation.

24. By contrast, a universal jurisdiction has been asserted by the Bavarian Higher Regional Court in respect of a prosecution for genocide (the accused in this case being arrested in Germany). And the case law of the United States has been somewhat more ready to invoke "universal jurisdiction", though considerations of passive personality have also been of key importance (*Yunis*, 1988; *Bin Laden*, 2000).

25. An even more ambiguous answer is to be derived from a study of the provisions of certain important treaties of the last 30 years, and the obligations imposed by the parties themselves.

26. In some of the literature on the subject it is asserted that the great international treaties on crimes and offences evidence universality as a ground for the exercise of jurisdiction recognized in international law. (See the interesting recent article of Luis Benavides "The Universal Jurisdiction Principle: Nature and Scope", *Anuario Mexicano de Derecho Internacional*, Vol. 1, p. 58 (2001).) This is doubtful.

27. Article VI of the Convention on the Prevention and Punishment of the Crime of Genocide, 9 December 1948, provides:

> Persons charged with genocide or any of the other acts enumerated in Article III shall be tried by a competent tribunal of the State in the territory of which the act was committed, or by such international penal tribunal as may have jurisdiction with respect to those Contracting Parties which shall have accepted its jurisdiction.

This is an obligation to assert territorial jurisdiction, though the *travaux préparatoires* do reveal an understanding that this obligation was not intended to affect the right of a State to exercise criminal jurisdiction on its own nationals for acts committed outside the State (A/C 6/SR, 134; p. 5). Article VI also provides a potential grant of non-territorial competence to a possible future international tribunal — even this not being automatic under the Genocide Convention but being restricted to those Contracting Parties which would accept its jurisdiction. In recent years it has been suggested in the literature that Article VI does not prevent a State from exercising universal jurisdiction in a genocide case. (And see, more generally, *Restatement (Third) of the Foreign Relations Law of the United States (1987)*, §404.)

28. Article 49 of the First Geneva Convention, Article 50 of the Second Geneva Convention, Article 129 of the Third Geneva Convention and Article 146 of the Fourth Geneva Convention, all of 12 August 1949, provide:

> Each High Contracting Party shall be under the obligation to search for persons alleged to have committed, or to have ordered to be committed, ... grave breaches, and shall bring such persons, regardless of their nationality, before its own courts. It may also, if it prefers, and in accordance with the provisions of its own legislation, hand such persons over for trial to another High Contracting Party concerned, provided such High Contracting Party has made out a *prima facie* case.

29. Article 85, paragraph 1, of the First Additional Protocol to the 1949 Geneva Convention incorporates this provision by reference.

30. The stated purpose of the provision was that the offences would not be left unpunished (the extradition provisions playing their role in this objective). It may immediately be noted that this is an early form of the *aut dedere aut prosequi* to be seen in later conventions. But the obligation to prosecute is primary, making it even stronger.

31. No territorial or nationality linkage is envisaged, suggesting a true universality principle (see also Henzelin, *Le principe de l'universalité en droit pénal international : Droit et obligation pour les Etats de poursuivre et juger selon le principe de l'universalité* (2000), pp. 354-6). But a different interpretation is given in the authoritative Pictet Commentary: *Geneva Convention for the Amelioration of the Condition of the Wounded and Sick in Armed Forces in the Field* (1952), which contends that this obligation was understood as being an obligation upon States parties to search for offenders who may be on their territory. Is it a true example of universality, if the obligation to search is restricted to the own territory? Does the obligation to search imply a permission to prosecute in absentia, if the search had no result?

32. As no case has touched upon this point, the jurisdictional matter remains to be judicially tested. In fact, there has been a remarkably modest corpus of national case law emanating from the jurisdictional possibilities provided in the Geneva Conventions or in Additional Protocol I. ...

[33-40: Authors review other treaties and conclude:]

41. The parties to these treaties agreed both to grounds of jurisdiction and as to the obligation to take the measures necessary to establish such jurisdiction. The specified grounds relied on links of nationality of the offender, or the ship or aircraft concerned, or of the victim. See, for example, Article 4 (1) Hague Convention; Article 3 (1) Tokyo Convention; Article 5, Hostages Convention; Article 5, Torture Convention. These may properly be described as treaty-based broad extraterritorial jurisdiction. But in addition to these were the parallel provisions whereby a State party in whose jurisdiction the alleged perpetrator of such offences is found, shall prosecute him or extradite him. By the loose use of lan-

guage the latter has come to be referred to as "universal jurisdiction", though this is really an obligatory territorial jurisdiction over persons, albeit in relation to acts committed elsewhere. …

42. Whether this obligation (whether described as the duty to establish universal jurisdiction, or, more accurately, the jurisdiction to establish a territorial jurisdiction over persons for extraterritorial events) is an obligation only of treaty law, *inter partes or*, whether it is now, *at least as regards the offences articulated in the treaties*, an obligation of customary international law was pleaded by the Parties in this case but not addressed in any great detail.

43. Nor was the question of whether any such general obligation applies to crimes against humanity, given that those too are regarded everywhere as comparably heinous crimes. Accordingly, we offer no view on these aspects.

44. However, we note that the inaccurately termed "universal jurisdiction principle" in these treaties is a principle of *obligation*, while the question in this case is whether Belgium had the right to issue and circulate the arrest warrant if it so chose.

If a dispassionate analysis of State practice and Court decisions suggests that no such jurisdiction is presently being exercised, the writings of eminent jurists are much more mixed. The large literature contains vigorous exchanges of views (which have been duly studied by the Court) suggesting profound differences of opinion. But these writings, important and stimulating as they may be, cannot of themselves and without reference to the other sources of international law, evidence the existence of a jurisdictional norm. The assertion that certain treaties and court decisions rely on universal jurisdiction, which in fact they do not, does not evidence an international practice recognized as custom. And the policy arguments advanced in some of the writings can certainly suggest why a practice or a court decision should be regarded as desirable, or indeed lawful; but contrary arguments are advanced, too, and in any event these also cannot serve to substantiate an international practice where virtually none exists.

45. That there is no established practice in which States exercise universal jurisdiction, properly so called, is undeniable. As we have seen, virtually all national legislation envisages links of some sort to the forum State; and no case law exists in which pure universal jurisdiction has formed the basis of jurisdiction. This does not necessarily indicate, however, that such an exercise would be unlawful. In the first place, national legislation reflects the circumstances in which a State provides in its own law the ability to exercise jurisdiction. But a State is not required to legislate up to the full scope of the jurisdiction allowed by international law. The war crimes legislation of Australia and the United Kingdom afford examples of countries making more confined choices for the exercise of jurisdiction. Further, many countries have no national legislation for the exercise of well recognized forms of extraterritorial jurisdiction, sometimes notwithstanding treaty obligations to enable themselves so to act. National legislation may be illuminating as to the issue of universal jurisdiction, but not conclusive as to its

legality. Moreover, while none of the national case law to which we have referred happens to be based on the exercise of a universal jurisdiction properly so called, there is equally nothing in this case law which evidences an *opinio juris* on the illegality of such a jurisdiction. In short, national legislation and case law, — that is, State practice — is neutral as to exercise of universal jurisdiction.

46. There are, moreover, certain indications that a universal criminal jurisdiction for certain international crimes is clearly not regarded as unlawful. The duty to prosecute under those treaties which contain the *aut dedere aut prosequi* provisions opens the door to a jurisdiction based on the heinous nature of the crime rather than on links of territoriality or nationality (whether as perpetrator or victim). The 1949 Geneva Conventions lend support to this possibility, and are widely regarded as today reflecting customary international law. (See, e.g., Cherif Bassiouni, *International Criminal Law, Volume III: Enforcement*, 2nd Edition, (1999), p. 228; Theodor Meron, I*nternational Criminalization of Internal Atrocities,* 89 *AJIL* (1995), at 576.)

47. The contemporary trends, reflecting international relations as they stand at the beginning of the new century, are striking. The movement is towards bases of jurisdiction other than territoriality. "Effects" or "impact" jurisdiction is embraced both by the United States and, with certain qualifications, by the European Union. Passive personality jurisdiction, for so long regarded as controversial, is now reflected not only in the legislation of various countries (the United States, Ch. 113A, 1986 Omnibus Diplomatic and Antiterrorism Act; France, Art. 689, Code of Criminal Procedure, 1975), and today meets with relatively little opposition, at least so far as a particular category of offences is concerned.

48. In civil matters we already see the beginnings of a very broad form of extraterritorial jurisdiction. Under the Alien Tort Claims Act, the United States, basing itself on a law of 1789, has asserted a jurisdiction both over human rights violations and over major violations of international law, perpetrated by non-nationals overseas. Such jurisdiction, with the possibility of ordering payment of damages, has been exercised with respect to torture committed in a variety of countries (Paraguay, Chile, Argentina, Guatemala), and with respect to other major human rights violations in yet other countries. While this unilateral exercise of the function of guardian of international values has been much commented on, it has not attracted the approbation of States generally.

49. Belgium — and also many writers on this subject — find support for the exercise of a universal criminal jurisdiction *in absentia* in the "*Lotus*" case. Although the case was clearly decided on the basis of jurisdiction over damage to a vessel of the Turkish navy and to Turkish nationals, it is the famous dictum of the Permanent Court which has attracted particular attention. The Court stated that:

> Far from laying down a general prohibition to the effect that States may not extend the application of their laws and the jurisdiction of their courts to persons, property and acts outside their territory, it leaves them in this respect a wide measure of discretion which is only limited in certain

cases by prohibitive rules; as regards other cases, every State remains free to adopt the principles which it regards as best and most suitable. (*P.C.I.J., Series A, No. 10*, pp. 18-19.)

The Permanent Court acknowledged that consideration had to be given as to whether these principles would apply equally in the field of criminal jurisdiction, or whether closer connections might there be required. The Court noted the importance of the territorial character of criminal law but also the fact that all or nearly all systems of law extend their action to offences committed outside the territory of the State which adopts them, and they do so in ways which vary from State to State. After examining the issue the Court finally concluded that for an exercise of extraterritorial criminal jurisdiction (other than within the territory of another State) it was equally necessary to "prove the existence of a principle of international law restricting the discretion of States as regards criminal legislation".

50. The application of this celebrated dictum would have clear attendant dangers in some fields of international law. (See, on this point, Judge Shahabudeen's dissenting opinion in the case concerning *Legality of the Threat or Use of Nuclear Weapons Advisory Opinion, I.C.J. Reports 1996*, pp. 394-396.) Nevertheless, it represents a continuing potential in the context of jurisdiction over international crimes.

51. That being said, the dictum represents the high water mark of *laissez-faire* in international relations, and an era that has been significantly overtaken by other tendencies. The underlying idea of universal jurisdiction properly so-called (as in the case of piracy, and possibly in the Geneva Conventions of 1949), as well as the *aut dedere aut prosequi* variation, is a common endeavour in the face of atrocities. The series of multilateral treaties with their special jurisdictional provisions reflect a determination by the international community that those engaged in war crimes, hijacking, hostage taking, torture should not go unpunished. Although crimes against humanity are not yet the object of a distinct convention, a comparable international indignation at such acts is not to be doubted. And those States and academic writers who claim the right to act unilaterally to assert a universal criminal jurisdiction over persons committing such acts, invoke the concept of acting as "agents for the international community". This vertical notion of the authority of action is significantly different from the horizontal system of international law envisaged in the "*Lotus*" case.

At the same time, the international consensus that the perpetrators of international crimes should not go unpunished is being advanced by a flexible strategy, in which newly-established international criminal tribunals, treaty obligations and national courts all have their part to play. We reject the suggestion that the battle against impunity is "made over" to international treaties and tribunals, with national courts having no competence in such matters. Great care has been taken when formulating the relevant treaty provisions not to exclude other grounds of jurisdiction that may be exercised on a voluntary basis. (See Article 4 (3)

Hague Convention for the Suppression of Unlawful Seizure of Aircraft, 1970; Article 5 (3) International Convention Against Taking of Hostages, 1979; Article 5 (3) Convention Against Torture; Article 9, Statute of the International Criminal Tribunal for the Former Yugoslavia and Article 19, Rome Statute of the International Criminal Court.)

52. We may thus agree with the authors of the Oppenheim, 9th Edition, at page 998, that:

> While no general rule of positive international law can as yet be asserted which gives to states the right to punish foreign nationals for crimes against humanity in the same way as they are, for instance, entitled to punish acts of piracy, there are clear indications pointing to the gradual evolution of a significant principle of international law to that effect...

53. This brings us once more to the particular point that divides the Parties in this case: is it a precondition of the assertion of universal jurisdiction that the accused be within the territory?

54. Considerable confusion surrounds this topic, not helped by the fact that legislators, courts and writers alike frequently fail to specify the precise temporal moment at which any such requirement is said to be in play. Is the presence of the accused within the jurisdiction said to be required at the time the offence was committed? At the time the arrest warrant is issued? Or at the time of the trial itself? An examination of national legislation, cases and writings reveals a wide variety of temporal linkages to the assertion of jurisdiction. This incoherent practice cannot be said to evidence a precondition to any exercise of universal criminal jurisdiction. The fact that in the past the only clear example of an agreed exercise of universal jurisdiction was in respect of piracy, *outside of any territorial jurisdiction*, is not determinative. The only prohibitive rule (repeated by the Permanent Court in the "*Lotus*" case) is that criminal jurisdiction should not be exercised, without permission, within the territory of another State. The Belgian arrest warrant envisaged the arrest of Mr. Yerodia in Belgium, or the possibility of his arrest in third States at the discretion of the States concerned. This would in principle seem to violate no existing prohibiting rule of international law.

55. In criminal law, in particular, it is said that evidence-gathering requires territorial presence. But this point goes to *any* extraterritoriality, including those that are well established and not just to universal jurisdiction.

56. Some jurisdictions provide for trial *in absentia*; others do not. If it is said that a person must be within the jurisdiction at the time of the trial itself, that may be a prudent guarantee for the right of fair trial but has little to do with bases of jurisdiction recognized under international law.

57. On what basis is it claimed, alternatively, that an arrest warrant may not be issued for non-nationals in respect of offences occurring outside the jurisdiction? The textual provisions themselves of the 1949 Geneva Convention and the First Additional Protocol give no support to this view. The great treaties on aerial

offences, hijacking, narcotics and torture are built around the concept of *aut dedere aut prosequi*. *Definitionally, this envisages presence on the territory*. There cannot be an obligation to extradite someone you choose not to try unless that person is within your reach. National legislation, enacted to give effect to these treaties, quite naturally also may make mention of the necessity of the presence of the accused. These sensible realities are critical for the obligatory exercise of *aut dedere aut prosequi* jurisdiction, but cannot be interpreted *a contrario so as to exclude a* voluntary exercise of a universal jurisdiction.

58. If the underlying purpose of designating certain acts as international crimes is to authorize a wide jurisdiction to be asserted over persons committing them, there is no rule of international law (and certainly not the *aut dedere* principle) which makes illegal co-operative overt acts designed to secure their presence within a State wishing to exercise jurisdiction…

59. If, as we believe to be the case, a State may choose to exercise a universal criminal jurisdiction *in absentia*, it must also ensure that certain safeguards are in place. They are absolutely essential to prevent abuse and to ensure that the rejection of impunity does not jeopardize stable relations between States.

No exercise of criminal jurisdiction may occur which fails to respect the inviolability or infringes the immunities of the person concerned. We return below to certain aspects of this facet, but will say at this juncture that commencing an investigation on the basis of which an arrest warrant may later be issued does not of itself violate those principles. The function served by the international law of immunities does not require that States fail to keep themselves informed.

A State contemplating bringing criminal charges based on universal jurisdiction must first offer to the national State of the prospective accused person the opportunity itself to act upon the charges concerned. The Court makes reference to these elements in the context of this case at paragraph 16 of its Judgment.

Further, such charges may only be laid by a prosecutor or *juge d'instruction* who acts in full independence, without links to or control by the government of that State. Moreover, the desired equilibrium between the battle against impunity and the promotion of good inter-State relations will only be maintained if there are some special circumstances that do require the exercise of an international criminal jurisdiction and if this has been brought to the attention of the prosecutor or *juge d'instruction*. For example, persons related to the victims of the case will have requested the commencement of legal proceedings…

60. It is equally necessary that universal criminal jurisdiction be exercised only over those crimes regarded as the most heinous by the international community.

61. Piracy is the classical example. This jurisdiction was, of course, exercised on the high seas and not as an enforcement jurisdiction within the territory of a non-agreeing State. But this historical fact does not mean that universal jurisdiction only exists with regard to crimes committed on the high seas or in

other places outside national territorial jurisdiction. Of decisive importance is that this jurisdiction was regarded as lawful because the international community regarded piracy as damaging to the interests of all. War crimes and crimes against humanity are no less harmful to the interests of all because they do not usually occur on the high seas. War crimes (already since 1949 perhaps a treaty-based provision for universal jurisdiction) may be added to the list. The specification of their content is largely based upon the 1949 Conventions and those parts of the 1977 Additional Protocols that reflect general international law. Recent years have also seen the phenomenon of an alignment of national jurisdictional legislation on war crimes, specifying those crimes under the statutes of the ICTY, ICTR and the intended ICC.

62. The substantive content of the concept of crimes against humanity, and its status as crimes warranting the exercise of universal jurisdiction, is undergoing change. Article 6 *(c)* of the Charter of the International Military Tribunal of 8 August, 1945, envisaged them as a category linked with those crimes over which the Tribunal had jurisdiction (war crimes, crimes against the peace). In 1950 the International Law Commission defined them as murder, extermination, enslavement, deportation or other inhuman acts perpetrated on the citizen population, or persecutions on political, racial or religious grounds if in exercise of, or connection with, any crime against peace or a war crime (*YILC* 1950, Principle VI *(c)*, pp. 374-377). Later definitions of crimes against humanity both widened the subject-matter, to include such offences as torture and rape, and de-coupled the link to other earlier established crimes. Crimes against humanity are now regarded as a distinct category. Thus the 1996 Draft Code of Crimes Against the Peace and Security of Mankind, adopted by the International Law Commission at its 48th session, provides that crimes against humanity *means any of the following acts, when committed in a systematic manner or on a large scale and instigated or directed by a Government or any organization or group*:

(a) Murder;

(b) Extermination;

(c) Torture;

(d) Enslavement;

(e) Persecution on political, racial, religious or ethnic grounds;

(f) Institutionalized discrimination on racial, ethnic or religious grounds involving the violation of fundamental human rights and freedoms and resulting in seriously disadvantaging a part of the population;

(g) Arbitrary deportation or forcible transfer of population;

(h) Arbitrary imprisonment;

(i) Forced disappearance of persons;

(j) Rape, enforced prostitution and other forms of sexual abuse;

(k) Other inhumane acts which severely damage physical or mental integrity, health or human dignity, such as mutilation and severe bodily harm.

63. The Belgian legislation of 1999 asserts a universal jurisdiction over acts broadly defined as "grave breaches of international humanitarian law", and the list is a compendium of war crimes and the Draft Codes of Offences listing of crimes against humanity, with genocide being added. Genocide is also included as a listed "crime against humanity" in the 1968 Convention on the Non-Applicability of Statutes of Limitation to War Crimes and Crimes against Humanity, as well as being included in the ICTY, ICTR and ICC Statutes.

64. The arrest warrant issued against Mr. Yerodia accuses him both of war crimes and of crimes against humanity. As regards the latter, charges of incitement to racial hatred, which are said to have led to murders and lynchings, were specified. Fitting of this charge within the generally understood substantive context of crimes against humanity is not without its problems. "Racial hatred" would need to be assimilated to "persecution on racial grounds", or, on the particular facts, to mass murder and extermination. Incitement to perform any of these acts is not in terms listed in the usual definitions of crimes against humanity, nor is it explicitly mentioned in the Statutes of the ICTY or the ICTR, nor in the Rome Statute for the ICC. However, Article 7 (l) of the ICTY and Article 6 (l) of the ICTR do stipulate that "any person who planned, instigated, ordered, committed or otherwise aided or abetted in the planning, preparation or execution of a crime referred to [in the relevant articles: crimes against humanity being among them] shall be individually responsible for the crime". In the *Akayesu* Judgment (96-4-T) a Chamber of the ICTR has held that liability for a crime against humanity includes liability through incitement to commit the crime concerned (paras. 481-482). The matter is dealt with in a comparable way in Article 25 (3) of the Rome Statute.

65. It would seem (without in any way pronouncing upon whether Mr. Yerodia did or did not perform the acts with which he is charged in the warrant) that the acts alleged do fall within the concept of "crimes against humanity" and would be within that small category in respect of which an exercise of universal jurisdiction is not precluded under international law.

JUDGE *ad hoc* VAN DEN WYNGAERT, dissenting.

44. There is no generally accepted definition of universal jurisdiction in conventional or customary international law. States that have incorporated the principle in their domestic legislation have done so in very different ways. Although there are many examples of States exercising extraterritorial jurisdiction for international crimes such as war crimes and crimes against humanity and torture, it may often be on other jurisdictional grounds such as the nationality of the victim. A prominent example was the *Eichmann* case which was in fact based, not on universal jurisdiction but on passive personality. In the Spanish *Pinochet* case, an important connecting factor was the Spanish nationality of some of the victims. Likewise, in thc case against Mr. Yerodia, some of the complainants were of

Belgian nationality, even if there were, apparently, no Belgian nationals that were victims of the *violence* that allegedly resulted from the hate speeches of which Mr. Yerodia was suspected (Judgment, para. 15).

45. Much has been written in legal doctrine about universal jurisdiction. Many views exist as to its legal meaning and its legal status under international law. This is not the place to discuss them. What matters for the present dispute is the way in which Belgium has codified universal jurisdiction in its domestic legislation and whether it is, as applied in the case of Mr. Yerodia, compatible with international law.

Article 7 of the 1993/1999 Belgian Act, which is at the centre of the dispute, states the following: "The Belgian courts shall be competent to deal with breaches provided for in the present Act, irrespective of where such breaches have been committed . . .".

46. Despite uncertainties that may exist concerning the definition of universal jurisdiction, one thing is very clear: the *ratio legis* of universal jurisdiction is based on the international reprobation for certain very serious crimes such as war crimes and crimes against humanity. Its *raison d'être* is to avoid impunity, to prevent suspects of such crimes finding a safe haven in third countries. ...

47. It may not have been the International Court of Justice's task to define universal jurisdiction in abstract terms. What it should, however, have considered is the following question: was Belgium under international law, entitled to assert *extraterritorial* jurisdiction against Mr. Yerodia (apart from the question of immunity) in the present case? The Court did not consider this question at all. ...

48. The leading case on the question of extraterritorial jurisdiction is the 1927 "*Lotus*" case [author proceeds to recite "famous dictum" mentioned in sep. op. *supra*].

49. ... A distinction must be made between prescriptive jurisdiction and enforcement jurisdiction. The above-mentioned *dictum* concerns *prescriptive jurisdiction*: it is about what a State may do *on its own territory* when investigating and prosecuting crimes committed abroad, not about what a State may do on the territory of other States when prosecuting such crimes. Obviously, a State has no *enforcement jurisdiction* outside its territory: a State may, failing permission to the contrary, not exercise its power on the territory of another State. This is "the first and foremost restriction imposed by international law upon a State". In other words, the permissive rule only applies to prescriptive jurisdiction, not to enforcement jurisdiction: failing a prohibition, State A *may*, on its own territory, prosecute offences committed in State B *(permissive rule)*; failing a permission, State A *may not* act on the territory of State B. ...

51. It follows from the "*Lotus*" case that a State has the right to provide extraterritorial jurisdiction on its territory unless there is a prohibition under international law. I believe that there is *no prohibition* under international law to

enact legislation allowing it to investigate and prosecute war crimes and crimes against humanity committed abroad. It has often been argued, not without reason, that the "*Lotus*" test is too liberal and that, given the growing complexity of contemporary international intercourse, a more restrictive approach should be adopted today. In the *Nuclear Weapons* case, there were two groups of States each giving a different interpretation of "*Lotus*" on this point and President Bedjaoui, in his declaration, expressed hesitations about "*Lotus*". Even under the more restrictive view, Belgian legislation stands. There is ample evidence in support of the proposition that international law clearly *permits* States to provide extraterritorial jurisdiction for such crimes. I will give reasons for both propositions in the next paragraphs. I believe that *(a)* international law does *not prohibit* universal jurisdiction for war crimes and crimes against humanity;*(b)* clearly permits it.

(a) International law does not prohibit universal jurisdiction for war crimes and crimes against humanity

52. The Congo argued that the very concept of universal jurisdiction presupposes the presence of the defendant on the territory of the prosecuting State. Universal jurisdiction *in absentia*, it submitted, was contrary to international law. This proposition needs to be assessed in the light of conventional and customary international law and of legal doctrine. …

54. There is no rule of *conventional international law* to the effect that universal jurisdiction *in absentia* is prohibited. The most important legal basis, in the case of universal jurisdiction for war crimes is Article 146 of the IVth Geneva Convention of 1949, which lays down the principle *aut dedere aut judicare*.. A textual interpretation of this Article does not logically presuppose the presence of the offender … Reading into Article 146 of the IVth Geneva Convention a limitation on a State's right to exercise universal jurisdiction would fly in the face of a *teleological interpretation* of the Geneva Conventions. The purpose of these Conventions, obviously, is not to restrict the jurisdiction of States for crimes under international law.

55. There is no *customary international law* to this effect either. The Congo submits there is a State practice, evidencing an *opinio juris* asserting that universal jurisdiction, *per se*, requires the presence of the offender on the territory of the prosecuting State. Many national systems giving effect to the obligation *aut dedere aut judicare* and/or the Rome Statute for an International Criminal Court indeed require the presence of the offender. This appears from legislation and from a number of national decisions including the Danish *Saric* case, the French *Javor* case and the German *Jorgic* case. However, there are also examples of national systems that do not require the presence of the offender on the territory of the prosecuting State. Governments and national courts in the same State may hold different opinions on the same question, which makes it even more difficult to identify the *opinio juris* in that State. And even where national law requires the presence of the offender, this is not necessarily the expression of an *opinio juris* to the effect that this is a requirement under international law. National

decisions should be read with much caution. In the *Bouterse* case, for example, the Dutch Supreme Court did not state that the requirement of the presence of the suspect was a requirement under international law, but only under domestic law. It found that, *under Dutch law*, there was no such jurisdiction to prosecute Mr. Bouterse but did not say that exercising such jurisdiction would be contrary to *international law*. In fact, the Supreme Court did *not* follow the Advocate General's submission on this point.

56. The "*Lotus*" case is not only an authority on jurisdiction, but also on the formation of customary international law as was set out above. A "negative practice" of States, consisting in their abstaining from instituting criminal proceedings, cannot, in itself, be seen as evidence of an *opinio juris*. Only if this abstinence was based on a conscious decision of the States in question can this practice generate customary international law. As in the case of immunities, such abstinence may be attributed to other factors than the existence of an *opinio juris*. There may be good political or practical reasons for a State not to assert jurisdiction in the absence of the offender.

It may be *politically* inconvenient to have such a wide jurisdiction because it is not conducive to international relations and national public opinion may not approve of trials against foreigners for crimes committed abroad. This does not, however, make such trials illegal under international law.

A *practical* consideration may be the difficulty in obtaining the evidence in trials of extraterritorial crimes. Another practical reason may be that States are afraid of overburdening their court system. This was stated by the Court of Appeal in the United Kingdom in the *Al-Adsani* case and seems to have been an explicit reason for the Assemblée nationale in France to refrain from introducing universal jurisdiction *in absentia* when adopting universal jurisdiction over the crimes falling within the Statute of the Yugoslavia Tribunal. The concern for a linkage with the national order thus seems to be more of a pragmatic than of a juridical nature. It is not, therefore, necessarily the expression of an *opinio juris* to the effect that this form of universal jurisdiction is contrary to international law.

57. There is a massive literature of learned scholarly writings on the subject of universal jurisdiction. I confine myself to three studies, which emanate from groups of scholars: the Princeton principles, the Cairo principles and the Kamminga report on behalf of the ILA, and look at one point: do the authors support the Congo's proposition that universal jurisdiction *in absentia* is contrary to international law? The answer is: no.

58. I conclude that there is no conventional or customary international law or legal doctrine in support of the proposition that (universal) jurisdiction for war crimes and crimes against humanity can only be exercised if the defendant is present on the territory of the prosecuting State.

(b) International law permits universal jurisdiction for war crimes and crimes against humanity

59. International law clearly permits universal jurisdiction for war crimes and crimes against humanity. For both crimes, permission under international law exists. For crimes *against humanity*, there is no clear treaty provision on the subject but it is accepted that, at least in the case of genocide, States are entitled to assert extraterritorial jurisdiction. In the case of *war crimes*, however, there is specific conventional international law in support of the proposition that States are entitled to assert jurisdiction over acts committed abroad: the relevant provision is Article 146 of the IVth Geneva Convention, which lays down the principle *aut dedere aut judicare* for war crimes committed against civilians.

From the perspective of the drafting history of international criminal law conventions, this is probably one of the first codifications of this principle, which, in legal doctrine, goes back at least to Hugo Grotius but has probably much older roots. However, it had not been codified in conventional international law until 1949. There are older Conventions such as the 1926 Slavery Convention or the 1929 Convention on Counterfeiting, which require States to lay down rules on *jurisdiction* but which do not provide an *aut dedere aut judicare* obligation. The 1949 Conventions are probably the first to lay down this principle in an article that is meant to cover both jurisdiction and prosecution.

Subsequent Conventions have refined this way of drafting and have laid down distinctive provisions on *jurisdiction* on the one hand and on prosecution *(aut dedere aut judicare)* on the other. Examples are the 1970 Convention for the Suppression of Unlawful Seizure of Aircraft (Arts. 4 and 7 respectively) and the 1984 Convention against Torture (Arts. 5 and 7 respectively).

60. In order to assess the "permissibility" of universal jurisdiction for international crimes, it is important to distinguish between *jurisdiction* clauses and *prosecution (aut dedere aut judicare)* clauses in international criminal law conventions.

61. The *jurisdiction* clauses in these Conventions usually oblige States to provide extraterritorial jurisdiction, but do not exclude States from exercising jurisdiction under their national laws. Even where they do not provide universal jurisdiction, they do not exclude it either, nor do they require States to refrain from providing this form of jurisdiction under their domestic law. The standard formulation of this idea is that "[t]his Convention does not exclude any criminal jurisdiction exercised in accordance with national law". This formula can be found in a host of Conventions, including the 1970 Convention for the Suppression of Unlawful Seizure of Aircraft (Art. 4, para. 3) and the 1984 Convention against Torture (Art. 5, para. 3).

62. The *prosecution* clauses *(aut dedere aut judicare)*, however, sometimes link the prosecution obligation to extradition, in the sense that a State's duty to prosecute a suspect only exists "if it does not extradite him". Examples are

Article 7 of the 1970 Convention for the Suppression of Unlawful Seizure of Aircraft and Article 7 of the 1984 Convention against Torture. This, however, does not mean that prosecution is *only* possible in cases where extradition has been refused. Surely, this formula cannot be read into Article 146 of the IVth Geneva Convention which according to some authors even prioritizes prosecution over extradition: *primo prosequi, secundo dedere*. Even if one adopts the doctrinal viewpoint that the notion of universal jurisdiction assumes the presence of the offender, there is nothing in Article 146 that warrants the conclusion that this is an actual requirement. …

67. Article 7 of Belgium's 1993/1999 Act, giving effect to the principle of universal jurisdiction regarding war crimes and crimes against humanity, is not contrary to international law. International law does not prohibit States from asserting prescriptive jurisdiction of this kind. On the contrary, international law permits and even encourages States to assert this form of jurisdiction in order to ensure that suspects of war crimes and crimes against humanity do not find safe havens.

NOTES AND QUESTIONS

1. For a thorough discussion and submission of universal jurisdiction, see International Law Association, *Final Report on the Exercise of Universal Jurisdiction in respect of Gross Human Rights Offences*, (Committee on International Human Rights Law and Practice 2000)(Kammenga Report); Princeton Project on Universal Jurisdiction, *The Princeton Principles on Universal Jurisdiction*, July 23, 2001 *available at* http://www.princeton.edu/~lapa/unive_jur.pdf; Africa Legal Aid (AFLA), *Preliminary Draft of the Cairo Guiding Principles on Universal Jurisdiction in Respect of Gross Human Rights Offenses: An African Perspective*, Cairo, 31 July 2001, http://www.afla.unimaas.nl/en/act/univjurisd/preliminaryprinciples.htm. *See also* M. Cherif Bassiouni, *Universal Jurisdiction for International Crimes: Historical Perspectives and Contemporary Practice*, 42 VA J. INT'L L. 81 (2001).

2. In what respects, exactly, do the separate opinion by Judges Higgins et al. and Judge Van den Wyngaert's dissent differ? How does each approach the *Lotus* case? Which opinion do you think better suits the jurisdictional system of international law?

3. Ceding to strong international pressure, in particular from the United States, the Belgian law at issue has been substantially modified, and universal jurisdiction over human rights abuses has been removed. Loi relative aux violations graves du droit humanitaire (Moniteur Belge du 7 août 2003), arts. 14-16; *see also* the report of the House Justice Committee, July 28, 2003, Parliamentary Doc. 51 0103/003, at 4-5, *available at* http://www1.dekamer.be/FLWB/pdf/51/0103/51K0103003.pdf [hereinafter Justice Committee Report]. For a thoughtful review of life and death of the Belgian universal jurisdiction statute, *see* Steven R. Ratner, *Belgium's War Crimes Statute: A Post-Mortem*, 97 AM. J. INT'L L. 888 (2003).

III. COMPETENCE TO APPLY LAW

A. THE PROBLEM

The competence to apply law, the exercise of judicial jurisdiction in its more conventional denotation, involves policies somewhat different from those about making law and is distributed by the international legal system in entirely different ways. With regard to prescriptive competence, the critical question is the degree of comparative interest or comparative need of the would-be prescriber as against other communities which seek to regulate the same persons, events or things and the effects on world public order of different systems of distributing law-making competence. With regard to application, the same dimensions of a common world community interest persist, but the peculiar concerns in relation to each other of putative plaintiffs and defendants, ameliorating both the inclusive and exclusive interest of their particular communities, become a major factor in many of the jurisdictional claims There are four basic grounds on which claims for applicative competence are made: consent of the parties, physical presence of the parties, location of property, and universal jurisdiction. As you proceed through the illustrative cases, propose policies to guide decision with regard to applicative competence and test the decision trends against those policies.

B. TRADITIONAL GROUNDS ON WHICH APPLICATIVE COMPETENCE HAS BEEN CLAIMED

1. Restatement (Third) of Foreign Relations Law of the United States (1987)

§ 421. Jurisdiction to Adjudicate

(1) A state may exercise jurisdiction through its courts to adjudicate with respect to a person or thing if the relationship of the state to the person or thing is such as to make the exercise of jurisdiction reasonable.

(2) In general, a state's exercise of jurisdiction to adjudicate with respect to a person or thing is reasonable if, at the time jurisdiction is asserted:

(a) the person or thing is present in the territory of the state, other than transitorily;

(b) the person, if a natural person, is domiciled in the state;

(c) the person, if a natural person, is resident in the state;

(d) the person, if a natural person, is a national of the state;

(e) the person, if a corporation or comparable juridical person, is organized pursuant to the law of the state;

(f) a ship, aircraft or other vehicle to which the adjudication relates is registered under the laws of the state;

(g) the person, whether natural or juridical, has consented to the exercise of jurisdiction;

(h) the person, whether natural or juridical, regularly carries on business in the state;

(i) the person, whether natural or juridical, had carried on activity in the state, but only in respect of such activity;

(j) the person, whether natural or juridical, had carried on outside the state an activity having a substantial, direct, and foreseeable effect within the state, but only in respect of such activity; or

(k) the thing that is the subject of adjudication is owned, possessed, or used in the state, but only in respect of a claim reasonably connected with that thing.

(3) A defense of lack of jurisdiction is generally waived by any appearance by or on behalf of a person or thing (whether as plaintiff, defendant, or third party), if the appearance is for a purpose that does not include a challenge to the exercise of jurisdiction.

2. Unterweser, Reederei G.m.b.H. v. Zapata Offshore Co.

[1968] 2 Lloyd's L. Rep. 158 (C.A.)

LORD JUSTICE WILLMER: ... The question at issue between the parties arises out of a marine casualty which took place in January, 1968. The plaintiffs are well-known towage contractors and owners of a tug called the *Bremen.* The defendants are a company incorporated in the United States of America who carry on business *inter alia* in the operation of oil rigs.

In November, 1967, the plaintiffs and the defendants entered into a contract in writing for the towage of an oil rig called the *Chaparral* belonging to the defendants from a place called Venice in Louisiana to Ravenna in Italy by the tug *Bremen.* We have been referred to a number of the clauses in the contract, only one of which need be mentioned now. The concluding provision of the contract was:

> Any dispute arising must be treated before the London Court of Justice.

The towage from Venice began on Jan. 4, 1968. By Jan. 9, when the tow was still within the Gulf of Mexico, disaster overtook it, and it was necessary to take refuge in the port of Tampa in Florida. Each party blamed the other for the disaster which occurred, and each has asserted a claim for damages. The plaintiff tug-owners say that the defendants were at fault in that the oil rig being towed was not in a seaworthy condition. The defendants on their part say that the tug was not seaworthy to undertake the voyage, and also that it was negligently operated. There are all the elements present for an interesting battle to ascertain whose fault it was. The defendants got their blow in first, because immediately upon arrival of the tug and tow at Tampa they instituted proceedings in Admiralty in the United States District Court at Tampa, and in the course of those proceedings the tug was arrested. The release of the tug was eventually obtained upon security being furnished satisfactory to the defendants in the sum of U.S. $3,500,000.

On Feb. 21, 1968, the plaintiffs issued the writ in the present action and sought leave to serve that writ out of the jurisdiction on the American owners of the oil rig. Leave to serve the writ out of the jurisdiction was obtained from the learned Registrar, and it was that matter which came before the learned Judge. The grounds upon which the plaintiffs sought leave to serve the writ out of the jurisdiction were, first, that the contract was one which "by its terms, or by implication, was governed by English law", and secondly, that the contract contained an express term to the effect that the High Court should have jurisdiction.

In the meantime, however, the present plaintiffs had taken steps to defend themselves in the proceedings which were being carried on in Tampa. Those proceedings involved taking depositions from a number of witnesses, and in that operation both the present plaintiffs and the present defendants took part. Depositions appear to have been taken from a considerable number of witnesses. But from an early date the plaintiffs took exception to the jurisdiction of the Court at Tampa, and instituted proceedings to set aside or stay the American action. Those proceedings came before the United States District Court in Tampa on Apr. 29, 1968, when judgment was reserved. Up to date, so far as we have been informed, no judgment has yet been delivered, and it is not, therefore, known whether the action instituted by the defendants in America will be set aside or stayed. At present, however, assuming that leave to serve this writ out of the jurisdiction stands, there is a situation when proceedings are on foot in both countries. The position is further complicated by the fact that, just before the matter came before Mr. Justice Karminski at the beginning of this month, the plaintiffs launched proceedings for exoneration or limitation of their liability in the United States of America. It is to be pointed out that that is a course which they had to take, if the American proceedings were allowed to continue, within six months of the institution of those proceedings. Time was running out against them, and they were, therefore, forced to institute those proceedings at the beginning of this month in order to preserve their rights.

The learned Judge knew of the institution of those proceedings but he did not actually know (although I have no doubt that he had good reason to suspect) that, immediately following the institution of those proceedings, an order would be made by the American Court which, among other things, enjoined the defendants against prosecuting any claim of theirs against the plaintiffs pending the determination of the plaintiffs' limitation proceedings. That, it has been said, would effectively prevent the defendants, if they were so minded, from putting forward a counterclaim in any proceedings in this country. That is a matter much relied upon by the defendants as showing that, as a matter of convenience, and in order to avoid duplication of proceedings, leave ought not to be granted to serve this writ out of the jurisdiction.

Reliance is also placed upon the fact that, under American procedure, it appears that a party sued as a defendant there (as are the present plaintiffs) who has a counterclaim against the plaintiff in that country, is compelled to assert that counterclaim within a certain limit of time, or he will be for all time barred. That is another reason why it is suggested on behalf of the defendants that, as a matter of convenience, proceedings ought not to be allowed to continue in this country, since it is said that it will be necessary for the present plaintiffs to assert their claim by way of counterclaim in the United States.

The law on the subject, I think, is not open to doubt, and I do not think that it is really necessary to cite the authorities to which we have been referred. It is always open to parties to stipulate (as they did in this case) that a particular Court shall have jurisdiction over any dispute arising out of their contract. Here the parties chose to stipulate that disputes were to be referred to the "London Court", which I take as meaning the High Court in this country. *Prima facie* it is the policy of the Court to hold parties to the bargain into which they have entered. *Prima facie* it is to be presumed, therefore, that the plaintiffs should have leave to prosecute their proceedings in this country, and in pursuance of that to serve their writ out of the jurisdiction. But that is not an inflexible rule, as was shown, for instance, by the case of *The Fehmarn:,* [1957] 1 Lloyd's Rep. 511; (C.A.) [1957] 2 Lloyd's Rep. 551, ... in which the Court in its discretion declined to give effect to a stipulation made by the parties in their contract conferring jurisdiction on a foreign Court.

I approach the matter, therefore, in this way, that the Court has a discretion, but it is a discretion which, in the ordinary way and in the absence of strong reason to the contrary, will be exercised in favour of holding parties to their bargain. The question is whether sufficient circumstances have been shown to exist in this case to make it desirable, on the grounds of balance of convenience, that proceedings should not take place in this country, the stipulated forum, but that the parties should be left to fight out their battles in the United States of America.

The learned Judge in his discretion came to the conclusion that it was proper to grant leave to serve the writ out of the jurisdiction so that the action might proceed in this country. We in this Court should not interfere with the Judge's exercise of his discretion unless it is shown that he acted on some wrong principle, or misapprehended the facts, or unless it is shown that his exercise of his discretion was plainly wrong.

It is said that the situation has to some extent altered since the time when the learned Judge had the matter before him, by reason particularly of the plaintiffs' institution of exoneration and limitation proceedings in the United States to which I have referred. That is the only new factor which has arisen since the time when the learned Judge delivered his judgment.

I am unable to see that the Judge acted on any wrong principle. I do not think that the new facts said to have been brought to light really alter the complexion of the case to any material extent, nor am I prepared to say that the learned Judge's exercise of his discretion is shown to have been plainly wrong.

I should record the fact that in an affidavit put in on behalf of the plaintiffs today, the offer is made (and Mr. Lloyd on behalf of the plaintiffs has renewed it in the course of the argument) to waive the provisions of the restraining order which has been obtained by the plaintiffs in the United States so as to relieve the defendants of any difficulty which they might otherwise have in putting forward a counterclaim in this country if they want to. I should also record the fact that an offer has been made on behalf of the plaintiffs (which still holds good) to hold the security which has been furnished in America as available to cover any counter-claim which may be brought in this country. I refer to those two circumstances because I think that they are in their turn relevant to the question whether it is right to allow these plaintiffs to pursue their action in this country in accordance with their contractual bargain. I think that it is, and that the learned Judge reached the right conclusion.

In the circumstances I think that the appropriate order for us to make is that the defendants be granted leave to appeal, but that the appeal be dismissed.

LORD JUSTICE DIPLOCK: I agree, and add very little.

It has long been recognized that the jurisdiction of the High Court to give leave for service of a writ, or notice of a writ, out of the jurisdiction under Order 11, r. 1, is one which should be exercised with caution, because there are circumstances set out in that rule in which service outside the jurisdiction is authorized which are in conflict with the ordinary rules of comity, that is to say, the Courts in this country assert a jurisdiction in themselves wider than that which they recognize in the Courts of other countries. …

Those observations should be read in relation to an application for service out of the jurisdiction under r. 1. Rule 2, which is a separate rule and applies to this case, authorizes service out of the jurisdiction where the contract contains a term to the effect that the High Court has jurisdiction to hear and determine any action in respect to the contract. This does not raise any question of conflict with ordinary comity because, so far as I know, it is the policy of the Courts of most countries, if it be reasonable at any rate to do so, to see that parties keep their word; and having had the privilege of reading a memorandum brief which has been accepted in the Federal District Court at Tampa on behalf of the plaintiffs in this action, it looks to me as if there is some ground at any rate for saying that the Federal Courts and State Courts in the United States take the same view.

When it comes to a case under Order 11 r. 2, as distinct from a case under Order 11 r. 1, I say again in this case, as I said in *Mackender (sup.,* at pp. 604 and 459 of the respective reports):

> Where parties have agreed to submit all their disputes under a contract to the exclusive jurisdiction of a foreign court, I myself should require very strong reasons to induce me to permit one of them to go back on his word. …

We should, I think, apply the same principle whether the forum of contractual choice is England or of some other country. The question arises more frequently before us where the forum of contractual choice is some other country, as in *Mackender's case, sup.,* where the choice was Belgium. In the present case the choice of the parties was the English Court, and as I say I should myself require strong grounds for saying that one of the parties should not keep his word.

There is, of course, undoubtedly a discretion on the part of the Court in this case to refuse to allow service of the writ outside the jurisdiction, despite the contractual term in the contract. The learned Judge from whom this appeal is brought recognized that he had a discretion. So far as I can see he applied his mind to all the relevant matters; and, even if I myself might have come to some other conclusion, I do not think that any ground has been put forward which would justify the Court in interfering with his discretion. Having said that, let me say, as must have been apparent during the course of this hearing, I agree entirely with his decision. I should have done the same myself.

LORD JUSTICE WIDGERY: I agree with both judgments.

The parties here have quite deliberately chosen that their dispute shall be decided in the Courts of this country, and it would need strong grounds in my view to deprive either party who sought to take advantage of that course from receiving the advantage which he expects from it. I also would put my decision on the footing that there is no reason here to suppose that the learned Judge exercised his discretion improperly. But, like my Lord, I feel that had I had to decide the matter myself, I should have reached precisely the same conclusion.

I also would dismiss this appeal.

3. M/S Bremen v. Zapata Off-Shore Co.

407 U.S. 1 (1972)

[This litigation arose out of the same series of events as the previous case. After the Bremen put into port in Florida, Zapata brought an action in rem against the ship for damage done to its towed drilling rig. Unterweser, the Bremen's owner, defended by invoking the forum clause discussed in the previous case. The federal district court denied Unterweser's motion to dismiss and enjoined it from continuing the action it had already begun in England. The Court of Appeals for the Fifth Circuit affirmed.]

Plainly, the courts of England meet the standards of neutrality and long experience in admiralty litigation. The choice of that forum was made in an arm's-length negotiation by experienced and sophisticated businessmen, and absent some compelling and countervailing reason it should be honored by the parties and enforced by the courts.

The argument that such clauses are improper because they tend to "oust" a court of jurisdiction is hardly more than a vestigial legal fiction. It appears to rest at core on historical judicial resistance to any attempt to reduce the power and business of a particular court and has little place in an era when all courts are overloaded and when businesses once essentially local now operate in world markets. It reflects something of a provincial attitude regarding the fairness of other tribunals. No one seriously contends in this case that the forum-selection clause "ousted" the District Court of jurisdiction over Zapata's action. The threshold question is whether that court should have exercised its jurisdiction to do more than give effect to the legitimate expectations of the parties, manifested in their freely negotiated agreement, by specifically enforcing the forum clause.

There are compelling reasons why a freely negotiated private international agreement unaffected by fraud, undue influence, or overweening bargaining power, such as that involved here, should be given full effect. In this case, for example, we are concerned with a far from routine transaction between companies of two different nations contemplating the tow of an extremely costly piece of equipment from Louisiana across the Gulf of Mexico and the Atlantic Ocean, through the Mediterranean Sea to its final destination in the Adriatic Sea. In the course of its voyage, it was to traverse the waters of many jurisdictions. The *Chaparral* could have been damaged at any point along the route, and there were countless possible ports of refuge. That the accident occurred in the Gulf of Mexico and the barge was towed to Tampa in an emergency were mere fortuities. It cannot be doubted for a moment that the parties sought to provide for a neutral forum for the resolution of any disputes arising during the tow. Manifestly much uncertainty and possibly great inconvenience to both parties could arise if a suit could be maintained in any jurisdiction in which an accident might occur or if jurisdiction were left to any place where the *Bremen* or Unterweser might happen to be found. The elimination of all such uncertainties by agreeing in advance on a forum acceptable to both parties is an indispensable element in international trade, commerce, and contracting. There is strong evidence that the forum clause was a vital part of the agreement, and it would be unrealistic to think that the parties did not conduct their negotiations, including fixing the monetary terms, with the consequences of the forum clause figuring prominently in their calculations. Under these circumstances, as Justice Karminski reasoned in sustaining jurisdiction over Zapata in the High Court of Justice, "[t]he force of an agreement for litigation in this country, freely entered into between two competent parties, seems to me to be very powerful."

Thus, in the light of present-day commercial realities and expanding international trade we conclude that the forum clause should control absent a strong showing that it should be set aside. Although their opinions are not altogether explicit, it seems reasonably clear that the District Court and the Court of Appeals placed the burden on Unterweser to show that London would be a more convenient forum than Tampa, although the contract expressly resolved that issue. The correct approach would have been to enforce the forum clause specifically unless Zapata could clearly show that enforcement would be unreasonable and unjust, or that the clause was invalid for such reasons as fraud or overreaching. Accordingly, the case must be remanded for reconsideration.

We note, however, that there is nothing in the record presently before us that would support a refusal to enforce the forum clause. The Court of Appeals suggested that enforcement would be contrary to the public policy of the forum under *Bisso v. Inland Waterways Corp.*, 349 U.S. 85 (1955), because of the prospect that the English courts would enforce the clauses of the towage contract purporting to exculpate Unterweser from liability for damages to the *Chaparral.* A contractual choice-of-forum clause should be held unenforceable if enforcement would contravene a strong public policy of the forum in which suit is brought, whether declared by statute or by judicial decision. See, e.g., Boyd v. Grand Trunk W. R. Co., 338 U.S. 263 (1949). It is clear, however, that whatever the proper scope of the policy expressed in *Bisso,* it does not reach this case. *Bisso* rested on considerations with respect to the towage business strictly in American waters, and those considerations are not controlling in an international commercial agreement. . . .

Courts have also suggested that a forum clause, even though it is freely bargained for and contravenes no important public policy of the forum, may nevertheless be "unreasonable" and unenforceable if the chosen forum is seriously inconvenient for the trial of the action. Of course, where it can be said with reasonable assurance that at the time they entered the contract, the parties to a freely negotiated private international commercial agreement contemplated the claimed inconvenience, it is difficult to see why any such claim of inconvenience should be heard to render the forum clause unenforceable. We are not here dealing with an agreement between two Americans to resolve their essentially local disputes in a remote alien forum. In such a case, the serious inconvenience of the contractual forum to one or both of the parties might carry greater weight in determining the reasonableness of the forum clause. The remoteness of the forum might suggest that the agreement was an adhesive one, or that the parties did not have the particular controversy in mind when they made their agreement; yet even there the party claiming should bear a heavy burden of proof. Similarly, selection of a remote forum to apply differing foreign law to an essentially American controversy might contravene an important public policy of the forum. For example, so long as *Bisso* governs American courts with respect to the towage business in American waters, it would quite arguably be improper to permit an American tower to avoid that policy by providing a foreign forum for resolution of his disputes with an American towee.

This case, however, involves a freely negotiated international commercial transaction between a German and an American corporation for towage of a vessel from the Gulf of Mexico to the Adriatic Sea. As noted, selection of a London forum was clearly a reasonable effort to bring vital certainty to this international transaction and to provide a neutral forum experienced and capable in the resolution of admiralty litigation. Whatever "inconvenience" Zapata would suffer by being forced to litigate in the contractual forum as it agreed to do was clearly foreseeable at the time of contracting. In such circumstances it should be incumbent on the party seeking to escape his contract to show that trial in the contractual forum will be so gravely difficult and inconvenient that he will for all practical purposes be deprived of his day in court. Absent that, there is no basis for concluding that it would be unfair, unjust, or unreasonable to hold that party to his bargain.

In the course of its ruling on Unterweser's second motion to stay the proceedings in Tampa, the District Court did make a conclusory finding that the balance of convenience was "strongly" in favor of litigation in Tampa. However, as previously noted, in making that finding the court erroneously placed the burden of proof on Unterweser to show that the balance of convenience was strongly in its favor. Moreover, the finding falls far short of a conclusion that Zapata would be effectively deprived of its day in court should it be forced to litigate in London. Indeed, it cannot even be assumed that it would be placed to the expense of transporting its witnesses to London. It is not unusual for important issues in international admiralty cases to be dealt with by deposition. Both the District Court and the Court of Appeals majority appeared satisfied that Unterweser could receive a fair hearing in Tampa by using deposition testimony of its witnesses from distant places, and there is no reason to conclude that Zapata could not use deposition testimony to equal advantage if forced to litigate in London as it bound itself to do. Nevertheless, to allow Zapata opportunity to carry its heavy burden of showing not only that the balance of convenience is strongly in favor of trial in Tampa (that is, that it will be far more inconvenient for Zapata to litigate in London than it will be for Unterweser to litigate in Tampa), but also that a London trial will be so manifestly and gravely inconvenient to Zapata that it will be effectively deprived of a meaningful day in court, we remand for further proceedings.

Zapata's remaining contentions do not require extended treatment. It is clear that Unterweser's action in filing its limitation complaint in the District Court in Tampa was, so far as Zapata was concerned, solely a defensive measure made necessary as a response to Zapata's breach of the forum clause of the contract. When the six-month statutory period for filing an action to limit its liability had almost run without the District Court's having ruled on Unterweser's initial motion to dismiss or stay Zapata's action pursuant to the forum clause, Unterweser had no other prudent alternative but to protect itself by filing for limitation of its liability. Its action in so doing was a direct consequence of Zapata's failure to abide by the forum clause of the towage contract. There is no basis on which to conclude that this purely necessary defensive action by Unterweser should preclude it from relying on the forum clause it bargained for.

For the first time in this litigation, Zapata has suggested to this Court that the forum clause should not be construed to provide for an exclusive forum or to include *in rem* actions. However, the language of the clause is clearly mandatory and all-encompassing; the language of the clause in the *Carbon Black* case was far different.

The judgment of the Court of Appeals is vacated and the case is remanded for further proceedings consistent with this opinion.

Vacated and remanded.

4. U.S. v. Alvarez-Machain

504 U.S. 655 (1992)

CHIEF JUSTICE REHNQUIST. The issue in this case is whether a criminal defendant, abducted to the United States from a nation with which it has an extradition treaty, thereby acquires a defense to the jurisdiction of this country's courts. We hold that he does not, and that he may be tried in federal district court for violations of the criminal law of the United States.

Respondent, Humberto Alvarez-Machain, is a citizen and resident of Mexico. He was indicted for participating in the kidnap and murder of United States Drug Enforcement Administration (DEA) special agent Enrique Camarena-Salazar and a Mexican pilot working with Camarena, Alfredo Zavala-Avelar. The DEA believes that respondent, a medical doctor, participated in the murder by prolonging Agent Camarena's life so that others could further torture and interrogate him. On April 2, 1990, respondent was forcibly kidnaped from his medical office in Guadalajara, Mexico, to be flown by private plane to El Paso, Texas, where he was arrested by DEA officials. . . .

Although we have never before addressed the precise issue raised in the present case, we have previously considered proceedings in claimed violation of an extradition treaty and proceedings against a defendant brought before a court by means of a forcible abduction. We addressed the former issue in *U.S. v. Rauscher,* 119 U.S. 407 (1886); more precisely, the issue whether the Webster-Ashburton Treaty of 1842, 8 Stat. 576, which governed extraditions between England and the United States, prohibited the prosecution of defendant Rauscher for a crime other than the crime for which he had been extradited. Whether this prohibition, known as the doctrine of specialty, was an intended part of the treaty had been disputed between the two nations for some time. Justice Miller delivered the opinion of the Court, which carefully examined the terms and history of the treaty; the practice of nations in regards to extradition treaties; the case law from the States; and the writings of commentators, and reached the following conclusion:

> [A] person who has been brought within the jurisdiction of the court *by virtue of proceedings under an extradition treaty,* can only be tried for one of the offenses described in that treaty, and for the offence with which he is charged in the proceedings for his extradition, until a reasonable time and opportunity have been given him, after his release or trial upon such charge, to return to the country from whose asylum he had been forcibly taken under those proceedings. *Id.,* at 430 (emphasis added).

In addition, Justice Miller's opinion noted that any doubt as to this interpretation was put to rest by two federal statutes which imposed the doctrine of specialty upon extradition treaties to which the United States was a party. *Id.,* at 423. Unlike the case before us today, the defendant in *Rauscher* had been brought to the United States by way of an extradition treaty; there was no issue of a forcible abduction.

In *Ker v. Illinois*, 119 U.S. 436 (1886), also written by Justice Miller and decided the same day as *Rauscher,* we addressed the issue of a defendant brought before the court by way of a forcible abduction. Frederick Ker had been tried and convicted in an Illinois court for larceny; his presence before the court was procured by means of forcible abduction from Peru. A messenger was sent to Lima with the proper warrant to demand Ker by virtue of the extradition treaty between Peru and the United States. The messenger, however, disdained reliance on the treaty processes, and instead forcibly kidnaped Ker and brought him to the United States. We distinguished Ker's case from *Rauscher,* on the basis that Ker was not brought into the United States by virtue of the extradition treaty between the United States and Peru, and rejected Ker's argument that he had a right under the extradition treaty to be returned to this country only in accordance with its terms. We rejected Ker's due process argument more broadly, holding in line with "the highest authorities" that "such forcible abduction is no sufficient reason why the party should not answer when brought within the jurisdiction of the court which has the right to try him for such an offence, and presents no valid objection to his trial in such court." *Ker, supra,* at 444.

In *Frisbie v. Collins*, 342 U.S. 519, rehearing denied, 343 U.S. 937 (1952), we applied the rule in *Ker* to a case in which the defendant had been kidnaped in Chicago by Michigan officers and brought to trial in Michigan. We upheld the conviction over objections based on the Due Process Clause and the federal Kidnaping Act and stated:

> This Court has never departed from the rule announced in *[Ker]* that the power of a court to try a person for crime is not impaired by the fact that he had been brought within the court's jurisdiction by reason of a 'forcible abduction.' No persuasive reasons are now presented to justify overruling this line of cases. They rest on the sound basis that due process of law is satisfied when one present in court is convicted of crime after having been fairly apprized of the charges against him and after a fair trial in accordance with constitutional procedural safeguards. There is nothing in the Constitution that requires a court to permit a guilty person rightfully convicted to escape justice because he was brought to trial against his will. *Frisbie, supra,* at 522 (citation and footnote omitted).

The only differences between *Ker* and the present case are that *Ker* was decided on the premise that there was no governmental involvement in the abduction, 119 U.S., at 443; and Peru, from which Ker was abducted, did not object to his prosecution. Respondent finds these differences to be dispositive, as did the

Court of Appeals in *Verdugo*, 939 F.2d, at 1346, contending that they show that respondent's prosecution, like the prosecution of Rauscher, violates the implied terms of a valid extradition treaty. The Government, on the other hand, argues that *Rauscher* stands as an "exception" to the rule in *Ker* only when an extradition treaty is invoked, and the terms of the treaty provide that its breach will limit the jurisdiction of a court. Therefore, our first inquiry must be whether the abduction of respondent from Mexico violated the Extradition Treaty between the United States and Mexico. If we conclude that the Treaty does not prohibit respondent's abduction, the rule in *Ker* applies, and the court need not inquire as to how respondent came before it.

In construing a treaty, as in construing a statute, we first look to its terms to determine its meaning. The Treaty says nothing about the obligations of the United States and Mexico to refrain from forcible abductions of people from the territory of the other nation, or the consequences under the Treaty if such an abduction occurs. Respondent submits that Article 22(1) of the Treaty, which states that it "shall apply to offenses specified in Article 2 [including murder] committed before and after this Treaty enters into force," evidences an intent to make application of the Treaty mandatory for those offenses. However, the more natural conclusion is that Article 22 was included to ensure that the Treaty was applied to extraditions requested after the Treaty went into force, regardless of when the crime of extradition occurred.

More critical to respondent's argument is Article 9 of the Treaty, which provides:

> 1. Neither Contracting Party shall be bound to deliver up its own nationals, but the executive authority of the requested Party shall, if not prevented by the laws of that Party, have the power to deliver them up if, in its discretion, it be deemed proper to do so.
>
> 2. If extradition is not granted pursuant to paragraph 1 of this Article, the requested Party shall submit the case to its competent authorities for the purpose of prosecution, provided that Party has jurisdiction over the offense.

According to respondent, Article 9 embodies the terms of the bargain which the United States struck: If the United States wishes to prosecute a Mexican national, it may request that individual's extradition. Upon a request from the United States, Mexico may either extradite the individual or submit the case to the proper authorities for prosecution in Mexico. In this way, respondent reasons, each nation preserved its right to choose whether its nationals would be tried in its own courts or by the courts of the other nation. This preservation of rights would be frustrated if either nation were free to abduct nationals of the other nation for the purposes of prosecution. More broadly, respondent reasons, as did the Court of Appeals, that all the processes and restrictions on the obligation to extradite established by the Treaty would make no sense if either nation were free to resort to forcible kidnaping to gain the presence of an individual for prosecution in a manner not contemplated by the Treaty.

We do not read the Treaty in such a fashion. Article 9 does not purport to specify the only way in which one country may gain custody of a national of the other country for the purposes of prosecution. In the absence of an extradition treaty, nations are under no obligation to surrender those in their country to foreign authorities for prosecution. Extradition treaties exist so as to impose mutual obligations to surrender individuals in certain defined sets of circumstances, following established procedures. The Treaty thus provides a mechanism which would not otherwise exist, requiring, under certain circumstances, the United States and Mexico to extradite individuals to the other country, and establishing the procedures to be followed when the Treaty is invoked.

The history of negotiation and practice under the Treaty also fails to show that abductions outside of the Treaty constitute a violation of the Treaty. As the Solicitor General notes, the Mexican Government was made aware, as early as 1906, of the *Ker* doctrine, and the United States' position that it applied to forcible abductions made outside of the terms of the United States-Mexico Extradition Treaty. Nonetheless, the current version of the Treaty, signed in 1978, does not attempt to establish a rule that would in any way curtail the effect of *Ker.* Moreover, although language which would grant individuals exactly the right sought by respondent had been considered and drafted as early as 1935 by a prominent group of legal scholars sponsored by the faculty of Harvard Law School, no such clause appears in the current Treaty.

Thus, the language of the Treaty, in the context of its history, does not support the proposition that the Treaty prohibits abductions outside of its terms. The remaining question, therefore, is whether the Treaty should be interpreted so as to include an implied term prohibiting prosecution where the defendant's presence is obtained by means other than those established by the Treaty.

Respondent contends that the Treaty must be interpreted against the backdrop of customary international law, and that international abductions are "so clearly prohibited in international law" that there was no reason to include such a clause in the Treaty itself. Brief for Respondent 11. The international censure of international abductions is further evidenced, according to respondent, by the United Nations Charter and the Charter of the Organization of American States. Respondent does not argue that these sources of international law provide an independent basis for the right respondent asserts not to be tried in the United States, but rather that they should inform the interpretation of the Treaty terms. The Court of Appeals deemed it essential, in order for the individual defendant to assert a right under the Treaty, that the affected foreign government had registered a protest. Respondent agrees that the right exercised by the individual is derivative of the nation's right under the Treaty, since nations are authorized, notwithstanding the terms of an extradition treaty, to voluntarily render an individual to the other country on terms completely outside of those provided in the treaty. The formal protest, therefore, ensures that the "offended" nation actually objects to the abduction and has not in some way voluntarily rendered the individual for prosecution. Thus the Extradition Treaty only prohibits gaining the defendant's presence by means other than those set forth in the Treaty when the nation from which the defendant was abducted objects.

This argument seems to us inconsistent with the remainder of respondent's argument. The Extradition Treaty has the force of law, and if, as respondent asserts, it is self-executing, it would appear that a court must enforce it on behalf of an individual regardless of the offensiveness of the practice of one nation to the other nation. In *Rauscher,* the Court noted that Great Britain had taken the position in other cases that the Webster-Ashburton Treaty included the doctrine of specialty, but no importance was attached to whether or not Great Britain had protested the prosecution of Rauscher for the crime of cruel and unusual punishment as opposed to murder.

More fundamentally, the difficulty with the support respondent garners from international law is that none of it relates to the practice of nations in relation to extradition treaties. In *Rauscher,* we implied a term in the Webster-Ashburton Treaty because of the practice of nations with regard to extradition treaties. In the instant case, respondent would imply terms in the Extradition Treaty from the practice of nations with regards to international law more generally. Respondent would have us find that the Treaty acts as a prohibition against a violation of the general principle of international law that one government may not "exercise its police power in the territory of another state." There are many actions which could be taken by a nation that would violate this principle, including waging war, but it cannot seriously be contended that an invasion of the United States by Mexico would violate the terms of the Extradition Treaty between the two nations.

In sum, to infer from this Treaty and its terms that it prohibits all means of gaining the presence of an individual outside of its terms goes beyond established precedent and practice. In *Rauscher,* the implication of a doctrine of specialty into the terms of the Webster-Ashburton Treaty, which, by its terms, required the presentation of evidence establishing probable cause of the crime of extradition before extradition was required, was a small step to take. By contrast, to imply from the terms of this Treaty that it prohibits obtaining the presence of an individual by means outside of the procedures the Treaty establishes requires a much larger inferential leap, with only the most general of international law principles to support it. The general principles cited by respondent simply fail to persuade us that we should imply in the United States-Mexico Extradition Treaty a term prohibiting international abductions.

Respondent and his *amici* may be correct that respondent's abduction was "shocking," and that it may be in violation of general international law principles. Mexico has protested the abduction of respondent through diplomatic notes and the decision of whether respondent should be returned to Mexico, as a matter outside of the Treaty, is a matter for the Executive Branch. We conclude, however, that respondent's abduction was not in violation of the Extradition Treaty between the United States and Mexico, and therefore the rule of *Ker v. Illinois* is fully applicable to this case. The fact of respondent's forcible abduction does not therefore prohibit his trial in a court in the United States for violations of the criminal laws of the United States.

JUSTICE STEVENS, with whom JUSTICE BLACKMUN and JUSTICE O'CONNOR join, dissenting:

... The law of nations, as understood by Justice Story in 1824, has not changed. Thus, a leading treatise explains:

> A State must not perform acts of sovereignty in the territory of another State. ... It is ... a breach of International Law for a State to send its agents to the territory of another State to apprehend persons accused of having committed a crime. Apart from other satisfaction, the first duty of the offending State is to hand over the person in question to the State in whose territory he was apprehended." 1 Oppenheim's International Law 295, and n. 1 (H. Lauterpacht 8th ed. 1955).

Commenting on the precise issue raised by this case, the chief reporter for the American Law Institute's Restatement of Foreign Relations used language reminiscent of Justice Story's characterization of an official seizure in a foreign jurisdiction as "monstrous":

> When done without consent of the foreign government, abducting a person from a foreign country is a gross violation of international law and gross disrespect for a norm high in the opinion of mankind. It is a blatant violation of the territorial integrity of another state; it eviscerates the extradition system (established by a comprehensive network of treaties involving virtually all states).

In the *Rauscher* case, the legal background that supported the decision to imply a covenant not to prosecute for an offense different from that for which extradition had been granted was far less clear than the rule against invading the territorial integrity of a treaty partner that supports Mexico's position in this case. If *Rauscher* was correctly decided—and I am convinced that it was—its rationale clearly dictates a comparable result in this case.

III

A critical flaw pervades the Court's entire opinion. It fails to differentiate between the conduct of private citizens, which does not violate any treaty obligation, and conduct expressly authorized by the Executive Branch of the Government, which unquestionably constitutes a flagrant violation of international law, and in my opinion, also constitutes a breach of our treaty obligations. Thus, at the outset of its opinion, the Court states the issue as "whether a criminal defendant, abducted to the United States from a nation with which it has an extradition treaty, thereby acquires a defense to the jurisdiction of this country's courts." That, of course, is the question decided in *Ker v. Illinois,* 119 U.S. 436 (1886); it is not, however, the question presented for decision today.

The importance of the distinction between a court's exercise of jurisdiction over either a person or property that has been wrongfully seized by a private citizen, or even by a state law enforcement agent, on the one hand, and the attempted exercise of jurisdiction predicated on a seizure by federal officers acting beyond the authority conferred by treaty, on the other hand, is explained by Justice Brandeis in his opinion for the Court in *Cook v. United States,* 288 U.S. 102 (1933). That case involved a construction of a Prohibition Era treaty with Great Britain that authorized American agents to board certain British vessels to ascertain whether they were engaged in importing alcoholic beverages. A British vessel was boarded 11½ miles off the coast of Massachusetts, found to be carrying unmanifested alcoholic beverages, and taken into port. The Collector of Customs assessed a penalty which he attempted to collect by means of libels against both the cargo and the seized vessel.

The Court held that the seizure was not authorized by the treaty because it occurred more than 10 miles off shore. The Government argued that the illegality of the seizure was immaterial because, as in *Ker,* the court's jurisdiction was supported by possession even if the seizure was wrongful. Justice Brandeis acknowledged that the argument would succeed if the seizure had been made by a private party without authority to act for the Government, but that a different rule prevails when the Government itself lacks the power to seize. Relying on *Rauscher,* and distinguishing *Ker,* he explained:

> *Fourth.* As the Mazel Tov was seized without warrant of law, the libels were properly dismissed. The Government contends that the alleged illegality of the seizure is immaterial. It argues that the facts proved show a violation of our law for which the penalty of forfeiture is prescribed; that the United States may, by filing a libel for forfeiture, ratify what otherwise would have been an illegal seizure; that the seized vessel having been brought into the Port of Providence, the federal court for Rhode Island acquired jurisdiction; and that, moreover, the claimant by answering to the merits waived any right to object to enforcement of the penalties. The argument rests upon misconceptions.

It is true that where the United States, having possession of property, files a libel to enforce a forfeiture resulting from a violation of its laws, the fact that the possession was acquired by a wrongful act is immaterial. *Dodge v. United States,* 272 U.S. 530, 532 [(1926)]. Compare *Ker v. Illinois,* 119 U.S. 436, 444. The doctrine rests primarily upon the common-law rules that any person may, at his peril, seize property which has become forfeited to, or forfeitable by, the Government; and that proceedings by the Government to enforce a forfeiture ratify a seizure made by one without authority, since ratification is equivalent to antecedent delegation of authority to seize. *Gelston v. Hoyt,* 3 Wheat. 246, 310 [(1818)]; *Taylor v. United States,* 3 How. 197, 205-206 [(1845)]. The doctrine is not applicable here. The objection to the seizure is not that it was wrongful merely because made by one upon whom the Government had not conferred authority to seize at the place where the seizure was made. The objection is that the Government itself lacked power to seize, since by the Treaty it had imposed a territorial limitation upon its own authority. The Treaty fixes the conditions under which a 'vessel may be seized and taken into a port of the United States, its territories or possessions for adjudication in accordance with' the applicable laws. Thereby, Great Britain agreed that adjudication may follow a rightful seizure. Our Government, lacking power to seize, lacked power, because of the Treaty, to subject the vessel to our laws. To hold that adjudication may follow a wrongful seizure would go far to nullify the purpose and effect of the Treaty. Compare *U.S. v. Rauscher,* 119 U.S. 407. *Cook v. United States,* 288 U.S., at 120-122.

The same reasoning was employed by Justice Miller to explain why the holding in *Rauscher* did not apply to the *Ker* case. The arresting officer in *Ker* did not pretend to be acting in any official capacity when he kidnaped Ker. As Justice Miller noted, "the facts show that it was a clear case of kidnapping within the dominions of Peru, without any pretence of authority under the treaty *or from the government of the United States.*" *Ker v. Illinois,* 119 U.S., at 443 (emphasis added). The exact opposite is true in this case, as it was in *Cook.*

The Court's failure to differentiate between private abductions and official invasions of another sovereign's territory also accounts for its misplaced reliance on the 1935 proposal made by the Advisory Committee on Research in International Law. As the text of that proposal plainly states, it would have rejected the rule of the *Ker* case. The failure to adopt that recommendation does not speak to the issue the Court decides today. The Court's admittedly "shocking" disdain for customary and conventional international law principles is thus entirely unsupported by case law and commentary.

Notes and Questions

1. Compare *Alvarez-Machain*, with *State v. Ebrahim* [1991] 2 S. Afr. L. Rep. 553 (S. Afr. Ct. App.). 31 I.L.M. 888 (1992), in which a member of the military wing of the African National Congress was forcibly abducted from Swaziland to South Africa. The South African Appellate Division found:

> The individual must be protected against illegal detention and abduction, the bounds of jurisdiction must not be exceeded, sovereignty must be respected, the legal process must be fair to those affected and abuse of law must be avoided in order to protect and promote the integrity of the administration of justice. This applies equally to the state. When the state is a party to a dispute, as for example in criminal cases, it must come to court with "clean hands." When the state itself is involved in an abduction across international borders, as in the present case, its hands are not clean.

> Principles of this kind testify to a healthy legal system of high standard. ... Society is the ultimate loser when, in order to convict the guilty, it uses methods that lead to decreased respect for the law.

2. In *Decision on the Motion for Release by the Accused Slavko Dokmanovi*, Case No. IT-1995-13a-PT, Trial Chamber, International Criminal Tribunal for the Former Yugoslavia (Oct. 22, 1997), the Trial Chamber denied the defendant's motion that asserted that his arrest was illegal. Dokmanovi had been tricked into crossing from Serbia into Croatia where he was arrested by U.N. forces. After canvassing a number of national judgments on the topic, the Court found that "'luring' is consistent with principles of international law" (para. 57). The Tribunal deliberately did not decide, however, the question raised in *Alvarez-Machain*: "whether the International Tribunal has the authority to exercise jurisdiction over a defendant *illegally* obtained from abroad" (para. 78).

3. It will be recalled that *U.S. v. Yunis*, 924 F.2d 1086 (D.C. Cir. 1991), which is set out in part at page 1449 *supra*, takes up another aspect of abduction.

C. Traditional Grounds on Which Exceptions to Applicative Competence Have Been Claimed

Customarily, international law makes a distinction between the governmental and non-governmental acts of states, requiring immunity from application of law by other states only for the former.

National courts frequently deny themselves the exercise of a jurisdiction allocated to them by international law because of national policies, deference to other states, or certain principles of judicial fairness, many of which are common to a wide number of states. Where states are potential defendants, the most common counter-principle is the claim of sovereign immunity. Private litigants frequently invoke principles of *forum non conveniens* and *lis alibi pendens* to evade the exercise of an internationally lawful national jurisdiction. States and private litigants may seek to invoke the so-called Act of State doctrine.

Consider each of these principles not only in terms of fairness to plaintiff and defendant but also in terms of its impact on the effectiveness of an international system of application in which national courts play by far the most significant role.

1. Foreign Sovereign Immunity

a. The Schooner Exchange v. M'Faddon

11 U.S. (7 Cranch) 116 (1812)

MARSHALL, Ch.J.: This case involves the very delicate and important inquiry, whether an American citizen can assert, in an American court, a title to an armed national vessel found within the waters of the United States.

The question has been considered with an earnest solicitude that the decision may conform to those principles of national and municipal law by which it ought to be regulated.

In exploring an unbeaten path, with few, if any, aids from precedents or written law, the court has found it necessary to rely much on general principles, and on a train of reasoning, founded on cases in some degree analogous to this.

The jurisdiction of *courts* is a branch of that which is possessed by the nation as an independent sovereign power.

The jurisdiction of the nation within its own territory is necessarily exclusive and absolute. It is susceptible of no limitation not imposed by itself. Any restriction upon it, deriving validity from an external source, would imply a diminution of its sovereignty to the extent of the restriction, and an investment of that sovereignty to the same extent in that power place which could impose such restriction.

All exceptions, therefore, to the full and complete power of a nation within its own territories, must be traced up to the consent of the nation itself. They can flow from no other legitimate source.

This consent may be either express or implied. In the latter case, it is less determinate, exposed more to the uncertainties of construction; but, if understood, not less obligatory.

The world being composed of distinct sovereignties, possessing equal rights and equal independence whose mutual benefit is promoted by intercourse with each other, and by an interchange of those good offices which humanity dictates and its wants require, all sovereigns have consented to a relaxation in practice, in cases under certain peculiar circumstances, of that absolute and complete jurisdiction within their respective territories which sovereignty confers.

This consent may, in some instances, be tested by common usage, and by common opinion, growing out of that usage.

A nation would justly be considered as violating its faith, although that faith might not be expressly plighted, which should suddenly and without previous notice exercise its territorial powers in a manner not consonant to the usages and received obligations of the civilized world.

This full and absolute territorial jurisdiction being alike the attribute of every sovereign, and being incapable of conferring extra-territorial power, would not seem to contemplate foreign sovereigns nor their sovereign rights as its objects. One sovereign being in no respect amenable to another; and being bound by obligations of the highest character not to degrade the dignity of his nation, by placing himself or its sovereign rights within the jurisdiction of another, can be supported to enter a foreign territory only under an express license, or in the confidence that the immunities belonging to his independent sovereign station, though not expressly stipulated, are reserved by implication, and will be extended to him.

This perfect equality and absolute independence of sovereigns, and this common interest impelling them to mutual intercourse, and an interchange of good offices with each other, have given rise to a class of cases in which every sovereign is understood to wave the exercise of a part of that complete exclusive territorial jurisdiction, which has been stated to be the attribute of every nation. . . .

The preceding reasoning has maintained the propositions that all exemptions from territorial jurisdiction must be derived from the consent of the sovereign of the territory; that this consent may be implied or expressed; and that when implied, its extent must be regulated by the nature of the case, and the views under which the parties requiring and conceding it must be supposed to act.

When private individuals of one nation spread themselves through another as business or caprice may direct, mingling indiscriminately with the inhabitants of that other, or when merchant vessels enter for the purposes of trade, it would be obviously inconvenient and dangerous to society, and would subject the laws to continual infraction, and the government to degradation, if such individuals or merchants did not owe temporary and local allegiance, and were not amenable to the jurisdiction of the country. Nor can the foreign sovereign have any motive for wishing such exemption. His subjects thus passing into foreign countries, are not employed by him, nor are they engaged in national pursuits. Consequently there are powerful motives for not exempting persons of this description from the jurisdiction of the country in which they are found, and no one motive for requiring it. The implied license, therefore, under which they enter can never be construed to grant such exemption.

But in all respects different is the situation of a public armed ship. She constitutes a part of the military force of her nation; acts under the immediate and direct command of the sovereign; is employed by him in national objects. He has many and powerful motives for preventing those objects from being defeated by the interference of a foreign state. Such interference cannot take place without affecting his power and his dignity. The implied license therefore under which such vessel enters a friendly port, may reasonably be construed, and it seems to the Court, ought to be construed, as containing an exemption from the jurisdiction of the sovereign, within whose territory she claims the rites of hospitality.

Upon these principles, by the unanimous consent of nations, a foreigner is amenable to the laws of the place; but certainly in practice, nations have not yet asserted their jurisdiction over the public armed ships of a foreign sovereign entering a port open for their reception.

Bynkershoek, a jurist of great reputation, has indeed maintained that the property of a foreign sovereign is not distinguishable by any legal exemption from the property of an ordinary individual, and has quoted several cases in which courts have exercised jurisdiction over causes in which a foreign sovereign was made a party defendant.

Without indicating any opinion on this question, it may safely be affirmed, that there is a manifest distinction between the private property of the person who happens to be a prince and that military force which supports the sovereign power, and maintains the dignity and the independence of a nation. A prince, by acquiring private property in a foreign country, may possibly be considered as subjecting that property to the territorial jurisdiction, he may be considered as so far laying down the prince, and assuming the character of a private individual; but this he cannot be presumed to do with respect to any portion of that armed force, which upholds his crown, and the nation he is entrusted to govern. …

This case of the Spanish vessels is, it is believed, the only case furnished by the history of the world, of an attempt made by an individual to assert a claim against a foreign prince, by seizing the armed vessels of the nation. That this proceeding was at once arrested by the government, in a nation which appears to have asserted the power of proceeding in the same manner against the private property of the prince, would seem to furnish no feeble argument in support of the universality of the opinion in favor of the exemption claimed for ships of war. The distinction made in our own laws between public and private ships would appear to proceed from the same opinion.

It seems then to the Court, to be a principle of public law, that national ships of war, entering the port of a friendly power open for their reception, are to be considered as exempted by the consent of that power from its jurisdiction.

Without doubt, the sovereign of the place is capable in of destroying this implication. He may claim and exercise jurisdiction either by employing force, or by subjecting such vessels to the ordinary tribunals. But until such power be exerted in a manner not to be misunderstood, the sovereign cannot be considered as having imparted to the ordinary tribunals a jurisdiction, which it would be a breach of faith to exercise. Those general statutory provisions therefore which are descriptive of the ordinary jurisdiction of the judicial tribunals, which give an individual whose property has been wrested from him, a right to claim that property in the courts of the country, in which it is found, ought not, in the opinion of this Court, to be so construed as to give them jurisdiction in a case, in which the sovereign power has impliedly consented to wave its jurisdiction.

The arguments in factor of this opinion which have been drawn from the general inability of the judicial power to enforce its decisions in cases of this description, from the consideration, that the sovereign power of the nation is alone competent to avenge wrongs committed by a sovereign, that the questions to which such wrongs give birth are rather questions of policy than of law, that they are for diplomatic, rather than legal discussion, are of great weight, and merit serious attention. But the argument has already been drawn to a length, which forbids a particular examination of these points.

The principles which have been stated, will now be applied to the case at bar.

In the present state of the evidence and proceedings, the Exchange must be considered as a vessel, which was the property of the Libellants, whose claim is repelled by the fact, that she is now a national armed vessel, commissioned by, and in the service of the emperor of France. The evidence of this fact is not controverted. But it is contended, that it constitutes no bar to an enquiry into the validity of the title, by which the emperor holds this vessel. Every person, it is alleged, who is entitled to property brought within the jurisdiction of our Courts, has a right to assert his title in those Courts, unless there be some law taking his case out of the general rule. It is therefore said to be the right, and if it be the right, it is the duty of the Court, to enquire whether this title has been extinguished by an act, the validity of which is recognized by national or municipal law.

If the preceding reasoning be correct, the Exchange, being a public armed ship, in the service of a foreign sovereign, with whom the government of the United States is at peace, and having entered an American port open for her reception, on the terms on which ships of war are generally permitted to enter the ports of a friendly power, must be considered as having come into the American territory, under an implied promise, that while necessarily within it, and demeaning herself in a friendly manner, she should be exempt from the jurisdiction of the country.

If this opinion be correct, there seems to be a necessity for admitting that the fact might be disclosed to the Court by the suggestion of the Attorney for the United States.

I am directed to deliver it, as the opinion of the Court, that the sentence of the Circuit Court, reversing the sentence of the District Court, in the case of the Exchange be reversed, and that of the District Court, dismissing the libel, be affirmed.

NOTES AND QUESTIONS

1. The problem of foreign sovereign immunity is essentially one of liberal constitutional systems in which courts have an independent role while the conduct of foreign relations is largely assigned to the Executive Branch. The issue of foreign sovereign immunity as a judicial problem does not arise in command economies and in systems in which the judiciary is not independent. In this regard, there is a certain anomaly in the International Law Commission taking up the project of codifying the diverse foreign sovereign immunity approaches into a single international standard. Many command economies, which themselves conduct foreign trade and are, hence, the beneficiaries of a broad and strict sovereign immunity, negotiated with liberal states in which foreign trade is conducted by individuals. The result was a set of legal conceptions that are not marked by their internal consistency. For the text of the Draft Articles on Jurisdictional Immunities of States and their Property together with understandings with regard to certain provisions, see *Report of the Ad Hoc Committee on Jurisdictional Immunities of States and Their Property*, U.N. GAOR, 58th Sess., Supp. No. 22, U.N. Doc. A/58/22 (2003).

b. Argentine Republic v. Amerada Hess Shipping Corp.

488 U.S. 428 (1989)

CHIEF JUSTICE REHNQUIST: Two Liberian corporations sued the Argentine Republic in a United States District Court to recover damages for a tort allegedly committed by its armed forces on the high seas in violation of international law. We hold that the District Court correctly dismissed the action, because the Foreign Sovereign Immunities Act of 1976 (FSIA), 28 U. S. C. § 1330 et seq., does not authorize jurisdiction over a foreign state in this situation.

Respondents alleged the following facts in their complaints. Respondent United Carriers, Inc., a Liberian corporation, chartered one of its oil tankers, the Hercules, to respondent Amerada Hess Shipping Corporation, also a Liberian corporation. The contract was executed in New York City. Amerada Hess used the Hercules to transport crude oil from the southern terminus of the Trans-Alaska Pipeline in Valdez, Alaska, around Cape Horn in South America, to the Hess refinery in the United States Virgin Islands. On May 25, 1982, the Hercules began a return voyage, without cargo but fully fueled, from the Virgin Islands to Alaska. At that time, Great Britain and petitioner Argentine Republic were at war over an archipelago of some 200 islands—the Falkland Islands to the British, and the Islas Malvinas to the Argentineans—in the South Atlantic off the Argentine coast. On June 3, United States officials informed the two belligerents of the location of United States vessels and Liberian tankers owned by United States interests then traversing the South Atlantic, including the Hercules, to avoid any attacks on neutral shipping.

By June 8, 1982, after a stop in Brazil, the Hercules was in international waters about 600 nautical miles from Argentina and 500 miles from the Falklands; she was outside the "war zones" designated by Britain and Argentina. At 12:15 Greenwich mean time, the ship's master made a routine report by radio to Argentine officials, providing the ship's name, international call sign, registry, position, course, speed, and voyage description. About 45 minutes later, an Argentine military aircraft began to circle the Hercules. The ship's master repeated his earlier message by radio to Argentine officials, who acknowledged receiving it. Six minutes later, without provocation, another Argentine military plane began to bomb the Hercules; the master immediately hoisted a white flag. A second bombing soon followed, and a third attack came about two hours later, when an Argentine jet struck the ship with an air-to-surface rocket. Disabled but not destroyed, the Hercules reversed course and sailed to Rio de Janeiro, the nearest safe port. At Rio de Janeiro, respondent United Carriers determined that the ship had suffered extensive deck and hull damage, and that an undetonated bomb remained lodged in her No. 2 tank. After an investigation by the Brazilian Navy, United Carriers decided that it would be too hazardous to remove the undetonated bomb, and on July 20, 1982, the Hercules was scuttled 250 miles off the Brazilian coast.

Following unsuccessful attempts to obtain relief in Argentina, respondents commenced this action in the United States District Court for the Southern District of New York for the damage that they sustained from the attack. United Carriers sought $10 million in damages for the loss of the ship; Amerada Hess sought $1.9 million in damages for the fuel that went down with the ship. Respondents alleged that petitioner's attack on the neutral Hercules violated international law. They invoked the District Court's jurisdiction under the Alien Tort Statute, 28 U. S. C. § 1350, which provides that "[t]he district courts shall have original jurisdiction of any civil action by an alien for a tort only, committed in violation of the law of nations or a treaty of the United States." Amerada Hess also brought suit under the general admiralty and maritime jurisdiction, 28 U. S. C. § 1333, and "the principle of universal jurisdiction, recognized in customary international law." Complaint of Amerada Hess para. 5, App. 20. The District Court dismissed both complaints for lack of subject-matter jurisdiction, ruling that respondents' suits were barred by the FSIA. A divided panel of the United States Court of Appeals for the Second Circuit reversed. . . .

In the FSIA, Congress added a new chapter 97 to Title 28 of the United States Code, 28 U. S. C. § 1602-1611, which is entitled "Jurisdictional Immunities of Foreign States." Section 1604 provides that "[s]ubject to existing international agreements to which the United States [was] a party at the time of the enactment of this Act[,] a foreign state shall be immune from the jurisdiction of the courts of the United States and of the States except as provided in sections 1605 to 1607 of this chapter." The FSIA also added § 1330(a) to Title 28; it provides that "[t]he district courts shall have original jurisdiction without regard to amount in controversy of any nonjury civil action against a foreign state . . . as to any claim for relief in personam with respect to which the foreign state is not entitled to immunity under sections 1605-1607 of this title or under any applicable international agreement." § 1330(a).

We think that the text and structure of the FSIA demonstrate Congress' intention that the FSIA be the sole basis for obtaining jurisdiction over a foreign state in our courts. Sections 1604 and 1330(a) work in tandem: § 1604 bars federal and state courts from exercising jurisdiction when a foreign state is entitled to immunity, and § 1330(a) confers jurisdiction on district courts to hear suits brought by United States citizens and by aliens when a foreign state is not entitled to immunity. As we said in *Verlinden*, the FSIA "must be applied by the district courts in every action against a foreign sovereign, since subject-matter jurisdiction in any such action depends on the existence of one of the specified exceptions to foreign sovereign immunity." *Verlinden B. V. v. Central Bank of Nigeria*, 461 U.S. 480, 493 (1983).

The Court of Appeals acknowledged that the FSIA's language and legislative history support the "general rule" that the Act governs the immunity of foreign states in federal court. The Court of Appeals, however, thought that the FSIA's "focus on commercial concerns" and Congress' failure to "repeal" the Alien Tort Statute indicated Congress' intention that federal courts continue to exercise jurisdiction over foreign states in suits alleging violations of international law outside the confines of the FSIA. The Court of Appeals also believed that to construe the FSIA to bar the instant suit would "fly in the face" of Congress' intention that the FSIA be interpreted pursuant to "'standards recognized under international law.'" Taking the last of these points first, Congress had violations of international law by foreign states in mind when it enacted the FSIA. For example, the FSIA specifically denies foreign states immunity in suits "in which rights in property taken in violation of international law are in issue." 28 U. S. C. § 1605 (a)(3). Congress also rested the FSIA in part on its power under Art. I, §

8, cl. 10, of the Constitution "[t]o define and punish Piracies and Felonies committed on the high Seas, and Offenses against the Law of Nations." See H. R. Rep., at 12; S. Rep., at 12. From Congress' decision to deny immunity to foreign states in the class of cases just mentioned, we draw the plain implication that immunity is granted in those cases involving alleged violations of international law that do not come within one of the FSIA's exceptions.

As to the other point made by the Court of Appeals, Congress' failure to enact a *pro tanto* repealer of the Alien Tort Statute when it passed the FSIA in 1976 may be explained at least in part by the lack of certainty as to whether the Alien Tort Statute conferred jurisdiction in suits against foreign states. Enacted by the First Congress in 1789, the Alien Tort Statute provides that "[t]he district courts shall have original jurisdiction of any civil action by an alien for a tort only, committed in violation of the law of nations or a treaty of the United States." 28 U. S. C. § 1350. The Court of Appeals did not cite any decision in which a United States court exercised jurisdiction over a foreign state under the Alien Tort Statute, and only one such case has come to our attention—one which was decided after the enactment of the FSIA.

In this Court, respondents argue that cases were brought under the Alien Tort Statute against foreign states for the unlawful taking of a prize during wartime. The Alien Tort Statute makes no mention of prize jurisdiction, and § 1333(2) now grants federal district courts exclusive jurisdiction over "all proceedings for the condemnation of property taken as a prize." In *The Santissima Trinidad*, 7 Wheat. 283, 353-354 (1822), we held that foreign states were not immune from the jurisdiction of United States courts in prize proceedings. That case, however, was not brought under the Alien Tort Statute but rather as a libel in admiralty. Thus there is a distinctly hypothetical cast to the Court of Appeals' reliance on Congress' failure to repeal the Alien Tort Statute, and respondents' arguments in this Court based on the principle of statutory construction that repeals by implication are disfavored.

We think that Congress' failure in the FSIA to enact an express pro tanto repealer of the Alien Tort Statute speaks only faintly, if at all, to the issue involved in this case. In light of the comprehensiveness of the statutory scheme in the FSIA, we doubt that even the most meticulous draftsman would have concluded that Congress also needed to amend pro tanto the Alien Tort Statute and presumably such other grants of subject-matter jurisdiction in Title 28 as § 1331 (federal question), § 1333 (admiralty), § 1335 (interpleader), § 1337 (commerce and antitrust), and § 1338 (patents, copyrights, and trademarks). Congress provided in the FSIA that "[c]laims of foreign states to immunity should henceforth be decided by courts of the United States in conformity with the principles set forth in this chapter," and very likely it thought that should be sufficient. § 1602 . . .

For similar reasons we are not persuaded by respondents' arguments based upon the rule of statutory construction under which repeals by implication are disfavored. This case does not involve two statutes that readily could be seen as supplementing one another, see *Wood v. United States*, 16 Pet. 342, 363 (1842), nor is it a case where a more general statute is claimed to have repealed by implication an earlier statute dealing with a narrower subject. See *Morton v. Mancari*, 417 U.S. 535, 549-551 (1974). We think that Congress' decision to deal comprehensively with the subject of foreign sovereign immunity in the FSIA, and the express provision in § 1604 that "a foreign state shall be immune from the jurisdiction of the courts of the United States and of the States except as provided in sections 1605-1607," preclude a construction of the Alien Tort Statute that permits the instant suit. The Alien Tort Statute by its terms does not distinguish among classes of defendants, and it of course has the same effect after the passage of the FSIA as before with respect to defendants other than foreign states. Respondents also argue that the general admiralty and maritime jurisdiction, § 1333(1), provides a basis for obtaining jurisdiction over petitioner for violations of international law, notwithstanding the FSIA. ... But Congress dealt with the admiralty jurisdiction of the federal courts when it enacted the FSIA. Section 1605(b) expressly permits an in personam suit in admiralty to enforce a maritime lien against a vessel or cargo of a foreign state. Unless the present case is within § 1605(b) or another exception to the FSIA, the statute conferring general admiralty and maritime jurisdiction on the federal courts does not authorize the bringing of this action against petitioner. Having determined that the FSIA provides the sole basis for obtaining jurisdiction over a foreign state in federal court, we turn to whether any of the exceptions enumerated in the Act apply here. These exceptions include cases involving the waiver of immunity, § 1605(a)(1), commercial activities occurring in the United States or causing a direct effect in this country, § 1605(a)(2), property expropriated in violation of international law, § 1605(a)(3), inherited, gift, or immovable property located in the United States, § 1605(a)(4), noncommercial torts occurring in the United States, § 1605(a)(5), and maritime liens, § 1605(b). We agree with the District Court that none of the FSIA's exceptions applies on these facts.

Respondents assert that the FSIA exception for noncommercial torts, § 1605(a)(5), is most in point. This provision denies immunity in a case "in which money damages are sought against a foreign state for personal injury or death, or damage to or loss of property, occurring in the United States and caused by the tortious act or omission of that foreign state or of any official or employee of that foreign state while acting within the scope of his office or employment." 28 U. S. C. § 1605(a)(5).

Section 1605(a)(5) is limited by its terms, however, to those cases in which the damage to or loss of property occurs in the United States. Congress' primary purpose in enacting § 1605(a)(5) was to eliminate a foreign state's immunity for traffic accidents and other torts committed in the United States, for which liability is imposed under domestic tort law. See H. R. Rep., at 14, 20-21; S. Rep., at 14, 20-21. In this case, the injury to respondents' ship occurred on the high seas some 5,000 miles off the nearest shores of the United States. Despite these telling facts, respondents nonetheless claim that the tortious attack on the Hercules occurred "in the United States." They point out that the FSIA defines "United States" as including all "territory and waters, continental and insular, subject to the jurisdiction of the United States," § 1603(c), and that their injury occurred on the high seas, which is within the admiralty jurisdiction of the United States, see *The Plymouth*, 3 Wall. 20, 36 (1866). They reason, therefore, that "by statutory definition" petitioner's attack occurred in the United States. We find this logic unpersuasive. We construe the modifying phrase "continental and insular" to restrict the definition of United States to the continental United States and those islands that are part of the United States or its possessions; any other reading would render this phrase nugatory. Likewise, the term "waters" in § 1603(c) cannot reasonably be read to cover all waters over which United States courts might exercise jurisdiction. When it desires to do so, Congress knows how to place the high seas within the jurisdictional reach of a statute. We thus apply "[t]he canon of construction which teaches that legislation of Congress, unless contrary intent appears, is meant to apply only within the territorial jurisdiction of the United States." *Foley Brothers v. Filardo*, 336 U.S. 281, 285 (1949). Because respondents' injury unquestionably occurred well outside the 3-mile limit then in effect for the territorial waters of the United States, the exception for noncommercial torts cannot apply.

The result in this case is not altered by the fact that petitioner's alleged tort may have had effects in the United States. Respondents state, for example, that the Hercules was transporting oil intended for use in this country and that the loss of the ship disrupted contractual payments due in New York. Under the commercial activity exception to the FSIA, § 1605(a)(2), a foreign state may be liable for its commercial activities "outside the territory of the United States" having a "direct effect" inside the United States. But the noncommercial tort exception, § 1605(a)(5), upon which respondents rely, makes no mention of "territory outside the United States" or of "direct effects" in the United States. Congress' decision to use explicit language in § 1605(a)(2), and not to do so in § 1605(a)(5), indicates that the exception in § 1605(a)(5) covers only torts occurring within the territorial jurisdiction of the United States. Respondents do not claim that § 1605(a)(2) covers these facts.

We also disagree with respondents' claim that certain international agreements entered into by petitioner and by the United States create an exception to the FSIA here. As noted, the FSIA was adopted "[s]ubject to international agreements to which the United States [was] a party at the time of [its] enactment." § 1604. This exception applies when international agreements "expressly conflic[t]" with the immunity provisions of the FSIA, H. R. Rep., at 17; S. Rep., at 17, hardly the circumstances in this case. Respondents point to the Geneva Convention on the High Seas, Apr. 29, 1958, [1962] 13 U. S. T. 2312, T. I. A. S. No. 5200, and the Pan American Maritime Neutrality Convention, Feb. 20, 1928, 47 Stat. 1989, 1990-1991, T. S. No. 845. Brief for Respondents 31-34. These conventions, however, only set forth substantive rules of conduct and state that compensation shall be paid for certain wrongs. They do not create private rights of action for foreign corporations to recover compensation from foreign states in United States courts. Nor do we see how a foreign state can waive its immunity under § 1605(a)(1) by signing an international agreement that contains no mention of a waiver of immunity to suit in United States courts or even the availability of a cause of action in the United States. We find similarly unpersuasive the argument of respondents and Amicus Curiae Republic of Liberia that the Treaty of Friendship, Commerce and Navigation, Aug. 8, 1938, United States-Liberia, 54 Stat. 1739, T. S. No. 956, carves out an exception to the FSIA. Article I of this Treaty provides, in pertinent part, that the nationals of the United States and Liberia "shall enjoy freedom of access to the courts of justice of the other on conforming to the local laws." The FSIA is clearly one of the "local laws" to which respondents must "conform" before bringing suit in United States courts.

We hold that the FSIA provides the sole basis for obtaining jurisdiction over a foreign state in the courts of this country, and that none of the enumerated exceptions to the Act apply to the facts of this case. The judgment of the Court of Appeals is therefore

Reversed.

c. Republic of Austria v. Altmann

124 S.Ct. 2240 (2004)

JUSTICE STEVENS delivered the opinion of the Court. ...

Born in Austria in 1916, respondent Maria V. Altmann escaped the country after it was annexed by Nazi Germany in 1938. She settled in California in 1942 and became an American citizen in 1945. She is a niece, and the sole surviving named heir, of Ferdinand Bloch-Bauer, who died in Zurich, Switzerland, on November 13, 1945.

Prior to 1938 Ferdinand, then a wealthy sugar magnate, maintained his principal residence in Vienna, Austria, where the six Klimt paintings and other valuable works of art were housed. His wife, Adele, was the subject of two of the paintings. She died in 1925, leaving a will in which she "ask[ed]" her husband "after his death" to bequeath the paintings to the Gallery. ... The attorney for her estate advised the Gallery that Ferdinand intended to comply with his wife's request, but that he was not legally obligated to do so because he, not Adele, owned the paintings. Ferdinand never executed any document transferring ownership of any of the paintings at issue to the Gallery. He remained their sole legitimate owner until his death. His will bequeathed his entire estate to respondent, another niece, and a nephew. ...

On March 12, 1938, in what became known as the "Anschluss," the Nazis invaded and claimed to annex Austria. Ferdinand, who was Jewish and had supported efforts to resist annexation, fled the country ahead of the Nazis, ultimately settling in Zurich. In his absence, according to the complaint, the Nazis "Aryanized" the sugar company he had directed, took over his Vienna home, and divided up his artworks, which included the Klimts at issue here, many other valuable paintings, and a 400-piece porcelain collection. A Nazi lawyer, Dr. Erich Führer, took possession of the six Klimts. He sold two to the Gallery in 1941 and a third in 1943, kept one for himself, and sold another to the Museum of the City of Vienna. The immediate fate of the sixth is not known. …

In 1946 Austria enacted a law declaring all transactions motivated by Nazi ideology null and void. This did not result in the immediate return of looted artwork to exiled Austrians, however, because a different provision of Austrian law proscribed export of "artworks ... deemed to be important to [the country's] cultural heritage" and required anyone wishing to export art to obtain the permission of the Austrian Federal Monument Agency. … Seeking to profit from this requirement, the Gallery and the Federal Monument Agency allegedly adopted a practice of "forc[ing] Jews to donate or trade valuable artworks to the [Gallery] in exchange for export permits for other works." …

The next year Robert Bentley, respondent's brother and fellow heir, retained a Viennese lawyer, Dr. Gustav Rinesch, to locate and recover property stolen from Ferdinand during the war. In January 1948 Dr. Rinesch wrote to the Gallery requesting return of the three Klimts purchased from Dr. Führer. A Gallery representative responded, asserting—falsely, according to the complaint—that Adele had bequeathed the paintings to the Gallery, and the Gallery had merely permitted Ferdinand to retain them during his lifetime. …

Later the same year Dr. Rinesch enlisted the support of Gallery officials to obtain export permits for many of Ferdinand's remaining works of art. In exchange, Dr. Rinesch, purporting to represent respondent and her fellow heirs, signed a document "acknowledg[ing] and accept[ing] Ferdinand's declaration that in the event of his death he wished to follow the wishes of his deceased wife to donate" the Klimt paintings to the Gallery. ... In addition, Dr. Rinesch assisted the Gallery in obtaining both the painting Dr. Führer had kept for himself and the one he had sold to the Museum of the City of Vienna. At no time during these transactions, however, did Dr. Rinesch have respondent's permission either "to negotiate on her behalf or to allow the [Gallery] to obtain the Klimt paintings."

In 1998 a journalist examining the Gallery's files discovered documents revealing that at all relevant times Gallery officials knew that neither Adele nor Ferdinand had, in fact, donated the six Klimts to the Gallery. The journalist published a series of articles reporting his findings, and specifically noting that Klimt's first portrait of Adele, "which all the [Gallery] publications represented as having been donated to the museum in 1936," had actually been received in 1941, accompanied by a letter from Dr. Führer signed " 'Heil Hitler.' " …

In response to these revelations, Austria enacted a new restitution law under which individuals who had been coerced into donating artworks to state museums in exchange for export permits could reclaim their property. Respondent—who had believed, prior to the journalist's investigation, that Adele and Ferdinand had "freely donated" the Klimt paintings to the Gallery before the war— immediately sought recovery of the paintings and other artworks under the new law.

... A committee of Austrian government officials and art historians agreed to return certain Klimt drawings and porcelain settings that the family had donated in 1948. After what the complaint terms a "sham" proceeding, however, the committee declined to return the six paintings, concluding, based on an allegedly purposeful misreading of Adele's will, that her precatory request had created a binding legal obligation that required her husband to donate the paintings to the Gallery on his death. ...

Respondent then announced that she would file a lawsuit in Austria to recover the paintings. Because Austrian court costs are proportional to the value of the recovery sought (and in this case would total several million dollars, an amount far beyond respondent's means), she requested a waiver. ... The court granted this request in part but still would have required respondent to pay approximately $350,000 to proceed. ... When the Austrian Government appealed even this partial waiver, respondent voluntarily dismissed her suit and filed this action in the United States District Court for the Central District of California. ...

Chief Justice Marshall's opinion in *Schooner Exchange v. McFaddon,* 7 Cranch 116, 3 L.Ed. 287 (1812), is generally viewed as the source of our foreign sovereign immunity jurisprudence. In that case, the libellants claimed to be the rightful owners of a French ship that had taken refuge in the port of Philadelphia. The Court first emphasized that the jurisdiction of the United States over persons and property within its territory "is susceptible of no limitation not imposed by itself," and thus foreign sovereigns have no right to immunity in our courts. *Id.,* at 136. Chief Justice Marshall went on to explain, however, that as a matter of comity, members of the international community had implicitly agreed to waive the exercise of jurisdiction over other sovereigns in certain classes of cases, such as those involving foreign ministers or the person of the sovereign.[9] Accepting a suggestion advanced by the Executive Branch, see *id.,* at 134, the Chief Justice concluded that the implied waiver theory also served to exempt the *Schooner Exchange*—"a national armed vessel ... of the emperor of France"—from United States courts' jurisdiction. *Id.,* at 145-146.[10]

In accordance with Chief Justice Marshall's observation that foreign sovereign immunity is a matter of grace and comity rather than a constitutional require-

---

[9] [The] "perfect equality and absolute independence of sovereigns, and th[e] common interest impelling them to mutual intercourse, and an interchange of good offices with each other, have given rise to a class of cases in which every sovereign is understood to wave *[sic]* the exercise of a part of that complete exclusive territorial jurisdiction, which has been stated to be the attribute of every nation." *Schooner Exchange,* 7 Cranch, at 137, 3 L.Ed. 287.

[10] Chief Justice Marshall noted, however, that the outcome might well be different if the case involved a sovereign's *private* property:

ment, this Court has "consistently ... deferred to the decisions of the political branches—in particular, those of the Executive Branch—on whether to take jurisdiction" over particular actions against foreign sovereigns and their instrumentalities. *Verlinden B.V. v. Central Bank of Nigeria,* 461 U.S. 480, 486 ... Until 1952 the Executive Branch followed a policy of requesting immunity in all actions against friendly sovereigns. 461 U.S., at 486. ... In that year, however, the State Department concluded that "immunity should no longer be granted in certain types of cases."... In a letter to the Attorney General, the Acting Legal Adviser for the Secretary of State, Jack B. Tate, explained that the Department would thereafter apply the "restrictive theory" of sovereign immunity:

> A study of the law of sovereign immunity reveals the existence of two conflicting concepts of sovereign immunity, each widely held and firmly established. According to the classical or absolute theory of sovereign immunity, a sovereign cannot, without his consent, be made a respondent in the courts of another sovereign. According to the newer or restrictive theory of sovereign immunity, the immunity of the sovereign is recognized with regard to sovereign or public acts *(jure imperii)* of a state, but not with respect to private acts (*jure gestionis*). ... [I]t will hereafter be the Department's policy to follow the restrictive theory ... in the consideration of requests of foreign governments for a grant of sovereign immunity." ...

As we explained in our unanimous opinion in *Verlinden,* the change in State Department policy wrought by the "Tate Letter" had little, if any, impact on federal courts' approach to immunity analyses: "As in the past, initial responsibility for deciding questions of sovereign immunity fell primarily upon the Executive acting through the State Department," and courts continued to "abid[e] by" that Department's " 'suggestions of immunity.' " 461 U.S., at 487 ... The change did, however, throw immunity determinations into some disarray, as "foreign nations often placed diplomatic pressure on the State Department," and political considerations sometimes led the Department to file "suggestions of immunity in cases where immunity would not have been available under the restrictive theory." *Id.,*

Without indicating any opinion on this question, it may safely be affirmed, that there is a manifest distinction between the private property of the person who happens to be a prince, and that military force which supports the sovereign power, and maintains the dignity and the independence of a nation. A prince, by acquiring private property in a foreign country, may possibly be considered as subjecting that property to the territorial jurisdiction; he may be considered as so far laying down the prince, and assuming the character of a private individual; but this he cannot be presumed to do with respect to any portion of that armed force, which upholds his crown, and the nation he is entrusted to govern. *Id.,* at 145.

at 487-488 ... Complicating matters further, when foreign nations failed to request immunity from the State Department:

> [T]he responsibility fell to the courts to determine whether sovereign immunity existed, generally by reference to prior State Department decisions. ... Thus, sovereign immunity determinations were made in two different branches, subject to a variety of factors, sometimes including diplomatic considerations. Not surprisingly, the governing standards were neither clear nor uniformly applied. *Ibid.*

In 1976 Congress sought to remedy these problems by enacting the FSIA, a comprehensive statute containing a "set of legal standards governing claims of immunity in every civil action against a foreign state or its political subdivisions, agencies, or instrumentalities." *Id.,* at 488 ... The Act "codifies, as a matter of federal law, the restrictive theory of sovereign immunity," *ibid.,* and transfers primary responsibility for immunity determinations from the Executive to the Judicial Branch. The preamble states that "henceforth" both federal and state courts should decide claims of sovereign immunity in conformity with the Act's principles. 28 U.S.C. § 1602.

The Act itself grants federal courts jurisdiction over civil actions against foreign states, § 1330(a), ... and over diversity actions in which a foreign state is the plaintiff, § 1332(a)(4); it contains venue and removal provisions, § § 1391(f), 1441(d); it prescribes the procedures for obtaining personal jurisdiction over a foreign state, § 1330(b); and it governs the extent to which a state's property may be subject to attachment or execution, § § 1609-1611. Finally, the Act carves out certain exceptions to its general grant of immunity, including the expropriation exception on which respondent's complaint relies. ... These exceptions are central to the Act's functioning: "At the threshold of every action in a district court against a foreign state, ... the court must satisfy itself that one of the exceptions applies," as "subject-matter jurisdiction in any such action depends" on that application. *Verlinden,* 461 U.S., at 493- 494. ...

This leaves only the question whether anything in the FSIA or the circumstances surrounding its enactment suggests that we should not apply it to petitioners' 1948 actions. Not only do we answer this question in the negative, but we find clear evidence that Congress intended the Act to apply to preenactment conduct.

To begin with, the preamble of the FSIA expresses Congress' understanding that the Act would apply to all postenactment claims of sovereign immunity. That section provides:

> *Claims* of foreign states to immunity should *henceforth* be decided by courts of the United States and of the States in conformity with the principles set forth in this chapter. 28 U.S.C. § 1602 *(emphasis added).*

Though perhaps not sufficient to satisfy *Landgraf's* "express command" requirement, 511 U.S., at 280, ... this language is unambiguous: Immunity "claims"—not actions protected by immunity, but assertions of immunity to suits arising from those actions—are the relevant conduct regulated by the Act;[17] those claims are "henceforth" to be decided by the courts. As the District Court observed, ... this language suggests Congress intended courts to resolve *all* such claims "in conformity with the principles set forth" in the Act, regardless of when the underlying conduct occurred.

The FSIA's overall structure strongly supports this conclusion. Many of the Act's provisions unquestionably apply to cases arising out of conduct that occurred before 1976. In *Dole Food Co. v. Patrickson,* 538 U.S. 468 ... (2003), for example, we held that whether an entity qualifies as an "instrumentality" of a "foreign state" for purposes of the FSIA's grant of immunity depends on the relationship between the entity and the state at the time suit is brought rather than when the conduct occurred. In addition, *Verlinden,* which upheld against constitutional challenge 28 U.S.C. § 1330's grant of subject-matter jurisdiction, involved a dispute over a contract that predated the Act. 461 U.S., at 482-483, 497. ... And there has never been any doubt that the Act's procedural provisions relating to venue, removal, execution, and attachment apply to all pending cases. Thus, the FSIA's preamble indicates that it applies "henceforth," and its body includes numerous provisions that unquestionably apply to claims based on pre-1976 conduct. In this context, it would be anomalous to presume that an isolated provision (such as the expropriation exception on which respondent relies) is of purely prospective application absent any statutory language to that effect.

Finally, applying the FSIA to all pending cases regardless of when the underlying conduct occurred is most consistent with two of the Act's principal purposes: clarifying the rules that judges should apply in resolving sovereign immunity claims and eliminating political participation in the resolution of such claims. We have recognized that, to accomplish these purposes, Congress established a comprehensive framework for resolving any claim of sovereign immunity:

> We think that the text and structure of the FSIA demonstrate Congress' intention that the FSIA be the sole basis for obtaining jurisdiction over a foreign state in our courts. Sections 1604 and 1330(a) work in tandem: § 1604 bars federal and state courts from exercising jurisdiction when a foreign state *is* entitled to immunity, and § 1330(a) confers jurisdiction

---

[17] Our approach to retroactivity in this case thus parallels that advocated by Justice SCALIA in his concurrence in *Landgraf:*

> "The critical issue, I think, is not whether the rule affects 'vested rights,' or governs substance or procedure, but rather what is the relevant activity that the rule regulates. Absent clear statement otherwise, only such relevant activity which occurs *after* the effective date of the statute is covered. Most statutes are meant to regulate primary conduct, and hence will not be applied in trials involving conduct that occurred before their effective date. But other statutes have a different purpose and therefore a different relevant retroactivity event." 511 U.S., at 291 (opinion concurring in judgment).

on district courts to hear suits brought by United States citizens and by aliens when a foreign state is *not* entitled to immunity. As we said in *Verlinden,* the FSIA 'must be applied by the district courts in every action against a foreign sovereign, since subject-matter jurisdiction in any such action depends on the existence of one of the specified exceptions to foreign sovereign immunity.' *Argentine Republic v. Amerada Hess Shipping Corp.,* 488 U.S. 428, 434-435 … (1989).

The *Amerada Hess* respondents' claims concerned conduct that postdated the FSIA, so we had no occasion to consider the Act's retroactivity. Nevertheless, our observations about the FSIA's inclusiveness are relevant in this case: Quite obviously, Congress' purposes in enacting such a comprehensive jurisdictional scheme would be frustrated if, in postenactment cases concerning preenactment conduct, courts were to continue to follow the same ambiguous and politically charged " 'standards' " that the FSIA replaced. …

We conclude by emphasizing the narrowness of this holding. To begin with, although the District Court and Court of Appeals determined that § 1605(a)(3) covers this case, we declined to review that determination. … Nor do we have occasion to comment on the application of the so-called "act of state" doctrine to petitioners' alleged wrongdoing. Unlike a claim of sovereign immunity, which merely raises a jurisdictional defense, the act of state doctrine provides foreign states with a substantive defense on the merits. Under that doctrine, the courts of one state will not question the validity of public acts (acts *jure imperii)* performed by other sovereigns within their own borders, even when such courts have jurisdiction over a controversy in which one of the litigants has standing to challenge those acts. See *Underhill v. Hernandez,* 168 U.S. 250, 252 … (1897); *Banco Nacional de Cuba v. Sabbatino,* 376 U.S. 398, 401 … (1964) ("The act of state doctrine in its traditional formulation precludes the courts of this country from inquiring into the validity of the public acts a recognized foreign sovereign power committed within its own territory"). Petitioners principally rely on the act of state doctrine to support their assertion that foreign expropriations are public acts for which, prior to the enactment of the FSIA, sovereigns expected immunity. … Applying the FSIA in this case would upset that settled expectation, petitioners argue, and thus the Act "would operate retroactively" under *Landgraf.* 511 U.S., at 280 ... But because the FSIA in no way affects application of the act of state doctrine, our determination that the Act applies in this case in no way affects any argument petitioners may have that the doctrine shields their alleged wrongdoing.

Finally, while we reject the United States' recommendation to bar application of the FSIA to claims based on pre-enactment conduct, Brief for United States as *Amicus Curiae,* nothing in our holding prevents the State Department from filing statements of interest suggesting that courts decline to exercise jurisdiction in particular cases implicating foreign sovereign immunity. The issue now before us, to which the Brief for United States as *Amicus Curiae* is addressed, concerns interpretation of the FSIA's reach—a "pure question of statutory construction ... well within the province of the Judiciary." *INS v. Cardoza-Fonseca,* 480 U.S. 421, 446, 448 … (1987). While the United States' views on such an issue are of considerable interest to the Court, they merit no special deference. See, *e.g., ibid.* In contrast, should the State Department choose to express its opinion on the implications of exercising jurisdiction over *particular* petitioners in connection with *their* alleged conduct, that opinion might well be entitled to deference as the considered judgment of the Executive on a particular question of foreign policy. See, *e.g., Verlinden,* 461 U.S., at 486 …; *American Ins. Assn. v. Garamendi,* 539 U.S. 396, 414 … (2003) (discussing the President's " 'vast share of responsibility for the conduct of our foreign relations'"). We express no opinion on the question whether such deference should be granted in cases covered by the FSIA. …

The judgment of the Court of Appeals is affirmed.

[JUSTICE SCALIA concurred on the ground that the application of a new jurisdictional statute to prior events is not an exercise in retroactivity.]

[JUSTICE BREYER, joined by JUSTICE SOUTER, concurred:] The sole issue before us is whether the "expropriation exception" of the Foreign Sovereign Immunities Act of 1976 (FSIA or Act), 28 U.S.C. § 1605(a)(3), withdrawing an otherwise applicable sovereign immunity defense, applies to this case. The exception applies to "foreign state[s]" and to any "agency or instrumentality" of a foreign state. §§ 1603, 1605(a)(3). The exception deprives the entity of the sovereign immunity that the law might otherwise entitle it "in any case," § 1605, where that entity "is engaged in a commercial activity in the United States" and the case is one "in which rights in property taken in violation of international law are in issue." § 1605(a)(3).

It is conceded that the Gallery is an "agency or instrumentality" of a foreign state, namely the Republic of Austria. Nor can Austria now deny that the Gallery is "engaged in commercial activity in the United States." The lower courts held that the Gallery's publishing and advertising activities satisfy this condition. …And our grant of certiorari did not embrace that aspect of the lower courts' decision. 539 U.S. 987 (2003).

Austria replies that, even so, this part of the statute is not "retroactive." Austria means that § 1605(a)(3), the expropriation exception, does not apply to events that occurred in 1948, almost 30 years before the FSIA's enactment. The upshot is that if the FSIA's general rule of immunity, § 1604, applies retroactively to events in 1948 (as is undisputed here), but the expropriation exception, § 1605 (a) (3), does not apply retroactively, then the Gallery can successfully assert its sovereign immunity defense, preventing Altmann from pursuing her claim. …

The question, then, is whether the Act's expropriation exception applies to takings that took place many years before its enactment. The Court notes that Congress, when enacting the FSIA in 1976, wrote that the Act should "henceforth" apply to any *claim* brought thereafter. § 1602. .... The dissent believes that there is no logical inconsistency between an act that applies "henceforth" and a reading of § 1605 (a) (3) that limits it to "rights in property *taken after this Act came into force.*" ... I agree with the dissent that the word "henceforth" (and similar words) cannot resolve this disagreement by themselves. Nonetheless several additional considerations convince me that the Court is correct. As Altmann argues, Congress intended the expropriation exception to apply retroactively, removing a defense of sovereign immunity where "rights in property" were "taken in violation of international law," irrespective of when that taking occurred. ...

JUSTICE KENNEDY, with whom THE CHIEF JUSTICE and JUSTICE THOMAS join, dissenting. To reach its conclusion the Court must weaken the reasoning and diminish the force of the rule against the retroactivity of statutes, a rule of fairness based on respect for expectations; the Court abruptly tells foreign nations this important principle of American law is unavailable to them in our courts; this is so despite the fact that treaties and agreements on the subject of expropriation have been reached against a background of the immunity principles the Court now rejects; as if to mitigate its harsh result, the Court adds that the Executive Branch has inherent power to intervene in cases like this; this, however, is inconsistent with the congressional purpose and design of the FSIA; the suggestion reintroduces, to an even greater degree than before, the same influences the FSIA sought to eliminate from sovereign immunity determinations; the Court's reasoning also implies a problematic answer to a separation-of-powers question that the case does not present and that should be avoided; the ultimate effect of the Court's inviting foreign nations to pressure the Executive is to risk inconsistent results for private citizens who sue, based on changes and nuances in foreign affairs, and to add prospective instability to the most sensitive area of foreign relations.

The majority's treatment of our retroactivity principles, its rejection of the considered congressional and Executive judgment behind the FSIA, and its questionable constitutional implications require this respectful dissent. ...

NOTES AND QUESTIONS

1. Compare *Princz v. Federal Republic of Germany*, 26 F.3d 1166 (D.C. Cir. 1993) (Ginsburg, J.) ("Assuming that the FSIA applies retroactively to events occurring in 1942-1945, no exception to the general grant of sovereign immunity in that statute applies in this case."); *Siderman de Blake v. Republic of Argentina*, 965 F.2d 699 (9th Cir. 1992) ("[A]lthough acts of torture were violations of jus cogens and customary international law, such violations did not supersede the FSIA. However, Argentina may have implicitly waived its immunity by earlier seeking the assistance of United States courts."). *See* cases and discussion on the ATCA and FSIA, *supra* Part Three, at 565-612. Does *Altmann* have any effect on cases such as *Princz*?

d. European Convention on State Immunity
11 I.L.M. 470, 471 (1972)

Article 2. A Contracting State cannot claim immunity from the jurisdiction of a court of another Contracting State if it has undertaken to submit to the jurisdiction of that court either:

(*a*) by international agreement;

(*b*) by an express term contained in a contract in writing; or

(*c*) by an express consent given after a dispute between the parties has arisen.

Article 3. (1) A Contracting State cannot claim immunity from the jurisdiction of a court of another Contracting State if, before claiming immunity, it takes any step in the proceedings relating to the merits. However, if the State satisfies the court that it could not have acquired knowledge of facts on which a claim to immunity can be based until after it has taken such a step, it can claim immunity based on these facts if it does so at the earliest possible moment.

(2) A Contracting State is not deemed to have waived immunity if it appears before a court of another Contracting State in order to assert immunity.

2. *Forum Non Conveniens* and *Lis Alibi Pendens*

Two counter principles which appear to be animated primarily by considerations of litigant fairness and administrative order in the prosecution of international suits are *forum non conveniens* and *lis alibi pendens.*

a. Gulf Oil Corp. v. Gilbert
330 U.S. 501 (1947)

[Applying the doctrine of *forum non conveniens*, a federal district court dismissed a tort action brought by Gilbert in New York. Gilbert was a resident of Virginia, and the events allegedly constituting a tort had taken place there. The Second Circuit reversed, and an appeal was taken to the Supreme Court on certiorari.]

MR. JUSTICE JACKSON: The questions are whether the United States District Court has inherent power to dismiss a suit pursuant to the doctrine of *forum non conveniens* and, if so, whether that power was abused in this case.

The respondent-plaintiff brought this action in the Southern District of New York, but resides at Lynchburg, Virginia, where he operated a public warehouse. He alleges that the petitioner-defendant, in violation of the ordinances of Lynchburg, so carelessly handled a delivery of gasoline to his warehouse tanks and pumps as to cause an explosion and fire which consumed the warehouse building to his damage of $41,889.10, destroyed merchandise and fixtures to his damage of $3,602.40, caused injury to his business and profits of $20,038.27, and burned the property of customers in his custody under warehousing agreements to the extent of $300,000. He asks judgment of $365,529.77 with costs and disbursements, and interest from the date of the fire. The action clearly is one in tort.

The petitioner-defendant is a corporation organized under the laws of Pennsylvania, qualified to do business in both Virginia and New York, and it has designated officials of each state as agents to receive service of process. When sued in New York, the defendant, invoking the doctrine of *forum non conveniens,* claimed that the appropriate place for trial is Virginia, where the plaintiff lives and defendant does business, where all events in litigation took place, where most of the witnesses reside, and where both state and federal courts are available to plaintiff and are able to obtain jurisdiction of the defendant.

The case, on its merits, involves no federal question and was brought in the United States District Court solely because of diversity in citizenship of the parties. Because of the character of its jurisdiction and the holdings of and under *Erie Railroad Co. v. Tompkins.* 304 U.S. 64, the District Court considered that the law of New York as to *forum non conveniens* applied and that it required the case to be left to Virginia courts. It therefore dismissed.

The Circuit Court of Appeals disagreed as to the applicability of New York law, took a restrictive view of the application of the entire doctrine in federal courts and, one judge dissenting, reversed. The case is here on certiorari. 328 U.S. 830.

I.

It is conceded that the venue statutes of the United States permitted the plaintiff to commence his action in the Southern District of New York and empower that court to entertain it. But that does not settle the question whether it must do so. Indeed, the doctrine of *forum non conveniens* can never apply if there is absence of jurisdiction or mistake of venue.

This Court, in one form of words or another, has repeatedly recognized the existence of the power to decline jurisdiction in exceptional circumstances. As formulated by Mr. Justice Brandeis, the rule is:

> Obviously, the proposition that a court having jurisdiction must exercise it, is not universally true; else the admiralty court could never decline jurisdiction on the ground that the litigation is between foreigners. Nor is it true of courts administering other systems of our law. Courts of equity and of law also occasionally decline, in the interest of justice, to exercise jurisdiction. where the suit is between aliens or non-residents or where for kindred reasons the litigation can more appropriately be conducted in a foreign tribunal. *Canada Malting Co., Ltd., v. Paterson Steamships, Ltd.,* 285 U.S. 413, 422-23.

We later expressly said that a state court "may in appropriate cases apply the doctrine of *forum non conveniens.*" *Broderick v. Rosner,* 294 U.S. 629, 643. Even where federal rights binding on state courts under the Constitution are sought to be adjudged, this Court has sustained state courts in a refusal to entertain a litigation between a nonresident and a foreign corporation or between two foreign corporations. ... It has held the use of an inappropriate forum in one case an unconstitutional burden on interstate commerce. ... On substantially *forum non conveniens* we have required federal courts to relinquish decision of cases within their jurisdiction where the court would have to participate in the administrative policy of a state. ... And most recently we decided *Williams v. Green Bay & Western R. R. Co.,* 326 U.S. 549, in which the Court, without questioning the validity of the doctrine, held it had been applied in that case without justification.

II.

The principle of *forum non conveniens* is simply that a court may resist imposition upon its jurisdiction even when jurisdiction is authorized by the letter of a general venue statute. These statutes are drawn with a necessary generality and usually give a plaintiff a choice of courts, so that he may be quite sure of some place in which to pursue his remedy. But the open door may admit those who seek not simply justice but perhaps justice blended with some harassment. A plaintiff sometimes is under temptation to resort to a strategy of forcing the trial at a most inconvenient place for an adversary, even at some inconvenience to himself.

Many of the states have met misuse of venue by investing courts with a discretion to change the place of trial on various grounds, such as the convenience of witnesses and the ends of justice. The federal law contains no such express criteria to guide the district court in exercising its power. But the problem is a very old one affecting the administration of the courts as well as the rights of litigants, and both in England and in this country the common law worked out techniques and criteria for dealing with it.

Wisely, it has not been attempted to catalogue the circumstances which will justify or require either grant or denial of remedy. The doctrine leaves much to the discretion of the court to which plaintiff resorts, and experience has not shown a judicial tendency to renounce one's own jurisdiction so strong as to result in many abuses.

If the combination and weight of factors requisite to given results are difficult to forecast or state, those to be considered are not difficult to name. An interest to be considered, and the one likely to be most pressed, is the private interest of the litigant. Important considerations are the relative ease of access to sources of proof; availability of compulsory process for attendance of unwilling, and the cost of obtaining attendance of willing, witnesses; possibility of view of premises, if view would be appropriate to the action; and all other practical problems that make trial of a case easy, expeditious and inexpensive. There may also be questions as to the enforcibility of a judgment if one is obtained. The court will weigh relative advantages and obstacles to fair trial. It is often said that the plaintiff may not, by choice of an inconvenient forum, "vex," "harass," or "oppress" the defendant by inflicting upon him expense or trouble not necessary to his own right to pursue his remedy. But unless the balance is strongly in favor of the defendant, the plaintiff's choice of forum should rarely be disturbed.

Factors of public interest also have place in applying the doctrine. Administrative difficulties follow for courts when litigation is piled up in congested centers instead of being handled at its origin. Jury duty is a burden that ought not to be imposed upon the people of a community which has no relation to the litigation. In cases which touch the affairs of many persons, there is reason for holding the trial in their view and reach rather than in remote parts of the country where they can learn of it by report only. There is a local interest in having localized controversies decided at home. There is an appropriateness, too, in having the trial of a diversity case in a forum that is at home with the state law that must govern the case, rather than having a court in some other forum untangle problems in conflict of laws, and in law foreign to itself. ...

Reversed.

NOTES AND QUESTIONS

1. In *Piper Aircraft Co. v. Reyno*, 454 U.S. 235 (1981), the representative of Scottish citizens killed in an airplane crash in Scotland brought wrongful-death actions against the U.S. manufacturer of the plane and propellers. Justice Marshall, writing for the Court, upheld the district court's dismissal on the ground of *forum non conveniens*. Marshall found that the "plaintiffs may [not] defeat a motion to dismiss on the ground of *forum non conveniens* merely be showing that the substantive law that would be applied in the alternative forum is less favorable to the plaintiffs than that of the present forum."

b. *In re* Union Carbide Corporation Gas Plant Disaster at Bhopal, India in December, 1984

809 F.2d 195 (2d Cir. 1987)

MANSFIELD, CIRCUIT JUDGE. This appeal raises the question of whether thousands of claims by citizens of India and the Government of India arising out of the most devastating industrial disaster in history—the deaths of over 2,000 persons and injuries of over 200,000 caused by lethal gas known as methyl isocyanate which was released from a chemical plant operated by Union Carbide India Limited (UCIL) in Bhopal, India—should be tried in the United States or in India. The Southern District of New York, John F. Keenan, Judge, granted the motion of Union Carbide Corporation (UCC), a defendant in some 145 actions commenced in federal courts in the United States, to dismiss these actions on grounds of *forum non conveniens* so that the claims may be tried in India, subject to certain conditions. The individual plaintiffs appeal from the order and the court's denial of their motion for a fairness hearing on a proposed settlement. UCC and the Union of India (UOI), a plaintiff, cross-appeal. We eliminate two of the conditions imposed by the district court and in all other respects affirm that court's orders.

The accident occurred on the night of December 2-3, 1984, when winds blew the deadly gas from the plant operated by UCIL into densely occupied parts of the city of Bhopal. UCIL is incorporated under the laws of India. Fifty and nine-tenths percent of its stock is owned by UCC, 22% is owned or controlled by the government of India, and the balance is held by approximately 23,500 Indian citizens. The stock is publicly traded on the Bombay Stock Exchange. The company is engaged in the manufacture of a variety of products, including chemicals, plastics, fertilizers and insecticides, at 14 plants in India and employs over 9,000 Indian citizens. It is managed and operated entirely by Indians in India.

Four days after the Bhopal accident, on December 7, 1984, the first of some 145 purported class actions in federal district courts in the United States was commenced on behalf of victims of the disaster. On January 2, 1985, the Judicial Panel on Multidistrict Litigation assigned the actions to the Southern District of New York where they became the subject of a consolidated complaint filed on June 28, 1985.

In the meantime, on March 29, 1985, India enacted the Bhopal Gas Leak Disaster (Processing of Claims) Act, granting to its government, the UOI, the exclusive right to represent the victims in India or elsewhere. Thereupon the UOI, purporting to act in the capacity of parens patriae, and with retainers executed by many of the victims, on April 8, 1985, filed a complaint in the Southern District of New York on behalf of all victims of the Bhopal disaster, similar to the purported class action complaints already filed by individuals in the United States. The UOI's decision to bring suit in the United States was attributed to the fact that, although numerous lawsuits (by now, some 6,500) had been instituted by victims in India against UCIL, the Indian courts did not have jurisdiction over UCC, the parent company, which is a defendant in the United States actions. The actions in India asserted claims not only against UCIL but also against the UOI, the State of Madhya Pradesh, and the Municipality of Bhopal, and were consolidated in the District Court of Bhopal.

By order dated April 25, 1985, Judge Keenan appointed a three-person Executive Committee to represent all plaintiffs in the pre-trial proceedings. It consisted of two lawyers representing the individual plaintiffs and one representing the UOI. On July 31, 1985, UCC moved to dismiss the complaints on grounds of *forum non conveniens*, the plaintiffs' lack of standing to bring the actions in the United States, and their purported attorneys' lack of authority to represent them. After several months of discovery related to *forum non conveniens*, the individual plaintiffs and the UOI opposed UCC's motion. After hearing argument on January 3, 1986, the district court, on May 12, 1986, 634 F. Supp. 842, in a thoroughly reasoned 63-page opinion granted the motion, dismissing the lawsuits before it on condition that UCC:

> (1) consent to the jurisdiction of the courts of India and continue to waive defenses based on the statute of limitations,
>
> (2) agree to satisfy any judgment rendered by an Indian court against it and upheld on appeal, provided the judgment and affirmance "comport with the minimal requirements of due process," and
>
> (3) be subject to discovery under the Federal Rules of Civil Procedure of the United States.

On June 12, 1986, UCC accepted these conditions subject to its right to appeal them; and on June 24, 1986, the district court entered its order of dismissal. In September 1986 the UOI, acting pursuant to its authority under the Bhopal Act, brought suit on behalf of all claimants against UCC and UCIL in the District Court of Bhopal, where many individual suits by victims of the disaster were then pending.

In its opinion dismissing the actions the district court analyzed the *forum non conveniens* issues, applying the standards and weighing the factors suggested by the Supreme Court in *Gulf Oil Corp. v. Gilbert*, 330 U.S. 501 (1947), and *Piper Aircraft Co. v. Reyno*, 454 U.S. 235 (1981). At the outset Judge Keenan concluded, in accordance with the Court's expressed views in Piper that, since the plaintiffs were not residents of the United States but of a foreign country, their choice of the United States as a forum would not be given the deference to which it would be entitled if this country were their home. Following the dictates of Piper, the district court declined to compare the advantages and disadvantages to the respective parties of American versus Indian Laws or to determine the impact upon plaintiffs' claims of the laws of India, where UCC had acknowledged that it would make itself amenable to process, except to ascertain whether India provided an adequate alternative forum, as distinguished from no remedy at all. Judge Keenan reviewed thoroughly the affidavits of experts on India's law and legal system, which described in detail its procedural and substantive aspects, and concluded that, despite some of the Indian system's disadvantages, it afforded an adequate alternative forum for the enforcement of plaintiffs' claims.

The Indian judiciary was found by the court to be a developed, independent and progressive one, which has demonstrated its capability of circumventing long delays and backlogs prevalent in the Indian courts' handling of ordinary cases by devising special expediting procedures in extraordinary cases, such as by directing its High Court to hear them on a daily basis, appointing special tribunals to handle them, and assigning daily hearing duties to a single judge. He found that Indian courts have competently dealt with complex technological issues. Since the Bhopal Act provides that the case may be treated speedily, effectively and to the best advantage of the claimants, and since the Union of India represents the claimants, the prosecution of the claims is expected to be adequately staffed by the Attorney General or Solicitor General of India.

The tort law of India, which is derived from common law and British precedent, was found to be suitable for resolution of legal issues arising in cases involving highly complex technology. Moreover, Indian courts would be in a superior position to construe and apply applicable Indian laws and standards than would courts of the United States. Third parties may be interpleaded under Order 1, Rule 10(2) of the Indian Code of Civil Procedure, and defendants may seek contribution from third parties. The absence in India of a class action procedure comparable to that in federal courts here was found not to deprive the plaintiffs of a remedy, in view of existing Indian legal authorization for "representative" suits under Order 1, Rule 8 of the Indian Code of Civil Procedure, which would permit an Indian court to create representative classes. Judge Keenan further found that the absence of juries and contingent fee arrangements in India would not deprive the claimants of an adequate remedy.

In two areas bearing upon the adequacy of the Indian forum the district court decided to impose somewhat unusual conditions on the transfer of the American cases to India. One condition dealt with pre-trial discovery. Indian courts, following the British pattern, permit parties to have pre-trial discovery of each other through written interrogatories, liberal inspection of documents and requests for admissions. Non-party witnesses can be interviewed and summoned to appear at trial or to produce documents. Witnesses unable to appear at trial are sometimes permitted to give evidence by means of affidavits. Discovery in India, however, as in Britain, is limited to evidence that may be admitted at trial. Litigants are not permitted to engage in wide-ranging discovery of the type authorized by Fed. R. Civ. P. 26(b), which allows inquiry into any unprivileged matter that could reasonably lead to the discovery of admissible evidence.

Judge Keenan, concluding that the Indian system might limit the victims' access to sources of proof, directed that dismissal of the actions on grounds of forum non conveniens must be conditioned on UCC's consent to discovery of it in accordance with the Federal Rules of Civil Procedure after the cases were transferred to India. He added, "While the Court feels that it would be fair to bind the plaintiffs to American discovery rules, too, it has no authority to do so."

Another condition imposed by the district court upon dismissal on grounds of forum non conveniens dealt with the enforceability in the United States of any judgment rendered by an Indian court in the cases. Judge Keenan, expressing the view that an Indian judgment might possibly not be enforceable in the United States, provided in his order that UCC must "agree to satisfy any judgment rendered by an Indian court, and if applicable, upheld by an appellate court in that country, where such judgment and affirmance comport with the minimum requirements of due process."

As the district court found, the record shows that the private interests of the respective parties weigh heavily in favor of dismissal on grounds of forum non conveniens. The many witnesses and sources of proof are almost entirely located in India, where the accident occurred, and could not be compelled to appear for trial in the United States. The Bhopal plant at the time of the accident was operated by some 193 Indian nationals, including the managers of seven operating units employed by the Agricultural Products Division of UCIL, who reported to Indian Works Managers in Bhopal. The plant was maintained by seven functional departments employing over 200 more Indian nationals. UCIL kept at the plant daily, weekly and monthly records of plant operations and records of maintenance as well as records of the plant's Quality Control, Purchasing and Stores branches, all operated by Indian employees. The great majority of documents bearing on the design, safety, start-up and operation of the plant, as well as the safety training of the plant's employees, is located in India. Proof to be offered at trial would be derived from interviews of these witnesses in India and study of the records located there to determine whether the accident was caused by negligence on the part of the management or employees in the operation of the plant, by fault in its design, or by sabotage. In short, India has greater ease of access to the proof than does the United States.

The plaintiffs seek to prove that the accident was caused by negligence on the part of UCC in originally contributing to the design of the plant and its provision for storage of excessive amounts of the gas at the plant. As Judge Keenan found, however, UCC's participation was limited and its involvement in plant operations terminated long before the accident. Under 1973 agreements negotiated at arm's-length with UCIL, UCC did provide a summary "process design package" for construction of the plant and the services of some of its technicians to monitor the progress of UCIL in detailing the design and erecting the plant. However, the UOI controlled the terms of the agreements and precluded UCC from exercising any authority to "detail design, erect and commission the plant," which was done independently over the period from 1972 to 1980 by UCIL process design engineers who supervised, among many others, some 55 to 60 Indian engineers employed by the Bombay engineering firm of Humphreys and Glasgow. The preliminary process design information furnished by UCC could not have been used to construct the plant. Construction required the detailed process design and engineering data prepared by hundreds of Indian engineers, process designers and sub-contractors. During the ten years spent constructing the plant, its design and configuration underwent many changes.

The vital parts of the Bhopal plant, including its storage tank, monitoring instrumentation, and vent gas scrubber, were manufactured by Indians in India. Although some 40 UCIL employees were given some safety training at UCC's plant in West Virginia, they represented a small fraction of the Bhopal plant's employees. The vast majority of plant employees were selected and trained by UCIL in Bhopal. The manual for start-up of the Bhopal plant was prepared by Indians employed by UCIL.

In short, the plant has been constructed and managed by Indians in India. No Americans were employed at the plant at the time of the accident. In the five years from 1980 to 1984, although more than 1,000 Indians were employed at the plant, only one American was employed there and he left in 1982. No Americans visited the plant for more than one year prior to the accident, and during the 5-year period before the accident the communications between the plant and the United States were almost non-existent.

The vast majority of material witnesses and documentary proof bearing on causation of and liability for the accident is located in India, not the United States, and would be more accessible to an Indian court than to a United States court. The records are almost entirely in Hindi or other Indian languages, understandable to an Indian court without translation. The witnesses for the most part do not speak English but Indian languages understood by an Indian court but not by an

American court. These witnesses could be required to appear in an Indian court but not in a court of the United States. Although witnesses in the United States could not be subpoenaed to appear in India, they are comparatively few in number and most are employed by UCC which, as a party, would produce them in India, with lower overall transportation costs than if the parties were to attempt to bring hundreds of Indian witnesses to the United States. Lastly, Judge Keenan properly concluded that an Indian court would be in a better position to direct and supervise a viewing of the Bhopal plant, which was sealed after the accident. Such a viewing could be of help to a court in determining liability issues.

After a thorough review, the district court concluded that the public interest concerns, like the private ones, also weigh heavily in favor of India as the situs for trial and disposition of the cases. The accident and all relevant events occurred in India. The victims, over 200,000 in number, are citizens of India and located there. The witnesses are almost entirely Indian citizens. The Union of India has a greater interest than does the United States in facilitating the trial and adjudication of the victims' claims. Despite the contentions of plaintiffs and amici that it would be in the public interest to avoid a "double standard" by requiring an American parent corporation (UCC) to submit to the jurisdiction of American courts, India has a stronger countervailing interest in adjudicating the claims in its courts according to its standards rather than having American values and standards of care imposed upon it.

India's interest is increased by the fact that it has for years treated UCIL as an Indian national, subjecting it to intensive regulations and governmental supervision of the construction, development and operation of the Bhopal plant, its emissions, water and air pollution, and safety precautions. Numerous Indian government officials have regularly conducted on-site inspections of the plant and approved its machinery and equipment, including its facilities for storage of the lethal methyl isocyanate gas that escaped and caused the disaster giving rise to the claims. Thus India has considered the plant to be an Indian one and the disaster to be an Indian problem. It therefore has a deep interest in ensuring compliance with its safety standards. Moreover, plaintiffs have conceded that in view of India's strong interest and its greater contacts with the plant, its operations, its employees, and the victims of the accident, the law of India, as the place where the tort occurred, will undoubtedly govern. In contrast, the American interests are relatively minor. Indeed, a long trial of the 145 cases here would unduly burden an already overburdened court, involving both jury hardship and heavy expense. It would face the court with numerous practical difficulties, including the most impossible task of attempting to understand extensive relevant Indian regulations published in a foreign language and the slow process of receiving testimony of scores of witnesses through interpreters.

Having made the foregoing findings, Judge Keenan dismissed the actions against UCC on grounds of forum non conveniens upon the conditions indicated above, after obtaining UCC's consent to those conditions subject to its right to appeal the order. After the plaintiffs filed their notice of appeal, UCC and the Union of India filed cross appeals.

Upon these appeals, the plaintiffs continue to oppose the dismissal. The Union of India, however, has changed its position and now supports the district court's order. UCC, as it did in the district court, opposes as unfair the condition that it submit to discovery pursuant to the Federal Rules of Civil Procedure without reciprocally obligating the plaintiffs and Union of India to be subject to discovery on the same basis so that both sides might be treated equally, giving each the same access to the facts in the others' possession.

Upon argument of the appeal, UCC also took the position that the district court's order requiring it to satisfy any Indian court judgment was unfair unless some method were provided, such as continued availability of the district court as a forum, to ensure that any denial of due process by the Indian courts could be remedied promptly by the federal court here rather than delay resolution of the issue until termination of the Indian court proceedings and appeal, which might take several years. UCC's argument in this respect was based on the sudden issuance by the Indian court in Bhopal of a temporary order freezing all of UCC's assets, which could have caused it irreparable injury if it had been continued indefinitely, and by the conflict of interest posed by the UOI's position in the Indian courts where, since the UOI would appear both as a plaintiff and a defendant, it might as a plaintiff voluntarily dismiss its claims against itself as a defendant or, as a co-defendant with UCC, be tempted to shed all blame upon UCC even though the UOI had in fact been responsible for supervision, regulation and safety of UCIL's Bhopal plant.

DISCUSSION

The standard to be applied in reviewing the district court's forum non conveniens dismissal was clearly expressed by the Supreme Court in *Piper Aircraft Co. v. Reyno*, 454 U.S. at 257, as follows:

> The *forum non conveniens* determination is committed to the sound discretion of the trial court. It may be reversed only when there has been a clear abuse of discretion; where the court has considered all relevant public and private interest factors, and where its balancing of these factors is reasonable, its decision deserves substantial deference.

Having reviewed Judge Keenan's detailed decision, in which he thoroughly considered the comparative adequacy of the forums and the public and private interests involved, we are satisfied that there was no abuse of discretion in his granting dismissal of the action. On the contrary, it might reasonably be concluded that it would have been an abuse of discretion to deny a forum non conveniens dismissal. Practically all relevant factors demonstrate that transfer of the cases to India for trial and adjudication is both fair and just to the parties.

Plaintiffs' principal contentions in favor of retention of the cases by the district court are that deference to the plaintiffs' choice of forum has been inadequate, that the Indian courts are insufficiently equipped for the task, that UCC has its principal place of business here, that the most probative evidence regarding negligence and causation is to be found here, that federal courts are much better equipped through experience and procedures to handle such complex actions efficiently than are Indian courts, and that a transfer of the cases to India will jeopardize a $350 million settlement being negotiated by plaintiffs' counsel. All of these arguments, however, must be rejected.

Little or no deference can be paid to the plaintiffs' choice of a United States forum when all but a few of the 200,000 plaintiffs are Indian citizens located in India who, according to the UOI, have revoked the authorizations of American counsel to represent them here and have substituted the UOI, which now prefers Indian courts. The finding of our district court, after exhaustive analysis of the evidence, that the Indian courts provide a reasonably adequate alternative forum cannot be labeled clearly erroneous or an abuse of discretion.

The emphasis placed by plaintiffs on UCC's having its domicile here, where personal jurisdiction over it exists, is robbed of significance by its consent to Indian jurisdiction. Plaintiffs' contention that the most crucial and probative evidence is located in the United States is simply not in accord with the record or the district court's findings. Although basic design programs were prepared in the United States and some assistance furnished to UCIL at the outset of the 10-year period during which the Bhopal plant was constructed, the proof bearing on the issues to be tried is almost entirely located in India. This includes the principal witnesses and documents bearing on the development and construction of the plant, the detailed designs, the implementation of plans, the operation and regulation of the plant, its safety precautions, the facts with respect to the accident itself, and the deaths and injuries attributable to the accident.

Although the plaintiffs' American counsel may at one time have been close to reaching a $350 million settlement of the cases, no such settlement was ever finalized. No draft joint stipulation in writing or settlement agreement appears to have been prepared, much less approved by the parties. No petition for certification of a settlement class under Fed. R. Civ. P. 23 has ever been presented. Most important, the UOI, which is itself a plaintiff and states that it now represents the Indian plaintiffs formerly represented by American counsel, is firmly opposed to the $350 million "settlement" as inadequate. Under these circumstances, to order a Rule 23 "fairness" hearing would be futile. The district court's denial of the American counsels' motion for such a hearing must accordingly be affirmed.

The conditions imposed by the district court upon its forum non conveniens dismissal stand on a different footing. Plaintiffs and the UOI, however, contend that UCC, having been granted the forum non conveniens dismissal that it sought and having consented to the district court's order, has waived its right to appellate review of these conditions. We disagree. UCC expressly reserved its right to appeal Judge Keenan's order. Moreover, it has made a sufficient showing of prejudice from the second and third conditions of the court's order to entitle it to seek appellate review. UCC's position is comparable to that of a prevailing party which, upon being granted injunctive relief, is permitted to challenge by appeal conditions attaching to the injunction that are found to be objectionable. *U.S. v. Bedford Assocs.*, 618 F.2d 904, 913-16 (2d Cir. 1980). Similarly, conditions imposed by the court upon dismissals without prejudice under Fed. R. Civ. P. 41(a)(2) may be appealed by the plaintiff when they prejudice the plaintiff.

All three conditions of the dismissal are reviewable since plaintiffs have appealed the district court's order and UCC has cross-appealed "from each judgment and order appealed in whole or part by any plaintiff." We therefore have jurisdiction over the entire case and may in the interests of justice modify the district court's order.

The first condition, that UCC consent to the Indian court's personal jurisdiction over it and waive the statute of limitations as a defense, are not unusual and have been imposed in numerous cases where the foreign court would not provide an adequate alternative in the absence of such a condition. The remaining two conditions, however, pose problems.

In requiring that UCC consent to enforceability of an Indian judgment against it, the district court proceeded at least in part on the erroneous assumption that, absent such a requirement, the plaintiffs, if they should succeed in obtaining an Indian judgment against UCC, might not be able to enforce it against UCC in the United States. The law, however, is to the contrary. Under New York law, which governs actions brought in New York to enforce foreign judgments, a foreign-country judgment that is final, conclusive and enforceable where rendered must be recognized and will be enforced as "conclusive between the parties to the extent that it grants or denies recovery of a sum of money" except that it is not deemed to be conclusive if:

> 1. the judgment was rendered under a system which does not provide impartial tribunals or procedures compatible with the requirements of due process of law;
>
> 2. the foreign court did not have personal jurisdiction over the defendant.

Art. 53, Recognition of Foreign Country Money Judgments, 7B N.Y. Civ. Prac. L. & R. §§ 5301-09 (McKinney 1978). Although § 5304 further provides that under certain specified conditions a foreign country judgment need not be recognized, none of these conditions would apply to the present cases except for the possibility of failure to provide UCC with sufficient notice of proceedings or the existence of fraud in obtaining the judgment, which do not presently exist but conceivably could occur in the future.

UCC, as a New York business corporation, would be subject to personal jurisdiction in a court sitting in New York. An Indian money judgment could be enforced against UCC in New York by means of either an action on the judgment or a motion for summary judgment in lieu of complaint. In either case, once converted into a New York judgment, the judgment would be enforceable as a

New York judgment, and thus entitled to the full faith and credit of New York's sister states.

UCC contends that Indian courts, while providing an adequate alternative forum, do not observe due process standards that would be required as a matter of course in this country.

As evidence of this apprehension it points to the haste with which the Indian court in Bhopal issued a temporary order freezing its assets throughout the world and the possibility of serious prejudice to it if the UOI is permitted to have the double and conflicting status of both plaintiff and co-defendant in the Indian court proceedings. It argues that we should protect it against such denial of due process by authorizing Judge Keenan to retain the authority, after forum non conveniens dismissal of the cases here, to monitor the Indian court proceedings and be available on call to rectify in some undefined way any abuses of UCC's right to due process as they might occur in India.

UCC's proposed remedy is not only impractical but evidences an abysmal ignorance of basic jurisdictional principles, so much so that it borders on the frivolous. The district court's jurisdiction is limited to proceedings before it in this country. Once it dismisses those proceedings on grounds of forum non conveniens it ceases to have any further jurisdiction over the matter unless and until a proceeding may some day be brought to enforce here a final and conclusive Indian money judgment. Nor could we, even if we attempted to retain some sort of supervisory jurisdiction, impose our due process requirements upon Indian courts, which are governed by their laws, not ours. The concept of shared jurisdictions is both illusory and unrealistic. The parties cannot simultaneously submit to both jurisdictions the resolution of the pre-trial and trial issues when there is only one consolidated case pending in one court. Any denial by the Indian courts of due process can be raised by UCC as a defense to the plaintiffs' later attempt to enforce a resulting judgment against UCC in this country.

We are concerned, however, that as it is written the district court's requirement that UCC consent to the enforcement of a final Indian judgment, which was imposed on the erroneous assumption that such a judgment might not otherwise be enforceable in the United States, may create misunderstandings and problems of construction. Although the order's provision that the judgment "comport with the minimal requirements of due process" (emphasis supplied) probably is intended to refer to "due process" as used in the New York Foreign Country Money Judgments Law and others like it, there is the risk that it may also be interpreted as providing for a lesser standard than we would otherwise require. Since the court's condition with respect to enforceability of any final Indian judgment is predicated on an erroneous legal assumption and its "due process" language is ambiguous, and since the district court's purpose is fully served by New York's statute providing for recognition of foreign-country money judgments, it was error to impose this condition upon the parties.

We also believe that the district court erred in requiring UCC to consent (which UCC did under protest and subject to its right of appeal) to broad discovery of it by the plaintiffs under the Federal Rules of Civil Procedure when UCC is confined to the more limited discovery authorized under Indian law. We recognize that under some circumstances, such as when a moving defendant unconditionally consents thereto or no undiscovered evidence of consequence is believed to be under the control of a plaintiff or co-defendant, it may be appropriate to condition a forum non conveniens dismissal on the moving defendant's submission to discovery under the Federal Rules without requiring reciprocal discovery by it of the plaintiff. Basic justice dictates that both sides be treated equally, with each having equal access to the evidence in the possession or under the control of the other. Application of this fundamental principle in the present case is especially appropriate since the UOI, as the sovereign government of India, is expected to be a party to the Indian litigation, possibly on both sides.

For these reasons we direct that the condition with respect to the discovery of UCC under the Federal Rules of Civil Procedure be deleted without prejudice to the right of the parties to have reciprocal discovery of each other on equal terms under the Federal Rules, subject to such approval as may be required of the Indian court in which the case will be pending. If, for instance, Indian authorities will permit mutual discovery pursuant to the Federal Rules, the district court's order, as modified in accordance with this opinion, should not be construed to bar such procedure. In the absence of such a court-sanctioned agreement, however, the parties will be limited by the applicable discovery rules of the Indian court in which the claims will be pending.

As so modified the district court's order is affirmed.

NOTES AND QUESTIONS

1. Consider the following from the WASHINGTON POST, Dec. 13, 1984, at A18:

> First the air was filled with poison. Then it was filled with lawyers—lawyers from other places, descending in airplanes with the hope of turning the awful misery to advantage. Where are you Mark Twain, Charles Dickens when we need you? Who else could do justice to the kind of "justice" being pursued in this unhappy scene. In the city, survivors of the chemical gas disaster mourn their dead. Hospitals and health centers struggle to treat the injured and dying. The bodies of dead animals litter the streets. Mother Teresa visits the sick and mourning and counsels forgiveness. And, in the midst of it all there they are: rival teams of American lawyers competing for clients.
>
> The best known of the would-be claimants' representatives is, of course, Melvin Belli. "You couldn't lose a case like this," Mr. Belli is quoted as saying, "... the only question is the amount of damages." Mr. Belli hopes to collect $15 billion for his clients in a class-action suit filed in West Virginia, where Union Carbide, which owns 51 percent of the Bhopal subsidiary corporation, runs a similar pesticide plant.
>
> Mr. Belli won't be without competitors. The Bhopal city government has hired a team of liability lawyers from this area to represent it in a Connecticut suit. That team—which has as its slogan "Get Union Carbide"—says it has already signed up 7,000 plaintiffs

> and is going for 20,000. Another legal group from Los Angeles is also organizing a suit to be filed in New York.
>
> Normally lawyers would prefer to sue in the jurisdiction where a disaster has occurred, since local juries are most sympathetic to the victims' plight, and where judges are most familiar with applicable law. But suits adjudicated by U.S. courts—even though they would typically apply Indian law and standards in assigning blame and assessing individual damages, are expected to produce much more lucrative punitive damage awards. If adjudication of the Bhopal claims plays out according to the usual U.S. model, you can expect three results: many victims will not be compensated for years; awards will vary in quixotic fashion depending on who was represented by whom in what suit; the lawyers will end up with anywhere from 30 to 50 percent of the take. Sizable punitive damages, which are not insurable, could also bankrupt the parent as well as the subsidiary company's 13 other Indian plants, thus further delaying and limiting payments.

2. In *Airbus Industrie G.I.E. v. Patel*, [1998] 2 All E.R. 257 (H.L.), the House of Lords refused to issue an anti-suit injunction against the claimants' Texas lawsuit that arose out of a airplane crash at the Bangalore, India airport in 1990. The Bangalore court had issued an injunction against the claimants' pursuit of the Texas claim but could not enforce it since they were residents of England. Forum non conveniens relief was not available in Texas. Lord Goff of Chieveley concluded:

> [For] the English court to come to the assistance of an Indian court, the normal process is for the English court to do so by enforcing a judgment of the Indian court. However, as the present proceedings have demonstrated, that is not possible here. ... So Airbus is relying simply on the English court's power of itself, without direct reliance on the Indian court's decision, to grant an injunction in this case where, unusually, the English jurisdiction has no interest in, or connection with, the matter in question. I am driven to say that such a course is not open to the English courts because ... it would be inconsistent with comity. In a world which consists of independent jurisdictions, interference, even indirect interference, by the courts of one jurisdiction with the exercise of the jurisdiction of a foreign court cannot in my opinion be justified by the fact that a third jurisdiction is affected but is powerless to intervene. The basic principle is that courts of an interested jurisdiction can act in the matter; and if they are powerless to do so, that will not of itself be enough to justify the courts of another jurisdiction to act in their place.

IV. Recognition and Enforcement

A. Recognition of Legal Acts

1. Legal Consequences for States of the Continued Presence of South Africa in Namibia (South West Africa) Notwithstanding Security Council Resolution 276 (1970)

1971 I.C.J. 16

[Review *supra*, Part Two, at 231.]

2. Act of State Doctrine

[Review *supra*, at 1398-1402.]

B. ENFORCEMENT OF JUDGMENTS

1. National Judgments

a. Hilton v. Guyot
159 U.S. 113 (1895)

MR. JUSTICE GRAY. ... International law, in its widest and most comprehensive sense—including not only questions of right between nations, governed by what has been appropriately called the law of nations; but also questions arising under what is usually called private international law, or the conflict of laws, and concerning the rights of persons within the territory and dominion of one nation, by reason of acts, private or public, done within the dominions of another nation—is part of our law, and must be ascertained and administered by the courts of justice, as often as such questions are presented in litigation between man and man, duly submitted to their determination.

The most certain guide, no doubt, for the decision of such questions is a treaty or a statute of this country. But when, as is the case here, there is no written law upon the subject, the duty still rests upon the judicial tribunals of ascertaining and declaring what the law is, whenever it becomes necessary to do so, in order to determine the rights of parties to suits regularly brought before them. In doing this, the courts must obtain such aid as they can from judicial decisions, from the works of jurists and commentators, and from the acts and usages of civilized nations. ...

No law has any effect, of its own force, beyond the limits of the sovereignty from which its authority is derived. The extent to which the law of one nation, as put in force within its territory, whether by executive order, by legislative act, or by judicial decree, shall be allowed to operate within the dominion of another nation, depends upon what our greatest jurists have been content to call "the comity of nations." Although the phrase has been often criticized, no satisfactory substitute has been suggested.

"Comity," in the legal sense, is neither a matter of absolute obligation, on the one hand, nor of mere courtesy and good will, upon the other. But it is the recognition which one nation allows within its territory to the legislative, executive or judicial acts of another nation, having due regard both to international duty and convenience, and to the rights of its own citizens or of other persons who are under the protection of its laws.

Mr. Justice Story, in his Commentaries on the Conflict Laws, treating of the question in what department of the government of any State, in the absence of any clear declaration of the sovereign will, resides the authority to determine how far the laws of a foreign State shall have effect, and observing that this differs in different States, according to the organization of the departments of the government of each, says: "In England and America, the courts of justice have hitherto exercised the same authority in the most ample manner: and the legislatures have in no instance (it is believed) in either country interfered to provide any positive regulations. The common law of both countries has been expanded to meet the exigencies of the times as they have arisen; and so far as the practice of nations, or the *jus gentium privatum*, has been supposed to furnish any general principle, it has been followed out." Story's Conflict of Laws, §§ 23, 24.

Afterwards, speaking of the difficulty of applying the positive rules laid down by the Continental jurists, he says that "there is indeed great truth" in these remarks of Mr. Justice Porter, speaking for the Supreme Court of Louisiana: "They have attempted to go too far, to define and fix that which cannot, in the nature of things, be defined and fixed. They seem to have forgotten that they wrote on a question which touched the comity of nations, and that that comity is, and ever must be, uncertain; that it must necessarily depend on a variety of circumstances which cannot be reduced to any certain rule; that no nation will suffer the laws of another to interfere with her own to the injury of her citizens; that whether they do or not must depend on the condition of the country in which the foreign law is sought to be enforced, the particular nature of her legislation, her policy, and the character of her institutions; that in the conflict of laws it must often be a matter of doubt which should prevail; and that, whenever a doubt does exist, the court, which decides, will prefer the laws of its own country to that of the stranger." Story's Conflict of Laws, § 28; *Saul v. His Creditors,* (1827) 5 Martin (N.S.) 569, 596.

Again, Mr. Justice Story says: "It has been thought by some jurists that the term *comity* is not sufficiently expressive of the obligation of nations to give effect to foreign laws when they are not prejudicial to their own rights and interests. And it has been suggested that the doctrine rests on a deeper foundation; that it is not so much a matter of comity or courtesy as a matter of paramount moral duty. Now, assuming that such a moral duty does exist, it is clearly one of imperfect obligation, like that of beneficence, humanity and charity. Every nation must be the final judge for itself, not only of the nature and extent of the duty, but of the occasions on which its exercise may be justly demanded." And, after further discussion of the matter, he concludes: "There is then not only no impropriety in the use of the phrase 'comity of nations,' but it is the most appropriate phrase to express the true foundation and extent of the obligation of the laws of one nation within the territories of another." Story's Conflict of Laws, §§ 33-38. . . .

In the case at bar, the defendants offered to prove, in much detail, that the plaintiffs presented to the French court of first instance and to the arbitrator appointed by that court, and upon whose report its judgment was largely based, false and fraudulent statements and accounts against the defendants, by which the arbitrator and the French courts were deceived and misled, and their judgments were based upon such false and fraudulent statements and accounts. This offer, if satisfactorily proved, would ... be a sufficient ground for impeaching the foreign judgment, and examining into the merits of the original claim.

But whether those decisions can be followed in regard to foreign judgments, consistently with our own decisions as to impeaching domestic judgments for fraud, it is unnecessary in this case to determine, because there is a distinct and independent ground upon which we are satisfied that the comity of our nation does not require us to give conclusive effect to the judgments of the courts of France; and that ground is, the want of reciprocity, on the part of France, as to the effect to be given to the judgments of this and other foreign countries.

In France, the Royal Ordinance of June 15, 1629, art. 121, provided as follows: "Judgments rendered, contracts or obligations recognized, in foreign kingdoms and sovereignties, for any cause whatever, shall have no lien or execution in our kingdom. Thus the contracts shall stand for simple promises; and, notwithstanding the judgments, our subjects against whom they have been rendered may contest their rights anew before our judges." Touillier, Droit Civil, lib. 3, tit. 3, c. 6, sect. 3, no. 77.

By the French Code of Civil Procedure, art. 546, "Judgments rendered by foreign tribunals, and acts acknowledged before foreign officers, shall not be capable of execution in France, except in the manner and in the cases provided by articles 2123 and 2128 of the Civil Code," which are as follows: By article 2123, "A lien cannot arise from judgments rendered in a foreign country, except so far as they have been declared executory by a French tribunal; without prejudice to provisions to the contrary which may exist in public laws and treaties." By article 2128, "Contracts entered into in a foreign country cannot give a lien upon property in France, if there are no provisions contrary to this principle in public laws or in treaties." Touillier, ub. sup. no. 84.

The defendants, in their answer, cited the above provisions of the statutes of France, and alleged, and at the trial offered to prove, that, by the construction given to these statutes by the judicial tribunals of France, when the judgments of tribunals of foreign countries against the citizens of France are sued upon in the courts of France, the merits of the controversies upon which those judgments are based are examined anew, unless a treaty to the contrary effect exists between the Republic of France and the country in which such judgment is obtained, (which is not the case between the Republic of France and the United States,) and that the tribunals of the Republic of France give no force and effect, within the jurisdiction of that country, to the judgments duly rendered by courts of competent jurisdiction of the United States against citizens of France after proper personal service of the process of those courts has been made thereon in this country. We are of opinion that this evidence should have been admitted. ...

Mr. Justice Story, already cited: "Holland seems at all times, upon the general principle of reciprocity, to have given great weight to foreign judgments, and in many cases, if not in all cases, to have given to them a weight equal to that given to domestic judgments, wherever the like rule of reciprocity with regard to Dutch judgments has been adopted by the foreign country whose judgment is brought under review. This is certainly a very reasonable rule, and may perhaps hereafter work itself firmly into the structure of international jurisprudence." Story's Conflict of Laws, § 618.

This rule, though never either affirmed or denied by express adjudication in England or America, has been indicated, more or less distinctly, in several of the authorities already cited. …

By the law of France, settled by a series of uniform decisions of the Court of Cassation, the highest judicial tribunal, for more than half a century, no foreign judgment can be rendered executory in France without a review of the judgment *au fond*—to the bottom, including the whole merits of the cause of action on which the judgment rests. …

[There follows a survey of the practice of various countries in recognizing foreign judgments.]

It appears, therefore, that there is hardly a civilized nation on either continent, which, by its general law, allows conclusive effect to an executory foreign judgment for the recovery of money. In France, and in a few smaller States—Norway, Portugal, Greece, Monaco, and Hayti [sic] — the merits of the controversy are reviewed, as of course, allowing to the foreign judgment, at the most, no more effect than of being ˜*prima facie* evidence of the justice of the claim. In the great majority of the countries on the continent of Europe—in Belgium, Holland, Denmark, Sweden, Germany, in many cantons of Switzerland, in Russia and Poland, in Roumania, in Austria and Hungary, (perhaps in Italy,) and in Spain—as well as in Egypt, in Mexico, and in a great part of South America, the judgment rendered in a foreign country is allowed the same effect only as the courts of that country allow to the judgments of the country in which the judgment in question is sought to be executed.

The prediction of Mr. Justice Story (in § 618 of his Commentaries on the Conflict of Laws, already cited,) has thus been fulfilled, and the rule of reciprocity has worked itself firmly into the structure of international jurisprudence.

The reasonable, if not the necessary, conclusion appears to us to be that judgments rendered in France, or in any other foreign country, by the laws of which our own judgments are reviewable upon the merits, are not entitled to full credit and conclusive effect when sued upon in this country, but are *prima facie* evidence only of the justice of the plaintiffs' claim.

In holding such a judgment, for want of reciprocity, not to be conclusive evidence of the merits of the claim, we do not proceed upon any theory of retaliation upon one person by reason of injustice done to another; but upon the broad ground that international law is founded upon mutuality and reciprocity, and that by the principles of international law recognized in most civilized nations, and by the comity of our own country, which it is our judicial duty to know and to declare, the judgment is not entitled to be considered conclusive.

By our law, at the time of the adoption of the Constitution, a foreign judgment was considered as *prima facie* evidence, and not conclusive. There is no statute of the United States, and no treaty of the United States with France, or with any other nation, which has changed that law, or has made any provision upon the subject. It is not to be supposed that, if any statute or treaty had been or should be made, it would recognize as conclusive the judgments of any country, which did not give like effect to our own judgments. In the absence of statute or treaty, it appears to us equally unwarrantable to assume that the comity of the United States requires anything more.

If we should hold this judgment to be conclusive, we should allow it an effect to which, supposing the defendants' offers to be sustained by actual proof, it would, in the absence of a special treaty, be entitled in hardly any other country in Christendom, except the country in which it was rendered. If the judgment had been rendered in this country, or in any other outside of the jurisdiction of France, the French courts would not have executed or enforced it, except after examining into its merits. The very judgment now sued on would be held inconclusive in almost any other country than France. In England, and in the Colonies subject to the law of England, the fraud alleged in its procurement would be a sufficient ground for disregarding it. In the courts of nearly every other nation, it would be subject to reexamination, either merely because it was a foreign judgment, or because judgments of that nation would be reexaminable in the courts of France.

b. Bi v. Union Carbide Chemicals & Plastics Co.

984 F.2d 582 (2d Cir. 1993)

NEWMAN, CIRCUIT JUDGE: This appeal presents an interesting issue of comity among nations in the resolution of claims arising from torts occurring within a foreign country. The precise issue is whether the federal and state courts of this country should defer to the judgment of a democratic foreign government that disputes arising from a mass tort occurring within its borders can be best resolved by according the foreign government exclusive standing to represent the victims of the disaster in the courts of the world. This question arises on an appeal by a class of tort victims from the March 4, 1992, judgment of the District Court for the—Southern District of New York (John F. Keenan, Judge) dismissing two complaints on the ground of *forum non conveniens*. We conclude that the plaintiffs lack standing and on that ground affirm. ...

In September 1986, the Indian Government, acting pursuant to its authority under the Bhopal Act, brought suit on behalf of all claimants in the District Court of Bhopal. The litigation continued in India for more than two years. By orders dated February 14 and 15, 1989, the Supreme Court of India approved a settlement of "all litigations, claims, rights and liabilities related to and arising out of the [Bhopal] disaster." Under the settlement, Union Carbide and UCIL agreed to pay $470 million to the Indian Government for the benefit of all victims of the Bhopal disaster. On May 4, 1989, the Supreme Court of India set forth its reasons for concluding that the settlement was just and reasonable. The Court was concerned primarily that the victims of the disaster receive immediate relief. On December 22, 1989, in a related decision, the Court upheld the constitutional validity of the Bhopal Act and confirmed the Indian Government's exclusive authority to compromise all claims arising out of the Bhopal disaster.

After settlement of the Indian lawsuit, two class actions were filed in Texas state courts in October 1990 seeking compensation for injuries caused by the Bhopal disaster. In one action, Abdul Wahid, as class representative, filed a suit against Union Carbide and UCIL. In the other action, Bano Bi, as class representative, filed a suit against Union Carbide, UCIL, Union Carbide Eastern, Inc., Enserch Corporation, Humphreys & Glasgow Consultants Pvt., Ltd., Humphreys & Glasgow, Ltd., and Ebasco-Humphreys & Glasgow, Inc. These class representatives, appellants on this appeal, contend that their collateral attack on the settlement of their claims by the Indian Government is proper because, among other things, the Indian Government had an unacceptable conflict of interest as part owner of UCIL, most of the victims oppose the settlement as grossly inadequate, and their due process rights were violated because they received inadequate notice and inadequate representation in the proceedings and because they could not opt out of the settlement.

Appellees removed these actions to two Texas federal district courts in November 1990. In the *Bi* action, Judge Fisher, of the Eastern District of Texas, dismissed as defendants Enserch Corporation, Humphreys & Glasgow Consultants Pvt., Ltd., Humphreys & Glasgow, Ltd., and Ebasco-Humphreys & Glasgow, Inc. He also denied Bi's motion to remand that action to the Texas state court. On January 30, 1991, the Judicial Panel on Multidistrict Litigation transferred these two actions to the Southern District of New York before Judge Keenan. Judge Keenan refused to reconsider Judge Fisher's rulings and denied Wahid's motion to remand his action to the Texas state court. Applying federal forum non conveniens law, Judge Keenan dismissed both actions; he held that the analysis and the results of his 1986 opinion were still appropriate.

This appeal presents an extraordinary collection of issues, but we have concluded that we need reach only the threshold issue of plaintiffs' standing to dispose of the appeal. That issue is whether the plaintiffs have standing to maintain this action in the courts of this country despite the Bhopal Act's delegation to the Indian Government of the exclusive right to represent those injured in the Bhopal disaster.

India passed the Bhopal Act to "secure that claims arising out of, or connected with, the Bhopal gas leak disaster are dealt with speedily, effectively, equitably and to the best advantage of the claimants." Preamble to Bhopal Act. To effectuate the swift and just resolution of claims, section 3 of the Act delegates to the Indian Government "the exclusive right to represent, and act in place of (whether within or outside India) every person who has made, or is entitled to make, a claim for all purposes connected with such claim in the same manner and to the same effect as such person." This delegation includes the right to institute or withdraw a suit and to enter into a compromise. Section 3 also provides that, in cases pending as of the effective date of the Act in courts outside of India, the Indian Government would "represent, and act in place of, or along with, such claimant, if such court or other authority so permits." Section 4 of the Act permits individual claimants a limited right to participate in the proceedings. Section 4 states that the Indian Government "shall have due regard to any matters which such person may require to be urged with respect to his claim and shall, if such person so desires, permit at the expense of such person, a legal practitioner of his choice to be associated in the conduct of any suit or other proceeding relating to his claim."

The Supreme Court of India, in a lengthy opinion, concluded that the Bhopal Act was constitutional under the Indian Constitution and that the Act violated no principles of natural justice. In so ruling, the Indian Court rejected many of the same arguments that appellants urge in this Court. The Indian Court held that the Indian Government's exclusive representation of all victims in its sovereign capacity would be constitutional as long as the Indian Government assumes the obligation to pay the victims interim relief or maintenance until monies are realized from Union Carbide, because the Indian Government's exclusive representation deprived the victims of their right to seek immediate relief from Union Carbide themselves. The Court excused the Indian Government's failure to give notice of the settlement to each of the several hundred thousand claimants prior to approving the settlement. It reasoned that although the lack of notice may affect the appearance of justice, justice was in fact done because the arguments against settlement were adequately advocated by those who were aware of the settlement and argued against it. In sum, the Court confirmed that as far as Indian law is concerned, the Bhopal Act's grant of exclusive standing to the Indian Government was proper.

We are faced with what we believe is an issue of first impression. We must decide whether we will give effect to the statute of a foreign government that purports to grant that government exclusive standing to represent the victims of a mass tort that occurred within its borders. India is a democracy. Its Constitution, which took effect in 1950, provides for a republican form of parliamentary government and guarantees the fundamental rights of the people, including equal protection and procedural due process. Its President is chosen for a five-year term by an electoral college consisting of the elected members of the Parliament and the state legislatures. The President selects the justices of the Supreme Court and other high courts. The de facto executive is the Prime Minister, who is elected by the parliamentary members of the majority party. The Parliament consists of two houses: the Council of States, which consists of state representatives chosen primarily by the state assemblies along with 12 members nominated by the President, and the House of the People, which is directly elected. Judicial independence is a basic principle of India's Constitution. The members of the Supreme Court are guaranteed tenure until age 65 and can be removed only for incompetence or misconduct by a vote of a majority of all the members of each house and two-thirds of those voting.

India has chosen a system to deal efficiently with a problem of mass proportions that occurred within its borders. It decided in an act passed by its democratic parliament to represent exclusively all the victims in a suit against Union Carbide and to use the money it received in settlement of that suit to fund a plan framed, pursuant to the Bhopal Act, to process the claims of all the victims. Union Carbide's negotiations with the Indian Government were conducted under the assumption that the settlement amount covered all claims. To grant the victims of the Bhopal disaster, most of whom are citizens of India, access to our courts when India has set up what it believes to be the most effective method of dealing with a difficult problem would frustrate India's efforts.

Under the act of state doctrine, we will not sit in "judgment on ... acts of a governmental character done by a foreign state within its own territory and applicable there." See 1 Restatement (Third) of the Foreign Relations Law of the United States § 443 (1987). Although the act of state doctrine is not precisely applicable here, the concerns underlying it support our result. That doctrine has "'constitutional' underpinnings" and "arises out of the basic relationships between branches of government in a system of separation of powers." *Banco Nacional de Cuba v. Sabbatino*, 376 U.S. 398, 423 (1964). Our Supreme Court was concerned that the Judicial Branch's "passing on the validity of foreign acts of state may hinder rather than further this country's pursuit of goals both for itself and for the community of nations as a whole in the international sphere." Here too, were we to pass judgment on the validity of India's response to a disaster that occurred within its borders, it would disrupt our relations with that country and frustrate the efforts of the international community to develop methods to deal with problems of this magnitude in the future.

It is not relevant to our determination whether, under our constitutional standards, our Government could pass an act similar to the Bhopal Act. We are deferring to the statute of a democratic country to resolve disputes created by a disaster of mass proportions that occurred within that country. Any challenge appellants may have to the settlement must be made through the legislative or judicial channels that are available in India. We hold that when a recognized democracy determines that the interests of the victims of a mass tort that occurred within its borders will be best served if the foreign government exclusively represents the victims in courts around the world, we will not pass judgment on that determination, and we will permit only the foreign government access to our courts to litigate those claims, subject of course to our own requirements for standing. This conclusion is especially compelling in a case such as this where almost all of the victims are Indian citizens. …

Because the Texas state courts, applying federal common law, would be obliged to reach the same conclusion regarding appellants' lack of standing that we have reached, a remand would be pointless. We therefore affirm the District Court's judgment of dismissal.

c. Uniform Enforcement of Foreign Judgments Act (1964)

1. Definition.

In this Act "foreign judgment" means any judgment, decree, or order of a court of the United States or of any other court which is entitled to full faith and credit in this state.

2. Filing and Status of Foreign Judgments.

A copy of any foreign judgment authenticated in accordance with the act of Congress or the statutes of this state may be filed in the office of the Clerk of any [District Court of any city or county] of this state. The Clerk shall treat the foreign judgment in the same manner as a judgment of the [District Court of any city or county] of this state. A judgment so filed has the same effect and is subject to the same procedures, defenses and proceedings for reopening, vacating, or staying as a judgment of a [District Court of any city or county] of this state and may be enforced or satisfied in like manner.

3. Notice of Filing.

(a) At the time of the filing of the foreign judgment, the judgment creditor or his lawyer shall make and file with the Clerk of Court an affidavit setting forth the name and last known post office address of the judgment debtor, and the judgment creditor.

(b) Promptly upon the filing of the foreign judgment and the affidavit, the Clerk shall mail notice of the filing of the foreign judgment to the judgment debtor at the address given and shall make a note of the mailing in the docket. The notice shall include the name and post office address of the judgment creditor and the judgment creditor's lawyer, if any, in this state.

In addition, the judgment creditor may mail a notice of the filing of the judgment to the judgment debtor and may file proof of mailing with the Clerk. Lack of mailing notice of filing by the Clerk shall not affect the enforcement proceedings if proof of mailing by the judgment creditor has been filed.

[(c) No execution or other process for enforcement of a foreign judgment filed hereunder shall issue until [ ] days after the date the judgment is filed.]

4. Stay.

(a) If the judgment debtor shows the [District Court of any city or county] that an appeal from the foreign judgment is pending or will be taken, or that a stay of execution has been granted, the court shall stay enforcement of the foreign judgment until the appeal is concluded, the time for appeal expires, or the stay of execution expires or is vacated, upon proof that the judgment debtor has furnished the security for the satisfaction of the judgment required by the state in which it was rendered.

(b) If the judgment debtor shows the [District Court of any city or county] any ground upon which enforcement of a judgment of any [District Court of any city or county] of this state would be stayed, the court shall stay enforcement of the foreign judgment for an appropriate period, upon requiring the same security for satisfaction of the judgment which is required in this state.

d. Restatement (Third) of Foreign Relations Law of the United States (1987)

§ 481. Recognition and Enforcement of Foreign Judgments

(1) Except as provided in § 482, a final judgment of a court of a foreign state granting or denying recovery of a sum of money, establishing or confirming the status of a person, or determining interests in property, is conclusive between the parties, and is entitled to recognition in courts in the United States.

(2) A judgment entitled to recognition under Subsection (1) may be enforced by any party or its successors or assigns against any other party, its successors or assigns, in accordance with the procedure for enforcement of judgments applicable where enforcement is sought.

§ 482. Grounds for Nonrecognition of Foreign Judgments

(1) A court in the United States may not recognize a judgment of the court of a foreign state if:

(a) the judgment was rendered under a judicial system that does not provide impartial tribunals or procedures compatible with due process of law; or

(b) the court that rendered the judgment did not have jurisdiction over the defendant in accordance with the law of the rendering state and with the rules set forth in § 421.

(2) A court in the United States need not recognize a judgment of the court of a foreign state if:

(a) the court that rendered the judgment did not have jurisdiction of the subject matter of the action;

(b) the defendant did not receive notice of the proceedings in sufficient time to enable him to defend;

(c) the judgment was obtained by fraud;

(d) the cause of action on which the judgment was based, or the judgment itself, is repugnant to the public policy of the United States or of the State where recognition is sought;

(e) the judgment conflicts with another final judgment that is entitled to recognition; or

(f) the proceeding in the foreign court was contrary to an agreement between the parties to submit the controversy on which the judgment is based to another forum.

2. International Judgments

a. Charter of the United Nations

Article 94

1. Each Member of the United Nations undertakes to comply with the decision of the International Court of Justice in any case to which it is a party.

2. If any party to a case fails to perform the obligations incumbent upon it under a judgment rendered by the Court, the other party may have recourse to the Security Council, which may, if it deems necessary, make recommendations or decide upon measures to be taken to give effect to the judgment.

NOTES AND QUESTIONS

1. The reinforced discretion assigned to the Security Council in Article 94 (2) represents a feeble commitment to enforcement. What are the policy reasons for this high amount of discretion? *See* J. Noelle Hicks, *Facilitating International Trade: The U.S. Needs Federal Legislation Governing the Enforcement of Foreign Judgments*, 28 BROOK. J. INT'L L. 155 (2002).

C. RECOGNITION AND ENFORCEMENT OF ARBITRAL AWARDS

1. Convention on the Recognition and Enforcement of Foreign Arbitral Awards

21 U.S.T. 2517, T.I.A.S. No. 6997, 330 U.N.T.S. 3, 9 U.S.C.A. § 201

Article II

1. Each Contracting State shall recognize an agreement in writing under which the parties undertake to submit to arbitration all or any differences which have arisen or which may arise between them in respect of defined legal relationship, whether contractual or not, concerning a subject matter capable of settlement by arbitration.

2. The term "agreement in writing" shall include an arbitral clause in a contract or an arbitration agreement, signed by the parties or contained in an exchange of letters or telegrams.

3. The court of a Contracting State, when seized of an action in a matter in respect of which the parties have made an agreement within the meaning of this article, shall, at the request of one of the parties, refer the parties to arbitration, unless it finds that the said agreement is null and void, inoperative or incapable of being performed.

Article III

Each Contracting State shall recognize arbitral awards as binding and enforce them in accordance with the rules of procedure of the territory whom the award is relied upon, under the conditions laid down in the following articles. There shall not be imposed substantially more onerous conditions or higher fees or charges on the recognition or enforcement of arbitral awards to which this Convention applies than are imposed on the recognition or enforcement of domestic arbitral awards. …

Article V

1. Recognition and enforcement of the award may be refused, at the request of the party against whom it is invoked, only if that party furnishes to the competent authority where the recognition and enforcement is sought, proof that:

(a) The parties to the agreement referred to in article II were, under the law applicable to them, under some capacity, or the said agreement is not valid under the law to which the parties have subjected it or, failing any indication thereon, under the law of the country where the award was made; or

(b) The party against whom the award is invoked was not given proper notice of the appointment of the arbitrator or of the arbitration proceedings or was otherwise unable to present his case; or

(c) The award deals with a difference not contemplated by or not falling within the terms of the submission to arbitration, or it contains decisions on matters beyond the scope of the submission to arbitration, provided that, if the decisions on matters submitted to arbitration can be separated from those not so submitted, that part of the award which contains decisions on matters submitted to arbitration may be recognized and enforced; or

(d) The composition of the arbitral authority or the arbitral procedure was not in accordance with the agreement of the parties, or, failing such agreement, was not in accordance with the law of the country where the arbitration took place; or

(e) The award has not yet become binding on the parties, or has been set aside or suspended by a competent authority of the country in which, or under the law of which, that award was made.

2. Recognition and enforcement of an arbitral award may also be refused if the competent authority in the country where recognition and enforcement is sought finds that:

(a) The subject matter of the difference is not capable of settlement by arbitration under the law of that country; or

(b) The recognition or enforcement of the award would be contrary to the public policy of that country.

2. Iran Aircraft Industries v. Avco Corp.

980 F.2d 141 (2d Cir. 1992)

LUMBARD, CIRCUIT JUDGE: [Avco, a United States party, brought arbitration before the Iran-United States Claims Tribunal on claims arising out of contracts of the repair and replacement of helicopter engines and replacement parts with Iranian parties the performance of which was interrupted by the Iranian Revolution. The Iranian parties counterclaimed and a final award was rendered allowing a net balance of $3,513,086 in favor of the Iranian parties. The favorable balance was arrived at largely because of the disallowal of a large part of Avco's claims on the basis that they were not sufficiently supported by invoices. Avco obtained summary judgment from the District Court declining to enforce the award and the Iranian parties appealed.]

On May 17, 1985, the Tribunal held a pre-hearing conference to consider, inter alia, "whether voluminous and complicated data should be presented through summaries, tabulations, charts, graphs or extracts in order to save time and costs." See *Avco Corp. v. Iran Aircraft Indus.*, Case No. 261, 19 Iran-U.S. Cl. Trib. Rep. 200, 235 (1988) (Brower, J., concurring and dissenting). At the conference, Avco's counsel, Dean Cordiano, requested guidance from the Tribunal as to the appropriate method for proving certain of its claims which were based on voluminous invoices, stating:

> In the interest of keeping down some of the documentation for the Tribunal we have not placed in evidence as of yet the actual supporting invoices. But we have those invoices and they are available and if the Tribunal would be interested in seeing them we can obviously place them in evidence or we can use a procedure whereby an outside auditing agency… certifies to the amounts of the… summaries vis-a-vis the underlying invoices. Both of those approaches can be taken. But I want to assure the Tribunal that all of the invoices reflected in our exhibits to the memorial ... exist and are available.

Id. at 235-36. After noting that the Iranian parties "obviously have had those invoices all along," Cordiano stated that he would:

> [l]ike the Tribunal's guidance as to whether… you would like this outside certifying agency to go through the underlying invoices and certify as to the summary amounts or that the Tribunal feels at this point that … you would rather have …the underlying invoices…
>
> *Id.* at 236.

The Chairman of Chamber Three, Judge Nils Mangard of Sweden, then engaged in the following colloquy with Cordiano:

> Mangard: I don't think we will be very, very much enthusiastic getting kilos and kilos of invoices.
>
> Cordiano: That, that's what I thought so . . .

Mangard: So I think it will help us . . .

Cordiano: We'll use . . .

Mangard: to use the alternative rather.

Cordiano: Alright . . .

Mangard: On the other hand, I don't know if, if any, if there are any objections to any specific invoices so far made by the Respondents. But anyhow...as a precaution maybe you could . . .

Cordiano: Yes. sir.

Mangard: Get an account made.

Id. at 236. Neither counsel for the Iranian parties nor the Iranian Judge attended the pre-hearing conference.

On July 22, 1985, Avco submitted to the Tribunal a Supplemental Memorial, which stated in part:

> In response to the Tribunal's suggestion at the Pre-hearing Conference, Avco's counsel has retained Arthur Young & Co., an internationally recognized public accounting firm, to verify that the accounts receivable ledgers submitted to the Tribunal accurately reflect the actual invoices in Avco's records.

Attached to the Supplemental Memorial was an affidavit of a partner at Arthur Young & Co. which verified that the accounts receivable ledgers submitted by Avco tallied with Avco's original invoices, with the exception of one invoice for $240.14. Id. at 237.

The Tribunal held its hearing on the merits on September 16-17, 1986. By that time, Judge Mangard had resigned as Chairman of Chamber Three and had been replaced by Judge Michel Virally of France. At the hearing, Judge Parviz Ansari of Iran engaged in the following colloquy with Cordiano:

Ansari: May I ask a question? It is about the evidence. It was one of the first or one of the few cases that I have seen that the invoices have not been submitted. So what is your position on this point about the substantiation of the claim?

Cordiano: Your Honor, this point was raised at the pre-hearing conference in May of last year.

Ansari: I was not there.

Cordiano: I remember that you weren't there. I think we were kind of lonely that day. We were on one side of the table, the other side was not there . . . We could have produced at some point the thousands of pages

> of invoices, but we chose to substantiate our invoices through . . . the Arthur Young audit performed specifically for this tribunal proceeding.
>
> *Id.* at 237.

The Tribunal issued the Award on July 18, 1988. Of particular relevance here, the Tribunal disallowed Avco's claims which were documented by its audited accounts receivable ledgers, stating, "The Tribunal cannot grant Avco's claim solely on the basis of an affidavit and a list of invoices, even if the existence of the invoices was certified by an independent audit." *Id.* at 211 (majority opinion).

Judge Brower, the American judge and the only judge of the panel who was present at the pre-hearing conference, filed a separate Concurring and Dissenting Opinion in which he stated:

> I believe the Tribunal has misled the Claimant, however, unwittingly, regarding the evidence it was required to submit, thereby depriving Claimant, to that extent, of the ability to present its case. ...
>
> Since Claimant did exactly what it previously was told to do by the Tribunal the denial in the present Award of any of those invoice claims on the ground that more evidence should have been submitted constitutes a denial to Claimant of the ability to present its case to the Tribunal.
>
> *Id.* at 231, 238.

A. *"Direct" Enforceability of the Award*

[The Court of Appeal rejected the Iranian parties argument that under the Algiers Accord all Claims Tribunal awards are "final and binding" and must be "directly" enforced by the U.S. courts without regard to the New York Convention and defenses thereunder.]

B. *The New York Convention*

Avco argues that the district court properly denied enforcement of the Award pursuant to Article V(1)(b) of the New York Convention because it was unable to present its case to the Tribunal. The New York Convention provides for nonenforcement where:

> The party against whom the award is invoked was not given proper notice of the appointment of the arbitrator or of the arbitration proceedings or was otherwise unable to present his case ...
>
> New York Convention, Art. V(1)(b). ...

We have recognized that the defense provided for in Article V(1)(b) "essentially sanctions the application of the forum state's standards of due process," and that due process rights are "entitled to full force under the Convention as defenses to enforcement." *Parsons & Whittemore Overseas Co., Inc. v. Soci-*

ete Generale de L'Industrie du Papier (RAKTA), 508 F.2d 969, 975-76 (2d Cir. 1974). Under our law, "the fundamental requirement of due process is the opportunity to be heard 'at a meaningful time and in a meaningful manner.'" *Mathews v. Eldridge*, 424 U.S. 319, 333 (1976) .... Accordingly, if Avco was denied the opportunity to be heard in a meaningful time or in a meaningful manner, enforcement of the Award should be refused pursuant to Article V(1)(b).

At the pre-hearing conference, Judge Mangard specifically advised Avco not to burden the Tribunal by submitting "kilos and kilos of invoices." Instead, Judge Mangard approved the method of proof proposed by Avco, namely the submission of Avco's audited accounts receivable ledgers. Later, when Judge Ansari questioned Avco's method of proof, he never responded to Avco's explanation that it was proceeding according to an earlier understanding. Thus, Avco was not made aware that the Tribunal now required the actual invoices to substantiate Avco's claim. Having thus led Avco to believe it had used a proper method to substantiate its claim, the Tribunal then rejected Avco's claim for lack of proof.

We believe that by so misleading Avco, however unwittingly, the Tribunal denied Avco the opportunity to present its claim in a meaningful manner. Accordingly, Avco was "unable to present [its] case" within the meaning of Article V(1)(b), and enforcement of the Award was properly denied.

Affirmed.

CARDAMONE, CIRCUIT JUDGE, dissenting:

The issue before us is whether Avco was denied an opportunity to present its case before the Iran-United States Claims Tribunal at the Hague. To rule, as the majority does, that it was denied such an opportunity renders the Tribunal's award unenforceable under article V(1)(b) of [the New York Convention]. I respectfully dissent because it seems to me that a fair reading of this record reveals that Avco was not denied such an opportunity. Thus, in my view the arbitral award is enforceable under the New York Convention.

I.

Avco's focus is on a pre-trial colloquy between its counsel and Judge Mangard of the Tribunal regarding the use of summaries in place of some of the invoices Avco needed to prove its claim. Judge Mangard stated the panel would not be very "enthusiastic about getting kilos and kilos of in voices," and added that there appeared to be no objection to using summaries of certain invoices, and suggested to counsel that "as a precaution" Avco might get an account summary made. Based on this brief exchange, Avco now makes the dubious argument that this colloquy constituted a binding pre-trial ruling by the Tribunal that summaries of those particular invoices could substitute for the invoices and would be sufficient evidence at trial.

At the time of trial Judge Mangard was no longer a member of the Tribunal. Another judge who was present at the pre-trial had also been replaced. The three-judge panel hearing the case retained therefore only one of the original judges present at the pre-trial exchange. These trial judges had different concerns than had the earlier panel. One of the new judges, Judge Ansari, questioned the adequacy of Avco's proof based only on summaries of invoices. He noted that it was "the first or one of the few cases" he had heard of in which none of the invoices were produced as evidence. In response, Avco's counsel stressed the massive number of invoices involved, mentioning that Avco "chose to substantiate [the] invoices through other methods," and stated, "we simply chose not to put in thousands of pages of documents." (emphases added.) Concluding that Avco's proof did not establish its claim, the Tribunal declined to grant Avco an award based only on summaries of its invoices.

II.

The New York Convention obligates U.S. courts to enforce foreign arbitral awards unless certain defenses provided in article V(1) of the Convention are established. The specific defense with which we deal in the case at hand appears in article V(1)(b). That section states that enforcement of an arbitral award may be denied if the court is satisfied that the party against whom the award is sought to be enforced was unable to present its case before the arbitration panel.

Based on the facts before us, Avco fails to meet the legal standard of being unable to present its case before the arbitral Tribunal so as to render the award unenforceable under the New York Convention. That standard, as the majority points out, essentially involves a due process inquiry to see whether the party against whom enforcement is sought has been put on notice and has had an opportunity to respond. See *Parsons & Whitmore Overseas Co. v. Societe Generale de l'Industrie du Papier (RAKTA)*, 508 F.2d 969, 975-76 (2d Cir. 1974). Unfortunately, only limited case law exists on this issue, and those cases that can be found merely note, in applying article V(1)(b), that due process serves as an interpretive guide.

One of the reasons for this dissent is because until today no federal or foreign case appears to have used article V(1)(b)'s narrow exception as a reason to refuse to enforce an arbitral award due to the arbitration panel's failure to consider certain evidence. Moreover, some decisions have rejected the article V(1)(b) defense under other, somewhat analogous circumstances. For example, in *Parsons & Whitmore Overseas Co.*, 508 F.2d at 975-76, we refused to use the defense to bar enforcement based on an arbitral Tribunal's refusal to accommodate a key witness' schedule, stating that the inability to present one's witness was "a risk inherent in an agreement to submit to arbitration." Similarly, another court has held that a party was not denied the opportunity to present its defenses under article V(1)(b) when it had notice of an arbitration, but chose not to respond. See *Geotech Lizenz AG v. Evergreen Systems*, 697 F. Supp. 1248, 1253 (E.D.N.Y. 1988). The court in Evergreen Systems ruled that the defendant's "failure to participate was a decision that was reached only after the Company had full knowledge of the peril at which it acted." Id. In the face of Judge Ansari's repeated questioning of Avco's counsel, Avco was plainly placed on similar notice of the possible risk that the panel would choose not to rely on invoice summaries in determining whether to grant it an award.

Further support for finding that Avco was not denied due process arises from a like exception to enforceability that appears in the Federal Arbitration Act, 9 U.S.C. § 10 (1988). That Act also provides an exception to enforcement for the inability to present one's case at arbitration. The more extensive case law available under § 10 supports the conclusion that Avco was not denied due process before the Iran-U.S. Claims Tribunal. Avco's protests that the events in this case were more "egregious" than in other cases involving the inability to present one's case at arbitration are unpersuasive. The ruling by the Hague Tribunal in the instant matter was not high-handed or arbitrary as are those cases, upon which Avco relies, arising under the Federal Arbitration Act. A reading of those cases reveals that they either involve arbitration hearings actually cut short and not completed before an award was rendered, ... or a panel's outright refusal to hear certain relevant evidence at all, ...

The present picture is vastly different. Avco had a full opportunity to present its claims, and was on notice that there might be a problem with its proof, especially given Judge Ansari's concerns voiced at trial. The earlier panel surely had never said that the invoices themselves would not be accepted or considered as evidence at trial. Nor did the pretrial colloquy clearly indicate that the earlier panel had issued a definitive ruling that account summaries would be sufficient substitute proof for the invoices. Avco did not declare, after hearing Judge Ansari's comments, that it had been precluded by the pretrial colloquy from producing the invoices, nor did it then attempt to introduce them before the panel. Rather than address Judge Ansari's concerns through producing the invoices themselves, Avco reiterated its "choice" to produce only a summary of the invoices. In so doing it took a calculated risk. Under these circumstances, Avco can scarcely credibly maintain that it was prevented from presenting its case before the Tribunal.

III.

When reviewing the grant of summary judgment which dismissed the action to enforce the award, we must view the facts in the light most favorable to the Iranian parties. When so viewed those facts fail to demonstrate that Avco was denied the opportunity to present its claims to the Tribunal. For the reasons stated I think the district court erred in reaching the opposite conclusion. Accordingly, I dissent and vote to enforce the award.

V. CONCLUSIONS

1. W. Michael Reisman, *What Are the Alternatives?*

in JURISDICTION IN INTERNATIONAL LAW xix, xix-xxi (Ashgate 1999)

Territorialism, as a decision theory, elects one state, in case of a conflict but presupposes a clearly territorial base to the activity that gives rise to the dispute.

In multi-national disputes, the nationality theory produces a stalemate. The effects theory and its various epicycles—contacts and interests—cut to the core issue in jurisdictional conflicts, but "effects" has proved to be less a theory for decision than a restatement of the essential problem. Moreover, the theory and its corollaries were premised on a bilateral paradigm: a dispute between two states over the competence to make or apply law to persons, things or events over which control was simultaneously or sequentially shared. The apparently inexorable advance of interdependences has rendered that paradigm obsolete as both an explanatory and deontological or prescriptive technique. Increasingly, effects are plurilateral or multilateral.

The theoretical and practical options available to the international community in the face of these developments are limited. The community could transcend the jurisdictional issue (i) by creating vastly expanded sectors of substantive international law that would always trump national law in cases of conflict; (ii) by establishing networks of international tribunals which would be exclusively competent to make jurisdictional decisions in cases of conflict and then remand the cases to the appropriate national courts; or (iii) by establishing private international law conventions that would allocate competences on the basis of a specific code, with applications of the conventions to be made by all national courts seised of the case. Each of these options would require significant political adjustments for implementation. Let us consider them *seriatim*.

1. Jurisdictional conflicts over whose law is to be applied can be substantially mitigated if a single law, common to the competing states, can be installed. The "uniform law" movement in the United States and comparable movements in other federations have, in the sectors in which they have "inter-legislated," substantially reduced conflicts of law problems. At the international level, uniformity may be achieved in two ways: First, by agreeing upon substantive international conventions which must be applied internally and externally or, at least, to all transactions involving a non-national. Second, by international prescriptions that effectively prohibit the application to transnational cases of certain species of national legislation or regulation, in order to achieve uniformity in a broad range of national practices. Examples of the first technique may be found in the UNCITRAL Conventions. Examples of the second may be found in the prescriptions of the World Trade Organization, or the EU, or NAFTA, which prohibit certain national governmental practices with the aim of securing uniform treatment at the national level.

Uniformizing legislation solves the conflicts problem by undermining the autonomy of many states. If the reduction in national autonomy were symmetrical or were at least proportionally reduced for all the states affected, it might be tolerable. But that is not likely to be the case. Law-making, whether domestic or international, is a quintessentially political activity in which preponderant power is translated into legislative instruments that discriminate in favor of the powerholder and ensure the continuation of that discrimination through authoritative application in the future. Were conferences to be convened to address the social and economic activities that generate most international jurisdictional conflict, the results would likely be substantive norms that favored the strongest states and deprived the weaker states not only of legislative autonomy but of the comparative economic advantages that their weaknesses might otherwise vouchsafe. In other words, uniformization may become a technique by which stronger states, under the seemingly beneficent symbol of internationalism, impose their policies on the internal legislation of weaker states. Precisely because uniformization would undermine autonomy, it has occurred in only marginal sectors, in sectors in which there already was substantial agreement and corresponding congruent national practices, or in sectors in which powerful transnational pressure groups perceived a compelling interest in securing a uniform regime. Even when uniformization can be achieved, its continuing uniformity and practice will depend upon faithful application by national courts. That is less likely, the more the international prescription affects, deprivationally, the internal process of the state concerned.

2. A second solution may be found in the establishment of networks of international tribunals which would, in cases of conflict, be competent to make the jurisdictional decisions and then remand the cases to the appropriate national courts for application. The Lotus case, which we considered earlier, is one of the few examples of such an international decision, but it was an essentially consensual adjudication and there are not likely to be many such voluntary submissions. The dispute resolution mechanisms of the World Trade Organization may assume some of these functions in trade disputes before them, insofar as they have to decide whether the law of one state or another is to be applied to a particular transaction. ...

National courts have, in the absence of international tribunals, been obliged to make jurisdictional decisions. In every case in which a national court defers its own application of jurisdiction and refers a case to the courts of another state, it is functioning as a type of international tribunal. But national judgments are likely to manifest international uniformity only when there are internationally prescribed standards for them to apply, which refers us back to the first option.

3. Private international law conventions that do not address the issue of a common substantive law, but develop authoritative criteria for allocating competences to different states may also serve as a conflict-resolutive technique. A number of private international law conventions, such as The Hague Convention of 1931, have adopted this method.

Challenges

The limited toolbox of the law of international jurisdiction appears barely adequate for current challenges. For the challenges even of the near future, the tools seem quite primitive. If the so-called globalization of many sectors of the economy does not, as suggested above, signal the end of the state, it certainly does signal an exacerbated identity crisis. Renato Ruggiero, Director-General of the World Trade Organization remarked:

> The electronic exchange of software, services or information takes place in the closest thing yet to a single, world market—one defined, not by products, paperflows and border checks, but by electronic bytes and laser beams. Several years ago Robert Reich asked the question "Who is Us?" in an age of global integration. In other words, will economic nationality matter any more in a world where the web of global value added can't be unravelled?

Yet enough of a sense of "us" remains for the demands for the autonomy of national communities to continue to be pressed. Thus the terrain is different and more difficult, but the essential problem of the international law of jurisdiction remains essentially the same. As in the past, particular constitutive norms about how to allocate competences for particular sectors or disputes are likely to be short-lived. For cases of the most major impacts, the constitutive norm will probably continue to be the negotiation of a political solution. The most urgent objective is the improvement of the world constitutive process.

INDEX

References are to pages